Reprints of Economic Classics

OFFICIAL CIRCULARS
OF
PUBLIC DOCUMENTS AND INFORMATION

Volumes I-VI

OFFICIAL CIRCULARS

OF

PUBLIC DOCUMENTS AND INFORMATION

DIRECTED BY THE

POOR LAW COMMISSIONERS TO BE PRINTED, CHIEFLY
FOR THE USE OF BOARDS OF GUARDIANS AND
THEIR OFFICERS

TEN VOLUMES IN TWO
Volumes I-VI

[1840-1851]

REPRINTS OF ECONOMIC CLASSICS

AUGUSTUS M. KELLEY · PUBLISHERS
NEW YORK 1970

First Published 1840 - 1851

(London: Knight & Co., *90, Fleet Street,* Publishers
by Authority to The Poor Law Board, 1840-1851)

Reprinted 1970 by

AUGUSTUS M. KELLEY · PUBLISHERS

REPRINTS OF ECONOMIC CLASSICS

New York New York 10001

. . . .

S B N 678 00581 8
Vol I 678 04009 5

L C N 68 56565

. . . .

PRINTED IN THE UNITED STATES OF AMERICA
by SENTRY PRESS, NEW YORK, N. Y. 10019

OFFICIAL CIRCULARS

OF

PUBLIC DOCUMENTS AND INFORMATION;

DIRECTED BY THE

POOR LAW COMMISSIONERS TO BE PRINTED, CHIEFLY FOR THE USE OF THE BOARDS OF GUARDIANS AND THEIR OFFICERS.

VOLS. I.—VI.

LONDON:

Printed, by Order of the Poor Law Board, by BLACKBURN & BURT, 90½, Holborn Hill.

PUBLISHED BY CHARLES KNIGHT, 90, FLEET STREET,

Publisher to the Poor Law Board.

GENERAL INDEX

TO

VOLS. I.—VI.

OF THE

OFFICIAL CIRCULARS.

GENERAL INDEX TO VOLS. I.—VI.

NOTE.—*The numerals, i., ii., &c., refer to No. of volume, and the figures, 1, 2, &c., to page. The Nos with a * affixed, refer to pages in vols. 1 & 4 where corresponding Nos. occur in the same volumes.*

C.

GENERAL INDEX.

GENERAL INDEX.

London: Printed, by Order of the Poor Law Board, by BLACKBURN & BURT, 90½, Holborn Hill, and Published by CHARLES KNIGHT, 90, Fleet Street.

VOLUME I
[1840]

AN

OFFICIAL CIRCULAR

OF PUBLIC DOCUMENTS AND INFORMATION:

DIRECTED BY THE POOR LAW COMMISSIONERS TO BE PRINTED, CHIEFLY FOR THE USE OF THE MEMBERS AND PERMANENT OFFICERS OF BOARDS OF GUARDIANS, UNDER THE POOR LAW AMENDMENT ACT.

No. 1. CIRCULAR ISSUED JANUARY 8TH, 1840.

Poor Law Commission Office, Somerset House, January 6, 1840.

THE Commissioners, on a review of their minutes, directed that the minutes and correspondence on the following subjects should be printed and circulated for the information of guardians and officers of the several Unions, viz.:—

By order of the Board,
EDWIN CHADWICK, Secretary.

I.—RETURNS OF THE EXPENDITURE OF POOR RATES FOR THE YEAR ENDED 25TH MARCH, 1839.

The Board took into consideration the quarterly abstracts, Form B. 11, from each Union, for the quarter ended Lady-day, and also the summaries of the parochial returns of expenditure for the year ended on the 25th March, 1839.

It appeared that (allowing that the expenditure for twelve Unions where the completion of the returns have been neglected was not beyond the general average) the total expenditure of poor's rates, during the year ended 25th March, 1839, was 4,412,500*l*., or 4 per cent. beyond the amount of the year ended 25th March, 1838.

In their Fifth Annual Report, the Commissioners had anticipated an increase of expenditure for the past year as a consequence of the increase in the price of provisions, which increase then amounted to 18 per cent. In that report, they stated—"In all the Unions supplied with provisions by contract, the contracts having been entered into during periods of low prices, and having been renewed in many instances at prices considerably advanced, the expense of maintenance will, in these instances, appear to have been greater during the succeeding quarters than during the period for which the return was made.

But it was gratifying to the Commissioners to observe, in respect to the chief test of the progressiveness of the system, the decrease of the number of paupers; whilst there had been a slight increase of the expenditure during the past parochial year, that there had been a decrease of 3 per cent. as compared with the number of paupers relieved during the year preceding. It was also highly satisfactory to perceive, that whilst in 238, or the majority, of the new Unions, there had been a considerable diminution of the numbers of paupers; in 115 Unions there had been a decrease in the expenditure as well as in the numbers of paupers, whilst relief was so well administered as to be free from any well founded complaints. (Table B.) These Unions are spread under such various circumstances all over the country as to sustain the inference that they were not exempted from any common pressure, and that the reductions were not attributable to any favourable facilities enjoyed by the majority of them, but were such as might equally well have been effected in all other Unions, by an equally extensive application of the pure workhouse principle. They are specified in the annexed list (A.):—

(A.)—List of Unions in which the Pauperism and Expenditure have *both decreased* during the year ended 25th March, 1839, as compared with the parochial year ended 25th March, 1838.

Unions.	Decrease per Cent. in Pauperism.	Decrease per Cent. in Expenditure.
Bedford—		
Leighton Buzzard	5	1
Luton	7	16
Berks—		
Abingdon	5	2
Buckingham—		
Aylesbury	36	1
Chester—		
Altrincham	9	9
Congleton	26	11
Macclesfield	25	8
Northwich	15	4
Cornwall—		
Launceston	3	2
Devon—		
Barnstaple	12	4
Torrington	7	2
Durham—		
Auckland	7	1
Chester le Street	4	2
Essex—		
Colchester	8	3
Romford	2	2
West Ham	10	3
Gloucester—		
Cirencester	6	3
Northleach	3	2
Stow on the Wold	3	4
Tetbury	18	6
Thornbury	7	2
Wheatenhurst	10	43
Hereford—		
Weobly	1	6
Hertford—		
St. Albans	3	1
Barnet	19	3
Hatfield	4	6
Hitchin	1	5
Ware	12	3
Kent—		
Dartford	20	2
Hoo	23	20
Lewisham	20	9
North Aylesford	..	8
Tenterden	14	4
Leicester—		
Ashby de la Zouch	14	1
Blaby	39	14
Hinckley	17	1
Leicester	22	17
Market Bosworth	11	3
Market Harborough	2	2
Melton Mowbray	11	8
Lincoln—		
Sleaford	8	4
Holbeach	..	10
Middlesex—		
Bethnal Green	20	13
Edmonton	11	5
Holborn	4	17
Stepney	22	23
Norfolk—		
Aylsham	4	1
Blofield	22	16
Henstead	16	19
Northampton—		
Northampton	7	3
Oundle	12	1
Peterborough	5	14
Northumberland—		
Alnwick	12	10
Bellingham	3	2
Berwick	11	4
Castle Ward	4	4
Glendale	3	1
Haltwhistle	10	7
Nottingham—		
Bingham	14	11
Nottingham	33	21
Oxford—		
Chipping Norton	14	4
Woodstock	9	4
Rutland—		
Oakham	9	9
Salop—		
Cleobury Mortimer	10	2
Southampton—		
Kingsclere	11	10
Petersfield	7	2
Romsey	13	1
Stafford—		
Lichfield	11	3
Suffolk—		
Hartismere	14	5
Surrey—		
Guildford	1	4
Reigate	7	5
Rotherhithe	6	1
Wandsworth & Clapham	7	10
Sussex—		
Rye	13	3
Warwick—		
Foleshill	16	12
Nuneaton	21	2
Westmoreland—		
Kendal	14	3
Wilts—		
Calne	4	1
Wilton	13	4
Worcester—		
Droitwich	19	1
Upton on Severn	20	1
Worcester	12	5
North York—		
Northallerton	..	8
Scarborough	1	4
Brecknock—		
Hay	21	2

The Commissioners, after examining the Union returns for the last quarter, as well as those submitted to them for the last week, expressed their satisfaction at the constant diminution which they appear to indicate of the *numbers* of the adult paupers and claimants of relief. From the reports of the Assistant Commissioners who have examined the inmates of the workhouses to which the returns relate, it appears that the workhouses, in an increasing proportion of their districts, are free from any but the most proper objects—cripples, or persons helpless from extraordinary diseases of an uncurable character. The examination of the out-relief lists is equally satisfactory.

On the other hand, the Commissioners regret to perceive from the same returns, the large numbers of pauper children, of an age capable of some useful employments, who still remain in the workhouses. The number of children between the ages of 9 and 16, at present in the Union workhouses, appears to be:—

Males	11,793
Females	10,509
Total . . .	22,302

These children constitute 19 per cent. of the pauper population of the workhouses. The cost of the maintenance of these children as paupers appears to be upwards of 160,000*l*. per annum. But unless, by the active aid of the Guardians, these children are got out into courses of productive industry, not only will the hereditary pauper stock be maintained, and possibly increased, but the produce obtainable from their well directed labour, of much greater value than the sums at present expended in maintaining them in idleness, will be entirely lost. The Commissioners earnestly invite the attention of the Guardians to the condition of this class of paupers, and the consideration of the best means of rendering them efficient workmen and good servants. The Board will avail itself of an early opportunity for promoting the practicable remedies which may appear to be available for this class of cases.

The Commissioners perceive that, in several well managed Unions, the number of able-bodied paupers who had received relief are greater than in other adjacent Unions, where the general administration of relief was less in advance. This increase the Commissioners believe to be chiefly in casual relief, attributable to the active and beneficial use of the system of tickets for the prevention of almsgiving and the extinction of mendicity.

The following is a synoptical view of the chief results indicated by the returns from the various Unions, presented to the Board:—

(B.)

Table showing the Increase or Decrease in Pauperism and Expenditure, during the year ended 25th March, 1839, as compared with the year ended 25th March, 1838, in 426 Unions, which have been in operation twelve months and upwards.

Pauperism.			Expenditure.		
No. of Unions.	Increase per cent.	Decrease per cent.	No. of Unions.	Increase per cent.	Decrease per cent.
	Between.			Between.	
1	. .	45 — 40	1	. .	45 — 40
3	. .	40 — 35	2	. .	25 — 20
1	. .	35 — 30	7	. .	20 — 15
3	. .	30 — 25	7	. .	15 — 10
11	. .	25 — 20	22	. .	10 — 5
20	. .	20 — 15	76	. .	5 — 0
44	. .	15 — 10	115		
60	. .	10 — 5			
95	. .	5 — 0			
238					
77	0 — 5	. .	144	0 — 5	. .
53	5 — 10	. .	94	5 — 10	. .
29	10 — 15	. .	41	10 — 15	. .
11	15 — 20	. .	16	15 — 20	. .
6	20 — 25	. .	11	20 — 25	. .
3	25 — 30	. .	3	25 — 30	. .
5	30 — 35	. .	1	30 — 35	. .
1	35 — 40	. .	1	35 — 40	. .
1	40 — 45	. .	311		
2	60 — 65	. .			
188			426		
426					

Pauperism.—Average *Decrease* per cent. in each of the 426 Unions.................... } 3

Expenditure.—Average *Increase* per cent. in each of the 426 Unions.................. } 4

Amongst other instances favourably noticed by the Board, was the following, stated in a communication from the clerk to the Board of Guardians of Stoke-upon-Trent.

"*Parish Office, November* 11*th*, 1839.

"GENTLEMEN,—In the discharge of my duty as clerk to the Board of Guardians of this parish, I now transmit you an analysis or recapitulation, for the year ending the 25th March, 1839, of the operation of the Poor Laws, as administered in this parish, under the rules and orders of the Poor Law Commissioners, and in doing so I have only to repeat the opinions I have before expressed to the Board of the benefits which have resulted in this parish from the system adopted, not only in diminution of the rates, but, what is of paramount importance, in the moral good effected, is every year more and more confirmed by the additional experience afforded me from the practical duties of my situation. The analysis will, I trust, be found to develope in detail an exposé of all classes of parochial applications for relief, and of the mode of dealing with them, and thus enable you to form a pretty correct judgment as to the administration of the law in this parish.

"I have the honour to be, gentlemen, yours, &c.

"THOMAS GRIFFIN, Jun.

"*To the Poor Law Commissioners.*"

"Number of Applications for Relief in the parish of Stoke-upon-Trent, Staffordshire, and how disposed of during the year 1838-39.

Applications.

No. of Applications.	Aged and Infirm.	Ablebodied.	Sickness.	Widows with Families.	Orphans.	Husbands absconded or transported, &c	Children under 16, relieved with their parents.
836	302	563	185	7	37	45	1241

How disposed of.

Orders for Workhouse given.	No. Admitted into Workhouse.	Provisions from Stores.	Out-Relief.	Clothing.	Medical Relief.	Total No. of Cases.
619	342	143	29	34	11	836

Total number of persons relieved, including their children, under 16 years of age.................. } 2380

Number of cases that did not accept the workhouse . 277

The parties who received provisions from the workhouse stores are as under:—

4 cases by way of loan.
6 { ,, refunded, being paupers belonging to other parishes.
15 ,, under orders of removal.
118 ,, sickness.

143

The parties who received out-relief were as under:

11 cases of aged and infirm.
5 ,, widows with families, &c.
2 ,, infirm, under orders of removal.
11 ,, sickness.

29

The parties who received clothing were as under:

12 cases of orphan children.
2 ,, idiots.
7 ,, aged and infirm.
4 ,, sickness.
9 ,, widows with small children, &c.

34

"Upon the revision of the out-door relief lists, out of 98 cases in which orders for the workhouse were given only two cases accepted."

The Board observed, with great satisfaction, that the amount of money expended for litigation during the year ended March 25, 1839, was 64,454*l*., being a reduction of 29,528*l*. on the charges for litigation of the year preceding. The charges for litigation in the year 1833-4, the year preceding the passing of the Poor Law Amendment Act, were 258,604*l*., which, compared with the amount expended in 1839, shows a reduction in 1839 of 194,150*l*., or an annual saving on this item of expenditure alone of more than three times the total expense of the Commission. The Commissioners believe, however, that the sum at present expended might, by means of legislative provisions, be greatly reduced, and a more satisfactory decision of disputed questions afforded to the Unions and the public. Amongst other means of reducing the charge, the Commissioners reverted to those suggested by the Guardians of the Frome Union, who had passed the following resolution:—

"That it appears to this committee, that the expenses of orders of removal, and of litigation consequent thereon, might be very materially lessened by an understanding between the different Unions, that no order of removal of any pauper shall be applied for until such pauper shall have made a statement, before the Board of Guardians of the Union in which he shall have become chargeable, of all the facts connected with his place of settlement, and a copy of such statement, under the sanction of such Board, shall have been transmitted to the clerk of the Union in which it shall appear, on such statement, that such pauper shall be then legally settled."

On this resolution, the Commissioners directed the following circular letter to be transmitted to the Assistant-Commissioners:—

"*Poor Law Commission Office, Somerset House,*
"*24th July*, 1839.

"SIR,—The Poor Law Commissioners enclose a copy of a resolution passed by the Board of Guardians of the Frome Union on the 5th instant, relative to a proposed examination of non-settled paupers by Boards of Guardians, previous to application being made to obtain orders of removal for such paupers.

"If such an arrangement as that described in the resolution could be universally adopted, the Commissioners entertain no doubt that the result would be very beneficial, especially in preventing improper removals and litigation; but the adoption of this arrangement must for the present be entirely voluntary, both as between the Guardians and the overseers of the parishes within their respective Unions in which the paupers reside, and between these functionaries and the Guardians and overseers of the Unions to which the paupers might be ultimately removed, the overseers now being exclusively responsible for the removal of paupers becoming chargeable to the poor-rates.

"The Commissioners would take no immediate steps by means of an order of the Board to give effect to the suggestion contained in the minute of the Guardians of the Frome Union, as a question might be raised as to the power of the Commissioners to compel obedience to such an order, until the Unions became Unions for settlement, but they would consider it a very satisfactory result, if, with a knowledge of the voluntary nature of the proposed arrangement, the Guardians and overseers of your district should follow the course specified in the resolution of the Board of Guardians of the Frome Union.

"Signed by order of the Board.
"GEORGE COODE, *Assistant Secretary.*

"*To*
"*Assistant Poor Law Commissioner.*"

The Commissioners invite the attention of the Guardians, and especially of the ex-officio Guardians, to the expediency of making every legitimate application of the new workhouses and staff of paid officers, for the repression of the evils of indiscriminate almsgiving, and of mendicity, in aid of any paid constabulary force that may be appointed under the County and District Constables Act. Should it appear to the magistrates desirable that any of the space at present unoccupied in the Union workhouse, but which it may be necessary to keep in reserve against any extensive influx of claims to relief, may be usefully occupied as station houses for any portion of a paid force, the Commissioners will be ready to consider of the best means of facilitating such objects.

In several instances in divisions where there has been no proper accommodation for holding petty sessions, and where the meetings have unavoidably been held at some expense and inconvenience at country inns, to the promotion of bad habits of drinking on the part of witnesses and others in attendance, the Commissioners have, on application, readily sanctioned the use of the board-rooms of the Union workhouse, for holding petty sessions, when they could be held without interfering with the meetings of the Guardians. The extent to which legal business, connected with the raising of rates, and the administration of relief to the poor, is transacted at the petty sessions, and the advantage of having such cases decided on the spot to officers and witnesses, appear to the Commissioners to justify the use of board-rooms of the Union workhouses for holding petty sessions, wherever the magistrates have thought fit to make use of them.

II.—RELIEF:—CAUSES OF SICKNESS AND DESTITUTION, AND OF CONSEQUENT CLAIMS TO RELIEF AMONGST THE LABOURING CLASSES.

The Commissioners having considered the winter quarter the fitting period for making arrangements to collect information for a report, to be laid before the House of Lords at the ensuing session of parliament, the following letter from Lord John Russell was read at a Board, held on the 28th of September last, and the steps to be taken thereon reconsidered:—

"*Whitehall, August* 21, 1839.

"GENTLEMEN,—The Queen having been pleased to comply with the prayer of an humble address presented to her Majesty, in pursuance of an order of the House of Lords, dated 19th Aug., 1839, that 'her Majesty will be pleased to cause inquiry to be made as to the extent to which the causes of disease stated in the Appendix A, No. 1, of the Poor Law Commissioners' Fourth Annual Report, and Appendix C, No. 2, of their Fifth Annual Report, to prevail amongst the labouring classes in the metropolis, prevail also amongst the labouring classes in other parts of England and Wales, and that her Majesty will be graciously pleased to cause the results of such inquiry to be communicated to the House,'—I have to desire that you will cause inquiry to be made accordingly, and that you will prepare a report upon the result of such inquiry, and transmit the same to me, in order that it may be laid before the House of Lords.

"I am, gentlemen, your obedient servant,

"J. RUSSELL."

The following instructions were prepared for the Assistant-Commissioners; and, as the inquiry appeared to the Commissioners to be one on which the especial aid of the Guardians in furtherance of their Lordships' order should be requested, such aid is by this minute requested:—

"The Commissioners request your particular attention to the subject, as one of great importance to the labouring classes; inasmuch as it may lead to the removal of the causes of prevalent and fatal diseases, and of consequent destitution and suffering.

"The steps which the Commissioners propose to take for obtaining the information required by the order of the House of Lords, are—

"1. To procure from the medical officers of Unions, returns of the number of cases of contagious or infectious disease, the spread of which within their respective districts has been promoted by the circumstances referred to in the order of the House of Lords, with their observations thereon, for which purpose the Commissioners will issue the necessary circulars to the medical officers.

"2. To obtain information from the Boards of Guardians of districts in which these diseases appear to have prevailed to a considerable extent, and where the Guardians have applied to municipal or other authorities for the removal of circumstances promoting the prevalence of such diseases.

"3 In large towns, to request some physician or general practitioner of eminent reputation to prepare a report (founded upon data obtained from the various dispensaries, infirmaries, fever hospitals, and other similar public establishments) respecting the circumstances promoting the prevalence of contagious and infectious diseases in such large towns.

"4. If the means already indicated should prove insufficient, to obtain a report from yourself, founded on personal examinations on spots where, from the returns or from other information, such examination by yourself or the medical officer of the district may appear necessary.

"Some of the chief considerations bearing upon the subject are set forth in the reports referred to in the resolution of the House of Lords; and if within your district there were any boards of health appointed during the prevalence of the cholera, it is probable that their reports, founded on an examination of the condition of those classes amongst whom the prevalence of that disease was apprehended, may furnish you with useful information.

"The Commissioners wish further to observe that the state of the dwellings occupied by the labouring classes exercises an important influence upon their health, and the nature and frequency of the diseases to which they are subject, as well as indirectly upon the moral state of themselves and their families.

"The Commissioners, therefore, request you to investigate the state of the dwellings of the labouring classes in your district, both in towns and the country, with reference to the following observations:—

"It will be desirable, generally, after informing yourself of the various descriptions of cottage tenements in your district, and the nature of the accommodation or comforts which they contain, to observe—

"1. What is the common cost of erection and the average cost of repairing each description of these cottages or tenements.

"2. What are the rents paid by the labourers for each description of these cottage tenements.

"3. What is the general proportion of the rent paid by the labourer to his total expenditure.

"You may find within your district instances where the employers of labour (whether agricultural or manufacturing) have erected on their own lands tenements of an improved description, for the residence of the labourers employed by them. You are requested to take notice of all such instances which may come before you, and examine them as standards of comparison with other tenements of an inferior kind. You will inquire as to the comparative health and condition of the inmates, and whether the advantage of improved dwellings has been observed to have any salutary influence on the moral habits of the inmates; whether the increased comforts of his house and home have tended to withdraw the labourer from the beer-shop, and from the habits of improvidence to which it leads; whether residents in separate and improved tenements are superior in condition as compared with the labourers who hold merely lodgings, or who reside with other families in the same house.

"Where you meet with remarkable instances of improved tenements of this description, you are requested to set them forth in your report, and obtain the loan of the plans or drawings of them, together with any information as to their cost and the probable returns in rent, and whether, on the whole, (other advantages than the pecuniary return being taken into consideration), they are deemed profitable; or what may be the extent of pecuniary loss upon them, or how far it may be countervailed by other considerations.

"Although the facts collected by you may not lead to the adoption of any legislative remedies, the publication of successful examples may be useful in stimulating to emulate the voluntary adoption of them.

"The Commissioners wish you, however, to consider whether any legislative measure in the nature of a Building Act (*i. e.*, an Act prescribing certain rules to be followed in the building of cottages) would tend to introduce generally the improvements which may have been adopted partially by public-spirited persons in your district.

"This may be considered—

"1. In the case of tenements intended for the residence of the labouring classes in towns.

"2. In the case of cottage tenements in rural districts.

"With regard to the former class of tenements, the wages of labourers in towns being commonly double those earned in the rural districts, they may be well able to afford to procure such an increase of comfort in their houses as may be obtained by means of a Building Act, even at the cost of an additional rent. You are also requested, in your observations on this subject, to bear in mind another question, namely, the expediency of exempting small tenements from the payment of rates, or, wherever rents are collected weekly, of collecting the rates from the landlord.

"It has been stated that the exemption from poor-rates tends to deteriorate the tenements of the labouring classes, inasmuch as many of such tenements are, for the purpose of obtaining the exemption, built of such quality and appearance as may bring them within the exempted class. It has been further stated that the benefit of the exemption goes to the landlord, the rents of cottages built for letting in towns being very high compared with rents obtained for other house property, and that such increased rents have been demanded expressly on the ground of exemption from rating.

"The causes affecting the construction of cottages are not expressly mentioned in the reports referred to in the resolution of the House of Lords, which treats chiefly of the external and immediately removeable causes of disease, such as stagnant pools, or other out-door nuisances with which the parochial officers had to some extent been heretofore accustomed to interfere; but the defective construction of the cottages themselves, and the imperfect protection they may afford against cold or damp, the want of means for the due regulation of warmth, or of conveniences for cleanliness, may often be the causes of the prevalence of disease; and the Commissioners consider not only that these subjects cannot with propriety be overlooked in any report on the sources of disease among the labouring classes, but that the beneficial moral results which may arise from the suggestion of improvements in the habitations of the labouring classes, justify the Commissioners in taking this occasion to direct your attention to the heads of inquiry which are noticed in this communication."

The following instructional letter was also directed to be sent to the medical officers of the Unions.

"*Poor Law Commission Office, Somerset House,*
"*12th November*, 1839.

"SIR,—With the view of ascertaining the extent of the existence of circumstances promoting the prevalence of contagious and infectious diseases described in the reports referred to in the order of the House of Lords, set forth in the letter from Lord John Russell, a copy of which is hereto annexed, you are requested to fill up from the medical relief lists the enclosed returns, and transmit them to the clerk of the Union, with such observations as occur to you thereon.

"You will observe that the object of the Commissioners is to ascertain the existence and extent of the visible and removeable agencies promoting the prevalence of such diseases as are commonly found connected with the defects in the situation and structure or internal economy of the residences of the labouring classes.

"The attention of the physicians who drew reports on the state of the metropolis was almost exclusively directed to the causes affecting the prevalence of various forms of *continued fever*, arranged under distinguishing names adopted by nosological writers; but in rural districts the prevalence of ague and of small-pox and scarlet fever may be worthy of notice when the causes promoting their prevalence may appear removeable.

"You will, in your observations on the class of cases returned, note the situation and character and quality of the tenements in which the diseases have occurred;—whether they are situated in a neighbourhood habitually infected with malaria;—whether there are occasional causes of malaria, such as floods, &c., and in such cases, whether you have any suggestions to make as to the best means of diminishing the evil;—whether they are drained or undrained, weather-tight or otherwise;—whether there are good means of securing ventilation with a due regard to warmth; whether there are accumulations of filth, and if so, whether they are ascribable to the slovenly or indolent habits of the inmates, or to the want of proper receptacles for refuse; whether the occurrence of disease amidst this part of the population is regular or otherwise, and what are the seasons at which it appears, and its characteristics.

"The Commissioners request that you will favour them with any information which you may have gained in the course of your medical experience, as to the condition of the inmates of such residences; whether there is a need of superior cottage accommodation, or to what extent the improvement of the residence would influence the habits beneficially; as for example—whether you have witnessed any beneficial effects on the habits of the inmates by providing cottages with a day-room, scullery, pantry, three bedrooms, and convenient receptacles for refuse and for fuel;—whether within your district there are other labourers of the like class, who occupy improved tenements in a superior situation, and what is the general health and condition of the inmates, as compared with the general health and condition of the inmates less advantageously situated;—whether you have seen any cottages constructed with a view to the most economical management of fuel both in cooking and maintaining a proper temperature in the rooms; and further, any observations that may occur to you on the subject of the health of the labouring classes in connexion with what may appear to you to be available sanitary regulations.

"The accompanying portions of the Report, and the Appendix referred to in their Lordships' Order, are transmitted for your information as to the causes of disease existing in the metropolis, which it is deemed necessary to investigate in other parts of the country.

"Signed by Order of the Board,
"EDWIN CHADWICK, *Secretary.*"

"To the Medical Officer of the
"District, Union."

"The following are the heads of the Returns alluded to in the above:—

"Number of Cases; Nosological Names of; Occupation of Applicants; Situation; State of Residence; Observations."

The Board accepted the honorary services of the following physicians, &c., who had expressed their willingness to examine and report on the causes of disease within the several districts specified; and the thanks of the Commissioners were directed to be given to them severally for their offers, and instructions were transmitted to them thereon:

ASHBY-DE-LA-ZOUCH	Dr. Kennedy
BARNSTAPLE	Dr. G. S. Britton
BATH	Dr. Harman
BEDFORD	Dr. Witt
Do.	Mr. Chapman
BIRMINGHAM	Dr. Palmer
Do.	Dr. Payton Blakiston
Do.	Mr. Hodgson
BRIGHTON	Dr. Jenks
BRISTOL	Mr. Brady
CAMBRIDGE	Dr. Haviland
Do.	Dr. Thackeray
Do.	Dr. Bond
CANTERBURY	Mr. Andrews
CHELMSFORD	Dr. Miller
CHIPPENHAM	Dr. Alexander
CLIFTON	Dr. Howell
COLCHESTER	Dr. Maclean
DERBY	Dr. Baker
DEVONPORT and PLYMOUTH	Dr. Rowe
GODMANCHESTER	Dr. Boungardenir
IPSWICH	Dr. Beck
LEEDS	Dr. Williamson
LICHFIELD	Dr. Rawson
LISKEARD	Mr. Fagoe
LINCOLN	Dr. Charlesworth
MALDON	Dr. Baker
MANCHESTER	Dr. R. B. Howard
NORTHAMPTON	Dr. Robertson
SHEFFIELD	Dr. A. Knight
STAFFORD	Dr. Knight
STAMFORD	Dr. Arnold
SWANSEA	Dr. Bird
WELLS	Dr. S. Macmullen
WOLVERHAMPTON	Dr. Dehane
TAUNTON	Dr. Woodford
TRURO	Dr. Charles Burham

III.—RELIEF TO THE MOTHERS OF BASTARD CHILDREN. THE OPERATION OF THE NEW ACT.

Oct. 3.—The Board took into consideration the applications arising from the operation of the new Act (2 and 3 Vict. c. 85), for giving to magistrates in petty sessions jurisdiction in cases of claims to relief on account of bastard children.

The following questions were stated from the Guardians of the Congleton Union:—

"1st. Whether, under the 2nd and 3rd Vict. c. 85, where any parish is in union, the overseers thereof can take any proceedings in procuring orders in bastardy, or whether the Guardians of the Union are the only persons authorized by that Act so to do?

"2nd. Whether a case of affiliation belonging to the parish of Biddulph, which s in the Congleton Union, although in the county of Stafford, can be heard before the magistrates of the Nantwich division (Cheshire), in which the township of Congleton, and the greater number of the townships in the Congleton Union, are situate?"

The Commissioners, in reply, stated that they were of opinion—

1st. That under the 2nd and 3rd Vict. c. 85, the Guardians of a Union are alone authorized to take proceedings in procuring orders at petty sessions on the reputed fathers. It is only where a parish is not under the control of Guardians that the overseers of such parish are competent to apply.

2nd. That a case of affiliation belonging to the parish of Biddulph, within the Congleton Union, though locally situate in the county of Stafford, may be heard, under the terms of the 1st section, by the justices holding petty sessions in and for the division in which the township of Congleton is situate. Under that section, it is sufficient that any part of the Union be within the division or borough for which the sessions are held, to give the justices jurisdiction.

The following question was stated from the Guardians of the Wincanton Union:—

"Whether the seven days' notice to the putative father, under the new Act, of the intention of the Guardians to apply for an order of maintenance, should be given under the common seal of the Board, or whether it should be signed by the presiding Chairman and two other Guardians?"

The Commissioners, upon this case, replied, that they were of opinion that the notice directed to be given by the Act 2nd and 3rd Vict. c. 85, should be given in the same manner, excepting only as to time (seven days being substituted for fourteen), as the notice provided for by the 73rd section of the Poor Law Amendment Act, to which the clause in the recent enactment has express reference.

Generally it may be observed that the signatures of the Chairman and two other Guardians are sufficient to authenticate orders and notices, the signature of the Chairman to express the concurrence of the majority, and the signature of two additional Guardians to show that at least three were present and concurring.

But whenever, as under the 73rd sec. 4th and 5th Wm. 4th, c. 76, notices are required to be given under *the hands* of the Guardians, the Commissioners are advised that they should be signed, and purport to be signed, by an actual majority of the Guardians present at the meeting, including the Chairman.

The following question was stated from the Guardians of the Easingwold Union:—

"Whether the usual formality in evidence will not have to be followed, as at the quarter sessions?"

The Commissioners, upon this point, stated that they were of opinion—

That the same formalities as to evidence appear to be necessary in applications under the recent enactment, as were required to be observed in applications to the quarter sessions under the Poor Law Amendment Act.

The following question was put by the Guardians of the Machynlleth Union:—

"Whether the application of the clerk to the justices, by the direction and on behalf of the Board of Guardians, would be a sufficient application of the Guardians within the meaning of the Act; or is it necessary for some of the Guardians to attend personally at the petty or special sessions?"

The Commissioners gave it as their opinion that—

Any person whom the Board might authorize is competent to make the application to the sessions; and the Commissioners consider that no officer is so suitable to make the application as the clerk.

The following question was stated in a letter from the Guardians of the Witney Union:—

"I am directed to ascertain whether you will sanction out-relief being given in kind to bastard children where an order of maintenance has been obtained against the putative father. It appears that, unless such relief is allowed, no benefit will be derived from the late Act of Parliament, as, though the expense of obtaining the order is reduced, the parishes will still be burthened with the maintenance of the mother in the workhouse; whereas, if out-door relief is allowed to be given to the child only, which will be repaid by the father, they will in most cases get rid of the burden altogether, as the mother will, in very few cases, remain in the house when she can get relief in kind for the child out."

The Commissioners stated in answer—

That, in Unions in which out-door relief to able-bodied persons has been prohibited, it would be illegal to give out-door relief to the bastard child of an able-bodied woman, because such relief is declared, by the 71st sec. of the Poor Law Amendment Act, to be relief to the mother.

The Commissioners consider it of paramount importance, that relief out of the workhouse should not be afforded under ordinary circumstances to able-bodied persons, and they deem it their duty to withhold their sanction from any arrangement which would be directly or indirectly a deviation from the intention of the legislature, in investing them with the power of directing that relief to paupers of this class should be restricted to the workhouse.

The following case was stated by the Guardians of the Weardale Union:—

"An application by the parish officers of Stanhope for an order of filiation having been entered and respited at the Midsummer sessions, the parish officers request to be informed, whether the exceptive clauses in the 1st sec. of the new Bastardy Act will enable them to proceed with their application, and to obtain an order upon the putative father at the ensuing Michaelmas sessions?"

The Commissioners, in reply to this case, stated that they were of opinion that—

Although the point is not free from doubt, that in every case of affiliation in which an application had been made to a court of quarter sessions before the 26th of August last, such court retains its jurisdiction, notwithstanding the 2nd and 3rd Vict. c. 85.

It is evident that the Act in question does not confer jurisdiction upon the court of petty sessions in any such case.

The Board, in consequence of the various applications for information on the subject, directed the following circular letter to be issued to the clerks of the several Unions:—

"*Poor Law Commission Office, Somerset House,*
"*November* , 18

"SIR,—In consequence of various applications on the subject of orders in bastardy under the statute 2 and 3 Vic. c. 85, the Poor Law Commissioners have deemed it advisable to have forms drawn by counsel of the notice required by the statute, and also of the order, and they herewith send you printed copies of such forms for the use and guidance of the Board of Guardians.

"At the same time, the Commissioners desire to state that no alteration has been made in the law relative to orders in bastardy as settled by the Poor Law Amendment Act, except as relates to the application for the order against the putative father, which is now to be made to the petty sessions within three calendar months after the chargeability of the child has accrued The order is to be as under the Poor Law Amendment Act, to reimburse the expense which has been incurred by the Union in the maintenance of such child, and is not to be granted in any case where the Union has not been put to some expense in its support and maintenance.

"The Commissioners desire to observe also, as some misapprehension has prevailed with reference to the nature of the alteration, that no part of the money recoverable under the order can be paid to the mother of the child, nor will any personal relief given to the mother be a sufficient ground to warrant the justices in making an order upon the putative father.

"The Commissioners desire further to observe, with respect to applications for orders in bastardy, that the Guardians possessed under the Poor Law Amendment Act the power of applying for such orders; and that the new Act neither increases that power nor extends it to any new class of cases. In every case where it was formerly proper to make an application for such an order, it will still be proper to do so; and in every case where it was proper to omit making such application, the like reasons will still require the like omission. The only material change effected by the latter statute (as has been already stated) is to transfer the jurisdiction from the quarter to the petty sessions. This transfer has been understood to have been made for the purpose of diminishing the trouble and expense attendant on the application to the quarter sessions, and of preventing the evil consequences supposed to follow from the publicity given by the examination in that court to the legal evidence required in the case, by referring such investigations to a less crowded tribunal.

"Signed by order of the Board.
"EDWIN CHADWICK, *Secretary.*"

IV.—RELIEF BY EMIGRATION.

On the 10th ultimo the Board took into consideration the various applications made since the last Board held for the consideration of loans for emigration.

A report on the subject of the present state of emigration, made by Mr. Parker, Assistant Commissioner, was read to the Board. The following are extracts:—

By a Parliamentary paper (255) recently printed, containing reports and correspondence respecting emigration to the colonies, it appears that the average annual emigration from England for the six years preceding 1838, was—

To the British North American Colonies	8,830
United States	26,819
Cape of Good Hope	318
Australian Colonies	2,808
	38,805

And that in 1838 it was—

To the British North American Colonies	1,572
United States	12,566
Cape of Good Hope	292
Australian Colonies	9,746
	24,176

Thus in the last year, when the Poor Law Amendment Act had been brought into operation over nearly the whole of England and Wales, notwithstanding the price of provisions had increased twenty per cent., and the demand for labour had become stronger in the colonies, there was less emigration by 14,629 persons than the average of the six preceding years. This difference there is every reason to suppose would have been much greater, had not emigration to the Australian colonies suddenly increased to its present extent, an increase attributable to the bounty now given to the labouring classes proceeding to that part of the British dominions. Previous to 1837, assistance was given to only single females between fifteen and thirty years of age proceeding to Australia; but since then, all persons deemed likely to prove eligible colonists have received gratuitous passages. This aid has naturaily operated as an encouragement to labouring people, who may fairly argue, that unless their services are required, the cost of their removal to a colony would not be defrayed from public funds set apart by the colonists for that purpose. The aid so given will account for the sudden increase of the numbers of persons who proceeded to the Australian colonies in 1838, and without which increase the emigration of the past year would have been insignificant in the extreme as compared with former years. It is to be regretted that the statistical information supplied in the tables contained in these reports does not supply the actual immigration to the different colonies and to the United States for each year since 1829, similar to the one prepared by the agent for emigration at Quebec. The table relating to Quebec shows conclusively that immigration to that port has materially diminished. In the four years preceding the passing of the Poor Law Amendment Act (including 1834, the Act having been passed after the season for emigration had terminated), there arrived in Quebec from England and Wales, 39,821 persons, whilst in the four years after the passing of the Act there arrived there 21,895, including upwards of 1,000 assisted by parochial funds, which a provision in the

Poor Law Amendment Act, for the first time, made applicable to emigration purposes. It has been frequently asked of witnesses before committees of the Houses of Parliament, what has become of the surplus labour existing before the Poor Law Amendment Act passed; and it has been broadly asserted by an influential journal, opposed to the provisions of the Poor Law Amendment Act, that that surplus has been reduced by shipping off thousands of poor persons to the colonies. The assertion, broadly as it has been made, is nevertheless negatived by the official returns from the United States, where it is presumed no one will say poor law influence prevails; as well as the British possessions in Asia, Africa, and America. It would be out of place, in a notice of a Parliamentary paper, to discuss the causes of the absorption of the surplus labour apparently existing before the operation of the Poor Law Amendment Act; yet from whatever cause the reduction in the number of unemployed labourers may proceed, it cannot fail to be an important consideration in ascertaining the causes, that the reduction has taken place at a time when the demand for the services of the productive classes is more than ever urgent in the colonies.

"The attempt of the journalist to account for the reduction in the number of unemployed labourers by asserting that it has been effected by emigration, may have been made upon the well-grounded supposition that the demand for labour in the colonies and United States might attract so many labourers from England as to give some colour to his assertion. If it was his intention to take advantage of any emigration created by such a demand for labour in the colonies, he must have now found that he has erred in consequence of his having overlooked the counteracting demand for labour in England, which has sprung up in the agricultural districts, if not from the operation of, at least since the Poor Law Amendment Act was passed.

"That the demand for the services of the productive classes has become more urgent in the colonies since the passing of the Poor Law Amendment Act, is clearly evinced by the reports. Mr. Buchanan, adverting to the Canadas, says:—'The great scarcity of labourers, and the high prices of wages, which farmers are obliged to pay for the necessary assistance required on their land, continue to weigh heavily on the new settler, who has not sufficient physical aid amongst the members of his own family.' And he further adds, that in the eastern townships good labourers can earn from 40*s.* to 50*s.* currency per month, with board and lodging found.

"In New South Wales demand for the services of the labouring classes exists equally as strong, if not more so, than it does in the Canadas. A committee of the Legislative Council, presided over by the Bishop of Australia, has reported that 'it cannot be assumed that the want of labour in the colony can be supplied by the introduction of a smaller number than 3,000 adult males every year—a number which will, allowing the average number of women and children, require the introduction of 12,500 persons annually.' The committee estimate the cost of introducing 12,500 persons to be 250,000*l.*, and without recommending that a loan of 2,000,000*l.* should be raised, advert to the communications suggesting a loan in such a manner as to lead the Governor, Sir G. Gipps, to remark, 'that the members of the committee are not unfavourable to it.' The Governor, adverting to the want of labour, says 'that immigration should be kept up at its present rate, and that if the funds prove insufficient, then recourse should be had to a loan rather than put a stop to it. The committee, in their report, say:—'As the foundation of every other inquiry, your committee naturally directed their first attention to ascertain, as nearly as in the nature of things might be possible, the actual demand for labour of various descriptions at this time prevailing in the colony. Their own private sources of information had sufficed to satisfy them that such demand was certainly urgent, and the supply highly insufficient to meet it; and that, generally speaking, every resident in the colony who had occasion to employ the services of others, was exposed to difficulties in conducting his pursuits, of whatever nature they might be, as well as in providing for the service of his domestic establishments. But until their inquiries were directed, in the course of this examination, to an actual investigation of individual wants, and of the losses, inconveniences, and disappointments to which entire classes are reduced through inability to obtain the extent of labour which their various operations require, your committee had not a due or distinct conception of the urgency of the prevailing distress.'

"In Van Diemen's land there exists so urgent a demand for female servants, that the governor (Sir J. Franklin) says, 'Not only is social intercourse at present very much restricted, especially in the interior, in consequence of the difficulty felt even by the wealthiest families to obtain female attendants for their children, and the additional domestic duties thereby imposed upon parents, but it has recently been found impossible even to procure in cases of sickness the requisite number of attendants, of sufficiently good character, however deficient in skill.'

"In Western Australia (Swan River), a memorandum presented to the governor states, that 'in the present state of the colony, there is such a deficiency of labour as to impede its advancement.

"'The prudent portion of the workmen have saved means, and are now in condition to extend their business, and to hire assistance, if they could procure it; but they cannot venture to undertake works in the existing scarcity of workmen, and the consequent high rate of wages. Under these circumstances the price of every product has risen; improvement is discouraged; capital prevented from finding investment here, must go elsewhere; and the colony is menaced with a return to its former state of unproductiveness, in the midst of every natural convenience for producing abundance.

"'The only remedy for these evils, is a steady and well regulated supply of labour from abroad, in proportion to the growth of capital within the settlement.'

"The council concurred in this, and pledged itself to a limited extent to any future measures tending to procure a supply of labour.

"At the Cape of Good Hope labour is also required, and a scheme to supply it from this country has been suggested in the colony; from which it would appear that some thousands of young people might be annually introduced with benefit to the colony.

"Great as the demand is for labour in all these colonies, and tempting as the inducements held out in the shape of remuneration are, and easy as it is to obtain a passage to the Australian Colonies, yet it is found that the demand cannot be supplied, because there exists no disposition amongst the labouring classes to emigrate. Before the passing of the Poor Law Amendment Act, when there was an apparent surplus population, emigration was extensive; now that there exists an urgent demand for the services of the productive classes in the colonies, the number of emigrants has fallen off. In the present year the disp sition to emigrate has not strengthened. Within the last few days, a vessel, chartered to convey emigrants gratuitously, has sailed with only two-thirds of its complement of passengers."

The following letter from the Agent-General for emigration was read to the Board :—

(Copy.)

"2, *Middle Scotland Yard, 29th October*, 1839.

"SIR,—In pursuance to instructions received from Lord John Russell, I have the honour to acquaint you that despatches have been received from the Lieutenant-Governor of Upper Canada, reporting the successful introduction into that colony of a body of 181 emigrants, who were sent out from Ennis, in the county of Clare, last summer, in the ship 'Waterloo,' through the liberality of Colonel Wyndham.

"On arriving at Quebec, the whole of the emigrants proceeded in a body, under the charge of Lieutenant Rubridge, to whom Colonel Wyndham had intrusted the care of them, to Cobourg, Upper Canada, where they were all immediately engaged, the men at 2*l.* 10*s.* per month, boarded and found, and the women at 1*l.* per month, boarded and fed.

"No sickness or accident of any kind occurred amongst them from the time of their leaving Ireland.

"In consequence of these favourable accounts of the result of Colonel Wyndham's liberal efforts in promotion of emigration, Lord John Russell has conveyed to me his desire that the officers of this department should give every advice and facility to landlords who may be desirous of following Colonel Wyndham's example.

"I have, &c.
(Signed) "T. FREDERICK ELLIOTT."

Several original letters of labourers who have emigrated to South Australia were brought to the notice of the Board as descriptive of their feelings and of the demand for labour in that colony.

EMIGRATION OF CHILDREN.

The following application was read from the Vice-Chairman of the Dursley Union:—

"*Wootton under Edge, January 28th*, 1839.

"SIR,—Will you be so good as to inform me if the Poor Law Commissioners would sanction the sending out to Australia or New South Wales any of the orphan boys from twelve to fifteen years of age now in our workhouse.

"At present we have a good many orphans who have received a fair education in the house, but for whom there appears no chance of providing work about this place, but who could be sent out with some emigrant families which we expect will leave this in April next.

"As I expect the Commissioner in about ten days, an early answer would much oblige, more particularly as I wish to bring the subject before the Board on Thursday next. Could you conveniently communicate with me by that day, please to direct to me at the Board, Dursley, or to Mr. A. Jackson, the clerk.

"I have the honour, &c.
(Signed) "T. S. CHILD,
"Vice-Chairman of the Dursley Union.

"*E. Chadwick, Esq., Secretary*," *&c.*

The Commissioners directed that the following reply should be sent to this application: "They are of opinion that it is not expedient to sanction the application of parochial funds to defray the cost of sending orphan children to the colonies, unless a desire be expressed by the children to go abroad, and there be some guarantee given that the children will be provided for in the colony."

EMIGRATION OF SOLDIERS' WIVES.

The following application was made from the parish of Issing, in the Midhurst Union:—

"*Midhurst Union.—Issing Parish.*

"GENTLEMEN,—I herewith send the forms A, B, and C, together with a list of persons desirous of emigrating from the above parish. The parties, Margaret Hutson, aged twenty, and her infant child, aged one year, have resided for several months in the Eastbourne workhouse, at a very considerable cost to the parish, and so will continue, unless the overseers are permitted to make the present outlay of 15*l.* for the purpose of enabling them to emigrate.

"I am, &c.
(Signed) "RICHARD WARDROPER.

"*To the Poor Law Commissioners.*"

"The husband of this woman, Thomas Hutson, is a private in Her Majesty's 70th regiment of foot, now stationed at the Island of St. Vincent, in the West Indies; and not being allowed to take her with him, she has been removed to the parish of Issing, where she and her child are now chargeable.

"The woman states that she could earn a good living by washing for the officers of her husband's regiment, if she could but join him."

To this application the Commissioners stated in reply:—"That they cannot sanction the application of parochial funds to defray the cost of sending the wives of soldiers to join their husbands who are serving with their regiments abroad, inasmuch as such emigrations would interfere with the regulations of the service, which only permit a limited number of females to accompany each regiment."

EMIGRATION TO NEW ZEALAND.

The following letter was read from the parish of Staplehurst, in the Maidstone Union:—

"*Staplehurst, 27th October*, 1839.

"GENTLEMEN,—I herewith forward the duplicate notice of vestry meeting, resolution passed thereat, and a certificate signed by the minister and parish officer, with a list of the paupers about to emigrate; and I am directed to request that as the vessel in which the emigrants are to proceed to New Zealand is appointed to sail on Friday next, you will lose no time in confirming the resolution and informing me thereof.

"I have, &c.
(Signed) "N. OTTAWAY, Clerk."

The Board, by Letter, requested information on the subject from Her Majesty's Under Secretary of State for the Colonies, and thereupon transmitted the following reply, in which they declined to sanction the loan:—"The Commissioners having in several instances considered it their duty to decline giving their sanction to parochial emigrations to New Zealand, felt anxious, before coming to any determination upon this case, to obtain information upon the subject from the Colonial Office; and they have therefore received from that department a communication to the effect that there is at present no British colony established at New Zealand.

"The Commissioners, under these circumstances, do not feel themselves warranted in confirming the resolution in question, and regret that it was not communicated to them earlier, that they might have prevented the disappointment likely to be caused to the parties who had proposed to emigrate. At the same the Commissioners desire to suggest that the Board of Guardians should endeavour to make arrangements with some of the emigration agents who undertake to convey emigrants to those colonies which are already established."

EMIGRATION OF CONVICTS' FAMILIES.

The following application was received from the parish of Thornbury, in the Thornbury Union.

"*January 7th*, 1839.

"SIR,—James Hayman, late a parishioner of Thornbury, was about three years ago transported to New South Wales for a term of seven years, leaving chargeable to the parish a wife and seven children under the age of nine, who have been ever since maintained in the Union workhouse, at an average weekly expense of 3*s.* 7*d.* per head.

"A few days since the man's wife received a letter from him, requesting that she and the children would go out to him, and stating that he was in a situation to support them, and that Government would give them a passage free of expense.

"The Board of Guardians being desirous to rid the parish of so heavy a burden, have directed me to request you will be pleased to inform them, whether, under the circumstances, Government will now send out this family, and if not, whether the cost of the passage could legally be paid by the parish.

"I am, &c.

"R. SCARLETT, Clerk."

The Commissioners stated in reply:—"That if the behaviour of convicts for a certain period (in the case of a person transported for

7 years	. . .	4 years
14 ,,	. . .	6 ,,
Life	. . .	8 ,,)

of their sentence, is satisfactory to the officers put over them, the colonial government rewards them with tickets of leave, entitling them to work on their own account, and in the cases of married men, of orders for the conveyance of their wives and families to the colony. As such an order is only given to a convict as a reward for good behaviour, it would defeat the object of the Government in holding out such an inducement to reformation, if the reward could be obtained from other sources.

"For this reason the Commissioners decline sanctioning the application of parish funds to discharge the cost of sending out the wives and families of convicts.

"The Commissioners also desire to inform you, that the Government will render no assistance to enable the woman and her children to join the convict, unless an order of the nature above referred to has been obtained by him, which it is impossible he can have obtained within three years of his sentence."

The following application was received from the parish of Michelmarsh, in the Romsey Union.

"*Romsey Union, Romsey.*

SIR,—I am desired by the Board of Guardians to request the favour of information from the Poor Law Commissioners, with reference to a large family desirous of emigrating to South Australia. The applicant, John Collins, is an agricultural labourer, aged forty, with a wife the same age, three daughters, twenty, ten, and seven years old; four sons, eighteen, sixteen, fourteen, and twelve years old; the whole of the family healthy and industrious.

"Collins has recently returned from Van Diemen's Land, whither he was transported for his unguarded conduct during the agricultural riots, but he has not been employed since his return. The parish are willing to contribute towards the emigration expenses, if the family could be sent out under the order of the Commissioners and the protection of the Government, so that employment might be insured on their arrival. Any information that this application may suggest, in addition to an answer to the above, will be conferring a favour on the parish, as they wish to send the family off as soon as possible.

"I am, &c.

(Signed) "J. LORDAN, Clerk.

"*To the Poor Law Commissioners.*"

The Commissioners in reply to this case stated:—"That they have been in communication with the Colonization Commissioners for South Australia on the subject, and now enclose a copy of the letter received from them in reply, from which it will be seen that the Colonization Commissioners decline affording a free passage to the above family, in consequence of John Collins (the father) having been transported."

"*South Australian Colonization Office,*
"*Adelphi Terrace.*

"SIR,—I have to acknowledge the receipt of your letter of the 20th instant, transmitting the copy of a letter from the clerk to the Board of Guardians of the Romsey Union, respecting the allowance of a free passage to South Australia for John Collins and family.

"I am directed by the Colonization Commissioners for South Australia to acquaint you in reply, that they must beg to decline affording a free passage to any person who has been transported.

"I have, &c.

(Signed) "JOHN GLIDDON, Assist. Secretary.

"*E. Chadwick, &c. &c.*"

EMIGRATION OF THE FAMILIES OF VAGRANT PAUPERS.

The following application was made from the Ulverstone Union.

"*Ulverstone Union.*

"GENTLEMEN,—In reply to your letter of the 22nd instant, requesting to be informed of the circumstances under which Anthony Hewitson emigrated from this country, leaving behind him his wife and children, I beg to give you the statement which I have received from Mr. Rigg, the chairman of the township meeting which passed the resolution to grant the money to enable the widow and children to emigrate. Mr. Rigg states, 'Anthony Hewitson made application to our township (Lower Holker) for a sum of money (I think 20*l.*) to take his family to New York, but the overseers refused the application; consequently he, finding he could not maintain his family by his own labour in this country, determined to leave them behind, and fetch them as soon as he had the means. On his arrival in America he took a farm, but that not answering his expectation, he sold his goods, and bound himself apprentice to a miller, and as yet his apprenticeship is not quite completed; but he hopes by the time his wife and children shall arrive there, he will be in a capacity to maintain them comfortably by the profits of his labour.'

"I have, &c.

"JOHN POSTLETHWAITE, Jun., Clerk."

In reply to which, the Commissioners stated:—"That they do not think it advisable to sanction the application of parish funds to defray the expense of the emigration of the wife and children of Anthony Hewitson, as the Commissioners consider that by adopting such a course, the man, whom it is the policy of the law to punish for deserting his family, would be rewarded, and other persons might be encouraged to follow his example, in the expectation of their families receiving assistance to join them."

GENERAL REGULATIONS ON EMIGRATION.

The Commissioners having, on other communications, taken into their consideration the present mode of expending the money raised and borrowed under their orders for the purposes of parochial emigrations, consider that it will be expedient, in every future case, to direct that such money, instead of being expended by the parish officers, as heretofore, shall be paid by them to the Treasurer of the Union, to be placed to the credit of the Board of Guardians; and that the Guardians shall thereupon open an account in their ledger, entitled, " . . . . Parish Emigration Account;" and also, that the Guardians shall not expend any part of such money unless the poor persons proposing to emigrate shall have settlements in the parish, and unless the following conditions be strictly observed:—

1. The parties emigrating shall go to some British Colony.

2. The churchwardens and overseers may expend not exceeding three-pence a mile in conveying each person above seven years of age to the port of embarkation: and each child under seven years, three half-pence.

3. The churchwardens and overseers may give to each emigrant clothing to the value of 1*l*., if the place of the said party's destination be not eastward of the Cape of Good Hope; and to the value of 2*l*. if the place of his destination be eastward of the Cape of Good Hope.

4. If the cost, or any part thereof, of conveying the emigrants from the port of embarkation to the port of discharge, shall be defrayed from the fund above directed to be provided, a contract, to be approved of by the Poor Law Commissioners, shall be entered into for conveying them to such port of discharge.

5. If no part of the cost of conveying the said parties shall be defrayed from the said fund, and no provision be made for their maintenance on arrival at the place of their destination, a contract, to be approved by the Poor Law Commissioners, shall be entered into for giving them money on their arrival, according to the following scale:—

	£.	s	d
To each person exceeding Fourteen Years of age	1	0	0
To each person exceeding Seven Years, and not Fourteen Years.	0	10	0
To each person not exceeding Seven Years	0	6	8

6. If no part of the fund above directed to be provided shall be expended in defraying the cost of conveying the said parties from the port of embarkation to the port of discharge, and no contract shall be entered into for giving them money to provide for their maintenance on arrival at the place of their destination, the churchwardens and overseers shall transmit to the Poor Law Commissioners, within ten days after the said parties shall have embarked, a list containing the names, ages, occupations, and places of destination of the said parties.

7. Every contract entered into for conveying the said parties from the port of embarkation, or for giving them money to provide for their maintenance on arrival at the place of their destination, shall be registered at the office of the Poor Law Commissioners, previous to the day on which the said parties shall embark.

The auditor will also be directed to disallow every payment made from the emigration fund, which shall not have been made in strict conformity with the above conditions.

V.—SALES OF PARISH PROPERTY, AND THE APPROPRIATION OF THE PROCEEDS OF THE SALE.

In regard to the appropriation of the produce arising from the sales of parish property, the Commissioners having considered it necessary to take the opinion of the Attorney and the Solicitor-General on one case, and the opinion of the Attorney-General on a second case, the following are the copies of their opinions: —

"CASE.

"Your opinion is requested upon the proper construction of the 1st and 2nd Vic. c. 25, s. 2, whether the Poor Law Commissioners can sanction the liquidation of any debts, liabilities, or engagements, incurred on behalf of any parish, which have not been incurred for any of the purposes of 'building, altering, enlarging, purchasing, and fitting up houses for the reception of the poor, or of purchasing or hiring land in order to erect buildings thereon, or for other purposes permanently beneficial to such parishes or townships,' but which the Poor Law Commissioners consider to constitute fair and just claims against such parish: in other words, whether the general language of the enactment is limited by the preamble?

"OPINION.

"We are of opinion that the Poor Law Commissioners cannot sanction the liquidation of debts not incurred for building, &c., &c., or purchasing or buying land, &c. *or for other purposes permanently beneficial to such parishes or townships.* It is difficult to understand how any sum borrowed by a parish can constitute a just claim against it, unless such sum was borrowed for a purpose permanently beneficial; if such a case should exist, we do not think it would come within the enactment in question, which is stated expressly to be for enabling the discharge of money borrowed *for the purposes aforesaid.*

"J. CAMPBELL,
"R. M. ROLFE.

"*Temple, May* 2, 1839."

"CASE.

"Previous to the passing of the Poor Law Amendment Act, in many parishes debts had been incurred by the parish officers and individual parishioners, in their own names, for money borrowed to enable paupers or poor persons to emigrate. They gave, in most instances, their own bonds or promissory notes as securities to the lenders, and the parish subsequently paid the interest from year to year as it accrued.

"Such borrowing being inoperative, as far as relates to the charging the poor-rates, the auditors, in most cases, have disallowed the payment of any more interest, and the holders of the securities are now proceeding against the parties to the instruments. This is a hardship upon them, and almost universally contrary to the feeling of the parish. The Commissioners are anxious, as much as possible, to relieve those parties, and to yield to the wishes of the parishioners.

"The 1st and 2nd Vic. c. 25, s. 2, has enabled them to discharge certain debts and liabilities, but the construction which you have given to it in the case of which a copy is sent herewith, has very much crippled their power.

"You will observe that the Legislature authorizes the Commissioners to sanction the appropriation of parish property proceeds in liquidation of any debt, liability, or engagement, incurred or made by or on behalf of any parish, which the Commissioners shall consider a fair and just claim against any such parish, though not capable of being legally enforced; and by the preamble of the section the debts are confined to such as were incurred before the passing of the Poor Law Amendment Act, for certain specified purposes, *or for other purposes permanently beneficial to such parishes.*

"Now, it is urged that the emigration of a pauper, or of a poor settled inhabitant likely to become a pauper, is a purpose permanently beneficial to the parish. The parishioners are for ever relieved from that which may be a perpetual burthen or a perpetual liability. The superabundant population of the parish is not temporarily reduced, but, so far as relates to the persons emigrating, is permanently relieved.

"The Legislature also, in the 4th and 5th Wm. 4, c. 76, s. 62, have treated emigration as a mode of relief which ought to be sanctioned, and have authorized parishes to borrow money on the rates to provide a fund for it.

"Again, by the 5th and 6th Wm. 4, c. 69, s. 3, the Guardians of any Union are authorized to apply the proceeds of the sale of any parish property to certain specified purposes, '*or in liquidation of any debt contracted by such parish or Union, or dissolved Union, or in such other manner, for the permanent advantage of such parish or Union, as the Poor Law Commissioners may approve.*'

"YOUR OPINION IS REQUESTED—

"1. I am of opinion that they may.	"1. Whether the Poor Law Commissioners can sanction the application of the sale proceeds under the 1st and 2nd Vic., c. 25, to the liquidation of debts contracted before the passing of the Poor Law Amendment Act, for the purpose of assisting paupers or settled inhabitants to emigrate?
"2. I am of opinion that they may.	"2. Whether, where a parish has contracted a debt for emigration purposes, under the 4th and 5th Wm. 4, c. 76, s. 62, the Commissioners can, under the 5th and 6th Wm. 4, c. 69, s. 3, sanction the application of such proceeds to liquidate that debt?
"3. I am of opinion that they may upon either supposition.	"3. Whether they can treat such emigration as a permanent advantage to the parish, within the meaning of the same section; whether the parish have or have not charged the future rates, as they were permitted to do by the 4th and 5th Wm. 4, c. 76, s. 62?
"4. I am of opinion that this would be a lawful application of the fund in question.	"4. Whether the Commissioners can sanction the application of sale proceeds to the erection or endowment of a parochial school, where the same is requested by the parishioners?

"J. CAMPBELL.
"*Temple, July 1st*, 1839."

The Board took into consideration the following applications for authority to sell parochial properties, which have been submitted to the Commissioners during the last month, upon which they directed investigations to be made, in order to ascertain the titles under which the properties were held:

"*Cambridge; North Witchford* Union; *Benwick* Parish. For the sale of the freehold premises lately used as the parish poor-house.
Five freehold cottages.
Seven acres of freehold land.
Estimated value 450*l*.

" *Devon; St. Thomas* Union; *Pinhoe* Parish. For the sale of four freehold cottages called 'the poor-house.'
Estimated value 90*l*.

" *Cornwall; St. German's* Union; *Maker* Parish. For the sale of the parish workhouse, with the garden belonging thereto.

" *Bedford; Bedford* Union; *Cardington and East-cotts* Parishes. For the sale of freehold premises lately used as the parish poor-house, with the garden ground belonging thereto.
Two freehold cottages with gardens.
Estimated value 250*l*."

Due investigation having been made in reference to applications for the Commissioners' sanction to sell the following parochial properties, they issued orders for convening meetings to obtain the consent of the rate-payers and owners to the sale thereof:—

" *Derby; Shardlow* Union; *Melbourne* Parish. Ten freehold houses and gardens lately used as the parish workhouse.

" *Devon; Taunton* Union; *Churchstanton* Parish. Three freehold cottages, containing six dwellings, with gardens.

" *Somerset; Wincanton* Union; *Charlton Horethorne* Parish. Two freehold cottages with gardens.

" *Stafford; Stone* Union; *Trentham* Parish. The interest of the parish in the premises lately used as the parish workhouse.

" *Sussex; Hailsham* Union; *Laughton* Parish.

A copyhold messuage with half an acre of land in Laughton.
A copyhold messuage in four tenements with a croft of land at Whitesmith Green, Laughton.
A copyhold cottage in two dwellings with a piece of land near Laughton Pound.
A copyhold cottage with a garden near Laughton Pound.
A copyhold messuage in two dwellings, with a piece of land containing one acre three roods, on Laughton Little Common.
A copyhold cottage in two tenements, with a garden at Shortgate.
A copyhold cottage, with a garden at Shortgate.
The leasehold premises lately used as the parish workhouse, now divided into six tenements.

" *York; Beverley* Union; *Elton* Parish. Five freehold cottages situate at Elton."

The consent of the rate-payers and owners (obtained in pursance of the Commissioners' directions) having been received to the sale of the parochial properties hereunder mentioned, the Commissioners issued orders sanctioning the sale thereof accordingly.

" *Gloucester; Dursley* Union; *Stinchcombe* Parish. A freehold cottage in two tenements with gardens adjoining the Stinchcombe church-yard.
Four freehold cottages adjoining Lurbin Lane.

" *Leicester; Barrow-upon-Soar* Union; *Ansty* Parish. A freehold messuage lately used as the parish workhouse.

" *Somerset; Axbridge* Union; *Winscombe* Parish. A freehold messuage, lately used as the parish poor-house, with three acres three roods and thirty-five perches of ground.

The reversion, in fee, of a piece of ground containing three roods thirty-three perches, with the six cottages erected thereon, situated at Woodborough Green.

" *Sussex; Midhurst* Union; *Lerwick* Parish. The interest of the parish in three cottages built on the waste, together with the gardens belonging thereto.

" *Sussex; Cuckfield* Union; *Ardingley* Parish. Two copyhold messuages, held of the manor of the borough of Lewes.

" *York; Beverley* Union; *Cherry Burton* Parish. Four freehold cottages, situate at Cherry Burton."

Conveyances of the following parochial properties were submitted to the Commissioners, when they caused the same to be registered and their seal to be affixed thereto:—

" *Somerset; Clutton* Union; *Farmborough* Parish. A leasehold cottage called the poor-house. Purchase money 28*l*.

" *Somerset; Clutton* Union; *Chew Stoke* Parish. Two freehold tenements, with a piece of garden ground. Purchase money 82*l*.

" *Hereford; Tenbury* Union; *Brimfield* Parish. A piece of freehold land, containing two roods twenty-nine perches, being part of a field called 'Sparnell Field.' Purchase money 32*l*.

A piece of freehold land called the 'Wetlands,' containing thirty perches. Purchase money 8*l*.

A piece of freehold land called 'Satchell Field,' containing thirty-five perches; and a piece of freehold land, being part of a piece of land called 'Dream Style,' containing one rood ten perches. Purchase money 22*l*.

"*Lincoln; Spilsby* Union; *Friskney* Parish. The parish workhouse, with four cottages and gardens. A piece of garden ground, containing one rood and thirty-five perches. Purchase money 238*l*.

"*Northampton; Uppingham* Union; *Gretton* Parish. Seven freehold cottages, situate in 'Little London,' together with the piece of ground occupied therewith. Purchase money 70*l*.

A freehold tenement, lately used as the parish workhouse, with a garden, and two other freehold tenements. Purchase money 138*l*."

The Commissioners issued the orders hereunder specified for the appropriation of the produce of the sale of parochial properties:—

"*Somerset; Yeovil* Union; *West Chinnock* Parish. For the application of 61*l*. 9*s*. 11*d*. in part payment of the proportion of the parish of the cost of building the Union workhouse.

"*Norfolk; Depwade* Union; *Tacolneston* Parish. For the investment of 101*l*. 12*s*. 6*d*. in the public funds.

"*Sussex; Steyning* Union; *New Shoreham* Parish. For the application of 37*l*. 6*s*. 8*d*. to defray the cost of a new valuation, and of 63*l*. 3*s*. 4*d*. towards the building of the Union workhouse.

"*Oxford; Banbury* Union; *Bodicott* Parish. For the application of 366*l*. 7*s*. to liquidate a debt under the provisions of the Act 1 and 2 Vic. c. 25, and of 78*l*. 9*s*. 4*d*. towards the building of the Union workhouse.

"*Norfolk; Aylsham* Union; *Heydon* Parish. For the application of 125*l*. towards the liquidation of a debt incurred under the provisions of the 22nd Geo. 3, c. 83.

"*Somerset; Langport* Union; *Langport* Parish. For the application of 45*l*. to defray the cost of a new survey, plan, and valuation, and for the investment of 42*l*. 17*s*. 6*d*. in the public funds.

"*Lincoln; Horncastle* Union; *Minningsby* Parish. For the application of 42*l*. 0*s*. 6*d*. in discharge of the proportion payable by the parish in respect of the cost of building the Union workhouse.

"*Devon; Torrington* Union; *Yarnscombe* Parish. For the application of 64*l*. 8*s*. in part payment of the proportion due from the parish in respect of the cost of building the Union workhouse.

"*Devon; Torrington* Union; *Langtree* Parish. For the application of 28*l*. 5*s*. 11*d*. as an investment in the public funds.

"*Essex; Maldon* Union. For the application of the several sums set opposite to the names of the under-mentioned parishes, towards the proportion payable by such parishes in respect of the cost of altering and enlarging the Union workhouse.

	£.	s.	d.
Stow Maries	26	12	5
Purleigh	284	6	6
Great Totham	109	9	1
Woodham Walter	132	12	7
Little Totham	95	12	8

"*Essex; Tendring* Union. For the application of the several sums, set opposite to the names of the under-mentioned parishes, towards the proportion payable by such parishes in respect of the cost of building of the Union workhouse.

	£.	s.	d.
Alresford	31	2	8
Ardleigh	271	19	5
Bentley, Little	46	18	5
Bradfield	40	15	4
Bromley, Little	65	10	0
Clacton, Great	176	18	8
Clacton, Little	13	13	10
Frating	44	13	6
Holland, Great	274	12	2
Kirby	247	19	0
Lawford	11	3	10
Manningtree	414	11	9
Mistley	278	6	4
St. Osyth	236	19	1
Tendring	277	13	2
Thorrington	57	16	0
Thorpe	204	12	10

And for the investment in the public funds of the sums set opposite to the names of the under-mentioned parishes—

	£.	s.	d.
Little Bromley	75	16	10
Manningtree	9	15	9"

LONDON:
Printed by order of the Poor Law Commissioners, by W. CLOWES and SONS, Stamford Street, and Published by CHARLES KNIGHT and Co., 22, Ludgate-street, Publishers to the Poor Law Commissioners.

AN

OFFICIAL CIRCULAR

OF PUBLIC DOCUMENTS AND INFORMATION:

DIRECTED BY THE POOR LAW COMMISSIONERS TO BE PRINTED, CHIEFLY FOR THE USE OF THE MEMBERS AND PERMANENT OFFICERS OF BOARDS OF GUARDIANS, UNDER THE POOR LAW AMENDMENT ACT.

No. 2. CIRCULAR ISSUED MARCH 9TH, 1840.

Poor Law Commission Office,
Somerset House,
March 6, 1840.

THE Poor Law Commissioners, on a review of their minutes, directed that the minutes and correspondence on the following subjects should be printed and circulated for the information of guardians and officers of the several Unions, viz.—

Signed, by order of the Board,
EDWIN CHADWICK, *Secretary.*

I. — RATING OF THE PROFITS OF STOCK IN TRADE TO THE RELIEF OF THE INDIGENT POOR.

Poor Law Commission Office,
Somerset House,
March 6, 1840.

THE Commissioners considered the effect of the decision in the case of Regina *v.* Lumsdaine, and the proceedings to be taken for the execution of the law as set forth in the decisions of the judges in other cases, which render stock in trade liable to be rated to the relief of the poor.

It appears to the Commissioners that the Overseers, in carrying the law into effect, and in framing new rates, will, unless they are informed, be in extreme danger of making illegal rates, and of creating serious inconvenience to the rate-payers, and incur much expense in litigation.

The evils generally incidental to the practice of rating stock in trade are stated by Lord Mansfield and others in the course of the arguments on the decided cases, and are otherwise well known; but the decision referred to leaves no discretion to the overseer on the subject. The Commissioners conceive, however, that the partial adoption of the law in isolated parishes will produce still further evils to such parishes. If, for example, stock in trade be rated in one place and not in another, the trade in the place where the stock is rated must be injured, since either profit must be diminished or the prices of goods must be increased in the particular place rated, and, consequently, trade be driven to those places where the stock is not rated. The tendency of the partial operation of the law, as the Commissioners conceive, would be ultimately to affect rents as well as trade mischievously; as it must follow that if the profits in trade in particular places are diminished by partial rating, the demand and the rent paid for shops in those places will also be ultimately affected.

The Board therefore directed that the following Circular Letter should be issued for the information of the Overseers of each parish throughout England and Wales:—

RATING OF STOCK IN TRADE.

Poor Law Commission Office,
Somerset House.
March 6, 1840.

GENTLEMEN,—Since the recent decision in the Court of Queen's Bench in the case of Regina *v.* Lumsdaine, in last Easter Term, it can no longer be doubted that inhabitants of parishes remain liable to the poor-rate in respect of stock in trade, in the like manner as they were before the passing of the Act to regulate parochial assessments, and that every rate may be successfully appealed against, if any inhabitant having productive stock in trade be omitted therefrom.

Since the decision of the above case, the Commissioners have been frequently applied to for instructions as to the form in which the rate in respect of stock in trade is to be made and the value estimated. This subject has always been one of the greatest practical difficulty, and the Commissioners regret that it is not in their power to obtain any advice on the subject which can be of much practical utility to the persons charged with the duty of making poor-rates. The Commissioners, however, conceive that the following remarks may be of some service:—

1st.—*The rate in respect of Stock in Trade can only be made upon persons who are actually inhabitants of the parish.* Persons not residing in the parish are in law frequently occupiers of lands, houses, &c., but no person can be rated for stock in trade unless he is *resident* within the parish. These are the words of Chief Justice Abbott in the case of Rex *v.* the Hull Dock Company (3 B. and C. 525), "Under the statute of Elizabeth there was no word applicable to personal property, and it was only on the ground of his being an *inhabitant* that any owner of personal property could be rated for that property, because there was no word in that statute to include him, except the word *inhabitant.* Under that statute, therefore, there was necessarily a distinction between residents and non-residents, *because the resident would be rateable for his personalty* within the place, the *non-resident not.* The distinction, however, under that statute applied only to those kinds of property which the statute did not specify, for the occupier of lands, houses, &c., and whatever the statute enumerated was rateable whether he were resident or not."

Those owners of stock in trade within the parish, who do not reside in the parish, must consequently be omitted from the rate in respect of stock in trade.

Residence, by reference to which the character of inhabitancy is to be determined, (see above, and also Rex *v.* Collinson, 12 East 342,) has been defined in the case of Rex *v.* North Currey, (4 B. and C. 953,) "to denote the place where an individual eats, drinks, and sleeps, or where his family or his servants eat, drink, and sleep."

2nd.—*The stock to be rated must be locally situate and visible within the parish in which its owner resides.* Earby's case, (2 Bulst. 354), Rex *v.* Shepheard, (1 B. and A. 109). It must not only be productive, but must be capable of being proved to be productive. Rex *v.* Macdonald, (12 East 324).

3rd.—It appears that it is not all the productive stock in trade which an inhabitant may be possessed of that is liable to the rate; it is only the clear liquidated surplus, after payment of all the owner's debts, which is considered to constitute his ability. "If personal property be rateable, it is not to be done at random, and to leave the party rated to get off as he can; but the officer making the rate must be able to support what he has done by evidence. And *no surplus property can be rated, but the clear liquidated surplus after paying all his debts.*" Rex *v.* White, (6 T. R. 777). Personal property, with reference to the poor-rate, was defined by Lord Mansfield in Rex *v.* Shalfleet, (2 Burr. 2001,) "the surplus of a man's estate and effects after payment of debts, the maintenance of his family, and necessary expenses." It is laid down that a trader may deduct the interest of borrowed capital, that being in the nature of an incumbrance upon his goods. Rex *v.* Dursley, (6 T. R. 53).

4th.—The determination of *the rateable value of stock in trade* is the chief subject of difficulty. The Parochial Assessments Act, which prescribes the rule for estimating the annual value of the various hereditaments, the subjects of occupation, and liable in that character to the poor-rate, has evidently no application to stock in trade, the nature of which does not admit of its being let at a rent.—It is, however, clear that the valuation of such stock in trade as may be rateable, must be made in respect of the profit which may be realized by its means, and not of its total present value as so much capital. Lord Ellenborough says, in Rex *v.* Macdonald (12 East, 324,) "Now, visible property in the place, such as stock in trade, merely as being *visible*, is not liable to be rated, but, to make it rateable, it must also be *productive;* but the justices have found that it was not productive, or, what is the same in effect, that it was not proved to be so to their satisfaction."

Generally, on account of the great difficulty of the subject, extreme caution must be used in determining the rateable value of stock in trade; and this is the more necessary, inasmuch as it is incumbent on the officers making the rate to show the grounds of their estimate. In R. *v.* Topham (12 East, 546), Lord Ellenborough says, that "when the question before the sessions is upon the quantum of the rate, the officers making it must show the justices some probable ground for the amount at which they charge the party in the rate."

5th.—It is a rule applicable to the rating, in respect of every kind of property, that the rate must show on its face the property in respect of which the rate is imposed. Rex *v.* the Undertakers of the Aire and Calder Navigation, (2 B. and C. 713).

The schedule to the Parochial Assessments Act (6 and 7 Wm. IV. c. 96) is generally inapplicable to the particulars which will be required to describe the assessment in respect to stock in trade. In such a rate the Commissioners would suggest that the persons rated should be placed together either at the beginning of the book or at the end before the declaration; that the entries should be numbered, as in the case of the rate on occupiers; that the persons rated should be described as inhabitants, and not as occupiers; that the property should be described as the "property in respect of which the inhabitant is rated;" and that against the name of the inhabitant the situation or locality, and the kind, and perhaps the quantity of stock, should be specifically described; that the annual value, or productiveness, or profit should be next estimated; and next, that the rate in the pound should be stated in the head of a column, and the sum assessed placed in that column opposite the inhabitant's name.

Signed, by order of the Board,

E. CHADWICK, *Secretary.*

II.—RELIEF OF DESTITUTION.

Correspondence of the Poor Law Commissioners with the Registrar-General on the subject of a passage in a Letter addressed to the Registrar-General by Mr. Farr, and published in the Appendix to the Registrar-General's First Annual Report.

Poor Law Commission Office,
Somerset House,
September 30, 1839.

SIR,—I am directed by the Poor Law Commissioners, to state that their attention has been drawn to the following passage in the letter from William Farr, Esq. on the registered causes of death, which is published in the appendix to your First Annual Report, p. 106.

"It will be seen with regret that in the half year the deaths of sixty-three individuals were ascribed (principally at inquests) to starvation; this is almost 1 annually, to a population of 111,000. The want of food implies a want of everything else, except water; as firing, clothing, every convenience, every necessary of life, is abandoned at the imperious bidding of hunger. Hunger destroys a much higher proportion than is indicated by the registers in this and in every other country, but its effects, like the effects of excess, are generally manifested indirectly, in the production of diseases of various kinds."

The statement that so many persons have in the course of six months perished of actual hunger, if left unexplained, appears to the Commissioners calculated to produce a belief that the provisions of the law, which are intended to bring relief within the reach of every one needing it, are either inadequate to their object or improperly administered; and I am therefore to request that the particulars of the cases on which such a statement is founded, may be communicated to them, in order that, if on inquiry, it should appear to be correct, some remedy for the evil may be provided, and if erroneous, means may be taken to remove the impression which it might otherwise serve to create.

The Commissioners also desire me to point out that in a subsequent passage of the same letter, p. 111, it is stated that the "Poor Law Inquiry, and Successive Parliamentary Committees, have shown that the families of agricultural labourers subsist upon a minimum of animal food, and an inadequate supply of bread and potatoes."

The Commissioners are not aware that there is any reason whatever for the belief that the agricultural labouring classes in this country are suffering from the want of an adequate supply of food, nor that the evidence taken by the Commissioners of Poor Law Inquiry, or before the Parliamentary Committees, would lead to such a conclusion, and they are desirous, therefore, of being informed of the particular portions of evidence on which the allegation contained in the passage above cited rests.

I have, &c.

EDWIN CHADWICK, *Secretary*.

J. H. Lister, Esq. &c.

The Poor Law Commissioners received from the Registrar-General, a copy of the registries described as those of the sixty-three cases above referred to, and also sixteen other additional cases, together with the following copy of a letter from Wm. Farr, Esq.

General Register Office,
29th November, 1839.

SIR,—I have examined the passages in my letter to which the attention of the Poor Law Commissioners has been directed, and submit to you "the particulars of the cases" which have been referred to the head "Starvation" in the abstracts.

It was considered that "starvation" would include the terms in the registers which imply death by privation, the want of warmth, and of proper food at all ages. It must not be understood to imply merely hunger.*

The passage in my letter (p. 106) states that sixty-three is not to be considered the true number of deaths from starvation, and that the want of proper food is generally accompanied with a want of all the other necessaries of life. To render the sense of the passage which Mr. Chadwick has quoted complete, the concluding sentence of the paragraph should have been given:—"*The privation is rarely if ever absolute;* the supply of food is inadequate to supply the wants of the organization, which requires daily animal or vegetable matter containing not less than nine ounces of carbon." Few die from the absolute want of food, while many die, or drag on a miserable existence upon insufficient, innutritious diet.

The effects of want vary at different ages, and in different circumstances, such as cleanliness, ventilation, and the extent to which the starvation is carried. But from the structure of the teeth and stomach, from all the experiments and facts, it appears that man requires a certain amount of *animal* and *vegetable* food; that the nature of this should be varied, and that the privation of proper food, according to the extent to which it is carried, produces death directly or indirectly by giving rise to diseases of various kinds.

In the present state of our knowledge it may be assumed that the quantity of food required by animals of every species, including man, is the average quantity of plain food that they consume in ordinary circumstances when the supply is not limited. The rations in the public service afford a fair standard. The English soldier's daily ration is bread, 16 ounces; beef or mutton, 12 ounces—16 ounces; besides vegetables, sugar, coffee, &c. The French soldier has bread, 26 ounces; meat, 8½ ounces. The carbon and nitrogen in the food represent its nutritive power (Prout, Bridgewater Treatise); the nitrogen should amount to 1¼ ounces—3 ounces, the carbon to 11 ounces. The carbon is converted into carbonic acid, is burnt, in fact; sustains the temperature of the body at blood heat, and escapes in respiration. The quantity of food should be proportional to the intensity and quantity of labour; the harvest-man will consume twice the amount of the soldier's ration, and twice as much as he requires in the short winter days. The human machine in this respect bears some resemblance to the steam-engine. But there are reservoirs of nutritive matter in the body, and a deficiency of a half or three-fourths, rarely produces any serious effect in less than 30 or 90 days, particularly if the place of nutritive matter be supplied by earth, &c., as it is in parts of America.

From a very able memoir, by Dalton, in the "Memoirs of the Manchester Philosophical Society," it appears that he consumed, on an average of 14 days, 23 ounces of bread, oatcake, and pastry; 2 ounces of potatoes; 4 ounces of butchers' meat; 9

* To starve, from the Anglo-Saxon, *starfan;* German, *sterben,* to die, to be destroyed, has the following acceptations according to Johnson:—

1. To perish.
2. To perish with hunger.
3. To be killed with cold.

"Have I seen the naked *starve* for cold."—Sandys.
"From beds of raging fire to *starve* in ice."—Milton.

4. To suffer extreme poverty.

"Sometimes virtue *starves* while vice is fed."—Pope.

5. To be destroyed with cold.

ounces of cheese; 31 ounces of milk; 22 ounces of tea; and beer daily. The whole containing 11½ ounces of carbon, 1½ ounces of nitrogen, nearly the same as the rations in the public service.

Assume, as we may very fairly, that full diet would contain carbon, 11 ounces; nitrogen, 2 ounces, = 13 ounces avoirdupois. Then the workhouse dietaries of the Poor Law Commissioners contain about 9¾ of these elements (8·7 ounces carbon, 1 ounce nitrogen), and the workhouse dietary is = 0·75 of full diet. Dr. Kay states that the average expense of maintenance in the workhouses of Norfolk and Suffolk would be "18*s*. a-week, or about 50*l*. a-year" for a man, his wife, and four children; and he found that of 120 families, whose number of children averaged 3·7 to a family, the annual income, including the earnings of the wife and children, was 35*l*. 9*s*. If the diet of the families out of the workhouses is in the same proportion, or = 0·8 of the workhouse dietary, it will follow that the families of agricultural labourers, in the employment of the great agriculturists of Norfolk and Suffolk, are upon but little better than half diet, = 0·6 of full diet. The gross income is 4*d*. *a-day* per head; and this furnishes the rent, firing, clothing, &c., as well as food.

From a series of facts before me, it appears that full diet cannot be procured by adults for less than 10*d*. a-day. Reduce it to 6*d*. for children, and the cheapness of coarse food, then the result will differ little from that stated above. The calculation proves to demonstration that the agricultural labourer can purchase scarcely any animal food. This appears to be the case, the family subsists upon potatoes, salt, bread (a limited quantity), and a small quantity of bacon.

In my letter, I state that "the food of the inhabitants of towns is as substantial as that of the agricultural labourer. The Poor Law Inquiry, and successive Parliamentary Committees, have shown that the families of agricultural labourers subsist upon a minimum of animal food, and an inadequate supply of bread and potatoes."

The "portions of evidence on which this allegation rests," will be found in the Appendix to the Poor Law Inquiry, answers to the question 29; whence it appears that the rate of labourers' wages is 5*s*. 10*d*., and seldom exceeds 9*s*. a-week. The labourers' family consists of about five individuals on an average; and the earnings of the wife and children can scarcely be estimated at 3*s*. a-week, if, indeed, they counterbalance with the harvest wages the labourers' loss of time by sickness and irregular employment.

The Parliamentary Papers furnish abundant evidence on the subject. It will be sufficient to refer to the evidence of the agricultural labourers themselves (probably the best judges), to Dr. Kay's valuable tables (14th Report, Appendix G.), to Mr. Turner's tables, and to those of Mr. Pearce and Mr. Marshall in the volumes of evidence taken in the last and previous sessions of Parliament.

I have the honour to be, Sir,
Your obedient Servant,

To the Registrar-General, WILLIAM FARR.
&c. &c. &c.

Poor Law Commission Office,
Somerset House,
February, 1840.

SIR,—The Poor Law Commissioners have had under their consideration the copy of a letter received by you from Mr. Farr, in explanation of his statement of the number of deaths which he reported to you as having been caused by starvation. They have also examined a copy of the particular cases on which he founds his statement. It appears to the Commissioners that the statement (in the sense in which it must have been understood by the public), is entirely unsustained by the facts from which it purported to be deduced. Mr. Farr, in his explanatory letter, says that the word "starvation," as used in the passage, "It will be seen with regret, that in the half-year, the deaths of 63 individuals were ascribed (principally at inquests) to *starvation*,"—"includes the terms in the register which imply death by privation, the want of warmth, and proper food at all ages. It must not be understood to imply merely hunger."

Although the word "starvation" may perhaps be considered to have the double sense of the privation of warmth as well as of food, Mr. Farr had himself supplied a definition which (whatever might be his own meaning), appears to the Commissioners to have restricted it to the understandings of others to cases of death caused by the inability to procure food.

"The want of food implies a want of everything else, except water; as firing, clothing, every convenience, every necessary of life, is abandoned at the imperious bidding of hunger. Hunger destroys a much higher proportion than is indicated by the registers in this and in every other country; but its effects, like the effects of excess, are generally manifested indirectly, in the production of disease of various kinds."

This description is further confirmed by the addition of the concluding sentence of the paragraph, which he states should have been given to render the sense of the paragraph complete. "The privation is rarely if ever absolute; the supply of food is inadequate to supply the wants of the organization, which requires daily animal and vegetable matter, containing not less than nine ounces of carbon."

On an examination of the particular cases the Commissioners observe, that instead of the sixty-three deaths having been ascribed "principally at inquests" to starvation, in only sixteen cases does it appear that any inquests were held; and it further appears that in the majority of the sixty-three cases the deaths were not ascribed in the registries to starvation, either in the sense of the privation of food, or the privation of warmth as usually understood. Not less than thirty-six of the cases appear to have been the cases of infants, of whom two were under the age of one week, seven under one month, eleven under two months, six under three months, and the rest under nine months, nearly all of whom died from various causes of mortality prevalent amongst the children of all classes, *e. g.*

Helen Elizabeth Thompson, aged three weeks, (condition of parent, a gentleman) died at No. 20, Whitmore-road, Hoxton. Cause assigned in the registry, "*Owing to malformation about the mouth, the child was incapable of deglutition, and gradually perished from want of sustenance.*"

Frederic Browning, aged eight months, father a woolcomber, died at Exeter workhouse. Cause assigned in the registry, "*Starved from malformation.*"

George Pugh, aged nine days, father a miller, died at Sutton-lane, Shrewsbury. Cause assigned in the registry, "*For want of nourishment after the death of the mother.*"

Edward Dopson, aged 19 days, father a carter, died at Stone-lane, Oxford, Ramsbury. Cause assigned in the registry, "*Want of proper nourishment, the mother having died in giving him birth.*"

Margaret Dalton, aged six weeks, parents' condition not stated, died at Aylesbury. Cause assigned in the registry, "*Brought up by hand, the mother diedin childbed.*"

George Chamberlain, aged three months, father a tailor, died at Mount Pleasant, Gosport. Cause assigned in the registry, "*Pined away for want of the breast; the mother died 16th of July, the child 23rd of August.*"

Henry Roberts, aged one month, parents' condition not stated, died at 16, Bury-street, Bloomsbury. Cause assigned in the registry, "*For want of the nourishment usually supplied by the mother.*"

The following are further exemplifications:—

Ellen Wombwell, aged six weeks and three days, the condition of parents not stated, died at West Hackney. Cause assigned in the registry, "*Atrophy from want of the breast-milk.*"

Andrew Austin, aged 14 weeks, father a shoemaker, died at West Hackney. Cause assigned in the registry, "*Atrophy from want of the breast-milk.*"

Thomas Ebenezer Edmonds, aged nine months, parents' condition not stated, died at 14, Albion-place, Newington. Cause assigned in the registry, "*Atrophy from weaning.*"

Sophia Browne, aged 16 weeks, parents' condition not stated, died at 33, Carnaby-street. Cause assigned in the registry, "*Occasioned through weaning.*"

John Owen, aged three weeks, parents' condition not stated, died at 9, United-buildings, Mary-le-bone. Cause assigned in the registry, "*Loss of the breast.*"

Of the remainder of the thirty-six cases of infants, the causes of death, in twelve cases, are ascribed simply to "inanition;" the deaths of two others are occasioned "through weaning;" seven "from the want of the nourishment usually supplied by the mother;" one, "probably, from want of proper food;" four to "atrophy for want of breast milk;" two others as follow:—

Ann Alcock, aged eight weeks, father a labourer, died at Swaffham. Cause assigned in the registry, "*Weak child, and had no breast-food.*"

Charlotte Clayden, aged seven months, father a shopkeeper, died at Henham. Cause assigned in the registry, "*Wasting away without fever after weaning.*"

The public could not have understood that cases such as these, casualties incidental to infant nurture, were denoted by the terms in which they and the whole of the sixty-three cases (including the thirty-six cases of infant mortality) are characterized as arising from one all-pervading cause, "the want of food:" and that "firing, clothing, every necessary of life" were abandoned by these infants "at the imperious bidding of hunger." The Commissioners are equally at a loss to comcomprehend the application of the following terms:—

"The privation is rarely, if ever, absolute; the supply of food is inadequate to the organization, which requires daily animal or vegetable matter, containing not less than nine ounces of carbon." To these thirty-six cases of infants whose natural food is stated to be a pint or a pint and a half of milk daily, containing, perhaps, one or two ounces of carbon in the whole quantity, and whose deaths in such cases as the following —

Harriet Parkin, aged 10 weeks, father a spectacle-frame maker, died in New George-street, Ecclesall Bierlow. Cause assigned in the registry, "*Weakness from want of natural sustenance from the mother.*"

—— Nash, aged six weeks, condition not stated, died at Croom's Hill, Greenwich. Cause assigned in the registry, "*Want of breast-milk.*"

might be ascribed, with more probability, not to the want of food, but to the extreme ignorance in administering proper nutriment to infants, which physicians represent as too often found in the labouring classes, many of whom, on the loss of the mother, offer broth, or even gin, instead of milk, as means of sustenance.

In such cases as those last cited of infant deaths, and also in such cases as the following of adults—

Susannah Waddington, aged 18 years, died at Halifax. Cause assigned in the registry, "*Inflammatory fever from exposure to cold,*"

there is nothing to show that indigence was a primary cause. So far from "privation," either of food or shelter being generally assignable in all the cases in which the term "starvation" is used, excess is distinctly assigned in several, as in the following, which are sent as cases of starvation in addition to those comprised in the sixty-three cases in question.

Charles Allen, a beggar, aged 46 years, died at the house for farmed poor, Lombard-street, St. George the Martyr. Cause assigned in the registry, "*Natural death, accelerated by intemperance and exposure to cold.*"

Sarah Page, a married woman, aged 50 years, died at Buxton. Cause assigned in the registry, "*Found dead; exposure to cold all night in a state of intoxication.*"

Benjamin Ollerinshaw, slater, aged 50 years, died at Longnor. Cause assigned in the registry, "*Intoxication and exposure to cold.*"

Gerrard Potter, shopkeeper, aged 89 years, died at Adlington. Cause assigned in the registry, "*Surfeit from exposure to cold, as sleeping in a wood.*"

Benjamin Dawson, woolcomber, aged 46 years, died at Warley. Cause assigned in the registry, "*Died from excessive drinking, and exposure to the weather.*"

On examination of the registered causes of the deaths of adults it appears that in a large portion of the remainder of the cases, death was ascribed, not to hunger, but to the exposure to cold from casualties such as wayfarers or persons of the labouring classes are exposed to from accident or want of caution, without reference to indigence, *e.g.*

William Cookham Ellis, a seaman, aged 19 years, died at Stockton on Tees. Cause assigned in the registry, "*Inclemency of the weather.*"

John Jones, farmer's servant, aged 14 years, died at Holywell. Verdict "*Found dead on the highway about* 9 *o'clock in the morning of the* 21*st of December*, 1837, *being starved in consequence of the very boisterous night of the* 20*th instant, in the parish of Ysceifiog.*"

Edward Marvin, a Chelsea pensioner, by trade a carpenter, aged 45 years, died at Deeping. Cause assigned in the registry, "*Found dead; died from natural cause, and from being exposed to the weather.*"

Male person, unknown, died at Brentwood. Cause assigned in the registry, "*Died in consequence of exposure to cold.*"

Dorothy Thorpe, a widow, aged 77 years, died at Boroughbridge. Cause assigned in the registry, "*Died from starvation, in consequence of exposure to the inclemency of the weather.*"

The Commissioners are glad to find that of the cases investigated before coroners' juries, in but one case is any blame attached by the verdict to the administrators of relief, and that that case had been brought to the notice of the Commissioners, and made the subject of a special inquiry, and of the application of such remedy for the prevention of the future occurrence of such cases as then appeared available.

Charlotte Leonard, pauper, aged 71 years, died at the workhouse, Bethnal-green, Middlesex, 26th of October, 1837. Cause assigned in the registry, "*Died from want, occasioned by the gross neglect of the parochial authorities of St. Luke, Middlesex, and St. Matthew, Bethnal-green.*"

Of the seven other cases classed as arising from hunger, and the voluntary abandonment of food, but ascribed by coroner's juries to various causes, one case is a case of murder:

Elizabeth Breadman, a bastard, aged two days, died at Kingsclere, Hants, 1st of September, 1837. Cause assigned in the registry, "*Pressure and exposure; verdict against the mother, 'Murder.'*"

and another is a case of manslaughter:

Benjamin Broadway, apprentice, aged 18 years, died at the workhouse, Islington, Middlesex, 10th of August, 1837. Cause assigned in the registry, "*Starvation; Manslaughter against Wm. Smith.*"

The Commissioners have directed inquiries to be made as to the particulars of several of the cases when the causes of death have been ascribed by coroner's juries to starvation in the sense of the privation of food; and they have received statements of evidence respecting them, from which it appears that no blame is justly imputable in the cases either to the parish or to the union officers, nor any defects in the administration of relief which has not always been sought by the deceased where it was available. On the face of the registry it appears that the deaths of several were either voluntary or wilful, or suicidal, *e. g.*

Benjamin Miller, late a soldier and pensioner, aged 46 years, died at Tuxford, Nottinghamshire, 24th of July, 1837. Cause assigned in the registry, "*Want and exposure, arising from insanity.*"

Of this class of cases are the two following:

Jane Morris (condition of life not stated), aged 47 years, died in the House of Industry, Oswestry, Salop, 18th of September, 1837. Cause assigned in the registry, "*For want of the common necessaries of life, refusing the protection of the house.*"

Esther Beaumont (condition not stated), aged 57 years, died at Sheffield, Brightside Bierlow, Yorkshire, 31st of August, 1837. Cause assigned in the registry, "*Want of the common necessaries of life.*"

The answer made to the inquiries of the Commissioners in this case by the clerk of the Union is as follows:

"Esther Beaumont resided in Brightside Bierlow, and was settled in Ecclesfield, from which parish she has been in the habit of receiving a small weekly allowance. Some time previous to her death (August, 1837) this allowance was discontinued by the overseers, who gave an order for the workhouse, from a desire to benefit the woman, but which she refused to accept. Her situation was not known to any of the officers of this Union until it was too late to render any assistance, and no blame was attached either to them or to the officers of Ecclesfield, which at that time was not in Union."

What may have been the influences which governed the two individuals, in the two last cases, the Commissioners have no means of knowing; but the false and mischievous statements propagated respecting the new modes of administering relief, which have in some instances occasioned the refusal of bread offered as out-door relief—refusals made on the supposition that it was poisoned, have prepared the Commissioners to expect the occurrence of such instances, as the natural effects of such statements upon weak and ignorant minds.

In respect to the use of the ambiguous term of "starvation" by coroners' inquests, the Commissioners find that it is applied on very uncertain conjecture, especially where the body is not opened and carefully examined. For example, in the following case:

Thomas Kitchen, formerly a servant, aged 43 years, died in the parish of St. Giles-in-the-Fields, and St. George, Bloomsbury, Middlesex, 8th of November, 1837. Cause assigned in the registry, "*Visitation of God, being at the time in great want of the common necessaries of life.*"

The Commissioners are informed that the deceased was a man who got his living by selling tracts; that on the night before his decease he left a beer-house in Drury-lane, where he had been drinking in company with two others with whom he took up his abode in the attic of a house occupied by some labouring people, and in the course of the forenoon he was found dead on the floor. He had some halfpence in his pocket, and had made no application for relief. He had been previously ill, and it was believed from a letter in his pocket that he had been the subject of medical examination. He was believed to be a common beggar of the description frequenting that neighbourhood. The neighbourhood where the death occurred is one inhabited by some of the most wretched of the population in the metropolis, and it is stated by the officer employed to collect evidence for the inquests in that neighbourhood, as well as by other witnesses, that such an occurrence as a death, proved to have arisen from the absolute privation of food, or from the inadequacy of the common necessaries of life, or from the inadequacy of legal relief which is known and open to all the destitute, has not occurred within that district, or been alleged on any coroner's verdict, during the last ten years.

In the following case:

Robert Laycock, a pauper, printer, aged 28 years, died at the workhouse, St. Sepulchre's, London, 30th of December, 1837. Cause assigned in the registry, "*Consumption and destitution.*"

the indefinite terms of the verdict would admit of various interpretations, but the evidence upon it is characteristic of the causes:

"Jordan Lynch, of King-street, Snow-hill, surgeon, says, 'I made a post-mortem examination of the body of the deceased to-day; I found him in an extreme state of emaciation; there were spots of secondary venereal disease on the legs, and I found the bones of the nose and larynx to have been moved by disease; I found the liver to have been diseased by drinking ardent spirits; I found the stomach small and contracted from want of food; I found the lungs in a high state of inflammation, and that was the approximate cause of death; want had diminished the powers of life, and exposure to the cold air was prejudicial to him; the inflammation of the lungs was the cause of his death; I think any relief in that stage was unavailing."

The Commissioners observe upon these last cited cases as exemplifications of their grounds for believing that the correct course is to restrain the inferences from such statements below the terms which happen to be used, rather than to extend them beyond their ordinary meaning. Thus instead of the returns proving the existence of one all-pervading cause of mortality, hunger, when examined, and so far as they serve as data, they prove the reverse. Of the 63 cases, it appears that there are, of the various casualties of

Infant mortality, malformation, inanition, weaning, inability to take proper nourishment, &c.	36
Murder	1
Manslaughter	1
Starvation, ascribed to cold by coroners' juries	6
———, by the Registrars	6
———, ascribed to hunger or want of proper food by coroners' inquests	7
———, by the Registrars	6
	63

In respect to the several cases of death from hunger which are not accounted for, the Commissioners find that from the great length of time which has elapsed since their occurrence, and from the administration of relief in the places where they occurred having been imperfectly organized, there was no probability of obtaining sufficiently correct results to repay the trouble of a special inquiry into them. But even as they appear on the face of the registries they do not sustain, but rather rebut, any inference as to the want of food having been a prevalent cause of death. Any cause of hunger or destitution equally pervading a whole class of the population at the same time and place must be attended with effects as extensive as the cause. Now the cases of death which are ascribed to the want of food (which want may possibly have arisen from indigence) will be seen to have occurred almost singly in different and distant places at various times, and that almost every individual who has so died is of a distinct class or occupation.

Taking these cases last specified to be cases where the want of food has arisen from accidental, isolated, and individual causes, the Commissioners, nevertheless, deem them the subject of very serious consideration. Whilst they consider it a duty to remove, as far as may be in their power to do so, false and exaggerated impressions as to the frequency of death by hunger, they would not diminish the feeling of anxiety on the occurrence of any single case of death arising from absolute want amidst a community in which so heavy a tax is paid for the prevention of such casualties. They conceive that, for the maintenance of the care for life and social feelings of anxiety for the relief of suffering, which characterize a civilized people, every such case should be the subject of a careful inquiry, with the view to the adopting of any available measures for the prevention of the recurrence of similar casualties. They are concerned to find, so far as appears from the copies of the registries you have supplied to them, that nearly as many cases of death from the want of the necessaries of life have passed without inquiry as have been the subject of inquiry before coroners' juries, *e. g.*

Mary Harkness, an itinerant vender of thread and tapes, aged 62 years, died at the Workhouse, Church-street, St. Paul, Deptford, Kent, 18th of December, 1837. Cause assigned in the registry, "*Frostbitten and want.*"

Joseph Copley, husbandman, aged 44 years, died at Armley, Yorkshire, 26th of July, 1837. Cause assigned in the registry, "*No particular disease; a want of proper support.*"

Rebecca Baker, lodging-house-keeper, aged 27 years, died at St. Botolph, Lincoln, 27th of October, 1837. Cause assigned in the registry, "*Said to die from want.*"

William Croupe, beggar, aged about 50 years, died at Garstang, Lancashire, 16th of December, 1837. Cause assigned in the registry, "*General debility and insufficiency of food and lodging.*"

Mary Bryant, a widow, age not stated, died in the Poorhouse, Swansea, Glamorgan, 13th of December, 1837. Cause assigned in the registry, "*Debility, occasioned by want of food.*"

The Commissioners believe that the new registration, under your superintendence, may be made to serve as a new and valuable additional security against the omissions of due inquiry in the class of cases in question, as well as in others.

For the due and efficient administration of the large amount of money still raised for the relief of destitution, it appears to the Commissioners to be highly desirable that all cases, where death may have been proximately caused by indigence, should be carefully investigated, to ascertain whether from the mode of administering relief it has failed of its effect, and if so, what measures may be used for the most certain prevention of the like evils. With this view, and for their own as well as the public satisfaction, the Commissioners request that you will give directions that copies of the registries of cases of death, apparently occurring from indigence, may be furnished to them.

They propose, as an additional security, themselves to institute inquiries as to the causes of the death in those cases which may appear not to have been made the subjects of coroners' inquests, and to ascertain whether any and what remedies may be applied for the future. The Commissioners will, at the same time, apprize the clerks of the Unions that those cases, when made known to the Board, will form the subject of special inquiries; and charge them that they bring all such cases which may come to their knowledge, whether as superintending registrars or otherwise, immediately before the Boards of Guardians. The Commissioners will request the Guardians, the representatives of the rate-payers, to make due inquiries as to the cause of the death, and whether any and what blame appears to be imputable to the parish or the union officers, or whether it is ascribable to any and what defects in the arrangements for the administration of relief. The Commissioners are prepared to make the proceedings on such cases an exception to the rule, which prohibits the admission of strangers to Boards of Guardians.

In respect to the general observations on the sufficiency of food of the agricultural population, contained in the letter transmitted with the returns, the Commissioners submit to you that, inasmuch as it is only from the particulars on the face of the returns that the stated conclusions must have been understood by the public to have been deduced, the different facts or speculations by Mr. Farr are inadmissible as justifications of the mis-statements of the causes of mortality set forth in the registers. When those registers specify several different causes, the Commissioners conceive that no reference to the facts or reasonings of the most eminent chemists will justify the representation that the registers assign the mortality to one all-pervading cause.

The Board do not doubt that Dr. Dalton and the other eminent men referred to would deduce correct conclusions from the facts before them, but the Commissioners have no means of judging of the correctness and adequacy of those facts, or of their applicability to any large proportion of the labouring population. The subject of the food of the independent labourers does not come within the Commissioners' province, otherwise than as the subject of observation and as a standard for comparison with the condition of those who are occasionally dependent on parochial relief.

The Commissioners, of course, desire that the labouring classes of this kingdom should enjoy the largest possible share of the comforts and necessaries of life, which is compatible with their condition; but the Commissioners cannot overlook the fact, that the labouring classes in many countries subsist in health and strength without the allowance of animal food which Mr. Farr declares to be necessary for the proper sustentation of life.

No ordinary man saves a shilling whilst he is subjected to the imperious call of hunger, or is in need of a loaf, or of what he deems the necessaries of life. The increasing amount of upwards of 20,000,000*l.* of deposits in the savings' banks, almost wholly from those of the labouring classes who are frugal, attest the amount of means at their disposal beyond a bare subsistence. Amongst the contributors to savings' banks are found many agricultural labourers, whose wages are not higher than the ordinary wages of their fellows of the same class. Amongst the contributors to the savings' bank of Exeter and Devon, as an example, though a distinguished one, there were, according to the last returns, 2,558 agricultural labourers and husbandmen, whose aggregate amount of deposits was 84,880*l.* But the surplus means of the great mass of the labouring population is unfortunately more strikingly marked by their expenditure for immediate gratification, than by their frugal reserves for more full comfort and enjoyment. A sum of 8,444,800*l.*, or nearly double the amount expended as poor rates, is annually paid as duty on gin, whiskey, rum, and other spirits, the ultimate cost of which to the consumer cannot (the Commissioners believe) be less than two-thirds more, or nearly 24,000,000*l.* per annum, for spirits chiefly consumed by the labouring classes, exclusively of upwards of 3,000,000*l.* of duty on tobacco, and of 4,000,000*l.* of duty on malt and hops; the cost of which commodities, and of the beer, to the consumers will be scarcely less in amount than the cost of spirits; making an aggregate of not less than between 40,000,000*l.* and 50,000,000*l.* per annum, (*i. e.* in one year, more than double the aggregate of deposits in savings' banks during more than 20 years,) expended as comforts and luxuries, principally by labouring men in England and Wales.

The Commissioners think that Mr. Farr's statements respecting the insufficient food of the labouring classes, are not supported by his references to the evidence taken before the Committee of the House of Commons, which sat in the Session of 1837-8. As he was some time in attendance before that committee as one of the principal medical witnesses against the administration of the New Poor Law, he might have been aware that the subject of the food of the labouring classes did not form a main or even a collateral part of the inquiry; and that, neither as respects the labouring classes, nor the paupers, was the subject of their diet introduced otherwise than incidentally. The only workhouse dietary on which, so far as the Commissioners recollect, any specific inquiries were made, was the dietary of the West Hampnet Union, on which the following evidence was given:—

"3633. Do you know whether, since this workhouse has been established, there has ever been any dearth of provisions?—Never.

"3634. Do you happen to know whether it has ever occurred, that all the provisions have not been consumed?—Certainly.

"3635. Do you know whether it has been calculated what amount of provisions has been left unconsumed?—I have for a period which I cannot from recollection speak to with great accuracy, whether it be a fortnight or three weeks, but it was from the information of the governor, that within a period, which he named, he had found a surplus of 60 loaves of four pounds each, which were not consumed."

The tables referred to by Mr. Farr, are tables not of the amounts of food, but of money obtained as wages by certain labourers, whose cases were adduced to prove that they had, by the change of the law, simply lost the amount of their former allowances from the parish; and with respect to whom it was proved, according to the Report of the Committee of the House of Commons, that the amount of employment has greatly increased, the wages of regular labour are substituted for parish pay for doing nothing or worse than nothing, and the amount received in wages is actually 8*l.* more than the parish pay under the former system.

The Commissioners believe that the proved tendency of the labouring classes to improvement would be arrested, and that any temporary distress or diminution of comforts amongst particular classes in particular places, caused by the fluctuations of trade, must only be ultimately aggravated by the practice of mendicity, by alms giving, or misdirected charity, which always creates greater evil than it cures:—that mendicity and its train of vices can only be promoted by unfounded representations of the existence of all-pervading causes of privation, suffering, and death—"hunger," which, it is alleged, destroys a much higher proportion than is indicated by the registers in this or any other country.

I have, &c.

EDWIN CHADWICK, *Secretary.*

III.—ADMISSION OF PAUPERS TO THE WORKHOUSE.

THE Board took into consideration the following application for advice from the Board of Guardians of the Honiton Union respecting their power to refuse admission of a pauper and his family into the workhouse:—

"*Honiton Union, Devon. Board Meeting, Monday,* "*1st January,* 1840.

"SIRS,—I am instructed by the Board of Guardians of the Honiton Union to request your opinion on the following cases:—

"1st. A pauper applied to the Board for an order for admission into the workhouse for himself and family; this was refused, but relief ordered for him out of the house. Had the Board power to refuse the application, his destitution being admitted by relief being ordered?

"2d. Have the Board power to refuse an order for the admission of a man and his family into the workhouse, and also refusing out-relief as they consider the man not in a state of destitution?

"3rd. There is an able-bodied man and his family in the house, who can be provided with sufficient work to maintain them in his own parish. Have the Board power to discharge him from the house without a residence being provided?

"I have the honour to be, Sirs,
"Your obedient Servant,
(Signed) "HENRY CHARLES MULES."

"*To the Poor Law Commissioners,*
"*Somerset House.*"

The Commissioners stated in reply:

1. As regards the first case submitted to them, the Commissioners are of opinion that if a pauper whose destitution is admitted, apply for admission into the workhouse for himself and family, the Guardians have the power to refuse the application, and to order out-door relief if they think fit, provided the latter mode of relief be not prohibited by any rule of the Commissioners.

2. The Commissioners are of opinion that the Guardians have the power to refuse an application for an order for the admission of a man and his family into the workhouse, and also to refuse out-door relief, if they consider the man and his family not to be in a state of destitution, so as to require relief.

The Commissioners, however, must observe, that this course of proceeding exposes the Guardians to serious responsibility if their decision should turn out to be erroneous, and if the destitution of the applicant, being real, should lead to death or permanent injury.

3. With respect to your third question, the Commissioners wish to state that being fully satisfied that in all ordinary cases a labourer will prefer the ordinary labour and wages of his class to a residence in the workhouse, they are extremely unwilling that relief in the workhouse should be refused to those who apply for it, or that any compulsion should be used in order to compel a labourer to quit the workhouse.

Extraordinary circumstances, however, do rarely occur in which either from obstinacy or peculiarity of disposition, a labourer in the workhouse prefers remaining therein to accepting an offer of work at adequate wages; and for such instances the laws appear to have provided a remedy.

If the pauper, upon being offered work at competent wages for the support of himself and family, refuses to accept the offer, he should be dealt with under the third section of the Vagrant Act, and his family should be relieved in the workhouse.

This course, however, cannot be adopted when the labourer is absolutely unable to find a habitation for himself and family within a reasonable distance from his work; although the fact of such residence being out of the parish in which the work is procurable is immaterial.

For such cases, which are necessarily rare, the Commissioners have only to suggest that the workhouse must be exclusively relied on, and the pauper should continue to be relieved therein, until an offer of work which would admit of the pauper's procuring the proper necessaries of life for himself and his family can be obtained.

IV.—THE NEW POSTAGE REGULATIONS:—FACILITIES AFFORDED TO LABOURERS FOR THE TRANSMISSION OF SMALL SUMS OF MONEY TO THEIR FAMILIES, OR TO FRIENDLY SOCIETIES, OR SAVINGS' BANKS.

THE Board having received a letter from the Lords Commissioners of Her Majesty's Treasury announcing to them that the privilege of official franking was discontinued, the Commissioners thereupon directed that the following letter should be sent to the Boards of Guardians:

Poor Law Commission Office,
Somerset House, January 8, 1840.

SIR,—I am to inform you that as the Commissioners' privilege of franking and of receiving letters free has been abolished by the New Post Office regulations, it will be desirable, inasmuch as the omission of pre-payment will subject the letters to double postage, that you should pre-pay all letters directed to them. You will ask of the Guardians a sum to enable you to defray the postage expenses, for the expenditure of which you will account and be allowed according to the number of letters which it may appear by your minutes or copies of correspondence, you may have sent. When arrangements for the issue of stamps shall have been made, the facilities for accounting will be much increased.

Signed by order of the Board,
E. CHADWICK, *Secretary.*
To the Clerk to the Board of Guardians.

The Commissioners desire to bring to the attention of the Guardians the enclosed copies of correspondence with the Guardians of the Stockport Union; and the Commissioners also request the Guardians to make known to the servants or labourers in their employment, and to the members of friendly societies of which they may be patrons, and to the contributors to savings' banks of which they may be trustees, the facilities now afforded for the transmission of small amounts of money as deposits, subscriptions, or otherwise. By the new regulations of the Lords Commissioners of Her Majesty's Treasury, parties may send in a small sheet of note paper, coin of the following amounts:—

In silver,	2*s.*	or	½ oz.	for 1 penny.
,,	4*s.* 6*d.*	,,	1 ,,	2 pence.
,,	9*s.* 6*d.*	,,	2 ,,	4 pence.
In gold, ½ sovereign and 1*s* in silver	11*s.*	or	½ oz.	for 1 penny.
,, 1½ sovereigns,	30*s.*		½ oz, ,,	1 penny.
,, 3 sovereigns			1 oz.	2 pence.
,, 6½ sovereigns			2 oz.	4 pence.

A 5*l.* note, or Bank of England note of any amount might be added to the above sums, or to a sum less in each case, the smallest coin, as 4*d.*

The Commissioners are informed that where it is necessary for the labouring classes to transmit pence or odd amounts of money for which there is no silver coinage, such as 1*d.* 2*d.* 3*d.* when the postage stamps are prepared, it will be a convenient arrangement available to the public to transmit stamps instead of coin.

THE following are copies of some correspondence on the subject between the Board of Guardians of the Stockport Union and the Poor Law Commissioners, and the Honourable E. J. STANLEY, one of the under-secretaries of the Treasury, on the subject of the conveyance of money through the post by the labouring classes:—

"Stockport, 1st of 8th Month, 1839.

"ESTEEMED FRIEND E. CHADWICK,—Allow me to hand thee, for the information of the Poor Law Commissioners, the annexed minute of the Board of Guardians of this Union, respecting the fees payable on taking out post-office orders:—

"The Board have had in view the great number of operatives working at a distance from their families, as well as the hundreds of labourers employed on the line of railway adjoining Stockport

"Of the latter, scarcely one-fourth belong to this neighbourhood, and many of these industrious men are, unhappily, surrounded by interested persons, who frequently tempt them to dissipate their earnings, to the injury of themselves and their families.

"It does, therefore, appear desirable to afford additional facilities to labouring men, whilst working remote from home, frequently to remit small sums to their families; and I hope ere long the plan may be yet further simplified, by allowing clerks of public works,* and respectable manufacturers and tradesmen, to grant money orders, payable at the respective post towns, and account for the same to the post-office in London, or those in the country.

"By these, or similar alterations in the system, it is likely the humbler classes of society would avail themselves of the means of sending monies to their connexions much more frequently than at present, and there is reason to hope the object of the Commissioners and Guardians would thereby be promoted.

"We shall be obliged by the assistance of the Commissioners in reference to this subject, and by being informed of the result.

"Thy friend, very respectfully,
(Signed) "JOS. CHRISTY."

"*Board of Guardians, Stockport Workhouse,*
"*July* 31, 1839

"POST-OFFICE ORDERS.

"The Money Order-office in London, and the country agencies therewith connected, are understood to have been established to enable mechanics, seamen, operatives, and others, to remit small sums of money to their families and poor relatives at a distance.

"Although this intention has no doubt been partially attained, yet the benefits of the plan would, it is believed, be greatly extended by a still further reduction of the fees payable on making small remittances; thereby giving additional encouragement to industrious men working at a distance from home, and thus exposed to increased temptations, to remit to their families from time to time portions of their earnings, which at present are too often wasted in dissipation. This remark applies particularly to the thousands of labourers employed on railways and other public works, many of whom have families at a great distance, often suffering by their absence.

"The fees charged at present on money orders and the proposed alterations are as follow:—

* The earnings of labourers on public works, &c. would often be saved from waste, if they could obtain Post-office orders at the time of receiving their wages.

"*Present Fees.*—On any sum not exceeding 20*s.*, 6*d.*; not exceeding 40*s.*, 1*s.*; afterwards, 6*d.* in the pound to £5.

"*Proposed Fees.*—On any sum not exceeding 10*s.*, 2*d.*; not exceeding 20*s.*, 3*d.*; not exceeding 30*s.*, 4*d.*; not exceeding 40*s.*, 6*d.*; afterwards, 3*d.* in the pound to £5.

"A minute having been read to this Board respecting the fees on post-office orders, this meeting approves the same; and the vice-chairman is desired to forward a copy thereof to the Secretary of the Poor Law Commissioners, in London, and request the aid of the Commissioners to carry the same into effect.

(Signed) "JOS. CHRISTY, Chairman."

Poor Law Commission Office,
Somerset House, October 14, 1839.

SIR,—I have submitted your letter of the 1st of August, and the minute of the Board of Guardians of the date of the 31st July, to the Poor-law Commissioners, and I am directed to convey their thanks to you and the Board for having called their attention to the subject.

"The Commissioners, considering this an appropriate time for submitting the facts to the consideration of the Lords Commissioners of her Majesty's Treasury, have directed that the Board's Minute, together with your letter, should be transmitted to them, together with the additional suggestions made by the Commissioners, and set forth in their letter, a copy of which I am directed to enclose for your information.

I have the honour to be, Sir,
Your obedient servant,
(Signed) E. CHADWICK, Secretary.

Jos. Christy, Esq., Vice-Chairman to the Stockport Union, Stockport.

(Copy.)

Poor Law Commission Office,
Somerset House, October 14, 1839.

SIR,—I am directed by the Poor-law Commissioners to request that you will move the Lords Commissioners of her Majesty's Treasury, that they will take into consideration the subject of the annexed copy of a letter from the Vice-Chairman of the Board of Guardians of the Stockport Union, and of a minute of the Board of that Union, in connexion with any measures which their Lordships may have in preparation for the establishment of a uniform penny postage.

Amongst the classes who claim relief from the poor-rates on the ground of temporary destitution are often found the wives and families of labourers who are alleged to be absent in work, or in search of work. Many of the migratory classes of labourers, when they obtain work at places beyond a day's journey from their own houses, do not transmit any portion of their earnings to their families for their support.

Whilst the Commissioners are compelled to ascribe much of such omissions to profligate habits, they have reason to believe that much more is ascribable to the want of facilities, and to factitious hinderances to the performance of the social and legal duties of those labourers who are in receipt of adequate earnings.

The labourers on railroads, who frequently earn nearly double the ordinary rate of wages, and others who are absent and engaged on particular descriptions of work, might even, after allowing for the increased cost of living at a distance from their own homes, set aside from their earnings such sums as a shilling, eighteen-pence, half-a-crown, or three shillings, which they might transmit weekly to their families, and render them material service by such additions to the earnings of their wives, or to other means; but hitherto the postage of a single letter (not to speak of the postage of a double letter, or the tax for the transmission of a money order), as it absorbs the whole, or a half, or a third of the most important savings to a labourer's family, has operated as an almost insuperable bar to the formation of frugal habits, or to the performance of the duties in question in such cases.

The like want of facilities for the transmission of small sums has operated as a bar to the exercise of filial affection in the transmission of contributions from labourers for the support or comfort of parents, or other relations.

In other respects the want of facilities for the transmission of small sums of money appears to operate as a serious obstacle to the formation of frugal habits by the labouring classes.

The savings' banks are situated at considerable distances from a large proportion of the population, especially in the thinly-populated districts. If the small sums saved—the one or two shillings or half-a-crown, which the labouring man may from time to time be able to set aside, be not immediately placed out of continually recurring and immediate temptation, they are soon lost But to transmit such sums to the savings' bank, at present a journey of five or six miles or more to the market town would be requisite, or an amount of labour which would go far to consume the amount of money saved.

Those savings' banks appear to have been the most prosperous where the clergy have undertaken to collect subscriptions, and avail themselves of the opportunities for going to the town to deposit them in the savings' banks. But it must be apparent that a large proportion of the population have not the means of obtaining such facilities, and others are reluctant to intrust any second person with the knowledge of their means of saving. It is observed of the savings' banks in the metropolis, that a large proportion of the depositors reside in the district in which other savings' banks are situated, and it is surmised that they make deposits in distant banks from a desire to maintain the privacy of their own affairs.

The Commissioners would request their Lordship's more particular attention to the inconvenience of the transmission of small sums of money by a money order as it is now given, though for such purposes it were given gratis. The money transmitted by a money order is only payable to the person in whose favour the order is made. The time of an artisan in work is commonly less easily spared than the time of a tradesman or of a wealthy person, for the purpose of going to receive a small payment at the Post-office. In the rural districts such a form of payment would frequently incur the necessity of a journey of several miles, or labour of the value of the payment itself. In the case of aged persons, such a form of payment would offer very serious obstacles—in the case of bed-ridden persons, to whom small sums might be transmitted by their children or natural relations, it would form an insuperable obstacle. Labouring men who are taken to a distance from their usual places of occupation, find the same difficulties in forwarding their contributions to their sick-clubs as to the savings' banks. When the member of a club falls sick at a distance from the club-house, equal difficulty is found in transmitting his payments to him.

The bulk of the distant subscriptions to sick-clubs, and of payments from them are sent by hand. Scarcely any instances are known where the money is transmitted through the post by money orders to the sick members of such clubs; and, for the reasons stated, the existing form of payment by money orders would be impracticable. Indeed, so far has this mode of transmission of small sums for payments to non-resident paupers been hitherto found ineligible by parishes, that they have generally transmitted them at much trouble by the coachmen or carriers, for the advantage of the direct delivery.

The Commissioners consider that, in all probability, the establishment of practical facilities for the transmission of small amounts of money would, in this class of cases, be attended with great moral as well as pecuniary advantages.

A large proportion of labourers have sufficient of self-restraint to set aside small sums weekly, who are unable to resist the temptations to spend larger sums when in their own possession.

If, from what is already done under difficulties by one small portion of the labouring population, an inference may be drawn of what may be done with facilities by the greater proportion of the population who possess the like means of exercising the same virtues, it appears probable that when the knowledge of the cheapness of such conveyance, and the trust-worthiness thereof is propagated, considerable sums would be saved and transmitted for the accomplishment of the highly desirable objects now seriously impeded.

The Commissioners take occasion to observe that the poorer classes of Irish labourers are distinguished by their manifestations of the strength of such affections, by their self-denial in saving and carrying money about them, at much personal risk, to convey it to relations or friends at home.

There appears to be no means of ascertaining the amounts of money transmitted to Ireland by Irish labourers in England and Wales; but from the known amounts of their earnings and the known frugality of the modes of living of a large proportion of the Irish labourers in this country, there is reason to believe that the amount of money meritoriously saved and carried back, or transmitted by them to Ireland, is in the total considerable.

The Commissioners conceive that, with the facilities which they hope a cheap postage may afford, such payments would often be made at more frequent and convenient intervals than in the comparatively larger sums now accumulated, to make the transmission worth the present cost. It is believed that the charge of 1*d.* would afford no serious obstacle to the transmission of sums amounting to 1*s*. or upwards, which form the greater proportion of the sums for which facilities appear to be highly desirable, and that the greater bulk of such postage would be entirely the creation of such facilities; the sums required to be transmitted would be rarely more than 5*s*., or 2*s*. 6*d*., or half-an-ounce, which weight is understood to be under their Lordship's consideration as the general scale for single letters.

In the transmission of sums for small payments in the immediate administration of the Poor Laws, the Commissioners believe that considerable advantage would frequently be derived from an improved system of postage.

Where it might appear to a Board of Guardians that a labourer in work in a distant county might contribute a small sum to the discharge of an obligation to the parish for the maintenance of his family or offspring, the want of facilities for the transmission of such sums would not longer operate, as it now does, as a bar to salutary arrangements on behalf of poor families.

The Commissioners take the occasion to notice, as within their own experience of the delivery of letters in remote and thinly populated districts, that letters containing notices and orders in the public service to the overseers of parishes in Wales, have been delayed for considerable periods, and on inquiry it has been found that it has not been the practice in such districts to deliver letters, but to allow them to remain in the window of the post-office, until, from some person seeing a letter in the window, the fact of the existence of such a letter came to the knowledge of the person to whom it was directed; and the Commissioners have had reason to believe that overseers or others, on seeing in the windows letters under the official frank, have concluded that the act of calling for them would involve some labour, and have purposely abstained from taking them. The Commissioners have therefore been advised that it is necessary to provide in such cases for the delivery of letters by some special agency, and they have, in such cases where it appeared necessary to insure the delivery of a letter to an overseer, forwarded it to the Clerk of the Union, with directions that it should be delivered by a relieving officer. In some instances these officers traverse their districts at regular intervals, and in places where the expense of the delivery would seriously outweigh the cost of providing a person to go on foot for the purpose. The Commissioners submit that it might be deserving of inquiry, whether the officers in such districts may not inform the postmaster of their ordinary routes, that he may avail himself of them, when special occasion arises, without any additional expense.

The Commissioners do not pretend to offer an opinion on the whole subject of the proposed change: they confine themselves to a request that the facts which they have indicated as coming within their own observation, and those set forth in the annexed communications from the Vice-Chairman of the Board of Guardians of the Stockport Union may be submitted to their Lordships' consideration.

(Signed) By order of the Board,
E. CHADWICK, *Secretary*.

Honourable E. J. Stanley, &c.

VI.—CLAIMS TO RELIEF OF ARMY AND NAVY PENSIONERS.

THE Commissioners having had before them frequent instances of loss and destitution, occasioned by payments to army and navy pensioners of money, in quarterly or other payments, in large amounts, presenting irresistible temptations to extravagance and mismanagement, which would not probably occur, if the payments were made in smaller amounts, and at shorter intervals, considered it expedient to make special inquiries, to enable them to form a more complete judgment of the nature and extent of the evil. With this view they directed the following queries to be issued to the officers of those Unions in which it appeared probable there would occur the greatest number of cases of the assignments of such pensions; but should the officers of any other Unions be in possession of any peculiar information with relation to the subject, they are requested to transmit it to the Commissioners.

1. Amongst the applicants for relief, have you had any and what cases of Greenwich and Chelsea out-pensioners, or of the wives and children of out-pensioners?
2. Number of such cases, if any on the list?
3. What are the circumstances under which the pensioners become applicants for relief?
4. In any of these cases has the necessity of applying for relief arisen from the want of self-control, or the power of expending frugally the money advanced in quarterly payments?
5. General observations?

LONDON:
Printed by order of the Poor Law Commissioners, by W. CLOWES and SONS, Stamford Street, and Published by CHARLES KNIGHT and Co., 22, Ludgate-street, Publishers to the Poor Law Commissioners.

nancing the opinion that stock in trade is liable to be rated.

The Commissioners have further to state that if stock in trade should still be held to be rateable, it should at all events be rated separately from the premises in which the trade is carried on. And it must be borne in mind that the stock must be visible stock, locally situate within the parish; that the person rated for the stock must actually inhabit the parish, Rex *v.* Hull Dock Company, (3 B. and C., 525.) And it must be susceptible of proof that it produces a *profit,* Rex *v.* Macdonald, (12 East, 324) after payment of all debts, Rex *v.* White, (C. and R., 777.)

In conclusion, the Commissioners have to observe that they have no authority to determine whether any kind of property shall be included in the rate or not, as such a power involves the power to tax the community, or to remit the tax. All they can do in such a matter is to advise upon what appears to them to be the intention of the Legislature, and upon the best means of carrying that intention into effect.

II.—ELECTION OF GUARDIANS.

Qualification of Guardian.

THE overseers of the parish of Aston, near Birmingham, submitted the following question to the Commissioners:—

"Whether a person who has removed to another house, but whose notice to quit his former residence does not expire till the 25th March, and who will be qualified as a Guardian by virtue of the two houses, on the day of nomination, which will take place on the 16th March, but will be disqualified on giving up possession of one of the houses on the 25th March, which is the day of election, can yet be admitted as a candidate for the office of Guardian by virtue of his qualification on the day of nomination; and, if so, what course is to be pursued to prevent his acting as a Guardian when he becomes disqualified?

In reply the Commissioners stated:—

"It is obligatory on the officers conducting the election to admit as candidates all persons who at the time of the election are duly nominated and qualified. The officers cannot act upon any expectations that the person nominated will be disqualified before the time for serving the office shall arrive.

"If, after the election, a person loses his qualification, without at the same time acquiring another, his place at the Board of Guardians becomes vacant, and after such disqualification he would be incompetent to act at the Board of Guardians. If the disqualification should take place after election, and before the return, it would be the duty of the officers making the return to omit the name of the person so disqualified, stating the reason."

Right of Tenants to vote where Rates are paid by Landlord.

In reply to the question,—

"Whether the tenants of small houses who are assessed, and whose names appear in the rate-book, but whose landlords regularly pay the poor-rates, are entitled to vote as rate-payers?"

The Commissioners stated:—

"If the landlords of the houses have been distinctly rated under the provisions of the 59th Geo. 3, c. 12, the occupiers would not in such case remain liable to the obligations of rate-payers, nor entitled to a rate-payer's peculiar rights and privileges. The case would, the Commissioners consider, be altogether different if by any voluntary or private understanding the landlords of the tenements undertook to pay the rates. Such an undertaking would not deprive the occupier of his rights as a rate-payer, as he would remain liable to all the obligations to pay, and the payment by the landlord would in such case confer the same rights as payments by the occupier himself."

Nomination of Guardians.

On the subject of a protest addressed to the Guardians of the Tavistock Union, and submitted to the consideration of the Commissioners, to the effect—

"1. That the parties who nominated the Guardians of the parish of Tavistock, had no right to do so, not having paid their rates.

"2. That the parties nominated were not qualified to act as Guardians, on the same ground of non-payment of rates.

The Commissioners stated:—

"1. That the proviso in the 40th section of the Poor Law Amendment Act, that no person shall be deemed a rate-payer, or be entitled to vote, or do any other act, matter, or thing as such, unless he shall have been rated to the relief of the poor for a whole year immediately preceding his so voting and acting, and have paid the parochial rates and assessments made upon him for that period, would undoubtedly prevent a person from proposing a Guardian who had not complied with the provision of the statute in regard to the payment of rates. And with regard to the term "parochial rates and assessments," the Commissioners are advised that it includes other rates besides poor-rates, and extends to every rate strictly of a parochial nature. The Commissioners are of opinion that a church rate is within the meaning of the term, and that the non-payment of that rate (where due) would disqualify a person from proposing a Guardian, or voting or doing any other act as rate-payer.

"2nd. The Commissioners are of opinion that it is not necessary, in order to qualify a person to serve the office of Guardian, that he be a rate-payer. It is sufficient that he be *rated* for property of a given value at the time of nomination, (see sec. 38 of the Poor Law Amendment Act,) it being immaterial how long he may have been rated, and whether he have paid any rates whatever."

Nomination Paper: as to the rejection of.

The following questions relative to the nomination of candidates at the election of Guardians were submitted to the Commissioners by the clerk of the Ely Union:—

"1. Whether a nomination paper should be rejected if, at the time of its delivery, the nominator has not paid all his parochial rates?

"2. Whether the lighting and watching rate, which is a local and partial rate, is one of the parochial rates which must be paid to qualify a person liable to pay it to nominate a Guardian."

To these questions the Commissioners replied:—

"1st. If a person be entitled to vote as *owner* he may in that capacity nominate a person as Guardian, though he may not have paid his rates, as required in the case of a rate-payer by the 40th sec. of the Poor Law Amendment Act. But if he claim to nominate in his capacity of rate-payer, then it must appear that he is duly qualified to vote in that capacity by having been rated for the prescribed period, and by having paid all the parochial rates and assessments made upon him for the year immediately preceding his so voting or acting, except such as may have become due within the last six months.

"2nd. If a rate is levied for a portion of the parish only, as in the case of the lighting and watching rate referred to in the second query, then it is not, the Commissioners consider, a "*parochial* rate or assessment," and payment of it, therefore, is not necessary to qualify a person to vote as rate-payer under the 40th sec. of the Poor Law Amendment Act."

As to Votes of Occupiers.

The following application for advice from a rate-payer of the Eastry Union was taken into consideration:—

"Whether a person having occupied previously in a parish and left that occupation, but afterwards gets into another occupation in the same parish, must not occupy and pay rates for one year before he is qualified to vote upon it?"

To this question the Commissioners replied: —"That if a person has been rated to the poor rate in any parish continuously for a whole year immediately preceding the election of Guardians, such person, if he have paid the parochial rates required by the 40th section of the Poor Law Amendment Act, is entitled to vote in such election, notwithstanding any change in his occupancy which may have taken place during that period."

As to the voting of Occupiers, Owners, and Proxies.

The following questions were submitted to the Commissioners by the clerk of the Kensington Union:—

"1st. Whether a householder can be deemed a rate-payer, who has not been rated to the poor-rate for twelve months?

"2d. Whether, not having been so rated for a rental of the qualifying amount, he can become a candidate for the office of Guardian?

"3d. Whether a proxy can vote on the appointment of an owner, who has not previously sent in his claim?

"4th. Is a proxy entitled to vote, if the proxy paper be not signed by him, admitting that he has filled up some of the blanks?

"5th. How are owners and proxies living out of the parish to be furnished with voting papers? Is application to be made at the clerk's office for the voting papers, or is he to send them to any house in the parish, if so required by the owner or proxy?

"6th. If a rate-payer, on account of being in arrear, be disqualified on the 22d instant (the day for delivering the voting papers), can he, by paying up his rate before the 25th instant, require a voting paper; and, if so, is it to be collected by the police constable, though not delivered by him, or must it be brought by the rate-payer to the clerk's office on the 25th instant, after which can any owner's or proxy's claim to vote be received?"

To these questions the Commissioners replied:—

"1. A householder cannot be deemed a "rate-payer" under the provisions of the Poor Law Amendment Act unless he have been rated for twelve months to the poor-rates.

"2. But it is not necessary in order to qualify a person to serve the office of Guardian that he be a "rate-payer." It is sufficient that he be rated for property of a given value, at the time of nomination, (see sec. 38 of the Poor Law Amendment Act,) it being immaterial how long he have been rated, and whether he have paid any rates whatever. The qualification to vote and act as rate-payer, and the qualification to be a Guardian, are thus materially different; the one consisting of the fact of having been rated at least a year, and of having paid all rates and assessments made on him up to the last six months, without reference to the relative value of the property rated, while that for the office of Guardian consists of the fact merely of the person being rated to the poor-rate (irrespectively of other rates and assessments) conjoined with a certain property qualification.

"3. The Commissioners consider that the 40th section enables either the owner or the proxy to make the statement of the qualifying property, and that the proxy's statement, and claim, and production of appointment, enables him to vote without any independent claim by the owner himself.

"4. It is not necessary, however desirable, that the statement should be signed by the proxy. The owner's appointment of proxy must be under the owner's hand, *i. e.*, either written or signed by him; but if written, it need not be signed with his name.

"5. If owners and proxies have any address *within* the parish, whether their respective residences or not, it is the duty of the returning officer to cause voting papers to be delivered at such address, and if the owners and proxies not resident and giving no such address apply on the day of delivery to the clerk or his assistants at the place of election, they should be supplied with papers, such place being fairly to be considered for the purpose their place of address within the parish. But no duty is imposed on the returning officer to distribute papers beyond the limits of the parish.

"6. To be entitled to vote, a rate-payer, owner, or proxy, must be fully and completely qualified on the day on which the voting-papers are to be delivered, the receipt of the voting-paper in the manner prescribed by the order being part of the mode of voting directed by the order; and if not qualified by that time, the party loses his opportunity to vote as given by the order."

Votes of Owners and Rate-payers in Cases of joint Ownership.

An application from the clerk of the Totnes Union, requesting advice on the following points, was read:—

"1. As to the votes of rate-payers in cases of co-partnership, and in cases of the subdivision of tenements.

"2. As to the votes of owners in cases of joint ownership."

To which the Commissioners directed that the following reply should be given.

"1st. That presuming there is no local Act in Totnes affecting the rateability of occupiers of property, it appears to the Commissioners that, under the general law lodgers occupying portions of houses cannot be rated or considered as "rate-payers," except in the cases to which the provisions of the 2nd and 3rd Wm. 4. (Reform Act,) sec. 30, and the 5th and 6th Wm. 4, c. 76, (Municipal Corporations Act,) sec. 11, apply.

"Under the general law, occupiers of "tenements" are not made rateable; but occupiers of lands, "*houses*," &c.; and as respects occupiers of houses, it is clear that it is the occupier of the whole house, not the several occupiers of several parts of houses, who must be rated.

"The express authority given by the Reform and Municipal Corporations Acts clearly shows what the law was presumed to be without such an authority.

"2nd. In the case of joint owners, the number of votes is not increased, but such owners would be entitled to divide between them the number of votes which any one owner of the same property would be singly entitled to give; so also in the case of joint owners who are the occupiers of a property which would yield seven votes to a single person, being owner and occupier, that number is not increased by the fact of joint ownership, but only, as before observed, divisible amongst the parties."

Number of Votes in Cases of joint Occupations.

In answer to a letter received from a candidate for the Guardianship of the parish of Bishopsteignton, requesting the attention of the Commissioners to a memorial addressed by him to the Guardians of the Newton Abbot Union, complaining of the incorrectness of the return of the parish officers of Bishopsteignton, and of illegality in the mode of conducting the election for that parish, the Commissioners replied:—

"1st. That in the case of joint occupations the number of votes is not increased, but the occupiers (if both were rated) would be entitled to divide between them the number of votes which any one occupier of the same property would be singly entitled to give.

"2nd. No person would be entitled to vote as owner in the election of Guardians unless he had sent to the churchwardens and overseers, before the day of election, his claim to vote as owner, together with the statement of the property as required by the 40th sec. Poor Law Amendment Act. But if such claim were made in sufficient time, the fact of there being no register of owners wherein the name of such owner appeared, would not disqualify him from voting, although it would subject the overseers to penalties for disobedience of the order of the Commissioners in not preparing such book, and entering such claims.

"3rd. As to the allegation that more votes were given by certain owners and occupiers than they were entitled to under the Poor Law Amendment Act, the Commissioners can only observe that if such were the case, such votes were improperly and unlawfully included in the calculation of votes by the parish officer."

As to the validity of Proceedings where Overseers neglect to publish the Names of Guardians, &c.

Application for advice from the Guardians of the Wolverhampton Union was read respecting the validity of the proceedings of the overseers for the township of Wednesfield, who had omitted to publish the names of the Guardians on the church-doors, and likewise to give notice to the Guardians elected in the prescribed form.

In reply to which the Commissioners stated, that

"The overseers appear to have been guilty of a great neglect of duty, in not publishing the list of elected Guardians by placing such lists upon the church-doors, and in likewise neglecting to give notice to the Guardians elected. The Commissioners are of opinion, however, that neither of these omissions are sufficient to void the election, although they would subject the overseers to penalties for disobedience of the orders of the Commissioners. If, therefore, the nomination of the parties was legally made, and if the Board are satisfied that the parties are possessed of a legal qualification, the return of the overseers should be received."

III.—CONTRACTS AND SUPPLIES FOR IN-MAINTENANCE, &c. AND LIABILITIES OF CONTRACTORS.

Contracts for the Supply of Bread.

THE Board took into consideration the following communication from the Guardians of the Bedford Union.

"*Bedford Union.*

"BREAD CONTRACT.

"SIR,—I am directed by the Board of Guardians of this Union to forward you a contract entered into by ——, of ——, baker, for the supply of bread to the workhouse and parishes therein named, and to request that the Poor Law Commissioners will, according to the terms therein stated, consent to put an end to the same.

"The Board, in making this application, do so in consequence of the bread which he supplies to the paupers being deficient in weight and quality, and they prefer that the contract should be put an end to in this manner, in order that some other person may be procured to supply the district with bread in a proper manner.

"I have, &c.
(Signed) "SAMUEL WING,
"Clerk of the Union.

"*E. Chadwick, Esq., Secretary to the Poor* "*Law Commissioners.*"

The following answer was directed to be sent to the Guardians:—

"The Commissioners desire to state in reply that, under the circumstances of the case, they are willing to comply with the application made by the Guardians, and they consent that the Guardians shall put an end to such contract in the manner therein provided."

Tenders for the Supply of Stationery.

The following letter was received from the Pershore Union:—

"*Pershore.*

"SIR,—The Guardians issued an advertisement in the newspapers for tenders from persons willing to supply them with articles of stationery, &c.

"On Tuesday last, the day appointed for opening the said tenders, one tender only was sent in; and a discussion arose whether, under the circumstances, that tender could be accepted, some of the Guardians suggesting that, being the only one, it could not be refused; and others, that the words of the resolution of the 2d July would justify such refusal.

"I am directed to request that the Poor Law Commissioners will favour the Board with an opinion at their earliest convenience.

"I have, &c.

(Signed) "E. MURRELL, Clerk.

"*To Edwin Chadwick, &c.*"

To this application the Commissioners directed the following answer to be returned:—

"The obligation of the Guardians of the Pershore Union to accept the only tender sent in for supplying stationery for the use of the Union depends upon the terms of the advertisement soliciting the tenders. If the advertisement did not expressly pledge the Guardians to accept the only tender sent in, the fact of a single tender only being received, so far from binding them to its acceptance, would generally be a good reason for seeking fresh tenders."

Contractors—Liability of, to serve Parochial Offices, and Disability to continue Contracts.

The following letter from the Guardians of the Guildford Union was read to the Board:—

"GENTLEMEN,—One of the contractors for the supply of provisions throughout the Union has, since he entered into his contract, been appointed one of the overseers of one of the parishes in the Union, and he has now some doubts whether he can fulfil his contract without running the risk of incurring a penalty. I shall, therefore, be obliged by your informing me what course you would recommend him to take previous to the meeting of the Board on Tuesday next.

"I am, &c.

(Signed) "GEORGE SMALLPIECE.

"*To the Poor Law Commissioners.*"

To this letter the following answer was returned:—

"The Commissioners, in reply, desire to state to you their opinion that the fact of the person holding such a contract does not exempt him from his liability to serve the office of overseer. The proper course the Commissioners consider to be taken by the contractor would be to get a release from his contract, his performance of which would subject him to the penalties of the statute 53 Geo. III. c. 187."

Contracts—Advertisements for.

The Commissioners received a copy of the following resolution from the Guardians of the Market Drayton Union:—

"Resolved,

"That (with the sanction of the Poor Law Commissioners) the advertisements for contracts in the local papers be discontinued, on account of the unnecessary expense incurred, as no tenders are received in consequence of such advertisements; and that bills be posted in the towns of Drayton and Hodnet, and circulated amongst the tradesmen in those towns in lieu thereof."

The Commissioners directed the following letter to be transmitted in reply:—

"The Poor Law Commissioners acknowledge the receipt of your letter of the 3rd instant, enclosing a resolution of the Guardians of the Market Drayton Union respecting the discontinuance of advertising for contracts in the local papers.

"The ground of this resolution is the alleged unnecessary expense which is produced by such advertisements, inasmuch as no tenders are received in consequence of them; and the Guardians accordingly propose that bills be posted in the towns of Drayton and Hodnet, and circulated in those towns in lieu of such advertisements.

"On comparing the expense of in-maintenance of the paupers in the Market Drayton Union with the same head of expense in other Shropshire Unions, it appears that whilst the average expense of the in-maintenance of the paupers in all the Unions in Shropshire is 2*s.* 8*d.* per head, in the Market Drayton Union it is only 2*s.* 2*d.* per head. The comparison of the stated prices of the articles obtained as supplies for the paupers in the workhouse is also on the whole confirmatory of the presumption raised by the fact first stated in favour of the general good economy exercised by the Guardians of the Market Drayton Union. The Commissioners, therefore, hesitate to abandon the practice of advertising contracts in some local publication, even in such a case, and with the security of the proposed substitution of the mode of advertisement by bills posted in the adjacent towns.

"One advantageous contract, obtained by means of an advertisement in the usual mode, may more than defray the cost of unsuccessful advertisements over a long period, and the knowledge of the fact of advertisements having been issued, and of competitors being induced to offer from a distance, may restrain the undue demands of contractors or combinations of persons in the immediate vicinity against the rate-payers, and will induce them to offer terms beneficial to the Union in proportion to the advantages which the contractors may possess in respect of proximity or otherwise. The abandonment of the practice of advertising in journals of unrestricted circulation would tend to narrow the market and the possible competition, and otherwise prejudice, not only the pecuniary expenditure, but the general administration of the law in such cases, for in the instances where there were no advertisements, or where the notifications for tenders were confined to narrow districts, or were merely formal notices read in the church or posted on the church-door, the supplies were frequently profuse in quantity, bad in quality, and exorbitant in price.

"The evil of the profuse expenditure was less than the evil of mismanagement arising from the temptations connected with the abusive distribution of relief. Tradesmen got parties elected, or elected each other in turns, to secure to themselves the monopoly of the supplies, and the supplies were distributed profusely to enhance the profits, which served also as a means of corruption to retain particular tradesmen as voters and canvassers in the interests of local parties. Some of the most violent opposition to the administration of the new law has been traced to the influence of such interests which had heretofore been predominant. In one instance a person in a Union who took a lead in breaking through the Commissioners' orders for the supply of groceries to the aged and infirm, on the ground that the supplies, though better than those usually obtained by aged persons of the labouring class living on their own means, were cruelly inadequate, was found to be a grocer who was shortly afterwards convicted of using short weights. In another Union a person who endeavoured to incite the populace against the relief in kind as inadequate, was a baker who was also convicted of the like offence. The sources of reports that the provisions distributed from the workhouse stores were poisoned, by which reports popular tumults against the distribution of relief in kind were excited in Devonshire, were in several instances traced to small shopkeepers who had heretofore been accustomed to supply paupers.

"Complaints have been frequently made to the Commissioners that the present mode of advertising for contracts is inadequate, and the different prices which are given in adjacent Unions in the same county appear to warrant the supposition that, even under the existing arrangements, the markets for the Union are frequently narrowed to the prejudice of the rate-payers, and suggest to the Commissioners the necessity of calling the attention of Boards of Guardians to the present modes of obtaining supplies, and of considering of new arrangements at some early opportunity. For example, it appears that whilst in the Market Drayton Union 3*s*. 8*d*. per stone is paid for meat, in other Unions in the same county the price paid is 4*s*. and 4*s*. 4*d*.; whilst in Market Drayton Union 5½*d*. per lb. is paid for soap, in other Unions 7½*d*. is given; and so with other articles. Tradesmen engaged in furnishing clothing and other articles used in the workhouse have complained to the Commissioners that from the irregular manner in which advertisements for contracts were inserted, they are precluded from making tenders to distant Unions of supplies of goods at from 15 to 20 per cent. below the prices at which they are now provided for the use of many of the Unions.

"The Commissioners trust that the preceding statements will satisfy the Guardians of the Market Drayton Union of the inexpediency of discontinuing the practice of advertising for tenders. The Commissioners recommend them to advertise in at least one local newspaper of the widest local circulation, and, in addition, to post notices in the manner proposed. But it is to be observed of the practice of giving notice by posting bills, that it is a very uncertain mode, inasmuch as it may be restricted by the common indolence or dishonesty of the persons employed to post the bills, and the notices may otherwise be restricted by design to a particular street or place in a manner which is not practicable with advertisements in a newspaper of general circulation. The Commissioners presume that the charges made for advertisements in the newspapers are reasonable, since they have hitherto had no complaints presented to them against the practice on the ground of the exorbitance of the charges."

IV. — DISEASE AND CONSEQUENT DESTITUTION; MEDICAL OFFICERS' RETURNS.

IN the course of the examination of the returns made on this subject, it appeared that frequent mistakes had been made by the medical officers in making up the returns, by which they have given themselves much unnecessary trouble, and frequently involved the necessity of sending back the documents for the preparation of amended returns. The common error is the mistake of the heading "Cases—No. of," as intending the reference number of each case in the medical relief book, instead of the total number of each class of the classes of cases designated, which the practitioner may have treated; as thus:—

CASES.

No. of	Nosological Names of
15	Variola.
17	Rubeola.*
20	Intermittent fever.
105	Synochus.
72	Typhus.
45	Scarlatina.

These five classes are those adverted to in the instructional letter of the 12th of November, in which it is stated, "That the attention of the physicians who drew reports on the state of the metropolis was almost exclusively directed to the causes affecting the prevalence of various forms of *continued fever*, arranged under distinguishing names adopted by nosological writers: but in rural districts the prevalence of ague, and of small-pox, and scarlet fever, may be worthy of notice, when the causes promoting their prevalence appear removable."

The medical officers who, from error or inattention to the tenour of the instructions, have not confined their returns to the classes of cases, have returned every case of every description which they have treated, embodying in several closely written sheets the information which ought to be set forth in a few lines, and proportionally multiplying their own labour unnecessarily. The following particulars from returns properly made will serve as exemplifications:—

* When epidemic.

AN EXEMPLIFICATION of a RETURN, showing the prevalent causes of Diseases among the Labouring Population.

Cases. No. of.	Cases. Nosological Names of.	Occupation of Applicants.	Situation and State of Residence.	Observations.
15	Cholera.	6 Dock labourers. 9 Fruit and fish women.	Small tenements, situate at ——— in a blind alley with broken pavement.	The cholera exhibited itself in a most malignant aspect here, and before other parts of the parish had been visited by it, which was attributed to the depression of the health of the inhabitants, by the accumulation of rain water and garbage, there being neither drains nor scavengers in this district. The want of free circulation of the air, the court being very narrow and bottle-shaped. And a frightful source of pestilence was discovered in the practice of the fish hawkers leaving their baskets of sprats, &c. often in a state of decomposition under their beds in their ill ventilated apartments. The number of tripe-boilers, tanneries, and size manufactories in the vicinity, as well as the extremely crowded state of the graves in the burial ground, and the meagre quantity of earth with which the heaps of coffins are covered, had doubtless an injurious influence on the neighbourhood.

An Exemplification of a Return, &c.—*continued.*

Cases.		Occupation of Applicants.	Situation and State of Residence.	Observations.
No. of.	Nosological Names of.			
19	Synochus.	3 Sugar bakers. 4 Market women. 12 Children of sailors.	Small, No. 4 class, tenements in a court, situate at ———.	A low description of fever always prevails in this district during the summer months; the court is fairly paved, but collections of filth are continually being made by the inhabitants; a water plug at the upper end of the court would remove a week's accumulation of filth easily, as the place slopes to the street. The dwellings are also extremely filthy, but, perhaps, would be cleaner if the court were constantly cleansed.
24	Typhus in a very intense form.	12 Butchers. 3 Labourers. 4 Jews (salesmen). 5 Children of the butchers.	Small houses, but not badly constructed if the inmates were but moderately cleanly, in —— and adjoining streets.	The typhus, which prevailed in this court, was very fatal, as nine persons died from it. The blood and offal from three of the largest slaughter-houses in this district runs through the street, and is often obstructed by accumulations of pig-stye filth. This was the case during July and August when this disease raged.
5	Typhus.	Tramps and costermongers.	Low lodging houses in —— street.	The spread of these cases of disease has been undoubtedly promoted by the crowded state of the rooms, which have from three to six or seven beds in them, and sometimes several persons in each bed—the lodgers pay from 2*d*. to 4*d*. for their night's accommodation. The effluvia arising from these crowded rooms, and the uncleanly state of the beds, bad at all times, with the frequent disturbances of sleep occasioned by the drunken and turbulent habits of the inmates, are among the causes of the rapid spread of typhus in these houses.
24	Variola.	Children of weavers.	Small tenements situate in dirty narrow streets; in —— street and those adjoining.	The children unable to assist in weaving are generally allowed to run about the streets, in a most filthy and squalid state; when the disease first showed itself it spread rapidly, as no means were taken to prevent the usual congregation of children in the streets.
14	Ague.	Agricultural labourers.	Ordinary cottages at ——.	A few wells have been lately dug and good water has been obtained. There is every probability, that if the water pits (from which the inhabitants obtain their supply) were filled up, and more wells dug and drainage completed, ague, which has so long infested this village and occasioned so much distress and expense, might be eradicated.
42	Scarlatina.	Chiefly children of agricultural labourers.	Small two-roomed thatched cottages at ——.	Scarlatina raged extensively in the village in which most of these cases occurred; the houses are chiefly situate in front of a pool of filthy stagnant water, and a dirty ditch runs behind them.

The clerks of the Unions are requested, before submitting the returns to the Guardians, or transmitting them to the Commissioners, to see to their conformity to the instructions referred to.

V.—MEDICAL RELIEF: REMUNERATION TO MEDICAL OFFICERS.

Copy of a Minute of the Poor Law Commissioners, dated 6th of June, 1839.

THE Board took into consideration the subject of the arrangements for affording Medical Relief to Paupers, so far as respects the remuneration of the Medical Officer: and the Reports of the Assistant Commissioners thereon were laid before the Board:—

Of the modes of remuneration which combine both a fixed salary and a payment per case, that which appears to the Commissioners to unite the advantages, and to avoid the disadvantages, of both of these systems, is the following:

That at the commencement of every parochial year a list of all the paupers in the receipt of relief within a district should be made out, and that for the medical care of these paupers a fixed sum, to be then determined, should be paid, which should be apportioned to the several parishes of the district according to the number of the paupers on the list belonging to such parishes respectively; and that the medical officers should attend these paupers when sick without any specific order from the Union or parish officers.

And that as respects all other persons to whom medical relief shall be ordered during the current parochial year, the medical officers shall receive a fixed sum per case.

By this arrangement, the further details of which are reserved for future consideration, the aged, infirm, and helpless would be placed directly under the care of the medical officer, who, in addition to the ordinary motives, which to the credit of the medical profession lead to their careful and humane attention to this class of patients, will find it to be his direct interest to attend promptly, and to treat effectively, any case of sickness which may arise amongst those who are thus committed to his charge.

As respects this class of paupers so included in the pauper list, the Board of Guardians and their officers, and the overseers, will be relieved from a part of the responsibility and trouble incidental to providing medical relief, and from the anxiety and obloquy they now undergo in reference to cases in which there has been any unavoidable delay or justifiable doubt in providing medical aid.

As regards the able-bodied labourers, whilst there will be no temptation to the Guardians to administer (as under the system of remuneration by a gross fixed salary) relief to individuals of this class indiscriminately at the expense of the medical officer, there will at the same time be no inducement to refuse it when really necessary, inasmuch as the system of payment per case admits of medical relief being granted by way of loan, an arrangement which inevitably operates to encourage the labourer to provide himself with medical aid on easier terms, by subscribing beforehand to a sick club or friendly society.

With regard to the amount of the remuneration, the Commissioners are disposed to give much weight to the concurrent testimony of the witnesses examined before the Committee of the House of Commons of last Session, in reference to medical relief; and they deduce from that testimony that the fixed remuneration to be paid in rural districts for the permanent list, should be such as to afford to the practitioner a payment of 6*s.* or 6*s.* 6*d.* per case on the average number of *bonâ fide* cases, subject to be augmented if the district is extensive.

The remuneration per case for those not on the pauper list may reasonably be on a somewhat higher scale; but the Board are inclined to think that it will not be found necessary to exceed 10*s.* per case.

In the arrangements which have been indicated, it is presumed that midwifery cases and surgical operations of a serious character will be paid for by a separate fixed charge for each case.

The Commissioners entertain no doubt that if the principle of the payment per case be thus adopted, it may be easily modified to suit the special circumstances of the Union, and that further experience of its operation will enable them to ascertain accurately whether the rates above alluded to, which at first will be of a somewhat experimental character, furnish an adequate and not unreasonable remuneration for the services performed.

VI.—VACCINATION EXTENSION,
MARCH 28.

THE Commissioners received the following copy of the Bill for the extension of vaccination, as it had been passed in the House of Lords, and read a first time in the House of Commons, intituled, "An Act to extend the Practice of Vaccination."

Clause 1.—That from and after the passing of this Act, it shall be lawful for the Guardians of every Parish or Union, and for the Overseers of every Parish in which relief to the poor shall not be administered by Guardians, in England and Wales, and they are hereby directed to contract with the medical officers of their several Unions or Parishes respectively for the vaccination of all persons who may come to them for that purpose.

Clause 2.—That such Guardians and Overseers shall, after consultation with such medical officers, from time to time appoint and give four days' notice of the appointment of such and so many convenient places and times, as to them may seem fit, at which such medical officers shall attend to vaccinate all persons who may come to them for that purpose: provided always, that not more than three calendar months shall in any case elapse between the times at which such medical officers shall so attend.

Clause 3.—That in making such arrangements as may be required for the execution of this Act, such Guardians and Overseers, and all other officers engaged in the administration of the laws for the relief of the poor, shall conform to the regulations which may from time to time be issued by the Poor Law Commissioners in that behalf, which regulations the said Commissioners are hereby authorized and required to make and issue.

Clause 4. That such medical officers shall make a report to such Guardians or Overseers, on the next day of the meeting of such Guardians or Overseers after every such time so appointed as aforesaid for the vaccination of persons, of the number of persons then vaccinated; and from time to time shall make such further report with respect to the persons so vaccinated, as such Guardians and Overseers, under the direction of the Poor Law Commissioners, shall require.

Clause 5.—That in case any such medical officer shall not be willing, during the pendency of any existing contract which may have been entered into by him with such Guardians or Overseers, to make a further contract for the vaccination of persons as hereinbefore mentioned, on such terms as to such Guardians or Overseers may appear reasonable; or in case there shall not be a medical officer appointed in any district of any Union or in any Parish, then it shall be lawful for such Guardians and Overseers, and they are hereby directed to make such contract as hereinbefore mentioned with any medical person, not being a medical officer of any such Parish or Union: provided always, that every such last-mentioned contract shall cease and determine at the same time as the contract entered into with such medical officer as aforesaid.

Clause 6. That every such medical person shall give the like attendance and make the like reports as is and are hereinbefore required from the medical officer of any Parish or Union.

Clause 7.—Provided always, that such Guardians or Overseers shall forthwith, after the conclusion of any such contract as before mentioned, transmit a copy thereof to the Poor Law Commissioners; and that it shall be lawful for such Commissioners to annul the same if the terms of such contract shall appear to them to be unreasonable or insufficient; and in all such cases, such contract so annulled shall be deemed to have been null from the beginning thereof: provided nevertheless, that if such Commissioners shall not annul such contract within fourteen days from the receipt thereof, such contract shall thenceforth not be liable to be annulled by such Commissioners.

Clause 8.—That as soon as may be after the passing of this Act, the Guardians of every Poor Law Union in Ireland shall (subject to the approbation of the Poor Law Commissioners) divide such Union into districts of convenient extent, and shall (subject to such approbation as aforesaid) contract with competent medical persons for the period of one year, and so from year to year as such contract may expire, for the vaccination of all persons who may come to such medical persons for that purpose.

Clause 9.—That all the provisions hereinbefore made with respect to England and Wales for the appointment and giving due notice of the appointment of the places and times at which such medical officers or medical persons shall attend to vaccinate such persons, and for the making of reports by such medical officers or medical persons, shall apply to all such contracts as may be made under this Act by the Guardians of any Poor Law Union in Ireland; and such Guardians, and all other officers engaged in the administration of relief to the destitute poor, shall conform to the regulations and instructions of the Poor Law Commissioners, in like manner as is hereinbefore directed with respect to Guardians, Overseers and other officers in England and Wales.

Clause 10.—That any person not being qualified by law to practise as physician or apothecary, or not being a member of the Royal College of Surgeons, who shall inoculate with variolous matter for the purpose of causing the disease of the small-pox, or use in any other manner any variolous matter for such purpose, shall be liable to be summarily proceeded against and convicted before a justice of the peace, on proof of such offence committed in England or Wales, or in case of such offence committed in Ireland, before the Magistrates assembled in petty Sessions; and for every such offence shall be liable to be imprisoned in the common gaol or house of correction for a term not exceeding one calendar month, with or without hard labour.

Clause 11.—That every person not hereinbefore prohibited from inoculating with variolous matter for the purpose of causing the disease of the small-pox, and from using in any other manner any variolous matter for such purpose, shall on the first day of January, April, July, and October in every year, transmit to the clerk of the Board of Guardians of the Union, or to the Guardians or Overseers of the Parish (as the case may be), in which such person may reside, a Report according to the Schedule annexed to this Act, and containing such further particulars as the Poor Law Commissioners may from time to time, by any regulation published in the Gazette, require of all persons so inoculated by him, or with respect to whom he shall have so used any variolous matter, in the three calendar months next preceding the day on which such Report shall be so transmitted; and every such Report shall be read at the first meeting of such Guardians or Overseers after the receipt thereof, and shall then be by them forthwith transmitted to the Poor Law Commissioners.

Clause 12.—That every word in such part of this Act as refers to England and Wales shall be interpreted in like manner as such word is directed to be interpreted in an Act passed in the fourth and fifth year of his late Majesty King William the Fourth, intituled, "An Act for the Amendment and better Administration of the Laws relating to the Poor in England and Wales;" and that every word used in such part of this Act as relates to Ireland shall be interpreted in like manner as such word is directed to be interpreted in an Act passed in the first and second year of the reign of Her present Majesty, intituled, "An Act for the more effectual Relief of the destitute Poor in Ireland."

SCHEDULE.

Name of Person inoculated, or otherwise affected with Small Pox by the use of Variolous Matter.	Age.	Condition.	Residence.	Date of Inoculation, or other communication of the Disease of Small Pox by the use of Variolous Matter,

Christian and Surname of Inoculator.

Residence of Inoculator.

VII.—POLITICAL MEETINGS: UNFITNESS OF BOARDS OF GUARDIANS FOR.

THE following application from a rate-payer of the Derby Union was read respecting the right of a Board of Guardians to meet to take into consideration the propriety of petitioning Parliament for a repeal of the Corn Laws.

"*Derby, February 28th*, 1840.

"GENTLEMEN,—I herewith send you a notice that has been delivered to a Guardian in the Derby Union. I shall feel obliged if you will inform me, through the medium of the Board of Guardians, whether they can hold such meeting, and who is to pay the expense of such proceedings, and whether you will see the rate-payers protected from such illegal practice.

"I remain yours, very respectfully,

"—— ——."

"*Derby Union Offices*, 19, *Wardwick, Derby, February 25th*, 1840.

"SIR,—I am directed to summon an extraordinary meeting of the Guardians of the said Union, to be held in the Board Room, 19, Wardwick, on Tuesday next, the 3rd day of March, 1840, at two o'clock in the afternoon, to take into consideration the propriety of petitioning both Houses of Parliament for a repeal of the Corn Laws, which meeting you are requested to attend.

"I am, sir, your most obedient servant,

"JOHN MOODY, Clerk.

"*To* ——."

The Commissioners addressed the following letter to the Clerk to the Board of Guardians.

"The Poor Law Commissioners have had before them the copy of a notice signed by you convening a meeting of the Board of Guardians of the Derby Union to take into consideration the propriety of petitioning Parliament for the repeal of the Corn Laws.

"The Commissioners regret that they have not been enabled to give you notice in time to apprize you of the error into which you have fallen in convening the meeting, in acting on an occasion foreign to your duties, and in not apprizing the Guardians that their Board is constituted for administrative purposes specified in the Statute under the authority of which they are created, and that its meetings can only be convened or held for those purposes.

"The Commissioners would observe, that if

the Boards of Guardians held meetings for political or other such purposes, inducements would be held out to parties to seek parochial offices not for the legitimate purpose of distributing relief to the poor, but for the purpose of furthering political or party objects. The obtrusion of the political feelings of any party, or of any sect, in the administration of relief, has generally been found to operate prejudicially in increasing the spread of pauperism amongst the labouring classes; in causing relief to be distributed for other objects than the simple object of relieving the destitute; and in occasioning the appointment of paid officers to be made, not for their fitness to perform the duties of their offices, but for their activity as political connexions or partisans. The retention of office, and abusive modes of administration at the expense of the rate-payers and to the prejudice of the poor for party purposes, has been frequently found by the Commissioners one of the most serious obstacles to a voluntary and beneficial change of system.

"The Commissioners hope that when the Guardians duly consider what must be the effects of the general intrusion of party feelings into Boards of Guardians, and the possible occupation of their time with contests on the various contested political questions which they could not be elected by their constituents to consider, they will be disposed to abstain carefully from such questions even though they were perfectly competent to entertain them.

"Should a petition upon the Corn Laws have been agreed upon at a meeting of the Board of Guardians, the Commissioners think it desirable that the petition should purport to emanate from the Guardians as private individuals exercising the undoubted right of every subject to petition Parliament. But this is widely different from the right to assemble a Board of Guardians, and occupy its time and the time of the officers for that purpose."

Similar letters have been sent to other Boards of Guardians respecting proposed petitions *in favour* of the Corn Laws.

VIII.—RELIEF TO MEMBERS OF FRIENDLY SOCIETIES.—*Copy of Minute of Poor Law Commissioners on the subject of.*

THE Poor Law Commissioners have carefully considered the question—In what cases and to what extent a man who, as a member of a friendly society, is entitled to certain advantages in respect of it, ought to receive parochial relief?

The chief principles of the Poor Law Amendment Act received their strongest corroboration from the examples set by the labouring classes themselves, in the administration of relief to the members of their own friendly societies. From the evidence received on this topic, especially from Mr. Tidd Pratt, the barrister charged with the revision of their rules, it appears that on no point was their opinion and practice more decided and unanimous than in the prohibition of partial relief. They constantly acted on the rule that, whatever were the apparent special circumstances of the particular case, entire and undivided reliance on one source or other should be rigorously enforced. They were well aware that where, by any arrangement, more than one source of relief is opened to the same individual at the same time, the vigilance of the dispensers of relief is weakened, their means of protecting the funds under their charge are diminished, and an increased and undue reliance on the divided and extended sources is created, which is moreover always attended by an influx of fraudulent claims. The labourers who act on the principles set forth in the best considered rules of the friendly societies, would, no doubt, decide that it were better that benefit societies should not exist at all, than that they should exist as means to eke out the amounts of a pauper's allowance, and add to the inducements to obtain and rely on such an allowance. In a communication received by the Commissioners from Mr. Tidd Pratt on this subject, he states—

"I have to observe, that a large proportion of the rules of friendly societies submitted to me from those formed by labouring men, contain express exceptions of granting relief to those who are in receipt of parochial relief, or are in a workhouse; and, perhaps with a view to ascertain that fact, the certificate of their being ill and unable to follow their usual employ, is directed to be signed by the clergyman or overseer.

"The rule in question appears to me to be considered by societies as of great importance; and their great object is, to prevent a member receiving relief from any other source than that from the funds of the society, and provides generally, that no member shall belong to any *other* society at the same time. Societies are quite sensible of the frauds which would be committed if partial relief were allowed; and seem of opinion that the best interests of the society and of the members are consulted by the adoption of such a rule, which I invariably recommend."

In illustration of the views entertained by the labouring classes, as to the impropriety of contributors to friendly societies receiving relief from the poor-rate, the Commissioners may cite the following passages of the report of the Commissioners of Inquiry, pp. 275, and 335, in which the evidence of working men, members of these societies, is given.

"Launcelot Snowden examined:—

"Are you acquainted with the operative classes? —Yes, having been a journeyman printer twenty years, and one-half of the time foreman; and, having been in different situations in our own societies, as well as connected with various other societies of operatives, I believe I am well acquainted with them.

"In what way do they regard the fact of any one of their body receiving parochial relief?—I know that none but the worst characters would ever think of applying for parish relief, and that the respectable workmen consider it disgraceful. The other day a list of those who received out-door parish relief was brought to a printing office to be printed. One of the men saw on the list the name and address of one of the journeymen in the same office. This man was challenged with the fact, which he did not attempt to deny. He had been receiving as much as six shillings or eight shillings a-week, out-door relief, during two years for four children, although he had been in receipt of thirty-six shillings a-week, steady wages, during the same time. The men stated the circumstance to the employer, and he was discharged.

"Do you find any effect produced by men obtaining parochial relief readily when they are out of work, or have anything the matter with them?—I have always seen that men who have had parish relief have been very careless of work and of their money ever afterwards. It has also acted very mischievously on the benefit societies, as these men would never contribute to them. We had a large and very good society of our own, which failed some time ago; and I have known the societies of other trades fail; and it has been a common complaint amongst us, that but for the parish they would have stood firm. I am myself confident that but for the parish they would have stood firm."

The form in which the question now under consideration most frequently presents itself is, whether any member of a friendly society ought to receive an order for the medical officer of the Union? Upon this point the Poor Law Commissioners must observe that, according to the letter of the statute of Elizabeth, relief was only to be given to those who had no means to maintain them, and not to those who had the means of partial self-support from any other source. This principle has unfortunately been very generally abandoned, and its re-establishment can only be effected gradually. In the mean time, when an application is made for relief by a person who possesses some means of supporting himself, whether from a friendly society or otherwise, the guardians will only have to consider what are the absolute wants of the applicant and his family which cannot be supplied from these partial resources. If the applicant has the right to the attendance of a medical man and medicines, in respect of his belonging to a friendly society, this will, of course, not be one of the wants to be provided for by the Guardians. If he has not this right, the Guardians will give him medical relief in the same manner as it would be given to any other person unable to provide it for himself.

With regard to the money allowance granted by the friendly society, the Guardians cannot but take into account this allowance in estimating the resources of the applicant and his family; and if they acted in consistency with universally admitted principles of poor-law administration, the Guardians would not grant further aid than would be sufficient, together with this allowance, to relieve the destitution of the applicant and his family to the same extent as they would relieve the destitution of any other applicant and his family not being a subscriber to a friendly society.

The Commissioners, however, believe that in practice, the Guardians have treated the friendly society allowance as in some degree more immediately destined for the restoration of the health and strength of the subscriber, and have, therefore, granted a larger allowance to the family than would have been given if no such consideration had presented itself. The Commissioners have not deemed it advisable for the present to interfere with this mode of proceeding; but they entertain no doubt that it will, at no distant period, be found to be more in accordance with the interest of the labouring classes to carry out the principles adverted to at the commencement of these observations, and not to permit the contributors of friendly societies to receive relief at the same time from the funds of the contributors and the poor-rates.

In the administration of medical relief in this class of cases, as well as in all other cases of medical relief, the Commissioners recommend to the Guardians that they should in general give the relief by way of loan, and enforce strict attention to the recovery of the loan by instalments, however small, after the party relieved has returned to his labour. This they will find to be an effectual course to prevent the full and liberal relief which they may naturally be disposed to give on the occasion of sickness, being invaded to the expense of the rate-payers, to the prejudice of the medical profession in general, and above all to the injury of the sick clubs and societies. By such associations, the prosperity, and even the existence of which depends almost entirely on the mode in which the Guardians administer relief, the labouring classes secure immediate relief without (necessary) preliminary inquiry, and disease being met more speedily, the medical attendant is enabled to apply more effectual remedies.*

If the system of giving medical relief by way of loan be gradually adopted, those who find that they will have ultimately to pay for the relief which they obtain from the poor's rates, will find it to be so obviously their interest to have recourse to medical clubs, or friendly societies, or other similar institutions, that the Commissioners look forward with confidence to the increase and prosperity of institutions of this nature, and to the consequent growth of forethought and frugality amongst the labouring classes.

The Commissioners finally remark that they think it desirable that the Guardians should furnish once a quarter to every friendly society in the Union a list of the persons receiving relief.

* *Note.*—The best and almost the only data we have to judge of the probable amount of sickness among the labouring classes in Great Britain are the returns obtained by the exertions of the Highland Society. This society procured returns from seventy-nine benefit societies situate in sixteen counties of Scotland. These returns were made up from the books kept during various periods, in some instances extending from 1750 to 1821. The aggregate number of members on the books of the respective societies was 104,218. The first table ever formed to exhibit the probable annual sickness which a labouring man will sustain through life is to be found in an able report drawn up by Mr. Oliphant for the society. The results stated are, that a workman will experience in a year at

21 years of age	4	days' sickness	
46 ,,	1	week's	,,
57 ,,	2	weeks'	,,
63 ,,	3	,,	,,
65 ,,	$4\frac{4}{10}$	,,	,,
66 ,,	$5\frac{4}{10}$	,,	,,
67 ,,	$6\frac{6}{10}$	,,	,,
68 ,,	8	,,	,,
69 ,,	9	,,	,,
70 ,,	10	,,	,,

The proportion, after that period, goes on increasing rapidly, at a rate that puts the individual beyond the means of assurance possessed by any of those institutions. The society endeavoured to ascertain also the different degrees of intensity to be expected in this sickness; and they state, as their nearest approximation, that of ten weeks' sickness among persons of all ages under seventy, two may be assumed as bed-fast sickness; five as walking; three as permanent sickness.

The Commissioners constituting the Central Board of the Commission appointed to inquire into the effects of labour in factories upon the general condition of the operative classes, obtained as a means of comparison, from the Directors of the East India Company, returns for ten years of the experience of the labourers in their service. The number of these labourers was at the commencement of the period of the service 2,461.

As the most accurate accounts had been kept, and a sum of 1*s*. 6*d*. had been paid to every man during sickness, the most exact return was obtained. The result, as calculated from this return, was as follows:—

Age.	Average duration of Sickness per annum for every man employed.	Average duration of Sickness per annum for every man sick.
	Days and decimal parts.	Days and decimal parts.
16 to 21	4·02	13·96
21 to 26	5·40	17·22
26 to 31	4·49	20·18
31 to 36	4·55	21·44
36 to 41	5·57	23·84
41 to 46	5·18	22·83
46 to 51	5·43	23·59
51 to 56	6·80	28·61
56 to 61	7·21	23·28
61 to 66	10·24	31·25
66 to 71	9·93	26·89
71 to 76	10·60	29·67
76 to 81	12·67	38·88

This experience of the labourers of the East India Company agrees as far as the age of forty-one with that of the societies of which account was taken by the Highland Society of Scotland, and is rather more favourable from forty-one to fifty-one. After that it is much more favourable, which is readily accounted for from the circumstance that the East India Company pensioned off all the men who had become invalid, and no account was kept of their sickness. It may appear surprising that the experience of a body of men living in London in a comparatively unhealthy district, and prone to habits of intemperance, should be as favourable as that of the Societies chiefly composed of persons living in rural districts. The causes are explained in the evidence of Mr. Lewis Leese, junior. The men were in the first instance select, nearly as much so as recruits going into the army; care was taken also to give men who became infirm such labour as they could perform without severe exertion; *"but, above all, they had the benefit of medical advice without any expense in the particular case; and being thereby induced to make early application, disease was cut short at once on its first appearance."*

LONDON:
Printed by order of the Poor Law Commissioners, by W. CLOWES and SONS, Stamford Street, and Published by CHARLES KNIGHT and Co., 22, Ludgate-street, Publishers to the Poor Law Commissioners.

AN

OFFICIAL CIRCULAR

OF PUBLIC DOCUMENTS AND INFORMATION:

DIRECTED BY THE POOR LAW COMMISSIONERS TO BE PRINTED, CHIEFLY FOR THE USE OF THE MEMBERS AND PERMANENT OFFICERS OF BOARDS OF GUARDIANS, UNDER THE POOR LAW AMENDMENT ACT.

No. 4. CIRCULAR ISSUED MAY 18TH, 1840.

Poor Law Commission Office,
Somerset House,
May 13, 1840.

THE Poor Law Commissioners, on a review of their minutes, directed that the minutes and correspondence on the following subjects should be printed and circulated for the information of guardians and officers of the several Unions, viz.—

By order of the Board,
EDWIN CHADWICK, *Secretary.*

I.—EMIGRATION.

THE Board, having received from the new Land and Emigration Commissioners a copy of their instructions, considered it desirable that the following portions of them should be made known to the members of Boards of Guardians for their information, in respect to the modes of conducting public emigration now sanctioned by the Government. The instructions, which are issued by Her Majesty's principal Secretary of State for the Colonies, state:—

"In your other capacity of a General Board for the sale of lands and for promoting emigration, your duties may be conveniently arranged under the four following heads: first, the collection and diffusion of accurate statistical knowledge; secondly, the sale in this country of waste lands in the colonies; thirdly, the application of the proceeds of such sales towards the removal of emigrants; and, fourthly, the rendering of periodical accounts, both pecuniary and statistical, of your administration of this trust. Of each of these in their order.

"First. There is no subject on which misapprehension and fallacies are more easily propagated, or with more fatal success, than in reference to the state, resources, and advantages of those numerous dependencies of this kingdom which are spread over every region of the American, African, and Australian continents and islands. Nor is there any subject on which the public at large can with equal reason demand that the Government should, as far as may be possible, supply the ignorant and unwary with authentic and unexaggerated intelligence. When the Crown, in the person of its officers, undertakes to dispose of lands at so vast a distance, and to remove emigrants thither, it is not competent to them to decline the duty of imparting a faithful account of all the material circumstances by which the choice of emigrants, especially of the poorer class, should be determined. The executive government cannot in this case, as in transactions confined within the limits of the United Kingdom, refer those with whom it has to treat to the ordinary sources of popular intelligence, knowing that those sources are often perverted, and unworthy of confidence,and that they are to be correctly appreciated only by laborious study. We have no right to interpose actively to promote emigration, and at the same time to leave the ignorant and helpless to explore, as chance may determine, questions so deeply affecting their future welfare. On the other hand, in undertaking to impart information for the guidance of men on such an occasion, we subject ourselves to a formidable responsibility. No diligence or sagacity can effectually guard against misconceptions, more or less material, as to the real state and prospects of colonies so numerous and so remote; and they to whom any erroneous statement may be made on such a subject by officers acting under the authority of the Crown, will ascribe to those errors any disappointment, from whatever cause arising, and will prefer claims for compensation, which it might be at once difficult to resist, and impossible to admit.

"It is therefore to be considered as a first principle of your official conduct that you are at once to be prompt in affording to all applicants the most easy access to all authentic means of knowledge, and resolute in abstaining from giving on behalf of the government any pledge or warranty as to the accuracy of the information which you may so impart. Nor will it be enough to abstain from such assurances. Every capitalist or emigrant with whom you may be brought into communication as an applicant for statistical knowledge for his guidance must be distinctly warned that you cannot warrant the exactness of the intelligence with which you may furnish him, nor be held responsible for more than for the communication of the truth according to your own apprehension of it, and that it will be his own duty to satisfy himself as to matters of fact of this nature from every other accessible quarter, before embarking his capital or his person in so serious an enterprise. The same precautions must be strictly enforced on all your subordinate agents, and must be carefully observed by them. Yet, with your utmost caution in this respect, you will recollect that information given to the poor and ignorant by a government officer respecting distant countries, will unavoidably be received in most cases with implicit confidence; you must therefore weigh and compare the statements you receive, and sift them scrupulously before you stamp them with any sort of authority.

"Subject to the preceding qualifications, it will be your duty to diffuse, either by oral or by written statements, a distinct and compendious account of whatever relates to the agriculture, the commerce, the natural products, the physical structure, and the ecclesiastical and political institutions of each of the colonies in which you may offer lands for sale, care being of course taken to present such facts in the most precise and determinate form, unaccompanied by any superfluous comment, and still more, to strip them of any language calculated to work on the imagination, or to interfere with the calm and dispassionate exercise of their own judgment on the part of those whom you may address. To enable you to execute aright the duty of thus diffusing accurate knowledge of the statistics of the British colonies, I have directed that all the official returns in this office bearing on the subject, with all printed books, maps and charts illustrative of it, and at present belonging to this department, or copies of them, should be deposited in your custody. Such defects as you may find in these sources of intelligence, it will be your duty to point out to me; and I shall be ready to instruct the various governors to use all the means in their power for supplying all such omissions. Your office will thus gradually become the depository of all this branch of statistical information, for the assistance, not of private adventurers only, but of this and of every other department of the state.

"Secondly. The next topic to be noticed is that of the sale in this country of the waste lands of the Crown in the British colonies.

"In every colonial possession of Great Britain, in which wild and unoccupied lands have been found, one general principle of law has been universally acknowledged. It is, that such lands are vested in the sovereign in right of the Crown, and that every private title must rest upon a royal grant as its basis. To what inconvenient consequences this abstract principle has formerly been urged it is needless to explain. In later times, and more especially since the year 1831, another principle, not less important, or in itself less clear, has been most distinctly acknowledged and inflexibly observed —it is, that the sovereign holds the lands in question in trust for the public good, and cannot, without a breach of that trust on the part of the responsible ministers of the government, be advised to make to any person a gratuitous donation of any such property. It must be appropriated to public uses and for the public benefit. Of those uses the first in order are such as respect the future improvement of the colony in which the lands are situate, by the dedication of all convenient tracts to public works, such as roads, quays, towing-paths, sites of public buildings and of military defences, sites of churches, school-houses, cemeteries, and places for public recreation and health. These and similar objects being provided for, the next use of the waste lands in the colonies is that of creating a public revenue by the sale of them. The appropriation of a part of that revenue to the ordinary exigencies of the public service will probably be found inevitable in every colony. Even in the case of South Australia, where the opposite principle was first maintained, the Colonization Commissioners found it necessary, after a short trial of the experiment, to apply to Parliament for an Act, which has authorized the application, even there, of the land revenue, in the first instance, to the support of the civil government; although indeed on condition that the sums so applied should be replaced to the emigration account, when the ordinary revenue of the colony may be adequate to meet that charge."

After referring to the state of various Colonies in respect to unoccupied lands, and setting forth that, from various causes, the Australian Colonies must be the principal field for the Commissioners' operations, the instructions thus proceed:—

"On this head I might, perhaps, content myself with a general reference to the instructions under which the agent-general for emigration has hitherto been acting. But, as this is a matter of deep interest and importance, I think it best to convey to you such explanations as have been suggested to me by the results of the experiment in which that officer has been engaged.

"1st. With regard to the manner of selecting and obtaining proper emigrants, it may be observed that two distinct methods have been pursued. The first is that of employing officers to travel through a particular district for the purpose. The second is that of establishing a resident local agency in different parts of the kingdom to enrol candidates for emigration, subject to the future approval of them.

"The first method has the advantage of accumulating experience in the hands of one person, of securing a uniformity of action, and of affording the means of personal inspection by an officer of trust, and of inquiry by him in the applicants' own neighbourhood before any steps at all are taken towards their acceptance. The plan of filling ships from given districts has the further advantage, as is remarked in one of the recently printed reports from the agent-general, of rendering it 'more likely that the people should agree on the voyage, and more likely that the deserving amongst them should carry to their new homes a pride in sustaining the good character they had borne in this country.' But times will occur when a transient interruption of the prosperity of some of the settlements, or an excessive competition amongst private parties to procure emigrants, may render it difficult to ensure a good complement for a ship from any single district; and this consideration has latterly led the agent-general to contemplate the other course of using local agents. That course has the convenience of giving a wider field to choose from, a greater command therefore over the assortment of the emigrants, and the means of having a large number of applicants enrolled at the same time, so as to be able with more confidence to form the shipping arrangements prospectively—a point of much importance, but attended with the hazard of great loss if the *data* on which they are based cannot be sufficiently ascertained. Between these different modes of proceeding, it will be for you to judge according to circumstances, using the one or the other, or blending the two, as you may find most compatible with effectiveness and economy.

"The next subject for consideration is, from what particular class of persons the choice of emigrants will be most advantageously made.

"There can be little doubt that, other circumstances being equal, the most desirable emigrants would be young married couples without children. Great anxiety is expressed on this subject in New South Wales; but it is found by experience that, generally speaking, unencumbered people will not leave their country, and that the encumbered will; and further, that even when young couples, without children, have said that they will emigrate, they are the most apt to desert at the last movement, and to cause a loss to the colony. Indeed, if the same migratory habits should spring up in the countries of Australia as prevail in those of America, it might be doubted how far it would be for the interest of each individual colony to spend its funds in the introduction of that description of persons who would find it the easiest to wander; certainly it would not be for the interest of any colony which enjoyed labour at a rate at all lower than its neighbours. For the present, however, it may be taken for granted, that the Commissioners should aim at sending out young people with few children, having always a due regard to other qualifications.

"I have next to advert to a point of some practical difficulty. It respects the security which can best be taken against the inconvenience arising from the default of persons who have pledged themselves to embark in fulfilling that engagement. The chance of defaulters at the last moment is one necessary attendant of a system of carrying passengers who have paid nothing for their conveyance. To supply some remedy for it, a deposit of 1*l.* has been taken in Ireland from each head of a family, or single adult who is accepted, returnable to him on reaching the colony. In Scotland the extreme poverty of the Highland emigrants has hitherto prevented this expedient; and in England it has not been resorted to, because, as most of the emigrants are at any rate supplied with part of their outfit by aid from their Unions, the extra 1*l.* would come from the same source, and constitute no additional motive in the labourer's own mind to keep his engagement. You will consider whether any better rules can be given under this head than those which have been practically followed.

"The mode of proceeding to hire ships for the voyage is another topic of much practical importance.

The shipping may either be engaged, and all the supplies purchased by the public, as has been the practice hitherto under the agent-general, or contracts may be made with ship-owners to take out the passengers at a rate per head, as used to be done when the London Emigration Committee acted under the authority of this department, and as has since been practised by the South Australian Commissioners. Convicts are sent out by the Transport Department of the Admiralty under the former plan: troops are sent to India by the Company under the latter. It will be for the Commissioners to choose between the two; or, if they think it expedient, to send some vessels on either plan upon trial, merely observing, in regard to those furnished by contract, that a strict check must be established, both upon the quality of the ship and also of the various provisions and stores for the use of the emigrants.

"The medical care of the emigrants on the voyage is a matter requiring the most careful attention. It will be a difficult question how the office of surgeon-superintendent may be best provided for in such numerous vessels as may be expected to be required for all the Australian settlements. The agent-general has, with propriety, endeavoured gradually to introduce a proportion of private surgeons into the service, as surgeons of the navy can hardly be permanently obtained in sufficient numbers, and must also not unnaturally be a more expensive class of officers. It is evident, however, of how much value they are rendered by their previous experience and attainments, and it is possible that the Commissioners will always find it expedient to retain as many of them as the exigencies of their own service will enable the Board of Admiralty to spare for this purpose.

"For the management of the people on board the emigrant ships, a code of instructions was prepared by the agent-general last year with much care and inquiry. As those rules have been adopted by the South Australian Commissioners, and by some of the largest private shipowners; and as the accounts up to this time of every vessel which sailed since its establishment, so far as they have reached me, appear to be far more favourable than were ever received before, I see reason to hope that the Commissioners may find this code to provide for all material points: some modifications, however, will probably be requisite if any vessels are sent out upon contracts; as for instance, stricter directions than before to the surgeon-superintendent, vigilantly to control the sufficiency and quality of the issues to the people under his charge, and to note any defects.

"I must also briefly advert to the proceedings to be adopted on the arrival of the emigrants at their place of destination. From that period, a month's board and lodging in public barracks was, for some time, allowed by the Government of New South Wales to emigrants in the Government vessels. It was in contemplation, at the date of the latest intelligence, to reduce the period to a fortnight, which I think would be enough in any ordinary circumstances. This must always remain, however, a point for the local authorities; and the proper course at home will be to apprize emigrants in the public ships, that either in barracks, or on board of their vessel, they will be sure of the option of a maintenance for not less than one week after arrival; but that any extension beyond that period must depend on circumstances at the time, and on the directions of the colonial government.

"Every information on the disposal of the emigrants, the addresses of their employers, and the rates of wages given to them, should continue to be obtained, as is the present practice, in returns to the office in this country.

"In an earlier part of this communication, I adverted to the facilities which would be derived by emigrants or capitalists from the plan of depositing sums of money on certificates producible in discharge of an equal sum of money to be bid at future auctions within the colony, where the lands are situate. It may, therefore, be desirable to explain, that the depositors of such money would have the advantage of the employment of it in the removal of emigrants of their own selection, subject to the approbation of the choice by yourselves. In effect, therefore, any man, or body of men, desirous of removing from this country a number of unemployed, but eligible labourers to lands in the colonies, might accomplish that purpose, to a very great extent, by merely advancing the amount of the passage-money, which would be repaid to them by an equivalent amount of land. There are, probably, large numbers of persons who, on these terms, would be willing to embark their property and their persons in such undertakings.

"You are probably aware, that a question of considerable importance has, for a long time past, been much discussed in the correspondence between this office and the agent-general, and the Governor of New South Wales, relating to what is termed 'The Bounty System'—that is, the system of paying from the Land Revenue bounties to persons, proportionate to the number of eligible emigrants whom they may introduce into the colony from this country, the candidates for such bounties being intrusted with the selection of the emigrants, and with whatever relates to the management of the voyage. How far it may be right to continue this system at all, and, if continued, what may be the regulations under which it ought to be placed, and in what proportion the proceeds of the sales of lands available for emigration should be divided between the recipients of the bounty on the one hand, and the conductors of emigration on behalf of the public on the other hand, and how security can be most effectually taken to prevent the undue interference of the one plan with the other,—these are all questions on which I am unwilling to express any final opinion, until I shall have received your report on them; but they are at the same time questions of so much importance, that your attention cannot be too soon, or too carefully, given to the right solution of them.

"It remains to make some remarks on those colonies which do not at present afford a revenue appropriated to the introduction of emigrants. To these the emigration which takes place is entirely voluntary, and subject to no other influence by any department of the Government, than from the diffusion of any information which it may appear expedient to publish, and the enforcement of any general rules which an Act of Parliament may supply for the regulation of passengers' ships. The Commissioners will find naval officers resident at the principal ports to perform the latter duty, over whom it will be the business of the Commissioners to exercise a general superintendence.

"You will further make twice in each year a report of your proceedings, exhibiting with all practical distinctness the progress of your labours—the results, whether favourable or otherwise, as far as they can be ascertained—the prospects of an increase or reduction in the sale of lands, and in the number of emigrants,—accompanied by any suggestions which you may be able to offer for the advancement of those objects, or for improving the efficiency of the institution, over which you are to preside."

The following letter and enclosure, from the Secretary to the Land and Emigration Commissioners, were also read to the Board:—

"2, Middle Scotland Yard, 12th
"February, 1840.

"SIR,—I am directed by the Commissioners of Land and Emigration to transmit to you, for the information of the Poor Law Commissioners, the enclosed copy of a recent report from Mr. Elliot to Lord John Russell, containing some general remarks on the emigration to New South Wales in government vessels during the last three years. Several Unions in the southern counties of England having promoted emigration to New South Wales in the government vessels, the information contained in this document may possibly be acceptable to the Poor Law Commissioners.

"I have the honour to be, Sir,
"Your obedient humble Servant,
"JOHN WALPOLE.

"*E. Chadwick, Esq.*

(Copy.)

"2, Middle Scotland Yard, 18th
"January, 1840.

"MY LORD,—I have the honour to transmit to your Lordship a return of last year's emigration in government ships to New South Wales, by which document it will be seen that seventeen ships were sent out, and that the number of persons they contained was 4,096. In consequence of the accounts of the continued drought and high prices of provisions, accompanied by a falling off in the land revenue of the colony, and by a temporary diminution of candidates to emigrate from home, it was not thought expedient to urge the numbers beyond that amount.

"At the date of the latest accounts, abundance of rain had fallen, and the crops were looking well. The wages of mechanics and domestic servants continued as high as ever, and agricultural labourers were receiving £25 per annum with board and lodging. All the emigrants of 1838 had obtained comfortable employments.

"As this is the last occasion on which I shall have to address your Lordship in my separate capacity, it may perhaps be permitted me to offer some observations on the government emigration of the past three years.

"There has been no want of strictures upon it; and it is perhaps due to the office just merged in a larger commission, not to withhold some general answers to those strictures, especially as it is happily in my power to afford them in the shape of a few decisive and undeniable facts.

"First. The shipping, including under that name the hire of vessels, the fitting up of them, and the purchase and regulation of the supplies, has been under this office from the beginning; and the shipping has been well spoken of by all.

"Secondly. The care and discipline of the people on board was during the years 1837 and 1838 confided to the surgeons of the respective ships, in pursuance of a proposal strongly recommended from the colony. Much sickness prevailed during those years, and was, very properly, rendered the subject of unsparing investigation in New South Wales. The plan of making each surgeon the exclusive manager of his own ship originated in the colony; and whatever may have been the dissatisfaction with the results of a fair and patient trial of it, the blame cannot attach to any department at home. My own opinion is that the plan was plausible, and worth trying, but that it has been proved to be unsuited to emigration on a large scale.

"At the end of 1838, therefore, I resolved to take the system on board under the immediate responsibility and control of this office. The 'Asia' having put into Plymouth about that time with sickness amongst the passengers, and in a state which was described to me as one of 'Mutiny,' I took the opportunity of a personal inspection to frame a code of regulations, which I required every grown man in the ship to sign in my presence. From that period, their vessel was kept in a state of cleanliness which was admitted to do them the highest credit. I afterwards extended the regulations to all other ships, accompanied by a general revision of every detail of the internal arrangements, the whole being embodied in a printed volume of instructions to surgeons superintendent. To state the experience that has occurred since that measure is the duty that now remains to me.

"The 'Asia' was the first ship. Having put into Plymouth from Scotland, with the commencement of a fever amongst her people, and in a condition of great disorder, this vessel completed her subsequent voyage from Plymouth to Sydney without the death of one person, man, woman, or child. The next ship that reached the colony was the 'Navarino' from Cork. Like her predecessor, this vessel also performed the whole voyage from the United Kingdom to New South Wales without a single death amongst the people embarked in her, the only casualty having been of an infant born on board.

"Ten other ships have been heard of at sea, most of them having been on their voyage a considerable time. Five out of the ten have not had a single death, and four of the remaining five have not had more than two deaths. It is enough to look at the Returns printed for Parliament last year (Commons' Paper, No. 580), to see that in 1837, and the first part of 1838, a ship might be accounted prosperous which did not lose as many as ten passengers. On the other hand, out of twelve ships in all that have been heard of since the new regulations, seven have not lost one passenger, and four have lost only two. These are facts which probably the warmest advocate would not have ventured to anticipate. It would be too much to expect that so singular a prosperity should continue unmixed, but the number of twelve ships will perhaps be deemed sufficient to show that the change is not owing to chance; and that the colony will scarcely have reason to complain of the part this office has taken in the system on board the ships.

"Thirdly. The next question I would advert to is that of selection. The remarks made on this subject in the colony are too apt to assume that there is an unlimited command of emigrants in this country. It may be natural for an officer at Sydney to point out that the persons who arrive are not the best that could be desired; but the duty to which the officers at home must attend is to send the best who can be procured; and it may be questioned how they should otherwise have succeeded in doubling and quadrupling the emigration to New South Wales within the last three years.

"The substantially satisfactory fact upon this head is, that by the last annual report of the agent for emigrants at Sydney, pointing out all the objections which he could state against the people in government vessels, it nevertheless appears that 'all the emigrants who arrived during the past year, 1838, are now comfortably settled, and at high wages throughout the colony.'

"Much unnecessary argument has been expended to prove that the most eligible emigrants would be young married couples without children. There is not any difference of opinion, that I am aware of, on that point; but experience has taught us that it is not people unburthened with families, but those who are burthened, who are willing to leave their country for a distant settlement. While for this reason it is not possible to get quit of children altogether, the following statement may serve to show that there has been no want of effectual and persevering endeavours to repress their numbers. The proportion of children under seven years of age in the government ships in 1837 was 34 per cent.; the proportion in 1838 was 23 per cent.; and the proportion in 1839, 11½ per cent: their numbers having been reduced, therefore, from more than a third of the whole of the passengers, to much less than an eighth.

"The three foregoing heads of the shipping, the discipline of the people during the voyage, and their selection before they start, embrace the principal duties involved in emigration.

"I am disposed to think that the employment of vessels entirely fitted out and supplied by government, was useful at the outset of so large an emigration to a new point, more distant than any to which equally extensive numbers of free passengers had been sent before. They afforded an example of what responsible servants of the public felt to be necessary, and they certainly did serve to establish confidence in some parts of the country from which people were not disposed to go by other opportunities. But I have no doubt that they could not be made the most economical means of conveyance, and I should feel every disposition to prefer, as the general rule in such cases, a recourse to private competition. I think that the time is come when it would be advantageous to substitute contracts for passengers, at a certain rate per head, in lieu of fitting out and victualling the ships immediately by the government.

"It was not surprising that two courses of proceeding so much resembling one another as the government emigration and that upon bounty, should not go on together without exciting some party spirit, especially as the latter involved in its favour a considerable commercial interest. But, however strenuously may have been urged every defect which could be found or supposed in the government emigration, it must always remain a satisfaction to the officers employed at home during the last three years, and will, I doubt not, weigh duly with the reflecting part of the community in New South Wales, that those officers found the emigrants assisted to proceed to Sydney going by hundreds, and that they have sent them by thousands; that they found the colony still inadequately known, and by no means popular; that they now see it very well known (as the extent itself of the new emigration sufficiently proves), and in many parts of the country preferred to all other places of resort.

"I have the honour to be, my Lord,
"Your Lordship's most obedient humble Servant,
(Signed) "T. FRED. ELLIOT.

"*The Lord John Russell,*
&c. &c. &c."

II.—THE DUTIES OF CLERKS TO BOARDS OF GUARDIANS IN REFERENCE TO PROCEEDINGS UNDER THE RECENT BASTARDY ACT, 2 AND 3 VIC. C. 85.

THE Board took into consideration the following letter upon this subject:

"LOUGHBOROUH UNION.

"*Loughborough.*

"GENTLEMEN,—I beg to inform you that by a resolution passed on the 14th instant, the Guardians of this Union have appointed me their solicitor, which appointment I request you to confirm.

"The circumstances which caused this appointment are as follow:—The Board on the same day passed a resolution to the effect of applying for orders of affiliation in all cases of bastardy; and on the supposition that these applications, according to the wording of the Act, emanate from the Board, and not from any parish officer, that my appointment as clerk did not involve the gratuitous rendering of my professional services, and that most, if not all, the cases of application would require the aid of a solicitor, they paid me the compliment of appointing me their solicitor with a view to my conducting those applications.

"I remain, Gentlemen,
"Faithfully yours,
"BEAUVOIR BROCK.

"*To the Poor Law Commissioners.*"

The Board directed the following reply to be made to this letter:—

"The Commissioners entertain great doubts whether they have the power to authorize the Board of Guardians to appoint a solicitor (*eo nomine*) as a paid officer of the Board, and the Commisioners see great objections to such an appointment, as it would tend to fetter the discretion of the Guardians in the case of any litigation arising in which, for any peculiar reasons, the services of some other professional gentleman might be preferable.

"Moreover, unless the solicitor's salary was previously fixed at a definite sum, it would expose his advice, as clerk, to the suspicion that in counselling a resort in any instance to litigation or other legal transactions, he was directed by his professional or personal interest. Such a suspicion would seriously affect the character for disinterestedness of the officer, who should always be regarded as the most confidential and disinterested adviser of the Guardians.

"The Commissioners have reason to be satisfied with the footing upon which the appointment of professional men as clerks to Boards of Guardians now rests. In making such appointments, and in giving the higher remuneration which usually accompanies such appointments, the Commissioners and the Guardians have secured for the Union the benefit of a professional intelligence and discretion in performing all the duties in which the Board of Guardians can act directly.

"In all cases in which the law regards the Board of Guardians as acting, their clerk, who is made inseparable from the Board and their immediate instrument, will practically be the agent of the whole body, and will be bound to exercise the best discretion of which he may be master.

"When he is appointed for his professional qualification, he will act with professional caution and discretion. This caution and discretion will in most cases supersede the necessity of resorting to other legal aid, and will enable the Guardians to transact with accuracy and safety many matters in which the Overseers were formerly liable to failure unless professional assistance was obtained by them.

"When a professional man is appointed clerk, the Commissioners consider the Board of Guardians is in strictness already supplied for the most part with professional advice, although where it is necessary that a title should be examined or a lease or other similar document prepared, or where proceedings are to be taken in any Court of Law or Equity, he cannot be called upon to transact that business in the capacity of clerk, unless under some such arrangement for the general performance of legal business as is above adverted to. But in cases such as are usually the applications to sessions for orders of affiliation, applications similar in almost all respects to those formerly made by overseers in person, the Commissioners can perceive no occasion for further assistance than that already possessed by the Guardians.

"The assistance to be given to the Boards by

their clerks will undoubtedly be an additional labour, and in that point of view will constitute a ground for an increase in the clerk's salary, when this addition may cause the clerk's duties in the whole to exceed those which he undertook at the original determination of the amount of salary.

"The Commissioners take occasion to observe with respect to applications for orders of affiliation, that the Guardians have always possessed under the Poor Law Amendment Act the power to apply for such orders, and that the occasion for making such applications is not increased by the recent statute, which was not intended to encourage the making of such applications in greater number, or to affect the Guardians with any increased motive to make such applications. When it was formerly right to make such applications, it will still be right to do so; when it was proper to omit the making such applications, the like reasons will still require the like omission. The statute was merely intended to diminish the trouble and expense attendant on the applications to quarter sessions in cases where such applications were judged proper, and to diminish the evil consequences supposed to follow from the delivery of evidence corroborative of the paternity of the party charged as father, in a court so thickly and promiscuously attended as the general quarter sessions usually are."

III. — RELIEF IN KIND — GENERAL REGULATIONS AS TO PAUPER CLOTHING.

THE Board having had before them information of much evil created by the mode in which relief was given in clothing to certain classes of paupers, passed the following minute thereon:—

"1. The practice of allowing clothing to adult paupers out of the workhouse appears to be so rare as not to call for any remarks on the part of the Commissioners.

"2. The practice of making allowances of clothing to the children of able-bodied labourers going into service appears to prevail in many Unions, and several applications have lately been made to the Commissioners to sanction allowances of this description.

"It is manifest that the practice of making allowances of clothing to the children of labourers going into service cannot increase the total amount of employment; that every person who obtains employment on account of the allowance of clothes from the parish must prevent another person who has not that advantage from obtaining employment; and consequently that such allowances are detrimental to the independent labourer. Such allowances are in the nature of premiums upon pauper apprenticeships, the evils of which have been already pointed out by the Commissioners on various occasions, and are particularly illustrated in a letter from Mr. Tufnell, published in the Appendix to their Third Annual Report.

"3. With respect to allowances of clothing to paupers in the workhouse, it is desirable that persons residing a short time in the workhouse should not, on leaving it, be furnished, except under very particular circumstances, with a fresh suit of clothes. In some places where such an allowance had been made, the result has been that able-bodied men, previous to entering the workhouse, have disposed of their clothes, and clothed themselves in rags not sufficiently decent to work in, knowing that they would receive a complete suit on leaving the workhouse: and no way has been found of preventing this evil, except by keeping to the strict rule of giving to a pauper who leaves the house no other clothes than those he had on when he entered it.

"Persons permanently domiciled in the workhouse, and especially children who have remained in it from an early age, must, on quitting it, be furnished with a decent outfit of clothing. Young persons who have been brought up in the workhouse, and who leave it for service or apprenticeship, ought, in the opinion of the Commissioners, to be furnished with such an outfit of clothing as is usually possessed by young persons, not being paupers, in a similar condition."

IV. — MODE TO BE PURSUED BY BOARDS OF GUARDIANS OR OFFICERS IN CORRESPONDING WITH EACH OTHER.

THE Commissioners took into consideration an application from the Brackley Union, as to the mode to be pursued by Boards of Guardians in corresponding with each other; to which the Commissioners stated their opinion as follows:—

"When a Board of Guardians or clerk of one

Union wishes to communicate with a relieving officer of another Union, or where a relieving officer of one Union wishes to communicate with a Board of Guardians or with the clerk of another Union, the letter should pass through the clerks of both Unions.

"The only cases in which the relieving officer of one Union can properly communicate directly with the relieving officer of another Union are, firstly, cases of special emergency, in which the delay in communicating through the Guardians might be productive of evil; and, secondly, cases in which the relieving officer of one Union, as an accommodation to the relieving officer of another Union, has undertaken to be the channel of transmitting relief to a pauper residing in his Union, but belonging to such other Union."

V.—POOR RATES.—NOTICES OF APPEALS AGAINST.

THE Commissioners took into consideration the following proposal from the Guardians of the Chailey Union, respecting Notices of Appeals against Poor Rates:—

"These notices are now sent by the clerk to the justices, at an expense of 6*l*. 12*s*. per annum. This charge is considered very objectionable, as appeals against poor rates seldom occur in any of the parishes of this Union.

"The Guardians propose that in future one precept should be sent from the justices to the clerk to the Union, who will be instructed by the Board to forward copies of the notices to the parishes, and by this means a saving of 6*l*. a-year will be effected in this Union.

"The Board of Guardians consider that the sending of these precepts is strictly a parochial duty, and one that may very properly be entrusted to their clerk; they therefore request that the Poor Law Commissioners will sanction the above arrangement, and, if necessary, will recommend that a clause be inserted in the Poor Law Amendment Act of this session, which may enable the Board of Guardians to direct the notices to be sent to parishes by the clerk as proposed."

In reference thereto, the Commissioners stated

"That the Parochial Assessments Act makes it the duty of the justices to give notice of the time and place of hearing appeals against poor rates, by causing each notice to be affixed to or near the door of the churches of the parish situate within the division for which such justices act. It appears to the Commissioners that the justices, in giving notices, are at liberty to pursue what course they think best for giving effect to the statute.

"The Commissioners consider the course suggested by the Board of Guardians of sending one precept to the clerk of the Union, that officer being instructed to forward copies of the notices to parishes concerned, is, in an economical point of view, a very desirable arrangement, and one which, if no objection be offered on the part of the justices, it would be proper to adopt.

"The Commissioners do not perceive that any reasonable objection can be made to the adoption of such a course, the object of which is to relieve the justices of trouble and to facilitate the working of the statute."

VI. — CONTRACTS. — EXECUTION OF BONDS FOR DUE PERFORMANCE OF.

THE Commissioners took into consideration the following extract from a letter addressed to them by a contractor for provisions, complaining of being charged 10*s*. 6*d*. for a bond he was required to execute for the due performance of his contract.

"I tender for some of the Unions near here in the grocery and provision line. Upon the 7th September last there appeared in a provincial newspaper an advertisement for tenders for a Union stating that the contractors would be required to find two sureties and enter into a bond, but nothing about *paying* for the bond. I obtained the contract, found the sureties required, and executed the *bond*, but when at the end of the quarter, I sent my bill in, I was stopped 10*s*. 6*d*. by the clerk of the Union for the bond.

"I tendered again last Lady Day, and represented that it was a very heavy tax upon the profits of goods supplied to pay for the *bond*, and tended to the disadvantage of the Union, as, if the bond is paid, contractors must have larger profits to make up for paying 10*s*. 6*d*., when the clerk replied 'I should not be charged *this* quarter,' which made an impression upon my mind that the charge was not legal, which was strengthened by a knowledge of some contractors, who, by holding out, have never paid the bond, while others have submitted to it. In the Union in which I reside and contract for, no such thing is required. I find two sureties, but have never been asked to execute a bond, although my contracts have been heavier than in the Union above referred to."

The Commissioners directed the following communication to be addressed to the clerk of the Union.

"The Poor Law Commissioners desire to inform you they have received a communication from a contractor for the supply of provisions for your Union, complaining of your having charged him 10*s*. 6*d*. for a bond he was required to execute for the due performance of his contract. Questions as to the propriety of charging for bonds of this nature have frequently been asked by clerks of Unions who are professional men, and by clerks who are not members of the legal profession;—the former supposing that they should be allowed to make specific charges for attending the execution of such bonds, and the latter that they should incur penalties by attending the execution of such documents. The Commissioners, in answer to these questions, have stated, that clerks to Unions, who are professional men, cannot charge for services which can be performed by non-professional persons of ordinary capacity; and that non-professional persons, who are clerks to Unions, do not expose themselves to penalties in filling up forms of bonds and attending their execution. In giving this opinion, the Commissioners have not supposed that clerks to Unions, who are professional men, can be called upon to perform duties which require the skill of a person who has had a legal education.

"Forms of bonds have been prepared, under the direction of the Commissioners, to meet the ordinary business of Unions; and such forms, when applicable, should not, in the opinion of the Commissioners, be charged for by you either for the drawing or execution."

VII.—RELIEF OF DESTITUTION.

Further Correspondence of the Poor Law Commissioners with the Registrar-General on the subject of a passage in a Letter addressed to the Registrar-General by Mr. Farr, and published in the Appendix to the Registrar-General's First Annual Report.

IN compliance with the request of the Registrar-General, the Poor Law Commissioners have directed the insertion of the subjoined letter from Mr. Farr, in vindication of the statement made in his letter of the 29th November, 1839.

The Commissioners see no grounds for altering the opinions they expressed in their first letter, with relation to the statement in question. They conceive that the inferences that the deaths of infants from inanition was occasioned by the destitution of the mothers, is entirely gratuitous as respects the cases cited. The Commissioners do not assert the impossibility of a death having occurred from the destitution of the mother in any of the cases of infant mortality, but no such cause was assigned on the face of the returns or appeared in evidence with relation to those cases, and the assumption could not, as it appears to them, be justified by any facts as to infant mortality having been occasioned by destitution in other cases occurring at other times and places, supposing the facts to be so. The Commissioners observe that Mr. Farr, on a gratuitous assumption that reference was made by them to the amount of deposits in the savings banks in 1837, which was 16,578,849*l*., denies the correctness of that part of their letter wherein it is stated that "the increasing amount of upwards of 20,000,000*l*. of deposits in the savings banks, almost wholly from those of the labouring classes who are frugal, attest the amount of means at their disposal beyond a bare subsistence." The reference was made in round numbers, not to returns of past years, but to what they were informed was the then present amount, which they believed was increasing. On inquiry which they have directed to be made at the National Debt Office as to the precise fact, they are informed that the balance due to the savings banks on the 20th of November, 1839, was 23,583,365*l*.

On the question raised by Mr. Farr as to the accuracy of the statement in respect to the amount expended by the labouring classes on spirits, the Commissioners observe that the data were stated in the letter, and that no one could be misled by the expression "two thirds more," or be led to understand otherwise than that the duty of eight millions formed one third of the cost of twenty-four millions to the consumer. The Commissioners do not feel themselves called upon to enter further into the examination of any of Mr. Farr's statements on the subject, but will feel it a duty to avail themselves of the facilities which the Registrar General may afford for the investigation of any cases of alleged starvation caused by destitution, which in future may be brought to their notice, and they trust that the investigation will be made in a manner as satisfactory to the public as to themselves.

"*General Register Office, March*, 1840.

"GENTLEMEN,—I have the honour to transmit to you the enclosed copy of a letter from Mr. Farr, in reply to the comments on his previous letters, contained in that which was addressed to me by your direction in the past month. As the preceding part of this correspondence has been published, while yet unfinished, in your Official Circular issued early in the present month, I trust you will give equal publicity to his reply, a copy of which I now enclose.

"I entirely concur with you in the belief you express 'that the new registration may be made to serve as a new and valuable additional security against the omissions of due inquiry in the class of cases in question' (namely, of deaths alleged to have been caused by want), 'as well as in others;' and I beg leave to assure you that it is my earnest desire to aid, by my co-operation, in the furtherance of that important object, and to take such means as shall enable you to be furnished with early information of every registered case of death which shall appear to have been caused by destitution.

"I have the honour to be, Gentlemen,
"Your obedient servant,
(Signed) "T. H. LISTER.

"*To the Poor Law Commissioners.*"

"(Copy.)

"*March 17th*, 1840.

"SIR,—I have read, at your request, the letter of the Poor Law Commissioners, dated 24th February, 1840. It contains remarks on two passages, published in the Appendix to your Report,* on the cases of starvation, registered in the year 1837, and on my letter of the 29th November, 1839: and it is intended to show that the passages in the first letter 'are entirely unsustained by the facts.' The question under dispute is starvation, considered as a cause of death; and the importance attached to the subject will justify me in discussing, more fully than I have hitherto done, its more important bearings.

"The 148,701 statements in the column, headed 'cause of death,' in the registers, were classed in the first abstract by me, without distinction of age, profession, or any other circumstance, except the sex, the registered cause of death, and the districts. The passage in my letter (Appendix, p. 106) was written with the tabular results of the abstracts before me, the facts under discussion having constituted rather more than 4 ten-thousandths of the number of entries. The 63 cases, ascribed to starvation, have since been extracted from the registers, with the time and place of death, the age, sex, rank, or profession, the cause of death as described in the registers, the names of the persons, and the names and descriptions of the informants. I stated, parenthetically, that the cases were ascribed to the cause in question, 'principally at inquests.' This is an error. I wrote from memory and was mistaken in the proportion of inquests. The coroner was not the 'informant,' or at least did not sign the registers, in the majority of instances; for, as the Poor Law Commissioners remark, it appears on the face of the registers that in the year 1837 'nearly as many cases of death, from the want of the necessaries of life, have passed without inquiry, as have been made the subjects of inquiry before coroners' juries.' With this exception, the passage in my letter is substantially correct.

"It is quite true that 36 of the cases were 'only infants' under one year of age; that 12 of them died 'simply of inanition;' and that the remaining 24 died for want of their natural nourishment—the mother's milk, or an adequate substitute for milk.

"From your Report, Sir, it appears that in the year ending June 30th, 1838, 71,888 infants died under one year of age, the greater part of them the children of the lower classes, and many of them the offspring of paupers. Is it not probable that out of these a much higher proportion than twice 36 were starved in the cold nights of winter, and on the coarse, innutritious, inadequate subsistence of impoverished parents?

"The Poor Law Commissioners profess their inability to understand how 'firing, clothing, every necessary of life, were abandoned by these infants at the imperious bidding of hunger.' They can have no difficulty in understanding that, if the mothers are ever reduced to extremities, the children will share and suffer their fate. In a recent work Dr. Alison supplies an illustration. 'During the inclement weather of the spring of 1838,' says this benevolent and scientific physician, 'I saw three young women with natural children on the breast, who were out of work, in a miserable state of destitution; after some weeks of severe suffering, *the children all died, certainly from the effects of cold and imperfect nourishment.*'*

"If infants die of starvation, the deaths will generally be ascribed in the registers to the want of the mother's milk. The informants are not likely to state that the want of the strong diet of adults was the cause of death in their cases.

"Infants are starved (1) on the thin milk of ill-fed mothers; or (2) in cases where the mother does not suckle the child, and the artificial food is coarse, and such as nature never intended for the food of infants.

"The experience of Foundling Hospitals shows that the want of the mother's breast is more fatal to

* Report of the Registrar-General, 1839, 8vo. Appendix, pp. 106, 111.

* Cited by the Editor of the Medical Gazette, February 28, 1840, in a series of articles on the diet of the poor, written in an excellent spirit.

infants than the want of sufficient food is to adults. The Abbé Gaillard states* that at Parthenay 54 of 153 foundlings died in the year after birth, or 35 out of 100 born. At X—— 197 out of 244 born, or 81 per cent., perished in the first year.

"He ascertained that as much care was taken of the children at X—— as at Parthenay; but at X—— the children were all brought up by hand (*au biberon*), and it is to the want of milk (*au défaut seul d'allaitement*) that the Abbé and the managers of the hospital ascribe the excessive mortality. The same fact is deduced by M. Villermé from three extensive returns, which he procured from the Foundling Hospitals of Rheims, Lyons, and Paris. In ordinary circumstances, when the children are suckled by the mother, the deaths in the first year out of 100 born alive, are 15 to 20; a proportion which, as has been seen, increases to 80 in the 100 when the children are deprived of milk. The privation of milk is the privation of food, and is equivalent to the starvation of adults.

"It is only when the child is deprived of milk and the event can be traced to no disease, that the death of infants is ascribed to starvation; and it will be perceived, upon the slightest reflection, that the 'want of nourishment usually supplied by the mother, weaning,' &c. &c., can be referred to no other head in the *abstract* than 'starvation.' 'Want of breast milk' is not a disease, but it is a cause of death. It is, in the strictest scientific sense, 'starvation.'

"I must notice one passage in the letter of the Poor Law Commissioners on this subject. It is this: 'Not less than 36 of the cases appear to have been the cases of infants, nearly all of whom died from various causes of mortality prevalent amongst the children of all classes, *e.g.* Helen Elizabeth ——, aged three weeks (condition of parent a *gentleman*), died at ——. Cause assigned in the registry, *Owing to malformation about the mouth, the child was incapable of deglutition, and gradually perished from want of sustenance.* Frederick ——, aged eight months, father a woolcomber, died at Exeter workhouse. Cause assigned in the registry, starved from malformation,' &c. &c. &c. &c.

"It is somewhat remarkable that neither of these two cases is included in the 36, or in the 63 cases, to which the Poor Law Commissioners say they belong, and of which they give them as examples. They were classed under 'malformations' in the abstract, and are not in the classified list of 63 cases, which the Poor Law Commissioners have forwarded to you as an appendix to their letters.†

"Twelve deaths were ascribed to cold. It will be seen, upon reference to the long list of cases in 1838, that 'death by starvation' has been understood by the registrars, informants, coroners, and juries, all over the country, in the sense that it has in the English classics, and as it has been defined by the lexicographers. It denotes death by cold, death by hunger, death by cold and hunger, accidental death by cold and hunger, death by want the result of destitution, or death by cold and hunger the result of destitution. The senses run imperceptibly into each other as the facts do in nature. The deaths by want, the result of destitution, make the strongest impression on the mind; they are, perhaps, the most frequent. Hence the accessary idea of destitution is often called up by 'starvation.'

"In the rigorous winters of this latitude, the human race requires artificial heat, and fuel in parts of England is so expensive, that very little fire can be procured by the poor. The 'tables of mortality' for the metropolis show that 997 persons died in the coldest week in January, and only 813 in the last mild week in February. Is it, then, extravagant to assert that of 148,701 deaths, 'a much higher proportion' than 12 had their source in starvation by cold, in too many instances unmitigated in intensity when it penetrated the bare chamber, gathered round the desolate hearth, and froze the veins of the infant, the sickly, or the old?

"Medical practitioners meet with many distressing cases of starvation in this metropolis. I will mention one. In the winter of 1838 I was requested, in the middle of the night, to see a woman, who, it was said, was dying for want of help. I followed the messenger through a labyrinth of narrow passages, near Fitzroy market, and found in the corner of an attic a young woman, thinly clad, lying on a straw bed spread upon the floor. She had given birth to a child, then at her feet. Three children lay on the same bed, under a single rug. It was intensely cold. She had no fire, no candle, no food, and, if I recollect right, had not more than three half-pence in money to meet the exigencies of child-birth. The lodgers in the room below had been aroused by her groans.

"The Poor Law Commissioners discuss, at great length, the question whether blame attaches to them and to the administration of the new Poor Law, in connection with the deaths of 14 adults, ascribed in the registers of the half year more specifically to starvation, in the sense of 'privation of food.' This may be a question well deserving investigation; but it is a question with which, as it appears to me, I have here nothing to do. In my letter I brought no charge against the administration of the new Poor Law, and neither mentioned nor alluded to the Poor Law Commissioners. The passage has never been made the handle of an attack by their enemies. It refers to a 'cause of death' existing 'in this *and in every other country*,' and it forms part of a *paragraph*, addressed almost exclusively to members of the medical profession, on deaths from intemperance,

* Résultats du défaut d'allaitement des nouveaux nés par M. L'Abbé Gaillard—Annales d'Hygiène, tome 19, p. 39.
† The list was not published in the Official Circular.

gout, debility, tumours, cancer, scrofula, mortification, abscess, inflammation, and hœmorrhage.*

"The abstract was a classification of the causes of death, and had no reference to the remote, incidental, or accessary circumstances in which the direct cause of death originated; for the reason that this would have led to endless subdivisions of the several heads, and could have yielded few satisfactory results. Thus every case of death by drowning was classed under 'Violent deaths;' yet drowning might either be suicide, accident, murder, or manslaughter. The same observation applies to deaths by blows, hanging, burns, wounds, poisons, &c. &c., which, after careful consideration and consultation with you, Sir, it was deemed advisable, in the present state of registration, to refer to one generic head, 'violent deaths.'

"Whether starvation occurred therefore in infants, or in the aged; whether it was accidental, inevitable, or the result of negligence, the fact itself remained unchanged; it was still starvation; and, unless other causes were mentioned, could only be referred to one head in the classification. In determining the connexion and origin of the facts, more particularly in tracing the circumstances of starvation with the view of criminating, or of exculpating, any class of individuals, it would be necessary to examine all the statements in the registers with this object in view. A list of the particulars of 79 cases, which appeared calculated to assist the Poor Law Commissioners, was transmitted to their secretary; and several of the cases referred to other heads in the abstract, are, perhaps, as interesting and as important for the purpose which they professed to have in view, as the 63 cases.

"Of the cases in addition to the 63, the Poor Law Commissioners have cited (incorrectly) the case of Helen Elizabeth ——, and another instance in which starvation was occasioned by 'malformation;' also four cases of intoxication, and death by exposure to cold. Of a pauper, aged 50 years, the registered cause of death was *mortification of the feet—starved with hunger and cold.* This case was entered in the abstract under 'mortification;' the cases of intoxication and starvation, by cold, under 'intemperance;' the starvation of insane persons under 'insanity.' Each case could be entered under only one head; and it was considered that intemperance, insanity, and malformation were the prior causes, although starvation was the direct cause of death. Mortification is a well defined disease; and the case was classed under it, although the mortification was the effect of 'hunger and cold.'

"When the starvation is not absolute it generally gives rise to disease. The informant may then either specify the starvation or the disease, as the cause of death; and it is often difficult to determine the influence of several concurring causes on that event, so that the registers can only be considered to indicate an approximation to the real number of deaths from starvation. In all statistical observations of this uncertain character there are errors on both sides; errors of omission and insertion. To correct the errors of the registers the investigation should not be restricted to one class of causes. Deaths from other causes may be included in the 63 ascribed to starvation; it is still more probable that cases of starvation were registered under the remaining 141,544 specified causes, or included in the 7,094 cases in which the cause of death was not stated.

"The following list of cases of starvation in the year 1838, in number 123, has been extracted, in continuation of the list which was furnished to the Poor Law Commissioners, and which they published in *the Official Circular* so far as it illustrated their views. It will be seen that the number of cases in the Appendix to your First Report was not above the average. All the entries have been extracted in which the death was ascribed to starvation by hunger or by cold; but no attempt has been made to distinguish the cases of death from destitution, hunger, or want of shelter and fuel (which apparently constituted the majority), from the accidental deaths in storms; or the death of the houseless outcast, from the deaths of persons in good circumstances. The list is exclusive of infants under one year of age, as the Poor Law Commissioners have objected to the inclusion of such cases under the head of starvation.

[The List of Cases is omitted.]

"It is difficult to say what proportion of the mortality in England should be ascribed to insufficiency of food. If the quantity of provisions and the supply of food to the great mass of the population could be augmented, the mortality would be reduced; but every improvement in the means of the working classes leads to ameliorations in their habits, clothing, dwellings: so that the effect of better food is mixed up almost inextricably with other elements. I believe that the amount of subsistence exercises a less *direct* influence upon the diseases, epidemics, and general mortality of the population than Mr. Malthus imagined. The Poor Law Commissioners have, however, directed Mr. Chadwick to inform you that my letter contains 'the representation that the registers assign the *mortality to one all-pervading cause —hunger.** They repeat the words three times, with little variation, and reserve them for the peroration of their letter. It might be inferred from this, that the greater part of my letter had been devoted to the 'all-pervading cause' in question, whereas it was only incidentally referred to in two passages of 40 lines. I stated that according to the registers 63, or less than *one hundred-thousandth* of

* Registrar-General's Report, App., p. 106.

* Official Circular, No. II. p. 10; also pp. 9, 11.

the people, die annually of starvation; and added, 'Hunger destroys a much higher proportion than is indicated by the registers in this and every other country; but its effects, like the effects of excess, are generally manifested indirectly in the production of diseases of various kinds.' Upon this ground, and this sentence, which they quote, they assert in their letter to you that I '*assign the mortality to one all-pervading cause—hunger.*' If 63 died of starvation, what did the words 'a much higher proportion' imply? Fifty per cent. would be 'a much higher proportion;' doubled, the number would be 126; decupled 630; and the reader could scarcely have extended the sense of the expression further. Now 148,701 deaths were registered in the half year, and if 630 deaths had been distinctly ascribed to the 'all-pervading cause,' 148,071 would have remained to be ascribed to other causes.

"A passage in the Appendix to your Report distinctly expresses my opinion as to the influence of external causes on the mortality.*

"'Different classes of the population experience different rates of mortality, and suffer different kinds of diseases. The principal causes of these differences, besides the sex, age, and hereditary organization, must be sought in three sources—exercise in the ordinary occupations of life, the adequate or inadequate supply of warmth and of food, and the different degrees of exposure to poisonous effluvia and to destructive agencies.'

"It is subsequently shown, that the number of deaths in 25 cities was 47,953; and in country districts, containing nearly the same population, 29,693. The low diet of agricultural labourers was adduced as evidence against the doctrine, that the high mortality of cities is to be ascribed to the deficiency of food, and not to the impurity of the air. I am quite at a loss, therefore, to understand, why the Poor Law Commissioners reiterate three times, that my letter ascribed the mortality of the people of England to 'one all-pervading cause;' the all-pervading cause being nothing more than a cause which indirectly produced a much higher proportion than 63 in 148,701 deaths.

"I have shown from the facts registered in 1837 and in 1838, that the number of deaths from starvation in any of its senses was not exaggerated; that the classification of the cases was accurate; and that the passage which has called down animadversion is substantially correct. I admit, without any hesitation, that it *may* have been misunderstood; and I may add that the meaning of the term 'starvation' was not well understood by the public: its complications at different ages, with hunger, cold, destitution, and human agency, could scarcely have been conjectured, much less well known, by persons who had thought but casually on the subject, before they were made acquainted with the facts that have been extracted from the registers by your direction.

"The ascertained low rates of wages in agricultural districts refute the observations in the Poor Law Commissioners' letter 'on the *surplus means* of the *great mass* of the labouring population.' This is an extensive question, and cannot be satisfactorily discussed here. I may nevertheless remark in passing, that the arguments drawn from the savings' banks, and the sale of spirits, are inaccurately stated and fallacious. The Report referred to England and Wales, during the half year ended December 31st, 1837. The amount of deposits in the savings' banks was 16,578,849*l.* on November 20th, 1837, and not 'upwards of 20,000,000*l.*' The number of depositors was 547,910. The population was about 15,880,000; so that only 3½ per cent. of the total population, or 7 per cent. of adults, above the age of 20, were depositors in the savings' banks: 93 adults in 100 held no deposits, which is surely no proof that the 'great mass' of the agricultural labourers had 'surplus means.' The Poor Law Commissioners enter into a calculation to show that the labourers of England and Wales expend from 40,000,000*l.* to 50,000,000*l.* a-year in 'comforts and luxuries.' The proof is arithmetical. 'A sum of 8,444,800*l.*,' they say, 'is annually paid as duty on gin, whiskey, rum, and other spirits, the ultimate cost of which to the consumer cannot (the Commissioners believe) be less than *two-thirds* more, or nearly 24,000,000*l.* per annum.* The duty on tobacco, malt, and hops is 7,000,000*l.*, the cost of which commodities and of beer to the consumer will be scarcely less than the cost of spirits; making an aggregate of not less than between 40,000,000*l.* and 50,000,000*l.* per annum.' Now 8,444,800*l.*, and the 'two-thirds of that sum,' namely, 5,629,867*l.* make 14,074,667*l.*, which, when multiplied by 2, gives as the product 28,149,334*l.*

"From the data supplied by the Poor Law Commissioners it is evident that they have committed an error in the calculation of from 12,000,000*l.* to 22,000,000*l.* per anuum; and this in a letter urging an accusation of inaccuracy and exaggeration in an affair of 63 in 148,701 facts.

"I do not believe that a knowledge of the fact, that a certain number of persons die from starvation can lead to evil, if it have the effect of stimulating the vigilance and charity of the English public.

"The Poor Law Commissioners state, that 'for the maintenance of the care for life and social feelings of anxiety for the relief of suffering which characterize a civilized people, every case of death from want should be the subject of a careful inquiry.' They deem the cases in the registers 'a subject of very serious consideration.' They engage to institute inquiries themselves, 'and to ascertain if any, and what, remedies may be applied *for the future*.' They

* Registrar-General's Report, Appendix P. p. 108.

* Official Circular, p. 11.

will apprize the clerks of Guardians that the cases of 'starvation will form the subject of special inquiries,' and will request the Guardians to make due inquiries as to the cause of death, and whether 'any and what blame attaches to the parish or Union officers, or whether it is ascribable to any and what defects in the administration of relief.'

"The measures which the Poor Law Commissioners propose to adopt 'for the future' will probably be viewed with satisfaction by the public; and I shall not regret that the facts in the registers, and the few lines in the letter, which you did me the honour to publish, in the Appendix to your Report, suggested inquiries which may ultimately diminish the chance of death from starvation. If there should be one death the less, 'for the future,' I ask no other vindication.

"I have the honour to be, Sir,

"Your very obedient and humble Servant,

(Signed) "WILLIAM FARR.

"*To the Registrar General.*"

VIII.—TRANSMISSION OF MONEY BY POST.

AT the request of the Post-Master-General the Commissioners directed the insertion of the following notification:—

"Notice to the Public, and Instructions to all Postmasters.

"*General Post Office*, 20*th December*, 1839.

"In consequence of the great increase of letters containing coin, it has become necessary, in order to prevent the total interruption of the service, to discontinue the system which has hitherto prevailed of *entering the addresses* of such letters, and taking receipts for them on delivery to the owners. The practice, therefore, of entering such letters as money letters will cease on and after the 1st of January, 1840; after which time, parties having occasion to transmit small sums in cash, are recommended to make use of the MONEY ORDER OFFICE, where they will incur no risk, while those who may desire to remit bank notes, or drafts payable to bearer, are requested to cut them in half, sending each half, if possible, by two different posts. In the case of bank notes, or bank post bills, being sent, the numbers, dates, and amounts should be carefully taken. Money orders for sums under £5 are granted by every *post town* upon every other *post town* in the United Kingdom on application at the various offices. By Command,

"W. L. MABERLY, *Secretary*."

IX.—SALE AND APPROPRIATION OF PARISH PROPERTY, EMIGRATION, &c.

PAROCHIAL resolutions, directing Churchwardens and Overseers to raise money for the purposes of emigration, having been taken into consideration by the Commissioners, they issued the orders hereunder specified, confirming such resolutions:—

Kent; Maidstone Union; *Yalding* Parish. An order to raise the sum of 30*l.*, to assist three persons to emigrate to South Australia; of whom two are adults and the other a child between seven and fourteen; the two adults are labourers.

Kent; Maidstone Union; *Hunton* Parish. An order to raise the sum of 50*l.*, to assist several poor persons to emigrate, the particulars respecting whom have not been furnished.

Wilts; Wilton Union; *South Newton* Parish. An order to raise the sum of 50*l.* 7*s.* 8*d.*, to assist fourteen persons to emigrate to South Australia, of whom seven are adults and seven are children, three between seven and fourteen, and four under seven; two of the males are shepherds, and two of them are agricultural labourers.

Wilts; Alderbury Union; *West Harnham* Parish. An order to raise the sum of 56*l.*, to assist a labourer, together with his wife and eight children, to emigrate to South Australia."

The Board took into consideration the following applications for their authority to sell parochial properties, upon which they directed investigations to be made, in order to ascertain the titles under which the properties were held:—

Denbigh; Wrexham Union; *Ryton* Parish. For the sale of three freehold cottages, and a quarter of an acre of land, bounded by the road leading from Cross lanes to the Cock Bank.
Estimated value 60*l.*
The produce to be applied towards defraying the cost of building the Union workhouse.

Durham; Darlington Union; *Coatham Mundeville* Township. For the sale of two freehold cottages and a garden.
Estimated value 60*l.*

Gloucester; Cheltenham Union; *Great Witcomb* Parish. For the sale of three freehold tenements, with the garden ground belonging thereto, adjoining the parish churchyard.
Estimated value 40*l.*
The produce to be applied towards defraying the cost of building the Union workhouse.

Gloucester; Chepstow Union; *Lidney* Parish. For the sale of a freehold dwelling-house.
Estimated value 100*l.*
The produce to be applied towards defraying the cost of building the Union workhouse.

Gloucester; Thornbury Union; *Ham and Stone* Parish. For the sale of a leasehold building, lately used as the parish workhouse, and the garden belonging thereto.

A freehold house in three tenements with thirty perches of garden ground.

Estimated value 350*l.*

The produce to be applied in part payment of a debt of 600*l.*, incurred about forty-five years ago to build the parish workhouse.

Hertford; Hertford Union; *St. John Hertford* Parish. For the sale of five freehold cottages, situate in Butchery Green, Hertford.

Estimated value from 300*l.* to 360*l.*

The produce is proposed to be applied to discharge a debt incurred under the authority of the Parochial Assessments Act.

Kent; Elham Union; *Lympne* Parish. For the sale of a freehold cottage, with the garden and appurtenances belonging thereto, situate near the Spout, in Lympne.

Estimated value 100*l.*

The produce to be applied towards defraying the cost of building the Union workhouse.

Leicester; Market Bosworth Union; *Twycross* Parish. For the sale of a freehold building, consisting of three dwelling-houses, with a garden belonging thereto.

Estimated value 100*l.*

The produce to be applied to discharge a debt incurred by the parish in 1819.

Leicester; Blaby Union; *Thurlaston* Parish. For the sale of two freehold cottages and one garden, situate in the parish.

Estimated value 130*l.*

The produce to be applied towards defraying the cost of building the Union workhouse.

Northampton; Peterborough Union; *Eye* Parish. For the sale of a freehold tenement, together with twenty-nine perches of land, situate at the west end of the town of Eye.

Estimated value 60*l.*

The produce to be applied towards defraying the cost of building the Union workhouse.

Stafford; Burton-upon-Trent Union; *Burton Extra* Parish. For the sale of a leasehold building, lately used as the parish workhouse, with the garden and appurtenances belonging thereto.

Estimated value 150*l.*

The produce to be applied towards defraying the cost of building the Union workhouse.

Suffolk; Thingoe Union; *Risby* Parish. For the sale of a freehold double tenement, with the garden and appurtenances belonging thereto, situate in Narrow Street, Risby.

Estimated value 160*l.*

The produce to be applied towards defraying the cost of building the Union workhouse.

Suffolk; Hartismere Union; *Mendlesham* Parish. For the sale of freehold premises now occupied by paupers.

The produce to be applied towards defraying the cost of altering the Union workhouse.

Sussex; Hailsham Union; *Warbleton* Parish. For the sale of:—

1. A copyhold cottage, and twenty-six roods of land, situate at Collins Green.
2. A house and one rood of land, situate near the parish church.
3. A house, and one rood and thirty-six perches of land, situate near Punnett's Town.
4. Cottages, and two roods and thirty perches of land called 'Mud Castle,' situate at Bodle Street Green.
5 Three cottages in four tenements, and four acres, one rood and thirty-six perches of land, situate near Downgate.
6. A cottage and two acres, three roods, and one perch of land, situate near Punnett's Town.
7. A cottage and thirty-six perches of land, situate near Punnett's Town.
8 A cottage and one acre, two roods, and thirty-six perches, situate near 'Mooreocks.'

Estimated value 700*l.*

The produce to be applied towards the liquidation of the sums of 300*l.*, 200*l.*, 150*l.*, 100*l.*, and 100*l.*, being debts incurred by the parish, before the passing of the Poor Law Amendment Act.

Westmoreland; Kendal Union; *Lambrigg* Parish. For the sale of a freehold messuage, called 'Lambrigg Park Low House.'

Two freehold closes of land, situate in Lambrigg, containing three acres.

A freehold close of land, also situate in Lambrigg, containing seven acres.

Estimated value 300*l.*

The produce to be applied to pay a debt of 60*l.* incurred for making a fence, and also to make roads.

Worcester; Evesham Union; *Bengeworth* Parish. For the sale of the freehold buildings, lately used as the parish workhouse, together with a cottage and a plot of land.

Estimated value 250*l.*

Produce to be applied towards defraying the cost of building the Union workhouse.

York; Goole Union; *Collington* Parish. For the sale of four freehold cottages.

Estimated value 50*l.*

The produce to be applied towards defraying the cost of building the Union workhouse.

York; Doncaster Union; *Conisborough* Parish. For the sale of—

Lot 1. A freehold messuage and garden.
2. A freehold messuage.
3. A freehold piece of land, containing about thirty-nine perches.

Estimated value 180*l.*

LONDON:
Printed by order of the Poor Law Commissioners, by W. CLOWES and SONS, Stamford Street, and Published by CHARLES KNIGHT and Co., 22, Ludgate-street, Publishers to the Poor Law Commissioners.

AN

OFFICIAL CIRCULAR

OF PUBLIC DOCUMENTS AND INFORMATION:

DIRECTED BY THE POOR LAW COMMISSIONERS TO BE PRINTED, CHIEFLY FOR THE USE OF THE MEMBERS AND PERMANENT OFFICERS OF BOARDS OF GUARDIANS, UNDER THE POOR LAW AMENDMENT ACT.

No. 5. CIRCULAR ISSUED JUNE 16TH, 1840.

Poor Law Commission Office,
Somerset House,
June 13th, 1840.

At a Board held on the 8th instant, the Commissioners directed that a copy of the Bill approved by Her Majesty's Government "for the further amendment of the laws relating to the relief of the poor in England," shall be printed in the "Official Circular," with references to such part of their report to the Marquis of Normanby, "on the continuance of the Poor Law Commission, and on some further amendments of the law relating to the relief of the poor," to which the provisions of the Bill may relate: and also any further information that may be useful with relation to those additional provisions.

By Order of the Board,
EDWIN CHADWICK, *Secretary*.

BILL FOR THE AMENDMENT OF THE LAW, AND REASONS FOR THE PROVISIONS.

"Clause 1.—That the Act passed in the session of Parliament holden in the fourth and fifth years of the reign of his late Majesty King William the Fourth, intituled 'An Act for the Amendment and better Administration of the Laws relating to the Poor in England and Wales,' and the Act passed in the session of Parliament holden in the fifth and sixth years of the reign of his said Majesty, intituled 'An Act to facilitate the Conveyance of Workhouses and other Property of Parishes and of Incorporations of Parishes in England and Wales,' and the Act passed in the session of Parliament holden in the sixth and seventh years of the reign of his said Majesty, intituled 'An Act to regulate Parochial Assessments,' and so much of an Act passed in the session of Parliament holden in the first and second years of the reign of her present Majesty, intituled 'An Act for the more effectual Relief of the Destitute Poor in Ireland,' as relates to the style of the Poor Law Commissioners, their appointment, the sittings of their board, their common seal, and the residence of one of their number in Ireland, and all Acts to amend or extend any of the said Acts, or the said provisions of the Act last recited, or the present Act, shall (except so far as the provisions of any former Act shall be expressly altered or amended by the provisions of any subsequent Act) be construed as one Act; and that in each and every such Act (except the said Act of the session holden in the first and second years of the reign of her present Majesty) the words 'auditor,' 'guardian,' 'justice or justices of the peace,' 'oath,' 'officer,' 'overseer,' 'owner,' 'rack-rent,' 'parish,' 'person,' 'poor,' 'poor laws,' 'laws for relief of the poor,' 'poor-rate,' 'general quarter sessions,' 'union,' 'united workhouse,' 'vestry,' 'workhouse,' and words importing the singular number or the masculine gender only, shall be interpreted as is provided in the first recited Act."

The Commissioners have submitted to Her Majesty's Government, that it is desirable to give to the whole series of Acts enumerated in this clause the same construction. In several subsequent Acts in which the terms of the Poor Law Amendment Act are used, the construction has been disputed for want of such a declaration as that contained in the present clause. For instance, it has been denied that the orders which the Commissioners are required to issue under the Parochial Assessments Act have any obligatory effect, because the latter Act makes no direct reference to the provisions of the Poor Law Amendment Act for enforcing obedience to the Commissioners' orders. The declaration in the present clause will prevent many repetitions and references which would otherwise be necessary in the present Bill.

General Rules and particular Orders defined.

"Clause 2.—That every rule, order, or regulation of the Poor Law Commissioners which shall be issued after the passing of this Act, and which shall apply to a class of cases, or to a series or succession of occasions, shall be deemed to be a general rule, subject to all the provisions relating to general rules contained in the Act first herein recited; and that every such rule, order, or regulation of the said Commissioners which shall apply only to a single case or a single occasion, or which shall suspend or rescind any previous rule, order, or regulation, or which shall amend any error of description or clerical error, or other error, through which the intention of any previous rule, order, or regulation whatsoever shall not have been accurately or completely expressed, shall be deemed a particular order, notwithstanding that such rule, order, or regulation shall at the time of issuing the same be addressed by the said Commissioners to more Unions than one, or to more parishes or places than one."

The reasons of the Commissioners for submitting this section are stated in their Report on the continuance of the Poor Law Commission, pp. 32 to 38; especially, pp. 36 and 37, 8vo. *ed.* and pp. 20 to 23 fol. *ed.*

Construction of the words "Rule," "Order," and "Regulation."

"Clause 3.—That whenever it shall have been or shall hereafter be made lawful for the Commissioners to issue any rule, order, or regulation, such rule, order, or regulation shall have every quality, incident, and effect of a rule, order, or regulation made under the provisions of the first recited Act and this Act."

This provision is considered necessary for the reasons stated with reference to section 1.

General Rules once allowed, to take effect thenceforth as particular Orders.

"Clause 4.—That where any general rule, signed and sealed by the said Commissioners, shall have been sent by them to one of Her Majesty's Secretaries of State, and shall have come into operation, it shall thenceforth be lawful for the said Commissioners to make any rule, order, or regulation of like import and effect, and to issue the same, to any parish or parishes, Union or Unions, or parishes and Unions not previously affected thereby, as a particular order, and the same shall be deemed to be a particular order and not a general rule, and shall take effect accordingly."

The grounds for this provision are specified in p. 37 of the Commissioners' Report.

Time of Operation of Rules and Orders.

"Clause 5.—That every order of the said Commissioners suspending any previous rule, order, or regulation, or suspending any paid officer from the exercise of his office, in which the said Commissioners shall declare that the urgency of the case requires that such order should take effect within the period of fourteen days, shall come into force at such time as the said Commissioners shall in such order direct, notwithstanding that fourteen days shall not have expired since a written or printed copy of the same shall have been sent by the said Commissioners, as required by the first recited Act."

The reasons for this provision are also stated in pp. 37 and 38 8vo. and p. 23 fol. of the Report.

Evidence of the Commissioners' Rules, &c.

"Clause 6.—And whereas it is provided by the said first recited Act that a written or printed copy of every rule, order, or regulation of the said Commissioners shall, before the same shall come into operation in any parish or Union, be sent by the said Commissioners by the post, or in such manner as the Commissioners shall think fit, sealed or stamped with their seal, addressed to the overseers of such parish, the guardians of such Union, or their clerk, and to the clerk to the justices of the petty sessions held for the division in which such parish or Union shall be situate. And whereas the proof of such sending is often attended with great expense and difficulty; be it enacted, That it shall not in any civil or criminal proceeding be necessary to prove such sending, except to the clerk of the guardians of the Union or of the parish, or, where there shall be no guardians, to the overseers of the parish within which such rule, order, or regulation is intended to have effect; and that it shall in no case be necessary to prove such sending, unless reasonable notice in writing be given to the party upon whom such proof would lie that such proof will be required; and whenever such sending shall be proved to the satisfaction of any court, such court shall order the reasonable expenses of the witness or witnesses proving the same to be paid by the party who shall have given such notice, and such expenses shall be recoverable as penalties and forfeitures under the first recited Act."

The reasons for this provision are set forth in the Preamble to the Clause.

Dissolution and Alteration of Unions.—Consent of Majority of Guardians required to Dissolution of Unions.

"Clause 7.—That so much of the first recited Act as provides that no dissolution or alteration of any Union, whether formed before or after the passing of the first recited Act, nor any addition to any such Union, shall take place, or be made, unless a majority of not less than two-thirds of the guardians of such Union shall concur therein, or as provides that no addition shall be made to any Union of parishes united for the purposes of settlement or rating, shall be repealed: Provided always, That it shall not be lawful for the said Commissioners to dissolve any Union, whether formed before or after the passing of the said firstly recited Act, unless a majority of the guardians thereof shall concur therein, except in the case of incorporations of guardians and Unions of parishes, made under the provisions of the Act passed in the twenty-second year of the reign of King George the Third, intituled 'An Act for the better Relief and Employment of the Poor,' which last-mentioned incorporations and Unions of parishes the said Commissioners shall be authorized to dissolve, as and when they shall see fit, without any consent whatever of guardians to such dissolution: Provided also, That in every case in which the said Commissioners shall declare any parish or parishes to be added to any Union for the purposes of settlement or rating, the parishes which shall have composed such Union for settlement or rating, before such addition, shall continue to defray the expense of their poor, and to contribute and be assessed to the common fund of the Union constituted by such addition, as if they had before such addition been one parish."

The reasons for this clause, as set forth in pp. 44 and 45 8vo. and p. 27 fol. of the Report, are as follows:—

"With respect to conferring on the Commissioners a power of modifying the constituent parts of existing Unions, we will extract the recommendations of the Committee of the House of Commons:—

'Your Committee have observed that several petitions complain of the too great size of Unions, and in some instances, of the selection of the parishes of which the Unions have been formed. It may have happened that, in the first arrangement of so great a proportion of the country into Unions, some may have been too large, and others, perhaps, too small; and in some instances parishes may have been attached to one Union which would have been more conveniently placed in another. To remedy this state of things, your Committee are of opinion that it would be desirable to give to the Commissioners a power to reconstruct the Unions where the inconveniences referred to may be found to exist. At present they can only do so with the consent of two-thirds of the Guardians of all the Unions affected by the change. But your Committee recommend that the Commissioners should have the power referred to, subject to this condition, that no parish should be taken from or added to a Union without its consent, expressed by its Guardian. Some pecuniary interests of the parish which may be transferred would remain to be adjusted, and your Committee think this may be safely left to the Guardian of the parish, whose consent is to be a necessary condition of the transfer, and to the superintendence of the Commissioners, who can have none but a public interest in the question. In all cases where it may be thought proper to alter the size of the Union, your Committee recommend that especial consideration be had to the easy access of the poor, and to the good attendance of the Guardians at the Board; these conditions being in their opinion of essential and paramount importance.'—pp. 34, 35.

"We may here remark that if the power of modifying existing Unions, which is recommended by the Committee, were conferred upon the Commissioners, we should think it our duty to use such a power with the utmost caution, and to abstain from altering the component parts of existing Unions without very cogent reasons."

To these may be added the fact, that when in various instances the position of single parishes in particular Unions has been found to be inconvenient, and application has been made to separate them from the Union, it has been found impracticable to obtain the consent of a majority of the Guardians. The other parishes would not, to save inconvenience or loss to the particular parish which they did not feel, consent to give up a source of contribution to their common expenses. The Commissioners consider that in this, as in other cases, power should be given to a disinterested authority to protect the interests or conveniences of the particular parish from being unduly sacrificed to the interests of any majority.

Parishes and Unions to be combined for Schools, Infirmaries, &c.

"Clause 8.—That it shall be lawful for the said Commissioners, as and when they shall see fit, by order under their hands and seal, to declare so many parishes or Unions, or parishes and Unions, as they may see fit, to be united for the management of any class or classes of infirm or infant poor, and from time to time to add thereto or separate therefrom any parish or Union, and to determine the mode in which a board of management of such poor shall be appointed by the guardians of the parishes or Unions, or parishes and Unions, so united, and the number and qualifications of the members of such board of management, and to define and specify and direct the execution of the duties of such board, and with the consent in writing of a majority of such board of management to direct such board of management to purchase or hire, or build, and to fit up and furnish a building of such size and description, and according to such plan and in such manner as the said Commissioners shall deem most proper for the purpose of being used or rendered suitable for the relief and management of such infirm or infant poor; and for the purpose of providing such building, it shall be lawful for such board of management to exercise the powers given to guardians by the said first recited Act, or any other Act or Acts, for the purchase and hire of lands and buildings, and to purchase, take, and hold such lands and buildings as a corporation, by such name as the Commissioners shall direct, and to borrow under the provisions of the said first recited Act, or of any other Act or Acts, such sum or sums of money as may be necessary for the purpose of purchasing, hiring, building, fitting up, and furnishing such building as aforesaid, and to charge the future poor rates of the parishes or Unions, or parishes and Unions, so united as aforesaid, with the payment of such sum or sums of money and interest thereon: Provided always, That the consent of any rate-payers or owners of property of any parish shall not be necessary to any sale, exchange, lease, or other disposal by guardians or overseers to or with any such board of management of any workhouse, tenement, building, or land: Provided also, That the principal sum or sums to be raised for the purpose of providing any such building or buildings as aforesaid shall in no case exceed one-fifth of the average annual amount of the rates made for the relief of the poor for three years, ending the twenty-fifth of March next preceding the raising of such money in the parishes or Unions, or parishes and Unions, so united as aforesaid."

The reasons in support of this provision are stated in pp. 55 to 61 8vo. and pp. 34 to 37 fol. of the Commissioners' Report, and also in Mr. Tufnell's Report, Appendix, p. 114 8vo. and p. 77 fol.

The Commissioners learn that objections have been made to the above provisions, on the ground of the expense which may be incurred.

The Commissioners are firmly persuaded that the arrangements practicable under these provisions will be amongst the most efficient that can be devised for obtaining considerable ultimate economy, and that the narrow objection of immediate expense will be found no more applicable to the exercise of the powers under these sections, than to the exercise of other powers created by the Poor Law Amendment Act, few or none of which would have been exercised had the consent of the districts benefited by the application of the law been required before they had experience of the effect of the law.

The number of children between 9 and 16 years of age chargeable to the Poor Rates of the several Unions according to the returns was upwards of twenty thousand.

The greater proportion of these children remain chargeable or become so at intervals, on account of defective education, which does not attain the objects of education in qualifying them to act as good servants or good workmen. It is found where children receive a proper industrial training, that they obtain situations as quickly as they attain the proper physical strength; without premiums or apprenticeships, they are taken from the schools so rapidly as to impede the full developement of industrial training, which can only have its complete effect with full-grown children or youths.

Effective industrial, moral, or religious instruction can only be communicated, at a reasonable expense, in classes sufficiently large to make it worth while to pay for competent teachers, and to carry out that effective industrial, moral, and religious instruction, which is found in the end to be the best means of saving expense to the Union.

In a large proportion of the Unions the numbers of children are too small to allow the formation of classes for appropriate tuition. If the savings of the expense of competent teachers were no object, the number of competent teachers is at present so small as to render the formation of classes desirable for the sake of the best tuition.

In many of the Unions it may be found that the training given to the children is satisfactory; but in all cases the practical tests of the appropriateness of the training and education are, first, in the fact of there being no children in the workhouse of the same ages as those at which other children are engaged in industrial occupations within the district; secondly, in the fact of such children being got out and maintaining themselves in service without the inducements of premiums or of apprenticeship fees; and thirdly, in keeping in places at weekly or other hirings for short periods, without coercion or threat of punishment, under any indenture.

There are few or no districts in which there is not a demand for good, trustworthy, and skilful servants, or in which servants of this kind are so numerous as to render emigration the sole resource as a means of getting children of good character into productive employment.

Board of Management to have the same powers as Guardians

"Clause 9.—That the board of management shall have such of the powers of guardians as the said Commissioners shall by order under their hands and seal direct, for the relief and management of the infirm or infant poor in such building, and for the appointment, payment, and control of paid officers; and the legal and reasonable orders of such board of management shall be obeyed, and obedience thereto enforced in the same manner and by the same remedies and penalties as the legal and reasonable orders of guardians."

Contributions by Parishes and Unions so combined.

"Clause 10.—That the said Commissioners shall from time to time ascertain and determine the proportions and rates of contribution of the parishes or Unions, or parishes and Unions, so united for the management of any class or classes of infirm or infant poor; and the board of management shall, unless such contributions be duly paid by the treasurers of such parishes or Unions, have the same remedy for recovery of the same from the overseers of the several parishes for which such board of management may act, as are given to guardians for the recovery of the contributions of parishes; and in case of any addition or separation of parishes or Unions, the said Commissioners shall ascertain the proportionate value of property and amount of obligations of every parish or Union affected by the change, and shall fix the amount to be received by, or paid, or secured to be paid, to every such parish or Union."

Definition of "Infirm" and "Infant Poor."

"Clause 11.—That in the construction of the preceding provisions the words 'infirm poor' shall be construed to include every person applying for or receiving relief who shall by reason of any bodily defect, or of any permanent ailment, or of the permanent effects of any ailment or bodily accident, be incapable of supporting himself; and the words 'infant poor' shall be construed to include every person under the age of sixteen, who may require or receive relief."

Board of Management for lewd and disorderly Poor.

"Clause 12.—That all the provisions in this Act contained relating to the management of infirm or infant poor, and to the constitution and powers of a board of management of such poor, shall extend to the purpose of providing workhouses within the counties of Middlesex and Surrey, and the cities of London and Westminster, and for relieving and setting to work therein of women of lewd or disorderly behaviour, and chargeable to any parishes within such counties and cities."

This is a provision rendered necessary in the metropolis for the treatment of lewd or refractory females who seek refuge in the workhouse, and disturb the older, and corrupt the younger inmates, and who can only be subjected to appropriate treatment under a separate management. The grounds for this provision are specified in the Report, p. 60, 8vo. and p. 37 fol., and in the Appendix, p. 287, 8vo. and p. 178 fol. One reason for the provision for the maintenance of children in separate buildings, consists in the necessity of preventing acquaintanceship within the house, or association out of it with the elder paupers, or contamination by the example their of habits.

Treatment in classes and separate buildings is often found necessary on medical grounds; and the general policy of the above clauses, which are needed as a means of improved treatment by improved classification, is founded on such circumstances as those stated in the Report of the Commissioners of Inquiry, pp. 303 to 313 8vo. The management arising from inadequate means of treatment and classification which formerly characterised most of the parish workhouses, still characterises many of the workhouses of the Unions. The Commissioners of Inquiry stated:—

"In such parishes, when overburthened with poor, we usually find the building, called a workhouse, occupied by sixty or eighty paupers, made up of a dozen or more neglected children (under the care, perhaps, of a pauper), about twenty or thirty able-bodied adult paupers of both sexes, and probably an equal number of aged and impotent persons, proper objects of relief. Amidst these the mothers of bastard children and prostitutes live without shame, and associate freely with the youth, who have also the examples and conversation of the frequent inmates of the county gaol, the poacher, the vagrant, the decayed beggar, and other characters of the worst description. To these may often be added a solitary blind person, one or two idiots, and not unfrequently are heard, from among the rest, the incessant ravings of some neglected lunatic. In such receptacles the sick poor are often immured.

"Even in the larger workhouses internal subdivisions do not afford the means of classification, where the inmates dine in the same rooms, or meet or see each other in the ordinary business of the place. In the largest houses, containing from 800 to 1000 inmates, where there is comparatively good order, and in many respects, superior management, it is almost impossible to prevent the formation and extension of vicious connexions. Inmates who see each other, though prevented from communicating in the house, often become associates when they meet out of it. It is found almost impracticable to subject all the various classes within the same house to an appropriate treatment. One part of a class of adults often so closely resembles a part of another class, as to make any distinction in treatment appear arbitrary and capricious to those who are placed in the inferior class, and to create discontents, which the existing authority is too feeble to suppress, and so much complexity as to render the object attainable only by great additional expense and remarkable skill."

Unions, &c., may contract with Guardians for maintenance of their Poor.

"Clause 13.—That it shall be lawful for the guardians of any parish or Union having a building suitable for the management of any class or classes of poor, or for such board of management as aforesaid, to contract respectively with the guardians of any parish or Union, or with any board of management, not interested in such building, for the maintenance and management of any such poor, in such manner and for such period not exceeding seven years, and on such terms as the said Commissioners may by any order under their hands and seal direct."

Since many Unions and parishes now have, and many more may eventually have, greater accommodation than is required for their own paupers, the Commissioners consider that the present clause will enable the Boards of Guardians to turn such accommodation to profitable account for themselves, or else to save an independent outlay for the purpose, and thus avoid the necessity of recurring to the machinery of a Board of management. The provision it is conceived will also be applicable to cases of extensive and emergent destitution, such as have sometimes arisen in particular Unions, where the workhouse accommodation is inadequate to meet an extraordinary influx of claims of able-bodied persons. In such cases it would enable the Guardians of adjacent Unions where there is workhouse room to spare, to accommodate, for the time, the Union in which the pressure takes place.

Wives liable in certain cases to maintain their Children.

"Clause 14.—That in all cases in which the husband of any woman shall be beyond the seas, or in custody of the law, or shall be a lunatic or idiot, or shall refuse or neglect to maintain his family, or shall leave his family chargeable, or so that it may become chargeable, or shall from any cause be unable to maintain himself, his wife shall, notwithstanding her coverture, be liable to maintain herself and her children in the like manner in all respects as a widow."

The grounds for this clause are stated in the Report, p. 101 8vo. and p. 36 fol., where it is, amongst other things, set forth that

"It is unquestionable that the desertion by men of their families, with the collusion of the wives, has much increased since the Commissioners of Inquiry adverted to the subject. The misconduct also of women whose husbands are absent at sea, or suffering the sentence of the law, is more often remarked, since it has become generally known that they can cast the burden of their children on the parish, without submitting, in their own persons, to the ordinary conditions attached to the receipt of relief by the able-bodied. A power to pay the costs of prosecution will operate largely to prevent the original evil, so far as it depends on the act of the man. In order not to diminish, by the operation of the Poor Laws, the reluctance of the wife to the absence of her husband, it appears to us to be sufficient to place her, during the absence of her husband, in that relation to her children in which a widow is placed by the present law. This, though a highly favourable situation for a married woman, will, we think, connect the wife with her children as effectually as can be done by the operation of a Poor Law.

"The want of a fund for the payment of the expenses incurred in apprehending and convicting men who have deserted their families, is very extensively known, and affords to all, who have any inducement to leave their families, a strong reason for hoping that they may do so with impunity. This expectation of impunity has recently been aided by many powerful inducements, especially by the increased means of obtaining work at high wages afforded by railroads and other large improvements, as well as by mining operations, in which the nature of the employment renders the discovery and apprehension of the offenders difficult. In addition to these influences, there are others operating on wives, which render them indifferent to the absence of their husbands, and often positively interested in it. A married woman is not generally considered to be liable to maintain her children during her husband's lifetime. The freedom from this liability involves the consequence that she is exempt from the obligation to accept relief with her children in the workhouse, and also from the liability to be punished for deserting them. A woman, therefore, whose husband is not to be found, is in a condition superior, so far as the claim to relief is concerned, to that of the woman who has a husband present, needing relief for his family, with whom she may be required to accept it in the workhouse."

Guardians' Control of Orphans, &c., under Sixteen.

"Clause 15.—That it shall be lawful for the guardians of any parish or Union to exercise the like guardianship, control, and custody of the body of any child under the age of sixteen, not having any natural or testamentary guardian, and chargeable to any parish, and requiring relief in such parish or Union, as might by law have been exercised by the natural guardians of such child."

The grounds for this clause are thus set forth in the Report, p. 60 8vo. and p. 36 fol.:—

"The powers of the Guardians for the custody of pauper children are not defined by any statutory enactment. Every adult pauper can at any time quit a workhouse, upon giving reasonable notice to the master; but it is manifest that the Guardians would not be justified in allowing children to leave the workhouse and roam about without a protector. When consulted on the subject, we have expressed an opinion that the Guardians of the poor stand in the relation of natural Guardians to the children in the workhouse. In order, however, to prevent the existence of any doubt on this important point, we recommend that the Guardians of the poor should be declared to possess the powers, with respect to pauper children under the age of 16, having no natural or testamentary Guardians, which are possessed at common law by a Guardian for nurture."

Management of Children within the Bills of Mortality.

"Clause 16.—That the said Commissioners shall from time to time, as they shall see occasion, make and issue all such rules or orders for the management of poor children by the guardians of the poor, elected under the said first recited Act, or by a board of management appointed under this Act, as they shall deem expedient, for attaining the objects of an Act passed in the seventh year of the reign of his late Majesty King George the Third, intituled 'An Act for the better Regulation of the Parish Poor Children of the several Parishes therein mentioned within the Bills of Mortality;' and while any such rule or order shall be in force in any parish or Union, the provisions of the said last-mentioned Act shall, so far as regards such parish or Union, cease to have effect."

The Poor Law Amendment Act, by the 15th section, requires the Commissioners to make regulations for the management of poor children, under the 7th Geo. III. (Jonas Hanway's Act). The 7th Geo. III., however, is in its provisions wholly irreconcileable with the management of the children by a Board of Guardians appointed under the Poor Law Amendment Act; and it keeps in nominal existence a body of persons independent both of overseers and of the Poor Law Guardians to act as visitors of the poor children. In other respects, the Act makes provision for the management of the children, which it may be still desirable to preserve. It is, therefore, only proposed by the clause to clear the power of the Commissioners from any liability to dispute by superseding the Act of 7th Geo, III. while those regulations shall be in operation.

Cost of obtaining Workhouses.

"Clause 17.—That, in addition to the principal sum or sums of money which guardians are empowered by the said first recited Act to raise or borrow for the purpose of purchasing, hiring, building, enlarging, or altering workhouses, or buildings to be converted into workhouses, the guardians of any parish or Union, any part of which may be situate within the metropolitan police district, may also raise or borrow and charge the future poor-rates of such parish or Union with such further or other sum or sums of money as may be necessary for the purchase of any land, or interest in land, required as the site of any such workhouse, or of additions to any such workhouse."

The limit fixed by the Poor Law Amendment Act to the expenditure which may be incurred in providing workhouses, is the average amount of poor-rates raised in the previous three years. For several reasons this sum is inadequate to the purpose of obtaining efficient workhouses in the metropolis and its neighbourhood. In that district, from the various character of the paupers sent to the workhouse, more complete arrangements are necessary than in places where the pauperism is of a more uniform and unvarying description. The expenditure about the erection itself also greatly exceeds the average expenditure in other parts of the country, all the materials being to be transported, and the cost of labour in all departments generally much higher.

But the chief cause of inequality is in the cost of building ground, which, in the country, can always be easily obtained at small cost, but in the neighbourhood of the metropolis must usually be obtained at the highest known price. The limit, therefore, which has not been found inconvenient in other parts of the country, operates in the metropolis and its neighbourhood to render ineffectual all attempts to procure proper workhouse accommodation; and the difficulty is much increased by the delay which has already taken place in building, inasmuch as by the reduction of rates which has been effected the averages have been reduced, and the sums applicable to the purpose thus made much less than would have been applicable had the requisite provision been earlier made, while the averages were higher in amount.

Parish Apprentices.

"Clause 18.—That the said Commissioners may, by order under their hands and seal, define the classes of poor children who may be apprenticed, the cases in which any premium or apprentice fee shall be paid with such poor children out of rates raised for the relief of the poor, and the amount and mode of payment thereof."

Apprenticeship by parishes is chiefly resorted to in order to get rid of burdens by means of the settlement which apprentices obtain by residing forty days in another parish. Thus the whole district of Spitalfields and Bethnal Green is burdened with a constant influx of pauper apprentices, adding in their turn to the misery of the artisans, who, in that district, have long been redundant. The premium given is so high as to be a strong inducement to any poor weaver, or other artisan or tradesman, to take an apprentice. If the practice were beneficial to the apprentice, the Commissioners submit that it would still be an unjust advantage given to the pauper over the children of the independent poor; but it is notorious, that the greater number of pauper apprentices are oppressed and maltreated during their term of apprenticeship, and usually fail to learn their trade. The whole operation of the law, as at present carried into execution, usually is, to shift a burden from one parish to another, by means of a present bribe to a poor man, eventually operating as oppressively to the master as to the child, and burdening the occupation of both by an additional rival of inferior habits and skill. But occasional opportunities arise for apprenticing a child lame or blind, or otherwise subject to some infirmity, rendering him, without a premium, wholly incapable of remunerating a master for instructing him. The existence of such cases may make it desirable not entirely to abolish the power of parish officers to apprentice; and the present clause would allow of the practice being confined within limits within which it may be beneficially continued.

Expenditure of Funds raised for Emigration.

"Clause 19.—And whereas it will be convenient for Boards of Guardians to undertake such arrangements as are incidental to the emigration of poor persons whose expenses are wholly or partly defrayed from parochial funds; be it therefore enacted, That every fund raised or borrowed in pursuance of the provisions in the said first recited Act contained, shall be paid to the treasurer of the Union in which the parish raising or borrowing the same is comprised, to the credit of the Board of Guardians of the said Union, and shall be expended by the said board, subject to the orders of the said Commissioners, in defraying the expenses of the emigration of poor persons belonging to the parish raising or borrowing such fund."

It is considered that when emigration is determined upon, it would be much better conducted by the paid and responsible officers of the Union than by the officers of the parish. The Boards of Guardians and their officers act with much more extensive and complete information for their guidance as to the places for emigration, and the times and mode of conducting it, and are less likely to be led into improper expenditure of the rates than the rate-payers and inhabitants. Appendix to the Report, p. 128 8vo. and p. 77 fol. The provision is considered to be within the policy of other provisions of the Poor Law Amendment Act for placing the administration of the rates under a more extended control than the parish.

Burials of Paupers.

"Clause 20.—That it shall be lawful for guardians to bury the body of any poor person who shall die within their parish or Union without effects of sufficient value to defray the expenses of the burial, and to charge the expense thereof to any parish under their control, to which such person may have been chargeable, or in which he may have died; and every body which the guardians or any of their officers duly authorized shall direct to be buried at the expense of the poor-rates shall, unless the guardians or such officer shall otherwise direct, be buried in the burying-ground of the parish, division of parish, chapelry, or place in which the death shall have or shall be considered to have occurred, and that a fee of five shillings and no more shall be payable out of the poor-rates for the burial of each such body, and such fee shall be paid to the clergyman who, according to the practice in the place, shall have been accustomed to receive fees for burial."

The occasion for this provision is thus stated in the Commissioners' Report, p. 55 8vo. and 33 fol.:—

"The English law does not (as we are advised) define precisely on what persons the obligation to bury a dead body is incumbent. It is probable that the person who has the custody of a dead body, or the occupier of the house in which it is deposited, is bound to inter it; and it is moreover probable that he is bound to give it Christian burial. But, whatever the law may be, it has been the practice for the parish to bury all paupers, including casual paupers, at its expense. This practice is not, as far as we are aware, liable to any serious objection; but it is important that the liability of the parish to bury should be precisely determined. We therefore recommend that, where a poor person dies within his Union, he should be buried at the cost of his own parish; and that, where a poor person does not die within his Union, he should be buried at the cost of the parish from which, if a pauper, he was receiving relief at the time of his death, or, if not a pauper, in which he died.

"A question has likewise arisen in many Unions respecting the liability of the parish to pay a fee to the clergyman for the burial of a pauper. When consulted by Boards of Guardians, we have recommended that, wherever it has been customary to pay a fee for burials to the clergyman, such fee should be paid by the parish on the burial of the pauper. There does not, however, appear to be any express authority for the exaction of such a fee in the case of a person dying within the parish. It is highly inexpedient that disputes should arise between clergymen and the Union or parochial authorities on such a subject; and we recommend that the question should be settled by an enactment, either that every pauper shall be buried, without the payment of a fee, in the parish where he dies, or that a certain fee shall be paid to the clergyman on the burial of every pauper, whether he be buried in the parish in which he died, or not."

Guardians may obtain Burial-grounds.

"Clause 21.—That all the provisions of the said firstly recited Act, or of any other Act relating to the purchase by guardians of land for the purpose of erecting a workhouse thereon, and to the raising or borrowing monies for such purchase, shall extend to the purchase by any Board of Guardians or of Management, of land for the purpose of being used as the burial-ground of any workhouse or building under their control, respectively."

Casual Poor chargeable to the whole Union

"Clause 22.—That the cost of the relief of poor persons not coming to settle, but becoming casually chargeable in any parish in a Union, and the cost of their removal, and all expenses incident thereto, shall be repaid from the common fund of such Union; and all poor persons becoming so chargeable (excepting such as become and remain chargeable by reason of sudden illness or accident) shall be removable in like manner as persons coming to settle; and, for the purpose of such removal, they shall be deemed chargeable to any parish in which they may receive relief."

One principal object of a compulsory provision for the relief of destitution, is the prevention of mendicancy. One effectual means of accomplishing this object is the distribution of tickets to the rate-payers, containing directions to the workhouses, where all really destitute persons are relieved. The Commissioners have already stated in their Report:—

"The full advantage of this practice cannot be obtained in the present state of the law relating to the relief and removal of casual poor. A destitute person is relievable wherever he is found in a state of destitution. With respect to habitual beggars and vagrants, the places in which they are found are usually the main roads passing through the Unions; and the places where the Union officers first ascertain their destitution, and where the relief is actually administered, are usually the parishes in which the workhouses, or the residences of the relieving officers, are situate. In proportion, therefore, as effectual measures are taken in any Union for the giving of all necessary relief to casual poor, the burdens on certain parishes in that Union are disproportionately increased; and other parishes out of the main road, though freed by these measures from the mendicants and vagrants who had previously circulated throughout the Union, cannot be charged with any portion of the burden. Besides this inconvenience, there arises from the present state of the law a great amount of unnecessary contest and litigation between parishes, as to their respective liabilities to give relief to the casual poor. The practice of considering that parish liable in which a destitute person last slept, is obviously inapplicable for the purpose of affording relief to the sudden wants of the mass of poor persons travelling on foot or by wagon, of habitual beggars and vagrants, of discharged prisoners travelling with passes, and similar classes of persons who may not have slept within the district in which their necessity arises. This practice likewise constitutes a strong inducement, especially in small parishes, to prevent destitute persons from obtaining shelter, and to drive them into some adjoining parish. Very lamentable cases are thus produced, even in the rich and populous parishes of the metropolis, inasmuch as the object is not confined to the escape from the costs of immediate relief, but extends also to the avoiding of the permanent charge of relief to the pauper, or the great expense and difficulty (very often in the case of vagrants insuperable) of establishing a settlement in some other parish, with a view to the removal of the pauper. When the claims to relief cannot be evaded, the same reasons operate as an inducement to parishes to afford insufficient relief to such unsettled paupers as cannot be placed immediately under orders of removal. By affording scanty relief, the burden is directly diminished, and an urgent motive created in the pauper to betake himself to any other parish in which he may hope to better himself. In this way casual paupers, whose settlements are in doubt, are frequently kept in a course of circulation amongst a number of parishes, to the cost and injury of each in its turn, and in a manner involving unnecessary hardship to the pauper, and frequently his serious demoralisation, by converting him into a common beggar or vagrant. Very numerous applications have been made by Boards of Guardians to the Commissioners, to be permitted to make the costs of relief and removal of casual poor an establishment charge; that is, a charge to be borne jointly by all the parishes of the Union. It appears to us that the change sought for in these applications can only be effected by the authority of Parliament; but we are satisfied that the alteration, with the corresponding modifications in the law of removal, would be of very large benefit, inasmuch as it would at the same time cause the adoption of much more general and effectual measures for the relief of all classes of casual poor, and would remove a great difficulty and constant source of contest in the administration of the Poor Laws. We may add, that the mode of charging the relief of casual poor which we have just recommended, does not involve any novel principle; for by 33 Geo. III. c. 35. s. 3, the relief of casual poor was made a common charge for parishes united under Gilbert's Act."

It is found that in proportion to the extension of the district on which the relief is charged, the burden on the whole is equalized, and falls in the nature of an insurance lightly on each parish included.

Notices of Removal may be served by Post.

"Clause 23.—That every notice of chargeability or relief of any poor person, every copy or counterpart or notice of any order (whether suspended or otherwise) for the removal of any poor person, every copy of examination upon which every such order shall have been made, every notice of appeal against such order, every bill or demand of costs incurred under or by reason of any such order, and every notice of appeal against any order for payment of costs incurred by reason of the suspension of any order of removal, shall be held to have been properly served or delivered, if it shall be proved that the same was properly addressed to the parties entitled to receive the same, and endorsed on the outside of the letter or packet with the name of the document as it is above described, and put into the post forty-eight hours at the least before the time when the same is required to be served or delivered."

The Poor Law Amendment Act makes transmission by the post of the notice of chargeability, of the examination of the pauper, and of the order of removal, sufficient service. These are the most essential documents connected with the removal of paupers, any irregularity in the receipt of which may expose a parish to be permanently burdened with a pauper not its own, without redress. But the convenience of adopting such service, instead of personal service, to be made between parishes sometimes at the opposite extremities of the kingdom, is obvious, and, in practice, has not been known to be productive of injustice in any one instance. The present clause merely extends the principle to the less material documents about which the expense of personal service is the most unnecessary.

Guardians to consent to exemption from Rates.

"Clause 24.—That no person shall be excused by justices on account of poverty from the payment of any poor-rate in any parish in which the relief of the poor shall be administered by a Board of Guardians, without the consent of such Board of Guardians."

This clause is merely declaratory of the law as it is believed to be at present, but is intended to remove some doubts which have been entertained by eminent counsel.

Workhouse to be deemed to be situate in every Parish of a Union.

"Clause 25.—That for the purposes of relief, removal, and burial of the poor, and the registration of births and deaths, and for all other purposes civil and ecclesiastical, connected with the relief of the poor maintained in or received into any workhouse of any Union, such workhouse shall be considered as situate in the parish to which each such poor person shall be chargeable."

There are many burdens which fall on parishes in which a pauper is found. Thus the fees connected with the registration of births and deaths is to be paid by the parish in which the birth or death occurs. Again: persons are to be buried where they die. These liabilities become very onerous to parishes in which the workhouses of Unions are situate; and the present clause is intended to relieve such parishes, by making the workhouse in law a part of each parish to which it belongs.

County, Borough, and Police Rates to be paid by Guardians.

"Clause 26.—That all county rates and borough rates, and all rates made in cities, boroughs, and towns, or in liberties and franchises, in the nature of county rates, and all police rates, shall be paid by the Boards of Guardians constituted under the said first recited Act; and upon like notice being given to the treasurer, and to the clerk of any Board of Guardians, as is required by law to be given to overseers and other parochial officers having the making of poor-rates, the same remedies for the recovery of the rates aforesaid shall and may be had against such guardians as might heretofore have been had against overseers; and for the purpose of obtaining the monies necessary for the payment of every such rate, the guardians shall have the same powers, authorities, and remedies as for obtaining contributions from parishes for the relief of the poor; and all precepts and warrants of justices for the levying, collecting, and paying of county rates, or other rates as aforesaid, shall be issued and addressed by such justices directly to the clerk and treasurer of each Board of Guardians required to pay the same."

This provision is for substituting a Union for a parochial collection; is one for substituting, in round numbers, 600 Unions for 15,000 parochial collections of contributions towards the county rates. It has been estimated that by the substitution of 26 Union collections in the county of Kent for 433 collections by constables from the separate parishes, about 1,000*l.* would be saved to the rate-payers in that county alone.

Costs of Apprehending and Prosecuting Vagrants, &c., to be paid out of Poor-rates.

"Clause 27.—That the reasonable costs of apprehending and prosecuting any person who shall refuse or neglect to maintain himself or his family, or who shall run away and leave his family chargeable, or so that such family may become chargeable, or who shall beg or gather, or endeavour to gather alms, or procure or encourage any child to do so, or who shall be guilty of misbehaviour in any workhouse, or of neglect or disobedience of the reasonable and lawful orders of justices or guardians, or of the orders of the Poor Law Commissioners, or who shall obstruct or assault any officer engaged in the administration of the laws for relief of the poor, or who shall fraudulently obtain, or shall steal, purloin, embezzle, waste, or injure, or wilfully misapply any property applicable to or connected with the relief of the poor, and the reasonable costs of apprehending and prosecuting any officer who may have been employed in the administration of the laws for the relief of the poor, for any neglect or breach of duty, and the costs of all legal proceedings for the protection of the poor-rates or property of any parish or Union (where the Board of Guardians shall have authorized or directed such prosecution or legal proceedings) shall, to the extent to which such costs shall not be repaid to the guardians by the offending or other party, or from the county or borough rates, be payable out of the poor-rates coming under the control of the guardians, either of the parish in which the offence may take place, or the rates of which may be affected by the offence, or out of the common fund of the Union in which such parish may be situate, as the guardians, having due regard to the circumstances of the case, shall direct."

The chief ground for this provision is stated in p. 101 8vo. and p. 61 fol., of the Report.

On formation of Unions, &c. the Commissioners may direct the re-appointment of pre-existing paid Officers.

"Clause 28.—That in every case in which there shall be any persons appointed to act as paid officers for any purpose connected with the administration of the laws for relief of the poor in any parish in which the said Commissioners shall direct that the relief of the poor shall be governed and administered by a Board of Guardians, or in any parish or parishes which the said Commissioners shall declare to be united for the administration of the laws for the relief of the poor, or which the said Commissioners may declare to be added to any Union, it shall be lawful for the said Commissioners to direct that such persons, or any of them, shall be re-appointed by the guardians to hold their offices, notwithstanding the constitution of such Board of Guardians or such union of parishes, or such addition of parishes to any Union: Provided always, That the said Commissioners shall have, with respect to such officers, the same powers for directing their appointment and continuance in office, their dismissal, and the re-appointment to their office, and the nature of the security to be given for the due performance of such offices, and for regulating the salaries payable to such officers, and that such officers shall be liable to the same penalties for neglect or misconduct in their offices as is provided with respect to paid officers appointed under the provisions of the said first recited Act."

The newly appointed Guardians, when newly assembled on the declaration of a Union, or the formation of a new Board, frequently find themselves pledged, upon a previous canvass, to the election of a new clerk, and are otherwise, before becoming acquainted with the qualifications requisite for the public service, impelled to new appointments, without regard to the experience of old, and possibly better qualified persons, who may be in office at the time of the change. In such cases the individuals suffer, and it is rarely found that the public gain by it. Much of the opposition and resistance to the introduction of the Poor Law Amendment Act has had its origin in the exertions of paid officers who expected to be displaced by the change, and who otherwise, from being acquainted with its advantages, would have given their aid to it. The Commissioners submit that they should, under such circumstances, be enabled to retain for the rate-payers the advantage of the services of properly qualified officers.

Accounts may be rendered half-yearly.

"Clause 29.—That so much of the said first recited Act as provides that accounts shall be made and rendered not less frequently than once in every quarter, shall be repealed; and such accounts shall be made and rendered at such times and as often as the said commissioners shall direct, but not less than once in every half year."

The accounts must now be audited quarterly. The interval is too close to allow of a large combination of Unions in one auditing district; it much increases the cost of the audit; and is not believed to be more effective than a half-yearly audit would be.

Guardians to appoint Collectors, &c.

"Clause 30.—That in all cases in which the said Commissioners shall declare or shall have declared any parishes to be united for the administration of the laws for the relief of the poor, or shall direct or shall have directed that the administration of the laws for the relief of the poor of any single parish shall be governed and administered by a Board of Guardians, the powers of any vestry, or parish officers, or of any persons other than the guardians of the Union or parish to appoint paid officers for any purpose whatever, connected with the administration of the laws for the relief of the poor in any such parishes, and all appointments under such powers, shall cease; and that the powers given by the said first recited Act to the said Commissioners for directing the execution by guardians of the laws for the relief of the poor, shall extend to the collection and distribution of poor-rates, and to the custody thereof, as well as to the relief, maintenance, and removal of the poor, and to the appointment of paid officers for the performance of the said duties, or any of them; and that every officer appointed by guardians of the poor, under the orders of the said Commissioners for the performance of any duty, shall have the like powers, authorities, privileges, immunities, protections, and remedies as are by law given to overseers of the poor in the performance of the like duty."

The grounds of this provision are detailed at length in pp. 84 to 97 8vo., and pp. 50 to 58 fol., of the Report, wherein it is stated,—

"This clause makes valid every order authorizing a Board of Guardians to appoint a collector of rates, which was issued by the Commissioners before the 6th of May last. The number of parishes to which such orders apply is about 4,600, and they naturally comprehend those places in which the services of a paid collector are most needed. But since the appointment of paid collectors by the Boards of Guardians appears, by unquestionable evidence, to have been generally beneficial, and since Parliament has sanctioned the orders for this purpose which had been issued by the Commissioners before the 6th of May last, we submit to your Lordship the propriety of generalizing the power, and of enabling the Commissioners to authorize Boards of Guardians in every case to appoint paid collectors of the poor-rates."

Overseers ineligible as Guardians.

"Clause 31.—That no person during the year for which he may serve the office of overseer, or hold the office of assistant overseer, of any parish, shall be capable of serving as a guardian for such parish."

On this clause the Commissioners have stated in their Report, pp. 39, 40 8vo. and pp. 24, 25 fol.:—

"This may not amount to the introduction of any new principle, but simply to a declaration of the effect of the law. It is doubtful whether overseers are now eligible as Guardians. The two offices are, so far as the administration of relief is concerned, precisely in the relation of controlling and subject offices. The overseers are required to obey the Guardians under penalties to be inflicted for disobedience, and the Guardians have express power to give orders to the overseers. There appears a clear inconsistency in the same person in one office giving directions to himself, and subjecting himself to penalties in another; and the two offices, would, as we are advised, be clearly incompatible in the same person, were it not for a doubt arising from the fact that a Guardian cannot individually give any order, and that all directions of the Guardians must be given by a

Board, at which three persons must be present and concur. This reason for doubt existing, it has been considered proper to incline in favour of the right of choice by the constituency, and overseers have therefore been considered eligible as Guardians, and many have been elected. There are, however, very conspicuous inconveniences and anomalies arising out of this course. It modified considerably the position of different parishes in a Union; some having the same person for both overseer and Guardian; others having the benefit of the subordination of these officers generally contemplated by the law. When the overseer is a member of the Board of Guardians, the effective control over him in his capacity of overseer, is greatly diminished by his being enabled to deliberate and vote in his own case on the instructions to be given to him, and the responsibility to be enforced of him. The effect is a practical accumulation of powers in overseers, and both a diminished responsibility in those officers, and less efficiency in the members of the Board of Guardians. The principal evil has hitherto been observed in the elections, in which overseers, being candidates for the office of Guardian, are frequently accused, and are sometimes guilty, of partiality in the admission of the claims and votes of the constituents, and in the general conduct of the election. Another striking evil is found in the difficulty with which contributions are enforced from the parishes whose overseers are members of the Board of Guardians. It therefore appears to us to be expedient that overseers should be declared ineligible to the office of Guardian. The only possibility of inconvenience from this declaration would be, that in some of the places too small or too little populous to provide both overseers and Guardians, the latter office may be unfilled, and the parish may, therefore, be unrepresented at the Board of Guardians. This inconvenience, however, can be partly provided against under the present law, which enables a parish to elect as its Guardian any person, whether a rate-payer of the parish or not, so that he be qualified in any place within the Union. The most effectual remedy, however, for this inconvenience (which can only arise in very small places which are now represented at the Board by the appointment of a Guardian for each such place) will be found in the provision recommended by the Committee, for enabling the Commissioners to combine a certain number of such places for the election jointly of one or more Guardians."

Votes of Owners and Proxies.

"Clause 32.—That no owner of property shall be entitled to vote as such, under the provisions of the said first recited Act, either in person or by proxy, until three months after he shall have given to the overseers the statement required by the said Act, nor unless such statement shall contain a description of the nature of the interest or estate he may have in such property, and a statement of the amount of all rent-service he may receive and pay in respect thereof, and of the persons from whom he may receive and to whom he may pay such rent-service; and no owner of property usually resident in any parish shall be entitled to appoint any person to vote as his proxy in such parish; and no person shall be entitled to vote as proxy until three months after he shall have made his claim so to vote in the manner required by the said Act; and no person shall be entitled to vote as proxy for more than four owners of property in any one parish (except he be a steward, bailiff, or land-agent, or collector of rents for the owners of property for whom he may be appointed to vote); and no appointment of proxy shall remain in force for a longer period than two years from the making thereof, excepting only in the case in which an owner shall appoint his bailiff, steward, land-agent, or collector of rents to be his proxy, in which case such appointment shall remain in force so long as the proxy shall continue to be such bailiff, steward, land-agent, or collector, and while such appointment shall remain unrevoked."

In p. 42 8vo. and p. 45 fol. of their Report, the Commissioners have stated,—

"By the 40th section of the Act it is provided, that 'it shall be lawful for any owner, from time to time, by writing under his hand, to appoint any person to vote as his proxy; and every such appointment shall remain in force until revoked or recalled by such owner.' The ground of allowing *owners* to vote by proxy was, that they are likely to be non-resident, which of course cannot be the case to any great extent with *occupiers*. The power given by the provision just cited is liable to the abuse, that any number of proxies may be accumulated in the hands of a single person; and if any person obtains a large number of them, he exercises an undue influence upon the election. For example, we have been informed that one person at the election of Guardians for the parish of Chelsea, in 1838, held 833 proxies; and that the candidate who stood at the head of the poll, and for whom all these proxies were given, had only 1,138 votes. The abuse in question is further facilitated by the procuration being unlimited in time; so that an absentee owner may almost lose sight of his vote. Since the powers of voting by proxy are given expressly by the Poor Law Amendment Act, they cannot be restrained by the Commissioners; we therefore recommend that the provision in question be amended by limiting the number of proxies to be holden by any one person to four, and by limiting the time for which a procuration shall be valid to two years. This limitation of the number of proxies to be holden by one person would be, we believe, in analogy with the rule which obtains respecting proxies in the House of Lords. If it should be thought inconvenient to make any express limitation by Act of

Parliament, the voting by proxy might be declared to be subject to the regulations of the Commissioners."

Payment of Poor-rates alone required of Rate-payers.

"Clause 33.—And whereas by the said first recited Act it is provided, that no person shall be deemed a rate-payer, or be entitled to vote, or do any other act, matter, or thing as such, under the provisions of that Act, unless he shall have been rated to the relief of the poor for the whole year immediately preceding his so voting, or otherwise acting as such rate-payer, and shall have paid the parochial rates and assessments made and assessed upon him for the period of one whole year, as well as those due from him at the time of so voting or acting, except such as shall have been made or become due within the six months immediately preceding such voting or acting; be it declared and enacted, That such parochial rates and assessments shall be deemed to extend only to rates made for the relief of the poor."

In pp. 41 and 42 8vo. and p. 25 fol. the grounds of this provision are thus stated:—

"By the 40th section of the Poor Law Amendment Act it is provided, that 'no person shall be deemed a rate-payer or be entitled to vote, or to do any other act, matter, or thing as such, under the provisions of this Act, unless *he shall have paid the parochial rates and assessments made and assessed upon him for the period of one whole year*, as well as those due from him at the time of so voting or acting, except such as shall have been made or become due within the six months immediately preceding such acting or voting.' A difficulty has arisen in practice respecting the extent of the terms 'parochial rates and assessments' in the provision just cited. It is manifest that they comprehend other rates than the poor-rate; but it is not manifest *which* of such other rates they comprehend. For example, they certainly comprehend church-rates, and probably comprehend highway-rates; whether they comprehend other rates, such as burial-ground rates. watching, lighting, and paving rates, and parochial rates of a local character, for the repair of wharfs, bridges, &c., is doubtful. A literal construction of the terms 'parochial rates and assessments' in the clause just cited, would in some cases have led to a very extensive disfranchisement of rate-payers. Conceiving that extensive disfranchisements, on such grounds as these, were not contemplated by Parliament, we have inclined to adopt a construction as favourable to the franchise as the terms of the Act would permit. We think, however, that the words are of inconveniently wide signification; and we recommend that a payment of poor-rates alone, in the manner prescribed by the Act, shall be held to qualify a rate-payer to vote in the election of Guardians."

Parishes may be divided into Wards.

"Clause 34.—That in every case in which a parish shall contain more than eight thousand persons, according to the then last enumeration of the population by authority of Parliament, it shall be lawful for the said commissioners, by order under their hands and seal, for the purpose of conducting the election of guardians or taking the votes of owners of property and rate-payers on any other lawful occasion, to divide such parish into such and so many wards as they shall deem expedient, and to determine the number of guardians to be elected for every such ward, which shall, for the purpose of every election of guardians, be considered as a separate parish."

The grounds for this provision are adverted to in p. 42 8vo. and p. 26 fol. of the Commissioners' Report:—

"It is likewise expedient that the Poor Law Commissioners should have a power of dividing parishes and townships into wards for the election of Guardians. This power would be particularly applicable to populous parishes situated in large towns; and it would introduce a mode of voting similar to that prescribed by the Municipal Corporations Act. The Committee of the House of Commons recommend that the Commissioners should be invested with this power, for reasons which are stated in the evidence taken by the Committee, and which we will shortly recapitulate. From the evidence of Mr. Power, our Assistant Commissioner, and Mr. Matthew Johnson, formerly one of the Guardians of the Poor at Leeds, it appears that, where the population is dense, elections of Guardians are carried on more cheaply and expeditiously, and with less danger of confusion and error, if the votes are taken by small districts, than if they are given for the entire parish. From the evidence of Mr. Hickson, one of the Guardians of the West London Union, it further appears that the system of voting simultaneously, for a large number of candidates whose names are circulated in a list, produces party elections, prevents a discriminating choice on the part of the voter, founded on personal knowledge, and causes the interests of minorities or peculiar localities to be represented imperfectly, or not at all. To these reasons it may be added, that where persons representing different constituencies meet in one body, each constituency has a powerful inducement to select discreet and respectable men, whose opinions and characters are likely to produce a favourable impression upon their colleagues. But where the whole of a body is elected by a single constituency, the predominant party is apt to run into extremes, and to disregard the character and moral worth of the candidates, knowing that the persons elected will all be agreed in their opinions."

Commissioners may alter number of Guardians.—Parishes may be combined for the election of one Guardian.

"Clause 35.—That in every case in which, since the first election of guardians, the relative population or circumstances of any parish included in a Union shall have changed, it shall be lawful for the said commissioners to alter the number of guardians to be elected for such parish; and that it shall be lawful for the said commissioners, having due regard to the circumstances and relative population of parishes in any Union, to combine two or more parishes for the election of one guardian, or of such number of guardians, being in a less proportion than one guardian for each such parish, as the said commissioners shall think fit, and without the consent of the majority of the owners of property and rate-payers of any such parish or Union."

This provision is founded on a recommendation of the Committee of the House of Commons that—

"The Commissioners should have the power of altering the number of Guardians, from time to time, as the proportions of population in the different parishes in the Union may vary; and that, in the case of very small parishes being contiguous, one Guardian should be allowed to serve for more than one parish (p. 37)."

The power here adverted to would be peculiarly applicable to some of the Unions in the northern conntics, where the townships, and not the parishes, usually relieve their poor, and where consequently, according to the present law, the Guardians are usually returned by townships and not by parishes. To this subject reference is also made in a Report by Sir John Walsham, inserted in the Appendix B, No. 3, p. 136 8vo. and 81 fol.

Appointment of Collectors of Votes, &c.

"Clause 36.—That the said Commissioners shall have power and authority from time to time to appoint or to direct guardians, overseers, or other officers to appoint persons to take, collect, and return, and to assist in taking, collecting, and returning, the votes of owners of property and rate-payers, and to fix the payments to be made to such persons out of the poor-rates, and from time to time to revoke or vary such appointments and payments as the said Commissioners may see fit."

The Commissioners are enabled, by the 40th section of the Poor Law Amendment Act, to direct the proceedings in election of Guardians; and they were advised that they had the power described in this clause; but the Court of Queen's Bench has recently decided that the Commissioners cannot appoint a returning officer, or his assistants, and that the appointment must be made by the Guardians or Overseers.

Determination of Disputes as to the Election, &c., of Guardians.

"Clause 37.—That in case any question shall arise as to the right of any person to act as an elected or *ex-officio* guardian, it shall be lawful for the Commissioners, if they shall see fit, to inquire into the circumstances of the case, and to issue such order or orders therein, under their hands and seal, as they may deem requisite for determining the question; and no such order shall be liable to be removed by writ of *certiorari* into the Court of Queen's Bench, unless the application for such writ shall be made during the term next after the issuing of such order."

This provision arises, as stated in the Report, p. 44 8vo. and p. 26 fol. that—

"It sometimes happens at present that a dispute arises respecting a person's title to act as an elected or an *ex-officio* Guardian. The Court of Queen's Bench has decided that it will not issue a writ of *quo warranto* to try the title of a Guardian of the poor; and consequently, the only means by which such a question can now be brought to trial is for the Guardians to turn the person out of their board-room, and for him to bring an action against them. In order to avoid the inconvenience caused by this circuitous proceeding, we propose that the Poor Law Commissioners should be empowered to determine every dispute of this nature by issuing an order under their hands and seal; and that this order should be liable to be brought before the Court of Queen's Bench by *certiorari*. We do not anticipate any serious objection to this arrangement, since it would furnish an immediate and inexpensive means of making a provisional settlement of the dispute, and would at the same time facilitate the legal remedy of the parties, if either should wish to obtain the decision of the Queen's Bench, upon the question."

Continuance of Guardians in Office.

"Clause 38.—That in every case in which a person shall not be nominated for the office of guardian at any annual election of guardians, the persons elected for the previous year shall be considered to be again elected, and shall continue to act as guardians until the next annual election."

Very serious inconvenience has been sustained by the change of the members of Boards of Guardians soon after they have become familiar with the principles of the law and with its proper administration. The relapse of many Unions, or the check to their progress in the abatement of pauperism, has been occasioned by the influx of new and uninformed members, who commonly are only prepared by information to exercise correctly the discretionary authority entrusted to them, when the period of their office has nearly expired, and when they are about to be succeeded by others, probably, who have had no better means of becoming fully acquainted with their duties. Many of the best qualified members of Boards of Guardians are persons who have no personal interests to serve, and have no care to be elected, and will not take the trouble to be re-elected. The Commissioners have submitted that when the constituents are so far satisfied with the services of a Guardian as not to propose another person for the office, neither the parishioners nor the Guardians should necessarily be put to the trouble of another election; and that this provision will tend greatly to the steadiness and uniformity of the proceedings of the Boards.

Commissioners may accept Resignation of any Guardian, and may order new Election.

" Clause 39.—That the said Commissioners may accept the resignation of any person proposed or elected as a guardian, tendered for any cause which the Commissioners may deem reasonable; and in every case of vacancy in any Board of Guardians, by death, resignation, or disqualification, the said Commissioners shall be and shall be deemed to have been empowered to order a new election for the completion of such board."

The grounds for this provision are stated in the Commissioners' Report, p. 43 8vo. and p. 26 fol.:—

" The resignation of an elected Guardian is alluded to in s. 38 of the Poor Law Amendment Act; but no mode or form of resignation is pointed out in the Act. Since the office is unpaid, a doubt has been entertained whether it is competent to a Guardian to resign, or whether the office is not compulsory, like that of overseer or constable. We have on many occasions accepted the resignations of Guardians; but we think it desirable that a power of resigning, with the consent of the Poor Law Commissioners, should be given expressly to the elected Guardians.

" A power of ordering a new election, in the event of the death, resignation, or other disqualification of a Guardian, or in the event of the irregularity of an election, has, from the necessity of the case, been exercised by the Commissioners, but without any express statutory authority. In order to obviate any doubt on this head, we recommend that the first part of sect. 25 of the Irish Poor Relief Act be extended to England."

Absent Guardians not to be considered as acting.

" Clause 40.—That in any case in which the consent or concurrence of any majority of guardians is necessary to the validity of any act or proceeding, no *ex-officio* guardian shall be considered as a member of the Board of Guardians, unless he shall attend at the board at which such consent or concurrence may be expressed, or such act or proceeding may take place; nor shall any elected guardian be considered as a member of such board in calculating any such majority, unless he shall have attended at the board within the two months preceding, if he shall have been so long elected; and no member of any Board of Guardians, except he shall be a peer or member of Parliament, shall have a vote in the appointment of any paid officer, unless such guardian shall have attended at least one-third of the ordinary meetings of such board held since the thirty-first day of March last preceding such appointment, or since his election or qualification, whichever shall have last happened."

De facto Guardians.

" Clause 41.—That no defect in the qualification or election of any person acting as a guardian at a Board of Guardians, the majority of persons assembled at which shall be entitled to act as guardians, shall be deemed to vitiate or make void any proceedings of such board in which he may have taken part."

Act limited to England and Wales.

" Clause 42.—That except so far as is hereinbefore expressly excepted, and so far as the continuance in office of the said Commissioners, their Assistant Commissioners, Secretary, Assistant Secretaries, and other officers and persons appointed by them, and the removal and re-appointment of the said Commissioners, no part of this Act shall extend to Ireland."

Act may be amended, &c. this Session.

" Clause 43.—That this Act may be amended or repealed in this present session of Parliament."

LONDON:
Printed by order of the Poor Law Commissioners, by W. CLOWES and SONS, Stamford Street, and Published by CHARLES KNIGHT and Co., 22, Ludgate-street, Publishers to the Poor Law Commissioners.

SUPPLEMENT
TO THE
FIFTH NUMBER OF THE OFFICIAL CIRCULAR,
CONTAINING
A COPY OF THE BILL FOR THE AMENDMENT OF THE POOR LAW, AND THE REASONS FOR THE SEVERAL PROVISIONS.

THE provisions contained in the Bill recently introduced into the House of Commons by Her Majesty's Government are substantially the same as those in the Bill introduced during the last session. Some alterations have been made in the present Bill which are chiefly to be found in Sections 9, 11, 12, 13, 14, 23, and are hereafter described. The explanations of the several clauses contained in the fifth number of the Official Circular were nearly all taken from the Commissioners' Report on the Further Amendment of the Poor Law, and on the continuance of the Commission, presented in December, 1839, and publicly circulated. The following is an extract from a part of the Report which was not given in the Official Circular, No. 5, and which sets forth some of the chief grounds for the continuance of the Commission.

Observations of the Committee of the House of Commons, which sat from March to July, 1836, and from November, 1837, to August 1838, in recommending the Continuance of the Commission.

" 'WITH respect to the powers of the Poor Law Commissioners, it is said that they are unconstitutional, and that they have deprived the rate-payers of all control over their own funds and the management of their own affairs. In some few instances, as in the petition from Nottingham, those powers are more specifically complained of, as enforcing a particular dietary and classification of the inmates of the workhouse; an objection has also been made by one witness, Mr. Bull, to the particular provisions contained in the 98th clause of the Poor Law Amendment Act. Your Committee have not felt it to be their duty to enter so much into any general examination of the principles of the law in question, as of the manner in which its administration has been conducted. The reasons for granting these powers to the Poor Law Commissioners are fully explained in the Report of the Commissioners of Inquiry in 1834. It is there stated, that any instances of good management under the former state of the law have been partial and accidental; that they have depended on the exertions of some individual of superior energy and intelligence; that the improved practice had not been adopted in the immediate neighbourhood of the parishes where its success had been most conspicuous, and that even in those parishes there was no security for its permanence. The great irregularity which so often prevailed in the administration of relief to the poor in parishes immediately contiguous, and under circumstances exactly similar, was felt to be both inconvenient and unjust, and it was hoped that this might be corrected by the superintendence of a Central Board. In some parishes it was said that the overseers required protection against intimidation; in others, the poor suffered from the partial distribution of relief; and for these evils a remedy was proposed in the authority of the Commissioners, and in the influence of general rules. It was felt, too, that any system which might be good for the ordinary state of circumstances would be unsuited to extraordinary emergencies, and that the Central Board, in constant communication with its Assistant Commissioners and the various Boards of Guardians, would be the best judge of the time and degree in which any modifications suited to those emergencies might be introduced. Your Committee entirely agree with the Commissioners of Inquiry (page 261 of their Report), that 'those modes of administering relief which had been tried wholly or partially, and have produced beneficial effects in some districts, should be introduced, with modifications according to local circumstances, and carried into complete execution in all;' and if, indeed, such an approach to uniformity in the administration of relief to the poor as the circumstances of different parts of the country will admit of, be thought desirable, and if the control of any central authority, invested with discretionary power, be objected to, it would seem necessary to have recourse to an Act of the Legislature, in which almost every variety of cases where relief should be either given or withheld, must be prescribed in detail. Such an attempt, if not impracticable, could only be enforced at the expense of the greatest hardship and injustice. Your Committee do not feel it necessary to make any further observations in defence of these provisions of the law; but they earnestly recommend the reasoning contained in the Report of the Commissioners of Inquiry to those who may be disposed to doubt the necessity of conferring those powers on some central authority. Your Committee believe the powers of the Central Board to be indispensable to the execution of the law; and that without some control of this kind, there could be no security against a recurrence to almost every variety of mismanagement or abuse; neither have they seen anything in the manner in which the powers have been exercised to lessen the force of those reasons which originally recommended their adoption by the Legislature. When the extent of the change, the number of individuals, and the variety of interests affected by it, are considered, it is impossible not to feel that the task imposed on the Poor Law Commissioners was one of the utmost difficulty. The arrangements made by them appear generally to have been skilful and judicious, and well adapted to the local peculiarities by which they have been modified; and your Committee feel much gratification in stating, that in no instance which has been brought under their notice do these powers appear to have been abused.*

* * * *

" 'Your Committee cannot quit this portion of their inquiry without expressing a favourable opinion of the clear form in which many of the regulations and public documents are issued by the Commissioners, as well of the practice hitherto pursued by them of stating fully, in their letters of instruction and answers to inquiries, the facts and reasonings on which their rules or recommendations are founded. On this part of the subject your Committee have agreed to the following resolution:—

" 'That in the important duties committed to them, the Commissioners have evinced zeal, ability, and great discrimination; and the Committee recommend the continuance of their power, in preference to any system which, by leaving the administration of the Poor Laws without the control and superintendence of a Central Board, might cause the recurrence of those abuses which existed in many counties previously to the passing of the Poor Law Amendment Act.'—pp. 26, 27.

Reasons urged by the Commissioners for the continuance of their powers.

"We are conscious of the delicacy of the task which a compliance with the instructions of Her Majesty's Government imposes upon us, and of the suspicions with which a statement of reasons in favour of the continuance of the Poor Law Commission, made by the Commissioners themselves, is likely to be received. Nevertheless, as our position has necessarily given us the widest and most exact knowledge of the operation of the new law, and of the means by which it has been carried into execution, we think that we should be wanting to our duty if we were deterred by a fear of the imputation of interested motives from laying before your Lordship those reasons in favour of the continuance of the Poor Law Commission which have not been adverted to by the Committee of the House of Commons. We feel the less hesitation about taking this course, as we shall confine ourselves to the statement of facts, and to the suggestion of obvious inferences from them.

"To the reasons stated in the passage from the Report of the Committee, which we have just quoted, the following considerations may, as it appears to us, be added."

Temporary purposes of Commission not yet fulfilled.

"1. Even upon the most limited view of the purposes of the Poor Law Commission, its functions have not yet been discharged. The change in the administration of the English Poor Law which it was intended to introduce, has not yet been completed. The machinery by which that change was to be effected is not yet in operation over the whole country. There still remain 799 parishes in England and Wales which have not been brought under the operation of the Poor Law Amendment Act, containing a population of 2,055,733 souls. Of these, some are formed into incorporations under Gilbert's Act, some are under Local Acts, and a few others have, for special reasons, been left under their former parochial management. Moreover, there are still about 70 Unions in which a central workhouse has not yet been built. Many other Unions (especially in the northern counties) have only been recently formed, and they still need the frequent guidance of the Commissioners and Assistant Commissioners, in order to bring them into a state in which they can give effect to the provisions of the new law."

Machinery still incomplete.

"The subject of the apprenticeship of pauper children has not yet been approached by the Commissioners; and the arrangements for their education (which will be adverted to in a subsequent part of our Report) are as yet far from being matured. Notwithstanding the large reduction in the expenditure for the relief of the poor, several of the abuses of the old system of administration still continue to exist. Relief in aid of wages is still given in almost every Union to all paupers except able-bodied males, and it is given even to paupers of this latter class in many Unions in which the workhouse arrangements are not completed. Relief is still given extensively to paupers resident out of their Unions. From a recent return which we obtained, it appears that, in the quarter ending 25th March, 1838, 94,852 persons were thus supported. There are likewise various matters connected with the keeping of accounts, the forms of contracts, and the regulations for the government of the officers of the Unions, which require the careful revision of the Commissioners, in order to place the administration of relief on a satisfactory footing as regards both the paupers and

* The passage here omitted is adverted to in a subsequent part of our Report.

rate-payers. No steps have been yet taken for carrying into effect the provisions of the Poor Law Amendment Act (ss. 33-34), respecting Unions for purposes of rating and settlement, by which a great improvement and simplification of management would be effected, and much fraud and litigation, now produced by contested settlements, and by partial and unequal rating, would be prevented.

Delay in the Progress of the Administration of the Law, not attributable to the Commissioners.

"We may here remark, that if less progress has been made towards the administrative changes intended to be introduced through the agency of the Poor Law Commission, in the five years which have elapsed since its creation, than some persons may have anticipated or desired; and if much still remains to be done in order to introduce and establish universally the mode of administration contemplated by the Poor Law Amendment Act, this delay has been owing, not to any remissness on the part of the Commissioners, but to the opinion of Parliament, Her Majesty's Government, and the public generally, which was opposed to a more rapid extension of the law, and to the employment of more decisive measures for carrying it into effect. The delay has also arisen in part from the want of certain additional facilities for administering the law, which have been recommended by the Committee of the House of Commons, and which will be adverted to in the present Report."

The Objects of the Commission permanent.

"2. It is evident, however, that the Poor Law Commission was not intended merely to introduce a new system of administering the Poor Laws, (as the Tithe Commission was created simply for the purpose of effecting a certain commutation of tithes,) but that it was intended also to maintain and regulate that system when introduced. The Commissioners of Inquiry recommended a permanent, and not a temporary Commission, as appears from their arguments repeated in the extract from the Report of the Committee of the House of Commons, which we have cited above;* and, in the Bill as originally introduced by the Government, the duration of the Commission was unlimited. The limitation of its duration was inserted in the Bill during its progress through Parliament; and it was probably rather adopted as a measure of precaution, and for the purpose of expressly subjecting the proceedings of the Commission to the revision of Parliament at the end of five years, than with an intention that the Commission should expire at the time designated in the Act."

Nature and Importance of these Objects apparent from the Business transacted.

"That the Poor Law Commission was constituted, not merely for the purpose of introducing the Poor Law Amendment Act, but also for the purpose of superintending the ordinary administration of this and the other laws relating to the relief of the poor, and that great confusion, disorder, and other serious inconveniences would arise from the extinction of a superintending authority, will, we think, appear conclusively from an examination of the business transacted by it.

"The business transacted by the Poor Law Commission is of two sorts:—First, the business which it originates;—and, secondly, the business which arises from the applications of Poor Law or other public officers, or of private persons, for information or advice. The business originated by the Commission consists mainly in orders issued for the purpose of introducing the mere machinery of the Act, and then for the gradual application of its provisions, as the district becomes from time to time prepared for their adoption: such as orders for the election of guardians, the regulation of workhouses, the authorizing the appointment of paid officers and the defining their duties, the restriction of money or out-door relief to certain classes of paupers, &c. The orders of the latter class require revision, emendation, and addition from time to time. The auditing of the Poor Law accounts is another important branch of the business initiated by the Commission. The power of dismissing the officers of Poor Law Unions likewise gives rise to much business of the same sort. The Parochial Assessment Act has moreover necessitated a survey and a new valuation of a large part of the real property of England and Wales, which has been carried on under the directions of the Poor Law Commissioners, their consent being made necessary for these operations. The Parish Property Act has besides imposed much additional business on the Poor Law Commissioners, which is necessary for giving effect to the provisions of that Act.

"All the business which we have just mentioned is necessary for the administration of the existing law; and if the Poor Law Commission were simply abolished, and no other authority substituted for it, the administration of the Poor Laws, as modified by the late Acts of Parliament, could in many places be scarcely carried on, and in all places it would only be carried on with great inconvenience.

Saving effected in Law Expenses.

"The second sort of business above adverted to, may be styled the *voluntary* business of the Poor Law Commission. It does not originate with the Commission, nor is it absolutely necessary for carrying the existing law into effect: but it consists in answers to applications made to the Commissioners for their opinion and advice in questions where the applicant is in doubt as to the legality or prudence of any course of conduct. A large number of ques-

* Page a.

tions on points of law, arising in the administration of relief, are submitted to the Commissioners, and are regularly answered by them. Many of the legal questions thus submitted to the Commissioners admit of an easy solution by persons whose attention is continually directed to the subject of the Poor Laws. Many, however, present considerable difficulty to persons who approach them even with this advantage. This may be considered a very valuable part of the business which is transacted by the Commission, inasmuch as the advice given in this manner has materially contributed to produce the great reduction in Poor Law litigation which has taken place since 1834, the last year before the passing of the Poor Law Amendment Act. The total amount of expenses for the removal of paupers and Poor Law litigation, in 1834, was 258,604*l.*; the total amount of the expenses for the same purposes, in 1839, was 64,510*l.*: showing a diminution, as compared with 1834, of 194,094*l.* From such a diminution of litigation, it may be inferred that a much greater proportion of injustice and illegality has been prevented; since of many cases of wrong, few could at any time have been the subjects of litigation.

"The whole of the business just described (in addition to the Irish business, of which we are not now speaking) is transacted by the Poor Law Commissioners, aided, chiefly for the purposes of local inspection and control, by their Assistant Commissioners."

Extent of Abuses existing prior to the Act.

"We would here beg leave to recall to your Lordship's memory the state of England immediately before the passing of the Poor Law Amendment Act, as described in the Report of the Commissioners of Inquiry. The amount of the Poor-rates had become grievously oppressive in most parts of the country, and in some places had become nearly intolerable, so as to threaten the abandonment of the land by the proprietors. But the heavy taxation was not so oppressive to the rate-payer as the mode of distributing the rates was pernicious to the paupers and the rest of the community. Various contrivances for confounding relief with wages had enabled the predominant interest in each locality to force their weaker neighbours to contribute to a common fund from which they did not derive an equal benefit, and had converted the state of the labourer into a condition little superior to that of predial servitude. The consequences of this perversion of the natural relations of employer and workman were developed in the agrarian disturbances and fires of 1830 and 1831, and in a general feeling of insecurity and alarm throughout the southern and eastern counties of England."

Extinction of under present Administration.

"Now, although the Poor Law Commission has existed for little more than five years, the causes of evil which we have just described have been extinguished. Systematic relief of able-bodied men in aid of wages, only exists in a few Unions which do not yet possess an efficient workhouse. All the other pernicious varieties of the old mode of relief, which are described by the Commission of Inquiry as being then in full vigour—the allowance system, the roundsman system, the labour-rate system—have ceased. That the Poor Law Commission has thus far executed the task prescribed to it by the Legislature cannot be disputed."

Evil habits thereby engendered, not eradicated.

"But notwithstanding the cessation of the vicious practices just described, it is not to be supposed that the habits which those practices had engendered can have been eradicated in the short course of a few years; or that new habits, more consistent with a sound practice, can have been established in their place. The reflecting part of the public may support the new Law from a conviction of its utility; but the unreflecting part can only be expected to be determined by usage."

Probability and Extent of Recurrence of Abuses on the expiration of the Commission.

"Hence it is to be feared that the amended system of Poor Laws would not be established permanently in the country, and would not continue to work beneficially, if the powers of the Poor Law Commissioners were to cease at the term fixed by the late Act. From the addresses of the Boards of Guardians, and from the opinions of persons practically conversant with the subject, it may be inferred that the superintending authority of the central Commissioners, combined with the local inspection and control of their Assistant Commissioners, is essential to the administration of the existing law. The modern workhouse furnishes (as we shall show hereafter) a mode, consistent with humanity, of making the condition of the pauper less desirable than that of the independent labourer, and consequently introduces a new principle into the ordinary administration of legal relief to the poor in this country. This principle, on the one hand, affords a satisfactory answer to those reasoners who object to all legal relief of the poor, on the ground that its abuses must always preponderate over its uses; and, on the other hand, furnishes an effective instrument to those who desire to administer legal and sufficient relief in a manner consistent with the preservation and accumulation of property, and with the maintenance of the rights of industry. Since the efficiency of the workhouse principle has, through the operation of the Poor Law Amendment Act, been understood by a large number of persons, the country would probably not relapse into all the abuses of its former administration of the Poor Laws, if the Poor Law Commission were abolished. Persons desirous to correct or guard against these abuses would henceforth, under any circumstances, know what to do, and would only be deterred by want of courage or energy from contending against the aggressions of pauperism. Formerly those who most desired to reform the administration of the Poor Laws knew not what to do, and despaired of finding a remedy for the evils which they deplored. If, therefore, the Poor Law Commission were to be suffered to expire at the time fixed by the late Act, the administration of the Poor Laws would probably not sink to quite its former level, and the poor-rates would probably not rise to quite their former height; but the force of the vicious habits and deep-rooted prejudices which were generated by the old system, and the struggles of interested classes and persons to revert to it, show that the deterioration would be general and rapid. The attempts which are constantly made to evade the law by indirect means, whenever there is a possibility of so doing, (as by voluntary rates, by the highway-rates,* and by the abuse of orders for food, &c., given by the medical officers,) confirm us in this anticipation. In expressing this opinion, we are not unmindful of the able and efficient support which the law and the Commissioners have received from many leading members of the Boards of Guardians; but we doubt whether even their zeal and intelligence would suffice to maintain the correct principles of the Poor Law Administration, if they were deprived of the support of a central superintending authority, ready to enforce the law without reference to local or personal consideration."

Commission necessary for the Irish Poor Relief Act.

3. "Another reason for prolonging the powers of the Poor Law Commissioners has been created by the passing of the Irish Poor Relief Act. This important measure received the royal assent on the 31st of July, 1838. The Bill was introduced by Her Majesty's Ministers after the elaborate inquiries of a Commission which continued its labours for several years; and it was passed after mature deliberation, having been discussed in two successive sessions of Parliament. This measure introduces into Ireland some innovations of great moment, viz., a compulsory rate for the relief of the destitute poor, and representative Boards of Guardians. It likewise authorizes the expenditure of considerable sums of public money in the construction of workhouses. The execution of this measure was deliberately confided to the Poor Law Commissioners; and the scheme of a separate Board of management was deliberately rejected. Now, if the Poor Law Commission were suffered to expire, and no provision were made for the exercise of the powers vested by the Irish Act in the Poor Law Commissioners, this Act would be virtually repealed. Since a Poor Law machinery does not exist in Ireland, and must be created in order to enable legal relief to be administered, the provisions of the Act would be perfectly nugatory. This result can hardly have been contemplated by the Legislature when it passed the Act in question at so late a period as the session of 1838.

"It may, perhaps, be said that the powers of the Poor Law Commission might conveniently be suffered to expire for England and Wales, and continued for Ireland alone. But this plan is utterly inconsistent with the views upon which the Irish Poor Relief Act was founded. The administration of that Act was intrusted to the English Poor Law Commissioners, for the very purpose of introducing into Ireland the system of legal relief which had been established in England. It was thought that this object would be best attained by vesting the administration of the Poor Laws of *both* countries in the same authority; that by this means a unity of management would, as far as circumstances would permit, be ensured on both sides of the Channel, and that the accumulated experience of the Commissioners for England would be made available for the benefit of Ireland. All these advantages would be sacrificed if the powers of the Commission were to expire for England, and were to be continued for Ireland alone. It may be added, that if the English Commission were to be suffered to expire on the ground of economy, little saving of public money would be produced by the measure. The addition made to the duties of the Poor Law Commission by the Irish Poor Relief Act has made little addition to its expenses. The salaries of the Commissioners have not been increased, and the increase of the establishment of their office has not been considerable."

Identity of the English and Irish Poor Laws.

"There is, moreover, another consideration in reference to this supposition, to which it is important to advert. The system of legal relief which actually exists in England, and the system which is about to be introduced into Ireland, may be considered as substantially identical; that is to say, both systems rest upon the workhouse. In both countries the struggle to obtain out-door relief on easy terms will be very great; in England, on account of habits created by the former profuse administration; in Ireland, on account of the depressed state of the great body of the peasantry. Now, the principal function of the Poor Law Commissioners is to resist the strong tendency of the local authorities to fall into a lax administration of relief, and to strengthen them in the performance of their duties when they are unable to stand alone against the heavy pressure to which they are subject. If, therefore, the Poor Law Commission were

* See the Evidence before the Select Committee of the House of Commons on the Highways Act, ordered to be printed 16th August, 1838.

e

abolished for England and continued for Ireland alone, the abuses of the former system would, to a great extent, return in England; and the existence of such practices in England would immediately serve as an argument for their introduction into Ireland. The authority of the practice in England would, in such a case, soon be too powerful for any resistance which the arguments or influence of the Poor Law Commissioners could oppose to it; and we leave your Lordship to consider what would shortly be the state of Ireland under the operation of a Poor Law administered as the English Poor Law was administered before the recent changes."

Objections to existence of Commission examined.

"Having stated the principal reasons in favour of the continuance of the Poor Law Commission, we proceed to examine the chief objections most commonly urged against its existence.

"The objection most commonly made to the existence of the Poor Law Commission consists in the assertion that its powers are *unconstitutional* or *arbitrary*. Stronger expressions, such as 'tyrannical,' 'despotic,' 'dictatorship,' 'star-chamber procedure,' &c., are sometimes used, but apparently to convey only the same general meaning.

"Expressions like those which we have just stated are sometimes applied to an exercise of the governing power which is really mischievous, and sometimes to any exercise of that power which the writer or speaker dislikes. But where these expressions have been applied to the Poor Law Commission with any precise meaning, we conceive that they have been intended to object to it, either that it introduces *a centralized administration*, or that it possesses *powers of subordinate legislation*. Upon this assumption we shall proceed to examine how much weight is due to each of the two latter objections."

Centralized Administration no innovation.

"1. With respect to the *centralized administration*, which is objected to the Poor Law Commission as an innovation inconsistent with the general spirit of the constitution, we may observe that this objection appears to assume that nearly the entire administration of the United Kingdom is conducted by local authorities, bound together by no common tie except the general law, and acknowledging no common superior except the Crown and the Parliament. This assumption, however, is not consistent with fact. Not to mention the army and navy, and also the Post-office, for which a centralized administration may be thought almost indispensable, it is to be observed that the administration of justice is as much centralized in this country as is consistent with the termination of civil and criminal actions. The judges of the superior courts of common law only move out of London twice in the year; and the sittings of the courts of equity, and of the superior ecclesiastical and admiralty courts, are permanently fixed in London. Besides the administration of justice, all the administrative machinery for the collection and protection of the public revenue is worked by central authorities, viz., the Boards of Customs, Excise, Stamps, and Taxes, and the chief office of the Preventive Service, which departments are again subject to the general control of the Lords Commissioners of the Treasury. The auditing of the public accounts is likewise carried on by a central board. These examples show that superintendence by a central administrative authority is no innovation in the English constitution. Indeed, the only important instances in which the English constitution has permitted a large outlay of public money without some responsibility to the general Government are the poor-rates, and the analogous cases of county and borough rates, highway rates, and the expenditure for the maintenance of turnpike roads. The want of adequate responsibility has, in these branches of expense, led to profuse outlays of public money, and to serious financial embarrassments. But the annual expenditure for the purposes defrayed out of the county and borough rates, and for the maintenance of roads, however large, falls very short of the expenses for the relief of the poor; nor is the tendency to abuse, or the difficulty of resisting a lavish expenditure, so great in the former as in the latter case. The government of England, and (as far as we are aware) the governments of the rest of the civilized world, can offer no parallel to the old Poor Law system, which annually levied and disbursed, in England and Wales alone, about seven millions sterling, by means of local, unconnected, and unpaid officers, abandoned to their own judgment, destitute of any central guidance or control, and subject to no effectual responsibility."

THE substance of those Clauses in which alterations have taken place is hereunder stated. The words printed in italics are those contained in the Bill of last session which do not appear in the present Bill—those printed between brackets are the words introduced in the present Bill and not included in the former one.

"Clause I.—[Empowers the Commissioners, &c. to hold office until the 31st December, 1851.]

"Clause III.—Defines general rules and particular orders; and provides, that every rule, order, or regulation, which shall apply only to a single case or a single occasion, or which shall suspend *or rescind* any previous rule, &c., shall be deemed a particular order.

"Clause IV.—And [whereas, by sundry Acts of Parliament, passed since the said Act of the fifth year of his late Majesty, power has been given to the said Commissioners to issue rules, orders, and regulations] Be it declared and enacted, that *whenever it shall have been or shall hereafter be made lawful for the Commissioners to issue any rule, order, or regulation, such* [every] rule, order, or regulation [so authorized, or which shall be so authorized by this or by any future Act of Parliament] shall have every quality, incident, and effect of a rule, order, or regulation made under the provisions of the *said* first recited Act and this Act [unless otherwise expressly provided in the Act authorizing the same].

" Clause V. Provides, that general rules, having been once allowed, may afterwards be issued as particular orders, and shall take effect *and operate* accordingly.

" Clause VI.—That every order of the said Commissioners, suspending any previous rule, order, or regulation, or suspending any paid officer from the exercise of his office, *and every order* in which the said Commissioners shall declare that the urgency of the case, &c., as required by the *said* first recited Act.

" Clause VII. line 42.—Be it enacted, that it shall not, in any civil or criminal, *or other legal* proceeding, be necessary to prove such sending except to the clerk of the Guardians [of the Union] or of the parish, or [where] *when* there shall be no Guardians to the Overseers of the parish within which *respectively* such rule, &c., is intended to have effect; and that it shall in no case be necessary to prove such sending unless reasonable notice in writing be given [by the party requiring such proof] to the party upon whom such proof would lie, &c., under the *said* recited first Act.

" Clause VIII.—And be it enacted, that so much of the *said* [first] recited Act as provides that no dissolution or alteration of any Union, whether formed before or after the passing of the *said* first recited Act, &c., shall be *and the same is hereby* repealed, &c.; which last mentioned incorporations and unions of parishes the said Commissioners [shall be] *are hereby* authorized to dissolve.

" Clause IX.—Empowers the Commissioners to unite parishes and Unions for the management of infirm [insane] or infant poor, &c. &c.; to determine the mode in which a Board of Management shall be appointed, and the number and qualifications of the members of such Board of Management [to be selected from the several Boards of Guardians], &c.; to direct such Board of Management to purchase, or hire, or [build] *erect*, and to fit up and furnish a building, &c. for the relief and management of such infirm [insane] or infant poor.

" Clause X.—That the Board of Management shall have such of the powers of Guardians as the Commissioners shall direct for the relief and management of infirm [insane] or infant poor.

" Clause XI.—[Proviso for counties where there are county lunatic asylums.]

" Clause XII.—[Visitation of lunatic asylums.]

g

" Clause XIII.—Provides for the contribution of parishes united for the management of infirm [insane] or infant poor.

" Clause XIV.—Is a definition of the terms ' infirm poor,' [' insane poor,'] and ' infant poor.'

" Clause XVII.—And be it declared and enacted, that [so long as] *in all cases in which* the husband of any woman shall be beyond the seas, or in custody of the law, or shall be a lunatic or idiot, *or shall refuse or neglect to maintain his family, or shall leave his family chargeable, or so that it may become chargeable, or shall from any cause be unable to maintain himself*, his wife shall, notwithstanding her coverture, be liable to maintain herself and her children in the like manner in all respects as a widow [and that relief to the children of any married woman whose husband shall refuse or neglect to maintain his family, or shall leave his family chargeable, or so that it may become chargeable, shall be considered relief to the mother.]

" Clause XX.—Provides, that in addition to the money which the Guardians are authorized by the first recited Act to borrow for building *or* enlarging or altering workhouses, the Guardians of any parish or Union which [is] *may be* situate within the metropolitan police district, may raise further sums for the purchase of land as the site of *any* such workhouse, &c.

" Clause XXI.—Enacts, that the Commissioners may define the classes of poor children who may be apprenticed [the trades or businesses to which they may be apprenticed] &c.

" Clause XXII.—Provides, that funds raised for emigration purposes under the authority of the first recited Act, shall be expended, subject to the orders of *the said Commissioners* [one of Her Majesty's Principal Secretaries of State.]

" Clause XXIII.—Provides for the burial of paupers, and that every [dead] body which the Guardians, &c. shall direct to be buried at the expense of the poor-rates, shall be buried in the burying ground of the parish &c., in which the death shall have *or shall be considered to have* occurred, and that [the fee or fees] *a fee of five shillings and no more, shall be* payable [by custom of the place in which the burial shall take place, or under the provisions of any Act of Parliament shall be paid] out of the poor rates for the burial of each such body [to the person or persons who by such custom, or under such Act, may be entitled to receive any fee, and that if any dispute shall arise, it shall be lawful for the Commissioners to declare whether any and what amount shall be payable out of the poor rates, provided that no fee exceeding shall be payable out of the poor rates to any one person for the burial of the body of a pauper] *and such fee shall be paid to the clergyman who, according to the practice in the place, shall have been accustomed to receive fees for burial.*

" Clause XXV.—Provides for the relief of poor

persons casually chargeable, and the cost of their removal, and all expenses incident thereto [and in case of their death and burial, by direction of the Guardians the cost of their burial] &c., and that for the purpose of [authorizing] such removal, they shall be deemed chargeable to any parish in which they may receive relief.

"Clause XXVIII.—Provides that for the purposes therein mentioned, the workhouse shall be considered as situated in the parish to which each *such* poor person [respectively to be relieved, removed, buried, registered, or otherwise concerned in any such purpose] shall be chargeable.

"Clause XXIX.—Provides that all county, borough, police rates, &c., [and all other rates whatever payable out of the rates made for the relief of the poor] shall be paid by [the] *any* Board[s] of Guardians constituted under the first recited Act; and that for the purpose of obtaining the monies for such payments, the Guardians shall have such powers, &c. as [they have] for obtaining contributions from parishes for the relief of the poor, [and all precepts, &c. for the levying of such money shall be addressed to the clerk and treasurer of each Board of Guardians required to pay the same.]

"Clause XXX.—Provides that the costs of apprehending and prosecuting vagrants, &c., or of persons guilty of neglect or disobedience of the reasonable and lawful orders of justices or Guardians [in the administration of the laws relating to the relief of the poor] &c. shall be paid from the county, [liberty], or borough, rates, &c., or out of the common fund of the Union, as the Guardians, having due regard to the circumstances of the case [and subject to the approval of the said Commissioners], shall direct.

"Clause .—*Empowering Commissioners to appoint auditors.*

"Clause .—*For the appointment of chaplains.*

"Clause XXXII.—Provides that where the Commissioners shall direct, or shall have directed parishes to be united for the relief of the poor, or that any single parish shall be under the management of a Board of Guardians, the powers of any vestry, or parish officers, or any persons other than the Guardians of the Union or parish to appoint paid officers for any purpose connected with the laws for the relief of the poor shall, *and shall be deemed to* cease; and that the powers given by the first recited Act to the Commissioners for directing the execution by Guardians of the laws for the relief of the poor, *shall be deemed to extend, and* shall extend to the collection and distribution of poor-rates, &c.

"Clause XXXIII.—That no person during the [time] *year* for which he may serve the office of overseer, or hold*ing* the office of assistant overseer of any parish [nor any paid officer engaged in the administration of the laws for the relief of the poor in any parish or Union] shall be capable of serving as a Guardian for such parish [or in such Union].

h

"Clause XXXV.—Provides that no person shall be entitled to vote as proxy for more than *four* [two] owners of property in any one parish, except in the case of a steward, &c.; and that no appointment of proxy shall remain in force longer than [one year] *two years.*

"Clause XXXVII.—And be it *further* enacted, that in every case in which a parish shall contain *a population, which according to the returns made under the then last parliamentary census, shall exceed* 8000, *it shall* [more than 8000 persons, according to the then last enumeration of the population by authority of parliament, it shall be lawful for the Commissioners, by order under their hands and seal] for the purpose of conducting the election of Guardians, or taking the votes of owners, &c., *be lawful for the said Commissioners by order under their hands and seal,* to divide such parish into wards, &c., and that every such ward shall be considered as a *single and* separate parish.

"Clause XXXVIII.—And be it *further* enacted, that in every case in which, since the first election of Guardians, the relative population or circumstances shall have changed, it shall be lawful for the Commissioners [with the consent of the greater number of the Guardians] to alter the number of Guardians, &c., and [with the consent of the greater number of the Guardians] to combine two or more parishes for the election of one Guardian, *anything in the said first-recited Act to the contrary notwithstanding.*

"Clause XXXIX.—Enacts that the Commissioners shall have, *and be deemed to have,* power to appoint collectors of votes.

"Clause XL.—Empowers the Commissioners to determine disputes as to the election of Guardians, and to issue orders accordingly, and provides that no such order shall be liable to be removed by certiorari, unless application be made [during] *within* the term next after the issuing of such order.

"Clause XLI.—Enacts that in every case in which [no] *a* person shall *not* be nominated as Guardian at the annual election, the person elected for the previous year shall be considered to be again elected.

"Clause XLIII.—Provides (inter alia) that no elected Guardian shall be considered as a member of the Board for the purposes therein mentioned, unless he shall have attended at the Board [since his election, and also] within the two months preceding.

"Clause XLVI.—And be it enacted, that this Act may be *altered,* amended, or repealed [by any Act to be passed] in this present session of Parliament."

LONDON:

Printed, by order of the Poor Law Commissioners, by W. Clowes and Sons, Stamford Street, and Published by Charles Knight and Co., 22, Ludgate Street, Publishers to the Poor Law Commissioners.

AN

OFFICIAL CIRCULAR

OF PUBLIC DOCUMENTS AND INFORMATION:

DIRECTED BY THE POOR LAW COMMISSIONERS TO BE PRINTED, CHIEFLY FOR THE USE OF THE MEMBERS AND PERMANENT OFFICERS OF BOARDS OF GUARDIANS, UNDER THE POOR LAW AMENDMENT ACT.

No. 6. CIRCULAR ISSUED JULY 2ND, 1840.

Poor Law Commission Office,
Somerset House,
June 29, 1840.

THE Poor Law Commissioners, on a review of their minutes, directed that the minutes and correspondence on the following subjects should be printed and circulated for the information of Guardians and officers of the several Unions, viz.—

By order of the Board,
EDWIN CHADWICK, *Secretary.*

I.—RATING.

RATING STOCK IN TRADE.

Copy of a Report from the Poor Law Commissioners to the Marquis of Normanby, on the expediency of an alteration of the Law in respect to the Rating of Stock in Trade, dated 14*th May*, 1840.

Poor Law Commission Office,
Somerset House,
14*th May*, 1840.

MY LORD,—In our report to your Lordship, dated the 30th April, we explained the present state of the law respecting the rating of stock in trade, and the steps which we have taken for instructing the parish officers as to the performance of their duties, in accordance with the recent decision of the Court of Queen's Bench in the case of Regina *v.* Lumsdaine.

Since the date of that report, the attention of Parliament has, as we perceive from the papers of the House of Commons, been directed to the subject; and we, therefore, propose to submit to your Lordship a fuller statement of the existing law, and the changes which appear to be desirable, than are contained in our report of the 30th ultimo.

Extent of Operation.

The observations which we are about to make are not to be confined to the poor-rates. The county-rates, the borough and police-rates, the highway-rates, and the whole system of local taxation, either form part of the taxation nominally imposed for the relief of the poor, or are immediately founded upon the assessment to the poor-rate. Any evil in the imposition of the poor-rate is, therefore, multiplied in all the local taxes; and any extension of the poor-rate to any kind of property not before burdened with it, is practically an extension to the same property of the burden of all the other local taxes.

Progress of the Tax on Stock in Trade.

The statute of Elizabeth, upon which the system of taxation to the relief of the poor is founded, renders three classes of persons liable to the rate:—

1. The parson or vicar, defined by the name of his office.
2. The occupiers of land, or of buildings, or of other species of real property. (The description of the property perfectly identifies this class of rate-payers.)
3. The other inhabitants.

The third class is not distinguished by any other words of description. It is on the use of the word "inhabitants" that the practice of rating stock in trade is founded. Like the rest of the rate-payers, the "inhabitants" are to be rated according to their ability.

For a century and a half after the passing of the statute, the liability of inhabitants to be rated for personal property was not agitated. The rate had been laid universally on the tithe-holders, and on the occupiers of the real property subject to the rate. But whether it was owing to the small relative value of stock in trade in the rural districts, or to other causes, the liability of inhabitants to be rated in respect of their stock in trade was not established for more than a century and a half after the passing of the statute of Elizabeth. Lord Mansfield, in the earlier cases before him, with the other judges, resolutely denied the general liability, and required a custom to be proved in each parish, in order to legalize the rate. Lord Mansfield strongly insisted on the impossibility, as well as the impolicy, of making the rate; and he described many of the anomalies, and anticipated most of the practical difficulties, which have since been experienced.

The general liability was, however, finally established by Lord Kenyon; and a practice of making rates on stock in trade was extensively adopted in the clothing districts of the west and south-west of England, after long contest and litigation, in which the interests of the declining manufacturers unsuccessfully opposed the interests of the occupiers of land and the owners of tithes. A tax so heavy as the poor-rates were in this district, which, after the commencement of the practice of rating stock in trade, rapidly became one of the most pauperized in England, the pauperism constantly increasing as the manufactures declined, must have operated very disadvantageously in diminishing the inducements to the application of capital, and may reasonably be supposed to have had a large share in turning the scale, notwithstanding the long possession by these districts of this staple industry, their superior skill, their proximity to the ports of London and Bristol, and their equal advantages in possession of coal, in favour of their rivals in the North of England, where industry was not subjected to the like burden.

The practice of rating inhabitants for their stock in trade was adopted but very partially as regards the whole of England and Wales, but, when once adopted, had usually been continued until the passing of the Parochial Assessments Act, in August, 1836. As that Act prescribes a criterion for rating real property, and is silent on the subject of personalty, it was supposed to discountenance the rating of stock in trade, and the practice of rating it was generally abandoned where it had before existed. The question having, however, been again agitated, the case of Regina *v.* Lumsdaine came before the Court of Queen's Bench for decision; and that court has again affirmed the general liability of inhabitants to be rated in respect of stock in trade.

Inconveniences and Anomalies.

Since this new promulgation of the law, attention has been excited to the subject in parts of England and Wales where the practice was before unknown. The inevitable difficulties of the subject will necessarily produce great irregularities in the application of the law, with the consequent contests and litigation between the manufacturing and landed interests; and even the most correct application of the law must produce great derangements in the profits of trade.

To prevent these evils, and the impediments which extensive litigation would create to the administration of the law generally, it appears to us that some legislative interference during the present Session would be of great benefit; and it is with a view to the passing of some measure on the subject, that we have determined to present to your Lordship the following short statement of some of the anomalies in the law as it now exists:—

Inequalities as to Persons.

By the statute of the 43rd Elizabeth, the relief of the poor was to be provided for by taxation on every "inhabitant," according to the ability of the parish. The Courts have decided that these words make an inhabitant rateable in respect of stock in trade. But, any rich possessor of stock in trade may escape the tax at his pleasure; it is only the poorer inhabitants who cannot escape the tax. If the owner's concerns are sufficiently extensive to allow of his warehousing his stock in trade in a parish in which he does not reside, or if he is sufficiently opulent to reside out of the parish where his stock is kept, he, not being a resident inhabitant there, is not rateable. Thus, three partners carried on business upon premises in which their foreman and his family resided, but they themselves resided in another parish: they were held not rateable.—R. *v.* N. Currey (4 B. and C. 953). The owners of ships, packet-boats, &c., in places where these are rated, contrive to escape the tax by taking up their residence out of the parish of the ship's home. A ship-owner whose ships were registered at Liverpool, and who had warehouses and a counting-house in the parish of Liverpool, but resided in a different parish, was held not rateable for his ships.—R. *v.* Liverpool (8 East. 455).

The tax is thus commonly escaped by the opulent owners of stock in trade, who do not reside in the parish in which their stock lies. The escape from the rate on a large stock would indeed often be more than sufficient to pay the expense of a country residence; while to the poorer owners of stock, who must reside in the place of their business, the tax is inevitable.

Even amongst persons of exactly the same condition, the operation of the tax is as strikingly unequal and anomalous. Thus, of several partners, one resided on the premises: he alone was rateable, as an inhabitant, for his share of the stock, to the extent of his interest in it.—R. *v.* Gosse (7 B. and C. 60).

The persons thus escaping the rate on their stock in trade in the parishes where it is kept, cannot be taxed for it in the parishes where they reside. — Earby's Case (2 Bulst. 354, 1 Bott, 124).

Inequalities as between different Trades.

Again: stock of one kind makes an inhabitant liable; stock of another kind does not. Thus, the stock in trade of common brewers and maltsters cannot be taxed, because, as is said by the courts, it cannot be sufficiently ascertained.—R. *v.* Ringwood (Cowp. 326).

Again: household furniture is not rateable, R. *v.* White, (4 T. R. 771,) although an obvious source of ability in the hands of a lodging-house keeper, a family hotel keeper, or an upholsterer letting furnished houses. Thus, the tax operates capriciously and as a discriminating tax against some kinds of stock in trade or industry, and in favour of others.

Indefiniteness of Saleable Value.

Another source of inequality in the imposition of the tax is contained in the rule laid down by the courts, that the profit is not to be presumed, but must be proved, and that it is not on the whole profit made, but on what is in excess after payment of all debts, R. *v.* White (4 T. R. 771). The rate on land, houses, &c., is laid on the reasonable net annual value; but this rate on stock in trade is only to be laid on what the overseers can prove to remain after payment of debts. Thus, he who can conceal his profits from the overseers, or he who by his imprudence is involved in debt, escapes a burden which will be thrown upon his neighbours, the nature of whose business, or whose openness of dealing, does not allow of concealment, or whose prudence keeps them out of debt.

Indefiniteness as to the Ability of the Rate-payer.

Another anomaly in the interpretation of the statute, is the distinction between the kinds of "ability" by which the inhabitants are rendered liable. Inhabitants are to be rated in respect of their ability; now, although nothing is said in the statute about stock in trade, the courts decided that profits derived from stock in trade constitute a rateable "ability;" but the courts also decided that other kinds of personal profits do not constitute a rateable ability. Thus, furniture, money, stock in the funds, money lent on real security, the profits of manufacturers, (as of silk throwsters,) where the materials wrought up may not be of the manufacturer's own stock, salaries, and professional earnings, (however large the ability constituted by them,) have been decided not to constitute a rateable ability of an inhabitant. We refer to these decisions, not as being in themselves objectionable, but as tending to show how capricious has been the operation of the tax which has no fixed relation either to persons or to income.

Thus, although inhabitants, without distinction, are, by the statute of Elizabeth, made rateable according to their ability, it will be seen that by the decisions of the courts, one class only of inhabitants is made rateable; that even within this class the liability is most unsettled, capricious, and unequal; that other classes, though of equal ability, are excepted; and that the test of the ability, in respect of which inhabitants are to be rated, that is to say, the amount of actual profit, after provision for payment of debts, is most difficult to ascertain.

Difficulties of Valuation.

To apply the law of rating to lands, houses, and other objects of occupation, is comparatively easy; and the rule for rating these objects according to a reasonable estimate of their net annual value, renders it unnecessary to institute inquiry into the personal concerns of the rate-payers, and makes an evasion of the tax by concealment of profits impossible.

But the rate on stock in trade, dependent on the amount of profit, as before described, cannot be made without minute investigations into the concerns of individuals;—investigations so difficult, and the results of which are so fallacious, that a right conclusion can scarcely be obtained; while to the rate-payers, every inequality, the result of a wrong estimate, is a subject of dissatisfaction, necessarily begetting disputes and litigation.

Consequent Inequalities.

From these difficulties, and from a desire to avoid appeals, another kind of injustice has ensued in places where stock in trade has been rated. Those who could most successfully conceal their profits, or could most easily reside elsewhere, or keep their stock away from the parish, have been able to make the best terms with the overseers, to which terms, rather than lose all, the overseers and other inhabitants are compelled to submit; and, as an inducement to avoid appeals by such as might be supposed to be capable of appealing successfully, it has been the practice of overseers to set the rate at sums, which, being much below the true amount of the liability, were likely to be undisputed by the rate-payers, and which the overseers were certain of being able to prove.

There is good reason to believe that there is no parish in the kingdom in which the overseers have ever been able fully to carry out the law. The instances which have come to our knowledge of attempts to carry it out, have been instances of compromise, and fully justify Lord Mansfield's enlightened views as to the impossibility of carrying the rating of stock in trade into effect.

His Lordship's views appear to be still entertained in the manufacturing districts and other parts of the country, since the recent communications on the rating of stock in trade which we have received express a stronger sense of the impracticability of the law than of its injustice or impolicy.

General Impolicy of the Tax.

It would appear to be unnecessary for us to make any remarks upon the general policy of a tax operating so unequally, affecting some trades and some classes of traders with inevitable burdens from which others are exempt, without any other reason for the difference than the merely accidental variety in the ease with which the tax can be imposed in one class of cases as compared with the other. But it is proper to call your Lordship's attention to the fact that the tax as yet has never been imposed on the parishes in the greater part of England and Wales, and is practically unknown in the districts which have become the great modern seats of manufactures. Thus its extension to these would operate with all the disturbing effects of a new tax, and with an effect which we are not prepared to estimate, but which may be considerable in changing the relations of our trade and manufactures, both as regards other parts of Her Majesty's dominions, as Scotland and Ireland, where no such tax can be laid, and as regards the competition of our countrymen with the trade and manufactures of other countries.

Effect of its Repeal.

On the other hand, as the tax has not yet been practically laid on these districts, the repeal of the law would not deprive the landed interest of any benefit now enjoyed by it in the taxation of the commercial and manufacturing classes,—the repeal of the liability would leave the whole class of rate-payers in those districts in their existing relative positions. In the districts in which the practice of rating stock in trade formerly prevailed, and has been recently resumed, the alteration by the repeal of the liability would be comparatively small, on account of the limited extent to which the liability has hitherto been, from the causes before adverted to, capable of being enforced.

It is likewise important to remark that rates are made by the parish overseers, who are unpaid officers, acting only for a single year; and, therefore, not likely to possess, or obtain the skill, or to bestow the labour which would be requisite for so difficult a task as that of making a fair and legal rate upon stock in trade.

It has been sometimes suggested as desirable, that the practice of rating inhabitants for stock in trade should be confined by legislative enactment to the places in which it has already been carried into effect. If this suggestion should be adopted, it would be right to couple it with another, namely, that the rate should be made only in the same proportions to the actual profits, as hitherto. For, as we have before stated, the practice has been such as to allow of a large escape of profits from the rate; and if ever a rate should be made in any place on the whole amount of profits legally liable to the rate, such a rate would, to the extent of this difference, be a new rate on the trade of the place. This provision, however, from the difficulty of discovering the proportion between the amount of profits which have been rated, and the amount of the true rateable profits, would be difficult of application.

Commissioners' Recommendation.

We think that it would be most beneficial to repeal altogether the effect of the word "inhabitant" in the statute of Elizabeth. Hitherto no inhabitants, simply as inhabitants, have been rated, other than the possessors of stock in trade; but, inasmuch as stock in trade was affected, with its liability, above a century and half after the passing of the statute of Elizabeth, and as the words of the statute would undoubtedly admit of a much wider signification than has yet been attributed to them, there is still danger that it may at some time or other have a wider practical effect given to it. It appears to us to be better to prevent such an extension, than to postpone the remedy until the evil has arisen; especially as this can now be done without any derangement beyond the repeal of the liability to be rated in respect of stock in trade.

It would, however, be sufficient for the immediate purpose, to repeal specifically the liability of inhabitants to be rated in respect of stock in trade.

Before we close the present Report, we think it right to add, that neither the repeal of the general liability of inhabitants to be rated according to their ability, nor the repeal of their specific liability to be rated in respect of their stock in trade, would at all affect the question now pending before the Court of Queen's Bench, (in the case Regina *v.* Capel,) concerning the extent of the respective liabilities to be rated of tithe owners and of occupiers of land.

We have the honour to be, &c.

J. G. S. LEFEVRE.
GEO. NICHOLLS.
G. C. LEWIS.

To the Marquis of Normanby,
&c. &c. &c.

2. DRAUGHT OF A BILL TO EXEMPT STOCK IN TRADE AND OTHER PERSONAL PROPERTY FROM LIABILITY TO BE RATED TO THE RELIEF OF THE POOR.

At a Board held on the 12th instant, the Commissioners having been informed that Her Majesty's Attorney-General desired to bring in a bill to exempt inhabitants from the liability to be rated in respect of profits derived from personal property, and having considered the terms of a draft of a bill for the purpose, Resolved, that the same should be transmitted to Her Majesty's Attorney-General, with a copy of the Commissioner's Report addressed to Lord Normanby on the "Expediency of an alteration of the law in respect to the rating of stock in trade."

The following is a copy of the Bill as laid before the House of Commons by the Attorney and Solicitor-General, and ordered to be printed.

"WHEREAS by an Act passed in the forty-third year of the reign of Queen Elizabeth, intituled, 'An Act for the Relief of the Poor,' it was amongst other things provided, that the overseers of every parish should raise, by taxation of every inhabitant, parson, vicar and other, and of every occupier of lands, houses, tithes impropriate, propriations of tithes, coal-mines, or saleable underwoods in the said parish, competent sums of money for and towards the relief of the poor, to be gathered out of the same parish, according to the ability of the same:

"And whereas by another Act, passed in the thirteenth and fourteenth years of the reign of King Charles the Second, intituled, 'An Act for the better Relief of the Poor of this Kingdom,' the provisions of the said Act of Elizabeth were extended to townships and villages:

"And whereas, by reason of the provisions of the said Acts, it has been held that inhabitants of parishes, townships, and villages, as such inhabitants, are liable, in respect of their ability, derived from the profits of stock in trade and of other personal property, to be taxed towards the relief of the poor, and it is expedient to repeal the liability of inhabitants, as such, to be so taxed:

"Be it therefore enacted, by the Queen's most excellent Majesty, by and with the advice and consent of the Lords spiritual and temporal, and Commons, in this present Parliament assembled, and by the authority of the same, that from and after the passing of this Act it shall not be lawful for the overseers of any parish, township or village, to tax any inhabitant thereof, as such inhabitant, in respect of his ability, derived from the profits of stock in trade or any other personal property, for or towards the relief of the poor."

3. RATING OF TITHE TO THE RELIEF OF THE POOR.

THE Commissioners having received and considered a report of the legal proceedings on this subject, directed the following circular should be issued for the information of overseers:—

The judgment of the Court of Queen's Bench has been delivered in the case of the Queen *v.* the Honourable and Reverend William Capel, clerk. The court has decided that the tithe owner is to be rated for his tithes upon the same estimate of their net annual value as is provided for all other rateable hereditaments by the 1st section of the Parochial Assessments Act (6 and 7 Wm. IV. c. 96), and that the tithe owner is not entitled, under the proviso in that section, to any deduction or allowance corresponding with the profits of occupiers of lands, houses, &c.

While the question as to the extent of the tithe owner's liability was in dispute, and with a view to prevent unnecessary litigation in the multitude of appeals which were then to be apprehended, the Poor Law Commissioners and Tithe Commissioners recommended, by a Minute of the 8th September, 1838, that a single case should be selected in some one parish for argument, and that in all other parishes provisional arrangements should be adopted between the overseers and the tithe owners, which would allow of an eventual settlement of the payments to be made by the tithe owners, in conformity with the principle of any decision which might be obtained upon the selected case.

The case of the Queen *v.* Capel was eventually selected to try the question in dispute; and, in accordance with the recommendation contained in the Minute of the Poor Law Commissioners and the Tithe Commissioners, the rates were in many parishes laid on the net annual value of tithes, and a portion only of such rates was collected, an arrear being allowed to remain proportionate to the amount of the deduction which the tithe owner claimed.

But rates on the whole net annual value being now, by the decision in the case of the Queen *v.* Capel, determined to be correct, it has become the duty of overseers to proceed to collect from the tithe owners any arrears which may have been allowed to accrue, and in future rates to assess the tithe owners on the whole net annual value, and to collect the whole rate so assessed.

Signed by order of the Board,
E. CHADWICK, *Secretary*.

II.—RELIEF.

1. PENSIONS PAYABLE TO BOARDS OF GUARDIANS UNDER 2 AND 3 VICT., c. 51.

Poor Law Commission Office,
Somerset House,
May 20, 1840.

SIR,—The Poor Law Commissioners desire to inform the Board of Guardians of the Union, that they have been in communication with the Lords Commissioners of Chelsea Hospital and the Paymaster-General, upon the subject of the pensions payable to the guardians of Unions, under the late Act 2 and 3 Vict., c. 51, in pursuance of the minutes of the board, or assignments by pensioners, or under magistrates' orders; and it has been agreed that the most convenient course to be adopted will be for the guardians to direct the relieving officers to apply to the Collectors of Excise for payment, and to receive the same. The Lords Commissioners and Paymaster-General require that the relieving officers should have a certificate of their being authorized by the Board of Guardians to give the receipt, and also of the existence of the pensioner.

It will probably be necessary for the Commissioners to issue an order imposing this additional duty upon the relieving officer; but the Commissioners will be better able to define the duty when they have ascertained from experience what is required to be done. The Commissioners, therefore, think it advisable for the present occasion, that you should appoint some one or more of the relieving officers of the Union to receive the pensions, and should deliver to him or them a document according to the accompanying form, authorizing the application for the payment of the pensions for the past quarter, and the same may be renewed every succeeding quarter. It will be perceived that the clerk will have to make out a list of the pensioners whose pensions are to be received before the warrant is delivered to the relieving officer, and the relieving officer should then be called upon to certify as to the existence of the pensioners.

The relieving officers so appointed should be directed to pay within a week the money to the treasurer of the Union to the account of the guardians, and to return to the guardians at their next meeting the document duly filled up and signed. The guardians will then ascertain what amount is to be retained by them, and what, if any, is to be paid to the pensioners.

In case there should be any balances payable to the pensioners, the Commissioners think it advisable that the pensioners should be required to attend at the next meeting of the board to receive the same; or where they cannot attend, the guardians will cause such balances to be forwarded to them as they may deem advisable.

As the amount received by the guardians is to reimburse the expenditure by them for relief, the respective parishes to which such relief has been charged should be credited with the sums so paid to the guardians in respect of the pensions.

Signed by order of the Board,
EDWIN CHADWICK, *Secretary.*

To the Clerk to the Board of Guardians.

______________ *UNION.*

This is to certify that Mr. Relieving Officer of this Union, has been appointed by the Board of Guardians to receive from the Collector of Excise the Pensions which have become payable to them at last under Assignments, Magistrates' Orders, and Minutes of Guardians, with reference to the Provisions of the Act 2 & 3 Vict. c. 51, and that his acquittance for the same is to be a sufficient warrant and discharge.

Given under our hands at at a meeting of a Board of Guardians on the day of 184

______________ *Chairman.*
______________ *Clerk.*

And I do hereby certify that the Pensions payable to

[*Here set out the names.*]

are to be received by the above mentioned.

______________ *Clerk.*

I, Relieving Officer of the Union, do certify that the several Pensioners above mentioned were all alive on the day of last.

Signed this day of 184 .

______________ *Relieving Officer.*

I, Collector of Excise, do hereby certify that I have this day paid to the above mentioned the following Sums on account of the Pensioners named below.

Names of Pensioners.	Amount. £.	s.	d.
Total . . .			

Signed this day of 184

Collector of Excise for the district.

To Relieving Officer.

You are required by the Board of Guardians to pay the above sum within the space of one week to the Treasurer of the Union on account of the said Guardians, and not to introduce the same in your Out-door Relief and Expenditure Book.

Chairman.

I, Treasurer of the Union, have this day received the above sum of from the Relieving Officer, on account of the Guardians of the said Union.

Treasurer.

2. MEDICAL RELIEF.—RIGHT OF GUARDIANS TO ORDER VACCINATION WITHOUT CONSENT OF PARENTS.

On the 19th ultimo, the Board took into consideration the following Report from their Assistant Commissioner Mr. Senior.

Loughborough,
May 18, 1840.

"GENTLEMEN,—In several workhouses in my district (Blaby, Hinckley, Basford, Nottingham, &c.) small-pox has broken out, which has obliged the Guardians to discontinue giving orders of admission to the house. To prevent a similar occurrence, I have recommended that the medical officer be instructed to vaccinate all children on their admission to the house.

"The Guardians of the Shardlow Union wish to adopt a similar course, but are doubtful whether the consent of the parent be not necessary, and have requested me to apply for your opinion.

"It appears to me that the Guardians can legally take such sanatory precautions as they may think necessary to prevent the spread of infectious diseases among the inmates of the house, and that vaccination should be included among those precautions.

"I have the honour to be, Gentlemen,
"Your obedient servant,
"EDWARD SENIOR, *Assistant Commissioner.*"

On the 20th ultimo the Commisioners directed the following reply to be sent.

"The Poor Law Commissioners have had under their consideration your report of the 18th inst., in which you submit the question whether a Board of Guardians can direct the medical officer to vaccinate all children on their admission into the workhouse, without the permission of their parents.

"The Poor Law Commissioners are of opinion that the Guardians have, without the permission of the parent, the right to vaccinate any child in their custody, during any danger of contagion from the small-pox.

"There can be no doubt that the Guardians are bound to prevent contagion, by keeping those who are labouring under contagious diseases from coming into contact with others who might contract the disease. Exposure in a public place, of children having the small-pox, is an indictable offence, and exposure to the inmates in a workhouse, the proper place for the reception of all destitute persons, would not seem to be essentially distinguishable from exposure in a public place.

"When the disease has once appeared in a workhouse, it is not safe to send out the inmates in which it may not have showed itself, but in whom it may be latent.

"On the other hand the Guardians are bound to protect all the inmates who may yet be protected from the danger, and the Commissioners see no limit to the medical, surgical, or other sanatory means which the Guardians may, and are bound to employ, provided the means are such as competent judges would hold to be proper.

"Thus, for more ordinary purposes of cleanliness, there is no question that the Guardians rightly exercise, without express permission from the parent, a constraint on the persons of the paupers, which if exercised by a stranger would amount to assaults,

"Again, as to medical treatment, this is often

very painful, is rarely pleasant, and can scarcely be afforded to the younger paupers without frequent instances of constraint. But there seems to be no reason to doubt that the Guardians would grossly neglect their duty to the patient, if they waited for a parent's permission to administer medicine; and every medicine operates so far like vaccination, as it expels one disorder by the introduction of another of a less violent or dangerous character.

"Then as to surgical treatment, there can be as little doubt that bleeding or other operations involving more personal violence, are as justifiable in the cases in which they can be beneficially applied, as less violent sanatory precautions.

"In-as-far then as the puncturing of the skin and the introduction of vaccine is a mere precaution against an apprehended disease, not a remedy for an existing disease, this would appear to constitute no essential distinction from the preceding cases, even if in other cases the medical and surgical care was never applied but when disorder had actually made its appearance. For, even in these cases, medical and surgical treatment is as much directed to the prevention or alleviation of the apprehended progress of a disorder, as to the cure or alleviation of the disease at its present stage.

"It seems to the Commissioners, therefore, that whenever medical men are agreed that any application is the specific or most proper prevention of any disorder immediately apprehended, the Guardians are fully justified in law in applying it; and more especially when the bad consequences of neglect would extend beyond the pauper to whom the application is proposed to be made; and that the fact that the consent of parents or of the pauper is wanting, that the appliance involves personal violence and the introduction of a specific disease, and that it is purely and exclusively precautionary, as in the case of vaccination when the small-pox is known to be prevalent, makes no difference in the duty and right of the Guardians in these respects."

---

3. EXPENSE OF CHRISTMAS AND FEAST DINNERS IN WORKHOUSES.

The Board took into consideration the following letter from the clerk to the Guardians of the St. Saviour's Union.

"27, *Bridge Street, Southwark,*
May 25, 1840.

"GENTLEMEN,—At the weekly meeting of the Board, on Thursday last, it was

"Resolved,

"That the usual dinner be provided at Whitsuntide, and that the master be instructed to discontinue all extra dinners, except at Christmas, Easter, and Whitsuntide.

"I have, &c.

"RICHARD CARPENTER SMITH.

"*To*
"*The Poor Law Commissioners.*"

In reply to which the Commissioners directed to be forwarded to the Guardians for their information, the following copy of a letter, which the Commissioners have thought it their duty to address to the auditors of the different Unions, relative to the payment of the expenses incurred in providing dinners at Christmas, and on other occasions, for the inmates of workhouses.

"*Poor Law Commission Office,*
Somerset House.

"SIR,—The Poor Law Commissioners forward for your information and guidance with reference to future cases of Christmas and other similar feasts in workhouses, the accompanying Copy of a Letter recently addressed by them on that subject to their Assistant Commissioners.

"With respect to any past instances in which expenses of this nature have already been incurred and shall not be objected to, the Commissioners have no wish to interfere.

"*To*
The Union Auditor."

"*Poor Law Commission Office,*
Somerset House.

"SIR,—The Poor Law Commissioners have perceived that on Christmas-day, and other recent festive occasions, the Guardians of various Unions have provided for the inmates of workhouses dinners which, both in quantity and quality of food, and its cost, have greatly exceeded the usual diet of the workhouse inmates, and even of many of the less prosperous portion of the rate-payers. The Commissioners admit that they are very unwilling to interfere with these proceedings, owing to their respect for the motives which have given rise to them.

"The Commissioners, however, cannot but perceive the injustice of applying the proceeds of a compulsory tax, raised only to relieve destitution, to provide for the inmates of a workhouse luxuries which are beyond the reach of those by whom the tax is paid. They have, therefore, determined to give positive instructions to the auditors to disallow in the accounts any expenditure which shall henceforth have been incurred in the extra allowances which shall be furnished on the occasions above alluded to.

"The Commissioners have only to add, that where the indulgences above mentioned are supplied to the inmates of the workhouse at the expense of private individuals, the question assumes altogether a different form, and, if strictly confined to extraordinary occasions, seems not to require the interference of the Commissioners.

"Signed, by order of the Board,
"EDWIN CHADWICK, *Secretary*."

---

4. APPRENTICESHIP OF PAUPER CHILDREN IN COLONIES.

The Board took into consideration the following letter from the clerk of the West London Union:—

"5, *St. Andrew's Court, Holborn, 20th April*, 1840.

"GENTLEMEN,—I am desired by the Board of Guardians of the West London Union to lay before you an application which has been made to them by a Mr. Sloper, to allow certain of their pauper children to enter the service of a Mr. Lawson, a resident in New South Wales.

"Mr. Sloper's application was made to the Board on the 26th of March last, and was prefaced by his stating, that he applied on behalf of his friend Mr. Lawson, who went out to Australia in the year 1800, with a capital of £350 only, which, by judicious management and persevering industry, has been converted by Mr. Lawson into about £400,000; that that person, who is now an opulent, influential, and a highly respected settler in the colony, is desirous of raising on his estates a small colony of farmers under his own immediate patronage and control, and for this purpose proposes to have out, should he meet with encouragement, parish boys in tens and twenties, who shall be articled to him for the term of five years, and at the expiration of such period to give each boy the sum of £30 to start him in life.

"Mr. Sloper, in answer to a question put by the Board, stated that not a single boy had as yet been sent out to Mr. Lawson, and undertook, should the Board assent to his application, to see the boys on a proper vessel, and to execute any guarantee or agreement that might be required for their proper care and maintenance.

"Mr. Sloper also stated that the passage out of each boy would be paid by Mr. Lawson, and that the only expense which the Board would be put to would be in furnishing the boys with proper bedding and clothing.

"Mr. Sloper also gave references as to his own and Mr. Lawson's respectability.

"The Board, after a careful attention to Mr. Sloper's statement, and deliberately considering all the circumstances connected with it, resolved that inquiry should be made by the school committee, whether there were any boys in the Union workhouse who were willing to go out to Australia; and that the relieving officers should inquire of the persons referred to as to the respectability of the parties.

"The result of these inquiries was, that there were ten boys who expressed themselves ready and willing to proceed to Australia, and that both Mr. Sloper and Mr. Lawson were gentlemen of undoubted respectability.

"Mr. Sloper attended the Board on the 9th instant, at their request, and inspected the boys, and also explained to them the nature of the duties they would be required to perform. The Board having, on this occasion, felt some difficulty as to the want of a permanent medium or officer, through whom the boys could communicate with the Board when at New South Wales, appealed to Dr. Kay, who happened to be at the Board, for his opinion, upon the propriety of their acceding to Mr. Sloper's application. Dr. Kay, after elaborately stating his views with regard to the migration of pauper children, intimated his opinion that the Commissioners would not confirm the agreement with Mr. Sloper, should any such be entered into; and that there were, he thought, certain legal difficulties which would prevent the Board from proceeding further in the matter.

"Under these circumstances the Board desired that all the particulars might be laid before the Commissioners, and their opinion requested as to the propriety of their agreeing with Mr. Sloper, and as to the power they possess for carrying such agreement into effect.

"I am also desired by the Board to forward you Mr. Sloper's written statement upon the subject of his application.

"I have, &c.,
"JOHN PONTIFEX,
"Clerk to the Guardians.

"*To the Poor Law Commissioners.*"

"*St Anne's Hill, Wandsworth Common, 14th April*, 1840.

"GENTLEMEN,—I beg to avail myself of your suggestion, that I commit to writing a statement explanatory of the application I have recently made to your Board, to supply *in the first instance*, ten boys of about the age of fourteen years, to be sent out to my friend, Mr. Lawson, in New South Wales, to be employed by him on his estates as agricultural servants, and in the care of his flocks of sheep, &c., as his convenience may suggest.

"Allow me, for your information, to mention that Mr. Lawson, in the year 1800, purchased an ensigncy in a foot regiment, (the seventy-third, I think) then in New South Wales, and quitted this country for the colony about that period. He afterwards obtained a lieutenancy in the veteran corps subsequently formed and stationed there, and since disbanded. He, from that period, has remained on the list as the retired lieutenant of that corps. He was one of the three gentlemen who volunteered to explore that part of the colony now known as Bathurst settlement. Their joint labours were rewarded by the discovery of that fertile and important part of the colony; after having, with unparalleled exertion, cut their way through the native bush for an uninterrupted period of about six weeks, when they effected a communication with the newly discovered land and Sydney, a distance exceeding 100 miles. He has directed his attention to agricultural pursuits, farms at Prospect, also at Bathurst, and beyond it, on a large scale, and, by his industry and perseverance, has become one of the most opulent, influential, and respectable settlers in the colony.

Desirous, also, to promote the public welfare of New South Wales, he has within the last few years been chiefly instrumental in the erection of a parish church, and the building a parsonage and parochial school houses, besides actively assisting in any patriotic undertaking for the benefit of the colony.

"He deeply laments the sad deficiency of honest and industrious labourers, to remedy which, he has requested me to send him out a supply of parish boys,—say ten in the first instance,—all of whom he will place on his farms and pastures, and with the care of his flocks of sheep, as he shall deem expedient. Of these he will assume the entire charge. They will be fed, and clothed, and taken care of, and he will prove himself to them a liberal and kind master. Mr. Lawson proposes that each boy shall be approved by the Board of Guardians, shall be in good health, of good character for honest and industrious principles, must be able to read and write, and possess some knowledge in ciphering. They will be required to be apprenticed to him for a period of seven years, by indentures containing covenants for kind treatment and a proper supply of food and clothing. At the expiration of their apprenticeship he will give to each boy the sum of 30*l*. as a reward for good and faithful service, and assist in their advancement in the world.

"These boys, now become men, will be the object of Mr. Lawson's continued care and patronage. He gives an instance in the case of a shepherd (Cheeseman by name) whom I sent out in the year 1826 in the charge of twenty valuable merino sheep. This man engaged to serve him for five years after his arrival in the colony. His conduct during the first four years was so satisfactory to Mr. Lawson, that he cancelled the agreement, and gave him his freedom. Cheeseman commenced business as a farmer, principally with the savings he made while in Mr. Lawson's service; and at the expiration of seven years he possessed an income of 500*l*. per per annum.

"These lads, by previous good conduct, will experience similar encouragement; and thus a new intercolony may be formed of industrious farmers, with honest labourers,—be multiplied and enlarged, as those in progressive service shall have opportunity also of starting in the world.

"It is expected these ten boys shall be put on board equipped with clothing proper for the passage, at the expense of the Union, which will not exceed seven guineas for each; all other charges for passage money and provision to be paid by Mr. Lawson. The captain of the vessel will be required to sign an agreement to provide proper accommodation and food for each lad, on a scale liberal and satisfactory; and medical care provided in case of sickness.

"I have the satisfaction of stating that I have secured the immediate superintendence of a gentleman who is in a short time going out to settle in Sydney, and who has kindly consented to take charge of the boys on the passage. He will attend to their daily instruction, their personal cleanliness, the repair of their clothing, the regularity of their meals, the airing of their bedding, the observance of their religious duties on Sunday, and never omit the reading of the Church service, once at the least, on that day, to attend and keep the oldest boy (who will act as monitor) to his daily school duty with the boys, washing their clothes and linen, and in the day-time only they can assist in the light work of the ship, but not to watch or work on deck at night, or in bad weather. On their arrival in the colony, the captain will report the same to Mr. Lawson, and they will be accompanied to his residence, about the distance of thirty miles from Sydney, by the gentleman who attended them on their passage. I am quite sensible of the propriety and utility of establishing a local agency, or committee of gentlemen to take the charge of the boys on their reaching the colony. I have written to Mr. Lawson, very strongly recommending that some five or seven gentlemen should be selected, who are willing to assume this duty, and of reporting periodically of their welfare for the information of the guardians and friends at home: that such committee should be composed of persons of known respectability in the colony, to whom all matters requiring investigation respecting either master or apprentice might with entire safety be referred; and that no boys be sent out but those for whom approved application shall have been made.

"I earnestly hope this application may be favourably received. Allow me to remark that, if properly encouraged, it may be regarded as the commencement of a system of transmigration capable of producing the happiest and most extensive results both in a private and national view. It is beyond question that honest labourers are required in the colony in terms of the loudest entreaty. Should this plan be steadily pursued, that great object can be accomplished; and by its beneficial progress, in the course of some 20 or 30 years, may establish the complete ascendancy of honesty and industry over immorality and crime. This happy result must diffuse its valuable influence over other portions of the country, and while the inter-colony of Bathurst is found to furnish the laudable example of good order and improvement to the rest of the settlement, and the complete success of the plan established, you will feel the high gratification that those lads whom you kindly fostered and protected through the helpless period of their early years, to whom you properly and humanely afforded the valuable opportunity of obtaining success and prosperity in after life, have by honesty and good conduct become useful and respectable members of society.

"I have the honour to be, &c.,

"JOHN SLOPER.

"*To the Board of Guardians of the*
"*West London Union.*"

To which the Commissioners directed the following reply to be sent:—

Poor Law Commission Office,
Somerset House,
April 28, 1840.

SIR,—The Poor Law Commissioners have had under their consideration the application of the Board of Guardians of the West London Union, for their advice, as to the propriety of agreeing to a proposal made by Mr. Sloper on behalf of Mr. Lawson, an opulent colonist at Bathurst, in New Holland, to take ten boys as apprentices on his farm, to instruct them in agricultural employment, and at the termination of their apprenticeship to give them a liberal outfit.

The Commissioners have in similar applications for their sanction to the migration of children to employments in different parts of England, considered it their duty to require that the children should be placed under the charge of a matron in whose respectability they could have confident reliance that the children would be provided with a comfortable home; and they have never permitted such migration to occur, even in England, excepting to districts in which the children could be visited from time to time by an agent appointed and paid by the Commission for that and other similar purposes.

The cases in which the Commissioners have acceded to applications for the migration of pauper children in England, have been exceedingly few; and their experience does not induce them to think that the interests of the children would be sufficiently protected even in this country, were they removed to a great distance from their parishes without the appointment of some agency directed by the Commission, or the Boards of Guardians, for the visitation of the children so put out to service.

The Commissioners conceive that the difficulty attending the success of the apprenticeship of pauper children in places remote from their parishes, is so greatly increased, when the place of their apprenticeship is removed to the British colonies, that in the absence of direct legal authority for the practice of a colonial agency for the right regulation of every thing relating to the interests of the children, and of sufficient means of enforcing the terms of the indenture of apprenticeship in the colony, the Commissioners consider it their duty to advise the Guardians that the proposed arrangement should not be carried into effect.

Signed, &c.

To John Pontifex, Esq, Clerk to the Guardians of the West London Union.

---

5. ON THE PUBLICATION OF A STATEMENT RESPECTING ALLEGED MISMANAGEMENT IN THE PEWSEY UNION WORKHOUSE.

At a Board held on the 1st of April, the attention of the Commissioners was called to the following paragraph in the "Times" newspaper.

"New Poor Law Cleanliness and Comfort. (From a Correspondent.) In the Union workhouse at Pewsey, Wilts, it has been accidentally discovered that few, if any, of the inmates, men or women, boys or girls, know the comfort of a clean pair of stockings or socks, for three, and in some cases four, months together. Flannels worn next the skin have retained, unchanged, one and the same position for even a much longer period! For the truth of these remarks we pledge ourselves, and are prepared to make good our words whenever called upon to do so."

A communication was also read from the clerk of the Union, who stated that he had applied twice to the Editor of the "Times" for the name of the author, but could obtain no answer or notice of his application.

The Commissioners directed the letter of the clerk and the newspaper to be forwarded to the Assistant Commissioner, with a request that he would make an investigation as to the truth of the allegations contained in the paragraph in question.

Mr. Adey, the Assistant Commissioner of the district, being unable to attend, Colonel A'Court, was directed to undertake the investigation, to whom all subsequent communications on the subject were referred.

The chaplain of the Union avowed himself to be the author, and Colonel A'Court having examined the persons named by the chaplain as having been his informants, reported the result to the Commissioners as follows:—

"In pursuance of your instructions, I yesterday attended a special meeting of the Pewsey Guardians for the purpose of ascertaining how far the statement in the 'Times' newspaper of the 27th March, of which the Rev. William Bleeck, chaplain to the Union, avows himself to be the author, is founded on fact; and secondly, to inquire into the conduct of the chaplain, in furnishing to the public press anonymous statements reflecting on the management of an establishment to which he belongs, without any previous communication with the Guardians, and without calling their attention to the abuses which he alleges to have existed. I first proceeded to take down the chaplain's statement, intimating to him that I should then expect him to produce the witnesses on whose evidence (as stated in his letter to you of the 3d April) the offensive paragraph in the 'Times' was founded.

"He informed me that he had other witnesses whom he wished to produce; and I at once expressed my readiness to receive any information he might desire to put before me; but that my first object must be to examine those witnesses mentioned in his letter of the 3d April, as on their evidence his assertions were confessedly made.

"Some little objection was made to this mode of proceeding; and some few of the witnesses had been examined, when Mr. Bleeck begged me to understand that his anonymous newspaper paragraph was not, as he had stated in his letter to you of the 3d April, the result of his examination of the witnesses mentioned, for some of them he had seen for the first time since the paragraph was published; but that he had acted principally on hearsay evidence only! satisfied that he could at any time establish the truth of his assertions.

"No less than fourteen witnesses were called before me,—two of whom did not attend; three were of such tender age as to render it very doubtful how far their evidence ought to be received, and two, * * * * * * were stated to be of such infamous characters that they could not be believed on their oaths.

"On completing Lucy Head's examination, Mr Bleeck stated that he did not wish to carry the case further;—'that he was much vexed at having been deceived by the parties who had furnished him with information respecting the alleged abuses in the Pewsey workhouse,—that their statements are in no way borne out by the evidence this day taken before the Assistant Poor Law Commissioner. 'That after what had taken place, he is of opinion that it will not be for the benefit of the Union, that he should retain his situation as chaplain to the workhouse, which he therefore begs to resign.'

"These words being noted by me, Mr. Bleeck assented to causing them to be inserted in the 'Times' newspaper, in order that the vindication of the Guardians might be as public as his assertions reflecting on them."

The Commissioners directed a letter to be written to the Board of Guardians, and a copy thereof to be transmitted to the chaplain, communicating the result of the investigation, and stating that—

"The Poor Law Commissioners concur in the opinion expressed by the chaplain, that it will not be for the benefit of the Union that he should retain his situation, and they accept the resignation which he has thus offered.

"They do not so, however, without some hesitation. They are of opinion that it is the bounden duty on the part of all the paid officers of any Union, if they suspect or become aware of the existence of any abuses in the workhouse or otherwise, in reference to the administration of relief to the poor of the Union, to call the attention of the Guardians thereto in the first place, and in case of any want of attention on their part, then to bring the matter under the notice of the Poor Law Commissioners; the Guardians and the Poor Law Commissioners, being the authorities to whom the law has confided the management and superintendence of the workhouse, and of the administration of relief.

"Instead of adopting this course, the chaplain, without adequate personal inquiry or examination on his part, and for the most part on hearsay evidence, denounced the defects which he supposed to exist in the Pewsey Union, in the manner most calculated to injure the character, and lessen the influence of the Guardians, and to promote as widely as possible dissatisfaction with the existing laws for the relief of the poor.

"The Commissioners entertain some doubt whether by accepting the Rev. Mr. Bleeck's resignation, instead of authoritatively ordering his dismissal, they have sufficiently marked their sense of the great impropriety of the course which that officer deemed it right to pursue. They trust, however, that the publication of Mr. Bleeck's resignation in the same channel through which his accusation was conveyed, will to some extent remedy the evil which he has caused, and will be a warning to other officers of Unions not to adopt a similar mode of proceeding."

6. EXTRACT FROM A REPORT ON THE COMPARATIVE STATE OF PAUPERISM OF THE PARISHES OF BIRMINGHAM AND ASTON.

GENTLEMEN.—In your Fourth Annual Report you drew the attention of the Secretary of State to the working of the Poor Law Amendment Act during a period of great distress in manufacturing districts, and in confirmation of your conclusions, amongst other instances, you quoted a Report from Mr. Earle, dated in June 1838, and in the Appendix you have added a comparative statement, framed by that gentleman, of the "Expenditure for the Relief of the Poor in the parish of Birmingham, and in the parish of Aston, during the years ending 25th March, 1837, and 25th March, 1838."

For the better understanding of the comparison intended to be exhibited by the report and statement I have before referred to, you premised,

"1st. That the *town* of Birmingham extends into Aston parish, the latter forming a suburb of at least one-fourth of the circumference of the town. According to the census of 1831, the parish of Birmingham contained a population of 111,000, Aston about 32,000. The population, therefore, then stood, and probably still is, in the proportion of 3½ to 1. Which of the two contains the greatest proportion of poor could not easily be determined; but there is no reason to suppose that fewer poor, either casual or settled, are to be found in the suburbs than in the centre of such a town as Birmingham, in proportion of the areas of each.

"2nd. That the labouring poor of both are engaged in like employments, equally affected by any interruption, or by the vicissitudes in trade, and are not to be distinguished from each other in any point which can affect the comparison.

"3rd. That the contrast can be drawn for a period during which has occurred a depression in trade almost unexampled in extent and duration, and sufficient to try the merits of the new system, under those very circumstances which, it has been predicted, would prove its insufficiency."

It may, perhaps, be well at the outset, to anticipate an objection that may be raised to the comparison, from the fact, that the parish of Aston, in addition to its manufacturing population, contains a considerable number of persons employed in agriculture, and that from that circumstance a diminution of pauperism may be expected. Experience, however, has convinced me that there is no foundation for this assumption, as I find that the expenditure calculated upon the population is very considerably greater in agricultural, than in manufacturing Unions, and on a comparison of the parish of Aston with the other parishes in the same Union, all of which are agricultural, I find that while the average cost per head on the population of those parishes, for the year ending Lady-Day, 1840, amounts to 4*s.* 5¼*d.*, in the parish of Aston it amounts only to 2*s.* 8½*d.*

At this time I feel it my duty to call your attention to the results of the last year's experience, corroborative of the former conclusions.

	In-door.	Out-door.	Total.	Proportion to Population.
The Average Number of Paupers who received Relief weekly, was in Aston	90	959	1,049	1 in 30·617 or rather more than 3 per Cent.
In Birmingham . . .	716	6,760	7,476	1 in 14·836 or nearly 7 per cent.

The Money expended was
In Aston . . £4,366, being 2*s.* 8½*d.* per head.
In Birmingham £30,358, being 5*s.* 5½*d.* per head.

The statement annexed to this Report, will show not only the expenditure for the parishes of Birmingham and Aston, and the number of paupers relieved, but a comparison of the state of pauperism in the two parishes, and I know of no other cause than a more effective system of management to which can be attributed the difference that must present itself to your notice; of this, however, I feel assured, that this contrast is not the effect of an oppressive system, but I am induced to believe, from an examination of the last Table (and to which I beg most particularly to call to your notice), that the strict investigation to which the different appeals for relief are now subjected, has prevented many fraudulent applications from being made, and, what is more gratifying, I am led to hope that those habits of provident care and forethought which the Poor Law Amendment Act was intended to engender, have been realized in some degree.

If I might refer to the experience of other districts than those in which I have been engaged, I would refer to the experience of the Nottingham Union and of Stoke upon Trent, as evidence of the peculiar protection afforded by the new law against the effects of extraordinary manufacturing pressure.

I may, however, support the case to which I recall your consideration, by reference to the parallel experience of Manchester, at present under the superintendence of my colleague, Mr. Mott. To those speculative persons, who knowing little or nothing of the real condition of the manufacturing districts or places to which the law has yet to be generally applied, who judging of the state of public feeling by the clamours of itinerant and trading agitators, and what they see in newspapers, advise that the introduction of the law into any part of those districts would be unsafe, we may offer the same answer which I am informed was given to an agitator in one of the manufacturing districts, who stated he was sure the inhabitants would rise to prevent its introduction—that the law has for a long time been introduced, and is working safely and satisfactorily. The Chorlton Union, is immediately adjacent to Manchester, and contains a part of the same population. The Salford Union comprehends a district on the side opposite to the Chorlton Union, and contains a more unmixed town population, and forms as integral a portion of Manchester itself as Lambeth or Stepney is of the metropolis. In both these Unions the experience is, in comparison with Manchester, highly favourable to the new law. In the Chorlton Union, which has been in operation longer than the Salford Union, notwithstanding the pressure of manufacturing distress, the expenditure on the claims to relief amply given was 2*s*. per head on the population, whilst in Manchester it was 3*s*. 11*d*. The Guardians of the Chorlton Union state in their printed report for 1839.

"The Guardians have great pleasure in referring to their financial statement for the present year, which will be found in the Appendix. It will appear from a careful examination, that notwithstanding the depressing circumstances before adverted to, and which, it must be borne in mind, have had their operation chiefly in the manufacturing districts of the Union, that, compared with the average of three years expenditure under the old system of poor laws, and those years periods of great prosperity, there results a considerable pecuniary advantage to the ratepayers under the present mode of affording parochial relief, which the Guardians fearlessly assert, is more discriminating as to its objects, and more liberal to the really deserving and necessitous poor, than any former one.

"No part of the Poor Law Amendment Act has excited more clamour than the vesting powers so great in the Poor Law Commissioners, yet in practice this is found to be exceedingly beneficial. The Commissioners, by their position, are entirely exempted from the operation of all local prejudices and partialities, and the controlling superintendence which they exercise, being guided by abundant practical knowledge, is admirably adapted to restrain Boards of Guardians from yielding to such influences." * * * * *

"The Guardians of the Chorlton Union have now had the experience of another year, in the actual working of the new law, and they are unanimously of opinion, that the result of their observations has been to strengthen their conviction of the excellence of the main principles on which it is founded."

The experience of parts of these large towns and of others to which I might refer, may be presented as the anticipation of the experience of the whole, and will accumulate in proof of the necessity of bringing them under one common system, and so far carrying out the original intentions of the Legislature. It was established by the Poor Law Amendment Act, that it should not be left to the discretion of any set of managers of any place by erroneous modes of administration to foster pauperism within that place; nor even to the inhabitants of that place, however unanimous, to prefer the same errors, to engender pauperism to the annoyance or disadvantage of the rest of the community. The inhabitants of great commercial towns are, however, too much engaged in their own business to attend closely to the administration of relief; and the respectable tradesmen who are engaged as officers, can scarcely be expected, voluntarily, to devote themselves to the study of new principles now spread over eight volumes, or attend to their operation, though so immediately within their view.

As to the operation of the law in such a town as Birmingham, in so far as it affects other places, it appears to me that there is one point of view in which the importance of setting aside the Local Acts, and introducing the new law has not yet been sufficiently brought before the attention of the Legislature, namely, as to the suppression of mendicity.

Mendicity can only be generally suppressed when it is suppressed in the larger towns. Mendicity can only be effectually abated by any exertions of the police, when alms-giving is prevented; and no other means of attaining that object has yet been found so efficient as that adopted under your orders, by appropriate workhouse regulations and arrangements for labour in return for food, vagrant's wards, and the distribution under proper care of mendicity tickets, which shall ensure to those who would otherwise give alms that the case will be properly treated. Birmingham is now a great centre or place of refuge for mendicants and vagrants who infest the surrounding country; and by a reference to the annexed table,* detailing the expenditure of Birmingham, you will observe the numbers of this class relieved during the year ended Lady-day, 1839, were 3,080; and in the year ended Lady-day, 1840, the numbers were increased to 4,605. Indeed, so great has been the evil arising from the increase in this class of applicants, that the parochial authorities have, within the last six months, called in a policeman to inspect the several persons relieved previously to their being allowed to depart. Whilst the maintenance of a defective system in this town entails the train of evils incident to mendicity, and amongst the rest juvenile delinquency in distant places, it has, amongst other things, been the means of introducing contagious disease amongst the inhabitants of the town itself. Mr. Hodgson, who is one of the most able and eminent members of the medical profession in the country, in some recent evidence which he has given before a committee of the House of Commons, has strongly represented the evils of the beggars' lodging-houses. In the course of his examination the following passages occur:

"Are there any other suggestions you would make referable to measures to promote the general health of the inhabitants?—I think that the great source of disease in Birmingham is the existence of lodging-houses; and not only of disease but of immorality and crime, and very great misery; that what are called beggar lodging-houses are the great sources of disease and crime, and demoralization in every way.

"Does fever frequently prevail there?—Fever is rare comparatively in Birmingham; Birmingham is a very healthy town; there is never any severe contagious fever in the town—a contagious fever rarely comes; but when there is any contagious disorder, it almost always begins in those beggar lodging-houses which abound in the town, which are the sources of all the disease and all the vice in the place. * * * * *

"Many of those persons are migratory in their habits, and therefore any contagion they receive is likely to spread to other parts of the country?—Certainly; it is important not only on account of the inmates themselves but the persons who live in the neighbourhood, and it is important in a moral point of view that those places should be under some inspection; they certainly are great nests and sources of crime."

These conclusions will, no doubt, be further corroborated in a report which Mr. Hodgson and several other able practitioners are preparing for you on the sanatory condition of the labouring population of that town. The reports from other districts will have shown you how necessary is the appropriate provision for the relief of destitution to the prevention of alms-giving, together with the provision included in the bill for the payment of the costs of prosecuting vagrants, to render effectual the exertions of a police in the extinction of mendicity and the evils adverted to.

* This Table is too voluminous for insertion.

LONDON:
Printed by order of the Poor Law Commissioners, by W. CLOWES and SONS, Stamford Street, and Published by CHARLES KNIGHT and Co., 22, Ludgate-street, Publishers to the Poor Law Commissioners.
WEIGHT UNDER HALF AN OUNCE.

AN

OFFICIAL CIRCULAR

OF PUBLIC DOCUMENTS AND INFORMATION:

DIRECTED BY THE POOR LAW COMMISSIONERS TO BE PRINTED, CHIEFLY FOR THE USE OF THE MEMBERS AND PERMANENT OFFICERS OF BOARDS OF GUARDIANS, UNDER THE POOR LAW AMENDMENT ACT.

No. 7. CIRCULAR ISSUED SEPTEMBER 1ST, 1840.

Poor Law Commission Office,
Somerset House,
August 29, 1840.

THE Poor Law Commissioners, on a review of their minutes, directed that the minutes and correspondence on the following subjects should be printed and circulated for the information of Guardians and officers of the several Unions, viz.—

I.—THE EXTENSION OF VACCINATION ACT.

The Poor Law Commissioners having conferred with the Royal Vaccine Board, and taken into consideration the testimony of the several medical practitioners whom they had consulted as to the best means of accomplishing the intentions of the Legislature in the extension of vaccination, directed the following circular letter to be sent to the Boards of Guardians, together with the Minute of Instructions and Form of Contracts.

"*Poor Law Commission Office,*
"*Somerset House,*
"*August* 21*st*, 1840.

"SIR,—The Poor Law Commissioners request that you will, at the first Board day, place the enclosed Circular Letter in the hands of the Chairman, that he may call the immediate and special attention of the Guardians to the provisions of the new Act for the extension of Vaccination.

"You will also examine the terms of the contract, and acquaint the medical practitioners therewith, and be prepared with any information in respect to the convenient or available Vaccination Stations, or otherwise, which may facilitate the arrangements which the Guardians may have to make thereon.

"You will, when the Guardians have determined on the contracts, fill them up and forward them to the Poor Law Commissioners for their approbation.

"When the contracts are completed, you will fill up the form of notification, and cause copies to be printed, of a small, convenient size, to be given to each of the registrars, that he may give a copy to each parent or other person as a notification on the occasion of the registration of a birth. You will also cause copies to be given by the relieving officers to each clergyman with the like request. You will take any other means that the local circumstances may render desirable, as being the most effectual for the complete promulgation of the knowledge of the law; such as causing the notification (A.) to be printed in a large type, and posted as a bill in places used for public notifications in each parish. You will also ask the opinion of the Guardians in respect to the expediency of causing the notification to be advertised in any paper of such circulation within the district as may warrant the expense.

"By Order of the Board,
"*To* "EDWIN CHADWICK, *Secretary.*
"*The Clerk to the Board of Guardians.*"

Poor Law Commission Office,
Somerset House.
August 20, 1840.

GENTLEMEN,—In the execution of the duty imposed upon them by the Act 3 and 4 Vict. cap. 29, for the Extension of the Practice of Vaccination, the Poor Law Commissioners consider it desirable to call the attention of the Guardians to the several provisions of the Act with a view to the understanding of their object, and the steps to be taken for its accomplishment.

1. The benevolent object of the statute is, by the general use of tried and efficacious means, to prevent, as far as possible, the mortality and sufferings occasioned by small-pox. From the valuable information recently obtained by the registration of the causes of death, it appears that in 1837 there were in England only four diseases by which more people were killed than by small-pox. The number of deaths registered, as caused by small-pox, during the two years and a half ended December 31, 1839, was 30,000, which gives about 12,000 deaths annually in England and Wales. It appears that the extremes of mortality at the Small-pox Hospital, in London, amongst those attacked by the disease have been 15 per cent. and 42 per cent. In some districts the mortality from small pox is stated to be one in six of those attacked. But if, according to other statements, the average mortality be taken at one in four, or 25 per cent. of those attacked, the number of persons attacked in England and Wales must amount, on an average, to nearly 50,000 persons, or about 12,000 persons killed and 36,000 persons who recover subjected to the sufferings of disease, including in the case of the labouring classes loss of labour and long-continued debility, and in respect to all classes often permanent disfigurement and occasionally loss of sight.

2. For the prevention of these evils the means prescribed by the new statute are,—first, the entire prohibition of inoculation with the small-pox; secondly, the general extension of vaccination. These means have heretofore been only partially applied. In the course to be adopted for their general application, the Commissioners have been mainly guided by the advice and practice of the Royal Vaccine Board in London, which is maintained by a public grant, and is constituted of the President of the Royal College of Physicians, Sir Henry Halford, and Dr. John Bright, senior Censor, J. P. Vincent, Esq., President of the Royal College of Surgeons, and Dr. Hue, Registrar, aided by the recorded experience of their predecessors in office. The Commissioners have also consulted the medical authorities in Dublin and Edinburgh, and several members of the profession who were recommended to them as having had peculiar opportunities of experience, or as having given great attention to the subject.

3. It appears that the practice of inoculating with the small-pox has been long abandoned by the whole of the respectable part of the medical profession, on the grounds, first, as respects the individual inoculated, that it is much more dangerous than the cow-pox; secondly, as respects others, that it makes the person inoculated a source of contagion, thus multiplying the chances of its spreading, and, without absolutely protecting the life of the one person inoculated, exposes to imminent risk the lives of others, who are the more entitled to protection as they have the less warning to protect themselves. The practice of inoculation with small-pox is mostly pursued by ignorant and unqualified persons, old women, and itinerant quacks. Excessive mortality from small-pox is frequently traceable to the proceedings of such persons. Even were it allowed to any person of the age of discretion voluntarily to incur the sufferings and dangers of the disease himself, it ought not to be allowed to any one to act against the experience of the medical profession and of the best informed persons in the country, and to do that which may spread disease, death, or the causes of disfigurement, and loss of sight, amongst the community. Hitherto it was in law a misdemeanour to endanger the public health by exposing in the public streets any person infected with the small-pox or any other infectious disease. The Legislature has, for the protection of the public, by the new statute entirely prohibited inoculation by the small-pox, and has made it an offence subjecting any one to imprisonment for one month who shall produce or attempt to produce small-pox in any person by inoculation with small pox matter, or wilfully, by any means whatsoever. In adopting this course, the Legislature has followed the example of several of the continental states. The Commissioners are informed that the prohibition of inoculation, conjoined with the general extension of vaccination, has, in several countries, effected nearly the entire cessation in them of

the contagion and mortality produced by this severe malady. Sir James Clark, Her Majesty's Physician, has informed the Commissioners of the instance of which he was a witness, when in Italy, of the state of Lucca, where vaccination having been generally adopted, small-pox was entirely banished, whilst the people in the surrounding territory still suffered from the disease.

4. Under these circumstances, the Commissioners would call the especial attention of the *ex-officio* Guardians to the 8th clause, which subjects to penalties every person who shall hereafter inoculate with the small-pox. In the instructions to medical officers the Commissioners will request, as an additional means of carrying out the provisions of the Act, that the officers will, in each case of small-pox which comes before them, inquire whether the party had been inoculated, and by whom, or whether the infection was taken from a person inoculated, and, on ascertaining by whom the offence had been committed, that they will inform the magistrates.

5. With the view of preventing the commission of the offence, the Commissioners have prepared the annexed form of notice (A.), which they request may be posted by the relieving officers, or otherwise promulgated in the several parishes of the Union. They suggest also that copies of that notice should be transmitted to each of the clergymen in the Union for his information. The Commissioners request that the officers of the Union who are registrars, on the occasion of the registration of a birth, will give or cause this notice to be given to the parents of the child registered, to inform them of the advantages and the time and mode of getting the child vaccinated.

6. It appears to the Commissioners to be important that the Guardians should be informed that certain erroneous impressions which have existed, both with respect to the nature of cow-pox and its efficacy as a protection against small-pox, have been recently removed. On this subject Dr. Baron, of Cheltenham, in a communication to the Commissioners, remarks,—"It has been proved both by historical evidence and by direct experiment, that the disease derived from the cow is of a true variolous character, human small-pox having been recently communicated by Mr. Ceely, of Aylesbury, to the cow, by inoculation, and the result having been the production of cow-pox. This direct confirmation of a great doctrine, if duly explained to the people, may tend very much to allay their prejudices, by proving to them that when they derive the disease from the cow, it is small-pox in its mildest form, instead of the fatal and pestilential variety which is generally communicated from man to man."

7. The nature of the protection having been thus demonstrated, the Commissioners would next call your attention to the degree of its permanency and completeness. They have made particular inquiries on this point, and they are informed that vaccine matter does not become deteriorated by being transmitted through many individuals, and if the vaccination has duly and regularly passed through all its stages, that it has an enduring influence, and will protect the constitution as much as if the person had had small-pox. Mr. Charles Aikin, a member of the College of Surgeons, and one of the vaccinators appointed in London by the Vaccine Board, was examined upon this point; and in reference to an allegation that the protective efficacy of the ordinary vaccine matter had diminished, he stated, "that having vaccinated persons side by side with vaccine matter renewed from the cow, on a fair experiment, no difference was observable between them; no person," he states, "would have been able to say this is the new, this is the old, vaccine matter; they were both perfectly good." This is corroborated by Mr. Gillham, the Inspector and Vaccinator of the Vaccine Board, who has tested the progressive cases of Vaccination at different periods from 1833 to 1839, when the number of cases through which the original vaccine matter had passed was upwards of 80,000 persons; and he states that the cases vaccinated with new matter from the cow were submitted to Sir Astley Cooper and other members of the Board who could discern no difference between them and the cases vaccinated with the original matter.

8. Instances are authenticated of persons having caught small-pox after vaccination, and having died, as there are also of persons having small-pox a second time and dying from it; but instances even of the former kind are extremely rare; and allowing that the sufferers had been properly vaccinated, a fact which is still more rarely proved, the proportion of such fatal cases is so small as scarcely to affect the value of a general vaccination as a measure of prevention. In the metropolis vaccination

stations have been appointed, at which, as well as at other places, and by a large proportion of the medical practitioners, vaccination has been performed gratuitously. The persons who have attended with their children to receive vaccination from the appointed officers are chiefly of the well-dressed, cleanly, and respectable classes of mechanics. From ignorance, indolence, and their habits of procrastination, and carelessness about their offspring, and sometimes from the influence of quacks, the more pauperized classes have not brought their children to be vaccinated in proportionate numbers. A large proportion of the population has thereby been exposed to the ravages of the small-pox. It nevertheless appears that in the metropolis this partial employment of vaccination has been attended by a considerable diminution of mortality. Sir Henry Halford has brought to the attention of the Commissioners, that before the discovery of vaccination as a means of prevention, the deaths from small-pox within the bills of mortality in the metropolis, amounted to between three and four thousand a year. During the year 1838, when the variolous disease was particularly prevalent, they amounted only to 780. The comparative rarity of cases of disfigurement since the extension of vaccination, has been observed by persons who recollect the population previously to that event. Heretofore there have been no exact or extensive registries, such as the Commissioners hope they may be able to institute and cause to be maintained for the information of the public and the profession, and for pointing out the extent of the omissions and insecurity in respect to the population not vaccinated, and the extent of any failures in vaccination itself from the mode of its performance or otherwise Such instances as have been observed of the comparative effects of small-pox upon persons who have been vaccinated or inoculated, and upon persons who have received no protection in any shape, tend to confirm the value of the security of vaccination. Three sets of such instances may be cited,—one observed by Dr. J. Thomson, of Edinburgh; another consisting of the experience of the Military Asylum at Chelsea; a third set of cases observed by Mr. Dodd, one of the secretaries of the vaccination section,—of the proportionate mortality from small-pox after vaccination, after inoculation, and in cases of casual infection taken by persons who had received no protecting care.

	Number of persons attacked with Small-pox.	Of whom had previously—		Of whom died.
1. Edinburgh . . .	586	Vaccination	310 . .	1
		Inoculation	71 . .	3
		Neither cow-pox nor small-pox	205 . .	50

	Number of Cases reported as having had, previously to admission,—		Were attacked with Small-pox.	
2. Experience at the Military Asylum at Chelsea.	Vaccination . . .	3,060 . .	24 . .	..
	Small-pox	2,532 . .	26 . .	3
	(Two children also died who had neither undergone small-pox nor vaccination.)			
	Vaccinated subsequently to admission	628 . .	3 . .	..

					Had the disease		
3. Cases observed by Mr Dodd in 1837.	Persons attacked . .	201	Vaccinated . .	114	Mildly . .	91	2
					Severely .	23	
			Unvaccinated .	87	Mildly . .	29	17
					Severely .	58	

9. In a letter to the Poor Law Commissioners, Dr. Thomson says—

"In reference to the above table of the results of my observations as to the proportionate mortality from small-pox after vaccination, inoculation, and natural small-pox, I beg to state, that my observation of the very severe small-pox epidemic which prevailed in Scotland from 1818 to 1823, was carried on till I had had an opportunity of seeing not fewer than 1,500 individuals affected with small-pox after vaccination; and of this number only three died, but none of them with the disease in that form which is termed malignant. I saw also about 85 cases of small-pox in persons who had previously passed through either natural or inoculated small-pox, and of this number three also died. In addition to these, I saw 400 cases of primary small-pox, out of which 100 died. These results gave me a confidence in the conservatory effects of vaccination, which nothing has since occurred to shake. Small-pox has twice prevailed epidemically in Scotland since 1823; and from all I have seen or heard, I am satisfied that the proportion of deaths in the several classes of patients I have mentioned, did not materially differ from that above specified. In the first of these epidemics, the deaths that occurred in the vaccinated were of adult males, and in the second, chiefly I believe of adult females."

10. In the course of a Report to the Poor Law Commissioners on the sanatory condition of the labouring classes in Manchester, by Dr. Baron Howard, the Physician to the Ardwick and Ancoats Dispensary, he observes—

"The indifference to vaccination which exists among the labouring classes is greatly to be lamented, and there is reason to fear it is an increasing evil. This indifference is most frequently observed in the case of Irish families, or those leading a vagrant life and residing in common lodging-houses. The number of children vaccinated at the various medical charities in Manchester during the last five years is only 4,324, whilst that for the five previous years was 4,868; a diminution of 544 has therefore taken place, which is very considerable when the increased population during that period is calculated, and shows a growing inattention to this important duty on the part of the poor. With a view of ascertaining the extent to which vaccination is neglected by the poor, I put a series of queries on the subject to all the mothers of families indiscriminately, who happened to present themselves at the Ardwick and Ancoats Dispensary, during several weeks, and the following is the result of my inquiries. My examination extended to 250 families, and comprised 1,341 children. Of this number 412 had never been vaccinated, and of these unvaccinated children, 192 had suffered attacks of small-pox, of which a great many had died; whilst out of the whole number (929) of those who had undergone the protective influence of vaccination, only 26 had been attacked with that disease, and in these, with the exception of about four cases, the malady was extremely mild and modified in character. In this calculation, children under three months old were excluded, earlier than which age vaccination is not generally performed. To account for the large average number of children to each family, it is necessary to state that I included those who were dead as well as the living, provided they had lived three months. This was requisite to accomplish the object of the inquiry, inasmuch as many of the children had fallen victims to small-pox in consequence of not having been vaccinated. The effects of the lamentable neglect of vaccination hereby shown to exist, will only be manifested gradually, and are not yet fully developed; but if the same negligence be allowed to continue, the ravages which small-pox must in a few years produce, cannot fail to be dreadful; and from the greater proportion of adults who will then be unprotected by vaccination, the consequences will be infinitely more serious. At present the mortality is almost entirely confined to children, but it will gradually extend to those of maturer years; and we shall then witness the more melancholy spectacle of the heads of families falling victims to the disease, and leaving their orphan offspring (bereft of parental care and protection) exposed to all the hardships and temptations of the world; results which will not only entail a heavy burden upon the Poor Rates, but, what is of still more serious import, will prove most disastrous to the moral as well as to the physical welfare of the community. This omission of vaccination is owing in some instances to a positive prejudice against the practice, or to a doubt of its efficacy as a protection against small-pox; but it is more generally attributable to indifference, procrastination, or thoughtless negligence. Though vaccination is performed gratuitously every week, and without the necessity of any recommendation, at the Royal Infirmary, Lying-in Hospital, and the various Dispensaries, the poor will not be at the trouble of taking their children to get the operation done."

11. It will be observed that the three statements above quoted ascribe very different degrees of protection to vaccination. That from the Chelsea Hospital shows that there were more cases of sm ll-pox, after small-pox, in that institution, than of small-pox after vaccination. The inference which may be deduced from this occurrence is, that in the more unfavourable examples, the deficiency of the protective influence may have arisen from some imperfection in the progress of vaccination. This inference is plainly justified by the fact mentioned at page 48 of the Report from which these details are taken, viz., that Mr. Dodd had not seen a single instance of small-pox in a patient whom he had vaccinated, though he had resided at Chichester ten years. The Commissioners have deemed it especially necessary to advert to events of this kind, inasmuch as it appears that a great majority of the most respectable medical men in the kingdom are inclined to ascribe as large an amount of the failures which have been reported, to some accidental irregularity, which, it is to be hoped, may hereafter be obviated by increased care and attention.

12. The Report above alluded to was drawn up by Dr. Baron, as chairman of a section of the Provincial Medical and Surgical Association, appointed to inquire into the present state of vaccination, and read at the Anniversary

Meeting at Liverpool, in July, 1839. The Commissioners have obtained permission to reprint and circulate this Report for the information of the medical practitioners, as it contains many facts strongly corroborative of these views, and well merits careful examination.

13. The Report gives many instances of the testimony of the medical profession on the subject, which appear to the Commissioners to be highly deserving of attention. It states—

"At a meeting of the College of Physicians of Dublin, held on the 18th of January, 1839, Dr. Montgomery advanced the opinion that vaccination affords only a temporary security, and that its protective influence is now less than it was when the practice commenced. This called forth important counter-statements from several of the physicians and surgeons of that city. Dr. Maunsell asserts that the real origin of the failures is to be found in the neglect of the careful performance of vaccination, and to the practice of small-pox inoculation, which is indirectly encouraged by the alarmists. Dr. Labatt, who, from the commencement, has bestowed the most unwearied attention to the character of vaccination, and watched its practice with equal care, thus delivers his sentiments:—'It is very true that many instances have from time to time been brought before the public of persons attacked with small-pox, who were believed to have regularly had the cow-pox; but from my experience of the manner in which the latter has been conducted, I assert, without fear of contradiction, that these reputed failures have almost invariably originated either from want of skill, or inattention of practitioners, from inoculation having been performed by unprofessional persons, or the extreme inattention of parents and others in not showing children at the several stages of the affection. I do not pretend to say that cow-pox, any more than small-pox, inoculation is infallible; but having been thirty-six years and upwards extensively engaged in the practice, without witnessing a single case of death from small-pox after regular vaccination during that period, nor more certainly than ten, if so many, in which small-pox (in four of whom the disease was severe, and in the remainder very mild) occurred in persons who previously had cow-pox, I feel justified in stating that cow-pox, if skilfully applied, and conducted with that attention which it requires, will almost invariably afford a permanent security against small-pox.' He further adds, 'My experience leads me to say with the immortal Jenner, that perfect vaccination is permanent in its influence.'

"Dr. O'Brien, senior physician to the Fever Hospital, which is the chief receptacle for small-pox among the poor of Dublin, asserts that no case had occurred in that institution during the last twelve months, and that for a period of twenty-five years a few incidental cases only of small-pox had been admitted into the hospital, and those were generally persons who had not been vaccinated. He does not recollect the disease being communicated to any of the surrounding attendants or patients, though it was sometimes of a malignant and confluent character. This he attributes to the immunity afforded by vaccination. It is his opinion that the cause why small-pox has increased in Great Britain to an alarming extent, while it is nearly extinct in Ireland, is to be found in the neglect or careless employment of vaccination in one country, and to its universal adoption, and more attentive, not to say scientific, performance in the other. We may observe in passing, that the report from Glasgow, noticed in another page, strikingly corroborates this opinion of Dr. O'Brien.

"One other testimony from the Dublin Foundling Hospital may be added. The late Professor Creighton introduced vaccination into that institution in the year 1800. Many of the children were at two different periods inoculated with small-pox virus under his inspection, and completely resisted it. * *

"In the year 1827 the small-pox appeared in one of the largest institutions in Dublin, the average number of inmates being between 2,000 and 3,000. The disease attacked 106 individuals, and was confined chiefly to the nursery, in which were 141 children, together with their mothers or nurses, many of the latter having been vaccinated during their infancy or childhood, and they all escaped the small-pox, though placed under circumstances most favourable for the reception of the infection. Up to the 28th March of the present year, thirty-eight cases of small-pox have occurred; and notwithstanding the close and constant intercourse which arises from the crowded state of the establishment, no instance of small-pox after vaccination was observed, excepting in one child, who was said to have been vaccinated two years ago in Liverpool, but on whose arm there was no trace of cow-pox."

14. But in point of fact there is no difference of opinion among medical men as to the value of vaccination. All, without exception, appear to be agreed that the practice is of the utmost importance as a protection from small-pox; and it must be obvious that when vaccination becomes universal, the risk to the community from any exposure to that disease must be greatly diminished.

15. On another point, namely, the expediency of re-vaccination, the Report expresses what appears to be the opinion of most of the members of the profession conversant with the subject:

"Upon the whole, we are of opinion that re-vaccination can only be required where doubts are entertained of the correctness of the first vaccination. This is also the decision of such of our correspondents who mention the subject. In reference to this point, Dr. Kendrick, of Warrington, says, 'that inasmuch as cases of modified small-pox have occasionally occurred in a few weeks after well ascertained vaccination, the practice of re-vaccination is superfluous, and in some cases may have proved injurious.'

"Systematic re-vaccinations appear to us uncalled for, and liable to several objections, which we will now briefly state. In the first place, the practice implies that the virtues of cow small-pox are less permanent than we believe them to be; and now that this point has been freed from all ambiguity, we are not inclined to do anything to shake the confidence which must ultimately spring from right views of this subject. In the next place, it is probable, if re-vaccination be looked upon as essential, that less attention may be paid to the first vaccination than it demands, persons believing that all imperfections may be rectified by the subsequent operation. Now, as we are firmly convinced that incomplete vaccination has been the cause of a large proportion of failures, we cannot help dreading that defects of this kind, which it is so needful to remedy, might become more frequent than they are at present."

16. Hitherto the Guardians have had no power to make, nor the Commissioners to sanction any payments out of the rates for vaccination, otherwise than as medical relief in cases of destitution. It has sometimes been erroneously represented that the restriction of vaccination to the cases of paupers to whom relief was authorized by statute was made solely on the discretion of the Commissioners. It will be observed from the terms of the present Act, that the Guardians are "directed to contract with the medical officers of their several Unions or parishes respectively, or with any legally qualified medical practitioner or practitioners *for the vaccination of all persons resident in such Unions or parishes respectively*: Provided always, that it shall be a condition of every such contract, that the amount of the remuneration to be received under the same shall depend on the number of persons who, not having been previously successfully vaccinated, shall be successfully vaccinated by such medical officers or practitioners respectively so contracting."

17. The provision for vaccination is now therefore legally extended to the whole of the population; to all those who are independent as well as to those who are still dependent on relief, or who may become so.

18. In many schools and public institutions where proper sanatory precautions are taken for the protection of the inmates, a certificate of the proper performance of vaccination is required as a condition of admission. The Commissioners will consider of the means which may be recommended for promoting the general extension of this security.

19. One advantage obtainable to an individual by vaccination under the provisions of the new law is, that he will obtain a public document, or authorized and registered certificate of the vaccination having been properly performed.

20. The Commissioners take occasion to observe to the honour of the medical profession that they have hitherto performed vaccination gratuitously to a large proportion of the poorer classes who come to them. For the proper execution of the new law, it will be requisite that the Guardians shall make various arrangements which are set forth in the Minute of Instructions and the form of Contract, a copy of which is herewith transmitted (B.)

21. In the regulations as to the medical contract, in the certificates and the new registries, will be seen the nature of the services to be performed by the medical officer or practitioner contracting for the performance of vaccination; these services will entitle them to extra remuneration governed by local circumstances, on which the Guardians will consider and report.

22. The Commissioners will, on the medical reports, which it is necessary to require for the information of the public and the profession, obtain the opinion of competent medical authority.

23. The Commissioners feel assured that, independently of the zealous performance of the duties required of them by the provisions of the Act, the Guardians will as private individuals in their respective neighbourhoods, voluntarily and extra-officially exert their influence to remove prejudice, and promote the general adoption of the practice of vaccination.

Signed by Order of the Board,
EDWIN CHADWICK, *Secretary.*

To

The Board of Guardians.

(A.)

FORM OF NOTIFICATION IN RESPECT TO THE EXTENSION OF VACCINATION.

It is requested that parents of children, and all other persons, will take notice of the provisions made by the new Act of the 4th and 5th year of the reign of Queen Victoria, for the extension of Vaccination with the cow-pox, and the prevention of the spread of small-pox, which latter disease, chiefly in consequence of the want of due care, and the proceedings of ignorant individuals, has occasioned, during the last two years and a half, the deaths of upwards of thirty thousand persons in England and Wales, and the suffering and disfigurement of a much larger number of persons who have been attacked by the disease, but have escaped death.

Cow-pox is merely a mild form of small-pox; vaccination with the cow-pox is perfectly free from danger, and will protect the child from small-pox as effectually as the small-pox itself. In nearly all the instances in which small-pox has attacked persons who have been vaccinated, the vaccination has been imperfectly performed, or the attack of small-pox has been in a very mitigated form and quite free from danger. By vaccination being made universal, small-pox would be entirely banished from the country: to secure the benefits of vaccination, it should be performed, and its progress be watched, by a medical man.

For the extension of vaccination, it is provided, under the authority of the Act, that the following duly authorized medical practitioners are appointed to vaccinate persons resident in the parishes here named: (*insert the names of the several medical practitioners who contract, with names of the parishes within the district of each.*)

It is appointed that, for the purpose of performing vaccination, (*insert the name of the practitioner or practitioners*) will attend on each (*insert the day or days and fixed times of attendance*), at (*insert the names of the places where children will be vaccinated*), when the fact of the person having been vaccinated will be registered, and, after a proper examination, a certificate of the child having been successfully vaccinated will be given gratuitously.

Every child should be taken to be vaccinated when it is six weeks old, unless it be delicate, or suffering from disease, when the operation may be deferred for a week or two; but during the prevalence of cases of small-pox in any neighbourhood, all persons who have not been vaccinated, and had the cow-pox or the small-pox, should be vaccinated without delay; even infants a few days after birth.

It is also to be observed, that in consequence of the great number of deaths, and of the evils, including blindness, which have been occasioned by the inoculation of children with small-pox, which has generally been done by ignorant persons, the Act of Parliament has made it an offence punishable with one month's imprisonment, for *any person, by any means*, to produce the disease of small-pox.

It is further to be noted, that whilst it is an offence to produce small-pox by inoculation, it is also an offence to endanger other persons by carrying about or exposing any person who may have caught the small-pox, whether naturally or by inoculation. For any one to endanger the safety of the public by causing persons who have any infectious disease, and who are in a state to communicate it, to be exposed or carried about at the risk of infecting others, is by the common law of this kingdom illegal, and punishable as a misdemeanour.

It is the duty of all persons, therefore, not only to avoid committing the offence of creating small-pox by inoculation or otherwise, but to give information to the magistrate, or some peace officer, of any persons who have been guilty of the offence, that effectual means may be taken for the protection of the public.

II.—MINUTE OF INSTRUCTIONS TO BE ISSUED WITH RESPECT TO THE PREPARATION OF CONTRACTS FOR THE EXTENSION OF VACCINATION.

(B.)

"CONTRACTS must be made under the Act to extend the practice of vaccination in order to carry its provisions into effect in every place in England and Wales maintaining its own poor, whether such places be included in a Union or not, and whether known by the name of parish, township, or vil, or by any other designation whatsoever. The officers who are immediately invested with the duty of making contracts are the Guardians of the poor in parishes, Unions, and incorporations, in which relief to the poor is administered by Guardians, and other officers having similar functions to those of Guardians but having different names of office, such as visitors, governors, directors, managers of the poor; and where there are no such Guardians or other officers, then the Overseers of the Poor. The extension of the provisions of the Act to all places maintaining their own poor and to all the officers besides Guardians and Overseers, is an effect of the ninth clause in the Act, by which the like meaning is given to the terms used in the Act, as is given to the terms used in the Poor Law Amendment Act.

"The Act is generally to be carried into effect under the direction of the Poor Law Commissioners. But the Commissioners prefer to leave, as far as may be possible, the introduction of the measure to the voluntary action of the local officers, and they will not issue compulsory orders except in cases where the provisions of the Act would otherwise fail of having their due effect given to them.

"The first duty of the Guardians and other local officers will be to take into consideration the circumstances of the district, the number of persons who will probably require to be vaccinated at the commencement of the measure, and the probable average in succeeding periods. These considerations will enable them to come to a determination on the following points:—

"1. The number and extent of the districts and the number of the persons to be contracted with.

"The Guardians not being limited to the medical officers of the Union, may make these as numerous as they think desirable: they may contract, if they think fit, with every legally qualified medical practitioner who may be willing to undertake the duty. But every addition to the number of medical practitioners will extend the number of returns and reports, and will probably, by diminishing the number of cases falling to the share of each, add to the amount of remuneration which each will require. Bearing these qualifications in mind, it will be desirable, for obtaining the objects of the Act (to the benefits of which all residents are entitled), to make the districts as small and the number of contractors as great as possible.

"2. The stations at which attendance should be given by the persons appointed to vaccinate.

"These should obviously be well known places, and so placed that convenience of access may practically render them central to the aggregate population of each district. Where the contractors are numerous there will be less difficulty in determining the stations, and the residence of the contractor will often be the most convenient that can be chosen.

"3. The number of attendances to be given in each quarter at the several stations.

"Even in the cases when the station fixed on is the residence of the contractor, some fixed days of attendance should be contracted for and notified to the public. In some cases it may be sufficient to fix days for the operation at long intervals apart, as on the 1st of each month for the operation and the 8th for the inspection. In such cases the days fixed should be such as will be easily remembered.

"In all cases it will be desirable, in addition to the regular attendances, to stipulate for the services of the contractor whenever he is personally applied to at his own residence. This stipulation will at the same time tend to the ease of the contractor, will provide for contingencies, and will take away all pretext from individuals for neglecting to avail themselves of the benefit of the contract.

"It will be of course understood that the contractor may if he should think fit visit any person at his own house and vaccinate him, on inspecting his case, there, and that the contractor having duly recorded and reported the case should be entitled to charge for it as for a case vaccinated at a station or at his residence.

"4. The remuneration to be paid to the persons to be contracted with.

"The Act prescribes the principle of remuneration. It is to depend on the number of persons who, not having previously been successfully vaccinated, shall be successfully vaccinated under the contract.

"But the amount to be paid per case will depend on the circumstance before, and hereafter to be adverted to. The Commissioners after having made inquiry of several medical practitioners, and also adverting to the customary fees paid to medical men for examinations and certificates in the case of factory children and recruits for the army, have arrived at the conclusion that a payment of 1*s.* 6*d.* for every case of successful vaccination will, under ordinary circumstances, be an adequate remuneration to the contractor. If extraordinary circumstances should induce the Guardians to agree with the contractor for a higher rate of payment, these extraordinary circumstances should be stated by the Guardians in transmitting the contract for the approval of the Commissioners.

"5. The various means which may be adopted to secure the most effectual carrying out of the measure.

"The check by which assurance is to be obtained of the effectual working of the measure, is a matter requiring the very sedulous attention of the Guardians. The Guardians must mainly depend on the Contractor's returns for evidence of the success in each case.

"The Commissioners will require in every case the adoption of returns in alternate books in the Form I. in the schedule to the form of agreement suggested below. And at every meeting of a Board of Guardians the Clerk having first made out a summary of all the Returns in the following form

Date.	New Cases reported by			Total.
	Mr. A.	Mr. B.	Mr. C.	
Sept. 1 .	5	3	6	14
" 4 .	4	4	7	15
Totals .	9	7	13	29

Successful Cases reported by			Total.
Mr. A.	Mr. B.	Mr. C.	
5	2	4	11
4	3	4	11
9	5	8	22

should read over, immediately after he has read the notices of marriages, the total number of new cases, and the total number of successful cases reported by each contractor, and should leave the books returned by each open during the meeting of the Board. At the end of each quarter the sum of the totals of successful cases thus reported in each week, will give the number of cases for which payment is to be made to the contractors.

"The certificate also set forth in Form II. in the same schedule, is indispensable. But the Register in the Form III., though very desirable, the Commissioners will not require to be provided for in any contract by a Board of Guardians, who may be of opinion that it may be dispensed with.

When a Board of Guardians or other competent officers shall have taken the general arrangements into consideration, and thus come to a conclusion as to the terms of the contracts they would be prepared to enter into, it will be desirable that they should record in their minutes the result of their deliberations, and transmit copies of such minutes to the Poor Law Commissioners, so far as relates to the terms and forms of the contracts. It is desirable that these contracts should be made in pursuance of an order under the hands and seal of the Commissioners, that they may be exempt from stamp duty. To facilitate this object, the Commissioners append a form of Minute of Terms of Contract, to which they would be prepared to give their sanction.

"*Copy of a Minute of the Board of Guardians of the Union held at on the day of in the year One thousand eight hundred and forty.*

"The Board having made arrangements, as before recorded in these minutes, for carrying into effect the provisions of the Act passed in the year one thousand eight hundred and forty, to extend the practice of vaccination, took into consideration the general terms of the contracts to be entered into with the medical officers of the Union and other legally qualified medical practitioners who may be willing to contract for the vaccination of all persons resident in the Union; and they are of opinion that the general terms of such contracts should be as is set forth in the following form :—

CONTRACT for VACCINATION.

3 & 4 *Vict.* c. 29.—*An Act to extend the Practice of Vaccination.*

ARTICLES OF AGREEMENT entered into this day of 184 , between[1]

of the one Part, and the Guardians[2] of the Poor of the[3] in the Count of of the other Part.

1. *Name and Address of the Medical Man contracting*, describing him as a Medical Officer of the Union, or of a legally qualified Medical Practitioner, as the case may be.
2. *Guardians*, *Overseers*, *&c.*, as the case may be.
3. *Union* or *Parish*, being the whole of the District over which the Guardians or Overseers contracting have authority.

IT IS HEREBY AGREED, and the said[1]

doth Contract with the said[2] and their Successors, that from and after the day of he will vaccinate all Persons resident within the said[3] who shall apply to him at any reasonable hour of the day at his own residence, or at the times and places at which he shall in conformity with the terms of this Contract attend.

And that he will, for the purpose of vaccinating all such Persons, attend on every day in every week, from the hour of in the noon, to the hour of at in the Parish of

And on every day in every week, from the hour of to the hour of at in the Parish of[4]

4. Repeat this clause for as many Stations as the Contractor may agree to attend at.

"And that he will, at all such times and places, duly vaccinate all such persons as may be present for the purpose of being vaccinated, and who may not before have been successfully vaccinated, and do and perform all such other acts and things as may be necessary for the immediate purpose of causing such vaccination to be successfully terminated.

"And that he will keep two books to be used respectively on alternate weeks, and will immediately after he shall have vaccinated any person, and also immediately after he shall have inspected the progress of vaccination in any person vaccinated previously by him under this contract, make the entries described in the Form I. in the schedule hereto annexed. And that he will on the day next before such day of weekly meeting of the Board of the said Guardians, deliver to their clerk the book in which he shall have made such entries during the preceding week.

And that in every case in which the result of Vaccination performed by him under this Contract on any person shall be successful, he will give to such Person, or to its Parent, Guardian, or Nurse, a Certificate of the fact, in the Form II. in the said Schedule. And that he will also keep a Register in the Form III. in the said Schedule, of all cases of Small-pox which he shall attend, and will deliver a copy of the same once in every Quarter of the Year to the Clerk of the said Guardians on the [5]

5. Days to be named, which will allow of the results to be forwarded to the Poor Law Commissioners, with the Quarterly Abstracts of the Union Accounts.

"And the said Guardians do, for themselves and their successors, contract and agree with the said to pay to the said his executors, administrators, or assigns, within one calendar month after the 1st of January, the 1st of April, the 1st of June, and the 1st of November respectively, during the subsistence of this contract, and within one month after its termination, the sum of for every person who, not having been previously vaccinated, shall have been successfully vaccinated under this contract by the said and with respect to whom the said shall have made the entries, and given the certificate hereinbefore described.

"And it is hereby further agreed between the said and the said Guardians, that this contract shall be liable to be put an end to by either of the parties hereto, on giving twenty-eight days' notice to the other party respectively, of the intention to put an end to the same.

"IN WITNESS whereof the said hath hereunto set his hand and seal, and the said Guardians their common seal, the day and year first above written.

"Signed, sealed, and delivered by the above-named in the presence of

L. S.

Guardians' Seal.

"The common seal of the Guardians of the above named Union, was hereunto affixed at a meeting of the Board of Guardians, held on the day of the date hereof, by Chairman of the Board at the said meeting, in the presence of

Clerk of the said Union.

FORM (I.)

SCHEDULE referred to in the above Articles of Agreement.

Book 1.—For the 1st, 3rd, 5th, 7th, 9th, 11th, and 13th Weeks in every Quarter.

NEW CASES.						CASES OF PRECEDING WEEK.					
Date.	Name.	Sex.	Age.	State of Health.	Where Vaccinated.	Date.	Name.	Successful.	Unsuccessful.	Observations.	Where observed.
8 Sept. 1840	Y. Z.	..	..	..	Station A..	1 Sept.	A. B.	S.	..		Station A.
,,	Z. Y.	..	..	..	..	,,	B. C.	..	U.		..
,,	W. V.	..	..	..	Station B..	,,	C. D.	S.	..		Station B.
,,	V. W.	..	..	..	Station C..	,,	D. E.	S.	..		Station C.
,,	T. V.	..	..	..	At my residence.	,,	E. F.	..	..		At my residence.
2 Sept.	S. T.	..	..	..	At his parents' house, 10, King-street.			3	1		

* If the state of Health be good, or not otherwise remarkable, this column may be left blank.

Book 2.—For the 2nd, 4th, 6th, 8th, 10th, and 12th Weeks, exactly similar.

FORM (II.)

CERTIFICATE.

aged , was vaccinated the 184
by me, and passed regularly and successfully through the disease.

(Signed)

You are desired to attend next that the Certificate may be filled up.*

* The above Certificate, in blank, should be given to the Person on whom the operation of Vaccination has been performed, or to the Parent, Nurse, or other Person having care of the Child, immediately after the operation.

FORM (III.)

Register of Cases of Small-pox attended by me during the Quarter ending in the Year 184

Date.	Name of Patient.	Sex.	Age.	Description of Case.	Result.	Patient had previously			When.	Where.	By whom.
						Had the Small-pox naturally; when.	Had the Small-pox by Inoculation; when.	Been Vaccinated			
	A. B.										
	C. D.					In 1804.					
	E. F.						In 1821.				
	G. H.							Yes.	In 1821.	At Manchester.	By Y. Z. Apothecary.

"Resolved :—That the clerk do transmit a copy of the said form to the Poor Law Commissioners, and that the Poor Law Commissioners be requested to issue an order that the same form be adopted in all contracts to be made in this Union under the provisions of the said Act until further order shall be made in that behalf.

"The Poor Law Commissioners will thereupon issue an order to the following effect :—

"Whereas the Board of Guardians of the Union are about to enter into contracts for carrying into effect the provisions of the Act passed in the session of Parliament held in the third and fourth years of the reign of Her Majesty Queen Victoria, intituled, '*An Act to extend the practice of Vaccination*,' and have requested that an order should be issued by us, directing that the said contracts should be made in the tenour and form above set forth.

"Now therefore, We, the Poor Law Commissioners, having considered and approved the said Form, do hereby order that the said Form of Contract shall, so far as the same may be applicable to the circumstances of each case, be adopted by the Guardians of the Union in making contracts with medical officers of the said Union, or other legally qualified medical practitioners, under the provisions of the said recited Act.

"Given under our hands and seal of office, this day of in the year of our Lord one thousand eight hundred and forty

"The above order, prescribing prospectively the form and general provisions of contracts, will not dispense with the necessity of transmitting a copy of each contract when entered into by the Guardians, under the 4th section of the Act, for the allowance of the Poor Law Commissioners."

III.—EXTENSION TO SCOTLAND OF THE INQUIRY AS TO THE SANATORY CONDITION OF THE LABOURING CLASSES.

THE Poor Law Commissioners having received from Her Majesty's Principal Secretary of State for the Home Department a communication with respect to the inquiry into the sanatory state of the labouring population, now in progress in England and Wales, stating that addresses had been presented to Her Majesty from the lord provosts, magistrates, and town councils of the cities of Edinburgh, Glasgow, and Aberdeen, praying that the inquiry might be extended to Scotland; in which communication his lordship requested to know whether the inquiry could be conveniently extended, the Board expressed their readiness to extend the inquiry to that part of the United Kingdom.

The Commissioners thereupon received directions to make the inquiry into the sanatory condition of the labouring classes in the towns of Scotland as complete as possible.

Circular leters, similar in purport to those which have been transmitted to the Boards of Guardians in England, were addressed to the provosts of the burgh towns of Scotland, requesting a list of the names of the medical officers of the public institutions and charities, and also the names of the medical practitioners within the towns to whom circular letters might be sent.

Communications were made accordingly to the Royal Colleges of Physicians and Surgeons at Edinburgh, and to the officers of the institutions, and medical practitioners, whose names were indicated to the Commissioners.

From the president of the Royal College of Physicians in Edinburgh, the Commissioners have received the following communication:—

Physicians' Hall, Edinburgh,
5th August, 1840.

"SIR,—I am instructed by the Royal College of Physicians to inform the Poor Law Commissioners of England, that on the documents sent to me not long ago as President of the College having been considered by the college yesterday at a quarterly meeting,—the college resolved to express to the Commissioners their strong conviction of the necessity of a careful inquiry into the circumstances connected with the spread of fever in Scotland; their satisfaction on understanding from several of the Fellows of the College that they had put themselves in communication with the Commissioners on the subject; and their readiness to contribute, either as a body, or as individuals, in any way which may be pointed out to them, towards supplying the Commissioners with the information required to enable them to determine what provisions should be recommended to Government, or other parties, for abating the prevalence of continued fever, and other epidemic diseases. The subject is one which has long engaged the attention of many Fellows of the College. They are all aware of its high importance, and they feel assured that every facility will be given by the Members of the Medical Profession to the Commissioners in conducting their inquiries.

"I have, &c.
"R. CHRISTISON, President, &c.

"*To the Secretary of the Poor Law Commissioners.*"

In furtherance of the inquiry, Dr. Traill, Professor of Medical Jurisprudence and Police, and Drs. Maclagan and Wm. Thomson, have consented to act as a local committee in Edinburgh, and draw up a report on the sanatory condition of that city. In Glasgow a committee has been formed for the like purpose, consisting of the lord provost, town council, and magistrates of the city, together with Mr. Sheriff Alison, Dr. Cowan, and the medical officers, &c., of the several public institutions, Mr. Davie, the town clerk, acting as secretary. In Aberdeen, St. Andrew's, and Paisley, the provosts have also formed local committees to act in aid of the general inquiry.

From the following towns, and medical and other gentlemen, the Commissioners have already received answers to their inquiries:—

ABERDEEN ....The Provost
Do..........Dr. Cuddie
ALLOA........Mr. Russell, Mr. Miller, and Mr. Syme, Surgeons
ARBROATH ....The Provost
Do..........Dr. Arrott
Do..........Mr. Trail, Mr. Wannan, Mr. Thomson, and Mr. Cochrane, Surgeons
AYR..........The Provost
Do..........Dr. Rankine
Do..........Dr. Sloan
Do..........Mr. Mitchell and Mr. Whiteside, Surgeons
BANFF........Dr. White
BERVIE.......The Senior Baillie
BURUTISLAND .The Provost
Do..........Mr. Cairns, Surgeon, Aberdour
CAMPBLETON...Mr. Hunter, Surgeon
COLDSTREAM ..Mr. Gillie, Mr. Turnbull, and Mr. McDonald, Surgeons
CRAILL.......Mr. Bouthrone, Surgeon
CULLEN ......A Committee of the Magistrates
CUPAR........Mr. Mackie, Surgeon
DUNDEE ......Mr. Johnston, Senior Baillie
Do..........Mr. Baxter, Town Chamberlain
Do..........Dr. Davidson
Do..........Dr. Arrott
Do..........Mr. Aitken, Surgeon
DUNFERMLINE.The Provost
EARLS FERRY .The Chief Magistrate
Do..........Mr. Todd, Surgeon, Colmsburgh
EDINBURGH ...The Lord Provost
Do..........The Royal College of Physicians
Do..........The Royal College of Surgeons
Do..........Dr. Handyside
Do..........Dr. W. P. Alison
Do..........Dr. Pagan
Do..........Dr. James Hunter
Do..........Dr. G. A. Borthwick

EDINBURGH....Dr. Christison
Do..........Dr. W. Adam
Do..........Dr. John Abercrombie
Do..........Dr. Adam Hunter
Do..........Dr. W. H. Thomson
Do..........Dr. Ransford
Do..........Dr. Young
Do..........Dr. Gardiner
Do..........Mr. Tait and Mr. Inglis, Surgeons
ELGIN........The Provost
FALKIRK......Ditto
FORFAR.......Ditto
Do..........Dr. Smith
Do..........Mr. Laird, Surgeon
FORRES.......The Provost
Do..........Mr. Bell, Surgeon
GALASHIELS ...Mr. Weir, Surgeon
GLASGOW .....The Lord Provost
Do..........Mr. Sheriff Alison
Do..........Mr. Davie, Town Clerk
Do..........Dr. Couper
Do..........Dr. Cleland
Do..........Dr. Macewan
Do..........Mr. Fleming, Surgeon, Anderston
Do..........Mr. Macewan, Surgeon
GREENOCK ....The Provost
HADDINGTON ..Ditto
Do..........Dr. Allison, Tranent
INVERARY.....The Provost
Do. ....Dr. Anderson
Do..........Dr. Mackechine
INVERKEITHING, The Provost
Do..........Mr. Fraser, Town Clerk
Do..........Dr. Bartholomew
IRVINE........Mr. King and Mr. Robertson, Surg.
KELSO........Dr. Wilson
Do..........Dr. James Douglas
Do..........Dr. F. Douglas
Do..........Dr. Stewart
Do..........Mr. Robertson and Mr. Purves, Surgeons
KIRKCALDY....Mr. Philp, Surgeon
KIRKWALL ....The Provost
Do..........Mr. Bremner, Surgeon
LANARK.......The Provost
Do..........Mr. Gibson, Surgeon
Do..........Mr. Frame, Surgeon, Lesmahagow
Do..........Mr. Affleck, Surgeon, Douglas
LILLIESLEAF ..Mr. Stevenson, Surgeon
LINLITHGOW...The Provost
LOCHMABEN ...The Provost.
Do. ....The Rev. T. Marjoribanks, Lochmaben
Do. ....The Rev. T. H. Thomson, Dalton
Do. ....Mr. Wilson, Surgeon, Lockerby
Do. ....Mr. Young, Surgeon, Ecclesfechan
MONTROSE ....The Provost
Do. ....Dr. Poole
Do. ....Dr. Ogilvy
Do. ....Dr. Ferguson

MONTROSE ....Mr. Niddrie, Mr. Duncan, and Mr. Arrott, Surgeons
NAIRN........The Provost
NORTHBERWICKThe Chief Magistrate
Do. ....Mr. Watson, Surgeon
QUEENSFERRY, SOUTH ..The Provost
Do. ....Mr. Greig and Mr. Lawrie, Surgeons
PAISLEY ......The Provost
PORTOBELLO ...The Provost
Do. ....Dr. Stephen
Do. ....Dr. Vallange
RENFREW .....The Provost
Do. ....Dr. Baird
Do. ....Mr. Patison, Surgeon
ST. ANDREW'S .The Provost
Do. ....Dr. Mudie
TAIN ....Dr. Ross
WICK.........The Provost
WIGTOWN .....Mr. M'Millan, Surgeon.

There being no practitioners engaged for the medical treatment of the destitute poor, or as medical officers, attached to any system of local administration in Scotland, analogous to the medical officers of the new Poor Law Unions in England, and there being consequently no analogous system of registration of the diseases occurring amongst those classes, from which statistical returns might be obtained, the queries transmitted to the medical officers belonging to the Poor Law Unions, were found to be inapplicable to Scotland. The Commissioners directed that in lieu of such statistical returns, the following form of queries should be transmitted:—

Questions for Information on the Inquiry as to the Prevalence of certain Causes of Disease amongst the labouring Classes of the Population.

1. HAVE diseases of the various forms of continued fever, and other contagious febrile diseases, been prevalent in any, and what, parts of your parish or district, and do such diseases recur at regular intervals, or are they rare and occasional only?

2. What are the seasons at which such diseases appear amidst any part of the population, and what are their characteristics?

3. Did the cholera, at the time of its general prevalence, prevail to any, and what, extent within the district?

4. What is the *external* condition, in the following respects, of the residences of the population amidst which such diseases occur?—

a. As to the contiguity of vegetable or animal substances in a state of decomposition, stagnant pools or undrained marshes, accumulations of refuse, either thrown from houses or otherwise?

b. As to the means adopted, or the means

available for the *removal* of such substances, or the prevention of the generation of malaria; whether there are sufficient drains or sewers, adequately well supplied with water to dilute, and sufficiently sloping to carry off, all such refuse; whether such drains are sufficiently *closed* to confine noxious exhalations from them; whether there is any regularly appointed service of scavengers, or otherwise, for the removal of such substances; whether there is sufficient ventilation around their residences to dissipate the noxious vapours apparently irremovable?

5. Describe the *internal structure and economy* of the residences of the population amidst which contagious febrile diseases arise,—

a. State whether they, as well as the surrounding land, are drained or undrained?

b. Whether they are properly supplied with water for the purposes of cleanliness of the houses, persons, and clothing?

c. Whether there are good means of ventilation, with a due regard to warmth?

d. Whether there are proper receptacles for filth in connexion with the cottages?

6. As to the internal economy of such residences, describe further,—

a. Whether they are unduly crowded, and several families or persons occupy the space which would properly suffice only for a less number?

b. Whether there are any inferior lodging-houses crowded by mendicants or vagrants?

c. Whether there is gross want of cleanliness in the persons or habitations of certain classes of the poor?

d. Whether there is a habit of keeping pigs, &c., in dwelling-houses, or close to doors or windows?

e. Whether there is an indisposition to be removed to the hospitals when infected with contagious disease?

7. Is the extension of the diseases described in Question 1, ascribable in any or what proportion to want of any of the necessaries of life; or to other causes than those specified in Questions 4, 5, and 6? if so, distinguish those other causes, so far as you are able, and the extent of diseases resulting from them.

8. What is the common cost of erection, and average cost of repairing, each description of the tenements or cottages inhabited by the labouring classes?

9. What are the rents paid by the labourers for each description of tenements or cottages?

10. What is the general proportion of the rent paid by the labourer to his total expenditure?

11. What is the common cost of the lodgings to persons of the labouring classes?

12. Are you of opinion that any, and what, legislative measures are desirable or available for remedy of any of the evils existing within your district?

13. Have any, and what, voluntary exertions been made to improve the external or internal economy of the residences of the labouring classes within your district, and if so, describe their nature and effects?

Name of the Parish or District to which the answers refer. } ____________

Name of the Medical Practitioner or other person by whom the answers are given. } ____________

The Commissioners directed that the same form of queries should be transmitted to the medical officers or practitioners in England, where the new law had not yet been brought into operation, or where the medical accounts have not yet been fully established in practice a sufficient length of time to furnish materials for statistical returns such as have been obtained from the medical officers of the new Unions.

Dr. Couper, of Glasgow, having stated, in the course of his answers to the Commissioners, that proper measures would cost the public less than is expended in treating the diseases of pauperism which the neglect of those measures occasion, he was requested to state more fully the grounds for this proposition. The Commissioners have received the following answer to their letter. Considering it desirable to ascertain how far the same proposition was applicable to other places, they have directed the attention of those gentlemen engaged in the preparation of sanatory reports to the particulars which it specifies, and have requested them to state how far they are applicable to their respective districts:—

"*Glasgow, August* 7, 1840.

SIR,—"I have received yours of the 30th July, marked 86 S., acknowledging receipt of my answers to your queries, and asking further for any proofs or illustrations that may occur to me in support of the proposition advanced by me, 'that proper sanatory measures would cost the public much less than is at present expended in treating the diseases and pauperism which the neglect of those measures occasions.' In reply I submit the following considerations:—

"1. In the year 1836, which may be taken as an example, there were treated in the Glasgow Fever House 3125 cases of fever, at an average expense of 1*l.* 10*s.* each, and at a total expense therefore to the public of 4,687*l.* 10*s.*

Note.—In this estimate nothing is allowed for the cost of the fever-house, which was erected a few years ago, at an expense to the public of more than 6,000*l.*

"2. Of the above number, 498 died, and of the latter at least three-fourths, or 373·5, must have been buried at the public charge, at an expense of 10*s*. each, or 186*l*. 15*s*.

"3. During the same year 716 pauper fever patients, exclusive of those sent to the fever house, were treated in their own houses, by the district surgeons, at an expense (including the salaries of the district surgeons, medicines, cordials, &c.) of, say, to the public, 8*s*. each, and at a total expense, therefore, of 286*l*. 8*s*.

"4. Of the above mentioned 716 patients at least one-tenth, or 71, must have died, and of the latter three-fourths, or 53·7, must have been buried at the public expense, at a charge of 10*s*. each, and at a total expense, therefore, of, 26*l*. 13*s*. 6*d*.

"*Note*.—This estimate of the proportion of paupers buried at public expense will not appear too great to any one who considers the fact stated in the Glasgow Mortality Bill for 1839, viz. that during that year 21·66 per cent. of all who died, of every class, in Glasgow, during that year, were buried at the public expense.

"The above estimate too, it is to be remarked, of paupers treated in their own houses, has reference to the *borough* of Glasgow only, which contains considerably less than one half of the whole population. The actual expense, therefore, under items 3 and 4 must have been more than double what is here stated.

"5. Of the above-mentioned 3841 paupers, treated in the fever house and in their own houses together, each (including disease and convalescence) must, on an average, have been rendered unfit for work for six weeks. The loss thus sustained would, at 5*s*. per week, amount to 5,761*l*. 10*s*.

"6. Of the above 3841 paupers, many must have been heads of families, and their children and other dependants must have been supported at public expense, during the six weeks' incapacity of their parents, &c. Of the 569 paupers who died, the children and other dependants must have become a more permanent burden on the public. It is impossible to estimate the amount, but it must have been considerable in the various shapes of increased poor-rates, police and bridewell assessments, contributions to charitable institutions, and private charity.

"7. But in 1836 the total deaths from fever in Glasgow were 841; if from this number we deduct the 569 deaths occurring among paupers treated at the public expense as above, there remain 272 deaths occurring among persons who, it is to be presumed, were treated at their own expense. It is not probable that the mortality in that class would exceed 1 in 10, and therefore 272 deaths imply the existence of 2720 cases which could scarcely be treated at a less expense for medical attendance, medicines, cordials, &c. than 3*l*. each, or double the expense of a pauper in the fever-house. The total expense, therefore, would be 8,160*l*.

"8. The funeral charges of the 272 persons of this class who died would amount, at 2*l*. each, to 544*l*.

"9. But the 2,720 persons treated at their own expense would, like the paupers, be rendered incapable of following their usual employment for a period averaging six weeks, and the value of their labour during that time would consequently be lost. The amount cannot be estimated, but that it must be great will be apparent, if it be recollected that this class begins with the poorest operative who can pay for his own medical treatment, and ends with the most opulent citizen of Glasgow, including, betwixt those extremes, all sorts of artificers, shopmen, overseers, clerks, professional men, managers, and proprietors of manufacturing and mercantile establishments, in the cases of many of whom an interruption of business for even one day is attended with serious pecuniary loss.

"10. It would be taking a very limited view of the subject, to suppose that typhus fever is the only disease, the prevalence of which is materially increased by the neglect of sanatory measures. The case is the same with small-pox, measles, scarlet-fever, hooping-cough, dysentery, scrofula, and a multitude of anomalous affections, all of which operate in the same manner as typhus fever, although to a less extent, in occasioning pecuniary loss to the public.

"It is scarcely necessary to add, that all the above estimates are merely approximations used to illustrate the opinion which I have advanced. The actual expenditure for a series of years under most of the above items could be ascertained by the Committee now sitting at Glasgow, and I have no doubt it would, as to the year 1836, more often exceed than fall short of that above stated. The items estimated amount, it will be observed, to nearly 20,000*l*., and half as much more may be added for those which are not estimated. Believing as I do that this large amount of loss has been inflicted in a single year on the inhabitants of a single town, by diseases capable of being prevented, to a great extent, by sanatory measures, the cost of which would probably not amount to one-tenth of the estimated loss, I cannot help thinking, without reference to human suffering at all, that a law compelling the inhabitants to contribute to defray the expense of those sanatory measures would be desirable on the score of economy alone.

"I have the honour, &c.

"*To E. Chadwick, Esq.* *&c.* *&c.*" "JOHN COUPER.

LONDON:
Printed by order of the Poor Law Commissioners, by W. CLOWES and SONS, Stamford Street, and Published by CHARLES KNIGHT and Co., 22, Ludgate-street, Publishers to the Poor Law Commissioners.

AN

OFFICIAL CIRCULAR

OF PUBLIC DOCUMENTS AND INFORMATION:

DIRECTED BY THE POOR LAW COMMISSIONERS TO BE PRINTED, CHIEFLY FOR THE USE OF THE MEMBERS AND PERMANENT OFFICERS OF BOARDS OF GUARDIANS, UNDER THE POOR LAW AMENDMENT ACT.

No. 8. CIRCULAR ISSUED SEPTEMBER 25TH, 1840.

Poor Law Commission Office,
Somerset House,
September 23, 1840.

THE Poor Law Commissioners, on a review of their minutes, directed that the minutes and correspondence on the following subjects should be printed and circulated for the information of Guardians and officers of the several Unions, viz.—

By order of the Board,
EDWIN CHADWICK, *Secretary.*

I.—COMPARATIVE OPERATION OF THE LAW IN MANUFACTURING AND AGRICULTURAL DISTRICTS.

The following Report from Mr. Weale, one of the Assistant Commissioners, on the comparative state of Pauperism in the Agricultural and Manufacturing Unions in his District was read to the Board.

GENTLEMEN.—In my recent report on the comparative state of pauperism in the parishes of Birmingham and Aston, I met an objection that I anticipated would be made against the comparison there instituted, that a decrease of pauperism might be expected to prevail in the latter parish from the fact of its containing a considerable number of persons employed in agriculture, by stating that my own experience had tended to convince me that there was no foundation for an assumption such as this; and I showed by a comparison of the expenditure for the relief of the poor in the purely agricultural parishes of the Aston Union with the parish of Aston itself, a result very favourable to the latter parish.

To convince you that I did not come to this conclusion without sufficient data, and again to support the assertion I have frequently made, that the principles of the Poor Law Amendment Act are beneficially applicable to manufacturing districts during a state of commercial depression, I have prepared the two following tables, the first containing the expenditure for the relief of the poor for the year ending Lady-day, 1840, in fourteen agricultural Unions, indifferently selected from my district, in several counties, and in the only seven Manufacturing Unions under my superintendence, and the other containing the number of paupers relieved in the same Unions during the quarter ending at Lady-day last. In selecting the particular quarter I have done in the last table, I was influenced by a desire to show the greatest amount of pauperism, and no difference of opinion can exist as to the quarter in which this is to be found. It must also be borne in mind, that in the manufacturing Unions a very great depression of trade was experienced during the whole of the period I have dilated on, and which was greatly increased during the last quarter.

A TABLE showing the Number of Paupers relieved in

	Name of Union.	County in which situate.	Population in 1831.	For the Qua								
				Number of Paupers relieved.								
				In-door.				Out-door.				Gr Tot
				Men.	Women.	Children.	Total.	Men.	Women.	Children.	Total.	
Agricultural.	Bedford	Beds	28,033	74	93	152	319	412	857	576	1,845	2,
	Woburn		10,633	69	67	126	262	191	366	445	1,002	1,
	Newport Pagnell	Bucks	22,087	45	55	93	193	292	777	559	1,628	1,
	Berkhampstead	Herts	9,871	40	31	44	115	162	385	492	1,039	1,
	Hemel Hempstead		9,910	62	42	43	147	97	205	263	565	
	Saint Albans		15,833	382	148	152	682	90	196	183	469	1,
	Brixworth	North-ampton	13,751	26	33	71	130	260	533	550	1,343	1,
	Daventry		19,137	39	40	89	168	299	593	479	1,371	1,
	Kettering		15,464	27	53	77	157	314	709	695	1,718	1,
	Oundle		13,517	36	33	77	146	148	390	286	824	
	Wellingborough		18,571	35	51	50	136	303	742	773	1,818	1,
	Rugby	Warwick	16,668	27	31	58	116	230	280	357	867	
	Solihull		11,433	38	33	45	116	107	200	179	486	
	Warwick		28,924	46	54	98	198	279	630	682	1,591	1,
			233,832	946	764	1,175	2,885	3,184	6,863	6,519	16,566	19,
Manufacturing and Mining. Iron. Coal. Hardware.	Walsall	Stafford	24,931	98	108	105	311	235	423	508	1,166	1,
	Wolverhampton		46,937	126	132	151	409	220	487	395	1,102	1,
	West Bromwich		34,616	65	85	89	239	311	761	880	1,952	2,
	Dudley	Worcester	66,009	49	82	76	207	450	1,027	1,073	2,550	2,
	Aston	Warwick	36,635	58	65	68	191	198	499	511	1,208	1,
Ribbon.	Foleshill		11,965	39	54	60	153	130	245	230	605	
	Nuneaton		12,868	57	89	78	224	356	670	806	1,832	2,
			233,961	492	615	627	1,734	1,900	4,112	4,403	10,415	12,

dermentioned Unions during the Quarter ended Lady-day, 1840.

ling Lady-day, 1840.

Per cent. of Paupers on Population.	Number of able-bodied Paupers relieved.											Per cent. of able-bodied Paupers relieved on Population.	Does the Union possess an efficient Workhouse?
	On account of Sickness or Accident.				Out of Work and other Causes.				Totals.				
	In-door.		Out-door.		In-door.		Out-door.						
	Men.	Women.	Men.	Women.	Men.	Women.	Men.	Women.	Men.	Women.	Total.		
·719	6	5	85	126	13	8	4	4	108	143	251	.895	Yes.
·887	8	6	90	110	23	19	..	..	121	135	256	2·407	Yes.
·244	5	2	53	68	3	5	2	34	63	109	172	·778	Yes.
·689	..	..	101	118	13	12	..	..	114	130	244	2·471	Yes.
·184	8	4	55	58	15	4	6	5	84	71	155	1·564	Yes.
·269	24	18	56	68	8	7	..	..	88	93	181	1·143	Yes. The number of vagrants relieved in this Union is very great; out of the total number of 682 relieved in the workhouse, 339 are of this class.
·711	1	..	84	103	5	17	10	11	100	131	231	1·679	Yes.
042	3	2	87	95	7	12	2	5	99	114	213	1·113	Yes.
124	1	..	130	142	10	21	6	9	147	172	319	2·062	Yes.
176	4	2	54	53	2	1	5	22	65	78	143	1·057	Yes.
521	5	2	105	178	4	13	6	12	120	205	325	1·750	Yes.
879	3	3	89	48	8	10	2	4	102	65	167	1·001	Yes.
265	8	6	32	45	..	3	4	5	44	59	103	·901	Yes.
184	8	1	67	75	4	14	19	21	98	111	209	·612	Yes.
318	84	51	1,088	1,287	115	146	66	132	1,353	1,616	2,969	1·269	
924	2	1	82	89	13	13	..	..	97	103	200	·802	Yes.
219	31	19	44	45	12	11	8	9	95	84	179	·381	Yes.
329	2	3	129	142	2	5	26	28	159	178	337	·973	These Unions possess two workhouses each, but they are entirely inefficient as a test; there is no classification, and no employment is provided; and the guardians have hitherto refused to erect suitable workhouses.
176	11	13	129	122	..	7	16	13	156	155	311	·471	
818	2	5	48	48	9	6	..	1	59	60	119	·300	Yes.
335	..	1	25	28	11	13	..	..	36	42	78	·651	Yes.
977	1	4	66	84	23	24	113	171	203	283	486	3·776	No; but a suitable workhouse is in the course of completion.
192	49	46	523	558	70	79	163	222	805	905	1,710	·730	

A TABLE showing the Average Expenditure for the Relief of the Poor in the undermentioned Unions, for the Thr

		NAME OF UNION.	County in which situate.	Population in 1831.	Average Expenditure for the Relief of the Poor for Three Years preceding the formation of the Union.	Average Cost per Head on the Population, calculated on the preceding column.	Expenditure for the Relief: In-maintenance.	Expenditure for the Relief: Out-relief.
					£.	£. s. d.	£. s. d.	£. s.
Agricultural.		Bedford	Beds	28,033	25,716	0 18 4	1,558 16 1¾	6,955 2
		Woburn	Beds	10,633	10,935	1 0 6¾	832 6 3	2,696 1
		Newport Pagnell	Bucks	22,087	17,277	0 15 7½	1,203 18 2¾	6,036 12
		Berkhampstead	Herts	9,871	7,750	0 15 8¼	552 11 2	2,677 7
		Hemel Hempstead	Herts	9,910	5,672	0 11 5¼	896 7 1	1,252 7
		St. Albans	Herts	15,833	8,488	0 10 8½	1,858 9 0	1,015 8
		Brixworth	North-ampton.	13,751	12,469	0 18 1½	649 14 9½	5,264 14
		Daventry	North-ampton.	19,137	16,554	0 17 3½	1,219 15 8¾	5,403 5
		Kettering	North-ampton.	15,464	15,754	1 0 3¾	1,048 10 0¾	7,096 16
		Oundle	North-ampton.	13,517	8,901	0 13 2	866 2 3	3,342 14
		Wellingborough	North-ampton.	18,571	14,782	0 15 11	819 15 0	5,897 19
		Rugby	Warwick	16,668	11,028	0 13 2¾	512 2 10½	2,985 7
		Solihull	Warwick	11,433	5,813	0 10 2	606 16 9	1,638 2
		Warwick	Warwick	28,924	12,245	0 8 5½	1,292 7 0¾	6,597 15
				233,832	173,384	0 14 9¾	13,917 12 4¾	58,859 16
Manufacturing and Mining.	Iron.	Wallsall	Stafford	24,931	5,297	0 4 2¾	1,528 8 10½	2,181 2
	Iron.	Wolverhampton	Stafford	46,937	9,021	0 3 10	2,056 17 5¼	2,695 7
	Iron.	West Bromwich	Stafford	34,616	6,584	0 3 9½	1,619 12 8	4,348 18
	Coal. Hardware.	Dudley	Worcester	66,009	11,455	0 3 5½	1,083 6 8¼	7,284 11
	Coal. Hardware.	Aston	Warwick	36,635	8,813	0 4 9½	909 13 0½	3,533 11
	Ribbon.	Foleshill	Warwick	11,965	5,621	0 9 4¾	564 18 4¼	1,442 1
	Ribbon.	Nuneaton	Warwick	12,868	6,971	0 10 10	1,097 19 6¾	3,712 14
				233,961	53,762	0 4 7	8,860 16 7½	25,203 7

(a) Including salaries to officers, rent of workhouses (when rented), interest on loans for building, and expenses of alterations and r this year, are not included in this amount; as money has been borrowed in some, and not in other instances, the insertion of these am

(b) In this column the same payments are included as were included in the averages taken on the formation of the Unions, so the columns under those heads.

previous to their formation, and the Expenditure in the same Unions for the Year ended Lady-day, 1840.

Poor for the Year ending Lady-day, 1840.			Average Cost per Head on the Population, calculated on the			Expenditure for the Year ended Lady-day, 1840, compared with the Averages.		Does the Union possess an efficient Workhouse?
	Totals.							
...blishment ...rges (a).	In-maintenance and Out-relief.	In-maintenance, Out-relief, and Establishment Charges (b).	In-maintenance and Out-relief.	Establishment Charges.	In-maintenance, Out-Relief, and Establishment Charges.	Decrease per Cent.	Increase per Cent.	
s. d.	£. s. d.	£. s. d.	s. d.	s. d.	s. d.			
2 6 5¾	8,513 18 9¼	10,176 5 3	6 0¾	1 2	7 3	60 4/10	..	Yes.
5 3 9	3,528 8 1¾	4,643 11 10¾	6 7½	2 1	8 8¾	57 5/10	..	Yes.
7 6 8	7,240 11 2¼	8,457 17 10¼	6 6½	1 1	7 7¾	51	..	Yes.
4 5 4½	3,229 18 5¼	3,974 3 9¾	6 6½	1 6	8 0½	48 7/10	..	Yes.
7 6 9¾	2,148 14 7½	3,326 1 5¼	4 4	2 4½	6 8½	41 3/10	..	Yes.
4 12 2	2,873 17 7	3,838 9 9	3 7½	1 2½	4 10	54 7/10	..	Yes.
0 15 3	5,914 9 6½	7,085 4 9½	8 7	1 8½	10 3½	43 1/10	..	Yes.
8 15 5	6,623 1 2¼	8,431 16 7¼	6 11	1 10½	8 9¾	49	..	Yes.
1 9 2½	8,145 6 6¼	9,426 15 8¾	10 6¼	1 7¾	12 2¼	40 1/10	..	Yes.
8 5 5½	4,208 17 1¼	5,517 2 6¾	6 2½	1 11	8 1¾	38	..	Yes.
8 17 8	6,717 14 0½	7,886 11 8½	7 2¾	1 3	8 5¾	46 6/10	..	Yes.
5 1 0	3,497 10 3¼	4,502 11 3¼	4 2¼	1 2¼	5 4¾	59 1/10	..	Yes.
1 5 10¾	2,244 19 1¼	3,066 5 0	3 11	1 5	5 4¼	47 2/10	..	Yes.
6 8 7	7,890 2 6	9,986 11 1	5 5¼	1 5¼	6 10¾	18 4/10	..	Yes.
1 19 8¾	72,777 9 0¼	90,319 8 9	6 2½	1 6	7 8½	47 9/10	..	
2 11 3	3,709 11 6	4,852 2 9	2 11½	0 10¾	3 10½	8 4/10	..	Yes.
9 17 8¾	4,752 4 11¼	6,812 2 8	2 0¼	0 10½	2 10¾	24 4/10	..	Yes.
9 10 7½	5,968 11 7	6,888 2 2½	3 5¼	0 6¼	3 11¾	..	4 6/10	These Unions possess two workhouses each, but they are entirely inefficient as a test; there is no classification, and no employment is provided; and the Guardians have hitherto refused to erect suitable workhouses.
3 19 9	8,367 18 0½	9,681 17 9½	2 6¼	0 4¾	2 11	15 4/10	..	
1 16 0	4,448 4 11¾	5,530 0 11¾	2 5	0 7	3 0	37 2/10	..	Yes.
4 15 2½	2,006 19 5¼	2,641 14 7¾	3 4¼	1 0½	4 4¾	53	..	Yes.
8 16 10½	4,810 13 9¼	5,519 10 7¾	7 5½	1 1	8 6¾	20 8/10	..	No; but a suitable workhouse is in the course of completion.
1 7 5¼	34,064 4 3	41,925 11 8¼	2 10¾	0 8	3 7	22	..	

khouses. The portion of the loans for building the workhouses and the cost of furnishing new houses which have been paid during have prevented me from making the comparison I wished.

rison may be fairly made as to the increase or decrease of expenditure since the formation of the Unions, and which will be seen by

To these tables I beg most respectfully to call your attention, and you will by the following analysis at once see the comparative state of pauperism in the agricultural and manufacturing Unions referred to.

Description of Unions.	Population.	Average Cost per Head on Population.	Per Cent. of Paupers on Population.
		s. d.	
Agricultural Unions .	233,832	7 8½	8·318
Manufacturing Unions .	233,961	3 7	5·192

It is not only for the sake of the comparison thus exhibited between the state of pauperism in the agricultural and manufacturing Unions that I call your attention to the annexed tables, but also as to the comparison between Unions of the same class. To attempt to account for the difference in the state of pauperism in the several Unions would occupy more time than I have at this moment at my disposal, but by a reference to the returns of the Unions of St. Albans and Wolverhampton you will perceive that the principles of the Poor Law Amendment Act have been kept more in view by the Guardians of those Unions than in others, by the proportion of relief they have afforded in their workhouses, and that the result of such an adherence has realized the expectations of those who advised the adoption of that measure.

Let me also draw your attention to the state of the Foleshill and Nuneaton Unions. The trade carried on in these Unions is the same, namely, the manufacture of ribbons; and the only disadvantage that I am aware of that the latter Union labours under, is its greater distance from Coventry, the principal seat of that branch of manufacture. In the former Union, relief to the able-bodied has been confined to the workhouse; in the latter, in consequence of the incomplete state of the workhouse, I was obliged to advise that the prohibitory order should be suspended, and the result will be seen by a reference to the tables appended to this report. On the suspension of the prohibitory order in the Nuneaton Union, the Guardians at my suggestion passed a resolution to the following effect:—

"That a committee be formed to consider the best means of providing employment for such paupers as are now applying for relief, and that they be empowered to take a stone pit and engage a person to superintend such work, it being a strong recommendation that no pauper to be employed in any work to be provided by this Board shall be engaged for a less period than a week, and that they be employed at task-work and paid one half of their wages in kind."

This resolution, from the fear of the expense it would entail on the several parishes, and from a feeling of opposition to the law, I could never get willingly carried out; and the consequence has been, that for the last half year a very large majority of the operative ribbon weavers have, at different periods, been brought to a state of pauperism. The manufacturers have at intervals given work to all the weavers, and the consequence has been almost universal pauperism amongst the population employed in this trade. Had a portion of such population been taken to the workhouse, and a portion employed in the way I suggested, it is not unfair to assume that those really required to supply the market with the goods required would have been saved from much suffering and degradation, and that a less expenditure of public money would have taken place. The Union workhouse at Nuneaton is now being enlarged, and I trust the day is not distant when not only pauperism will be reduced to the same ratio as at Foleshill, but that the distress which prevails will not (as it now does) by many degrees exceed in the former Union that which prevails in the latter.

Now, as the Unions of St. Albans, Wolverhampton, and Foleshill have been favourably noticed by me in this report, in comparison with other Unions, it becomes necessary that I should, in the first instance, state that the Guardians adopted the practice of applying the workhouse in the cases they now do previous to the issue of the prohibitory order to them by your Board; and, in the next, make a few observations as to the operation of the law, so far as the poor themselves are concerned; and as to the first named Union, I shall dismiss this part of my subject by giving you an extract from a Report made by the Board of Guardians itself to your Board on the 10th day of April last:—

"Among many proofs which may be adduced of the improvement gradually taking place in the general character of the labouring classes, arising from this change in the system of administering relief (*i. e.* the general application of the workhouse principle in all new permanent cases), a very gratifying one is the progress made by the benefit society established at St. Albans in 1836 for provision in sickness and old age. Although there are several other local clubs, the number of members of this society, consisting chiefly of young people of both sexes, now amounts to 203, and the stock of the society to upwards of 300*l*. Much, however, yet remains to be done before the poor can be entirely weaned from that reliance upon parochial aid (so detrimental to habits of industry and forethought) on which they had been so long accustomed to depend, and which the system of out-door relief so greatly encouraged. It is only by carefully guarding against any recurrence to this pernicious practice, by a strict adherence to the principles of the present law, that a relapse into all the evils of the former system can be effectually prevented."

And as to the Unions of Wolverhampton and Foleshill, I assure you I have never heard the least complaint, so far as the poor are concerned; but, on the contrary, it has been frequently communicated to me that their condition has been improved by the change made in the administration of relief, both in a moral and physical point of view. And I would particularly observe, with reference to the former Union, that the comparison of the workhouse which the Guardians have provided themselves with, with those of the Unions of Dudley and West Bromwich, where the Guardians, in consequence of their hostility to the law, have refused to build, is highly favourable to the course they have adopted.

In the Wolverhampton workhouse, the classification of the inmates is complete; the aged and the sick are placed apart from the young and healthy, and every comfort is secured to them; the youth of both sexes are separated, and each preserved from the contamination of associating with the adult population (and amongst which class, in every workhouse, are to be found many of abandoned and profligate characters), and means of education are provided for them; the able-bodied are well provided for, and only kept under such restraint and regulations as are sufficient to make them feel that a maintenance derived from honest industry is preferable to a dependence on that which is afforded at the public cost.

At West Bromwich and Dudley, from the very construction of the wretched premises used as workhouses, any attempt at classification would prove fruitless, and it is needless for me to observe that in these workhouses a very opposite state of things prevails to that which I have described as existing at Wolverhampton. So very strongly has this been impressed on my mind, that I have on several occasions protested to the Guardians, that neither yourselves nor myself can be held to be responsible for any moral or physical disaster that may occur to the inmates of either of their workhouses. And I will here just observe, that on my first entering on my present district, in September, 1838, I found that portions of the workhouses in the Unions of Dudley and West Bromwich were used for the purpose of confining prisoners, and that communication with them and the paupers was not only easy, but could not be avoided. On one occasion, in one of the workhouses in the latter Union, I saw a prisoner in chains seated in the ordinary day-room with the paupers. On my bringing this matter before the Boards of Guardians at Dudley, they so far altered their cells as to prevent any communication with the inmates; and at West Bromwich the Guardians, after much trouble with the parochial authorities at Wednesbury, disallowed entirely the practice of sending prisoners to the workhouse.

It would, indeed, be well if some of the declaimers against the Poor Law Amendment Act were, by personal inspection of well-regulated workhouses, to convince themselves of the state of things they exhibit; and I am sure no candid or impartial visitor to the workhouses I have now described could come to any other conclusion than that those Guardians who have acted up to the spirit of that law, have secured for their poorer neighbours moral and physical advantages which those who take credit for a greater share of humanity have not been able to provide for those of the same class under their charge.

The chief objections raised to the workhouse principle are on the score of humanity, and the great expense it is calculated to entail on the parishes. To the first objection so much has been said and written, that I shall in this place only refer you to my previous statement on the Wolverhampton Union, and the comparison I have hinted at between that and the Unions of Dudley and West Bromwich, and I am sure it would be no difficult task to find many parallel instances; and as the best answer to the latter,

I again venture to draw your attention to the comparative state of the Unions of Wolverhampton and St. Albans (where, as I have before observed, the workhouse principle is more strictly enforced), with the other Unions referred to in the annexed table, and you will not fail to notice that these Unions (although so considerable a reduction has been made in their expenditure) were not previously so heavily pauperised as many others.

The following table will exhibit the results and comparisons I have last referred to:—

Description of Unions.	Average Cost per Head on Population calculated on the Average Expenditure previous to the formation of the Union.	Average Cost per Head on Population calculated on the Expenditure for the Year ended Lady-day 1840.	Proportion per Cent. of Expenditure of the Relief given in the Workhouse.	Decrease per Cent. of Expenditure for the Year ended Lady-day 1840, compared with the Averages previous to the formation of the Union.
	s. d.	s. d.		
Total of Agricultural Unions (including St. Albans) . .	14 9¼	7 8½	19·122	47 9-10ths
St. Albans (separately) where the Workhouse principle is strictly applied	10 8½	4 10	64·671	54 7-10ths
Total of Manufacturing Unions (including Wolverhampton) . . .	4 7	3 7	26·009	22
Wolverhampton (separately) where the Workhouse principle was strictly applied . . .	3 10	2 10¾	43·265	24 25ths

I have the honour to be, Gentlemen,
Your most obedient servant,
ROB. WEALE,
July 31, 1840. *Assist. Commissioner.*

II.—RELIEF:—PROHIBITION OF, OUT OF THE WORKHOUSE, TO ABLE-BODIED AND NON-RESIDENT PAUPERS.

THE Board took into consideration the several orders issued on the subject of relief to the able-bodied and non-resident paupers, together with the reports of the Assistant Commissioners in reference to various points of construction and matters of practice which have arisen at different periods; and it was ordered that the following Instructional Letter and Amended Prohibitory Order should be issued to the undermentioned Unions:—

INSTRUCTIONAL LETTER *as to Amended Prohibitory Order.*

Poor Law Commission Office,
Somerset House,
August, 1840.

SIR,—The Poor Law Commissioners have had under their consideration their orders regulating the relief of able-bodied and non-resident paupers, in reference to various points of construction and matters of practice which from time to time have arisen.

The Commissioners have embodied in the accompanying order the various exceptions and provisions which experience has shown to be now advisable; and they propose not only to issue the order, as thus framed, in future cases, but to substitute it in those Unions to which any of the previous orders prohibiting out-door relief have been issued.

The Commissioners request the attention of the Board of Guardians to the following remarks, in reference to those parts of the order which appear to require explanation; and they are desirous that if the Guardians perceive any difficulty unexplained, they should communicate with the Commissioners accordingly, and make such suggestions as may occur to them.

Relief of Able-bodied.

1.—ARTICLE I.—The only remark on the prohibitory clause which the Commissioners need make is, that the Guardians under this clause are not bound to require any child of an able-bodied person who can support itself to accompany its parent into the workhouse, if it appear expedient that such child should continue in employment.

2.—[*Exception* 1.]—By "sudden and urgent necessity" (which words are used in § 54 of the Poor Law Amendment Act,) the Commissioners understand any case of destitution requiring instant relief, before the person can be received into the workhouse; as for example, when a person is deprived of his usual means of support, by means of fire, or storm, or inundation, or robbery, or riot, or any other similar cause which he could not control when it had occurred, and which it would have been impossible or very difficult for him to foresee and prevent.

It is to be remarked further, that the present exemption does not authorize *permanent* out-door relief in any case. A case originally of sudden and urgent necessity, which subsequently requires continued relief, loses its character of suddenness and urgency. The relief subsequently required will be either ordinary relief, and therefore to be given in the workhouse, or it may be extraordinary, and given, for example, under the second exception of Article I.

3.—[*Exception* 2.]—The second exception provides for the case of any able-bodied man who is himself insane or temporarily sick, or who has met with an accident, or any of whose family require to be relieved on the ground of insanity, infirmity, accident, or sickness.

4.—[*Exception* 3.]—In most Unions to which the prohibitory order has been issued, relief has been given to able-bodied male persons for the funerals of their families, without requiring them to come into the workhouse; and the Commissioners, although not unaware of the possibility of abuses arising as to this branch of relief, are not prepared to prohibit it. The Commissioners think, therefore, that it is better to admit it as an express exception, than to allow it to be given under a lax construction of the term "*sudden and urgent necessity,*" in Exception 1.

5.—[*Exception* 4.]—The exception of widows during the first six months of their widowhood is adopted in conformity to the practice of a very well managed Union in Sussex, and with a view of enabling persons thus unfortunately situated to have an adequate interval for the purpose of making such arrangements for their support as their altered condition may require.

6.—[*Exception* 5.]—The exception in favour of widows with children, so far as it relates to able-bodied widows in employment, is one respecting which the Commissioners themselves entertain strong doubts, and they request that the Guardians will exercise great circumspection in applying it in practice. The Commissioners request the Guardians, when administering relief under it, to take into account, that when small weekly allowances in aid of wages are made, they too commonly serve to excuse relations from the payment of contributions to a much larger amount; and that the out-door allowances when given indiscriminately in widowhood tend to put an end to provident habits, in respect of insurances in sick clubs or otherwise. It should, moreover, be borne in mind that allowances made by the parish to able-bodied widows in employment do not always confer the advantages intended, inasmuch as their wages, as in the case of able-bodied men, are commonly reduced in consideration of the allowance from the parish; and that such reduction of the wages, combined with the excuse furnished to relations or friends for withholding their contributions, together with the pauper habits thus engendered, often renders such allowances to widows in aid of wages an injury rather than a benefit to them; whilst in some districts this class of able-bodied widows is so numerous that their labour (thus depreciated at the expense of the rate-payers) is substituted for the more highly paid labour of independent labourers.

7.—The Commissioners trust, that the Guardians will seldom find that the ordinary rate of earnings of women is so low as not to enable them to support one child at the least; and that the Guardians will not adopt any such general rule as that of relieving all widows with one, or with any fixed number of children, without careful inquiry into every case thus to be relieved.

8.—[*Exception* 6.]—It sometimes happens that a person is confined for debt in a prison where no provision is made out of a prison-fund, or out of the county-rates, for his maintenance. In such a case as this, it is advisable that the Guardians of his Union should be empowered to relieve him. It is further necessary that the Guardians should be empowered to give relief to the wife and children in cases where the husband cannot be required to enter the workhouse.

9.—[*Exception* 7.]—The state of the law in reference to married women explained in *par.* 10, and the peculiar rights and obligations of soldiers, sailors, and marines, render it desirable to give great latitude to the proceedings of the Board of Guardians in respect of the families of persons in these departments of the Queen's service. The seventh exception, therefore, allows of relief of any kind being given to the wife or children of a soldier, sailor, or marine, whether in or out of the workhouse, without requiring the husband to come into the workhouse.

10.—[*Exception* 8.]—The eighth exception provides for the case of a wife whose husband is absent from her, either by desertion or otherwise, and it is necessary, in consequence of the state of the law applicable to women thus situated. It is held that in such cases relief to the children is not relief to the wife; consequently, the wife cannot be compelled to come with her children into the workhouse. If, however, she require relief for herself, the Guardians may require her to receive it in the workhouse; and if she require relief for her children, the Guardians may require such of them as are above the age of nurture to receive it in the workhouse, whether she do or do not come into the workhouse. As regards, however, children under the age of nurture who may be living with the mother, the Guardians cannot remove them from her; so that if she require relief for them and them only, and she will not come into the workhouse, the Guardians must give out-relief if relief be necessary.

11.—ARTICLE II.—The regulation which requires the entry on the minutes of the medical officer's report, or a medical certificate in case of relief being given to an able-bodied pauper on account of sickness, accident, &c., has been suggested to the Commissioners, in consequence of a tendency which has displayed itself in various parts of the country, to make exceptions to the prohibitory order on too slight grounds, and the Commissioners think that this provision will have the useful effect of calling the special attention of the Guardians to every such case.

If the pauper should not have been attended by a medical officer of the Union, a certificate may be given either by the medical practitioner who may have attended him, or by a medical officer of the Union who may visit him for the purpose.

12.—Upon the portion of the order which relates to the relief of the able-bodied, the Commissioners have only further to observe, that, although the exceptions introduced in it are larger and better defined than those contained in the previous orders, yet it is upon the whole more restrictive than most of the previous orders, inasmuch as it extends to single women, including those with illegitimate children, and to widows without children.

Relief of Non-residents.

13.—ARTICLE III.—As respects the portion of the order which relates to the relief of non-residents, the Commissioners desire to point out that after the date of the order it will prevent new cases of non-resident relief, with the exceptions therein mentioned. On the other hand, it does not require that a pauper, in order to receive relief, should reside in the parish to which he is chargeable, provided that he be resident in the Union; and in this respect it is rather less strict than the fifth rule in the original regulations, under which new cases of widows could not permanently be relieved, unless they resided within their parishes. [See First Annual Report, 8vo. Appendix, page 85.]

14.—Under the rule as now framed, the Guardians may relieve a pauper residing within the Union, though not residing in the parish to which he belongs; the Commissioners, however, are far from wishing to encourage even this species of non-resident relief. It is true that the frauds and evils which are incidental to non-resident relief, in consequence of the want of inspection, and the difficulty of transmitting the relief, do not occur with reference to paupers resident within the Union, who are within the reach of the relieving officers: but, nevertheless, the rate-payers of the parish charged with the relief, who by means of the quarterly lists of paupers can, by personal observation of those who reside in their parish, ascertain whether they are fit objects for relief, are deprived of this protection where the pauper for whom they pay is resident at a distant part of the Union. Moreover, relief of non-residents is almost always *partial* relief; and therefore liable to the objections to which partial relief is liable. The relief of paupers out of their parish and out of the relieving district in which the parish is comprised is not unattended with difficulties both of a legal and practical nature, which are sufficient to make it desirable that the Guardians should not, without sufficient ground, permit new cases of this nature even within the Union.

15.—[Article III. *Exception* 1.]—The Commissioners have not introduced into the second branch of the order an exception on account of sudden and urgent necessity. [See above, paragraph 2.] Cases of sudden and urgent necessity manifestly require the prompt attention and vigilant inspection which can only be exercised by the Guardians and their officers in the district where the necessity arises.

The Commissioners have introduced the present exception in order to meet the cases of vagrants, who may become casually destitute within the Union. It is the duty of the Guardians to relieve persons so situated, without reference to the place of their settlement or residence. The Commissioners have had occasion to address several communications to the Metropolitan Boards of Guardians, on the duty of the locality to relieve all cases of urgent destitution. [See the Commissioners' Fourth Annual Report, 8vo. pages 154, 155, 156, and 157, Appendix A., No. 2; and Fifth Annual Report, 8vo. page 87, Appendix A., No. 10.]

16.—[*Exception* 2.]—This exception is intended to permit poor persons to be sent to establishments out of the Union, intended for the treatment of their respective infirmities, as to hospitals for the sick, asylums for the insane, and schools for the blind or deaf and dumb.

17.—[*Exception* 3.]—The second exception is intended expressly to except from the operation of the order the cases of relief given to non-resident lunatics in asylums under orders of justices, to debtors confined under mesne process entitled to relief under the 52 Geo. III., c. 160, s. 1, and to persons under orders of removal.

18.—[*Exception* 4.]—This exception is similar to Exception 4 in Article I, the reasons for which are stated above in paragraph 5.

19.—[*Exception* 5.]—This exception permits the Guardians to send pauper children to a workhouse or establishment for the training of pauper children, which may be situated out of their Union. On the advantages of combining Unions for the education of pauper children, the Commissioners have made some remarks in their Report on the further Amendment of the Law, (Dec. 1839.) p. 55—59.

20.—[*Exception* 6.]—This exception resembles Exception 8, Article I., the reasons for which are stated above in paragraph 10.

21.—[*Exception* 7.]—This exception permits the continuance of non-resident relief to all paupers (not being able-bodied persons within Article I.), who were in the receipt of such relief from some parish in the Union, within the twelve calendar months next preceding the date of the order. Consequently, it permits the continuance of non-resident relief to the infirm through age or any other cause, and to able-bodied widows with a child or children, who were in the receipt of parochial relief from the Union within that period.

Cases of peculiar Urgency.

22.—ARTICLE IV.—It is possible, although not probable, that cases may occasionally arise which present very peculiar circumstances, and which do not fall within any of the exceptions contained in the present order. The Commissioners think it desirable in cases of that kind, in which the immediate withdrawal or denial of out-door relief might appear likely to produce serious evil to the applicant, that the Guardians should give out-door relief, or take a portion of the applicants' family into the workhouse, and report the case within fifteen days to the Poor Law Commissioners, as a case of peculiar urgency, in order that the Commissioners may give their opinion thereupon. The Commissioners have accordingly introduced a proviso at the end of the order, enabling the Guardians to pursue this course with respect to exceptional cases of this description.

Relief by way of Loan.

23.—ARTICLE V.—The first part of Article V. is introduced in order to put an end to a misapprehension which existed in some Boards of Guardians, viz.—that although the prohibitory order prevented them from *giving* out-door relief, they might nevertheless *lend* it. The second part of the article enables the Guardians to make all the relief which may be given to persons above twenty-one years of age, or their families, a loan, under the 59th section of the Poor Law Amendment Act.

Signed by order of the Board,
EDWIN CHADWICK, *Secretary*.

To the Clerk of the Board of Guardians.

Amended Prohibitory Order.

To the Guardians of the Poor of The UNION, in the Count of

To the Churchwardens and Overseers of the several Parishes and Places comprised within the said Union.

To the Clerk or Clerks to the Justices of Petty Sessions, held for the Division or Divisions in which the Parishes and Places comprised within the said Union are situate;—and to all others whom it may concern.

WHEREAS by a certain Order bearing date the day of in the year of our Lord One thousand eight hundred and the Poor Law Commissioners did, amongst other matters, make certain regulations concerning the administration of relief to be given to able-bodied poor persons, and to poor persons not resident in their Parish or Union, in the Union, in the Count of ;

And whereas it is now expedient that the regulations contained in the present Order should be substituted for the said regulations contained in the above recited Order;

Now, therefore, in pursuance of the powers and authorities vested in us under and by virtue of an Act passed in the fifth year of the reign of his late Majesty King William the Fourth, intituled, "An Act for the Amendment and better Administration of the Laws relating to the Poor in England and Wales," we, the Poor Law Commissioners, do hereby rescind the said regulations contained in the above recited Order.

ARTICLE I. And we do hereby order, direct, and declare, that from and after the day of every able-bodied person, male or female, requiring relief within the said Union, shall be relieved wholly in the workhouse of the said Union, together with such of the family of every such able-bodied person as may be resident with him or her, and may not be in employment, and together with the wife of every such able-bodied male person, if he be a married man, and if she be resident with him; save and except in the following cases:—

1st. Where such person shall require relief on account of sudden and urgent necessity.

2nd. Where such person shall require relief on account of any sickness, accident, or bodily or mental infirmity, affecting such person, or any of his or her family.

3rd. Where such person shall require relief for the purpose of defraying the expenses, either wholly or in part, of the funeral of any of his or her family.

4th. Where such person, being a widow, shall be in the first six months of her widowhood.

5th. Where such person shall be a widow and have a legitimate child or legitimate children dependent upon her, and incapable of earning his, her, or their livelihood, and no illegitimate child born after the commencement of her widowhood.

6th. Where such person shall be confined in any gaol or place of safe custody.

7th. Where the relief shall be required by the wife, child, or children of any able-bodied man who shall be in the service of Her Majesty as a soldier, sailor, or marine.

8th. Where any able-bodied person, not being a soldier, sailor, or marine, shall not reside within the said Union, but the wife, child, or children of such person shall reside within the same, the Board of Guardians of the said Union, according to their discretion, may afford relief in the workhouse to such wife, child, or children, or may allow out-door relief for any such child or children being within the age of nurture, and resident with the mother within the said Union.

ARTICLE II. And we do further order and direct, that in every case in which out-door relief shall be given on account of sickness, accident, or infirmity, to any able-bodied male person resident within the said Union, or to any member of the family of any able-bodied male person, a special entry shall be made in the minutes of the proceedings of the Board of Guardians of the day on which the relief is ordered or subsequently allowed, which entry shall contain an extract from the medical officer's weekly report (if any such officer shall have attended the case), stating the nature of such sickness, accident, or infirmity, or, if the Board of Guardians shall think fit, a certificate under the hand of a medical officer of the Union, or of the medical practitioner in attendance on the party, shall be laid before the Board, stating the nature of such sickness, accident, or infirmity, and a copy of the same shall be entered in the minutes of the proceedings of the said Board of the day on which the relief is ordered, or subsequently allowed.

ARTICLE III. And we do further order and direct, that from and after the said day of , no relief shall be given from the poor-rates of any parish or place comprised in the said Union, to any person who does not reside in some parish or place comprised therein, save and except in the following cases—

1st. Where such person, being casually within such parish or place, shall become destitute.

2nd. Where such person shall be maintained in any hospital, asylum, or other establishment for the treatment of any bodily or mental disease, not being situate within the said Union.

3rd. Where such person shall be entitled to receive relief from any parish or place in which he may not be resident, under any order which justices may by law be authorized to make.

4th. Where such person, being a widow, shall be in the first six months of her widowhood.

5th. Where the relief shall be allowed for a child under the age of sixteen maintained in a workhouse or establishment for the education of pauper children not situate within the said Union.

6th. Where any person shall not reside within the said Union, and the wife, child, or children of such person shall reside within the same, relief may be afforded to such wife, child, or children, by the Guardians of the Union, as they shall think fit.

7th. Where such person shall, within the twelve calendar months next preceding the date of this order, have been in the receipt of relief from some parish in the said Union not being then resident in the parish in which he or she was settled.

ARTICLE IV. Provided always, and we do hereby declare, that in case the Guardians of the said Union shall depart in any particular instance from any of the regulations hereinbefore contained, and shall within fifteen days after such departure report the same and the grounds thereof to the Poor Law Commissioners, and if the Poor Law Commissioners shall approve of such departure, then the relief granted in such particular instance shall, if otherwise lawful, not be deemed to be unlawful or be subject to be disallowed.

ARTICLE V. And we do further order and direct, that no relief which shall be contrary to any regulation in this order shall be given by way of loan; and that every relief which may be given to or on account of any person above the age of twenty-one, or to his wife or any part of his family under the age of sixteen under Article I., or any of the exceptions thereto, or under any of the exceptions to Article III., or under the proviso in Article IV., may, if the Guardians shall think fit, be given by way of loan.

Given this day of , &c. &c.

LIST of UNIONS to which the above Order has been issued.

Bedford—Ampthill, Biggleswade.

Cambridge—Cambridge, Caxton and Arrington, Chesterton, Ely, Linton, Newmarket, North Witchford, Whittlesea, Wisbeach.

Chester—Nantwich, Wirrall.

Cornwall—Austel, St., Columb, St. Major, German's, St., Launceston, Liskeard, Penzance, Redruth.

Cumberland—Brampton.

Devon—Axminster, Bideford, Crediton, East Stonehouse, Honiton, Kingsbridge, Newton Abbott, Okehampton, Plympton St. Mary, Tavistock, Thomas, St., Tiverton, Torrington, Totnes.

Dorset—Beaminster, Blandford, Bridport, Cerne, Dorchester, Poole, Shaftesbury, Sherborne, Sturminster, Wareham and Purbeck, Weymouth, Wimborne and Cranborne.

Durham—Auckland, Chester-le-Street, Darlington, Durham, Lanchester, Sedgefield, South Shields, Stockton, Teesdale, Weardale.

Essex—Billericay, Braintree, Chelmsford, Colchester, Dunmow, Epping, Halstead, Lexden and Winstree, Maldon, Ongar, Orsett, Rochford, Romford, Saffron Walden, Tendring, West Ham, Witham.

Gloucester—Chipping Sodbury, Cirencester, Clifton, Dursley, Stroud, Tetbury, Thornbury, Wheatenhurst.

Herts—Barnet, Bishop Stortford, Buntingford, Hertford, Hitchin, Royston, Ware, Welwyn.

Hunts—Huntingdon, Ives, St., Neots, St.

Kent—Ashford, East, Ashford, West, Cranbrook, Dartford, Elham, Faversham, Gravesend and Milton, Hollingbourn, Hoo, Maidstone, Malling, Medway, Milton, North Aylesford, Romney Marsh, Sevenoaks and Penshurst, Sheppey, Tenterden, Tonbridge.

Leicester—Melton Mowbray.

Lincoln—Caistor, Horncastle.

Norfolk—Guiltcross, Henstead, Loddon and Clavering, Tunstead and Happing, Wayland, Yarmouth, Great.

Northampton—Peterborough.

Northumberland—Alnwick, Belford, Berwick upon Tweed, Castle Ward, Glendale, Tynemouth.

Nottingham—Bingham.

Rutland—Oakham, Uppingham.

Salop—Atcham, Bridgnorth, Church Stretton, Clun, Drayton, Ellesmere, Madely, Newport, Shiffnall, Wellington, Wem.

Somerset—Axbridge, Bath, Bedminster, Bridgwater, Chard, Clutton, Frome, Keynsham, Langport, Shepton Mallett, Taunton, Wellington, Wells, Williton, Wincanton, Yeovil.

Southampton—Alresford, Alton, Andover, Basingstoke, Catherington, Christchurch, Droxford, Fareham, Fordingbridge, Hartley Wintney, Havant, Kingsclere, Lymington, New Forest, Petersfield, Portsea Island, Ringwood, Romsey, Stockbridge, Whitchurch, Winchester.

Suffolk—Blything, Cosford, Hartismere, Hoxne, Ipswich, Mildenhall, Plomesgate, Risbridge, Samford, Stow.

Surrey—Croydon, Dorking, Epsom, Godstone, Guildford, Hambledon, Reigate.

Sussex—Battle, Chailey, Cuckfield, Eastbourne, East Grinstead, Hailsham, Hastings, Horsham, Lewes, Midhurst, Newhaven, Petworth, Rye,

Steyning, Thakeham, Ticehurst, Uckfield, Westbourne, Westfirle.
Westmoreland—East Ward.
Wilts—Alderbury, Amesbury, Bradford, Calne, Chippenham, Cricklade and Wootton Bassett, Devizes, Highworth and Swindon, Malmsbury, Marlborough, Melksham, Mere, Pewsey, Tisbury, Warminster, Westbury and Whorwellsdown, Wilton.
Worcester—Worcester.
Denbigh—Wrexham.

Orders similar to the above, and varying only in a few particulars, have been issued to the following Unions:—

Bedford—Bedford, Leighton Buzzard, Luton, Woburn.
Berks—Abingdon, Bradfield, East Hampstead, Faringdon, Hungerford, Newbury, Reading, Wantage, Wokingham.
Bucks—Amersham, Aylesbury, Buckingham, Newport Pagnell, Winslow, Wycombe.
Chester—Altrincham, Northwich.
Derby—Chesterfield, Derby, Shardlow.
Devon—Barnstaple, South Molton.
Gloucester—Cheltenham, Gloucester, Newent, Northleach, Stow-on-the-Wold, Tewkesbury, Westbury-on-Severn, Wheatenhurst, Winchcombe.
Hereford—Bromyard, Dore, Hereford, Kington, Ledbury, Leominster, Ross, Weobly.
Hertford—Albans, St., Berkhamstead, Hemel-Hempstead, Watford.
Kent—Blean, Bridge, Bromley.
Leicester—Ashby-de-la-Zouch, Barrow-upon-Soar, Billesdon, Blaby, Hinckley, Loughborough, Lutterworth, Market Bosworth, Market Harborough.
Lincoln—Boston, Bourn, Gainsborough, Glanford Brigg, Grantham, Holbeach, Lincoln, Louth, Sleaford, Spalding, Spilsby, Stamford.
Monmouth—Abergavenny, Chepstow, Monmouth, Newport, Pontypool.
Norfolk—Aylsham, Blofield, Depwade, Docking, Downham, Erpingham, Faith, St., Flegg, East and West, Forehoe, Freebridge Lynn, Mitford & Launditch, Swaffham, Thetford, Walsingham.
Northampton—Brackley, Brixworth, Daventry, Hardingstone, Kettering, Northampton, Oundle, Potterspury, Thrapstone, Towcester, Wellingborough.
Nottingham—Basford, East Retford, Mansfield, Newark, Southwell, Worksop.
Oxford—Banbury, Bicester, Chipping Norton, Headington, Henley, Thame, Witney, Woodstock.
Salop—Cleobury Mortimer, Ludlow.
Southampton—South Stoneham.
Stafford—Burton-upon-Trent, Cheadle, Leek, Lichfield, Newcastle-under-Lyme, Penkridge, Seisdon, Stafford, Stone, Tamworth, Uttoxeter, Walsal, West Bromwich, Wolverhampton.
Suffolk—Bosmere and Claydon, Thingoe, Wangford, Woodbridge.
Sussex—Westhampnett.
Warwick—Alcester, Aston, Atherstone, Foleshill, Meriden, Nuneaton, Rugby, Solihull, Southam, Stratford-on-Avon, Warwick.
Worcester—Bromsgrove, Droitwich, Dudley, Evesham, Kidderminster, King's Norton, Martley, Pershore, Shipston-on-Stour, Stourbridge, Tenbury, Upton-on-Severn.
Anglesey—Anglesey.
Brecknock—Brecknock, Crickhowell, Hay.
Cardigan—Aberaeron.
Carmarthen—Carmarthen, Llandilo Fawr, Llandovery, Llanelly, Newcastle on Emlyn.
Carnarvon—Conway.
Glamorgan—Neath, Swansea.
Merioneth—Dolgelly.
Montgomery—Machynlleth.
Pembroke—Haverfordwest.
Radnor—Knighton.

The total number of Unions in England and Wales under the operation of the rules and regulations of the Commissioners is 586 in 412, of which, therefore, out-relief is prohibited to the able-bodied and non-resident, except in cases of sickness, and other cases which are specified in the order.

III.—RATING OF TITHES:—FURTHER INSTRUCTIONAL LETTER TO CHURCHWARDENS AND OVERSEERS THEREON.

The Commissioners having received since the recent decision of the Queen *v.* Capel, numerous applications for their advice and opinion respecting the course to be pursued in rating tithes, directed the following circular to be prepared, and a copy to be transmitted to the churchwardens and overseers of the several parishes in England and Wales.

"*Poor Law Commission Office,*
Somerset House, Sept. 16, 1840.

GENTLEMEN,—Since the decision of the case of the Queen *v.* Capel, the Poor Law Commissioners have received many applications for statements of their views as to the rating of tithes under the provisions of the Parochial Assessments Act, 6 and 7 Wm. IV., c. 96.

I. Previously to that decision, they had recommended that a provisional arrangement should be made, for the purpose of preventing immediate litigation, and arrangements were accordingly made in many parishes, by which the tithe-owner was rated upon the entire net annual value of the tithe—but a smaller sum than the rate so made was collected, and an arrear was allowed to accumulate until the Queen *v.* Capel should be settled, with the understanding that such arrear was to be remitted to the tithe-owner, or paid up by him in whole or in part, according to the event of the decision.

The decision having been come to, and its effect being that the tithe-owner is rateable in respect of his tithe upon its full net annual value, according to the terms of the Parochial Assessments Act—nothing more remains to be done with respect to the arrear in question, but for the overseers to collect so much as appears by the rate-books to have been allowed to accumulate.

II. But the Commissioners learn that in some cases instead of rating the tithe-owner upon the whole net annual value, and then collecting a less amount, according to the suggestions of the Commissioners, the overseers have adopted another course—that, namely, of rating the tithe-owner in a sum less than the net annual value, and collecting the whole of such less sum. In such cases there will be no arrear appearing upon the rate-books, and consequently no arrear now to be collected, and the tithe-owner will be entitled to the benefit of the overseers' arrangement, as by another result of the case he might have been exposed to a prejudice, by the same arrangement.

III. In some cases the Commissioners have been applied to by tithe-owners to recommend a portion of the arrear to be now remitted, on the ground that, besides the objection raised in the Queen *v.* Capel, the tithe-owners had other objections to the rates. The Commissioners cannot make any such recommendation to overseers. The arrears, which have been allowed to accumulate provisionally, had reference solely to the intended trial of the questions raised in the Queen *v.* Capel, and if other objections, not intended to be raised in that case, existed in any instance, the usual remedies should have been resorted to for the relief of the party grieved.

IV. With reference to future rates — the Commissioners now take occasion to state their understanding of the effect of the first section of the Parochial Assessments Act.

1. Tithes, whether they constitute a part of the liability of a parson or vicar, or be in the hands of an appropriator or impropriator, are hereditaments, and are therefore subject to be rated on the estimate of their net annual value, as defined in that clause.—(Regina *v.* Capel.)

2. The gross annual value of the hereditaments is the entire sum which might be received in rent from a tenant, exempt from rates, taxes, or any of the other outgoings described in the first clause of the Act. Where the tithe has been commuted, and the tithe-owner is in the receipt of the tithe commutation rent-charge, the gross annual value will be the gross amount of the commutation rent-charge, including the sum allotted for rates and taxes. But until the tithe-owner is in the enjoyment of the commutation rent-charge, he must continue to be rated in respect of his ability arising from his tithe in the manner in which he actually enjoys it.

This gross annual value, ascertained by reference to the rent-charge, will vary every year, according to the average prices of corn, and the overseers will be bound to rate the tithe-owner on the value of the rent-charge of the current year, just as they are bound to rate all other rate-payers upon the value of the rateable property, estimated at the time of the rate being made.

3. The estimate of the *net annual value* is founded on the supposed rent which might be realized by the letting of the rateable hereditaments. This will entitle the tithe-owner to an advantage which the Commissioners believe he has not in all cases had the benefit of. The rent which a tenant would consent to pay for the rent-charge, supposing the rent-charge to be let, would obviously be a sum which would remunerate him for the trouble of collection, and insure him against all risks of loss of rent-charge itself, and of loss of interest incurred by the obligation to advance rent, and by occasional delays in recovering the rent-charge, and against all incidental expenses incurred in enforcing his rights.

The compensation of the tenant taking those risks will obviously exceed the payment which the tithe-owner would make to an agent or collector, who incurs no risks, and is not bound to insure and pay to the tithe-owner a certain fixed sum at fixed times.

To the benefit involved in this distinction, the Commissioners consider the tithe-owners to be clearly entitled by the express terms of the definition of *net annual value* in the Parochial Assessments Act.

4. Having ascertained the rent at which the rent-charge might be reasonably expected to let, it will next be the duty of the overseers to ascertain the amount of deductions which are to be made in respect of rates and taxes, and other outgoings (if there be any such), which may be necessary for keeping up the value of the hereditament.

The rates and taxes required by the Act to be deducted from the estimate of the gross annual value, are only such as tenants are, by law, liable to. Land-tax, sewer-rates, and the like rates and taxes, being landlord's charges, cannot be deducted.

The value of the rent-charge is known prospectively, and such value constitutes the gross annual value, but no means exist for determining the amount of rates prospectively; these can only be estimated by reference to the amount in the year or years preceding. It would perhaps be most satisfactory in all cases to estimate the probable rates of the ensuing year at the exact amount of the year expiring immediately before the making of a rate; but no objection could be maintained if the estimate was founded on an average of years immediately preceding (as for instance, three years), provided that the average was always founded on the same number of years, terminating always at the time of making the rate, and that the same calculation was applied to all the rateable property in the same parish. The Commissioners consider, however, that the calculation made on the year immediately preceding, will be preferable to any other.

Tithe commutation rent-charge, being a charge to which tithe itself is not liable—no deduction is to be allowed for this. Neither does the tithe commutation rent-charge appear to be a subject of repairs or insurance, or of any other expense for keeping up its value. If no such liability exists, no deduction can be allowed for such outgoings.

Having made these deductions from the supposed rent, the estimate of the *net annual value* will be complete, and the amounts of the *gross annual value* and the *net annual value* thus estimated, are to be inserted in the rate-book in the columns respectively headed "Gross estimated rental" and "Rateable value."

Thus, for example, in the case of the Queen *v.* Capel, in which the rate was held to be free from the objections stated by the appellant, as the grounds of his appeal, the tithe for which the appellant, as vicar of the parish of Watford, received composition, was rated in the following manner:—

	£.	s.	d.	£.	s.	d.
The gross annual value of the tithe compositions was estimated at				660	0	0
From this were deducted—						
1. For the compensation of a lessee undertaking to collect the tithe composition, and to pay a fixed net rent to the tithe-owner . .	37	5	0			
2. For usual tenant's rates and taxes . . . . . } 3. For ecclesiastical dues . }	82	15	0			
Total deductions				120	0	0
Leaving a *net annual value*, or *rateable value*, of				£540	0	0

The foregoing remarks apply equally to the case of tithes in the hands of ecclesiastical and of lay persons and corporations.

5. There are many payments of ecclesiastical tithe-owners consequent upon the receipt of tithe, but which, not being necessary to maintain the value of the tithe, do not appear to constitute subjects for deduction for the gross value of their tithe.

Instalments of payments to Queen Anne's Bounty for advances for improvement of the living, are not allowable, any more than similar charges incurred by other owners of hereditaments for the improvement of their property. Nor are divisions of the net value of the tithe between the tithe-owner and other persons, such as fee-farm rents, allowable.

Expenses of providing for the performance of the duties of incumbency, as for a curate's salary, cannot be deducted; see R. *v.* Joddrell (1 B. and Ad. 403). But ecclesiastical dues, payable by the tithe-owner, were decided by the same case to be a subject of deduction, inasmuch as they diminish the ability of the tithe-owner in respect of which he is by the statute of Elizabeth rateable. The Commissioners believe that this would still be held to be lawful since the passing of the Parochial Assessments Act, and they also believe that an allowance to the tithe-owner for the expense of repairing the chancel would, for the same reason, still be held to be lawful in all cases in which the tithe-owner is liable to that expense.

Signed, &c., GEO. COODE, *Assist. Sec.*

LONDON:
Printed by order of the Poor Law Commissioners, by W. CLOWES and SONS, Stamford Street, and Published by CHARLES KNIGHT and Co., 22, Ludgate-street, Publishers to the Poor Law Commissioners.

AN

OFFICIAL CIRCULAR

OF PUBLIC DOCUMENTS AND INFORMATION:

DIRECTED BY THE POOR LAW COMMISSIONERS TO BE PRINTED, CHIEFLY FOR THE USE OF THE MEMBERS AND PERMANENT OFFICERS OF BOARDS OF GUARDIANS, UNDER THE POOR LAW AMENDMENT ACT.

No. 9. CIRCULAR ISSUED NOVEMBER 10TH, 1840.

Poor Law Commission Office,
Somerset House,
November 6, 1840.

THE Poor Law Commissioners, on a review of their minutes, directed that the minutes and correspondence on the following subjects should be printed and circulated for the information of Guardians and officers of the several Unions, viz.—

By order of the Board,
EDWIN CHADWICK, *Secretary.*

I.—RELIEF, OUT-DOOR: DANGERS OF ITS MISAPPLICATION.

THE Commissioners having taken into consideration the report of their Assistant-Commissioner and various papers with relation to the case of Stephanus Jeffery, a pauper child on whom a coroner's inquest was held in the Axminster Union, directed that the following letter should be sent thereon:—

SIR,—The Poor Law Commissioners have had under their consideration the Report of their Assistant Commissioner, Mr. Gilbert, and the evidence on which it was founded as to the cause of the death of a boy named Stephanus Jeffery, of the parish of Hawkchurch, in the Axminster Union, who is declared by the verdict of a coroner's jury to have died "through the want of the common necessaries of life."

From the best consideration the Commissioners have been enabled to give to the case it appears to them that there is a case of strong suspicion that the death of the deceased was occasioned by a deficiency of food, but not a case of clear proof that such deficiency was the immediate cause of the death.

It appears that Robert Jeffery, the father of the deceased, was a hurdle maker, in the receipt of wages from 12*s*. to 18*s*. per week, renting a cottage and garden and other premises at 9*l*. a year, and in a position of better comfort than most labourers in the same neighbourhood.

It appears that he was member of a sick club, from which he received during his illness 5*s*. per week for the first two weeks of his illness, and 2*s*. 6*d*. per week afterwards, during the three months' illness to which he was subjected, and that he was in receipt of relief from the Union, to which the Commissioners will hereafter advert. The account which he himself gives of his means of maintaining his family is as follows:

"My wages are usually 12*s*. or 14*s*, and I have made as much as 18*s*., but I think not since the winter. My wife used to earn something, about 1*s*. per week, as a lace-mender. One of my children, the eldest boy, 12 years old, works with me at the hurdle making, and the wages I have named are the joint earnings. I belong to a club at Hawkchurch, from which I had for two weeks of my illness 5*s*. a-week as bed-pay, and the rest of the time 2*s*. 6*d*. as walking-pay. I had from the Union surgeon, and by his order, sugar and groats from a shop, two loaves of bread, and some candles; and the relieving officer, after I had received that from the overseers, gave me a note, the value of 4*s*. to be got at More's shop, and three pounds of meat for three weeks My wife during her illness could earn nothing, but my boy earned his victuals. I have often heard the children ask for food, and we most times gave it them, but sometimes we had to go to the shop for it when we had not got it. My wife is ill and in bed, and cannot attend here to-day. I do not recollect any day this last six weeks in which we have not had food in the house, or money to buy it, with a credit on which it could be got. I have got friends well off in the parish, who would never deny me food, if I sent for it; and I have never sent but once, and then I got it; but I always get milk or cream, or something from them, whenever my children go up."

From this account, which is corroborated by other evidence, there appears to have been no general deficiency of means to maintain the children of his family in the same state and condition, and indeed a better state, than that in which other labourers from lower wages maintain their children.

The following is the account which the pauper gives of the deceased child:—

"I had a son Stephanus Jeffery, nearly six years old. He died a fortnight come yesterday. For about two years after his birth he was a very fine child. At that time a cock flew at him and picked his eye out. From that time the child was always ailing in a weak way, and never thrived. He continued thus till the day of his death."

It is asserted by the father that the child had the common food on which the family lived, and that on the night before the morning on which he was found dead in his bed, his mother had given him some gooseberry cake. One of the neighbour's wives who laid out the corpse on the morning on which it was found dead in its bed, states that there was then bread in the house.

It appears that at the time of the death there was no deficiency of means to maintain the child, nor is it alleged by the father that there were, neither is there any reasonable ground for the suggestion that if at that time there had happened to have been a deficiency in the house, proper supplies were not immediately procurable.

But it is stated in evidence that during several years previously to the eleven weeks of illness of the father, and whilst he was in receipt of his full wages and was living as an independent labourer, the neighbours believed that the children were stinted in their allowance of food. Elizabeth Denning, a married woman, and a neighbour, states,

"I have known Robert Jeffery for many years before he was married. I never knew anything of the management of his family, except what I have heard the last twelve months. I have heard it said by different people that the children were very badly off; this is about six months ago; about the same time one of the children came near my window to the door, the boy who has been examined to-day. He sat down in my kitchen; I said, you don't grow, my boy He said no, I have not food enough; he said his father and mother did not give it to him. I gave him a good bit of cake and cheese. He took it as if he was very hungry and ate it; he then went away. and I heard a few days afterwards he was in the Union; he came to my house, I found, from the copse where he had been at work. I never went to the cottage. Robert Jeffery, a few days after I had relieved his son, said he understood I did harbour the boy to my house. I told him that I heard that his children were quite destitute, and I said, for God's sake, if you can't keep them, apply for relief to the Union, and get some of your children taken in, for from what I have heard I thought it would come to this. He was very angry with me, said he did not do as other people, buy up a parcel of bad wheat, but he bought the best, and gave his children plenty. He was very angry. He said people gave the boy, and encouraged him to go about, instead of staying at home."

Another witness states that she has seen one of the children eating turnip-rind out of a gutter with an appearance of hunger; and one of the man's sons states of himself and the other children, that their parents did not give them sufficient food, and that on that account he had frequently ran away from his home. The boy examined was taken to the Union workhouse, and, according to the evidence of a neighbour, looked much better, more healthy and strong, than he used to do when living at home with his own parents.

On the whole, the Commissioners are inclined to concur with the opinion of one of the medical witnesses, who states, "I consider this to be a case rather of scantiness than abstinence of food;" that the parents, having at the time the means of giving to their children an adequate supply of food, having also, in the case of the failure of such means, the resource of full and certain relief by obtaining admission to the workhouse, such scantiness of food and its consequences are attributable to the culpable neglect of the parents.

No blame appears to have been imputed to the guardians, to the Union officers, or to the overseer, by the pauper or his neighbours, or by those with whom the investigation originated. Nor do the Commissioners consider that blame is justly imputable to them in this particular case whilst acting under a recognised mode of relief. In this view the Commissioners now feel it to be their duty to point out to the Guardians the case of the death as an example of the dangers attendant upon any system of out-door relief, especially of partial relief, in aid of other means.

The Guardians were probably induced in this case to give out-door relief to the head of the family with a view to a greater economy of the funds of the rate-payers, and the better satisfaction of the applicant, the out-door relief given being perhaps one-half the immediate cost of the maintenance of the family; and such out-door relief being probably considered more appropriate in the cases of destitution arising from sickness than in the cases of destitution arising from the failure of work. The Commissioners are not informed of the exact nature of the illness sustained by the head of the family in this particular case, but it will generally be found that the view to immediate economy by the grant of the smaller amount of out-door relief (usually partial relief) is defeated by the greater duration of the sickness, as well as more frequent death, occasioned by the unavoidable absence of proper medical appliances in the treatment of out-door cases. With the advantages of the superior cleanliness and the better regulated warmth and ventilation of the appropriate rooms or a sick ward; with the power which it gives the medical officer of prescribing an appropriate diet, and of securing its adoption, together with the due administration, by an experienced nurse, of the medicines he may prescribe; the head of a family, or any sick person, may in the course of weeks in a workhouse be restored to work and relieved of an illness which would be protracted over months, with the additional danger of terminating fatally, in the cottage. The Commissioners might cite extensive evidence and illustrations of this fact from the most eminent medical authorities. They only deem it necessary to request the attention of the Guardians to the following passage from a Report of the Guardians of the Strand Union, where in-door relief is the general rule in all new cases:—

"That new cases of sudden and urgent necessity will still occasionally occur in which immediate relief may be indispensable, is too obvious to be denied; but these cases will chiefly arise from accidents, sickness, and destitution, cases which no description of 'out-relief' would so effectually reach as that which would be administered within the workhouse. It is the decided opinion of the medical officers of this Union that it would be far better, in all cases of sickness and infirmity, that the parties should be immediately removed into the house, where they would receive that care and attention which it would be impossible for them to obtain in their own half-furnished and miserable lodgings. In short, the medical officers have often complained that their remedies have little chance of success, and that it was a waste of medical appliances to administer them unaided by those essential auxiliaries, warmth, cleanliness, and good nursing, which would certainly be administered in the workhouse, but which few indeed of their pauper patients were able to obtain out of it. It is also well known that during the prevalence of the late epidemic, numerous persons were removed into the Portugal-street workhouse of this Union in a state of sickness and destitution, where they were restored to health, who must in all human probability have perished out of it. In fact, experience has shown, in the Strand Union at least, that in cases of sickness, disease, or even infirmity, out-relief cannot be so administered as to meet the wants or necessities of the pauper."

It may be that the head of the family, having a prejudice against the workhouse, objected to being taken there. In like manner, many of the labouring classes strongly object to being taken into hospitals; and many lives are lost in consequence, and much misery and loss is occasioned, for which those are morally responsible who misrepresent the intention and operation of the beneficent provisions made for the destitute poor, and create unfounded prejudices against them. But whilst it is the duty of the Guardians to do all that may be in them to remove such prejudices, they are bound to act on their own superior information and adopt what they know to be the most beneficial course.

The Guardians should be made aware that by the preference of out-door relief to in-door relief, besides the protraction of the illness, and the increased danger of a fatal result, they also incur other dangers, consisting chiefly of the dangers of the misapplication and failure of the money or food intended to be given as relief.

Cases have come before the Commissioners which show that one danger incident to out-door relief in such cases, is the misapplication of the relief, from error or otherwise, by the relieving officer. A short time since the Commissioners felt it their duty to direct the dismissal of a relieving officer of the Newcastle Union, who in the case of an aged female had insisted upon giving her only out-door relief, (some bread which she could not eat, she being in a state of illness, of which she died,) instead of giving an order for her reception into the workhouse, where she would have received appropriate medical treatment.

In giving out-door relief as partial relief, on the presumption of other resources being available to the pauper, the guardians incur the constant danger of the failure of those other casual resources, and extreme suffering by the parties partially relieved. In the case under consideration, the amount of relief given was 2*s*. 6*d*. per week in kind, and 2*s*. 6*d*. per week in money. By reference to the dietary, and estimating the quantity of food allotted to each person, such an allowance will be found to have been inadequate for the maintenance of a family of eight persons. The average cost of the maintenance of paupers in the Axminster Union being, according to the quarterly abstract of the June quarter, 1840, 2*s*. 2¼*d*. per week for food only, the cost of the maintenance of a family of eight persons on that scale, would be 17*s*. 6*d* per week. The relief given must, therefore, have been really partial relief in aid of that presumed to have been obtainable by the pauper from other sources. It appears to have so happened that such relief was available to the family; but had the extraneous and casual resources failed, the Guardians would have been exposed to the imputation of having contributed to the death of the child by the scantiness of the out door relief allowed to the family. The inadequacy of such partial relief is moreover frequently held out, as the justification of much mendicancy, and fosters almsgiving, which it is the object of the law to prevent. On the other hand, if full out-door relief be given, bounties in proportion to the relief are held out for improvidence, imposture, and pauperism.

By this mode of relief the Guardians also incur all the dangers of misapplication of the relief by the paupers to whom relief is given, the dangers of misapplication arising from simple incapacity to apply it, or, in the case of children, misapplication from such culpable neglect as that manifested in the particular case under consideration.

The mismanagement of wages is the unfailing indication of the probability of the mismanagement of relief. The improvidence which begets the pauperism is commonly extended to the children, and is too frequently accompanied by culpable and unnatural neglect of them.

In another case which occurred in January last, in which the feelings of the people of Newcastle had been strongly excited, the Guardians and the law which they administered were similarly subjected to imputations, on the ground that the death of two children had been occasioned by the inadequate relief given to the family. In that case, which was also properly made the subject of a coroner's inquest, the following description was given of the place where the head of the family resided with his children:—

"It is almost impossible to convey the slightest idea of the wretched hovel in which the deceased child was found. The room was low and naturally dark. The first object that attracted attention was the dead body of the child, the object of the visit of the jury, lying on a board which had been placed on a table; it had apparently been a good looking child, but was greatly emaciated. On the other side of the fire was a quantity of straw, and, when the inspector handed a light, a sick child was discovered in a very weak state, covered with old rags. A partition was seen at one part of the room, as if the former possessor had been a person of substance and had kept an ass: the stench was most intolerable; and impure as was the air in the narrow passage from the filth that everywhere abounded, it was a great relief after being for a few moments within the dwelling."

In this case it appeared that ample means of relief in food and medicines had been given to the family, who had neglected to apply them. In the course of the examination of the parent the following evidence occurred:—

"The dispensary doctor said it was a fever, but I cannot say whether Mr. Mason agreed with him. The dispensary doctor said it was a fever, brought on by cold and hardship. Bridget died last night; we knew ourselves that the hooping cough was the matter with her; the doctor attended her. I suppose it is a fever that Ellen has (the other child lying ill). Mr. Wilson wanted to take her to the workhouse this morning, but her mother would not let her go."

The Coroner.—"Did the doctor not tell you, that if she remains where she is, it will kill her?—Yes; he did many a time.

"And you will not let her go?—(No answer.)

"Did he not tell your wife so too?—Yes.

"Still your wife will not let her go?—No; she will not. She thought she could take as good care of her, and she eats nothing.

"What have you been living on? Were you ever short of meat?—Yes; I eat very little."

It appears from the following statement that whilst the children were kept in a state of neglect and destitution as to food, the parents were in possession of abundant means.

"Mr. Gibson, inspector of police, was informed by police constable 119, M'Leod, that the woman Groke had applied to him for advice, stating that they were again in a state of starvation. Mr. Gibson took police constable 26, Dodds, along with him to see in what state they were previous to his applying to the relieving officer on their behalf. On inquiring how they were, the woman said they were very poorly, and that they were nearly dying of hunger; that she had not tasted food from ten o'clock on the previous day, and that all her husband had got from that time was a roasted potato, and that they had not a bit to eat in the house. Mr. G., finding the woman to smell strong of rum, had his doubts about the truth of her statement. On searching he found something on a shelf in a dark corner of the room, and he desired Dodds to hand down what was on it. The following is what was found:—A soup-plate full of beefsteaks, the lap of a loin of mutton, a piece of boiled bacon, a loaf of bread just cut, a plate with slices of bread and butter eight or nine inches high, and a bag containing oatmeal. Besides these articles, she had a plentiful supply of tea, sugar, &c."

The verdict of the jury in this case was in the following terms:—

"'That Bridget Groke had died a natural death. They also expressed their opinion, 'that although sufficient relief in money had been given to provide food, they could not separate without expressing their regret that, although the relieving officer had not the power of himself to furnish the necessary bedding for the family, he did not take an earlier period of laying their destitute situation in this respect before the Board of Guardians.'"

It appears to the Commissioners that if bedding had been granted it would have been equally neglected and misapplied with the food and medicines provided as out-door relief, and that the only correct course was to have given relief in the workhouse, where only the Guardians could ensure the appropriate treatment to the children. Had the state of the poor-house been such as to have enabled the Guardians to take this course, and had it been taken in the first instance, it is highly probable that the lives of both the deceased children would have been saved. It is proved by extensive experience that where the parents are improvident they are generally negligent of their children and selfish; and that no amount of money or goods given as out door relief will prevent such consequences as those displayed in the case last cited, or in the case more especially under their consideration; inasmuch as it was proved in the case of Jeffery, that the children had suffered as much from scantiness of food whilst he was in receipt of full earnings of from 16*s*. to 18*s* per week, as whilst he was dependent on the parish, they would in all probability have continued to suffer as much if the family had been allowed out-door relief to the amount of 16*s*. or 18*s*. per week. The time at which he would have returned to obtain the same amount of money by labour that he obtained as relief without labour, would naturally be protracted by him, and the family be kept in pauperism at the expense of the rate-payers during as long a period as possible. The increased health and strength gained in the workhouse by the boy, who was ultimately taken there, renders it a matter of certainty, so far as the death was occasioned by scanty food, that had the children been taken with the parent into the workhouse in the first instance, the child who died would in this instance also have been saved.

In respect to the relief of the children of pauperized parents, but especially of the children of the vagrants who may require more than temporary relief, the Commissioners further observe; that if the workhouse school be in a proper condition, and the religious instruction and the industrial and moral training of the children of the destitute be properly provided for, the Guardians, by adopting the alternative of giving out-door relief, voluntarily create future public burthens by adding to the number of paupers, vagrants, or delinquents, those children who, if rescued by the use of the opportunity of conferring fit instruction and training, would be added to the number of good servants, productive and independent labourers. The source of a large proportion of the existing mass of juvenile delinquency is found in the mismanagement of the poor's-rates.

The Commissioners have compared the expenditure of the rates in the Axminster Union with the expenditure in a Union where as a general rule full relief is given in the workhouse instead of partial relief out of the house, and the Guardians will perceive from the comparison in the enclosed table that the last mode is ultimately the most economical.

For these and other reasons which have been set forth in various published reports, and are established by the practical experience of the Unions where the administration of the relief is the most advanced, the Commissioners trust that the Guardians will in future endeavour to make out-door relief the exception instead of the general rule.

Signed by order of the Board,
EDWIN CHADWICK, *Secretary.*

II.—RELIEF OF DESTITUTION OCCASIONED BY DISEASE; SANATORY MEASURES.

THE following application for advice and instructions from the Radford Union was read to the Board:—

"*Radford, 3d October*, 1840.

"GENTLEMEN,—I am directed by the Board of Guardians of this Union to request your instructions on the following minute entered upon the minutes of the Guardians at the weekly meeting of the Board on Thursday last, and to beg your early reply:—

"The medical officer having represented that a great amount of low fever has existed for some months, and is still spreading in some parts of this Union owing to want of food, want of clothing, and want of cleanliness in the houses and neighbourhood in which it prevails; and having stated that lime-washing the houses might tend to mitigate, remove, and prevent the spread of the disease; and this Board having on a former occasion authorized the purchase of lime-brushes to be lent to the poor for this purpose, the clerk be directed to inquire of the Poor Law Commissioners if such an expenditure, or if any other steps, and of what character, will be considered as falling within the province of this Board in discharge of their duties as Guardians of the Poor.

"I am, Gentlemen, &c.

"*To the Poor Law Commissioners.*"

In reply to which the Commissioners stated that the subject of the minute of the Board of Guardians, namely, the relief of the destitution occasioned by disease, and the means of its prevention by sanatory measures, is one to which the Poor Law Commissioners have long given anxious attention, and is now the subject of their inquiry under a special reference in England, Wales, and Scotland, with a view to a report to the Legislature on the remedial measures that may appear to be expedient and practicable.

Although it appears from the information received by the Commissioners, that expenditure requisite for the adoption of general sanatory measures, in respect to the external situation and structure of the dwellings of the labouring classes, would frequently be good economy for the prevention of burthens on the poor-rates, the law as it stands does not authorize an expenditure of a general preventive character. Sanatory measures can only be adopted as medical relief to those who are diseased, and apply for relief by reason of their destitution. In these cases the Board of Guardians may adopt measures, such as those specified, of lime-washing, &c., to mitigate and remove the disease; though this course is at present liable to the abuse of incurring charges to the parish, in the improvement of tenements, which ought to be incurred by the landlord. For the prevention of this abuse, and for the enforcement of general sanatory measures, a provision was included in the Metropolitan Police Act, 2 and 3 Vic., c. 71, s. 41, authorizing magistrates, on application of the Guardians with the medical officers of a Union, to direct any house which is in such filthy and unwholesome condition, that the health of the inmates is thereby affected or endangered to be cleansed. It may be requisite to submit to the Legislature the expediency of extending similar provisions to the Unions in other districts.

In the case of persons actually destitute, it will be proper for the Guardians to adopt such sanatory measures as the medical officer may report to be necessary for the mitigation or removal of the disease.

The Commissioners would direct the attention of the Guardians to the expediency of employing as many of the able-bodied paupers as may be usefully employed, in whitewashing and cleansing the infected tenements occupied by persons who are not in employment, and are in a state of destitution.

Amongst the causes of disease adverted to in the minute of the Board of Guardians are specified, 1. The want of food; 2. The want of clothing: and 3. The want of cleanliness.

The Commissioners suggest with respect to the cases where the disease appears to result from the want of food and clothing, as they are cases which *prima facie* come within the ordinary rules for relief, that it will be the duty of the relieving officer to make close inquiry into such cases, and to report to the Guardians in the form prescribed in the Pauper Examination and Report Book. Where it shall appear that the utmost earnings of any person are insufficient for his maintenance, that person is, within the meaning of the law, a destitute person, and relief should be given accordingly. But the relief given should be entire, not partial relief, or relief in aid of wages; keeping up unremunerative employment at the expense of the rate-payers. The person relieved should be taken wholly upon the parish, and if he be sick as well as destitute, it will probably be found that he could nowhere be placed under circumstances so favourable to his recovery in respect to cleanliness, appropriate food, and medical treatment, as in the workhouse.

So in respect to the persons whose illness and destitution arise from want of personal cleanliness. It will occur to the Guardians, that where persons are so indolent and of such depraved habits as to incur disease by their want of cleanliness, there is no security for the proper application of any remedies or means of relief at their own homes, and that the only safe and effectual course will be to order them to be relieved in the workhouse, where they may be properly cleansed, and the application of appropriate remedies may be insured.

If the want of personal cleanliness be a prevalent vice amongst those claiming out-door relief, the Commissioners suggest that the Guardians should enforce as a rule that no widow or other able-bodied person should receive relief otherwise than in the workhouse who did not attend to receive the relief himself or herself, with his or her children, in a state of personal cleanliness. The Commissioners consider it a vulgar error that personal filth is a necessary incident of poverty and destitution, or an indication of any other than indolent and vicious habits in persons who are not in a state of idiotcy or mental imbecility.

The Commissioners observe that they have not yet received from the medical officers of the Radford Union their answers to the circular letter of queries transmitted to them on the sanatory inquiry.

Signed by order of the Board,
E. CHADWICK, *Secretary.*

The following letter on the same subject from W. Wilson, Esq., one of the Guardians of the Radford Union, was also read to the Board:—

"*Radford*, 1*st October*, 1840.

"GENTLEMEN,—For some time past a serious amount of mortality and disease has been prevalent in some parts of this Union, and understanding that the medical officer would bring the subject before the Board to-day, I felt it my duty to be present, although circumstances have previously prevented my attendance since the last election. Having heard the statement of the medical officer, and being more conversant with the circumstances than other Guardians from residing near the seat of the disease, I felt it my duty to move a resolution, which was unanimously carried, and will be transmitted to you to-day.

"The history of the last two months in this neighbourhood will, I believe, prove, that the prevalent disease has caused numbers of applications for medical relief from parties who would ordinarily be unwilling to apply to a parish. The medical officer has been obliged to order that support which the case has required, and it is to be feared that having in this way become accustomed to parochial relief many will not in future feel disposed, under other, and it may be, more ordinary circumstances, to make the effort they would otherwise have made to maintain an independence of such relief.

"In many houses several inmates have been, and still are, at once laid prostrate by the disease, and the earnings of the family being small at all times, they are immediately compelled to throw themselves on the parish.

"Heads of families, too, removed by such fatal maladies, frequently leave families at once dependent on the parish.

"I could mention other reasons, but I doubt not these, and others, will suggest themselves to you in favour of any measures which shall act as preventives of the evils arising from so many individuals becoming pauperized. As a question of economy merely, I imagine prevention will be found better than cure; but, on higher grounds, I deem it the duty of every man, and still more of the *Guardians of the poor*, to do what is possible to alleviate and prevent the spread of such distress as, under the circumstances I have stated, prevails here.

"There seems no prospect of any other kind of relief for the poor in the districts alluded to, as with the exception of myself, and a respectable miller, there are scarcely any persons, *if any*, who may be considered able to afford individual relief. The inhabitants consist of manufacturers, colliers, and mechanics, whose earnings are usually very small and inadequate; and small shopkeepers, &c., who supply their wants. For myself, the circumstances of extreme depression under which all around me are placed, puts it out of my power to make any individual efforts beyond those which the wants and necessities of my own work-people involve. The owners of the small tenements, in which the poor people reside, obtain so little rent, that they would, I imagine, feel that *they already* bear a large share of the burden; and the amount of distress in parts not visited by this disease would render it useless, I fear, to make any attempt to raise money by subscription for this neighbourhood exclusively.

"On all these accounts I am certainly very desirous to find you able to suggest some steps which the Board may take, which must be my apology for addressing you.

"If no steps of a preventive character can be taken the mischief will, I fear, spread, the increase of pecuniary burthen become considerable, and the great increase of suffering and mortality be such as deeply to afflict all acquainted with the facts. This augmentation of mischief may, I imagine, be prevented, and with no increase of expense to the Union, by the adoption of some means to *check the spread of the disease*, which, I trust, you will be able to sanction and suggest.

"Early soliciting your best attention to the subject, in haste

"I am, Gentlemen, yours respectfully,

"W. WILSON.

"*To the Poor Law Commissioners.*"

SANATORY MEASURES.—CIRCULAR LETTER THEREON TO THE GUARDIANS OF THE PARISHES AND UNIONS IN THE METROPOLIS.

To the Clerk to the Board of Guardians.

SIR,—The Commissioners request that the attention of the Board of Guardians may be directed to the provisions of the Act 2 and 3 Vict, c. 71, sec. 41, with respect to the powers conferred by law for the cleansing of houses which are in an unwholesome condition.

The Commissioners desire to recall to the attention of the Guardians the facts which have from time to time been brought to the attention of the Legislature in respect to the sanatory condition of the labouring population in the metropolis, and remind them of the circumstance made apparent in the course of the investigations instituted, that a large proportion of the claims to relief on account of destitution arise from sickness, attributed chiefly to the defective internal and external economy of the dwellings of the labouring classes, and to the want of proper cleanliness in them. From returns made in 1838 by the medical officers of twenty Unions and parishes in the metropolis, it appeared that 13,972 cases of claims to relief on the ground of destitution were created during that year by attacks of fever alone, and that in 1,281 cases the attacks proved fatal. The general deaths from fever in the metropolis during that year appear from the summary of the Superintendent Registrar's returns to have been 5,634. A considerable proportion of other cases of sickness and mortality were ascribed to the operation of the like causes, which the physicians and medical officers by whom the Commissioners are advised consider to be preventible by the enforcement of proper sanatory regulations.

Powers for the enforcement of means for preventing within the metropolis those evils that may be guarded against by proper cleansing, are given by the section of the New Police Act to which the Commissioners desire to call the attention of the Guardians. The Commissioners take this opportunity of calling the attention of the Guardians of parishes and Unions in the Metropolitan Police District to the provisions of the Act, because at this season the places where the effects of the want of proper cleanliness are prevented by the greater ventilation of open doors or windows during the summer, are frequently manifested in diseases which arise from filth or damp, and the stoppage of ventilation by the doors and windows being closed to prevent cold in winter.

The following are the terms of the section of the New Police Act:—

And be it further enacted:—

1. "That if the Guardians of the Poor of an Union or Parish,
"Or the Churchwardens and Overseers of the Poor of any parish within the Metropolitan Police District,
"Together with the Medical Officer for any such Parish or Union,
"Shall be of opinion, and shall certify under the hands of two or more of such Guardians, Churchwardens, or Overseers, and also of such Medical Officer,
"That any house or part of any house within such Union or Parish is in such filthy and unwholesome condition that the health of the inmates or of the public is thereby affected or endangered;
2. "It shall be lawful for any Magistrate, acting within the district in which such Union or Parish is situate, if he shall think fit, to cause notice to be affixed on the door or other conspicuous part of such house requiring the occupier or occupiers of such house, or part thereof, to appear before him to answer such complaint,
3. "Or to cause the same to be cleansed within seven days of the date of affixing such notice:
4. "And if, within the said seven days, such house or part thereof shall not be cleansed to the satisfaction of such Medical Officer,
"And if such occupier or occupiers being duly summoned shall not appear before the Magistrate and show sufficient cause to the contrary,
5. "Such Magistrate is hereby empowered, on proof thereof, to issue an order under his hand and seal, to the Guardians of the Poor or the Churchwardens and Overseers aforesaid, to cause such house or part thereof to be cleansed at the expense of such occupier or occupiers,
"And to cause the amount thereof to be levied, in case of non-payment, by distress and sale of the goods and chattels of such occupier or occupiers by warrant under the hand and seal of such Magistrate."

The course which the Commissioners recommend to the Guardians for carrying the provisions of the law into operation, is first to promulgate the knowledge of them in the districts where the cases of fever or of epidemic and contagious diseases and claims to relief have been most frequent. The places to which the special attention of the Guardians should be directed will, of course, be indicated by the pauper application and relief lists, in which will be found the names of those places from whence the greatest number of applications have been made for relief, from parties who have laboured under epidemic or contagious diseases. But the more full and correct indications of the places for examination will be afforded by reference to the mortuary registers kept by the clerk to the Board, as the superintendent registrar, in which will be found the registration of the whole of the places in which deaths from epidemic or contagious diseases have occurred, including the general population as well as those occupied by the persons who are subject to casual destitution. The Commissioners request that a notification in the form annexed, or any similar form which the Guardians may on consultation with the medical officer deem more closely applicable to the general state of the district,(or to any part of it which may appear to require special notice,). directing the attention ofthe occupier to the law, and the state of their dwellings, calling upon them to take steps for the removal of any masses of filth on the premises, of stagnant fluids in the gutters; to amend the state of the cesspools, &c.; and to whitewash the houses inside and out, and the walls of the courts; to cleanse, that is, to remove whatever may clearly endanger the health of the inmates or of the public. After due notice given, the medical officer should be instructed whenever he is required to visit any case of illness requiring his attendance, and he finds the house in such a condition that the health of the inmates or of the public is thereby endangered, to call the attention of the Guardians to the fact, that they, or a committee of them, may view the spot, and make a certificate of the condition of the premises, with a view to a proper notice being obtained from a magistrate acting within the district.

The Commissioners have seen frequent occasion to regret that the abodes of the labouring classes, and more particularly those in which the greatest proportion of cases of destitution arise, are rarely visited, and in many districts are entirely unseen and unknown, by their superiors in station. The facts set forth in the medical reports, to which the Commissioners refer, were received with surprise by persons who were not aware of the condition in which their own labourers were living, or of the neglected and dangerous condition of their own immediate neighbourhoods. The Commissioners have been informed, that the knowledge already promulgated on the subject has led to much voluntary and beneficial exertion for amendment, in draining and cleansing, and in various other improvements in the external economy of the labourers' residences. In the administration of relief, the Guardians act upon imperfect information, when they have not the knowledge of the habits and important circumstances influencing the condition of the pauperised classes, which can only be obtained by a personal inspection of their common places of residence.

The Commissioners, therefore, consider it desirable, that as many of the Guardians as conveniently can, should examine the spot, although the certificates of two only of the Guardians (which certificate must be given on view and not on report) are necessary to enable the magistrate to take the requisite proceedings for the protection of the inmates and the public.

It is to be observed of the terms of the Act, that it does not restrict the powers of the authorities for the enforcement of cleanliness to houses which are inhabited, but enables them to proceed with respect to any house, or to the part of any house, whatsoever, whether inhabited or not, which is in such unwholesome condition that the health of the inmates or of the public is thereby endangered; neither is it necessary to show that the condition of the house does at the time actually affect the health of the inmates or the public, but it will be sufficient if it be shown on competent authority that it may affect it, and thereby endangers it.

It is not necessary that the proceedings should be originated by the medical officer: and his attention may in the first instance be called to the state of any house by any of the Guardians who may be ready to certify as to the condition of the premises, or by the relieving officer or by any other person who may be aware that the health of the inmates, or of the public, is there endangered by the want of proper cleansing.

In respect to what is to be deemed part of any house, the Commissioners apprehend that everything may be included as part of the house for remedial purposes that is by law included in it in respect to burglaries, that is to say, the curtilage, or any place enclosed with the house, and having an immediate communication with it.

The Commissioners are aware from the information they have received that the statutory provisions to which they have called the special attention of Guardians will not prevent much disease arising from the defects of the internal structure of many of the dwellings of the labouring classes, and from their external condition in respect to drainage, where proper drains have not yet been formed, but the Commissioners are led to believe that the proper enforcement of the provisions in question will, in all cases, diminish the evils which they may not remove, and will tend to render manifest the precise practical remedies that may yet be needed, to which the Commissioners have every reason to believe that Her Majesty's Government and the Legislature will give the most favourable attention.

By order of the Board,

EDWIN CHADWICK, *Secretary*.

The Commissioners directed that copies of the above circular should be forwarded for the information of each medical officer and relieving officer in the several Unions and parishes to which it was addressed.

IV.—VACCINATION EXTENSION ACT.

1 VACCINATION UNDER THE ACT NOT RELIEF.

The Commissioners took into consideration a letter, addressed to them by direction of the Board of Guardians of the Stamford Union, in which the clerk states:—

"I am directed to inform you, that the Guardians are still of opinion, that if parents who are voters voluntarily take their children to be vaccinated, and suffer the fee of 1*s*. 6*d*. to be paid out of the Poor-rates, it would be considered by Revising Barristers under the Reform Act, and by the Assessors under the Municipal Corporations Act, as Parochial Relief, and would therefore, if objected to, disqualify them from voting. The Guardians consider that Stephens, in his recently published work, fully bears them out, and that there is no pretence for considering this as extraordinary relief."

To which the Commissioners directed the following reply to be sent:—

The Commissioners desire to state, that they see the same objection to the conclusion that vaccination, under the 3d and 4th Vict., c. 29, is "extraordinary relief," as to the conclusion that it is ordinary relief; the Commissioners believe it not to be relief in any legal sense whatever, Parliamentary or other.

The election cases which have been cited on this subject were entirely beside the matter; those cases occurred when it was unlawful to expend the poor-rates for the benefit of any but the poor. As the poor are defined by the statute of Elizabeth, it was only as "Poor" that persons could receive the benefit of vaccination, or other sanatory service, at the expense of the poor-rates; and the expenditure could only be allowed as "relief;" and in any other view than as "relief" it would have been an unauthorized and illegal expenditure.

But even when such expenditure (if admitted at all as legal) could not by any possibility be regarded otherwise than as "relief" to the "poor," it was still held in the cases cited not to disqualify voters; and as it was impossible to refuse to it the character of "relief," without denying its legality altogether, it was held to be "extraordinary relief," and thus the voter's franchise was preserved.

But the recent statute has entirely changed the character of this benefit and expenditure. It extends the benefit to all "residents," without distinction of rich or poor; that is, with small exceptions, to the whole population of England, Wales, and Ireland.

It is not for residents as residents, and especially not for rich residents, that the statute of Elizabeth provides "necessary relief."

It is, therefore, no longer necessary to assume that those who may be vaccinated at the expense of the poor-rates are "poor," and that the benefit of vaccination is received as "relief of the poor." On the contrary, as it is extended to all "residents," it is as residents and not as poor that they receive it; and all that can be inferred from the receipt is, not that the party requiring was "poor," but that he was a "resident."

Moreover it may be observed, that it is not allowable to call all benefits enjoyed by parishioners by means of the expenditure of poor-rates "relief." The poor-rates have been, before the last Act, applied to many purposes of general convenience, such as the maintenance of bridges, gaols, stocks, lock-up houses, and constables' expenses, without the least justification for considering such application as "relief" to those who enjoy the benefit of the expenditure.

Without adverting to the improbability that it was intended by the Legislature that the benefit of vaccination should be received by all the residents in England, Wales, and Ireland, as relief to the poor, with its enormous consequences of universal disfranchisement, but bearing in mind these facts that "relief" and "poor" are legally correlative; that is to say, that relief can only be lawfully given to the poor as poor, and that it is only the poor as poor who can lawfully partake of it; and the further fact that the vaccination is provided for those for whom relief is unnecessary, for the whole of that very class who at the time the Act was passed was actually coextensive with the largest description of rate-payers (the inhabitants resident), and that the nature of the benefit is thus immediately coextensive with the contributors of the tax, not with the recipients of relief; and the yet further fact that its object is the protection of the whole community, fully as much as the protection of the patients, the Commissioners come to the conclusion that all these considerations satisfactorily negative any supposition that to accept the benefit of vaccination is to accept relief in any sense; and justify the assurance that no such consequence is to be apprehended as the pauperization or disfranchisement of residents availing themselves of it.

The question whether vaccination is relief when performed on paupers in the receipt of ordinary relief is not material, inasmuch as the ordinary relief would of itself disfranchise them, and additional relief (if vaccination were relief) would not add to their disqualification as paupers. But the Commissioners are firmly of opinion that if vaccination be not relief to the rich residents, it is not relief to the poor; that the poor, equally with their richer neighbours, will receive this benefit not as poor, but as residents, and that their chargeability as poor is, therefore, not increased by partaking of the benefit of vaccination.

Signed by order of the Board,
EDWIN CHADWICK, *Secretary.*

2.—POWER OF GUARDIANS TO PAY THE EXPENSES OF VACCINATION OUT OF THE POOR-RATES.

Copy of a Minute of the Poor Law Commissioners, dated 28th September, 1840.

The Vaccination Extension Act is imperative upon the Guardians of every parish or Union to contract with medical men for the vaccination of all persons resident; and it imperatively prescribes the mode in which the remuneration to be received under the contract is to be settled.

Every contract in the English law necessarily implies mutuality of consideration. In providing for a contract, the statute therefore necessarily provides for the parties to the contract incurring mutual obligations. It would have been mere tautology if, in addition to the instruction to enter into contracts, the parties had been expressly empowered to perform the mutual considerations, or if any other necessary legal incident of a contract had been expressly provided for.

On the other hand, if anything so anomalous had been intended as that the medical officers were to incur obligations without mutual considerations, or that persons, not parties to the contracts (as the residents who were to be vaccinated), were to pay the remuneration stipulated, or that parties contracting in one character, as the Guardians do in their official character, were to incur obligations in another character, as an obligation to pay for a public service in their personal character out of their private means; in any such case this anomaly would have required the most explicit and positive expressions in the statute to render it legal.

The Commissioners cannot doubt that on a further reference to the terms of the Act, the Guardians will perceive that the entering into contracts is obligatory on them. That in the performance of this duty they are only referred to in their official and public character; that in conforming to the directions of the Act in entering into contracts, the obligations they incur will only be in their public capacity, and that the nature of the transaction which they are required to enter into for the benefit of all the inhabitants of the Union, quite as much as the express terms of the statute, removes all reason for any suspicion that the Guardians are to incur any private responsibility.

It seems, therefore, to follow by necessary implication, that the Guardians are to discharge the obligation which they have officially incurred out of the funds of which they have officially possession as Guardians, namely, the funds which they have derived from the various parishes in the Union.

As to the mode in which these funds are to be applied towards the costs of vaccination, the Commissioners have expressed their opinion in a Circular Letter of the 17th instant, a copy of which has been already sent to the Board of Guardians.

In answer to other applications on this subject, the Commissioners have stated in addition, that if any doubt should be found generally to be entertained on this important subject it may be corrected by an explanatory Act in the ensuing session of Parliament, so framed as to apply not only to future contracts but to all contracts made under the Act as at present framed.

3.—CIRCULAR LETTER ON THE MODE OF PAYING AND CHARGING VACCINATION EXPENSES.

Poor Law Commission Office,
Somerset House,
September 17, 1840.

SIR,—The Poor Law Commissioners have had under their consideration various communications requesting information as to the manner in which the expenses incurred in Unions under the Act for the Extension of Vaccination are to be defrayed, and more especially whether such expenses should be charged to the several parishes according to their averages, or according to any other proportion.

Having regard to the terms of the 1st and 2d sections of the Vaccination Extension Act, and also such portion of the Poor Law Amendment Act as defines that class of expenses which are to be defrayed out of the common fund to be contributed by the several parishes according to their respective averages, the Commissioners are of opinion—

1st. That the common fund is more especially provided for the payment for such objects and services as are to be obtained for the whole of the parishes in a Union, —such as the structure and repairs of the workhouse, the services of the clerk of the Union,—the separate benefit of which objects and services to each several parish cannot be accurately ascertained.

2dly. That although the contracts for vaccination which the Commissioners have recommended for adoption may be considered as, to some extent, made for the benefit of all the parishes of such Union; nevertheless, the services to be rendered under such contracts, and for which, and not for the contract itself, the remuneration is to be paid to the medical contractor, are such that the exact amount of the cost incurred for the immediate benefit of the inhabitants resident in each parish can be ascertained with perfect accuracy.

3dly. That, moreover, the extent of the benefit which may be enjoyed by the inhabitants resident in each parish cannot be assumed to be in any proportion to the pre-existing pauperism which decides the average contributions in such parish.

The Commissioners, therefore, conclude that the common fund of each Union is not applicable to the present purpose, and that the Guardians of each Union should pay out of the separate funds, and charge to the separate account of each parish in such Union, the remuneration which accrues to the medical contractor under the Vaccination Extension Act, in respect of the successful vaccination of persons resident in such parish at the time of vaccination. And the Commissioners recommend that for this purpose the Guardians should require the medical contractor to insert in his register the place of residence of each person whom he shall report to have been successfully vaccinated.

Signed by order of the Board,

GEORGE COODE, *Assistant Secretary.*

To the Clerk of the Board of Guardians.

4.—CIRCULAR LETTER ON THE PERSONS TO BE COMPRISED IN THE RESPECTIVE DISTRICTS.

Poor Law Commission Office,
Somerset House,
25*th September*, 1840.

SIR,—The Poor Law Commissioners perceive, from the resolutions and drafts of contracts relating to vaccination which they have recently received from various Unions, that in some instances the Boards of Guardians in contracting with medical practitioners for their services at the stations within certain of the districts, have also, by the terms of the contract, proposed to limit their services to the residents within such districts, instead of extending the benefit of each several contract, as proposed in the printed form which the Commissioners appended to their minute of the 20th August last, to all the residents within the Union who may resort to the stations within the district. It is an obvious advantage to decide, before contracts are entered into, upon certain districts, with a view to the fixing of convenient stations for the attendance of the medical contractors and of the persons who may have to resort to them, and with a view of making an approximate estimate of the probable number of attendances which may be necessary during each year, and of the probable number of cases by which the total remuneration of the contractor will be determined. But it is not equally obvious that the residents within such district ought to be prevented from resorting to the contractor for another district, where they may be willing to take on themselves all the trouble which this would involve.

The first object of the Guardians will be to conquer, by every legitimate means, any repugnance or prejudice which persons may entertain against the practice of vaccination. With all the care which the Guardians can use, objections, well and ill founded, will occasionally exist against certain contractors, and these objections will diminish the inclination or increase the disinclination of the persons who entertain them, to avail themselves of the arrangements made by the Guardians. Where a well founded objection to any contractor may exist, it is clear that his district would be under great comparative disadvantage if the residents were strictly limited to his services.

On the other hand, the trouble to the residents involved in their attending in a district other than their own will prevent any light or groundless objections being made to a contractor; and the contractor therefore will, when the respective districts are conveniently arranged for the residents, have nearly a moral certainty that by proper attention he will retain the whole of his district.

Practically, therefore, the system of contracting with each contractor to attend a certain district, to vaccinate all the residents within the Union, whether resident within his district or not, who may resort to him, will not involve any real subtraction of remuneration.

The contractors, moreover, being conscious of the possession of character and ability, and of an intention fully to perform their duty, will not object to the Guardians giving this opportunity to the residents, subject as it is to the impediments before adverted to, to select whichever of the contractors they may prefer.

Such are the considerations which appear to the Commissioners chiefly to apply to the respective cases of the residents and of the contractors. But as regards the execution of the more immediate duties of the Guardians, the system of contracting in each case for residents in all parts of your Union appears to the Commissioners to be recommended by the following considerations:—

In the first place, the Act requires the Guardians to make contracts with medical officers, and other medical practitioners, "for the vaccination of all persons resident within the Unions or parishes respectively."

Although the Commissioners believe that the Act will be satisfied by the making of contracts for the vaccination of all residents within districts, if all the districts together make up the whole of a Union; still a literal as well as a virtual compliance with a statute is obviously preferable in all cases to a merely virtual compliance. In the present case more especially, the duty of the Guardians being to give the whole of the residents in the respective Unions the benefit of the measure, contracts framed on the system thus recommended by the Commissioners will best provide at all times against the occurrence of those casualties amongst contractors, by which particular districts may be deprived of the services of their contractors.

Where no preponderating reasons exist for a different course, the Commissioners, therefore, trust that the Guardians will frame their contracts so as to follow the words of the Act, and to provide for the vaccination by each contractor of all persons resident not only in some district, but in the Union, who may come to him at the places and times specified.

But where preponderating reasons may exist, as may possibly be the case in some instances, the Commissioners request to be informed of them when the contract is sent up for their approval, as in such cases they will not be disposed to withhold their sanction on that ground.

The Commissioners have, in conclusion, to remark that the form of contract appended to the order recently issued to the Union will admit of either of the modes of contracting above alluded to.

Signed by order of the Board,
EDWIN CHADWICK, *Secretary*.

To the Clerk to the Board of Guardians.

5.—NECESSITY FOR NEW CONTRACTS WHERE VACCINATION IS PROVIDED FOR TO PAUPERS IN EXISTING MEDICAL CONTRACTS.

Poor Law Commission Office,
Somerset House,
September 23, 1840.

SIR,—The Poor Law Commissioners having received from the Boards of Guardians of various Unions communications, stating that the medical contracts in such Unions already provided for the vaccination of the poor, and expressing doubts whether it would be necessary for them to take any steps in reference to the Vaccination Extension Act until these contracts should have determined, deem it advisable to make known their views on this subject.

The Act for the extension of vaccination is not confined either to actual paupers or to those who, although able to provide for themselves in other respects, ordinarily require and receive medical aid from the parish. It extends to all classes who choose to take advantage of its benevolent provisions.

The Guardians will not, therefore, have fulfilled, by anticipation, the requirements of the Act by the contracts which they have entered into with their medical officers, which, in their widest sense, cannot lawfully extend beyond the two classes of poor persons above mentioned.

Under these circumstances, several alternatives appear open to the Guardians, and the Commissioners will, in describing them, offer some observations on each, leaving it to the Guardians themselves to decide which they shall adopt.

I. The Guardians can enter into contracts with the medical officers to vaccinate at so much per case all persons resident within the Union, not coming within the terms of the existing medical contracts.

If this plan be followed, it will be most important that the Guardians should define accurately the persons to whom the existing medical contract extends. This may be done by an order of the Board of Guardians (made in pursuance of the medical contract, and which order should be recited or noticed in the vaccination contract), requiring the medical officers to vaccinate—

1. All persons named in a schedule and their families; or,
2. All persons and their families who, at the time of the order being issued, are in the receipt of relief; or,
3. All persons and their families who are at the time of the order being issued, or who during the remainder of the term of the medical contract may be, in receipt of relief.

The Commissioners do not recommend the latter of these three modes of defining the medical contract: they think that it may lead to differences of opinion between the Guardians and the medical officer as to the persons not now receiving relief, but who hereafter may be in the receipt of relief. This class of persons will, until they receive relief, be within the terms of the vaccination contract, and will afterwards be transferred to the medical contract,—an arrangement which may produce disputes and confusion.

Having regard to the fact that the legislature has now provided means of vaccination without the disadvantageous consequences which result from the acceptance of relief, the Commissioners recommend that the Guardians should treat the existing contract (if kept on foot at all) as confined to paupers actually in the receipt of relief, and should direct the medical officers to vaccinate those paupers and their families, and should not add to that list any families who are not now paupers.

II. The Guardians may contract with legally qualified medical practitioners, whether medical officers or not, to vaccinate at so much per case all persons resident within the Union, not immediately within the terms of the existing contract.

This alternative only differs from the first in the extension of the vaccination contract to other persons beyond the medical officers: upon that point the Commissioners have already expressed their views to the Guardians in their circular of the 20th of August last.

The definition of the medical contract as above suggested, would of course be absolutely necessary in the event of this alternative being adopted; and in the new contracts entered into with practitioners, not being medical officers, exception should be made of all persons whom the medical officers would be bound to vaccinate as paupers, otherwise those persons for whom sufficient provision would already have been made at the cost of the Union might cause a double expense to be incurred by being vaccinated under the new contracts.

III. The Guardians may come to an agreement with the medical officers to rescind the medical contracts, so far as respects vaccination, upon fair terms, and may enter into vaccination contracts either with these medical officers or with other persons.

The following reasons may be urged in favour of this mode of proceeding. The vaccination contracts will be so framed as to furnish greater securities for the success of the operation, and for certifying that success, than are provided by the medical contracts; and it seems right that the pauper class, as well as others, should have the full benefit of these securities.

The provisions of the Act will be more rigidly complied with in a contract expressly founded on it, especially in regard to the remuneration of the medical contractor, and his obligations consequent upon the contract, and his subjection to the directions of the Guardians; and the contracts will be more accurately understood and more uniform, as being determined by the Act, than can possibly be the case under any contract passed before the Act was contemplated.

When the medical contracts were entered into, neither the Guardians nor the medical officers could have contemplated the general measure passed by the legislature for the extension of vaccination; it seems not unreasonable, therefore, to relieve the medical officers from a contract which was framed under a totally different state of circumstances, and which, if the performance be now insisted on, even with the most limited of the definitions above pointed out, will involve the medical officer in duties widely differing from those which were contemplated by either party.

The whole of these observations, however, do not apply to those medical contracts in which the remuneration for vaccination is at a fixed sum per case equal to or greater than the sum contemplated to be given in the contracts under the Vaccination Extension Act.

If the medical contracts terminate in March, there is a further reason for not enforcing them to their full extent: namely, that a great portion of the intervening period is deemed by many practitioners to be the season least favourable for vaccination.

IV. A fourth alternative has been suggested, which partakes both of the advantages and disadvantages of the other modes of proceeding above pointed out; namely —that the medical officers should contract to vaccinate all persons resident within the Union, at so much for each case of successful vaccination, but that they should not be remunerated for those cases which are fairly comprised within their medical contracts.

This, although securing for the paupers the benefits intended to be provided for them, may, unless the medical contract be accurately defined, as before suggested, be the cause of dispute and litigation.

The Commissioners think that it would be better for both contracting parties to abandon the medical contract as respects vaccination, and, in consideration thereof, to adopt a lower amount of remuneration per case.

The Commissioners trust that the preceding remarks, which are offered as suggestions only, and are not to be deemed of a directory character, will aid the Guardians in coming to a satisfactory decision on their vaccination arrangements.

Signed by Order of the Board,
GEORGE COODE, *Assistant Secretary*.

To the Clerk to the Board of Guardians.

EMIGRATION. NOTIFICATION FROM THE EMIGRATION COMMISSIONERS OF THE NAMES AND DUTIES OF THEIR AUTHORIZED AGENTS.

Colonial Land and Emigration Office,
9, *Park Street*, *Westminster*,
31*st August*, 1840.

SIR,—In consequence of the frauds that are frequently practised at several of the ports of embarkation on intending emigrants, it has occurred to the Commissioners of Land and Emigration that the best mode in their power of guarding against such impositions would be to make known as widely as possible to parish authorities and the poorer class generally the existence and residence of a body of officers whose especial duty it is to protect poor emigrants, and to afford gratuitously, to those who may require it, every information as to the facilities for emigration from the ports to which they are severally appointed. With this view, I am directed to forward the enclosed memorandum to the Poor Law Commissioners, and to suggest, should they see no objection, that its publication in one of their early Circulars might be attended with advantage.

I have the honour to be, Sir,
Your most obedient servant,
S. WALCOTT, *Secretary*.

E. Chadwick, Esq., *&c. &c.*

List of the Government Agents for Emigration, and of the Ports at which they reside.

Lieut. Lean, R.N.	East Smithfield, London.
Lieut. Henry, R.N.	Liverpool.
Lieut. Forrest, R.N.	Leith.
Lieut. Hemmans, R.N. .	Greenock.
Lieut. Hodden, R.N. ...	Dublin.
Lieut. Friend, R.N.	Cork.
Lieut. Starke, R.N......	Belfast.
Mr. Lynch, R.N........	Limerick.
Lieut. Shuttleworth, R.N.	Sligo
Lieut. Ramsay, R.N. ...	Londonderry.

These officers act under the immediate directions and control of Her Majesty's Commissioners for Colonial Land and Emigration, No. 9, Park-street, Westminster, and the following is a summary of their duties:—

They are to correspond with any magistrates, clergymen, parish-officers, and others, who may apply to them for information as to the facilities for emigration from their respective stations. They are to procure and give, gratuitously, information as to the sailing of ships, means of accommodation for emigrants, &c.; to receive, if required, remittances of money for the purposes of defraying the passages of emigrants recommended to their care, and, whenever applied to for the purpose, to see that all agreements between shipowners, agents, or masters, and intending emigrants, are duly performed. They are also to see that the provisions of the Passengers' Act are strictly complied with; that passenger vessels are seaworthy, that they have on board a sufficient supply of provisions, water, medicines, &c., and that they sail within a reasonable time from the date first fixed.

They are to attend personally at their offices during a certain fixed time on every week day, and they are generally to afford, gratuitously, all the assistance in their power to protect intending emigrants against fraud and imposition, and to obtain redress where oppression or injury has been practised on them.

LONDON:
Printed by order of the Poor Law Commissioners, by W. CLOWES and SONS, Stamford Street, and Published by CHARLES KNIGHT and Co., 22, Ludgate-street, Publishers to the Poor Law Commissioners.

AN

OFFICIAL CIRCULAR

OF PUBLIC DOCUMENTS AND INFORMATION:

DIRECTED BY THE POOR LAW COMMISSIONERS TO BE PRINTED, CHIEFLY FOR THE USE OF THE MEMBERS AND PERMANENT OFFICERS OF BOARDS OF GUARDIANS, UNDER THE POOR LAW AMENDMENT ACT.

No. 10. CIRCULAR ISSUED DECEMBER 24TH, 1840.

Poor Law Commission Office,
Somerset House,
December 21, 1840.

THE Poor Law Commissioners, on a review of their minutes, directed that the minutes and correspondence on the following subjects should be printed and circulated for the information of Guardians and officers of the several Unions, viz.:—

By order of the Board,

EDWIN CHADWICK,

Secretary.

I.—RELIEF; ADMINISTRATION THEREOF TO ABLE-BODIED LABOURERS DURING PERIODS OF MANUFACTURING DISTRESS.

The Commissioners took into consideration the following resolution of the Board of Guardians of the Hinckley Union:—

"GENTLEMEN,—I beg leave most respectfully to submit the following resolution of the Guardians of this Union, agreed upon on Monday last, for your consideration; and at the same time to inform you of the circumstance which led to it. The case, as it is stated in the minute book, is as follows:—

"'Thomas Cleaver, William Hackett, James Leigh, and Thomas Ireland, attended the board on behalf of the framework knitters, and stated that Mr. John Glover had tendered an offer of work to his hands (most of whom are now breaking stones at the workhouse) at sixpence per dozen under the statement price; and it is the opinion of this deputation that the carrying out of this will prove seriously detrimental to the interests of the Union, if adopted. Our other employers have considerable stocks on hand; and if the men are *forced* to work at the reduced price, Mr. Sills (a very extensive house in the town) will turn off his hands; Mr. Clarke (the chairman of the Board, also an extensive manufacturer, and who is now giving out work) will do the same; Mr. Woodcock, hosier, the same: and Mr. Spencer, hosier, of Earl Shilton, likewise. We (the deputation) know of no other hosier in this town besides Mr. Glover who attempts to do it; and we desire to know from the Board whether, if the men refuse to accept the work from Mr. Glover at a reduced price, they may be allowed to come and work in the stone-yard as heretofore.'

"The Board having taken the matter into their most serious consideration, and having judged that by forcing the men to submit to a reduced price of wages they should be acting contrary to the spirit of the new Poor Law, unanimously resolved,

"'That the poor men shall not be compelled to go to work under the statement price, and can come down here to work as usual.'

"The Board will be most happy to receive advice in what way they had better continue to act, as the resolution can only be said to stand good until your answer is known. Awaiting which,

"I have the honour, &c.

"*To the Poor Law Commissioners.*"

In reply, the Commissioners stated that they are unaware of the precise nature of the statement prices, but they apprehend that the only question open for the consideration of the Guardians is whether the men are in such a state of destitution as to entitle them to relief; and they are not destitute, or in law entitled to relief, whenever an offer is made to them of such wages as will yield them subsistence, or the necessary food, clothing, and shelter. But if such wages were offered as only to yield a part of the absolute necessaries of life, then the deficiency of the part is equivalent to a deficiency of the whole; the person comes within the meaning of the old law as a destitute person, and the Guardians are bound to set the person at work and give him relief in return. The chief error to be avoided is that of giving partial relief in aid of partial wages, and of thus aiding the manufacturer for a time, and then reducing both wages, and ultimately the price of the commodity, at the expense of the rate-payers. The only immediate question for the Guardians is, whether work at the statement prices will afford to the persons employed the absolute necessaries of life. It forms no part of their duty as Guardians to consider what will be the effect of such prices upon the market. If they give relief whilst wages, which ensure the means of subsistence, are offered to the parties relieved, such relief will be liable to be disallowed; and Mr. Glover or any other ratepayer may appeal against the expenditure for the relief of persons who, in the words of the Statute of Elizabeth, have "means to maintain them," and the Poor Law Commissioners have not authority to prevent its disallowance.

The Commissioners can state as the result of wide experience, that if the law left open the consideration of the operation of such an offer as that in question upon the labourers, and the interests of other employers, that all factitious interferences to keep up prices against a falling demand, in the end operate mischievously on the interests of the labouring classes; and that if it were allowable, it would be ultimately prejudicial to them, to permit the use of the poor-rates as a trades' union fund, either by the workmen or by the employers, to raise wages. All factitious stoppages of work against a falling market—all stoppages of the employment of capital, only reduce the fund from which wages are paid; they only diminish that fund, the abundance of which is the cause of increased demand, and the means of giving an increase of wages.

The Commissioners have directed some of the evidence bearing on the subject to be reprinted, and they will forward copies to you for the information of the Board of Guardians.

Signed by Order of the Board,

EDWIN CHADWICK, *Secretary*.

In a subsequent communication, the clerk to the Board stated, that a number of the operatives having declared that the wages offered to them were inadequate to their subsistence, they were directed to be taken wholly on the parish.

The Guardians also passed the following resolution:—

RESOLVED—"That the able-bodied out of employ be cautioned, that it is the intention of this Board not to allow any man, after Saturday next, to come into the stone-yard on account of non-employment, until he has first sent home the stocking frame to his employer, the Guardians having reason to believe that frauds have been practised upon the Union by men coming here to work during a time their frames have been employed at home."

This proceeding of the Guardians might be represented as one of a harsh nature towards the workpeople: yet in its ultimate operation it has been, as it was anticipated it would be, found the most beneficial that could be adopted in preventing the labour market being depressed at the expense of the labourers.

The Commissioners received from Mr. Edward Senior a report on the case, which is in substance as follows:—

I am now desirous of reporting to you the result of this decision. Mr. Law, the clerk of the Union informs me that "the workmen of this town (Hinckley) have got employment from those same masters who offered reduced wages, at the former rate, and the result of the attempt at reduction has been that, owing to the sanction and assistance of the Guardians in affording labour, in breaking stones, and relief in bread, the prices of the workmen have for the present been sustained, and the masters have been prevented from reducing their workmen."

"The object of the Guardians is good, and their intention is to prevent wages from sinking to that depressed state in which it would be necessary to afford relief, to supply the deficiency, even to those fully employed, as was the case in this town before the New Poor Law came into operation."

The Guardians have, during the present year, granted out-door relief to able-bodied persons quite without employment, in return for task-work (stone breaking) with the advantage of an efficient workhouse; whereas during a similar depression of trade in the year 1837, able-bodied persons, partially employed, were relieved; no labour test was made use of, and the workhouse accommodation was extremely deficient. I annex a tabular statement, showing the greatest number who received both in-door and out-door relief in the year 1840, during a period of five weeks, as compared with the corresponding period of the highest amount of relief in 1837.

This table shows that, as a mere matter of cost, the saving has been from 238*l.* to 81*l.*, or a saving of two-thirds in out-relief; but the more important result is, that instead of 2073 persons being pauperized, or one-third of the whole population, under the present system only 468 heads of families have received relief, or about one-fourth of the previous number.

The circumstance of a considerable number of labourers having been withdrawn from the labour market must also have prevented the accumulation of goods in the warehouses of the hosiers, and have led to a more speedy revival of trade.

Mr. Law further observes: "From the daily and constant experience that I have had in both instances, of the effect produced by giving relief without a labour test, and by refusing relief to all except in return for labour performed, I have no hesitation in declaring the latter to be the safer and surer plan, and one that is better calculated both to prevent imposition (which in such times will be attempted) and to ensure to the really deserving and industrious poor a means of living by their own labour.

"I have the honour to be, Gentlemen,
"Your obedient servant,
"EDWARD SENIOR,
"*Assistant Commissioner.*"

The Commissioners conceived it to be of importance that the attention of the Guardians should be directed to the ultimate operation of the principles of administration, as proved by practical experience. With this view they directed to be reprinted for circulation the following instructive portion of evidence of the effects of the administration of relief on correct principles in elevating the general condition of a single parish—a result effected with a machinery comparatively inefficient to that at the disposal of Boards of Guardians, acting by a staff of paid officers:—

Mr. John Ashworth, jun.:—"What is your profession?—I am a land-agent.

"As a land-agent, have you occasion to examine the condition of the neighbourhood generally as to property?—Yes; extensively.

"During what period have you been so engaged?—Prior to the year 1826, and since.

"Do you remember the circumstances of the distress which occurred in the manufacturing districts in the year 1826?—Yes; very well.

"Will you state what was the nature of the distress that occurred at that time, and how it visited your neighbourhood?—It was the master manufacturers were in difficulties. They restrained their manufacture of cotton goods, and all that neighbourhood is principally employed, or was at that time, in the manufacture of cotton goods, chiefly those called calicoes, the lowest quality of cotton goods. The labouring people, especially those in the neighbourhood of Darwen, were principally employed in that occupation, and, in consequence of the distress of the master manufacturers, a great number were thrown out of employment, consequently they came upon the parish for relief. I, as representing the lord of the manor, along with many of the other landowners, as well as the farmers, were called together at the town's office, to devise some means of affording immediate relief. The overseer declared that he could not collect money to pay the paupers; that there was not a sufficiency of money among the rate-payers to pay them with. Consequently there were very large subscriptions made by the landowners in the neighbourhood, and we were called upon, on behalf of Samuel Duckworth, Esq., the owner of the manor, to contribute towards the fund to relieve the poor for the then occasion. It was found that that relief was not the sort of relief that was effectual.

"What was the sort of relief?—They gave it in money first, and they afterwards gave it in provision.

"When they gave it in money what effects were produced?—A great many of them, after they had got a little money, came again and were more clamorous, and the continued receipt of money brought others, until the number was so large that they could not find money to pay them with—not out of the subscription. They came threatening to distress Mr. Robert Knowles, a considerable farmer; they threatened to take his cows, to milk his cows, and sell his cows, and take what he had, if he did not give them money; they said they would sell him up, and all the rest of the farmers, and make them equal to themselves; they would live out of them as long as they had anything left. Then they threatened to beat them, and, in fact, reduce everything to a common level. In the midst of the distress these paupers summoned the overseers before the magistrates, and the magistrates, anticipating some disturbance in the neighbourhood, were not so prompt as they should have been; they leant to the poor people, and even allowed summonses to be issued without any payment of fees, to bring the overseers before them to give relief to those paupers. The overseer went away and was not heard of for some time. He left the farmers to make the best they could of it, for he could not satisfy the paupers. He went away in a fright, and staid away several days. He left the select vestry to manage the best they could, he got so tired of it, and the paupers threatened several times, that if he did not give them relief they would do for him, as they called it,—meaning that they would kill him,—and he was glad to get away. About this time many of these people joined the rioters at Blackburn (four miles off), and went about the country breaking power-looms, supposing power-looms to have been the cause of their distress. After the overseer refused to act, a respectable landowner volunteered his services as overseer, and served the office of overseer for several years, till things took a turn, and till the poor people got into other employments. Referring to what I have said, that the continued receipt of money brought others, and that the numbers became so large that they could not find money to pay them out of the subscription, I would observe, that it was then proposed that they should offer them employment. A great many were taken to the highways to repair the roads. Those were nearly all weavers, at least nine-tenths of them. Of course there were some few individuals of other occupations, but the majority of them were weavers. It was then proposed to buy tools, and to set them quarrying stone in the stone-quarries.

"Are you still speaking of the distressed weavers? —Yes? a few hands—labourers in the neighbourhood, that could quarry stone and use the spade—were set as overlookers, to direct those weavers what they were to do; but it was determined that they should none of them receive any relief, unless they did some sort of work before they received it. It was found that there were too many hands to go into the quarry. Employment in other modes was provided. When this had passed over two or three weeks, some of those men began to find other employment for themselves. Having been confined to the house in weaving, they did not like out-door work for long together; but they were glad to get hold of it at the time, thinking that the parish officers or the select vestry would find some employment for them in weaving. That continued about six weeks. Afterwards, some of the men finding other employment, and the summer advancing, work of other descriptions began to be more plentiful, the numbers lessened, and the thing came about gradually of itself.

"What other descriptions of work did they find than those you have specified?—I do not at present remember anything; but the paper-makers took a lot of them to make a reservoir for the purposes of their works.

"Were there any difficulties found in getting those weavers to adapt themselves to that sort of work—quarrying?—Many of them said they would not work unless they would find them weaving to do, and the same sort of work as they had been used to; and, not in Darwen, but in the adjoining township, the overseer became a manufacturer, and bought materials for the men to work. This was talked about amongst the Darwen vestry, and these weavers were kept employed at anything they could find them to do, with some expectation when they could get the weaving to do. In Darwen they were kept draining, quarrying, and things of that kind, and still this work was supposed to be arranging for them, and therefore they were content for a while in the expectation of a return to their work. At length, in consequence of Mr. Duckworth's saying that the parish officers could not become legally manufacturers, the thing was put an end to, and all that while the paupers kept in good humour, in the hope of getting their own business instead of being quarriers.

"How was it, except for the mere purposes of getting relief, that they were glad of the parish becoming manufacturers—had they any expectation that their task-work would be easier or their employment more certain?—It was a great deal easier work than working in the fields to persons that had never been used to work at the quarrying or digging.

"In persevering in enforcing this work in Darwen, did you find much difficulty?—In the commencement, before they got sufficient tools to work with, one of the farmers volunteered to take a number of those paupers and find them stone to carry out of the quarry, because the applicants were so numerous that they could not find tools. In a day or two I saw myself, I should think, thirty or forty standing at the distance of about a yard from each other, carrying stones out of the quarry, for which they received a shilling a-day; but if they did not work a day, they received no pay. If they worked only half a day and went away, they received nothing for what they had done; but at the end of the day they received a shilling in money. Out of the thirty or forty sent there, only six or seven remained till five o'clock in the afternoon.

"Then did they find work for themselves?—They

did not apply to the parish, and we concluded that they had found work or other means.

"Then the relief given was given determinately on the principle of not making it eligible for them to continue, by making the relief given to be such as not to be preferable to ordinary employment, and not to diminish the motive to seek it. The motive to seek employment was vigorously sustained?—Yes.

"Did they work with alacrity?—They did not come to the parish afterwards, they found employment for themselves. I do not know that all the individuals did not come, but they found employment or other occupations, which lessened the relief offered to them by the overseer. After they had been worked in the fields at draining, getting turf or peat on the common, and other work, they began to find work for themselves as the summer advanced. This was from about February to about May, and in May they found other employment, and consequently there was only a very few left.

"This was the bulk of the labouring population who were in distress, and applied for relief?—Yes.

"The weavers, those who had been accustomed to use the shuttle and the shuttle only, now handled the spade or the pick-axe?—Yes; or other stronger occupations than they had been used to.

"Did the great bulk of those weavers eturn to their old occupation of weaving?—No; they did not one-half of them. Many that could not use the spade before were taught to use the spade, and have been useful labourers since. Even in the neighbourhood, some of those, weavers at that time, have never woven since, but have continued labourers, working on the road or quarrying in the stone-quarry, or assisting builders. After a bad trade it generally happens that it is so.

"And those weavers that did return, were they found to be as good weavers as ever?—Yes; not the least diminished. They returned to their weaving, and we heard no complaint of any personal deficiency.

"Do you believe that any such occupation to a weaving community would permanently deteriorate them?—I do not think it would. Many of the cotton-weavers took silk to weave, and they never had silk manufactured in that neighbourhood previously; they made the best sort of plain silk weavers. The silk manufacturers wanted the silk goods made as light as they possibly could be, and the manufacturers said they were better silk weavers than those that had been in similar occupations in the neighbourhood of Manchester. It took a few days or a week to get their hands into proper condition for the handling of the cotton and silk when they resumed their weaving. It must take a few days after the skin had been torn and made rough with the stone-breaking or handling the rougher tools, or in hay-making (instances are quite common of weavers becoming hay-makers), to get their hands smooth again. They are awkward for a day or two on returning to the loom.

"How was it that they made better silk than the people of Manchester?—I had it from a manufacturer that they made better weavers of common plain silk goods than those about Manchester. The reason given was, that the best class of silk weavers in Manchester preferred the fancy work, and those in Manchester who undertook plain common work were not generally as expert as the cotton weavers of Darwen; because the weavers of Darwen had been accustomed to weave very thin, light calicoes, and consequently could weave light thin silks for linings, &c. much better.

"Besides what took place in Darwen, did you observe what took place in respect to the distribution of the relief or the alleviation of this distress in other townships at that time?—In our own township, the township of Turton, and the next adjoining township, the paupers came to the town's office in the same way almost as in Darwen, but not to threaten, because the farmers were more respectable men: they were a higher class of people. At Turton there were a great number of the paupers weavers who applied for relief. The relief was handed to them for a day or two, and then work was offered to them. The overseer had orders to buy tools for them—to furnish every man that came for relief with a wheelbarrow and spade, to wheel a certain quantity of sand in lowering a hill for the improvement of a turnpike-road. The meetings were generally held on the Wednesday, and, out of thirty-two that applied, only four accepted that work; at the end of that day only two remained; at the end of two days only one remained, and that one continued to work for several weeks.

"What became of the others?—They found work for themselves, and consequently they had no relief from the parish.

"So that the mode of meeting this influx of claims for relief was quite effectual?—It was; they found work for themselves, and the parish had not occasion to furnish them with relief at that time. Some of them have applied since, but it has been from sickness or unforeseen accidents.

"Do you happen to know what was the course pursued in other townships than those you have mentioned?—I do not know of any but one; that was Eccleshill, the next township to Darwen, and there the overseer had unlimited directions from the parish officers to furnish such work as he thought best suited for the applicants; and he bought cotton to work into manufactured goods, and sold those goods. He also provided other work for them. That was the township that participated to the largest extent in the government money, because the parish officers left it entirely to his discretion to act as he thought proper, and they acted with him and afforded him all the necessary orders and aid. He took them to the magistrates, or to M'Adam, the road-surveyor, who took a house in the neighbourhood, and he resided in the neighbourhood for some time, and countersigned the orders after they had been signed. In Bolton there was great distress, and the same course of dealing with it was adopted there. The extent of the distress was such, that a large number of the rate-payers met together at the town's office to consult what should be done, and some suggested one thing and some suggested another. But the clergyman and one or two others advised that they should take a length of new turnpike-road to make. There was one set out between Bolton and Chorley. In fact, the road was shaped but not the stones broken, and they discussed this measure a good while what they should do about it. A good many of them were sanguine that to undertake this road-making would be an excellent thing to furnish them employment, and my father attended. He advised the measure, as it succeeded in Turton. He told them, 'I tell you, gentlemen, you may take this road to do, and you may set paupers to do it; but I advise you, before you begin, that if you burthen your hands with an undertaking of that kind your paupers will leave you, and you will have to employ other people to finish it; they will not stick to it, and you will have it left on your hands unfinished.' Some laughed at it. It created a little speculation whether he was wrong or right. They, however, went so far as this: they undertook some stone-breaking. They set those weavers with hammers to break stones, and the clergyman went to stimulate them, and watch and encourage them to go on getting their living. Wherever he went they were grumbling at the hard work and sore fingers; there was nothing but grumbling. They thought he would be soft-hearted, and that he would make interest for them to have the money on easier terms. They tired themselves out, found other employment, and gave over the job; very little road-making was done.

"And it was left on their hands?—I think they did not take it. I think they engaged the stone-breaking. If they had contracted for the road, they would have had it left on their hands. The work was there to go to, and they would not go to it.

"You mentioned that the government advanced money upon this occasion. Now what was the effect of that distribution of money; was all of it properly applied?—I think it was. I think there was no complaint on that score. A balance was left, and it is now agreed to give it to enlarge the dispensary at Bolton.

"This, which you have stated with regard to Darwen, and Turton, and Bolton, is the limit of what came within your own knowledge as to the state of pauperism within your district?—Yes.

"Now, confining yourself to Darwen, will you state how the labouring population got on after the immediate pressure of the distress had subsided, or how it was that they got out of it? Did the weavers' wages fall upon the occasion of the pressure of this distress?—They were very much reduced; as much as from 4*s.* to 1*s.* 6*d.* per piece of twenty-eight yards. They dropped gradually from 4*s.* to 3*s.*, then to 2*s.* 6*d.*; and there was one manufacturer, it was said, got some advantage by the employment of those paupers at a less price through the overseer; that he sent paupers to get work from him, and then he had some benefit out of it; but that I cannot tell, not knowing how it was done. It is so stated that a cotton manufacturer extended his business with the assistance of the parish officer making him some allowance to induce him to employ those paupers.

"That is, rates in aid of wages?—Yes; he made a larger quantity of goods in that distressed time than any other person in the neighbourhood. He would not employ any of those paupers but with the consent of the overseer, and I leave you to judge that he had some allowance from the overseer to induce him to employ them. When the effects of that distress became complete, the wages of the weaving reduced themselves from 4*s.* to 1*s.* 6*d.* When they got to that extremity, the quantity of redundant labour, and the distress spoken of as existing in that neighbourhood began to attract the notice of persons engaged in trade, and then the manufacturers of cotton and silk goods began to see a more extensive opening for their productions: they could produce them at so much less money, that Darwen, instead of being scantily supplied with work, had almost a redundancy of work brought to it to be worked; and the silk people, as well as the cotton people, brought employment into the neighbourhood.

"That is, the silk manufacturers, as well as those capitalists who were attracted by the cheap labour to come and give employment in cotton?—Yes.

"Both were attracted to the neighbourhood by it?—Yes; as soon as trade revived, they came near it. Other manufacturers came and gave work in the neighbourhood, finding that they could have it worked at a less price. They sent carts with work; a man with a spring cart and a horse could come from Manchester to Darwen and go back again in one day; and it was stated that the quantity of work the horse and cart would take and bring back would save them 6*l.* in wages, and the work would be better done.

"Was this increased demand for labour followed by the restoration of the condition of the labourers?—Yes; it gradually improved. The wages advanced after they had got to that low point; and there arose a competition among the manufacturers for them, and then the wages increased.

"Did the wages come up to the full amount that they were before?—No, they did not; because they discontinued manufacturing that sort of cloth in the neighbourhood. The manufacturers introduced a different and finer sort of cotton goods, as well as silk.

"Did the rate of wages per week increase?—It did; they got more than double wages by the silks and the different sorts of cotton than they did previously by their other work.

"What wages had the weavers got before the distressed times in that neighbourhood?—The average was from 6*s.* to 10*s.* a-week.

"When trade was restored, and, in consequence of this influx of capital, the demand for employment also, what wages did they get then?—Some of them got more than a pound a-week. One man in particular said he would not work unless he could get more than a guinea a-week. He wove silk; they doubled their wages quite.

"And all that in consequence of the energies of the people being brought out?—Yes. At the same time it must be kept in mind, that the lowest description of cotton goods they were accustomed to make before is now manufactured by the power-loom; and of course the power-loom beats the hand-loom weavers; and then these poor hand-loom weavers of low calicoes become weavers of silk and finer goods: by that means they improved their wages. But it also happened that the extension of the cotton manufacture and power-loom weaving became so general, and the capitalists became so alive to the advantages of cheap labour, that Darwen became an object of attraction to them, and more than 100,000*l.* of capital has been employed there in cotton-spinning and weaving; also property to near the same amount in paper-mills and other works. I should think more than 200,000*l.*, including cottages built, and other things connected therewith.

"Could you form any estimate or notion of the amount of fixed capital, previous to the occurrence of this period of distress in Darwen?—Scarcely anything; I should think not 20,000*l.* in the whole parish; and there is now probably 250,000*l.* of capital expended.

"Was there any mischief done by that manufacture of the overseer?—There was a loss at the commencement of the distressed times; and one man had thirty power-looms broken on his premises.

"But the point was as to the operation of the overseer's becoming manufacturer: was that prejudicial in any way?—No; it was not. It was beneficial to the parish, because it employed people who would not have got employment otherwise. It is true that the goods that were manufactured by the paupers in that sort of way were not so good as those manufactured in the regular manufactories; and there was a great loss in the disposal of them.

"Did the parish officer dispose of those goods with as much zeal and fidelity as he would have done with his own?—A great many hints were thrown out that there was partiality shown; I do not think the goods were so well worked, he not understanding the business. He took the goods if they were only put together in the shape of cloth; that was all he knew of it; and he had little or no interest in disposing of them again.

"Then the weavers did not weave so well, the man did not superintend the manufacture so well, nor so vigilantly, nor dispose of the goods so well as a person in the trade would have done?—No.

"Was the amount of money spent in that way considerable?—No; it was not considerable.

"But inconsiderable as it was, its prejudicial tendencies were manifest in the idleness on the part of the workmen, the bad superintendence on the part of the overseer, and bad sales?—Yes.

"Besides this amount of advance in the fixed capital, and this advance in the wages, did the landlord participate in any advantage in the way of advance in the rent from the increased industry, and consequent increased prosperity?—Yes; numbers doubled their rental: but that rental is increased by letting the land for the purposes of works, and for building cottages; and some coal-mines were opened that would, perhaps, never have been opened if those works had not been established, and that field makes upwards of 400*l.* a-year. The rental has been nearly doubled upon the estate in consequence of the increase of works.

"Concurrently with the advance in the several ways mentioned, has there been any increase of the population?—Yes; this place, that ten years ago had so redundant a population that the parish officers could not get employment for the surplus, has now been so greatly improved that they have been obliged to import labourers from the south. There has been a migration of labourers in addition from the southern parishes: and this place, which was all but eaten up with paupers ten years ago, borrowed a sum of money, with the subscriptions that were raised by the landowners, and built a large house of industry, what is called a workhouse; and that workhouse was not finished till after the times had began to improve again. The paupers were put in before the house was finished; but the consequence was, that that workhouse brought about a reform in the paupers sooner than it would otherwise have done, in this way:—they put over these paupers placed in the workhouse a sharp man—a man who understood how to manage them; and after the head of a family had been in a week or so, and found he must work before he ate, he found work for himself, and went out: the consequence was, that a man who was very outrageous, and used bad language to the overseers and officers who had the management of the affairs of the town, and who would not work nor provide his children with work, was actually hired out to a master manufacturer as a dresser, at 8*s.* a-week; before he had been there six months he got his family out of the workhouse. The master paid him 1*l*. 6*s*. a-week, and then he increased it. They could get 2*l*. a-week; and he actually left his master and went to Robert Orrell's and engaged to work there at higher wages than what his master at Darwen had given him; and all that took place in less than two years, and, from being the lowest of the low, he changed to a man that could get nearly 2*l*. a-week. This parish was formerly notorious for the low and brutish habits of the working classes—many of them were accustomed to poach, &c.—since their condition has been improved their habits are also improved.

"Then in the administration of relief there you have uniformly done it on what may technically be called the earn-before-you-eat principle?—Yes.

"Had not the workhouse principle been in operation in Darwen before the occurrence of this distress?—It had not; they had no workhouse before that.

"Had there been any at Bolton or Turton?—Yes; at Turton they had been well managed on the workhouse principle for above thirty years.

"The circumstance of their having witnessed the effect of the workhouse principle has already been stated in the evidence. Was it their having witnessed its effects that facilitated its full adoption in the instances which you have mentioned?—Yes, it was. The governor was sent over to Turton to see the system before he entered upon his situation at Darwen.

"Supposing, judging from past experience, the occurrence of wide-spread or general distress amongst the manufacturing population of yours, or of any other district, is there any modification of your own practice that you would suggest for the future, or do you believe that that practice is applicable to the present times, or to any apprehended visitation of similar distress?—So far as work could be had for the paupers, I think it is applicable to the present times, or to any future distress, or to any distress anywhere. I am quite of opinion that, whatever relief you hand to the able-bodied man, it is wrong if he should not do something first before he has it.

"Then you would not hesitate to enforce now, or in future, what you enforced formerly with these results, namely, spade labour or any other labour, however different from the ordinary labour of the weavers?—No; I do not think there need be any hesitation about it. If the present crisis were to come to the same extremity as in 1826, I do not think there is any better practice to be adopted than by the various parishes in our neighbourhood offering work, and money for work.

"And not letting the reliance upon the parish be the most eligible course; giving relief, but not to such an extent, or of such a nature, as to make the parish the easiest taskmaster of the two?—Of course, let them shun the parish as soon as they could. In this case, before they gave them the shilling a-day, they made them work for it. Now, the wages of the man would have been 1*s*. 6*d*. or 2*s*. They would naturally endeavour to induce people to employ them; they would ask for it; and if they could not find better employment, or come to any other place, then they would come to the parish for the shilling a-day and work. They would do draining or digging, or anything of that kind; they would very soon turn their labour towards that. They would very soon begin to think that for the parish they had to do a great deal of work for a very little money, and they would get a better kind. There was a manufacturer at Darwen, of common calicoes; that man was giving 4*s*. a-piece for weaving those calicoes. He was a well-known seller; sell he would. If he went to market, and found he could not get for his calicoes as much as he had got on a previous day, he would go home and tell his weavers that they must do it for sixpence less. He would say, I cannot make anything of you; what is the matter; why, whatever I give you, I give you too much: last week I gave you so much; I take it into the market, and lose as much by it; it is no use making it; we must give over. Well, the weavers would say, we might as well take the work out at so much as go to the parish quarrying and draining; we may as well take half-a-crown as go home and hunger; and by and by, without appearing to attempt to reduce the wages, for which other manufacturers would have blamed him, and thus reducing the value of stock, he makes an observation or two, leaning towards the necessity of lessening the wages, and those wages got quietly reduced from 4*s*. to 1*s*. 6*d*., and when reduced to the lowest point they begin to start up. The moment a man gets a profitable trade, which he does at these low wages, others come in, and by and by a number of others come; then the people say, there is so much stirring I will have 1*s*. 9*d*. and 2*s*., and the thing adjusts itself in a few months. It was not longer than from this time of year to Midsummer, before Darwen was active again after that serious depression.

"Then you would recommend or enforce that course, judging from past experience, and having regard solely to the welfare, not the immediate but ultimate welfare of the labouring classes, acted upon by such a system; meaning the adoption of the workhouse principle, giving them spade labour, or any other labour?—Yes.

"The workhouse system, or relief within it, and spade labour out of it, if you cannot get that?—Yes.

"Is there anything that you should judge in the Spitalfields labourer, or anything of any kind, that would induce you to recommend any variation in the treatment with them, as to employing them with rough tools, stone-breaking, or anything else?—No the least. The sensation of the skin upon the fingers would be impaired a little by the difference of labour, but that would soon return, and skin grow again."

Other more recent evidence of the same character is cited in the Commissioners' Sixth Annual Report, 8vo. edition, pp. 2–6.

II.—RELIEF: IN THE AGRICULTURAL DISTRICTS, TO ABLE-BODIED LABOURERS DURING PERIODS OF THE STOPPAGE OF WORK BY CONTINUED FROST OR SNOW, OR THE INCLEMENCY OF THE WEATHER.

THE Commissioners considering that many of the newly-appointed Guardians might not have had opportunities of the experience or observation of the operation of sound principles of relief when administered in the agricultural districts in the winter season, in periods of the stoppage of ordinary employment, when claims for exception flow in from the more pauperized parishes, deemed the present a fitting season for the republication of the following instructional letter in their Official Circular.

Poor Law Commission Office,
Somerset House,
January 4, 1837.

SIR,—1. The Poor Law Commissioners for England and Wales have to acknowledge the receipt of your letter of the 29th ultimo, stating that many labourers had made application for temporary relief in consequence of their being deprived of employment by the then state of the weather; and, also, that it was the opinion of the Guardians of the Union, that there existed a necessity for some provision for their wants in consequence thereof.

2. The Commissioners have to express their regret that such vicissitudes of the seasons as the occurrence of a frost, or heavy fall of snow, should still be considered as entailing as a necessary consequence that the labourers must be immediately thrown out of employment, and as a further consequence, that they should be maintained as paupers out of the rates levied for the relief of destitution.

3. The Commissioners had confidently hoped that the principles of Poor Law Administration so clearly set forth, and so widely disseminated by the Poor Law Commissioners of Enquiry, and so frequently explained by themselves, and by the several Assistant Commissioners in the county of Sussex, would have been too well understood to have rendered it necessary at the present time, under unfavourable circumstances, to explain the advantages of the workhouse system, and to point out the evils which always accompany the practice of giving out-door relief to able-bodied labourers.

4. The Commissioners consider that the adherence to the workhouse system on occasions like the present, is essentially protective of the real interests and happiness of the labouring classes.

5. In the districts in which happily the number of labourers does not exceed the demand for labour, and where consequently the wages of a labourer employed for broken and uncertain periods, are sufficiently high to maintain him through such part of the year as does not afford him occupation, the practice of giving an able-bodied labourer parochial relief out of the workhouse, is a direct bounty on improvidence. The certainty of parish support at his home extinguishes in his mind all motive for husbanding the summer earnings, the harvest money, the profitable results of job-work, and induces him too often to spend the superfluous moneys arising from his occasional but adequately paid employment, not in promoting the comfort of his family, but in selfish indulgence at the beer-house.

6. The Commissioners know of but one mode of puting an end to this evil; namely, the adoption of the workhouse system, as contemplated by the legislature.

7. As soon as the labourer is aware that the only form in which he can receive parochial relief is as an inmate of the workhouse, together with his family, subject to the restrictive discipline of that establishment, he will gradually, if not immediately, be supplied with motives of a totally opposite character and forethought, and increased industry will take the place of extravagance and indulgence.

8. In this effect of the workhouse system the Commissioners have the fullest confidence, increased by the facts which are daily developed throughout the country; and they have only to wish that they could impress the Guardians with as strong a conviction of its successful results as they themselves entertain.

9. It is true that there are districts to which the preceding observations are less applicable,

and in which the wages of the labourer, during those intervals in which he is employed, are insufficient to supply the wants of himself and family during the whole year. This is more especially the case in the most pauperised parts of England, in which the practice of regarding the poor-rates as the natural and obvious means of supporting the labourer was carried to such an extent, that the employers of labour were accustomed to discharge their labourers, and throw them upon the rates as paupers, on every interruption of the work on which they were engaged, occasionally even on the interruption caused by a rainy day.

10. It is unnecessary to enlarge on the miserable condition of the labourers in parishes such as these. There, however, the application of the workhouse system is equally salutary in its results, and restores to them their independence and comfort, either by leading to their permanent employment, or to such an increased rate of wages, as would enable them to subsist without aid from the poor-rates; it operates both on the feelings and interests of the employers of labour, as an inducement to resort to the ancient and excellent practice of hiring labourers for the year certain, rather than suffer the labourers' home to be broken up, and the labourer and his family to be placed in a workhouse, so as to render it difficult for his employers to regain his services, although they may be urgently required.

11. The continuance, moreover, of any number of labourers in the workhouse under these circumstances affords a decisive proof that their number in the district exceeds the demand for their services, and furnishes them with a powerful motive for seeking employment elsewhere, and thus contributing to raise the condition of those whom they leave behind.

12. To suggest, in such cases, the districts in which they are most likely to find work; to facilitate their migration; or if they should prefer seeking a livelihood in the British colonies, to afford every assistance in going there, are the most pleasing portion of the duties of the Commissioners, and will be promptly and cheerfully performed.

12. The Commissioners have to point out to the Guardians, that the results which follow a steady adherence to the workhouse system are no longer a matter of conjecture, but of experience, which, although not long in point of duration, is ample in point of extent.

14. The same system, which the Guardians in several of the Sussex Unions are trying to revive, existed in parts of East Kent, Berks, and Oxfordshire; the same rule, which is now sought to be relaxed, has been applied in those counties; and the Guardians of the several Unions therein are so aware of its essential importance, and of its salutary consequences, that not a single application for its relaxation has been received by the Commissioners.

15. The conviction which the Commissioners entertain of the advantages and practicability of adhering to the rule, preventing out-door relief being given to able-bodied labourers, a conviction which they have endeavoured to communicate to the Guardians, renders the Commissioners very unwilling to undertake the responsibility of foregoing the beneficial results adverted to, or of reviving a pernicious practice by sanctioning or encouraging any departure from that regulation.

16. They recommend, therefore, that, to the extent to which workhouse accommodation is available, the claims of those able-bodied persons who are really destitute, should be met by the offer of relief in the workhouse, to themselves and to their families, where they will be sheltered from the inclemency of the weather, and receive a sufficient supply of nutritious food, in return for such labour as can there be provided for them.

17. For those able-bodied paupers, for whom no accommodation can be provided in the workhouse, for whom no work can be provided by themselves, or by their employers, and who are wholly destitute, out-door relief, chiefly in kind, should be given, but, as far as possible, in return for work.

18. If the applications for relief are numerous, it becomes of the highest importance, especially when, from the workhouse being full, it can no longer be used as a test of destitution, that the Guardians should exercise the greatest watchfulness as to the cases which come before them, in order that they may be fully satisfied that the destitution is real.

19. Whenever an able-bodied agricultural labourer applies for relief on account of the stoppage of his work by his employer, the relieving officer should be sent to the employer to ascertain the circumstances.

20. In cases of destitution in consequence of marked improvidence of the person's earnings, the relief should be administered by way of loan, with a notice that the loan, or a fixed portion of it, will be recovered by attachment of wages when the period of full employment returns.

21. It is desirable, moreover, that the Guardians should be careful not to suggest relief from the poor-rates as a resource in any case by the appearance of preparation for relief before the relief is absolutely demanded.

22. Although the Commissioners have deemed it their duty to decline sanctioning any relaxation of their rules on the present occasion, yet when they consider how much of the defects in the conduct or character of the labouring classes has arisen from causes over which they had themselves no control, they cannot but feel the strongest conviction that every possible assistance should be afforded to them by their employers in the struggle to regain their independence.

23. It should be borne in mind that the increased facilities for obtaining parish relief, so far from operating as assistance, is directly the reverse; and that the best and almost the only aid, which can be safely afforded, is by providing employment at fair wages.

24. The saving effected by the stoppage of out-door relief, must have left in the hands of the employers a sum precisely equal to such saving. From this source the employers have the means, and they will have doubtless the inclination, to support their labourers when the weather makes work less abundant, without placing them on the poor-rate.

25. Although such employment may not always return immediate profit, yet it rarely happens that it does not produce a result equivalent to the expenditure, the more especially when it is considered that in default of such employment the maintenance of the labourers in the workhouse will fall upon the occupiers.

26. The question, in fact, now is, whether they shall be maintained out of the poor-rate in comparative idleness, or on the farms of their former masters, at such work as the inclemency of the weather still renders it possible to perform; that is, whether the labourer shall be supported in a way that demoralizes his character by weakening all motive to industry and foresight, or (at no greater expense) by the spontaneous determination of their employers to resort to the better system of yearly hiring, which has been pursued in unpauperized counties.

27. The Commissioners trust that the Guardians will themselves, as employers of labourers, set an example to their neighbours and constituents, by their exertion in providing useful work for the labourers at this season, and where work absolutely fails, it is hoped the Guardians will not be backward in rendering neighbourly assistance or temporary aid from individuals as loans, or otherwise using every means to make the poor-rates the last, instead of as heretofore the first, resource in cases of emergency.

28. The Commissioners would impress upon the Guardians and rate-payers that gratitude and kindly feelings must be generated between individuals for assistance rendered on such occasions; and that though a false popularity may be gained by individual distributors of relief in distributing the money of others, no gratitude is ever created (for relief received as a right), towards a numerous body, invested with a corporate character and official functions.

29. The Commissioners, in the preceding observations, have confined themselves to the cases of able-bodied labourers and their families.

30. With regard to the aged and infirm, they are well aware that it needs no recommendation from the Commissioners to ensure a careful attention to the wants of that class of claimants during the inclement season, and that the Guardians will cheerfully give all the relief which is needful to supply the deficiencies of the exertions of natural relations or private beneficence.

31. The Commissioners have only to add, that if any case should occur by reason of the state of the weather, or from any other cause which the Guardians might consider a particular case of emergency, and shall deem it right to afford out-door relief as an exceptional case, the Commissioners will not withhold their sanction, provided that the claim for relief, and the grounds thereof shall be reported to them, and that it shall appear that a proper discretion has been exercised in such departure from the rule.

Signed by order of the Board,

E. CHADWICK, *Secretary*.

The following statements of practical exemplifications of the rule are extracted from their Third and Fourth Annual Reports :—

"Mr. Hawley reported to us of the further proceedings in Sussex—that in the Petworth Union, where the instructions issued prevented a relaxation of the rule which the Guardians were on the point of ceding, 'the second board-day after the snow, at which I attended, twelve applications were made by able-bodied paupers, and all were offered the workhouse, with even a more striking result than that which followed the offers at Cuckfield, for none accepted them.'

"Towards the end of November the Guardians of the Highworth and Swindon Union, who had scarcely commenced acting upon the order for withholding out-door relief from able-bodied males, received in one day applications for relief, in aid of wages, from nineteen able-bodied labourers, who with their wives and families numbered about ninety-five persons. The Guardians had the firmness and judgment not to relax in their determination. All were offered the house. Rather, however, than incur the heavy expense of their maintenance there, the farmers of the parish to which they belonged (for nearly all belonged to one place, where an effort was making to reduce the already low rate of wages) in a few hours agreed to increase their wages; and only four or five families ultimately came into the house.

"Mr. Hall reported as follows concerning the Unions in Berkshire, Oxfordshire, and a part of Gloucestershire :—

"'The periodical Returns will best exhibit the effects of the workhouse system on able-bodied pauperism. I may, however, instance one Union, that of Hungerford. When I aided in the formation of this Union, in the summer of 1835, I ascertained that the three parishes of Lambourne, Hungerford, and Ramsbury supported, during every winter, more than three hundred able-bodied men, of whom one-half might be men with wives and families. On the 11th January, 1837, the number of able-bodied men relieved by the eighteen parishes comprised in the Union was eight, there being, in all, only twenty-one men whom the Guardians would permit to be set to work at the hand corn-mill. This Union commenced with two workhouses; within the first year of its existence it dispensed with one of them, and in the autumn of 1836 it contracted to receive into its remaining house the paupers of the adjacent Union of Andover, by which arrangement I am informed that Union is dispauperized, more than four hundred able-bodied men having disappeared from the relief-lists since the agreement was formed.

"'I perceive everywhere the most satisfactory proofs that the compulsion to depend upon his own resources exercised on the labourer by the workhouse system, not only does not place him in a hopeless condition as to his means of subsistence, but guards against mischief by multiplying those resources, and by working effectually on those by whom, in its proper shape, that subsistence is supplied. Permanent employment is now given to a far greater extent than formerly: during the recent sudden fall of snow, it was found difficult to procure hands to clear the high-roads and dig out the vehicles which had been buried in the drift; and nowhere have I heard of an increase in the applications for relief arising from the inclemency of the whether.

"'At the Board of Guardians of the Bradfield Union, on the 9th day of this month (January, 1837), when the snow was but partially melted, an application was made, in my hearing, by a respectable farmer, to one of the relieving officers for men to do farm-work; the answer was—"That he knew of none disengaged whom he could recommend." Another relieving officer then informed me that he had given the same answer to a similar application, two days previously; this announcement produced a declaration from all the Guardians present,—that they knew of no men out of employment, whose character was not so notoriously bad, that the farmers could not venture to set them to work; and they also were very few in number.'

"Mr. Gulson reported to us (23d January) as follows, of the districts under his superintendence :—

"'During the severe weather I attended those Boards where I anticipated the greatest falling back upon the poor-rate by the labouring population; and, I am happy to say, I am aware of no case in which your rules have been infringed, or in which hardship has been created by a steady adherence to them in this season of severity.

"'In the visits which I have paid to the Boards of Guardians since the fall of snow, I have found that wherever the workhouse accommodation has been complete, the applications for relief during the "severe blast," as it is here called, have been few and unimportant; where the accommodation has been limited and imperfect, the demands have been more numerous and pressing; and in those Unions where no workhouse yet exists, the labourers have endeavoured to fall back upon the parish purse for support, with a determination which no single parish officer could possibly have withstood.'

"In illustration of the effects of this system in developing the energies of the labourers who had been pauperized, Mr. Gulson adduces the following instances :—

"'On Thursday, the 29th of December, the frost having continued and become more intense, Mr. ——— was not a little surprised to find his drainers again at work, and proceeding nearly as well as before the frost. He went to them and said, "How is this? It appears you can go on very well, notwithstanding the weather?" "Yes," rejoined the men, "we have found it out this morning." "Why then," said Mr. ———, "were you absent on Monday, Tuesday, and Wednesday?" "Because," added they, "we thought we could not go on; but as we cannot obtain relief as we used to do, necessity has made us try, and we have this morning discovered that we can proceed with the draining without much difficulty."'

"Suffolk and Norfolk have been of late years amongst the most pauperized counties, and we are gratified in being enabled to state to your Lordship, that the effects produced by the introduction of the new law have been highly satisfactory. Dr. Kay, in a Report to us, cites the testimony of several of the able Guardians of the Unions in those counties.

"The Rev. Jex Blake, Chairman of the Aylsham Union, says:—'I have the pleasure to state, that during the late inclement weather the Board of Guardians of the Aylsham Union steadily persevered in their discontinuance of out-door relief to all able-bodied males. We had rather an increase in the number of applications from that class during the month, but I really believe most of them were experiments on the Board, suggested by small occupiers to their able-bodied labourers, for whom, during the snow-storm, they could not readily find employment.

"'These men, however, on the refusal of out-door relief, either returned to their masters, or found immediate employment in the removal of snow from the roads, &c. &c.

"'In this part of the country, where the roads are narrow, I think a drifting snow-storm, like that which we have just experienced, creates during the first fortnight as much work as it hinders; hundreds of men might have been usefully employed, if magistrates would only have issued orders for the more immediate clearance of the highways, but generally speaking, there are no good labourers out of work at this moment.

"'I repeat, Sir, that relaxation of our important (and in the end I may say our merciful) regulation was not for one moment entertained by the Aylsham Board, the only deviation in any part of our course was the allowances of a few sixpences weekly to the extremely aged paupers. You will have learnt by the returns you receive from the clerk, that during the snow-storm our inmates at Buxton Workhouse decreased; the return a fortnight ago was—Admitted, 7.—Discharged, 38.'

"The Rev. Henry Owen, chairman of the Hoxne Union, states:—'That the late heavy fall of snow did not occasion us in this Union to deviate in the smallest degree from our resolution of May last, the effect of which was to discontinue from that period all out-door relief to able-bodied male paupers. Indeed, so rare, during the whole winter (the period of the snow even inclusive), have been the applications for relief from this class of persons, and so invariably has the offer of the workhouse been refused by the few applicants who have appeared, that our Board has experienced no difficulty whatever in continuing to adhere strictly, unless in cases of sickness, to the resolution to which I have referred.

"'I was much struck with the spirit of independence manifested by the labourers of many of our parishes during the time of the snow. Aware that the surveyors had received orders from the magistrates to clear the roads within a given time, they very fairly availed themselves of the opportunity thus afforded them of endeavouring to make a particularly good bargain before they would commence operations. In fact, there was a general strike for one day; and I have reason to believe that the surveyors would have been unable to hire labourers at all, had they not consented (which they were at length obliged to do) to pay beyond the customary wages of the district.'

"The Rev. F. Calvert, the chairman of the Cosford Union, states:—'No relaxation whatever in the rule of giving relief to able-bodied males only in the workhouse was thought to be admissible by the Board of Guardians of the Cosford Union, in consequence of the late snow. The sure consequence of a relaxation would have been, that a great number of employers would have turned off hands, whom, without the prospect of out-door relief for them, they would, and no doubt did, continue to employ throughout the season of snow.'

"We find in all these districts that the employers, who once believed that the former system was advantageous to them, now begin to perceive that their ultimate interest in the independence of the labourers is coincident with the interest of the labourers themselves.

"Robert Newton Shawe, Esq., the chairman of the Woodbridge Union, stated to Dr. Kay, that several of the most intelligent and wealthy yeomen of the district called upon him about the period of the snow-storm, and earnestly entreated that he would use his utmost personal influence to prevent the Union from relapsing into the evils of the allowance system.

"Dr. Kay concludes his report from these two counties in the following terms:—

"'From the tables containing an account of the various classes of paupers relieved in the workhouses of the Unions in Norfolk and Suffolk, which I forward with this Report, you will perceive that the numbers relieved in the workhouses of Unions, containing a population of 336,166 persons in the week before the snow-storm, were 2,491, including all classes, or about 3-4ths of 1 per cent. upon the population; that in the week of the snow-storm the number decreased to 2,461, or about 7-10ths of 1 per cent. upon the population; the week after the snow-storm the numbers increased to 2,558, or about 3-4ths of 1 per cent. upon the population; and in the succeeding week they amounted to 2,696, or were about 4-5ths of 1 per cent. upon the population. You will therefore perceive that this extraordinary fall of snow had but a very slight effect upon the numbers relieved in the Union workhouses, the total increase in the course of an entire month in the depth of the winter season being barely 200 persons of all classes in a population of 336,166, or about 1 person in 1,700.'

"Mr. Tufnell stated (4th Report, 8vo. p. 219) 'That large sums in charity were given away in the Isle of Thanet during the snow, yet, during that period, the circumstance of two labourers' balls at least being given, came to my knowledge, and one pauper in receipt of out-relief, actually gave a ball. Great distress was said to exist at Canterbury, though the poor refused to take much of the soup that was made for them, and in consequence fifty gallons were thrown into the river. In Romney Marsh, I found that the wife of a man receiving relief attended a "grand fancy masquerade ball," at which the tickets were either 3*s.* or 4*s.* There is also reason to believe that the subscriptions to relieve the distress were sometimes positively injurious. In one parish in East Kent, the surveyor was unable to clear the roads of snow, on account of a considerable subscription collected to relieve the poor. The observation of the men was, "Why should we work, is not the subscription for us?" and accordingly a landholder, who was desirous of carting manure across a road obstructed by the snow, was compelled to send to his own farm for men to clear the way, while those who should have done it were living in idleness.'"

Most of the Unions in this district that had for some time acted on the principle of giving no out-relief to able-bodied, steadily adhered to it during the winter, many of the Guardians being well convinced that to depart from it in a very few cases would have the effect of throwing hundreds out of service who were kept in employ solely by the operation of this rule.

Similar instances were adduced from other counties.

III.—RELIEF IN WORKHOUSES:

ILLEGALITY OF THE INFLICTION OF PUNISHMENT ON UNCHASTE WOMEN.

Copy of a Minute of the Poor Law Commissioners, dated March 5, 1839.

THE Poor Law Commissioners are informed that in several Union workhouses single women, mothers of children or pregnant, are compelled to wear a dress of a peculiar colour as a mark of disgrace.

The Commissioners are aware that such a regulation has originated solely in a desire on the part of the Guardians to repress vice; and it is only because they are convinced that principles of considerable importance are involved in this practice that they feel called on to express an opinion on the subject.

The following are the principal grounds on which they have arrived at the conclusion that such distinction in dress, or any equivalent mark of disgrace, is inexpedient.

It was the obvious intention of the legislature in the Poor Law Amendment Act to carry into effect the views of the Commissioners of Enquiry, "that a bastard should be what Providence appears to have ordained that it should be—a burthen on its mother." The woman by her imprudence has become charged with the maintenance of a child, without having previously secured for herself and her offspring the protection of a husband and a father. The amended law, most properly, as the Commissioners conceive, removed the punishment which by the statutes of the 7 Jas. I., c. 4, and the 50 Geo. III., c. 51, placed such conduct in the class of *crimes*, and simply left the mother to bear the natural consequences of *vice*. These consequences are—the burthen of supporting the child, and she becomes an inmate of the workhouse, because she is destitute of means to bear this burthen. Whatever the cause of her destitution may be, it ought not, as the Commissioners think, to affect her treatment there. Any attempt to inflict disgrace or punishment on the mother of a bastard, as such, appears to be in opposition to the principles which guided the legislature in the alteration of the law on this subject.

Even if the penal provision against mothers of bastards, contained in the 50 Geo. III., c. 51, had not been repealed, it would not, in the opinion of the Commissioners, be expedient to inflict any punishment on unchaste women, as such, in workhouses. The statute in question empowered two justices to commit the mother of a bastard child to a house of correction for any time not exceeding twelve months, nor less than six weeks; but it did not direct that mothers of bastards, when inmates of workhouses, should be subject to any punishment. The sole object of the workhouse is to give relief to the destitute poor in such a manner as shall satisfy their necessary wants, without making pauperism attractive, or otherwise injuring the industrious classes. The workhouse is not intended to serve any penal or remuneratory purpose; and it ought not to be used for punishing the dissolute, or rewarding the well-conducted pauper. If it is attempted by means of the workhouse to attain comparatively unimportant ends for which it is not fitted, there is a danger of not attaining the important end for which it is fitted.

Many, probably a majority, of the inmates of a workhouse have become such by want of prudence on their own part: but it is manifestly impossible to distinguish in the mode of relief the various shades of character which have led to pauperism. In administering relief through a workhouse, necessary food, raiment, and lodging, are all that can safely be offered in *any* case; and *less* than such necessaries can be afforded in *none*.

The following objections may be raised in reply to these arguments:—

1st. That the Commissioners have repeatedly pressed on Boards of Guardians the expediency of relieving women with bastard children in the workhouse only.

2nd. That it is sometimes necessary in towns to separate the women of infamous and thoroughly abandoned character from the other female inmates.

The Commissioners feel convinced that relief to able-bodied women of any class should, as far as possible, be given in a workhouse; not only because of the evils which would result from relief in aid of wages, but because in the case of an able-bodied woman, her means of support are uncertain, and far more difficult to determine with precision than those of other paupers. The Commissioners, however, have forborne from pressing this opinion on Boards of Guardians with regard to widows with families; believing that in general the Boards of Guardians, from not thoroughly apprehending the evils of out-door relief, would be disposed to consider as severe any regulation withholding relief of this nature from a class of persons whose circumstances justly excite their sympathy.

The separation of certain abandoned persons from the other inmates rests, not on the consideration of their *past* conduct, but on that of their *present* habits and character. Their separation from the other inmates is necessary for the maintenance of order in the workhouse; and it has even been suggested that it would be expedient to form a central receptacle in which the riotous and abandoned prostitutes from the several London Unions might be congregated, and subjected to peculiar regulations.

It will be evident, therefore, that if, on the one hand it is inexpedient that the necessary support of the destitute should be converted into an apparent reward of good character, but a real premium on improvidence; so, on the other hand, it was not the intention of the legislature to constitute the Board of Guardians a tribunal for the punishment of past profligacy by any varieties in the mode of administering in-door relief.

IV.—LIABILITY OF OFFICERS OCCUPYING APARTMENTS IN THE WORKHOUSE TO PAY ASSESSED TAXES.

The following application from the Guardians of the Tonbridge Union for the opinion of the Commissioners was read to the Board:—

"*Tonbridge Union.*

"GENTLEMEN,—A claim is made on the Guardians for assessed taxes for the workhouse, as under:—

"Windows . . . . 1*l.* 16*s.*

"In the assessors' instructions under the 43 Geo. III., in the lists of exemptions from duties on windows, appears,

"'3. Any hospital, charity school, or house, provided for the reception and relief of poor persons, except such apartments therein as are or may be occupied by the officers or servants thereof, which shall severally be assessed and be subject to the said duties as entire dwelling houses.'

"The separate apartments occupied by the officers or servants of this workhouse contain windows, as under:—

"Guardians and clerk's room . . .	3
Governor's apartments	5
Schoolmaster's and schoolmistress's do.	3
Porter's do.	1
Total . .	12

"It appears that windows under the number of eight, in separate dwelling houses, are not liable to duty, and the Guardians think there is a question whether the workhouse windows are liable, as it appears neither of the apartments, if considered as entire (or separate) dwelling houses contain eight windows. The guardians think it likely this point may have been brought under your notice, and they request the favour of your opinion on the subject.

"I am, gentlemen,
"Your most obedient servant,
"JOHN SCOONES, *Clerk*

"*To the Poor Law Commissioners.*"

The Commissioners directed a copy of the letter to be sent to the Commissioners of Stamps and Taxes, requesting their view of the law upon the subject. The following is the reply, a copy of which the Commissioners directed to be sent to the Guardians of the Tonbridge Union; and from which it will be seen that the windows in a workhouse are exempt from duty, and that none of the officers are chargeable with duty, unless the apartments occupied by them individually contain more than seven windows.

"*Stamps and Taxes.*

"SIR,—The Board having had before them your letter of the 19th instant, respecting a claim for window-duty made on the Guardians of the Tonbridge Union in respect of windows in the workhouse, and in apartments occupied by the various officers,

"In reply I am directed to state that the board are of opinion that the windows in the workhouse are exempt from duty under the 2nd Case of Exemptions, Schedule A, of the 48th Geo. III., cap. 55, and that as none of the officers individually occupy apartments containing more than seven windows, they are not chargeable with duty with reference to the 6th Geo. IV., cap. 7.

"I am, Sir,
"Your most obedient servant,
"CHARLES PRESSLY.

"*To E. Chadwick, Esq.*"

V.—SUPPLIES BY CONTRACTORS:—

ILLEGALITY OF ANY GUARDIAN SUPPLYING ANY CONTRACTS.

The Commissioners took into consideration the following application from the Clerk of the Chesterfield Union:—

Chesterfield, 22nd October, 1840.

SIRS,—It having been represented to the Board of Guardians that an individual Guardian was in the habit of supplying the contractor with part of the milk consumed in the Workhouse, I was desired to state my opinion to the Board whether such was or was not an illegal act. The facts are, such Guardian keeps a considerable number of cows, and is a dealer in milk, and he does not deny that he sells to the contractor supplying the workhouse a proportionate share of the quantity of milk daily consumed, but he contends as he is not the contractor, he can sell to any individual who may apply to him for milk, and that he is not bound to know that the milk he sells to a contractor is for the use of the Workhouse. The opinion I gave to the Board was that I considered that no Guardian could legally supply the Workhouse, either directly or indirectly, with any article, and that in this case the milk had been indirectly, and consequently illegally, supplied. I shall be obliged by your informing me at your earliest convenience whether you consider the opinion I have given is correct.

I have the honour to remain, Sirs,
Your obedient servant,
JOHN MARSH.

The Poor Law Commissioners.

To which the Commissioners stated in reply that they were of opinion that a Guardian of the Poor in supplying the contractor with the milk consumed in the Workhouse would be liable to the penalties imposed by the 55th Geo. III. c. 137, for being concerned indirectly in furnishing a supply of provisions for the use of the Workhouse. The Commissioners cannot distinguish between the present case and that of West *v.* Andrews, reported in 5 B and A, 328. There a Guardian furnished provisions to the master of the Workhouse, who had the contract for providing for the poor of the parish for which such Guardian acted; the Guardian, in conjunction with others, appointed the contractor to his situation, and it was their duty to superintend the conduct of such contractor. The Court held that the Guardian was liable to the penalty. Abbott, Chief Justice, observing, "Under these circumstances it seems to me, that all the mischief which was contemplated by the Legislature would arise if we were to hold that it was lawful; I am, therefore, clearly of opinion that the defendant's case falls both within the words and spirit of the Act of Parliament, and that the rule for a new trial must therefore be made absolute."

(Signed) E. CHADWICK,
Secretary.

LONDON:
Printed by order of the Poor Law Commissioners, by W. CLOWES and SONS, Stamford Street, and Published by CHARLES KNIGHT and Co., 22, Ludgate-street, Publishers to the Poor Law Commissioners.

VOLUME II
[1841-1842]

AN

OFFICIAL CIRCULAR

OF PUBLIC DOCUMENTS AND INFORMATION:

DIRECTED BY THE POOR LAW COMMISSIONERS TO BE PRINTED, CHIEFLY FOR THE USE OF THE MEMBERS AND PERMANENT OFFICERS OF BOARDS OF GUARDIANS, UNDER THE POOR LAW AMENDMENT ACT.

No. 11. CIRCULAR ISSUED FEBRUARY 6TH, 1841.

Poor Law Commission Office,
Somerset House,
February 2, 1841.

THE Poor Law Commissioners, on a review of their minutes, directed that the minutes and correspondence on the following subjects should be printed and circulated for the information of Guardians and officers of the several Unions, viz.—

By order of the Board,

EDWIN CHADWICK, *Secretary*.

I.—EXTENSION OF VACCINATION.

1.—MEASURES RECOMMENDED TO BE TAKEN TO CHECK THE SPREAD OF SMALL POX IN THE METROPOLIS.

Poor Law Commission Office,
Somerset House,
19th January, 1841.

SIR,—The Poor Law Commissioners deem it right to call the special attention of the Guardians, to the prevalence of small-pox in the metropolis, as exhibited in the weekly returns of the mortality, and in the number of cases which are sent to the Small-pox Hospital.

The Commissioners are informed by Dr. Gregory, the physician of that establishment, that the number of cases sent to the Small-pox Hospital is so great that the establishment will soon be filled, and that it may shortly be necessary to provide wards in the Union houses for the reception and appropriate treatment of such cases.

The Commissioners are informed that nearly the greater proportion of the persons received into the Small-pox Hospital are (in the proportion shown in the annexed return) adults who have not received the protection of vaccination.

The Commissioners feel assured that this

announcement will be sufficient to induce the Board of Guardians to avail themselves to the utmost extent of the powers placed at their disposal by the Vaccination Extension Act, and of the influence which they possess, in order to arrest the progress of this fatal disease.

They would recommend the Board of Guardians to confer with the vaccinators on the subject, without loss of time, to ascertain from them, 1. Whether the measures for vaccination already adopted in compliance with the Commissioners' instructional letter of the 20th day of August, 1840, and the recommendations and orders subsequently issued, are sufficient to meet the present emergency. 2. Whether the inhabitants of the Union avail themselves of the opportunities afforded to them, or whether any means can be suggested of removing their objections (if such exist) or of stimulating their apathy.

The Commissioners would recommend that at all events a fresh notification of the *times* and *places* of attendance, in large characters, (and that in case the increase of small-pox should have extended to the ——— Union, the notification should be headed "*Increase of small-pox* in the parish of ———") should be placed in conspicuous places in the Union, and it should be particularly stated therein that the arrangements are not confined to children only, but are also intended for the benefit of adults.

The Commissioners would also suggest for the consideration of the Guardians and the vaccinators, whether, under existing circumstances, it might be expedient for the vaccinators to visit from house to house in their several districts, and thus to bring to the homes of the inhabitants the means of vaccination.

Under ordinary circumstances the Commissioners would hesitate to recommend such an arrangement; but feeling that on the present occasion, by energy and promptitude on the part of the Guardians and the vaccinators, the progress of the small-pox may be arrested, and its attacks rendered comparatively innocuous, the Commissioners think it well worthy the consideration of the Guardians.

The Commissioners think moreover that if the extra exertions of the vaccinators should require further remuneration, the Guardians would be perfectly justified in giving it.

The Commissioners are desirous that, in order that no time may be lost, you would, if possible, request the vaccinators to be in attendance to-morrow at the meeting of the Board of Guardians, in order that they may be at hand when you lay this communication before the Guardians.

The Commissioners also wish that you will not fail to apprize the Guardians of any facts relating to the spread of small-pox which may come to your knowledge as Superintendent-Registrar, and that in addition to other steps and precautions which may be decided on, you would yourself inform the vaccinators of any particular parts of the Union in which you may have ascertained the small-pox to be prevalent, and that you will specially call the attention of the residents in those parts of the Union by handbills, or by the agency of the relieving officer, to the measures provided for vaccination.

Signed by order of the Board,
EDWIN CHADWICK, *Secretary.*

Return of the Number of Cases (and Deaths) admitted into the Small-Pox Hospital during the year 1840.

	Numbers.	Whereof Died.
Patients wholly unprotected	194	87
——— previously vaccinated	120	8
——— supposed to have had small pox previously	2	..
——— not having small pox	11	..
Total	327	95

Return of the Number, and Ages, and Deaths of the Cases admitted into the Small-Pox Hospital in 1840.

	Numbers.	Whereof Died.
Patients under 5 years of Age	49	28
——— between the Ages of 5 and 15 (inclusive).	46	9
Adults	232	58
Total	327	95

Jan. 18, 1841. G. GREGORY, M.D.

The Secretary read a letter from Sir James Clarke, her Majesty's physician, expressive of his satisfaction at the progress of vaccination. In that letter Sir James stated—

"The Princess Royal was vaccinated yesterday; Her Majesty and the Prince Albert considered it right to have the Princess vaccinated at the early age of one month in consequence of the prevalence of small-pox in the metropolis. Should the vaccination fail, it is the intention of Her Majesty and the Prince to have it repeated at short intervals until it succeeds, being fully persuaded of its efficacy as a preventive of small-pox."

The Commissioners were subsequently informed that the Princess Royal was vaccinated three times, namely, on the 21st of November, the 28th of December, and the 12th of January, before the vaccination took effect.

II.—EMIGRATION.

2.—DESCRIPTION OF PERSONS APPROVED OF BY THE COMMISSIONERS FOR COLONIAL LANDS AND EMIGRATION.

THE Commissioners took into consideration the Report of a Committee of the Cork Board of Guardians, containing a list of inmates of the workhouse whom the Guardians were desirous should have assistance afforded them to emigrate. The Commissioners directed the following letter, enclosing a copy of the Report, to be forwarded to the Right Honourable Lord John Russell, Her Majesty' Secretary for the Colonies:—

Poor Law Commission Office,
Somerset House,
13th November, 1840.

MY LORD,—We have the honour of transmitting to your Lordship a copy of a Report of a Committee of the Cork Board of Guardians, containing a list of inmates of Cork workhouse whom the Guardians consider fit for emigration, and of whom it is unquestionably desirable, if it be possible, to relieve the Cork workhouse. We also transmit some remarks upon this Report by Mr. Voules, the Assistant Commissioner for the Cork Union.

The building now used by the Cork Guardians as the workhouse of the Cork Union was formerly a house of industry for the county of Cork; and at the period of its declaration as the Union workhouse it contained a large number of inmates, many of whom had not before their admission been residents in the Union. All these persons are now a burden upon the rate-payers of the Cork Union; and, moreover, they occupy space which would otherwise be allotted to persons who, according to the provisions of the Irish Relief Act, would be considered as having a prior claim to relief in the Cork workhouse.

The present is a peculiar case, and cannot recur; inasmuch as there is no other Union in Ireland similarly situated. The emigration of a portion of the inmates of the Cork workhouse at the expense of the general Government would relieve the rate-payers of the Cork Union of a burden which has been, if not unfairly, at least unfortunately, cast upon them; and it would facilitate the working of the Irish Relief Act in the important Union of Cork.

For the preceding reasons we recommend this application to your Lordship's favourable consideration, in case Her Majesty's Government should have any funds applicable to purposes of emigration.

We have the honour to be,
My Lord,
Your Lordship's obedient servant,
(Signed) J. G. S. LEFEVRE.
G. C. LEWIS.

To the Right Hon. Lord John Russell,
&c. &c. &c.

"*Emigration Committee Report.*

"*Office of Poor Law Guardians, Cork,*
"*26th October*, 1840.

"The Emigration Committee, in preparing this amended Report of their inquiry, have adhered strictly to the instructions of the Board in the classification of applicants for emigration. To prevent the multiplication of documents, they repeat here briefly the principles which guided them as contained in their former report.

"The *first and largest class comprises the members of the old house of industry;* the second class, those charged to the general Union, but not belonging to the house of industry. A third class is composed of those charged to the several electoral divisions. Each class is divided into sexes, and those within and beyond the age of thirty.

"They have admitted, *from special causes*, a few who entered the house since the 17th August. The names of those parties are mentioned, and their cases are referred by the Committee to the consideration of the Board. They have rejected very many who appeared to have come into the house merely for the purpose of emigrating. While making their inquiry, they had peculiar opportunities of judging how just are the claims advanced by the Board of Guardians for Government aid to relieve the Cork workhouse by emigration. They have ascertained *that there were nearly* 400 *persons inmates of the house of industry when surrendered to the Board, who had no claim on the Union.* A considerable number of those are still in the house; there are also within its walls *hundreds admitted since the Union was declared, not fairly claimants by birth or residence,* but forced on the house by the circumstance of this being the first Union declared in the south of Ireland. Another cause has added greatly to our numbers: the large immigration of other paupers sent to our city by the English workhouses. It will be in the recollection of the Board that it was compelled repeatedly to pass resolutions against the admission of strange paupers, in consequence of the influx from these several causes; notwithstanding which resolutions, the feelings of humanity often prevailed over considerations of mere prudence, and scores were admitted to our over-crowded house who would otherwise have perished from starvation.

"In this branch of the Report it may not be irrelevant to state, *that though several of the parties selected by your Committee for emigration were not inmates of the old house of industry, and were born within this Union, they do not nearly equal the number of those belonging to the old house of industry* who were unwilling to emigrate, or incapacitated from infirmity or other causes: and who, though strangers to the Union, will remain for life a burthen on its resources.

"The Committee conclude their Report by handing the Board the classified list of applicants for emigration, which they believe will be found to contain in a simple form all the requisite information connected with their inquiry.

RECAPITULATION of the Numbers, Names, &c. of Inmates of the Cork Union Workhouse for Emigration.

	15 to 30 Years.		Over that Age		Families.			Total.		
	Men.	Women.	Men.	Women.	Men.	Women.	Children.	Men.	Women.	Children.
House of Industry Cases . .	12	98	4	11	10	38	66	26	147	66
General Union .	..	9	..	..	..	..	..	.	9	..
Cork Eastern Division . . .	5	17	..	2	4	8	11	9	27	11
Cove Eastern Division . . .	..	..	1	..	..	..	..	1	..	..
Glanmire Eastern Division . .	..	..	..	..	..	1	3	..	1	3
Total (300) .	17	124	5	13	14	47	80	36	184	80

In reply, the following letter and enclosure were received from Mr. Vernon Smith, one of the Under Secretaries of State for the Colonial Department:—

Downing-street, November 30, 1840.

GENTLEMEN,—I am directed by Lord John Russell to acknowledge the receipt of your letter of the 13th instant, suggesting that facilities should be afforded by Her Majesty's Government to the emigration of a number of paupers, who are at present a charge on the Cork Poor Law Union.

The subject having been referred for the consideration of the Commissioners for Colonial Lands and Emigration, a report has been received from them, of which a copy is enclosed for your information. The opinions expressed in it meet with Lord John Russell's entire concurrence, and his Lordship regrets that it is, therefore, out of his power to promote the object which you had in view, in bringing the state of the Cork Union under his notice.

As it is desirable that publicity should be given to the remarks contained in the enclosed report, in order to apprize the public of the description of persons approved for emigration, Lord John Russell requests that you will cause the substance to be inserted as early as possible in your Official Circular.

I have the honour to be, Gentlemen,
Your most obedient Servant,
R. VERNON SMITH.

To the Poor Law Commissioners.

Colonial Land and Emigration Office,
9, Park-street, Westminster.
November 23, 1840.

SIR,—We beg to acknowledge the receipt of your letter of the 19th instant, enclosing to us, by Lord John Russell's directions, a letter from the Poor Law Commissioners recommending that Government aid should be afforded towards the emigration of a number of the inmates of the Cork Workhouse, and requiring us to report our opinion how far it may be practicable to comply with this recommendation.

We have at the present moment no funds at our disposal applicable to emigration, except some recent deposits for the purchase of land in Australia, in consideration of which we have given to the purchasers a right of nominating such emigrants for a free passage, as they wish to send to the colony. This right is in the course of being exercised, and until the period for its exercise has expired, we are unable to apply the money to the emigration of persons not nominated by these purchasers.

With regard to other means, it has been so repeatedly communicated to us in the course of the present year, that it is not the intention of Her Majesty's Government upon any consideration to advance money out of the public funds of this country in aid of emigration, that we have always considered the point as finally decided, and answers to that effect are always returned to the numerous applications of a kind similar to the one before us, which are made directly to this office. If, however, we are at liberty to suppose that Her Majesty's Government might be induced, upon applications of a totally different character from those which they have hitherto rejected, to relax the rule which we have above adverted to, we should yet be unable to report that the present case was so special as to call for such extraordinary intervention. The circumstances of the case are of course peculiar to itself, but not so the principle upon which it rests, which is that of relieving a particular district, which may be over-peopled in proportion to the demand for labour, by means of the general revenue of the country. It is the principle upon which the distressed inhabitants of the highlands and islands of Scotland, and upon which artisans and operatives in places where employment has failed, have so repeatedly urged upon the Government their claim to be assisted in emigrating. And although the Commissioners state that there is no Union in Ireland under the same circumstances as the Cork Union, at the same time it is perhaps not improbable, that a certain amount of pauperism has been established in the country, which it will be deemed unadvisable to throw upon the relief fund at the first introduction of the new system,—and that there will be felt a necessity for emigration on too extensive a scale to be carried on by the funds which could be raised in the respective Unions.

We, therefore, are of opinion, should the Government grant pecuniary assistance towards emigration in the present instance, that there would be established a precedent for relieving local hardships out of the general revenue,—and that innumerable claims from Scotland and England, as well as Ireland, would be founded upon the precedent, which it might be difficult with consistency to reject.

Under these circumstances, we suppose that Her Majesty's Government would not consider it expedient to advance the money required, and we can see no source from which it can be raised, unless some portion of the funds, out of which the inhabitants of the house of industry have been heretofore maintained, could be made available for the purpose.

If, however, there should be found the means of providing the necessary sum out of some public fund, there would yet remain for consideration what may be called the Colonial Question, viz., the fitness of the individuals to become settlers in a new country. This is a consideration which we find to be almost entirely overlooked in this country, and which we consequently consider it to be our duty, in an especial manner, to keep in view.

On referring to the description of the persons in whose favour the present application is made, we find that for the most part they have been, previously to the passing of the Irish Poor Law, dependent, not on their own exertions, but upon public charity; that they have been the habitual inmates of a house of industry; and that they constitute, in fact, what the Assistant Commissioner calls "the old stock of paupers in Cork," from whom, as he says, it is desirable to clear the new Union house. Mr. Voules further remarks, that other individuals in the list of applicants, though not themselves of the old stock, are "the immediate connexions of and dependent on those who were actually the old stock."

We entertain a strong conviction that the emigration of individuals with the established habits and feelings of paupers, is not likely to be advantageous to themselves, and is almost certain to be prejudicial to the colony in which they settle. It is reasonable to expect that every settler in a new country will, to a certain extent, have to encounter hardships and difficulties; some fortitude and some self-denial will be requisite for enduring the one, and much patient and persevering industry for overcoming the other. But these are the qualities which we believe that habitual pauperism never fails to eradicate from the human character. Those, therefore, who have been established paupers in this country will remain so in the colony, and prove a burden upon the industrious settlers which it is unjust to impose upon them.

In practical illustration of the view we have here taken, we would beg to refer to the following extracts of a report which we have recently received from the governor of South Australia, and the colonial emigration agent. It may be right to mention, that in the South Australian emigration it is contrary to the regulations that a free passage should be allowed to paupers. It is only through ignorance or inadvertence that they have ever obtained it.

The emigration agent having classified the objectionable emigrants, makes the following observations upon the first class:—

"*Paupers sent out by the Guardians of Parishes or Unions.*

"In most ships from England several families of miserably poor, squalid-looking creatures come out. Accustomed to mendicant habits, they are generally indolent and improvident; and immediately on the occurrence of sickness, or any difficulty arising from their new situation, they throw themselves a burden on the department. When the father and principal members are not able-bodied, the whole family must either be assisted or perish; and as by the public instructions the emigration agent is charged to prevent destitution, a considerable part of all the rations ordered through this office is consumed by persons of the above description."

Colonel Gawler says,—

"The evil to which I would so earnestly request attention is this, *that actual parish paupers* are forwarded from Great Britain to this colony, sometimes on system by Poor Law Unions, and sometimes by the improper conduct of agents, at the expense, of the immigration fund. Mr. Smillie's report gives some instances of these kinds.

"The consequences of such a practice to the colony need scarcely be described. For the clearing of a new country, and the labours of a new settlement, energy of mind and body are especially required; while the unhappy beings to whom I have referred generally possess none of either, and their minds are also but too frequently as demoralized as their bodies are weak. After being thrown on our shores, they remain a burden and a disgrace to society, hopeless in themselves and endless in their offspring, who probably inherit their vices, their debility, and their diseases."

Agreeing as we do with these opinions, and believing the facts to be correctly stated, we never can recommend that aid from the public funds should be given to the emigration of habitual paupers.

We have dwelt at this length upon the subject, because we have had much reason to perceive, during the past year, that Boards of Guardians, in considering the subject of emigration, are apt to direct their minds exclusively to ridding their district from the worthless characters who prey upon the parochial funds; and because we think it especially incumbent upon a government department to take a wider view of the subject, and consider the prospects and future fate of the emigrants, and also the interests of the colony as affected by their emigration.

Before concluding, we would mention that on referring to the list of applicants in the present instance, we find an extreme disproportion of the sexes. The total gives 36 men and 184 women. The preponderance being on the side of women, the disproportion might appear less objectionable, from the deficiency of women which usually exists in new settlements. But in all the emigration which is under our management, there is one rule invariably adhered to, which is, never to take unmarried females unless they are under the protection of their families, and near married relatives, or unless they go as servants to cabin passengers by the same ship. Experience has shown that a contrary course is attended with the worst consequences; and when we see in the list before us, that out of the whole number proposed, there are no less than 124 females between the ages of 15 and 30 years not included under the head of families, we cannot but be apprehensive that the emigration of these individuals, if we are correct in considering that a proportion of them are unprotected, might prove the means of introducing a large amount of vice into the colony.

Upon the whole, therefore, we have to report that there are no funds at our disposal applicable to the emigration in question, and that should Her Majesty's Government feel disposed to provide them, we would recommend that the lists of applicants be minutely scrutinized with the view of removing from them all who are likely to prove unprofitable settlers to themselves and to the colony.

We have, &c.

(Signed) ROBERT TORRENS.
EDWARD E. VILLIERS.

The Commissioners directed a copy of the above Report to be forwarded to their Assistant Commissioner, Mr. Tufnell, for his observations thereon. The following is Mr. Tufnell's reply:—

21*st December*, 1840.

GENTLEMEN,—In obedience to your direction I have perused the letter from the commissioners for Colonial Lands and Emigration with reference to the emigration of paupers from Cork. You are of course aware that more emigrants have departed from the counties of Kent and Sussex during the last few years, than from any other part of England of equal extent; in some years more than a third of the whole of the voluntary emigration to Australia having been supplied from this district. Hence the point as to what classes are best fitted for colonization is perpetually brought under my notice, and all that I can see or learn on the subject induces me fully to concur in the observations of the Emigration Commissioners, that *habitual* paupers should never be assisted to emigrate. The remarks of Colonel Gawler are, I submit, too general and sweeping, as they would lead a reader to infer that any one who has received or is receiving parish relief should be considered thereby disqualified from being sent out at the expense of the colonial emigration fund. This rule would have excluded perhaps at least three-fourths of the labouring population of these counties from the benefits of emigration, as under the habits engendered by the old system of poor law relief there were but few labourers who did not at times receive some assistance from the rates, and even now, in many parts, a labourer, whatever may have been his earnings, runs to the relieving officer at the first hint of an ailment to himself, or to any part of his family. Yet they are not habitual paupers, and many of them, when placed under new circumstances in a colony, display all the hardihood, patience, and self-reliance, which are so necessary to face and overcome the difficulties of a new country. I happen to know that the Kentish and Sussex emigrants, many of whom are of this class, have been most favourably received by the Australian farmers, and bear generally a high character for probity, industry, and zeal. I have perused numerous letters from the emigrants, and they almost invariably speak in the most glowing terms of the high wages they are earning, the kindness with which they are treated, and their general satisfaction at the change of their condition. Far different is the conduct of *habitual* paupers. These unhappy victims of the old mismanaged poor law are well described in Colonel Gawler's letter, "as possessing neither energy of mind nor body, as persons whose minds are but too frequently as demoralized as their bodies are weak." I have often seen instances of a disposition in the Union authorities to get rid of these persons by emigration, and have always objected to such a course. Some of these characters have at times been included among the emigrants, and the result is, that they are always dissatisfied with the provisions on board ship, with the accommodation, and with the captain; on landing, they are dissatisfied with the work, the climate, their employers; they seem totally unable to bear the slightest variation from their usual habits, have no power of adaptation to circumstances, or of putting forth energy to overcome obstacles, and send home letters full of complaints of everything and everybody. Letters of this sort do infinite harm to the cause of emigration, and in fact one such letter will suddenly stop the emigration from a large district, and thus, whatever advantage might be anticipated as likely to result from getting rid of a pauperized family of this description, is far more than counteracted by the check which such reports give to all future emigration. Those unfortunate persons who have been victimized by the Old Poor Law, had far better remain at home, than be cast upon shores where they can only prosper through the virtues of self-reliance, and high and independent spirit, and where they would remain, in the words of Colonel

Gawler, of the truth of which I have little doubt, "a burden and disgrace to society, hopeless in themselves, and endless in their offspring, who frequently inherit their vices, their debility, and their diseases!" Therefore, to encourage such persons to emigrate is bad policy, both as respects themselves, their country, and the colony to which they proceed. The letter of the Emigration Commissioners preserves this distinction between habitual and casual paupers, which it is so important in this question never to lose sight of.

I beg further to observe, that the neglect to attend to this distinction was, in my opinion, the main reason why the migration to the manufacturing districts, which was carried on a few years ago under your auspices, was in many cases found to answer badly. At least I know, that in every case where I made the inquiry, I found that those migrants who had met with difficulties in their new position were of the pauper class, and these, after causing their parishes infinite expense and trouble, had frequently to be returned home. No wages were a sufficient recompense for the change of some habit that their new station made necessary. In the last case of this sort into which I inquired, a man who was earning 22*s.* a week, or nearly double what he could in Kent, returned from the North, where he had been employed in the same occupation as in his native county, because he did not like the air. It rained more in Lancashire than in Kent. He was an habitual pauper. Those who were untainted with the vice of pauperism, according to my experience, invariably got on well, and sent home the most encouraging accounts of their altered circumstances, and their satisfaction at their change of condition. This conclusion was confirmed to me by the statements of several large manufacturers, who had employed many of these migrants in their establishments.

I have the honour to be,
Gentlemen,
Your obedient servant,
E. CARLETON TUFNELL.

To the Poor Law Commissioners.

2.—NOTIFICATION OF THE CONDITIONS OF SALE OF LAND IN THE COLONIES.

The Board took into consideration the following letter from the secretary to the Commissioners of Land and Emigration.

"*Colonial Land and Emigration Office,*
"9, *Park Street, Westminster,*
"6*th January*, 1841.

"SIR,—It having been suggested by Lord John Russell, to the Commissioners of Land and Emigration, that in order to make known as extensively as possible the terms and conditions upon which they contract for the sale of lands in the colonies, it might be expedient that one of their advertisements should be published in the "Official Circular," issued from your Office, I am directed by the Board to apply to the Poor Law Commissioners, through you, and to request that, should it not be inconvenient, as displacing matter of greater importance, the enclosed statement on the subject of the sales of land may be inserted in their next publication.

"I have the honour to be,
"Sir,
"Your most obedient servant,
"S. WALCOT, *Secretary.*

"*To E. Chadwick, Esq.,*
&c. &c. &c.

"Her Majesty's Colonial Land and Emigration Commissioners—Hereby give notice, that they are prepared to contract for the sale of Crown Lands in the following British settlements, and upon the following terms, viz.:—

Port Philip District of New South Wales..... New Zealand........... Western Australia.......	In sections of not less than 320 acres, at a uniform price of 1*l.* per acre.

"In Port Philip, or New Zealand, the purchaser of eight square miles, or 5,120 acres, will be allowed to select land in any part of the colony, without reference to the progress of the surveys; but the land is to be chosen in one block, of which only the outer boundaries will be surveyed by the government, and it will be subject to all regulations which may be established on the spot, respecting the proportion of front to depth, water frontage, reserves for roads, and other conditions of a similar nature.

"In the Sydney district of New South Wales land is sold by auction at an upset price of 12*s.* per acre, and the Commissioners receive deposits from persons desirous of purchasing land there, and give in return orders entitling the holders to credit for a corresponding sum in the acquirement of land in the colony.

"In all cases, and previously to the issue of any land order, the money must be paid into the Bank of England to the credit of Mr. Barnard, Agent-General for Crown Colonies, No. 2, Parliament-street, Westminster; and the fact notified to him and to the Commissioners.

"Every purchaser will be entitled to name a number of persons of the labouring class, subject to the approval of the Commissioners, for a free passage to the colony in which he has purchased land, in proportion to the amount of the deposit, and after the rate of about one adult emigrant for every 20*l*. of his purchase money.

"Further information, as to the conditions for the sale of land, and the introduction of labourers in the different colonies, may be had at the office of the Commissioners, No. 9, Park-street, Westminster.

"By order of the Board,
"S. WALCOT, *Secretary*.

"1 *January*, 1841.

"N.B. The following is a list of the Commissioners' agents in different parts of the country :—

Capper and Gole	11, Park-street, Westminster, and 151, Fenchurch-street, City.
Angas and Co.	2, Jeffrey-square, St. Mary Axe, City.
Mr. C. Jacob	Ingram-court, Fenchurch-street, City.
Mr. S. Ritherdon	13½, Bishopsgate-street, City.
Tinkler and Hancock	17, St. Dunstan's Hill, Tower-street, City.
Mr. W. Claxton	9, Clare-street, Bristol.
Mr. H. Lear	Arundel.
Mr. A. B. Duckham	Falmouth.
Mr. J. B. Thorngate	Gosport.
Mr. J. Alger	Plymouth.
Mr. G. Whiting	Maidstone.
Mr. D. Holt	Manchester.
Mr. G. H. Davenport	Oxford.
Mr. W. Roberts	Sherborne, Dorsetshire.
Mr. John Gealne	Launceston.
Mr. R. H. Hartley	Halifax.
Mr. J. Latimer	Truro.
Messrs. R. and B. Webb.	1, Marine Parade, Brighton.
Mr. F. W. Sargent	Brigg.
Mr. Patrick Just	Dundee.
Mr. Francis Reid	Glasgow.
Mr. A. B. Watson	Leeds.
Messrs. Adamson and Co.	Leith.
Mr. T. Wallace	Market-street, St. Andrew's.
Mr. G. Rae	Stirling.
Dr. Bernard	47, Lower Mount-street, Dublin."

3. EXPENSE OF SENDING A FAMILY TO CANADA OR VAN DIEMEN'S LAND.

THE following application from the Guardians of the Tonbridge Union respecting the expenses of sending out a family to Canada or Van Diemen's Land was read to the board :—

"*Tonbridge*, 11*th September*, 1840.

"GENTLEMEN,—A vestry meeting was held yesterday for the parish of Tonbridge, to consider as to raising a sum of money for defraying the expenses of emigration of certain parties wishing to emigrate, and the meeting was adjourned to Thursday next, for the purpose of ascertaining, in the mean time, what would be the expense of sending out a family to Canada or Van Diemen's Land. Assuming that you might be able to furnish this information, or refer the parish officers to the proper channel for obtaining it, we were directed by the vestry to communicate with you thereon, and request you would have the goodness to favour us with such information as you may be able to afford thereon. There are probably agents to vessels conveying emigrants to those colonies from whom the information might be obtained, and to whom, had we known their address, our application would perhaps have been more properly made. As the vestry meeting is next Thursday, we shall feel obliged by your answer before that day.

"We have the honour to remain, gentlemen,
"Your most obedient servants,
"SCOONES and ALLEYNE.

"*To the Poor Law Commissioners*."

The Commissioners directed a letter to be written to the Land and Emigration Commissioners, requesting them to favour the Commissioners with such information as might enable them to give an answer to the application. The following is the answer received, a copy of which was forwarded to the Guardians of the Tonbridge Union :—

"*Colonial Land and Emigration Office*,
"9 *Park Street, Westminster*,
"16*th September*, 1840.

"SIR,—I am directed by the Commissioners of Land and Emigration to acknowledge the receipt of your letter of the 12th instant, respecting an inquiry which has been received by the Poor Law Commissioners from the Board of Guardians of the Tonbridge Union, relative to the expense of sending out a family from thence to Canada or Van Diemen's Land; and I am directed to acquaint you in reply, for the information of the Poor Law Commissioners, that the usual price of a steerage passage, exclusive of provisions, to Canada from London, is about 5*l*. for an adult, and half for each child. It is not usual at this port for the ship to find provisions for steerage passengers to North America, and the cost of finding them for themselves would probably amount to about 3*l*. for each adult.

"The price of a steerage passage to New South Wales or Van Diemen's Land, *including* provisions, is about 20*l*. for adults. In some ships half that sum is charged for all children under fourteen years, while in others the charge is 7*l*. for every child not exceeding four years, and 1*l*. more for each year of age above four.

"Should the Board of Guardians finally determine to defray the expense of conveying any parties from Tonbridge to the Colonies, Lieut. Lean, the Government Emigration Agent at the Port of London, will answer any inquiries which they may address to him on the subject, and will be able to give them further information respecting the cost of passage.

"I have the honour to be,
"Your most obedient servant,
"JOHN WALPOLE, *Assistant Secretary.*
"*To the Poor Law Commissioners.*"

PAID OFFICERS.

COPY OF A MINUTE OF THE POOR LAW COMMISSIONERS ON THE REDUCTION OF SALARIES, DATED 31ST OCTOBER, 1840.

1. The Poor Law Commissioners have recently received several proposals from Boards of Guardians for reducing the salaries of the paid officers of the Unions, particularly of the master and matron, and the clerk to the Guardians. The Commissioners, therefore, deem it expedient that they should state, in a connected form, the reasons by which they have guided, and intend to guide, their conduct respecting the determination of the amount of such salaries.

2. By sec. 46 of the Poor Law Amendment Act, the Poor Law Commissioners are empowered, by order under their hands and seal, to direct the Overseers or Guardians of any parish or Union to appoint paid officers, with such qualifications as the Commissioners shall think necessary, for superintending or assisting in the administration of the relief and employment of the poor, and for the examining and auditing, allowing or disallowing the accounts in such parish or Union, and otherwise carrying the provisions of the Act into execution. By the same section, the Commissioners are further empowered, when they may see occasion, to regulate the amount of salaries payable to such officers respectively, and the time and mode of payment thereof.

3. It follows, from the provisions just recited, that the Commissioners can authorize the Guardians to appoint paid officers, but that the appointment of the officers is made by the Guardians; and that the power of determining the amount of the salaries of such officers is vested in the Commissioners. It is not incumbent on the Commissioners to justify any of the provisions of the Poor Law Amendment Act; but they cannot forbear from calling the attention of the Guardians to the obvious advantages of the arrangement, that the same authority should not fix the salary and make the appointment.

4. Since the power of fixing the salaries of the paid officers of Unions has been vested in the Commissioners, it is their duty to exercise this power according to the best of their judgment respecting the circumstances of each case. The opinion of the Guardians of the Union, as to the amount of the salaries of their officers, will always have great weight with the Commissioners: nevertheless, such opinion will not be conclusive with them; and although they will always have much reluctance to depart from it, yet they will consider themselves bound to satisfy themselves of the grounds of the recommendation of the Guardians, before they decide upon adopting it.

5. The Commissioners have recently observed a disposition in some Boards of Guardians to depress the salaries of the Union officers beyond what the Commissioners consider to be their proper amount; and they likewise perceive that the Guardians have in some cases wished to receive tenders, stating the lowest salary at which a candidate will undertake to perform the duties of an Union office. The Commissioners proceed to state their reasons for thinking that great caution ought to be exercised in the reduction of the salaries of Union officers, and that the method of requiring tenders of salary from the candidates ought very rarely to be adopted.

6. It is difficult to over-rate the importance to a Union of possessing a body of efficient paid officers. Without efficient paid officers, no Union, of whatever size, can conduct its Poor Law business in an economical and satisfactory manner. Although the vigilant superintendence of the Guardians is necessary to the well-working of the Union, it is not alone sufficient; and without able instruments for carrying the directions of the Guardians into effect, even a closer and more constant attention to details than can fairly be expected of a body of unpaid officers, would fail to accomplish the desired purpose.

7. Many of the results produced by efficient Union officers are positive and apparent:— such as the order, cleanliness, and salubrity of the workhouse; the good discipline of its inmates; the progress of the workhouse children

in industrial, moral, and religious acquirements; the regular keeping and accuracy of the Union accounts; a frequent inspection of the out-door paupers; a reduction of out-door pauperism, and of vagrancy. On the other hand, many of the results produced by efficient Union officers are merely negative, and therefore, although they may be equally important with the others, they are likely to escape the attention of many persons, and their existence can always be disputed by uncandid reasoners. Thus the great diminution in the law expenses of parishes which has taken place since the passing of the Poor Law Amendment Act* is partly to be attributed to the changes in the law effected by that Act, and partly to the measures and the advice of the Poor Law Commission; but it is also, to a large extent, to be attributed to the management of parochial business by a class of officers superior to the parish overseers; officers, many of whom (particularly the clerks of Unions) have had a professional education, and can therefore save parishes from the rashness, the ignorance, and the carelessness which, directly or indirectly, produced so much of the vexatious and expensive litigation which took place under the unreformed system. In like manner, when pauperism has been diminished, or prevented from increasing, by the exertions of the Union officers, the small quantity of their apparent business (which is owing to their efficiency), is made an argument for reducing their salaries, or even for dismissing them altogether. A similar mode of reasoning has been sometimes employed respecting policemen, who have been thought useless, in the exact proportion in which they were successful in preventing the commission of crimes.

8. Now since the salaries of the Union officers were in general fixed, only a few years ago, after careful consideration and comparison, and at moderate rates, it cannot be doubted that a system of reducing them below their existing rates would tend to prevent the Unions from obtaining good officers. Here and there an individual candidate well fitted for an Union office, may, from peculiar circumstances, be willing to accept it for an inadequate salary; but even he will, probably, after a short time become dissatisfied, and will desire to transfer his services to some other Union, or to seek some other sort of employment. Moreover, frequent changes in the salaries of Union officers are inexpedient, as depriving the Union service of the character of stability and certainty, which forms one of the strongest temptations to persons seeking employment.

9. It is further to be borne in mind, that some of the Union officers, as the master and matron, and the relieving officers, are intrusted with the custody of valuable stores, and of considerable sums of money; consequently, if their salaries are depressed to the lowest point, and if, besides, the persons employed were tempted by their necessities to accept the office at an insufficient remuneration, it is to be feared that they will be induced to commit peculation or embezzlement, or, at any rate, that they will abuse the powers and opportunities afforded to them by their office, for the purpose of obtaining some pecuniary advantage, at the cost of the rate-payers and paupers.

* Expenditure in Suits of Law, Removal of Paupers, &c.

Years ended 25th March.		Average.	Years ended on the 25th March.					Average.
1833.	1834.		1835.	1836.	1837.	1838.	1839.	
£. 254,412	£. 258,604	£. 256,508	£. 202,527	£. 172,432	£. 126,951	£. 93,982	£. †64,510	£. 132,080
Decrease compared with the Average of 1833 and 1834			53,981	84,076	129,557	162,526	191,998	124,428

The Total Expenditure for the 5 years ended 5th March, 1839, was £660,402.

† Removal of Paupers and Travelling Expenses of Overseers not included in this Sum.

10. The system of requiring from the candidates for a Union office tenders of the salary at which they are willing to accept such office, has been pursued, to a considerable extent, with respect to medical officers. The system (which was rendered unavoidable at the outset of the proceedings of the Commission, the wide and irreconcilable difference of opinion as to the extent of the remuneration for medical services) was however loudly complained of by the medical profession; and the Commissioners having weighed the arguments for and against it, have arrived at the conclusion, that it ought now to be abandoned. (See the arguments stated in their Report on the further Amendment of the Law, pp. 76, 77, ed. 8vo.) The Commissioners think that the objections to a system of tender, which were made with respect to the medical officers, apply still more strongly to the offices of clerk, master and matron, and relieving officer; and they have no doubt that its general adoption would provide the Unions with a set of officers, deficient in nearly all the qualities which they ought to possess, and tempted by their straitened circumstances, or their failure in other callings, to accept the lowest amount of pay on which they could hope to subsist in decency. For these reasons, the Commissioners disapprove of the method of requiring tenders of salaries from candidates for Union offices; and in fixing the salary of an officer who may have been elected upon tender, they will not consider themselves concluded by the understanding which may have existed between him and the Board of Guardians as to the amount of such salary.

11. The Commissioners are conscious that a little temporary popularity might be obtained at the cost of the general efficiency of the system, by depressing the salaries of Union officers to the lowest point at which the services of a person capable of getting through the necessary duties of his office could be procured. But although the judgment of the Commissioners in following a different course may be called in question, they rejoice to think that their conduct cannot, with any show of probability, be attributed to interested motives; since the appointments of the officers are not vested in them, and they never interfere in any way to recommend candidates (unless specially requested by the Guardians), or otherwise to influence the decision of the Board of Guardians, with whom the choice of the officers, both in law and in practice, exclusively resides.

2.—EMBEZZLEMENT: PROSECUTION OF CLERK OF THE STROUD UNION.

The Commissioners took into consideration a communication from the Board of Guardians of the Stroud Union, in which they informed the Commissioners that the clerk to the Union had cashed and appropriated to his own use a cheque of 22*l.* 10*s.* 8*d.*, instead of paying it to the party in whose favour it was drawn, and that they had in consequence passed the following resolution:—

RESOLVED—"That the clerk be forthwith suspended, and the grounds of such suspension be notified to the Poor Law Commissioners, and they be requested to send down a man to undertake the duties of clerk temporary; that Mr. Brotherton be appointed clerk in the mean time, and that Mr. Burgh, Mr. Bucknall, Mr. John Stanton, and Mr Ricardo be requested to assist him."

The Commissioners acknowledged the receipt of this communication, and expressed their approval of the course pursued by the Guardians in suspending the clerk, and expressed regret that they were unable to send down any one to perform the duty of clerk as requested by the Guardians, but that they would direct an Assistant Commissioner immediately to visit the Union and inquire into and report upon the charge against the clerk.

The Commissioners accordingly transmitted the communication of the Guardians to their Assistant Commissioner, Mr. Parker, with directions to investigate and report upon the case.

The following is Mr. Parker's report of the result of his investigation:—

"*Highgate, November 9th*, 1840.

"GENTLEMEN,—I have the honour to inform you that in pursuance of your instructions communicated to me by your letter dated the 5th instant, I proceeded to Stroud without delay, and there investigated the charges against the clerk of that (Stroud) Union. A committee of Guardians had previously compared the entries in the minute book and ledger, and having discovered only one case of criminal misconduct, although there were several instances of irregularities apparent, I confined my attention to that case, and elicited, in the investigation which ensued, the following circumstances:— At a meeting of the Board of Guardians held on the 18th September a cheque duly signed was given to the clerk for the payment of a bill, which was cashed by the treasurer of the Union on the 22d September, having the name of the party in whose favour it was drawn on the back of it; an endorsement rendered necessary by a resolution of the Guardians, that no payment shall be made except by cheques endorsed by the person in whose favour they may be drawn. On the 24th October the audit of the preceding quarter's accounts commenced, when the auditor discovered no irregularity respecting this cheque, which was for 22*l*. 10*s*. 8*d*., and passed the account. The auditor says that he well remembers the clerk producing to him a receipt for the amount of the cheque, signed for A, but that he cannot recollect the initial prefixed to the name A. Having thus ascertained from the auditor that the transaction when submitted to him presented no irregularity, I obtained the cheque from the bankers, and have now traced evidence showing the endorsement thereon to be a forgery.

"With regard to the receipt produced to the auditor as the authority for his passing the item, there is evidence of the clerk having had an opportunity to destroy it after the Guardians' suspicions had been excited; an opportunity of which it is not improbable that he availed himself, inasmuch as he was seen to draw a slip of paper from a bundle of receipts and throw it into the fire, and the auditor has since missed one of the receipts from that bundle.

"Thus the charges against the clerk are threefold:—

"1st. That he embezzled the sum of 22*l*. 10*s*. 8*d*.

"2dly. That he forged the name of one of the persons to whom it was to be paid.

"3dly. That he forged a receipt for it.

"The charges having assumed this serious character, I did not think proper to examine the clerk, but after cautioning him that I should take down in writing whatever he might say, inquired if he wished to offer anything by way of explanation, when he remarked that he did not intend to make use of the cheque to defraud the Union, and that he had paid the money before any question arose.

"This observation that he had paid the money is correct, for it appears that on the day the discovery took place, he wrote to the parties, informing them that he had paid the money to their credit, and requesting a receipt, which was duly returned. This receipt has been produced to me, but it is evident that it is not the receipt upon which the auditor passed the item in the Union accounts, inasmuch as it is dated subsequently to the audit.

"The prevailing opinion with the Guardians, now that the money has been paid, is that the loss of his situation will operate as a sufficient punishment for the offence of which the clerk has been guilty, and holding this opinion, it is not probable they will institute a prosecution for the embezzlement and forgery.

"I have the honour to be, Gentlemen,
"Your obedient servant,
"H. W. PARKER,
"*Assistant Poor Law Commissioner.*
"*To the Poor Law Commissioners.*"

The Commissioners did not think that it would be consistent with their duty simply to dismiss the clerk, and they gave directions that he should be proceeded against for embezzlement of one of the smaller sums, thinking that a summary conviction, under the circumstances, would answer the object of a prosecution. With this view their Assistant Commissioner laid an information against him, under the 97th section of the Poor Law Amendment Act, for embezzling and wilfully misapplying 5*l*. 12*s*. 6*d*., one of the sums misapplied by him. To this information the clerk pleaded guilty, and he was fined 5*l*. and treble the sum misapplied, making together 21*l*. 17*s*. 6*d*.

Mr. Parker subsequently informed the Board of Guardians of the steps taken by him, and advised them that the conviction incapacitated him for holding any office connected with the relief of the poor; and the Guardians advertised their intention of appointing another clerk in his place. The Guardians subsequently appointed Mr. Alfred John Driver to be their clerk, which appointment has been confirmed by the Commissioners.

The Commissioners referred to various communications they had received from different parts of the country respecting an irregular and improper practice which has arisen in the mode of paying tradesmen. It appeared from these communications, that on the days appointed for the quarterly payment of the tradesmen's bills, it is seldom that the whole of them attend, either by their representatives or in person. Cheques for the amount due, sometimes in separate draughts, but sometimes in the gross, are given to the clerk, who usually pays them into his banker's hands, and is credited for the amount. Frequently in such cases there is great irregularity in the payments to tradesmen. This may arise partly from the difficulty of communication in rural districts, and partly from habits of procrastination. The practice may also be increased by the clerks having a running account with a banker, and he be thus tempted to increase his own available balance by delaying payments, or be indisposed to diminish it by prompt payments to the tradesmen; and although the latter may be dissatisfied, and may make complaints in private, yet inasmuch as the delay may not occasion any serious loss to them, they may conceive it to be for their interest to keep on good terms with an influential officer, and make no complaint in public. This practice is, in its ultimate effects, fraught with much mischief to the administration of relief, and danger to the funds of the rate-payers. It appears to the Commissioners to be irregular, if not directly illegal; first, as making the clerk a treasurer without sureties, and diminishing the balance held by the treasurer of the Union as a remuneration for the labour and responsibility which he undertakes; and secondly, as tending to deprive tradesmen of the advantages of ready money, and increase the ultimate charge on supplies at the expense of the rate-payers.

3.—RETURN OF THE NUMBER DISMISSED OR WHO HAVE RESIGNED, AND CAUSES OF DISMISSAL AND RESIGNATION.

On a review of the minutes of the proceedings of the Board during the past year, it appears that orders have been issued within the year for the dismissal of 78 officers for offences hereafter specified:—

14 Masters of Workhouses, for
- Pecuniary malversation 1
- Neglect of duty . . . 2
- Drunkenness. . . . 2
- Indecent behaviour. . 4
- General incompetency. 1
- Irregularity in accounts 1
- Peculation and mismanagement of workhouse 1
- Want of cleanliness. . 1
- Ill-treatment of paupers 1

6 Matrons of Workhouses, for
- Drunkenness . . . 1
- General incompetency. 1
- Ill treatment of a pauper 1
- Refusing to admit female pauper in labour into the workhouse . . 1
- Want of cleanliness . 1
- Insubordination to the Board of Guardians . 1

6 Medical Officers, for
- Neglect of duty . . . 6

22 Relieving Officers, for
- Pecuniary malversation 15
- Neglect of duty . . . 2
- Irregularity in accounts 3
- General incompetency. 1
- Drunkenness . . . 1

6 Assistant Overseers, for
- Pecuniary malversation 1
- Neglect of duty . . . 1
- Irregularity and fraud in accounts . . . 3
- Illegal removal of pauper 1

5 Collectors, for
- Pecuniary malversation 5

1 Treasurer, for
- Pecuniary malversation 1

12 Schoolmasters, for
- Neglect of duty . . . 2
- Drunkenness . . . 1
- For indecent behaviour 2
- General incompetency . 1
- Making false charges and misconduct . . 1
- Lying, drinking, and general bad conduct. 1
- Undue harshness to children 2
- Attempt to incite insubordination. . . 1
- General misconduct . 1

2 Schoolmistresses, for
- Neglect of duty . . . 2

4 Porters, for
- Pecuniary malversation 1
- Indecency towards a female pauper . . . 1
- Want of cleanliness. . 1
- Ill-treatment of pauper boy 1

The following officers have during the year resigned in consequence of the recommendation of the Commissioners:—

3 Clerks to Guardians, under charges of—
- General incompetency 1
- Breach of trust. . . 1
- Neglect of duty . . 1

4 Masters of Workhouse, under charges of—
- General incompetency 2
- Fraud 1
- Irregularity of accounts (negligence) . . 1

5 Matrons of Workhouse, under charges of—
- General incompetency 4
- Fraud 1

3 Medical Officers, under charges of—
- Neglect of duty . . 3

5 Relieving Officers, under charges of—
- General incompetency 3
- Apparent defalcation in accounts . . . 1
- Irregularity in accounts 1

1 Assistant Overseer—
- General incompetency 1

2 Auditors, under charges of—
- General incompetency 1
- Drunkenness . . . 1

1 Chaplain—
- Intemperance . . . 1

1 Schoolmaster—
- General incompetency 1

1 Schoolmistress—
- General incompetency 1

The following officers have resigned:—

11 Clerks to Guardians:—
- 2 Not stated.
- 3 No account.
- 1 Additional trouble without remuneration.
- 1 Inadequate salary.
- 3 On private business.
- 1 Difference of opinion with the Guardians.

22 Masters of Workhouses:—
- 11 For causes not stated.
- 2 On expression of want of confidence.
- 5 No account.
- 1 Domestic circumstances.
- 1 Ill health.
- 1 Another Union appointment.
- 1 Disagreement with chaplain.

21 Matrons of Workhouses:—
- 10 Not stated.
- 1 Under a charge of negligence.
- 4 No account of cause.
- 1 Domestic circumstances.
- 1 Consequence of husbands (masters) resignation.
- 1 Ill health.
- 1 Misconduct of husband.
- 1 Another Union appointment.
- 1 Disagreement with schoolmaster.

3 Medical Officers:—
- 1 Not stated.
- 1 No account.
- 1 Difference with Guardians.

16 Relieving Officers:—
- 8 Not stated.
- 4 No account.
- 1 Appointment as master in another Union.
- 1 Improper conduct to the poor.
- 1 Accession of property.
- 1 Ill health.

9 Collectors and Assistant Overseers:—
- 5 Not stated.
- 3 No account.
- 1 Inadequacy of salary.

1 Treasurer:—
- 1 Failure of bank.

12 Auditors:—
- 7 Not stated.
- 1 Reduction of salary £20 to £12 per annum.
- 2 Disqualified, being in another situation.
- 1 No account of cause.
- 1 Ill health.

10 Chaplains:—
- 4 Not stated.
- 1 Honorary appointment resigned on the appointment of a paid chaplain.
- 2 No account.
- 1 In consequence of disagreement with master.
- 1 Ditto with Board.
- 1 Insanity.

12 Schoolmasters:—
- 9 Not stated.
- 1 Obtained a better situation.
- 1 Insanity.
- 1 Appointed as master of workhouse in another Union.

7 Schoolmistresses:—
- 6 Not stated.
- 1 Appointment as mistress of workhouse to another Union.

1 Porter:—
- 1 Not stated.

1 Nurse:—
- 1 Not stated.

The following Table exhibits an account of

the total Number of Officers dismissed since the establishment of the Commission :—

	1835	1836	1837	1838	1839	1840
Assistant Overseers	..	1	1	..	2	6
Auditor	..	..	..	..	1	..
Chaplain	..	..	..	..	1	.
Collectors	..	..	2	5	4	5
Clerks to Guardians	..	1	1	4	2	..
Masters of Workhouses	7	12	10	12	14	14
Matrons of ditto	..	6	4	5	8	6
Medical Officers	..	1	..	4	2	6
Porters	..	1	2	1	3	4
Relieving Officers	5	9	15	23	16	22
Schoolmasters	..	1	4	5	8	12
Schoolmistresses	..	..	1	2	2	2
Treasurer	..	..	..	..	..	1
Totals	12	32	40	61	63	78
Grand Total			286			

Of whom about 6 were restored on special grounds on application by the Guardians.

The following Table exhibits an Account of the Total Number of Paid Officers employed in the New Unions, and the proportion which they bear to the Average Annual Number of Dismissals.

Description of Officer.	Number of Employed.	Total Number Dismissed during the six years ended 31st Dec. 1840.	Average Annual Dismissed.	Proportion of Average Annual Dismissals to Total Employed.
Collectors and Assistant Overseers	271	26	4	1 in 68
Auditors	479	1	..	..
Chaplains	335	1	..	..
Clerks to Guardians	579	8	1	1 in 579
Masters of Workhouses	614	69	12	1 in 51
Matrons of ditto	542	29	5	1 in 108
Medical Officers	2,327	13	2	1 in 1,164
Porters	301	11	2	1 in 150
Relieving Officers	1,245	90	15	1 in 83
Schoolmasters	223	30	5	1 in 45
Schoolmistresses	323	7	1	1 in 323
Other Officers	278	1	..	..
Total	7,517	286	48	1 in 157

The Commissioners observe upon these cases of dismissals, that they illustrate the difficulty of obtaining at the present salaries good officers possessing the various qualifications required for the performance of arduous duties, and the necessity in the actual condition of the labour market of the Guardians seeking for competent officers, rather than limiting their choice to those who present themselves, or determining upon the claims of different sets of local canvassers. Nevertheless it may be observed that with all existing precautions a proportion of cases must be anticipated in the appointment of such officers, where the individuals have failed to perform the duties intrusted to them. The Commissioners believe that the appointments to the metropolitan police have been as care fully made as it was possible to make them with so numerous a force requiring high qualifications for moderate payment; yet the dismissals, as set forth in the Report of the Constabulary Force Commissioners, appear to have been as follows, up to the year 1838 :—

	Superintendents.	Inspectors.	Sergeants.	Private Constables.
The establishment of the Metropolitan Police, when completed in May, 1830, consisted of	17	67	318	2,896
Of this number, who joined previous to the 1st of June, 1830, there remained serving at the end of the year 1838. The greater part of the superintending inspectors and sergeants were in May, 1830, serving in subordinate grades.	16	57	162	352
Dismissals up to 31st Dec. 1838	1	16	..	4,858
Resignations	11	78	..	6,046
Deaths	7	5	35	239
N.B.—In the dismissals and resignations, the sergeants and constables have been included in the total.				

Of the 6,000 cases of resignations of police constables, nearly one-half or three-sevenths appear to have been resignations under charges of misconduct.

The Commissioners apprehend that it will be found that the difference between the past and present Poor-law management is that cases of misconduct are now brought under public examination that formerly passed without notice.

The Commissioners think it convenient to recall the attention of the Boards of Guardians to the following instructions respecting the choice of paid officers, extracted from the Commissioners' Circular of the 31st December, 1837.

"Next in order is the consideration of the appointment of the paid officers. On this, much of the success of the Union depends. It will therefore be necessary carefully to consider the character of the candidates. You should particularly avoid pledging yourselves on a canvass; and thereby committing injustice and doing injury to the public, by appointing a person less fit than some other, who would perform the required duty for the same remuneration.

"The Guardians should look to evidence of ability and good conduct in previous situations as the security for future good service; general testimonials to fitness, without such evidence, being of little weight, especially from persons unacquainted with the new duties to be performed. All canvassing should be repressed, as an attempt to induce the Guardians to injure the public service, and commit injustice by pledging themselves in favour of one candidate without an examination of the claims of the others, amongst whom there might be persons better qualified for the office. The circumstance of a person having been a bankrupt or an insolvent, or of having failed in other pursuits, is regarded by the Commissioners as presumptive evidence of unfitness.

"It should be borne in mind, in selecting the paid officers, that the duties of the Guardians will ultimately be reduced, in a great measure, to the general superintendence and control of those officers to whom the detailed business of the Union will be intrusted. But whenever improper appointments are made, where an officer is wanting in intelligence or in energy, either his deficiencies must be made up by the personal exertions of the Guardians, or the public service will be injured, and the relief of the destitute will be neglected.

"The qualifications especially requisite in the relieving officers, as well as in masters of workhouses, are diligence, firmness, and mildness, together with a knowledge of the habits of the indigent classes. The poor are far more sensitive to the behaviour of persons in authority, and of their superiors in rank, than is generally imagined, and they feel the manner of rejecting their claims almost as powerfully as the rejection itself. Each of the Union officers should, therefore, be especially cautioned as to his conduct towards the claimants of relief; he should be reminded that it is his duty to treat the sick, the aged, and the infirm, with tenderness and care; that many of the claims which it will be his duty to reject, have been created by abuses heretofore prevalent; and that in rejecting even such claims he must not use harsh language or show an angry deportment. He must so conduct himself as to obtain the respect and confidence of the claimants of relief; and he should be warned, that the Poor Law Commissioners will visit any instances of harshness, severity, inattention, or incompetency, with immediate dismissal. In case of tumult or resistance amongst the paupers, explanation will be required from the officer whose authority is resisted; and a repetition or continuance of insubordination or resistance to the new regulations, will be deemed to be strong evidence of incompetency on the part of the officer who may thus have failed in enforcing them.

"The Commissioners have occasionally been called upon to repair the error of a precipitate local appointment, made under the improper influence of previous canvass, or otherwise, by withholding their sanction to such appointment. But it is important to remark, that every such instance has arisen in the case of the appointment of some individual who was resident, or who had previously held office in some parish of the Union; and whose local connexions, rather than his fitness, had unduly influenced the Guardians in making the appointment.

"These observations upon the appointment and qualifications of relieving officers apply, even in a stronger degree, to those of the master of the workhouse, his office being comparatively permanent, and the strict management of the workhouse being the point on which the whole system rests. Besides a large measure of the qualifications prescribed for the relieving officers, he must understand the economical management of provisions, and the proper regulation of the labour and diet of such of the able-bodied paupers as may from time to time become inmates of the workhouse. Where no able masters can be found amongst the candidates who have been masters of well-managed workhouses, the best appointments have been made from amongst the non-commissioned officers of the army or navy.

"The choice of a proper schoolmaster is of great importance. Where the character of the master is good, and his habits are regular and correct, and he pays due attention to the moral and religious education of the children, it is found that a corresponding effect is produced in their habits; situations in service are easily obtained for them, and they retain them permanently. Where the teacher is a pauper or a person of indifferent character, or of indolent habits, the habits of the children become bad; they do not continue in service, but return to the parish, and remain permanently burthensome."

LONDON:
Printed, by order of the Poor Law Commissioners, by W. CLOWES and SONS, Stamford Street, and Published by CHARLES KNIGHT and Co., 22, Ludgate-street, Publishers to the Poor Law Commissioners.

AN

OFFICIAL CIRCULAR

OF PUBLIC DOCUMENTS AND INFORMATION:

DIRECTED BY THE POOR LAW COMMISSIONERS TO BE PRINTED, CHIEFLY FOR THE USE OF THE MEMBERS AND PERMANENT OFFICERS OF BOARDS OF GUARDIANS, UNDER THE POOR LAW AMENDMENT ACT.

No. 12. CIRCULAR ISSUED OCTOBER 14TH, 1841.

Poor Law Commission Office,
Somerset House,
October 12, 1841.

THE Poor Law Commissioners, on a review of their minutes, directed that the minutes and correspondence on the following subjects should be printed and circulated for the information of Guardians and officers of the several Unions, viz.—

By order of the Board,
EDWIN CHADWICK, *Secretary.*

I.—RELIEF:—PROHIBITION OF, OUT OF THE WORKHOUSE, TO ABLE-BODIED AND NON-RESIDENT PAUPERS.

THE Board took into consideration the subject of out-relief to able-bodied and non-resident paupers, and with the view of rendering the practice in the different Unions as uniform as circumstances permit, the Board directed the following Instructional Letter and General Prohibitory Order to be issued to the several Unions and places mentioned in the schedule annexed to the order:—

INSTRUCTIONAL LETTER AS TO GENERAL PROHIBITORY ORDER.

Poor Law Commission Office,
Somerset House,
2nd August, 1841.

SIR,—The Poor Law Commissioners have thought it expedient, for the sake of rendering the practice of the different Unions as uniform as circumstances permit, to issue their order regulating the relief of able-bodied and non-resident paupers as a general order.

Separate orders, containing provisions nearly identical with, or closely resembling, those contained in the general order now issued, are already in force in most of the Unions and incorporations to which this order is addressed.

The Commissioners request the attention of the Board of Guardians to the following remarks, in reference to those parts of the order which appear to require explanation.

Relief of Able-bodied.

1.—ARTICLE I.—The only remark on the prohibitory clause which the Commissioners need make is, that the Guardians under this clause are not bound to require any child of an able-bodied person who can support itself to accompany its parent into the workhouse, if it appear expedient that such child should continue in employment.

2.—*Article I. Exception* 1.]—By " sudden and urgent necessity " (which words are used in section 54 of the Poor Law Amendment Act,) the Commissioners understand any case of destitution requiring instant relief, before the person can be received into the workhouse; as, for example, when a person is deprived of his usual means of support by means of fire, or storm, or inundation, or robbery, or riot, or any other similar cause which he could not control when it had occurred, and which it would have been impossible or very difficult for him to foresee and prevent.

It is to be remarked further, that this exception does not authorize *permanent* out-door relief in any case. A case originally of sudden and urgent necessity, which subsequently requires continued relief, loses its character of suddenness and urgency. The relief subsequently required will be either ordinary relief and therefore to be given in the workhouse, or it may be extraordinary and given, for example, under the second exception to Article I.

3.—*Exception* 2.]—The second exception provides for the case of any able-bodied man who is himself insane or temporarily sick, or who has met with an accident, or any of whose family require to be relieved on the ground of insanity, infirmity, accident, or sickness.

4.—*Exception* 3.]—Under this exception relief may be given to able-bodied persons for the funerals of their families, without requiring them to come into the workhouse.

5.—*Exception* 4.]—The exception of widows during the first six months of their widowhood is adopted with a view of enabling persons thus situated to have an adequate interval for the purpose of making such arrangement for their support as their altered condition may require.

6.—*Exception* 5.]—The exception of widows with children, so far as it relates to able-bodied widows in employment, is one respecting which the Guardians ought to exercise great circumspection in applying it in practice. The Guardians when administering relief under it ought to take into account, that when small weekly allowances in aid of wages are made, they too commonly serve to excuse relations from the payment of contributions to a larger amount; and that the out-door allowances when given indiscriminately in widowhood tend to put an end to provident habits, in respect of insurances in sick clubs or otherwise. It should, moreover, be borne in mind that allowances made by the parish to able-bodied widows in employment do not always confer the advantages intended, inasmuch as their wages, as in the case of able-bodied men, are commonly reduced in consideration of the allowance from the parish; and that such reduction of the wages, combined with the excuse furnished to relations or friends for withholding their contributions, together with the pauper habits thus engendered, often renders such allowances to widows in aid of wages an injury rather than a benefit to them; whilst in some districts this class of able-bodied widows may be so numerous that their labour (thus depreciated at the expense of the ratepayers) may be substituted for the more highly paid labour of independent labourers,

7.—The Commissioners trust, that the Guardians will seldom find that the ordinary rate of earnings of able bodied women is so low as not to enable them to support one child at the least; and that the Guardians will not adopt any such general rule as that of relieving all widows with one, or with any fixed number of children, without careful inquiry into every case thus to be relieved.

8.—*Exception* 6.]—It sometimes happens that a person is confined for debt in a prison where no provision is made out of a prison-fund, or out of the county-rates, for his maintenance. In such a case as this, it is advisable that the Guardians of the Union should be empowered to relieve him. It is further necessary that the Guardians should be empowered to give relief to the wife and children in cases where the husband cannot be required to enter the workhouse on account of his being in a place of legal confinement.

9.—*Exception* 7.]—The state of the law in reference to married women explained in par. 10, and the peculiar rights and obligations of soldiers, sailors, and marines, render it desirable to give great latitude to the proceedings of the Board of Guardians in respect to the families of persons in these departments of the Queen's service. The seventh exception, therefore, allows of relief of any kind being given to the wife or children of a soldier, sailor, or marine, whether in or out of the workhouse, without requiring the husband to come into the workhouse.

10.—*Exception* 8]—The eighth exception provides for the case of a wife whose husband is absent from her, either by desertion or otherwise, and it is necessary, in consequence of the state of the law applicable to women thus situated. It is held that in such cases relief to the children is not relief to the wife; consequently, the wife cannot be compelled to come with her children into the workhouse. If, however, she require relief for herself, the Guardians may require her to receive it in the workhouse; and if she require relief for her children, the Guardians may require such of them as are above the age of nurture to receive it in the workhouse, whether she do or do not come into the workhouse. As regards, however, children under the age of nurture who may be living with the mother, the Guardians cannot remove them from her; so that if she require relief for them and them only, the Guardians must give out-relief if relief be necessary.

11.—ARTICLE II.—The regulation which requires the entry on the minutes of the medical officer's report, or a medical certificate in case of relief being given to an able-bodied pauper on account of sickness, accident, &c., has been introduced in consequence of a tendency which has displayed itself in various parts of the country, to make exceptions to the prohibitory order on too slight grounds, and the Commissioners think that this provision will have the useful effect of calling the special attention of the Guardians to every such case.

If the pauper should not have been attended by a medical officer of the Union, a certificate may be given either by the medical practitioner who may have attended him, or by a medical officer of the Union who may visit him for the purpose.

Relief of Non-residents.

12.—ARTICLE III.—As respects the portion of the order which relates to the relief of persons not resident within their Union, the Commissioners desire to point out that it prohibits new cases of relief of this sort, with the exceptions therein mentioned.

13.—Under the provisions of this article, the Guardians may relieve a pauper residing within the Union, though not residing in the parish to which he belongs; the Commissioners, however, are far from wishing to encourage even this species of non-resident relief. It is true that the frauds and evils which are incidental to non-resident relief, in consequence of the want of inspection and the difficulty of transmitting the relief, do not occur with reference to paupers resident within the Union, who are within the reach of the relieving officers; but, nevertheless, the rate-payers of the parish charged with the relief, who by means of the quarterly lists of paupers, can, by personal observation of those who reside in their parish, ascertain whether they are fit objects for relief, are deprived of this protection where the pauper for whom they pay is resident at a distant part of the Union. The relief of paupers out of their parish and out of the relieving district in which the parish is comprised is not unattended with difficulties both of a legal and practical nature, which are sufficient to make it desirable that the Guardians should not, without sufficient ground, permit new cases of this nature even within the Union.

14.—The Commissioners have stated fully their views on the subject of non-resident relief, as respects both its legality and expediency, in a minute dated 26th of January, 1841, which is reprinted in the Appendix to their Seventh Annual Report, 8vo. Edit., (App. A., No. 2, p. 106.)

15.—*Article III. Exception* 1.]—The Commissioners have introduced this exception in order to meet the cases of vagrants, who may become casually destitute within the Union. It is the duty of the Guardians to relieve persons so situated, without reference to the place of their settlement or residence. The Commissioners have had occasion to address several communications to the Metropolitan Boards of

Guardians, on the duty of the locality to relieve all cases of urgent destitution. (See the Commissioners' Fourth Annual Report, pp. 154, 155, 156, and 157, Appendix A. No. 2; and Fifth Annual Report, page 87, Appendix A. No. 10.)

The Commissioners have not introduced into this article an exception on account of sudden and urgent necessity. (See paragraph 2.) Cases of sudden and urgent necessity manifestly require the prompt attention and vigilant inspection which can only be exercised by the Guardians and their officers in the district where the necessity arises.

16.—*Exception* 2.]—This exception corresponds to exception 2 to Article I. (See paragraph 3.) The Commissioners omitted this exception in the forms of the prohibitory order which they have recently issued, but they have restored it in the present order, on account of the difficulty which a want of the power of giving temporary relief to non-residents in case of sickness has been found to create in some parts of the country. The Commissioners, however, desire to caution the Guardians against giving temporary relief in cases of sickness to persons not resident within the Union, unless they are able to obtain accurate information concerning the case, and can ensure adequate and prompt relief, both medical and otherwise. It may be observed that this exception permits poor persons to be sent to establishments out of the Union, intended for the treatment of their respective infirmities, as hospitals for the sick, asylums for the insane, and schools for the blind or deaf and dumb.

17.—*Exception* 3.]—The third exception is intended expressly to except from the operation of the order the cases of relief given to non-resident lunatics in asylums under orders of justices, to debtors confined under mesne process entitled to relief under the 52 Geo. III., c. 160, s. 1, and to persons under orders of removal.

18.—*Exception* 4.]—This exception is similar to the fourth exception to Article I, the reasons for which are stated above in paragraph 5.

19.—*Exception* 5.]—This exception permits the Guardians to send pauper children to a workhouse or establishment for the training of pauper children, which may be situated out of their Union. Some remarks on the advantages of combining Unions for the education of pauper children, may be seen in the Report of the Commissioners on the further Amendment of the Law, (Dec. 1839), p. 55—9, and in their Report on the Training of Pauper Children, (21st January, 1841,) with the Appendix.

20.—*Exception* 6.]—This exception enables the Guardians to relieve the resident family of a non resident man, provided he be not able-bodied, without requiring them to come into the workhouse.

21.—*Exception* 7.]—This exception permits the continuance of non-resident relief to all paupers (not being able-bodied persons within Article I.), who were in the receipt of relief from some parish in the Union, within the twelve calendar months next preceding the date of the order. Consequently, it permits the continuance of non-resident relief to the infirm through age or any other cause, and to able-bodied widows with a child or children, who were in the receipt of parochial relief from the Union within that period.

Cases of peculiar Urgency.

22.—ARTICLE IV.—It is possible, although not probable, that cases may occasionally arise which present very peculiar circumstances, and which do not fall within any of the exceptions contained in the present order. The Commissioners think it desirable in cases of that kind, in which the immediate withdrawal or denial of out-door relief might appear likely to produce serious evil to the applicant, that the Guardians should give out-door relief, or take a portion of the applicant's family into the workhouse, and report the case within fifteen days to the Poor Law Commissioners, as a case of peculiar urgency, in order that the Commissioners may give their opinion thereupon. The Commissioners have accordingly introduced a proviso at the end of the order, enabling the Guardians to pursue this course with respect to exceptional cases of this description.

Relief by way of Loan.

23.—ARTICLE V.—The first part of Article V. is introduced in order to put an end to a misapprehension which existed in some Boards of Guardians, viz., that although the prohibitory order prevented them from *giving* out-door relief, they might nevertheless *lend* it. The second part of the Article enables the Guardians to make all the relief which may be given to persons above 21 years of age, or their families, a loan under the 59th section of the Poor Law Amendment Act.

Interpretation.

24.—ARTICLE VI.—The last clauses of this Article are introduced because the order is addressed to four Unions of parishes formed not under the Poor Law Amendment Act, but under local Acts of Parliament, viz., East and West Flegg, Forehoe, Samford, and Tunstead and Happing.

Signed by order of the Board,
GEORGE COODE, *Assistant Secretary.*

To
The Clerk of the Board of Guardians.

GENERAL PROHIBITORY ORDER.

To the Guardians of the Poor of the several Unions named in the schedule hereunto annexed.

To the churchwardens and overseers of the several parishes and places comprised within the said Unions.

To the clerk or clerks to the justices of the petty sessions held for the division or divisions in which the parishes and places comprised within the said Unions are situate; aud to all others whom it may concern.

WE, the Poor Law Commissioners, in pursuance of the authorities vested in Us by an Act passed in the fifth year of the reign of His late Majesty King William the Fourth, intituled "*An Act for the Amendment and better Administration of the Laws relating to the Poor in England and Wales,*" do hereby rescind so much of any order or orders heretofore issued by the Poor Law Commissioners as relates to the administration of relief to be given to able-bodied poor persons, and to poor persons not resident in their parish or Union, in the several Unions named in the schedule hereunto annexed.

And we do hereby order, direct, and declare, with respect to each and every of the Unions named in the said schedule, as follows:—

ARTICLE I. Every able-bodied person, male or female, requiring relief from any parish within any of the said Unions, shall be relieved wholly in the workhouse of the Union, together with such of the family of every such able-bodied person as may be resident with him or her, and may not be in employment, and together with the wife of every such able-bodied male person, if he be a married man, and if she be resident with him; save and except in the following cases:

1st. Where such person shall require relief on account of sudden and urgent necessity.

2nd. Where such person shall require relief on account of any sickness, accident, or bodily or mental infirmity affecting such person, or any of his or her family.

3rd. Where such person shall require relief for the purpose of defraying the expenses, either wholly or in part, of the burial of any of his or her family.

4th. Where such person, being a widow, shall be in the first six months of her widowhood.

5th. Where such person shall be a widow, and have a legitimate child or legitimate children dependent upon her, and incapable of earning his, her, or their livelihood, and no illegitimate child born after the commencement of her widowhood.

6th. Where such person shall be confined in any gaol or place of safe custody.

7th. Where the relief shall be required by the wife, child, or children of any able-bodied man who shall be in the service of Her Majesty as a soldier, sailor, or marine.

8th. Where any able-bodied person, not being a soldier, sailor, or marine, shall not reside within the Union, but the wife, child, or children of such person shall reside within the same, the Board of Guardians of the Union, according to their discretion, may afford relief in the Workhouse to such wife, child, or children, or may allow out-door relief for any such child or children being within the age of nurture, and resident with the mother within the Union.

ARTICLE II. In every case in which out-door relief shall be given on account of sickness, accident, or infirmity, to any able-bodied male person resident within any of the said Unions, or to any member of the family of any able-bodied male person, an extract from the medical officer's weekly report, (if any such officer shall have attended the case,) stating the nature of such sickness, accident, or infirmity, shall be specially entered in the minutes of the proceedings of the Board of Guardians of the day on which the relief is ordered or subsequently allowed.

But if the Board of Guardians shall think fit, a certificate under the hand of a medical officer of the Union, or of the medical practitioner in attendance on the party, shall be laid before the Board, stating the nature of such sickness, accident, or infirmity, and a copy of the same shall be in like manner entered in the minutes.

ARTICLE III. No relief shall be given from the poor-rates of any parish comprised in any of the said Unions, to any person who does not reside in some place within the Union, save and except in the following cases:—

1st. Where such person, being casually within such parish, shall become destitute.

2nd. Where such person shall require relief on account of any sickness, accident, or bodily or mental infirmity, affecting such person, or any of his or her family.

3rd. Where such person shall be entitled to receive relief from any parish in which he may not be resident, under any order which justices may by law be authorised to make.

4th. Where such person, being a widow, shall be in the first six months of her widowhood.

5th. Where the relief shall be allowed for a child under the age of 16 maintained in a workhouse or establishment for the education of pauper children not situate within the Union.

6th. Where any person, not being able-bodied, shall not reside within the Union, and the wife, child, or children of such person shall reside within the same, relief may be afforded to such wife, child, or children, by the Guardians of the Union, as they shall think fit.

7th. Where such person shall, at some time within the 12 calendar months next preceding the date of this order, have been in the receipt of relief from some parish in the Union, being settled in such parish, and not being resident therein.

ARTICLE IV. Provided always that in case the Guardians of any of the said Unions shall depart in any particular instance from any of the regulations hereinbefore contained, and shall, within 15 days after such departure, report the same and the grounds thereof to the Poor Law Commissioners, and if the Poor Law Commissioners shall approve of such departure, then the relief granted in such particular instance shall, if otherwise lawful, not be deemed to be unlawful, or be subject to be disallowed.

ARTICLE V. No relief which shall be contrary to any regulation in this order shall be given by way of loan; and every relief which may be given to or on account of any person above the age of 21, or to his wife or any part of his family under the age of 16, under Article I., or any of the exceptions thereto, or under any of the exceptions to Article III., or under the proviso in Article IV., may, if the Guardians shall think fit, be given by way of loan.

ARTICLE VI. Whenever the word "Parish" is used in this order, it shall be taken to signify any place separately maintaining its own poor;

Whenever the word "Union" is used in this order, it shall be taken to include not only an Union of parishes formed under the provisions of the hereinbefore recited Act, but also any Union of parishes incorporated or united for the relief or maintenance of the poor under any local Act of Parliament;

Whenever the word "Guardians" is used in this order, it shall be taken to include not only Guardians appointed or entitled to act under the provisions of the said hereinbefore recited Act, but also any governors, directors, managers, or acting Guardians entitled to act in the ordering of relief to the poor from the poor-rates under any local Act of Parliament.

Whenever the words "Board of Guardians" are used in this order, they shall be taken to mean not only a Board of Guardians competent to act under the provisions of the said hereinbefore recited Act, but also such Guardians, or such a number of any Guardians as are competent to order relief to the poor from the poor-rates under any local Act of Parliament.

SCHEDULE,

Containing the Names of the Unions to which the present Order applies.

Aberaeron	Atcham
Abergavenny	Atherston
Abingdon	Auckland
Albans, St.	Austell, St.
Alcester	Axbridge
Alderbury	Axminster
Alnwick	Aylesbury
Alresford	Aylesford, North
Alton	Aylsham
Altrincham	
Amersham	Bakewell
Amesbury	Banbury
Ampthill	Barnet
Andover	Barnstaple
Ashby-de-la-Zouch	Barrow-on-Soar
Ashford, East	Basford
Ashford, West	Basingstoke
Aston	Bath

Battle
Beaminster
Bedale
Bedford
Bedminste
Belford
Belper
Bellingham
Berkhampstead
Berwick-on-Tweed
Beverley
Bicester
Bideford
Biggleswade
Bellericay
Billesdon
Bingham
Bishops Stortford
Blaby
Blandford
Blean
Blofield
Blything
Bosmere and Claydon
Boston
Bourn
Brackley
Bradfield
Bradford (Wilts)
Braintree
Brampton
Brecknock
Bridge
Bridgenorth
Bridgewater
Bridport
Brixworth
Bromley
Bromsgrove
Bromyard
Buckingham
Buntingford
Burton-on-Trent

Caistor
Calne
Cambridge
Cardiff
Cardigan
Carmarthen
Castle Ward
Catherington
Caxton and Arrington
Cerne
Chailey
Chapel-en-le-Frith
Chard
Cheadle
Chelmsford
Cheltenham
Chepstow
Chesterfield
Chesterton
Chester-le-Street
Chippenham
Chipping Norton
Chipping Sodbury
Christchurch
Church Stretton
Cirencester
Cleobury Mortimer
Clifton
Clun
Clutton
Colcheste.
Columb Major, St.
Cookham
Cosford
Cranbrook
Crediton
Crickhowel
Cricklade and Wootton Bassett
Croydon
Cuckfield

Darlington
Dartford
Daventry
Depwade
Derby
Devizes
Docking
Doncaster
Dorchester
Dore
Dorking
Dover
Downham
Drayton
Driffield
Droitwich
Droxford
Dudley
Dunmow
Durham
Dursley

Easingwold
Eastborne
East Grinstead
Easthampstead
East Retford
East Ward
Eastry
Elham
Ellesmere
Ely
Epping
Epsom
Erpingham
Eton
Evesham

Faith, St.
Fareham
Faringdon
Faversham
Flegg, East and West
Foleshill
Fordingbridge
Forehoe
Freebridge Lynn
Frome

Gainsboroug
Germans, St.
Glanford Brigg
Glendale
Glossop
Gloucester
Godstone
Goole
Grantham
Gravesend and Milton
Guildford
Guiltcross
Guisborough

Hailsham
Halstead
Haltwhistle
Hambledon
Hardingstone
Hartismere
Hartley Wintney
Hastings
Havant
Haverfordwes
Hay
Hayfield
Headington
Hemel Hempstead
Henley
Henstead
Hereford
Hertford
Hexham
Highworth and Swindon
Hinckley
Hitchin
Holbeach
Hollingbourn
Holywell
Honiton
Hoo
Horncastle
Horsham
Houghton-le-Spring
Howden
Hoxne
Hungerford
Huntingdon
Hursley

Ipswich
Ives, St.

Kettering
Keynsham
Kidderminster
Kingsbridge
Kingsclere
Kings Norton
Kington
Knighton

Lanchester
Langport
Launceston
Ledbury
Leek
Leighton Buzzard
Leominster
Lewes
Lexden and Winstree
Leyburn
Lichfield
Lincoln
Linton
Liskeard
Llandilo Fawr
Llandovery
Llanelly
Loddon and Clavering
Loughborough
Louth
Ludlow
Luton
Lutterworth
Lymington

Madeley
Maidstone
Maldon
Malling
Malmsbury
Malton
Mansfield
Market Bosworth
Market Harborough
Marlborough
Martley
Medway
Melksham
Melton Mowbray

Mere
Meriden
Midhurst
Mildenhall
Milton
Mitford and Launditch
Monmouth
Morpeth

Nantwich
Narberth
Neath
Neot's, St.
Newark
Newbury
Newcastle in Emlyn
Newcastle under Lyne
Newent
New Forest
Newhaven
Newmarket
Newport (Monmouth)
Newport (Salop)
Newport Pagnell
Newton Abbot
Northampton
Northleach
Northwich
North Witchford
Nuneaton

Oakham
Okehampton
Ongar
Orsett
Oundle

Patrington
Pembroke
Penkridge
Penrith
Penzance
Pershore
Peterborough
Petersfield
Petworth
Pewsey
Pickering
Plomesgate
Plympton St. Mary
Pont-y-pool
Poole
Portsea Island
Potterspury

Reading
Redruth
Reeth
Reigate
Ringwood
Risbridge
Rochford
Romford
Romney Marsh
Romsey
Rothbury
Ross
Royston
Rugby
Rye

Saffron Walden
Samford
Scarborough
Sculcoates
Sedgefield
Seisdon
Selby
Sevenoaks
Shaftesbury
Shardlow
Sheppey
Shepton Mallet
Sherbourne
Shiffnal
Shipston-on-Stour
Skirlaugh
Sleaford
Solihull
Southam
South Molton
South Shields
South Stoneham
Southwell
Spalding
Spilsby
Stafford
Staines
Stamford
Steyning
Stockbridge
Stockton
Stone
Stourbridge
Stow
Stow-on-the-Wold
Stratford-on-Avon
Stroud
Sturminster
Sudbury
Swaffham
Swansea

Tamworth
Taunton
Tavistock
Teesdale
Tenbury
Tendring

Tenterden
Tetbury
Tewkesbury
Thakeham
Thame
Thanet, Isle of
Thetford
Thingoe
Thirsk
Thomas, St.
Thornbury
Thorne
Thrapston
Ticehurst
Tisbury
Tiverton
Tonbridge
Torrington
Totness
Towcester
Tunstead and Happing
Tynemouth

Uckfield
Uppingham
Upton-on-Severn
Uttoxeter
Uxbridge

Wallingford
Walsal
Walsingham
Wangford
Wantage
Ware
Wareham and Purbeck
Warminster
Warwick
Watford
Wayland
Weardale
Wellingborough
Wellington (Somerset)
Wellington (Salop)
Wells
Welwyn
Wem
Weobly
Westbourne
West Bromwich
Westbury-on-Severn
Westbury and Whorwelsdown
West Firle
West Ham
West Hampnett
West Ward
Weymouth
Wheatenhurst
Whitby
Whitchurch
Williton
Wilton
Winborne and Cranborne
Wincanton
Winchcombe
Winchester, New
Windsor
Winslow
Wirrall
Wisbeach
Witham
Witney
Woburn
Wokingham
Wolverhampton
Woodbridge
Woodstock
Woolstanton and Burslem
Worcester
Worksop
Wrexham
Wycombe

Yeovil.

Given under our hands and seal of office this second day of August, in the year of our Lord One thousand eight hundred and forty-one.

(Signed) J. G. S. LEFEVRE.
L.S. G. C. LEWIS.

Orders exactly similar to the above have been issued to the Boards of Guardians of the undermentioned parishes.

Alston with Garrigill
East Stonehouse
Stoke-upon-Trent
Whittlesea, St. Mary and St. Andrew, Great Yarmouth.

II.—VAGRANTS:—1. COURSE TO PURSUE TO CHECK IMPOSITION OF.

The Commissioners took into consideration an application for advice from the Board of Guardians of the parish of Lambeth respecting the number of travellers and mendicants, as stated in the following letter addressed to the Guardians, by Mr. Luke Teather, one of their relieving officers.

"*Lambeth Workhouse, August 31st*, 1841.

"GENTLEMEN,—It has been the constant practice lately for all travellers and mendicants to come to my house at all hours of the evening requesting admission into the house for the night, and knocking at the door and laying about, refusing to go away without their request being complied with. These occurrences have taken place so frequently within the last few weeks, and particularly the last week, as to threaten a serious interruption to my duties.

"When I am out after leaving business at the house visiting my cases, or making inquiries or other business, I have been obliged to request my son to attend to these applications at home, and he has told me frequently, and which I find the case when I am at home myself, that if one order is given from fifteen to twenty more applications are immediately made, and these being sent, the ward they sleep in, the master informs me, is a scene of riot and noise throughout the night, which has induced him to request me to admit none but ill and destitute characters not known, excepting all belonging to our parish. I sent my son last night to the police station, and the superintendent informed him that their orders were to take all parties of this description to the workhouse, leaving us to find out all the rest. The question will arise, gentlemen, whether the workhouse is to be a lodging-house, and filled with vagrants night after night (in the probationary ward reserved for persons ill and unable to proceed on their journies), or not. All cases of illness and accident of our own would be admitted by the master from the police without an order, but the able-bodied ought to be removed by them from annoying in the way they do any officer of the parish by collecting in crowds about their houses that no one can scarcely pass. Requesting your instructions hereon,

"I am, Gentlemen,
"Your obedient humble Servant,
(Signed) "LUKE TEATHER.
"*Relieving Officer.*

"*To the Guardians of the Poor of the*
"*Parish of Lambeth.*"

The Commissioners also took into consideration the following letter on the same subject addressed to their Assistant Commissioner, Mr. Twisleton, by the clerk of the Colchester Union.

"*Colchester Union, September 3rd*, 1841.

"DEAR SIR,—My attention has been called by the Guardians to the subject of the admission of vagrants into our Union-house, and the question being altogether a most difficult one, I request you will favour me at your convenience with such suggestions as may appear applicable to the case.

"We are positively inundated with these trampers; five or six at a time apply late in the evening to the master, and, exhibiting destitution, he admits them; they are lodged for the night, and in the morning every article in their room swarms with vermin; they give three hours' notice, leave the house for the day, and again retrace their steps in the evening to the Union-house, and are admitted. The most horrible and loathsome diseases pervade most of them, and it is by such persons as these that fevers, cutaneous disorders, &c., are communicated to the regular inmates. It is impossible to ascertain, although no doubt of it exists, whether these vagrants have been guilty of punishable acts of vagrancy within the jurisdiction, and thus they make the Union-house a lodging-house, and interrupt greatly the working of the in-door establishment.

"They are searched, but it is believed the produce of their begging is 'planted,' as it is called, before they apply for admission, and when they leave the house they go to their hoard.

"What is to be done, I know not; but this I am well aware of, that unless a most efficient check can be placed against the present system we had need have an additional master and Union-house, and, in fact, a supernumerary establishment.

"Pray give the subject your best consideration, and favour me with your suggestions.

"I am, dear Sir, yours faithfully,
(Signed) "F. G. ABELL.

"*Edward Twisleton, Esq.*"

This letter was answered by Mr. Twisleton.

In reply to the application from Lambeth, the Commissioners stated:—The Commissioners are deeply sensible of the importance and difficulty of the subject to which these papers refer, and in the present state of the law they feel it impossible to offer advice which can be wholly satisfactory either to the Guardians or to themselves. The first and paramount duty of those to whom the administration of the relief of the poor is entrusted must be to provide effectually and instantly for all cases of urgent want. This object the Commissioners feel confident will always be kept in view by the Guardians at whatever risk or at whatever cost it may be attained.

The Commissioners know by experience that too easy and indiscriminate a reception of all applicants who present themselves for a night's lodging often affords to street mendicants or impostors that portion of food and shelter which should be reserved for the really destitute. Prostitutes have been known to have gone forth to their occupation in the streets every morning, and to have returned at night for a fortnight in succession to the vagrant ward of a workhouse, which was thus wholly misapplied and rendered a place of contamination to those whom misfortune and not vice might bring thither. For these evils the only effectual remedy would be an establishment for the reception of persons casually destitute separate from the workhouse, conducted on different principles of discipline, and with a power of temporary detention as a test of the urgency of the want which brought the applicant to seek shelter in it.

In the mean time the Commissioners hope that the erection of a handmill in your workhouse, which should be applicable to casual poor, might do much to diminish the number of able-bodied male applicants.

There can be no objection to the Guardians affixing a notice to the gate of the workhouse and at the residence of the relieving officer to the effect that no order for admission to the vagrant ward will, under *ordinary circumstances*, be given after a certain hour, remembering, of course, that *really urgent cases* must form an exception to every rule, and be admitted on application at the workhouse at all times. In general the fact of an applicant being brought by any of the police force should be taken as *primâ facie* evidence of real and urgent want, inasmuch as it is the duty of that body to treat as offenders under the Vagrant Act any impostors or persons committing acts of vagrancy within their district. The Commissioners have every reason to believe that the inspectors of police will take care that proper caution is exercised by the constables under their control, so that the shelter and relief, intended for the destitute, may not be absorbed by wilful and habitual mendicants.

The Commissioners directed a copy of this correspondence to be transmitted to Sir James Graham, Her Majesty's Secretary of State for the Home Department, and to the Commissioners of the Metropolitan Police.

2. VAGRANTS: POWER OF JUSTICES TO COMMIT.

The Commissioners took into consideration the following application from the clerk of the Stafford Union.

"*Marston Stafford, June* 11, 1840.

"*Casual Poor.*

"GENTLEMEN,—I am directed by the Board of Guardians, to state the following Case, and request your opinion as to the power of justices to commit vagrants under the 55th Geo. III., c. 137, s. 5, on being convicted of idleness, or on refusing to perform a task of work proportionate to his or her capacity.

"*Case.*

"Henry Swift, an able-bodied vagrant, on the 3d instant, about 6 o'clock, P.M., under the regulations adopted in this Union for the relief of mendicants, after receiving such a meal of food as is provided for the regular pauper inmates of the workhouse was set to work for one hour. At the expiration of the hour he was found idle, and ordered to continue at work for a further period of half an hour, and was then provided with lodgings for the night, and resumed his work at half-past 6 o'clock next morning. On being remonstrated with for idleness, (not having performed one-fourth of the task allotted to him,) the pauper intimated to the governor that he had lodged in a workhouse before, that he knew the law, and as he wanted no more food, he would not break another stone.

"The pauper was taken before the justices, the case submitted to a barrister-at-law, and dismissed under the impression that there was no Act of Parliament to authorize the punishment of casual paupers, on the ground of their being idle, or refusing to perform a task of work, and further, that the work performed by the pauper was in the opinion of the justices adequate to the value of the relief afforded.

"Your opinion is therefore requested—

"1st. Under the circumstances above named, had the magistrates the power, or were they justifiable in dismissing the case?

"2d. Is it lawful under any circumstances to commit casual paupers to the House of Correction, on being convicted of idleness, or refusing to perform a task of work suited to his or her strength or capacity?

"3d. Is a casual pauper subject to the regulation of giving three hours' notice of his or her intention to quit the house?

"4th. Is a casual pauper liable to punishment on refusing to work during the said period of three hours, after having given notice of his or her intention to quit the house.

"I have the honour to be, &c.

"(Signed) PETER LOWE,

"*To the Poor Law Commissioners.* *Clerk.*"

In reply the Commissioners stated, 1st. That the grounds stated were not such as would justify the dismissal of this case.

The 55 Geo. III. c. 137, extends to every person maintained in any workhouse. No exception is made as to the settlement of the persons so maintained, whether belonging to the parish or Union to which the workhouse belongs or not, nor is there any limit as to the time during which the person shall be so maintained, whether it be for one hour, or for the remainder of the pauper's life. Neither is the value of the work to which the pauper is set material, as the work may be utterly valueless, except as a means of discipline, and such therefore, as would never enable the pauper to repay the cost of his maintenance, or it may be very easy and comparatively valuable, but these circumstances in no way affect the question. The only point for the magistrates to consider with reference to the quality of the work, is that described in the statute, namely, whether it be "*work, occupation, or employment, suited to his, her or their age, strength and capacity.*"

2. The Commissioners know of no distinction between casual and others, with reference to the liability to be committed for refusing to work or for other misbehaviour in workhouses. As is stated above, the statute extends to all persons maintained in the workhouse without distinction as to the causes or circumstances of their admission, and therefore, to vagrant poor, as much as to any other, and judging from the objects and purview of the clause, the provision is more applicable as a restriction upon vagrant and occasional poor, who are, as a class, the most disorderly, than to the settled and more permanent inmates of workhouses.

The only material distinction of casual and settled poor, is in the rules applicable to their removal, especially the rule in favour of the casual poor rendered chargeable by any sudden and grievous hurt. There is no distinction that the Commissioners are aware of in favour of vagrant casual poor. The casual poor rendered destitute by any grievous bodily hurt would, as regards the liability to work in a workhouse, be in the same condition as any other pauper suffering under the like bodily disability, namely, the work given to the pauper must, in each case, be suited to his age, strength, and capacity, and it would not be on account of his being casual poor, that he would be excused, but on account of his bodily inability, which would excuse any other pauper.

3. The Commissioners know of no distinction between the cases of casual and other poor, as respects their liability to submit to the discipline of the workhouse, except the greater necessity of a strict discipline being applied to the former class according to the strength and capacity of the respective persons. The Commissioners' orders in their terms apply equally to all.

During the term of their detention in the workhouse, whether before or after notice to leave, all paupers are subject to the same discipline; the three hours during which they are kept after notice is in nowise distinguished from the rest of the time of their stay in the house, nor is any relaxation of discipline at all desirable during those hours.

III.—GUARDIANS:—1. POWERS OF EX-OFFICIO GUARDIANS TO ACT MAGISTERIALLY IN CASES ARISING WITHIN THE UNION.

The Commissioners took into consideration an application from their Assistant Commissioner, Mr. Weale, requesting them to obtain counsel's advice in the following case.

Case.

"By the Poor Law Amendment Act, 4 and 5 Will. IV., cap. 76, sec. 38, it is provided, 'That 'except for the purpose of consenting to the disso'lution or alteration of any Union for the purposes 'of settlement or rating, no ex-officio or other 'Guardian of any such Board (of Guardians) shall 'have power to act in virtue of such office, except as 'a member, and at a meeting of such Board.'

"In consequence of the above proviso ex-officio Guardians within Unions generally feel a delicacy, and refuse to act in cases of the removal of paupers to their settlement; in punishing disorderly paupers; in affiliating illegitimate children, and other matters arising out of the Poor Law, considering themselves in their capacity of ex-officio Guardians in some measure as being complainants, and also as judges of matters in which they so become personally interested; consequently their decision is looked at with great jealousy by the public, and it is very difficult and often expensive in having to bring matters arising in a Union under the cognizance of justices who reside a considerable distance from, and unconnected with, such Union.

"Counsel will therefore be pleased to advise whether under the above section of the Act, or otherwise, ex-officio Guardians are prohibited from acting in their capacity of Justices in all cases arising within the Union in which they reside, and if not in all cases—

"What particular case or cases they are incapacitated from so acting.

In reply the Commissioners stated:—In the Case attention is directed to the proviso contained in section 38 of the 4th and 5th Will. IV. cap. 76, namely, "That except for the purposes "of consenting to the dissolution or alteration of "any Union for the purposes of settlement or "rating no ex-officio or other Guardian of any "such Board shall have power to act in virtue "of such office, except as a member, and at a "meeting of such Board." The Commissioners observe that the question raised in the case is not in any way affected by this proviso. The proviso relates to the power of Guardians, whether ex-officio or elected, to act in that capacity, and it restrains them from acting as such, except as members, and at a meeting of the Board. On the other hand the question submitted to the Commissioners involves the power of justices of the peace, being by virtue of their office Guardians of a Union, to act magisterially in certain cases arising within the Union. The proviso, therefore, although it restrains a justice of the peace from acting as Guardian, except at a meeting of the Board, yet it does not in any way affect his power to act magisterially within the Union, his power to do which depends upon other considerations.

The Commissioners would observe that the question proposed is one of jurisdiction, upon which the justices themselves are properly competent to form a judgment, and upon which they should satisfy themselves before they perform an act of a magisterial character. But, in the opinion of the Commissioners, justices are not restrained by any rule of law from adjudicating upon matters brought before them relating to the Union, such as the removal of paupers to their settlement, or to the punishment of paupers charged with offences under any statute.

As regards making orders in bastardy,—the subject is not free from doubt, but the Commissioners are disposed to think that a justice can adjudicate upon applications for orders in bastardy, though arising in any of the parishes or townships of the Union of which such justice might be an ex-officio Guardian. The Commissioners are aware of the decision in the case of Rex *v.* Great Yarmouth, 6 Barn. and Cres. 646, in which it was held that an order of removal signed by a justice, who was likewise a complaining churchwarden of the parish, on whose behalf the order was applied for, was invalid on the ground that the same person could not be the complainant and the person hearing the complaint. The Commissioners, however, think the case under consideration as distinguishable from that above cited. In the case under consideration the remedy is sought on behalf of the parish to which the child is chargeable. Now the justice is not a Guardian of the parish but of the Union, and has therefore no immediate interest in affording the remedy.

The Commissioners have been referred to a decision of Lord Denman's in a case of an indictment for disobeying an order of maintenance in bastardy, tried at the Durham summer assizes. From the report which the Commissioners have seen of that case it appeared that both the magistrates who made the order were ex-officio Guardians of the Union from which the application proceeded, and that *one* of them signed the notice of application. Lord Denman held, that where an ex-officio Guardian signs the notice of application he cannot sit to determine the application, and if he does so the order is bad. The case in no way decides that a justice who does not sign the application, and is not therefore a party to the complaint, is disqualified from hearing and determining the application.

---

2. GUARDIANS: POWERS OF, AND OF VISITING COMMITTEES.

The Commissioners took into consideration the following application for advice from the Vice-Chairman of the Thirsk Union:—

"To the Poor Law Commissioners.

"The arrangement regarding the Visiting Committee and the power of individual Guardians appointed members of the committee, have been frequently discussed at our Board, and as the subject will be again debated in an approaching meeting of the Guardians, I take the liberty of writing to you respecting it.

"In the order for governing the workhouse, it is stated 'The Board of Guardians shall appoint from their own body a committee, to be called a Visiting Committee, whose duty it shall be to visit the workhouse or workhouses of the Union once a week at the least, and after a careful inspection to write such answers as the facts may warrant to the following queries,' &c. Several questions have arisen on this regulation, amongst which are the following:—As no mention is made as to the number of Guardians to be present before proceeding to business, is it intended that all the members of the committee are on each visit to be present—if not, has the Board a power of deciding as to the number to form a quorum? Is it intended that any Guardian, if a member of the committee, should inspect the house individually at any time, or in the absence of any arrangement made by the Board, can any portion of the committee visit and inspect the house without informing the other members of the committee of such intention? Is there any regulation which can by any construction give a power to individual Guardians, whether members of the committee or not, to inspect the house without permission of the master?

"Some of our Guardians also entertain the opinion that three Guardians may meet as directed, in cases of emergency, and inspect the workhouse.

"I have at various times expressed my own sentiments on several of these different queries, but I find it so difficult to convince some of our Guardians, that I am anxious to obtain your opinion, that a final arrangement may be made. The proper conducting of the Visiting Committee is an essential point in the government of the workhouse, and therefore I am the more desirous that the present discussion may terminate in the introduction of a judicious plan, whether it be in accordance with my own views or those of others. An early reply will oblige me, as will also any suggestion you may be inclined to make.

"I remain, very respectfully,
"(Signed) THOMAS SMITH,
"*Vice Chairman, Thirsk Union.*
"*Thirsk, June* 3, 1840.

In reply the Commissioners stated that any number of the Visiting Committee may visit the workhouse at any time, at which the committee could visit it collectively, unless the Guardians should have given the committee only a limited authority to visit it, so as to confine that authority to a majority or any fixed number or proportion of the members of the committee.

The Commissioners have further to state, that there is no regulation issued by the Commissioners which confers a power to individual Guardians, whether members of the committee or not, to visit the workhouse without permission of the master, but the Commissioners consider that it is competent to the Guardians to effect an arrangement of this nature by a bye-law.

The Commissioners also desire to state, that if a Board composed of three Guardians is duly assembled, in case of emergency, in accordance with the directions of the regulations, it is within the power of such Board to inspect the workhouse, their acts however will be subject to the revision of the Board at the next weekly meeting.

IV.—PAID OFFICERS:—FALSE TESTIMONIALS OF CANDIDATES FOR THE SITUATION OF.

The Commissioners took into consideration the following communication from the clerk of the Chertsey Union.

"*Chertsey, Surrey, September 8th,* 1841.

"GENTLEMEN,—The Board of Guardians, in pursuance of a public advertisement, received applications and testimonials from persons desirous of becoming schoolmaster and schoolmistress in the workhouse, and, amongst others, the two enclosed testimonials were sent.

"On inquiries they appear to be complete forgeries, and the Board of Guardians have desired me to forward them to your office, thinking that you would not only like to be informed of the means resorted to to obtain situations in Unions, but also that you might like to punish them for their deception.

"I am, your obedient Servant,
(Signed) "HENRY G. GRAZEBROOK,
"*Clerk.*
"*The Poor Law Commissioners.*"

"This is to certify that we have known Mr. and Mrs. Chillman some years, and believe them to be capable of instructing children, they having been engaged for upwards of six years in a school of their own in New Kent Road.

(Signed) "JOHN LAWRENCE, New Kent Road.
"J. GOVER, Dover Road.
"E. WATKINS, Borough.
"J. TREVALLIEN, Bishopsgate.
"C. COX, St. Ann's, Blackfriars.
"F. WOODHAM, Roupell Street, Lambeth.
'R. RETSON, Aldersgate Street."

"We, the undersigned Guardians of the Bromsgrove Union, can with confidence recommend Richard Harnian to the situation of clerk of the works to any Union, he having been so employed by this Board for two years past, we having had sufficient proof of his honesty and punctuality in the time to warrant our signing on his behalf, and for the benefit of any Union requiring his services.

(Signed)

" W. A. Greening,	" G. M. Noel,
" Henry Hickman,	" Henry Edwards,
" George Addis,	" William Godwin,
" G. M. Merry,	" Charles Cresswell,
" W. Aston,	" Thomas Greening,
" Thomas Phelps,	" William Wright,
" William Freeman, jun.,	" Alfred Neale,
" Henry Iddens,	" Henry Turner,
" Thomas Fielding,	" E. Addis,
" George Thomas,	" Alexander Hunt."

In reply, the Commissioners stated that they would make known the information contained in the letter by circulating it amongst the Guardians of Unions in order to put them on their guard against attempts at deception.

The deception in question, however, does not come within the legal definition of forgery, nor within that of fraud at common law, and the Commissioners are not aware of any means of punishing the parties who have made the attempts to impose on the Guardians in the manner described.

V.—FUNDS:—Contributions of Parishes to Union; Mode of filling up Orders for.

The Board took into consideration the following application from the Clerk of the Brecon Union:—

" *Brecon*, *June* 29, 1840.

" Gentlemen,—On 9th May last I prepared, in the usual way, and filled up, the orders, &c., for a call on the several parishes in this Union, and laid the same before the Board for signature, there being at that time a balance *due* to the treasurer of upwards of 150*l.* One of the guardians objected to issue a call then, as the Board expected to receive the 500*l.* to be refunded the parishes out of the loan of 1,200*l.* The call was, consequently, refused, and my orders made useless, as the dates had been put in.

" On Saturday, the 20th June instant, I again laid before the Board the state of the treasurer's accounts, by which there appeared to be a balance of about 980*l.* due to him; but deducting the 500*l.* which was expected that day to be received by the treasurer, the actual balance due to him would be about 480*l.*

" *An order was then entered in the minutes for a call on the parishes*, to be paid on the 6th July next; but as this Union consists of forty-two parishes, I could not possibly get the orders properly filled up for immediate signatures *at the Board.* However, on the Tuesday following the orders were signed by the chairman, vice-chairman, and an *ex-officio* guardian, separately at their respective residences; these calls have been since served upon the overseers. Now this same guardian, who objected, as before, states that he will advise the overseers not to pay, as the orders were not signed *at a meeting.*

" I beg you will favour me, personally, with your opinion if these orders have been legally signed, and can this call be legally enforced.

" I am, Gentlemen,

" Your obedient servant,

(Signed) " John Davies,

" *Clerk to the Union.*

" *To the Poor Law Commissioners.*"

In reply, the Commissioners stated that under the 38th section of the Poor Law Amendment Act, no Guardians have any power to act in virtue of that office, except as a member and at a meeting of the Board.

In the form of order prescribed by the rules and regulations of the Commissioners, it purports to be made at a meeting of the Guardians. The order runs—" Given under our hands at a meeting of the Guardians of the said Union, &c."

VI.—ACCOUNTS:—Power of Auditors in respect to the Taxation of Attorneys' Bills for the transaction of Parochial Business.

The Commissioners took into consideration the following application for advice from the Clerk to the Magistrates of the Hundred of Bosmere and Claydon:—

" *Bosmere and Claydon*,
" *Needham Market*, *April* 11, 1840.

" Gentlemen,—I will thank you to inform me, at your earliest convenience, whether any order has been made by you, in pursuance of the powers vested in you by the Poor Law Amendment Act, or any other Act of Parliament, directing the auditors of Unions to disallow all taxable bills of attornies and solicitors for business done and transacted on behalf of any parish or parishes in a Union (with or without the sanction of the Board of Guardians), until taxed; and whether all payments of fees to justices' clerks must be made in the quarter in which they are incurred; and that no attorney's bill can be paid by any parish or Union until the same has been taxed; and if so, by whom the costs of taxation should be paid?

"If such order, or any similar one, should have been made, I beg to request you will forward me a copy for the guidance of the magistrates in this hundred.

"I am, Gentlemen,
"Your very obedient servant,
(Signed) "FREDERICK HAYWARD,
"*Clerk to the Magistrates.*
"*To the Poor Law Commissioners.*"

In reply, the Commissioners stated that they have instructed the auditor, under the authority of the Poor Law Amendment Act, in cases where law expenses are charged in the overseer's accounts, to require the taxation of the attorney's bill, where it may be taxable, before he allows such bill. The Commissioners refer you to their Circular, containing the instructions referred to. Whether the sanction of the Board of Guardians to the payment of the bill be necessary, will depend upon whether the business in respect of which the charge is made be business of the Union or of the parish, and if the latter, whether it is such as the Guardians can control.

All charges lawfully incurred in any quarter should be, as far as possible, paid within the quarter within which they are incurred, whether the charge relate to justices' clerks' fees, or otherwise.

With regard to the taxing of an attorney's bill, the Commissioners wish to observe, that though they have instructed the auditor to require the production of it, taxed by the proper officer, they think that some latitude may be allowed in this respect, and that such taxation can only be considered necessary where the amount of the bill will justify the expense of taxation, because the costs of such taxation must be borne by the respective parties, according to the general rules of law prescribed by the statute 2 Geo. II. c. 23, or the practice of the particular courts in which the business is done.

VII.—PENSIONS—NAVAL OR MILITARY:—FRESH ASSIGNMENTS MUST BE MADE EACH QUARTER FOR THE CURRENT EXPENSES OF RELIEF.

The Commissioners took into consideration the following application from the Guardians of the Wolverhampton Union:—

"*Wolverhampton, June* 16, 1840.

"SIR,—We have a few pensioners of the Royal Hospital, Chelsea, whose pensions were assigned in February last past, that is, the pension due 1st April was in February assigned to the guardians of the Wolverhampton Union.

"The said pensions have only been received within the last fortnight, owing to some delay occasioned by instructions to the Excise, as such it would appear by the Pension Assignment Act 2 and 3 Victoria, c. 51, that all relief given by the Union should be charged to the pensioner when he settles, a record of the same being entered in the minutes of the Board. May I trespass upon your attention for a reply to the following case, illustrative of my inquiry:—

"A. B. enters the Union workhouse last February; he assigns his pension the same month; that pension (due the 1st April) has been received in this month (June, 1840); from the period of A. B. entering the house to June, there will have elapsed more than one quarter of a year,—the cost of relief afforded for such time being more than the value of the pension above referred to. Is it proper to refund the pensioner the balance of his pension up to 1st April, leaving the Union to be remunerated for any keep subsequent to 1st of April from his pension, receivable in July next; or on the other hand, is it justifiable to cover all relief given up to the period of settlement from the pension first assigned. If, without inconvenience, your answer can reach here next Friday morning, it will be of considerable importance to the Board.

"I have the honour to be,
"Sir,
"Your's very respectfully,
(Signed) "H. N. PAYNE.
"*Edwin Chadwick, Esq.*,
&c. &c. &c."

In reply, the Commissioners stated that the Guardians of the Wolverhampton Union can only deduct the expense incurred up to the 1st April, and must take a fresh assignment of the next quarter's pension for the expense of the current quarter.

VIII.—EMIGRATION:—COURSE TO BE PURSUED IN ISOLATED CASES OF.

The Commissioners took into consideration the following application from the Guardians of the East Retford Union for advice as to the course to be pursued in isolated cases of Emigration:—

"*East Retford.*

"GENTLEMEN,—I am led to expect that isolated cases will arise in which an individual, or family, in a particular parish, will be tempted, by the offers now advertised by emigration agents, to exchange this country for another, in which the parish will be disposed to assist in instances when the individual is, or threatens hereafter to become burthensome.

"It is not anticipated that the emigration of several families will take place together from one parish, so as to make it necessary to resort to the provisions you have made for such an exigency; but the object of my letter is to inquire how the Board should deal with an isolated case,—as, where an orphan girl is invited to accompany friends to Australia, and would want 4*l*. or 5*l*. aid from the parish, which the parish would be willing to advance out of the current rates, without wanting a loan.

"I beg the favour of an early answer, as the case just suggested as an instance is likely to occur at the next meeting of the Board.

"I am, Gentlemen,

"Your very obedient servant,

(Signed) "THOS. BIGSBY.

"*To the Poor Law Commissioners.*"

In reply, the Commissioners stated that in cases where the proposed emigration is limited to a single individual, or family, and the relief required is trifling in amount, the Guardians can advance the sum required, provided the parishioners agree to the payment and assent to the same at a meeting convened for the purpose, in accordance with the 62nd section of the Poor Law Amendment Act

---

IX.—BASTARDY:—NOTICE UPON PUTATIVE FATHER SHOULD BE SIGNED BY A MAJORITY OF THE GUARDIANS PRESENT AT A BOARD, INCLUDING THE CHAIRMAN.

The Commissioners took into consideration the following application for advice, from one of the Relieving Officers of the Aylesbury Union:—

"*Aston Clinton, May* 4, 1840.

"GENTLEMEN,—On the 22nd of April, at a meeting of the Board of Guardians of this Union, I was directed to take proceedings against one John Watson, of Upper Winchendon, to compel him to maintain an illegitimate child. I accordingly served a notice on him personally on the 24th of April, stating that I intended to apply for an order of affiliation at the Petty Sessions, in Aylesbury, on the 2nd of May, thereby giving him a clear seven days' notice, according to the Act 2 and 3 Vict., cap. 85, clause 1. When the case came on for hearing, Watson employed Mr. Benson, a solicitor, to defend him. Mr. Benson took an objection to the notice on Watson, because it was not signed by every Guardian in the Union. I contended that the majority being present at the Board having signed, it was sufficient to all intents and purposes, and that the notice was a true copy of a form sent by you, the Commissioners, and which was drawn by counsel for the express purposes of different Unions. The magistrates have adjourned the case until Saturday week, the 16th instant, in order that we may get fresh notices served, signed by the Guardians of the parish,—the words of the Act being 'the Guardians of the parish, *or of the Union in which any parish may be situate.*' The magistrates, therefore, holding Mr. Benson's objection to be good, I shall, therefore, feel extremely obliged if you would give me your opinion in this matter, as if this objection is good it will seriously affect the business of the Union, as the same words are used in many parts of the Poor Law Amendment and other Acts, and in many cases the Guardian of a single parish will object to sign documents which he may be required to do. This will, therefore, cause great confusion and dissatisfaction in the business of the obtaining orders, &c.

"Waiting your answer,

"I am, Gentlemen,

"Your most humble and obedient servant,

(Signed) "HUMPHREY BULL,

"*Relieving Officer.*

"*To the Poor Law Commissioners.*"

In reply the Commissioners stated, that they entertain no doubt that the notice directed to be served on the supposed father of a bastard child, by the 2nd and 3rd Vic. c. 85, should be signed by the Board of Guardians, and that such notice will be good if signed by an actual majority of the Guardians present at a Board, including the Chairman.

The Commissioners are of opinion, that it is not necessary that the Guardians of the parish to which the child is chargeable should sign the notice, where the parish is in Union.

LONDON:
Printed, by Order of the Poor Law Commissioners, by W. CLOWES and SONS, Stamford Street, and Published by CHARLES KNIGHT and Co., 22, Ludgate Street, Publishers to the Poor Law Commissioners.

AN

OFFICIAL CIRCULAR

OF PUBLIC DOCUMENTS AND INFORMATION:

DIRECTED BY THE POOR LAW COMMISSIONERS TO BE PRINTED, CHIEFLY FOR THE USE OF THE MEMBERS AND PERMANENT OFFICERS OF BOARDS OF GUARDIANS, UNDER THE POOR LAW AMENDMENT ACT.

No. 13. CIRCULAR ISSUED NOVEMBER 16TH, 1841.

Poor Law Commission Office,
Somerset House,
November 13, 1841.

THE Poor Law Commissioners, on a review of their minutes, directed that the minutes and correspondence on the following subjects should be printed and circulated for the information of Guardians and officers of the several Unions, viz.—

By order of the Board,
EDWIN CHADWICK, *Secretary.*

I.—GUARDIANS:—1. POWERS OF, IN RESPECT TO THE INSTITUTION OF LEGAL PROCEEDINGS.

The following is a copy of a letter received from the Clerk of the Skipton Union:—

"*Skipton.*

"GENTLEMEN,—This Board have had occasion to employ their clerk as their solicitor, in bringing actions for money withheld by parties, in taking opinions of counsel on cases, in conducting appeals, &c., in all which instances the Guardians for the several townships immediately interested have concurred. In paying the bills incurred, which the

Board has done after submitting them to the Guardians of the townships, some strong observations have been made by individuals as to the power assumed by the Board, and the improper exercise of it, insinuating that these bills should have been laid before towns' meetings, and the overseer or relieving officer received his instructions from the ratepayers and not the Guardians.

"We shall be glad to be favoured with your sanction to our proceedings, in order that the aspersions, which continue to be cast upon the Board, may be met by a public denial of the truth of them.

"I am, Gentlemen,
"Your most obedient humble Servant,
"(Signed) CHARLES CARR.

"*To the Poor Law Commissioners,*
"*Somerset House, London.*"

In reply, the Commissioners stated that in all matters which constituted the business of the Union, and which came under the control of the Guardians, the Board were competent to give sanctions as to conducting any legal proceedings which might arise out of such matters, and where the circumstances of the case might render necessary the taking of such proceedings.

In matters which were not the business of the Union, but of the separate parishes or townships, as in the case of appeals against orders of removal, the Guardians could not in such cases direct the proceedings, which was a matter within the discretion of the overseers of the several parishes or townships.

In every case in which it was proposed to have recourse to legal proceedings, the Commissioners considered it highly desirable that the advice and direction of the Guardians should be first obtained, and parishes would materially consult their own interests in leaving such matters to the determination of the Board of Guardians; but, as before observed, the Guardians could not compel the overseers of parishes to act according to their views in things which were solely within the discretion of the overseers.

---

2 MINUTES OF: GUARDIAN CANNOT LAIM AS A MATTER OF RIGHT THAT HIS UNSECONDED MOTION SHOULD BE INSERTED IN.

The Commissioners took into consideration the following application from the Clerk of the Aston Union:—

"*Aston Road, Birmingham, March 27th,* 1839.
"ENTRIES IN THE MINUTE BOOK.

"GENTLEMEN,—I shall feel obliged if you will have the kindness to inform me whether it would be acting consistent with my duty for me, at the request of an individual Guardian, in opposition to the wishes of a majority of the meeting, to enter upon the minute-book every resolution moved by a member of the Board, although not seconded. The following statement will explain my reason for seeking your advice. On different occasions, the Rev. W. R. Bedford, ex-officio Guardian for Sutton Coldfield, has moved resolutions which no one seconded, and the Board have directed me not to enter them on the minutes. In consequence of such a refusal Mr. Bedford, at a meeting held February 19th last, moved 'That for the future, whenever a motion be made in writing by a member of this Board, and the motion is not seconded, still the said motion shall be entered in the minute-book.' This motion was negatived.

"At a numerous meeting of the Guardians, held yesterday, Mr. Bedford again moved a resolution which was not seconded; he afterwards required me, as he stated, upon my own responsibility, to record it among the minutes of the day, while several Guardians exclaimed against my doing so in direct opposition to the resolution above quoted; they argued that a motion did not become the property of the meeting till seconded, and consequently ought not to be entered; also that if such a procedure were allowed any Guardian may impede the business of the meeting, and unnecessarily encumber the minute-book, while, on the contrary, Mr. Bedford contended that it was my duty to enter every motion made, whether seconded or not, and that the responsibility of not doing so would rest with me, and not the Guardians. Under these circumstances I am unable to act in the case to the satisfaction of all, and as the subject will no doubt be discussed again when the minutes are read at the next meeting, I take the liberty of soliciting the favour of your advice, which, I trust, will satisfactorily set the subject at rest.

"I am, Gentlemen,
"Your obedient Servant,
(Signed) "E. PEARSON,
"*Clerk of the Union.*

"*The Poor Law Commissioners.*"

In reply the Commissioners stated, that a Guardian cannot claim, as a matter of right, that his unseconded motion should be inserted in the minute book, presuming it to be the practice of the Board, as is the case with other deliberative bodies, not to discuss or decide on any unseconded motion. The minutes should, as far as possible, be confirmed resolutions or acts of the Board; but an unseconded motion would seem to lead to no act or resolution, and therefore not to be a proper subject for entry in the minute book.

3. ELECTION OF: OUT OF WHAT FUND CLERK TO BE COMPENSATED FOR SERVICES IN.

The following letter was received from the clerk of the Shepton Mallet Union:—

"*Shepton Mallet, August 3rd*, 1841.

"SIR,—I am instructed to acquaint you that the Board of Guardians, at their meeting of the 2nd instant, agreed to allow me the sum of 3*l.* 8*s.* (including the expenses of persons employed in assisting me), as a remuneration for the election of Guardians, as directed by the Poor Law Commissioners in their orders of the 10th of June and the 2nd of July last, viz.:—Evercreech, West Cranmore, Doulting, Emborough, Hornblotton, East Lydford, West Lydford, and Pilton. The Board wishes to be informed, whether the said sum of 3*l.* 8*s.* is to be placed to the establishment charges, or paid in equal proportions by those parishes for which the Guardians were severally elected? not excluding West Cranmore, from which there was no nomination made, although the parishioners were duly advised of the election.

"I am, Sir,
"Your obedient servant,
(Signed) "ROBERT NORTON.

"*Edwin Chadwick, Esq.*,
"*Secretary to the*
"*Poor Law Commissioners.*"

In reply, the Commissioners stated that they are of opinion that the compensation so awarded should be charged not to the parishes in which the elections occurred, but should be defrayed out of the common funds of the Union, pursuant to Article 3 of the Election Expenses Order.

The following is a copy of a further letter received from the clerk:—

"*Shepton Mallet, August 25th*, 1841.

"SIR,—I am instructed to draw the attention of the Poor Law Commissioners to the direction of their letter of the 12th instant, 8,501 B, regarding the remuneration of 3*l.* 8*s.* to the clerk for the election of Guardians, by the Commissioners' orders of the 19th June and 2nd July. The Board trust, on the explanation as below, the Commissioners will direct the remuneration to be borne by those parishes only for whom the elections were made, and not by the general fund of the Union, as those elections were occasioned generally by the neglect of the officers and rate-payers of the parishes at Lady-day.

"Emborough . .	No nomination return.
West Cranmore .	Ditto.
Doulting . .	Ditto.
Hornblotton .	Ditto.
East Lydford .	Ditto.
West Lydford .	Ditto.
Evercreech . .	One Guardian resigned after his election.
Pilton . . .	One Guardian resigned on 7th June last, in consequence of his removing out of the Union.

"I am, Sir,
"Your obedient servant,
(Signed) "ROBERT NORTON.

"*Edwin Chadwick, Esq.*,
"*Secretary to the*
"*Poor Law Commissioners.*"

In reply, the Commissioners stated that they have given much consideration to the subject, but do not feel themselves justified in sanctioning the course suggested by the Guardians of apportioning the general charges of those elections among the particular parishes on whose account they are supposed to have been incurred.

Although the Commissioners admit that it is for the benefit of a parish that it should have its representative at the Board of Guardians, they nevertheless consider that the Union itself is generally interested in having that Board complete, and therefore that the elections in question cannot be considered as exclusively for the benefit of the parishes which were unrepresented at the Board.

But independently of this consideration the Commissioners can find no authority for charging the expenses incurred by the officer of the Union among any particular parishes, and there is this practical difficulty, that the Commissioners cannot ascertain in what proportions they would have to contribute to those expenses.

II.--PAID OFFICERS:—1. RELATIVE DUTIES AND PRIVILEGES OF THE SEVERAL UNION OFFICERS.

The following is a copy of a letter from the Clerk of the Chesterfield Union, enclosing copy of resolution of the Board of Guardians respecting the relative duties and privileges of the several officers of the Union:—

"*Chesterfield.*

"SIRS,—I am directed by the Guardians of the Chesterfield Union to send you the enclosed copy of a resolution, passed at the Board held on Saturday last, and to request your opinion on the subject matter thereof at your earliest convenience; and, as a difference of opinion prevails amongst the Guardians as to the relative duties and privileges of the clerk, and of the governor, porter, and other officers of the house, the Guardians are desirous that the same should be more particularly defined.

"1st. With regard to the clerk—

"Whether he is entitled, at all reasonable hours, to have free access to the house, particularly the porter's lodge, governor's office, and school-rooms, by the interior communication through the board-room and paupers' waiting-room, or by the exterior communication, through the porter's gates, and thereby exposed to the weather? Has the clerk a right to a master-key of the exterior gate leading to his office, or of any and what doors of the house? particularly the room doors leading from his office to the governor's office through the board-room?

"2nd. As to the officers of the workhouse—

"Has the governor or matron, or their children, or any other of the inmate officers, a right to pass through the porter's lodge without the time of their going out and coming in being put down in the porter's book?

"I have the honour to remain,
"Sirs,
"Your obedient Servant,
(Signed) "JOHN MARSH, *Clerk to the Union.*"

In reply, the Commissioners observed, that as the clerk is not an officer of the workhouse establishment, they consider that he is not entitled to enter all parts of the workhouse, but the Commissioners think that the clerk should be permitted to have free access to the Board-room and his own office at all reasonable hours, and that that access should be allowed to him by means of the most convenient entrance.

The Commissioners do not think that the clerk should be possessed of a master-key, by which he could enter the workhouse, or the rooms or wards contained in it, whenever he may choose to do so.

The Commissioners have further to state, that they do not consider it part of the porter's duty to record in his book the times at which the officers of the establishment leave or enter the workhouse, although the Guardians could by a bye-law render it incumbent upon him to make such an entry in his book if they found it necessary or expedient.

---

2. NOTICES UPON PUTATIVE FATHERS OF BASTARD CHILDREN—DUTIES OF CLERK IN RESPECT OF.

The following is an application for advice from the Clerk of the Brecon Union:—

"*Brecon.*

"GENTLEMEN,—By the 2nd and 3rd Victoria, c. 85, it is enacted, that the notice of application to justices for an order upon the putative father of a bastard child, for its maintenance and support, must be signed by a majority of the Guardians present at a meeting of the Board. I beg you will be pleased to favour me with your opinion, whether it is absolutely necessary that I, a clerk, should attend the Petty Sessions to prove to the signatures of the Guardians, and also to the majority having signed? I consider it my duty, as clerk, to fill up the application and procure the signatures at the Board; but, if I am obliged to attend the Petty Sessions, who is to pay me for my loss of time and expenses?

"In the first clause of this Act it states, 'that the Guardians may, if they think proper, apply to justices for an order,' &c. In the second, 'that justices may summons any witness to appear and give evidence on behalf of the Guardians,' &c. Will you also be pleased to inform me whose duty it is to collect evidence, obtain summonses, and to conduct the proceedings before the justices?

"Your answer will oblige,
"Gentlemen,
"Your obedient Servant,
"JOHN DAVIES, *Clerk to the Union.*"

In reply, the Commissioners stated the understanding of the Commissioners—and they have no doubt that the same is the understanding in Parliament—is, that whenever any duty is imposed on the Guardians, the execution is supposed, where it is possible and compatible with the general appointment of their officers, to be imposed on those officers. This is more especially the case with the clerk, who is the immediate agent and instrument of the Guardians, who, being a Corporation and capable of acting only as a Board, are precluded from executing immediately many of the duties with which Parliament has invested them.

The application for orders on putative fathers of bastard children, and all steps incidental to the application, appear to the Commissioners to be in all respects such as should be performed by the Guardians by the agency of their clerk.

But the Commissioners do not understand that the new duties from time to time imposed on Guardians are to be performed by the clerk without additional remuneration, on the contrary, the Commissioners consider that the clerk being a paid officer, is considered, with respect to new duties imposed, as being in the same condition as with regard to the older duties of his office; and that his salary, being capable of being varied, should be the subject of reconsideration whenever his duties are materially changed in character or extent.

Whenever the total duties of a clerk appear, whether by addition of new duties or increase of the older duties, to be permanently increased beyond the extent of duty contemplated when his salary was last fixed, it becomes proper again to take his salary into consideration. When his general duties have so far diminished as not to exceed with the addition of duties newly imposed the extent of duty contemplated at the time his salary was last fixed, the additional duties will obviously constitute no reason for an increase of salary.

---

3. AS TO POWER OF MEDICAL OFFICER TO EXAMINE ANATOMICALLY THE BODIES OF PAUPER INMATES OF A WORKHOUSE.

The following is a copy of a resolution of the Guardians of the Chipping Ongar Union, transmitted to the Commissioners for their opinion thereon by the Clerk of that Union:—

"Resolved, That the clerk do apply to the Poor Law Commissioners for information, whether the medical officer of the workhouse is empowered, either with or without the sanction of the Board of Guardians, to examine anatomically the body of any pauper inmate dying in the workhouse?"

"(Signed) THOMAS STOKES,
"*Presiding Chairman.*"

In reply, thereto, the Commissioners stated that nothing further is required by them in their order, directing that the medical officer of the Union should "ascertain and certify the cause of death" in the case of a pauper dying in the workhouse, than a statement of what, from apparent circumstances, and such information as can be obtained from nurses and attendants, may be considered the probable cause of death.

In no case do the Commissioners desire a post-mortem examination to take place solely for the purpose of satisfying their rule. Excepting by the direction of a coroner when holding an inquest, or of the Board of Guardians for any special, urgent, and peculiar reason, which they may deem of sufficient importance to render such an examination necessary, or at the request of the nearest relatives of the deceased, the Commissioners deem that the medical officer would not be justified in making a post-mortem examination.

The Commissioners have further to add, that they think that the Board of Guardians would hardly be justified in directing in any particular case that a post-mortem examination should take place, if the nearest relatives of the deceased objected clearly and decidedly to the course; and the Commissioners need hardly add, that the Guardians would, so far as circumstances will permit, do well to satisfy themselves of the necessity for such an examination before they took upon themselves to authorize it.

---

4. IS MEDICAL OFFICER ENTITLED TO FEE FOR GIVING EVIDENCE ON INQUEST HELD ON PAUPER IN THE WORKHOUSE.

The Commissioners took into consideration the following application from the Auditor of the Leighton Buzzard Union:—

"*Leighton Buzzard.*

"SIR,—I trust you will excuse the liberty I take in requesting an answer to the following question:—

"When a coroner's inquest is held in the poorhouse upon the body of an inmate, is the medical officer of the Union who gives his evidence entitled to the usual fee, if there be no special clause in his contract to exclude him from the receipt of it?

"If you will be so kind as to favour me with an answer, which is solicited on behalf of a medical officer, I shall feel obliged to you.

"I am, Sir,
"Your very obedient servant,
(Signed) "JOSEPH KIPLING,
"*Auditor of the Leighton Buzzard Union.*
"*E. Chadwick, Esq.,*
"*&c. &c. &c.*"

In reply the Commissioners stated, that where the medical officer's contract does not require him to attend to give evidence at inquests, as one of the duties for the performance of which the salary is the consideration, there is nothing to prevent his receiving the usual fee allowed by the Coroner in such a case.

---

5. REMOVAL OF MEDICAL OFFICER.

The Commissioners took into their consideration a report from their Assistant Commissioner, Mr. Weale, on a charge against one of the medical officers of the Loughborough Union, of having refused to attend the daughter of Thomas Hickling, of the parish of East Leake, although he had received a written order from the relieving officer requiring him to do so.

The Commissioners had also before them a letter from the Board of Guardians, enclosing a copy of a resolution passed by them respecting the medical officer's conduct in the case, and stating that the Board considered that his neglect did not arise from any malicious or improper feeling, but merely from an error of judgment; that he had always been thought a very efficient officer, and had treated the poor with the greatest kindness, and that having acknowledged the error under which he had acted, and expressed his determination, as he now knew his duty, to act agreeably to it, it was the wish of the Board of Guardians that he should be continued in his office.

The material facts of the case (as to which there appeared to be no doubt) are thus stated by Mr. Weale in his report:—

"Thomas Hickling, a frame-work knitter, on the 29th of June, had a wife and three children, the eldest of whom, a girl, named Eliza, aged twelve years, being ill, he applied to the relieving officer for an order for the attendance of the medical officer. After making the usual inquiries, the relieving officer felt called on to give the order, and the medical officer refused to attend. On the following day, the wife of Hickling saw Mr. Brown, a medical officer of an adjoining district, passing by her house, and called him in. He saw the child, pronounced it to be suffering from scarlet fever, and in a state of danger, and after giving a few directions, urged the father again to go to the medical officer, and claim his attendance. On the next day Hickling again applied to him, but he still refused to attend, and during the whole of the poor child's illness, she never received any other medical advice than that which Mr. Brown afforded on being called in as he was passing by. The child died early in the morning after the Board had given a peremptory order to the medical officer to attend."

The following is the account given by Mary Hickling, of the circumstances under which she delivered the order of the relieving officer to the medical officer, and of his remarks and conduct thereupon.

"I received this order about seven o'clock in the morning. Between eight and nine I saw the medical officer passing, and I gave him the order. He then asked who it was for, and I told him my daughter. He said, 'Your husband is at work;' and I said he was. And he said, 'He is able to maintain his family;' and I said, 'No, Sir, he is not, for he has only had part work for several weeks.' He then said, 'I shall not stand such work as that,' and put the order in his pocket, and walked off. He never did call to see my child."

The reasons which the medical officer stated to Mr. Weale at the inquiry, for his not attending Eliza Hickling, are the following:—

"1st. Because Hickling, the father, was earning more than he stated to the relieving officer. I believed him to be earning 7*s*. 8*d*. per week at that time.

"2d. That he was an able-bodied man, and able to maintain his family, and that his wife was also earning 1*s*. 6*d*. a-week by lace-running.

"3d. That a woman lodging with them was also earning 1*s*. 6*d*. per week, and that she paid Hickling for her lodgings."

It is not disputed that the relieving officer gave Mary Hickling an order upon the medical officer, to attend her sick child; that Mary Hickling presented the order to him at a reasonable hour, and at a place near her dwelling, and that he refused to attend her child, because he considered the order to have been improperly given. His reasons for not attending the child, as stated by himself, are in substance that the weekly earnings of the family were so large, (amounting, according to his view, to 7*s*. 8*d*. for the man, and 1*s*. 6*d*. for the woman, besides a payment by a lodger,) as to render the child an unfit subject for medical relief, and that the man had understated the amount of his earnings in the answers which he made to the inquiries of the relieving officer.

The following are the statements, bearing on the earnings of the family, in the evidence taken by Mr. Weale.

William Hardstaff, the relieving officer, states, that when the wife applied to him for relief, she said her husband only earned 5*s*. 6*d*. a-week, and that she herself got nothing; that not being satisfied with the statement of the wife, as to the earnings, on the day but one following the day he gave the order, he applied to Thomas Hickling himself on the subject, who told him (the relieving officer) that he sometimes earned more than 5*s*. 6*d*. but never so high as 8*s*.

Thomas Hickling states, that for the two or three months before his daughter's illness he was short of work and ill, and his average earnings did not amount to more than 7*s.* weekly, clear of deduction.

Mary Hickling states, that she told the medical officer on the Saturday following her daughter's death, that her husband had that week earned about 8*s.*, and that when she ran lace, she could herself earn 1*s.* 6*d.* a-week. She could not work when her daughter was ill.

It appears from these statements that the earnings of the family at the time in question, did not exceed 7*s.* or at the most 8*s.*; that the account which the relieving officer obtained from Mary Hickling, before giving the order, was not very wide of the truth; and that the account which he obtained from John Hickling, after having given the order, was substantially correct.

The Commissioners directed the following communication of their opinion on the facts of the case as above detailed to be made to the Board of Guardians.

If a medical officer can satisfy himself that a medical order is obtained from a relieving officer by substantially false representations as to the condition of an applicant, and that the case is one in which the discretion of the relieving officer has been improperly exercised, he would be justified in disobeying the order, and refusing to attend the case; but in every such case, it is incumbent on him to ascertain exactly the nature of the representations made by the applicant to the relieving officer, as well as the applicant's circumstances, and if he acts without this caution, or if having used this caution, he forms an erroneous judgment upon the facts, he is responsible for his refusal and its consequences.

In the present case the Commissioners cannot see that the medical officer acted with the caution which the circumstances of the case demanded, or that he had sufficient grounds for supposing the order to have been improperly given.

The Commissioners are always desirous, whenever they can do so consistently with their duty, to act in accordance with the views of the Boards of Guardians, respecting the conduct of their officers, and they duly appreciate the testimony of the Board of Guardians to the efficiency of the medical officer, and his kind behaviour towards the poor.

Nevertheless, as the medical officer acted in this case deliberately, and as the deliberate refusal of a medical officer to comply with a medical order might, if overlooked, constitute a dangerous precedent for other medical officers, as well in the Loughborough Union, as in other Unions, the Commissioners conceive themselves bound to terminate his official connexion with the Union, and they therefore request that he will resign his office to the Guardians, so as to enable them to proceed to the election of his successor.

III.—PAUPERS:—1. IMPORTANT THAT REMOVALS SHOULD TAKE PLACE WITH ALL THE FORMALITIES REQUIRED BY LAW.

The Commissioners took into consideration the following correspondence between the Boards of Guardians of the Frome and Bradford Unions respecting the removal of a pauper:—

"*Poor Law Union Office, Frome,*
"*August* 18, 1841.

"*Orders of Removal.*

"SIR,—I am directed by the Board of Guardians of this Union to forward to the Poor Law Commissioners the enclosed copy of a resolution of this Board, and also a copy of correspondence between it and the Bradford Union, relative to the removal of a pauper.

"I have the honour to be, Sir,
"Your obedient servant,
(Signed) "L. HAGLEY, *Clerk.*

"*To E. Chadwick, Esq.*"

"*Frome Union, August* 17, 1841.

"The Board being of opinion that the proceedings of the master of the workhouse of the Bradford Union, in sending paupers from such workhouse to a parish in this Union where they were supposed to belong, without any order of removal or any previous communication with this Board, is evidently irregular and highly prejudicial to the proper carrying out of the Poor Law; and such proceedings being acknowledged to have the sanction of the Guardians of the Bradford Union, Resolved—'That the resolution of this Board of the 27th ultimo, together with the reply of the Bradford Board of Guardians and a copy of this resolution, be transmitted to the Poor Law Commissioners, and that they be requested to state their opinion on such proceedings.'"

"*Frome Union, July* 27, 1841.

"Resolved—'That the clerk write to the Bradford Union, informing them another case has occurred similar to one which happened in March last,—the master of the workhouse of that Union having recently sent a man of the name of Job Penny and his wife to the parish of Woolverton without any order of removal, or any authority from the Board; and requesting to be informed, whether such proceeding has the sanction of the Bradford Union.' "

" *Bradford, Wilts, August* 4, 1841.

" SIR,—Your letter of the 28th July was laid before the Guardians of the Bradford Union at their meeting yesterday, and they direct me to inform you in reply that Job Penny and his wife were sent to their parish of Woolverton by the master of the Union workhouse under the sanction of the Guardians of the Bradford Union, there being no doubt that Woolverton is the pauper's parish.

" I am, Sir,
" Your's obediently,
" WILLIAM TIMBRELL, *Clerk.*

" *To Mr. Hagley, Clerk to the Union,*
" *Frome, Somerset.*"

The Commissioners directed a copy of the communication made to them by the Guardians of the Frome Union to be transmitted to the Guardians of the Bradford Union, with a request that they would inform the Commissioners of the grounds upon which they gave directions to the master of the workhouse to remove the pauper, in the manner alluded to, to the parish of Woolverton. The following is the answer of the Guardians:—

" *Bradford, Wilts, August* 30, 1841.
" ORDERS OF REMOVAL.

" SIR,—Your letter of the 23rd instant, together with the resolution of the Board of Guardians of the Frome Union, and accompanying correspondence relative to the removal of a pauper by the master of the workhouse of this Union to the parish of Woolverton, in the Frome Union, was laid before the Guardians of this Union at their last meeting; and I am directed by them to state in reply, that when the pauper (Job Penny) was brought up before the Board on the 20th of July last, with the paupers who had been admitted into the house the preceding week, he was examined by the chairman as to his place of settlement, when it clearly appeared that Woolverton was the place of his lawful settlement. The chairman asked him why he had not gone to his own parish of Woolverton (which is only about four miles distant from the Bradford Union workhouse) instead of troubling the parish of Bradford for relief, when the pauper said he was aware that Woolverton was his parish, and that he should not have troubled the parish of Bradford, but having an attack of rheumatism he was not able to walk so far as Woolverton;—that one of the guardians said, there are plenty of empty coal-carts passing within half a mile of the workhouse every morning, going close to Woolverton, on their way to the coal-pits, and that he could ride in one of them; that the pauper seemed very willing to go, and the Board thereupon directed the master to discharge him and his wife on the following morning after breakfast.

" I am, Sir,
" Your most obedient servant,
(Signed) " WILLIAM TIMBRELL, *Clerk.*

" *To E. Chadwick, Esq.*"

The Commissioners transmitted a copy of the above letter to the Guardians of the Frome Union, and in compliance with their request, that the Commissioners should state their opinion on the case, the Commissioners remarked as follows:—

It is generally of great importance that removals of paupers should take place in the manner and with all the formalities required by law; and that these should not be dispensed with. And the Commissioners even doubt whether any exception should be made when a parish may be willing to receive a pauper in the less regular manner, with a view to avoid the expense incidental to the obtaining and execution of an order of removal.

When a parish or Union officers remove a pauper in any other manner, or do anything to prevent his becoming chargeable to another parish, so as to deprive this other parish of its legal protections against the charge, it is an obvious injustice, destructive of that spirit of co-operation which is of such great mutual advantage; and, when it is done with a fraudulent intention to cast a burden on another parish, it appears to expose the parties to the act to penal consequences.

On the other hand there can be no legal objection, nor do the Commissioners know of any other objection, to a pauper's returning voluntarily to the place which he supposes to be his place of settlement. Nor does it appear to be a duty of any officer to prevent him from doing so if he desires it; though, even in this case, it is clear to the Commissioners that they should subject him to no extrinsic inducement to do so. For if an inducement however slight, supposing it to be sufficient, is held out to the pauper, it is as much a wrong to the other parish as if the inducement constituted ever so violent a motive; and the removal must be considered morally, and would probably be considered legally, to be effected irregularly by those who offered such inducement.

As regards the present case, however, assuming the facts to be correctly understood and reported by the Guardians of the Bradford Union, it would appear, first, that inasmuch as the settlement is unquestioned there was no corrupt motive to charge the parish of Woolverton with the burden of a pauper settled elsewhere, or whose settlement was so in doubt as to render his legal removal a matter of difficulty to any parish to which he might happen to be chargeable; that, accordingly, Woolverton could experience no injury in the case in question, unless it can be considered to be an injury to be deprived of the chance of defeating an order of removal in a case in which there are good grounds of removal; and that Bradford obtained no benefit except the saving of the cost of removal, which was not a benefit to be obtained by the prejudice of another parish. So far the circumstances as stated would negative any imputation of a corrupt or unfair object.

Next, as to the nature of the means by which the removal of the pauper in the parish of Woolverton was effected. If money or other advantage had been offered to the pauper, or threats held out to him, such facts would make the removal an act of the parties holding forth the inducement. But the mere discharge of the pauper from the workhouse does not appear to be such an inducement; nor does the casual suggestion by a Guardian present of the means of conveyance, without actually providing these means, contemplate such an inducement, being merely information to the pauper of the means by which he could himself effect a proposed end without superadding a motive to effect that end.

Moreover there would, undoubtedly, be some extenuation even where some irregularity had been committed by parish officers or Guardians in cases where the proximity of the parish of the settlement was such as to suggest the question, why a pauper had proposed to become chargeable to another parish. The latter might reasonably enough inquire why the pauper had selected it, and bid him apply to his own parish.

Though the Commissioners think the statement of facts has the effect of exonerating the Guardians of the Bradford Union from blame, the Commissioners feel that the distinctions between such a case, in which even positive inducements might have been held out to the pauper, are so subtle as to make such conduct as that of the Board of Guardians in the present instance of very dangerous example, tending strongly to bring about cases which, by very easy and almost imperceptible transition, would become liable to all the objections and penal consequences before adverted to. And the Commissioners, therefore, cannot refrain from recommending that, in all cases, the Guardians should not only not encourage, but should, as far as possible, prevent removals of persons who have become chargeable which are not to be effected under orders in the regular manner.

The Commissioners directed a copy of this letter to be transmitted to the Bradford Union Board of Guardians.

---

2. English and Scotch Poor Laws: No provision made for the removal of an English Pauper resident in Scotland.

The following is a copy of a letter received from the clerk to the heritors of Yetholm.

" *Yetholm.*

"Gentlemen,—The heritors of Yetholm, at a meeting held here on the 23rd of May last, entered on their records the following minute, which I extract as an apology for troubling you with this communication.

"'In respect to the money advanced to Henry Luke's family while in a state of destitution in the course of last winter, the meeting, considering that Luke's settlement is in the township of Howtal, in the county of Northumberland, and that proper and repeated notice respecting the state of the said family was given to the overseer of said township, and by him disregarded, instruct the clerk to make out an account of the money advanced by this parish in relief of Luke's family, and to transmit the same, with a request for repayment, to the Board of Guardians, Woolar Union, and in the event of this application being refused, to state the whole circumstances of the case to the Poor Law Commissioners in London.'

"As instructed by the heritors, the account referred to in the preceding minute was sent to the Guardians on the 13th of June last, along with a letter, of which the following is a copy.

"' *Yetholm.*

"' *To the Guardians for the Poor in the Woolar Union.*

"'Gentlemen,— I have received instructions from the heritors of the parish of Yetholm, to forward to you the prefixed account, and in their names to demand repayment of the same.

"'It will not be denied that Luke's family, though resident in Yetholm, belong to the township of Howtal, and that they were actually at the point of starvation when the money was advanced for their relief. Due notice was given to the overseer of the township at the time they got into distress, but as no attention was paid to the intimation, the overseer in this parish was in consequence compelled to relieve the family, on his own responsibility, to prevent them from absolutely starving.

"'I have therefore to request that you will not only order repayment of the money advanced as per account, but will also instruct the overseer of the poor in the township of Howtal to take care that the family be not burdensome to the parish of Yetholm in future.

"'I am, Gentlemen, with much respect,
"'Your most obedient servant,
(Signed) "'WILLIAM HENDERSON,
"'*Heritors' Clerk.*'

"This letter, to which no answer has been returned, was not, as may be presumed, the first intimation in respect to this case made to those who are charged with the management of the Howtal poor. The family became burdensome to the parish of Yetholm on the 15th of January last, and their destitution and distress were immediately made known to the overseer, and subsequently to the Guardians, by means of a petition for relief, presented by Luke's wife, and by a letter from the Yetholm overseer, describing the state of the family, and stating what he had done in their case, and claiming repayment of the money he had meantime advanced. Their petition in this form was refused, and the family of their own free will, on the 9th of March, with the exception of Luke himself, whose health rendered exposure to the inclemency of the weather dangerous to him at that time, removed from Yetholm to Howtal, and presenting themselves before the overseer, begged from him that aid which their circumstances required, and the law authorized. But as their removal had not been effected by legal warrant, (an instrument which cannot be obtained in Scotland,) the overseer would not receive them, or grant them relief in any form whatever. In this way they were in a manner driven back to Yetholm, where they rented a house but had no settlement, and where they might have perished had not the overseer of Yetholm supplied their wants.

"The object of the heritors of Yetholm, in making this statement, is in the first place to ascertain, if there be a process by which the money they have advanced in support of Luke's family can be recovered from the township of Howtal, supposing the case to be as here described; and in the next place, as Yetholm is a border parish, and likely to have to deal with such cases, the course which must be followed in order to secure the benefit of an English settlement for a person who falls into a state of pauperism in Scotland, but has no settlement, excepting in England.

"The information here desired from you will, I doubt not, be given, and will be of much service to the heritors of this parish.

"I am, Gentlemen, with the greatest respect,
"Your most obedient servant,
(Signed) "WM. HENDERSON,
"*Heritors' Clerk.*"

"*Yetholm by Kelso.*"

In reply, the Commissioners stated that the case described is not contemplated by the English Poor Laws, under which nothing can be claimed by one parish or township for relief given to the settled poor of another, unless the first parish or township protects itself by procuring an order of removal.

Under the English Poor Laws, every pauper is entitled to relief whenever he is found destitute, and the parish of his settlement is not bound to supply him with relief when resident elsewhere.

This statement will indicate to you the conclusion that the case you described is an omitted case in the English Poor Laws, and that, for the protection of Scotch parishes, a like legal remedy in regard of English paupers is required as that provided by the English law for the removal of Scotch and Irish paupers.

---

3. WHAT PROCEEDINGS TO BE TAKEN AGAINST PAUPER ABSCONDING WITH WORKHOUSE CLOTHING.

The following is a copy of a letter received from the Clerk of the Ruthin Union:—

"*Ruthin.*

"GENTLEMEN,—The Guardians have directed me to request that you will advise them what proceedings they should adopt against a pauper who, while wearing the Union clothing, runs away from the workhouse with the clothing on.

"I have the honour to be,
"Gentlemen,
"Your most obedient Servant,
"JOSEPH PEERS."

In reply, the Commissioners directed the attention of the Guardians to the 2nd section of 55th Geo. III. c. 137, which authorizes justices to commit persons to the common gaol, &c. for the space of three calendar months, on conviction of the offence of absconding from the workhouse, and taking with them the workhouse clothes.

IV.—RELIEF:—1. THE MERE FACT OF GIVING RELIEF CONFERS NO RIGHT TO TAKE POSSESSION OF ANY PROPERTY BELONGING TO A PAUPER.

The following application for advice was received from the clerk of the Chelmsford Union.

"*Chelmsford, October* 5, 1841.

"GENTLEMEN,—One of the overseers of Chelmsford having reason to suspect that an infirm old man who had recently been admitted into the Union workhouse, had left some money or other property in his hutches or boxes left in the house in which the old man had been residing, took upon himself to open and search the boxes. In one box he found five sovereigns belonging to the old man. The Board of Guardians are desirous of having your opinion, whether the overseer of Chelmsford will be fully authorized and justified in handing over the five sovereigns to the overseer of the parish (Great Baddow) to which the old man belongs, and to deduct his maintenance in the house on this and former occasions, as well as some out-door relief which has been charged; and whether on his doing this, the overseer of Chelmsford will be entirely free from all claim or risk of proceedings at law at the suit of the old man.

"I remain, Gentlemen, &c.,
"(Signed) ROBERT BARTLETT,
"*Clerk.*

"*To the Poor Law Commissioners.*"

In reply the Commissioners stated, that the mere fact of giving relief confers with it no right to take possession of money or other property belonging to a pauper. The Commissioners are of opinion in reference to the inquiry upon this point, that the overseer of Chelmsford will not be authorized in handing over the money to the overseers of *Great Baddow*, in which parish it is stated the pauper is chargeable, but is bound to restore the money to its lawful owner. As regards the future, relief, if necessary, might be granted as a loan, and the overseers could then pursue any of the prescribed remedies for recovering relief given by way of loan.

2. TO TRAMPS:—APPLICATION TO ALLOW A PAUPER TO LEAVE THE WORKHOUSE AND GO ON THE TRAMP.

The following case was submitted to the Commissioners by the Guardians of the Plympton St. Mary Union for their opinion and directions thereon:—

"*September 24th*, 1841.

"Edward Howard, his wife, and four children, were removed from a parish in Kent to the parish of Compton Gifford, in this Union, being the place of his last legal settlement, and were received into the Union workhouse, where they have remained ever since, a period of six weeks. Howard is a paper-maker by trade, able bodied, and unable to gain his living in any other way. He appears industrious, aad states that, before he applied for parish relief, he vainly endeavoured for fourteen weeks, after losing his employment by the failure of his master during the last winter, to get work in other manufactories.

"He now applies to the Board of Guardians for permission *to quit the workhouse without his wife and children*, in order that he may go into the counties of *Kent* and *Somerset* to seek employment, and on his succeeding, promises to send for his family.

"He belongs to a certain society of paper-makers in the counties of *Kent* and *Somerset*, and is in possession of a card which entitles him to receive relief at any manufactories in these counties at which he applies for employment unsuccessfully, so that, after quitting the workhouse, he will not be destitute even should he fail in procuring employment; and the fact of his belonging to that society quite excludes him from employment in Devonshire.

"The Guardians *wish to accede to his request*, as he and his family will otherwise remain a burthen on their parish for many years, but they find themselves precluded by the Prohibitory Order.

"What are they to do? Is the man with his family to remain in the house, or is it expedient to relax the prohibitory order as regards him, although the Guardians run the risk of the man absconding and deserting his family.

(Signed) "MORLEY, *Chairman.*"

In reply, the Commissioners stated that they have directed their more particular attention to that part of the case in which it is stated "that the pauper now applies to the Board of Guardians for permission to quit the workhouse without his wife and children in order that he may go into the counties of Kent and Somerset to seek employment, and, on his succeeding, to send for his family. He belongs to a certain society of paper-makers in the counties of Kent and Somerset, and is in possession of a card which entitles him to receive relief at any manufactories in those counties to which he applies for employment unsuccessfully, so that after quitting the workhouse he will not be destitute, even should he fail in procuring employment, and the fact of his belonging to that society quite excludes him from employment in Devonshire. The Guardians wish to accede to his request, as he and his family will otherwise remain a burthen on their parish for many years, but they find themselves precluded by the Prohibitory Order.

In some cases an able-bodied pauper is permitted to quit the house for the day to search for work; but the cases where the pauper has been allowed to go out for the day have not been cases of an entire separation from his family. The Commissioners consider that the mere promise of the pauper to return to his family, or to send for them as soon as he finds work, is not a security the Guardians would be justified towards the rate-payers in acting upon.

It appears that the pauper has been already removed from a parish in Kent. If after having been once relieved there, he return again, and become chargeable, he will be punishable as a vagrant. If he were allowed by the Guardians to separate himself from his family, they would apparently have no security against his returning and becoming chargeable to the parish from whence he was removed.

But the fact of the pauper belonging to a trade in which there is an organized system of tramping indicates peculiar danger in yielding to such an application. The relief of this one member of the trade from the burthen of maintaining his family whilst he is on the tramp holds out to all the rest of the married men of that trade an inducement to throw their wives and families into the workhouse whilst they absent themselves for as long a period as they please, and neglect their duties as long as they please, for not even the Board of Guardians, still less the rate-payers of any particular parish, have the means of following throughout the country each individual pauper to ascertain when he says he is on the tramp, whether his statement is true, and whether he is not in work, and in receipt of wages. The demoralization of a workman who goes upon the tramp appears to be certain. All the information with relation to such societies of their demoralizing and injurious effects on the workmen themselves would justify the presumption that any refusal on the part of masters in Devonshire to employ a man connected with such societies was well founded.

The Commissioners suggest that the relieving officers should be directed to inquire how the case stands in this respect, and whether employment would be given to the pauper if he did not voluntarily exclude himself by attaching himself to the association in question.

The evil of the neglect and desertion of families chiefly on the pretext of a search for work is so great as to call for the utmost vigilance of the Guardians for the protection of the rate-payers against the pecuniary burthens and the neglect and demoralization of children which it entails. The number of individuals, women and children, who appear to have been chargeable to the Plympton St. Mary Union, by the desertion of the husband during the year 1840 appear to have been 37. In the county the number of wives relieved as deserted in that year appears to have been 152, and their children 358.

The Commissioners are of opinion that the case can only be dealt with prudently with reference to the ultimate as well as the present operation of the rule, not only upon the single case, but on the whole class of cases.

They observe further, that the reduction of postage now affords a means of making inquiries for work from distant places in a mode much cheaper than by going on the tramp, and that this mode is now in practice by independent labourers, and is a mode of obtaining information in behalf of the pauper from distant places that may properly be resorted to.

For the reasons above stated the Commissioners advise the Guardians to continue to relieve the man and his family in the workhouse.

The Commissioners enclose, for the information of the Guardians, an extract from some evidence bearing on the habits of wandering artisans:—

Extract from Evidence received by the Poor Law Commissioners.

"When a boy is apprenticed, I understand he is compelled to subscribe to what is called the club belonging to the trade, out of his wages, which subscription continues, if he has work, after his apprenticeship. The club has places of resort, generally beer shops or public houses, where the members meet. When the boy is past his apprenticeship, he goes to the secretary of the club; he states he is going on the tramp, that he is to wander over the country in search of work. Some forms are gone through before the secretary, with a view to ascertain his right to support him from the club, and then the secretary gives him a card, which contains the names of the towns through which he purposes to pass, and the names of the public houses, and the keepers of them, which are the places of resort of the trade club. On presenting his card at any one of these houses, he is entitled to a shilling, bread and cheese for supper, and a bed for a certain number of nights; and after that period has expired, he wanders to another town. So far I do not see any harm in the principle, but it almost invariably results, as far as my inquiries enable me to judge, in a young man who sets off on the tramp never settling to business after three months' wandering. The public houses are generally of a low character, and, however well he may have been educated in the Sunday-schools, the associates he meets with lead him on to crime, or else into habits of professional beggary."

---

3. CASUAL POOR AND VAGRANTS: DIFFICULTIES RESPECTING RELIEF TO.—POWERS OF MAGISTRATES IN RESPECT OF.

The Commissioners took into their consideration the subjoined letter from the Board of Guardians of the parish of Camberwell on the subject of the relief of casual poor and vagrants.

"*Camberwell, September* 23, 1841.

"SIR,—I am requested by the Board of Guardians of the parish of Camberwell, to lay before the Poor Law Commissioners the following case:—

"On Friday, the 17th instant, two boys, whose names have since been ascertained to be Thomas Seddon, 15 years of age, and Richard Woodnut, 14 years of age, appeared at the workhouse for admission, between the hours of ten and eleven o'clock at night. Experience having shown that applications from the really destitute are rarely made at so late an hour, the usual examination with the view to learn if they were of the class of casually destitute or habitual vagrants was made in the presence of a police constable, in the course of which the boys convicted themselves by a variety of false statements, and as they had evidently been some time on the tramp, and could not give a good account of themselves, the officers of the workhouse considered them to be of that class deserving punishment at the hands of a magistrate rather than relief in a workhouse, and accordingly handed them over to the custody of the police as vagrants, believing they would be dealt with as usual without their further interference.

"On the following day the sitting magistrate at Union-hall, Mr. Cottingham, sent for the master of the workhouse, and censured him for refusing to receive the boys, and without hearing his explanation of the ground upon which his refusal was made, declared that the order under which he had acted, by attempting to draw a line of distinction between the casually destitute and common vagrants, was illegal, and that he would fine those who made it and him too. Mr. Cottingham then desired the master and relieving officer (who was present) to understand that they had no right to use any distinction whatever in the relief of such cases, it being sufficient for them to be told by the policeman, that the person presented is destitute, without putting a single question to the boys. He then desired they might be taken back to Camberwell workhouse, and be passed home to their parishes.

"I should here mention that the order alluded to by the magistrates is one given by the Board of Guardians to the master of the workhouse in July last, a copy of which, together with a letter addressed by me to the superintendent of the P division of police is hereto annexed.

"And in order further to assure the Commissioners how earnestly the Board desire to have all cases of actual want promptly attended to, I have annexed copies of two handbills published by the Guardians in November, 1838, and January, 1840, respectively. They have had also a male and female ward set apart for the casual poor.

"To proceed with the case in point, the boys were re-examined by the officers of the workhouse, when they contradicted all they had previously said, and it was not until closely pressed that they gave what we now believe to be a true account of themselves, from which it appears that Seddon was apprenticed by Bethnal Green parish to a shoemaker, from whom he has absconded several times, and been once imprisoned for so doing, he admits that he has lived during twelve months past by begging. Woodnut has been tramping about the country without visible means of support, for the last fifteen months, they have lately found the lodging afforded to them in the Union houses cheaper and better than any they could procure elsewhere, and of which they have invariably availed themselves; 4*d*. in money was found concealed upon one of them, and 2*d*. upon the other, their clothes were in the most filthy and tattered state, and covered with vermin.

"In bringing these circumstances under the notice of the Poor Law Commissioners, I am desired to request their particular attention to the uncalled-for interference of the police magistrate with the orders of the Board of Guardians, by taking upon himself to stultify in the practice of their officers the use of that discretion which the Board consider most essential in protecting the public interest, and preventing the casual wards of their workhouse from becoming the nightly resort of thieves and prostitutes, either to the entire seclusion (or what is equally bad, the corruption) of the deserving door, as they are convinced that much of the existing vagrancy is produced by the indiscriminate admixture of those classes, which it is their anxious desire to distinguish by giving to each according to their merits.

"It will thus be seen that the Board of Guardians have not given those directions to their officers without being first satisfied not only of the legal right, but of the moral benefit to be derived from the enforcement of them, and in the conscientious discharge of their duties they are not at all disposed to submit to such unauthorized interference as that of which they have now to complain, and they trust the Poor Law Commissioners will take up the subject in such a manner as cannot fail to prevent a recurrence of the same.

"I am, Sir, &c.

"(Signed) THOMAS PLUM,

"*Clerk of the Board.*"

Extracts from the Minutes of the Board of Guardians, July 28, 1840.

"The master reported to the Board that the police were accustomed to bring cases of *vagrancy* to the workhouse for relief and lodging, after 9 and 10 o'clock at night, and that in general he had refused to admit them, considering that as *vagrants* they should be kept in custody by the police in order to be dealt with as the law directs. Cases of real *destitution*, and of *emergency*, he had always at once admitted, but desired to have particular instructions of the Board with regard to the treatment of a class of cases upon which he felt there was much responsibility attached to his office.

"The Board were of opinion, that a wide distinction existed between cases of *destitution* and *vagrancy*, and instructed the master that while they wished him invariably to pay the most prompt attention to applicants of the former class, they should consider him justified in refusing the latter admission, *except* in cases of *emergency*, and instructed the clerk to communicate to the superintendent of police the nature of the orders now given to the master.

"*Camberwell, July* 31, 1841.

"SIR,—It has been represented to the Board of Guardians of the parish of Camberwell, that the constables of your division of police, employed in this parish, are in the habit of bringing vagrants to the workhouse in the Peckham Road for admission after 9 and 10 o'clock at night.

"The Board desire me to inform you that they have instructed the master of the workhouse not to admit such cases after that time at night, unless under some special and urgent circumstances.

"They beg to be understood, that it is not their wish to have cases of destitution refused, on the contrary, they would much regret that a single case should be rejected; they consider, however, that a wide distinction exists between cases of casual destitution and of vagrancy, that while the former should have their wants properly ministered to, the latter should be kept in custody and be taken before a magistrate for punishment.

"They trust, therefore, that you will have the goodness to cause the men to be directed to use the distinction between the two classes of cases, as it will in general save them, as well as the officers of the workhouse, much unnecessary trouble.

"I am, Sir,

"Your very obedient Servant,

"(Signed) THOMAS PLUM,

"*Clerk of the Board.*

"*The Superintendent of the P. Division*
"*of the Metropolitan Police.*"

"The Board of Guardians beg to inform the rate-payers of this parish, that tickets for distribution to beggars will be issued upon application to their clerk, at the Vestry Hall, which tickets will entitle the 'bearer,' *if really destitute*, to such temporary relief as may be required, from the master of the workhouse, upon the simple condition of the performance of a task of work proportioned to the capacity of the applicant.

"The Board of Guardians request that these tickets, instead of food or money, be given to all persons who, on the plea of destitution, shall beg relief.

"By order of the Board,

"(Signed) T. PLUM, *Clerk.*

"*St. Giles, Camberwell, November*, 1838."

"*St. Giles Camberwell.*—DESTITUTION.

"The Board of Guardians beg again to notify to the rate-payers, that all poor travellers and others found in the streets, who are really destitute, will, on their own application at the workhouse, receive relief, and, in case of sickness, medical assistance; they will be lodged, if necessary, and provided with an ample supply of simple but nutritious food, and set to such work as may be suitable to their strength and condition.

"For the convenience of the inhabitants, tickets (which it is requested may be given to beggars instead of food or money) continue to be issued, and may be obtained by personal or written application to the relieving officer at the Vestry Hall, the master of the workhouse, Havil Street, or of either of the beadles.

"By order of the Board,

"(Signed) THOMAS PLUM, *Clerk.*

"*Vestry Hall, January*, 1840."

The Commissioners addressed the following letter to the Guardians in reply.

The Commissioners are fully convinced that it is the wish of the Guardians of Camberwell parish to relieve real cases of urgent want, without encouraging mendicity, and that the directions given to the master of their workhouse had no object but this in view.

As a general rule, the Commissioners have been accustomed to consider, that the fact of a party being brought to a workhouse by a police constable is evidence of two things.

1st. That the applicant appears in urgent want.

2ndly. That he has not committed within the knowledge of the police, any such act of vagrancy as would render him liable to be detained in custody, and dealt with under the provisions of the Vagrant Act.

A person under such circumstances is, without doubt, a proper object for relief by admission into the vagrants' ward of a workhouse, and it is desirable that such admission should take place with the least possible risk of contamination to others, or of encouragement to imposture.

The Commissioners believe that it would be impossible to hope for complete success in their endeavours to secure these objects, unless by the formation of distinct establishments for the reception of trampers, and mendicants in or near the metropolis, in which a power of detention for a few hours might be exercised, and the discipline would be of a somewhat different character from that of an ordinary workhouse.

The difficulty of which the Camberwell Board complain really originates in the want of some arrangement of this kind.

As things now stand, however, persons in urgent want, whatever may be their character, and whatever may be the presumption of a dishonest and wandering course of life on their part, must, without doubt, be relieved. The risk incurred by their reception into a workhouse is the lesser evil of the two. The Commissioners doubt the possibility of arriving at the conclusion, that a particular applicant is one who ought to be dealt with as an offender, simply on the ground of a cross examination by the master of the workhouse, in which that officer may have elicited from the party himself, circumstances such as to excite a suspicion of habitual mendicancy and imposture. To transfer a person on these grounds only from the class of paupers to that of criminals, appears to be in some degree an encroachment on the functions of the police magistrates. A confession of an act of vagrancy, if made to the magistrate himself, is sufficient evidence for detention and conviction under the Vagrant Act, but would certainly not be enough in itself when made to some other party.

The Commissioners, therefore, cannot wholly concur in the views taken by the Camberwell Board with reference to these cases, although they are fully sensible of the evils necessarily attendant on the indiscriminate reception of vagrants, and would gladly see some such change in the arrangements now adopted as might secure the relief of destitution without its present inconveniences.

The Commissioners believe that they shall best forward the views of the Camberwell Board, by transmitting a copy of this correspondence to the Secretary of State for the Home Department, and to the metropolitan Commissioners of Police.

V.—BASTARDY:—MONEY DUE FROM PUTATIVE FATHERS, WHOSE DUTY TO COLLECT.

The Commissioners took into consideration the following application from the Clerk of the Halifax Union:—

"*Halifax.*

"SIR,—I am directed by the Board of Guardians of this Union to request the opinion and directions of the Poor Law Commissioners upon the following points:—

"1st. Is it the duty of the overseers to collect the money due from putative fathers, under orders of maintenance, obtained pursuant to 2 and 3 Vict. cap. 85,—the orders being obtained by, and the money made payable to, the Guardians?

"2nd. If so, can any steps be adopted by the Guardians to compel the overseers to perform that duty?

"3rd. If it is not the duty of the overseers, upon whom does the duty devolve, and in what form is the money to be accounted for?

"The same questions will also apply to the receiving of pensions, under 2 and 3 Vict., cap. 51.

"I am, &c.

(Signed) "CHARLES BARSTOW,

"*E. Chadwick, Esq.*,
"*&c. &c. &c.*"

In reply the Commissioners stated,—

1st. It appears to the Commissioners to be the strict legal duty of the putative father to apply to the Guardians, and to pay the amount to them; but, as this can hardly be expected to be done, the Guardians may appoint any person, such as the relieving officer or the overseers of the poor, or the collector of poor rates, if they have one, to apply for and receive these payments from the putative father; and when they are received by such agent he must account for the receipt to the Guardians, and they will pay the amount into the hands of their treasurer, and give the parish officers credit in their accounts for the amounts so received.

2nd. The Commissioners are of opinion, that the overseers cannot be compelled to collect the amounts referred to.

The above remarks will apply as well in respect to the receipt of money advanced to pensioners as to sums payable by putative fathers.

VI.—DESERTION OF FAMILIES:—Expenses incurred in apprehending persons deserting their families cannot be paid out of the Poor Rate.

The following letter was received from the clerk of the Watford Union:—

Watford.

"SIR,—I am desired by the Guardians of this Union to call your attention to a circumstance which frequently happens in this, and, most probably, in every Union in the kingdom. I mean, that of parents running away and leaving members of their family chargeable, or whereby they become chargeable, to the parish in which they are left.

"The party running away goes a considerable distance from the parish where the family or members thereof are left. The Guardians conceive they have not power to incur and pay expenses in searching; or, if it be known where the person leaving the family is, in sending for the party who has run away. The parish to which the parties are left and become chargeable, have the power to reimburse the constable reasonable expenses incurred by them in certain cases, but they have not the power of remunerating the constable for his loss of time. In this way parents running away and leaving their families escape punishment, and leave the members thereof a burthen on the parish.

"There are several families now in the workhouse here chargeable to parishes within the Union, and we have reason to believe the fathers are working on rail-roads now in progress; and in one case, we have been informed that the father is working on a rail-road. Would you allow me to suggest, whether bills incurred in seeking for and apprehending persons running away, and leaving their families chargeable, might not be paid by the relieving officer and charged to the parish as out-relief?

"I have, &c.

(Signed) "RICHARD PUGH, Jun. *Clerk*,

"*Edwin Chadwick, Esq.*"

In reply thereto, the Commissioners stated that any payment out of the poor-rate for the apprehension of persons offending under the Vagrant Act would be unlawful.

The Commissioners fully admit the inconvenience resulting from the inadequacy of the provision made by law for the payment of the expenses unavoidably incurred in the apprehension of offenders under the Vagrant Act, and they regret the loss to which parishes are subject in consequence by such offenders escaping with impunity.

The Commissioners do not perceive any means of remedying the inconvenience except by a legislative enactment, which it is felt is necessary.

But in cases where the desertion is committed by a person who may be rendered liable for relief to his family as for a loan, the relief should be so advanced, and all expenses of recovering the loan and of committing the party in default of payment will be payable out of the poor-rates.

VII.—TRANSMISSION OF MONEY BY POST.

At the request of the Postmaster-general the Commissioners have directed the insertion of the following notification, in order that the Guardians and officers of the several Unions may give it the widest circulation possible amongst overseers, and the humbler classes, among whom the practice of forwarding coin in letters extensively prevails.

NOTICE AND CAUTION TO THE PUBLIC.

"*General Post Office, November*, 1841.

"THE public are particularly cautioned *not to forward coin, Bank notes, cheques, bills, and documents payable to bearer, jewellery*, or other articles of value in *unregistered letters.*

"Any letter sent from one part of the United Kingdom to another may be registered for the fee of *one shilling*, and small sums can be remitted through the post by means of *money orders*, without risk, at the following low rates of charge, viz., *threepence for any sum not exceeding two pounds, and sixpence for any sum above two pounds and not exceeding five pounds.*

"If, however, notwithstanding this caution, notes, cheques, or bills payable to bearer and at sight are sent by post they should *be cut in halves*, and the second halves should not be despatched until the receipt of the first has been acknowledged. The numbers, dates, amounts, and other particulars of all documents of value so sent by post should also be preserved by the senders."

LONDON:
Printed, by Order of the Poor Law Commissioners, by W. CLOWES and SONS, Stamford Street, and Published by CHARLES KNIGHT and Co., 22, Ludgate Street, Publishers to the Poor Law Commissioners.

AN

OFFICIAL CIRCULAR

OF PUBLIC DOCUMENTS AND INFORMATION:

DIRECTED BY THE POOR LAW COMMISSIONERS TO BE PRINTED, CHIEFLY FOR THE USE OF THE MEMBERS AND PERMANENT OFFICERS OF BOARDS OF GUARDIANS, UNDER THE POOR LAW AMENDMENT ACT.

No. 14. CIRCULAR ISSUED DECEMBER 27TH, 1841.

Poor Law Commission Office,
Somerset House,
December 21, 1841.

THE Poor Law Commissioners, on a review of their minutes, directed that the minutes and correspondence on the following subjects should be printed and circulated for the information of Guardians and officers of the several Unions, viz.—

By order of the Board,
EDWIN CHADWICK, *Secretary.*

I.—STRAYED CHILDREN AND INSANE PERSONS.

The Commissioners having conferred on the above subject with the Metropolitan Commissioners of Police, and the Commissioner of Police for the City of London, directed the following Circular and Order to be issued.

Poor Law Commission Office,
Somerset House,
December 3, 1841.

SIR,—I am directed by the Poor Law Commissioners to request that you will call the early attention of the Board of Guardians, to which you act as clerk, to the subject of the means which the Commissioners have determined to adopt for effecting the restoration of strayed children and insane persons found wandering abroad, to their friends and relatives.

After conferring with the Metropolitan Commissioners of Police, and the Commissioner of Police for the City of London, the Poor Law Commissioners have determined on issuing the order, of which three copies are herewith transmitted to you.

You are requested to place one of those copies in the hands of the master of your Workhouse, and direct his attention to its provisions.

The Commissioners of Police for the Metropolis and for the City of London will respectively take care that all possible publicity is given to the notices forwarded to them by affixing the same at the principal police stations, and the Poor Law Commissioners do not doubt that the Guardians will zealously co-operate in promoting the speedy restoration of children and helpless persons to their parents or friends. Independently of the obvious humanity of such a measure, the Poor Law Commissioners conceive that it will have a tendency to prevent the prolonged chargeability of parties found destitute under such circumstances.

The need of some measure for this purpose is proved by the fact, that in the six months of the year 1840, from March to August inclusive, no less than 349 children were found by the police and sent to different workhouses within the Metropolitan Police district.

A printed list of all the stations of the Metropolitan and City Police is given on the other side.

It will be necessary that the master of the Workhouse and the clerk to the Guardians should be furnished with a sufficient number of printed notices in the proper form.

The Commissioners will take care to give due publicity to this circular, and to their order, by advertisement in the public papers.

I have the honour to be, Sir,
Your most obedient servant,
(Signed) E. CHADWICK, *Secretary.*

To the Clerk to the Board of Guardians,
of the

METROPOLITAN POLICE STATIONS.

Name of Division.	Local Name of each Division.	Name of Superintendent.	Police Stations.
A.	Whitehall	Mr. John May . . .	Great Scotland-yard, Whitehall. 2, Gardener's Lane.
B.	Westminster . . .	Mr. Edward Lowry .	New-way, Tothill-street. Roberts'-buildings, Ebury-square.
C.	St. James's	Mr. Thomas Baker .	Little Vine-street, Piccadilly.
D.	St. Mary-le-bone . .	Mr. John Lincoln . .	Mary-le-bone-lane. 5, Little Harcourt-street, Mary-le-bone. Hermitage-street, Paddington.
E.	Holborn	Mr. W. E. Grimwood .	George-street, St. Giles'. Hunter-street, Brunswick-square.
F.	Covent Garden . . .	Mr. J. H. Sandrock .	34, Bow-street.
G.	Finsbury	Mr. George Maisey .	Rosoman-street, Clerkenwell. Bagnigge Wells-road. Featherstone-street, St. Luke's.

METROPOLITAN POLICE STATIONS—*continued.*

Name of Division.	Local Name of each Division.	Name of Superintendent.	Police Stations.
H.	Whitechapel . . .	Mr. W. F. Pierse . .	1, Chapel-yard, Spital-square. Denmark-street, St. George's, East.
K.	Stepney.	Mr. Edward Young .	1, Devon's-lane, Bromley. Green Bank. King David's-lane. Great Ilford. Newby-place, Poplar. Mile End.
L.	Lambeth	Mr. S, D. C. Grinsell .	Tower-street, Waterloo-road. High-street, near the old Church.
M.	Southwark	Mr. W. Murray . .	4, Southwark-bridge-road. Paradise-street, Rotherhithe.
N.	Islington	Mr. James Johnson .	High-street, Kingsland. Church-street, Hackney. Robert-street, Hoxton. Islington-green, Islington. Green-street, Enfield Highway. Stoke Newington. Hornsey. Walthamstow. Tottenham. Edmonton. Enfield. Cheshunt. Waltham Abbey.
P.	Camberwell . . .	Mr. Andrew Mc Lean	Park-house, Lock's-fields, Walworth. Camberwell-green. Brixton-road. Mitcham. George-street, Croydon.
R.	Greenwich	Mr, F. M. Mallalieu .	Blackheath-road, Greenwich. Woolwich. Lee-road, Lee. Rushey-green, Lewisham. Chislehurst. Bexley. Bromley. Foot's Cray. Farnborough.
S.	Hampstead . . .	Mr, John Carter . .	High-street, Highgate. Stone-bridge, Willesden. Edgeware-road, 8, Mile-street. 52, Albany-street, Regent's-park. Junction-place, Kentish-town. Heath-street, [1] Hampstead. 52, Salisbury-street, Portman-market. Phœnix-street, Somers-town.

METROPOLITAN POLICE STATIONS—*continued.*

Name of Division.	Local Name of each Division.	Name of Superintendent.	Police Stations.
S. *continued.*	Hampstead . . .	Mr. John Carter . .	High-street, Chipping Barnett. Bushey, High-street. South Mimms.
T.	Kensington. . . .	Mr. D. Williamson .	Kensington. Hammersmith. Brentford. Hanwell. Hillingdon and Uxbridge Hounslow. Staines. Harrow. Ealing. Acton [occasionally].
V.	Wandsworth . . .	Mr. Thomas Bicknell .	London-road, Kingston. Epsom. Hampton Sunbury. The Plain, Wandsworth. Millman's-row, Chelsea. Clapham Common. Prince's-street, Richmond. High-street, Mortlake. Salvador, Lower Tooting. Merton. Priest-bridge, Barnes.
T. D.	River Thames . . .	Mr. J. Evans . . .	Wapping and Blackwall, near the river. Port Mahon, lying off Strand-lane.

CITY OF LONDON POLICE STATIONS.*

Chief Office (at present) No. 83, Basinghall Street.
1st Division.—Moor Lane, Cripplegate.
2nd Division.—Smithfield.
3rd Division.—Black Horse Court, Fleet Street.
4th Division.—Watling Street.
5th Division.—Tower Street.
6th Division.—Bishopsgate Street, adjoining the Churchyard.

To the Guardians of the Poor of the several Unions and Parishes under a Board of Guardians named in the schedule hereunto annexed.

To the churchwardens and overseers of the several parishes and places comprised within the said Unions, and of the several other parishes named in the said schedule.

To the clerk or clerks to the justices of the petty sessions held for the division or divisions in which the parishes and places comprised within the said Unions and the other Parishes named in the said schedule are situate; and to all others whom it may concern.

In pursuance of the authorities vested in Us by an Act of Parliament passed in the fifth year of the reign of King William the Fourth, intituled "*An Act for the Amendment and better Administration of the Laws relating to the Poor in England and Wales,*" We, the Poor Law Commissioners, do hereby order and direct, as follows:—

Art. 1.—Whenever any child supposed to

* Of these Stations those in Smithfield and Moor Lane only are permanent. The chief office will shortly be at No. 26, Old Jewry.

have strayed, or any insane person wandering abroad, whose friends or relations are unknown, shall have been received into any Workhouse belonging to any of the Unions or parishes mentioned in the schedule hereunto annexed, the master or other person having charge of such workhouse shall properly fill up four notices in the forms marked A or B respectively, hereto annexed, and shall forthwith cause one of such notices to be affixed on the outer gate of the said workhouse, and shall forward one other of the same so filled up to each of the three police stations, whether of the Metropolitan or City Police, nearest to the place where such child or insane person shall be understood to have been found.

Art. 2.—If at the expiration of 24 hours from the reception of such child or insane person into such workhouse, no claim or inquiry respecting the same shall have been made at the workhouse in which such child or insane person shall have been received, the master or other person having charge of such workhouse shall send a copy of the notice already filled up as hereinbefore directed to the clerk to the Guardians of the parish or Union to which such workhouse may belong, and such clerk shall immediately cause to be prepared 48 copies of the notice so filled up and forwarded to him, and shall forthwith transmit 36 copies of such notice to the Commissioners of the Metropolitan Police at their chief office, and 12 copies of such notice to the Commissioner of Police for the city of London at his office.

Art. 3.—In the construction of this present order:—

1.—The word "child" shall be taken to signify every person being or appearing to be under 12 years of age.

2.—The words "insane person" shall be taken to signify any idiot or other person of unsound mind.

FORM A.

Child Found.

Where
When
Sex
Name (if known)
Apparent Age
Complexion
Hair (colour of)
Particular Marks on the person
Dress and Marks thereon
Any Statement made by the Child as to its abode

Now in Workhouse
Day of 184

FORM B.

Insane Person Found.

Where
When
Sex
Name (if known)
Apparent Age
Complexion
Hair (colour of)
Particular Marks on the Person
Dress and Marks thereon
Any Statement made by the Insane Person as to his or her abode

Now in Workhouse
Day of 184

SCHEDULE CONTAINING THE NAMES OF THE UNIONS AND PARISHES TO WHICH THE PRESENT ORDER APPLIES.

List of Unions and Parishes.

UNIONS.	PARISHES.	
Hackney.	George, Saint, in the East.	In the County of Middlesex.
Holborn.	Martin, Saint, in the Fields.	
Kensington.	Matthew, Saint, Bethnal Green.	
London, City of.		
London, East.		
London, West.		
Olave's, Saint.	George, Saint, the Martyr, Southwark.	In the County of Surrey.
Poplar.	Giles, Saint, Camberwell.	
Saviour's, Saint.	Mary, Saint, Lambeth.	
Stepney.	Mary, Magdalen, Saint, Bermondsey.	
Strand.	Mary, Saint, Rotherhithe.	
Wandsworth and Clapham.		
Whitechapel.		

Given under our hands and seal of office, this third day of December, in the year One thousand eight hundred and forty-one.

(Signed) G. C. LEWIS,
EDMUND W. HEAD.

II.—RATING OF PROPERTY; DEDUCTIONS FOR "TENANTS' RATES AND TAXES."

Copy of Minute of the Poor Law Commissioners thereon, dated 29th November, 1841.

The Commissioners inserted in their Circular of the 16th September, 1840, relating to the valuation of tithes, for the purpose of rating them to the Poor Rate, an example of the sums deducted from the gross value of the tithe commutation rent-charge in the case of *The Queen* v. *The Honourable and Rev. W. Capel, Clerk*. This example was chosen because those deductions had in principle been supported by the decision of the Court of Queen's Bench in that case. But the calculation, by means of which the sum of 82*l*. 15*s*. (allowed in that case for usual tenants rates and taxes, and for ecclesiastical dues) was ascertained, did not appear to the court, and was not referred to in the Poor Law Commissioners' Circular.

It is desirable, not only with regard to tithes, but with reference to every other kind of rateable property, to determine how the deduction for rates and taxes is to be made. It appears that this deduction is sometimes made from the gross estimated rental. This practice is not apparently in accordance with the principle upon which the estimate is to be made, and it will cause injustice in its application to property in proportion as the amount of outgoings for repairs, renovation, or insurance, is greater or less. For example, supposing that 100*l*. is the sum which is supposed will be required in the next year, to be raised by rates and taxes on tenants, and supposing that the parish consists of three different properties, for the occupation of each of which a tenant would pay 100*l*., and that the expenses of repairs of each of these properties varies from a high amount, as would be the case with some perishable erections, to nothing, as is the case with tithe; *e. g*.

—	1. Gross estimated Rental.	2. Repairs, &c.	3. Gross estimated Rental, diminished by Repairs, &c.
	£.	£.	£.
1. House .	100	25	75
2. Land .	100	10	90
3. Tithe .	100	..	100
Total .	300		265

Now the amount estimated to be required for rates during the next year being 100*l*., would be after the rate of 6*s*. 8*d*. in the 1*l*., upon 300*l*. the total of the gross estimated rental of rateable property in the parish, or would be after the rate of 7*s*. 6*d*.$\frac{30}{53}$ in the 1*l*. on the sum of 265*l*., which is the total of the gross estimated rental after it has been diminished by the cost of repairs, &c.

First case.—If the deductions for the estimate of rates and taxes are to be made from the gross rental, the deductions will, at 6*s*. 8*d*. in the 1*l*., amount in each case to 33*l*. 6*s*. 8*d*., and the case of the three properties will stand thus:—

	£.	s.	d.	£.	s.	d.
1. House.—Gross estimated rental....				100	0	0
Deduct for repairs, &c....	25	0	0			
For estimated rates at 6*s*. 8*d*. per £ on the 100*l*.	33	6	8			
				58	6	8
Net annual or rateable value ..				41	13	4
2. Land.—Gross estimated rental.....				100	0	0
Deduct for repairs, &c....	10	0	0			
For estimated rates at 6*s*. 8*d*. per £........	33	6	8			
				43	6	8
Net annual or rateable value...				56	13	4
3. Tithes.—Gross value.............				100	0	0
Deduct for repairs, &c....	0	0	0			
For estimated rates at 6*s*. 8*d*. per £........	33	6	8			
				33	6	8
Net annual or rateable value...				66	13	4

Second case.—If, on the other hand, the deductions for tenant's rates are to be made on the gross rental after it is reduced by allowance for repairs, &c., the deductions at 7*s*. 7*d*. in the pound, will, in that case, vary as below:—

	£.	s.	d.
1. House.—Gross estimated rental....	100	0	0
Deduct for repairs................	25	0	0
	75	0	0
For estimated rates at 7*s*. 6*d*.$\frac{30}{53}$ per £ on 75*l*....................	28	6	0½
Net annual or rateable value.	46	13	11½
2. Land.—Gross estimated rental.....	100	0	0
Deduct for repairs, &c............	10	0	0
	90	0	0
For estimated rates at 7*s*. 6*d*.$\frac{30}{53}$ per £ on 90*l*....................	33	19	3
Net annual or rateable value.	56	0	9

	£	s.	d.
3. Tithe.—Gross estimated rental	100	0	0
Deduct for repairs, &c.	0	0	0
	100	0	0
For estimated rates at 7*s*. 6*d*.$\frac{30}{33}$ per £ on 100*l*.	37	14	8½
Net annual or rateable value.	62	5	3½

The difference in the two cases is thus seen to be as shown below:—

—	Gross estimated Rental.	Deductions for Repairs, &c.	For estimated Tenant's Rates, &c.	Net Annual or Rateable Value.
	£.	£.	£. s. d.	£. s. d.
1. House . . .	100	25		
First Case .	..	..	33 6 8	41 13 4
or			or	or
Second Case .	..	..	28 6 0½	46 13 11½
Difference .	..	..	..	5 0 7½
2. Land . . .	100	10		
First Case .	..	..	33 6 8	56 13 4
or			or	or
Second Case .	..	..	33 19 3	56 0 9
Difference .	..	..	..	0 12 7
3. Tithe . . .	100			
First Case .	..	..	33 6 8	66 13 4
or			or	or
Second Case .	..	..	37 14 8½	62 5 3½
Difference .	..	..	..	4 8 0½

It appears clear to the Commissioners that the second case is that which is conformable with the Parochial Assessments Act. For as rates cannot lawfully be made on the gross estimated rental, it would seem necessarily to follow, that the estimate should not make an allowance for deductions of rates, on the false assumption that such rates will be made on the gross estimated rental. Neither can the deductions for rates be made from the "net annual value," as defined by the Parochial Assessments Act; for that net annual value is the result to be obtained as the effect of deducting the estimated rates, and does not preexist as a sum from which this deduction can be made. It remains as the only possible conclusion,—that the sum from which the estimated rates and taxes is to be deducted, in order to arrive at the "net annual value," or "rateable value," is the gross estimated rental of the property, less the expense of repairs and renovation. This also is the only constant fund out of which, in fact, the rates and taxes can possibly be paid; the only permanent taxable revenue from property being that profit which remains after the necessary outlay for the preservation of the property.

Practical Directions.

The course which the persons making the rate should adopt in giving effect to the above views is as follows:—

1st.—To estimate the sum which will be required during the next year in the parish or township for all the rates and taxes payable by the tenant.

(In the examples which will be given below, it will be assumed that the estimated sum of the whole of the rates for the ensuing year is 100*l*.)

2nd.—To put in the proper column in the rate-book the "gross estimated rental" of each property. This the valuation will always supply.

1. Description of Property rated.	2. Gross estimated Rental.
	£.
1. House	100
2. Land	100
3. Tithe Rent-charge of £110, less £5. 10*s*. for Tenant's Composition, and £4. 10*s*. for Ecclesiastical Dues	100

In the case of tithes, the "gross estimated rental" is not the gross value of the rent-charge, supposed here, by way of example, to be 110*l*.; but the rental which a tenant would pay, taking upon himself the risk and trouble of collecting it. It will, therefore, be the value of the rent-charge diminished by this compensation to the tenant, which being here supposed to be 5*l*. 10*s*., makes the supposed "gross estimated rental" 104*l*. 10*s*.; from which sum it will be necessary to make a further deduction for ecclesiastical dues, here supposed to be 4*l*. 10*s*., making the "gross estimated rental" 100*l*.

3rd.—To estimate the reasonable expenses supposed to be incurred in respect of each rateable property for repairs, insurance, and other expenses necessary to maintain the condition of the property.

This will also be supplied by the valuation.

1. Description of Property Rated.	2. Gross estimated Rental.	3. Repairs, Insurance, &c.
	£	£.
1. House	100	25
2. Land	100	10
3. Tithe Rent-charge of £110 . .	100	..

4th.—When these particulars have been ascertained in every case, the following further operations must be performed.

First.—Deduct the amount of these expenses, in each case, from the gross rental of the particular property; the remainder will be the sum from which the allowance for tenant's rates and taxes is to be made.

1. Description of Property Rated.	2. Gross estimated Rental.	3. Repairs, Insurance, &c.	4. Remainder.
	£.	£.	£.
1. House	100	25	75
2. Land	100	10	90
3. Tithe Rent-charge of £110	100	..	100

Secondly.—Add together the whole of these remainders, and subtract from that total the total amount of the estimated tenant's rates and taxes, the remainder will be the total net annual value of the whole of the rateable property in the parish or township; thus,—

1. Description of Property Rated.	2. Gross estimated Rental.	3. Repairs, Insurance. &c.	4. Remainder.
	£.	£.	£.
1. House	100	25	75
2. Land	100	10	90
3. Tithe Rent-charge of £110	100	..	100
Total .			265
Subtract estimated Tenant's Rates and Taxes .			100
Total "Net Annual Value" of all the Rateable Property of the Parish			165

Thirdly,—Now as the total 265*l.* is to bear the taxation of 100*l.*, by which it will be reduced to 165*l.*, the amount of the total "net annual value," it will follow that each of the sums 75*l.*, 90*l.*, and 100*l.*, must be reduced by their respective proportions of 100*l.*

The calculation to be made will now be,—as 265*l.* is reduced to a net annual value of 165*l.*, to how much will 75*l.* be reduced; and so for the other sums: thus,—

	£.		£.		£.		Net Annual Value. £. s. d.
1. House	265	:	165	::	75	:	46 13 11⅓
2. Land	265	:	165	::	90	:	56 0 9
3. Tithe	265	:	165	::	100	:	62 5 3½

The case will now stand thus:—

1. Description of Property Rated.	2. Gross estimated Rental.	3. Repairs, &c.	4. Remainder.	5. Rateable Value.
	£.	£.	£.	£. s. d.
1. House .	100	25	75	46 13 11⅓
2. Land . .	100	10	90	56 0 9
3. Tithe . .	100	..	100	62 5 3½
Total Net Annual Value of Rateable Property in the Parish				165 0 0

The total of column 5 should be the same as the result before obtained by deducting the estimated rates and taxes from the total of column 4. The one result will therefore serve to check the other.

5th.—Now enter in the rate-books, in their proper places, columns 1, 2, and 5, and proceed to lay your rate on the sum contained in the latter column.

The information contained in columns 3 and 4, and the calculation made in reference to the latter column should be carefully preserved for the purpose of satisfying rate-payers as to the amounts allowed for repairs, and for rates and taxes, as well as for the purpose of affording evidence in case of appeal. While the relations of property and the estimate of prospective rates remain the same, those calculations will, of course, serve for future rates, and save the necessity of re-calculation.

It must be borne in mind that the sums mentioned above are only assumed hypothetically; and the proportions of the gross rental and of the several deductions are not to be understood as having any application to any actual case in making a rate. The value of the property and the amount of the deductions must in every case be determined by the circumstances of each individual property.

III—RATING OF STOCK IN TRADE.—
CONTINUANCE OF ACT RESPECTING.

The Commissioners received an application from the clerk to the Guardians of the Dorking Union requesting to be informed whether any provision has been made to assess "Stock in Trade," to the poor rate after Dec. 31, 1841.

In reply, the Commissioners informed the clerk that the provisions of the Act 3 and 4 Vict. c. 89, exempting stock in trade from liability to poor rate have been extended until the 31st July, 1842, by the continuance Act 5 Vict. c. 7. s. 1.

IV.—GUARDIANS:—As to power of, to continue a pregnant unmarried Woman in the Workhouse after her confinement.

The following is a copy of a letter received from the Eastry Union:—

"*Eastry Union.*

"SIR.—The Guardians of this Union are desirous, as far as it is within their power, to discharge the duty imposed upon them by the 2nd and 3rd Vict. c. 85, relating to cases of bastardy, but as difficulties present themselves to prevent the possibility of casting the expense of maintenance upon the putative father, I have been instructed to request the advice of the Commissioners on the subject.

"The most prominent is the short period which a woman, giving birth to an illegitimate child, continues in the workhouse after her confinement, as it frequently occurs, that soon after the expiration of the second or third week the mother makes application to the governor for the discharge of herself and child, thereby preventing the possibility of an examination by the Board of Guardians, unless it be taken at a time when decency forbids such an occurrence, the power of the Guardians to inquire into the matter appearing to expire when the chargeability ceases.

"To remedy this evil, on the admission of Mary Beake, belonging to the parish of Preston, on the 8th October last, the Guardians inquired whether the applicant *would agree to continue in the workhouse six weeks after her confinement, which she consented to.*

"The object of the Guardians in the above stipulation arose from a desire, if possible, to prevent the workhouse being resorted to as a perfect convenience for women of bad character, who generally apply for admission when they are incapable of performing scarcely any work, and have the power of demanding their discharge after their confinement whenever they think proper to do so, thereby securing to themselves all the indulgence and attention their cases require, giving no assistance in the work of the house in return for the care and attention they have received, also avoiding the inconvenience of an examination in almost every instance which occurs.

"Mary Beake was delivered of an illegitimate child on the 22d instant.

"A few days since, the governor intimated to the woman, that, before leaving the workhouse, she would be required to attend before the Board of Guardians, to undergo an examination respecting the father of her child, and in reply to an inquiry respecting the nature of the relief he might be required to contribute, was informed, that the father of the child could not be compelled to pay for its maintenance while in the workhouse, when she immediately determined she would not name the father to the Guardians.

"The governor, in the expectation that the above declaration will shortly be followed by an application from the pauper for the discharge of herself and child from the workhouse, requested the Board of Guardians at the last weekly meeting to inform him whether, in the event of an application, the Board would authorize him to detain the woman until he received the consent of the guardians for her discharge, he being bound by the regulations to attend to her request within three hours.

"Under all the circumstances, I considered it to be my duty to suggest to the Board that, for the present, it would be adviseable to withhold the guarantee required by the governor, and that the case should be submitted to the Commissioners.

"I have the honour to be, &c.

(Signed) "EDW. GREEY, *Clerk of the Union.*

"*E. Chadwick, Esq.*"

The Commissioners in reply stated, in answer to this question, that any such stipulation as that described in your letter appears to them to be illegal, and neither binding upon the guardians nor on the woman. Every destitute person has by law an absolute right to relief, and the guardians cannot, in administering relief, annex any such condition to it as that suggested in your letter, nor can they lawfully extend the relief beyond the time for which it is needed.

It appears moreover to the Commissioners that if the guardians were to induce the mother of a bastard child to receive relief in the workhouse after the time when she wished to quit it, and if an application were made to the sessions for an order upon the putative father of such child, the person against whom the order was applied for could lawfully object to being charged with the expenses of the relief of the child which were incurred after the time when the mother was desirous of taking it out of the workhouse.

You state in your letter that "the guardians

desire, if possible, to prevent the workhouse being resorted to as a perfect convenience for women of bad character, who generally apply for admission when they are almost incapable of performing any work, and have the power of demanding their discharge after their confinement whenever they think proper to do so, thereby securing to themselves all the indulgence and attention which their cases require, giving no assistance in the work of the house in return for the care and attention which they have received, and avoiding the inconvenience of an examination in almost every instance which occurs."

The Commissioners have received complaints similar to this from other parts of the country, but it does not appear to them that the evil complained of can be prevented by applying for orders against the putative fathers. If a woman who is delivered of a bastard child be in a state of destitution, the expenses of her confinement must fall upon the Union; and the Commissioners believe that, not only will the women receive better medical and other assistance if they are invariably received into the workhouse, but that the number relieved will be smaller, and the period of their receiving relief will be shorter than if they were relieved at their own cottages.

On this account the Commissioners think that it is expedient to relieve the mothers of bastard children during their confinement in the workhouse rather than at their homes; and with regard to the recovery of the expenses of such relief from the putative fathers, all experience has shown that only a small portion of the expenses incurred is in general recovered by the parishes under orders made by sessions on the putative fathers.

---

2. LEGALITY OF PROCEEDINGS OF GUARDIANS AT A BOARD NOT AFFECTED BY THE FACT OF ANY PARTICULAR GUARDIAN PRESIDING OR NOT PRESIDING.

The Commissioners took into consideration the following copy of a Minute of the Board of Guardians of the Tonbridge Union.

"*Tonbridge Union, October* 29, 1841.

"GENTLEMEN,—I am directed by the Board of Guardians to transmit the subjoined copy of a Minute of the Board at their meeting this day.

"I am, &c.

(Signed) "JOHN SCOONES.

"*The Poor Law Commissioners.*"

"Mr. Delves having, in the absence of the chairman and vice-chairman, taken the chair, and part of the business of this meeting having proceeded, the vice-chairman entered into the room, when the question arose, whether it became necessary, in order to legalize the further proceedings of the Board, that Mr. Delves should vacate the chair in favour of the vice-chairman; and considerable doubt being entertained, and opposite opinions expressed by various Members of the Board it was—

"Resolved,—That the case as above stated, be submitted by the clerk to the Poor Law Commissioners, referring them to their order of 2d March, 1836, and requesting their instructions for our future guidance."

In reference thereto the Commissioners stated, that, as the Commissioners have by an order of 2d March, 1836, prescribed that, if the chairman and vice-chairman should be absent at any meeting, the Guardians present should elect a chairman of that meeting, it might admit of a question, whether the Guardians could strictly appoint a chairman for a period less than the whole of the meeting. Accordingly the Commissioners have advised in other cases that the Guardian appointed to preside in the absence of the chairman and vice-chairman should continue to preside during the whole of that meeting, and should not vacate the chair on the arrival of the chairman or vice-chairman of the Board. At the same time, the Commissioners do not consider that the legality of the meeting could generally be affected by the fact of any particular Guardian presiding or not presiding.

The legality of the decision of the Board might, however, be questioned on any particular decision when the Board was equally divided in opinion, and when the chairman had given a casting vote. In such a case, his right to preside and to give such casting vote would obviously affect the validity of the decision of the Board.

V.—PAID OFFICERS:—DISMISSAL OF ONE OF THE RELIEVING OFFICERS OF THE MELKSHAM UNION.

The Board took under their consideration the report of their Assistant Commissioner, Colonel A'Court, and the evidence taken by him on an enquiry which he made into the conduct of the relieving officer for the parish of Trowbridge, in the Melksham Union, in reference to the case of Harriet Hulbert, a pauper, who died in that parish of typhus fever, and on whose body an inquest was held; the jury in their verdict expressing their opinion, "that the disease and its fatal termination appear to have been accelerated by the refusal of the relieving officer of Bradford to relieve her during her sickness;" also the evidence of John Forster, the relieving officer of the Bradford Union, transmitted to them by the guardians of that Union.

The Commissioners addressed a letter to the guardians of the Melksham Union, conveying to them the Commissioners' opinion and decision on the case, in which the Commissioners observed,

The relieving officer in his examination states as follows:—

"I know the family of John Hulbert. In April last Hulbert and his family were removed by an order of magistrates to the parish of Bradford, the supposed place of their settlement. I lost sight entirely of the family until the 1st September last, when John Hulbert called at my house, stated that his wife was very ill, and asked for a medical order for her. I believe I did not give him an order, but referred him to the surgeon. I referred him also to the relieving officer of Bradford, and I asked him whether he was aware of the situation which he placed himself in if he applied for relief to me, he having been removed by an order to Bradford. He replied, I do not ask for relief, I only ask for the doctor. I saw Mr. Stapleton on that or the following day, and found that he had attended Hulbert's wife. He said she had a malignant fever. I did not visit the family, the surgeon, Mr. Stapleton, having advised me not to do so, for fear of infection. I neither gave nor ordered relief to the family, but a day or two afterwards Hulbert called upon me again with a doctor's certificate which he was going to take to Bradford. I asked him why he brought it to me, and he said he merely showed it to me, for he was going to Bradford with it. I did not tell him that I ought to relieve him, neither did I relieve him, as I made sure the Bradford Officer would do so. I thought that as Bradford was so near, the relieving officer of that Union ought to have relieved him. I stated this opinion at the coroner's inquest. Harriet Hulbert died on the 7th, on which day she had some brandy by order of the doctor. To the best of my belief this is all the relief she had during her illness, with the exception of medicine. On the 7th September, the case of Hulbert's wife appears in the medical officer's book. On the 14th I reported it in my book. I did not report it before, as it was only on the 7th that the doctor ordered the brandy to the wife."

It also appears from the statement of the relieving officer of the Bradford Union, that about the 12th May last, Harriet Hulbert, together with her husband, John Hulbert and their two children, was removed by order of justices from Trowbridge to Bradford, that on their arrival at Bradford, John Hulbert was offered an order for the admission of himself and family into the workhouse of the Bradford Union, which the husband was willing to accept, but of which the wife resolutely refused to avail herself, and that they subsequently returned to Trowbridge; that on the 24th May John Hulbert again applied to the relieving officer of the Bradford Union for an order for the admission of himself and family into the workhouse, which the relieving officer gave him, and they were admitted into the workhouse accordingly, where they remained for a few days only, and then went again to reside at Trowbridge; that on the 4th September, Hulbert (being then resident in Trowbridge) again applied to the relieving officer of the Bradford Union for relief for his wife, and stated that she was ill, when he was told by the Bradford relieving officer, "that he could not relieve him, as he was residing out of the Union, and that if his wife required relief, he must apply to the relieving officer at Trowbridge, who was bound to attend to his case;" that upon being so informed, Hulbert went away, and he (the Bradford relieving officer) heard no more of the case, until after the wife's death, which occurred on the 8th instant.

The Commissioners are of opinion that the relieving officer for the parish of Trowbridge is censureable,—

1st. For not giving a medical order, but referring him to the medical officer.

2nd. For referring him to the relieving officer of the Bradford Union, and for threatening him with penal proceedings in consequence of his applying for relief in Trowbridge parish after removal from it.

3rd. For not visiting the family upon the application for medical relief, and upon the receipt of the statement of the medical officer that he had visited Harriet Hulbert and found that she had a malignant fever.

4th. For not visiting the family and affording relief when John Hulbert called upon him with a medical certificate, and stated his intention of applying to the Bradford relieving officer for relief.

5th. For not reporting the case to the Board of Guardians.

The Commissioners do not remember to have met, in the course of their official experience, with a more remarkable instance of neglect and misapprehension of duties on the part of any relieving officer than the case now before them. They will, therefore, issue an order for his dismissal, and they request that the guardians will proceed to the election of his successor.

The Commissioners observe that, in his evidence, the relieving officer states himself to have been advised by Mr. Stapleton, the medical officer, not to visit Harriet Hulbert, lest he should catch the infectious fever under which she was suffering. The Commissioners do not know whether Mr. Stapleton admits that he gave this advice, but they think that if the advice was given, it was calculated to mislead the relieving officer as to the extent of his duties. The relieving officer is bound to visit all applications for relief, whether medical or otherwise; and the Commissioners cannot admit it to be a valid excuse for the omission of any such visit that the applicant or any of his family is afflicted with an infectious disease. The relieving officers accept their office with a knowledge of their liability to visit applicants for relief, and those visits must be made whatever may be the risk of infection to which the relieving officer may expose himself in making them. In this respect there is no difference between the duties of a relieving officer and those of a medical officer.

The Commissioners, in conclusion, will advert to the conduct of the relieving officer of the Bradford Union, who has been, by an error which he had no means of preventing, mixed up with the present transaction. The relieving officer of the Melksham Union improperly referred John Hulbert to the Bradford Union, in which he was not then resident, and the coroner's jury which sat upon Harriet Hulbert's body expressed in their verdict their opinion "that her disease and its fatal termination appear to have been accelerated by the refusal of the relieving officer of Bradford to relieve her during her sickness."

It appears, however, that John Hulbert and his wife were resident during the whole time of her sickness in the Melksham Union, and therefore (although their settlement may have been in the Bradford Union) the Bradford guardians and their officers were not answerable for her relief. The information which John Forster, the relieving officer of the Bradford Union, according to the evidence transmitted by the Bradford guardians, states that he gave to John Hulbert, on being referred to by the relieving officer of the Melksham Union, was perfectly correct:—

"He told me that his wife was ill, and that he wanted some relief for her. I told him that I could not relieve him, as he was residing out of the Union; and that if his wife required relief, he must apply to the relieving officer at Trowbridge, who was bound to attend to his case."

The Commissioners trust that the facts of this case will serve to impress upon the minds of the relieving officers of the Melksham Union the necessity of their instantly relieving all cases of destitution which arise within the Union, although the destitute person may have returned from a parish to which he had been removed in due course of law, or may otherwise have come into the Union under circumstances which would bring such person within the operation of the Vagrant Act.

---

2. RELIEVING OFFICER—GUARDIAN NOT DISQUALIFIED TO BECOME SECCURITY FOR.

The Commissioners received the following letter from the clerk of the Ludlow Union:—

"*Ludlow Union, Ludlow*, 18*th Nov.*, 1841.

"SIR,—I am desired by the Board of Guardians to request the Poor Law Commissioners will acquaint them if a guardian is disqualified to be the surety for a relieving officer; and if so, under what section of the Poor Law Amendment Act, or otherwise, such disqualification arises.

"I am, dear Sir,
"Your obedient Servant,
(Signed) "ROBERT THOMAS.

"*Edwin Chadwick, Esq.*"

In reply, the Commissioners stated that they are not aware that any legal disqualification exists to prevent a guardian from becoming security for a relieving officer; but the Commissioners think it very undesirable that such an arrangement should be made; and they therefore advise the Board of Guardians of the Ludlow Union to require their relieving officer to find some person as surety for him who is not a guardian of the Union.

---

3. RELIEVING OFFICER—INSOLVENCY OF—IF A DEFAULTER WITH THE UNION FUNDS, WHO TO SUSTAIN THE LOSS.

The Commissioners received the following letter from the clerk of the Halsted Union :—

"*Halsted Union, Halsted, 4th Sept.*, 1841.

"SIR,—I am directed to inform you that Thomas Cardinall, the late relieving officer of the first district of this Union, has died insolvent; and that, on the investigation of his accounts with the Union, it appears that he had neglected to repay to various persons who had, *with the sanction of the Board*, advanced monies to paupers residing out of the Union, but respectively belonging to seven of the parishes of the Union, amounting together to the sum of 21*l*. 16*s*. 5*d*.

"Unfortunately, on the formation of the Union, it was not thought necessary to call upon the relieving officers to give securities for the faithful discharge of their duties, and therefore this money is lost.

"Under these circumstances, the Poor Law Commissioners are requested to suggest the proper mode of paying this demand—whether by the individual parishes to which the paupers belong, or out of the general fund of the Union.

"I have the honour to be, Sir,
"Your very obedient Servant,
(Signed) "O. HUSTLER, *Clerk*.
"*The Poor Law Commissioners.*"

In reply, the Commissioners remarked that, when money is advanced by the Board of Guardians, generally to an officer, and not on behalf of any particular parish or district, if loss were incurred, it would fall on the whole Union. But when money is advanced specifically for the relief of certain paupers or individual parishes, or for defined purposes of individual parishes, this money must be regarded as the money of those parishes, and the loss will fall on them, and not on the Union generally, nor on the officer's district generally. Accordingly, the Commissioners consider the loss described in your letter to be the loss of the seven parishes respectively to which the several paupers belonged, and whose funds were alone applicable to the relief of those paupers.

The Commissioners will add, for your general guidance in similar cases, that if money be advanced to the relieving officer of a district generally for the purposes of the district, and if this money be lost without any particular default in respect of any one parish, the loss would, in the Commissioners' opinion, be to be borne by the whole of that district, and, as the Commissioners conceive, not by the Union generally.

4. RELIEVING OFFICER—ORDERS OF MEDICAL OFFICER OUGHT TO BE COMPLIED WITH LITERALLY BY, UNTIL NEXT MEETING OF GUARDIANS.

The following letter was received from the clerk of the Thame Union :—

"*Thame Union, Thame* 29, 1841.
"MEDICAL RELIEF.

"SIR,—The wife of a tramper in the lodging-house in this place applied to the relieving officer for relief on behalf of her husband, whom she stated to be unable to travel from his feet being frost-bitten. The relieving officer gave her a medical order, when the medical officer ordered the man two pounds of mutton. The woman, on presenting the order to the relieving officer, stated that the mutton would be of no use to her without bread, when he substituted some other articles of provision for her immediate want.

"The medical officer complained to the guardians at their weekly meeting on Wednesday last of the relieving officer not obeying his order, which he considered ought to have been attended to by him; and I am directed by the guardians to request the opinion of the Poor Law Commissioners, whether the relieving officer was justified in refusing the mutton ordered by the medical officer, and substituting other articles; and whether a relieving officer has any and what discretionary power in refusing to provide articles for sick paupers ordered by medical officers.

"I have the honour to be, Sir,
"Your most obedient servant,
(Signed) "JOHN HOLLIER,
"*Clerk to the Guardians.*
"*To E. Chadwick, Esq.*"

In reply the Commissioners stated, that the relieving officer ought to have complied literally with the recommendation of the medical officer until the next meeting of the Board of Guardians, and that he ought not to have substituted other articles at the request of the pauper, though he might have added them at his own discretion.

5. CENSURE OF MASTER OF THE FAREHAM UNION WORKHOUSE FOR NEGLECT OF DUTY.

The Commissioners took into consideration a Report from their Assistant Commissioner, Colonel A'Court, containing the result of an investigation made by him respecting the following complaints preferred against the master of the Fareham Union workhouse by a pauper inmate, James Earwaker:—

1st. That his wife had not received proper nourishment after her confinement, and that beer, which had been ordered for her by the medical officer, had been withheld from her by the master.

2nd. That two idiot boys who had the itch, and were in the ward appropriated to patients of that description, had been neglected.

The Commissioners also took into consideration a memorial from the master of the workhouse, containing his observations and statements in reference to these complaints.

The Commissioners, in their letter addressed to the guardians in reference to this subject, stated that they were of opinion,—

1st. That the complaint relating to James Earwaker's wife was disproved.

2nd. That the two idiot boys were by the master given in charge to other pauper inmates, and were neglected.

The Commissioners, in reference to the latter case, wish to observe, that it is the duty of the master to superintend personally all the arrangements he may make for the proper care and treatment of the inmates; and that, if he entrust the performance of any portion of his duties to other persons, he is nevertheless responsible for the acts of those whom he employs.

Adverting to the observations made by the master in giving his evidence to the effect that he "considered that the schoolmaster ought to have attended to them (the boys)," the Commissioners wish to remark that the master, and not the schoolmaster, has charge of the health of the boys, although it is his (the schoolmaster's) duty to call the master's attention to any sickness of the children under his care which he may observe.

It appears that this case occurred ten weeks before the charge was brought forward against the master, and the boys are stated to be now in good health.

The master admitted his error to the guardians, and also admits it to the Commissioners. In his memorial he states as follows:—

"Your memorialist, though he respectfully submits that he did frequently visit the boys during their confinement, and regularly served their food himself, sending to them by the hands of their sister, he at the same time feels fully conscious of his error in not personally seeing his orders daily executed, and expresses deep regret at this neglect, and begs to assure your Board that, should he be honoured by a continuance in his office, he will take every care that any such error shall not occur again."

The neglect of the master in this case is of so serious a character that the Commissioners doubt whether they ought not to consider it as a proof of his unfitness for his office; but, looking to the master's generally good character, and to the manner in which he has admitted his misconduct in the present case, the Commissioners will be satisfied to allow him to continue in his office, at the same time that they express their strong disapprobation of his neglect on the occasion in question. The Commissioners take this opportunity of expressing their opinion that a candid admission of misconduct by an officer, accompanied by assurances of future amendment, will always be considered by the Commissioners as an extenuation of the offence, while a false or disingenuous defence against a well-founded charge will always be considered by them as an aggravation of the officer's original misconduct.

---

6. MASTER OF THE WORKHOUSE NOT ENTITLED TO ANY PERQUISITES, AND TO ACCOUNT FOR THE PROCEEDS OF THE SALE OF BONES OR OTHER REFUSE.

The Commissioners took into consideration a report from the auditor of the Romford Union on the audit of the accounts for that Union for the Lady-day and Midsummer quarters of the present year. The Commissioners in acknowledging the receipt of the report, requested to be informed whether the master of the workhouse has been in the habit of bringing the produce of bones sold, and other refuse to account.

In reply, the auditor stated, that the master has not been in the habit of so doing.

The Commissioners thereupon directed a letter to be written to the auditor, stating that the Commissioners do not think that the master of a Union workhouse is entitled to any perquisites, and that all bones, hogwash, or other refuse from the workhouse shall, when sold, be accounted for by him.

---

7. CHAPLAIN—EXTENT TO WHICH HE MAY PROPERLY MAKE REPORTS TO THE GUARDIANS.

The Commissioners took into consideration an application from the chaplain of the Tendring Union requesting the opinion of the Commissioners as to the extent to which he, as chaplain, might properly make reports to the Board of Guardians.

The Commissioners in reply observed, that it is the duty of the chaplain of a workhouse to examine and catechise the children at least once every month, and after each of such examinations to record the same and state the general progress and condition of the children, and the moral and religious state of the inmates generally, in a book to be kept for that purpose, to be laid before the Board of Guardians at their next meeting; and that it is likewise the chaplain's duty to watch over the moral and religious conduct of all the individuals of the establishment.

The Commissioners are of opinion that these duties would confer upon the chaplain the privilege of reporting to the Board of Guardians, if he thinks fit, on the moral and religious state of the inmates generally, and on the moral and religious conduct of all the individuals of the establishment; but the Commissioners do not consider it as part of the duties of a chaplain that he should otherwise report on the general management of a workhouse.

At the same time the Commissioners do not doubt that the Board of Guardians of the Tendring Union would willingly receive any well considered suggestion for the improvement of their workhouse management which you might desire to offer. If, however, an objection is entertained by any guardian to your offering any such suggestions, the Commissioners are of opinion that you would exercise a sound discretion in refraining from offering them to the Board of Guardians in your official capacity as chaplain; but that if you see anything in your occasional visits to the workhouse which you may think wrong, or at any rate susceptible of improvement, in matters not relating to the moral and religious condition of the inmates generally, or to the moral and religious conduct of individuals of the establishment, the Commissioners would recommend you to take a favourable opportunity of communicating on the subject as a private individual with the chairman of the Board of Guardians, or with some member of the visiting committee.

8. AUDITORS—AS TO THE RIGHT OF, TO BE PRESENT AT MEETINGS OF BOARDS OF GUARDIANS.

The Commissioners took into consideration a letter from their Assistant Commissioner, Mr. Senior, requesting the opinion of the Commissioners as to the right of an auditor to be present at the meetings of Boards of Guardians.

The Commissioners in reply stated that they consider the office of auditor does not confer on the person who holds it any right to be present at the meetings of the Board of Guardians. There is no doubt that it is competent to the Board to exclude any person (other than a Guardian) from their deliberations, saving of course the power of the Commissioners or their assistants to attend any such meeting under the 21st Section of the Poor Law Amendment Act. The Commissioners are nevertheless sensible of the advantage to be derived from the occasional attendance of auditors at meetings of the Board. By this means the auditor being made acquainted with the circumstances, under which relief is given, or expenditure incurred, is the better able to fulfil the object of his appointment in judging of lawful and unlawful expenditure.

The Commissioners do not anticipate that any objection would be offered by a Board of Guardians to an application of an auditor to be present at their deliberations whenever the auditor might think that the interest of the Union, or of the parishes, would be promoted by his doing so.

VI.—PAUPERS.—1. ABSCONDING OF, WITH WORKHOUSE CLOTHES.

The Commissioners took into consideration the following extract from the minutes of the Board of Guardians of the Union:—

"The master of the workhouse reported, that John Bendle, an inmate of the workhouse, scaled the walls and absconded on Thursday last, wearing the Union clothes, and having in his possession a pair of stockings and a knife belonging to the Union; and that he and the porter pursued him, and brought him back. In consequence of which report, John Bendle was called before the Board, and being unable to give any excuse, the Board decided that his conduct was highly disorderly; and it was ordered that he be allowed no other diet during the next seven days except bread and water, and that he be locked up in the refractory ward for the space of four hours during some part of each of such seven days."

The Commissioners, in reference thereto, observed that the pauper was guilty of an offence distinctly recognized and provided for by the 55th Geo. III. c. 137, s. 2, that of absconding from the workhouse, and taking with him the Union property. The Commissioners think, therefore, that the course pointed out by the statute should have been pursued instead of that which was taken. The Commissioners are of opinion that neither the master, porter, nor any other officer of the establishment had any authority to capture the pauper, and to compel him to re-enter the workhouse. The pauper had committed an offence, for which he could have been taken before justices upon a warrant, and that authority should have been procured. The Commissioners, therefore, think that the master and the porter exceeded their powers in the proceeding which they adopted, though the Commissioners entertain no doubt upon a misconception of what was their duty in such a case.

The Commissioners do not see that the guardians were authorized by anything contained in the workhouse regulations to administer such punishment as was ordered by them for the offence. The pauper was not disorderly within the meaning of Rule 26, nor did he commit any of the offences described in Rule 27, for which he could be deemed refractory and punished accordingly.

Moreover if the offence had been within the workhouse regulations the punishment would have been excessive and otherwise objectionable, inasmuch as it was spread over seven days, and the total period of confinement for the same offence 28 hours.

The Commissioners think it desirable, in order that the guardians may be informed of their duties and powers in regard to any cases of a like nature which may occur in future, that you should put them in possession of the views of the Commissioners on the subject.

2. DECEASED PAUPERS' EFFECTS—HOW TO BE APPLIED.

The following is an application for advice from the guardians of the Glanford Brigg Union:—

" *Glanford Brigg Union,*

" *Brigg, Nov.* 11, 1841.

" GENTLEMEN,—The master of the workhouse of this Union yesterday stated to the Board, that he had in his hands some small sums of money which had been found in the possession of the inmates of the workhouse at their death, and wished to take the directions of the Board as to the manner in which the money should be applied. The Board directed me to state the circumstance for your consideration. It is apprehended that the expense of the funeral of the paupers might be discharged out of the money found upon them, even though the remainder of the money might not be legally the property of the parish to which the paupers belonged.

" I shall feel obliged by a reply before the meeting of the Board on the 25th instant.

" I am, Gentlemen,

" Your most obedient servant,

(Signed) " JOHN HETT.

" *To the Poor Law Commissioners,*
&c. &c. &c."

In reply the Commissioners stated, that they consider that any personal effects found upon a deceased inmate of the Union workhouse should be applied to defray the funeral expenses, the property of a deceased person being, in the first place, applicable in this matter.

Where relief has not been advanced by way of loan, and the value of the effects exceeds the expenses of the care of the pauper's body after his decease and those incurred in burying the body, the guardians could not refuse to return the residue to any executor or administrator legally appointed; but until applied for by a lawful representative it should be retained in their hands, but not disposed of for six years, after which, if no lawful claim is made, it may be disposed of in ease of the current rates of the parish at whose expense the pauper was relieved.

LONDON:
Printed, by Order of the Poor Law Commissioners, by W. CLOWES and SONS, Stamford Street, and Published by CHARLES KNIGHT and Co., 22, Ludgate Street, Publishers to the Poor Law Commissioners.

AN

OFFICIAL CIRCULAR

OF PUBLIC DOCUMENTS AND INFORMATION:

DIRECTED BY THE POOR LAW COMMISSIONERS TO BE PRINTED, CHIEFLY FOR THE USE OF THE MEMBERS AND PERMANENT OFFICERS OF BOARDS OF GUARDIANS, UNDER THE POOR LAW AMENDMENT ACT.

No. 15. CIRCULAR ISSUED JANUARY 31st, 1842.

Poor Law Commission Office,
Somerset House,
January 28, 1842.

THE Poor Law Commissioners, on a review of their minutes, directed that the minutes and correspondence on the following subjects should be printed and circulated for the information of Guardians and officers of the several Unions, viz.—

By order of the Board,
EDWIN CHADWICK, *Secretary.*

I.—GUARDIANS EX-OFFICIO:—1. AS TO QUALIFICATION OF MAGISTRATES OCCUPYING FURNISHED APARTMENTS ONLY TO ACT AS.

The following is an extract of a letter received from one of the Guardians of the Cheltenham Union:—

"*Cheltenham, December* 24, 1841.

"GENTLEMEN,—An election for a paid officer of this Union is about to take place, when I presume, the *ex-officio* Guardians will, for that occasion, attend the meeting of the Board. There are several magistrates who only occupy furnished lodgings in the town, and my object in troubling you now is to beg the favour of your opinion as to the right of magistrates so circumstanced to vote in the appointment.

"I believe in the month of June or July, 1836, a similar application was made to you, but what the result of your decision was, I am not aware of.

"As the election takes place on Thursday next, the 30th instant, I shall feel particularly obliged by an answer before that day."

The Commissioners stated in reply, that they thought with reference to the qualification to act as *ex-officio* Guardian under the 38th section of the Poor Law Amendment Act, that a justice was not the less a resident in a parish because the house or lodgings which he occupied was hired by him ready furnished; and consequently that his qualification as an *ex-officio* Guardian was not affected by that fact.

Neither did it appear to be material whether a person resided in a lodging or occupied a house, the extent of the tenement or place of residence not being essentially connected with residence, nor adverted to in the Poor Law Amendment Act (section 38.)

With respect, however, to the permanency of the residence, the Commissioners observed that the Act did not specify any particular period for which the justice should reside, nor were the Commissioners aware of any decision of the Courts of Law which determined the point. In the absence of any decision the Commissioners could not undertake to determine the degree of permanency which would be required to constitute a person resident within the meaning of the 38th section.

2. AS TO QUALIFICATION OF BOROUGH MAGISTRATES TO ACT AS GUARDIANS EX-OFFICIO.

The following is a copy of a letter received from the Mayor of Bridgenorth:—

"*Bridgenorth, December* 10, 1841.

"GENTLEMEN,—I shall feel obliged if you will have the kindness to inform me as soon as possible whether, according to section 38 of the Poor Law Amendment Act, borough magistrates are entitled, if they think fit, to officiate as members of any Board of Guardians, provided they reside within the borough or parishes comprehended within any union of parishes. It appears from the interpretation clause (section 109) that the words 'justice or justices of the peace shall be construed to include justices of the peace of any county, division of a county, riding, borough, division of a liberty, precinct, county of a city, county of a town, cinque port, or town corporate, unless where otherwise provided by this Act'

"I have the honour to remain,
"Gentlemen,
"Your obedient servant,
"(Signed) JAMES MILMAN COLEY,
"*The Poor Law Commissioners.* *Mayor*."

In reply, the Commissioners stated that they had been advised, and were of opinion, that the magistrates of a corporate town were not entitled to be considered nor to act as ex-officio guardians. By the 38th section, Poor Law Amendment Act, the ex-officio Guardians were required to be justices of the peace residing in any such parish and acting for the county, riding, or division in which the same might be situate. The word "division," when used in conjunction with county and riding, as decided by the case of Evans *v.* Stephens, 4 T. R. 224, 459, did not include cities, boroughs, cinque ports, and such jurisdictions.

With regard to the supposed effect of the definition of the words justices of the peace in the 109th section, Poor Law Amendment Act, the Commissioners considered that no authority was afforded by that definition for the construction in favour of the right of justices of boroughs or towns (not being counties) to be ex-officio Guardians. That section, provided that the words "justice or justices of the peace" should be construed to "include justices of the peace of any county, division of a county, riding, borough, liberty, division of a liberty, precinct, county of a city, county of a town, cinque port, or town corporate, *unless where otherwise provided by this Act*." If the word "justices" in the 38th section had been used without any limitation or qualification, the Commissioners thought that it might with reference to the 109th section have been reasonably held to include every species of justice, and therefore justices of a corporate town. But it *was* "otherwise provided," in the 38th section, the justices therein referred to being termed "justices of a division." It appeared, therefore, to the Commissioners that the word "justices," as there used, having a specific meaning or qualification attached to it, did not include justices who were not within the limitations, *i. e.*, who were not "justices of the division."

II.—PAID OFICERS:—1. ELECTION OF, NUMBER OF VOTES NECESSARY TO CONSTITUTE A VALID APPOINTMENT.

The following is a copy of a letter received from the Chairman of the Barnstaple Union:—

"*Barnstaple*, 29*th October*, 1841.

"GENTLEMEN,—The election of a Registrar for the Ilfracombe district in this Union having been fixed for this day, 57 Guardians attended at the Board.

"The candidates having been named, the votes were thus divided: for the first 25, for the second 2, for the third 26, and for the fourth 2; the remaining two Guardians declining to vote, but not withdrawing from the Board.

"As chairman, I stated to the Board, that the third candidate was elected, having 26 votes. Before I had an opportunity of declaring to the candidate his appointment, my decision was protested against, on the ground that the candidate had not a majority of the Guardians present. This having occasioned a difference of opinion in the Board, I have deferred declaring the appointment until I have had the opinion of the Poor Law Commissioners as to what in their judgment would, under the circumstances stated, be a majority of the Board.

"I would request the favour of an early reply, and

"Have the honour to be,
"Gentlemen,
"Your obedient servant,
"A. S. WILLETT, *Chairman*.

"*The Poor Law Commissioners*."

In reply, the Commissioners stated they were of opinion that it was necessary to the validity of the appointment of any officer of a Union, that he should be elected by a majority of the whole number of Guardians present at the meeting at which the election takes place. In the present instance it did not appear that the candidate who had the largest nnmber of votes was elected by a majority of the Board. It was stated that there were 57 Guardians present, two of whom declined to vote. There remained, therefore, 55 Guardians who took part in the election. But the greatest number of votes given to any candidate was 26, which was not a majority of the Guardians present who took part in the election.

The Commissioners, under the circumstance, thought it would be necessary to proceed to a new election.

2. DISMISSAL OF THE CLERK AND RELIEVING OFFICER OF THE GLOSSOP UNION.

The Board took into consideration the Report of their Assistant Commissioner, Mr. Gilbert, on the result of the inquiry made by him into the complaint preferred by the Guardians of the Hayfield Union against the clerk to the Board of Guardians and relieving officer of the Glossop Union, alleging that he had caused a woman of the name of Ann Hyde, having three bastard children, and whose settlement was in the Glossop Union, to intermarry with a man of the name of James Chadwick, a parishioner of a parish in the Hayfield Union, whereby the burthen of maintaining the woman and her children was improperly cast upon the latter Union. The Board also perused and considered the evidence taken by Mr. Gilbert in the inquiry.

The facts detailed in the evidence clearly showed that this was one of those cases of compulsory marriages so common before the passing of the Poor Law Amendment Act, but happily so rare since; and that the clerk was a principal promoter of it.

The Commissioners addressed a letter to the Guardians of the Glossop Union, conveying to them the Commissioners' opinion and decision on the case, in which they stated as follows:—

"The Commissioners are of opinion, that the facts detailed in Mr. Gilbert's Report, and which are contained in the evidence adverted to, clearly proved that the clerk, although a responsible paid officer under a Board of Guardians, constituted under the provisions of the Poor Law Amendment Act, was, contrary to the letter and spirit of that enactment, actively concerned in promoting, by improper means, a marriage between the parties above mentioned, with the view of unfairly shifting the burthen of maintaining the woman and her three children from the parish in the

Glossop Union in which they were settled, and to which they were chargeable, to another parish in the Hayfield Union.

"Entertaining this opinion, the Commissioners consider that they could not consistently with their duty permit the clerk to continue to hold his offices; and they have, accordingly, decided on issuing an order forthwith removing him from the office of clerk to the Guardians and relieving officer of the Glossop Union."

---

3. DISMISSAL OF ONE OF THE RELIEVING OFFICERS OF THE PETERBOROUGH UNION.

The Commissioners took into consideration a letter from the clerk of the Peterborough Union, enclosing a copy of a resolution of the Board, with a copy of an entry in the medical officer's report, and of a statement made by a female pauper, the subject of that entry, who, it appears, notwithstanding her being extremely ill and destitute, was refused relief by one of the relieving officers of the Peterborough Union.

The Commissioners transmitted the several papers relating to the case to their Assistant Commissioner, Mr. Weale, directing him immediately to inquire into and report to the Commissioners the circumstances of the case.

In compliance with the Commissioners' directions, Mr. Weale reported the results of his investigation. The defence set up by the relieving officer was:—

"1st. That he had no funds for relief of vagrants.

"2nd. That he offered the workhouse because he considered it to be the most proper place.

"3rd, That he was confirmed in his judgment, that he had no funds, and that the workhouse was the only relief he could give, from the fact, that the Board had refused to allow a sum of 1*s*. given to a vagrant by Mr. Thompson, his colleague.

"4th. That Thompson had been ordered to refuse out-relief to vagrants, and to send them to the workhouse."

The statement of the pauper, however, was corroborated by that of Mr. Forvague, the constable, who deposes to having accompanied her to the house of the relieving officer, when, on the constable telling him that the woman was in great distress, was very ill and likely to die, he replied that he could do nothing for her. Mr. Forvague further deposed, that the relieving officer took no steps to relieve her, and that he omitted to see the woman, who was waiting outside his door.

The Commissioners, after a careful consideration of the whole of the case, and of the defence of the relieving officer, stated, in their communication to the Guardians of the Peterborough Union, that it appeared to them proved beyond a doubt, that the woman was utterly destitute—that her case required immediate relief—that application for relief was made directly to the relieving officer—that it was refused without investigation—that, that refusal was repeated even when the relieving officer's attention was specially called to the case, by the constable, and that too, perhaps, without the offer of the workhouse. If this offer was in fact made, it is immaterial to the defence. It is, undoubtedly, the duty of a relieving officer to provide lodging as well as food and clothes, whenever it may be necessary. The relieving officer had the means of affording immediate relief; he ought to have known (if he was not in fact aware) that he possessed those means, and he should have had immediate recourse to those means in Mary Ann Hurlinstone's case. Supposing that the offer of the workhouse was actually made, and that there had been no other legal mode of relieving the woman, still the relieving officer would have been highly culpable for not *immediately* conveying the woman there, instead of saying that he would give her an order of admission on the following day, provided she came to him again.

The Commissioners, however, think it impossible that the relieving officer should have been ignorant of his power immediately to afford relief to Mary Ann Hurlinstone out of the workhouse. It is reported to the Commissioners that he had often previously given out-relief to casual paupers who had become destitute whilst in lodging-houses, and that the expenses of the lodgings for those paupers, when paid by him, had been allowed by the Guardians.

With regard to his statement, that the Board of Guardians had refused to allow the sum of 1*s*. given to a vagrant by Mr. Thompson, another relieving officer of the Union, the Commissioners find the circumstances under which that refusal occurred were so dissimilar to that of the case of Mary Ann Hurlinstone, that the fact cannot be adduced either in justification or extenuation of his offence.

The examination of Mr. Thompson by the Assistant Commissioner, shows that Mr. Thompson was aware of his powers to give out-relief to vagrants and casual paupers, and that he was aware how he should have treated the case under consideration had it arisen in his district.

The Commissioners feel it necessary to call the attention of the Guardians to the deposition of Sarah Hales, of Eye, who states that she went to the place of the Guardians' meeting to complain of the cruelty and neglect with which Mary Ann Hurlinstone had been treated by the relieving officer, but that she was refused access to the Guardians by him. This statement is not contradicted by the relieving officer.

The Commissioners, therefore, deem the relieving officer highly censurable:—

1st. For not attending to the application of Mary Ann Hurlinstone, and for not personally investigating her case.

2nd. For not immediately giving the relief which the pressing emergency of her case rendered imperatively necessary.

3rd. For repelling Sarah Hales and preventing her access to the Guardians, when she attended for the purpose of preferring a charge against him.

On these grounds the Commissioners deem it their duty to issue an order dismissing the relieving officer from the service of the Union, and they request the Board of Guardians to take the earliest proceedings for the election of his successor in office.

---

4. MEDICAL OFFICER—IF DISMISSED BY AN ORDER OF THE COMMISSIONERS IS INELIGIBLE TO RETAIN THE SITUATION OF REGISTRAR.

The following is a copy of correspondence on this subject between the Poor Law Commissioners and the Registrar-general.

Poor Law Commission Office,
Somerset House,
November 15, 1841.

SIR,—I am directed by the Poor Law Commissioners to state that they have been applied to, to be informed whether a surgeon, who has been dismissed by an order of the Commissioners from the office of medical officer of a Union, is eligible to retain the office (which he now holds) of registrar of births and deaths, for a temporary registration district in a city adjoining such Union.

The Commissioners request that you will be good enough to obtain for them the opinion of the Registrar-general on the point.

I have the honour to be, Sir,
Your most obedient Servant,
(Signed) E. CHADWICK,
Secretary.

Thomas Mann, Esq.
&c. &c. &c.
General Register Office.

General Register Office,
November 17, 1841.

SIR,—I am directed by the Registrar-general to acknowledge the receipt of your letter of the 15th instant, and in reply to inform you that a medical officer of a Poor Law Union, who being also a registrar of births and deaths has been dismissed from his office of medical officer by an order of the Poor Law Commissioners, is, in the Registrar-general's opinion, clearly ineligible to retain the situation of registrar for a temporary district adjoining such Union, it being provided by the 8th section of the Registration Act, that any person so removed shall "cease to hold office" under that Act and be incapable of re-appointment thereto.

I have the honour to be, Sir,
Your obedient Servant,
(Signed) THOMAS MANN,
Chief Clerk.

E. Chadwick, Esq.
&c. &c. &c.
Poor Law Commission Office.

---

5. CHAPLAIN:—AS TO THE POWER OF, TO CHRISTEN CHILDREN AND CHURCH WOMEN IN THE WORKHOUSE.

The following is a copy of a letter received from the clerk of the Lichfield Union:—

"*Lichfield, January* 8, 1842.

"SIR,—I am directed by the Guardians of this Union to inquire whether the chaplain of the workhouse has power to christen children and church women in the chapel of the workhouse; or, whether it is the duty of the minister of the parish church in which the workhouse is situate?

"I am, Sir,
"Your obedient servant.
"(Signed) P. DYOTT, JUN., *Clerk.*

"*E. Chadwick, Esq.*"

In reply, the Commissioners stated, that previously to the receipt of his letter, they had communicated with the Bishop of London, in reference to a similar question to that above stated, which arose in another Union, and the Commissioners were informed that his Lordship's opinion was, that when infants born in a workhouse were in such a state of health that they could not be safely taken to church, they might then be privately baptized, according to the form prescribed in such cases, in the house; but that where no such impediment to their being publicly baptized existed they ought to be taken to church for that purpose.

The Commissioners considered it their duty to concur in this opinion; and they thought that the mothers of the children should be churched in the church when the children were taken to be baptized.

---

6. AUDITOR AND COLLECTOR.—AS TO LIABILITY OF COLLECTOR TO ACCOUNT TO AUDITOR.

The following is a copy of a letter received from one of the Guardians of the West Bromwich Union:—

"*West Bromwich Union, Handsworth,*
"*near Birmingham, 19th August*, 1841.

"GENTLEMEN,—As one of the Guardians of the Union above mentioned, I beg leave to state to you, that the auditor of this Union fixed the 22d day of July last for the audit of the accounts; that the clerk and the assistant-overseer of the parish of Olabury were the only officers who attended at the time and place appointed. In consequence, the auditor adjourned the audit to this day, but none of the officers attended besides the clerk.

"The auditor stated to me to-day, when I attended the audit, that he considered he had no power to summon the collectors to attend and produce their books for his inspection; that the overseers never attended his audits, and he thought it was the business of the clerk and the Board of Guardians to examine the collectors' accounts. This neither the clerk nor the Guardians do.

"I shall be glad if you will send me by the post of Saturday a copy of the instructions which you have issued relative to the duty of the collectors. The auditor mentioned his having received a copy from you some months ago, but he had lent it to one of the late overseers, who had not returned it.

"The collector of Handsworth is also the assistant-overseer, and if the collectors are not to produce their books, &c. to the auditor, he, Corbet, in his office as overseer, ought to have attended the audit on 22d July, or to-day.

"I beg to add, that the debts now due by this Union are equal in amount to about the expenditure of two quarters, and therefore it is desirable that the collectors should be urged to an active discharge of their duty.

"I am,
"Your obedient servant,
(Signed) "SAMUEL KENRICK.
"*The Poor Law Commissioners.*"

In reply thereto the Commissioners stated, that a collector of poor rates was an officer who under the 47th section of the Poor Law Amendment Act, and the order for keeping accounts, (rule 8, section 6), was bound to submit his accounts to the auditor for his examination. The 47th section rendered every person, having the collection or receipt of the monies assessed for the relief of the poor, liable to account to the auditor.

If, therefore, the collectors, overseers, or any other officer liable to account, failed to attend at the time and place appointed for the audit, they subjected themselves to be convicted in penalties for the neglect. The Commissioners considered it matter of great importance that the auditor should satisfy himself that the duties imposed upon the collectors by the orders of the Commissioners were properly and efficiently performed,

---

III.—TREASURER:—1. FAILURE OF BANK WITH WHICH HE ACCOUNTED.—INABILITY OF, IN CONSEQUENCE, TO MEET THE CALLS UPON HIM.—COURSE TO BE PURSUED UNDER THE CIRCUMSTANCES.

The Commissioners took into consideration the following copy of a letter, addressed to their Assistant Commissioner, Sir John Walsham, Bart, by the clerk of the Berwick-on-Tweed Union.

"*Berwick, January 6th*, 1842.

"SIR,—I regret to say that the failure of the Tweed Bank is likely to involve the officers of this Union in some confusion. At the time of the failure, the Treasurer had in the Bank somewhere about 500*l.*, and though he managed to meet the cheques issued upon him at the meetings of the 7th and 21st ultimo, he found himself unable to pay those issued at the meeting on Tuesday last. This not being known until after the meeting, great inconvenience was likely to be the result, as the relieving officers could not get cash to pay their poor, but fortunately Mr. Atkinson, as collector for Berwick, had sufficient in his hands to enable him to assist his brother relieving officers in their time of need. On consulting with the guardians resident in the town, it has been thought right to call an extraordinary meeting of the Board on Tuesday next. At this meeting I presume the first thing to be ascertained is, whether the Treasurer has yet enabled himself to meet the demands of the Union to the extent of the balance in his hands, and if on finding that he is not prepared, to take immediate steps for supplying the present wants. This, I suppose, can only be done by issuing orders on the overseers, but very few of them will be prepared for probably two or three weeks to meet the orders. To whom must the orders be made payable, as our Board will be most unwilling to issue them in favour of the present Treasurer? I gather from those with whom I have spoken on the subject, that a difference of opinion is entertained as to holding the Treasurer and his sureties liable for the amount in the Bank. It is urged, I understand, that the bond was only taken to secure the guardians against any misappropriation of his own, and that he should not be held liable in such a case as the present; he having used the bank which was of the best repute in the town as a place of safe keeping for the money.

The question, however, is, can the guardians, if they are even so disposed, exercise any such power or judgment with respect to public money? I should think not, but on the contrary, that they are bound to recover the amount from the Treasurer and his sureties.

"I shall be glad to hear from you before the meeting,

"And remain, Sir,
"Your most obedient Servant,
"(Signed) E. WILLOBY.

"*Sir John Walsham, Bart.*"

In reply, the Commissioners stated that the guardians appeared to have been advised to pursue the course which was most proper under the circumstances, namely, to issue orders for contributions immediately, with a view to supplying themselves with funds for the emergencies of the Union. But as to the payment of such contributions there was an obvious irregularity in the lodgement of them with any other person but the treasurer, unless he was suspended or removed previously. The Commissioners, however, would not consider it necessary to object to the course advised, if he satisfied himself that adequate provision was made for the safe custody of the funds when they came to hand.

With respect to the bond of the treasurer and his sureties it appeared to the Commissioners that the guardians could not dispense with their duty of enforcing it under the circumstances stated. The blamelessness or misfortune of the treasurer in having placed the funds, so that loss was incurred, was no discharge of him or his sureties from their liability in respect of the funds intrusted to him, unless he so placed the money at the express request of the guardians, or under circumstances proving that the guardians were to be at the risk.

It was certainly not in the power of the guardians to abandon the rights of the Union to the benefit of this security; the object of which was quite as much to guard against the involuntary, as against the voluntary default of the treasurer.

---

2. BANKRUPTCY OF TREASURER.—GUARDIANS CANNOT PROPERLY FOREGO MAKING THEIR CLAIM IMMEDIATELY ON THE SURETIES.

The following is a copy of a letter received from the clerk of the Cambridge Union:—

"*Cambridge*, 4*th December*, 1841.

"SIR,—In the event of the Guardians proving against the estate of Mr. ——— for the two sums of 1,117*l.* 10*s.* 7*d.* and 468*l.* 19*s.* 6*d.*, they understand they have their remedy against the sureties *for the balance which may appear due after the receipt of the dividends.* Should such be the case in the opinion of the Poor Law Commissioners, it is their wish so to act, as they are anxious not to inconvenience the sureties further than there is any real occasion for, and a dividend will be received before the money can well be obtained from the sureties, and provided they do not lose their remedy against the sureties by proving under the bankruptcy, there appears no reason why they should not do so.

"But as to the proof, they wish to be informed who is the proper person to prove, the chairman, clerk, or the bankrupt treasurer himself? and whoever proves whether it must not be done under a power of attorney, stamped with the Union seal, at a meeting of the Guardians? and whether (in order to give a valid power of attorney) the seal must be affixed in the presence of a majority of the whole Guardians, or only a majority of the number present at the meeting?

"The early answer of the Poor Law Commissioners is requested, Thursday next being the day appointed for a meeting of creditors to prove their debts.

"I am, Sir,
"Your obedient servant,
"(Signed) FREDERIC BARLOW, *Clerk.*

"*To E. Chadwick, Esq.*"

The Commissioners in reply observed, that it was true that the Guardians would have their remedy against the sureties for the balance which might appear due after receipt of the dividend.

But, although the Commissioners quite concurred in the wish of the Guardians that the sureties should not be subjected to unnecessary inconvenience, it appeared to the Commissioners that the Guardians could not properly forego making their claim immediately on the sureties. The Guardians were bound to proceed in such a way as best protected the interests of the Union, and no private consideration for the sureties should be allowed to interfere with this duty. The Guardians would eventually be entitled to receive money both from the sureties and under the fiat; but it was obvious that by delaying their claim against the sureties they prejudiced the rights of the Union, whereas, if the Guardians took the course suggested by the Commissioners, they would secure the Union to the utmost as regarded the sureties, and have a clear claim to whatever might be the residue of their demands upon the estate of the bankrupt—an estate which could not be diminished, as the ability to pay of the sureties might.

The debt would best be proved by the clerk of the Union, who might, without warrant of attorney, be constituted an agent for the Guardians for the purpose, by the mere direction of the Board at an ordinary meeting: any agent so appointed would have to swear that he was such agent, and was therefore entitled to prove the debts of any body politic or corporate, such as the Guardians were. See the 46th section of the 6 Geo. 4, cap. 16.

---

3. AS TO GRATUITY TO TREASURER AND ALLOWANCE OF INTEREST ON MONEY ADVANCED BY.

The following is a copy of a letter received from the clerk to the Board of Guardians of the parish of Great Yarmouth:—

"*Great Yarmouth Parish.*

"GENTLEMEN,—At the weekly meeting of the Board of Guardians of this parish, held yesterday, and which was specially summoned and numerously attended, a resolution was unanimously passed, voting to D. Turner, Esq., the treasurer of the parish, the sum of 50*l.* as a gratuity for the services he has performed in that office.

"It may be necessary to recall to your attention that two or three years since the rate under the new valuation for this parish was quashed, and a rate lost, and in consequence of that dilemma, and of the fact of the new building and fixtures having exceeded the amount borrowed of the Exchequer Loan Commissioners, the parish has always been in debt to the treasurer, sometimes considerably, and the auditor has refused to allow any interest.

"There would be no objection made by the auditor to the payment of the 50*l.* as a gratuity to the treasurer, as he has not received any salary, and the interest, if paid to this quarter, would exceed the sum. I am, therefore, directed by the Guardians to request your approval of this payment, in order that we may now be enabled to settle that portion of the treasurer's account. Mr. Twisleton, your Assistant-Commissioner, is fully acquainted with our situation.

"I have the honour to be,
"Gentlemen,
"Your most obedient servant,
"(Signed) J. L. CUFAUDE.

"*The Poor Law Commissioners.*"

In reply, the Commissioners observed that there appeared to be no doubt entertained that the auditor had taken a correct view of his duty in refusing to allow interest on money overdrawn by the Guardians and advanced by the treasurer. But it was suggested that he might be compensated by a gratuity instead of the interest, which it would not be lawful to pay. The Commissioners did not think that this could properly be done. They saw a wide difference between the case in which gratuities had on some occasions been allowed to officers performing duties, the extent and burden of which bad been found to be much greater than was contemplated when the salary was fixed (as in the case of a medical officer during an epidemic, where, if the case had been anticipated, it would have been lawful and right to have provided for a higher salary), and cases such as the *present*, where the compensation was intended for a supposed service, payment for which to any extent is unlawful.

The Commissioners would not dismiss this subject without observing on the importance of the Guardians withholding all encouragements and facilities for irregularity in the contributions of parishes towards the expenses of the Union. The legitimate and proper compensation to the treasurer would be the benefit of the use of the balance which would constantly be in his hands, if the contributions of every parish were regularly called for and enforced.

IV. — RELIEF:—1. To Non-Residents—Robbery of a Pauper of Five Pounds.

The Commissioners received the following letter and enclosure from their Assistant-Commissioner, Sir John Walsham:—

"*North Allerton, 28th October*, 1841.

"Non-Resident Relief.

"Gentlemen.—I have the honour to inclose for your information a note attached to my monthly return of progress, that the Clerk of the Darlington Union (who is also Clerk of the Magistrates) has forwarded to me illustrative of the abuses of non-resident relief.

"I remain,
"Your very obedient Servant,
"(Signed) John Walsham.

"*The Poor Law Commissioners.*"

"Darlington Union.
"*Darlington, 25th October*, 1841.

"Sir John,—On the other side you have a statement, viz. Monthly Average of Weekly Expenditure: to-day we had a case before the Magistrates which proves the difficulty of dispensing relief to non-resident paupers. A person applied to the Bench for a warrant against a woman for picking his pocket of five sovereigns, which could not be proved against her. The man is in the receipt of 2*s.* 6*d.* per week from Stokesley Union, and applied a week ago for an increase, stating he was in distress. The R. O. and the Union are put in possession of the fact.

"I am, Sir John,
"Your obedient Servant,
"(Signed.) Jervis Robinson.

"*To Sir John Walsham, Bart.*"

2. Relief to Mendicants:—Course to be adopted with respect to.

The following is a copy of a letter received from the clerk of the Warminster Union:—

"*Warminster*,
"*January* 3, 1842.

"Sirs,—There has been in the town of Warminster for some years past a society for the relief of mendicants, which, within the last two months, has been done away with, owing to their want of funds to continue it. The county police have refused to interfere in the matter. The mendicants have, therefore, applied to Mr. Jones (the relieving officer for the parish of Warminster, whose duties for his district are already sufficient without any additional ones) for relief. Many of the applicants he has relieved to the amount of 2*d.* or 3*d.* each to pay for a bed, and a great many he has refused. Under these circumstances, and taking into consideration that the parish of Warminster alone of all the parishes in the Union is burdened with such relief, what course should you recommend to be adopted by the Guardians with regard to such mendicants, and in what manner should the relief given be charged.

"I am, Gentlemen,
"Your obedient Servant,
"(Signed) J. Book, *Clerk.*

"*To the Poor Law Commissioners.*"

In reply, the Commissioners stated, that they thought that the Guardians should cause the relief to mendicant or vagrant poor to be given in the workhouse, and that some apartment in the workhouse, separated, as far as circumstances would permit, from the other parts of the establishment, should be exclusively kept for the reception and use of such persons. All persons who were destitute were entitled to be relieved where they were destitute, and in the case of wandering or vagrant poor the Commissioners considered it important that relief should be given in that form which afforded the greatest security that the persons who accepted it were in the condition which constituted the title to relief. The Commissioners thought that relief in the workhouse afforded this security.

In the present state of the law the parish where the destitution occurred, and in which application was made for relief, was alone liable for the relief which might be given. But as a very heavy burden was thus cast upon particular parishes in a Union, while others were in a great measure exempt, the Commissioners thought that a more equal distribution of the burden would be desirable. They had, therefore, recommended in the report on the amendment of the Poor Laws (page 102,) that the relief in such cases should be made a charge on the common fund of the Union.

3. Relief in cases of Sudden and Urgent Necessity—Duty of Guardians in respect to the payment of expenses of.

The following letter was received from the clerk of the Chepstow Union:—

"*Chepstow Union*,
"*Chepstow, Nov.* 8, 1841.

"Gentlemen,—I am directed by the Board of Guardians to ask you, whether in case of relief given by overseers and reported to the Board it is the duty of the Board to order payment out of the funds under their control, or simply to receive the fact as information, leaving the overseer to pay the value of the articles given out of the funds in his hands, or to bring it before the auditor as an item in his own accounts and not those of the Union.

"I am, Gentlemen,
"Your obedient servant,
"(Signed) W. E TOYE.
"*To the Poor Law Commissioners.*"

In reply the Commissioners stated, that the relief given by an overseer in a case of "sudden and urgent necessity" is given on his own responsibility; his authority to relieve in such cases is quite independent of the judgment or sanction of the Board of Guardians. The relief so given, therefore, should be submitted to the auditor in the overseers' accounts, and not in those of the agent of the guardians,—the relieving officer. The effect of the practice of repaying to the overseer the cost of the relief granted, and placing the amount in the relieving officer's weekly relief list, is to withdraw these cases of urgent necessity from efficient cognizance on the part of the auditor.

---

4. RELIEF IN CASES OF ACCIDENT:—AS TO PAYMENT OF EXPENSES OF.

The following is a copy of a letter received from the clerk of the Uppingham Union.

"*Great Easton Parish, Uppingham Union,*
"*4th November*, 1841.

"GENTLEMEN,—On the 18th October last, Robert Yates, an able-bodied man, not a pauper, belonging to the parish of Great Easton, in this Union, was struck by the shaft of a cart at Uppingham, which caused his death on the 25th. The person who was driving the cart was an apprentice to a druggist in Uppingham, and had been sent out by his master on business, but that business did not require the apprentice to be where the accident occurred. A coroner's inquest was held, and a verdict of 'accidental death' returned.

"The deceased was carried to a public-house in Uppingham by the persons who saw the accident, unknown to the parish authorities, and could not from the violence of the blow be afterwards removed.

"The Board of Guardians on the 21st October granted relief to the family of the deceased.

"The innkeeper has sent in to the parish of Great Easton a bill to the amount of about 6*l.* 10*s.* for nurses, leeches, wine ordered by the medical officer, board and lodging of the deceased, his wife and nurse, &c. &c.

"The Board of Guardians will feel obliged by your informing them who, in your opinion, is liable under the circumstances to pay this bill, by Thursday next.

"I have the honour to be,
"Gentlemen,
(for William Gilson)
"Your obedient servant,
"(Signed) JOHN WILMOT.
"*The Poor Law Commissioners.*"

The Commissioners requested to be informed whether the medical officer ordered the wine, &c. to be supplied in the case of Robert Yates, upon his own responsibility, and without the knowledge and concurrence of the Board of Guardians, and if not, whether the articles were such as the Board of Guardians would have authorized him to order.

In reply the clerk stated:—

"I beg to say that the wine, &c. was ordered by Mr. Greaves, the medical officer who attended Yates, and I have no hesitation in saying that if the Guardians had been asked they would have allowed it."

The Commissioners thereupon addressed a communication to the Guardians in reply, in which they observed, that it appeared from the statements that the case was admitted to be one for relief by the Board of Guardians of the Uppingham Union. It appeared equally that it was properly a case for the medical officer of the Union.

The doubts entertained by the Guardians on the subject were not stated. The Commissioners conceived that they must be one or more of the following:—

1. Was it competent to the medical officer to order nurses, leeches, and wine of an innkeeper where the deceased lay disabled by the accident.

2. Was it competent to the innkeeper to charge the Board of Guardians for board and lodging of the deceased, his wife, and nurse.

3. Who was amenable for such charges as were incurred,—the apprentice who caused the accident or the Board of Guardians,—and if so, on behalf of the parish of Uppingham, where the accident happened, and the deceased remained, or of the parish of Great Easton, to which he belonged, or was the medical officer answerable for anything he might have ordered, not being within the scope of his authority, or

was the innkeeper bound to look to the representatives of the deceased only for payment in whole or in part.

It appeared to the Commissioners that the apprentice was not liable either to the Guardians or the innkeeper, but would only have been liable at the suit of the deceased; that it was competent to the medical officer to order the diet, medicines, and nurse for the deceased while the necessity was urgent, and until those things could be supplied by himself and the relieving officer, or under the direction of the Board of Guardians; but that he could not order such things continuously without authority from the Board of Guardians; still, supposing that he did not report the case, if the Guardians did not then disapprove of his conduct, the Commissioners thought that in a case of such urgency it would not be desirable to dispute the bill of the innkeeper, merely on the ground of want of continuous authority in the medical officer. The board of the nurse would appear to be governed by the like considerations as the diet and medicine of the deceased; but the board and lodging of the wife at the inn was not a matter which the medical officer could authorize, and which the innkeeper should have had direct authority for, in order to charge the guardians. Supposing the medical officer to have countenanced the lodging and board of the wife, he would still not be liable to the innkeeper without express guarantee in writing, and he could not in fact have intended or been understood to be responsible in his private capacity.

The Guardians would judge from the above observations as to their general liability to the several items of the innkeeper's charge. As regards the burden of that charge by the one parish or the other, the Commissioners entertained no doubt of the liability of Uppingham to the expense incurred about the deceased himself, in consequence of the accident which happened there, and for which he was there attended, the case being clearly within the decisions applicable to casual poor. But as regards the relief of the wife, who was not casual poor in Uppingham, the relief to her would be chargeable to Great Easton, unless she had abandoned her residence in Great Easton before she received that relief.

---

5. AS TO AN ALLOWANCE TO THE WIFE OF A PRIVATE SOLDIER, TO ENABLE HER TO JOIN HER HUSBAND.

The following letter was received from the clerk of the Hertford Union:—

"*Hertford Union, Hertford, Nov. 5, 1841.*

"SIR,—A private in the army, who is now stationed in Norfolk Island, has left a wife with a young child chargeable to the parish of Watton, in this Union. She is quite an able-bodied woman.

"Several applications have been made by her for out-relief, but the Board of Guardians have invariably refused out-relief, (although her request was backed by the oft-expressed wish of the vestry,) on the ground that if she was allowed out-relief the guardians must allow relief to the wives of all soldiers or sailors in Her Majesty's service. She is now in the workhouse with her child.

"She wishes very much to get out to her husband, and he has written two lettters urging her to go to him; and, in consequence, the guardian for Watton wishes an allowance to be made to assist her out to her husband. The guardians have doubts of their power to do so, and would be glad of the advice of the Poor Law Commissioners upon the subject; and if the principle be admitted, they would also like to know about the amount which would be sanctioned by the Commissioners.

"I am, Sir,
"Your most obedient servant,
"(Signed) THOMAS SWORDER, *Clerk.*
"*To E. Chadwick, Esq.*"

In reply the Commissioners stated that, a similar application having been made to them a short time ago, they made inquiries of the authorities of the War Office and the Horse Guards on the subject, and they were informed in reply that, in cases where regiments are ordered upon foreign service six women are selected to accompany every 100 men sent out from this country, and that these selected women only are permitted to live with their husbands in barracks, and to be rationed at the public expense.

In the event of the proportion of soldiers wives, according to Her Majesty's regulations being now present with the service companies of the regiment, to which your letter refers, it is not in the power of the general commanding in chief to sanction any further embarkation until vacancies shall occur. In such a case, any woman desiring to join her husband would be instructed to apply through the officer commanding the depôt companies, who can alone judge of her eligibility, according to the established regulations of the service, for the indulgence.

The Poor Law Commissioners are further informed that, any women sent out by the parish authorities, or by private subscription, or who find their way out as servants or by paying for their passages, not only become incumbrances to the regiments, but, as they are in excess of the regulated number, are subject to very great privations by being excluded from barracks and not allowed any rations by the public.

Under these circumstances, the Commissioners are unable to advise the interference of the guardians for the purpose of sending out the wife of the soldier to whom your inquiry relates to join her husband; and the Commissioners request that the guardians will make known to her the hardships and privations to which she would probably be exposed were she to join her husband whilst on foreign service.

---

6. As to the liability of a Husband to support his Wife after she has committed Adultery.

The following is a copy of a letter received from a Mr. Henry Trotman, of Shepton Mallet:—

" *Shepton Mallet*, 16*th December*, 1841.

" Sir,—Upwards of three years since a mutual separation took place between a man and his wife, inhabitants of this town, the husband allowing the wife a weekly sum for her maintenance, and the husband having the custody of the children. The wife subsequently became a common prostitute in the town, and continued so, and in consequence thereof, about a month since, the husband, acting under the advice of his friends, discontinued the weekly allowance, and the wife has now become chargeable to the parish, and been admitted an inmate of the Union house. The husband is to be summoned before the magistrate by the parish authorities, to show cause, it is presumed, why he refuses to support his wife. You will, therefore, very greatly oblige me by saying whether upon the fact of adultery being substantiated against the wife the husband will any longer be liable to support her. I hope you will pardon the liberty I am taking in thus addressing you.

" I have the honour to be, Sir,
" Your most obedient servant,
(Signed) " Henry Trotman.

" *E. Chadwick, Esq.*"

In reply, the Commissioners observed that it was to be collected from the decisions in Govier *v.* Hancock, 6. T. R. 603, Rex *v.* Flintorn, 1. B. and Ad. 227, that a husband was not bound to receive and support his wife after she had committed adultery; nor to be punished under the 5 Geo. IV., cap. 83, sec. 3, if he refused, and his wife became chargeable.

But the Commissioners conceived that no general allegation of adultery having been committed by the wife would be sufficient to warrant the justices in holding the husband exonerated from the charge of maintaining her. The proofs in support of the allegation ought to be of the clearest and most cogent description. And presuming that adultery could be proved, the Commissioners thought it should be further shown that there had been no condonation, and that the husband had not received his wife since the separation, and subsequently to the commission of the offence imputed to her.

V.—PAUPERS:—1. Illegal Removal of Casual Paupers.

The Commissioners took into consideration the following letter and enclosures transmitted to them by their Assistant Commissioner, Mr. Senior:—

" *Cuckney, December* 24, 1841.

" Gentlemen,—I have to draw your attention to the enclosed copy of an extract from a letter addressed to Sir John Walsham, by the Rev. J. T. Monson, the chairman of the Bedale Union, respecting the illegal removal of a pauper from the Sculcoates Union, to the Bedale Union, together with the observations of the Guardians of the Sculcoates Union thereon, addressed to myself.

" I am, Gentlemen,
" Your obedient Servant,
" (Signed) Edward Senior,
" *Assistant Commissioner.*

" *To the Poor Law Commissoners.*"

" *December* 7, 1841.

" My dear Sir John,—Eli Robinson, an able-bodied man, wife able-bodied, and three healthy children, arrived in Bedale late on Saturday evening in a state of destitution, and applied for relief, claiming a settlement at Bedale. They were duly admitted into the workhouse, their case was examined into yesterday at our Board, when the pauper made the following statement:—

" 'I have lived the two last years at Hull within the district of the Sculcoates Union, and supported my wife and family by daily labour. On Tuesday the 23rd of November last, being out of work, I applied to the Board of Guardians of that Union for relief. I told them I belonged to Bedale. I was ordered to call upon the relieving officer at three o'clock, who would report to me the decision of the Board. I did so; when the relieving officer told me that the Board thought that I had better go home to my parish, and that he would give me money to carry me on the road. He asked me what would do, proposed 10*s.*; I said that was not enough. At last we agreed for 16*s.*, which he promised should be paid before I set off. When I was on the pier, just getting into the packet, a man with one hand, who I know to be always in attendance on the Board, gave me the money.'

" Now we do not think ourselves either legally or fairly treated in this proceeding, and feel much inclined to lay the case before the Commissioners, or to act in any way you would recommend, if you will favour us with your opinion. What gives additional hardness to the case is, that Robinson's settlement at Bedale is a very doubtful one, and will probably entail an expensive litigation upon the township. Neither do I see how the Guardians of the Sculcoates Union, being included in the prohibitory order, could direct out-relief to so considerable an amount, to be paid to an able-bodied pauper and his family; and *above all*, is it not *enticing*, *taking*, conveying, or removing a poor person from one parish to another without an order of removal, thereby offending against the law.

" (Signed) I. J. T. MONSON.

" *Sir John Walsham,*
" *Assistant Poor Law Commissioner.*"

" *George Street, Hull, December* 21, 1841.

" SIR,—I have to acknowledge the receipt of your letter of the 14th instant, with its enclosure, which was laid before the Board of Guardians of this Union at their meeting to-day. In reply, I am desired to state that the circumstances relative to Eli Robinson, as detailed in the letter of the Rev. I. J. T. Monson to *Sir John Walsham is substantially correct.*

" The Guardians, although aware that the practice of assisting paupers on their way home is not exactly countenanced by the law, yet, not being advised that it is directly contrary to any statute, have in one or two instances adopted the plan.

" This has been when it has been the pauper's desire to return to his parish, and when it appeared no injury could possibly be done to the place of his destination; the settlement being clear, and the pauper at all events removable under an order.

" This mode of proceeding does not come within the scope of the 22nd Geo. III., c. 83, s. 41, to which clause the Rev. Mr. Monson probably alludes in his letter.

" The Board, however, having no wish to persevere in an improper course, will feel obliged by any suggestions you will be good enough to offer on the subject, and particularly by your pointing out in what manner the law is infringed in the present instance.

" I am, Sir,
" Your obedient servant,
" (Signed) WM. CHATHAM,
" *Clerk to the Board.*

" *Edward Senior, Esq.,*
" *Assistant Poor Law Commissioner.*"

In reference thereto the Commissioners directed the following letter to be transmitted to the Board of Guardians of the Sculcoates Union.

Poor Law Commission Office,
Somerset House,
January 22, 1842.

SIR,—I am directed by the Poor Law Commissioners to state that they have received from their Assistant Commissioner, Mr. Senior, a copy of an extract from a letter addressed to Sir John Walsham by the chairman of the Bedale Union, respecting the illegal removal of a pauper (Eli Robinson) from the Sculcoates Union to the Bedale Union, and a copy of a letter addressed by you to Mr. Senior, containing the observations of the Guardians of the Sculcoates Union upon the case.

The Guardians therein admit that the circumstances detailed in the letter are substantially correct. The Commissioners desire to point out that the course pursued in the case of Eli Robinson was decidedly illegal. The pauper it appears was resident in the Sculcoates Union when he became chargeable. The proper mode of dealing with the case was to have ascertained the pauper's settlement, and if not settled where he was residing, to have removed him by order of justices to the place to which he did belong. But instead of this, money was given to the pauper by direction of the Guardians to enable him to journey to another parish without the liability of such parish to maintain the pauper, having been established in a legal way. The Guardians cannot fail to perceive that this was illegally casting a burthen upon another parish, besides applying the poor rates in a manner not authorised by the law or the regulations of the Commissioners.

The Commissioners think it probable that the attention of the Guardians may not have been directed to a Circular issued by the Commissioners on the 13th February, 1839, as to the illegal removal of casual poor. The Commissioners enclose, for the consideration of the Guardians, a copy of the circular referred to.

The condemnation of the practice therein expressed of inducing casual paupers to quit the parish in which the chargeability has arisen, applies in greater force to such a case as the present. The pauper was, it seems, resident in Hull when he became chargeable. That parish therefore was bound to relieve him, and could only relieve itself by establishing in a legal manner that the pauper was settled elsewhere.

I am, Sir, &c.

The Clerk to the Guardians of Sculcoates Union, Hull.

Circular to Boards of Guardians as to the illegal Removal of Casual Paupers.

Poor Law Commission Office,
Somerset House,
13th February, 1839.

SIR,—The Poor Law Commissioners have had under their consideration a report transmitted by their Assistant Commissioner, Sir John Walsham, from which it appears that, in several of the Unions under his superintendence, there lately occurred frequent instances in which the parish officers of these Unions have resorted to the very reprehensible course of bribing or otherwise inducing casual paupers (who from sickness or other accidental causes have appeared likely to become burthensome), to quit the parish in which the chargeability has arisen, from some other place, so as unfairly to impose upon the parish to which the paupers may proceed the charge of either investigating their settlements (if they have any), and procuring their legal removal, or of supporting them so long as their necessities may require.

The Commissioners learn with regret that so obviously indefensible a method of shifting off a legal liability (extensively as such method might have obtained under the former system of parochial administration), should have been adopted by any of the responsible officers to whom the working of the system of poor laws has been confided; but in order that there may be henceforth no pretence for doubting the illegality of the course of proceeding to which reference has been made, the Commissioners request that the Board of Guardians will admonish all the paid officers of the Union, that they are on no account to remove a pauper, or induce a pauper to remove (whether he have a settlement in England or not), except by a proper warrant of justices, or with the sanction of the parish to which the removal is effected, and if the latter, then only with such precautions as may secure the completion of the journey, and prevent the possibility of the pauper becoming during the journey unfairly chargeable to a third parish. And with the view of discountenancing to the extent of their ability the improper practice to which they have adverted, the Commissioners desire in conclusion to observe that in every case where it shall be proved that any paid officer shall have been instrumental in removing (otherwise than by due course of law), a pauper who has become chargeable to his Union or parish, the Commissioners will feel it their duty to take very serious notice of the officer so offending.

Signed, &c.

---

2. AS TO COMPLETION OF PUNISHMENT OF PAUPERS WHEN NOTICE TO QUIT THE WORKHOUSE HAS BEEN GIVEN.

The following is a copy of a letter received from the clerk of the East London Union:—

"*30th December*, 1841.

"GENTLEMEN,—I am desired by the Board of Guardians of this Union to request that you will be good enough to favour them with your opinion on the following points:—

"1st. Whether the master of the workhouse would be justified in detaining any inmate after receiving the usual three hours' notice of discharge, such inmate being at the time in confinement as 'refractory?'

"2nd. Whether, in case of the discharge of such inmate, and his or her return to the workhouse, the master would then be justified in inflicting the punishment which had been previously prescribed?

"I have the honour to be,
"Gentlemen,
"Your most obedient servant,
"(Signed) A. J. BAYLIS, *Clerk.*

"*The Poor Law Commissioners.*"

In reply the Commissioners stated, that when a pauper had committed an offence, or been guilty of a misbehaviour in the workhouse, punishable by confinement, his giving the proper notice to quit the workhouse would not prevent the completion of such punishment when lawfully imposed, provided the confinement did not extend beyond the period mentioned in the 7th section of 54 Geo. 3, cap. 170, namely, twenty four hours, or such further space of time as might be necessary, in order to bring such pauper before a justice of the peace.

If an inmate be discharged from the workhouse, the punishment prescribed for any offence he might have committed not having been inflicted, the master would not be justified in inflicting such punishment upon the return of such pauper to the workhouse.

3. AS TO CLOTHING OF PAUPERS ON LEAVING THE WORKHOUSE.

The following is a copy of a letter received from the clerk of the Alderbury Union:—

" *Alderbury Union, Salisbury,*
" *January* 14, 1842.

" SIR,—I am directed by the Guardians of the above Union to request the opinion of the Poor Law Commissioners as to the course they should adopt under the following circumstances.

By a bye law of the Union (sanctioned by the Commissioners) if a pauper come into the house in a filthy state, upon the recommendation of the medical officer, the clothes of the pauper are burned; in this case, when the pauper wishes to leave the house, are the Guardians obliged to provide him with other clothes or not? The guardians are particularly desirous of the opinion of the Commissioners on this point, inasmuch as they find by experience, that paupers come into the house in a filthy state for the mere purpose of getting an outfit of clothing.

" I am, Sir,
" Your obedient Servant,
" (Signed) W. D. WHITMARSH, *Clerk.*
" *E. Chadwick, Esq.*"

In reply, the Commissioners stated that they thought the guardians should not, in any such case, refuse to furnish such clothing as might be necessary for the immediate use of the pauper.

The original clothes of the pauper had been burnt by direction of the guardians, for a salutary and proper reason certainly; but still on their own judgment that such a course was necessary. If the guardians could direct the clothes of a pauper to be burnt, and afterwards refuse clothes when such pauper desired to leave the house, it might be argued that the guardians could detain any person there as long as they pleased, since decency and comfort required that the pauper should wear some clothes when he quitted it.

The Commissioners thus pointed out the reasons why they thought that the Guardians could not be justified in absolutely refusing clothing under the circumstances. They were aware of all the inconveniences which might ensue, and they recommended that the clothes given should not be new or of a description to tempt persons to seek relief in the condition, and for the objects described in the clerk s letter.

VI.—ACCOUNTS:—1. PARISH READY RECKONER.

The Commissioners received the following letter from the auditor of the Wrexham Union, with a book of tables to facilitate the calculation of church, highway, police, and poor-rates; published by Simpkin and Marshall.

" *Wrexham Union*, 23*rd October*, 1841.

" GENTLEMEN,—I have taken the liberty of presenting for the honour of your approbation and acceptance the enclosed book of tables. Comprehensiveness of arrangement and perspicuity of the page form the only merit that can be claimed for such a work. The latter feature I have endeavoured to attain by a novelty in the art of typography, which is the rejection of *cyphers* where they usually stand alone, and the substitution of dashes instead of them.

" My object in the publication is to remove many of the irregularities that overseers of the poor, especially in our Welsh districts are ignorantly committing, and to secure more accurate accounts, with less cost of time to themselves, than can be usually accomplished without it.

" If you should think that I have succeeded in the former attempt, I shall feel both honoured and obliged by your aid in promoting the latter, which your favourable notice will certainly ensure.

" I have the honour to be, Gentlemen,
" Your very humble Servant,
" (Signed) BARTHO. C. DILLON, *Auditor.*
" *The Poor Law Commissioners.*"

With reference thereto the Commissioners stated that they were of opinion that the principle upon which the " Parish Ready Reckoner" was constructed was an exceedingly good one, and calculated to avoid fractional errors; and that if the limits of the tables were sufficiently extensive, the Commissioners did not think that neater or more useful tables for the purposes intended could be constructed. Assuming that the tables were accurately printed, the Commissioners thought that, with the exercise of ordinary care, it would be almost impossible to make a mistake in calculating the rates, &c.

---

2. ATTORNEY'S BILLS—WHO TO BE TAXED BY.

The following letter was received from the Peterborough Union:—

"*Peterborough, October* 7, 1841.

"GENTLEMEN,—With regard to the taxation of our bills against some of the parishes in the Peterborough Union for conducting appeals, making applications for orders of affiliation, &c. before the justices in Quarter Sessions and in Petty Sessions, we submit that the clerk of the peace is the proper officer to tax those bills. The expense of taxing before him is less than before a master in the Queen's Bench. We should be glad if the questions of the Board of Guardians upon this subject were settled, as we have several accounts against different parishes in this Union, for business, in the progress of which we have advanced several sums of money, which in the aggregate, amount to a considerable sum.

"We are, Gentlemen,
"Your very obedient servants,
"(Signed) ATKINSON and JENKINS.
"*The Poor Law Commissioners.*"

In reply, the Commissioners stated that the bill must be taxed in the Court where the business is done. Therefore when the business is done at the Quarter Sessions the clerk of the peace is the proper officer to tax the bill.

At the same time the masters of the Crown Office in London are accustomed to tax all bills for business done in criminal or Crown proceedings, but the taxation before them, would be more expensive than before the officers alluded to.

---

3. CENSUS EXPENSES—HOW TO BE INSERTED IN QUARTERLY ABSTRACT.

The following is a copy of a letter received from the clerk of the Guildford Union:—

"*Guildford, 7th December*, 1841.

"GENTLEMEN,—The payments on account of taking the census within this Union have been made, and will therefore be charged in the Union accounts for the present quarter; will you, therefore, have the kindness to inform me how you would have them inserted in the Union Quarterly Abstract, (Form No. 11,) whether before the column intituled 'Total Expenditure for the Relief of the Poor,' or after that intituled 'Vaccination Fees.'

"I have the honour to be,
"Gentlemen,
"Your most obedient servant,
"(Signed) G. S. SMALLPEICE.
"*The Poor Law Commissioners.*"

The Commissioners in reply stated, that payments on account of the recent census should be inserted in the Quarterly Abstract, schedule B. form 11, immediately after the column headed "Vaccination Fees," and ought not to be included in the column headed "Total Expenditure for the relief of the Poor."

The following is a copy of a Circular Letter on this subject transmitted to the clerks of Unions by direction of the Commissioners:—

Poor Law Commission Office,
Somerset House,
October 28th, 1841.

Population Enumeration Expenses.

SIR,—I am directed by the Poor Law Commissioners to state, that as it is very desirable that the expenses incurred under the Acts for taking the account of the Population of England and Wales, should be distinguished from the expenditure upon the relief of the poor, they recommend that a separate account should be opened in the ledger, to be entitled "Population Enumeration Expenses." In this account the clerk should enter all the sums paid by the Guardians under the provisions of the 5th Vict. c. 9, and the Commissioners think it will be expedient that when the Guardians shall have apportioned the total sum paid by them to the Superintendent Registrar among the several parishes of the Union, the apportionments charged to the parishes should be entered in a separate column in the quarterly abstract forwarded to the Commissioners.

I am, Sir, &c.
To the Clerk to the Guardians

LONDON:
Printed, by Order of the Poor Law Commissioners, by W. CLOWES and SONS, Stamford Street, and Published by CHARLES KNIGHT and Co., 22, Ludgate Street, Publishers to the Poor Law Commissioners.

AN

OFFICIAL CIRCULAR

OF PUBLIC DOCUMENTS AND INFORMATION:

DIRECTED BY THE POOR LAW COMMISSIONERS TO BE PRINTED, CHIEFLY FOR THE USE OF THE MEMBERS AND PERMANENT OFFICERS OF BOARDS OF GUARDIANS, UNDER THE POOR LAW AMENDMENT ACT.

No. 16. CIRCULAR ISSUED FEBRUARY 28TH, 1842.

Poor Law Commission Office,
Somerset House,
February 26, 1842.

THE Poor Law Commissioners, on a review of their minutes, directed that the minutes and correspondence on the following subjects should be printed and circulated for the information of Guardians and officers of the several Unions, viz.—

By order of the Board,

EDWIN CHADWICK, *Secretary.*

I.—ELECTION OF GUARDIANS.

THE order issued by the Poor Law Commissioners, dated January 25, 1841, placing the conduct of the election of Guardians under the superintendence of the Union clerks, under which order it may be observed the election of Guardians will continue to be conducted in the Unions and parishes to which that order has been issued until altered or rescinded by the Commissioners, was issued by them in consequence of the numerous irregularities, which took place in the progress of the election of Guardians, when conducted by churchwardens and overseers; and because the clerk is a paid and highly responsible officer, and has an opportunity of becoming better acquainted with the necessary forms of an election than the churchwardens and overseers,—has ordinarily less strong local interest than these officers in the result of the election, and, unlike them, cannot be a candidate for the office of a Guardian.

By their order the Commissioners have invested the clerk to the Guardians with all authority to conduct the election upon his own legal discretion and responsibility, without reservation of any appeal to themselves. They therefore confine themselves in any communication upon the subject of the order to a mere explanation of their views for the clerk's information only, and not for the purpose of controlling him in the exercise of his authority according to his own judgment.

The following are the days fixed by the order on which the several proceedings in reference to the election of Guardians in Unions are to be taken:—

1st March.—Last day for publishing notice of election.
10th March.—Time expires for overseers to distinguish in the rate-books, the persons who have paid their rates.
10th March.—Last day for sending in nomination papers.
14th March.—Time expires for persons nominated, to state their unwillingness to serve.
20th March.—Day for delivering voting papers.
23d March.—Day for collecting voting papers.
24th March.—Time for application to the clerk for voting papers (by persons who have not received such papers) expires.

Note.—Voting-papers so obtained must not be taken away, but must be filled up by the voter in the presence of the clerk, and delivered to him.

25th March.—First day of clerk's attendance at the Board-room to ascertain the validity of votes.

*** If any of the above dates happens to fall on a Sunday or Good Friday, the act required is to be done on the following day. The above dates do not apply to the orders issued to some of the parishes under Boards of Guardians.

The following are statements of opinions expressed by the Commissioners in reply to various questions which have been submitted to them with respect to the construction of the order and to the law affecting the election of Guardians generally.

Completion of arrangements at the times mentioned in the Order.

Every possible effort to complete the necessary arrangements at the times mentioned in the order should be made, as the mere convenience or expediency of a postponement would not justify it, and nothing short of an absolute impossibility duly to perform the several acts required by the order, would legally justify the delay.

Right of persons to be present at the Election.

It is generally desirable that the election should be conducted in such a manner as to prevent the possibility of any suspicion attaching to the officer conducting it so far as this is compatible with the progress of the election.

With this limitation the admission of all interested persons to be present at the election, is desirable. But the admission should only be for the purpose of witnessing the acts of the officer, and not with the view of determining his decisions otherwise than as he would make them in the conscientious and deliberate exercise of his individual judgment.

If, therefore, the clerk thinks fit to admit persons, it is proper that they should not interfere with his responsibility, nor even take any part in his deliberations, further than as he may invite them to afford him information or to give him the benefit of their opinions.

The Commissioners see little objection to the presence of any Guardian at the proceedings, and no objection at all if such Guardian be present, not to participate in them, but merely as a witness.

With reference to the admission and hearing of objections and arguments upon the allowance of votes, the clerk is not precluded from hearing anything which he thinks calculated to afford him information in the execution of his duties, but in doing so must exercise his individual judgment in each case, and if he decides upon hearing such objections or arguments, must take care that it does not involve a delay in the progress of the election, as provided for by the Commissioners' order.

Appointment of Officers to assist in the Election.

It will be proper for the clerk at any early period to bring the subject of the appointment of the persons necessary to assist him in conducting the election under the notice of the Guardians.

Qualification of Guardians.

1. The order does not in any way affect or vary the qualification of a guardian as prescribed in the order of election first issued.

2. To be qualified for the office of guardian a candidate must be rated in respect of rateable property of an annual rental of the amount stated in the order of declaration of union. It is the actual annual rental or value of the premises for which a person is rated that gives him a qualification as guardian; provided, therefore, that the value or rental is of the required amount, the sum at which the property is rated is immaterial.

The mere fact of being rated for premises of the required amount without occupation is sufficient to qualify a person to be elected.

It is not requisite that a person should reside in any particular parish in an union to render him eligible to be elected guardian for such parish; provided he be rated to the poor in some parish in the union, he will, if duly qualified in all other respects, be eligible as guardian for any of the said parishes.

The property composing the qualification may be dispersed through every parish in an union, and so that its aggregate annual value amount to the sum fixed as a qualification the qualification is perfect according to the provisions of the 38th section of the Poor Law Amendment Act.

3. In the case of joint occupations or partnerships, if the property be of such yearly value that it would yield, when divided amongst the partners interested in it, an amount to each equivalent to that fixed as the qualification for a guardian, each of such partners or occupiers would, if distinctly rated, be eligible to be elected guardian; where the property is not sufficient to yield a qualification for all the partners, that partner would be eligible who should be distinctly rated in respect of such property.

4. The clerk is empowered by the recently issued order to inquire into the qualification of any person proposed as guardian, and to hear and determine objections concerning the same.

5. Holding the office of registrar of births and deaths does not disqualify a person from being elected guardian. But a registrar by becoming a guardian becomes disqualified as a registrar, except in the case provided by the general rule issued by the registrar-general on the 10th October, 1836, which is in the following terms:—" A registrar shall not be a member of any Board of Guardians by whom he shall be appointed registrar, unless, upon a representation to be made in writing and signed by two-thirds of the remaining members of such board, it shall be made to appear to the satisfaction of the registrar-general, to be signified under his hand, that there is no other person resident within the district capable and willing to undertake the said office of registrar."

Nomination Papers. Who to receive. Duties of Clerk, &c.

1. It is not desirable to cast upon overseers or any other unpaid officer where it can be avoided, the duty of receiving nomination papers. It will be proper to employ any paid officer of the Union, as relieving officer, workhouse master, or paid officers of the parish, such as collectors of rates. The clerk as superintendent-registrar will in some cases find it convenient, under the sanction of the guardians, to employ the registrars and the deputy registrars. In some cases, paid officers of police, or the local paid officers resident in the parish will undertake the receipt of the nomination papers. It is only when all these means fail, that it will be necessary to appoint a private person. It will, however, usually be easy to select in every parish in which such selection may be necessary, a person fit and competent to perform so easy a service as the mere receipt and delivery to the clerk of nomination papers.

2. The persons appointed to receive nomi-

nation papers, and to collect voting papers, need not be the same. The latter may be appointed, when it has been ascertained by the nominations in what parishes the elections will be contested. Still it is advisable generally, that the persons employed in one duty, should be employed in the other.

3. There is no objection to a person being appointed to receive the nominations for his own parish, and for others adjoining, provided there be a place named in each parish, at which nominations will be received by the persons employed to receive them. But it would not be in conformity with the intention of the Commissioners' order, if parishioners should be required to deliver their nominations at any place out of the parish.

4. The fact of a nomination paper being delivered at the residence of the clerk instead of the person appointed by the clerk to receive such papers, or at the place named for their reception, does not vitiate the nomination. The Commissioners consider that such nomination would properly be admitted, presuming that it was delivered within the prescribed time.

5. A nomination paper left with the person appointed to receive nominations within the time named in the order, but not forwarded by the latter to the clerk until after the expiration of that time should be admitted.

6. Though a nomination paper may differ from the prescribed form, still, if it contains all the material particulars required by that form, it may be considered valid.

Nomination of Candidates. Who qualified to Nominate. Duties of Clerk, &c.

1. It is the duty of the clerk to ascertain (whether objection be made or not) the qualification of the parties respectively nominating and proposed as Guardians, and to reject any nomination where either party is disqualified. He must inform himself of the fact of qualification, according to the means available for that purpose, and by what he can ascertain from any documents which it is in his power to consult, as the rate-book for instance.

2. If a person be entitled to vote as owner, he may in that capacity nominate a person as Guardian, though he may not have paid his rates as required by the 40th section of the Poor Law Amendment Act, in the case of a rate-payer.

But if he claim to nominate in his capacity as rate-payer, then it must appear that he is duly qualified to vote as rate-payer by having been rated for the prescribed period, and having paid all the parochial rates and assessments made upon him for the year immediately preceding his so voting or acting (except such as may have become due within the last six mon hs).

3. An owner or rate payer qualified to vote in a parish is entitled to nominate for the office of Guardian any person or number of persons legally qualified to be elected for that office not exceeding the number of Guardians to be elected for such parish. If a person nominates more, then such nomination is void as to all for uncertainty.

4. Though it might appear in the published list of candidates that certain persons were proposed by a person in the capacity of owner when such person was not qualified in law to vote as owner, (not having complied with the 40th section of the Poor Law Amendment Act,) the Commissioners do not think that such an inaccuracy would invalidate the nomination, provided the proposer was, at the time of the nomination, legally entitled to vote as a rate-payer in the parish for which the nomination was made.

5. If the calling of the person nominated be omitted, but he can still be identified throughout the parish, and distinguished from all other persons by the description in the nomination, the nomination is good.

6. The form of nomination requires that the address of the proposer should be inserted, and where it is omitted, the clerk is justified in treating the nomination as informal.

7. A rate-payer can only propose a Guardian for that parish in which he is entitled to vote as rate-payer.

8. Where in any case there has been a total omission to nominate candidates within the time prescribed by the order, or where the proper number has not been nominated, the order does not give any discretion to the clerk to receive nominations after such period.

9. If more than the proper number be nominated, and all above such number signify to the clerk their unwillingness to act, the names of all the candidates proposed must nevertheless

be put to the vote. But the clerk should, in such case, state in the voting paper opposite to the names of the persons so declining to act, that they are unwilling to serve the office.

10. If only the proper number of candidates be nominated, and some of them declare their unwillingness to act, they must nevertheless be all returned; and in such case the nomination stands in place of election by the whole constituency, and, with the return, will constitute the election of the candidates.

11. If less than the proper number of guardians are nominated for a parish, then those guardians who are properly nominated will be returned as elected, and the parish will be represented by those guardians instead of the full number which it was entitled to elect.

12. If no nomination has taken place, it is evident that no return can be made by the clerk for the parish; the affairs of the parish will in such case be attended to by the remaining members of the Board of Guardians.

13. When a person has been once nominated, the nomination cannot be withdrawn, although the person proposed should consent to the withdrawal by the proposer: but the election must proceed.

The Commissioners have always recognized the importance of the power to receive resignations of candidates, but nevertheless they are satisfied it is not competent to any proposer of a candidate to withdraw his nomination. When once duly nominated, the right to elect a candidate is the right of the whole constituency, and no individual can claim the right to withdraw him. If such a withdrawal were allowed, it is obvious that in addition to the legal anomalies it would introduce, the greatest opportunity would be afforded for frauds, inasmuch as parties might propose candidates who would be most likely to be returned with the intention of withdrawing the nomination when it was too late for any other party to nominate them again.

14. Neither the overseer nor any other officer of the parish can be required to nominate a guardian; an overseer can only do so in his capacity of owner or rate-payer, and whether he thinks fit to exercise his right or not is altogether a matter within his own discretion.

15. In the case of the whole of a parish being in the possession of one person, the usual form of nomination, and all other forms of election, should be gone through before that person can take his seat at the Board, as any owner or rate-payer is entitled to propose himself as guardian.

Voting Papers. Who to deliver and collect. How to be filled up. Duties of Clerk.

1. The paid officers of the Union should be employed in distributing or collecting the voting papers in preference to the overseers.

2. It is not the intention of the order to cast upon the clerk the duty of delivering voting papers to rate-payers not supplying the clerk with some address (which need not be the place of residence of the rate-payer) within the parish in which the election takes place; but it is competent to the clerk, and, indeed, desirable, that he should, if it be possible, announce that non-resident (but none other) rate-payers may name an address at which the voting papers may be left and collected. As this course may, however, when many voting papers are left at one address, lead to irregularities, it will be necessary that the clerk should give an especial attention to the voting papers so left and collected.

3. If owners and proxies have any address within the parish, whether their respective residences or not, it is the duty of the clerk to cause voting papers to be delivered at such address. And if the owners and proxies, not resident and giving no such address, apply on the day of delivery to the clerk or his assistants at the place of election they should be supplied with papers, such place being fairly to be considered for the purpose their place of address within the parish. But no duty is imposed on the clerk to distribute papers beyond the limits of the parish concerned.

4. The names of all the proposers should, if practicable, be inserted in the voting papers; but, if the space will not allow of this being done, the name of one proposer will be sufficient, adding thereto the words "and others."

5. Voting papers, filled up with all the material particulars and duly signed, are not invalidated by the addition of any superfluous matter. If defective in any material particular, as for instance, if not duly signed, or if the voter has omitted to place his initials opposite the name of the person for whom he votes, it must be disallowed.

6. Votes ought not to be admitted where the voting-papers have been filled up by the wives of the voters.

7. Any voting papers collected in any other manner than that directed by the order of the Commissioners, and by the person authorized to collect, ought not to be received by the officers conducting the election, or if received should not be included in the calculation of votes.

8. In the case of the clerk or his assistants either not filling up the voting papers or filling them up erroneously by inserting a wrong number of votes, the omission or the inaccuracy in nowise affects the right to vote of the constituency. The number of votes is not to be ascertained by the voter, but to be inserted in the voting papers before the papers are issued.

9. When the voter cannot write, the initials of the witness must be placed opposite the names of the chosen candidates, but the mark of the person voting must be attested by the witness.

In the case of proxies, the initials of the proxy, not of the principal, must be placed against the names of the persons for whom the proxy votes.

Owners' Votes—Owners' and Proxies' Claims—Duties of Clerk.

1. The clerk, under the recent order, is to decide whether persons have properly established their claim to vote as owners by making the statement required of them under the 40th section of the Poor Law Amendment Act. The overseers are bound to enter in the rate-book, or in some book to be provided for the purpose, the names of the parties making such statements.

The clerk, however, is not concluded by that book, but is at liberty to receive other evidence as to an owner having made a statement, and as to the correct insertion of his name in the registry.

2. Any owner of rateable property is entitled to vote who complies with the directions as to owners, contained in the 40th section Poor Law Amendment Act. By rateable property the Commissioners understand property which is legally liable to be assessed to the poor-rate, as distinguished from property which is not the subject of assessment, and they do not consider it essential, as far as the owner's right to vote is affected, that the property should be actually assessed at the time of voting. The fact therefore of a house being unoccupied, or not rated at the time of voting would not affect the right of the owner to vote in respect of it provided he had complied with the 40th section of the Poor Law Amendment Act.

3. Owners who have once made their claim to vote in the manner required by the 40th section of the Poor Law Amendment Act, need not renew such claims every year to entitle them to vote, but such claims remain in force.

4. Where an overseer may have omitted to enter in the rate, or some other book to be provided for the purpose, the claims of owners, or the proxies of such owners in the manner directed by the 40th section of the Poor Law Amendment Act, such overseer is subject to penal consequences for the neglect; but the rights of the parties are in no way prejudiced by the omission of the overseer, and the claims of such owners and proxies, if otherwise valid, should be allowed in the calculation of votes.

5. Owners under the Poor Law Amendment Act are entitled to the same number and proportion of votes as is provided by the Acts 58 Geo. III. c. 69, and 59 Geo. III. c. 85. The number of votes is to be estimated according to the amount at which the property is assessed, not at the amount which is to be collected.

6. The Poor Law Amendment Act only authorizes the appointment of a proxy by owners and does not allow such an appointment by occupiers. A person therefore who is both owner and occupier of property cannot appoint a person to vote for him in both capacities; and unless he vote himself in his capacity of rate-payer, the vote of another on his behalf could not be received or allowed.

7. Where a proxy omits to sign his own name, and to state in writing the person for whom he is proxy, such omission will invalidate the vote.

8. The appointment of proxy supersedes the owner's claim to vote until that appointment is revoked.

9. The 40th section of the Poor Law Amendment Act enables either the owner or the proxy to make the statement of the qualifying

property, and the proxy's statement, claim, and production of appointment, enables him to vote without any independent claim by the owner himself.

10. It is not necessary, however desirable, that the proxy's statement of the property, as proxy to the owner whereof he claims to vote, should be signed by the proxy. The owner's appointment of proxy must be under the owner's hand, that is, either written or signed by him; but if written by him it need not be signed with his name.

11. Where nothing appears to show the portion of the charge borne by respective joint owners or occupiers, it is to be presumed that each is equally interested, and their votes should be allowed accordingly. But where either claims a preponderant share in the property, and shows his liability to a greater charge in respect of it than another joint occupier, he will be entitled to a proportionate increase in the votes where the number of votes conferred by the property allows of it. In such case the principle of the 58th Geo. III. c. 69, sec. 3, which must in this matter be considered and construed as part of the Poor Law Amendment Act, clearly applies.

Votes of Occupiers.

1. If the occupiers' names are inserted in the rate, any voluntary and private understanding by which the landlords may undertake to pay would not deprive the occupier of his rights as a rate-payer, as he would remain liable to all the obligations to pay, and all the consequences of non-payment, and the payment by the landlord would confer the same rights as payment by the occupier himself or by his agent. This has been so held when the subject of paying rates was in question as conferring a settlement.

The case would be different if the landlord has been rated under the provision of the 59th Geo. III., c. 12. or any local Act; the occupiers in such case would not remain liable to the obligations of rate-payers nor entitled to their rights and privileges.

Upon the first supposition, therefore, viz., that the occupier is rated, the Commissioners conceive that a payment of the rate by the landlord would be considered a sufficient payment by the tenant, to entitle the latter to vote.

2. Presuming that there is no local Act affecting the rateability of occupiers of property, it appears to the Commissioners, that under the general law, lodgers occupying portions of houses cannot be rated or considered as "rate payers," except in the cases to which the provisions of the 2nd and 3rd Wm. IV. (Reform Act) sec. 30, and the 5th and 6th Wm. IV. cap. 76 (Municipal Corporation Act), sec. 11, apply. Under the general law occupiers of "tenements" are not made rateable, but occupiers of "lands, houses, &c.;" and as respects occupiers of houses, it is clear that it is the occupier of the whole house, not the several occupiers of several parts of the house, who must be rated, and would, consequently, be the party to vote at the election of guardians.

Votes of Paid Officers.

1. Although the clerk of a Union is not expressly prohibited by the order of election from nominating or voting for candidates, or otherwise taking a part in the election of guardians, yet, inasmuch as the management of the election is entrusted to him by the order, the Commissioners think that he would act very improperly if he were to do anything which showed a preference for any candidate.

2. Considering the relation in which an auditor stands to the Board of Guardians, the Commissioners think that he would act wisely in abstaining from giving his vote in any contest for an election of guardians.

The Commissioners are of opinion that public canvassing by an auditor for a guardian (even though the canvass should be made in behalf of another person) is more objectionable than his voting, and the Commissioners would advise an auditor to abstain, while he holds the office of auditor, from taking any public part in any election of guardians.

The Commissioners would be prepared to take very serious notice of the conduct of any officer of a Union employed in the election against whom any act of partiality or undue interference should be proved.

Voting—Miscellaneous.

1. To be entitled to vote, a rate-payer, owner, or proxy must be fully and completely qualified on the day on which the voting papers are to be delivered, the receipt of the voting papers

in the manner prescribed by the order being part of the mode of voting directed by the order; and if not qualified by that time the party loses his opportunity to vote, as given by the order.

2. A person having one vote as owner or rate payer in a parish electing more guardians than one, is entitled to give one vote to each of the candidates (to the amount of the number of guardians to be elected); and if he have six votes as owner, and three as rate payer, he may give the whole number of nine votes to each candidate A person having nine votes cannot, under any circumstances, give more than nine votes to any one candidate; but he may, if he think fit, vote only for one candidate, and refrain from voting for any of the other candidates.

3. Female rate payers and owners of property not married are entitled to vote in the election of guardians.

4. Married women, being owners of property in their own right, are not entitled to vote in the election of Guardians under the Poor Law Amendment Act. The Commissioners do not think it would make any difference as regards the right to vote if the property were settled, on the marriage, to the separate use of the wife.

The fact of the marriage, in the opinion of the Commissioners, revokes all proxies appointed by a woman prior to the marriage.

5. In the case of two candidates having an equal number of votes, neither candidate can be returned as having been duly elected.

6. The clerk is bound to disallow every vote which he may consider not to have been given by a person entitled to vote. The delivery of the voting paper to a person not otherwise entitled to vote, cannot confer on such a party a right to vote, or to have his vote allowed.

7. If any person entitled to vote has not received a voting paper, and the failure has not occurred through his own default, it would be proper for the clerk to allow the party to vote, provided he apply for and fill up a voting paper in the manner required by Article 21 of the order.

8. If the clerk has good reason to consider any person entitled to vote who may not have been declared so by the churchwardens and overseers, he may properly deliver to such person a voting paper and receive his vote.

9. There is nothing in the Poor Law Amendment Act, or in the rules of the Commissioners, to prevent a person from voting, who may have received relief, provided such person is in other respects qualified to vote as a rate-payer.

10. A person is only entitled to vote as a rate-payer in the election of guardians for the parish in which he is a rate-payer. In like manner an owner can only vote for the parish in which the property is situate.

11. It is the amount of assessment which, in the case of owners and rate-payers, determines the number of votes to which they are respectively entitled. The gross value of property is not the subject of the assessment, and the number of votes should be calculated on the net value, which is the subject of the assessment, or, in other words, on the "rateable value."

Construction of the word Month.

The construction of the word 'month' in Acts of Parliament appears to be settled, beyond a doubt, and where the word 'month' is alone used without the word 'calendar,' or anything else in the Act to show that 'calendar month' is intended, the rule is clear that the word must be understood to mean a 'lunar' month.

Expenses of conducting the Election.

1. It was contemplated by the order providing for the payment of election expenses, that the compensation to be awarded to the clerk under Article 3, and the allowance upon the population in case of contests under Article 4, should cover all the expenses for services or assistance in carrying the order into effect.

2. The cost of providing the forms B. and C. contained in the order of election should be charged to the persons who apply for such forms. Where the overseers of a parish may not themselves procure a book for registering the statement of owners, it would be proper for the clerk to see that one is provided and charged to such parish.

II.—CONTRACTS. — APOLOGY AND COMPENSATION BY A CONTRACTOR FOR SUPPLYING ADULTERATED SUGAR AND TEA THAT HAD BEEN IMMERSED IN SALT WATER.

The Board of Guardians of the West Ham Union have placed in the hands of the Poor Law Commissioners the following letter from

J. Percival, a person who formerly contracted for the supply of tea and sugar to their workhouse. The Commissioners have thought it right to print this letter, together with that addressed to the Board of Guardians by the Poor Law Commissioners on the 24th day of February instant.

"*Valentine Place, Blackfriars Road,*
"*January* 20, 1842.

"GENTLEMEN,—I beg to express my regret for having supplied the West Ham Union with tea that had been immersed in salt-water and sugar that had been adulterated; and, in consideration of the Board of Guardians withdrawing their action, and abstaining from proceedings against me, I hereby agree to pay the bill of costs of their solicitor, as between attorney and client, incurred in and previous to such proceedings against me, and to pay 5*l.* to any charitable purpose the Board of Guardians may point out. But the Board of Guardians of the West Ham Union are not to publish this letter further than by transmitting the same, (if they think proper,) or a copy of it, to the Poor Law Commissioners, to be made such use of as they the Poor Law Commissioners may think fit, but not for the purpose of prosecution, or of taking other proceedings.

(Signed) "J. PERCIVAL.

"*To the Guardians of the*
"*West Ham Union.*"

Poor Law Commission Office,
Somerset House,
February 24, 1842.

SIR,—The Poor Law Commissioners have received, through the hands of Mr. W. S. Fry, the letter addressed by J. Percival to the Board of Guardians of the West Ham Union, acknowledging the fraud committed by him in supplying damaged tea and adulterated sugar to the guardians, and offering to pay the costs incurred, together with a sum of 5*l.* to any charitable purpose, if the guardians would consent to compromise the action commenced against him.

When a deputation of the Board of Guardians waited on the Poor Law Commissioners in the month of August last, for the purpose of consulting them as to the course to be pursued, the Commissioners felt great pleasure in witnessing the readiness of the guardians to defend the interests of the rate-payers and of the poor, and recommended the adoption of legal proceedings against Mr. Percival.

The Commissioners now rejoice to find that the proceedings in question are brought to a satisfactory termination, and they will consider the expediency of printing Mr. Percival's letter in their "Official Circular" as a warning to contractors similarly circumstanced, and as a proof that Boards of Guardians have the means, if they exercise proper vigilance, of effectually protecting their own body and the poor against any frauds which may be attempted.

I am, Sir,
Your most obedient servant,
(Signed) E. CHADWICK, *Secretary.*

S. Richardson, Esq.,
Clerk of West Ham Union,
Leytonstone, Essex.

III.—GUARDIANS — EXPENSES INCURRED BY, IN TAKING OPINION OF COUNSEL AS TO THE RATING OF CERTAIN PROPERTY—DISALLOWANCE OF BY AUDITOR.

The Commissioners took into consideration a letter from the clerk to the guardians of the Ulverstone Union upon the subject of certain expenses incurred by the Board of Guardians of the Ulverstone Union in taking the opinion of counsel as to rating property belonging to the Ulverstone Canal Company, and stating that an objection has been made to the allowance of such costs by the auditor, in consequence of a notice from the churchwardens and overseers of Ulverstone, setting forth that the expenditure was not incurred with their sanction, but contrary to their wishes.

The Commissioners also took into consideration a resolution of the guardians with respect to the conduct of the professional business of the several parishes and townships in the Union.

In reference thereto the Commissioners stated that it appeared to them that the matter was not one which came within the province of the guardians, or in which they could give any directions which could bind the parish officers of Ulverstone. The question was as to the liability of certain property to be rated to the poor rate of that parish, and was therefore one for the exclusive consideration of those persons to whom the law has entrusted the duty of making the rate. The guardians are not those persons.

Although the Commissioners entertain no doubt that the guardians pursued the course indicated in the clerk's letter, from a desire of setting a doubtful question at rest, and of avoiding litigation, and of benefiting the poor rates of the parish of Ulverstone, the Commissioners cannot say, for the reason above expressed, that the guardians were justified in ordering the opinion to be taken, and the expenses to be paid out of the poor-rates of Ulverstone. The Commissioners think therefore, that, considered in a legal point of view, the objection taken to the allowance must prevail.

The Commissioners have to add with respect to the resolution passed by the guardians as to the conduct of the professional business of the several parishes and townships, that the guardians cannot, in the present state of the law, give any directions as to the management of legal proceedings, which exclusively affect individual parishes or townships, which will be binding upon the overseers of such parishes or townships.

IV.—PAID OFFICERS:—1. AS TO POWER OF CLERK TO INTERFERE WITH THE MANAGEMENT OF THE WORKHOUSE.

The following is a copy of a letter received from the master of the Croydon Union workhouse:—

"*Croydon Union, Duppas Hill,*
"*January* 13, 1841.

"GENTLEMEN,—Permit me in the most respectful manner to ask you how far the clerk of the Union has power to interfere with the interior of the house over which I preside as master? Can he give an order for persons to be admitted into the house to see paupers against the wish of the master?

"I have the honour to be,
"Gentlemen,
"Your most obedient humble servant,
(Signed) "HUNGERFORD LUTTRELL.

"*The Poor Law Commissioners.*"

The Commissioners referred the letter to the Board of Guardians, and in reply stated, that the office which the clerk holds does not of itself confer upon him any power to interfere with the management or discipline of the workhouse, or to admit persons to see paupers maintained in the house.

But the clerk, as the officer or agent of the Board, may interfere to see that the orders of the guardians, as regards the management of the house, are carried out, if authorized by the guardians to do so.

---

2. ALLEGED NEGLECT OF ONE OF THE MEDICAL OFFICERS OF THE CHARD UNION IN THE CASE OF A DECEASED PAUPER.

The Commissioners took into consideration a copy of depositions taken by Colonel Wade upon an inquiry into a charge of neglect against Mr. Mules, one of the medical officers of the Chard Union, in the case of Ann Robins, a deceased pauper.

In reference thereto, the Commissioners directed the following letter to be written to the Board of Guardians.

"The statements of Thomas Binham, the brother of the deceased, being contradicted in different particulars, not only by Dr. Mules, the father of the medical officer, but also by Daniel Edward Hamilton, his apprentice, and by the daughter of the relieving officer, the Commissioners think that the accuracy of his evidence cannot be relied on.

"The Commissioners are of opinion that Mr. Mules was not aware of the application made by Thomas Binham on the afternoon of 1st November, and that on hearing of the case the following morning, when Binham first brought an order from the relieving officer for his attendance, he took immediate steps to prescribe for and visit Ann Robins. Unfortunately, however, as is proved by the evidence, the poor woman was actually dead at the time the case was first mentioned to him.

"With regard to the application made by Thomas Binham at the surgery of Mr. Mules on the 1st November, it appears that he did not bring an order from the relieving officer for Mr. Mules's attendance, although directed by the apprentice of Mr. Mules to procure it, and that he did not represent the case to be a very urgent one. There was, therefore, no legal obligation on Mr. Mules to have visited the case, which indeed was not reported to him by his apprentice.

"On these grounds, the Commissioners are of opinion, that no charge of neglect is established personally against Mr. Mules.

"It remains to consider whether the neglect or the defective arrangements of the officers of the Union prevented Thomas Binham from making his application in the proper form, so as to have procured earlier attention to his sister's case.

"It is alleged by him—

"1. That he did apply on the 1st November to the relieving officer for an order, but that he could not procure it, the relieving officer not being at home.

"2. That on returning to the surgery of Mr. Mules a second time he found no one there, and could make no one hear.

"On the first point, the discrepancy between the evidence of Thomas Binham as to the time and circumstances under which the alleged application to the relieving officer was made, and that of Dr. Mules and of D. E. Hamilton, throws great doubt upon the statement of the former respecting his application to the relieving officer, and it is positively denied by the daughter of the relieving officer, who was examined by Colonel Wade upon the point, that any such application was made. It is admitted, however, that the relieving officer was from home during part of the evening in question, and the Commissioners think it indispensable that the relieving officer should leave directions with regard to any applications which may be made during his absence. They request that the Guardians will see that this is attended to in future.

"On the second question, it is acknowledged by D. E. Hamilton, that about three quarters of an hour after Thomas Binham's first application he went away, leaving no one in the surgery, and that there is no bell or knocker to the surgery. It is alleged that the surgery was not locked, and that the servants were in the house which adjoins; but the Commissioners think that this is not sufficient, and that some one should always be left in charge to give an answer to any person who may apply at the surgery in the absence of Mr. Mules or his apprentice.

"The Commissioners are also of opinion that every application, although it may not be accompanied by an order of the relieving officer, should, if made during the absence of the medical officer, be reported to him on his return.

"The Commissioners trust that such precautions will be taken for the future as will give every facility to persons applying for medical relief.

"It is painful to consider, that in the case adverted to in this letter, the poor woman died without medical assistance being afforded to her, although the Commissioners think that if Thomas Binham had been aware of the urgency of the case, and had made greater exertions, he might have procured it."

V.—RELIEF.—1. EFFECTS OF THE PROHIBITORY ORDER ON A MANUFACTURING POPULATION DURING A DEPRESSION OF TRADE.

The following is a copy of a Report received from Mr. Senior, one of the Assistant Commissioners, on the effects of the Prohibitory Order, recently issued by the Commissioners.

"*Cuckney, January* 20, 1842.

"*Effects of Prohibitory Order*

"GENTLEMEN,—I think it desirable to bring under your notice an additional illustration of the pecuniary results of a strict adherence to the provisions of the Prohibitory Order in a manufacturing population during a period of depression in trade.

"It appears that, in the Radford Union, 121 able-bodied persons, either males or deserted wives, have applied for relief to the Radford Board of Guardians from September 25, 1838, to September 25, 1841, and been offered the workhouse. Of the above number, 76 stated themselves to be totally out of work; 29 partially employed; 16 deserted women. Total number of persons comprising the families of the above number of cases 455.

"Of the previous number of (121) cases to whom the workhouse was offered—

12 have accepted it, stating themselves to be totally out of work.
2 partially employed.
5 deserted women.

Total 19, or one person in six to whom the offer was made.

"Total cost in the workhouse of the 19 persons during the period they remained in it, including the cost of their families, amounting to 70, was 137*l.* 12*s.*, or an average of 7*l.* 4*s.* 10*d.*

"But the amount given to 13 cases in out-door relief previous to the completion of the workhouse, to all of whom the house was then offered, and accepted only by four, their cases being included in the 121 before mentioned, was 95*l.* 2*s.* 2*d.*, or on an average of 7*l.* 6*s.* 4*d.* per case.

"Now, had the Union been unprovided with a workhouse, or had the Guardians acted on that common fallacy of granting out-door relief on its supposed superior economy, the usual argument being that, as a family of seven persons will accept a weekly allowance of 12*s.*, and that in-door relief would cost 21*s.*, that the former would be the cheapest to the parish, forgetting that experience shows, as in the present instance, that but few able-bodied persons accept the workhouse, and that those few usually remain there but a short time; and assuming even that no fresh applications had been made to the Board in consequence of the easy terms on which the relief was afforded, the cost of the out-relief on the previous average of 7*l.* 6*s.* 4*d.*, deducting the actual expenses of the in-maintenance, would have been 700*l.* instead of 137*l.*

"But the most remarkable point in the table is, the very small number of able-bodied who have applied to the Board for relief during the three years, (of a bad state of trade,) the applications averaging less than one per week, showing that the labouring classes had learnt that they must rely on their own exertions for their support.

"It is also worthy of observation, that so bad was the previous management prior to the change of the law in the parishes of Radford, Lenton, and Snenton, which now comprise the Radford Union, that the Guardians of the late Basford Incorporation stipulated in writing with the then Assistant Commissioner, previous to consenting to the dissolution of the incorporation, that neither of those parishes was to form part of the New Basford Union.

"On the formation of the Radford Union the Guardians immediately consented to build a new workhouse, and have since most ably administered the law; whereas the Guardians of the adjoining Basford Union, with a population precisely similarly employed, having declined to make the necessary additions to their workhouse, have been obliged to grant out-relief to the able-bodied; and the increase on the last quarter's expenditure, as compared with that of the corresponding quarter of the previous year, was 1,521*l*, and the weekly out-door relief being 248*l.*, or more than double the weekly relief of two years ago: and so difficult has it been found to collect the rates, that the relieving officers have been obliged to borrow money on their personal security to relieve the poor.

"I have the honour to be,
"Gentlemen,
"Your obedient servant,
(Signed) "EDWARD SENIOR,
"*Assistant Commissioner.*

"*The Poor Law Commissioners.*"

2. RELIEF OF CASUAL POOR—TO WHAT PARISH, AND HOW TO BE CHARGED.

The following is a copy of a resolution of the Board of Guardians of the Foleshill Union:—

"Resolved—That the clerk write to the Commissioners, requesting their opinion whether a casual pauper applying to the relieving officer for relief on the ground of destitution must be considered as belonging to the parish in which he slept the night preceding such application; and if such parish be situated out of the Union, to what parish within the Union must the expense of relieving such casual poor be charged—must it be considered an establishment charge? And supposing an order of removal become necessary, to what parish within the Union must the expense of litigation be charged; or must this also be an establishment charge?

(Signed) "RICHARD DEWES,
"*Clerk to the Board.*"

In reference thereto, the Commissioners stated that the relief given to casual poor cannot in the present state of the law be made an establishment charge, as the law undoubtedly requires that such poor should be relieved at the cost of the parish in which the destitution occurs.

The parish in which the pauper sleeps the night preceding the application may not always be the parish liable for the relief. The fact of the pauper being destitute in any given parish, and not that of his having slept therein, creates the liability of such parish to afford relief. But where both parishes are situate in the same Union, and the destitution seems to have existed in the parish in which the pauper slept, and application is made for relief in another parish, which the pauper only enters for that purpose on account of the relieving officer residing there, or the workhouse being situated there, the proper and legal course appears to be to charge the relief to the parish in which the pauper slept. The accidental circumstance of the application for relief being made in the parish where the relieving officer may reside, or the workhouse be situate, does not relieve the parish in which the destitution occurs from the obligation which is cast upon it to maintain its own poor, whether settled or casually chargeable, and the application is virtually made in such parish.

Where a pauper applies to the relieving officer for relief, having slept the preceding night in a parish not within the Union, there appears to be no alternative but to treat the pauper as destitute where the application is made for relief, as the guardians cannot enforce the liability against the parish where the pauper slept.

VI.—OPERATION OF THE NEW POOR LAW IN THE DUNMOW UNION.

The following is a communication received from the Rev. J. P. H. Chesshyre, chairman of the Dunmow Union.

"*Lower Easton Rectory, Dunmow,*
"*February* 7, 1842.

"GENTLEMEN,—It was my intention to have published a sheet pamphlet on the beneficial results of the Poor Law in this neighbourhood, in the improvement of the condition and habits of the labouring poor; but I found that the public was already encumbered by pamphlets on this subject, so that I gave up my intention: but, as some facts may be interesting to you, I venture to trouble you with a short detail of them.

Even under the old system of organized pauperism, which existed in this neighbourhood 12 years ago, there were some benevolent individuals who indulged the hope that the labouring class, in spite of the strong inducements to improvidence which that system held out, might be persuaded into an honest desire of independence, and into habits of economical prudence. In the year 1832, the then vicar of Dunmow,* aided by the exertions of some of his reverend brethren and several influential tradesmen and farmers, established a Friendly Society on the improved system of mutual assurance. This society, carried on by the contributions and voluntary services of the honorary members, offers to its ordinary members the advantages of a provision in sickness and old age for a very low annual payment. Some (and I confess that I was one) thought the success of this society hopeless under existing circumstances; for we had seen most of the old friendly societies broken up or fallen into decay, and it did not appear probable that the labouring class could be persuaded to lay up a provision for that for which they knew the parish would provide. The individuals, however, who had commenced the undertaking would not despair, and by the best arrangements and most indefatigable exertions, as will be seen by the following statement, enrolled in the first year 164 members.

"STATEMENT of the Funds and Numbers of the Members of the Dunmow Friendly Society, from its commencement in 1832.

	Capital.			Numbers.	Description of Members.		
					Females.	Labourers	Artisans.
	£.	s.	d.				
Oct. 1833 .	174	18	2½	164	9	78	77
April, 1834	241	0	8½	159	10	75	74
" 1835	330	15	0½	188	9	85	94
" 1836	462	8	0¾	222	16	100	106
" 1837	607	10	2½	357	26	193	138
" 1838	1,004	11	10¾	497	38	300	159
" 1839	1,339	17	0¼	556	39	343	174
" 1840	1,618	15	3¼	556	43	344	169
" 1841	1,932	15	3¼	616	49	388	179
Oct. 30,	2,163	14	4	687	56	427	204

"To this statement I request particular attention. Observe, in the second year, a decrease of the number of the members. In the year 1836, the New Poor Law was in full operation; and, in 1837, we find an addition of 135 members, 93 of whom were labourers: whereas, up to this time, the majority of the new members were artisans. In 1838 there was an addition of 140, of whom 107 were labourers; in 1839, 59, of whom 43 were labourers. During this period the society had taken in one new district; but, at the same time, various friendly clubs, either on the old principle or offering greater advantages from higher gratuitous contributions, had sprung up in the neighbourhood. In 1839, a misunderstanding with some distant members, and their withdrawal in consequence, gave a check to the increase of numbers; but we find the society immediately rallying, and, in the last return, 427 labourers are enrolled, being more than double the number of artisans, which class, shortly after the commencement, was the most numerous. As the society is unwilling to extend its operations, its increase in numbers must now be slow; for, in some parishes, every young labourer is enrolled in this or some other similar society.

"In the returns of the Dunmow Savings' Banks, although not materially depending on the savings of the labouring class, an increase is found in these years wherein the Poor Law had become generally known, and might be supposed to warn the poor that the improvident could no longer command a provision on their own terms from the poor rates.

Dunmow Savings' Bank.—Open Deposit Accounts.

1834	385	£12,222
1835	407	12,982
1836	437	13,753
1837	485	15,157
1838	523	15,247
1839	571	16,121
1840	605	17,641
1841	609	18,293

"Under the old Poor Law, few of the labourers' wives either earned anything or saved anything; they looked to the parish or charitable individuals to furnish them with the necessaries of apparel. Clothing clubs had been established in several parishes, but with small success. In the two parishes under my own care, I was disappointed in all my applications to the poor to lay by something for this purpose; the constant answer was that they were never allowed extra earnings, the parish allowance being always withheld in hay and gleaning times. As soon as the new law was fully known, I made another attempt to bring the labourers and their wives to a sense that they must depend on themselves, or expect no clothing from the parish rates, except that which would be provided for them in the workhouse. This year, out of a population of less than 400, 56 women have laid out their savings, averaging each 13*s*., with the addition of 3*s*. 9*d*. from the contributions of charitable individuals to the fund. Among the above are the

* The Rev. J. Smith, a brother-in-law to the Bishop of London.

wives of two labourers not earning more than 10*s.* a-week, each with five very small children. These women have paid their subscriptions regularly for the last four years. On my asking one of them how she could afford to pay to the clothing club better now than under the old law, her answer was, 'We work all we can, and lay by all we can; and my husband often gives me a shilling which, if not for the club, might be spent at the beer-house.'

"In the above observations I have confined myself to facts about which I am certain. Clothing clubs are general in every parish, and in some are more successful than in my own.

"The success, then, of friendly societies, the increase in the savings' banks, the spread and popularity among the lower classes of clothing clubs, coal clubs, and medical clubs, all taking place in the same years, and all evidently receiving an extraordinary impulse in these very years in which the new Poor Law had become generally known, may fairly be looked upon as results of the operation of that law; and, from my experience, I am quite convinced that, were the law repealed, or a system of out-door relief again encouraged, an immediate decrease in all these beneficial institutions would follow; and in the course of a very few years the habits of industry and providence which the poor have already adopted would be discarded and forgotten.

"Among the happiest results of the amended administration of the laws of relief I must reckon the tendency that it has to direct the charity of benevolent individuals into a proper channel. Instead of relieving destitution, the great object now is to prevent it: and no money can be so well bestowed as that which assists the labourer in his own endeavours to provide for the future: here beneficence renders that possible which would often be impossible without it. The labourer never feels the value of a charitable donation so sensibly as when it is given in consequence of and in proportion to some savings of his own; because he feels a consciousness of having in some measure deserved it; he looks upon it as a reward more than a mere gratuity; and instead of being tempted as by common alms-giving to appear destitute, he is encouraged to be industrious and saving.

"I have the honour to be,
"Your obedient Servant,
(Signed) "J. P. H. CHESSHYRE.

"*The Poor Law Commissioners.*"

VII.—UNION ADVERTISEMENTS—AS TO THE PRINCIPLE WHICH OUGHT TO GUIDE THE CONDUCT OF GUARDIANS IN SELECTING NEWSPAPERS FOR THE INSERTION OF.

The Commissioners took into consideration a letter from Mr. Pike, of the Reporter Office, Derby, complaining that the Guardians of the Shardlow Union gave the whole of their advertisements to the "Derby Mercury" newspaper, and do not advertise in the "Reporter," which "is the oldest of the three newspapers which have the greatest circulation in North Derbyshire." In reference thereto, the Commissioners addressed a letter to the Guardians of the Shardlow Union, in which the Commissioners stated, that they do not wish to interfere with the discretion of the Guardians in the present case, but they will state, for the information of the Guardians, the opinion which the Commissioners have formed as to the principle which ought to guide the conduct of the Guardians in selecting newspapers for the insertion of the Union advertisements.

Since the purpose of inserting Union advertisements in newspapers is to obtain the utmost publicity for them, they consider that the advertisements ought to be inserted in the newspaper which circulates the most widely among the class of persons who are likely to make the desired tenders, or to whom the advertisements may be in other respects addressed.

The Commissioners think that the choice of a newspaper ought to be determined by the considerations just mentioned, without any reference to the opinions either on the administration of the Poor Laws or any other subject which may have been expressed in the newspapers.

VIII.—FUNDS—CONTRIBUTIONS OF PARISHES TO UNION.

The following is a copy of a letter received from one of the Guardians of the Godstone Union:—

"*Stone Hall, 25th December*, 1841.

"GENTLEMEN,—Permit me, as a Guardian of the Godstone Union, to lay the following case before you, and to request your reply. Myself, with three or four others, were deputed as a committee of Guardians for accounts; we commenced the duty by examining the accounts of expenditure for the quarter now ended, and recommended warrants to be made out to the overseers of the several parishes giving them credit for any balances in hand, or charging them, in addition to the usual call, the amount of deficiency, in manner as instanced in the parish of Godstone as below:—

"GODSTONE PARISH.

Dr.	£.	s.	d.	Cr.	£.	s.	d.
Out relief . . .	97	4	8½	Paid Treasurer between 29th Sept. and 24th Dec. .	217	0	0
In Maintenance .	19	19	1¾	Balance due to parish 29th Sept. .	24	14	10¼
Establishment .	50	0	0	Warrant required.	144	18	6
Registration . .	1	17	6				
Proportion to raise 1,272*l.* for ensuing quarter . .	217	12	0				
	386	13	4¼		386	13	4¼

"It was contended that the warrant should be made out for 217*l.* 12*s.*, and not for the 144*l.* 18*s.* 6*d.*, or *vice versâ*, where the parish expenditure had exceeded its payments.

"I am, Gentlemen,
"Your humble servant,
(Signed) "EDWARD KELSEY.

"*The Poor Law Commissioners.*"

In reply, the Commissioners stated hat where there might be a balance due to a parish, at the termination of the quarter, such parish in any future call should have credit for that balance, and the amount of the warrant diminished to that extent. Where a parish is in debt to the Union at the termination of the quarter, the amount in arrear should be added to the proportion which might be required for the support of its poor for the ensuing quarter.

It was to be observed, that the estimate of the sums which would be required from the whole of the parishes for the next quarter would be made independently of the fact, that certain parishes were in advance to the treasurer and others in arrears. But in making out the warrants, the parishes which were in advance would be credited with the amount of such advance, and the parishes in arrear debited with the deficiency.

IX.—RENTS OF TENEMENTS—NEGLECT OF OVERSEERS TO COLLECT.—AUDITORS' DUTY IN SUCH CASES.

The following is the copy of a letter received from Mr. Senior, Assistant Commissioner.

"*Cuckney, January* 3, 1842.

"ENFORCEMENT OF COLLECTION OF RENTS BY OVERSEERS.

"GENTLEMEN,—As the collection of rents for tenements belonging to the several parishes in the Louth and Wakefield Unions, has generally been neglected by the overseers, and not enforced by the auditor, I have to recommend that the usual communication be made to the auditors on the subject.

"I have the honour to be, Gentlemen,
"Your obedient Servant,
(Signed) "EDWARD SENIOR.

The Poor Law Commissioners."

In reference thereto, the Commissioners directed the following letter to be written to the auditor:—

Poor Law Commission Office,
Somerset House,
14th January, 1842.

SIR,—It has been represented to the Poor Law Commissioners by their Assistant Commissioner, Mr. Senior, that the collection of rents for tenements belonging to the several parishes in the Wakefield Union, and applicable in aid of Poor Rates, of such parishes has been generally neglected by the overseers, who have not been required to account for the same at the passing of their accounts.

The Commissioners observe, that it is the duty of the overseers to see that all rents or other sources of income belonging to the parish, and applicable in diminution of the Poor Rates, are collected, the overseers being accountable for the same under the 47th section of the Poor Law Amendment Act. Where the overseers fail to collect and account for rents arising from the parish houses, it will be your duty in auditing the accounts to charge them with the omission.

I am, Sir,
Your most obedient Servant,
(Signed) E. CHADWICK, *Secretary.*

To the Auditor of the Wakefield Union,
Yorkshire.

X.—PENSIONS.—1. AS TO POWER OF MAGISTRATES TO ORDER PART PAYMENT OF TO PARISH OFFICERS FOR THE SUPPORT OF A CHILD AGED 32 YEARS.

The Commissioners took into consideration the following letter from Mr. Anderson, of the office of Her Majesty's Paymaster-General:—

"*Office of Her Majesty's Paymaster-General,*
"*January 7th*, 1842.

"SIR,—I am directed to submit for the consideration of the Poor Law Commissioners, the enclosed copy of a letter from Samuel Lovenewton, a naval claimant on this department, and to request that you will acquaint me, for the information of the Paymaster-General, whether the Commissioners are of opinion, that under the provisions of the Poor Law Amendment Act, or of any other Act, Magistrates are justified in ordering the half-pay, or any portion of a man's pension, to be paid to parish officers for the support of a child who shall have attained the age of 32 or 42 years, as appeared to be the case in the present instance, or whether the power extends to such children only as are under the age of 16 years.

"I am, Sir,
"Your obedient Servant.
(Signed) "W. G. ANDERSON.
"*E. Chadwick, Esq.*"

(Copy.)

"*Rich Street, Limehouse, January 4th*, 1842.

"HONOURED SIR,—With feelings of the deepest humility, I write in hope you will take my unfortunate case into consideration. I have the misfortune to have two sons both deprived of their senses, *one forty-two, the other thirty-two* years of age; they got past my management about nine months since; they were committed to the County Kent Lunatic Asylum by Mr. Groves, the magistrate of Greenwich; since that, one is sent to Devonport, the other to Durham, the counties where they were born. I had the honour of serving in the royal navy upwards of 32 years, 28 years of that time a carpenter. I served in the actions of Trafalgar and Algiers. I received 75*l.* per annum until yesterday, being the day appointed to receive my pension in Deptford dock-yard, to my surprise I received through my agent one half of my quarter's pension, the sum of 9*l.* 7*s.* 6*d.* instead of 18*l.* 15*s.*, which has thrown me into the deepest distress, not being aware the parish officers were established to stop one half of my pension. I have ever supported them at my own expense, until nine months since, and am now left with an afflicted wife in the deepest distress. Would you, Sir, take my most unfortunate case into your consideration, and get me a situation on board one of the convict ships, or any other that I can take to assist me in my embarrassed state, you will confer a lasting obligation on

"Your obedient servant,
(Signed) "SAMUEL LOVENEWTON.
"*The Secretary of the Admiralty.*"

In reply, the Commissioners stated that there was no provision in the Poor Law Amendment Act which applied to the case. But the 4th section of 2d and 3d Victoria, cap. 51, authorized justices to make orders respecting pensions in certain cases where the wife or family of any person entitled to or in the receipt of any pension were left or were suffered to become chargeable to any Union or parish. The Commissioners presumed therefore that the justices had construed this provision as authorising them to make the order in the case of Samuel Lovenewton.

Looking to the whole of the 4th section of the Act in question it seemed to the Commissioners to contemplate that the child in respect of whose chargeability an order might be made, should be a part of the family of the person whose pension was attached. In the present instance the sons were not living with their father when they became chargeable, and their ages, 32 and 42 years respectively, lead to the inference that they were not a part of his family in the sense of the statute; the presumption in such a case being in favour of their being emancipated. But, independently of that, the Commissioners were of opinion that the word child as used in the fourth section would not be held to apply to a person who had attained the age of 21 years. The Commissioners were the more inclined to that view from the construction put by the Courts upon the 56th Geo. III., cap. 139, in Rex *v.* the inhabitants of St. John Bedwardine, 5 Barn. and Adol. 169. That statute which authorized the binding of "poor children" apprentices by parish officers, was there held not to extend to a person of the age of 21 years.

The Commissioners observed that the father might be required under the 43d Eliz. cap. 2, sec. 9, to maintain his children, if of sufficient ability to do so. But before the justices could make an order under that statute they must satisfy themselves that the person intended to be charged had the requisite ability.

XI.—WORKHOUSE AND OTHER REGULATIONS—PUBLICATION OF.

The Commissioners have authorized their publishers, Messrs. Charles Knight and Co., to print in book form the New Workhouse Regulations and Instructional Letter thereon issued by the Commissioners, and as the Commissioners intend shortly to issue other general regulations, they have directed Messrs. Knight and Co. to keep the type standing, in order that when all the regulations are issued they may be able, for the convenience of the guardians and the paid officers of Unions, to print and publish the whole of them in one volume.

LONDON:

Printed, by Order of the Poor Law Commissioners, by W. CLOWES and SONS, Stamford Street, and Published by CHARLES KNIGHT and Co., 22, Ludgate Street, Publishers to the Poor Law Commissioners.

AN

OFFICIAL CIRCULAR

OF PUBLIC DOCUMENTS AND INFORMATION:

DIRECTED BY THE POOR LAW COMMISSIONERS TO BE PRINTED, CHIEFLY FOR THE USE OF THE MEMBERS AND PERMANENT OFFICERS OF BOARDS OF GUARDIANS, UNDER THE POOR LAW AMENDMENT ACT.

No. 17. CIRCULAR ISSUED APRIL 12TH, 1842.

Poor Law Commission Office,
Somerset House,
April 8, 1842.

THE Poor Law Commissioners, on a review of their minutes, directed that the minutes and correspondence on the following subjects should be printed and circulated for the information of Guardians and officers of the several Unions, viz.—

By order of the Board,
EDWIN CHADWICK, *Secretary.*

I.—PAID OFFICERS:—RELATIVE RESPONSIBILITY OF. CENSURE OF RELIEVING OFFICERS FOR NEGLECT OF A FEMALE PAUPER WHO DIED AT YARMOUTH.

The Commissioners took into consideration a letter from Samuel Palmer, Esq. J. P., Great Yarmouth, forwarding, for the consideration of the Commissioners, a copy of evidence taken before the mayor and magistrates of Great Yarmouth, on the 31st of January and 2nd of February last, relative to the case of Clementia Nickerson, a pauper belonging to Caistor, in the incorporated hundreds of East and West Flegg, but who died at Yarmouth on the 15th of January last.

In reference thereto the Commissioners observed in reply:—

The facts, as the Commissioners gather them from the evidence, are as follows—On the 24th December, 1841, Mary Ann Nickerson, who was residing with her mother, Clementia Nickerson, in the town of Yarmouth, applied to Mr. Thornton, the relieving officer of Yarmouth, for relief for her mother.

Mr. Thornton visited the case immediately and relieved her for the time. The first question which he asked seems to have been, "Where the woman belonged to?" Finding that she belonged to the parish of Caistor, in the incorporated hundreds of East and West Flegg, and knowing that Mr. Clowes was a large proprietor in Caistor, and had had some money transactions with Clementia Nickerson, Mr. Thornton went to Mr. Clowes who admitted her settlement, and promised to place the case in the hands of Mr. Beare the relieving officer for the district in which Caistor is situated.

This, it appears, Mr. Clowes did the first time, after his interview with Mr. Thornton, that he chanced to see Mr. Beare.

It appears, that at some time after the daughter's application for the mother, an application was made to Mr. Thornton on behalf of the daughter herself by Mrs. Carman with whom they lodged. Mr. Thornton seems to have thought both cases provided for so far as regards general relief by his reference to Mr. Beare through Mr. Clowes.

He sent Mr. Worship, the medical officer of

Yarmouth, to attend them on the 27th December. Mr. Worship did accordingly attend, and on the 3rd January (Monday) he delivered to the daughter an order for two pounds of mutton and four pints of porter weekly, to be given to Clementia Nickerson the mother. This order was put by and was not given to Mr. Beare (who was in fact the only relieving officer attending to the case) till, as Mary Ann Nickerson says, Saturday 15th January, but, as Beare himself says, Saturday 22nd January.

It is to be observed, that Mr. Lucas's account of what Beare stated to the Directors and acting Guardians of East and West Flegg, on the 25th of January, goes to confirm Beare's assertion that the 22nd of January (that is three weeks after it was dated) was the day on which he received the order of the medical officer of Yarmouth, and Mrs. Carman would appear to have stated to the Directors and acting Guardians that she delivered it on the 21st.

A good deal turns on this date, and the Commissioners are inclined to think that the evidence preponderates in favour of the later day.

To return to Mr. Beare's treatment of the case: when he was called in, in pursuance of Mr. Clowes's request, he seems to have given 2*s.* 6*d.*, and to have obtained a weekly allowance to that amount, as he asserts, for *Clementia Nickerson only.* He denies any application on the part of Mary Ann Nickerson, and her settlement appears to be in dispute; at any rate Mr. Clowes's communication to him could only refer to Clementia Nickerson, for when Mr. Thornton saw Mr. Clowes (on the 24th December), application had only been made for the mother.

When Beare received Mr. Worship's (the medical officer) order, he did not comply with it, he left 2*s.* 6*d.* with Mrs. Carman on Saturday 22nd, which was to last till Tuesday, when he intended to come again; as it was, he did not return till Wednesday 26th, having been detained on the preceding day by the auditor. On the Wednesday morning the Commissioners suppose that the mother died.

Mr. Worship, the medical officer, who continued to attend the case from December 27th to the death of the mother, was not aware that the nourishment ordered by him had not been given until after the order had been delivered to Beare, that is, probably on the 21st or 22nd.

Before determining the question as to the degree of blame attaching to all or any of the officers concerned in this case, it is desirable distinctly to set out the obligations which respectively attach to persons so situated, under the simple circumstances of a pauper residing in one Union and belonging to a parish situated in another. The proximity of one of these Unions to the other makes no sort of difference in the duty which the law casts on the persons charged with the administration of relief.

In the first place, as regards Mr. Thornton.

From the moment that application was made to him, on December 24th, by Mary Ann Nickerson, *on him*, as relieving officer of Yarmouth, rested the whole responsibility of inquiring into the circumstances and of relieving the wants of the family.

The parties brought their destitution under his notice: they then resided and continued to reside in his district.

The obligation on him to attend to their wants was complete in a legal and moral point of view.

The next question is, how did he discharge himself of this obligation? He did three things.

1st. He gave temporary relief in kind, (two pounds of groats, half a pound of sugar, and a loaf of bread.)

2nd. He sent the medical officer to the house.

3rd. He communicated with Mr. Clowes, and obtained his promise to put the case in the hands of Mr. Beare.

In the two steps first named, as far as they went, Mr. Thornton discharged his duty for the time. If by the third he considered he was free from all further responsibility respecting the case, as the Commissioners infer from his answers to the mayor, he was, to say the least, most grossly mistaken. At page 4 of the Evidence, Thornton says, "My direction from the clerk and the guardians is to apply to the parishes, and if they accept the case *to leave them to take it.*

The observations of the mayor on this answer clearly show that he at least entertained serious doubts of the removal of the responsibility from the relieving officer of Yarmouth.

At pages 7 and 8 of the evidence, Thornton answers the questions put to him as follows:—

"You turn the pauper over to the officer of the adjoining hundred?—Yes, if they take the case.

"You did not tell us if you had any interview with the relieving officer whatever?—That was left to Mr. Clowes; he said he would write to Beare, and order him to attend the case.

"You never called to know if our relieving officer (*i. e.* Beare) had attended the case?—No; I understood that Beare allowed her half-a-crown a-week.

Mr. Thornton, moreover, admits that he knew that Mr. Clowes was in no official situation, but yet states distinctly,—

"I consider my duty ceased when Mr. Clowes said he would order the officer to attend. If Mr. Clowes had rejected the applicant I should have put her on the books; but when the parishes take the case and acknowledge it, we leave the case."

Now, even admitting for a moment that Mr. Thornton's view of his duty were the right one, how did the parish of Caistor take the case? Why, by Mr. Clowes, *who was not an officer at all*, saying that he would communicate with the relieving officer. A communication which was, in fact, left to the chance of his falling in with the relieving officer, (see page 10, Evidence,) and which did not take place for some days.

But the Commissioners are, moreover, of opinion that no acceptance of the case by the "*parish*," who are not entitled to give relief, nor even by the guardians, who are entitled in such cases as that of Clementia Nickerson to make non-resident allowances, can exonerate the relieving officer of the district in which a pauper resides from the distinct duty of watching the case and supplying the wants of the destitute person.

Moreover, there is a very serious aggravation of Mr. Thornton's neglect in the fact, that Mary Anne Nickerson's (the daughter) case never appears, as he calls it, to have been "taken by the parish of Caistor" at all, or in any sense, not even by the mere promise of a third non-official party, to communicate with the relieving officer when he might happen to see him; yet Mary Anne Nickerson had applied to Mr. Thornton for relief, and continued to be resident in his district.

It is to be observed, too, that Mr. Thornton took no trouble to ascertain whether the case was properly attended to by Beare; and, when examined by the mayor himself, asserts the insufficiency of the allowance,—an insufficiency for which, in the eye of the law, he, and he only, was primarily responsible.

As regards Mr. Beare, no *primâ facie* obligation to attend to a pauper residing out of his district, though settled in it, rested on him by law.

If the Board of Guardians directed him to visit a case so situated, he would, of course, be bound to do so; and such an order would only be given within reasonable distance, so as not to interrupt the due performance of his usual duties.

In this case, however, he did, on Mr. Clowes's application, visit the case, administer relief, and adopt it as belonging to his district.

It appears to the Commissioners that he thus voluntarily created a moral, though not a legal obligation to supply the wants of *Clementia Nickerson*, an obligation which, though not sufficient to relieve Mr. Thornton from blame, is sufficient in case of neglect to subject Beare himself to censure. As regards *Mary Anne Nickerson*, Beare denies that application was made to him on her behalf, at any rate there is no evidence of any recognition of her case as belonging to his district.

The important question is, what did Mr. Beare's neglect amount to? Three points are charged against him:—

1. The insufficiency of the allowance, 2*s*. 6*d*. a-week.
2. The neglect of the medical order.
3. The inattention to Mary Anne Nickerson's case.

With regard to the first, 2*s*. 6*d*. a-week was decidedly insufficient for both mother and doughter; but the allowance seems to have been made wholly for the former, in which case its insufficiency is not so clear, though the Commissioners pronounce no opinion on this point in a case of illness.

As to the medical order, if it was only delivered to Mr. Beare on the 22nd of January, some doubt might reasonably arise as to his executing it then; but in that case the Commissioners think that he ought to have done one of two things,—either have supplied the meat and beer until the meeting of the Board of Directors, or have seen the medical officer and consulted him as to the course to be pursued.

He ought to have done this, because he had voluntarily, in the first instance, and afterwards by the direction of the Board of Directors and Guardians, taken on himself the care of *Clementia Nickerson's* case; not because such an obligation originally rested on him,—having assumed it, he was morally, though not legally bound to have acted in every respect as the relieving officer of the district in which the pauper lived would have been bound to act. The Commissioners are inclined to believe, however, that, in thus postponing the compliance with a medical order which was only delivered three weeks after date until he had received the orders of the Board of Directors and Guardians, though guilty of an error of judgment, he did not wilfully neglect a case which he considered as urgent.

The third point is, whether he ought not to have taken cognizance of the case of Mary Anne Nickerson.

There are two suppositions:—

1st. That Mary Anne Nickerson did apply to Beare, and was refused in the terms alleged by her, viz., "that he did not give relief to single women."

2ndly. That she did not apply to him; but that, in his visits to the mother, he must have become aware of her destitute condition.

On the first supposition, the answer was an improper one; and Beare having accepted the mother's case was morally bound to report the application of the daughter to the Board of Directors and Guardians.

On the second supposition, the Commissioners think he ought, at any rate, to have called Thornton's attention to the daughter's state; saying at the same time that, although he had undertaken to relieve the mother, the duty of attending to the daughter's wants still rested on the relieving officer of the district in which she resided.

As a general principle, the Commissioners will never, under any circumstances, recognize the validity of *any private arrangement whatever, even when made in the most express terms, between the Officers themselves or the respective Board of Guardians, as extinguishing the universal duty cast by the law on the officer of the place where a destitute person is found, fully to relieve and attend to the case in every respect*—much less can they admit such an excuse in this case, where a mere verbal message is sent through a third party invested with no official character, and where no subsequent trouble is taken to ascertain if the case is attended to.

The Commissioners therefore, in the first place, feel called on severely to censure Mr. Thornton. On him, in the first instance, the blame of neglecting the case of mother and daughter must necessarily fall.

If the Commissioners find it expedient to dismiss Mr. Beare, as suggested by the magistrates of Yarmouth to the guardians and directors of East and West Flegg, they must, at the same time, and on still stronger grounds, dismiss Mr. Thornton, and they are inclined to think that an example of this kind would go very far towards removing any inclination to substitute an ambiguous moral responsibility for the distinct and admitted legal obligation which the locality alone in every instance imposes, and about which no sort of doubt can possibly exist.

They were, at first, the more inclined to adopt this course because Mr. Beare is, for the reason above stated, most certainly to blame, though, legally speaking, not by any means so much so as Mr. Thornton.

On reconsidering the whole case, however, and taking into consideration the fact that Mr. Thornton may have misunderstood, or have been misled by some directions of the Board of Guardians of the parish of Yarmouth, (see evidence, p. 4), the Commissioners are induced to hope that the censure conveyed in this letter, and the distinct expression of their view of the respective duties of officers so situated, will effectually prevent the recurrence of anything of the same kind.

The Commissioners must further add, that it appears singular that Mr. Worship, who thought that Clementia Nickerson's death was accelerated by want of nourishment, should never have detected any symptoms during three weeks' attendance (from January 3rd to 22nd) which would induce him to think she had not taken the nourishment ordered.

It seems probable that the appearances presented by her complaint would have been different from what they were had she consumed, as Mr. Worship supposed her to have done, two pounds of meat and four pints of porter weekly. At any rate it would have exhibited greater care and attention on the part of the medical officer to his patient, had he ascertained the fact that she had received the food recommended rather than have trusted implicitly to the official routine of the relieving officer duly furnishing whatever the medical officer had ordered as requisite.

II.—COMPARATIVE STATEMENT of EXPENDITURE for the RELIEF of the POOR, &c., during the Year ended 25th March, 1841, with the preceding Years.

Counties.	Expended for the Relief and Maintenance of the Poor, during the Years ended 25th March.			Amount of Decrease in 1841, compared with		Amount of Increase in 1841, compared with 1840.	Decrease per Cent. in 1841, compared with		Increase per Cent. in 1841, compared with 1840.
	1834.	1840.	1841.	1834.	1840.		1834.	1840.	
	£.	£.	£.	£.	£.	£.			
Bedford	77,819	39,889	41,063	36,756	..	1,174	47	..	3
Berks	100,183	70,125	74,308	25,875	..	4,183	26	..	6
Buckingham	124,200	72,367	74,007	50,193	..	1,649	40	..	2
Cambridge	96,497	75,745	72,158	24,339	3,587	..	25	5	..
Chester	92,640	75,895	77,698	14,942	..	1,803	16	..	2
Cornwall	93,037	77,633	85,063	7,974	..	7,430	9	..	10
Cumberland	43,067	37,006	36,867	6,200	139	..	14	..	..
Derby	72,721	53,635	55,238	17,483	..	1,603	24	..	3
Devon	210,825	194,361	195,402	15,423	..	1,041	7	..	1
Dorset	84,293	81,373	80,097	4,196	1,276	..	5	2	..
Durham	79,399	67,331	66,639	12,760	692	..	16	1	..
Essex	239,946	165,340	171,356	68,590	..	6,016	29	..	4
Gloucester	161,449	125,168	130,321	31,128	..	5,153	19	..	4
Hereford	56,683	42,226	43,512	13,171	..	1,286	23	..	3
Hertford	85,799	56,126	61,250	24,549	..	5,124	29	..	9
Huntingdon	35,844	25,123	25,329	10,515	..	206	29	..	1
Kent	343,878	193,526	208,786	135,092	..	15,260	39	..	8
Lancaster	253,405	239,491	262,227	*8,822	..	22,736	*3	..	9
Leicester	100,857	63,604	70,423	30,434	..	6,819	30	..	11
Lincoln	161,074	99,860	103,894	57,180	..	4,034	35	..	4
Middlesex	582,412	407,670	435,606	146,806	..	27,936	25	..	7
Monmouth	27,626	21,897	24,819	2,807	..	2,922	10	..	13
Norfolk	306,787	181,058	182,229	124,558	..	1,171	41	..	1
Northampton	140,179	83,171	86,148	54,031	..	2,977	39	..	4
Northumberland	71,983	65,416	64,649	7,334	767	..	10	1	..
Nottingham	66,030	53,407	57,721	8,309	..	4,314	13	..	8
Oxford	120,616	74,585	76,474	44,142	..	1,889	37	..	3
Rutland	9,008	7,246	7,453	1,555	..	207	17	..	3
Salop	82,493	55,022	57,571	24,922	..	2,549	30	..	5
Somerset	176,286	156,059	157,022	19,264	..	963	11	..	1
Southampton	203,466	141,694	142,507	60,959	..	813	30	..	1
Stafford	120,512	92,835	95,242	25,270	..	2,407	21	..	3
Suffolk	245,509	141,536	138,228	107,281	3,308	..	44	2	..
Surrey	261,501	169,952	199,477	62,024	..	29,525	24	..	17
Sussex	246,626	144,128	145,013	101,613	..	885	41	..	1
Warwick	158,159	109,522	102,828	55,331	6,694	..	35	6	..
Westmorland	22,283	16,532	17,607	4,676	..	1,075	21	..	7
Wilts	173,925	133,468	133,573	40,352	..	105	23	..	..
Worcester	81,612	60,530	62,958	18,654	..	2,428	23	..	4
York, East Riding	91,111	67,093	68,182	22,929	..	1,089	25	..	2
York, North Riding	75,810	59,352	58,308	17,502	1,044	..	23	2	..
York, West Riding	251,821	217,217	245,676	6,145	..	28,459	2	..	13
Totals of England	6,029,371	4,315,214	4,494,929	†1,534,442	‡179,715		25	..	4
WALES.									
Anglesey	15,542	16,511	17,268	*1,726	..	757	*11	..	5
Brecknock	18,974	15,085	15,648	3,326	..	563	18	..	4
Cardigan	18,625	18,532	17,856	769	676	..	4	4	..
Carmarthen	33,755	32,160	32,004	1,751	156	..	5	..	..
Carnarvon	20,136	21,327	20,893	*757	434	..	*4	2	..
Denbigh	33,136	30,735	31,401	1,735	..	666	5	..	2
Flint	19,566	17,470	19,980	*414	..	2,510	*2	..	14
Glamorgan	40,306	32,596	33,753	6,553	..	1,157	16	..	4
Merioneth	14,977	14,362	15,005	*28	..	643	*..	..	4
Montgomery	34,201	28,937	28,365	5,836	572	..	17	2	..
Pembroke	25,593	24,183	23,812	1,781	371	..	7	2	..
Radnor	13,072	9,853	10,015	3,057	..	162	23	..	2
Totals of Wales	287,883	261,751	66,000	†21,883	‡4,249		8	..	2
Totals of England and Wale	6,317,254	4,576,965	4,760,929	1,556,325	183,964		25	..	4

* Increase. † Decrease, after deducting increase. ‡ Increase, after deducting decrease.

Comparative Statement of Expenditure for the Relief of the Poor, &c.—*continued.*

Counties.	Expended in Law Charges, &c., during the Years ended 25th March.		Amount of Decrease in 1841, compared with 1834.	Decrease per Cent. in 1841, compared with 1834.	Expended for purposes other than the Relief of the Poor during the Years ended 25th March.		Amount of Decrease in 1841, compared with 1835.	Decrease per Cent. in 1841, compared with 1835	Total Expenditure for the Relief of the Poor, Law Charges, and other purposes (exclusive of Payments under the Registration, Parochial Assessments, and Vaccination Acts) during the Years ended 25th March.		Amount of Decrease in 1841, compared with 1834.	Decrease per Cent. in 1841, compared with 1834.
	1834.	1841.			1835. (*a*)	1841.			1834.	1841.		
	£.	£.	£.		£.	£.	£.		£.	£.	£.	
Bedford	1,866	72	1,794	96	5,864	747	5,117	87	85,549	41,882	43,667	51
Berks	3,458	1,044	2,414	70	11,597	2,456	9,141	79	115,238	77,808	37,430	32
Bucks	3,140	489	2,651	84	12,543	4,245	8,293	66	139,883	78,741	61,142	44
Cambridge	3,427	913	2,514	73	10,561	4,719	5,842	55	110,485	77,790	32,695	30
Chester	8,570	1,320	7,250	85	17,229	6,884	10,345	60	118,439	85,902	32,537	27
Cornwall	4,182	1,722	2,460	59	11,914	5,938	5,976	50	109,133	92,723	16,410	15
Cumberland	2,316	340	1,976	85	5,130	2,239	2,891	56	50,513	39,446	11,067	22
Derby	4,163	839	3,324	80	13,818	4,687	9,131	66	90,702	60,764	29,938	33
Devon	7,507	3,516	3,991	53	18,052	8,977	9,075	50	236,384	207,895	28,489	12
Dorset	2,635	1,804	831	31	6,999	3,045	3,954	56	93,927	84,946	8,981	10
Durham	5,245	912	4,333	83	9,167	4,180	4,987	54	93,811	71,731	22,080	24
Essex	6,898	1,593	5,305	77	23,716	6,768	16,948	71	270,560	179,717	90,843	34
Gloucester	7 064	2,384	4,680	66	21 634	15,641	5,993	28	190,147	148,346	41,801	22
Hereford	2,245	769	1,476	66	5,481	1,322	4,159	76	64,409	45,603	18,805	29
Hertford	2,057	465	1,592	77	12,187	3,463	8,724	72	100,043	65,178	34,865	35
Huntingdon	1,146	560	586	51	3,968	660	3,308	83	40,958	26,549	14,409	35
Kent	15,340	2,021	13,319	87	47,743	17,620	30,123	63	406,961	228,427	178,534	44
Lancaster	15,776	6,856	8,920	57	64,888	48,219	16,669	26	334,069	317,302	16,767	5
Leicester	5,472	1,330	4,142	76	12,091	3,811	8,280	68	118,420	75,564	42,856	36
Lincoln	8,674	1,504	7,170	83	25,856	5,192	20,664	80	195,604	110,590	85,014	43
Middlesex	20,427	5,322	15,105	74	187,045	170,590	16,455	9	789,884	611,518	178,366	23
Monmouth	2,557	189	2,368	93	2,856	1,361	1,495	52	33,039	26,369	6,670	20
Norfolk	9,535	1,326	8,209	86	29,322	13,565	15,757	54	345,644	197,120	148,524	43
Northampton	3,311	782	2,529	76	13,123	3,895	9,228	71	156,613	90,825	65,788	42
Northumberland	4,651	1,015	3,636	78	6,776	3,560	3,216	47	83,410	69,224	14,186	17
Nottingham	3,980	823	3,157	79	13,824	3,916	9,908	72	83,834	62,460	21,374	25
Oxford	4,441	809	3,632	82	11,695	2,845	8,850	76	136,752	80,128	56,624	41
Rutland	237	81	156	66	1,959	516	1,443	74	11,204	8,050	3,154	28
Salop	4,082	741	3,341	82	7,267	4,169	3,098	43	93,842	62,481	31,361	33
Somerset	6,710	2,004	4,706	70	21,080	4,893	16,187	77	204,076	163,919	40,157	20
Southampton	6,546	1,421	5,125	78	22,251	5,488	16,763	75	232,263	149,416	82,847	36
Stafford	6,894	2,111	4,783	69	20,829	7,460	13,369	64	148,235	104,813	43,422	29
Suffolk	7,746	784	6,962	90	19,775	6,234	13,541	68	273,030	145,246	127,784	47
Surrey	8,862	2,604	6,258	71	71,021	31,947	39,074	55	341,384	234,028	107,356	31
Sussex	7,873	2,003	5,870	75	30,937	9,654	21,283	69	285,436	156,670	128,766	45
Warwick	5,935	2,283	3,652	62	22,092	50,176§	28,084*	127*	186,186	155,287	30,899	17
Westmorland	510	561	*51	* 10	2,037	865	1,172	58	24,830	19,033	5,797	23
Wilts	3,587	859	2,728	76	15,888	6,282	9,606	60	193,400	140,714	52,686	27
Worcester	3,781	1,963	1,818	48	10,589	3,223	7,366	70	95,982	68,144	27,838	29
York, East Riding	4,049	799	3,250	80	10,081	3,851	6,230	62	105,241	72,832	32,409	31
York, North Riding	3,015	1,203	1,812	60	7,888	1,936	5,952	75	86,713	61,447	25,266	29
York, West Riding	13,436	6,946	6,490	48	39,675	26,670	13,005	33	304,932	279,292	25,640	8
Totals of England	243,346	67,082	†176,264	72	908,448	513,909	394,539†	43	7,181,165	5,075,920	2,105,245	29
WALES.												
Anglesey	1,441	335	1,106	77	2,003	1,034	969	48	18,986	18,637	349	2
Brecknock	737	159	578	78	1,639	690	949	58	21,350	16,497	4,853	23
Cardigan	688	298	390	57	1,905	1,305	600	31	21,218	19,459	1,759	8
Carmarthen	1,850	358	1,492	81	2,594	1,638	956	37	38,199	34,000	4,199	11
Carnarvon	1,367	386	981	72	2,149	1,510	639	30	23,652	22,789	863	4
Denbigh	1,440	183	1,257	87	3,981	1,731	2,250	57	38,557	33,315	5,242	14
Flint	1,853	84	1,769	95	2,442	1,197	1,245	51	23,861	21,261	2,600	11
Glamorgan	1,939	357	1,582	82	4,228	1,949	2,279	54	46,473	36,059	10,414	22
Merioneth	708	109	599	85	890	209	681	77	16,575	15,323	1,252	8
Montgomery	1,315	248	1,067	81	2,162	1,122	1,040	48	37,678	29,735	7,943	21
Pembroke	1,444	121	1,323	92	2,327	1,178	1,149	49	29,364	25,111	4,253	14
Radnor	476	222	254	53	593	245	348	59	14,141	10,482	3,659	26
Totals of Wales	15,258	2,860	12,398	81	26,913	13,808	13,105	49	330,054	282,668	47,386	14
Totals of England and Wales	258,604	69,942	†188,662	73	935,361	527,717	407,644†	44	7,511,219	5,358,588	2,152,631	29

(*a*) There being no separate head for this item of expenditure in the year ended 25th March, 1834, the comparison is made with the year ended 25th March, 1835. * Increase. † Decrease, after deducting increase.

§ The large increase under this head, in the county of Warwick, may be accounted for by the payments on account of the Constabulary Police Force being included in the amount expended in 1841.

Comparative Statement of Expenditure for the Relief of the Poor, &c.—*continued.*

Counties.	Ratio of Expenditure per Head to Population.						
	1831.			1841.			Decrease in the Rate per Head in 1841, as compared with 1831.
	Population.	Expenditure for the Relief of the Poor (only).	Rate per Head.	Population.	Expenditure for the Relief of the Poor (only).	Rate per Head.	
		£.	s. d.		£.	s. d.	s. d.
Bedford	95,483	81,016	17 0	107,937	41,063	7 7	9 5
Berks	145,389	115,070	15 10	160,226	74,308	9 3	6 7
Bucks	146,529	137,356	18 9	155,989	74,007	9 6	9 3
Cambridge	143,955	98,522	13 8	164,[illegible]09	72,158	8 9	4 11
Chester	334,391	103,572	6 2	395,300	77,698	3 11	2 3
Cornwall	300,938	102,151	6 9	341,269	85,063	5 0	1 9
Cumberland	169,681	46,167	5 5	177,912	36,867	4 2	1 3
Derby	237,170	78,717	6 8	272,202	55,238	4 1	2 7
Devon	494,478	223,074	9 0	533,731	195,402	7 4	1 8
Dorset	159,252	90,668	11 5	174,743	80,097	9 2	2 3
Durham	253,910	81,862	6 5	324,277	66,639	4 1	2 4
Essex	317,507	272,593	17 2	344,995	171,356	9 11	7 3
Gloucester	387,019	168,288	8 8	431,307	130,521	6 1	2 7
Hereford	111,211	62,622	11 3	114,438	43,512	7 7	3 8
Hertford	143,341	94,336	13 2	157,237	61,250	7 9	5 5
Huntingdon	53,192	40,474	15 3	58,699	25,329	8 8	6 6
Kent	479,155	345,512	14 5	548,161	208,786	7 7	6 10
Lancaster	1,336,854	293,226	4 5	1,667,064	262,227	3 2	1 3
Leicester	197,003	113,951	11 7	215,855	70,423	6 6	5 1
Lincoln	317,465	174,055	11 0	362,717	103,894	5 9	5 3
Middlesex	1,358,330	681,567	10 0	1,576,616	435,606	5 6	4 6
Monmouth	98,130	26,613	5 5	134,349	24,819	3 8	1 9
Norfolk	390,054	299,358	15 4	412,621	182,229	8 10	6 6
Northampton	179,336	150,816	16 10	199,061	86,148	8 8	8 2
Northumberland	222,912	74,092	6 8	250,268	64,619	5 2	1 6
Nottingham	225,327	72,717	6 5	249,773	57,721	4 7	1 10
Oxford	152,156	130,043	17 1	161,573	76,474	9 7	7 7
Rutland	19,385	8,809	9 1	21,340	7,453	7 0	2 1
Salop	222,938	87,111	7 10	239,014	57,571	4 10	3 0
Somerset	404,200	178,048	8 10	436,002	157,022	7 2	1 8
Southampton	314,280	215,229	13 8	354,940	142,507	8 0	5 8
Stafford	410,512	132,887	6 6	510,206	95,242	3 9	2 9
Suffolk	296,317	270,651	18 3	315,129	138,228	8 9	9 6
Surrey	486,334	265,389	10 11	582,613	193,477	6 10	4 1
Sussex	272,340	263,908	19 5	299,770	145,013	9 8	9 9
Warwick	336,610	161,212	9 7	402,121	102,828	5 1	4 6
Westmorland	55,041	26,586	9 8	56,469	17,607	6 3	3 5
Wilts	240,156	198,194	16 6	260,007	133,573	10 3	6 3
Worcester	211,365	83,513	7 11	233,484	62,958	5 5	2 6
York, East Riding	204,253	100,976	9 11	231,998	68,182	5 10	4 1
York, North Riding	190,756	83,931	8 10	204,662	58,308	5 8	3 2
York, West Riding	976,350	274,586	5 7	1,154,924	245,676	4 3	1 4
Totals of England	13,091,005	6,509,466	9 11	14,995,508	4,494,929	6 0	3 11
WALES.							
Anglesey	48,325	16,247	6 9	50,890	17,268	6 9	..
Brecknock	47,763	18,542	7 9	53,295	15,648	5 10	1 11
Cardigan	64,780	17,591	5 5	68,380	17,856	5 3	0 2
Carmarthen	100,740	33,598	6 8	106,482	32,004	6 0	0 9
Carnarvon	66,448	21,205	6 5	81,068	20,893	5 2	1 3
Denbigh	83,629	35,126	8 5	89,291	31,401	7 0	1 5
Flint	60,012	20,559	6 10	66,547	19,930	6 0	0 10
Glamorgan	126,612	38,751	6 1	173,462	33,753	3 11	2 2
Merioneth	35,315	14,865	8 5	39,238	15,005	7 8	0 9
Montgomery	66,482	34,815	10 6	69,220	28,365	8 2	2 4
Pembroke	81,425	24,552	6 0	88,262	23,812	5 5	0 7
Radnor	24,651	13,571	11 0	25,186	10,015	7 11	3 1
Totals of Wales	806,182	289,422	7 2	911,321	266,000	5 10	1 4
Persons ascertained to have been travelling during the night of the 6th June, 1841	. . .	. . .	..	4,896	. . .	..	..
Totals of England and Wales	13,897,187	6,798,889	9 9	15,911,725	4,760,929	6 0	3 9

III.—GENERAL MEDICAL ORDER;— INSTRUCTIONAL LETTER THEREON.

The following is a copy of an Instructional Letter and General Order on the subject of Medical Relief, transmitted by direction of the Commissioners to the several Unions enumerated in the Schedule annexed to the Order.

Poor Law Commission Office,
Somerset House,
12th March, 1842.

SIR,—One of the most important subjects considered by the select committee of the House of Commons, which in 1838 enquired into the operation of the Poor Law Amendment Act, was the medical relief of the poor.

After examining numerous witnesses on this subject, the Committee decided to recommend no legislation by Parliament on medical relief, but having expressed their opinion that the existing arrangements might in several points be ameliorated, and having indicated several improvements, they left the introduction of these and other alterations to the discretion of the Poor Law Commissioners.—(Report, p. 25.)

The Commissioners, having given the entire subject a mature consideration, fully stated their views upon it in their report on the further Amendment of the Poor Laws (31st of December, 1839), p. 73—81. They subsequently, by a circular letter, dated the 6th of March, 1841 (see 7th Annual Report, p. 8), called the attention of the Boards of Guardians to their suggestions in this report; and requested to be informed of the opinion of the Boards as to the expediency of adopting those suggestions.

The answers which were returned by the Boards of Guardians to this circular (which are partially abstracted in the Seventh Annual Report of the Commissioners, p. 9—14), shewed, however, that no extensive change in the existing arrangements was likely to originate with the Boards of Guardians. Accordingly, as much dissatisfaction continued to prevail amongst many members of the medical profession, and as little progress had been made towards carrying into effect some of the recommendations of the Committee, the Commissioners have thought themselves called upon to select the most important points of the subject, and to issue generally to the Unions such regulations upon these points as appear to be needful and prudent.

The following are the heads of the accompanying order:—

1. Tenders for medical attendance.
2. Qualifications of medical officers.
3. Maximum amount of area and population of medical districts.
4. Rates of payment of medical officers in certain surgical and midwifery cases.
5. Substitutes for medical officers during their incapacity to act.
6. Arrangement for affording medical relief to permanent paupers without a special order in each case.
7. Continuance in office of medical officers.

The Commissioners subjoin some explanatory remarks upon the main provisions of the order.

ARTICLES I. and II. are intended to abolish the system of requiring tenders for the services of medical officers; according to the views of the Commissioners, explained in their report on the further Amendment of the Law, p. 76—8. These articles, however, do not prohibit advertisements for the services of medical officers, provided such advertisements specify the remuneration fixed or approved by the Commissioners. It is the wish of the Commissioners that the competition of the candidates should turn upon their respective characters and skill, and not on the sum at which they may be severally willing to undertake the office.

ARTICLES III.—V. relate to the qualifications of medical officers.

The Commissioners think it desirable that every medical officer should possess both a medical and a surgical qualification, and, therefore, they have required the three sorts of double qualification which are specified in Article 3, Nos. 1, 2, and 3.

With respect to the second qualification in No. 3, see 55 Geo. 3, c. 194 (the Apothecaries' Act).

The Commissioners thought themselves bound to consider the qualification stated in Article 3, No. 4, as virtually a double qualification, according to the decision of the Court of Exchequer, in Stevenson *v.* Oliver, 8 Meeson and Welsby, 234. The qualification is limited to warrants or commissions, dated previously to 1st August, 1826; inasmuch as the Act of 6 Geo. 4, c. 133 (which brought persons possessing this qualification within the benefit of the Apothecaries' Act), expired on that day.

ARTICLE IV. provides a means by which a duly qualified medical man not possessing any of the four qualifications required by Article 3, may, in case of necessity, be appointed a medical officer: and Article 5 enables an exception to be made in favour of existing medical officers.

The Commissioners have limited the provisions of their order to medical qualifications proceeding from an English source. In case, however, any medical man possesses an English qualification of physician or apothecary, together with a Scotch or Irish surgical qualification, the Commissioners will consider such person as virtually possessing a double qualification: and they will admit him as an officer (if otherwise fit for the office), under Article 4, upon application from the Guardians for that purpose.

ARTICLES VI.—IX. relate to the maximum area and population of medical districts.

The Committee of 1838 expressed an opinion that the medical districts seemed to be in some instances inconveniently large, and that they should be of such a size as to admit of an easy access of the medical man to his patients. (Report, p. 25.) The Commissioners have constantly borne in mind this recommendation of the Committee, and have already required the division of many medical districts which seemed to have too large an area. A considerable improvement has thus been already effected in many individual cases; but the Commissioners think that the time is now arrived when it is desirable for them to make a general regulation on the subject, and they have accordingly inserted one in these Articles, accompanied with such limitations and exceptions as the circumstances of the case appeared to require.

The Commissioners are aware that in many districts containing almost exclusively a poor population, even the limit of 15,000 persons may admit of a number of patients too large for the care of one medical officer; especially if the district consist partly of a town and partly of rural parishes. Under such circumstances, it would generally be practicable for the Guardians to divide the district between two or more duly qualified medical practitioners. In like manner, it may happen that a district consisting of an area less than 15,000 acres, may contain a large population, and that the Guardians may be able to divide it with advantage. The Commissioners, therefore, do not, by the limits fixed in Article 6, imply that no district is objectionable, or that every district will be sanctioned by them, which is within these limits.

With respect to Article 9 it may be observed, that the measure of acreage adopted in Article 6 cannot be applied to Wales, as there are no available means of obtaining the requisite information in that part of the country: and the Commissioners have accordingly prescribed for Wales a limit, not of area, but of distance, which, though less convenient, is the best which the case permits Moreover, the physical circumstances of Wales, and the small number of resident medical practitioners, render it necessary to permit the formation of medical districts larger than those in most parts of England.

ARTICLES X.—XIII. It is the earnest wish of the Commissioners to carry into effect the recommendation of the Committee, that "the remuneration of medical officers should be such as to ensure proper attention and the best medicines" (Report, p. 25); and the Guardians will doubtless perceive, that unless the medical officer be adequately remunerated, no vigilance on their part will suffice to secure proper attendance and medicines to the poor under his care.

The Commissioners still retain the opinions expressed in their report on the further Amendmend of the Law, p. 78—80, and since repeated to the Boards of Guardians in their circular of March, 1841, as to the advantages of a joint system of fixed salary and payment per case for medical officers: and they will remark incidentally, that unless a system of payment per case is adopted, the recommendation of the Committee, that the medical relief should be a Parochial and not a Union charge (Report, p. 24), cannot be carried into effect.

The wide differences between the circumstances of different Unions, especially in respect of the density and character of the population, render it, however, nearly impossible for the Commissioners to prescribe the universal introduction of this or any other mode of payment.

It appeared, nevertheless, to the Commissioners, that it was possible for them to furnish a universal scale of payment for the surgical and obstetrical services specified in Articles 10—13; the nature of which is such that they might, under certain circumstances, be properly excluded from the salary of the medical officer, and be paid at higher rates than ordinary medical cases. The Guardians will thus be enabled to approximate to the views of the Committee, by making these cases a Parochial charge.

The operations enumerated in Article 10, are intended to provide for cases of urgency (principally those arising from accidents), which cannot be sent to a public hospital with safety and propriety. The payments for operations are limited to operations on outdoor poor, and do not include those performed in the workhouse. It appears to the Commissioners that the continued attendance at the house of the patient in severe surgical cases, usually forms the most burdensome part of the extra service of the medical man: whereas the constant visits of the medical officer to the workhouse enable him to attend a patient in the workhouse without always making a visit for that express purpose. Moreover, when a patient can be removed to a workhouse, or when he has long been the subject of medical treatment in the workhouse, he may in general be removed with safety or propriety to an infirmary or hospital; and the Commissioners think it desirable that, where the distance or other circumstances do not present serious obstacles, paupers should enjoy the practised skill and combined judgment of the medical men usually connected with such establishments. While, therefore, the Commissioners would discourage the performance of important surgical operations in workhouses, they are ready to sanction any reasonable subscription to a hospital or similar establishment by a Board of Guardians for the Union.

The payments are intended to cover not only the operation, but also the attendances after the operation, which in severe cases of this sort ought usually to be numerous; and, therefore, they are limited to cases in which the patient survives the operation more than thirty-six hours, and receives several subsequent attendances. Cases in which the patient does not survive the operation thirty-six hours, or in which he does not receive several subsequent attendances, may be included in the contract of the medical officer with the guardians.

ARTICLE XV. If any medical officer has a partner or assistant who is a duly qualified medical man, he may name such partner or assistant under this article.

The medical officer will be considered by the Commissioners as responsible for the skill and diligence of the person named by him as a substitute.

ARTICLES XVI.—XIX. are intended to facilitate the obtaining of attendance and medicines by the permanent paupers; a class whose destitution is acknowledged, and which necessarily includes the most helpless portion of the community.

ARTICLE XX. places the medical officer on the same footing with the other officers, as to the period of his office, unless such period be specially limited at the time of his appointment. It does not seem desirable to exclude the guardians from the opportunity of improving the arrangements respecting medical relief as the circumstances of the several districts may permit, and therefore it is not advisable to deprive them of the power of limiting the period of the medical officer's services.

The Commissioners intend, in a short time, to issue a general order prescribing the adoption, by the medical officers, of the nomenclature of diseases now in use under the authority of the registrar general, which will ensure greater uniformity and precision of language in the returns made by the medical officers, and will furnish a convenient interpretation of many of the more obscure scientific names of diseases.

Signed, &c.

The Clerk to the Guardians
of the *Union.*

MEDICAL ORDER.

To the Guardians of the Poor of the several Unions named in the schedule hereunto annexed.

To the clerk or clerks to the justices of the petty sessions held for the division or divisions in which the parishes and places comprised within the said Unions are situate; and to all others whom it may concern.

WE, the Poor Law Commissioners, in pursuance of the authorities vested in Us by an Act passed in the fifth year of the reign of His late Majesty King William the Fourth, intituled "*An Act for the Amendment and better Administration of the Laws relating to the Poor in England and Wales,*" do hereby order, direct, and declare, with respect to each and every of the Unions named in the schedule hereunto annexed, as follows:—

Tender.

ARTICLE I. It shall not be lawful for the Board of Guardians of any of the said Unions, by advertisement, or other public notice, printed or written, to invite tenders for the supply of medicines, or for the medical attendance on any of the paupers within any such Union, unless such advertisement or notice shall specify the district or place for which such supply of medicines and such attendance is required, together with the amount of salary or other remuneration fixed or approved by the Poor Law Commissioners, as the consideration for such supply of medicines and such attendance, or either of them.

ARTICLE II. All salaries or other payments to any medical man, fixed by any of the said Boards of Guardians, and every contract made by any of the said Boards of Guardians with any medical man, in pursuance of any advertisement or other notice, inviting medical men to tender their services at a sum or sums not named in such advertisement, or notice, shall be deemed to be fixed or made in opposition to the rules and regulations of the Poor Law Commissioners in force in this behalf, and all payments made towards such salary, or in fulfilment of such contract, shall be disallowed in the accounts of the parties authorizing or making the same.

Qualification.

ARTICLE III. It shall not be lawful for any of the said Boards of Guardians to appoint any person to be a medical officer, unless such person, at the time of his appointment, shall possess one of the four following qualifications; that is to say,—

1st. A diploma from the Royal College of Surgeons in London, together with a degree in medicine from an University in England, legally authorized to grant such degree, or together with a diploma or licence of the Royal College of Physicians of London.

2nd. A diploma from the Royal College of Surgeons in London, together with a certificate to practise as an Apothecary from the Society of Apothecaries of London.

3rd. A diploma from the Royal College of Surgeons in London — such person having been in actual practice as an apothecary on the first day of August, one thousand eight hundred and fifteen.

4th. A warrant or commission as surgeon or assistant-surgeon in Her Majesty's Navy, or as surgeon or assistant-surgeon or apothecary in Her Majesty's Army, or as surgeon or assistant-surgeon in the service of the Honourable East India Company, dated previous to the first day of August, one thousand eight hundred and twenty-six.

ARTICLE IV. Provided always, that if it shall not be practicable for the Board of Guardians to procure a person residing within or near the district in which he is to act, and duly qualified in one of the four modes recited in Article 3, to attend on the poor in such district, or that the only person resident in or near such district, and so qualified, shall have been dismissed from office under the seal of the Poor Law Commissioners, or shall be judged by the Poor Law Commissioners to be unfit or incompetent to hold the office of medical officer, then and in such case the Board of Guardians shall cause a special minute to be made and entered on the usual record of their proceedings, stating the reasons which, in their opinion, make it necessary to employ a person not qualified as required by Article 3, and shall forthwith transmit a copy of such minute to the Poor Law Commissioners for their consideration; and the Poor Law Commissioners may, if they think fit so to do, permit the employment by such Board of Guardians of any person duly licenced to practise as a medical man, although such person shall not be qualified in one of the four modes required by Article 3.

ARTICLE V. Provided also, that it shall be lawful for the Board of Guardians, with the consent of the Poor Law Commissioners first had and obtained, to continue in office any medical officer duly licensed to practise as a medical man already employed by any such Board of Guardians, although such medical officer may not be qualified in one of the four modes required by Article 3.

Maximum Area and Population of Medical Districts.

ARTICLE VI. It shall not be lawful for the Board of Guardians to assign to any medical officer, to be by them hereafter appointed, a district which shall exceed in extent the area of fifteen thousand statute acres, or which shall contain a population exceeding the number of fifteen thousand persons, according to the then last enumeration of the population published by authority of Parliament.

ARTICLE VII. Provided, always that where any medical officer may on the day on which this order shall come in force, hold any district exceeding either in area or population the limits fixed in Article 6, and such medical officer may have been appointed to such district for any time not exceeding twelve calendar months, he shall continue to hold his office, if not otherwise removed therefrom, up to the expiration of the time for which he was so appointed; but that where any medical officer shall have been appointed to any district exceeding the said limits in area or population for any space of time longer than twelve calendar months from the day in which this order shall come into force, the continuance of such officer in his office shall cease and determine on the twenty-fifth day of March, one thousand eight hundred and forty-three, or whenever the term of such appointment may expire, whichever shall first happen.

ARTICLE VIII. Provided also, that if it shall be impracticable for the Board of Guardians to divide any Union into districts containing respectively an area and population less than is specified in Article 6, then and in such case the Board of Guardians shall cause a special minute to be made and entered on the usual record of their proceedings, stating the reasons which in their opinion make it necessary to form a district exceeding the said limits, and shall forthwith transmit a copy of such minute to the Poor Law Commissioners for their consideration, and if the Poor Law Commissioners shall signify their approval thereof to such Guardians, then and in such case, but not otherwise, such Guardians may proceed to appoint a medical officer for the said district.

ARTICLE IX. Provided also, that the limits of fifteen thousand statute acres, prescribed in Article 6, shall not apply or be in force in respect to any medical district situate wholly, or in part, within the Principality of Wales; but no medical district situate wholly, or in part, within that Principality, shall be assigned to any medical officer residing more than seven miles from any part of any parish included within such district, unless the formation of such district shall have been specially sanctioned by the Poor Law Commissioners in the same manner as is directed in Article 8.

Rates of payment of Surgical and Midwifery cases.

ARTICLE X. No salary of any district medical officer, or contract made by any Board of Guardians with a district medical officer, shall include the remuneration for the operations and services of the following classes performed by such medical officer in that capacity for any out-door pauper, but such operations and services shall be paid for by the Board of Guardians, according to the rules specified in this Article.

	£	s.	d.
1. Amputation of Leg, Arm, Foot, or Hand..... 2. The operation for strangulated Hernia....... 3. The operation of Trephining for Fractured Skull 4. Treatment of Compound Fractures of the Thigh 5. Treatment of Compound Fractures, or Compound Dislocations of the Leg..............	5	0	0
6. Treatment of simple Fractures or simple Dislocations of the Thigh or Leg	3	0	0
7. Treatment of Dislocation or Fractures of the Arm	1	0	0

The above rates to include the payment for the supply of all kinds of apparatus and splints.

Provided that in every such case the patient survives the operation not less than thirty-six hours, and that he has required and has received several attendances after the operation by the medical officer, who has performed the same.

Provided also, that except in cases of sudden accident immediately threatening life, no medical officer shall be entitled to receive such remuneration for any amputation or for the operation of trephining unless he shall before performing such amputation or operation have obtained at his own cost, the advice of some member of the Royal College of Surgeons of London, or some fellow or licentiate of the Royal College of Physicians of London, and shall produce to the Board of Guardians a certificate from such member of the Royal College of Surgeons, or such fellow or licentiate, stating that in his opinion it was right and proper that such amputation or operation should be then performed.

ARTICLE XI. All trusses furnished by a medical officer in consequence of any contract with or direction of a Board of Guardians, shall be charged by such medical officer at the cost price, including carriage, and be paid for accordingly by such Board of Guardians.

ARTICLE XII. The delivery of any woman in childbirth and the subsequent medical attendance upon her by any medical officer, in that capacity, whether in or out of the workhouse, shall be paid for by the Board of Guardians in the manner specified in this and the following Article; that is to say:

In cases in which any such medical officer shall be called on by order of any person legally qualified to make such order, to attend any woman in or immediately after childbirth, or shall be required, under circumstances of difficulty or danger, without any order, to visit any such woman actually receiving relief, or whom the Board of Guardians may subsequently decide to have been in a destitute condition, such medical officer shall be paid for his attendance and medicines by a sum of not less than ten shillings, nor more than twenty shillings, as the Board of Guardians may determine, regard being had to the distance from the residence of such medical officer.

ARTICLE XIII. Provided that in any special case in which great difficulty may have occurred in the delivery, or long subsequent attendance may have been requisite, such medical officer shall receive the sum of two pounds; and if in any such case, any dispute shall arise between the Board of Guardians, and such medical officer, such medical officer shall not receive the said sum until the Poor Law Commissioners shall have signified their approval of such payment on a report made by such medical officer and transmitted to them through the Board of Guardians of the said Union.

Substitutes for Medical Officers.

ARTICLE XIV. Every medical officer appointed, or to be appointed, in pursuance of the rules, orders, and regulations of the Poor Law Commissioners, shall be bound to visit and attend personally the poor persons entrusted to his care, and shall be responsible for such visits and attendances, and shall so keep any weekly return prescribed by the orders of the Poor Law Commissioners, as to show when the visit or attendance made, or given to any pauper was made, or given by any person other than himself.

ARTICLE XV. Every medical officer to be hereafter appointed, shall if practicable, within twenty-one days of the time of his appointment, name to the Board of Guardians, some legally qualified medical practitioner to whom application for medicines or attendance may be made, in the case of his absence from home, or other hindrance to his personal attendance, and who will supply the same at the cost of such medical officer; and the name and residence of every medical practitioner so named shall be forwarded by the clerk to the Guardians to each relieving officer, and to the overseers of every parish in the Union.

Mode of obtaining Medical Relief by permanent Paupers.

ARTICLE XVI. The Board of Guardians shall, once in every six months, cause to be prepared a list of all such aged and infirm persons, and persons permanently sick or disabled, as may be actually receiving relief from such Board of Guardians, and residing within the district of each medical officer of the Union, and shall from time to time furnish to each medical officer a copy of the list aforesaid.

ARTICLE XVII. Every person whose name shall be inserted in such list, shall receive a ticket in the following form, and shall be entitled on the exhibition of such ticket to the medical officer of his district to obtain such advice, attendance, and medicines, as his case may require, without any order from the relieving officer, overseer, or other authority.

FORM OF TICKET.

______________________ UNION.

Date ______________________

Good until the ____________ day of ____________ 184

Name of Pauper ______________________

Residence of Pauper ______________________

Name of Medical Officer ______________________

Residence ______________________

Usual hour at which he is at Home ______________________

ARTICLE XVIII. Such medical officer shall, on the exhibition to him of the said ticket, and on application made on behalf of the party to whom such ticket was given, be held responsible for affording such advice, attendance, and medicines, as he may be bound to supply, in the same manner as if he had received in each case a special order from the Board of Guardians, or from any officer, to afford such advice, attendance, and medicines.

ARTICLE XIX. Provided always that if on complaint of any medical officer it be made to appear to the Board of Guardians, that any poor person who may have been furnished with a ticket in the aforesaid form shall have wilfully applied to, or sent for the medical officer on frivolous grounds, such poor person shall for the first time be admonished by the Board of Guardians, and on a repetition of such frivolous application, such poor person shall be deprived of his ticket, and thenceforth until the next half-yearly list be made out, shall not be empowered, except in cases of sudden and urgent necessity, to demand advice, attendance, or medicines, from such medical officer without an order of the Board of Guardians, a relieving officer, or an overseer of some parish in the Union.

Continuance in office of Medical Officers.

ARTICLE XX. Every medical officer duly appointed in pursuance of the orders and regulations of the Poor Law Commissioners shall, unless the period for which he is appointed be expressly entered on the Minutes of the Guardians at the time of making such appointment, or be expressly inserted in a written contract entered into by such medical officer, and such period have been subsequently approved by the Poor Law Commissioners, continue in office until he may die or resign, or become legally disqualified to hold such office, or be removed therefrom by the Poor Law Commissioners.

Explanation of Terms.

ARTICLE XXI. Whenever the word "Union" is used in this order, it shall be taken to include not only an Union of parishes formed under the provisions of the hereinbefore recited Act, but also any Union of parishes incorporated or united for the relief or maintenance of the poor under any local Act of Parliament.

ARTICLE XXII. Whenever the word "Guardians" is used, in this order, it shall be taken to include not only Guardians appointed or entitled to act under the provisions of the said hereinbefore recited Act, but also any governors, directors, managers, or acting Guardians entitled to act in the ordering of relief to the poor from the poor-rates under any local Act of Parliament.

XXIII. Whenever the words "Board of Guardians" are used in this order, they shall be taken to mean not only a Board of Guardians competent to act under the provisions of the said hereinbefore recited Act, but also such Guardians, or such a number of any Guardians as are competent to order relief to the poor from the poor-rates under any local Act of Parliament.

ARTICLE XXIV. Whenever the word "Parish" is used in this order, it shall be taken, to signify any parish, township, vill, or other place separately maintaining its own poor.

ARTICLE XXV. Whenever the word "Medicines" is used in this order, it shall be taken to include all medical and surgical appliances, and whenever the words "medical attendance" are used in this order, they shall be taken to include surgical attendance.

ARTICLE XXVI. Whenever the words "Medical Officer" are used in this order, they shall be taken to include any person duly licensed as a medical man, who shall have contracted with any Board of Guardians for the supply of medicines, or for medical attendance.

ARTICLE XXVII. Whenever, in describing any person or party, matter or thing, the word importing the singular number or the masculine gender only is used in this order, the same shall be taken to include, and shall be applied to, several persons or parties as well as one person or party, and females as well as males, and several matters or things as well as one matter or thing, respectively, unless there be something in the subject or context repugnant to such construction.

ARTICLE XXVIII. Whenever in this order any article is referred to by its number, the article of this order bearing that number shall be taken to be signified thereby.

Schedule containing the Names of the Unions to which the present Order applies.

Aberaeron
Abergavenny
Aberystwith
Abingdon
Albans, St.
Alcester
Aldeibury
Alnwick
Alresford
Alton
Altrincham
Amersham
Amesbury
Ampthill
Andover
Anglesey
Asaph, St.
Ashby-de-la-Zouch
Ashford, East
Ashford, West
Aston
Atcham
Atherstone
Auckland
Austel, St.
Axbridge
Axminster
Aylesbury
Aylesford, North
Aylsham
Bakewell
Bala
Banbury
Bangor & Beaumaris
Barnet
Barnstaple
Barrow on Soar
Basford
Basingstoke
Bath
Battle
Beaminster
Bedale
Bedford
Bedminster
Belford
Bellingham
Belper
Berkhampstead
Bermondsey
Berwick-on-Tweed
Beverley
Bicester
Bideford
Biggleswade
Billericay
Billesdon

Bingham
Bishop Stortford
Blaby
Blackburn
Blandford
Blean
Blofield
Blything
Bodmin
Bolton
Bootle
Bosmere & Claydon
Boston
Boughton, Great
Bourn
Brackley
Bradfield
Bradford (Wilts)
Bradford (York)
Braintree
Brampton
Brecknock
Brentford
Bridge [bridge
Bridgend and Cow-
Bridgnorth
Bridgewater
Bridlington
Bridport
Brixworth
Bromley
Bromsgrove
Bromyard
Buckingham
Builth
Buntingford
Burnley
Burton-on-Trent
Bury
Bury St. Edmunds
Caistor
Calne
Cambridge
Camelford
Cardiff
Cardigan
Carlisle
Carmarthen
Carnarvon
Castle Ward
Catherington
Caxton & Arrington
Cerne
Chailey
Chapel-en-le-Frith
Chard
Cheadle
Chelmsford

Cheltenham
Chepstow
Chertsey
Chesterfield
Chester-le-Street
Chesterton
Chippenham
Chipping Norton
Chipping Sodbury
Chorley
Chorlton
Christchurch
Church Stretton
Cirencester
Cleobury Mortimer
Clifton
Clitheroe
Clun
Clutton
Cockermouth
Colchester
Columb, St. Major
Congleton
Conway
Cookham
Corwen
Cosford
Cranbrook
Crediton
Crickhowel
Cricklade & Wootton
Croydon [Bassett
Cuckfield
Darlington
Dartford
Daventry
Depwade
Derby
Devizes
Dewsbury
Docking
Dolgelly
Doncaster
Dorchester
Dore
Dorking
Dover
Downham
Drayton
Driffield
Droitwich
Droxford
Dudley
Dulverton
Dunmow
Durham
Dursley
Easington

Easingwold
Eastbourne
East Grinstead
Easthampstead
East Retford
Eastry
East Ward
Ecclesall Bierlow
Edmonton
Elham
Ellesmere
Ely
Epping
Epsom
Erpingham
Eton
Evesham
Faith, St.
Falmouth
Fareham
Faringdon
Faversham
Festiniog
Flegg, East & West
Foleshill
Fordingbridge
Forehoe
Freebridge Lynn
Frome
Fylde
Gainsborough
Garstang
Gateshead
Germans, St.
Glanford Brigg
Glendale
Glossop
Gloucester
Godstone
Goole
Grantham
Gravesend & Milton
Greenwich
Guildford
Guiltcross
Guisborough
Hackney
Hailsham
Halifax
Halstead
Haltwhistle
Hambledon
Hardingstone
Hartismere
Hartley Wintney
Haslingden
Hastings
Hatfield

Havant
Haverfordwest
Hay
Hayfield
Headington
Helmsley Blackmoor
Helston
Hemel-Hempstead
Hendon
Henley
Henstead
Hereford
Hertford
Hexham [don
Highworth & Swin-
Hinckley
Hitchin
Holbeach
Holborn
Hollingbourn
Holsworthy
Holywell
Honiton
Hoo
Horncastle
Horsham
Houghton-le-Spring
Howden
Hoxne
Huddersfield
Hungerford
Huntingdon
Hursley
Ipswich
Ives, St.
Keighley
Kendal
Kensington
Kettering
Keynsham
Kidderminster
Kingsbridge
Kingsclere
King's Lynn
King's Norton
Kingston-on-Thames
Kington
Knighton
Lampeter
Lancaster
Lanchester
Langport
Launceston
Ledbury
Leek
Leicester
Leigh
Leighton Buzzard

Leominster
Lewes
Lewisham
Lexden & Winstree
Leyburn
Lichfield
Lincoln
Linton
Liskeard
Liverpool
Llandilo Fawr
Llandovery
Llanelly
Llanfyllin
Llanrwst
Loddon & Clavering
London, city of
London, East
London, West
Longtown
Loughborough
Louth
Ludlow
Luton
Lutterworth
Lymington
Macclesfield
Machynlleth
Madeley
Maidstone
Maldon
Malling
Malmsbury
Malton
Manchester
Mansfield
Market Bosworth
Market Harborough
Marlborough
Martley
Medway
Melksham
Melton Mowbray
Mere
Meriden
Merthyr Tidvil
Midhurst
Mildenhall
Milton
Mitford & Launditch
Monmouth
Morpeth [land
Mutford & Lothing-
Nantwich
Narberth
Neath
Neot's, St.
Newark
Newbury

Newcastle-in-Emlyn
Newcastle-under-
Lyne [Tyne
Newcastle-upon-
Newent
New Forest
Newhaven
Newmarket [mouth)
Newport (Mon-
Newport (Salop)
Newport Pagnell
Newton Abbott
Newtown & Llanid-
Northallerton [loes
Northampton
Northleach
Northwich
North Witchford
Nottingham
Nuneaton
Oakham
Okehampton
Olave's, St.
Ongar
Ormskirk
Orsett
Oundle
Pateley Bridge
Patrington
Pembroke
Penkridge
Penrith
Penzance
Pershore
Peterborough
Petersfield
Petworth
Pewsey
Pickering
Plomesgate
Plympton St. Mary
Pocklington
Pont-y-pool
Poole
Poplar
Portsea Island
Potterspury
Prescot
Presteigne
Preston
Pwllheli
Radford
Reading
Redruth
Reeth
Reigate
Rhayadar
Richmond (Surrey)
Richmond (York)
Ringwood

Ripon
Risbridge
Rochford
Romford
Romney Marsh
Romsey
Ross
Rothbury
Rotherham
Royston
Rugby
Runcorn
Ruthin
Rye
Saffron Walden
Salford
Samford
Saviour's, St.
Scarborough
Sculcoates
Sedbergh
Sedgefield
Seisdon
Selby
Settle
Seven Oaks
Shaftesbury
Shardlow
Sheffield
Sheppey
Shepton Mallet
Sherborne
Shiffnal
Shipston-on-Stour
Skipton
Skirlaugh
Sleaford
Solihull
Southam
South Molton
South Shields
South Stoneham
Southwell
Spalding
Spilsby
Stafford
Staines
Stamford
Stepney
Steyning
Stockbridge
Stockport
Stockton
Stone
Stokesley
Stourbridge
Stow
Stow-on-the-Wold
Strand
Stratford-on-Avon

Stratton
Stroud
Sturminster
Sudbury
Sunderland
Swaffham
Swansea
Tamworth
Taunton
Tavistock
Teesdale
Tenbury
Tendring
Tenterden
Tetbury
Tewkesbury
Thakeham
Thame
Thanet, Isle of
Thetford
Thingoe
Thirsk
Thomas, St.
Thornbury
Thorne
Thrapston
Ticehurst
Tisbury
Tiverton
Todmorden
Tonbridge
Torrington
Totnes
Towcester
Tregaron
Truro
Tunstead & Happing
Tynemouth
Uckfield
Ulverstone
Uppingham
Upton-on-Severn
Uttoxeter
Uxbridge
Wakefield
Wallingford
Walsal
Walsingham [ham
Wandsworth & Clap-
Wangford
Wantage
Ware [beck
Wareham and Pur-
Warminster
Warrington

Warwick
Watford
Wayland
Weardale
Wellingborough
Wellington (Salop)
Wellington (Somer-
Wells [set)
Welwyn
Wem
Weobly
Westbourne
West Bromwich
Westbury-on-Severn
Westbury & Whor-
welsdown
West Derby
West Firle
West Ham
West Hampnett
West Ward
Weymouth
Wheatenhurst
Whitby
Whitchurch
Whitehaven
Whitechapel
Wigan
Wigton
Williton
Wilton [Cranborne
Wimborne and
Wincanton
Winchcombe
Winchester, New
Windsor
Winslow
Wirrall
Wisbeach
Witham
Witney
Woburn
Wokingham
Wolstanton and
Burslem
Wolverhampton
Woodbridge
Woodstock
Worcester
Worksop
Wortley
Wrexham
Wycombe
Yeovil
York

Given under our Hands and Seal, &c., &c.

LONDON: Printed by Order of the Poor Law Commissioners, by W. CLOWES and SONS, Stamford Street, and Published by C. KNIGHT and Co., 22, Ludgate Street.

AN

OFFICIAL CIRCULAR

OF PUBLIC DOCUMENTS AND INFORMATION:

DIRECTED BY THE POOR LAW COMMISSIONERS TO BE PRINTED, CHIEFLY FOR THE USE OF THE MEMBERS AND PERMANENT OFFICERS OF BOARDS OF GUARDIANS, UNDER THE POOR LAW AMENDMENT ACT.

No. 18. CIRCULAR ISSUED MAY 9TH, 1842.

Poor Law Commission Office,
Somerset House,
May 5, 1842.

THE Poor Law Commissioners, on a review of their minutes, directed that the minutes and correspondence on the following subjects should be printed and circulated for the information of Guardians and officers of the several Unions, viz.—

By order of the Board,
EDWIN CHADWICK, *Secretary*.

I.—WORKHOUSE—REPORTS ON BAKING BREAD IN.

The Commissioners took into consideration a letter from the Board of Guardians of the West Ham Union, requesting the Commissioners to furnish them with any information in their possession as to the several Unions that grind their own corn and bake their own bread.

The Commissioners, in compliance with the request of the Guardians, transmitted for their information the following reports which the Commissioners had received on the subject from the Barnstaple, Hoxne, Redruth, and Tendring Unions, but without pledging themselves to the entire accuracy of the details, as statements of this kind are often open to controversy, and are not always to be implicitly relied on, as it is possible that items, such as the original cost of the oven and wear and tear, may have been omitted which ought to have been included in the estimate.

From the statements it would appear that there is, on the whole, a saving in point of expense in baking in the workhouse, but perhaps the strongest reasons in favour of baking are that paupers in a workhouse certainly appear to prefer home-baked bread to that purchased of common bakers, and that the Guardians may be certain both as to the quantity and quality of the loaf which never can be the case under a contract.

On the other hand, when bread is baked in a workhouse, the door is opened to irregularities and malversations on the part of the baker and master of the workhouse; with a really good master and a skilful baker there may be no reason for complaints on this head, but it is desirable where the system is adopted that a return should be required by the Guardians from time to time of the quantity of flour and other materials consumed, and of the number of loaves supplied, or a check otherwise provided, whereby any loss by waste or from any other cause may be discovered and prevented.

"REPORT on BAKING BREAD in the BARNSTAPLE UNION WORKHOUSE, in the county of Devon, for the use of the Paupers of the said Union.

"The Board commenced baking for the workhouse only at Lady-day, 1838.

"This was done merely as an experiment, for although many of the guardians considered that all the bread for the Union might be advantageously baked in the house, others were of opinion that any attempt to carry this object into effect must fail, and that even in baking for the in-door paupers *only* success was very problematical.

"The principal argument urged by the advocates for baking the out-door bread was furnished by the fact, that scarcely a Board-day passed without one or another of the contractors being called before the guardians charged with having sent out loaves of a bad quality, added to which it was notorious that the relieving officers had frequently to wait about at their different stations for the bread, and were sometimes obliged to go away without delivering it at all in consequence of the non-arrival of the contractor.

"On the other hand, whilst the existence of these evils was acknowledged and deplored, it was argued that baking for the entire Union would be attended with difficulties exceedingly great, if not altogether insurmountable. It was first shown that it would be necessary to produce about 70,000 loaves annually, and then contended that a business of such magnitude, involving an expenditure of from sixteen to eighteen hundred pounds a-year, would require a system of superintendence and of accounts which the Board could not calculate on being able to establish. It was also urged that great difficulties would arise in distributing the out-door bread in the several parishes of the Union.

"A most unwearied advocate for the baking system was found in the then chairman of the visiting committee (the Rev. James Arthur, of Atherington,) to whose persevering exertions it was owing (mainly, if not altogether) that the guardians consented to bake for the in-door paupers only for one quarter of a-year.

"On the adoption of this resolution contracts for materials were immediately entered into, and a baker was engaged, who undertook to bake such quantities of bread as might be wanted, and to provide the necessary quantity of yeast, at 4*s*. per sack (of flour). Forms of accounts were also prepared, of which copies are hereto subjoined.—(See Appendix F and G.)

"During this quarter occasional inconvenience was felt from the irregular attendance of the baker; but upon the whole the experiment was so far successful, that it was determined to prosecute it still further. As to the out-door bread, however, no idea was entertained of baking that for the present, and contracts for providing it in the usual way during the following quarter had been entered into, when the accidental occurrence of the following circumstance induced the Board to make immediate arrangements for baking a large portion of the out-door, in addition to the in-door, bread. One of the contractors for the Midsummer quarter, 1838, had entered into a fresh contract for supplying 35 parishes during the ensuing quarter; but before the latter could commence, such heavy complaints were made as to the quality of the bread which he supplied, and such strong representations of his inability to complete his new engagement satisfactorily, that the Board determined at once to vacate his contract and to bake in the workhouse for the parishes he had engaged to supply.

"The arrangements necessary for carrying out this resolution were speedily completed, and at the proper time were put in operation with so much success, that at the end of one quarter the guardians unanimously resolved to bake thenceforth the whole of the bread for the Union.

"These first arrangements, however, having been rather hastily concocted, were unavoidably defective in some of their details. No further reference will, therefore, be made to them in this Report; but the improved arrangements now in operation (the result of time and experience) will be given at full length hereafter. It may, however, be here stated, that during the three probationary months the new system (as promotive of the ends of economy) was properly tested, for whilst the Board had engaged, under the dissolved contract, to pay 7*d*. per 4 lb. loaf, by baking their own bread, it was ascertained that a loaf of the same size and of superior quality cost (including every expense) a fraction less than 6½*d*.

"The baking for the whole Union has proceeded ever since with complete success, having been attended with the following undoubted advantages: first, the certainty of providing good bread for the poor; secondly, regularity in its delivery; and thirdly, a considerable saving to the rate-payers.

"Such is the history of the baking business in the Barnstaple Union. The following details will show the system at present in operation:—

"*Materials*.—These, consisting of flour, coals, yeast, and potatoes, are all supplied by contract (if possible). In this Union, at first, the baker was permitted to find yeast; but the Board soon saw the propriety of discontinuing this practice. Whilst on this branch of the subject, and in order to prevent misapprehension, perhaps a word or two may be desirable as to the use of potatoes in bread-baking. It is asserted by bakers as a fact, that no person in their trade prepares, or can satisfactorily prepare, his "sponge" without the aid of this esculent. By a particular process, the nutritive portion, or "flour" of it is extracted and used as an auxiliary to the fermenting principle, and the true method of doing this is regarded, it is said, as one of the principal secrets in "the art and mystery" of a baker.

"*The Baker*.—This individual is a strong able-bodied man, of exceedingly steady habits, and possessing a thorough knowledge of his business. Any deficiency in these qualifications (especially in the second or third) would be fatal to the success of the system. He devotes his whole time to the service of the Union, examines all materials and sees that they are of the proper quality, and has to bear the loss of a bad batch of bread when caused by the use of inferior articles, or by his own negligence or carelessness. To secure this desiderata, it is obvious that he must be remunerated liberally. In this Union the baker is paid a guinea per week, the average rate of a journeyman's wages being only 12*s.* or 13*s.* A copy of the contract between the baker and the Board of Guardians will be found in the Appendix (H).

"*Delivering Bread.*—The relieving officers carry round and distribute the bread in their respective districts in light vehicles capable of holding from 100 to 150 loaves each, and so constructed as to keep the bread dry and compact. They attend at the workhouse either daily, on alternate days, or at more distant intervals (as may be necessary) for such bread as they require. One of the relieving officers, the extremity of whose district is 20 miles from the bakehouse, gets his loaves conveyed to two or three distant parishes by carriers. But all arrangements of this kind must be governed in a great measure by local circumstances. In consideration of the extra expenses to which the relieving officers are put, and the additional labour entailed on them in distributing the bread, they receive 20*l.* a-year each in addition to their salary *as relieving officers.*

"*The Master of the Workhouse.*—This officer keeps the accounts, receives and gives out all materials, takes into store all the bread when baked, and delivers out loaves to the relieving officers when they apply for them, receives all reports as to improper materials from the baker, and returns the same to the contractors. He has the general superintendence of the whole concern, being in point of fact, emphatically, *the master.* He is paid for his additional labour and responsibility 15*l.* a-year.

"*The Porter.*—In the event of the master being absent, or otherwise particularly engaged, it is the porter's duty to see that all materials sent in are of the proper weight. He assists the master generally in all matters, except making up the accounts. He receives 5*l.* a-year extra.

Accounts for the whole Union.—These accounts consist of five forms given in the appendix, and marked A, B, C, D, and E,—Form A, called the "Production Account," shows the value of all materials used daily, and the number of loaves produced. It is made up at the end of each week. Form B, (the "Consumption Account,) exhibits the number of loaves taken out of the store daily for each relieving district, and also for the workhouse. This also is made up and balanced weekly. Form C, is the account of materials received, and D, that of materials consumed, one line only in each being required for one week. These accounts are made up and balanced quarterly. Before any remark is offered on Form E, it will be necessary to show how the cost per loaf is *estimated* (for it cannot be ascertained with certainty) at the beginning of each quarter.

	£.	s.	d.
" Suppose a sack of flour to cost	2	2	0
Coals	0	1	0
Yeast	0	1	0
Potatoes	0	0	6
Wages and salares . . .	0	3	6
Altogether	£2	8	0

This sum must be divided by the average number of loaves which a sack of flour will produce (say 95) thus:—

2*l.* 8*s.* = 576 pence ÷ 95 = 6*d.* $\frac{6}{95}$

or a fraction above 6*d.* per loaf. But as it is obvious that fractions cannot be admitted into the Union accounts, a charge of 6¼*d.* per loaf must be made, and hence the necessity of Form E; in one column of which is inserted the cost of production, and in the other the amount charged to the Union: the difference between the totals being carried quarterly to the credit of 'establishment' as compensation for the use of the bakehouse and store-rooms, and for wear and tear of the baking apparatus.

"*Accounts for the Workhouse only.*—These accounts are exceedingly simple. The cost per loaf need not be calculated; for supposing 95 loaves to be made in one week at an expense of 2*l.* 5*s.* 8¼*d.*, the whole of these loaves are taken by the master of the workhouse into the store, and proper entries made in the provision-book under the heads 'new stock,' and 'cost of new stock.' Then, should it turn out, that only 84 of those loaves are consumed in the course of that week, their value is ascertained by the rule of simple proportion, thus:—

As 95 : 2*l.* 5*s.* 8¼*d.* : : 84 : 2*l.* 0*s.* 4½*d.*

and the columns in the provision-book, under the head of 'articles consumed' 'in the house,' are filled up accordingly.

"Perhaps this report may not be inappropriately concluded with an anecdote. One complaint (and *only* one) has been made of the quality of the bread baked in the workhouse, and that was by a pauper of Georgeham, who carried a piece of one of her loaves to her clergyman, telling him that from the peculiar sensations it created in her stomach she was quite sure it contained deleterious ingredients. The clergyman took the bread from her, and caused it to be forwarded (through an agent in Barnstaple) to Mr. Herepath, the eminent chemist of Bristol, to be analyzed. The result of that gentleman's experiments will be found in the annexed letter (see page 262.)

FORM A.

Bread Production Account for the Week of the Quarter ending 184 .

Days of the Week.	Flour used.		Cost of Potatoes.	Cost of Coals.	Cost of Yeast.	Total Cost.	Loaves produced.	Cost per Loaf.
	Sacks.	Cost at £ per sack.						
		£. s. d.	£. s. d.	£. s. d.	£. s. d.	£. s. d.		
Totals . .								

FORM B.

Bread Consumption Account (with Abstract of Production) for the Week of the Quarter ending 184 .

Production.		Consumption.										
Number of Loaves.	Value at per Loaf.	In what District.	Number of Loaves delivered on						Total.	Value at per Loaf.	Officers' initials, acknowledging the receipt of Loaves.
			Fri.	Sat.	Mon	Tu.	We.	Th.			
In Store at the beginning of the Week . Made during the Week											
		Totals delivered In Store .									
Totals . . .		Totals .									

FORM C.

Materials for Bread received during the Quarter ending 184 .

Week.	Flour.				Potatoes.			Coals.				Yeast.			Totals.
	No. of Invoice.	Sacks.	Price.	Cost.	Quantity.	Price.	Cost.	No. of Invoice.	Tons.	Price.	Cost.	Quarts.	Price.	Cost.	
				£. s. d.			£. s. d.				£. s. d.			£. s. d.	£. s. d.
In Store .															
Total Received . . Total Used .															
In Store .															

FORM D.
Quarter ending 184 .

Bread Materials taken out of Store.

Weeks.	Flour.		Potatoes.	Coals.	Yeast.	Totals.
	Sacks.	Cost.	Cost.	Cost.	Cost.	
		£. s. d.	£. s. d.	£. s. d.	£. s. d.	£. s. d.
Totals						

FORM E.

Summary of

Weeks.	Production.		Consumption.	
	Loaves	Cost.	Loaves	Charged.
		£. s. d		£. s. d.
Salaries				
Totals				
Deduct Cost of Production				
Difference carried to Establishment . .				

FORM F.
Account of Bread Materials received in the Quarter ending 184 .

Weeks.	No. of Invoice.	Flour.		Coals.		Potatoes.		Total Cost.
		Quantity.	Cost.	Quantity.	Cost.	Quantity.	Cost.	
			£. s. d.		£. s. d.		£. s. d.	£. s. d.
Totals .								

FORM G.
Bread Account for the Quarter ending 184 .

Weeks.	Flour consumed.		Coals.	Potatoes.	Labour and Yeast.	Total Cost.	Number of Loaves produced.
	Quantity.	Cost.	Cost.	Cost.	Cost.		
		£. s. d.	£. s. d.	£. s. d.	£. s. d.	£. s. d.	
Totals .							

"FORM H.

"An agreement made and entered into the twenty-third day of November, one thousand eight hundred and thirty-eight, between George French, of Barnstaple, in the county of Devon, baker, of the one part, and the Board of Guardians of the Barnstaple Union, of the other part, as follows (that is to say), the said George French (in consideration of the payments to be made to him as hereinafter mentioned), agrees with the said Board of Guardians to work for them in the capacity of a baker from the twenty-first day of December next until this agreement shall be duly put an end to, in the manner hereinafter mentioned; and during the continuance of the same agreement shall and will devote, and give his whole time and attention to the service of the said Board of Guardians, not following, carrying on, or being concerned in any other trade, employment, or occupation whatsoever; and shall adopt and use the best and most appropriate and economical means and methods with which he is or shall be acquainted for converting the flour and materials which may be confided to him into bread; and shall, without fear, favour, or partiality, inspect, examine, and ascertain the nature and quality of the flour that shall from time to time be supplied for the use of the said Union, and faithfully report thereon to the said Board of Guardians, or to the visiting committee, or to the master of the said workhouse; and shall daily and every day make into bread such reasonable quantities of flour as he shall be required to do by the master of the said workhouse; and shall find and provide all such yeast as may be necessary for the purpose of converting the said flour into good wholesome bread.* And that in case any bread, flour, or other materials belonging to the said guardians shall receive or sustain any damage or injury by reason of the inattention, negligence, or carelessness of the said George French, he, the said George French, shall bear, allow, and make good to the said Board of Guardians the full cost and amount of such damage or injury, and the said guardians shall have full power to keep back the same from any money that may be due from them to the said George French. And the said Board of Guardians agree to pay to the said George French (for and in consideration of his work and labour as before mentioned) the wages of one pound per week during the continuance of this agreement. And also to pay to the said George French for all such yeast as shall be required as aforesaid, at and after the rate of one shilling for the quantity used in making each sack of flour into bread. And it is hereby mutually agreed by and between the said parties hereto, that in case either of them shall at any time be desirous of putting an end to this agreement, the said Board of Guardians shall be at liberty so to do upon giving to the said George French one month's previous notice thereof in writing; and the said George French shall be at the like liberty upon giving to the said Board of Guardians three months' previous notice thereof in writing: Provided always, that in case the said George French shall be guilty of inattention, wilful negligence, or any other impropriety in the performance of his duties under this agreement, the said Board of Guardians shall have full power and authority to discharge the said George French without giving him any previous notice thereof whatsoever. In witness whereof the said parties have hereto set their hands the day and year first above written.

"GEORGE FRENCH.

"Witness, JOHN BARRY."

"'*Mansion House, Old Park, Bristol,*
June 19th, 1839.

"'DEAR SIR,—Taking it for granted that the sensations described by you to have followed eating the bread sent, were not illusory, I closely examined it; first, by obtaining the soluble parts in various menstrua, and submitting the solutions to the necessary re-agents; and, secondly, by incinerating the bread to obtain any insoluble mineral substances. By the latter process 100 grains gave of ashes $\frac{73}{100}$ of a grain; of these water dissolved 33, which were composed of common salt, potassa resulting from the decomposed acetate of potassa, and phosphate of potash; the remaining $\frac{40}{100}$ were all phosphate of lime. As all these substances are natural to wheat flour, and are not in an unusual proportion, I think you will agree with me that no fixed insoluble mineral substance could have been present. I demonstrated to my own satisfaction that the watery solution contained nothing unnatural which could be discovered in the present state of chemical knowledge. But not being satisfied with this, I ate a large slice of the bread, and found no inconvenience from the experiment. I am therefore sceptical as to the sensations having been felt by the parties who have made such representations of the guardians, and this I should not be surprised at after the experience I have had with 4,000 paupers of Bristol.

"'I am, dear Sir,
(Signed) "'WILLIAM HERAPATH.

"'*Mr. G. K. Cotton, Chemist, &c.,*
"'*Barnstaple.*

(Signed) "'J. S. CLAY,
"'*Clerk to the Barnstaple Union.*

"'*Barnstaple, 13th October*, 1841.'"

* This part of the contract was subsequently rescinded.

TENDRING UNION.

Flour Account from Midsummer to Michaelmas, 1841.

When received.	Of whom.	Quantity.			Price per Sack.	Total Value.		
		sacks.	lbs.	oz.	s.	£.	s.	d.
June 12, 1841	Mr. May	10	0	0	44	22	0	0
June 19 ,,	,,	10	0	0	44	22	0	0
July 10 ,,	,,	10	0	0	44	22	0	0
July 31 ,,	,,	10	0	0	44	22	0	0
Aug. 14 ,,	,,	10	0	0	44	22	0	0
Sept. 4 ,,	,,	5	0	0	44	11	0	0
		55	0	0	44	121	0	0
Deduct for Puddings		4	148	8	44	9	19	4
Used for Baking		50	131	8	44	111	0	8
Total Cost of Flour for Baking						111	0	8
Add Expenses of Baking:—								
Baker, 13 weeks' wages, at 6s. per week						3	18	0
Ditto, 13 weeks' board, at 5s. per week						3	5	0
Coals, 1½ tons						1	16	4
Salt. 56 lbs.						0	1	6
Potatoes, 1 sack						0	4	0
Yeast for the quarter						0	19	6
Total Expense						121	5	0

Loaves Baked in the House from Midsummer to Michaelmas, 1841.

Week of Quarter.	Number of Loaves.	Price as per Contracts.		Total Value.		
		s.	d.	£.	s.	d.
1st	468	..		..		
2nd	372	..		..		
3rd	359	..		..		
4th	369½	..		..		
5th	363	..		..		
6th	368	..		..		
7th	272	..		..		
8th	383½	..		..		
9th	300½	..		..		
10th	346½	..		..		
11th	333½	..		..		
12th	170½	..		..		
13th	509½	..		..		
Total	4,615½	0	6½	129	19	0¾*
				121	5	0
Balance in favour of Baking				8	14	0¾

* Expense of loaves at contract price.

HOXNE UNION, November 29, 1841.

Extract from Minute Book.—" The Governor produced a Report, setting forth the quantity of Flour consumed for Bread, the cost of same, and all incidental expenses: showing a comparison with the same and the probable Contract Price, had Bread been bought for consumption in the House, viz.:—

—	Flour consumed.			Price per Sack.		Total Value.			Calculated produce, Ninety 4 lb. Loaves to the Sack.	Calculated Contract Price of Bread.		Cost of Bread.		
	sacks.	st.	lbs.	s.	d.	£.	s.	d.	Loaves.	s.	d.	£.	s.	d.
From October 24, 1840, to the end of March quarter, 1841, being 22 weeks	75	4	7	42	0	160	0	0	6,770	0	7½	211	4	3
Quarter ending June—13 weeks	36	0	0	44	0	79	4	0	3,240	0	7½	101	5	0
Quarter ending September—13 weeks	33	3	7	42	6	70	10	0	2,985	0	7½	93	5	7½
First four weeks of quarter ending December	7	5	9	47	0	17	3	2	656	0	8	21	19	0
Total value of Flour						326	17	2	Cost of Bread			427	13	10¼
Coals, at 8 cwt. per month						7	4	6						
Yeast, 9d. per week						1	19	0						
Wages—Extra for Baker, 3s. 6d. per week						9	2	0						
Wear and tear of Utensils						2	0	0	Ditto of Flour and Baking			349	14	8
Interest on Capital						2	12	0						
Total Expense						349	14	8	Balance			77	19	2½

REDRUTH UNION.—UNION BAKERY.

Dr. 1841.				£.	*s.*	*d.*
To Materials and Expenses attending baking of Bread, in the Union House during the quarter ending Midsummer, 1841, as follows:—						
103½ sacks Flour . .	£222	7	3			
135 bushels Barley . .	73	19	0			
1½ bushel Malt . . .	1	14	6			
1½ lb. Hops . . .	0	3	0			
3 cwt. Salt	0	7	6			
70 cwt. Coals . . .	3	10	0			
Baker's Wages . . .	7	14	0			
Baker's Rations . . .	2	12	0			
Paid for Carriage out . .	4	14	0			
				317	1	3
To ditto for the quarter ending Michaelmas, 1841, as follows:—						
90½ sacks Flour . .	£201	7	3			
129 bushels Barley . .	70	19	0			
64 cwt. Coals . . .	3	0	8			
1¼ bushel Malt . . .	1	7	6			
1¼ lb. Hops	0	2	6			
3 cwt. Salt	0	7	6			
Baker's Wages . . .	7	3	0			
Baker's Rations . . .	2	12	0			
Hay, Corn, and Grass for Horse, and Toll-gates carrying out	6	10	0			
				293	9	5
To ditto for the quarter ending Christmas, 1841:—						
98 sacks Flour . .	£208	5	0			
133 bushels Barley . .	69	16	6			
65 cwt. Coals . . .	3	1	9			
1¼ bushel Malt . . .	1	7	6			
1¼ lb. Hops	0	2	6			
3 cwt. Salt	0	7	6			
Baker's Wages and Rations	9	15	0			
Hay, Corn, and Bran . .	6	0	0			
Tolls	1	4	3			
Paid Cash carrying out .	2	1	0			
				302	1	0
To Balance gained in nine months by baking Bread at the Union House .				287	9	7¾
				£1,200	1	3¾

1841.	£.	*s.*	*d.* *Cr.*
By Bread produced during the quarter ending Midsummer, 1841, at the contract price for the corresponding quarter, 1840, when Flour was 10 per cent lower in price:—			
2,685 white Loaves, at 7¼*d.*	81	2	2¼
13,052 brown ditto, at 6¼*d.*	339	17	11
By Bread produced during the quarter ending Michaelmas, 1841, at the contract price for the corresponding quarter, 1840. Flour same price:—			
2,720 white Loaves, at 7¼*d.*	82	3	4
11,790 brown ditto, at 6¼*d.*	307	0	7½
By Bread produced during the quarter ending Christmas, 1841, at the contract price for the corresponding quarter, 1840. Flour same price:—			
3,135 white Loaves, at 7*d.*	91	8	9
11,937 brown ditto, at 6*d.*	298	8	6
45,319 Loaves.	£1,200	1	3¾

Union House, 23rd January, 1842.

JAMES ROGERS, *Governor.*

II.—ARTICLE XI., OF THE GENERAL WORKHOUSE RULES.

Copy of Minute of the Poor Law Commissioners thereon, dated 5th April, 1842.

"Article 11. The guardians shall, within fourteen days after this order shall have come into force, after consulting with the medical officer, report to the Poor Law Commissioners, the greatest number of paupers which ought to be admitted into the workhouse; and when such number shall have been approved or fixed by the Poor Law Commissioners, it shall not be lawful for the guardians to admit into the workhouse, or retain therein, a larger number of paupers, and the fact of any excess above such number so approved of, or fixed by the Poor Law Commissioners, which shall be made known by the visiting committee, or the master of the workhouse, to the Board of Guardians, shall be forthwith reported to the Poor Law Commissioners by the clerk to such guardians, and entered on the minutes of the meeting at which such fact was so made known, and the clerk to the said guardians shall take the direction of the Board for summoning within seven days a special meeting of the guardians for the purpose of considering the steps necessary to be taken for hiring, or otherwise providing additional workhouse accommodation.

"Provided that if any alteration in the arrangements of the said workhouse, or any addition thereto shall have been made, which may render such workhouse capable of accommodating a number of inmates larger than the number already approved, or fixed by the Poor Law Commissioners, the guardians shall, after consulting their medical officer, report to the Poor Law Commissioners the additional number which the workhouse may be deemed capable of accommodating, in order that the number already fixed or approved may be altered by the said Commissioners as occasion may require."

With reference to this article of the workhouse rules the Board ordered:—

1st.—That a register be prepared and kept in the office, to be lettered "Workhouse Accommodation," ruled in the following form.

2nd.—That as the reports in pursuance of Article 11 are successively received, entries be made in the registers in conformity with such reports, and the numbers sanctioned by the Commissioners be, in like manner registered from time to time.

3rd.—That there be transmitted to each Assistant Commissioner, as soon as it is complete, an extract from the register of workhouse accommodation, containing a list of the workhouses under his superintendence, and the maximum number to be respectively received into each workhouse, and that any change in such number be notified to each Assistant Commissioner from time to time, as it may occur.

4th.—That each Assistant Commissioner be instructed to take care that the clerks of the several Unions punctually transmit to him the returns of the numbers in the workhouse, and other matters prescribed by the orders of the Poor Law Commissioners, or required by him, and that he do compare such returns with the extract from the register of workhouse accommodation, as forwarded to him from this office, corrected from time to time.

Whenever any excess above the maximum number shall appear on the face of the return or whenever the Assistant Commissioner may have reason to apprehend a pressure of any particular class in the workhouse, although the maximum number is not exceeded, or whenever he may learn the prevalence of any disease in the workhouse, he will immediately visit the Union in question, when there he will inspect the workhouse, and will confer with the guardians and their medical officer on the steps to be taken, and will then apprise the Commissioners with the least possible loss of time, of any matters connected with the conduct of the officers, or of any circumstances in the district which may render a deviation from the ordinary rules and regulations necessary, and will advise the Commissioners as to the nature of such deviation. He will in all cases bear in mind that the first object is to remedy any defect in the local management which may affect the health of the poor, and the efficiency of the relief to be afforded to them, and that all forms are of secondary importance to this end: so far, at least as the law has invested the Commissioners with a discretionary power of dispensing with them.

Number of Work-houses.	Old or New.	Where situ-ated.	Number of Persons which each Workhouse is capable of receiving according to the report of the Guardians.	Number of Persons to be received in each, as fixed by the Poor Law Commissioners.	Reference to correspondence fixing the Number of Persons to be received in each.		Nature of any subsequent alterations in the arrangements, or of any addition to the Workhouse leading to a change in the Number.	Total Number when so changed.	Reference to correspondence altering the Number.		OBSERVATIONS.
					No. of Letter.	Date.			No. of Letter	Date.	

III.—SUMMARY of the RETURNS of the Amount of Money Levied, &c., and Expended for the Relief and Maintenance of the Poor, and for other purposes, during the Year ending 25th March, 1841.

Names of Counties.	Amount of Money Levied by Assessment.	Received from all other sources in aid of Poor Rate.	Total Amount of Money received for Relief, &c. of the Poor.	Amount of Money expended in Relief, &c. of the Poor.	Amount of Money expended in Law Charges, (Parochial and Union).	Payments under the Vaccination Extension Act.	
						Amount of Fees paid to the Vaccinators.	Outlay for Register and Certificate Books, &c.
	£.	£.	£.	£.	£.	£.	£.
Bedford	51,876	841	52,717	41,063	72	..	6
Berks	92,109	2,994	95,103	74,308	1,044	460	22
Buckingham	92,955	7,686	100,641	74,007	489	37	10
Cambridge	90,238	1,791	92,029	72,158	913	253	20
Chester	104,607	6,075	110,682	77,698	1,320	105	30
Cornwall	103,947	3,321	107,268	85,063	1,722	302	37
Cumberland	49,993	1,884	51,877	36,867	340	94	24
Derby	81,194	2,715	83,909	55,238	839	228	14
Devon	225,780	4,100	229,880	195,402	3,516	89	64
Dorset	98,769	1,596	100,365	80,097	1,804	142	3
Durham	92,995	3,005	96,000	66,639	912	147	26
Essex	213,715	3,669	217,384	171,356	1,593	71	35
Gloucester	182,857	5,232	188,089	130,321	2,384	211	100
Hereford	52,838	727	53,565	43,512	769	300	11
Hertford	71,361	1,427	72,788	61,250	465	124	17
Huntingdon	32,439	596	33,035	25,329	560	74	10
Kent	265,352	6,955	272,307	208,786	2,021	514	54
Lancaster	429,017	32,729	461,746	262,227	6,856	519	52
Leicester	95,316	2,293	97,609	70,423	1,330	172	23
Lincoln	140,513	3,306	143,819	103,894	1,504	505	79
Middlesex	668,527	34,523	703,050	435,606	5,322	364	163
Monmouth	39,182	731	39,913	24,819	189	73	1
Norfolk	236,079	5,038	241,117	182,229	1,326	100	35
Northampton	102,810	1,705	104,515	86,148	782	226	8
Northumberland	81,289	2,145	83,434	64,649	1,015	72	17
Nottingham	83,205	2,365	85,570	57,721	823	197	44
Oxford	88,268	2,626	90,894	76,474	809	90	10
Rutland	9,114	382	9,496	7,453	81	154	
Salop	79,233	1,592	80,825	57,571	741	202	36
Somerset	199,569	2,879	202,448	157,022	2,004	235	56
Southampton	182,453	2,937	185,390	142,507	1,421	332	30
Stafford	127,820	3,055	130,875	95,242	2,111	910	32
Suffolk	175,795	4,780	180,575	138,228	784	159	26
Surrey	263,597	19,446	283,043	199,477	2,604	451	57
Sussex	168,806	4,695	173,501	145,013	2,003	260	36
Warwick	171,435	9,202	180,637	102,828	2,283	324	22
Westmorland	22,629	1,235	23,864	17,607	561	68	2
Wilts	176,750	3,067	179,817	133,573	859	366	24
Worcester	96,185	2,026	98,211	62,958	1,963	239	66
York, East Riding	83,018	3,207	86,225	68,182	799	23	43
York, North Riding	65,718	2,560	68,278	58,308	1,203	64	18
York, West Riding	320,211	20,743	340,954	245,676	6,946	471	83
Totals of England	6,009,564	223,881	6,233,445	4,494,929	67,082	9,727	1,446
WALES.							
Anglesey	19,864	143	20,007	17,268	335	..	..
Brecknock	19,228	313	19,541	15,648	159	51	6
Cardigan	23,221	209	23,430	17,856	298	20	2
Carmarthen	40,888	277	41,165	32,004	358	15	7
Carnarvon	28,703	181	28,884	20,893	386	..	..
Denbigh	41,713	159	41,872	31,401	183	31	2
Flint	24,184	283	24,467	19,980	84	..	..
Glamorgan	42,251	497	42,748	33,753	357	147	3
Merioneth	16,807	124	16,931	15,005	109	55	10
Montgomery	42,044	268	42,312	28,365	248	112	6
Pembroke	29,758	379	30,137	23,812	121	..	8
Radnor	13,603	270	13,873	10,015	222	13	3
Totals of Wales	342,264	3,103	345,367	266,000	2,860	444	47
Totals of England and Wales	6,351,828	226,984	6,578,812	4,760,929	69,942	10,171	1,493

SUMMARY of the RETURNS of the Amount of Money Levied, &c.—*continued.*

Names of Counties.	Payments on Account of the Registration Act.		Payments under the Parochial Assessments Act (for Surveys, Valuations, &c.) and Loans repaid under the same.	Payments for or towards the County Rate.	Money Expended for all other purposes.	Total Parochial Rates, &c. expended.	Medical Relief.	Lunatics.	
	Fees to Clergymen and Registrars.	Outlay for Register Offices, Books, and Forms, and other incidental Expenses.						Number maintained in Asylums.	Amount Expended in their Maintenance, &c.
	£.	£.	£.	£.	£.	£.	£.	£.	£.
Bedford	353	2	297	9,701	747	52,241	1,533	59	962
Berks	498	114	777	11,373	2,456	91,052	3,285	99	1,899
Buckingham	453	23	680	10,344	4,245	90,288	2,463	45	827
Cambridge	614	17	200	8,496	4,719	87,390	2,607	33	600
Chester	1,215	142	216	20,724	6,884	108,334	2,220	126	1,420
Cornwall	1,009	36	438	11,270	5,938	105,815	1,960	124	1,736
Cumberland	506	12	109	8,694	2,239	48,885	922	67	856
Derby	864	34	402	16,955	4,687	79,261	1,227	42	811
Devon	1,441	71	735	17,346	8,977	227,641	5,564	215	3,558
Dorset	461	33	999	8,763	3,045	95,347	2,921	158	1,990
Durham	1,004	104	284	19,641	4,180	92,937	1,344	116	1,661
Essex	1,052	165	3,587	32,520	6,768	217,147	8,747	94	1,803
Gloucester	1,306	169	1,390	38,204	15,641	189,726	3,902	203	4,010
Hereford	367	33	155	5,992	1,322	52,461	1,810	35	620
Hertford	447	3	804	9,171	3,463	75,744	3,126	85	1,447
Huntingdon	204	39	15	4,929	660	31,820	1,062	17	376
Kent	1,603	209	3,647	33,126	17,620	267,580	7,018	251	5,209
Lancaster	5,938	161	1,258	132,570	48,219	457,800	6,911	537	7,565
Leicester	715	45	421	21,619	3,811	98,559	2,296	107	1,524
Lincoln	1,128	162	637	26,737	5,192	139,838	3,253	106	2,386
Middlesex	4,650	188	401	102,136	170,590	719,420	13,354	1,236	22,880
Monmouth	438	45	87	12,764	1,361	39,777	1,086	42	787
Norfolk	1,374	96	2,708	29,747	13,565	231,180	6,122	246	2,418
Northampton	685	116	410	12,942	3,895	105,212	2,460	112	1,919
Northumberland	746	106	101	8,765	3,560	79,031	1,317	143	2,287
Nottingham	812	60	125	20,413	3,916	84,111	2,083	118	2,665
Oxford	484	32	294	9,617	2,845	90,655	2,622	77	1,414
Rutland	66	10	..	1,050	516	9,330	313	12	286
Salop	657	120	973	15,832	4,169	80,301	2,721	104	1,889
Somerset	1,260	12	1,036	25,801	4,893	192,319	5,841	191	3,534
Southampton	989	175	2,449	30,046	5,488	183,437	6,366	207	3,525
Stafford	1,749	43	1,456	18,271	7,460	127,274	2,875	190	2,359
Suffolk	959	138	3,232	26,861	6,234	176,621	5,352	334	3,249
Surrey	1,862	200	2,841	44,960	31,947	284,399	5,988	377	7,522
Sussex	800	194	905	16,378	9,654	175,243	5,576	128	2,452
Warwick	1,267	91	2,421	31,567	50,176	190,979	3,287	114	2,620
Westmorland	167	2	40	3,929	865	23,241	553	15	316
Wilts	742	166	1,406	24,713	6,282	168,131	4,324	197	3,328
Worcester	719	86	701	23,992	3,223	93,947	3,042	131	2,283
York, East Riding	720	138	197	9,790	3,851	83,743	1,586	126	2,399
York, North Riding	624	97	235	6,190	1,936	68,675	1,436	69	1,107
York, West Riding	3,840	482	3,301	50,966	26,670	33[illegible],435	4,854	543	7,140
Totals of England	46,788	4,171	42,370	974,905	513,909	6,155,327	147,329	7,231	119,599
WALES.									
Anglesey	115	12	..	1,167	1,034	19,931	261	..	..
Brecknock	194	4	..	2,975	690	19,727	541	9	158
Cardigan [2]	178	4	20	2,767	1,305	22,450	559	2	42
Carmarthen	322	15	165	5,603	1,638	40,127	706	10	201
Carnarvon	211	80	16	4,079	1,510	27,175	692	3	64
Denbigh	220	22	92	6,272	1,731	39,954	515	..	..
Flint	150	25	156	3,207	1,197	24,799	482	..	..
Glamorgan	540	33	77	5,413	1,949	42,272	843	32	648
Merioneth	85	12	28	1,298	209	16,811	475	2	14
Montgomery	195	9	5	10,887	1,122	40,949	772	8	181
Pembroke	259	9	188	4,484	1,178	30,059	680	13	236
Radnor	69	6	40	2,978	245	13,591	199	1	7
Totals of Wales	2,538	231	787	51,130	13,808	337,845	6,725	80	1,551
Totals of England and Wales	49,326	4,402	43,157	1,026,035	527,717	6,493,172	154,054	7,311	121,150

IV.—OPERATION OF THE NEW POOR LAW I

The Commissioners took into consideration the following comparative statement of the Recei and Expenditure of the parish of Stoke-upon-Trent for six years previous, and subsequent to New Poor Law being brought into operation, transmitted to them by the Chairman of the Boar Guardians.

The Commissioners also took into consideration, communications on the subject from the clerk the Board of Guardians, and from their Assistant Commissioner, Mr. Gilbert.

With reference thereto, the Chairman observed:—"These savings have not been effected flourishing, but in most difficult times; not by lessening relief to the destitute poor, but by admi tering it with discretion, and by teaching those who were able to depend upon themselves; though the system admits, and indeed needs farther improvement, enough has been done to prove value, and to show the good it is capable of doing."

The clerk stated that, "It should be borne in mind, that the six years since the introduction of

PARISH OF STOK

COMPARATIVE TABLE of RECEIPT and EXPENDITURE for the Relief of the Poor for the six yea of the Poor Law Commissione

RECEIPTS.				DISBURSEMENTS.					
Comprising Money received on Account of "Rates," "Pensioners," "Loan Money," "Paupers' Earnings," "Bastardy," "County Voters," &c.				Establishment Charges, under which have been included "Salaries of Officers," "Law Expenses," "Printing and Stationery," Rent, Insurance," &c.; "Loan Money Repaid," "County Rate," "Additional Buildings and new Workhouse," "Old Debts," and "Miscellaneous."				Tot In-Maintenan	
Years ended March.	Total Receipts.	Years ended March.	Total Receipts.	Years ended March.	Total Establishment.	Years ended March.	Total Establishment.	Years ended March.	Total In-Maintenanc
	£. s. d.		£. s. d.		£. s. d.		£. s. d.		£. s.
1831	18,418 13 5½	1837	12,329 6 5½	1831	4,649 4 5½	1837	4,143 17 4	1831	1,689 5
1832	19,654 1 6	1838	9,683 0 11¼	1832	7,670 11 8¼	1838	4,430 1 11	1832	1,866 11
1833	19,822 2 9	1839	9,585 14 3	1833	7,849 14 11	1839	5,003 19 7½	1833	1,218 7
1834	18,422 16 8	1840	9,391 14 0	1834	7,730 6 11	1840	4,246 10 8¾	1834	1,813 19
1835	16,034 14 3½	1841	9,377 0 5¾	1835	6,045 3 4	1841	5,469 2 0¼	1835	1,924 10
1836	13,693 13 4¾	1842	9,777 10 6½	1836	4,364 14 4¼	1842	4,801 10 4	1836	1,903 19
Totals, 6 Years.	106,076 2 0¾		60,144 6 8¼		*38,309 15 8¼		†28,095 1 11¾		10,416 13

* In this amount the following items are included, Loan Money repaid, 4,097*l.* 3*s.* 7¼*d.*—County Rate, 6,203*l.* 16*s.* 1½*d.*—Additi Building and New Workhouse, 1,623*l*, 5*s.* 2*d.*—Old Debts, 11,998*l.* 1*s.* 1½*d.*—Making a total of 23,922*l.* 6*s.* 0½*d.*

HE PARISH OF STOKE-UPON-TRENT.

, have been years of unprecedented distress, and that the six years previous were years of a d and flourishing trade; still under every disadvantage, we show a saving of 40,000*l.* and upwards, had I time to go more into particulars, it would be found that a greater number of deserving r had been relieved."

Mr. Gilbert, the Assistant Commissioner, in his observations upon the statement, directed the nmissioners' attention to the circumstance, that "during the former and more expensive six years, trade in the potteries was considered to have been as flourishing and prosperous as at any known iod, whilst during the six years subsequently, the trade has been depressed beyond any former time own to the oldest inhabitant. I am informed by those whose experience and judgment entitle their nion to respect, that had the former system of parochial management continued during the last years, instead of so great a decrease, there must have been an increase at the least of 100,000*l.*"

ON-TRENT.

evious to the Administration of the Law in the above Parish, being placed under the orders d for the six years subsequently.

DISBURSEMENTS.

harges.		Total Out-Relief Charges.				Grand Totals.			
ears nded arch.	Total In-Maintenance.	Years ended March.	Total Out-Relief.	Years ended March.	Total Out-Relief.	Years ended March.	Total.	Years ended March.	Total.
	£. s. d.		£. s. d.		£. s. d.		£. s. d.		£. s. d.
837	2,441 18 1¾	1831	12,268 3 9½	1837	5,575 7 8¼	1831	18,606 13 7½	1837	12,161 3 2
838	2,027 2 11½	1832	10,220 4 10	1838	3,107 10 2	1832	19,757 8 3	1838	9,564 15 0½
839	2,357 11 3¾	1833	10,679 1 0½	1839	2,737 7 3	1833	19,747 3 2	1839	10,098 18 2¼
840	2,292 15 1¼	1834	8,980 9 7	1840	2,341 5 10	1834	18,524 16 1	1840	8,880 11 8
841	2,335 7 9	1835	7,889 16 6½	1841	2,911 17 3	1835	15,859 10 2	1841	10,716 7 0½
842	2,271 13 11	1836	7,160 8 0	1842	2,947 13 4½	1836	13,429 1 7¾	1842	10,020 17 7½
	13,726 9 2¼		57,198 3 9½		19,621 1 6¾		105,924 12 11¼		61,442 12 8¾

In this amount the following items are included, Loan Money repaid, 3,141*l.* 4*s.* 9*d.*—County Rate, 4,830*l.* 11*s.* 3*d.*—Additional lding and New Offices, 1,363*l.* 8*s*, 3*d.*—Old Debts, 611*l.* 2*s.* 6*d.*—Registration, Vaccination, and Census Expenses, 1,112*l.* 13*s.* 4*d.*, king a total of 11,058*l.* 10*s.* 1*d.*

V.— RATING.— 1. OVERSEERS NOT AT LIBERTY TO ALTER A RATE WHEN ALLOWED AND SIGNED BY MAGISTRATES.

The following is a copy of a letter addressed to the Commissioners by the clerk to the borough justices of Lyme Regis:—

" *Lyme, October* 18, 1841.

" GENTLEMEN,—At the late registration for this borough a case of an alteration of a poor-rate, apparently for party purposes, having been discovered, the mayor has instructed me to apply to you, requesting to be informed whether it is not the duty of the overseers to see that no alteration is made in the poor's-rate after signature by the justices and publication ; and whether they be not liable to punishment if such occurs through their inattention or otherwise ; and further, whether the rules of the Poor Law Commissioners are not to that effect, and provide a remedy for the evil complained of?

" I have the honour to be,
" Gentlemen,
" Your humble servant,
" GEORGE HINGESTON,
" *Clerk to the Borough Justices of*
" *Lyme Regis, Dorset.*

" *The Poor Law Commissioners.*"

In reply, the Commissioners stated that they have not issued any direction or regulation upon the subject. The question whether a rate, when once made and allowed, can be altered by the overseers, is a question unaffected by the regulations of the Commissioners. The Commissioners are of opinion that, after a rate has been duly allowed and published, the overseers are not at liberty to alter the rate, except in the cases in which they are expressly authorized by statute to do so. Under the 2nd and 3rd William IV. c. 45, the overseers are required to put the name of occupiers who claim to be rated upon the rate for the time being. They are likewise required to do so where like claims are made under 5th and 6th William IV. c. 76, s. 11 (Municipal Corporation Act).

But, except in the cases thus especially provided for, the overseers are not justified in altering the rate. If any corrupt or improper motive can be shown on the part of the overseer, the Commissioners apprehend he may be subject to an indictment for the improper alteration. See R. *v.* Barrett, 2 Dang, 465.

2. PRINCIPLE UPON WHICH RAILWAYS SHOULD BE RATED.

The following is an extract of a letter received from the overseer of the parish of Stretton :—

" The North Midland Railway, from Leeds to Derby (72½ miles in length), runs for the space of nearly a mile through this township. The railway was opened throughout on the 1st June, 1840 ; but had been partially opened two months before. The question we submit for your consideration is, in rating this railway to the poor, ought we to go upon an estimate of the clear profits derived by the company for the use of the said railway on a *mileage calculation* throughout the whole line, or ought we to base our estimate on the amount of *profits earned in our township ?*

" In answering this question, we beg leave to draw your attention to a clause in the Railway Act, 6th and 7th William IV. cap. 107, sec. 203, which runs thus : 'And be it further enacted, that in all cases in which the said company shall carry for their own profit any passengers, cattle, or other animals, goods, wares, or merchandise, articles, matters, or things, a separate account shall be duly kept, showing the amount of rates or tolls which have been received by the said company, or which would have been received by them for the use of the said railway in respect of such passengers, cattle, or other animals, goods, wares, or merchandise, articles, matters, or things, if carried by any other party or parties ; and the overseers of the poor of the several parishes and townships through which the said railway shall pass shall have free access to, and liberty to inspect, the same at any time during the first fourteen days in the months of February and August in each year.' And by a subsequent Act, 7th William IV. cap. 23, sec. 17, the above clause is re-enacted *verbatim*, with this addition : 'And if the said company shall neglect or refuse to keep such accounts, or to permit the inspection thereof as aforesaid, they shall forfeit and pay for every such neglect or refusal the sum of three hundred pounds, and a further sum of fifty pounds for every day during such neglect or refusal may continue.'

" We beg leave here to observe that we are not aware of any case having been decided which settled the principle of rating canals or railways, so as to ascertain whether such rating shall be by a mileage calculation throughout the whole line or by a calculation of the amount of profits arising in each township through which they pass. Some of the arguments made use of in the cases of Rex *v.* the Mayor and Aldermen of Bath, Rex *v.* Milton, Rex *v.* the Trent and Mersey Canal Company, Rex *v.* Oxford. 10 Barn. and Cress. 163, and some others, seem to favour the latter principle ; but, independent of other arguments, the rate and toll clause in the

Railway Acts before quoted appears to be very strong in favour of the former principle. The framer of that clause must have had some object in view at the time he drew it, and if that object was not to enable overseers of townships to act upon a *mileage* calculation, it is difficult to see what other object could possibly be had in view; for, on any other supposition, the whole section becomes nugatory. A mileage calculation is also by far the more convenient and intelligible in practice; for it would be exceedingly difficult, and next to an impossibility, for overseers ever to arrive at anything like a just calculation as to the amount of profit derived in each township.

"We have, however, been informed that on an appeal before a special sessions of magistrates lately held at Wakefield, on precisely a similar case, that it was then and there determined that the calculation ought not to have been on a mileage calculation throughout the whole line, but by the amount of clear profit earned in each township; but, at the same time, we were given to understand that the rate and toll clause above quoted was not then adverted to, perhaps not thought of.

"It may also be argued that, on various parts of the line there are large and commodious station-houses erected for the purpose of booking passengers, collecting the tolls, dues, &c., but that there is nothing of this sort in Stretton. To this it may be answered that a station-house, *solely occupied* for the purpose of booking passengers, parcels, and receiving tolls, dues, &c. is not such a 'beneficial occupancy' as to render such station-houses liable to poor's rates. No profit is derived by these station-houses independent of the railway; they are necessary expenses, and may be considered as drawbacks from the profits rather than as sources of profit themselves. There are great numbers of bridges on the line; and it is certain that bridges are rateable where a profit is made by them; but in the case of railway bridges no profit is made from them separate and distinct from the railway itself, and therefore not separately rateable; and in this point of view it is not easy to distinguish between a station-house and a bridge.

"As we fully expect that the Railway Company will appeal against any rate we may make upon them, it behoves us to be exceedingly cautious and particular how we proceed; and we shall feel very grateful for your opinion on the above case, or for any information you can give us as to our general mode of proceeding as regards this subject.

"I am, Gentlemen,
"For self and brother Officers,
"Your most obedient and humble Servant,
"(Signed) FRANCIS BRADLEY, *Overseer.*
"*The Poor Law Commissioners.*"

In reply, the Commissioners stated that the principle upon which a railway was to be rated appeared to the Commissioners to be the same as that which had been laid down as proper to be followed in the case of canals. The rule by which canal companies were to be rated was expressed in Rex *v.* Kingswinford, 7 Barn. and Cress. 242, in these words: "A canal company is to contribute to the relief of the poor in each parish through which the canal passes, in proportion to the profit which they derive from the use of the land in that parish." In like manner, the Commissioners thought the overseers should rate the railway company according to the profit derived from the use of the land occupied by the part of the line which was within the township. This would depend upon the local traffic and expenditure within the township. If the traffic should be equal on all parts of the line, and an equal profit thence derived, then (by analogy to the case of a canal) the proportion of the township of Stretton might be ascertained by a mileage calculation, with reference to the whole line; Rex *v.* Woking, 4 A. and E. 40. But if, as was probably the case, the traffic was not equal, and a different profit was derived from any portion of the line in which the township of Stretton was included, then the proportion of the township (in respect of such portion) might be ascertained by a mileage calculation, with reference to the distance on which the profit was derived.

VI.—ACCOUNTS.—AS TO APPLICATION OF THE PRODUCE OF PAUPER LABOUR.

The following is a copy of a letter received from the clerk to the guardians of the Hexham Union:—

"*Hexham, May* 26, 1840.

"GENTLEMEN,—In reference to the order respecting the application of the produce of pauper labour contained in page 43 of the General Orders for keeping, examining accounts, &c. in this Union, I am directed by the Board of Guardians to inquire whether you will permit the fund created by such labour to be credited rateably to the township to which the paupers who have produced such fund belong, instead of to the establishment generally, as ordered heretofore? And if so, whether the labour of the paupers employed in domestic capacities in the workhouse household may be considered as productive labour applicable as aforesaid?

"I am, Gentlemen,
"Your most obedient servant,
"(Signed) JOHN STOKOE,
"*Clerk to the Guardians.*
"*The Poor Law Commissioners.*"

In answer thereto the Commissioners stated that they would not deem themselves justified in permitting the produce of pauper labour to be credited to the respective parishes in the mode suggested by the guardians.

The following considerations appear to the Commissioners to justify the course generally pursued while they exhibit the difficulties in practice which would attend the placing the earnings of paupers to the credit of the individual townships.

1. By the 28th section of the Poor Law Amendment Act, the utensils and materials for setting the poor on work, are to be provided at the charge of the common fund, and every parish in the Union being thus subject to the cost of providing (in the proportion of the declared averages) the material and stock, whether it have poor maintained in the workhouse or not, is entitled in common with other parishes, to have that cost diminished in its fair proportion, by the profit which may be realized by the work or labour performed.

2. It appears almost impossible to ascertain the profit of the labour of any particular pauper, and where this could be ascertained in a particular case it could scarcely be fixed for all the paupers of the township, and it is obviously necessary that in case the profit of any individual labourer is given to the particular township, the loss should also be borne by the township of all its paupers not profitably engaged.

3. The profit is not made by the arrangements of the single township but by the arrangements of the whole Union establishment, and is due to the superintendence and arrangements of all the officers of the Union.

VII.—PAUPERS—REMOVAL OF.

The following is an extract of a letter received from the chairman of the Ledbury Union:—

"Is it the recommendation of the Commissioners that all formularies of law should be implicitly attended to, in giving relief, in respect to removal of applicants for relief? (supposing the settlement not disputed.)

"In the Ledbury Union there are some parishes wherein several of the poor are prevented from residing, through a deficiency of tenements, who reside in adjacent parishes, or in the town of Ledbury. Supposing an individual whose settlement to Coddington parish is not disputed, reside in Ledbury, and be compelled through temporary illness to apply for relief, is this individual to be regularly passed on by Ledbury parish to Coddington parish? if so, this difficulty seems to present itself; supposing that individual to be regularly passed on to Coddington, he must, upon recovering his health and ability to support himself without aid, either quit the parish of Ledbury, or return to his residence in it, at the risk of being committed as a vagrant, should he at any future time be again obliged to seek relief.

"The adoption of the system, it need hardly be observed, will entail considerable expense upon such parishes as Ledbury for example, in which very many persons reside, who are settled to small and adjacent parishes, which have not sufficient accommodation for their parishioners.

"Do the Commissioners object to the practice hitherto pursued by the Ledbury Board of Guardians, of making every applicant for relief, whose settlement is not disputed, at once chargeable to the parish to which such applicant belongs, when resident within the district?

In reply, the Commissioners stated that the circular (OFFICIAL CIRCULAR, No. 15) the terms of which are adverted to, relates only to cases where the actual removal of the pauper is to be effected. The case where relief is given to the pauper of one parish resident in another parish was not intended to be considered in the circular.—It would doubtless have made the circular more clear if the latter class of cases had been expressly considered.

In your letter you state that the practice hitherto pursued by the Ledbury Board of Guardians, has been that of making every applicant for relief whose settlement is not disputed, at once chargeable to the parish to which such applicant belongs, where resident within the district.

The Commissioners are of opinion that where the settlement of a pauper has been actually adjudged or acknowledged, the guardians are justified in charging the relief to the parish in which such pauper has been received or acknowledged, unless the charge be formally protested against by the officers of the parish. Where it is so protested against, the less convenient but more strictly legal course must be taken, namely, that of charging the parish where the pauper is destitute, with the support of such pauper, until a second time acknowledged by or removed to the parish to which he belongs.

LONDON:
Printed, by Order of the Poor Law Commissioners, by W. CLOWES and SONS, Stamford Street, and Published by CHARLES KNIGHT and Co., 22, Ludgate Street, Publishers to the Poor Law Commissioners.

AN

OFFICIAL CIRCULAR

OF PUBLIC DOCUMENTS AND INFORMATION:

DIRECTED BY THE POOR LAW COMMISSIONERS TO BE PRINTED, CHIEFLY FOR THE USE OF THE MEMBERS AND PERMANENT OFFICERS OF BOARDS OF GUARDIANS, UNDER THE POOR LAW AMENDMENT ACT.

No. 19. CIRCULAR ISSUED JUNE 4TH, 1842.

Poor Law Commission Office,
Somerset House,
May 28, 1842.

THE Commissioners directed the following documents to be printed and circulated for the information of Guardians and officers of the several Unions, viz.—

By order of the Board,
EDWIN CHADWICK, *Secretary.*

I.—POOR LAW AMENDMENT BILL.

ARRANGEMENT OF CLAUSES.

Clause — Page of Bill

by the Guardians, and the Guardians may bury a pauper in the churchyard of the parish in which he dies, or of that to which he belongs 13

31 & 32. For the purpose of relief, settlement, removal, and committal of offenders, the workhouse is deemed to be situate in the parish to which the pauper is chargeable 13 & 14

Provisions respecting Removals of Paupers under Orders of Justices.

33. Guardians may apply for orders of removal 14
34. Notices of removal, &c., may be served by post 14
35. Paupers removed may be delivered to the proper officer at the workhouse of the Union 15
36. Penalty on officers for causing or procuring improper removals without the order of justices 15
37. Persons becoming chargeable through sickness are to be relieved where resident, and and are not to be removed until they have been chargeable for forty days consecutively 15

Costs of certain Legal Proceedings to be paid out of the Poor Rates.

38. The costs of apprehending and prosecuting vagrants, and of certain other civil and criminal proceedings connected with the administration of the Poor Laws, are to be paid by the Guardians out of the poor rates, subject to the approval of the Commissioners 16

Appointment of paid Collectors of Poor Rates, and Enforcement of Collection by Overseers.

39. Upon application from a Board of Guardians, the Commissioners may direct the appointment of a paid collector of rates; and in such case the power of the vestry to appoint a collector is to cease 17
40. If overseers do not pay sufficient monies to the Guardians, and the relief of any poor person is delayed in consequence for seven days, every such overseer is to be guilty of a misdemeanour 17

Remedy against the person of a Putative Father of a Bastard Child.

41. If a putative father does not pay the money due from him under an order of affiliation and maintenance, the same may be recovered by distress and sale of his goods; and if sufficient distress cannot be had, he may be committed to gaol for any term not exceeding three months. But no order is to be made upon any putative father for any expenses in respect of the child otherwise than for its maintenance within a workhouse, and in conformity with the regulations of the Commissioners 17

Audit of Poor Law Accounts.

42. Auditors are to be appointed for districts of Unions, by the chairmen and vice-chairmen of Boards of Guardians; such auditors are to have the powers necessary to compel the attendance of persons accountable, and to recover the balances struck 18
43. Any person aggrieved by any allowance or disallowance of an auditor, may remove such allowance or disallowance, by certiorari into the Court of Queen's Bench . . . 2
44. Where district auditors have been appointed, the power of justices to audit Poor Law accounts is to cease; the existing district auditors may be continued 20
45. The audit of Poor Law accounts may be held half-yearly instead of quarterly . . . 20

Scale of Voting for Election of Guardians.

46. The existing scales of voting of owners or occupiers for the election of Guardians are to be repealed, and a new scale is to be substituted 21

The following are the existing Scales:

Scale for Rate-payers.

4 & 5 Will. IV. c. 76, s. 40.

If a rate-payer be rated at any sum under 200*l.*, He will have one vote.
If at 200*l.*, but under 400*l.*, He will have two votes.
If at 400*l.* or more . . He will have three votes.

Scale for Owners.

58 Geo. III. c. 69; 59 Geo. III. c. 85; and 4 & 5 Will. IV. c. 76, s. 40.

If the aggregate amount of the assessment, for the time being, of any property belonging to such owner in such parish, or on any person or persons in respect of the same, to the Poor-rates, shall not amount to 50*l.*, He will have one vote.
If the same shall amount to 50*l.* and not to 75*l.*, He will have two votes.
If the same shall amount to 75*l.* and not to 100*l.*, He will have three votes.
If the same shall amount to 100*l.* and not to 125*l.*, He will have four votes.
If the same shall amount to 125*l.* and not to 150*l.*, He will have five votes.
If the same shall amount to 150*l.* or upwards, He will have six votes.

The following is the proposed Scale for Owners and Rate-payers.

If the property in respect of which the owner or rate-payer is entitled to vote be rated upon a rateable value of less than 50*l.*,
He shall have one vote.

If such rateable value amount to 50*l.* and be less than 100*l.* . . . . He shall have two votes.

If such rateable value amount to 100*l.* and be less than 150*l.* . . . He shall have three votes.

If such rateable value amount to 150*l.* and be less than 200*l.* . . . He shall have four votes.

If such rateable value amount to 200*l.* and be less than 250*l.* . . . He shall have five votes.

If such rateable value amount to or exceed 250*l.*,
He shall have six votes.

Regulations as to Claims of Owners, and as to Proxy Votes.

Clause — Page of Bill

47. The owner is to give in a statement of his property fourteen days before he votes. No person is to hold more than four proxies, unless he be the steward, bailiff, land-agent, or collector of his principal. No appointment of a proxy is to remain in force for more than two years, except of steward, &c. 21

Division of large Parishes into Wards for Election of Guardians.

48. Parishes exceeding 20,000 persons may be divided into wards for the election of Guardians. No ward is to contain less than 400 rated houses 22

49. Every person qualified for the parish is to be qualified for any ward in the parish; but no person is to be elected for more than one ward. The candidate may elect which ward he will stand for 22

50. The aggregate number of votes given in all the wards by any one person shall not exceed the number which he is entitled to give in the whole parish; nor in any one ward, the number of votes to which he is entitled, by property, in that ward; subject to these limitations the voter may elect which ward he will vote in 22

Miscellaneous Provisions as to Appointment, Resignation, and Competency of Guardians.

51. Disputes as to the election of Guardians may be determined by the Commissioners, subject to removal of their decision by certiorari into the Court of Queen's Bench . . . 23

52. Candidates declining to serve the office of Guardian, not to be put in nomination . 23

53. Where no person is elected to the office of Guardian at an annual election of Guardians,

Clause — Page of Bill

the Guardian for the previous year is to continue to act 23

54. The Commissioners may accept the resignation of a Guardian, and may authorize new elections 23

55. In case of the full number of Guardians not being elected, the remaining Guardians may act 23

56. Defects in the qualification or election of a Guardian not to make void the proceedings of a Board of Guardians 24

57. Paid officers and persons deriving profit from the poor-rates are to be disqualified from being Guardians, and dismissed officers to be disqualified for five years 24

Ex-officio Guardians competent to act as Justices.

58. Ex-officio Guardians not to be disqualified to act as justices on the ground of being members of the Board of Guardians . . . 24

Powers for Boards of Guardians to sue and be sued, and to make Applications to Justices.

59. Boards of Guardians and District Boards may hold property as a corporation, and sue and be sued in their corporate name . . . 24

60. Boards of Guardians and District Boards may make complaints or applications to justices, and orders in writing, signed by their chairman, and countersigned by their clerk. Guardians may depute an officer to make applications or complaints before justices . 25

---

61. Interpretation clause 25

62. Act limited to England and Wales . . . 26

63. Act may be amended this session . . . 26

II.—GENERAL ORDERS.

1. LETTER ACCOMPANYING GENERAL ORDERS REGULATING THE PROCEEDINGS OF GUARDIANS, AND THE DUTIES OF CLERK, TREASURER, DISTRICT MEDICAL OFFICER, AND RELIEVING OFFICER.

Poor Law Commission Office,
Somerset House,
22nd April, 1842.

SIR,

The Poor Law Commissioners have issued to the Unions and single parishes under a Board of Guardians, two general orders: one regulating the proceedings and principal functions of the Board of Guardians; the other directing the mode of appointment and defining the duties of the clerk, treasurer, district medical officers, and relieving officers. The regulations in these orders agree substantially with the regulations relating to the same subjects which are already in force; but they have received such amendments and additions as a careful revision, aided by the experience of the Commissioners, has suggested; and their simultaneous issue, in the form of general orders, to all the Unions, will insure greater uniformity in the practice of the several Boards of Guardians, and in the ordinary administration of the law.

The first order, dated the 20th day of April, relates to the following subjects:—

ARTICLES 1—11, contain regulations respecting the meetings of the Board of Guardians.

12—14, direct the mode of proceeding at such meetings, and the order in which the business is to be transacted.

15—20, prescribe the manner in which contracts for goods and work are to be made by the Guardians.

21—23, regulate the manner in which orders for contributions and payments are to be made by the Guardians.

24 and 25, direct the Guardians to require security from certain officers.

26—30, contain explanations of terms used in the order.

The power of the Poor Law Commissioners to make the regulations contained in this order is derived partly from Sec. 15 of the Poor Law Amendment Act, which authorizes and requires the Commissioners from time to time, as they shall see occasion, to make and issue rules, orders, and regulations for the guidance and control of all guardians, vestries, and parish officers, so far as relates to the management and relief of the poor, and the keeping, examining, auditing, and allowing of accounts, and making and entering into contracts in all matters relating to such management or relief or to any expenditure for the relief of the poor; and partly from Sec. 38, which enacts that the Commissioners shall prescribe the duties of the Guardians to be elected in each Union.

The Commissioners subjoin the following remarks upon certain articles of this order, for the information of the Guardians:—

Article 1.] Sec. 38 of the Poor Law Amendment Act provides that "except where otherwise ordered by the Poor Law Commissioners, and also except for the purpose of consenting to the dissolution or alteration of any Union, or any addition thereto, or to the formation of any Union for the purposes of settlement or rating,—no *ex officio* or other Guardian of any such Board as aforesaid [*i. e.* Board of Guardians] shall have power to act in virtue of such office, except as a member and at a meeting of such board."

4.] Sec. 38 of the Poor Law Amendment Act provides, that "No act of any such meeting [*i. e.* of a Board of Guardians] shall be valid unless three members shall be present and concur therein."

13.] If the meeting consist of only three Guardians, no act can be done by it if the Guardians are not unanimous. See Art. 4, and the note. It is to be observed that the Chairman will not, under the provisions of this order, be in any case entitled to a casting vote.

14.] The order of business indicated by this article is not obligatory on the Guardians, but the Commissioners believe that it will in general be found convenient.

15.] Concerning the validity of contracts made by or on behalf of any parish or Union, not in conformity with the regulations of the Commissioners, see Sec. 49 of the Poor Law Amendment Act.

16—20, require the Guardians to purchase goods, &c., upon tender. The Commissioners are aware that the system of purchase by tender is sometimes productive of inconvenience, and that goods may occasionally be obtained on more advantageous terms without a recourse to this method. They believe, however, that on the whole it affords the best security to the public; and the practice of the administrative bodies which make the largest purchases of goods (viz., the military and naval departments), strongly confirms them in this conclusion. Article 20 allows of an exception being made in extraordinary cases, with the consent of the Commissioners.

21.] It is important that the Guardians should be careful to keep constantly a sufficient balance in the Treasurer's hands to defray the current expenses of the Union; and for this purpose that they should make, from time to time, sufficient orders for contributions upon the overseers of the several parishes, and enforce the orders in case the payment should be delayed. The Guardians ought, in general, to call for contributions from each parish fully sufficient to meet the expenditure incurred in respect of it; and no such arrears should be allowed to accrue, in any case, as would cast the burdens of one parish on the other parishes of the Union.

If the parish officers should fail to pay the money required, the Guardians may proceed against them before the justices for a disobedience to the orders of the Commissioners, under Sec. 98 of the Poor Law Amendment Act; or they may have recourse to the remedy afforded to the Guardians by the 2nd & 3rd Vic. cap. 84, sec. 1. In case of its being necessary for the Guardians to proceed adversely against the parish officers, the Commissioners recommend a recourse to the remedial proceeding afforded by the latter statute rather than to the penal proceeding authorized by the former.

The powers conferred on the Guardians by the 2nd & 3rd Vic. cap. 84, render them responsible for securing a sufficient supply of funds from the parish officers; and if the Guardians should fail to obtain from the parish officers funds sufficient to defray the current expenditure of the parish, they are without any legal power to procure funds to supply the deficiency. The Guardians are not in general empowered to borrow money on the security of the rates (except in the cases and for the purposes specially provided for by the statutes, such as the building of or procuring workhouses under 4th & 5th Wm. IV. cap. 76—and enabling poor persons to emigrate, under the same Act—and the making a survey or valuation of a parish, under 6th & 7th Wm. IV. cap. 96), or to pay interest for the money borrowed.

By Article 18, No. 4, of the second order, the treasurer is required, whenever there should not be funds belonging to the Guardians in his hands, to report in writing the fact of such deficiency to the Poor Law Commissioners.

Article 24 requires the Guardians to take proper security from the treasurer, the master of the workhouse, and the relieving officers, and to renew the security from time to time: and Article 25 renders it necessary that the bonds so taken by the Guardians should be produced once a-year for the inspection of the auditor. The latter provision is highly desirable, in order to ensure the preservation of the bonds in the proper hands.

The second order, dated the 21st of April, relates to the following subjects:—

Articles 1—3 authorize the appointment of a clerk to the Guardians, a treasurer of the Union, of district medical officers, and of relieving officers, with assistants to these several officers.

4—15 regulate the mode of appointment, qualification, and salaries of these officers,—the security which they are to give,—their continuance in office,—the appointment of substitutes,—and the filling up of vacancies.

16—20 define the duties of the above-named officers.

21—25 contain explanations of terms used in the order.

The Commissioners subjoin the following remarks upon several of the articles in this order:—

Articles 1—15.] This series of Articles is similar to Articles 60—72, in the general workhouse order (5th February, 1842); and the Commissioners, therefore, refer the Guardians to the notes on those articles in their explanatory letter, where the subjects of them are fully illustrated, and the sections in the Poor Law Amendment Act, conferring on the Commissioners their powers with respect to paid officers, are cited.

Article 5 is intended to prevent surprises in the appointment of the officers, and to secure to the Union the advantages of allowing time for candidates to come forward and obtain a consideration of their claims. In addition to the regulations in this article, the Commissioners suggest to the Guardians the expediency of making a bye-law requiring that special notice of every intended election should be sent by the clerk to all the Guardians some days before the day of election. All regulations made by the Guardians must, in order to be legally valid and binding, be submitted to and confirmed by the Commissioners. See sec. 22 of the Poor Law Amendment Act.

By the proviso in Article 2, every regulation applying to officers holding their office under this order, applies to officers of the like denomination appointed before the order comes into force.

6.] With respect to the general qualification of a medical officer, see note on Article 64 of the workhouse order; and with respect to the qualifications prescribed by the regulations of the Commissioners, see the medical order, dated the 12th of March, 1842.

7.] The insertion of the proviso in this

article is not intended to relax the rule as to residence within the district, or any other of the restrictions therein enumerated; but to meet certain rare cases, which require a special consideration.

10.] See Articles 22 & 23 of the former order. Under this Article the Guardians can require the treasurer, relieving officer, and any other Union officer, to give security; and as the security is given in pursuance of the regulations of the Commissioners, the instrument by which it is given is exempt from stamp duty. (Sec. 86 of Poor Law Amendment Act.)

11.] By the exception in this Article, the Commissioners do not intend to advise that the medical officer should be appointed only temporarily. The exception is made for the reasons stated in their remarks in their explanatory letter on Article 20 of their medical regulations. It will be observed in reference to that order, that the medical officer will be presumed to be appointed for an indefinite period, unless the Guardians expressly limit the time of his appointment.

The regulation requiring that the dismissals of assistants, and the grounds of them, should be reported to the Commissioners, is inserted in order to enable the Commissioners to judge if a person so dismissed from one Union should be allowed to be appointed in another Union. See Art. 4, requiring the appointments of assistants to be reported to the Commissioners.

13.] With respect to substitutes for the medical officer, see Articles 14 and 15 of the medical regulations.

17, No. 1.] The minutes are intended to be a true record of the proceedings of the Board; and the confirmation of the minutes by the succeeding Board will merely authenticate the accuracy of the record, without affecting the acts of the previous meeting, which in general require no subsequent confirmation.

17, No. 2.] As to the production of officer's bonds to the auditor, see Article 23 of the former order.

17, No. 4.] See Articles 9 and 10 of the first order.

17, No. 5.] See Articles 21—3, of the same order.

17, No. 7.] With respect to the payment of the clerk for applications for orders in bastardy, see the letter of the Commissioners to the clerk of the Loughborough Union, inserted in their official circular, No. 4.

It is to be observed that business relating to the survey and valuation of parishes, and the sale of parish property, and the application of the sale proceeds, is the business of the Guardians under the statutes relating thereto, and, therefore, the clerk is not entitled to make an extra charge for conducting the correspondence which arises out of it, or for advising or assisting the Guardians in the performance of any of the acts or duties which become necessary in the furtherance of this business.

17, No. 8.] Form A. is not intended to diminish the quantity of weekly information sent by the clerk to the Assistant-Commissioner in Unions where the form used has been fuller than that prescribed by this order. Moreover, there may be special circumstances in a Union which may render it necessary for the Assistant-Commissioner to require the periodical transmission to him of certain particulars which are not included in Form A.

Where there are several workhouses occupied by the Guardians, the account required by the first part of the form should be repeated separately for each workhouse.

18.] The treasurer ought not to allow his account with the Guardians to be overdrawn; and if he advances money to them, he does so at his own risk, as the Guardians cannot legally borrow money for their current expenses upon the security of the rates, or pay interest upon money so borrowed. See remarks on the first order, Article 21. The regulation in No. 4 is introduced for the purpose of enabling the Commissioners to warn the Guardians of their duty, in case they should have failed to obtain the requisite supplies of money from the overseer. It is also desirable that when the funds in his hands are low, the treasurer should communicate the fact to the Guardians.

When any parish of a Union has an account with the treasurer, independent of the Union account, the treasurer ought not to transfer money from the former to the latter without an order of the overseers.

Money in the treasurer's hands, arising from the sale of parish property, ought not to be appropriated without an order under the seal of the Commissioners. See 5 & 6 Wm. IV., cap. 69, sec. 3.

19.] Upon the appointment of any medical

officer, his attention should be specially called to the regulations, dated 12th of March, 1842, as well as to the duties specified in this Article.

19, No. 4.] Concerning information to be given by the medical officer to the relieving officer, see Article 20, No. 4.

20, No. 2.] It is important for the relieving officer to observe that it is his duty to visit at their dwellings all persons who have applied for relief, as soon as possible after he has received the application.

The relieving officer should moreover observe that he is responsible for all persons who apply for, or receive relief in his district; and that he cannot discharge himself of this responsibility by any agreement or understanding between himself or the Guardians, and the Guardians or relieving officer of another Union. See the Minute of the Commissioners on the relief of non-resident paupers, in their Seventh Annual Report, p. 106, ed. 8vo.

20, No. 4.] In case the medical officer should have attended any paupers without an order from himself (as, for example, under an order from the Board of Guardians, or from an overseer, or without an order under Articles 16—19 of the medical regulations), it will be the duty of the relieving officer to ascertain the names of such paupers, and to visit them.

20, No. 6.] In cases of sudden and urgent necessity, it is the duty of the relieving officer to administer the appropriate relief needed (such as food, lodging, or medical assistance), and not to save his own trouble by giving money to a pauper at a moment when he may be unable to use it.

The Commissioners think it desirable that the attention of the treasurer, medical officers, and relieving officers, should be specially directed by the Guardians to the definitions of their duties in this order.

The Commissioners have not included in this order the duties of the auditor; inasmuch as they intend in the course of the year to issue their accounts' order in an amended form, and it will be convenient to include the duties of the auditor in that order.

In addition to the two orders above mentioned, the Commissioners have issued an order, dated the 22nd of April, prescribing certain duties of the overseers of parishes, in relation to relief in cases of sudden and urgent necessity, the election of Guardians, the keeping of the rate-books, the payment of money to the Guardians, and the auditing of their accounts.

Signed by Order of the Board,

EDWIN CHADWICK,

Secretary.

To the Clerk to the Guardians of the Union.

2.—GENERAL ORDER—PROCEEDINGS OF BOARDS OF GUARDIANS.

To the Guardians of the Poor of the several Unions named in the Schedule hereunto annexed;

To the Churchwardens and Overseers of the several parishes and places comprised within the said Unions;

To the Clerk or Clerks to the Justices of the Petty Sessions held for the Division or Divisions in which the parishes and places comprised within the said Unions are situate;

And to all others whom it may concern.

WE, the Poor Law Commissioners, in pursuance of the authorities vested in us by an Act passed in the fifth year of the reign of His late Majesty King William the Fourth, intituled "*An Act for the Amendment and better Administration of the Laws relating to the Poor in England and Wales,*" do hereby rescind so much of any order or orders heretofore issued by the Poor Law Commissioners to the several Unions named in the Schedule hereunto annexed, as is in any way affected or altered by the regulations herein contained, except so far as the same may have authorized the making of any contract not yet executed, or the making of any orders for contributions and payments not yet obeyed.

And we do hereby order, direct, and declare, with respect to each of the Unions named in the said Schedule, as follows:—

Meetings of the Guardians.

Article 1. No Guardian shall act in virtue of his office, except as a member, and at a meeting of the Board of Guardians, except as in the said Act is excepted.

2. The Guardians shall upon the day of the week, and the hour of the day, and at the place already appointed for holding the ordinary meetings, hold an ordinary meeting once at the least in every week for the execution of their duties; or so often as shall have been already prescribed by any orders of the Poor Law Commissioners, and may, when they think fit, change the period, time, and place, with the consent of the Poor Law Commissioners previously had and obtained.

3. The Guardians shall at the first meeting after every annual election of Guardians, elect out of the

whole number of Guardians a chairman and a vice-chairman, who shall continue respectively to act as such until the next annual election of Guardians shall take place, if they so long continue respectively to be Guardians.

4. If the Guardians shall at any time deem fit, they may elect two vice-chairmen, and shall determine the precedence of such vice-chairmen; and according to such precedence the said vice-chairmen shall thenceforth preside and act as in the case when only one vice-chairman is elected.

5. If a chairman, or a vice-chairman, cease to be a Guardian, or refuse, or become incapable, to act as chairman, or vice-chairman, before the expiration of the term of office, the Guardians shall, within one month after the occurrence of the vacancy, refusal, or incapacity, elect some other Guardian to be chairman or vice-chairman, as the case may be.

6. No act of any meeting of the Guardians shall be valid unless three Guardians be present and concur therein.

7. If three Guardians be not present at any meeting, an entry of that fact shall be made in the minute book by the clerk to the Guardians, and the time for holding such meeting shall be deemed to have expired as soon as the said entry shall have been made. But one hour at least shall be allowed to elapse from the time fixed for the commencement of the meeting, before such entry shall be made.

8. If three or four or more Guardians be present at any ordinary meeting, such three, or the majority of such four or more Guardians, may adjourn the same, to the day of the next ordinary meeting, or to some other day previous to the next ordinary meeting.

9. An extraordinary meeting of the Guardians may be summoned to be held at any time, upon the requisition of any two Guardians, addressed to the clerk of the Guardians. Every such requisition shall be made in writing, according to the Form A. hereunto annexed, and no business, other than the business specified in the said requisition, shall be transacted at such extraordinary meeting.

10. Notice of every change in the period, time, or place of holding any meeting, and notice of the adjournment of any meeting, and notice of every extraordinary meeting, shall be given in writing to every Guardian. Every such notice shall be respectively according to the Forms B., C., and D., hereunto annexed, and shall be given or sent by the clerk to every Guardian, or left at his place of abode two days, if practicable, before the day appointed for the meeting to which it relates.

11. If any case of emergency arise, requiring that a meeting of the Guardians should immediately take place, they, or any three of them, shall meet at the ordinary place of meeting, and take such case into consideration, and may make an order, or orders, thereon.

Proceedings of the Board.

12. At every meeting the chairman, or, in his absence, a vice-chairman, shall preside; and if at the commencement of any meeting the chairman and vice-chairman or vice-chairmen be absent, the Guardians present shall elect one of themselves to preside at such meeting as chairman thereof, until the chairman or a vice-chairman may take the chair.

13. All questions at any meeting consisting of more than three Guardians, shall be determined by a majority of the votes of the Guardians present thereat.

14. At every ordinary meeting of the Guardians, the business shall, as far as may be convenient, be conducted in the following order:—

Firstly. The minutes of the last ordinary meeting, and of any other meeting which may have been held since such ordinary meeting, shall be read to the Guardians and signed by the chairman presiding at the meeting at which such minutes are read, and an entry of the same having been so read, shall be made in the minutes of the day when read.

Secondly. The Guardians shall dispose of such business as may arise out of the minutes so read, and shall give the necessary directions thereon.

Thirdly. They shall read the report of the state of the workhouse or workhouses, and shall proceed to give the necessary directions respecting all applications for relief made since the last ordinary meeting, and also respecting the amount and nature of relief to be given and continued to the paupers then in the receipt of relief, until the next ordinary meeting, or for such other time as such relief may be deemed to be necessary.

Fourthly. They shall hear and consider any application for relief which may be then made, and determine thereon.

Fifthly. They shall examine all books and accounts relative to the relief of the paupers of the Union, give all needful directions concerning the management and discipline of the workhouse or workhouses of the Union, and the providing of furniture and stores and other articles.

Sixthly. They shall make the necessary orders on the overseers or other proper authorities of the several parishes in the Union, for providing such sums as may be lawfully required by the Guardians on account of the respective parishes.

Seventhly. They shall give the necessary directions respecting applications to justices for orders of bastardy, and respecting pensions payable to paupers of the Union.

Eighthly. They shall transact any such business as may not fall within any of the above classes.

Contracts.

15. All contracts to be entered into on behalf of the Union relating to the maintenance, clothing, lodging, employment, or relief of the poor, or for any other purpose relating to or connected with the general management of the poor, shall be made and entered into by the Guardians.

16. The Guardians shall require tenders to be made in some sealed paper for the supply of all provisions, fuel, clothing, furniture, or other goods, or materials, the consumption of which may be estimated, one month with another, to exceed 10*l.* per month, and all provisions, fuel, clothing, furniture, or other goods, or materials, the cost of which may be reasonably estimated to exceed 50*l.* in a single sum, to be paid for by the Guardians, and shall purchase the same upon contracts to be entered into after the receipt of such tenders.

17. Any work or repairs to be executed in the workhouse, or the premises connected with the workhouse, or any fittings to be put up therein, which shall respectively be reasonably estimated to exceed the cost of 50*l.* in one sum shall be contracted for by the Guardians, on sealed tenders, in the manner prescribed in Articles 16 and 18.

18. Notice of the nature and conditions of the contract to be entered into, of the last day on which tenders will be received, and the day on which the tenders will be opened, shall be given in some newspaper circulating in the Union, not less than ten days previous to the last day on which such tenders shall be received, and no tender shall be opened by the clerk, or any Guardian, or other person, prior to the day specified in such notice, or otherwise than at a meeting of the said Guardians.

19. When any tender shall be accepted, the party making the tender shall, in pursuance of these regulations, enter into a contract, in writing, with the Guardians, containing the terms, conditions, and stipulations mutually agreed upon, and whenever the Guardians shall deem it advisable, the party contracting shall in like manner find one or more surety or sureties who shall enter into a bond in such penalty as the Guardians shall think fit, conditioned for the due performance of the contract, or shall otherwise secure the same.

20. Provided always, that if from the peculiar nature of any furniture, goods, materials, or fittings to be supplied, or of any work or repairs to be executed, it shall appear to the Guardians desirable that a specific person or persons be employed to supply or execute the same, without requiring sealed tenders as hereinbefore directed, it shall be lawful for the Board of Guardians, with the consent of the Poor Law Commissioners first had and obtained, to enter into a contract with such person or persons as may be deemed best qualified to supply or execute the same, and to require such sureties and securities as are specified in Article 19.

Orders for Contributions and Payments.

21. The Guardians shall make orders on the overseers or other proper authorities of every parish of the Union, from time to time for the payment to the Guardians of all sums which may be required by the Guardians for the relief of the poor of the parish, and for the contribution of the parish to the common fund of the Union, and for any other expenses chargeable by the Guardians on the parish.

22. Every such order shall be given according to the Form E. hereunto annexed. It shall be signed by the presiding chairman of the meeting, and two other Guardians present thereat, and shall be countersigned by the clerk to the Guardians.

23. The Guardians shall pay every sum greater than 3*l.* by an order, which shall be drawn upon the treasurer of the Union, and shall be signed by three of the Guardians at a meeting, and shall be countersigned by the clerk of the Guardians.

Security of Officers.

24. The Guardians shall require every person appointed, or to be hereafter appointed, to the offices of treasurer, master of the workhouse, or relieving officer, to give a bond in such penal sum as the Guardians shall think fit, with two sufficient sureties, conditioned for the due and faithful performance of the duties of the office; and shall from time to time call upon such officers to supply a fresh surety in place of any such surety who may die, or become bankrupt or insolvent, or be released from his obligation.

25. The Guardians shall, once in every year, that is to say, at the audit next after the 25th day of March, cause every person having the custody of bonds given by any officer of the Union to produce such bonds to the auditor for his inspection, and the fact of such inspection and any defects apparent in the said bonds, shall be reported by the auditor to the Board of Guardians.

Explanation of Terms.

26. Whenever the word "Union" is used in this order, it shall be taken to include not only an union of parishes formed under the provisions of the hereinbefore recited Act, but also any union of parishes incorporated or united for the relief or maintenance of the poor under any Local Act of Parliament.

27. Whenever the word "Guardians" is used in this order, it shall be taken to include not only guardians appointed or entitled to act under the provisions of the said hereinbefore recited Act, but also any governors, directors, managers, or acting guardians entitled to act in the ordering of relief to the poor from the poor-rates under any Local Act of Parliament.

28. Whenever the word "Parish" is used in this order, it shall be taken to include any place maintaining its own poor, whether parochial or extra parochial.

29. Whenever, in describing any person or party, matter or thing, the word importing the singular number or the masculine gender only is used in this order, the same shall be taken to include, and shall be applied to, several persons or parties as well as one person or party, and females as well as males, and several matters or things as well as one matter or thing, respectively, unless there be something in the subject or context repugnant to such construction.

30. Whenever in this order any article is referred to by its number, the article of this order bearing that number shall be taken to be signified thereby.

FORM A.

To the Clerk to the Guardians of the Union.

Requisition for an Extraordinary Meeting of Guardians.

We, the undersigned, being two of the Guardians of the Poor of the Union, do hereby require an extraordinary meeting of the Guardians of the said Union to be summoned, to be holden at on the day of 18 , at o'clock in the forenoon, to take into consideration [*set out the motion.*]

____
__________________ } Guardians.

FORM B.

Notice of Change of Period, Time, or Place of Meeting.

To *A. B.*
Guardian of the Poor of the Union.

SIR,—You are hereby informed that the next ordinary meeting of the Guardians of the Poor of the Union will take place at on the day of 18 , at o'clock in the forenoon, for the transaction of business; and that meetings of the said Guardians will henceforth be held [*weekly or fortnightly, as the case may be*] at the same place, on in every week, at the same hour of in the

____
Signature of Clerk to the Guardians.

FORM C.

Notice of an Adjourned Meeting of Guardians.

To *A. B.*
Guardian of the Poor of the Union.

SIR,—This is to give you notice that an adjourned meeting of the Guardians of the Poor of the Union will be held at on the day of 18 , to take into consideration [*set out the motion*] which meeting you are hereby requested to attend.

____
Signature of Clerk to the Guardians.

FORM D.

Notice of an Extraordinary Meeting of Guardians.

To *A. B.*
Guardian of the Poor of the Union.

SIR,—I am directed by *C. D.* and *E. F.*, two of the Guardians of the Poor of the Union to summon an extraordinary meeting of the Guardians of the Poor of the said Union at on the day of 18 , at o'clock in the forenoon, to take into consideration [*set out motion*]; which meeting you are hereby requested to attend.

____
Signature of Clerk to the Guardians.

FORM E.

To *A. B.* and *C. D.*, Overseers (or) of the Parish of

You are hereby ordered and directed to pay to *F. G.*, of on behalf of the Guardians of the Poor of the Union on the day of at the sum of pounds, shillings, and pence, from the poor-rates of the parish of towards the relief of the poor thereof, and to the contribution of the parish to the common fund of the Union, and such other expenses as are chargeable by the said Guardians on the said parish, and to take the receipt of the said *F. G.* for the said sum of £

Given under our hands, at a meeting of the Guardians of the Poor of the said Union, held on the day of 18 .

(Signed) X. Y. *Presiding Chairman.*
W. X. } *Guardians.*
U. V. }

(Counter-signature of the Clerk to the Guardians.)

3.—GENERAL ORDER—DUTIES OF OFFICERS.

To the Guardians of the Poor of the several Unions named in the Schedule hereunto annexed;

To the Churchwardens and Overseers of the several parishes and places comprised within the said Unions;

To the Clerk or Clerks to the Justices of the Petty Sessions held for the Division or Divisions in which the parishes and places comprised within the said Unions are situate;

And to all others whom it may concern.

WE, the Poor Law Commissioners, in pursuance of the authorities vested in us by an Act passed in the fifth year of the reign of His late Majesty King William the Fourth, intituled "*An Act for the Amendment and better Administration of the Laws relating to the Poor in England and Wales,*" do hereby rescind so much of any order or orders heretofore issued by the Poor Law Commissioners to each of the several Unions named in the Schedule hereunto annexed as is in any way affected or altered by the

Regulations herein contained, except in so far as the said orders, or any of them, may have authorized the appointment of the existing Officers.

And we do hereby order, direct, and declare, with respect to each and every of the Unions named in the said Schedule, as follows:—

Art. 1. The Board of Guardians shall, whenever any of the under-mentioned offices may be vacant, appoint a fit person to perform respectively the duties specified by the rules and regulations of the Poor Law Commissioners, in force at the time, to belong to each of the two following officers:—

1. Clerk to the Guardians.
2. Treasurer of the Union.

And also whenever such vacancy shall occur, or it may otherwise be requisite, so many fit persons as may be required for performing respectively the duties specified as aforesaid to belong to each of the following officers:—

1. District Medical Officer.
2. Relieving Officer.

And also such assistants as the Board of Guardians with the consent of the Poor Law Commissioners shall deem necessary for the efficient performance of the duties of the several offices above enumerated.

Art. 2. The said officers shall respectively perform such duties as may be required of them by the rules and regulations of the Poor Law Commissioners in force at the time, together with all such other duties conformable with the nature of their respective offices as the said Board of Guardians may lawfully require them to perform.

Provided always that every regulation applying to any officer holding his office under this Order shall apply to any officer of the like denomination appointed by the Guardians, although such officer may have been appointed before this Order shall have come into force.

Art. 3. The Board of Guardians shall, from time to time, on any change in the division of the Union into districts for general and medical relief, or in the assignment of relieving officers and medical officers to such districts, report every such change to the Poor Law Commissioners for their approbation.

MODE OF APPOINTMENT.

Art. 4. Every officer and assistant, to be appointed under this Order, shall be appointed by a majority of the Guardians present at any meeting of the Board, consisting of more than three Guardians, and every such appointment shall, as soon as the same shall have been made, be reported to the Poor Law Commissioners by the clerk to the Guardians.

Art. 5. No appointment to the office of clerk, treasurer, district medical officer, or relieving officer, shall be made under this Order, unless notice that such appointment will be made shall have been given at one of the two ordinary meetings of the Board next preceding the meeting at which the appointment shall be made, or unless an advertisement giving notice of such appointment shall have appeared in some public paper by the direction of the Guardians at least seven days before the day on which such appointment shall be made.

QUALIFICATION OF OFFICERS.

Art. 6. No person shall be appointed a district medical officer who shall not be at the time of such appointment duly licensed to practise as a medical man, and be otherwise qualified, as may be required by the rules and regulations of the Poor Law Commissioners in force at the time.

Art. 7. No person shall be appointed a relieving officer unless he shall be able to keep accounts, and unless he reside in the district for which he may be appointed to act, devote his whole time to the performance of the duties of his office, not follow any trade or profession, or enter into any other service, and undertake to give one month's notice previous to resigning the office or quitting the service, or to forfeit one month's amount of salary, to be deducted as liquidated damages from the amount of salary due at the time of such resignation.

Provided always that the Guardians may, with the consent of the Poor Law Commissioners previously obtained, dispense with any of the conditions specified in this Article, which the said Commissioners may deem inexpedient.

SALARIES OF THE OFFICERS.

Art. 8. The Board of Guardians shall pay to the several officers and assistants appointed to or holding any office or employment under this Order, such salaries or remuneration as the Poor Law Commissioners may from time to time direct or approve.

Art. 9. The salary of every officer or assistant appointed to or holding any office or employment under this Order, shall be payable up to the day on which he ceases to hold such office or employment, and no longer.

SECURITY.

Art. 10. Every person appointed to, or holding the office of, treasurer or relieving officer, and every other officer whom the Board of Guardians shall require so to do, shall respectively give a bond in such penal sum as the Board of Guardians shall think fit, with two sufficient sureties, conditioned for the due and faithful performance of the duties of the office; and every such officer shall give immediate notice to the Board of Guardians of the death, insolvency, or bankruptcy of either of such sureties, and shall, when required by the Guardians, supply a fresh surety in the place of any such surety who may die, or become bankrupt, or insolvent.

CONTINUANCE IN OFFICE AND SUSPENSION OF OFFICERS—SUPPLY OF VACANCIES.

Art. 11. Every officer appointed to or holding any

office under this Order, other than a district medical officer, shall continue to hold the same until he shall die, or resign, or be removed by the Poor Law Commissioners, and every assistant may be dismissed by the Board of Guardians without the consent of the Poor Law Commissioners; but every such dismissal and the grounds thereof shall be reported to the Poor Law Commissioners.

Art. 12. The Board of Guardians may, at their discretion, suspend from the discharge of his duties any district medical officer or relieving officer, and shall in case of every such suspension, forthwith report the same, together with the cause thereof, to the Poor Law Commissioners for their decision thereon.

Art. 13. If any officer, or assistant, appointed to or holding any office or employment under this Order, be at any time prevented by sickness or accident, or other sufficient reason, from the performance of his duties, the Guardians may appoint a fit person to act as his temporary substitute, and may pay him a reasonable compensation for his services, and every such appointment shall be reported to the Poor Law Commissioners as soon as the same shall have been made.

Provided always, that if any district medical officer be temporarily incapacitated from performing his duties, it shall be competent to him to recommend to the Guardians a duly qualified medical practitioner in order to perform his duties during his temporary incapacity.

Article 14.—The Vice-chairman, or some Guardian to be appointed by the Board of Guardians, may perform any of the duties assigned to the clerk until any vacancy in the office shall have been filled, or until a substitute be appointed in the case of the sickness, accident, or absence of the clerk.

Article 15.—When any officer appointed to or holding any office specified in Article 1, shall die, or resign, the Board of Guardians shall, as soon as conveniently may be after such death, or resignation, give notice thereof to the Poor Law Commissioners, and shall proceed to make a new appointment in the manner prescribed by the above regulations.

DUTIES OF THE OFFICERS.

Article 16.—And we do hereby define and specify the duties of the several officers appointed to or holding their offices under this Order, and direct the execution thereof, to be as follows:—

Duties of the Clerk to the Guardians.

Article 17.—The duties of the clerk to the Guardians shall be:—

No. 1. To attend all meetings of the Board of Guardians, and to keep punctually minutes of the proceedings at every meeting, to enter the said minutes in a book, and to submit the same so entered in the said book to the presiding chairman at the succeeding meeting, to be confirmed by the Board, and authenticated by the signature of such chairman, as a true record of the proceedings of the Board.

No. 2. To keep all accounts, books of accounts, minutes, books, and other documents, as required of him by the Regulations of the Poor Law Commissioners, or relating to the business of the Board of Guardians, and from time to time to produce all such books, other documents, and vouchers for the same, together with the bonds of any officers which may be in his custody, to the auditor of the Union, at such place and time, and in such manner, as may be required by the regulations of the said Commissioners in force at the time.

No. 3. To peruse and conduct the correspondence of the Board of Guardians according to their directions, and to preserve the same, and all letters, books, papers, and documents belonging to the Union, or entrusted to him by the Board of Guardians, and to make all necessary copies thereof.

No. 4. To receive all requisitions of Guardians for extraordinary meetings, and to summon such meetings accordingly, and to make, sign, and send all notices required to be given to the Guardians by any Order of the Poor Law Commissioners.

No. 5. To countersign all orders legally made by the Board of Guardians on overseers for the payment of money, and all orders legally drawn by the Board of Guardians upon the treasurer of the Union.

No. 6. To communicate to the several officers and persons engaged in the administration of relief within the Union, all orders and directions of the Poor Law Commissioners, or of the Board of Guardians; and so far as may be, to give the instructions requisite for the prompt and correct execution of all such orders and directions, and to examine and report on any neglect or failure therein which may come to his knowledge.

No. 7. To conduct all applications necessary to be made by or on behalf of the Board of Guardians, to any justice or justices at their special petty, or general sessions; and if he be an attorney or solicitor, to perform and execute all legal business connected with the Union, or in which the Board of Guardians shall be engaged, except actions at law or suits in equity, without charge for anything beyond disbursements.

No. 8. To prepare, after every ordinary meeting of the Board of Guardians, a statement in the Form A. hereunto annexed, and punctually to transmit the same to the Assistant Poor Law Commissioner having the superintendence of the Union.

No. 9. To prepare and transmit all answers or

returns, as to any question or matter connected with or relating to the administration of the laws for the relief of the poor in the Union, or to any other business of the Union which the Poor Law Commissioners, or any Assistant Commissioner, may lawfully require from the Board of Guardians, or from himself.

No. 10. When required by the regulations of the Poor Law Commissioners, to conduct duly and impartially, and in strict conformity with the said regulations in force at the time, the annual or any other election of Guardians.

No. 11. To observe and execute all orders and directions of the Board of Guardians applicable to his office.

Duties of the Treasurer.

Article 18. The duties of the treasurer shall be:—

No. 1. To receive all monies tendered to be paid to the Board of Guardians, and to place the same to their credit.

No. 2. To pay out of any monies for the time being in his hands belonging to the Board of Guardians, all orders for money which shall be drawn upon him, on behalf of such Guardians, and shall be signed by the chairman and two other of such Guardians, and shall be countersigned by the clerk, or the person for the time being acting as the clerk, as and when the same shall be presented at the house or usual place of business of the treasurer.

No. 3. To keep an account, under the proper dates, of all monies received and paid by him as such treasurer, and to render an account thereof to the Board of Guardians, when required by them to do so.

No. 4. Whenever there should not be funds belonging to the Guardians in his hands as treasurer of the Union, to report in writing the fact of such deficiency to the Poor Law Commissioners.

No. 5. To submit the above-mentioned account to the auditor at the periods of audit, duly notified in pursuance of the regulations of the Poor Law Commissioners in force at the time.

Duties of a District Medical Officer.

Article 19. Every district medical officer shall comply with the regulations and provisions of an order of the Poor Law Commissioners, bearing date the twelfth day of March, in the year of our Lord One thousand eight hundred and forty-two, or any other order of the Poor Law Commissioners in force at the time, and shall also perform the following duties:—

No. 1. To attend duly and punctually upon all poor persons requiring medical or surgical assistance within the district of the Union to which he shall be appointed, and to supply the requisite medicines, and medical and surgical appliances to such persons, whenever he shall be thereunto required by a written or printed order of the Board of Guardians, or of any relieving officer of the Union, or of an overseer of the poor in cases of sudden and urgent necessity, or by the production of a ticket on the part of any poor person whose name shall be included in any list of persons actually receiving relief, directed to be prepared by Article 16 of the said order of the Poor Law Commissioners, bearing date the twelfth day of March, in the year One thousand eight hundred and forty-two, or by any other order of the said Commissioners in force at the time.

No. 2. To give a certificate under his hand in every case to the Board of Guardians, or the relieving officer, or the pauper on whom he is attending, of the sickness of such pauper or other cause of his attendance, when required to do so.

No. 3. To make a weekly return to the Board of Guardians in a book prepared according to the Form B, hereunto annexed, and to insert therein the date of every attendance, and to make an annual index to the same, with the names arranged alphabetically, according to the Form C. hereunto annexed, and to deliver the same when completed to the Board of Guardians.

No. 4. To give to the Board of Guardians, or to any relieving officer, when required, any reasonable information respecting the case of any pauper under his care; to make any such written report relative to any sickness prevalent among the paupers in the workhouse as the Board of Guardians or the Poor Law Commissioners may require of him, and to attend the Board of Guardians when summoned by them.

Duties of a Relieving Officer.

Art. 20. The duties of every relieving officer shall be:—

No. 1. To attend all ordinary meetings of the Board of Guardians, and to attend all other meetings when summoned by the clerk.

No. 2. To receive all applications for relief made to him within his district, or relating to any parish situated within his district, and forthwith to examine into the circumstances of every case by visiting the home of the applicant (if situated within his district), and by making all necessary inquiries into the state of health, the ability to work, and the means of such applicant, and to report the result of such inquiries in the prescribed form to the Board of Guardians at their next ordinary meeting.

No. 3. In any case of sickness or accident requiring medical or surgical relief, to procure medical or surgical assistance by giving an order on the district medical officer, or by such other means as the urgency of the case may require.

No. 4. To ascertain from time to time from the district medical officer, the names of any poor persons whom such medical officer may have attended, or supplied with medicines, without having received an order from himself to that effect.

No. 5. In every case of sickness or accident of any poor person receiving medical relief, as soon as may be, and from time to time afterwards, to visit the home of such sick person, and until the next ordinary meeting of the Board of Guardians, to supply such relief (not being in money) as the case on his own view, or on the certificate of the district medical officer, may seem to require.

No. 6. In every case of sudden and urgent necessity to afford such relief to the destitute person as shall be requisite, either by giving such person an order of admission to the workhouse, and conveying him thereto if necessary, or by affording him relief out of the workhouse, provided that the same shall not be given in money, whether such destitute person be settled in any parish comprised in the Union or not.

No. 7. To report to the Board of Guardians, at their ordinary meetings, all cases reported to him by an overseer of the poor of any parish in the district for which he shall be appointed to act, in which relief shall have been given by such overseer.

No. 8. To give all reasonable aid and assistance at the request of any other relieving officer of the Union, by examining into the case of any applicant for relief, or administering relief to any pauper, whose name has been entered on the books of such other relieving officer, and who may be within his own district.

No. 9. If required by the Board of Guardians, to apply to the persons appointed to pay the pensions payable to out-pensioners, and to receive the amounts which shall be payable to the Board of Guardians, and forthwith to pay the same to the treasurer on their account.

No. 10. Duly and punctually to supply the weekly allowances of all paupers belonging to his district, and to relieve all paupers within his district to the amount and in the manner in which he may have been ordered to pay and relieve such paupers respectively by the Board of Guardians.

No. 11. To keep a separate, full, and true account of all monies received and disbursed by him for or on account of the relief of the poor of each parish in the district for which he shall be appointed to act, and also of all articles received and given out by him for the relief of the outdoor poor; to balance such account weekly, and to present the same to the clerk for his inspection and authentication before every ordinary meeting of the Board of Guardians, and to the Board of Guardians, at such meeting, for their approval.

No. 12. In no case to take credit in his accounts, or enter as paid or given, any money or other articles which shall not have been paid or given previously to the taking of such credit, or the making of such entry; and not to take credit in such accounts for any money paid to any tradesman or other person without producing, at the next ordinary meeting of the Guardians, a bill from such tradesman or other person.

No. 13. To submit to the auditor of the Union all his books, accounts, and vouchers, at such place and time, and in such manner, as may be required by the regulations of the said Commissioners in force at the time.

No. 14. To assist the clerk to the Guardians in conducting and completing the annual or other election of Guardians, according to the regulations of the Poor Law Commissioners in force at the time.

No. 15. To observe and execute all lawful orders and directions of the Guardians applicable to his office.

EXPLANATION OF TERMS.

Art. 21. Whenever the word "Union" is used in this Order, it shall be taken to include not only an union of parishes formed under the provisions of the hereinbefore recited Act, but also any union of parishes incorporated or united for the relief or maintenance of the poor under any local Act of Parliament.

Art. 22. Whenever the word "Guardians" is used in this Order, it shall be taken to include not only Guardians appointed or entitled to act under the provisions of the said hereinbefore recited Act, but also any governors, directors, managers, or acting guardians entitled to act in the ordering of relief to the poor from the poor-rates under any local Act of Pariament.

Art. 23. Whenever the word "Parish" is used in this Order, it shall be taken to include any place maintaining its own poor, whether parochial or extra-parochial.

Art. 24. Whenever in describing any person or party, matter or thing, the word importing the singular number or the masculine gender only is used in this Order, the same shall be taken to include, and shall be applied to, several persons or parties as well as one person or party, and females as well as males, and several matters or things as well as one matter or thing respectively, unless there be something in the subject or context repugnant to such construction.

Art. 25. Whenever in this Order any Article is referred to by its number, the Article of this Order bearing that number shall be taken to be signified thereby.

FORM A.

________________ *Union.*

Day of Meeting________________day of________________ 184

Day and hour to which adjourned________________

Number of Guardians present.____________ ____________Chairman.

Amount of Treasurer's balance due to the Union. ____________

Weekly Return of the In-door and Out-door Paupers.

____________ Week of the____________Quarter.

Workhouse.	In the house at commencement of the week.	Admitted.	Discharged.	Dead.	Remaining.
Men.					
Able-bodied					
Temporarily disabled by sickness or accident . . .					
Old and infirm					
Youths.					
From 7 to 15 Years					
Boys.					
From 2 to 7 Years					
Women.					
Able-bodied					
Temporarily disabled					
Old and infirm					
Girls.					
From 7 to 15 Years					
From 2 to 7 Years					
Infants.					
Born					
Totals . . .					

Number of Paupers belonging to each Relieving Officer's District in the Union.

	In-door.	Out-door.	Out-relief in Kind.	Out-relief in Money.
District No. 1.—Mr.____________Relieving Officer				
District No. 2.—Mr.____________Relieving Officer				
District No. 3.—Mr.____________Relieving Officer				
Total Relief in Kind . . .				
Ditto Money . . .				
Total . . £				

1. Is there any Remark in the Visiting Committee's Book concerning any defect in the discipline or internal economy? If so, furnish a copy of the remark . . . .
2. Does the Number of Paupers in the house exceed that fixed or sanctioned by the Poor Law Commissioners? . . . .
3. Copy of any special minute made or notice of motion on the books . . . .

Signed,

____

Clerk to the Guardians.

To

____

Assistant Poor Law Commissioner.

Sent this____________day of____________184

FORM B. Week ending day of 184

Name.	Age.	Residence.	Parish to which chargeable.	Nature of Disease.	Days when attended.							Necessaries ordered to be given to the Patient.	Present State or Termination of the Case.	Observations.
					S.	M.	T.	W.	Th.	F.	Sat.			

FORM C.

Index.

Name of Patient.	Page of Form B. in which the Name of the Patient first appears.	Day of Termination of Disease, and Event.

3.—GENERAL ORDER :—DUTIES OF OVERSEERS.

To the Guardians of the Poor of the several Unions named in the Schedule hereunto annexed;

To the Churchwardens and Overseers of the several parishes and places comprised within the said Unions;

To the Clerk or Clerks to the Justices of the Petty Sessions held for the Division or Divisions in which the parishes and places comprised within the said Unions are situate;

And to all others whom it may concern.

WE, the Poor Law Commissioners, in pursuance of the authorities vested in us by an Act passed in the fifth year of the reign of His late Majesty King William the Fourth, intituled "*An Act for the Amendment and better Administration of the Laws relating to the Poor in England and Wales,*" do hereby order, direct, and declare, with respect to each and every of the Unions, named in the Schedule hereunto annexed, as follows :—

Duties of the Overseers.

1. If any overseer of the poor of any parish shall, in any case of sudden and urgent necessity, have given temporary relief to any poor person in articles of necessity, or in any case of sudden and dangerous illness, shall have given an order for medical relief, the said overseer shall forthwith report such case in writing to the relieving officer of the district or to the Board of Guardians of the Union, and the amount of such relief or the fact of having made such order.

2. If any overseer of the poor of any parish receive an order under the hands and seal of two justices, according to the provisions of the said Act directing relief to be given to any aged or infirm person, without such person being required to reside in any workhouse, he shall forthwith transmit the same to the relieving officer of the district to be laid before the Guardians at their next meeting, that they may be enabled without delay to give to the relieving officer the necessary directions as to the amount and nature of the relief to be given.

3. If any overseer receive an order for medical relief from any justice in case of sudden and dangerous illness, he shall, as soon as may be after complying with such order, report the fact of his having received the same, and the manner in which he has complied with it, in writing to the relieving officer of the district, or to the Board of Guardians of the Union.

4. To perform such duties in connexion with the election of Guardians for the Union as may be imposed upon the overseers by any regulations of the Poor Law Commissioners in force at the time.

5. And we do further order and direct the overseers of the poor of every parish in the Union—

Firstly. From time to time to provide *Rate-Books* according to the Form A. hereunto annexed; and duly and punctually to make the entries therein of the several matters mentioned in the headings of the several columns of the said Form: and to cause every rate for the relief of the poor in the township, and the allowance of such rate by the justices, to be recorded in the said Rate-Book.

Secondly. To pay over from time to time out of the poor-rates collected, all such sums as by any order of the Guardians expressed to them in writing, according to the Form set forth in the order of the Poor Law Commissioners, bearing date the twentieth day of April instant, shall be directed to be provided from the poor-rates of the parish ; and to pay over such sums to such person or persons, at such times and places as by the same order shall be directed, and to take the receipt of such person or persons; and to produce such order and such receipt as their vouchers for such payments before the auditor of the said Union in passing their quarterly accounts.

Thirdly. To submit, within forty days after each of the following days, namely, Lady-day, Midsummer-day, Michaelmas-day, and Christmas-day, to the auditor of the Union, a distinct account and balance-sheet, exhibiting the amount collected by them, and the amount disbursed by them during the previous quarter, together with the proper vouchers for the same.

Fourthly. To enter in some book, to be from time to time provided for that purpose, the names and addresses of the owners and proxies, who shall send statements of their claims to vote, and the assessment of the poor-rate on the property, in respect whereof they respectively claim to vote, which book may be kept in the Form marked (B) hereto annexed.

Explanation of Terms.

6. Whenever the word "Union" is used in this order, it shall be taken to include not only an union of parishes formed under the provisions of the hereinbefore recited Act, but also any union of parishes incorporated or united for the relief or maintenance of the poor under any local Act of Parliament.

7. Whenever the word "Guardians" is used in this order, it shall be taken to include not only Guardians appointed or entitled to act under the provisions of the said hereinbefore recited Act, but also any governors, directors, managers, or acting guardians entitled to act in the ordering of relief to the poor from the poor-rates under any local Act of Parliament.

8. Whenever the word "Parish" is used in this order, it shall be taken to include any place maintaining its own poor, whether parochial or extra-parochial.

9. Whenever the word "Overseer" is used in this order, it shall be taken to include any person acting or legally bound to act in the discharge of any of the duties usually performed by overseers of the poor, so far as such duties are referred to in this order.

FORM A.

RATE-BOOK.

No.	Name of Occupier.	No. of Votes.	Name of Owner.	No. of Votes.	Description of Property rated.	Name or Situation of Property.	Estimated Extent.	Gross estimated Rental.	Rateable Value.	Rate at — in the Pound.	Arrears due, or if excused.	Total Amount to be collected.	Amount actually collected.	Present Arrear.	Amount not recoverable, or legally excused.

FORM B.

Book for Registry of Owners of Property and Proxies.

Union. Parish of

No.	Name of Owner.	Address.	Property in respect whereof right to vote is claimed.	No. of Reference to Rate-Book.	Aggregate Amount of Assessment.	Name of Proxy.	Address of Proxy.	No.	Date on which Claim received.

We do certify that the above is a full and correct register and entry of the claims to vote of owners of property and proxies in the said parish.

(Signed) } *Overseers.*

Given under our hands, &c. &c.

Schedule containing the Names of the Unions to which the foregoing Orders apply.

Aberaeron
Abergavenny
Aberystwith
Abingdon
Albans, St.
Alcester
Alderbury
Alnwick
Alresford
Alton
Altrincham
Amersham
Amesbury
Ampthill
Andover
Anglesey
Asaph, St.
Ashby-de-la-Zouch
Ashford, East
Ashford, West
Aston
Atcham
Atherstone
Auckland
Austel, St.
Axbridge
Axminster
Aylesbury
Aylesford, North
Aylsham
Bakewell
Bala
Banbury
Bangor & Beaumaris
Barnet
Barnstaple
Barrow on Soar
Basford
Basingstoke
Bath
Battle
Beaminster
Bedale
Bedford
Bedminster
Belford
Bellingham
Belper
Berkhampstead
Berwick-upon-
Beverley [Tweed
Bicester
Bideford
Biggleswade
Billericay
Billesdon
Bingham
Bishop Stortford
Blaby
Blackburn
Blandford
Blean
Blofield
Blything
Bodmin
Bolton
Bootle
Bosmere & Claydon
Boston
Boughton, Great
Bourn
Brackley
Bradfield
Bradford (Wilts)
Bradford (York)
Braintree
Brampton
Brecknock
Brentford
Bridge [bridge
Bridgend and Cow-
Bridgnorth
Bridgewater
Bridlington
Bridport
Brixworth
Bromley
Bromsgrove
Bromyard
Buckingham
Builth
Buntingford
Burnley
Burton-on-Trent
Bury
Bury St. Edmunds
Caistor
Calne
Cambridge
Camelford
Cardiff
Cardigan
Carlisle
Carmarthen
Carnarvon
Castle Ward
Catherington
Caxton & Arrington
Cerne
Chailey
Chapel-en-le-Frith
Chard
Cheadle
Chelmsford
Cheltenham
Chepstow
Chertsey
Chesterfield
Chester-le-Street
Chesterton
Chippenham
Chipping Norton
Chipping Sodbury
Chorley
Chorlton
Christchurch
Church Stretton
Cirencester
Cleobury Mortimer
Clifton
Clitheroe
Clun
Clutton
Cockermouth
Colchester
Columb, St. Major
Congleton
Conway
Cookham
Corwen
Cosford
Cranbrook
Crediton
Crickhowel
Cricklade & Wootton
Croydon [Bassett
Cuckfield
Darlington
Dartford
Daventry
Depwade
Derby
Devizes
Dewsbury
Docking
Dolgelly
Doncaster
Dorchester
Dore
Dorking
Dover
Downham
Drayton
Driffield
Droitwich
Droxford
Dudley
Dulverton
Dunmow
Durham
Dursley
Easington
Easingwold
Eastbourne
East Grinstead
Easthampstead
East Retford
Eastry
East Ward
Ecclesall Bierlow
Edmonton
Elham
Ellesmere
Ely
Epping
Epsom
Erpingham
Eton
Evesham
Faith, St.
Falmouth
Fareham
Faringdon
Faversham
Festiniog
Flegg, East & West
Foleshill
Fordingbridge
Forehoe
Freebridge Lynn
Frome
Fylde
Gainsborough
Garstang
Gateshead
Germans, St.
Glanford Brigg
Glendale
Glossop
Gloucester
Godstone
Goole
Grantham
Gravesend & Milton
Greenwich
Guildford
Guiltcross
Guisborough
Hackney
Hailsham
Halifax
Halstead
Haltwhistle
Hambledon
Hardingstone
Hartismere
Hartley Wintney
Haslingden
Hastings
Hatfield
Havant
Haverfordwest
Hay
Hayfield
Headington
Helmsley Blackmoor
Helston
Hemel-Hempstead
Hendon
Henley
Henstead
Hereford
Hertford
Hexham [don
Highworth & Swin-
Hinckley
Hitchin
Holbeach
Holborn
Hollingbourn
Holsworthy
Holywell
Honiton
Hoo
Horncastle
Horsham
Houghton-le-Spring
Howden
Hoxne
Huddersfield
Hungerford
Huntingdon
Hursley
Ipswich
Ives, St.
Keighley
Kendal
Kensington
Kettering
Keynsham
Kidderminster
Kingsbridge
Kingsclere
King's Lynn
King's Norton
Kingston-on-Thames
Kington
Knighton
Lampeter
Lancaster
Lanchester
Langport
Launceston
Ledbury
Leek

Leicester
Leigh
Leighton Buzzard
Leominster
Lewes
Lewisham
Lexden & Winstree
Leyburn
Lichfield
Lincoln
Linton
Liskeard
Llandilo Fawr
Llandovery
Llanelly
Llanfyllin
Llanrwst
Loddon & Clavering
London, city of
London, East
London, West
Longtown
Loughborough
Louth
Ludlow
Luton
Lutterworth
Lymington
Macclesfield
Machynlleth
Madeley
Maidstone
Maldon
Malling
Malmsbury
Malton
Manchester
Mansfield
Market Bosworth
Market Harborough
Marlborough
Martley
Medway
Melksham
Melton Mowbray
Mere
Meriden
Merthyr Tidvil
Midhurst
Mildenhall
Milton
Mitford & Launditch
Monmouth
Morpeth [land
Mutford & Lothing-
Nantwich
Narberth
Neath
Neot's, St.
Newark
Newbury
Newcastle-in-Emlyn
Newcastle-under-
Lyne [Tyne
Newcastle-upon-
Newent
New Forest
Newhaven
Newmarket [mouth)
Newport (Mon-
Newport (Salop)
Newport Pagnell
Newton Abbott
Newtown & Llanid-
Northallerton [loes
Northampton
Northleach
Northwich
North Witchford
Nottingham
Nuneaton
Oakham
Okehampton
Olave's, St.
Ongar
Ormskirk
Orsett
Oundle
Pateley Bridge
Patrington
Pembroke
Penkridge
Penrith
Penzance
Pershore
Peterborough
Petersfield
Petworth
Pewsey
Pickering
Plomesgate
Plympton St. Mary
Pocklington
Pont-y-pool
Poole
Poplar
Portsea Island
Potterspury
Prescot
Presteigne
Preston
Pwllheli
Radford
Reading
Redruth
Reeth
Reigate
Rhayadar
Richmond (Surrey)
Richmond (York)
Ringwood
Risbridge
Rochford
Romford
Romney Marsh
Romsey
Ross
Rothbury
Rotherham
Royston
Rugby
Runcorn
Ruthin
Rye
Saffron Walden
Salford
Samford
Saviour's, St.
Scarborough
Sculcoates
Sedbergh
Sedgefield
Seisdon
Selby
Settle
Seven Oaks
Shaftesbury
Shardlow
Sheffield
Sheppey
Shepton Mallet
Sherborne
Shiffnal
Shipston-on-Stour
Skipton
Skirlaugh
Sleaford
Solihull
Southam
South Molton
South Shields
South Stoneham
Southwell
Spalding
Spilsby
Stafford
Staines
Stamford
Stepney
Steyning
Stockbridge
Stockport
Stockton
Stokesley
Stone
Stourbridge
Stow
Stow-on-the-Wold
Strand
Stratford-on-Avon
Stratton
Stroud
Sturminster
Sudbury
Sunderland
Swaffham
Swansea
Tamworth
Taunton
Tavistock
Teesdale
Tenbury
Tendring
Tenterden
Tetbury
Tewkesbury
Thakeham
Thame
Thanet, Isle of
Thetford
Thingoe
Thirsk
Thomas, St.
Thornbury
Thorne
Thrapston
Ticehurst
Tisbury
Tiverton
Todmorden
Tonbridge
Torrington
Totnes
Towcester
Tregaron
Truro
Tunstead & Happing
Tynemouth
Uckfield
Ulverstone
Uppingham
Upton-on-Severn
Uttoxeter
Uxbridge
Wakefield
Wallingford
Walsal
Walsingham [ham
Wandsworth & Clap-
Wangford
Wantage
Ware [beck
Wareham and Pur-
Warminster
Warrington
Warwick
Watford
Wayland
Weardale
Wellingborough
Wellington (Salop)
Wellington (Somer-
Wells [set)
Welwyn
Wem
Weobly
Westbourne
West Bromwich
Westbury-on-Severn
Westbury & Whor-
welsdown
West Derby
West Firle
West Ham
West Hampnett
West Ward
Weymouth
Wheatenhurst
Whitby
Whitchurch
Whitehaven
Whitechapel
Wigan
Wigton
Williton
Wilton [Cranborne
Wimborne and
Wincanton
Winchcombe
Winchester, New
Windsor
Winslow
Wirrall
Wisbeach
Witham
Witney
Woburn
Wokingham
Wolstanton and
Burslem
Wolverhampton
Woodbridge
Woodstock
Worcester
Worksop
Wortley
Wrexham
Wycombe
Yeovil
York

Given under our Hands and Seal, &c., &c.

LONDON: Printed by Order of the Poor Law Commissioners, by W. CLOWES and SONS, Stamford Street, and Published by C. KNIGHT and Co., 22, Ludgate Street.

AN

OFFICIAL CIRCULAR

OF PUBLIC DOCUMENTS AND INFORMATION:

DIRECTED BY THE POOR LAW COMMISSIONERS TO BE PRINTED, CHIEFLY FOR THE USE OF THE MEMBERS AND PERMANENT OFFICERS OF BOARDS OF GUARDIANS, UNDER THE POOR LAW AMENDMENT ACT.

No. 20. CIRCULAR ISSUED JULY 30TH, 1842.

Poor Law Commission Office,
Somerset House,
July 25, 1842.

THE Poor Law Commissioners, on a review of their minutes, directed that the minutes and correspondence on the following subjects should be printed and circulated for the information of Guardians and officers of the several Unions, viz.—

By order of the Board,
EDWIN CHADWICK, *Secretary.*

I. — RELIEF IN CASES OF EMERGENCY—DUTIES OF MEDICAL AND RELIEVING OFFICERS AND OVERSEERS IN RESPECT OF.

The Poor Law Commissioners having had their attention called, in February last, to the case of Alban May, a travelling man, who was taken ill in the parish of Yalding, and subsequently removed to the workhouse of the Maidstone Union at Coxheath, where he died; they requested the Guardians to furnish them with information relative to the case; also to obtain and transmit to them the written explanation of the medical officer who had visited the sick man, previous to his removal to the workhouse; and on the 22d of March last, the Guardians transmitted to the Commissioners a copy of the depositions of the witnesses examined by the coroner at the inquest held on the body of Alban May, together with a letter from Mr. Pout, the medical officer referred to, containing his explanation relative to the case.

The facts of the case, so far as they affect the officers for the administration of relief to the poor, appear from these depositions to be as follows:

That Alban May, deceased, was first seen by Stephen Bowles, of Yalding, labourer, between 3 and 4 P.M., on Tuesday, the 1st of February, in an open lodge, at Mr. Martin's farm, in Yalding parish, to whom he complained of illness, and of inability to proceed further; that between 10 and 11 o'clock the same evening, S. Bowles, by direction of his master, Mr. Hartridge, went to Mr. Pout, the medical officer, and informed him that there was a man very ill in Mr. Martin's barn, and that Mr. Hartridge had sent him for Mr. Pout,—that Mr. Pout declined to go that night to visit the deceased, but sent some medicine for him, and promised to see the deceased in the morning; that Mr. Pout visited the sick man on the following day about noon, and finding him in a dangerous state, and apparently suffering from apoplexy, and considering the place in which the deceased was, an unfit place for him to be in, although he was hardly in a fit state to be removed, he applied to the overseer for an order of admission to the workhouse, and the deceased was conveyed to the workhouse accordingly, where he was attended by Mr. Kennett, the medical officer of the workhouse,—that although every attention was then paid him, and every means used for his recovery, he continued to get worse, and died on Thursday, the 3d of February.

The Commissioners having perused the above-mentioned depositions, and Mr. Pout's explanation, directed their Assistant Commissioner, Mr. Power, to attend the Board of Guardians of the Maidstone Union, for the purpose of expressing the opinion of the Commissioners upon the conduct of Mr. Pout.

The annexed Report of Mr. Power contains an account of his proceedings, in pursuance of the above-mentioned direction, and, together with the notice appended thereto, which he has submitted to the Board of Guardians, expresses the opinion of the Commissioners on the conduct of Mr. Pout, and their views on the points urged in Mr. Pout's explanation (also appended to that Report) as to his not being bound, in the absence of an order from some competent authority, to attend the sick man, and on the duty of overseers, in cases of emergency like the present one, and the proper course to be followed by rate-payers or inhabitants who may become aware of the existence of such a case before any of the officers of the Union, or the overseers have been made acquainted with it.

"*London*, 8*th April*, 1842.

"GENTLEMEN,—I attended the meeting of the guardians of the Maidstone Union yesterday, in pursuance of your instructions, for the purpose of expressing the opinion of your Board upon the conduct of Mr. Pout, a medical officer of that Union, in reference to the circumstances connected with the death of Alban May, as detailed in the depositions given before the coroner's jury on the 5th February last.

"I stated to Mr. Pout in the presence of the Board of Guardians, that upon view of the depositions made on the inquest, and his (Mr. Pout's) own letter to the clerk of the Union, the Commissioners considered that relief had not been effectively administered in this case, and that his, Mr. Pout's, conduct was by no means free from blame; but that before I proceeded to pass any censure upon him, I was desirous to hear any statement he might wish to make upon certain points, in regard to which his conduct had appeared to require explanation.

"The following were the points to which I drew Mr. Pout's attention:—

"1. That he did not attend on the evening of Tuesday, the man having been reported to him to be then 'insensible,' but sent medicines promising to see him early the next day.

"2. That he did not personally attend the man before 12 o'clock the next day.

"3. That he advised the overseer to have the man removed to the Union workhouse, a distance of seven miles, although fearing, as he expressed himself before the jury, that he might die on the road, and did not make any endeavour to have him removed to a nearer place of accommodation.

"I took down in writing Mr. Pout's statements in explanation of his conduct in these several particulars, and the statements he made are attached to this report.

"It will be seen that Mr. Pout's main vindication on the first two points is that he was not called on to attend the case as medical officer, having received no order to do so; and in regard to the third, he pleads ignorance that either he himself or the overseer had authority to remove the man to any other place than the Union workhouse, or to provide a lodging for him elsewhere. It appears that the Duke of Wellington public-house, alluded to in Mr. Pout's statement as only half a mile from the spot where the man lay, is not the house referred to in the depositions on the inquest, the latter being only a beer-shop, and that no application was made by any person to have the man received and lodged in the Duke of Wellington public-house.

"After hearing Mr. Pout's statements in explanation of his conduct, I said that I was now prepared to say on behalf of the Commissioners, 'that if a medical officer was sent for to attend a poor person, and he accepted the case, and treated the person in any way as his patient, and as being under his care, the Commissioners would not allow the circumstance that there was no written order from a relieving officer, overseer, or other authority, to be a justification of neglect of the case by the medical officer, or to protect him from the consequences of such neglect; and I cautioned Mr. Pout not to act upon any such supposition for the future. The reasons for this construction I stated to be as follows; namely, that if the medical officer makes no objection to attending the case, but proceeds, or promises to proceed, in the treatment of it, he causes reliance to be placed upon his services by those who apply for his assistance, and so prevents their obtaining an order from some competent authority or from applying for assistance in some other quarter.

"With regard to Mr. Pout's plea of ignorance that it was in the power of the overseer to provide lodging in such a case, and therefore that he himself was competent to advise that step, many of the guardians present assured me that such a doctrine was quite new to them, and unknown, as they believed, to the overseers of the several parishes in the Union.

"It seems not improbable, therefore, that Mr. Pout shared in the general want of knowledge existing in the Union on this point, and it will be seen that he refers to this erroneous impression, both in his evidence on the inquest, and his letter to the clerk of the Union. I begged Mr. Pout to understand that in all future similar cases he must give his advice to the overseers as to persons fully competent, in cases of urgency, to incur any reasonable expense in providing lodging as well as other necessaries.

"I next drew the attention of the guardians to the fact, that although this poor man was discovered in a destitute and helpless state at 3 o'clock in the afternoon of the Tuesday, and although several persons who appeared humanely disposed, were acquainted with the circumstances, the attention of an overseer of the poor was never drawn to the case, until the afternoon of the day following, when Mr. Pout himself informed Mr. Beadle, and gave instructions for the removal of the man.

"This appeared to have arisen from ignorance of what ought to be done under such circumstances, and I accordingly urged the Board of Guardians to take some step for the purpose of giving clear information to the inhabitants of each parish as to the real state of the law and the steps which ought to be taken in such cases, and for the purpose also of pointing out to each successive set of overseers the true extent of their powers and responsibilities under the Poor Law Amendment Act.

"In a Union like Maidstone where the great bulk of the population is at a distance of several miles from the only workhouse, it seems of the last importance that the overseers of parishes as well as the other officers should understand that in cases of urgency, affecting life, it is in their power to provide lodging as well as other necessaries.

"I recommended the Board of Guardians therefore to have a short placard printed in very plain language, explaining the true state of the law in regard to cases of urgent distress, and to publish such notice annually in each parish after the new appointment of churchwardens and overseers, inserting the names and residences of each of those officers, as well as those of the relieving officer of the district.

"The guardians present appeared to concur in the tenor of the observations which I had occasion to make, and more especially in the expediency of taking the step suggested for the purpose of making the actual state of the law known to the overseers and other inhabitants of each parish, and I stated that I would forward to the clerk of the Union a form of notice for that purpose to be laid before the guardians for their consideration at some future meeting.

"It is necessary to state in justice to Mr. Pout, the medical officer, tha tafter the termination of the meeting, the Chairman of the Board informed me that he considered that one very material circumstance in explanation of Mr. Pout's conduct was, that the man who came to fetch him to attend Alban May had not sufficiently represented to him the dangerous nature of the case; and that he believed, if Mr. Pout had understood the man's illness to be of a serious nature, he would not have neglected to attend him merely on the ground that there was no medical order; for that it was by no means Mr. Pout's practice to insist on the production of any order to attend his pauper patients. It is right to add that the chairman, Mr. Whitaker, had been present at the inquest.

"I am, Gentlemen,
"Your very obedient Servant,
(Signed) "A. POWER.

"*The Poor Law Commissioners.*"

Mr. Pout's Explanation of his Conduct as Medical Officer.

Mr. Pout states on his own behalf, and in explanation of his conduct, as follows:—

"First, with reference to my not attending Alban May on the evening of Tuesday, I did not consider myself called upon as medical officer to attend the case, having received no order from any parochial or other authority."

In what capacity then did you consider yourself as treating this case?

"As the case of any other private patient. I could not tell what the circumstances of the man were, not having seen him or heard more of him than that he was a railroad labourer, and it is, I have since learnt, usual for medical attendance to be provided by the contractor making an engagement with some medical man on the part of the workmen. I did not by any means consider myself bound to attend the case as an officer of the Union.

"As to the circumstance of my not personally attending in this case before 12 o'clock the next day, I was engaged the early part of the morning attending to Union patients, that being the day on which the relieving officer attends at Galding, which is the means of bringing an unusual number of paupers, as they take the opportunity of meeting the relieving officer and seeing me at the same time; and on this point again I should wish to observe that I did not feel myself called upon to attend the case as medical officer of the Union."

In regard to the removal of the sick man to the Union workhouse, did you take any step for the purpose of endeavouring to obtain accommodation for him on the spot?

"I felt that I had no authority myself to direct his removal to any other place than the Union workhouse, and I expressed my regret to the bystanders at the time that I had no such authority. The nearest overseer was Mr. Beadle, who lived three or four miles from the spot where the man lay. He resides near my house, and I saw him on going home."

Did you suggest to him to endeavour to find accommodation for the man on the spot?

"I do not think I did; but, as I said before, I did not think I had authority to direct the removal to any place but the Union workhouse."

What was the distance of the nearest public-house from the spot where the man lay?

"The Duke of Wellington public-house was from a quarter to half a mile off."

It did not occur to you to recommend his removal to the public-house?

"No, I was not aware that the overseer had authority to remove him to any place but the Union house."

Maidstone Union, } th day of ,
Parish of ——— } 184 .

RELIEF OF THE POOR.

Take Notice,

The Relieving Officer for this district is ——— ———, who lives at ———, and he will attend on ——— in every week at the hour of in the [forenoon or afternoon] at ———, to pay the poor and to receive applications for relief for the parish of ———; and all persons requiring relief in that parish should apply to him, if possible, at the above time and place.

Take Notice also,

That ——— ———, of ———,
——— ———, of ———,
——— ———, of ———,
——— ———, of ———,

are churchwardens and overseers of the poor of the parish of ——— for the present year, and that each of them has power and authority, in any case of sudden and urgent necessity, to give temporary relief in articles of absolute necessity, such as food, clothing or lodging; or in any case of sudden illness or accident, requiring instant medical assistance, to provide the same immediately.

In any case of sudden and urgent necessity requiring immediate medical or other relief, the relieving officer should be informed thereof, if possible, or in his absence immediate information should be given to some one of the churchwardens or overseers of the parish in which the person requiring immediate relief may be.

If any churchwarden or overseer shall refuse or neglect to provide relief in any such case of sudden and urgent necessity, application should be made to the nearest magistrate.

If any churchwarden or overseer shall be called upon to give relief in any such case of sudden and urgent necessity, he will be expected to attend to the case himself; and, if he shall find it necessary to make any order for medical attendance, to make such order in writing. He must also send immediate information of the case in writing to the relieving officer of the district.

Signed, by order of the Board of Guardians,

——— ———,

Clerk of the Union

II.—MEDICAL RELIEF.—APPROVAL OF COMMISSIONERS OF RESOLUTION OF GUARDIANS OF POPLAR UNION TO SEND TO THE HOSPITAL ALL CASES REQUIRING EXTRAORDINARY SURGICAL AID.

The Commissioners took into consideration a letter from the clerk of the Poplar Union, communicating to the Commissioners the particulars of the case of an Asiatic seaman who was admitted into the Poplar Union Workhouse, with a disease in his legs, which it was feared would have rendered amputation necessary, and forwarding to them the following copy of a resolution thereon passed by the Guardians:—

"That all cases requiring extraordinary surgical aid should be sent to the London Hospital at the earliest possible opportunity (if the circumstances of the cases will, in the opinion of the medical officer, admit of such removal), the Board considering that the hospital affords superior means for the general treatment of surgical cases to that which can be rendered in a workhouse."

In reply, the Commissioners stated that they fully concurred in the view taken by the Guardians in this matter, and very much prefer the removal of a patient whose case may require the performance of a capital operation of surgery to some good hospital, to the performance of such an operation in a workhouse.

III.—WORKHOUSE.—1. AS TO POLICY OF INSURANCE OF FROM FIRE.

The following is a copy of a letter received from the clerk of the Ecclesall Bierlow Union:—

"*Ecclesall Bierlow, 6th January*, 1842.

"GENTLEMEN,—The Board of Guardians being desirous of insuring the new Union Workhouse from loss by fire forthwith, have directed me to inquire of you in whose name the policy should be made out.

"I have the honour to be,

"Gentlemen,

"Your most obedient servant,

"(Signed) B. SLATER.

"*The Poor Law Commissioners.*"

In reply, the Commissioners stated that the policy for insuring the workhouse from fire should be made out in the corporate name of the Union.

2. WORKHOUSE OFFICERS OCCUPYING APARTMENTS CONTAINING LESS THAN SEVEN WINDOWS EXEMPT FROM PAYMENT OF ASSESSED TAXES.

The following is a copy of a letter received from the clerk of the Holbeach Union.

"ASSESSED TAXES.

"*Holbeach, 13th December*, 1841.

"SIR,—I am directed by the Board of Guardians to inform you that they have received notice from the Surveyor of Taxes again charging the Governor of the House with duty for 27 windows.

"A similar charge was made last year, and in reference to my inquiry as to the liability of a Union Workhouse to be assessed, you forwarded me copy of a letter from the Secretary of the Board of Stamps and Taxes on the subject,* and wherein it appeared that it was the opinion of the Commissioners of Stamps and Taxes that the windows in the Workhouse were exempt from duty under the second case of exemption, Schedule A, of the 48 Geo. III., cap. 55, and that as none of the officers individually occupied apartments containing more than seven windows they were not chargeable with duty with reference to the 6 Geo. IV., cap. 7.

"The Surveyor of Taxes was then satisfied, and did not press the charge.

"I should be glad to be informed whether any thing has transpired during the year to induce the Board of Stamps and Taxes to come to any other conclusion than that stated in their letter above referred to.

"I am, Sir,

"Your obedient servant,

(Signed) "E. KEY.

"*E. Chadwick, Esq.*"

In reply, the Commissioners stated that they had communicated with the Commissioners of Taxes on the subject, and they were informed in reply that the charge in question was made by the surveyor under an erroneous view of the law, conceiving the master of the workhouse to be liable for all the windows except those in the rooms occupied by the paupers, but as it seemed that neither the master of the workhouse, nor any of the officers of the Union, occupied individually apartments containing

* See Official Circular, No. 10, p. 144.

more than seven windows, they were exempt from duty, and the Commissioners of Taxes had accordingly given instructions that the charge should be withdrawn.

---

3. EMPLOYMENT OF ABLE-BODIED PAUPERS IN THE WORKHOUSE—BEST KIND OF MILL TO BE USED FOR.

The following is a copy of a letter transmitted by the Commissioners to the Board of Guardians of the Bicester Union, in reply to an application made by that Board for directions as to the best plan to adopt in erecting a mill to employ the able-bodied men:—

Poor Law Commission Office,
Somerset House,
5th March, 1842.

SIR,—I am directed by the Poor Law Commissioners to inform you that they have caused enquiries to be instituted as to the best kind of mill for the employment of the inmates of a workhouse. The mills most commonly used are of steel, but as it is found, that the flour from them is not so smooth as from mills having French burr stones; the mills with stones are generally preferred.

The difference in the quality of the meal has been ascertained by competent persons, who find that flour from the steel mills takes up, or drinks, as it is technically called by bakers, about one-fourth less of water than flour from the same corn ground by the other mills.

It would seem, therefore, that the steel mill produces an inferior article, and that poor persons with small allotments, or others who have gleaned a little wheat would, on that account, abstain from bringing their corn to such a mill; and that the labour would not be so profitable if the Board of Guardians provided wheat, and manufactured their own flour. At the Frome Union Workhouse, employment at an expensive steel mill has been discontinued, notwithstanding that the flour consumed in the workhouse, would require more labour to manufacture it than the inmates of the workhouse could perform.

At the Hungerford Union Workhouse, there is an excellent mill, with French burr stones, manufactured by Weir, of Oxford-street, London. It is calculated to employ twenty-eight persons, and can be worked by seven. It is, however, too heavy, except for a very pauperized district, and too expensive for general use. When completed, it cost 182*l.*

At the workhouse of the Reading Union, there is a very good mill, complete in every respect; erected by Phillips, of Reading. It has two pair of burr stones, and performs its duties in a most satisfactory manner. It affords employment for about nine paupers, but can be worked by two. The cost of this mill, including fixing, was 42*l.*

The number of inmates of the Bicester Union Workhouse has been hitherto so limited, as to induce the Commissioners to recommend to the notice of the Board, a mill similar to that at Reading, inasmuch as it would afford sufficient labour for the paupers who are likely to enter the workhouse.

I have the honour to be, Sir,
Your most obedient Servant,

---

4. REPORTS ON BAKING BREAD IN WORKHOUSES.—ERROR IN ACCOUNT OF IN TENDRING UNION, PUBLISHED IN "OFFICIAL CIRCULAR," No. 18.

The following is a copy of a letter received from one of the Guardians of the Tendring Union, pointing out certain inaccuracies contained in the account of the pecuniary results of baking bread in the Tendring Union Workhouse, published by the Commissioners in their Official Circular, No. 18.

"*Frating Lodge*, 18*th May*, 1842.

"GENTLEMEN,—The well-known anxiety of the Poor Law Commissioners for correct information on all subjects relating to the details of Poor Law management, whether in or out of Union houses, must be my apology for intruding myself on your valuable time at the present moment. In the 'Official Circular' issued on the 9th instant there is a detailed account of the result of 'Baking Bread' for the use of the *Tendring Union* house for the quarter ending Michaelmas, 1841, which, I think, in some respects, is not strictly correct; and as the Commissioners furnished the information for the guidance of other Unions, it may be well to notice them. In the first place, then, the sum of 129*l.* 19*s.* 0¾*d.*, assumed to be the cost of 4615½ loaves, at 6½*d.*, is incorrect, it should only be (as I calculate it) 125*l.* 0*s.* 0¾*d*, *lessening* the balance in favour of baking by 4*l.* 19*s.* Again, there is no reason why the contract price is assumed to be 6½*d.* I have made the following extract from the Minute Book, dated June 9th, 1841:—

" 'Mr. G. Pattrick contracts to supply bread for the Harwich District of the Tendring Union, for the ensuing quarter, at 6½d.

" 'Mr. John Rivers, ditto, ditto, for the Ardleigh District, at 6½d.

" 'Mrs. Bones, ditto, ditto, for the Thorpe District, at 6d.'

" And on reference to other quarters, when the bread for the house *was* contracted for, we always got that ¼d. or ½d. lower on account of it being all delivered at one place; and as Mrs. Bones supplied the Thorpe District at 6d., taking the expense of sending it round to the different places, I have no doubt the like contract might have been made for the house: but of this the Commissioners will be the best judges. As the Commissioners themselves state 'that statements of this kind are not always to be implicitly relied on, as it is possible the original cost of wear and tear of oven and implements of trade are omitted, which ought to be included,' I would forbear to insist on it (although it is noticeable); that there is nothing in the published account of the Tendring Union allowed for these things, nor for interest of original outlay, as there is in the account of Hoxne Union, published in the same 'Official Circular.'

" The account might very fairly stand thus, viz.—

	£.	s.	d.
" 4615½ loaves baked in the house, cost	121	5	0
4615½ loaves contracted for at 6d.	115	7	9
Loss by baking per quarter .	£5	17	3

" And this is assuming that all the expenses are correctly stated, which I think is open to doubt, as the system has never been fairly tested.

" I am,
" Your obedient servant,
" ALEXANDER DAVIDSON,
" *Guardian for the Parish of Frating.*"

The Commissioners directed an examination to be made of the printed statement, and the original MS., and found that the account as printed in their Official Circular, corresponded with the MS. Table received from the Union.

The Commissioners thereupon transmitted a copy of Mr. Davidson's letter to the clerk of the Union, who informed the Commissioners that the statement had been prepared by the master of the workhouse, from whom the Commissioners received the following explanatory letter:—

" *Tendring Union House, 3rd June*, 1842.

" HONOURED SIRS,—Finding that the clerk of this Union has been blamed for the incorrectness of the account of baking in this house, I consider it my duty to free him from that charge, as he had no part in it. E. Twisleton, Esq., when here, before we began baking, on talking with me on the subject, expressed a wish to have an account of the receipts and expenditures therein.

" I am very much grieved to find that I did not render a correct account; but as everything connected with baking was quite new to me, I trust, Honoured Sirs, you will not think me very culpable in this affair, but I assure you it will cause me to be more careful for the future.

" I believe I am at liberty to state that when our Board of Guardians thought of baking, their chief motive was to secure a good wholesome article for the paupers, and in this I think they have succeeded, therefore I could have no motive in attempting to show a profit on baking.

" I am, Honoured Sirs,
" Your very obedient and humble servant,
" JOHN ALLOWAY."

IV.—WORKHOUSE DISCIPLINE.—REFUSAL OF PAUPERS TO SUBMIT TO MEDICAL TREATMENT.—COURSE TO BE ADOPTED.

The following is a copy of a correspondence on the above subject between the Guardians of the Hertford and Maidstone Unions and the Poor Law Commissioners:—

" HERTFORD UNION.

" *Hertford, 23rd February*, 1842.

" SIR,—I am directed to request the advice of the Poor Law Commissioners under the following circumstances:—

" William Walls, aged 36, with Agnes his wife, aged 31, James, aged 12, and Robert, 20 months, were admitted into the workhouse of this Union on the 10th January, at the charge of the parish of All Saints, Hertford. Walls is a hatter by trade, and had been at work for a year or two at Mr. Judd's, a hatter here, up to July 3rd, when, in consequence of his coming very late of a morning to work, Judd, after several complaints, discharged him. He worked by the piece, and has earned from 1*l.* to 2*l.* per week; generally from 30*s.* to 35*s.* Walls states that his settlement is in Cannonbury parish, Mary Port, Cumberland, where he is very anxious to be removed, but the Guardians do not think fit to incur the expense of removal, and prefer to keep him for a time in the workhouse, in the hope that he may, before long, get work, and Mr. Judd stated this morning to me that the trade was better, and he had no doubt of his getting plenty of work in the course of a month, if he wished.

" Inclosed I send the minutes made by the medical officer and the workhouse keeper, by which you will learn that he refuses to let the medical officer examine his leg, although he has been repeatedly requested to do so; the consequence of his refusal is that all discipline with him is at an end. He has an ulcer on his leg, and, in consequence of his inability to examine it, the medical officer dare not order him to be set at work, nor does he know whether he ought to have a more generous diet or not.

"By the direction of the Guardians, he was taken before the magistrates for disobeying the legal orders of the master of the workhouse; but the magistrates felt so much difficulty, that although they reprimanded him, yet they refused to punish him in any way until the facts were laid before the Poor Law Commissioners, and their opinion was taken as to the precise charge which could be made against Walls, and as to the Act of Parliament under which he could be punished.

"The Guardians meet on Saturday next, by which day I hope for an answer.

"I am, Sir,

"Your obedient servant,

"THOMAS SWORDER, *Clerk*.

"*To Edwin Chadwick, Esq.*,

"*Secretary to the Poor Law Commission*."

In reply, the Commissioners stated that they entertain a doubt whether the refusal of an adult pauper to submit to a medical examination, when there is no reasonable ground to suspect that he labours under any contagious disorder, by which the other inmates of the workhouse might be endangered, is so distinct a general misbehaviour within the meaning of the 55 Geo. 3, c. 137, sec. 5, as to justify a conviction on that ground.

The Commissioners also doubt whether, in the absence of any reason to suspect a contagious disorder, the master of the workhouse has any such legal authority to compel an adult pauper to submit to a medical examination after he has been removed from the probationary ward as to constitute the refusal, of the pauper, a disobedience of the regulations of the Poor Law Commissioners.

But in the present case, the pauper is stated to have refused to work on the 3rd February, alleging as an excuse for such refusal, the state of his leg. Any disabling disorder would undoubtedly be a good defence to a charge of refusing to work under the statute before referred to. But, unless the pauper should prove this excuse by competent medical or other evidence, especially when the opportunity of obtaining medical evidence is offered him gratuitously by the Guardians, the Commissioners think he ought to be convicted of refusal to work under the 5th sec. of 55 Geo. 3, c. 137.

"MAIDSTONE UNION.

"*Staplehurst*, 15*th April*, 1842.

"GENTLEMEN,—I am directed by the Board of Guardians to inform you that a pauper in the Union workhouse, Ann Miller, lately entered the house, and was reported by the medical officer as having the itch. She, however, positively denies this, and refuses to submit to the medical treatment prescribed in such cases.

"The Guardians directed her to be punished as disorderly, and they desire to be informed what power of punishment they have, in case she should persist in her refusal to submit to medical treatment, which they expect she will do, after she shall have been also punished as refractory.

"I remain, Gentlemen,

"Your most obedient servant,

"W. N. OTTAWAY, *Clerk*."

In reply, the Commissioners stated that they presumed that the pauper was an adult of sound mind, and she was as stated in the above letter, reported, by competent authority, the medical officer, to have a contagious disorder.

Under these circumstances, the Commissioners entertain no doubt that it is the duty of the Guardians to take effective means of protecting the other inmates of the workhouse from infection. The means of doing this consists of two distinct courses of proceeding—first, in the keeping of the pauper out of communication with the other paupers; secondly, in the medical treatment of the pauper, with a view to his or her own cure. The first is an imperative duty of the Guardians, which they are bound to perform without reference to the individual pauper's choice. The second is not essential to the protection of the other inmates of the workhouse. It is true that the Guardians cannot neglect it; but on the other hand, it is not clear that they can compel the pauper to submit to medical treatment which has only her own cure in view. For, although she can only have relief on the conditions imposed by the existing regulations, she is, being an adult of sound mind, at liberty to refuse any additional relief which may be offered to her, but which is not required by the regulations to be taken as a condition of receiving the relief she requires. Medical relief is only an additional species of relief, the receipt of which relief is not made a condition of receiving other necessary relief.

The Commissioners, therefore, conclude that according to the existing regulations, a pauper, having a contagious disorder, who resists the being placed in such a ward as is provided for the class of such persons, or as the Guardians or the proper officers, exercising a sound discretion, consider necessary for the protection of the inmates of the workhouse, is disorderly, and may be dealt with accordingly, but that an adult pauper of sound mind who refuses medical treatment, having his own cure only for its object is not disorderly, and is not liable to be punished on that account.

V.—WORKHOUSE DIETARIES.—REPORT THEREON BY MR. PARKER, ONE OF THE ASSISTANT COMMISSIONERS.

"*Southampton*, 9*th July*, 1842.

"GENTLEMEN,—Numerous inconveniences and much expense result from allowing the inmates of workhouses a certain number of ounces of tea and sugar; the provision of separate teapots and cups and saucers; the difficulty of inducing the inmates to take their tea at a fixed hour; the impossibility of bringing all the inmates, with their teapots and saucers, to a common dining-hall; and the frequent passings to and fro for hot water,—all combine to interfere with the discipline of a public establishment.

"In a workhouse visited by me during this week there were no less than three fires in the day ward, lighted merely to heat as many kettles, and this expense was incurred to avoid giving the inmates the opportunity of mixing together when the doors were opened.

"The simple remedy is to allow a certain quantity of liquid tea, which, if made in a large tea-urn, will be of much better quality than if the same quantity of tea were used separately to make the same number of pints. This plan is adopted in the Windsor Union workhouse, and is attended with no inconvenience whatever.

"It is also desirable to avoid making any weekly allowance of butter or other articles, inasmuch as the inmates are in the habit of placing their allowance in their beds and other places, and the master of the workhouse cannot take back the allowance if the inmates desire to go out of the workhouse before the expiration of a week.

"I have the honour to be,
"Gentlemen,
"Your obedient servant,
"H. W. PARKER,
"*Assistant Poor Law Commissioner.*

"*The Poor Law Commissioners.*"

VI.—WORKHOUSE RULES.—PAUPERS REQUIRING TO LEAVE THE WORKHOUSE.—CONSTRUCTION OF ARTICLE 23.

The following is a copy of a letter received from the master of the workhouse of the Ellesmere Union:—

"*Ellesmere Union, July* 9, 1842.

"GENTLEMEN,—I beg leave most respectfully to refer you to the 23rd article of your General Workhouse Rules, of the 5th of February last, wherein it is stated that in the event of any able-bodied pauper having a family quitting the workhouse, the whole of such family shall be sent with him, unless the guardians shall otherwise direct. I should therefore feel particularly obliged by your informing me at your earliest convenience how I am to act in the event of a pauper who may not be able-bodied, having a family, and wishing to leave the workhouse without taking such family with him.

"I named the subject to William Day, Esq., your Assistant Commissioner, who thought the definition of the article was not very clear, and advised me to take your opinion respecting the same.

"I have the honour to be,
"Gentlemen,
"Your most obedient humble servant,
(Signed) "JOHN P. PRITCHARD,
"*Master of the Workhouse.*"

In reply, the Commissioners stated that the general rule is that when the head of the family, whether able-bodied or not, requires to leave the workhouse, he should only be allowed to do so on the condition that he takes his family with him. But the Board of Guardians, under the 23rd article of the Workhouse Rules, can dispense with this condition without special directions in the case of the families of paupers not able-bodied; whereas, in the case of able-bodied paupers, they can only let them out without their families in special cases and for special reasons.

As regards the workhouse master, his rule of conduct, under the 23rd article, is this:—1st. With regard to the families of paupers not able-bodied, in the absence of all instructions from the Guardians, they must accompany the head of the family if he or she leave the house; but the master may receive and act upon a general instruction to the contrary, either to let a particular family or a class of families remain in the house when the head is allowed to go out. 2nd. With regard to the able-bodied, the rule is now that the master cannot receive a general instruction to let a particular person leave the house from time to time without his family, but must have a special instruction in every case, which instruction the article 23 enables the Guardians to give wherever special reasons apply.

VII.—CONTRACTOR — PENALTY PAID BY, AS A FORFEITURE UNDER HIS BOND.

The Commissioners took into consideration a communication from the clerk of the Huntingdon Union, in reference to previous correspondence with the Commissioners respecting a penalty of 100*l.* paid by a contractor as a forfeiture under his bond, on account of his having supplied bread deficient in weight to the poor of the Union, and stating that the Board of Guardians wish to return to the contractor the sum of 80*l.* out of such 100*l.* penalty as the Guardians "never contemplated the retention of the whole amount forfeited by the contractor and his sureties, but were induced to institute proceedings at law for the recovery thereof, for the purpose of giving publicity to the powers of Guardians, and the liability of a contractor in such a case of injustice towards the poor, in preference to accepting from the contractor in the first instance any sum by way of compromise," and "that the retention by them of the whole amount forfeited, will, in their opinion, entirely ruin the contractor, who is a tradesman of small capital, and has already suffered much in his business by this occurrence."

In reply, the Commissioners stated that they think it desirable clearly to explain to the Board of Guardians, that there is no provision either in the law itself, or in the regulations issued to the Union, under which the approval or the dissent of the Commissioners is required to meet the proposition which the Guardians have made to them. If the Commissioners were to express either their sanction or objection to the payment of 80*l.* to Mr. ——— neither the legality of that payment, nor the responsibility of the Guardians duly to account for it, would in any way be affected.

The Guardians have put the case to the Commissioners for their opinion, and on purely legal grounds the Commissioners have stated, that the money cannot be paid. Having given this opinion, at the request of the Guardians, an opinion, the correctness of which the Guardians do not doubt, the Commissioners must leave the Guardians to take that course which they may finally determine to adopt, subject, of course, to their legal liability to account.

The Commissioners exceedingly regret that they see no means by which they could give effect to the Guardians' wishes, and which the Commissioners are fully sensible are to be attributed solely to the desire of the Guardians to avert the serious consequences which will attend upon Mr. ——— delinquency.

VIII.—POOR LAW RETURNS.

The following is a List of Returns relating to the administration of the Poor Law in England, presented to Parliament during the present Session:—

Copies or Extracts of Reports from Sir John Walsham to the Poor Law Commissioners upon the state of the Burnley Union during the months of May and June, 1842; and also of Copy of a Letter from the Poor Law Commissioners to the Guardians of the Burnley Union, dated the 26th of May.—(*House of Lords*, 175.)

Copies of any communications addressed from Bolton to the Home Office, during the late recess, on the subject of Mr. Mott's Report; together with any reports presented by Mr. Mott in answer to such communications.—(*House of Commons*, 77.)

A Copy or Extract of any Report made by Mr. Tufnell, or other Assistant Commissioner, to the Poor Law Commissioners, in October, 1841, as to the State of the Poor in the Borough of Rochdale.—(*House of Commons*, 89.)

A Copy of the Evidence taken, and Report made, by the Assistant Poor Law Commissioners sent to inquire into the State of the Population of Stockport.—(*House of Commons*, 158.)

Copy of the Report of Sir John Walsham, Bart., to the Poor Law Commissioners, relating to the Keighley Union.—(*House of Commons*, 347.)

Copy of the Report of Mr. Mott, the Assistant Poor Law Commissioner, of the Proceedings of the Board of Guardians of the Keighley Union, and of the Magistrates' interference therewith.—(*House of Commons*, 359.)

A Copy of all the Correspondence relating to the granting of Out-door Relief which has passed between the Poor Law Commissioners and the Board of Guardians of the Easingwold Union, in the County of York; also Copy of the Minutes of the Board, relating to their proceedings upon the Poor Law Commissioners having refused to allow the same, so far as Copies of such Minutes are in the possession of the Commissioners.—(*House of Commons*, 292.)

Copy of a Correspondence between the Board of Guardians of the Depwade Union and the Poor Law Commissioners, which took place in May, 1841, or about that time, relating to the case of a widow named Booty, who was then residing at Eaton, near Norwich.—(*House of Commons*, 343.)

A Copy of all the Orders issued by the Poor Law Commissioners to the Board of Guardians of the Settle Union since the 1st day of January last, and of the Resolutions adopted by the Board thereon; together with the Correspondence between the Poor Law Commissioners and the said Board of Guardians with respect to the said Orders up to the present time.—(*House of Commons*, 422.)

Copies of all Correspondence which has taken place between the Poor Law Commissioners and all Guardians and Officers of the Basford Union, relative to the payment out of the Poor's-rates of the costs of a Rule Nisi, &c., against three of the Guardians, for an illegal libel on a Magistrate of the County of Nottingham, &c.

Copies of the Statement of Grounds for the Exemption of the Parish of Liverpool from Administration by a Board of Guardians, forwarded to the Secretary of State for the Home Department by the Churchwardens and Guardians of the Parish of Liverpool; and of the Report of Mr. Mott and of the Poor Law Commissioners on that Statement; and of the Answer of the Churchwardens and Overseers to Mr. Mott's Statement; and of the further Statements, if any, of Mr. Mott.—(*House of Commons*, 232.)

A Copy of Minute of the Poor Law Commissioners upon the admissibility of Scotch and Irish Medical Practitioners to Union Offices in England.—(*House of Commons*, 278.)

A Copy of a Circular Letter, dated the 26th day of May, 1842, addressed by the Poor Law Commissioners to the Guardians of certain Unions in the Coal-mining Districts, on the subject of apprenticing poor Children to work in a Coal-mine; together with Copies of the Answers returned thereto.—(*House of Commons*, 393.)

Return of the Poor Law Unions, distinguishing the County of each, to which no Order has been issued by the Commissioners, prohibiting Out-door Relief to Able-bodied Paupers; also a similar Return of Unions to which such Orders have been issued by the Commissioners.—(*House of Commons*, 205.)

A Return of all Debts, Liabilities, and Engagements claimed against the Poor-rates of any Parish at the time of the passing of the Act 4 and 5 Will. IV. c. 76, for which securities had been given and interest was then paid; distinguishing such as were duly secured and were legally charged upon the Poor-rates, and such as were secured by notes or engagements of Parish Officers or other persons on behalf of such Parishes; with a statement of the consideration given for such Debts, and the purposes for which they were incurred; whether paid, and, if so, how paid, or if unpaid; and in such case the names of the parties to whom the same are now due, and the parties responsible upon the securities.—(*House of Commons*, 84.)

An Account of the Money levied by Assessment for Poor-rates and County-rates in each County in England and Wales for the Year ending 25th March, 1826.

Return of the Average Annual Expenditure of the Parishes comprised in each Union in England and Wales, for the Relief and Maintenance of the Poor, in the Three Years prior to the Declaration of the Union; of the Sum expended in every Union for the Year ending the 25th day of March, 1840, specifying the Sum expended in Salaries and Establishment Charges; the Sum expended in Out-door Relief, and the Sum expended in In-door Relief; Orders for Relief out of the House, given, since the passing of the said Act, by Justices of the Peace, and communicated to Boards of Guardians, specifying on whom the Orders were made, and what Relief was given.—(*House of Commons*, 145.)

Returns of each Parish and Township in England and Wales in which the Poor are managed under the Provisions of the Act 22 Geo. III. c. 83, commonly called Gilbert's Act; distinguishing whether incorporated in any Union, or governed separately; and stating the Population of each Parish or Township, and of each Union respectively, according to the last Census, and also according to the Census of 1831; of each Parish and Township subject to the Provisions of any Local Act for the Management of its Poor, with the Amount of Population according to the last Census, and also according to the Census of 1831.—(*House of Commons*, 156.)

Abstract of Returns showing the Annual Value of Real Property in each County in England and Wales, assessed to the Poor-rates, for the Year ended Lady-day, 1841; distinguishing landed Property, Dwelling-houses, and all other kinds of Property; also the total Amount levied for Poor-rates and County-rates in that Year, and the Rate in the Pound of such Levy on the annual Value of Real Property; and also the Population of each County, according to the Census of 1841; with the Area of each County in English Statute Acres; together with the total annual Value of Real Property in 1815.—(*House of Commons*, 235.)

IX.—REAL PROPERTY.

RETURN to an ORDER of the Honourable the House of Commons, dated 3rd May, 1842.

Names of Counties.	Total Annual Value of Real Property in 1815.	Net Rental, or Annual Value of Real Property, Assessed to the Poor Rates for the Year ended Lady-day, 1841.			
		Landed Property.	Dwelling Houses.	All other Kinds of Property.	Total Annual Value of Real Property Assessed.
ENGLAND.	£.	£.	£.	£.	£.
Bedford	343,683	326,684	159,816	8,896	495,396
Berks	652,082	477,570	199,999	54,547	732,116
Buckingham	644,130	545,157	95,757	33,420	674,334
Cambridge	655,221	581,761	239,079	47,844	868,684
Chester	1,083,084	778,560	447,034	198,241	1,423,835
Cornwall	916,060	603,119	190,408	115,952	909,479
Cumberland	705,446	497,573	147,920	50,859	696,352
Derby	887,659	625,396	160,777	80,315	866,488
Devon	1,897,515	1,241,523	490,528	120,093	1,852,144
Dorset	698,396	550,567	148,125	36,542	735,234
Durham	791,359	516,971	213,986	200,391	931,348
Essex	1,556,836	1,018,650	445,953	121,116	1,585,719
Gloucester	1,463,260	898,957	739,201	144,039	1,782,197
Hereford	604,614	552,383	102,921	25,931	681,235
Hertford	571,107	386,341	220,076	61,293	667,710
Huntingdon	320,188	236,633	71,221	9,864	317,718
Kent	1,644,179	1,044,999	878,472	188,204	2,111,675
Lancaster	3,087,774	1,402,208	2,449,196	1,415,202	5,266,606
Leicester	902,217	690,914	221,771	21,114	933,799
Lincoln	2,061,830	1,766,740	300,348	60,219	2,127,307
Middlesex	5,595,537	304,653	6,680,202	308,514	7,293,369
Monmouth	295,097	251,019	119,974	50,057	421,050
Norfolk	1,540,952	1,209,181	486,758	197,885	1,893,824
Northampton	942,162	748,116	158,621	33,658	940,395
Northumberland	1,240,594	740,609	324,159	261,646	1,326,414
Nottingham	737,230	563,840	252,230	40,605	856,675
Oxford	713,147	528,242	149,658	17,852	695,752
Rutland	133,487	106,119	9,104	3,911	119,134
Salop	1,037,988	874,316	213,251	82,441	1,170,008
Somerset	1,900,651	1,361,547	567,776	121,193	2,050,516
Southampton	1,130,952	723,087	541,229	97,710	1,362,026
Stafford	1,150,285	900,102	683,762	422,896	2,006,760
Suffolk	1,127,404	912,062	302,059	83,835	1,297,956
Surrey	1,579,173	376,644	1,409,180	141,669	1,927,493
Sussex	915,348	611,320	472,443	85,467	1,169,230
Warwick	1,236,727	713,390	300,427	595,930	1,609,747
Westmoreland	298,199	221,054	37,374	7,907	266,335
Wilts	1,155,459	899,878	219,931	55,807	1,175,616
Worcester	799,605	605,610	323,007	66,625	995,242
York, East Riding	1,190,326	760,942	271,258	79,607	1,111,807
York, North Riding	1,145,252	845,547	131,681	34,657	1,011,885
York, West Riding	2,392,406	1,449,007	1,414,800	460,995	3,324,802
Totals of England	49,744,622	30,448,991	22,991,472	6,244,949	59,685,412
WALES.					
Anglesey	92,589	164,637	15,785	11,191	191,613
Brecon	146,539	170,397	52,911	19,355	242,663
Cardigan	141,889	143,330	16,929	6,852	167,111
Carmarthen	277,455	285,188	31,853	21,362	338,403
Carnarvon	125,198	125,587	34,924	22,655	183,166
Denbigh	225,464	262,635	42,563	30,341	335,539
Flint	153,930	147,876	40,561	25,634	214,071
Glamorgan	334,192	226,652	69,043	80,787	376,482
Merioneth	111,436	99,281	12,936	4,248	116,465
Montgomery	207,286	247,350	25,688	9,302	282,340
Pembroke	219,589	221,167	39,115	15,830	276,112
Radnor	99,717	112,046	12,621	5,986	130,653
Totals of Wales	2,153,801	2,206,146	394,929	253,513	2,854,618
Totals of England and Wales	51,898,423	32,655,137	23,386,401	6,498,492	62,540,030

ABSTRACT of RETURNS showing the ANNUAL VALUE of REAL PROPERTY—*continued.*

Names of Counties.	Total Amount of Money Levied for Poor Rates, for the Year ended Lady-day, 1841.	Rate in the £. on Annual Value of Real Property Assessed.	Population according to the Census of 1841.	Rate per Head of Annual Value of Real Property.	Area in English Statute Acres.	Annual Value of each Acre.
ENGLAND.	£.	s. d.		£. s. d.		£. s. d.
Bedford	51,876	2 1	107,937	4 12 10	297,632	1 1 11
Berks	92,109	2 6	160,226	4 11 5	472,270	1 0 3
Buckingham	92,955	2 9	155,989	4 6 6	463,820	1 3 6
Cambridge	90,238	2 1	164,509	5 5 7	536,853	1 1 8
Chester	104,607	1 6	395,300	3 12 0	649,050	1 4 0
Cornwall	103,947	2 3	341,269	2 13 4	854,770	0 14 1
Cumberland	49,993	1 5	177,912	3 18 3	969,490	0 10 3
Derby	81,194	1 10	272,202	3 3 8	663,180	0 18 10
Devon	225,780	2 5	533,731	3 9 5	1,636,450	0 15 2
Dorset	98,769	2 8	174,743	4 4 2	627,220	0 17 7
Durham	92,995	2 0	324,277	2 17 5	679,530	0 15 3
Essex	213,715	2 8	344,995	4 12 0	979,000	1 0 10
Gloucester	182,857	2 1	431,307	4 2 8	790,470	1 2 9
Hereford	52,838	1 7	114,438	5 19 1	543,800	1 0 4
Hertford	71,361	2 2	157,237	4 4 11	400,370	0 19 4
Huntingdon	22,439	2 1	58,699	5 8 3	241,690	0 19 7
Kent	265,352	2 6	548,161	3 17 1	972,240	1 1 6
Lancaster	429,017	1 8	1,667,064	3 3 2	1,117,260	1 5 1
Leicester	95,316	2 0	215,855	4 6 6	511,340	1 7 0
Lincoln	140,513	1 4	362,717	5 17 4	1,663,850	1 1 3
Middlesex	668,527	1 10	1,576,616	4 12 6	179,590	1 14 0
Monmouth	39,182	1 10	134,349	3 2 8	324,310	0 15 6
Norfolk	236,079	2 6	412,621	4 11 10	1,292,300	0 18 8
Northampton	102,810	2 2	199,061	4 14 6	646,810	1 3 2
Northumberland	81,289	1 3	250,268	5 6 0	1,165,430	0 12 9
Nottingham	83,205	1 11	249,773	3 8 7	525,800	1 1 5
Oxford	88,268	2 6	161,573	4 6 1	467,380	1 2 7
Rutland	9,114	1 6	21,340	5 11 8	97,500	1 1 9
Salop	79,233	1 4	239,014	4 17 11	864,360	1 0 3
Somerset	199,569	1 11	436,002	4 15 8	1,028,090	1 6 6
Southampton	182,453	2 8	354,940	3 16 9	1,018,550	0 14 2
Stafford	127,820	1 3	510,206	3 18 8	736,290	1 4 5
Suffolk	175,795	2 9	315,129	4 2 5	918,760	0 19 10
Surrey	263,597	2 9	582,613	3 6 2	474,480	0 15 11
Sussex	168,806	2 11	299,770	3 18 0	907,920	0 13 6
Warwick	171,435	2 1	402,121	4 3 1	567,930	1 5 1
Westmoreland	22,629	1 8	56,469	4 14 4	485,990	0 9 1
Wilts	176,750	3 0	260,007	4 10 5	869,620	1 0 8
Worcester	96,185	1 11	233,484	4 5 3	459,710	1 6 4
York, East Riding	83,018	1 6	231,998	4 15 10	763,800	0 19 11
York, North Riding	65,718	1 4	204,662	4 18 11	1,275,820	0 13 3
York, West Riding	320,211	1 11	1,154,924	2 17 7	1,629,890	0 17 9
Totals of England	6,009,564	2 0	14,995,508	3 19 7	31,770,615	0 19 2
WALES.						
Anglesey	19,864	2 1	50,890	3 15 4	173,440	0 19 0
Brecon	19,228	1 7	53,295	4 11 1	482,560	0 7 1
Cardigan	23,221	2 9	68,380	2 8 11	432,000	0 6 8
Carmarthen	40,888	2 5	106,482	3 3 7	623,360	0 9 2
Carnarvon	28,703	3 2	81,068	2 5 2	348,160	0 7 3
Denbigh	41,713	2 6	89,291	3 15 2	405,120	0 13 0
Flint	24,184	2 3	66,547	3 4 4	156,160	0 18 11
Glamorgan	42,251	2 3	173,462	2 3 5	506,880	0 8 11
Merioneth	16,807	2 11	39,238	2 19 4	424,320	0 4 8
Montgomery	42,044	3 0	69,220	4 1 7	536,960	0 9 3
Pembroke	29,758	2 3	88,262	3 2 7	390,400	0 11 4
Radnor	13.603	2 1	25,186	5 3 9	272,640	0 8 3
Totals of Wales	342,264	2 5	911,321	3 2 8	4,752,000	0 9 3
Totals of England and Wales	6,351,828	2 0	*15,906,829	3 18 8	36,522,615	0 17 11

NOTE.—The Returns from which the above Abstract is made, were obtained by the Poor Law Commissioners from the overseers of each parish or other place in England and Wales maintaining its own poor.

The annual value of real property in 1815, is taken from the Parliamentary Document, No. 444, Session, 1835.

* Exclusive of 4,896 persons ascertained to have been travelling by railways and canals during the night of 6th June, 1841.

2nd May, 1842.

GEORGE COODE, Assistant Secretary.

X.—PAID OFFICERS.

1. RETURN OF THE NUMBER OF PAID OFFICERS DISMISSED OR WHO HAVE RESIGNED, AND CAUSES OF DISMISSAL OR RESIGNATION, DURING THE YEAR 1841.

On a review of the minutes of the proceedings of the Board during the past year, it appears that orders have been issued within the year for the dismissal of 85 officers for causes hereafter specified:—

3 Clerks to Guardians: for—
- Embezzlement . . . 1
- Withholding cheque from medical officer and receiving per centage on a contract for supply of workhouse . . . 1
- Misconduct 1

15 Masters of Workhouses: for—
- Improper punishment of pauper children . . 1
- Ill treatment of female pauper 1
- Intoxication, inattention to duty, and general misconduct 1
- Intemperance . . . 2
- Improper conduct with reference to female paupers 5
- Neglect of duty . . . 1
- Insolvency 1
- Drunkenness and absence without leave . 1
- Unfitness. 1
- Unfounded accusations against clerk . . . 1

2 Matrons of Workhouses—
- Neglect of duty . . 1
- Impropriety of conduct 1

10 Medical officers: for—
- Neglect of duty and drunkenness . . . 1
- Neglect of duty . . . 8
- Insanity 1

23 Relieving officers: for—
- Neglecting to relieve paupers in a state of destitution 2
- Consequent on dismissal from another office . 2
- Misconduct 1
- Malversation . . . 8
- Imperfectly reporting on relief cases, breach of confidence, and personally insulting the vice-chairman . . . 1
- Absence from district without leave and procuring a false certificate of illness to account for such absence 1
- Absconding 3
- Neglect of duty . . . 3
- Omitting to distribute out-relief monies . . 1
- Misapprehension and neglect of duties . . 1

14 Collectors and assistant Overseers: for—
- Defalcation 4
- Absconding 2
- Neglect of duty . . . 5
- Embezzlement and absconding 1
- Drunkenness and incompetency. . . . 1
- Neglect of duty and defalcation 1

2 Auditors: for—
- Neglect of duty . . . 1
- Incompetency . . . 1

1 Chaplain—
- Insanity 1

12 Schoolmasters: for—
- Absence without leave and general misconduct 1
- Calumniating certain officers, and one of the paupers of the Union . 1
- Excessive punishment of children 2
- Drunkenness . . . 1
- Returning to the workhouse intoxicated after having absented himself without leave . . 1
- Absence without leave. 2
- Immoral conduct in the presence of the children 1
- General misconduct . 1
- Improper conduct with reference to female pauper 1
- Causing the exposure of the person of a male idiot pauper . . . 1

2 Schoolmistresses—
- Immoral conduct in the presence of the children 1
- Improper behaviour with a boy in the workhouse 1

1 Porter: for—
- Improper conduct with reference to female pauper 1

The following officers have during the year resigned in consequence of the recommendation of the Commissioners:—

2 Clerks to Guardians: under charges of—
- Negligence in conducting correspondence . 1
- Misconduct 1

11 Masters of Workhouses: under charges of—
- Tearing leaves out of visiting book, leaving workhouse without permission of Guardians or visiting Committee. 1
- Neglect in reference to two idiot boys . . . 1
- Making a groundless charge against medical officer, and showing an insulting behaviour to the Guardians on their lecturing him on the subject 1
- Incompetency and inefficient discharge of duties 1
- Irregularity in accounts 1
- Intoxication 1
- Incompetency . . . 2
- Indecent conduct . . 1
- Neglect of duty . . . 1
- Confinement in gaol for debt 1

2 Matrons of Workhouses: under charges of—
- Neglect of duty . . 1
- Unfitness 1

5 Medical officers: under charges of—
- Negligent attendance on pauper who died . 3
- Neglect of duty . . . 1
- Inefficient discharge of his duties , . . . 1

8 Relieving officers: under charges of—
- Incompetency and irregularity 1
- Defalcation 1
- Incompetency and negligence 2
- Inattention to duties . 2
- Inefficiency 2

2 Collectors: under charges of—
- Irregularity in collection of rates 1
- Inefficient discharge of duties 1

1 Auditor: under charge of—
- Inefficient mode of keeping accounts . . 1

1 Chaplain: under charge of—
- Entrusting his duties to his curate, who is not responsible to the Guardians; and infrequent attendance on the aged and infirm . 1

5 Schoolmasters: under charges of—
- Insulting conduct to the chairman 1
- Making serious charges against the master and matron which were not substantiated . . . 1
- Inefficiency 3

5 Schoolmistresses: under charges of—
- Inefficiency 2
- Making serious charges against the master and matron which were not substantiated . . . 1
- Dismissal of her husband the schoolmaster 1
- Theft 1

1 Porter: under charge of—
- Incompetency . . . 1

2 Nurses: under charges of—
- Unfitness 1
- Incompetency . . . 1

The following officers have resigned:—

17 Clerks to Guardians:—
- Not stated 13
- Obtaining another appointment 1
- Ill-health 3

21 Masters of Workhouses:—
- Not stated 19
- On being called to account for keeping his sister in the workhouse 1
- Not having given satisfaction to the guardians 1

21 Matrons of Workhouses:—
- Not stated 16
- On her husband (the master) being called to account for keeping his sister in the workhouse 1
- Death of husband, the master of the workhouse 2
- Incompetency of her husband, (the master of the workhouse) . 1
- Not having given satisfaction to the guardians 1

20 Medical Officers:—
- Not stated 13
- Leaving the neighbourhood 2
- Ill-health 2
- Purchasing another practice 1
- Question as to validity of election 1
- Increase of private practice 1

51 Relieving Officers:—
- Not stated 41

On succeeding to the occupation of a farm . 1
On taking a farm which will occupy his whole time 2
Failure in business . 1
Entering into business. 1
In consequence of charge of neglect of sick pauper 1
On obtaining another appointment . . . 3
On being appointed clerk 1

7 Collectors:—
Not stated 6
Removal to London . 1

1 Assistant Collector:—
On being appointed collector 1

3 Assistant Overseers:—
Not stated 2
In consequence of charges made against him 1

8 Treasurers:—
Not stated 5
Failure of bank in which he was a partner . . 1
Being appointed a Guardian 1
Default in providing the requisite security . . 1

14 Auditors:—
Not stated 10
Illness 2
Appointed clerk . . 1
On account of opposition against him . . 1

26 Chaplains:—
Not stated 21
Insanity 1
Leaving the neighbourhood 2
Ill-health 2

30 Schoolmasters:—
Not stated 22
On being appointed master 1
On obtaining another appointment . . . 2
Ill-health 3
About to keep a private school 1
On entering into business 1

30 Schoolmistresses:—
Not stated 24
To obtain a more lucrative situation . . . 1
Disagreement with master and matron . . . 2
Ill-health 1
About to keep a private school 1
On her husband (the schoolmaster) entering into business . . . 1

28 Porters.—
Not stated 20
Differences with the master 1
His wife (the nurse) not liking her situation . 1
Ill-health 3
To obtain a more eligible situation . . . 1
Old age 2

7 Nurses:—
Not stated 4
To obtain a more eligible situation . . . 1
Not liking her situation 1
Ill-health 1

4 Registrars:—
Not stated 3
Duties of the office interfering with his other engagements . . . 1

Yardman:—
Not stated 1

Baker:—
Not stated 1

Messenger:—
Not stated 1

Cook:—
Not stated 1

The following Table exhibits an account of the total Number of Officers dismissed since the establishment of the Commission:—

	1835	1836	1837	1838	1839	1840	1841
Assistant Overseers and Collectors	..	1	3	5	6	11	14
Auditor	..	..	..	..	1	..	2
Chaplain	..	..	..	..	1	..	1
Clerks to Guardians	..	1	1	4	2	..	3
Masters of Workhouses	7	12	10	12	14	14	15
Matrons of ditto	..	6	4	5	8	6	2
Medical Officers	..	1	..	4	2	6	10
Porters	..	1	2	1	3	4	1
Relieving Officers	5	9	15	23	16	22	23
Schoolmasters	..	1	4	5	8	12	12
Schoolmistresses	..	..	1	2	2	2	2
Treasurer	..	..	..	..	..	1	..
Totals	12	32	40	61	63	78	85
Grand Total				371			

2. RELIEVING OFFICER — ABSCONDING OF.—APPORTIONMENT OF EXPENSES INCURRED IN APPREHENDING.

The following is a copy of a letter received from the clerk of the Anglesey Union:—

"ANGLESEY UNION.

"*Llangefni*, 13*th January*, 1840.

"SIRS,—I am requested by the Board of Guardians of the above Union to state that expenses have been incurred in the apprehension of ———, the relieving officer who had absconded, and of bringing his case before the magistrates; and to beg that you will be pleased to inform them whether those expenses are to be paid by the Union generally, or from what other fund.

"Mr. ——— has again been remanded until Saturday the 18th instant.

"I have the honour to be,
"Sirs,
"Your obedient, humble servant,
"SAMUEL DEW,
"*Clerk to the Guardians.*

"*To the Poor Law Commissioners.*"

In reply, the Commissioners stated that as the proceedings taken against the officer, were for the protection of the Union generally, and not for any individual parish, the expenses should be charged to the establishment.

3. CLERK AND AUDITOR.—EXAMINATION OF ACCOUNTS OF THE MASTER OF THE WORKHOUSE.—EXTENT OF CLERK'S DUTY IN RESPECT OF.

The following is a copy of a letter addressed to Sir John Walsham, Bart., one of the Assistant Commissioners, and transmitted by him to the Commissioners.

"*Examination of the Accounts of the Master of the Workhouse.*

"*Berwick*, 16*th October*, 1841.

"SIR,—A matter arising out of the late audit of the books, &c., of this Union has been discussed between the auditor and myself, and the one not being satisfied with the view taken of it by the other, it has been agreed between us that the matter should be stated to you, and that you should be requested to favour us with your opinion thereon. The question is connected with the provision books kept by the master of the workhouse, and is this:—Whether, at the weekly examination of these books, I am required to test the accuracy of them to the extent of seeing that each pauper in the house has received his or her quantity of food, as specified in the dietary.

"To enable you to judge, I give the following detail of the mode in which the examination of these books has hitherto been conducted by us:—

"I first examine the entries in the Admission and Discharge Book for the purpose of ascertaining that the paupers therein mentioned are properly admitted or discharged; that the entries in the In-door Relief List and Provision Check Account agree with the entries in that book; and that the total number of days in the Abstract of the In-door Relief List agrees with the collective number of days in the Provision Check Account. I then cast up the additions of the provisions consumed by the several classes in the workhouse, and find that they agree with the quantities charged in the Consumption Account; that the quantities of provisions are correctly brought forward from the previous week; that the prices charged for these provisions on both receipt and consumption sides of the book, are the proper contract prices, and that the values are correctly extended; and also that the quantities shown as remaining on hand are the correct balances.

"This plan of examination has hitherto been adopted, being, as I conceive, all that is required by the 12th rule of the 2nd section of the Order for keeping and auditing the Accounts of this Union, dated the 23rd February, 1837. It does not appear by that rule that the clerk is called upon to see that the paupers are fed according to the dietary, but it is conceived that that is a question simply between the master of the workhouse and the auditor at his quarterly audit. If such be a clerk's duty, a very onerous one will be imposed upon him, while it will entirely relieve the master from any responsibility for the correctness of these books, and will in a great degree render their examination by the auditor a matter of form. It will also entail upon the clerk the necessity of being present at the audit of these books by the auditor, which would not otherwise be the case, as it is presumed that that officer would only require the attendance of the clerk while engaged with the Ledger and Minute Book, those being the only books kept by him.

"I am, Sir,

"Your most obedient servant,

"E. WILLOBY.

"*Sir John Walsham, Bart.,*
&c. &c. &c.

"P.S.—It may afford you satisfaction to know that the auditor has seen and approved of this letter.
"E. W."

In reply, the Commissioners stated that by Rule 6, sec. 3, of the order of keeping accounts of the Berwick-upon-Tweed Union, the master of the workhouse is directed to keep a book, called the Provision Check Book (Form 19, A), which shall contain, amongst other entries, an account of the number of paupers daily supported in the workhouse, and the provisions weekly consumed by them according to the quantities allowed per diet table.

By Rule 12, sec. 2, of the same order, the clerk is required previous to the weekly meeting of the Guardians, to ascertain the accuracy of the several entries made by the master of the workhouse in the weekly in-door relief list, (Form 18, A), and Abstract (Form 18, B), and the *Provision Check Account* (Form 19, A), (the book upon which the present question arises;) and he is to *authenticate* the entries by his signature.

The question is, whether the direction to the clerk to ascertain the accuracy of the entries in the provision check account involves the duty of seeing that each pauper in the house has received his or her quantity of food as specified in the dietary.

It appears to the Commissioners that the clerk's duty upon this matter is as follows;—the clerk is required to see that the number of paupers charged for and entered in Form 19, A. as maintained during the week in the workhouse is correct, and corresponds with the entry in the in-door relief list. Having done this, he must next assume that the several classes of paupers are maintained, and fed according to the diet table. For instance, if it be shown that 50 men have been maintained for a week, what the clerk will have to do (knowing what one man is entitled to receive for a week in the several articles of meat, bread, &c, according to the diet table), will be to multiply such quantities by 50, which will give the comsumption of 50 paupers for a week; and so as regards all the other classes.

To this extent the clerk is required to see that the paupers are fed according to the dietary, otherwise he cannot certify as to the correctness of the entries made by the master. But he is not in the terms of the question required to see that any pauper has actually received his or her quantity of food as specified in the dietary.

LONDON:
Printed, by Order of the Poor Law Commissioners, by W. CLOWES and SONS, Stamford Street, and Published by CHARLES KNIGHT and Co., 22, Ludgate Street, Publishers to the Poor Law Commissioners.

VOLUME III
[1842-1843]

AN

OFFICIAL CIRCULAR

OF PUBLIC DOCUMENTS AND INFORMATION:

DIRECTED BY THE POOR LAW COMMISSIONERS TO BE PRINTED, CHIEFLY FOR THE USE OF THE MEMBERS AND PERMANENT OFFICERS OF BOARDS OF GUARDIANS, UNDER THE POOR LAW AMENDMENT ACT.

No. 21. CIRCULAR ISSUED NOVEMBER, 23, 1842.

Poor Law Commission Office,
Somerset House,
November, 1842.

The Poor Law Commissioners, on a review of their Minutes, directed that the Minutes of Correspondence on the following subjects be printed and circulated for the information of Guardians and Officers of the several Unions, viz.:—

By Order of the Board,

Edwin Chadwick, *Secretary.*

I.—ACCOUNTS.

1. Advertising for situations for Children in the Union Workhouse.

18*th May*, 1842.

A letter from the clerk of the Guardians of the Thetford Union, was read, enquiring whether the Guardians may charge, in the Union accounts, the expense of advertising in the local newspapers for situations for the children in the Union workhouse, when the Commissioners stated in reply, that they are not aware of any legal objection to the adoption of the course proposed by the Guardians, and that they think the Guardians may charge such expenses in the Union accounts.

2. Application of the Rates of the present Year to satisfy a demand made in the past Year.

4*th August*, 1842.

A letter from the auditor of the Stroud Union, in reference to the accounts of the parish of Horsley, was read, in which he stated as follows:—

" The present overseers of this parish have brought into account in this year a sum of 42*l*. 14*s*. 5*d*., paid for county rate on the 11th of April last. This amount of rate was due from the parish and demanded of them at about the end of January or beginning of February last, but was not paid in the last parochial year. The last rate for the parish in last year was made on the 8th of January last. A balance of 31*l*. 11*s*. 3*d*., money in hand, was handed over by the late to the present overseers. No uncollected rate was turned over. Under these circumstances I consider that I must disallow so much of the sum of 42*l*. 14*s*. 5*d*., as the balance handed over would not satisfy, and I should feel obliged to your Board if you would inform me whether I propose to take the proper course."

And the Commissioners directed the following reply to be made thereto:—

" The rule that the demands of the year must be supplied by the rates of the year, has a different application according as the payment to be made, is for a benefit which the parish has already enjoyed, or for one which is still to be obtained by the payment.

" Thus the rate of the present year cannot be applied to repay relief given in the past year. But where the payment is merely to supply some officer with the funds necessary for future expenditure, the verbal demand made in the past year, may be satisfied in the present year. Thus if the Guardians in last year required contribution, it would be lawful and requisite, if not before supplied, to supply it in the present year, and as the money thus supplied this year, would be applied to the burdens of the year, the rule would be kept inviolate. The same application of the rule must be made, where any officer requires to be supplied with a fund under the denomination of a tax, such as the county rate, which is applicable to the future exigencies of the district during the coming year.

" The Commissioners conclude that the payment of county rate by the present overseers, ought to be allowed."

3. Fire Rewards.

11*th August*, 1842.

A letter from Mr. Burnell, the auditor of some of the metropolitan Unions, stating that at the late audit, his attention was called to the large and increasing sums paid for fire rewards, most of them paid for attending to extinguish fire in chimneys, was read, and the Commissioners directed the following letter to be sent to him on the subject:—

" The Commissioners desire to thank you for calling their attention to this subject. The 14 Geo. III., c. 78, sections 76 and 81, appears to be the authority under which these rewards are rendered payable out of the poor rates. With respect to the expediency of an alteration of the law, the Commissioners are not at present prepared to express an opinion, but they wish to draw your attention to the 78th section of the statute, which provides for the recovery of the money so paid by the churchwardens and overseers, and declares that the occupiers of the house or premises where the fire breaks out, shall reimburse and repay to the churchwardens and overseers the reward or other payment made by them as the justices, before whom the case may be brought, may order and direct, and the latter part of the same section provides a summary remedy for the recovery in case of default of repayment.

"The Commissioners have reason to believe that great laxity prevails in this respect, and that parishes are subject to a great annual charge, by reason of the non-enforcement of the recovery of the sums paid out of the poor rates under the authority of the statute.

"The Commissioners are of opinion that you should require in every case in which an overseer takes credit in his accounts for sums paid for fire rewards, and does not account for the repayment of the money, the order of the justices to be produced, discharging the occupier of the premises from his liability in this respect."

II. — APPRENTICING OF PAUPER CHILDREN—DUTY OF OVERSEERS IN REGARD TO.

9th August, 1842.

The Commissioners took into consideration a letter received from the clerk of the Wem Union, stating that the overseers of some of the parishes in that Union, refuse to obey the orders of the Guardians directing them to place out as apprentices pauper children maintained in the Union workhouse, and enquiring whether the overseers by such refusal are not liable to a penalty of 5*l*., under the 95th section of the 4 and 5 Will. IV. c. 76; and the Commissioners directed the following reply to be made thereto:—

"In answer the Commissioners wish to state, that the apprenticing of a poor child is relief within the statute of the 43rd Elizabeth. The guardians have the exclusive ordering of all relief by the 54th section of the Poor Law Amendment Act. The overseers on the other hand, are the proper persons to carry into execution the apprenticeship of the child.

"It appears, therefore, to the Commissioners, that if the Guardians, in the exercise of their discretion, direct a child to be bound apprentice, it is a legal and reasonable order, and the Commissioners entertain no doubt that the 95th section of the Poor Law Amendment Act, was intended to provide a penalty for the breach of such an order.

"The words of that section have, however, given rise to doubts in some persons' minds. It describes the offence as 'disobeying the legal and reasonable orders of such Justices and Guardians,' and it has been in some cases supposed that the provision only applies where the justices and Guardians join in making an order. On the other hand there are orders to be made by the justices singly, on overseers and others under the Act (sec. 27, 54, &c.), and orders to be made by the Guardians singly, as incidental to their duties under the Act, and the Commissioners' regulations. The Commissioners, therefore, entertain no doubt that the operation of the 95th section, is to enact a penalty, for a breach of such an order of the Guardians, as is in question in the present case."

III.—CONSTABLE.—AS TO WHETHER FEES PAID BY A COUNTY OR DISTRICT CONSTABLE ON THE PROSECUTION OF VAGRANTS, ETC., ARE REPAYABLE OUT OF THE POOR RATES.

25th July, 1842.

1. The Commissioners took into consideration a letter received from Mr. Wicks, solicitor for the parish of Chelmsford, enclosing a bill delivered to the overseers, by Mr. May, the superintendent of the New Police force, in Chelmsford, for fees which he had paid to the clerk of the magistrates, on the prosecution of vagrants and disorderly persons, and stating that the parishioners in vestry having refused to allow such fees, the churchwardens and overseers had received notice to the effect, that on the 26th July, the justices would proceed to examine, and to hear and determine any objection that should be made to certain accounts of John May, a constable appointed under the authority of the 1 and 2 Wm. IV., c. 41, of sums expended by him, on account of the parish of Chelmsford, for the three months, ending 30th June last, the same having been laid before the inhabitants, as directed by the Statute, and disallowed; and requesting the Commissioners' opinion as to the liability of the parishioners

to the payment of such fees, when the Commissioners directed the following answer to be given thereto:—

"The Commissioners, in reply, desire to state that they do not understand the nature of the claim as set forth in the notice signed 'Thomas Brooksby,' and in the Bill annexed to your letter.

"If the constable in question has been appointed, as stated in the notice, under the 1st and 2nd Wm. IV., c. 41, it could only be as a special constable, and any allowance to be made to him, could only be paid under the 13th section of that Act, out of the county rate; or if the parish where the constable was appointed, do not contribute to the county rate, the allowance could still only be claimed from some rate, for purposes similar to the county rate, and from officers having the collection and disbursement of that fund, and not from overseers as overseers.

"The Commissioners conceive that possibly the constable may be a local constable appointed under the 2nd and 3rd Vic., c. 93, in which case he would be entitled to fees as settled by a table of fees, approved by the Secretary of State, (3 and 4 Vic., c. 88. sec. 17,) but even in this case the overseers would only be liable to pay fees for things done at the instance of the parish, and the proceedings referred to in vestry, which appear to be of the kind provided for by the 18th Geo. III., c. 19., sec. 4, would be inapplicable.

"As far as the Commissioners understand the case, it appears to them that the notice discloses no ground of claim upon the poor rate."

10th August, 1842.

2. The Commissioners took into consideration a further communication received from Mr. Wicks, respecting the claim made on the parish of Chelmsford, for the fees referred to above, wherein he stated that the case came on before the justices at the Petty Sessions, according to the notice also adverted to above, when they determined that the objection taken to the claim must be overruled, and settled the amount at 6*l*. 4*s*. 6*d*.; and the Commissioners directed the following letter to be written to Mr. Wicks on the subject:—

"When the Commissioners before wrote to you they were, as they described, not aware of the nature of the appointment of the constables who claimed the payment in question. The Commissioners now gather from the Chelmsford Chronicle, enclosed by you, that the constables are county or district constables, appointed and acting under the provisions of the Acts 2 and 3 Vic., c. 93, and 3 and 4 Vic., c. 88.

"Assuming this to be so, the Commissioners are able to state their opinion more decidedly than before, that the charges contained in the bill cannot be lawfully paid out of the poor rates.

"Whatever is a duty of such constables seems to be provided for by the 18th section of the 2 and 3 Vic., which authorizes payments not only for salaries and ordinary expenses, but expressly authorizes reasonable allowances for extraordinary expenses, necessarily incurred by the chief constable, or by constables under his orders, instancing especially the apprehension of offenders, a term which includes vagrants, and including all other expenses incurred in the execution of the Act. The Act makes these allowances a charge on the county rate; the subsequent Act 3 and 4 Vic., c. 88, s. 3, as clearly includes them as charges on the police rate, authorized by that Act.

"There is nothing in either Act to give these constables the remedies given to parish constables by the 18 Geo. III. c. 19, s. 4.

"The opinion* of Sir N. Tindal, referred to on the other side, does not in any way relate to the claims of county and district constables, but solely to parish constables. The reasoning on which Sir N. Tindal's conclusion is founded,

* The following is the opinion (together with the case) here referred to:—

CASE.—"A considerable number of persons are apprehended by the constable as vagrants, detained in custody until they can be taken before a magistrate, and on examination, if convicted, are committed to prison. The constable pays the fees to the clerk of the Magistrates, and for the maintenance of the vagrants while in custody.

"Your opinion is requested, whethert he overseers of the poor are compellable or justified in paying the constable the expenses of maintaining, and the fees of the magistrate's clerk on the examination, conviction, and commitment of these vagrants, out of the poor's rate."

OPINION.—"The expenses above mentioned were expressly directed by the 3 Geo. IV. c. 40, s. 18, to be paid out of the county rate; but this statute was repealed by the 5 Geo. IV., c. 38, under which the law relating to vagrants is now regulated; and as the latter statute altogether omits the 18th Section of the 3 Geo. IV. it follows, that the justices have no authority to order the expenses of apprehending and maintaining the vagrant, and the fees of the clerk, to be paid out of the county rate; and as these expenses cannot be borne by the constable himself, I conceive they fall within the provision of the 18 Geo. III. c. 19, as part of the charge and expenses of his office, and are payable out of the poor's rate."

"(Signed) N. C. TINDAL,
"*August* 9, 1827. *Lincoln's Inn.*"

is, as the Commissioners understand, clearly against the present claim, inasmuch as he only infers that the parish is liable, because the county had ceased to be so, evidently implying that if the county had continued liable, as it is in the present case, there was no foundation for a claim on the parish.

"The Commissioners think that it is the duty of the parish officers to obtain the decision of the highest tribunal before they submit to this demand."

22nd October, 1842.

3. A letter received from Mr. Wicks this day was read, stating that the parish of Chelmsford having appealed to the Quarter Sessions against the allowance of the claim mentioned in the foregoing correspondence, the appeal was heard on the 19th October, and disallowed, but that a case was granted for the decision of the Court of Queen's Bench on this point.

IV.—CLERK'S DUTIES.—CONSTRUCTION OF No. 7, ART. 17, OF THE GENERAL ORDER RELATING TO THE DUTIES OF OFFICERS.

8th June, 1842.

1. The Commissioners took into consideration the following letter received from the clerk to the Guardians of the Chesterton Union on this subject:—

"I beg to call the attention of the Poor Law Commissioners to Article 17, No. 7, of the 'New Regulations—Duties of Officers,' and to request them to favour me with their explanation of this article, enumerating the different matters to be included under the head of 'All applications to any Justices at their Special, Petty, or General Sessions:' for instance,—whether it includes the conducting applications for orders of removals and appeals against them; applications for orders of maintenance upon relations; applications in cases of bastardy against overseers for non-payment of contributions; all indictments for disobedience of any justices' order upon the above matters; applications or indictments, as the case may be, for vagrancy or indictments of officers or other persons for embezzlement, &c., &c., &c.; and generally whether it includes any other application, &c., &c., to justices which the Guardians or parish-officers of any parish within the Union might feel it necessary and proper to make; and whether it will be the duty of the clerk under this article to travel out of his Union to attend any special, petty, or general sessions.

"In conclusion, I again beg the favour of the Poor Law Commissioners to enumerate separately and distinctly every *particular case*, as far as their recollection of the cases which come before justices will carry them; and to add such a general explanation as will show generally what other cases as they arise may be considered as coming within the operation and meaning of this article."

And the Commissioners directed the following reply to be made thereto:—

"The Commissioners desire to state that they think it would be mischievous to attempt to enumerate each individual case included in the description of the duties to be performed by the clerk, inasmuch as some omissions could scarcely be avoided, and such omissions would operate to mislead the clerk and the Guardians more than the present general description could do. Nevertheless, the Commissioners are desirous of explaining their general meaning in the regulation in question, so as to enable persons to make more easy application of it to the individual cases as they arise. First, as to conducting all applications to be made by, or on behalf of the Board of Guardians, to any justice or justices at Special, Petty, or General Sessions. This, of course, does not include applications for orders of removal, and appeals on them; such applications and appeals being overseers' business, not that of the Guardians of any Union not a Union for settlement. On the other hand, it does include applications in cases of bastardy, which Guardians are expressly empowered to make,—for orders of maintenance, which they may make equally with overseers,—for compelling payment of contribution by overseers, which is specifically a remedy of the Guardians, and generally it includes all those cases, incapable of enumeration without extensive research, in which summary remedies, through the intervention of justices, are given generally, and which the Guardians may, in the course of their business, have to avail themselves of.

"In making these applications, it will be the duty of the clerk to attend the justices whenever the attendance may be required, according to the circumstances affecting the jurisdiction of justices, whether within or out of the Union.

"Where criminal proceedings are the peculiar means provided for protection of the Guardians in the exercise of their official duties, or the enforcement of their authority, as in the case of departing from the workhouse with clothes, or of misbehaviour in the workhouse, or in the case of penalties imposed by the Poor Law

Amendment Act, upon officers purloining, embezzling, wasting, or misapplying the property of the Union, or upon officers disregarding the orders of the Guardians, or upon persons for introducing spirituous liquors into the workhouse; these proceedings are on behalf of the Guardians in their official character, and are within the scope of the regulation. But where the criminal proceeding, either by complaint or indictment, is one open to the whole public, and not specifically provided for the protection of the Guardians, and the enforcement of their authority, such applications are not considered by the order; thus it would not extend to the case you describe as 'all indictments for disobedience of justices' orders on the above matters,' but only to indictments for disobedience of such of the orders as were made on the applications on behalf of the Guardians.

"The above observations will have contemplated the reply to your last enquiry, whether the regulation extends to all applications to justices, which the Guardians or parish officers within the Union would think it proper to make. It does not extend to applications made on behalf of a single parish, unless the Board of Guardians have specific authority to make that application. The clerk is under no obligation to make applications for the individual parishes or their officers; and is only under an obligation to make applications on behalf of the Guardians when the business is peculiarly that of the Board of Guardians."

10*th June*, 1842.

2. The Commissioners took into consideration a letter received from the auditor of the ——— Union, wherein he requested their opinion as to whether the clerk was entitled to charge professionally for business done by him for the Union in certain cases, when the Commissioners directed the following observations to be made in reply:—

"The duties of the clerk, as prescribed by the General Order of the Commissioners of the 21st April, 1842, require the clerk to conduct all the correspondence of the Board, and to observe and execute all orders and directions of the Board of Guardians applicable to his office. The Guardians, therefore, can require the aid and assistance of their clerk in the performance of acts within the scope of their authority, which form a part of the official duty of the Guardians. Under the Act 2 and 3 Vic., c. 85, the Guardians are the parties to apply for orders of maintenance on putative fathers. There is nothing to prevent the Guardians directing their clerk to make and conduct the application on their behalf. If the Guardians direct him to do this, it appears to the Commissioners that he is bound to do it, and that he cannot claim specific remuneration for his services in this respect. As to sums actually paid by the clerk out of pocket, in respect of the service of notices, or to witnesses, he is, of course, entitled to be reimbursed those expenses. But as the duty of attending to applications in bastardy may be considered, if not created by the recent statute, still to have been greatly increased by it, and could not have been contemplated by the Guardians when the amount of the clerk's salary was settled, the Commissioners, if the applications should be numerous hereafter, and the Guardians should be disposed, in consequence, to increase the amount of his salary, would be ready to entertain any proposal that might be made to them in this respect.

"The Commissioners agree with you that the whole of the business in negotiating the loan with the Royal Exchange Assurance Office, came within the clerk's ordinary duties, for which the salary was the consideration.

"The preparation of the indentures of apprenticeship was for a particular parish, and not for the Union; the Commissioners think, therefore, if the clerk was employed professionally to prepare such indentures, he is entitled to make a charge against the overseers."

16*th June*, 1842.

3. A letter from the clerk to the Guardians of the Gainsborough Union, in reference to Art. 17, No. 7, of the General Order as to the duties of officers, was read, and the Commissioners directed the following answer to be given thereto:—

"I am to state, in reply, that it is not intended by that section that the clerk should conduct appeals against orders of removal, the same not being legal business connected with the Union, or in which the Board of Guardians are engaged, but the business of the overseers of the respective parishes.

"So in any other case where the Board of Guardians are not parties to the proceedings, the clerk will not be required to conduct such proceedings as a part of his duty."

V.—EMIGRATION.

6th August, 1842.

The following communication from the Colonial Land and Emigration Commissioners was read:—

"*Colonial Land and Emigration Office,*
"*9, Park-street, Westminster,*
"*August*, 1842.

"SIR,—I am directed by the Colonial Land and Emigration Commissioners to transmit to you, for the information of the Poor Law Commissioners, a list of the vessels which have been reported by Mr. Buchanan to have arrived at Quebec with emigrants sent out by their respective parishes between the 29th May and the 18th of June.

"I am, Sir,
"Your most obedient servant,
(Signed) "JOHN WALPOLE,
"*E. Chadwick, Esq.* "*Assistant Secretary.*

Vessel's Name.	Where from.	When arrived.
Lord Canterbury.	Bristol.	June 2nd.

"Among the passengers in this vessel were eight families, 54 in number, who were assisted by their respective parishes; they are proceeding to the western section of the province. The remaining families are all in good circumstances, and have brought out a good deal of money with them: they intend settling in the Johnston, Midland, and Home Districts.

Vessel's Name.	Where from.	When arrived.
Emmanuel.	Bristol.	May 31st.

"In this vessel were three families, 19 in number, also sent out by their parish; they were forwarded to Montreal at ship's expense, and are going to their friends at Prescott.

Vessel's Name.	Where from.	When arrived.
Voluna.	Padstow.	11th June.

"The emigrants from England are from Padstow, Bideford, and Aberystwith; they are all able to pay their way to their destination, and many of them have brought out a good deal of money. They all emigrated on their own account, with the exception of one family, eight in number, sent out in the 'Voluna' by parish relief.

Vessel's Name.	Where from.	When arrived.
Minstrel.	Liverpool.	16th June.

"By this vessel one family, seven in number, and a number of young men and women, were assisted by their parish.

Vessel's Name.	Where from.	When arrived.
Irvine.	Bristol.	16th June.

"In this vessel were four families, 32 in number, sent out by their parish.

Vessel's Name.	Where from.	When arrived.
Pusey Hall.	Cowes.	16th June.

"One hundred and seventy-one passengers in this vessel, from London and Cowes, were sent out under the sanction of the Poor Law Commissioners. They were well supplied during the voyage, and the sum of 116*l.* 10*s.* sterling was paid to them on landing, with a free passage to Montreal."

13th August, 1842.

The following document, forwarded to the Commissioners by the Colonial Land and Emigration Commissioners, was read:—

EXTRACT from Mr. Buchanan's Returns of Emigrants arrived at Quebec in the week ended 2d July, 1842.

Vessel's Name.	Where from.	Number of Emigrants.				Date of Arrival.	If sent out by Parishes, or Government aid.	If voluntary.	Remarks.
		Males.	Females.	Children under 14.	Total.				
Dependent.*	Bridgewater	31	23	44	98	1842. 27th June	52	46	Gone to settle in St. Catherines, Whitby, Coburg, and Guelph.
Orbit† . .	London .	80	41	96	217	1st July .	194	23	Proceeded to Kingston, Toronto, and Winchester.

* Ninety-eight passengers in the "Dependent" from Bridgewater arrived in good health; 52 of whom are sent out by the Chard Union, in Somersetshire. These people were found in provisions by the ship, and received the 20*s.* sterling on landing. The remaining passengers were of the better class, and possess good means; they intend going to the western section of the province to settle. A good many of the paupers intend to proceed to the United States.

† One hundred and ninety-four passengers in the "Orbit," from London and Gravesend, were sent out under the direction and superintendence of the Poor Law Commissioners. There were five deaths during the voyage—one old man, the others children, and left a number of cases at Gross Isle. These people were forwarded to Montreal at ship's expense, and received 20*s.* sterling each adult on landing here.

VI.—GUARDIANS.

1. AS TO WHETHER THE CHAIRMAN OF A BOARD OF GUARDIANS CAN GIVE A DOUBLE VOTE. *8th August*, 1842.

The Commissioners took into consideration a letter received from the clerk of the Dorking Union, wherein he states as follows:—

"Previous to your order of the 20th April last, Art. 13, the chairman had, I believe, the same right as any other Guardian, to give his vote in the first instance, and then in case of an equality of votes, to give the casting vote in addition to his original vote on the question. Since your order above alluded to, the power of the chairman to give the double vote in the cases above-mentioned, is questioned, and I should be glad if you would favour me with your opinion on the point."

And the Commissioners directed the following reply to be made thereto:—

"In reply I am to state that the term, 'casting vote,' used without qualification, may signify one of two things, viz., either the single vote of a person who never votes but in the case of an equality, or the double vote of a person who first votes with the rest, and then upon an equality, creates a majority by giving a second vote.

"The right to give a second vote must be expressly given by statute or immemorial usage, and the Commissioners do not find that the law confers any such power on the chairman of a Board of Guardians, constituted under the 4th and 5th William IV. c. 76, though the rules issued by the Commissioners in the first instance to the Dorking Union assumed to give such a power to the chairman."

2. A CORONER, AS SUCH, IS NOT ENTITLED TO ACT AS AN EX-OFFICIO GUARDIAN.

13th August, 1842.

The Commissioners took into consideration a letter received from the clerk to the Anglesey Union, inquiring whether the coroner for the County of Anglesey, has a right, by virtue of his office of Coroner, to sit as a member of the Board of Guardians of the Union, and the Commissioners directed the following answer to be given thereto:—

"In reply I am to state that the Commissioners cannot infer from your statement, what are the grounds upon which the coroner claims to act as ex-officio Guardian.

"Only justices of the peace of counties, are ex-officio Guardians. The coroner is not a justice of the peace by virtue of his office. He is a conservator of the peace within his own court, as every judge of record is, and as the sheriff is in his court and county. These and many other officers are conservators of the peace; amongst others, justices of the peace are so. But the being conservator of the peace does not make a coroner a justice of the peace, or a justice of the peace a coroner. As coroner, therefore, for all that the Commissioners are at present informed of, a person has no right to claim to act as an ex-officio Guardian of a Union."

3. PERSONS INCAPABLE OF SERVING AS GUARDIANS—14 sec. of 5 and 6 Vic., c. 57.

The following Circular has been addressed by the Commissioners to the clerks of the several Boards of Guardians on this subject:—

"*Poor Law Commission Office,*
"*Somerset House, 2d August*, 1842.

"SIR,—I am directed by the Poor Law Commissioners to call the attention of the Board of Guardians to the 14th Clause in the Act for the Continuance of the Poor Law Commission, which is in the following words:—

"And be it enacted, that no person, during "the time for which he may serve or hold the "office of assistant-overseer of any parish, nor "any paid officer engaged in the administra- "tion of the laws for relief of the poor, nor "any person who, having been a paid officer, "shall have been dismissed within five years "previously from such office, under the pro- "visions of the said first recited Act, shall be "capable of serving as a Guardian; and no "person receiving any fixed salary or emolu- "ment from the poor rates in any parish or "union shall be capable of serving as a Guardian "in such parish or union."

"The Commissioners desire me to state that if in consequence of this enactment any vacancy is created in the Board, they will upon the application of the Guardians, be ready to issue an order for a new election.

"The Commissioners deem it right to observe that if any person to whom the above clause is applicable shall henceforth wilfully act as a Guardian, he will render himself liable to the usual penalties of violating the provisions of a statute. I am, your obedient servant,

"GEORGE COODE,
"*Assistant Secretary.*

"*To the Clerk to the Guardians.*"

4. AS TO WHETHER CLERGYMEN AND REGISTRARS ARE INCAPABLE OF SERVING AS GUARDIANS.

8th November, 1842.

The Commissioners took into consideration a letter addressed to them by J. Parrott, Esq., the chairman of the Totnes Union, requesting their opinion whether a registrar of births and deaths, who is entitled to certain fixed fees for registration under the 29th section of the 6 and 7 Wm. IV. c. 86, and a clergyman, who is also entitled to certain fixed fees for certified copies of marriages under the 27th section of the 1 Vic. c. 22, payable in the manner provided by those Acts, are disqualified thereby for serving the office of Guardian; and the Commissioners directed the following answer to be given thereto:—

"With regard to the latter case I am to state that if a clergyman be supposed to be rendered incompetent to serve the office of Guardian by the 14th section of the 5th and 6th Vic., c. 57., it must be by effect of the words 'no person receiving any fixed salary or emolument from the poor-rates in any parish or Union shall be capable of serving as a Guardian.'

"Before they make any observations on these words, the Commissioners will remark that the principle of such disqualifying provisions is well known, namely, that persons having an interest in increasing or continuing their emolument, or in diminishing their duty, or return for emolument, shall not hold an office in which they can secure their personal objects by neglect of their public duty. It is obvious that a clergyman acting as Guardian cannot by any misuse of that office increase the number or amount of fees payable to him for the quarterly register for marriages, nor secure impunity for himself in the improper performance of that duty. It appears clearly to follow as a matter of principle that there is no reason to suppose that the clause was intended to disqualify a clergyman on account of the receipt of these fees, and that the terms of the clause would not be extended in their construction for the purpose of effecting such disqualification.

"As to the terms of the clause, it is clear that the emolument is not a fixed salary, neither does the payment at the rate of sixpence per marriage appear to be a fixed emolument in the sense of the Act; the total emolument is not fixed, but the rate for each article is fixed. This, however, is the case with almost every article which could occasionally be purchased or obtained by the parish officers or Guardians, especially every fee of any officer of justice, and most of the fees of professional men of every description. But these occasional payments, though fixed in the individual instance, do not appear to be within the meaning of the term 'fixed emolument.'

"It is further to be remarked that the payment, though ultimately derived from the poor-rates, is made immediately by the superintendent registrar, and in this is like payments out of the county rate, or hundred rate, &c., and is therefore placed out of the control of the Guardians as Guardians, and has, in fact, ceased to be poor-rate when in the hands of the superintendent registrar.

"As regards the case of the registrar, the reasons for deeming him not to be disqualified for the office of Guardian under the 5th and 6th Vic., c. 57, are not so strong as those in the case of the clergyman. He is appointed by the Guardians to his office, and, what is more important, he is immediately paid by them out of the monies which are at the time of payment unquestionably poor-rates. (See 6th and 7th Wm. IV., c. 86, s. 29.) The strongest of the reasons, therefore, in favour of the clergyman's right, that namely, which the Commissioners last referred to, fails as regards the registrar. Still the other reasons stated in regard to the clergyman apply to the registrar also.

"On the whole the Commissioners think there is nothing to prevent the clergyman from acting, but that there is sufficient doubt as regards the registrar to render it unadvisable that he should act until a legal decision can be obtained on the point."

VII.—LUNATICS, ANNUAL RETURN OF.

1. The following is a copy of a Circular on this subject addressed by the Commissioners to the clerks of the several Boards of Guardians in England and Wales:—

"*Poor Law Commission Office,*
"*Somerset House, 4th August*, 1842.

"SIR,—I am directed by the Poor Law Commissioners to inform you, that by the 6th Clause of the Act (5 and 6 Vic., c. 57) passed for the continuance of the Poor Law Commission, it is enacted, that the clerk to every Board of Guardians shall on the 15th day of

August in every year, or as soon after as may be, make out and sign two true and faithful lists of all insane persons chargeable to the parish or Union in the form in the schedule thereunto annexed, and shall on or before the first day of September next succeeding transmit one copy of such list to the clerk of the peace acting in and for the county within which the parish to which each such insane person is chargeable is situated, or to his deputy, to be by him laid before the justices acting for such county at their next general quarter sessions, and the other copy of such list to the said Commissioners; and from and after the passing of the Act, the overseers of any such parish, or of any parish within any such Union, shall not be required to make the annual return required of them by the 9 Geo. IV., c. 40:—The form prescribed is annexed.

"As the time will soon arrive for the preparation of this return, it will be necessary that you should make immediate enquiry for the requisite information from the relieving officers and other persons.

"I am, Sir, your obedient servant,
"GEORGE COODE,
"*Assistant Secretary*.
"*To the Clerk to the Guardians*."

2. And a Circular, of which the following is a copy, was addressed by the Commissioners to the Overseers of every parish and township comprised in any Union or under a Board of Guardians.

"*Poor Law Commission Office*,
"*Somerset House*, 2*d August*, 1842.

"GENTLEMEN,—I am directed by the Poor Law Commissioners to inform you that under the provisions contained in the sixth Section of the Act passed on Saturday last, for the continuance of the Poor Law Commission, the Overseers of every parish or township, situate in any Union formed under the Poor Law Amendment Act, or subject to a Board of Guardians appointed under the same Act, are exempted from making the annual return of lunatics, heretofore required from them by the 9 Geo. IV. c. 40.

"I am, your obedient Servant,
"GEORGE COODE.
"*To the Overseers*. "*Assistant Secretary*."

3. LUNATIC RETURNS.—VISITING LUNATICS.
12*th August*, 1842.

The Commissioners took into consideration a letter received from the Clerk of the Poplar Union, inquiring upon whom the duty of visiting lunatics devolved, in order to prepare the annual return of lunatics under the Act 5 and 6 Vic., c. 57, and the Commissioners directed the following reply to be made thereto:—

"I am to state, in reply, that when a visit is necessary beyond the information supplied by the relieving officer, power is given to the Guardians by the 6th section of the statute cited, to contract with a person duly licensed to practise as a medical man to certify as to the state and condition of insane persons. The 9th Geo. IV., c. 40, gives to the medical man appointed by an overseer under the authority of that Act the power to examine insane persons, and to visit any asylum or hospital for that purpose, as a consequence of the appointment. The Guardians under the recent Act have the like powers as to insane persons as overseers, therefore the same power to confer authority; consequently any medical man who may be appointed by the Guardians for the purpose will have the same authority as a medical practitioner under 9th Geo. IV., c. 40, s. 40."

VIII.—PENSIONS.—ASSIGNMENT OF.

2*nd August*, 1842.

The Commissioners took into consideration a letter received from the clerk of the Bedford Union, inquiring whether the Act 2 and 3 Vic., c. 51, regulating the payment and assignment of pensions, authorizes the Board of Guardians to retain and apply any portion of a pension to repay the Union an excess of charges for relief given in a previous quarter, over and above the amount of pension then received; when the Commissioners directed the clerk to be informed that they were of opinion that the Act of Parliament does not authorize such a course to be taken, and consider that there must be a minute or an assignment in respect of each quarter's pension.

IX.—RATING.

1. MANUFACTORIES PARTIALLY OCCUPIED.

The Commissioners took into consideration a letter, addressed to them by the clerk of the Sheffield Union, in which he submitted the following points for their opinion:—

"First,—Whether any entire building thrown out of use can be returned 'Empty' where the whole property is situated within an inclosure?

"Second,—If so, what kind of division is necessary to make a part of one building an entire tenement? so as to leave one part of such building rateable, and the other entitled to an abatement, or total exemption.

"Third,—Whether every thing of the nature of personalty, or tenant's fixtures, or working tools must be removed before the tenement can be allowed for?

"Fourth,—Whether, in the case of a building of two stories, where every thing is removed from the second story, and the staircase built or blocked up, so that access is given only to the low story, and no entrance effected to the chamber, the lower story can be rated and the upper returned 'Empty?'"

And the Commissioners directed the following observations to be communicated to the clerk thereon:—

"There is an obvious distinction between a tenement not occupied, and a tenement occupied, but not used, or only partially used, by the occupier. A property is not ratable according to the extent of the use an occupier may actually make of it; but it is ratable whenever occupied, according to the value which it would be of, supposing that the occupier made full use of it.

"It appears to the Commissioners that the property described by you is not unoccupied, but that it is unused, or rather only partially used, by the occupier.

"It appears, therefore, that there is no such failure of an occupation as to do away with the liability in respect of the property.

"As to what may be sufficient to constitute a separate tenement or occupation, is a matter of great difficulty, even if it were possible to anticipate or enumerate all the circumstances which might be held sufficient to distinguish one occupation from another.

"As regards buildings, however, generally, every property held by one person or by the joint tenants, coparceners, or tenants in common, is considered as one occupation, if it has one distinct entrance, common to all the property held by the same person or persons.

"The occupation of such a property by the use and control of the common entrance seems to be an occupation of the whole. The use or non-use of a part of occupied property has never been considered as a ground of exemption from rates. The entire abandonment of the use of the whole by removal of all property from it, and of all persons except such as are left merely to guard the property, or to show it with a view to letting it, is admitted, in practice, to exempt the tenant from the rate.

"The Commissioners, therefore, consider that the first question in your letter of the 11th of May, must be answered in the negative.

"With regard to your second question,—what kind of division is necessary to make a part of one building an entire tenement, so as to leave one part of such building ratable, and the other entitled to an abatement, or total exemption, the Commissioners think that no division will have this effect, but a mode of access, excluding the occupation of the rest of the tenement, and allow of its being occupied by some one else. This, as in the case of chambers, makes a separate occupation.

"Where the property is so held and appointed as to make a distinct occupation, all property must be removed, except fixtures, (landlord's and tenant's fixtures,) before the occupation is so abandoned as to bring the property within the ordinary exemption.

"The building or blocking up an entrance without transferring the right of instant entrance to some other tenant, is no greater abandonment of the occupation than when the door is closed. The non-use of an apartment in a building has never been admitted as a ground of exemption of the occupier of the rest of the building, unless where a distinct occupation is created in favour of some other person, as a lodger, to the exclusion of the right of entrance of the occupier of the rest of the building."

---

2. RATING RENT-CHARGE.—LAND-TAX.

4th August, 1842.

The Commissioners took into consideration a letter received by them from the Rev. G. E. Webster, the rector of Grundisburgh, claiming a deduction from a rent-charge on account of land-tax, wherein he states:—

"The land tax on my benefice is not a Government tax; it is redeemed. But though redeemed, it has not returned to the benefice from which it was taken. It was bequeathed by will by that predecessor in the living, who did redeem it. It now forms (if I may so call it) a separate private property, being the present property of a merchant in London, to whom the land-tax is now paid annually.

"The land-tax on the other estate in this parish

being redeemed, was left by will to the parish itself, or is now parish property for certain purposes specified in the will.

"In my own case the contract for the redemption of the land-tax specifies three distinct properties on which it was first laid and afterwards redeemed, viz.:—1. Parsonage house and buildings adjoining. 2. Tithes. 3. Glebe, enumerating the acres of which it consists. The warrant also for collecting the land-tax, issued to the assessors, distinctly mentions tithes. It cannot, therefore, be alleged that the land-tax was laid on the parsonage-house and glebe alone, and the proportion of it which I claim a right to deduct, is that only which may be fairly estimated and adjudged to have been upon the tithes.

"Full proof, then, being made of the fact that the land-tax is redeemed, and being redeemed, has *not* returned to this benefice again so as to become part and parcel of it, but remains absolutely severed from it, I respectfully ask, do you, in such case, oppose your authority to the claim made by me of a deduction to be made from the rent-charge on account of part of the land-tax previous to the rate being made."

And the Commissioners directed the following reply to be made thereto:—

"The Commissioners' opinion that land-tax cannot be deducted in estimating the net annual value of any property, is founded on the terms of the Parochial Assessments' Act, which defines the net annual value, or ratable value, as 'the rent at which the hereditaments might reasonably be expected to let from year to year, free from all usual tenants' rates and taxes,' &c. The express mention of tenants' rates and taxes, by the common rule of legal construction, operates, as the Commissioners are advised, as an exclusion of landlords' taxes, such as the land-tax is.

"But in the case you describe the land-tax has been redeemed, and the amount of it is charged on the property in favour of a private person.

"In this case a reduction in the net annual value cannot, as the Commissioners conceive, be claimed as a deduction from a tax at all. The receipt of the sum has become a private right by which the entire net profit of the property is so far enjoyed by two persons. It is like any other participation of the entire net value of property by different persons, as in the case of annuities and rents of various denominations charged on property. For the portions of the entire net value of property thus foregone by the tenant of the property, no deduction can be claimed consistently either with any statute or any practice."

3. RATING TITHES.—ECCLESIASTICAL DUES.

4th August, 1842.

The Commissioners took into consideration the following letter, addressed to them by the Rev. H. W. Simpson, the vicar of Bexhill:—

"In the rating of tithe you state that certain deductions are to be made from the gross rental for risk and trouble of collecting, and for *ecclesiastical dues*.

"I suppose this latter term to include tenths and procuration fees, and, at the first rate on a new incumbent, the first fruits.

"This is a vicarage endowed with great tithes, which latter originally belonged to the bishoprick; and there is a yearly sum, called the bishop's tax and pension, payable by the vicar. I shall be obliged by your informing me if I am right in supposing that this sum falls within the description of ecclesiastical dues."

And the Commissioners directed the following answer to be given thereto:—

"The Commissioners desire to state, in reply, that tenths and procuration fees are ecclesiastical dues, for which deduction is allowable on the gross value of the tithes upon an estimate of their average annual amount.

"First-fruits are an ecclesiastical due, for which deduction should be made during the period over which the payment is spread.

"The Commissioners do not know of any ecclesiastical due of the denomination of the bishop's tax, or pension. They infer from the fact that the great tithes of the vicarage belonging originally to the bishoprick, that it is a reservation somewhat in the nature of a fixed rent-charge on the tithe, and that it is, therefore, only a participation by the bishop in the profits of the tithe, fixed in its amount as to the bishop, but not a matter of common due by way of contribution towards general ecclesiastical expenses, or as fees for common ecclesiastical officers. The Commissioners, on this assumption, conclude that they are not ecclesiastical dues for which deduction can be made in the estimate of the ratable value of the tithe."

4. RATING TITHES.—INCOME TAX.

17th August, 1842.

The Commissioners took into consideration a letter addressed to them by the Rev. Ellis

Anwyl Owen, rector of Llanystundwy, enquiring whether the income tax is to be deducted out of the amount of tithes, or rent-charge, in rating the same to relief of the poor, when they directed the following reply to be made thereto:—

"The Parochial Assessments' Act, 6 and 7 Wm. IV., c. 96, s. 1, allows the deduction of *all usual tenants' rates and taxes* from the gross value of ratable property; but the tax referred to by you (property and income tax) is imposed under the 5 and 6 Vic., c. 35, schedule A, upon the *property* of the party liable to that tax, and is a charge not upon the tenant but upon the owner or landlord. Hence it appears to the Commissioners that it is not a subject of deduction in the estimate of the net annual value of property ratable to the poor rate."

X.—RELIEF.

1. RELIEF TO ABLE-BODIED PAUPERS WHERE THE UNION WORKHOUSES ARE FULL.

20th August, 1842.

The Commissioners took into consideration a letter received from the clerk of the Wellington Union (Salop), informing the Commissioners that the Guardians, at their meeting held on the 18th of August, were under the necessity of departing from the regulations contained in the *Prohibitory Order* in respect of the cases of certain able-bodied paupers, in consequence of both the workhouses of the Union being full, and unable to receive any more inmates; when the Commissioners directed the following reply to be made thereto:—

"In reply I am to state that the Commissioners, under the circumstances stated by you, sanction the relief to the paupers in question whose cases are reported in your letter.

"With regard to the numerous applications anticipated by the Guardians, the Commissioners recommend, that if possible, some sort of stone-breaking or other work should be offered to the able-bodied, that the Guardians should proceed to afford assistance to the relieving officers, and if necessary to appoint some person or persons temporarily to superintend the work, and that the relief given should, as far as possible, be given in kind.

"A difficult question may arise as to men refusing to work at fair wages, and applying for relief, and on this subject the Commissioners will offer the following observations.

"The poor rates constitute a fund for the relief of destitution. The amount so levied is withdrawn from the capital which must itself furnish employment to the labouring classes, and form a severe burthen on the middle classes, who are themselves liable to be reduced to poverty by the contingencies of trade, or the excess of public burthens.

"So long, however, as real and involuntary destitution exists, so long must the Guardians, in discharge of their public duties, require from the rate-payers, and distribute to the applicants for relief, that sustenance which the necessities of the latter class demand.

"But the question becomes a different one when the destitution is self-imposed, and when the Guardians are satisfied that individuals supported by the poor rates, may obtain employment at wages adequate for the maintenance of themselves or families.

"With the dispute between masters and workmen, or with the agreements of either class among themselves, the Guardians have nothing to do. It is not the object of the poor rates to aid either class in their struggle against the other, and it must be assumed that the law will be found sufficiently strong to protect those willing to work, from the prolonged action of forcible interference.

"If, therefore, the Guardians are in a situation to say, the men now applying for relief may obtain work within their reach, at wages sufficient for their maintenance, or that of their families, and it only depends on themselves to accept it, they are justified in refusing relief to those persons, simply because they can no longer be considered as destitute. It is not, however, sufficient that they should say vaguely to the whole mass 'employment may be had,' but they must be able to state definitely that at a certain place, employment at wages sufficient for the support of the man and his family can be obtained; all cases of great and temporary urgency would of course be treated as exceptions."

2. TEMPORARY RELIEF TO ABLE-BODIED PAUPERS UNTIL THEY CAN AVAIL THEMSELVES OF ORDERS OF ADMISSION INTO THE WORKHOUSE.

11th May, 1842.

The Commissioners took into consideration the following letter received from the clerk of the Walsall Union:

"Very frequently able-bodied men apply to the relieving-officer, and afterwards to the Board of Guardians, for relief, stating that their families have had no food for a day or two, and were then sinking for want, whereupon a loaf, two, or three, of bread, has been given on such statements, when believed to be true, together with an order to admit the family into the workhouse; but some of the Guardians were of opinion that the Poor Law Commissioners' General Order, dated the 2nd August, 1841, prohibited the officers and Board from giving such relief for the sudden necessities of the family, and that it was not lawful to give other than in-door relief, without reporting the particulars thereof to the Commissioners under Article 4 of the same Order.

"One portion of the Board were of opinion that the bread was lawfully given under clause 1 of Art. 1 of that Order, and that as soon as that sudden necessity ceased to exist, the admission order was the only proper relief then to be afforded, and if the bread had been refused, the applicants might, probably, have died from want before they could make arrangements to enter the workhouse.

"I am directed to inquire from the Commissioners whether, in their opinion, the Guardians have acted properly in giving out-door and in-door relief at the same time, in those cases of necessity."

And the Commissioners directed the clerk to be informed they were of opinion that in such cases as those described in his letter, the Guardians or the relieving officer were authorised in administering relief in food, under the first exception to Article 1. of the *prohibitory order*, until the paupers could be admitted into the workhouse, and therefore that it was not necessary in such cases to report the relief so given for the Commissioners' special sanction, as is requisite in cases of departure from the order under Article 4.

---

3. MEDICAL RELIEF TO A PERSON NOT IN RECEIPT OF OTHER RELIEF.

9th August, 1842.

The Commissioners took into consideration a letter received from the clerk of the Wrexham Union, inquiring whether the Board of Guardians were liable to pay a bill delivered to them by one of the medical officers of the Union for attending on a person who was not in receipt of other relief under an order from the relieving officer; when the Commissioners directed the following answer to be given thereto:—

"The Commissioners think the medical officer is bound to attend upon any person whom the Guardians, or other authority competent to give relief, may deem to want and be properly entitled to receive relief at the cost of the Union. The Commissioners do not understand this power to order medical relief to be limited to parties already in the receipt of other relief. It is immaterial as regards constituting a person a pauper, what may be the description of relief which may be ordered him, whether it be food or money, or medicine, if to be furnished at the cost of the poor rates. It is the application of the person to be relieved, coupled with the fact of relief being granted, which renders a person a pauper. It appears, therefore, to the Commissioners, that if a person who may not previously have received relief, apply for medical aid, and the Guardians, or the relieving officer, or (in a case of sudden and urgent necessity,) the overseer see fit to order it, the medical officer is bound to attend upon such case. The obligation upon those who have the administration of relief to supply necessary medical assistance to a person labouring under dangerous illness, though such person may not have received, or stood in need of relief previous to his illness, is established by the decision in R. *v.* Warren, Russ. and R., Cr. cases 48. With respect to the demand made by the medical officer in the present case, the Commissioners are of opinion that the Guardians are not liable to pay any portion of such demand.

"Whether or not the person was destitute, so as to make him a proper object for the gratuitous attendance of the medical officer, the Commissioners express no opinion. This point would appear at least to be doubtful, and the Commissioners need not say that care should be taken not to inflict an injury on the medical men by improper orders, in addition to the injustice of causing such attendance to be paid for from the poor rates."

4. MEDICAL RELIEF. — CONSTRUCTION OF ARTICLES 16 AND 17 OF THE GENERAL MEDICAL RELIEF ORDER.

26th April, 1842.

The Commissioners took into consideration a letter addressed to them by the clerk of the Chipping Norton Union, inquiring whether it is intended by these articles, that separate tickets should be made out for the wives of aged and infirm persons, and persons permanently sick or disabled, or whether the ticket of the husband will be sufficient to authorize attendance on the wife; the wife not being a "person actually receiving relief;" when the Commissioners directed the following answer to be given thereto:—

"The Commissioners wish to observe that it does not follow that because all relief to a wife or child, is chargeable to the husband, the wife or child, therefore, is not also receiving relief. The former is often chargeable only constructively; the words 'actually receiving relief,' were used in the order, in opposition to any such constructive chargeability.

"The Commissioners consider that the parties actually sick or infirm, and actually relieved, should be placed on the list required by the order."

5. MEDICAL RELIEF. — CONSTRUCTION OF ARTICLES 16 AND 17 OF THE ABOVE ORDER.

24th June, 1842.

A letter from the clerk of the Llanelly Union was read, inquiring whose duty it is to prepare the lists and tickets referred to in these articles, when the Commissioners directed that the clerk should be informed in reply that they consider it to be *his* duty to prepare such lists and tickets; but that the relieving officers should be required to furnish him with any information which might be necessary to enable him to prepare the same, and which they might be able to give.

6. MEDICAL RELIEF.—BOOKS TO BE KEPT BY THE MEDICAL OFFICER.

28th April, 1842.

The Commissioners took into consideration a letter received from the clerk of the Bridgewater Union, inquiring whether the medical officer of the Union workhouse is required to keep the Medical Relief Book, Schedule E, Form 28, and the Register of Sickness and Mortality Book, Form 27, of the same schedule, as directed by the Accounts Order, dated the 4th of August, 1836, in addition to the books required to be kept by the general workhouse rules; when the Commissioners directed the clerk to be informed, in reply, that the duty of keeping the first-mentioned books is rescinded by those rules.

XI.—SETTLEMENT BY ESTATE.

3rd August, 1842.

The Commissioners took into consideration the following letter, received from Mr. Wm. Antwis, overseer of Eddisbury:—

"I respectfully beg leave to ask the favour of your opinion on the following cases:—

"1st. Some years ago C. N. became settled in the township of D. by the purchase of property of more than 30*l*. value and residence thereon, having several children born to him during such residence. That property being sold, he purchased other premises of greater value in this township of E, where he resided for several years. Being reduced in circumstances, and having disposed of this property, he has frequently received relief from this township. He is now residing more than ten miles from this township (in the township of R). The following are the relative positions of the townships and residences of the pauper in each respectively:—

"The distance from the nearest point of township E. to the nearest point of township R., by the nearest legal footpath, is nine miles and a half. The distance of the present residence of C. N., in township R. to the nearest point of township E., by the nearest legal footpath, is eleven miles. The distance by any highway is considerably more.

"2nd. H. N., a daughter of the pauper C. N., having been in service during his residence in E., returned (not being removed with an order of justices, nor having gained a settlement in her own right,) to her father's house, and was delivered of a bastard child previous to the passing of the Poor Law Amendment Act, and another since; both of which, with H. N., have become chargeable to this township of E.

"First. Please to state whether either of the distances before mentioned come within the meaning of the 68th section of the 76th of 4 and 5 Wm. IV.

"Second. If the section 68 operates, and the settlement of C. N. is not retained in the township of E., how far are the settlements of the daughter H. N., and her two bastard children, affected by this circumstance? Do they, or any of them, take the original settlement of C. N. *previous* to his coming into the township of D. (which is farther from his present residence than E.); or does the birth of any of C. N.'s children, during his residence in D., confer a settlement on the children so born.

"Your answers will, probably, prevent considerable litigation, and will be gratefully received."

And the Commissioners directed the following reply to be made thereto:—

"The 68th section of the Poor Law Amendment Act declares that a settlement gained by virtue of an estate, or interest in a parish, shall not be retained by any person after he ceases to inhabit within ten miles thereof.

"Where the person inhabits at a distance from the parish, greater than ten miles by the nearest public footpath, but less than ten miles in a straight line, from his residence to the nearest point of the parish, there is considerable difficulty at present in determining the manner in which the distance is to be calculated. In the cases which have been decided upon contracts, preventing a party from trading within a certain distance, the distance has been calculated by the nearest common footpath, (Woods *v.* Dennett, 2 Starkie 89, and Leigh *v.* Hind, 9 B and C 774;) but in the latter case Mr. Justice Parke inclined to the opinion that the proper mode of measuring, was by a straight line from point to point. In these cases the contracts involved a prohibition of trading under a penalty, neither of which would usually be extended by the construction of courts of law, and the measurement by the pathway, which contracts the extent of the prohibition, may have been preferred on that account, to a measurement from point to point by a straight line, which would have extended the operation of the prohibition and penalty. Moreover, the contracting parties having reference to a particular place of business, and a particular neighbourhood surrounding it, may have been reasonably considered to have especial reference to the means of access by the common pathway. These considerations do not so strongly apply in the present case. The legislature cannot have had any particular roads in view, there is no restriction or penalty imposed, which would induce the courts to adopt a narrow or strict construction, and it is not, therefore, improbable that the views expressed by Mr. Justice Parke in the case last cited, which would give a more fixed rule than the measurement by footways would do, would prevail in construing the 68th section.

"No argument, one way or the other can be founded on the definition of the settlement by estate, for though the settlement be lost in one place, it is given in another.

"On the whole, however, the Commissioners think a measurement by the nearest footpath is most accordant with such decisions as seem in any way to bear on the subject.

"Next as to the points, from which, and to which the measurement is to be made. The point from which the measurement is to be made, is evidently not the land in which the pauper had his estate or interest; for the property is not referred to, but only the estate or interest in it, which have not a local existence, but the parish in which the settlement by estate was gained. The part of the parish boundary from which the measurement would be made, would probably differ as either one or the other of the above constructions was adopted. If the measurement were by the straight line from point to point, one of the points would most probably be that point in the parish boundary nearest to the place of the subsequent inhabitancy; if the measurement by the footway was adopted, the point in the parish boundary accessible by the nearest footway, would undoubtedly be the proper point from which to measure. The place to which the measurement is to be made, is the place of subsequent residence, the dwelling, not the boundary of the parish in which that dwelling is situate; for the terms of the 68th clause has no reference to this parish.

"On considering the whole of this matter, the Commissioners, although they cannot express a decided opinion on a matter upon which the courts have expressed these doubts, are of opinion that the settlement of C. N. in the township of E. has been lost by residence in the township of R.

"Enough is not stated to enable the Commissioners to judge whether the daughter was emancipated at the time of entering service, or at any other time.

"If she were emancipated at any time she would retain the settlement she had then derived from her father; and if this were a settlement by estate, which the father might subsequently forfeit under the 68th section of the Poor Law Amendment Act, the Commissioners are of opinion that the daughter's settlement would not be affected by that forfeiture;—the section as they consider only defeating the settlement originally gained by estate, not settlements communicated by marriage, parentage or other mode by which derivative settlements are conferred.

"If she be not emancipated when her father forfeits his settlement, she will follow the change of her father's settlement.

"Whichever result applies to the daughter, the same will apply to her bastard until sixteen."

LONDON:
Printed, by Order of the Poor Law Commissioners, by W. CLOWES and SONS, Stamford Street, and Published by CHARLES KNIGHT and Co., 22, Ludgate Street, Publishers to the Poor Law Commissioners.

AN

OFFICIAL CIRCULAR

OF PUBLIC DOCUMENTS AND INFORMATION:

DIRECTED BY THE POOR LAW COMMISSIONERS TO BE PRINTED, CHIEFLY FOR THE USE OF THE MEMBERS AND PERMANENT OFFICERS OF BOARDS OF GUARDIANS, UNDER THE POOR LAW AMENDMENT ACT.

No. 22. CIRCULAR ISSUED JANUARY 25, 1843.

Poor Law Commission Office,
Somerset House,
25th January, 1843.

THE Poor Law Commissioners, on a review of their Minutes, directed that the Minutes of Correspondence on the following subjects be printed and circulated for the information of Guardians and Officers of the several Unions, viz.:—

By Order of the Board,
EDWIN CHADWICK, *Secretary.*

I. BASTARDS.—AS TO THE LIABILITY OF MOTHERS TO PUNISHMENT FOR DESERTING THEIR BASTARD CHILDREN. REG. *v.* MAUDE.—TOTNES UNION.

24th September, 1842.

The Commissioners took into consideration a letter addressed to them by J. Parrott, Esq., the chairman of the Board of Guardians of the Totnes Union, referring to the case of Reg. *v.* Maude, recently decided by the Court of Queen's Bench, and inquiring whether the mothers of bastard children can be punished for deserting them, under the 3rd section of the 5th Geo. IV. c. 83; and the Commissioners directed the following reply to be made thereto:—

"In reply I am to point out to you, that the decision in the case of Reg. *v.* Maude turns on the particular terms of the 4th section of the Vagrant Act, (5 Geo. IV., c. 83) in which the word 'child' is used in juxtaposition with the word 'wife,' and it is, therefore, inferred that the provisions of that section extend only to cases where legitimate children are deserted. Such being the construction put on the words of the 4th section of the Act, there is no provision in the Poor Law Amendment Act having the effect of identifying in this respect a bastard with a legitimate child.

"But such is not the case with the 3rd section of the Vagrant Act; the words describing the objects in respect of which a father's or mother's obligation attaches, are quite different from those of the 4th section, viz., 'himself, herself, or any of his or her *family.*' Family is of itself a much more comprehensive term than 'wife or child,' and the Poor Law Amendment Act, section 71, expressly declares that the mother of a bastard child 'shall be bound to maintain such child as a part of her family, until,' &c. By this provision the liability of mothers, whether of legitimate children or illegitimate children, so far as the 3rd section of the Vagrant Act is concerned, appears to be completely assimilated. Such has been hitherto the understanding of the justices of the peace in all parts of the country, and there is obviously nothing in the decision of Reg. *v.* Maude bearing on this construction."

II.—CLERK'S DUTIES—AS TO WHETHER THE CLERK CAN APPOINT A SUBSTITUTE.—MACHYNLLETH UNION.

19th November, 1842.

The Commissioners took into consideration a letter addressed to them by Sir John Edwards, Bart., inquiring whether the clerk to the Board of Guardians of the Machynlleth Union had a right to appoint a substitute to attend the meetings of the Board, and, in case he had no such right, whether any Guardian could object to such substitute being present; and the Commissioners directed the following reply to be given to the inquiry:—

"The Commissioners desire to point out, that by Article 17, clause 1, of the Commissioners' General Order of the 21st April, 1842, relating to the duties of officers, the clerk is required 'to attend all meetings of the Board of Guardians, and to keep punctually the minutes of the proceedings at every meeting,' &c. Article 13 of the same Order provides, that 'if any officer or assistant appointed to, or holding any office or employment under this Order, be at any time prevented by sickness or accident, or other sufficient reason, from the performance of his duties, the Guardians may appoint a fit person to act as his temporary substitute, and may pay him a reasonable compensation for his services;' and under Article 14, 'the Vice-Chairman, or some Guardian to be appointed by the Board of Guardians, may perform any of the duties assigned to the clerk until any vacancy in the office shall have been filled, or until a substitute be appointed, in the case of sickness, accident, or absence of the clerk.'

"Unless, therefore, where the arrangement is formally agreed to by the Board of Guardians, and sanctioned by the Commissioners, it would not be lawful for the clerk to appoint a substitute. The office of clerk to the Guardians is one entirely of personal trust and confidence. If the Guardians should sanction the absence of the clerk on any occasion, and accept the services of some substitute, it would not be competent to a single Guardian to enforce the withdrawal of that substitute."

III.—INTEREST.—AS TO THE PAYMENT OF, ON ADVANCES BY A TREASURER TO A BOARD OF GUARDIANS.—STOURBRIDGE UNION.

24th November, 1842.

The Commissioners took into consideration a resolution passed by the Board of Guardians of the Stourbridge Union, applying for the sanction of the Commissioners, to allowing interest to be paid to the treasurer of the Union on money to be advanced by him to the Guardians'; and the Commissioners directed the following letter to be addressed to the Guardians in reference thereto:—

"The Commissioners are desirous that it should be clearly understood by the Guardians, that the question, whether the Guardians are, or are not, justified in borrowing money, and charging the poor-rates with interest, is one which depends entirely upon legal considerations; and is wholly unaffected by any sanction, or disapproval of the Commissioners.

"The Commissioners trust, therefore, it will be borne in mind that they are expressing, not what their wishes, or inclination might suggest, but what they are instructed to consider as the only view sanctioned by law; and, consequently, the only one which they are justified in promulgating, or the Guardians in adopting as public officers.

"If the law permitted the borrowing of money by the Guardians, the disapproval of the Commissioners would not render such a proceeding on the part of the Guardians unlawful; on the contrary, if the law did not allow of it, any sanction, or acquiescence, on the part of the Commissioners would not have the effect of rendering the act of the Guardians valid, or of shielding them from a disallowance of the charge or other consequences.

"The views which the Commissioners entertain upon the legal question are as follow:—

"The law, it may be observed, has furnished the Guardians with the requisite powers to obtain, beforehand, the funds required for the relief of the poor. The Guardians are not, in general, empowered to borrow money on the security of the rates, or to pay interest for the money borrowed. There are, however, purposes or cases, for which express statutory provision is made, in which such a power can be lawfully exercised by the Guardians. Such are the building of, or procuring workhouses under the 4th and 5th Wm. IV., c. 76; enabling poor persons to emigrate under the same Act; and the making a survey or valuation of a parish under the 6th and 7th Wm. IV., c. 96. Whether under any other circumstances, (as for instance, where the Guardians having had recourse to all the legal remedies, and completely exhausted all the stringent powers at their disposal to obtain funds from the overseers, such endeavours may have proved ineffectual,) the Guardians would be justified in borrowing money, is a point upon which no Court has as yet given a decision.

"It may be observed, however, that the necessity for a statutory enactment in these special cases, of itself raises a presumption, that no such power can exist, when not *expressly given:* and this view is strictly in conformity with the principle asserted by the Court in Tawney's case. Salk 531. 2 Ld. Raym. 1013.

"The Commissioners are thus of opinion, that where an unlimited power of demanding funds as between the Guardians and the Overseers, and an equally unlimited power to compel payment of rates, as between the overseers and ratepayers, is acknowledged to exist, and where no express statutory authority to borrow is given to either party, it cannot be safely held, that any charge can be thrown on future ratepayers by borrowing, or that interest can be charged upon the poor-rates.

"However the Commissioners may regret the present depression in trade, and the distress consequent upon that depression, the Commissioners are obliged to repeat their conviction, that this affords no valid reason in law for not compelling, by legal means, a compliance with the orders of contribution made upon the overseers. The duties of those officers to furnish, when required by the Guardians, the funds for the relief of the poor remains the same, though the difficulties in collecting the rates may be enhanced by the prevalent distress.

"Nothing can be further from the wish of the Commissioners, than to suggest or recommend harsh measures in the collection of the rates in a time of difficulty; yet, when appealed to, they can but reply, that the overseers are invested with ample powers for enforcing payment of poor-rates; and that apparent indulgence (if legal) would often terminate in causing the accumulation of an arrear to fall with double weight, in addition to the current expenditure, on ratepayers, who may be different parties from those who were parties to the charge when incurred."

IV. — PAROCHIAL DEBTS. — THE PROVISIONS OF THE ACT 5 AND 6 VIC., C. 18, IN REGARD TO THE OUT-STANDING DEBTS OF PARISHES.

The following circular is sent by the Commissioners to the Overseers of such Parishes as are known to have outstanding debts, apprizing the Overseers of the provisions made by the recent Act (5 and 6 Vic. c. 18.) for the payment of such debts.

Poor Law Commission Office,
Somerset House,
1842.

GENTLEMEN,—I am directed by the Poor Law Commissioners to call your attention to the provisions contained in the Act, 5 & 6 Vic., c. 18, for the discharge of debts, liabilities, and engagements incurred by or on behalf of parishes.

The 8th section provides that the payment out of the poor rates, either of principal or interest, in respect of any debt, liability, or engagement, not being at the time of the passing of the Act a subsisting legal charge on the rates, without the order of the Commissioners, shall be *unlawful*, and as such *disallowed* in the accounts of the officer paying the same.

The statute, however, provides a mode for the discharge of any debt heretofore *bonâ fide* entered into by parish officers or other persons on behalf of any parish, which shall have been recognized in the year before the passing of the Poor Law Amendment Act, (that is, in the year previous to August 14, 1834,) as a parish debt, by the inhabitants assembled in vestry, or by the payment of the interest out of the poor rate.

The mode is as follows:—A meeting of rate payers and owners of property must be held, after public notice duly given, who must pass a resolution expressive of their consent to the Poor Law Commissioners issuing an order directing the Overseers to pay or discharge the debt, either in full, or by equal annual instalments, not exceeding ten.

Such resolution should state whether the Overseers are to pay the debt at once, or borrow the amount, and charge the same on the poor rates.

A copy of the resolution under the hands of the overseers must be forwarded to the Poor Law Commissioners, and they will issue an order directing the payment of the debt accordingly, provided they shall be satisfied that it constitutes a fair and just claim against the parish, and shall approve of and sanction its discharge.

The Commissioners learn from the return, a copy of which is sent to you on the other half sheet (see Return, p. 21), that there is an outstanding debt claimed against the poor rates of your parish, and the Commissioners wish to know whether the particulars given in such Return are correct, and whether the rate-payers are willing to provide for the discharge of the debt in the manner already pointed out. If such be the wish of the rate-payers, the Commissioners will, upon hearing from you, transmit to you the forms (see pp. 21—23) necessary to be observed, in order to meet the provisions of the Statute.

But I am to caution you that the debt in question appears to be one, the payment whereof, or of any interest thereon, out of the poor rates, will be unlawful, unless an order be obtained as mentioned above.

I am, &c.
W. G. LUMLEY *Assistant Secretary.*

To the Overseers of the Poor.

COPY RETURN.

County of ______________ Parish, Township, or other Place* . . } of ______________

Hundred, or other similar Division } of ______________ ______________ *Union.*

Whether any, and if any, what Amount of Debt was claimed against the Poor-Rates on the 14th of August, 1834, the date of the passing of the Poor Law Amendment Act.	Whether secured by Gilbert's Bond or other legal Charge on the Poor Rates.	Whether secured by Note or Bill given by Parish Officers or others, on behalf of the Parish, not being a legal charge on the Poor Rates.	Consideration of the Debt.	Purpose for which the Debt was incurred.	If the Debt has been paid, how and when was it paid.	If not paid, Names of the holders, and Names of parties liable.

Signed this 　　 *day of* 　　 184

____

Overseers of the Poor.

The following are the forms referred to in the above circular :—

A.

Proceedings under 5 and 6 Vic., c. 18.

Notice of Meeting to consent to Liquidation of Debt.

* ______________ *of* ______________ }
______________ '*Union*, }
County of ______________ }

NOTICE is hereby given, that a Meeting of the Rate-payers in this* and of the Owners of Property therein entitled to vote in person, or (as respects Owners) by proxy, pursuant to the provisions of an Act passed in the 5th year of the reign of his late Majesty King William IV., intituled "*An Act for the Amendment and better Administration of the Laws relating to the Poor in England and Wales,*" will be held at 　　 in this* 　　, on† 　　 the 　　 day of 　　, at 　　 o'clock in the 　　 noon, for the purpose of giving the consent of such Meeting to the Poor Law Commissioners issuing an Order under their hands and seal directing the Overseers to pay out of the Poor-rates the following debt, that is to say—‡

Dated this 　　 day of 　　, 184

______________ } *Churchwardens.*
______________ }

______________ } *Overseers.*
______________ }

* Insert here "parish" or "township" as the case may be.
† Three clear days' notice is requisite: the notice being affixed on the church door on a Sunday, the meeting cannot be legally held earlier than the following Thursday.
‡ Here state the debt, and the party to whom it is now due.

B.

Resolution of Meeting consenting to discharge a Debt, to be entered in the Vestry Book.

* ______________ *of* ______________
______________________________ *Union,*
County of ______________________________

AT a Meeting of the Rate-payers of the * of , and Owners of Property therein entitled to vote pursuant to the provisions of an Act passed in the 5th year of the reign of His late Majesty King William IV., intituled, "*An Act for the Amendment and better Administration of the Laws relating to the Poor in England and Wales,*" held at in the said* on the day of 184 pursuant to Notice of such Meeting duly given, ______________________ *Chairman,*

It was Resolved, that this Meeting do consent to the Poor Law Commissioners issuing an Order under their hands and Seal, directing the Overseers of the Poor of the said* under the power given by the several statutes in this behalf † the following debt, that is to say ;—‡

For the above Resolution.

Signatures.	Number of Votes as Owner or Proxy.	Number of Votes as Rate-payer.

Against the above Resolution.

Signatures.	Number of Votes as Owner or Proxy.	Number of Votes as Rate-payer.

(Signed) ______________________ *Chairman.*

____
______________________ *Churchwardens.*

____
______________________ *Overseers.*

* Insert here "parish" or "township," as the case may be.

† *If it be intended to pay the debt at once out of the poor rates, insert here* " to pay out of the poor rates of the said* forthwith."

Or,

† *If it be intended to pay the debt out of the poor rates by annual instalments, insert* " by equal annual instalments," *which instalments must not exceed* TEN.

Or,

† *If it be intended to borrow the sum requisite to discharge the debt, insert* " to borrow the sum of , and to charge the poor rates of the said* with the repayment thereof, and the interest thereof by equal annual instalments, and thereupon forthwith to apply the said sum in payment of " *The annual instalments in this case must not exceed* TEN *in number.*

‡ Here state the debt, to whom and how it is secured, when and for what purpose it was incurred, and the party to whom it is now due.

C.

Certificate of Minister, Churchwardens, and Overseers of the Forms of Act having been complied with.

* ______________ *of* ______________
______________ *Union,*
County of ______________

WE hereby certify, that at a Meeting of the Rate-payers of the said* , and Owners of Property therein entitled to vote, held at in the said* , on the day of the Resolution, of which a true copy is hereunto annexed, was duly passed. And we do further certify and declare, that such Meeting was duly convened and held for the purpose expressed in such Resolution, after public notice of the time and place of holding such Meeting, and the purpose for which the same was intended to be held, had been given in like manner as Notices of Vestry Meetings are given in the said* . And we further certify, that the paper marked A, hereunto annexed, and signed by us, is a true copy of the Notice of such Meeting, and that such Notice, fairly† , was affixed on the day of on the principal door of the‡ of the said* ; and that the paper hereto annexed, marked B, and signed by us, is a true extract from the Vestry Books of the said* .

Dated this day of , 184

______________ *Minister.*

____
______________ *Churchwardens.*

____
______________ *Overseers.*

* Insert here "parish" or "township," as the case may be. † "Written" or "printed." ‡ "Church" or "Chapel."

V.—PAUPERS.—AS TO THE POWER TO CONVICT PAUPERS ABSCONDING FROM THE WORKHOUSE WITH UNION CLOTHING NOT MARKED WITH THE WORD "WORKHOUSE."—NEWPORT UNION, SALOP.

19*th September*, 1842.

The Commissioners took into consideration a letter, addressed to them by the clerk of the Newport Union, Salop, of which letter the following is an extract:—

"Two boys of the name of Cadman, in the month of February last, absconded from the workhouse, taking with them, not only the Union clothing, but also clothes belonging to paupers then in the house. They have eluded the officers from that time till this last week, when they were apprehended. This is their second offence. The clothes they had on were marked 'Newport Union.' I applied to the magistrates to have them summarily convicted under the 55th Geo. III. c. 137, s. 2, but it was objected, that as the word 'workhouse' was not marked also on the clothes, that the magistrates had not any jurisdiction: on reference to that section of the Act, you will see that the 'goods,' &c. are to be marked, stamped, or branded with the word 'workhouse,' and such other mark, &c. The magistrates upon this refused to convict; but have adjourned the case at my request until I could write and obtain from you your opinion whether such omission of the word 'workhouse' on the clothes took the case out of the operation of the statute.

"Arising out of the above case, is the following, upon which also, you will oblige me by letting me have your opinion:—

"The mother of the two boys lives at Stafford; and she is a most abandoned character. It appears from the evidence, that the two boys some time after their desertion, or immediately after it, went home to her: I have no doubt but that they absconded at her instigation. Amongst the articles of clothing taken by the boys when they absconded, was a smock frock marked also 'Newport Union' very plainly. This smock frock, the mother of the boys, (and as they say unknown to them) took to a pawn shop, and exchanged for a shirt, which she applied to her own purposes. Upon this coming to the knowledge of the Guardians, at their request, I have had her apprehended also; and I applied to the magistrates at the same time to have her summarily convicted under the 2nd section of the 55th Geo. III. c. 137, but the same objection was taken, namely, that as the word 'workhouse' was not marked on it, the magistrates had not jurisdiction. This case was at my request also adjourned; and as was also the charge against the pawnbroker who received the smock frock, and who under that section is liable to a penalty of 5*l*., or, in default, to two months' imprisonment.

"Should you be of opinion that as the word 'workhouse' is not marked on the clothes, that the magistrates have no jurisdiction, then, with regard to the mother, could not she be proceeded against for illegally pawning; or, would it be best to commit the boys for stealing, and the mother for receiving, or cannot they be convicted under the Vagrant Act."

The Commissioners directed the following reply to be made to this letter:—

"I am to state for the information of the Guardians, that the Commissioners are decidedly of opinion that both the classes of penalties provided by the 2nd section of the 55 Geo. III, c. 137, apply to the 'goods,' 'clothes,' 'wearing apparel,' and other things enumerated, whether they be marked, or be not marked, or be not capable of being marked.

"The first provision in the section casts a duty on overseers and others to mark such goods, &c. 'capable of being marked, and from time to time belonging to such overseers.' The marking is a substantive duty cast by the clause on the overseers, and is evidently no part of the description of the 'goods,' &c. with respect to which the duty is imposed.

"The second provision in the section, by which persons receiving, knowingly, any 'goods,' &c. are rendered liable to penalties, does nothing to make the marking a part of the description of the 'goods,' &c. as it might easily have done if such had been the intention, by the insertion of the words 'so marked;' but on the contrary, it provides quite a new description of the 'goods,' &c.much larger than the description in the preceding provision. It does not by any words of reference, 'such,' or, 'aforesaid,' adopt the preceding description; it omits the restriction to such kinds of goods as are 'capable of being marked;' and it enlarges the class beyond the goods 'belonging to the overseers,' so as to include all the goods 'provided for the use of the poor;' whether such goods belong or not to the overseers. The reason of this enlargement of terms is also very apparent, for if a person 'knowingly' receive such 'goods, &c.' it would certainly be unreasonable to afford him impunity merely on the ground that the goods were not capable of being marked, or had not yet been marked, through want of time or attention in the overseers. The Commissioners think, therefore, that this provision clearly extends to 'goods,' &c. whether marked, or not marked, or not capable of being marked; in fact, that the marking is immaterial to the offence.

"If this be so, then it seems to follow, partly for the same reasons, and partly for the additional reason that the words, 'as aforesaid,' are, by the established rules of construction, to be referred to the antecedent immediately preceding, that the offence of carrying away 'goods,' &c. applies to the whole of the more ample description given in the second provision, and not to the more limited description given in the first. But even if this provision applied to the description of goods, &c. given in the first, that would not involve the necessity that the goods should be marked: that, as before observed, not being part of the description of the goods, &c. given in the first provision, but the substantive matter of enactment in that provision.

"And there is no apparent reason why the offence should be dependent on the marking: an inmate of the workhouse can be made no more conscious of the right of the Union to the goods, &c. by the marking, than he is without the marking; and certainly the danger to be guarded against is greater in the case of unmarked, and unmarkable goods, than in others more easily identified. If the entire absence of the mark is immaterial to the offence, the informal marking must be immaterial. The Commissioners conclude, therefore, that in the case stated an offence has been committed under the statute by the paupers, in carrying away the clothes; by the mother, in receiving them; and by the pawnbroker, in taking them in pledge; notwithstanding the informal marking of the clothes.

"But as regards the evidence of the offence, the Commissioners think that the clothes were not marked in compliance with the statute; that the omission of the word 'workhouse,' is informal; and, therefore, that other proof besides the mark is necessary to establish the property of the overseers in the goods, if proceedings be taken involving the question of property. This remark, however, does not apply to the offence under the statute, as that is complete if the goods were 'provided for the use of the poor,' although they do not belong to the overseers.

"If a summary conviction should not, however, be obtained, it appears to the Commissioners that the taking away of the smock frock not given to the paupers, was a larceny; and that they are indictable for that, and their mother, probably, as an accessary.

"The 30 Geo. II., c. 24, s. 7, as to pawning of stolen goods, does not appear to apply to the mother's case. The Commissioners do not know of any provision in the Vagrant Act under which the parties could be convicted."

VI.—POOR-RATE.—As to the Duty of Justices to allow the Rate.—Wigan Borough.

9th March, 1842.

The Commissioners took into consideration the following letter, addressed to them by John Acton, Esq., of Wigan:—

"As a magistrate for this borough, I am called upon occasionally by the overseers of the poor to sign a new rate when a preceding rate may not have been wholly collected; and I have always understood, that magistrates are bound to allow such new rate, whether the old rate has been fully collected or not.

"A Treatise by a Mr. Thomas Newbold, published in 1839, has been handed to me, in the Appendix to which appears an 'instructional letter to the churchwardens, overseers, and other officers required to account for the expenditure of the poor-rate,' and purporting to have been issued from the 'Poor Law Commission Office, Somerset House.'

"The 12th section of that letter (in page, of the Treatise, 164) after speaking of deductions in collection of rates, and as to arrears, proceeds thus:—

"You must be prepared with evidence to establish the grounds for these deductions from the full amount of the rate allowed; and until the rate already allowed has been fully collected, no new rate must be applied for; and if applied for in any case, *the justices are bound to withhold their sanction, and to require that the whole of the old rate should be first collected and accounted for.*

"This appears to be so much at variance with what has been hitherto, here, considered to be the law of the case, that I should feel obliged if you would inform me, by what authorities the Commissioners have been guided, in stating that justices are bound to withhold their sanction as mentioned in the instruction above referred to."

And the Commissioners directed the following answer to be given thereto:—

"In the concise directions contained in the instructional letter cited by you, the duty of the justices to withhold their allowance of a new rate while a previous rate is uncollected, is stated in too broad and unqualified a manner.

"The more complete expression of what the Commissioners are advised is the law on the subject is as follows:—

"The duty of the justices is, except as to the duty of seeing that a rate is made on the estimate of net annual value defined by the 6 and 7 Wm. IV., c. 96, s. 1, (Parochial Assessments Act,) still ministerial, that is to say, the justices must allow the rate whenever the occasion arises for a rate, and such rate is presented for allowance in proper form by persons entitled to make it; and they cannot withhold their allowance on any grounds tryable judicially. But this does not involve the consequence that the justices are to allow every rate which overseers may please to bring before them, whether there be occasion for a rate or not. A ministerial duty in the case of a justice is not distinguished by any statute or decision nor by principle from any other merely ministerial (*i. e.* non-judicial) duty of any other officer. The duty of all officers is to act when the legal necessity or occasion for their acting arises, and it is at their peril that they then refuse to act. But without express provision to the contrary, every independent officer is bound to satisfy himself of the occasion to act; and is not to be governed in that by the pleasure of any other person. To act without occasion, often as much exposes the officer to penalty, as to refuse to act when there is occasion. In this sense it is the duty of the justices to see that the occasion for the allowance of a rate has arisen before they allow it; but being satisfied that some rate is reasonably required, they cannot use a judicial discretion, anticipating the remedy by appeal, and disallow it on any ground of which judicial cognizance can be taken, and on which a judicial remedy can be afforded.

"According to this view is the practice with regard to the compulsion of justices of the peace, by writs of *mandamus*, to allow a rate. The overseers show by their affidavits that they have authority, or right, generally to make a rate, and to claim the intervention of the Court. It is always upon a suggestion on oath of the party injured of his own right, and of the denial of justice, that the writ of mandamus is issued. The overseers' right is to raise competent sums of money for and towards the necessary relief of the poor; but not to raise any sums when and how he may please, more than is in reason competent. For instance, the overseers cannot show any right to make a new rate while another is in force, and only partially collected—Reg. *v.* Fordham, 3 P. and D. p. 103. If the overseers, however, can in any case show their title and the right to make a rate, and if this is not rebutted by the justices, and none but judicial reasons are stated for non-allowance of the rate by the justices, the writ is made peremptory. But if the want of right in the overseers to make a rate at all on the occasion is established by the justices, there is no provision, decision, or principle, that the Commissioners are aware of, to take the ministerial duty of justices out of the rule applicable to all other ministerial acts of public officers.

"The Commissioners are not aware of any decision expressly relating to the allowance of poor-rates by justices to the above effect. But the general rules with relation to the writ of mandamus, and all the cases on the subject of the justices' ministerial duties in relation to the allowance of poor-rates, appear to involve the reasoning stated above.

"Thus the cases, like that of *R.* v. *the Justices of Dorchester*, 1 Str. 393, where the returns of justices have been disallowed, have been cases where the justices have refused their consent to a rate on grounds tryable on appeal, *i. e.* on grounds purely judicial.

"The cases where justices have neglected or evaded the performance of their duty, without reason assigned by them, as in R. *v.* Edwards, 1 Black. Rep. 637, of course imply and admit that at least a *primâ facie* case for the performance of their duty had been made out.

"On the other hand there are cases showing that, although their duty be ministerial, the justices are bound to see that the overseers and themselves are qualified and entitled, the one to make and the other to allow the rate—R. *v.* Folly, 1 Bott. 86.

"In R. *v.* Gordon, 1 B. and Ald. 524, the Court disallowed the return of the justices, on the ground that the overseers *were* competent; but the decision implies that if they had not been competent, the justices' return to the mandamus would have been good, and their refusal to allow the rate justified.

"It is not, therefore, the ordinary ministerial discretion which justices are excluded from the use of by the decision that their duties are merely ministerial; they are only excluded by that rule from the exercise of a judicial authority.

"But the necessity of a rate, so that it be fair and equal in its imposition, is not tryable at sessions, or in any other judicial manner, and seems, like every other legal necessity for acting, to be the proper subject of consideration by the person called on to act ministerially.

"In allowing or disallowing a rate, the justices of course act on their responsibility; and it cannot be denied that, whatever may be their legal duty and responsibility for refusing their consent to a rate made by overseers without authority, justices are practically much less likely to be called on to justify an improper allowance of a rate, than to justify a proper refusal."

VII.—PROPERTY AND INCOME TAX ACT.—1. AS TO THE PAYMENT OF THE EXPENSE OF MAKING A COPY OF THE POOR RATE FOR THE PURPOSES OF THE ACT.

The following circular has been addressed by the Commissioners to the clerks of Boards of Guardians upon this subject:—

"*Poor Law Commission Office,*
"*Somerset House, 7th December,* 1842.

"SIR,—I am directed by the Poor Law Commissioners to transmit to you the accompanying copy of a letter which they have received, communicating to them the decision of the Lords Commissioners of Her Majesty's Treasury on the subject of the payment of the expense of making a copy of the last poor rate, where required, in any case, for the use of the surveyors or inspectors under the Income Tax Act.

"The Poor Law Commissioners transmit this letter to the Board of Guardians for their information, and in order that they may be enabled to make known the effect of it to the overseers, auditor, and other persons interested in the matter.

"I am, Sir,
"Your most obedient servant,
"EDWIN CHADWICK, *Secretary.*
"*The Clerk to the Guardians.*"

" *Treasury, 29th November*, 1842.

"GENTLEMEN,—The Lords Commissioners of Her Majesty's Treasury having considered your memorial, requesting to be informed whether the overseers are 'officers employed in the execution of the Property Tax Act;' and also, whether the words 'incident charges and expenses attending the execution of the Act,' apply to expenses which the overseers may incur in giving effect to certain sections of the Act, I am directed to acquaint you, that their lordships are of opinion, that overseers of the poor do not come within the term of 'officers employed in the execution of the Act,' and that neither do the expenses which such overseers incur, in giving effect to the 75th and 76th section of the Act, fall within the meaning of the words 'incident charges and expenses attending the execution of the Act.' My lords, nevertheless, consider it but reasonable that where the overseers have been called upon by the surveyors of taxes for a copy of the last rate made for the relief of the poor, and have actually furnished the same, to assist the surveyor in checking the assessment, the amount of the expenses of such copy should be paid, and their lordships have authorized the Commissioners of Stamps and Taxes to pay the same accordingly.

" I am, Gentlemen,
" Your obedient servant,
(Signed) " C. E. TREVELYAN.

" *The Poor Law Commissioners.*"

---

2. ASSESSMENT OF THE SALARIES OF UNION OFFICERS, AND THE INTEREST ON WORKHOUSE LOANS, TO THE INCOME TAX. — BOSTON UNION.

5th October, 1842.

The Commissioners having received a letter from the clerk of the Guardians of the Boston Union, respecting the mode in which the salaries payable to the several officers of that Union were to be brought into charge under the Property and Income Tax Act, and in what manner the interest payable on account of the workhouse loan was to be assessed, referred the inquiry to the Commissioners of Stamps and Taxes, who sent the following letter in reply, which the Commissioners directed should be communicated to the clerk of the Guardians:—

" *Stamps and Taxes, London,*
" *14th September*, 1842.

" SIR,—Having laid before the Board your letter of the 3rd instant, I am directed to inform you that if an assessment is not made on the clerks of the several Unions by the Commissioners appointed by the Poor Law Commissioners for assessing the duties on the salaries of their several officers, such clerks must make a return of their salaries and emoluments, and be assessed at the places where the duties of the office are executed.

" With respect to your other question, I have to state that, if the interest of the money is not paid out of profits and gains liable to be assessed to the property tax, it must be paid in full, and the mortgagee or creditor must return and be assessed for the same, unless the money is charged on the poor rates, in which case you will find, on reference to section 102 of the Act, that the officer having the management of the accounts must be charged with the duty on the interest.

" I am, Sir,
" Your obedient servent,
(Signed)" T. SARGENT, *for the Secretary.*

" *W. G. Lumley, Esq.*"

---

3. AS TO THE ASSESSMENT OF THE UNION WORKHOUSE TO THE PROPERTY TAX.—TICEHURST UNION.

30th December, 1842.

The Commissioners took into consideration a letter received from the clerk of the Ticehurst Union, inquiring, first, whether the workhouse of the Union, and the land belonging thereto, are liable to be assessed under the Property Tax Act; second, and, if so, whether the sum at which the same are assessed to the poor-rates is the amount at which they should be assessed to the property tax; and the Commissioners directed the following answer to be given thereto:—

" I am to state, in reply, that there is no express exemption of workhouses, or of any similar property, from the tax referred to; and they appear to be included in the general terms of the descriptions, in sec. 1, of the properties liable, under Schedule A, in respect of the *proprietorship;* and of the properties liable, under Schedule B, in respect of the *occupation.* Under these general provisions, the workhouse seems to be taxable in the hands of the Guardians of the Ticehurst Union, both as proprietors and occupiers; in the former character, at *7d.* in the pound, and in the latter, at *3½d.* in the pound. With regard to the question, whether the sum at which the workhouse is assessed in the valuation to the poor-rate is the proper sum at which such workhouse should be charged, I am to state, that it is liable, under sec. 60, Schedule A, No. 1, to be assessed on the rack-rent: the Commissioners understand this to be such a rent as the Guardians would pay to a landlord for the use of the workhouse, supposing it were let to them; the Guardians paying the tenants' rates and taxes, and tithe commutation rent-charge, if any."

---

4. AS TO WHETHER A WORKHOUSE MASTER IS LIABLE TO PAY THE INCOME TAX IN RESPECT OF HIS OCCUPATION OF PART OF THE WORKHOUSE, &c.—WINDSOR UNION.

3rd December, 1842.

The Commissioners took into consideration a letter on this subject, addressed to them by the clerk to the Windsor Union, and they directed the following reply to be given thereto:—

"I am to state that the fact that the workhouse was mortgaged,* would make no difference in the liability of the Guardians unless the mortgagee were in possession; in which case, such mortgagee would be chargeable as landlord, and if also in occupation, then also as occupier.

"As regards the claim on the master of the workhouse of duty on his occupation, it may be the case that the workhouse master may have such an exclusive use given to him of some portion of the workhouse, as to constitute him an occupier of a tenement within the ordinary sense of the word, and of the meaning of the 63rd section, schedule B, No. IX., Art. 2 [of the Income Tax Act]: but generally, the occupation of workhouse master is such only as amounts to the occupation by the Guardians; like the occupation of ordinary servants. It is rarely that his occupation is of any hiring which could be considered as a separate tenement. In these cases the Commissioners presume that the claim could not be supported. But supposing that the master is liable for his occupation of any tenement, distinct from the occupation of the Guardians, it is clear that in that case, the Guardians are not also occupiers of the same tenement, and would be entitled as occupiers to a reduction of the charge on them to the same extent as the workhouse master would be liable."

* This refers to the charge on the poor rates for the money expended in building the workhouse.

VIII.—RATING.—AS TO THE LIABILITY OF OCCUPIERS OF COUNTING HOUSES TO BE RATED TO THE RELIEF OF THE POOR.—ALLHALLOWS, LONDON WALL.

12th December, 1842.

The Commissioners took into consideration the following letter addressed to them by Mr. Barton, the vestry clerk of the parish of Allhallows, London Wall:—

"Certain occupiers of counting-houses in this parish, some time since, claimed to be rated to the relief of the poor in respect of such counting-houses under the 30th section of the Reform Act, 2nd Wm. IV. cap. 45, for the purpose of entitling them to vote for Members of Parliament, under the 27th section, and the overseers considered they were bound to assess them in pursuance of such claim, and did accordingly assess them in three several rates, which were duly allowed and published, but without making any alteration in the assessment on the tenants of the whole house.

"The poor-rate in the City of London is made under the 43rd Eliz., cap. 2, and there is no provision made in that Act for rating parts of a house, such as counting-houses, &c.; but the Reform Act, 2nd Wm. IV., cap. 45, it is contended, has established a new species of rating in respect of such persons claiming to be rated, and that unless the Act intends that such parties should be *bonâ fide* rated and actually pay the rate, it means nothing. On the other hand, it is contended by the claimants that when a claim is made by any occupier of a counting-house, the overseers are either to rate them jointly with the occupier of the whole house, or to rate them for the counting-houses at *10l.*, whatever the rent paid for the same may be, and deduct that rating from the rating of their lessor, or that the name of such claimant is to be put on the rate, but without any assessment being made on them.

"The overseers contend, that they would not be justified in rating an occupier of a counting-house jointly with his immediate lessor for the whole house, inasmuch as they are not joint tenants, and could not be sued jointly for the rate. In the second case, that independently of the occupiers of counting-houses not being assessed upon an estimate of the net annual value, as required by the Parochial Assessment Act, 6th and 7th Wm. IV. cap. 96, if the occupiers of counting-houses quit without paying the rate, there are no means of recovering from the lessor more than the amount to which he individually is rated; and thirdly, if the name of the claimant is merely placed on the rate, without any assessment being made on him, it is not a compliance with the 30th section of the Reform Act; the proviso at the end of that section, 'that where by virtue of any Act of Parliament the landlord shall be liable to the payment of the rate in respect of premises occupied by his tenant, such liability shall still continue,' does not apply in this instance, inasmuch as there is no local Act for this parish, nor are they (the landlords) liable under the 19th section of 59th Geo. III. cap. 12.

"There are now three rates due from the occupiers of these counting-houses, amounting in the whole to upwards of 50*l*., and the overseers request to be informed—

"1st. Whether they are to proceed to enforce the rate, and if not, how the rate is to be got rid of, the overseers having no power to excuse or abandon the rate, nor have the justices any such power, except in cases of poverty. No appeal against either of the rates have been made to the Quarter Sessions; and

"2ndly. How the occupiers of these counting-houses are to be placed on the future rates."

And the Commissioners directed the following answer to be given thereto:—

"1st. The Commissioners will first advert to the duties of the overseers in this matter, as the Commissioners understand the provisions of the Act, 2nd Wm. IV., c. 45, s. 30, with a view to the guidance of the overseers for the future.

"In the cities and boroughs referred to in the Act, it is open to every person occupying a counting-house, shop, &c., to claim to be rated.

"But it is not made the duty of the overseer to put the name of such an occupier on the rate, until the latter has paid, or tendered the amount of rate due. Moreover, the duty of rating such an occupier only extends to the rate for *the time being*, when the claim and tender of payment is made.

"It is, therefore, wholly within the overseers' power for the future to protect the parish from loss, by abstaining from putting the occupiers of the class in question on the rate, until a full tender is made of the current rate.

"2nd. Next, as to the case where an occupier of a shop, counting-house, &c., has once claimed under the provision of the Act, and his claim has been acquiesced in, and he has been rated accordingly in the then current rate but he has not paid that rate.

"The Commissioners think there is no ground whatever for doubting that the occupier of such a shop, counting-house, &c., is liable to pay the rate. His claim is 'to be rated to the relief of the poor, &c.' It is a condition expressly imposed on him that he should pay, or tender to pay, the full amount of the rate in force.

"The intention that such occupier should pay the rate appears, therefore, to be manifest and indisputable.

"You state that the occupiers in arrear contend, that they should be rated jointly with the occupier of the whole house. The Commissioners can discover no such intention in the Act; but, on the contrary, the terms of the Act show that the payment is to be several and personal to the occupier of the shop, &c., and, as you observe, the occupier and the occupiers of the rest of the house are not joint tenants or tenants in common, and cannot be therefore sued jointly.

"As regards the claim of those occupiers to be rated at only 10*l*. per annum, whatever may be the value of the part of the house they occupy, this again appears to be entirely inconsistent with the terms of the Act, which require, as a condition of their being rated, a tender of the rate or rates due in respect of their premises.

"With respect to the proviso at the end of the 30th clause, it is evidently applicable only to cases where landlords, not being the occupying tenants, are rateable either under the 59th Geo. III., c. 12, s. 19, or under a Local Act, and has no reference whatever to cases where the *occupying* tenant of the whole house remains rateable.

"The Commissioners, therefore, think that the occupiers of shops, counting-houses, &c., in the cases described, can be proceeded against for arrears under the 43rd Eliz., c. 2, s. 4, in the same manner as if they were occupiers of an entire and distinct property of the same value. The Commissioners are also of opinion that the proviso not applying to those cases, if the occupier of a shop or counting-house neglect to pay, the occupier of the rest of the house cannot be made liable for the rate in respect of the shop or counting-house.

"3. But where an occupier has claimed to be rated in one rate, and has, without a subsequent claim, been rated by the overseers in a subsequent rate, it appears to the Commissioners that there is great doubt whether the sum for which such occupier has been so subsequently rated is recoverable.

"Without an actual claim to be rated, and tender of payment of rate, an occupier of a part of a house is not rateable. The overseer has no general power to rate such an occupier but on that claim. The claim can only be made to be rated on the current rate. The claim to be rated in the rate would not appear to give an authority to the overseer to rate the same person in any subsequent rate, whether that person desired it or not.

"If the overseers have no authority to rate such an occupier in a rate made subsequently to his claim, then it would appear that such rating is void. It does not require to be appealed against, but the person so rated may have his action if he be distrained on for the rate.

"In such a case the overseers cannot claim to be paid by the tenant of the whole house, inasmuch as he is not rated.

"Accordingly, the Commissioners are of opinion that, in such a case, the rate is wholly irrecoverable."

IX. — RELIEVING OFFICER'S DUTIES.—As to the Power of a Relieving Officer to vary Relief ordered by the Guardians.—Kingsbridge Union.

28th November, 1842.

The Commissioners took into consideration a letter received from W. J. Clark, Esq., the chairman of the Board of Guardians of the Kingsbridge Union, requesting the Commissioners' opinion whether a relieving officer can, upon his own authority, alter or discontinue the amount of relief ordered in any case by the Board of Guardians without first obtaining their permission to do so; and the Commissioners directed the following answer to be given thereto:—

"I am to state in reply, that the Commissioners were aware of the possibility of the question arising, as to the power of the relieving officer to vary the relief ordered by the Guardians during the intervals between the meetings of the Board, when they framed Article 10 of the relieving officer's duties, by which the relieving officer is required to supply to the paupers the amount of the weekly allowances ordered by the Board.

"The intention of that Article, was to make it the duty of the relieving officer to fulfil the legal orders of the Guardians, and it follows from that, that the officer can only justify a departure from those orders by shewing either,

"1st, Obvious and manifest fraud on the part of the pauper; or,

"2nd, A cessation of the circumstances under which the relief was given, as in the case of illness.

"If the relieving officer withhold the relief, he must be prepared to prove most clearly that one of these two reasons existed to justify him in doing so; and he must, like other functionaries, occasionally incur some responsibility in unforeseen circumstances. The Commissioners think a medical certificate would be almost indispensable when the ground for withholding the relief ordered was the cessation of the illness of the pauper.

"With regard to increasing the relief, in any case he has the power to allow additional relief, in kind, in cases of sudden and urgent necessity."

X.—RELIEVING OFFICER'S DIARY.—St. Columb Major Union.

23rd February, 1842.

The Commissioners took into consideration a resolution passed by the Board of Guardians of the St. Columb Major Union, in which they expressed their opinion that it was not necessary for the relieving officer of that Union to keep a diary; and the Commissioners directed the following reply to be sent to the clerk of the Board:—

"I am to state that the Commissioners have not required, by their Order, that a diary should be kept by each relieving officer; but they still consider such a record of his proceedings generally desirable, as affording some check upon the officer in the performance of his duties, and exhibiting to the Guardians, from time to time, the course of his proceedings more explicitly and satisfactorily than a verbal explanation to the Board would be likely to do. The Commissioners have no wish to prescribe any particular form of diary; and if that which has been submitted to the Guardians is considered too voluminous, they would request their attention to a form given in the Appendix to their Seventh Annual Report (p. 190), which may be more simple, and may nevertheless be sufficient to answer the intended object."

XI.—REMOVAL.—OFFICERS INDICTABLE FOR CAUSING AN UNLAWFUL REMOVAL.—KEYNSHAM UNION.

20*th December*, 1842.

The Commissioners took into consideration a letter addressed to them by the clerk of the Keynsham Union, charging the relieving officer of the Pontypool Union, and one of the overseers of the parish of Usk, in that Union, with having given money to a pauper who had been deserted by her husband (whose settlement was unknown), to induce her to remove with her children to the parish of Mangotsfield, in the Keynsham Union, which was alleged to be her maiden parish, and inquiring whether an indictment could be sustained against the parties for a conspiracy to get rid of the pauper without taking the legal steps for that purpose; and the Commissioners directed the following answer to be given to the letter:—

"The Commissioners think it only necessary to observe that the application of that course of proceeding [an indictment] to a case like the present, appears to be decided by the cases of Rex *v.* Edwards, 1 Bott. 374; Rex *v.* Busby, 1 Bott. 375; Rex *v.* Tarrant, 1 Bott. 379; Rex *v.* Compton, 1 Bott. 383.

"But, in framing an indictment, reference should be had to the case of Rex *v.* Seward, Ad. and Ell. 706. It is true, that that case is not founded on the misconduct of officers in applying poor-rates to a purpose to which they are not legally applicable, and thereby bringing about immediately an unlawful charge on another parish, but was a case, where private parishioners gave from their private income a sum to encourage a pauper to marry a woman constructively chargeable, with a view to enable her to obtain a legal settlement in another parish, whereby a possibility of additional burden was incurred by that parish. The case is different in its nature from the present, but it will indicate the necessity of showing in the indictment that the means employed (the payment of parochial money for the purpose) was itself unlawful, and perhaps also of showing that the result sought (the effecting of a burden without a preceding settlement) was unlawful."

XII.—WORKHOUSE RULES.—1. DUTIES OF CHAPLAIN.—MODIFICATION OF THE COMMISSIONERS' REMARKS ON ARTICLE 31.—EASTRY UNION.

20*th December*, 1842.

The Commissioners took into consideration a letter addressed to them by the Rev. Charles Chambers, the chaplain of the Eastry Union workhouse, on the subject of the Commissioners' remarks on Article 31 of the General Workhouse Rules, and the Commissioners directed that the following answer should be given thereto:—

"I am directed by the Commissioners to state that they are prepared to modify those remarks in the following manner:—

"The Commissioners think that the pauper inmates of a workhouse should be allowed to receive the Holy Communion at the parish church, if not always, at least on the great festivals of Easter and Christmas; and that where there is no workhouse chapel used exclusively for the purpose of divine worship, this rite should not be administered in the workhouse, except to sick and disabled paupers.

"Where, however, there is a workhouse chapel, the Commissioners think that the Communion might be celebrated in it without impropriety, with the consent of the bishop of the diocese; but even in that case the Commissioners think that those inmates who desire it, should be allowed to attend the parish church to receive the sacrament at Easter and Christmas. At the same time, if the bishop of the diocese sanction the administration of the sacrament exclusively in the workhouse, the Commissioners consider this approbation a sufficient authority for the chaplain."

2. DUTIES OF MASTER.—CONSTRUCTION OF ARTICLE 23.—ELLESMERE UNION.

19*th July*, 1842.

The Commissioners took into consideration a letter addressed to them by the master of the Ellesmere Union Workhouse, inquiring how he should act in the case of a pauper who is not able-bodied, having a family, and wishing to quit the workhouse, leaving such family behind him, Article 23 of the general workhouse rules, appearing to apply only to the cases of able-bodied paupers having families; and the Commissioners directed the following reply to be given thereto:—

"The general rule is, that when the head of the family, whether able-bodied or not, requires to leave the workhouse, he should only be allowed to do so on the condition that he take his family with him. But the Board of Guardians, under the 23rd Article of the Workhouse Rules, can dispense with this condition, without special directions, in the case of the families of paupers not able-bodied; whereas in the case of able-bodied paupers, they can only let them out without their families in special cases, and for special reasons.

"As regards the workhouse master, his rule of conduct, under the 23rd Article, is this:—1st, With regard to the families of paupers not able-bodied: in the absence of all instructions from the Guardians, they must accompany the head of the family, if he or she leave the house; but the master may receive and act upon a general instruction to the contrary, either to let a particular family, or a class of families, remain in the house when the head is allowed to go out. 2nd, With regard to the able-bodied: the rule is, now that the master cannot receive a general instruction, to let a particular person leave the house from time to time without his family, but he must have a special instruction in every case, which instruction the Article 23 enables the Guardians to give wherever special reasons apply."

---

3. DUTIES OF PORTER. — CONSTRUCTION OF ARTICLE 79, NO. 2.—BAKEWELL UNION.

25th April, 1842.

The Commissioners took into consideration a letter addressed to them by the master of the Bakewell Union Workhouse, inquiring whether the master and matron come within the operation of No. 2, Article 79, of the General Workhouse Rules, which requires the porter to keep a book in which he shall enter the name and business of every officer and other person who shall go into the workhouse; when the Commissioners directed the inquiry to be answered in the affirmative.

---

4. DUTIES OF SCHOOLMISTRESS.—PUNISHMENT OF FEMALE CHILDREN.

27th May, 1842.

The Commissioners having taken into consideration a letter on this subject, received from the clerk of the Abingdon Union, directed the following communication to be addressed to him in reply:—

"The Poor Law Commissioners acknowledge the receipt of your letter of the 19th instant, in reply to their letter of the 14th instant, in which they inquired, what portions of the workhouse regulations were supposed to have caused the derangement of discipline in the Abingdon Union Workhouse, and stating that the compliance of the schoolmistress with the 12th rule which prohibits corporal punishment on female children in the workhouse having been made known to them, has caused such inmates to be exceedingly refractory and ungovernable, and that they have gone so far as to say that they dare not be chastised, even though they had committed an offence which called for correction.

"Upon such a representation of the state of the workhouse school, the Commissioners must observe, that they would be led to suppose one or both of two things, either that an undue use had been made of corporal punishment before the issue of their rules, and too much reliance placed on what ought to be last resorted to, or that the schoolmistress is incapable of acquiring that influence over the minds and tempers of the children which is essential to a proper fulfilment of her duties. In either case, it is apparent to the Commissioners that her competence would be, at least, doubtful.

"In prohibiting corporal punishments of female children, the Commissioners know that some difficulty will arise from time to time; but they think this difficulty a less evil than the risk of undue punishment of this class, or even of the apprehension of such punishment in the case of children whose comparatively friendless state, requires great vigilance on the part of those who act as their legal guardians."

LONDON:

Printed, by Order of the Poor Law Commissioners, by W. CLOWES and SONS, Stamford Street, and Published by CHARLES KNIGHT and Co., 22, Ludgate Street, Publishers to the Poor Law Commissioners.

AN

OFFICIAL CIRCULAR

OF PUBLIC DOCUMENTS AND INFORMATION:

DIRECTED BY THE POOR LAW COMMISSIONERS TO BE PRINTED, CHIEFLY FOR THE USE OF THE MEMBERS AND PERMANENT OFFICERS OF BOARDS OF GUARDIANS, UNDER THE POOR LAW AMENDMENT ACT.

No. 23. CIRCULAR ISSUED FEBRUARY 13, 1843.

Poor Law Commission Office,
Somerset House,
13*th February*, 1843.

THE Poor Law Commissioners, on a review of their Minutes, directed that the Minutes of Correspondence on the following subjects be printed and circulated for the information of Guardians and Officers of the several Unions, viz.:—

By Order of the Board,
EDWIN CHADWICK, *Secretary.*

I.—ACCOUNTS.

1. AS TO THE ALLOWANCE OF BILLS FOR LAW EXPENSES IN PAROCHIAL ACCOUNTS.

May 30th, 1842.

The Commissioners took into consideration a report of Mr. Johnson, district auditor of Unions in Devonshire, respecting his late audit, in which he remarks as follows:—

"During my late audit I have had to pass several bills for law charges, incurred in cases of disputed settlements of paupers. They have all been brought to me, sanctioned by the ratepayers legally convened at vestry meetings, but not taxed. Finding on inquiry that it is not usual to tax bills of costs between attorney and client, or between party and party; and, that the reason given is the great expense of taxation, I have ventured to pass the bills, and hope you will not disapprove of what I have done, as I observe in one of your authorized publications that auditors have a discretionary power to do so, when the bills of costs are small, as they were in those cases to which I have alluded."

And the Commissioners directed the following communication to be made to Mr. Johnson in regard to this part of his report:—

"With reference to your observations on the subject of the taxation of the bills of attornies employed by parish officers, I am to state, that the Commissioners have had frequent occasions to consider the relative advantages and disadvantages of the advice which they have given to auditors, not to pass such bills unless they have been taxed by the proper officer, where they are taxable. The Commissioners are aware that since the promulgation of this advice the bills sent in by attornies to parish officers, have been so much reduced, that for the most part the parish has had to bear the cost incurred in the taxation of the bills. Yet that reduction justifies the Commissioners in the view which they originally took of this matter, and induces them to retain the advice which they so gave. As this taxation is of general application, no remark can be justified in any particular case of the conduct of the overseers being invidious; or that they are actuated by any improper feeling or motive, and the success, of course, depends entirely upon the generality of the practice.

"The Commissioners have thought at one time, that the auditor might exercise a discretion in the case, and take upon himself to determine whether a bill did or did not require taxation. But they have since felt that such a course would necessarily place him in a situation of unpleasantness, and expose him to invidious remarks, while the possibility or probability of the bills not being taxed, would let in the mischief of improper or extravagant charges in bills for professional business; which the Commissioners consider has been removed by the general directions which they have given to auditors and parish officers."

2. AS TO THE EXPENSES OF DEFENDING A POOR RATE, IN WHICH SEVERAL TOWNSHIPS WERE INTERESTED.—TODMORDEN UNION.

18th July, 1842.

The Commissioners took into consideration the following letter addressed to them by Mr. Gledhill, the Auditor of the Todmorden Union:—

"Some time ago the Manchester and Leeds Railway Company appealed against the Poor's Rate for the township of Stansfield in the Todmorden Union. The case was put to reference at the Quarter Sessions, and the rate ultimately confirmed. The overseers made out several bills of charges and expenses, amounting altogether to 64*l.* 0*s.* 2½*d.*, in addition to the attorney's bill of 135*l.* and upwards. Several townships through which the railway passes have contributed 78*l.* 9*s.* 4*d.* towards the expenses of establishing the principle of rating the said railway; and the overseers have, out of this sum, deducted the bills above alluded to, and accounted merely for the balance of 14*l.* 9*s.* 1½*d.*, without inserting in their accounts the several amounts of the said bills.

"When the assistant overseer submitted the accounts for audit, I required the production of these bills in order to ascertain whether they are proper and legal; and the overseers have now furnished them, copies of which I enclose I presume (as in ordinary cases) I cannot allow the overseers any charges for their loss of time or trouble, but simply their expenses paid out of pocket.

"The overseers have also some bills of charges of parties who have assisted them to assess the new property in the township (being chiefly the railway) previous to laying the rate so appealed against.

"With respect to all the above charges however, since they chiefly relate to the valuation of the railway and the appeal case, the overseers may contend, that they have a right to deduct and reimburse themselves the amount thereof (although not legal items) from the contributions of the other townships, and which sums I should think would not be legal payments in the accounts of the overseers of such townships."

And the Commissioners directed the following answer to be given thereto:—

"When a bill is defrayed, whether in whole or in part, at the expense of a parish, or township, the auditor is bound to satisfy himself as to the whole bill; and the overseers or other officers are bound to produce it. The Commissioners therefore, think that you are bound to examine the entire bill and all the items, amounting to 78*l.* 9*s.* 4*d.*

"With regard to the manner of proceeding with the items, the Commissioners do not think so strict a rule applicable as when the money would be payable by the township or parish for which the overseer is appointed. For that township he is bound to act gratuitously, but he is not bound so to act for any other township; and if any other township should engage his services, and should pay him or other persons for their services, a payment made to him, or to those other persons, might be retained by him and them: and this, although the other township had no authority to make the payment. But although the Commissioners do not consider so rigid a rule applicable so far as extra services were performed by the overseer, or by others for other townships; still, so far as the services were requisite for the appeal of the overseer's own township, he was bound to perform them gratuitously; necessary reasonable charges out of pocket being allowed him. And as any payment made by other townships in respect of these charges, must have been intended strictly in discharge of the burden of the litigation of the overseer's own township, such payments must be considered as the money of the latter, and accounted for accordingly. The result will be, that for services which were necessary for his own township, he must account rigidly; for extra services in the interest solely of other townships, greater latitude may be allowed, the overseer being considered in their matters a private agent.

"Again, as regards the contributing townships, the payment of contributions may not in strictness be lawful, unless they were wholly engaged in appeals, and abided by the result of reference; but so far as the contribution has been made with a bonâ fide intention of saving expense to the respective townships, the Commissioners think a rigid strictness not desirable."

II.—AUDITOR'S DUTIES.—ANDOVER UNION.

29th April, 1842.

The Commissioners took into consideration a letter, addressed to them by the Clerk of the Andover Union, requesting their opinion on the following point;—

"Whether it is the duty of the auditor of the Union at the quarterly audits to cast up each rate brought to him by the overseers, and satisfy himself that the amount of each rate as debited to the overseers is the correct total amount of such rate; or, if it is only necessary or sufficient for him to debit the overseers with what appears on the face of the rate to be the gross amount of it, as signed and allowed by the magistrates, without casting it up to test that such gross amount is really correct."

And the Commissioners directed the following reply to be given thereto:—

"I am directed by the Poor Law Commissioners, in reference to the case submitted in your letter of the 26th instant, to point out that the duty of the auditor, under the order relating to the accounts, is to ascertain 'that all sums received, or which ought to have been received, are brought to account.'

"The Commissioners consider it is requisite that the auditor should cast up each rate; that is, the column 'amount to be collected,' in order to ascertain whether that which appears on the face of the rate to be the gross amount, is the true amount.

"What the overseers are liable to account for (as is justly remarked by the auditor in his observations appended to your letter) is the rate as made, and subsequently allowed, by the justices. But the Commissioners understand this to be, the sums which are set against the names of the several occupiers included in the rate.

"Supposing the sum entered as the gross amount of the rate, to fall short of the true aggregate of the several assessments, this would not prevent the enforcement of those several proportions of the rate.

"It appears clear that it is the duty of the overseer to collect each assessment which is recoverable; it is equally his duty to account for everything he collects; and, it follows, that the auditor cannot know whether the overseer properly performs his duty in this respect, unless he ascertains the accuracy of the entry in the rate-book, which purports to be the total amount to be collected."

III.—BURIAL OF PAUPERS.—As to the Payment of Fees.—Ware Union.

25th July, 1842.

The Commissioners took into consideration a letter addressed to them by the Rev. John Gibson, of Furneux Pelham, stating that the parish of Brent Pelham had refused to pay the customary fees for the interment of paupers dying in that parish, and inquiring whether, in a case of such poverty as justified the overseers in granting the coffin, the clergyman was entitled to receive his fee from the poor rates; and the Commissioners directed the following reply to be given thereto :—

"The Poor Law Commissioners wish to explain to you, that in a Union formed under the provisions of the Poor Law Amendment Act, it is only under circumstances of sudden and urgent necessity, that it would be legally competent for an overseer to provide for the interment of persons dying in a destitute condition: under ordinary circumstances, and such cases will of course be by far the most numerous, the Board of Guardians, and not the overseers, are the authority to give directions, and pay for the cost of the funeral.

"You are, doubtless, aware that the Commissioners, owing to the state of the law as it affects this question, are unable to do more than to express their views to the Guardians; and it is entirely open to them either to act on the opinion of the Commissioners or otherwise, as they may think fit.

"The Commissioners entertain the general wish that the fee payable by the custom of the parish should be paid on the interment of any pauper. The Commissioners, however, refrain from making any remark as to the probable result of any attempt to enforce from the Guardians payment of such fees, whether customary or otherwise, as, from the law on the subject, the legal responsibility of the Guardians seems extremely doubtful."

IV.—CLERK'S DUTIES.

As to form "A" prescribed by the General Order—Duties of Officers.—East Stonehouse.

16th July, 1842.

1. The Commissioners took into consideration a letter addressed to them by the Clerk to the Board of Guardians of East Stonehouse, conveying to them the request of the Board that the Commissioners would dispense with the transmission to the Assistant Commissioner of the weekly return in the Form A, prescribed by the General Order relating to the duties of officers, which the Guardians object to on account of the expense it would occasion to the parish; and the Commissioners directed the following answer to be given thereto :—

"The Commissioners are desirous of explaining to the Guardians the grounds on which they have required this Return to be made. The Assistant Poor Law Commissioners have hitherto been in the habit of receiving returns from the clerks of Unions in order to keep them informed of the state of pauperism in the Unions, and of other particulars; and it appeared to the Commissioners advisable that these returns should be made on a uniform plan. They therefore took occasion on the issue of their general order respecting the duties of officers, to prescribe a form in which they should be made. These returns have become more necessary, in consequence of the diminution of the number of Assistant Commissioners; and the Commissioners think that the form contains nothing unreasonable, as it merely requires that timely notice of any special business (such as the complaints of paupers against officers, steps to be taken in consequence of the prevalence of an infectious disease, and the like) should be transmitted to the Assistant Commissioner in the same manner as notices of special business are sent to members of Boards of Guardians.

"With regard to the expense which the return will occasion, as the cost of the form is only 2*s*. per quire, the charge, including postage, cannot amount to more than a few shillings annually."

DITTO.—WELLINGBOROUGH UNION.

16th June, 1842.

2. The Commissioners took into consideration a letter received from the Clerk of the Wellingborough Union, inquiring, with reference to the general order respecting the duties of officers, whether in the weekly statement of Form A, given in the schedule of that order, he was to state as the "Number of Paupers belonging to each Relieving Officer's District in the Union," the number of heads of families to whom the relief is given, or the number including the children relieved with their parents: and the Commissioners directed that he should be informed that he should state the number of individuals receiving relief, and not the number of the heads of families only.

V.—COUNTY RATE.—AS TO THE PAYMENT OF THE RATE FOR A BY-GONE PERIOD.—WREXHAM UNION.

1st June, 1842.

The Commissioners took into consideration a letter, of which the following is an extract, received from Joseph Pierce, Esq., clerk of the peace for the county of Denbigh:—

"In the year 1837 some townships in the Wrexham Union neglected to pay the high constable their quota to the county rate. In the year 1838 the payments were made regularly, and have been so since; and the high constable (who is still in office), in the receipts which he has (since the arrears became due) given to the overseers, states that the sums paid were 'on account of the county rate due.' The treasurer of the county, when he received any money, placed it to the earliest account due, showing by his accounts that the sums now due are for the current year.

"The parish officers have been summoned, and have been ordered to pay, and are willing (as well as the inhabitants) to pay, but have requested the magistrates to adjourn and to delay issuing the distresses, in order to have your opinion, whether the auditor will be justified in allowing the payments under the foregoing circumstances. The auditor thinks that he ought not to allow them, as four quarterly payments have been made since 1837; thus showing, on the face of the overseers' accounts audited since that period, that the county rate has been liquidated, though the receipts given by the high constable specify that the payments were 'on account of the county rate due.' Had the receipts specified that the sums received were in liquidation of the claims for each current quarter, the auditor might have been right in his view of the matter; but when it is admitted that the demand was made quarterly for the arrears, as well as for the current quarter's quota, and that the receipts were successively given on account of county rate due, the magistrates think that the auditor would be justified in allowing the payments when presented to him in the overseers' accounts."

And the Commissioners directed the following answer to be given thereto:—

"In reply, I am to state that it is a principle thoroughly established, that the poor's rate and the county rate are charges on the rate-payers of the time; that is, of the year in which the charges on the respective rates are incurred. As to the poor's rate, see Tawney's case, 2 Salk, 531; Rex *v.* Goodcheap, 1 Bott. 115. As to the county rate, it is asserted by the court in general terms in the case Rex *v.* Justices of Flintshire, 5 B. and A., 761, 'that the justices have no right, except by following the provision of particular Acts of Parliament, &c. to make the expense ultimately fall on different persons from those who were by law liable at the time it was incurred.'

"The Commissioners conceive that the power here denied to the justices is not possessed by high constables or overseers; yet, if the rate-payers of the present year, who appear to have paid all the county rates made on them during the present year, can be compelled to pay the rates of 1837, which were allowed to get into arrear by the negligence of the overseer of that year, or rather by the neglect of the high constable to use the power which the County Rate Acts invests him with for the recovery of the rates, the result would be, that the overseer, or high constable, could effect that by their own negligence which the justices have not power to effect.

"The Commissioners think that the terms of the County Rate Acts, especially of the 12 Geo. II. c. 29, s. 2, and 55 Geo. III. c. 51, s. 12, leave no doubt that the rate is to be paid by the 'overseer for the time being,' within the time named in the warrant of the justices, and within 30 days after the demand of the high constable; and that neither the overseers nor the high constable has any right to dispense with this provision; and consequently, that the high constable cannot by any form of receipt reserve to himself a right of claiming in some subsequent year, the rates due in a preceding year.

"The Commissioners, therefore, think that the present overseers can only pay such rates to the high constable as become due in their time, including in that time 30 days before the commencement of their year of office, if within that 30 days a demand was made by the high constable for any rate then recently imposed by the justices, and also any further amount of county rate as their predecessors may have enabled them to pay, by having made sufficient rates, or transferred sufficient balances for the purpose.—17 Geo. II. c. 38, s. 11; Tawney's case, 2 Salk, 531."

VI.—GUARDIANS.

1. THE READING OF A MARRIAGE NOTICE NOT TO BE ENTERED ON THEIR MINUTES.—SAFFRON WALDEN UNION.

13*th May*, 1842.

The Commissioners read the following letter addressed by the Registrar-General to Mr. R. D. Thurgood, of Saffron Walden, and forwarded by him to the Commissioners for their information:—

"*General Register Office, May* 13, 1842.

"SIR,—I am directed by the Registrar-General to acknowledge the receipt of your letter of the 12th instant, and, in reply, to inform you that, on referring to the 'Act for Marriages in England,' he can discover nothing to warrant the practice of entering upon the minutes of the proceedings of the Board of Guardians the fact of a marriage notice having been read before the Board, nor does he consider that such an entry is at all requisite, or within the contemplation or spirit of that Act.

"I am, Sir, your obedient servant,
(Signed) "THOMAS MANN, *Chief Clerk*.

"*R. D. Thurgood, Esq., Superintendent Registrar, Saffron Walden*."

2. DUTIES OF THE CHAIRMAN OF A BOARD OF GUARDIANS IN REGARD TO ILLEGAL MOTIONS OR AMENDMENTS.—NEWCASTLE-ON-TYNE UNION.

15*th June*, 1842.

The Commissioners took into consideration a letter addressed to them by Henry Ingledew, Esq., the chairman of the Board of Guardians of the Newcastle-on-Tyne Union, requesting the Commissioners' opinion as to the correctness of the position assumed by him as chairman of the Board of Guardians of the Newcastle-on-Tyne Union in a case where out-door relief was ordered by the Guardians to able-bodied paupers, in having stated, on its being moved, that half of the relief ordered be in kind, in accordance with Article 1 of the Out-door Labour Test Order, and an amendment being moved that the whole of such relief be given in money (which amendment was carried), that those Guardians who had voted for the whole relief being given in money, and no part in food, contrary to the Order, had thrown away their votes, and that the decision of the minority, that one-half of the relief should be given in food, constituted a valid order of the Board, and should be acted on; and the Commissioners directed the following reply to be made thereto:—

"I am to state that there is no doubt that the amendment was illegal, it being directly in contravention of the Order. The amendment, by being put, acquired no legal character; but every supposed vote in its favour was a mere nullity, and the amendment, when voted for by a majority of the Guardians, had no more effect than when it was illegally proposed.

"The Commissioners, therefore, entertain no doubt of the entire correctness of your decision as against the amendment. As regards the carrying of the original motion, that one-half of the relief should be in food, the Commissioners also think your decision to be correct: there was but one legal motion before the Guardians, which might have been lawfully opposed by an amendment to increase the proportions of relief in kind, or to include other relief in kind besides food. As no such amendment was proposed, the Guardians were bound to determine the amount on the original motion. It was not competent to them to reject the motion altogether; accordingly, no votes being against the original motion on a lawful amendment, and none being receivable to reject the motion altogether, the motion must be considered as carried.

"If the motion had been one which the Guardians could have negatived absolutely, as in any case where they are not bound to act, but have a power to do so or not at their discretion, the Commissioners think it would not have been so clear that the original motion was carried; inasmuch as it would have been necessary in any such case to take the votes in the negative as well as in the affirmative of such a motion; and as the illegal amendment could not be regarded as the proper negative of the motion, it could not be said that the motion had been properly voted on for and against. The Commissioners would therefore recommend, generally, that when an illegal amendment is proposed, it should not be put from the chair; but that the chairman should put the legal motions and legal amendments only, and go through the regular steps of voting on these alone, taking the votes in the affirmative, and when the case allows it, on the negative also, of each of them. And that, in cases where the legality of an amendment is doubtful, and the chairman cannot undertake the responsibility of rejecting it, he should first take the votes for the original motion, next (if the motion is one that can be absolutely rejected) against the motion; and last, the votes on the amendment; explaining at the same time the purpose of this course to be to enable the amendment to prevail if it be found to be legal, and if it have in its favour a greater number of votes than the motion."

VII.—LAND TAX.—AS TO THE COURSE TO BE PURSUED WHEN THE UNION WORKHOUSE IS OVER-ASSESSED TO THE TAX.—CHIPPING SODBURY UNION.

3rd February, 1842.

The Commissioners took into consideration the following letter addressed to them by the Clerk of the Chipping Sodbury Union:—

"The collector of land tax made, some time back, a charge upon the Union for half a year's land tax, due September 20th, of 2*l*. 7*s*. 11*d*. The previous payment for land tax was 3*s*. 9*d*. a half year: this advance he made in consequence of the improved value by the erection of the workhouse.

"The Guardians were unanimously of opinion, that the charge made upon the workhouse was much higher than on any other property in the parish, and refused to pay it as unjust; and directed me to make a tender of 1*l*. 5*s*. 10*d*. for the half year, which, by their estimate, was equal to the charges upon other property in the parish, and which was refused.

"The assessment was in the usual way placed on the church door, with the day of appeal.

"Mr. Parker, the Assistant Poor Law Commissioner, was at the Board on the 7th instant, and concurred with the Board, that the demand was unjust when shown that a mansion that cost more than the workhouse, with 50 acres of good land, was charged for land tax but 4*s*. a year more, but could not decide what remedy.

"The collector this morning made a distress and took away several chairs, which he has impounded, and will sell in four days, unless redeemed by paying the money and expenses.

"The Board beg to request your opinion upon the following points:—

"Is not the collector obliged to give notice in writing to the parties when he has made an alteration?

"If the charge can be proved to be higher in proportion on the workhouse than on other property in the parish, has the Board any remedy against the payment if they neglect to appeal?

"If they have any remedy, please inform them what?

"If the collector have paid the money for the parish, has he still the power of distraining, or has he made it a private debt?

"The Board beg to request your advice for the future, whether you would recommend them to appeal next year, or continue to pay this sum."

And the Commissioners directed the following answer to be given thereto:—

"1st. The Commissioners suppose that the alteration was made by the Commissioners of Land Tax upon the return of the assessors, and not by the collector, who has no authority of himself to make an alteration; and who would, therefore, be liable to an action if he should distrain for a sum charged on his own authority.

"Assuming that the alteration has been made by the proper persons, the notice required to be given is only the annual notice which appears to have been given.

"As no authority exists for subsequent alteration during the year, except by the Commissioners upon appeal, there can be no occasion for any further notice.

"2nd and 3rd. Supposing that (as appears to be clear) the workhouse is subject to some land tax, there is no remedy against an overcharge, when made by the persons having authority, but by appeal.

"If the workhouse were exempt, or if an amount were imposed by persons wanting authority, as by the collector, and a distress were made, a remedy by action would exist, as by replevin or action of trespass.

"4th. The Poor Law Commissioners think that the fact that the collector had paid in the money assessed on the workhouse, would not deprive him of the power to distrain for the amount.

"5th. The Poor Law Commissioners are only informed that the workhouse is considered to be over-rated by reference to some other property; and not being informed of the annual value of the rest of the property in the district, are not in a condition to advise the Guardians either to acquiesce in the demand or to appeal on the first occasion. However, the Poor Law Commissioners infer, from the statement, that it is advisable for the Guardians to appeal on the first opportunity, when it will probably appear whether there were sufficient grounds or not for the assessment; and when, according to the result, the Guardians or the Poor Law Commissioners will be better enabled to judge whether another appeal or acquiescence is the more desirable course."

VIII.—LUNATIC PAUPERS.

1. AS TO THEIR ADMISSION INTO A WORKHOUSE.—CHESTERTON UNION.

14th July, 1842.

The Commissioners took into consideration a letter received from the Clerk of the Chesterton Union relating to the cases of two lunatic paupers, and requesting the Commissioners to inform the Guardians whether the relieving officer acted rightly in ordering one of the lunatics into the workhouse until the next Board day, and, generally, whether the workhouse is the proper place for such persons to be taken to until orders can be obtained for their admission to some lunatic asylum, not exceeding the fourteen days allowed by the Act: and the Commissioners directed the following reply to be given thereto:—

"The Commissioners think, as a rule, that the workhouse is not the proper place for lunatic paupers. The 9th George IV., c. 40, sec. 38, points out the course which ought to be taken for the care and safe custody of insane persons who become chargeable to the parish, viz. by causing them to be conveyed to an asylum or licensed house under the order of justices.

"But there may be cases in which some short delay must occur before the necessary order of justices can be procured, and the other arrangements made for the conveyance of such lunatics to an asylum. In these instances it may be desirable for the security, as well of the public as of the insane person, that temporary admission of the latter into the workhouse should be resorted to. The 45th section of the Poor Law Amendment Act, however, forbids the detention of a dangerous lunatic in a workhouse for any longer period than fourteen days; and the Commissioners on every ground, both as regards the lunatic and the other inmates of the workhouse, disapprove of the detention for any longer period than absolute necessity may warrant."

2. AS TO WHETHER PERSONS OF WEAK INTELLECT CAN BE DETAINED IN THE WORKHOUSE. —BERWICK-UPON-TWEED UNION.

9th June, 1842.

The Commissioners took into consideration a letter, of which the following is an extract, addressed to them by the Clerks of the Berwick-upon-Tweed Union:—

"It frequently occurs, that persons of weak intellect, (but not to the extent to necessitate any restraint or even much personal care or vigilance) and others of confirmed vagrant habits, after remaining for a short period in the workhouse, give the required notice to leave; making it a practice to return again after a short absence, generally in a most abject and loathsome state.

"Have the Board, with or without the previous sanction of the Poor Law Commissioners, power to detain such individuals in the house?"

And the Commissioners directed the following answer to be given thereto:—

"I am to state in reply that the Commissioners think that the Guardians have not, and that the law does not enable the Commissioners to confer on the Guardians, the power to detain any person of weak intellect in the workhouse, except where in any case there may be reasonable grounds to suppose that such person is incapable of taking proper care of himself, and that harm to the person of the pauper is to be apprehended from his being at large."

IX. OVERSEER.

1. AS TO WHETHER HE IS BOUND TO MAKE A PERSONAL DEMAND OF POOR RATES.—AXBRIDGE UNION.

14th July, 1842.

The Commissioners took into consideration a letter received from Mr. J. Yeatman, Uphill, Somerset, inquiring whether an overseer was not bound to apply personally, or by a person duly appointed, for payment of the poor rates; and also whether the overseer could enforce payment of rates which ought to have been collected in 1841; and the Commissioners directed the following answer to be given thereto:—

"I am to state that there is no express provision for a personal demand of poor rates by an overseer. The effect of the decisions on the subject is not perfectly clear: but it would appear that the demand required previous to a distress, consists, not exclusively of a personal demand, but that the thing essentially necessary is, that information should be given to the rate-payer of the precise amount claimed. Hurrell *v.* Wink, 2 J. B. Moore, 417.

"The Commissioners are of opinion, that when this information can be shown to have been given in a way to inform the party fully of the demand, a levy can be made without a personal demand where the ratepayer is out of the parish, where the overseer would not be bound to follow him. But the Commissioners are not enabled to come to the conclusion, that a demand by the overseer can be dispensed with when the ratepayer resides within the parish.

"In answer to your concluding inquiry, I am to state, that payment of rates lawfully made by the overseers of 1841 can be enforced by the overseers of the present year."

---

2. BANKRUPTCY OF OVERSEER.—LEIGHTON BUZZARD UNION.

26th July, 1842.

The Commissioners took into consideration a letter addressed to them by Mr. Kipling, the Auditor of the Leighton Buzzard Union, stating that the late overseer of the parish of Bellington, who had a balance in hand on going out of office, had become bankrupt, and had not obtained his certificate, and requesting to be informed how to proceed to recover such balance; and the Commissioners directed the following answer to be given thereto:—

"I am to state that it was decided in the case of Rex *v.* Tucker, 5 M. and Sel. 508, that the balance due from an overseer was a debt proveable under the commission within the Statute of Bankruptcy, and the overseer was in that case held discharged by his bankruptcy and certificate from a debt due in respect of a sum of money in his hands, as overseer, at the time of his bankruptcy.

"In the present instance, the overseer has not obtained his certificate, and is, therefore, not discharged from his debt to the parish. The Commissioners think there is nothing to prevent the justices issuing their warrant on the complaint of the present overseers, and committing the defaulter under 17th Geo. II. c. 38, and 50th Geo. III. c. 49, in case he should not pay over the balance.

"The Commissioners, upon the whole, think it would be proper that the overseers should make the application to the justices."

X.—PAUPERS.

1. OUT-DOOR LABOUR TEST.—NEWCASTLE-UPON-TYNE UNION.

31st July, 1842.

The Commissioners took into consideration the following letter, addressed to them by the Clerk of the Newcastle-upon Tyne Union:—

"I am directed by the Board of Guardians to submit to the Poor Law Commissioners the following statement, and to request their advice and directions thereon.

"In carrying out the provisions of the Out-door Labour Test Order, with reference to able-bodied men applying for relief, the Guardians have ordered relief, one half in money and one half in food, to such amount as, in the opinion of the Board, the number of the family and the wants of each applicant required; annexing to each such order the condition of the applicant's performing, in the stone-yard, labour in breaking stones, to such an amount as it appeared he could reasonably perform.

"This relief has been given, along with the other relief, to the out-door paupers in advance, at the beginning of the week, or rather on the Saturday, being the first day after the sitting of the Board.

"In some cases the paupers, after receiving relief, have never attended the stone-yard to perform any labour; and in other cases they have refused to perform it.

"The overseers of the poor of one of the parishes to which two or three of the parties so neglecting or refusing to work are chargeable, have applied to the magistrates to have them punished under section 3 of the Vagrant Act, as recommended by the Poor Law Commissioners' Instructional Letter; but the magistrates refuse to entertain the case, alleging that, as relief has been given to the man, his offence of refusing to labour does not come within the meaning of the Act in question.

"This determination of the magistrates places, as it will be seen, the Guardians, with reference especially to the worst description of able-bodied paupers, who are unwilling to work, in such a position, that they feel much difficulty in carrying out the provisions of the Order; and therefore the Board has deemed it necessary to resort to the Poor Law Commissioners for instructions how to act."

And the Commissioners directed the following answer to be given thereto:—

"I am to state in reply, that the Commissioners cannot concur in the view of the case taken by the justices. The 3rd section of the 5th Geo. IV. c. 83, provides that every person being able, wholly, or in part, to maintain himself, or herself, or his or her family, by work, or by other means, and wilfully refusing or neglecting to do so, by which refusal or neglect, he or she or any of his or her family, whom he or she may be legally bound to maintain, shall have become chargeable to any parish, &c. &c., shall be deemed an idle and disorderly person within the true intent and meaning of the Act.

"It will be observed that the statute does not require a *full ability* to maintain, but the offence is complete if there be an ability in *part* to maintain, &c. by work, and a refusal to do so.

"In the present instance, the pauper is able to maintain himself, or his family, *in part*, since the produce of his work would in part go to repay the parish the cost of the relief given. In so far, therefore, as the parish has to forego the indemnity to be derived from the share of his work, his family become chargeable by his refusal to perform such work, since the charge to the parish would be less if he did perform it. The Commissioners do not admit the force of the objection, that no offence was committed because the giving of relief preceded the refusal to work; the performance of which was the condition upon which the relief was granted.

"The Commissioners think it desirable to offer one or two suggestions in reference to a point, which may, probably, have presented itself as a difficulty to the minds of the justices in dealing with the case, viz., whether the pauper, or his family, could be considered as having become chargeable in consequence of the refusal to work.

"From what has been already stated, it will be apparent to the Guardians, that the Commissioners do not entertain any doubt that the pauper may, by a fair and reasonable construction of the terms of the Vagrant Act, be considered as having become chargeable in consequence of the refusal to work.

"But the adoption of the following course will avoid all question on the point. If the pauper will not work, all relief to him or his family should be refused, and his name erased from the relief book. He would then cease to be chargeable. If he again apply to be relieved, relief should be refused, and an offer made to pay him the same sum as would have been given in relief, in exchange for his work. If he refuse this, relief may then be given to the pauper's wife and children, and himself proceeded against under the Vagrant Act.

"The Commissioners suggest this course as a means of dealing with exceptional cases of refractory paupers, and not as a mode of proceeding desirable to be adopted in ordinary cases where there is no indication of an indisposition to labour. In these cases the Guardians should adhere to the terms of the order of the Commissioners, and insist upon the performance of work as the condition of receiving food, or money, to be considered as relief.

"The Commissioners have thus gone fully into the question raised in your letter; but in the cases in which the pauper manifestly refuses work with an intention of remaining chargeable, or acts with bad faith in declining to complete the task required of him, the shortest mode of dealing with him would be to select that case for an offer of the workhouse."

---

2. AS TO THE EMPLOYMENT OF ABLE-BODIED PAUPERS.—HONITON UNION.

18th February, 1842.

The Commissioners took into consideration a letter addressed to them by the clerk of the Honiton Union, stating that the Board of Guardians find much difficulty in fixing on any employment for the able-bodied men in the workhouse; that they have tried stone-breaking, but find it very unproductive, besides not being a sufficient test, and requesting the suggestions of the Commissioners on the subject; and the Commissioners directed the following answer to be given thereto:—

"I am to inform the Guardians that the Commissioners cannot suggest any kind of labour which is likely to be productive of much profit; nor is that the object which ought to be kept in view in pauper labour; stone-breaking under proper superintendence, is generally found to answer.

"Besides this mode of employing able-bodied paupers, the following have frequently been adopted:—

"In some Unions a hand corn mill, by which flour is ground for the use of the house, is provided, and it is certainly effectual as a test.

"A machine for pounding, or grinding bones for manure is occasionally used.

"Oakum picking has also been tried in several Unions, but it is less effectual, depends more on the locality of the Union, and is exposed to some other disadvantages."

3. CASUAL POOR.—WEST HAM UNION.

28th March, 1842.

The Commissioners took into consideration a letter addressed to them by W. C. Streatfield, Esq., the Chairman of the West Ham Union, of which the following are extracts:—

"Reference to 'Archbold's Justice,' to the Mendicity Regulations approved by you, as published in the third Report, and lastly, to the Official Circulars, have made a point of some difficulty, incomprehensible to me. * * * *

"Archbold, vol. iii. p. 163, where it is clearly laid down that casual poor are not removeable, the cases, however, cited are only those of sickness or accident; and I should have been satisfied to advise our Guardians to pass mendicant poor, or such persons as, though in a state of health, on account of destitution, make use of our house for a month at a time, but that, when I refer to the Mendicity Regulations, as published in your third Report, p. 135, octavo edition, I find (clause 5) that every destitute person is to be treated as casual poor; and if so, of course, cannot be passed; but then, again, on my reading clause 8, I find special directions to the clerk to take the orders of the Guardians concerning the removal of this same class. The notification to rate-payers also, which follows, clearly supposes a power to pass. Again, in p. 57 of your Official Circular, in your remarks upon clause 22 of the amended Bill, as proposed two years since, you clearly write under the impression that parties admitted as casual poor may be removed. Again, p. 171, at the bottom of the first column, you seem clearly to read the law against the removal of casual poor, as including those only who are chargeable through sudden or grievous hurt. * * *

"The more I look into the matter, the more persuaded I become, that in passing to their settlements persons who made use of our house for any length of time, being in health, but who are yet casual poor, we have acted legally and wisely. Without, therefore, further tasking your time, I would request answers to the following questions:—

"1st. A person going from place to place in search of work, but finding none, enters a workhouse for a night's lodging; he is to all appearance destitute, and inclines to remain (more than one instance I could produce at this time where, under these circumstances, the party has been chargeable for more than a month); is such person casual poor, and to be treated as such?

"2nd. If not, but you answer mendicant poor; where have you authority for treating mendicant poor differently to casual poor?

"3rd. If you show authority, where do you draw the line between the two?

"Having drawn such line, I will suppose, strictly according to the cases cited in Archbold, a case occurs of a person who is thus casual poor, but he recovers, and refuses then to leave the house; at what stage does he pass from casual to mendicant poor, thus legalizing a removal? Of this, again, I can produce cases.

"I think it well to be satisfied also on the following point:—The same authority told me that if a person received as a mendicant determines after twenty-four hours not to leave the house, he should be removed to his proper class in the body of the house. We have mendicant wards built for the purpose, one for males, another for females."

And the Commissioners directed the following reply to be given thereto:—

"The Commissioners are not able to verify your references to Archbold's Justice, a book which they had not in the office, and the edition of which, published by Shaw and Son, 1842, which they have procured for the purpose, not containing the passages you refer to.

"The Commissioners, however, think there will probably be no difficulty in reconciling the apparent discrepancies in the several expressions you refer to. In the first place, the words 'casual poor' are often used in terms which ought to be discriminated. The poor who are detained in a parish by consequence only of a casualty, which renders them chargeable, such as the breaking of a limb or other unexpected injury or sudden illness while passing through the parish, and without any intention of staying there for any time, however short, are held to be irremovable, as not coming *animus morandi;* and it is to these, and these only, that the decisions in the cases by which it is held that casual poor are irremoveable apply.

"On the other hand, the words 'casual poor'

are often used to denote all poor not permanently resident. But there is no decision nor good authority that the Commissioners are aware of to the effect that those are irremoveable: mendicants and vagrants intending to sleep or to rest in a parish, and becoming chargeable there voluntarily and not by reason of some irresistible and unexpected casualty, have an *animus morandi*, and have a design on the stock of the parish, although not for any long continuance, which quite distinguish these cases from those above described, and accordingly Lord Ellenborough thus delivers the judgment of the Court in R. *v.* Birmingham, 14 East, 251.—'This was the case of a starving vagrant, in whichever of the two parishes she was, who was going backwards and forwards between them, and would have been starved if she had not received temporary relief from one or the other; she was liable to be removed from either,' &c.

"The Commissioners would, moreover, refer you to the more recent case of R. *v.* Woolpit, 4 A. and E. 205, in which a majority of the judges appear to have held that the length of the intended stay was immaterial.

"Mr. Justice Coleridge, however, dissented, and this difference of opinion shows that it is impossible at present to give such an answer to your questions as is wholly satisfactory, and that the points involved in those questions are very doubtful.

"On the whole, the Commissioners think there is no sufficient authority to the effect that mendicants and vagrants becoming chargeable temporarily and not by compulsion of any grievous casualty, but of their own will, are irremoveable.

"The Commissioners trust that the above remarks render it unnecessary for the Commissioners to make application of them to the several cases which you have specifically stated."

---

4. AS TO CHARGING RELIEF GRANTED to CASUAL POOR.—YORK UNION.

14th July, 1842.

The Commissioners took into consideration the following resolution, passed by the Board of Guardians of the York Union:—

"That the clerk send to the Commissioners a copy of the resolution passed by this Board, 'That all paupers having been once relieved by a parish as casual poor, shall again be charged to the same parish if the pauper become again chargeable within a short period;' this Board being of opinion, that as soon as a casual pauper becomes chargeable to any parish, it is the duty of such parish to remove the pauper."

And the Commissioners directed the following communication to be made to the Guardians in regard thereto:—

"With reference to this resolution I am to state, that the Commissioners think it is not in accordance with the law, and that the Guardians are not empowered to direct, according to the terms of the resolution, that where a pauper has once been relieved by a parish as casual poor, the relief of such pauper shall again be charged to the same parish if the pauper become chargeable within a short period.

"If the second chargeability should arise in the same parish as that in which the first arose, there can be no difficulty as to the liability, and as to the mode in which the relief should be charged. But where a person, having been relieved as a casual pauper by one parish, subsequently goes into some other parish within the same Union, and becomes destitute therein, it is clear that such latter parish is legally liable for the relief of such pauper, upon the very same grounds that the parish in which the first chargeability arose was liable. Where the overseers of the parish to which the pauper first became chargeable may admit the settlement of the pauper, or their liability to relieve him, and consent to the charge being transferred to their parish, there can be no objection to that course being adopted. But, where the overseers may not consent, the Commissioners are of opinion that the Guardians are not legally authorized to transfer the relief; and, moreover, that the Commissioners have no power to authorize them so to do."

XI. PENSIONERS.—RELIEF GRANTED TO DECEASED PENSIONERS NOT RECOVERABLE.—MERE UNION.

8th July, 1842.

The Commissioners took into consideration the following minute of the Board of Guardians of the Mere Union:—

"The relieving officer reported that he had advanced 6*s*. 2*d*. weekly to William Hill, a Chelsea pensioner, belonging to Bourton parish, on account of his pension, which pensioner died ten days previous to his pension becoming due; consequently, the parish of Bourton will be the losers of the sum advanced. The clerk is directed to send a minute thereof to the Poor Law Commissioners and ask the favour of their informing the Board of Guardians whether they can put them in a position to recover the amount so advanced."

And the Commissioners directed the following reply to be given to the inquiry:—

"I am to state that the Commissioners understand, that the pensions of soldiers and sailors are paid in advance; consequently, nothing was due to the pensioner alluded to in the minute of the Guardians at his decease; and the Guardians cannot recover the amount of the relief advanced to the pensioner."

XII. RATING TITHES.

10th June, 1842.

The Commissioners took into consideration a letter addressed to them by the Rev. Edward Nicholson, Pentridge Rectory, Dorset, complaining of the manner in which the estimate for the poor rate was made by the overseer of the parish of Pentridge, in so far as the deductions from the tithe rent charge were concerned; and the Commissioners directed the following answer to be given thereto:—

"I am to state that the Commissioners conceive, that it is the duty of the overseers in levying the rate to estimate as near as possible, under all the existing circumstances, the net value of property at the time the rate is imposed on its owner or occupier.

"In the case of the tithe commutation rent charge, this can be done with certainty, so far as the gross value is concerned, by taking the sum determined by the even corn averages.

"But as regards the deductions to be made from the gross rental, these are not so fixed before hand; and it appears to be necessary to estimate these amounts for the succeeding period, by reference to some previous period: and it is obvious that the period taken into consideration, whether it be the year immediately preceding, or a series of years, should be the same for all properties affected by the rate. It is also obvious, that if the period be constantly of the same extent, say for one year, or for three years, each property must eventually, after the expiration of each period, have the benefit of the calculation of all its burdens, however much these may have fluctuated within the period.

"It appears, therefore, to the Commissioners, that the rule for calculating the deductions must be such as eventually to give to each property the benefit of the allowance for all fluctuations in the amount of rates and other burdens: but that it is not legally necessary, and is not indeed allowable where the value of a property for the current year can be remotely fixed, that the usual period taken for estimating the deductions for rates should be abandoned in respect of that property."

XIII.—RELIEF.

1. TO PERSONS POSSESSING SMALL PROPERTIES. —AXMINSTER UNION.

7th July, 1842.

The Commissioners took into consideration the following letter addressed to them by the clerk of the Axminster Union:—

"Cases often occur of persons applying for relief by reason of sickness, or of a numerous family of children, or of some other cause, who are owners of the houses they occupy, to which is attached a garden plot, and, probably, from a quarter to half an acre of orchard ground. In some instances the property might be worth from 5*l.* to 10*l.* per annum, and, if sold, might produce from 100*l.* to 200*l.* In most of these cases the applicants state the property of little value, merely saving them from paying rent, and the owners, generally, owe a sum of money on mortgage of the premises.

"The Board is desirous of knowing how you would advise the Guardians to deal with cases of this description; as, on the one hand, it would seem inconsistent to grant relief to individuals possessing landed property; and, on the other hand, the actual benefit of this property might not probably extend beyond 4*l.* or 5*l.* per year."

And the Commissioners directed the following answer to be given thereto:—

"I am to state that, as a general rule, persons possessed of property cannot be considered as coming within the class of destitute persons for whose benefit and relief the poor rate is provided. In some cases, however, it may be that the possession of the property (from the incumbrances, or charges to which it may be subject) is an actual disadvantage to the owners; in others, that the benefit derived is very inconsiderable. In these cases, where the owners may apply for relief, having no means of support derived from other sources, the Commissioners are not prepared to advise the Guardians to refuse to grant relief to such persons, except upon the condition that they should dispose of their interest in the property.

"In some instances it might be proper to require this. The difficulty of discriminating between cases in which it might be proper to grant, and those in which it would be right to withhold relief, is no doubt considerable. The Commissioners would only observe, that it appears to them that relief in the workhouse would be the least objectionable mode in which relief could be granted in doubtful cases of this description; as it affords the surest guarantee, that the persons receiving the relief are in the condition which alone constitutes a title to relief."

---

2. THE RIGHT OF JUSTICES TO ORDER RELIEF.—CHORLEY UNION.

1st July, 1842.

The Commissioners took into consideration a letter addressed to them by the Clerk of the Chorley Union, of which letter the following is an extract:—

"I shall feel greatly obliged by the favour of your opinion as to the legality of certain orders for relief, issued by one of the magistrates in this Union. The gentleman in question is in the habit of giving orders upon the overseers of the different townships in favour of persons who are settled parishioners, as well as those who are not so; and contends that he has a right to do so, under the 54th section of the Poor Law Amendment Act. I find that in the 48th page of Theobald's treatise on the Poor Laws, there is a statement which appears to agree with this view of the case, but I must confess that I cannot so read the statute. I have stated my opinion to the Board, but as some of the magistrates present appeared to differ from me, I shall feel greatly obliged by your informing me whether you are of opinion that an order, such as the one enclosed, in favour of a person residing in the township to which such overseer belongs is legal."

And the Commissioners directed the following reply to be given thereto:—

"I am to state in reply, that the Commissioners are decidedly of opinion that the power assumed by the justice in the cases you describe has no foundation in law.

"The power of justices with respect to the administration of relief in parishes under the government of Guardians of the poor rests on the provisions of the 4th and 5th Wm. IV., sec. 27 and 54. The former of these sections has obviously no application in the present case. The latter enables a justice to order relief where the following circumstances exist:—1st, where in any case of sudden and urgent necessity, the overseer may neglect to give necessary relief, a justice can order the overseer to give such relief in articles of absolute necessity; provided the necessitous person be *not settled, nor usually residing* in the parish to which the overseer belongs. 2d. A justice can, where any case of sudden and dangerous illness may require it, give an order for medical relief (*only*) to any parishioner, as well as out-parishioner; *i. e.* to any settled, as well as non-settled person.

"The case described in your letter does not, from the facts stated, appear to have been a case of sudden and urgent necessity; and, therefore, not a case for which the 54th section provides. But, assuming the emergency to have existed which would have justified an overseer in giving temporary relief, it is clear that as the pauper is settled in the township of Chorley, the overseers of which were ordered to give the relief, the case was not one in which a justice could legally make such an order; the pauper not being a person not settled, nor usually residing in the parish. As the pauper was a parishioner of Chorley, medical relief (*only*), if the nature and urgency of the case required it, might indeed have been ordered; but the case was not one requiring medical aid, and the order made in the present instance is not for medical relief.

"The Commissioners think it necessary to call attention to the 96th section, Poor Law Amendment Act, which provides that no overseer shall be liable to a penalty for not carrying into effect any illegal order of justices."

---

3. RELIEF BY WAY OF LOAN.—CIRENCESTER UNION.

25th January, 1843.

The Commissioners took into consideration the following letter, addressed to them by the Rev. Thomas Maurice of Harnhill rectory:—

"I am induced to take the liberty of asking your opinion on the following case: The Board of Guardians at Cirencester, of which I am a member, determined that able-bodied single men becoming applicants for admission to the house, should receive relief in the house only by way of loan; the payment of which should be enforced on their again obtaining employment; and although on the last Board day, by urging the ill consequences which I thought likely to ensue from adopting such a course, I was successful, on a division, in negativing the proposal in the cases then before us; still the question will undoubtedly be again mooted; and a knowledge of the opinion of the Commissioners will be a great satisfaction, and a guide to myself and many others.

"The objections which I pressed on the notice of the Guardians were, briefly, that by relieving the rate-payers from the expense of maintaining paupers in the house, an inducement to find them work would be removed; that by making this distinction between single and married men, the single men would be generally dismissed when labour became scarce, and improvident marriages be thereby promoted."

And the Commissioners directed the following answer to be given thereto:—

"The Commissioners at once perceive the full force of the objections which you have pointed out to the Guardians, as attending on any established and undeviating practice of giving out-relief by way of loan to single men, as such, whilst relief given to other labourers was afforded free of such condition, solely on the ground of their being married.

"The Commissioners conceive, that in determining whether relief should, or should not be given by way of loan, in any particular case, a Board of Guardians should bear in mind that they must decide with reference to the man's general ability to repay the relief advanced to him; and in determining whether he is capable of refunding the loan, the Guardians should not be guided by any one particular circumstance, connected with the case, but by a full consideration of *all* the circumstances, of which the question of a man's being single or married must obviously form a part only.

"Undoubtedly the cases of single men will often be those in which the ability to repay will be most apparent; but this is an adventitious circumstance over which the Guardians have no control: but the course by which the Guardians can, as far as possible, avoid the evils of which you are apprehensive, will be that above indicated; namely, a consideration of *all* the circumstances of the applicant's case, of which his marriage would be one only; and more especially, a careful forbearance from the announcement of any general principle, expressly referring to the fact of the man being married or single, as likely to guide them in their ultimate determination."

XIV.—REMOVAL.—TAVISTOCK UNION.

3rd March, 1842,

The Commissioners took into consideration the following letter, addressed to them by Messrs. Robins and Son, Tavistock:—

"The workhouse belonging to the Tavistock Union is, as you are aware, situate within the parish of Tavistock; and paupers who become chargeable to any of the parishes in the Union are frequently placed in this workhouse.

"A pauper has lately become chargeable to the parish of Lamerton, and is now in the workhouse in Tavistock; her examination has been taken, and it is found that her settlement is in the parish of Tavistock; and it has been intimated by one of the Guardians of the Union, but on what authority we know not, that an order of removal cannot legally be made, inasmuch as the pauper is already in the parish of Tavistock, and that it would be an anomaly to make an order to remove from one parish to the same.

"We cannot see the force of such objection, as in the examination it is stated that the pauper is chargeable to Lamerton; and the parish officers of that parish are directed by the order to remove her to Tavistock.

"We shall thank you for your opinion on the point at your earliest convenience."

And the Commissioners directed the following answer to be given thereto:—

"The Commissioners, from the facts of the case as stated by you, observe that the pauper, though maintained in the Tavistock Union, which is situate in the parish of Tavistock, is chargeable to Lamerton. The Commissioners see nothing to prevent the latter parish procuring an order to remove the pauper to Tavistock. It is not necessary that the pauper should be locally within the parish by which the order is obtained, but only that he should be chargeable. But even if it were, the pauper being in the workhouse, is constructively within the parish to which the relief is charged; and the 79th section of the Poor Law Amendment Act authorizes the removal from any workhouse; all that is requisite is, that the provisions of the 79th section of the Poor Law Amendment Act should be complied with, as to sending the notice of chargeability, and copy of the order and examination, and causing the pauper to be delivered to the overseers of Tavistock at the expiration of the period of notice.

"Tavistock will have its remedy by appeal if there are grounds for disputing the settlement.

"The Commissioners think it would be unfair of the parish of Tavistock, to delay or obstruct *bonâ fide* proceedings by such an objection as that referred to, even if it had any weight."

XV.—WITNESSES.—SUBPŒASN TO COMPEL THE ATTENDANCE OF.—OKEHAMPON UNION.

19*th July*, 1842.

The Commissioners, in consequence of a letter addressed to them by W. Ponsford, Esq., an ex-officio Guardian of the Okehampton Union, inquired of the Master of the Crown Office whether that office would be prepared to grant subpœnas to compel the attendance of witnesses before justices out of sessions to give evidence on applications for orders of removal, and the Commissioners received from him the following reply:—

"*Crown Office, Temple,*
22*d July*, 1842.

"SIR,—In answer to your letter of the 19th inst., inquiring 'Whether the Crown Office would be prepared to grant subpœnas to compel the attendance of witnesses before justices out of sessions to give evidence on applications for orders of removal,' I beg to state for the information of the Poor Law Commissioners, that subpœnas have frequently been issued from the Crown Office to compel the attendance of witnesses before justices of the peace, as well on applications for orders of removal as for other matters. It is not for me to say how, and in what manner the disobedience of such process would be punished; but, whenever a writ of subpœna is required for what appears to be a legal purpose, I do not consider that I have any right to withhold it.

"I am, Sir,
"Your most obedient servant,
(Signed) "PERE. DEALTRY.

"*Edwin Chadwick, Esq.*"

The Commissioners directed a copy of the above communication to be forwarded to Mr. Ponsford.

XVI. WORKHOUSE RULES.

1. PAUPERS ABSCONDING FROM THE WORKHOUSE. — TEESDALE UNION.

21*st February*, 1842.

The Commissioners took into consideration a letter addressed to them by the clerk of the Teesdale Union, respecting the punishment of paupers absconding from the workhouse (without giving notice) by climbing a wall, or dropping from a window; which offence is stated by the Commissioners in the instructional circular accompanying the general workhouse order, not to be punishable unless the paupers carry off or injure clothes, or other property of the Guardians; and referring to the 5th section of the 55 Geo. III., c. 137, which gives justices of the peace power to commit to gaol for a specified period any person maintained in a public workhouse who may be guilty of drunkenness or other misbehaviour; and stating that the Commissioners' opinion, as expressed in the above-mentioned circular, seems to be at variance with that statute, and requesting to be informed whether any decision had taken place in support of the Commissioners' views on the subject; and the Commissioners directed the following reply to be given thereto:—

"In reply I am directed to state, that the word '*misbehaviour*' is a general word, and must be limited in meaning by the particular word preceding it. The Commissioners expressed the opinion referred to by you, because they think the point doubtful, and they are most anxious in such a matter to keep on the safe side; especially as no practical difficulty can result, as the rules of the Commissioners require that the paupers should be clothed in the Union clothing, and therefore they would always be punishable under the statute referred to by you."

2. AS TO WHO IS TO DECIDE UPON THE CLASS IN WHICH A PAUPER IS TO BE PLACED.—DOVER UNION.

13*th July*, 1842.

The Commissioners took into consideration a letter received from the master of the Dover Union workhouse, requesting to be informed, with reference to the workhouse rules, as to the classification of the inmates, who is the party to decide whether a man is infirm or not, or to which class of paupers in the workhouse he is to be assigned: and the Commissioners directed the following answer to be given thereto:—

"In reply I am to state that the Commissioners consider, that the governor of the workhouse decides in the first instance to which class of paupers an inmate shall be assigned; but in the event of any doubt arising as to the class to which a pauper belongs, the Commissioners think it desirable, that the governor should be guided by the opinion of the medical officer of the workhouse, until the case is brought before the Board of Guardians for their decision."

LONDON:
Printed, by Order of the Poor Law Commissioners, by W. CLOWES and SONS, Stamford Street, and Published by CHARLES KNIGHT and Co., 22, Ludgate Street, Publishers to the Poor Law Commissioners.

AN

OFFICIAL CIRCULAR

OF PUBLIC DOCUMENTS AND INFORMATION:

DIRECTED BY THE POOR LAW COMMISSIONERS TO BE PRINTED, CHIEFLY FOR THE USE OF THE MEMBERS AND PERMANENT OFFICERS OF BOARDS OF GUARDIANS, UNDER THE POOR LAW AMENDMENT ACT.

No. 24. CIRCULAR ISSUED MARCH 30, 1843.

Poor Law Commission Office,
Somerset House,
30th March, 1843.

The Poor Law Commissioners, on a review of their Minutes, directed that the Minutes of Correspondence on the following subjects be printed and circulated for the information of Guardians and Officers of the several Unions, viz.:—

By Order of the Board,
Edwin Chadwick, *Secretary.*

I.—AUDITOR:—Claim of to Exemption from serving the Office of Overseer.—Launceston Union.

April 9, 1842.

The Commissioners took into consideration a letter addressed to them by Mr. Badcock, auditor of the Stratton Union, stating that he had been appointed overseer of the poor of the parish of St. Stephen, by Launceston, in the Launceston Union, and that he had an impression that his being auditor of the Stratton Union exempted him from the office, and requesting to be informed if he was correct; and the Commissioners directed the following reply to be given thereto:—

"The Commissioners do not see in what way the circumstance of your being auditor of one Union would confer a legal exemption from being appointed overseer for a parish in another Union, of which you are not the auditor. If you had been appointed overseer for some parish in the Stratton Union, the question would have been raised how far the two offices of overseer and auditor are compatible, and can be held by the same person. The Commissioners apprehend that the grounds upon which it was held that a justice could not be appointed overseer, because of the incompatibility of the two offices, the overseer having to account to the justices, might be held to apply to an auditor: see Rex *v.* Patemen, 2 Term Rep. and Lord Kenyon's observations referring to the case of Rex *v.* Gayer, 1 Burr. 245."

II.—AUDITORS' DUTIES.

1. BLEAN UNION.

The Commissioners took into consideration a letter addressed to them by Mr. Abbott, district auditor, Canterbury, stating, that having received a notice from a rated inhabitant of the parish of Herne, in the Blean Union, that the poor-rate of that parish contained some errors which required to be investigated by him, he wished to have the instruction of the Commissioners, as to how far he could interfere in the matter; and the Commissioners directed the following reply to be given thereto:—

"I am to state in reply that the Commissioners are of opinion that the power of the auditor of a Union does not extend to the investigation of any alleged inaccuracies in a rate made for the relief of the poor. This is a power which belongs to the justices on appeal against the rate. The rate as made by the overseers, and allowed by the justices, must be deemed to be a good and lawful rate, until the contrary is shown on appeal.

"It is the duty of the auditor to ascertain, not how the rate has been made, or whether all the property in the parish has been properly assessed in such rate, but that the rate has been collected by the overseers, and the sums collected duly brought to account."

2. DITTO.—STAINES UNION.

12th November, 1841.

The Commissioners took into consideration a report made to them by Mr. Mitchiner, district auditor, in regard to the allowance by him of certain items in the accounts of the overseers of the parish of Harmondsworth, to which objections had been urged by the churchwardens and principal rate-payers of that parish; and the Commissioners directed a communication, of which the following are extracts, to be addressed to him on the subject of his report, and that a copy of such communication should be forwarded to the churchwardens of the parish:—

"The Commissioners' think it necessary to make the following remarks upon certain passages which occur in the report in question.

"1st. As to overseers' travelling charges:—

"Upon this subject, the Commissioners have to point out to you, that when an overseer is put to unavoidable charges in performing the duties of his office, the law allows of his being reimbursed those expenses out of the poor-rates. Thus, when an overseer in the exercise of his office is required to travel to a distance from his parish, and is under the necessity of hiring a conveyance, the expense, being unavoidable, may, so far as it is reasonable, be allowed him. But the Commissioners would observe, that the law does not allow of any compensation for the personal exertion of an overseer; or for loss of time; nor does it allow a fixed charge in lieu of the actual expenses incurred on the occasion.

"The Commissioners cannot undertake to enumerate the particular occasions or duties, in performing which charges of this nature might be allowed the overseers. The general rule above expressed will govern each of these cases; in applying which the auditor will bear in mind,—

"1. That there was a reasonable necessity for incurring expense; and,

"2. That the sum charged is reasonable, or such as the occasion justified;

"3. When the charge relates to travelling expenses, that such expenses can only be reimbursed when incurred in travelling beyond the limits of the parish or district for which the overseer is appointed.

"With respect to the question whether, when an overseer has a conveyance of his own, he can use such conveyance, and charge the cost to the parish, the Commissioners consider an overseer is only bound to perform personal services, and is not bound to use his own horse or carriage in doing business which may require him to travel beyond reasonable walking distances.

"If in such case he hires a conveyance, he is entitled to be repaid his reasonable expenses; but if he choose to use his own horse or carriage, in such a case he is incurring in the business of the parish an expense which has either been discharged by anticipation, or will fall upon him afterwards; although he may not at the time make an immediate outlay of money. It may be difficult to ascertain in such cases the real expense to an overseer. But whatever the true expense is, that would be allowable, and it is the duty of the auditor to be vigilant in preventing unreasonable charges in such cases. It is obvious that a charge for more than the true expense would be unreasonable and unlawful, as would also a charge for more than the amount at which the means of conveyance could have been hired.

"2nd. As regards the objection, that charges for payment of county rate and police constables' bills were allowed, the Commissioners observe with respect to the former, that it is the duty of the overseers, under the 2nd section, 12 Geo. II., c. 29, to pay to the high constable the sums assessed upon the parish for the purposes of the county rate, within the space of thirty days after demand thereof, made in writing, shall be given to such overseers, or left at their dwelling-houses. It does not appear necessary that the high constable should collect it from the overseers after demand made, and the overseers would subject themselves to have the amount levied on them by distress of their goods, in case of their refusal, or neglect, to pay the sum so demanded (See 55 Geo. III. c. 51, s. 12).

"But it would seem that if an overseer, in paying county rates in obedience to the precepts served upon him, should incur any expenses, the quarter sessions may order him an allowance or compensation out of any county rate (55 Geo. III. c. 51, s. 16). The Commissioners are not aware of any authority for paying such expenses out of the poor-rate. * * * *

"3rd. With respect to the charges made on exempting poor persons from payment of their poor rate, to which objection has been made, the Commissioners observe, that there is no doubt of the right of the justice's clerk to demand a fee upon such exemption taking place, if a fee be fixed by the authorized table of fees. The exemption takes place under the 54 Geo. III. c. 170, s. 11. That statute authorizes justices (with the requisite consent) to discharge poor persons from the payment of their poor rate, upon the application of such persons. The order is made, therefore, on the application of the person rated; and on this ground the Commissioners conceive that the fee would be payable by that person, and not by the parish. The parish cannot be regarded either as offending parties, or parties resisting a right (for the consent of the overseers or guardians is a necessary condition to the discharge) and cannot, therefore, even equitably, be charged with the cost of the proceeding which does not originate with the parish, and is not for its benefit. The Commissioners are, therefore, of opinion that the fee, where it is lawfully demandable, can only be demanded of the person applying to be excused.

* * * *

"5th. As regards the cost of writing out the jury list, the Commissioners think, that as the statute 6 Geo. IV. c. 50, which casts the duty of preparing the jury lists on the overseers, only provides for the payment out of the poor rate of the costs of printing the jury lists; any further charge is illegal.

"6th. As regards the objection to allowing 'receipt accounts without accounting for the whole rate,' and your remarks thereon, the Commissioners are of opinion that the overseers are required by law, as well as by the order for keeping the accounts, to bring into the debtor side of the account the full amount of the rate as allowed by justices, and not the amount only which they collect.

"7th. Upon the objection, that summonses repaid, and monies received for expense of paupers are not accounted for, the Commissioners observe, that the auditor's duty in this respect is, undoubtedly, to charge the overseer with any omission to account. The Commissioners are aware that it may be difficult to ascertain in all cases whether an overseer has duly accounted for such receipts; but the knowledge of this difficulty obviously calls for an increased vigilance on the part of the auditor to see that the rates are duly protected."

III. — BREAD. — Prosecution of Bread Contractor.—Wincanton Union.

3rd March, 1843.

The following letter, addressed to the Commissioners by the Clerk of the Wincanton Union, was read, when they directed that their thanks should be conveyed to him for the communication:—

"I beg to state, for the information of the Poor Law Commissioners, that, on Wednesday last (22nd February, 1843), it was reported to the Board of Guardians that Thomas Criddle, the bread contractor for the Castle Cary and Bruton districts of this Union, had delivered bread for the use of the poor in those districts under the weight contracted for by him; and, that at the time of the delivery, he he had not in his bread-cart the weights and scales, or other just balances, as directed by the statute, which subjected him to a penalty of 5*l*. And the Guardians having received other complaints of short weight, they directed me to make an example of Criddle, that the law might become generally known, and that bakers might at all times hereafter be compelled to carry with them just and proper balances according to the standard in the Exchequer.

"As directed by the Guardians I commenced immediate proceedings, and brought the case on for hearing at the Wincanton Petty Sessions yesterday, when Criddle was fined in the full penalty of 5*l*. This I trust will have a salutary effect in this part of the country upon every baker contracting to supply the poor with bread; and if the Commissioners deem it of sufficient importance to give it general publicity, it may induce the respective Boards of Guardians throughout the country to prosecute summarily every contractor who neglects to have in his cart just and proper balances when delivering bread to the poor."

IV. — BURIAL OF PAUPERS. — Bury Union.

13th May, 1842.

The Commissioners took into consideration a letter addressed to them by the Clerk to the Bury Union, requesting their opinion as to whether the Guardians of the Union should continue to pay out of the poor rates, the dues on the burial of poor persons dying out of the workhouse, which he stated they had lately in one or two instances paid; and the Commissioners directed the following answer to be given thereto:—

"I am to call the attention of the Guardians to the decision in Reg. *v.* The Overseers of St. George, Hanover Square; [Reg. *v.* Steward and another, 12 A. and E. 773;] in which the law in respect to the supposed obligation on parishes to bury destitute paupers is clearly explained. The result of the decision is, that the overseers, and consequently the Guardians, have no general obligation as to the burial of dead bodies found within the parish or union.

"The Court, however, stated, that the common law cast upon some one the duty of carrying to the grave, decently, the dead body of every person whose representatives or relations do not possess the means of defraying the expenses of the burial. It is difficult, as the Commissioners stated in their report on the further amendment of the law, to determine the person on whom the obligation is incumbent; but the Commissioners conceive, that it is in general incumbent on the person who has the custody of the dead body. Now, if this person be destitute, and be unable to defray the expenses of the burial, the Guardians may, as the Commissioners think, give him relief for that purpose.

"With respect to burial fees, where the claim to them in respect of the burial of a person not being a pauper is either admitted or established, the Commissioners are not prepared to say, that the circumstance of the person interred being dependent on the poor rates at the time of his decease, would make any difference as to the right of the incumbent or sexton, &c. to claim a fee for the interment.

"If, therefore, the claim of the incumbent be in any case well founded, the burial fees would form part of the necessary expenses attendant on the funeral, and the Guardians, in advancing relief to the person who has the custody of the body, would no doubt duly consider this necessity."

V.—COOKING APPARATUS.

October 21, 1840.

The Commissioners read a letter, received from the Clerk of the West Ham Union, applying for information on the subject of Steam-cooking Apparatus, and the Commissioners directed the letter to be referred to their Assistant-Commissioner Mr. Parker.

October 29, 1840.

The following report of Mr. Parker on this subject was read, and directed to be communicated to the Clerk of the West Ham Union:—

"*Highgate, October* 28, 1840.

"GENTLEMEN,—I have the honour to acknowledge the receipt of your letter, dated the 21st instant, requesting me to report the names of the Unions in which cooking by steam has been tried and been found to answer, the nature and cost of the apparatus, and whether this mode of cooking has proved economical, or in other respects advantageous, and to acquaint you that cooking by steam has been tried and found to answer in the Abingdon, Amersham, and Windsor Unions.

"The apparatus erected in the kitchen of the Abingdon workhouse, is a boiler (with a safety valve) from which steam is conveyed into the kettles. This apparatus is simple in its construction, and not likely to be injured by any neglect on the part of the cook. It is not, however, adequate for every purpose, inasmuch as the kettles are not calculated for making the gruel for the breakfasts of the able-bodied inmates; which, in consequence, is cooked in a copper, heated by a separate fire. It is also worthy of remark, that the surplus steam created is not applied to any useful purpose. Thus, a separate fire for cooking gruel is rendered necessary, and much steam applicable to useful purposes is wasted.

"The apparatus in the Windsor Union workhouse was completed about a fortnight since, and was selected by the Guardians after inspecting the cooking apparatus at the Amersham Union workhouse, from which it varies in one or two respects, affecting in no way the principle of construction, though highly judicious, inasmuch as copper kettles are substituted for wooden tubs, which are liable to injury by the action and force of steam.

"The apparatus in each of these houses is intended to cook food for 300 persons; but is calculated to cook for a much larger number. The master of the Windsor Union workhouse feels confident that the apparatus in that house will cook sufficient food for 500 persons, with no more fuel than is required to cook for 200. I have requested him accurately to ascertain the quantity of fuel daily consumed in the course of the next week, and to give me his opinion of the apparatus, which has already been tried in the presence of the Guardians, and found to answer their fullest expectations; producing sufficient steam to cook food in two large coppers and a long range of large saucepans, and to heat the water in the cistern from which the boiler feeds itself, supplying hot water to the scullery as well as to the male and female infirmaries, which are detached several hundred feet from the building. The master informs me that on this occasion the steam was raised in twenty-five minutes from the time the fire was lighted, notwithstanding the freshness, and therefore unfavourable state of the brick work of the boiler to receive heat, and that less than half a bushel of coals was consumed in experiments lasting for three hours.

"He has also expressed an opinion that the food cooked by it is superior to food cooked in the ordinary way, and that the cooking is attended with less waste.

"For this apparatus complete, together with a large copper, Mr. Young, of Barnstaple, the inventor, charges 85*l*.

"I am, Gentlemen,
"Your obedient servant,
(Signed) "H. W. PARKER,
"*Assistant Poor Law Commissioner.*
"*The Poor Law Commissioners.*"

4th November, 1840.

The following letters also on this subject were read, and copies directed to be sent to the Clerk of the West Ham Union:—

"*Highgate, 2d November*, 1840.

"GENTLEMEN,—In reference to my observations on the steam-cooking apparatus in use in three of the workhouses in my district, I have the honour to enclose you a copy of a letter from Mr. Nicholls, the Master of the Windsor Union workhouse.

"I have the honour to be, &c.
"H. W. PARKER, *Assistant Commissioner.*
"*The Poor Law Commissioners.*"

"*Windsor Union Workhouse,*
30th October, 1840.

"SIR,—In reply to your request as to the steam-cooking apparatus in this house, I beg leave to say, for the short time it has been in operation, I find it to answer every purpose, with a great saving. I can cook for 300 paupers with the same ease as 100. It takes about three-fourths of an hour to get up the steam, and in ten minutes the gruel is made; the steam is turned off to boil the water for washing up. To cook the dinner, it takes two hours, and the same steam will supply the baths with hot water, if required. All this is done with three-fourths of a cwt. of coals.

"The provisions thus cooked are equal to, if not preferable, to those which have been prepared by boiling. The management is simple, and perfectly safe, with little trouble to the cook, and the kitchen always clean.

"I have, &c.

"(Signed) WM. NICHOLLS.

"*H. W. Parker, Esq.*,

"*Assistant Poor Law Commissioner.*"

VI.—GUARDIAN.

1. A HIGH SHERIFF CANNOT ACT AS EX-OFFICIO GUARDIAN.—LICHFIELD UNION.

14th February, 1843.

The Commissioners took into consideration a letter addressed to them by the Clerk to the Lichfield Union, requesting their opinion as to whether the high sheriff for a county, being a justice of the peace for the same county, and consequently an ex-officio Guardian for the Union within which he resides, can, during the period of his shrievalty, legally act as such ex-officio Guardian at the Board of Guardians: and the Commissioners directed the following answer to be given thereto:—

"In reply, I am to state that the Commissioners consider that a person, while holding the office of high sheriff of a county, is disqualified to act as ex-officio Guardian within that county. To be an ex-officio Guardian of a Union, under the 38th section of the Poor Law Amendment Act, the justice must reside within the Union, and act for the county in which it is situate. By statute 1 M. sess. 2, c. 8, sec. 12, no sheriff shall exercise the office of a justice of the peace during the time he acts as sheriff. As he cannot, therefore, act as justice for the county, it follows that he has not the qualification of a Guardian ex officio, prescribed by the 38th section of the Poor Law Amendment Act."

2. ELECTION OF.—WAREHAM AND PURBECK UNIONS.

16th February, 1843.

The Commissioners took into consideration a letter addressed to them by the Clerks of the Wareham and Purbeck Union, inquiring whether, under Article 12 of the election order, they were enabled to require that the nomination papers should be sent to them in every case direct, or if it was imperative on them to name a person to receive the papers in each parish; and observing that the former plan would have the advantage of preventing collusion, and would save trouble: and the Commissioners directed the following answer to be given thereto:—

"I am to state in reply that the Commissioners think, that the election order contemplates that the clerk to the Union should appoint some person to receive nomination papers in each parish. Sending the papers direct to the clerk is an alternative, and a course which it is in the discretion of the proposer to adopt; but the obligation to appoint persons to receive the nomination papers is not thereby dispensed with."

3. DITTO.—YEOVIL UNION.

16th February, 1843.

The Commissioners took into consideration a letter, of which the following is an extract, addressed to them by the Clerk of the Yeovil Union:—

"The Form E, No. 6, states the course to be pursued if more than the required number of persons be nominated, viz., to cause on the 20th voting-papers to be issued; and No. 5 states that no limit is set during the election to a person nominated sending a refusal. *Query*—If the person or persons more than required send a refusal prior to the 20th, will it be at all necessary to cause voting-papers to be issued, as in such a case there would be no contest?

"If after the voting-papers shall have been issued a similar circumstance occur, what course must the clerk take, as No. 5 says, the election, so far as regards that person, will be no further proceeded with, seems to imply that it is to proceed as regards the others on the list: and in this last case, having proceeded thus far, to issue the voting-papers, would he be entitled to claim as for a contested election, although thus late all but the number required had testified their unwillingness to act?"

And the Commissioners directed the following reply to be given thereto:—

"I am to state that, in the first case supposed by you, where the candidate or candidates above the number of Guardians to be elected for the parish declare in writing their unwillingness to serve the office previously to the time appointed for issuing the voting papers, it will not be necessary to issue such papers.

"In the second case supposed, where the refusal to serve is not given until after the voting papers are issued, the votes given for the candidate so refusing will be thrown away. The Commissioners think that such a case would not be a contested election, within the meaning of the order of the Commissioners, so as to entitle the clerk to the remuneration provided in cases of contested elections, provided the remaining number of candidates, after the withdrawal of the one who resigned, did not exceed the number to be elected for the parish.'

4. DITTO.—CHELMSFORD UNION.

13*th February*, 1843.

The Commissioners took into consideration a letter addressed to them by the clerk to the Chelmsford Board of Guardians, inquiring as follows, in reference to the approaching election of Guardians for the parish of Chelmsford, or any other parish for which two or more Guardians are to be elected:—

"If one person, or any other number of persons *less* than the number of Guardians to be elected, be duly put in nomination, such person or persons not being either of the Guardians of the present year, and neither of the Guardians of the present year signifying his intention to resign, what course is to be pursued as to the election? Must the person or persons so put in nomination be returned as duly elected? And in that case, could all or any, and which of the Guardians of the present year, continue to act for the next year?"

And the Commissioners directed the following reply to be given thereto:—

"I am directed by the Poor Law Commissioners to acknowledge the receipt of your letter of the 9th instant, and in answer thereto to state that, in the case supposed, the person duly put in nomination will be returned. But notwithstanding that the full number of Guardians to which the parish may be entitled be not elected, neither of the Guardians of the previous year can continue to act. Section 10 of 5th and 6th Vic. c. 57, provides for the case where *no* person shall be elected for the office of Guardian in any parish. This is not the case to which your question applies, in which a Guardian is elected, but not the full number of Guardians."

VII.—LUNATICS.

The following Abstract of Returns showing the number of pauper lunatics and idiots chargeable to parishes comprised in 589 Unions in England and Wales in the month of August, 1842, distinguishing the number of each sex, whether dangerous to themselves or others, where maintained, and the average weekly cost per head for maintenance and clothing, &c., was read:—See pp. 57—59.

VIII.—MEDICAL RELIEF.

1. IN URGENT CASES.—LEOMINSTER UNION.

16*th February*, 1843.

The Commissioners took into consideration a letter, addressed to them by the Rev. J. Edwards, rector of Croft with Yarpole, calling their attention to a case of urgent sickness, which a medical officer of the Leominster Union had refused to attend on the order of an overseer, alleging that he was not bound to do so unless an order from the relieving officer was obtained; and the Commissioners directed the following answer to be given thereto:—

"I am to inform you in reply, that the order of the Commissioners issued on the 21st of April, 1842, renders it the duty of the medical officer to attend duly and punctually upon all persons requiring medical or surgical assistance, and to supply the requisite medicines and appliances, whenever they are required to do so by a written or a printed order of the Board of Guardians, or of a relieving officer, *and, in cases of sudden and urgent necessity, by an order of the overseers of the poor.*

"The Commissioners consider it of great importance that this portion of the medical officers' duties should be clearly and fully understood, and the Commissioners will address a communication to the Board of Guardians of the Leominster Union, calling their especial attention to the circumstances you have been good enough to make known to the Commissioners."

And the Commissioners directed the following communication to be made on this subject to the clerk of the Leominster Union:—

"I am directed by the Poor Law Commissioners to transmit for the consideration of the Board of Guardians of the Leominster Union, the accompanying copy of a letter which the Commissioners have received from the Rev. J. Edwards, together with a copy of their reply thereto.

The Commissioners wish especially to direct

the Guardians' attention to that portion of Mr. Edward's letter, in which he alludes to an existing impression on the minds of the medical officers of the Union, that they are not bound to attend cases of sickness, however urgent, on the order of an overseer. The Commissioners think it important that this misapprehension should be at once removed, and they suggest to the Guardians the expediency of their addressing an official letter to each of the medical officers of the Union, calling attention expressly to Article 19, Section 1, of the Order of the 21st April last, whereby it is rendered the duty of medical officers, duly and punctually to attend cases of sickness under urgent circumstances, on the order of an overseer of the poor, as well as on the direction of a relieving officer, or of the Guardians themselves."

2. DITTO.—CHESTER-LE-STREET UNION.

8th March, 1843.

The Commissioners took into consideration a letter addressed to them by the Clerk to the Chester-le-Street Union, of which the following is an extract:—

"The enclosed bill for surgical and medical attendance was sent in to the Board of Guardians at their meeting yesterday by Mr. Linton, who is not a district officer, and was disallowed by them. The pauper is residing in, but not belonging to, this Union.

"Mr. Linton was called in immediately upon the occurrence of the accident, as the relatives of the pauper did not know who was the district medical officer, nor had they the means of obtaining a medical order immediately.

"As this is a district peculiarly liable to such accidents, from the number of collieries and railways in and traversing it, and as in many of the cases immediate medical assistance is necessary for the preservation of the patient's life, and the attendance of the district medical officer may, through unforeseen circumstances, be delayed, I would wish to be informed how far the Commissioners would sanction the allowance, by the Board, of payment of charges made by medical gentlemen who may be called upon to attend paupers in cases of sudden accident or extreme emergency, where, from the before-stated causes, the attendance of the district medical officer cannot be so readily obtained."

And the Commissioners directed the following reply to be given thereto:—

"The Commissioners are of opinion, that in cases of sickness or accident requiring immediate medical or surgical attendance, and when the services of the medical officer cannot be promptly obtained, the relieving officer may employ any other medical man to attend the case. (*Vide* General Order of the 21st April, 1842, Art. 20, No. 3.) They also think, that in a case of urgency of this nature, in which, in the absence of the medical officer, another medical man attends without any order, the Guardians would be justified in paying him for such attendance; provided they subsequently decide that the person so attended was at the time in a destitute condition.

"As to the amount of the charge for the medical attendance in such a case, that must depend upon the circumstances of each case, and must be settled between the medical man and the Guardians. The fees prescribed by Articles 10 and 13 of the General Medical Order refer to medical officers only.

"The Commissioners wish to add, that, when a medical man (not being the medical officer) attends a pauper under the circumstances above described, the relieving officer should visit the case as soon as he is made acquainted with it; and the medical officer should be directed to attend the case, and relieve the medical man who had attended in his absence from the charge of it as soon as practicable."

IX.—MEDICAL OFFICER.—QUALIFICATION OF.

16th July, 1842.

The Commissioners took into consideration a letter, received by them from Mr. George Crutch, of Old-street, St. Luke's, Middlesex, inquiring whether a person holding the diploma of Bachelor of Medicine, or Doctor of Medicine, of the London University, in conjunction with a diploma of the Royal College of Surgeons of London, is eligible as a medical officer under the Poor Law Amendment Act; and the Commissioners directed the following answer to be given thereto:—

"In reply I am to state, that the senate of the London University have, by the Queen's Charter of 26th December, 1837, the power to confer the degrees of Bachelor of Medicine and Doctor of Medicine. There appears, therefore, to be no question that persons holding the diploma of Doctor or Bachelor of Medicine of this University, together with a diploma from the London College of Surgeons, are qualified under the Commissioners' Order, Article 3, paragraph 1, to be a medical officer of a parish or Union."

Name of County.	Population of the Unions in each County in 1841, some of which comprise parts of several Counties.	Number of LUNATICS and IDIOTS chargeable to Parishes in each Union, in the month of August, 1842.							
		Number of Lunatics and Idiots.							
		Lunatics.			Idiots.			Total Lunatics and Idiots.	Proportion per Cent. to Population.
		Males.	Females.	Total.	Males.	Females.	Total.		
ENGLAND.									
Bedford	112,379	32	36	68	28	39	67	135	·1
Berks	190,367	50	66	116	56	69	125	241	·1
Buckingham	149,352	28	39	67	28	32	60	127	·09
Cambridge	171,848	33	43	76	47	36	83	159	·09
Chester	371,331	53	58	111	72	90	162	273	·07
Cornwall	340,728	63	99	162	80	70	150	312	·09
Cumberland	177,912	42	41	83	37	41	78	161	·09
Derby	220,028	27	28	55	58	51	109	164	·07
Devon	430,221	97	129	226	158	144	302	528	·1
Dorset	167,874	55	71	126	35	45	80	206	·1
Durham	325,997	48	48	96	65	49	114	210	·1
Essex	320,818	55	81	136	93	96	189	325	·1
Gloucester	330,562	103	108	211	87	100	187	398	·1
Hereford	110,675	26	42	68	41	38	79	147	·1
Hertford	176,173	34	48	82	66	66	132	214	·1
Huntingdon	55,573	13	16	29	13	14	27	56	·1
Kent	534,882	105	155	260	95	110	205	465	·09
Lancaster	1,543,449	274	281	555	179	245	424	979	·06
Leicester	220,232	59	62	121	59	64	123	244	·1
Lincoln	356,347	77	73	150	80	66	146	296	·08
Middlesex	841,402	268	399	667	106	111	217	884	·1
Monmouth	150,222	24	27	51	24	30	54	105	·07
Norfolk	343,277	70	112	182	101	118	219	401	·1
Northampton	197,197	47	75	122	64	83	147	269	·1
Northumberland	265,988	60	68	128	89	104	193	321	·1
Nottingham	270,719	43	87	130	58	73	131	261	·1
Oxford	141,330	32	36	68	51	53	104	172	·1
Rutland	23,150	8	4	12	6	6	12	24	·1
Salop	191,052	42	46	88	72	84	156	244	·1
Somerset	454,446	77	151	228	146	198	344	572	·1
Southampton	311,413	94	144	238	89	78	167	405	·1
Stafford	442,348	78	87	165	105	114	219	384	·09
Suffolk	314,722	96	110	206	73	82	155	361	·1
Surrey	512,580	132	185	317	100	104	204	521	·1
Sussex	223,435	44	50	94	76	81	157	251	1
Warwick	220,029	42	50	92	58	75	133	225	·1
Westmoreland	56,469	3	12	15	13	22	35	50	·09
Wilts	233,246	80	106	186	84	87	171	357	·1
Worcester	336,108	64	78	142	64	78	142	284	·08
York, East Riding	180,218	45	57	102	38	33	71	173	.1
York, North Riding	180,527	35	43	78	29	37	66	144	·08
York, West Riding	790,751	168	174	342	154	168	322	664	·08
Totals of England	12,978,377	2,826	3,625	6,451	2,977	3,284	6,261	12,712	·1
WALES.									
Anglesey	38,105	11	20	31	18	19	37	68	·2
Brecon	55,399	8	13	21	20	23	43	64	·1
Cardigan	75,136	28	23	51	23	45	68	119	·2
Carmarthen	110,404	28	44	72	42	51	93	165	·1
Carnarvon	86,728	25	24	49	42	57	99	148	·2
Denbigh	68,483	4	14	18	34	31	65	83	·1
Flint	64,355	9	13	22	21	21	42	64	·1
Glamorgan	178,041	33	52	85	25	37	62	147	·08
Merioneth	50,696	11	14	25	28	16	44	69	·1
Montgomery	58,709	11	11	22	36	50	86	108	·2
Pembroke	78,563	16	18	34	25	44	69	103	·1
Radnor	19,554	2	4	6	7	7	14	20	·1
Totals of Wales	884,173	186	250	436	321	401	722	1,158	·1
Totals of actual Returns from 589 Unions in England and Wales.	13,862,550	3,012	3,875	6,887	3,298	3,685	6,983	13,870	·1
Estimated Totals for the whole of England and Wales	15,906,053	3,456	4,446	7,902	3,784	4,228	8,012	15,914	·1

Name of County.	Number of LUNATICS and IDIOTS chargeable to Parishes in each Union, in the month of August, 1842.											
	Where Maintained.											
	In County Lunatic Asylum.			In Licensed House.			In Union Workhouse.			With their Friends, elsewhere.		
	Males.	Females.	Total.	Males.	Females.	Total.	Males.	Females.	Total.	Males.	Females.	Tc
ENGLAND.												
Bedford	30	21	51	1	4	5	21	31	52	8	19	
Berks	1	3	4	47	60	107	32	28	60	26	44	
Buckingham	5	4	9	19	23	42	11	19	30	21	25	
Cambridge	12	13	25	12	15	27	19	19	38	38	31	
Chester	46	55	101	..	..	..	22	30	52	57	63	
Cornwall	51	59	110	..	1	1	48	70	118	44	39	
Cumberland	8	6	14	26	22	48	31	31	62	14	23	
Derby	4	2	6	20	11	31	21	30	51	40	36	
Devon	7	6	13	51	50	101	69	91	160	128	126	
Dorset	44	52	96	8	10	18	16	36	52	22	18	
Durham	..	4	4	49	36	85	27	22	49	37	35	
Essex	6	4	10	42	58	100	44	57	101	56	58	
Gloucester	73	70	143	15	9	24	52	64	116	51	64	
Hereford	..	5	5	11	14	25	9	13	22	48	47	
Hertford	31	24	55	11	15	26	25	37	62	30	41	
Huntingdon	9	10	19	4	4	8	12	7	19	1	9	
Kent	92	105	197	19	38	57	57	74	131	32	48	
Lancaster	223	220	443	..	..	..	148	197	345	82	109	
Leicester	45	37	82	3	..	3	38	55	93	32	34	
Lincoln	34	28	62	17	17	34	56	47	103	50	47	
Middlesex	188	255	443	72	122	194	99	118	217	15	15	
Monmouth	5	5	10	17	12	29	7	16	23	19	24	
Norfolk	73	91	164	3	3	6	50	41	91	45	95	
Northampton	33	44	77	5	5	10	27	42	69	46	67	
Northumberland	1	1	2	54	58	112	57	59	116	37	54	
Nottingham	39	59	98	..	..	..	36	64	100	26	37	
Oxford	2	2	4	28	34	62	21	26	47	32	27	
Rutland	5	2	7	1	..	1	3	6	9	5	2	
Salop	6	7	13	23	15	38	36	49	85	48	60	
Somerset	5	9	14	68	102	170	54	86	140	96	152	
Southampton	..	..	..	82	112	194	53	56	109	48	54	
Stafford	81	62	143	1	6	7	68	92	160	33	41	
Suffolk	87	89	176	6	11	17	57	32	69	39	60	
Surrey	119	151	270	11	39	50	84	72	156	17	28	
Sussex	1	1	2	45	38	83	27	29	56	47	63	
Warwick	9	9	18	33	31	64	27	40	67	31	45	
Westmoreland	4	3	7	2	6	8	5	12	17	5	13	
Wilts	4	5	9	71	91	162	37	50	87	52	47	
Worcester	19	20	39	35	37	72	36	56	92	38	43	
York, East Riding	9	14	23	32	32	64	19	28	47	23	16	
York, North Riding	14	5	19	17	25	42	15	22	37	18	28	
York, West Riding	124	122	246	2	3	5	105	121	226	91	96	
Totals of England	1,549	1,684	3,233	963	1,169	2,132	1,661	2,075	3,736	1,628	1,983	3,
WALES.												
Anglesey	..	..	..	..	..	..	..	..	..	29	39	
Brecon	1	..	1	4	2	6	1	3	4	22	31	
Cardigan	1	1	2	..	1	1	..	..	..	50	66	
Carmarthen	1	..	1	6	5	11	5	8	13	58	82	
Carnarvon	1	1	2	..	..	..	1	..	1	65	80	
Denbigh	3	4	7	..	..	..	5	2	7	30	39	
Flint	3	1	4	..	..	..	8	5	13	19	28	
Glamorgan	1	..	1	16	21	37	8	17	25	33	51	
Merioneth	1	..	1	..	..	..	2	3	5	36	27	
Montgomery	5	1	6	1	..	1	3	5	8	38	55	
Pembroke	10	6	16	..	..	..	2	12	14	29	44	
Radnor	..	..	..	..	..	..	1	2	3	8	9	
Totals of Wales	27	14	41	27	29	56	36	57	93	417	551	
Totals of actual Returns from 589 Unions in England and Wales.	1,576	1,698	3,274	990	1,198	2,188	1,697	2,132	3,829	2,045	2,534	4,
Estimated Totals for the whole of England and Wales	..	..	..	..	..	..	..	..	..	..	..	

Number of Lunatics and Idiots chargeable to Parishes in each Union, in the month of August, 1842.

	Ages.								Dangerous to themselves or others.	Of Dirty Habits.	Average Weekly Cost per Head of Maintenance and Clothing.			
	5 to 10	10 to 20	20 to 30	30 to 40	40 to 50	50 to 60	60 to 70	70 and upwards.			In County Lunatic Asylum.	In Licensed House.	Elsewhere.	Average.
											s. d.	s. d.	s. d.	s. d.
..	..	6	38	21	25	23	17	5	27	20	7 11½	9 0	2 9¼	4 11½
..	2	20	53	38	56	41	24	7	76	48	7 6	8 6½	2 10¼	5 5¾
..	..	5	19	24	27	24	20	8	20	10	9 0	9 3	3 2	5 7¼
..	..	9	29	40	44	18	15	4	37	45	8 6	9 6	3 1¼	5 0½
..	2	21	50	63	63	42	25	7	58	41	4 10¼	..	2 4½	3 3½
3	..	31	43	53	67	63	30	22	85	66	6 0	10 6	2 4½	3 8¼
1	..	8	46	40	27	19	15	5	37	36	8 8¾	7 11¾	2 7	4 8¾
..	..	11	30	48	38	22	11	4	26	33	9 8¼	9 9½	2 6¾	4 2¼
..	3	30	101	100	113	86	69	26	98	95	8 8½	10 3	2 11	4 5½
..	..	11	26	37	47	42	24	19	53	34	7 0	7 3¼	2 8¾	5 1¼
..	..	10	38	58	43	29	20	12	71	42	7 0	7 6¾	2 6¾	4 8
..	5	37	72	63	58	52	24	14	64	56	9 6½	9 3½	3 1¼	5 2½
..	1	22	79	110	63	60	44	19	108	80	9 0¼	8 5½	2 8¾	5 4½
..	2	11	23	28	33	25	20	5	22	27	12 0	10 10	2 7	4 3¾
..	..	12	53	40	43	43	21	2	52	25	8 8¼	8 7¼	3 0	5 1¾
..	1	4	10	9	15	8	9	..	13	11	9 0½	8 6	3 1½	5 10¾
..	2	22	90	99	116	74	43	19	144	94	8 5¾	9 1	2 9¾	5 11¾
..	4	53	189	248	220	134	113	18	321	85	7 8	..	2 5½	4 9¾
..	1	19	39	53	49	47	25	11	48	45	9 2½	10 0	2 10¼	5 0¾
..	..	24	53	65	62	52	25	15	72	59	10 9	10 5¼	3 1¼	5 6¾
..	1	44	145	204	230	138	89	33	226	114	9 0	9 5¾	3 8	7 7
..	..	2	28	15	26	20	10	4	20	23	9 6	8 6¼	2 7	4 10½
..	..	22	75	76	81	68	52	27	133	101	5 3½	8 6	2 8	3 10
..	1	20	46	49	75	38	27	13	61	83	9 8	8 11½	3 4¼	5 4¼
1	1	18	60	62	78	53	32	16	74	48	11 0	8 2½	2 9	4 8¼
..	..	17	46	64	55	51	21	7	55	40	9 0¼	..	3 0½	5 3½
..	3	21	23	41	33	31	10	10	40	29	9 0	8 9½	2 11½	5 2½
..	..	1	1	4	8	3	4	3	7	3	11 9¾	10 3	3 10½	6 5½
..	..	16	60	59	52	36	11	10	33	33	12 0½	11 0¼	2 7½	4 5¼
..	3	36	131	117	115	80	64	26	137	119	8 10¼	8 0	2 6¾	4 4
..	2	31	61	78	85	77	51	20	106	71	..	8 4¾	3 0½	5 7½
..	..	29	94	81	75	62	30	13	61	43	6 1¼	9 9	2 8¾	4 1¼
..	1	25	63	87	81	48	43	13	123	113	6 5½	10 3¼	2 5¼	4 9
..	3	16	93	116	135	74	63	21	90	136	9 0	9 4	3 8	6 11½
..	3	30	49	56	56	31	21	5	56	55	..	9 9	3 1¾	5 3¾
..	1	14	40	58	45	31	24	12	78	50	9 10¾	9 9¾	2 11¼	5 5¼
..	..	2	2	9	16	9	6	6	3	6	10 0	8 6	2 5½	4 5¾
1	1	19	59	52	87	64	50	24	127	69	8 1¼	7 11½	2 6¾	5 1¾
..	..	15	50	56	64	48	39	12	71	66	7 10¼	10 4¼	2 11	5 5¾
..	..	5	32	49	38	20	22	7	67	42	8 6¼	8 8¾	3 3	6 0
..	..	6	23	32	34	25	12	12	56	43	8 0¼	7 3¾	2 11	4 10½
..	2	36	134	136	152	121	63	20	197	123	7 0	9 0	2 8¼	4 4
6	45	791	2,396	2,738	2,830	2,032	1,338	536	3,259	2,371	7 11	8 10¾	2 10	5 1¾
..	..	2	13	18	5	11	13	6	6	11	..	..	2 6¼	2 6¼
..	..	3	12	17	10	9	11	2	13	16	13 2	11 6	3 0¼	3 11¾
..	..	10	17	23	25	20	17	7	5	19	7 2	9 9	2 4¼	2 6
1	2	12	28	41	37	21	14	9	14	12	12 0	8 6	2 2½	2 8¼
..	..	6	19	26	35	28	26	8	7	33	13 0	..	2 5¼	2 7½
..	1	7	20	17	17	12	6	3	9	7	11 7¾	..	2 4½	3 2
..	..	8	16	7	12	9	8	4	10	10	11 1½	..	2 11½	3 5½
..	..	8	32	31	29	25	14	8	14	22	9 0½	8 9¼	3 1¼	4 8
..	..	2	12	12	11	18	7	7	13	29	12 0	..	2 8	2 9½
..	..	3	28	14	21	16	21	5	13	37	11 0	12 0	2 6½	3 1
..	..	13	22	16	17	16	14	5	1	9	7 0½	..	2 3½	3 0½
..	..	3	2	3	9	1	2	..	2	5	..	..	2 7½	2 7½
1	3	77	221	225	228	186	153	64	107	210	9 6½	9 1	2 6½	3 1¼
7	48	868	2,617	2,963	3,058	2,218	1,491	600	3,366	2,581	7 11¼	8 10¾	2 9½	4 11¾
..	..	..	..	..	..	..	..	..	..	..	7 11¼	8 10¾	2 9½	4 11¾

X.—MENDICITY SOCIETY.—POOR-RATES CANNOT BE APPLIED TOWARDS THE SUPPORT OF.—STRATFORD-ON-AVON UNION.

11th January, 1842.

The Commissioners took into consideration a letter addressed to them by the Clerk to the Stratford-on-Avon Union, stating that the Guardians were desirous of subscribing a sum of 10*l.* annually towards the support of a mendicity society, established in the town of Stratford-on-Avon and the neighbourhood, (almost co-extensive with the Union,) under the conviction that such society would tend very materially to relieve the poor-rate from the payment towards the support of persons obtaining assistance from the society, who would otherwise have to be relieved by the Guardians as casual paupers; and requesting the opinion and direction of the Commissioners on the subject; and the Commissioners directed the following answer to be given thereto:—

"I am to state in reply, that the Commissioners concur with the Guardians in thinking the object sought to be effected by the proposed subscription a beneficial one, and one which, so far as it can be promoted by private means, should be encouraged.

"But the Commissioners apprehend that the proposal, as affecting the poor-rates, is, legally considered, subject to objections. Viewing the contribution from the poor-rates to a mendicity society as a means of relief, it is clear that such application is unauthorized, as the Guardians are thereby transferring to others that control of the fund raised for the relief of destitute persons, which the law has vested in them, and leaving the duty of relieving such persons to be discharged by others who have no legal responsibility in the performance of such duty. But viewing the measure as a means of preventing chargeability, the proposed payment, as it seems to the Commissioners, is equally objectionable. The poor-rate being a statutable fund, is to be applied to statutable purposes. The support of a society whose object, by relieving destitution, is to prevent chargeability, is not one of those purposes. The poor-rates can only be applied to the relief of destitution when it actually occurs, and the relief must then be given by the persons and in the form provided by law.

"The Commissioners regret that the opinion which they have felt it their duty to convey in this letter, should interfere with the benevolent object which the Guardians wished to attain by the proposed subscription."

XI.—OVERSEERS.—LIABILITY OF IN REGARD TO THE CALLS OF BOARDS OF GUARDIANS.—STOURBRIDGE UNION.

1st March, 1842.

The Commissioners took into consideration a letter addressed to them by Mr. Henry Fernie, one of the overseers of the borough of Hales Owen, stating that the Board of Guardians of the Stourbridge Union had unexpectedly made a call upon the overseers for 131*l.*, whose term of office was nearly expired, and inquiring, as they found it impossible to satisfy the call, whether they were compelled to pay the whole amount of the call; or, if they collected a part only of the amount and paid it to the treasurer, whether their successors would be obligated to pay the remainder; also, whether in case they made a rate sufficient to cover the call, but did not collect the whole of it, and advanced the deficiency themselves, their successors would be bound to reimburse them; and further, whether the overseers would have power to collect any rates after the 25th March: and the Commissioners directed the following answer to be given thereto:—

"I am to state in reply, that the order of the Board of Guardians being made upon the present overseers, such order is enforceable against them, and not against their successors. The order being made for a specific sum, payment of a part would not be an obedience to the order, and would leave the overseers subject to penalties under the 98th section of the Poor Law Amendment Act.

"The proper course appears to be, for the present overseers forthwith to make a rate sufficient to meet the whole amount required by the order. If the overseers can, before their period of office expire, collect sufficient to meet the demand of the Guardians, none of the difficulties suggested by your inquiries will arise. But if the overseers are not able to collect under the new rate sufficient to satisfy the order, and the Guardians insist upon payment by the present overseers, it would be perfectly legal and proper for the succeeding overseers to collect the arrears of the rate, and reimburse the present overseers any sums they may advance on account of the parish beyond what they may have been able to collect. But the present overseers will not themselves be empowered, after their period of office expires, to collect the arrears of rate."

XII.—PAID OFFICERS.—How THEIR EXPENSES, WHEN ATTENDING AS WITNESSES, SHOULD BE CHARGED.

18th July, 1842.

The Commissioners took into consideration a letter addressed to them by Mr. Abbott, district auditor, respecting the fund to which the expenses of Union officers, when attending the justices as witnesses on parochial business, should be charged; and the Commissioners directed that he should be informed that they agreed with him in thinking, that such expenses should be defrayed by the overseers of the particular parish on whose account the attendance of the officers might be required.

XIII.—RELIEF.

1. TO A WOMAN LIVING APART FROM HER HUSBAND.—MARKET BOSWORTH UNION.

21st July, 1842.

The Commissioners took into consideration the following letter, addressed to them by the Clerk of the Market Bosworth Union:—

"I am directed by this Board to lay before you the following case which came before them at their last weekly meeting:—About twenty-seven years ago a person named John Ballard, residing at Dadlington, married a wife, by whom he had twin children; but in consequence of his ill-treatment she left him about twelve months after their marriage, and up to the present time she has been able to maintain herself, the children being dead. In consequence of depression and age, she has become chargeable to the parish, and the overseer gave her a ticket of admission to the workhouse, where she now is, the man having another woman living with him.

"Application has been made to the man to allow her a separate maintenance, but he refuses, and offers to take her into his house and keep her; but the woman refuses to go, partly from fear and partly from his having another woman residing with him. On the other hand, the parish refuse to maintain her in the workhouse, as the man offers to keep her, and is in circumstances so to do. The Board have inquired into the character of the man, and he is represented as being of a violent disposition and likely to ill-treat her again. The parish officers have applied to the magistrates on the subject, but they refuse to interfere, saying they have no power to act, the man offering to receive her.

And the Commissioners directed the following answer to be given thereto:—

"In reply the Commissioners have to observe, that the general violent character of the husband, as represented in your letter, would not justify the Guardians in giving relief to the wife, when he is able and expresses his willingness to maintain her. If, in fact, he should ill treat her, either by violence or by refusing sufficient maintenance to her, he would, in the one case, be liable to be bound by articles of the peace, and, in the other, to be dealt with under the Vagrant Act, in case she become chargeable through being insufficiently maintained by him.

"But under the present circumstances of his offering to maintain his wife in his own house, the Commissioners think the magistrates have no ground for interference, nor the Guardians for giving relief."

2. BY OVERSEERS IN CASES OF SUDDEN OR URGENT NECESSITY.—BLEAN UNION.

12th April, 1842.

The Commissioners took into consideration the following letter, addressed to them by the Clerk of the Blean Union:—

"The Board of Guardians of the Blean Union have directed me to lay the following case before the Poor Law Commissioners:—

"In your Official Circular, issued January 31, 1842, in reply to Mr. Toye, of the Chepstow Union, you state that the authority of the overseers to relieve, in cases of sudden and urgent necessity, is quite independent of the judgment or sanction of the Board of Guardians; and in a communication from Mr. Chadwick to Mr. Abbott, auditor of the Blean Union, dated 24th March, 1842, and laid before the Board, it is stated that 'the Commissioners require the relief (so given) to be reported to the Board of Guardians; and the Guardians may in doubtful cases refuse payment, and apprize the auditor in order that he may deal with the case at the next audit.'

"Will the Commissioners be good enough to reconcile these opinions, and inform the Board of Guardians—

"1st. If they can compel an overseer to produce those items of expenditure which come under the head of 'relief given in cases of urgent necessity;'

"2ndly. Whether, in case the Board of Guardians refuse to certify as to the correctness of the amount disbursed by an overseer, the auditor has power to allow it at the quarterly audit."

And the Commissioners directed the following answer to be given thereto:—

"In reply I am directed to state, that the opinions of the Commissioners, expressed in their letter to the clerk of the Chepstow Union, which is published in the Official Circular of the 31st January last, and in the letter dated 24th March, 1842, which they addressed to Mr. Abbott, the auditor of the Blean Union, relative to the authority of overseers to relieve in cases of sudden and urgent necessity, are in no way opposed to each other.

"The Commissioners require the relief given by overseers to be reported to the relieving officer, and through him to the Board of Guardians. If not so reported, the overseers will be liable to a penalty for disobedience to the Commissioners' orders, under section 38 of the Poor Law Amendment Act; but it does not follow that the relief, if given by the overseers in a *bonâ fide* case of urgent necessity, in conformity with section 54 of the Poor Law Amendment Act, would necessarily be disallowed by the auditor, on the ground that it had not received the sanction of the Guardians.

"The refusal of the Board of Guardians to certify the correctness of the items would not render the relief liable to be disallowed, if otherwise legal, because the overseer is authorized to give it by the statute.

"The Commissioners stated, that the Guardians might adopt the relief given by the overseers and repay it, if they thought proper so to do. Such a course is convenient, because it is desirable that the out-relief account in the ledger should be as nearly complete as possible, by including all that comes under that name. It follows, from what has been already said, that the overseer is compellable under the rules of the Commissioners to report the relief; and it only remains to add, that in a case in which the Guardians disapprove of the relief, although they cannot ensure its disallowance by the mere refusal to repay it, they may and ought to call the special attention of the auditor to it; who, if legal, will allow it, and if illegal, will disallow it in the overseers' accounts."

3.—TO WIDOWS IN THE FIRST SIX MONTHS OF THEIR WIDOWHOOD.—STROUD UNION.

20th July, 1842.

The Commissioners took into consideration a letter addressed to them by Peter Leversaye, Esq., an ex-officio Guardian of the Stroud Union, inquiring, in reference to the 4th exception in the General Order of the Commissioners, dated 2nd August, 1841, prohibiting out-door relief, which relates to widows in the first six months of their widowhood, whether the Board of Guardians had a discretionary power of affording relief in such cases in the workhouse, if they deemed it expedient to do so; and the Commissioners directed the following answer to be given thereto:—

"In reply, I am to state, that the Prohibitory Order of the Commissioners does not make it imperative on a Board of Guardians to grant out-door relief in the several exceptions to that Order. The giving of such relief is discretionary with the Guardians, except in so far as it is prohibited by the Order. The Guardians may offer the workhouse if they think proper; although the allowance of out-door relief in the case to which you refer would be legal. The Commissioners desire, in addition, to call your attention to the 27th section of the Poor Law Amendment Act."

XIV.—REMOVAL.—CARDIGAN UNION.

28th May, 1842.

The Commissioners took into consideration the following letter, addressed to their Assistant Commissioner, Mr. Day, by Lieut.-Colonel Vaughan, vice-chairman of the Cardigan Union:—

"William Jenkins, a tailor, with his wife and family, residing in the parish of Llechryd, were sent to the workhouse from that parish. After a short period the overseers, considering they did not belong to that parish, obtained an order of removal to the parish of Kilgerran. The latter parish gave notice of appeal at the next court of Quarter Session; but there not being sufficient time, according to law, to serve the notice of appeal, Kilgerran applied to have it respited till the next court of Quarter Session, which was granted. The paupers remained in the poor-house till last week, when William Jenkins demanded to quit the house, taking with him his family. Of course the master did not consider himself authorized to detain them, and so let them out. Now, I wish to know whether the pauper ought to have been discharged, pending the order of removal; for suppose he abscond about the time the court of Quarter Session is to be held, how is the order of removal from Llechryd to Kilgerran to be carried out? Suppose the said William Jenkins has property left him, can he be made to pay up all the expenses that have been incurred by the parish of Llechryd for the support of his family?"

And the Commissioners directed the following reply to be given thereto:—

"The Commissioners entirely concur in the effect of the opinion expressed by Mr. Day, that there is no authority for detaining the pauper in the workhouse of the appellant parish, pending the determination of the appeal. Whatever effect the order of justices directing the removal of a pauper may have, as regards giving the parish officers to whom the order is directed the legal custody of the pauper, and in a case where such pauper may desire to avoid the execution of the order by absenting himself from the house, the authority to detain such pauper, the Commissioners entertain no doubt, that after the execution of the order, the detention of such pauper against his will for the purpose of giving evidence at the trial would be wholly unlawful.

"The Commissioners apprehend that the appellant parish can only compel the attendance of a pauper, upon the hearing of the appeal, by the ordinary process which is necessary to secure the attendance of other material witnesses at the Sessions.

"With respect to the further question asked concerning William Jenkins as to whether, upon the supposition of his having property left him, he can be compelled to repay the parish of Llechryd the expenses incurred in the support of his wife during his absence, I am to state, that the parish would have no legal claim to repayment unless the relief had been granted expressly as a loan to the wife of the pauper."

XV.—TITHES.—RATING OF.—ST. ASAPH UNION.

1st June, 1842.

The Commissioners took into consideration a letter, of which the following is an extract, addressed to them by Mr. S. Edwardes, solicitor, Denbigh:—

"The tithes of Abergele belong to the Bishop of St. Asaph, as rector, and to the Rev. Richard Jackson, as vicar of the parish. In some townships, the bishop has the corn and the vicar the hay; in a few, the bishop has two-thirds of the corn and hay and the vicar the remaining third; and the tithes of some particular districts belong entirely to one or the other of them. The origin of this arrangement it is unnecessary to observe upon.

"It is the practice in Abergele, and other parts of North Wales, to set the tithes of a parish by auction, subject of course to conditions. The conditions premise the nature of the tithes to be let, and that the same were to be let from the 29th of June to the 29th of June following; and provide for the payment of all taxes imposed during the year. In cases where the bishop and vicar have the corn and hay-tithes separately, they are let apart; when they own the tithes in different proportions, they are let together, and each has his separate security for his proportion of the joint letting; and when either party has the entire tithes, they are let for, of course, the benefit of the exclusive owner. On the highest bidder being declared, he is considered the taker or lessee; and, together with a surety, signs a memorandum to the following effect:—'We, A. B., of &c., and C. D., of &c., (the latter being surety,) have bid for and do take the tithes of the township of Grwych at the sum of 60*l.*, subject to the foregoing conditions.' They also sign a promissory note for the sum bid. The memorandum is not usually stamped, but the promissory note is. A formal lease of the tithes is never executed.

"In signing the memorandum and promissory note, the takers consider themselves to be the lessees and occupiers of the tithes for the year commencing the 29th of June and ending the 29th of June, and act accordingly.

"The tithes are generally collected by the takers in kind; but sometimes they set them to the occupiers of the land they arise from, though the latter cases are exceptions to the rule. All rates and taxes have been invariably paid by the takers as tenants for the year, irrespective of the date of the poor rate assessment, and even, if only a few days from the end of the year, without any claim for a proportion of the rate from their successors, under the powers of the 17th Geo. II., c. 38, sec. 12.

"In July, 1840, Mr. John Hughes took the tithes' hay of the townships of Bottegwal Bodorin, and 'in the remainder of the parish;' and the corn tithe of Grwych, Hendreissa, and Abergele, for the year commencing the 29th of June, 1840, to the 29th of June, 1841; subject to the usual conditions that the taker should pay 'all taxes, highway duties, and other levies and charges in respect of the said tithes, commencing and ending as aforesaid.' He signed a memorandum, *mutatis mutandis*, in the terms of the memorandum above copied; and Thomas Williams, a surety, stands in the place of C. D.

"Mr. J. Hughes, as had been the previous practice, was not called upon to contribute to the last poors' rate charged upon his predecessor, and granted only a few days before his (Hughes') year commenced, under the 17th Geo. II., if applicable.

"Mr. J. Hughes has paid all the poor-rates charged in his time, up to the 12th day of June, 1841, but declines paying more than a proportion of that rate, corresponding with his occupation of the tithes relatively to the period elapsing after his occupation, and before the next assessment was made upon his successor; the takers under the same circumstances of the tithes in 1841 claiming the advantage of the 17th Geo. II.

"The disputed assessment is thus headed:—'An assessment for the relief of the poor of the parish of Abergele, in the county of Denbigh, and for the purposes chargeable thereon according to law, made this twelfth day of June, in the year of our Lord one thousand eight hundred and forty-one, after the rate of 12 pence in the pound.' This heading is not signed at the foot of it by either the churchwardens or overseers, or by any other person; nor is the assessment signed at the end by the parish officers, as is usually done, after the word 'assessors,' (see vol. iv. B. J., 26 ed., p. 131;) but the declaration required by the Commissioners is inserted and duly signed, though that amounts merely to a certificate of the introduction of certain facts they require to be inserted, and does not amount to an assessment of the property referred to.

"Under all the circumstances, your advice and opinion is desired for the guidance of the parish officers on the following points:—

"1st. Whether the taker or lessee, entering upon the collection, &c., of the tithes in the manner before stated, is such an occupier under the written memorandum, for tithes cannot be let verbally, as will, under the laws now in force, make him liable to be rated as occupier of the tithes taken by him? The takers have always been so rated since the tithes have been let by auction.

"2nd. Whether the assessment of June, 1841, not being signed either under the heading, or as is more usual, under the word 'assessor,' at the end of it, is a valid rate, it being regular as respects the allowance and publication? This question is one of great importance, and affects many rates in this part of Wales.

"3rd. Whether it is required that the churchwardens and overseers should be together when the assessment is signed; the making of one being *quasi* a judicial Act? This is also a very important question, and is a point seldom attended to.

"4th. Whether if the rate be valid, must the application of the overseers to the magistrates be for a summons against Mr. John Hughes for the recovery of the rate against him as the party assessed; and can the overseers legally obtain the warrant of two magistrates to levy the amount wholly from him; or are they bound to enter into the question between Mr. J. Hughes and his succeeding occupier of the tithes before a warrant is issued; or, is the latter question to be a matter for the decision of the magistrates upon the application of Mr. J. Hughes for relief, as against his succeeding taker or lessee, without reference to the parish officers?"

And the Commissioners directed the following reply to be given thereto:—

"The Commissioners desire to state that there is a distinction between the tithes of a parson, or vicar, and the tithes appropriate or impropriate.

"The parson and vicar are personally rateable for their ability; these tithes are not made by express terms rateable, but are only rateable as part of the ability of the parson or vicar. Their being let does not diminish that ability, and there is no authority to show (although the suggestion has been thrown out) that the parson or vicar can avoid being rated, or that lessees of their tithes become rateable when these tithes are even let by deed. The statute 43 Eliz. c. 2, s. 1, enumerates the occupiers of tithes impropriate and propriations of tithes, but does not refer to lessees of tithes of the parson or vicar as persons liable to be taxed. There does not, therefore, appear to be any authority by which the overseers are either obliged or enabled to tax the lessees of the parson's or vicar's tithe, or to take notice of the private contracts between such parsons or vicars and their lessees.

"With regard to tithes impropriate and propriations of tithes, the law is different. The *occupiers* of these are expressly made liable to the tax. The occupiers, therefore, of the bishop's tithe, which is apparently an appropriation, are liable to be rated for it.

"The question, who is an occupier of an incorporeal hereditament might be difficult, but the courts have recognized the application of the word in the statute of Elizabeth, to the person taking the tithe under a valid title; but in order to make a person an occupier of tithe, whether appropriate or impropriate, the tithe must be let by deed. Therefore,

"1. If the tithe be not let by deed, the supposed occupier has no such possession or occupation as would render him liable to be rated.

"2. A book not signed by the overseers is not a rate, although allowed as such by the justices, and afterwards published as such.

"3. The making a rate is not a judicial or quasi-judicial act. It is entirely ministerial, and it is not necessary that the overseers signing it should be together when they do so.

"4. When a rate is valid, the occupier of tithes appropriate or impropriate is entitled to the benefit of the 17 Geo. II. c. 38, s. 12. The overseers should adjust the rate between the occupiers respectively coming into or going out of occupation. It is only in case of dispute that application is to be made to justices, but it is evidently the duty of the overseers, if possible, to adjust the rate before the justices are applied to."

LONDON:
Printed, by Order of the Poor Law Commissioners, by W. CLOWES and SONS, Stamford Street, and Published by CHARLES KNIGHT and Co., 22, Ludgate Street, Publishers to the Poor Law Commissioners.

AN

OFFICIAL CIRCULAR

OF PUBLIC DOCUMENTS AND INFORMATION;

DIRECTED BY THE POOR LAW COMMISSIONERS TO BE PRINTED, CHIEFLY FOR THE USE OF THE MEMBERS AND PERMANENT OFFICERS OF BOARDS OF GUARDIANS, UNDER THE POOR LAW AMENDMENT ACT.

No. 25. CIRCULAR ISSUED MAY 23, 1843.

Poor Law Commission Office,
Somerset House,
23*d May*, 1843.

THE Poor Law Commissioners, on a review of their Minutes, directed that the Minutes of Correspondence on the following subjects be printed and circulated for the information of Guardians and Officers of the several Unions, viz.:—

By Order of the Board,
EDWIN CHADWICK, *Secretary*.

I.—ACCOUNTS.—AS TO MODE OF APPORTIONING MEDICAL RELIEF WHEN PAID BY THE CASE.—UPTON-ON-SEVERN UNION

31st March, 1843.

The Commissioners took into consideration a letter received from the Clerk of the Upton-on-Severn Union, stating that since the dismissal of the medical officer of the Malvern district, the medical relief afforded to paupers therein has been paid for by the case, instead of by a fixed salary, and inquiring how he is to apportion this charge in the accounts; and the Commissioners directed the following answer to be given thereto:—

"When a medical officer is remunerated by the case, the sum paid for each case will be debited to the account of the parish to which the pauper might be chargeable at the time the attendance of the medical officer was given."

II.—AUDITORS' DUTIES.—AS TO EXAMINATION OF OFFICERS' BONDS.—WOLVERHAMPTON UNION.

22d February, 1843.

The Commissioners took into consideration the following letter, addressed to them by Mr. Simkiss, Auditor of the Wolverhampton Union:

"I shall feel obliged by the Commissioners' instructions for my guidance, in reference to that portion of their General Order (No. 7, art. 25), which directs, 'that the officer's bonds shall be produced to the auditor for his inspection.'

"Is it intended that the auditor shall confine his duties to examining that the bond is properly drawn up, and properly executed; or is he to require the officer to satisfy him that the persons who have executed it are still living, and that they have not, since the time of the execution, been either insolvent or bankrupt?"

And the Commissioners directed the following answer to be given thereto:—

"The Commissioners refer you to the words of the order, 'Any defects apparent in the said bonds,' as showing that the object was—

"1st. To ascertain that the bonds are in existence, and in proper custody.

"2nd. That there are no defects apparent upon the face of them.

"The auditor is not bound to inquire whether the sureties are alive or solvent. That is the business of the Board of Guardians, whom he may, however, apprise of any facts which he happens to know or learn, on such points as may affect the validity or sufficiency of such bonds."

III.—BAPTISM:—FEE FOR REGISTERING THE BAPTISM OF PAUPER CHILDREN. — EAST GRINSTED UNION.

6th March, 1843.

The Commissioners took into consideration a letter addressed to them by the Rev. Christopher Melvill, inquiring how unmarried women who brought their infant pauper children from the East Grinsted Union Workhouse to his church to be baptized, were to pay the shilling for registering their infants' baptism, and referring the Commissioners to the 6 & 7 William IV., c. 86, sec. 49. The Commissioners directed the following reply to be made thereto:—"The Commissioners have referred to section 49 of the 6 & 7 Will. IV., c. 86, which they perceive reserves the right of any officiating minister to receive the fees usually paid at the time of the passing of the Act, for the performance of registration of any baptism, burial, or marriage. There can be no doubt, therefore, in the case put by you, of your right to a fee: the only question is, from what fund the fee is to be paid. The Commissioners can only say, that in those cases in which the Board of Guardians may think fit to order that a pauper child in the workhouse should be baptized, the Commissioners would not feel themselves justified in raising any objection to the payment of the customary fee by the Guardians. The Commissioners are bound to add, however, that the Guardians are under no obligation to do so."

IV.—BASTARDY.

1. LIABILITY OF FATHER TO MAINTAIN THE ILLEGITIMATE CHILD OF HIS DAUGHTER.—ASTON UNION.

6th March, 1843.

The Commissioners took into consideration a letter addressed to them by the Clerk to the Guardians of the Aston Union, inquiring whether a person of sufficient ability can be compelled to maintain his daughter *and her illegitimate infant child*, and if not, whether, as the child cannot be admitted into the workhouse without the mother, he could be compelled to contribute towards his daughter's maintenance in the workhouse. The Commissioners directed the following reply to be given thereto:—

"The Commissioners had occasion to consult the late Attorney-General on the liability of a father to support the illegitimate child of his daughter, under the 43rd Eliz., c. 2, sec. 7, and the Commissioners were advised that the father was not liable. The Commissioners concur in that opinion. As regards the case stated in your letter, if the mother be admitted with her child into the workhouse, the Commissioners think the father of the woman (if a person of sufficient ability) would be liable to have an order made on him under the statute to maintain her."

2. CHARGEABILITY OF BASTARDS. — NEWTOWN AND LLANIDLOES UNION.

23rd February, 1843.

The Commissioners took into consideration a letter received from the Clerk to the Guardians of the Newtown and Llanidloes Union, inquiring whether, in a case where the mother of a bastard child is admitted into the workhouse with her child, and stays only a few days, the child being supplied with spoon-food, there is sufficient ground of chargeability to warrant an application for an order in bastardy, and also whether the circumstance of the child receiving nurture *only* from the mother in the workhouse, would be a sufficient ground of chargeability. The Commissioners directed the following answer to be made thereto:—

"In the first case, where the mother and child are relieved in the workhouse only for a few days, there is no doubt of the legal chargeability of the child; because the child is stated to be directly relieved with food, and the shortness of the period during which the child is maintained is immaterial. In the second case, also, the Commissioners think there is a legal chargeability; because, although no food be given, yet the child is directly relieved by the shelter afforded to it in the workhouse."

3. DITTO.—HUNDRED OF FOREHOE.

7th March, 1843.

A letter from Mr. Ecclestone, a relieving officer of the hundred of Forehoe, was read, stating, that a young woman, with her illegitimate child, born within the last four months, became chargeable to the city of Norwich, and an order was obtained on the 21st December, 1842, for their removal to the parish of Cossey, and on the 11th January last they were admitted into the workhouse of the hundred of Forehoe, of which that parish forms a part, and inquiring which of the two dates should be taken as the date on which the child became chargeable to the parish of Cossey. The Commissioners stated in reply, that they were inclined to think that it could not be considered that the child became chargeable to the parish of Cossey until the order of removal was executed, and the child, with its mother, received into the workhouse.

V.—CLERK'S DUTIES.—IN OBTAINING ORDERS, &c.—HUNTINGDON UNION.

24th February, 1843.

The Commissioners took into consideration a letter received from the Clerk to the Guardians of the Huntingdon Union, inquiring whether the proceedings necessary to be taken in reference to orders of removal, orders of maintenance, appeals against orders of removal, and the like, were within the province of the parish officers alone, or whether they were under the control of the Board of Guardians, and ought to be conducted by their clerk. The Commissioners directed the following reply to be given thereto:—

"As regards orders of removal and appeals

against such orders, the control of such matters is not vested in the Guardians.

"The overseers are the proper parties to give the directions as to the conduct of an appeal. But with respect to applications for orders upon persons to maintain their relations, it is within the province of the Guardians to give directions as to procuring such orders."

VI.—COLLECTOR. — POWER OF, TO GIVE RECEIPTS.—REDRUTH UNION.

2d March, 1843.

A letter from Mr. Robert Blee, jun., was read, stating that he had been called upon by the collector of poor rates for the parish of Redruth, for the payment of poor rates due on certain properties which he (Mr. Blee) held in trust for three orphan children, but that he had declined to pay such rates, unless he was furnished with a churchwarden's or overseers' receipt for the same. The Commissioners directed the following reply to be given thereto:—

"The Commissioners conclude that the collector who acts for the parish of Redruth, was duly appointed by the Board of Guardians of the Redruth Union under an order of the Commissioners. If so, he is legally authorized to demand the rate; and his receipt is, to all intents and purposes, as good a discharge of the liability of a rate-payer as the receipt of the overseer (See 2 and 3 Vict., c. 84, sec. 2). The ground, therefore, that the collector did not produce a receipt signed by the churchwardens and overseers, was not in itself a valid reason for withholding payment of the rate."

VII.—GUARDIANS.

1. THE ELECTION OF AN ADDITIONAL GUARDIAN FOR A PARISH.—BROMSGROVE UNION.

4th March, 1843.

The Commissioners took into consideration a memorial of the inhabitants of the parish of Redditch, in the Bromsgrove Union, forwarded to the Commissioners by the Guardians of that Union, requesting the Commissioners to authorize the election of an additional Guardian for that parish; and the Commissioners directed the following answer to be given thereto:—

"The Commissioners desire to call the attention of the Guardians and the memorialists to the terms of the 41st section of the Poor Law Amendment Act, and to point out to them that, after a careful consideration of the operation of that section, the Commissioners are of opinion that when an alteration is to be made in the number of Guardians to be elected by any parish in a Union, it is necessary that the consent of a majority of the owners and rate-payers of the *whole* Union should be first obtained thereto. The chief reasons for this conclusion are as follow:—

"1st. As to the construction of the 41st section, the Commissioners understand the consent of the owners and rate-payers of a parish to be required when the alteration affects only the Guardians of a parish; and the consent of the owners and rate-payers of a Union to be required when the alteration affects the Guardians of a Union. Now, when Guardians are elected in a parish comprised within a Union, such Guardians are, in the language of the Act, Guardians not of the parish but of the Union (see the terms of the 38th section); and it is only in the case in which a Board of Guardians is constituted for a single ununited parish, under the 39th section, that the Guardians are described as Guardians of a parish. In the present case it is the number of the Guardians of the Union which is proposed to be changed, the benefit being in favour of a particular parish in that Union, the remaining parishes in the Union being proposed to be left with a representation which will be relatively diminished by the alteration.

"In this last consideration consists the second reason of the Commissioners for the conclusion which they adopt; for, it being clear that the alteration in favour of one parish proportionally involves a disadvantage to the remaining parishes, the consequence would follow, that it would be those remaining parishes whose consent should be obtained, and not that of the parish which must necessarily be in favour of the change."

---

2. CHAPLAIN OF UNION WORKHOUSE INCAPABLE OF SERVING AS GUARDIAN.—BRIDGNORTH UNION.

25th February, 1843.

A letter from the Rev. W. K. Marshall, St. Mary, Bridgnorth, in reference to the operation of the 14th section of the 5 and 6 Vic., c. 57, was read, and the Commissioners directed the following answer to be given thereto:—"The Commissioners are of opinion that a chaplain to a Union workhouse, in the receipt of a fixed salary, is clearly within the terms 'paid officer engaged in the administration of the laws for the relief of the poor,' and the terms 'person receiving any fixed salary or emolument from the poor-rates in any parish or Union;' and therefore that he is, under the 14th section of the 5 and 6 Vic. c. 57, incapable of serving as a Guardian in such parish or Union."

3. PAYMENT OF RATES AS A QUALIFICATION IN THE ELECTION OF GUARDIANS.—WEST BROMWICH UNION.

6th March, 1843.

The Commissioners took into consideration a letter addressed to them by Mr. Samuel Kenrick, of Handsworth, Birmingham, inquiring if the non-payment of a church-rate, alleged to have been informally made on the 18th March, 1842, would disqualify him from either nominating candidates or voting for them at the ensuing election of Guardians for the West Bromwich Union, although he had paid all other rates except those made during the last six months. The Commissioners directed the following reply to be given thereto:—

"I am to state that whether the church-rate made on the 18th March, 1842, was or was not a legal rate is a question of fact which it is not the province of the Commissioners to determine, but belongs to the ecclesiastical courts. Assuming, however, that the rate was valid, it appears to the Commissioners that as a parochial rate and assessment due, and not coming within the exception expressed in the 40th section of the Poor Law Amendment Act, viz., except such as shall have been made or become due within the six months immediately preceding such voting or acting, payment of the rate would be necessary to enable a person to vote in the election of Guardians for the West Bromwich Union, or to do any other act as a rate-payer; as, for instance, to 'nominate' a candidate for the office of Guardian."

4. PROVENDER FOR GUARDIANS' HORSES CANNOT BE PAID FOR OUT OF THE POOR-RATES.—LLANFYLLYN UNION.

28th February, 1843.

A letter addressed to the Commissioners by the clerk to the Guardians of the Llanfyllin Union was read, inquiring whether the Guardians of that Union, several of whom travel a distance of from 12 to 14 miles to attend the meetings of the Board, and whose horses are obliged to remain four or five hours in the stables without any hay or corn, would be justified in buying provender for the use of the stables adjoining the workhouse, and charging the same to the poor-rates; and the Commissioners directed that the clerk should be informed that such a course would resolve itself into a payment of part of the cost of the conveyance of the Guardians to the workhouse, and appeared to the Commissioners one which would be entirely unlawful to charge to the poor-rates.

VIII.—LUNATIC PAUPERS.—BY WHOSE AUTHORITY TO BE REMOVED FROM AN ASYLUM.—DORE UNION.

8th March, 1843.

The Commissioners took into consideration a letter addressed to them by the clerk of the Dore Union, stating that the overseers of Abbey Dore some years since placed a pauper lunatic in a licensed asylum; that the Guardians were desirous of removing the pauper to another asylum; but the keeper of the asylum in which the pauper is confined refused to deliver him up, although repeatedly requested to do so, and desiring the Commissioners' opinion as to the means to be adopted for obtaining the delivery of the lunatic. The Commissioners directed the following answer to be given thereto:—

"I am to state that as the lunatic pauper was originally placed in the asylum by an order of justices, the Commissioners think that the Guardians are restrained from removing the pauper from the asylum without an authority similar to that by which the pauper was confined. Section 38, 9 Geo. IV., c. 40, provides (and the provision is made applicable to Guardians by the Act 5 and 6 Vic. c. 57), 'and the said last-mentioned overseer shall not remove such poor person from the said house without an order for that purpose made by two justices of the peace, &c., unless such person shall have been discharged as cured.'"

IX.—MEDICAL ORDER.

1. CONSTRUCTION OF ART. 10.

21st April, 1843.

The Commissioners took into consideration certain inquiries which had been submitted to them in regard to the construction of Article 10, No. 7, of their general Medical Order, and directed the following minute to be made in reference thereto:—

"In the construction of Article 10 of their General Medical Order, the Commissioners understand that a dislocation of the arm includes a dislocation of the elbow, or of the wrist, as well as of the shoulder.

"In the same article the Commissioners understand that a fracture of the arm includes a fracture of the humerus, radius, or ulna, but not a fracture of the scapula or clavicle."

2. QUALIFICATION OF MEDICAL OFFICERS' SUBSTITUTES.—BRENTFORD UNION.

16th February, 1843.

A letter from the Clerk to the Guardians of the Brentford Union was read, stating that on calling on the newly appointed medical Officers for the several districts in that Union, to name their substitutes in case of an unavoidable absence, &c., difficulty was experienced by them in offering gentlemen with the double qualifications required by the Commissioners' order, and inquiring what qualifications such substitutes were required to possess: and the Commissioners directed the Clerk of the Guardians to be informed, that it was not necessary that the substitutes should have any of the double qualifications required by the order, in the case of the Medical Officers themselves; it being sufficient that the substitutes should be legally qualified to practise medicine.

X.—OVERSEERS.—A CHARGE FOR ENTERING THE NAMES OF OWNERS AND PROXIES IN A BOOK CANNOT BE ALLOWED.—BATH UNION.

6th March, 1843.

The Commissioners took into consideration a letter addressed to them by the Auditor of the Bath Union, stating that the overseers of the parish of Walcot, in that Union, had inquired of him whether he would allow a charge for filling up a book with the names and addresses of the owners and proxies who send statements of their claims to vote, and the assessment of the poor-rate on the property, in respect whereof they claim to vote; and requesting the Commissioners' instructions in the matter. The Commissioners directed the following reply to be given thereto:—

"The duty imposed upon overseers, by the 40th section of the Poor Law Amendment Act, of entering the names of owners and proxies in a book to be provided for that purpose, is like any other personal duty which the law casts upon overseers; it must be performed gratuitously, unless special provision is made for paying other persons to perform it. The Poor Law Amendment Act does not make any such provision, as regards the particular duty in question, neither are the Commissioners empowered to order that the expence of making out the register should be cast upon the poor-rates. The Commissioners think you could not lawfully allow the charge in the accounts."

XI.—PAUPERS.—HOW TO CHARGE RELIEF GRANTED TO CASUAL PAUPERS.—YORK UNION.

18th February, 1843.

The Commissioners took into consideration the following resolution, passed by the Board of Guardians of the York Union:—"That casual paupers, when they first become chargeable to any parish, and remove to another parish, shall be chargeable to the first parish, unless they have ceased to become chargeable for three months;" and the Commissioners directed the following communication to be addressed to the Guardians, in reference thereto:—

"The Commissioners think the resolution above adverted to, to be entirely opposed to the law. The law does not confer upon the Guardians the power to charge a parish with the relief of a pauper after the chargeability in that parish has ceased, and a fresh liability has arisen in some other parish, by the pauper becoming destitute therein. The law, as respects a casual pauper, is, that he is to be relieved where he is destitute; and it may occur that he may become chargeable to all the parishes in a Union successively. But there is no provision, that having become chargeable to one parish and ceasing to be so, that he shall, upon his again requiring relief in some other parish, be relieved at the charge of the first parish, where three months have not elapsed from the termination of the first chargeability.

"The difficulty of ascertaining in some cases the parish liable for the relief of a casual pauper, may be considerable; and the object of the Guardians in adopting the resolution may have been to lessen that difficulty, to render their practice uniform, and to equalize the burden of relieving casual paupers.

"Whatever advantages might attend the operation of the rule, as tending to secure all or any of these results, the Commissioners trust it will be sufficient for the Guardians to be informed of the want of legal authority for the course now adopted, to induce them to alter it."

XII.—POLICE RATE.—PAYABLE OUT OF THE POOR RATE.

6th March, 1843.

The Commissioners took into consideration a letter addressed to them by Mr. J. Waterall, churchwarden of Alton, Staffordshire, stating that he had received an order from the High Constable to pay the township's proportion of the police-rate for the rural police district of the county of Stafford, and inquiring whether such rate could be legally paid out of the poor-rates; and the Commissioners directed the following reply to be given thereto:—

"The Commissioners presume that the police force for the rural police district of the county of Stafford, was established under the provisions of the 2 & 3 Vic., cap. 93. If so, the salaries and allowances of such police constables are, under section 20 of that Act, to be paid out of the county rates; and by section 21, the justices at quarter sessions are empowered to order the county-rate levied within the police district to be increased for this purpose. A county-rate is by law payable out of the poor-rate; and the demand which has been made upon you is, as the Commissioners understand, in the nature of a county-rate, though the order you may have received from the High Constable may specify the purpose for which the money is required to be the maintenance of the police."

XIII.—POOR-RATES.—OVERSEERS TAKING CREDIT FOR POOR RATES IRRECOVERABLE, BUT NOT EXCUSED UNDER THE STATUTE.—SPALDING UNION.

24th February, 1843.

The Commissioners took into consideration a letter addressed to them by Mr. Bonner, auditor of the Spalding Union, calling their attention to the circumstance of the overseers of several parishes in the Union taking credit in their accounts for poor-rates, alleged to be irrecoverable, but not excused by the justices under the 54 Geo. III., c. 170, sect. 11, and requesting the Commissioners' instructions upon the subject. The Commissioners directed the following communication to be sent to Mr. Bonner in reference thereto:—

"The Commissioners are not prepared to say that it is only such rates as have been excused by the justices, under the statute with the requisite consent, that the overseers are entitled to take credit for in their accounts. There are, doubtless, cases in which, through deaths, removals, or other causes, the overseers are prevented recovering the rate, though the cases are not those to which the 54 Geo. III., c. 170, sec. 11 applies. The question is, what evidence is admissible to show that the rate is irrecoverable, so as to justify the auditor in allowing the overseer to take credit for the amount.

"The Commissioners are aware of the difficulty of laying down any particular rule or principle for guidance in such a case. It appears, however, to the Commissioners, that as it is impossible that the auditor should himself know the exact circumstances of each case, or should have the opportunity of making that local investigation which would give him the information, he must be content to take the explanation of the overseers in connexion with any other evidence which can be procured, as that of the relieving officer, or collector; allowing, where the explanation appears fair and satisfactory; and pursuing a contrary course where there is reasonable ground for supposing that the rate might have been recovered, if proper caution and ordinary diligence had been used."

XIV.—RATING.

1. POOR RATE.—COUNTY RATES.—CHERTSEY UNION.

6th March, 1843.

The Commissioners took into consideration a letter addressed to them by the Clerk to the Guardians of the Chertsey Union, explaining that the overseers of Byfleet were desirous of obtaining an order from the Commissioners for the readjustment of the valuation of the parish, because the valuer had, in order to find the gross estimated rental, added to the rent a property would let for, the tithes, insurance, and repairs,and stating that this was contrary to instructions given by the Court of Quarter Sessions, held at Reigate, 5th April, 1842, to parish officers, on the subject of assessing property to the county-rate, in which the gross estimated rental is declared to be the sum a property might reasonably be expected to let for, and that the inhabitants were paying a higher proportion to the county-rate, than other parishes which were assessed according to the rules laid down by the quarter-sessions. The Commissioners directed the following reply to be given thereto :—

"In reference to this explanation I am to point out, that the county-rate is not assessed on a gross rent, but on the full and fair annual value,(55 Geo. III., c. 51, s. 1). or full and fair estimated annual productive value (ib. s. 2.) This, of course is very different from the gross annual value, and is not exactly the net annual value required to be ascertained for the poor-rate by the Parochial Assessment Act; but it may easily be ascertained by the overseers in adding to the net rent in the valuation for the purpose of the poor-rate, the amount of tenants' taxes and repairs. But it would be wholly illegal to make the valuation for poor-rate to accord with the valuation for the county-rate.

"The Commissioners cannot, therefore, issue the order required. If the overseers have returned the gross rental of the parish, instead of the fair annual value to let, it is probable that the justices would, on the facts being correctly represented to them, make the proper alteration in the next county-rate, without compelling the parish to resort to an appeal."

2. MANUFACTORIES.—STOKE-UPON-TRENT PARISH.

6th March, 1843.

The Commissioners took into consideration a letter addressed to them by the Clerk to the Board of Guardians of the parish of Stoke-upon-Trent, stating, that at special sessions held in pursuance of the Parochial Assessment Act, it was decided, in a case in which the parish was the respondent, and Messrs. Copeland and Garrett were the appellants, that the principle upon which manufactories ought to be rated, is the number of ovens which they have ; the respondent, however, contended, that the proper guide in assessing such property was the admeasurement, local situation, conveniencies, and state of repair of the property, and requesting the Commissioners' opinion upon the subject. The Commissioners directed the following reply to be given thereto :—

"I am to state, that it does not clearly appear from your letter, upon what grounds the decision of the justices proceeded in the case referred to.

"The Commissioners consider, however, that all difficulty would be avoided by following the simple rule prescribed by the Parochial Assessment Act, sec. 1, viz., by ascertaining the rent which a tenant from year to year would be willing to pay for the premises, to occupy them for the particular purpose for which they are adapted. That rent would obviously be greater or less, according to the situation of the premises, their extent, condition, and the convenience afforded for carrying on the business. If the premises have machinery attached to them, the letting value is increased, and the rate should be increased in like proportion."

3. POWER OF OVERSEERS TO ALTER ASSESSMENT TO THE POOR RATE. — WREXHAM UNION.

28th February, 1843.

The Commissioners took into consideration a letter addressed to them by Mr. C. Poyser, jun., of Summer Hill, Wrexham, stating that being overseer of his township for the last year, he had altered the assessment wherever he had found it clearly wrong, and requesting the Commissioners' opinion as to whether he was authorized in doing so; and the Commissioners replied as follows:—

"Assuming that in the cases which you mention the houses were rated below the net annual value, it was proper that in future rates the assessment should be altered so as to conform to the law, which requires property to be rated at its net annual value, which is its value to let from year to year. But no alteration should be made in a rate after it has been signed by the justices; and where an alteration in the assessment is made before the rate is allowed, it should be done with the concurrence of a majority of the churchwardens and overseers."

XV.—RELIEF.

1. To a Person possessed of Property.—Shepton Mallet Union.

4th March, 1843.

The Commissioners took into consideration a letter addressed to them by the Clerk of the Guardians of the Shepton Mallet Union, stating that James Edwards, an agricultural labourer, not of the first class, aged 44, and generally healthy, who has a wife and five children, under the age of 16, was possessed of, and in the actual occupation of, a freehold cottage and garden, and had received temporary relief at different times, and inquiring whether the Guardians could, as the family was likely to require permanent relief, take the property and dispose of it, and apply the proceeds to the relief of the family; or whether the Guardians could refuse relief until the pauper had himself disposed of the property; and the Commissioners directed the following reply to be given thereto:—

"The law does not give to Boards of Guardians, or parish officers, any power to take possession of property belonging to a pauper, or to dispose of it, and apply the proceeds in the manner suggested in your letter.

4 "As regards the question, whether the Guardians should refuse relief to the pauper alluded to by you, until he has disposed of his freehold property, I am to state that, as a general rule, persons possessed of property cannot be considered as coming within the class of destitute persons, for whose benefit and relief the poor rate is provided. In some cases, however, it may be that the possession of property, from the incumbrances or charges to which it may be subject, is an actual disadvantage to the owner; in others, that the benefit derived is very inconsiderable. In those cases where owners of property may apply for relief, having no means of support derived from other sources, the Commissioners are not prepared to advise the Guardians to refuse relief to such persons, except upon the condition that they should dispose of their interest in the property.

"In some instances it might be proper to require this. The difficulty of discriminating between cases in which it might be proper to grant, and those in which it would be right to withhold relief, is, no doubt, considerable. The Commissioners would only observe, that it appears to them that relief in the workhouse would be the least objectionable mode in which relief could be granted in doubtful cases of this description, as it affords the surest guarantee that the persons receiving the relief are in the condition which alone constitutes a title to relief."

2. To Illegitimate Children. — How charged.—Wareham and Purbeck Union.

27th February, 1843.

The Commissioners took into consideration a letter received by them from the Clerk to the Guardians of the Wareham and Purbeck Union, stating that James Court, belonging to the parish of Holy Trinity, Wareham, had lately married Maria Parker, a single woman with three illegitimate children, belonging to the parish of Corfe Castle; that James Court was chargeable to the parish of the Holy Trinity on account of his wife's illness; and inquiring whether relief given on account of the illegitimate children, who were born subsequent to the passing of the Poor Law Amendment Act, either in or out of the workhouse, should be charged to the parish of Corfe Castle, the place of their mother's settlement at the time of her marriage, or to the parish of the Holy Trinity, in which parish she is now settled; and referring to the case of Rex *v.* Walthamstow. The Commissioners directed the following answer to be given thereto:—

"The parish of the Holy Trinity is liable for the relief of the illegitimate children of the wife of the pauper alluded to in your letter, that being the parish in which the husband is settled. The children, by the circumstance of the marriage of the mother, and the operation of the 71st section of the Poor Law Amendment Act, which enacts that every illegitimate child born since the passing of that Act (14th August, 1834), has and follows every settlement the mother may acquire until the child attains the age of 16, take the settlement of the mother acquired by her marriage.

"The Commissioners are advised that the case where the mother acquires a settlement by marriage, is not an exception to the rule; and that the settlement so acquired is communicated to her illegitimate child. They think that the decisions in the cases Reg. *v.* Wendron, 7 Ad. & Ell. 819, and Reg. *v.* Walthamstow, 6 Ad. & Ell. 301, are not applicable to the case of illegitimate children born since the passing of the Poor Law Amendment Act, the mother acquiring a settlement by marriage subsequent to the birth of the children."

---

3. POWER OF JUSTICES TO ORDER OVERSEERS TO RELIEVE CASUAL POOR. — FALMOUTH UNION.

7th March, 1843.

The Commissioners took into consideration the following letter, received from the Clerk to the Guardians of the Falmouth Union:—

"About noon of the 7th February, William Deakin, formerly a marine in her Majesty's service, and a pensioner, residing in the parish of Mylor, accompanied by Elizabeth Deakin, his wife, came into the town of Falmouth; whilst there the latter became noisy, and brought together a considerable number of persons. A magistrate of the borough of Falmouth, who happened accidentally to be passing, directed the constable to place the woman in the Town gaol for safe custody. On the same evening Deakin and his wife were brought before two of the magistrates for the borough, who remanded Deakin to the gaol until the next day, and at the same time issued a written order for the admission of the wife into the Falmouth Town workhouse, alleging that they had no power to send her to the prison. The woman was then noisy, and showed symptoms of insanity. On her being brought to the workhouse for admission, the master applied to a Guardian and to myself, to ascertain whether he would be justified in acting on the magistrate's order. He was made acquainted with the power of justices in such cases, and it was thought proper to confer with the borough justices and their clerk on the matter. On which the magistrates sent for one of the overseers of Falmouth, and, without taking any evidence on oath, withdrew their order on the master, and made the following order on the overseers:—

"*To the Overseers of the Town of Falmouth.*

"We hereby order you to grant temporary relief to Elizabeth Deakin, she being unable to take care of herself and destitute.

"Dated the 8th day of February, 1843.

"JOSEPH FOX, *Mayor.*
"JOHN HILL, *J. P.*"

Stating at the same time, that it was intended to cause the woman to be brought before them on the next day with the husband. On this the overseer (it being then nearly eleven o'clock at night) issued this order:—

"*Falmouth Union.*

"To Mr. T. Smith, Master of the Workhouse at Falmouth.

"Admit Elizabeth Deakin, aged 50 years, wife of William Deakin, conditionally to abide the determination of the Board of Guardians at their next meeting.

"This 8th day of February, 1843.

"JOHN BROMACOMB.
"*Overseer, Falmouth Town.*"

And upon this the party has been admitted and her maintenance charged to Falmouth. She is still in the workhouse, and is deemed insane. Deakin was brought before the justices who made the remand on the morning of the 9th instant, and set at liberty. The wife, however, was not again had before these authorities.

"An answer to the following questions will oblige the Board:—

"1st. Had the magistrates, under the circumstances stated, power to make an order on the overseer?

"2nd. Supposing they had such power, is the order made in this case a valid one?

"3d. To what parish ought the maintenance of the woman to be charged?

"4th. What steps would you advise the Board to adopt for the future provision of the woman, she being now considered insane?

"Elizabeth Deakin's maiden name was Worsdale. She was, before her marriage with Deakin, which took place about a month since, an acknowledged pauper of the borough of Penryn. Deakin, it is reported, had a wife living at the time of his recent marriage."

And the Commissioners directed the following reply to be made thereto:—

"1st. That whether the justices had power to make an order on the overseers for the temporary relief of the pauper, depends upon whether the case was one of sudden and urgent necessity, and if so whether there had been a previous neglect or refusal on the part of the overseer to relieve; because it will be seen, on referring to the 54th section of the Poor Law Amendment Act, that it is only in this case that the justices have power to order relief. The Commissioners are not able to say, that the facts stated by you lead them to the conclusion that the case was either sudden or urgent, within the meaning of the statute; but the Commissioners are far from expressing confident opinion upon this point. As regards the second condition—the neglect or refusal of the overseer to relieve, the Commissioners do not find it stated that any application was made to the overseer for relief before the making of the order; and if there were no application, there could be no refusal or neglect.

"2d. As regards the order itself, the Commissioners think it is open to objection on the score of informality, as not showing sufficiently the jurisdiction of the justices. The Commissioners think the order could not be sustained on two grounds—1st, because it does not set forth that the case was one of sudden and urgent necessity; 2d, that there was a refusal or neglect on the part of the overseer to give relief; both of which must exist before the justices can interfere under the 54th section of the Poor Law Amendment Act.

"3d. Whether the order were or were not enforcible against the overseer, it would seem that the pauper was relieved under it, and has continued to be relieved. The Commissioners think that as the destitution occurred in Falmouth, that parish is liable.

"4th. It would appear desirable that an order of justices should be procured, to place the pauper in some suitable asylum. If that course be taken, two justices are empowered under 9th George IV., c. 40, to ascertain the settlement of the pauper, and to make an order upon the parish of the settlement, to pay the costs of maintenance."

---

4. RELATIVE DUTIES OF GUARDIANS AND THEIR OFFICERS, AS TO THE RELIEF OF POOR PERSONS SETTLED IN ONE UNION AND RESIDING IN ANOTHER.—ERPINGHAM UNION. NORWICH CORPORATION.

2d May, 1843.

The Commissioners took into consideration the case of John Daniels, brought under their notice through a letter from a physician attached to the Norwich Dispensary, of which institution the pauper, a lad 16 years of age, was a patient, he having received a severe injury from a kick, and to whose case it was alleged that the Guardians and officers of the Erpingham Union, in which he was settled, had exhibited some degree of inattention; and that the officers of the corporation of the poor of Norwich had thrown some impediments in the way of the lad's obtaining relief, until the period when a mutual understanding was come to with the Erpingham Union.

The Commissioners, upon taking into consideration the facts of the case, as elicited from the correspondence, and the report of their Assistant-Commissioner thereon, directed a letter to the following effect to be sent to the Corporation of the Poor of the City of Norwich, on the relative responsibilities of Guardians and of their officers, in cases of poor persons residing in one Union, whose settlement was elsewhere:—

"The obligation to relieve a poor person in a state of destitution, is complete by the mere fact that such person applies for relief where he is at the time, without any reference to the question where he is settled. This obligation, of course, rests on the Board of Guardians, or other authorities of the parish or Union where the destitution exists.

"The only difference between settled and non-settled paupers is, that in the case of the former the charge is permanent—in the case of the latter, it may be transferred, by obtaining an order of removal to the place of settlement.

"But sometimes (as in Daniels' case) the Board of Guardians or officers acting for the place where a non-resident pauper is settled, may take the case on themselves in a certain sense, by giving non-resident relief, or authorizing its being given, to a certain amount.

"Where this is done, a moral obligation is, no doubt, created on their part to inquire into and attend to the case; but this moral obligation in no wise changes the duty imposed by the law on the officers of the place where the pauper is.

"As a general principle, the Commissioners will never, under any circumstances, recognise the validity of any private arrangement whatever, even when made in the most express terms, between the officers themselves or the respective Boards of Guardians, as extinguishing the universal duty cast by law on the officer of the place where a destitute person is found, fully to relieve and attend to the case in every respect. On the contrary, they wish distinctly to deny the possibility of substituting an ambiguous moral responsibility, for the admitted and distinct legal obligation which the locality alone in every instance imposes, and about which no sort of doubt can possibly exist.

"If a non-resident case is neglected by the Guardians or officers of a distant Union, after they have engaged to attend to it, or if the relief given turns out insufficient, or be not duly administered, still the officers on the spot are the parties to whom the law would look, as answerable for any evil consequences arising from such negligence.

"The officers of the place of settlement may, by undertaking the care of a non-resident case, implicate themselves in fresh responsibilities of a moral kind, not incumbent on them by law; but the only result would be, that two persons would be liable to be called to account—viz., the officer who had engaged to attend to a case at a distance, and the officer of the place of residence, from whose shoulders that engagement had not removed the pre-existing obligation to relieve destitution within the limits of his own district or parish.

"Now, the Poor Law Commissioners are not desirous of applying all this specially to the case of Daniels, feeling certain that the Norwich board will deal with all such matters in the spirit of humanity to the poor, and justice to the rate-payers, which is really the spirit of the law. The Commissioners are, nevertheless, anxious to impress forcibly on the minds of the Guardians, that, it is, above all, desirable that no suspicion should exist, in such cases, that the relief given to a non-settled case has been niggardly or defective, before any engagement has been entered into on the part of a distant board or parish; and has become comparatively lax or liberal, when the persons determining its amount are not ultimately liable to the charge.

"Honesty and humanity require that what the necessities of the case demand should be given, equally before and after any correspondence with the place of settlement, and without any reference to the chance of repayment."

---

5. The following TABLE, showing the number of paupers relieved in England and Wales during the quarters ended at Lady-day, 1840, 1841, and 1842 respectively; also the amount of money expended for in-maintenance and out-relief, during each of the years ended Lady-day, 1840, 1841, and 1842, was read:—

Quarters ended Lady-day.	Number of Paupers relieved.			Proportion per Cent. on Population, 1841.	Years ended Lady-day.	Expenditure for In-Maintenance and Out-Relief.			Rate per Head of Expenditure on Population in 1841.	Average Price of Wheat per Quarter during each Year.
	In-door.	Out-door.	Total.			In-Maintenance.	Out-Relief.	Total.		
						£.	£.	£.	s. d.	s. d.
1840	169,232	1,030,299	1,199,529	8	1840	808,151	2,931,263	3,739,414	4 8	68 6
1841	192,106	1,106,942	1,299,048	8	1841	890,883	2,995,330	3,886,213	4 11	65 3
1842	221,687	1,207,402	1,429,089	9	1842	928,086	3,108,367	4,036,453	5 1	64 0
Average	194,342	1,114,880	1,309,222	$8\frac{2}{100}$	..	875,707	3,011,653	3,887,360	4 11	65 11

Population in 1841—15,906,829.

NOTE.—In the above Table an estimate is made for those places which are not under the orders of the Commissioners.

XVI.—SETTLEMENT.

1. BY APPRENTICESHIP.—UCKFIELD UNION.
6th March, 1843.

The Commissioners took into consideration a letter received from Mr. W. Elphick, requesting their opinion as to whether a widow and her children could claim a settlement in the parish of Newhaven, Sussex, under the following circumstances:—John Mepham, of the parish of Hellingly, Sussex, was apprenticed, in September, 1831, to Mr. Edward Sheldrick, of Newhaven, who was master of a vessel trading from that place to London, for the term of four years. On the expiration of the term of his apprenticeship in 1835, Mepham married Jane Greene, by whom he had three children. He subsequently deserted his family, and he is believed to have died at Bombay. The wife and the children are now chargeable to the parish of Newhaven. The Commissioners directed the following answer to be given thereto:—

"With respect to the question whether John Mepham, under the circumstances related in your letter, gained a settlement in the parish of Newhaven, I am to state that this depends upon whether he completed a residence of 40 days as an apprentice in that parish before the passing of the 4 and 5 Wm. IV. c. 76. If he served his master, and resided in the parish so as to have gained a settlement in that parish before the passing of the 4 and 5 Wm. IV. c. 76, that statute does not defeat the settlement, though the term of the apprenticeship was not completed at the time the statute was passed. This was so decided in Reg. *v.* The Inhabitants of St. Giles, Middlesex, reported in 2 Gale & Dav. 542, to which case the Commissioners would direct your attention."

2. OF A BASTARD CHILD.—DURHAM UNION.

2d March, 1843.

The Commissioners took into consideration a letter addressed to them by the Clerk to the Guardians of the Durham Union, inquiring whether a bastard child born four years since, who is now chargeable to the Union, and whose mother has lately died, will keep its mother's settlement until it is 16, or will it now be entitled to its birth-settlement, which is not the place of the mother's settlement, and calling the Commissioners' attention to section 71 of the 4 and 5 Wm. IV. c. 76. The Commissioners directed the following answer to be given thereto:—

"The Commissioners are of opinion, on the case stated in your letter, that the child would probably retain the last parentage settlement, which it received from its mother; and that it does not, upon the decease of the mother, revert to its birth settlement. The Commissioners think the word 'have,' in the 71st section of the Act above-mentioned, must be construed to mean to 'take;' and that the limitation in the subsequent part of the clause, viz., 'until,' has reference to the word 'follow,' but will not deprive the pauper of the settlement already acquired."

XVII.—VAGRANTS.—EMPLOYMENT OF, IN THE WORKHOUSE.—LEOMINSTER UNION.

3d March, 1843.

The Commissioners took into consideration a minute passed by the Board of Guardians of the Leominster Union, that able-bodied male vagrants relieved in the Union workhouse should be detained by the master for a period not exceeding four hours on the morning after their admission, and that they should be required to perform such work as the master should allot them to perform. The Commissioners directed the following communication to be made to the clerk in reference to such minute:—

"The Commissioners doubt the legality of this delegation on the part of the Guardians to the master, to assign the quantity and nature of the work to be done by the vagrants. They think that the Guardians should themselves direct the nature and quantity of the work to be performed; and they therefore suggest for the adoption of the Guardians a form to the following effect, which would remove this objection, *e. g.*:—

'That all able-bodied men shall do work at the mill, or at the , or pick lbs. of oakum, &c., the same to be subject to and superintended by the master of the workhouse [enumerating thus all the species of work provided in the workhouse, with a reservation], unless the workhouse-master should see fit to dispense, in any case, with such task or any part of it.'

"A form of a similar nature might be adopted for the other classes — able-bodied women, boys, girls, &c., the infirm, &c."

XVIII.—WITNESSES.—POWER OF JUSTICES TO COMPEL ATTENDANCE OF.—MACHYNLLETH UNION.

6th March, 1843.

The Commissioners took into consideration a letter received from the Clerk to the Guardians of the Machynlleth Union, stating that the Guardians of that Union had recently made an order upon the overseers of Llanbrynmair, to apply to the magistrates for an order for the removal of a person chargeable to that parish; that the overseers had attended at the petty sessions accordingly, and as a material witness declined to attend, they requested the justices to enforce his attendance. The justices, however, considered themselves unauthorized to compel the attendance of an unwilling witness; and the Guardians wished, therefore, to have the advice of the Commissioners as to the course to be pursued. The Commissioners directed the following answer to be given thereto:—

"In the case Reg. *v.* Lydiard St. Lawrence, 11 A. & E. 627, Lord Denman was represented to say that the justices had a power to compel the attendance of witnesses within their jurisdiction; but the Commissioners are not aware of any other authority in favour of the power of two justices, or of justices of petty sessions, to summons witnesses, except in those cases where it is expressly given by Act of Parliament, and there is no express statutory authority of the kind given to summon witnesses for examination previous to the making of an order of removal. Mr. Justice Coleridge, in the same case, appeared to admit that there was no such power in the justices; and the statements in the text-books generally treated it as non-existent, except where expressly authorized. (See Paley on Convictions, 23 Burns' Justice, Evidence, s. 1 (6); Dickinson's Quarter Sessions, 4th edit., 116, 117, note 1.

"The Commissioners desire to add that the common practice of obtaining a Crown Office order seems strongly to confirm the view expressed by Mr. Justice Coleridge, that the justices have no such power to compel the attendance of witnesses."

XIX.—WORKHOUSE.

1. PAUPERS LEAVING THE WORKHOUSE FOR IMPROPER PURPOSES.—YEOVIL UNION.

10th February, 1843.

A letter from the clerk to the Guardians of the Yeovil Union was read, stating that in consequence of some of the able-bodied women in the workhouse, who have illegitimate children, being in the habit of giving to the master notice, and quitting the workhouse for improper purposes, and after remaining out a short time applying for re-admission, the Guardians had passed a resolution that in future, when the master should have reason to believe that notice given to him to quit the house was given merely for a temporary purpose, and with intention to return again, he should refuse such notice till he had brought it before the Board of Guardians for their decision. The Commissioners directed the following communication to be addressed to the clerk in reference to such resolution:—

"The Commissioners desire to point out to the Guardians, that (except in the case of orphan children) there is no power to detain a person in a workhouse against his will, after he has given reasonable notice to the master of his intention to quit it. The above-cited resolution is, therefore, unauthorized by law, and consequently cannot be legally acted upon. The Commissioners refer the Guardians to Article 23 of the General Workhouse Rules, relating to this subject, and to the observations of the Commissioners thereon in their Instructional Letter relating to those Rules.

"The Commissioners are well aware of the great inconvenience arising from the practice above alluded to, having frequently had their attention called to it; but in the present state of the law they are unable to suggest any effectual remedy.

"The Commissioners think that in such cases it might be well to warn the parties, that unless under circumstances of urgent necessity, the relieving officer would not give an order for their re-admission into the workhouse without a direction from the Board of Guardians, and that in all cases, when re-admitted, they should be placed in the probationary ward, and be treated in the same manner as paupers admitted for the first time into the workhouse. The Commissioners also think that all such paupers should be kept to hard work under strict discipline and superintendence.

"If, however, the parties are in urgent necessity, the fact of their having recently quitted the workhouse under the circumstances above described will not justify an absolute refusal of relief."

2. WHETHER THE MOTHER OF A LEGITIMATE CHILD IS LIABLE TO PUNISHMENT FOR LEAVING HER CHILD IN THE WORKHOUSE. —HUNGERFORD UNION.

7th March, 1843.

The Commissioners took into consideration a letter addressed to them by the Clerk to the Guardians of the Hungerford Union, inquiring whether there is any law which renders the mother of a legitimate child, left by her in the workhouse, liable to punishment; and the Commissioners directed the following reply to be given thereto:—

"If the mother be a widow, there can be no doubt of her obligation to maintain the child; and that she accordingly would be punishable under 5th Geo. IV., c. 83, sec. 3, for the refusal or neglect to maintain it. But if the husband be alive, the obligation to maintain attaches to him, as the head of the family; and the Commissioners consider that the wife would not be punishable for leaving the child in the workhouse, unless it amounted to a running away within the meaning of the 4th section. The terms of the 4th section do not, as is the case with the 3d, involve the question of the liability to maintain."

3. WHETHER GUARDIANS CAN SEND A PAUPER OUT OF THE WORKHOUSE. — BRAINTREE UNION.

24th February, 1843.

The Commissioners took into consideration a letter received from the Clerk to the Guardians of the Braintree Union, submitting to the Commissioners the following statement:—

"John Ridgewell, an able-bodied labourer of the parish of Histed, was in the course of last spring, with his family, consisting of a wife, a son, and two younger children, admitted into the workhouse. About the 19th of April they gave notice, and left the house; immediately after which, the man (taking with him his son) deserted his wife and the younger children. The wife then having no residence removed out of the Union, leaving the two younger children homeless, and they were again admitted into the workhouse, where they have continued ever since. The man, about the middle of November, returned to the Union, with the son, in a state of destitution, and they were again admitted into the workhouse, his wife being then residing out of the Union separately from him, and maintaining herself;" and inquiring whether, under these circumstances, the Guardians would be justified in turning the man and his three children out of the workhouse. The Commissioners directed the following reply to be given to the inquiry:—

"The Commissioners are of opinion that the Guardians would not be justified in turning the man, or any of his children, out of the workhouse. With regard to any intention of punishing the parties under the Vagrant Act for the neglect to maintain their children, the Commissioners would observe, that though the wife would not be liable under the 3d section of the 5 Geo. IV., c. 83, to maintain the children during the continuance of her husband's liability, she appears, as well as her husband, to be liable under the 4th section, for running away and leaving the children chargeable—a question which does not involve the liability, or the ability, to maintain the deserted family."

4. AS TO THE RIGHT OF PERSONS FINDING A DEAD BODY TO PLACE THE SAME IN A UNION WORKHOUSE.—WISBECH UNION.

3d February, 1842.

The Commissioners took into consideration a letter received by them, through their Assistant-Commissioner, Mr. Twisleton, from the Rev. Henry Fardell, the chairman of the Board of Guardians of the Wisbech Union, stating that, before the erection of the Union Workhouse, it was customary for persons finding a dead body to remove the same, sometimes before and sometimes after an inquest had been held, into the old workhouse; and inquiring whether persons had a right to demand the use of the dead house in the New Union Workhouse for such a purpose: and the Commissioners directed the following answer to be given to the inquiry:—

"There is no common law on the subject; workhouses and poor laws being of too recent institution to admit of any common law rule as to their disposition for any special purpose; neither is there any statutory provision upon the subject of holding inquests in workhouses. The Commissioners consider that there is no ground, therefore, for claiming the right to the use of the workhouse, or any part of it, for the purpose of holding an inquest on any person found dead not within the walls.

"There may, however, be particular cases in which the Guardians would be justified in allowing the inquest on such a body to be held in the workhouse, as where the inconvenience of a refusal would be great. In such cases the Guardians would, no doubt, think it their duty to allow of the inquest being so held; but whenever they do so, it will be proper that they should give the permission as a voluntary act, and not as the admission of a right."

5. PUNISHMENT FOR OFFENCES COMMITTED IN WORKHOUSES.—BARROW-UPON-SOAR UNION.
21st February, 1842.

The Commissioners took into consideration a letter addressed to them by the Clerk of the Barrow-upon-Soar Union, inquiring whether the inmates of Union workhouses are subject to be punished for offences committed in the workhouse under the 22 Geo. III., c. 83, s. 40: and the Commissioners directed the following answer to be given thereto:—

"The Act of 22 Geo. III., c. 83, is still in operation; but the powers given by the 40th section to justices relative to the punishment of persons for embezzling, or wasting goods provided for the use of 'such house,' only extend to poor-houses or workhouses established under the authority of that Act. This provision, therefore, has no application to workhouses established under the authority of the 4 and 5 Wm. IV., c. 76. The provision in the 50 Geo. III., c. 50, which imposes a penalty for embezzling goods, is general, and extends to any poorhouse or workhouse. The Commissioners are of opinion, that proceedings may be taken under that statute in regard to any embezzling or wasting of goods committed in Union workhouses."

6. PAUPERS ABSCONDING FROM THE WORKHOUSE.—BROMSGROVE UNION.
24th March, 1842.

The Commissioners took into consideration a letter addressed to them by the Clerk of the Bromsgrove Union, inquiring whether or not a pauper who absconds from the workhouse, by climbing over a wall, and who returns again of his own accord, is to be deemed disorderly, and is punishable for neglecting to observe the workhouse regulations (Article 23), which are applicable and binding on him; and stating that the Guardians cannot reconcile with the workhouse rules, the observations made by the Commissioners on this point in the last section of Article 24, at page 10 of their instructional letter; and the Commissioners directed the following reply to be given thereto:—

"The object of Article 23, is to show the circumstances under which a pauper may regularly leave the house. It enumerates his right, and the workhouse master's obligation, so far as leaving the house is concerned; but it does not purport to impose a restriction on the pauper, nor make his leaving it in other manners than that indicated an offence. The mere leaving the house without reasonable notice is not, therefore, made to be of itself an offence. The observations in the instructional letter upon Article 24 merely expresses this fact.

"But, practically, the leaving the house without notice can rarely take place without there being also some decided misbehaviour, or other irregularity for which the pauper would be punishable; especially, it will be almost certain, that he will carry away some of the workhouse clothing, and thus be liable to the penalties of the 55 Geo. III. c. 137."

7. DUTIES OF PORTER.—WEST HAM UNION.
7th April, 1842.

The Commissioners took into consideration a letter received from the Clerk of the West Ham Union, inquiring whether the porter ought to enter the following cases of ingress to and egress from the workhouse, in the book which he is required to keep under the General Workhouse Regulations:—

"The Guardians on Board or other days.—The Clerk and those having business at his office.—The Relieving Officers.—The Master, Matron, and other officers, and their friends visiting them.—Persons coming in with goods, fuel, &c.—Paupers admitted into the house.—Ditto discharged therefrom.—Mendicants admitted and discharged.—Persons attending funerals.—Applicants on Board days.—The Chaplain.—The Medical Officer.—All persons going to church or chapel."

And the Commissioners directed the following reply to be given thereto:—

"I am to state, that it appears to the Commissioners that the entries in question should be made.

"It sometimes happens that it is of great importance, for the justification of an officer, or for confuting a false statement of a pauper, that facts of this nature should be recorded somewhere. No one can say beforehand the particular case in which this may be required. Moreover, the book thus kept presents the Guardians with a complete history of the visits to and discharges from the workhouse, and has been found of the greatest use."

LONDON:
Printed by Order of the Poor Law Commissioners, by W. CLOWES and SONS, Stamford Street, and Published by CHARLES KNIGHT and Co., 22, Ludgate Street, Publishers to the Poor Law Commissioners.

AN

OFFICIAL CIRCULAR

OF PUBLIC DOCUMENTS AND INFORMATION:

DIRECTED BY THE POOR LAW COMMISSIONERS TO BE PRINTED, CHIEFLY FOR THE USE OF THE MEMBERS AND PERMANENT OFFICERS OF BOARDS OF GUARDIANS, UNDER THE POOR LAW AMENDMENT ACT.

No. 26. CIRCULAR ISSUED JUNE 30, 1843.

Poor Law Commission Office,
Somerset House,
June 29, 1843.

THE Poor Law Commissioners, on a review of their Correspondence, directed that the following abstract thereof should be printed and circulated for the information of Guardians and Officers of the several Unions, viz.:—

By order of the Board,
EDWIN CHADWICK, *Secretary.*

I.—FRIENDLY SOCIETIES.—RELIEF TO MEMBERS OF.

14*th June*, 1843.

Clerk of Bourn Union.—Several benefit or friendly societies in that neighbourhood have resolved to withhold their usual allowances to their members in case of sickness, as often as parochial relief is refused or discontinued, in consequence of such allowances rendering them independent of the poor-rate. How should the Guardians act in such cases?

Ans. The Commissioners exceedingly regret the existence of a misunderstanding of the object of benefit societies, which, instead of promoting independence, under the circumstances stated will encourage and give a permanent character to the pauperism of the Union; and in compliance with the Guardians' request for advice, the Commissioners desire to remark, that the Guardians cannot do otherwise than deal with each case as it arises according to their view of the destitution of the applicant at the time he seeks relief, from whatever source his means may be derived. The Guardians, in all cases admitting of removal to the workhouse, may offer relief in that shape if they think fit. Such a mode of dealing with these cases would, in many instances, prevent the evil consequences apprehended by the Guardians. A little consideration will serve to show, that the difficulty connected with these cases is one which no contrivance can wholly remove. It must be borne in mind that one evil necessarily attending any poor law is, that the provident labourer does not appear to stand in a position, so far superior to that of his improvident neighbour as to compensate for the privations and difficulties which have attended the self-denial of saving on his part. This, neither the Guardians, nor the Commissioners, nor, in fact, any legislative provision consistent with a poor law, can wholly remove. It is an evil, but it has been rightly assumed to be a less evil than the constant recurrence of the extreme consequences which the absence of all provision would entail on the imprudent.

The Commissioners called the attention of the Guardians to No. 3 of the *Official Circular*, section 8, as relating to the relief of members of friendly societies.

II.—GUARDIANS.—ELECTION OF.

1. DESCRIPTION OF NOMINATOR.

10*th March*, 1843.

Clerk of Cambridge Union.—Is the nomination valid, the nominator having described himself as a "householder," instead of a "ratepayer" or "owner of property?"

Ans. The Commissioners are of opinion that the insertion of the words "*a householder*," in the nomination paper, instead of the words "a ratepayer," renders the nomination invalid.

2. DATE OF NOMINATION PAPER.

11*th March*, 1843.

Clerk of Cambridge Union.—He has received a nomination paper signed Thomas Wood, and dated 1844. Is the error sufficient to invalidate the nomination?

Ans. The Commissioners are of opinion that the error in the date of the nomination paper, signed by Thomas Wood, must be regarded as clerical only, and that such error does not invalidate the nomination.

3. ADDRESS OF NOMINATOR OMITTED.

15*th March*, 1843.

Clerk of Weardale Union.—He has received a nomination paper, in which the address of the nominator has not been inserted. Is such a nomination valid?

Ans.—The Commissioners think the address of the proposer material, and that the nomination paper is invalid, such address having been omitted.

4. ADDRESS OF CANDIDATE AND NOMINATOR OMITTED.

16*th March*, 1843.

Clerk of Huddersfield Union.—1. Is the omission of the name of the township in the address of a candidate material? 2. Does the omission of the name of the township in the address of a nominator invalidate the nomination?

Ans. 1. The Commissioners are of opinion that this would not render the nomination invalid. 2. The Commissioners do not think that the fact of the proposer merely inserting his name, and the street he lives in, without adding "Huddersfield," would invalidate the nomination.

5. DESCRIPTION OF NOMINATOR OMITTED.—CLAIMS OF OWNERS, WHEN TO BE DELIVERED.—NOTICE OF REFUSAL TO ACT, WHEN TO BE RECEIVED.

15*th March*, 1843.

Clerk of Kidderminster Union.—1stly. Is the nomination paper marked "A" valid, the nominator having omitted to state in what capacity he nominates? 2ndly. Is the nomination paper marked "B," which is intended to be for the borough of Bewdley, although described as for the "Parish of Ribbesford, Borough of Bewdley Union," valid? The candidate's calling is also omitted; and the nominator describes himself to be a ratepayer of the parish of Ribbesford, although he is, in point of fact, a ratepayer of the borough of Bewdley. 3rdly. Should the claims of owners of property to vote be delivered before the 20th of March, or on or before what other day? 4thly. Should a notice in writing from a candidate, declining to act, and delivered on the 11th of March, be considered as delivered during the election, and ought the Clerk to omit his name from the voting paper?

Ans. 1stly. The Commissioners consider the nomination marked "A" invalid, in not showing by what title the proposer assumes to nominate. 2ndly. The Commissioners consider the nomination marked "B" cannot, consistently with the Clerk's explanation, be treated as valid. 3rdly. The statements of owners, showing their title to vote, should be delivered to the overseers before the 20th instant, or the day fixed for delivering the voting papers. 4thly. Yes.

6. SUBSTITUTION OF NAMES IN NOMINATION PAPER.

23*rd March*, 1843.

Clerk of Chelmsford Union.—The Rev. E. Edison nominated John Clarke for the office of Guardian; but supposing afterwards that he was not rated at the necessary amount, Mr. Edison erased his name from the nomination paper, and substituted that of Jordan. Upon its being ascertained subsequently that Clarke was qualified, Jordan requested Mr. Edison to withdraw his name, and restore that of Clarke, and Mr. Edison directed him to give the requisite instructions to the overseer, which he did. Mr. Edison's nomination paper was given to the overseer on the 5th instant, at a large meeting of the parishioners; and on the 9th instant, a few of the ratepayers met, and put the name of Mr. W. Moss (as being nominated by Mr. Homer) on Mr. Edison's nomination paper, without restoring the name of Mr. Clarke. What course should be pursued under the above circumstances?

Ans. The Commissioners think that Mr. Edison could give no authority to the overseer to withdraw Mr. Jordan's name, and to substitute the name of some other person. It is, therefore, to be considered that Mr. Jordan was the person, and the only person in nomination at that time. But subsequently the name of another person (Mr. Moss) is added, and it would seem improperly so. There were then two persons proposed for the parish in the same nomination paper, whereas the parish was only entitled to one Guardian. This renders the nomination void for uncertainty, and the Commissioners think it should be rejected.

---

7. NAME OF TOWNSHIP OMITTED IN NOMINATION PAPER.

23*rd March*, 1843.

Mr. R. Liddell, Huddersfield.—Does the omission of the name of the township, at the head of a nomination paper, render the nomination invalid, the name of the township being inserted at the foot of the paper?

Ans. The Commissioners are disposed to think that the omission of the name of the township at the head of the nomination, is cured by the insertion of it at the foot of the form. When, however, a nomination is in any respect informal, the Commissioners, by their order, have left to the clerk to decide, upon his own responsibility, whether the informality is of a nature to invalidate the nomination or not.

---

8. NEGLECT TO NOMINATE.—PLURALITY OF VOTES.

18*th March*, 1843.

Clerk of Evesham Union.—1st. Some of the parishes have neglected to nominate a Guardian. May the Guardians for last year continue to act? 2ndly. Is it legal to nominate a person for the office of Guardian after the 10th of March? 3rdly. Is a person who is both owner and occupier of property to the amount of 40*l.*, entitled to two votes?

Ans. 1st. Where parishes neglect to nominate Guardians for the ensuing year the Guardians for the present year may continue to act as such, under sec. 10, of 5 and 6 Vic. c. 57. 2ndly. A person cannot be legally nominated for the office of Guardian after the 10th March, unless the Commissioners issue a special order for that purpose. 3rdly. A person who is both owner and occupier of property to the amount of 40*l.* is legally entitled to two votes.

---

9. NOMINATION OF A PERSON FOR TWO PARISHES.—REFUSAL TO ACT.

18*th March*, 1843.

Clerk of Williton Union.—The parishes of Lilstock and Kilton are each entitled to one Guardian. Mr. John Govett has been nominated for Lilstock. He has also, together with Mr. C. Addams, been nominated for Kilton, consequently the rate-payers of Kilton must proceed to an election, unless one of the candidates withdraw. Mr. Govett is willing to represent Lilstock, and Mr. Addams to represent Kilton. Can Mr. Govett, under the 9th sec. of 5 and 6 Vic., c. 57, decline to serve for Kilton; and can he then be returned for Lilstock, and Mr. Addams for Kilton?

Ans. The Commissioners are of opinion that the 9th sec. of 5 and 6 Vic., c. 57, enables the Clerk to accept Mr. Govett's refusal to serve as Guardian for the parish of Kilton, and that he can be returned for the parish of Lilstock.

---

10. CANDIDATE REFUSING TO ACT.—VALIDITY OF CHURCH-RATE.—NON-PAYMENT OF HIGHWAY-RATE.

18*th March*, 1843.

Clerk of Cambridge Union. — 1st. Mr. Edward Litchfield, and Mr. John Harvey (Guardians for the present year,) were, with Mr. John Dumvill, nominated as Guardians for the parish of Holy Sepulchre for the ensuing year. Mr. Litchfield's nomination being invalid, and Mr. Dumvill having sent in a refusal in writing, to act, Mr. Harvey is the only person now in nomination; If Mr. Harvey decline to act under the present nomination, will he and Mr. Litchfield be entitled to act as Guardians for the ensuing year, under sec. 10 of 5 and 6 Vic. c. 57? 2ndly. A church-rate was made in the parish of St. Michael, in June last, but has never been allowed by the Surrogate. Is such allowance necessary to render it valid? 3rdly. A highway rate was made in the parish of St. Andrew the Less, on the 14th April last, and Mr. Cooper (who has nominated two persons as Guardians for the parish,) did not pay the amount of his assessment thereunder until the 10th inst., no demand having been made upon him, in consequence of the parish Surveyors' being indebted to him in a larger sum for professional business transacted for them; the nomination paper is dated the 2nd inst. Is the nomination valid?

Ans. 1stly. The Commissioners think that if Mr. Harvey were to send in his refusal to serve as Guardian, under the circumstances stated, he could not continue to act under the 10th sec. of 5 and 6 Vic., c. 57, by virtue of his former appointment. In such case, however, there would be nothing to prevent Mr. Litchfield acting. 2ndly. By the case of Knight and Littlejohn *v.* Gloyne, 3 Add. 53, it appears to be decided that though it is usual and proper to have the rate confirmed by the Archdeacon, or other authorized ordinary, yet it is not essential to the validity of a church rate that it be confirmed by the ordinary. 3rdly. The party nominating should, at the time of nomination, have been entitled to vote as rate-payer, under the 40th sec. of the Poor Law Amendment Act. The Commissioners think this was not the case with Mr. Cooper, as the highway rate (a parochial rate) must be considered as owing by him, when he assumed to nominate.

11. NON-PAYMENT OF RATES BY NOMINATOR.

22*nd April*, 1843.

Clerk of West Derby Union.—Mr. James Williams was returned Guardian for the township of Little Crosby: an objection has been made to his return, on the ground that the person who nominated him, had not, at the time of the nomination, paid the church-rates due to the parish of Sefton, in respect of property which he occupied in the township of Great Crosby—Little Crosby and Great Crosby being distinct townships in that parish; but he had paid the whole of his parochial rates in respect of Little Crosby; was the nomination valid?

Ans. If the nominator of Mr. Williams was entitled to vote as a rate-payer in the township of Little Crosby, he was duly qualified to nominate a person to the office of Guardian for that township. The fact of his not being a rate-payer, *i. e.* of his not having paid his rates in the township of Great Crosby, would not affect his right to vote and nominate for Little Crosby township, the order of the Commissioners enabling those townships each to appoint a Guardian.

12. DITTO.

23*rd March*, 1843.

Clerk of Wakefield Union.—1st. A church-rate was laid on the 6th of August, 1840, for several townships in the Union, which was but partially paid, and there has been no subsequent church-rate legally made. It is contended that the rate, being more than a year old, the non-payment of it does not disqualify a person from voting. 2. In the townships of Alverthorpe and Thornes, cottages have not been rated at all to the church-rate, nor do their names appear in the rate books. 3. In Wakefield the cottagers' names are entered in the church-rate books, but it has not been usual to collect the rate from persons paying a less rent than 5*l.* per annum. Should the votes, in these cases, be accepted or rejected?

Ans. 1. The Commissioners understand the words in the 40th section of the Poor Law Amendment Act, "shall have paid the parochial rates and assessments made and assessed upon him for the period of one whole year, as well as those due from him at the time of so voting or acting," as extending to any parochial rate and assessment made previously to the year immediately preceding the time of voting, and which may not have been paid; such a rate must be considered as "due" from the person rated. 2. There is nothing to prevent such cottagers voting, if they have been rated to the poor-rate for the prescribed period, and paid the poor-rate. 3. It appears to the Commissioners that the rate is still due.

13. EMPLOYMENT OF PAUPERS TO DELIVER VOTING PAPERS.

18th March, 1843.

Clerk of Calne Union.—Would two or three of the better informed paupers, of steady character in the workhouse, be proper parties to distribute and collect voting papers?

Ans. The Commissioners are of opinion that paupers are not suitable persons to be employed in delivering and collecting voting papers in the election of Guardians.

14. DESCRIPTION OF PROPERTY IN CLAIMS.

23rd March, 1843.

Clerk of Lutterworth Union.—The overseers of Bruntingthorpe have received certain claims of owners and appointments of proxies, in which the property in respect whereof the parties claim to vote is described as consisting of "houses and land." Is this description such as is required by the 40th sec. of the Poor Law Amendment Act?

Ans. The description of the property is not, in the Commissioners' opinion, such as is contemplated by the 40th sec. of the Poor Law Amendment Act. The Commissioners think it ought to be a description which would enable those conducting the election to identify the property, so that, upon reference to the rate books, the proper number of votes might be assigned; as the particular name of the property, if known by any such name; the particular locality in a parish; or the names of the parties in occupation.

15. CLAIMS OF JOINT OWNERS.

23rd March, 1843.

Clerk of Petersfield Union.—The overseers of Eastmeon have sent in a register of owners of property in that parish, in which Mr. William Weeks has inserted his own name, as owner, as follows:—"William Weeks, jun., joint proprietor of Lower House Farm, occupier John Weeks, assessment, 115*l.* 7*s.* 6*d.* No. of votes 4." The voting papers are issued, stating the number of votes, according to the register, wherein Mr. Weeks' claim as owner runs thus:—"Joint proprietor with John and James Weeks for Lower House Farm." In the rate-book the property is rated as follows: "John Weeks occupier, executors of James Weeks, owners." What steps should be taken in casting up the votes, so far as regards the allowance of the four votes claimed by Mr. Weeks?

Ans. In the case of joint owners of property, where there is nothing to show the interest of each owner respectively, it is to be presumed that all are equally interested. The votes, therefore, which the entire property would yield to an individual owner, should in the case supposed, be apportioned according to the individual interest. If one owner claims a preponderant share in the property, and shows that his interest is greater than another joint owner, he will be entitled to a proportionate increase in the votes, where the number of votes conferred by the property allows of it. The Commissioners arrive at this conclusion, from the analogy furnished by the 58th Geo. III., c. 69, s. 3, in the case of occupiers jointly rated. The Commissioners think that the above principle should be observed in dealing with the particular case instanced in the clerk's letter.

16. CLERK MAY CALL FOR ORIGINAL STATEMENTS OF OWNERS AND PROXIES.

24th March, 1843.

Clerk of Headington Union.—In the parish of Headington the overseers have received several owners' statements and appointments, and statements of proxies, and have registered them in the rate-book, but have not forwarded the original documents. The proxies are given to one of the overseers, who is also a candidate for the office of Guardian. Should the votes be allowed without comparing the original documents with the register in the rate-book?

Ans. The clerk is entitled to call for the production of the original statements made by owners and proxies, and is not concluded by the register produced by the overseers. He can, therefore, where he feels any doubt as to the validity of any entry in the register, refuse to issue a voting paper, unless he is furnished with the original statements.

17. PERSONS WHO HAVE QUALIFIED SUBSEQUENT TO THE DELIVERY OF VOTING PAPERS.

24*th March*, 1843.

Clerk of Nottingham Union.—Some of the rate-payers, not being qualified to vote in the election of Guardians, on the day on which the voting papers were delivered, from not having paid the highway rate; but having subsequently paid the rate, and applied for voting papers, is he empowered to enforce the attendance of the collectors of the highway rate, with the rate-books, for the purpose of ascertaining if the rates have been paid, and when? Would he be justified in refusing voting papers to persons who have obtained the qualification subsequent to the general delivery of the voting papers?

Ans. The Commissioners consider that the clerk could not compel the attendance of the collector of the highway rate, nor the production of the rate-book, if such collector should be unwilling to attend when required, and to produce such book. With regard to persons to whom voting papers were not issued, upon the supposition that they had not paid the highway rate in sufficient time, and who may apply for voting papers under Art. 21 of the Order of Election, the Clerk should require such persons to show that they had paid the rate in due time (*i. e.* before the 20th instant), and to that end should require the production of the receipt in discharge of payment.

18. CLAIMS NOT REQUIRED TO BE RENEWED.

25*th March*, 1843.

Clerk of Calne Union.—Is it necessary that parties duly registered, two or three years back, as owners claiming to vote at the election of Guardians, should claim and be registered again previous to voting at a subsequent election?

Ans. Owners who have once made their claim to vote, in the manner required by the 40th section of the Poor Law Amendment Act, need not renew their claims every suceeding year, but such claims remain in force.

19. STATEMENT, &c., OF PROPERTY BY OWNER.

25*th March*, 1843.

Clerk of Newport Pagnell Union.—Can an owner of property, of which he is also the occupier, vote in respect of his ownership, without giving to the overseers a statement and description of the property for which he claims to vote?

Ans. The Commissioners are of opinion that whether the owner be or be not in the occupation of his own property, the 40th section of the Poor Law Amendment Act renders it in either case necessary, as the condition of voting as owner, that he should have delivered to the overseers the statement and description of his property previously to the day on which he claims to vote.

20. CLAIMS, WHEN TO BE RECEIVED.—NOT ADVISABLE FOR CLERK TO VOTE.

25*th March*, 1843.

Clerk of King's Lynn Union.—Can he receive claims of owners to vote on or after the day fixed for the delivery of the voting papers (20th instant)? Is it his duty to abstain from voting at the election of Guardians?

Ans. The Commissioners think the owner should be duly entitled to vote on the day on which voting papers are delivered; *i. e.*, by the order, the 20th instant. To be entitled to vote, the owner must, previously to that day, have delivered to the overseers the statement of his property, required by the 40th section of the Poor Law Amendment Act. The Commissioners are of opinion that, although the Clerk of a Union is not expressly prohibited by the order of election from voting for candidates, or otherwise taking a part in the election of Guardians, yet, inasmuch as the management of the election is entrusted to him by the order, the Commissioners think that he would act very unadvisedly if he were to do anything which showed a preference for any candidate.

21. OCCUPIERS CANNOT APPOINT PROXIES.

25*th March*, 1843.

Clerk of Patrington Union.—Can a non-resident owner of property, which he also occupies, appoint a proxy to vote for him in right of his occupancy, as well as owner of the property?

Ans. The Poor Law Amendment Act only authorizes the appointment of a proxy by owners, and does not allow of such an appointment by occupiers. A person, therefore, who is both owner and occupier of property cannot appoint a proxy to vote for him in both capacities.

22. VOTING PAPERS INFORMALLY SIGNED.

27th March, 1843.

Clerk to the Guardians of the Parish of Chelsea.—Several voters, in filling up their voting papers, instead of writing their initials against the names of the persons for whom they intend to vote, and signing the voting paper at the foot, have written their names in full opposite the names of the persons for whom they intend to vote, and have omitted to sign at the foot. Should such votes be allowed?

Ans. The Commissioners are of opinion that voting papers, filled up in the way described by the clerk, cannot be considered as duly signed by the voters, which it is essential they should be to allow of their being taken into the calculation of votes.

23. NAME OF CANDIDATE MIS-SPELT IN VOTING PAPER.

25th March, 1843.

Clerk of Wheatenhurst Union.—The name of one of the candidates for the office of Guardian for the parish of Arlingham has been spelt in the voting papers "Tooly," instead of "Tooby:" there is no person in the parish of the former name, and the address of the candidate is given; so that it is understood by every one who is meant. Will the mis-spelling of the name vitiate the proceedings?

Ans. The inaccuracy in the spelling of the name of Mr. Tooby in the voting paper, will not invalidate the proceedings, as the variance is not likely to mislead the persons entitled to vote in the parish, the residence and calling of Mr. Tooby being accurately stated.

24. VOTING.—PERSONS OCCUPYING SEPARATE ROOMS IN A DWELLING-HOUSE.

28th March, 1843.

Clerk of Hexham Union.— A dwelling-house, containing six rooms, is let out into tenements to six different persons, each person renting and occupying his own room separately; but they are rated to the relief of the poor as joint tenants. Can each of these six tenants give one vote in the election of Guardians, or can any one of them vote for this property according to the manner in which it is rated, rented, and occupied? And have the overseers the power to rate this house in the way it is rated?

Ans. The Commissioners presume that the several occupiers referred to have been rated, on their own application, under the 2d Wm. IV., c. 45, s. 3 (the Reform Act), or the 5th and 6th Wm. IV., c. 76, s. 11 (the Municipal Corporations Act). If the occupiers of the apartments are not rated under one of these provisions, they are not duly rated, there being no authority for rating the occupier of a part of a house, where there is a private occupier of the whole house. The occupier of the whole house, whether he himself resides in it or not, is the only person lawfully rateable for it, unless where the landlord is rated under the 59th Geo. III., c. 12, s. 19; and the claims to vote of all other persons in respect of the occupancy of the house and payment of rates must be disallowed.

25. VOTING PAPERS IN CASE OF A FIRM.

28th March, 1843.

Clerk of Barnstaple Union.—In the poor-rate, the overseers, instead of assessing the actual occupiers of warehouses by name, have, in some instances, inserted the designation of the firm under which the business is carried on: thus, "William Arter and Co.;" the occupiers being Thomas Arter and William Arter the younger. To whom should the voting paper be sent?

Ans. The voting paper should be sent to the party whose name appears upon the rate, viz., William Arter.

26. STATEMENTS OF OWNERS, &c., DELIVERED IN 1837, ON MEETING FOR SALE OF PARISH PROPERTY.

28th March, 1843.

Mr. C. Walford, overseer, Kidderminster.—1. Supposing two or more persons to be joint occupiers of property rated under 200*l.*, would they be entitled to more than one vote in the election of Guardians, and could such vote be exercised by any of them? 2. If any one of such joint occupiers were rated for other property, would he be entitled to vote for such separate rating independent of the partnership? 3. Are the statements of owners and appointment of proxies, delivered to overseers in 1837, on occasion of a meeting to consent to the sale of parish property, sufficient for the ensuing election of Guardians; or must new statements and appointments be delivered under the last election order, which varies the forms of such statements, &c., from those before delivered? 4. Will persons be entitled to vote who have not paid their church and highway rates, due more than six months previous to the election?

Ans. 1. Where two or more persons are joint occupiers of the same property, which is rated at a sum under 200*l.*, such joint occupiers will not be entitled to more than one vote between them. 2. If any of such occupiers should happen to be rated for any other property, he will be entitled to a separate vote in respect of that independent rating. 3. The statements of owners and appointments of proxies, delivered to the overseers in 1837, on the occasion of a meeting to consent to the sale of parish property, continue valid, and may be acted upon with reference to the election of Guardians, notwithstanding that the form in which they were given may differ from that set forth in the Election Order now in force, and notwithstanding that they were made for another purpose, and not with a view to the election of Guardians. It will be seen that the present Election Order does not render it obligatory upon owners to adopt the form of statement (marked A.) therein contained, but leaves it open to them to make the statement in any form which contains the particulars required by the Poor Law Amendment Act. 4. A person who has not paid the church and highway rates, which were due from him more than six months preceding the time of voting, is disqualified for voting as a ratepayer at the election of Guardians.

---

27. VOTER CHANGING RESIDENCE WITHIN THE SAME TOWNSHIP.

31*st March*, 1843.

Rev. Edward Edwards, Wrexham.—In February last he changed his place of residence, but still lives in the same township, which returns two Guardians. He paid his parochial rates for the property which he formerly occupied, and one poor-rate since he has occupied his present dwelling-house. He is informed that he cannot vote in the election of Guardians for the ensuing year in consequence of having changed his residence since July last, though he has not changed the parish, township, or district. Is he disqualified from voting in the election of Guardians for the ensuing year?

Ans. Assuming that Mr. Edwards has been rated continuously in the same parish for the period required by the 40th sect. of the Poor Law Amendment Act, viz., one whole year prior to the time of voting, and paid the rates for that period, except such as may have been made or become due within the last six months, the Commissioners think the fact of his not having been rated for the same premises, but for different premises in succession, would not deprive him of his right to vote at the annual election of Guardians, as a ratepayer of the parish for which the election takes place.

---

28. OMISSION OF PROXY TO STATE BY WHOM APPOINTED.

1*st April*, 1843.

Mr. George Edwards, Bath.—Having been appointed proxy by a considerable number of owners of property, the necessary claims were duly served on the overseer. The voting papers were headed, "George Edwards, for John Allen," or for such other persons as he claimed to vote as proxy. He signed the voting papers with his name only, omitting to state the names of the persons who had appointed him their proxy. He has been informed that the clerk has rejected a vote in a similar case; and he trusts that the Commissioners will not allow a large number of owners, who had appointed him their proxy, to be disfranchised merely on account of a technical omission.

Ans. The directions in the voting paper, prescribed by the order of election, distinctly require that the proxy, in addition to his own signature, should state in writing the person for whom he is proxy; where this is omitted to be done, the Commissioners think it is not a compliance with the order of directions issued by them, under the 40th section of the Poor Law Amendment Act, for the giving and returning of votes; and the Act directs that "persons who shall not comply with the directions to be made by the said Commissioners for the giving or returning of votes shall be omitted in the calculation of votes."

---

29. A PERSON NOT ASSESSED WITHIN THE UNION MAY BE PROXY.

6*th April*, 1843.

Clerk of Halsted Union.—Can a person who is not rated to the relief of the poor in any parish within the Union be appointed a proxy, and vote as such for owners of property?

Ans. It is not necessary that a person should be rated to the poor rate of any parish in the Union to enable him to vote and act as proxy for an owner of property.

30. VALIDITY OF VOTES.

28th April, 1843.

Clerk of Preston Union.—1. Would the circumstance of one or more of the initials on the voting paper being struck out with the pen, or erased with the knife, render the vote void as to the remaining initials? 2. Ought the vote to be rejected where the signature is not placed in its proper place—the name of the voter being written where the initials ought to be placed, and the initials placed opposite the names of the succeeding candidates? 3. Can the vote of a female be rejected on the ground that the handwriting is of a masculine character? 4. Where the initials had apparently been written at twice, with some little difference in the appearance of the ink, ought the vote to be rejected altogether, or retained, or only as to the initials first made? 5. Ought the vote to be rejected on the ground that the initials are in printed Roman capitals, instead of in written characters? 6. Where a married woman who has a settlement, and is separated and living apart from her husband, voted as a rate payer and owner in respect of property which she possessed, independent of her husband, ought the vote to be rejected? 7. Where the aggregate assessment amounted to 1,300*l.* a-year, are each of *three* partners entitled to three votes as occupiers, and to six as owners, they having separately claimed to vote as owners? 8. Has the Board of Guardians the power to call upon the clerk to amend the return of Guardians according to any recommendation of a Committee appointed to examine the voting papers and return?

Ans. 1. If the alteration is not certified by the voter, the clerk should obtain an explanation from him as to the fact of his alteration before he allows the vote. 2. Not being fully signed, the voting paper ought to be rejected. 3. Unless there is some other cause of doubt besides the general character of the writing, the paper cannot be rejected. 4. It is no objection that the initials were written at different times. The paper cannot be rejected, or any of the votes for the several candidates disallowed, on the ground stated. 5. The paper ought not to be rejected on the ground that the initials are in Roman capitals. 6. As regards the case of the married woman with a settlement and living apart from her husband, if she is directly rated in the rate-book, she can vote as *occupier*, but the Commissioners doubt her right to do so as *owner*. 7. The Commissioners believe that the three partners can only divide between them the three votes as occupiers, and six as owners; but all the facts of the particular rating should be before the Commissioners to give a satisfactory opinion. 8. A committee of Guardians, or the Board of Guardians, cannot direct the clerk to amend his return. The Commissioners would observe upon the necessity of using due caution in applying the foregoing answers to particular cases. Their application must depend upon the facts of any case being coincident with those upon which the answer is given. There is an obvious inconvenience in replying to hypothetical cases; and the Commissioners wish that in future, the particular facts of any case upon which their advice may be desired, should be furnished.

31. PRESENCE OF CANDIDATES DURING THE CASTING-UP OF VOTES.

25th March, 1843.

Clerk of Yarmouth Parish.—Are candidates for the office of Guardian entitled to be present at the examination and casting up of the votes?

Ans. The order of election does not confer upon any of the parties interested in the election of Guardians, either proposers or candidates, any right to be present at the examination and casting up of the votes. The Commissioners see no objection to the clerk, in his discretion, allowing the presence of any parties who may desire to witness the proceedings, provided they abstain from all interference in the conduct of the proceedings.

32. BANKRUPTCY DOES NOT DISQUALIFY A PERSON FROM ACTING AS GUARDIAN.

9th March, 1843.

Clerk of Hinckley Union.—Does bankruptcy disqualify a Guardian from acting? Is a person who is compounding with his creditors (but who is in other respects properly qualified) eligible as a candidate for the office of Guardian?

Ans. If the Guardian continue to be rated to the relief of the poor, in respect of hereditaments of the annual value fixed by the Commissioners as constituting a qualification for that office, the fact of such Guardian becoming a bankrupt, does not legally disqualify him from acting as Guardian. A person compounding with his creditors, is not, by such composition, legally ineligible as a candidate for the office of Guardian, assuming that he is rated in respect of hereditaments of the annual value conferring a qualification.

33. QUALIFICATION IN RESPECT OF PROPERTY IN DIFFERENT PARISHES IN THE UNION.

18*th March*, 1843.

Clerk of Honiton Union.—Is an owner of property, whose tenant is rated, and whose name appears merely as owner, eligible for the office of Guardian? Will the qualification of 25*l.* in different parishes of the Union, be sufficient to render a candidate eligible for the office of Guardian; or must he be rated in some one parish for the whole sum?

Ans. The owner, in the case described cannot be considered as rated to the poor-rate. The Commissioners are of opinion that if the aggregate rental of property for which a person may be assessed, in different parishes in the Union, is equal to the amount fixed by the order of the Commissioners, such person will be qualified. The words of the 38th section of the Poor Law Amendment Act are, "such qualification to consist in being rated to the poor-rate of some *parish* or *parishes* in such Union."

34. WHETHER ANNUAL VALUE OR ASSESSMENT SHOULD DETERMINE A GUARDIAN'S QUALIFICATION.

18*th March*, 1843.

Clerk of St. Asaph Union.—Are persons who occupy premises of the annual value of 25*l.*, though they are not assessed to that amount, eligible for the office of Guardian? and if so, how is the annual value to be ascertained, particularly in cases where parties occupy their own premises, or do not pay any rent?

Ans. The actual rental is the criterion by which to ascertain whether a person is qualified for the office of Guardian; not the net annual value of the premises. Where parties occupy their own premises, and pay no rent, the clerk, in forming his decision, should act upon the best evidence he can obtain as to the premises upon which the rate is imposed, being of the annual rental prescribed by the order of election. The poor-rate will be some guide, but the net annual value of the property for the purposes of the poor-rate, if correctly estimated, will rarely be identical with the rental, but will generally be below it, inasmuch as the occupier will rarely do the whole of the repairs, or pay the insurance, and will, therefore, pay the equivalent for these as rent.

35. DITTO.

4*th May*, 1843.

Richard Oxford, Esq., Stockport.—A Guardian has been elected for a parish in the Hayfield Union, whose property in the parish is assessed to the poor-rates at a lower sum than that specified in the Commissioners' election order: ought not the poor-rate assessment be the only guide for determining the qualification of a candidate for the office of Guardian?

Ans. The qualification for Guardian does not depend upon the amount of the assessment, but upon the actual rental of the property for which the individual is assessed. A person, therefore, may be qualified as Guardian by the order of the Commissioners as regards rental, who is rated to the poor-rate at an amount below that named in the order as a qualification. The rate-book is only *prima facie* evidence of the value of the property, and in doubtful cases, therefore, recourse must be had to other evidence to determine the question of legal qualification.

36. QUALIFICATION.—JOINT OCCUPIERS.

18*th March*, 1843.

Clerk of Ampthill Union.—Joseph March Morris has been nominated for the office of Guardian; but his name does not appear in the rate-book except in the firm of "Morris and Son." Does the word "Son" sufficiently identify the individual? And as there are two persons meant by "Morris and Son," should not half the rental amount to the sum of 25*l.* in order to entitle one of them to act as Guardian, which in this case it does not?

Ans. In the absence of anything showing the proportion borne by each, of the charge to the rate, it must be assumed, from the entry in the rate, that the father and son are equally interested. If so, the rental, when divided between them, ought to yield to each an amount equal to that fixed by the order as a qualification.

---

37. DITTO.—ASSISTANT OVERSEERS.

18th March, 1843.

Clerk of Warrington Union.—Are parties who at the time of the election, are Assistant-Overseers, but who will probably cease to hold that office, shortly after the 25th of March, disqualified from being elected Guardians; or, are they disqualified only from acting whilst they continue assistant-overseers?

Ans. The Commissioners think that if the persons alluded to cease to be assistant-overseers at the time when their office of Guardian commences, they are not disqualified for serving such office under sect. 14 of the 5 & 6 Vict. c. 57.

---

38. DITTO.—PARTNER OF AUDITOR.

24th March, 1843.

Norton I. Knatchbull, Esq., Provender.—Faversham Union.—Is the partner of a district auditor, who is a solicitor, legally qualified to act as Guardian?

Ans. The Commissioners are not aware of any disqualification attaching to the partner in such a case. The Commissioners think that he is not a person receiving any fixed salary or emolument from the poor-rates, within the meaning of the 14th section of 5 & 6 Vic., c. 57. The auditor is the only person entitled to the salary; the partner, not being an officer, has no claim on the Guardians. The Commissioners consider that no indirect participation by the partner, under any private arrangement, in the emolument received by the auditor, would affect his capability of serving as Guardian.

---

39. DITTO.—WAYWARDEN.—NON-PAYMENT OF CHURCH-RATES.

30th March, 1843.

6. *J. J. Cox, Esq., Honiton.*—1st. Four persons have been nominated as Guardians for the parish of Honiton, one of whom is the waywarden of the parish. Is he not disqualified from holding the office of Guardian? And, if so, are not the remaining three (being the number the parish is entitled to return) duly elected? 2ndly. A church-rate was made on the 23d of June, 1842, but the several amounts due upon the rate were not delivered to the ratepayers until the 20th instant. Will non-payment of the rate disqualify persons from voting at the election of Guardians?

Ans. 1st. A person filling the office of waywarden is not thereby disqualified from serving the office of Guardian. 2ndly. The Commissioners consider that non-payment of the church-rate, made as described in Mr. Cox's letter, would disqualify the parties omitting to pay it, for voting as rate-payers.

---

40. DITTO.—A PERSON WHO CANNOT READ OR WRITE.

25th March, 1843.

The Rev. John Lister, Stanley, Wakefield.—Is a person who is unable to read or write qualified to become a Guardian?

Ans. The law requires that a person should be rated to the poor rate at a certain annual rental (fixed by the order of the Commissioners) in order to be qualified to serve the office of Guardian: but it is not necessary that he should be able to read or write, or possess any particular mental acquirements; although, it must be admitted, that a person who can read and write, is so far a more suitable person for the office than one who cannot. The Commissioners have no power to impose any qualification upon a Guardian, except a qualification of rating.

---

41. DITTO.—SURETY FOR RELIEVING OFFICER.

31st March, 1843.

Clerk of Northallerton Union.—An objection has been taken to Mr. Naisby acting as Guardian, on the ground that he is surety for one of the relieving officers, which it is contended renders him ineligible.

Ans. The Commissioners do not think the objection valid in point of law. The Guardians being a corporation, there would be nothing to prevent their enforcing the bond against the sureties should it become necessary, notwithstanding that one of the sureties was a member of their own body.

---

42. GUARDIAN CEASING TO HOLD HIS QUALIFICATION.

6th April, 1843.

Rev. R. C. Taunton, Ashley. — Stockbridge Union.—If a Guardian, in the course of his year of office, should sell, or otherwise part with his estate in the Union on which his qualification is founded, does he thereby (*ipso facto*) cease to be a Guardian, so that his signature (in that character) would be of no effect?

Ans. If a person cease to retain the qualification which he had at the time of his election as a Guardian, *i. e.* if he cease to be rated to the poor-rate in some parish or parishes in the Union, in respect of hereditaments of the annual rental prescribed by the order of the Commissioners, as a qualification for a Guardian, he becomes thereby disqualified from acting as Guardian, though the period for which he otherwise might have continued to act is not expired.

43. ELECTION RETURN.

25th March, 1843.

Clerk of Wakefield Union.—Two persons have been nominated as Guardians for the township of Flockton, both of whom have sent in written refusals to serve. In consequence of this, Mr. William Woffenden, the Guardian for the current year, has sent in a written claim to act as Guardian for the township for the ensuing year. Should the return for Flockton be "no election," or should Mr. Woffenden's name be inserted in the list?

Ans. The Guardian for the present year of the township of Flockton, who may continue to act for the ensuing year, under sec. 10 of 5 & 6 Vic., c. 57, cannot be included in the return of Guardians elected for the ensuing year. The Commissioners think the names of the persons nominated, who have refused to serve, should be entered in the return, and the reason assigned why no election has taken place.

44. DITTO.

1st April, 1843.

Clerk of Frome Union.—Are the names of the Guardians who may continue to serve for the ensuing year, under sec. 10 of 5 & 6 Vic., c. 57, to be inserted in the return form I, of the Election Order? Should the names of *all* the persons nominated, whether qualified or not, or who have given notice of their unwillingness to serve, be inserted in the return?

Ans. The names of those Guardians who may continue to serve for the ensuing year, under sec. 10 of 5 & 6 Vic., c. 57, need not appear in the return form I, required by Art. 26 of the Commissioners' Order; neither should the names of persons proposed, but not duly qualified, be inserted therein. The Commissioners see no objections to the names of persons duly proposed, and declining to serve, being inserted in the return.

45. ELECTION EXPENSES.

18th March, 1843.

Clerk of St. German's Union.—The Guardians entertain an opinion that the Commissioners' General Order of the 21st April, 1842, relating to the duties of officers, repealed their order dated the 20th January, 1841, respecting the payment of election expenses; and that Art. 10 of the former order deprives the Clerk of the right to remuneration, to which he was entitled under the latter, for conducting the election of Guardians.

Ans. The provisions of the Commissioners' General Order of the 21st of April, 1842, do not in any way affect the claim which the Clerk to the Guardians has, under the previous order issued by them as to the election expenses, to remuneration for his services in conducting the election of Guardians. The General Order of the Commissioners, Art. 10, only directs that it shall be part of the clerk's duty when required by the regulations of the Commissioners, to conduct the election of Guardians according to the regulations which may be in force at the time; and he will continue to be entitled, for performing those services, to the remuneration assigned to him by the Election Expenses Order.

46. DITTO.

6th April, 1843.

Clerk of Hastings Union.—Is the Clerk, as returning officer in the election of Guardians, entitled to a fee, under Art. 3 of the Commissioners' Order of the 5th February, 1841, there having been no contest, for the present year, in any parish of the Union?

Ans. The clerk will be entitled to remuneration, under the article of the Order cited in his letter, though no contest in the election of Guardians may have taken place. The Guardians, in fixing the amount of remuneration, will, of course, do so with regard to the actual amount of trouble incurred.

47. GUARDIANS DECLINING TO ACT.

30th March, 1843.

Clerk of West Derby Union.—One of the Guardians has given notice that he will not act. Should notices be transmitted to him, whenever notices are sent to the other Guardians?

Ans. It will not be necessary to send any notice to the Guardian who refuses to serve, on occasions when notices are sent to the Guardians generally.

48. DITTO.

6th April, 1843.

Clerk of Clifton Union.—Two persons were nominated as Guardians for the parish of St. James and St. Paul, on the 10th of March, which being the number the parish was entitled to return, the election, so far as regards that parish, was completed on that day. Can a refusal of one of these Guardians to serve, sent in on the 23rd of March, be received, so as to affect the election which took place on the 10th?

Ans. The election is not completed until the return is made; and a declaration of a refusal to serve, tendered before the making of the return, is in time under the 9th section of 5 & 6 Vic., c. 57.

49. DITTO.

15th April, 1843.

Clerk of Blean Union.—Mr. J. Wotton, who was returned on the 25th of March, as being duly elected a Guardian for the parish of Swalecliffe, sent in a written refusal to act on the 29th March. Can he decline to act, not having sent in such refusal till after the day of the election?

Ans. It was competent to Mr. Wotton to refuse to act as Guardian for the parish of Swalecliffe, notwithstanding the clerk had returned him as duly elected. But the candidate who had the smallest number of votes, is not now entitled to be returned.

50. GUARDIAN ELECTED FOR THE PREVIOUS YEAR CANNOT ACT FOR THE SUCCEEDING YEAR, WHERE NO GUARDIAN IS ELECTED FOR SUCH YEAR.

1st April, 1843.

Clerk of Hereford Union.—By the 10th section of 5 & 6 Vic., c. 57, it is enacted "that in every case in which no person shall be *elected* for the office of Guardian in any parish at any annual election, the persons *elected* for the previous year may continue to act as Guardians until the next annual election." 1st. Does the word "elected," in the above clause, apply only to cases where there has been a contest, or a nomination sent in without a contest; or is a Guardian who continues in office for the present year, no one having been proposed in opposition to him, to be considered as "elected," so as to continue in office for two years from the 25th of March instant, provided no fresh election should take place on the 25th of March, 1844? 2ndly. Where there are two or more Guardians for a parish, and the requisite number of persons are nominated to supply their places, but it is found that one of the candidates is disqualified, which of the old Guardians is to continue in office? 3rdly. The Board day fell on the 25th instant, upon which day the clerk issued the notices to the new Guardians intimating their election, and requiring their attendance at the first meeting of the new Board on the 1st of April—was this correct? 4thly. In issuing the list of Guardians appointed, would it not be advisable to have two columns—one for the names of the Guardians elected, and the other for the Guardians continuing in office?

Ans. 1st. The word *elected* in sec. 10 of 5 & 6 Vic, c. 57, applies as well to the case where the election has taken place upon the nomination, and where no voting papers have been issued, as where voting papers have been issued. 2ndly. It is only the person who has been "*elected*" for the previous year that under section 10 of 5 & 6 Vic., c. 57, can continue to act for the succeeding year, where no Guardian is elected for such year. In the case supposed, the Guardian who may continue to act for the year ending March, 1844, will not (in the event of no election taking place in March, 1844) be entitled to act for the succeeding year, *i. e.* the year ending March, 1845, as he would not be, in the terms of the section, "the person elected for the previous year," and that section only enables a Guardian to serve until "the next annual election," *i. e.* for one year beyond that for which he was originally appointed. 3rdly. The Commissioners think the Clerk did right in issuing the notices to the Guardians elected for the present year, to attend the meeting to be held on the 1st of April. 4thly. The names of those Guardians for the previous year, who may continue to serve for the present year, under section 10 of 5 & 6 Vic., c. 57, need not appear in the list of Guardians required to be made out by Art. 26 of the Order of Election.

---

51. JUSTICES WHO HAVE NOT QUALIFIED.—POWER TO ACT AS EX-OFFICIO GUARDIANS.

26*th April*, 1843.

Clerk of Maidstone Union.—Requesting the Commissioners to refer him to any recent Act of Parliament, or regulation of the Commissioners, relating to the eligibility of *ex-officio* Guardians who may not have qualified as magistrates; or who having qualified, have omitted to attend the Board for a given length of time.

Ans. Unless a Justice of the Peace resides in some parish in the Union, and *acts* for the county, &c., in which that parish lies, he is not qualified to act as an *ex officio* Guardian of the Union (s. 38 of Poor Law Amendment Act); and unless he has taken the necessary oaths, he is not qualified to act as a justice. There is no enactment whereby the omission of a justice of the peace to attend to the Board of Guardians for any particular period, is made to affect his right to attend and act as an *ex-officio* Guardian when he may see fit to do so.

---

52. POWER OF A GUARDIAN, WHO IS AN OVERSEER, TO ACT.—GUARDIANS WHO DECLINE TO VOTE, HOW TO BE CONSIDERED.

19*th April*, 1843.

Clerk of Witney Union.—1st. Can a Guardian, who has been appointed an overseer for his own or any other parish in the Union, sit and act as Guardian? 2ndly. Can a Guardian, who has been appointed an overseer subsequent to his election as Guardian, decline to act as overseer? 3rdly. Should Guardians, who decline to vote when an amendment has been put, be considered as voting for the original motion?

Ans. 1st. The appointment of a person as overseer, does not nullify the appointment of such person to the office of Guardian, unless he be appointed a *paid* overseer. (See section 14 of the Act 5 & 6 Vic, c. 57.) 2ndly. The Commissioners are not aware that the fact of a person being a Guardian has ever been recognized as a ground of exemption or disqualification from serving the office of overseer. 3rdly. Guardians present, and declining to vote, must be reckoned as voting with the majority. (See Oldham *v.* Wainwright, 2 Burr. 1017.) It seems, moreover, to have been even held, that if a majority dissent from an election, but vote for no one else, the election by the minority is good.

---

53. A GUARDIAN ELECTED FOR TWO TOWNSHIPS HAS ONLY ONE VOTE.

22*nd March*, 1843.

Mr. James Williams, Great Crosby.—Has a Guardian who has been elected for two townships a double, or only a single vote as a member of the Board of Guardians?

Ans. He has only a single vote.

III.—LUNATIC.—LIABILITY OF HUSBAND TO MAINTAIN HIS WIFE IN A LUNATIC ASYLUM.

9*th March*, 1843.

Clerk of Wells Union.—About seven years ago, the wife of a parishioner of the out-parish of St. Cuthbert, in Wells, being a lunatic, was sent to the Union Asylum, and her husband paid 2*s.* a week, for about four years, toward the expense of her maintenance, but he is now upwards of two years in arrear, and declines paying any more. He is an agricultural labourer, without any family, and has a small income from some cottages, which, with his wages, would enable him, without inconvenience, to contribute towards the expenses of his wife; but there seems to be a difficulty in compelling payment, the magistrates being of opinion that the case does not come under the Vagrant Act, and some doubt is entertained whether the case comes under 4 & 5 Wm. IV., c. 76, s. 56. Can the husband be compelled to contribute towards the support of his wife?

Ans. As regards the past relief, there is no power of compelling the husband to repay it. But future relief to the wife may be made a loan to the husband, and his wages attached under the 58th section of the Poor Law Amendment Act. The Commissioners think the case is one to which the 3rd section of the 5th Geo. IV., c. 83, applies; as the husband allows his wife to continue chargeable to the parish, he being able, wholly or in part, to maintain her.

IV.—POOR-RATES.—CAN PAYMENT BE ENFORCED WHEN MADE FOR AN ILLEGAL PURPOSE.

29th March, 1843.

Mr. R. Wane, Hill House, Faringdon.—About four years ago certain open and arable fields, authorized to be enclosed by the 6 & 7 Wm. IV., c. 115, were allotted amongst the several persons interested therein, and the parties immediately took possession of their allotments. Two of the parties afterwards, thinking themselves aggrieved, appealed to the quarter sessions, and the churchwardens and overseers in consequence declined to make any poor-rate, but borrowed the sums necessary for the maintenance of the poor. In November last they made and collected a rate of 4*s*. in the pound, and they have now made a rate of 6*s*. in the pound, to repay the money borrowed by them during the last four years. Can payment of the rate be enforced?

Ans. The Commissioners consider that if the rate be good upon the face of it, *i. e.*, if it purport to be made for the relief of the poor, and if it be duly allowed in manner prescribed by law, the parties assessed cannot legally refuse to pay it, on the ground of any apprehension which they may entertain that it will be applied to unlawful purposes; see R. *v.* The Mayor of Gloucester, 5 T. R. 346. If any portion of it should be so applied, the remedy of the rate-payers will consist in objecting to the allowance of the improper charge in the overseers' accounts. The Commissioners think that such an objection would probably be sustainable in this instance, inasmuch as overseers are not empowered to borrow money for the relief of the poor; see Tawney's case, Viner's Abr. tit. "Poor."

V.—PROPERTY TAX.

1. ASSESSMENT OF WORKHOUSES TO THE PROPERTY TAX.

24th June, 1843.

The Commissioners have addressed the following circular upon this subject to the clerks of Boards of Guardians:—

"*Poor Law Commission Office, 24th June*, 1843.

"SIR,—I am directed by the Poor Law Commissioners to transmit, for the information of the Board of Guardians, the following extract from a circular dated the 10th April last, and addressed by the secretary of the Commissioners of Stamps and Taxes to the surveyors under the Property and Income-Tax Act, in reference to the assessment of workhouses to that tax:—

"'I have to acquaint you that the Lords of the Treasury have lately had under consideration the assessment, which should be made to the property-tax upon buildings used for workhouses, and that they have directed that the tax shall not be charged upon the whole premises, but confined to such portions only as may be occupied by the officers of the establishment as a residence. I am therefore to desire, that if there is any case in your district in which the tax has been charged on the whole premises, you will take the necessary steps for having the assessment reduced according to the Treasury direction, and any duty which may have been paid beyond that amount repaid to the parties; and if the total income of the officers occupying apartments in such workhouses is under 150*l*. (including the value of such occupation), the assessment may be altogether discharged.'

"I am, &c.,

"EDWIN CHADWICK, *Secretary*.

"*To the Clerk of the Board of Guardians.*"

VI. RELIEF.—JUSTICES NOT EMPOWERED TO FIX AMOUNT OF RELIEF, UNDER 4 & 5 WM. IV. c. 76, s. 27.

20th April, 1843.

Clerk of Alcester Union.—Are justices empowered to direct the *amount* of relief to be given in those cases in which they are authorized, by the 27th section of the Poor Law Amendment Act, to make orders for out-relief?

Ans. The Commissioners are of opinion that the 27th section of 4 & 5 Wm. IV. c. 76, does not enable the justice to determine or fix the amount of relief, but merely to direct that a pauper whose age or condition is that which the section contemplates, shall be relieved out of the workhouse if the pauper so desire. The Commissioners think that the amount of relief is a matter to be judged of by the Guardians, and by them alone. It should be borne in mind, however, that any nominal sum, so small as virtually to afford no support (such for instance as 2*d*. a-week) would not be held to be "relief," but would amount to an evasion of the obligation.

VII.—VALUATION AND PLAN.—THE PAYMENT OF THE EXPENSE OF.

15*th March*, 1843.

Clerk of Newmarket Union.—A new plan and valuation of the parish of Wicken have been made under an order of the Commissioners, at an expense of 145*l.*, which the Guardians are now called upon to pay. An appeal is pending against the poor's rate of Wicken, and the appellants have intimated to the Guardians and overseers that they will not, unless compelled by law, pay any rate for raising the 145*l.* for the expenses of the valuation and plan. Under these circumstances it has been found impossible to borrow the 145*l.*, so as to make a charge on the rates. The Guardians propose, therefore, to raise the 145*l.* by a separate rate, and the overseers are willing to cooperate with them. 1. Can the Guardians issue an order of contribution upon the parish officers of Wicken, of sufficient amount to cover the 145*l.*, and so pay that sum to the parties who made the plan and valuation, debiting the parish of Wicken with the amount; the overseers, upon receiving such order, taking care to make a separate rate, and to levy 145*l.* and no more? 2. If this proposal is objectionable, who is to make the rate, the Guardians or the overseers? 3. Is the form of the rate to be as usual, for the relief of the poor, or for the specific purpose required? 4. If not made in the common form, by what remedy can it be enforced, as no magistrate would risk an action of trespass by issuing a distress warrant? 5. If the money could be borrowed, is it quite clear that the Guardians can enforce the payment of the sum charged on the rates, and how; and within how short a period of time may the loan be made repayable? 6. Would the overseers be justified in paying the Guardians 145*l.* out of any general rate made for the relief of the poor, upon receiving the Guardians' order to raise that sum by a rate?

Ans. There are such difficulties as to the making of a separate rate, that the Commissioners have in no case advised a resort to that course where the amount required could be borrowed, or where there was a probability that the payment out of the ordinary funds coming to the hands of the Guardians from the general poor's rate would not be objected to. The intimation of the appellants against the rate, that they will not pay any rate for raising the 145*l.* for the expenses of the valuation and plan, affords a reason for not resorting to a separate rate. But the intimation suggests no reason why the money required should not be borrowed, nor any reason for making a lender doubt his security. The difficulties as to the repayment of the loan, if the Guardians and overseers join in the security, are not increased by the threat: the persons objecting cannot appeal against a general rate, because it is known to be the intention to apply that rate, or part of it, to a lawful purpose; they cannot resist a distress against a poor's rate because of such an intention, nor can they appeal, or support an objection against the overseers or Guardians' accounts, in consequence of such a payment when it has been made. But there appears to be no desire to avoid the immediate payment, if it were practicable to make a separate rate: this being so, it would facilitate the borrowing of the money, and probably the treasurer would feel no difficulty in lending it, if the loan were made to be repaid within the current year, which would be quite consistent with the provisions of the Parochial Assessments Act, as to the repayment of money borrowed. If that course were taken, the Guardians would immediately be authorized to repay the amount from the monies of the parish, and no legal objection could be made by the present appellants.

VIII.—WORKHOUSE.—MASTER'S DUTY IN CASE OF THE DANGEROUS ILLNESS OF A PAUPER.

9*th June*, 1843.

Clerk of Aston Union—Communicates the following resolution passed by the Board of Guardians:—"Resolved, that in accordance with the advice of the Poor Law Commissioners, the master and matron be instructed in future to send a written communication to the medical officer, in any dangerous case requiring his immediate attendance; and that the master be furnished with a printed checkbook for that purpose."

Ans. The Commissioners approve of the resolution.

LONDON:
Printed by Order of the Poor Law Commissioners, by W. CLOWES and SONS, Stamford Street, and Published by CHARLES KNIGHT and Co., 22, Ludgate Street, Publishers to the Poor Law Commissioners.

AN

OFFICIAL CIRCULAR

OF PUBLIC DOCUMENTS AND INFORMATION:

DIRECTED BY THE POOR LAW COMMISSIONERS TO BE PRINTED, CHIEFLY FOR THE USE OF THE MEMBERS AND PERMANENT OFFICERS OF BOARDS OF GUARDIANS, UNDER THE POOR LAW AMENDMENT ACT.

No. 27. CIRCULAR ISSUED AUGUST 26, 1843.

Poor Law Commission Office,
Somerset House,
August 26, 1843.

THE Poor Law Commissioners, on a review of their Correspondence, directed that the following abstract thereof should be printed and circulated for the information of Guardians and Officers of the several Unions, viz.:—

Page

By order of the Board,
EDWIN CHADWICK, *Secretary*.

I.—ACCOUNTS.

1. EXPENSES OF COMMITMENT FOR OFFENCES IN WORKHOUSE, OF MIDWIVES EMPLOYED IN WORKHOUSE, AND OF FUNERALS OF PERSONS DYING IN WORKHOUSE,— HOW TO BE CHARGED.

10th March, 1843.

Clerk of Depwade Union.—Would it be legal to charge magistrates' clerks' fees, and such other expenses as may arise from the commitment of persons in the workhouse, for misbehaviour, running away with clothing, &c., under the 55 Geo. III., c. 137, ss. 2 and 5, the 51 Geo. III., c. 80, s. 4, and the recent Poor Law Amendment Act, to the several parishes to which the paupers respectively belong, instead of to the establishment? Also, would it be legal to charge the expenses of midwives employed to deliver paupers in the workhouse, as well as the funeral expenses of paupers dying within the workhouse, to the several parishes to which such paupers respectively belong?

Ans. The Commissioners think the costs incurred in the commitment of persons for misbehaviour in Union workhouses, or running away with clothing, under the statutes cited by the clerk, cannot lawfully be charged to the particular parish to which the pauper may belong, but should be defrayed out of the common fund of the Union; the proceeding in such case being taken, not for the protection of any particular parish, but in defence of the authority of the Guardians and the protection of the Union property, in which all the parishes in the Union are equally interested. As regards the expense of midwives employed to deliver persons in the workhouse, the Commissioners are of opinion that the cost would be properly placed to the account of the parish liable for the maintenance of the pauper. As regards the funeral expenses of persons dying in the workhouse, the Commissioners think they should be charged to the parish liable for the relief of such persons while living, and not to the common fund.

2. OVERSEERS' EXPENSES IN DEFENDING RATE APPEALED AGAINST MAY BE CHARGED IN THEIR ACCOUNTS.

6th April, 1843.

Mr. R. Flawn, Rounds Lodge, near Higham Ferrers; Thrapstone Union.—The overseers have incurred considerable expenses in defending a rate which they knew that five out of every six of the ratepayers were decidedly opposed to. Can the overseers charge these expenses in their accounts?

Ans. The overseers are bound to make a good rate, and, when the rate is good, to support it; and as the support of it is not a personal, but an official matter, they are entitled to pay the expense of defending it out of the poor rate. The Commissioners understand from Mr. Flawn's letter that the poor rate to which he refers was, upon appeal against it, established as a good rate; and the Commissioners accordingly consider that the reasonable expenses incurred in maintaining it may be allowed in the overseers' accounts.

II.—BASTARDS.

1. LIABILITY OF HUSBAND TO MAINTAIN HIS WIFE'S ILLEGITIMATE CHILDREN: CUSTODY OF ORDER IN BASTARDY.

30th March, 1843.

Mr. R. Weaver, Guardian, Great Boughton Union.—Two young women belonging to the Union, who have had bastard children, are now married; and, as he construes the 57th section of the Poor Law Amendment Act, the husbands are bound to maintain the children until they arrive at the age of 16; but the clerk to the Guardians has expressed a doubt as to the liability of the husbands. The relieving officer, at his request, applied to the clerk for an order which he has in his possession, made some time ago on the putative father of a bastard child, but the clerk has not given it to him, because the overseer will require it for the purpose of collecting the money payable under it.

Clerk of Great Boughton Union.—As to the first part of Mr. Weaver's letter:—On the 18th instant the case of a bastard, aged seven years, was entered in the relieving officer's book as in want of clothes. On the case being considered by the Guardians it was stated that the mother was married; and on his opinion being asked as to whether the child followed the new settlement gained by the mother on her marriage, he stated that he did not consider the law quite settled on the point, but that he was of opinion the husband of the mother was bound to maintain his wife's children, legitimate or illegitimate, if able to do so, until they arrived at the age of 16. As regards the order in bastardy, Mr. Weaver spoke to him on the subject on the 18th instant, and he told him he would look for it against the next Board day; and although Mr. Weaver attended on that day he did not allude to the subject. He has some difficulty in advising the Guardians as to Bastardy Orders; the money is made payable to the Guardians, and he does not know the proper mode either of demanding or enforcing payment of it. The Guardians allow 1*s*. a-week towards the bastard's maintenance when probably the magistrates have ordered 1*s*. 8*d*., the mother being most likely in service. The order in bastardy appears, from its form, to belong to the Guardians.

Ans. to the Clerk of Great Boughton Union.—With respect to the first point referred to under section 71 of the Poor Law Amendment Act, every bastard, born after the passing of that Act, is to "have and *follow*" its mother's settlement until it shall attain the age of 16 years, or gain a settlement in its own right. The Commissioners are advised that a settlement acquired by the marriage of the mother is no exception to this rule; but, equally with any other settlement, is communicated to her illegitimate child. Moreover, the Commissioners concur with the clerk in the opinion that, under section 57 of the Poor Law Amendment Act, the husband, in the case referred to, is bound to maintain the illegitimate child, if able to do so, until the child arrives at the age of 16 years, or until the mother dies. With regard to the order in bastardy to which Mr. Weaver alludes, the Commissioners think that, as it is made in favour of the Guardians, they are the parties in whose custody it ought properly to remain, and whose duty it is to see to its enforcement. At the same time, the Commissioners are not aware of any objection to the Guardians selecting, if they think fit to do so, the overseers of the parish as their agents, for the purpose of collecting the money due from the putative father. With respect to the clerk's remark, as to the difference often occurring between the amount of the relief given and of the money ordered to be paid in cases of bastardy by the reputed father, the Commissioners deem it right to add that, assuming the relief to be legally afforded according to statute, and under the Commissioners' regulations, the Guardians will be entitled to recover the actual amount of it, but no more, of course within the limits of the order.

[A reply of a similar purport was sent to Mr. Weaver.]

---

2. NEGLECT OF SINGLE WOMAN TO SUPPORT HER BASTARD CHILDREN.

7th March, 1843.

Clerk of Braintree Union.—Elizabeth Ann Dawson, of the parish of Rayne, and living with her parents, had a bastard child, which is now between two and three years of age. She left this child some time since with her parents, and went to reside with a widower of the name of Owers, also belonging to the parish of Rayne, but living out of the Braintree Union; and recently she has had another bastard child. The woman's parents finding themselves unable to support the first child any longer, applied to the parish for relief for it, and an order was given, and the child was admitted into the workhouse. The grandparents parted with the child reluctantly, and would have kept it if the Guardians would have allowed out-relief to the amount of about half what it would have cost in the house; but the Guardians did not consider they would be acting up to the spirit and intention of the Poor Law by granting out-relief. The parish officers of Rayne took the woman before the justices, who decided that one child was as much as she could maintain, and left the case exactly where they found it. The Guardians have uniformly acted upon the principle that relief to a bastard child is relief to the mother, and therefore all relief to that class has been in the workhouse, except in cases of illness, when they could not be removed, or where they were of temporary duration. The Guardians feel that they are not acting justly towards some others, who have two or more bastard children, if this woman is to have her child maintained at the expense of the parish; and they, therefore, request the Commissioners' advice as to how they should act.

Ans. The ability, wholly or in part, of the mother to maintain her illegitimate children, is of course a point upon which the justices who are applied to to punish the mother for her refusal or neglect to maintain, must be satisfied before they can convict under 5 Geo. IV., c. 83. As the grounds upon which the justices decided the case of Elizabeth Ann Dawson are stated by the clerk, the Commissioners do not concur in the views of the justices, or think the reason assigned valid. The Commissioners think the ability of the parent to maintain, wholly or in part, spoken of in section 3; and where that exists the consequent obligation to maintain is not divisible in the manner contended for, but has reference to the entire family. There cannot be any obligation to maintain *one* child in preference to *another*. The obligation is equal as to all; and the means or earnings of the mother applicable, as far as they will go, to the maintenance of all: because the means or earnings of the mother may be sufficient *adequately* to maintain one child *only*, it cannot be said that she is therefore released altogether from the obligation to maintain any other portion of her family in part, or is not liable to punishment if she deserts them or refuses to maintain. As regards the course pursued by the Guardians in relieving such cases, the Commissioners think the Guardians pursue an expedient course in confining the relief to workhouse relief. The Commissioners recommend the Guardians to adhere to this rule in future cases.

III.—BENEFIT SOCIETIES.—RELIEF TO MEMBERS OF.

3d *June*, 1843.

Clerk of Hardingstone Union:—Edward Underwood, belonging to Yardley, Hastings, in the Hardingstone Union, was, with his wife and five children, received into the Union workhouse in December last. Shortly after he entered the workhouse he applied to the Board of Guardians for 1*s*. 6*d*., and for leave to go home, stating that he belonged to a benefit society, and that unless he paid his subscription that day, he would lose his claim on the society in case of sickness. The Board gave him the money, and he went to Yardley and paid it, and then returned to the workhouse. A similar circumstance took place in the months of January, February, March, and April. In the month of May, the pauper was taken ill and placed in the workhouse hospital, where he now remains. During his sickness he has received from the club 8*s*. per week, amounting on the whole to 32*s*. The Board have called on him to pay over this sum in part repayment of the expenses of himself and family in the workhouse, which he has refused to do. Can the Board receive this money from the benefit society without its passing into the pauper's hands?

Ans. The relief afforded by the Guardians in this case to pay the pauper's subscription to a benefit society, was not justified by law, nor is it desirable that such institutions should be supported out of the poor-rates. The value of these institutions (which cannot be over-rated) consists in the character of independence and self-support which ought necessarily to belong to them. If the relief in the workhouse granted in this case was not given by way of loan, the Guardians cannot compel repayment from the man, nor can they receive the money from the society and apply it to the pauper's maintenance. Such a system of paying the subscription and receiving the allowances, would be in fact to make the Board of Guardians in its corporate capacity a member of the benefit society on behalf of a particular parish, and under the name of an individual pauper.

IV.—BURIAL OF PAUPERS.

1. LIABILITY TO BURY THE CHILD OF A PAUPER.

16*th March*, 1843.

Clerk of Catherington Union:—John Marchant was some years since removed under an order of justices from the parish of Stoughten, in the Billesdon Union, to the parish of Idsworth, in the Catherington Union, and has not since obtained a settlement elsewhere. The man having obtained employment in his parish and neighbourhood, was obliged (from a scarcity of houses,) to take a house within the parish from whence he was removed, where he is still living, and where he has been occasionally relieved, during sickness, by the Guardians of the Catherington Union. About a fortnight ago, one of the pauper's children was taken ill, and on application to the relieving officer of Stoughten, medical aid was granted, but before the medical officer arrived the child died. The pauper then applied to the relieving officer for a coffin, which was refused, on the ground, that as he had been legally removed to Idsworth, it was illegal to give him relief in this case, and that he had rendered himself liable to imprisonment for seeking relief in the parish from whence he had been removed. Could the parish of Stoughten legally refuse to bury the child upon the grounds stated?

Ans. Although there was no obligation upon the parish of Stoughten to bury the child of John Marchant, yet there was an obligation on that parish to relieve John Marchant, if (as there seems to be no doubt) he was destitute. The obligation lay upon the pauper to see to the interment of his child, and as his necessities were increased by that circumstance, the Commissioners consider the Board of Guardians of the Billesdon Union might have granted relief proportionate to the necessity so occasioned, under exception 3 to Article 1 of the General Prohibitory Order. The fact that the pauper had returned to Stoughten after having been removed by order of justices, did not release the parish of Stoughten from the obligation to relieve the pauper on his again becoming destitute, though the pauper might have subjected himself to be convicted, under the 9th Geo. IV., c. 83, for returning to the parish from which he had been removed. As regards the Catherington Union, the Guardians of that Union could not, under the Prohibitory Order, have given non-resident relief to an able-bodied man.

2.—FEES ON THE BURIAL OF OUT-PARISHIONERS DYING IN THE UNION WORKHOUSE.

27*th March*, 1843.

Rev. James Blatch, Basingstoke:—The Guardians of the Basingstoke Union have passed a resolution, that "In future no other than the usual fees, for recognised parishioners in the parish of Basing, buried there, be paid in respect of paupers dying in the workhouse, and interred in the churchyard of Basing parish, to whatever parish they may have been chargeable while in the house." Since the establishment of the workhouse in the parish of Basing up to the present time, the paupers dying there and settled in other parishes, have been considered out-parishioners, and their parishes have paid the fee for burial customary under the circumstances. He requests the Commissioners' interference in the matter, as affecting his interest, as well as that of every minister in whose parish a Union house may be situate.

Clerk of Basingstoke Union.—The Guardians consider that the extra payment is not founded in law, and it is their intention to resist it.

Ans. If a person die within the parish in which it is proposed to bury him, and his body is brought to the churchyard for interment, the clergyman is bound by law to bury him; and this obligation is in no way affected by the distinction to which Mr. Blatch adverts, with respect to the settlement of the deceased. Consequently, assuming that Mr. Blatch is entitled in law to any fee upon the burial of any person, the Commissioners do not perceive any authority to justify his demanding a higher fee on the funeral of paupers not settled in Basing than in respect of those belonging to the parish, in cases in which the pauper whose interment is required has died in that parish. The Commissioners, in fact, consider that as Mr. Blatch is equally bound to bury a settled and a nonsettled person, if such person die in his parish, and is brought to him for interment, he is not entitled to make any distinction as regards the rate of payment. If a nonsettled person who had died in another parish were brought to be interred in the churchyard of Basing, a different question would arise.

V.—CLERK.—VALIDITY OF CERTIFICATE SIGNED BY HIS SUBSTITUTE.

10*th March*, 1843.

Clerk of St. Thomas Union.—Is a certificate of chargeability, to which is affixed the signature of a person acting for the clerk during his unavoidable absence, a valid certificate?

Ans. The Commissioners think the certificate is properly countersigned, within the meaning of the 17th section of 5 and 6 Vic., c. 57. The Commissioners construe the words "or person acting as their clerk," as extending to any person who, on any occasion of the clerk's absence, may, by permission of the Guardians, attend at the Board, and perform temporarily the duties of clerk.

VI.—CONSTABLES.

1. THE CASE OF THE QUEEN AGAINST THE CHURCHWARDENS AND OVERSEERS OF CHELMSFORD.

(Circular.) *Poor Law Commission Office, Somerset House,*
28*th July*, 1843.

SIR,—I am directed by the Poor Law Commissioners to send to you, on the other side, a Report, with which they have been furnished, of the judgment delivered by the Court of Queen's Bench, on the 29th of June last, in the case of the Queen against the Churchwardens and Overseers of Chelmsford.

This decision appears to the Commissioners to establish, that expenses necessarily incurred by district constables appointed under the Acts of 2 and 3 Vict., c. 93, and 3 and 4 Vict., c. 98, in relieving a parish from the burthen of vagrants, are not extraordinary expenses to be paid by the district, but are common and ordinary disbursements, to be defrayed out of the Poor-rates of the parish, and within the meaning of 18th Geo. III., c. 19, sec. 4.

The Commissioners have deemed it right to call attention to this decision, because it seems to apply to expenses incurred by constables in proceedings before justices against men who have deserted or neglected to maintain their families, and because the Commissioners have on several occasions stated, under legal advice, that they did not consider that such expenses were legally chargeable on the Poor rates.

I am, Sir,
Your obedient servant,
GEORGE COODE, *Assistant Secretary.*

To ———,
Auditor.

"*Westminster Hall*, 28*th June*, 1843.

"In the Queen's Bench.

"The Queen *v.* the Churchwardens of Chelmsford.

"JUDGMENT.

"*Lord Denman.*—In the Queen *v.* the Churchwardens of Chelmsford, an appeal against the Order of two Justices under the 18th of George the Third, cap. 16, sect. 4, allowing one John May, the sum of six pounds nine shillings and fourpence, expended by him as constable in doing the business of the parish of Chelmsford, as he alleged. May was a superintendent constable under the statute of the 2nd and 3rd Victoria, cap. 93, and 3rd and 4th Victoria, cap. 98; the sums in question had been paid by him for the fees of the justices' clerk, in respect of proceedings against vagrants apprehended in the parish of Chelmsford. May was superintendent for a division comprehending several other parishes, as well as that of Chelmsford: the 8th section of the 2nd and 3rd of Victoria, in fact, puts the constable appointed under that Act in the same position as parish constables.

"It is stated in the case, the sums so expended had always been allowed to the parish constable, prior to the Act of the 2nd and 3rd Victoria, and we are of opinion that such statement is sufficient to show a general authority from the parish officer to the constable to make such necessary disbursements: but it is contended for the parish, that these payments came within the 18th section of the 2nd and 3rd Victoria, which provides for allowance to constables under that Act for extraordinary expenses in the execution of their duties beyond their fees and salaries, which allowances, by the 3rd Victoria, are to be paid by the division.

"We are of opinion the sums are not extraordinary expenses within that section, but are the common and ordinary disbursements necessary for the relieving of the parish from the burden of vagrants, whom the constables are bound by the several provisions of the Vagrant Act to apprehend themselves, or to receive and take charge of when apprehended by others—expenses, therefore, which the constable could not avoid. They are manifestly incurred on behalf, and for the benefit of the parish, and in doing the business of the parish—not of the divisions; and this is an attempt by the parish officers of Chelmsford, to shift from themselves, an expense which properly belongs to them, and not to the parish, in common with other parishes included in their division, who have nothing to do with it.

"The cases cited, the King *v.* Bird, 2 Barn. and Adol. The King *v.* Seville, 5 Barn. and Ald., are entirely distinguishable; they were cases of expenses incurred voluntarily, and not in doing the business of the parish, as these are. For these reasons, we are of opinion the order of Quarter Sessions should be affirmed."

---

2 FEES FOR SWEARING IN CONSTABLES, UNDER 5 & 6 VIC. c. 109.

14*th March*, 1843.

Auditor of Haverfordwest Union.—The clerk to the magistrates for the hundred of Rose has sent in a claim to the overseers of West Walton, of 2*l.* 17*s.* 10*d.*, for fees (approved by the Secretary of State) for swearing in constables appointed under 5 and 6 Vic., c. 109. Should the item be allowed in the overseer's accounts?

Ans. The statute of last session, 5 and 6 Vic., c. 109, which regulates the appointment of parish constables, provides that the justices of the county may (with the approval of the Secretary of State) settle a table of fees and allowances to the clerks to the justices for the performance of their duties under the Act. And such fees and allowances can then be paid out of the poor rates. If a table of fees has been so settled and approved for the county of Pembroke, and if such table provides for taking a fee for swearing in parish constables, the auditor would do right in allowing the fees demanded, if in accordance with the table, but not otherwise.

VII.—GUARDIANS.

1. SUFFICIENCY OF REFUSAL TO SERVE AS GUARDIAN.

27*th April*, 1843.

Clerk of Nottingham Union.—Mr. Reckless, one of the persons nominated as Guardians for the parish of St. Mary, Nottingham, for the present year, placed his initials, in the margin of the voting paper, against the names of the persons for whom he intended to vote, signed the paper, and then added at the foot, "I beg leave to say that I am not willing to serve.—Jonathan Reckless." The voting papers, including the one in question, were collected on the 23rd March; but the intimation of Mr. Reckless's unwillingness to serve, was not observed by him (the clerk) until the 25th, when he was examining and recording the votes. Mr. Reckless having a majority of votes, he disregarding the intimation, certified him to be duly elected Guardian. Requests the Commissioners' opinion as to the legality of the course he adopted.

The Rev. W. J. Butler, Chairman of the Nottingham Union.—On the same subject.

Ans. The question is whether this addition to the voting paper ought to have been regarded by the officer conducting the election, as a tender of the writer's refusal to serve the office of Guardian, within the meaning of section 9 of 5 and 6 Vic., c. 57. If it could, the fact of its not having attracted the notice of the clerk until the 25th, would not make any difference, as regards stopping the election, so far as Mr. Reckless was concerned.

The Commissioners are of opinion that the clerk pursued a proper course in refusing to regard it as a compliance with the statute. The tender of the refusal ought to have been made in such a clear and unambiguous manner as to have left no doubt in the mind of the officer conducting the election. The voting paper was obviously not the place for making the announcement, and it had nothing to do with the act of voting, and was in fact mere surplusage. Moreover, the memorandum in which the supposed refusal is conveyed, does not in words express that the writer refuses to serve the office of Guardian, it omits all mention of the office intended. The clerk was not bound to supply this omission by any conjecture of his own. But if it had been free from this ambiguity, and could otherwise be regarded as a refusal, it was not tendered to the clerk in the manner which could enable that officer to take official notice of it under the 9th section.

---

2. MAY BE APPOINTED TO MAKE A VALUATION.

11*th March*, 1843.

Clerk of Belper Union.—Can a Guardian be appointed to value the ratable property of a township within the Union of which he is a Guardian?

Ans. The Commissioners are of opinion that the compensation for the performance of the valuation is not such a fixed emolument from the poor rates of the township as renders any Guardian, from the time of accepting such contract to the payment for its completion, incapable of serving the office of Guardian.

VIII.—OVERSEER.

1. CANNOT BE EMPLOYED TO MAKE A SURVEY AND VALUATION OF HIS OWN TOWNSHIP.

6th March, 1843.

Clerk to Wortley Union.—Can a Guardian, who is also overseer of the township for which he is returned as Guardian, legally contract with the Guardians to make a new survey, map, and valuation of his own township?

Ans. The Commissioners think it will be decidedly illegal for a person to be appointed to value, for a pecuniary consideration, the township to which he is overseer. As overseer it is already his duty to estimate, to the best of his ability, without charge or compensation, the rateable value of all properties subject to the rate; this being necessary to the correct performance of the duty of making a fair and equal rate. It is only where the overseers are unable to do this that the Commissioners are, upon representation of the fact, empowered to order a new valuation to be made at the cost of the poor rates.

2. MAY BE PUNISHED FOR MISAPPROPRIATING A RATE NOT ALLOWED BY MAGISTRATES.

10th March, 1843.

Clerk of Louth Union.—Can an overseer who has collected a rate, which was not allowed and signed by magistrates, from several parishioners who were ignorant of that fact, and appropriated the money so collected to his own use, be proceeded against for embezzling parish money, under the provisions of the Poor Law Amendment Act?

Ans. The Commissioners consider the overseer would be punishable, under the circumstances stated in the clerk's letter, under the 97th section of the Poor Law Amendment Act, for misapplication of the monies belonging to the parish. It appears to the Commissioners that, whether the overseer was legally entitled to demand the money is not a point which affects his liability to account. Whether the money were received under a good or under a void rate, it was in either case raised for the purposes of the poor, and in virtue of the insolvent's official character as overseer. And being monies assessed for the relief of the poor, it is clear he was liable to account for the same under the 47th and 109th sections of the Poor Law Amendment Act. To embezzle or misapply that for which an overseer is bound both to apply lawfully and to render an account of, is the offence to which the 97th section of the Poor Law Amendment Act applies.

3. RECOVERY OF BALANCE DUE FROM PRECEDING OVERSEER.

28th March, 1843.

Mr. D. Mountague, Churchwarden, Leigh; Rochford Union.—What course should the present overseers adopt for the recovery of certain deficiencies in the accounts of their predecessors; the magistrates having declined to grant a summons, saying they had no jurisdiction, as the account had been signed by the auditor and themselves, and the application should have been made within fourteen days after the passing of the account?

Auditor of Rochford Union.—The overseers who took office in March last, debited themselves with a balance of 61*l.* 6*s.* 1½*d.*, but afterwards took credit for 5*l.* 13*s.* 1*d.*, their predecessors having paid over to them only 55*l.* 13*s.* 0½*d.*

Ans. The 50th Geo. III., c. 49, s. 1, contains the following provisions:—" In case such churchwardens and overseers, or any of them, shall refuse or neglect to pay to their successors, within fourteen days from the signing and attesting such account, any sum or sums of money, or arrearages, which on the examination and allowance of such account in manner aforesaid, shall appear or be found to be due and owing from such churchwardens or overseers, or any of them, or remaining in their hands, it shall and may be lawful for the subsequent churchwardens and overseers, by warrant from any two or more justices of the peace, to levy all such sum or sums of money by distress and sale of the offender's goods, rendering to the parties the overplus; and in default of such distress, it shall be lawful for any such two justices of the peace to commit the offender or offenders to the common gaol of the county, there to remain without bail or mainprize, until payment of such sum or sums of money or arrearages as aforesaid." It appears to the Commissioners that, under this provision, the present overseers, instead of being obliged to apply for a summons against the previous overseers within fourteen days from the time of passing the accounts, cannot, in fact, do so until the expiration of that period. The outgoing overseers are required "to pay to their successors within fourteen days" the balance found against them; and consequently, until the end of the fourteen days the offence of refusing or neglecting to pay is not complete; after that time, the succeeding overseers may apply to the justices for a warrant of distress; and, if they decline, they may be compelled by mandamus to grant it. The Commissioners are, therefore, of opinion that the parish officers of Leigh should again apply to the justices, to enforce the payment of that portion of the balance which still remains due from the overseers of that parish for last year; inasmuch as the present overseers are bound to account for the whole of the balance as found, both by the auditor and by the magistrates, against their predecessors.

IX.—PAUPERS.

1. Punishment of Disorderly Paupers by Magistrate on the Information of Workhouse Master, without the Authority of the Guardians.

30*th March*, 1843.

Vice-Chairman of the Woodbridge Union.—He is in the commission of the peace, and has been in the habit of committing disorderly inmates of the workhouse at once to the house of correction for twenty-one days, on the information of the master. The clerk to the magistrates is of opinion that paupers should not be committed, under such circumstances, without an order from the Board of Guardians, under the 17th section of 5 and 6 Vic., c. 57.

Ans. The Commissioners do not consider it legally necessary that the order of the Board of Guardians, in the mode prescribed by the 17th section of the Act, should be obtained before the justices can convict a pauper charged with misbehaviour in the workhouse, punishable under the statute. It appears to the Commissioners that the statute does not confine the application in such a case to the Guardians, or the person whom they may authorize; but that, being an offence, it is open to the master to prosecute, on his own responsibility. When the circumstances allow of the delay, the Commissioners think the master would exercise a sound discretion in taking the instructions of the Guardians.

2. Apprenticing Pauper Boys to the Sea Service.

7*th March*, 1843.

Mr. Etheredge, Chairman of the Board of Guardians of the Depwade Union.—There are in the workhouse about seventy boys, between the ages of seven and fifteen, besides many others, classed as able-bodied men, who have just attained the age of sixteen. Every endeavour has been made, both by the Board and by the Guardians of the several parishes to which the boys belong, to find situations or employment for them. Can the Commissioners point out any method by which some of these boys may be employed, either in Her Majesty's navy or in the general merchant service?

Ans. The Commissioners direct Mr. Etheredge's attention to the provisions of the Act 5 and 6 Will. IV., c. 19, which authorizes the binding out by indenture of boys who have attained the age of thirteen years as apprentices to the sea service, with the consent of such boys, but not otherwise. The statute confers this power on the overseers of the poor of any parish, or other persons having the authority of overseers of the poor, or in whom the duty of overseers or Guardians of the poor shall or may be vested. The Commissioners will be glad to be informed of the result of any endeavours to act upon this provision, assuming that the Guardians think it desirable to resort to it.

X.—POOR RATES.—A Discharge under the Insolvent Debtors' Act extends to a Claim for Poor-rates.

30*th March*, 1843.

Auditor of Preston Union.—Will a discharge under the Insolvent Debtors' Act operate against the recovery of the poor-rate from the discharged debtor?

Ans. There appears to the Commissioners to be nothing in the nature of a debt for poor-rate, or of a warrant of distress or commitment in execution of the debt, to take it out of the class of debts which may be entered in an insolvent's schedule, under the Insolvent Debtors' Act. A discharge obtained under that Act appears to the Commissioners to be applicable to such a debt.

XI.—RATING.

1. ALTERATION OF RATE — PROPERTY ASSESSED BELOW ITS VALUE.

17th March, 1843.

Mr. W. Walford, Overseer, Brackley.—A new brewery has been erected in the parish, and not knowing how to assess it (from being unacquainted with the value of buildings and machinery), he called a vestry, at which the premises were assessed at 15*l.* gross rental and 12*l.* rateable value. The rate-payers generally have expressed their dissatisfaction at the amount at which this property has been rated, the expense of erecting the premises having been above 1,500*l.* Would he be justified in altering the assessment on this property to 40*l.* gross rental, and 32*l.* rateable value?

Ans. The overseer will not be justified in altering the present rate: but if he is of opinion that the property referred to is rated below the net annual value, *i. e.*, the value to let from year to year, he will do right, in any future rate, in assessing the property at its true value.

2. RATEABILITY OF CURATE'S SALARY.

25th March, 1843.

Rev. J. Compton, Minesteed Rectory, Lyndhurst; *New Forest Union.*—Lyndhurst and Minesteed are distinct parishes, but they constitute one ecclesiastical benefice; and they must, therefore, be always under one rector. There must, however, always be a curate at Lyndhurst, licensed by the bishop. Is he liable to be assessed to the poor-rate on the salary he pays to such curate?

Ans. The Commissioners think the case of Rex *v.* Joddrell, 1 B. and Ad. 403, is decisive that the expense of providing for the duties of incumbency is, under no circumstances, an allowable deduction from the gross value of the rent-charge.

3. RATING OF TITHES.

15th March, 1843.

Rev. E. Pughe, Llanidloes.—1stly. Is the gross estimated rental of farms and tenements the sum at which they let from year to year, or that sum *plus the poor rates?* 2ndly. Is not the rent paid to a landlord from year to year (where tenants invariably pay the poor rates themselves) the *net annual value?* 3rdly. If the valuation of a parish be made proportionally, at the rate of 30*l.* per cent. lower than such net rental, are not tithes to be valued on a similar principle, and in the same proportion; and moreover subject to a further deduction on account of poor rates, &c., if valued only at 30*l.* per cent. lower than the gross settings? Our assessment is made on this principle, viz., farms at 30*l.* per cent. lower than the net yearly rent, with a deduction for repairs; tithes 30*l.* per cent. lower than the gross settings, without any further deduction whatever.

Ans. 1stly. The gross estimated rental is the reasonable rent which a tenant would pay, *plus the poor rates*, and plus any other taxes, repairs, or insurances which the occupier would pay or provide. 2ndly. The rent paid to a landlord, if a reasonable one, when the tenants pay the tenants' taxes, and do repairs, is the net annual value. 3rdly. The tithe owner is entitled to deduction from the gross annual value of his tithe or rent-charge, for the whole amount of his poor's rate, and other tenants' taxes in respect of his tithe and of his ecclesiastical dues, and of a lessee's compensation. But since the Parochial Assessment Act, it is not lawful to rate at less than the net annual value. Therefore the tithe-owner cannot, on the ground that others are underrated, claim to be underrated also. He can only lawfully claim that the others should be put to their full value. The Commissioners have no doubt that the rate Mr. Pughe describes is wholly unlawful, in as far as the farms are valued at less than their net annual value, and that the rate ought, on appeal, to be quashed, on the ground that it is universally made on a wrong rateable value. Still the objection is one which is the proper subject of appeal.

4. PROPERTY RATED HIGHER THAN THE RENT PAID BY THE OCCUPIER.

25*th April*, 1843.

Rev. W. J. Rees, Cascob Rectory, Presteigne.—When the proceedings for effecting the tithe commutation for the parish of Cascob were taking place, a new valuation of the rateable property in the parish was made. An occupier of a farm objects to pay the rate assessed on his farm, because it is rated higher than his rent. The estimated rental of his farm is 179*l.* 8*s.* 11*d.*, the rateable value 166*l.* 0*s.* 5*d.*, and the rent paid by the occupier 140*l.* Can the occupier object to the payment of the rate made according to the surveyor's report on the grounds stated? And is the rent which he pays the highest sum at which he should be rated?

Ans. Over assessment is not a valid objection to the payment of the rate, where the party aggrieved has failed to appeal. The question of fairness or unfairness in the rate is a matter for the determination of the justices on appeal. Whether the fact of a person being assessed at a sum beyond the rent is a good ground of appeal must depend upon circumstances, and particularly upon whether the rent paid by the tenant be or be not, under the circumstances, a fair and reasonable rent. Where the rent paid is a fair and reasonable rent, an assessment of the premises at or beyond that amount, could not, with reference to the provisions of the 6th and 7th Wm. IV., c. 96, be supported. Where the rent paid is clearly less than the fair value of the premises to let from year to year, an assessment of the property at a sum beyond the rent could be supported. In Rex *v.* Chaplin, 1 B. and Ad. 927, it was observed by Mr. Justice Patteson, "where the land is let the actual rent is the criterion, unless it can be clearly shown that that is too small."

XII.—REGISTRATION OF PARLIAMENTARY VOTERS.

11*th March*, 1843.

Mr. J. Procter, Overseer of Brompton-upon-Swale, Richmond Union, Yorkshire.—The township of Brompton-upon-Swale is one of the four townships of the parish of Easby, which parish is included in the borough of Richmond for the election of members to serve in parliament. Twenty-six persons are entitled to vote in respect of property occupied within that township; but of this number, two are also inhabitants of the township of Easby in the same borough, with a like qualification. Are the voters liable to the payment of one shilling annually so long as they remain upon the register? And if so, are the two voters, who have a double qualification, liable to the same payment, as the other voters in each of the townships?

Ans. The provision in question is expressed to be made for the purpose of defraying the expenses to be incurred by the parish officers of the city and borough, and by the overseers of the several parishes and townships in the city and borough. For this purpose the elector is declared to be liable to the "payment of one shilling annually," which sum is to be levied and collected, in addition, and as part of the money payable as poor-rate, and is to be applicable to the same purposes as the poor-rate; 2 Will. IV., c. 45, s. 56. When an elector has qualifications in two or more parishes in the same borough, the question is raised, whether he is to pay a shilling annually in each of such parishes or whether he is to pay amongst the two or more parishes only one shilling annually. The Commissioners are of opinion that he must pay the shilling annually in each of such parishes; first, because the trouble and expense incurred in respect of him, is equally incurred in each of the parishes, and cannot be divided between them, or escaped by any of them; and, secondly, if any one only of the parishes received the shilling, there is no authority to that one to pay a part to any other parish. If one should, though without authority, divide the shilling, they must all. And, moreover, if any one could be preferred, there is no means of determining which should have the preference in levying it.

XIII.—RELIEF.

1. OUT-RELIEF TO MOTHERS OF BASTARDS, AND RECOVERY OF ARREARS OF RELIEF FROM PUTATIVE FATHER.

13*th March*, 1843.

Clerk of Ware Union.—About two months since, an order of affiliation was obtained against a tradesman, in good circumstances, as the putative father of the illegitimate child of Elizabeth Edwards, then recently confined, and chargeable to the parish of Ware. The infant is now about six months old, and therefore cannot be removed from the mother. The Guardians have allowed the mother 1*s.* 6*d.* a-week out-relief, and it is understood that she is able to earn a trifle in addition, so as to prevent her being chargeable to the parish on her own account. The Guardians are informed that the putative father intends to resist payment of the arrears of allowance, due under the order of affiliation, and any future relief given; and the Guardians request the Commissioners to sanction and legalize the weekly allowance; and desire to know whether the arrears are recoverable from the putative father.

Ans. The Commissioners do not consider that any sufficient grounds are stated in the clerk's letter for a departure, in the case of Elizabeth Edwards, from the mode of relief applicable to able-bodied persons and their families, whose case does not fall within any of the exceptions to Art. 1 of the Prohibitory Order. The present case does not appear to come within any of those exceptions. The Commissioners do not regard the fact, that the reputed father would be bound, under the order, to repay the out-relief given to the child, (if given with the sanction of the Commissioners,) as a valid ground for giving relief in the manner proposed, when the case is one of a class which it is desirable, on every account, should be dealt with on general principles, rather than with a view to any immediate saving in the individual instance. Seeing no good reason for thus exempting this case from the operation of the general rule, the Commissioners must withhold their sanction to the relief of the child out of the workhouse. The question whether the arrears are or are not recoverable from the putative father, depends upon whether the relief which has already been given has been lawfully given. The Commissioners apprehend that it is only where a lawful charge has been occasioned to the parish that the putative father can be called upon to indemnify the parish. To create a lawful charge, the relief given must be lawful relief. Relief can only be lawful when in conformity with the orders of the Commissioners. In the case of able-bodied persons and their families, this relief must, under Art. 1 of the Prohibitory Order, be given in the workhouse. The Commissioners understand Elizabeth Edwards to be an able-bodied pauper. If so, the out-relief heretofore given, on account of her child, not being in conformity with Art. 1, would appear to have been unlawful; and, therefore, not recoverable from the putative father under the order.

2. RELIEF TO NON-RESIDENT PAUPERS.

21st July, 1843.

In regard to a difference of opinion which existed between two Boards of Guardians, as to the proper mode in which the amount of relief advanced to non-resident paupers should be remitted by one Union to another, the Commissioners wrote to their Assistant Commissioners, Mr. Weale and Mr. Clements, as follows :—

"The Commissioners consider that the Clerk of the Union has nothing whatever to do with the advancement or repayment of the relief given by a distant Union, to a pauper residing in the Union of which he is Clerk. In advancing relief to a pauper belonging to another Union, at the request of the Board of Guardians giving non-resident relief, the relieving officer of the Union in which the pauper resides, acts as agent for the Union to which the pauper belongs. The relieving officer, however, should in all cases receive the direction of his own Board to pay the relief for the other Union. The Commissioners are further of opinion that the relieving officer who actually pays the pauper should be reimbursed; and this, as a general rule, should be done by a post-office order, made payable to *him* or to *his* signature. At the same time the money-order may be sent to, and correspondence be carried on through, the clerk of the Union; but the money must be made payable to the relieving officer of the Union."

XIV.—REMOVAL AND RELIEF.

1. OUT-RELIEF TO AN ABLE-BODIED PAUPER NOT RESIDING IN THE PARISH WHERE HE IS SETTLED. REMOVAL OF A PAUPER IN THE UNION WORKHOUSE, NOT CHARGEABLE TO THE PARISH IN WHICH THE WORKHOUSE IS SITUATE.

5th May, 1843.

Clerk of Howden Union.—1. Can an able-bodied pauper be legally relieved out of the workhouse where the settlement of such pauper is not in the parish in which he is resident; and in case the Guardians give out-relief, would it constitute a lawful chargeability upon which such pauper could be removed to his place of settlement? 2. Can a pauper in the Union workhouse, chargeable to a parish in which the workhouse is not situate, be removed to his place of settlement, by an order obtained by the overseers of the parish to which she is chargeable?

Ans. 1. The Commissioners consider that the General Order prohibitory of out-relief, applies equally, without regard to settlement, to all able-bodied persons requiring relief from any parish within the Union; and that, therefore, relief to any able-bodied person in the Union, not residing in the parish of his settlement, and not coming within any of the exceptions to the order, would be unlawful if given to him out of the workhouse. 2. The 1st section of 35 Geo. III., c. 101, prevents the removal of any poor person from the place where he is inhabiting to the parish of his settlement, unless such person shall have become actually chargeable to such place. Even without the provision made by Sect. 79, of the Poor Law Amendment Act, as to removal from a "workhouse," the Commissioners would have been disposed to think that a workhouse erected for the common use of a Union must be considered as a part of the parishes to which it so belongs; and for the purposes of relief and maintenance, as locally situate in each of such parishes, according to the view expressed by Lord Mansfield, in R. *v.* St. Peter and St. Paul, Cald. 213, 2 Bott. 691. But the 79th section of the Poor Law Amendment Act, contemplates a removal from any "workhouse," as well as from any "parish." Unless intended to meet the case of paupers maintained in a workhouse, the use of which might be common to all the parishes in a Union, it is not easy to say for what reason the word "workhouse" was used in addition to the word "parish." As regards the parish in which the workhouse might be situate, the addition was not necessary, as the removal from the workhouse would be a removal from the parish. The Commissioners think that the reasonable construction is, that it was intended to meet the case of a pauper relieved in the workhouse, but chargeable to a parish other than that in which the workhouse stands; so as to avoid the difficulty which might otherwise have been raised, as to the paupers not inhabiting in the parish chargeable with his relief, within the meaning of 35 Geo. III., c. 101.

---

2. RECOVERY OF COST OF RELIEF PENDING AN ORDER OF REMOVAL.

3rd June, 1843.

Clerk of Cockermouth Union.—At the last Michaelmas Sessions for Cumberland an appeal against an order of removal of Joseph Bell and wife and six children from the parish of Greysouthen to the parish of Eaglesfield, both in the Cockermouth Union, was tried; when the order was quashed on a technical ground, subject to a case. The overseers of Greysouthen have not, however, availed themselves of a case; and the overseers of Eaglesfield have applied to them for payment of the amount expended by the former in relief to the paupers from the date of the order of removal to the determination of the appeal; but the overseers of Greysouthen have refused to pay them the amount. The opinion of the Commissioners is requested as to the best mode of proceeding to obtain payment of the same. It is understood that the authorities of Greysouthen are apprehensive that the auditor would refuse to allow the sum, if paid, when passing their accounts.

Ans.—The costs of relief and maintenance pending an order of removal are recoverable under the 84th section of the Poor Law Amendment Act independently of the 82nd; and it is not necessary in order to recover such costs, that the court trying an appeal should order them. The objection, therefore, of the parish of Greysouthen on this ground appears to the Commissioners to be of no weight. The pauper's "*settlement was in question at the time of granting the relief*," and by the parish of Greysouthen's neglect to avail itself of the opportunity of trying the question further by means of a special case, the decision of the sessions is final; in other words, the parish of Greysouthen is that to which the pauper is "finally adjudged to belong." Whether the final adjudication was on a technical point, or on one ever so material, the result appears to be the same. The parish of Greysouthen is therefore liable to repay the relief under the general words of the 84th section. It is not understood that Greysouthen makes any objection founded on the proviso in that section.

As regards Greysouthen, as the expense is lawfully charged against that parish, the auditor will, unless other facts not stated to the Commissioners, are made known to him, see it to be his duty to allow the amount in the overseers' accounts.

---

3. THE POWER OF REMOVAL CANNOT BE EXERCISED OVER A PERSON ACCIDENTALLY INJURED IN A PARISH OF WHICH HE IS NOT A RESIDENT.

11*th March*, 1843.

Clerk of Knighton Union.—James Roberts, belonging to Beguildy in the Knighton Union, was employed by a cattle dealer, who occasionally engaged him to assist in driving some sheep to Welshpool fair, where he was ridden against by a man on horseback, his ribs fractured, and he was otherwise seriously injured. Could the parish of Welshpool place the man under a suspended order of removal, and charge the expense to the parish of Beguildy; or was not the man, in consequence of the accident, a casual pauper upon the parish of Welshpool, and as such were not the whole of the expenses of his relief chargeable to that parish?

Ans. The Commissioners do not think that the facts mentioned afford any evidence that the pauper went into the parish of Welshpool to inhabit, within the meaning of the statute 13 and 14 of Car. II., c. 12. The power of removal can only be exercised over those who come to inhabit, and does not extend to persons who meet with accidents in a place in which they may happen to be, not having gone there to reside (See Rex *v.* Woolpit, 4 A. and E., 205; Rex *v.* Oldland, 4 A. and E., 929). The pauper does not appear to have gone to Welshpool with that intention, but only in pursuit of his business, *i. e.*, with a view of attending the fair, and of leaving it when the cattle which he was employed to drive there had been disposed of. The Commissioners are of opinion that the parish of Welshpool was under the circumstances liable to relieve the pauper as casual poor.

---

4. THE COSTS OF SUBMITTING A CASE, RELATIVE TO A REMOVAL, TO THE COURT OF QUEEN'S BENCH CANNOT BE PAID FROM THE COMMON FUND OF THE UNION.

10*th March*, 1843.

Clerk of Garstang Union.—An appeal was made to the Quarter Sessions, held at Preston on the 4th of January last, against an order for the removal of a pauper and her child from the township of Preston to the township of Inskip-with-Sowerby, in the Garstang Union. The order was quashed, subject nevertheless to the opinion of the Court of Queen's Bench. The Guardians have decided upon submitting a case for the opinion of the Court, and have resolved that the expense of obtaining such opinion (which will be about 11*l.* or 12*l.*) shall be defrayed from the common fund of the Union; and they request the Commissioners' sanction thereto.

Ans. The Commissioners consider the law does not enable the Guardians to give any directions respecting the trial of questions arising upon cases of settlement; and that it would be illegal to charge any portion of the costs which may be incurred in taking the opinion of the Court of Queen's Bench upon the case granted by the sessions, out of the establishment, or common fund of the Union.

---

5. SUFFICIENCY OF MEDICAL RELIEF TO AUTHORIZE ORDER OF REMOVAL.

30*th March*, 1843.

Clerk of Halstead Union.—Is medical relief alone such a chargeability as to authorize justices granting an order of removal?

Ans. The Commissioners consider that medical relief only, afforded to an applicant for such relief, and for that alone, is such a constructive chargeability as may authorize justices to grant orders of removal.

XV.—SETTLEMENT.

1. WHAT AMOUNTS TO AN ACKNOWLEDGMENT OF SETTLEMENT.

17*th June*, 1843.

Mr. W. Richards, Guardian of Gelligare, Merthyr Tydfil Union.—In November last, one William Williams was removed under an order of removal from the parish of Gelligare to the parish of Merthyr Tydfil. The parish of Gelligare, on the order being appealed against, gave notice of abandonment; and the order was quashed at the last Quarter Sessions. This parish subsequently offered to take back the pauper; but the Guardians of the parish of Merthyr Tydfil, who were a majority at the Board, ordered the relieving officer of Gelligare to relieve him, although he was residing in Merthyr Tydfil. This may hereafter be construed into an acknowledgment of a settlement. Was the proceeding legal?

Ans. The principle in all the cases relating to the acknowledgment of a settlement, by granting relief to a pauper while resident in another parish, is founded on the presumption that a parish would not relieve a pauper residing elsewhere unless it recognized the settlement of such pauper; because the parish in such case is under no obligation to relieve at all. And if the pauper were not settled, and not liable to be removed to it, could have no motive or justification for affording such relief.

But the grounds for this presumption do not apply where a pauper resident in one parish of a Union is relieved by the Board of Guardians at the expense of another parish in the same Union; for, in the first place, the Guardians are bound to relieve the pauper at the expense of some parish; which the overseers in the other case are not bound to do at all. In the next place, the Guardians do not exclusively represent the particular parish, as the overseers do, and may have as much motive to charge the one parish as the other. Therefore, their affording of relief at the expense of one parish is not so necessarily against the interest of the whole Board as to involve any such presumption as applies to overseers in the class of cases in question. The Commissioners, therefore, are of opinion, that there is no reason to apprehend that what the Guardians have done can be construed as an acknowledgment of settlement by the parish of Gelligare. But, nevertheless, the Commissioners are of opinion that the more strictly regular course would have been for the Guardians to have relieved the pauper at the expense of Merthyr Tydfil, where he was resident. After the order of removal was quashed, it would then be competent to the overseers of that parish to remove him by an order, not on the ground of settlement, but an order in execution of the decision of the Sessions (See the cases cited, 2 Nolan's Poor Laws, p. 246, n. 3), against which order no appeal would lie.

---

2. SETTLEMENT OF BASTARD CHILD WHOSE MOTHER IS DEAD.

2nd March, 1843.

Clerk of Durham Union.—By section 71 of 4 and 5 Will. IV., c. 76, a bastard is to have and follow the settlement of its mother until sixteen years of age. The mother of a bastard, born four years ago, has lately died, and the child has now become chargeable. Will it retain its mother's settlement till it is sixteen, or will it now be entitled to its birth settlement, which was not the mother's?

Ans. The Commissioners are of opinion that the child would probably retain the last parentage settlement which it received from its mother, and that it does not, upon the decease of the mother, revert to its birth settlement. The Commissioners think the word "have," in the 71st section of the Act, must be construed to mean, to "take," and that the limitation in the subsequent part of the clause (viz. "until") has reference to the word "follow," but will not deprive the pauper of a settlement already acquired.

XVI.—TREASURER. — CHARGE OF COMMISSION BY UNION TREASURER.

6th March, 1843.

Auditor of Stockport Union.—In auditing the accounts for the quarter ended Christmas, 1842, he finds that the treasurer has charged the sum of 105*l.* 13*s.* 3*d.* for "Commission;" which sum includes both interest and commission. He disallowed sums previously charged for interest and commission, from a conviction of their illegality, but the chairman of the Union states that the Assistant Commissioner for the district has told him that commission is a legitimate item, and as such can be charged by the treasurer. Should he allow this item?

Ans. With regard to so much of the item as relates to a charge for interest, the Commissioners think it is unlawful, for the reasons given in the correspondence contained in the enclosed number of the Official Circular (No. 22). The Commissioners are not certain that they correctly understand what is meant by the term "Commission," as used in the auditor's letter. Commission, used in its more strict sense, means compensation for the services of an agent, and is therefore a pro rata salary, when the agent is appointed an officer under the Poor Law Amendment Act. On the other hand, the word "Commission" is sometimes used to apply only to overdrawn accounts, so as to be a sort of composition for interest. To this extent it is certainly an illegal item in the accounts of the Guardians, upon the same grounds as those which render interest itself unlawful. On the first supposition, however, the charge may be lawful, if the Guardians made such an arrangement with the treasurer, with the view of compensation for services with the sanction of the Commissioners.

XVII.—WORKHOUSE.

1. Arrangement respecting the Workhouse Refuse.

9*th March*, 1843.

Clerk of West Bromwich Union.—Resolution of the Board of Guardians "that the refuse made at each workhouse be considered as the perquisite of the respective governors, by charging each governor at the rate of 6*d.* per week, to be carried to the credit of the establishment, and debit of each governor," submitted to the Commissioners for their sanction.

Ans. It appears to the Commissioners that there is a great objection to an arrangement of the nature of that proposed by the Guardians in their resolution, as it might naturally be supposed that it would create an interest in the master of the workhouse to waste the provisions of which he has the charge, and make more refuse than is necessary. On these grounds the Commissioners deem it their duty to withhold their sanction to the arrangement proposed in the resolution of the Guardians. The Commissioners prefer that the refuse should be sold by the master, and brought to account for the benefit of the establishment.

2 Punishment of Paupers in Workhouse.

15*th April*, 1843.

Clerk of Weardale Union.—Does the column "Date of punishment," in the pauper punishment book, refer to the punishments inflicted by the master as well as to that ordered by the Guardians? And should the initials of the clerk be affixed in both cases?

Ans. The column for the date of punishment in the punishment book refers to the punishment inflicted by the master of the workhouse as well as that ordered by the Guardians; and the initials of the clerk refer to the punishment ordered by the Guardians only.

3. Boys who Abscond with Workhouse Clothes: How to be dealt with.

19*th June*, 1843.

Clerk of Aylsham Union.—The Guardians have lately been much annoyed by boys absconding from the workhouse, and after a day or two returning again. In two or three instances they have been punished by the magistrates; but if the boys are very young,—not more than 13 or 14 years of age,—the justices express a reluctance to punish the offenders in the manner prescribed by law. The Guardians, therefore, request the Commissioners' advice in the matter.

Ans. The Commissioners think that in dealing with such cases the ages of the offenders should chiefly be taken into consideration. If the boys be under the age of 16, they can be punished by the Guardians at their discretion, regard being had to the Articles 44 to 49 of the workhouse rules. But if above the age of 16, there seems no alternative but to take youths absconding with the workhouse clothing before the magistrates, to be punished under the 2nd or 5th section of the Act 55 Geo. III., c. 137, as the case may be. As regards, however, offences of this nature, the Commissioners would remark generally, that it is found that a strict and efficient management of the school and the workhouse according to the regulations in force prevents, in a great degree, the occurrence of the annoyances of which the Guardians complain.

LONDON:

Printed by Order of the Poor Law Commissioners, by W. Clowes and Sons, Stamford Street, and Published by Charles Knight and Co., 22, Ludgate Street, Publishers to the Poor Law Commissioners.

AN

OFFICIAL CIRCULAR

OF PUBLIC DOCUMENTS AND INFORMATION:

DIRECTED BY THE POOR LAW COMMISSIONERS TO BE PRINTED, CHIEFLY FOR THE USE OF THE MEMBERS AND PERMANENT OFFICERS OF BOARDS OF GUARDIANS, UNDER THE POOR LAW AMENDMENT ACT.

No. 28. CIRCULAR ISSUED OCTOBER 7, 1843.

Poor Law Commission Office,
Somerset House,
October 7, 1843.

THE Poor Law Commissioners, on a review of their Correspondence, directed that the following abstract thereof should be printed and circulated for the information of Guardians and Officers of the several Unions, viz.:—

By order of the Board,
EDWIN CHADWICK, *Secretary.*

I. ACCOUNTS.

1. EXPENSE INCURRED BY CONSTABLES IN ATTENDING TO BE SWORN IN.

14*th July*, 1843.

Auditor of Malton Union.—Should he allow in the overseers' accounts, sums paid by them to constables, appointed under 5 and 6 Vic., c. 109, for attending before the magistrates to be sworn in?

Ans. If a parish constable incurs any necessary expenditure in attending before the justices to be sworn in, the Commissioners think that he may charge the same in his accounts, under 18 Geo. III., c. 19, s. 4. It must be borne in mind that this provision is limited to the repayment of actual expenses, and does not extend to the remuneration of the constable for services or loss of time.

---

2. POWER OF AUDITOR TO DISALLOW ITEMS IN A BILL WHICH HAS BEEN TAXED. CUSTODY OF RECEIPT AND PAYMENT BOOK.

27*th July*, 1843.

Auditor of West Ham Union.—1. After taxation by the clerk of the peace, of law charges in a bill for services by a party acting both as solicitor to the parish and as clerk to the select vestry, has the auditor any authority, or is he required, to take notice of the objections of ratepayers to such charges? 2. What is the proper course to be adopted for obtaining payment of such sums as may be disallowed by him in bills brought to account by the overseers? 3. In case of a disagreement between the select vestry and the parish officers, who is the proper person to have the custody of the receipt and payment book, directed to be kept by the Commissioners' general order for keeping the accounts of the Union? And if the party entitled be the overseer for the current year, has he a right to demand the custody of the book before his predecessor has passed his accounts?

Ans. 1. The taxation of the bill by the authorized officer, is only a settlement of the amount which an attorney may receive in case his client be liable; but it does not determine that a party is liable if there be any question on that point. The auditor, if he considers that on any occasion the employment of an attorney was proper, will be guided by the taxation; but he remains, notwithstanding the taxation, invested with the duty of judging whether any expense was necessarily or reasonably incurred; and he is bound to receive objections of ratepayers as to any item of such expense, consider of these objections, and decide on them. 2. The recovery would be the duty of the overseers and their successors, either in the manner indicated in the 47th section of the Poor Law Amendment Act, or any person might cause the money to be refunded by application to the Court of Chancery. See Attorney-General *v.* Compton, 1 Yo. and Coll. New Chancery Cases, 418. 3. The receipt and payment book is a book for the keeping of which the overseers are personally responsible, and is not, while open for the entry of current or further accounts, a book which the vestry have, under the 58th Geo. III., c. 69, s. 6, any power to take out of the overseers' hands, or to dispose of, by investing any other person with the custody of it. When closed, the vestry have a right to give directions for its custody under that Act. The overseers cannot enforce the delivery of the book in question by their predecessors, until ten days after the signing of the accounts of the latter, 17 Geo. II., c, 38, s. 2; 50 Geo. III., c. 49, s. 1.

II. BASTARDY.—COSTS TO BE ALLOWED ON AN APPLICATION IN.

21*st July*, 1843.

Clerk of Stow-upon-the-Wold Union.—A solicitor, who appeared for the alleged putative father in a case of bastardy, in which the application was dismissed, has applied to the magistrates, by whom the case was heard, for an order upon the Guardians for the costs incurred by his client. The magistrates acting for the Stow-upon-Wold division have suggested, that the Commissioners' opinion should be obtained as to the nature of the costs to be allowed.

Ans. The point turns upon the words contained in the 73rd section of 4 and 5 Wm. IV., c. 76, "if upon the hearing of such application the Court shall not think fit to make any order thereon, it shall order and direct that the *full costs and charges* incurred by the person so intended to be charged shall be paid by the overseers or Guardians," &c., it being argued, and the Commissioners think rightly, that by the 2 and 3 Vic., c. 85, the same power as to awarding costs is vested in the justices in

Petty or Special Sessions, as by the first cited Act was given to justices in Quarter Sessions. The Commissioners remark that the question raised, as it involves the exercise of a power by the justices, is in strictness one which the justices should determine on their own responsibility. As, however, the advice of the Commissioners is sought, they wish to state, for the information of the justices, that some time since the Commissioners had occasion to consult counsel upon the interpretation of the term "full costs and charges" used in the 73rd section of the Poor Law Amendment Act. The Commissioners were then advised that the words "full costs and charges" were not intended to sanction the allowance of any unreasonable charges, but that the party successfully resisting such an application, should be indemnified as to such costs and charges incurred by him, as a man of ordinary prudence would fairly and reasonably incur in his defence. The Commissioners are disposed to agree in this view of the meaning of the words. It would seem, therefore, that the legal or professional costs incurred by the putative father in resisting the application might be allowed. The Commissioners think the justices would probably deem it right to have the exact amount which they are to order to be paid settled by their officer; who, from his office as clerk, must be conversant with the proper amount of professional charges incurred in such cases.

III. BURIAL OF PAUPERS.

1. HOW TO CHARGE EXPENSES OF.

8th July, 1843.

Clerk of Wigton Union.—A lead-miner rented a dwelling-house in the parish of S—, and with his family resided and slept therein at nights. During the day-time he worked in a lead mine in the parish of C—. Whilst working in the lead-mine, about three weeks ago, part of the roof of the mine fell in and killed him; and his family being unable to defray the expenses of his funeral, the same have been paid by the relieving officer. Should such expenses be charged to the parish of S—, where the man resided, or to the parish of C—, where the accident happened?

Ans. Referred to the case of Reg. *v.* St. George, Hanover Square, 12 Ad. and Ellis, 773; and stated the expenses of the burial, which must be regarded as relief to the widow, upon whom the obligation to bury rested, should be charged to the parish in which the widow was resident at the time.

2. THE TERM "PARISHIONER," HOW TO BE UNDERSTOOD IN REFERENCE TO BURIAL.

12th July, 1843.

A Clergyman states that C——— T——— was delivered of an illegitimate child in the M——— workhouse where she remained for some months, her relief being charged to the parish of D———, which has never disputed her claim. She afterwards wandered about the country as a vagrant, during which time her child died. Eventually she returned to M———, resided in a lodging-house, and there died. The Guardians of the M——— Union directed her body to be buried in the churchyard of the parish of St. Mary, M———, of which he is the vicar, and the body was accordingly buried there. He states also that she was not a parishioner of M———, although that parish was made chargeable with her funeral expenses. That the customary fee for the burial of a pauper *parishioner* is 4*s.* 6*d.*, but for the funeral of any person *not being a parishioner* the charge is 11*s.* 6*d.*; which latter fee the Guardians refused to pay, but offered 4*s.* 6*d.* He adds that he used the term "parishioner" in the sense in which he finds it in the Ecclesiastical law—"If a vestry meeting is called, every *parishioner* should attend:" Clutton *v.* Cherry, 2 Phill. R., p. 380, quoted in Maddy's Digest, p. 160. "Every *parishioner* has a right to be buried in the churchyard of his parish:" Gilbert *v.* Buzzard and Boyer, 2 Phill. R., p. 352, quoted in Maddy's Digest, p. 160. In this sense he presumed that the term means a person having a settlement in the parish.

Ans. The Commissioners by no means admit that the word parishioner as used in the cases cited by the Clergyman must receive the construction contended for. On the contrary it seems to them that settlement is in no way intended. As regards the first of the decisions cited, it may be observed that the word "parishioners" could not be used in the sense of persons having a legal settlement in the parish, because, as the authorities show, before the passing of the 58 Geo. III, c. 69, any person who paid to the church-rates, or scot and lot, had at the common law a right to attend vestries. It is manifest that a person might pay church-rates, or scot and lot, without acquiring a settlement in the parish in the meaning of the statute of 13 and 14 Car. II. And since the passing of the 58 Geo. III., c. 69, any person is entitled to attend a vestry who is rated to the poor-rate and pays the poor-rate, but he may be both rated to and may pay the poor-rate without acquiring a settlement. With respect to the second of the cases cited, the Commissioners remark that the right of burial, being a common law right, was long antecedent to any law of settlement, which was not in existence until the 13 and 14 Car. II. When, therefore, it is said, as in the case last referred to, that a parishioner is to be buried in the churchyard of his parish, it is obvious that circumstances or considerations are involved wholly distinct from those on which a legal settlement, *i. e.*, a right to be permanently relieved at the charge of a parish, depends. In the case of the Attorney-General *v.* Parker, Ves. 577, Lord Hardwicke said " Parishioners is a very large word, takes in, not only inhabitants of the parish, but persons who are occupiers of lands, that pay the several rates and duties, though they are not resident, nor do contribute to the ornaments of the church." It would, therefore, seem that the word parishioner is one of varying import, and must be explained as circumstances will allow, and with reference to the subject matter. Though, therefore, for the reasons assigned, it appears very clearly to the Commissioners that the word parishioners in the instances given is used in a sense wholly irrespective of that settlement, the Commissioners cannot undertake to determine what particular meaning attaches to that word, or whether any or all of the persons spoken of by Lord Hardwicke in Attorney-General *v.* Parker, are to be understood as designated by or included in that word, when the question is as to the right of the incumbent to demand an extraordinary fee for the performance of the rite of burial. That meaning would in fact be one of the principal points to be determined in any suit for the recovery of those fees. In the mean time, under the 68th canon, the Commissioners apprehend that the obligation to bury the body of a person dying in the parish is sufficiently clear.

IV.—CLERK.

26*th July*, 1843.

Clerk of South Molton Union.—Can he charge a fee for furnishing parish officers with certificates of chargeability under 5 & 6 Vic. c. 57?

Ans. The Commissioners are of opinion that the issuing of the certificate under 5 & 6 Vic., c. 57, is business transacted on account of the Union, as it is the Guardians who are required to certify, and the making out such certificate, and counter-signing it, is a part of the clerk's ordinary duty, for the performance of which the salary is the consideration.

V.—GUARDIANS.—As to whether Guardians signing Cheques on the Treasurer are liable for the Amounts.

16*th September*, 1843.

Clerk of Dudley Union.—Inquires whether the amount of a cheque upon the treasurer of the Union, signed in the usual way by the Chairman, two of the Guardians, and the clerk, is recoverable from any one of those parties in case the cheque is dishonoured by the treasurer.

Ans. The Chairman and Guardians who sign the cheque, only do so officially; and do not pledge their own credit. The cheque is accepted as affecting the Guardians' funds: the claim of the holder still subsists against those funds; and if the draft is dishonoured, the Guardians remain still liable in the same way as before the draft was made.

Clerk of the same Union:—States that the above answer is not sufficiently satisfactory to induce the Chairman of the Board of Guardians to sign any more cheques upon the treasurer; and requests further information in regard to the liability of the Chairman, in case he is proceeded against upon cheques drawn on the treasurer, to pay the expenses of any such proceedings.

Ans. The orders upon the treasurer of the Union not being negotiable, and the parties who sign them acting only in their public capacity as representing the corporate body of the Guardians of the Union, to which corporation alone the credit has been given by the creditors of the Guardians, the Commissioners cannot see how any legal claim upon those orders can be raised by any person against the Guardians who sign them. But the Commissioners are desirous of stating, that if there are not funds in the hands of the treasurer belonging to the Union, and no such prospect of his being in funds as to warrant him in paying the orders when presented to him, the Guardians ought not to give the orders. It is incumbent upon them in such a state of things to enforce the immediate payment of contributions from the different parishes of the Union, until there are such funds in the treasurer's hands, as to enable the Guardians to meet the outstanding demands upon them. The Commissioners think, that probably the urgent pressure upon the Guardians, when communicated to the overseers, will produce such an attention to the calls of the Guardians as will restore their credit. But if this should not be the case, the Guardians will be bound to use such means as the law has entrusted to them for the purpose of obtaining the requisite funds, by proceeding against the officers who shall be in default.

VI.—JUSTICES.—JURISDICTION OF COUNTY JUSTICES OVER OFFENCES COMMITTED IN A UNION WORKHOUSE SITUATE WITHIN A BOROUGH.

31*st July*, 1843.

Clerk of Okehampton Union:—The Union workhouse is locally situated within the borough of Okehampton, which has a corporation, consisting of a mayor, justices, and burgesses. The mayor and justices possess, by charter, exclusive jurisdiction over all offences *committed within the borough*. If a pauper chargeable to the parish of Belstone, which is out of the borough, absconds from the workhouse, taking with him the workhouse clothes, can he be apprehended, in that parish, under a warrant granted by a *county* justice acting for the division within which that parish is situated, and be committed by him to bridewell (the borough prison) for such offence; or must such pauper, although out of the borough, be apprehended under a warrant from the mayor and justices, and be brought before them to be committed for the offence? Hitherto the county justices have acted in apprehending and committing paupers who have been guilty of such offences, although they have been apprehended in parishes *out* of the jurisdiction of the borough; the justices conceiving that they were warranted in so doing under the 4th section of the 50th Geo. III., c. 51 and 52, which, for all such offences, in their opinion, treats the workhouse as situated in the respective parishes of the Union, and thereby gives them, as county justices, jurisdiction over such offences.

Ans. The statute referred to by the clerk, and described as the 50th Geo. III.. c. 51 and 52, appears to be the 50th Geo. III., c. 50. The latter Statute, section 4, gives jurisdiction to the justices acting for the district in which "such parish" is situate. As there is no previous reference in the clause to any parish, the preceding section (the 3rd) must be looked to, in which the word parish is used as denoting the parish to which the workhouse belongs. The question substantially is, whether this has the effect in the case of a Union workhouse of giving jurisdiction, in regard to offences committed in such houses, to justices acting for districts in which the workhouse is not situated, but in which a parish forming part of the Union may be comprised. On one side, it may be said that the jurisdiction has relation to the parish having property in the workhouse, and therefore to all the several parishes having a joint property in a Union workhouse; this is supposed to be the ground for the conclusion which the justices of the county have come to on the subject. But, on the other hand, it is not to be supposed that a change of the principle of jurisdiction is to be effected by words which could not, at the time they were used, have the effect now proposed to be deduced from them. The word parish in the 3rd clause of the Act only denotes single parishes having separate workhouses. It has no reference to Union houses. In the 4th clause, therefore, the "said parish" would appear to have been used in no other sense than as denoting the parish which at the same time had property in the workhouse, and comprehended it within its limits. In such a sense, the word would not have the effect of disturbing the ordinary practice as to jurisdiction of justices. But to give jurisdiction to the justices of the county with reference to offences committed in the workhouse of the Okehampton Union, it is necessary to assign a more extensive sense to the word "parish" in the 4th and 3rd clauses than it could have had in the contemplation of the legislature at the time.

VII.—LUNATIC.—POSSESSED OF PROPERTY NOT AVAILABLE.

19*th July*, 1843.

Overseers of Littleham, Exmouth.—A man named Rowell having been reported by two medical men to be a "dangerous lunatic," and that he ought immediately to be confined in a lunatic asylum, his wife applied to them, as overseers, to place some one over her husband capable of controlling him. Rowell is possessed of two freehold cottages, producing about 10*l.* per annum, and also of 300*l.*, which is in a bank in Exeter. As parish officers, they considered it their duty to place some person, at the expense of the parish, to watch over Rowell until steps could be taken to place him in an asylum; but doubts have arisen as to whether the case comes within the provisions of the 38th or 44th of the 9th Geo. IV., c. 40. Can Rowell be considered a "*poor person chargeable*" to the parish in consequence of the necessity of the overseers employing a person to watch him at the expense of the parish, and there being no person authorized to receive any of his money whilst he is in this situation? Or, can he be considered as "*wandering about and at large*," and thus be brought under the power of confinement? Or, what other proceeding can the parish officers adopt to place him in confinement as a lunatic?

Ans. The Commissioners do not think that Rowell can, in his present circumstances be considered a poor person, so as to bring the case within the 38th section of 9 Geo. IV., c. 40. But it is possible that he, or his wife and children, may become poor or destitute in the event of his property not being available for his support, from the fact of no one being authorized to draw the money from the bank, or to receive the interest accruing thereon. If he thus become chargeable, by relief being afforded either to himself or his family, the 38th section would at once apply. With regard to the 44th section, it is for the justices to determine, on the facts of the case, whether it is or is not applicable.

VIII.—MEDICAL OFFICERS.—CIRCULAR RELATING TO QUALIFICATIONS OF.

"*Poor Law Commission Office,*
Somerset House,

"SIR, 31*st August*, 1843.

"In consequence of a communication made to them by Her Majesty's Principal Secretary of State for the Home Department, the Poor Law Commissioners have consulted the Attorney-general and another Counsel on the competency of medical practitioners possessing Scotch and Irish qualifications to act as officers in a Union or parish under the Poor Law Amendment Act.

"The effect of this opinion (a copy of which is annexed for your information) is as follows:—

"1. That persons having a surgical diploma or degree from a Royal College or University in Scotland or Ireland, are legally as competent to be medical officers under the Poor Law Amendment Act, as persons having the diploma of the Royal College of Surgeons in London.

"2. That persons having only Scotch and Irish medical qualifications are not, as such, competent to practise pharmacy in England and Wales.

"The Commissioners think that they are by this opinion justified in admitting persons having a surgical diploma or degree from a Royal College or University in Scotland or Ireland, to the same rights under the Poor Law Amendment Act, as members of the Royal College of Surgeons of London.

"The Commissioners will therefore be prepared to consent to such arrangements, and to make such modifications in their general order of the 12th March, 1842, as may be necessary to give effect to the above recited opinion of the Attorney-General.

"I am, Sir,
"Your very obedient Servant,
"E. CHADWICK, *Secretary.*

"*To the Clerk to the*
Guardians of the Union."

"*Question arising out of the Case submitted to Counsel.*

"Whether persons on whom medical degrees, diplomas, or licences, have been conferred by the universities or other medical authorities in Scotland and Ireland are competent to be appointed and to act as medical officers under the 4th and 5th Wm. IV., c. 76?

Opinion.

"We are of opinion that as far as the question of *surgery* is concerned, those persons who have a *surgical* diploma or degree from a Royal College or University in Scotland or Ireland are (in point of law) as competent to be appointed and to act as medical officers under the Statute referred to as the persons who have the diploma of the Royal College of Surgeons in London.

"With respect to *pharmacy*, the right to practise (in England and Wales) is confined to those who have the licence or certificate of the Apothecaries Company and other persons whose rights are saved by the Apothecaries Acts; and in our opinion persons having Scotch and Irish *medical* degrees are not among such last-named persons.

"FREDERICK POLLOCK.
SAMUEL MARTIN.

"*Temple,*
8th August, 1843."

IX.—MEDICAL ORDER.

1. CONSTRUCTION OF.

5th July, 1843.

Mr. Thomas Robinson, Medical Officer, Settle Union.—Is a fracture of the malleolus externus or the coronoid process of the malleolus externus a fracture of the leg? And will attendance in such a case entitle the medical officer to the fee provided in the General Medical Order?

Ans. The Commissioners are of opinion that the fracture of the malleolus externus must be considered as a simple fracture of the leg, and that the medical officer would be entitled to the fee of 3*l.* for his attendance in such a case.

2. REPAYMENT OF FEES UNDER ART. 10 FOR OPERATIONS ON NON-RESIDENT PAUPERS.

10th July, 1843.

Clerk of Mansfield Union.—Would the Guardians be justified in reimbursing, along with other relief afforded, in the case of a non-resident pauper belonging to this Union, whose settlement is acknowledged, the cost of any operation for which a fee is allowed by Art. 10 of the General Medical Order, to the Board of Guardians of the Union in which the pauper resides, and who have advanced the relief? And, on the other hand, could the Guardians of this Union recover such amount of extra remuneration from any other Union, under similar circumstances? Also, should the payments in such cases be made by cheque drawn by the Board of Guardians, and debited in the ledger to the parish on which the expense may fall; or, be paid by the relieving officer, and charged to the parish in his out-relief list.

Ans. As the remuneration for operations and services contemplated by Article 10 of the Order cited should be charged to the parish on account of which the pauper is relieved, the Commissioners see nothing to prevent the Guardians of the Mansfield Union reimbursing the Guardians of another Union the cost of any such operation, in addition to the cost of any other relief afforded by the latter to a pauper settled in the former. In like manner there would be nothing to prevent the Guardians of any other Union reimbursing the Guardians of the Mansfield Union the cost of any similar operation performed on a pauper residing in and relieved by the latter Union, but settled in such other Union. But the right to recover such cost must depend upon the nature of the authority to relieve, or the undertaking which may have been given in any particular case. If such authority were general, and not limited to any particular amount or description of relief, it would include all relief necessarily afforded to the pauper, medical or otherwise, and would, therefore, include the cost of any operation. On the other hand, an undertaking to repay a specific amount of weekly relief given to a pauper, and for a particular period, would not involve, as regards the Union giving the undertaking, the liability to repay the cost of any other relief given to the pauper, though unavoidably given, or for a more extended period. As regards the mode in which the cost of an operation, or of other service rendered under Article 10, should be charged, the Commissioners think it had better be paid directly by cheque delivered to the medical officer at the meeting of the Board.

X.—OVERSEERS.

1. CAN HAVE ONLY ONE RATE-BOOK.

27th July, 1843.

Overseers of High Offly, Newport Union; Salop.—The Assistant-Overseer for the parish having recently died, it was resolved at a vestry meeting that each of the overseers should have a rate-book, and collect the rate for his own part of the parish. This has been done, but on the books being taken before the auditor, he refused to pass them, unless the rate be made out in one book. Can the overseers have two rate-books as proposed?

Ans. There should be but one rate-book; *i. e.*, the book which is signed by the justices, and which contains the declaration of the overseers as to the truth of the particulars contained in the rate. But for the purpose of collection there is no objection to each of the overseers having a copy of the rate-book which is so signed by the justices. But although these copies may be used for the personal convenience of the Overseers, it is necessary, and the law requires, that the several columns of the rate-book (as to the sums collected, arrears, &c.) should be filled up by the overseers from time to time, and previously to each audit, so that it may distinctly appear in one book what is the collective liability of the overseers, in regard to rates assessed, received, and not received. The auditor is fully empowered to call for this book.

2. POWER OF OVERSEERS TO GIVE ORDERS FOR THE WORKHOUSE TO PARTIES WHO HAVE BEEN REFUSED ORDERS BY THE RELIEVING OFFICER.

14th July, 1843.

Clerk of Thirsk Union.—Have the Guardians the power to refuse admission into the workhouse to vagrants who have received tickets of admission from the overseers of a township, after having been refused tickets by the relieving officer, such vagrants being, in a large majority of cases, persons by no means in destitute circumstance, or standing in need of such relief?

Ans. The Commissioners consider that the authority, given by Article 1, of the Workhouse Rules, for the admission of paupers to the workhouse on a provisional order from an overseer, cannot be withdrawn by any direction or resolution of the Board of Guardians; even in those cases in which orders for admission have been previously applied for and refused by a relieving officer. The case of a pauper received in the house by a provisional order is, in accordance with Article 3, to be brought before the Guardians at their next meeting, and the Guardians will then decide on the propriety of the pauper's continuing in the workhouse, or otherwise, and make order accordingly. With reference to the statement that a large majority of the vagrants admitted to the house, under provisional orders from overseers, are by no means in need of such relief, the Commissioners would remark that overseers are only empowered to give relief under circumstances of "*sudden and urgent necessity.*" An order for the workhouse is undoubtedly "relief," and the overseers will, the Commissioners consider, be bound to use the same discretion in giving orders for the workhouse as they would be bound to exercise in giving relief, "in articles of absolute necessity," in cases of "sudden and urgent necessity," occurring out of the workhouse.

XI.—POOR-RATES.—EXPENSES OF DEFENDING, UPON APPEAL.

12th July, 1843.

Mr. Jas. Young, Sunderland.—He is professionally employed by the overseers of Bishops Wearmouth in certain appeals against the poor-rate under 6 and 7 Wm. IV. c. 96; and although it appears both proper and necessary that the overseers should call builders and engineers for the purpose of proving or maintaining the accuracy of several of the assessments appealed against, he does not feel himself at liberty to advise the overseers that they would be entitled to charge in their accounts the expenses of such builders and engineers. The Commissioners' opinion is, therefore, requested on that point.

Ans. The propriety of paying from the poor-rates the costs incurred by the overseers in defending a poor-rate upon appeal must, as it seems to the Commissioners, depend upon the circumstances of each individual case. Where the poor-rate is confirmed by the justices, the Commissioners consider that the reasonable costs incurred by the overseers, if not recoverable from the appellants, may be lawfully charged in the overseers' accounts. Where the poor-rate is amended or quashed, the Commissioners think that the power of charging the expenses upon the poor-rates will depend upon the question, whether the circumstances of the case were such as to raise a reasonable probability of a successful defence, and thus to justify the overseers in endeavouring to support the rate. In corroboration of the opinion above expressed, the Commissioners would refer Mr. Young to the decision of the Court of Queen's Bench in the case of R. *v.* Fouch (1 Gale and Dav. 585); which decision appears to involve the principle, that although the overseers may not be entitled in every case to litigate questions of rating at the expense of the parish, yet there may be cases in which they would be justified in doing so, and that the propriety of fixing the charge upon the poor-rates in any particular instance is a matter for the justices (and consequently the auditor) to decide at the audit of the overseer's accounts. The Commissioners would add, that if a builder or valuer were called on, in case of an appeal, to give evidence in support of the rate, it would not be a case within the 6 and 7 Wm. IV. c. 96, in which the authority or sanction of the Commissioners would be necessary, but the payment made to such builder or valuer as a witness would be a lawful charge upon the poor-rates, subject to the limitation expressed above, that the case was one in which the defence was properly undertaken.

XII.—RATING.

1. OF MARKETS, TURNPIKES, AND FARM HOUSES.

8th July, 1843.

Overseers of Yeovil.—1. Should a market be rated on the gross estimated rental of the tolls and buildings, or on the buildings only?

2. Should turnpikes be rated on the actual amounts they are severally let for, or on the turnpike-houses only? 3. Are farm-houses separately rateable?

Ans. 1. The Commissioners could not express an opinion as to the market referred to, without a fuller statement of the particulars of the case: for example, as to the occupation of the buildings, the receipt of the tolls, &c. The general rule as to rating tolls is this;—tolls are not rateable as tolls and by themselves, but where they give additional value to real property occupied within the parish, such property is liable to increased assessment accordingly. 2. The 51st section of 3 Geo. IV. c. 126, provides that neither the tolls taken on turnpike roads, nor the toll-houses "erected for the purpose of collecting the same," shall be rateable to the poor-rate. But if such toll-houses afford accommodation beyond what is necessary for the mere collection of the tolls, the occupiers would seem to be rateable in respect of such excess of accommodation. 3. It is usual to rate together whatever may be considered as one occupancy. Where the house and buildings on a farm are such only as are necessary for the beneficial occupation of the farm itself, for the residence of the farmer, the security of the crops, the protection of the cattle, and so forth, the assessment should be laid upon the land, according to its value at so much an acre, including the advantages of these various erections. But where the house affords an accommodation beyond what is necessary for the beneficial occupation of the land, as for example in the case of a mansion occupied with a farm, the excess of accommodation would be a fit subject of additional rating.

---

2. AS TO WHETHER OWNER OF RENT-CHARGE CAN CLAIM TO HAVE THE OCCUPIERS RATED.

11th July, 1843.

Mr. H. Symons, Guardian of Plympton St. Mary Union.—A valuer has been employed to prepare an assessment, in which the rent-charges, vicarial and rectorial, are charged to the respective owners in one sum each; to this an objection has been taken by the vicar, who claims under the Tithe Commutation Act, 6 and 7 Wm. IV. c. 71, and the Commutation Amendment Act, 1 Vic. c. 69, s. 8, to have the rates charged on the occupiers of the rent-charge; which, in this, as in many other cases of rating rent-charges, will be exceedingly troublesome to effect; inasmuch as there are many rent-charges as low as 1*s*., and no doubt many still less. Is the vicar's objection valid, and how can it be best provided against?

Ans. The 8th section of the 1st Vic. c. 69, enables the overseers, if they see fit, to rate the owner of the rent-charge directly. Previously to the passing of that Act, and under the 6th and 7th Wm. IV. c. 71, the rate to which the rent-charge was subject could only be assessed upon the occupier of the land. The overseers are not, therefore, bound to assent to the claim of the vicar to have the rates charged on the occupiers of the land. If, however, the overseers prefer the course of rating the vicar as the owner of the rent-charge directly, as being the more simple and convenient course, it will be seen, on referring to the 8th section of 1 Vic. c. 69, that, in default of payment of the rate by the owner of the rent-charge, the occupier of the whole or any part of the lands out of which the rent-charge issues, is liable to pay the whole rates assessed upon the entire rent-charge; subject, however, to certain conditions which the section specifies.

XIII.—RELATIVES.—ORDERS FOR THE SUPPORT OF.

12*th July*, 1843.

1. *Clerk of Newtown and Llanidloes Union.*—Two farm-bailiffs in the receipt of high wages were summoned before the magistrates, in order to compel them to aid in the support of their parents, who are paupers chargeable to parishes in the Union. One of the bailiffs employed an attorney, who contended that the magistrates had no power to attach the wages of a servant under the circumstances. Have the magistrates jurisdiction in the matter, and power to attach wages?

Ans. The Commissioners presume that the proceedings to compel the persons in the situations of bailiffs to support their parents were taken under the 43 Eliz. c. 2, s. 7, and 59 Geo. III. c. 12, s. 26. The Commissioners are of opinion, with regard to the recovery of sums due under orders of justices made under those statutes, that the proceeding by attachment of wages is not available.

Clerk of the same Union.—Can the bailiffs mentioned in his previous letter be proceeded against, under the 43 Eliz. c. 2, s. 7, and 59 Geo. III. c. 12, s. 26, by distress, and in default, by commitment, if it is apparent to the magistrates that the parties have the means wherewith to contribute towards the support of their aged parents?

Ans. With respect to orders made under 43 Eliz. c. 2, s. 7, and 59 Geo. III. c. 12, the remedy by distress and commitment is applicable to the recovery of monies due under such orders. By sec. 78 of 4 and 5 Wm. IV. c. 76 (Poor Law Amendment Act), sums assessed under the statute of Eliz., and subsequent Act, are made recoverable in the same manner as penalties and forfeitures under the Poor Law Amendment Act. By section 99 of the latter Act penalties and forfeitures are recoverable by distress and sale of the goods of the offender, or in default of sufficient distress, by commitment.

5*th September*, 1843.

2. *Clerk of Calne Union.*—1. Can a brother be compelled, under the 43 Eliz., c. 2, s. 7, to contribute towards the maintenance of a brother? 2. Can a daughter, after marriage, be compelled to maintain her father?

Ans. On the first point, the Commissioners desire to remark, that a brother is not among the relatives enumerated in the statute; which applies only to fathers, grandfathers, mothers, grandmothers, and children. Consequently, a brother is not liable under the statute for the maintenance of his brother. And, accordingly, this point was so decided in the case of R. *v.* Smith, (2 Car. and P. 449.) With respect to the second question, the Commissioners think that a woman whose husband is living is not compellable to maintain her father. Having no property of her own, she herself is clearly not a person "of sufficient ability," within the meaning of the statute. And it has been decided, in similar cases, that the husband is not liable, on the ground that the statute extends only to natural relations, and not to relations by marriage (See R. *v.* Munden, 1. Bott. 447; R. *v.* Munday, 1 Bott. 448.)

XIV.—RELIEVING OFFICER.—Whether he can be appointed Churchwarden.

10*th July*, 1843.

Rev. Henry Clarke, Jun., Guisborough.—He has appointed the relieving officer of the Guisborough Union to act as churchwarden; but has been informed that he cannot be compelled to serve. Is the relieving officer exempt from acting as churchwarden?

Ans. There is no exemption from, or disqualification for, the office of churchwarden in the holding of the appointment of relieving officer. Whether the doing of the duties of churchwarden would impede the performance of the duties of relieving officer, or be in any way incompatible with the latter, is another question, and one for the consideration of the Commissioners. If the holding of the two offices by the same person should produce these results, it would, of course, affect the retention by such person of the office of relieving officer.

XV.—RELIEF.

1. To a Discharged Prisoner.

17*th July*, 1843.

Clerk of Bedford Union.—Ann Butler was committed for seven days, as a vagrant to the house of correction, which is situate in the parish of St. Paul, Bedford, At the expiration of her term of imprisonment, it was ascertained that she was wholly unable to travel, and the governor of the prison requested the relieving officer for Bedford, to remove her from the house of correction, and provide for her as a casual pauper; to which the relieving officer objected, until he had received instructions from the Guardians. On the matter being brought before the Guardians, they resolved not to admit the liability of the parish of St. Paul to the relief applied for; and they request the Commissioners' opinion thereon.

Ans. It appears to the Commissioners that the relieving officer was under no legal obligation to remove Ann Butler from the House of Correction, and to provide for her; and therefore, that he properly objected to do so upon the application made by the governor. If upon Ann Butler being turned out of the house of correction, she was destitute in the parish of St. Paul, and made application to the relieving officer, no doubt the latter would have been bound to have given such relief as the case required, at the charge of St. Paul's parish. The case does not appear to have been one, in which the power given by 5th Geo. IV., c, 85, to justices of affording to discharged prisoners the means of returning to their place of settlement, could have been *properly* exercised.

2. To the Child of a Woman deserted by her Husband.

1*st July*, 1843.

Clerk of Bodmin Union.—A woman deserted by her husband, lives in service in Bodmin, and her child, aged two years, resides with his grandfather at Endellion, in the Union. The mother has applied for relief for this child. Would such relief be relief to the mother; or should it be charged in the child's name?

Ans. The Commissioners are of opinion that the relief to the child could not be charged in the books to the mother, because, her husband being alive, relief to the child is constructively relief to the father (sec. 56, Poor Law Amendment Act); and the relief to the child would bring with it the same legal consequences as though the relief were given directly to the father on his application. But the Commissioners are of opinion, as regards the mode of charging the relief in the Union books, that in the father's absence the relief might be charged in the child's name.

3. To an Illegitimate Child born since the transportation of the Mother's Husband.

13*th July*, 1843.

Clerk of Bingham Union.—A woman now residing in the workhouse, whose husband was transported for life in July, 1838, and who has two children, one legitimate, aged nine years, and the other illegitimate, aged three years, has applied to the Guardians for out-relief for the illegitimate child. Such relief has been refused for the present, some of the Guardians considering that she comes under the same class as widows having a bastard child born since the commencement of their widowhood. Can the Guardians give out-relief in this case?

Ans. The Commissioners in the first place, desire to point out that, if the woman's husband is still living (and there is nothing in the clerk's communications to lead to a contrary supposition), she is clearly not a widow; nor do the circumstances of her husband's transportation, and of the birth of her illegitimate child, bring her even constructively within the class of widows. Consequently, it is not as a widow having an illegitimate child that she is precluded (if precluded at all) from receiving out-door relief. But as she and her legitimate child are resident within the Union, while her husband is not so resident, her case comes within the 8th exception to Article I. of the Prohibitory General Order. Under that exception, the Guardians, in such a case, may either afford relief *in the workhouse* to the wife and child of the absent husband, or else afford relief *out of the workhouse* for the child alone, if it be within the age of nurture, and resident with its mother within the Union. But, in this instance, the legitimate child is not within the age of nurture; and, therefore, according to the letter of the rule, the Guardians can adopt only the former alternative, and if they relieve the wife and the legitimate child at all, must relieve them in the workhouse. As regards the illegitimate child, the case is different. This child is not itself within the provisions of Art. I. of the above-named order. Moreover, as its mother is neither unmarried nor a widow, she is not bound to maintain it under the 71st section of the Poor Law Amendment Act. Consequently, relief to the child would not be relief to the mother, and Art. I. of the Prohibitory Order would not affect such relief, although the mother be able-bodied. Under these circumstances the Guardians, if they think fit, may grant out-door relief for the illegitimate child, while resident within the Union. The practical result of the whole is that the case is a complicated one, but the Commissioners are quite willing to rely on the discretion of the Guardians in the matter, and will sanction any departure from the letter of the rule which may appear necessary in the case. Care should be taken, however, not apparently to give the woman any advantages on account of her own misconduct.

---

4. AN APPLICANT FOR RELIEF HAVING MONEY, HOW TO BE DEALT WITH.

11*th September*, 1843.

Clerk of the Windsor Union.—Inquires whether in the event of a person coming to the workhouse with an order from the relieving officer, or other competent authority, who, upon being searched is found to have money on him, the master would be justified in refusing to admit him; and also, whether such person, becoming chargeable, would not be punishable under 3 sec. 5 Geo. IV., c. 83?

Ans. If the money found upon the person admitted to the workhouse, under the circumstances supposed, were sufficient for his present maintenance, the master would be justified in refusing to keep such person in the house. The justification will depend upon the circumstances of each case; and the circumstances that would justify, would be such as to show that the person seeking relief was not destitute. If such an applicant, as is described, becomes chargeable, the Commissioners are of opinion that he would be punishable under the statute referred to, as a person being able, wholly or in part, to maintain himself, or herself, or his family by work, or *other means*, and wilfully refusing or neglecting to do so.

XVI.—REMOVAL.

1. POWER OF OVERSEERS TO SELECT THE JUSTICES TO WHOM TO APPLY FOR ORDERS OF REMOVAL.

27*th July*, 1843.

Overseers of Hyde, Stockport Union.—The Guardians of the Stockport Union meet at the town of Stockport, where there are also magisterial sessions held for the Stockport division. The town and township of Hyde are in the Stockport Union, but in a separate magisterial division, called the division of Hyde, and the magistrates hold a weekly session for that division in the town of Hyde. Hyde is six miles distant from Stockport, and there are many orders for the removal of paupers from that township. The Guardians of the Stockport Union have appointed a removal officer, who takes all the removal cases from Hyde before the magistrates of Stockport, instead of before the magistrates at Hyde; by this practice the rate-payers of Hyde are put to additional expense in conveying witnesses, &c., in these cases to Stockport. 1. Can the overseers require these orders to be made at the Hyde Bench? 2. Can the overseers legally refuse to sign notices of chargeability upon orders made at Stockport, and refuse to recognize such orders? 3. Would the removal officer, whose salary is paid by the whole Union, be bound to act on a notice that the overseers will prefer complaints only before the bench at Hyde and to give the same attention in getting up evidence for, and obtaining and carrying into effect, orders made at Hyde, as if the same were made at Stockport?

Ans. 1. The overseers are by law charged with the duty of obtaining orders of removal, and of seeing to their execution. In the exercise of this duty they appear to be unquestionably entitled to select the justices to which they will make application, supposing always that such justices have the necessary jurisdiction. 2. When, however, an order has been made for the removal of a pauper, that order generally is binding like any other order of justices on the overseers to whom it is directed. So far as the Commissioners are informed, the question whether such order would be void if granted without an actual complaint of the overseers, has never arisen for decision, such complaint being alleged in the order, but having in fact been made by some other officer. The Commissioners cannot undertake to express any confident opinion that such an order would be void. If not void, it is the duty, and for the interest of the overseers to comply with it, unless they see ground to apply to the justices to supersede it. 3. The removal officer, having no legal authority in the matter of removal, cannot act in that matter contrary to the directions of the overseers. But he may legally conform to their directions in any way not incompatible with the proper duties of his office as removal officer.

---

2. COST OF MAINTENANCE UNDER SUSPENDED ORDER OF REMOVAL.

13*th September*, 1843.

Clerk of Hay Union.—States that on the 2nd October, 1839, an order was made for the removal of a pauper and his wife and children from Lambeth, Surrey, to the parish of Clyro, in the Hay Union; and in consequence of the man's illness was, on the same day, suspended. The order was duly served on the 10th of the same month, and nothing whatever was heard of the order or the paupers until the 21st July, 1843, when the overseers of Clyro received a letter from the clerk to the Guardians of Lambeth, stating that the pauper was suffering from a spinal affection, and still unable to be removed; that the relief afforded amounted to 87*l.* 6*s.* 4*d.*, and requesting payment of the sum. It is considered unfair towards the present rate-payers of Clyro to call on them to pay this large amount.

Clerk of Lambeth Parish.—To whom the Commissioners referred the above communication states, that, from the date of the order until the pauper's admission into the Homœpathic Medical Institution, about six weeks previous, the pauper has been under the care of a medical officer of the parish except during short intervals, who has repeatedly expressed his opinion that it would endanger the life of the pauper to remove him to Clyro, a distance of 156 miles.

Ans. to the Clerk of Hay Union.—The Commissioners do not see that they have any power to interfere further in the matter; they can only direct the attention of the Guardians to what they conceive to be the effect of the 2nd sec. of the 35 Geo. III. c. 101., and must leave it to the Guardians themselves to decide on the course to be pursued.

The section referred to, enables the justices to order repayment of the charges incurred by the suspension of the order, in case "any removal shall take place, or in case of the death of such poor person before the execution of such order." But it does not provide for repayment in any other event than the removal or the death of the pauper. This was held to be its effect, in Reg. *v.* Chagford (4 B. and A 235). As in the present case, the pauper has not been removed, and is still living, the justices have no power to order repayment, and consequently the Guardians of Hay Union are under no obligation to comply with the demand in question. Whether they will do so, is a point which the Commissioners (as before remarked) must leave to themselves to determine.

XVII.—WORKHOUSE.

1. POWER OF GUARDIANS TO LIMIT THE HOURS FOR THE ADMISSION OF PAUPERS INTO THE WORKHOUSE.

20*th July*, 1843.

Clerk of Colchester Union.—Can the Guardians legally make and act upon the following resolution, namely:—"That the hours for the admission [into the workhouse] of paupers be as follow,—for wayfarers till 8 o'clock at night, and for paupers resident in the town till 7 o'clock at night; and if either class of paupers be admitted at later hours, such (admission) is only to be on their giving satisfactory reasons to the governor why they did not apply earlier?"

Ans. The workhouse rules (Art. 74) render it the duty of the master "to admit paupers into the workhouse in obedience to the orders specified in Art 1." Article 1 provides for the admission of paupers, either by an order of the Board of Guardians, by a provisional order from a relieving officer or an overseer, or by the master himself, without any order, if the case be sudden and urgent. The effect of the resolution proposed, would be to direct that, after a certain hour, the master should *not admit* a pauper or vagrant to the workhouse who might be the bearer of any such order. The workhouse rules do not contemplate the exclusion of any person who presents such an order for his admission, or who applies without one, under urgent circumstances; and it is for this reason the Commissioners think that it would not be competent for the guardians to give instructions of the nature of those indicated in the suggested resolution.

2. PROVISION ACCOUNT.

8*th July*, 1843.

Mr. Day, Assistant Commissioner.—Is there any general mode of charging the numbers of the inmates in a workhouse in the daily entries in the provision account, with reference to the entries in the admission and discharge book? Are both the paupers who are discharged, and the paupers who are admitted on the *same* day, to form part of the gross number of the paupers who are placed on the provision book? The way he has always

checked the account has been, to take the *difference* of the admissions and discharges each day, and add, or subtract, from the daily numbers in the provision check account accordingly. He is not sure that he is right, as it is evident that the correctness of his mode must depend upon the equality, both in number and *quality*, of the meals gained one way and lost the other.

Ans. The only remedy for the inconvenience alluded to by Mr. Day, that the Commissioners are aware of, is the making out the provision account according to the actual number of meals consumed: that is, according to the number of paupers actually present at each meal; and the Commissioners have considered this question with reference to the improvement of the form of accounts. In the mean time the shortest practical remedy is to reckon the dinner as the test, and charge all who are present at dinner for the whole day; and if greater accuracy is desirable, the master must make an entry at the foot of each day's admissions and discharges, specifying the numbers who received one or two meals only.

XVIII.—RETURNS RELATING TO THE ADMINISTRATION OF THE POOR LAW IN ENGLAND AND WALES, PRESENTED TO PARLIAMENT DURING THE SESSION OF 1843:—

A RETURN of the Number, Names, and Ages of all Persons committed to any Prison in England or Wales for any offence in a Union Workhouse established under the provisions of the Poor Law Amendment Act; stating the nature of the offence, the period of punishment, the name of the Union, and the number for each Union and for each year, from the 25th day of March, 1835, to the 25th day of March, 1842; with the population of each Union, according to the last Census.

Similar Return for Offences in Workhouses of Parishes and Unions governed by Guardians, Vestrymen, or Parish Officers, under Local Acts and 22 Geo. III., c. 83, known as Gilbert's Act, or not included in any Poor Law Union. (63.)—*Moved for, by Captain Pechell. Presented, 27th February.*

COPY OF THE DIET TABLE in use at the Belper

Union Workhouse, and at the Derby Union Workhouse, on the 31st day of January, 1843. (65.)—*Moved for, by Mr. Ferrand. Presented, 28th February.*

A RETURN of the Number of Persons who have been assisted to Emigrate by Funds derived from the Poor Rate. (90.)—*Moved for, by Mr. Wm. Smith O'Brien. Presented, 13th March.*

1. A COPY OF THE MINUTES and Proceedings, as well as the Resolutions adopted by the Board of the Halifax Union on the 1st day of March, so far as they relate to the administration of the new Poor Law within the said Union; likewise, Copy of any Resolution for the erection of a Mill within the Workhouse, on the day aforesaid, or any other day.

2. A Copy of the Report of Mr. Clements to the Poor Law Commissioners, upon inmates of the Skipton Workhouse sent to a Factory; dated 6th day of March, 1843. (143.)—*Moved for, by Mr. Ferrand. Presented, 24th March.*

A RETURN showing the Number of In-door and Out-door Paupers relieved in each Union in England and Wales during the quarter ended Lady-day, 1842; distinguishing the Adult able-bodied from all other classes, including Children. (144.)—*Moved for, by Mr. Wallace. Presented, 24th March.*

A RETURN of the Sum expended in every Poor Law Union in England and Wales, in each of the years ended Lady-day, 1841, and 1842; specifying the Sum expended in Salaries and Establishment Charges, the Sum expended in In-door Relief, the Sum expended in Out-door Relief, and the aggregate amount of the same; also, the Number of Persons who received In-door Relief, and the Number of Persons who received Out-door Relief in those years. (144.)—*Moved for, by Mr. William Williams. Presented, 27th March.*

A COPY OF INSTRUCTIONS of the Poor Law Commissioners to their Assistant Commissioners to inquire into the state of the Gilbert's Act Incorporations, dated the 23d day of December, 1842; and Reports of the Assistant-Commissioners made in pursuance of those Instructions. (172.)—*Moved for, by Mr. Colville. Presented 6th April.*

A RETURN of the name of each Union in England and Wales, formed in pursuance of the Poor Law Amendment Act, according to the Districts of the Assistant Commissioners; with the name of each Assistant-Commissioner; the Number of Parishes in each Union; the Area in Statute Acres (excepting the Welsh Unions); the Population of each Union; the Weekly average Number of Paupers relieved in the Workhouse during the year; the Number of Medical Officers employed in each Union; the aggregate amount of Money paid to them; the rate per head of Medical Expenses on the Population of each Union; and any augmentation of the Salaries of Medical Officers since the 25th day of March, 1842. (182.)—*Moved for, by Colonel Thomas Wood. Presented, 7th April.*

COPIES OF AN ORIGINAL LETTER addressed to Edwin Chadwick, Esq., Secretary to the Poor Law Commission, by Robert Hyde Greg, Esq., dated Manchester, September 17th, 1834; and of an original Letter to Edwin Chadwick, Esq., by Henry Ashworth, Esq., dated Turton, near Bolton, Lancashire, 2nd Month, 13th day, 1835.

Copy of the Correspondence relating to, and a Return of, the Number of Persons who were removed from their Parishes in the Agricultural Districts into the Manufacturing Districts, under the authority and sanction of the Poor Law Commissioners; with the dates and mode of their removal, the names of the Parishes from which they were taken, and the names and residences of the Persons to whom they were assigned, with a particular Account of the Numbers, Sexes, and Ages in each Family, when they were removed; and also, of the Number of Deaths, by accident or otherwise, which have since taken place among them; also, an Account of those who have been maimed in their employment; and a Statement of the Amount of the Wages agreed upon when consigned, with the actual Wages they received; and also, an Account of their present Residences, Employment, and Wages. (254.)—*Moved for, by Mr. Ferrand. Presented, 3d May.*

REPORT made by H. W. Parker, Esq., Assistant Poor Law Commissioner, relative to the East Preston Gilbert's Incorporation. (247.)—(*House of Commons.*) *Presented* (*by Command*), *9th May.*

STATEMENTS in Columns, of the Number of Unions in England and Wales, and the average Number of Paupers relieved; distinguishing the In-door from the Out-door recipients of relief; showing, also, the Amount of Expenditure for maintenance, and for Out-door assistance, as well as the total Expenditure for the separate years ending at Lady-day, from 1837 to 1843. (Not ordered to be printed.)—*Moved for, by Dr. Bowring. Presented,* 10*th May.*

NINTH ANNUAL REPORT of the Poor Law Commissioners. (*House of Commons*)—*Presented* (*by Command*), 19*th May.*

A RETURN of the Names of Persons who have been appointed Governors of the Skipton Union Workhouse during the last two years, with the reasons why they resigned or were dismissed from the office. Also a copy of all communications addressed to, or received from, the Poor Law Commissioners by the Board of Guardians, relating to any charges brought against Mr. C. Mottram, Master of the said Union Workhouse, with the Proceedings of the Board thereon.

A Return of the Names and Ages of all Inmates of the said Union Workhouse (as well as of the names of their parents), who are now, or who have been employed in, any Factory since the 1st day of January last, with the number of hours per day they have been compelled to work, as well as of the amount of their wages, and of the names of the persons to whom the same have been paid; and stating whether the Owner of the Factory is a member of the said Board of Guardians, and whether the employment of the said Inmates was sanctioned by the Board of Guardians, by the Poor Law Commissioners, or by any Assistant Poor Law Commissioner. Also a Copy of all contracts for Food, Clothing, Coals, and Timber, which have been entered into by the said Board of Guardians since the formation of the Union, with any Member, or with any one in partnership with any Member, of the said Board. (438.)—*Moved for, by Mr. Ferrand. Presented* 13*th July.*

REPORTS of Special Assistant Poor Law Commissioners, on the Employment of Women and Children in Agriculture. (*House of Commons.*)

COPY OF REPORT of the Special Assistant Poor Law Commissioners upon the treatment of the Infant Pauper Children in the Marylebone Workhouse; together with the correspondence relating thereto. (483.)—*Moved for, by Mr. Manners Sutton. Presented* 24*th July.*

REPORT of the Poor Law Commissioners on Local Taxation, with Appendices. (*House of Commons.*) *Presented* (*by Command*) 31*st July.*

ACCOUNT of the Prices of the following Articles of Consumption at the Poor Law Unions throughout England and Wales, in March, 1842 and March, 1843: Flour, Bread, Meat, Butter, Cheese, Potatoes, Peas, Oatmeal, Candles, Soap, Coals, Tea, Coffee, Sugar, Salt, Rice, and Milk. (554.)—*Moved for, by Mr. Irving. Presented* 11*th August.*

MARYLEBONE WORKHOUSE:—Copy of Proceedings of the Directors and Guardians of the Poor relative to the Infant Pauper Children in the Workhouse subsequently to the 1st January, 1843. (559.)—*Presented by Command. Ordered to be printed* 4*th August.*

A RETURN, showing the Number of In-door and Out-door Paupers relieved during the first week of the month of April, 1843, in the several Unions comprised in each Assistant Poor Law Commissioner's District. (*House of Commons.*) (591.)—*Moved for, by Mr. Manners Sutton. Presented* 17*th August.*

COPIES OF ALL LISTS OF INSANE PERSONS chargeable to Parishes, returned by the Overseers of the Poor, in the year 1842, to the respective Clerks of the Peace acting in and for the several Counties of England and Wales, or their Deputies, pursuant to the Act 9 Geo. 4. c. 40, s. 36.

Of all Lists of Insane Persons chargeable to Parishes or Unions returned by the Clerks of Boards of Guardians to the respective Clerks of the Peace, acting in and for the several Counties of England and Wales, pursuant to the Act 5 and 6 Vict., c. 57, s. 6.—*Moved for, by Lord Ashley. Presented* 24*th August.*

LONDON:
Printed by Order of the Poor Law Commissioners, by W. CLOWES and SONS, Stamford Street, and Published by CHARLES KNIGHT and Co., 22, Ludgate Street, Publishers to the Poor Law Commissioners.

AN

OFFICIAL CIRCULAR

OF PUBLIC DOCUMENTS AND INFORMATION:

DIRECTED BY THE POOR LAW COMMISSIONERS TO BE PRINTED, CHIEFLY FOR THE USE OF THE MEMBERS AND PERMANENT OFFICERS OF BOARDS OF GUARDIANS, UNDER THE POOR LAW AMENDMENT ACT.

No. 29. CIRCULAR ISSUED NOVEMBER 30, 1843.

Poor Law Commission Office,
Somerset House,
November 30, 1843.

THE Poor Law Commissioners, on a review of their Correspondence, directed that the following abstract thereof should be printed and circulated for the information of Guardians and Officers of the several Unions, viz.:—

By order of the Board,

EDWIN CHADWICK, *Secretary*.

I. ACCOUNTS.

1. CONSTABLES' CHARGES AND FEES FOR SWEARING IN—WHETHER TO BE ALLOWED IN AUDIT OF ACCOUNTS. 21*st August*, 1843.

Auditor of Ampthill Union—Stated, that the overseers of several of the parishes in the Ampthill Union had recently entered in their accounts a charge of 11*s*. 6*d*. paid by them to justices' clerks for fees on constables being sworn into office; also the following charges of constables, "for making assessors' lists, and attending at Petty Sessions with same, 3*s*. 6*d*.;" "attending at Ampthill, to be sworn in as constable, 5*s*.;" and "justices' clerk's fee on overseers quitting office, and appointment of new overseers, 8*s*." And inquired whether he could legally pass charges made by justices' clerks and constables, for fees under the 5th and 6th Vic., c. 109, without their being first made into distinct bills, and an order or allowance by justices for the overseers to pay the same be first obtained. [Forwarded five bills as specimens.]

Ans. The Commissioners think that the auditor ought not to allow in the overseers' accounts any charges for such fees, unless the payment has been made in accordance with the 17th section of 5 and 6 Vic., c. 109, "upon the order of the justices in Petty Sessions assembled for the division." With regard to the particular bills enclosed in the auditor's letter, the Commissioners will point out the general principles which they conceive should regulate the allowance of constables' charges in the overseers' accounts, and will leave it to the auditor to apply those principles to the accounts submitted to him. When provision has been made, by an authorized Table of Fees, under 5 and 6 Vic., c. 109, s. 17, for payments to a constable for specified services, the Commissioners consider that such payments are chargeable on the poor-rates, in those cases in which the constables' services have been lawfully required in respect of the parish, but not otherwise. Where, however, the constable incurs expenses on account of the parish, for which the Table of Fees does not provide, the Commissioners think that he is still entitled to be reimbursed, under the 18th Geo. III., c. 19, s. 4. For example,—if the constable, in attending before the magistrate to be sworn in, should be put to any necessary charges (such as travelling expenses), it appears to the Commissioners that he might claim repayment accordingly. But this provision does not authorize the allowance of any remuneration to the constable for services or loss of time.

---

2. RECOVERY OF BALANCES FROM PAID OFFICERS.—POWER OF JUSTICES. 24*th August*, 1843.

Clerk of —— *Union*— Stated, that one of two justices who had signed a distress-warrant under the 47th section of the Poor Law Amendment Act, against the goods of a collector who was a defaulter, had since left the country, and was not expected to return for two years; and requested the Commissioners' opinion as to whether the future proceedings under the warrant must be taken before the same justices who granted it; or whether any other two justices acting for the division can legally commit the collector to prison for want of sufficient distress.

Ans. Balances recoverable under the 47th section of the Poor Law Amendment Act are to be recovered according to the provisions of the 99th section. The persons empowered by the latter section to commit to prison, in case of insufficient distress, are "*any* such justices as aforesaid, as the case may be." The Commissioners think that this expression includes *any* justices answering to the description contained in the earlier portion of the section; consequently, it is *not* necessary that the justices who commit to prison should be the same persons who issued the warrant of distress.

II. BASTARDY.

1. SUFFICIENCY OF NOTICE OF APPLICATION IN BASTARDY, AND PAYMENT OF COSTS THEREOF. 11*th and* 25*th August*, 1843.

Clerk of Whitchurch Union—Stated, that L. M., widow, belonging to the parish of Hurstbourne Priors, in the Whitchurch Union, was, on the 6th of May last, delivered of a male bastard child in the Union workhouse, where she has since remained, and was likely to continue. The whole of the Guardians present at a meeting of the Board on the 17th instant, signed a notice of an intended application for an order of bastardy upon Mr. G. O., who was charged as being the father of the child. On the hearing of the application, Mr. O.'s attorney contended that the notice was informal and insufficient, on account of its not having the common seal of the Board of Guardians affixed to it, and referred to some case reported in "The Justice of the Peace" in support of his argument, which the magistrates considered to be applicable, and that the seal should have been affixed; and, therefore, declined to make any order. Mr. O.'s attorney then applied to the magistrates for costs, under the 73rd section of the Poor Law Amendment Act, which the magistrates considered they were bound to allow, although the case had not been heard and decided on the merits. Inquired whether the decision of the magistrates, as to the necessity of affixing the common seal of the Guardians to the notice was correct. And also whether the Guardians were bound to pay the costs.

Ans. The Commissioners do not know what case the clerk alludes to as having guided the magistrates to the conclusion they came to. But, unless it has been expressly decided that the notice of an application for an order in bastardy must, in order to be valid, be sealed with the Union seal, the Commissioners are of opinion that such sealing is not requisite. The 73rd section of the Poor Law Amendment Act requires the notice to be "given *under the hands* of such overseers or Guardians;" and the 2 and 3 Vic., c. 85, s. 1, makes no difference in this respect. The 5 and 6 Vic., c. 57, s. 17, which regulates to a certain extent the mode in which Guardians shall make applications to justices, and requires the seal of the Guardians to be attached to certain documents connected with such applications, does not refer in any way to the notice to be given to the putative father, under 4 and 5 Wm. IV., c. 76, s. 73, and 2 and 3 Vic., c. 85, s. 1. With regard to the clerk's inquiry as to the payment of the costs, the Commissioners desire to advert to the terms of the proviso in the 73rd section, which are as follows:—"If upon the hearing of such application the Court shall not think fit to make any order," &c. It appears, from the clerk's statement of the circumstances, that in this case the application was heard, and that the Court did not think fit to make any order thereon. The Commissioners do not perceive that the grounds on which the Court decided to refuse the order would at all affect the question; and the Commissioners therefore consider that the Guardians are liable to defray the costs referred to.

Clerk of the same Union—Inquired, whether the costs ordered to be paid to Mr. O. as above should be paid out of the funds of the Union, or by the parish of Hurstbourne Priors: and stated that the magistrates were much influenced in this case by the statement in the "Justice of the Peace" of the 10th September, 1842, p. 556.

Ans. Under 2 and 3 Vic., c. 85, the duty of applying for an order of affiliation devolves upon the Guardians of the Union; but the resort to that remedy is, nevertheless, the concern of the individual parish, and the costs incurred cannot be charged to the other parishes of the Union not interested in the matter. The Commissioners therefore think that the costs in question should be paid by the Guardians of Whitchurch Union, out of any funds in their hands belonging to the parish of Hurstbourne Priors, and charged in the ledger accordingly. The Commissioners have referred to the passage to which the clerk alludes, in "The Justice of the Peace," but they do not see anything therein to induce them to modify the views expressed in their letter of the 11th instant. Indeed, it seems to the Commissioners that the opinion given in "The Justice of the Peace" refers to the mode of "preferring complaints" or of making applications to the justices, and not to the mode of giving the notice to the putative father.

---

2. WHETHER A SECOND APPLICATION FOR AN ORDER IN BASTARDY CAN BE MADE, THE FIRST BEING INFORMAL.

7th October, 1843.

Clerk of Beaminster Union — Inquired, whether the Board of Guardians can make a fresh application to the justices in Petty Sessions for an order in bastardy, within three months from the commencement of the chargeability, the first application having been dismissed through informality.

Ans. The Commissioners are of opinion, that

where an application for an order on the reputed father has been made to the justices under 2nd and 3rd Vic., c. 85, within three months from the commencement of the chargeability, and that application has been dismissed through informality, a second application may be made, provided the three months have not expired.

III. BURIAL GROUND.—RIGHT OF UNION CHAPLAIN TO TIMBER TREES GROWING IN THE WORKHOUSE BURIAL-GROUND.

4th August, 1843.

Clerk of —— *Union*—Stated, that there were a few poplar trees growing in the burial-ground attached to the workhouse; and in consequence of one or two injuring the foundation of the Infirmary, and in order to obtain more room for burials, they were, by direction of the Guardians, cut down; since which, the chaplain of the workhouse had claimed the trees as his property, stating that he had a right to them as chaplain there. The Guardians, however, were of a different opinion, and requested the Commissioners' advice as to whom the timber belonged.

Ans. The chaplain of the workhouse has no freehold in the burial-ground, as the rector or vicar has in a churchyard; and the produce of the burial-ground of a workhouse is, like that of other private burying places, the profit of those who are the occupiers of the freehold: in the present case, the produce is the legal property of the Guardians, for the use of the entire Union.

IV. CONTRACTS.—COURSE TO BE PURSUED WHERE NO TENDERS ARE MADE.

25th October, 1843.

Clerk of Bury (*Lancashire*) *Union*—Inquired, what course the Board of Guardians should adopt when, after advertising for tenders to contract for the supply of any articles required for the use of the Union workhouse, no tenders are received.

Ans. If the contract were properly advertised, and there was no tender offered, there appear to the Commissioners to be two courses open to the Guardians, viz.:—1st, to advertise again; or, 2nd, to contract with the former contractor or any other respectable person on the best terms which can be made. The Commissioners would recommend the Guardians in the case stated to adopt one of the courses above suggested.

V. GUARDIAN.—VACCINATOR TO THE UNION INELIGIBLE FOR THE OFFICE OF GUARDIAN.

19th October, 1843.

Mr. —— Inquired, whether a medical man who received payments for the performance of vaccination under the usual vaccination contract entered into by him with the Board of Guardians of the —— Union, is to be regarded as receiving a "fixed salary or emolument from the poor-rates," so as to be incapable of serving as a Guardian in such Union under the 14th section of the Act 5 & 6 Vic., c. 57.

Ans. The Commissioners entertain very little doubt on this subject; the source of the payment is unquestionably the poor-rates; the payment is unquestionably an "emolument," and "fixed" in proportion to the service, although not as to the whole amount. The principle on which the disqualification is founded appears also to be in every respect applicable to the case,—the office of Guardian being one which involves the duty of seeing to the performance of the duty of the person who contracts to vaccinate, and consequently one which enables a Guardian, if so inclined, to give effect to his partiality to the contractor to the disadvantage of the public.

VI. EMIGRATION TO NEW SOUTH WALES.

The Colonization Circular, issued by the Colonial and Land Emigration Commissioners on the 30th October last, announces that the contracts for carrying on the new emigration on bounty to New South Wales have been taken up by *Messrs. Carter and Bonus*, No. 11, Leadenhall-street, London; *Messrs. William Smith and Sons*, Liverpool; and *Mr. William Glen Anderson*, Glasgow. The circular also states that "it cannot be too distinctly understood that the contractors are held strictly responsible to the Colonial Government for the fitness of their selections, and forfeit the amount of the passage-money of persons judged ineligible; and that therefore justice requires them to have the whole power of accepting or rejecting applicants, and that no Government department will consent to interfere on the subject." The following, which are stated to be some of the principal regulations issued by the Commissioners upon the manner of carrying out this scheme, are also set out in the Circular:—

SHIP.

1. The ship must be of the first class in Lloyd's Register, not lower than the red diphthong, with a star. When a ship is selected, she is to be immediately notified to the Commissioners, and to their officer at the port where she is, that he may report upon her to the Board. It will be competent to the Commissioners, when they see occasion, to order a survey, at the contractor's expense, in dry-dock. No ship can be taken which is of less height than 6 feet 4 inches between decks, or 5 feet 6 inches from deck to beam.

2. The ship should be thoroughly cleared of all kinds of vermin; the hold properly cleansed; and, if the ballast used be shingle, it should be washed and screened to prevent injurious effects in hot weather from the dirt and sand which it is liable to contain. The between decks to be painted white, including the under part of the upper deck and beams.

3. The crew is to be in the proportion of five men and a boy to each 100 tons of the old registered burthen of the ship.

4. The cargo not to include salt or gunpowder, or other articles of known deleteriousness to health or danger to the vessel. Horses and cattle cannot be allowed to be taken on freight in ships carrying emigrants under Government. This will not of course interfere with a proper supply of live stock, and a cow for milk.

5. The fittings to be according to a specification, of which a printed form may be had at the office of the Commissioners, or at the office of the Government Emigration Agent at the port.

7. Due notice must be given to the Government Emigration Agent of the intended plan of laying out the fittings.

8. The decks are not to be lumbered, but to be kept duly clear for the working of the ship and the exercise of the people. All provisions are to be stowed under hatches, and only sufficient water for immediate use (never exceeding two tons) to remain on deck. A proper space, at the rate of not less than 15 cubic feet for each adult, is to be reserved in the hold for the emigrants. Baggage subject to no charge whatever.

12. Water being the article which it is most important to preserve sweet on a long voyage, great care should be taken to put on board the purest filtered water that can be procured; and the water-casks are to be sweet and *substantial*, properly charred, and constructed of staves of not less than one inch in thickness.

THE EMIGRANTS' PREPARATIONS.

The contractors will be at liberty to take a sum not exceeding 1*l.* per statute adult, from the emigrants themselves; and where this has been done, the money may be forfeited if the parties do not come forward to embark. No further payment whatever is to be taken from the passengers.

The emigrants are to be provided by the contractors with new mattresses, bolsters, blankets, and counterpanes; and with a small lock-up box, 15 inches square, per adult, intended to contain one month's linen, &c.; also with a knife and fork, two spoons, a metal plate, and a drinking mug; the whole of which articles, including the bedding, are to be kept by the emigrants after arrival in the colony.

The contractors are also to provide the necessary mess utensils for the emigrants.

But the emigrants must bring their own clothing and linen for the voyage,—not less than two suits of outside clothing, two pairs of strong shoes or boots, eight shirts or shifts, six pairs of worsted stockings, three towels, two pounds of marine soap, combs, &c.

BERTHING.

16. The emigrants ought to be berthed according to their natural connexions, and so as to place in the neighbourhood of one another those whose relative circumstances and habits render it most likely that they will agree. The names of the parties should be affixed to each berth.

17. Married people are not to be separated; their berths are to be interposed between those of the single men and single women; and separate hospitals are to be fitted for males and females, as provided for in the specification mentioned in Clause 5. No more than three children are on any account to be placed in one berth; and, as far as possible, not more than two children above the age of 10 years ought to be in the same berth; and boys and girls above that age must not be berthed together.

SURGEON.

18. The Commissioners have undertaken the appointment of the surgeon. But in cases where the contractors, who are to be the losers by any sickness or mortality, wish to point out a tried surgeon who already has their confidence, the Commissioners will be prepared to lend every due weight to their recommendation, subject to the necessary inquiries by the Commissioners themselves.

SELECTION OF EMIGRANTS.

25. The responsibility for the selection of the emigrants, and the providing of sufficient proof of their fitness, is left entirely to the contractors, and the judgment upon the emigrants will remain as heretofore with the colonial authorities.

26. The former regulations on bounty, dated at Sydney, 3d March, 1840, and 11th October, 1841, remain in force as far as regards the selection of emigrants; and for the convenience of parties concerned, the substance is subjoined in the six follow-

ing articles of such parts of those regulations as relate to this subject :—

27. The eligible classes are stated in the Sydney Regulations as follows :—

Agricultural labourers,
Shepherds,
Carpenters,
Smiths,
Wheelwrights,
Bricklayers,
Masons,
Female domestic and farm servants.

28. The age of married couples, not having children above the age of 10 years, is not to exceed on embarkation 40 years.

29. But if accompanied by one or more children above 10 years, and still hale and capable of work, the age of the parents may be increased according to the following scale :—

	Years.			
If the age of the Father or Mother, or both, be above 40, but under	42	they must be accompanied by	1 child	above 10 Years.
	44		2 children	
	46		3 ditto	
	48		4 ditto	
	50		5 ditto	

But if either parent be above 50 years of age, no bounty will be paid on account of any member of the family, unless qualified as a single man or woman under the regulations. Parties between the ages of 40 and 50 years, admissible under the preceding rule, will not be considered ineligible if also accompanied by children under 10 years of age, nor will bounty be withheld on such children, provided that the family be in all other respects qualified according to the regulations.

30. Unmarried females are to be domestic or farm servants, not below 15 nor above 30 years of age at the time of embarkation, and are to go out under the protection of a married couple as forming part of the family, and destined to remain with it until such female be otherwise provided for.

31. Unmarried males are to be agricultural labourers or mechanics of any trade or calling above enumerated, not below 18 nor above 30 years of age at the time of embarkation. Their number is not to exceed the number of females who are brought out at the same time by the same party.

32. The wives and families of soldiers of regiments in the colony, or in Van Diemen's Land, and of persons serving under sentence of transportation in either colony, are not eligible for bounty.

NOTE.—Of the two rules numbered 30 and 31, the following constructions have been sanctioned.

So far as regards protection, it will suffice that a single woman, if not younger than 18, be placed under the bonâ fide protection of a married couple, who may be willing to undertake that she shall form part of their family during the voyage, and at least a fortnight after its termination. The written engagement of the married man to this effect, and the acknowledgment of it by both parties before the Commissioners' agent at the port of embarkation, and the surgeon superintendent, will be admitted as evidence of the arrangement, but will not avail against such misconduct on the part of the single female as shall constitute a presumption that the protection must have been illusory, or her previous character bad.

With regard to equality in the numbers of single men and single women, the contractors will be allowed to balance the numbers upon the result of their whole emigration, and not upon the numbers in each ship. The disallowance of bounty on a single female judged objectionable, will not involve the rejection of a single man as having on that account become in excess of the regular number.

MISCELLANEOUS.

35. All publications by which poor persons are invited by the contractors to emigrate are to be submitted to the Commissioners.

38. No emigrants to be despatched from the 1st of January to the 15th of February, inclusive.

VII. INCOME TAX.—LIABILITY OF THE JOINT EMOLUMENT OF MASTER AND MATRON, BEING HUSBAND AND WIFE, TO BE ASSESSED TO THE TAX.

17*th August*, 1843.

Clerk of —— *Union*—Stated, that a difficulty had arisen as to the amount at which the master of the workhouse should be assessed to the income-tax. His salary was 65*l.* a-year, besides his rations and apartments; and his wife, who held, under a distinct appointment, the office of matron, had a salary of 55*l.* a-year, besides her rations and apartments. The apartments occupied by the master and matron had been assessed under Schedule A. at 15*l.*, and the profits of offices and emoluments under Schedule E. at 145*l.* The master considered that even if he be chargeable for his wife's salary, he was clearly not chargeable for the value of her rations and apartments, which were personal privileges enjoyed by her in return for the duties she was obliged personally to perform, and from which he derived no direct benefit. Requested the opinion of the Commissioners upon the subject.

Ans. The Commissioners apprehend that the case of the matron comes within the proviso of section 45 of the Income Tax Act, viz.—"That the profits of any married woman living with her husband shall be deemed the profits of the husband, and the same shall be charged in the name of the husband." The master of the workhouse, therefore, would be chargeable, as the matron's husband, in respect of her salary and her rations, as constituting the profits of her office. With regard to the occupation of the apartments, the Commissioners refer the clerk to the circular issued by the Commissioners of Stamps and Taxes, of which the Commissioners sent him an extract on the 24th June last. [See 'Official Circular,' No. 26, p. 111.] The Commissioners presume that the master will be subject to assessment, on account of the apartments occupied by his wife in the Union workhouse, as well as those occupied by himself.

VIII. MEDICAL ORDER.—DEFINITION OF THE TERM "CHILDBIRTH" IN THE ORDER.

13*th August*, 1843.

Mr. E. Copeman, Coltishall, Aylsham Union—Inquired, whether the term "*childbirth*," in the General Medical Order, included abortions, miscarriages, or premature births; or whether the remuneration prescribed by the order in cases of the delivery of women in childbirth, was only to be given in cases of childbirth at the full period of pregnancy.

Ans. The term "childbirth," as used in the Commissioners' General Medical Order of 12th March, 1842, is intended to apply only to cases in which the child was or might have been born alive.

IX. OVERSEERS.—OMISSION TO ACCOUNT FOR ALL THE RATES RECEIVED—HOW TO BE PROCEEDED AGAINST.

9*th August*, 1843.

Auditor of Anglesey Union—Stated, that the overseers of the parish of Llanwenllyfo had collected eleven rates, but had only accounted for seven in their accounts; and seven were all that appeared by the regular rate-book to be collected. The others were entered in a small book kept for that purpose. The latter account contained many items that were illegal and would not be allowed in the accounts. Inquired what course he should, as auditor, adopt in this case.

Ans. The course which it would be most advisable for the auditor to adopt, in reference to this matter, would be, that he should call upon the overseers to account for the rates in question, and require them specifically to make oath, or to declare, that the accounts rendered by them include all monies received by them relating to the relief of the poor (Poor Law Amendment Act, section 47). If they refuse, or declare falsely, they might then be proceeded against penally, under the provisions of the Poor Law Amendment Act, or they might be indicted. See R. *v.* Maston, 2 Camp. 268; and Townson *v.* Wilson, 1 Camp. 396. The Commissioners desire to add that they would consider the expediency of taking proceedings against the overseers, in the event of their refusal to account.

X. PAUPERS.—EMPLOYMENT OF, IN REPAIRING PARISH ROADS, CANNOT BE SANCTIONED.

6*th October*, 1843.

Clerk of Bradford (Wilts) Union—Stated, that the Board of Guardians wished to be informed whether it would be in accordance with the out-door labour test order to employ the able-bodied paupers in repairing the parish roads generally throughout the Union, they having hitherto been employed in altering and improving certain roads only.

Ans. The Commissioners think the proposed mode of employing the able-bodied paupers very objectionable, on account of its direct interference with independent labourers. The parishes are bound to repair the roads, and to defray the expenses out of the highway rate. Under the proposed arrangement the Guardians would be doing by pauper labour what ought to be done by independent labour, and the persons thus employed would be subjected to the demoralizing influence of pauperism. Hitherto the out-door employment of pauper labour in the Bradford Union appears to have been very properly confined to making such alterations and improvements of roads as would not otherwise have been effected at all; such as cutting down hills on parish roads, which, however desirable that it should be done, it is not likely that the parishes would have thought of attempting by the employment of independent labour at the expense of the highway rate. The Commissioners are aware how desirable it is to provide some suitable employment for the able-bodied paupers. They are likewise aware that almost all out-door employment for paupers is open to some kind of objection, but the Commissioners consider the mode of employing them now proposed by the

Guardians very questionable on the grounds above stated, and the Commissioners therefore doubt whether they can, consistently with their public duty, give their sanction to its adoption.

XI. PENSIONS.—Assignment of Arrears of Pension to reimburse Parish for Relief granted.

17*th August*, 1843.

Mr. S. Smithers, Ashford, Bakewell Union —Stated, that Francis Howard, who belonged to the parish of Ashford, and who was formerly a serjeant in the Marines, in November, 1836, being at that time entitled to a pension of 4*l*. 9*s*. per quarter, left his wife and family chargeable to the parish. From that period up to the present time the family have received relief, which, with the expenses incurred in endeavouring to apprehend Howard, amounted to 109*l*. 3*s*. 2*d*. The overseers took steps to prevent the receipt of the pension by Howard, the arrears of which amounted, on the 27th of March last, to 115*l*. 14*s*. In April last the overseers succeeded in discovering Howard, when he was apprehended and taken before a magistrate to assign over the arrears of his pension to the township, which he accordingly did. Application had since been made to the office of the Paymaster of Greenwich Pensioners for the payment of the amount; but as there appeared some difficulty in making the payment, the Commissioners' instructions were requested as to the course to be pursued.

Ans. The Commissioners presume that Howard was taken before a magistrate with a view to the procuring of an order of justices for the payment of his pension under the provisions of 2 & 3 Vic., c. 51, s. 4. Mr. Smithers's letter does not afford the Commissioners any information, either as to the effect of this order, if any such were made, or as to the nature of the difficulty which prevents the observance of it. If, however, it was an order for the payment of the *arrears* of Howard's pension for the benefit of the township, the Commissioners think that it would not be valid. The section referred to enacts, that when a pensioner suffers his wife or family to become chargeable, the justices may direct that one-half (or two-thirds, according to circumstances) of "the *next* payment *which shall become due* of such pension or allowance" shall be made to the Guardians for the reimbursement of the parish. The provisions of the section, therefore, do not extend to *arrears* of pensions, or payments other than the "next payment which shall become due."

XII. POLICE RATE.—Enforcement of, when levied as a distinct Rate.

4*th August*, 1843.

Clerk of Calne Union—Stated, that since the establishment of the rural police, it had been the practice to make a police-rate entirely separate and distinct from the poor-rate, and entered in a separate book. The rate had been made at vestry-meetings in the same way as the poor-rate, and the book had been signed by the churchwardens and overseers, and allowed by the magistrates as a distinct rate. The rate was made out in this manner, because all property liable to the payment of poor-rate within the boundaries of the municipal borough of Calne is exempt from payment of the police-rate. A person who had been summoned for the amount of his police-rate positively refused to pay it. The magistrates, finding that the rate had always been made out separately from the poor-rate, were of opinion that they had no authority to grant a distress-warrant for the amount as police-rate; but that had the amount been included in and formed part of the poor-rate, and been demanded and collected as poor-rate, there would have been no difficulty. Inquired whether the payment of the police-rate, as a separate and distinct rate, could be enforced by distress-warrant.

Ans. In the first place the levy of the police-rate is identified with that of the county-rate, it being provided (3 & 4 Vic., c. 88, s. 5), that it shall be collected from the persons liable to contribute, with and as part of the county-rate. But it appears to be clearly provided, as to county-rate, that it may be raised, either as poor-rate under the 12th Geo. II., c. 29, s. 2, or as a separate and distinct rate on the estates and property rateable to the relief of the poor, under the more recent and more operative statute, 55 Geo. III., c. 51, s. 12. There appears, under this statute, to be no necessity that the rate should be entitled as a rate for the relief of the poor; but it appears to be beyond question that a rate entitled, according to the true state of the facts, "a rate to raise county-rate assessed on the parish," or "a rate to raise the moneys necessary to reimburse the overseers the sums they have paid on account of county-rate," &c., would be a good title for the rate, according to the provisions of the 55th Geo. III., c. 51; and that the justices would be bound to enforce the payment of it, as if it were poor-rate. This being so, and the provisions of the 3rd and 4th Vic., c. 88, incorporating and identifying the provisions for county-rate, for the purpose of the police-rate, it appears that the course described as being adopted in the Calne Union is quite correct, and that the rate ought to be levied and enforced as if it were actually poor's-rate.

XIII. POOR'S RATE.—RIGHT OF OVERSEERS TO MAKE AND COLLECT TWO RATES CONCURRENTLY.

15*th August*, 1843.

Auditor of Pershore Union—Stated, that the overseers of St. Andrew, Pershore, on the 10th of March last, made a rate of 1*s*. in the pound, which they afterwards considered insufficient to cover their liabilities; and they therefore, on the 24th of the same month, and whilst the first was in force, and only partially collected, made another rate of 2*s*. in the pound. The latter rate was believed to have been made for the purpose of paying a bill of costs incurred in litigation with the hamlet of Pensham. His attention was drawn to the subject by the decision in Reg. *v*. Fordham, 11 A. & E. 73, 3 P. & D. 95. Inquired whether two rates could exist at the same time, both having been made in the same month, the first being only partially collected when the second was made, and the sums remaining uncollected of the former not being carried into and embodied in the latter.

Ans. The rates in the case of Reg. *v*. Fordham, to which the auditor adverts, were intended to raise the same sum; the one being in substitution for the other, and not additional to it. In the present case, the rates are to raise different sums, the one being in addition to the other; the first intended to raise 1*s*. in the pound, the second 2*s*. in the pound; the latter one being made fourteen days after the first, and before the first was collected. It is obvious that these rates are not concurrent in the full sense in which the rates referred to in Reg. *v*. Fordham were said to be concurrent. The observations made by the judges in that case were therefore applicable to a state of things not found in the present case. The rates were made at an interval of fourteen days apart; the 43rd Eliz. authorised the raising of money weekly, the rate was not therefore liable to objection on the ground of mere time. Were the sums to be raised by the rates, then, such as to constitute an objection to the validity of the rate? It would appear not, inasmuch as the amount to be raised by a rate is a matter for the discretion of the overseers, 43 Eliz., c. 2, s. 1. It remains then to be considered whether the fact that a portion of one rate is uncollected when another is made, rendering it inevitable that a part of the collection of both will go on concurrently, will vitiate the latter rate. The observations of the judges in Reg. *v*. Fordham do not appear to imply this conclusion; and, as such a conclusion would be adverse to what is believed to be the universal practice of making rates while some portion of preceding rates is uncollected, and would consequently render every rate illegal, and introduce a mode which would, in most cases, make it impossible ever to make a new rate, it is most reasonable to suppose that the language of the judges was not intended to convey this conclusion. In the present case it is true that, when the second rate was made, a portion of the previous rate, larger than is usual, remained uncollected. Still there is no rule for fixing the amount of arrears which may be outstanding when a fresh rate is made; and if any arrear uncollected will invalidate a new rate, the smallest amount of such arrear must have the same legal consequences. The Commissioners therefore think that the money assessed under two rates, both having been made during the same month, for the purpose of liquidating expenses incurred by the overseers during their year of office, may be lawfully collected, the first rate being only partially collected when the second was made.

XIV. RATING.

1. INCUMBENT'S LIABILITY TO BE ASSESSED IN RESPECT TO THE CHURCHYARD.

11*th August*, 1843.

Rev. G. G. Beadon, Axbridge—Inquired, if he was rateable to the poor-rate for the churchyard, as he paid 10*s*. 6*d*. a-year for it, in consideration of the grass, which was made into hay, and of the walnuts growing on a tree therein.

Ans. A churchyard, held by the parson for

the benefit of the parish, is not, when used only for burial, a subject for rating to the relief of the poor, chiefly on the principle that the occupation by the parson is, in this respect, for the benefit of the parish, and is not a beneficial occupation to him, the fees he may receive for burials not being the profits of the land, but the profits of his office. But, so far as such a churchyard may be glebe, the Commissioners consider that the parson is rateable in respect of the profit he may derive from it as land.

---

2. WHETHER CHARITY SCHOOLS ARE RATEABLE.

15*th November*, 1843.

Mr. ——, *All Saints, St. Pancras*—Inquired, whether a building situated in Mortimer market, Tottenham Court-road, and used exclusively for charity schools connected with the district church of All Saints, and in which no one resided, was liable to be rated to the poor-rate.

Ans. Several cases which have been decided by the Courts appear to establish the principle that where premises are appropriated exclusively to a charitable object, and no profit whatever is derived from them, they are not rateable to the relief of the poor. The Commissioners refer you especially to the case of R. *v.* Waldo (1 Bott.), in which a house, built by Mr. Waldo, and used solely for the maintenance and education of ten poor girls, supported by his charity, was held to be not rateable. But where a profit is made from the property, although applied to charitable purposes, it would seem, on the authority of R. *v.* Sterry (12 Ad. and Ell. 84), to be liable to assessment. In that case a charity-school at Croydon, belonging to the Society of Friends, was held rateable, on the ground that, as the parents or friends of every child received into the school were required to contribute a certain sum towards the costs of its maintenance and education, there was a revenue derived from the property, and consequently a beneficial occupation of it. Lord Denman observed, "This sum, it is true, is not adequate to the expense, and, in a popular sense, does not make the occupation of the premises beneficial, *i. e.* gainful; but still it is a revenue which the building produces; and actual gain on a balance of profit and loss is not needful, it is enough if a revenue be produced."

XV. RELIEF.

1. POWER OF GUARDIANS TO COMPEL THE RELATIVE OF AN ORPHAN CHILD TO SEND IT TO THE WORKHOUSE.

25*th August*, 1843.

Clerk of Kingsclere Union—Stated, that a bastard child, of the age of eight years, whose mother had deserted her, and who received parochial allowance, had been hitherto living in the Kingsclere Union with a grandmother, who had just died. The child was then removed to her mother's brother, who resided out of the Kingsclere Union, a situation of which the Guardians did not approve. Application had been made to the Guardians to grant some allowance towards the child's maintenance, which they declined to do; and the uncle refused to allow the child to be placed in the workhouse. Inquired whether the Guardians could compel the sending of the child to the workhouse.

Ans. The Commissioners know of no legal means by which the Guardians can compel the uncle to surrender the child, and to permit its reception into the workhouse. The only course which appears to be open to the Guardians to adopt for the purpose, is to refuse any other relief than maintenance in the workhouse. Indeed, by the Commissioners' General Order of 2nd August, 1841, the Guardians are precluded from affording relief to the child while resident out of the Union, except under some one of the exceptions contained in the Order.

---

2. BURIAL MONEY NOT ATTACHABLE FOR RELIEF GRANTED TO THE CHILDREN OF THE DECEASED.

13*th July and* 2*nd August*, 1843.

Clerk of Market-Drayton Union—Stated, that four children of the late S. M., who died on the 17th May last, had been for some time in the workhouse, and were then receiving out-relief. The father was a member of the Cheswardine benefit club, and his representatives were entitled, on his death, to the sum of 13*l.* out of the society. The ages of the children were nine, seven, four, and two years. No relief was given during the father's lifetime, neither was any relief given by way of loan. The wife died two years before her husband; she was the mother of the children, and they were born in wedlock. Inquired whether the Guardians had any legal claim upon that sum for the cost already incurred, or to be incurred, in the maintenance of the children.

Ans. The Commissioners are of opinion that the Guardians have no legal claim on the fund mentioned. But the Guardians will properly bear in mind the existence of this fund in granting relief to the persons entitled to the enjoyment of the money.

---

3. AT WHAT RATE TO CHARGE THE COST OF MAINTENANCE OF A PAUPER BELONGING TO ONE UNION IN THE WORKHOUSE OF ANOTHER UNION.

7th October, 1843.

Clerk of Honiton Union—Stated, that the sum of 3*s.* 6*d.* a-week had been charged for twenty-one days for the maintenance of a pauper in the *Tiverton Union* workhouse, under an order of removal. It appeared that the average weekly cost per head was 2*s.* 0½*d.* only; and it was thought that that sum only should have been charged in this instance. It was, however, contended that the actual cost of maintaining each adult was equal to 3*s.* 6*d.* per week, and that the paupers of other Unions maintained in the Tiverton Union workhouse had therefore been always charged at that rate. Requested the opinion of the Commissioners on the propriety of the demand.

Clerk of Tiverton Union—Explained that the average cost per head, as shown by the quarterly abstract of the Tiverton Union, was the average of adults and *children*, and that, in addition to the amount of such cost, should be considered the expense of lodging and of the officers of the establishment, and of the wine and other necessaries supplied to the pauper under the order of the medical officer, which together exceeded the 3*s.* 6*d.* per week claimed in respect of his maintenance.

Ans. The Commissioners consider the question to be one of much difficulty. The 84th section of the Poor Law Amendment Act, provides for the payment of the "cost and expense" of the relief and and maintenance of the pauper. The Commissioners think that these terms might possibly include, not only the cost of the food and clothing actually consumed by the pauper, but also a proportion of the charges incurred in supporting the establishment of the Union. For the shelter of the workhouse is as much an advantage enjoyed by the pauper as the food he eats, or the clothing he wears; and the services of the Union officers are also beneficial to him, in ministering to his relief. But the difficulty here arises, in estimating the proportion of those charges which is to be assigned to the individual case. This difficulty may possibly induce some parishes to forego this part of their legal claim; whilst it may lead others to found their demand upon merely an approximate calculation. Again, there is great difficulty in ascertaining, with anything like exactness, the actual cost incurred for each individual pauper, even as regards the food and clothing. The maintenance of children, especially infants, is of course less expensive than that of adults; and that of adults must vary with the circumstances of different cases,—as, for example, the distinctions of sex, of sickness and health, and the like. Having regard to these difficulties, and to the apparently reasonable amount of the charge made in the present case, the Commissioners would not feel themselves justified in recommending the Guardians of Honiton Union to persevere in resisting the payment. Indeed it is obvious that all Unions have a common interest in adopting the simplest and readiest mode of approximating to the cost of relief thus charged; and that the ordinary weekly rate of maintenance and clothing on which the distribution of the charge is made among the parishes of the same Union is, in common cases, the best guide to what should be demanded on one side and paid on the other.

---

4. RELIEF BY OVERSEERS IN CASES OF SUDDEN AND URGENT NECESSITY: RELATIVE POWERS OF MEDICAL AND RELIEVING OFFICERS IN CERTAIN CASES.

9th November, 1843.

Clerks of Berwick-upon-Tweed Union—Forwarded a letter of Mr. Robertson, the chairman of the Board of Guardians, wherein he inquired, 1. How sums paid by overseers in cases of sudden and urgent necessity were to be debited by, or re-imbursed to them: 2. What were the relative powers and duties of medical and relieving officers in cases where the former ordered not merely medical relief, wine, &c., but ordinary relief—common necessaries. With regard to the first point, he referred the opinions given by the Commissioners in the Official Circulars, No. 15, p. 218, and No. 24, p. 62, which he conceived to be apparently opposed to each other.

Ans. Upon the former of these points Mr. Robertson, in his letter, places in juxta-position two opinions or instructions from the Commissioners, extracted from the Official Circulars, Nos. 15 and 24, which instructions he considers apparently opposed to each other. The only point on which, as it seems to the Commissioners, the two opinions conflict, is as to the expediency of the practice of the Guardians repaying to the overseers the cost of the relief granted in a case of sudden and urgent necessity, which practice, in the letter contained in the Official Circular, No. 15, is spoken of as likely to withdraw these cases of urgent necessity from official cognizance on the part of the auditor. In other respects the instructions, though the terms employed are different, lead to the same conclusion, viz., that the auditor is the ultimate judge of the propriety and legality of the relief entered in the accounts of the overseers as having been given in cases of sudden and urgent necessity. As regards, therefore, the question of the repayment to the overseers by the Guardians of the relief given by the former in cases of this nature, though such repayment, whether made or not by the Guardians, does not affect the validity of the relief or the auditor in any way, the Commissioners are disposed on reconsideration to adhere to the view expressed in the later communication as to the expediency of the practice of repaying the relief in cases in which the Guardians think that it has been properly given. The overseers are bound under the orders of the Commissioners to report the relief to the Guardians; by this the important object of keeping the Guardians informed of the proceedings of the overseers, under the 54th section of the Poor Law Amendment Act, is attained. But by the Guardians adopting such relief and repaying it through the relieving officer, the additional advantage is, as far as practicable, secured, of bringing into one account (at all times accessible to the Guardians) the total amount of relief given to the pauper of a particular parish. Further, the fact of such repayment will assist the auditor's judgment in dealing with cases of this description, and will enable him at once to distinguish those in which the Guardians have recognized the propriety of the expenditure or have withheld such approbation. The course of proceeding will be this; the overseer will give relief, report it to the Guardians, and debit the parish with the amount. If the Guardians approve, they will order the relieving officer to pay the amount to the overseers, who, in their accounts, will credit the parish with the amount so received. The relieving officer will in the meantime, in his account affecting the particular parish, have taken credit for the repayment made by him to the overseers. If the Guardians refuse to recognize the relief, it will only appear as an item for which he claims credit against the parish in the overseer's accounts, and in that form the attention of the auditor can be called to it. With respect to the second point raised by Mr. Robertson, I am to state generally that the medical officer is not empowered by the orders of the Commissioners, or by his contract with the Guardians, to *order* food or articles of diet; such a power would be equivalent to the power of giving relief, which the law has vested generally in the Guardians. Any direction that the medical officer may give to this effect will not amount to more than an expression of opinion upon his part, that relief in food or other necessaries is required. No doubt such opinion is entitled to the greatest weight, both with the Guardians and their officers; and the relieving officer would in the intervals of the meeting of the Board incur serious responsibility in refusing food or other necessaries recommended by a medical officer, professedly on the ground that the health of the paupers required it.

XVI. RELIEVING OFFICER.

1. COURSE FOR HIM TO ADOPT WHEN GUARDIANS OMIT TO MEET AND TO FURNISH HIM WITH FUNDS.

31*st August*, 1843.

Clerk of Saffron-Walden Union—Inquired in what way, in case a sufficient number of Guardians should not arrive at any time to form a Board, the relieving officers could be supplied with money wherewith to pay the paupers until the next meeting of the Guardians.

Ans. No one is empowered to draw cheques upon the treasurer of the Union, except the Board of Guardians; and no one could act in their place. In such an event as that suggested, the relieving officer should relieve the poor by provisional orders for the workhouse, or by the means at his own command (such as any balance in hand), until the next meeting of the Guardians. It would, moreover, be the duty of the overseers, under the 54th section of the Poor Law Amendment Act, to provide for any cases which might arise of "sudden and urgent necessity." It is obvious that the responsibility for any defect occurring in the mode in question would rest with the Guardians themselves, and that no power of drawing money from the Union funds could be safely vested in other hands.

---

2. CANNOT BE APPOINTED BY ONE UNION TO RELIEVE PAUPERS RESIDING IN ANOTHER UNION.

24th October, 1843.

Clerk of West Ward Union—Forwarded a resolution of the Board of Guardians, appointing Mr. Thomas Castley to be relieving officer for superintending and paying the *paupers of the West Ward Union residing in Penrith*, subject to the approval of the Commissioners.

Ans. Mr. Castley, it appears, is a relieving officer of the West Ward Union, and under the proposed arrangement, would have to act in another Union, that is to say, in a district over which, territorially, the Guardians of the West Ward Union have no authority, and in which another Board of Guardians have duties to discharge in respect of the very same persons, at least whilst they continue to reside therein. This alone would appear exceedingly objectionable. He would, moreover, have to quit his own district in the West Ward Union, and thus run the risk of neglecting his duties there, as cases might arise in his own district requiring his immediate attention, at the very time he was absent attending to his duties in Penrith. It may be further remarked, that non-resident relief is not contemplated by the existing law, and appears to be inconsistent with the constant design of the statutes, which make no provision for any machinery for dispensing it. In this respect the Poor Law Amendment Act in no degree altered the law as it existed previous to that statute. The law has (very properly, as the Commissioners consider) made the persons invested with the administration of relief in the parish in which a pauper resides primarily responsible for the due relief of such pauper, if destitute, and until removed by due course of law to the parish of his settlement; and no undertaking on the part of a distant Board of Guardians can destroy the legal responsibility of any parish to relieve the destitute persons resident therein. The Commissioners, therefore, think it very inexpedient to attempt to interfere with this responsibility by any systematic arrangements for the relief of non-resident paupers, which arrangements must necessarily be incomplete and unsatisfactory, and would be contrary to the theory of the law as respects the duties of the respective Boards of Guardians and their officers. The Commissioners having regard to the above considerations, would not feel justified in sanctioning the proposed arrangement, and they request the attention of the Guardians to the enclosed Copy Minute of the Commissioners, dated 26th January, 1841, on the relief of persons not resident within their Union.—[See Seventh Annual Report, p. 106.]

XVII. REMOVAL.

1. FRESH ORDERS WHERE PAUPERS BECOME CHARGEABLE MORE THAN ONCE IN THE SAME PARISH.

3rd August, 1843.

Mr. W. H. Cave, Thatcham, Newbury Union—Stated that, in the year 1815, a pauper named Wheatland, together with his wife and one child, became chargeable to the parish of Thatcham, and were removed, under an order of justices, to the parish of Ecchingswell, now in the Kingsclere Union, such order never having been appealed against. The pauper did not remain long in Ecchingswell, but again returned to Thatcham. Within the last few months, Wheatland, together with his wife and three younger children, again became chargeable to the parish of Thatcham, and the overseers of Ecchingswell were requested to admit the settlement of the paupers. The overseers, of themselves, did not object to do this; but the Guardians of the Kingsclere Union refused to relieve the paupers. The overseers of Thatcham had applied to the justices to commit Wheatland to the house of correction as a vagrant, for having returned to Thatcham; but the justices refused to commit him, on the ground of his being afflicted with dropsy. They have also refused to grant a fresh order of removal, stating that, as the former was duly executed and not appealed against, it was conclusive and binding between the two parishes, and that a new order could not be taken out by the parish officers of Thatcham. Inquired—

1. Whether a fresh order of removal could, under the circumstances, be obtained by the overseers of Thatcham. 2. Whether the fact of the three children (then under the age of sixteen, and chargeable) not being included in the previous order of removal, would be a sufficiently good ground for the parish officers of Ecchingswell refusing to receive the pauper Wheatland and his family.? 3. Whether, if a fresh order could be obtained, the Commissioners would (should there be any other mode of proceeding) recommend the parish officers of Thatcham to take out an order, as it was liable to be appealed against, which would occasion litigation and expense. 4. Whether, in case a fresh order could be obtained, the Commissioners would advise the parish officers of Thatcham to proceed by mandamus against the parish officers of Ecchingswell; or could they in any other way be compelled to receive the paupers; or what other course would the Commissioners recommend to be adopted.

Ans. 1. It is true that the first order, unappealed against in this case, is conclusive up to the time at which it was made; but this is as matter of evidence. Its being conclusive, as regards all the world, does not prevent other orders being made for removing the pauper again to the same place, whenever he again becomes chargeable either to the parish which first removed him, or to any other parish. 2. The parish officers of Ecchingswell are not bound to receive the pauper without a fresh order of removal. The first order, which they were bound to obey, they have obeyed by receiving the pauper on the first occasion. That order was not founded on the present chargeability, and does not of itself bind them again to receive the pauper; accordingly, it does not bind them to receive the pauper's family subsequently born; but a fresh order would properly include them, if they have not obtained settlements on their own account. 3. The propriety of taking out an order depends on circumstances not known to the Commissioners. If there be no strong reasons for believing that no settlement has been gained since the last order of removal, the probability of an appeal is proportionally small; and the motive to abstain, from apprehension of appeal and expense, comparatively slight; and *vice versâ*. 4. The Commissioners do not know of any authority for proceeding against the officers of Ecchingswell by mandamus; nor do they know of any other remedy for the parish of Thatcham, under the circumstances, except a fresh order of removal.

---

2. RELIEF GIVEN WHERE ORDER OF REMOVAL MADE AND DELAYED TO BE EXECUTED BEYOND TWENTY-ONE DAYS,—BY WHICH PARISH TO BE BORNE.

2nd and 21st August, 1843.

Clerk of Rye Union—Inquired whether a parish removing paupers, under an order of justices, to their settlement parish, can, under the 79th and 84th sections of the Poor Law Amendment Act, claim from the latter parish the cost of more than the twenty-one days' maintenance of the paupers, although no notice of appeal against the order had been given, the paupers having been maintained for several weeks after the expiration of the twenty-one days prior to removal.

Ans. The Commissioners are of opinion that the removing parish cannot, under sections 79 and 84 of the Poor Law Amendment Act, be reimbursed the cost of any relief given to a pauper, under an order of removal, after the expiration of the twenty-one days. Any charge arising in such case, from the delay in executing the order of removal, after the twenty-one days, must be borne by the removing parish.

Clerk of Romney Marsh Union—Requested to be informed of the grounds upon which the Commissioners founded the opinion given in the above letter to the clerk of the Rye Union.

Ans. The 84th section of the Poor Law Amendment Act provides for the repayment of relief in those cases only in which the pauper's settlement is in question at the time of granting the relief. Consequently, where a claim is made for such repayment, the point to be ascertained is, whether the pauper's settlement was in question when the relief for which the claim is made was granted. And this is to be ascertained by reference to the 79th section. Where an order of removal is taken out, that section requires the fact to be notified to the parish of the alleged settlement, and makes the actual execution of the order contingent upon subsequent events. If the parish consent to receive the pauper, he may be removed immediately; if the parish do not give such consent, he is not to be removed until the expiration of twenty-one days; if the parish within that time give notice of appeal, he is not to be removed until the abandonment or determination of such appeal. The Commissioners think that, under this provision, whenever the twenty-one days expire without notice of appeal, or the appeal is abandoned or determined, the pauper's settlement virtually ceases to be in question, and he then becomes properly removable to the parish to which he is admitted or judged to belong. The Commissioners entertain this opinion notwithstanding the difference which exists between the consequences of these events as regards the order. The absence of notice of appeal only raises a presumption that the settlement is not questioned. The admission or final adjudication of the settlement (if on the merits) of course terminates the case. Still it would appear, that as no one has questioned the settlement, and the order is now by law operative, the settlement is not "*in question*" at the time, whatever it may be if notice of appeal is given subsequently. If the pauper be not thereupon removed, it appears to the Commissioners that the consequences of the delay (such delay not being connected with the question of settlement) must be borne by the removing parish.

---

3. CHARGE FOR MEDICAL RELIEF GIVEN UNDER A SUSPENDED ORDER OF REMOVAL, WHETHER RECOVERABLE.

3rd October, 1843.

Clerk of Hartismere Union—Stated, that amongst the charges made by the corporation of the poor of the city of Norwich, in respect of Robert Websdale and wife, who had been removed from thence to the parish of Thorndon All Saints, in the Hartismere Union, under a suspended order of removal, was one of 12*l*. 8*s*. 6*d*. for "medical attendance on Websdale and wife from February to August." The demand being an unusual one, the Board of Guardians wished the opinion of the Commissioners as to whether it could be legally enforced. By a letter of Mr. Kerrison, of Norwich, a copy of which accompanied the clerk's letter, it appeared that the charge in question had been proved upon oath before the justices, who had directed the same to be paid by the parish adverted to under the second section of the Act 35 Geo. III., c. 101.

Ans. The Guardians of Hartismere Union, on reference to the second section of the 35th Geo. III., c. 101, will perceive that the parish of Thorndon is bound to repay, if ordered by the justices to do so, the charges proved upon oath to have been incurred by the suspension of the order of removal. There can be no doubt that the medical relief afforded to the pauper is a charge incurred by Norwich in consequence of the suspension of the order. It appears from Mr. Kerrison's letter that the charge for such relief has been proved upon oath before the justices, and that the justices have ordered it to be paid by the parish officers of Thorndon. Under these circumstances the Commissioners do not see that the payment can be properly resisted, inasmuch as presuming the reasonableness of the charge to be questioned, the case is not one in which the statute 35th Geo. III., c. 101, gives the right of appeal. The fact to which you advert, that the Guardians of the Hartismere Union have never either made such charges themselves, or been subjected to them by other Unions, does not affect the legality of the claim in this particular instance. The Commissioners' regulations as to medical relief are not in force in the city of Norwich; and it is stated by Mr. Kerrison that the salaries of the medical officers for that city do not include cases of this description. The Commissioners, however, fully approve of the course pursued by the Hartismere Guardians, and they trust that no occurrence of isolated cases of this description will induce them to deviate from their present practice, except as regards surgical fees or extra payments of that nature.

XVIII. SETTLEMENT—ACQUISITION OF BY RENTING A HOUSE.

5th August, 1843.

Overseer of All Saints, York Union—Inquired, whether a woman who rented a house at upwards of 10*l*. a year, and paid the assessed taxes; but being unable to pay the whole of the rent, gave the landlord a Bible, which he considered equivalent to the amount of rent deficient, gained a settlement under these circumstances. Inquired also, if the occupier of a house, who paid a rent of 10*l*. a year as well as taxes, and let out a portion of such house in lodgings, was prevented from gaining a settlement.

Ans. 1. There is no decision on the first point. At the same time there is no reason apparent to the Commissioners why any payment by other things, of sufficient value to satisfy the rent, should not be equally a payment of the rent as a payment in money. The

Commissioners are of opinion that if the rent was satisfied by the payment of the money and the delivery of the Bible, the payment was sufficient for the purpose of the statutes relating to the acquisition of settlements by renting a tenement. 2. The underletting of a portion of a house as lodgings, does, since the 30th March, 1831, prevent the occupier of the house from acquiring a settlement by renting such house: Rex *v.* St. Nicholas, Rochester, 5 B. and Ad. 209.

XIX. TREASURERS — APPOINTMENT OF, FOR EACH PARISH IN THE UNION.

24th August, 1843.

Clerk of Carnarvon Union.—Stated, that the Guardians wished the Commissioners' permission to appoint a treasurer for each of the parishes in the Union, instead of one for the whole Union; so that those parishes which have no money in hand may not make use of the money of those that have, for the relief of their paupers.

Ans. The Commissioners cannot consent to the appointment of a Union treasurer for each parish for such portion of the funds as are paid into the Guardians' hands; but the overseers of each parish may keep an account at any bank they may please as regards the funds in their own hands. The order of the Commissioners, under which Union officers are appointed, only authorises the appointment of one treasurer for the Union, and it is not competent for the Guardians to appoint more. Any money paid into other hands than those of the treasurer lawfully appointed, would be improperly paid, and individual responsibility would be incurred by any parties co-operating in so paying monies to unauthorised persons. No such inconvenience, as the Guardians appear to refer to, would exist, if the Guardians cause the necessary funds to be paid in for each parish as they are wanted; and there is nothing to prevent their directing the clerk to state, at each meeting of the Board, the balance for or against each parish, when the Guardians will be enabled, should there be no funds in the hands of the treasurer, on account of any individual parish, to make fresh calls upon the overseers of that parish, if necessary, or to proceed against them to enforce payment of the calls already made.

XX. WORKHOUSE.

LETTERS, ETC., TRANSMITTED TO WORKHOUSE INMATES—CONTROL OF UNION OFFICERS IN RESPECT TO.

16th October, 1843.

Clerk of the —— Union—Stated, that the attention of a member of the visiting committee having been called to a letter addressed to one of the inmates of the Union workhouse, that gentleman was induced to open it, and the circumstance having been discussed by the Board of Guardians, the Board passed the following resolution in regard thereto:—"That the letter now produced addressed by —— to —— be forwarded to the Poor Law Commissioners, with a request that they will instruct the Board whether the terms of the said letter are such as justified the detention and opening of it, and also whether money may be received weekly by the inmates of the workhouses from any of their friends or relatives."

Ans. The Commissioners are of opinion, that there was no right on the part of the master or other authorities of the workhouse to open the letter. The case does not come within Art. 26 of the workhouse rules, or Art. 79, No. 5, and the Commissioners cannot but disapprove of the letter having been opened. It is the master's duty to prevent any opportunities for improper conduct on the part of any inmate presenting themselves while the party is in the workhouse. But there is nothing to prohibit the transmission of letters to the inmates under ordinary circumstances. As to the receipt of money transmitted to inmates of the workhouse by any of their friends and relatives, the master has no power to seize the money; but he should report the fact of its receipt by a pauper to the Guardians, who will determine whether the person in possession of it is destitute in such a sense as to be entitled to continue an inmate of the workhouse. No opportunities for spending the money in any manner inconsistent with the discipline of the workhouse can occur while the rules for the government of the workhouse are duly observed.

LONDON:

Printed by Order of the Poor Law Commissioners, by W. CLOWES and SONS, Stamford Street, and Published by CHARLES KNIGHT and Co., 22, Ludgate Street, Publishers to the Poor Law Commissioners.

AN

OFFICIAL CIRCULAR

OF PUBLIC DOCUMENTS AND INFORMATION:

DIRECTED BY THE POOR LAW COMMISSIONERS TO BE PRINTED, CHIEFLY FOR THE USE OF THE MEMBERS AND PERMANENT OFFICERS OF BOARDS OF GUARDIANS, UNDER THE POOR LAW AMENDMENT ACT.

No. 30. CIRCULAR ISSUED DECEMBER 30, 1843.

Poor Law Commission Office,
Somerset House,
December 30, 1843.

THE Poor Law Commissioners, on a review of their Correspondence, directed that the following abstract thereof should be printed and circulated for the information of Guardians and Officers of the several Unions, viz.:—

By order of the Board,
EDWIN CHADWICK, *Secretary.*

I. ACCOUNTS. — LIABILITY OF PARISH, WHERE PAUPER IS CHARGEABLE, FOR MEDICAL RELIEF.

9th November, 1843.

Mr. Gilbert, District Auditor—Stated that a young woman, living in the parish of Sevenoaks, with her father, who is an acknowledged parishioner of Kemsing, and who, it is alleged, has never been from under his roof, was taken suddenly in labour, and was in danger of losing her life. An order for the medical officer was applied for, and immediately given by the overseers of Sevenoaks. The case proved to be an extremely difficult one, and the medical officer claimed the fee of 2*l.* under Article 13, of

General Medical Order, which the Guardians, under the circumstances of the case, have allowed; and they are about to charge the parish of Kemsing with the amount. But the Guardian for that parish objects, on the ground that no order of removal has been obtained by the parish of Sevenoaks. The auditor has been asked, whether, if the expense is charged to Kemsing, and the charge is objected to before him at the audit, as an illegal charge upon that parish, he should admit the objection. It is urged, that the Board of Guardians, having all the powers of overseers under the old law to relieve, can charge the expense of any pauper in the Union to any parish which the pauper may appear to them to belong to. The auditor replied, that he considered the Board of Guardians undoubtedly had that power where there were no objecting parties; but that in this case one of the parishes interested did object; and that as under the old law no parish could be compelled to relieve out of the parish, unless under an order of removal, he conceived this exemption was not taken from them in the case alluded to, particularly as the case of the young woman may not be regarded as an entirely new case, distinct from that of her father; and, therefore, he considered that it must be looked upon as a casualty belonging to Sevenoaks, and the expense charged to that parish. Requested the Commissioners' opinion on the point.

Ans. It would have been desirable if there had been sufficient time, that the Commissioners should have been informed whether before, and at the occasion for the medical relief to the woman, the father was in receipt of relief; and whether that relief was granted in contemplation of the burden of maintaining his family, including the daughter whose case gives rise to the question. Before the particulars of this case are considered, it is proper to state the Commissioners' general views upon the principle applicable to the whole class of such cases. There is no doubt of the liability of each parish to relieve primarily at its own charge the destitute poor resident therein. Consequently, where proper relief in a case of destitution is given to a non-settled, but resident pauper, it is perfectly lawful, and the auditor, although he has cognizance of the case to judge of the reasonableness in amount, and of the lawfulness of the relief, could not lawfully disallow the relief on the ground of the non-settlement of the pauper. On the other hand, the power to give relief to a person settled and destitute, but not resident, (assuming that the power does exist,) is a discretionary one; and it is not a compulsory legal obligation. In giving such relief, Guardians and other competent officers are bound to act with caution. It is obviously proper that in such a case they should not act contrary to the views of the parish officers more particularly interested in the question of settlement, without having good reasons for what they do. In this case, since the *primâ facie* ground of residence in the parish to which the relief is charged would be wanting, the auditor, although approving of the kind and amount of relief, would, if satisfied that the Guardians had improperly charged the alleged parish of the settlement, be bound to disallow the charge as against that parish. As regards the particular case, if the father was receiving such relief at the expense of the parish of Kemsing, the increased necessity of the daughter, involving a necessity for additional relief of another kind, did not make a new case; and the Guardians, if justified before in giving outdoor non-resident relief to the family, at the expense of the parish of Kemsing, were justified also in giving the increased relief required by the daughter, at the expense of the same parish. But if no relief were at the time given to the father, in consideration of his family, there appears to be good ground for considering the necessity of the daughter as constituting a new case for relief. In this case the necessity arises in the parish of Sevenoaks, which is legally bound to relieve it, while the parish of the settlement is certainly not under the same legal obligation, the person being non-resident. Assuming that before the Poor Law Amendment Act, the overseers had the legal power of relieving a non-resident case, although not bound to do so, it only remains to consider, whether the Board of Guardians, in their collective capacity, have the same power as overseers formerly exercised in this respect. The Commissioners think it is almost certain, that whatever lawful power of this description the overseers had, the Guardians, subject to the regulations of the Commissioners, may now exercise. Then do the objections made by the Guardians of the particular parish of the alleged settlement diminish that power? The Commissioners think that it does not, but that every Guardian has an equal and undistinguishable power with respect to all the parishes in the Union, as well that which he is elected to represent as those for which he is not elected, except with regard to special matters expressly specified in the Poor Law Amendment Act.

The Commissioners, therefore, think that if the case is one which requires relief, and if the pauper was previously receiving relief at the expense of the parish, the Guardians were, according to the ordinary practice, justified in increasing the relief at the expense of the same parish. Also, if not previously receiving such relief, but if the pauper is clearly settled in such parish, the Commissioners think, though not so confidently, that the Guardians have the same authority as overseers previously exercised of giving non-resident relief at the expense of the parish of the settlement.

But if the parish, at the expense of which the relief is given by the Guardians, be neither the parish of the settlement, nor of the pauper's residence, both the *primâ facie* grounds for the charge referred to above would appear to fail, and the Guardians would seem to have no power to give relief at the charge of the parish. In this case, it would seem to be the duty of the auditor to disallow the relief given, as charged against that parish, especially if objections were made on the part of any ratepayer.

II. APPRENTICESHIP.—EXPENCE OF INDENTURE OF PARISH APPRENTICE, AND PARTIES THERETO.

4th December, 1843.

Clerk of Eastry Union—Stated that an orphan boy, aged 13, had been sent from the Union workhouse to a grocer and outfitter at Ramsgate, with a view to his being ultimately apprenticed. The boy and the master having had some trial of each other, were desirous of executing the necessary indentures of apprenticeship. An expense of 30*s*. must be incurred for the indenture, which will carry a 20*s*. stamp. Inquired, first, whether the Guardians can defray the cost of the indenture, beyond the usual allowance for clothing granted to children whose condition requires it on their leaving the workhouse for service: secondly, whether the Board of Guardians must be a party to the indenture, and if so, whether they can, under the 17th section of the 5 and 6 Vic., c. 57, empower one of their officers to execute the indenture on their behalf: or, thirdly, whether the parish officers were the parties who should join in the indenture.

Ans. The Commissioners see no objection, under the circumstances, to the Guardians allowing the cost of the indenture beyond the usual allowance of clothing to children who leave the workhouse for service. But assuming that the Guardians are at the charge of providing the indenture and the clothing, the case is not one in which any stamp duty is payable, as the 40th section of 8 Anne, c. 9, provides that the stamp duties shall not extend to cases in which the apprentice is placed out at the common, or public, charge of any parish or township. A further consequence of the proposed provision from the poor-rates would be, that the indenture would require to be allowed by the justices. The 56 Geo. III., c. 139, s. 11, enacts, that no indenture, by reason of which any expense shall be incurred by the parochial funds, shall be valid unless approved by two justices under their hands and seals, according to the provisions of that Act, and the Act of 43 Eliz. With respect to the second and third inquiries, I am to observe, that the Commissioners understand the proposed binding to be a voluntary one on the part of the apprentice, and not a binding by the parish. If so, the apprentice must execute the deed; and the execution by the overseers will not be necessary. If the case were that of a binding by the parish, the overseers, and not the Guardians, would still be the proper parties to the indenture. The overseers could not, however, since the passing of 4 and 5 Wm. IV., c. 76, in any case lawfully incur any cost at the charge of the poor-rates, in respect of the apprenticeship of a poor person, unless the Guardians had sanctioned the proceedings; apprenticeship being relief, and the administration of relief being, by the 54th section of the above statute, vested in the Guardians.

III. BASTARDY.—DEMAND UPON PUTATIVE FATHER PRIOR TO ENFORCEMENT.

6th November, 1843.

Clerk of Chertsey Union—Stated that the father of a bastard child, on whom an order for the payment of 3*s*. per week had been made, had left that part of the country. The Board of Guardians being about to take proceedings to obtain the arrears then due, wished to be informed whether ulterior proceedings by warrant, distress, &c. could be taken before the arrears due have been demanded by the overseers.

Ans. Although the ordinary practice, and that which appears to the Commissioners the expedient one, is to demand of the putative father the sums due under an order of justices, before any proceeding is taken to compel payment, the Commissioners do not perceive, with reference to the 76th section of the Poor Law Amendment Act, that such demand is legally requisite. It would seem that under that section, the fact of the payments directed by the order to be made not having been made (if such fact is made to appear upon the oath of the Overseers or Guardians), is sufficient to enable the justices to proceed to issue the warrant to cause the reputed father to be brought before them. The warrant, in such case, would be in the nature of a demand, and would, on its return, enable the putative father to show that he had paid, or that he was not liable, or make any other defence which the circumstances of the case might allow of. Then if, upon the hearing, the parties should see fit to issue the warrant of distress, the whole proceeding would have been in conformity with the general principle of law, viz., that a person should not be punished (the warrant of distress being in the nature of an execution) until he has had the opportunity of being heard. Where the order directs the payments to be made to the Guardians, the Guardians can empower the overseers, or any of their officers, to receive the sums which may from time to time become due.

IV. CONSTABLES.—CONSTRUCTION OF SECTION 17 of 5 AND 6 VICT. c. 109. (PARISH CONSTABLES' ACT.)

The following is a case submitted by the Poor Law Commissioners to the Solicitor-General and Mr. Tomlinson, as to what fees are properly payable to parish constables out of poor's-rate, under the 17th section of the 5 and 6 Vict., c. 109, together with the opinion of those gentlemen thereon:—

"The Act 5 and 6 Vict., c. 109, contains the following provision for the payment of parish constables appointed in pursuance of that statute:—

"Section 17. That the justices of the county in general or quarter sessions assembled, shall from time to time, subject to the approval of one of Her Majesty's principal Secretaries of State, settle tables of fees and allowances to the clerks to the justices for the performance of their duties under this Act, and to the constables for the service of summonses and execution of warrants, and for the performance of such other occasional duties which may be required of the said constables, for which the said justices shall think that fees ought to be allowed, and whenever any duty for which any such fee or allowance shall have been settled, and for which the payment is not by law charged upon the county rates, shall have been performed by any clerk, or by any constable appointed under this Act, the amount of the fee or allowance shall be paid by the overseers of *the parish in respect of which such fee has become payable* out of any monies in their hands collected for the relief of the poor, upon the order of the justices in petty sessions assembled for the division, and under such regulations as shall be made from time to time by the justices in general or quarter session assembled, subject to the approval of the Secretary of State.

"Upon this section a question arises, whether the fees payable to the constables under the above provisions, are, when not chargeable on the county rates, to be paid out of the poor-rate in *all* cases; or whether they are to be so paid in those cases in which the constables' services have been required in a matter of parochial concern.

"In favour of the latter view, it is to be observed, that the section provides for the payment of the fee by the overseers of the parish in respect of which 'such fee has become payable.' It is, perhaps, difficult to conceive on what ground the fee can become payable 'in respect of the parish,' except as being due on account of services required and rendered specifically on behalf of the parish. Suppose A. assaults B. in the parish of C., B. complains to a magistrate, who issues his warrant for the apprehension of A. A. is taken by the constable of C. before two magistrates, who convict him in a penalty of 20*s.*, which is paid by A.; the magistrates at the same time make an order on the overseers of C. professedly under the 5 and 6 Vict., c. 109, s. 17, for the payment from the poor-rates of the constables' fee for the apprehension of A. Can the constables' fee in such a case be said to be payable 'in respect of the parish?' And how can any distinction be drawn on this point between the constables' fee and the costs of the magistrates' clerk?

"If this construction of the phrase in question be correct, it seems to follow, that the constables' fees are payable from the poor-rates, only when the constables' services have been required in parochial matters, and it may be presumed, that in other cases the fees will be payable by the particular parties at whose instance the constables may have been employed.

"Upon this point, the case of *Rex* v. *Bird*, 2 *B. & A.* 522, and *Rex* v. *Seville*, 5 *B. & A.* 180, which arose upon the 18 Geo. III. c. 19, s. 4. (passed expressly for the better indemnification of constables, the charges incurred by them in doing the business of the *parish or township*,) may be referred to as a judicial interpretation of what is to be considered the matter or business of the parish. In the former case, the costs incurred in prosecuting an assault committed on the constable in the execution of his office, were held not to be sums expended *on account of the parish.*

"In favour of the view, that the constables' fees when not chargeable upon the county, are payable from the poor-rates in all cases, it is contended, that parish constables were originally unremunerated officers; but one of the objects of the 5 and 6 Vict., c. 109, was, as expressed in its title and preamble, to make provision for their remuneration, and that the 17th section, in making such provision, refers in specific terms to the poor-rate alone, save in so far as it creates an exception with regard to the county rate. It is therefore inferred, that the intention of the legislature was to cast upon the poor-rate (with the exception above mentioned), the charge of the constables' compensation, and that the expression 'the parish in respect of which such fee has become payable,' must be read as equivalent to the words, 'the parish for which the constable is appointed.' It is moreover maintained, that the 18th, 19th, and 20th sections of the Act, which provide for the appointment of parish constables with salaries, and for the payment of such salaries out of the poor-rates, are confirmatory of the foregoing view. It is thought, that as the salaried constables will be paid for the whole of their duties out of the poor-rates, the same fund was probably intended to be charged in the case of constables remunerated by fees.

"It may, however, be argued on the other hand, that as no mention of the poor-rates, or indeed of any source of payment whatever is made in the title or preamble, the intention of the legislature as to the fund or party to be charged, can be gathered only from the body of the statute, and that although the poor-rate alone is expressly charged in the 17th section, the extent of the charge thus cast upon it is nevertheless limited by the phrase 'in respect of the parish,' and that such limitation cannot be legitimately held to include matters which are not of parochial concern. It may, moreover, be remarked, that the argument deduced from the analogy of the provisions in sections 18, 20, being merely an argument from analogy, is of course by no means conclusive; that different intentions may be readily conceived as existing, in regard to the two modes of payment, and that the adoption of the system of remuneration by fees may have been designed as a means of fixing the charge on the parties actually concerned in each individual case. It may be added, that this system is prescribed by the Act as the one for general adoption, while the payment by salary is admissible only under certain conditions. Again, supposing that the fees demandable by the constable according to the table are payable *out of the poor-rates*, how, or upon what principle is the liability of a particular parish to pay such fees to be ascertained! Is it the parish for which the constable is appointed, the parish in which the offence is committed, or the parish in which the offender is apprehended? By the 15th section of 5 and 6 Vict., c. 109, a constable may act not only in any part of the county in which the parish for which he is appointed is situated, but also in every county adjoining thereto. Suppose the constable of A. is called upon to act in the parish of B., which he does, and ultimately apprehends the offender in C. In such case, which of the parishes, A., B., or C., is to be considered the parish '*in respect of which the fee has become payable?*'

"You are requested to advise,

"*First.* Whether, under the 17th section of the above cited Act, the fees payable to parish constables are, when not chargeable on the county rates, to be paid out of the poor-rates in all cases, or in those cases only in which the constables services *are rendered in matters of parochial concern.*

"*Secondly.* Assuming that the poor-rates

are liable in all cases, how is that liability to be determined as between different parishes concerned ?

"OPINION.

"We are of opinion that all the fees which are payable to parish constables under the 17th section of the above cited Act, are, when not chargeable on the county rates, to be paid out of the poor-rates. The only exception which runs through the section is of the duties for which the payment is by law chargeable upon the county rate. Subject to this exception, the constables are to be paid for the service of summons and execution of warrants without reference to the subject matter to which they apply, and for the performance of such other occasional duties required of them as the justices shall think ought to be compensated by fees. The only limitation here is the discretion of the justices. The reference to the parishes who are to pay does not appear to have been intended to qualify the preceding enactment with respect to the subject-matter for which fees were to be paid to constables by parishes, but only to point out the particular parish upon which the liability is to be fixed. No power is given to settle a scale of fees as between constables and individuals setting them in motion, and the preamble shows that the intention was by rewarding constables to increase the security of persons and property generally. This object would be defeated if the payment to constables were limited to parochial concerns.

"*Secondly.* The general intention of the legislature, as indicated by the preamble and other sections of the Act, appears to have been to tax the parochial funds of each parish for the security of persons and property within such parish; but it is impossible to lay down any rule of construction of universal application for determining the liability as between different parishes concerned. Reference must be had in each particular case as it arises to the table of fees and allowances, and the duties for the performance of which they may be allowed, as applicable to the services performed, and the peculiar circumstances under which they may have been performed.

(Signed "W. W. FOLLETT.
T. TOMLINSON.

"*Temple,* 1*st December*, 1843."

V. LUNATIC PAUPERS—VISITATION OF, WHEN IN LUNATIC ASYLUM.

9*th November*, 1843.

Clerk of Alnwick Union—Forwarded the following resolution passed by the Board of Guardians, and requested the Commissioners' approval thereof:—" That a medical officer or officers be appointed to inspect from time to time the paupers belonging to this Union who shall be in a lunatic asylum, and report to the Board their condition."

Ans. The Guardians, if they think fit, can agree with any medical man to inspect and report to them on the state of the lunatic paupers belonging to the Union who are confined in asylums; and the Commissioners approve of such a course; but they do not think that the Guardians can appoint officers specially for such a purpose: the main result, however, in either case is the same.

VI. MEDICAL OFFICER.

1. INSUFFICIENT ATTENDANCE.

22*nd December*, 1843.

Sheffield Union—The Commissioners having on the 17th November received from the registrar for the district of South Sheffield, Barkerpool, a certificate of the death of Fanny Blackburn, from want of sufficient food, requested the Board of Guardians to inquire into the circumstances under which her death occurred. On the 24th November, a meeting of the relief committee of the Guardians was held for this purpose, when the following evidence was taken by them:—

William Blundell, of Sheffield, relieving officer, stated that on the 15th September last deceased applied to him for relief, her husband being in Beverley prison. She was relieved on her first application with 1*s.* in money, and six pounds of bread; and again on witness visiting the case. The relief ordered by the Guardians on the Wednesday following was 2*s.*, and 12 pounds of bread per week. Deceased never applied to come into the workhouse, and did not complain to witness of being unwell till the 2nd October, when she asked for a note to the medical officer, which witness gave her. No complaint was ever made that deceased or her family suffered from want of food. About the 30th October application was made for a nurse, whom witness sent; but before she arrived at the house the woman was dead. The husband returned before the death of his wife, and made application in his own behalf. Relief was ordered, but was never paid. The woman died on the 2nd, and witness furnished a coffin and funeral dues. The husband stated, that he did not expect his wife to die so suddenly, and never mentioned that she had wanted food.—*John Porter, surgeon,* stated that on the 3rd October he received Mr. Blundell's note; saw deceased the same day; reported her case, and ordered medicine. He saw her again on the 8th, and again on the 13th, at the workhouse dispensary, where he also saw her on the 24th. He visited her at her own house on the 26th, when she was confined to bed. On the 29th (Sunday), witness saw her again at her own house. He ordered medicine for her on the 31st, but is not certain that he saw her at that time. He called on the 2nd November, and found her dead. Does not remember that she asked for better support. Witness would have ordered it if he had thought it necessary. He has no doubt that she died from ulceration of the bowels.—*Ann Beckett,* sister of deceased, stated that she saw her nearly every day for 10 days previously to her death. She complained of violent pain and purging. Witness gave her 2*s*., but she did not complain of want of food, and witness does not believe that she died from that cause.—*Mary Selby,* a neighbour, stated that she saw her every day for some weeks before she died. Witness thinks she was badly off, but did not die from want of sufficient food.—*John Blackburn,* the husband, stated that on the 19th October he came home, and received the relief ordered for his wife and children, and believes relief was ordered for himself on his going to work; but from his wife's illness he stayed at home with her. He told the registrar that she died from "clamming and trouble of mind." Witness now believes that she died from the bowel complaint, and not of starvation. The Commissioners, on receiving this evidence, requested that they might be supplied with a copy of the entries in the medical officer's weekly report of his visits to the deceased between the 3rd October and her death; together with a fuller history of the case, and of his attendance upon it, than was given in his evidence; and that he would explain why he did not visit her between the 3rd and 8th of October, the 8th and 13th, the 13th and 24th, the 29th and her death. Moreover, that he would state precisely on which days he visited her at her own house. The Guardians accordingly transmitted to the Commissioners a copy of such weekly report, together with the following explanation of the medical officer:—"I received an order to attend Fanny Blackburn on Tuesday, October 3rd; this order was presented by Fanny Blackburn herself at the workhouse dispensary, where attendance is given twice a week (viz. Tuesday and Friday) by the medical officers, when all those patients who are able to attend are required to do so, and are prescribed for. She was labouring under diarrhœa and debility, and had not been well for some weeks. I prescribed medicine for her, and gave her a card, on which was specified the days when out-patients are required to attend. She attended again on Friday, October 6th. She neglected attending on the following Tuesday, but came on Friday, October 13th, when she was prescribed for. She did not attend again at the dispensary, nor did I hear anything of her until the 24th, when I was requested to see her at her own house, which I did, and found her very much reduced from diarrhœa. I prescribed medicine, and visited her again on the 26th; medicine seemed to have no effect, though the most powerful remedies had been employed to check the diarrhœa. I again visited her on the 29th, the case was hopeless. On the 31st, I either prescribed medicine or visited her at her house, but I cannot positively state which; I called on the morning of the 2nd of November, and I found she had died a short time before my visit." The Commissioners on consideration of the case addressed to the Guardians the following letter:—

The Commissioners observe that the patient was labouring under diarrhœa and debility; that she was requested (as is stated to be the case with all paupers able to do so) to come to the workhouse dispensary for advice and medicine, where the medical officers attend two days in the week; that she attended on Friday, October 6, neglected attending on the following Tuesday, but came on Friday the 13th, after which she did not attend again; but that the medical officer, on a request being conveyed to him to see her at her own home, visited her on the 24th October, and found her much reduced; that he saw or prescribed for her three times afterwards, and that she died on the 2nd November. The Commissioners think this explanation by no means satisfactory, and they can come to no other conclusion than that the woman had not sufficient medical attendance. Under the Commissioners' General Medical Order, Art. 14, the medical officer is bound to visit and attend personally the poor persons entrusted to his care. The practice which is pursued in the Sheffield Union, of requiring the patients to come to the workhouse is certainly not a full compliance with this rule. In chronic, or slight cases of illness, such a practice may not be objectionable. But when it is borne in mind that in such a complaint as Fanny Blackburn was suffering from, the patient was left unseen and unprescribed for, probably at the most critical time, from the 13th to the 24th of October, it is evident that the system does not ensure in all cases adequate medical relief. It appears, indeed, that application was not made to the medical officer to attend the pauper at her own house until the 24th, and that he then attended immediately. This exonerates the officer in a great measure from a charge of neglect. Had it been otherwise, the Commissioners would have been under the necessity of taking more serious notice of the case. The Commissioners request, however, that the Board of Guardians will draw the attention of the medical officers to the rule requiring them personally to visit the sick poor entrusted to their care. Should evil consequences ensue in any case from a neglect to comply with this rule, the Commissioners could not admit as an excuse for such neglect that the medical officer had acted in pursuance of the practice usually followed in the Sheffield Union.

——

2. THE ORDERING OF RELIEF IN KIND TO SICK PAUPERS BY MEDICAL OFFICERS.

5th December, 1843.

St. Faith's Union.—The Board of Guardians of the St. Faith's Union having reported to the Commissioners certain resolutions passed by them, relative to the ordering of relief in kind to sick paupers, the Commissioners have deemed it advisable to publish the same for the information of the Boards of Guardians of other Unions.

Resolutions: "That all relief in kind to the sick poor be ordered in future by the Board of Guardians according to the recommendations in the weekly reports of the medical officers, subject to the following exceptions only, viz.:

1st. Urgent cases of sickness, where such relief shall be considered necessary by the medical officers, previous to the next meeting of the Guardians.

2ndly. Extreme urgent cases of sickness, where any medical officer, on visiting any sick person, considers such relief to be immediately required.

" In the first case, the relief to be given on a recommendation of a medical officer, through an order made by the relieving officer or the overseer of the parish in which the person to whom such relief is recommended resides; and in the second case, the relief required to be ordered by the medical officer himself. And that the medical officers be required to enter in their weekly reports all cases of relief in kind which had been recommended through the relieving officers or overseers, or ordered by themselves."

The Board of Guardians, on passing the above resolutions, addressed a letter to each medical officer of the Union, setting forth the resolutions and conveying instructions for carrying the same into effect. The following is an extract from the letter:—

"As much inconvenience might possibly result to the sick poor from any accidental irregularity, either on the part of the medical officer, or the Board in recommending, or ordering this form of relief, it is unnecessary to remind you, that the greatest attention will be necessary in forwarding regularly, your weekly report to this Board for their inspection and guidance; and in stating therein particularly, the kind and quantity of such relief, which may be recommended by you for any patient or patients under your care for the following week, or such other period of time as you may name.

" In all cases of urgency where relief in kind has been recommended through an order by the relieving officer or overseer, or received by your own order, it is the desire of the Board that the same should be entered in your weekly reports."

The following is the form of order for relief in kind for sick paupers, used in the St. Faith's Union:—

No. ____
To Mr. ____
of ____
for ____
of ____

MEAT ORDER.

for ____ weeks.

____ Medical Officer.

No. ____ SAINT FAITH'S UNION.

To Mr. ____
Butcher, ____

On delivery of this Order, you are requested to supply ____ ____ of ____ (being Sick), ____ lbs. of Mutton during the Week ending Tuesday next, and a *similar* quantity per Week for the ____ *Weeks following.*

By Order of the Board of Guardians,

Board Room, Union House ____ 184

____
Chairman, Clerk, or Relieving Officer.

Note.—This and all similar Orders for Meat, Porter, Wine, &c., must be returned to the Relieving Officer of the District, with the Tradesmen's Bills for the same, during the first week of every Quarter, that they may be immediately discharged.

No.
To Mr. ____
of ____
for ____
of ____

PORTER & WINE ORDER.

for ____ weeks.

____ Medical Officer.

No. ____ SAINT FAITH'S UNION.

To Mr. ____
Publican ____

On delivery of this Order, you are requested to supply ____ ____ of ____ (being Sick),

____ pints of Porter, ____ pints of Wine during the Week ending Tuesday next, and a *similar* quantity per Week for the ____ *Weeks following.*

By Order of the Board of Guardians,

Board Room, Union House, ____ 184

____
Chairman, Clerk, or Relieving Officer.

Note.—This and all similar Orders for Meat, Porter, Wine, &c., must be returned to the Relieving Officer of the District, with the Tradesmen's Bills for the same, during the first week of every Quarter, that they may be immediately discharged.

VII. MEDICAL RELIEF.—FEES UNDER ART. 10 OF MEDICAL ORDER TO WHOM CHARGED.

15*th November*, 1843.

Clerk of Lymington Union—Stated that since the General Medical Order came into operation, the medical officers (who were under contracts to attend to all cases within their districts, except vaccination and midwifery cases), claim to be paid, in addition to their salaries, which continue the same as before, the sums mentioned in article 10 of the Order for the cases there enumerated, and as several of those cases have occurred, a considerable increase has taken place in the expense of medical relief in the Union. The following cases have occurred within the six months from the 25th March, 1843:—Widow M'Donald, belonging to the parish of Lymington, fractured arm, 1*l.*; John Whitehorn's son, belonging to the parish of Lymington, fractured arm, 1*l.*; Edward Croucher, belonging to the parish of Milford, fractured collar-bone, 1*l.*; John Colborne's son, belonging to the parish of Boldre, fractured collar-bone, 1*l.*;

John Cooper's child, non-parishioner, fractured thigh, 3*l.*; Thomas Gregory's son, belonging to the parish of Boldre, fractured arm, 1*l.*; Joseph Matthews's son, non-parishioner, compound fracture of thigh, 5*l.*; William Sherry's child, non-parishioner, fractured thigh, 3*l.*; John Sibley's child, non-parishioner, fractured thigh, 3*l.*—Inquired, 1. Whether the medical officer could make any claim in respect of a pauper not belonging to the Union, where the case occurred within it.—2. If he could, whether the amount paid could be claimed from the parish to which the pauper belonged, without an order of removal being obtained.—3. If it could not be claimed without an order of removal, whether it was such relief as would authorize an application for an order, and whether, if an order should be obtained subsequently to the payment by the Union, the amount could be recovered under the order.—4. If such relief would authorize an application for an order of removal, but could not be recovered under an order subsequently obtained, whether on the order being given to the medical officer to attend the case of a non-parishioner, an order to remove him could be obtained and its execution suspended, and the medical relief then recovered under such order.—5. And if the medical relief could not be recovered from the parish to which the pauper belonged, on which parish ought the payment in the case of Matthews's son, above named, to fall,—the accident having taken place in the parish of Milford, but the pauper's residence being in the parish of Lymington, and he having been removed to Lymington immediately after the accident occurred, and attended by the medical officer of the latter parish.

Ans. 1. The payments contemplated by article 10 of the General Medical Order of the Commissioners, are to be made in respect of "any out-door paupers for whom the services of the medical officers are rendered; whether such paupers be settled in any parish within the Union or not." 2. The amounts so paid cannot be recovered from the parish of the pauper's settlement, where an order of removal has not been obtained, unless a previous undertaking to repay the charge has been entered into on behalf of such parish. 3. If the pauper receiving this description of relief is not a casual pauper, his chargeability arising from the reception of such relief, would be a sufficient ground for an order of removal. But relief given to him prior to the making of the order, would not be recoverable from the parish of his settlement, except in pursuance of such an undertaking as that above referred to. 4. As soon as the pauper becomes chargeable to the parish, an application may be made for an order of removal. If such an order be made and suspended, "the charges proved upon oath to have been incurred by such suspension," may, under 35 Geo. III., c. 101, s. 2, be recovered from the parish of the settlement. 5. Assuming that Matthew's son was taken without fraud to his father's house in Lymington, as being the most proper place to which, under the circumstances, he could be taken, his relief on the authority of Lamb *v.* Bunce (4 M. and S. 275,) would be chargeable to Lymington. That case decided that there is no exclusive liability to give relief attaching to the parish where the accident occurs; but that the law raises an obligation against the parish where the pauper lies sick to look to the supply of his necessities. The Commissioners desire to add (with reference to the cases of Edward Croucher and John Colborne's son,) that none of the fees mentioned in article 10 applies to the treatment of a fractured collar bone.

VIII. OVERSEERS. — PROCEEDINGS TO COMPEL PAYMENT OF CONTRIBUTIONS.

5th December, 1843.

Clerk of Torrington Union—Stated that the overseers to some of the parishes in the Union, not situate in the petty sessional division in which the Board of Guardians meet, neglect to pay their contributions; and inquired whether the overseers could legally be summoned to attend at the petty sessions for that division, instead of at petty sessions held within the divisions in which such parishes are situate.

Ans. The question refers apparently to proceedings under the 4th and 5th Will. IV., c. 76, s. 95, or ss. 98 and 99. Overseers may be summoned to answer for their disobedience under these sections, before any two justices having jurisdiction within the county; and not exclusively before the justices of the petty sessional division in which their parish is situated. But the 2nd and 3rd Vict., c. 54, for compelling payment of arrears, is not so clear in its designation of the justices to act at special sessions. There appears, however, to be nothing in that Act to confine the jurisdiction to the justices of the division in which the parish is situate, or to exclude the jurisdiction of justices assembled anywhere within the county.

IX. POOR-RATE.

1. POWER OF JUSTICES TO ORDER THE PAYMENT OF COSTS ON COMMITMENT FOR NON-PAYMENT OF POOR-RATE.

7th November, 1843.

Clerk of Stourbridge Union—Stated that in the several parishes composing the Union great difficulty had arisen in collecting the poor-rate from the small rate payers, in consequence of a doubt existing as to the power of the justices to order the payment of costs on the commitment of a person for non-payment of his poor-rate, and upon whose goods no sufficient distress could be levied. The Act of the 43 Eliz., c. 2, which gives authority to justices to commit in default of sufficient distress, says nothing in regard to costs; and the justices had great doubt whether the 18 Geo. III., c. 19, which gives justices power to award costs in summary proceedings, is applicable to the present case; and, therefore, decline to order costs in the warrant of commitment. Requested the Commissioners' opinion on the subject.

Ans. Except that a doubt was entertained by the justices on this subject, the Poor Law Commissioners would have entertained none. The Commissioners will not enter upon the general question, whether, under the statute of Elizabeth, which provides for the levy, not only of the said sums of money rated, but also of all arrearages, the costs incurred by default of the offender, are not recoverable by the operation of the statutes relating to costs generally. It appears sufficient for the purpose to consider the statute of the 18 Geo. III., c. 19, s. 1. That statute provides for the award of costs by justices, in cases which the Commissioners are not able to distinguish in any respect from the present; the application is a "*complaint;*" the two justices act "*out of sessions;*" in the cases described, "*a warrant issues*" in consequence of the complaint. There appears, therefore, to be full authority to the same justices to make their award of costs under the statute. The Commissioners think it desirable, as the committal of the offender differs under the two statutes, that the several determinations on the 43 Eliz. and on the 18 Geo. III., should be kept distinct.

2. LIABILITY OF THE POOR-RATE TO BEAR THE COST OF TAKING A POLL ON DISCONTINUING THE PROVISIONS OF THE WATCHING AND LIGHTING ACT.

8th November, 1843.

Clerk of Settle Union—Stated that a poll had been taken by the churchwardens of the town of Settle, as to whether the provisions of the Watching and Lighting Act, 3 and 4 Will. IV., c. 7, (which had been in operation three years,) should be continued; and various expenses had thereby been incurred; an account of which had been sent in by the churchwardens to the overseers. The Board of Guardians, to whom the overseer brought the accounts, had declined to interfere in the matter, and there was a probability that the churchwardens would institute proceedings against the overseer if the accounts were not paid. Forwarded copies of the accounts, and requested the opinion of the Commissioners as to what amount ought to be paid to the churchwardens.

Ans. If the poll above referred to had been the original poll taken to ascertain the determination of the parish to adopt, or not to adopt, the provisions of the Lighting and Watching Act, there would be no doubt that the lawful expenses of taking the poll would be payable out of the poor-rates. But once adopted, the Act continuing in force without any determination so to continue it, the determination to continue must be on a question whether the Act shall be abandoned. Now, the determination of the inhabitants to abandon the Act is to be expressed at a meeting to be called in the manner before directed (s. 15), that is, as directed by clauses 5, 6, 7, and 8. No provision is here made for a poll, and, consequently, the proviso in s. 12, enabling the churchwardens to pay the expense of the poll, and charge the expenses to the poor-rate, does not appear in strictness to apply. Nevertheless, the expenses of calling the meeting, and giving notices of it, with a view to abandon the Act, appear to be payable in the way described, by virtue of the combined provisions of the 15th and 12th clauses. At the same time, as there is a common law right to claim a poll whenever the inhabitants are enabled to decide any matter by their votes, it is not improbable that the power to abandon, which is given to the meeting of inhabitants by s. 15, would be held to involve the poll by implication; and the Courts might, by a remedial construction, hold that the proviso in clause 12 applied, not only to this meeting, but also to the poll which might be taken on the resolution put to it. The Commissioners, therefore, doubt whether the fair expenses of the poll on this resolution should be refused by the overseers; and incline to think that it would be better to pay such expenses as would be lawfully payable on the poll, to determine on the original adoption of the Act. Proceeding on this view, the Commissioners now have to make the following observations on the items of the bill of the churchwardens. Generally, it is to be remarked, the churchwardens would not be entitled to be repaid charges incurred for doing the official business which the Act casts on the churchwardens themselves. So far as the expenditure might be for hired assistants, and regarded as part of their remuneration while engaged on those duties, the expense would be lawfully charged on the poor-rates; but not for the officers, who are personally bound to execute their office at their own charges. The charge for the time of the churchwardens themselves is wholly unlawful. The Commissioners would recommend the overseers, when they have considered of the effect of the above observations on such items as are illegal, or of doubtful legality, to make a tender to the churchwardens of such a sum as appears on the whole to be lawfully payable, and to resist any further claim.

---

3. RATE CANNOT BE AMENDED BY INSERTION OF OCCUPIER'S NAME, AFTER ALLOWANCE.

9*th December*, 1843.

Overseers of Rochdale—Stated that when the last poor's rate was made and allowed they were ignorant of the name of the occupier of some of the rateable property, and a blank was left in the column for names in the rate-book. They had since discovered his name, and were desirous of knowing whether he could lawfully be distrained on for the rate, and whether the rate could be amended by inserting his name therein, as surveyors of highways may under 5 and 6 Will. IV., c. 50, s. 31.

Ans. The Commissioners are of opinion that upon the facts stated the rate cannot be lawfully recovered from the person in occupation of the property, but who was not charged in the rate either by name or as occupier. The Commissioners are not aware of any power to amend the rate by the insertion of the omitted name. The case is not that provided for by 17 Geo. II., c. 38, s. 12, of a person coming into the parish to occupy since the making of the last rate.

X. REMOVAL.

1. ILLEGAL PROCEEDINGS IN THE REMOVAL OF AN AGED AND INFIRM PAUPER.

10*th October*, 1843.

Droitwich and Strand Unions.—The Commissioners having had their attention directed to a paragraph in the public newspapers, relating to the case of Jemima Moncton (an aged and infirm woman who, it was alleged, had been illegally removed from Droitwich to the metropolis, and had been refused admission into two Union workhouses at which she had applied, but afterwards admitted into the workhouse of the Strand Union), requested the guardians of the Droitwich Union to inquire into the circumstances of her removal, and report thereon to the Commissioners. The Commissioners afterwards received a communication from the clerk of the Strand Union, forwarding the copy of a statement made by Jemima Moncton touching her place of settlement and the circumstances attending her removal from Droitwich, and also accompanied by copies of correspondence which had passed prior to such removal between the officers of the Strand Union and the relieving officer of the Droitwich Union. The Commissioners thereupon called upon Mr. Davis, the assistant overseer of St. Nicholas Droitwich, and Mr. Morgan, relieving officer of the Droitwich Union (who appeared to have been concerned in the removal of the pauper), for an explanation of their conduct. Such explanation not being completely satisfactory to the Commissioners, they directed their Assistant Commissioner, Mr. Austin, to enter into a full inquiry of the case.

It appeared that Jemima Moncton, an aged married woman, paralytic, and of rather unsound mind, after living in Droitwich, without her husband, during a great number of years, became chargeable to the parish of St. Nicholas, in that town, at the beginning of the present year; and, owing to her infirmities she was allowed out-door relief, and was receiving such relief at the time of her removal to London. Inquiries were set on foot to ascertain her settlement, with the view of relieving the parish from the burthen of her support; and on one occasion she was taken by the assistant overseer before two of the borough magistrates, to be examined respecting the parish to which she belonged; but she could give no satisfactory account of it. The assistant overseer having obtained possession of a letter written to the pauper by her son, communicated with the relieving officer, who wrote to the officers of the Strand Union, with a view to ascertain whether the woman was settled in any parish of that Union. This correspondence not having produced the desired result, the assistant overseer, to avoid personal responsibility in any steps taken for her removal, called a parish meeting, at which it was resolved to take legal steps for ascertaining the settlement. On the following day, or the day after, it was alleged that Mr. Wood, a parishioner, informed the assistant overseer that the pauper was going to London, and asked him (the assistant overseer) to take care of her as far as Birmingham, at the same time handing over to him money to pay the woman's fare to London; and the assistant overseer accompanied her to Birmingham and paid her fare accordingly. It appeared that the money to pay the woman's fare was subscribed by seven or eight persons at the house of Mr. Wood, with the view to relieve the parish from the burthen of supporting the pauper.

The Commissioners, upon receiving the report of their Assistant Commissioner, directed a letter to be sent to the clerk to the Guardians of the Droitwich Union in the following terms:—

"The Commissioners have fully considered the circumstances relating to the case, and they desire to state, with reference to the conduct of Mr. Morgan, the relieving officer, that, although they acquit him of all participation in the illegal removal of Jemima Moncton, yet they consider that the fact of his writing to an officer of an Union for information of the description, relative to the settlement of the pauper, he sought from the clerk and master of the workhouse of the Strand Union, without specifically stating the object he had in view, was an indirect proceeding in a matter not strictly within his own official duties, and therefore deserving of censure. With respect, however, to the conduct of the assistant overseer, Mr. Davis, in the matter, the Commissioners consider that the circumstances of the case go far to show that he was an active party in the removal of the poor woman. The Commissioners are willing to admit that the course taken by him in this case was not for the purpose of serving any private object; but, looking to the facts admitted by him, that at the time he left Droitwich with the poor woman to conduct her to Birmingham, he knew that she was receiving parochial relief, and that she was not in a condition to pay the expenses of a journey to London; that he received the money from Mr. Wood to pay those expenses, without making any inquiry, or without being informed whence it came, or the purpose for which it was raised; and that he accompanied the poor woman to Birmingham, and saw her off by the train to London, without making any inquiries as to where she was going in town; and having, moreover, himself endeavoured during some months to discover her settlement, and been present on the Thursday previously at a parish meeting convened for the purpose of obtaining legal evidence respecting her settlement; the Commissioners certainly consider that he allowed himself to be made use of by third parties in effecting an illegal removal. The Commissioners can regard the circumstance of his abstaining from making inquiries in no other light than either a wilful design of remaining ignorant of facts which, if he knew them, must prevent the removal of the woman in an illegal manner, or a great neglect of his duty under the peculiar circumstances within his knowledge. In either case, the Commissioners fear that Mr. Davis is not a person in whom the confidence of a parish ought to be placed. Illegal removals of this nature are so common, that the Commissioners find themselves compelled to check the practice, as far as lies in their power, by punishing any paid officer who may be a party to any arrangement by which he casts, or assists in casting, the burthen of maintaining a pauper from one parish to another, by the illegal removal of such pauper. In this case, Mr. Davis must have known that by his conduct in the matter he was facilitating and abetting an irregular and illegal removal. Under these circumstances, the Commissioners do not see how they can allow Mr. Davis to continue in his office of assistant overseer of the parish of St. Nicholas Droitwich, and they have accordingly required him to resign his situation."

The Commissioners subsequently received a letter from the clerk of the Droitwich Union, reporting the resignation of Mr. Davis accordingly.

2. REMOVAL OF AN UNEMANCIPATED CHILD, WITHOUT THE PARENTS—COURSE OF PROCEEDING.

2nd December, 1843.

Clerk of Bury St. Edmund's Incorporation—Stated that E. M., aged nineteen years, was living with her parents in the parish of St. Mary, and had gained no settlement in her own right. She was very ill, unable to bear removal, and there was no prospect of her being better, though she might live for a long time. Application for relief for her had been made, which had been given, her father not being able to maintain her. The father belonged to the parish of Cockfield, in the Cosford Union; he had applied to the Board of Guardians of that Union for relief for the daughter, and was informed that it could not be granted unless he lived in some parish within the Union. There were several other children at home with the parents, but relief was required for this daughter only. The Guardians, therefore, wished to be informed whether the daughter, being with her parents, and unemancipated, could be legally removed (or an order for that purpose be made) without interfering with the rest of the family. The Guardians wished also to be informed whether a copy of the minutes of the Board of Guardians, certificate of chargeability, or authority to take proceedings, as mentioned in 5 and 6 Vic. c. 57, s. 17, or any of them, would be requisite on applying for the order of removal, as the overseer and the relieving officer would attend personally to make the complaint, and prove the chargeability, and one of the Guardians would also be present.

Ans. The Commissioners are not aware of any judicial determination of the question, whether the relief of an unemancipated child above the age of sixteen years, renders the father liable to be removed. The decisions with regard to certificated persons seem, however, to involve the principle upon which such a question must be decided. In the case of R. *v.* Framlingham (Burr S. C. 748), Aston, J., gave it as his opinion, "that if several persons resided in a parish under the same certificate, the asking relief by a single one of them would not render the rest removable." This conclusion would no longer be tenable with respect to children under sixteen, since the passing of the Poor Law Amendment Act (sec. 56); but it appears to be still applicable to all children above that age receiving relief without their parents. The Commissioners, therefore, think it probable that E. M. might be legally removed alone, and separated from her father's family. The Commissioners, in addition to the above remarks, direct the Guardians' attention to the case of R. *v.* Mile End Old Town, 5 Nev. and Man. 581, in which a similar point was raised, though no decision was given in it. With reference to your second question, the Commissioners desire to point out that the 17th section of the 5 and 6 Vic. c. 57, has not made any alteration in the law as to the complaint upon which an order of removal is to be made, or as to the parties who are to make the complaint. The proper parties to apply for the order are still the overseers of the parish to which the pauper is chargeable. The recent statute defines and declares what shall be deemed sufficient proof of the chargeability. But it by no means declares that what was legal evidence of chargeability before its passing, shall not be deemed legal evidence now, although it simplifies the proof. The Commissioners, therefore, while they consider it obviously desirable, as a general rule, that the course pointed out by the statute should be followed, as being a more simple and convenient one, nevertheless think it quite clear that the justices may proceed upon any other legal proof of the chargeability which may be tendered to them. There may be cases in which the mode of proof provided for by the statute would not be applicable; as, where the overseers give relief under circumstances of urgent necessity, and the case has not yet come before the Guardians at the time of applying for the order.

3. WHETHER REMOVING PARISH CAN RECOVER EXPENCES BEYOND TWENTY-ONE DAYS.

15th December, 1843.

Clerk of Darlington Union. — Inquired whether, in case a pauper be kept by the removing parish for more than three weeks, under an order of removal not suspended, such parish can legally recover the relief given to him beyond that period.

Ans. The Commissioners are of opinion that, in such a case, the relief in question is not legally recoverable, if during the 21 days no notice of appeal against the order has been given. Under the 84th section of the Poor Law Amendment Act, the relief is recoverable only when the pauper's settlement is in question at the time of granting the relief. Under the 79th section, his settlement is in question during 21 days from the notification of the chargeability, unless he be removed with the consent of the receiving parish; and if, during that period, notice of appeal be given, then it is in question, until the abandonment or determination of such appeal. If no such notice be given, the order of removal becomes operative at the close of the three weeks, and the pauper's settlement is not then "in question," whatever it may be if an appeal be entered subsequently. Again, it is clear that the obligation to keep the pauper, either during the 21 days, or pending the appeal, imposed upon the removing parish by the Poor Law Amendment Act, is the ground on which that parish is empowered to recover the relief in the event of a removal. The detention is not a matter of option with the removing parish, but an express obligation. But the Commissioners see no reason for supposing that the removing parish may, at its pleasure, indefinitely extend the period of the pauper's detention, and thus accumulate the charges of the receiving parish, without the consent of such latter parish, and without any statutory authority.

§ XI. VAGRANTS.

1. RELIEF GRANTED TO VAGRANTS, HOW TO BE CHARGED.

31*st August*, 1843.

Clerk of Pembroke Union—Stated that vagrants apply to the relieving officer, at his residence in the parish of St. Mary, Pembroke, for orders to be admitted into the workhouse; some of such vagrants having slept the previous night in parishes within, and others in parishes out of the Union: and inquired whether the cost of their maintenance should be debited to the parish of St. Mary, or to the respective parishes in which they slept the preceding night, or to the establishment.

Ans. The relief of casual paupers cannot, in the present state of the law, be charged upon the common fund of the Union. A clause to render such relief so chargeable was introduced into the Bill for the further Amendment of the Poor Laws, but it has not received the sanction of the legislature. With regard to the relative liability of particular parishes in cases of this description, the Commissioners wish to point out that a pauper is properly chargeable to that parish in which, being destitute, he applies for and obtains relief. Where, however, a person destitute in one parish is compelled by the situation of the relieving officer's residence, or other similar causes, to make his application for relief in another parish, he will nevertheless, in most cases, be chargeable to the former parish, in which his destitution occasioned his seeking relief, and in which he must be constructively considered as having sought it. From these considerations it follows, that the parish in which a casual pauper sleeps during the night before he applies for relief will not necessarily in all cases be the parish chargeable with such relief; although, under certain circumstances, it may be so. Where, however, the parish in which the pauper sleeps, and that in which he applies for relief, lie within different Unions, there appears to be no alternative but to treat the pauper as destitute in the parish wherein he applies for relief; as the Guardians of the Union including such latter parish could not, under these circumstances, enforce the liability against the parish in which he slept. Where the pauper becomes destitute in another parish, after having left the parish in which he slept, and applies for and obtains relief in such other parish, the parish in which he passed the night would not be liable for such relief. The common opinion, that a person is chargeable to the parish in which he slept, very possibly arose from the fact, that a person is only removable where he can be said to have come to settle, and it may have been supposed that the duty to give relief, and the right to get rid of the burthen, went together. This view, the Commissioners have already stated, has no foundation in law, even admitting that the mere act of sleeping in a parish was necessarily a coming to settle, within the words of the statute.

2. REIMBURSEMENT OF CONSTABLE FOR MAINTENANCE OF VAGRANTS IN CONFINEMENT.

21*st August*, 1843.

Clerk of Luton Union—Inquired whether the cost of the subsistence of mendicant vagrants, under confinement previous to their committal to gaol, could be legally charged in the overseers' accounts.

Ans. If the relief in these cases be afforded by a parish constable, that officer might, in default of provision by the county-rate, provide for the expense by a constables' rate. But as the making of a constables' rate is almost everywhere abandoned, the Commissioners think that the constable would be held entitled to charge in his accounts, under 18 Geo. III., c. 19, s. 4, the relief in question, as money expended on account of the parish. If the relief be afforded by district constables appointed under 2 & 3 Vic., c. 93, and 3 & 4 Vic., c. 88, it appears to result from a recent decision in the case of the Queen against the churchwardens and overseers of Chelmsford that the expense is in like manner chargeable on the poor rates.

---

3. PRESCRIBING TASK OF WORK TO BE DONE BY VAGRANTS.

The Commissioners having received communications on this subject from several Unions, forwarded to such Unions the circular and form of resolution, of which the following are copies:—

Poor Law Commission Office,
Somerset House,
December, 1843.

SIR,—I am directed by the Poor Law Commissioners to refer to your letter of on the subject of the setting vagrants in the workhouse on work, and to state, that the Commissioners consider it will be desirable that the determination of the Guardians should be expressed in a formal manner. They have instructed me, therefore, to enclose a form of resolution, to be adopted by the Guardians, and to state, that when the same shall have been adopted, and the maximum amount of work to be performed by each vagrant settled, a copy of the resolution should be transmitted to the Commissioners for their sanction and approval, under the 5th sect. of the 5th and 6th Vict., c. 57.

I am, sir, &c.
E. CHADWICK,
Secretary.

To the Clerk to the Guardians of the Union.

Ordered by the Guardians of the Union, at a meeting of the Board this day of , 184 .

THAT the master of the workhouse of the Union do set every adult person not suffering under any temporary or permanent infirmity of body, being an occasional poor person, who shall be relieved in the said workhouse, in return for the food and lodging afforded to such person, to perform the following task of work—that is to say:*

[* Here insert the kind and amount of work to be performed.]

Provided that no such person shall be detained against his will for the performance of such task of work for any time exceeding four hours from the hour of breakfast on the morning next after admission.

And provided also that such amount of work shall not be required from any person to whose age, strength, and capacity it shall appear not to be suited.

A. B.
Clerk to the Guardians.

We, the Poor Law Commissioners, do consent to and approve of the said order of the Board of Guardians.

This day of

Notice.—Any such person as above who shall while in such workhouse refuse or neglect to perform such task of work suited to the age, strength, and capacity of such person, will be deemed an idle and disorderly person, and be liable to be imprisoned in the house of correction with hard labour for one calendar month.

LONDON:
Printed by Order of the Poor Law Commissioners, by W. CLOWES and SONS, Stamford Street, and Published by CHARLES KNIGHT and Co., 22, Ludgate Street, Publishers to the Poor Law Commissioners.

VOLUME IV
[1844]

AN

OFFICIAL CIRCULAR

OF PUBLIC DOCUMENTS AND INFORMATION:

DIRECTED BY THE POOR LAW COMMISSIONERS TO BE PRINTED, CHIEFLY FOR THE USE OF THE MEMBERS AND PERMANENT OFFICERS OF BOARDS OF GUARDIANS, UNDER THE POOR LAW AMENDMENT ACT.

No. 31. CIRCULAR ISSUED JANUARY 31, 1844.

Poor Law Commission Office,
Somerset House,
January 31, 1844.

THE Poor Law Commissioners, on a review of their Correspondence, directed that the following abstract thereof should be printed and circulated for the information of Guardians and Officers of the several Unions, viz.:—

By order of the Board,
EDWIN CHADWICK, *Secretary*.

I. ACCOUNTS.—FEES TO MAGISTRATES' CLERKS IN THE CASES OF SUMMONSES AGAINST DEFAULTERS IN THE PAYMENT OF THE POOR RATES, WHEN THE SUMMONSES ARE NOT ENFORCED.

15*th January*, 1844.

Assistant Overseer, Redruth, Redruth Union – Stated, that at the hearing of summonses obtained against persons who had made default in the payment of their poor rates, before the magistrates at the petty sessions, many of the defaulters were excused as poor. Others by proving a change of occupancy during the collection of the rate were considered by the magistrates as not liable, and some were charged in error, and of course did not pay. The magistrates' clerks insisted on payment of fees for every person summoned, as well those against whom the summonses were not enforced, as those who were excused or not liable, and the fees were in consequence paid by the overseers. The auditor having objected to allow those fees, inquired whether the magistrates' clerks were entitled to fees in the cases of persons who were excused, or who were not considered by the magistrates to be liable. Or, if the fees were properly payable in such cases, whether they ought not to be allowed in the overseers' accounts.

Ans.—The cost of the summons is in the first place demandable of the person at whose instance, or on whose application, the summons is obtained; and it is recoverable, or not, against the party summoned, according to the nature of the case and the discretion of the justices. Where the justices, upon the hearing of the case, do not see fit to order payment of the costs by the party in arrear, the overseers will be answerable for them; but the overseers if they had fair grounds for applying to the justices, will be at liberty to pay such costs out of the poor rates, and charge the amount in their accounts. On the other hand, if the overseers were not justified in making the application, the charge would not be allowed by the auditor in their accounts.

II. AUDITOR.—THE PERIOD AT WHICH AN AUDITOR'S SALARY OUGHT TO COMMENCE.

1*st January*, 1844.

Clerk of Truro Union—Stated that Mr. Dryden, the late auditor of that Union, died on the 7th day of July last, without having audited the accounts of the quarter ended 24th June, but his representatives were paid the salary due to him up to that date. Mr. Clyma was elected on the 13th day of September last to succeed Mr. Dryden, and having since audited the accounts between the 25th March and 24th June, conceived that his salary ought to commence from the former period. Requested the Commissioners' opinion as to the period at which Mr. Clyma's salary ought to commence.

Ans. The salary of the auditor is, like that of any other Union officer, an annual salary, and not a payment of a certain sum for each audit, and the auditor is therefore only entitled to his salary from the date of his appointment. He also takes the office subject to the performance of all the duties required to be done subsequently to his appointment, and is consequently bound to audit all the accounts left unaudited by his predecessor, and he is not entitled to claim any extra payment on that account.

III. EDUCATION OF PAUPER CHILDREN.

23*rd December*, 1843.

Clerk of the Berwick-upon-Tweed Union—Transmitted a copy of a report made to the Board of Guardians by the School Committee of the Union, together with the following resolution passed by the Board of Guardians in reference to such report:—"That the following arrangement be submitted to the Poor Law Commissioners for their approval:—That an allowance not exceeding twopence per week as a school wage be added in favour of each child in the pauper list of an age to attend school, and not residing within one mile of the workhouse school; such allowance, or school wage, to be paid each quarter to the schoolmasters by the relieving officers of the respective districts in which the schools may be situated, certificates stating the number of days' attendance being previously handed by the schoolmasters to the relieving officers, and the allowance or school wage being computed at a rate not exceeding twopence per week for each period of five days' attendance, certified as above. And further, that at the end of each quarter such certificates, with full particulars of the payments in respect thereof, be laid before the Board."

Ans.—The objection to the proposed arrangement which occurs to the Commissioners is, that there is no legal authority to charge the poor rates for the purpose. When children are maintained in the workhouse, under the immediate care and control of the Guardians, it is undoubtedly competent to the Guardians to provide suitable training and instruction for such children; and the Poor Law Amendment Act (sec. 15) expressly enables the Commissioners to make and issue regulations for the attainment of these objects. But the education of children relieved out of the workhouse, and placed under other control, is not a matter within the purview of the Poor Laws; and however desirable it may be that the means of instruction should be extended to this class, the Commissioners are bound to say, that in the present state of the law it is not competent to the Guardians to effect this object directly or indirectly at the charge of the poor rates.

IV. MEDICAL ORDER.

1. Dislocation of the Ankle.

22*nd January*, 1844.

Clerk of the Tewkesbury Union—Inquired, whether a medical officer is entitled to the fee of three pounds for attending to a dislocation of the ankle.

Ans. The Commissioners consider a dislocation of the ankle to be a dislocation of the leg, within the meaning of the Medical Order, and that therefore the fee of three pounds ought to be paid to the medical officer for the treatment of such a dislocation.

2. Definition of the term "Child-Birth" in the Medical Order.

6*th January*, 1844.

Medical Officer and Clerk of the Plomesgate Union—Stated, that Susan Baker was taken in labour December 5, 1843, and after a difficult and preternatural labour (in which surgical attendance was required for about three hours) was delivered of a full-grown seven months (or rather over seven months) child, supposed to have been dead about three days. That the Board of Guardians had deducted the medical officer's charge (ten shillings) for attending on the case, in consequence of the opinion expressed by the Commissioners, in their Official Circular, No. 29, Art. VIII; viz. that the term "child-birth," as used in their General Medical Order, was intended to apply only to cases in which the child was, or might have been, born alive.

Ans. The Guardians have apparently not attached the same meaning to the opinion quoted as that which the Commissioners intended to convey. It is perfectly clear, that in one sense the child of Susan Baker, having died before delivery, could not have been born alive; but the view of the Commissioners is, that whenever pregnancy is so far advanced that it was possible that the child might have been born alive; then the delivery of such a child (although still-born) would entitle the medical officer to the usual fee. In the case in question, as the child was "a seven months' child," it "might have been born alive," and for this reason the Commissioners think the medical officer should be paid the fee.

V. MEDICAL OFFICER.—Workhouse Medical Officer entitled to a Fee on attending a Coroner's Inquest therein.

9*th January*, 1844.

Medical Officer, Richmond Union, Yorkshire—Inquired, whether the circumstance of his being medical officer to the Union workhouse prevented him from having the usual remuneration for attending coroner's inquests in that establishment when duly summoned.

Ans.—The Commissioners do not consider that the fact of a medical man being medical officer of a Union workhouse precludes him from receiving such remuneration as he may be legally entitled to, for giving evidence on a coroner's inquest.

VI.—PAU-

1. A RETURN showing the Number of In-door and Out door Paupers relieved in 584 Unions in England and Wales, during the relief during each of the years ended Lady-Day, 1842 and 1843; together with the estimated Number of Paupers Relieved, and

COUNTIES.		Population* in 1841.	Number of Paupers Relieved Quarters ended						Proportion per Cent. of Number of Paupers Relieved to Population, Lady day, 1843.
			Lady-day, 1842.			Lady-day, 1843.			
			In-door	Out-door.	Total.	In-door.	Out-door.	Total.	
ENGLAND	Bedford	112,379	2,378	10,182	12,560	2,484	10,562	13,046	12
	Berks	190,367	4,187	14,833	19,020	4,682	15,263	19,945	10
	Buckingham	140,352	2,479	15,996	18,475	2,703	15,755	18,458	13
	Cambridge	171,848	4,125	14,022	18,147	3,895	15,118	19,013	11
	Chester	371,331	2,803	25,904	28,707	2,736	24,912	27,648	7
	Cornwall	340,728	2,599	19,702	22,301	2,688	20,419	23,107	7
	Cumberland	177,912	1,935	10,064	11,999	2,182	9,045	11,227	6
	Derby	220,028	1,949	10,004	11,953	2,203	10,636	12,839	6
	Devon	430,221	4,444	36,860	41,304	4,827	37,033	41,850	10
	Dorset	167,874	2,298	19,007	21,305	2,508	20,083	22,591	13
	Durham	325,997	1,866	22,663	24,529	2,229	25,362	27,591	8
	Essex	320,818	9,717	32,849	42,566	9,149	35,545	44,694	14
	Gloucester	330,562	4,546	24,305	28,851	4,622	24,751	29,373	9
	Hereford	110,675	1,454	8,478	9,932	1,430	8,716	10,146	9
	Hertford	176,173	3,864	13,873	17,737	4,334	13,735	18,069	10
	Huntingdon	55,573	844	4,965	5,809	1,059	4,445	5,504	10
	Kent	534,882	11,353	36,944	48,297	11,762	38,128	49,890	9
	Lancaster	1,186,882	10,737	99,156	109,893	11,612	109,322	120,934	10
	Leicester	220,232	3,662	20,683	24,345	3,776	23,296	27,072	12
	Lincoln	356,347	4,047	17,342	21,389	5,315	19,649	24,964	7
	Middlesex	841,402	21,378	45,277	66,655	20,515	43,815	64,330	8
	Monmouth	150,222	1,227	7,586	8,813	1,205	8,846	10,051	7
	Norfolk	343,277	6,889	27,987	34,876	7,817	29,849	37,666	11
	Northampton	197,197	2,674	16,227	18,901	3,134	17,481	20,615	10
	Northumberland	265,988	1,705	19,202	20,907	2,246	21,185	23,431	9
	Nottingham	270,719	2,982	21,663	24,645	3,317	19,149	22,466	8
	Oxford	141,330	2,487	13,991	16,478	2,699	16,344	19,043	13
	Rutland	23,150	363	1,421	1,784	418	1,510	1,928	8
	Salop	191,052	2,623	9,128	11,751	3,526	11,185	14,711	8
	Somerset	454,446	6,942	42,165	49,107	7,122	46,764	53,886	12
	Southampton	269,642	5,085	24,284	29,369	5,191	24,558	29,749	11
	Stafford	442,348	6,127	19,886	26,013	7,851	26,500	34,351	8
	Suffolk	314,722	5,757	30,003	35,760	7,726	31,763	39,489	13
	Surrey	512,580	10,846	27,492	38,338	10,478	29,685	40,163	8
	Sussex	223,435	5,479	24,015	29,494	6,121	25,102	31,223	14
	Warwick	220,029	2,147	12,522	14,669	2,375	13,481	15,856	7
	Westmoreland	56,469	1,002	5,113	6,115	1,113	6,157	7,270	13
	Wilts	233,246	5,457	30,370	85,827	5,763	30,972	36,735	16
	Worcester	336,108	2,927	19,748	22,675	3,312	26,372	29,684	9
	York, East Riding	180,218	1,465	12,619	14,084	1,628	14,639	16,267	9
	York, North Riding	180,527	2,054	12,273	14,327	1,959	12,783	14,742	8
	York, West Riding	790,751	4,685	61,459	66,144	5,467	83,214	88,681	11
	Totals of England	12,580,039	183,588	942,263	1,125,851	197,179	1,023,129	1,220,308	9
WALES	Anglesey	38,105	..	4,951	4,951	..	5,120	5,120	13
	Brecon	55,399	495	4,487	4,982	506	4,462	4,968	9
	Cardigan	75,136	183	6,228	6,411	178	6,124	6,302	8
	Carmarthen	110,404	1,156	8,609	9,765	934	8,311	9,245	8
	Carnarvon	86,728	101	8,246	8,347	114	8,700	8,814	10
	Denbigh	68,483	443	7,312	7,755	502	6,785	7,287	11
	Flint	64,355	533	4,929	5,462	419	4,938	5,357	8
	Glamorgan	178,041	664	11,779	12,443	757	11,900	12,657	7
	Merioneth	50,696	126	5,839	5,965	176	6,050	6,226	12
	Montgomery	58,709	614	7,415	8,029	565	7,916	8,481	14
	Pembroke	78,563	416	5,181	5,597	504	5,333	5,837	7
	Radnor	19,554	135	2,339	2,474	93	2,394	2,487	13
	Totals of Wales	884,173	4,866	77,315	82,181	4,748	78,033	82,781	9
Totals of 584 Unions in England and Wales		13,464,212	188,454	1,019,578	1,208,032	201,927	1,101,162	1,303,089	10
Estimated Totals of Unions not included, and of places not united		2,442,617	34,188	184,967	219,155	36,633	199,768	236,401	10
Estimated Totals of England and Wales		15,906,829	222,642	1,204,545	1,427,187	238,560	1,300,930	1,539,490	10

* Some of the Unions are composed of parishes situate in different counties, which cause

PERISM.

Quarters ended Lady-Day, 1842 and 1843, respectively: also, the Amount of Money Expended for In-maintenance and Out-
Amount Expended for Relief, in the Unions not included, and places not under the provisions of the Poor Law Amendment Act.

Expenditure for In-maintenance and Out-relief.						Increase per Cent. of Expenditure in 1843 compared with 1842.	Decrease per Cent. of Expenditure in 1843 compared with 1842.	COUNTIES.	
Year ended Lady-day, 1842.			Year ended Lady-day, 1843.						
In-maintenance.	Out-relief.	Total.	In-maintenance.	Out-relief.	Total.				
8,639	25,037	33,676	8,829	26,898	35,727	6	..	Bedford	
19,353	50,699	70,052	18,044	51,071	69,115	..	1	Berks	
10,382	44,305	54,687	9,971	45,080	55,051	1	..	Buckingham	
12,404	46,333	58,737	11,795	47,625	59,420	1	..	Cambridge	
10,997	53,783	64,780	11,562	60,782	72,344	12	..	Chester	
11,045	54,738	65,783	10,812	55,360	66,172	1	..	Cornwall	
6,808	22,805	29,613	6,948	23,302	30,250	2	..	Cumberland	
5,908	22,909	28,817	6,928	24,184	31,112	8	..	Derby	
17,379	120,611	137,990	17,643	122,597	140,240	2	..	Devon	
9,906	52,708	62,614	9,910	53,763	63,673	2	..	Dorset	
8,528	51,607	60,135	8,718	59,987	68,705	14	..	Durham	
28,177	88,707	116,884	28,915	88,230	117,145	..	..	Essex	
18,280	60,159	78,439	18,297	62,812	81,109	3	..	Gloucester	
4,951	27,226	32,177	4,718	27,924	32,642	1	..	Hereford	
16,816	36,678	53,494	16,886	38,577	55,463	4	..	Hertford	
3,220	16,080	19,300	3,241	15,523	18,764	..	3	Huntingdon	
53,542	90,751	146,293	52,711	93,205	145,916	..	..	Kent	
43,098	137,026	180,124	50,626	171,812	222,438	23	..	Lancaster	
11,738	50,645	62,383	12,736	60,110	72,846	17	..	Leicester	
16,192	64,290	80,482	17,798	67,294	85,092	6	..	Lincoln	
121,259	102,352	223,611	116,186	108,811	224,997	1	..	Middlesex	ENGLAND.
3,951	17,754	21,705	4,726	20,534	25,260	16	..	Monmouth	
22,560	101,347	123,907	24,725	100,868	125,593	1	..	Norfolk	
11,583	53,667	65,250	11,997	57,349	69,346	6	..	Northampton	
7,889	51,654	59,543	8,796	54,201	62,997	6	..	Northumberland	
12,601	45,166	57,767	13,793	50,416	64,209	11	..	Nottingham	
9,346	49,744	59,090	8,810	50,343	59,153	..	..	Oxford	
1,211	4,654	5,865	1,320	4,585	5,905	1	..	Rutland	
8,994	25,953	34,947	10,964	29,860	40,824	17	..	Salop	
24,113	112,130	136,243	23,992	118,535	142,527	5	..	Somerset	
23,958	69,733	93,691	22,897	71,096	93,993	..	..	Southampton	
19,394	41,490	60,884	25,708	54,945	80,653	32	..	Stafford	
20,204	87,863	108,067	21,642	88,453	110,095	2	..	Suffolk	
64,794	68,209	133,003	64,492	72,760	137,252	3	..	Surrey	
26,230	64,065	90,295	26,252	65,418	91,670	2	..	Sussex	
9,823	38,028	47,851	9,858	39,370	49,228	3	..	Warwick	
3,700	11,886	15,586	3,684	13,226	16,910	9	..	Westmoreland	
18,934	81,211	100,145	18,930	85,571	104,501	4	..	Wilts	
12,048	50,195	62,243	13,235	56,045	69,280	11	..	Worcester	
5,616	39,734	45,350	6,105	40,889	46,994	4	..	York, East Riding	
5,569	38,459	44,028	6,101	40,099	46,200	5	..	York, North Riding	
23,289	134,352	157,641	24,365	174,099	198,464	26	..	York, West Riding	
776,429	2,406,743	3,183,172	795,666	2,593,609	3,389,275	6	..	Totals of England.	
..	12,651	12,651	..	12,506	12,506	..	1	Anglesey	
1,238	13,742	14,980	1,195	14,992	16,187	8	..	Brecon	
358	17,327	17,685	520	16,990	17,510	..	1	Cardigan	
2,050	26,004	28,054	2,275	26,538	28,813	3	..	Carmarthen	
107	22,529	22,636	131	22,942	23,073	2	..	Carnarvon	
2,026	16,745	18,771	2,097	16,896	18,993	1	..	Denbigh	WALES.
1,110	15,083	16,193	1,263	15,069	16,332	1	..	Flint	
2,901	29,367	32,268	2,768	34,817	37,585	16	..	Glamorgan	
329	15,542	15,871	351	14,918	15,269	..	4	Merioneth	
2,376	18,624	21,000	2,686	19,682	22,368	7	..	Montgomery	
1,262	16,123	17,385	1,415	16,436	17,851	3	..	Pembroke	
525	5,775	6,300	573	6,070	6,643	5	..	Radnor	
14,282	209,512	223,794	15,274	217,856	233,130	4	..	Totals of Wales.	
790,711	2,616,255	3,406,966	810,940	2,811,465	3,622,405	6	..	Totals of 584 Unions in England and Wales.	
143,447	474,629	618,076	147,117	510,043	657,160	6	..	Estimated Totals of Unions not included, and of places not united.	
934,158	3,090,884	4,025,042	958,057	3,321,508	4,279,565	6	..	Estimated Totals of England and Wales.	

the population of counties to differ from that published by the Census Commissioners.

2. COMPARATIVE STATEMENT of the Number of Adult Able-bodied Paupers relieved during the Years ended

	NAMES OF COUNTIES.	NUMBER OF ADULT ABLE-						
		Quarter ended Lady-day, 1842.						
		In-door.			Out-door.			Total In-door and Out-door.
		On Account of Sickness or Accident.	All other causes, including Vagrancy.	Total.	On Account of Sickness or Accident.	All other causes, including Vagrancy.	Total.	
ENGLAND	Bedford	203	833	1,036	2,024	885	2,909	3,945
	Berks	180	1,337	1,517	2,180	1,171	3,351	4,868
	Buckingham	119	757	876	2,791	1,741	4,532	5,408
	Cambridge	129	2,036	2,165	2,348	1,167	3,515	5,680
	Chester	101	844	945	2,028	6,199	8,227	9,172
	Cornwall	153	606	759	2,010	2,521	4,531	5,290
	Cumberland	70	485	555	708	1,887	2,595	3,150
	Derby	91	560	651	1,301	1,441	2,742	3,393
	Devon	361	1,304	1,665	4,682	2,402	7,084	8,749
	Dorset	172	580	752	2,886	1,641	4,527	5,279
	Durham	81	520	601	1,472	5,962	7,434	8,035
	Essex	382	5,064	5,446	5,960	2,938	8,898	14,344
	Gloucester	269	1,258	1,527	3,121	2,857	5,978	7,505
	Hereford	110	298	408	1,151	522	1,673	2,081
	Hertford	236	1,319	1,555	2,817	1,800	4,617	6,172
	Huntingdon	26	308	334	759	412	1,171	1,505
	Kent	663	3,294	3,957	4,323	5,373	9,696	13,653
	Lancaster	1,006	3,058	4,064	5,240	26,480	31,720	35,784
	Leicester	122	1,250	1,372	2,696	3,158	5,854	7,226
	Lincoln	165	1,424	1,589	2,233	1,753	3,986	5,575
	Middlesex	870	6,448	7,318	3,109	12,341	15,450	22,768
	Monmouth	91	396	487	715	1,559	2,274	2,761
	Norfolk	189	2,291	2,480	3,143	2,098	5,241	7,721
	Northampton	92	809	901	2,669	1,440	4,109	5,010
	Northumberland	131	392	523	1,040	4,557	5,597	6,120
	Nottingham	109	1,092	1,201	2,710	4,166	6,876	8,077
	Oxford	76	783	859	2,519	936	3,455	4,314
	Rutland	5	155	160	153	127	280	440
	Salop	131	944	1,075	1,154	823	1,977	3,052
	Somerset	304	2,568	2,872	5,801	3,302	9,103	11,975
	Southampton	227	1,525	1,752	4,027	2,512	6,539	8,291
	Stafford	278	2,200	2,478	2,334	4,650	6,984	9,462
	Suffolk	177	1,894	2,071	4,403	2,150	6,553	8,624
	Surrey	587	4,170	4,757	3,422	6,166	9,588	14,345
	Sussex	197	1,645	1,842	3,375	1,739	5,114	6,956
	Warwick	78	654	732	1,627	1,289	2,916	3,648
	Westmoreland	30	402	432	338	1,117	1,455	1,887
	Wilts	192	1,915	2,107	4,134	4,652	8,786	10,893
	Worcester	223	913	1,136	2,272	2,840	5,112	6,248
	York, East Riding	53	535	588	1,125	2,111	3,236	3,824
	York, North Riding	50	984	1,034	904	2,162	3,066	4,100
	York, West Riding	357	1,482	1,839	3,130	16,904	20,034	21,873
	Totals of England	9,086	61,332	70,418	106,834	151,951	258,785	329,203
WALES	Anglesey	..	..	..	661	790	1,451	1,451
	Brecon	13	230	243	310	524	834	1,077
	Cardigan	9	67	76	567	653	1,220	1,296
	Carmarthen	29	504	533	979	790	1,769	2,302
	Carnarvon	10	29	39	618	1,307	1,925	1,964
	Denbigh	24	129	153	891	927	1,818	1,971
	Flint	10	174	184	502	692	1,194	1,378
	Glamorgan	3	90	93	1,056	2,733	3,789	3,882
	Merioneth	..	38	38	292	579	871	909
	Montgomery	36	124	160	734	910	1,644	1,804
	Pembroke	22	95	117	307	476	783	900
	Radnor	3	35	38	215	251	466	504
	Totals of Wales	159	1,515	1,674	7,132	10,632	17,764	19,438
Totals of 584 Unions in England and Wales		9,245	62,847	72,092	113,966	162,583	276,549	348,641
Estimated for Unions not included, and places not in Union		1,677	11,402	13,079	20,675	29,495	50,170	63,249
Estimated Totals of England and Wales		10,922	74,249	85,171	134,641	192,078	326,719	411,890

Lady-day 1842 and 1843; distinguishing those relieved on account of temporary sickness or accident.

BODIED PAUPERS RELIEVED.

Quarter ended Lady-day, 1843.								
In-door.			Out-door.				NAMES OF COUNTIES.	
On Account of Sickness or Accident.	All other causes, including Vagrancy.	Total.	On Account of Sickness or Accident.	All other causes, including Vagrancy.	Total.	Total In-door and Out-door.		
179	869	1,048	1,932	1,232	3,164	4,212	Bedford	ENGLAND.
190	1,705	1,895	2,270	997	3,267	5,162	Berks	
148	1,100	1,248	2,768	1,653	4,421	5,669	Buckingham	
126	1,744	1,870	2,505	1,320	3,825	5,695	Cambridge	
79	942	1,021	1,944	5,899	7,843	8,864	Chester	
179	683	862	2,077	2,595	4,672	5,534	Cornwall	
64	699	763	849	1,432	2,281	3,044	Cumberland	
84	758	842	1,437	1,318	2,755	3,597	Derby	
375	1,637	2,012	4,502	2,301	6,803	8,815	Devon	
156	726	882	3,232	1,909	5,141	6,023	Dorset	
109	763	872	1,870	6,870	8,740	9,612	Durham	
392	4,728	5,120	6,081	3,419	9,500	14,620	Essex	
250	1,398	1,648	2,974	3,000	5,974	7,622	Gloucester	
97	317	414	1,207	517	1,724	2,138	Hereford	
208	1,732	1,940	2,568	1,921	4,489	6,429	Hertford	
12	480	492	700	279	979	1,471	Huntingdon	
673	3,896	4,569	4,615	6,119	10,734	15,303	Kent	
979	3,391	4,370	5,339	29,661	35,000	39,370	Lancaster	
87	1,523	1,610	3,150	3,412	6,562	8,172	Leicester	
175	2,157	2,332	2,729	2,361	5,090	7,422	Lincoln	
971	7,139	8,110	3,131	11,629	14,760	22,870	Middlesex	
88	374	462	1,085	1,718	2,803	3,265	Monmouth	
149	3,122	3,271	3,399	2,428	5,827	9,098	Norfolk	
87	1,030	1,117	2,973	1,418	4,391	5,508	Northampton	
144	848	992	1,342	5,546	6,888	7,880	Northumberland	
96	1,068	1,164	2,685	2,679	5,364	6,528	Nottingham	
88	1,002	1,090	3,151	1,359	4,510	5,600	Oxford	
4	213	217	165	161	326	543	Rutland	
147	1,421	1,568	1,611	1,390	3,001	4,569	Salop	
296	2,724	3,020	6,892	3,900	10,792	13,812	Somerset	
209	1,573	1,782	4,321	2,170	6,491	8,273	Southampton	
268	3,558	3,826	2,850	6,773	9,623	13,449	Stafford	
134	3,335	3,469	4,909	2,458	7,367	10,836	Suffolk	
673	4,117	4,790	3,421	7,448	10,869	15,659	Surrey	
145	2,238	2,383	3,841	1,928	5,769	8,152	Sussex	
85	762	847	1,618	1,441	3,059	3,906	Warwick	
18	556	574	357	1,751	2,108	2,682	Westmoreland	
169	2,461	2,630	4,963	3,277	8,240	10,870	Wilts	
226	1,048	1,274	2,792	5,482	8,274	9,548	Worcester	
55	588	643	1,375	2,882	4,257	4,900	York, East Riding	
79	798	877	995	2,480	3,475	4,352	York, North Riding	
324	2,004	2,328	4,073	26,495	30,568	32,896	York, West Riding	
9,017	73,227	82,244	116,698	175,028	291,726	373,970	Totals of England.	
..	..	..	594	805	1,399	1,399	Anglesey	WALES.
12	284	296	338	477	815	1,111	Brecon	
7	69	76	464	584	1,048	1,124	Cardigan	
19	408	427	912	720	1,632	2,059	Carmarthen	
30	26	56	641	1,538	2,179	2,235	Carnarvon	
24	140	164	1,009	777	1,786	1,950	Denbigh	
23	95	118	490	657	1,747	1,265	Flint	
11	92	103	1,151	2,607	3,758	3,861	Glamorgan	
5	57	62	415	623	1,038	1,100	Merioneth	
28	136	164	641	1,079	1,720	1,884	Montgomery	
31	129	160	312	482	794	954	Pembroke	
2	26	28	228	319	547	575	Radnor	
192	1,462	1,654	7,195	10,668	17,863	19,517	Totals of Wales.	
9,209	74,689	83,898	123,893	185,696	309,589	393,487	Totals of 584 Unions in England and Wales.	
1,671	13,550	15,221	22,476	33,688	56,164	71,385	Estimated for Unions not included, and places not in Union.	
10,880	88,239	99,119	146,369	219,384	365,753	464,872	Estimated Totals of England and Wales.	

3. SUMMARY OF RETURNS, showing the Number of Paupers relieved in England and Wales during the Quarters ended at Lady-day, 1840, 1841, 1842, and 1843; and the Amount of Money expended for the Maintenance and Out-relief during the Years ended Lady-day 1840, 1841, 1842, and 1843 respectively. Also the Proportion per Cent. which the Number of In-door and Out-door Paupers relieved bear to the Total Number; and the Proportion per Cent. of the amount expended for In-maintenance and Out-relief to the total; with the rate per head of Expenditure to the Population of 1841; and the Average Price of Wheat per Quarter in each Year.

Quarters ended Lady Day.	Number of Paupers Relieved. In Door.	Proportion per Cent. to Total.	Out-Door.	Proportion per Cent. to Total	Total In-Door and Out-Door.	Rate per Cent. on Population, 1841.	Years ended Lady Day.	Expenditure for In-maintenance and Out-relief. In-Maintenance.	Proportion per Cent. to Total.	Out Relief.	Proportion per Cent. to Total.	Total of In-maintenance and Out Relief.	Rate per Head of Expenditure to Population, 1841. s.	d.	Average Price of Wheat per Quarter for each Year. s.	d.
								£.		£.		£.	s.	d.	s.	d.
1840	169,232	14	1,030,297	86	1,199,529	8	1840	808,151	22	2,931,263	78	3,739,414	4	8	68	6
1841	192,106	15	1,106,942	85	1,299,048	8	1841	890,883	23	2,995,330	77	3,886,213	4	11	65	3
1842	222,642	16	1,204,545	84	1,427,187	9	1842	934,158	23	3,090,884	77	4,025,042	5	1	64	0
1843	238,560	15	1,300,930	85	1,539,490	10	1843	958,057	22	3,321,508	78	4,279,565	5	5	54	4
Average	205,635	15	1,160,679	85	1,366,314	9	Average	897,812	22	3,084,746	78	3,982,558	5	0	63	0

Population in 1841, 15,906,829.

NOTE.—An estimate is made for those places not under the provisions of the Poor Law Amendment Act.

4. RETURN showing the Number of In-door and Out-door Paupers Relieved in England and Wales, during the Year ended at Easter, 1803, and the Quarter ended Lady-day, 1843, respectively, with the Rate per Cent. on the Population at each period; also showing the Number that would have been Relieved in the Quarter ended Lady-day, 1843, assuming the rates of Paupers to the Population to have been the same as it was in 1803.

Population of England and Wales in 1801.	Number of In-door and Out-door Paupers Relieved, including Children, during the Year ended Easter, 1803.	Rate per Cent. of number of Paupers Relieved on the Population of 1801.	Population of England and Wales in 1841.	Number of In-door and Out-door Paupers Relieved, including Children, during the Quarter ended Lady-day, 1843, being the Quarter of the Year in which the largest number were Relieved.	Rate per Cent. of number of Paupers Relieved on the Population of 1841.	Number of Paupers that would have been Relieved in the Quarter ended Lady-day, 1843, assuming the ratio of Paupers to the Population to have been the same as it was in 1803.
8,872,980	1,040,716	12	15,906,829	1,539,490*	10	1,908,819

* An estimate is made for places not under the Poor Law Amendment Act.

5. COMPARATIVE STATEMENT of the Number of In-door and Out-door Paupers relieved in England and Wales, during the Quarters ended Michaelmas, 1842 and 1843, and the Amount expended for In-maintenance and Out-relief during the Half-years ended Michaelmas, 1842 and 1843 respectively.

Quarters ended Michaelmas.	Number of In-door and Out-door Paupers relieved.	Decrease per Cent.	Half-year ended Michaelmas.	Amount expended for In-maintenance and Out-relief.	Decrease per Cent.
1842	1,372,642	..	1842	£2,121,763	..
1843	1,294,574		1843	1,981,837	
Decrease.	78,068	6	..	139,926	7

6. COMPARATIVE STATEMENT of the Amount of Money expended for In-maintenance and Out-relief, in 584 Unions in England and Wales, during the Half-years ended Michaelmas, 1842 and 1843 respectively, in which the Counties are placed according to their highest rate of Expenditure.

COUNTIES.	Expenditure for In-maintenance and Out-Relief. Half-year ended Michaelmas 1842	Expenditure for In-maintenance and Out-Relief. Half-year ended Michaelmas 1843	Increase per Cent. in 1843, compared with 1842.	Decrease per Cent. in 1843, compared with 1842.
	£.	£.		
Salop	19,668	21,658	10	.
Rutland	2,854	2,971	4	.
Durham	33,574	34,445	3	.
York, East Riding	22,833	23,465	3	.
Flint	7,964	8.192	3	.
Lincoln	41,345	42,189	2	.
Northumberland	31,121	31,814	2	.
Brecon	8,229	8,319	1	.
Worcester	33,858	33,877	.	.
York, North Riding	22,956	22,828	.	1
Cambridge	28,762	28,059	.	2
Monmouth	12,500	12,285	.	2
Northampton	33,853	33,334	.	2
Westmoreland	8,070	7,888	.	2
Glamorgan	18,840	18,440	.	2
Merioneth	7,836	7,661	.	2
York, West Riding	97,585	94,889	.	3
Buckingham	26,761	25,814		4
Derby	15,504	14,957	.	4
Oxford	28,912	27,622	.	4
Anglesey	6,342	6,103	.	4
Carnarvon	11,762	11,297	.	4
Wilts	51,272	48,623	.	5
Berks	33,566	31,598	.	6
Gloucester	40,382	38,021	.	6
Hereford	16,330	15,323	.	6
Somerset	71,535	67,165	.	6
Suffolk	54,409	51,114	.	6
Montgomery	11,493	10,759	.	6
Huntingdon	9,272	8,628	.	7
Kent	71,168	66,362	.	7

COUNTIES.	Expenditure for In-maintenance and Out-Relief. Half-year ended Michaelmas 1842	Expenditure for In-maintenance and Out-Relief. Half-year ended Michaelmas 1843	Increase per Cent. in 1843, compared with 1842.	Decrease per Cent. in 1843, compared with 1842.
	£.	£.		
Norfolk	62,350	58,195	.	7
Warwick	24,631	22,994	.	7
Cardigan	8,978	8,350	.	7
Cornwall	33,413	30,891	.	8
Dorset	32,109	29,600	.	8
Essex	56,931	52,593	.	8
Hertford	26,705	24,552	.	8
Southampton	46,471	42,618	.	8
Surrey	68,196	62,521	.	8
Sussex	44,654	40,935	.	8
Denbigh	9,554	8,797	.	8
Pembroke	9,165	8,399	.	8
Cumberland	15,348	13,945	.	9
Bedford	17,412	15,681	.	10
Devon	71,129	64,356	.	10
Stafford	40,328	36,471	.	10
Radnor	3,406	3,062	.	10
Chester	36,382	32,489	.	11
Leicester	37,116	32,679	.	12
Middlesex	112,006	98,582	.	12
Carmarthen	15,075	13,256	.	12
Nottingham	32,663	27,769	.	15
Lancaster	111,372	93,076	.	16
Totals of 584 Unions	1,795,950	1,677,511	.	7
Estimated for Places not in Union	325,813	304,326	.	7
Estimated for England and Wales	2,121,763	1,981,837	.	7

7. COMPARATIVE STATEMENT of the number of In-door and Out-door Adult able-bodied Paupers relieved in England and Wales, during the Quarters ended Lady-Day, 1842 and 1843, respectively.

Quarters ended at Lady-Day.	Number of ADULT able-bodied Paupers relieved. In-door. On account of temporary sickness or accident.	Proportion per cent. to Total.	All other causes, including Vagrants	Proportion per cent. to Total.	Total In door.	Out-door. On account of temporary sickness or accident.	Proportion per cent. to Total.	All other causes, including Vagrants.	Proportion per cent. to Total.	Total Out-door.	Total In-door and Out-door.	Total number of In-door and Out-door relieved on account of temporary sickness or accident.	Proportion per cent. to total In-door and Out-door.
1842	10,922	13	74,249	87	85,171	134,641	41	192,078	59	326,719	411,890	145,563	35
1843	10,880	11	88,239	89	99,119	146,369	40	219,384	60	365,753	464,872	157,249	34

NOTE.—An estimate is made for places not in union under the Poor Law Amendment Act.

8. COMPARATIVE STATEMENT of the Amount of Money Levied and Expended in England and Wales, during the Nine Years prior, and the Nine years subsequent, to the Passing of the Poor Law Amendment Act.

Years ended Lady-day.	Total Amount of Money Levied.	Expended in Relief and Maintenance of the Poor.	Law Charges, Removals, &c.	County Rate.	All other Purposes.	Total Parochial Rates Expended.	Rate per Cent. of Increase or Decrease on Amount Expended in Relief to the Poor, in each Year, compared with the preceding. Increase.	Decrease.	Average Price of Wheat per Quarter.
NINE YEARS BEFORE THE PASSING OF THE POOR LAW AMENDMENT ACT.									
	£.	£.	£.	£.	£.	£.			s. d.
1826	6,965,051	5,928,502	..	743,111	503,034	7,174,647	2	..	58 9
1827	7,784,352	6,441,088	..	762,187	600,191	7,803,466	9	..	56 9
1828	7,715,055	6,298,000	..	721,308	651,125	7,670,433	..	2	60 5
1829	7,642,171	6,332,410	..	714,308	566,021	7,612,739	1	..	66 3
1830	8,111,422	6,829,042	..	726,800	605,439	8,161,281	8	..	62 10
1831	8,279,218	6,798,889	..	772,966	767,232	8,339,087	..	..	67 8
1832	8,622,920	7,036,969		799,414	847,079	8,683,462	4	..	63 4
1833	8,606,501	6,790,800	* 254,412	745,270	949,400	8,739,882	..	4	57 3
1834	8,338,079	6,317,255	258,604	691,548	1,021,941	8,289,348	..	7	51 11
NINE YEARS SINCE THE PASSING OF THE POOR LAW AMENDMENT ACT.									
1835	7,373,807	5,526,418	202,527	705,711	935,362	7,370,018	..	13	41 2
1836	6,354,538	4,717,630	172,432	699,845	823,213	6,413,120	..	15	39 5
† 1837	5,294,566	4,044,741	126,951	604,203	637,043	5,412,938	..	14	52 6
1838	5,186,389	4,123,604	93,982	681,842	§ 569,271	5,468,699	2	..	55 3
1839	5,613,938	4,406,907	‡ 63,412	741,407	602,855	5,814,581	7	..	69 4
1840	6,014,605	4,576,965	67,020	855,552	567,889	6,067,426	3	..	68 6
1841	6,351,828	4,760,929	69,912	1,026,035	‡ 636,266	6,493,172	4	..	65 3
1842	6,552,890	4,911,498	68,051	1,230,718	501,504	6,711,771	3	..	64 0
1843	7,084,759	5,207,457	84,793	1,294,774	446,707	7,033,731	6	..	54 4

* The amount expended for Law, &c., was not distinguished until 1833, previous to which time the expenditure under that head was included partly with Relief, &c., to the Poor, and partly under the head of "Other Purposes."
† The Year in which the Expenditure for Relief, &c., to the Poor was at the minimum.
‡ In this and the following Years the expenses incurred in removal of Paupers is included under the head of "Other Purposes."
§ Including in this and following Year's Expenses under Registration and Parochial Assessments Acts.
Decrease in 1837 compared with 1834 on Relief, &c., to the Poor, 36 per cent.
Increase in 1843 compared with 1837 on Relief, &c., to the Poor, 29 per cent.
Decrease in 1843 compared with 1834 on Relief, &c., to the Poor, 18 per cent.
|| Including in this and subsequent Year's Expenses under the Vaccination Extension Act.

9. TOTAL AMOUNT of Money Levied and Expended, under the following heads, in England and Wales, during the Nine Years prior, and the Nine years subsequent, to the passing of the Poor Law Amendment Act.

Years.	Amount of Money Levied.	Amount of Money Expended in Relief and Maintenance of Poor.	Proportion per Cent. to Total.	Expenditure in Law Charges, Removals, &c.	Proportion per Cent. to Total.	Expenditure for County Rate.	Proportion per Cent. to Total.	Expended for all other Purposes.	Proportion per Cent. to Total.	Total Parochial Rates Expended.
	£.	£.		£.		£.		£.		£.
1826 to 1834	72,064,769	58,772,955	81	*513,016	..	6,676,912	9	6,511,462	9	72,474,345
1835 to 1843	55,827,320	42,276,149	74	949,110	2	7,840,087	14	5,720,110	10	56,785,456
Decrease	16,237,449	16,496,806	..	..	..	..	..	791,352	..	15,688,889
Increase	..	..	..	..	..	1,163,175	..	..	..	..

* Total of two Years only.

VII. PAUPER.—Refusing to leave the Workhouse.

4th January, 1844.

Clerk of Malmsbury Union — Stated that James Clifford, a pauper, belonging to the parish of Little Somerford, in the Malmsbury Union, with his wife and five children, all under ten years of age, was admitted into the Union workhouse about three weeks previous; being, as he asserted, unable to maintain his wife and family upon his then earnings, viz. 7*s*. per week. Since that time, the Guardians of Little Somerford had offered to guarantee him 8*s*. per week, and find him a lodging free of rent, upon his leaving the workhouse, and taking with him his family. This, however, Clifford refused to do, unless one of his children was provided for in the house, or the parish would guarantee him 10*s*. per week, being 2*s*. more than ordinary labourers could obtain there. The magistrates, upon being applied to, refused to interfere in the matter, and the Board, being at a loss to know how to act therein, requested the advice of the Commissioners.

Ans. The Commissioners are of opinion that if any pauper be offered work, at competent wages, for the support of himself and family, and refuses to accept such offer, remaining at the same time chargeable to his parish, he would be liable to be dealt with under the 3rd section of the Vagrant Act. That section provides, "that any person, being able, wholly, or in part, to maintain himself or herself, or his or her family, by work or other means, and wilfully refusing or neglecting so to do, by which refusal or neglect, such person, or any of his or her family, shall have become chargeable, &c. &c. shall be deemed an idle and disorderly person." The Commissioners do not think it advisable that any means should be used, in order to compel the pauper to quit the workhouse. The law has undoubtedly invested the Guardians with full power to withhold relief, if they are satisfied that any applicant is of ability and has the means to maintain himself and those dependent on him, "or uses ordinary or daily trade of life to get his living by," (see 43 Eliz., c. 2.) They might therefore discharge a pauper from the workhouse to whom suitable employment might be offered, but refused by such pauper. Such a course of proceeding, however, might expose the Guardians to serious responsibility, if their decision should turn out to be erroneous, and any ill consequences should ensue from the discharge of the pauper. The Commissioners would therefore suggest that the pauper should be allowed to remain in the workhouse, and they advise the Guardians to keep him constantly at work, so long as he remains in the workhouse.

VIII.—POOR RATE. — Not legally assessed.

15th January, 1844.

Auditor of Market Drayton Union—Stated that in auditing the accounts for last Lady-day for the parish of Mucclestone, he found there was a balance due to the late overseers of 239*l*. and it not appearing at the Midsummer audit that such balance had been paid over to them, he doubted the correctness of the accounts, and consequently summoned, not only the present, but the former overseers, before the magistrates. It then appeared that the assistant overseer had collected a rate not signed or allowed by the magistrates, and which was not produced to the auditor, which would be sufficient to repay the balance appearing to be due to the former overseers. The present overseers were satisfied that this voluntary rate had been properly applied, and it seemed no wrong had been sustained in consequence. The auditor felt a difficulty in allowing this rate, and the magistrates requested him to obtain the sanction of the Commissioners to the assessment.

Ans. The Commissioners in reply desire to point out that their sanction is wholly unnecessary. If the voluntary rate to which you refer has been applied towards the relief of the poor, the assistant-overseer is accountable to you for it, under the 47th section of the Poor Law Amendment Act. That section includes every person holding any sum of money relating to the relief of the poor; and even if it were not so, the term "poor-rate," as used in that section is interpreted by the 109th section as extending, not only to a rate legally assessed, but to any subscription or contribution for the relief of the poor.

IX.—RATING.—A Manganese Mine.

11th January, 1844.

Assistant Overseer, Lamberton — Inquired whether the proprietor of a manganese mine, from which he received the sum of 1*l*. per ton, amounting to upwards of 800*l*. a-year, was rateable to the poor-rate.

Ans. The mine in question is certainly not rateable *as a mine*, the exclusive mention of coal-mines, in the 43 Eliz. c. 2, having been held by the Courts to exempt from the rate all other descriptions of mines. The Company occupying the mine is therefore not rateable: nor is the owner rateable, inasmuch as he receives from the Company a money rent, and not a rent consisting of any portion of the unwrought produce of the mine. With regard to the question of the owner's liability, the Commissioners direct your attention to the case of R. *v.* Tremayne (4 B. and Ad. 162), in which the proprietor of a manganese mine, who received, as rent from the occupiers, 1*l.* 15*s.* per ton, was held not to be rateable.

X.—REGISTRATION LISTS.

1. AS TO THE EXPENSES WHICH THE REVISING BARRISTER IS EMPOWERED TO CERTIFY FOR.

25*th October*, 1843.

Mr. Binyon, Auditor, East London Union—Inquired whether the Revising Barrister's certificate for the expenses incurred by overseers in making out the registration lists under the Act 8th Vic., c. 18, was a sufficient authority to the auditor to allow in the parish accounts the amount comprehended in such certificate; or, whether expenses so certified were to be subject to revision by the auditor.

Ans. The 6th Vict., c. 18, s. 57, appears to effect this. 1. It enables the overseers to lay an account before the revising barrister of all expenses incurred by the overseers in carrying into effect the provisions of the Act. It even seems to contemplate the probability of such expenses being put into this account, as may not be proper for allowance. It cannot be inferred from any thing apparent in the clause that the overseers are prevented from putting into the account any expenses actually incurred, however unreasonably or unlawfully.—2. It enables the barrister to certify the sum he may allow to be due to the overseers. This may, as it appears, be a different sum from that stated in their accounts. It is not a mere allowance of those accounts as presented to the barrister. The barrister appears in this to be invested with a judicial function, and to be made a competent authority, as he is undoubtedly from his position most perfectly acquainted with those exigencies of the case which may have justified the incurring of expense.—3. It enables the overseer to receive the sum so certified out of the poor-rates next to be collected. This appears to make the certificate of the barrister final and conclusive, as an authority for the receipt of the money by the overseers. The Commissioners conclude that the auditor cannot reverse the decision of the revising barrister, but must regard his certificate as a final settlement of the claim of the overseers, by a competent tribunal, subject to no appeal.

2. AS TO WHETHER EXPENSES OF REGISTRATION LISTS COULD BE ALLOWED WHERE NO CERTIFICATE HAD BEEN OBTAINED.

Auditor of the Pershore Union—Stated that several overseers, not knowing that it was required, neglected to lay the accounts of their expenses before the revising barrister at the Court at which their lists of voters were revised, and consequently by this neglect they had not obtained certificates of the sums due to them according to the provisions of the 57th section of 6 Vic. c. 18. Inquired whether he could properly allow at his next audit the sums expended by the overseers for the last registration of voters, and for which they could produce proper vouchers, but without any certificate from the revising barrister.

Ans. The sum which the overseers are to be allowed from the poor-rates under section 57, 6 Vic. c. 18 (the only statutory authority for charging the poor-rates at all in this matter), is the sum which the revising barrister shall allow to be due to them in respect of the expenses incurred by them. It appears to the Commissioners that there is no authority for paying anything from the poor-rates, on account of registration expenses, until the revising barrister has exercised the discretion, with which the Act invests him, of declaring what is due. The Commissioners feel bound, therefore, to say that, in the absence of the certificate, the auditor could not lawfully allow any payments entered in the accounts of the overseers as having been incurred for the purposes of the parliamentary voters' registration.

XI.—REGISTRATION OF DEATHS.—

DEMAND OF A FEE FOR A CERTIFICATE OF THE CAUSE OF DEATH.

1*st January*, 1844.

Tiverton Union.—The registrar for the Silverton district of this Union stated that he had been applied to by a nurse to register the death of one Robert Thomas; but the nurse not being able to state the name of the complaint of which the deceased had died, she was requested to bring a note from the medical man (Mr. Puddicombe) who had attended him. The nurse called on the registrar afterwards, and stated that Mr. Puddicombe declined to give the required note without being paid a fee. Mr. Puddicombe, who was stated to be a medical officer of this Union, on being written to by the Poor Law Commissioners, explained that he had attended the deceased as a private, not as a pauper patient, and requested to be informed whether he was legally bound to give certificates of disease whenever the registrar called on him to do so The Commissioners, in reply, addressed to Mr. Puddicombe the following letter:—

"The Registrar-General, in his instructions to the registrars, has recommended them to obtain, whenever it can be done, information from the medical man attending the deceased as to the complaint of which he died. This course is recommended, as being the one calculated to ensure the greatest accuracy in registering the cause of death, a matter of considerable importance both as regards medical and statistical science. If, however, the medical man does not sign the entry of a death in the register, as the informant, he cannot be compelled to furnish the information. But the Commissioners request your attention to the paper* signed by the President of the Royal Colleges of Physicians and Surgeons, and the Master of the Apothecaries' Company, at page 5 of the enclosed pamphlet, in which they invite all medical practitioners to assist in establishing a better registration of the causes of death throughout England. As regards the cases of paupers, the Commissioners are prepared to state that they think the information required ought to be given by the medical officers."

* The paper referred to is as follows:—"We, the undersigned, President of the Royal College of Physicians, President of the Royal College of Surgeons, and Master of the Worshipful Society of Apothecaries, having authority from the several bodies whom we represent, do resolve to fulfil the intentions of the legislature in procuring a better registration of the causes of death, being convinced that such an improved registration cannot fail to lead to a more accurate statistical account of the prevalence of particular diseases from time to time.

"We pledge ourselves therefore to give, in every instance which may fall under our care, an authentic name of the fatal disease.

"And we entreat all authorised practitioners throughout the country to follow our example and adopt the same practice, and so assist in establishing a better registration in future throughout England; for which purpose we invite them to attend to the subjoined explanatory statement, in which they will see set forth the provisions of the recent statute, and the means whereby the important object we have recommended may most effectually be attained.

"(Signed) HENRY HALFORD, *President of the Royal College of Physicians.*

"(Signed) ASTLEY COOPER, *President of the Royal College of Surgeons.*

"(Signed) J. HINGESTON, *Master of the Society of Apothecaries.*

"*1st May*, 1837."

XII.—RELIEF.

1. RELIEF TO NON-RESIDENT PAUPERS, WHERE CHARGEABLE.

8th January, 1844.

1. *Clerk of the Hay Union*—Stated that on the 19th day of December last, W. W., aged 59, called upon John Mills, relieving officer of the Hay Union, at his residence in the parish of Talgarth, and asked for relief; at the same time, stating he was travelling from the iron-works to his parish (Glasbury), which is in Mills's district. Mills refused relief, under the impression that the man was not in a state of destitution. W. W. proceeded on to Hay, and there applied to Thomas Perks, the other relieving officer of the Union, stating again that he belonged to Glasbury, and that he had seen Mills, who had referred him to Perks. Perks gave W. W. an order of admission into the workhouse, as a pauper belonging to Glasbury. W. W. came into the house, but on the case coming before the Board for confirmation on the 21st of Dec., the guardian of Glasbury objected to admit him to be a parishioner.—Inquired, to what parish should W. W. be charged; whether to Talgarth, the parish in which the first application for relief was made; to Hay, where the second application was made and relief obtained; or, to Glasbury, the parish on behalf of which the relief was granted.

Ans.—The Commissioners can perceive no good ground for charging the relief of W. W. to the parish of Talgarth: although he applied for relief in that parish he did not obtain it, and the Commissioners are not aware of any reason for supposing that the circumstance of merely soliciting, without receiving, relief, is a sufficient ground for chargeability. Then he applied for relief in Hay, and was thereupon admitted into the Union workhouse. Under these circumstances the primary liability, in respect of his relief, rested with Hay. He does not appear to have been resident in any particular place, but to have been travelling to Glasbury; consequently, he was not in the position of a person, who being resident in one parish in the Union, goes into another parish, (where the relieving officer lives or where the workhouse stands,) solely for the purpose of applying for relief. But, notwithstanding the primary liability of Hay, the Commissioners think that the guardians of the Union, if they are satisfied that the pauper is legally settled in Glasbury, might, if they should deem it fit, give him non-resident relief, that is to say, they might charge his relief to Glasbury, although at the time he applied for it he happened to be in Hay, both the parishes being included in the same Union. It appears, however, that the guardian for Glasbury refuses to acknowledge his settlement therein, and the guardians of the Union ought therefore to be particularly cautious in charging the relief to that parish, as the charge would of course be subject to the revision of the auditor should any objection on behalf of Glasbury be made against it at the audit.

---

2. DITTO.

16*th January*, 1844.

Clerk of the Penzance Union—Stated that William Tredinnick resided at St. Ives, one of parishes of the Penzance Union, for several years, and until within a few days of his coming to the workhouse on the 30th November. After leaving St. Ives, he spent two or three days in Uny Lelant, another of the parishes of the Union, and on the 29th November he came to Penzance, and slept there one night; and, on the following day, he attended at the Union-house, where the Board were then sitting, and applied for an order of admission into the workhouse, which was granted to him. He had made no previous application for relief to any overseer or relieving officer. The Board, therefore, on referring to the Commissioners' letter of the 4th May last,* in the case of Elizabeth Stodden, directed the pauper to be charged to the parish of Madron, in consequence of his first application having been made at the board-room, which is situate therein. It was contended, however, by some of the Guardians, that this case differed from Elizabeth Stodden's in this respect, viz., that Tredinnick had been immediately, prior to his admission, a resident in one of the parishes in this Union, while Elizabeth Stodden had not been so, but merely passed from an adjoining Union through, and slept one night in Penzance, on her way to the workhouse. Tredinnick stated that he left St. Ives with the intention to go to the workhouse, and merely stopped at a friend's in Uny Lelant, and slept one night in Penzance on the way thither.

Ans. The Commissioners conceive that the general rule for determining the chargeability of paupers is this, that a pauper is chargeable to that parish in which, being destitute, he applies for and obtains relief. There is, however, one class of cases which present an apparent exception to this rule, namely, those cases in which the pauper, being destitute in one parish, is compelled to go into another parish where the workhouse stands, or the Guardians meet, or the relieving officer lives, in order to make his application for relief. In this class of cases the application must be constructively regarded as having been made in the parish where it became necessary, and where it would have been actually made but for the situation of the workhouse, the Guardians' place of meeting, or the relieving officer's residence, and the relief will be accordingly chargeable to that parish. With regard to Elizabeth

* The following is the case referred to above:—

4th May, 1843.

Clerk of the Penzance Union—Stated that Elizabeth Stodden, an infirm woman, who lately resided with her son at Redruth, in an adjoining Union, came on the 16th April to the Union workhouse whilst the Board was sitting, and applied to be admitted into the workhouse. She claimed St. Hilary, in the Penzance Union, as her legal settlement, which the overseers of that parish did not admit. It appeared that she had left Redruth on the 13th April to come to Penzance for the purpose of obtaining relief, and came on to Camborne in the same Union, where she slept that night and the next. On the 15th she came on to Penzance, where she expected to find the relieving officer for St. Hilary; but finding that he lived in Gulval, she felt unable to go there, and slept that night in Penzance. On the following morning she applied to the Board at the Union workhouse, which is in the parish of Madron, and was ordered to be admitted as an inmate of the house.

Ans. As Elizabeth Stodden first applied for relief (being destitute) in the parish of Madron, the Commissioners think that she must be considered as chargeable to that parish. The fact of her having slept the night before at Penzance would not render that parish liable to receive her. The Guardians would not have been justified in sending her back to the place of her previous residence. She was destitute in Penzance Union, and therefore entitled to receive relief from the authorities charged with its administration in that Union, whatever might have been the circumstances under which she entered the Union.

Stodden, the Commissioners saw nothing in your communication to show that she was so far destitute as actually to require relief until she applied for it in Madron, and the Commissioners therefore considered that parish liable for her relief, as being the parish in which, when destitute, she applied for and obtained it. With respect to William Tredinnick, likewise, it appears to the Commissioners that the chargeability, *primâ facie*, rests on the parish of Madron. The Commissioners conceive that there is no ground for deeming St. Ives liable; for, although Tredinnick had resided there for several years previously, he had nevertheless left it some days before he applied for relief. The Commissioners presume there is no doubt that Uny Lelant is not chargeable; and the mere circumstance of the pauper's having slept at Penzance the night before he made the application for relief would not of itself prove that he was destitute in that parish, but rather the reverse, as he probably provided himself with a lodging from his own resources. If, however, it can be shown that he was actually destitute in Penzance so as to need relief, and that he went into Madron for the sole purpose of soliciting such relief because the Guardians were sitting there, then the Commissioners think that Penzance, and not Madron, would be the parish chargeable.

---

3. NON-RESIDENT RELIEF—DEATH OF PAUPER.
22nd January, 1844.

Bradford Union (York).—In reference to the case of Martha Robinson, a pauper belonging to the township of Wilsden, Bradford Union, but residing at the time of her death in the township of Bingley, Keighley Union, on whose body an inquest was held, when the jury returned a verdict that she had died by the visitation of God from natural causes, but that her death had been accelerated by the want of proper and sufficient food, care, and attention, the Poor Law Commissioners have addressed the following letter to the Guardians of the Bradford Union, and have transmitted a copy of the letter to the Guardians of the Keighley Union:—

"The Commissioners very much regret the circumstances of distress in which this poor woman died, but they see no reason to attribute neglect to any of the officers of the Bradford Union in the case. It appears that Martha Robinson and her daughter, with two illegitimate children of the latter, having been inmates of the Bradford workhouse, were upon their own application allowed by the Guardians to leave the workhouse about four months ago, and to receive out-relief to the amount, at first, of 3*s*., and afterwards of 3*s*. 6*d*. per week, which was paid to them by the relieving officer of the Bradford Union, the paupers residing some little distance out of the Union, at Harden Beck, which is in the Keighley Union. The daughter of Martha Robinson, on the Monday before she died, applied to the relieving officer for further relief, on the ground that her mother was ill; and was told by the relieving officer, who was not aware of the serious nature of the illness, that if more relief was wanted before the next Board-day than had been ordered by the Bradford Guardians, she must go to the relieving officer for the Bingley District of the Keighley Union, in which the pauper resided. She did not, however, make any application to the Bingley relieving officer, and on the following Friday her mother died. Upon this statement of facts, the Commissioners think it is much to be lamented that the pauper did not remain in the Bradford workhouse, where she would have been properly taken care of, and would have received such medical assistance as her case required. Or if on leaving the workhouse she had gone to reside within the Bradford Union, it would then have been the duty of the relieving officer (Art. 20, No. 5, Duties of Officers' Order), on being informed of her illness, to have visited her, and supplied, until the next meeting of the Guardians, such relief as she might have needed. But as she resided in the parish of Bingley, in the Keighley Union, the legal liability for her relief rested upon that township. That she was actually in receipt of some relief from the Bradford Union would make no difference in the case, as regarded any further relief she might require, and the relieving officer, therefore, did not act otherwise than correctly in referring her daughter to the Bingley relieving officer. The Commissioners think it cannot be too clearly understood or widely known, both by the poor and by Union officers, that the place in which a destitute person resides is that liable for his relief. The importance and humanity of this provision of the law, whereby the question as to whom a destitute person can legally claim relief from, is decided by a fact of which no doubt can be entertained, instead of by the settlement of the party or any other circumstance which might admit of dispute, is obvious; and the Commissioners think that the practice of allowing relief to non-resident paupers, in addition to other inconveniences, is objectionable on this ground, that it cannot fail to raise doubts in the minds of the Union officers, and also of the poor, to whom the latter are entitled to look for relief. The Commissioners have no reason to suppose that the Bingley relieving officer, if applied to in this case, would not have afforded relief; but as they are aware that non-resident relief is commonly allowed in the district, they think it desirable that the Guardians of that Union, as well as of the Bradford Union, should draw the attention of their officers to what their duty is in such cases, and for that purpose they will transmit a copy of this letter to the Keighley Board."

XIII.—REMOVAL.—OUT-RELIEF WITH A VIEW TO REMOVAL.

25*th January*, 1844.

Clerk of Bath Union—Requested the Commissioners' sanction to out-door relief, which the Guardians had directed to be given to Sarah Gooding, Thomas Viles, and Caroline Davies, respectively, with a view to their removal to the parishes to which they belonged, such paupers being chargeable to different parishes from that in which the Union workhouse stood.

Ans. The Commissioners refer to their Official Circular, No. 27, which contains an expression of their opinion that a pauper is removable from a Union workhouse, notwithstanding he may be chargeable to a different parish from that in which the workhouse stands. The Commissioners arrived at this conclusion some time ago, after a careful consideration of the question, and they see no reason to alter the view which they then adopted. They have long thought it desirable, however, that all doubt on the subject should be removed, and accordingly a clause designed to obviate the difficulty was inserted in the Bill for the further amendment of the poor laws, which was intended to be brought forward in the last session of Parliament. The Commissioners are not prepared to modify their general rules in respect to the relief of able-bodied paupers, on account of the difference of opinion which appears to prevail upon this subject; nevertheless they are ready to consider in any special case the propriety of allowing out-door relief for a day or two previous to the pauper's removal, until at least the doubt as to the law shall have been set at rest by the superior courts or by the legislature. They accordingly sanction the out-door relief reported in your letters of the 5th and 16th instant.

XIV. — VACCINATION. — CIRCULAR ADDRESSED TO THE METROPOLITAN BOARDS OF GUARDIANS.

Poor Law Commission Office,
Somerset House,
29*th January*, 1844.

SIR,—The Poor Law Commissioners have had their attention drawn to the fact that small pox at present prevails to a considerable extent in several districts of the metropolis. It appears from the weekly tables of mortality published by the Registrar-General, that the deaths from this cause have within the last few weeks been much beyond the average deaths of previous weeks, and that the greater portion of the parties who died from the disease had not been vaccinated.

The Commissioners feel it their duty to call the attention of the Board of Guardians of the several Unions and parishes in the metropolis to these facts, and to suggest that immediate steps be taken to make known to the residents the arrangements of the Guardians in regard to vaccination, under the Vaccination Extension Act, and the names and addresses of the several vaccinators. This can best be done by the Guardians causing hand-bills in the usual form to be extensively posted on the church-doors and other public places in the district.

In addition to this, the Commissioners would suggest that the several vaccinators be instructed to visit the houses of the poorer classes, when they have reason to believe that there are any children unvaccinated, and to urge upon the parents of such children the expediency of the operation being performed forthwith.

I am, Sir, &c.
GEORGE COODE, *Assistant Secretary.*

The Clerk to the Board of

LONDON:
Printed by Order of the Poor Law Commissioners, by W. CLOWES and SONS, Stamford Street, and Published by CHARLES KNIGHT and Co., 22, Ludgate Street, Publishers to the Poor Law Commissioners.

AN

OFFICIAL CIRCULAR

OF PUBLIC DOCUMENTS AND INFORMATION:

DIRECTED BY THE POOR LAW COMMISSIONERS TO BE PRINTED, CHIEFLY FOR THE USE OF THE MEMBERS AND PERMANENT OFFICERS OF BOARDS OF GUARDIANS, UNDER THE POOR LAW AMENDMENT ACT.

No. 32. CIRCULAR ISSUED FEBRUARY 29, 1844.

Poor Law Commission Office,
Somerset House,
29th February, 1844.

THE Poor Law Commissioners, on a review of their Minutes, directed that the Minutes of Correspondence on the following subjects be printed and circulated for the information of Guardians and Officers of the several Unions, viz:—

By Order of the Board,
EDWIN CHADWICK, *Secretary.*

I.—REPORT OF THE POOR LAW COMMISSIONERS TO SIR JAMES GRAHAM ON THE LAW CONCERNING THE MAINTENANCE OF BASTARDS.

Poor Law Commission Office,
Somerset House,
31st January, 1844.

SIR,

WE take the liberty of submitting to you a Report on the present condition of the Law concerning the Maintenance of Bastard Children, with reference to the Bill for making some further amendments in the Poor Laws, which Her Majesty's Government intend, we believe, to introduce into Parliament during the approaching Session.

The remarks which we feel it our duty to lay before you will be contained within a narrow compass, and will be limited almost exclusively to the period subsequent to 1834, the year of the passing of the Poor Law Amendment Act (6 & 7 Will. 4, c. 76).

The law concerning the Maintenance of Bastards is, so far as it is connected with the Poor Laws, exclusively of statutory origin. The Commissioners of Poor Law Inquiry have deduced its history down to the year 1834 (Report, edit. 8vo. p. 165—178), and have shown, by copious evidence, the manner of its practical operation, as it had been established at that time.

It is needless for us to repeat the perspicuous explanation of the Commissioners of Inquiry; we will merely state that the *purpose* of the law, as it then stood, was to indemnify the parish for the cost of the relief given by it to a bastard child, by enabling it to compel the putative father to contribute to the child's maintenance; but that the *operation* of the law was to enable the mother to recover from the putative father a weekly payment which the parish transferred to her as of course. The parish went even further, for it often guaranteed to the mother the payment ordered by the justices; and if the father omitted to pay, the parish made the money good. "Whatever is received by the man," say the Commissioners of Inquiry, "is paid over by the parish to the woman; and in almost every case the parish pays to the woman the sum, whatever it may be, that has been charged on the man, whether paid by him or not."—(Page 167.) In *form*, therefore, the proceeding was against the putative father for the indemnification of the parish, and the mother was not a material party to it; but in *substance*, it was a proceeding of the mother against the putative father, the benefit of which accrued to her, and to which the parish was little more than a nominal party, except when it made good the father's default. It was, in truth, an action of the mother against the putative father for a contribution towards the expenses of their common child, in which, by a fiction of law, the parish was plaintiff.

The Commissioners of Inquiry set forth the various evils resulting from the law as thus administered; and they recommended that the mother of a bastard should be rendered liable for its maintenance, but that she should be exempted from punishment under 30 Geo. 3, c. 51, and that all enactments charging the putative father of a bastard should be repealed. (Report, pp. 346—351.)

The Bill for amending the Poor Laws as introduced into Parliament in the Session of 1834, was framed in accordance with these suggestions; but a clause authorising the making of orders of affiliation in petty sessions, was introduced into the Bill in the House of Commons. In the House of Lords, the Bill was amended, in the manner in which it ultimately received the Royal Assent. (*See* ss. 72—76.) According to the Act as thus altered, the parish might apply to the quarter sessions for an order upon the putative father; but the proceeding was of such a nature, and was accompanied with so many onerous conditions, that it could not be extensively available.

The effects of this mode of legislation soon began to be felt. In April, 1835, the magistrates for the county of Nottingham, assembled in general quarter sessions, transmitted to Lord John Russell, then Her Majesty's Principal Secretary of State for the Home Department, a memorial respecting the recent alterations of the Bastardy Law, in which, (after having expressed their opinion that the liability of the mother to maintain her bastard, and the exemption of the putative father from imprisonment for want of securities, were wise and salutary measures), they objected to the operation of the 72nd section of the Act, which contained the principal enactments on the subject. These objections, as stated in their own words, were, "First, the very great expense of bringing all the parties and their witnesses to the general quarter sessions, however distant, instead of the nearest petty sessions; Secondly, the very great difficulty of obtaining corroborative evidence; Thirdly, the want of power of charging the defendant with costs, in case of the parish officer succeeding in obtaining an order of filiation; Fourthly, the payment of 'full costs' to the defendant without limitation of amount, if the order is not made; Fifthly, the impossibility, in most cases, of compelling obedience to the order, from want of goods to seize, or wages to attach, and from want of power to attach the person in default." (First Annual Report of the Poor Law Commissioners, Appendix, p. 358, ed. 8vo.) As remedies for these evils, the magistrates of the county of Nottingham proposed—

1. That the putative father should be permitted to appeal to the quarter sessions, on giving security for costs; but that where there was no defence and no objection, the case should be decided by the magistrates at the nearest petty sessions.

2. That the person of the putative father should be attachable in default of payment, and that his liability should continue so long as the child was chargeable, but no longer.

By the direction of Lord John Russell, this memorial was referred to the Poor Law Commissioners, who reported upon it shortly afterwards to his Lordship. Their Report (dated 13th May,

1835) states, that with respect to the four first objections in the memorial (cited above), "It must be observed, that as the change in the law, which transferred the jurisdiction in bastardy cases from the petty to the general quarter sessions, necessarily produced increase of expense, and increase of trouble to all parties, the Legislature must be presumed to have contemplated these obvious results. The giving of full costs to the person charged, and none against him, must be held also to indicate that the object of the Legislature was to impede, rather than encourage, the application to quarter sessions, and, by so doing, to conform partially to the recommendation of the Commissioners of Inquiry, that the remedy against the supposed father should be abolished altogether." With respect to the fifth objection, the Commissioners remark, that "the want of power to attach the person was deliberately established by the Legislature, under the impression that all severe proceedings against the father might be used as a means of compelling a marriage where the man was reluctant; and it is apparent that the imprisonment of the father, whether immediate or after default of payment, would always be an evil, from the occurrence of which he might relieve himself by marriage." After some further remarks, they proceed to say, "The expediency, therefore, or the inexpediency of making the proposed alteration in the law, depends altogether on the determination it may be thought right to take on the main question at issue. Is or is it not desirable to revert to the principle on which the bastardy laws stood prior to the Poor Law Amendment Act? Or is it better to follow out the recommendations contained in the Poor Law Report, and abandon orders of affiliation altogether?"

With respect, however, to the probable success of the indirect means for discouraging affiliation, adopted in the Poor Law Amendment Act, the Commissioners proceed to observe as follows: "It should be borne in mind, that though more money may be expended in the applications to the magistrates at quarter sessions than can ever be recovered from the fathers of the children, it does not seem likely that the practice will soon yield to the discouragement to which it is exposed.

"The mother of the child endeavours by every means in her power to induce the overseers to make the application; with the overseers themselves such applications have become habitual, and with them the necessity of making them is hardly a matter of doubt.

"The prevailing wish to inflict, if possible, some punishment on the father of the child, influences the judgment and opinion of all the parties interested, and the overseers themselves (with whom the decision as to the appeal mainly rests) are in many instances not liable to any considerable share of the expense to be incurred by the prosecution. There appears to be no ground for expecting, therefore, that the practice of applying to the magistrates at quarter sessions for orders of affiliation will be speedily and voluntarily abandoned.

"Whenever consulted on the subject, the Commissioners have thought it their duty to point out the certainty of expense and inconvenience, and the little chance which exists of indemnification, by resorting to the court of quarter sessions."

They add, however: "When unions shall be established, and the workhouse system be brought into operation, the bastardy clauses in the Poor Law Amendment Act will, it may be hoped, in great measure, fall into desuetude; but until those arrangements are completed, the operation of the Act will be justly liable to the objections so clearly stated by Mr. Rolleston, and to which, in fact, all legislative enactments are liable, which, instead of pointing at once to their object, are designed to accomplish it by indirect means."

The same course of remark is followed up in the First Annual Report of the Commissioners, (dated 8th August, 1835, pp. 58—61). In this Report the Commissioners state their opinion that in order to remove the remaining evils of the Bastardy Laws, it would be desirable to repeal all the statutory provisions under which proceedings can be taken by the parish against the putative father. "The ground (the Commissioners there observe) most strongly urged for the process against the father is founded on the notion that it may serve as a means of punishing the seducer. We participate in the feelings of detestation of the crime of seduction; but the principle that Poor Law administration should be the administration of relief alone, cannot be departed from by the introduction of anything having a view to punishment, without at the same time creating far greater evils than those which it is intended to repress."

Some remarks tending to show that the practice of affiliation was gradually diminishing under the influence of the Act, are made in the Second Annual Report of the Commissioners (dated 17th August 1836, pp. 17—19); and the following passage there occurs: "There are no clauses in the Act, which, in comparison with their importance, have occasioned so little correspondence with the office as those which relate to Bastardy. We occasionally receive letters containing inquiries as to the mode of relieving bastards born before the passing of the Act. More frequently we receive complaints that the expense which a parish is put to by applying to the quarter sessions for an order of affiliation is so great, that it is not worth while to incur it. To these statements we can only reply, that we believe this to be the result which the Legislature intended to produce."

The Law relating to Bastardy was one of the subjects which occupied the attention of the Select Committee of the House of Commons, which reported on the operation of the Poor Law Amendment Act, in August, 1838. After adverting to the recommendations of the Commissioners of Inquiry on the Maintenance of Bastards, and also to the Report of the Poor Law Commissioners on the Nottinghamshire Memorial, they proceed to state as follows:

"Your Committee are disposed to agree with the general views expressed on this subject by the Commissioners of Inquiry, and by the Poor Law Commissioners; they think it desirable that relief to the poor should be mixed up as little as possible with matters which seem to be more properly and directly connected with the administration of justice; and that relief to the mothers of bastard children, and to the children themselves, should be granted or refused on considerations arising out of their necessities, and not on any other grounds, or with a view to other objects; and if objections are entertained to the impunity of the man, it would appear to be desirable that the woman should be authorised to appeal to some easily accessible and unexpensive tribunal, such as has been suggested by Mr. Power, for redress in cases of seduction, or of breach of promise of marriage. This would, in the opinion of your Committee, be free from some of the objections to which all parochial interference in these questions is liable; and they have agreed to the following resolution:

"'That it is the opinion of the Committee, that many of the abuses arising under the former administration of the Laws relating to Bastardy have been corrected by the clauses in the Poor Law Amendment Act relating to this subject, an end having been put to the compulsory marriages, and the facilities to perjury, formerly prevalent; but that the remedy afforded by that Act leads, in many instances, to great expense in the trials in Courts of Quarter Sessions, which are often offensive to public decency; and that the law being rendered generally inoperative by those inconveniences attending it, requires the further consideration of the Legislature, especially with a view of inflicting some punishment for the crime of seduction.'"—*Report, p.* 34.

The motives for retaining the system of affiliation, which were adverted to by the Commissioners in their Report on the Nottinghamshire memorial, continued to exercise so much influence, that the obstacles to obtaining orders in bastardy, created by the provisions of the Poor Law Amendment Act, instead of repressing applications for orders, produced irritation and complaints; and on the 23d of July, 1839, Lord John Russell introduced a Bill for transferring the power of making orders in bastardy from the quarter to the petty sessions. The Bill thus introduced became the Act of 2 and 3 Vict. c. 85, which after reciting that "it is expedient to give more speedy and effectual means for obtaining orders upon the putative fathers of bastard children for their support and maintenance," proceeds to enable any two justices in petty sessions to make such orders.

This Act indicated an entire change in the views of Parliament with respect to orders of affiliation for the indemnity of the parish. Instead of discouraging orders of affiliation by indirect means, it gave facilities for obtaining them.

In our Sixth Annual Report (dated 30th April, 1840), we stated, that shortly after the passing of that statute, we addressed a letter to the Boards of Guardians, explaining the change which it had effected in the law; and we added the following reasons for sending this letter:—"The indemnification of the parish or union from the expenses incurred by it in the relief of the bastard, is the sole purpose and effect of the orders made under the statute in question; but we perceived a frequent wish among the local authorities to divert this proceeding from its proper purpose, and to employ it sometimes as a civil remedy for the mother, and at other times as a penal proceeding against the supposed father. We therefore thought it important for the guardians to bear constantly in mind that the indemnification of the parish is the sole purpose of orders in bastardy made under the recent statute; and that in applying to the justices for such orders, they ought not to seek to attain other and different ends."—P. 37.

We likewise remarked, "that if it be expedient to give to the mother of a bastard a civil remedy against the supposed father, or if it be expedient to make illicit connexion with the mother of a bastard a crime, and to proceed penally against the supposed father on account of it, these purposes ought to be effected directly, and not obtained indirectly and partially by the perversion of a law established for a different purpose. But whether the Legislature should give remedies to parishes, or to mothers of bastards, against the putative fathers, or enable putative fathers to be proceeded against criminally, it ought to be remembered that every law which, directly or indirectly, enables an unmarried woman to impose on an unmarried man the obligations of paternity, contravenes the principle on which the institution of marriage is founded, and tends inevitably to encourage concubinage and forced marriages, and to introduce the numerous and extensive evils which attend a disturbance of the conjugal and parental relations as established by the general law of marriage."

We believe that, by keeping the attention of the proper local officers alive to the precise nature of the remedy afforded by the statutes, we have generally succeeded in repressing any tendency which may have existed since the passing of the 2 and 3 Vict. s. 85, to pervert the law to illegal purposes. We believe that in general the payments made under orders in bastardy have been limited to the cost of the relief actually given, and that they have been made *bonâ fide* to the parish; and therefore that the parish has not been a purely formal party to the proceeding, and a mere screen to the woman.

The very fact, however, that there was in existence a controlling authority, charged with the duty of preventing the misapplication of the statutory provisions, has tended powerfully to increase the demand for further changes. The perversion of the remedy of the parish which we were bound to counteract, was the very object which the public seemed to desire. The indemnity of the parish, by the putative father, for the cost of relief in case of the child's destitution,—the only purpose recognized by the statutes, or having any affinity with the poor laws,—appeared to be generally considered as a matter of comparative indifference. The object really aimed at was to compel the putative father to bear an equal share with the mother in the expenses of the maintenance of the child; whether the child might or might not be chargeable.

The feeling to which we allude is generally expressed in the formula that "the putative father ought to be *punished*." We believe, however, that the persons who use this phrase do not intend to express an opinion that the putative father should be subject to any criminal proceeding by way of information or indictment; and that they merely refer to a civil remedy, such as we have above described, to be enforced, when necessary, by imprisonment.

The desire of obtaining an efficient legal remedy against putative fathers is particularly prevalent in Lancashire, Yorkshire, and the other northern counties; and we have likewise long had reason to know that a similar opinion is generally entertained in Wales. The prevalence of this feeling in South Wales at the present time is proved by the evidence recently taken by the Commissioners of Inquiry; a large part of which we have had an opportunity of inspecting.

We retain unaltered the opinions which are expressed in our Sixth Annnal Report, with respect to the tendencies of any system of affiliation; and we still anticipate that those tendencies will be more surely developed, in proportion as the system is extended. We are however fully conscious of the difficulties which have grown up under the course of legislation which we have above described. The result of these changes is, as it seems to us, that the present Bastardy Law rests on the acknowledgment of no definite or consistent principle. The Poor Law Amendment Act was intended to discourage parishes from attempting to indemnify themselves by orders on putative fathers: the Act of 2 and 3 Vict. c. 85, is shown, both by its recital and its provisions, to tend in the opposite direction. It is not therefore to be wondered that the inefficiency of the present law should be complained of, or that additional facilities for enforcing the remedy against the putative father should be demanded.

Assuming that affiliation is to be further facilitated, we think that the best mode of accomplishing this end, is to give an independent civil remedy to the mother of a bastard, as such, and not as a pauper, against the putative father; and thus to remove the barrier which the necessity of chargeability now interposes between the woman and her means of legal redress.

In order to effect this purpose, it would be necessary to repeal the existing remedy of the parish against the putative father, and to give to the justices a power of making, on the application of the mother, an order for a weekly sum to be paid towards the maintenance of the bastard.

In such a state of the law, the mother of a bastard would be in the same condition as any other pauper, being bound to maintain her child to the best of her ability, and being entitled to relief if destitute; whilst she would have against the putative father a direct and summary remedy, independent of the chargeability of her bastard, and founded on a proceeding in which she was both formally and substantially the plaintiff.

Although the parish would lose its remedy against the putative father, it would be no sufferer by the loss; for if the mother obtained an order upon the putative father, and the money was paid under it, she would have the means of supporting her child, and would not require relief. At the same time, proper provision should be made for prohibiting the interference of the parish officers in the proceedings; in order to prevent the demoralising system of forced marriages, for the supposed interest of the parish, which prevailed under the old system, and which might be renewed indirectly by their influence over the mother.

If the proceeding is to be instituted by the mother, it ought to be the cheapest and most direct which can be afforded, consistently with the protection which is due to the party charged. For this purpose it appears most convenient that such applications for orders in bastardy should, as at present, be heard and decided by the justices in petty sessions.

We append to this Report a copy of a letter relating to the Law of Bastardy in Scotland, which one of the members of our board has received from Mr. Twisleton, now acting as a Commissioner of Inquiry into the Administration of the Laws relating to the Poor in Scotland.

We have the honour to be, Sir,
Your very faithful and obedient servants,
GEORGE NICHOLLS.
GEORGE CORNEWALL LEWIS.
EDMUND WALKER HEAD.

---

27 *January*, 1844.

My dear Sir,

The chief distinction between the English and Scotch bastardy laws consists in this, that in England the putative father of an illegitimate child can only be required to contribute towards its maintenance in case it becomes chargeable to a parish, so that the bastardy laws are inseparably connected with the poor laws; whereas in Scotland the putative father is liable without any such previous chargeability, and it is only indirectly and occasionally that the poor laws are brought under consideration at all, as connected with the bastardy laws.

The mother of an illegitimate child in Scotland may at once bring an action for aliment in the Sheriff's Court against the putative father, and if she proves her case, the sheriff decrees that the father shall pay a certain sum yearly for the maintenance of the child until seven years of age if it is a boy, and until ten years of age if it is a girl. The sum thus decreed by the sheriff is a debt to the mother, and can be recovered in the same way as any other debt under the Scotch laws. The parish, for reasons which may be easily inferred from facts which will be mentioned in the course of this letter, interferes very rarely in behalf of the mother.

The oath of the woman may be received against the putative father, provided that some other evidence tending to inculpate him is previously adduced. This evidence is technically called "*Semiplena probatio*," and may be regarded as substantially the same as the "corroborative evidence" in the English law.

I am unable to state the average number of actions for aliment which are instituted annually by the mothers of illegitimate children, but I have been assured that such information would convey no correct idea of the extent to which the present law operates in inducing putative fathers to contribute towards the maintenance of their illegitimate children, inasmuch as the general law on the subject is said in many instances to cause the father to enter into an arrangement with the mother without the interference of the sheriff.

With regard to the practical effect of the law, either in promoting or discouraging illicit connexions, it is difficult to form an accurate opinion, as so very many circumstances ought to be taken into consideration in endeavouring to arrive at a correct judgment in matters of this kind, and there are not even data for knowing the exact proportion of illegitimate to legitimate births in Scotland. It seems certain, however, that the principle of the law gives general satisfaction; and as far as the being in unison with the popular sentiment is a recommendation, the law may be considered as eminently successful. Various complaints have been raised in this country against the Law of Settlement, and other important enactments in the Scotch poor laws; but I have not hitherto met a single individual who has objected to the main principle of the Scotch bastardy laws. Any suggestions or inquiries as to the possible effect which the making the putative father legally liable may have in weakening the motives to resistance on the part of the woman, are usually met by an assertion of its being unjust that the whole burden of maintaining the child should be thrown upon the mother; and reference is made to the plain principle of equity, that when two persons are equally concerned in the commission of an offence, they should both be held equally responsible for its consequences.

It is proper however to remark, on the supposition of there being a tendency in this law to encourage bastardy, that there are certain peculiarities in Scotland which are calculated to counteract such tendency. In the first place, incontinency subjects the offending parties to ecclesiastical censures, which in Scotland are not obsolete, and the fear of which may still occasionally have a restraining power on a certain class of minds. The minister and elders of a parish in kirk session call before them the mother, and the putative father (when discovered) of an illegitimate child, admonish them seriously for their misconduct, and exclude them from participation in the ordinance of bread and wine, until they have expressed contrition for their offence. A fine likewise is sometimes imposed upon the man. In the next place, it is the practice in many parishes of Scotland to refuse all relief to the mothers of illegitimate children, partly on the principle that the granting such relief would offer a premium to immorality, and partly under the idea that the withholding it altogether has the effect of inducing the putative father to come forward more readily for the maintenance of his offspring. And in many other parishes, where such relief is not altogether refused, the obtaining it is made a matter of considerable difficulty, and the sum given is of comparatively small amount. Moreover, in some parishes, the rule is laid down of refusing relief to able-bodied widows with only one child; a rule, which by parity of reasoning would exclude an able-bodied single woman from relief, unless she had at least two children. Now, as it is often by no means easy for the mother to produce evidence before the sheriff which amounts to a "*semiplena probatio*," as even when a decree is obtained against the father, there is certain expense, if he is obstinate, in maintaining him as a debtor in prison, and as the decree only extends to a period of life when children at the present day are not usually able to earn their own livelihood, the known fact that either no relief, or very scanty relief is to be expected from the parish on account of an illegitimate child, must render it highly improbable that a single woman, if she reflects at all, can do otherwise than regard her giving birth to such a child as a source of future embarrassment and expense.

Hence, taking into consideration all these various circumstances, I am inclined to doubt whether the present Scotch law practically encourages bastardy; while at the same time, as I have already mentioned, it has succeeded in a remarkable manner in satisfying the popular feeling.

Yours very truly,

(Signed) EDWARD TWISLETON.

G. C. Lewis, Esq.

P.S. In order not to convey a false impression by what I have above stated, respecting the absence of any objection to the main principle of the Scotch Bastardy Laws, I would mention that one or two witnesses have recommended that a putative father, if he refused to obey the sheriff's decree for aliment, should be penally incarcerated, instead of being merely imprisoned as a debtor. This, however, does not seem to me to affect the *main principle* of the laws; by which expression I understand the legal recognition, without reference to poor laws, that the mother and the putative father of an illegitimate child are jointly liable for its maintenance. I may add, that an approximation to the number of illegitimate births might perhaps be obtained from the baptismal registers in rural parishes, although certainly not in towns.

II.—ABSTRACT OF A BILL FOR THE FURTHER AMENDMENT OF THE LAWS RELATING TO THE POOR IN ENGLAND, prepared and brought in by Sir James Graham and Mr. Manners Sutton, 10th February, 1844.

Repeal of existing Remedy of Parish against the Putative Father, and Enactment of Remedy for the Mother of a Bastard against the Putative Father.

CLAUSE 1.—All powers of making order on putative Father shall cease, except in pursuance of this Act.

2.—The Mother of a Bastard may apply for a summons to be served on the alleged Father, for the next petty Sessions.

3.—The Justices in petty Sessions may, after hearing proper evidence, make an order on the putative Father to pay to the Mother a weekly sum, not exceeding Four Shillings and Costs, and may enforce such order by distress and imprisonment.

4.—The hearing in petty Session may be adjourned; but every application must be determined within Forty Days from the service of the original summons. The putative

Father may, on giving security, appeal to the Quarter Sessions.

5.—Money payable under the order shall be paid to the Mother, or, if she be incapacitated, to a person to be appointed by the Justices to have the custody of the Child. The Child must not be chargeable, and the Order is to cease when the Child reaches the age of Thirteen, or at the Marriage of the Mother.

6.—The Mother of a Bastard neglecting to maintain it, or deserting it, is to be punishable under the Vagrant Act (5 Geo. 4, c. 83.)

7.—No Officer of any Parish or Union is to receive the money from the putative Father, or to interfere in making the application to the Justices. If the Mother is dead or incapacitated, the Guardians or Overseers may apply to enforce the Order.

8.—Any person conspiring to cause false evidence to be given shall be guilty of Perjury. Any Parish or Union Officer endeavouring to promote Marriage by threat or promise relating to an order in Bastardy shall be guilty of a misdemeanor. Any person having the custody of a Bastard misapplying the money for its support, or ill-treating it, may be fined Ten Pounds.

9.—Orders already made, and proceedings pending not to be affected by this Act; but no Order made before the 14th of August, 1834, shall be in force after the 1st of January, 1849.

10.—The Clerk to the Justices in Petty Sessions to transmit to the Clerk of the Peace a List of Orders made, &c. Copies of these Lists are to be forwarded to the Secretary of State for the Home Department.

Regulation of Parish Apprenticeship, and Abolition of Compulsory Apprenticeship.

11.—The Commissioners may regulate the trades, premium, &c. of Parish Apprentices, and prescribe conditions to be inserted in their Indentures.

12.—Compulsory Apprenticeship of Paupers to be abolished.

Scale of Voting for Election of Guardians.

13.—The existing Scales of voting of owners or occupiers for the election of Guardians are to be repealed, and a new Scale is to be substituted.

The following are the existing Scales :

Scale for Rate-payers.

4 & 5 Will. IV., c. 76, s. 40.

If a Rate-payer be rated at any sum under 200*l.*—He will have One vote.

If at 200*l.*, but under 400*l.*—He will have Two votes.

If at 400*l.* or more—He will have Three votes.

Scale for Owners.

58 Geo. III., c. 69; 59 Geo. III, c. 85; and 4 & 5 Will. IV., c. 76, s. 40.

If the aggregate amount of the Assessment, for the time being, of any property belonging to such Owner in such parish, or on any person or persons in respect of the same, to the Poor-rates, shall not amount to 50*l.*—He will have One vote.

If the same shall amount to 50*l.* and not to 75*l.*—He will have Two votes.

If the same shall amount to 75*l.* and not to 100*l.*—He will have Three votes.

If the same shall amount to 100*l.* and not to 125*l.*—He will have Four votes.

If the same shall amount to 125*l.* and not to 150*l.*—He will have Five votes.

If the same shall amount to 150*l.* or upwards—He will have Six votes.

The following is the proposed Scale for Owners and Rate-payers.

If the Property in respect of which the Owner or Rate-payer is entitled to vote, be rated upon a rateable value of less than 50*l.*—He shall have One vote.

If such rateable value amount to 50*l.* and be less than 100*l.*—He shall have Two votes.

If such rateable value amount to 100*l.* and be less than 150*l.*—He shall have Three votes.

If such rateable value amount to 150*l.* and be less than 200*l.*—He shall have Four votes.

If such rateable value amount to 200*l.* and be less than 250*l.*—He shall have Five votes.

If such rateable value amount to, or exceed 250*l.*—He shall have Six votes.

Regulations as to Claims of Owners, and as to Proxy Votes, and Time of Election of Boards of Guardians, and Power of altering the Number of Guardians for a Parish.

14.—The Owner is to give in a statement of his Property Fourteen Days before he votes. No person is to hold more than Four Proxies, unless he be the Steward, Bailiff, Land-agent, or Collector of his Principal.

No appointment of a Proxy is to remain in force for more than Two Years, except of Steward, &c.

15.—Annual Election of Guardians may take place within Forty Days of the 25th of March, instead of within Fourteen Days of the same.

16.—The number of Guardians for any Parish may be altered in reference to its relative population or circumstances.

Division of large Parishes into Wards for Election of Guardians.

17.—Parishes exceeding 20,000 persons may be divided into Wards for the election of Guardians. No Ward is to contain less than 400 rated houses.

18.—Every person qualified for the Parish is to be qualified for any Ward in the Parish; but no person is to be elected for more than one Ward. The candidate may elect which Ward he will stand for.

19.—The aggregate number of votes given in all the Wards by any one person, shall not exceed the number which he is entitled to give in the whole parish; nor in any one Ward, the number of votes to which he is entitled, by property, in that Ward; subject to these limitations the voter may elect which Ward he will vote in.

Miscellaneous Provisions.

20 & 21.—Townships not now relieving their own poor, are not to appoint separate Overseers, under 13 & 14 Car. 2, c. 12; and orders of the Commissioners determining the number of Guardians, or ascertaining the averages of Townships which have been separated since the passing of the Poor Law Amendment Act, declared valid.

22.—Justices of the Peace who reside in extra-parochial places, or parishes situate within a Union, to be *ex officio* Guardians.

Relief of Wives whose Husbands are beyond the Seas, &c.

23.—The relief of a woman whose husband is beyond the seas, or in custody of the law, or lunatic, to be subject to the same conditions as if she were a widow.

Recovery of the cost of Relief of Lunatics.

24.—Two Justices may make an order, directing the Overseers to take the money or goods of any Lunatic chargeable to their Parish.

If any Trustee of a Pauper Lunatic pays any money of his *cestui que* trust to Guardians or Overseers, to defray the charges of the Parish, their receipt to be a good discharge.

Miscellaneous Powers of Guardians.

25.—Power to the Guardians to apply money for emigration.

26.—Power to Guardians within the limits of the Metropolitan Police to borrow money for the cost of the site of the Workhouse.

Burial of Paupers.

27.—Funeral expenses and burial fees may be paid by the Guardians, and the Guardians may bury a Pauper in the churchyard of the Parish in which he dies, or of that to which he belongs.

Audit of Poor Law Accounts.

28.—Auditors are to be appointed for Districts of Unions, by the Chairmen and Vice-chairmen of Boards of Guardians; such Auditors are to have the powers necessary to compel the attendance of persons accountable, and to recover the balances struck.

29.—The Accounts of Overseers, Assistant-Overseers, and Collectors, are to be deposited for inspection Seven Days before the audit.

30.—Any person aggrieved by any allowance or disallowance of an Auditor, may remove such allowance or disallowance by Certiorari into the Court of Queen's Bench.

31.—Where District Auditors have been appointed, the power of Justices to audit Poor Law accounts is to cease; the existing District Auditors may be continued.

32.—The audit of Poor Law accounts may be held half-yearly instead of quarterly.

33.—Law Bills to be taxed by the Clerk of the Peace upon the application of Overseers, Guardians, or Attorneys-at-Law.

District Pauper Schools, and Asylums for occasional Poor, in London and other Large Towns; Mode of charging Relief of occasional Poor.

34.—Parishes may be combined for the formation of District Schools, with a maximum diameter of Fifteen miles.

35.—Parishes may be combined for providing Asylums for the temporary relief of destitute houseless poor, within the District of the Metropolitan Police or the City of

London, or the Cities and Boroughs named in the Schedule; [viz., Liverpool, Manchester, Bristol, Leeds, and Birmingham]

36.—District Boards for the management of Schools and Asylums to be elected from the Rate-payers of the Districts, by the Guardians or Overseers; the Chairman of each Board of Guardians to be *ex officio* a Member of the District Board.

37.—Power to the District Board to manage the inmates of the School or Asylum; to appoint, pay and control the paid officers; to provide and fit up the requisite building. Power to the Commissioners to alter the District with consent of the District Board; to regulate the proceedings of the District Board, and to make rules for the government of the School or Asylum. No inmate of a School or Asylum to be obliged to attend a religious service celebrated in a mode contrary to the religious principles of such inmate or of his parents. Inmates to be visited by licensed ministers of their persuasion.

38.—The District Board to have the powers given to Guardians for obtaining land and buildings, and for borrowing money; the principal sum borrowed not to exceed one-fifth of the average annual expenditure for the relief of the poor of any Union in the District. Money to be repaid in twenty years.

39.—District Board incorporated.

40.—District Board to give notice in writing of their calls for contributions, and on default of payment, to have the same power for recovering contributions from Overseers as the Guardians have.

41.—Common expenses of schools to be paid by the Unions and Parishes within the District, in proportion to their last declared averages. Relief to individual children to be charged separately to their Parishes or Unions.

42.—Expenses of Asylums to be charged on Parishes and Unions, in proportion to the value of property therein rated to the County or Borough Rate.

43.—Power to the Commissioners to appoint some Parish or Union Auditor to be Auditor of the District. Powers of the Auditor; his salary; his removal. District Boards and their Officers to account twice a year. Recovery of Balances. Abstract of Accounts to be forwarded to each Board of Guardians, and to Parish Officers.

44.—Parishes not contained in a District may, if not distant more than Twenty Miles from the District School, send children to such School.

45.—The 2 Geo. 3, c. 22, and the 7 Geo. 3, c. 39 (Jonas Hanway's Act), to be repealed.

46.—Definition of the class of Poor to be relieved in Asylums; mode of their admission and relief.

47.—Inmates of Asylums punishable for misbehaviour therein, in like manner as the inmates of workhouses.

48.—Inmates of Asylums remaining chargeable more than Four Days, or relieved a second time, liable to be removed to their places of settlement like other Paupers, subject to the like appeal against the order of removal.

49.—Persons removed from Asylums and returning, and again becoming chargeable thereto, liable to punishment, provided by the 5 Geo. 4, c. 83, s. 3.

50.—The cost of the relief of certain Poor in Unions not included in such districts, to be chargeable to the common fund of the Union; and persons so chargeable may be removed.

Constructive Situation of Workhouse.

51 & 52.—For the purposes of relief, settlement and removal, and also a committal of Offenders, the Workhouse is deemed to be situate in the Parish to which the Pauper is chargeable.

Costs of certain Legal Proceedings to be paid out of the Poor Rates.

53.—The costs of apprehending and prosecuting Offenders under 5 Geo. 4, c. 40, and of certain other civil and criminal proceedings connected with the administration of the Poor Laws, are to be paid by the Guardians out of the Poor Rates, subject to the approval of the Commissioners.

Collectors of Poor Rates may be appointed to perform Duties of Assistant Overseers; Enforcement of Contributions by Overseers.

54.—Collectors appointed by Guardians may be appointed to perform the duties of Assistant Overseers; and in such case the power of the vestry to appoint a Collector is to cease.

55.—If Overseers do not pay sufficient monies to the Guardians, and the relief of any poor person is delayed in consequence for Seven Days, every such Overseer is to be guilty of a misdemeanor.

Parishes under Local Acts.

56.—Commissioners may direct Guardians under Local Acts to act as a Board, to appoint a Chairman and hold their Meetings in like manner as Guardians appointed under 4 & 5 Will. 4, c. 76. No parish under a Local Act containing a Population of more than 20,000, may be united with another Parish, without the consent, in writing, of Two-thirds of the Guardians. Exception as to School, Vagrant, and Audit Districts.

Miscellaneous Provisions.

57.—Repeal of 55 Geo. 3, c. 137, s. 7, as to notices of contracts for supplying Workhouses.

58.—Mode of making application, &c., by District Board.

59.—After Fourteen Days' notice to a Board of Guardians, any person to whom any sum of money is due by such Board may apply to the next Quarter Sessions, and the Justices may make an order for the payment thereof. The Treasurer of the Guardians to pay the said sum upon a certified copy of the order being served upon him.

60.—If any civil or criminal proceeding the sending of the orders of the Commissioners need not be proved without notice.

61.—Interpretation Clause.

62.—Act limited to England and Wales.

63.—Act may be amended this Session.

III.—ACCOUNTS.

1. As to the Taxing of Bills for Law Expenses when payable out of the Poor-Rates.

13*th January*, 1844.

Clerk of the Stafford Union —Stated, that the attorney employed by the overseers of the united parishes of St. Mary and St. Chad, Stafford, in an appeal against an order for the removal of Mary Healey and family from Salford to Stafford, in the year ending March, 1842, and in an appeal against an order for the removal of Sarah Smith and child, from Willenhall to Stafford, in the year ending March, 1843, had delivered to them his bill of costs, amounting to about 120*l*. The overseers had since paid the attorney 80*l*. on account of his bill, and had entered the amount in the accounts of the quarter ending September last. The auditor disallowed the amount, on the ground that the bill had not been taxed, and because the overseers had omitted to certify the allowance of the bill by their signatures; and he requested the overseers to have the bill taxed by the proper officer previous to the next audit. The overseers had taken the opinion of counsel as to the necessity of taxing the bill, and they were advised, that if the churchwardens and overseers were satisfied with the several items in the bill, there was no Act of Parliament to compel them to tax it. The auditor wished, under the circumstances, to have the Commissioners' opinion as to whether he would be justified in dispensing with the taxation of the bill, on the allowance of the overseers being certified on the face of the account.

Ans.—It appears that the debts were incurred in 1841 and 1842, or at least before the commencement of the present overseers' year of office. The payment of them is illegal, as being a payment of debts of a bygone year, unless, indeed, their predecessors turned over to them a sufficient sum of money to meet these particular demands, in which case the overseers would have been justified in paying what was lawfully due. In regard to the taxation of the bills, the Commissioners readily admit that the parish officers, who are personally responsible to the attorney for the business performed by him, may pay the amount of his bills without requiring them to be taxed. But when it is sought to pay those bills out of the poor-rates of the parish, the case assumes a different character. The parish officers are trustees of the parish funds, and the Commissioners consider that parish officers are not justified in adopting a different course of proceeding from that which is prescribed to other trustees. The Commissioners believe that it is the usual course in the Court of Chancery, for trustees to submit their solicitors' bills to the masters to be taxed, previous to obtaining their allowance. The bills of attorneys for professional business are of a character not ordinarily to be understood by parish officers, and therefore it is highly desirable that the correctness of the charges should be ascertained in the manner pointed out by the law, before they are paid out of the poor-rates. It moreover appears to the Commissioners to be perfectly competent to the auditor to require such bills to be taxed before he allows them, and where he lays down this principle, and refuses to allow any untaxed bills, his audit is final, and no question can be raised upon the subject.

IV.—MEDICAL ORDER.

1. REMUNERATION UNDER SEVERE SURGICAL CASES NOT NAMED IN THE ORDER.

1st Jan. 1844.

Medical Officer, Tamworth Union—Inquired, 1. Whether the guardians were empowered to remunerate the medical officer for surgical attendance, or for any severe surgical cases not specifically named in the Commissioners' Medical Order, such as severe cases of burns, &c.; such cases frequently involving a greater outlay of time and trouble than the generality of surgical cases. 2. Whether an agricultural servant, regularly hired for twelve months, and meeting with a severe accident in his master's service, or becoming incapable from sickness or any other cause from following his usual employment, could be made chargeable to the Union before the expiration of his servitude.

Ans. 1. As a general rule, the medical officer's remuneration for his attendance in all surgical cases not mentioned in Article X. of the Medical Order, must be considered as included in his fixed salary. If, however, in any special case, not mentioned in that Article, the guardians should be of opinion, that the medical officer is fairly entitled to some extra remuneration, the Commissioners think that the guardians would be justified in paying the medical officer such additional remuneration as the circumstances of the case might render proper. 2. Sickness does not put an end to the contract of service, but it has been decided that a master is not bound (in the absence of any agreement to that effect) to provide medical or surgical assistance for his servant. There may be cases, therefore, in which persons in service as agricultural labourers, or otherwise, may be unable to obtain medical aid at their own charge, and destitute of friends who are able or willing to assist them. In any such case, if application be made to the guardians for medical relief, the Commissioners cannot say that the application should be refused. If the guardians, or other competent authority, order the relief, the medical officer would be bound to afford it.

2. CIRCULAR ADDRESSED TO THE MEDICAL OFFICERS OF UNIONS.

Poor Law Commission Office,
Somerset House,
8th February, 1844.

SIR,

With reference to the Books required by the Regulations of the Poor Law Commissioners to be kept by the Medical Officers of Unions and Parishes under Boards of Guardians (Form A. in the General Workhouse Rules, and Form B. in the Order on Duties of Officers), I am directed to call your attention to the Provision in Article 14 of the General Medical Order,* which directs that every Medical Officer shall so keep any weekly return prescribed by the Orders of the Commissioners, as to show when the visit or attendance made or given to any Pauper was made or given by any person other than himself. The Commissioners are, therefore, desirous of reminding you that the report of attendances in the columns headed "Days when attended," is intended only to apply to cases in which the patient is seen by the Medical Officer, or his authorised substitute. If an Apprentice, or unqualified Assistant, has visited or seen the patient, and "Attendance" is recorded, it must be distinguished from that given by the Medical Officer himself. The Medical Officer is bound to visit his patients at their own homes; but whether the patient is seen at his own home, or attends voluntarily at the Medical Officer's house or a station, provided he is seen, and examined personally, attendance may be entered.

This explanation may seem unnecessary,—but misapprehension has been alleged to exist as to the meaning of the column in question, and attendances in certain cases have been recorded, when medicine was merely sent by some third person.

* ARTICLE 14.—*General Medical Order, dated 12th March,* 1842:—

"Every Medical Officer appointed, or to be appointed, in pursuance of the Rules, Orders, and Regulations of the Poor Law Commissioners, shall be bound to visit and attend personally the poor persons entrusted to his care, and shall be responsible for such visits and attendances, and shall so keep any Weekly Return prescribed by the Orders of the Poor Law Commissioners, as to show when the visit or attendance made or given to any pauper was made or given by any person other than himself."

The Commissioners would deem it their duty to treat any case of false entry in the Medical Books as a Breach of their Rules and Regulations.

I am, Sir,
Your most obedient Servant,
EDWIN CHADWICK, *Secretary*.

To
Medical Officer.

V.—PAUPER.—DEATH OF AN INFANT PAUPER AND CHARGE OF IMPROPER TREATMENT.

15*th Feb*. 1844.

Eton Union.—The Commissioners noticed in the *Times* and the *Morning Chronicle* newspapers of the 1st February, the report of an Inquest held at the Uxbridge Union workhouse, on the body of John Murrell, aged six months, who was with its mother removed on the 25th January, from the Eton Union workhouse to the workhouse of the Uxbridge Union, where it died from natural causes on the following day—a removal which the Jury of the Inquest characterised as "cruel in the highest degree, and disgraceful to the management of the Eton Union workhouse." The Commissioners in consequence requested the Board of Guardians of the Eton Union to furnish them with such information as they might be able to procure in reference to the case, and especially in regard to the discharge of the mother of the deceased child from the Eton workhouse, and their removal to the Uxbridge workhouse. The Clerk of the Eton Union, on the 8th February, transmitted to the Commissioners an extract from the Minutes of the weekly meeting of the Board of Guardians, together with the written statements referred to in such Extract, viz., The Statement of James Stratton, the Relieving Officer of the Iver District of the Eton Union; the Statement of Thomas Aitken, the Master of the Eton workhouse; and the Statement of Mr. Hammond, the Surgeon of the Eton workhouse. The Commissioners having carefully considered these statements, on the 15th February addressed the following letter to the Board of Guardians of the Eton Union:—

From the statements of the above-named officers, the Commissioners gather that the following are the principal circumstances connected with this removal. It seems that Martha Murrell and her two children were admitted to the Eton Union workhouse on the 20th of December last; that the youngest child (the deceased John Murrell) was placed on the Medical Officer's list, according to the account of the Master, on the 7th of January, but according to the account of the Medical Officer, on the 14th of January last, for an affection of the chest; that he was regularly visited by the Medical Officer, and its mother regularly supplied with medicines for her child up to the day on which they left the workhouse. During their stay in the workhouse it appears that the family were carefully attended to, and that the mother acknowledges the kind treatment she and her children had received. Martha Murrell, however, was legally settled in the Uxbridge Union, and an order for her removal having been made out by the Magistrates, and acceded to by the Overseers of the parish to which she was ordered to be removed, Mr. Stratton was directed to convey her to the workhouse of the Uxbridge Union. For this purpose he called at the Eton workhouse, on the 25th ult., and having no previous knowledge of the sickness of any of the family, he requested that they might be got ready for the journey. The mother and her children were then dressed for that purpose, in their own clothes; and Martha Murrell was then asked whether she did not think it would hurt the child to take it out? She answered, "No; I think the child is better, and that the journey will do it good." She was asked whether she thought the child was in a fit state to be removed? Her answer was, "Oh, it will take no hurt." The question was subsequently repeated, and an answer to a similar effect returned. The Matron even pressed her to remain, if she had any doubt of the propriety of removing the child; and she was told, that no attempt would be made to remove her, if she had the slightest objection on account of her child's health. The Matron having cautioned her to be careful of her child, and offered her the use of some cloaks to keep it warm, which were rejected, attended her to the waiting hall, and put her under the care of Mr. Stratton, the relieving officer. When in the cart, Mr. Stratton lent her his great coat, which she wrapped round herself, but seemed negligent of the child, and a "rug" was provided, "that would cover round the front." Mr. Stratton left the Union Workhouse about half-past one, stopped on his way, for a short time, at his own residence—offered Martha Murrell refreshment, which she refused—gave the eldest child some biscuits—and arrived at the workhouse of the Uxbridge union about a quarter before three. The Poor Law Commissioners, on a consideration of these circumstances, although they think that the removal of the child was highly improper, and much to be regretted, acquit the Matron and Relieving Officer of the Eton Union, of any cruelty which may have been imputed to them in the case. They think that it is shown that the woman and her children met with due attention and proper treatment whilst inmates of the Eton Union Workhouse; that the Matron evinced a kindness and solicitude for the health and care of the sick child, which certainly (in the evidence before the Commissioners) does not seem to have been more than faintly manifested by the mother herself; and that when the mother and children were placed under the temporary care of Mr. Stratton, the relieving officer, he showed his humane consideration, by the personal attention to their comfort which he paid to them during their journey. The only additional remark which the Commissioners think it necessary to make on this case is, that as in cases of severe illness, they think that no removal should take place, except upon a written certificate of its safety from a medical officer, Mr. Hammond, if he was aware of the intended removal of the child, ought to have given a certificate stating its impropriety; and if the intended removal had not been made known to him, then the Master ought to have communicated the fact to the medical officer, and have requested his written opinion as to its safety. Whilst the Commissioners fully acquit the officers of any cruelty or harsh treatment, they think that blame attaches either to the Master, or to the medical officer, as the case may be, in regard to the removal in the absence of a medical certificate.

VI.—RATING REGISTER OFFICES.

13*th Dec.* 1843.

Clerk of the Teesdale Union—Stated that the guardians of that Union rented as tenants from year to year a register office, under the provisions of the Act for Registering Births, Deaths, and Marriages. Inquired, whether the guardians were rateable to the relief of the poor for such office to the township of Barnard Castle, within which township it is situate. The register office is not connected with the workhouse. Submitted, that the guardians had no beneficial occupation; and that the benefit of the register office, as a depôt of registers, was not confined to the Union, as in cases of workhouses, but was available and beneficial for the public generally throughout the kingdom.

Ans.—The attention of the Commissioners has been particularly directed to the case of Reg. *v.* the Guardians of the Wallingford Union, 2 Perry & Dav. 226, which establishes the liability of the guardians to be assessed in respect of a Union workhouse to the relief of the poor in the parish in which it is situate. But for that decision the Commissioners would certainly have considered that the providing and upholding a register office for the preservation of registers, in pursuance of the statute, is an object, or purpose, so essentially public, and so entirely unproductive of any private "utility" to the guardians as occupiers, as to exempt it from liability to the rates under the 43rd Eliz., c. 2. But since the Court has decided that a workhouse is rateable, the Commissioners see no such essential distinction between a workhouse and a register office, as to afford any reason to doubt that the rule laid down as to the former, would be extended to the latter. But assuming the liability, some difficulty will probably be felt in ascertaining the persons liable to be assessed. The guardians, it may be observed, do not occupy the register office as they do the workhouse for the performance of any of their own functions, nor does the registrar (though he may happen to be the clerk) use it in subordination to the guardians, so as to render them liable for the occupation of their servant or agent. The Commissioners therefore cannot see how the guardians can be rated as occupiers, neither can they discover any such personal benefit to the registrar by the occupation as to make him liable. The Commissioners have intimated these doubts in order to enable the guardians the better to judge of the bearings of the subject. The Commissioners regret that the state of the law does not enable them to give a more clear and decided opinion.

VII.—REMOVAL.

IN THE CASE OF A PAUPER BELONGING TO A DIFFERENT PARISH TO THAT IN WHICH THE UNION WORKHOUSE IS SITUATE.

15*th Dec.* 1843.

Clerk of the Yeovil Union—Inquired, whether the Union workhouse, which was the property of the parishes comprising the Union, was or was not to be considered as such for the purposes of settlement, recent decisions at quarter sessions having decided that it could not be so considered, and an order of removal from the workhouse quashed on that ground. If such decision be held good, it would materially affect the parish in which the house stood, as every illegitimate child born in the house, after sixteen, would take its birth settlement in that parish; which the Board of Guardians deemed would be unjust, and therefore inquired further whether, in the event of the Commissioners' opinion being in conformity to recent decisions, the guardians would not be justified in giving to the mothers of bastards out-relief for a period before confinement, and for the first month after, instead of ordering them into the house. Stated, that there was another difficulty involved in the same decision, in regard to the able-bodied becoming destitute where they had no settlement; if out-relief should be given, and a removal took place, the order would be in danger of being quashed; and if in accordance with the prohibitory order of the Commissioners, such able-bodied persons were admitted into the house, and from thence removed, the order would in that case also be liable to be quashed.

Ans. It has come to the knowledge of the Commissioners, that in a case which was tried at the late Somerset session, (in which the parish of Buckland St. Mary was appellant, and the parish of Otterford respondent,) the Court held that the justices had no jurisdiction to order the removal of a pauper, where, at the time of making the order, such pauper was residing in the Union workhouse, situate in a different parish from that to which the pauper was chargeable. The Commissioners presume that this is the decision to which you refer. The Commissioners do not, however, understand that the decision involved any question as to the settlement of paupers, as affected by their residence in the workhouse. The fact of a pauper's residing in a Union workhouse does not in any way affect or vary his settlement; though if the decision of the quarter sessions be right, it may render the pauper irremoveable from the parish to which he is chargeable for so long a time as he may continue to reside in the workhouse situate in a different parish. [The Commissioners here referred to the Official Circular, No. 27, page 124, Article XIV.] I am to add, that the Commissioners do not concur in the view which you have expressed, that illegitimate children, on arriving at the age of sixteen, revert to their birth settlement.

VIII.—TRUCK SYSTEM.—CIRCULAR TO THE CLERKS OF BOARDS OF GUARDIANS.

Poor Law Commission Office,
Somerset House,
30th January, 1844.

SIR,—I am directed by the Poor Law Commissioners to forward to you the accompanying printed copies of the 7th, 18th, 19th, and 20th sections of the Act of the 1st and 2nd of Wm. IV., c. 37, intituled "An Act to prohibit the payment in certain Trades of Wages in Goods or otherwise than in the current Coin of the Realm;" and I am to request that you will take an early opportunity of calling the attention of the several overseers of the parishes in the Union for which you are the clerk to the provisions contained in those sections. The object of this communication would be to suggest to the overseers the propriety of their availing themselves of the powers conferred upon them by the Act, in the event of any poor persons becoming chargeable, under circumstances in which it would be competent to the overseers to proceed for the recovery of the wages not paid in the current coin of the realm.

I am, Sir,
Your most obedient Servant,
EDWIN CHADWICK, *Secretary.*

To the Clerk to the Board of Guardians.

Copies of Sections 7, 18, 19, and 20, *of Act* 1 and 2 *Wm. IV.*, c. 37.

VII. "And be it further enacted, That if any such artificer as aforesaid, or his wife or widow, or if any child of any such artificer, not being of the full age of twenty-one years, shall become chargeable to any parish or place, and if within the space of three calendar months next before the time when any such charge shall be incurred, such artificer shall have earned, or have become entitled to receive, any wages for any labour by him done in any of the said trades, which wages shall not have been paid to such artificer in the current coin of this realm, it shall be lawful for the overseers or overseer of the poor in such parish or place to recover from the employer of such artificer, in whose service such labour was done, the full amount of wages so unpaid, and to proceed for the recovery thereof by all such ways and means as such artificer himself might have proceeded for that purpose; and the amount of the wages which may be so recovered, shall be applied in reimbursing such parish or place all costs and charges incurred in respect of the person or persons to become chargeable, and the surplus shall be applied and paid over to such person or persons.

XVIII. "And be it further enacted, That out of any penalty or forfeiture incurred by any offence committed against this Act, it shall be lawful for the court or justices imposing the same, to award any sum to the informer not exceeding in any case the sum of twenty pounds; and the rest of any such pecuniary penalty or forfeiture shall go to the treasurer of the county in which the offence shall be committed, in aid of the rates of such county: Provided always, that every proceeding whatsoever for any offence against this Act shall be commenced within three calendar months after such offence shall have been committed.

XIX. "And be it further enacted, That nothing herein contained shall extend to any artificer, workman, or labourer, or other person engaged or employed in any manufacture, trade, or occupation, excepting only artificers, workmen, labourers, and other persons employed in the several manufactories, trades, and occupations following; (that is to say), in or about the making, casting, converting, or manufacturing of iron or steel, or any parts, branches, or processes thereof, or in or about the working or getting of any mines of coal, ironstone, limestone, salt-rock; or in or about the working or getting of stone, slate, or clay; or in the making or preparing of salt, bricks, tiles, or quarries; or in or about the making or manufacturing of any kinds of nails, chains, rivets, anvils, vices, spades, shovels, screws, keys, locks, bolts, hinges, or any other articles or hardwares made of iron or steel, or of iron and steel combined, or of any plated articles of cutlery, or of any goods or wares made of brass, tin, lead, pewter, or other metal, or of any japanned goods or wares whatsoever; or in or about the making, spinning, throwing, twisting, doubling, winding, weaving, combing, knitting, bleaching, dyeing, printing, or otherwise preparing of any kinds of woollen, worsted, yarn, stuff, Jersey, linen, fustian, cloth, serge, cotton, leather, fur, hemp, flax, mohair, or silk manufactures whatsoever; or in or about any manufactures whatsoever, made of the said last-mentioned materials, whether the same be or be not mixed with one another; or in or about the making, or otherwise preparing, ornamenting, or finishing of any glass, porcelain, China, or earthenware whatsoever, or any parts, branches, or processes thereof, or any materials used in any of such last-mentioned trades or employments; or in or about the making or preparing of bone, thread, silk, or cotton lace, or of lace made of any mixed materials.

XX. "And be it further enacted, That nothing herein contained shall extend to any domestic servant, or servant in husbandry."

IX.—WORKHOUSE.—PUNISHMENT OF PAUPERS WILFULLY BREAKING WINDOWS OF WORKHOUSE.

12th January, 1844.

Clerk of the Beaminster Union—Inquired, 1. Whether or not the magistrates had the power to commit persons for wilfully breaking windows in the Union workhouse, for more than twenty-one days after the first, second, or third offence. 2. Whether section 4 of 50 Geo. III. c. 50, contemplated the breaking of windows, furniture, &c., under the terms "wilfully waste, spoil, or damage, any of the clothing, goods, or materials," —"provided for the use of such poorhouse." 3. Whether section 5 of 55 Geo. III. c. 137, relating to misbehaviour in workhouse, and section 4 of 50 Geo. III. c. 50, cannot be taken together, so as to enable the magistrates, on the two offences being proved before them, to commit for three months.

Ans.—1. If any person do wilful damage to the property of the guardians, he may be proceeded against in the manner provided by 7 and 8 Geo. IV., c. 30, s. 24; but if he be proceeded against for the offence of misbehaviour in the workhouse, he is only liable, on conviction, to be committed to the house of correction for a period not exceeding 21 days, (see 55 Geo. III., c. 157, s. 5,) whether it be for a first or second offence. 2. The Commissioners are of opinion that section 4 of 50 Geo. III., c. 50, which renders punishable persons sent to poor-houses, for wilfully wasting, spoiling, or damaging any of the clothing, goods, or materials, committed to their care, does not extend to breaking windows of the Union workhouse, or the furniture belonging to the guardians. 3. The Commissioners desire to reply to your last inquiry in the negative.

LONDON:
Printed by Order of the Poor Law Commissioners, by BLACKBURN and PARDON, 6, Hatton Garden, and Published by CHARLES KNIGHT and Co., 22, Ludgate Street, Publishers to the Poor Law Commissioners.

AN

OFFICIAL CIRCULAR

OF PUBLIC DOCUMENTS AND INFORMATION:

DIRECTED BY THE POOR LAW COMMISSIONERS TO BE PRINTED, CHIEFLY FOR THE USE OF THE MEMBERS AND PERMANENT OFFICERS OF BOARDS OF GUARDIANS, UNDER THE POOR LAW AMENDMENT ACT.

No. 33. CIRCULAR ISSUED MARCH 30, 1844.

Poor Law Commission Office,
Somerset House,
30th March, 1844.

THE Poor Law Commissioners, on a review of their Minutes, directed that the Minutes of Correspondence on the following subjects be printed and circulated for the information of Guardians and Officers of the several Unions, viz :—

By Order of the Board,

Edwin Chadwick, *Secretary*.

I.—AVERAGES.—Whether Excused Rates ought to be brought into Account on taking Averages.

6th January, 1844.

Mr. C. Hill, Buxhall, Stowmarket—Inquired, whether the amount of "Excused Rates" were to be taken into account in ascertaining the averages of a parish.

Ans.—The conclusion which the Commissioners have formed on this subject is, that the amount of Excused Rates ought not to be so included. The ground of this conclusion is, that an Excused Rate is not an *expense* incurred by a parish for the relief of the poor, within the meaning of the 28th section of the Poor Law Amendment Act. The remission of the rate no doubt diminishes the produce of the rate, but it appears to the Commissioners that the statute contemplated that the calculation should only have reference to actual expenditure, *i. e.*, to sums paid out of the fund when raised and collected.

II.—CONSTABLES' FEES. — Under 5 and 6 Vic. c. 109.

7th Feb. 1844.

Clerk of the Bootle Union—Inquired, whether the fees payable to Parish Constables by virtue of the 5th and 6th Vic. c. 109, sec. 17, were to be charged to the parish in those cases only where the parties ordered to pay costs were supposed to be unable to pay; or, whether those costs ought to be charged to the parish in the first instance, without regard to the supposed ability or inability of the parties. Referred to the opinion of Sir William Follett and Mr. Tomlinson* on the above section.

Ans.—The Commissioners, in construing the section in question, are guided by the opinion of Sir William Follett and Mr. Tomlinson, with which you appear to be acquainted. Although the particular point raised in your letter was not specially brought under the notice of those learned Counsel when they gave that opinion, it nevertheless seems to the Commissioners to be met by the general principles on which that opinion was founded. Sir William Follett and Mr. Tomlinson took this view : That the Act intended to provide for the remuneration of Constables, in order to promote the general security of persons and property ; and that the 17th section effected this object, by casting the charge upon the Poor Rate, except only in those cases in which the County Rate would be liable for the payment under the general law. One sentence of their opinion is as follows : "No power is given to settle a scale of fees as between Constables and individuals setting them in motion, and the preamble shows that the intention was, by rewarding Constables, to increase the security of persons and property generally." Again : "The only exception which runs through the section is, of the duties for which the payment is by law chargeable upon the County Rate." In these remarks the Commissioners see nothing to justify an inference that the question as to the liability of a private individual to pay these fees would be in any way affected by his ability to pay them.

III.—CONVEYANCES OF PARISH PROPERTY—Exempt from Stamp Duty.

The Commissioners have read the report of the case of the Guardians of the Banbury Union against Robinson, published in the Law Journal, vol. 12, New Series, Queen's Bench, page 327, to which the Commissioners deem it right to refer Boards of Guardians, as leading to the conclusion

* See this opinion in the *Official Circular*, No. 30, p. 164.

that Conveyances made in pursuance of orders of the Commissioners, are within the exemption from Stamp Duty contained in the 86th section of the Poor Law Amendment Act.

IV.—COUNTY RATE.—EXPENSES OF VALUATION FOR.

6th March, 1844.

Clerk of the Neath Union—Stated that the Hamlet of Coedfrank had recently been surveyed for a county valuation by order of the Quarter Sessions. The Overseer necessarily attended the Surveyor during twelve days, to point out the land to him, for which the Overseer made a charge of £3; being at the rate of 5*s*. a day. The account was allowed by the Vice-chairman of the Board of Guardians, but the Auditor refused to allow the item in the Overseer's account, except with the Commissioners' sanction.

Ans.—The Commissioners are of opinion that the Auditor acted quite rightly in refusing to allow the item, to which you allude in the accounts of the Overseers of Coedfrank. By the 6th section of the 55 Geo. 3, c. 51, the Justices, in General or Quarter Sessions, are empowered to employ persons to value parishes for the purpose of the County Rate, in case the Overseers of such parishes fail to make the requisite returns; and the "said Justices so assembled," (*i. e.* in General or Quarter Sessions,) are further empowered to charge the expenses of such valuations on the parishes concerned, the amount thereof to be levied in the same way as the County Rate, though distinguished from it. The item alluded to in your letter, does not appear to be founded on the provisions of the above-named Section, but to have been charged irregularly in the Overseer's accounts.

V.—ELECTION OF GUARDIANS.—1. GUARDIAN'S QUALIFICATION—PAYMENT OF RATES.

19th March, 1844.

Clerk of Newtown and Llanidloes Union—Inquired whether a person who occupied his own house and premises, for which he was rated at a net annual value of £10 a year, and who occupied also other premises, for which his landlords were rated, was eligible for the office of Guardian.

Ans.—It is that property for which the person nominated is *himself* assessed, and not that in respect of which he is neither rated, nor pays rates, which can be taken into consideration in determining the legal qualification of such person for Guardian.

2. GUARDIAN'S QUALIFICATION.—AN INFANT.

22nd March, 1844.

Clerk of North Witchford Union—Stated, that one of the persons nominated for the office of Guardian was a minor (aged 20,) but as he was a considerable Rate-payer, and a young man of business habits, there could be no objection to his being returned as a Guardian, if his age did not legally disqualify him.

Ans.—The office of Guardian is one of public trust, and involves the liability to account for the monies of the Union. The Commissioners are, therefore, of opinion that an infant is not capable of exercising the office (see Claridge *v.* Evelyn and others, 5 B. and A. 81 Selw. N. P. 1043.)

3. GUARDIAN'S QUALIFICATION—OCCUPIER NOT RESIDING IN THE PARISH.

20th March, 1844.

Clerk of the Boston Union—Stated, that A. B. had been proposed as one of the Guardians for the parish of Swineshead. He occupied very largely in that parish, but resided on a small plot of extra-parochial ground immediately adjoining, and almost wholly surrounded by the parish for which he was nominated. Inquired, whether A. B. could act as Guardian.

Ans.—It is presumed that A. B. is rated for the land he occupies in the parish of Swineshead. It is immaterial where he resides. His qualification to be elected Guardian consists alone in his being rated in some parish in the Union, in respect of a property of the prescribed annual value, (4 and 5 Wm. 4 c. 76, s. 38.)

4.—NOMINATOR'S QUALIFICATION — PAYMENT OF A CHURCH-RATE.

14th March, 1844.

Clerk of the Wakefield Union—Stated, that a Church-rate for the township of Wakefield having been refused by a majority of the inhabitants in vestry assembled, the Vicar, Churchwardens, and the minority of the meeting, made a Church-rate, which had since been partly collected; that the legality of this rate had been questioned by a great majority of the inhabitants, who had refused to pay it; amongst whom were several rate-payers, who had nominated persons for the office of Guardian. Inquired, whether such nominations should be rejected.

Ans.—The clerk has omitted to state the precise time when the rate was made. The Commissioners presume, however, that it was not made within the six months immediately preceding the time of voting at the ensuing election; because payment of a rate made within the last six months (assuming it to be free from legal objection) would not be necessary to enable a person to vote as rate-payer under the 40th section of the Poor Law Amendment Act. The question whether the Churchwardens and a minority in a vestry are competent to make a valid Church-rate, where the majority may have refused, has very recently been before the Courts. There are conflicting decisions upon the point; but the highest court hitherto appealed to is in favour of the legality of a rate made by the Churchwardens and the minority. (See the case of Veley and Joslin, Churchwardens of Braintree *v.* Gosling, decided by the Court of Arches, 27th March, 1843, reported in *The Justice of the Peace*, No. 29, July, 1843.) What the ultimate decision of the Judicial Committee may be, of course cannot be anticipated; but, in the mean time, it appears to the Commissioners that the judgment in the Court of Arches must be taken to be law, and therefore authoritative, until set aside. The Commissioners, of course, do not mean to assert that all the necessary formalities were observed in making the rate, in the particular case which the clerk has brought before them, but simply that (according to the decision referred to) a rate made by the Churchwardens and a minority of the parishioners is a good and valid rate, assuming this to be the only point in dispute in the present case. Therefore, if there be no other objection to the rate affecting its validity, the Commissioners think that payment of such rate is necessary to enable a person to vote as rate-payer under the 40th section of the Poor Law Amendment Act. A person, at the time he assumes to nominate, must be duly qualified to vote as rate-payer, otherwise the nomination is invalid.

19*th March*, 1844.

Clerk of the same Union—Stated, that there were eight Churchwardens for the parish of Wakefield, (four elected by the vicar and four by the inhabitants in vestry,) and that four only of the eight had signed the rate-book. The rate was laid on the 8th of August, and after the majority had refused the rate; the Vicar, who was in the chair, and whilst all the Churchwardens and the meeting still remained, saying, "I shall now, in accordance with the last decision, along with the Churchwardens and a minority of the meeting, proceed to lay a rate of one penny in the pound." The rate-books were then produced and signed by the Vicar, four of the Churchwardens, and a minority of the meeting; all the opponents of the rate, and the other Churchwardens, being still there, and the latter offering no objection or remark. The resolution making the rate was entered in the Vestry Minute Book, and signed by the Vicar, as chairman of the meeting; and all the eight Churchwardens had actually collected some parts of the rate. Inquired, whether the rate-books should have been signed by all the Churchwardens.

Ans.—Although a minority of Vestry, concurring with the Churchwardens, may make a rate, it does not appear to follow that a number less than a majority of the Churchwardens in such a case would be sufficient. It appears to be consistent with the usual practice, with regard to joint and equal officers, that there should be a majority of Churchwardens concurrent to bring the question before the vestry, and that otherwise it would not be the act of the Churchwardens. The Commissioners perceive much difficulty with this subject, on account of the absence of any distinct decision on the point; and they, therefore, wish to avoid expressing any opinion on the validity of the rate. But having regard to the doubts, they think that the more prudent course, and one most favourable to the franchise, and therefore most accordant with the general principle of the law, would be for the returning officer to accept the nomination and votes of persons to whose vote no other objection is made besides the non-payment of such a church-rate. The Commissioners state this as their opinion upon the additional facts mentioned in the clerk's present letter, without withdrawing anything of what was said in their former letter.

5.—NOMINATIONS—JOINT NOMINATORS.

22*nd March*, 1844.

Chairman of King's Lynn Union—Inquired, if more than one person wished to nominate the same individuals as Guardians for a parish in the Union, in one nomination paper, the nominators might substitute the word "*We*" for "*I*," and "*Rate-payers*" for "*Rate-payer*," at the foot of such nomination paper, and sign the same conjointly.

Ans.—The Commissioners perceive no objection to the same nomination being signed by several nominators, provided that the wording of the form be altered so as distinctly to meet the case.

6. NOMINATION—VALIDITY OF.

16*th March*, 1844.

Clerk of Sedbergh Union—Stated, that he had received two nomination papers, each containing the full number of names of persons entitled to act as Guardians for the township of Dent; one of the papers having the signature of "Richard Sutton" at the bottom, which signature there was reason to believe was a forgery. Inquired, in case the nomination should be objected to, as to the proper time for making such objection, and by whom it should be made.

Ans.—1. Any time after the delivery of the supposed nomination, an objection made thereto may be entertained; and when reasonable ground for the objection appears to the Returning Officer, he ought to satisfy himself at once, so as to avoid the taking of further proceedings, if they should prove to be unnecessary. It is not requisite that any party interested, or having any peculiar character, should make the objection. The Returning Officer, acting on his own responsibility, should be guided by his knowledge, however obtained.

7. NOMINATION—VALIDITY OF,—THE PERSON NOMINATED HAVING PREVIOUSLY PASSED BY ANOTHER NAME.

16*th March*, 1844.

Clerk of Northallerton Union—Stated that a person residing in Northallerton had served the office of Guardian at different times, for that township, under the name of "Henry Naisby;" that a person had been nominated to be Guardian for the ensuing year, under the name of "Henry Naisbitt;" and that he believed those two names might be intended for the same person. Inquired, whether he should not reject the nomination for uncertainty.

Ans.—If the case should be that the real name of the person referred to, is *Naisbitt*, it would not be safe to reject his nomination on the ground of his having been previously known by another name. If, on the other hand, the true name should be that by which he was previously known, and which he has before used, then the name newly assumed would be an uncertain indication of the party, which would warrant the Returning Officer in rejecting the nomination.

8. NOMINATIONS—VALIDITY OF GUARDIAN'S QUALIFICATION—A MEMBER OF A FIRM WHOSE NAME DOES NOT APPEAR IN THE RATE-BOOK.

19*th March*, 1844.

Clerk of the Todmorden Union—1. Stated, that a Rate-payer nominated two persons for the township of Erringden, (which returns two Guardians,) and afterwards made a second nomination of the like number, but included one of the persons named in the first nomination; thus nominating in all, three individuals. Inquired, whether both or either of the nominations are valid. 2. The name of R. C., who was a nominator, did not appear in the rate-book, but that of "C——, brothers," (of which firm R. C. claims to be a partner,) was entered in the rate. Inquired, whether the nomination made by him was good. 3. The name of W. O., who had been nominated as a Guardian, was not in the rate-book, but that of "O——, brothers," (of which firm he stated himself to be a partner,) appeared in the rate. Inquired, whether he was eligible for the office of Guardian.

Ans. 1.—The first case stated, is not without difficulties; but the Commissioners on the whole, are disposed to think that the second nomination should, under the circumstances, be rejected. In the first place, the Commissioners are of opinion that a nominator is not at liberty to withdraw a nomination once sent in by him, and consequently, that the first nomination in the present case, (if good in itself,) must stand, unless it be revoked indirectly by the second. The Commissioners further think, that the second nomination is not necessarily inadmissible. If, for example, the first nomination had contained only one name, and the second only one, the Commissioners think that the second might have been received as an addition to the first. But in this particular instance, the whole number of candidates proposed by the two nominations exceeds the prescribed number of Guardians for the parish, and consequently, if each of the nominations be deemed good in itself, they must, when combined, be pronounced void for uncertainty. The result is, that, as the first cannot be withdrawn, either the second must be rejected, or else it will indirectly invalidate the first; and it is because of the latter effect that the Commissioners incline to its rejection; for the same objections in principle, which apply to a direct withdrawal of a nomination, may be urged with equal force against an indirect withdrawal. The one would afford as much facility for fraud as the other; and the right of the whole constituency to elect the nominee would be alike defeated by both. 2. The Commissioners think that, if R. C. is really one of the firm, assessed as "C——, brothers," he may be deemed, as far as such description is concerned, sufficiently rated for the purposes of the election of Guardians. 3. The Commissioners entertain a similar opinion with respect to the eligibility of W. O. to serve as Guardian.

---

9. NOMINATIONS—VALIDITY OF.

20th March, 1844.

Mr. E. W. Scott, Kendal Union—Stated, that certain nominations of Guardians had been objected to; in one instance, on the ground of the name of the street in which the candidate resided not having been inserted in the nomination paper; and in another, because the name of the street only, (and not the parish,) was inserted in the nomination paper. Inquired whether these objections were valid.

Ans.—The Commissioners are disposed to consider that the Clerk is not bound to treat a nomination paper as invalid, merely on the ground of its describing the address of the candidate by the name of the street, without that of the parish, or by the name of the parish, without that of the street, in which he lives, provided there is no uncertainty created by the omission.

---

10. NOMINATIONS—VALIDITY OF.

22nd March, 1844.

Clerk of Isle of Thanet Union—Stated, that Richard Brice had been nominated for the office of Guardian by Benjamin Bushell and Thomas Coleman; that Benjamin Bushell's nomination had been objected to, on the ground of another person having written his (Bushell's) name to it, though with his consent; and that Thomas Coleman had not paid his Poor-rate, due more than six months. Inquired, whether either of the above nominations are legal.

Ans.—If Thomas Coleman was not duly entitled to vote at the time the nomination was made, he was not legally entitled to nominate. In nominating a Guardian, Mr. Coleman was doing an act as a rate-payer, and section 40 of the Poor Law Amendment Act prevents any person voting or doing any act as a rate-payer, until he has complied with the conditions of that section as to the payment of rates for the prescribed period. As regards Mr. Benjamin Bushell, the nomination it seems was not signed by him, but by another person with his consent. The Commissioners think that this is not a compliance with article 12 of the election order, and that the nomination cannot be admitted.

---

11. NOMINATIONS—VALIDITY OF.

15th March, 1844.

Clerk of Cambridge Union—Inquired as to the validity of the following nominations for the office of Guardian. In the first, the residence of Mr. Bishop (the person nominated,) was described as "King's Parade," whereas he lived at "51, Regent Street," the former being only the place in which he conducted his business. In the second, the candidate was nominated as "George Fowler," his name being "Frederick Gordon Fowler." And in the third, the nominator having written his name "Jeremiah Garner," and added his correct address, but his real name was Jeremiah Banks Garner."

Ans.—1. As it appears Mr. Bishop occupies the premises at "King's Parade" for the purposes of business, and his name appears in the rate-book as the occupant, it may, the Commissioners think, fairly be deemed to be his residence. The object of inserting the residence of the person proposed in the nomination paper was identification, and that appears to be attained by such a description as the present. 2. In the case of the person nominated by the description of "George Fowler," his real name being "Frederick Gordon Fowler," the Commissioners consider that the name given is so entire a misdescription, that the nomination cannot be received. 3. In the case of "Mr. Jeremiah Banks Garner," who has written his name "Jeremiah Garner," with a correct address, the Commissioners think the nomination should be treated as valid, if there is no doubt of the identity of the party.

12. NOMINATIONS—VALIDITY OF.

20th March, 1844.

Clerk of Battle Union—Inquired, whether a nomination made by a rate-payer, who did not state that he was either a rate-payer or owner, but merely "I being a resident of the parish," was good. And also, whether a person who had lately removed from one house to another in the same parish, was qualified to vote, such person having been rated twelve months, but not in respect of the property actually occupied by him at the present time.

Ans. — First, Residence does not entitle a person to nominate,—a person is only entitled to perform that act in the capacity of owner, or rate-payer. Where he omits to state in the nomination in which of these characters he nominates, the nomination is rendered invalid by the omission. Secondly, to entitle a person to vote as rate-payer, he need not be rated and pay the rates for the same premises for a year; it will be sufficient if he occupy different premises in the same parish in succession; so that there be a year's rating, and the proper payment of rates.

13. NOMINATIONS—VALIDITY OF—PAPER BEING DELIVERED TO THE WRONG PERSON, &c.

16th March, 1844.

Clerk of Sevenoaks Union—Stated that, in the notice of Election of Guardians for the ensuing year, persons living in *each* of the parishes were appointed to receive nomination papers for such parishes respectively. In one case, a nomination for the parish of *S.* was left with the person appointed for, and living in, the parish of *B.*, and in another case, a nomination paper was brought on the evening of the 11th inst. to the person appointed to receive it, after he and all his family were in bed, and he refused to take it in. The party who brought it, however, afterwards knocked at the servant's window, and left the paper with her. Inquired, whether either of the nominations ought to be admitted.

Ans. 1.—A nomination may be sent, under article 12 of the Election Order, either to the Clerk or to the person appointed to receive it; but if it is sent to any other person, it will not be receivable. Under article 10, the Clerk is to give notice of the persons by whom the nomination papers in respect of *each* parish are to be received. Consequently, a nomination in respect of one parish, sent to a person appointed to receive nominations for another parish, would not be delivered in compliance with the regulations, and therefore would not be receivable by the Clerk. 2.—A nomination delivered to the person appointed to receive it, before midnight on the last day on which nominations are receivable, would, as it appears to the Commissioners, be delivered in time; and of course, a delivery to the person's servant at his own house, is tantamount to a delivery to himself.

14. NOMINATION—VALIDITY OF—PAPER DELIVEED ON THE 11TH MARCH.

20th March, 1844.

Clerk of Newport Pagnel Union—Inquired, whether a nomination paper received on the 11th inst. is valid; the 10th of March (the day appointed for their being sent in) having fallen on a Sunday.

Ans.—The Commissioners think that, under articles 12 and 30 of the Election Order, the last day for receiving nominations was, in the present year, the 11th of March, and consequently that the nomination referred to, as far as the date of its receipt is concerned, was good.

15. NOMINATIONS—VALIDITY OF, WHEN MADE ON A SUNDAY.

16th March, 1844.

Clerk of Fareham Union—Inquired, whether two nominations of candidates for the office of Guardians, made on Sunday, the 10th inst., were valid.

Ans.—The act of nomination is not business of the person's ordinary calling, nor is the nomination a service or execution of any suit, process, warrant, or decree. It does not, therefore, appear to be void under the statute of Car. 2, c. 7; nor does there appear to the Commissioners to be any other authority under which the nomination can be held void, on the ground of its having been made on a Sunday.

16. NOMINATION—WHETHER NOMINATOR CAN WITHDRAW HIS NOMINATION.

20th March, 1844.

W. S. Leicester—Inquired, whether a Nominator could withdraw the list of candidates nominated by him for the office of Guardian.

Ans.—The Nominator is not at liberty to withdraw his nomination; but any of the parties nominated may, under the 5th and 6th Vic. c. 57, s. 9, refuse to serve as Guardian, and thus terminate the election as regards himself.

17. PROXY'S APPOINTMENT — EXEMPT FROM STAMP-DUTY.

13*th March*, 1844.

Clerk of Bridgwater Union—Inquired, whether the document for the appointment of a proxy to vote in the election of Guardians should be stamped.

Ans. — The 86th section of the Poor Law Amendment Act expressly exempts from liability to stamp duty, any "mortgage, bond, instrument, or any assignment thereof, given by way of security, in pursuance of the Rules, Orders, or Regulations of the said Commissioners, and conformable thereto, or any contract or agreement, or appointment of any officer, made or entered into, in pursuance of such Rules, Orders, or Regulations, and conformable thereto, *or any other instrument made in pursuance of the Act.*" The question is, whether the writing appointing a person to vote as proxy for an owner, given in pursuance of the 40th section, is an instrument made in pursuance of the Act, such as is contemplated by the 86th section. The Commissioners entertain no doubt whatever that it is, and that no stamp is necessary, in order to render the votes tendered by the proxy appointed by the writing receivable. But for the provision in the 86th section, the Commissioners think it probable that the appointment of a proxy by an owner, *i. e.*, a general authority to vote as the party thinks right, would have been regarded as "a letter or power of attorney, or procuration," within the statute 55th Geo. 3, c. 184, schedule part 1; so that in the absence of a stamp, no valid vote could have been given by the party named in the instrument of appointment (see Reg. *v.* Kelk, 12 A. and E. 559.)

18. WHETHER AN UNCERTIFICATED BANKRUPT CAN VOTE AS PROXY.

8*th March*, 1844.

Clerk of Leicester Union—Stated, that it was probable an objection might be raised to a person voting as proxy for several owners, in consequence of his being an uncertificated bankrupt. Inquired, whether such objection would be valid.

Ans.—There is nothing in the fact of a person being an uncertificated bankrupt, which would prevent his voting and acting as the proxy or representative of an owner of property.

19. VOTING PAPERS — ARRANGEMENT OF CANDIDATES' NAMES.

19*th March*, 1844.

Clerk of Strand Union—Stated, that by article 12 of the Election Order, the Clerk is directed to endorse every nomination paper with the date of its receipt, and also to number it according to the order of its receipt. Inquired, whether the names of the candidates should be placed in the voting papers according to the order in which they are received.

Ans.—The Election Order does not prescribe any course to be observed by the clerk in regard to the order in which the names of candidates should be inserted in the voting papers. As a matter of general convenience, and to avoid disputes and imputation of partiality, the Commissioners are disposed to think that the desirable course would be to follow the order of receipt. Still, however, if the clerk should consider that any other arrangement of the names (an alphabetical one, for instance) would, upon general grounds of convenience or utility, be preferable, it is open to him to adopt that arrangement.

20. VOTING—JOINT OCCUPIERS.

25*th March*, 1844.

Clerk of the Cambridge Union—Enclosed a communication, addressed to him by Mr. John Bentley, of which the following is a copy:—"I see by a voting paper left at my house this morning, that I have been put in nomination to fill the office of one of the Guardians for the parish of All Saints; it being done without my consent, I beg leave to decline filling that office, if elected." Inquired, whether this communication was a sufficient *refusal* under the 9th section of the 5th and 6th Vic. c. 57. Also requested the Commissioners' reply to the following queries:—

1. Whether a person in arrear of a Church-rate made upwards of six months, was entitled to vote by paying the same after the delivery of the voting papers.

2. Whether, in a case where two or more persons were members of a firm, and jointly assessed as occupiers of premises which, if held by one person, would confer only one vote, each partner was entitled to a vote and a separate voting paper.

3. Whether it was necessary that each partner

should sign the voting paper, or was the usual signature of the firm sufficient.

4. Whether, where the statements of Owners and Proxies had been entered in the register, and the Overseer represented that such statements had been lost, the Clerk was bound by such entries, without the production of the documents themselves.

Ans.—The Commissioners think, that the communication from Mr. Bentley (of which you enclose a copy) is a sufficient refusal to act as Guardian, within the 9th section of the 5th and 6th Vic. c. 57.

In replying to your other inquiries, *seriatim*, the Commissioners desire to state—

1. If a rate-payer pays his rates at any time before the day on which the voting papers are issued, it would be sufficient, but not otherwise.

2. The 4th section of the Poor Law Amendment Act provides that *the rate-payers* under £200 shall *each* have "a single vote." The Commissioners do not think that a firm can be regarded collectively as being a single rate-payer, and entitled as such to one vote only. It appears to them that each individual member of the firm is virtually as much a separate rate-payer, to the extent of his individual interest in the concern, as if he were separately rateable for property equal in value to such interest; and, consequently, that each such member is entitled to vote independently of the rest, according to the extent of his interest.*

3. The Commissioners think that each member of the firm who votes, should do so in a separate voting paper.

4. The original documents themselves are of course the best evidence which the Clerk can have, as to the statements made by Owners and Proxies; but in the event of their loss, the Commissioners consider that he might properly rely upon the registry, where no objection is made against it. If any objection is made, he must exercise his own judgment in the case.

21. VOTING—JOINT OWNERS.

25th March, 1844.

Clerk of the Cambridge Union—Requested the Commissioners' opinion on the following points:

1.—Whether an owner's statement, signed "Hawkes and Co.," there being five members composing the firm, was a good signature of all the owners.

2.—Whether an owner's statement in the handwriting of the owner, but without his signature, was valid.

3.—Whether a proxy's notice to the Overseers of his appointment as proxy, in the handwriting of the proxy, but without his signature, was good.

4.—As the Clerk would commence on Monday, [25th March,] at 11 P. M., at the Board-room, to cast up the votes, up to what hour in the day might the Clerk adjourn the performance of his duties to the following morning.

5.—As the weekly meeting of the Board of Guardians was appointed to be held on a Wednesday, and there were eight parishes contested, would the clerk be justified (in the event of the casting up of the votes not being completed at a sufficiently early hour on the Tuesday, to give the requisite notice to the newly-elected Guardians,) in forthwith making his return; the effect of which would be to prevent the present board from transacting the business of the Union on the Wednesday, and several of the new members might be prevented attending, in consequence of the Clerk's inability to furnish them with a fair and reasonable notice of their election.

6.—What proportion of votes, (if any,) the Clerk ought to assign to a person appointed proxy by three persons, whose interest appeared by their several owners' statements to be one-sixth each in an undivided portion of an estate which would, if the property belonged to one individual, give two votes to the owner thereof.

Ans. 1. The 40th s. of the Poor Law Amendment Act, in adverting to the statements to be made by owners, does not expressly provide for the case of joint ownership. Where, however, joint owners claim to vote in respect of any property, the Commissioners think that the claim of each should be made distinctly apparent, either by being made separately from the rest, or by the attachment of the signature of each of the claimants to a statement made in common by them all.

2. The 40th s. requires the owner to make a statement in writing of his name and address, &c. If an owner makes such a statement in his own hand-writing, the Commissioners do not think it absolutely necessary that he should subjoin his signature.

3. The Commissioners likewise think that a proxy's signature is not indispensable, if his statement is made in his own handwriting.

4. The time for the adjournment of the calculation of votes, if such an adjournment be necessary, is a matter within the Clerk's discretion.

* See note at the foot of page 58.

5. The Commissioners are of opinion that the Guardians elected on the 25th or 26th instant, should constitute the board to be held on the 27th.

6. The 40th s. of the Poor Law Amendment Act provides that owners "shall have the same number and *proportion* of votes," as is given to inhabitants in vestry, by the 58th Geo. 3, c. 69, the third section of which enacts, that "in cases where two or more of the inhabitants present [in vestry] shall be jointly rated, each of them shall be entitled to vote according to the proportion and amount which shall be borne by him of the joint charge." Applying this provision analogically to the case of owners, it would seem that the three persons alluded to in your sixth question, are severally entitled to vote on account of their respective shares of the estate. You state, however, that their interest appears to be "one-sixth each, in an undivided portion, of an estate which would, if the property belonged to one individual, give two votes to the owner thereof." The Commissioners presume you to mean that the share of each of these three persons is an undivided portion, and amounts to one-sixth of the whole estate, and that the whole estate is of such value as would give two votes to an individual owner of the whole. Then, the question is, whether, notwithstanding the plurality of owners, the total number of votes in respect of the entire property remains no more than two. The Commissioners think not. The clause above cited, from 58 Geo. 3, c. 69, provides that *each* of the joint owners shall be entitled to vote according to *his* proportion of the estate. It appears to the Commissioners that, if six persons are held entitled to only two votes amongst them, it cannot be said that each of them has a vote. Supposing the entire property to give only one vote, it is manifest that, if a difference of opinion should exist among the six proprietors, the single vote could not be made to represent them all. And even with two votes, each of the six could not individually vote according to the proportion of his separate interest in the estate. The only construction, therefore, which the Commissioners can put upon the section in question, is, that in the case of joint owners, each is entitled to vote independently of the rest, and each is also entitled to such a number of votes in respect of his share of the joint estate, as he would derive from a separate estate equal in value to that share. It may be added, that the section does not contain any express limitation of the number of votes derivable from *property*, though it provides that no *inhabitant* (or owner) shall have more than six votes. This limitation as to six votes would of course apply to each of the joint owners. The proxy appointed by each of the three persons you refer to, will, if the above view be correct, be entitled to act separately for each.*

---

22. VOTING—AS OWNER IN RESPECT OF PROPERTY OF WHICH HE WILL NOT OBTAIN POSSESSION TILL THE 25TH MARCH.

13th March, 1844.

Mr. J. Shephard, Stonehouse, Devon—Stated, that he had just purchased a house, and paid the deposit, but would not obtain possession until the 25th March. And inquired whether he, who had just bought the property, or the person who had sold it, was entitled to vote for the election of Guardians in respect of it.

Ans.—The Commissioners refer Mr. Shephard to the 109th section of the Poor Law Amendment Act for a definition of the word owner. That section provides that "the word owner shall be construed to include any person, for the time being, in the actual occupation of any property rateable to the relief of the poor, and not let to him at rack rent, or any person receiving the rack rent of any such property, either on his own account or as mortgagee, or other incumbrancer in possession." From Mr. Shephard's statement it would appear that he is not entitled to vote as owner under the first clause of the definition, as he is not in the actual occupation of the property. Neither will he (as the Commissioners collect) be in the receipt of the rents of the property at the time when the act of voting is to take place under the order of the Commissioners. If this be so, the Commissioners think Mr. Shephard will not be entitled to vote under the second clause of the definition. It appears to the Commissioners that that person will be entitled to vote as owner, who, at the time fixed for voting, may be in the actual occupation of the property, (the same not being let to him at rack rent,) or who may be in the actual receipt of the rents.

---

* *Note.*—On some former occasions the Commissioners expressed an opinion at variance with that contained in these communications. A reconsideration of the statutory provisions bearing on the question, however, disposes them to think that the view now taken, would be held to be the correct one.

23. VOTING—TRUSTEES AND EXECUTORS.

24th Feb. 1844.

Clerk of the Strand Union—Inquired, whether Executors or Trustees were entitled to vote as Owners in the Election of Guardians.

Ans.—A Trustee or Executor not receiving the rent of the property on his own account as mortgagee or other incumbrancer in possession, is not within the definition of owner, contained in the 109th section of the Poor Law Amendment Act, and is consequently not entitled to vote in that capacity.

24. VOTING — NON-PAYMENT OF TOWN-RATE, OR HIGHWAY-RATE.

16th March, 1844.

Clerk of Wolverhampton Union—Inquired, first, whether a town-rate, raised under the powers of a Local Act, for the purpose of paving, lighting, &c., and which only embraced a part of the township of Wolverhampton, could be deemed a parochial rate, disqualifying the party who might not have paid it from voting in the election of Guardians. And, secondly, whether the highway rate, which was not a general rate, (owing to the town-rate preventing its application to parties within the limits of the Town Act,) should also disqualify the party not paying it from voting.

Ans.—Unless the district for which a rate is made is co-extensive with the limits of the parish or township in which the election takes place, such a rate is not, as the Commissioners consider, a parochial rate, within the meaning of the 40th section of the Poor Law Amendment Act; and payment of such rate is, therefore, not necessary to enable a person to vote as rate-payer at the annual election of Guardians.

25. VOTING—COLLEGIATE BODY.

20th March, 1844.

E. B., Cambridge—Inquired, whether the Master, President, or authorised Officer of the several Colleges could vote on the Election of Guardians in respect of property rated in the different parishes and belonging to such Colleges.

Ans.—Any Collegiate Body is able to make its claim to vote, and may appoint any one of its officers to vote for it, in respect of any rateable property in the ownership of the college, (4 and 5 Wm. 4, c. 76, s. 4, last proviso.) The governing body is determined by the deed, charter, or other act of foundation; but, whoever is the governing body may make their claim and appointment in any manner apparently, in which they may give any authoritative direction, or in which they may exercise other acts of ownership.

26. REFUSAL TO SERVE—FURTHER PROCEEDING TO ELECT AFTER.

16th March, 1844.

Clerk of Ringwood Union—Stated, that the parish of Ringwood returned five Guardians, and ten persons had been nominated, five of whom had sent in written notices of their unwillingness to serve the office. Inquired whether he was to issue voting papers for the parish of Ringwood, or to certify the five persons, from whom he had received notices, as duly elected.

Ans.—As, under the 9th section of the 5th and 6th Vic. c. 57, the election is to be no further proceeded with, as regards a candidate for the office of Guardian, after he has refused to serve; the Commissioners are of opinion that the Clerk ought not to issue voting papers in the case of the parish of Ringwood, under the circumstances described in his letter, but that he ought to act in that case in accordance with Article 13 of the Election Order.

27. GUARDIANS CONTINUING TO ACT, UNDER SECTION 10 OF 5 AND 6 VIC. c. 57.

16th March, 1844.

Clerk of Walsingham Union—Stated, that he had not received nomination of Guardians for the ensuing year in eight of the parishes of the Union, and that, therefore, the Guardians for the previous year will continue to act, under section 10 of 5 and 6 Vic. c. 57; and inquired what steps should be taken with regard to the notices to the Guardians of such parishes, and the publication of the list of Elected Guardians, pursuant to articles 25 and 26 of the Election Order.

Ans.—The names of those Guardians who may continue to serve under section 10 of 5 and 6 Vic. c. 57, need not be inserted in the return of Elected Guardians (Form I.) required by article 26 of the Election Order. The order does not provide for the notification to such Guardians of the omission to elect Guardians for the present year.

28. VALIDITY OF ELECTION OF A GUARDIAN.

1st Feb. 1844.

Clerk of the Corwen Union—Inquired, whether an objection could now be made to the vote of a person acting as Guardian of the Corwen Union on the ground that his nomination had not been received by the Clerk or his agents within the time specified in the notice of election. The Guardian had continued to act on the nomination since March, 1842.

Ans.—The question as to the right of any person to act as an elective Guardian may be raised and determined by the Commissioners under the 8th section of 5 and 6 Victoria, c. 57. But assuming that the person to whom the objection applies was included in the official declaration or return made by you of persons duly elected, that return being *primâ facie* evidence of due election, the parties included in it must, as the Commissioners consider, be regarded as entitled to act as Guardians until the question of their right to act has been raised in a legal manner, and determined under the provision in the statute above cited.

VI.—GUARDIAN—1. If appointed a Valuer, incapable of serving the office of Guardian.

27*th March*, 1844.

Belper Union.—The Commissioners having referred to a correspondence between themselves and the Clerk of the Belper Union in March, 1843, relative to the appointment of a Guardian as Valuer to the township for which he acted as Guardian, and inserted in the Official Circular, No. 27, page 119, discovered that by the insertion of the word "*not*" in the Commissioners' answer, they were made to express an opinion which is exactly the reverse of that which they really entertain; they therefore directed a letter to be written to the Clerk of the Belper Union, informing him that although there is no legal objection to the appointment of a Guardian as Valuer of a parish, yet they are of opinion that the compensation allowed for the performance of the valuation *is* such a fixed emolument from the Poor-rates of the parish, as renders any Guardian, from the time of accepting such contract till the payment for it is completed, incapable of serving the office of Guardian—(5 and 6 Vic. c. 57. s. 14.)

---

2. A Guardian cannot be concerned in the Maintenance of Lunatics chargeable to the Union for which he acts.

13*th March*, 1844.

Mr. R—— L—— Inquired whether the circumstance of his having Lunatic Paupers in his Asylum belonging to the P—— Union disqualified him from being a Guardian of the parish of P—— in that Union. His agreement with the Board of Guardians was, that he should receive a certain sum per week for each pauper; which sum was paid quarterly.

Ans.—If you were elected a Guardian, and if, after your election to that office, you still continued to be concerned in the maintenance of the Lunatics chargeable to the P—— Union, you would, in the opinion of the Commissioners, be liable to the penalties imposed by the 55 Geo. 3, c. 137, and 4 and 5 Wm. 4, c. 76, sec. 51, on persons who, having the management of the poor, supply and furnish for their own profit goods and provisions for the support and maintenance of the poor.

VII.—JUSTICES' CLERKS' FEES—When payable.

20*th Jan.* 1844.

Auditor of the West Ham Union—Stated, that the Assistant Overseers in this Union had occasionally, when the persons making default in the payment of the Poor Rates were very poor, applied to a single magistrate, at his private residence, to hear informations and grant summonses against them, which the magistrate had done gratuitously; and this course had been adopted for the purpose of preventing a disproportionate expense attaching to the recovery of rates of small amount. The Clerk to the Petty Sessions having become acquainted with this circumstance, charged his fees (three shillings) on each information and summons, which charge the auditor had disallowed in the Overseer's accounts. Inquired, if the Justices' Clerk had a right to charge his fees in these cases, seeing that the business was not done at the Sessions, nor by him.

Ans.—The Commissioners are disposed to concur with you in thinking that the Justices' Clerk, under the circumstances which you describe, is not entitled to any fee. The Commissioners do not think that the Justices' Clerk has any such interest in his office as would entitle him to be paid at all events, whether he performed the work or not. They consider that the fees included in the table are intended to be assigned to the Justices' Clerks for services rendered by them; and that consequently, when the service is not rendered by the Clerk, he has no valid claim to the remuneration.

VIII. — LUNATIC PAUPER—How to be disposed of.

7th Feb. 1844.

Clerk of the Liverpool Select Vestry—Forwarded a letter addressed to the sitting magistrate of Liverpool, by the authorities of Jersey, stating that John Duckworth, a prisoner charged with theft, then in Her Majesty's gaol there, having been declared to be labouring under monomania, with lucid intervals, the Royal Court had directed that Duckworth should be sent to his parish, Blackburn, near Liverpool, and requesting that a pass might be given him for that purpose. The Clerk stated, that Duckworth was then in the Liverpool workhouse, and inquired how the Select Vestry were to proceed in disposing of him.

Ans.—The Commissioners, in reference to the future disposition of the pauper, stated, that it appeared to them that the proper course to be pursued would be this : If there are grounds for supposing the pauper to be insane, he should be taken before Justices under the 9th Geo. 4, c. 40, sec. 38, with a view to an order being made for his confinement in some suitable asylum. Should the Justices see fit to make such order, they can then proceed, under the same section, to ascertain the settlement of the pauper, and make order on the parish of the settlement to reimburse the cost of maintenance. If the Justices should not be satisfied upon medical evidence of the insanity of the pauper, it will of course be for the parish of Liverpool to relieve the pauper so long as he may continue destitute, unless the authorities can procure the necessary legal evidence to remove him to Blackburn, as the place of his legal settlement.

IX.—OVERSEERS.—1. For an Extra-Parochial Place.

9th March, 1844.

Clerk of the Billesdon Union—Inquired, whether an extra-parochial place, not having Overseers, could be compelled to appoint Overseers, there being inhabitants there capable of filling that office : and if so, what course must be adopted in the matter.

Ans.—Overseers may be appointed for an extra-parochial place, if it be a town or a vill, Rex *v.* Rufford, 1 Str. 512, 1 Bott. 47, but not otherwise, Rex *v.* Welbeck, 1 Bott. 50. If the extra-parochial place to which your inquiry refers is entitled to have Overseers appointed for it, the Justices should be applied to, to appoint ; and if they refuse, the case of Rex *v.* Rufford shows that the Court of Queen's Bench will grant a mandamus to compel the appointment.

---

2. Overseer of a Parish cannot be at the same time Churchwarden of the same Parish.

7th March, 1844.

Mr. R. Hughes, Anglesey—Inquired, whether a person could at the same time serve the offices of Churchwarden and Overseer for the same parish. Also, whether an Overseer of the Poor had of himself, the power to appoint an Assistant Overseer.

Ans.—On the authority of Reg. *v.* All Saints, Derby, (13 East 143,) the appointment of the same person as Churchwarden and Overseer for the same parish during the same year, would seem to be void ; as the statute of the 43rd Eliz. c. 2, s. 1, which requires the appointment of at least two persons as Overseers, distinct from the Churchwardens, would not in such a case be satisfied. The only authority for the appointment of an Assistant Overseer, with a salary payable from the Poor Rates, is the 59th Geo. 3, c. 12, s. 7 ; which vests in the Justices the power of appointing such an officer, upon the nomination of the vestry. An appointment by an Overseer alone, would be of no force.

---

3. The Recovery of Parochial Monies from an Overseer in Default.

21st Nov., 1843.

Overseer of St. Giles, Reading—Stated that four Overseers were appointed for the parish of St. Giles, Reading; three by the borough Justices for that part of the parish which is within the borough, and one by the Justices for that part which is without the borough, and which is called the hamlet of Whitley. The Overseer appointed for the hamlet had collected the rates for that district, but had only accounted for a portion of the amount, there being, it was believed, a balance in his hands of upwards of £90. This balance ought to have been paid into the general account of the Overseers for the whole parish, but they had failed to obtain it, and the Overseer in default had absented himself, and his goods were being removed. The Overseers were in consequence unable to make out their accounts, and they did not know how to proceed. The Auditor had served a notice on the Overseers, requiring them to render to him an account within three days.

Ans.—As a general rule, Overseers are not liable for the defalcations of their colleagues. In the case of R. *v.* the Justices of Essex, 3 B. & Ad. 941, Lord Tenterden observed, "When there are two Overseers, it may be laid down generally, that the one is not answerable for the malversation or misappropriation of the other." The principle thus laid down appears to be applicable to such a default on the part of one Overseer, as has occurred in the present case. If the defaulting Overseer can be found, he may be required by the Auditor to account for what he has received on behalf of the parish. If another Overseer be appointed in his room, under the 17th Geo. 2, c. 38, s. 3, the Overseers may proceed to enforce under the 47th section of the Poor Law Amendment Act, payment of the balance which the Auditor may find to be due from the defaulter.

9th Jan. 1844.

The same Overseer—Stated that the Auditor left a notice at the house of the defaulting Overseer previous to his quitting the parish, requiring him to account for the parochial monies received by him. The Overseer however failed to do so, and immediately left the parish. The amount in his hands was ascertained to be £94 12*s.* 9¼*d.*, besides his own rate, £8 14*s.* Inquired whether there was any summary proceeding which could be adopted for the recovery of either or both of these amounts.

Ans.—It appears to the Commissioners, that as Mr. H. has removed altogether from the parish, he is bound, under the 3rd section of the 17th Geo. 2, c. 38, to "deliver over to some Churchwarden, or other Overseer of the same place, his accounts verified as aforesaid (*i. e.* before the Justices, see s. 1,) with all rates, assessments, books, papers, sums of money, and other things concerning his office, under the like penalties as are inflicted by the Act on an Overseer refusing to do the same after the expiration of his office." The punishment thus referred to, consists in committal to the common jail until the requirements of the statute be complied with by the offender, (see s. 2.) But this provision would not apply to the sum of £8 14*s.* due from Mr. H. in respect of the poor rate assessed upon himself; as that assessment is made upon him in his private, not in his official capacity. It has, however, been recently decided (Skingley *v.* Surridge and another, 12 L. I. R. n. s. M. C. 122,) that, where the poor rate due from one Churchwarden (or Overseer) has been duly demanded of him, and he has refused payment, his colleagues may proceed against him before Justices to recover the rate by warrant of distress, in the usual way; supposing he has not charged himself with the amount, and has not himself applied it to parochial purposes.

---

4. OVERSEER NOT ELIGIBLE FOR THE OFFICE OF ASSISTANT OVERSEER.

12th February, 1844.

Overseer of Swanscombe, Kent.—Inquired whether, being an overseer of the poor of the parish of Swanscombe, he was eligible for the office of assistant overseer for that parish.

Ans.—The Commissioners think that, although the vestry is empowered, by the 59th Geo. 3, c. 12, s. 7, to elect "any discreet person to be assistant overseer," yet the offices of overseer and assistant overseer are of such a nature as necessarily to place a limitation upon the powers of the vestry in the matter, and to prevent the appointment of the same individual to both those offices at once. You are, as overseer, already bound to perform all the duties which you could be required to discharge as assistant overseer. Your appointment to the latter office would not invest you with any new powers, or impose upon you any new obligations. Moreover as overseer, you are bound to discharge all the duties of your office without remuneration for your services, (R. *v.* Gwyer, 4 Nev. and Man, 158.) Consequently, the only effect of your appointment as assistant overseer would be, to do that indirectly, which the law forbids to be done directly, by paying you in one character for the discharge of those duties which you are in another character bound to perform gratuitously. Again, an assistant overseer may and ought to be required to give security for the due execution of his office. The bond is to be made to the churchwardens and overseers, and on breach of its conditions, to be put in suit by them. An individual holding the two appointments of overseer and assistant overseer would therefore stand in the double relation of giver and taker of the same bond; and might, perhaps, be under the necessity of joining in proceedings against himself.

X. — PAUPERS. — ABSCONDING WITH THE WORKHOUSE CLOTHES, &c.

6th Feb. 1844.

Clerk of the Selby Union—Stated, that two boys had absconded from the workhouse, taking with them some school-books. They were both under the age of sixteen years. One of them had several times absconded. On one occasion of his doing so, he was taken up and tried for a larceny at the Sessions; and he was thought a fit object for prosecution under 55 Geo. 3, c. 137, s. 2, for the present offence. The Clerk had referred to the Letter in the Official Circular, No. 27, page 128, and it seemed to him that a difficulty would arise in laying the property; for how could it be called the property of the Overseers? Perhaps the clothing might be described as the property of the Overseers of the township to which the boy belonged; inasmuch as the Overseers were charged with the proportion of the cost of the clothing. If so described, the proceedings, he presumed, must be in the names of the Overseers, and not of the Guardians. The school-books would seem to be the property of the Guardians, and might, he thought, be so laid. The Board of Guardians wished the opinion of the Commissioners on the subject.

Ans.—The Commissioners think that the property ought to be described in the information as belonging to the Guardians of the Union. It appears to the Commissioners quite immaterial whether the property be that of an individual parish or of the Union; in both cases it seems equally, in the sense of the statute, to belong to the Guardians, their title being the same to property in their possession, whether obtained at the joint or several expense of the parishes in the Union. The Commissioners would further observe, that there are terms used in the 2d section of 55 Geo. 3, c. 137, which accurately describe the Guardians of Unions formed under the Poor Law Amendment Act: the terms of the section are prospective, and apply not to "such Guardians" only, but the reason and policy of the enactment are quite as applicable to Guardians of Unions as to any officers or districts for relief known at the time the Act was passed.

XI.—POOR RATES.—1. CANNOT BE APPLIED TO THE PAYMENT OF A DEBT INCURRED IN A BYGONE YEAR.

6th January, 1844.

Mr. Jos. Child, Soothill Grange, Dewsbury—Stated, that in the year 1837 a new survey and valuation of the Township of Soothill Grange were made under the Parochial Assessments Act. Considerable delay occurred in making the new valuation, during which time the rates were made on the old valuation. On the new valuation being completed, the valuer intimated to the Overseers that he was ready to deliver the document up to them on being paid his charges, or receiving security for the amount. The Overseers not being in possession of funds to discharge the valuer's claim, they could not obtain the new valuation, and a rate being required, they made it on the old valuation. However, on presenting the rate to the Justices, they refused to allow it, on the ground that it ought to have been made on the new valuation. Shortly after this, the valuation was delivered to the Overseers, but it was found on examination to be so incorrect, that a rate could not be made upon it in its then state. A meeting of the Rate-payers was therefore called to consider what means should be adopted for raising money, until a rate could be made on the new valuation. At this meeting a resolution was passed to the effect, that the Overseers, together with several Rate-payers, should give security to the West Riding Union Banking Company, for the advance of such sum of money as should be necessary for the use of the Township, until a rate could be made on the new valuation. From the depression of trade, the whole of the money borrowed in pursuance of this resolution had not been repaid at the time stipulated for its repayment, and a balance of £49 5*s.* 6*d.* then remained owing to the Bank. Wished the Commissioners' sanction for the payment of this amount out of the Poor Rates.

Ans.—The Commissioners are of opinion that the law settled in Tawney's case, (Salk. 531, 2 Lord Raymond,) clearly establishes the principle that Overseers having the power to make rates for the current and prospective expenses of relieving the poor, have no authority to borrow money. The Commissioners do not perceive from the statements contained in your letter, that any such impediment existed as prevented the Overseers of Soothill Grange from making a rate. Notwithstanding the incorrectness of the valuation, the Overseers ought to have made the best rate they could, rendering it as conformable as possible to the Parochial Assessments Act. Such a rate might have been the subject of appeal, but it might nevertheless have been collected, pending the determination of the appeals, provided the sums sought to be recovered did not exceed the amounts assessed in the last effective rate (41 Geo. 3, cap. 23, sec. 2.) The Commissioners therefore consider that the Overseers were not authorised in borrowing money instead of making a rate, and that consequently they cannot charge the interest upon the Poor Rates. The Commissioners regret the course which has been taken in this matter; but you will perceive that the obstacle to the payment from the rates is entirely of a legal character, and is not in any way dependent upon the Commissioners' sanction or disapproval.

EXCUSAL FROM PAYMENT OF POOR RATES.

6th January, 1844.

Clerk of the West Derby Union—Inquired, whether the Board of Guardians, or the Overseers of the several townships, were the parties whose consent was requisite to enable Justices to excuse poor persons from the payment of the poor rates.

Ans.—The Commissioners are inclined to think that the Churchwardens and Overseers of a parish are still empowered, by the terms of 54 Geo. 3, c. 170, s. 11, to give a valid consent to the excusal from the rate, notwithstanding such parish may be in Union, and under the control of Guardians. The Commissioners, however, have been advised, that the words in the section referred to, " with the consent of the Churchwardens and Overseers of such district, &c., or of such other person or persons as is or are competent to act, under the authority of any Act or Acts of Parliament, for the ordering, management, control, or direction of the poor of any such district," &c. empower the Guardians where they exist for the management of the poor, to give the required consent.

XII.—RATING.—LIME KILNS.

7th Feb. 1844.

Mr. Thomas Hawkes, Williton, Somerset—Stated that in the parish of Luxmore, the Poor Rate of which he was making, there were several lime kilns, burning from two thousand to three thousand hogsheads of lime a-year for sale for manure. The lime works were rented with the farms, and not separately, so that their value to rent was not distinctly known. He presumed that lime kilns which would let at a rent separate from a farm, whether used for the benefit of the farm to which it was attached or for general sale, was rateable for the fair rental to let.

Ans.—It appears from your statement, that the kilns in question are let, not separately, but in

conjunction with farms. The letting value, and consequently the rateable value, of such farms is of course increased in proportion. Any special advantage of this nature attendant upon the occupation of the land, is to be taken into account in estimating the rent which the property may be reasonably expected to fetch.

XIII.—RELATIONS—MAINTENANCE OF.

9th February, 1844.

Clerk of the South Stoneham Union—Stated that Mary Light, who was upwards of seventy years of age, was in the receipt of out relief from the South Stoneham Union, on account of the parish of Hamble, one of the parishes comprised therein, and in which parish she was residing. Her son, Stephen Light, was considered by the guardians to be in receipt of wages to an amount which would enable him to contribute to the support of his mother, and they had determined that application should be made to the magistrates under the 43 Eliz. c. 2, s. 7. As it appeared, however, that the mother was not totally unable to work, but on the contrary actually did work on two or three days in the week, a doubt had arisen whether the son was, under sec. 7 of the above statute, liable to maintain, or in any way contribute to the support of his mother, or in other words, whether the words " not able to work" applied to the whole class of persons enumerated in that section.

Ans.—In every case in which an order on a person for the support of a relation is sought to be obtained under the 43 Eliz. c. 2, it appears to be necessary to show that such relation is not only poor, but also unable to work (R. *v.* Gulley, 1 Bott;) but the Commissioners believe that it has never been required that the state of the pauper should be one of absolute inability to work,—it being always considered, and acted on in practice, that if the party is not able to work to the extent of getting his own living, he comes within the reason and effect of the provision. The Commissioners, therefore, think that the case of Mary Light is one in which the justices can lawfully make an order of maintenance under the above-mentioned statute.

LONDON:
Printed by Order of the Poor Law Commissioners, by BLACKBURN and PARDON, 6, Hatton Garden, and Published by CHARLES KNIGHT and Co., 22, Ludgate Street, Publishers to the Poor Law Commissioners.

AN

OFFICIAL CIRCULAR

OF PUBLIC DOCUMENTS AND INFORMATION:

DIRECTED BY THE POOR LAW COMMISSIONERS TO BE PRINTED, CHIEFLY FOR THE USE OF THE MEMBERS AND PERMANENT OFFICERS OF BOARDS OF GUARDIANS, UNDER THE POOR LAW AMENDMENT ACT.

No. 34. CIRCULAR ISSUED APRIL 30, 1844.

Poor Law Commission Office,
Somerset House,
30th April, 1844.

THE Poor Law Commissioners, on a review of their Minutes, directed that the Minutes of Correspondence on the following subjects be printed and circulated for the information of Guardians and Officers of the several Unions, viz:—

(Signed) By Order of the Board,

EDWIN CHADWICK, *Secretary*.

I.—APPRENTICE—RUNNING AWAY FROM HIS SITUATION, HOW TO BE PUNISHED.

19*th Feb.* 1844.

Clerk of Croydon Union—Stated that Henry Letts, aged 14, a pauper in the workhouse of the Croydon Union, having been instructed and considerably advanced in the knowledge of the trade of a tailor, was taken by a respectable person of that trade, residing at Islington, on trial as an apprentice. He went very willingly to his place, on the 2nd Feb. On the 5th Feb., however, he made his appearance at the workhouse, and told the master that he had that morning run away from Islington, and would not go back. He stated, he had nothing to complain of, as his master had behaved exceedingly kind to him; but that he had been sent of errands, which he did not like, and that he was away from his mother, and brother, and sister, who were then in the workhouse. The master at Islington declined taking him again. Inquired, whether the boy could be legally punished for such conduct; and, if so, in what manner.

Ans.—It appears to the Commissioners that the boy was able, wholly or in part, to maintain himself, if he had kept his place; and that he has rendered himself subject to the provisions of the Vagrant Act by wilfully neglecting or refusing to do so. The Commissioners therefore think that proceedings might be taken by the Guardians to punish him under that statute.

II.—AUDITOR'S DUTIES.—CERTIFYING THE AMOUNT OF RATES NOT RECOVERABLE OR EXCUSED.

19*th Feb.* 1844.

Mr. Yarker, District Auditor—Stated, that the column in the Abstract of the Parochial Accounts (B. 12) of the —— and —— Unions, headed "Amount of Rates not recoverable, or legally excused," had hitherto never been filled up. This omission had been occasioned by the absence of any head in the Quarterly Statements of receipts and payments of the parishes, adapted to contain the information necessary to fill up the column in the abstract above alluded to, and the omission rendered it impossible to get the items supplied from the Quarterly Statements. The certificates at the foot of the abstract state that it is made from such statements; he had not, therefore, considered it correct to fill up the column from any other source. Requested to be informed in what way the column mentioned could be filled up consistently with the certificates at the foot of the abstract; and also whether it was his duty, or that of the Clerk of the Union, to fill up the abstract from the Quarterly Statements, he (the Auditor) only ascertaining that it was correctly filled up, and certifying that such was the fact.

Ans.—If the quarterly accounts of the overseers are presented in proper form, they will furnish the information necessary to be inserted in the abstract (B. 12.) The Commissioners consider that the order of accounts imposes upon the Auditor the duty of seeing, not only that all the sums actually received by the overseers on account of poor-rates are placed to their debit, but also of ascertaining what other sums ought to have been received by them on account of the parish. It would, therefore, be his duty to require the overseers to present such an account as would distinctly exhibit what portion of the entire rate was uncollected, and what portion of the amount so uncollected was legally irrecoverable. The law does not, it is true, enable the Auditor himself to charge the overseers in their accounts (as for sums received) with monies which have not in fact come into their hands; and, therefore, the balance recoverable from the overseers will not be affected by the amount of uncollected or irrecoverable rates. Nevertheless, the amount of the uncollected or excused rates at the time of the audit should be stated in the receipt and payment book; and the overseers may be required to make a declaration of the truth of such statement. If this be done, there will be no difficulty in transferring the results to the appropriate column in the Abstract of the Parochial Accounts, or in signing the certificates appended to the Abstract.

It may further be observed that the 43 Eliz. c. 2, s. 1, expressly requires the overseers to "make and yield up *** a true and perfect account of all sums of money by them received, or *rated and cessed and not received.*"

III.—BAKING—IN WORKHOUSES.

Bury St. Edmunds,
27th April, 1844.

Gentlemen,

As the Official Circulars have more than once indicated the interest taken by you (in reference to economical management) on the subject of baking in the workhouse, I transmit for your information a clear (and I believe a trustworthy) report, which I have just received from the master of the Kenninghall workhouse.

I am not, however, favourable myself to baking in the workhouse: the operation, to be fully successful, depends too much on the watchfulness and cleverness of the master; and I doubt, even under the most favourable circumstances, whether the bread is better, or supplied cheaper, than when contracted for. As an auxiliary to the hand-mills, baking in the house is perhaps advantageous; but not, I think, otherwise.

JOHN WALSHAM,
Assistant Commissioner.

To the Poor Law Commissioners.

Abstract of the Bread Account of the Guiltcross Union, for the Quarter commencing December 24th, 1843, *and ending* 23rd *March,* 1844.

Weeks.	Number of stones of flour used, at 1s. 9d. per stone.	Number of pounds of bread made.	Cost of flour used for baking bread.			Number of stones of coals.	Cost of coals, at 2¼d. per st., used for baking bread.		Pints yeast, at 3½d. per pt.	Cost of yeast.		Total cost.		
			£.	s.	d.		s.	d.		s.	d.	£.	s.	d.
1	80	1348	7	0	0	20	3	9	4	1	2	7	4	11
2	80	1362	7	0	0	20	3	9	4	1	2	7	4	11
3	140	2240	12	5	0	28	5	3	7	2	0½	12	12	3
4	80	1362	7	0	0	20	3	9	4	1	2	7	4	11½
5	140	2316	12	5	0	28	5	3	7	2	0½	12	12	3
6	80	1362	7	0	0	20	3	9	4	1	2	7	4	11
7	80	1347	7	0	0	20	3	9	4	1	2	7	4	11
8	160	2747	14	0	0	30	5	7½	8	2	4	14	7	11½
9	100	1734	8	15	0	20	3	9	5	1	5½	9	0	2
10	80	1340	7	0	0	20	3	9	4	1	2	7	4	11
11	120	1969	10	10	0	24	4	6	6	1	9	10	16	3
12	120	2013	10	10	0	24	4	6	6	1	9	10	16	3
13	72	1252	6	9	4	20	3	9	4	1	2	6	14	3
	4	22392										129	9	0
		5598												

5598 4lbs. loaves, at 5⅛*d.* per loaf, is £119. 10*s.* 9¾*d.*, or a fraction exceeding 1*s.* 8½*d.* per stone of 16lbs., or 5*s.* 2*d.* per dozen 4lbs. loaves.

The oven has not cost anything for repairs for two years.

IV.—BASTARDY.

1. APPLICATION FOR ORDER IN.

6th March, 1844.

Clerk of Newcastle-Emlyn Union—Stated, that an application had been made by the Guardians of the Newcastle-Emlyn Union to the justices in petty sessions, at Treleach, in Carmarthenshire, for an Order of Affiliation of a male bastard child of Mary Davies, on Thomas Howell,—the notice stating the chargeability to be in the parish of Kilrhedin, to which parish Mary Davies was then chargeable. The application was dismissed by the justices, on the ground that it was not preferred within three months from the time of the chargeability first occurring. It was proved that Thomas Howell kept out of the way to avoid service within the three months. Mary Davies subsequently became chargeable to the parish of Kenarth, and was sent by the Relieving Officer to the Union Workhouse, being then chargeable to that parish. The Guardians made application on behalf of the parish of Kenarth to the justices in petty sessions, at Newcastle-Emlyn, for an Order of Affiliation. On the hearing, the counsel for Thomas Howell objected that it was not competent for the justices to entertain the case, it having been dismissed when the chargeability was to the parish of Kilrhedin.—Requested the Commissioners' opinion upon the case.

Ans.—Although the terms of the 1st section of the 2nd and 3rd Victoria, c. 85, are by no means free from doubt, the Commissioners, looking to the object of that Statute, are disposed to think, that an Order of Affiliation cannot now be made on Thomas Howell, in respect of the bastard child of Mary Davies, under the circumstances stated in your letter. As both the parishes of Kilrhedin and Kenarth are in the Newcastle-Emlyn Union, and as the Guardians of the Union, and not the Overseers of the respective parishes, are the parties to apply for the Order, the application might have been made within three months from the commencement of the first chargeability; and as the object of the statute was, to enforce some limitation of time on application for Orders, it would in fact be defeating its intention, and doing away with the restriction, to hold that the Guardians could apply, on a chargeability occurring in another parish in the same Union, after omitting or failing to obtain the Order in the first instance. At the same time, the Commissioners admit that the expressions in the Act—"when any child, &c. shall become chargeable to *any* parish, &c."—certainly leave room for doubt; and it remains, of course, for the justices themselves to act according to their own view of the intent and purport of the Statute.

---

2. EVIDENCE OF AUTHORITY TO MAKE APPLICATION IN BASTARDY.

7th Feb. 1844.

Clerk of Skipton Union—Inquired, whether in applications in bastardy it was competent for the solicitor for the putative father, under 5 and 6 Vict. c. 57, to call for the production of a copy of the Board of Guardians' minute, signed by the chairman, sealed with their seal, and countersigned by the clerk, authorising the application to be made. It had not been the clerk's practice to produce a copy of such minute; and in cases of removal his *viva voce* evidence of the fact of chargeability had been deemed to be sufficient.

Ans.—In the opinion of the Commissioners the putative father might very properly request, and the justices might also very properly require, the production of a copy of the Guardians' minute, duly signed and sealed, authorising the application for the filiation order. The statute (5 and 6 Vict. c. 57) expressly points out a mode of proceeding in such cases, calculated to remove all doubt as to the authority for the application to the justices; and the Commissioners are not aware of any reason why that course should not be followed. With regard to the proof of chargeability, the statute does not declare that what was legal evidence of chargeability before its passing is not to be deemed legal evidence now, although it simplifies the proof. It appears to the Commissioners that the Justices may proceed upon any other legal proof of the chargeability, besides that referred to in the above-mentioned statute.

---

3. BASTARD—COST OF MAINTENANCE.

24th Feb. 1844.

Clerk of Market Drayton Union—Stated, that application had been made to the Guardians for relief for Henry Chesters, an illegitimate child, aged fourteen years, who was then ill; an order of affiliation had been obtained prior to the passing of the Poor Law Amendment Act, and the putative father had paid towards the maintenance of the child till some time after the passing of that Act, since which time the mother married. Inquired,—whether the Guardians ought to apply, in the first instance, to the putative father, or to the husband of the child's mother, for its maintenance; and if the application ought, in the first instance, to be made to the mother's husband,—whether in the event of his being unable to maintain the child, the putative father could be called upon to do so.

Ans.—Having regard to the decision in Lang. *v.* Spicer, (1 M. & W. 129,) the Commissioners apprehend there can be no doubt, that the step-father of Henry Chesters is primarily liable for the child's support. Whether in the event of the step-father being unable to maintain the child, the putative father can be called upon to contribute to its support, is not so clear. But, looking to the tenor of the remarks made by the judges in the case of Lang *v.* Spicer, the Commissioners think it, at least, very doubtful whether the putative father would be held liable, in such a case as that of Henry Chesters.

4. RECOVERY OF RELIEF TO THE MOTHER.

15th Feb. 1844.

Clerk of Hursley Union—Stated, that on the 27th Dec. 1842, a pregnant young woman was received into the workhouse of the Hursley Union; on the 13th June, 1843, she gave birth to the child who had been previously affiliated. The father of the child had been absent until recently, and he, the clerk, was now called upon to make out an account for the maintenance of the mother and child, including the fee paid to the midwife, to be presented to the justices with the view of enforcing payment from the putative father. A doubt having been suggested as to the liability of the putative father to the expense of *maintaining the mother*, and to the midwife's fee, requested the Commissioners' opinion on the subject.

Ans.—The Commissioners call your attention to the second and third provisos in the seventy-second section of the Poor Law Amendment Act; from which you will perceive that the amount recoverable from the putative father, under an order of affiliation, is in no case to exceed the actual expense incurred for the maintenance of the bastard child while chargeable to the parish; and that no part of the money paid by the putative father, in pursuance of the order, is to be applied in any way to the support of the mother. The midwife's charge being an expense incurred on the mother's behalf, is not recoverable under the order.

V.—CLERK'S DUTIES.

MINUTES OF THE BOARD OF GUARDIANS.

22nd March, 1844.

Clerk of Saint Saviour's Union. — Inquired, whether he was to enter anything except resolutions come to by the Board of Guardians; and also, if, in the case of a pauper making a complaint against an Officer to the Board of Guardians, he ought to enter the ex-parte statement of the pauper on the minutes, or any subsequent examination which might take place in consequence thereof.

Ans.—It is impossible for the Commissioners to say, precisely, what ought or ought not to be entered on the minutes of the proceedings of a Board of Guardians. Generally speaking, the discussion of any subject at a meeting of the Board, should result in a resolution, and the subject would thus be placed on record in the minutes. In the case supposed in your letter, there is no doubt that any complaint of a pauper against an officer, should be entered on the minutes when made,—that it should always be entertained, and the decision of the Guardians upon it should also be entered upon the minutes, as well as notes of the evidence of witnesses, so that a sufficient account of the case should be on record; and every occurrence, whether an ex-parte statement or otherwise, and whether finally disposed of or not, should be placed on the minutes of the meeting at which it came under the notice of the Board.

VI.—EMIGRATION.—WIFE AND FAMILY OF A TRANSPORTED CONVICT.

20th Feb. 1844.

Clerk of Sudbury Union—Forwarded a copy of minute of the Board of Guardians, whereby it appeared that James Pearman, late of Glemsford, in the Sudbury Union, who had been transported to Van Diemen's Land about sixteen years ago, had written requesting that his wife Frances and her son David would go out to him, and stating that he had paid the passage money for them. It further appeared, that after James Pearman was transported, a daughter had been born to him in due time, who was now about sixteen years of age. The mother was of very respectable character, and she and her daughter were desirous of going out to him as requested. The Board of Guardians, on the application of the parish of Glemsford, consented, subject to the sanction of the Commissioners, to the appropriation of part of the sum of £43. 8*s*., remaining in the hands of the treasurer, being the residue of the "Glemsford Emigration Fund Account," for the purpose of assisting the parties to emigrate accordingly.

Ans.—The Commissioners have made inquiries, and find that the practice on the part of the Government of granting free passages to the Colony of Van Diemen's Land to the wife and family of a transported convict has been abolished, and that their proceeding thither under any other circumstances is discouraged by the Government. The Commissioners cannot, therefore, feel justified in sanctioning any assistance being rendered towards the emigration of any persons in the situation of the family referred to.

VII.—EVIDENCE—LIABILITY OF RELIEVING OFFICER TO PRODUCE HIS BOOKS BEFORE JUSTICES, UNDER A CROWN OFFICE SUBPŒNA.

12*th Feb.* 1844.

Clerk of Eastbourne Union—Stated, that one of the Relieving Officers of the Eastbourne Union had been served with a Crown Office subpœna duces tecum, to attend before the Justices, and to produce the application and report books, weekly relief lists, and any other documents containing entries of relief to one Elizabeth Stevens, or otherwise relating to the settlement of Daniel Stevens and Sarah his wife. The Board of Guardians considered that they were not justified in allowing the books and documents required to be produced, as the Board regarded them to be of a privileged nature, and not liable to be called for as evidence in cases of settlement. The Overseers of a parish could not be required to produce their books in evidence against themselves, or their own parish, and the Board of Guardians felt that they ought not to place parishes in a worse situation than they would have been, if the relief of the poor had not been taken out of the hands of the Overseers. Requested the Commissioners to advise the Board how to act in the matter.

Ans.—The Commissioners think it incumbent on the Relieving Officer to attend the Justices, in obedience to the subpœna, and to produce such books and documents enumerated as are in his power and custody. The Commissioners apprehend that, under the like authority, the Overseers of any parish in the Union, would be bound to attend and produce any documentary evidence in their power, though the production of such evidence might be to establish a settlement in their parish. It will be for the Justices, before whom the parties attend, to decide whether any of the evidence produced under such authority, is privileged.

VIII.—GUARDIANS, ELECTION OF.

1. GUARDIANS' MEETING, HELD ON 26TH MARCH, BEFORE THE COMPLETION OF THE ELECTIONS, OF WHOM TO BE COMPOSED.

25*th March*, 1844.

Clerk of Frome Union—Inquired, whether in the event of the elections in some of the parishes not being completed by the 26th March, the usual Board-day, the first meeting of the Guardians, elected for the present year, could be held on that day; and also, whether he would be justified in adjourning the election over Tuesday, the 26th March, the Board-day, if not completed on the Monday.

Ans.—The meeting of the Guardians of the Frome Union, to be held on the 26th instant, should be composed of the Guardians whose election is complete on the 25th March, and who, on casting up the votes, or otherwise, may then be ascertained to be duly elected. Such Guardians will be entitled to act, though the election of certain parishes may not have terminated. The Commissioners think the Clerk should proceed with the casting up of the votes on Tuesday, the 26th, *pro forma*, and adjourn the proceedings, if necessary, to the following day.

2. NOMINATION—VALIDITY OF.

15*th March*, 1844.

Clerk of Northampton Union—Forwarded a nomination paper, in which the nominator had not stated in what capacity he nominated, having omitted to strike out either the words "rate-payer," or the words "owner of property;" and observed that the Commissioners' answer to the Clerk of the Kidderminster Union, in No. 26, page 98, of the Official Circular, and which declared such a nomination as the above to be invalid, seemed to be in point.

Ans.—Where the nominator is both "owner of property" *and* "rate-payer," the nomination would seem to be valid, whichever is taken; the rest of the description may be omitted as surplusage. Where he is only one of these, and has not said which, it appears to the Commissioners, that it is not the Clerk's business to inquire, and the nomination should be treated as invalid, on the ground of uncertainty.

3. NOMINATION—VALIDITY OF, WHERE THE NOMINATOR HAD NOT PAID A CHURCH-RATE UNTIL AFTER THE DAY OF NOMINATION.—GUARDIAN'S QUALIFICATION.

20*th March*, 1844.

Clerk of Saint Saviour's Union—Stated, that in going through the nominations, it occurred to him, that one of the nominators had not paid a Church-rate, made in August last, and on sending to ascertain the fact, he was informed that it was paid; but he found, on further inquiry, that it was paid *subsequently* to the day of nomination. Inquired, whether he should retain the names of the persons nominated by this nominator in the voting papers. Also, whether an owner of property, who did not reside in the Union, and had no place of business therein, was eligible for the office of Guardian.

Ans.—Assuming the person, to whom your first question relates, nominated in the capacity of rate-payer, it was undoubtedly necessary that, at the time of doing the act, he should be legally qualified to vote as rate-payer; *i. e.*, that he should have previously paid the Parochial Rates and Assessments made and assessed upon him, except those made or which became due within six months immediately preceding his so acting as a rate-payer, (see 40th sec. Poor Law Amendment Act). The Commissioners are advised that the term "Parochial Rates and Assessments" includes Church-rates. The qualification for Guardian does not depend upon residence. A person who is rated to the Poor-rate in the Union, in respect of a sufficient annual rental, will be eligible for the office, though he may not reside in the Union. If in any case, and under any express authority, an owner, as such, should be legally rated to the Poor-rate, in lieu of the occupier, he would be eligible as Guardian.

---

4. NOMINATION—VALIDITY OF WHEN SIGNED BY OTHERS THAN THE NOMINATOR.

13th March, 1844.

Clerk of Westbourne Union—Stated, that he had received a nomination made by a person who was unable to write his name, and that he knew the handwriting of the person who had subscribed the nomination. It was believed, however, that this person had filled up, signed, and delivered the paper, at the request of the person purporting to nominate.—Inquired whether such nomination was valid.

Ans.—The order of election (Art. 12,) requires that the nomination shall be in writing, and signed by the party nominating. If the clerk knows that the nomination made in the case referred to is not signed by the party by whom it purports to have been made, the Commissioners think that he will have no alternative, with reference to Art. 12, but to reject the nomination as not made in conformity with the order.

---

5. GUARDIANS' QUALIFICATION—A RATE-PAYER WHOSE NAME HAS BEEN OMITTED IN THE RATE-BOOKS.

4th April, 1844.

Clerk of Merthyr Tydfil Union—Stated, that subsequent to the return of the voting papers for the election of Guardians in one of the parishes of the Union in March, 1843, he discovered that the name of one of the candidates did not appear upon the Rate-books, although he was a rate-payer and had held his qualification for years, his name having been omitted by accident. He had notwithstanding been included in the return of the Guardians elected in 1843, and had acted accordingly. Inquired whether he could act as Guardian for the present year.

Ans.—In the case of Reg. *v.* the Inhabitants of Hulme, (12 L. J. R. n. s. M. C. 100,) it was held that where the name of an occupier of rated property has been omitted from one of the rates, but he actually paid that rate and the following ones, being assessed by name for the latter, there was a sufficient rating to satisfy the terms of the 66th section of the Poor Law Amendment Act, which, for the purpose of gaining a settlement by occupying a tenement, requires that the occupier "shall have been *assessed* to the poor-rate, and shall have paid the same," &c. The 38th sec. of the Poor Law Amendment Act, provides that the qualification of a Guardian of the Poor shall consist in being "*rated*" to the poor-rate, &c. The Commissioners do not perceive any essential distinction between the terms "assessed" and "rated," but it is to be observed that in the present case another name was substituted for that of the person liable. The Commissioners think however that the principle of the decision in Reg. *v.* Hulme may perhaps be applied to the present case, and the Guardian in question consequently held to have been sufficiently qualified to act when elected in March, 1843. Under these circumstances the Commissioners are of opinion that he may continue to serve under the 10th sec. of the 5 and 6 Vic. c. 57, if no person has been elected for the parish at the annual election just concluded.

---

6. VOTING—STATEMENT OF OWNER IN CASES OF VOTING BY PROXIES.

16th March, 1844.

Overseers of St. Anne, Limehouse—Inquired whether proxies must hand in to each succeeding set of Overseers, previous to the election of Guardians, a statement in writing, &c.; or having once sent in such a statement, say in 1840, whether that will suffice for 1844. And if such statement be required from year to year, how are the Overseers to know whether the owner has withdrawn his proxy; or, where property has changed hands, and the new owner neglects to claim his right to vote, whether the proxy may not be voting for some owner who is no longer entitled to vote.

Ans.—It is not necessary that a proxy should deliver to the Overseers, previously to the election, in each year, a statement, in writing, of his name and address, &c.; he having once made the statement required by the 40th sec. Poor Law Amendment Act, and his appointment as proxy not having been revoked. The Commissioners think, as a general rule, that it must be assumed that the appointment of proxy still exists, where the owner appoints no other person as his proxy, (which subsequent appointment would operate as a revocation of the one previously made,) and where the owner does not vote himself in person. So also where no subsequent appointment is made, (and no notice is given to the Overseers, by the owner, of the fact of revocation,) it must still be presumed that the original appointment continues in force. Of course the power of the proxy to act will cease when the person by whom he was appointed ceases to possess the qualification of an owner. It will therefore cease upon the death of an owner. If, in any case, information should be afforded to the Overseers, which may show that an owner, who may have appointed a proxy to vote for him, has parted with his interest in the property, or is dead, the Overseers would be bound to act upon that information, and exclude the name of the proxy from the register. When a proper notice has been given, by the person appointing a proxy, the presumption is, that such proxy is entitled to vote; unless it be known that the right of the principal is changed, or the authority expressly or impliedly revoked.

7. VOTING—RIGHT OF VOTING AS OWNER AND OCCUPIER.

23*rd March*, 1844.

Mr. Walmsley, Preston—Stated, that he was owner of property in the Township of Preston, in respect of which he had six votes, as owner; the property consisted of cottages, occupied by weekly tenants; he was assessed to, and charged with the Poor-rates, and all other rates, which he paid, in respect of such cottages, the occupiers becoming tenants upon the express stipulation that they should be free from all rates. Inquired whether he was entitled to vote as Rate-payer, as well as owner.

Ans.—Under the 40th section of the Poor Law Amendment Act, you are entitled to vote, on account of this property, *as owner;* if you were also the *occupier*, you would be entitled to vote in respect of such occupation. The section does not expressly provide for the case of an owner rated but not occupying; nevertheless, the Commissioners are disposed to consider that, assuming you are lawfully assessed as owner, under the 59th Geo. 3, c. 12, s. 19, you might vote as Rate-payer under the 40th section of the Poor Law Amendment Act, if you have complied with the conditions contained in that section, as to the period of assessment and the payment of the rates.

8. VOTING—NON-PAYMENT OF HIGHWAY RATE, BY PERSONS NOT RATED TO THE POOR RATE.

29*th March*, 1844.

Clerk of West Bromwich Union—Stated that a number of persons claiming to vote at the election of Guardians had refused to pay a Highway rate granted in April, 1843, on the ground that they were never rated to the Poor rate until the 5th of August, 1843, and therefore not liable to pay a Highway rate granted in the previous April.

Ans.—If the parties referred to were occupiers in the parish when the Highway rate was made, viz.—in April, 1843, they were no doubt liable to that rate. In such case the fact of the same persons not having been rated to the Poor rate of the parish until August in the same year does not in any way affect their liability in respect of the former rate. You will observe that to constitute a person a rate-payer under the 40th section of the Poor Law Amendment Act, he must have been rated for the period of one whole year prior to the time of voting, and have paid the parochial rates made and assessed on him for that period except those which were made and became due within the last six months. If the persons to whom your inquiry refers, were assessed for the first time in August last, they are not entitled to vote as rate-payers, not having been rated to the Poor rate for a year.

9. VOTING—OWNERS' NAMES IMPROPERLY OMITTED FROM THE LIST OF VOTERS.

3*rd April*, 1844.

Clerk of Leicester Union—Stated that on examination of the voting papers for the Election of Guardians, complaints were made that certain owners had not had voting papers furnished to them, as usual at all former Elections: that he found on inquiry that the Overseers of St. Margaret's had employed a person to make out the list of owners and proxies, and that the person so employed had erased (by scratching with a knife,) upwards of 100 names previously standing on the list as owners, taking upon himself to decide the question of their ownership. Requested to be informed what remedy the parties aggrieved had under the circumstances.

Ans.—If the persons who have been deprived of their votes were in fact entitled to such votes, the person who illegally deprived them of them would be liable to an action on the case, or an indictment for a misdemeanour. It is the duty of the Overseers to make out the list of owners, and there seems to be no reason to suppose that they are not to use their best judgment as to placing any persons on that list, or that they are not to alter the list as they learn that parties already placed there have been placed there without title: neither does it appear that they must make or alter this list by their own hands alone, or that they may not obtain advice or assistance. If therefore the erasures described were done by their authority or with their concurrence, or adopted by them, there is no objection in law to the obliteration of the names. But if they were obliterated without the authority of the Overseers, the person who erased the names would be liable to a fine of £50 under the 58 Geo. 3, c. 69, s. 6.

10. VOTING—REVOCATION OF PROXY APPOINTMENT.

23*rd March*, 1844.

Clerk of Swansea Union—Inquired, 1st, whether the fact of an owner sending in a fresh claim to vote as owner (at the present election) would amount to a revocation of a proxy given at a former election. And, 2ndly, whether the same person can vote as a rate-payer himself, and give a proxy, as owner, to another person to vote at the same election.

Ans.—1st. The Commissioners think that the fact of the owner sending in a fresh claim to vote, as owner, would be a sufficient revocation of a proxy given at a former election. 2ndly. The commissioners see nothing to prevent a person from voting as owner by proxy, and as rate-payer in person.

11. VOTING.—TIME FOR RECEIVING VOTING PAPERS AND CASTING UP VOTES.

23*rd Feb.* 1844.

Clerk of Eastbourne Union—Inquired, whether he would be acting right in receiving a voting paper, (under article 22nd of the Election Order), delivered before twelve o'clock on the 25th March, the 24th being Sunday; and if so, whether he would be justified, under article 23rd of the same Order, in casting up the votes on the 26th March, instead of the 25th.

Ans.—The Commissioners think the day for receiving voting papers in the ensuing Election of Guardians for the Eastbourne Union, will, under article 22nd of the Order for the Election of Guardians, be the 25th of March. The casting up of the votes must, under article 23rd of the same Order, be begun on the 25th of March; but having been so begun, may be continued on the 26th and following days, under the same article.

12. CONSTRUCTION OF SECTION 10 OF 5 & 6 VIC. c. 57.—NO ELECTION.

16*th March*, 1844.

Clerk of Llanfyllin Union—Stated that he had received a nomination for one Guardian only, for the parish of Llanfair Caereinion, which is entitled to return three; and inquired which of the three Guardians of the past year should go out of office.

Ans.—The 10th sec. of the 5 and 6 Vic. c. 57, provides only for the case in which *no* person shall be elected as Guardian for a parish: as under the circumstances described in your letter *one* Guardian will be elected, it is clear that such a case would not come within the above-named section.

13. A GUARDIAN ELECTED IN 1842 CANNOT, UNDER 5 AND 6 VIC. c. 57, CONTINUE TO ACT DURING 1844 WITHOUT BEING RE-ELECTED.

16*th March*, 1844.

Clerk of Romford Union—Inquired whether, under the 10th Section of the 5 and 6 Vic. cap. 57,—which provides "that in every case in which no person shall be elected for the office of Guardian in any parish at any annual election of Guardians the persons elected for the previous year may continue to act as Guardians until the next annual election,"—Mr. Samuel Francis, the Guardian for the parishes of Great Warley and Cranham, who was duly elected at the annual election in 1842, and who acted as Guardian for those parishes during the present year, would be at liberty to act as such Guardian during the ensuing year; no Guardian having been nominated, and consequently none elected, for either of those parishes since 1842.

Ans.—The Guardian elected in 1842, for the Parishes of Great Warley and Cranham, cannot continue to act (without being re-elected) as

Guardian for those parishes, beyond the present parochial year. The 10th Sec. of the 5 and 6 Vic. c. 57, applies only to persons *elected* for the year previous to 1844,—i.e. of course for 1843; but he was elected in 1842, and continued to act in 1843.

14. AS TO WHETHER THE RETURNING OFFICER IS BOUND TO DISCLOSE THE NAMES OF CANDIDATES.

13*th March,* 1844.

Clerk of the Cheltenham Union—Inquired, whether he ought to disclose the names of the candidates for the office of Guardian, upon being applied to for that purpose, if the person making the application, is not one of the persons nominated for the office.

Ans.—It is entirely in the Clerk's discretion to inform any one else than the persons put in nomination, of the fact of such nomination. The Commissioners could not advise that the information should be refused, if application be made by the person proposed.

20*th March,* 1844.

Ditto.—Forwarded resolution of the Board of Guardians, stating, that by the Clerk's refusal to disclose the names of the persons nominated, the rate-payers had no opportunity of avoiding the excitement, trouble, and expense of a contest for the parish of Cheltenham, which the Guardians were anxious to avoid, especially as they believed the parties nominated, would, if known, withdraw till the proper number was left.

Ans.—It is impossible for the Commissioners to say, that the Clerk is bound to disclose the names of persons nominated for the office of Guardian in every case, inasmuch as they might be asked for, for very different reasons from those which actuate the Cheltenham Board of Guardians.

15. A NOMINATOR CANNOT WITHDRAW HIS NOMINATION.

20*th March,* 1844.

Clerk of Leicester Union—Stated, that having received two nomination papers for the parish of St. Margaret, each containing the number of names the parish was entitled to return as Guardians, he had directed voting papers to be prepared; but that he had since received a written notice from the nominator of one of the lists, wishing to withdraw it altogether, to save the expense of a contest. Inquired whether he could allow the withdrawal of the list.

Ans.—Although any of the candidates nominated may, under sec. 9th of the 5 and 6 Vic. c. 57, refuse to serve, and thus end the election as regards himself, yet it is not competent to a nominator to withdraw his nomination of any candidate, after it is once sent in: the right to elect a person duly nominated is the right of the whole constituency, and it is obvious that to grant to the nominator the privilege of withdrawing any candidate would open a wide door for fraud.

IX.—MEDICAL RELIEF.

1. WHAT ARTICLES OF DIET A MEDICAL OFFICER MAY ORDER.

22*nd Dec.* 1843.

Clerk to the East Retford Union—Referred to the *Official Circular*, No. 29, p. 156, wherein it is stated that "generally, the medical officer is not empowered by the orders of the Commissioners, or by his contract with the Guardians, to order food or articles of diet." Inquired, whether the terms "food or articles of diet" included meat, milk, and wine, or porter. The Guardians were quite sensible of the weight to be attached to the opinion of the medical officers, that meat, &c. might be proper in particular cases; but they wished to be satisfied as to where the power to order such articles rested.

Ans.—The Commissioners consider that a medical officer is not empowered by their orders to order food or articles of diet for sick paupers, and that meat, milk, wine, or porter would be such articles of diet as the medical officer is not empowered to order *authoritatively*. Any direction that the medical officer may give to this effect will not, as stated in the *Official Circular* to which you refer, amount to more than an expression of opinion upon his part that relief in food or other necessaries is required. No doubt such an opinion is entitled to the greatest weight, both with the Guardians and their officers; and the Relieving Officer would, in the intervals of the meetings of the Board, incur serious responsibility in refusing food or other necessaries recommended by a medical officer, on the ground that the health of the paupers required it.

2. JUSTICES' POWER TO ORDER MEDICAL RELIEF.

1*st March,* 1844.

Chairman of the Bedford Union—Inquired, 1. Whether a justice of the peace was empowered to give an order for medical relief in a case of sudden and dangerous illness, before the overseer had been applied to for an order, and had refused or neglected to give one. 2. Whether a justice of the peace, when required to give an order for medical relief, in a case of sudden and dangerous illness, and after the overseer had been applied to for an order, and had refused to give one, ought to address his order to the overseer, or immediately to the medical officer of the district. 3. Whether a justice of the peace, before he grants an order for medical relief, in a case of sudden and dangerous illness, was required to summon the overseer, to show cause why he refused to give one.

Ans.—1. The Commissioners think that the 54th section of the Poor Law Amendment Act enables a justice of the peace to give an order for medical relief (only) in any case of sudden and dangerous illness in which such relief may be requisite, whether the overseers have or have not previously refused to give such relief. The first proviso in the section clearly refers to the immediately antecedent clause, requiring overseers to give relief "in cases of sudden and urgent necessity;" and it limits the justice's power in such cases to those instances in which the overseer refuses or neglects to perform his duty: but the second proviso has reference to a different class of cases, and empowers the justice to give an order for medical relief, &c., "where *any* case of sudden and dangerous illness may require it." Some doubt may possibly arise from the description of the order, in the second proviso, as a "similar order;" but the Commissioners apprehend that this expression was intended to indicate merely the character of the order itself, and not the occasion for its issuing. 2. The Commissioners consider that the phrase "similar order" has the effect of requiring that the order for medical relief, under the second proviso, should be like the order for temporary relief in articles of necessity, authorised by the first proviso; that is to say, that it should be made upon the overseer of the parish, by a justice of the peace, in writing under his hand and seal. This view is placed beyond doubt by the subsequent clause, "And any *overseer* shall be liable to the penalties as aforesaid for disobeying such order." 3. The Commissioners' answer to your first inquiry will intimate their opinion that the justice, before granting an order for medical relief, need not call upon the overseers to show cause why he refused to give such relief; although of course the justice will be bound to satisfy himself that the case is really one of illness so sudden and dangerous as to justify his making an order on the overseers.

3. QUALIFICATION OF MEDICAL OFFICER.

11th March, 1844.

Mr. N. Blythe, Haltwhistle—Inquired, whether the certificate of the Apothecaries' Company was a necessary qualification for a Medical Officer of a Union; and whether a person, who possessed only a diploma of the College of Surgeons of Edinburgh, was equally qualified for such an appointment with one who had the diploma of the Royal College of Surgeons of London, and the license of the Apothecaries' Company. Stated, that he was aware that, by the recent opinion of counsel, an Edinburgh and a London Surgeon were placed upon an equality, but he wished to know, whether both must possess the license of the Apothecaries' Company, in addition to the Surgeon's diploma.

Ans.—As regards the qualification for the office of Medical Officer, the fact of a person possessing a diploma of the College of Surgeons of Edinburgh, merely places such person in the position of one who is a member of the Royal College of Surgeons of London. The opinion of counsel, to which you refer, only went to the extent of placing persons having English, Scotch, or Irish surgical diplomas, on an equality in this respect.

16th March, 1844.

Ditto.—Inquired, whether a person, who possessed no other qualification, than the diploma of the College of Surgeons of Edinburgh, and who was not in actual practice as an apothecary on the 1st August, 1815, was qualified for the office of Medical Officer.

Ans.—A person who possesses the diploma of the College of Surgeons of Edinburgh, but who has no other qualification, is not qualified under the General Medical Order of the Commissioners, to be appointed a Medical Officer, except under circumstances, such as would justify the appointment of a member of the Royal College of Surgeons of London, not otherwise qualified, and which are described in Articles 4 and 5 of the Order.

4. MEDICAL RELIEF TO PERSONS ENTITLED TO MEDICAL ASSISTANCE FROM AN INDEPENDENT SOURCE.

13th Feb. 1844.

The Clerk of Abergavenny Union—Stated, that it was the custom at the different iron-works situate in the Abergavenny Union, to stop from time to time, from the workmen employed therein, a penny or twopence in the pound, for the surgeon attached to the works. Four of the medical officers of the Union were surgeons connected with iron-works, and were paid out of the funds so raised, for their attendance upon the workmen and their families employed in those works. In the Blaenavon district this was the case, and an accident which recently happened to one of the workmen, whilst employed at his work, was immediately attended to by the surgeon. The man and his family also became immediately chargeable to the parish, and the surgeon claimed the fee allowed by the Medical Order, for his attendance on the man. Requested the opinion of the Commissioners as to whether, under similar circumstances, which were of frequent occurrence, the medical officers were entitled to be paid the fees specified in the Medical Order. In this case, the Relieving Officer had given no order for the attendance of the medical officer.

Ans.—It appears to the Commissioners to be clear, that a person labouring under dangerous illness, and unable to obtain the medical assistance he requires, is legally entitled to medical relief. (R. *v.* Warren, R. & Ry. 48. a.) The Commissioners understand by this, however, that he must be destitute of the means of procuring the necessary medical assistance. If, therefore, he belongs to a club, or has made other provisions, through which he can *actually* obtain medical assistance, in cases of urgency, the Commissioners consider that, when such a case arises, he is not destitute in the above sense. In the case in which the opinion of the Commissioners is requested, they think that if the man is properly attended to by the surgeon of the works, in that capacity, medical or surgical relief may be refused by the Union, so long as he is entitled to, and actually obtains, the assistance of that surgeon. Whether other relief is required or not, does not affect the question. That the surgeon attended the man as surgeon of the works, is to be inferred from his attending without a medical order, and also from the circumstance that he is the surgeon of the works to which the man belonged.

X.—OVERSEER—1. SUPPLYING GOODS TO A BOARD OF GUARDIANS.

24th April, 1844.

Overseer of ———— : Stated, that previous to his appointment as overseer he had been in the habit of supplying the Board of Guardians of the Union in which his parish was situate, with stationery, and he had been also employed in printing for them. Inquired, whether he could legally continue to do so whilst holding the office of overseer.

Ans.—The 55th Geo. 3, c. 137, s. 6, imposes a penalty on any overseer who supplies "for his own profit, any goods, materials, or provisions for the use of any workhouse or otherwise for the support and maintenance of the poor." The Commissioners are disposed to consider that stationery and printed documents supplied to the Guardians of a Union, being auxiliary to the administration of relief, and probably used by the Guardians at the workhouse, would be held to be within the words of the statute referred to above: at any rate the same objections in principle apply to the furnishing of such goods by an overseer as of articles used for more immediate consumption by the paupers themselves. The Commissioners think you might therefore be exposed to the penalties enacted by the 55th Geo. 3, c. 137, if you continued to supply the goods in question during your year of office.

2. RECOVERY OF CONTRIBUTIONS FROM OVERSEERS.

22nd April, 1844.

Clerk of Great Boughton Union—Stated, that the townships of Great Boughton, Kelsall, and Burrow, (Little,) within the Great Boughton Union, had neglected to pay their contributions for the last quarter, and the Board of Guardians had directed application to be made to the justices, to recover the amounts from the respective Overseers. The Overseer for Great Boughton, who had been in office two years, positively refused to pay; and alleged that, as he was no longer Overseer, payment could not be enforced; he had not, however, passed his accounts, and the auditor had been requested not to pass them without production of the Treasurer's receipt for the contribution.

Ans.—The Commissioners are of opinion that the Guardians of Great Boughton Union cannot now avail themselves of remedial proceedings, for the recovery of contributions, against the late Overseers of any parish; who, being no longer in office, would have no power to reimburse themselves the sums levied on them. The Commissioners think, however, that in such cases penal proceedings may be adopted; as the offence of disobedience to the Guardians' order was completed by the Overseers during their period of office; and the mere fact of their ceasing to hold such office, does not purge them of that offence, or oust the jurisdiction of the justices.

XI.—PAUPER.—Punishment of Pauper under the Vagrant Act.

1st Feb. 1844.

J. H. Rees, Esq., J.P., Llanelly Union—Stated, that a man, with his wife and family, were admitted into the workhouse of the Llanelly Union; after being there some time, the man left without leave, and leaving his family in the workhouse. In a few days he was discovered in the town of Llanelly, within a mile of the workhouse, working as a labourer: he had not reported himself at the workhouse during his absence, and though his wife had obtained leave to go out, and had seen him, she denied knowing where he was. The man's defence, on being brought before the Llannelly Petty Sessions was, that he intended, as soon as he had earned enough to maintain his family, to take them out of the workhouse; but that, though he was then at work, he could not get his pay till the expiration of a fortnight, which was true. Qu. 1st—Was the man punishable under the Vagrant Act, title, "Idle and Disorderly Persons"? 2nd. Or under the same Act, title, "Rogues and Vagabonds"? The objection under the first, seems, that his family had not become chargeable by *reason of neglecting* to maintain them—the family being chargeable already. And under the second, that the act he committed could hardly be called a *running away*, as he stated his intention of taking his family out, when able, and he was at work openly so near to the workhouse. Qu. 3d.—Was he punishable under any provision in any other Act?

Ans.—It appears to the Commissioners at all events doubtful, whether the case of the pauper to whom your letter refers, could be regarded as coming within the third section of the Vagrant Act. But the Commissioners are disposed to think, that the case falls within the provisions of the fourth section. It seems to them that quitting the workhouse secretly, the family remaining therein, was a "running away" on the part of the pauper, within the meaning of the Statute. The short distance to which he thought fit to flee, and his intention of eventually maintaining his family, even if true, would not, in the Commissioners' opinion, alter the fact of his having run away from the workhouse, and left his family chargeable therein.

XII. POOR-RATE—1. Apportionment of the Rate between an Out-going and In-coming Tenant.

23rd Feb. 1844.

Clerk of the Fylde Union—Stated, that throughout the whole of the Fylde Union, which was principally an agricultural district, it had time immemorial been the custom for terms of occupation in farms to end on the 2nd day of February with respect to the land, and on the 1st day of May following with respect to the farmhouse and buildings, and one close of land or other small proportion of the farm for outlet for cattle. The reason for this distinction in the time of quitting farms, was owing to a great proportion of the fodder (the produce of the farm) not being consumed by the 2nd of February, and the inconvenience of removing the fodder, as well as the injury which would be done to the farm by such removal would be very great. The parochial year, previous to the passing of the Poor Law Amendment Act, generally ended at Easter, and in that district nominally on the 5th of April. The custom of paying poor-rates between the off-going and on-coming tenants, for the quarter ending 5th of April, was invariably one-third of the rate by the off-going and two-thirds thereof by the on-coming tenant, which was very near the proportion between the tenants for the time of occupation, pursuant to 17th Geo. 2, c. 38, s. 12. Since the passing of the Poor Law Amendment Act, the parochial year had ended on the 25th March, being eleven days earlier; and the custom of paying poor-rates in the Union, between the off-going and on-coming tenants, for the quarter ending 25th March, had been one-half of the rate by each party—being nearly an equitable proportion of the rate, pursuant to the statute, taking into consideration the eleven days before mentioned, and also the off-going tenant's liability to a proportion of a subsequent rate, for the farmhouse, buildings, and outlet. The magistrates of the district were of different opinions respecting the proportions of the rate, for the quarter ending 25th March, to be paid between the off-going and on-coming tenants of a farm; some deciding that the rate for the whole quarter must be paid; others, that the proportion last before-mentioned only ought to be paid—thus placing the collectors in a situation of difficulty. Requested the Commissioners to advise how the collectors ought to proceed in the matter.

Ans.—The case referred to is one to which the provision in the 17th George 2, c. 38, as to the division of the rate between the out-going and the in-coming tenant, appears to be applicable. But the proportion of rate payable in any such case (where there is any dispute between the parties concerned) is to be ascertained by the justices. The matter is therefore one entirely in the discretion of the justices. But as the opinion of the Commissioners has been asked on the subject, they are not prepared to say that the division which, since the passing of the Poor Law Amendment Act, has been made, is, under the circumstances, an unfair division.

---

2. POOR RATE IRREGULARLY MADE.

22nd *April*, 1844.

Clerk to the Justices, Mansfield—Stated, that the Overseers of a township in the Mansfield petty sessional district had collected a Poor-rate, without having it allowed by the Justices. Some weeks previous, the rate was presented to the Justices for their allowance, but being very imperfectly made out, they refused their signatures to it. In a few days the Overseers would present their accounts for allowance by the Justices. Requested the Commissioners to suggest the course which the Justices ought to adopt in the matter. The irregularity, if not stopped now, in all probability would be continued.

Ans.—Notwithstanding any irregularity which may have occurred in laying a Poor-rate, the Overseers are bound to account to the Justices for all sums collected under it by them. It appears from your statement, that the Overseers have not only disobeyed the Statute, but probably also the Commissioners' regulations, (see the General Order—Duties of Overseers, Art. 5 ;) and they might accordingly be punished, under the 98th section of the Poor Law Amendment Act. Clearly such a rate as the one you describe, could not be enforced.

---

3. EXCUSAL OF POOR RATE.

6*th March*, 1844.

Auditor of Lymington Union—Inquired as to the mode in which the payment of Poor-rates could be legally excused.

Ans.—All the rateable property in a parish should be assessed in every Poor-rate, and no person assessed can be lawfully excused from payment of the rate on account of poverty, except in accordance with the provisions of the 54th Geo. 3rd, c. 170, s. 11. Under that section, the Justices alone have power to excuse the payment ; and such excusal can be granted only upon the application of the party rated, (though the Commissioners believe such application need not be made in person,) and with the consent of the Overseers of the Parish, or the Guardians of the Union. Some doubt prevails as to whether the Parish Officers are still competent to give such consent, or whether they are not superseded in that function by the Board of Guardians; and while such doubt remains, it must rest, of course, with the Justices themselves to determine whose consent they will receive.

---

4. LEVYING A SECOND RATE WHILST THE FIRST IS IN COLLECTION.

22*d March*, 1844.

Clerk of Stoke-upon-Trent Parish—Inquired, whether the overseers could levy a second rate whilst the first was in collection, there being some small sums remaining unpaid which could be recovered only by summons, or by allowing time for payment.

Ans.—Where a poor-rate has been for the most part collected, the Commissioners think that the fact of its not being immediately recoverable in some few instances, would not prevent the making of a new rate, supposing a necessity to arise for obtaining further funds, and provided that the two rates be not concurrent rates, *i. e.* laid for the same period of time. The schedule annexed to the 6th and 7th William 4, c. 96, (Form of Rate,) which requires the "arrears" to be brought forward, clearly contemplates the case of a former rate being partially uncollected when a new one is made ; and the 43d Eliz. c. 2, s. 4, provides for the recovery, not only of the current rate, but likewise of "all arrearages."

XIII.—RELIEF—1. CHARGEABILITY OF.

7*th Feb.* 1844.

Clerk of the Auckland Union—Stated, that Robert Stewart, a coke-burner at Hunwick colliery, had fractured his thigh, and he was in consequence confined to his lodgings, situate in the township of Hunwick, in the Auckland Union, and had become chargeable to that township.

Stewart had a wife and four children, who were residing four miles distant from Hunwick, in the township of Bishop Auckland, in the same Union, where they had become chargeable, in consequence of Stewart's inability to support them. Stewart lived with his family in Bishop Auckland, but had lodgings at Hunwick for the convenience of his work, where he remained from Monday morning till Saturday evening, spending the rest of the time with his family at Bishop Auckland. Inquired which of the two townships were liable to maintain Stewart and his family, or if the duty of maintaining them rested with the townships in which they respectively resided.

Ans.—The Commissioners are of opinion that, under the circumstances stated in your letter, the relief of Robert Stewart should be charged to the township of Hunwick, where he was abiding at the time of the accident (see Gent. *v.* Tomkins, T. T. 1822, and Tomlinson *v.* Bentall, 1 Bott. 396,) and where he has since remained; and that the relief of his wife and family should be charged to the township of Bishop Auckland, in which they live. The 56th s. of the Poor Law Amendment Act certainly provides that the relief given to the wife and children shall be considered as given to the head of the family; but this provision does not appear to the Commissioners to interfere with the primary liability, cast by the general law upon each parish, to afford relief to every person destitute within its boundaries. The result will be, that Stewart will be chargeable to Hunwick, in respect of his own relief, and to Bishop Auckland, in respect of the relief afforded to his wife and family.

---

2. OUT-DOOR RELIEF TO BASTARD CHILDREN.

22nd Feb. 1844.

Clerk of Ticehurst Union—Requested the opinion of the Commissioners on the following points—1. Whether Out-Relief may (if the Guardians think proper) be granted to an illegitimate child, born *before* the passing of the Poor Law Amendment Act, 4 and 5 W. 4, c. 76, such child being resident with its mother. 2. Whether in such case, the power to give Out-Relief to such child would be altered, by the fact of the mother having had another illegitimate child, born since the passing of the Poor Law Amendment Act. The Clerk presumed that the ground upon which Out-Relief to an illegitimate child, born *subsequent* to the passing of the act referred to, was illegal was, that under the 71st section of that Act—"all relief granted to such child, while under the age of sixteen, shall be considered as granted to such mother," and she being able-bodied, could not legally receive Out-Relief, under the Commissioners' order relating to Out-Relief. A question had been asked, whether such child would be entitled to Out-Relief, in case the mother was *not* able-bodied, or *certified as labouring under sickness or illness.*

Ans.—You have correctly stated the grounds on which Out-Relief to a bastard child becomes illegal, viz.—that under the 71st section of the Poor Law Amendment Act, relief to such child, if born subsequently to the passing of the Act, is relief to its mother, and under the Commissioners' regulations, Out-Relief to able-bodied persons is unlawful. These being the only grounds for the illegality, it is needless to remark that, where these grounds do not exist, the illegality will not prevail. Consequently, the replies to your several questions will be as follows:—1. Out-Relief may (if the Guardians think fit) be granted to an illegitimate child, born *before* the passing of the Poor Law Amendment Act, whether such child be resident with its mother or not. 2. The power to give Out-Relief to such child would not be affected by the circumstance of the mother's having had another illegitimate child, born *since* the passing of the Poor Law Amendment Act. Out-Relief, even to a bastard born *since* the passing of the Act, would not be unlawful, if the mother be not able-bodied, or if her case fall within any of the exceptions to the Commissioners' Order as to Out-door Relief.

XIV.—RELIEVING OFFICERS—AUDITING OF THEIR ACCOUNTS.

24th April, 1844.

Clerk of Doncaster Union—Inquired, whether it was the duty of the Relieving Officers to present their accounts quarterly to the auditor for examination, or whether the auditor should in the first instance require them to do so.

Ans.—By the order for keeping accounts issued to the Doncaster Union, dated 18th July, 1837, it is provided by Article 7, No. 4, "that the auditor shall also examine the several auxiliary books and accounts in use in the Union and parishes, and shall ascertain whether they be kept in the prescribed form, and that the several entries correspond with and balance each other, where such balance may be required, and that the number of paupers relieved accord with the several entries of the amount and description of relief administered, and he shall certify the accuracy of such books and accounts, by affixing his signature to each, and the date of such credit." As the accounts of the Relieving Officer are "auxiliary books and accounts in use in the Union," it follows, that not only is it the duty of the auditor to examine such accounts, but that it is the duty of the Relieving Officer to render them, both under the Regulations of the Commissioners, (see Order, Duties of Officers, Article 20, No. 13,) and under the 47th section Poor Law Amendment Act, the terms of which include "every person holding or accountable for any balance or sum of money in any Union." It appears to the Commissioners, that the duty of the Relieving Officers in this respect, is not contingent upon the receipt of the auditor's notice of audit, but that they are bound to inform themselves of the time of the audit, of which notice will be given by the clerk, in pursuance of Article 2, No. 8.

XV.—TREASURER—APPOINTMENT OF TREASURER AS OVERSEER.

24*th April*, 1844.

Treasurer of the Shaftesbury Union—Inquired whether, as Treasurer of the Shaftesbury Union, he was exempt from serving the office of Overseer for a parish in that Union.

Ans.—The Commissioners are not aware that the Treasurer of a Union is exempt as such from serving the office of Overseer. Whether there is any such incompatibility between the two offices, as would render it undesirable for the same person to hold both, is a question for the justices to consider, when appointing the Overseers.

XVI.—WORKHOUSE—PAUPER REFUSING TO QUIT WORKHOUSE.

12*th Feb.* 1844.

Mr. Kearsey, Warnford, Droxford Union—Stated, that James Adams, a young stout, able-bodied pauper, belonging to the parish of Warnford, was in the Droxford Union Workhouse, where he had taken shelter during several winters, under pretence that there was no house for him in the parish. In summer, Adams left the workhouse with his family, and was employed in brickmaking, and earned from twenty to thirty shillings per week. He had recently offered to take Adams out of the workhouse, provide him with a house, and give him constant work, either till next Michaelmas, or for twelve months, at the same rate of wages as was paid to other labourers in the parish. This offer Adams had rejected.

Clerk of Droxford Union—Stated, that Adams had been repeatedly urged by the Guardians to accept the work offered by Mr. Kearsey, but his objection to doing so was, that Mr. Kearsey would not employ him unless he consented to hire himself till Michaelmas next; to this he objected—no doubt for the reason, that he could earn considerably more in the summer months by brickmaking. Adams would be willing to leave the workhouse and go into Mr. Kearsey's service by the week or month, but he would not bind himself for any lengthened fixed period; and on the other hand, Mr. Kearsey would not take him on any other terms than his binding himself till Michaelmas. The Guardians were desirous of knowing how far they were empowered, under the above circumstances, to insist on Adams leaving the workhouse, the man having a wife and four children dependent on him.

Ans.—The Commissioners would be disposed to infer, from the reluctance of Adams to leave the workhouse, that the management of the workhouse, as regards work to the able-bodied, and the discipline of the house, is not such as might be desired. The Commissioners think, however, that the case referred to is a peculiar one. The great object of the Guardians should be to administer the poor-rates so as not to interfere between employer and labourer. The Commissioners, looking to the condition of a permanent engagement, which Mr. Kearsey requires the man to enter into, would not advise that he should be turned out of the workhouse; but this course might be pursued,—warning might be given to him, that after a given day application will be made to the justices for their decision, whether he is, or is not, punishable, under the 3d section of the Vagrant Act, for refusing to work, being able to do so. The offer of employment must be proved. It appears to the Commissioners, that it is open to any rate-payer, at present, if he can prove the facts, to originate proceedings under this section.

LONDON:
Printed by Order of the Poor Law Commissioners, by BLACKBURN and PARDON, 6, Hatton Garden, and Published by CHARLES KNIGHT and Co., 22, Ludgate Street, Publishers to the Poor Law Commissioners.

AN

OFFICIAL CIRCULAR

OF PUBLIC DOCUMENTS AND INFORMATION :

DIRECTED BY THE POOR LAW COMMISSIONERS TO BE PRINTED, CHIEFLY FOR THE USE OF THE MEMBERS AND PERMANENT OFFICERS OF BOARDS OF GUARDIANS, UNDER THE POOR LAW AMENDMENT ACT.

No. 35. CIRCULAR ISSUED MAY 31, 1844.

Poor Law Commission Office,
Somerset House,
May 31*st*, 1844.

THE Poor Law Commissioners, on a review of their Minutes, directed that the Minutes of Correspondence on the following subjects be printed and circulated for the information of Guardians and Officers of the several Unions, viz. :—

By Order of the Board,

EDWIN CHADWICK, *Secretary.*

I.—ACCOUNTS.

1. AUDITING OVERSEERS' ACCOUNTS.

January 11th, 1844.

Mr. ——, *Auditor*—Submitted the following cases for the advice and instructions of the Commissioners. 1. The overseer of T— had credited his account with £3 as paid to the medical officer of the —— Union for setting the leg of a man who met with an accident in that parish. The overseer having been told that the man did not belong to the parish of T., went to a magistrate for the purpose of obtaining his attendance on the man, to take his examination with a view to placing him under a suspended order of removal. The magistrate objected to attend unless the clerk of the Petty sessions who lived at C—, ten miles off, accompanied him. The overseer neglected to procure the clerk's attendance, and the order was therefore not made. Under the impression that the above sum, together with the relief to the pauper, would (had the overseer done his duty) have been returned to the parish under a suspended order, he, the auditor, had disallowed the medical officer's fee, and informed the overseer that his account would be debited with the relief as soon as the next quarter's accounts for the union were audited, and he, the auditor, could ascertain the amount. 2. The overseer of St. B—, having removed a pauper to W—, under a suspended order extending over a period of forty-two months, and credited his account with the expenses, he, the auditor, inquired why the overseer had not debited himself with the amount of relief: he replied, because he had not received, though he believed that the parish of W— had paid the money to the attorney employed to recover it; but he had since died, and it was feared it could not now be obtained. He, the auditor, had therefore felt it his duty to debit the overseer's account with the amount of the relief, £35. 15*s*. 6*d*. For this purpose, he had requested the relieving officer of the district to extract from the out-relief list the various sums charged quarterly, which being done, the overseer stated, the amount was certainly more than that mentioned in the order. The relieving officer being required to account for the difference, alleged that he could not find one of the out-relief lists when he made the extract for the parish, and consequently the amount of relief in three quarters (£6. 16*s*. 6*d*.) was omitted in his certificate of amount upon which to obtain the order of removal on the suspension being taken off, thereby causing, under any circumstances, a loss to the parish of St. B—, to that amount. The relieving officer above referred to had since been dismissed by an order of the Commissioners. In order that the parish of St. B— might not sustain a loss by the inattention of a paid officer, he, the auditor, proposed to debit the relieving officer's account with the £6. 16*s*. 6*d*. and to give the overseer credit for the sum so received against the whole amount debited to him. Requested the Commissioners' instructions as to the course he should take in case it should be found that the attorney adverted to had died insolvent, and the overseer was not able to recover the sum received by the attorney for the parish. It was doubted whether the parishioners were consulted as to the propriety of employing an attorney in the matter, and also whether the money might not have been obtained on the application of the overseers themselves. Remarked, that it had always been his practice to debit the officers generally with sums which they neglected to obtain.

Ans.—1. The Commissioners think that you

acted rightly in disallowing in the accounts of the overseers of T——, the charge for the medical officer's fee in a case of accident. But they come to this conclusion, on different grounds from those on which you rested your decision. The neglect on the part of the overseer, to take such proceedings as might have led to a repayment of the charge, does not appear to the Commissioners to afford a valid reason for disallowing the charge itself. But the payment was one which ought not to have been made by the overseer at all. You will perceive, that under Article x. of the General Medical Order, the fees mentioned in that article are to be paid by the board of guardians, and by them alone. When an overseer gives an order for medical relief, he is required by the 1st article of the General Order, relating to the Duties of Overseers, to report the fact in writing either to the relieving officer of the district, or to the board of guardians of the union. It will then rest with the board of guardians to pay the fee that may be due to the medical officer. 2. With regard to the expenses incurred under the suspended order for the removal of the pauper from St. B——, the Commissioners desire to make the following remarks. It does not appear certain whether the case was of such a character, as to require the aid of an attorney, nor whether the attorney employed by the overseers ever recovered the money from the parish liable to repay it, nor (if he did) whether the amount can now be obtained by the overseers. These points are important. The Commissioners presume there is no doubt that the money has not come to the hands of the overseers, and they are of opinion that you are not empowered as auditor to insert in the accounts a charge against the overseers, for sums which they have not actually received; nevertheless the Commissioners think that under the order of accounts (Art. vii. sec. 2,) which directs you to *ascertain* that all sums received or which *ought to have been received*, are brought to account, you acted quite rightly in ascertaining the amount which ought to have been recovered under the suspended order of removal above referred to; and the Commissioners further consider that it is the duty of the overseers to pursue the matter to take all such measures as may yet be available for the recovery of the sum due to the parish, and to render an account thereof. With regard to the amount (£6. 16*s*. 6*d*.) which the relieving officer's negligence has rendered irrecoverable, the Commissioners think that, notwithstanding that negligence, you have no power to charge it against the relieving officer, and that in fact there are no means of compelling him to indemnify the parish. His negligence did not amount to embezzlement, or misapplication of moneys belonging to the parish; and although such negligence might have deserved severe censure, or even more serious notice from the Commissioners, they do not consider that the officer in fault could be proceeded against penally: as he has been dismissed on other grounds, no further steps seem possible.

---

2. CONSTABLE'S EXPENSES IN PROSECUTING DRUNKARDS, HOW CHARGEABLE.

March 2nd, 1844.

Auditor of Pershore Union—Stated that four men committed a breach of the peace in the parish of C—, and were apprehended and conveyed before the justices in petty sessions, by a police constable. The justices directed the police constable, who had been appointed under the 2 and 3 Vic. c. 88, to prosecute the offenders; and they were severally convicted of drunkenness, and committed to the county gaol, in default of finding sureties. The justices intended to make an order upon the overseers of the parish of C—, under the 18 Geo. 3, c. 19, s. 4, for the payment of the expenses incurred by the police constable in the prosecution. Inquired whether such expenses could be allowed in the accounts of the overseers.

Ans.—The Commissioners observe that, in the case of Reg. *v.* Chelmsford, part of the expenses in question in that case consisted of fees paid to the justices' clerk in respect of drunkards (12. L. J. R., n. s., M. C. 139). But as Lord Denman, in delivering judgment, did not advert to these, but confined his remarks exclusively to the charges for vagrants, the Commissioners presume that the point raised in the Auditor's letter cannot be regarded as directly decided by that case, though it may be affected by it indirectly. The Commissioners are disposed to think that the costs of prosecuting vagrants, and those of prosecuting drunkards, stand upon a similar footing. By the 6th section of the Vagrant Act, the constable, or other peace officer of the place, is bound to take into custody offenders against that Act; and by the 7th section of the 4th Jac. 1, c. 5, the constable, &c., are required to present the offences contrary to that statute. In Reg. *v.* Chelmsford, the circumstance of the constable's being bound to apprehend the vagrants, and being consequently unable to avoid the attendant expenses, seems to have formed a prominent part of Lord Denman's argument. The like obligation, and the like consequence, occur with regard to drunkards. By a similar analogy the expenses in question, in the present case, though incurred by a county or district constable appointed under the 2 and 3 Vic. c. 93, and 3 and 4 Vic. c. 88, would appear to be payable by the parish and not by the division. The Commissioners observe that the expenses specified in the auditor's letter are not restricted to justices' clerks' fees. They incline to think, however, that the decision in Reg. *v.* Chelmsford, supposing it to justify inferentially the payment of any such costs at all, would authorise the payment of all such costs in the matter as the constable unavoidably incurs. How far the payments to the witnesses are, under the circumstances of the particular case, expenses of this kind, the Commissioners express no opinion; but they apprehend that the item described "Paid to the police 8*s*.," is not the reimbursement of an expense, but the payment of a remuneration to the constable. If so, it would not come within the scope of the 18th Geo. 3, c. 19, s. 4.

II.—AUDITOR.—HIS DUTIES.

March 27th, 1844.

Auditor, Halifax Union—Requested the Commissioners' opinion in reference to the apportionment by him, the Auditor, of the debt due from F. N., late relieving officer in the Halifax Union, who was a defaulter. The board of guardians, in accordance with a resolution passed by them, had paid all the debts due to other Unions, including a considerable amount of tickets given by the relieving officer to paupers for relief in kind, which had been borrowed and held by shopkeepers in the neighbourhood, the aggregate amount of which had been passed to the debit of F. N.'s account; as the clerk of the Union had intimated his intention, at the close of the quarter, of apportioning to the debit of each township in the relieving officer's district, according to the averages, the debt standing against him, requested to be informed, 1st, Whether that could be legally done, without first enforcing the bond against the relieving officer's sureties: 2ndly. Whether an appeal against the allowance by any rate-payer could be successfully maintained: and, 3dly, Whether a written notice of objection against such allowance would be valid, in the event of the objector failing to appear in person at the audit.

Ans.—With regard to the apportionment of the debt due from F. N., it is lawful to apportion any loss to which the townships of the Union are temporarily liable, before the sureties are sued. It is presumed that the loss is in fact incurred before the sureties are called on to pay. But the loss in this case consists in the relief paid a second time in respect of certain paupers, who must have been relieved on account of certain townships; and accordingly the loss should be charged to those townships, each for the amount of relief supplied to its own paupers, and not according to the averages. 3. No appeal can be maintained. 4. When the Auditor learns, by any means, of an objection to the accounts, it is his duty to examine into such objection; and to cause the accounts to be properly made out. It is not absolutely necessary that any person should appear to support an objection before the Auditor, in order to impose on him the obligation to enforce correctness in the accounts.

III.—BAPTISM.

DUTY OF CHAPLAIN IN RESPECT OF REGISTRY OF BAPTISMS IN WORKHOUSE.

January 18th, 1844.

Clerk of Hollingbourn Union—Inquired, on behalf of the chaplain, whether it was necessary to transmit to the registrar of the diocese copies of the entries of the several baptisms which had been solemnised in the Union workhouse agreeably to the provisions of 52 Geo. 3, cap. 146; and if it was necessary to do so, by whom were the copies to be attested, as pointed out in the 6th section of the above statute; and whether they should be sent with the copies belonging to the parish of Hollingbourn, in which the workhouse is situate.

Ans.—The case appears to the Commissioners to be provided for by section 4 of 52nd Geo. 3, c. 146. By that section, when baptisms are performed in any other place than the parish church of any parish, and such ceremony is performed by any minister, not being the rector, vicar, or curate of such parish, the minister performing the ceremony is, on the same or next day, to transmit to the rector, vicar, or curate (as the case may be) a certificate of such baptism in the form provided by the Act. On receipt of such certificate the rector, vicar, or curate, is to enter the baptism in the book kept for that purpose, pursuant to the Act. In this way the baptisms taking place in the workhouse, being private baptisms, would find their way into the ordinary register of the parish in which the workhouse is situate. The 7th section regulates the mode in which copies of the register books are to be returned to the registrar of the diocese, having been first verified by the rector, vicar, or curate of the parish, as the case may be. It appears to the Commissioners that the chaplain of the workhouse has no duty to perform under the statute cited in transmitting an account of baptisms performed in the workhouse to the registrar of the diocese.

IV.—CHAPLAIN—

Whether liable to Toll in Journeying to and from the Workhouse.

February 13th, 1844.

Clerk of Stroud Union — Stated, that the chaplain of the Stroud Union Workhouse was charged toll at the turnpike-gates through which he had to pass in going to the workhouse to perform his duties on Sundays and other days; the workhouse being situate in the parish of Stroud, while the chaplain lived in the parish of Leonard Stanley, of which he was the curate. Inquired whether the demand for toll was legal.

Ans.—The Commissioners have referred to the 3rd Geo. 4, c. 126, which relates to public turnpike-roads. Sec. 22 enumerates the exemptions from tolls on such roads. Amongst the exemptions is "any Rector, Vicar, or Curate, going to or returning from visiting any sick parishioner, or on other his parochial duty within his parish." The Commissioners think that the case of the Chaplain to the workhouse is clearly not within the terms of this exemption, as he is not, when going to the workhouse, performing a parochial duty within his parish. Neither is the case met by the exemption contained in a preceding part of the same section, "as to persons going to or returning from his, her, or their *proper parochial church or chapel*." The workhouse is obviously not the proper parochial church or chapel of the chaplain in the sense of the statute. The Commissioners are not therefore aware of any legal ground of exemption from toll in the case submitted to them.

V.—CONSTABLES—

Power of Auditor to investigate their Accounts.

January 15th, 1844.

Clerk of Gainsborough Union — Inquired, whether it was necessary that the particulars of the charges allowed to parish constables under the recent statute (5th and 6th Vic. c. 109) should be produced to the auditor for his examination, and how far he was required to investigate the particulars.

Ans. — The particulars of the constables' charges, under the 17th section of the 5th and 6th Vic. c. 109, ought to be laid before the auditor. That section enables the justices to order payments to the constables, not at discretion, but only under certain conditions; and it is impossible for the auditor to ascertain that those conditions have been complied with (in other words, to determine whether the charge is a legal charge upon the poor-rates) unless he is furnished with the details of the account, as well as informed of the total sum which the justices have ordered to be paid. The Commissioners think that on the authority of Reg. *v.* the Overseers of Halifax (10 L. J. R. (n. s.) M. C. 81) the auditor might disallow the gross item, if the particulars should be withheld.

VI.—CONTRACTOR—

Liability of to serve the Office of Overseer.

February 29th, 1844.

Mr. C. Frampton, Wimborne — Inquired, whether he could be compelled to serve the office of overseer of the parish of Wimborne, while under contract with the guardians of the Wimborne and Cranborne Union, to supply articles of clothing for the use of the poor: and if he could be compelled to serve the office, whether he was at liberty to forego his contract.

Ans.—The fact of your having entered into a contract to supply articles of clothing to the guardians for the use of the poor would not constitute an exemption from serving the office of overseer, if the justices should see fit to appoint you. In the event of your being appointed by the justices, the effect of the appointment would be to subject you to the penalties imposed by the statutes 55 Geo. 3, c. 137, and 4 and 5 Wm. 4, c. 76, if you should continue to supply, under the contract, goods to the Union in which the parish for which you are appointed overseer, is situate. As regards your liability to the guardians for the non-performance of the contract, the Commissioners consider that, as your appointment to the office of overseer, under the circumstances, would be an act of the law which would interfere with, and prevent, the performance of the contract by you, no penalty could be claimed under the contract for such non-performance.

VII.—JUSTICES—

1. JURISDICTION OF, IN PROCEEDINGS AGAINST OVERSEERS FOR NEGLECTING TO PAY CONTRIBUTIONS TO UNION FUNDS.

March 2nd, 1844.

Clerk of Machynlleth Union—Stated that the guardians proposed to take proceedings under the 95th sec. of the Poor Law Amendment Act, against the overseers of the parish of Towyn, for disobedience to the guardians' contribution order. The parish of Towyn being situated in the county of Merioneth, and the union treasurer, to whom the money was ordered to be paid, resided in the county of Montgomery; inquired whether the proceedings should be taken before the justices of Merionethshire, or the justices of Montgomeryshire.

Ans.—The Commissioners are disposed to think that the proceedings should be taken before the justices for Merionethshire. If the offence of the overseers had consisted in the *commission* of some specific act, it would of course be only necessary to ascertain the place where the act was done; and the question as to the justices having jurisdiction in the matter would at once be determined accordingly. But as the offence consists merely in the *omission* of a duty, the same mode of settling the question is not available. It appears to the Commissioners, however, that the neglect occurs where the overseers are,—not at the place where they ought to do something, and whither they neglect to go. It seems difficult to conceive how the overseers can commit an offence where they are not. True, they are ordered to make the payment in Montgomeryshire; but they do not go into that county, and consequently do not offend there. They disobey in Merionethshire. The Commissioners, however, in thus expressing their views on the subject, think it right to repeat that the matter is one for the justices themselves to decide.

2. POWER OF JUSTICES TO HEAR COMPLAINTS MADE BY BOARDS OF GUARDIANS, OF WHICH THEY ARE MEMBERS.

February 1st, 1844.

Chairman of Thame Union — Requested the Commissioners' opinion as to the construction of sec. 15 of 5 and 6 Vic. c. 57; and generally as to the power of an individual justice to hear complaints made by guardians, where such justice may be an *ex-officio* member of the board on behalf of which the complaint is preferred.

Ans.—So far as the 15th sec. of 5 and 6 Vic. c. 57 is concerned, it certainly only extends to remove any incompetency on the part of justices to act as such at petty, special, or quarter sessions, in any matter, merely on the ground that such justice is an *ex-officio* member of the board of guardians complaining, interested, or concerned in the matter. No authority is derived from that section to enable a justice to act singly or out of sessions. The question is whether, independently of that provision, a justice could act in the cases referred to. In the case of Reg. *v.* Cant, (2 Moody's Crown Cases, 271) it was decided by the fifteen judges that an order in bastardy was binding, though made by two justices, one of whom was an *ex-officio* guardian of the Union in behalf of which the order was made, but had not taken any step in the case at the board. Probably, on the same grounds upon which it may be conceived that case was decided, it might now be held that a single justice who had not taken any step at the board of which he was an *ex-officio* member, in reference to any proceeding which might subsequently come before him as a justice, would not be disqualified from acting by the mere circumstance of the interest he might be supposed to have as a member of the board. Still from the fact of the legislature having made express provision, removing the doubts as to the power of justices to act in certain cases and not in another, it may be readily conceived that the omission was intentional, and the established rule of construction, *expressio unius exclusio alterius*, may be considered as applying in such a case. Upon the whole, the Commissioners think sufficient doubt attaches to the point to render it undesirable that justices should act singly in the determination of any matter or complaint preferred by boards of guardians, of which such justices may be members.

VIII.—LUNATIC.

CHARGEABILITY OF NON-RESIDENT PAUPER FOR THE PURPOSE OF BEING REMOVED TO A LUNATIC ASYLUM.

March 28th, 1844.

Clerk of Presteign Union—Stated, that the wife of a labourer, living in Presteign, (Radnor) had of late been afflicted with a severe mental affection. The husband had been for some years in the receipt of relief from the parish of Hopesay, in the Clun Union (Salop.) The medical officer of the Presteign Union visited the woman in his private capacity, and finding that the husband received parochial aid from the Clun Union, he reported his attendances in the Medical Weekly Return, remarking that it was a most proper case for a lunatic asylum : he also stated to the guardians, at their meeting, that the woman was dangerous both to herself and others. Inquired, whether the lunatic was chargeable to the township of Presteign within the meaning of the 5 and 6 Vict. cap. 57, and whether she should be reported as such by the relieving officer to some justice, according to the provisions of sec. 6 of that statute.

Ans.—The Commissioners perceive considerable difficulty in dealing with the case; as the statutes 9 Geo. 4, c. 40, and 5 and 6 Vict. c. 57, do not appear to have contemplated the case of a lunatic pauper receiving relief from a parish not within the county in which he is residing. Under the 5 and 6 Vict. c. 57, it is provided that, whenever any insane person is relieved by any board of guardians, or any of their officers, the relieving officer within whose district the parish is situate to which such person may be chargeable, or in which such person may be found destitute, shall give the like information to some justice of the peace, acting for the division of the county within which such parish is situated, as is required to be given by overseers, under the 9th Geo. 4, c. 40. The Commissioners, in the first place, think it extremely doubtful whether the mere visit of the medical officer to the woman, alluded to in your letter, can be considered as rendering her chargeable to the parish of Presteign. At all events, they could not recommend any steps to be taken upon such uncertain ground. Nor does it appear practicable to regard her as a person "found destitute" in that parish, whilst she is receiving all necessary relief from the guardians of the Clun Union. On the other hand, there can be no doubt that she is chargeable to the parish of Hopesay, from which she is receiving relief. But if the relieving officer of the district comprising that parish were to give the required information to some justice of the division in which that parish is situate, what would be the result? The justices for Shropshire would have no authority, either under the 38th sec. of the 9th Geo. 4, c. 40, or otherwise, to cause the woman to be brought before them out of the county of Radnor; and consequently no further proceedings could be adopted in the matter. So that, as she is not chargeable to the parish in which she is living, the officers of that parish have no power to act in the case; and as she is not living in the county comprising the parish to which she is chargeable, the justices of that county are without jurisdiction. These difficulties would of course be got over were she to become in any manner chargeable to the parish of Presteign. In that event she might either be removed by an order of removal to the parish of her settlement, or else be sent by the justices of Radnor to a lunatic asylum, at the instance of the Presteign relieving officer.

IX. MEDICAL OFFICER—

1. PAYMENT TO FOR REDUCING A FRACTURE WHERE PATIENT IS REMOVED TO A HOSPITAL IMMEDIATELY AFTERWARDS.

February 22nd, 1844.

Clerk of Stroud Union—Inquired whether a medical officer was entitled to any fee under the General Medical Order for setting the broken limb of a patient, who immediately afterwards was removed to a hospital, and no longer attended by such officer. If he is not entitled to a fee, would the Commissioners sanction the payment of £1 to the medical officers in such cases?

Ans.—The Commissioners do not think that the medical officer could claim a fee as a right for the service mentioned by the clerk. The fee provided by the 10th Article of the Order is for the "*treatment*" of the fracture; and there is a proviso, as a condition to the payment, that the patient shall have required, and have received, *several attendances* after the operation by the medical officer. The patient, in the case submitted to the Commissioners, was removed to the hospital *immediately* after the operation, and was not subsequently attended by the medical officer at all. In reply to the guardians' second inquiry, the Commissioners desire to state that they would be prepared to acquiesce in the propriety of the payment of such additional remuneration, as mentioned by the clerk, under the circumstance described, whenever it should be recommended by the guardians.

2. LIABILITY OF MEDICAL OFFICER TO SUPPLY LEECHES TO MEMBERS OF SICK CLUBS.

May 8th, 1844.

Clerk of Walsall Union—Inquired, whether the medical officer is bound to provide leeches for a pauper, when prescribed necessary by a club surgeon, the patient not having the means, nor the club-surgeon the liability to procure them. If the medical officer had been the only person called upon to attend, and he had prescribed leeches, there would have been no question as to who should pay for them.

Ans.—The Commissioners think that, when the medical officer is bound to furnish medical and surgical appliances, he is bound to furnish leeches, as falling within this description. But the medical officer must exercise his own discretion as to the cases in which leeches are requisite; and the Commissioners think that the medical officer is not bound to furnish leeches, or any particular surgical appliance or medicine, in a case which was not regularly under his care. The Commissioners are therefore of opinion that the medical officer was justified in his refusal to supply leeches in the case in question.

---

3. QUALIFICATION OF MEDICAL OFFICER.

April 20th, 1844.

Dr. Brookes, London—Requested the Commissioners to inform him whether they considered the extra-licentiate physicians' degree of the Royal College of Physicians, London, came within the meaning of the English medical qualification referred to in their Medical Order.

Ans.—From inquiry made at the College of Physicians, the Commissioners learn that the term "extra-licentiate physicians" applies to licentiates of the college who may practise in any part of England, excepting the precinct of London. As the Commissioners understand, the power of extra-licentiates to practise physic within the limits specified, is as full and as complete as that possessed by licentiates who may practise within the precinct of London, it appears to the Commissioners that they come within the meaning of the Medical Order (Article 3, No. 1) *i. e.* that the license to practise physic, coupled with the diploma of the Royal College of Surgeons, would confer on the persons possessing them the legal qualification for medical officer in any union or parish in England or Wales, in which the Medical Order is in force, and which is not included in the precinct of London, (*i. e.* in the city of London and within seven miles round it.)

X.—MEDICAL RELIEF.

FEE UNDER MEDICAL ORDER, BY WHAT PARISH PAYABLE, WHEN SUSPENDED ORDER OF REMOVAL IS OBTAINED.

February 24th, 1844.

Clerk of Malmsbury Union—Stated, that T. W., a pauper, belonging to Alderley, in the Chipping Sodbury Union, accidentally broke his leg on the 21st of August last, while working for a farmer in the parish of Malmsbury; and having thereby become chargeable to that parish, he was attended by one of the medical officers of the Malmsbury Union. On the 22nd of September a suspended order of removal was obtained, and served on the parish officers of Alderley; and the pauper was removed to Alderley on the 30th of October. Inquired whether any, and what portion of the fee, to which the medical officer of the Malmsbury Union was entitled, under the Medical Order, could be included in the expenses incurred under the suspended order of removal, and charged to the parish of Alderley.

Ans.—It appears to the Commissioners extremely doubtful whether any part of a fee of this kind would be recoverable under such circumstances. The fee being given in one undivided payment (according to the provisions of the Commissioners' Order) for the medical officer's whole attendance on the case, it would seem to be properly regarded as a single indivisible sum, recoverable either in its entirety, or not at all. But even supposing the fee to be not altogether indivisible, it is difficult to suggest any principle of apportionment which could be successfully maintained by the one parish against the dissent of the other. Should the distribution be made according to the number of days over which the whole attendance may have spread; or according to the number of attendances given within the entire period; or according to the degrees of importance in the services rendered in the different portions of the period? The first of these methods would be liable to the objection that the amount of the fee was settled in the Commissioners' Order, with reference chiefly to the nature, and not to the extent, of the service; and, consequently, this mode of apportioning the amount would be at variance with the principle according to which it was originally fixed. The second method would also be open to the like objection. And the third would be exposed to the difficulty, in each individual case, of assigning to the different portions of the period their relative degrees of importance. Again, whatever mode the one parish might adopt, the other parish might demand (and perhaps with equal reason) that a different plan should be followed; and it would probably not be easy to decide in favour of either. These various considerations prevent the Commissioners from giving the guardians a conclusive answer.

XI.—OFFICERS.

PRELIMINARY STEPS TO BE TAKEN BEFORE THE ELECTION OF PAID OFFICERS.

November 9th, 1843.

Vice-Chairman of —— *Union*—Stated, that the election of schoolmistress took place on the 3rd November: there had been no advertisement whatever in any public paper for candidates for the vacancy; but a notice to the following effect was given to the guardians five or six weeks previously, viz.: "*The board will meet on the 3rd November, to consider the propriety of electing Miss P. to the office of Governess.*" He did not consider the election valid, and requested the Commissioners' opinion thereon. It had been the invariable custom of the Board of Guardians to advertise for all their paid officers.

Ans.—The Commissioners have referred to Art. 63, of the General Workhouse Rules, wherein it is prescribed that no appointment of workhouse officers shall be made, unless notice is given at *one of the two ordinary meetings of the board next preceding the meeting at which the appointment shall be made,* or unless an advertisement in some public paper shall have appeared seven days before the day of appointment. As notice of the intended appointment of a schoolmistress was not duly given in either of the modes prescribed by the Article adverted to, the appointment of Miss P. was invalid; and the guardians must therefore proceed to a new election, after due notice has been given of their intention to do so.

November 13th, 1843.

Clerk of —— *Union.*—Stated that, on the 6th October, it was resolved that notice should be given that Miss P.'s appointment, as schoolmistress, be taken into consideration on that day month. At the next meeting of the board that minute was read, and the notice and minute-book was upon the board-room table during both the next meetings, and the appointment was made on "the day month" according to the notice. It was apprehended that the intention of the Workhouse Rules was, that no appointment of Union officers should take place unless the whole of the guardians should be made acquainted with it, either by seeing a notice thereof upon the minute-book *at least* one week (if present at one of the ordinary meetings of the guardians) before the appointment, *or* by public advertisement. In this case, not only was the notice upon the book in due time, but each guardian had *written* notice of the special meeting for the purpose of the appointment. Contended that, for the above reasons, the appointment was valid, and requested the Commissioners to reconsider their decision.

Ans.—It appears that the only distinct notice given to the board of guardians, of the intended appointment, was that given on the 13th October, by the reading of the minutes. This was a meeting, third in order, preceding the 3rd November, the day of the supposed appointment. Therefore the notice was not "given at one of the two ordinary meetings of the board next preceding the meeting at which the appointment was made." But it is urged that three weeks' notice is more notice than one or two. If this were so, it would not dispense with the distinct terms of the regulation. But, in fact, in a case like this, the more remote the period of notice from the time of action, the less is the effect of the notice, because of the probability that the circumstance will be forgotten, or the dates confounded. Considering, therefore, that the notice of the 13th of October was not in compliance with the regulation, it remains to be determined whether the fact that the minute-book, in which the notice had been entered, was lying on the board-room table during both the meetings next preceding that at which the appointment took place, was equivalent to a notice to the board of guardians on either of those days. It appears to the Commissioners impossible to admit this on any principle applicable to notices. The mere presence of the book certainly could not be regarded as notice to those whose attention was not specifically drawn to the entry. Notice does not mean the opportunity afforded to a person to inform himself, but means something done to direct his attention specifically to the subject. The Commissioners do not, therefore, consider that notice was given in the manner provided by the regulation, and are, therefore, of opinion that the appointment is void.

December 14th, 1843.

Second Letter from the Clerk of the same Union—Inquired in what way the Commissioners considered a notice should be given, of an appointment under their regulations.

Ans.—The most orderly and formal course would be, for the chairman of the meeting at which the notice is to be given, to announce the proposal to elect, stating precisely whether at the next meeting or the next but one. The time for making the announcement would be, after directions had been given respecting applications to justices for Orders of Bastardy, and respecting pensions payable to paupers of the Union. Of course the chairman would make the announcement in such a way as to draw the attention of all the guardians present to its purport; and it would be right to inform any guardians who might be about to leave the meeting before the notice should be given, that such an announcement would be made; but this is not a matter of necessity. The fact of the announcement being so made should be entered on the minutes of the guardians.

XII.—PAUPER—

1. CHARGEABILITY OF.

March 23rd, 1844.

Clerk of St. Faith's Union—Stated, that M. A. U., a widow, removed under an order of justices, dated 1st December last, with her three children, from the parish of Edmonton, Middlesex, to the parish of St. Faith in the St. Faith's Union, had applied to the board of guardians, at their last meeting, for relief for herself and children: the pauper, on her removal, was received into the Union workhouse, and her maintenance was charged to the parish of St. Faith, but she now resided in the adjoining parish of Catton. A question had arisen whether the relief to be granted should be charged to the parish of Catton or to the parish of St. Faith; and, after some discussion, it was decided by a majority of the board that the relief should be charged to the parish of Catton. Inquired, whether this decision was correct. Added, that the pauper's settlement was alleged to be in Catton, and not in St. Faith's; and that it was the intention of Catton parish to appeal against the order of removal.

Ans.—The Commissioners desire, with relation to this case, to direct the attention of the guardians of St. Faith's Union to their Official Circular, No. 30, in which (in a letter to Mr. Gilbert, District Auditor) they have stated their views as to the power of guardians to give non-resident relief. In accordance with those views, the Commissioners consider that, as both the parishes of St. Faith and Catton were in St. Faith's Union, it was a matter of discretion with the guardians to charge her relief either to St. Faith's (if they were satisfied of her settlement being in that parish) or to Catton, in which parish she was living. They decided, it appears, upon charging it to Catton. The Commissioners think that, as the alleged settlement of the pauper had been, as far as any proceedings had then gone, adjudged to be in St. Faith's, the proper presumption was that such adjudication was good. At any rate it constituted a *primâ facie* ground for charging the parish of St. Faith, until it was quashed. The Guardians, however, as has been said, had a discretion in the matter. In neither case does it appear to the Commissioners that the charge would have been illegal, but they think it would have been more proper to have made it against St. Faith's, whilst that order remained untouched.

---

2. PROPERTY OF PAUPERS.

January 16th, 1844.

Clerk of Headington Union—Stated, that a pauper, who had become chargeable to the parish of Stanton St. John, in the Headington Union, had many years ago built a cottage on land given to him for that purpose by the warden and fellows of New College, Oxford, on condition of his paying a small quit-rent—seven-pence per annum. He had been compelled, from age and infirmity, to apply for relief, which the Board of Guardians had afforded him; and it was proposed that he should convey the cottage, &c., to the parish officers, conditionally that he and his wife should be allowed to occupy it during their lives. The expense of the conveyance would be about eight pounds. Requested the Commissioners' sanction to the expenditure of that sum.

Ans.—The parish officers cannot lawfully purchase any real property without the consent of the Poor Law Commissioners, under the 21st section of the Poor Law Amendment Act, for any purpose relating to the relief of the poor, and the Commissioners have not authorised any parish officers to purchase property where the parish is in Union. The Commissioners, moreover, consider it highly objectionable that the parish should become possessed of the cottages of paupers.

XIII.—POOR'S - RATE—

WHETHER CHARGEABLE WITH THE EXPENSES OF A VALUATION FOR THE COUNTY-RATE.

March 22nd, 1844.

Mr. Wm. Lowther, Neath—Stated that in 1842, the magistrates in quarter sessions directed a valuation of the hamlet of B—— to be made, for the purposes of the county-rate. The overseers wished to charge the cost of making the valuation upon the poor-rates, but were informed by the auditor of the Neath Union that this could not be allowed. A vestry was then summoned, by which a rate was ordered to be levied for payment of the expenses. The rate, duly allowed and signed by the magistrates for this purpose, was then in course of collection, but the auditor stated that the money could not be appropriated to the purpose for which the rate was made without the permission of the Commissioners. The Commissioners were requested to instruct the overseers how they should act.

Ans.—The auditor of Neath Union is quite right in his view that the expenses of a valuation for the purposes of the county-rate, are not lawfully payable from the poor-rates. By the 6th section of the 55th Geo. 3, c. 51, the justices, in general or quarter sessions, are empowered to employ persons to value parishes for the purposes of the county-rate, in case the overseers of such parishes fail to make the requisite returns; and "the said justices so assembled" (*i. e.* in general or quarter sessions) are further empowered to charge the expenses of such valuations on the parishes concerned, the amount thereof to be levied in the same way as the county-rate, though distinguished from it.

XIV.—RATING—

1. TIMBER, LIME, STONE QUARRIES, NEW ASSESSMENTS.

February 1, 1844.

Mr. J. England, Uplyme (Axminster) Union.)—Inquired whether Scotch firs, planted 50 years

and then cut down, were assessable to the poor-rate; and also whether limestone-quarries were assessable to the poor-rate. Inquired also whether parish officers could alter an old, or make a new assessment of a parish, if they considered it expedient to do so.

Ans.—The express mention of "saleable underwoods," in the 43rd Eliz. c. 2, has been held to exempt, by implication, all other kinds of wood from liability to assessment for the relief of the poor. Consequently, the Scotch firs to which you allude, not being underwood, are not rateable. On a similar principle, it has been decided that, as "coal-mines" alone are mentioned in the statute, all other mines are exempt from the rate. Thus it has been held that limestone-mines are not rateable (R. *v.* Sedgeley, 2 B. and Ad. 65.) But where the same material is raised out of pits or excavations which are not mines, the property is then considered rateable; as, for example, lime-works and stone-quarries not worked as mines. (R. *v.* Alderbury, 1 East, 534; R. *v.* Dunsford, 4 Nev. and Man. 349.) Presuming the limestone-quarries mentioned in your letter to be neither mines, nor worked as mines, they would seem to be liable to the rate. Their rateable value should be ascertained according to the rule prescribed by the 1st section of the Parochial Assessments Act; viz., by estimating the rent for which the property would let to a tenant for the purpose for which it is occupied. The parish officers are bound to lay each poor-rate upon the several properties in the parish, according to their rateable value at the time of making the rate. They ought not to adhere to an old assessment where they are satisfied that it is not in accordance with the present value.

2. OF BRICK-FIELDS.

March 6th, 1844.

Overseers of Northfleet, North Aylesford Union—Stated, that a brick-field at Northfleet, containing about five acres, and working nine stools, had, for the last five years, been rated at £35 per stool, each stool being calculated to make 700,000 bricks annually. The present occupiers of the field intended to appeal against the rate, on the ground that it was much too high, and that it was customary to assess brick-fields by the acre, at about £4 or £5 per acre,—and not by the quantity of bricks made. The Commissioners' advice was requested as to the principle on which the rating should be fixed.

Ans.—The Parochial Assessments Act (6 and 7 Wm. 4, c. 96) prescribes a general rule of rating, applicable to all properties subject to the poor-rate. The rate is to be made upon an estimate of the net annual value of the property, that is to say, of the rent at which it might be reasonably expected to let for from year to year; this rule is therefore applicable to a brick-field, which is no doubt rateable at a larger amount in consequence of the advantage derived from its being worked as a brick-field, and which enables the owner to obtain a higher rent. Where the actual rental paid by the occupier of a brick-field cannot be ascertained, it will be necessary to have recourse to other data upon which to estimate the rateable or letting value. The Commissioners cannot, however, undertake to express an opinion as to which of the modes mentioned in the overseer's letter, it would be the best to adopt for this purpose. It appears to the Commissioners to be a case in which the overseers would do well to consult a surveyor, or person accustomed to the valuation of properties.

3. LIABILITY OF VICAR TO PAY A RATE MADE PREVIOUS TO HIS PRESENTATION TO THE LIVING.

February 20th, 1844.

Mr. John Aldborough, Loddon and Clavering Union—Stated, that between the 1st and 26th of October last, a communication was made by the agent of the late vicar of B., to the overseer of that parish, to the effect that the then vicar would derive no benefit from the rent-charge, in lieu of the vicarial tithes of the parish, after the 1st of October, as the benefice was about to be presented to the Rev. T. B., who would take the rent-charge from the 1st of October, and for that reason the late vicar would not be liable to any further poor-rate. On the 26th of October, a poor-rate of 1*s.* in the pound was made by the overseers, and instead of the late, the name of the present vicar was inserted in the poor-rate assessment. Such rate was afterwards allowed by the magistrates. Application had been made to the new vicar for his quota of the rate; but he declined paying it, on the ground that he was not presented to the benefice until November, which was after the rate was made. Inquired what course should be pursued for the recovery of the vicar's rate.

Ans.—If in fact the present vicar of B. was not presented to the benefice when the rate in question was made, it was not lawful to include him in it. When a person comes into the occupancy of any hereditament during the currency of a rate, the respective shares of himself and the previous occupier may be settled between themselves and the overseers, or in case of dispute, by two justices, under the 17th Geo. 2, c. 38, s. 12. A vicar is not occupier of the tithe in the strict sense of the term; but he would probably be considered so under the statute. But he is occupier of the living, which constitutes his ability under the statute, and which is apparently a tenement within the terms of the 17th Geo. 2; and therefore liable, as it seems, to the abovementioned provisions. The Commissioners, however, do not consider the question to be entirely free from doubt.

4. EXCUSAL OF POOR PERSONS FROM PAYMENT OF RATES.

Feb. 16th, 1844.

Auditor of Ampthill Union—Stated, that in the parish of Ampthill there were several tenements rated to the poor-rate, which were occupied by poor persons *not* settled in the parish, and some of whom were receiving relief from other parishes in the union. The overseers, finding it impossible to recover such rates, except by distraining, and being unwilling to resort to that measure, had inserted the names of these parties in the list of persons excused from payment of rates, and such list had been sanctioned by the justices. Some of the rate-payers having objected to this course, the Commissioners' opinion was requested upon the subject.

Ans.—The Commissioners are of opinion that the excusal of a poor person from the payment of rates should not be influenced by any consideration as to the party's settlement. The liability to be rated arises solely from the occupation of property within the parish; and the only ground of exemption from payment recognised by the 54 Geo. 3, c. 170, s. 11, is "inability through poverty to pay the rate."

XV.—RELATIONS—

1. MAINTENANCE OF.

February 8th, 1844.

Clerk of Peterborough Union—Stated, that R. S. an able-bodied person, with a wife and family, belonging to the parish of Stilton, had applied to the board of guardians of the Peterborough Union for relief, and they had ordered out-door relief to be given to him in consequence of his wife's illness. The pauper's mother occupied a considerable farm in the parish of Stilton, and the overseers were directed to apply for an order on the mother for the son's maintenance. The justices to whom the overseers applied, however, refused to grant a summons for the mother to appear to show cause why such an order should not be made, considering that the son was not "poor, old, blind, lame, or impotent, or other *person not able to work*," within the meaning of the 43rd Elizabeth, c. 2, s. 7. Requested the Commissioners' opinion on the point.

Ans.—The Commissioners concur in the view taken by the justices on the case in question. They consider, that in order to render the mother liable for the son's maintenance, under the 43rd Eliz. c. 2, s. 7, it must be shown that the son is not able to work on account of some bodily or mental defect; not merely that he is out of employment whilst capable of labour. (R. *v.* Gulley, 1 Bott.) If there are young children *not able to work*, the mother of R. S. might, however, be liable for their support as their grandmother.

---

2. AN ILLEGITIMATE SON NOT COMPELLABLE TO MAINTAIN HIS MOTHER.

February 26th, 1844.

Clerk of St. Luke's, Middlesex—Stated, that a woman, who had been chargeable to this parish for many years, had an illegitimate son, who was in good business, and quite able to maintain his mother, but refused to do so on the plea of non-liability. Inquired, whether an illegitimate child came within the provisions of the 7th section of the 43rd Eliz. c. 2, which defined the liability of relations.

Ans.—The Commissioners are of opinion that an illegitimate child is not compellable under the 43rd Eliz. c. 2, section 7, to maintain his mother.

XVI.—RELIEF.

1. ADMISSION INTO WORKHOUSE OF ABLE-BODIED MEN WITH PART ONLY OF THEIR FAMILIES.

February 10th, 1844.

The Vice-Chairman of Warminster Union—Inquired what course ought to be pursued where an able-bodied man applied to be admitted into the workhouse with some of his children, leaving his wife and other part of his family, who were in work, and required no relief, out. And inquired also what would be proper to be done in the case of a man who applied for the admission into the workhouse of himself, his wife, and some of his children, the remainder being in work, and desirous of stopping out.

Ans.—The guardians will perceive that under Article 1 of the General Prohibitory Order, it is required, as a general rule, that the family of an able-bodied person, except such members of the family as are in employment, should accompany him or her into the workhouse, and in the case of a married man, that his wife also should do so. It appears to the Commissioners generally inexpedient to receive part of a family into the workhouse, or to treat the members of a family as if the interests of all were not bound up together. On the other hand, if children, able to support themselves, are in work, and taken care of, it would be unadvisable to require them to come into the house because the father entered. It appears to the Commissioners there can be no doubt that the husband should enter the workhouse if the wife is received therein; and that as a general rule, the wife should, in like manner, follow her husband. This the husband, by his marital control, is supposed by the law to be capable of enforcing. Children not able to support themselves, should, of course, accompany their parents. In cases of this nature, however, answers to general questions must necessarily be vague: particular exceptions will present themselves, in which the relation of husband and wife is not practically what the law supposes it to be; and the Commissioners would not, in these exceptional instances, think it right that the risk of neglecting to relieve destitution on mere theoretical grounds should be incurred.

---

2. RE-PAYMENT OF NON-RESIDENT RELIEF.

February 13th, 1844.

Clerk of Downham Union—Requested the advice of the Commissioners as to the propriety of the guardians of the Downham Union adopting the following account sent to them by the guardians of the Orsett Union:—"For the maintenance of George Towson, thirty-one weeks, from May 18th to Dec. 23rd, 1843, at 3*s.* per week, £4 13*s.* 0*d.* During that period, gin, two and a half gallons, £2 2*s.* 7*d.*; wine, half a pint daily, sixty-seven bottles, £13 8*s.* 0*d.*; coffin and burial expenses, £1 13*s.* 6*d.* Total, £21 17*s.* 1*d.*" This account was accompanied by a certificate from the medical officer, that the gin and wine charged for were necessary. It appeared that George Towson, a year or two ago, had been removed, under an order of justices, from the Orsett Union to the parish of Southery, in the Downham Union. He subsequently left Southery, and returned into the Orsett Union, and was there taken ill. Application was thereupon made to the overseers of Southery, to repay any expense that might be incurred in the pauper's maintenance without fresh order of removal; and the overseers of Southery, on this, wrote to the guardians of the Orsett Union, consenting to repay any such expense; but never reported the case to the guardians of the Downham Union, nor to their relieving officer, who knew nothing of it until the account adverted to was received by them.

Ans.—The Commissioners think that, as the control of all relief, except in cases of sudden and urgent necessity, is, by the 54th section of the Poor Law Amendment Act, taken away from the overseers and vested in the guardians, the overseers of Southery had no power to authorise non-resident relief in the case of George Towson. It, therefore, rests with the guardians of the Downham Union now to decide whether, under the circumstances, they will adopt the act of the overseers of Southery, and repay the relief in question. With regard to the amount of the charge, the Commissioners presume that the certificate of the medical officer of the Orsett Union workhouse must be deemed conclusive as to the necessity for the allowance of the wine and gin. The Commissioners are not aware of any circumstance in the case which prevented the overseers from bringing it before the guardians, and therefore afforded any justification of the course which they pursued. Moreover, the long continuance of the relief renders the conduct of the overseers less intelligible. The Commissioners can see no ground for advising the guardians to adopt this payment. The circumstance of the pauper being resident out of the Union renders the proceeding of the overseers more objectionable and irregular than if the pauper had been resident within its limits.

---

3. RELIEF TO PRISONERS TAKEN IN EXECUTION FOR DEBT.

February 22*nd*, 1844.

Clerk of Radford Union—Stated, that a debtors' prison, not being a county gaol, is situate in the Radford Union, and the prisoners being generally of the poorer class, required relief. The custom formerly pursued, had been to allow each prisoner 6*d*. per diem, and apply for repayment from the parishes to which such prisoners respectively belonged. This had been done under the provisions of 52 Geo. 3, c. 160; but it was discovered that the act only authorised payment to prisoners confined under *mesne* process, whereas the prisoners confined in the prison in question were all taken in *execution*. Inquired, whether the guardians were bound to relieve such prisoners, on application being made on their behalf by the gaoler, as heretofore.

Ans.—The Commissioners, on a former occasion, very carefully considered the subject to which you have called their attention. The importance of it led the Commissioners to take the opinions of the late Solicitor-General (Sir Thomas Wilde) and Mr. Tomlinson, by whom they were advised that prisoners in execution for debt, and in a state of destitution, had no legal claim upon the poor-rates for maintenance or relief; but were (except as to persons confined in county gaols) left dependent upon casual benevolence and charity. As regards debtors confined in county gaols, it would seem, from the several statutes relating to the subject, that they may be maintained, if necessary, out of the county rates. The Commissioners concur in the effect of the above opinion; and they would add that, as the poor-rates are not subject to the liability of relieving persons so confined, the law imposes no obligation on the guardians to entertain any application for relief that may be made on behalf of such persons.

---

4. RELIEF BY WAY OF LOAN TO A SINGLE WOMAN — WHETHER AFTER MARRIAGE HER HUSBAND IS LIABLE TO REPAY IT.

March 2*nd*, 1844.

Clerk of Evesham Union—Stated that a young woman named Vernon, who for many years prior to her marriage was supported in the Union workhouse at the expense of the parish of Ashton Underhill, and who after leaving the house was allowed by the guardians £2, as a loan, had since her marriage, become entitled to a sum of money, but her husband refused either to repay the parish for her maintenance in the workhouse or the amount of the loan advanced. Inquired whether he could be compelled to do so.

Ans.—The Commissioners are of opinion that though the loan granted by the board of guardians to the young woman adverted to by the clerk becomes the debt of her husband, by his subsequent marriage with her, he is neither liable to the remedy provided by the 59th Geo. 3, c. 12, s. 39, nor to that of attachment of wages under the 4th and 5th Wm. 4, c. 76, s. 9. The

Commissioners consider that the only remedy which the guardians have is by action, or if there be a local court having jurisdiction in cases of debts of the amount in question, by proceeding there.

XVII.—RELIEVING OFFICERS' DUTIES.

January 29th, 1844.

Clerk of Godstone Union—Stated, that the guardians of the Godstone Union had, in some cases, given to applicants for relief, orders of admission to the workhouse, which they refused to use; and the relieving officer, finding them afterwards in absolute distress, had given them out-relief. The guardians wished to be informed whether the relieving officer was justified in giving such relief, and also whether he would be responsible in case any fatal effects followed his refusal.

Ans.—A relieving officer in any case of sudden and urgent necessity, is bound by Art. 20, No. 6, of Duties of Officers, to afford such relief to the destitute person as shall be requisite, either by giving such person an order of admission into the workhouse, and conveying him thereto, if necessary, or by affording him relief out of the workhouse, provided that the same shall not be given in money. If, therefore, a relieving officer should repeat the offer of the workhouse, and afford the means of conveyance to it, he must be considered to have furnished adequate relief, provided the person be in a state fit for removal, and be not in actual want of food. In the latter cases it would be necessary for the relieving officer to give immediate out-relief in kind. Under any circumstances, the case would be brought by the relieving officer before the board of guardians at their next meeting.

XVIII.—REMOVAL—
WHETHER AN ORDER CAN BE OBTAINED AFTER CHARGEABILITY HAS CEASED.

March 8th, 1844.

Clerk of Fordingbridge Union—Stated, that S. W., aged nine years, son of T. W., belonging to a parish in another Union, but residing in the Fordingbridge Union, had broken his thigh about two months before, and was attended by the medical officer of the Fordingbridge Union, who was entitled, under Art. 10 of the Medical Order, to a fee of £3. The guardians of the Union in which the father was settled having been applied to for payment of the fee, declined payment, in consequence of having doubts as to the father's legal settlement. The father being an able-bodied man, and not having received relief in money or necessaries, inquired whether an order could be obtained for his removal.

Ans.—The Commissioners see no reason to doubt that T. W. and his family might have been placed under an order of removal, while S. W. was actually in the receipt of medical relief. There is nothing in the 35 Geo. 3, c. 101, to limit the time during which an order may be obtained, after the time when the pauper became chargeable. Still the Commissioners are of opinion that, as the purpose of the order of removal is the relief of the parish from continuance of the burden of maintaining the pauper, it would be exceeding the intention of the statute to remove a person who had ceased to be chargeable before the order was obtained. Such appears to be the general view, inasmuch as the orders of removal universally state that the pauper is at the time of the making of the order chargeable. In the present case, therefore, the Commissioners are of opinion that as the relief has been discontinued, and T. W. is therefore no longer chargeable to the parish, he cannot now be removed.

XIX.—SETTLEMENT—
BY HIRING AND SERVICE.

February 15th, 1844.

Clerk of Fordingbridge Union—Stated, that E. S. went, in July 1831, to live, as under-servant, with Mrs. M., at Fordingbridge, receiving for her services, for the first year, her clothes, board, and lodging, but no wages. At the end of the first year Mrs. M. agreed to give her 6*d*. a week wages, in addition, and she remained another year and two days, when she left in consequence of receiving a month's notice to do so. She went to her parents for two or three weeks, and then hired herself to Mr. S., at Kingston, in the parish of Ringwood, at 5*l*. a year, and remained in his service two years and a quarter, when she left and again went home; but afterwards went to live with Mr. T., of Avon, in the parish of Christ Church, at 5*l*. 10*s*. a year, and was with him one year and ten months. Requested the Commissioners' opinion as to whether E. S. had gained a settlement at Fordingbridge.

Ans.—The Commissioners presume (although the dates are not precisely stated) that the 65th sec. of the Poor Law Amendment Act would interpose to prevent E. S. from gaining any settlement in Ringwood, by her service with Mr. S. The question then is, whether she gained a settlement in Fordingbridge by her service with Mrs. M. The Commissioners are disposed to think that she did; though there is some room for doubt. She states:—" I went to *live as under-servant* to Mrs. M.,—to have my clothes, board, and lodging, but no wages *the first year. I served the first year;* and Mrs. M. then agreed to give me 6*d* a week wages in addition." From this statement, it may perhaps be inferred that there was, if not expressly a hiring for a year, at least a general hiring tantamount to it (See R. *v.* Wincanton, Burr. S. C. 299; R. *v.* Worfield, 5, T. R. 506); that there was also a service for the year, and a residence for forty days in the parish during the year. The second year's service, the Commissioners think, could not be relied on as the foundation of a settlement, without further particulars. The stipulation for weekly wages is adverse to the presumption of a yearly hiring; though the month's warning might possibly show that the hiring in fact was not weekly.

XX.—WORKHOUSE.

1. A Rate-payer cannot visit a Workhouse as a matter of right.

January 8th, 1844.

Mr. ——— — Inquired, 1. Whether as a rate-payer he had a right to visit the inmates of the Union workhouse, at a seasonable hour, any day he thought proper. 2. Whether he was at liberty to ask the inmates questions in regard to their treatment.

Ans.—1. As a rate-payer you cannot, as a matter of right, visit the Union workhouse; but if you are in the commission of the peace, you have such an authority. 2. If admitted to the workhouse, you cannot insist, as a matter of right, upon examining the inmates with reference to their treatment, or any other matter, nor oblige them to answer your inquiries. The control of the workhouse is immediately vested (subject to the orders and general rules of the Commissioners) in the hands of the representatives of the rate-payers, that is to say, the Guardians of the Poor, as a board.

2. Provisional order for admission into the Workhouse.

February 24th, 1844.

Clerk of Bridge Union — Inquired, what was meant by the " Provisional Order," which an overseer was authorised to make under the Workhouse Rules, for the admission of paupers into the workhouse. And, also, whether the workhouse-master was bound to admit every applicant who presented such an order.

Ans.—The Commissioners refer the guardians to Art. 3 of the Workhouse Rules, which will explain the meaning of the word " provisional," as used in Art. 1, with reference to an order made by an overseer for the admission of a pauper into the workhouse. The order is called provisional, because it is valid only for the interval from the time it is given to the next ordinary meeting of the board of guardians, when the admission of a pauper by such an order is required by Art. 3 to be brought before the guardians, who are then to decide on the propriety of the pauper's continuing in the workhouse, or otherwise, and make an order accordingly. The master of the workhouse is bound, under Art. 1, to admit any pauper by a provisional written or printed order, signed by an overseer.

3. Powers of Visiting Committee.

February 27th, 1844.

Clerk of St. Faith's Union — Requested the Commissioners to empower the visiting committee, both collectively and individually, to inspect the Union workhouse as often as they might think fit.

Ans.—According to the 56th Article of the General Workhouse Rules, the visiting committee is to examine the workhouse " once in every week at the least." The Workhouse Rules certainly apply only to the committee as such; but the guardians, as a board, have the control of the workhouse (subject to those Rules), and nothing prevents their ordering that each individual member of the committee should at all times be admitted to inspect the workhouse. The Commissioners cannot alter the Workhouse Rules, which are a general order, without considerable inconvenience; but they consider that the provisions of the order are perfectly compatible with the course suggested above.

LONDON:
Printed by Order of the Poor Law Commissioners, by Blackburn and Pardon, 6, Hatton Garden, and Published by Charles Knight and Co., 22, Ludgate Street, Publishers to the Poor Law Commissioners.

AN

OFFICIAL CIRCULAR

OF PUBLIC DOCUMENTS AND INFORMATION:

DIRECTED BY THE POOR LAW COMMISSIONERS TO BE PRINTED, CHIEFLY FOR THE USE OF THE MEMBERS AND PERMANENT OFFICERS OF BOARDS OF GUARDIANS, UNDER THE POOR LAW AMENDMENT ACT.

No. 36. CIRCULAR ISSUED JUNE 29, 1844.

Poor Law Commission Office,
Somerset House,
29th June, 1844.

THE Poor Law Commissioners, on a review of their Minutes, directed that the Minutes of Correspondence on the following subjects be printed and circulated for the information of Guardians and Officers of the several Unions, viz:—

By order of the Board,
EDWIN CHADWICK, *Secretary.*

I.—ACCOUNTS.

1. CONTRIBUTIONS TO UNION FUNDS—COSTS OF RECOVERING, HOW TO BE CHARGED.

June 11th, 1844.

Clerk of the Lichfield Union—Inquired, to what fund the justices' clerk's fees attendant upon an application from the board of guardians, against overseers for non-payment of calls in cases where justices had given the parish officers time for payment, and no warrant of distress had been granted, should be charged, — whether to the Union establishment, the separate parish funds in the hands of overseers, or to the overseers on their own account. In the latter case, if the overseers were out of office there would be no remedy.

Ans.—Where the guardians proceed against overseers under the 2nd and 3rd Vict. c. 84, for the recovery of their required contribution to the Union fund, and the justices do not issue any warrant of distress, the Commissioners can suggest no remedy for the recovery of the costs from the overseers. The Commissioners consider that the costs incurred in such cases by the guardians should not be charged on the common fund of the Union, but to the parish, the default of whose officers was in fact the occasion of the proceedings.

---

2. COST OF OBTAINING COUNSEL'S OPINION ON RATING LIGHTHOUSE.

June 7th, 1844.

Auditor of Eastbourne Union—Inquired, as to the propriety of allowing, in the accounts of the overseers of East Dean, certain charges incurred by them, under the authority of the vestry, in obtaining counsel's opinion, with regard to the assessment of the dues derivable in respect of a lighthouse situated in that parish.

Ans.—There is no fixed rule for determining the occasions on which overseers may properly employ professional persons; but it may be observed generally, that when the difficulties of any case are such, that it is not to be expected that overseers can proceed without professional advice or assistance, any reasonable expense incurred for such advice or assistance, would be allowable in the overseers' accounts, as a charge incidental to the due execution of their office. Having thus stated the general principle applicable to such cases, the Commissioners must leave it to yourself to determine, in the present instance, whether under all the circumstances, there was sufficient doubt or difficulty in the matter to justify the overseers in seeking professional advice. The Commissioners themselves will merely remark, that they do not perceive any circumstances which could have occasioned any such difficulty; that is to say, they do not see that the case of the lighthouse in question was in any material respect distinguishable from the cases in which lighthouse dues had been expressly held to be not rateable,—nor do they consider that there was any good ground for supposing that those decisions would be likely to be reversed, and a new principle of rating adopted, with regard to this description of property. The overseers of East Dean were fully aware of those decisions. The Commissioners think it right to add, that if the overseers were not justified by the circumstances of the case in obtaining the opinion of counsel, the sanction of the vestry would not of itself be sufficient to authorise the proceeding. The decision in R. *v.* Gwyer (4 Nev. and Man. 158) shows, that where the law does not authorise the charging of any particular payment on the poor-rate, the mere concurrence of the vestry will be no protection to the overseers.

---

3. RELIEF TO BASTARD CHILDREN, HOW TO BE ENTERED IN THE ACCOUNTS.

June 3rd, 1844.

Clerks of Wareham and Purbeck Union—Inquired, whether in the case of a single woman receiving out-relief on account of her bastard child, born before the passing of the Poor Law Amendment Act, and resident with her, the relief should appear in the out-relief list as given to the child, to be entered in the Quarterly Abstract, under class 3, or to the mother, to be entered under class 8, and her child placed in the column headed "Gross number of children under sixteen relieved with their parents."

Ans.—Relief of the description mentioned above should be entered in the columns of the class marked 3 of the Quarterly Abstract, and headed "Illegitimate children under sixteen without their mothers." The mothers should not be included at all in the Abstract, where the relief given is solely for the child.

II.—ASSISTANT OVERSEER.

MODE OF PROCEEDING WHEN A POLL DEMANDED ON THE ELECTION OF.

June 7th, 1844.

A Rate-payer of the parish of Bangor—Stated, that at a vestry meeting for the election of an assistant overseer, where there were two candidates, a poll was demanded on the part of the candidate who was in the minority on the show of hands; that a poll was accordingly granted by the senior churchwarden, who was presiding chairman, to be taken on the following Monday in the market-place. Inquired, whether the chairman was competent to order the proceedings, and whether the election was not illegal from the poll having been taken elsewhere than at a vestry meeting.

Ans.—The show of hands at the meeting alluded to was not necessarily conclusive; and if a poll was demanded, it was proper to grant it. The Commissioners are not aware of any legal objection to the adjournment of the meeting to another place and day, for the purpose of taking the poll. At such poll, however, the votes should have been calculated according to the provisions of the 58 Geo. 3, c. 69, and 59 Geo. 3, c. 85; but whether they were so calculated appears, from the statement, to be doubtful. The 2nd section of the 58 Geo. 3, c. 69, provides that, in the absence of the rector, vicar, or perpetual curate, the vestry shall elect a chairman for the occasion. If the senior churchwarden, in the case referred to, was so elected to preside, it became his duty to regulate the proceedings, including the poll; but if he was not so elected, the Commissioners do not know under what authority he could claim to assume the direction of the matter.

III.—CLERK'S DUTIES.—SERVICE OF CONTRIBUTION ORDERS.

May 2nd, & *June 25th*, 1844.

Relieving Officer, Alnwick Union—Transmitted the following resolution, passed by the board of guardians of the Alnwick Union,—"That as great irregularity has heretofore occurred in the service of the money orders, the relieving officers shall in future deliver the money orders to the overseers personally, and keep a minute of the time when the persons to whom the same are delivered;"—and inquired, whether the delivering of such orders formed part of his duties.

Ans.—It does not appear to the Commissioners to be the duty of the relieving officer to deliver the contribution orders of the guardians to the several overseers personally: that duty is expressly imposed upon the clerk of the Union by Article 17, No. 6, of the General Order, dated April 21, 1842.

Clerk of Alnwick Union stated, that it had been the practice, since the Union was established, for the relieving officers to deliver the contribution orders to the overseers within their respective districts. The resolution adverted to by the relieving officer was passed, with the view of preventing some irregularity which the relieving officers had fallen into in regard to the delivery of these orders. The board of guardians considered, that they had the power of passing the resolution, under Article 20, No. 15, of the General Order of the 21st April, 1842.—Represented the great increase to his (the Clerk's) duties, which the serving of these orders would occasion.

Ans.—The Commissioners certainly think that is the effect of the article in question, [*i. e.* to convey to the overseers the contribution orders.] Personal service of the order is, as the Commissioners are advised, necessary to enable the justices to convict in case of the order being disobeyed. But the Commissioners consider, that any unavoidable expenses in effecting personal service ought not to fall upon the clerk, but should be defrayed out of the common fund of the Union. The Commissioners see no objection to the relieving officer delivering the orders of contribution, if he does not object to do so, and it does not interfere with his ordinary business, but it is no part of his prescribed duty.

IV.—CONTRIBUTION ORDERS.

SERVICE OF.

June 15th, 1844.

Clerk of Great Boughton Union—Inquired whether it was necessary that the notices of the contributions required from the several townships in Great Boughton Union should be served upon every overseer of each such township, or whether service upon one of them was sufficient.

Ans.—The Commissioners some time ago, had occasion to consult counsel on this point, who inclined to the opinion, in which the Commissioners coincide, that as great strictness is required in proceedings of a penal nature, all the overseers of the township ought to be served with the guardians' order, to enable the justices to convict any one of them of disobedience to it.

V.—FIRE-ENGINE.

EXPENSES OF REPAIRING, NOT PAYABLE OUT OF THE POOR RATES.

May 25th, 1844.

Overseers of Botesdale, Hartismere Union—Stated, that there was belonging to the parish of Botesdale a fire-engine, which for many years past had been kept in repair by voluntary contributions; but this means of preserving it in a state of efficiency had entailed an annual expense on a few individuals, while others, claiming the use of the instrument, refused their assistance; so that at length the overseers were without any funds wherewith to pay for keeping it in a proper and useful state. Requested to know whether charges for needful repair, and other necessary expenses, might not be paid out of the poor-rate, in which case all would bear a proportion of the burden.

Ans.—The only enactments of which the Commissioners are aware, authorising the provision and repair of fire-engines at the charge of the poor-rates, are the 12th Geo. 3, c. 73, and 14 Geo. 3, c. 78; and these statutes extend only to the cities of London and Westminster, certain parishes in Middlesex specially named, and other parishes within the bills of mortality. The Commissioners fully recognise the utility and importance of maintaining such engines in a state of efficiency, but they are nevertheless constrained to state, that however desirable the object in question may be in itself, there does not appear to be any lawful authority for charging the expense upon the poor-rates, in parishes which do not come within the range of the above-named statutes.

VI.—GUARDIANS' ELECTION.

QUALIFICATION OF VOTERS.

June 24th, 1844.

Mr.—— —Stated that parties claimed to vote at the election of guardians in March 1844, who were rated to the relief of the poor in the August rate of 1843, being the only rate made during the year immediately preceding their tendering their votes. There was only one highway rate made during the same year, to which they were not rated. They duly paid the August poor rate. Inquired whether these parties were entitled to have their votes recorded. Remarked that by the 40th section of Poor Law Amendment Act, it is provided that no person shall be entitled to vote, unless he shall "have been rated to the relief of the poor for the whole year immediately preceding his so voting." Did this mean that such person must be actually on a rate during the whole of the year, or only on the rates that are made during the year? The parties in the present case could not show that they were on a rate in the course of the year preceding their tendering their votes, previous to the August rate.

Ans.—The section cited provides that no person shall be deemed a rate-payer nor be entitled to vote "unless he shall have been rated to the relief of the poor for the whole year immediately preceding his so voting," nor "unless he shall have paid the parochial rates and assessments made and assessed upon him for the period of one whole year." The Commissioners construe these words as meaning, that a person must be charged in the rate book for the entire period of a year, and pay the rate for that period, (except as to the last six months.) It does not appear to the Commissioners that the terms of the section are satisfied by a person having been charged to all the rates made during the year preceding the 25th March, in case those rates do not extend over the entire period of a year. Where a person has been rated to, and paid a rate made prior to the 25th March, 1843, and no subsequent rate has been made in the parish until the August following, in which, as well as in every succeeding rate made up to the following March, the name of such person has been included, he will have been rated to the relief of the poor for a whole year. In such a case there will have been a continuous rating, as the rate made prior to the 25th March, 1843, continued in force until the succeeding rate was made, and it was in law the existing rate of the parish during the interval which occurred between the making of the two rates. But a person who was in the occupation of premises in any parish for one year prior to the 25th March last, and was assessed for the first time to the poor rate made in August 1843, will obviously not have been rated for one whole year, but he will have been rated to a rate made for, and having reference to a portion of a year only, (the poor rate being made prospectively) *i. e.* to that portion subsequent to the month of August.

VII.—GUARDIANS' QUALIFICATION.

PAID OFFICER OF ONE UNION NOT QUALIFIED TO ACT AS GUARDIAN OF ANOTHER UNION.

May 14th, 1844.

Clerk of Carlisle Union—Inquired, whether the circumstance of his being a paid officer in the Carlisle Union disqualified him from acting as guardian of the Longtown Union.

Ans.—The Commissioners are of opinion that the prohibition contained in the 14th section of the 5th and 6th Vict. c. 57, as to serving the office of guardian, is not confined to the Union of which the person is a paid officer, but is general; so as to make it unlawful for a paid officer of one parish or Union to act as guardian of any other parish or Union.

VIII.—LUNATIC.

MAINTENANCE OF.

June 8th, 1844.

Clerk of the Bingham Union—Stated, that Sarah the wife of Henry Richardson, about eight years ago, being a confirmed lunatic, and chargeable to the parish of St. Peter, Nottingham, was placed by that parish in the Nottingham Lunatic Asylum. An order of justices was then obtained under the 9th Geo. 4, c. 40, for the maintenance of the lunatic in the asylum by the parish of Tollerton, (in the Bingham Union,) where her settlement was adjudged to be. The parish of Tollerton did not at the time investigate the lunatic's settlement, but paid for her maintenance under the order, until about five years ago, when the same was continued to be paid by the board of guardians, and charged to the parish. In September, 1843, Henry Richardson became chargeable to the parish of St. Peter, Nottingham, and an order for his removal to Tollerton was obtained. The parish officers of Tollerton then investigated the matter of the settlement of the parties, and found that neither of them had any settlement there. In consequence of this, the parish officers gave notice of appeal against the order of removal, which was eventually quashed, but *not on the merits*, and they therefore gave notice to the board of guardians, not to make any further payment, on account of the lunatic's maintenance in the asylum. The board of guardians, and the parish officers respectively also gave notice to the managers of the asylum, that no such payment would in future be made; the managers of the asylum, however, disregarded these notices, alleging that they held an order for the maintenance of the lunatic by the parish of Tollerton, and they had accordingly made a demand on the guardians of the Bingham Union, for the quarter's maintenance, due the 25th of March last. Requested the Commissioners' advice under the above circumstances.

Ans.—An order of removal unappealed against, has been decided by the courts to be conclusive evidence, as to the pauper's settlement, up to the date of such order. The Commissioners are not aware of any case in which this principle has been expressly held to be applicable to orders of maintenance under the 9th George 4, c. 40. But where such an order has been made, and notice of it has been given to the parish of the alleged settlement, and that parish has submitted to it, allowing the time of appeal to go by, without appealing, the Commissioners are disposed to consider that the principle above referred to would apply to such a case, in the same manner as it does to orders of removal. The Commissioners, therefore, think that, as the parish officers of Tollerton, in the present instance, acquiesced in the order for the wife's maintenance under 9th George 4, c. 40, and did not appeal against it as they might have done, they were concluded by it with regard to the settlement up to that time. Then, there is nothing to show that any subsequent settlement has been obtained by the pauper. The order for the removal of the husband to Tollerton was quashed, but not (it is stated) on the merits. Consequently, it proves nothing, one way or other: as to the settlement, if it had been quashed on the merits, there might have been a question, how far the former order, under 9th George 4, c. 40, being unappealed against, could be affected by it. Under the circumstances stated, the Commissioners see no reason to suppose that the order of maintenance could now be successfully resisted by the parish officers of Tollerton.

IX.—MEDICAL OFFICER.

Fees payable to him for Midwifery Cases at the Workhouse.

June 25th, 1844.

Clerk of the South Molton Union—Inquired, with reference to Art. 12 of the Medical Order, whether the medical officer is entitled to a fee for every midwifery case which occurs in the workhouse, whether he has been specially called upon or not, or whether he has been present at the time of delivery or not. The medical officer contended that he had attended all midwifery cases at the workhouse at or soon after the delivery, and that frequently women, after their confinement, required attention.

Ans.—The Commissioners consider the medical officer to be entitled to a fee in every case in which he has been sent for by the master or the matron of the workhouse to attend a woman in the workhouse, either in or immediately after childbirth.

X.—MEDICAL ORDER.

Fees for Surgical Cases, to whom payable when a change of Medical Officers takes place.

April 22nd, 1844.

Clerk of the Ludlow Union—Stated, that on the 11th of March last, Mr. M., a medical officer of the Union, was called to a case of fractured thigh, which he set and attended until the 25th of March, the expiration of the year for which he had been appointed; when the case was handed over, with all others of his pauper patients, to Mr. S., who had been elected to succeed him. Mr. M. claimed the fee of £3 under the Medical Order of the Commissioners; but as the patient in question (who still had Mr. M.'s splints upon her thigh) would require close and constant attention for a period of perhaps a month, the guardians deferred paying the whole amount of the fee claimed to Mr. M., considering that it should be apportioned between the two officers. Inquired the Commissioners' opinion thereon, as similar cases must frequently occur at the end of the parochial year and the termination of medical contracts.

Ans.—The Commissioners think that Mr. M. is entitled to the entire fee, and that it cannot be apportioned between the two officers. The Commissioners would observe, that in cases of this sort an arrangement ought to be made by the guardians that the former medical officer should complete his attendance on the case, notwithstanding the change of officers.

2. Poultices not included under Medical and Surgical Appliances.

June 10th, 1844.

Chepstow Union—The Commissioners addressed the following letter to the guardians of the Chepstow Union,—"A copy of the resolution passed by the board of guardians of the Chepstow Union, that the board consider all poultices to come under the words 'Medical and Surgical appliances,' mentioned in Art. 19, No. 1, of the General Medical Order, has been forwarded to the Commissioners by one of the medical officers of the Union, and in reference thereto, the Commissioners desire to state that as bread for poultices is not supplied by medical men to private patients, and is in fact a household article, they are of opinion that it does not come within the meaning of the words 'Medical and Surgical appliances' as used in the Medical Order, and that it ought therefore to be supplied by the relieving officer."

XI.—OVERSEERS.

1. Bound over to Prosecute in a Case of Manslaughter—Costs not payable out of the Poor-Rates.

June 28th, 1844.

Messrs. Collins and Son, Bodmin—Stated that, in the month of October, 1842, two men, whilst returning from a fair at Wadebridge in a drunken state, rode over and killed a poor woman, who was a pauper of the parish of Egloshayle; a coroner's inquest was held on the body, when a verdict of manslaughter was returned. The coroner then summoned the overseers of the parish of Egloshayle before him, and bound them in heavy penalties to prosecute at the next assizes, and committed one of the men to prison to answer the charge. The overseers being thus bound to prosecute, employed them (Messrs. Collins and Son) for that purpose, and the party was accordingly tried at the March assizes, 1843. The overseers and the parishioners were desirous that the costs of the prosecution should be paid, but the auditor objected to allow the amount in the overseers' accounts, considering it a charge which should not have been incurred by them. The overseers had no discretion in the matter after being bound in heavy penalties to prosecute, and without it no prosecution would have taken place. Requested the Commissioners' sanction to the overseers, under the circumstances, paying these costs out of the poor-rates. The coroner stated, that the course always pursued by him in all cases where the party injured is a pauper, was the one adopted in the present instance, in order to secure the proper prosecution of the offenders, and he contended that he had a legal right to do so.

Ans.—The Commissioners do not doubt the power of the coroner, under 7th George 4, c. 64, to bind over by recognizance any person to prosecute in a case of manslaughter, who may know or declare anything material touching the matter to be tried. But his power does not extend to binding over persons to prosecute in their official capacity. There is no obligation or duty attaching to overseers, as such, to prosecute charges of murder or manslaughter. They, in common with other persons, are liable to be bound over, but it is not as overseers, but as individuals. It consequently follows, that if they are bound over in any case, they cannot lawfully apply the funds which come to their hands for a specific purpose (viz. the relief of the poor) to the payment of any costs incurred in the prosecution which may not be allowed by the county. The practice, therefore, of binding over overseers in such cases (inasmuch as it proceeds upon the erroneous assumption that they have public funds at their disposal applicable to the payment of the costs of the prosecution) is much to be regretted. The Commissioners consider that the auditor would have no alternative, but to disallow as unfounded any payment of this nature which might be entered in the accounts of the overseers.

2. RECOVERY OF BALANCES FROM A DEFAULTING OVERSEER, WHO BECAME INSOLVENT.

June 27th, 1844.

Clerk of the Alton Union—Forwarded resolutions of the vestry of Bentworth parish, whereby it appeared that the overseer, who had become insolvent, was in default with the parish, and that the vestry considered it inexpedient to proceed against him for the recovery, on account of the expense of the proceeding and the uncertainty of the result, and requested to have the Commissioners' opinion thereon.

Ans.—The Commissioners cannot, of course, express any opinion as to the probable success of any proceeding which might be taken against the defaulting overseer, with a view to the recovery of the balance in his possession. It nevertheless appears to the Commissioners a case in which it would be proper that some endeavour should be made to protect the parish from loss. Such proceedings may not be effectual, but the present overseers will have discharged their duty in instituting them. If the defaulting overseer has not accounted to the justices, he can be required to do so, under 50th Geo. 3, c. 49. If he has accounted, and the justices have found a balance due from him, and such balance has not been paid over to the succeeding overseers, such overseers can apply to the justices to issue their warrant for the recovery of the balance; and in default of a sufficient distress, the defaulting overseer can be committed until the balance is paid, (50th George 3, c. 49.) On the other hand, the overseer who is represented to have misapplied the monies of the parish can be proceeded against, under the 97th section of the Poor Law Amendment Act, for such misapplication. If the justices should convict, the offender will be liable to pay treble the amount or value of the money misapplied. The Commissioners think it necessary to add, that in case the balance in hand, or any portion of it, should be recovered, the present overseers will of course be bound to charge themselves in their accounts with the monies so obtained.

XII.—PAUPER.

1. CHARGEABILITY OF, IN CASE OF ACCIDENT.

April 22nd, 1844.

Mr. —— *Axminster Union*—Stated, that a pauper named William Newton, a short time since broke his leg whilst residing in the parish of Seaton, in the Axminster Union. On his case being brought before the board of guardians, they ordered the relief to be given to him, to be charged to the parish of Colyton, the board believing that he belonged to that parish: the pauper still remained at Seaton, where he met with the accident. The parish of Colyton, however, on inquiry found that the pauper belonged to the parish of Lyme Regis. Inquired whether the parish of Colyton could under these circumstances apply for an order for the pauper's removal to Lyme Regis.

Ans.—The guardians of Axminster Union are at liberty, as it seems to the Commissioners, to give non-resident relief to paupers within the union; that is to say, to give to a pauper residing in one parish of the union, relief at the charge of another parish within the same union, supposing the pauper to be legally settled in such other parish. If however, he be not settled in such other parish, the guardians could not lawfully charge that parish with his relief, while resident elsewhere. It is, therefore, in the present case, a question of fact, whether William Newton is, or is not, settled in Colyton,—and if not, then whether he is, or is not, settled in Lyme Regis. Assuming him to belong to the latter parish, the former parish will have been wrongfully charged with his relief by the guardians; and, consequently, as he is neither inhabiting therein, nor properly chargeable thereto, the Commissioners think that Colyton could not resort to an order of removal in the case. On the supposition that he is settled in Lyme Regis, the guardians may charge his relief to that parish. The primary liability, however, to provide for his relief rests upon the parish of Seaton, where he is living; and if there should be any doubt as to his settlement, the guardians will certainly do well to cast upon Seaton the burden of his maintenance; which there can be no doubt that parish is in the first instance liable to bear.

---

2. DITTO—MOTHER WITH HER BASTARD CHILD.

June 27th, 1844.

Clerk of Penzance Union—Stated, that Mary Edwards, with her bastard child, on the 13th of May, were removed to the workhouse of the Penzance Union, and charged in the books of the house to St. Erth parish. Her settlement not being in that parish, the overseers, by direction of the board of guardians, applied to the magistrates to adjudicate on the settlement, and order her removal; but there being some difficulty, on the evidence adduced by the overseers, in determining whether she belonged to Uny Lelant or St. Ives, two other parishes in the same Union, the magistrates adjourned the hearing of the case to Thursday, the 13th June. The pauper, however, in the mean time, viz. the 12th June, left the workhouse with her child, on her own notice, stating that she was going to try to get a place of service, and her name was discharged from the books of the house. She failed to attend before the magistrates on the 13th respecting her settlement, and the case was therefore again adjourned. In the evening of that day, she applied to the relieving officer of the eastern district (in which are all the three litigating parishes) at Penzance, which is not his residence, but where he happened to be on parochial business, for an order for the readmission of herself and child to the house. He gave her an order accordingly, but stating therein that he could not say what parish they should be charged to. The master, however, on receiving them, charged them to the parish of St. Erth, in consequence of their having been charged to that parish before, and having been out only one day. To this the guardians of St. Erth objected, alleging, that with her discharge from the house, all connexion with St. Erth ceased; whilst Penzance, the parish in which the pauper made her last application for relief, contended that she only came there for the purpose of seeing a relieving officer, and that St. Erth, having taken measures for ascertaining the settlement, and the paupers having been so lately chargeable thereto, ought to continue to maintain the paupers until their settlement was ascertained; at all events, that the burden should not be thrown on Penzance, as the destitution did not take place there, the pauper having come there for the express purpose of seeing a relieving officer. It appeared, by the pauper's statement, that on her leaving the workhouse on the 12th June, she went to the parish of Uny Lelant, hoping to get a place of service. She slept there that night, and on the following day, not being able to get a place, she was obliged to return to the house, and came to Penzance in search of the relieving officer, to obtain a ticket for admission. Under these circumstances the board were uncertain to which of the three parishes, viz., St. Erth, Penzance, or Uny Lelant, the parties should be charged, and requested the Commissioners' advice.

Ans.—A pauper is chargeable to that parish in which, being destitute, he applies for and obtains relief. To this general rule, however, an apparent exception occurs in the case of persons who, being destitute in one parish, are compelled to go into another for the purpose of making the application for relief, in consequence of the relieving officer's dwelling, the guardians' place of meeting, or the Union workhouse being situate in such other parish. In these cases, the relief is chargeable, not to the parish in which the application is *actually made*, but to the parish in which the necessity for it arose, and in which it must be deemed to have been constructively made. As the facts are stated, there appears to be no ground for charging St. Erth with the relief granted to Mary Edwards on her second application. The original chargeability to St. Erth ceased, upon the pauper quitting the workhouse on her own notice, and the facts do not show either that she was subsequently destitute in St. Erth, or that she made application for relief in that parish. The question therefore to be determined in the present case appears to be this,—was Mary Edwards so far destitute in the parish of Uny Lelant, in which she slept on the night of the 12th, as to need relief then and there, and did she go into the parish of Penzance solely for the purpose of seeking such relief, that parish being the place of the relieving officer's residence? If this question can be answered in the affirmative, the Commissioners think that Uny Lelant ought to be charged with the relief given upon the second application. But, if not, there appears to be no alternative but to charge the relief to Penzance in which the pauper actually applied for relief, and obtained it. The Commissioners must leave the point to the decision of the guardians, who are better able, from their knowledge of the circumstances of the case, to draw the conclusion as to the fact of the pauper's being destitute in Uny Lelant.

---

3. DITTO—OF A MENDICANT,

June 24th, 1844.

Clerk of Lincoln Union—Stated, that James Smith, a mendicant, was admitted into the workhouse of the Lincoln Union, on the 4th of April, by a ticket from the relieving officer. The following morning he complained of being unwell, and the master desired him to remain where he was until the surgeon visited on that day; but he refused to do so, and left the house immediately, and went and applied at the dispensary in that city for medical advice. The physician there advised him to go to the relieving officer, and obtain an order for re-admission into the workhouse. He went accordingly, but the relieving officer declined to give him an order, in consequence of having given him one on the day previous. The applicant then went to the workhouse, and the master admitted him without an order. He still remained in the workhouse, and the question was, to what parish he was to be charged. The workhouse is situate in the parish of St. Peter, in Eastgate, and the residence of the relieving officer, where the order for the first admission was obtained, is in the parish of St. Martin, and the dispensary is in the parish of St. Mary-le-Wigford. The guardians desired to know, also, whether, in the event of a person not belonging to any parish in the Union applying for and obtaining an order for admission into the workhouse from the relieving officer, he was to be charged to the parish in which the relieving officer resided.

Ans.—The Commissioners are disposed to consider that the parish of St. Martin, the parish in which the relieving officer resided, was, under the circumstances, the parish properly chargeable with the relief. It may fairly be presumed that the pauper, when he applied to the relieving officer for assistance, was destitute; as, immediately after the refusal of relief by the relieving officer, the pauper was taken into the Union workhouse upon the responsibility of the master; and being destitute in St. Martin, and having made application for relief in that parish, the legal obligation to afford it lay upon that parish. The Commissioners do not think that the refusal of the relieving officer to grant relief in such a case would justify the charging the parish in which the workhouse stands with the relief. With respect to your general inquiry, the Commissioners are not prepared to say that the parish in which the relieving officer resides would, in all cases, be liable to the relief afforded by him to a person, by the admission of such person into the Union workhouse, where it might appear that such person did not belong to any parish in the Union. If the facts of the case should show that the pauper was destitute in some other parish, prior to his making application to the relieving officer, and left that parish solely for the purpose of finding the relieving officer, the circumstance of the application being made where the relieving officer resided would not relieve the parish in which the destitution occurred from the obligation which is cast upon it to maintain its own poor, whether settled or casually chargeable. But if there be no evidence of the pauper being destitute, until application be made for relief to the relieving officer, the parish in which the relieving officer resides would probably be liable. The obligation on the latter parish ought not to be increased by the fact of the relieving officer residing there, but, on the other hand, such parish cannot be exonerated from the ordinary liability imposed by law.

---

4. DITTO—OF A MAN AND HIS FAMILY IN DISTINCT PARISHES, WHERE HIS PLACE OF SETTLEMENT CANNOT BE ASCERTAINED.

June 11th, 1844.

Clerk of the Eastry Union — Requested the Commissioners' advice upon the following case:

John Marten, seventy-six years of age, was in the early part of his life a soldier. On obtaining his discharge he settled in the parish of St. Peter, Sandwich, and shortly afterwards married Ann his present wife, and the result of the marriage was a numerous family, who were all born in St. Peter's parish. During the last two years he was allowed out-relief, and several attempts were made to prove his settlement, but, either in consequence of loss of memory, the result of his age, or a disinclination to give the information requisite to prove his original settlement, proceeding from a desire to avoid returning to it, no satisfactory statement could be obtained to enable the justices to order his removal. In the month of March last, in consequence of his increasing infirmities, and being unable to continue any longer his usual calling, that of a collector of manure, he applied to the guardians for admission into the workhouse, and from that time he had been an inmate. Shortly afterwards possession of the house in which he had resided for so many years, was given up by his wife, who removed into the parish of St. Mary, Sandwich. Since her residence there she applied to the guardians for out-relief, and being a woman of industrious character, and far advanced in life, the board felt a desire to give her trifling assistance; but a difference of opinion having arisen as to which of the two parishes should be charged with the cost of her out-relief if allowed, some adopting the opinion that the parish which from necessity was obliged to relieve the husband should also relieve the wife, and others that in consequence of her having obtained no settlement in the parish of St. Peter, the parish of St. Mary in which she then resided should bear the charge in the event of relief being allowed to her. It was determined to offer her an order for the workhouse, which she declined; but as there was no reason to expect that she could maintain herself long without parochial relief, the guardians were desirous of being advised in what manner they should treat her case when she became chargeable, and in the event of any of the family requiring relief, whether they must fall to the parish of St. Peter, being the place of their birth, as there could be no expectation entertained of discovering the legal settlement of John Marten, the father. Ann, the wife, stated, that she was born in the workhouse of St. Mary, Sandwich, that she never knew her father, but understood that he died about five months before her birth, and that he was a foreigner, and that she never gained a settlement by servitude.

Ans. — If John Marten has no settlement, or if his settlement cannot be ascertained, his wife will retain her maiden settlement, if she had one, and their children will take such maiden settlement, or in default thereof will be settled in the parish of their birth. With Marten's consent the wife and children may be removed to the parish of their settlement; but without his consent it would seem that they cannot be separated from him for the purpose of such removal. (R. *v.* Carleton, Burr, 813; R. *v.* Eltham, 5 East, 113. With regard to the chargeability, there can be no doubt that as Marten himself was residing in St. Peter's, Sandwich, when he applied for relief, and was received into the workhouse, he is chargeable to that parish. If his wife or any of the children should require relief hereafter, the parish in which she or they then reside will be primarily liable to provide such relief. If, however, she or they be settled in any other parish in the Eastry Union, the guardians might charge the relief to such other parish if they should think fit. The Commissioners are not aware of any ground for supposing that the parish in which the man himself was residing when he required relief will be necessarily liable for the relief of the wife and family, should they become destitute elsewhere.

XIII.—POOR RATE.

COSTS OF ENFORCING THE PAYMENT OF THE POOR RATE, BY WHOM TO BE PAID.

June 11th, 1844.

Clerk of Westbury-on-Severn Union—Inquired whether in the case of parties summoned for the non-payment of the poor rate, the expenses of the applications as well as the rate were recoverable against the defaulters; or whether such expenses must be borne by the overseers.

Ans.—The cost of a summons for non-payment of poor rate, is in the first place, demandable of the person at whose instance or on whose application such summons is obtained, and it is recoverable or not against the party summoned, according to the nature of the case and the discretion of the justices. Where the justices upon the hearing of the case, may not see fit to order payment of the costs of the summons, by the party in arrear, the overseers will be answerable for it.

XIV.—RATING.

1. COAL-MINES.

June 15th, 1844.

Assistant Overseer, Kirkburton — Inquired as to which township a coal-mine should be rated, the pit being sunk and the coals wound up in Kirkburton, though the coals were obtained in the adjoining township, fifty yards being the distance of the mouth of the pit from the boundary line of the two townships.

Ans.—The Commissioners direct your attention to the case of R. *v.* Foleshill (2 Adol. and Ellis, 593) in which a coal-mine extended under the surface into the parishes of Exhall and Foleshill, but the pits, engines, and fixed machinery for working the mine were all situated in Foleshill alone; and it was held that the proprietor of the mine could not be rated in Foleshill for that part of the mine which lay in Exhall. Lord Denman observes—"It is too great a refinement to say that there was no mine there (*i. e.* in Exhall) because all the works for raising the coal were not within that parish. According to that argument, if a coal-mine extended into twenty parishes, and all the coal was brought to the surface in one, the proprietor must be rated in that only. The difficulty of ascertaining what is raised in each parish may be great, but here the sessions have ascertained it." According to this decision, the Commissioners apprehend that the proprietor of the coal-mine to which you allude is rateable in Kirkburton for so much of the property, whether mine or works, as is situated in that parish, and that he is rateable in Stockton for so much of the property as lies therein. The distribution of the property between the two parishes is a question of fact, to be ascertained according to the circumstances of the individual case.

---

2. COURSE TO BE PURSUED IN LEVYING A RATE WHERE THE EXISTING ASSESSMENT IS UNFAIR.

June 17th, 1844.

Overseer of Kingswalden, Hitchin Union—Stated that a rate, made in February last, was quashed by the justices on appeal, for unfairness in the assessment: in consequence of which there was a balance due to the preceding overseer, and the calls of the guardians for contributions to the Union funds could not be met: the parish officers could not make a rate to the best of their judgment and ability, as the two churchwardens were opposed to the two overseers. Requested to have Commissioners' instructions how to proceed under the circumstances; and also inquired whether the money which had been collected under the rate that had been quashed, should be considered as payments on account.

Ans.—If the overseers of Kingswalden are in want of funds for the purposes of their office, it is their duty to levy a rate upon as fair and equal an assessment of the rateable property in the parish as they can make, according to the best of their judgment. If the churchwardens and overseers cannot agree amongst themselves with regard to such an assessment, they must abide the consequences, for the guardians of Hitchin Union must not be kept out of the requisite funds for the relief of the poor, by such disagreements. The Commissioners desire to point out that, under the 1st section of the 41st Geo. 3, c. 23, the sums paid under the rate, which you describe as having been quashed on appeal, are to be taken as payments on account of the next effective rate.

XV.—REGISTRATION.

EXPENSES OF REGISTRATION OF PARLIAMENTARY VOTERS.

April 3rd, 1844.

Auditor of Malmesbury Union, &c. — Stated, that by virtue of the Acts, 2 Wm. 4, c. 45, s. 34, and 6 Vict. c. 18, s. 21, persons whose rights were reserved to vote for members of Parliament for the Borough of Cricklade, in respect of freeholds situated in the parishes of Malmesbury, St. Paul, The Abbey, and St. Mary Westport, within the new borough of Malmesbury, were registered at Norton, the next adjoining parish in the borough of Cricklade. By the first-mentioned statute, s. 56, each borough elector had to pay 1*s.* annually for registering his vote, and the overseers of Norton collected the shillings from the electors, claiming in respect of freeholds in the other three parishes above-mentioned; but by the latter statute, s. 58, the annual payment of 1*s.* by each elector was abolished, and the parish of Norton deprived of its former claim on the individual electors for contributions towards the expenses of registration. By the same statute, s. 55, the expenses incurred by the town-clerk, or returning officer, of any city or borough, in carrying into effect the provisions of the Act, were to be defrayed out of the monies to be collected for the relief of the poor in the several parishes and townships *within the same city or borough;* and he, the auditor, could not discover any provision in the Act to enable the overseers of Norton to compel contributions from the overseers of the other parishes above-named towards the expenses of the register. Requested the opinion of the Commissioners for his guidance.

Ans.—As the recent statute, 6 and 7 Vict. c. 18, provides (s. 57) that the expenses incurred in this matter by the overseers of every parish or township shall be paid from the poor-rates of the *same* parish or township, and (s. 55) that the expenses incured by the town-clerk of any city or borough shall be paid according to a certain rule of proportion from the poor-rates of the several parishes and townships within the *same* city or borough, the Commissioners apprehend that the expenses incurred, whether by the overseers or by the town-clerk, in respect of the registration of voters for the parish of Norton, in the borough of Cricklade, whether such voters derive their qualification within that borough or from freeholds situate in the borough of Malmesbury, must be paid from the poor-rates of the said parish, and cannot be levied or recovered from any parish within the last-named borough. With regard to the propriety of this state of the law, it is beyond the province of the Commissioners to express any opinion.

XVI.—RELATIVES.

NON-LIABILITY OF A WIFE TO MAINTAIN HER HUSBAND AND CHILD.

June 20th, 1844.

Clerk of the Cuckfield Union—Stated, that a man and his wife and child had been removed under an order, to a parish in the Union: they were inmates of the workhouse for a time, when the wife escaped, leaving her husband and child behind: the husband was partially a lunatic, and wholly unable to support himself and family, whilst the wife was capable of maintaining herself and child, and offered to do so if she had been permitted to leave the house with her child. Inquired whether the wife was liable to a conviction under the Vagrant Act for deserting her husband and child.

Ans.—A wife is not liable to be proceeded against under the Vagrant Act for refusing or neglecting to maintain her husband, inasmuch as she is not under any legal obligation to support him. So also as regards the child, the legal obligation to maintain it attaches to the husband as the head of the family, and the wife cannot therefore be proceeded against for the desertion.

XVII.—RELIEF.

MEDICAL RELIEF IN CASES OF URGENT NECESSITY, TO WHAT PARISH TO BE CHARGED.

May 24th, 1844.

Clerk of the Bedminster Union—Stated, that Edward Watts, settled in Yatton, but resident in Clevedon, both in the Bedminster Union, before the confinement of his wife, made application for an order for the attendance of the medical officer on her during her confinement, which application the guardians, taking into consideration the husband's circumstances, (being an able-bodied man not in receipt of relief, but constantly employed,) refused to accede to. Subsequently the overseers of Clevedon, in which parish the family resided, gave an order to the medical officer to attend the woman; and under such order application was made to the guardians for payment of the fee for the attendance. The guardians considered they were liable to pay this fee, but requested to have the Commissioners' opinion as to whether it should be charged to the settlement parish (Yatton,) or to Clevedon, where the woman was resident, and the overseer of which directed the medical officer to attend the case.

Ans.—Assuming that the case was one of sudden and urgent necessity, in which the overseer of Clevedon was justified in giving an order for the medical officer's attendance, under Art. 1 of the Commissioners' General Order, relating to the duties of overseers, (22nd April, 1842,) the guardians are bound to pay the medical officer the fee authorised by the General Medical Order. The parish of Clevedon, where the woman was residing, is clearly liable in the first instance to provide the relief. The Commissioners, however, are of opinion that the guardians may, at their discretion, afford non-resident relief to paupers within the Union; that is to say, they may give relief to a pauper residing in one parish of the Union, at the charge of another parish in the same Union, if the pauper be settled in such other parish. Supposing Watts to belong to Yatton, the guardians may therefore, if they think fit, charge the medical officer's fee to that parish. The Commissioners do not consider that this discretionary power of the guardians would be affected, by the circumstance of the order for the medical officer's attendance having been given by the overseer of Clevedon; for, although the order was given by him, the fee will be paid by the guardians, and it will consequently rest with them to charge the payment in the accounts.

XVIII.—RELIEVING OFFICERS.

EMPLOYED IN REMOVING LUNATICS TO ASYLUMS.

April 25th, 1844.

Clerk of St. Thomas's Union—Stated, that a doubt was entertained by the board of guardians as to the propriety of permitting relieving officers to be absent from their districts for one or more days, for the purpose of conveying lunatic paupers to asylums, and requested the opinion and instructions of the Commissioners on the subject.

Ans.—The Commissioners think it generally undesirable that the relieving officers should leave their districts, particularly for any long period; and certainly no duties should be assigned to them which would materially interfere with their more immediate duty of administering relief to the poor. At the same time, if their absence from their district should not exceed a single day, and would occasion no material inconvenience, the Commissioners do not say that the guardians might not employ them in conveying lunatic paupers to asylums, care being taken to provide for any emergency that might arise during their absence. The Commissioners do not think it necessary that the relieving officers should be solely entrusted with the conveyance of lunatic paupers to an asylum. Any other person might, in the opinion of the Commissioners, be employed by the guardians for this purpose. The Commissioners refer the guardians to the provisions of section 6 of 5 and 6 Vict. c. 57.

XIX.—REMOVAL.

1. COSTS OF APPEAL AGAINST AN ORDER OF.

March 29th, 1844.

The Overseers of St. James, Dover—Stated, that John Betts and his wife became chargeable to the parish of St. Sepulchre, in the city of London: an examination of the pauper was taken, wherein he stated he had been a yearly servant to Mr. Richard Marsh, of Farthlingoe, in the parish of St. James, Dover; and an order was made for his removal to that parish. Farthlingoe, however, is in the parish of Hougham, and the parish of St. James therefore appealed against the order, and although information was given to St. Sepulchre of the above fact, they had the appeal tried at the City of London Quarter Sessions, on the 30th of June last, and of course were defeated. A bill of charges in the matter had been delivered to the overseers by the vestry clerk, the Lord Mayor and Recorder of the city of London having, as it was alleged, refused to allow any expenses to the parish of St. James. Inquired whether there was any appeal from the decision of the Lord Mayor and Recorder.

Ans.—The ordering of costs in cases of appeals against orders of removal appears to be a matter within the discretion of the justices. In a case which occurred apparently under the 8th and 9th Will. 3, c. 30, s. 3, a writ of mandamus requiring the justices of Nottingham to allow costs, was quashed upon the ground that the court held it reasonable for the justices to have the power of judging whether costs should be allowed or not, (R. *v.* Justices of Nottingham, 2 Bott.) The terms of the eighty-second section of the Poor Law Amendment Act are more extended even than those of the third section of the above-named statute,—it provides that the justices "*shall* award and order the party for whom, and in whose behalf such appeal shall be determined, such costs and charges in the law, as by the said justices in their discretion shall be thought most reasonable and just;" the former enacts, that the justices "shall, and may, if they think fit, order and direct," &c. The Commissioners therefore think that as the magistrates in the present case have refused to award costs, the parish of St. James has no remedy in the matter as against the parish of St. Sepulchre.

---

2. COST OF SERVING NOTICE OF A SUSPENDED ORDER OF REMOVAL, BY WHOM TO BE PAID.

June 8th, 1844.

Clerk of the Stow-on-the-Wold Union—Stated, that the guardians of the Stow-on-the-Wold Union had received from the parish officers of St. Margaret Leicester, a demand for £10. 9*s*. 10*d*. the cost of "relief given to John Johns, of Stow parish, under orders of removal suspended from October last;" and for £2. 11*s*. 6*d*. the cost of "serving notice of the same." The guardians admitted the pauper's settlement, and did not object to repay the cost of the relief; but they considered that they were not legally bound to pay the cost of serving the notice, and requested the Commissioners' opinion on the point.

Ans.—The expense attendant on a personal service of a suspended order of removal, is recoverable under the 2nd sec. of the 35th Geo. 3, c. 101, as one of the charges incurred in consequence of the suspension of the order. The 84th sec. of the Poor Law Amendment Act, requires the notice of a suspended order to be "given" to the overseers; whereas, the 79th sec. expressly allows a common order to be "sent by post." This difference in the phraseology of the two sections renders it advisable that notice of a suspended order should be served personally; and the expenses incurred therein, appear to the Commissioners to be recoverable accordingly. But the Commissioners do not consider the expense of removing the pauper, to be recoverable from the receiving parish. It is clear that the removal does not take place in consequence of the suspension of the order, and that therefore the expense of the removal is not a charge incurred by reason of the suspension.

---

3. BY WHOM THE REMOVAL OF PAUPERS TO THEIR PLACES OF SETTLEMENT IS TO BE UNDERTAKEN.

June 14th, 1844.

Clerk of the Guardians of St. Mary, Rotherhithe—Inquired, whether the guardians could authorise any other persons than their paid officers to take the charge of the removal of paupers to their place of settlement; lately the assistant relieving officer had done this duty, but much inconvenience had arisen by his absence whilst so engaged. A pauper was about to be removed to Berwick-upon-Tweed, which would take four or five days to effect: the master of the vessel might be induced to take the charge and delivery of the pauper to the overseers at Berwick, provided the guardians could sanction such a proceeding, of the legality of which they were doubtful.

Ans.—The removal of paupers is a matter within the province of the overseers, and one in which the law does not impose any duty upon the guardians. The overseers, however, may, under the 10th section of the 54th Geo. 3, c. 170, employ any proper person or persons whomsoever to carry, remove, and deliver any pauper or paupers ordered to be removed by any justices; and the removal of the pauper by such person or persons shall be as effectual as if made by the overseers themselves.

---

4. WHETHER ONE MEMBER OF A FAMILY, WHO HAS BECOME CHARGEABLE, CAN BE REMOVED WITHOUT THE HEAD OF THE FAMILY.

June 21st, 1844.

Clerk of the Cirencester Union—Stated, that an order had been obtained for the removal of H., his wife, and five children, and that the order had been suspended on account of the sickness of the eldest daughter, aged twenty years. The removal was to take place in consequence of relief to this daughter, as neither the father nor any other part of his family had received or required relief. Inquired whether by reason of her age the daughter is not emancipated, and whether the order of removal should not be confined to her alone; and if there are good grounds of appeal against the order.

Ans.—If the daughter in question is unmarried, and has resided with her father from infancy, and has not acquired any settlement in her own right, she is not emancipated by reason of her age. The Commissioners are not aware of any judicial determination of the question, whether the relief of an unemancipated child, above the age of sixteen years, renders the father liable to be removed. The decisions with regard to certificated persons seem, however, to involve the principle upon which such a question must be decided. In the case of R. *v.* Framlingham (Burr. T. C. 748) Aston, J. gave it as his opinion, "That if several persons resided in a parish under the same certificate, the asking relief by a single one of them would not render the rest removeable." This conclusion would no longer be tenable with respect to children under sixteen years of age, since the passing of the Poor Law Amendment Act (see section 56) ; but it appears to be still applicable to all children above that age receiving relief without their parents. The Commissioners, therefore, think it probable that the young woman you refer to might be legally separated from her father, and removed alone. The Commissioners will add, that this question was suggested in the case of R. *v.* Mile End Old Town (5 Nev. and Man. 581,) though no decision was given upon it. In that case the immediate question at issue was of a similar character, but it was raised with reference to the removal of a pauper to Ireland, under 3 and 4 Wm. 4, c. 40. In delivering judgment, Patteson, J., observed—"We are of opinion that the provision in the 55th section of 4 and 5 Wm. 4, c, 76, as to the age up to which the parent is to be deemed answerable for relief given to a child, viz., sixteen (*whatever might have been its effect upon relief given to a child above that age, as to the chargeability of the parent, if the parties had been English, on which we give no opinion,*) does not apply to the present case, depending, as it has already been stated it does, on the 3rd and 4th Wm. 4, c. 40, s. 2."

XX.—SETTLEMENT.

1. Of Bastard, where the mother afterwards married, and her husband had died.

June 8th, 1844.

Clerk of the Docking Union—Stated, that Mary Williamson, widow, aged 31, (formerly Mary Roy,) on the 21st April, 1834, was confined with an illegitimate child in the parish of Burnham Westgate, where she then lived, and in which she was settled. In the year 1837 she married Thomas Williamson, of Burnham Sutton, farm-labourer, on which she, with the child, followed her husband's settlement. In March, 1843, the man died, since which time the parish officers of Burnham Sutton considered the child to belong to Burnham Westgate, and claimed a year's maintenance of the latter parish for the child. Inquired, whether the child actually belonged to Burnham Westgate; and, if so, whether the parish of Burnham Sutton could claim a year's maintenance.

Ans.—As the bastard child alluded to was born before the passing of the Poor Law Amendment Act, it will not follow its mother's settlement under the 71st section of that Act, but it still belongs to the parish of its birth, which appears to be Burnham Westgate. The child being above the age of nurture, may now be removed to that parish ; but the Commissioners know of no authority under which the parish of Burnham Sutton can recover from Burnham Westgate the relief already afforded to the child, which while it was residing in Burnham Sutton that parish was bound to provide.

2. By renting a Tenement and Garden separately.

June 20th, 1844.

Mr. Smith, Relieving Officer, South Hetton—Inquired, whether A., who occupied a tenement for upwards of four years at £8 per annum, and paid rates and taxes in respect thereof, and also a garden, by a separate holding, for which he paid £6 per annum, both holdings being in the same township, had gained a settlement in that township.

Ans.—The Commissioners see no reason to suppose that the house rented at £8 and the garden rented at £6 per annum, cannot be added together for the purpose of conferring a settlement upon the tenant. The 59th Geo. 3, c. 50, the 6th Geo. 4, c. 57, and the 1st Wm. 4, c. 18, all hold the same language upon this point. They all require the tenement to consist "of a dwelling-house or building, or of land, *or of both.*" In R. *v.* North Collingham (a case very similar to the present) a man rented a house and garden in North Collingham at £6 6*s.* a year, and also a piece of garden-ground in the same parish at £3 15*s.* a year ; and in reference to the terms of the 59 Geo. 3, c. 50, this was deemed sufficient to confer a settlement, (1 B. and C. 578.)

XXI.—TREASURER.

1. Payments under contribution orders.

Clerk of ——— *Union*—Stated, in replying to an inquiry of the Commissioners, as to the account on which the treasurer held the separate monies of certain parishes in the ——— Union at the time of the suspension of payment by the bank in which he deposited the Union funds, that such separate monies were held by him on account of the overseers of those parishes which had paid *instalments* only in respect of the orders of contribution made upon them ;

his practice having been to place such payments to the account of the overseers until the whole of the amounts mentioned in the orders were paid, when they were transferred to the general account of the Union.

Ans.—The course adopted by the treasurer in this matter was not the correct one. Though the treasurer may, perhaps, decline to receive payment of orders for contributions by instalments, the Commissioners think that if he receive any instalments, he can only receive them on account of the Union at large; and therefore that the monies in question ought to be treated as belonging to the Union. The consequence will be, that if they are actually lost, the loss must fall on the Union at large, and not on the particular parishes by whose overseers the sums were paid.

---

2. WHETHER AN UNPAID TREASURER IS ELIGIBLE AS GUARDIAN.

June 19*th*, 1844.

Clerk of the Stow Union—Stated that Mr. Hart, who held the office of treasurer, but without deriving any emolument therefrom, was elected guardian of a parish in the Union, and requested the Commissioners to issue an order for a fresh election, as it was considered illegal that a treasurer should hold the office of guardian.

Ans.—According to the bond given by the treasurer, it is clear that Mr. Hart is treasurer of the Union. He has no salary, and derives no profit from holding that office. Under the circumstances, there is no reason for Mr. Hart's resigning the office of guardian because of his being treasurer; neither is he incompetent to act as guardian.

XXII.—VALUATION.

NO LICENCE OR STAMP REQUIRED UNDER THE PAROCHIAL ASSESSMENTS ACT.

June 15*th*, 1844.

Mr. J. Edwards, Overseer, Lampeter Union—Inquired, whether by the Parochial Assessments act a licence is required by the valuation of property to the poor's rate, in case of an appeal, and whether the valuation should be stamped.

Ans.—Guided by the decision in the case of Atkinson *v.* Fell, (5 M. and S. 240,) the Commissioners consider that a person appointed under the 6 and 7 Wm. 4, c. 96, to make a valuation of the rateable property of a parish, need not take out an appraiser's license; and that a valuation made by a person so appointed does not require a stamp. In Atkinson *v.* Fell, it was held that a valuation of the parish lands, made by two parishioners appointed by the parish officers, with a view of assisting them to equalise the poor-rate, did not require a stamp. It was intimated by the court that, had such valuation required a stamp, then the persons making it ought to have had a licence, which, it appears, they had not. It would seem from that decision that a person need only take out a licence where the valuation to be made by him is intended to be binding between parties, or where a certain benefit, or right of action, is to result from it, and not where the valuation is not obligatory upon parties, but merely designed for their private information. A valuation made in pursuance of the 6 and 7 Wm. 4, c. 96, is intended for the guidance of the overseers, and is not binding upon them, (see Reg. *v.* Lord Yarborough, 12 A. and E. 416.)

XXIII.—WORKHOUSE.

REFUSAL OF PAUPERS TO QUIT WORKHOUSE.

June 5*th*, 1844.

Chairman of the Llanelly Union—Referred to the case of James Adams, Droxford Union, (Official Circular, No. 34) and the inadequacy of the existing provisions for the punishment of paupers who refused to leave the workhouse when employment was offered to them, and requested the Commissioners' directions as to how guardians and justices were to act under such circumstances.

Ans.—No change was made by the Poor Law Amendment Act in the law affecting the power of the authorities to refuse relief. Wherever the overseers could refuse relief, the guardians have power to refuse now, but in both cases that power of refusal is exercised under a certain responsibility. No doubt exists, if it was to be shown before justices that a man neglected or refused to maintain his family, being able wholly or in part so to do, and by such neglect or refusal became chargeable to the parish, that he would be punishable under section 3 of the Vagrant Act.

LONDON:

Printed by Order of the Poor Law Commissioners, by BLACKBURN and PARDON, 6, Hatton Garden, and Published by CHARLES KNIGHT and Co., 22, Ludgate Street, Publishers to the Poor Law Commissioners.

AN

OFFICIAL CIRCULAR

OF PUBLIC DOCUMENTS AND INFORMATION:

DIRECTED BY THE POOR LAW COMMISSIONERS TO BE PRINTED, CHIEFLY FOR THE USE OF THE MEMBERS AND PERMANENT OFFICERS OF BOARDS OF GUARDIANS, UNDER THE POOR LAW AMENDMENT ACT.

No. 37. CIRCULAR ISSUED JULY 31, 1844.

Poor Law Commission Office,
Somerset House,
31*st July,* 1844.

THE Poor Law Commissioners, on a review of their Minutes, directed that the Minutes of Correspondence on the following subjects be printed and circulated for the information of Guardians and Officers of the several Unions, viz:—

By Order of the Board,

EDWIN CHADWICK, *Secretary.*

ASSISTANT OVERSEER.—AS TO WHETHER HE IS EMPOWERED TO GRANT ORDERS FOR MEDICAL RELIEF.

6th June, 1844.

Mr. J. Mayes, Send, near Ripley—Inquired, whether an assistant-overseer had the same powers as overseers in granting orders for medical relief.

Ans.—An assistant-overseer appointed under the statute (59 Geo. 3, c. 12,) has such of the powers and duties of an overseer of the poor as are named in his warrant of appointment. The order of the Commissioners of the 22nd April, 1842, (duties of overseers,) enables an overseer to give orders for medical relief in any case of sudden and dangerous illness. Article 9 of that order would extend the same power to an assistant-overseer, assuming that the giving of relief was one of the duties assigned to him by the warrant of appointment. And generally the Commissioners would observe, that where an assistant-overseer is by the terms of his appointment authorised to perform such duties as appertain to an overseer of the poor, it would be competent to such assistant-overseer to give relief in any case in which an overseer could lawfully do so, under the 54th section of the Poor Law Amendment Act.

II.—AUDITOR.

1. ELIGIBILITY OF A PERSON IN THE SERVICE OF THE CLERK TO BE AUDITOR.

25th May, 1844.

Mr. ——— —Stated, that he held a situation in the office of the clerk of the Union; and inquired whether that circumstance would be an objection to his holding the office of auditor to the Union.

Ans.—The Commissioners think there is an obvious objection to allowing the appointment of auditor of a Union to be held by any one who fills a situation in the office of the clerk of the Union, and who would thus have to audit the accounts of the gentleman in whose service he is engaged. The Commissioners could not, therefore, consent to such an arrangement.

---

2. POWERS OF AUDITORS APPOINTED UNDER THE ORDERS OF THE POOR LAW COMMISSIONERS.

The following circulars have been issued by the Poor Law Commissioners on this subject:—

11th July, 1844.

Sir,

I am directed by the Poor Law Commissioners to transmit for the information of the guardians, a copy of a circular letter which the Commissioners have caused to be sent to all auditors appointed under their orders.

The guardians will probably deem it expedient to communicate to the several parish officers within their union the general purport of that letter.

I am, Sir,
Your obedient Servant,
W. G. LUMLEY, *Assistant Secretary.*

To the Clerk to the Guardians of the Union.

8th July, 1844.

Sir,

I am directed by the Poor Law Commissioners to transmit to you for your guidance, a copy of a judgment pronounced during the last term by the Court of Queen's Bench, in a case of *The Queen on the prosecution of the Poor Law Commissioners v. The Governors and Directors of the Poor of St. Andrew Holborn above Bars, and St. George the Martyr.*

You will observe from this decision that it is your duty to inquire into the expenditure by the overseers, or other parochial officers, within your district, of the whole of the monies raised by them under the name of the poor-rate, whether the expenditure by them be strictly confined to the relief of the poor or relate to any other object, and that if the accounts of such expenditure have not hitherto been laid before you, you must henceforth require them to be produced.

It is right, at the same time, to notice that these officers are not responsible for the expenditure by other parties of such sums as they are called upon by law to pay out of the poor-rates to such parties for specific application; thus, the overseers are not answerable for the expenditure by the guardians, of the contributions which they have called for, or by the Justices, of the sums paid to the county-rate, or for the application of the sums paid to the Police Commissioners, or to the treasurer of the borough, where police or borough-rates are made.

In these cases you will only require the production of the proper orders upon the overseers, or other vouchers, by which the amounts paid by them are legally demanded.

I am, Sir,
Your obedient Servant,
W. G. LUMLEY, *Assistant Secretary.*

To the Auditor of the Union.

IN THE QUEEN'S BENCH.

Westminster Hall,
8th June, 1844.

THE QUEEN, *v.* THE GOVERNORS AND DIRECTORS OF ST. ANDREW, HOLBORN ABOVE BARS, AND ST. GEORGE THE MARTYR.

JUDGMENT.

LORD DENMAN.—In the case of the Queen against the Governors and Directors of St. Andrew Holborn above Bars, and St. George the Martyr, and their Collector, there were two questions proposed for our consideration—first, whether the defendants, having accounted to the auditor under the local Act of the 6th of George the 4th, were also bound to account to the auditor appointed under the order of the Poor Law Commissioners; — secondly, whether, if they were bound to account to the auditor, the account rendered by them as stated in the case is sufficient.

With respect to the first question, the powers of the auditors under the local Act are so inadequate to the performance of the duties required of the auditor appointed under the order of the Poor Law Commissioners, having no power to disallow any of the items in the account, that we are clearly of opinion that the defendants were bound to account to the latter auditor, although they had already accounted to the auditor under the local Act. This part of the case was indeed scarcely contested on the part of the defendants, and was in effect settled by the decision of this court in the case of the Alstonfield Union, in the 11th Adolphus and Ellis, p. 558.

With respect to the second question, it was contended on the part of the defendants that they were not bound to render an account to the auditors appointed under the order of the Poor Law Commissioners of *all the money* collected by them under the rate denominated *the poor-rate*, which is partly applicable to other purposes than the relief of the poor, but only so much of the produce of the rate as was raised for and applied to the purposes of the relief of the poor.

The defendants made a rate of one shilling and two-pence in the pound for the relief, maintenance, lodging, and employment of the poor, which by estimation would produce a sum of upwards of £6000, but of this not much more than half was applied or intended to be applied to the relief of the poor, the residue was applied, and intended to be applied to the police-rate and county-rate, and in payment of principal and interest due in respect of debts contracted under the authority of the local Act, and salaries and expenses attending the carrying of the local Act into effect.

The defendants did account for so much of the money raised under the rate as had been applied and was intended to be applied to the relief and maintenance of the poor, but objected to account for the residue which was raised for and applied to other purposes, and whether they are bound to do so, is in fact the question.

It is not necessary to refer to the local Act, as the question turns entirely on the Poor Law Amendment Act, and applies undoubtedly to every parish in England, where the poor-rate is in part applicable to the payment of the county-rates, police-rate, or *any other expenses*, than the relief and maintenance of the poor.

By the 46th section of the Poor Law Amendment Act, the Commissioners may direct the guardians of any parish or union to appoint an officer for the examining, auditing, and allowing or disallowing of accounts of such parish or union, or united parishes; and may define, and specify, and direct the execution of the duties of such officers, and the places or limits within which the same shall be performed.

In pursuance of this power, the Commissioners did direct the guardians of the Holborn Union, of which the district in question forms a part, to appoint an auditor, whose duties were specified to be, among others, to audit the accounts of the said union, and of the several parishes comprised therein, at proper times, and to examine whether the expenditure in all cases was such as might lawfully be made, and to strike out such payments and charges as were not authorised by some provision of law or the order of the Commissioners.

By the 47th section of the Poor Law Amendment Act, every person having the collection, receipt, or distribution of the monies raised for the relief of the poor in any parish or union; or holding or accountable for any balance relating to the relief of the poor, or the collection or distribution of the poor-rate of any parish or union, shall, where the orders of the Commissioners shall have come in force, as often as the said orders shall direct, make and render to the guardians, auditor, or such other persons as by virtue of any statute or custom, or of the said orders, may be appointed to examine, audit, allow, or disallow such accounts, a full and distinct account in writing of all monies, matters, and things committed to their charge; or received, held, or expended by them on behalf of any such parish or union; and all balances due from any person having the control and distribution of the poor-rate, or accountable for such balances, may be recovered in the same manner as any penalties are recoverable under the Act.

Two things may be observed in this section—first, the accounts are to be rendered to a person appointed either by statute, custom, or order of the Poor Law Commissioners, to examine, audit, allow, or disallow such accounts; and secondly, that the account is to be made of *all monies*, matters and things committed to their charge, or received, held, or expended by them on behalf of the parish or union, and the balance may be recovered under the Act.

The auditors under the local Act do not, as already observed, possess the power required for an auditor under this section: they have no power to disallow accounts, but the auditor appointed under the order of the Commissioners does possess the power, and is therefore the person to whom the accounts should be rendered under the terms of the 47th section.

With respect to the accounts themselves, the terms of the 46th and 47th sections of the Act include *all monies* held by the parties accounting on behalf of the parish or union, and would therefore apply to all money raised by the poor-rate. And it is also to be observed, that in the description of the persons who are to account given in the beginning of the early part of the 47th section, persons holding or accountable for any money or balance relating to the relief of the poor, or the collection or distribution of the poor-rate are mentioned.

It appears to us therefore, that by the terms of the 46th and 47th sections of the Poor Law Amendment Act, as applied to this case, the defendants were bound to account to the auditor appointed under the order of the Poor Law Commissioners *not only for so much of the money raised by the poor-rate, as was raised for and applied to the relief and maintenance of the poor, but for the whole amount of the money raised by the poor-rate*, and that the auditor may insist on ascertaining the amount of balance of the whole rate in the hands of the accountant.

There is but one rate levied, and that professedly for the relief, maintenance, lodging, and employment of the poor; and even although the inquiry into the mode of disposing of the proceeds of the rate may introduce matters foreign to the direct and avowed object of the rate, this is but a necessary incident in the inquiry, and seems to have been contemplated by the legislature when a remedy is provided for the recovery of the balance in the hands of the accountant, obviously meaning the balance of the whole rate levied for the relief, maintenance, lodging, and employment of the poor.

We are therefore of opinion that the verdict which has been entered for the prosecutors should stand.

III.—BASTARDY.

PROSPECTIVE PAYMENT BY PUTATIVE FATHER.

29th January, 1844.

Churchwarden, Luxborough, Williton Union—Stated, that the parish of Luxborough had just received £50 from the putative father of a bastard child, to defray the cost of its maintenance, and inquired whether the money could be applied to the use of the parish in lieu of collecting a poor-rate for the current quarter.

Ans.—The taking of a sum of money in gross, as a discharge of the future liability of the putative father of a bastard child, has been decided to be altogether an illegal transaction; and the balance of any sum so paid, remaining unexpended in the relief of the child, may at any time be recovered back by the putative father in an action at law, (Cole *v.* Gower, 6 East 110; Clarke *v.* Johnson, 11 Moore 319.)

IV.—BURIAL OF PAUPERS.

24th Feb. 1844.

Clerk of Wellington Union, (Salop.)—Stated, that an able-bodied man, out of work, had applied for relief, to enable him to bury his child; the man came from Bishop's Castle (his settlement) to Wellington, where he then resided. Inquired, which parish should bear the expense of the funeral of the child; and whether relief of this kind was sufficient chargeability upon which to ground an order of removal.

Ans.—Relief given to a pauper to enable him to provide for the burial of his child, seems to the Commissioners to stand on the same footing as all other relief; consequently, the parish in which the pauper resides, is primarily liable to furnish it; the parish to which he belongs is under no obligation to repay it; and if he receives it from the parish of his residence, thereby becoming chargeable, he will be removable to the parish of his settlement.*

V.—CLERKS.

1. DISMISSAL OF CLERKS OF BOARDS OF GUARDIANS BY ORDERS UNDER THE HANDS AND SEAL OF THE POOR LAW COMMISSIONERS.

July, 1844.

The Commissioners took into their consideration the obstruction to the public business which was experienced from the want of attention on the part of the clerks of two Unions to letters addressed to them by the Commissioners, and also from their habitual failure to transmit to the Commissioners the abstracts of accounts and other returns in due time; and the Commissioners felt it to be their duty to remove these officers, for which purpose they issued orders under their hands and seal, dated the 17th and 22nd July, 1844.

The Commissioners read a report made by one of their Assistant-Commissioners, on an inquiry instituted by him into the conduct of the clerk of a board of guardians, together with the evidence taken by the Assistant-Commissioner on such inquiry, by which it appeared, that the clerk had neglected to see that certain contracts had been duly executed, and at the proper time,—that he had procured the irregular execution of contracts,—and that he had attempted to deceive the auditor in regard thereto. It further appeared, that the attention of the Commissioners had been, on a previous occasion, called to the conduct of the clerk as returning officer on the election of guardians, which was characterised by great carelessness, and that he was then warned of the consequences which would follow any subsequent failure in the proper discharge of his duties. The Commissioners after carefully considering the circumstances of the case, were of opinion that the interest of the public service called for the removal of this officer, and they issued an order for that purpose, under their hands and seal, dated 26th July, 1844.

2. PROFESSIONAL REMUNERATION TO CLERKS.

16th April, 1844.

Clerk of Winslow Union—Stated, that he had sent in a bill to one of the parishes in the Winslow Union, for professional services in a case of removal, as attorney to the parish, and for fees, as magistrates' clerk; but an objection had been raised to the bill, on the ground that the charges ought to be considered as satisfied by his salary as clerk to the Union. Requested, the Commissioners' opinion as to whether the charges were such as ought fairly to be placed to the account of the parish.

Ans.—Although the clerk of a Union who is a solicitor is bound by the Commissioners' General Order of 21st April, 1842, Art. 17, No. 7, to conduct the legal business of the Union, he is under no such obligation to act professionally for the several parishes in the Union. The removal of paupers is a matter within the province of the overseers, and not of the guardians, and the Commissioners accordingly consider, that if the overseers employ in such a matter the Union clerk, he is entitled to be paid in the same way as any other solicitor would be. In like manner, the Commissioners think that the offices of clerk to the guardians and of clerk to the justices being essentially distinct, the accident of their being held at any time by the same person would not affect his right to the distinct emoluments of each, or render the salary attached to the one a remuneration for the duties connected with the other.

* See sec. 31 of 7 and 8 Vic. cap. 101.

VI.—CONSTABLES' CHARGES.

9th Feb. 1844.

Clerk of Todmorden Union. — Stated, that a late constable of the township of Todmorden and Walsden had presented to the Board of Guardians an account against the overseers of that township, which contained a charge of £5. 9*s.* for the expenses of juries in five cases of inquest; and a charge of 18*s.* for attending the Petty Sessions, by order of the magistrates. The remainder of the charges were for small sums advanced by way of relief to persons in want and travelling through the township. The sum of £2. 9*s.* 7*d.* was paid to the constable, on account of the bill, about a year ago. Inquired, whether the overseers could legally discharge the balance of the bill out of the poor-rates: and added, that the practice of paying these expenses in the township had been discontinued.

Ans.—The expenses of holding coroners' inquests (which are expressly made a charge upon the county rate by the 1st Vict. c. 68,) cannot be lawfully defrayed out of the poor-rate. The usage to which you refer in this matter, does not affect the illegality of the payment; nor have the Commissioners any power to remove that illegality, by any sanction of theirs. The Commissioners are not aware that the constable has any authority to give relief from the poor-rates. And as, in the present case, the relief was given before the commencement of the present parochial year, the Commissioners think that the Guardians could not burden the present rate-payers with the charge, by adopting the acts of the constable. The legality of the payment for attendance at the Sessions, would depend upon the table of fees established for the district, and the order of the justices in the case.

VII.—GUARDIAN.

1. QUALIFICATION OF EX-OFFICIO GUARDIAN.

11th June, 1844.

Mr. ———, *Lichfield* — Inquired, first, whether an acting Magistrate of a county, residing in an extra-parochial place, was, by reason of such residence, qualified to sit as an ex-officio Guardian of the Union within which such extra-parochial place was situate; and, secondly, whether a Magistrate for a borough, being a city and county, but who did not reside within the county of the city or borough for which he acted, was entitled to sit as an ex-officio member of a Board of Guardians, the parishes comprising the city or borough forming a part of the Union.

Ans.—1. If the extra-parochial place be a place maintaining its own poor, it would probably be held to come within the meaning of the word "Parish," as used in the 38th section of the Poor Law Amendment Act; and that, consequently, if such place be included in any Union, any Justice of the Peace residing in such place, and acting for the county, &c., in which the same is situate, would be entitled to act ex-officio as a Guardian of such Union. If, however, it be not a place maintaining its own poor, the Commissioners conceive that residence within it would not serve to qualify a Justice to act as an ex-officio Guardian. 2. The Commissioners entertain no doubt that a Justice who does not reside in the county, &c. for which he acts, is not qualified to be an ex-officio Guardian, according to the 38th section of the Poor Law Amendment Act. That section requires as the qualification of an ex-officio Guardian, that he should be a Justice of the Peace, residing in some parish, and acting for the county, &c., in which that parish is situate. If, therefore, he does not reside within the county, &c. for which he acts as Justice, he does not come within the description given in the statute.*

2. COMPATIBILITY OF OFFICES OF EX-OFFICIO GUARDIAN AND CHURCHWARDEN.

16th May, 1844.

Clerk of Leamington Union—Stated, that one of the ex-officio guardians had lately been appointed churchwarden of a parish, within the division for which he acted as magistrate. Inquired, whether the office of churchwarden and that of a justice of the peace are compatible; and also, whether he could not act as an ex-officio guardian whilst holding the office of churchwarden.

Ans.—Looking to the fact, that a churchwarden is, by virtue of his office, an overseer of the poor, the Commissioners are disposed to think that the offices of justices of the peace and churchwardens are probably incompatible, on the view expressed by Lord Kenyon in Rex *v.* Pateman, 2 T. R. 779, as to the effect of Rex *v.* Gwyer, 1 Burr. 245, 1 Bott. 14. The Commissioners are not aware of anything to prevent the gentleman, to whom the clerk refers, from acting as an ex-officio guardian during his year of office as churchwarden, if he is capable of taking the latter office at all.

---

* See sec. 24 of 7 and 8 Vic. cap. 101.

VIII.—LUNATIC.

Maintenance of a Criminal Lunatic.

20*th May*, 1844.

Clerk of Kettering Union—Stated, that the Guardians had been informed that the care and expenses incident to the confinement of criminal lunatics usually devolve upon the Government; and inquired what course the Guardians should pursue in order to get Thos. Briggs, a criminal lunatic, who had been confined for several years in the Asylum near Nottingham, at a considerable expense to the parish of Kettering, placed under the Government charge.

Ans.—The Commissioners are not aware of any general liability attaching to the Government to provide for the maintenance of criminal lunatics. The statutes on the subject (within whose provisions the case mentioned in the Clerk's letter appear to fall,) cast the burden of the maintenance on the parish of the lunatic's settlement, or, in lack of a settlement, on the county. (See 9th Geo. 4th, c. 40; 1st Vic. c. 14; 3rd and 4th Vic. c. 54.)

IX.—MARRIED WOMAN.

Deserting her Husband and Family.

26*th Feb.* 1844.

Clerk of Bridge Union—Stated, that the wife of an able-bodied man had left him on the ground of cruelty, and refused to return to him; and he had, from the want of some one to attend to his children, become a pauper. The man offered to take his wife back; she, however, refused to go, but sought for no relief. Inquired, what course the Guardians should pursue in such a case, further than take the man and his children into the house.

Ans.—The only remedy in the case above referred to, is a suit for restitution of conjugal rights; and this, the *Guardians* cannot take advantage of.

X.—MEDICAL OFFICER.

Whether bound to supply cotton, wool, and calico, for pauper patients.

6*th May*, 1844.

Clerks to Haltwhistle Union—Stated, that an in-door pauper, belonging to the Union, had, for upwards of a year been afflicted with cancer in his face, to dress which, a considerable quantity of cotton-wool and calico was required, the expense of which, amounting to about 1*s.* 6*d.* per week, had hitherto been charged to the establishment, the medical officer not considering himself bound to provide such articles. Inquired, whether the medical officer was bound to find these appliances.

Ans.—The Commissioners are of opinion that, as the articles in question are not such as a medical man would furnish to a private patient, they are not within the terms "medical and surgical appliances," in the General Order of the Commissioners on "duties of officers;" and, therefore, that they should be furnished at the expense of the Union.

XI.—OVERSEERS.

Duties of Overseers in assessing to the Poor-rate.

16*th April*, 1844.

Overseer of Coed Frank, Neath Union—Stated that there were several coal and copper works in the hamlet, which had of late years considerably increased in size and in the extent of their operations. In consequence of these works being rated much too low, a new valuation was made in September last, which occasioned them to be assessed at double the sum at which they were rated under the old valuation. The proprietors of the works were anxious for the appointment of overseers for the ensuing year, who would cancel the new valuation. Requested the Commissioners, therefore, to take some steps for compelling the adoption of the new valuation.

Ans.—The appointment of overseers is a matter within the discretion of the justices, with which the Commissioners have nothing to do. Nor can the Commissioners express any opinion with regard to the amount at which the property in question (presuming them to be rateable) ought to be assessed. With regard to the adoption of the new valuation, the decision in the case of the Queen *v.* the Earl of Yarborough, and another, (12 A. and E. 416; 2 Lumley 51,) shows that it is not imperative on the overseers to follow the valuation, if they deem it inaccurate. Lord Denman observed: "The valuation makes no difference. It is certainly convenient that the overseers should be furnished with such means of knowledge; but still they are to exercise their judgment." And Mr. Justice Littledale: "The parish officers may do wisely to adopt the valuation, but they are not bound to do so; they may find gross mistakes in it." At the same time, if the overseers, in laying the poor-rate, assess any property at an amount below that at which it ought to be rated, any rate-payer aggrieved thereby, or having any material objection to urge against the sum so charged, may appeal against the rate under the 17th Geo. 2, c. 38, s. 4, and if the overseers depart from an authorised valuation without sufficient ground, they would incur considerable responsibility.

XII.—PAUPERS.

1. CHARGEABILITY OF.

8th June, 1844.

Chairman of the Wellington Union, Somerset—Stated, firstly, that the turnpike road leading from Beam-bridge, the present extreme western station of the Bristol and Exeter railway, passed through the parishes of Culmstock, Burliscombe, and Uffculm, towards all the West of England: in that road, within the distance of a mile and half, or thereabouts, were situated two public inns, and one licensed beer-house; one in each parish: an accident happened to a man in the parish of Burliscombe, and he was carried to the Lamb Inn in the parish of Uffculm, and was there supplied with all necessaries and surgical attendance. Inquired, which parish was to pay the expenses and the surgeon's bill, Burliscombe or Uffculm. Referred to the cases of Tomlinson *v.* Bentall, 5 B. and C., 738, and Lamb *v.* Bunce, 4 M. and S. 275. Secondly. A pauper belonging to the parish of Ashbrittle, in the Wellington Union, but residing in the town of Taunton in the Taunton Union, met with an accident in Taunton. Inquired, whether he should be treated as casual poor, and be relieved by the guardians of Taunton Union, or whether he was a proper subject for a suspended order of removal, and as such, to be relieved by the Wellington Union. - R. *v.* St. James Bury St. Edmunds, 10 East, 25.

Ans.—Firstly. It is presumed that the pauper referred to, was not settled in either of the parishes where the accident happened, or where he was removed to, though this does not affect the case as stated. The liability to relieve, in such cases, does not lie exclusively on the parish where the accident happens; but, if removed without fraud to a place, such as an inn, where the pauper can be most conveniently or readily attended to, he is apparently entitled to be relieved at the expense of the poor-rates of that place. In the present case, the inn was a more proper place of reception, as well as nearer than the beer-house. The carrying to the inn was, therefore, justifiable; and being, apparently, without fraud on the part of the parish of Burliscombe, it would seem that the burden lawfully falls on the parish of Uffculm. The Commissioners need not remark, that the question is one of great nicety, and often depends on some minute point in the individual case. The decisions of the court are, perhaps, somewhat difficult to reconcile. The view just expressed is as precise as the Commissioners can undertake to give, without having all the circumstances of the individual case more fully before them. Secondly. The pauper was resident where the accident occurred. He was there, therefore, with the intention to settle, according to the terms of the statute 13 and 14 Car. 2. c. 12, s. 1. His case was not one of those falling within the rules applicable to casual poor; but he was liable to be placed under an order of removal, to be suspended before execution, if, at the time for its execution he remained unfit to be removed. R. *v.* Oldland, 4 Ad. and E. 929.

2. CHARGEABILITY OF PAUPER, HOW TO BE PROVED.

29th May, 1844.

Clerk of Honiton Union—Transmitted a copy of a certificate of chargeability which had been used by the guardians of the Honiton Union, under the provisions of the 5th and 6th Vic. cap. 57, and called the attention of the Commissioners to the decision in "The Queen, *v.* the Inhabitants of High Bickington," by which it seemed that the word "chargeable" was not sufficient. In the 17th section of the above Act "a certificate of such pauper having become so chargeable," &c. are the words used; and there might be a question whether a certificate, stating that the pauper was receiving relief, would be deemed evidence of that fact. The guardians wished the Commissioners to send them such a form of certificate as they would recommend the guardians to adopt, to meet the case; and at the same time say whether they thought the chargeability could be legally proved in any other manner than by the relieving officer.

Ans.—The Commissioners have referred to two authentic reports of the case of the Queen *v.* High Bickington, one in 8 Jurist, p. 377, and the other in the 13 Law Journal, (n. s.) M. C. 74, and find that the question raised was as to the sufficiency of the examinations of the pauper and the relieving officer, both of whom stated that the former was *chargeable*, but no fact was alleged of relief having been given. The court decided that there should have been evidence of relief having been given, and that the allegation by the witnesses of chargeability merely, was not sufficient. The court had not before them a certificate of chargeability given in conformity with the provisions of the 5 and 6 Vic. c. 57, and it may be a question whether the court would consider such a certificate of itself evidence of chargeability. If not, it does not appear to the Commissioners that the guardians can give that effect to the certificate by introducing any other words into it, not warranted by the statute. It is right, however, to refer to the statute, and it will be seen, that the legislature authorise the reception of the certificate, not as proof of the fact of chargeability, but as sufficient proof *to what parish* and *at what time* the pauper became and was chargeable, in cases where it shall be necessary to prove to what parish a pauper has become chargeable. The Commissioners observe, that the form of the certificate submitted to them goes beyond the terms of the statute; as, besides stating when the pauper became chargeable, it avers the continuance of the chargeability to the date of the certificate. Whether this be an important extension of the terms of the statute or not, the Commissioners cannot undertake to say. They have reason to believe, that certificates so framed have been rejected by Justices, and they have seen other forms of certificates without these terms. As no decision has been pronounced upon the sufficiency of the certificate, for the purpose provided in the statute, the Commissioners are not prepared to recommend the adoption of any particular forms. In reference to the mode of proving the chargeability, it appears to be only necessary to prove the actual giving of relief to the pauper by the officer of the parish. This can generally be proved by the relieving officer, but it may also be proved in many cases by the pauper, or by the master of the workhouse, or other persons. All that the Commissioners can say is, that there is no rule of law which requires that the relieving officer alone can prove the chargeability.*

XIII.—POOR-RATE.

1. Overseers not empowered to enter into an agreement to return any Portion of a Rate collected by them.

13*th May*, 1844.

Auditor of Wakefield Union.—Stated, that about three years ago Messrs. S. and B., thinking themselves assessed too highly upon their colliery, in the township of Shitlington, gave notice of appeal; in consequence of which a meeting of rate-payers was held, when it was determined that a re-valuation of the township should take place, and overtures were made to S. and B. to the effect, that if they would withdraw their appeal, and any reduction should be made by the new valuation, in their assessment, such reduction should be retrospective. Upon this understanding S. and B. stopped all proceedings, and paid the rate, but under a written agreement with the then Overseer, that should the new valuation of their colliery be lower than the existing one, the reduction should apply to the rate then paid, as well as to all future rates. The new valuation in S. and B.'s case was a reduction upon the former one, and they therefore claimed a deduction pursuant to the agreement, which was accordingly made and sanctioned by a majority of the rate-payers. Inquired whether he (the Auditor) would be justified in allowing such deduction in the Overseer's accounts.

Ans.—When a poor-rate is duly made and allowed, the Overseers are bound to collect it from every person assessed to it, except in any cases in which it may be reduced by the Special or General Sessions on Appeal, or in which the amount may be excused by the Justices on the ground of poverty. The Commissioners accordingly consider that the Overseers of Shitlington had no lawful authority to enter into such an agreement as that described in the Auditor's letter as having been made with Messrs. S. and B., or to return to Messrs. S. and B. any portion of the sums collected from them in pursuance of rates duly made and allowed, against which they did not in fact appeal.

2. Costs of recovering Poor-Rate, by whom payable.

13*th February*, 1844.

Mr. J. Duncumb, Skeffling, Patrington Union—Inquired, whether the overseer of a parish was entitled to be paid the cost of summoning a party for the nonpayment of his poor-rates, and also the expenses of attending before the justices. Inquired, also, whether the expenses should be paid by the defaulter or the parish.

Ans.—The cost of the summons is in the first place demandable of the person at whose instance it is obtained; and is recoverable, or not, against

* See, however, 7 and 8 Vic. cap. 101, sec. 69.

the party summoned, according to the nature of the case, and the discretion of the justices. Where the justices may not, upon the hearing of the case, see fit to order payment of the costs by the party in arrear, the overseers will be answerable for the payment. If they had fair grounds for applying to the justices, they may charge the expense upon the poor-rates; but if they were not justified in making application, the poor-rates would not be liable. The allowance of the overseer's travelling expenses in such a case from the poor-rates will, of course, be governed by the same rule which is applicable to such expenses in all other cases—that is to say, by a consideration of the necessity of the occasion, and the reasonableness of the amount.

XIV.—PROPERTY TAX.

Liability to assessment of interest on loan.

24*th Feb.* 1844.

Clerk of Ellesmere Union—Inquired whether the guardians were bound to give the surveyor of taxes a statement of the amount of interest which was paid annually by the Ellesmere Old Incorporation, for money borrowed upon bonds; and stated, that the guardians had already paid one year's property-tax upon the assessment; but in consequence of the Commissioners' circular of the 24th of June, 1843, relative to the property-tax charged upon workhouses, the clerk was directed to appeal against any further charge, and endeavour to get the duty which had been already paid, returned; the surveyor of the tax required to be furnished with an account of the interest payable by the guardians on mortgage or bond, stating that the property-tax should be charged upon the interest, to be repaid by the parties to whom it was payable, and not upon the assessment on the workhouse.

Ans.—The Commissioners consider the interest referred to in your letter, is assessable to the income-tax, under schedule C of 5 and 6 Vict. c. 35; and by the rule in sect. 88, the guardians who have the payment of that interest, must be charged therewith, and are to retain the same, according to section 93, out of the amount payable to the bondholders. The guardians of the Ellesmere Union will thus see that the poor-rates are not affected by these payments, and the circular of the Commissioners dated the 24th June, to which you refer, relative to property-tax upon workhouses, does not apply to this case.

XV.—RATING.

1. Machinery.

11*th June,* 1844.

Clerk of Stourbridge Union—Stated that the iron masters in that Union contended that they were not liable to be assessed to the poor-rate on the annual value of their works, *including* the steam-engines and other machinery, but only on buildings *without reference* to the steam-engines and other machinery; and requested the Commissioners' opinion on the point.

Ans.—In deciding the case of Reg. *v.* Guest, (7 A. and E. 951,) Lord Denman laid down the rule, "that real property ought to be rated according to its actual value, as combined with the machinery attached to it, without considering whether the machinery be real or personal property, so as to be liable to distress or seizure under a *fieri facias,* or whether it would descend to the heir or executor, or belong, on the expiration of a lease, to the landlord or tenant."

2. Owners of Cottages.

16*th May,* 1844.

Overseer, St. Mary's, Newmarket — Stated, that it had been resolved in vestry to assess the owners of certain cottages in the parish to the poor-rate instead of the occupiers; and inquired whether the 59 Geo. 3, c. 12, s. 19, applied to cottages let weekly or quarterly for sums between £6 and £20 a-year.

Ans.—The provision of the 59 Geo. 3, c. 12, s. 19, applies to rents, the rate of which, when estimated for the whole year, would not be less than £6, nor more than £20, a-year; and to no other rents. As regards the letting, if it be by the week, month, or quarter, or for any other term less than a year, and the rent is within the described limit, the provision of the act applies. Or if the letting is for a whole year, or any longer term, and the rent being within the limit described, is made payable at periods shorter than three months, the provision likewise applies.

XVI.—RELIEF.

By way of loan in midwifery cases.

6*th May,* 1844.

Clerk of Croydon Union—Stated, that many persons resident in the Croydon Union, who in the opinion of the guardians were in the receipt of a sufficiency to maintain themselves and families and provide medical assistance, applied to the board for midwifery orders on the expected accouchement of their wives, which after due inquiry into the applicants' circumstances, and mature consideration, the guardians refused. The parties however did not provide for such event, but late in the evening, sometimes at midnight, made applications to the medical officer to "come immediately, as it is too late to apply to the relieving officer for an order;" the medical officer was thus prevailed upon in some cases to attend, without the slightest chance of obtaining his fee from the parties calling for him, as they invariably referred him to the board of guardians for payment: in other cases, the medical officer refused to attend without an order from the relieving officer, and he at that late hour of the night was induced to give the order, even after the refusal by the guardians, rather than incur any risk to the patient by the reckless conduct of the husband, in not securing the requisite assistance at his own expense; and thus the decision of the guardians was frustrated, and the rate-payers burthened with an expense which the guardians submitted it was not the intention of the law to provide for. Inquired whether such an order could be granted by way of loan, and the amount recovered afterwards from the applicant. And also whether the tendering of an order on such conditions and not accepted by the applicant, would be considered by the Commissioners as a refusal by the guardians or relieving officer to relieve a case of urgent necessity and illness.

Ans.—1st. The Commissioners think, that an order for medical relief in the cases under consideration may be given by way of loan in the same manner as if the order were given for any other sort of relief. 2nd. The Commissioners are of opinion, that the offer of relief by way of loan, cannot with propriety be considered as equivalent to a refusal of relief. If the pauper is unable to repay the cost of the relief afterwards, he can represent his inability to the guardians, and it is competent to them not to enforce the repayment.

XVII.—RELATIONS.

1. LIABILITY OF CHILDREN TO MAINTAIN PARENTS.

6th June, 1844.

Clerk of Selby Union—Stated, that Richard Liddell, a poor man belonging to the township of Cawood, had, with his wife, become chargeable to that township; and that he had two sons, either of whom was able to maintain his parents, but both refused to do so. Inquired, first, whether justices could include both sons in an order on them for maintenance, under the 43rd Eliz. and 59 Geo. 3, c. 12, s. 26, or whether the order should be confined to one son only; or, whether it should be made upon one son for one moiety of the maintenance, and upon the other son for the remaining moiety. Secondly, whether the sons should be summoned before the justices.

Ans.—Firstly. Both of the sons of Richard Liddell are liable to contribute to the support of their parent, if they are of sufficient ability. The justices can, therefore, in their discretion, make an order on each of the sons to contribute such weekly sum, as, in the opinion of the justices, might be his fair proportion of the charge of maintenance. The order should be several. Secondly. The Commissioners think the most advisable course will be to summon the parties upon whom it is sought to make the order of maintenance, to appear before the justices.

2. MAINTENANCE OF RELATIONS.

25th April, 1844.

Clerk of Bromsgrove Union—Inquired, whether Boards of Guardians were legally competent to institute proceedings, or to order overseers to do so, against persons, to compel them, under the 43 Elizabeth, c. 2, s. 7, to maintain their relatives; or whether the overseers, of their own authority, were the proper persons to make the complaint.

Ans.—In the cases which have come before the courts, and which are to be found in the reports, it would seem that the orders, under the 43rd Eliz. c. 2, have been made on the complaint of the churchwardens and overseers; and the general practice is, as the Commissioners believe, in accordance with the course pursued in those cases without objection; (see the recent case of Reg. *v.* Toke, 8 A. and E. 227.) Still, the statute does not, in terms, confine the power of making the application to any particular person; and it would probably, therefore, be held competent to any person acquainted with the facts, and able to prove the chargeability, to make and support the application.

XVIII.—REMOVAL.

1. OF A PAUPER NOT INHABITING IN THE REMOVING PARISH.

25th June, 1844.

Clerk of Wellington Union, Somerset—Stated,

that William Coleman, a pauper, resided with his wife and five children in the parish of West Buckland, in the Wellington Union, but his settlement was in the parish of North Curry, in the Taunton Union. He had become chargeable to West Buckland in consequence of want of work. Being an able-bodied man, the guardians could only administer relief to him through the medium of the workhouse. The workhouse was locally situate in the parish of Wellington. It has been stated, that by a recent decision of the quarter sessions in the county of Somerset, it had been held, that where a pauper, at the time of the making of an order of removal, was an inmate of a workhouse, such workhouse not being situate in the removing parish, it was not such a constructive inhabitancy in the removing parish as would support the order. Out-door relief to the pauper being illegal, and a residence in the workhouse being in that case considered not to be an inhabitancy, the guardians wished the Commissioners to suggest to them how the difficulty besetting the removal of the pauper and his family might be obviated. A similar difficulty presented itself to the removal of William Blackmore and his family, then inmates of the Union workhouse, and chargeable to the parish of Sampford Arundel, in the Wellington Union, but belonging to Staplefitzpaine, in the Taunton Union.

Ans.—The Commissioners have always entertained the opinion that the Union workhouse is, in respect of the several parishes whose paupers are relieved therein, to be deemed to be a part of those respective parishes, so that the relief therein will support the allegation of chargeability to any parish from which the paupers may be removed to the Union workhouse. Although the Commissioners are aware that a different opinion is held by justices in some parts of the country, they think that the recent decision of Queen *v.* St. Giles-in-the-fields, 8 Jurist, p. 467, and 1 Dav. and Mer. 110, strongly supports the view which they entertain. A question there arose as to the effect of relief to a pauper chargeable to the parish of St. Giles-in-the-fields, which was given in the house of a person who was contractor to maintain paupers, which house was situate in another parish. It was contended that this was relief to a non-resident pauper, and was therefore evidence of the settlement of the pauper in the parish of St. Giles. But the Court of Queen's Bench decided that it had not such effect, and held that the house out of the parish to which the pauper was removed in this case, was to be considered as a house of the parish, and Lord Denman stated, that it was exactly similar to the case of R. *v.* St. Peter's and St. Paul's, Bath. Cald. 213. If the house locally situated out of the parish is to be considered with reference to the settlement as virtually within it, the Commissioners can see no ground for applying a different principle in regard to the question of chargeability to any particular parish in the Union having a central workhouse. The Commissioners make these remarks upon the difficulty which has been referred to by you on the subject of paupers, and they wish at the same time to state, that if the guardians should think fit to give temporary relief out of the workhouse, under article 4 of the Prohibitory Order, in particular cases, for the purpose of satisfying the supposed legal requirements to establish the chargeability, the Commissioners will be prepared to give their sanction to it, on the cases being duly reported to them.*

2. REMOVAL OF A PAUPER WHO HAS A SETTLEMENT BY ESTATE.

2nd March, 1844.

Clerk of Aberayron Union—Stated, that a pauper of Trefilan parish had given notice of marriage with a widow of Dihewid parish, who was, with her children, then chargeable to the latter parish, in which she rented a cottage as a yearly tenant: the male pauper would, by the marriage, gain a settlement, by estate, in Dihewid, if he resided in his wife's cottage for forty days. Inquired, what steps could be taken to remove him to his parish before he completed his forty days' residence, in case the family became chargeable during that time; and whether, if the forty days should expire after the making of an order of removal, but before the twenty-one days' notice had expired, the family would be removable.

Ans.—The principle on which a settlement is derivable from the possession of an estate, is this,—that a man cannot lawfully be removed from his land, and consequently, if he reside while thus irremovable, for forty days in the parish, he will, by the operation of the 13 and 14 Car. 2, c. 12, gain a settlement therein. It has been held, as you seem to be aware, that a husband, acquiring by marriage an interest in a leasehold, will thereby gain a settlement, although such leasehold would not have been sufficient, before her marriage, to confer a settlement on the

* See sec. 56 of 7 and 8 Vic. cap. 101.

wife. According to the principle above referred to, the husband, in the present case, is irremovable from his property, and his residence upon it for forty days will give him a settlement. The circumstance of the husband's becoming chargeable will not render him removable from the estate derived from his wife, (R. *v.* Martley, 5 East 40; R. *v.* North Cerney, 4 B. and A. 463.)

3. A FRESH ORDER OF REMOVAL MUST BE TAKEN OUT WHERE A PAUPER HAS RETURNED TO THE PARISH FROM WHICH HE HAD BEEN REMOVED.

17th Feb. 1844.

Overseer, Whitchurch, Monmouth Union—Inquired, whether it was necessary to take a second order for the removal of a pauper from a parish from which he had previously been removed by order, but to which he had subsequently returned and again become chargeable.

Ans.—Although a pauper may have been once removed, by an order of Justices, to his place of settlement, if the pauper subsequently return to the parish from which he was so removed, and again become chargeable, the parish can only lawfully get rid of the burden by obtaining a second order of removal. A pauper however, who returns to the parish from which he has been removed, under an order of Justices, and becomes chargeable without certificate, is liable to be punished under the Vagrant Act.

4. REMOVAL OF AN IRISH MOTHER AND CHILDREN.

24th July, 1844.

Clerk of East Retford Union—Stated that an Irishman deserted his wife, an Irishwoman, and three infant children, about eight years ago. The woman had since resided in a parish in the East Retford Union, and had had three children born during her husband's absence since 1834. Inquired, whether the mother and her child (as well those born while the husband and wife lived together, as those born during his absence,) might be removed to Ireland. Observed that it is laid down in 3 Archbold's Justice of the Peace (ed. 1844,) that the bastard children of Irish mothers are not so removeable; and some doubt is suggested whether the Poor Law Amendment Act applies (as respects the settlement of bastards) to the children of Irishwomen.

Ans.— The woman being an Irishwoman by birth, and not having any settlement in England, is removeable to Ireland under 3 and 4 Wm. 4, c. 40, with such of her legitimate children as are not emancipated. The case is distinguishable from Rex *v.* Cottenham, 7 B. & C. 615. There the wife was not born in Ireland, and had a maiden settlement in this country; and the court held that in the absence of her husband she could not be removed to Ireland, but was properly removed to her maiden settlement. In the case stated in your letter, the woman has no maiden settlement, but is directly within the terms of the 1st section of 3 and 4 Wm. 4, c. 40, viz., a person born in Ireland, not having gained any settlement in England. With regard to the children alleged to be illegitimate, having been born during the absence of the husband, and since the 14th of August, 1834, Rex *v.* Mile End Old Town, 4 A. & E. 196, shows that they cannot be removed with the mother to Ireland. It must be observed, however, that as the woman is a married woman, the principle of course is that the children are legitimate, unless non-access on the part of the husband be proved; and this fact must be shown by some other evidence than the oath of the wife herself. (See R. *v.* Reading, quoted in Burn's Justice, i. 327.)

XIX.—SERVANTS.

MAINTENANCE OF IN SICKNESS.

11th June, 1844.

Clerk of Bedminster Union—Stated, that application had been made to the guardians by a ratepayer for an allowance of weekly relief and a nurse for his domestic servant, she being confined to her bed in his house by illness. The guardians doubted whether they ought to grant relief to a domestic servant, under such circumstances, and wished the Commissioners' advice upon the subject.

Ans.—In the absence of any agreement on the subject, a master is not bound to provide his servant with medical attendance, if the latter fall sick during the period of service. There may be cases in which the earnings of a yearly-hired servant are so small as to be obviously insufficient to enable him to procure medical attendance at his own cost. The question, whether the guardians, in any particular case, can grant medical relief to a domestic servant, must be determined upon a consideration of the circumstances of such case,—for example, the liability of the master under any agreement, or the ability of the servant himself, to provide or procure medical aid, independently of the parish. This is a question for the guardians themselves to decide, upon their knowledge of the facts, though it may be observed generally, that the circumstance of a person being in service and earning wages, raises a presumption against the necessity of his resorting to the parish.

XX.—SETTLEMENT.

1. BY BIRTH—PROOF.

22nd *April*, 1844.

Rev. Henry Eley, Broomfield Vicarage, Chelmsford—Inquired whether the register of baptism at the parish-church was, in itself, sufficient evidence to prove the settlement of the parties baptized.

Ans.—The register of baptism is not, of itself, sufficient evidence to prove the place of birth of any person, with a view to ascertaining his settlement, although it may be adduced as one of the circumstances tending to prove it, (R. *v.* North Petherton, 5 B. and C. 508; R. *v.* Lubbenham, 5 B. and Ad. 968.)

2. SETTLEMENT—VALIDITY OF MARRIAGE.

23*rd Feb.* 1844.

Clerk of Stow-on-the-Wold Union—Inquired as to the validity of the marriage of Sarah Upstone, the same having taken place about three years ago, at Cheltenham, by banns, neither of the parties living at that place either at the time the banns were published, or when the marriage took place.

Ans.—The Commissioners presume that the objection which the statement of facts has suggested to the guardians, is, that the marriage is invalidated by the fact that neither of the parties was actually resident in the parish in which the banns were published and the marriage was solemnised. The Commissioners would direct the attention of the guardians to the 4th Geo. 4, c. 76, by which, section 26, it is provided that after the solemnization of any marriage under a publication of banns, proof of the actual residence of the parties is not necessary to the validity of the marriage; and that in any suit touching the validity of any such marriage, evidence in support of non-residence is not admissible.

XXI.—VESTRIES.

1. VOTING AT.

22*nd April*, 1844.

Messrs. C. Sanders and W. Hill, junr., Bickland, Budock, near Penryn—Stated, that the larger rate-payers of the parish outvoted the smaller rate-payers, by claiming and exercising the right of voting at a higher scale in proportion to their rental, contending that persons whose rental was under £200 were entitled only to one vote, those under £400 to two votes, and so on, according to the 40th section of the Poor Law Amendment Act. Requested the Commissioners' opinion upon the subject.

Ans.—The scale of voting fixed for rate-payers by the 40th section of the Poor Law Amendment Act, is expressly confined to cases of the election of guardians under that Act, or in which "the consent of the owners of property or rate-payers in any parish or union shall be required for any of the purposes of that Act." The voting at vestries is still regulated by the Vestries' Act, 58 Geo. 3, c. 69.*

2. DITTO.

12*th June*, 1844.

Rev. ——— — Stated, that A. B. entered upon a rateable house on the 29th October, 1843: an assessment was made on the 2nd November, 1843, in which A. B.'s name was omitted by the overseer, consequently no rate was demanded from him on that assessment: previous to the next assessment, A. B. claimed to have his name put on the rate-book, and to have the privilege of giving a vote at a vestry meeting, under sections 4 or 5, or both, of 59 Geo. 3, c. 69. Inquired, whether A. B. was entitled to a vote under either of the above sections.

Ans.—After a careful consideration of the case, the Commissioners cannot come to any other conclusion than that, according to the strict letter of the statute, the individual in question was not entitled to vote in vestry, under the circumstances which you describe. The 3rd section of the 58 Geo. 3, c. 69, applies only to inhabitants "who shall, by the last rate which shall have been made for the relief of the poor, have been assessed and charged," &c. In the case put, the party was not assessed in the last poor-rate made before he came to vote, and therefore, as it appears to the Commissioners, he is not within that section. The 4th section of the same statute refers to those cases only, in which "any person shall have become an inhabitant of any parish, or become liable to be rated therein, since the making of the last rate for the relief of the poor thereof." The person

* See 8 Vict. cap. 101, sect. 14.

alluded to, became an inhabitant of the parish, and became liable to be rated therein, on the 29th October; the last rate being made before he claimed to vote, was made on the 2nd November; consequently, he became an inhabitant and became liable to assessment before, not after, the making of such rate. The Commissioners do not see that the 5th section in any way bears on the question.*

XXII.—VESTRY CLERKS.

16*th July*, 1844.

Mr. James Grant, Skirlaugh—Stated that he had been, in the month of April last, elected vestry clerk of the parish of Skirlaugh, at a salary of £15 per annum, and inquired whether such salary could be legally paid out of the poor-rates, and placed in the overseers' accounts.

Ans.—Whatever powers may belong to the vestry to appoint a clerk to record their proceedings, the law does not appear to have made any provision for the payment of a salary to that officer out of the poor-rates; this appears clear from the judgment of Lord Kenyon, in Rex *v.* Churchwardens of Croydon, 5 T. R. 714. It is true that by the 109 section Poor Law Amendment Act the word officer is construed to extend amongst others to a vestry clerk. But though the effect of this section is to bring any person acting as a vestry clerk, so far as he may be aiding in carrying the laws for the relief of the poor into execution within the control of the Commissioners, it does not thence follow that he is such an officer as the Commissioners have authority to direct the overseers of a parish, or the guardians of any Union, to appoint at a salary to be paid out of the poor-rates. The construction which the word officer used in the 46th section 4 and 5 Wm. 4, c. 76, as explained by the 109th, has received in Reg. *v.* The Poor Law Commissioners, in Re the Cambridge Union, 2 P. and D. 323, where it was held not to extend to a collector of poor-rates, seems plainly to show that a less restricted interpretation would not be given if the question were as to the appointment under the section referred to of a vestry clerk, whose ordinary duties and functions are still more foreign to the objects and purposes of the act than those of a collector.

* See 7 and 8 Vic. cap. 101, sec. 14.

XXIII.—WORKHOUSE.

1. HOW TO CHARGE THE PRODUCE OF LABOUR, &C. IN THE WORKHOUSE.

21*st May*, 1844.

Hon. C. S. Clements, Assistant Commissioner—Stated, that a good-sized garden was attached to the Lancaster Union Workhouse: the implements for cultivating the garden and the seeds for cropping it were charged to the establishment, as were also the pigs, which were fed upon the refuse of the garden and the offal of the house; the produce of the garden and the pigs, when killed, were charged to the provision account, and credited to the establishment, according to the market price of the day. The consequence was, that the charge for the maintenance of the paupers was in no way diminished by this branch of the management, but the establishment charges were very much reduced; and those townships that contrived to avoid sending their paupers to the workhouse, enjoyed the advantage derived from the labour and maintenance of the paupers of other townships, by the reduction of the establishment charges. If the charge for maintenance were less in the workhouse, the same reluctance to give an order for it would not be evinced. There were various works going on in the workhouse, and the amount credited to the establishment from these sources was by no means inconsiderable. Requested the Commissioners' opinion on the point.

Ans.—The Commissioners do not see how the profits arising from the work done in the house can be disposed of, otherwise than by placing it to the credit of the establishment account. But, with regard to the garden-stuff and the pigs, the better way will probably be, to open a distinct account for them, and to carry the cost price, instead of the market price, to the provision account. The result of this arrangement will be, that there will be no balance credited to the establishment, and the profit will go to diminish the cost of maintenance.

2. PROCEEDINGS FOR ABSCONDING FROM, WITH THE WORKHOUSE CLOTHES

4*th May*, 1844.

Clerk of South Molton Union—Stated, that a pauper, who had frequently absconded with the workhouse clothes, (for which different proceedings had been taken against him,) again absconded on the 25th February last, after having committed an assault, taking with him the workhouse clothes: a warrant was taken out for his apprehension, but he could not be found: he was subsequently re-admitted into the workhouse under a Relieving Officer's order, and on the 1st April he was convicted by the Magistrates of the assault, and sentenced to one month's imprisonment: the Guardians intended to proceed against him for absconding with the workhouse clothes; and as the proceedings would be taken under the 55th Geo. 3rd, c. 137, s. 2, they wished to know whether the operation of that statute was confined to parochial workhouses in existence at the time it passed, or extended to workhouses established under the Poor Law Amendment Act; also, if the statute in question applied to Union workhouses, who were the proper parties to conduct the proceedings against the pauper, and out of what fund the expenses of such proceedings were to be defrayed.

Ans.—1. Where there is a general description in an Act of Parliament, the rule of construction is, not to limit it to the persons and things coming within it, and existing at the time of the passing of the Act; but to extend it to all persons and things coming within it, whether existing before the passing of the Act, or coming into existence afterwards; unless, indeed, the reason or policy of the measure would not apply to such persons or things,—in which case, it is usually presumed they were not intended to be affected by the Act. In the 2nd section of the 55th Geo. 3rd, c. 137, there are general terms which accurately describe the Guardians of Unions formed under the Poor Law Amendment Act. These terms, moreover, are themselves prospective;—" the Overseers of the Poor, or other person or persons who may be appointed for the ordering, &c. the poor of any parish." And not only do the terms apply to the Guardians, but the reason and policy of the enactment are quite as applicable to them, as to any officers for the relief of the poor known at the time the Act was passed. 2. The Commissioners entertain no doubt that the workhouse clothing is the property of the Guardians. It appears to the Commissioners to be immaterial in relation to this matter, whether the property in the possession of the Guardians was obtained at the joint, or the several cost of the parishes in the Union. The interest which one, or several, or all, of the parishes may have in the property, does not appear to the Commissioners in any way to change the title of the Guardians, as a board, to its possession. The Commissioners, therefore, consider that the ordinary form of information, describing the property as belonging to the Guardians, should be followed in such cases. 3. The Commissioners think that proceedings, under the 2nd section of the statute, may be taken by the Guardians; and that as they would be taken for the protection of the property belonging to the Guardians as a Board, and for the benefit of the Union generally, the expenses should be charged upon the common fund.

---

3. PAUPER ESCAPING FROM WORKHOUSE LEAVING BEHIND HIM HIS WIFE AND CHILDREN.

10th July, 1844.

Vice-Chairman of Warminster Union—Inquired how far a man who, with his wife and family, was in the Union workhouse, and escaped from thence, leaving them behind, was liable to punishment under the Vagrant Act, the chargeability not being consequent on his desertion, it having preceded it. Observed, that there would have been no difficulty started but from the remarks in the Commissioners' Report for 1843, page 385, " Minute on out-door labour test."

Ans.—The case put appears to be one for which the 4th section of 5 Geo. 4, c. 83, in terms provides, viz., that of a person running away and leaving his wife, or his or her child or children, " chargeable to any parish," and one which renders the individual liable to be punished as a rogue and vagabond. The Commissioners are ready to admit that there may be some doubt whether the case comes within the 3rd section of the above statute. They are nevertheless disposed to consider that upon a reasonable construction of that section, the family of the pauper might be considered as having become chargeable in consequence of his refusal to work. The statute does not require a full ability to maintain, the offence being complete if there be an ability in part to maintain by work, &c., and a refusal to do so. In the case supposed, the pauper, by continuing in the house and performing the work there required of him, would be able to maintain his family in part, since the produce of his work (however small) would in fact go to repay the parish the cost of the relief given. In so far, therefore, as the parish has to forego the indemnity which it is entitled to derive from the pauper's work, his family become chargeable by his refusal to perform such work, since the charge to the parish would be less if he did perform it.

LONDON:
Printed by Order of the Poor Law Commissioners, by BLACKBURN and PARDON, 6, Hatton Garden, and Published by CHARLES KNIGHT and Co., 22, Ludgate Street, Publishers to the Poor Law Commissioners.

AN

OFFICIAL CIRCULAR

OF PUBLIC DOCUMENTS AND INFORMATION:

DIRECTED BY THE POOR LAW COMMISSIONERS TO BE PRINTED, CHIEFLY FOR THE USE OF THE MEMBERS AND PERMANENT OFFICERS OF BOARDS OF GUARDIANS, UNDER THE POOR LAW AMENDMENT ACT.

No. 38. CIRCULAR ISSUED AUGUST 31, 1844.

Poor Law Commission Office,
Somerset House,
31*st August*, 1844.

THE Poor Law Commissioners directed that the following Bill, brought into the House of Commons on the 8th of August instant, by Sir James Graham, and Mr. Manners Sutton, be printed and circulated for the information of Guardians and Officers of the several Unions.

By Order of the Board,
EDWIN CHADWICK, *Secretary*.

A BILL TO CONSOLIDATE AND AMEND THE LAWS RELATING TO PAROCHIAL SETTLEMENT, AND TO THE REMOVAL OF THE POOR.

CONTENTS OF THE BILL.

I. REPEALS:

Section 1. Repeal of so much of former Acts of Parliament as relates to Settlement in Parishes, and to the Removal of the Poor, whether English, Scotch, or Irish, or of the Isles of Man, Scilly, Jersey, or Guernsey.

II. SETTLEMENT:

Section 2. Settlements which, before the Act, had been ascertained by warrants of removal, or by admissions in writing, to be retained. But warrants of removal made before the passing of this Act may still be appealed against, as if the Act had not been passed.

Section 3. Other Settlements declared; namely, 1st. Birth Settlement; or, 2nd. Father's Settlement; or, 3rd. Mother's Settlement. No Settlement to be derived from Grandfather, Grandmother, or more remote ancestor.

— 4. Place of Birth proved by Register of Birth or Baptism.

— 5. Proviso, that Children born in Union Workhouses shall be settled where their mothers are chargeable: Children born in Hospitals, Prisons, &c., or while their Mothers are under orders of removal, shall not have a Birth Settlement, but shall take their Parent's Settlement.

Replaces with modifications, 9 Geo. 1, c. 7, s. 4, proviso; 13 Geo. 3, c. 82, s. 5; 20 Geo. 3, c. 36, s. 2; 54 Geo. 3, c. 17, s. 2, 3; 9 Geo. 4, c. 40, s. 49; and the effect of, Dalton, 168, and the cases R. *v.* Astley, 2 Bott., 17; Suckley *v.* Whitborn, 2 Bott., 3.

— 6. Declaration, that there shall be no other manner of Settlement.

III. CHARGEABILITY:

Section 7. Declaration, that unsettled persons are to be relieved at the charge of the 'Parish' where they are destitute, as if they were settled there, until they are lawfully removed, or their destitution there is lawfully at an end.

IV. REMOVAL:

Section 8. Persons chargeable to a 'Parish' in which they are not settled, declared liable to be removed to the parishes of their settlement, with a Salvo for the cases of—

1. Married women, who are not to be removed from their husbands.
2. Legitimate children, who are not to be removed from their fathers' parish.
3. Legitimate and bastard children, who are not to be removed from their mothers.
4. Widows and their families, who are not to be removeable for a year after the husband's death.
5. Widows are not to be removed from the place of their husband's settlement and death.
6. Persons chargeable through sickness, not to be removed until relieved Forty Days.
7. Labourers and others who have maintained themselves by their labour in the place for Five Years, not to be removeable.

— 9. Declaration, that, except wives and children who are before made removeable to the husband's or parent's parish, and persons removeable to Scotland, Ireland, &c., no person shall be removeable to any other parish than that in which they are settled.

— 10. Power to Overseers to admit settlements, and agree to amicable removals.

— 11. Summons of persons liable to be removed; their examination; the warrant for their removal. Proviso for the examination of persons who cannot attend the summons.

Replaces 13 and 14 Car. 2, c. 12, s. 1, as to power to remove; as to complaint to One Justice, R. *v.* Westwood, 2 Bott., 782; summons, R. *v.* Wykes, 2 Bott., 818; hearing by Two Justices, ib.; examination of infirm persons, 49 Geo. 3, c. 124, s. 4; and of prisoners, 59 Geo. 3, c. 12, s. 28.

Section 12. No removal to be made until after Forty Days' notice, unless the removal be previously submitted to. In case of appeal, the removal not to be made until such appeal is ended.

Replaces 4 and 5 Will. 4, c. 76, s. 79.

— 13. Overseers, or persons employed by them, may execute the Warrant of Removal.

Replaces 54 Geo. 3, c. 170, s. 10.

— 14. Persons procuring removals without warrants made subject to penalties.

— 15. Delivery of Paupers under warrants of removal, at the Workhouse of a Parish or Union, to be regarded as delivery to the Overseers.

— 16. Suspension of the Removal; recovery of the charges incurred by such suspension; Appeal where such charges exceed Twenty Pounds.

Replaces 25 Geo. 3, c. 101; as to sick persons, R. *v.* Everdon, 2 Bott., 878; and as to the whole family, 49 Geo. 3, c. 124, s. 3; as to Justices' jurisdiction, 49 Geo. 3, c. 124, s. 1; as to notice of the warrant and suspension, 4 and 5 Will. 4, c. 76, s. 84.

— 17. Overseers may abandon a Warrant of Removal, paying the costs caused to the other party.

— 18. The Clerk of the Justices to transmit a duplicate of every warrant of removal and the original depositions to the Clerk of the Peace.

— 19. The Clerk of the Peace, on application, to furnish copies to the Overseers of the Parish to which the removal is directed to be made.

V. APPEAL AGAINST WARRANT OF REMOVAL:

Section 20. The Parish aggrieved by a Warrant of Removal may appeal, giving notice of the grounds of their appeal.

Replaces 13 and 14 Car. 2, c. 12, s. 2; and 3 Will. 4, c. 11,

s. 10; and as to statement of periods of appeal, 4 and 5 Will. 4, c. 76, s. 81.

Section 21. And may have access to the Pauper touching his Settlement.

Replaces 4 and 5 Will. 4, c. 76, s. 80.

— 22. Quarter Sessions held Fourteen Days after notice of Appeal, to hear the Appeal, no grounds to be gone into, but such as have been set forth in the Respondents' and Appellants' statements.

Replaces 8 and 9 Will. 3, c. 30, s. 6, giving, however, jurisdiction to sessions of places, not counties; restriction to the grounds of removal and appeal, 4 and 5 Will. 4, c. 76, s. 81.

— 23. On the trial of the appeal, the duplicate of the warrant, and the original depositions transmitted to the Clerk of the Peace, may be referred to for certain purposes.

— 24. Costs incurred by reason of notice of removal, or of appeal, and costs of trial, and costs caused by statements of frivolous or vexatious grounds of removal or appeal, to be awarded and certified by the Court; recovery of such costs.

Replaces 8 and 9 Will. 3, c. 30, s. 3, and 4 and 5 Will. 4, c. 76, s. 82.

— 25. Costs may be taxed by the proper officer at any time, although the Court be not sitting.

See Regina *v.* Long, 1 Q. B. 740.

VI. Maintenance of Paupers under Warrants of Removal and during Appeal:

Section 26. The cost of relief and maintenance of persons under warrant of removal incurred from the time that notice of chargeability was sent, till the time when the warrants might lawfully be executed, to be repaid to the Parish. Proviso saving the provisions in clause 15, respecting suspended warrants.

Replaces 4 and 5 Will. 4, c, 76, s. 84.

VII. Service of Notices:

Section 27. Notices of Removal, Appeal, &c. may be sent by post.

VIII. Removal of Poor born in Scotland, Ireland, and the Islands of Man, Scilly, Jersey, and Guernsey.

Section 28. Natives of Scotland, Ireland, and the Islands of Man, Scilly, Jersey, and Guernsey, not settled in England, may be removed to the places of their birth.

Replaces, as to natives of Scotland, Ireland, Man, and Scilly, 3 and 4 Will. 4, c. 40, s. 2; of Jersey and Guernsey, 11 Geo. 4, c. 5. s. 2.

— 29. Justices in Quarter Sessions to make regulations for such removals.

Replaces 3 and 4 Will. 4, c. 40, s. 3 and 4.

— 30. The expenses incurred by Parishes in such removals to be repaid out of County Rates.

Replaces 3 and 4 Will. 4, c. 40, s. 5, with addition of natives of Jersey and Guernsey.

— 31. Or in London, by the Chamberlain of the City, and levied by a Special Rate.

Replaces 3 and 4 Will. 4, c. 40, s. 6.

— 32. And in other Cities and places not contributing to a County Rate, by a General Rate.

Replaces 3 and 4 Will. 4, c. 40, s. 7.

— 33. Guardians of Unions in Ireland, and the Heritors and Kirk Sessions or Borough Magistrates in Scotland, may appeal against such Warrants. Removing Parish may abandon its Warrant, on payment of all costs incurred, including those of sending the Pauper back to such Parish.

IX. Guardians invested with powers for Removal of Poor Persons:

Section 34. Boards of Guardians may apply for Warrants of Removal, and execute such Warrants.

Section 35. Paid Officers may be appointed to conduct removals.

X. CONSTRUCTION AND LIMITATION OF THE ACT:

Section 36. This Act to be construed as one Act with the Poor Law Amendment Acts.

— 37. The Act limited to England and Wales.

— 38. The Act may be amended this Session.

SCHEDULE.

Forms.

[Note.—The Words printed in *Italics* in the body of the clauses, are proposed to be inserted in the Committee.]

REPEALS.—*Preamble.*—1. *Repeal of so much of former Acts as relates to Parochial Settlement or the removal of the Poor, except so far as they repeal preceding Acts.*

WHEREAS it is expedient that the Law of Settlement should be rendered more simple, and that the Laws relating to the Removal of the Poor should be consolidated and amended; Be it therefore Enacted, by the Queen's most excellent majesty, by and with the consent of the Lords spiritual and temporal, and Commons, in this present Parliament assembled, and by the authority of the same, That from and after the passing of this Act, so much of the following Acts of Parliament as relates to the settlement of persons in parishes, or the removal of poor persons from the parishes to which they are chargeable, except so far as any of the said Acts may repeal the provisions of any former Act, shall be, and the same is hereby repealed; (namely) an Act made in the thirteenth and fourteenth years in the reign of King Charles the Second, "For the better Relief of the Poor of this Kingdom;" (13 and 14 Car. 2, c. 12, ss. 1, 2, 3;) an Act made in the third year of the reign of King William and Queen Mary, "For the better explanation and supplying the defects of the former Laws for the Settlement of the Poor;" (3 Will. and M., c. 11, ss. 3, 4, 5, 6, 7, 8, 9, 10;) an Act made in the eighth and ninth years in the reign of King William the Third, "For supplying some defects in the Laws for the Relief of the Poor of this kingdom;" (8 and 9 Will. 3, c. 30, ss. 1, 3, 4, 6, 7;) an Act made in the ninth and tenth years of the reign of King William the Third, "For explaining an Act made the last Session of Parliament, intituled, 'An Act for supplying some defects in the Laws for the Relief of the Poor of this kingdom;'" (9 and 10 Will. 3, c. 11, s. 1;) an Act made in the twelfth year in the reign of Queen Anne, "For making perpetual the Act made in the thirteenth and fourteenth years of the reign of the late King Charles the Second, intituled, 'An Act for the better relief of the poor of this kingdom, and that persons bound apprentices to, or being hired servants with persons coming with certificates, shall not gain settlements by such services or apprenticeships;' and for making perpetual the Act made in the sixth year of her present Majesty's reign, intituled, 'An Act for the importation of cochineal from any ports in Spain during the present war, and six months longer;' and for reviving a clause in an Act made in the ninth and tenth years of the reign of the late King William, intituled, 'An Act for settling the trade to Africa, for allowing foreign copper bars imported, to be exported;'" (12 Anne, c. 18, ss. 1, 2;) an Act made in the ninth year of the reign of King George the First, "For amending the laws relating to the settlement, employment, and relief of the poor;" (9 Geo. 1, c. 7, ss. 4, 5, 6, 8, 9;) an Act made in the third year of the reign of King George the Second, "For continuing and amending an Act for regulating the price and assize of bread; for relief of bankrupts whose certificates were not allowed before the expiration of a late Act for the better preventing frauds committed by bankrupts; for allowing further time for enrolment of deeds and wills made by Papists, and for relief of Protestant purchasers and lessees; and for making further provision concerning certificates relating to the settlements of poor persons, and the charges of maintaining and removing certificated persons;" (3 Geo. 2, c. 29, ss. 8, 9;) an Act made in the thirty-first year of the reign of King George the Second, "To amend an Act made in the third year of the reign of King William and Queen Mary, intituled, 'An Act for the better explanation, and supplying the defects of the former laws for the settlement of the poor, so far as the same relates to apprentices gaining a settlement by indenture; and also to empower Justices of the Peace to determine differences between masters and mistresses and their servants in husbandry, touching their wages, though such servants are hired for less time than a year;' " (31 Geo. 2, c. 11, ss. 1, 2;) an Act made in the thirteenth year in the reign of King George the Third, " For the better regulation of lying-in hospitals, and other places appropriated for the charitable reception of pregnant women, and also to provide for the settlement of bastard children born in such hospitals and places;" (13 Geo. 3, c. 82, ss. 5, 6, 7;) an Act made in the twentieth year of the reign of King George the Third, "For obviating doubts touching the binding and receiving of poor children apprentices, in pursuance of several Acts of Parliament made for the relief of the poor within particular incorporated hundreds or districts, and for ascertaining the settlement of bastard children born in the Houses of Industry within such hundreds or districts;" (20 Geo. 3, c. 36, s. 1, 2;) an Act made in the twenty-second year of the reign of King George the Third, " For the better relief and employment of the poor;" (22 Geo. 3, c. 83, s. 39;) an Act made in the twenty-third year of the reign of King George the Third, " To prevent prisoners in the King's Bench Prison, or the rules thereof, or their families or servants, gaining settlements in the parish of Saint George the Martyr, in the Borough of Southwark, and county of Surrey; and for the relief of the said parish, with respect to the families of prisoners in the said King's Bench, or the Marshalsea Prison, or in the County Gaol, or House of Correction, belonging to the said county; for regulating the manner of choosing the Overseers of the Poor; and for appointing collectors of the Poor's Rates within the said parish;" (23 Geo. 3, c. 23, s. 1;) an Act made in the thirty-fifth year of the reign of King George the Third, " To prevent the removal of poor persons until they shall become actually chargeable;" (35 Geo. 3, c. 101, ss. 1, 2, 3, 4, 6;) an Act made in the forty-ninth year of the reign of King George the Third, " For altering, amending, and explaining certain Acts relative to the removal of the poor, and for making regulations in certain cases touching the examination of Paupers, as to their Settlement; and for extending to all parishes certain rules and orders in workhouses, under an Act of the twenty-second year of his present Majesty, intituled, ' An Act for the better relief and employment of the poor;' " (49 Geo. 3, c. 124, ss. 1, 2, 3, 4;) an Act passed in the fifty-second year of the reign of King George the Third, " For the better cultivation of navy timber in the forest of Alice Holt, in the county of Southampton;" (52 Geo. 3, c. 72, s. 8;) an Act made in the fifty-fourth year of the reign of King George the Third, " To render valid certain indentures for the binding of parish apprentices, and certificates of the settlement of poor persons;" (54 Geo. 3, c. 107, s. 1, 2, 3;) an Act passed in the fifty-fourth year of the reign of King George the Third, " To repeal certain provisions in Local Acts for the maintenance and regulation of the poor, and to make other provisions in relation thereto;" (54 Geo. 3, c. 170, ss. 1, 2, 3, 4, 5, 6, 10;) an Act made in the fifty-sixth year of the reign of King George the Third, "To regulate the binding of parish apprentices;" (56 Geo. 3, c. 139, s. 5); an Act made in the fifty-ninth year of the reign of King George the Third, " To amend the laws for the relief of the poor;" (59 Geo. 3, c. 12, s. 28;) an Act made in the first and second years of the reign of King George the Fourth, " For declaring valid certain indentures of apprenticeship, and certificates of settlements of poor persons in England;" (1 and 2 Geo. 4, c. 32, ss. 1, 2;) an Act made in the third year of the reign of King George the Fourth, " To amend the general laws now in being for regulating turnpike roads in that part of Great Britain called England;" (3 Geo. 4, c. 126, s. 51;) an Act made in the sixth year of the reign of King George the Fourth, "For the amendment of the law respecting the settlement of the poor, as far as regards renting tenements and paying parochial taxes;" (6 Geo. 4, c. 57, ss. 1, 2;) an Act made in the eleventh year of the reign of King George the Fourth, " To repeal the provisions of certain Acts relating to the removal of vagrants and poor persons born in the isles of Jersey and Guernsey, and chargeable to parishes in England, and to make other provisions in lieu thereof;" (11 Geo. 4, c. 5, ss. 1, 2;) an Act made in the first year of the reign of King William the Fourth, "To explain and amend an Act of the sixth year of his late majesty King George the Fourth, as far as regards the settlement of the poor by the renting and occupation of tenements;" (1 Will. 4, c. 18, ss. 1, 2;) an Act made in the second year of the reign of King William the Fourth, "To amend an Act of the fifty-ninth year of his majesty King George the Third, for the relief and employment of the poor;" (1 and 2 Will. 4. c. 42, s. 5;) an Act made in the second year of the reign of King William the Fourth, "To enable churchwardens and overseers to inclose land belonging to the crown for the benefit of poor persons residing in the parish in which such crown land is situated;" (1 and 2 Will. 4, c. 59, s. 2;) an Act made in the fourth year of the reign of King William the Fourth, "To repeal certain Acts relating to the removal of poor persons born in Scotland and Ireland, and chargeable to parishes in England, and to make other provisions in lieu thereof, until the First day of May, one thousand eight hundred and thirty-six, and to the end of the then next session of parliament," and all Acts to continue the same; (3 and 4 Will. 4, c. 40; 7 Will. 4, c. 10; 3 and 4 Vict. c. 27;) an Act made in the fifth year of the reign of King William the Fourth, "For the amendment and better administration of the laws relating to the poor in England and Wales;" (4 and 5 Will. 4, c. 76, ss. 64, 65, 66, 67, 68, 79, 80, 81, 82, 83, 84.)

SETTLEMENTS.—2. *Persons to retain their Settlements ascertained by Warrants of Removal, or admissions in writing made before this Act.—Appeal preserved against Warrants of Removal made before this Act.*

Provided always, and be it enacted, That every person who, before the passing of this Act, has, on the ground of his own settlement, been removed, or directed to be removed to any parish under any warrant of removal not abandoned or quashed before or after the passing of this Act, or been expressly admitted by any writing under the hands of the majority of the Overseers of any parish to be settled therein, shall, after the passing of this Act, be deemed to be settled in such parish: provided also, That when any person has, before the passing of this Act, been placed under a warrant of removal, it shall be lawful for any person to appeal against such warrant, in like manner and with the like effect in all respects, as if this Act had not been passed: Provided also, That where any appeal against a warrant of removal has been finally decided upon before the passing of this Act, such decision shall have the like effect in all respects as it would have had if this Act had not been passed: Provided also, That where any appeal against a warrant of removal has been made, but not finally decided upon before the passing of this Act, nothing in this Act contained shall in any way affect the decision to be given upon such appeal.

3. *Other persons to have—1st. Birth settlement; or, 2nd. Father's settlement; or, 3rd. Mother's settlement.*

And be it enacted, That every person with regard to whom no such warrant or admission has been made, shall be settled in the parish in which he was born; or if the parish in which he was born cannot be ascertained, or if he was not born in England, he shall, if born in wedlock, be settled in any parish in which his father would, if living after the passing of this Act, be settled, or if his father would not be settled in any parish in England, or if the parish in which his father would be settled cannot be ascertained, or if he was not born in wedlock, he shall be settled in any parish in which his mother would, if living after the passing of this Act, be settled; but no person shall be settled in any parish on the ground that his grandfather or grandmother, or any more remote ancestor was settled there.

4. *Register of birth, or certified register of baptism, evidence of the place of birth.*

And be it enacted, That in any case in which the place of birth of any person may be in question before any Justices, or any Court, under the provisions of this Act, such Justices, or Court, shall admit a certified copy of the register of the birth of such person made under the provisions of the Act passed in the seventh year of the reign of King William the Fourth, intituled, "An Act for registering Births, Deaths, and Marriages in England," containing a statement of the place of birth of such person as *primâ facie* evidence of the place of birth of such person; or if such person were born before the said Act came into operation, or if the place of birth is not stated in such register, such justices, or court, shall admit a copy of the register of the baptism of such person, certified by the incumbent, officiating curate, parish clerk, or any churchwarden of the parish to which such register belongs, and witnessed by one witness, as *primâ facie* evidence of the birth of such person in the place in which he appears by such register, or such copy thereof, to have been baptized, unless the contrary appear on the face thereof.

5. *Proviso for Settlements of Children born in Union Workhouses, &c., or under Warrants of Removal.*

Provided always, and be it enacted, That if any child have been born in the workhouse of any Union, such child shall be deemed to have been born in the parish to which the mother of such child was, at the time of the birth, chargeable; and if any child have been born in any house licensed for the reception of pregnant women, or in any hospital for the reception and cure of persons suffering from disease or bodily injury, or in any county lunatic asylum, or in any house licensed for the reception of insane persons, or in any prison, if the mother of such child were not, before her admission into such house, hospital, asylum, or prison, respectively, resident in the parish in which such birth occurred, such mother not being settled in that parish, such child shall not, for the purposes of this Act, be deemed to have been born therein; and if any child have been born in any parish while his mother was under any warrant of removal, not executed at the time of the birth, nor afterwards abandoned or quashed, such child shall not, for the purposes of this Act, be deemed to have been born in such parish.

6. *No other mode of Settlement.*

And be it enacted, That no person shall be deemed to be settled in any parish in any other than one of the several manners herein provided.

Chargeability of Persons not settled.
7. *Declaration that persons are to be relieved at the charge of the parish where they are destitute, until removal or lawful cessation of their destitution.*

And be it declared and enacted, That the overseers and guardians of every parish, and the guardians of every union, shall take order for the relief, according to the laws in force for the time being, of every poor person destitute therein, but not settled therein, in like manner as if he were settled therein, until he is lawfully removed therefrom, or until he ceases by other lawful means to be destitute therein.

Removal.— *Person chargeable to a parish in which he is not settled, liable to be removed to the parish of his Settlement.*

And be it enacted, That every person who has become chargeable to any parish in which he is not settled, shall be liable to be removed therefrom to any parish in which he is settled, subject to the provisions next hereinafter made; (that is to say,)

Salvo, 1. *For married women not to be removed from their husbands' parish.*

Every woman during her marriage shall be liable to be removed to the parish in which her husband is deemed to be settled, if the same can be ascertained, and shall not be liable to be removed from such parish, or from her husband;

2. *For legitimate children not to be removed from fathers' parish.*

And every legitimate child under the age of *sixteen* years, whose father is living, shall be liable to be removed to the parish in which his father is settled, if the same can be ascertained, and shall not, while resident anywhere with his father, be liable to be removed from him;

3. *For legitimate and bastard children not to be removed from their mothers.*

And every child, under the age of *sixteen* years, being legitimate, whose father is dead and whose mother is living, or being a bastard, whose mother is living, shall be liable to be removed to the parish to which his mother would, if chargeable, be liable to be removed, and shall not, while resident anywhere with his mother, be liable to be removed from her;

4. *For widows and their families not to be removed for one year after the husbands' death.*

And no widow who at the time of her husband's death was residing with him, nor the children of such widow, whether legitimate or bastard, under the age of *sixteen* years, shall be liable to be removed from the parish where she was so residing until the expiration of *one year* after her husband's death.

5. *For widows not to be removed fvom the place of their husbands' settlement and death.*

And no widow, who at the time of her husband's death was residing with him in the parish in which he was settled, shall be liable to be removed therefrom.

6. *For persons chargeable through sickness, not to be removed until relieved forty days.*

And no person who becomes chargeable to any parish on account of sickness, or accident, shall be liable to be placed under a warrant of removal until he has received relief *bonâ fide* for the space of *forty* days, without any interval of more than *seven* consecutive days.

7. *For labourers, &c. resident five years not to be removable.*

And no person who has resided the *five* years last preceding in any parish, and has ordinarily maintained himself in or near thereto as a labourer, artificer, mechanic, servant, or tradesman, and has not been convicted of felony or misdemeanor, and has not during such *five* years been removed from such parish under a warrant of removal, shall be liable to be removed; but no residence in any prison, barrack, lunatic asylum, or public hospital, or while receiving relief, shall be considered either as an interruption, or as a portion of such *five* years.

9. *Persons only to be removed to the parish where settled. Exceptions.*

And be it declared and enacted, That no person, except such as is hereby made liable to be removed to the parish of the husband's, or father's or stepfather's settlement, and except persons born in Scotland, Ireland, the Isles of Man, Scilly, Jersey, or Guernsey, and their families, shall be removed to any parish other than the parish in which such person is, under the provisions of this Act, deemed to be settled.

10. *Amicable removal.*

And be it enacted, That if the overseers of any parish, by writing under the hands of any two or more of them, signed in the presence of any justice of the peace, and certified under his hand to be so signed, admit that any person is settled in such parish, or is liable to be removed thereto, and thereby agree to receive such person, such person shall be deemed to be settled in such parish, or removable thereto accordingly.

11. *Summons and examination of persons liable to be removed: warrant of removal. Proviso for examination of infirm persons and prisoners.*

And be it enacted, That if the overseers of any parish shall complain to any one justice of the peace for the county, borough, or place in which such parish is situate, that any person is liable to be removed from such parish, such justice may summon such person to come before any two justices of the peace of such county, borough, or place, at a time and place to be named in such summons; and at such time and place any two justices of the peace of such county, borough, or place, may hear and examine into the matter of such complaint, and if they see fit, they may make and issue a warrant, under their hands and seals, to remove such person to the parish in which he is deemed to be settled, or to which he is liable to be removed: Provided always, That if any such person be, by reason of age, illness, or infirmity, unable to be brought up before such two justices, or if the husband, or father, mother, or stepfather of any person liable to be removed, be a prisoner in any gaol, or house of correction, or in the custody of any constable or peace officer, under or by virtue of any warrant of commitment, then any one justice of the peace may take the examination of such person, husband, father, mother, or stepfather, where he or she may be, in writing, touching his or her settlement; and such examination, signed by such justice, shall be received and admitted as evidence of the facts therein stated, in the same manner and to the same extent as if the same facts were orally deposed to, before any two justices empowered to inquire into such settlement, who may thereupon make and issue their warrant of removal as effectually as if such person, husband, father, mother, or stepfather had appeared, and been examined before such two justices.

12. *Persons not to be removed under warrant till after forty days' notice; unless the removal be submitted to. In case of appeal, pauper not to be removed while it is pending.*

And be it enacted, That where any person has been directed by warrant of justices to be removed from any parish, if the overseers of such parish, within *seven* days after the making of such warrant, send notice, by post or otherwise, to the overseers of the parish to which such person is to be removed, that such person has become chargeable, and also within the said seven days send to the overseers last-mentioned, a copy or counterpart of such warrant of removal, and a statement of the grounds upon which the same was made, the overseers of the parish to which such person is so chargeable, may, after the expiration of *forty* days after the sending of such notice and copies or counterparts, remove such person, but not otherwise: Provided always, that if the overseers of the parish to which such person is to be removed agree, by writing under their hands, to receive such person before the expiration of such *forty* days, the overseers of the parish from which such person is to be removed may remove such person, although such forty days have not expired: Provided also, that if notice of appeal against the warrant for the removal of such person be received by the overseers of the parish on whose behalf such warrant was obtained, they shall not remove such person until after the time for prosecuting such appeal has expired, or if such appeal be prosecuted, until the final determination thereof.

13. *Overseers, or persons employed by them, may execute the warrant of removal.*

And be it enacted, That such overseers may employ any proper person to carry, remove, and deliver any pauper directed by such warrant to be removed, and that the delivery by such person of any such pauper shall be as good, valid, and effectual, to all purposes whatsoever, as if such pauper were delivered by any overseer.

14. *Penalty for procuring removals of poor persons without warrants of justices.*

And be it enacted, That if any officer of any parish or union do for the purpose and with the intent of causing any poor person to become chargeable to any other parish or union to which such person was not before chargeable, convey any poor person out of such parish or union, or cause or procure any poor person to be so conveyed, or give directly or indirectly any money, or other relief, or assistance, or afford or procure to be afforded any facility for such conveyance, or make any offer or promise, or use any threat to induce any poor person to depart from such parish or union, and if, in consequence of such conveyance or departure, any poor person become forthwith chargeable to any other parish or union, to which such poor person is not at the time removable under a warrant of removal, or admission of settlement in writing as aforesaid, such officer, on conviction thereof before any two justices (either of the place from whence such poor person has been conveyed, or had departed as aforesaid, or of the place where such poor person has so become chargeable) shall forfeit and pay for every such offence any sum not exceeding *five pounds*, and not less than *forty shillings*.

15. *Delivery of paupers under orders of removal.*

And be it enacted, that the delivery of any pauper under any warrant of removal to any officer of the workhouse of any parish, or of any union in which such parish is comprised, at such workhouse, shall be deemed to be a delivery of such pauper to the overseers of the said parish.

16. *Suspension of the execution of warrants of removal.—Recovery of expenses incurred by such suspension.—Appeal given where such charges exceed ten pounds.—Award of costs.*

Provided always, and be it enacted, That where any warrant has been made for the removal of any person, if it appear to the justices who made such warrant, or to any other two justices of the same county or jurisdiction, that such person is unable to travel, by reason of sickness or other infirmity, or that it would be dangerous for him to do so, such justices shall suspend the execution of such warrant, as well with respect to such person as with respect to every other person thereby directed to be removed, until the same may be executed without danger to any person who is the subject thereof, and shall indorse such suspension on the said warrant of removal, and shall sign the same; and when such justices, or any other two justices of the same county or jurisdiction, are satisfied that such warrant may be executed without danger to any person who is the subject thereof, such justices shall direct such warrant to be executed, and shall indorse such direction on the said warrant of removal, and shall sign the same; and if it be proved on oath before such last-mentioned justices that any expenses of relief or maintenance, other than of medical relief, have been incurred by such suspension, such justices may order the overseers of the parish to which such person is directed to be removed, to pay such expenses of relief and maintenance, other than of medical relief; and if the overseers of the parish in whose behalf such warrant was made have, within *seven* days after such suspension, sent, by post or otherwise, to the overseers of the parish to which such person is directed to be removed, notice of such warrant of removal, and of the suspension thereof, and have also within such *seven* days sent to the overseers last-mentioned a copy or counterpart of such warrant and suspension, and a statement of the grounds upon which such warrant was made, and if such person be afterwards removed under such warrant, or if such person die before the execution of such warrant, then the overseers of such last-named parish shall pay such expenses; and if they refuse or neglect to pay the same within *three* days after the demand thereof, and if they do not within such *three* days give notice of appeal against the order to pay such expenses, then the overseers of the parish on whose behalf such warrant was made may recover such expenses, together with cost of recovering the same, in the same manner as penalties and forfeitures; and when the sum so ordered to be paid on account of such charges exceeds the sum of *ten pounds*, if the overseers of the parish ordered to pay the same think such parish aggrieved thereby, and if within *three* days after demand made of payment under such order, they give notice to the overseers of the parish on whose behalf such order was made, of their intention to appeal against the same, then the overseers of the parish ordered to pay such sum, may appeal to the general or quarter sessions of the peace, held next after the expiration of *fourteen days* from the giving of such notice, for the county, city, borough, or place wherein the parish on whose behalf such order was made doth lie; and if such court be of opinion that the sum so ordered is more than of right ought to have been paid, such court shall strike out the sum contained in the order, and insert therein the sum which in the judgment of such court ought to be paid; and upon such appeal before such court, or upon proof made before such court that notice of such appeal has been given, although such appeal has not been prosecuted, such court shall award to the party in whose favour such appeal is determined, or to whom such notice was given, such costs and charges in the law as such court in their discretion think just and reasonable, to be paid by the party against whom such appeal is determined, or by whom such notice was given; and the party to whom such costs and charges are awarded may recover the sum inserted in such order by such court as aforesaid, and the costs and charges awarded by such court as aforesaid, in the same manner as penalties and forfeitures: Provided always, That if in any case it appear to the justices ordering payment of such costs and charges, or to the court of quarter sessions on appeal against such order, that the removal of any such person was negligently or improperly delayed after he was in a fit state to be removed, such justices or such court may reduce the amount of the costs and charges so to be paid, as to them may seem fit.

17. *Overseers may abandon a warrant of removal, paying the other parties' costs.*

And be it enacted, That in any case in which a warrant has been made for the removal of any person from any parish, and notice thereof sent as aforesaid, if at any time after such notice, whether notice of appeal against such warrant have or have not been then given, the overseers of such parish give notice in writing under the hands of any two or more of them to the overseers of the parish to which such person is directed to be removed, that they abandon such warrant, then such warrant, and all proceedings consequent thereon, shall become and be null and void to all intents and purposes, as if the same had not been made; and shall not be given in evidence in case any warrant be afterwards obtained for the removal of any person who may have been affected by such first-mentioned warrant; and the overseers abandoning such warrant shall pay to the overseers of the parish to which the removal was thereby directed to be made, the costs incurred by such last-mentioned overseers, by reason of such warrant, and of all subsequent proceedings thereon; and if such last-mentioned overseers apply to the proper officer of the court before whom any appeal against such warrant, if it had not been abandoned, might have been brought, and if they produce to him the notice of such abandonment, and if they satisfy him that such reasonable notice of taxation has been given to the overseers abandoning such warrant as in his judgment the distance between the parishes requires, such officer shall tax such costs; and may thereupon charge and receive the usual costs of taxation; and shall indorse the sum allowed by him as costs, and the amount of the said costs of taxation upon the notice of abandonment; and if such costs, being lawfully demanded, be not paid within *ten* days after taxation, the overseers entitled to the same may recover them as penalties and forfeitures.

18. *Duplicate of warrant of removal, &c. to be transmitted to the Clerk of the Peace, who is to preserve the same.*

And be it enacted, that the clerk to the justices, or, if there be no such clerk, then one of the justices, who have made any warrant of removal, shall transmit within days from the making of such warrant a duplicate of such warrant, and also all the original depositions upon which such warrant was made to the clerk of the peace for the county, borough, or place of which the said justices are justices, and that such duplicate and depositions shall thenceforward be kept by the said clerk of the peace.

19. *Clerk of the Peace to furnish copies.*

And be it enacted, That if the overseers of the parish to which any person is by such warrant ordered to be removed, do, by writing delivered to such clerk of the peace, require such clerk of the peace to furnish them with a copy of such duplicate and depositions, or either, such clerk of the peace shall within a reasonable time after the delivery to him of such written requisition, furnish a copy of such duplicate or deposition, as the case may be, on being paid therefor at the rate of

APPEAL AGAINST WARRANT OF REMOVAL.—20. *Overseers of the parish aggrieved by warrant of removal may appeal.*

And be it enacted, That, if the overseers of the parish to which any person is by any warrant directed to be removed as aforesaid, consider such parish to be aggrieved thereby; and if within *twenty-one* days after they have received the statement of the grounds upon which the same was made, and the copy or counterpart of the warrant, such overseers give to the overseers of the parish on whose behalf such warrant was obtained, notice in writing, under the hands of any two or more of them, of their intention to appeal against such warrant, together with a statement in writing, under the hands of any two or more of them, of the grounds of such appeal, the said overseers of the parish to which such person is directed to be removed, may appeal to the general or quarter sessions of the peace to be held for the county, city, borough or place wherein the parish on whose behalf such order was obtained, or any part thereof, doth lie.

21. *And may have access to the pauper, touching his settlement, or liability to removal.*

And be it enacted, That the overseers giving such notice of appeal, or their attorney, or any other person authorised by them may, until such appeal is heard and decided, at all proper times have free access to the person directed to be removed, for the purpose of examining him touching his settlement or liability to be removed; and if it be necessary for the more effectual examination of such person, that he should be taken out of the parish in whose behalf the warrant was obtained, such overseers may remove him therefrom for the time which may be necessary for that purpose; and in such case the said overseers shall defray the expense of such removal, and of the maintenance of such person during the same.

22. *Quarter Sessions to hear appeal; no grounds to be gone into, but those set forth in the respondents' and appellants' statements.*

And be it enacted, that the justices of the peace at the general or quarter sessions of the county, borough, or place wherein the parish is situate from which the warrant appealed against has directed the removal to be made, held next after the expiration of *fourteen* days from the day on which the notice of appeal was given, shall hear and determine such appeal upon the grounds set forth respectively in the respondents' statement of the grounds of the warrant of removal, and in the appellants' statement of the grounds of their appeal; and neither the respondents nor appellants shall, on the hearing of such appeal, go into, or give evidence of, or be heard upon, any other grounds of removal or of appeal than those set forth in their respective statements as aforesaid.

23. *On trial of Appeal, the duplicate of warrant and the depositions transmitted to the Clerk of the Peace, may be referred to for certain purposes.*

And be it enacted, That upon the trial of any appeal against any such warrant of removal, the court trying such appeal, or either party, shall be at liberty to refer to the said duplicate and depositions so transmitted as aforesaid to the clerk of the peace; but such depositions shall not be considered as furnishing evidence of the facts therein deposed to, except only for the purpose of showing that the person or persons making such depositions has or have made the statements therein contained, and except only where evidence of the fact of such statements having been made is by law admissible: Provided nevertheless, That where any party who has made such depositions is dead at the time of trying the appeals, the deposition of such party shall be admissible at such trial as evidence of the facts therein stated, in the same way and to the same extent as such statement would have been admissible at such trial if then orally deposed to by such person: Provided nevertheless, That on the trial of any such appeal no warrant of removal shall be quashed or set aside, either wholly or in part, on the ground that such depositions do not furnish sufficient evidence to support, or that any matter therein contained raises an objection to, the warrant or the statement of the grounds of removal, except when such objection to the warrant or statement arises upon depositions given in evidence, in consequence of the death of the party making such depositions, and in that case such objection shall have the same weight and effect as if it were raised by the oral evidence of such party.

24. *Costs to be awarded.*

And be it enacted, that upon any appeal against any warrant of removal being heard before any court of general or quarter sessions, or upon proof before any such court, of notice of such appeal having been given, though such appeal were not afterwards prosecuted, such court shall order either party to pay to the other, such costs and charges as they consider just and reasonable, and shall certify the amount thereof; and if either of the parties have included in their respective statements, any grounds of removal or of appeal which, in the opinion of the court determining such appeal, are frivolous or vexatious, such court may, at their discretion, direct such party to pay the whole or any part of the costs incurred by the other party in disputing any such grounds, and shall certify the amount thereof; and if the amount so certified in any of the cases aforesaid be demanded of the overseers, liable to pay the same, and if such certificate thereof be produced to them, and if they refuse or neglect to pay the same, the overseers entitled thereto may recover the same as penalties and forfeitures.

25. *Costs may be taxed by the proper officer at any time, although the court be not sitting.*

And be it enacted, that where, either by this act or any preceding acts, costs are incidental to any warrant or removal, or any appeal therefrom, or any proceedings touching the same, such costs may be taxed by the proper officer in that behalf at any time; and such taxation, when duly made in other respects, shall be valid and effectual, whether or not the court to which such officer belongs be sitting at the time of the taxation, in the same manner as if such court were actually sitting at the time of the taxation.

Maintenance of Paupers under Warrant.—26. *Cost of relief of persons under warrant of removal to be repaid.*

And be it enacted, that where a warrant has been made for the removal of any person from any parish, and the liability of such person to be removed under such warrant has been admitted by submission to the warrant, or adjudged upon appeal, the overseers of such parish may recover from the overseers of the parish to which such person was by such warrant directed to be removed, the charges and expenses of his relief and maintenance lawfully incurred from the time when notice was sent that he had become chargeable, until the time when he might lawfully have been removed; and if the same be not paid within *three* days after a demand thereof, the overseers entitled thereto may recover the same in the same manner as penalties and forfeitures: Provided always, That no charges or expenses of relief or maintenance incurred by reason of the suspension of any such warrant shall be recoverable, except upon the conditions hereinbefore prescribed.

Service of Notices.—27. *Notices of removal may be served by post.*

And be it enacted, That every notice of any poor person being chargeable, and every copy or counterpart or notice of any warrant (whether suspended or otherwise) for the removal of any poor person, and every statement of the grounds upon which any such warrant is made, and every agreement in writing to receive a person under a warrant of removal, and every notice of appeal against any such warrant, and every notice containing the grounds of any such appeal, and every notice of the abandonment of such warrant, and every bill or demand of costs incurred under or by reason of any such warrant, and every notice of appeal against any order for payment of costs incurred by reason of the suspension of any warrant of removal, shall be held to have been properly served or delivered, if it be proved that the same was properly addressed to the parties entitled to receive the same, and indorsed on the outside of the letter or packet with the name of the document as it is above described, and put into the post-office, and registered according to any regulations in force at the time, under the authority of Her Majesty's postmaster-general seven days at the least before the time when the same is required to be served or delivered, unless the party to be affected by such notice or other document prove that the same has not been duly received; and if any person make oath that he so put such letter or packet into the post-office, and if he produce a receipt for the same, purporting to be signed by the postmaster or other person authorised to register letters, and state upon oath to the satisfaction of the court before which he produces the receipt, the circumstances under which and the person from whom he received the receipt, the posting and registering of such letter or packet shall be deemed to be sufficiently proved.

Removal of Poor of Scotland, Ireland, &c.—28. *Provision for removal of natives of Scotland, Ireland, and the Isles of Man, Scilly, Jersey, and Guernsey.*

Provided always and be it enacted, That if any person born in Scotland or Ireland, or in the Isle of Man, or Scilly, or Jersey, or Guernsey, not deemed to be settled in England, nor being temporarily or permanently exempted from the liability to be removed under the provisions of this Act, become chargeable, by himself, herself, or any of his or her family, to any parish in England, such person, his wife, and any of his or her children so chargeable shall be liable to be removed therefrom to Scotland, Ireland, the Isle of Man, Scilly, Jersey, or Guernsey, respectively, according as he or she may belong thereto; and if the overseers of such parish complain thereof to any one justice of the peace, such justice may summon such person to come before any two justices of the peace, at any time and place to be named in the summons; and at such time and place any two justices may hear and examine into the matter of such complaint, and if they see fit they may make and issue a warrant under their hands and seals, in the form in the schedule hereunto annexed, to remove such person forthwith, at the expense of such parish in the first instance.

29. *Justices in quarter sessions to make new regulations for removal of Scottish and Irish poor, &c. to their respective places of birth or residence.*

And be it enacted, That the justices of the peace of every county, city, borough or place shall at their general or quarter sessions of the peace to be holden next after the passing of this Act, or some adjournment thereof, and from time to time thereafter, as they may see occasion, make regulations for the more effectually carrying into effect the provisions of this Act for the removal of such persons, their wives and children, whether by land or sea, or part of the way by land and part by sea; and as regards persons born in Scotland or Ireland, and their families, such justices shall, in such regulations, provide, so far as may be, for the removing of such persons to parts or places nearest to the respective places where such persons were born or have resided; and such regulations, when approved by the poor law commissioners, shall be observed and carried into effect by all justices of the peace, overseers, constables, and other persons charged with or concerned in such removal into such respective county, city, borough or place; and when any such regulations have been so approved, all rules, orders, regulations, and directions heretofore made for the removal of persons born in Scotland, Ireland, or the Isles of Man, Scilly, Jersey, or Guernsey, shall cease to have effect.

30. *Expenses of parishes to be repaid out of county rates.*

And be it enacted, That in case the overseers of the parish on whose complaint such last-mentioned warrant of removal was made, bring or send to the clerk of the peace, or town clerk of the county, city, borough or place in which such parish is situate, such warrant of removal, accompanied with an affidavit sworn before some justice of the peace of such county, city, borough or place (who is hereby authorised to adminster the same), of the amount of the expenses bonâ fide incurred and paid by such overseers on account of such removal, and also a statement of the several items comprised in such amount, such justice of the peace or town clerk shall lay the same before the justices of the peace assembled at the quarter sessions, or adjournment thereof, holden for such county, city, borough or place next after he has received the same; and the said justices, so assembled as aforesaid, shall, if the regulations in force in regard to such removal have been duly complied with, order the amount of such expenses to be paid out of the county rate raised in such county, city, borough or place.

31. *How such expenses are to be defrayed within London.*

And be it enacted, That all such expenses as last aforesaid properly and reasonably made out of the rates of any parish within the City of London, shall be charged against the said City of London; and when the justices of the said City of London assembled at any quarter sessions or adjourned sessions have audited and allowed such expenses, the chamberlain of the said City of London shall repay such expenses to the overseers of the said parish; and the justices of the said City of London shall, at such times as they may think fit, order a rate to be made in the several wards of the said city for the repayment of such expenses, and thereupon such rate shall be made in the same manner and with the same powers and authorities as the rates made for the relief of the poor in such parishes.

32. *How such expenses are to be defrayed by cities, &c. not contributing to county rate.*

And be it enacted, That in any city, borough, town corporate, division or liberty which does not contribute to the county rate, or in which no county rate, or rate in the nature of a county rate, is raised, but comprises more than one parish, the justices of the peace for such city, borough, town corporate, division or liberty, assembled at any quarter or adjourned sessions of the peace, shall order a general rate to be made in the parishes within such city, borough, town corporate, division or liberty, at such time as such justices think fit, for the repayment of the expenses incurred for the removal of persons born in Scotland, Ireland, or the Islands of Man, Scilly, Jersey, or Guernsey, and their families as aforesaid; and thereupon such rate shall be made in each of such parishes in the same manner and with the same powers and authorities as the rates made for the relief of the poor in such parishes.

33. *Appeals against such removals may be lodged at the instance of Boards of Guardians in Ireland, and of Kirk Session, Heritors, or Borough Magistrates in Scotland.*

And be it enacted, That if any board of guardians of any union in Ireland, or the heritors and kirk session, or borough magistrates in Scotland, think themselves aggrieved by any removal of any poor person under the provisions of the said Act; and if they forward to the poor law commissioners a statement of the case, and of any grounds for concluding that such poor person is to be deemed to be settled in any parish in England, or was liable to be removed to any parish in England, or was not in law liable to be removed from the parish from which he was in fact removed; and if they, or any persons on their behalf, give good security, in England, to the said commissioners, for the payment of all costs which may be incurred in any appeal against the warrant for the removal of such poor person, such commissioners, if satisfied that it will be expedient so to do, may appeal, on behalf of the persons so aggrieved, to the justice of the peace at any quarter sessions holden for the county, city, borough or place from which such removal was made, held at any time within *six* calendar months after such removal was completed; and such court shall proceed therein as in any case of appeal against a warrant of removal under this Act; and if the warrant of removal is reversed by such court, the overseeers of the parish on whose behalf the same was obtained shall pay the necessary expenses and charges of conveying the poor person removed under the same back to such parish; and if they refuse or neglect to pay the same within *three* days after demand thereof, the persons on whose behalf such appeal was brought, or any person authorised by them, may recover the same as penalties and forfeitures: Provided always, That the overseers of the parish on whose behalf such warrant was obtained, may at any time after such appeal give notice in writing, under the hands of any two or more of them, to the said commissioners, and to the persons on whose behalf such appeal was brought, that they abandon such warrant; and if they thereupon pay to such persons or to any person authorised by them, the expenses incurred by such persons by reason of such warrant, and in any proceedings consequent thereon, and the necessary expenses and charges of conveying the person removed under the same back to such parish, such appeal shall be no further prosecuted.

GUARDIANS INVESTED WITH POWERS FOR REMOVAL.—34. *Boards of Guardians may apply for warrants of removal in certain cases.*

And be it enacted, That if any person be liable to be removed from any parish under a Board of Guardians, or from any union, or from any parish in a union, it shall be lawful for justices of the peace to make a warrant for the removal of such person upon the complaint of the Board of Guardians of such parish or union, in like manner as such justices might do upon the complaint of the overseers of the parish to which such person may be chargeable; and such Board of Guardians shall have the like powers as overseers for the removal of such person.

35. *Appointment of a paid removing officer.*

And be it enacted, That the provisions of the said Act of the fifth year of the reign of King William the Fourth, intituled, "An Act for the amendment and better administration of the laws relating to the poor in England and Wales," relating to the appointment of paid officers, their duties, payment, continuance in office, and removal, shall extend and apply to the appointment of paid officers for the purpose of obtaining and executing warrants of removal, and the duties incident thereto or consequent thereupon.

CONSTRUCTION AND LIMITATION OF THE ACT.—36. *The Poor Law Amendment Act and this Act to be construed as one Act.*

And be it enacted, That the said Act of the fifth year of the reign of King William the Fourth, "for the amendment and better administration of the laws relating to the poor in England and Wales," and all Acts to amend and extend the same, and the present Act, except so far as the provisions of any former Act are altered, amended, or repealed by any subsequent Act, shall be construed as one Act.

37. *Act limited to England and Wales, except so far as relates to persons born in Scotland, &c.*

And be it enacted, That this Act shall apply so far as the same is applicable to the removal of poor persons born in Scotland and Ireland, and the Isles of Man, Scilly, Jersey, and Guernsey, and their families; but in other respects this Act shall extend only to England.

38. *Act may be amended this Session.*

And be it enacted, That this Act may be amended or repealed by any Act to be passed in this present Session of Parliament.

SCHEDULE

TO WHICH THE FOREGOING ACT REFERS.

FORM of WARRANT of REMOVAL of Persons born in Scotland or Ireland, or in the Isle of Man, or Scilly, or Jersey, or Guernsey.

To the Constable of the [parish or township] of in the County of

to wit. } WHEREAS complaint hath been made by the [churchwardens and overseers of the poor or guardians of the poor], of the parish, township, union [or as the case may be], in the said county of unto us, whose names are hereunto set, and seals affixed, two of Her Majesty's justices of the peace acting in and for the said county, that a person born in Scotland, [or Ireland, or the Isle of Man, or Scilly, or Jersey, or Guernsey], hath become and is now chargeable to the said parish and [or, to the parish of in the said union]: And whereas, upon examination of the said taken upon oath before us (which examination is hereto annexed), it doth appear, and we do adjudge that the hath not a settlement in England, and is not exempted temporarily or permanently from the liability to be removed from the said parish, and is not liable to be removed to any parish in England; and that he hath a wife named and children, videlicet neither of which children has any settlement in England.

These are therefore to require you, the said constable of aforesaid, in the county of aforesaid, to convey the said his wife and family aforesaid, to Scotland, [&c.] in the manner directed by the regulations of the justices of the said county, and approved by the Poor Law Commissioners, in pursuance of the provisions of a certain Act made and passed in the year of the reign of Queen VICTORIA, intituled [the title of this Act.]

Given under our hands and seals this day of in the year of our Lord one thousand eight hundred and

[Here copy the regulations of the justices of the county approved by the Poor Law Commissioners as applicable to the removal of the party.]

FORM OF EXAMINATION.

to wit. } The examination of taken on oath before us, two of Her Majesty's justices of the peace acting in and for the [county, riding, city, borough, town corporate, division or liberty] aforesaid, this day of in the year of our Lord one thousand eight hundred and , who on oath saith, that according to the best of [his or her] knowledge and belief, [he or she] born in in that part of the United Kingdom called Scotland [or Ireland, or in the Isle of Man, or Scilly, or Jersey, or Guernsey], which [he or she] left about years ago, and hath no settlement in that part of the United Kingdom called England, and hath actually become and is now chargeable to the [parish] of in the [county, township, &c. as the same may be], of and that he is not exempt from the liability to be removed therefrom [and that he hath a wife named and children, neither of which children have gained a settlement in England.]

Sworn the day and year first above written, before us

LONDON:

Printed by Order of the Poor Law Commissioners, by BLACKBURN and PARDON, 6, Hatton Garden, and Published by CHARLES KNIGHT and Co., 22, Ludgate Street, Publishers to the Poor Law Commissioners.

AN

OFFICIAL CIRCULAR

OF PUBLIC DOCUMENTS AND INFORMATION :

DIRECTED BY THE POOR LAW COMMISSIONERS TO BE PRINTED, CHIEFLY FOR THE USE OF THE MEMBERS AND PERMANENT OFFICERS OF BOARDS OF GUARDIANS, UNDER THE POOR LAW AMENDMENT ACT.

No. 39. CIRCULAR ISSUED SEPTEMBER 30, 1844.

Poor Law Commission Office,
Somerset House,
September 30, 1844.

THE Poor Law Commissioners, on a review of their Minutes, directed that the following Circular and Minutes of Correspondence explanatory of the provisions of the recent Act for the Amendment of the Poor Laws (7 & 8 Vic. c. 101,) should be printed and circulated for the information of Parish and Union Officers.

I.—THE OPERATION AND CONSTRUCTION OF THE ACT (7 & 8 VIC. c. 101,) *FOR THE FURTHER AMENDMENT OF THE LAWS RELATING TO THE POOR IN ENGLAND.*

This Act came into operation on the 10th of August, 1844, the day after it received the Royal Assent. (s. 76.)

It is to be construed as if it and the Poor Law Amendment Act (4 & 5 Wm. 4, c. 76) and the series of Acts amending and extending the latter were one Act. (s. 74.)

II.—RELIEF OF THE POOR.

The duty of relieving the poor is in no instance diminished, except by the abolition of compulsory apprenticeship, a mode of relief for poor children, but rarely resorted to in later times. Even in those instances in which new modes of relief are provided for particular classes of poor, the duty of relieving such poor in the manner required by the previous law is in no case dispensed with, and, in some instances, is expressly retained. Thus, in places where special provision may be made for the relief of houseless poor in Asylums, for large districts, the obligation imposed by previous Statutes or the regulations of the Commissioners, upon Guardians, Overseers, Relieving Officers, and Masters of Workhouses of the respective Parishes and Unions within those districts, to afford relief in cases of sudden and urgent necessity, or dangerous illness, is expressly retained. (s. 54.) Thus, also, although it is provided that non-resident relief may, in certain cases, be given to Widows, it is at the same time expressly provided, that the obligation to afford relief, previously imposed on the places where such Widows are resident, shall continue in full force. (s. 26.)

i.—*The Classes of Poor.*

Poor children can no longer be put out as apprentices under the 43 Eliz., or the 8 & 9 Wm. 3, c. 30, to parishioners unwilling to receive them; all provisions in those Acts, and in all other Acts, general or local, for this purpose, being repealed. (s. 13.)

But poor children may still be bound apprentices to persons willing to take them. Overseers, however, are, after the first day of October, 1844, deprived of the power of binding or assigning apprentices where there is a Board of Guardians, and their powers are transferred to such Guardians. (s. 12.)

The Poor Law Commissioners, in addition to their power to regulate the apprenticing of poor children under the 4 & 5 Wm. 4, c. 76, s. 15, which did not appear to extend to the controlling of the masters, are enabled by the present Act to prescribe the duties of the masters, and the terms and conditions to be inserted in the indentures; for breach of which the masters are made subject to a summary penalty not exceeding twenty pounds. (s. 12.)

Where there are Guardians, they are to execute the indenture of apprenticeship which, as a corporation under the 5 & 6 Vic., c. 57, s. 16, they will do by affixing their common seal; and in this case the allowance of the Justices of the Peace is dispensed with. The Guardians must cause their clerk to register all apprentices bound or assigned by them in the following form, so far as it is applicable to the case. (s. 12.) It is desirable that the Clerk should sign his name against each entry.

Form of the Register of Apprentices bound or assigned by the Board of Guardians of the ______________ Union.

Number	Date of Indenture	Name of Apprentice	Sex	Age	His or her Parents' Names	Their Residence	Name of the Persons to whom bound or assigned, as the case may be	His or her trade	His or her residence	Term of the Apprenticeship or Assignment	Apprentice or Assignment fee

Where there are no Guardians, the Overseers must still obtain the allowance of the Justices, and must in all other respects conform to the law previously in force.

The provisions of the Act do not extend to apprentices to be bound to the sea service, who must still be bound under the 5 & 6 Wm. 4, c. 19, until the 1st January, 1845. After that date they must be bound under the 7 and 8 Vic. c. 112, ss. 32—36.

The other provisions relating more particularly to the relief of children are of a local character. The more important of these are the powers for the formation of school districts for the management of orphan or deserted children, or children whose parents consent to their being placed in the district schools. The limit as to the size of these districts is such as to prevent them from being formed in any but a very few extremely populous places, and there only at the discretion of the Poor Law Commissioners (ss. 40 to 51.) These provisions, therefore, are too partial in operation to interest the great majority of parishes and unions. When school-districts are formed, however, it will be competent to the Board of Guardians of any parish or union, any part of which is within 20 miles from the district school, by arrangement with the district board, to send the children of their respective parishes or unions to the district school, upon such terms as are mutually agreed upon. (s. 51.)

The provisions of the Acts 2 Geo. 3, c. 22, and 7 Geo. 3, c. 39, relating to parish poor children within the city of London, and a certain district in its immediate vicinity, which provisions had for the most part been disregarded in practice, are now repealed. (s. 52.)

The changes in the law of bastardy, which will be hereafter more fully adverted to, make no difference in the legal obligation on parishes to relieve bastard children, whenever their necessities require relief.

Widows in certain cases are made the subject of a provision entirely new to the statute law. The provision is as follows :—

"In the case of any person being a widow—
having a legitimate child dependent on her for support—
and no illegitimate child born after the commencement of her widowhood—
and who at the time of her husband's death was resident with him, in some place other than the parish of her legal settlement, and not situate in any Union in which the parish of such settlement is comprised—
it shall be lawful for the Guardians of such parish or union, if they see fit, to grant relief to such widow, although not residing in such parish or union." (s. 26.)

It is to be observed that the widow must have been resident with her husband at the time of his death, not only out of the parish of her settlement, but also out of the Union in which that parish may be comprised. The object of the clause appears to be to avoid the disturbance of those connections and mode of life, at a distance from the Union, to which the family may have become accustomed, and which existed at the time of the husband's death.

Where all the conditions exist which would enable the Guardians to grant non-resident relief, they are still to use their discretion, as to whether non-resident relief to the widow is in each particular case desirable. The general objections to such relief, such as the difficulty of ascertaining the circumstances of paupers beyond the power of inspection of the Guardians or their officers, and the further difficulties attendant on the transmission of relief to places where the Guardians have no authority and no official agency, will be weighed by the guardians.

This power is one entrusted to Boards of Guardians only. Overseers acquire no authority under this provision to administer non-resident relief to the class of widows described.

It must be borne in mind by Guardians and their Officers that they are in no wise exempted from their previous obligation to relieve any widow who may be in their parish or Union requiring relief, by the power thus given to the Guardians of the place of her settlement to afford her non-resident relief. And even when that power is exerted, if, notwithstanding the relief sent to her by her parish, she or her children require additional or further relief, the officers of the place where she is, are still bound as heretofore to afford her the relief which the circumstances require. (s. 26.)

Married Women, whose children required and received relief, were not before the passing of this Act liable to any conditions in respect of such relief, and could cast off their children upon the parish, however well such women might be able to maintain their children, or to contribute to their maintenance. Widows, on the other hand, were liable to the like conditions and consequences of relief afforded to themselves and their children, as the fathers of legitimate children are. The present Act declares that while the husband of any woman is beyond the seas (that is, out of Great Britain), or in custody of the law, or in confinement in any licensed house or asylum as a lunatic or idiot, all relief given to the wife, or to her child or children shall, notwithstanding her coverture, be given to her, in the same manner and subject to the same conditions as if she were a widow. (s. 25.)

Insane Poor, in places where the Poor Laws are administered under Local Acts, are placed under the control of the Guardians and Officers appointed under such Local Acts, in the same manner as if they were appointed under the Poor Law Amendment Act. (s. 28.) The Guardians under such Local Acts will therefore exercise all the duties and powers in respect to insane persons, as Overseers were previously invested with. The Guardians may contract with a medical man to certify as to the state of insane persons. The Officers, who under such Local Act, exercise the functions of Relieving Officers, must give to the Justices the information heretofore required of Overseers. The Officer performing the duties of Clerk to the Guardians, must on the 15th of August, in every year, make out two lists of all the insane persons chargeable, and transmit one copy to the Clerk of the Peace of the County, and the other copy to the Poor Law Commissioners. (5 & 6 Vic., c. 57, s. 6.)

Houseless Poor are for the first time particularly provided for by the general law. The asylums for their reception and relief can only be established in the Metropolis, and in five other populous cities and towns. (ss. 40 to 55.)

ii.—*Modes of Relief.*

Relief, with the above exception in the case of certain widows, remains subject in all cases to the regulation of the Poor Law Commissioners, and is to be administered by Guardians and their officers, and the Overseers of the Poor, in all respects as before the passing of the Act.

The administration of *relief in the Workhouse* is freed from some technical difficulties. Relief in a Union Workhouse is to be deemed relief in the parish to which the pauper is chargeable. There will, therefore, be no further doubt as to the power of executing an order of removal from the Workhouse. (s. 56.) The punishment for offences in the Workhouses, or in relation to the property therein, under the 2nd and 5th sects. of the 55th Geo. 3, c. 137, is in the first case made capable of mitigation, at the discretion of the Justices; and in the last case, if the offence be repeated, may be increased. (s. 58.) Persons convicted before Justices of any offence in a Workhouse, or absconding from any workhouse with parish property, could only be committed to the gaol of the place where the offence was committed; that is to say, of the place where the Workhouse was situated. Now they may be committed to the gaol of the place where they were chargeable. (s. 57.)

Emigration. — The Guardians appointed under the Poor Law Amendment Act, are exclusively to apply money raised or borrowed under that Act for the purpose of emigration. (s. 29.)

Burial. — Guardians and Overseers have hitherto been without legal authority to provide directly for the burial of paupers dying out of the Workhouse. Guardians, and Overseers in places where there are no Guardians, are now enabled to bury the dead body of any poor person being within their parish or union. The churchyard or other consecrated burial-ground belonging to the parish, or place in which the death occurred, is to be the ordinary place of burial, for the bodies, both of persons who have been chargeable in their lifetime, and of those who have not. If, however, a deceased person in his lifetime, or the husband or wife, or next of kin of deceased have otherwise desired, it would appear that the Guardians may have regard to such desire, and may arrange and pay for the burial elsewhere. In any case where the deceased has been chargeable to any other parish than that in which he died, the Guardians are enabled, either in compliance with any desire expressed by the deceased, or by any of his relations, or for any other cause, to direct authoritatively that the body be buried in the churchyard or burial-ground of the parish to which the deceased was so chargeable. (s. 31, see also s. 56.) This latter provision is intended for the benefit of parishes where Union Workhouses are situate, upon whom the burden has hitherto fallen of providing ground for the burial of the paupers of other parishes dying in the Workhouse.

III. — LIABILITIES OF PERSONS RELIEVED.

Generally the obligations of persons to maintain themselves, of parents to maintain their children, of husbands to maintain their wives, and of such persons, parents, and husbands to repay the cost of relief to themselves, their children, or wives; of grandfathers and grandmothers to contribute to the maintenance of their grandchildren; and of children to contribute to the maintenance of their parents, remain undiminished.

The estates of *Insane Persons and Idiots* were only liable in a very imperfect manner to the repayment of relief afforded them. Now to the extent to which their property may be more than sufficient to maintain their families, such property is made liable generally to repay the costs incurred by parishes in respect of such persons, and Trustees and all other persons in possession of property belonging to insane or idiot persons, are indemnified for any payments they may make to Guardians or Overseers. (s. 27.)

The Fathers of Legitimate Children remain liable for the relief of such children as heretofore, and their liabilities are continued unimpaired in the cases where their wives are made responsible in respect of the same relief. (s. 25.)

The wife of a man beyond the seas, (that is, out of Great Britain,) or in the custody of the law, or in confinement as a lunatic or idiot, in a licensed house or asylum, is to receive relief for herself and her children in the same manner and subject to the same conditions as if she were a widow. (s. 25.) Where widows are obliged to receive relief for their children within the Union or within the Workhouse, these married women will be subject to the like condition. Relief may be afforded to such married women or their children as a loan, repayable by such married women, notwithstanding the ordinary exemption of married women from similar liabilities.

The Mothers of Bastards, and *the Putative Fathers of Bastards* are the subjects of the most considerable change in the policy of the law effected by the present Act. (ss. 1—11.)

The principle of the Law for charging the putative fathers of bastard children is wholly different from that of any law which has heretofore been in force in England, either before or since the Poor Law Amendment Act. Formerly the remedy was intended exclusively for the Parish: now the mother alone can obtain it, and the Parish is expressly prohibited from originating any proceedings for obtaining the order or payment under it to themselves. Formerly the chargeability of the child, either in fact or in prospect, was the ground of the remedy: now the actual or probable chargeability of the child is made wholly immaterial.

It is very necessary that Guardians and Overseers should make themselves fully aware of the nature of so much of this change as effects them as officers, inasmuch as their powers for the enforcement of the liabilities of putative fathers are abrogated, and their interference in the matter in which they were formerly exclusively concerned is now made criminal.

All the pre-existing powers for making orders on putative fathers for the maintenance of bastard children are abrogated from the 10th of August, 1844 (s. 1), except only in the cases where proceedings before Justices were pending on that day, in which cases the proceedings may be continued, and orders made as if the Act had not passed. (s. 9.)

Orders previously made (and apparently orders afterwards made in cases pending on the 10th of August, 1844) remain valid according to their effect. But orders made before the 14th of August, 1834, (the date of the passing of the Poor Law Amendment Act) which had, as to the time of their operation, no defined limit, are not to remain in force after the 1st of January, 1849, at which date the most recent of such orders will have been in force more than fourteen years and four months. (s. 9.) Orders made since the passing of the Poor Law Amendment Act remain in force only until the child attains the age of seven years, and the last of these Orders must expire some time before the 9th of August, 1851.

The parish is deprived of the power to apply for any order on the putative father.

The mother alone of the bastard is entitled to apply for such an order.

No officer of any parish or union may conduct any application to make or enforce any such order, or in any way interfere in causing such an application to be made, or in procuring evidence to support such application, or in receiving money under such an order. If he does so he is subject to a penalty of 40*s*. But after the death of the mother, or when she becomes legally incapable of receiving the money under an order, if a child for whose maintenance an order has been made, becomes chargeable to a parish or union through the neglect of the putative father to make the payments due from him under the order, in such a case the Guardians, or if there are no Guardians, the Overseers, may so far interfere as is necessary to compel a compliance with the order; but even in this case they must not receive the money, but it must be paid to some person appointed to have the custody of the child, who is to receive it on the condition that the child is to cease to be chargeable. (s. 7.)

Any officer of a union or parish who endeavours to induce any man to contract marriage, by means of threat or promise respecting any application for an order, or enforcement of an order, is declared guilty of a misdemeanour. (s. 8.)

The *Mothers of Bastards* remain, as heretofore, liable while unmarried, or in the state of widowhood, to maintain such bastards up to the age of 16, or the previous marriage of their female bastards (Poor Law Amendment Act, s. 71.) By the recent Act such mothers are expressly subjected to the punishment of idle and disorderly persons under the Vagrant Act, for neglecting to maintain such bastards, and permitting them to become chargeable, and to the punishment of rogues and vagabonds for offending in the same way a second time, or for deserting such children, and so permitting them to become chargeable. (s. 6.)

IV.—POOR RATES—THEIR ASSESSMENT, COLLECTION AND APPROPRIATION.

Assessment.—The Act referred to makes no alteration in the law relating to the assessment to the Poor Rate. The Act 7 and 8 Vic., c. 40, continues the exemption of stock in trade for another year.

Collection.—Provisions are made for the better collection of Poors' Rates, with the view more especially of connecting the Guardians more closely with the operation, and of giving them a better security for the supply of the funds they require for the performance of their duties. On the application of any Board of Guardians, the Poor Law Commissioners can issue an order for the appointment by such Guardians of a Collector of Poors' Rates, who is to be subject to the laws and regulations applicable to other paid officers appointed by Guardians. When such order is issued, the powers of all other persons to appoint officers to collect Poors' Rates in the same parish are to cease. (s. 62.)

As regards the Collectors and Assistant Overseers heretofore appointed under the orders of the Poor Law Commissioners, confirmed by the 2nd and 3rd Vic., c. 84, any such Collector or Assistant Overseer may be appointed by the inhabitants in Vestry, of any parish in which he was acting, on the 10th of August, 1844, to discharge all the duties of an Assistant Overseer, in addition to the collection of Poors' Rates. Every Collector and Assistant Overseer is to obey in all matters relating to the duties of Overseers the directions of the majority of the Overseers, and the Overseers' responsibility for the provision and supply of money for the relief of the poor and other lawful purposes is, notwithstanding the appointment of the Assistant Overseer, still retained. (s. 61.)

If the Overseers of any parish neglect to make or collect sufficient rates for the relief of the poor, or to pay such monies to the Guardians, as the Guardians may require, and if in consequence any relief directed by the Guardians be withheld during a period of seven days, every such Overseer is liable to a penalty of £20. (s. 63.)

Appropriation.—The appropriation of the Poors' Rates is in no instance restricted, though their due appropriation is better secured. On the other hand the appropriation to new or extended purposes is authorised in several instances by the present Act, as in the case of—

The costs and fees for burial of poor persons. (s. 31.)

The providing of district schools. (s. 47.)

The providing of district asylums. (s. 48.)

The payment of the salaries of auditors of districts for schools or asylums. (s. 49.)

The extension of the amount to be expended on workhouses in the Metropolis and Liverpool. (s. 30.)

Expense of recovering balances on accounts, and of the auditor in defending his decisions (ss. 35, 39,) and, where the court orders it, of the party impugning his decision. (s. 35.)

The apprehension and prosecution of persons under the Vagrant Act, being chargeable or making their families chargeable. (s. 59.)

or disobeying the regulations of the Poor Law Commissioners. (s. 59.)

guilty of offence or misbehaviour in workhouses. (*ib.*)

absconding from workhouses with clothes, &c. (*ib.*)

disobeying the lawful and reasonable orders of Justices or Guardians, or district boards. (*ib.*)

obstructing or assaulting officers engaged in administering the Poor Laws. (*ib.*)

unlawfully obtaining or misapplying property applicable to the relief of the poor. (*ib.*)

guilty of any offence directly affecting the administration of the Poor Laws. (*ib.*)

The apprehending and prosecuting of officers employed in the administration of the Poor Laws for neglect or breach of duty. (*ib.*)

All these payments under s. 59, are to be made by Guardians or district boards, and are to be charged, subject to the approval of the Poor Law Commissioners, to the particular parishes or unions concerned, or to the common fund of the union or district. (*ib.*)

The making out, preparing, printing, and collecting the lists of persons to serve on juries. (s. 60.)

The perambulation of parishes, not more than once in 3 years, and the setting up and maintaining boundary stones. (s. 60.)

In addition to these new and extended purposes, a new mode of appropriating the Poors' Rate to the purposes of the County, Hundred, Police, and other like rates, is authorised to be levied in Counties and parts of Counties, provided by another Act, the 7 and 8 Vic., c. 33. This Act enables Justices, after the 1st of October, 1844, so soon as any vacancy occurs in the Office of High Constable, to issue their precepts for the payment of such Rates to the Guardians at once, by Post or otherwise, without the intervention of the High Constable. The Guardians are required to raise and pay such Rates. (s. 1.) If they fail to do so the monies may be levied from the Overseers, with an addition of One Shilling in every ten. (s. 2.) The provisions of the whole of this Act should be carefully examined by the Guardians and Overseers.

V.—ACCOUNTS—AUDIT—RECOVERY OF BALANCES.

Important changes are made by the 7 and 8 Vic., c. 101, for the purpose of increasing the efficiency of the Audit, and of the remedies against defaulters.

Accounts.—The Accounts are no longer required by Statute to be rendered every quarter of the year; they are to be rendered as often as the Commissioners may direct, but not less than once in every half year. (s. 38.) The subsisting orders of the Commissioners which remain in force, still require the Accounts to be rendered quarterly, and until these are revoked, the Accounts must be so rendered.

In order to clear the future accounts from the embarrassment, caused by old disputed Accounts, and by the bringing forward of balances found before the passing of the Act, against Officers now out of office, and which, in many cases, are not recoverable from the persons who were originally in default;—there is a power given to the Auditor, with the consent of the Poor Law Commissioners, to discharge existing Officers from responsibility in respect of such balances. Old balances not so discharged are to be recovered as found by the Auditor (s. 34); and the persons against whom they were originally struck may be proceeded against for them under this act.

In future the Overseers and other Officers of Parishes are required to make up and balance their books of account, seven clear days before the Audit, (s. 33,) of which they will have had notice from the Auditor fourteen days before the Audit. (*ib.*) The Overseers and other Officers are to deposit such books at the house of one of the Officers of the parish for such seven days to be inspected, between the hours of eleven and three, by any person liable to be rated to the relief of the poor. Notice is to be affixed at the usual places for giving notices, stating the place where the books are deposited, and the time and place of Audit. (*ib.*) If any Overseer or Officer neglect to make up his account, or to give notice of the time and place of Audit or inspection, or alter his account, or refuse to allow it to be inspected, he is made liable to forfeit 40*s*. (s. 33.)

It will be observed, that all these provisions are in force at once without any reference to the appointment of a district Auditor, or any orders of the Commissioners.

Audit.—Every Rate-payer is entitled to be present at the Audit, and, if he thinks fit, to make any objection. (s. 33.)

The Auditor may require any person holding, or accountable for any money or property relating to the relief of the poor, to produce accounts and vouchers, and to make and sign a declaration with respect to such accounts. (s. 33.)

If any person required by the Auditor to attend his audit fails to do so, or to produce his accounts or vouchers, or refuses to make or sign a declaration as to his accounts if required, he is made liable to a penalty of Forty Shillings, and if he make a false declaration, to the penalties of perjury.

District Auditors.—With the exception of certain places under local Acts (s. 65), it is intended that the whole of England and Wales should be comprised in more extensive districts of audit, consisting of combinations of Unions, or of Unions and parishes. The Commissioners are enabled from time to time to form and alter such districts. Thereupon the Chairman and Vice-Chairman of Boards of Guardians, or where there are no Guardians, the Overseers are to elect the Auditor of the District, in a manner to be prescribed by the Commissioners. (s. 32.) But Auditors of districts existing at the time of the passing of the Act may be retained. Where districts are altered, the Auditor's office is not vacated. (s. 37.)

Such Auditor has full power to audit, allow, and disallow of accounts, and is invested with a new and important authority of charging any person accounting, with deficiencies and losses, caused by the negligence of such person, or with any sums for which he may be accountable. (s. 32.)

The Auditor is to certify on the face of the account the sums which he finds to be due. (*ib.*)

The person from whom any money is so certified to be due, notwithstanding that he may continue in office, and would hitherto have been still entitled to hold the balance, is now bound, within seven days, to pay the money into the hands of the Treasurer of the Guardians, where there is such an officer. In the case of a Union the Guardians are to apply such sum for the benefit of the parishes respectively interested in the money. (*ib.*) The importance of this provision is very great, as rendering the audit operative immediately, and preventing officers from still keeping in their hands the balances found to be due from them. Overseers and other officers leaving office must actually pay over the balances due from them, and the law can no longer be evaded by a mere entry to their credit in their successors' accounts.

If there is no treasurer, the money certified to be due must be paid over within seven days, to the person authorised to receive it. (*ib.*)

If the money be not duly paid, it is to be

recovered, as certified, on the application of the auditor, or any person authorised to receive it, that is, by the Treasurer; or, if there is no such Treasurer, by the officer succeeding the Accountant. The expenses of the recovery, if not obtained from the person accounting, are to be repaid to the Auditor by the Guardians. (*ib.*)

If any person refuse to deliver over other property, he is liable to the same penalties and proceedings as Overseers who neglect to deliver over the property of the parish to their successors. (*ib.*)

In order to prevent the practice occasionally resorted to by parish officers, of making up from other rates the sums disallowed in the accounts of Poors' Rate, it is provided that if any Churchwarden, Surveyor of Highways, Overseer, or other officer of any parish or union, wilfully makes any illegal payment from any rate or fund of a parish or union, or any unlawful entry in his accounts, for the purpose of making up to himself or any other person, any sums disallowed or surcharged in account, the offender, on conviction before two Justices, shall forfeit three times the amount of such payment, or of the sum wrongfully entered in the account, in addition to a penalty not exceeding £20. (*ib.*)

Any person aggrieved by the decision of the Auditor may require the Auditor to state his reasons for his decision, and may have a certiorari in the Court of Queen's Bench, to try the legality of the Auditor's decision, (s. 35); or in lieu of applying at once for a certiorari, may apply to the Poor Law Commissioners to decide upon the question, which they may do by order under their hands and seal, and this order may then be removed into the Queen's Bench by certiorari. (s. 36.)

In every district for which an Auditor is appointed under this Act, the power of Justices of the Peace, and of all other persons, to audit the same accounts, is repealed. (s. 37.)

VI.—APPOINTMENT AND ELECTION OF PARISH AND UNION OFFICERS.

Overseers.—The power to appoint separate Overseers *for Townships or Villages*, which had not separate Overseers appointed before the 10th of August, 1844, is repealed. (s. 22.)

Election of Guardians.—Powers are given for altering the number of Guardians to be elected for a Parish (s. 18,) and for dividing parishes for purposes of election into Wards (ss. 19, 20, 21,) and for adding Parishes to Unions or separating Parishes from Unions, and constituting Boards of Guardians for the Parishes so separated. (s. 66.) But nothing is to be done in these matters until orders are issued by the Commissioners for the purpose.

Considerable changes are made in the *Constituency* who elect the Guardians.

In the first place, as regards the *Rate-payers*—in order to vote they are not required to have paid any other parochial rates and assessments besides the rates made for the relief of the poor. (s. 16.) The periods for which they must have been rated, and have paid their Poors' Rate, remain unchanged.

They are hereafter to have the same number of votes in proportion to the value of property as owners (s. 14); namely:—

For less than	£50	1 Vote
For £50 and less than	£100	2 Votes
For £100 ———	£150	3 Votes
For £150 ———	£200	4 Votes
For £200 ———	£250	5 Votes
For £250 and upwards.	. . . .	6 Votes

The votes of *Owners of Property* are reduced in proportion to their property, and

The scale of their voting is identified with that on which rate-payers vote, as just before stated. (s. 14.)

It is necessary that before the 1st of February in each year, Owners should make statements containing particulars set forth in the present Act. Statements of owners once made will remain good while the circumstances described in the statement remain the same. But no statement will operate during any year unless made before the 1st of February in that year.

The statement must contain—

- a description of the interest or estate the owner has in the property—
- a statement of the amount of all rent service (*i. e.* rent not being rent charges, or rents sec., annuities, incumbrances, &c.,) which he may receive in respect of the property, and of the persons from whom he receives it—
- a like statement of the amount of all rent service he may pay in respect of the same property, and of the persons to whom he pays it (s. 15.)—

Owners may appoint *proxies* as heretofore, but no person can vote as proxy until fourteen days after he has made his claim to vote. And no person can vote as proxy for more than four owners of property, unless he be a Steward, Bailiff, Land Agent, or Collector of Rents for such owners. And no appointment of proxy is to remain in force for more than two years, excepting only in the case where an owner appoints his Tenant, Bailiff, Steward, Land Agent, or Collector of Rents, in which case the appointment will remain in force while such relation between the owner and the proxy continues.

It is important, in order to prevent the disfranchisement of many owners, that this information should be conveyed to them by any means which the Guardians can resort to for the purpose. An extract from this circular might be affixed to the church-door in every parish about the 1st of January next.

The statements of owners are to be *registered* by Overseers as heretofore. But in parishes containing a population exceeding 2000 persons, they must complete the registry before the 5th of February in each year, and allow any person to inspect it without fee, between the 5th and the 10th of February. Any person who has claimed as owner or proxy, and any Rate-payer, may object to any other person as not being entitled to vote as an owner, by delivering to the Clerk to the Guardians notice in writing of the grounds of his objection. Provisions are made for revising the registries in such parishes, and the persons whose names are left in the Register by the Revising Officer are to be alone entitled to vote as owners in the year following the then next 25th of March. (s. 15.)

The time for the *annual election* of Guardians, is now extended to forty days after the 25th of March. (s. 17.)

Ex-officio Guardians.—Justices of the Peace residing in extra-parochial places, whose boundary line is included within that of the Union, or for the greater part coincident with it, are to be declared to be *Ex-officio* Guardians of the Union. Every Justice also residing in any parish in a Union, although that parish is not within his jurisdiction as a Justice, is declared to be an Ex-officio Guardian. (s. 24.)

VII.—DISTRICTS FOR ADMINISTRATION OF THE POOR LAWS.

The prohibition of the further division of parishes for the appointment of Overseers, the power to divide parishes into wards for the election of Guardians, the powers to add to Unions or diminish them, the power to combine parishes and Unions into districts for the maintenance of schools and asylums, and for audit, have been adverted to before.

VIII.—SIMPLIFICATION OF LEGAL PROCEEDINGS.

Various provisions are made for avoiding formal and technical difficulties, and occasions for expense, in the conduct of the legal business of parishes and Unions.

Such is the declaration that the Workhouse for all purposes of relief, settlement, and removal, and for the burial of the poor, shall be considered as situated in the parish to which the person relieved or removed, or whose body is to be buried, is or was chargeable. (s. 56.)

The Clerk, or any other officer empowered by a Board of Guardians, is enabled to take, resist, and conduct proceedings on behalf of the Board before Justices of the Peace acting singly, or in Petty or Special Sessions, although such clerk or officer is not an attorney. (s. 68.) This removes the question which was raised upon this subject in reference to the Act for amending the law relating to Attornies (6 and 7 Vic., c. 73,) so far only as relates to business before Justices out of Quarter or General Sessions. As regards other business, the right of Clerks of Guardians who are not professional men, to act for the Guardians in legal proceedings, remains on the same footing as before.

Another Act, the 7 and 8 Vic., c. 33, before referred to, contains (s. 7) a provision of great importance to Guardians as regards the enforcement of their orders on Overseers for the payment of the contributions of parishes. Any person may apply to any one Justice acting for a division, for a notice of a Special Sessions to be holden. Such Justice may sign such notice, which, being sent by post, a reasonable time before the day for holding the sessions, to the address of each Justice residing and usually acting within the division,—the Special Sessions may thereupon lawfully proceed in the matter.

In all proceedings before Justices in Petty or Special Sessions, or out of Sessions, any Justices may, on the request of a party, summon any person to appear as a witness. If the person summoned having been paid or tendered his expenses do not appear, he may be brought up by the warrant of one Justice. Any person before Justices in Petty or Special Sessions or out of Sessions refusing to give evidence, may be committed to gaol for fourteen days, unless he previously submits to be examined. (s. 70.)

The evidence of proceedings of the Guardians, and of facts in which they are interested is, in several matters, made more cheap and easy by the 69th sect. of the 7 and 8 Vic., c. 101. The Guardians' Certificate of the chargeability of a pauper is made evidence of that fact. Copies of the minutes of the Guardians under their seal, signed by the Chairman and counter-signed by their Clerk, are to be received in evidence, without proof of the seal being that of the Guardians, or the signatures being those of the Chairman and Clerk. (s. 69.)

The Rules, Orders, and Regulations of the Poor Law Commissioners, when printed by the Queen's Printer, are to be received in evidence, and taken notice of judicially by all Courts and Judges, when so printed. (s. 71.)

Evidence of the transmission of the Rules, Orders, and Regulations of the Poor Law Commissioners to any other person than the Clerk of the Guardians, or where there are no Guardians, to the Overseers, is also dispensed with in all civil and criminal proceedings, unless special notice is given that proof of the transmission will be required. (s. 72.)

IX.—SUMMARY OF DUTIES OF GUARDIANS AND THEIR OFFICERS, AND OF OVERSEERS.

It may be well shortly to indicate the powers and duties which Guardians and their Officers, and Overseers, are called on to exercise and perform under the Act, without previous order or intimation from the Poor Law Commissioners. Such powers and duties as depend on some previous act of the Commissioners will be best explained on the occasions when the Commissioners may be called on to act.

The Guardians—

To abstain from interference on applications in bastardy. Proviso (s. 7.)

After the 1st of October, 1844, to bind apprentices, exclusively of the Overseers, (s. 12), and to cause their Clerk to keep a Register, (*ib.*)

To apply the money raised for the purposes of emigration (s. 29)—

To bury the bodies of poor persons within their parish or union (s. 31)—

To pay various expenses of legal proceedings (s. 59)—

To put in suit bonds and securities given by Assistant Overseers to Overseers (s. 61)—

And under the 7 and 8 Vic., c. 33, s. 1, on receipt of the precepts of Justices of the Peace, to pay County Rate, Hundred Rate, Police or other like Rates.

The Clerk to the Guardians—

To abstain from interference in applications in bastardy (s. 7)—

After the 1st October, 1844, to keep a register of children apprenticed or assigned by the Guardians (s. 12)—

To receive notice of grounds of objection to persons voting as owners (s. 15)—

And on or before the 20th of February, to send notice of revision of the register of owners (*ib.*)—

When empowered by Guardians, to conduct their legal proceedings before Justices out of Quarter or General Sessions (s. 68).

The Auditor—(whether he be a district auditor, or an auditor already appointed, and acting under the 4th and 5th Wm. 4, c. 70.)

To send 14 days' notice of Audit to Overseers and other Officers of parishes, by post or otherwise (s. 33)—

Such Notice may be in the following form :—

To the Overseers of the Parish [or Township, &c.] of

In pursuance of the Act of Parliament 7 and 8 Vic., c. 101, for the further Amendment of the Laws relating to the Poor in England,

THIS IS TO GIVE YOU NOTICE, that I shall attend as Auditor of the to Audit the Accounts of your [Parish, &c.] at on day, the th day of

You are required by the above-named Act of Parliament to have your Rate Books and other Accounts made up and balanced, Seven clear Days before the day fixed for the Audit. You are likewise to deposit them for the inspection of all persons liable to be rated to the relief of the Poor, at the house of a Churchwarden, Overseer, Collector, or Assistant-Overseer, or some other Parish Officer, and you are, as soon as such books are ready for inspection, to affix at the usual places of giving Parish Notices, Notice of the time and place of Audit, as above notified by me, and of the place where the Rate Books and Books of Account are deposited.

To receive objections of Rate-payers at the Audit—

On application of Parish Officers or Guardians, and with the consent of the Commissioners, to discharge old or disputed balances (s. 34)—

To state reasons for his decisions, if required, and to defend them on Certiorari (s. 35)—

To decide on legality of Law Bills, and where such bills are not taxed, on the reasonableness of the particular items (s. 39).

Overseers—

To abstain from interference in applications in bastardy. Proviso (s. 7)—

To abstain after the 1st of October, 1844, from apprenticing or assigning poor children (s. 12)—

Where there are no Guardians, to bury the bodies of poor persons within the parish (s. 31)—

To receive statements of owners and proxies (s. 15)—

And where the population exceeds 2000, to keep a register of owners' statements, to allow inspection of it, to publish notice of revision, and to attend the revising officer (s. 15)—

Seven days before audit, to make up their rate books and books of account, to deposit them for inspection, and immediately give notice thereof, and of the time and place of audit.—

Such Notice may be in the following form :—

To the Rate Payers, and persons liable to be rated to the relief of the poor of the Parish [or Township, &c.] of

We, the Churchwardens and Overseers of the Parish [Township, &c.] of HEREBY GIVE NOTICE, that the Auditor of the has notified to us, that he will attend to Audit the Accounts of the Officers of this Parish [&c.] at on day the th day of

AND that the Rate-books of the said Parish, and the book of Account of the said Officers, are deposited at the house of at within the Parish [&c.]

AND that the said books will be there open for the inspection of every person liable to be rated to the relief of the Poor of the said Parish [&c.,] until the day of Audit, between the hours of 11 in the Forenoon, and 3 of the Afternoon of each day.

} CHURCHWARDENS.

} OVERSEERS.

Under the 7 and 8 Vic., c. 33, if the Guardians fail to pay the County Rate or any similar rate required by the Justices, the Overseers are to pay the same, with an addition of one shilling in every ten shillings (s. 2, 3.) In certain parishes payment is to be made without a previous precept issuing to Guardians (s. 5.)

Correspondence.

I.—BASTARDY.—MODE OF ESTABLISHING LIABILITY OF PUTATIVE FATHER. (7 & 8 Vic. c. 101, s. 2.)

September 7th, 1844.

Clerk of the Atherstone Union—Referred to the 2nd clause of the recent act, and stated that considerable doubt existed as to its proper meaning. The wording and punctuation would seem to imply that in every case in which a woman was permitted to summon the putative father, it must be upon proof that the man had within twelve months next after the birth paid money for the child's maintenance, and failing in the preliminary proof, no summons could be granted ; if this was the legal construction, the act would in most cases be inoperative, as few women ever have or can give proof of payment of money. But it was suggested, that, notwithstanding the ordinary reading and punctuation, the intention of the legislature was to confine the proof of payment of money solely to those cases which should not be made within twelve months from the birth of the child, and that the words "or at any time thereafter upon proof that the man, &c. has paid money, &c.," must be taken as one sentence and referable only to applications made beyond the period of twelve months from the birth.

Ans.—The Commissioners are of opinion that the construction suggested is the true one, viz. that the words "upon proof that the man alleged to be the father of such child, has within the twelve months next after the birth of such child paid money for its maintenance," do not govern the whole of the preceding part of the section, but are restricted to the case provided by the words which immediately precede, "or at any time thereafter," (*i. e.* when the application is made after a lapse of twelve months from the birth.) Consequently that in cases where the application is made within the twelve months from the birth of the child, it will not be necessary in support of such application to give proof that money has been paid by the reputed father towards the child's support.

II.—CLERK.—POWER TO ACT PROFESSIONALLY, IN HIS PRIVATE CAPACITY, IN BASTARDY CASES. (7 & 8 Vic. c. 101, s. 7.)

August 29th, 1844.

Clerk of the Ulverstone Union — Inquired whether in his private capacity as an attorney (and not as clerk to the guardians) he could properly, on behalf of the mother of a bastard child, conduct, assist in, advise on, or otherwise interfere in any application for an order on the putative father, under the 7th sec. of the recent act.

Ans.—By section 7 of the New Act, 7 & 8 Vic. c. 101, the clerk of the guardians is prohibited from interfering *as Clerk*, in matters of this nature; this does not, however, seem to extend to his private capacity.

The Commissioners at the same time add, that as you will be liable to a penalty for contravention of that section, they must leave you to act on your own judgment.

III.—GUARDIAN.

EX-OFFICIO, QUALIFICATION OF—(7 & 8 Vic. c. 101. s. 24.)

September 30th, 1844.

Clerk of the L— Union—Stated, that the parish of A—— was, for the purpose of supporting the poor, divided into two parts, one part being in the L—— Union, and the other part in the K—— Union. That a county magistrate acting in both parts of the parish, and residing in the L—— Union, was desirous of acting as *ex-officio* guardian in both the said Unions, which he considered himself intitled to do under 7 & 8 Vic. c. 101, s. 24, which enacted that "every justice of the peace residing in any parish within such a union, and acting for any county, riding, or division in which any part of such union is situated, shall be, *ex-officio*, a guardian of such union." Requested Commissioners' opinion thereon.

Ans.—Although you state merely that the magistrate referred to "resides in the L—— Union," the Commissioners presume, from the nature of the question, that he in fact lives in that portion of the parish of A—— which is situated within that union. But whether this be so or not, if he resides in any parish in the L—— Union, and acts for the county in which any part of that union lies, he is, *ex-officio*, a guardian of such union. With regard to the K—— Union, the question seems to be, whether he can act as an ex-officio guardian for that Union, in respect of his residence in that portion of the parish of A—— which is in the L—— Union,—the remaining portion of that parish being in the K—— Union. The Commissioners are of opinion that he cannot so act. The latter part of the 24th sec. of 7 and 8 Vic. c. 101, relates to the cases where unions are situated in two or more counties. In such cases a justice residing in any parish within such union, although the parish is not within the county for which he acts, is nevertheless enabled to act as *ex-officio* guardian of the union if he is in the commission of the peace for any of the counties. The terms of this provision are not more favourable to the present claim than the terms of the Poor Law Amendment Act, s. 38. As regards the terms of the 24th sec. of 7 and 8 Vic. c. 101, it is in the first case obvious that the ecclesiastical parish of A——— is not in an ordinary sense, within the K——— Union, being only partly within the union. Now there is nothing in the provision of the Act to get over this difficulty. The Act only treats as parishes those places that maintain their own poor separately. (sec. 109 of the Poor Law Amendment Act.) It is only in this sense that the word parish is used in the 38th section of the Act; and the 7 and 8 Vic. c. 101, s. 74, requires both Acts to be construed as one Act. There is every reason, therefore, why the word "parish" in the 24th section should be construed as having the sense in which it is used in the 38th sec.

of the Poor Law Amendment Act, both clauses being concerned about precisely the same matter. It therefore does not seem to the Commissioners that the justice of the peace in question complies with the condition to entitle him to act as *ex-officio* guardian of the K—— Union, *i.e.* they do not consider him to be a "justice of the peace residing in any parish in K—— Union." If by "parish" is understood the whole parish of A——, that is not in the K—— Union. If by parish is understood the township or division maintaining its own poor, in which he resides, that is in the L—— Union only. The Commissioners therefore consider that a justice who lives in the one division of the parish cannot be regarded as residing in the other division, within the meaning of the 24th sec. of 7 and 8 Vic. c. 101. It appears to the Commissioners that this view is supported by the consideration that, as the parochial concerns of the two divisions are quite distinct, a resident in one has no such interest in the affairs of the other as constitutes the ground of the privilege of acting as a guardian *ex-officio*, and has no more interest in them, in fact, than he has in the affairs of any other parish.

IV.—LUNATICS.

LIABILITY OF THE WIFE OF A LUNATIC PAUPER TO CONTRIBUTE TO HIS SUPPORT.—(7 and 8 Vict. c. 101, s. 27.)

19th August, 1844.

Rev. T. I. Bumpstead, Chairman of Vestry, Burrington—Stated, that in the month of October last, James David, a pauper, was removed from Burrington parish to the asylum at Bailbrock, near Bath, as a dangerous lunatic, under an order of magistrates; his wife being a washerwoman, and, in the opinion of the vestry, in such a position that she was fully capable of contributing a share of her earnings towards the support of her husband. He had no young family; and in addition to his wife, there was only one lad of 17 or 18, who earned quite sufficient for his own support.

Ans.—The Commissioners do not perceive that the law furnishes any remedy for such a case. The earnings of the wife are in law the earnings of the husband; but there are no means of which the Commissioners are aware, of compelling the wife to pay them, or any portion of them, over for the support of her insane husband. The Commissioners do not think, as the facts are reported to them, that the case falls within the 26th section of 7 and 8 Vic. c. 101, which enables the expenses incurred in the maintenance of insane paupers, in certain cases, to be levied off their estates.

V.—RELIEF.

TO WIDOWS, NON-RESIDENT, UNDER 7 AND 8 VICT., C. 101, S. 26.

26th August, 1844.

Clerk of the Louth Union—Inquired, whether relief given to widows, under the 26th section of 7 and 8 Vic. cap. 101, must be given by the overseers of the parish where they are resident, or by the overseers of the parish to which they belong. It appeared to him that the intention of the provisions was to ensure regular payment of relief by the overseers of the parish where the paupers are resident, to be repayable by the overseers of the parish to which they belonged.

Ans.—The intention of the proviso contained in the 26th section of the act, relating to the relief of widows non-resident, is not in any way to provide for the transmission of non-resident relief, but to leave untouched the responsibility cast by the law on the authorities of the place where a pauper resides, supposing that from the refusal or insufficiency of non-resident relief, or from any accidental cause, the pauper is destitute.

LONDON:
Printed by Order of the Poor Law Commissioners, by BLACKBURN and PARDON, 6, Hatton Garden, and Published by CHARLES KNIGHT and Co., 22, Ludgate Street, Publishers to the Poor Law Commissioners.

AN

OFFICIAL CIRCULAR

OF PUBLIC DOCUMENTS AND INFORMATION:

DIRECTED BY THE POOR LAW COMMISSIONERS TO BE PRINTED, CHIEFLY FOR THE USE OF THE MEMBERS AND PERMANENT OFFICERS OF BOARDS OF GUARDIANS, UNDER THE POOR LAW AMENDMENT ACT.

No. 40. CIRCULAR ISSUED OCTOBER 31, 1844.

Poor Law Commission Office,
Somerset House,
October 31st, 1844.

THE Poor Law Commissioners, on a review of their Minutes, directed that the Minutes of Correspondence on the following subjects be printed and circulated for the information of the Guardians and Officers of the several Unions, viz.: —

By Order of the Board,
EDWIN CHADWICK, *Secretary*.

ACCOUNTS.

1. ALLOWANCE OF SALARIES PAID TO PARISH CONSTABLES.

July 6th, 1844.

Mr. ———, *Auditor* — Inquired, whether salaries paid to parish constables appointed under the Act of 5 and 6 Vic. c. 109, could be allowed in the overseers' accounts, where the parishes were comprised in rural police districts.

Ans.—The Commissioners do not see anything in the 5th and 6th Vict. c. 109 (Parish Constables' Act) to prevent a paid constable or constables being appointed at a yearly salary, for a parish included in a district, formed under the Act 2nd and 3rd Vict. c. 93, for the establishment of County and District Constables. The auditor cannot, of course, enter into the question of the expediency of the appointment in any case, provided the power to appoint is clear, and provided that the formalities of the statute have been observed in making the appointment.

2. AUDIT.—(Sec. 33 of 7 and 8 Vic. c. 101.)

October 12th, 1844.

Clerk of Keynsham Union—Requested the Commissioners' opinion as to whether sec. 33 of the Act 7 and 8 Vic. c. 101, applied to the audit of accounts for the quarter ended at Michaelmas last. It appeared to him that this section was to be taken in connexion with sec. 32, but some

of the guardians were of opinion that the operation of sec. 33 was immediate.

Ans.—Although the 32nd section of the act applies only to district auditors appointed in pursuance of that section, the 33rd sec. applies generally to all auditors of Union and parish accounts; and the latter section came into operation immediately after the passing of the act.

3. DITTO.

October 12th, 1844.

Clerk of Kingsclere Union—Inquired, whether notices of audit for the Michaelmas quarter were to be given by the clerk as theretofore, or should the notice under the late act be given.

Ans.—As the 33rd sec. of the 7th and 8th Vic. c. 101, came into operation upon the passing of the act, the notice to overseers, and other officers, should be given in conformity with that sec. The notice should be given by the auditor both in obedience to the terms of the statute and the order of the Commissioners in force in the Union. (art. 1. sec. 7, order for keeping accounts.) If the notices to the overseers were theretofore given by the clerk, such a course was not in conformity with the order. The clerk would still continue to give the notice required by art. 8, sec. 2, of the order adverted to.

4. PAYMENT OF REWARD ON THE APPREHENSION OF A MOTHER FOR DESERTING HER CHILD.

October 17th, 1844.

Clerk of Epping Union—Forwarded a handbill whereby a reward was offered by the guardians for information which might lead to the apprehension of a mother who had deserted her child. Stated that the mother had gone into Kent after deserting the child, and her place of abode there was discovered by the police, but that when she found she was pursued, she returned to the Epping Workhouse and claimed the child. There she was detained and taken before the justices, who sentenced her to one month's imprisonment and hard labour. The guardians had determined to whom the reward was to be paid, and that the amount should be charged to the establishment. Requested Commissioners' approval thereof.

Ans.—Referring to the 59th section of 7 and 8 Vic. c. 101, which authorises the guardians to defray out of the funds in their hands the costs of civil and criminal proceedings in certain cases, the Commissioners think the words, "costs of apprehension," would probably be held to include any payment as a reward offered for the taking or securing the offender, or for information which might lead to the discovery and apprehension of the offender. Whether in the present instance the circumstances justified the offering of a reward, and if so, whether the sum offered was or was not excessive, and further, whether under the particular circumstances of the case, any one can be fairly considered as entitled to the reward, are points upon which the Commissioners offer no opinion. The proceedings taken against the mother being criminal proceedings, and for the sake of example rather than for the protection of the parish charged with the burden of maintaining the child, it seems, therefore, to the Commissioners that the reward (if payable at all) should be charged to the common fund.

---

5. COSTS OF PROSECUTING FOR A BURGLARY IN A WORKHOUSE, WHETHER PAYABLE OUT OF THE RATES.

October 22nd, 1844.

Clerk of Kensington Union—Stated, that two men were remanded by the justices on a charge of burglary committed at the union workhouse on the previous Saturday night, and inquired whether, in the event of the men being committed for trial, the guardians were authorised to employ an attorney and counsel to conduct the prosecution, if the adoption of that measure should be considered expedient.

Ans.—As the prosecution in this case must take place in a court in which attorneys and counsel may by right be employed, there appears to be no doubt that the reasonable expenses of so employing them may be paid out of the funds in the hands of the guardians.

II.—BASTARDY—

RELIEF TO THE MOTHERS OF BASTARDS.

October 11th, 1844.

Clerk of Penzance Union—Called the Commissioners' attention to the subject of the relief of bastard children, born before the passing of the recent act (7 and 8 Vic. c. 101) for the support of whom orders of affiliation were in existence. Under the present regulations such children could be relieved only in the workhouse; and to enforce an order for maintenance, it was necessary to maintain both mother and child in the workhouse. Suggested, that as the new law recognised the principle of payment in money to the mother, it would be desirable that the same principle should be applied to cases under the old law; and that this alteration might be effected by the withdrawal of the prohibitory order, so far as concerned the mothers of bastards provided for under the old law, and granting them out-relief to the amount that the father was bound to repay.

Ans.—The policy of the law both before and since the passing of the Poor Law Amendment Act, until the act of last session, is entirely different in principle from that adopted in the latter act. In the former state of the law the payment made by the putative father, under an order of affiliation, was an indemnity to the parish for the expense it might be put to in the support of the child; in the latter it is a direct payment to the woman wholly independent of the question whether she is, or is not, a pauper. The Commissioners cannot see any mode in which this present principle, entirely new in the law of England, can be made a reason for altering their regulations, which have reference to a different practice, and which relate to the mothers of bastards as able-bodied females in need of relief. The Commissioners do not think it expedient to change the prohibitory order for the reason suggested.

III.—GUARDIANS' ELECTION—

1. EXPENSES OF.

7th Sept. 1844.

Clerk of —— Union—Stated, that on the election of guardians for the —— Union, for the current year, the relieving officers of the union were appointed to assist the clerk in conducting the election. The late clerk received the full amount allowed for his services under the Commissioners' Order, but did not pay the relieving officers therefrom, the sum agreed to be given them for such assistance. Inquired, therefore, whether, under the provisions of the Election Order, the relieving officers have now any claim upon the union for the amount detained from them by the late clerk; and also whether it was intended by Articles 6 and 7 of such order, and Article 3 of the Expenses of Election Order, that the services of the paid officers of the union should be made available in assisting the clerk for the purposes of the election, without further remuneration; or if otherwise, whether the amount so paid to them from the sum allowed to the clerk, was intended to be apportioned and awarded by the board of guardians, or left to the direction of the clerk as a matter of private arrangement between him and the relieving officers.

Ans.—As it is the duty of the relieving officers under Article 20 of the general order "Duties of Officers," No. 14, to assist the clerk to the guardians in conducting and completing the annual election of guardians, for the performance of which duty, as well as for the whole time of the officers, the salary annexed to the office is the consideration. These officers, therefore, have no legal claim against the guardians for remuneration for the specific service rendered by them in the case to which your letter applies. Other persons when required to assist the clerk are to be appointed by the guardians, (see Election Order Articles 6 and 7 ;) the guardians are not, however, to satisfy the claims of such persons, but are to leave the clerk to do so, out of the remuneration which the guardians may award to that officer under Article 3 of the Election Expenses Order. That article, undoubtedly, contemplates that the guardians, in fixing the remuneration, will have regard to the services rendered by persons appointed to assist in the election, with a view to enabling the clerk to make reasonable compensation to such persons. The object of this arrangement was, that persons thus employed should be under the immediate control of the clerk, as the returning officer ; at the same time, that he should not select any one whom the guardians might disapprove of. The remuneration, though paid through the clerk, should not be uncontrolled by the guardians.

---

2. THE CLERK'S DUTY IN REGARD TO NOMINATIONS OF OR BY DISQUALIFIED PERSONS.

July 23*rd*, 1844.

Clerk of Clun Union.—Inquired whether it was competent for him, as the officer charged with the conduct of the election of guardians for the borough of Bishop's Castle, to refuse to take any votes for candidates nominated who appeared to be disqualified for the office ; or whether it was his duty to take all the votes that might be tendered for any candidate, leaving the question of qualification to be afterwards decided by the Commissioners. And whether also, if a candidate who was not in the judgment of the clerk qualified, should have a majority of votes, such candidate ought to be declared the elected guardian, leaving the qualified candidate, with a minority of votes, to establish his claim by appealing to the Commissioners.

Ans.—The Commissioners consider that it is your duty, in conducting an election of guardians under the order of the Commissioners, to ascertain, as far as you can, the validity of each nomination that is made previously to issuing the voting papers ; and this can only be done by inquiry into the legal capacity of the persons respectively proposing and proposed—the one to nominate and the other to be elected. The attention of the Commissioners has been called to the case of Reg. *v.* Ledeard, 8 Ad. and E. 535, and to the observations made by Mr. Justice Patteson in the course of his judgment, to the effect that the duty of a returning officer under the Municipal Corporation Act is ministerial only for the purpose of summing up the votes, and that it is no part of his business to decide on the qualification of candidates. But the observations ascribed to Mr. Justice Patteson do not apparently go further than to show what the duties of a returning officer are with reference to the particular provisions of the statute under which the case arose ; and the Commissioners do not understand them as defining what the duty of a person acting as returning officer in respect to the point in question in other circumstances, and acting under different powers. That decision, therefore, appears to the Commissioners to leave the law as to the conduct of elections not occurring under the Municipal Corporation Act untouched.

---

3. ELECTION OF GUARDIANS, IN A PARISH WHERE NO RATE IS MADE.

March 19*th*, 1844.

Clerk of City of London Union—Stated that in parish A. no poor-rate had been made for the last ten years, and C. D., had nominated himself for the office of guardian for the parish. Although C. D. had been a householder in the parish for four years, he had not been rated during that time. Inquired, 1. Whether C. D. was qualified to be elected guardian. 2. Whether every resident householder in the parish, of more than one year's standing, who was liable to be rated, was qualified to vote in the election of guardian. 3. And whether the nomination of C. D. was valid, he having described himself in the nomination paper as a "householder," instead of a ratepayer,—no rates having been made.

Ans.—If no person be rated in a parish, and

if it be held in consequence that no person in that parish is qualified to be elected a guardian under the Poor Law Amendment Act, it will not follow that the parish must remain unrepresented, for the 38th sec. of the Poor Law Amendment Act enables any person to be elected who is rated in respect of the proper amount in any of the parishes of the union. In the same manner, if it be held that where no rate has been made there are no ratepayers qualified to vote under the 40th sec., it will not follow that the parish cannot elect; for the owners of property will still be able to vote. It is therefore not strictly necessary, for the representation of a parish, that persons in the parish should be deemed to be rated under the 38th sec., or deemed to be "ratepayers" under the 40th sec. It is clear that the Poor Law Amendment Act assumed that a rate, or something which could be construed to be a rate, under the interpretation clause sec. 109, would exist in every parish. Such a case as that described, where no rate has been made for many years, is therefore a *casus omissus*. As the constituency of the ratepayers, with their accumulated votes, is not a common law constituency, and as the inconvenience arising from their non-qualification does not prevent the great purpose of representing the parish, the Commissioners are of opinion—First, that the returning officer cannot, in the face of the express terms of the act, and especially the strong prohibition in the proviso of the 40th section, admit any person not actually rated at the time of nomination to be qualified to be elected guardian; secondly, that the returning officer cannot admit any person to vote or act as a ratepayer who has not actually been charged to some rate, or contribution in the nature of a rate, for the relief of the poor within the last year; thirdly, that the nomination in question cannot be admitted as valid, it not describing the proposer in any capacity in respect of which he is entitled to vote.

4. WHETHER A MEDICAL OFFICER'S SUBSTITUTE IS ELIGIBLE FOR THE OFFICE OF GUARDIAN.

March 29th, 1844.

Clerk of Launceston Union—Inquired whether Mr. W. P. was rendered ineligible for the office of guardian in consequence of his partner, one of the medical officers of the Launceston Union, having named him as his substitute, under Article 15 of the General Medical Order.

Ans.—The circumstances described do not, in the opinion of the Commissioners, render Mr. W. P. incapable of serving as a guardian. He is not a person receiving any fixed salary or emolument from the poor-rates, within the meaning of the 14th section of the 5 and 6 Vic. c. 57. The medical officer is the only person entitled to the salary. Mr. W. P., not being an officer, has no claim on the guardians. Again, the contract is with the medical officer, and he alone is responsible for the performance of the contract. It may be doubted whether a contract entered into by a medical officer with the guardians to furnish medicines and appliances to sick paupers, the supply being merely incidental to the performance of the duty of attending the poor, would be considered as coming within the 6th section of 55 Geo. 3, c. 137, so as to render such officer (upon acting as guardian) subject to the penalties of that statute as extended by 4 and 5 Wm. 4, c. 76, s. 51. But, assuming that it should be so held, the Commissioners would nevertheless be disposed to think that no liability would attach to the partner of the medical officer, if he acted as a guardian, as the contract, not being made with him, he could not be said to be concerned in a contract for the supply of goods or provisions for the support and maintenance of the poor.

IV.—LUNATICS.

1. JUSTICES' ORDER FOR A LUNATIC'S ADMISSION INTO AN ASYLUM.

September 3rd, 1844.

——— *Axminster Union*—Stated, that a pauper was brought into the workhouse of the Axminster Union, who was certified by a medical officer to be a lunatic, in order that he might be removed to an asylum. One magistrate signed the usual order for conveying the pauper to an asylum; but another magistrate who was applied to refused to sign it without seeing the pauper; and having seen him, decided that he was not insane, and therefore declined altogether to sign the order. A third magistrate, however, thinking that the medical man's certificate gave to the magistrate no option, signed the document. The question was, which of the magistrates acted correctly, those who relied simply on the medical officer's testimony, or the one who refused to sign, from a conviction that the pauper was not insane. Requested the Commissioners' opinion on the point.

Ans.—Under the 38th section of the 9th Geo.

4, c. 40, the justices cannot make an order for the conveyance of a pauper to a lunatic asylum, unless from "view and examination of the said poor person, or from other proof, the said justices shall be satisfied that such poor person is insane." Where, therefore, the justices are not satisfied of the pauper's insanity, they not only may, but are bound to refuse to make the order. The 45th section of the Act also contemplates such a refusal, and expressly prescribes the course to be followed in the event of its occurring; and the 46th section makes provision for an appeal against the decision of the justices in such a case. With regard to the effect of the medical man's certificate, it is to be observed, that the 38th section only requires the justices "to call to their assistance" a physician, &c.; and this expression appears to the Commissioners to show that the opinion of such professional adviser was intended merely as an aid to the justices in forming their own judgment on the case, and was not meant to be necessarily binding upon them. The Commissioners, therefore, consider it to be a question which each individual justice must determine for himself, how far the evidence in the particular case is sufficient to satisfy him that the pauper is insane. In determining this question, each justice of course will be required to decide for himself what degree of importance belongs to the testimony of the professional adviser consulted in the case. Having made these general remarks, the Commissioners need scarcely express their opinion, that in the instance stated in your letter, the justice who refused to sign the order, had the discretion of so refusing, if he was satisfied that the pauper was not insane; and that the justice who subsequently signed it acted rightly in so signing if he was satisfied of the pauper's insanity, by the evidence of the medical man, or otherwise.

---

2. LIABILITY TO PAY EXPENSE OF A LUNATIC'S MAINTENANCE.

July 24th, 1844.

Clerk of Buntingford Union—Stated that several years since, a man of the name of Scaife came to reside in the parish of Throcking, in the Buntingford Union, and married a woman legally settled in the parish of Layston, also in that Union, by whom he had several children: Scaife himself was illegitimate, supposed to have been born in a parish in Cambridge, and upon his becoming chargeable, was removed from Throcking to Cambridge; but the order of removal being appealed against, was quashed, the parish of Throcking not being able to produce sufficient evidence of his birth: some time afterwards, Scaife, with his wife and one or two children, were in the Union workhouse: the wife becoming insane was sent to Bethlem, where she remained for a year, when she was discharged as incurable: she had for upwards of two years past been confined in a lunatic asylum at Hoxton, at the expense of the parish of Throcking: the husband had absconded, and neither of the children were chargeable to, or resident in, the parish of Throcking; but some little time since, two of them became chargeable, whilst resident in the parish of Layston, and were relieved at the expense of the latter parish. The parish of Throcking was desirous of relieving itself from the expense of maintaining the woman, and had purposed sending for her from the asylum, considering that she was so far harmless as to justify that course; but it had occurred to the board of guardians, that by giving her an allowance whilst at large, out of the parish of Throcking, they might furnish evidence of a settlement in that parish; and as there was no pretence for saying that Scaife, or any part of his family, were legally settled in that parish, they might either shift the expense of maintaining the wife as a lunatic on to the county; or if not, that they might remove her to her maiden settlement, that of her husband being unknown. But before taking any step in the matter, the guardians wished the Commissioners' opinion as to whether the guardians could properly remove her from the asylum; and if not, whether they could throw the expense of maintaining her on the county; and if they could so remove her, whether they could remove her to her birth settlement.

Ans.—The propriety of removing the pauper in question from the lunatic asylum, must depend upon the state of her health, and ought not to be determined by reference to any question of her chargeability or liability to removal. The Commissioners cannot, without more detailed information, undertake to express an opinion, whether in the particular case, the lunatic is in a condition to be removed. They can only say, that in their opinion great responsibility will rest on the parties removing her, without proper medical advice, and a full knowledge of how she is to be disposed of afterwards. It appears clearly by the statement, that the woman has a settlement, namely, her maiden settlement, in case her husband has no discoverable settlement. Her maintenance cannot therefore be lawfully cast upon the county. The justices of the county, where the lunatic is kept, can make an order on the overseers of the place of the woman's settlement, to repay the cost of her maintenance under the 9th Geo. 4th, c. 40, s. 42.

September 7th, 1844.

Clerk of the same Union—Stated, that it appeared that the lunatic was originally sent to Bethlem upon the usual petition of the parish officers of Throcking; and in consequence of the hospital authorities requiring her removal at, or soon after, the expiration of the twelvemonth, she then being uncured, she was removed to a licensed lunatic asylum at Hoxton, there being no county lunatic asylum in Hertford; and this removal was consequently made without the intervention of justices. The parish authorities were desirous of having the Commissioners' opinion, as to whether they still thought that an order could be obtained, under the 42nd section of 9th Geo. 4, c. 40, for the expenses of her maintenance being borne by the parish in which her maiden settlement appeared to be, (that of her husband being unknown,) notwithstanding the want of an order of two justices for the confinement of the lunatic.

Ans.—The Commissioners consider that no order can, under existing circumstances, be made under the 42nd sec. of 9 Geo. 4, c. 40, upon the parish in which Scaife is settled, to defray the costs of her maintenance as a lunatic. That section applies only to the case of persons confined in any county asylum, or licensed house, under an order of two justices; and it is stated in your letter, that the removal of Scaife to Hoxton, was effected without the intervention of justices.

---

3. DITTO.

26th August, 1844.

Clerk of Newcastle-upon-Tyne Union—Stated, that on or about the 13th July last a person named Hans Lourinson, a native of Norway, was apprehended by the police, having been found wandering about in the township of Byker, in the Newcastle upon-Tyne Union, apparently in an insane state of mind, and was delivered up to the relieving officer of the district, by whom he was sent for safe custody to the vagrant ward, at the charge of Byker, whereby he became chargeable to that township. On the 16th, the assistant overseer of Byker, in conformity with the 9 Geo. 4, c. 40, sec. 37, gave information to one of the justices of the borough, of the state of this person, and the justice on the same day issued his warrant according to sec. 38 of the above act, directed to the overseers of Byker, and requiring them to bring the lunatic before two justices on the same day. He was accordingly brought before two justices, who, having called to their assistance a surgeon, adjudged him to be lunatic and insane, and by their warrant directed the overseers to cause the lunatic to be conveyed to a licensed asylum situate in the borough of Newcastle, there being no county asylum, and the lunatic was conveyed by the overseers to the asylum accordingly. It being ascertained that the lunatic was a foreign seaman, and had not gained a settlement in England, no adjudication as to a settlement was made by the justices, nor was any order made by them upon the overseers for payment of the charges of conveying the lunatic to the asylum, and for his maintenance therein. But the overseers having conveyed the lunatic there, the keeper would charge the township of Byker with the maintenance of the lunatic, and his name, so long as that charge continued, would remain upon the out-door relief list of that township. On the 20th July, the overseers of Byker made an application (no application having been previously made) to two justices of the borough in petty sessions, under sec. 42 of the above act, for an examination into the lunatic's settlement, and in the event of its not being ascertained, (which it was obvious must be the case,) for an order, under sec. 41, upon the treasurer of the borough for the charges of removal, maintenance, &c. of the lunatic. The justices objected to proceed under these sections, alleging that there not being a county treasurer within their jurisdiction, and that as the Municipal Act, 5 & 6 Wm. 4, c. 76, did not give them authority, they could not legally make an order upon the treasurer of the borough. On behalf of the overseers the attention of the justices was called to the 59th section of the statute last mentioned. And it was contended, that as by 9th Geo. 4, c. 40, sections 41 & 42, a justice of the peace, acting in and for a county, might, in a case similar to the present, make (or join in making) an order upon the treasurer of the county, so might a justice of a borough under the authority of the 59th section of 5 & 6 Wm. 4, c. 76, make (or join in making) a like order upon the treasurer of the borough. The justices however stated that they entertained so much doubt as to this being the right construction of the 59th section of the Municipal Corporations Act, that they must, and they did accordingly refuse the application; at the same time they recommended that, in preference to any more expensive mode of determining this point a case should be stated, and the opinion of counsel taken at the joint expense of the parishes and townships in the borough, the justices having no funds wherefrom to defray such expense.

Ans.—Although the 38th section of the 9th Geo. 4, c. 40, speaks of the justices of counties only, the Commissioners presume that by virtue of the interpretation clause, (s. 61,) the justices of Newcastle might act under the 38th section as being justices of a "town corporate" (see Reg. *v.* St. Laurence, Ludlow, 11 A. & E. 170;) upon the like ground the Commissioners conceive, that the justices of Newcastle might, where the lunatic has no settlement, make an order on the treasurer of the borough, under the 41st section, for the payment of the charges of maintenance, &c. out of "any funds assessed upon, or raised in, or belonging to the town corporate, in the nature of county rates, and applicable to the purposes to which county rates are applicable." You state, however, in the case of Newcastle, that there is a "borough fund raised from the property of the corporation," but that "no borough rate has as yet been made." The Commissioners think it doubtful whether the borough fund, if it be not in the nature of a county rate, could lawfully be charged with the expenses in question under the 9th Geo. 4, c. 40, s. 41. But the Commissioners do not perceive any such difficulty with regard to the construction of the 59th section of the 5 & 6 Wm. 4, c. 76; that section appears to the Commissioners to render it the duty of the borough treasurer to make such payments as he may be ordered to make by "a justice of the peace acting in and for the borough in the discharge of his judicial duty, in such case as a justice of the peace, acting in and for a county in the discharge of his judicial duty, may make an order for the payment of money on the treasurer of such county." The Commissioners conceive that as in the class of cases under consideration, a justice of the peace, acting for a county, may make, or (as you observe) join in making an order for payment on the county treasurer, a justice of the peace acting for a borough may likewise, in the same class of cases, make (or join in making) an order for payment on the borough treasurer. Then the 59th section of the Municipal Corporations Act does not limit or specify the particular portion of the borough funds, out of which the payments shall be made, whether raised from existing property, or by rates; and the Commissioners are therefore disposed to consider that the justices of Newcastle might lawfully direct the borough treasurer to make the payments in question from the funds belonging to the borough, whatever they may be, which may happen to be in his hands. With regard to the question, whether counsel's opinion may be taken on the point at the joint expense of the parishes and townships in the borough, or at the sole expense of the township of Byker, the Commissioners desire to observe that they do not see that either the parishes and townships collectively, or even the township of Byker individually, have any such direct interest in the matter as would justify them in obtaining the opinion of counsel at the charge of the poor-rates. The question appears to the Commissioners to be one affecting the jurisdiction of the justices or the corporation of Newcastle, on whom the duty of ascertaining the extent of the justices' powers or the liability of the borough funds respectively devolves. The Commissioners would observe that, according to the view which they take of the provisions of the 9th Geo. 4, c. 40, the township of Byker is not chargeable with Hans Lourinson's maintenance in the asylum. The Commissioners consider that when a pauper is removed to an asylum under the 38th section, one of two courses may be pursued; either the justices may at once make an order under that section, on the parish of the pauper's settlement (if discoverable) for the payment of the charges incurred in the case, or if the settlement cannot be ascertained, they may make an order for the payment under the 41st section upon the county treasurer. In either case, the parish to which the pauper, when sent to the asylum, was chargeable, is relieved from liability in regard to his maintenance, and where neither of the above alternatives is adopted, the Commissioners are not aware of any authority for casting the charge on that parish. This view is supported by the case of Reg. *v.* Darton (12 A. & E. 78;) in which Mr. Justice Patteson remarked, "the statute does not enact that the expenses shall be first paid by the overseers, where the settlement is not known their duty in such a case, is not to pay, but to let the magistrates make a proper order."

4. DITTO.

September 6th, 1844.

Clerk of Bedminster Union—Stated, that a man who had been employed by a soap manufacturer of the city of Bristol, against whom a charge was preferred, before the magistrates of Bristol, for defrauding the excise, was examined as a witness in the case, and in the course of such examination conducted himself with so much violence, and appeared to be labouring under so much excitement, that the magistrates ordered a policeman to take him to the asylum at St. Peter's Hospital, the poor-house of Bristol, as insane, where it was alleged he had repeatedly been confined before. The lunatic being settled in the parish of Bedminster, the governors of the poor of Bristol claimed to be paid ten shillings a week for his maintenance. Inquired whether the payment of this sum could be enforced, or only the actual expense incurred by the governors in the maintenance of the lunatic. It was believed that no written order was made by the magistrates, but as they had power to inquire into the lunatic's settlement, and to make a retrospective order for his maintenance, this fact did not appear to be material for the decision of the question as to the right of the authorities to charge ten shillings weekly for the lunatic's maintenance. The governors fixed the payment at ten shillings weekly, that being the amount the magistrates usually directed to be paid when applied to for orders.

Ans.—The Commissioners presume, from the circumstances stated in your letter, that this lunatic was sent to St. Peter's Hospital, under the 44th section of the 9th Geo. 4, c. 40, as being a person so far disordered in his senses that it was dangerous for him to be permitted to go abroad. It would seem that he was not chargeable to the parish at the time, and consequently could not have been sent to the asylum under the 38th section. The decision in R. *v.* St. Nicholas, Leicester, (3 A. & E. 79) is an authority to show, that, where the justices adjudge the settlement when the insane person is sent to the asylum, under the 44th section, they cannot subsequently make a retrospective order for the cost of maintenance, &c. The Commissioners, however, are not prepared to say that, where the settlement is not adjudged when the lunatic is sent to the asylum, under that section, the justices could not subsequently make a retrospective order under the 42nd section. If a retrospective order may be made in the present instance, under the 42nd section, it will be an order "for the repayment of the *reasonable* charges, &c. incurred within twelve calendar months, &c., such charges having been first proved to the satisfaction of the justices," &c. Whether the sum of ten shillings weekly be a *reasonable* charge in the case of the lunatic referred to in your letter, is a question for the justices to determine. The Commissioners, of course, can express no opinion on this point. Any prospective order, whether made under the 44th section, or under the 42nd section, must be made according to the directions of the 38th section, which empowers the justices, where the pauper is sent to a county asylum, to order the overseers to pay such weekly sum to the treasurer, as shall be from time to time fixed upon by the visitors. If the sum so fixed in the present case is ten shillings weekly, the Commissioners do not see that the overseers can properly resist the payment, if an order be duly made.

MEDICAL RELIEF.

RECOVERY OF NON-RESIDENT MEDICAL RELIEF.

July 29th, 1844.

Clerk of Malton Union—Stated that in the month of January last, G. H., residing at Norton, in the Malton Union, made application to the guardians of that union for relief, in consequence of the illness of his wife. From G. H.'s statement it appeared, that he belonged to the Banbury Union, and the clergyman of the parish of Norton, the Rev. E. Day, wrote to the chairman of the Banbury Union, informing him of G. H.'s case; and on the 10th of January Mr. Day received a letter from the clerk of that union, of which the following is a copy:—"Banbury, 10th January, 1844.—Sir, Your letter, addressed to Colonel North, of Wraxton Abbey, was laid before the board of guardians of the Banbury Union, on the 4th instant, and the board agreed to pay any relief that may be advanced to the pauper during his wife's illness. I am, Sir, yours, &c., G. Moore, Clerk of the Union." The board of guardians of the Malton Union, on the case being brought before them, ordered an allowance of 10*s.* per week to be made, which was reduced from time to time, as the circumstances of the case would permit; and up to the quarter ending in March last, the amount of relief granted was £4. 11*s.* This sum was repaid to the Malton relieving officer by the Banbury relieving officer. Relief was continued to the pauper until his wife's recovery; and on the 24th June last, the Malton relieving officer forwarded to the Banbury relieving officer an account amounting to £2.8*s*.; viz. £1.12*s*. for relief advanced to the pauper up to that period, and 16*s*. for medical relief, including a fee of 10*s*. for medical attendance on the pauper's wife in child-birth. From the 24th March last, the Malton guardians agreed with the medical officer for the Norton district (who was previously paid by a fixed salary) to attend the poor within the district, on being paid the cost of the medicines and journeys: and his charge for medicine supplied to the pauper's wife, from the 24th of March to the period of her recovery, amounted to 6*s*. No charge for medical relief to the woman had been made prior to the 25th March last. On the 8th July, the Malton relieving officer received a letter from the Banbury relieving officer, of which the following is a copy:—"Horley, 6th July, 1844, Banbury.—Sir, Annexed is a post office order, £1 12*s*. for relief advanced to G. H. and family. Our board refuses to allow the charge of 16*s*. for medicine and attendance at the confinement of his wife, as a similar charge would not be made by us, if a case of yours was placed in our hands. Yours, &c. Edward Charlton." The Malton guardians requested the opinion and advice of the Commissioners on the case, referring them to the "Official Circular," No. 28, p. 135, (Mansfield Union case,) upon the authority of which the guardians contended that the amount of medical relief in the present instance must be repaid to them by the Banbury guardians.

Ans.—The question raised in your letter appears to be, whether the guardians of Malton Union can recover from the guardians of Banbury Union the cost of the medical relief afforded to G. H.'s wife, subsequently to the 25th March last. This question turns entirely on the construction to be put upon the letter written on the 10th January last, by the clerk of Banbury Union to the Rev. C. Day. In that letter the Banbury guardians agree to repay "*any* relief that may be advanced to the pauper during his wife's illness." These terms are certainly very wide; but, notwithstanding their apparent unrestrictedness, the Commissioners think that the Banbury guardians, if disposed to do so, may fairly require that they should be construed with reference to the arrangements for relief at that time existing in Malton Union. It appears from your statement that, before the 25th of March, the medical officer in charge of the district in which G. H. resided, was paid by a fixed salary; but that, after that date, the Malton guardians entered into a new arrangement, agreeing to remunerate him thenceforth by the case. While he was paid by a fixed salary, it was not practicable for the Malton guardians to make any separate charge for the medical relief afforded to G. H.; and, consequently, up to the 25th March the medical relief was not included in the amount demanded of and repaid by the Banbury guardians. If the Malton guardians had then apprised the Banbury guardians of the alteration in their arrangements as to medical relief, and had obtained from the latter a promise of repayment, there would, of course, be now no question on the point; but as the Malton guardians did not do this, the Commissioners are not prepared to say that the Banbury guardians are bound to such repayment by the terms of the letter of the 10th January, written during the existence of arrangements, under which such repayment would not have been claimed.

———

August 13th, 1844.

Clerk of Malton Union—Stated that previous to the 25th March last, although the medical officer of the Norton district, in which G. H. resided, was paid by a fixed salary, such salary did not include the fees for attending cases of midwifery allowed by the medical order, and which are charged to the parish on account of which the pauper is relieved, and therefore form no part of the establishment charges. The arrangement which commenced on the 25th March last with the medical officer of the Norton district, did not affect the fees allowed for cases of midwifery by the medical order, the same being charged to the parish on account of which the pauper is relieved, as was the case prior to that date; and, therefore, as regarded the fee of 10*s*. payable on the confinement of the pauper's wife, the arrangement remained the same as when the authority was given by the Banbury guardians, and inasmuch as the latter agreed to pay *any* relief that might be advanced to the pauper during his wife's illness, the Malton guardians considered it to be a general authority to relieve, and as such, according to the case in the "Official Circular" before referred to, would include all relief, medical or otherwise. Requested the Commissioners to reconsider the case; and if they should still be of opinion that the arrangement made subsequently to the 25th March last destroyed the right of the Malton guardians to recover the 6*s*. for medical relief, whether it would equally affect the midwifery fee of 10*s*. Should the Commissioners think that the Banbury guardians were not liable to pay the latter charge, it was presumed the charge would fall on the parish of Norton, where the pauper was resident at the time he became chargeable.

Ans.—The distinction pointed out in your [second] letter between the midwifery fee and the rest of the medical charge, in the case of G. H., appears to the Commissioners to be a valid ground for considering that the principle laid down in their letter to yourself of the 29th ultimo, does not apply to the midwifery fee, though it does apply to the remaining portion of the charge. The Commissioners accordingly consider that the former expense is recoverable from the Banbury guardians, under the letter of the 10th January last; but that the latter is not. With regard to the chargeability of that part of the pauper's relief, which is not recoverable from the Banbury guardians, the Commissioners desire to point out that, as the medical officer, under the present arrangement, is paid by the case, it appears to them that the payments made to him should be charged respectively to the parishes liable to provide for the relief of the several paupers he attends. In this instance, the parish of Norton, where G. H. resided when the relief was afforded, was the parish liable to provide such relief, and should of course be charged with it accordingly.

VI.—NUISANCES.

1. POWER OF GUARDIANS TO PROCEED TO SUPPRESS NUISANCES.

October 23rd, 1844.

Clerk of Ware Union—Transmitted a copy of a minute of the guardians relating to the nuisances arising from the bad state of the drains in Kibes Lane and Caroline Court, Ware, and inquired the Commissioners' opinion as to the best course to be adopted by the guardians,—whether to proceed against the surveyor, or the owners or occupiers of the premises. The medical officer of the district had reported the necessity for remedying the nuisances in question.

Ans.—It does not appear to the Commissioners that the law invests the guardians with any power to take any proceedings in their official character for the suppression or removal of the nuisances in question, unless indeed it should appear that the property of the union is injured by the existence of such nuisances. If this be the case the interference of the guardians would seem to be warranted by 7 and 8 Vic. c. 101, s. 59. The powers given to justices by the 2 and 3 Vic. c. 71, to remove nuisances upon the application of the union authorities, is confined to parishes within the metropolitan police district.

VII.—ORPHAN CHILDREN—

CUSTODY OF.

August 21st, 1844.

Clerk of Mitford and Launditch Union—Stated that two orphan children, under the age of seven years, belonging to that Union, were then living with their grandfather and grandmother, who were poor people, and unable to maintain the children without parochial assistance. The board of guardians had hitherto given out-relief to the children, but having lately heard reports prejudicial to the character of the grandmother, some of the guardians were desirous of separating them from their grandparents, and relieving them in the workhouse. The grandparents, however, were unwilling to have the children taken from them. Inquired whether the guardians had the power of compelling the separation of the children, under the circumstances.

Ans.—The law does not allow a child under the age of nurture, to be separated from its mother or father; but the Commissioners are not aware of any decision which lays down any such doctrine in respect of the grandparents. The Commissioners therefore consider that it is quite competent for the guardians, if they deem it proper, to refuse to relieve the children in question, whilst resident with their grandparents.

VIII.—OVERSEERS—

1. DUTY OF IN REFERENCE TO THE RENTS OF PARISH COTTAGES.

August 22nd, 1844.

Auditor of Louth Union—Pointed out (in regard to a letter addressed to the Commissioners by an overseer of the parish of Strubby, in the Louth Union, and referred to the Auditor for his observations) the great objection entertained by overseers to bringing into account the rents of parish cottages.

Ans.—However unwilling the overseers or parishioners may be that the rents of the cottages adverted to should be brought into account, it is nevertheless the duty of the overseers to bring them into account. It is likewise your duty to insist upon such rents being brought into account; and this duty is materially enforced by the provisions of the Act, which has recently passed, for the further amendment of the Poor Laws.

---

2. ASSISTANT OVERSEER'S CONTINUANCE IN OFFICE.—(7 and 8 Vic. c. 101, sec. 61.)

October 12th, 1844.

Assistant Overseer, Weymouth — Stated, that by his appointment as assistant overseer, which was made under the 59th Geo. 3, c. 12, his duties were confined to the clerical duties of the overseers, in making rates, keeping accounts, making out lists, &c. and that he had nothing to do with the collection of rates, &c. and inquired whether section 61 of the 7th and 8 Vic. c. 101, would have any effect on his appointment, and whether it would be necessary that he should be appointed by the board of guardians.

Ans.—Section 61 of the recent statute (7 and 8 Vic. c. 101) does not operate to determine the appointment of any assistant overseer, duly appointed under the 59th Geo. 3, c. 12, except where the Commissioners may in any case direct that such appointment should cease.

IX.—PAUPER.

1. PAYMENT FROM RATES OF COSTS OF RECOVERING PROPERTY BELONGING TO A PAUPER, (7 and 8 Vic. c. 101, s. 27.)

October 12th, 1844.

Clerk of ——————— *Board of Guardians* —Stated that a pauper inmate of the workhouse was supposed to be entitled to some freehold property, and inquired whether the cost of procuring a copy of a will, and of other legal proceedings to recover possession of the property, could be defrayed out of the poor-rates. Inquired also whether he was entitled to remuneration for his professional services in the matter, as he had been employed solely as clerk, and not as solicitor for the parish.

Ans.—It does not appear whether the pauper alluded to is insane. If he is not, the Commissioners do not see that the guardians could lawfully take any proceedings in the matter at the expense of the poor's rates. If he be insane, the claim which the guardians would have on his estate, under the 27th section of the 7 and 8 Vic. c. 101, might justify them in incurring the expense of obtaining a copy of the will, though they could not litigate the claim beyond the tribunal appointed by the above-named section, viz. that of the two justices empowered to make the order. With regard to the question whether you are entitled to any remuneration for your professional services, having been employed solely as clerk, and not as solicitor, for the parish, the fact that you have been so employed as clerk, and not as solicitor, appears to the Commissioners to involve the consequence that you have no claim for remuneration as solicitor.

---

2. PROOF OF CHARGEABILITY OF PAUPERS, UNDER 7 AND 8 VIC. C. 101, S. 69.

October 16th, 1844.

Clerk of Presteign Union—Stated, that considerable difference of opinion existed whether the chargeability of a pauper could be proved by any other mode than the certificate set forth in the schedule to the 7 and 8 Vic. c. 101, and inquired the Commissioners' opinion as to the construction of the 69th section of that act; the words, "no further or other evidence of chargeability than such certificate shall be required," would seem to imply, that until the certificate be given, further evidence of chargeability may be required.

Ans.—The fact of chargeability may still be proved by other evidence than that of the certificate which the guardians may make under the 69th section of 7 and 8 Vic. c. 101. The statute does not, as the Commissioners consider, render it indispensable that that mode of proof should be resorted to, though where it is resorted to the words cited, "no further or other evidence of chargeability than such certificate shall be required," have clearly the effect of making the certificate conclusive of the fact of chargeability, and of restraining the justices from calling for further evidence of that fact.

---

3. REPAYMENT OF COST OF RELIEF GIVEN TO A PAUPER, WHO HAS BECOME POSSESSED OF PROPERTY.

July 1st, 1844.

Clerk of Tavistock Union—Stated that an aged woman, then in the Tavistock Union workhouse, and chargeable to the parish of Tavistock, had lately become entitled, jointly with a sister, who also had until lately been in the workhouse, to the income arising from a leasehold estate of the value of about £20 per annum. The woman was desirous of remaining in the house, and was willing to repay the cost of her maintenance out of her income. The property was believed to be in the hands of trustees. Inquired in what way the expense of the woman's maintenance could be secured to the parish; and also, whether the repayment of the cost of maintaining the other sister, whilst in the workhouse, could be enforced.

Ans.—The Commissioners are not able to point out any way in which, under the circumstances mentioned in your letter, the parish can be secured the payment of the cost of maintaining the pauper, assuming that she continue to reside in the workhouse. As the facts are stated, it would seem that the pauper alone is entitled to receive the rent, (*i. e.* the moiety) and to give a valid discharge to the trustees. The guardians can only trust to the pauper's fulfilling any engagement to repay the cost of her maintenance into which she may enter. If the past relief has been given unconditionally (which the Commissioners suppose to have been the case) the parish has no legal claim to be repaid the cost of such relief.

X.—REMOVAL.

1. COST UNDER SUSPENDED ORDER OF REMOVAL.

September 6th, 1844.

Mr. ——— — Stated, that an order was made for the removal of a woman, who had become chargeable to the parish of A., to the parish of B., and was suspended in consequence of the pauper having been delivered of a child in the Union workhouse. The parish of A. paid to the Union the sum of £4 19*s.* 6*d.* in respect of the woman, but could obtain repayment of only £3 19*s.* 6*d.*, it being alleged that the parish of B. was not chargeable with a sum of £1, which had been paid to the medical officer for extra attendance on the pauper, occasioned by an attack of fever subsequent to her delivery. Requested the Commissioners' opinion on the point.

Ans.—If the £1 in question was included among the expenses sworn to have been incurred in the case you allude to, under the 2nd section of the 35th George 3, c. 101, it is of course recoverable, like the rest of the charges so sworn to; but if it was not included among the costs thus proved on oath, the Commissioners are not aware of any mode in which it could be compulsorily recovered from the parish to which the pauper has been removed, assuming that there was no undertaking on the part of that parish to repay it.

---

2. REMOVAL OF A DESERTED WIFE AND FAMILY.

October 23rd, 1844.

Clerk of Newtown and Llanidloes Union—Stated, that a woman had for some time been deserted by her husband, whose settlement was in Berriew, a parish out of the Newtown and Llanidloes Union. One child, the issue of the marriage, was then maintained at the cost of that parish. The woman also had occasionally, in her deserted state, been relieved by that parish; but being a native of Llanwrog, in the Newtown and Llanidloes Union, she had come to reside in that parish with her mother, at the cost of which parish she, and two of her children, one legitimate and the other illegitimate, were then maintained in the union workhouse. The parish officers of Berriew did not object to relieve her in their own union, but she refused to go there, unless legally removed. Inquired whether, in the absence of the husband, the guardians could remove the wife and family, taking the best evidence available as to the husband's legal settlement in Berriew.

Ans.—The Commissioners see nothing in the statement of the case to prevent the woman's removal to the parish of Berriew, if that be the parish of her husband's settlement, and consequently her own. The mere circumstance of the husband being absent, would not, of itself, prevent the removal of the wife. (Rex *v.* Ironacton, Burr, S. C. 153, 2 Bott. 81.) With regard to her children, if the child, which you describe as "legitimate," be the offspring of her present and not of any former marriage, such child will belong to Berriew, the parish of its father's settlement, and will be removable with its mother to that parish accordingly. But the settlement and removal of the illegitimate child will depend upon the questions, whether it was born before or after the passing of the Poor Law Amendment Act, and whether it is above or under the age of nurture, *i. e.*, the age of seven years.

XI.—SCHOOLS.

LIMITS OF DISTRICTS FOR SCHOOLS, UNDER 7 AND 8 VIC. C. 101, S. 40.

October 15th, 1844.

Clerk of Aylsham Union—Stated, that the guardians contemplated establishing a district school under 7 and 8 Vic. c. 101, s. 40, but some doubt had arisen as to the construction of the section: there were two parishes in the proposed district so situated, that a part of one of them was more than fifteen miles distant from a portion of the other parishes. Requested Commissioners' opinion whether parishes so situated could be included in the same school district.

Ans.—Inasmuch as it is enacted by the 40th section that the Commissioners shall not include in any district, for educational purposes, any parish any part of which would be more than fifteen miles from any other part of such district, the Commissioners think that the provisions of the section alluded to will prevent in general any combination of country unions for the purpose of forming school districts.

XII.—SETTLEMENT—

BY RENTING TENEMENT AND PAYMENT OF RATES.

August 8th, 1844.

Clerk of Stow-in-the-Wold Union — Stated that William Townsend rented a house in the parish of Oddington, at the yearly rent of £10. He was duly assessed to the rates and taxes, and paid them, but it was expressed in the agreement between him and his landlord, that the landlord, on payment of the rent by the tenant, should pay back to the tenant the amount of rates and taxes, which repayment had been regularly made. On an application for an order for the removal of the man and his family, the justices decided that he had not gained a settlement in Oddington, while it was contended by the parish to which he was to be removed, that he had gained a settlement there. Requested Commissioners' opinion thereon.

Ans.—Upon the single point whether the payment of the rates and taxes, by the pauper himself, in the first instance, was a sufficient payment with reference to gaining a settlement, notwithstanding that the amount was afterwards allowed to the pauper by his landlord, out of the rent, the Commissioners are of opinion that such payment was sufficient. If the landlord had himself personally paid the rates and taxes the case might have been different, but all the decisions on the subject seem to establish that when a pauper himself pays them, the payment is sufficient, whatever private arrangement may exist between him and his landlord, with regard to the subsequent reimbursement of the amount. (See R. *v.* Fulham, Burr. 488; R. *v.* Chidingford, Burr. 415; R. *v.* Openshaw, Burr. 522.)

2. SETTLEMENT OF BASTARD CHILDREN.

October 2nd, 1844.

Clerk of Saffron Walden Union—Stated that a female pauper belonging to Saffron Walden parish, then an inmate of the Cambridge Union workhouse, was ordered to be removed to Saffron Walden with her two illegitimate children, both under seven years old, neither of whom were born in that parish, consequently, when sixteen years of age, the place of their birth will be the place of their settlement. Inquired whether it was not necessary that the overseers of Saffron Walden should appeal against this order of removal, or what steps should be taken to prevent the children becoming permanently settled in Saffron Walden.

Ans.—The Commissioners do not concur in the view, that the illegitimate children, referred to in your letter, will revert to their birth settlement, on attaining the age of sixteen years. The Commissioners admit that the point is not free from doubt; but they are disposed to consider that the word "have," in the 71st section of the Poor Law Amendment Act, must be construed to mean "take," and that the limitation in the subsequent part of the clause (viz. "until" &c.) has reference to the word "follow;" but will not deprive the bastard at sixteen of a settlement then actually acquired from its mother. The Commissioners, therefore, think that the children in question will probably retain, at the age of sixteen, the last parentage settlement derived from their mother.

XIII.—VAGRANTS—

PAYMENTS TO CONSTABLES FOR THE APPREHENSION OF.

August 27th, 1844.

Overseer, Bicester—Inquired if he should be justified in paying the expense incurred by the constable of the township in apprehending some persons under the Vagrant Act, for running away and leaving their families chargeable, whom he apprehended in London; and also if the constable could in such a case charge the mileage allowed by the county for the apprehension of prisoners, or should he be paid only the reasonable expenses for such apprehension.

Ans.—Assuming the parties adverted to, to

have been apprehended before the passing of the recent Act, 7 and 8 Vic. c. 101, the Commissioners consider that the decision in the case of Reg. *v.* Chelmford, (3 Gale and Dav. 357,) would be an authority to the constable to include in his accounts, under the 18 Geo. 3, c. 19, s. 4, such expenses as he may have necessarily incurred on the occasion. It must be borne in mind, however, that that statute does not entitle the constable to any remuneration for services or loss of time. With regard to the payment of such expenses in future, the Commissioners direct your attention to the 59th section of the 7 and 8 Vic. c. 101, which empowers boards of guardians to pay out of the funds in their hands the reasonable costs of the apprehension and prosecution of certain classes of offenders, including offenders of the kind now under consideration.

XIV.—VAGRANT ACT—

CONSTRUCTION OF.

July 1st, 1844.

Caxton and Arrington Union.—The questions following having been submitted to the Commissioners by their Assistant-Commissioner, Sir John Walsham, on behalf of the Board of Guardians of the Caxton and Arrington Union, the answers appended to the questions were sent to that Union.

Q.—1. Whether in the case of a man who being wholly, or in part, unable to maintain himself and family from want of employment, goes to the hay-country, with the (presumed) *bonâ fide* intention of obtaining work, and whose family, during his absence, become chargeable to the Union, (the 3rd section of the Act, 5th Geo. 4, c. 83, being here apparently inapplicable,) it is a running away from his family, under the 4th section of the Vagrant Act; and whether the fact of his refusal upon return to repay the relief ordered by way of loan to his family, would have any legal effect in bringing him more clearly within the statute.—*Ans.* The Commissioners think it is not a running away within section 7th of the 5th Geo. 4, c. 83. The relief might be granted by way of loan, and the repayment enforced; but the man's refusal to repay relief, whether granted by way of loan or not, would not operate retrospectively to make his conduct penal, nor serve as evidence of an original criminal intention.

Q.—2. Whether the circumstance of the board of guardians having given relief by way of loan to the wife and children of an absent able-bodied man, would preclude them from proceeding against him under the Vagrant Act, so far of course as its provisions would otherwise apply to the case.—*Ans.* It is no answer to a claim by the guardians for repayment of a loan that the party liable did not apply personally for the relief, or was not in fact cognisant of the grant of such relief. The husband or father is considered by the 56th section Poor Law Amendment Act, as the person to whom the relief of his family is given, and under the 58th section of the Poor Law Amendment Act, he is liable, not only for relief given to him, but given on his account. This section places the condition of the grant of the relief at the discretion of the guardians without the concurrence of the pauper in the condition. The grant of relief to a man's family, by way of loan to him, would not in any way interfere with any proceedings to which he might otherwise be subject under the Vagrant Act, inasmuch as his liability to repay the relief would not prevent the relief when given, and while unpaid, from being a charge on the parish.

XV.—VALUATION.

POWER OF OVERSEERS TO DEPART FROM, IN THE MAKING OF RATES.

October 16th, 1844.

——— *Esq., Lymington Union*—Inquired whether it was the duty of the board of guardians to enforce a strict adherence to a valuation made during the present year by a surveyor, under their authority, of a parish in the Union; the parish officers, in making a poor-rate, having deviated from the valuation by reducing it.

Ans.—The law does not confer any power upon the board of guardians to compel an adherence upon the part of the overseers to a valuation made by a surveyor acting under the authority of the former. The case of Reg. *v.* The Earl of Yarborough, 12 A. and E. 416, shows that a valuation so made is not conclusive on the overseers, who, notwithstanding the information furnished by means of an authorised valuation, are still free to exercise their own judgment in making the poor-rate, although the valuation might form a material portion of the evidence in cases of an appeal against the rate.

XVI.—VESTRIES—

VOTING IN.

October 4th, 1844.

Mr. H. Thomas, St. Leonard, Shoreditch—Inquired whether the provisions of the 14th, 15th, and 16th sections of 7 and 8 Vic. c. 101, which relate to voting, applied only to parishes comprised in poor law unions, or whether they applied to every parish in England and Wales.

Ans.—The operation of the 14th section of 7 and 8 Vic. c. 101, is confined, in express terms, to "cases in which by the said act, or by any act amending or extending the same, owners of property and rate-payers are entitled to vote;" the act thus referred to being the Poor Law Amendment Act, and the subsequent statutes affecting it. The voting in vestry is still regulated by the 58 Geo. 3, c. 69.

XVII.—WORKHOUSE REGULATIONS.

1. VISITS TO SICK INMATES.—CIRCULAR.

Poor Law Commission Office,
October 31st, 1844.

SIR,—The Poor Law Commissioners, by Article 25 of their Workhouse Rules, have provided that—

"Any person may visit any pauper in the workhouse by permission of the master, or (in his absence) of the matron, subject to such conditions and restrictions as the board of guardians may prescribe; such interview to take place, except where a sick pauper is visited, in a room separate from the other inmates of the workhouse, in the presence of the master, matron, or porter."

The Commissioners find, from a case which has recently occurred, that the master of a union workhouse understood the purport of the latter clause of this rule (as regards visits to the sick) to be—that although such visits were excepted from the condition that they should take place in a room separate from the other inmates of the workhouse, they are still required to be in the presence of the master, matron, or porter.

The Commissioners think it right to explain that this is an erroneous view of the intent and effect of the rule. The object of the Commissioners was to allow communication, with as few impediments as possible, between the sick inmates and their friends, especially in dangerous cases, and with this view to except these cases from the conditions which, for the purpose of preventing visits for improper purposes, the Commissioners have thought it right generally to lay down. The exception applies not only to the room in which such visits take place, but also to the presence of the master or other officer.

The meaning of the rule appears to the Commissioners so obvious, that if an actual case of misapprehension had not occurred, they would have thought any explanation on the subject superfluous, especially after the full explanation afforded in the Instructional Letter appended to the Workhouse Regulations. As, however, it appears to them of importance that no possibility of a misunderstanding of the rule in question should exist on the part of any workhouse officers, they request that the board of guardians will communicate to their officers the real intent of the rule as stated in this letter.

I am, Sir, &c.

EDWIN CHADWICK, *Secretary.*

The Clerk to the Board of Guardians.

---

2. AS TO WHO HAS THE POWER TO ORDER THE DISCHARGE OF A PAUPER OUT OF A WORKHOUSE.

October 14th, 1844.

Clerk of Bath Union—Inquired, whether the master of the workhouse could legally discharge a pauper (who was unwilling to quit the workhouse) on the order of a parish officer, or any other party, except the board of guardians or their relieving officer.

Ans.—The guardians alone have the ordering of relief to paupers who are in the workhouse. It is obviously in conflict with their power that a parish officer, or other party, not acting as the delegate of the guardians, should countermand the order, and put an end to the relief they had ordered. The relieving officer could only have such power by the delegation of the guardians.

LONDON:
Printed by Order of the Poor Law Commissioners, by BLACKBURN and PARDON, 6, Hatton Garden, and Published by CHARLES KNIGHT and Co., 22, Ludgate Street, Publishers to the Poor Law Commissioners.

AN

OFFICIAL CIRCULAR

OF PUBLIC DOCUMENTS AND INFORMATION:

DIRECTED BY THE POOR LAW COMMISSIONERS TO BE PRINTED, CHIEFLY FOR THE USE OF THE MEMBERS AND PERMANENT OFFICERS OF BOARDS OF GUARDIANS, UNDER THE POOR LAW AMENDMENT ACT

No. 41. CIRCULAR ISSUED NOVEMBER 30, 1844.

Poor Law Commission Office,
Somerset House,
30th November, 1844.

The Poor Law Commissioners, on a review of their Minutes, directed that the Minutes of Correspondence on the following subjects be printed and circulated for the information of Guardians and Officers of the several Unions, viz :—

By Order of the Board,
Edwin Chadwick, *Secretary.*

I.—APPRENTICING POOR CHILDREN.

1. Notice to Overseers not now necessary.—Construction of 7 and 8 Vic. c. 101, sec. 12.

November 5th, 1844.

Clerk of Wolstanton and Burslem Union—Stated, that the board of guardians were desirous of apprenticing four or five orphan boys, who had been for periods of three or four months on trial with persons willing to take them as apprentices. Requested to be furnished with the Commissioners' instructions with reference to the binding; and inquired whether, in cases where it is sought to bind boys apprentice to persons resident in other parishes, not in this Union, the *notice to the overseers* of such parish required by the 56th Geo. 3, c. 139, &c. was still to be given by the guardians of their "intention of so binding," &c.

Ans.—The Commissioners have not as yet prepared the regulations and conditions which they are empowered to issue on the subject of apprenticing poor children, but they have them at present under their consideration. In regard to the question whether the notice required by the 59th Geo. 3, c. 139, s. 2, to be given by the overseers of the parish into which a poor child is to be bound, will be now necessary, the Commissioners think that in all cases where the binding takes place by the guardians of any Union or parish, under the 12th section of the new statute (7 and 8 Vic. c. 101) such notice will not be required. It will be observed that the 2nd section of the 56th Geo. 3, c. 139, provides that the notice shall be given before the justices shall *allow* the indenture, and that, if not admitted it shall be proved before such justices shall *sign* such indenture. But the 12th section of the 7th and 8th Vict. c. 101, expressly enacts that the indentures shall be executed by the guardians, and shall not require to be *allowed*, assented to, or *executed*, by any justice of the peace. As the allowance and execution by the justices is thus dispensed with, the notice which was a preliminary to such *allowance* and *execution* ceases to be available, and consequently to be requisite.

2.—ORDER OF JUSTICES NOT NOW NECESSARY. CONSTRUCTION OF 7 & 8 VIC. c. 101, SEC. 12.

November 30th, 1844.

Clerk of the City of London Union.—Inquired, whether the order of justices, which was necessary under 56th Geo. 3, c. 139, s. 1, in cases of apprenticing by overseers was requisite, previously to the binding of an apprentice by a board of guardians, under the 12th sec. of the recent Act, 7th and 8th Vic. c. 101.

Ans.—There are two things which, after the 56th Geo. 3, c. 139, while overseers had the power of binding apprentices, the justices were required to do: First, to examine into the fitness of the binding, and thereupon, if they approved of it, to issue their order to authorise the overseers to bind (56th Geo. 3, c. 139, s. 1); Secondly, to allow the indentures. By the 18th section of the same act, the provisions applicable to overseers are extended to the officers of all incorporated or other districts for the maintenance of the poor, where those officers have power to bind apprentices. The 7th and 8th Vic. c. 101, s. 12, declares, that indentures of apprenticeship, executed by the guardians, shall not need to be *allowed, assented to*, or *executed* by any justices; but it makes no express reference to the preliminary inquiry by justices and order thereupon. The question which arises is, whether the order for the allowance of the apprenticeship, under the 1st section of the 56th Geo. 3, c. 139, is dispensed with. The Commissioners have arrived at the conclusion, that it is dispensed with, and upon the following grounds:—The power now given to guardians by the 7th and 8th Vic. c. 101, is a new power, and apparently a power complete in itself, and is one not contemplated by the 56th Geo. 3, c. 139; and in some matters is expressly at variance with the provisions of that act as applicable to overseers and to the officers of districts within the contemplation of that act. The power is given equally to guardians of Unions and guardians of single parishes, while the 56th Geo. 3, c. 139 would, if it applied at all, apply unequally, as it would not affect the guardians of single parishes, and would thus give a different operation to the same enactment, under circumstances in which it has clearly been the object of the legislature, that the administration should be identical. (Compare 4th and 5th Wm. 4, c. 76, s. 26—39, and the 7th and 8th Vic. c. 101, s. 74.) Further, the power is given to the guardians by the 7th and 8th Vic. c. 101, generally and absolutely to bind any poor child to be an apprentice. The words are as wide as those given by the 43rd Elizabeth, which gave the power to overseers without the restriction imposed by the express provisions of subsequent statutes. At the same time, the recent enactment omits the assent of justices expressly provided for by the statute of Elizabeth. The power to bind appears, therefore, to be given unreservedly to the guardians, and the justices' right to interfere at this stage does not appear to exist. Next, the guardians are invested with all the powers of overseers to bind. This provision does not appear to be meant restrictively as confining the guardians to such powers only, and as subjecting them to all the conditions imposed on overseers; and this view is confirmed by the next provision, which requires the guardians to cause the register of apprentices to be kept,—a direction altogether unnecessary, if the words investing the guardians with the powers of overseers were also intended to subject the guardians to the same conditions and restraints as overseers. It is also to be noticed, that if the order of the justices be requisite, it must be required for some purpose, and accordingly the purpose set forth in the statute of the 56th Geo. 3, c. 139 is, that it may be a warrant for the binding of the apprentice; so that the order is in effect an assent to the indenture, which is expressly rendered unnecessary by the terms of the statute. And if, the order being refused, the guardians are precluded from proceeding with the binding, it must be because the justices refuse to allow the binding. It is true, that the words which are used are, that the indenture need not be *allowed, assented to*, or *executed*, by the justices; and some inference is raised as though only the formal allowance of the indenture is dispensed with; but although the 56th Geo. 3, c. 139 required that the indenture should be *allowed* by the justices, no statute required that the indenture should be *assented to* by them, while the

43rd Elizabeth, c. 2, required that the *binding* should be with the assent of two justices. On the whole, therefore, the effect of the 12th section of the 7th and 8th Vic. c. 101, appears to be but a developement of the policy of the 54th section of the Poor Law Amendment Act (4th and 5th Wm. 4, c. 76), which entrusted guardians with the ordering of relief exclusively of overseers and justices, apprenticeship being itself the special relief provided in certain cases for children.

II. MEDICAL RELIEF.

ARRANGEMENTS RESPECTING MEDICAL RELIEF IN THE WAYLAND UNION.

November 20th, 1844.

Sir John Walsham, Bart., Assistant Commissioner—Stated, that in his evidence before the Select Medical Relief Committee of the House of Commons, he alluded more particularly to the medical arrangements in force in the Wayland Union; and as those arrangements (that were introduced, in 1841, into the Wayland Union by its late chairman, Sir Thomas Beevor) appeared to him to be upon the whole better calculated to deal satisfactorily with the great practical difficulties which necessarily beset the important question of medical relief, than any other of the many schemes which had come under his knowledge, he requested the Commissioners' re-consideration (previously to the termination of the present parochial year) of the resolutions adopted by the guardians of the above-named union, nearly four years ago, and since successfully carried out by them under the Commissioners' sanction.

COPY OF RESOLUTIONS REFERRED TO ABOVE.

Medical Relief, Wayland Union, 1841.

Resolved—that, subject to the approbation of the Poor Law Commissioners, from and after the 25th March, 1841, the medical officers be remunerated, partly by a fixed salary, of which the amount shall have reference to the number of persons in receipt of permanent relief, and partly by a payment per case, at an uniform rate. The fixed salaries (including that for the workhouse), to be, as at present, an establishment charge, and apportioned as such; the cases to be charged to the parish to which the pauper belongs, if belonging to any parish in the union, or receiving relief from this board, on behalf of any other board of guardians, or under suspended orders of removal; otherwise to the parish in which such pauper shall be resident as in other cases of persons casually chargeable.

That it appears that the whole sum annually paid for medical relief up to the present time, no extras whatever being allowed, is £240, which is charged by three medical men, and is thus apportioned:—

First district (including workhouse)			£110
Second	,,	,,	£80
Third	,,	,,	£50

That it further appears that the average number of persons in receipt of permanent relief from this board during the year from March, 1839, to March, 1840, at which latter period these calculations were commenced, was,—

Separate cases	379, exclusive of
Wives	68
Children, part of families .	119

Making a total of 566 individuals;

and that on these numbers a payment of 3*s*. for each individual separately allowed, 5*s*. for a man or wife, and 1*s*. for each child under 16, would amount to £69. 12*s*.

That considering the distance at which the workhouse is situated from any place in which a medical man is resident, the sum of £35 per ann. is a moderate compensation for attendance there.

That the following be the amount of the fixed salaries of the medical officers:—

First district (including workhouse)			£65
Second	,,	,,	£25
Third	,,	,,	£15
			£105

That the whole number of cases of sickness amongst persons not in receipt of permanent relief during the same period as reported by the several medical officers, was 346, which at 7*s*. 6*d*. per case, would amount to £129. 15*s*., and added to the proposed salaries would be £234. 15*s*., or within a trifling amount of the present salaries.

That the relieving officers at the commencement of each year, shall severally prepare a list of all persons in receipt of permanent relief resident in each medical district, and shall deliver such list as soon as prepared to the medical officer of such district; and shall, further, from time to time give notice to the medical officer of any alterations which may take place in such list, and that all persons whose names shall be upon such list for the time being, shall be attended in case of sickness by the medical officer of the district in which they shall be resident, in consideration of the fixed salary, without special order.

That no other person shall receive medical relief, except by order of the board of guardians, or of some officer or other person duly authorised by law to order the same to be given.

In all cases in which such order shall be given by any officer of the union or parish officer, the same must be reported to the board of guardians at their next weekly meeting, as in all other cases of provisional relief, or the person giving the same will be held to be individually liable for the payment.

If such order shall be then confirmed by the board, the medical officer shall receive, for his attendance on the same, the sum of seven shillings and sixpence, which sum shall be considered due, and be payable at the close of the quarter in which the sickness shall have commenced.

If however, the board shall not think fit to confirm any provisional order for medical relief, which shall have been duly reported by the person giving the same, the clerk shall forthwith give notice thereof to the medical officer, who shall in that case be entitled to *2s. 6d.* for his past attendance, provided the case shall appear in the weekly return of cases previously to such notice, but not otherwise.

That no case of relapse shall be considered as a separate case for payment, unless the case shall have been reported as cured, or as not having again been seen or applied to be seen by the

Parish

Name

Age

Occupation

Family

Date

WAYLAND UNION, *Parish of*

SIR,

You are requested to visit the under-mentioned case.

Name.	Age	Occupation.	To what Parish belonging.	Nature of Disease.	
				Sickness.	Accidents requiring immediate attention.

Dated the day of 184

Overseer

To Mr. Medical Officer.

Parish of

To the Board of Guardians of the Wayland Union.

This is to inform you that on last, the day of the under-named received from me a provisional order for Medical Relief on Mr.

Name.	Age	Occupation.	Particular and No. of Family.	Parish to which belonging.	Whether Sickness or Accident.

Given under my hand, this day of 184

Overseer.

This Notice must be forwarded to the next meeting of the board after the giving of the order, or delivered to the relieving officer, in sufficient time to be brought by him to the Meeting.

medical officer, and shall continue well, or make no fresh application for the space of three weeks from the date of such report.

That vaccination being provided for under a separate contract, no attendance in connexion with the progress of that disorder will, of course, be considered a case within the meaning of these resolutions.

That the salaries and payments above-mentioned shall include all journeys, medicines, and appliances whatever, except trusses, which shall be provided when necessary by the medical officer, and charged to the Union at cost price.

That the medical officers shall, as at present, attend any person belonging to any parish in the Union, and resident within one mile of the limits thereof, on the same terms as if such persons were resident within such limits.

That all certificates which may be required by the board of guardians shall be given without fee, except where the medical officer may be required to visit any person at his or her own residence for that purpose, in which case, if no further order be made thereon, he shall be entitled to the same fee as if such person were attended under a provisional order.

That the medical officer of the workhouse be required to give his attendance there at least three times in every week at such intervals, that not more than two whole days shall elapse between any two visits; or if, from any unavoidable cause, a greater interval shall so elapse, the same must be regularly reported by him to the board at its next weekly meeting.

III.—REPORT OF THE HON. C. CLEMENTS, ASSISTANT POOR LAW COMMISSIONER, ON THE COMPARATIVE EXPENDITURE IN 1838 AND 1843, BETWEEN THREE UNIONS IN THE MANUFACTURING DISTRICT, MANAGED BY OVERSEERS AND VESTRIES ACCORDING TO THE OLD SYSTEM, AND OTHER UNIONS IN THE SAME DISTRICT, MANAGED BY BOARDS OF GUARDIANS UNDER THE REGULATIONS OF THE POOR LAW COMMISSIONERS.

To the Poor Law Commissioners.

Didsbury, November 26th, 1844.

Gentlemen, — The preliminary arrangements required for bringing the Ashton-under-Lyne, Oldham, and Rochdale Unions, hitherto formed for registration purposes only, under the management of boards of guardians according to your regulations, having drawn my attention to the great increase which has taken place in the expenditure within those unions, as compared with others in the district, where the relief of the poor has been administered by boards of guardians under the regulations of your board, I have thought it right to enter into an examination of the expenditure of all the unions in the manufacturing district before and since the introduction of the new system, the result of which I have now the honour to submit.

I have been led to make this examination by the dissatisfaction generally expressed in the district at the great increase which has taken place in the expenditure. Though I am convinced that this increase has been solely caused by the necessities created during a period of unprecedented distress, the public have, I know, been led to believe the contrary, and it has been confidently asserted that, great as that distress has been, the expenditure would not have been so heavy under the old, as it has been under the new system. To refute such a position, founded on mere hypothesis, must always be difficult; but the returns now submitted enable me to do so conclusively by analogy. It will be seen that in the three unions of Ashton-under-Lyne, Oldham, and Rochdale, which have hitherto been formed for registration purposes only, where the relief of the poor has been left completely under the control and management of the overseers and vestries, and has not been interfered with in the slightest degree by your board,—the expenditure has increased no less than 147 per cent, in the same period that the increase throughout the rest of the district, where the distress has been far more severe, amounts to the comparatively small proportion of 68½ per cent. Such a marked difference may, I think, be held to settle the question of the comparative merits of the two systems in an economical point of view.

The comparison I draw is derived from the annual returns of poor-rate expenditure, laid before parliament every year, and included in the appendices to your reports. I have extracted from those returns the gross expenditure from the poor-rate of each union in the manufacturing district, showing the different purposes for which that expenditure has been incurred in the years ended 25th March, 1838 and 1843.

I have selected the year 1838 for comparison with 1843, when the expenditure had reached the maximum, because 1838 is the first year in which the returns for the different parishes or townships were brought together, according to the unions of which they formed a part, so that the particulars have been more readily obtained, and can be more readily referred to by any person who may desire it; and as the administration of relief by boards of guardians had only been *commenced* in the manufacturing district in a few unions at the latter end of 1837, the expenditure for the year ended 25th of March, 1838, may fairly be said to have been principally incurred under the old system.

The distress which has prevailed during the periods between which I have made my comparison is notorious, and I must observe that the places where the suffering has been greatest, have all been under the management of boards of guardians, while I am not aware that the three unions managed by overseers and vestries, have suffered even an average amount of distress as compared with the district at large.

The unions between which the comparison is drawn, are, first, the unions of Ashton-under-Lyne, Oldham, and Rochdale, hitherto formed, as already stated, for registration purposes only, and managed wholly upon the old system, by overseers and vestries, without any interference whatever from your board; secondly, all the other unions in the manufacturing district, thirty-eight in number, comprising the county of Lancaster, the manufacturing part of the West Riding of Yorkshire, and of Cheshire, with that part of Derbyshire adjoining Cheshire, and running into the district and the parish of Liverpool. The particulars of the expenditure in each union are detailed in the return which I have the honour to append. It will be found that the increase in the expenditure for the relief of the poor, which has taken place in the unions managed by boards of guardians, is in no one instance as great as the increase which has taken place in the unions managed by overseers and vestries. In almost every one of the former the increase is considerably less than in the Rochdale Union, which, of the three managed by overseers and vestries, exhibits the smallest increase; but even in the Stockport, Bolton, and Sheffield Unions, where the distress was intense, the relative increase does not come near to that of Oldham, the highest in point of increase, where there was nothing like an equal pressure of distress.

It is remarkable that the only two unions managed by boards of guardians, where the distress was not particularly great, in which the comparative increase at all approaches that of Oldham, are those of Todmorden and Haslingden. The opposition which has notoriously been offered to the law in the former, renders it no fit criterion of the new system of management; and though the same description of opposition has not been evinced in Haslingden, the guardians of that union have always endeavoured to render the management as similar as possible to that previously existing, and they have only lately been induced to make out their accounts in the proper form.

The following summary will, however, afford a more general view of the matter.

The aggregate expenditure in the three unions of Ashton-under-Lyne, Oldham, and Rochdale, during the years ended Lady-day 1838 and 1843, respectively was—

	1838.	1843.	Increase per cent in 1843.
	£.	£.	
In relief to the poor . . .	15,349	37,928	147.1
Payments under Parochial Assessments Act	47	76	61.7
All other purposes, including law charges	4,358	4,438	1.8
Totals . .	19,754	42,442	114.8
County and Police Rate . .	6,008	14,589	142.8
Registration & Vaccination	137	951	594.1
Totals . . . £	6,145	15,540	152.8

The Aggregate Expenditure in all the other Unions in the Manufacturing District, during the years ended Lady-day, 1838 and 1843, respectively was—

	1838.	1843.	Increase per Cent. in 1843.
	£.	£.	
In relief to the poor .	325,742	549,380	68.6
Payments under Parochial Assessments Act	5,100	1,760	187.7 (Decrease.)
All other purposes, including law charges .	65,236	65,153	.1 (Decrease.)
Totals . . . £	396,078	616,293	55.6
County and Police Rate	78,380	170,680	117.7
Registration and Vaccination	3,193	10,752	236.7
Totals . . . £	81,573	181,432	122.4

It will be perceived that the expenditure in relief to the poor in the three unions, managed according to the old system, increased from £15,349 in 1838, to £37,928 in 1843, or 147 per cent.; while the increase in the other unions during the same period, was from £325,742 to £549,380, or 68½ per cent. Had the expenditure in the other unions increased in the same ratio as those first named, it would have reached to £804,897; thus showing from the best data left us, that through the establishment of the new system a saving has been effected in the manufacturing district of £255,517.

To prevent misconception, it is necessary to observe that, under the item of relief to the poor, are included the much abused establishment charges, the instalments and interest on all loans for building or altering workhouses, and all expenses connected with the relief of the poor, except those of their removal, disputed settlements, &c., which are entered under the head of expenditure "for all other purposes."

Under the item, "expended for all other purposes," which is the only other with which the administration of relief is in any way connected, are included "law charges," entered separately in the printed returns. I have put them together, because the return for 1838, included under the head of law charges, the expenses of the removal of paupers, and the travelling expenses of overseers, which having since been transferred to the column "for all other purposes," the comparison between the two years is better made by placing them together. The other expenses, included under this item, are those before magistrates, constables' expenses, printing jury lists and lists of voters, expenses on account of parish property, &c., all of which are beyond the control of the guardians, but not of the auditor, to whose examination of the accounts and check on illegal disbursements, may probably be attributed the great reduction which has taken place in this branch of expenditure in the majority of the unions enumerated. In some of the large towns there has, however, been a considerable increase, attributable, no doubt, to some expenditure for municipal purposes; but for this the aggregate expenditure under this head in the unions, managed by boards of guardians, would have exhibited a considerable reduction; as it is, the reduction amounts only to £83. There is an increase of £80 in the same item in the three unions, managed by overseers and vestries, to which I draw your attention, to show that the great comparative increase in the expenditure for the relief of the poor, cannot have been effected by any misapprehension on the part of the officers of any of the unions in question, as to the mode of entering their expenditure; for the aggregate expenditure "for all other purposes," of the three unions managed by overseers and vestries and of all the other unions is, as is apparent above, very nearly the same in 1843 as in 1838.

It may possibly be contended in the district, that the great increase of expenditure in the three unions under the old, as compared with the others under the new system of management, arises from the superior liberality displayed by the overseers and vestries in the former as compared with the boards of guardians in the latter unions. Upon the degree of liberality evinced by the overseers and vestries I cannot speak; but I can confidently assert, that in the unions, managed by boards of guardians under your regulations, (though in many there is still room for improvement,) the poor have been better attended to, and their wants have been more fully and more regularly supplied than ever they were before. In my opinion, the comparatively small rate of increase can only be attributed to the superior management, which, though frequently not as good as could be wished, is yet an improvement on that previously existing. Under a board of guardians every item of expenditure is more strictly scrutinized, and the real circumstances of each applicant for relief more accurately ascertained. The result is, that while imposition is detected, the really destitute, the helpless, the aged and infirm, and the sick, are more adequately relieved. The essential feature of the old system, with, of course, some bright exceptions, was the employment of assistant overseers, whose only idea of good management too often consisted in an accurate knowledge of the smallest modicum of relief which would stop the importunity of each applicant; and though the prejudice existing in the district still prevents boards of guardians from taking a proper view of the necessity of administering relief to the able-bodied on sound principles, by which alone adequate relief can be given to that class of persons, yet the relief of all other classes, such as those previously enumerated, though still in many places not what it should be, is, notwithstanding, I am confident, far more adequate than it used to be. This has been fully proved in more instances than one, where an opposition to the "new law" having been created by the increased expenditure, the first attempt made by those put forward as friends of the "old system" has been *to reduce the amount of relief given in each individual case.* I can, therefore, confidently assert, that the increase in the expenditure in the unions under the management of boards of guardians, which my examination of the returns has shown to be so much less in comparison to the increase in those unions still under the management of overseers and vestries, does not arise from less adequate relief being afforded to those in want.

Nor does it arise from the wants of the poor being less attended to in the workhouses. That they have been better provided for there scarcely needs demonstration, though in this, as in other branches of management, much has still to be done. There are still, even in the unions, managed by boards of guardians, several old workhouses, in a very discreditable state, the guardians neglecting to improve them, notwithstanding the repeated representations made to them on the subject. One of the reasons alleged as an excuse is, an unwillingness to separate respectable married couples. The same reasons for opposing the "new law," as it is called, is constantly held up to those whose better judgment would lead them to support the improved management, which they cannot fail to perceive. But I have yet to learn that there is anything in the regulations issued by your board, or in the advice given under your instructions, which would ever cause the guardians to oblige respectable married couples, who require relief, to enter a workhouse. The extension of out-door relief in such cases has invariably followed the introduction of the Poor Law Amendment Act. But in these old workhouses, which the guardians are so averse to improve, I always find that in proportion to the absence of all arrangement for the classification, or even decent separation of the sexes, so is there a marked absence of all necessary provision for the preservation of cleanliness, or for the care and proper comfort of the sick. The old and young, the idle, profligate, and sick, are all mixed up together in one confused mass. That such a state of things has always existed in this district is well known, and though it still exists to a far greater extent than it ought to do, yet it is undoubted that considerable improvement has taken place, and is still going on. This improvement, from which has resulted the superior comfort of the sick and aged, has been mainly derived from the exertions emanating from your board. That similar improvements have not taken place in the three unions left to the management of the overseers and vestries is, I believe, pretty well known; but not having actually inspected the workhouses of these unions, I will not attempt a comparison.

Before closing this report, it is right that I should request your attention to another point, which my examination of the poor-rate returns indicates, viz., the great increase in the charge on the rates for purposes in no way connected with the relief of the poor.

That a great increase had taken place in the county-rate was well known, but these returns exhibit the precise state of the case. It will be perceived, that in the unions managed by boards of guardians, the increase is 117 per cent., thus exceeding the increase in the relief of the poor by 49 per cent.

The expenses on account of registration and vaccination also require notice. The former commenced in 1838, and the latter in 1841, and being therefore unknown before the introduction of the Poor Law Amendment Act into the district, the increased expenditure created thereby, which, in 1843, amounted to £10,752, is unfortunately attributed pretty generally to the new

EXTRACT FROM THE RETURNS OF POOR-RATE EXPENDITURE,

FOR THE YEARS ENDED MARCH, 1838 AND 1843,

Showing the Expenditure from the Poor-rate for all purposes in those years, in the several Unions comprising the Manufacturing District.

UNIONS.	YEAR ENDED MARCH, 1838.						YEAR ENDED MARCH, 1843.					
	Expended in Relief of Poor.	County and Police Rate.	Registration Expenses.	Payments under the Parochial Assessment Act.	Expended for all other purposes, including Law Charges.	TOTAL.	Expended in Relief of Poor.	County and Police Rate.	Registration & Vaccination Expenses.	Payments under the Parochial Assessment Act.	Expended for all other purposes, including Law Charges.	TOTAL.
	£. s.	£. s.	£. s.	£. s.	£. s.	£. s.	£. s.	£. s.	£. s.	£. s.	£. s.	£. s.
Ashton-under-Lyne	5,339 4	2,337 17	...	16 1	2,105 0	9,798 2	11,776 7	4,824 9	398 12	13 18	1,494 15	18,508 1
Oldham	4,676 10	1,630 15	0 10	30 9	1,107 2	7,445 6	14,658 9	4,065 8	310 17	...	1,557 1	20,591 15
Rochdale	5,333 15	2,039 15	136 6	...	1,145 11	8,655 7	11,493 1	5,699 1	241 15	62 4	1,386 12	18,882 13
	15,349 9	6,008 7	136 16	46 10	4,357 13	25,898 15	37,927 17	14,588 18	951 4	76 2	4,438 8	57,982 9
Blackburn	9,864 0	2,066 0	112 6	23 11	2,605 19	15,171 16	15,773 8	4,046 9	307 19	...	1,491 2	21,618 18
Bolton	8,889 7	2,849 19	112 9	15 19	3,063 16	14,931 10	24,698 13	9,178 1	460 11	...	2,897 16	37,235 1
Bradford	10,705 17	2,192 18	70 19	95 6	3,669 5	16,834 5	21,852 14	4,446 3	548 16	37 10	3,559 18	30,445 1
Burnley	11,553 7	1,788 5	60 0	11 10	1,750 18	15,164 0	17,929 10	3,219 11	187 0	...	1,455 13	22,791 14
Bury	6,580 17	2,237 7	101 5	49 3	1,716 13	10,685 5	13,659 5	5,099 2	378 11	295 0	2,469 2	21,901 0
Chapel-en-le-Frith	2,063 12	498 10	12 14	60 6	660 4	3,295 6	3,122 12	738 17	41 2	...	273 19	4,176 10
Chorley	5,728 5	1,763 11	75 3	52 13	1,096 1	8,715 13	9,964 5	3,067 19	136 9	...	374 7	13,543 0
Chorlton	8,744 5	2,427 14	202 14	2 1	1,789 16	13,166 10	13,083 18	13,604 3	434 5	...	1,350 15	28,473 1
Clitheroe	5,546 9	1,451 4	2 19	110 11	995 7	8,106 10	10,304 3	2,557 8	77 5	...	667 3	13,605 19
Congleton	7,717 2	1,522 17	27 19		793 4	10,061 2	6,853 12	2,207 5	148 4	26 1	738 1	9,973 3
Dewsbury	8,547 7	1,163 9	12 5	122 15	767 17	10,613 13	14,148 13	2,656 0	298 2	...	906 12	18,009 7
Ecclesall Bierlow	6,012 16	700 10	37 14	1 1	882 7	7,634 8	12,424 17	1,486 8	129 11	...	1,688 2	15,728 18
Fylde	3,138 4	1,308 14	0 18	9 15	744 17	5,202 8	4,905 9	2,337 8	65 13	...	380 2	7,688 12
Garstang	3,350 5	988 1	19 10	46 15	533 12	4,938 3	5,242 17	1,619 19	30 7	...	116 19	7,010 2
Glossop	908 0	385 14	25 10	265 17	180 9	1,765 10	1,909 15	459 6	55 15	...	177 8	2,602 4
Halifax	11,295 4	1,916 6	38 12	1,012 12	2,902 1	17,164 15	19,650 7	4,580 18	522 2	8 0	1,928 13	26,690 0
Haslingden	3,177 11	1,083 15	55 9	69 1	1,072 19	5,458 15	7,655 1	2,287 13	215 6	388 5	252 16	10,799 1
Hayfield	1,475 9	310 1	9 1	...	253 12	2,048 3	2,444 11	441 9	32 7	...	451 17	3,370 4
Huddersfield	11,665 12	2,045 18	3 0	294 17	2,546 2	16,555 9	21,171 0	4,279 13	481 3	...	5,583 8	31,515 4
Keighley	4,589 11	781 0	25 1	16 3	452 19	5,864 14	8,189 18	1,652 3	77 5	...	859 6	10,778 12
Lancaster	5,627 9	1,203 17	51 5	101 0	1,133 15	8,117 6	7,514 19	2,273 17	88 10	..	524 1	10,401 7
Leigh	3,971 3	1,043 18	59 7	...	712 18	5,787 6	6,784 13	1,719 9	104 7	24 3	351 6	8,983 18
Liverpool	36,564 6	5,078 16	251 4	...	8,001 17	49,996 3	42,536 3	13,967 16	1,348 17	210 0	4,923 13	62,986 9
Macclesfield	12,354 10	2,358 12	77 18	...	1,762 1	16,553 1	11,233 15	3,007 11	223 3	...	987 16	15,452 5
Manchester	31,993 14	10,738 7	362 16	...	2,480 7	45,575 4	50,621 13	25,716 18	1,083 6	...	5,253 2	82,674 19
Ormskirk	5,619 14	2,668 0	105 6	...	1,120 19	9,513 19	5,028 10	3,858 2	156 8	...	208 0	9,251 0
Prescot	5,439 16	2,792 8	1 15	80 8	1,515 17	9,830 4	8,215 14	4,544 16	227 13	...	391 8	13,379 11
Preston	12,085 6	3,051 11	13 14	36 0	2,110 6	17,296 17	23,455 18	6,272 4	335 16	...	1,726 8	31,790 6
Rotherham	5,049 12	1,129 10	55 9	...	655 5	6,889 16	9,537 1	2,168 5	126 6	...	660 18	12,492 10
Salford	7,796 10	2,393 7	104 0	...	2,890 13	13,184 10	10,270 8	5,505 7	332 5	...	1,679 1	17,787 1
Sheffield	14,687 7	2,129 2	478 17	515 18	707 2	18,518 6	42,576 16	4,535 10	375 6	108 9	4,196 0	51,792 1
Skipton	8,897 11	1,682 4	71 0	...	1,925 7	12,576 2	10,705 6	2,757 3	119 17	...	1,537 11	15,119 17
Stockport	7,785 4	2,548 17	54 18	1,293 2	2,391 3	14,073 4	22,694 3	4,739 9	358 2	509 19	2,054 12	30,356 5
Todmorden	3,025 0	467 15	...	2 9	349 1	3,844 5	9,038 15	1,141 1	94 8	1 17	686 3	10,962 4
Wakefield	9,994 6	1,206 14	89 3	42 18	1,723 15	13,056 16	13,829 2	2,813 10	221 0	150 7	1,509 14	18,523 13
Warrington	5,490 3	1,970 13	72 13	10 19	1,312 13	8,857 1	9,375 12	3,082 2	124 12	...	2,532 5	15,114 11
West Derby	6,542 9	2,597 6	103 1	...	3,295 18	12,538 14	9,777 5	5,575 12	401 17	...	3,336 10	19,091 4
Wigan	6,800 12	3,078 18	101 4	88 6	1,579 9	11,648 9	14,520 16	5,395 14	298 1	...	1,042 4	21,256 15
Wortley	4,464 5	758 5	34 2	69 8	1,090 13	6,416 13	6,679 2	1,640 4	104 13	...	3,929 6	12,353 5
	325,741 17	78,379 13	3,193 0	5,100 4	65,236 17	477,651 11	549,379 19	170,680 5	10,752 0	1,759 11	65,152 17	797,724 12

Note—The particulars of those Unions not formed, or not in operation in 1838, are taken from the returns furnished by the Overseers of each township.
The return for Chorlton Union includes the townships added to it in 1841.

law. The payments under the Parochial Assessment Act may also be placed under the same category, though there has been a decrease of £3340 in this item in 1843, as compared with 1838, but the charge itself is quite a new one.

It will thus be perceived, that in the unions managed by boards of guardians, the expenditure in matters wholly beyond the control of the guardians, and irrespective of relief, has increased from £81,573, in 1838, to £181,432, in 1843, or 122 per cent. It must not be supposed that in making these remarks I wish to cast the slightest reflection upon the administration of the county funds, or to induce an opinion that the additional charges recently imposed on the poor-rate are in any way unnecessary. My only object has been to explain the position in which that portion of the poor-rate, allotted to the relief of the poor, stands in connexion with other portions of that fund appropriated to other purposes. I have shown that in the unions managed by boards of guardians, while the expenditure in the relief of the poor has increased 68½ per cent., other expenses quite unconnected with it, but derived from the same fund, have increased 122 per cent. And as regards the increase in the expenditure for the relief of the poor, which has taken place since the introduction of the new system, I think I have shown incontestably, that no saving, but on the contrary, a considerable increase of expense, would have been the result, had the unprecedented distress, which has prevailed in the district, appeared before the new system had been brought into operation.

I have the honour to be, Gentlemen,
Your very obedient servant,
(Signed) CHAS. S. CLEMENTS,
Assist. Poor Law Commissioner.

IV.—PAUPER.

1.—INQUEST ON A PAUPER—UXBRIDGE UNION—CORRESPONDENCE RESPECTING THE CASE.

November 6th, 1844.

The Poor Law Commissioners to the Clerk of the Uxbridge Union.—The Poor Law Commissioners are desirous of bringing under the consideration of the board of guardians of the Uxbridge Union the accompanying *report* of proceedings at an inquest, held on the body of William Terry.* The Commissioners request that they may be furnished with the observations of the guardians on this case, and also on the subject of the arrangements for allowing to sick paupers the extra articles of diet ordered by the medical officer.

November 15th, 1844.

Clerk of the Uxbridge Union to the Poor Law Commissioners.—* * * William Terry, a labourer, was a parishioner of Uxbridge, but had for upwards of two years past resided at Pinner, which is in the Hendon Union: he was a man of drunken and dissolute habits, and had twice been in the Uxbridge Union workhouse, viz., from the 19th of November, 1841, to the 5th of February, 1842, and from the 11th of February, to the 20th of March, 1842. He was, on Wednesday morning, the 30th of October last, brought in a cart to his sister's house at Ruislip, in the Uxbridge Union, but his case was not reported, nor any applica-

* *Times, October 31st*, 1844.—*Death from Starvation.*—Yesterday an inquest was held before Mr. Wakley, M.P., coroner, at the Six Bells, Ruislip-common, near Uxbridge, on the body of *William Terry*, a labourer.—*Mary Lavenden*, the sister of the deceased, said the deceased was in no regular employ, having obtained his living by jobbing about, sometimes getting money for what he did, and at other times a little food. He had no house or lodgings. He had slept in a loft over an outhouse for two years past. He had no bed, but lay on straw or hay. He had been brought to her house from where he had slept, about four miles off, on Wednesday morning last, about ten o'clock, in a dung-cart, driven by a boy. He could not walk. Witness, her son, and the boy helped him into her cottage. He was quite sensible. He said that they saw he was going to die, and he thought that they wanted to get rid of him. He said that the owner of the loft where he was lying had come to him on the night before, and given him some gruel. He said he had not asked for any doctor to be sent for, nor had he applied to any overseer. He was with witness on Sunday last, and left her in the afternoon. He used to come to her and her husband on Sundays sometimes to get a bit of dinner. He said that he did not believe he had got out of the loft from Sunday night until he was put into the cart on Wednesday morning. He said that he had not any pain, but was very low and feeble, and got weaker and weaker. Witness and her son helped him into a chair. He almost fainted and fell from it two or three times. He was helped up to bed, such a bed as witness could let him have. It was made of chaff. She had no other. She got him a little milk. He drank a little of it. He could not eat any bread in it. She herself had no money in the house at the time, as her husband and son were out of work. Sixpence was sent home with him by the boy who drove the cart. The deceased had often not a shilling a-week to live upon. He did not ask for anything after he was in bed. He was very low, and continued in that state all that day. She hardly knew what to do; she was in great distress herself. She knew that she could not get any relief without going to the relieving officer, who lived four miles off, at Hillingdon. Next morning she went to the relieving officer. It was

tion made on his behalf, till Thursday morning, when Mary Lavenden, his sister, went to the relieving officer's house, but not finding him at home, proceeded to Mr. Rayner, the medical officer at Uxbridge, who visited the poor man the same afternoon, and pronounced him to be in a dying state, and he died soon after the medical officer had seen him. It will be observed by the evidence of Mary Lavenden, as reported in the *Times*, that this pauper, when brought to her house, was unable to eat any solid food. After the inquest, Mr. Rayner called on the chairman of the Uxbridge board of guardians, and stated that when he saw the pauper, he was in a dying state,—that nothing could have saved him,—but if he had been able to take anything, he would (as it was his duty to have done) immediately have had it procured for him. If Mr. Rayner had stated this fact at the inquest, the case would not have produced so unfavourable an impression on the public, as from misrepresentation and suppression of the facts, it appears to have done.

The above short narrative of simple facts, exhibits this case divested of the unfair gloss thrown over it by parties who, for purposes of their own, do not wish a just view to be taken of the circumstances. I submit, that there is not the slightest ground on which the least blame can be imputed to the guardians, or to any of the officers of the union, unless indeed to Mr. Rayner, for not having immediately supplied the pauper with such articles of diet (if any) as he considered necessary. That the pauper's death was hastened by destitution, the guardians are apprehensive cannot be doubted; but it must be remembered that he was living out of this union till the day before his death—that no notice was given of the pauper's illness—no application was made until too late, either to the relieving officer (who visits each parish of the Union twice every week,) or to the overseers, who, in cases of emergency, have the power of ordering immediate relief. Under such circumstances, how can the Poor Law system, the Uxbridge Union, or the officers conducting it, be fairly made responsible for the consequences? As to the time which elapsed between the application to the medical officer, and his visit to the pauper, it is merely necessary to observe, that all the residents in the parish (the wealthiest as well as the poorest,) are liable to the same inconvenience, having to send to Uxbridge for medical assistance.

With regard to the observation that the pauper was afraid to go into the workhouse again, the

---

raining fast, but she went as quick as she could go, as she thought that deceased was getting worse. She reached his house at about ten o'clock, but she had the sorrow of hearing that he was not at home. She was told by one of the children, that if she made haste she might find him at Uxbridge church. She did make haste there, but he had left before she could reach it. She then hardly knew what to do, but she thought she would go to Mr. Rayner, the union doctor, who attends on her parish. She went and saw him, and he said that he was coming to Ruislip, and that he would call. She got back to her cottage again at twelve o'clock. Had left her daughter with deceased during her absence. On her return he could not speak. Had no wine or cordial—in fact, nothing in the house to give him. All that she had was some bread and a bit of butter. He kept moaning, but did not move hand or foot. Mr. Rayner came in the afternoon, and examined him, and said he was dying. He was then so far gone that he could take nothing. He continued to get weaker and weaker, and died three hours after the doctor's visit. He had been in the Uxbridge Union twice. The last time was about three years ago. He said he would never go there again if he could only get one meal a-day out of it. He had no property of any kind, neither bed, stool, nor anything in the world but the clothes on his back, and they were not worth a shilling. He had not applied for relief from the union since he came out of the house three years ago. He was afraid to go in there again. He then went in through a bad leg. He made no complaint about being brought here in the cart. It was his own wish to come.—*The Jurymen* stated that they knew the deceased, and firmly believed that every word the witness had stated was true.—*Mr. Rayner*, the district union surgeon for the parishes of Ickenham and Ruislip, confirmed the last witness's evidence.—*The Coroner.* To what cause do you attribute the man's death?—*Mr. Rayner* said, he feared that the man had died from exhaustion and want of food and the other necessaries of life.—*The Coroner.* Have you any doubt in such a case?—*Mr. Rayner* had no doubt that the man had died from the effects of destitution.—*The Coroner.* If you find it necessary in such an instance of extreme destitution to order wine, jelly, arrowroot, or other nourishment, what course is adopted?—*Mr. Rayner.* Is it necessary that I should answer that question?—*The Coroner.* Undoubtedly. Everything on such a subject ought to be generally known. Although the law provides that in cases of emergency the churchwardens and overseers can grant orders for relief, yet the poor woman has stated that she knew that she could not obtain any without applying to the relieving officer. Now, sir, what I want to know is this,—suppose you had found it necessary in the case of the deceased to order for him nourishing food, how soon and where could the woman have obtained it?—*Mr. Rayner.* I grant an order for whatever I think is necessary.—*The Coroner.* That is not a full answer to the question. What I want to know is, to whom is the order addressed, and how soon the nourishment could be obtained?—*Mr. Rayner.* The order is addressed to the relieving officer, and if he thinks that it is right, whatever is directed in the order he can cause it to be supplied. *The Coroner.* "If the relieving officer thinks that it is right!" "If the relieving officer thinks that it is right!" Good heavens! do you not grant the order medically?—*Mr. Rayner.* Yes. *The Coroner.* And do you mean to say, that in such a case the relieving officer can have an authority superior to yours? Pray let us understand this matter distinctly. In fact it ought not only to be understood here, but throughout the whole empire. Every human being in the kingdom ought to comprehend it. 'What is the form of order you employ?—*Mr. Rayner* (producing a blank form.) This is one. "To Mr. Francis Stockwell, relieving officer of the Uxbridge Union. Supply with , unless you know he is in such circumstances that can h self provide the same. Dated the day of 184 . ———, medical officer." *The Coroner.* If guardians have anxiously endeavoured to make the pauper residents in it comfortable; but it is obvious that the necessary restraints of such an institution will always be unpalatable to persons of loose and irregular habits. Mr. Wakley, the coroner, has several times, on occasions of holding inquests at the Uxbridge Union workhouse, (when every opportunity was afforded him to inspect the institution,) expressed his satisfaction at the comfortable appearance of the inmates, and particularly of the healthy and happy condition of the children.

Respecting the mode in which the extra diet, ordered by the medical officers, has hitherto been supplied, I enclose a printed *form* (A), by which it will be perceived that the orders are addressed to the relieving officer, who gives directions to the different tradespeople to furnish the articles, unless he knows that the parties are in such circumstances that they can themselves provide the same, which some of the paupers are in a condition to do when supplied with medical attendance and medicine gratuitously. The relieving officer, however, has very rarely exercised the discretion thus given him, and the guardians seldom interfere, though they deem it proper to retain the power of doing so when necessary.

It may at first sight be supposed, that the Rules under which the extra diet has been supplied, might frequently occasion delay, and consequent injury to the patients; but when it is considered that the relieving officer each week visits every parish of the union twice, at fixed times and places, and that in case of emergency, the overseers, as well as the medical officers, have power to afford immediate relief, it will be seen that the risk of inconvenience is very slight; the guardians, however, anxious to avoid this remote contingency, have revised their regulations, and I enclose a copy of the amended *Rules* (B).

As the manner in which Mr. Ratcliff has stated another case at the inquest, is calculated to give a wrong impression, I beg to observe, that the relief there referred to, was afforded upwards of four years ago by Mr. Ratcliff, a butcher and publican, who took upon himself, whilst overseer of his parish, to supply articles of meat and beer from his own shop, for the period of three weeks, to the *wife of James Bunce*, a labourer, in constant work, at the weekly wages of 12*s.*; and as the wife had medical attendance and medicine supplied by the union, her husband was supposed to be able to procure the extra diet for his wife, as so many other labourers do without applying to the

---

you fill up the blank for half-a-pound, or a pound, of meat, do you mean to say that before the meat can be procured by the poor person, he must present it to the relieving officer, who in this case lives four miles from the cottage?—*Mr. Rayner.* Yes, that is the practice. *The Coroner.* There must be some mistake. You surely misunderstood me.—*Mr. Rayner.* What I have stated is the strict truth. *A Juryman.* It is quite true. A poor woman brought one of the orders to me. *The Coroner.* I will hear you directly, sir. (To Mr. Rayner.) At what distance do some of your profession live from the relieving officer?—*Mr. Rayner.* Six miles. *The Coroner.* And do you positively mean to state, that before the food can be procured, the order must, in some cases, be taken five or six miles to the relieving officer?—*Mr. Rayner.* Yes, in some cases. *The Coroner.* And then that the relieving officer can exercise a discretion whether it shall be obeyed or not?—*Mr. Rayner.* I do. *The Coroner.* But suppose that any tradesman living on the spot supplied the food directed in the order, would there be any objection to such a proceeding?—*Mr. Radcliffe* (the juryman who had before spoken.) It was on that point, sir, that I wished to address a word or two to the court. Some time since, one of these orders was signed by Mr. Rayner, which directed that half-a-pound of mutton, and a pint of beer, daily, should be supplied to a poor woman named Lawrence, who was then confined in childbirth. I furnished her with the articles for about three weeks, and when I asked the relieving officer for payment, I was told that it could not be paid; and the debt has not been discharged to this day, either by the relieving officer or the board. The ground of refusal was, that the order was from the medical gentleman, and not from the relieving officer. *The Coroner.* The case is now clear enough. Even the terms of the order show that the authority of the relieving officer is paramount to that of the medical gentleman, by whom the food is directed, although the food be ordered medicinally. This is monstrous. Why might not the relieving officer be permitted to interfere with the administration of drugs? The food is prescribed medically, yet the medical authority is not supreme! I wonder that my medical brethren submit to such an arrangement, which is most cruel to the poor. *A Juryman.* And when half-a-pound of meat a-day is ordered, they never allow but three pounds in the week, not thinking, I suppose, that the poor ought to eat on Sunday. *The Coroner*, in his charge to the jury, said, that he feared that the cause of the poor man's death was but too plain, and that he had fallen a victim to extreme destitution. The picture presented by the evidence was of an appalling description. The contrast that had arisen in this country between the destitute poor and the criminals in our gaols had become most striking and extraordinary. They had heard the ordeal which a sick person, or his friend, must undergo, and the miles that must be travelled before a medical order for food was obeyed. To-morrow he might hold an inquest at the House of Correction, Coldbath fields, on a prisoner, and what should he find? Why, that the medical treatment of the sick prisoner was entirely under the direction of the medical officer of the gaol; that the governor, the magistrates, or the Secretary of State, did not interfere with his medical authority; that he had power to cause to be given instantly, and without stint or restraint, wine, jellies, fish, fruit, arrowroot, sago, or any other thing that might be necessary for a sick person under his treatment. The jury had now been informed what was passing with reference to the management of the unoffending poor within view of their own dwellings, and he must say that such statements, unless they were verified as they had been, could scarcely obtain credence. (The facts disclosed were absolutely revolting.) *The Coroner* then asked if the jury wished to retire? The jury said, they had no wish to do so, as there were not two opinions amongst them. Their verdict was, "That the death of William Terry had been caused by a want of food and the other necessaries of life."

union for any, who have not the gratuitous medical assistance granted them. The case clearly was not one of emergency, and the relieving officer had no notice of the supply until after the expiration of many weeks. Most persons are aware that if the overseer had been paid for the articles so furnished, he would by the 55th Geo. 3, c. 157, have subjected himself to the penalty of £100.

As to the case of *William Haynes*, a labourer, of Ruislip parish, who lately destroyed himself, the proceedings at the inquest held on him are given in the *Times*, of Saturday, the 9th instant, and commented on in the same journal of the 12th with the acrimonious spirit, the prejudiced views, and exaggerated inferences, by which all articles of that journal on the Poor Law are characterised. This pauper was in receipt of 6*s.* a week from his club, and of 2*s.* and 3lbs. of mutton a week from this union, and (as is asserted by the treasurer of the club) they have £600 in the Bank of England, he must have been under some delusion in supposing the club was going to break up. He had 9*s.* 6*d.* in his pocket when he destroyed himself. With respect to his fear of being brought into the union-house and being separated from his wife, the circumstance of the guardians having given him an allowance in addition to his club-money, ought to have satisfied him that there was no danger of his being ordered into the workhouse: indeed, (unless under very peculiar circumstances) out-door relief is never refused to aged couples.

FORM (A) REFERRED TO ABOVE.

To the Rel. Offic.	*To Mr. Rel. Officer of*
	the Uxbridge Union. Supply
to supply	*with unless you*
	know he is in such circum-
with Dated	*stances that he can h*
	self provide the same.
184	*Dated the day of*
	184
Med. Officer.	*Medical Officer.*

RULES (B) REFERRED TO ABOVE.

Uxbridge Union. Resolved—That when the medical officers of the union order any articles of diet for persons whom they are attending by direction of the board, such order, signed by the medical officer, is to be immediately complied with; and the relieving officer will explain to the tradespeople of the different parishes, that articles supplied on such orders will be paid for by the board until they receive notice from him to discontinue doing so.

The relieving officer is to report all such orders on the next board day, and intermediately is not to interfere with them.

The above resolution to be communicated to the several medical officers, with the board's request that in giving these orders to their patients they will explain to them, that it will no longer be necessary for them to take the orders to the relieving officer, but to deliver them to him when he visits the parish, and that in the mean time the tradespeople will supply the articles therein ordered.

November 28th, 1844.

The Poor Law Commissioners to the Clerk of the Uxbridge Union.—The Commissioners will first take the case of William Terry. You state that William Terry, a labourer, was a parishioner of Uxbridge, but that he has for upwards of two years resided at Pinner, in the Hendon Union, and that he was a man of drunken and dissolute habits; that he was brought in a cart to his sister's house, at Ruislip, on Wednesday, the 30th October, but that no application was made on his behalf till the next day, when his sister went to the relieving officer's house, but not finding him at home, she proceeded to Mr. Rayner, the medical officer at Uxbridge, who visited the man the same afternoon, and pronounced him to be in a dying state; and that he in fact died shortly afterwards.

The Commissioners regret to observe from your letter, that it is feared destitution may have accelerated the man's death; but it will be seen from the above statement of facts, that he was not within the Union until brought to his sister's house the day before his death, and that no application was made until too late, either to the relieving officer, or to the overseers, who would have had, as is well known, the duty of affording relief, in a case of sudden and urgent necessity.

The Commissioners also observe from your letter, that after the inquest Mr. Rayner called on the chairman of the Uxbridge board of guardians, and stated, that when he saw the pauper he was in a dying state; that nothing could have saved him; but that if he had been able to take anything, he would (as it was his duty to have done) immediately have had it procured for him.

With regard to the general arrangements of the Union, the Commissioners learn that Ruislip parish is situated three miles from Uxbridge, and that there is no medical man nearer than that town. The parish is also the same distance from the residence of the relieving officer; and taking the extreme out-skirts of the parish, a pauper may live five miles from the relieving officer. It is evident, however, that ready access may be had to the overseers of the parish itself, and they are bound, under the provisions of section 54 of the Poor Law Amendment Act, to give, in cases of sudden and urgent necessity, such temporary relief as each case shall require, in articles of absolute necessity, but not in money, and whether the applicant for relief be settled in the parish where he shall apply for relief, or not. If the recommendation of a medical officer, for articles of food, in a case marked by him as one of sudden and urgent necessity, were taken to an overseer, he would, to say the least, be fully justified in obeying it; indeed, if the party were destitute, he would be bound to do so. It may be said, that he is bound by the Commissioners' Regulations to report the relief afforded, to the board of guardians. He is so, but it does not follow that the guardians have the power of disallowing the cost of it. If they refuse to repay him, he may still charge it in his accounts, and it can be disallowed by the auditor alone. Against this disallowance, moreover, (if made) there will be, by sections 35 and 36 of 7th and 8th Vic. c. 101, an appeal to the Court of Queen's Bench, or the Poor Law Commissioners.

It is clear, therefore, that at least the same facility for obtaining articles of food recommended, in a case of emergency, by a medical officer, exists now as existed before the passing of the Poor Law Amendment Act.

The Commissioners believe that in practice such articles are much more readily and much more abundantly supplied to the poor, than they were under the old system.

The guardians say that the orders for extra diet given by the medical officers, "are addressed to the relieving officer, who gives directions to the different trades-people to furnish the articles, unless he knows that the parties are in such circumstances that they can themselves provide the same, which some of the paupers are in a condition to do, when supplied with medical attendance and medicine gratuitously,—that the relieving officer, however, has very rarely exercised the discretion thus given him, and that the guardians seldom interfere, though they deem it proper to retain the power of doing so when necessary." On this the Commissioners will only observe that, although a medical man is, without doubt, the best judge of what is required for the health of his patient, they do not know that he is in like manner the most competent person to decide on his pecuniary means. For a relieving officer, or a board of guardians, to refuse to comply with the recommendation of a medical man, is on the part of either to incur a very considerable responsibility; the benefit of any doubt ought always to be given to the pauper, and in all ordinary cases the nourishment should be furnished at once: inquiry can be made afterwards. The Commissioners do not see the propriety or necessity of expressly inserting in the form of recommendatiou by the medical officer the words "unless you know he is in such circumstances that he can himself provide the same."

The Commissioners have, however, no doubt that, as the trustees of the ratepayers, the guardians are not only justified in making such inquiry, but are bound by their trust to do so, nor can they renounce the controlling power thus placed in their hands. The guardians may and ought to exercise such control with the greatest regard to the wants of the sick poor, and with the greatest confidence in the professional skill and integrity of those officers whom they have thought fit to appoint. But they cannot, as it appears to the Commissioners, entirely renounce all power of control over those officers without transferring the power of giving relief to hands other than those in which the legislature has placed it. If the medical man is to judge (as he alone can and ought to do) who is sick and who is not sick, and is moreover to judge, without appeal or the possibility of control, what relief is to be given in every case in which the health of the pauper may be affected, then, as it appears to the Commissioners, the administration of relief now vested by law in the board of guardians, would be transferred to the medical officers. Now whether it be desirable thus to transfer this discretion in the matter of relief from the board of guardians to the medical men, without any control on the part of the former, the Commissioners do not feel called upon to decide. They can only say that, under the existing law, they themselves have no power to effect the transfer. The legislature only can authorise such a change.

With regard to the statement made at the inquest by Mr. Ratcliffe, a juryman, on the subject of some relief which he had allowed to a pauper, and which the guardians had refused to repay him for, the Commissioners observe that the relief referred to was afforded upwards of four years ago, by Mr. Ratcliff, a butcher and publican, who took upon himself, whilst overseer of his parish, to supply articles of meat and beer from his own shop, for the period of three weeks, to the wife of James Bunce, a labourer, in constant work, at the weekly wages of 12*s.*, and as the wife had medical attendance and medicine supplied by the Union, her husband was supposed able to procure the extra diet of his wife, as so many other labourers do without applying to the Union for any, who have not gratuitous medical assistance granted to them. The case clearly was not one of emergency, and the relieving officer had no notice of the supply until after the expiration of many weeks.

The Commissioners think, if the circumstances were as you have stated them, the disallowance of the relief given by Mr. Ratcliff was perfectly right. By the statute 55 Geo. 3, c. 157, he was liable to a penalty of £100 for supplying, for his own profit, goods to the poor, being himself an overseer. It is unnecessary to say that any act to which a penalty is attached, is to be considered as forbidden. Lord Holt stated, in Bartlett *v.* Vinor, Carth 252, "that a penalty implies a prohibition, though there are no prohibitory words in the statute."

As regards the case of William Haynes, you state that this pauper was in receipt of 6*s.* a week from his club, and of 2*s.* and 3 lbs. of mutton a week from the Union, and that (as is asserted by the treasurer of the club) they have £600 in the Bank of England, and that he must therefore have been under some delusion in supposing the club was going to break up; that he had 9*s.* 6*d.* in his pocket when he destroyed himself; and with respect to his fear of being brought into the Union house, and being separated from his wife; the circumstance of the guardians having given him an allowance in addition to his club money, ought to have satisfied him that there was no danger of his being ordered into the workhouse,—indeed (unless under very peculiar circumstances) out-door relief is, you say, never refused to aged couples.

The Commissioners see nothing in this case that calls for any observations from them.

It gives the Commissioners much satisfaction to state that, neither in Terry's case, nor in that of Haynes, does any blame appear to attach to the officers or guardians of the Uxbridge Union.

---

2. CHARGEABILITY OF PAUPER.

Sept. 21*st*, 1844.

Clerk of Newton Abbot Union—Stated, that a man who had been residing in London some time, where he had left a sick wife, came into the parish of Ilsington, in the Newton Abbot Union, (his alleged parish) in order to apply for relief, but was told, unofficially, that he had better go to Ashburton (where the relieving officer for that parish resided) and have his application for relief taken down previous to his appearing at the following meeting of the guardians. He went to Ashburton accordingly, where he slept. He saw the relieving officer on the next morning, who told him to go back to Ilsington and see the overseer, and procure a note from him, admitting that he (the applicant) belonged to that parish, and bring it with him to the board of guardians on the following day. The overseer declined giving the note, but the poor man, in order to attend the board on the following morning, came to Newton Abbot the same evening, where he slept. The board gave an order for his going into the workhouse, which is situate in Newton Abbot. The board being in doubt to which of the three parishes the man's relief should be charged, requested the Commissioners' advice upon the subject.

Ans.—The Commissioners in the first place desire to point out that, if the man is clearly settled in the parish of Ilsington, the guardians of Newton Abbot Union may, if they think fit, charge his relief to that parish. If, however, the guardians do not think fit to charge his relief to Ilsington, in consideration of his alleged settlement therein, it will be necessary to consider to what parish, under the circumstances stated in your letter, such relief is properly chargeable. The Commissioners conceive that the 26th section of the Poor Law Amendment Act, which provides that each of the parishes in a union shall, notwithstanding such union, "be separately chargeable with and liable to defray the expenses of its own poor," had for its object, that every pauper in a union should be charged to that parish to which he would have been lawfully chargeable, supposing that the union had not been formed. The Commissioners admit that cases may arise in which it may be difficult to apply this principle in all its strictness; but they are nevertheless of opinion that it ought to be taken as the guiding consideration, and followed as far as practicable. Bearing this in mind, the Commissioners consider that in the present instance, the pauper is chargeable to the parish of Ilsington. In that parish he was destitute, and intended to apply for relief, and he would, in fact, have made the application there if the arrangements for the administration of relief in the union had allowed of his adopting such a course; but as the relieving officer to whom it was right that he should, under ordinary circumstances, address his application, resided in Ashburton, the pauper went thither in order to seek him, and the Commissioners therefore think that his application to that officer must be regarded as virtually made in Ilsington. Then it appears that the relieving officer, not deeming the case to be one of such urgency as to need immediate relief, referred the pauper to the board of guardians, who were to meet on the following day, and who, accordingly, on that day, took the case into their consideration and granted relief. The circumstance that the man went into Newton Abbot in order to attend the board of guardians, the Commissioners think must be looked at in the same light as the previous circumstance of his going from Ilsington into Ashburton in order to seek the relieving officer. All the steps of the process between the time when the man entertained the intention of applying for relief in Ilsington, and the time when he actually obtained it in Newton Abbot, being thus made to occur as they did solely in consequence of the existence of the union, the Commissioners are of opinion that they ought not to be regarded as affecting the question of the pauper's chargeability, and that as Ilsington is the parish to which, putting the union out of consideration, the pauper would have become chargeable, so it is the parish to which, under the actual circumstances of the case, his relief ought to be charged.

V.—VAGRANTS—REMOVAL OF.

1844.

Mr.——— detailed the circumstances of a case which involved the removeability of vagrants, and requested the Commissioners' opinion thereon.

Ans. The general question touching the removal of vagrants is certainly surrounded with considerable difficulty; but on the whole, the effect of the decisions which have been given upon this subject seems to be as follows:—There appears to be some doubt entertained, whether a tramp or vagrant who becomes chargeable in a parish is liable to be removed from that parish under an order of removal. It appears to be supposed that such persons do not come within the description of persons "coming to settle themselves," or of persons "coming to inhabit," within the 13 and 14 Car. 2, c. 12; and therefore, that they are not removeable under that statute. The rule which distinguishes "casual poor," that is to say, occasional poor who are irremoveable from the parish in which they are chargeable, is this: Where a person is in a parish, on his way through it, or under circumstances which show that he has an intention of leaving it, and no intention to become chargeable,—then if any casualty, such as sudden sickness, or bodily accident, renders him chargeable to the parish, contrary to, or independently of any intention on his part to become so, he is held, in obvious consistency with the terms of the statute, not to have come to settle or inhabit, and not to be removeable. But where a person comes into a parish, and while he stays there does so of his own choice, and becomes chargeable, without the intervention of any casual disaster, there is no statute, decision, rule, or practice, that the Commissioners are aware of, that prevents such person from being removeable, however short may have been his sojourn to the parish. No defined length of residence is necessary under the statute of Charles to render a person removeable; but on the contrary, length of residence constituted a settlement under that statute; a party being removeable under that statute only during the first forty days' sojourn, and if permitted to reside forty days, being consequently made irremoveable. It appears, therefore, that whatever may be the mode in which a person may remain in a place, if his remaining there and his chargeability are his own voluntary acts, and not the result of casualties, he is on becoming chargeable liable to be removed. Thus in the case of the King *v.* St. James in Bury, 10 East, p. 29, in which it was established that a pauper, chargeable through a casualty, could not be removed, Lord Ellenborough observed that "the expression *coming to settle* denotes that a party comes *animo morandi* or *manendi*," and upon this he remarks that "it may be for a temporary purpose." In the case of R. *v.* Birmingham, 14 East, 251, the court did not consider that the question admitted of discussion, and dispensed with all argument to establish the removeability of a vagrant, holding that a pauper, or starving vagrant, kept in a parish against his will, and desirous during all the time of his residence there of going into a neighbouring parish, did nevertheless, on receiving temporary relief there, become removeable.

LONDON:
Printed by Order of the Poor Law Commissioners, by BLACKBURN and PARDON, 6, Hatton Garden, and Published by CHARLES KNIGHT and Co., 22, Ludgate Street, Publishers to the Poor Law Commissioners.

AN

OFFICIAL CIRCULAR

OF PUBLIC DOCUMENTS AND INFORMATION:

DIRECTED BY THE POOR LAW COMMISSIONERS TO BE PRINTED, CHIEFLY FOR THE USE OF THE MEMBERS AND PERMANENT OFFICERS OF BOARDS OF GUARDIANS, UNDER THE POOR LAW AMENDMENT ACT.

No. 42. CIRCULAR ISSUED DECEMBER 31, 1844.

Poor Law Commission Office,
Somerset House,
December 31st, 1844.

THE Poor Law Commissioners, on a review of their Minutes, directed that the Minutes of Correspondence on the following subjects be printed and circulated for the information of the Guardians and Officers of the several Unions, viz.:—

By Order of the Board,

EDWIN CHADWICK, *Secretary.*

PAUPER.

DEATH OF PAUPER IN WORKHOUSE, AND CHARGES IN REFERENCE THERETO AGAINST THE WORKHOUSE OFFICERS.

Eton Union—The case of John Shaw, deceased.—The Commissioners have addressed the following letter to the Clerk of the Eton Union on the subject of charges made against the officers of the union workhouse in regard to the treatment of John Shaw, deceased, whilst in the workhouse, and also to the facilities given to the relations and friends of the deceased to visit him there.

October 26th, 1844.

The Poor Law Commissioners to the Clerk of the Eton Union.—The Poor Law Commissioners have received and carefully perused the report of their Assistant Commissioner, Mr. Parker, on the inquiry made by him into the case of John Shaw, deceased, whilst an inmate of the Eton Union workhouse; also the voluminous evidence accompanying that report.

The two main points which this evidence suggests for consideration appear to the Commissioners to be—1. The treatment of John Shaw in the workhouse of the Eton Union, including the medical treatment of the case, and the attention paid by the officers of the workhouse generally. 2. The facilities given to the wife and sister, or other friends of Shaw, to visit and converse with him whilst in the workhouse of the Eton Union.

Shaw was brought to the workhouse of the Eton Union on the afternoon of Monday, the 5th of August, having met with an accident of the most serious character, by which his thigh was fractured. Mr. Nordblad, a medical man residing at Slough, happened to be passing, and attended to the man immediately. He saw him placed on a proper bed, in a room on the ground-floor, and caused some brandy and water to be given to him. On the same afternoon, Dr. James Bryan, a surgeon and physician residing at Slough, set the thigh, having been sent for by the sons of Mr. Hammond, the medical officer, who was accidentally absent from home. The next day Mr. Hammond attended the case, and saw him again on the 7th, 8th, 9th, and 10th, and twice on the 11th. He continued to attend him daily till his death, sometimes twice a-day and once three times, excepting on the 12th, 16th, 18th, 23rd, 25th, and 27th of August.

Mr. Hammond held consultations with regard to Shaw's case with Dr. Stanford, Mr. Holderness, Mr. Waite, of Wokingham, and Mr. Wood, of Oxford. Dr. Stanford, who was an army surgeon throughout the peninsular war, and is a physician of eighteen years' standing, and Mr. Holderness, who has practised at Windsor for twenty years, were both examined on the present inquiry. The former states, that the bed was of the proper description; that he saw the nurses "put on the poultices, and that they put them on with all the care of experienced nurses." He also says expressly, that tea and broth were the proper diet in the early stage of the case, and adds, "Having looked over the book containing the medical officer's dietetic directions relating to this case, the diet ordered was perfectly suitable.—I think it is very likely that the man felt hungry, although stimulant food would have been improper for him in the first instance.—Having looked over the entries of these attendances on John Shaw by Mr. Hammond, the medical officer, I think the attendance was ample. No poor person out of the workhouse could have obtained anything equal to the attendance.—The object of the medical man was to save the limb; there was enormous swelling, and the medical man would wait until that subsided, and then judge of the case.—The opinion that I gave to Mr. Hammond at the time of the consultation was, that no operation could save his life; indeed, the man appeared to be sinking when I saw him; no surgeon could venture to operate under the circumstances. I understood at the time of my visit the man was taking porter, meat, and wine, and I recommended that they should be increased in quantity. I have heard that part of the evidence of William Todd read, relating to the washing of the ward in which John Shaw was placed. In apartments where patients with gangrenous limbs are, it is usual to wash the room every day, and to use chloride of lime. I have again examined the ward in which John Shaw was placed; it is about seventeen feet square, and I think a very excellent ward. I think it was more proper to place him in a room on the ground-floor than to carry him up the winding-stair in the state of the limb. Perhaps more water was used to cleanse the room than was necessary, but I suppose the quantity was used to wash the room rapidly. I cannot imagine that the man's death was hastened by the steam which would arise from the water."

At this later stage of the case, when the discharge from Shaw's leg became highly offensive, Peveril distinctly proves that "chloride of lime and vinegar were used abundantly; there was a jar full of chloride of lime used; the jar contained chloride of lime in a liquid state; we sprinkled it about the room, and dipped a cloth in it and hung the cloth up by the side of Shaw's bed. The cloth was wetted and hung up three or four times. The sprinkling took place ten, or a dozen, or twenty times. There was a great deal of vinegar used. Shaw's forehead was bathed with vinegar; his hands were washed with vinegar; we got a sponge and washed his hands with vinegar."

Mr. Holderness visited Shaw three times, in company with Mr. Hammond. The tenor of his evidence is to the same effect as Dr. Stanford's. He states—"The limb itself was kept perfectly clean. The nurses appeared to be attentive, and anxious, and expert. I saw the matron every time I came here. I saw the master and matron, and they both gave us every assistance they could in the case.—Having had opportunities, on the frequent occasions that I have been to this workhouse, to see the master and matron, I may say they always appear extremely kind and attentive to the sick poor.—The ward was always well aired and perfectly clean; there was no offensive smell when I was there."—This testimony appears to the Commissioners to be highly satisfactory as regards Mr. Hammond's treatment of the case, and the great care and attention bestowed on the man. It must be remembered that the case was brought without any notice, and was a peculiar one, such as would have required the utmost attention, even in the wards of an hospital expressly devoted to the reception of accidents of any moment.

Mr. Hammond's own evidence is also clear with regard to the conduct of the nurses and officers of the workhouse.—I know Peveril, the nurse, and have known him as a nurse several years. I think he is a very steady, careful man, who will take your directions and carry them into execution. I think him attentive, and decidedly kind and considerate. I do not think him capable of harshness. All that I want of a nurse to perform, he can perform satisfactorily. —When I visited the ward, I always found it clean and comfortable, had it not been so I should have immediately applied to the master and matron. I have understood that on the Tuesday, there were maggots found on the poultices, and on the bed. That is not at all unusual in cases where mortification occurs in the extremities. The bed always appeared to me to be clean. Any quantity of linen, or any other thing, the man could have been supplied with by my order. There was an abundance of warm water; at night there was a fire in the room, for the purpose of providing warm water to foment the leg. When I visited the ward at two o'clock in the morning of the 9th of September, I found the fire in the grate, and the room appeared very comfortable. Peveril did not expect me at that time; I took him quite unawares.—I should say, that I never saw greater kindness or more attention bestowed than is shown by the master and matron towards the inmates of this house. I have invariably found it to be the case; I have no reason to doubt, that all my directions in Shaw's case were strictly complied with by the nurses, as well as by the master and matron.—I saw Shaw's wife twice—she made no complaint to me."

The following extracts from the evidence of the Rev. Dr. Dodsworth, chaplain to the workhouse, appears to the Commissioners to confirm what has been stated by the other witnesses with regard to Shaw's general treatment:—"When I visit the sick for the purpose of prayer, the master and matron do not accompany me. I have free access to the sick at all times. I very often saw John Shaw when the master and matron were not present. If he had been ill-treated in the workhouse, I think it very probable, that he would have communicated it to me. When I saw him on the 11th of September, he was perfectly sensible. He was aware that his dissolution was approaching. In the early stage of my visiting him, he made a remark, that Mr. Hammond had not visited him. I have found it expedient not to seek out, and create grounds of complaint from the inmates of the workhouse. When he mentioned that he had been neglected by Mr. Hammond, I mentioned it to Mr. Aitken, who said, he had been seen by Dr. Bryan. I am sure I mentioned it either to Mr. Aitken or Mrs. Aitken, and that the reply was, the poor man had been seen by Dr. Bryan in Mr. Hammond's absence; that was the only complaint that he made to me. He made no complaint to me whatever of the treatment he received from the master and matron of the workhouse.—From my observations, it appeared to me, that the room, bed, and linen, were clean. I saw nothing to the contrary; there was an offensive odour perceptible during the last three or four days of the man's life, but more particularly the last day, when I was obliged through it to leave the room earlier than I should have done. On the last day of the man's life, the room bore its usual appearance of cleanliness."

The Commissioners will add, it is clearly proved, (so far as such a point can admit of proof,) that Shaw received the articles of food ordered for him. The evidence of the persons who prepared the food, or who saw it prepared in the kitchen, and the nurses who administered it to him, taken together with that of the medical officer, by whose directions it was regulated, leave no reasonable doubt on this matter. It is manifest, from the evidence of Shaw's wife and sister, as well as that of others, that Shaw himself in the early stage of his case, wished for a larger quantity of food, and for more nourishing food than was thought proper for him by the medical officer. The evidence of Dr. Stanford already quoted is material as to the propriety of the course pursued by Mr. Hammond. Unfortunately, however, the expressions used by the poor man to his relatives with reference to the food at first allowed him, joined to their natural mistrust of the attendance of strangers, appear to have created a prejudice in their minds as to his general treatment in the workhouse; for this prejudice, it appears to the Commissioners, from the full and clear testimony of the most competent witnesses, some indeed connected with the union, but others wholly independent of the board of guardians, there was not the smallest foundation.

The Commissioners are satisfied that the general treatment of John Shaw, whilst he was an inmate of the Eton workhouse, was kind and judicious. Nothing appears to have been denied him which the medical man thought it right that he should have. The latter, indeed, complains naturally enough of the conduct of his relations in introducing secretly, and without the knowledge of the workhouse authorities, improper articles of food. "I think it was a very imprudent thing on the part of his friends to give him plum-pudding, and a very unfair thing towards me. I think the diet for the sick ought to be entirely under the control of the medical officer, and particular care ought to be used to guard against persons introducing food to their sick friends in the house. In ordinary cases, the introduction of food might defeat the medical officer's treatment."

The Commissioners will now address themselves to the consideration of the second question, that is to say—The facilities given to the wife and sister of Shaw to visit and converse with him whilst in the workhouse of the Eton Union.

There are two points involved in this question. 1st, Whether the wife and sister were refused access to Shaw; and, if so, under what circumstances. 2ndly. Whether any hinderance was improperly thrown in the way of the wife and sister, or other person, communicating with Shaw, when they were admitted to see him.

There appear to have been two instances in which the wife of Shaw was not allowed to see her husband when she applied for permission to do so.—Mary Cripps, the wife of the man with whom Shaw had lodged in Slough, says in her evidence—"She once complained of having been refused admission, that was at twelve o'clock in the day. She was not admitted at all that day. Mr. Thornton told me that. He said she could not be admitted that day at all, and she returned the next morning by the train. He said she could not be admitted that day, because it was after the regular hours.

Mrs. Shaw's own account of this application is as follows—(the day referred to was Saturday, August 24th, upwards of a fortnight before Shaw's death)—"Mr. Aitken was at the door. It was then about five minutes before twelve o'clock, and he said he could not let me in. I said, I thought it was very hard if they would not let me go in, if it was only till the clock struck twelve. He said he did not think it worth while to let me in, as the man was in good health. I begged of him to let me in for half-an-hour, and he would not; and he said, what I had to leave should be taken to my husband by the porter. I said, I have nothing to take in. He said, My good woman, I do not see it is necessary for you to go in, as he is in good health. He said, If you have any message for your husband here is the porter, tell him. I said, what I had to tell my husband I could tell him myself, without sending in a message by a man. I then went to Mrs. Cripps; I did not return to the workhouse, because I had begged of him hard, and cried to him, too, to let me look at him, and he would not. I went home in the evening with Mr. Thornton. I sent in word to my husband that I would come again on the Monday."

The master's explanation of this refusal is given in the following words:—"Before Shaw was considered dangerously ill, I recollect Mrs. Shaw on one occasion coming just as the dinner was being served up; I refused to admit her. I said, There is a man now lying in the room in which your husband is, who taunted me with allowing you to come to see your husband after the regular hour, and, therefore, in future I should adhere strictly to the regulations. I went into the room where the man was immediately afterwards, and told John Shaw that I had refused his wife, and that I was very sorry, but that it was entirely owing to the conduct of the man (Brown) by the side of him. I had not adhered strictly to the rule when parties had come from a distance."

On this refusal the Commissioners must observe that they think persons suffering from injuries so serious as those of Shaw should not be prevented from seeing their friends, by the mere inconvenience of breaking through the hours which may be properly limited for the reception of visits under ordinary circumstances, even although they may not be in imminent danger at the moment. The master in such special cases might properly take the directions of the board of guardians, whether he should abide by the ordinary regulations or not. The consideration of inconvenience to other paupers, or apparent inconsistency, will no doubt occasionally interfere, as it appears to have done in this case. The Commissioners regret, however, that Mrs. Shaw was refused admittance on this occasion.

The other occasion in which Mrs. Shaw was refused admittance to her husband was under different circumstances. Mr. Aitken, the master of the workhouse, says—"In Article 74, paragraph 14, of the Regulations relating to the master's duties, the master is required, 'in the case of dangerous sickness, to send for the chaplain, or any relative or friend of the pauper, resident within a reasonable distance, whom the pauper may wish to see.' On the 1st of September, Mr. Hammond reported to me that Shaw's case had assumed a dangerous appearance. Betwixt one and two o'clock, Hitchcock, who was then an inmate, said to me that the man was getting worse, and wished to see his wife; I have no objection to go for her, if you will permit me to go. My answer was, that I expected the doctor every minute, and as soon as he arrived, and gave his opinion on the subject, I would determine whether he should go or not. Dr. Hammond came shortly after two o'clock, and after having visited the man, he said he was getting worse. Immediately sent for Hitchcock, and told him to go for Shaw's wife. I expected Hitchcock to be back with the wife before nine o'clock. He went off in sufficient time to be back by nine o'clock, the usual hour for closing the house." In taking this step, the Commissioners think that Mr. Aitken acted most properly. The residence of Mrs. Shaw was, they believe, twelve or thirteen miles distant from Slough, but under the circumstances he did quite right in apprising her of her husband's danger, according to the provisions in the regulations of the Commissioners. Hitchcock gives the following account of what passed when they arrived at the workhouse, which substantially agrees with the account given by Mrs. Shaw and her sister, and by the witness Scott—It was after twelve o'clock when we got to the workhouse. I rapped at the porter's window, and Scott came to it, and threw the letter-sash up. I said to Scott, How is Shaw? and he said, He is a little better. The women who were with me heard him say so. I asked if they were all gone to bed, and said his wife wanted to see him. He said, they could not get in; that Shaw was much better; that the matron had sat up till ten o'clock. Scott then came to the door and let me in. Mrs. Shaw asked me if I would go to the master and ask him if he would allow them to come in to see Shaw. I went to the master's bed-room door, and told him Mrs. Shaw was come, and wanted to see Shaw. Master said that Shaw was better, and that he had sat up till ten o'clock, and thought they would not be down here to-night. The master said it was late, and he did not see any necessity for it; that Shaw was better, and she could come in as early in the morning as she liked, I do not recollect the master saying anything about the medicine Shaw had taken. I went down and told Mrs. Shaw they could not come in before morning, but then they might come in as soon as daylight."

There is, however, one inconsistency between Mrs. Shaw's evidence and that of William Cripps, Shaw's friend, and his wife, to whose house they went after being refused admission at the workhouse. Mrs. Shaw says—"We did not like to wake Mrs. Cripps, and we walked about the fields till half-past two o'clock, when the child cried so with the cold, that we went to Mrs. Cripps and knocked her up, and she made some tea." This is confirmed by the sister, who, however, says they "walked the streets." Mrs Maddox, Mrs. Shaw's mother, states expressly that it was half-past two when they went to Mrs. Cripps. They all appear, however, by their evidence, to have doubted whether Mrs. Cripps would take them in. Now, William Cripps himself states—"The man's wife and sister came to lodge at my house at twelve o'clock at night, on the night I saw the man at the workhouse; the wife remained there Monday and Tuesday, and I think another day, but I am not quite sure. Whenever they came my house was open to them, they knew that." Mrs. Cripps says—"His wife, and mother, and sister, came to my house at twelve o'clock the same night, and called me up, and said they could not be let in here before the morning. I got up, and made them some tea, and kept them there till the morning." The Commissioners cannot reconcile these discrepancies, and the point is material only so far as it shows the extent of the inconvenience caused by the refusal to admit them into the workhouse.

The reason for this refusal remains to be considered. It is thus stated by Mr. Aitken, the master—"After Hitchcock left, Mr. Hammond returned to the workhouse and prepared a composing dose, and desired it to be given to Shaw, and expressed a wish that Shaw should not be disturbed that night. Mr. Hammond expressed that wish with the knowledge that the wife had been sent for. I sat up till ten o'clock that night, and at that hour I went to bed. I left directions with Scott, the person at the door; I said, when Hitchcock returned he was to be let in; and I told him it had been represented to me that her husband had told Mrs. Shaw that she could get lodgings at Cripps' at any time she chose to come, and that he was to tell Mrs. Shaw she was to go there. I meant that I knew she could get lodgings, if she went there. When it grew so late I did not expect Mrs. Shaw that night; I did not even expect Hitchcock back that night. About half-past twelve o'clock Hitchcock came to my bed-room door, and said three women had come to Shaw, and I told him to tell them they could find lodgings at Cripps's. I believe I did say to Hitchcock that the man was much better, and that he had had a composing draught; I am not quite certain that I said so, but I believe I did." This is confirmed by Mrs. Aitken, and by Peveril, the nurse. The former says :—" Mr. Hammond gave me, on the Sunday night, a composing draught for Shaw, and I gave it to him, according to Mr. Hammond's directions, the last thing at night. That was about ten o'clock."

The evidence of Mr. Hammond is still more important :—" On Sunday, the 1st September, I visited Shaw in the morning, and I thought him considerably worse; I again visited him in the afternoon, between two and three o'clock, and finding him still worse, I informed the master of it, and the master proposed to send for his wife. The master called the man, Hitchcock, and told him to go to Brentford, before I left the room. I prepared for Shaw a composing draught of laudanum, and gave it to the matron, with directions to give it him in the evening. The object of the medicine was to quiet him, and give him a tranquil night. I should say it was most desirable to keep him quiet during the night. I do think that if the man's wife and family had been admitted to him in the middle of the night, he might have been disturbed, and the good effect likely to be obtained from the medicine destroyed; it would have undone just what I was doing."

The fact that such medicine had been given, was in itself a reason amply sufficient to refuse admittance, especially since, although the man was getting worse, there was no reason to apprehend such immediate danger as made it necessary to admit his friends at midnight. Had the danger been imminent, the Commissioners would wish it to have been done at any hour. They do not, however, believe that it is usual in the metropolitan hospitals, to permit the friends of the patient to remain in the house all night, or to admit them at all times. Such an arrangement would be obviously impossible in many cases, and would lead to the greatest inconvenience.

The Commissioners do not blame the master for refusing to admit Shaw's wife, sister, and mother-in-law, on the night of the first of September. They think he was perfectly justified in refusing such admission, when the state the man was then in, the lateness of the hour, and the fact that the man had taken a composing draught, which made it expedient he should not be disturbed, are all considered together. They think that he acted under the full conviction that they would be received at Cripps's; a conviction justified by Cripps's own evidence already referred to, and by the knowledge that they constantly were received there without difficulty.

There is one point in this matter, however, which the Commissioners do not think satisfactory. The nature of the medicine taken by Shaw was, as they have said, a perfect justification of the refusal to allow his being disturbed; but why was not this reason stated at the time, for the satisfaction of the wife? Mr. Aitken, indeed, says he thinks he did allude to it. Hitchcock has no recollection of its being alluded to. Of the fact itself that such medicine was administered, no doubt can exist; but when there was a good and sufficient cause for an apparently harsh proceeding, it was exceedingly injudicious not to allege that cause, and thereby remove the irritation most naturally arising in the mind of the wife, and those who accompanied her. The Commissioners, then, must express great regret that this reason for refusing admission to Mrs. Shaw, on the night of the 1st of September, was not distinctly explained to her at the time such refusal was given.

It remains to consider the interference with the visits of the friends and relatives of Shaw. This interference took place either by limiting the time of their stay, or by the presence of other parties in the room with them whilst they were conversing with Shaw. When Mrs. Shaw visited her husband on the day after the accident, she was allowed to remain half-an-hour only. On another occasion, when she had been there, as she states, hardly half-an-hour, a little boy was sent to tell her it was time to go. The same thing is stated to have occurred at the next visit. On the 26th, when she came to the workhouse, the master very properly interfered to prevent her taking in food to her husband, of which the medical officer might not have approved. On one occasion Shaw asked the master to let her stop an hour, which he allowed her to do. On the 7th of September, Mrs. Shaw complained to Sergeant, that she was not allowed to stop all night. These instances occurred before the man was in imminent danger.

John Scott's evidence, as to the visits of the wife and sister, is as follows :—" I cannot tell the days on which she was at the workhouse, she was here so often. One or another came daily—his wife, his sister, or fellow-workmen. I recollect the wife coming more than once in the same day, the day she asked the master if she might come in the afternoon, and the master said 'Yes.' In that afternoon she said she was going home, and she would like to see him again. I do not know that a boy was sent to tell her to go away. I remember, on one occasion, a boy was sent to me to tell me to go into the hall, because the baker had brought bread. I had to assist in weighing the bread. I did not go immediately; I delayed a little; I then said to Mrs. Shaw, 'Now, then, the master is waiting for me.' 'Be so good as to say what you have got to say, because the master is waiting for me.' She then said she would go. I was not always in the room with her. I did not speak to her harshly. I said the master might be sending for me again. There is a general order, that I am to wait whilst persons are visiting the inmates. One day I was with her two hours. On another, I left her, and she remained in the ward till twelve o'clock. I have accompanied other people to the room; I have accompanied Mr. Sears. I go with people to their friends, to see that they pass no liquors, beer, and other things. They are always allowed to take in fruit, and sweetmeats, and such like."

Peveril, the nurse, states:—"After Shaw was taken worse, and his wife came to see him, she stopped on the Monday morning from nine till twelve o'clock. She came again on the same day, at three o'clock, and stopped till betwixt seven and eight o'clock. On the Tuesday morning she came again, and stopped the same time till twelve o'clock. In the afternoon she returned, at three o'clock, and stopped till mealtime, that is six o'clock. On the Wednesday she came again, betwixt eight and nine o'clock, and stopped till twelve o'clock. In the afternoon she returned, between three and four o'clock, and stopped till six at night. I think it was as late as six o'clock. On the Thursday and Friday she was not at the workhouse. She returned on the Saturday; I don't justly mind whether she came in the morning, but I think she did, and said she had come in a waggon as far as Datchet Lane End. She left, and returned in the afternoon, about three or four o'clock, and stopped till supper-time, and partook of a mutton chop supplied to him. The matron came in, and said it was not right she should eat the food from him. She said she had only a little bit; and he said he had given her only a little bit to taste. The matron said, as she had come so far, if she was hungry, she would send her some bread and cheese. Mrs. Shaw said, No, I thank you, when I go out I can get some. She left the house soon after seven o'clock. On the Sunday she visited him in the morning, and stopped till twelve o'clock. She returned on Sunday afternoon, soon after prayers in chapel; prayers are over at three o'clock. She left with Mr. Cripps about six or seven o'clock. On the Monday she came in, in the fore part of the day, and stopped till dinner-time, twelve o'clock. She returned again in the afternoon, and left in the evening, just before supper-time, six o'clock. On the Tuesday morning she came again, and stopped till nearly dinner-time. In the afternoon she returned about three o'clock, and stopped till nearly five; she said she was to start at five to go to Brentford. She did not see her husband alive after that. The last three days the man was alone with his wife half-an-hour or an hour at a time. His sister came three times or four, but I think only three. She was talking to him alone. The nurses were outside the room. When we left the room for the man to converse with his wife, neither the master nor matron was in the ward. The man and his wife were then alone together. As the leg required so much attention, the matron was constantly in and out of the room, five or six times every day, and sometimes nine or ten times. I think the matron was very anxious about him."

Thomas Brown, who was an inmate in the same ward with Shaw until the three last days of his life, says—"I was not in the room the first time Shaw's wife came. I saw her once in the room. I was only once, I think, in the room when Shaw's wife was there. Shaw's sister was there with the wife. That night they remained there till eight o'clock. I was not there all the time they were in the room; I dare say they were some hours. The matron came in. The matron did not remain there all the time, not quite. When I used to be sitting in the yard, I used to see the matron going backwards and forwards into Shaw's ward very often."

On the other hand, it is clear that in the early part of Shaw's case the matron was almost always present at her interviews with her husband. The nurses were constantly in the room, and the time she was allowed to stop with him was limited.

Shaw's other friends seem to have been admitted to see him without difficulty. Sears, the master of the bricklayer with whom Shaw had worked, says he saw him after the accident nearly daily; he was never refused admittance, but when he saw him there was always some one in the room.

Mr. Aitken, the master, states as follows:—"There were no restrictions on the wife and sister visiting the man, after the man was pronounced to be dangerously ill; they came in at what time they liked, and left at what time they liked, except being in the house at meal-time. I sent only one message to them whilst they were in the workhouse. I told Scott, or Hitchcock, but which I forget, to let these people (meaning Mrs. Shaw and her sister,) out, dinner was going to be served; and tell them to go and get their own dinners, and come back again. That is the only message I ever sent to them."

The matron's evidence respecting the interview on Monday, September the 2nd, is to the following effect:—"I did not see Mrs. Shaw, Mary Shaw, and Mrs. Maddox until half-past eight o'clock; I went to them in the front hall, and took them into the infirmary. Mrs. Maddox asked me if she could see the leg, and Peveril removed the cloths with which he was fomenting it, and showed it to them. I was present and saw it. I left the room to go to my breakfast, and they remained there. I saw nothing more of them until twelve o'clock, when I saw them pass the window, whilst I was engaged cutting the food for the inmates' dinners. I did not leave the porter in the room with them. If they went out and returned, it was without my knowledge. In the afternoon, Mrs. Shaw and Mary Shaw returned a little before four o'clock. I took them into the room, and left them there; I do not think they left until between seven and eight o'clock. When I went into the room, I heard them say the beds were full at Cripps'. John Shaw said, Can't you let my wife and sister stop here all night? I said, That is impossible, there are other men in the room. The wife and sister came in the next morning about nine o'clock, and stayed at the workhouse till twelve o'clock. I think Scott took them to the room. I told Scott to leave them. They left at twelve o'clock. They returned again in the afternoon betwixt two and three o'clock, and went away again about four o'clock. I went with them to the room, but did not remain with them, and I did not see them go away. I heard that they remained until four o'clock."

Mary Shaw, the sister, states—"On the Saturday we received a letter from my brother; this is the letter. In consequence of that letter, I went down to Slough by the train, from the Southwell station. When I got to the workhouse, I found my brother's wife there; she was sitting by the bed-side. The governor and matron were standing at the hall-door when I got to it. The matron took me into the ward. The two nurses and my sister-in-law were in the ward, nobody else. I sat down by the side of the bed. He said he was glad to see me, and said, I thought you would come, my girl, to see me. I asked him how he felt himself, and he said he knew he was dying, he had not many hours to live. He begged of us not to leave him. We sat talking until it was nearly dark; the porter Hitchcock came in, and said it was time for us to go. That was the first time we ever could get to be by ourselves with him; that was when he began to smell so. The nurses were there, but I mean the matron was away. The matron had never been away so long before. When the matron came to the door my brother said, My dear wife ought not to leave me now; I shall not be here long; thinking the matron would let her stop in the union. On the Sunday we went in again, between nine and ten o'clock, and stopped till twelve o'clock. Whilst we were there the inmates went to chapel, but the nurses did not go." Mrs. Shaw complains—"The matron came in there sometimes whilst I was there. After the smell got so bad, she used to come in with her apron up to her nose. The nurses were always there, if the matron was not. I was never alone with him; one or other was always there. If he had anything to tell me, he could not do so without them hearing of it."

These statements are not all perfectly reconcileable one with the other. It is evident that Mrs. Shaw and her sister were suspicious as to Shaw's treatment, and were irritated against the matron; amongst other causes of offence which they allege is, that she held her apron to her nose when she came into the room; the smell from the discharge in the latter stage of the case being very disagreeable. Upon the whole it is clear, that the authorities of the workhouse acted upon the supposition, that some one ought always to be present at the interview between the man and his friends. The Commissioners do not think it is proved, that any attempt to listen or interrupt the conversation was made; but no means were taken, when the matron herself was absent, for causing the nurses to leave the ward, so as to afford Shaw's wife and sister a private interview. Whether this would have been done in any of the large London hospitals, the Commissioners are unable to state.

It must be said, that no complaint appears to have been made to the master or matron on this subject by Shaw's wife, and she expressly states--"I never asked the master or matron to allow me to have a private conversation with my husband." Mary Shaw, his sister, says—"I never made any request to the master or matron to let me have a private conversation with my brother. I never heard that such a request was made by any one. The nurses, Peveril and Todd, were present when the matron went to my wife's sister. I think Peveril and Todd were kind and as attentive to him as they could be." Still, the fact is evident that no facilities were given for that kind of private intercourse, between Shaw and his family, which might naturally and properly have been desired by them on the eve of his death.

It is necessary to put this matter in a clear light with reference to the workhouse regulations. The rule of the Commissioners with regard to visits to inmates of workhouses, is as follows:—

"Any person may visit any pauper in the workhouse by permission of the master, or (in his absence) of the matron, subject to such conditions and restrictions as the board of guardians may prescribe, such interview to take place, except where a sick pauper is visited in a room, separate from the other inmates of the workhouse, in the presence of the master, matron, or porter."

The explanation of this rule, the Instructional Letter which accompanies the workhouse regulations, is—"This article allows any pauper in the workhouse to receive the visit of a stranger, but requires that (except in the case of a sick pauper) the interview shall take place in a separate room, and in the presence of the master, matron, or porter. The necessity for this restriction arises from several causes, among which the following may be specified, as the most prominent, namely, a fear of the introduction of spirits by visitors—the abuses which would ensue if the female inmates of the workhouse were generally permitted to have private interviews with men—the probability that the minds of young persons in the workhouse would be perverted by persons who might visit them—accordingly, this restriction is not intended to offer any obstacle to the innocent and proper visits of relations and friends--and the master or other officer present ought not to listen to the conversation between the visitor and the pauper, unless there should be a reasonable ground for suspecting the conversation to be of an improper character."

Mr. Aitken, the master, before the Assistant Commissioner in this inquiry, made the following statement—"From my reading of that order, I think it means that one of the officers shall attend on visitors whether the visited be sick or well. I think the exception extends to the room, that a sick person is not to be taken into a separate room, but that the visitors are to go into the room where the sick persons are, but still accompanied by the master, matron, or porter. When I attended the coroner's inquest I had this book with me. I did not read the rule. I examined it, and satisfied myself that it was my duty to attend visitors to the sick poor in the workhouse, and I told the coroner it was one of the duties prescribed by the Commissioners. The coroner asked for the book, and I said I would read the rule. I said the man had been kindly treated, and there was a great uproar in the room, and a cry, 'answer the question!'—The question was, whether it was my regulation or a rule of the Commissioners. I looked at the rule, and I said, The only thing is, the man has been treated kindly." He adds, that he is of opinion the Instructional Letter bears the same construction as the article of the rules, that is to say, that the exception of sick persons refers only to the fact, that the interview need not take place in a separate room. This construction he supports by saying, that the mischief which might be done in a case of sickness, by bringing in spirits or improper articles of food, was at least as great as in the case of healthy inmates.

The Commissioners will only say that it is the duty of the master of the workhouse to abide by the clear and obvious construction of the regulations: there may be reason for or against a certain regulation, the first question for him is whether the words admit of the construction which these reasons would support.

In this case it is obvious, that had the Commissioners intended to convey the meaning supposed by Mr. Aitken to attach to the rule, the concluding words, instead of running—"Such interview to take place, except where a sick pauper is visited in a room separate from the other inmates of the workhouse, in the presence of the master, matron, or porter," would have been arranged as follows—"Such interview to take place in the presence of the master, matron, or porter, and (except where a sick pauper is visited) in a room separate from the other inmates of the workhouse."

The Commissioners think, moreover, that in an extreme case such as that of Shaw, a doubtful construction of a rule (even if it were doubtful) should not have been rigidly acted upon without soliciting the directions of the board of guardians, or through them of the Commissioners themselves. Shaw's residence in the workhouse was of sufficient duration to admit of this being done long before his death. The presumption in a doubtful case, of such a nature, should have been in favour of the pauper. It appears, however, that no private interview having been sought for, and no complaint made, the master was content to act on what he alleges himself to have considered as the letter of the rule. The Commissioners do not deny that some discretion is necessary even in the case of sick inmates, but they wish it to be clearly understood that Mr. Aitken has mistaken the tenor of these regulations respecting the visits paid to sick inmates. They wish, moreover, most distinctly to express that they entirely disapprove of all needless impediments thrown in the way of the visits of friends or near relations of inmates of the workhouse who are *dangerously* ill—they think in such cases the usual restraints as to hours and the presence of third parties should be relaxed, and that all the privacy and all the opportunity for confidential communication should be given which the condition of the patient will permit. They do not say that it would be possible to allow the friends or relations to stop all night—they do not believe that this is the practice at any hospital—but if the danger be imminent, they would wish them to be admitted at any hour, unless it be objected to by the medical officer.

If the introduction of food, such as is disapproved of on account of the health of the patient, be attempted, the friends should be distinctly told the grounds of the objection, and the medical man should be got to state in writing the impropriety of admitting such articles. If this attempt be renewed after such a warning, the officers must, of course, adopt other means to guard against its repetition.

It is not sufficient that everything should be done which the medical care of the case may require, and ordinary kindness would dictate—every effort should be made to explain to the relatives the reason for any obstruction to their visits which may seem in itself vexatious, if unexplained, as in the case of the visit to Shaw, at twelve o'clock at night.

The Commissioners have now fully gone into the whole case, and have set forth their views on each point raised by the evidence.

They wish that the tenor of these observations should be communicated to the master and matron, and that in so far as blame is cast on them, they should be made aware of the necessity for pursuing a different course hereafter. The Commissioners feel bound to add, that the testimony already referred to with regard to the general character of Mr. and Mrs. Aitken for kindness and attention to the inmates is most satisfactory to them, and must be so to the board of guardians.

---

2. CHARGE AGAINST A WORKHOUSE SCHOOL-MISTRESS OF PUNISHING WITH UNDUE SEVERITY A PAUPER CHILD.

St. Matthew, Bethnal Green, Parish.—The attention of the Poor Law Commissioners having been directed to certain charges made against the school-mistress, and also against the master, of the Bethnal Green workhouse, the Commissioners instructed their assistant commissioner, Mr. Hall, to investigate such charges, and to report to them thereon. This having been done, the Commissioners, after carefully considering the facts of the case, addressed the following letter to the clerk of the board of guardians of the parish :—

December 5th, 1844.

The Poor Law Commissioners to the Clerk of Bethnal Green Board of Guardians.—The Poor Law Commissioners have had under consideration a charge against Mrs. Brassington, the school-mistress of the Bethnal Green workhouse, of having, with undue severity, punished a girl, Jane Kingston, under her care. The case was brought under the notice of the Commissioners, as well by the representation of William Dowling and his wife, Jane Dowling, the mother of the girl, (who is an illegitimate child,) as by the published report of proceedings at the Worship-street Police-office, on the hearing of their complaint.

The case involves a charge against the master of the workhouse of impeding William and Jane Dowling in their design of complaining at the police-office of Mrs. Brassington's conduct, and threatening them on their return from the office with confinement in the workhouse, as if they had infringed some regulation of the establishment. It also contains a statement, that the children in the school are not allowed water at their supper, and that it was in an attempt to procure some water after supper, to quench their thirst, that Jane Kingston committed the offence for which she was, as is alleged, too severely punished.

The Commissioners instructed their assistant commissioner, Mr. Hall, to inquire into the facts, and they believe them to be as follows:—It has been found necessary to prohibit generally the girls from going into the scullery, which adjoins the room in which they have their meals. This prohibition was well known to all the girls; but had been often disregarded by Jane Kingston, whose conduct in the school is habitually insubordinate, a cause of trouble to the school-mistress, and of annoyance to the other children. On the evening of the 15th of October last, immediately after supper, the school-mistress was informed by one of the girls, who had charge of the scullery, that Jane Kingston was repeating the offence of going into the scullery, in violation of the rule. The school-mistress immediately called her down to the school-room; she refused to go, and began to threaten loudly that she would revenge herself on the girl who had informed against her, by "slapping her little sister's chops," and "serving her out;" after calling her in vain several times, the school-mistress went up stairs, took her by the arm, and compelled her to go down to the school-room. Jane Kingston repeated her threats on the stairs and in the school-room, and began to cry out vociferously as if hurt by the school-mistress, though it is positively stated that she was not shedding tears, and that up to that time she was not struck; she herself asserted the contrary; but could not produce any witness who saw blows inflicted, although she stated that all the girls were in the school-room at the time. The school-mistress then took Jane Kingston with her into her private room, where she reasoned with her for some time on her habitual bad conduct; but her expostulations were only met by pert answers, by a repetition of threats against the sister of the girl who informed of her, by loud outcries, and by declarations that she (Jane Kingston) would complain to her mother against the school-mistress. Upon this the school-mistress required her to beg her pardon, and on her refusing, or hesitating to do so, she struck her three or four blows on the back, open-handed; she did not remove the child's clothes, nor use any instrument of correction; and she positively states that she did not strike her after she begged her pardon.

No person besides the school-mistress and the child having been present at this interview, any conclusion as to what actually occurred must depend upon the opinion formed of the credibility of the statements made by the parties. If the punishment inflicted had been so severe as is alleged on the one side, evident traces of it must have been afterwards observable on the child's body; accordingly it is asserted by Jane Dowling, that her daughter's back was on the following day covered with sores and bruises. The Commissioners feel compelled to observe, that Jane Dowling's character is not such as to entitle any statement of hers to an unhesitating reception; she is a person of violent impulses, and ungovernable conduct: she has been committed to prison for an assault on the workhouse master; on another occasion she was imprisoned and bound over to keep the peace for an assault on a relieving officer; during the interval between her recent complaint at the police-court and the final hearing, she was seen to knock her daughter, Jane Kingston, off a form on to the floor for some supposed offence, and kick and beat her so violently, that, to use the language of an inmate of the same ward, who witnessed the transaction, "if another pauper had not interfered, she (the girl) would have been well-nigh murdered;" her husband too, who joins her in the charge against the school-mistress, has been three times committed to prison for offences against the discipline of the workhouse. But as regards the indications of severe treatment visible on the person of the child, she herself could or would name no girl who saw the marks of the blows; the master of the workhouse saw the girl's back the day after the correction was administered, it was then slightly discoloured with finger-marks; the visiting committee, consisting of three guardians, saw it on the day following, they observed in one spot a mark which looked like the effect of an open-handed slap; the matron of the workhouse saw it the third day, there was then no mark at all. The Commissioners are satisfied that the descriptions which have been given by the child's mother of the state of her back are greatly exaggerated, and that the marks observable afterwards did not really indicate a degree of corporal chastisement more severe than that which the school-mistress admits that she inflicted.

The Commissioners have felt it their duty to refer to the temper and conduct of Jane Kingston's mother, and that of Jane Kingston herself; on the other hand, they are bound to state, that Mrs. Brassington is represented to them to be a woman of unimpeachable character, of mild temper, and quiet deportment; she was formerly school-mistress in the Walsall Union Workhouse, which situation she left, with unexceptionable testimonials, to enter upon that which she now holds. Jane Kingston bears reluctant testimony to the general kindness with which Mrs. Brassington has treated her; and it is represented to the Commissioners that Mrs. Brassington's mild and judicious management of the children under her care, in the workhouse at Bethnal Green, is evidenced by their regard and affection for her.

Taking this view of the facts of the case, (so far as it relates to the punishment of Jane Kingston,) the Commissioners are of opinion that the punishment inflicted by Mrs. Brassington amounted to much less than the personal chastisement which school-mistresses frequently feel justified in using, where punishment of that kind is not prevented by some local or special regulation similar to the rule of the Commissioners, which prohibits the corporal punishment of any female child in a workhouse; and, under all the circumstances of the case, the Commissioners bearing in mind the disobedience and contumacy of the child, the nature and extent of the punishment, and the respectability and good character of Mrs. Brassington, consider it sufficient that they should take this opportunity of requesting the guardians to inculcate on their school-mistress the utmost caution with reference to the rule referred to.

Such is the conclusion at which the Commissioners arrived, as soon as they were put in possession of the facts of the case; but having been informed that the complaint had been remanded by the sitting magistrate to the Middlesex sessions, and that it was intended to indict Mrs. Brassington for an assault upon Jane Kingston, the Commissioners refrained from communicating with the board of guardians while the proceedings were pending, lest they should in any respect prejudice any party concerned. The indictment has been tried, and a verdict of guilty given against Mrs. Brassington, accompanied, however, with a recommendation to the merciful consideration of the court. The Commissioners have perused the note of the trial, taken by a short-hand writer, and forwarded to Mr. Hall by you; it appears that the assistant judge, presiding in the Sessions Court, received the verdict of the jury, and passed sentence in the following terms: "I conclude from the verdict, that although the punishment was more than the offence itself demanded, yet, that it was very slightly so. With respect to the sentence of the court, as to imprisonment, it is quite out of the question, and not to be thought of for a moment. The difficulty is to know what fine to impose. Here is a school-mistress, who has a rebellious child, and she gives her two or three more slaps than is necessary. You are fined 5*s.* and discharged." The Commissioners need hardly observe, that the conclusion they had previously and independently arrived at, as to the merits of the case, is strengthened by the result of the trial.

The Commissioners will now advert to the other points involved in this case:—With reference to the charge against the workhouse master, the Commissioners are of opinion that it is unfounded: so far from throwing impediments in the way of the complainants, he gave facilities to William and Jane Dowling for conferring together as to the course they would take; and when she, in opposition to the advice of her husband, determined on making a complaint to the magistrate, the master of the workhouse gave them a letter to an officer of the police-court, with the object of obtaining for them an immediate hearing. Neither did he threaten them with punishment on their return; William Dowling was at once sent to his usual ward to bed; Jane Dowling was required to remain with her children in the receiving ward, a boarded room, twenty-four feet long by twelve wide, the accommodation and furniture of which is in no respect inferior to that of the ablebodied women's wards in the workhouse.

The master thought it right that Jane Dowling should remain in the receiving ward until he could take the special directions of the board on her case; besides the circumstances of her complaint being then unadjudicated, which might have rendered it desirable that neither she nor her daughter should have free intercourse with other paupers who were to be witnesses in the case (the marks on the girl's back having then disappeared,) the master thought her seclusion necessary for the security of Mrs. Brassington; Jane Dowling had threatened that "if she could get at the school-mistress she would go to prison for her," and her past conduct in the workhouse gave good ground for apprehending that she would attempt to act upon the meaning of her threat. It appears that she refused to remain in the receiving ward, and insisted on leaving the workhouse. At the moment, the master said that (in obedience to the regulations) she must take her family out with her; but on reflection, he spontaneously, and not by reason of the interference of a guardian, as stated in the petition of William and Jane Dowling, suggested that the children should be allowed to remain, though the parents left the workhouse. This statement is confirmed by the vice-chairman of the board of guardians, the guardian alluded to, who also states that the allegation in the same petition of a threat on the part of the master that he would employ three men to effect by force the separate confinement of William and Jane Dowling, is untrue. The Commissioners are of opinion that the master of the workhouse stands acquitted of all blame.

With reference to the supply of water to the girls at supper, the Commissioners understand the case to be as follows:—They will, however, first observe, that this point arises upon the excuse made by Jane Kingston for going into the scullery, she is reported to have stated to the magistrate that her supper consisted of dry bread and cheese, and that, as no water is placed on the table, she was compelled, being thirsty, to go into the scullery for it. It appears, on the admission of the child herself, as well as by other evidence, that the supper of the children on this night consisted of bread and broth, not bread and cheese, as was erroneously stated to the magistrate, so that on this particular occasion the necessity of obtaining the means of quenching her thirst could hardly be pleaded in extenuation of a breach of discipline.

But it appears that it was formerly the practice to place a supply of water on the table, for the children at supper, but that for reasons connected with their health, and the comfort of many of them at night, the practice has been disused. The children, however, are not debarred from the means of quenching their thirst. They have always access after supper to the yard attached to their school-room, in which there is a lavatory furnished with drinking-cans, at which water can be obtained: it is also an instruction to the elder girls who are employed in the scullery, to give a proper supply of water at the door to any child who may ask for it, but to allow no child to go in and help herself. The Commissioners are not prepared to find fault with these arrangements. To return to the particular case before them, the Commissioners will only add, that there was the same access to water on the night when Jane Kingston offended, as at other times; the door of the yard was not locked; she had not been down stairs to try, but went at once from the supper-room into the scullery, and in fact, there were children in the yard when she was in the scullery,—she could have obtained water in a legitimate way; and there is no doubt that she justly incurred punishment by an unnecessary act of wilful disobedience, and that her fault was aggravated by her contumacy afterwards.

II.—RETURNS RELATING TO THE ADMINISTRATION OF THE POOR LAW, MADE TO PARLIAMENT DURING THE SESSION OF 1844.

Auditors.—Returns of the names, addresses, professions, and occupations of the several auditors appointed under the Poor Law Amendment Act; together with the date of their respective appointments. (272.) Moved for by Mr. Jervis. Presented 13th of May.

Bastardy—Report on.—"Copy of the report of the Poor Law Commissioners to Sir James Graham, on the law concerning the maintenance of bastards." (31.) Moved for by Sir James Graham. Presented 14th of February.

Brassington Incorporation.—Copies of all correspondence which has passed between the Poor Law Commissioners and the guardians of the Brassington Incorporation; together with copies of all orders which have been issued to the said guardians by the said Poor Law Commissioners, from the passing of the New Poor Law Act, to the present time. (483.) Moved for by Mr. Colville. Presented 11th of July.

Brassington Incorporation. — Copy of Mr. Weale's reports to the Poor Law Commissioners, relating to the parishes calling themselves the Brassington Incorporation. (614.) Moved for by Mr. Barneby. Presented 5th of August.

Chaplains of Workhouses.—A return of the total number of Unions in England and Wales, stating in which of them chaplains have been appointed, the different rates of salary severally paid to those chaplains, the number of unions in which the poor in the workhouse, or any classes of them, are not allowed to go out of the workhouse on Sunday to attend divine service, no chaplains having been appointed to such unions. (144.) Moved for by Viscount Clive. Presented 25th of March.

Chaplains of Workhouses.—A return of the number of unions in England and Wales, in which no chaplains had been appointed on the 1st day of January last, and the number of inmates in such unions at that period. (231.) Moved for by Mr. S. O'Brien. Presented 30th of April.

Cirencester Union—Dietary Table.—A copy of the dietary table issued by the Poor Law Commissioners for the Cirencester union, on the 10th day of December, 1836; and of an amended table issued for the same union from that date to the present time. (102.) Moved for by Mr. Thomas Duncombe. Presented 12th of March.

County Rate.—An account of the latest valuation of every parish, township, or place, upon which the county rates have been laid in the respective counties of England and Wales, stating the year in which such valuation was taken, showing also the total valuation of each hundred and county. Abstract of the said accounts, (presented 15th of April, 1844,) showing the total valuation of each county; also the amount of county rate, levied in 1842, the proportion which such rate bears to the valuation, the rate per acre, and the rate per head upon the population. (268.) Presented 13th of May.

Dudley Union—Relieving Officer.—Copy of the report of Mr. Austin, Assistant Poor Law Commissioner, on the conduct of Mr. Benjamin Prince, the relieving officer of the parish of Dudley; and copies of all letters and communications which have passed between him, or the Commissioners, and the board of guardians of the Dudley Union, and of the surgeon and relieving officer, in reference to this matter. (117.) Moved for by Mr. Thornley. Presented 14th of March.

Dudley Union—Deaths in Workhouse.—Copy of the evidence taken by Mr. Austin, in the cases of *post mortem* examination of paupers, who died in workhouses belonging to the Dudley Union; together with his report, and the proceedings of the Poor Law Commissioners thereon. (385.) Moved for by Mr. Barneby. Presented 14th of June.

Extra-Parochial Places.—A return of all extra-parochial lands, houses, and tenements in each county and borough of England and Wales, exempted from the payment of poor's rates; together with the population and acreage of each such place, and its assessment to the county or borough rate, so far as the same can be ascertained. (209.) Moved for by Mr. Thomas Duncombe. Presented 16th of April.

Gilbert's Incorporations.—A return of the date of incorporations of all Gilbert's Unions, whether dissolved or not. (578.) Moved for by Mr. Barneby. Presented 3rd of August.

Gilbert's Incorporations.—Report of Committee for inquiring into the administration and operation of the law for the relief of the poor in unions, formed under the Act 22 Geo. 3. c. 83; together with the minutes of evidence. (543.) Presented (H. of C.) 25th of July.

Keighley Union—Sir John Walsham, Bart.—Copy of a letter from Sir John Walsham to the Poor Law Commissioners, dated the 11th day of June inst. [1844], relative to his report on the Keighley Union, and of the answer of the Commissioners thereto, dated the 19th day of June inst. (437.) Moved for by Mr. Bolton Clive. Presented 2nd of July.

Kensington Union, and Parish of Chelsea—Henry Osman.—Copy of a correspondence which passed between Mr. J. B. Ryder, the chairman of the Chelsea board of guardians, and the Poor Law Commissioners, in July and August last, relating to the removal of Henry Osman, a pauper, from the Kensington Union workhouse to the Chelsea workhouse, during the time he was in a dying state. (349). Moved for by Mr. Ferrand. Presented 5th of June.

Lunatic Paupers.—A return of the number of pauper lunatics and idiots, chargeable to each of the unions in England and Wales, in the month of August, 1842 and 1843 respectively, (in pursuance of the Act 5 and 6 Vic. c. 57) distinguishing those maintained in county lunatic asylum, in licensed house, and elsewhere, with the average weekly cost per head of maintenance and clothing, together with the population of each union in 1841, and the estimated number of lunatics and idiots for places not in union. (172.) Moved for by Mr. Manners Sutton. Presented 1st April.

Medical Relief.—First Report of Committee on Medical Poor Relief, on the petition of Thomas King, late an inmate of Woodbridge Union workhouse. (312.) Presented (H. of C.) 22nd May.

Medical Relief.—Second Report of Committee on Medical Poor Relief, on the petition of John Bromfield Ryder, Sloane-street, Chelsea, relating to the case of Henry Osman, deceased. (387.) Presented (H. of C.) 17th June.

Medical Relief.—Report of Committee on Medical Poor Relief, together with the minutes of evidence. (531.) Presented (H. of C.) 29th July.

Medical Relief.—Return of the names of each union in England and Wales, formed in pursuance of the Poor Law Amendment Act, according to the districts of the assistant Commissioners, with the name of each assistant Commissioner, the number of parishes in each union, the area in statute acres, (excepting the Welsh unions,) and the population of each union.—For each year, from 1840 inclusive, of the weekly average number of paupers relieved in the workhouse during each year, the number of medical officers employed in each union, the aggregate amount of midwifery and surgical fees, the total amount paid to the medical officers in each year, the rate per head of medical expences, on the population of each union in each year, and any augmentation or diminution of the salaries of medical officers since the 25th day of March, 1843. (602.) Moved for by Mr. Manners Sutton. Presented 7th August.

Orphan Children.—Widows.—A return of the number of orphan children, i.e., having lost one or both parents, under fourteen years of age, at present in the Poor Law Union workhouses of England and Wales, distinguishing the males from the females. The like return in respect to children who have been deserted by their parents.

A return of the number of orphan children, under fourteen years of age, at present in the parish workhouses of England and Wales, not incorporated in the Poor Law Unions, distinguishing the males from the females. The like return in respect to children who have been deserted by their parents.

A return of the number of widows at present receiving out-door relief from the various parishes and unions in England and Wales, stating the number of their children, under fourteen years of age, who are dependent upon them for subsistence. (534.) Moved for by Mr. Thomas Duncombe. Presented 23rd July.

Pauper Children sent to the Army, &c.—Returns of all children who have been removed from union houses into the army, and into the navy, distinguishing the two classes, their names, their ages, names of unions from which removed, and date of such removal, and whether by consent of their parents or not. (467.) Moved for by Mr. Hindley. Presented 9th July.

Pauperism.—Return showing the number of in-door and out-door paupers relieved in each county, in England and Wales, during the quarters ended Lady-day, 1842 and 1843 respectively, with the amount of money expended for in-maintenance and out-relief, during each of the years ended Lady-day, 1842 and 1843; also of the number of adult able-bodied paupers relieved, in each county in England and Wales, for the same periods.

Return of the amount of money expended for in-maintenance and out-relief, in each county, in England and Wales, during the half-years ended Michaelmas, 1842 and 1843, with comparative statements for England and Wales.

Return of the total amount of money levied and expended in England and Wales during the nine years prior and subsequent to the passing of the Poor Law Amendment Act. (42.) Moved for by Sir James Graham. Presented 19th February.

Pauperism.—Bastardy.—Return of the average annual expenditure of the parishes comprised in each of the unions in England and Wales during the three years prior to union, and the amount expended for the relief and maintenance of the poor in each of the years ended Lady-day, 1841, 1842, and 1843; also the number of in-door and out-door paupers relieved during each of the quarters ended Lady-day, 1841, 1842, and 1843, together with the number of illegitimate children relieved during the same periods, stating the per centage as compared to the other paupers and the present population in the different unions, specifying the number of unions now without workhouses. (241.) Moved for by Mr. H. O. Stanley. Presented 3rd May.

Pauperism.—Prohibitory Order.—Return of the number of able-bodied persons and their families (not being sick) for whom, or by whom, application for relief has been made to the board of guardians of any union in the counties of Dorset, Wilts, Berks, Oxford, Buckingham, and Bedford, in which the prohibitory order as to out-door relief is in force for six months, ending the 25th day of March, 1843,—of the number of such persons to whom relief has been refused—of the number of such persons to whom relief has been offered in the workhouse, of the number of such persons who have taken orders to go into the workhouse, and of the number of such persons who have gone into the workhouse. (118.) Moved for by Mr. Henley. Presented 14th March.

Pauperism.—In-door Paupers.—Returns respecting paupers in union workhouses in England and Wales, viz. :—

— Of the number of married paupers now in the union workhouses of England and Wales, established under the Act of 4 and 5 Will. 4, c. 76, who have been in such workhouses for a longer period than five years, also of the number of such paupers being above and under 50 years of age, stating how many of them may be considered as able-bodied men. Also,

— Of the number of married paupers at present in the union workhouses who have been in such workhouses for a period less than five years, stating whether any, and how many, of such paupers have been admitted more than once, and the number of times each of such paupers has been admitted. Also,

— Of the number of union workhouses that have been open for more than five years, and the number that have been open for a shorter period. Also,

— Of the number of married paupers, distinguishing male and female, that have died in the respective union workhouses since the passing of the Act. Also,

— From the several parishes in England and Wales, for the year ending 30th June, 1843, and for the four preceding years, of the number of persons charged with absconding, and leaving their wives or children chargeable to the parish, distinguishing such as absconded from within the workhouse, from such as absconded from without; and also,

— Of the number of such persons, during the same period, as have been apprehended, and of such as are known to have been re-united to their families without being previously apprehended, so far as the same can be ascertained. (72.) Presented (H. of L.) 18th of April.

Penzance Union—Appointment of Chaplain.—Copies or extracts of all correspondence between the Guardians of the Penzance Union and the Poor Law Commissioners, relative to the appointment of a chaplain in that union. (61.) Presented (H. of L.) 1st of April.

Poor Law Commission.—Tenth Annual Report of the Commission, together with App. A. B. and C. Presented (H. of C.) by command.

Poor Rate.—Property assessed.—Return showing the total value of property assessed to the poor-rates for the year ended Lady-day, 1841, with the amount of money levied for poor-rates for the years ended Lady-day, 1839 to 1842, on each parish in England and Wales. (63.) Moved for by Mr. George Palmer. Presented 26th of February.

Wandsworth and Clapham Union.—Treatment of Female Paupers.—Copy of all communications between the Poor Law Commissioners and the chairman of the Board of Guardians of the Wandsworth Union, with regard to the treatment of female paupers in the workhouse of that union. (76.) Presented (H. of L.) 22nd of April.

Wells Union.—Medical Officer.—Copy of correspondence between the Poor Law Commissioners and the guardians of the Wells Union relative to the dismissal of Mr. George Newman from medical superintendence of the poor of the Glastonbury districts. (26.) Moved for by Lord Robert Grosvenor. Presented 13th of February.

Wells Union.—Medical Officer.—A copy of so much of the minutes of the board of guardians of the Wells Union, at their meeting, on the 30th day of August, 1843, as relates to the dismissal of Mr. G. Newman, by the Poor Law Commissioners, from his office of surgeon to the poor in the Glastonbury district, or to any other proceeding taken upon that occasion relative to that gentleman ; and

A copy of such letter, or letters, as may have been addressed to the Wells board of guardians by any of the four clergymen who memorialised the Poor Law Commissioners in June last, explanatory of their object in requiring the removal of Mr. G. Newman from the situation of medical officer of the Glastonbury district. (132.) Moved for by Mr. Neville and Lord Robert Grosvenor. Presented 19th of March.

Workhouse Regulations of Poor Law Commissioners.—Copy of Articles 9, 10, 11, and 12 of the General Workhouse Rules, issued by the Poor Law Commissioners, bearing date the 5th day of February, 1842 ; together with the passages explanatory of those Articles contained in the letter of the Commissioners which accompanied the general workhouse rules, also dated the 5th day of February, 1842. (45.) Moved for by Mr. Ferrand. Presented 20th of February.

LONDON:

Printed by Order of the Poor Law Commissioners, by BLACKBURN and PARDON, 6, Hatton Garden, and Published by CHARLES KNIGHT and Co., 22, Ludgate Street, Publishers to the Poor Law Commissioners.

VOLUME V
[1845]

AN

OFFICIAL CIRCULAR

OF PUBLIC DOCUMENTS AND INFORMATION:

DIRECTED BY THE POOR LAW COMMISSIONERS TO BE PRINTED, CHIEFLY FOR THE USE OF THE MEMBERS AND PERMANENT OFFICERS OF BOARDS OF GUARDIANS, UNDER THE POOR LAW AMENDMENT ACT.

No. 43. CIRCULAR ISSUED JANUARY 1, 1845.

Poor Law Commission Office,
Somerset House,
January 1st, 1845.

THE Poor Law Commissioners, on a review of their Minutes, directed that the following general orders and instructional letters be printed and circulated for the information of the Guardians and Officers of the several Unions, viz.:—

By Order of the Board,
EDWIN CHADWICK, *Secretary.*

I.—APPRENTICING POOR CHILDREN—

1. GENERAL ORDER.

To the Guardians of the Poor of the several Unions and of the several Parishes under a Board of Guardians, named in the Schedule hereunto annexed, and the Officers of such Unions and Parishes;—

To the Churchwardens and Overseers of the several Parishes and Places comprised within the said Unions, and of the several other Parishes named in the said Schedule;—

To the Clerk or Clerks to the Justices of the Petty Sessions held for the Division or Divisions in which the Parishes and Places comprised within the said Unions, and the said other Parishes named in the said Schedule, are situate;—

And to all others whom it may concern.

In pursuance of the powers vested in us by an Act passed in the fifth year of the reign of his late majesty King William the Fourth, intituled "*An Act for the Amendment and better Administration of the Laws relating to the Poor in England and Wales,*" and an Act passed in the seventh and eighth year of the reign of her present majesty Queen Victoria, intituled "*An Act for the further Amendment of the Laws relating to the Poor in England,*" We, the Poor Law Commissioners, do make the following rules and regulations in regard to the apprenticing of poor children by the guardians of the poor of the several unions named in the schedule A. hereunto annexed, and of the parishes named in the schedule B. hereunto annexed.

The Parties.

Article 1.—No child under the age of n years shall be bound an apprentice;

And no child that cannot read and write hn own name.

No child shall be so bound to a person who is not a housekeeper, or assessed to the poor rate in his own name;

Or who is a journeyman, or a person not carrying on trade or business on his own account;

Or who is under the age of twenty-one;

Or a married woman.

The Premium.

Article 2.—No premium other than clothing for the apprentice shall be given upon the binding of any person above the age of *fourteen*, unless such person be maimed, deformed, or suffering from some permanent bodily infirmity, so that the nature of the work or trade which such person is fit to perform or exercise is restricted.

Article 3.—Where any premium is given it shall consist in part of clothes supplied to the apprentice at the commencement of the binding, and in part of money, one moiety whereof shall be paid to the master at the binding, and the residue at the termination of the first year of the binding.

Term.

Article 4.—No apprentice shall be bound for more than *eight* years.

Consent.

Article 5.—No person above *fourteen* years of age shall be so bound without his *consent;*

And no child under the age of *sixteen* years shall be so bound without the consent of the father of such child, or if the father be dead, or be disqualified to give such consent, as hereinafter provided, or if such child be a bastard, without the consent of the mother, if living, of such child.

Provided, that where the parent of such child whose consent would be otherwise requisite, is transported beyond the seas, or is in the custody of the law, having been convicted of some *felony*, or for the space of six calendar months before the time of executing the indenture has deserted such child, or for such space of time has been in the service of her majesty, or of the East India Company, in foreign parts, such parent, if the father, shall be deemed to be disqualified as hereinbefore stated, and if it be the mother, no such consent shall be required.

Place of Service.

Article 6.—No child shall be bound to a master whose place of business, whereat the child to work and live, shall be distant more than *thirty* miles from the place in which the child is residing at the time of the binding;

Unless in any particular case the Poor Law Commissioners shall, on application to them, otherwise permit.

Preliminaries to the Binding.

Article 7.—If the child, whom it is proposed to bind apprentice, be in the workhouse, and under the age of *fourteen*, the guardians shall require a certificate in writing from the medical officer of the workhouse as to the fitness in regard to bodily health and strength of such child to be bound apprentice to the proposed trade, and shall also ascertain from the master of the workhouse the capacity of the child for such binding in other respects.

Article 8.—If the child be not in the workhouse, but in the union or parish by the guardians of which it is proposed that it shall be bound, the relieving officer of the district in which the child shall be residing shall examine into the circumstances of the case, the condition of the child, and of his parents, if any, and the residence of the proposed master, the nature of his trade, the number of other apprentices, if any, then bound to him, and generally as to the fitness of the particular binding, and shall report the result of his inquiry to the board of guardians.

Article 9.—If the board of guardians think proper to proceed with the binding, they shall, when the child is under the age of *fourteen*, direct the relieving officer to take the child to the medical officer of the district, to be examined as to his fitness in respect of bodily health and strength for the proposed trade or business; and such medical officer shall certify in writing according to his judgment in the matter, which certificate shall be produced by the said relieving officer to the next meeeting of the guardians.

Article 10.—If the child be residing in some other parish or union, the guardians who propose to bind him shall not proceed to do so unless they receive such a report as is required in Article 8, from the relieving officer of the district in which such child is residing, and a certificate from some medical practitioner of the neighbourhood of the child's residence to the effect required in Article 9.

Article 11.—When a premium is proposed to be given, in a case within the provision of Article 2, the guardian shall require a certificate in writing of some medical practitioner, certifying that the person is maimed, deformed, or disabled, to the extent specified in such article, and shall cause a copy of such certificate to be entered on their minutes before they proceed to execute the indenture.

Article 12.—When such certificate, as is required by Articles 7, 9, and 10, is received, or in case from the age of the child no such certificate is required, the guardians shall direct that the child, and the proposed master, or some person on his behalf, and in case the child be under the age of *sixteen*, the parent or person in whose custody such child shall be then living, shall attend some meeting of the board to be then appointed.

Article 13.—At such meeting, if such parties appear, the guardians shall examine into the circumstances of the case; and if, after making all due inquiries, and hearing the objections (if any be made) on the part of the relatives or friends of such child, they shall deem it proper that the binding shall be effected, they may forthwith cause the indentures to be prepared, and, if the master be present, to be executed; but if he be not present they shall cause the same to be transmitted to him for execution; and when executed by him, and returned to the guardians, the same shall be executed by the latter, and shall be signed by the child, as herein-after provided.

Article 14.—If the proposed master reside out of the union, but in some other union or parish under a board of guardians, whether formed under the provisions of the first-recited Act, or of the Act of the twenty-second year of the reign of King George the Third, intituled, *"An Act for the better Relief and Employment of the Poor,"* or of any local Act, the guardians shall, before proceeding to effect the binding, communicate in writing the proposal to the guardians of such other union or parish, and request to be informed whether such binding is open to any objection; and if no objection be reported by such guardians within the space of one calendar month, or if the objection does not appear to the guardians proposing to bind the child to be sufficient to prevent the binding, the same may be proceeded with; and when the indentures shall have been executed, the clerk to the guardians who executed the same shall send notice thereof in writing to the guardians of the union or parish wherein the said apprentice is to reside.

Indentures.

Article 15.—The indentures shall be executed in duplicate, by the master and the guardians, and shall not be valid unless signed by the proposed apprentice, without aid or assistance, in the presence of the said guardians; and the consent of the parent, where requisite, shall be testified by such parent signing with his name or mark, to be properly attested, the foot of the said indenture; and where such consent is dispensed with under the provision contained in Article 5, the cause of such dispensation shall be stated at the foot of the indenture, by the clerk to the said guardians.

Article 16.—The indenture shall contain mention of the place or places at which the apprentice is to work and live.

Article 17.—One part of such indenture, when executed, shall be kept by the guardians; the other shall be delivered to the master.

Duties of the Master.

Article 18.—And we do hereby prescribe the duties of the master to whom such poor child may be apprenticed, and the terms and conditions to be inserted in the said indentures, as follows:—

No. 1.—The master shall teach the child the trade, business, or employment set forth in the indenture, unless the board of guardians authorise the substitution of another trade or business.

No. 2.—He shall maintain the said child with proper food and nourishment.

No. 3.—He shall provide a proper lodging for the said child.

No. 4.—He shall supply to the said child one suit of proper clothing every year during the term of the binding.

No. 5.—He shall, in case the said child be affected with any disease or sickness, or meet with any accident, procure, at his own cost, adequate medical or surgical assistance, to be supplied by some duly qualified medical man for such child.

No. 6.—He shall, once at least on every Sunday, cause the child to attend some place of divine worship, if there be any such within a reasonable distance, according to the religious persuasion in which the child has been brought up, so, however, that no child shall be required by the master to attend any place of worship to which his parents, or surviving parent may object, nor, when he shall be above the age of *sixteen*, any place to which he may himself object.

No. 7.—Where such parents or parent or next of kin shall desire it, he shall allow the said child, while under the age of *sixteen*, to attend any Sunday or other school which shall be situated within the same parish or within *two* miles distance from his residence, on every Sunday; and, if there be no such school which such child can attend, shall, at some reasonable hour on every Sunday allow any minister of the religious persuasion of the child to have access to such child, for the purpose of imparting religious instruction.

No. 8.—Where the apprentice continues bound after the age of *seventeen* years the master shall pay to such apprentice, for and in respect of every week that he duly and properly serves the said master, as a remuneration, a sum to be inserted in the indenture, or to be agreed upon by the guardians and the said master when that time arrives; or, if they cannot agree, to be settled by some person to be then chosen by the said master and the said guardians, and, until such sum be agreed upon or settled, not less than one *fourth* of the amount then commonly paid as wages to journeymen in the said trade, business, or employment.

No. 9.—The master shall, by himself or by his agent, produce the apprentice to the board of guardians by whom such apprentice was bound, at their ordinary meeting next preceding the end of the first year of the binding, and before the receipt of the remainder of the premium, if any be due, and shall in like manner produce the said apprentice at some one of their ordinary meetings, to be held at or about the middle of the term, and whenever afterwards required to do so by the said guardians.

Provided that if the apprentice reside out of the union by the guardians whereof he was bound, the apprentice shall be produced, as hereinbefore directed, to the board of guardians of the union or parish, as described in Article 14, in which the apprentice may be residing.

No. 10.—The master shall not cause the said apprentice to work or live more than *ten miles* from the place or places mentioned in the indenture, according to article 16, without the leave of the guardians so binding him, to be given under their common seal.

Article 19.—These duties of the master shall be enforced by covenants and conditions to be inserted in the said indenture so to be executed by him.

Article 20.—The master shall also covenant not to assign nor to cancel the indenture, without the consent of the guardians, under their common seal, previously obtained, under a penalty to be specified in the said covenant, and to pay to the said guardians all costs and expenses that they may incur in consequence of the said apprentice not being supplied with medical or surgical assistance by the master, in case the same shall be at any time requisite.

Article 21.—The indenture shall be made subject to the following provisoes:—

1.—That if the master take the benefit of any Act for the relief of insolvent debtors, or be discharged under any such act, such indenture shall forthwith become of no further force or effect.

2.—That if, on a conviction for a breach of any one of the aforesaid covenants before a justice of the peace, in pursuance of the provisions of the statute in such case made and provided, the guardians who may be parties to the said indenture shall declare by a resolution that the indenture shall be determined, and shall transmit a copy of such resolution, under the hand of their clerk or the person for the time being acting as such, by the post or otherwise, to the said master, such indenture shall, except in respect of all rights and liabilities then accrued, forthwith become of no further force or effect.

Explanation of Terms.

Article 22.—Whenever the word *Parish* is used in this order, it shall be taken to include any place maintaining its own poor, whether parochial or extra-parochial; and the word *Guardians* shall include the select vestry of the parish of *Liverpool.*

Article 23.—Whenever, in describing any person or party, matter or thing, the word importing the singular number, or the masculine gender only, is used in this order, the same shall be taken to include, and shall be applied to, several persons or parties, as well as one person or party, and females as well as males, and several matters or things, as well as one matter or thing, respectively, unless there be something in the subject or context repugnant to such construction.

Article 24.—Whenever in this order any article is referred to by its number, the article of this order bearing that number shall be taken to be signified thereby.

Article 25.—Provided that nothing herein contained shall apply to the apprenticing of poor children to the sea service.

Given under our hands and seal of office, this thirty-first day of December, in the year one thousand eight hundred and forty-four.

(Signed) GEO. NICHOLLS.
G. C. LEWIS.
EDMUND W. HEAD.

This order applies to all the unions and parishes named in the schedules A. and B. (pages 15 and 16), excepting those marked thus †.

Orders relating to the apprenticing of poor children will shortly be issued to parishes not in unions governed by Boards of Guardians, and also to parishes and incorporations governed by Boards of Guardians under local acts.

---

2. LETTER ACCOMPANYING THE APPRENTICING ORDER.

Poor Law Commission Office,
Somerset House,
January 1st, 1845.

SIR,—I am directed by the Poor Law Commissioners to forward to you a copy of a general order, which they have issued for regulating the proceedings to be taken in the binding of parish apprentices.

The Commissioners were empowered by the 4 and 5 W. IV., c. 76, (*the Poor Law Amendment Act,*) to make regulations upon this subject, which were to be enforced by the justices in the indentures which they might allow after the issue of the regulations. But they had not issued any such regulations previous to the passing of the act of the last session, which gives a more precise and summary remedy for the enforcing, against the masters, of the regulations which they may prescribe.

That statute having also taken the binding of parish apprentices away from the overseers, and removed the control of the justices over it, has substituted the board of guardians in the place of those respective parties. The Commissioners have, therefore, felt it expedient forthwith to prescribe and promulgate the regulations, which they think ought to be laid down for the control and guidance of the guardians upon this subject.

Their object has been to secure a careful attention, on the part of the guardians who are to bind out the children, to the fitness and propriety of the step which is to affect permanently the future condition of those children, and a due performance afterwards by the masters of the duties which appear naturally to result from the relation of master and apprentice.

I am to call the attention of the guardians to the fact, that the apprenticeship is a species of relief, and consequently can only be given subject to the regulations which may exist in any particular union or parish, with regard to the relief in such union or parish generally.

In conclusion, I have to observe, that the Commissioners by no means desire to express any opinion as to the propriety of the guardians extending the practice of parish apprenticeship. There is no doubt that the compulsory apprenticeship of poor children, which has been abolished by the 13th section of the 7 and 8 Vict. c. 101, has been found productive of great evils and mischief; and there are not wanting authorities of weight against the system of parochial apprenticeship in general.

That system, however, not having been abolished by the legislature, will doubtless continue to be practised in those districts where it has hitherto prevailed; but the Commissioners do not wish that the guardians in those parts of the country where the system has not been generally pursued, should infer that they entertain any desire to promote its introduction in consequence of their having issued the order above referred to.

I am, Sir,
Your obedient servant,
EDWIN CHADWICK, *Secretary.*

To the Clerk of the Guardians.

II.—NON-RESIDENT RELIEF—

1. GENERAL ORDER.

To the Guardians of the Poor of the several Unions and Parishes named in the Schedules hereunto annexed;—

To the Churchwardens and Overseers of the Poor of the several Parishes and Places comprised in the said Unions;—

To the Churchwardens and Overseers of the Poor of the said other Parishes;—

To the Clerk or Clerks to the Justices of the Petty Sessions held for the Division or Divisions in which all such Parishes and Places are situate;—

And to all others whom it may concern.

Whereas it is expedient that certain regulations should be made, with respect to the mode in which relief is to be transmitted to poor persons who reside in parishes or unions, but are not settled therein, and respecting the accounts to be kept and rendered with regard to such relief.

Now, therefore, we, the Poor Law Commissioners, in pursuance of the authorities vested in us by an Act passed in the fifth year of the reign of his late Majesty King William the Fourth, intituled "*An Act for the Amendment and better Administration of the Laws relating to the Poor in England and Wales,*" do hereby order, direct, and declare, with respect to each and every of the unions named in the schedule A. hereunto annexed, and of the parishes named in the schedule B. hereunto annexed, that from and after the twenty-fifth day of March next—

Article 1.—If any board of guardians undertake or agree to administer relief allowed to a non-settled poor person living within the parish or union for which they act, on behalf of the officers, or of the board of guardians, of the parish or union in which such pauper is deemed to be settled, every such undertaking or agreement shall be made in conformity with the rules and regulations of the Poor Law Commissioners in force at the time.

Article 2.—No relieving officer, or other officer of any board of guardians, nor any assistant overseer or collector, shall receive money for the relief of any non-settled pauper on behalf of any officer, or of the board of guardians, of any other parish or union, nor shall he constitute himself in any way the agent of the officers or board of guardians of such other parish or union, except as provided in this order.

Article 3.—Every relieving officer shall be bound to visit, relieve, and otherwise attend to non-settled poor, being within his district, according to the directions of the board of guardians whose officer he is, and in no other way, subject always to the obligation imposed on him in cases of sudden and urgent necessity, and to the rules, orders, and regulations of the Poor Law Commissioners; and every such relieving officer shall set apart one or more pages in his out-door relief list, in which he shall duly and punctually enter up the payments made by authority of his own board of guardians to non-settled poor, and shall take credit for such payments under the head of non-settled poor in his receipt and expenditure book.

Article 4.—No money shall be transmitted by any board of guardians or parish officers to the relieving officer or other officer of any union, or any parish, in which the relief is administered by a board of guardians, in order to be applied to the relief of any non-settled pauper, except in conformity with the provisions of this order; but if any money be so transmitted contrary to the provisions of this order, such officer shall forthwith pay such money into the hands of the treasurer to the guardians of the parish or union whose officer he is, and shall report to the board of guardians at their next meeting the fact that such money has been so received and paid, and shall make a true entry accordingly on both sides of his receipt and expenditure book.

Article 5.—If the board of guardians of any parish or union undertake or agree to administer relief through their officer to any non-settled pauper on behalf of the officer or guardians of any other parish or union, the clerk to such first-mentioned board of guardians shall open an account, in their ledger, to be headed "Non-settled Poor Account," and he shall debit such account with the cost of all relief paid to such non-settled poor, and shall credit such account by all payments from time to time actually made to the treasurer on account of the parish or union to which such non-settled poor are supposed to belong.

Article 6.—If any board of guardians authorise the administration of relief by any other board of guardians on their behalf to a non-resident pauper, the clerk to such first-mentioned board of guardians shall open an account in their ledger, to be headed "Non-resident Poor Account," and he shall debit such account with the amount of all money actually transmitted to any other parish or union in payment of non-resident relief, such amount to be credited to the treasurer or other officer by whom the same is paid, and the clerk shall credit the said Non-resident Poor Relief Account with the sums reported to have been paid as aforesaid, such sums to be carried to the debit of out-relief against the respective parishes for which the same were paid.

Article 7.—The clerk to every board of guardians shall at the first meeting of the guardians in each quarter lay before the board of guardians, or some committee appointed by such board, the Non-settled Poor Account, and the Non-resident Poor Account, posted in his ledger to the end of the preceding quarter, and shall take the directions of the board of guardians respecting the remittance of cheques or post-office orders to the guardians of any other union or parish, or the transmission of accounts due from other unions or parishes, and requests for payment.

Article 8.—The clerk shall, within fourteen days from the close of each quarter, transmit by post all accounts of relief administered in the course of the preceding quarter to non-settled poor to the guardians of the unions and parishes on account of which such relief was given; and every account so transmitted shall state the names and class of the several paupers to whom the relief in question has been administered; and all accounts for the relief duly administered to non-resident poor shall be discharged before the end of one calendar month from the receipt of such accounts, by the transmission of the amount due in one of the modes prescribed in this order.

Article 9.—No money shall be paid to the officer of any union or parish in which the relief is administered by a board of guardians on account of non-resident poor, except in one of the three following ways:—

No. 1.—By post-office order payable to the treasurer or the banker of such treasurer of the union or parish to the account of which the money is to be paid.

No. 2.—By cheque or order payable to the treasurer of such parish or union, or to his order.

No. 3.—By cheque payable to bearer (where the same may lawfully be drawn,) and crossed as payable through the treasurer of such parish or union, or his banker, or through the agent of such treasurer or banker; and every such cheque shall be so crossed by the clerk to the guardians before it is signed by the presiding chairman.

Article 10.—The clerk to the board of guardians shall, in making up his account before each audit, include the cost of all relief to non-resident poor, the payment on account of which has been actually made, in the cost of relief given by the board of guardians of the parish or union for which he is clerk.

He shall in like manner enter the non-resident poor, on account of whom the cost of relief has been transmitted, in their proper classes as paupers relieved by the board of guardians for which he is clerk, and shall deduct from the number of paupers so relieved all poor persons on account of whom any remittance may have been actually received from any other parish or union in the course of the period to which the account refers, notwithstanding that such poor persons may have received relief over and above the value of the remittance so made.

Article 11.—The clerk to every board of guardians shall immediately after each audit lay before the board of guardians a statement of the following particulars, which shall be signed by the auditor in testimony that it appears consistent with the accounts audited by him, so far as is apparent on the face of such accounts:—

No. 1.—The number of non-resident poor, and of the persons composing their families, on account of whom money has been actually transmitted during the period to which the accounts last audited relate, and the sum so transmitted, distinguishing the amount to each parish or union.

No. 2.—The number of accounts for relief given during the same period supposed to be outstanding on account of non-resident poor, but not yet received, distinguishing the parishes or unions from which they should have been sent.

No. 3.—The number of non-settled poor, divided into their proper classes, actually relieved in the course of the same period on account of other parishes or unions, and the sum expended in such relief, distinguishing the amount on account of each parish or union.

No. 4.—The sum actually received during the same period in repayment of relief to non-settled poor, distinguishing the sum for each parish or union.

No. 5.—The number of accounts for non-settled poor relieved during the same period, not yet discharged by other parishes or unions although sent in, distinguishing the amount due from each parish or union, and also distinguishing those cases in which the account has been sent in more than fourteen days before the audit.

Article 12.—Nothing in this order shall be taken to discharge any board of guardians, or any officer of a parish or union, from any legal obligation now incumbent on such board of guardians, or on such officer, to relieve poor persons destitute in such parish or union, but not settled therein, and nothing in this order shall be taken either to authorise the allowance of relief to any poor person in any case in which such relief may otherwise be unlawful, or to prohibit the allowance of relief to any poor person in any case in which the same may otherwise be lawfully made, or to affect any repayment of relief administered under a suspended order of removal.

Article 13.—The term *non-resident poor* in this order shall be taken to mean all paupers in receipt of relief allowed on account of any parish or union in relation to which the term is used, but not residing therein.

The term *non-settled poor* in this order shall be taken to mean all paupers residing in the parish or union in relation to which the term is used, but to whom relief has been or is to be allowed on account of some parish or union other than that in which they reside.

The terms "*allowance of relief*" and "*to allow relief*" in this order shall be taken to refer to the order or authority of the board of guardians, or other persons, making themselves liable for the ultimate payment of such relief, or undertaking to repay the same.

The terms "*administration of relief*" and "*to administer relief*" in this order, shall be taken to refer to the payment or actual giving of relief to the pauper who is to receive the same.

The word "*Union*" in this order shall be taken to include not only an union of parishes formed under the provisions of the hereinbefore recited Act, but also an union of parishes incorporated or united for the relief or maintenance of the poor under any local act of parliament.

The word "*guardians*" in this order shall be taken to include not only guardians appointed or entitled to act under the provisions of the said hereinbefore recited Act, but also any governors, deputy governors, assistants, directors, managers, acting guardians, trustees of the poor, or select vestrymen, entitled to act in the ordering of relief to the poor from the poor rate under any local act of parliament, and the churchwardens and overseers of the poor of the several parishes in the city of Salisbury.

The word *"parish"* in this order shall be taken to include any place maintaining its own poor, whether parochial or extra-parochial.

Whenever in describing any person or party, matter or thing, the word importing the singular number or the masculine gender only is used in this order, the same shall be taken to include, and shall be applied to, several persons or parties as well as one person or party, and females as well as males, and several matters or things as well as one matter or thing respectively, unless there be something in the subject or context repugnant to such construction.

Given under our hands and seal of office, this twenty-first day of December, in the year one thousand eight hundred and forty-four.

(Signed) GEO. NICHOLLS,
G. C. LEWIS,
EDMUND W. HEAD.

This order applies to all the unions and parishes named in the schedules A. and B., (pages 15 *and* 16).

---

2. LETTER RESPECTING THE NON-RESIDENT RELIEF GENERAL ORDER.

Poor Law Commission Office,
Somerset House,
December 21, 1844.

Sir,—I am directed by the Poor Law Commissioners to enclose a copy of an order which they have issued on the subject of non-resident relief, which will come into operation on the twenty-fifth day of March next.

The guardians will observe that the order in question is entirely confined to regulating the agency by which the relief of non-resident poor in certain cases, and the mode in which the accounts respecting them, shall be managed, and that it does not permit or forbid the allowance of non-resident relief in any case in which such relief is not now permitted, or is not now forbidden.

The order, moreover, does not prevent the guardians of any union from transmitting relief to a poor person who is non-resident in cases where the same may lawfully be given, through any private channel, or any means other than the officers of another union or parish, however objectionable such a course may generally be. When a course of this description is voluntarily resorted to by the guardians, they cannot hereafter complain if cases of imposition and peculation on the part of the paupers, and of the persons conveying the money, should occur.

All that is done by the present order is, to require that when the agency of another board of guardians is employed, certain rules shall be adhered to. Whether the board of guardians who allow the non-resident relief choose to employ that agency, is a matter for their own consideration, and whether the board of guardians of the union where the pauper resides choose to act in the capacity of agents, and direct their officers to administer the relief, is again a matter of choice.

If two boards do so agree to act together, these regulations must be observed, since no contract in opposition to them could be enforced by one party against the other, and the officers of the respective unions are of course bound to act in conformity with law.

The guardians will see that the relieving officer is expressly prohibited from acting as the agent of any board other than that whose officer he is. The Commissioners are persuaded that the guardians will have seen and felt the inconveniences which have arisen in many places from a different practice too well to be surprised at a restriction of this kind.

These inconveniences indeed form the principal reasons on account of which the Commissioners have thought it expedient to issue this order.

They have found that relieving officers were apparently placed in an anomalous position, receiving orders as it were from more than one board of guardians, and often being liable in two ways for the relief of the same pauper; that is to say, in their capacity of agent to some distant board, and in their position as relieving officers of their own district in which that pauper resides.

For reasons, in some measure similar to those which apply to the relieving officers, and for others of a more general character, the prohibition is extended to assistant overseers and collectors.

It is always to be remembered, that no undertaking to give relief to a pauper residing at a distance has any legal effect in lessening the obligation cast by the law on the guardians and officers of the spot where the pauper dwells or becomes destitute. The board of guardians at a distance may incur a moral responsibility, by promising to provide for the case, and may transmit from time to time the means of subsistence; but if by neglect, or error, or peculation, those means fail, or owing to any change of circumstances, become insufficient, it is on the authorities at the place where the pauper is, that the weight of legal responsibility will fall. A voluntary act on the part of one person, or one body, does not remove the positive legal duty already cast on another. Much of the ambiguity on this head will cease when this order is acted upon, since the relieving officer can only act as the officer and agent of his own board, though some misapprehension is inseparable from any system of non-resident relief.

A further advantage contemplated is, the removal of those opportunities for fraud and for wilful detention of money thus entrusted to a distant officer, which have so often acted as a temptation and a snare to persons who would otherwise have preserved an honest and trustworthy character. And as the money thus misapplied, does not come into the officer's hands in the capacity of officer of the parish or union in which he acts, but as a private agent for distant boards, and for overseers of other parishes in general, in case of peculation, such money could not be recovered from his sureties, since they were answerable for him only in the capacity of relieving officer.

Another benefit, will be the avoiding of errors and mis-statements of a statistical nature which now occur, in consequence of the same persons and the same relief being charged in the accounts of two unions.

The Commissioners feel satisfied, that the regulations will insure a better understanding of the duties and responsibilities connected with the relief of non-resident poor—that they will act as a powerful obstacle to peculation and fraud, and that they will prevent error in the returns of expenditure and the enumeration of paupers, which are now unavoidable. The relief of non-resident and non-settled poor administered under this order, will of course become the subject of correspondence between the board of guardians of the unions where they are relieved, and where they reside; and this correspondence will be conducted by the clerks of the unions concerned. The Commissioners regret that they should impose some trouble on the clerks to the guardians, but they believe that the amount of *additional* trouble is greater in appearance than in reality. Wherever non-resident relief is now given, either the ordinary correspondence with reference to these cases is conducted by the clerk, or difficulties arise from time to time, which produce long and tedious disputes, by letter, leading probably to appeal to the Poor Law Commissioners, and terminating in no satisfactory result, the matter devolving upon the clerk in the more advanced stages, and when complicated by previous misunderstandings.

The return after the audit of the number and amount of accounts outstanding, and other particulars, will enable the guardians to call the attention to any acts of gross neglect on the part of a distant union or parish, and will probably in the end be the means of saving much trouble to the clerk.

I am, Sir,

Your obedient Servant,

EDWIN CHADWICK, *Secretary.*

The Clerk to the Guardians.

III.—OUT-DOOR RELIEF—

1. GENERAL PROHIBITORY ORDER.

To the Guardians of the Poor of the several Unions named in the Schedule hereunto annexed;—

To the Churchwardens and Overseers of the Poor of the several Parishes and Places comprised within the said respective Unions;—

To the Clerk or Clerks to the Justices of the Petty Sessions held for the Division or Divisions in which the Parishes and Places comprised within the said respective Unions are situate;—

And to all others whom it may concern.

We, the Poor Law Commissioners, in pursuance of the authorities vested in us by an Act passed in the fifth year of the reign of his late Majesty King William the Fourth, intituled "*An Act for the Amendment and better Administration of the Laws relating to the Poor in England and Wales,*" do hereby rescind an order, being a general rule of the Poor Law Commissioners, bearing date the second day of August, in the year of our Lord one thousand eight hundred and forty-one, except so far as the same rescinds any order or orders theretofore issued by the Poor Law Commissioners.

And we do hereby also rescind the orders relative to the relief of able-bodied poor persons, issued by the Poor Law Commissioners to the several unions hereunder mentioned, except so far as the same rescind any order or orders theretofore issued by the said Commissioners, or relate to the out-door labour test for able-bodied male paupers; that is to say :—

The order bearing date the ninth day of December one thousand eight hundred and forty-one, and issued to the guardians of the poor of the Burgh of Bury Saint Edmunds;

The order bearing date the tenth day of January one thousand eight hundred and forty-two, and issued to the guardians of the poor of the Aberystwith Union;

The order bearing date the fifteenth day of April one thousand eight hundred and forty-two, and issued to the guardians of the poor of the Ruthin Union;

The order bearing date the thirtieth day of April one thousand eight hundred and forty-two, and issued to the guardians of the poor of the Llanfyllin Union;

The general order bearing date the thirtieth day of July one thousand eight hundred and forty-two, and issued to the guardians of the poor of the Longtown Union, the guardians of the poor of the Whitehaven Union, and the guardians of the poor of the Wigton Union.

The order bearing date the fifth day of August one thousand eight hundred and forty-two, and issued to the guardians of the poor of the Cockermouth Union;

The order bearing date the ninth day of September one thousand eight hundred and forty-two, and issued to the guardians of the poor of the Richmond Union, in the county of York;

The order bearing date the thirtieth day of November one thousand eight hundred and forty-two, and issued to the guardians of the poor of the Ormskirk Union;

The order bearing date the seventeenth day of December one thousand eight hundred and forty-two, and issued to the guardians of the poor of the Hailsham Union;

The order bearing date the twenty-first day of January one thousand eight hundred and forty-three, and issued to the guardians of the poor of the Chard Union;

And the general order bearing date the twenty-seventh day of June one thousand eight hundred and forty-three, and issued to the guardians of the poor of the Saint Asaph Union; the guardians of the poor of the Bala Union; the guardians of the poor of the Bridgend and Cowbridge Union; the guardians of the poor of the Corwen Union; the guardians of the poor of the Festiniog Union; and the guardians of the poor of the Pwllheli Union;

Provided that nothing herein contained shall apply to any relief given under or prohibited by any of the said orders hereby rescinded.

And we do hereby order, direct, and declare, with respect to each and every of the unions named in the schedule hereunto annexed, as follows:

Article I.—Every able-bodied person, male or female, requiring relief from any parish within any of the said unions, shall be relieved wholly in the workhouse of the union, together with such of the family of every such able-bodied person as may be resident with him or her, and may not be in employment, and together with the wife of every such able-bodied male person, if he be a married man, and if she be resident with him; save and except in the following cases :—

1st.—Where such person shall require relief on account of sudden and urgent necessity.

2d.—Where such person shall require relief on account of any sickness, accident, or bodily or mental infirmity affecting such person, or any of his or her family.

3d.—Where such person shall require relief for the purpose of defraying the expenses, either wholly or in part, of the burial of any of his or her family.

4th.—Where such person, being a widow, shall be in the first six months of her widowhood.

5th.—Where such person shall be a widow, and have a legitimate child or legitimate children dependent upon her, and incapable of earning his, her, or their livelihood, and have no illegitimate child born after the commencement of her widowhood.

6th.—Where such person shall be confined in any gaol or place of safe custody, subject always to the regulation contained in Article IV.

7th.—Where such person shall be the wife, or child, of any able-bodied man who shall be in the service of Her Majesty as a soldier, sailor, or marine.

8th.—Where any able-bodied person, not being a soldier, sailor, or marine, shall not reside within the union, but the wife, child, or children of such person shall reside within the same, the board of guardians of the union, according to their discretion, may, subject to the regulation contained in Article IV., afford relief in the workhouse to such wife, child, or children, or may allow out-door relief for any such child or children being within the age of nurture, and resident with the mother within the union.

Article II.—In every case in which out-door relief shall be given on account of sickness, accident, or infirmity, to any able-bodied male person resident within any of the said unions, or to any member of the family of any able-bodied male person, an extract from the medical officer's weekly report (if any such officer shall have attended the case), stating the nature of such sickness, accident, or infirmity, shall be specially entered in the minutes of the proceedings of the board of guardians of the day on which the relief is ordered or subsequently allowed.

But if the board of guardians shall think fit, a certificate under the hand of a medical officer of the union, or of the medical practitioner in attendance on the party, shall be laid before the board, stating the nature of such sickness, accident, or infirmity, and a copy of the same shall be in like manner entered in the minutes.

Article III. No relief shall be given from the poor-rates of any parish comprised in any of the said unions to any person who does not reside in some place within the union, save and except in the following cases :—

1st.—Where such person, being casually within such parish, shall become destitute.

2nd.—Where such person shall require relief on account of any sickness, accident, or bodily or mental infirmity, affecting such person, or any of his or her family.

3rd.—Where such person shall be entitled to receive relief from any parish in which he or she may not be resident, under any order which justices may by law be authorised to make.

4th.—Where such a person, being a widow, shall be in the first six months of her widowhood.

5th.—Where such person is a widow, who has a legitimate child dependent on her for support, and no illegitimate child born after the commencement of her widowhood, and who at the time of her husband's death was resident with him in some place other than the parish of her legal settlement, and not situated in the union in which such parish may be comprised.

6th.—Where such person shall be a child und the age of sixteen, maintained in workhouse or establishment for the education of pauper children not situate within the union.

7th.—Where such person shall be the wife or child residing within the union, of some person not able-bodied, and not residing within the union.

8th.—Where such person shall have been in the receipt of relief from some parish in the union from which such person seeks relief, at some time within the twelve calendar months next preceding the date of that one of the several orders herein-before recited which was applicable to that union, being settled in such parish and not being resident within the union at the time of the allowance of the relief.

Article IV.—Where the husband of any woman is beyond the seas, or in custody of the law, or in confinement in a licensed house or asylum as a lunatic or idiot, all relief which the guardians shall give to his wife, or her child or children, shall be given to such woman, in the same manner, and subject to the same conditions, as if she were a widow.

Article V.—It shall not be lawful for the guardians, or any of their officers, or for the overseer or overseers of any parish in the union, to pay, wholly or in part, the rent of the house or lodging of any pauper, or to apply any portion of the relief ordered to be given to any pauper in payment of any such rent, or to retain any portion of such relief for the purpose of directly or indirectly discharging such rent, in full or in part, for any such pauper.

Provided always, that nothing in this article contained shall apply to any shelter or temporary lodging, procured in any case of sudden and urgent necessity, or mental imbecility, or shall be taken to prevent the said guardians, in regulating the amount of relief to be afforded to any particular person, from considering the expense to be incurred by such person in providing lodging.

Article VI.—Provided always, that in case the guardians of any of the said unions depart in any particular instance from any of the regulations herein-before contained, and within fifteen days after such departure report the same, and the grounds thereof, to the Poor Law Commissioners, and the Poor Law Commissioners approve of such departure, then the relief granted in such particular instance shall, if otherwise lawful, not be deemed to be unlawful, or be subject to be disallowed.

Article VII.—No relief which may be contrary to any regulation in this order shall be given by way of loan; and any relief which may be given to, or on account of, any person above the age of twenty-one, or to his wife, or any part of his or her family under the age of sixteen, under Article I., or any of the exceptions thereto, or under any of the exceptions to Article III., or under Article IV., or under the proviso in Article VI., may, if the guardians think fit, be given by way of loan.

Article VIII.—Whenever the word "parish" is used in this order, it shall be taken to include any place separately maintaining its own poor, whether parochial or extra-parochial.

Article IX.—Whenever the word "union" is used in this order, it shall be taken to include not only an union of parishes formed under the provisions of the herein-before recited Act, but also any union of parishes incorporated or united for the relief or maintenance of the poor under any local Act of Parliament.

Article X.—Whenever the word "guardians" is used in this order, it shall be taken to include not only guardians appointed, or entitled to act, under the provisions of the said herein-before recited Act, but also any governors, directors, managers, or acting guardians entitled to act in the ordering of relief to the poor from the poor-rates under any local Acts of Parliament.

Article XI.—Whenever in this order any article is referred to by its number, the article of this order bearing that number shall be taken to be signified thereby.

Given under our hands and seal of office, this twenty-first day of December, in the year of our Lord one thousand eight hundred and forty-four.

(Signed) GEO. NICHOLLS.
G. C. LEWIS.
EDMUND W. HEAD.

*This order applies to all the unions and parishes named in the schedule A. (page 15), excepting those marked thus *.*

---

2. INSTRUCTIONAL LETTER AS TO THE GENERAL PROHIBITORY ORDER.

Poor Law Commission Office,
Somerset House,
December 21, 1844.

Sir,—In consequence of the provisions contained in the statute of the last session, relative to the relief of able-bodied women under certain circumstances and non-resident poor, the Commissioners have deemed it advisable to make some alterations in their General Order, of the second of August, 1841, usually known as their General Prohibitory Order. They have, as the most convenient course, rescinded that order, and also several orders containing the same provisions, which had been issued to individual unions since its date, and have issued the former order again, with the slight modifications which appear to them to have been rendered necessary.

Although, doubtless, the guardians have a general acquaintance with the explanation of that order, contained in the instructional letter which accompanied the issue of the order, the Commissioners think it desirable to repeat some portion of their former remarks.

Relief of Able-bodied.

1.—Article I.—The only remark on the prohibitory clause which the Commissioners need make is, that the guardians under this clause are not bound to require any child of an able-bodied person, who can support itself, to accompany its parent into the workhouse, if it appear expedient that such child should continue in employment.

2.—Article I. *Exception* 1.]—By "sudden and urgent necessity" (which words are used in section 54 of the Poor Law Amendment Act,) the Commissioners understand any case of destitution requiring instant relief.

It is to be remarked further, that this exception does not authorise *permanent* out-door relief in any case. A case originally of sudden and urgent necessity, which subsequently requires continued relief, loses its character of suddenness and urgency. The relief subsequently required will be either ordinary relief, and therefore to be given in the workhouse, or it may be extraordinary, and given, for example, under the second exception to Article I.

3.—*Exception* 2.]—The second exception provides for the case of any able-bodied man, who is himself insane or temporarily sick, or who has met with an accident, or any of whose family required to be relieved on the ground of insanity, infirmity, accident, or sickness.

4.—*Exception* 3.]—Under this exception relief may be given to able-bodied persons for the funerals of any members of their families, without requiring them to come into the workhouse.

5.—*Exception* 4.]—The exception of widows during the first six months of their widowhood is adopted with a view of enabling persons thus situated to have an adequate interval for the purpose of making such arrangements for their support as their altered condition may require.

6.—*Exception* 5.]—The exception of widows with children, so far as it relates to able-bodied widows in employment, is one respecting which the guardians ought to exercise great circumspection in applying it in practice. The guardians when administering relief under it ought to take into account, that when small weekly allowances in aid of wages are made, they too commonly serve to excuse relations from the payment of contributions to a larger amount; and that the out-door allowances, when given indiscriminately in widowhood, tend to put an end to provident habits, in respect of insurances in sick clubs or otherwise. It should, moreover, be borne in mind, that allowances made by the parish to able-bodied widows in employment do not always confer the advantages intended, inasmuch as their wages, as in the case of able-bodied men, are commonly reduced in consideration of the allowance from the parish; and that such reduction of the wages, combined with the excuse furnished to relations or friends for withholding their contributions, together with the pauper habits thus engendered, often renders such allowances to widows in aid of wages an injury rather than a benefit to them; whilst in some districts this class of able-bodied widows may be so numerous, that their labour (thus depreciated at the expence of the rate-payers,) may be substituted for the more highly paid labour of independent labourers.

7.—The Commissioners trust, that the guardians will seldom find that the ordinary rate of earnings of able-bodied women is so low as not to enable them to support one child at the least; and that the guardians will not adopt any such general rule as that of relieving all widows with one, or with any fixed number of children, but will make a careful inquiry into every case thus to be relieved.

8.—*Exception* 6.]—It sometimes becomes necessary that the guardians should be empowered to give relief to the wife and children in cases where the husband cannot be required to enter the workhouse, on account of his being in a place of legal confinement.

9.—*Exception* 7.]—The state of the law, in reference to married women, explained in par. 10, and the peculiar rights and obligations of soldiers, sailors, and marines, render it desirable to give great latitude to the proceedings of the board of guardians, in respect of the families of persons in these departments of the queen's service. The seventh exception, therefore, allows of relief of ny kind being given to the wife or children of a oldier, sailor, or marine, whether in or out of the workhouse, without requiring the husband to come into the workhouse.

10.—*Exception* 8.]—The eighth exception provides for the case of a wife whose husband is absent from her, either by desertion or otherwise, and is necessary, in consequence of the state of the law, applicable to women thus situated. It had been held that in such cases relief to the children was not relief to the wife; consequently, the wife could not be compelled to come with her children into the workhouse, although a new provision has been made by the statute 7 Vic. c. 101, sec. 25, to be noticed at full hereinafter, in respect of certain women separate from their husbands. If, however, under any circumstances she require relief for herself, the guardians may require her to receive it in the workhouse; and if she require relief for her children, the guardians may require such of them as are above the age of nurture to receive it in the workhouse, whether she do, or do not, come into the workhouse. As regards, however, children under the age of nurture, who may be living with the mother, the guardians cannot remove them from her; so that if she require relief for them, and them only, the guardians must, except in the case hereafter provided for, give out-relief, if relief be necessary.

11.—Article II.—The regulation which requires the entry on the minutes of the Medical Officer's Report, or a medical certificate in case of relief being given to an able-bodied pauper on account of sickness, accident, &c., has been introduced in consequence of a tendency which has displayed itself in various parts of the country, to make exceptions to the prohibitory order on too slight grounds; and the Commissioners think that this provision will have the useful effect of calling the special attention of the guardians to every such case.

If the pauper should not have been attended by a medical officer of the union, a certificate may be given either by the medical practitioner who may have attended him, or by a medical officer of the union who may visit him for the purpose.

Relief of Non-residents.

12.—Article III.—As respects the portion of the order which relates to the relief of persons not resident within their union, the Commissioners desire to point out that it prohibits new cases of relief of this sort, with the exceptions therein mentioned.

13.—Under the provisions of this article, the guardians may relieve a pauper residing within the union, though not residing in the parish to which he belongs; the Commissioners, however, are far from wishing to encourage even this species of non-resident relief. It is true that the frauds and evils which are incidental to non-resident relief, in consequence of the want of inspection and the difficulty of transmitting the relief, do not occur with reference to paupers resident within the union, who are within the reach of the relieving officers; but, nevertheless, the rate-payers of the parish charged with the relief, who by means of the quarterly lists of paupers, can, by personal observation of those who reside in their parish, ascertain whether they are fit objects for relief, are deprived of this protection where the pauper for whom they pay is resident at a distant part of the union. The relief of paupers out of their parish, and out of the relieving district in which the parish is comprised, is not unattended with difficulties both of a legal and practical nature, which are sufficient to make it desirable that the guardians should not, without sufficient ground, permit new cases of this nature even within the union.

14.—The Commissioners have stated fully their views on the subject of non-resident relief, as respects both its legality and expediency, in a minute, dated January 26th, 1841, which is reprinted in the Appendix to their 7th Annual Report, (App. A. No. 1.)

15.—Article III. *Exception* 1.]—The Commissioners have introduced this exception in order to meet the cases of vagrants, who may become casually destitute within the union. It is the duty of the guardians to relieve persons so situated, without reference to the place of their settlement or residence. The Commissioners have had occasion to address several communications to the Metropolitan Boards of Guardians, on the duty of the locality to relieve all cases of urgent destitution. [See the Commissioners' Fourth Annual Report, pages 154, 155, 156, and 157, Appendix A. No. 2—and Fifth Annual Report, page 87, Appendix A. No. 10.]

The Commissioners have not introduced into this article an exception, on account of sudden and urgent necessity. [See *paragraph* 2.] Cases of sudden and urgent necessity manifestly require the prompt attention and vigilant inspection which can only be exercised by the guardians and their officers in the district where the necessity arises.

16.—*Exception* 2.]—This exception corresponds to Exception 2 to Article I. (see *paragraph* 3.) The Commissioners introduced this exception on account of the difficulty which a want of the power of giving temporary relief to non-residents in case of sickness has been found to create in some parts of the country. The commissioners, however, desire to caution the guardians against giving temporary relief, in cases of sickness, to persons not resident within the union, unless they are able to obtain accurate information concerning the case, and can insure adequate and prompt relief, both medical and otherwise. It may be observed, that this exception permits poor persons to be sent to establishments out of the union, intended for the treatment of their respective infirmities, as hospitals for the sick, asylums for the insane, and schools for the blind, or deaf and dumb.

17.—*Exception* 3.]—The third exception is intended expressly to except from the operation of the order, the cases of relief given to non-resident lunatics in asylums under orders of justices, and to persons under orders of removal.

18.—*Exception* 4.]—This exception is similar to the fourth exception to Article I. the reasons for which are stated above in paragraph 5.

19.—*Exception* 5.]—This exception is that which the legislature has introduced in the 7th and 8th Vic. c. 101, sec. 26, and upon which the Commissioners have already made their remarks in their Circular Letter to Boards of Guardians, dated the 17th October last.

20.—*Exception* 6.]—This exception removes the restriction upon guardians from sending children to a workhouse or establishment for the training of pauper children, which may be situated out of their union, where, but for the prohibition of relief to non-residents contained in the order, they might lawfully do so.

21.—*Exception* 7.]—This exception enables the guardians to relieve the resident family of a non-resident man, provided he be not able-bodied, without requiring them to come into the workhouse.

22.—*Exception* 8.]—This exception permits the continuance of non-resident relief to all paupers (not being able-bodied persons within Article I.) who were in the receipt of relief from some parish in the union, within the twelve calendar months next preceding the date of the several orders issued to the different unions set forth in the schedule. Consequently, it permits the continuance of non-resident relief to the infirm through age, or any other cause, and to able-bodied widows with a child, or children, who were in the receipt of parochial relief from the union within that period.

23.—Article IV.—This Article is introduced in

conformity with the new provision contained in the 7 and 8 Vic. c. 101, s. 25, in regard to the relief of women separated from their husbands, in certain cases particularly specified, who are by that provision to be treated as widows in respect to relief to be afforded to them by guardians. The Commissioners refer again to their observations in the Circular Letter of the 17th of October last upon this subject.

24.—Article V.—This Article is intended to prevent a practice which has prevailed in some parts of the country, whereby the poor-rates have been made a fund for the payment of rents directly to the landlords. In all cases where the pauper is so far destitute as to require a lodging, or the means of paying for one, if the guardians do not deem it expedient in the particular case to require the party to come into the workhouse, they should supply to the pauper the means of paying for such lodging.

Cases of peculiar Urgency.

25.—Article VI.—It is possible, although not probable, that cases may occasionally arise which present very peculiar circumstances, and which do not fall within any of the exceptions contained in the present order. The Commissioners think it desirable in cases of that kind, in which the immediate withdrawal or denial of out-door relief might appear likely to produce serious evil to the applicant, that the guardians should give out-door relief, or take a portion of the applicant's family into the workhouse, and report the case within fifteen days to the Poor Law Commissioners, as a case of peculiar urgency, in order that the Commissioners may give their opinion thereupon. The Commissioners have accordingly introduced this proviso, enabling the guardians to pursue this course with respect to exceptional cases of this description.

Relief by way of Loan.

26.—Article VII.—The first part of Article VII. is introduced in order to put an end to a misapprehension of the law which existed in some boards of guardians, viz.:—that although the prohibitory order prevented them from *giving* out-door relief, they might nevertheless *lend* it. The second part of the Article enables the guardians to make all the relief which may be given to persons above twenty-one years of age, or their families, a loan under the 58th section of the Poor Law Amendment Act of 1834.

27.—Articles IX. and X.—These Articles are introduced because the order is addressed to four unions of parishes formed not under the Poor Law Amendment Act, but under local Acts of Parliament, viz.—East and West Flegg, Forehoe, Samford, and Tunstead and Happing.

Signed by order of the Board,
EDWIN CHADWICK, *Secretary.*

To the Clerk of the Board of Guardians.

Schedule A.

Aberaeron, Abergavenny, Aberystwith, Abingdon, St. Albans, Alcester, Alderbury, Alnwick, Alresford, Alton, Altrincham, Amersham, Amesbury, Ampthill, Andover, *Anglesey, St. Asaph, Ashby-de-la-Zouch, East Ashford, West Ashford, Aston, Atcham, Atherstone, Auckland, St. Austel, Axbridge, Axminster, Aylesbury, North Aylesford, Aylsham, Bakewell, Bala, Banbury, *Bangor and Beaumaris, Barnet, Barnstaple, Barrow-upon-Soar, Basford, Basingstoke, Bath, Battle, Beaminster, Bedale, Bedford, Bedminster, Belford, Bellingham, Belper, Berkhampstead, Berwick-upon-Tweed, Beverley, Bicester, Bideford, Biggleswade, Billericay, Billesdon, Bingham, Bishop's Stortford, Blaby, *Blackburn, Blandford, Blean, Blofield, Blything, *Bodmin, *Bolton, *Bootle, Bosmere and Claydon, Boston, *Great Boughton, Bourn, Brackley, Bradfield, Bradford (Wilts), *Bradford (York), Braintree, Brampton, Brecknock, *Brentford, Bridge, Bridgend and Cowbridge, Bridgnorth, Bridgwater, *Bridlington, Bridport, †*Bristol, Brixworth, Bromley, Bromsgrove, Bromyard, Buckingham, *Builth, Buntingford, *Burnley, Burton-upon-Trent, *Bury, †Bury Saint Edmunds, Caistor, Calne, Cambridge, *Camelford, †*Canterbury, Cardiff, Cardigan, *Carlisle, Carmarthen, *Carnarvon, Castle Ward, Catherington, Caxton and Arrington, Cerne, Chailey, Chapel-en-le-Frith, Chard, Cheadle, Chelmsford, Cheltenham, Chepstow, *Chertsey, †*Chester, Chesterfield, Chester-le street, Chesterton, *Chichester, Chippenham, Chipping Norton, Chipping Sodbury, *Chorley, *Chorlton, Christchurch, Church Stretton, Cirencester, Cleobury Mortimer, Clifton, *Clitheroe, Clun, Clutton, Cockermouth, Colchester, Columb St. Major, *Congleton, *Conway, Cookham, Corwen, Cosford, †*Coventry, Cranbrook, Crediton, Crickhowel, Cricklade and Wootten Bassett, Croydon, Cuckfield, Darlington, Dartford, Daventry, Depwade, Derby, Devizes, *Dewsbury, Docking, *Dolgelly, Doncaster, Dorchester, Dore, Dorking, Dover, Downham, Drayton, Driffield, Droitwich, Droxford, Dudley, *Dulverton, Dunmow, Durham, Dursley, *Easington, Easingwold, Eastbourne, East Grinstead, Easthamptead, East Retford, Eastry, East Ward, *Ecclesall Bierlow, *Edmonton, Elham, Ellesmere, Ely, Epping, Epsom, Erpingham, Eton, Evesham, †*Exeter, St. Faith, *Falmouth, Fareham, Faringdon, Faversham, Festiniog, †East and West Flegg, Foleshill, Fordingbridge, †Forehoe, Freebridge Lynn, Frome, *Fylde, Gainsborough, *Garstang, *Gateshead, St. German's, Glanford Brigg, Glendale, Glossop, Gloucester, Godstone, Goole, Grantham,

Gravesend and Milton, *Greenwich, Guildford, Guiltcross, Guisborough, *Hackney, Hailsham, *Halifax, Halstead, Haltwhistle, Hambledon, Hardingstone, Hartismere, Hartley Wintney, *Haslingden, Hastings, *Hatfield, Havant, Haverfordwest, Hay, Hayfield, Headington, *Helmsley Blackmoor, Helston, Hemel Hempstead, *Hendon, Henley, Henstead, Hereford, Hertford, Hexham, Highworth and Swindon, Hinckley, Hitchin, Holbeach, *Holborn, Hollingbourn, *Holsworthy, Holywell, Honiton, Hoo, Horncastle, Horsham, Houghton-le-Spring, Howden Hoxne, *Huddersfield, Hungerford, Huntingdon, Hursley, Ipswich, St. Ives, *Keighley, *Kendal, *Kensington, Kettering, Keynsham, Kidderminster, Kingsbridge, Kingsclere, *King's Lynn, King's Norton, *Kingston-upon-Thames, Kington, Knighton, *Lampeter, *Lancaster, Lanchester, Langport, Launceston, Ledbury, Leek, *Leicester, *Leigh, Leighton Buzzard, Leominster, Lewes, *Lewisham, Lexden and Winstree, Leyburn, Lichfield, Lincoln, Linton, Liskeard, Llandilo Fawr, Llandovery, Llanelly, Llanfyllin, *Llanrwst, Lodden and Clavering, *City of London, *East London, *West London, Longtown, Loughborough, Louth, Ludlow, Luton, Lutterworth, Lymington, *Macclesfield, *Machynlleth, Madeley, Maidstone, Maldon, Malling, Malmsbury, Malton, *Manchester, Mansfield, Market Bosworth, Market Harboro', Marlborough, Martley, Medway, Melksham, Melton Mowbray, Mere, Meriden, *Merthyr Tidvil, Midhurst, Mildenhall, Milton, Mitford and Launditch, Monmouth, Morpeth, †*Mutford and Lothingland, Nantwich, Narberth, Neath, St. Neots, Newark, Newbury, Newcastle-in-Emlyn, Newcastle-under-Lyne, *Newcastle-upon-Tyne, Newent, New Forest, Newhaven, Newmarket, Newport (Monmouth), Newport (Salop), Newport Pagnell, †*New Sarum (otherwise Salisbury), Newton Abbot, *Newtown and Llanidloes, *Northallerton, Northampton, Northleach, Northwich, North Witchford, *Nottingham, Nuneaton, Oakham, Okehampton, *St. Olave's, Ongar, Ormskirk, Orsett, †*Oswestry, Oundle, †*Oxford, *Pateley Bridge, Patrington, Pembroke, Penkridge, Penrith, Penzance, Pershore, Peterborough, Petersfield, Petworth, Pewsey, Pickering, Plomesgate, Plympton St. Mary, *Pocklington, Pont-y-Pool, Poole, *Poplar, Portsea Island, Potterspury, *Prescot, *Presteign, *Preston, Pwllheli, *Radford, Reading, Redruth, Reeth, Reigate, *Rhayadar, *Richmond (Surrey), Richmond (York), Ringwood, Risbridge, *Rochdale, Rochford, Romford, Romney Marsh, Romsey, Ross, Rothbury, *Rotherham, Royston, Rugby, *Runcorn, Ruthin, Rye, Saffron Walden, †*St. Margaret and St. John the Evangelist, (Westminster), †*Salisbury (otherwise New Sarum), *Salford, †Samford, *St. Saviour's, Scarborough, Sulcoates, *Sedbergh, Sedgefield, Seisdon, Selby, *Settle, Sevenoaks, Shaftesbury, Shardlow, *Sheffield, Sheppey, Shepton Mallett, Sherborne, Shiffnall, Shipston-upon-Stour, *Skipton, Skirlaugh, Sleaford, Solihull, Southam, †*Southampton, South Molton, South Shields, South Stoneham, Southwell, Spalding, Spilsby, Stafford Staines, Stamford, *Stepney, Steyning, Stockbridge, *Stockport, *Stockton, *Stokesley, Stone, Stourbridge, Stow, Stow-on-the-Wold, *Strand, Stratford-upon-Avon, *Stratton, Stroud, Sturminster, Sudbury, *Sunderland, Swaffham, Swansea, Tamworth, Taunton, Tavistock, Teesdale, Tenbury, Tendring, Tenterden, Tetbury, Tewkesbury, Thakeham, Thame, Isle of Thanet, Thetford, Thingoe, Thirsk, St. Thomas, Thornbury, Thorne, Thrapston, Ticehurst, Tisbury, Tiverton, *Todmorden, Tonbridge, Torrington, Totnes, Towcester, *Tregaron, *Truro, Tunstead and Happing, Tynemouth, Uckfield, *Ulverstone, Uppingham, Upton-upon-Severn, Uttoxeter, Uxbridge, *Wakefield, Wallingford, Walsal, Walsingham, *Wandsworth and Clapham, Wangford, Wantage, Ware, Wareham and Purbeck, Warminster, *Warrington, Warwick, Watford, Wayland, Weardale, Wellingborough, Wellington (Salop), Wellington (Somerset), Wells, Welwyn, Wem, Weobly, Westbourne, West Bromwich, Westbury-upon-Severn, Westbury and Whorwelsdown, *West Derby, West Firle, West Ham, West Hampnett, West Ward, Weymouth, Wheatenhurst, Whitby, Whitchurch (Southampton), *Whitechapel, Whitehaven, *Wigan, Wigton, Williton, Wilton, Wimborne and Cranborne, Wincanton, Winchcombe, New Winchester, Windsor, Winslow, Wirral, Wisbeach, Witham, Witney, Woburn, Wokingham, Wolstanton and Burslem, Wolverhampton, Woodbridge, Woodstock, Worcester, Worksop, *Wortley, Wrexham, Wycombe, Yeovil, *York.

Schedule B.

*Alston with Garrigill, †*Birmingham, *East Stonehouse, *Great Yarmouth. *Leeds, *Liverpool, *St. George the Martyr (Southwark), *St. George in the East, *St. Giles, Camberwell, †*St. Leonard, Shoreditch, *St. Luke, Chelsea, †*St. Luke, Middlesex, †*St. James, Clerkenwell, *St. Martin in the Fields, *St. Mary, Lambeth, *St. Mary Magdalen, Bermondsey, *St. Mary, Rotherhithe, *St. Matthew, Bethnal Green, *Stoke-upon-Trent, †*Whitchurch (Salop), *Whittlesea, St. Mary and St. Andrew.

*** *The order relating to the apprenticing of poor children applies to all the above unions and parishes, excepting those marked thus †; the order relating to non-resident relief applies to all the above unions and parishes; and the prohibitory order applies to all the above unions, excepting those marked thus *.*

LONDON:
Printed by Order of the Poor Law Commissioners, by BLACKBURN and PARDON, 6, Hatton Garden, and Published by CHARLES KNIGHT and Co., 22, Ludgate Street Publishers to the Poor Law Commissioners.

AN OFFICIAL CIRCULAR OF PUBLIC DOCUMENTS AND INFORMATION:

DIRECTED BY THE POOR LAW COMMISSIONERS TO BE PRINTED, CHIEFLY FOR THE USE OF THE MEMBERS AND PERMANENT OFFICERS OF BOARDS OF GUARDIANS, UNDER THE POOR LAW AMENDMENT ACT.

No. 44. CIRCULAR ISSUED FEBRUARY 1, 1845.

Poor Law Commission Office,
Somerset House,
January 31*st*, 1845.

THE Poor Law Commissioners, on a review of their Minutes, directed that the following general orders and instructional letter be printed and circulated for the information of the Guardians and Officers of the several Unions, viz.:—

By Order of the Board,

EDWIN CHADWICK, *Secretary*.

I.—ACCOUNTS.

TAXATION OF ATTORNEYS' BILLS.—GENERAL ORDER.

To the Clerks of the Peace of the several Counties, Ridings, Divisions, and Places, in England and Wales;—
To the Guardians of the Poor of the several Unions and Parishes in England and Wales;—
To the Overseers of the Poor of the several Parishes and Places in England and Wales;—
And to all whom it may concern.

Whereas it was enacted by the Act passed in the last session of parliament, intituled "*An Act for the further Amendment of the laws relating to the Poor in England*," that, on application of any overseer, or of any board of guardians, or of any attorney at law, it should be the duty of the clerk of the peace of the county, or place, or his deputy, if thereunto required, to tax any bill due to any solicitor or attorney in respect of business performed on behalf of any parish or union situate wholly, or in part, within such county, or place; and that the allowance of any sum on such taxation should be *primâ facie* evidence of the reasonableness of the amount, but not of the legality of the charge; and that the clerk of the peace should be allowed for such taxation after the rate to be fixed from time to time by the master of the crown office, and declared by an order of the said Commissioners.

And whereas the master of the crown office has fixed the rate of allowance to the clerk of the peace in respect of such taxation as herein declared.

Now, therefore, We, the Poor Law Commissioners, in pursuance of the statute aforesaid, do hereby declare, that the clerk of the peace of every county, or place in England and Wales, shall be allowed for the taxation of every bill due to any solicitor or attorney, in respect of business performed on behalf of any parish or union, after the rate of *four-pence per sheet*, or folio, of *seventy-two words* each.

Given under our hands and seal of office, this twenty-first day of November, in the year one thousand eight hundred and forty-four.

(L. S.) (Signed) GEO. NICHOLLS,
EDMUND W. HEAD.

II.—APPRENTICING POOR CHILDREN.

GENERAL ORDER ADDRESSED TO UNIONS AND PARISHES GOVERNED BY BOARDS OF GUARDIANS, UNDER LOCAL ACTS.

TO THE GUARDIANS OF THE POOR of the several Unions and of the several Parishes named in the Schedule hereunto annexed, and the Officers of such Unions and Parishes;—

To the Churchwardens and Overseers of the several Parishes and Places comprised within the said Unions, and of the several other Parishes named in the said Schedule;—

To the Clerk or Clerks to the Justices of the Petty Sessions held for the Division or Divisions in which the Parishes and Places comprised within the said Unions, and the said other Parishes named in the said Schedule, are situate;—

And to all others whom it may concern.

IN PURSUANCE of the powers vested in us by an Act passed in the fifth year of the reign of his late majesty King William the Fourth, intituled "*An Act for the Amendment and better Administration of the Laws relating to the Poor in England and Wales,*" and an Act passed in the seventh and eighth year of the reign of her present majesty Queen Victoria, intituled "*An Act for the further Amendment of the Laws relating to the Poor in England,*" We, the Poor Law Commissioners, do make the following rules and regulations in regard to the apprenticing of poor children of the several unions named in the schedule A. hereunto annexed, and of the parishes named in the schedule B. hereunto annexed.

The Parties.

Article 1.—No child under the age of *nine* years shall be bound apprentice;

and no child that cannot read, and write his own name.

No child shall be so bound to a person who is not a housekeeper, or assessed to the poor rate in his own name;

or who is a journeyman, or a person not carrying on trade or business on his own account;

or who is under the age of twenty-one;

or a married woman.

The Premium.

Article 2.—No premium other than clothing for the apprentice shall be given upon the binding of any person above the age of *fourteen*, unless such person be maimed, deformed, or suffering from some permanent bodily infirmity, so that the nature of the work or trade which such person is fit to perform or exercise is restricted.

Article 3.—Where any premium is given it shall consist in part of clothes supplied to the apprentice at the commencement of the binding, and in part of money, one moiety whereof shall be paid to the master at the binding, and the residue at the termination of the first year of the binding.

Term.

Article 4.—No apprentice shall be bound for more than *eight* years.

Consent.

Article 5.—No person above *fourteen* years of age shall be so bound without his *consent*.

And no child under the age of *sixteen* years shall be so bound without the consent of the father of such child, or if the father be dead, or be disqualified to give such consent, as hereinafter provided, or if such child be a bastard, without the consent of the mother, if living, of such child.

Provided that where the parent of such child whose consent would be otherwise requisite, is transported beyond the seas, or is in the custody of the law, having been convicted of some *felony*, or for the space of six calendar months before the time of executing the indenture has deserted such child, or for such space of time has been in the service of her Majesty, or of the East India Company, in foreign parts, such parent, if the father, shall be deemed to be disqualified as herein-before stated, and if it be the mother, no such consent shall be required.

Place of Service.

Article 6.—No child shall be bound to a

master whose place of business, whereat the child is to work and live, shall be distant more than *thirty* miles from the place in which the child is residing at the time of the binding ;

Unless in any particular case the Poor Law Commissioners shall, on application to them, otherwise permit.

Preliminaries to the Binding.

Article 7.—If the child, whom it is proposed to bind apprentice, be in the workhouse, and under the age of *fourteen*, the guardians shall require a certificate in writing from the medical officer of the workhouse, or from some medical man duly licensed to practise, as to the fitness in regard to bodily health and strength of such child to be bound apprentice to the proposed trade, and shall also ascertain from the master of the workhouse the capacity of the child for such binding in other respects.

Article 8.—If the child be not in the workhouse, but in the union or parish by the guardians of which it is proposed that it shall be bound, a relieving officer or some other person authorised by the persons proposing to bind such child, shall examine into the circumstances of the case, the condition of the child, and of his parents, if any, and the residence of the proposed master, the nature of his trade, the number of other apprentices, if any, then bound to him, and generally as to the fitness of the particular binding, and shall report the result of his inquiry to the board of guardians.

Article 9.—If the board of guardians think proper to proceed with the binding, they shall, when the child is under the age of *fourteen*, direct such child to be taken to a medical man duly licensed to practise, to be examined as to his fitness in respect of bodily health and strength for the proposed trade or business ; in order that such medical man may certify in writing according to his judgment in the matter, which certificate shall be produced previously to the binding to the guardians.

Article 10.—If the child be residing in some other parish or union, the guardians who propose to bind him shall not proceed to do so unless they receive such a report as is required in Article 8 from the relieving officer or some other officer administering the relief of the poor of the district in which such child is residing, and a certificate from some medical practitioner of the neighbourhood of the child's residence, to the effect required in Article 9.

Article 11.—When a premium is proposed to be given, in a case within the provision of Article 2, the guardians shall require a certificate in writing of some medical practitioner, certifying that the person is maimed, deformed, or disabled, to the extent specified in such article, and shall cause a copy of such certificate to be entered on their minutes before they proceed to execute the indenture.

Article 12.—When such certificate, as is required by Articles 7, 9, and 10, is received, or in case from the age of the child no such certificate is required, the guardians shall direct that the child, and the proposed master, or some person on his behalf, and in case the child be under the age of *sixteen*, the parent or person in whose custody such child shall be then living, shall attend some meeting of the board to be then appointed.

Article 13.—At such meeting, if such parties appear, the said guardians shall examine into the circumstances of the case ; and if, after making all due inquiries, and hearing the objections (if any be made) on the part of the relatives or friends of such child, they shall deem it proper that the binding shall be effected, they may forthwith cause the indentures to be prepared, and in such manner and with such sanction as the law shall require, to be executed, provided that when the same shall have been executed by the master and the other parties lawfully authorised, the same shall be signed by the child as herein-after provided.

Article 14.—If the proposed master reside out of the union or parish on account of which the binding is to be effected, but in some other union or parish under a board of guardians, whether formed under the provisions of the first-recited act or of the act of the twenty-second year of the reign of King George the Third, intituled "*An Act for the better Relief and Employment of the Poor*," or of any local act, the guardians shall, before proceeding to effect the binding, communicate in writing the proposal to the guardians of such other union or parish, and request to be informed whether such binding is open to any objection, and if no objection be reported by such guardians within the space of one calendar month, or, if the objection does not appear to the guardians proposing to bind the child to be sufficient to prevent the binding, the same may be proceeded with ; and when the indentures shall have been executed, the guardians who executed the same shall cause notice thereof in writing to be sent to the guardians of the union or parish wherein the said apprentice is to reside.

Indenture.

Article 15.—The indenture shall be executed in duplicate, by the master and the guardians, or the persons lawfully authorised to do so, and shall not be valid unless signed by the proposed apprentice, without aid or assistance, in the presence of the said guardians; and the consent of the parent, where requisite, shall be testified by such parent signing with his name or mark, to be properly attested, at the foot of the said indenture, and where such consent is dispensed with under the provision contained in Article 5, the cause of such dispensation shall be stated at the foot of the indenture, by any clerk or other officer acting as clerk to the said guardians.

Article 16.—The indenture shall contain mention of the place or places at which the apprentice is to work and live.

Article 17.—One part of such indenture, when executed, shall be kept by the guardians; the other shall be delivered to the master.

Duties of the Master.

Article 18.—And we do hereby prescribe the duties of the master to whom such poor child may be apprenticed, and the terms and conditions to be inserted in the said indentures, as follows:—

No. 1.—The master shall teach the child the trade, business, or employment set forth in the indenture, unless the board of guardians authorise the substitution of another trade or business.

No. 2.—He shall maintain the said child with proper food and nourishment.

No. 3.—He shall provide a proper lodging for the said child.

No. 4.—He shall supply to the said child one suit of proper clothing every year during the term of the binding.

No. 5.—He shall, in case the said child be affected with any disease or sickness, or meet with any accident, procure, at his own cost, adequate medical or surgical assistance to be supplied by some duly qualified medical man, for such child.

No. 6.—He shall, once at least on every Sunday, cause the child to attend some place of Divine worship, if there be any such within a reasonable distance, according to the religious persuasion in which the child has been brought up, so, however, that no child shall be required by the master to attend any place of worship to which his parents or surviving parent may object, nor, when he shall be above the age of *sixteen*, any place to which he may himself object.

No. 7.—Where such parents or parent or next of kin shall desire it, he shall allow the said child, while under the age of *sixteen*, to attend any Sunday or other school which shall be situated within the same parish or within *two* miles distance from his residence on every Sunday, and, if there be no such school which such child can attend, shall at some reasonable hour on every Sunday allow any minister of the religious persuasion of the child to have access to such child for the purpose of imparting religious instruction.

No. 8.—Where the apprentice continues bound after the age of *seventeen* years the master shall pay to such apprentice, for and in respect of every week that he duly and properly serves the said master, as a remuneration, a sum to be inserted in the indenture, or to be agreed upon by the guardians and the said master when that time arrives, or, if they cannot agree, to be settled by some person to be then chosen by the said master and such guardians, and until such sum be agreed upon or settled, not less than one *fourth* of the amount then commonly paid as wages to journeymen in the said trade, business, or employment.

No. 9.—The master shall, by himself, or by his agent, produce the apprentice to the board of guardians by whom such apprentice was bound, or to their successors in office, at their ordinary meeting next preceding the end of the first year of the binding, and before the receipt of the remainder of the premium, if any be due, and shall in like manner, produce the said apprentice at some one of their ordinary meetings, to be held at or about the middle of the term, and whenever afterwards required to do so by the said guardians or their successors.

Provided that if the apprentice reside out of the union or parish by the guardians whereof he was bound, the apprentice shall be produced, as herein-before directed, to any board of guardians of the union or parish, as described in Article 14, or if there be no such board of guardians, then to the overseers of the parish in which the apprentice may be residing.

No. 10.—The master shall not cause the said apprentice to work or live more than *ten miles* from the place or places mentioned in the indenture, according to Article 16, without the leave of the guardians so binding him, or their successors.

Article 19.—These duties of the master shall be enforced by covenants and conditions to be inserted in the said indenture so to be executed by him.

Article 20.—The master shall also covenant not to assign nor to cancel the indenture, without the consent of the guardians or their successors, previously obtained, under a penalty to be specified in the said covenant, and to pay to the said guardians or their successors all costs and expenses that they may incur in consequence of the said apprentice not being supplied with medical or surgical assistance by the master, in case the same shall be at any time requisite.

Article 21.—The indenture shall be made subject to the following provisoes :—

1.—That if the master take the benefit of any act for the relief of insolvent debtors, or be discharged under any such act, such indenture shall forthwith become of no further force or effect.

2.—That if on a conviction for a breach of any one of the aforesaid covenants before a justice of the peace in pursuance of the provisions of the statute in such case made and provided, the guardians who may be parties to the said indenture, or their successors, shall declare by a resolution that the indenture shall be determined, and shall transmit a copy of such resolution, under the hand of their clerk or the person for the time being acting as such, by the post or otherwise, to the said master, such indenture shall, except in respect of all rights and liabilities then accrued, forthwith become of no further force or effect.

Explanation of Terms.

Article 22.—The word *union* in this order shall be taken to include any union of parishes incorporated or united for the relief or maintenance of the poor under any local act of parliament.

Article 23.—The word *guardians* in this order shall be taken to include any governors, deputy governors, assistants, directors, managers, acting guardians, trustees of the poor, or select vestrymen, entitled to act in the ordering of relief to the poor from the poor-rate under any local act of parliament.

Article 24.—Whenever the word *parish* is used in this order, it shall be taken to include any place maintaining its own poor, whether parochial or extra-parochial.

Article 25.—The word *child* in this order shall signify any person under the age of twenty-one years.

Article 26.—Whenever, in describing any person or party, matter or thing, the word importing the singular number or the masculine gender only is used in this order, the same shall be taken to include and shall be applied to several persons or parties as well as one person or party, and females as well as males, and several matters or things as well as one matter or thing, respectively, unless there be something in the subject or context repugnant to such construction.

Article 27.—Whenever in this order any article is referred to by its number, the article of this order bearing that number shall be taken to be signified thereby.

Article 28.—Provided that nothing herein contained shall apply to the apprenticing poor children to the sea service.

Article 29.—And, in pursuance of the provisions contained in the said first-recited act, we do direct, that whenever any justice or justices shall, under any authority of law, assent or consent, order or allow, of the binding of any poor child as apprentice, such justice or justices shall certify at the foot of the indenture and the counterpart thereof, in the form and manner following ; that is to say,

" I, *or* we, *(as the case may be)* justice *or* justices of the peace of and in the county *(or other jurisdiction, as the case may be)* of , who have assented to, ordered, *or* allowed the above binding, do hereby certify that we have examined and ascertained that the rules, orders, and regulations of the Poor Law Commissioners, for the binding of poor children apprentices, and applicable to the above-named parish, *(or other place, as the case may be)* contained in their general order bearing date the twenty-ninth day of January, one thousand eight hundred and forty-five, have been complied with.

" Signed this day of

——————— Signature."

SCHEDULE A. containing the Names of the Unions to which the present Order applies.

Bury St. Edmunds	Chichester
Canterbury	Coventry
Chester	Exeter

Flegg, East and West Hundred
Forehoe Hundred
Mutford and Lothingland Hundred.
Norwich
Oswestry
Oxford
Plymouth
St. Giles in the Fields and St. George Bloomsbury
Samford Hundred
Southampton
Tunstead and Happing Hundred
Wight, Isle of

SCHEDULE B. containing the Names of the Parishes to which the present order applies.

Birmingham
Kingston-upon-Hull
St. George Hanover Sq.
St. Mary Islington
St. Mary-le-bone
St. Mary Newington
St. Pancras
Stoke Damerell
Whitchurch (Salop)

Given under our hands and seal of office this twenty-ninth day of January, in the year one thousand eight hundred and forty-five.

(Signed)

(L. S.) GEO. NICHOLLS,
G. C. LEWIS.

III.—ELECTION OF GUARDIANS—

1. GENERAL ORDER.

TO THE GUARDIANS OF THE POOR of the several Unions named in the Schedule hereunto annexed;—

To the Churchwardens and Overseers of the Poor of the several Parishes comprised in the said several Unions;—

To the Clerk or Clerks to the Justices of the Petty Sessions held for the Division or Divisions in which the said several Parishes are situate;—

And to all others whom it may concern.

WE, THE POOR LAW COMMISSIONERS, do hereby, under the authority of an Act passed in the fifth year of the reign of His late Majesty King William the Fourth, intituled, "*An Act for the Amendment and better Administration of the Laws relating to the Poor in England and Wales,*" rescind all such of the provisions contained in any order, or orders, under the hands and seal of the Poor Law Commissioners, as direct the manner of conducting the election of guardians of the poor for the several parishes comprised in the several unions named in the schedule hereunto annexed.

And we do hereby order and direct henceforth in regard thereto, with reference to each of the unions named in the said schedule, as follows:

Article 1.—The overseers of every parish shall before the *twenty-sixth day of March* in every year, distinguish in the rate-books, or enter in some other book to be provided for the purpose, the name of every rate-payer in their parish, who has been rated to the relief of the poor for the whole year immediately preceding the said day, and has paid the poor-rates made and assessed upon him for the period of one whole year, except those which have been made or become due within the six months immediately preceding the said day.

Article 2.—The clerk to the board of guardians shall at every future annual election of guardians perform the duties hereby imposed upon him, and all other duties suitable to his office which it may be requisite for him to perform in conducting and completing such election; and in case the office of clerk shall be vacant at any time when any proceeding is to be taken under this order, or in case the clerk, from illness or other sufficient cause, shall be unable to discharge such duties, the guardians shall appoint some person to perform such of the duties imposed by this order upon the clerk as shall then remain to be performed, and the person so appointed shall perform such duties.

Article 3.—The guardians shall, before or during every such election, appoint a competent number of persons to assist the clerk in conducting and completing the election in conformity with this order, but if the guardians shall not make such appointment within the requisite time, the clerk shall take such measures for securing the necessary assistance as he shall deem advisable.

Article 4.—In selecting such persons, the guardians shall choose such of the paid officers of the union as may be willing, and as may appear to the guardians to be able to afford such assistance, without interruption to the proper discharge of their other duties.

Article 5.—The persons appointed under Articles 3 and 4, shall obey all the directions which may be given by the clerk for the execution of this order.

Article 6.—The overseers of every parish in the union, and every officer having the custody of the poor-rate books of any such parish, shall attend the clerk at such times as he shall require their attendance, until the completion of the election of guardians, and shall, if required by him, produce to him such rate-books, and the registers of owners and proxies, together with the statements of owners, and appointments and statements of proxies, and all books and papers relating to such rates in their possession or power.

Provided that where any register of owners shall have been prepared in any parish containing a population exceeding two thousand persons, it shall not be necessary to produce the statements of owners.

Mode of conducting the Election.

Article 7.—The clerk shall prepare and sign a notice, which may be in the form marked (A.), hereunto annexed, and which shall contain the following particulars:—

1st. The number of guardians to be elected for each parish in the union.
2nd. The qualification of guardians.
3rd. The qualification of voters.
4th. The persons by whom, and the places in each parish where, the nomination papers in respect of such parish are to be received, and the last day on which they are to be sent.
5th. The mode of voting in case of a contest, and the days on which the voting papers will be delivered and collected.
6th. The time and place for the examination and casting up of the votes.

And the clerk shall cause such notice to be published on or before the *fifteenth day of March,* in the following manner:—

1st. A printed copy of such notice shall be affixed on the principal external gate or door of every workhouse in the union, and shall from time to time be renewed, if necessary, until the *ninth day of April.*
2nd. Printed copies of such notice shall likewise be affixed on such places in each of the parishes in the union as are ordinarily made use of for affixing thereon notices of parochial business.

Article 8.—Any person entitled to vote in any parish, may nominate for the office of guardian thereof, himself, if legally qualified, or any other person or number of persons (not exceeding the number of guardians to be elected for such parish) legally qualified to be elected for that office.

Article 9.—Every nomination shall be in writing, in the form marked (B.), hereunto annexed, and be signed by one person only, as the party nominating, and shall be sent on or before the *twenty-sixth day of March* to the clerk, or to such person or persons as may have been appointed to receive the same, and the clerk or such person or persons, shall, on the receipt thereof, mark thereon the date of its receipt, and also a number according to the order of its receipt; provided that no nomination sent after the said *twenty-sixth day of March* shall be valid.

Article 10.—If the number of the persons nominated for the office of guardian for any parish shall be the same as, or less than, the number of guardians to be elected for such parish, such persons, if duly qualified, shall be deemed to be the elected guardians for such parish for the ensuing year, and shall be certified as such by the clerk under his hand as hereinafter provided.

Article 11.—But if the number of the duly qualified persons nominated for the office of guardian for any parish shall exceed the number of guardians to be elected therein, the clerk shall cause voting-papers, in the form marked (C.), hereunto annexed, to be prepared and filled up, and shall insert therein the names of all the persons nominated in the order in which the nomination papers were received, and shall on *the fifth day of April* cause one of such voting papers to be delivered by the persons appointed for that purpose, to the address in such parish of each rate-payer, owner, and proxy qualified to vote therein.

Article 12.—If the clerk shall consider that any person nominated is not duly qualified to be a guardian, he shall state in the voting paper the fact that such person has been nominated, but that he considers such person not to be duly qualified.

Article 13.—If any person put in nomination for the office of guardian shall tender to the officer conducting the election, his refusal, in writing, to serve such office, and if, in consequence of such refusal the number of persons nominated for the office of guardian for such parish, shall be the *same as,* or *less* than, the number of guardians to be elected for such parish, all or so many of the remaining candidates as shall be duly qualified shall be deemed to be the elected guardians for such parish for the ensuing year, and shall be certified as such by the clerk under his hand as hereinafter provided.

Article 14.—Each voter shall write his initials in the voting paper delivered to him against the name or names of the person or persons (not exceeding the number of guardians to be elected in the parish) for whom he intends to vote, and shall sign such voting paper; and when any person votes as a proxy, he shall in like manner write his own initials and sign his own name, and state also, in writing, the name of the person for whom he is proxy.

Article 15.—Provided that if any voter cannot write, he shall affix his mark at the foot of the voting paper in the presence of a witness, who shall attest the affixing thereof, and who shall write the initials of such voter against the name of every candidate for whom the voter intends to vote.

Article 16.—If the initials of the voter shall be written against the names of more persons than are to be elected guardians for the parish, or if the voter shall not sign or affix his mark to the voting paper, or if his mark shall not be duly attested, or if a proxy do not sign his own name, and state in writing the name of the person for whom he is proxy, such person shall be omitted in the calculation of votes.

Article 17.—The clerk shall cause the voting papers to be collected by the persons appointed for that purpose, on the *seventh day of April*, in such manner as he shall direct.

Article 18.—No voting paper shall be received or admitted unless the same shall have been delivered at the address in each parish of the voter, and collected by the persons appointed or employed for that purpose, except as is provided in the following article.

Article 19.—Provided that every person qualified to vote, who shall not on the *fifth day of April* have received a voting paper, shall, on application before the *eighth day of April* to the clerk at his office, be entitled to receive a voting paper, and to fill up the same in the presence of the clerk, and then and there to deliver the same to him.

Article 20.—Provided also, that in case any voting paper duly delivered shall not have been collected through the default of the clerk, or the persons appointed or employed for that purpose, the voter in person may deliver the same to the clerk before twelve o'clock at noon on the *eighth day of April*.

Article 21.—The clerk shall, on the *ninth day of April*, and on as many days immediately succeeding as may be necessary, attend at the board room of the guardians of the union, and ascertain the validity of the votes, by an examination of the rate-books, and the registers of owners and proxies, and such other documents as he may think necessary, and by examining such persons as he may see fit; and he shall cast up such of the votes as he shall find to be valid, and to have been duly given, collected or received, and ascertain the number of such votes for each candidate.

Article 22.—The candidates, to the number of guardians to be elected for the parish, who being duly qualified, shall have obtained the greatest number of votes, shall be deemed to be the elected guardians for the parish, and shall be certified as such by the clerk under his hand.

Article 23.—The clerk, when he shall have ascertained that any candidate is duly elected as guardian, shall notify the fact of his having been so elected, by delivering or sending, or causing to be delivered or sent, to him a notice in the form (D.), hereunto annexed.

Notice of the Election of Guardians.

Article 24.—The clerk shall make a list containing the names of the candidates, together with (in case of a contest) the number of votes given for each, and the names of the elected guardians according to the form marked (E.), hereunto annexed, and shall sign and certify the same, and shall deliver such list, together with all the nomination and voting papers which he shall have received, to the guardians of the union, at their next meeting, and shall cause copies of such list to be printed, and shall deli.er or send, or cause to be delivered or sent, one or more of such copies to the overseers of each parish, and to the Poor Law Commissioners.

Article 25.—The overseers shall affix, or cause to be affixed, copies of such list, at the usual places for affixing in each parish, notices of parochial business.

Explanation of Terms.

Article 26.—Whenever the word "parish" is used in this order, it shall be taken to signify any place separately maintaining its own poor.

Article 27.—Whenever in describing any person or party, matter or thing, the word importing the singular number, or the masculine gender only, is used in this order, the same shall be taken to include, and shall be applied to, several persons or parties as well as one person or party, and females as well as males, and several matters or things, as well as one matter or thing respectively, unless there be something in the subject or context repugnant to such construction.

Article 28.—Whenever in this order any article is referred to by its number, the article of this order bearing that number shall be taken to be signified thereby.

Article 29.—Whenever the day appointed in this order for the performance of any act shall be a Sunday, or Good Friday, such act shall be performed on the day next following.

Article 30.—The word "clerk" shall extend in this order to the person who may be appointed under Article 2, to act as such in the performance of the duties hereby prescribed.

(A.)

Election of Guardians of the Poor.

________ Union.

I, clerk to the guardians of the poor of the Union, with reference to the ensuing election of guardians of the poor for the several parishes in the said union, do hereby give notice,—

1.—That the number of guardians of the poor to be elected for the parishes in the said union is as follows :—

For the parish of One guardian.
For the parish of Two guardians.

2.—That any person not otherwise disqualified by law who shall be rated to the poor-rate in any parish in the union, in respect of hereditaments of the annual rental of pounds, is qualified to be nominated for the office of guardian at the said election, by any person then qualified to vote.

3.—That any rate-payer who shall have been rated to the poor-rate in any parish in the union for the whole year immediately preceding his voting, and shall have paid the rates made and assessed on him, for the relief of the poor for one whole year, as well as those due from him at the time of voting, except those which had been made or become due within six months immediately preceding such voting ; and that every owner of rateable property situated within the said parish, who shall have given to the overseers thereof, before the first day of February, the statement in writing required by law, will be entitled according to the provisions of the 7 and 8 Vic. c. 101, s. 14, to have the number and proportion of votes at the election of the guardians for the said parish, according to the following scale :—

If the property in respect of which he is entitled to vote be rated upon a rateable value of less than £50, he shall have one vote. If such rateable value amount to £50, and be less than £100, he shall have two votes. If it amount to £100, and be less than £150, he shall have three votes. If it amount to £150, and be less than £200, he shall have four votes. If it amount to £200, and be less than £250, he shall have five votes. If it amount to or exceed £250, he shall have six votes.

Any owner of such property who has made such statement may, by writing under his hand, appoint any person to vote as his proxy, but such proxy must, fourteen days previously to the day on which he shall claim to vote, give to one of the overseers of such parish, a statement in writing of his own name and address, and also the name and address of the owner appointing him such proxy, and a description of the property as proxy to the owner whereof he claims to vote, and also the original or an attested copy of the writing appointing him such proxy.

4.—Nominations of guardians must be made according to the form below, which is the form prescribed by the Poor Law Commissioners. Such nominations must be sent on or before the day of March, to me, or to Mr. at for the parish of or to Mr. at for the parish of who alone are authorised to receive the same. Nominations sent after that day, or sent to any other person, will be invalid.

5.—That I shall, if more than the above-mentioned number of guardians be nominated for any parish, cause voting papers to be delivered on the day of , at the address in such parish of each rate-payer, owner, and proxy, qualified to vote ; and that on the day of , I shall cause such voting papers to be collected.

6.—That on the day of , I shall attend at the board room of this union at the hour of , and that I shall on that day, and, if necessary, the following days, proceed to ascertain the number of votes given for each candidate.

7.—That any person put in nomination for the office of guardian may, at any time during the proceedings in the election, tender to me in writing his refusal to serve the office, and the election, so far as regards that person, will be no further proceeded with.

(A. *continued.*)

Form of Nomination Paper.

Parish of ______________ }
______________ Union. } This day of 184 .

Names of Persons nominated to be Guardians.	Residence of the Persons nominated.	Quality or Calling of Persons nominated.

I, being * duly qualified to vote in the *parish* of nominate the above to be guardian (*or* guardians) for the said *parish*.

______________ Signature }
______________ Address } of Nominator.

* *Note.*—Only one person is empowered to sign this paper, and after the word *being* must insert (*a rate-payer*) or (*owner of property*,) according to his qualification.

Given under my hand, this day of 184
______________ Clerk to the guardians of the poor of the Union.

(B.)

Nomination Paper.

Parish of ______________ }
______________ Union. } This day of 184

Names of Persons nominated to be Guardians.	Residence of the Persons nominated	Quality or Calling of Persons nominated.

I, being * duly qualified to vote in the *parish* of , nominate the above to be guardian (*or* guardians) for the said *parish*.

______________ Signature }
______________ Address } of Nominator.

* *Note.*—Only one person is empowered to sign this paper, and after the word *being* must insert (*a rate-payer*,) or (*owner of property*,) according to his qualification.

(C.)

Voting Paper.

__________ Union.

Voting paper for the *parish* of

No. of Voting Paper.	Name and Address of Voter.	Number of Votes.	
		As Owner.	As Rate-payer.

Directions to the Voters.

The voter must write his initials against the name of every person for whom he votes, and must sign this paper.

If the voter cannot write, he must affix his mark, but such mark must be attested by a witness, and such witness must write the initials of the voter against the name of every person for whom the voter intends to vote.

If a proxy vote, he must in like manner write his initials, sign his own name, and state in writing the name of the person for whom he is proxy; thus, *John Smith* for *Richard Williams.*

This paper must be carefully preserved by the voter, as no second paper will be given. When it is filled up it must be kept ready for delivery to Mr. , who will call for the same on the day of

No other person is authorised to receive the voting paper.

If the voting paper be not ready for the person appointed to collect it when called for, the vote will be lost. It will also be lost if more than name be returned in the list, with the initials of the voter placed against such name , or if the voting paper be not signed by the voter, or if the mark of the voter be not attested when attestation is required.

Initials of the Voter against the Name of the Person for whom he intends to vote.	Names of the Persons nominated as Guardians.	Residence of the Persons nominated.	Quality or Calling of the Persons nominated.	Names of the Nominators.	Address of the Nominators.	Opinion of the Clerk as to Disqualification.

I vote for the persons in the above list against whose names my initials are placed.

Signed __________ (*or the mark of*) __________

Witness to the mark __________

or __________ for __________

(D.)

Notice to the Guardians elected.

__________ Union.

Parish of __________

Sir,—I do hereby give you notice, and declare, that you have been duly elected a guardian of the poor for the *parish* of in the Union, and that the next meeting of the board of guardians of the said union will be held at on next, at the hour of

Signed this day of

__________ Clerk to the guardians of the poor of the Union.

To Mr. __________ of __________

27

(E.)

____________ Union.

I do hereby certify, that the election of guardians of the poor for the several parishes in the Union was conducted in conformity with the order of the Poor Law Commissioners, and that the entries contained in the schedule hereunder written are true.

PARISHES arranged alphabetically.	Names of Persons nominated as Guardians.	Residence.	Quality or Calling.	No. of Votes given for each Candidate.	Names of the Guardians elected.

Given under my hand, this day of

____________ Clerk to the guardians of the poor of the Union.

[*This order applies to all the unions named in schedules A. and B. at pages* 31 *and* 32.]

Given under our hands and seals of office, this sixteenth day of January, in the year one thousand eight hundred and forty-five.

(L. S.) (Signed) GEO. NICHOLLS.
G. C. LEWIS.
EDMUND W. HEAD.

---

2. INSTRUCTIONAL LETTER ACCOMPANYING THE ELECTION ORDER.

Poor Law Commission Office,
Somerset House,
16*th January*, 1845.

Sir,—I am directed by the Poor Law Commissioners to transmit to you a copy of a general order which they have issued to regulate the election of guardians in parishes now in union.

The statute of the last session of Parliament has introduced some alterations in regard to this matter, the most important of which affect the scale of voting, and those alterations have rendered it necessary for the Commissioners to modify some parts of the orders hitherto in force which regulate the mode and manner of elections of guardians.

They have, therefore, deemed it advisable to rescind all those orders, and to issue the present as a general order, containing the few alterations which appear to them to be requisite.

The plan which the Commissioners established several years back for the conduct of these elections, having worked with success, and having in a satisfactory manner effected the election of the guardians in the great number of parishes now combined in unions, has not been departed from in the present order, and it will be seen, therefore, that it contains little more than verbal alterations, and some few changes in the details.

The Commissioners have, however, thought it expedient to alter the dates on which the several proceedings are to take place, and thus to avail themselves of the provision contained in the seventeenth section of the 7 and 8 Vict. c. 101, which continues the guardians in office for forty days after the twenty-fifth of March, if a new election do not previously take place.

The Commissioners have not set out in this order any forms for the statement of owners of property, for the appointment of proxies, the statements of proxies, and the register of those statements and appointments, which in the orders now rescinded appeared as forms A. B. C. and D. At the same time, as the Commissioners believe that it will be convenient if some forms be suggested for general use, they have re-considered those formerly prepared, with reference to the alterations made by the late statute; and think that forms to the following effect might be safely used in place of the first three of those forms.

(A.) *Owner's Statement.*

To the Churchwardens and Overseers of the poor of the *Parish* of ______________ in the County of ______________.

This day of 184 .

I, the undersigned, claim to be entitled to vote, according to the provisions of the statutes of the fifth year of the reign of King William the Fourth and the eighth year of the reign of Her present Majesty, relating to the Administration of the Laws for the Relief of the Poor (4 and 5 W. 4. c. 76, and 7 and 8 Vict. c. 101), as owner of the property hereinafter described, which is situated in the *Parish* of , that is to say,*

I do also state that the interest or estate which I have in such property, and the amount of all the rent service which I receive or pay in respect thereof, and the names of the persons from whom I receive or to whom I pay such rent service, are set forth in the form hereunder written.

Description of Property.[a]	In respect of which I have an Estate or Interest of[b]	And in respect of which I receive in Rent-service the sum of[c]			From[d]	And in respect of which I pay in Rent-service the sum of[e]			To[f]
		£.	s.	d.		£.	s.	d.	

Signature of Claimant ______________

Address of Claimant ______________

* Here insert a clear statement of the property, as house, building , house and acres of land.

[a] Describe the property by its name, situation, or the name of the occupier, or any other designation by which it may be identified.

[b] Describe the estate or interest, as *an estate in fee simple, a freehold, a term of years,* and also whether it is held by the claimant solely or jointly with others.

[c] If the property is let by the owner, insert the amount of rent received from each tenant.

[d] Insert name of tenant or tenants.

[e] If the owner is a lessee paying rent, insert the amount of all the rent he pays.

[f] Insert the name of the lessor.

(B.) *Appointment of Proxy.*

To the Churchwardens and Overseers of the Poor of the *Parish* of ______________ in the County of ______________.

This day of 184 .

I, the undersigned, being owner of the property hereinafter described, which is situated in the *Parish* of do hereby appoint of to vote as my proxy in all cases wherein he may lawfully do so, under the provisions of the statutes of the fifth year of the reign of His late Majesty King William the Fourth, and the eighth year of the reign of Her present Majesty, relating to the Administration of the Laws for the Relief of the Poor. And I do hereby state that the description of the said property is as follows, viz.[*]

______________ Signature of Owner.

______________ Address of Owner.

[*] Describe the property by its name, situation, or the name of the occupier, or any other designation by which it may be identified. It is not necessary here to set out the description of the estate or interest of the owner, nor the statement of the amount of rent received or paid by him.

(C.) *Proxy's Statement.*

To the Churchwardens and Overseers of the Poor of the *Parish* of ________________ in the County of ________________

This day of 184

I, the undersigned, having been appointed by of owner of the property hereinafter described, which is situated in the *Parish* of to vote as His proxy, under the provisions of the statutes of the fifth year of the reign of His late Majesty King William the Fourth, and of the eighth year of the reign of Her present Majesty, relating to the Administration of the Laws for the Relief of the Poor, do hereby give you notice, that I am entitled to vote as such proxy. I herewith transmit to you[a] the writing under the hand of the said appointing me such proxy.

The following is a description of the property in respect of which the said is entitled to vote as owner, and in respect of which I am entitled to vote as his proxy, viz.[b]

________________ Signature of Proxy.
________________ Address of Proxy.

[a] If the appointment itself be not sent, insert the words *an attested copy of.*

[b] Describe the property by its name, situation, or the name of the occupier, or any other designation by which it may be identified. It is not necessary here to set out the description of the estate or interest of the owner, nor the statement of the amount of rent received or paid by him.

I am to observe that the adoption of these forms is by no means compulsory upon any owner or proxy, and consequently any forms which may contain in substance the information herein set forth, which appears to be what is required by the statutes, will be fully available for the purposes of the election.

The form of register of owners and proxies is directed by the general order as to the duties of overseers, bearing date the 22nd of April, 1842, and addressed to the overseers of all parishes now in union; and such order being still in force, it is not necessary to set out the form in this place.

The Commissioners believe that the general provisions of the former law respecting the election of guardians are now well known, and they have in their memorandum of the 31st ult., which has been very widely circulated, pointed out the new provisions relative to the claims of owners; while in the form of the notice of election, contained in the order, of which the copy is herewith forwarded, they have set for that full the new scale of votes for owners and rate-payers.

It does not, therefore, appear to them to be necessary to make any further remarks on this subject in the present circular.

I am, Sir, your obedient servant,
EDWIN CHADWICK, Sec.

To the Clerk to the Guardians.

3 ELECTION EXPENSES—GENERAL ORDER.

TO THE GUARDIANS OF THE POOR of the several Unions named in the Schedules hereunto annexed;—

To the Churchwardens and Overseers of the Poor of the several Parishes comprised in the said several Unions;

To the Clerk or Clerks to the Justices of the Petty Sessions held for the Division or Divisions in which the said several Parishes are situate;—

And to all others whom it may concern.

WE, THE POOR LAW COMMISSIONERS, do hereby, under the authority of an act passed in the fifth year of the reign of his late majesty King William the Fourth, intituled "*An Act for the Amendment and better Administration of the Laws relating to the Poor in England and Wales,*" rescind all such of the provisions contained in any order or orders under the hands and seal of the Poor Law Commissioners, as direct the payment of expenses to be incurred in the election of guardians of the poor for the several parishes comprised in the several unions named in the schedules hereunto annexed.

And whereas by a general order under the hands and seal of the Poor Law Commissioners, bearing date the sixteenth day of January instant, addressed to the guardians of the poor of the said several unions, the said Commissioners have prescribed the manner of conducting the future election of guardians of the poor for the several parishes comprised in the said unions; and it is expedient that provision should be made for the payment of the expenses to be incurred in such elections.

Now, therefore, we, the said Poor Law Commissioners, do hereby order and direct henceforth in regard thereto, with reference to each of the said unions named in the said schedules as follows:—That the expenses of every future election of guardians of the poor of the several parishes comprised in the said unions shall be defrayed by the guardians of the said unions in the manner herein-after set forth; that is to say,

Article 1.—The cost of providing the several forms marked (A.) (D.) and (E.) contained in the said order, being the notice of election, the notice to the guardians elected, and the certificate of the election, shall be defrayed out of the common fund of the union.

Article 2.—The cost of providing the form marked (C.) contained in the said order, being the voting paper, shall be defrayed out of the funds in the possession of the said guardians belonging to the respective parishes to which the voting papers shall relate.

Article 3.—The compensation which shall be paid to the clerk, or to the person appointed under the authority of the said recited order to act as such in the performance of the duties thereby prescribed, shall include the remuneration of the persons who may have been appointed or employed to assist him in conducting and completing the election, and shall, in respect of the several unions named in the following schedule marked (A.) be such sum, not exceeding *ten pounds*, as the guardians shall determine, and shall, in respect of the several unions named in the following schedule marked (B.) be such sum, not exceeding *fifteen pounds*, as the guardians shall determine, and such sums respectively shall be defrayed out of the common fund of the unions.

Article 4.—And in the case of every contested election one farthing per head on the population of the parish in which the contest shall have taken place, if the population shall be more than five hundred, and one halfpenny per head on the population of the parish in which the contest shall have taken place, if the population be not more than five hundred, shall be paid to the said clerk or other person as aforesaid in addition to such compensation, and shall be defrayed out of the funds in the possession of the said guardians belonging to such parish. And for the purpose of ascertaining the last-mentioned sums, the population of the parish shall be taken to be as stated in the census which at the time of such election shall have been last made under the authority of any act of parliament.

And we do hereby declare, that wherever the word "parish" is used in this order, it shall be taken to signify any place in the union separately maintaining its own poor.

[*This order applies to all the unions named in the schedules A. and B. at pages* 31 *and* 32.]

Given under our hands and seal of office, this twenty-seventh day of January, in the year one thousand eight hundred and forty-five.

(L. S.) (Signed). Geo. Nicholls.
G. C. Lewis.

Schedule (A.)

Aberaeron, Abergavenny, Aberystwith, St. Albans, Alcester, Alderbury, Alresford, Alton, Amersham, Amesbury, Ampthill, St. Asaph, Ashby-de la-Zouch, East Ashford, West Ashford, Aston, Atherstone, St. Austel, Axminster, Aylesford, North.

Bala, Bangor and Beaumaris, Barnet, Barrow-upon-Soar, Bath, Battle, Beaminster, Bedale, Bedminster, Berkhampstead, Berwick-upon-Tweed, Bideford, Biggleswade, Billericay, Bishop's Stortford, Blaby, Blackburn, Blean, Bodmin, Bolton, Bootle, Boston, Brackley, Bradfield, Bradford (Wilts), Bradford (York), Braintree, Brampton, Brentford, Bridge, Bridgnorth, Bridport, Bromley, Bromsgrove, Buckingham, Buntingford, Burnley, Bury.

Calne, Cambridge, Camelford, Cardigan, Carlisle, Carmarthen, Carnarvon, Catherington, Caxton and Arrington, Cerne, Chailey, Chapel-en-le-Frith, Cheadle, Cheltenham, Chertsey, Chester-le-street, Chippenham, Chipping Sodbury, Chorley, Chorlton, Christchurch, Church Stretton, Cleobury Mortimer, Clifton, Clun, Clutton, Colchester, Columb St. Major, Conway, Cookham, Corwen, Cosford, Cranbrook, Crediton, Crickhowel, Cricklade and Wootten Bassett, Croydon, Cuckfield.

Dartford, Daventry, Derby, Devizes, Dewsbury, Dolgelly, Dore, Dorking, Dover, Downham, Drayton, Droitwich, Droxford, Dudley, Dulverton, Dunmow, Durham, Dursley.

Easington, Easingwold, Eastbourne, East Grinstead, Easthampstead, Eastry, East Ward, Ecclesall Bierlow, Edmonton, Elham, Ellesmere, Ely, Epping, Epsom, Eton, Evesham.

St. Faith, Falmouth, Fareham, Faversham, Festiniog, Foleshill, Fordingbridge, Frome, Fy'de.

Garstang, Gateshead, St. German's, Glossop, Godstone, Goole, Gravesend and Milton, Greenwich, Guildford, Guiltcross, Guisborough.

Hackney, Hailsham, Halifax, Halstead, Haltwhistle, Hambledon, Hardingstone, Hartley Wintney, Haslingden, Hastings, Hatfield, Havant, Hay, Hayfield, Headington, Helston, Hemel Hempstead, Hendon, Henley, Hertford, Highworth and Swindon, Hinckley,

Hitchin, Holbeach, Holborn, Hollingbourn, Holsworthy, Holywell, Honiton, Hoo, Horsham, Houghton-le-Spring, Hoxne, Hungerford, Hursley.

Ipswich, St. Ives.

Keighley, Kettering, Keynsham, Kidderminster, Kingsbridge, Kingsclere, King's Lynn, King's Norton, Kingston-upon-Thames, Kington, Knighton.

Lampeter, Lancaster, Lanchester, Langport, Launceston, Ledbury, Leek, Leicester, Leigh, Leighton Buzzard, Leominster, Lewes, Lewisham, Lichfield, Linton, Liskeard, Llandilo Fawr, Llandovery, Llanelly, Llanfyllin, Llanrwst, East London, West London, Longtown, Loughborough, Luton, Lymington.

Machynlleth, Madeley, Maidstone, Malling, Malmsbury, Manchester, Mansfield, Market Bosworth, Marlborough, Martley, Medway, Melksham, Mere, Meriden, Merthyr Tidvil, Midhurst, Mildenhall, Milton.

Neath, St. Neots, Newbury, Newcastle-in-Emlyn, Newcastle-under-Lyne, Newcastle-upon-Tyne, Newent, New Forest, Newhaven, Newmarket, Newport (Salop), Newtown and Llanidloes, Northampton, Northleach, North Witchford, Nottingham, Nuneaton.

Oakham, Okehampton, St. Olave's, Ongar, Ormskirk, Orsett.

Pateley Bridge, Patrington, Pembroke, Penkridge, Penzance, Petersfield, Petworth, Pewsey, Pickering, Plympton St. Mary, Pont-y-Pool, Poole, Poplar, Portsea Island, Potterspury, Prescot, Presteign, Preston.

Radford, Reading, Redruth, Reeth, Reigate, Rhayadar, Richmond (Surrey), Ringwood, Risbridge, Rochdale, Rochford, Romford, Romney Marsh, Romsey, Ross, Rotherham, Royston, Ruthin, Rye.

Salford, St. Saviour's, Sulcoates, Sedbergh, Sedgefield, Seisdon, Selby, Sevenoaks, Shaftesbury, Sheffield, Sheppey, Shepton Mallett, Sherborne, Shiffnall, Solihull, Southam, South Molton, South Shields, South Stoneham, Spalding, Stafford, Staines, Stepney, Steyning, Stockbridge, Stockport, Stokesley, Stone, Stourbridge, Stow-on-the-Wold, Strand, Stratton, Stroud, Sturminster, Sunderland, Swansea.

Tamworth, Tavistock, Tenbury, Tenterden, Tetbury, Tewkesbury, Thakeham, Isle of Thanet, Thornbury, Thorne, Thrapston, Ticehurst, Tisbury, Tiverton, Todmorden, Tonbridge, Torrington, Totnes, Towcester, Tregaron, Truro, Tynemouth.

Uckfield, Ulverstone, Upton-upon-Severn, Uttoxeter, Uxbridge.

Wakefield, Wallingford, Walsal, Wandsworth and Clapham, Wangford, Ware, Wareham and Purbeck, Warminster, Warrington, Watford, Wayland, Weardale, Wellingborough, Wellington (Salop), Wellington (Somerset), Wells, Welwyn, Wem, Weobly, Westbourne, West Bromwich, Westbury-upon-Severn, Westbury and Whorwelsdown, West Derby, West Firle, West Ham, West Ward, Weymouth, Wheatenhurst, Whitby, Whitchurch, Whitechapel, Whitehaven, Wigan, Wilton, Wimborne and Cranborne, Winchcombe, Windsor, Winslow, Wisbeach, Witham, Woburn, Wokingham, Wolstanton and Burslem, Wolverhampton, Worcester, Worksop, Wortley.

Schedule B.

Abingdon, Alnwick, Altrincham, Andover, Anglesey, Ashbourne, Atcham, Auckland, Axbridge, Aylesbury, Aylsham.

Bakewell, Banbury, Barnstaple, Basford, Basingstoke, Bedford, Belford, Bellingham, Belper, Beverley, Bicester, Billesdon, Bingham, Blandford, Blofield, Blything, Bosmere and Claydon, Great Boughton, Bourn, Brecknock, Bridgend, and Cowbridge, Bridgwater, Bridlington, Brixworth, Bromyard, Builth, Burton-upon-Trent.

Caistor, Cardiff, Castle Ward, Chard, Chelmsford, Chepstow, Chesterfield, Chesterton, Chipping Norton, Cirencester, Clitheroe, Cockermouth, Congleton.

Darlington, Depwade, Docking, Doncaster, Dorchester, Downham, Driffield.

East Retford, Erpingham.

Faringdon, Freebridge Lynn.

Gainsborough, Glanford Brigg, Glendale, Gloucester, Grantham.

Hartismere, Haverfordwest, Helmsley Blackmoor, Henstead, Hereford, Hexham, Horncastle, Howden, Huddersfield, Huntingdon.

Kendal.

Lexden and Winstree, Leyburn, Lincoln, Lodden and Clavering, City of London, Louth, Ludlow, Lutterworth.

Macclesfield, Maldon, Malton, Market Harboro', Melton Mowbray, Mitford and Launditch, Monmouth, Morpeth.

Nantwich, Narberth, Newark, Newport, (Monmouth), Newport Pagnell, Newton Abbot, Northallerton, Northwich.

Oundle.

Penrith, Pershore, Peterborough, Plomesgate, Pocklington, Pwllheli.

Richmond (York), Rothbury, Rugby, Runcorn.

Saffron Walden, Scarborough, Settle, Shardlow, Shipston-upon-Stour, Skipton, Skirlaugh, Sleaford, Southwell, Spilsby, Stamford, Stockton, Stow, Stratford-upon-Avon, Sudbury, Swaffham.

Taunton, Teesdale, Tendring, Thame, Thetford, Thingoe, Thirsk, St. Thomas.

Uppingham.

Walsingham, Wantage, Warwick, West Hampnett, Wigton, Williton, Wincanton, New Winchester, Wirral, Witney, Woodbridge, Woodstock, Wrexham, Wycombe.

Yeovil, York.

LONDON:
Printed by Order of the Poor Law Commissioners, by BLACKBURN and PARDON, 6, Hatton Garden, and Published by CHARLES KNIGHT and Co., 22, Ludgate Street, Publishers to the Poor Law Commissioners.

AN

OFFICIAL CIRCULAR

OF PUBLIC DOCUMENTS AND INFORMATION;

DIRECTED BY THE POOR LAW COMMISSIONERS TO BE PRINTED, CHIEFLY FOR THE USE OF THE MEMBERS AND PERMANENT OFFICERS OF BOARDS OF GUARDIANS, UNDER THE POOR LAW AMENDMENT ACT.

No. 45. CIRCULAR ISSUED MARCH 1, 1845.

Poor Law Commission Office, Somerset House, March 1st, 1845.

THE Poor Law Commissioners directed that the following Bill, brought into the House of Commons on the 17th Feb. 1845, by Sir James Graham, and Mr. Manners Sutton, be printed and circulated for the information of Guardians and Officers of the several Unions. By order of the Board,

EDWIN CHADWICK, *Secretary.*

A BILL TO CONSOLIDATE AND AMEND THE LAWS RELATING TO PAROCHIAL SETTLEMENT, AND TO THE REMOVAL OF THE POOR.

CONTENTS OF THE BILL.

I. REPEALS:

Section 1.—Repeal of so much of former Acts of Parliament as relates to Settlement in Parishes, and to the Removal of the Poor, whether English, Scotch, or Irish, or of the Isles of Man, Scilly, Jersey, or Guernsey.

II. SETTLEMENT:

Section 2.—Persons born before the Act to retain their settlement.

Section 3.—Other Settlements declared; namely, 1st. Birth Settlement; or, 2d. Father's Settlement; or, 3rd. Mother's Settlement. No Settlement to be derived from Grandfather, Grandmother, or more remote ancestor.

Section 4.—Place of Birth proved by Register of Birth or Baptism.

Section 5.—Proviso, that Children born in Union Workhouse shall be settled where their Mothers are chargeable: Children born in District Asylums, Hospitals, Prisons, &c., or while their Mothers are under orders of removal, shall not have a Birth Settlement, but shall take their Parent's Settlement.

Replaces, with modifications, 9 Geo. 1. c. 7, s. 4, proviso; 13 Geo. 3, c. 82, s. 5; 20 Geo. 3, c. 36, s. 2.; 54 Geo. 3, c. 17, s. 2, 3; 9 Geo. 4, c. 40, s. 49; and the effect of, Dalton, 168. and of the cases R. *v.* Astley, 2 Bott., 17; Suckley *v.* Whitborn, 2 Bott. 3.

III. CHARGEABILITY:

Section 6. Declaration, that unsettled persons are to be relieved at the charge of the 'Parish' where they are destitute, as if they were settled there, until they are lawfully removed, or their destitution there is lawfully at an end.

IV. REMOVAL:

Section 7.—Persons chargeable to a 'Parish' in which they are not settled, declared liable to be removed to the parishes of their settlement, with a reservation in the cases of—

1. Married women. Such women are not to be removed from their husbands.
2. Legitimate children. Such children are not to be removed from their fathers' parish.
3. Legitimate and bastard children. Such children are not to be removed from their mothers.
4. Widows and their families. These are not to be removeable for a Year after the husband's death.
5. Widows. They are not to be removed from the place of their husband's settlement and death.
6. Persons chargeable through sickness. They are not to be removed until relieved Forty Days.

Section 8.—Declaration, that, except wives and children who are before made removable to the husband's or parent's parish, and persons removable to Scotland, Ireland, &c., no person shall be removable to any other parish than that in which they are settled.

Section 9.—Power to Overseers to admit settlements, and agree to amicable removals.

Section 10.—Summons of persons liable to be removed; their examination: the warrant for their removal. Proviso for the examination of persons who cannot attend the summons.

Replaces 13 & 14 Car. 2, c. 12, s. 1, as to power to remove; as to complaint to One Justice, R. *v.* Westwood, 2 Bott., 782; summons, R. *v.* Wykes, 2 Bott., 818; hearing by Two Justices, ib.; examination of infirm persons, 49 Geo. 3, c. 124, s. 4; and of prisoners, 59 Geo. 3, c. 12, s. 28.

Section 11.—No removal to be made until after Forty Days' notice, unless the removal be previously submitted to. In case of appeal, the removal not to be made until such appeal is ended.

Replaces 4 & 5 Will. 4, c. 76, s. 79.

Section 12.—Overseers, or persons employed by them, may execute the Warrant of Removal.

Replaces 54 Geo. 3, c. 170, s. 10.

Section 13.—Persons procuring removals without warrants made subject to penalties.

Section 14.—Delivery of Paupers under warrants of removal, at the Workhouse of a Parish or Union, to be regarded as delivery to the Overseers.

Section 15.—Suspension of the Removal; recovery of the charges incurred by such suspension; Appeal where such charges exceed *Ten* Pounds.

Replaces 25 Geo. 3, c. 101; as to sick persons, R. *v.* Everdon, 2 Bott., 878; and as to the whole family, 49 Geo. 3, c. 124, s. 3; as to Justices' jurisdiction, 49 Geo. 3, c. 124, s. 1; as to notice of the warrant and suspension, 4 & 5 Will. 4, c. 76, s. 84.

Section 16.—Overseers may abandon a Warrant of Removal, paying the costs caused to the other party.

Section 17.—The Clerk of the Justices to transmit a duplicate of every warrant of removal and the original depositions to the Clerk of the Peace.

Section 18.—The Clerk of the Peace, on application, to furnish copies to the Overseers of the Parish to which the removal is directed to be made.

V. APPEAL AGAINST WARRANT OF REMOVAL:

Section 19.—The Parish aggrieved by a Warrant of Removal may appeal, giving notice of the grounds of their appeal. Appeal to be respited only on affidavit of special circumstances. Warrants of removal made before the passing of this Act may still be appealed against, as if the Act had not been passed.

Replaces 13 & 14 Car. 2, c. 12, s. 2, and 3 Will. 4, c. 11, s. 10; and as to statement of periods of appeal, 4 & 5 Will. 4, c. 76, s. 81.

Section 20.—Overseers may have access to the Pauper touching his Settlement.

Replaces 4 & 5 Will. 4, c. 76, s. 80.

Section 21.—Quarter Sessions held Fourteen Days after notice of Appeal, to hear the Appeal, no grounds to be gone into, but such as have been set forth in the Respondents' and Appellants' statements.

Replaces 8 & 9 Will. 3, c. 30, s. 6, giving, however, jurisdiction to sessions of places, not counties; restriction to the grounds of removal and appeal, 4 & 5 Will. 4, c. 76, s. 81.

Section 22.—On the trial of the appeal, the duplicate of the warrant, and the original depositions transmitted to the Clerk of the Peace, may be referred to for certain purposes.

Section 23.—Costs incurred by reason of notice of removal, or of appeal, and costs of trial, and costs caused by statements of frivolous or vexatious grounds of removal or appeal, to be awarded and certified by the Court; recovery of such costs.

Replaces 8 & 9 Will. 3, c. 30, s. 3, and 4 & 5 Will. 4, c. 76, s. 82.

Section 24.—Costs may be taxed by the proper officer at any time, although the Court be not sitting.

See Regina *v.* Long, 1 Q. B. 740.

VI. MAINTENANCE OF PAUPERS UNDER WARRANTS OF REMOVAL AND DURING APPEAL.

Section 25.—The cost of relief and maintenance of persons under warrant of removal incurred from the time that notice of chargeability was sent, till the time when the warrants might lawfully be executed, to be repaid to the Parish. Proviso saving the provisions in Clause 15, respecting suspended warrants.

Replaces 4 & 5 Will. 4, c. 76, s. 84.

VII. SERVICE OF NOTICES:

Section 26.—Notices of Removal, Appeal, &c. may be sent by Post.

VIII. REMOVAL OF POOR BORN IN SCOTLAND, IRELAND, AND THE ISLANDS OF MAN, SCILLY, JERSEY, AND GUERNSEY:

Section 27.—Natives of Scotland, Ireland, and the Islands of Man, Scilly, Jersey, and Guernsey, not settled in England, may be removed to the places of their birth.

Replaces, as to natives of Scotland, Ireland, Man, and Scilly, 3 and 4 Will. 4, c. 40, s. 2; or Jersey and Guernsey, 11 Geo. 4, c. 5, s. 2.

Section 28.—Justices in Quarter Sessions to make regulations for such removals.

Replaces 3 and 4 Will. 4, c. 40, ss. 3 and 4.

Section 29.—The expenses incurred by Parishes in such removals to be repaid out of County Rates.

Replaces 3 and 4 Will. 4, c. 40, s. 5, with addition of natives of Jersey and Guernsey.

Section 30.—Or in London, by the Chamberlain of the City, and levied by a Special Rate.

Replaces 3 and 4 Will. 4, c. 40, s. 6.

Section 31.—And in other Cities and places not contributing to a County Rate, by a General Rate.

Replaces 3 and 4 Will. 4, c. 40, s. 7.

Section 32.—Guardians of Unions in Ireland, and the Heritors and Kirk Session or Borough Magistrates in Scotland, may appeal against such Warrants. Removing Parish may abandon its Warrant, on payment of all costs incurred, including those of sending the Pauper back to such Parish.

IX. CONSTITUTION OF UNIONS FOR SETTLEMENT:

Section 33.—Poor Law Commissioners to declare Unions for Settlement.

Section 34.—Commissioners may in certain cases delay Declaration of any Union for the purposes of Settlement.

Section 35.—Commissioners may declare Unions under Local Acts to be Unions for Settlement.

Section 36.—Unions for Settlement to be as one Parish for Settlement and Removal.

Section 37.—Declaration of such Unions to be notified to Clerks of the Peace, and published in the Gazette.

Section 38.—Guardians and their Officers to proceed in matters of Settlement and Removal.

Section 39.—Guardians to take up such proceedings commenced before this Act.

Section 40.—Commissioners to declare the averages of such Unions.

Section 41.—Proviso for cases where Monies have been irregularly applied in relief of the Poor.

Section 42.—After the declaration of averages, the expenses of the Union to be charged on the respective Parishes according to such averages.

Section 43.—Overseers to continue to relieve in sudden and urgent cases. Such relief to be charged to the respective Parishes.

Section 44.—Proviso for the repayment of Loans, already partly discharged, but in different proportions by different Parishes.

Section 45.—Certain penalties for offences against Parishes extended to Unions for Settlement.

X. GUARDIANS OF PARISHES INVESTED WITH POWERS FOR REMOVAL OF POOR PERSONS.

Section 46.—Boards of Guardians of single Parishes may act in matters relating to the Settlement and Removal of the Poor.

XI. CONSTRUCTION AND LIMITATION OF THE ACT:

Section 47.—This Act to be construed as one Act with the Poor Law Amendment Acts.

Section 48.—Forms set forth in the Schedule to be sufficient in law, in proceedings under this Act.

Section 49.—The Act limited to England and Wales.

Section 50.—The Act may be amended this Session.

SCHEDULE.

Forms.

[Note.—The Words printed in *Italics* are proposed to be inserted in the Committee.]

REPEALS.—Preamble.—1. Repeal of so much of former Acts as relate to Parochial Settlements or the removal of the Poor, except so far as they repeal preceding Acts.

WHEREAS it is expedient that the Law of Settlement should be rendered more simple, and that the laws relating to the Removal of the Poor should be consolidated and amended; Be it therefore enacted, by the Queen's most excellent majesty, by and with the advice and consent of the Lords spiritual and temporal, and Commons, in this present Parliament assembled, and by the authority of the same, That from and after the *passing of this Act*, so much of the following Acts of Parliament, and of all Acts to amend or continue the same, as relates to the settlement of persons in parishes, or the removal of poor persons from the parishes to which they are chargeable, except so far as any of the said Acts may repeal the provisions of any former Act, shall be, and the same is hereby repealed; (namely) an Act made in the thirteenth and fourteenth years in the reign of King Charles the Second, "For the better Relief of the Poor of this Kingdom;" (13 and 14 Car. 2, c. 12, ss. 1, 2, 3;) an Act made in the first year of the reign of King James the Second, "For reviving and continuance of several Acts of Parliament therein mentioned; (1 Jac. 2, c. 17, ss. 2, 3;) an Act made in the third year of the reign of King William and Queen Mary, "For the better Explanation and supplying the Defects of the former Laws for the Settlement of the Poor;" (3 Will. and M. c. 11, ss. 3, 4, 5, 6, 7, 8, 9, 10;) an Act made in the eighth and ninth years in the reign of King William the Third, "For supplying some Defects in the Laws for the Relief of the Poor of this Kingdom;" (8 and 9 Will. 3, c. 30, ss. 1, 3, 4, 6, 7;) an Act made in the ninth and tenth years of the reign of King William the Third, "For explaining an Act made the last Session of Parliament, intituled, 'An Act for supplying some Defects in the Laws for the Relief of the Poor of this Kingdom;'" (9 and 10 Will. 3, c. 11, s. 1;) an Act made in the twelfth year, in the reign of Queen Anne, "For making perpetual the Act made in the thirteenth and fourteenth years of the reign of the late King Charles the Second, intituled, 'An Act for the better Relief of the Poor of this Kingdom, and that Persons bound Apprentices to, or being hired Servants with Persons coming with Certificates, shall not gain Settlements by such Services or Apprenticeships;' (12 Anne, c. 18, ss. 1, 2;) and for making perpetual the Act made in the sixth year of her present majesty's reign, intituled, 'An Act for the Importation of Cochineal from any Ports in Spain during the present War, and Six Months longer;' and for reviving a clause in an Act made in the ninth and tenth years of the reign of the late King William, intituled, 'An Act for settling the Trade to Africa, for allowing Foreign Copper Bars imported to be exported;'" an Act made in the ninth year, in the reign of King George the First, "For amending the Laws relating to the Settlement, Employment, and Relief of the Poor;" (9 Geo. 1, c. 7, ss. 4, 5, 6, 8, 9;) an Act made in the third year of the reign of King George the Second, "For continuing and amending an Act for regulating the Price and Assize of Bread; for Relief of Bankrupts, whose certificates were not allowed before the expiration of a late Act for the better preventing Frauds committed by Bankrupts; for allowing further Time for Enrolment of Deeds and Wills made by Papists, and for Relief of Protestant Purchasers and Lessees; and for making further Provisions concerning Certificates relating to the Settlements of Poor Persons, and the Charges of maintaining and removing certificated Persons;" (3 Geo. 2, c. 29, ss. 8, 9;) an Act made in the thirty-first year of the reign of King George the Second, "To amend an Act made in the third year of the reign of King William and Queen Mary, intituled, 'An Act for the better Explanation, and supplying the Defects of the former Laws for the Settlement of the Poor, so far as the same relates to Apprentices gaining a Settlement by Indenture; and also to empower Justices of the Peace to determine Differences between Masters and Mistresses, and their Servants in Husbandry, touching their Wages, though such Servants are hired for less time than a year;" (31 Geo. 2, c. 11, ss. 1, 2;) an Act made in the thirteenth year, in the reign of King George the Third, "For the better Regulation of Lying-in Hospitals and other places appropriated for the charitable reception of Pregnant Women, and also to provide for the Settlement of Bastard Children born in such hospitals and places;" (13 Geo. 3, c. 82, ss. 5, 6, 7;) an Act made in the twentieth year of the reign of King George the Third, "For obviating doubts touching the binding and receiving of Poor Children Apprentices, in pursuance of several Acts of Parliament made for the Relief of the Poor within particular Incorporated Hundreds or Districts, and for ascertaining the Settlement of Bastard Children born in the Houses of Industry within such Hundreds or Districts," (20 Geo. 3, c. 36, ss. 1, 2;) an Act made in the twenty-second year of the reign of King George the Third, "For the better Relief and Employment of the Poor;" (22 Geo. 3, c. 83, s. 39;) an Act made in the twenty-third year of the reign of King George the Third, "To prevent Prisoners in the King's Bench Prison, or the Rules thereof, or their Families or Servants, gaining Settlements in the Parish of Saint George the Martyr, in the Borough of Southwark, and County of Surrey; and for the Relief of the said Parish, with respect to the Families of Prisoners in the said King's Bench, or the Marshalsea Prison, or in the County Gaol, or House of Correction, belonging to the said County; for regulating the Manner of choosing Overseers of the Poor; and for appointing Collectors of the Poor's Rates within the said Parish;" (23 Geo. 3, c. 23, s. 1;) an Act made in the thirty-fifth year of the reign of King George the Third, "To prevent the Removal of Poor Persons until they shall become actually chargeable;" (35 Geo. 3, c. 101, ss. 1, 2, 3, 4, 6;) an Act made in the forty-ninth year of the reign of King George the Third, "For altering, amending, and explaining, certain Acts relative to the Removal of the Poor, and for making Regulations in certain Cases touching the Examination of Paupers, as to their Settlement; and for extending to all Parishes certain Rules and Orders in Workhouses, under an Act of the Twenty-second year of his present Majesty, intituled, 'An Act for the better Relief and Employment of the Poor;'" (49 Geo. 3, c. 124, ss. 1, 2, 3, 4;) an Act passed in the fifty-second year of the reign of King George the Third, "For the better Cultivation of Navy Timber in the Forest of Alice Holt, in the County of Southampton;" (52 Geo. 3, c. 72, s. 8;) an Act passed in the fifty-fourth year of the reign of King George the Third, "To render valid certain Indentures for the binding of Parish Apprentices, and Certificates of the Settlement of Poor Persons;" (54 Geo. 3, c. 107, ss. 1, 2, 3;) an Act passed in the fifty-fourth year of the reign of King George the Third, "To repeal certain Provisions in Local Acts for the Maintenance and Regulation of the Poor, and to make other Provisions in relation thereto;" (54 Geo. 3, c. 170, ss. 1, 2, 3, 4, 5, 6, 10;) an Act made in the fifty-sixth year of the reign of King George the Third, "To regulate the Binding of Parish Apprentices;" (56 Geo. 3, c. 139, s. 5;) an Act made in the fifty-ninth year of the reign of King George the Third, "To amend the Laws for the Relief of the Poor;" (59 Geo. 3, c. 12, s. 28;) an Act made in the first and second years of the reign of King George the Fourth, "For declaring valid certain Indentures of Apprenticeship, and Certificates of Settlements of Poor Persons in England;" (1 and 2 Geo. 4, c. 32, ss. 1, 2;) an Act made in the third year of the reign of King George the Fourth, "To amend the General Laws now in being for regulating Turnpike Roads in that part of Great Britain called England;" (3 Geo. 4, c. 126, s. 51;) an Act made in the sixth year of the reign of King George the Fourth, "For the Amendment of the Law respecting the Settlement of the Poor, as far as regards renting Tenements and paying Parochial Taxes;" (6 Geo. 4, c. 57, ss. 1, 2;) an Act made in the eleventh year of the reign of King George the Fourth, "To repeal the Provisions of certain Acts relating to the Removal of Vagrants and Poor Persons born in the Isles of Jersey and Guernsey, and chargeable to Parishes in England, and to make other Provisions in lieu thereof;" (11 Geo. 4, c. 5, ss. 1, 2;) an Act made in the first year of the reign of King William the Fourth, "To explain and amend an Act of the sixth year of his late Majesty King George the Fourth, as far as regards the Settlement of the Poor by the Renting and Occupation of Tenements;" (1 Will. 4, c. 18, ss. 1, 2;) an Act made in the second year of the reign of King William the Fourth, "To amend an Act of the fifty-ninth year of his Majesty King George the Third, for the Relief and Employment of the Poor;" (1 and 2 Will. 4, c. 42, s. 5;) an Act made in the second year of the reign of King William the Fourth, "To enable Churchwardens and Overseers to inclose Land belonging to the Crown for the Benefit of Poor Persons residing in the Parish in which such Crown Land is situated;" (1 and 2 Will. 4, c. 59, s. 2;) an Act made in the fourth year of the reign of King William the Fourth, "To repeal certain Acts relating to the Removal of Poor Persons born in Scotland and Ireland, and chargeable to Parishes in England, and to make other Provisions in lieu thereof, until the First day of May One Thousand Eight Hundred and Thirty-six, and to the End of the then next Session of Parliament," and all Acts to continue the same; (3 and 4 Will. 4, c. 40; 7 Will. 4, c. 10; 3 and 4 Vict., c. 27;) an Act made in the fifth year of the reign of King William the Fourth, "For the Amendment and better Administration of the Laws relating to the Poor in England and Wales;" (4 and 5 Will. 4, c. 76, ss. 64, 65, 66, 67, 68, 79, 80, 81, 82, 83, 84.)

SETTLEMENTS.—2. Proviso, that persons born before this Act shall retain their Settlements.

Provided always, and be it enacted, That every person who was born on or before the day of the *passing of this Act*, shall on the day succeeding the *passing of this Act* be deemed to be settled by this Act in the parish in which he was or would have been lawfully settled if this Act had not been passed.

3. Other persons to have—1st, Birth settlement; or 2nd, Father's settlement; or 3rd, Mother's settlement.

And be it enacted, That, except as hereinbefore provided, every person shall be settled in the parish in which he was born: or if the parish in which he was born cannot be ascertained, or if he was not born in England, he shall, if legitimate, be settled in the parish of his father's last settlement before such person attains the age of *Sixteen* years, or if his father has not, before such person attains the age of *Sixteen* years, any settlement which can be ascertained, or if such person be not legitimate, he shall be settled in the parish of his mother's last settlement before such person attains the age of *Sixteen* years; but no person shall be settled in any parish on the ground that his grandfather or grandmother or any more remote ancestor was settled there.

4. Register of Birth, or certified register of Baptism, evidence of the place of birth.

And be it enacted, That in any case in which the place of birth of any person may be in question before any Justices or any Court, with relation to settlement or removal, such Justices or Court shall admit a certified copy of the register of the birth of such person made under the provisions of the Act passed in the seventh year of the reign of King William the Fourth, intituled, "An Act for Registering Births, Deaths, and Marriages in England," containing a statement of the place of birth of such person as *primâ facie* evidence of the place of birth of such person; or if such person were born before the said Act came into operation, or if the place of birth is not stated in such register, such Justices or Court shall admit a copy of the register of the baptism of such person in which the place of birth is stated, certified by the incumbent, officiating curate, parish clerk, or any churchwarden of the parish to which such register belongs, and witnessed by One Witness, or the register of any church, chapel or meeting-house of persons professing the Roman Catholic religion or dissenting from the Church of England, as *primâ facie* evidence of the birth of such person in the place in which he appears by such register, or such copy thereof, to have been born, unless the contrary appear on the face thereof; but if the place so stated to be the place of birth be a parish comprising more than one township, vill, or place separately maintaining their own poor, such register or copy shall not be admitted as evidence of the birth of such person in any such township, vill, or place, unless such township, vill, or place, or some locality wholly within such township, vill, or place, be also expressly named as such place of birth.

5. Proviso for Settlements of Children born in Union Workhouses, &c., or under Warrants of Removal.

Provided always, and be it enacted, that if any child have been born in the workhouse of any Union, such child shall be deemed to have been born in the parish to which the mother of such child was, at the time of the birth, chargeable; and if any child have been born in any Asylum for the relief of houseless poor, or in any house licensed for the reception of pregnant women, or in any hospital for the reception and cure of persons suffering from disease or bodily injury, or in any county Lunatic Asylum, or in any house licensed for the reception of insane persons, or in any prison, if the mother of such child were not, before her admission into such house, hospital, asylum, or prison, respectively, resident in the parish in which such birth occurred, such mother not being settled in that parish, such child shall not, for the purposes of this Act, be deemed to have been born therein; and if any child have been born in any parish while his mother was under any warrant of removal, not executed at the time of the birth, nor afterwards abandoned or quashed, such child shall not, for the purposes of this Act, be deemed to have been born in such parish.

CHARGEABILITY OF PERSONS NOT SETTLED.—6. Declaration that persons are to be relieved at the charge of the parish where they are destitute, until removal or lawful cessation of their destitution.

And be it declared and enacted, That the overseers and guardians of every parish and the guardians of every union shall take order for the relief, according to the laws in force for the time being, of every poor person destitute therein, but not settled therein, in like manner as if he were settled therein, until he is lawfully removed therefrom, or until he ceases by other lawful means to be destitute therein.

REMOVAL.—7. Person chargeable to a parish in which he is not settled, liable to be removed to the parish of his settlement.

And be it enacted, That every person who has become chargeable to any parish in which he is not settled, shall be liable to be removed therefrom to any parish in which he is settled, subject to the provisions next hereinafter made; (that is to say)

Salvo 1. For married women not to be removed from their husband's parish.

Every woman during her marriage shall be liable to be removed to the parish in which her husband is deemed to be settled, if the same can be ascertained, and shall not be liable to be removed from such parish, or from her husband;

2 For Legitimate Children not to be removed from father's parish.

And every legitimate child under the age of *Sixteen* years, whose father is living, shall be liable to be removed to the parish in which his father is settled, if the same can be ascertained, and shall not, while resident anywhere with his father, be liable to be removed from him;

3. For Legitimate and Bastard Children not to be removed from their mothers.

And every child, under the age of *Sixteen* years, being legitimate, whose father is dead and whose mother is living, or being a bastard, whose mother is living, shall be liable to be removed to the parish to which his mother would, if chargeable, be liable to be removed, and shall not, while resident anywhere with his mother, be liable to be removed from her;

4. For Widows and their families not to be removed for One Year after the husband's death.

And no widow who at the time of her husband's death was residing with him, nor the children of such widow, whether legitimate or bastard, under the age of *Sixteen* years, shall be liable to be removed from the parish where she was so residing until the expiration of *One Year* after her husband's death;

5. For Widows not to be removed from the place of their husbands' settlement and death.

And no widow, who at the time of her husband's death was residing with him in the parish in which he was settled, shall be liable to be removed therefrom.

6. For persons chargeable through sickness, not to be removed until relieved forty days.

And no person who becomes chargeable to any parish on account of sickness or accident, shall be liable to be placed under a warrant of removal until he has received relief *bonâ fide* for the space of *Forty* days, without any interval of more than *Seven* consecutive days.

8. Persons only to be removed to the parish where settled. Exceptions.

And be it declared and enacted, That no person, except such as is hereby made liable to be removed to the parish of the husband's or father's or mother's or stepfather's settlement, and except persons born in Scotland, Ireland, the Isles of Man, Scilly, Jersey or Guernsey, and their families, shall be removed to any parish other than the parish in which such person is, under the provisions of this Act, deemed to be settled.

9. Amicable removal.

And be it enacted, That if the Overseers of any parish by writing under the hands of any Two or more of them, signed in the presence of any Justice of the Peace, and certified under his hand to be so signed, admit that any person is settled in such parish, or is liable to be removed thereto, and thereby agree to receive such person, such person shall be deemed to be settled in such parish, or removable thereto accordingly, without any warrant of Justices for such removal.

10. Summons and examination of persons liable to be removed; Warrant of removal.—Proviso for examination of infirm persons and prisoners.

And be it enacted, That if the Overseers of any parish shall complain to any One Justice of the Peace for the county, borough, or place in which such parish is situate, that any person is liable to be removed from such parish, such Justice may summon such person to come before any Two Justices of the Peace of such county, borough, or place, at a time and place to be named in such summons; and at such time and place any Two Justices of the Peace of such county, borough, or place, may hear and examine into the matter of such complaint, and if they see fit, they may make and issue a warrant, under their hands and seals, to remove such person to the parish in which he is deemed to be settled, or to which he is liable to be removed: Provided always, That if any such person be by reason of age, illness, or infirmity, unable to be brought up before such Two Justices, or if the husband or father, mother or stepfather, of any person liable to be removed, be a prisoner in any gaol or house of correction, or in the custody of any constable or peace officer, under or by virtue of any warrant of commitment, then any One Justice of the Peace may take the examination of such person, husband, father, mother, or stepfather, where he or she may be, in writing, touching his or her settlement; and such examination, signed by such Justice, shall be received and admitted as evidence of the facts therein stated, in the same manner and to the same extent as if the same facts were orally deposed to, before any Two Justices empowered to inquire into such settlement, who may thereupon make and issue their warrant of removal as effectually as if such person, husband, father, mother, or stepfather had appeared and been examined before such Two Justices.

11. Persons not to be removed under warrant till after forty days' notice; unless the removal be submitted to. In case of appeal, pauper not to be removed while it is pending.

And be it enacted, That where any person has been directed by warrant of Justices to be removed from any parish, if the Overseers of such parish within *Seven* Days after the making of such warrant send notice, by post or otherwise, to the Overseers of the parish to which such person is to be removed, that such person has become chargeable, and also within the said *Seven* Days send to the Overseers last-mentioned, a copy or counterpart of such warrant of removal, and a statement of the grounds upon which the same was made, the Overseers of the parish to which such person is so chargeable may, after the expiration of *Forty* days after the sending of such notice and copies or counterparts, remove such person, but not otherwise: Provided always, That if the Overseers of the parish to which such person is to be removed agree, by writing under their hands, to receive such person before the expiration of such *Forty* Days, the Overseers of the parish from which such person is to be removed may remove such person, although such *Forty* Days have not expired: Provided also, That if notice of appeal against the warrant for the removal of such person be received by the Overseers of the parish on whose behalf such warrant was obtained, they shall not remove such person until after the time for prosecuting such appeal has expired, or if such appeal be prosecuted, until the final determination thereof.

12. Overseers, or persons employed by them, may execute the warrant of removal.

And be it enacted, That such Overseers may employ any proper person to carry, remove and deliver any pauper directed by such warrant to be removed, and that the delivery by such person of any such pauper shall be as good, valid and effectual, to all purposes whatsoever, as if such pauper were delivered by any Overseer.

13. Penalty for procuring removals of Poor Persons without warrants of Justices.

And be it enacted, That, except as is provided by this Act, if any officer of any parish or union do for the purpose and with the intent of causing any poor person to become chargeable to any other parish or union to which such person was not then chargeable, convey any poor person out of the parish or union for which such officer acts, or cause or procure any poor person to be so conveyed, or give directly or indirectly any money or other relief or assistance, or afford or procure to be afforded any facility for such conveyance, or make any offer or promise, or use any threat to induce any poor person to depart from such parish or union, and if, in consequence of such conveyance or departure, any poor person become chargeable to any other parish or union, such officer, on conviction thereof before any Two Justices (either of the place from whence such poor person has been conveyed, or had departed as aforesaid, or of the place where such poor person has so become chargeable) shall forfeit and pay for every such offence any sum not exceeding *Five Pounds*, nor less than *Forty Shillings*.

14. Delivery of Paupers under orders of removal.

And be it enacted, That the delivery of any pauper under any warrant of removal to any officer of the Workhouse of any parish, or of any union in which such parish is comprised, at such Workhouse, shall be deemed to be a delivery of such pauper to the Overseers of the said parish.

15. Suspension of the execution of warrants of removal.—Recovery of expenses incurred by such suspension.—Appeal given where such charges exceed Ten Pounds.—Award of Costs.

Provided always, and be it enacted, That where any warrant has been made for the removal of any person, if it appear to the Justices who made such warrant, or to any other Two Justices of the same county or jurisdiction, that such person is unable to travel, by reason of sickness or other infirmity, or that it would be dangerous for him to do so, such Justices shall suspend the execution of such warrant, as well with respect to such person as with respect to every other person thereby directed to be removed, until the same may be executed without danger to any person who is the subject thereof, and shall indorse such suspension on the said warrant of removal, and shall sign the same; and when such Justices, or any other Two Justices of the same county or jurisdiction, are satisfied that such warrant may be executed without danger to any person who is the subject thereof, such Justices shall direct such warrant to be executed, and shall indorse such direction on the said warrant of removal, and shall sign the same; and if it be proved on oath before such last-mentioned Justices that any expenses of relief or maintenance, other than of medical relief, have been incurred by such suspension, such Justices may order the Overseers of the parish to which such person is directed to be removed, to pay to the Overseers of the parish from which such person is directed to be removed, such expenses of relief and maintenance, other than of medical relief; and if the Overseers of the parish in whose behalf such warrant was made have, within *Seven* Days after such suspension, sent, by post or otherwise, to the Overseers of the parish to which such person is directed to be removed notice of such warrant of removal, and of the suspension thereof, and have also within such *Seven* Days sent to the Overseers last-mentioned a copy or counterpart of such warrant and suspension, and a statement of the grounds upon which such warrant was made, and if such person be afterwards removed under such warrant, or if such person die before the execution of such warrant, then the Overseers of such last-named parish shall pay such expenses; and if they refuse or neglect to pay the same within *Fourteen* Days after the demand thereof, and if they do not within such *Fourteen* Days give notice of appeal against the order to pay such expenses, then the Overseers of the parish on whose behalf such warrant was made may recover such expenses, together with cost of recovering the same, in the same manner as penalties and forfeitures; and when the sum so ordered to be paid on account of such charges exceeds the sum of *Ten Pounds*, if the Overseers of the parish ordered to pay the same think such parish aggrieved thereby, and if, within *Fourteen* Days after demand made of payment under such order, they give notice to the Overseers of the parish on whose behalf such order was made, of their intention to appeal against the same, then the Overseers of the parish ordered to pay such sum, may appeal to the General or Quarter Sessions of the Peace, held next after the expiration of *Fourteen* Days from the giving of such notice, for the county, city, borough or place wherein the parish on whose behalf such order was made doth lie; and if such court be of opinion that the sum so ordered is more than of right ought to have been paid, such court shall strike out the sum contained in the order, and insert therein the sum which in the judgment of such court ought to be paid; and upon such appeal before such court, or upon proof made before such court that notice of such appeal has been given, although such appeal has not been prosecuted, such Court shall award to the party in whose favour such appeal is determined, or to whom such notice was given, such costs and charges in the law as such Court in their discretion think just and reasonable, to be paid by the party against whom such appeal is determined, or by whom such notice was given; and the party to whom such costs and charges are awarded may recover the sum inserted in such order by such Court as aforesaid, and the costs and charges awarded by such Court as aforesaid, in the same manner as penalties and forfeitures: Provided always, That if in any case it appear to the Justices ordering payment of such costs and charges, or to the Court of Quarter Sessions on appeal against such order, that the removal of any such person was negligently or improperly delayed after he was in a fit state to be removed, such Justices or such Court may reduce the amount of the costs and charges so to be paid, as to them may seem fit.

16. Overseers may abandon a warrant of removal, paying the other parties' costs.

And be it enacted, That in any case in which a warrant has been made for the removal of any person from any parish, and notice thereof sent as aforesaid, if at any time after such notice, whether notice of appeal against such warrant have or have not been then given, the Overseers of such parish give notice in writing under the hands of any two or more of them to the Overseers of the parish to which such person is directed to be removed, that they abandon such warrant, then such warrant, and all proceedings consequent thereon, shall become and be null and void to all intents and purposes, as if the same had not been made; and shall not be given in evidence in case any warrant be afterwards obtained for the removal of any person who may have been affected by such first-mentioned warrant; and the Overseers abandoning such warrant shall pay to the Overseers of the parish to which the removal was thereby directed to be made, the costs incurred by such last-mentioned Overseers, by reason of such warrant, and of all subsequent proceedings thereon; and if such last-mentioned Overseers apply to the proper officer of the Court before whom any appeal against such warrant, if it had not been abandoned, might have been brought, and if they produce to him the notice of such abandonment, and if they satisfy him that such reasonable notice of taxation has been given to the Overseers abandoning such warrant as in his judgment the distance between the parishes requires, such Officer shall tax such costs; and may thereupon charge and receive the usual costs of taxation; and shall indorse the sum allowed by him as costs, and the amount of the said costs of taxation upon the notice of abandonment; and if such costs, being lawfully demanded, be not paid within *Ten* Days after taxation, the Overseers entitled to the same may recover them as penalties and forfeitures.

17. Duplicate of Warrant of Removal, &c., to be transmitted to the Clerk of the Peace, who is to preserve the same.

And be it enacted, That the Clerk to the Justices, or, if there be no such Clerk, then One of the Justices, who have made any warrant of removal, shall transmit within Days from the making of such warrant a duplicate of such warrant, and also all the original depositions upon which such warrant was made to the Clerk of the Peace for the county, borough or place of which the said Justices are Justices, and that such duplicate and depositions shall thenceforward be kept by said Clerk of the Peace.

18. Clerk of the Peace to furnish Copies.

And be it enacted, That if the Overseers of the parish to which any person is by such warrant ordered to be removed, do, by writing delivered to such Clerk of the Peace, require such Clerk of the Peace to furnish them with a copy of such duplicate and depositions, or either, such Clerk of the Peace shall, within a reasonable time after the delivery to him of such written requisition, furnish a copy of such duplicate or depositions, as the case may be, on being paid therefore at the rate of

APPEAL AGAINST WARRANT OF REMOVAL.—19. Overseers of the parish aggrieved by warrant of removal may appeal.—Appeal only to be respited on affidavit of special circumstances.—Appeal preserved against Warrants of Removal made before this Act.

And be it enacted, That, if the Overseers of the parish to which any person is by any warrant directed to be removed as aforesaid, consider such parish to be aggrieved thereby; and if within *Twenty-one* Days after they have received the statement of the grounds upon which the same was made, and the copy or counterpart of the warrant, such Overseers give to the Overseers of the parish on whose behalf such warrant was obtained, notice in writing, under the hands of any Two or more of them, of their intention to appeal against such warrant, together with a statement in writing, under the hands of any Two or more of them, of the grounds of such appeal, the said Overseers of the parish to which such person is directed to be removed, may appeal to the General or Quarter Sessions of the Peace to be held for the county, city, borough or place wherein the parish on whose behalf such order was obtained, or any part thereof, doth lie; and no appeal against any warrant of removal shall be entered at any Sessions of the Peace by the appellant parish, and respited to the next Sessions, save only upon an affidavit of the special circumstances to the satisfaction of the Court, and upon such terms as to costs and otherwise as to the Court may seem fit; Provided always, That when any person has, before the passing of this Act, been placed under a warrant of removal, it shall be lawful for any person to appeal against such warrant, in like manner and with the like effect in all respects as if this Act had not been passed: Provided also, That where any appeal against a warrant of removal has been made, but not finally decided upon before the passing of this Act, nothing in this Act contained shall in any way affect the decision to be given upon such appeal; and such decision shall have the like effect as to the settlement of the persons named in such warrant, as if it had been given before the passing of this Act.

20. Overseers may have access to the Pauper touching his Settlement or liability to Removal.

And be it enacted, That the Overseers giving such notice of appeal, or their attorney, or any other person authorised by them, may, until such appeal is heard and decided, at all proper times have free access to the person directed to be removed, for the purpose of examining him touching his settlement or liability to be removed; and if it be necessary for the more effectual examination of such person, that he should be taken out of the parish in whose behalf the warrant was obtained, such Overseers may remove him therefrom for the time which may be necessary for that purpose; and in such case the said Overseers shall defray the expense of such removal, and of the maintenance of such person during the same.

21. Quarter Sessions to hear appeal; no grounds to be gone into, but those set forth in the respondents' and appellants' statements.

And be it enacted, That the Justices of the Peace at the General or Quarter Sessions of the county, borough or place wherein the parish or any part thereof is situate from which the warrant appealed against has directed the removal to be made, held next after the expiration of *Fourteen* Days from the day on which the notice of appeal was given, shall hear and determine such appeal upon the grounds set forth respectively in the respondents' statement of the grounds of the warrant of removal, and in the appellants' statement of the grounds of their appeal, and neither the respondents nor appellants shall, on the hearing of such appeal, go into, or give evidence of, or be heard upon, any other grounds of removal or of appeal than those set forth in their respective statements as aforesaid.

22. On trial of Appeal, the Duplicate of Warrant and the Depositions transmitted to the Clerk of the Peace, may be referred to for certain purposes.

And be it enacted, That upon the trial of any appeal against any such warrant of removal, the Court trying such appeal, or either party, shall be at liberty to refer to the said duplicate and depositions so transmitted as aforesaid to the Clerk of the Peace; but such depositions shall not be considered as furnishing evidence of the facts therein deposed to, except only for the purpose of showing that the person or persons making such depositions has or have made the statements therein contained, and except only where evidence of the fact of such statements having been made is by law admissible: Provided nevertheless, That where any party who has made such depositions is dead at the time of trying the appeals, the deposition of such party shall be admissible at such trial as evidence of the facts therein stated, in the same way and to the same extent as such statement would have been admissible at such trial if then orally deposed to by such person: Provided nevertheless, that on the trial of any such appeal no warrant of removal shall be quashed or set aside, either wholly or in part, on the ground that such depositions do not furnish sufficient evidence to support, or that any matter therein contained raises an objection to, the warrant or the statement of the grounds of removal, except when such objection to the warrant or statement arises upon depositions given in evidence, in consequence of the death of the party making such depositions, and in that case such objection shall have the same weight and effect as if it were raised by the oral evidence of such party.

23. Costs to be awarded.

And be it enacted, That upon any appeal against any warrant of removal being heard before any Court of General or Quarter Sessions, or upon proof before any such Court, of notice of such appeal having been given, though such appeal were not afterwards prosecuted, such Court shall order either party to pay to the other, such costs and charges as they consider just and reasonable, and shall certify the amount thereof; and if either of the parties have included in their respective statements, any grounds of removal or of appeal which, in the opinion of the Court determining such appeal, are frivolous or vexatious, such Court may, at their discretion, direct such party to pay the whole or any part of the costs incurred by the other party in disputing any such grounds, and shall certify the amount thereof; and if the amount so certified in any of the cases aforesaid be demanded of the Overseers, liable to pay the same, and if such certificate thereof be produced to them, and if they refuse or neglect to pay the same, the overseers entitled thereto may recover the same as penalties and forfeitures.

24. Costs may be taxed by the proper Officer at any time, although the Court be not sitting.

And be it enacted, That where, either by this Act or any preceding Acts, costs are incidental to any warrant or removal, or any appeal therefrom, or any proceedings touching the same, such costs may be taxed by the proper officer in that behalf at any time; and such taxation, when duly made in other respects, shall be valid and effectual, whether or not the court to which such officer belongs be sitting at the time of the taxation, in the same manner as if such court were actually sitting at the time of the taxation.

MAINTENANCE OF PAUPERS UNDER WARRANT.—25. Cost of relief of persons under Warrant of removal to be repaid.

And be it enacted, That where a warrant has been made for the removal of any person from any parish, and the liability of such person to be removed under such warrant has been admitted by submission to the warrant, or adjudged upon appeal, the Overseers of such parish may recover from the Overseers of the parish to which such person was by such warrant directed to be removed, the charges and expenses of his relief and maintenance lawfully incurred from the time when notice was sent that he had become chargeable, until the time when he might lawfully have been removed; and if the same be not paid within *Three* Days after a demand thereof, the Overseers entitled thereto may recover the same in the same manner as penalties and forfeitures: Provided always, That no charges or expenses of relief or maintenance incurred by reason of the suspension of any such warrant shall be recoverable, except upon the conditions hereinbefore prescribed.

SERVICE OF NOTICES.—26. Notices of Removal may be served by Post.

And be it enacted, That every notice of any poor person being chargeable, and every copy or counterpart or notice of any warrant (whether suspended or otherwise) for the removal of any poor person, and every statement of the grounds upon which any such warrant is made, and every agreement in writing to receive a person under a warrant of removal, and every notice of appeal against any such warrant, and every notice containing the grounds of any such appeal, and every notice of the abandonment of such warrant, and every bill or demand of costs incurred under or by reason of any such warrant, and every notice of appeal against any order for payment of costs incurred by reason of the suspension of any warrant of removal, shall be held to have been properly served or delivered, if it be proved that the same was properly addressed to the parties entitled to receive the same, and endorsed on the outside of the letter or packet with the name of the document as it is above described, and put into the post-office, and registered according to any regulations in force at the time, under the authority of Her Majesty's Postmaster-General, *Seven* Days at the least before the time when the same is required to be served or delivered, unless the party to be affected by such notice or other document prove that the same has not been duly received, and if any person make oath that he so put such letter or packet into the post-office, and if he produce a receipt for the same, purporting to be signed by the Postmaster or other person authorised to register letters, and state upon oath to the satisfaction of the Court before which he produces the receipt, the circumstances under which and the person from whom he received the receipt, the posting and registering of such letter or packet shall be deemed to be sufficiently proved.

REMOVAL OF POOR OF SCOTLAND, IRELAND, &C.—27. Provision for removal of natives of Scotland, Ireland, and the Isles of Man, Scilly, Jersey and Guernsey.

Provided always, and be it enacted, That if any person born in Scotland or Ireland, or in the Isle of Man, or Scilly, or Jersey, or Guernsey, not deemed to be settled in England nor being temporarily or permanently exempted from the liability to be removed under the provisions of this Act become chargeable, by himself, herself, or any of his or her family, to any parish in England, such person, his wife, and any of his or her children so chargeable shall be liable to be removed therefrom to Scotland, Ireland, the Isle of Man, Scilly, Jersey, or Guernsey, respectively, accordingly as he or she may belong thereto; and if the Overseers of such parish complain thereof to any one Justice of the Peace, such Justice may summon such person to come before any Two Justices of the Peace, at any time and place to be named in the summons; and at such time and place any Two Justices may hear and examine into the matter of such complaint, and if they see fit they may make and issue a warrant under their hands and seals, to remove such person forthwith, at the expense of such parish in the first instance.

28. Justices in Quarter Sessions to make new regulations for removal of Scottish and Irish Poor, &c. to their respective places of birth or residence.

And be it enacted, That the Justices of the Peace of every county, city, borough or place, shall at their General or Quarter Sessions of the Peace to be holden next after the passing of this Act, or some adjournment thereof, and from time to time thereafter, as they may see occasion, make regulations for the more effectually carrying into effect the provisions of this Act for the removal of such persons, their wives and children, whether by land or sea, or part of the way by land and part by sea; and as regards persons born in Scotland or Ireland, and their families, such Justices shall, in such regulations, provide, so far as may be, for the removing of such persons to parts or places nearest to the respective places where such persons were born or have resided; and such regulations, when approved by the Poor Law Commissioners, shall be observed and carried into effect by all the Justices of the Peace, Overseers, Constables, and other persons charged with, or concerned in such removal into such respective county, city, borough or place; and when any such regulations have been so approved, all rules, orders, regulations, and directions heretofore made for the removal of persons born in Scotland, Ireland, or the Isles of Man, Scilly or Guernsey, shall cease to have effect.

29. Expenses of parishes to be repaid out of county rates.

And be it enacted, That in case the Overseers of the parish on whose complaint such last-mentioned warrant of removal was made, bring or send to the Clerk of the Peace, or Town Clerk of the county, city, borough, or place, in which such parish is situate, such warrant of removal accompanied with an affidavit sworn before some Justice of the Peace of such county, city, borough, or place, (who is hereby authorised to administer the same), of the amount of the expenses, bonâ fide incurred and paid by such Overseers on account of such removal, and also a statement of the several items comprised in such amount, such Justice of the Peace or Town Clerk shall lay the same before the Justices of the Peace assembled at the Quarter Sessions, or adjournment thereof, holden for such county, city, borough, or place, next after he has received the same; and the said Justices, so assembled as aforesaid, shall, if the regulations in force in regard to such removal have been duly complied with, order the amount of such expenses to be paid out of the county rate raised in such county, city, borough, or place.

30. How such expenses are to be defrayed within London.

And be it enacted, That all such expenses as last aforesaid properly and reasonably made out of the rates of any parish within the City of London, shall be charged against the said City of London; and when the Justices of the said City of London assembled at any Quarter Sessions or adjourned Sessions have audited and allowed such expenses, the Chamberlain of the said City of London shall repay such expenses to the Overseers of the said parish; and the Justices of the said City of London shall, at such times as they may think fit, order a rate to be made in the several wards of the said City for the repayment of such expenses, and thereupon such rate shall be made in the same manner and with the same powers and authorities as the rates made for the relief of the poor in such parishes.

31. How such expenses are to be defrayed by cities, &c., not contributing to county rate.

And be it enacted, That in any city, borough, town corporate, division or liberty which does not contribute to the county rate, or in which no county rate, or rate in the nature of a county rate, is raised, but comprises more than one parish, the Justices of the Peace for such city, borough, town corporate, division or liberty, assembled at any Quarter or adjourned Sessions of the Peace, shall order a general rate to be made in the parishes within such city, borough, town corporate, division or liberty, at such time as such Justices think fit, for the repayment of the expenses incurred for the removal of persons born in Scotland, Ireland, or the Islands of Man, Scilly, Jersey or Guernsey, and their families as aforesaid; and thereupon such rate shall be made in each of such parishes in the same manner and with the same powers and authorities as the rates made for the relief of the poor in such parishes.

32. Appeals against such removals may be lodged at the instance of Boards of Guardians in Ireland, and of Kirk Session, Heritors, or Borough Magistrates in Scotland.

And be it enacted, That if any Board of Guardians of any Union in Ireland, or the

Heritors and Kirk Session, or Borough Magistrates in Scotland, think themselves aggrieved by any removal of any poor person under the provisions of the said Act; and if they forward to the Poor Law Commissioners a statement of the case, and of any grounds for concluding that such poor person is to be deemed to be settled in any parish in England, or was liable to be removed to any parish in England, or was not in law liable to be removed from the parish from which he was in fact removed; and if they, or any persons on their behalf, give good security, in England, to the said Commissioners, for the payment of all costs which may be incurred in any appeal against the warrant for the removal of such poor person, such Commissioners, if satisfied that it will be expedient so to do, may appeal, on behalf of the persons so aggrieved, to the justices of the Peace at any Quarter Sessions holden for the county, city, borough or place from which such removal was made, held at any time within *Six* calendar Months after such removal was completed; and such Court shall proceed therein as in any case of appeal against a warrant of removal under this Act; and if the warrant of removal is reversed by such Court, the Overseers of the parish on whose behalf the same was obtained shall pay the necessary expenses and charges of conveying the poor person removed under the same back to such parish; and if they refuse or neglect to pay the same within *Three* Days after demand thereof, the persons on whose behalf such appeal was brought, or any person authorised by them, may recover the same as penalties and forfeitures: Provided always, That the Overseers of the parish on whose behalf such warrant was obtained, may at any time after such appeal give notice in writing, under the hands of any Two or more of them, to the said Commissioners, and to the persons on whose behalf such appeal was brought, that they abandon such warrant; and if they thereupon pay to such persons or to any person authorised by them, the expenses incurred by such persons by reason of such warrant, and in any proceedings consequent thereon, and the necessary expenses and charges of conveying the person removed under the same back to such parish, such appeal shall be no further prosecuted.

33. Recital of 4 and 5 Will. 4, c. 76, s. 33.—Poor Law Commissioners to declare Unions for Settlement.

And whereas by the said Act made in the fifth year of the reign of his late Majesty King William the Fourth, for the Amendment and better Administration of the Laws relating to the Poor in England and Wales, it is enacted, "That in any Union already formed or which may hereafter be formed in pursuance of or under the provisions of this Act, it shall and may be lawful for the Guardians elected by the parishes forming such Union, by any writing under the hands of all such Guardians, to agree, subject to the approbation of the said Commissioners, for or on behalf of the respective parishes forming such Union, that for the purposes of settlement such parishes shall be considered as one parish: And whereas it is expedient that such Unions for the purposes of settlement should be formed as soon as conveniently may be after the passing of this Act; be it enacted, That the Poor Law Commissioners shall, as soon as may be, without any such agreement by the Guardians as is required by the said recited Act, proceed, by an order under their hands and seal, to declare every Union of parishes constituted or to be hereafter constituted under the said recited Act, a Union for the purposes of settlement, and shall specify in every such order the day, being not less than *Fourteen* days after the date thereof, when the same shall come into force.

34. Commissioners may in certain cases delay Declaration of any Union for the purposes of Settlement.

And whereas under the said recited Act it will not, after the time that any Union is declared to be united for the purposes of settlement, be lawful for any parish to be added to or taken from such Union; be it enacted, That the said Commissioners shall, in declaring such Unions for the purposes of Settlement, as aforesaid, have regard to the expediency or propriety of any alteration to be made in such Union before the same is declared, and may delay the declaration of the same, or the coming in force of their order, when it is necessary to effect any such alteration.

35. Commissioners may declare Unions under Local Acts to be Unions for Settlement.

And be it enacted, That it shall be lawful for the Poor Law Commissioners, if they see fit, but not otherwise, to declare any Union of parishes under any local Act to be a Union for the purposes of settlement, in the same manner and with the same consequences as if such Union were constituted under the provisions of the said recited Act.

36. Every Union for Settlement to be as one Parish.

And be it enacted, That from and after the day on which the declaration of any Union for the purposes of settlement, as hereinbefore provided, comes into force, the whole of the parishes in such Union shall become as one parish for the purposes of settlement and removal; and every pauper who would otherwise be deemed to be settled in any parish in the Union, shall be deemed to be settled in such Union, and not in any parish; and every pauper who would otherwise be liable to be removed from or to any parish in the Union shall be liable to be removed from or to such Union, and not from or to such parish; and no pauper shall thereafter acquire or be deemed to have any settlement in any parish of such Union, or shall be liable to be removed from one parish in such Union to another parish in such Union.

37. Declaration to be notified to Clerks of the Peace, and published in the London Gazette.

And be it enacted, That when any Union is declared to be an Union for the purposes of settlement under this Act, the said Commissioners shall forthwith notify the same to the Clerk of the Peace of every county in which any part of the said Union is situated, and shall forthwith cause the same to be published in the London Gazette.

38. Guardians and their Officers to proceed in matters of Settlement and Removal.

And be it enacted, That every notice of any poor person being chargeable, and every copy or counterpart or notice of any warrant (whether suspended or otherwise) for the removal of any poor person, and every statement of the grounds upon which any such warrant is made, and every agreement in writing to receive a person under a warrant of removal, and every notice of appeal against any such warrant, and every notice containing the grounds of any such appeal, and every notice of the abandonment of such warrant, and every bill or demand of costs incurred under or by reason of any such warrant made, and every notice of appeal against any order for payment of costs incurred by reason of the suspension of any warrant of removal, and every other document whatsoever relating to the settlement or removal of the poor, which might otherwise be lawfully sent to or served on the Overseers of any parish in such Union, shall, after the day on which such declaration of a Union for the purposes of settlement comes in force, be sent to and served on the Clerk to the Guardians of such Union; and subject to the regulations of the Poor Law Commissioners, the Board of Guardians of such Union, or the Clerk to the Guardians of such Union, or any other person properly authorised thereunto by such Board of Guardians, shall be authorised to pay such expenses, and, as the case may be, empowered or obliged to take all such measures whatsoever with respect to the settlement or removal of any pauper as any Overseers might otherwise have lawfully paid, or have been empowered or obliged to take, with respect to the settlement or removal of such pauper in relation to the parish for which they are Overseers; and it shall be lawful for the Poor Law Commissioners, by order under their hands and seal, to authorise and direct any such Board of Guardians to appoint paid officers for discharging all duties and attending to all questions and proceedings relating to the removal or to the settlement of paupers; and the said Commissioners shall exercise the same powers with regard to all officers employed in relation to the settlement or removal of the poor, which they may exercise under the said recited Act, and under any other Act or Acts, with regard to the qualifications, salaries, districts, or continuance in office of paid officers; and for the purpose of regulating the mode in which removals and all proceedings relating thereto are to be conducted by Guardians, Overseers and other officers, whether in Unions or single parishes, it shall be lawful for the Poor Law Commissioners to require any returns or information, and to make and issue rules and regulations for carrying this Act into effect.

39. Guardians may take up proceedings commenced before the declaration of the Union.

And be it enacted, That whenever any warrant of removal has been obtained before the day on which the declaration of a Union for the purposes of settlement, comprising either of the two parishes affected by such warrant, comes in force, and the settlement of the pauper removed or to be removed by such warrant is not finally determined before such day, it shall be lawful for the Board of Guardians of such Union to take up and continue any proceedings connected with such warrant of removal, as if the said warrant had been obtained by or served upon them under the provisions of this Act.

40. Commissioners to ascertain and declare the averages of such Unions.

And be it enacted, That the said Commissioners shall, before declaring any such Union for the purposes of settlement, ascertain the amount of Poor-rate levied in each parish in such Union, for the *Seven* Years ending the Twenty-fifth of March One thousand eight hundred and Forty-five, and after deducting from such amount all sums actually paid for county, borough or police-rate, or for contributions in the nature of county, borough or police rate, they shall, by an order under their hands and seal, fix and declare the said average amount of rates levied for each parish in such Union.

41. Proviso for the case where Monies have been misapplied in the relief of the Poor.

Provided always, and be it enacted, That in ascertaining such average amount as aforesaid, if it be alleged, in writing, by any Guardian, Overseer or Rate-payer of any parish in the Union, that any parish in such Union has defrayed the cost of its poor irregularly from the highway-rate, church-rate or other fund, or has applied any such rate or fund in such a manner as to operate unfairly and to the prejudice of the other parishes, in determining the average amount of rates levied as hereinbefore enacted, it shall be lawful for the said Commissioners or any of their Assistant-commissioners to inquire into the circumstances, by examining any Surveyor of the Highways, Churchwarden or other person, on oath or otherwise, and by calling for any books, deeds, papers or other documents which they may deem necessary; and such Commissioners may, if they see fit, after considering all the circumstances of the case, but before declaring the said average amount, make such addition to the average amount to be declared in respect of the said parish, as to them may seem fair and just, with reference to the other parishes of the said Union.

42. Expenses thenceforth to be charged according to the declared averages.—Overseers, &c. to levy and pay the Sums ordered by the Guardians.

And be it enacted, That in every Union declared under this Act for the purposes of settlement, all expenses whatsoever paid by the Board of Guardians or their officers for the maintenance, relief, burial or removal of the poor, for the salaries of officers, and all other purposes connected with the administration of the laws for the relief of the poor, as well as for vaccination, shall from the date of such declaration coming in force, be charged and continue to be charged on the several parishes included in such Union, in proportion to the average amount of rates so declared by the said Commissioners; and the Board of Guardians of each such Union, in order to defray such expenses, shall from time to time as they may deem necessary, make and issue orders on the Overseers of the several parishes included in such Union in the form given in the Schedule to this Act (marked F.;) and all such Overseers shall be bound to assess, levy and collect the rates of their respective parishes, and at the time and in the manner prescribed in such order to pay the contributions thereby required; and if such order be served on all the Overseers of the parish, not being Churchwardens thereof, within *Three* Days of the date thereof, and if such Overseers neglect so to pay such contributions within a period of *Four* Weeks from the date of such order, any Two Justices shall issue a warrant under their hands and seal, empowering the said Guardians to recover such contributions by distress and sale of the goods of the Overseers so neglecting to pay the same: Provided always, That if it appear to the said Justices, that any Assistant Overseer or Rate Collector has neglected to levy and collect the rates and to discharge his duties in respect of such rates as by law required, and that the default in paying such monies to the Guardians is caused by such neglect of the said Assistant Overseer or Collector, then the said Justices shall cause the money to be levied as aforesaid by distress and sale of the goods of the said Assistant Overseer or Collector, and not of the Overseers.

43. Relief to be given by Overseers in sudden and urgent necessity, and to be charged to the Parish.

And be it declared and enacted, That every Overseer shall continue to be bound to afford such and the same temporary or medical relief in cases of sudden and urgent necessity, or in cases of sudden and dangerous illness, as he is now by law bound to afford, anything in this Act contained to the contrary notwithstanding; and the cost of all such relief given by an Overseer of any parish, and of all medical relief afforded by any person not being a Medical Officer of the Union or parish in case of sudden and urgent necessity by order of an Overseer and the cost of all relief given by order of any Justice of the Peace addressed to an Overseer, shall be entered in the accounts of such Overseer, and shall be charged by him against the parish for which he acts, and if lawfully given shall be allowed by the Auditor in the accounts of such Overseer.

44. Proviso for Contributions for Repayment of Loans already discharged by different Parishes in unequal proportions.

Provided always, and be it enacted, That when any sum of money has been lawfully borrowed by such Union for the building of a Workhouse or other purpose, and any of the parishes in such Union have, from the proceeds of the sale of parish property or any other fund, repaid any of such money in any greater proportion than the rest of such Union, such parish shall be liable to be charged only with its respective share of the principal money remaining unpaid, and the interest accruing thereon, as it would if such Union had not been declared an Union for the purposes of settlement; but with regard to all parishes not having so repaid any of such money in a greater proportion than the rest of the Union, all ordinary charges in respect of such borrowed money, whether for principal or interest, shall be charged on such parishes, in proportion to the average amount of rates declared by the said Commissioners as hereinbefore directed.

45. Penalties for offences against Parishes, extended to Unions.

And be it enacted, That any person returning to any Union for the purposes of settlement without a certificate, after removal from such Union, and becoming chargeable to such Union, shall be liable to punishment in the same manner as if he returned without a certificate to any parish after removal therefrom, and became chargeable to such parish; and all officers or persons making, causing or aiding any illegal removal from or to a Union, shall be liable to the same penalties as if the same removal were from or to a parish; and all officers or persons guilty of any misconduct in relation to any removal of a pauper from or to any Union, shall be liable to the same proceedings and the same punishment as such officer would be liable to if he were guilty of such misconduct in relation to the removal of any pauper from or to any parish; and subject to the express provisions hereinbefore contained, all removals to or from a Union, and all warrants for such removals and all acts, proceedings or documents relating to such removals, or warrants, or connected therewith, shall, so far as the same are applicable, operate in the same manner and carry the same consequences as if such removal were a removal from or to a parish, and such acts, proceedings, warrants, orders and documents had reference to a removal from or to a parish.

46. Guardians of Parishes to have the like powers as to settlement and removal as the Guardians of Unions.

And be it enacted, That every Board of Guardians constituted for a single parish under the provisions of the said first-recited Act, or of any local Act, shall act in the like manner in all matters relating to the settlement and removal of the poor; and the said Commissioners may direct the Guardians of any such parish to appoint paid officers, and shall exercise the like powers with regard to such paid officers as is hereinbefore provided in the case of Guardians of Unions for the purposes of settlement.

CONSTRUCTION AND LIMITATION OF THE ACT.—47. The Poor Law Amendment Act and this Act to be construed as one Act.

And be it enacted, That the said Act of the fifth year of the reign of King William the Fourth, "for the Amendment and better Administration of the Laws relating to the Poor in England and Wales," and all Acts to amend and extend the same, and the present Act, except so far as the provisions of any former Act are altered, amended or repealed by any subsequent Act, shall be construed as one Act.

48. Forms in the Schedule may be used in proceedings under this Act.

And be it enacted, That in all proceedings under this Act it shall be sufficient in the law to use, with such changes only as the facts of each case may require, the forms contained in the Schedule to this Act annexed, for the purposes in the Titles to such forms respectively specified.

49. Act limited to England and Wales, except so far as relates to persons born in Scotland, &c.

And be it enacted, That this Act shall apply so far as the same is applicable to the removal of poor persons born in Scotland and Ireland, and the Isles of Man, Scilly, Jersey and Guernsey, and their families; but in other respects this Act shall extend only to England.

50. Act may be amended this Session.

And be it enacted, That this Act may be amended or repealed by any Act to be passed in this present Session of Parliament.

SCHEDULE

TO WHICH THE FOREGOING ACT REFERS.

SCHEDULE (A.)

FORM of ADMISSION of SETTLEMENT, &c.

WE, Two of the Overseers of the Parish, &c. of do hereby admit that is now settled in the said parish, &c. [*or*, is now liable to be removed thereto,] and we do hereby agree to receive h without any warrant of Justices for h removal. Given under our hands this day of in the year One thousand eight hundred and

Signature of Overseers

I, being a Justice of the Peace of and for the county of, &c. do hereby certify that the above named and being two of the Overseers of the parish, &c. of did sign the above admission in my presence. Given under my hand on the day above written.

Signature of Justice of the Peace

SCHEDULE (B.)

FORM of WARRANT of REMOVAL.

County of } To the Churchwardens and Overseers of the Poor of the parish of in the said county of and to the Churchwardens and Overseers of the poor of the parish of in the county of and to each and every of them.

Upon complaint of the Churchwardens and Overseers of the poor of the parish of aforesaid, in the said county of unto us, whose names are hereunto set and seals affixed, being two of Her Majesty's Justices of the Peace in and for the said county of that has become chargeable to the said parish of We, the said Justices, upon due proof made thereof, as well upon the oath of the said as otherwise, do adjudge the same to be true: And we do likewise adjudge that the lawful settlement of the said is in the said parish of in the county of and that he, &c. is liable to be removed thereto; we do, therefore, require you the Churchwardens and Overseers of the said parish of or some one of you, to convey the said from and out of the said parish of to the said parish of and him to deliver to the Churchwardens and Overseers of the poor there, or to some or one of them, together with this our order; and we do also hereby require you the said Churchwardens and Overseers of the parish of to receive and provide for him according to law.

Given under our hands and seals this day of One thousand eight hundred and

A. B. (L. S.)
C. D. (L. S.)

SCHEDULE (C.)

FORM of SUSPENSION of a WARRANT of REMOVAL to be indorsed on the back of such Warrant.

WHEREAS it doth appear to us and being Two of Her Majesty's Justices in and for the county of that the pauper within ordered to be removed, is at present unable to travel, by reason of sickness and infirmity, [*or*, that it would be dangerous for him to do so;] we do therefore hereby suspend the execution of the within Warrant of Removal, until it be made to appear to us that the same may be executed without danger.

Given under our hands the day of One thousand eight hundred and

A. B.
C. D.

SCHEDULE (D.)

FORM of a PERMISSION to execute the WARRANT of REMOVAL to be indorsed thereon, and ORDER of Payment of EXPENSES incurred by the suspension.

WHEREAS it hath been now made to appear to us, A. B. and C. D., being Two of Her Majesty's Justices, in and for the County of and we are satisfied that the within Warrant of Removal may be executed without danger, we do therefore hereby direct such Warrant to be forthwith executed accordingly.

And whereas it is duly proved to us upon oath, that the sum of hath been necessarily incurred by the suspension of the within Warrant of Removal, in the relief, not being medical relief, of who is directed by the said Warrant to be removed to the parish of we do therefore order the Churchwardens and Overseers of the poor of the said parish of to pay the said sum of to upon demand.

Given under our hands the day of One thousand eight hundred and

A. B.
C. D.

SCHEDULE (E.)

FORM of WARRANT of REMOVAL of Persons born in Scotland or Ireland, or in the Isle of Man, or Scilly, or Jersey, or Guernsey.

To the Constable of the [parish or township] of in the

County of } to wit, } WHEREAS complaint hath been made by the [Churchwardens and Overseers of the poor, or Guardians of the poor,] of the parish, township, union [or as the case may be,] in the said county of unto us, whose names are hereunto set, and seals affixed, Two of Her Majesty's Justices of the Peace acting in and for the said county, that a person born in Scotland [or, Ireland, or the Isle of Man, or Scilly, or Jersey, or Guernsey,] hath become and is now chargeable to the said parish and [or, to the parish of in the said union:] And whereas, upon examination of the said taken upon oath before us (which examination is hereto annexed,) it doth appear, and we do adjudge that the hath not a settlement in England, and is not exempted temporarily or permanently from the liability to be removed from the said parish, and is not liable to be removed to any parish in England; and that he hath a wife named and children, videlicet neither of which children has any settlement in England.

These are therefore to require you, the said constable of aforesaid, in the county of aforesaid, to convey the said his wife and family aforesaid, to Scotland [&c.] in the manner directed by the regulations of the Justices of the said County, and approved by the Poor Law Commissioners in pursuance of the provisions of a certain Act made and passed in the year of the reign of Queen VICTORIA, intituled [the title of this Act]

Given under our hands and seals this day of in the year of our Lord One thousand eight hundred and

[Here copy the Regulations of the Justices of the County approved by the Poor Law Commissioners as applicable to the removal of the party.]

FORM of EXAMINATION to which the above Warrant refers.

} to wit, } THE Examination of taken on oath before us, Two of Her Majesty's Justices of the Peace acting in and for the [county, riding, city, borough, town corporate, division or liberty] aforesaid, this day of in the year of our Lord One thousand eight hundred and , who on oath saith, that according to the best of [his or her] knowledge and belief, [he or she] born in in that part of the United Kingdom called Scotland [or, Ireland, or in the Isle of Man, or Scilly, or Jersey, or Guernsey,] which [he or she] left about years ago, and hath no settlement in that part of the United Kingdom called England, and hath actually become and is now chargeable to the [parish] of in the [county, township, et cætera, as the same may be,] of and that he is not exempt from the liability to be removed therefrom [and that he hath a wife named and children, neither of which children have gained a settlement in England.]

Sworn the day and year first above written, before us

SCHEDULE (F.)

ORDER of BOARD of GUARDIANS on OVERSEERS for Payment of Contributions.

To the Overseers of the parish, &c. of You are hereby ordered and directed to pay to F. G. of on behalf of the Guardians of the poor of the Union, on the day of at the sum of pounds, shillings and pence, from the poor-rates of the parish, &c. of towards the relief of the poor thereof, and to the contribution of the parish, &c. of towards the relief thereof, and to the contribution of the parish, &c. to the common fund of the union, and such other expenses as are chargeable by the said Guardians on the said parish, &c., and to take the receipt of the said F. G., for the said sum of pounds shillings and pence.

Given under our hands at a meeting of the Guardians of the poor of the said union, held on the day of One thousand eight hundred and

(signed) X. Y. Presiding Chairman.
W. X. } U. V. } Guardians.

(Counter-signature of the Clerk to the Guardians.)

LONDON:
Printed by Order of the Poor Law Commissioners, by BLACKBURN and PARDON, 6, Hatton Garden, and Published by CHARLES KNIGHT and Co., 22, Ludgate Street, Publishers to the Poor Law Commissioners.

AN OFFICIAL CIRCULAR

OF PUBLIC DOCUMENTS AND INFORMATION:

DIRECTED BY THE POOR LAW COMMISSIONERS TO BE PRINTED, CHIEFLY FOR THE USE OF THE MEMBERS AND PERMANENT OFFICERS OF BOARDS OF GUARDIANS, UNDER THE POOR LAW AMENDMENT ACT.

No. 46. CIRCULAR ISSUED APRIL 1, 1845.

Poor Law Commission Office,
Somerset House,
April 1, 1845.

THE Poor Law Commissioners, on a review of their Minutes, directed that the Minutes of Correspondence on the following subjects be printed and circulated for the information of Guardians and Officers of the several Unions, viz.:—

(Signed) By Order of the Board,
EDWIN CHADWICK, *Secretary.*

I.—APPRENTICING POOR CHILDREN.

GENERAL ORDER ADDRESSED TO PARISHES NOT IN UNIONS, AND NOT GOVERNED BY BOARDS OF GUARDIANS.

TO THE CHURCHWARDENS AND OVERSEERS of the several Parishes and

Places named in the Schedule hereunto annexed;—

To the Clerk or Clerks to the Justices of the Petty Sessions held for the Division or Divisions in which the Parishes and Places named in the said Schedule are situate;—

And to all others whom it may concern.

In pursuance of the powers vested in us by an Act passed in the fifth year of the reign of his late majesty King William the Fourth, intituled "*An Act for the Amendment and better Administration of the Laws relating to the Poor in England and Wales,*" and an act passed in the seventh and eighth year of the reign of her present majesty Queen Victoria, intituled "*An Act for the further Amendment of the Laws relating to the Poor in England,*" We, the Poor Law Commissioners, do make the following rules and regulations in regard to the apprenticing of the poor children of the several parishes named in the schedule hereunto annexed.

The Parties.

Article 1.—No child under the age of *nine* years shall be bound apprentice;

And no child that cannot read and write his own name.

No child shall be so bound to a person who is not a housekeeper, or assessed to the poor rate in his own name;

Or who is a journeyman, or a person not carrying on trade or business on his own account;

Or who is under the age of twenty-one;

Or a married woman.

The Premium.

Article 2.—No premium other than clothing for the apprentice shall be given upon the binding of any person above the age of *fourteen,* unless such person be maimed, deformed, or suffering from some permanent bodily infirmity, so that the nature of the work or trade which such person is fit to perform or exercise is restricted.

Article 3.—Where any premium is given, it shall consist in part of clothes supplied to the apprentice at the commencement of the binding, and in part of money.

Term.

Article 4.—No apprentice shall be bound for more than *eight* years.

Consent.

Article 5.—No person above *fourteen* years of age shall be so bound without his *consent.*

And no child under the age of *sixteen* years shall be so bound without the consent of the father of such child, or if the father be dead, or be disqualified to give such consent, as hereinafter provided, or if such child be a bastard, without the consent of the mother, if living, of such child.

Provided, that where the parent of such child, whose consent would be otherwise requisite, is transported beyond the seas, or is in the custody of the law, having been convicted of some *felony,* or for the space of six calendar months before the time of executing the indenture has deserted such child, or for such space of time has been in the service of Her Majesty, or of the East India Company, in foreign parts, such parent, if the father, shall be deemed to be disqualified as herein-before stated, and if it be the mother, no such consent shall be required.

Place of Service.

Article 6.—No child shall be bound to a master whose place of business, whereat the child is to work and live, shall be distant more than *thirty* miles from the place in which the child is residing at the time of the binding;

Unless in any particular case the Poor Law Commissioners shall, on application to them, otherwise permit.

Preliminaries to the Binding.

Article 7.—If the child, whom it is proposed to bind apprentice, be in the workhouse, and under the age of *fourteen,* the overseers shall require a certificate in writing from some medical man duly licensed to practise, as to the fitness in regard to bodily health and strength of such child to be bound apprentice to the proposed trade, and shall also ascertain from the master of the workhouse the capacity of the child for such binding in other respects.

Article 8.—If the child be not in the workhouse, but in the parish by which it is proposed that it shall be bound, the overseers shall examine into the circumstances of the case, the condition of the child, and of his parents, if any, and the residence of the proposed master, the nature of his trade, the number of other apprentices, if any, then bound to him, and generally as to the fitness of the particular binding.

Article 9.—The overseers shall, when the child is under the age of *fourteen,* direct such child to be taken to a medical man duly licensed to practise, to be examined as to his fitness in respect of bodily health and strength for the proposed trade or business, in order that such medical man may certify in writing according to his judgment in the matter, which certificate shall be obtained by the said overseers previously to the binding.

Article 10.—If the child be residing in some other parish or union, the overseers who propose to bind him shall not proceed to do so unless they receive such a report as is required in Article 8, from the relieving officer or some other officer administering the relief of the poor of the district in which such child is residing, and a certificate from some medical practitioner of the neighbourhood of the child's residence to the effect required in Article 9.

Article 11.—When a premium is proposed to be given, in a case within the provision of Article 2, the overseers shall require a certificate in writing of some medical practitioner, certifying that the person is maimed, deformed, or disabled, to the extent specified in such article, before they proceed to execute the indenture; and shall cause such certificate to be deposited with the books and documents of the parish.

Article 12.—When such certificate, as is required by Articles 7, 9, and 10, is received, or in case from the age of the child no such certificate is required, the overseers shall direct that the child, and the proposed master, or some person on his behalf, and in case the child be under the age of *sixteen*, the parent or person in whose custody such child shall be then living, shall attend some meeting of the overseers to be appointed for such purpose.

Article 13.—At such meeting, if such parties appear, and the said overseers, after making all due inquiries, and hearing the objections, (if any be made) on the part of the relatives or friends of such child, shall deem it proper that the binding shall be effected, they may forthwith cause the indentures to be prepared, and to be executed in such manner and with such sanction as the law shall require, provided that when the same shall have been executed by the master and the other parties lawfully authorised, the same shall be signed by the child, as herein-after provided.

Article 14.—If the proposed master reside out of the parish on account of which the binding is to be effected, but in some union or parish under a board of guardians, whether formed under the provisions of the first-recited act, or of the act of the twenty-second year of the reign of King George the Third, intituled *"An Act for the better Relief and Employment of the Poor,"* or of any local act, the overseers shall, before proceeding to effect the binding, communicate in writing the proposal to the guardians of such union or parish, and request to be informed whether such binding is open to any objection, and if no objection be reported by such guardians within the space of one calendar month, or, if the objection does not appear to the overseers proposing to bind the child to be sufficient to prevent the binding, the same may be proceeded with; and when the indentures shall have been executed, the overseers who executed the same shall cause notice thereof in writing to be sent to the guardians of the union or parish wherein the said apprentice is to reside.

Indenture.

Article 15.—The indenture shall be executed in duplicate by the master and the overseers, and shall not be valid unless signed by the proposed apprentice, without aid or assistance, in the presence of the said overseers; and the consent of the parent, where requisite, shall be testified by such parent signing with his name or mark, to be properly attested, the foot of the said indenture, and where such consent is dispensed with under the provision contained in Article 5, the cause of such dispensation shall be stated at the foot of the indenture by the said overseers.

Article 16.—The indenture shall contain mention of the place or places at which the apprentice is to work and live.

Article 17.—One part of such indenture, when executed, shall be kept by the overseers; the other shall be delivered to the master.

Duties of the Master.

Article 18.—And we do hereby prescribe the duties of the master to whom such poor child may be apprenticed, and the terms and conditions to be inserted in the said indentures, as follows:—

No. 1.—The master shall teach the child the trade, business, or employment set forth in the indenture, unless the overseers or their successors, or the guardians of any union in which the parish may hereafter be comprised, or of the parish itself, in case it shall be placed under a board of guardians, shall authorise the substitution of another trade or business.

No. 2.—He shall maintain the said child with proper food and nourishment.

No. 3.—He shall provide a proper lodging for the said child.

No. 4.—He shall supply to the said child one suit of proper clothing every year during the term of the binding.

No. 5.—He shall, in case the said child be affected with any disease or sickness, or meet with any accident, procure, at his own cost, adequate medical or surgical assistance, to be supplied by some duly qualified medical man, for such child.

No. 6.—He shall, once at least on every Sunday, cause the child to attend some place of Divine worship, if there be any such within a reasonable distance, according to the religious persuasion in which the child has been brought up, so, however, that no child shall be required by the master to attend any place of worship to which his parents or surviving parent may object, nor, when he shall be above the age of *sixteen*, any place to which he may himself object.

No. 7.—Where his parents or parent or next of kin shall desire it, he shall allow the said child, while under the age of *sixteen*, to attend any Sunday or other school which shall be situated within the same parish, or within *two* miles distance from his residence, on every Sunday, and, if there be no such school which such child can attend, shall at some reasonable hour on every Sunday, allow any minister of the religious persuasion of the child, to have access to such child for the purpose of imparting religious instruction.

No. 8.—Where the apprentice continues bound after the age of *seventeen* years, the master shall pay to such apprentice, for and in respect of every week that he duly and properly serves the said master, as a remuneration, a sum to be inserted in the indenture, or to be agreed upon by the overseers for the time being, or the guardians of the union in which such parish may then be included, or of the parish, if it shall be under a board of guardians, and the said master, when that time arrives, or, if they cannot agree, to be settled by some person to be then chosen by the said master and such overseers or guardians, and, until such sum be agreed upon or settled, not less than one *fourth* of the amount then commonly paid as wages to journeymen in the said trade, business, or employment.

No. 9.—The master shall, by himself or by his agent, produce the apprentice to the overseers by whom such apprentice was bound, or to their successors in office, at the end of the first year of the binding, and at the middle of the term, and whenever afterwards required to do so by the said overseers or their successors.

Provided that if the said parish shall at any time after the execution of the said indenture be comprised in any union, or be placed under a board of guardians, the child shall be produced at such times to such guardians instead of the overseers of the parish.

Provided also, that if the apprentice reside out of the parish by the overseers whereof he was bound, the apprentice shall be produced, as herein-before directed, to any board of guardians of the union or parish, as described in Article 14, or if there be no such board of guardians, then to the overseers of the parish in which the apprentice may be residing.

No. 10.—The master shall not cause the said apprentice to work or live more than *ten miles* from the place or places mentioned in the indenture, according to Article 16, without the leave of the overseers so binding him, or their successors.

Article 19.—These duties of the master shall be enforced by covenants and conditions to be inserted in the said indenture so to be executed by him.

Article 20.—The master shall also covenant not to assign nor to cancel the indenture, without the consent of the overseers or guardians, as mentioned in the next Article, or their respective successors, previously obtained, under a penalty to be specified in the said covenant, and to pay to the said overseers or guardians or their respective successors, all costs and expenses that may be incurred on account of the said parish, in consequence of the said apprentice not being supplied with medical or surgical assistance by the master, in case the same shall be at any time requisite.

Article 21.—The master shall also further covenant, that if the parish shall at any time after the execution of the said indenture be comprised in any union, or be placed under a board of guardians, he will discharge all the obligations incurred by him under the said indenture, in reference to the overseers, according to the directions of the guardians of such union or parish, as though such guardians had been the parties to the said indenture instead of the overseers.

Article 22.—The indenture shall be made subject to the following provisoes :—

1.—That if the master take the benefit of any act for the relief of insolvent debtors, or be discharged under any such act, such indenture shall forthwith become of no further force or effect.

2.—That if, on a conviction for a breach of any one of the aforesaid covenants before a justice of the peace, in pursuance of the provisions of the statute in such case made and provided, the overseers who may be parties to the said indenture, or their successors, shall declare by a notice that the indenture shall be determined, and shall transmit a copy of such notice, under the hands of the majority of them, by the post or otherwise, to the said master, such indenture shall, except in respect of all rights and liabilities then accrued, forthwith become of no further force or effect.

Explanation of Terms.

Article 23.—Whenever the word *parish* is used in this order, it shall be taken to include any place maintaining its own poor, whether parochial or extra-parochial.

Article 24.—The word *overseers* shall include churchwardens, where there are any such for the parish.

Article 25.—The word *child* in this order shall signify any person under the age of twenty-one years.

Article 26.—Whenever, in describing any person or party, matter or thing, the word importing the singular number or the masculine gender only is used in this order, the same shall be taken to include, and shall be applied to several persons or parties as well as one person or party, and females as well as males, and several matters or things as well as one matter or thing, respectively, unless there be something in the subject or context repugnant to such construction.

Article 27.—Whenever in this order any Article is referred to by its number, the article of this order bearing that number shall be taken to be signified thereby.

Article 28.—Provided that nothing herein contained shall apply to the apprenticing of poor children to the sea service.

Article 29.—And, in pursuance of the provisions contained in the said first-recited act, we do direct, that wherever any justice or justices shall, under any authority of law, assent or consent, order or allow of the binding of any poor child as apprentice, such justice or justices shall certify, at the foot of the indenture and the counterpart thereof, in the form and manner following; that is to say,

"I, *or* we, (*as the case may be,*) justice *or* justices of the peace of and in the county (*or other jurisdiction, as the case may be,*) of , who have assented to, ordered, *or* allowed the above binding, do hereby certify that we have examined and ascertained that the rules, orders, and regulations of the Poor Law Commissioners, for the binding of poor children apprentices, and applicable to the above-named parish, (*or other place, as the case may be,*) contained in their general order, bearing date the twenty-ninth day of January, one thousand eight hundred and forty-five, have been complied with.

"Signed this day of

——————— Signature."

The SCHEDULE containing the names of the Parishes and Places to which the present Order applies.

DERBY.

High Peake Hundred.

Blackwell
Rowland
Wormhill
Youlgrave

Wirksworth Hundred.

Elton

GLOUCESTER.

Bristol City.

All Saints
Augustine, St.
Castle Precincts
Christ Church
Ewin, St.
James, St.
John, St.
Leonard, St.
Mary-le-port, St.
Mary Redcliffe, St.
Michael, St.
Nicholas, St.
Paul, St.
Peter, St.
Philip and Jacob, St.
Stephen, St.
Temple
Thomas, St.
Werburg, St.

LANCASTER.

Lonsdale Hundred.

Arkholm-with-Cawood
Bare
Bolton-le-sands
Borwick
Burrow-with-Burrow
Cansfield
Caton
Claughton
Dalton-with-Hutton
Farleton
Gressingham
Halton-with-Aughton
Heysham
Hornby
Ireby
Kellet, Nether
Kellet, Over
Leck
Melling-with-Wrayton
Poulton
Quernmoor
Roburndale
Slyne-with-Hest
Tatham, Lower End
Tatham, Upper End
Torrisholme
Tunstal
Wennington
Whittington
Wray-with-Bolton

Salford Hundred.

Clifton
Worsley

LEICESTER.

Sparkenhoe Hundred.

Higham-on-the-Hill.
Ratcliffe Culey
Sibson
Stapleton
Stoke Golding
Sutton Cheney
Witherley

MIDDLESEX.

Saint James, and Saint John, Clerkenwell
Saint James, Westminster
Saint Leonard, Shoreditch
Saint Luke
Saint Margaret and St. John the Evangelist

NORFOLK.

Holt Hundred.

Brinton
Melton Constable and Burgh Parva

SALOP.

Chirbury Hundred.

Brompton and Riston
Chirbury
Worthen

Shrewsbury Town.

Alkmond, St.
Chad, St.
Holy Cross and St. Giles
Julian, St.
Mary, St.
Meole Brace

SOUTHAMPTON.

Bramshott
Dockenfield
Kingsley
Headley
Aldershott
Cove
Farnborough
Hawley
Long Sutton
Yateley
Avington
Laverstoke
Alverstoke

STAFFORD.

Offlow, North Hundred.

Haselour
Ronton Abbey
Alstonefield
Grindon
Butterton
Wetton

SURREY.

Farnham
Frensham
Seal and Tongham
Puttenham
Frimley
Ash and Normanby

SUSSEX.

Rape of Arundel, Arundel Hundred.

Arundel

Avesford Hundred.

Climping
Ford
South Stoke and Offham
Tortington

Bury Hundred.

Bignor
Bury and West Burton
Coates
Fittleworth
Houghton

Poling Hundred.

Angmering
Burpham
Ferring
Goring
Kingston
Leominster
Littlehampton
North Stoke
Poling
Preston, East
Rustington
Warningcamp

Rotherbridge Hundred.

Barlavington
Burton
Duncton
Egdean
Sutton

Westeaswrith Hundred.

Amberly
Greatham
Rackham
Wiggenholt

Rape of Bramber, Brightford Hundred.

Broadwater
Clapham
Durrington
Heene
Lancing

Patching Hundred.

Patching

Tarring Hundred.

West Tarring

Rape of Chichester, Aldwick Hundred.

Slindon
South Berstead

Eastbourne Hundred.

Heyshott

Rape of Leeds, Whales.

Brighthelmstone

WARWICK.

Hemlingford Hundred, Atherstone Division.

Hartshill

Knightlow Hundred, Kirby Division.

Bedworth
Brinklow
Pailton
Wolvey

YORK, EAST RIDING

Ouse and Derwent Wapentake.

Menthorpe-with-Bowthorpe

Liberty of Saint Peter, York.

Helperby

Ainstey of the City of York.

Acaster Selby
Acomb
Angram
Appleton Roebuck
Askam Bryan
Bickerton
Bilbrough
Bilton
Bolton Percy
Catterton
Colton
Helaugh
Hessay
Hutton
Knapton
Long Marston
Moor Monkton
Oxton
Poppleton, Nether
Poppleton, Upper
Rufforth
Steeton
Tadcaster, East
Thorp Arch
Tockwith
Walton
Wighill
Wilstrop

YORK, NORTH RIDING.

Allertonshire Wapentake

Norton Conyers

Bulmer Wapentake.

Shipton
Skelton
Tollerton
Warthill
Youlton

Halikeld Wapentake.

Asenby
Baldersby
Cundall and Leckby
Dishforth
Humberton
Kirby-on-the-Moor, or Kirby Hill
Langthorpe
Marton-le-Moor
Melmerby
Middleton Quernhow
Norton-le-Clay
Rainton-with-Newby
Sutton-with-Howgrave
Tanfield, East
Tanfield, West
Thornton Bridge
Wath

Hang, West, Wapentake.

Abbotside, Higher
Abbotside, Lower
Askrigg
Aysgarth
Bainbridge
Bishop Dale
Burton and Walden
Carperby
Hawes
Newbiggen

Thoralby
Thornton Rust

Langburgh Liberty, West Division.

Picton

YORK, WEST RIDING.

Agbrigg Wapentake.

Acton
Altofts
Crofton
Lofthouse and Carlton
Methley
Middleton
Normanton
Rothwell
Saddleworth-with Quick
Snydale
Whitwood

Barkston Ash Wapentake Lower Division.

Birken
Burton Salmon
Byrome-with-Poole
Haddlesey, West
Hambleton
Hillam
Monk Fryston
Ryther-with-Ozendike
Sutton

Barkston Ash Wapentake Upper Division.

Barkston
Bramham
Brotherton
Clifford-with-Boston
Fairburn
Fenton-with-Biggin
Grimston
Huddleston and Lumby
Kirkby Wharf with Milford
Kirk Fenton
Lead
Ledsham
Ledstone
Lotherton-with-Aberford
Micklefield
Micklethwaite
Milford, South
Newthorpe
Newton Kyme with Toulston
Saxton-with-Scarthingwell
Sherburn
Sutton-with-Hazlewood
Tadcaster, West
Towton
Ulleskelf

Claro Wapentake, Lower Division.

Aldborough
Aldfield
Arkendale
Azerley
Bilton-with-Harrowgate
Birstwith
Blubberhouses
Boroughbridge
Brearton
Burton Leonard
Clifton-with-Norwood
Clint
Copgrove
Farnham
Felliscliffe
Ferensby
Fewston
Grewelthorpe
Hampsthwaite
Killinghall
Kirby Hall
Kirkby Malzeard
Knaresborough
Laverton
Milby
Minskip
Ouseburn, Great
Pannall
Rocliffe
Scotton
Scriven-with-Tentergate
Skelding
Stainley, South, with Clayton
Staveley
Studley Roger
Thornville
Timble, Great
Winksley

Claro Wapentake, Upper Division.

Allerton Mauleverer with Hopperton
Askwith
Beamsley-in-Skipton
Castley
Cattall
Clareton
Coneythorpe
Cowthorpe
Deighton, North
Denton
Dunkeswick
Dunsforth, Lower
Dunsforth, Upper, with Branton Green
Farnley
Flaxby
Follifoot
Goldsborough
Greenhammerton
Hunsingore
Kirkby-with-Netherby
Kirk Deighton
Kirby Overblows
Kirk Hammerton
Leathley
Lindley
Linton
Marton-with-Grafton
Middleton
Nesfield-with-Langbar
Newhall-with-Clifton
Nun Monkton
Ouseburn, Little
Plumpton
Ribston, Great, with Walshford
Ribston, Little
Rigton
Ripley
Sicklinghall
Spofforth
Stainburn
Thorpe Green or Underwood
Timble, Little
Weeton
Weston
Wetherby
Whixley
Widdington

Morley Wapentake.

Churwell
Eccleshill
Gildersome

Osgoldcross Wapentake, Lower Division.

Baln
Beaghall
Cridling Stubbs
Eggborough
Heck
Hensall
Kellington
Smeaton, Little
Walden Stubbs
Whitley
Womersley

Osgoldcross Wapentake, Upper Division.

Ackworth
Badsworth
Carleton
Castleford
Darrington
Elmsall, North
Elmsall, South
Featherstone
Ferry Frystone
Hardwick, East
Hardwick, West
Hessle
Hilltop
Houghton Glass
Kirkby, South
Kirksmeaton
Knottingley
Monkhill
Nostel, Huntwick, and Foulby
Pontefract
Purston Jaglin
Skelbrooke
Stapleton
Tanshelf
Thorp Audlin
Upton

Skyrack Wapentake, Lower Division.

Abberford
Allerton Bywater
Austhorpe
Bardsey-with-Rigton
Barwick-in-Elmet

Collingham
Garforth, West
Guiseley
Keswick, East
Kippax
Parlington
Preston, Great and Little
Roundhay
Scarcroft
Seacroft
Shadwell
Sturton Grange
Swillington
Temple Newsham
Thorner
Wothersome

Skyrack Wapentake, Upper Division.

Addle-with-Eccup
Allwoodley
Arthington
Baildon
Bramhope
Burley
Carlton
Esholt
Harewood
Hawkesworth
Horsforth
Ilkley
Menstone
Otley
Pool
Rawden
Weardley
Wigton
Wike
Yeaden

Staincliffe and Ewcross Wapentake, E. Division.

Silsden

Staincross Wapentake.

Ardsley
Barnesley
Baraugh
Brierley-with-Grimsthorpe
Carlton
Cawthorne
Chevett
Clayton, West
Cudworth
Darton
Denby
Dodworth
Gunthwaite
Havercroft-with-Cold Hiendley
Hemsworth
Hiendley, South
Hoyland, High
Kexborough
Monk Bretton
Notton
Roystone
Ryhill
Shafton
Silkstone
Stainborough
Wintersett
Woolley
Worsborough

Strafforth and Tickhill Wapentake, N. Division.

Billingley
Darfield
Hamphall Stubbs
Hoyland
Houghton, Great
Houghton, Little
Wombwell

Liberty of Ripon.

Aismunderby-with-Bondgate
Bishop Monkton
Bishop Thornton
Bishopton
Hewick Bridge
Hewick Copt
Clotherholme
Eavestone
Givendale
Grantley
Ingerthorpe
Markington-with-Wallerthwaite
Newby-with-Mulwith
Nidd-with-Killinghall
Nunwick-with-How-grave
Ripon, Borough
Sawley
Sharrow
Skelton
Stainley, North, with Sleningford
Sutton Grange
Westwick
Whitcliffe-with-Thorpe

Borough of Leeds.

Armley
Beeston
Bramley
Chapel Allerton
Farnley
Headingley-with-Burley
Holbeck
Hunslet
Potter Newton
Wortley

WALES.

DENBIGH.

Chirk Hundred.

Chirk
Llansilin

MONTGOMERY.

Cawse Hundred, Lower Division.

Forden
Leighton
Middletown
Rhos Goch
Trelystan
Uppington

Cawse Hundred, Upper Division.

Castle Caereinion, Upper and Lower
Cyfronydd

Montgomery Hundred, Lower Division.

Aston
Castlewright
Churchstoke
Montgomery

Newton Hundred, Lower Division.

Berriew

Newton Hundred, Upper Division.

Llandysil
Llanmerewig

Pool Hundred.

Guilsfield

Pool Borough.

Cletterwood
Hope
Pool, Lower
Pool, Middle
Pool, Upper
Trewern

Given under our hands and seal of office, this twenty-ninth day of January, in the year one thousand eight hundred and forty-five.

(Signed) Geo. Nicholls,
G. C. Lewis.

II.—AUDITOR.

Whether the Office can be held by a Clerk to Justices.

January 30, 1845.

——————— Inquired, whether any objection existed to the office of auditor being held by a person also holding the office of clerk to a bench of magistrates.

Ans.—The Commissioners are inclined to think that it would be inconvenient that the two offices should be held concurrently; if the petty sessional district should be within the audit district, inasmuch as the auditor might be called on to audit payments made to himself as clerk to the justices.

III.—BASTARDS.

RELIEF TO THE MOTHERS OF BASTARDS.

Dec. 13th, 1844.

Chairman and Vice-Chairman of Cardiff Union.—Observed that under the previous state of the law in reference to bastards, when the mother was unable to maintain herself and child, the practice in the Cardiff Union had been, to afford no relief to either, out of the workhouse. Instances, then, were not unfrequent of the mother leaving the child in the workhouse chargeable to the parish, whilst she ran away to seek employment. Under the provisions of the act, 7 and 8 Vic. c. 101, justices in their orders of affiliation, often adjudged that the father of the child should pay the mother 1*s.* 6*d.* weekly towards the child's support. The mother in that case applied to the board of guardians for 6*d.* or 1*s.* weekly, to enable her to make up the 2*s.* 6*d.* required to place her child with a nurse, leaving herself free to go to service. The rate-payers in small agricultural parishes being mostly tenants-at-will, felt it to be an unreasonable pressure on them, to order the mother and child into the house when 6*d.* or 1*s.* weekly relief added to the sum ordered to be paid by the father, would enable her to place the child at nurse, and then, to gain her own livelihood in service. Sometimes the justices were unable to make any order of affiliation owing to the want of some evidence to corroborate the testimony of the mother. In that case the mother usually proposed to the parish to apply all the wages she could obtain in service, (except what was necessary to purchase clothes,) towards the maintenance of the child, provided the guardians made a weekly allowance of 1*s.* or 1*s.* 6*d.* to enable her to pay a nurse. In such instances, also, the contributors were anxious not only to save themselves the cost of maintaining mother and child in the workhouse by the payment of so small a sum, but they felt disposed to give the mother an opportunity of re-establishing her character by good conduct in service. Inquired whether under the altered state of the law, the Commissioners would recommend an adherence to the practice of ordering mother and child into the workhouse, or affording partial relief to the mother in the manner referred to.

Ans.—After carefully considering the Act, 7 and 8 Vic. c. 101, the Commissioners are of opinion, that its operation in bastardy cases was intended to be kept entirely distinct from the administration of the Poor Law. The ground on which relief is to be administered remains just what it was before the passing of that act,—namely, the inability of the applicant to maintain herself and her family: and the regulations of the Commissioners respecting able-bodied women receiving out-door relief, also remain just what they were before: nor do the Commissioners think it would be right to relax them on the ground that the mothers of bastard children are now placed in a better position as regards obtaining redress from the father than they had hitherto been. It follows, therefore, that if the woman, whether before or after an order is made by the justices, is unable to maintain herself, she should be relieved, and if able-bodied, relieved in the workhouse. The refusal of all relief could only be justified by clear proof that she was not destitude. If she deserts the child she is, of course, liable to punishment.

IV.—BURIAL OF PAUPERS.

1. CONSTRUCTION OF 7 AND 8 VIC. C. 101, SECT. 31 AND 56.

The Vicar of ———. — Stated, that the churchyard of ———, in which parish the Union workhouse is situate, was inconveniently crowded by the interment of its own population; and during the last seven years the evil had been increased, by the burial of all the paupers dying in the workhouse. Under the 56th section of the 7th and 8th Vic. c. 101, it is provided "That, for the purpose of *burial,* the workhouse shall be deemed to be situated *in every parish* of the Union;" and by the 31st section "that the guardians are empowered to send paupers, who die in the workhouse, to be buried in the parish to which they are chargeable, at the expense of such parish." Being desirous of saving his parishioners from the necessity of purchasing new ground, for the interment of persons belonging to other parishes, he had intimated to the board of guardians that he should require the fee, due by custom for the interment of non-parishioners, on the burial of every pauper brought to be buried in the churchyard of the parish, such persons being at the period of their decease actually chargeable to other parishes of the Union. The guardians having expressed a doubt as to his right to demand such fee, he requested the Commissioners' opinion on the subject.

Ans.—According to the 68th canon, and the common law, there is a *primâ facie* obligation on the clergyman to bury any person actually dying in the parish. The question is, whether the 56th section of the 7 and 8 Vic. c. 101, has substituted for this actual place of death a constructive place of death? If it has not, this obligation remains where it was. The 31st and 56th sections must be read together. In the 31st, the ordinary rule laid down is clearly that a body is to be buried in the churchyard of the parish where the death occurred; that is, *actually occurred*, for the case of the parish to which the person is chargeable is provided for specially just before. The exceptional cases contemplated by section 31 are those in which a pauper may in his lifetime have desired to be buried in the parish to which he was chargeable, or where his relations may have so desired, or where the guardians for any other cause, shall direct the body to be buried in the parish to which the person was chargeable or elsewhere. This they are authorised to do; and it is with reference to these cases that section 56 steps in, and enables the guardians to treat the death as having occurred constructively in the parish of the chargeability. In this manner the two sections are perfectly consistent with each other. Neither the clergyman of the parish where the death actually occurred, nor the clergyman of the parish to which the person was chargeable, can refuse to bury. The one, because the death *actually* occurred in his parish; the other because it *constructively* occurred in his. To either of them, as the case may be, a fee will be payable, viz.:—the fee due by the legal custom of the place, in the case of a person dying in the parish; and this fee the guardians are, by section 31 of the Act, bound to pay. The Commissioners will only add, that the word parishioner, in an ecclesiastical sense, may mean something wholly different from a person settled in the parish, in the poor-law sense of the word, or chargeable to the parish.

2. CONSTRUCTION OF THE WORD "CUSTOM," IN THE 31ST SECT. 7 AND 8 VIC. C. 101.

May 15th, 1845.

Clerk of Braintree Union—Inquired the opinion of the Commissioners as to the import of the word "custom," as used in the 31st section of the Act 7 and 8 Vic. c. 101.

Ans.—The Commissioners are advised that the statute, in alluding to the "custom of the place," refers to such a custom as would be held good at common law. This view appears to the Commissioners to be borne out by a case reported in

1 Ventris, 274; and the further case of the Dean and Chapter of Exeter, reported in Salk. 334. The common law (it is scarcely needful to add) requires a custom, to be good, to be of immemorial usage.

V.—CHURCHWARDENS — OF A PARISH DIVIDED INTO TOWNSHIPS — WHETHER EMPOWERED TO ACT WITH THE OVERSEERS.

Nov. 16th, 1844.

Mr. Thomas Burn, Sunderland—Stated, that the parish of Bishop Wearmouth was comprised of five townships, each of which maintained its own poor, and had its own overseers. Two churchwardens were appointed for the whole parish, and the townships had no separate churchwardens. Inquired, whether the churchwardens of the parish were entitled to act with the overseers of each township.

Ans.—If the five townships to which you allude, in the parish of Bishop Wearmouth, separately maintain their own respective poor, under the provisions of the 21st section of the 13th and 14th Car. 2, c. 12, the churchwardens of the parish have no authority to act as overseers for such townships respectively. The above-mentioned section provides, that in cases of this kind the relief of the poor shall be administered by "two or more overseers of the poor within every of the said townships;" but there is no allusion to churchwardens, as there is in the 1st section of the 43rd Eliz. c. 2. The Commissioners direct your attention to the case of R. *v.* Nantwich (16 East. 228.)

VI.—CLERKS' DUTIES—1. PREPARING CERTIFICATES OF CHARGEABILITY.

Nov. 4th, 1844.

Guardians of the Holywell Union—Inquired, whether the clerk could properly make a charge for drawing certificates of chargeability, in his capacity of attorney; or if it formed part of his duty, as clerk to the guardians, to prepare those documents.

Ans.—The Commissioners are of opinion that the issuing of the certificate of chargeability under the recent statute is business transacted on account of the Union, as it is the guardians who are required to certify. The making out of such certificate, and countersigning it, are a part of the clerk's ordinary duty for the performance of which his salary is the consideration.

2. WHETHER THE CLERK IS BOUND TO COUNTERSIGN A CHECK FOR AN ILLEGAL PAYMENT.

Feb. 3, 1845.

——— Inquired, whether the clerk to a board of guardians had power to refuse to countersign a check ordered by the board to be drawn for a payment which he considered to be illegal, and contended that, if he possessed such a power, he would be able to control the board.

Ans.—Where a check is drawn for an illegal purpose, the Commissioners consider that the clerk is not bound to countersign it. As the officer of the board, he is bound to give effect to what they resolve legally. But conformity to law is a tacit condition implied in every obligation to obedience; and with regard to the argument that the clerk would control the board of guardians by refusing his signature, it appears to the Commissioners to amount only to the general assertion that whenever persons exceed their powers they can command no obedience. Within the guardians' powers the clerk is their officer; beyond those powers he is not controlled by them.

VII.—GUARDIAN.

1. THE RIGHT OF AN INDIVIDUAL GUARDIAN TO EXAMINE TRADESMEN'S BILLS.

Nov. 9th, 1844.

Mr. ———, ——— *Union*—Inquired whether the guardians of a union had individually an ex-officio right to examine the bills of tradesmen supplying goods to the Union. Complained that the right of examining such bills was in the ——— Union confined to a visiting committee appointed quarterly, instead of being open to all the guardians.

Ans.—Strictly speaking an individual guardian has no several right to the possession or use of the papers or bills of the Union, and he can only have them by the permission or acquiescence of the whole body; unless the paper or bill be at the moment before the board, under the consideration of the guardians assembled thereat. It would, however, be obviously objectionable, if the guardians should use their power as a board to the exclusion of any member, or practically to divest the majority of the body of the power of inspecting all papers, by appointing a committee or otherwise. The Commissioners have no reason however, to doubt, that any individual guardian might obtain access to documents of the kind described in your letter on reasonable grounds.

2. WHETHER AN ATTORNEY CAN ACT FOR A PARISH IN THE UNION OF WHICH HE IS A GUARDIAN.

August 12, 1844.

A Guardian of ——— *Union*—Inquired whether an attorney, who is a guardian of the Union, can legally receive from the poor-rates of a parish in the Union the amount of his bill for professional business done for such parish.

Ans.—The Commissioners are not aware that any attorney, who is a guardian, is thereby prevented from being employed by the overseers of any parish in the Union in his professional capacity, or receiving from the poor-rate the fair and reasonable costs arising from his being so employed.

3. ELECTION OF GUARDIANS—MEMORANDUM.

Poor Law Commission Office,
Somerset House,
December 31st, 1844.

The Act 7 and 8 Vict. c. 101, requires—

1. Every owner, in order to be entitled to vote either as owner or by proxy, at the election of guardians, should, before the 1st day of February, have given to the overseers a statement of his name and address, together with a description of the property in the parish for which he claims to vote. Such description must show the nature of the interest or estate he may have in such property; it must also show the amount of rent service (if any) which he may receive or pay in respect of such property; and the names of the persons from whom he may receive, or to whom he may pay, such rent.

2. If this has been done, the owner may vote himself, or he may vote by proxy; but if he vote by proxy, the proxy must, fourteen days at least before he votes, send to the overseers the original, or an attested, copy of his appointment as proxy; together with a statement of the owner's name and address, and the property in respect of which he claims to vote as proxy.

3. On or before the 5th of February, the overseers of parishes containing a population exceeding 2000, according to the last census, are to prepare a registry of the names and addresses of the owners and proxies who have given the statement, or made the claim above referred to, before the 1st of the month.

4. This registry is to be open to the inspection of all persons any time between the 5th and 10th

of February; and any owner or proxy who has given in his statement, or made his claim to vote, or any rate-payer, may object to the vote of an owner, by delivering, before the 15th of February, a notice, in writing, of the grounds of his objection to the clerk of the guardians; and also at the address of the person objected to.

5. On or before the 20th of February the clerk is to provide for the revision of the list, so far as regards owners objected to, which will be revised on some day between the 24th of February and 1st of March. Any objection to be held valid must be supported by the person objecting at the time of revision.

VIII.—MEDICAL ORDER.

FEES UNDER ARTICLE 10.

January 30, 1845.

Clerk of Uckfield Union—Inquired, what fee a medical officer was entitled to in a case which he described as a "fracture of the leg and dislocation of the ankle."

Ans.—If in the case described there were a dislocation, and also a fracture of bones of the leg, constituting two independent injuries, the medical officer is entitled to a fee of £3 for each, under Art. 10 of the Commissioners' General Medical Order.

IX.—MEDICAL OFFICER.—1. AS TO VISITING THE SICK POOR.

April 3, 1844.

Dr. Corbet, Medical Officer, Orsett Union—Requested an explanation of the following paragraph in the Commissioners' circular, dated 8th Feb. 1844. [See Official Circular, No. 32.] "The medical officer is bound to visit his patients at their own homes; but whether the patient is seen at his own home, or *attends voluntarily* at the medical officer's home, or a station, provided he is seen and examined personally, attendance may be entered." He observed that, by his contract with the board of guardians, patients who were able were obliged to call at his surgery between nine and ten in the morning, and he was bound to visit at their own homes only those who could not come to him, or who would be injured by coming. For example, must he ride after a patient in good health, but with a bad hand, if he refused to come to his surgery?

Clerk of the Orsett Union—Stated that no positive arrangement had ever been entered into by the board of guardians with Dr. Corbet in reference to the visitation of pauper patients at their own homes, but that his attendance had always been satisfactory to the board.

Ans. to Dr. Corbet—In the performance of your duty as a medical officer, you will be guided generally by the orders of the Commissioners and their instructions. A medical officer is bound, if necessary, to visit his patients at their own homes; and if serious inconvenience is caused to any pauper by coming to the medical officer, the visits should be so made. For the Commissioners to prohibit any *attendance*, except at the patients' homes, would be unreasonable and unnecessary; but if the medical officer refuses or neglects to visit, he must be prepared to show that he was justified in the particular case.

2. WHETHER BOUND TO SUPPLY BOTTLES.

January 22, 1845.

Clerk of Hailsham Union—Inquired whether, under the Commissioners' General Order, "Duties of Officers," Art. 19, No. 1, it was the duty of the medical officers to provide bottles for the medicines supplied by them to their pauper patients.

Ans.—The Commissioners think that it is the duty of the medical officer to supply the medicines in such a state that they admit of being conveyed to his pauper patients. If the medicine is fluid, it ought to be in a bottle, or some other vessel; if solid, it ought to be in a box, &c. The Commissioners think that the medical officer is bound by Art. 19, No. 1, of the order on the duties of officers, to furnish these bottles, boxes, &c., so long as they are needed. They ought, if the medical officer should require it, to be preserved by the pauper, and restored to the medical officer. These remarks are made on the supposition that the contract of the medical officer contains no provision on the subject. If any doubt on this point is likely to arise hereafter, the Commissioners advise that it should be specifically provided for in the contract with the medical officer.

X.—MEDICAL RELIEF.—TO NON-RESIDENT POOR.

July 1, 1844.

Clerk of Preston Union—Inquired whether, under the General Medical Order, it was obligatory in the guardians, in all surgical and midwifery cases, to relieve the non-resident poor in that Union, without being entitled to claim the cost of the relief from the parish, or union, to which the parties might belong, unless placed under an order of removal at the time.

Ans.—The guardians are bound to give medical as well as all other relief which may be necessary to destitute persons resident in the Union, whether they belong to any parish of the Union or not. But with regard to the fees payable to the medical officers for their attendance on poor persons not settled in the Union in surgical cases, and cases of midwifery, these can only be recovered from the parish of the settlement, when the pauper is under a suspended order of removal, or where there is an agreement on the part of such parish to repay the same.

XI.—OFFICERS.—WHETHER CLERK CAN BE SURETY FOR TREASURER.

March 16*th*, 1844.

Clerk of —— *Union*—Inquired whether he can act as one of the sureties of the person about to be appointed treasurer of the —— Union.

Ans.—The Commissioners think it very objectionable that any one holding the office of clerk to a board of guardians should become surety for another officer of the same union. The Commissioners could not, therefore, approve of the clerk of the —— Union doing so in the present case. At the same time they desire to inform him that they have come to this decision on general principles only, and not because they entertain any doubt of the perfect respectability of the parties in the present case.

XII.—POOR-RATE.—1. EXCUSAL FROM PAYMENT OF.

November 11*th*, 1844.

Clerk of Llanfyllin Union—Stated that the board of guardians had experienced some difficulty in consequence of the numerous lists of persons recommended by parish vestries, to be excused from the payment of the poor-rates, on account of poverty and other reasons. Inquired,—1. Whether the receipt of parish relief should be considered a sufficient reason for excusing paupers from the payment of poor-rate. 2. Whether *any* circumstances should be considered to form a sufficient ground for such excusal, as, if the rate on any tenement is excused, it would only have the effect of increasing the value of the tenement, and be giving an advantage to the landlord at the expense of the rate-payers generally. 3. If *any* circumstances form sufficient grounds for excusing parties from payment of poor-rate, inquired what those circumstances are.

Ans.—The Commissioners in the first place desire to remark, that the only authority for the excusal of poor persons from the payment of the rates to which they are assessed, is the 11th section of the 54 Geo. 3, c. 170. The only consideration mentioned in that section as the ground of the excusal, is the parties' "inability, through poverty, to pay such rate." You speak of excusals on account of poverty, "or for other reasons." The Commissioners need scarcely add, that excusals "for other reasons" are not authorised by the statute. The Commissioners also think it right to observe, that the parish vestries have no authority in the matter; although, of course, there can be no objection to their affording advice or information to the overseers or guardians on the subject. In reply to your first inquiry, the Commissioners desire to state that it is properly a question for the justices to consider, whether the receipt of parish relief is such an evidence of poverty, as to justify an excusal of the rate, under the statute. With regard to your second question, the Commissioners can only say, that the statute expressly recognises "inability to pay" as a ground for excusal; though it mentions no other ground. The Commissioners at the same time, quite concur in your remarks as to the probable result of the practice referred to, in raising the rents in proportion to the remission of the rates. In reference to your third inquiry, the Commissioners wish to point out that the statute, in requiring the consent of the overseers, (or board of guardians,) as well as the sanction of the justices, to the excusal, seems to contemplate that the excusal shall not necessarily take place in every case of apparent inability to pay, but that the overseers, (or board of guardians,) as well as the justices, will exercise a discretion in the matter. It is obviously impossible to lay down any general rule as to the exercise of this discretion. The Commissioners, in conclusion, direct your attention to the remarks on this subject generally, in their Report on Local Taxation, (8vo edit. pp. 60, 61.)

---

2. RECEIPTS FOR THE POOR-RATE NOT EXEMPT FROM STAMP DUTY.

December 10, 1844.

Clerk of Macclesfield Union—Forwarded a copy

of a correspondence between the solicitor of stamps and taxes and one of the collectors of poor-rates for the township of Macclesfield, with reference to the necessity for giving stamped receipts on the payment of the poor-rates.

By this correspondence it appears that the solicitor of stamps and taxes, by a letter, dated 20th Sept., 1844, addressed to the collector, acquainted him that an unstamped receipt, which was said to have been given by him on the 4th Sept. for the sum of £5. 8*s*., had been lodged at his (the solicitor's) office, for the purpose of a prosecution being commenced against him, the collector, in the Court of Exchequer, for the recovery of the penalty of £10 incurred by him in respect of such receipt.

The collector having subsequently explained to the board of stamps and taxes the circumstances under which he had given the unstamped receipt in question, the board mitigated the penalty to 10*s*. which he paid.

XIII.—PUBLICATIONS.

POOR-LAW DOCUMENTS—CIRCULAR.

Poor Law Commission Office,
Somerset House,
January 31st, 1845.

Sir,—The Poor Law Commissioners have learned that some misapprehension exists as to the extent of the responsibility attached to them in reference to the Poor Law publications of Messrs. C. Knight and Co., and the Commissioners think it necessary, therefore, to state that the only publications which they have authorised Messrs. C. Knight and Co. to issue, and for which the Commissioners hold themselves responsible, are the following :—The Annual and other Reports of the Commissioners, presented to Parliament; their Official Circular, published monthly; Mr. Lumley's Abridgment of Poor Law Cases, in two volumes, 1840, and 1843; the Books and Forms prescribed by the Commissioners' Order for keeping Accounts; the Books and Forms prescribed by any other Orders and Circulars of the Commissioners; their General Orders; together with the Forms of Contracts under the Parochial Assessments Act, the Forms of Contracts for Building and Altering Workhouses, and the Forms of Charges on the Poor Rates, to secure Money borrowed for Building and Altering Workhouses, and for Emigration purposes.

The Commissioners are aware that besides the above, various Books and Forms have been published by Messrs. C. Knight and Co. The Commissioners do not doubt that these Books and Forms have been found to be useful to persons engaged in the administration of the Poor Law; but the Commissioners are in no way responsible for them.

The Commissioners are aware also that Messrs. Shaw and Sons have likewise published Books and Forms connected with the Poor Law; the Commissioners consider it right, however, to state, for general information, that they have given no authority to Messrs. Shaw and Sons to publish any Books or Forms.

Signed, by Order of the Board,
EDWIN CHADWICK, *Sec.*

To the Clerk to the Board of Guardians.

XIV.—RATING—OF LAND TAKEN TO FORM A RAILWAY.

October 2, 1844.

Mr. Reed, Noxton, Malton Union—Stated, that the York and Scarborough Railway Company had taken possession of some land which they would require for the line. The company were paying the occupiers for the damage done to their crops, but they had not paid the owners for the land; and the line would not be completed for eight or ten months. Inquired, whether the occupiers or the company should be rated to the poor-rate in respect of this land.

Ans.—As it appears, from your letter, that the railway company is in possession and occupation of the land, the Commissioners are of opinion that the company is alone liable to be rated for it. The right of the former occupiers or proprietors of the land to compensation is not a subject of assessment. The chief caution to be observed while the railway is in progress of formation, is to rate the land only on its present net annual value. This, until the railway is in profitable operation, will doubtless be less than the previous value of the land while under cultivation. As soon as rails are laid and become serviceable in the operations of the railway, the rateable value will increase, and when they are used in the conveyance of passengers or luggage, the rateable value will be ascertained by reference to the income and expenditure of the company.

XV.—RELATIONS—ORDERS FOR MAINTENANCE OF, BY WHOM TO BE OBTAINED.

Auditor of —— *Union*—Stated that, in the Union accounts, there was a charge against the parish of £6. 6s. paid to a solicitor for law expenses, under the following circumstances :

A person named J—— G——, who had a wife and seven children, having applied for relief, the Guardians directed an application to be made to the Justices, for an order of maintenance on the grandfather of the children. The clerk of the Guardians attended the Justices for that purpose, when they refused to grant a summons, the clerk not being the proper party to make the application. Upon this, the Assistant Overseer applied for a summons, which was granted. On the hearing, however, the summons was dismissed, the Assistant Overseer not being capable of examining the witnesses, and the Justices not allowing the clerk who was in attendance to examine them. The defendant was represented by his attorney. At the next meeting of the Guardians, they gave directions for the employment of an attorney to renew the application to the Justices for an order of maintenance against the grandfather. The application was accordingly made, but without success, and the Guardians directed a cheque for £6. 6s. to be drawn for payment of the attorney's charges in the matter, the amount to be charged to the parish where the parties were chargeable. The Clerk has therefore debited the parish with the amount in the union accounts; but it appearing that there is no statute which authorises the Guardians to employ an attorney for parochial matters, inquired whether his proper course would not be to strike out the charge from the accounts which he was then auditing, and direct it to be charged to the common fund for "establishment charges." In equity, however, he was of opinion that it should be borne by the parish, and charged in a similar manner to the expenses of orders of removal.

Ans.—The Commissioners in the first place desire to point out that the power to apply to the Justices for an order of maintenance, under the 43 Eliz. c. 2, s. 7, is not confined by the terms of that section to overseers, nor even to the case where the poor person is chargeable to a parish; and the Commissioners are disposed to consider that it is open to any one interested in the matter, the poor person himself, or the overseer of the parish to which he is chargeable, or any other parties concerned in the relief of the poor of such parish, such as the guardians of the Union in which it is included, to make the application to the Justices. It is true that, in the cases relating to this subject which have come before the courts it would seem that the orders have usually been made on the complaint of the Overseers; and the Commissioners believe that this is the general practice. But, looking to the terms of the section itself, and to the nature of the proceeding, the Commissioners see nothing to prevent the Guardians from making the application, or authorising it to be made. Entertaining the foregoing views, the Commissioners of course do not concur with the Justices, in the present instance, in refusing to receive the application from the Clerk to the Guardians. If the Clerk had been allowed by the Justices to conduct the proceedings, no expense would have been incurred by the Guardians for professional assistance; and the question is, whether the cost of such assistance, which was rendered necessary by the refusal of the Justices to receive the application from the Clerk, can lawfully be paid by the Guardians, and charged upon the poor-rates. The Commissioners are inclined to think that, under these circumstances, this may be done, assuming the case to have been of so much difficulty in itself, as to have required professional management. The Commissioners, of course, express no opinion as to the reasonableness of the expenses in point of amount. They are clearly of opinion, however, that if the Guardians charge the payment upon the poor-rates at all, they must charge it as against the particular parish concerned, and not upon the common fund of the Union,—the Union being, in fact, in no way interested in the matter.

XVI.—RELIEF—TO A PERSON RESIDING IN AN EXTRA-PAROCHIAL PLACE.

August 13th, 1844.

Clerk of Hereford Union—Stated that there was in the Hereford Union an extra-parochial piece of land, called "The Haywood Forest," which had never contributed to the poor-rates of any parish, or been assessed to the relief of the poor. A widow and her family residing in this extra-parochial hamlet had become destitute, and required relief. The relieving officer had relieved them, and carried the amount to a separate account. Requested to be informed to whom the relief ought to be charged.

Ans.—If the person to whom the inquiry relates is not settled in any parish in the Hereford Union, the guardians have no authority to relieve her, or her family, while residing in an extra-parochial place, which does not maintain its own poor: for whatever may be the local situation of such district, it is not within the union for the purposes of relief. Moreover, if the applicant is settled in some parish in the union, the guardians cannot lawfully relieve her while residing in such extra-parochial district, unless the case comes within the exceptions to Article 3 of the Prohibitory Order, or within the provisions of the 7 and 8 Vic. c. 101, sec. 26, relating to widows. If the case comes within those exceptions, the guardians may relieve the pauper while residing in "the Haywood Forest," and charge the relief to that parish in the union in which she is legally settled. But although the guardians may do this, it must be observed that they are under no obligation to do so. If the pauper is not settled in any parish in the union, or if so settled, the case does not fall within any of the exceptions to Article 3 of the order referred to, it follows (there being no authority to relieve) that the guardians cannot charge the amount already given by the relieving officer to any parish in the Hereford Union, nor to the account of the common fund.

XVII.—SETTLEMENT—MARRIAGE BETWEEN A PERSON AND HIS DECEASED WIFE'S SISTER.

Nov. 2, 1844.

Clerk of Tenterden Union—Stated that J. M., a widower, married E. C., his late wife's sister, at the parish church of Folkestone, on the 1st of August, 1842, and inquired whether the marriage was legal, and whether the children, the issue of the marriage, followed the mother's settlement.

Ans.—By the 2nd sec. of the 5th and 6th Wm. 4, c. 54, (passed August 31st, 1835,) it is enacted, "That all marriages which shall hereafter be celebrated between persons within the prohibited degrees of consanguinity or affinity, shall be absolutely null and void to all intents and purposes whatsoever." The marriage of a man with his deceased wife's sister, is a marriage between persons within the prohibited degrees of affinity; and as the marriage of J. M. and E. C. was a marriage of that kind, and took place on the 1st of August, 1842, subsequently to the passing of the above-named statute, it follows that such marriage was null and void to all intents and purposes whatsoever. It is clear, therefore, that the offspring of such marriage are illegitimate, and being born since the passing of the Poor Law Amendment Act, will follow their mother's settlement, under the 71st section of that statute.

XVIII.—WORKHOUSE.

PAUPERS ABSCONDING FROM A WORKHOUSE TEMPORARILY.

November 23, 1844.

———— Inquired, whether any circumstances had occurred since the issue of the workhouse rules (as explained in the Instructional Letter which accompanied them) that could justify the punishment, either by the guardians or the magistrates, of pauper inmates who shall have misconducted themselves in the following manner: that is to say, who shall have climbed over the walls of the workhouse during the night, for the purpose of attending a fair, and, having remained out during the greatest part of the night, shall have returned to the workhouse before daylight, and got back again into their ward without their absence having been discovered until some days afterwards.

Ans.—Although (as explained in the Instructional Letter accompanying the General Workhouse Rules) the Commissioners think that the guardians themselves are not empowered to punish a pauper who quits the workhouse clandestinely, and returns shortly afterwards voluntarily,—and although the Commissioners doubt whether the pauper's wearing the Union clothing on such an occasion would render him liable to punishment under the 2nd sec. of the 55th Geo. 3, 137,—the Commissioners, nevertheless, are disposed to consider that the conduct in question might be deemed a misbehaviour in the workhouse, under the 5th section of that statute; inasmuch as leaving the wards, climbing the walls, &c., must take place within the precincts of the workhouse.

LONDON:
Printed by Order of the Poor Law Commissioners, by BLACKBURN and PARDON, 6, Hatton Garden, and Published by CHARLES KNIGHT and Co., 22, Ludgate Street, Publishers to the Poor Law Commissioners.

AN

OFFICIAL CIRCULAR

OF PUBLIC DOCUMENTS AND INFORMATION:

DIRECTED BY THE POOR LAW COMMISSIONERS TO BE PRINTED, CHIEFLY FOR THE USE OF THE MEMBERS AND PERMANENT OFFICERS OF BOARDS OF GUARDIANS, UNDER THE POOR LAW AMENDMENT ACT.

No. 47. CIRCULAR ISSUED MAY 1, 1845.

Poor Law Commission Office,
Somerset House,
May 1, 1845.

THE Poor Law Commissioners have directed that their Eleventh Annual Report be printed and circulated for the information of Guardians and Officers of the several Unions.

By Order of the Board,
EDWIN CHADWICK, *Secretary*.

To THE RIGHT HON. SIR JAMES GRAHAM, BART. Her Majesty's Principal Secretary of State for the Home Department.

Poor Law Commission Office, Somerset House,
May 1, 1845.

PROCEEDINGS IN ENGLAND.

SIR,—1. In our last Annual Report we stated, upon the authority of the Returns which we received from the Unions and parishes of England and Wales, the amount of the expenditure for the relief of the poor, in the year ending at Lady-day, 1843; and we accompanied that statement with some details relative to the number and classes of paupers relieved during the same period. We proceed now to submit to you a similar statement with respect to the parochial year, ending at Lady-day, 1844.

Amount of Poor-rate levied in 1844, *and mode in which it was expended.*—2. The following statement exhibits the total amount of money levied in England and Wales under the denomination of poor's rate, in the parochial year 1844, together with the monies received from other sources in aid of the poor's rate.* These two sums amounted in that year to somewhat more than seven millions sterling. It likewise exhibits the manner in which this money was expended. Of the seven millions disposable as poor's rate, nearly five millions were applied to the relief of the poor. The payments made for the county and borough-rate amounted to above 1,350,000*l*. The law charges incurred by Unions and parishes a little exceeded 100,000*l*.; and the payments made, under the Parochial Assessments Act, for surveys and valuations of parishes, were about 30,000*l*. The expenses under the Vaccination Act were about 16,000*l*., and those under the Act for registering births, deaths, and marriages, were about 56,000*l*. The money returned to us as expended for "other purposes," not comprised in the preceding heads, amounts to 359,106*l*. We believe that the payments included in this unspecified item were principally made for the following purposes: viz. 1. Removals of paupers, and travelling expenses of overseers; 2. Constables' expenses; 3. Expenses of proceedings before magistrates; 4. Expenses on account of parish property; 5. Printing lists of voters, and making out lists of juries.

An Account of the Receipt and Expenditure of the Poor's Rate for the year ended Lady-day, 1844.

Receipt.	£.
Amount of money levied by assessment . .	6,847,205
Received from other sources in aid of poor-rate .	219,592
Total receipt .	7,066,797
Poor-rate expenditure.— *Expenditure.*	
For relief to the poor	4,976,093
Law charges, parochial and Union . . .	105,304
Payments under the Parochial Assessments Act (for surveys, valuations, &c.) and loans repaid under the same	30,083
Expenses under the Vaccination Act . . .	16,980
Expenses under the Act for Registering Births, Deaths, and Marriages	56,094
Payments for county and borough-rate, and for county and local police forces	1,356,457
Money expended for all other purposes . .	359,106
Total expenditure .	6,900,117

3. We likewise annex at the end of this Report a comparative statement, shewing the receipt and expenditure for all the above items since the year 1834. [This statement has been omitted from the want of room.]

4. Both the amount received as poor's rate, and the expenditure for the relief of the poor, were less in the parochial year 1844, than in the preceding year. The amounts are as follows:—

---

* The following are the principal sources of this subsidiary revenue: viz., 1. Rents of parish estates; 2. Income of funds of parishes; 3. Payments by relations of paupers; 4. Payments by fathers and mothers of bastards; 5. Re-payments of loans to out-pensioners; 6. Payments under orders of removal; 7. Fines, &c., paid over by magistrates; 8. Parliamentary registration shillings and lists of voters sold.

Years ending Lady-day	Total Amount of Monies received as Poor's Rate.
1843	£7,304,601
1844	7,066,797
Diminution	237,804

Years ending Lady-day	Total Expenditure for the Relief of the Poor.
1843	£5,208,027
1844	4,976,093
Diminution	231,934

5. The expenditure for the relief of the poor, which diminished during the years 1835, 1836, 1837, began to increase in 1838, and continued to increase in each successive year until Lady-day, 1843. The parochial year 1844 is the first year since 1837 which did not exhibit an increase of expenditure over the preceding year. As compared with the expenditure of the year 1834, the last parochial year previous to the passing of the Poor Law Amendment Act, the following is the amount for 1844 :—

Years ending Lady-day	Total Expenditure for the Relief of the Poor.
1834	£6,317,255
1844	4,976,093
Diminution .	£1,341,162

6. The diminution in the expenditure for the parochial year 1844, as compared with 1843, is distributed with tolerable equality over all the counties. The highest rates of reduction are in Lancashire, Cheshire, and the West Riding of Yorkshire; owing to the improvement in manufactures, which took place in the latter year. In some counties the expenditure of 1844 was slightly greater than that of the preceding year. The principal of these are Lincolnshire, Shropshire, Durham, and Northumberland. The increase of expenditure in the two latter counties was owing to the state of employment among the colliers: with regard to Lincolnshire, the cause is probably to be sought in a circumstance to which we shall advert in the course of our Report (par. 51).

7. The chief items of which the expenditure for the relief of the poor is composed, are shown in the following table, which relates to the two last parochial years, and comprises the Unions and parishes under the Poor Law Amendment Act. From the remaining parishes we receive no such returns as furnish the information contained in this table.

Years ended Lady-day	Expenditure of 585 Unions and Parishes under Boards of Guardians						Rate per Head of Total on Population
	In-Maintenance.	Out-Relief.	Estab. Charges and Salaries	Work-house Loans Repaid.	Other Charges connected with Relief to the Poor.	Total Expend. for Relief, &c. to the Poor.	
	£.	£.	£.	£.	£.	£.	s. d.
1843	810,372	2,818,843	786,148	167,103	7,092	4,589,558	6 9½
1844	705,253	2,726,451	748,985	183,898	5,584	4,370,171	6 5½
In.	...	...	...	16,795	...	...	...
De.	105,119	92,392	37,163	...	1,508	219,387	0 4

Decrease on Total Union Expenditure in 1844, compared with 1843 . . 4·8 per cent.

Number of persons relieved.—8. The diminution in the expenditure for the relief of the poor, with stationary prices of food, is naturally accompanied by a diminution in the number of the persons relieved. The following table exhibits the number of persons relieved during each of the Lady-day quarters in 1843 and 1844.

Comparative Statement of the Number of In-door and Out-door Paupers relieved in England and Wales, during each of the Quarters ended Lady-day, 1843 and 1844.

Quarters ended Lady-day	Number of Paupers Relieved.			Rate per Cent. of Total Number of Paupers on the Population in 1841.
	In-door.	Out-door.	Total.	
1843	238,748	1,307,642	1,546,390	9·7
1844	230,818	1,246,743	1,477,561	9·3
Decrease in 1844	7,930	60,899	68,829	·4

Population in 1841 . . . 15,906,741.

From this statement it appears that the total number of persons relieved in the three months ending Lady-day, 1844, amounted to nearly a million and a half, and were about 9⅓ per cent. of the entire population, according to the census of 1841. Of the million and half persons thus relieved, a large proportion were permanent paupers; but the number of new cases in the other three quarters may be safely estimated at half a million; so that the number of persons relieved in England and Wales, in the course of the parochial year 1844, may be taken at about two millions, or nearly one-eighth part of the actual population. In other words, about one person in eight, through the entire population, received relief from the poor's rate at some time during that year.

9. The same table shows that out of 1,477,561 paupers relieved in the quarter ending Lady-day, 1844, the number who were relieved in the workhouse was 230,818, and the number who received out-door relief was 1,246,743; that is to say, those who were relieved in the workhouse were 16 per cent., and those who received out-door relief were 84 per cent.; or, in other words, those who were relieved in the workhouse were to those who received out-door relief about as 1 to 5.

10. The following table shows the number of adult able-bodied paupers relieved during each of the quarters ending Lady-day 1843 and 1844; from which it appears, that although the number of those who received relief, both in and out of the workhouse, on account of sickness or accident, was greater in the second of these two periods, the number of those who were relieved on other grounds was considerably less. The decrease in the number of this class of able-bodied paupers was not less than 20 per cent.; a result highly gratifying, when it is remembered that the saving was not obtained by any change in the administration of the law, but arose solely from the improved state of the country.

Quarters ended at Lady-day.	In-door.			Out-door.			Total In-door and Out-door.
	On Account of temporary Sickness or Accident.	All other Causes, including Vagrants.	Total In-door.	On Account of temporary Sickness or Accident.	All other Causes, including Vagrants.	Total Out-door.	
1843	10,888	88,308	99,196	146,704	220,685	367,389	466,585
1844	11,458	86,327	97,785	158,280	175,419	333,699	431,484
Increase per Cent.	5·2	...	...	7·9	...	...	...
Decrease per Cent.	...	2·2	1·4	...	20·5	9·2	7·5

NOTE.—An estimate is made for places not in Union under the Poor Law Amendment Act. The above results are obtained from the Union Quarterly Abstracts.

11. On the other hand, the number of persons of both sexes, partially or wholly disabled by age or infirmity, who received out-door relief in the quarter ending Lady-day, 1844, is greater than the number who received similar relief in the corresponding quarter of 1843.

Aged and Infirm Paupers receiving Out-door Relief in 585 Unions.

Quarters ended Lady day	Wholly unable to Work.		Partially able to Work.		Total.		Grand Total.
	Males.	Females	Males.	Females	Males.	Females	
1843	64,246	117,806	34,716	74,306	98,962	192,112	291,074
1844	67,262	119,655	34,407	73,258	101,669	192,913	294,582

Variation in expenditure.—12. It may be observed, that the variation of the expenditure for the five years ending at Lady-day, 1844, leads, on the whole, to a satisfactory view of the manner in which the administration of the fund for the relief of the poor has been conducted by the local authorities. During the early part of this period, particularly during the year 1841, severe distress prevailed in most of the manufacturing districts, including that important part of the country where the manufactures of cotton are carried on.* The depression of the manufacturing districts was, as a natural consequence, soon followed by distress in the agricultural parts of the country.† In the year ending Lady-day, 1844, however, the demand for labour both in the manufacturing and agricultural districts had revived, and the number of able-bodied persons incapable of obtaining employment was not considerable.‡ Owing to this state of things, the expenditure for the relief of the poor increased steadily in the parochial years 1839—1843; but diminished in the year 1844. This fact proves that the amount of the poor-rate is not (as some persons have feared) governed by a law of constant and irresistible progression; but that, when subjected to proper control, the amount of the expenditure may be adapted to the varying exigencies of the people; that after having increased with the augmentation of distress, it can be diminished upon the return of comparative prosperity.

* See Sixth Annual Report, p. 1. Eighth Annual Report, pp. 7 and 8, ed. 8vo.
† Ninth Annual Report, pp. 1—3.
‡ Tenth Annual Report, p. 1.

Amount of local taxation.—13. Before we close our remarks upon the expenditure for the relief of the poor, we are desirous of again calling your attention to the magnitude of the sums annually levied in England and Wales for the purposes of local taxation. The total amount received for the poor's rate (which includes the county rate and part of the borough rate, and other miscellaneous items), was, as we have already seen, 6,847,205*l.* in the parochial year 1844. The amount of borough rate imposed by the municipal boroughs, (independently of the payments made out of the poor's rate, and the produce of the borough property and borough tolls and dues,) exceeds 200,000*l.* per annum.* The entire expenditure of the municipal boroughs is about 1,000,000*l.* sterling a year. The annual expenditure of the turnpike trusts is about 1,500,000*l.*; and that defrayed out of the highway rate is about 1,200,000*l.* The sums annually levied in towns for sewers rate, and for watching, lighting, and paving rates, have never been ascertained and returned to Parliament; the annual amount of the former is about 75,000*l.*; as to the latter, there is not, we believe, any information on which even an approximate estimate can be founded. The annual expenditure of the church rate appears to be nearly 500,000*l.* sterling. Adding some other branches of local taxation (which it is unnecessary to specify,†) the total amount of the local taxes annually levied and expended in England and Wales cannot, upon the most moderate computation, be placed at a less amount than 10,000,000*l.* sterling.

14. Now the amount of the revenue of the general government of the United Kingdom which is expended under the annual control of Parliament, may be measured by the sums included in the Appropriation Act. In the Appropriation Act for the year 1844, these sums amounted to 17,719,485*l.* Of this amount five-sixths may, in round numbers, be considered as having been contributed by England; the remaining sixth being paid by Ireland and Scotland. While therefore the share of the expenses of the general government, under the annual control of Parliament, which is borne by England, does not exceed 15,000,000*l.*; the sum which is annually expended in England out of the local taxes amounts to at least 10,000,000*l.* This comparison, we think, places in a clear light the magnitude and importance of the expenditure out of the local rates, and proves the expediency of bringing

* See Tables of Revenue, Population, and Commerce for 1843. Sess. Paper, vol. 55, p. 366.
† See the Report of the Poor Law Commissioners on Local Taxation, pp. 27, 28, ed. 8vo.

their amounts under the periodical observation of Parliament.

15. We are aware that the system of our local taxation is generally organised on the assumption that the imposition of the tax and its disbursement, as well as the audit of its expenditure, are committed to the discretion and control of the local authorities; and that *their* inspection is a sufficient security against abuse or mismanagement, without the interference of Parliament. Experience, however, has shown the advantage of ascertaining the aggregate amount of the public income and expenditure of the various local bodies, and of submitting these accounts, properly arranged and classified, to the frequent review of Parliament. As an illustration of this advantage, we may cite the returns of the Poor Law expenditure which have been annually made to Parliament since 1813: the annual accounts of the expenditure of the turnpike trusts returned under the 3 and 4 Wm. IV. c. 80, since 1834; and the accounts of the expenditure of the county rate, prepared from the returns of the county treasurers, which have for the last few years been annually printed for the use of the House of Commons. The reason of this advantage is, we think, apparent. So long as the local expenditure is stated exclusively for each parish, township, or other small division, the produce of the rate is viewed for one of these separate portions singly; and thus the aggregate importance of the tax is likely to be overlooked. The expense actually considered is small; while the amount of the expenses incurred by all the other divisions, which, taken together, would form an important sum, is unknown, and perhaps unthought of. The apparent amount of some of the most productive of the taxes imposed by the general government, might be reduced by a similar process of insulation. If, for example, an estimate were made of the amount of the tax on sugar, or tea, or spirits, which is contributed by a single rural parish, and if this sum was looked at by itself, without reference to the amount levied in the rest of the country, its importance would seem inconsiderable.

16. Amongst the local taxes, the fund levied under the denomination of poor's rate stands first in magnitude. The monies expended from this fund have, since the passing of the Poor Law Amendment Act, been subjected to a regular audit by paid auditors; which will we trust, be rendered still more effective by the provisions in the Poor Law Act of last session. The expenses for the survey and valuation of parishes, for vaccination, and for the registration of births, deaths, and marriages, which have been created by Acts of Parliament passed subsequently to 1834, have been imposed upon the poor's rate, and form a new charge upon that fund. Their aggregate annual amount is about 100,000*l.*; and although this expenditure may be justly considered as of great public utility, the fact of its recent creation ought not to be overlooked in comparing the present amount of the poor's rate with its amount in former years. With respect to the law charges incurred by parishes and Unions, (which are not included in the expenditure for the relief of the poor,) it is to be observed that they have undergone a great diminution since the passing of the Poor Law Amendment Act. Their amount in 1834 was not less than 258,604*l.*; in 1842 it had fallen to 68,051*l.*; in 1844 it had risen to 105,304*l.*, which, however, is less than half the amount in 1834. A further important saving due to the operation of the same Act is that which has taken place in the miscellaneous item returned to us under the unspecified head of "*other purposes*," as is shown in the following account:—

Years ended Lady-day	Money expended out of the Poor's Rate for all other Purposes.	Years ended Lady-day	Money expended out of the Poor's Rate for all other Purposes.
1834	£1,021,941	1840	£466,698
1835	935,362	1841	527,717
1836	823,213	1842	318,092
1837	637,043	1843	346,007
1838	507,929	1844	359,106*
1839	493,703		

The large reduction in this item must be attributed mainly to the exclusion of irregular and illegal expenses of a miscellaneous nature, which has been effected by the auditors appointed under the Poor Law Amendment Act. Upon this subject we refer to a passage contained in a report which was made to us in the year 1840 by our Assistant Commissioner, Mr. Power, when he was in charge of Lancashire and the West Riding of Yorkshire, and which was printed in the Appendix to our Sixth Annual Report.†

17. The decrease in the expenditure for law charges, and in the miscellaneous item just mentioned, ought

* The metropolitan police rate (which amounts to nearly 200,000*l.* per annum) is included in this item for the years 1834—1841; but not in the three subsequent years.

† "The item entitled 'other purposes,' in the Annual Parliamentary Returns, demands a few observations in reference to its enormous amount in the earlier years of the comparison, and the considerable reductions of this item effected in later years show the value of that part of the new system of management, whereby the expenditure of 20 or 30 townships, instead of being left separately in the hands of as many paid assistant overseers, is brought into one focus, a clear and distinct system of accounting introduced, and the whole submitted to the searching and effectual examination of an auditor every quarter. In the year 1835, no less a sum than 64,883*l.* was included in the Parliamentary Returns for Lancashire, under the head of 'other purposes;' and the sum of 39,675*l.* under the same head, for the West Riding of York.

"This item appears to have undergone a gradual decrease immediately from the passing of the Poor Law Amendment Act, the improper and illegal disbursements of which it partly consisted, having begun to be discontinued by the overseers, through fear of the impending change in the mode of examining and auditing the accounts. Much, however, was left to be effected by the auditors of the Unions, which, from time to time, have been brought into operation; and the labours of these officers have been attended with most important effect in the exclusion of improper items of expenditure."—(Mr. Power on the Poor-rate Expenditure of Lancashire and the West Riding; Sixth Annual Report, Appendix B., No. 2.)

to be added to the decrease in the expenditure for the relief of the poor, in order to obtain a complete view of the saving produced by the operation of the Poor Law Amendment Act.

Years ended Lady-day	Total Expenditure for the Relief of the Poor.	Law Charges, &c.	Money expended for all other Purposes.	Total.
1834	£6,317,255	£258,604	£1,021,941	£7,597,800
1844	4,976,093	105,304	359,106	5,440,503
Decrease	1,341,162	153,300	662,835	2,157,297

The actual reduction in the expenditure out of the poor's rate, under these three heads, for the year 1844, as compared with the year 1834, therefore exceeds two millions sterling.

County and Borough Rates.—18. The only expenditure charged upon the poor's rate, which has undergone a large increase since 1834, is that for the county and borough rates. The payments out of the poor's rate for county and borough rates, which amounted only to 604,203*l.* in the year 1837, had, in the year 1844, reached the sum of 1,356,457*l.*, that is to say, they have more than doubled in seven years. It is not within our province to inquire into the causes of this increase, or to consider whether the additional advantages afforded to the public service do not more than compensate the increased expenditure. We will, however, remark that in consequence of the manner in which the payments for the county and borough rates are mixed up in the returns made to us, and the imperfect accounts of the borough rate expenditure which have been laid before Parliament, it is impossible to make the payments for these two rates balance the expenditure. We have compared the sums returned from the Unions and parishes as paid for county and borough rate in the three years ending Lady-day 1840, 1841, 1842, with the sums acknowledged by the county treasurers to have been received as county rate in the three years ending Michaelmas, 1840, 1841, 1842, as stated in the returns made to the House of Commons.* From these authorities it appears that the payments made for the county and borough rate during the above three years ending at Lady-day, amounted to 3,177,005*l.* or to an average sum of 1,059,002*l.* per annum; whereas the sums received as county rate by the county treasurers, during the three years ending at Michaelmas, amounted only to 2,376,473*l.*, or to an average sum of 792,158*l.* per annum. We presume, therefore, that the difference between these two sums, that is, about 260,000*l.* per annum, was paid by the overseers, out of the poor's rate, to the town councils in the municipal boroughs. The exact amount of this payment cannot be ascertained from the returns of the expenditure of boroughs which have been presented to Parliament.† It is to be observed that the payments made from the poor's rate for the county rate are less than the county rate expenditure; inasmuch as an annual contribution to certain of the expenses charged upon the county rate is made by the general government. The sum thus allowed amounted in 1842 to 114,734*l.*

Diminution in pressure of poor rate as measured by its ratio to the population.—19. But, notwithstanding the recent increase in the amount of the county and borough rates, and the creation of new expenses charged upon the poor's rate, the sum levied as poor's rate in the year 1844 is less than the sum levied as poor's rate in 1834. Moreover, the sum levied as poor's rate in 1844 is less than the sum levied as poor's rate in any year from 1813 to 1834, except the year 1824, when the amount was slightly inferior. This fact becomes the more important when the great increase of population, since 1813, is taken into the account. The following table shows the population, the amount levied as poor's rate, and the ratio which this amount bore to the population, in each of the four years 1813, 1824, 1834, and 1844.

Years ended Lady-day	Population of England and Wales.	Total Money levied for Poor Rates, and County and Borough Rates.	Rate per Head on the Population.
		£.	£. s. d.
1813	10,505,886	8,646,841	0 16 5
1824	12,517,921	6,836,505	0 10 11
1834	14,105,645	8,338,079	0 11 9
1844	16,543,010	6,847,205	0 8 3

If therefore the pressure of the sum levied as poor's rate is measured by the ratio of its amount to the population, its burden in 1844 would be half its burden in 1813, and only two-thirds of its burden in 1834.

If it should be objected, that the pressure of this tax ought to be estimated by its ratio to property, and not to population, this comparison leads to an equally satisfactory result. There is no doubt that the yearly produce of the rateable property of England has undergone a very great increase since 1813; and that its annual progress is now rapid. The total annual value of real property assessed to the property tax in 1815 in England and Wales, was 51,898,423*l.** whereas the amount in 1843 was 85,802,735*l.*† It is further to be observed, that the increase in the annual value of rateable property arises, not only from the improved cultivation of the land, and its consequently increased productiveness, but also, to a great extent, from the large number of new houses and other buildings, (such as manufactories and warehouses,) as well as railways, canals, wharfs, &c., which are constructed from year to year. Accordingly, land, as such, pays a smaller proportion of the local rates in each successive year; and a larger proportion falls on the other sorts of rateable property. This fact ap-

* For the receipt and expenditure of the county rate, see Parliamentary Papers, No. 434, Sess. 1842, and No. 76, Sess. 1844.

† Return of Parochial and Borough Rates, &c. (England and Wales), No. 635, Sess. 1844.

* Parl. Paper, No. 444, Sess. 1835.

† Parl. Paper, No. 102, Sess. 1845. In the Parl. Paper, No. 316, Sess. 1844, this amount for the same period is returned at 82,253,844*l.* We presume that the latest return is most correct.

pears from the table inserted in our Ninth Annual Report, par. 27, which shows, that whereas the proportion of the poor's rate falling upon land was 69 per cent., and that falling on other property was 31 per cent. in 1826; the proportion falling on land was only 52 per cent., and on other property 48 per cent. in 1841. The following is the statement to which we refer:—

Years.	On Landed Property.	Proportion per Cent.	Dwelling Houses.	Proportion per Cent.	All other Property.	Proportion per Cent.	Total Amount of Poor Rate levied.
	£.		£.		£.		£.
1826	4,795,482	69	1,814,228	26	356,447	5	6,966,157
1841	3,316,593	52	2,375,221	37	660,014	11	6,351,828

20. The expenditure of the poor's rate and the county rate may, as it appears to us, be taken generally as affording some approximation to an index of the amounts of destitution and crime in the country; the former being applied solely to the relief of want, and the latter principally expended in the detection, prosecution, and punishment of crime. Tried by this test, the state of the country must be considered as presenting a favourable aspect; inasmuch as the ratio of this expenditure to population and property is at least as low as in any recent year; and is only half the amount at which it stood about the year 1813.

Expediency of establishing all practicable securities against abuse of local taxes.—21. But although the pressure of the most important of the local taxes in England may be less at present than in previous years, it is nevertheless highly expedient that all practicable securities against the abuse or mismanagement of those taxes should be established, and that the mode and amount of their levy and expenditure should be brought periodically under the observation of Parliament. We have already stated that complete accounts of the expenditure of the poor's rate are annually presented by us to Parliament; and that similar accounts are presented of the county rate expenditure from the returns of the county treasurers. Some returns of the borough rate expenditure have likewise been made; but the information which they afford is not complete. Ample returns of the expenses of the Turnpike Trusts are transmitted annually under the 3 and 4 Wm. IV. c. 80, to Sir James M'Adam, by whom they are digested for presentation to Parliament. We believe that the accounts thus obtained have been productive of much public benefit. On the other hand, there is no periodical return of the highway rate—a rate which is liable to great abuse, and is, we fear, in not a few parishes converted into a subsidiary poor's rate for the relief of able-bodied labourers. No return has ever been made to Parliament of the amounts levied and expended for the sewers rate, or for lighting, watching, and paving rates. Nor is any regular return made of the sums expended as church rate.

22. We have, perhaps, dwelt longer on this portion of our Report than was consistent with our strict duty; but we trust that the importance of the subject, and our official connexion with the poor's rate, the largest of the local taxes, as well as the intimate connexion which subsists between most of these taxes, will serve as a sufficient excuse for our venturing to submit to you the above remarks. We will merely state, in addition, that the general survey which we have taken of the present state of our system of local taxation seems to us to authorise the two following conclusions: viz. 1. That an account of the receipt and expenditure of all the more considerable local taxes ought to be annually prepared and laid before Parliament. 2. That the expenditure of all such taxes ought to undergo a strict and regular audit by competent auditors.

Relief of the Poor during the last year.—23. We are unable, on account of the delay which occurs in the transmission of the annual returns to our office, to state the amount of the expenditure for the parochial year ending at Lady-day, 1845. Indeed, the audit of the Poor Law accounts for the Lady-day quarter is, in many Unions, not yet completed. We can, however, say generally that the year since the 1st of May, 1844, has on the whole been favourable to the poorer classes of this country. In the manufacturing districts, the demand for labour has been extensive and constant; and even the iron and coal districts, which were the last to recover from the general depression, were prosperous during the last twelve months. The drought of last summer, and the length and severity of the cold during last winter, were unfavourable to the employment of agricultural labourers; but we rejoice to say that the number of rural Unions in which difficulty arose from the applications of unemployed able-bodied men was not considerable. Amongst those in which the workhouses were filled, and it became necessary to give out-door relief to the able-bodied, subject to a condition of labour, we may specify the Caxton and Arrington Union in Cambridgeshire, the Rye Union in Sussex, and the Highworth and Swindon Union in Wiltshire. The Guardians of the latter Union have, in order, as far as possible, to prevent a recurrence of the same state of things, agreed to build a new and enlarged workhouse. Moreover, in several Unions it has been necessary to give out-door relief to all applicants for a time, on account of the existence of small-pox in the workhouse. We have, however, the satisfaction of being able to state that, during the last year, the administration of the Poor Law, under the amended statutes and the regulations of the Commissioners, was conducted with general regularity on the part of the local authorities, and acquiescence on the part of the public.

Measures for giving Effect to 7 and 8 Vic., c. 101.—24. An important part of our proceedings, since the date of our last annual Report, has consisted in the execution of the additional duties imposed upon us by the Poor Law Act of last session, the statute of the 7 and 8 Vic., c. 101, and in the measures which we took for giving effect to its provisions.

25. Our first step, after the conclusion of the session of Parliament, was to place in the hands of the Guardians and Officers throughout the country a circular letter, calling attention to the enactments contained in that statute. We did not attempt to affix an authentic interpretation to that which the superior courts are alone competent to interpret; our purpose was to state, as plainly and as briefly as we could, any new duties and liabilities imposed on Guardians, Overseers, and paid Officers, as well as to explain the principal changes effected by the recent statute. This circular letter will be found in the Appendix to this Report.

Alteration of order regulating Out-door relief.—26. Our next duty appeared to be to modify any of our own regulations which might either really or apparently conflict with the new statute. The only order which seemed to require alteration on this account was that which regulates the administration of out-door relief. Sections 25 and 26 of the Act placed married women whose husbands were absent under certain conditions, and a peculiar class of widows, in a position somewhat different from that in which they had previously stood. We have, therefore, so modified our regulations as to make them consistent with these clauses, and have reissued the General Order with no other change in its provisions than was requisite for this purpose. The Order, as amended, will be found in the Appendix.

Order relating to Non-resident relief.—27. In connexion with this subject we may state that, in December last, we issued an Order, of considerable importance, with reference to the administration of relief to paupers not residing within the Union from which the relief is received. This order imposes no fresh restrictions as to the class of paupers to whom such relief may lawfully be given; nor does it diminish, in any degree, the discretion previously exercised by Boards of Guardians with reference to the persons who are to receive relief. Its sole object is to regulate the mode in which the money is to be transmitted from one Union to another, and that in which the accounts relating to it are to be kept, in cases in which a Board of Guardians voluntarily undertakes to administer relief for another Board.

28. It often happened that a relieving officer, acting for a large district in a manufacturing town, had constantly passing through his hands large sums payable to paupers belonging to other Unions, which were intrusted to him by the Officers or Guardians of these distant Unions to pay the paupers residing in his district. Now, for the due administration of all money placed in his hands by his own Board of Guardians, this officer had given security, and he and his sureties were accountable, under his bond, for any fraud or misapplication; but in respect to the money thus forwarded to him by Officers or Guardians with whom he was not officially connected, there existed no effectual responsibility of any kind. He was, to all intents and purposes, their private agent; and although, like any other private agent, he was liable to the ordinary proceedings for fraud, whether civil or criminal, there could not exist the same security against peculation, as in the case of monies delivered into his hands, as a public officer, by his official superiors.

29. These evils of agency are inseparably connected with any system of non-resident relief; they were not created by the Poor Law Amendment Act; on the contrary, we believe that they have been in every respect much diminished under the operation of that statute. We have found, however, by experience, that the opportunity thus thrown in the way of relieving officers not unfrequently led to misapplication of money over which no effectual control could be exercised. An officer was intrusted with a considerable sum to be paid away in half-crowns or shillings to a number of paupers living at a distance from the only persons who had any direct interest in ascertaining that he fulfilled his trust; he was not the officer of those paupers, and it was optional with him whether he undertook to distribute relief on their behalf. A temptation of this kind would often lead a man, hitherto honest, to keep back, at first, perhaps, for a short time with the intention of replacing it, some portion of the money in his hands; months might elapse before a complaint reached the distant Board of Guardians, and even then it was not easy for them to ascertain all the facts of the case.

30. These difficulties are in a great degree inseparable from a system in which the recipient lives at a distance from the persons making the allowance. We have, so far as we could, from time to time, lent our aid in detecting and punishing by dismissal any cases of fraud brought to our notice; but we became satisfied of the necessity of applying some more general remedy to the evils arising from this state of things. To do so was not easy, inasmuch as a relieving officer of one Union cannot be treated as the officer of another Union; he cannot be the servant of two different Boards at the same time; and a complete official responsibility extending to his sureties can only be enforced in the cases in which he misconducts himself in his capacity of a public servant. It followed that such a responsibility could only be created by causing him to distribute, under the authority and direction of his own Board, the relief originally allowed by distant Boards of Guardians; but for this purpose it became necessary that the former body should constitute themselves the agents of the authorities transmitting the money on account of the parish in which the pauper was settled. We did not conceive that we were empowered to compel a Board of Guardians to act as the agents of another Board which requested them to do so. All we could do was

to prohibit the officers from accepting such agency without the sanction of their own Board, and to regulate the mode of transmitting the money and keeping the accounts where they were directed to administer relief on behalf of other Unions or parishes.

31. The result is, that no officer can now lawfully administer relief to non-settled poor as from the parish of their settlement without being responsible for the proper application of monies, in the same manner as if he were relieving paupers settled and residing in his own district. Our Order (as is stated in the Instructional Letter sent with it) does not prohibit Boards of Guardians from employing any other agency, if they think proper to run the risk; all we have done is to regulate the proceedings of the Board of Guardians when the agency is accepted, and thus to secure the paid officers against the continual temptation to fraud thrown in their way by the extreme laxity of the system previously pursued. This Order, and the Instructional Letter accompanying it, will be found in the Appendix.

Order relating to Apprenticeship of Poor Children.—32. In the Poor Law Amendment Act certain powers of making rules and regulations respecting parish apprentices were intrusted to the Commissioners; but some doubt existed as to the possibility of so exercising these powers as effectually to bind the masters who undertook the care of children thus situated. By the 12th section of the Act of last Session these doubts were removed; and specific authority was given to the Commissioners to prescribe the duties of the masters, as well as the terms and conditions to be inserted in the indentures of parish apprentices. In pursuance of this section we have issued a General Order, which will be found in the Appendix.

33. In this Order we have, among other provisions, directed that no child shall be apprenticed until he can read and write; and we have endeavoured, so far as such an object can be attained by regulations, to protect the apprentice, and to prevent that risk of his maltreatment which is, to a certain extent, inseparable from every system of parish apprenticeship.

34. Certain provisions of this Order have been objected to by some parishes and Unions. These are more especially the limitations as to premiums for apprentices above the age of 14 (Art. 2,) the proposed payment to be made by the master to his apprentice after he is 17 years of age (Art. 18, No. 8,) and the prohibition of causing the boy to be taken more than 10 miles from the place of apprenticeship without the licence of the Guardians (Art. 18, No. 10.) The principal ground on which these provisions are objected to is, that they are calculated seriously to impede apprenticeship, by imposing responsibilities on masters such as will deter a great number of persons from taking parish apprentices at all.

35. We certainly entertain opinions unfavourable to that state of servitude which is created by the apprenticeship of parish children; and we should not regret to find that the regulations imposed by us tended gradually to diminish the number of children thus dealt with. We feel satisfied that greater attention to the education and industrial training of poor children would more than compensate for any supposed inconvenience arising from an indisposition to take apprentices, and that the results of such an improvement would be beneficial both to the master and the child. We think we are fully justified in arriving at this conclusion by the evidence embodied in Mr. Kay Shuttleworth's Report* on "The improvement in Training of Pauper Children, and on Apprenticeship in the Metropolitan Unions." This Report will be found in the Appendix to that which in the year 1841 we had the honour to make to the Marquis of Normanby on the general subject of the training of pauper children, and we confidently refer to it as establishing the unsatisfactory results of pauper apprenticeship with a premium.

36. At the same time it is not our wish to inflict any great or sudden inconvenience on large and populous parishes by regulations which may appear vexatious to the future masters, and thereby impede the placing out of children now fit for service. We have, therefore, collected such information on the probable operation of the Order as we could readily procure; we have, also, received a deputation from the parish of St. Marylebone, as well as one from the clerks to the Guardians of the Unions in the neighbourhood of London on the subject. We shall proceed to consider the representations of these parties, whose practical experience necessarily gives great weight to any expression of their opinion; and we are prepared to make such changes in the regulations now issued as may appear advisable.

Alteration of Law relating to Bastardy.—37. Perhaps the most important change effected by the Act of 7 and 8 Vict., c. 101, was that relating to bastardy. It is unnecessary for us to recite the various alterations in the law respecting the affiliation of bastard children, which had been made previously to the last session of Parliament. We expressed our views with reference to further legislation on the subject, in a special Report, which we had the honour of presenting to you on the 31st day of January, 1844. (See Tenth Ann. Rep., App. A, No. 7.)

38. The Legislature, in the Act of last Session, departed entirely from the principle on which the affiliation of bastard children had previously been based. In all former provisions on this subject, from the Act of Elizabeth downwards, the sole object avowed by the statutes was indemnity to the parish for the charge of supporting the bastard. This indemnity was to be supplied both by the putative father and by the mother; practically, it depended on the former of the two. In no Act had the principle

* "Report on Training of Pauper Children," 1841, 8vo., Appendix, pp. 127 to 194.

been recognised that redress to the woman for a wrong inflicted on her was the object of the Legislature. The fact, therefore, that the protection afforded was, in the eye of the law, given solely for the purpose of meeting the charge upon the rate-payers, necessarily connected the affiliation of bastard children with the question of relief.

Alteration of Law ralating to Bastardy.—39. We have always believed, and we still think, that the indirect use of what professed to be a remedy for the parish only, as a means of redressing any wrong supposed to be inflicted on the woman, was in every way most mischievous and embarrassing in its operation. The question, how far direct redress in such cases could properly be given, is not one which we were called upon to raise. If redress were to be given at all, it ought, in our opinion, as we had the honour of reporting to you, to be direct only; and such it was made by the statute of last session. The result of this enactment, therefore, has been that the affiliation of bastards stands altogether unconnected with the laws for the relief of the poor. Parish and Union officers are forbidden to take part in the proceedings relating to it, and an entirely new principle has been established by the law; that is to say, it is now admitted that the mother of a bastard, not the parish, is the party by whom redress is to be sought from the putative father, and to whom indemnity is to be awarded for the charge of maintaining the child. The means placed at her disposal for obtaining such redress are the cheapest and most accessible known to the laws of this country; that is to say, a proceeding in petty sessions.

Its effect as regards the Laws for relief of the Poor.—40. Our only duty, in this Report, is to state in what manner this new principle has been found to work in relation to the laws for the relief of the poor, with the administration of which we are intrusted.

41. We have been consulted on various points of bastardy law, arising under the recent statute, by Union and parish officers as well as by justices; and we have, in consideration of the former connexion of the subject with the Poor Laws, endeavoured to afford advice and assistance, even where it did not appear strictly within our province to do so. To Boards of Guardians we have uniformly stated that a bastard and the mother of a bastard were, like any other persons, entitled to relief when destitute; that the fact of the latter having affiliated the child did not of itself deprive her of such a right, although any payment made by the putative father to her necessarily formed part of those means the amount of which it was the duty of the Guardians to consider when they proceeded to decide on the fact of her destitution. We have no reason to think that any embarrassment or difficulty of importance will occur in administering the laws for the relief of the poor in the cases of illegitimate children or their mothers in consequence of the Act of last session.

Erection of District Schools.—42. We were, by the Act of last session, empowered to combine Unions and parishes, within certain limits, for the erection of district schools to be used for the education of pauper children. We accordingly proceeded, soon after the passing of the Act, to consider the arrangements which it would be expedient to make for the purpose of giving effect to this provision; and we have to express much regret that we have hitherto been unable to declare any such district. This has arisen mainly from the fact that when we had caused the probable cost of the buildings to be appropriated to such schools to be accurately calculated, we saw reason to fear that the limit imposed on the money to be raised or borrowed by the 44th section of the statute, viz., one-fifth of the average annual expenditure, would in most instances, though not perhaps in all, preclude our obtaining such a sum as would be adequate for the proper construction of the building in question.

43. We feel bound also to state that we find existing among the members of the various Boards of Guardians in and about the metropolis considerable reluctance to avail themselves of the powers conferred on them by the Legislature. This indisposition, we make no doubt, would, on further consideration of the subject, be greatly diminished, provided the preliminary obstacle of the narrow limit fixed for the cost of the building and site were previously enlarged by the authority of Parliament. It is clear that this might easily be done without authorising the expenditure of any such sum as would cast a serious burthen on the rate-payers; and it will be remembered that the Commissioners have no power conferred on them to order the erection of any school without the consent of the majority of the Board to be constituted for each district.

Formation of Districts for Relief of Casual Poor.—44. With regard to the other class of districts authorised by 7 and 8 Vic., c. 101, those, namely, for the relief of casual poor within the limits of the metropolitan police, we have framed a scheme for the division of the whole of the metropolitan district in such a manner as will, we think, enable us to carry out the intention of the Legislature. In this case, the cost to be actually incurred will probably fall very far short of that authorised by the Act; and we shall proceed to declare the districts in question at as early a period as possible. We have caused them to be arranged, as much as practicable, with reference to great lines of road along which mendicants and vagrants find their way into the metropolis; and our hope is that they will be found such as will enable the metropolitan police to discharge, without inconvenience, the duties imposed upon them in connexion with these asylums.

Appointment of District Auditors.—45. Among the provisions of the Act of last session, to which we are required to give effect, some of the most important are those relating to the appointment of District Auditors throughout England and Wales.

46. In the Report to the Marquis of Normanby on the further amendment of the Poor Laws, which the Commissioners had the honour to present in 1839, attention was called to the following recommendations of the Select Committee of the House of Commons on the Poor Law Amendment Act, in 1838:—1. That Auditors should not be confined to one Union, but should act for large districts. 2. That the Poor Law Commissioners should have the power of appointing District Auditors.

The Commissioners, in that Report, proceeded to dwell on the importance of the duties of an Auditor, and on the qualifications which appeared necessary for the discharge of those duties. In our Report of last year, we recurred to the defect in the existing system of audit, and to the cumbrous nature of the proceedings to which, in certain cases, we had been compelled to resort in order to protect the rate-payers from illegal expenditure of their funds. It was therefore with sincere satisfaction that we saw the Legislature, in the last session of Parliament, proceed to make such changes in the system of audit as will, in our opinion, secure far more efficient protection against fraud and illegality in the administration of the poor-rate than has ever yet existed in the case of any local fund in this country. The authority to form districts was conferred on the Commissioners, the powers of District Auditors were fixed and settled, and the method of their appointment to a certain degree defined by the Act. The appointment, however, was not, as recommended by the Select Committee of the House of Commons, vested in the Commissioners, but was placed in the hands of the Chairman and Vice-Chairman of each Board of Guardians included in a district. We think it right to state that we entertain no doubt of the superior advantages of the mode of appointment selected by the Legislature; and the experience of the elections which have taken place, though limited, has satisfied us that no preferable mode of appointment could have been devised. The Chairmen and Vice-Chairmen of Unions are usually gentlemen of such weight and experience in the despatch of business as to inspire a reliance on their judgment and their integrity. The Guardians, the rate-payers, and the officers must all alike feel that an Auditor, selected by such persons, is in the first instance entitled to public confidence. Should it be afterwards proved, by his misconduct or inefficiency, that such confidence has been misplaced, the Commissioners are empowered to remove the officer thus failing in the discharge of his duty.

47. At the same time, although the nomination of the Auditors generally is not vested in the Commissioners, they were authorised to deal with certain peculiar cases in which Auditors were already acting for more than one Union. In these instances, the Commissioners have the power to continue the existing Auditor in office, and to add to or alter his district as they see fit. We have considered this provision as intended to effect two objects;—1. It enabled us, in the case of persons who had already devoted a large part of their time to the performance of the duties of Auditor, and whose salary was not inconsiderable in amount, to secure to them a continuance of their present situation, provided that they had proved themselves competent to perform its duties, and that the existence of their district was not incompatible with the main object of the Legislature; that is to say, the general establishment of proper audit districts throughout the whole country. 2. It enabled us at once to extend the services of a tried and meritorious officer, acting for a small district, to one of larger extent, instead of exposing that officer to the risk of a fresh election, and of causing a new and perhaps inexperienced auditor to be elected for Unions which might properly be annexed to an existing district.

48. It will be observed that this power of continuance and of annexation does not prejudice the right of the Chairmen and Vice-chairmen to elect in the event of any future vacancy; and we only regret that the considerations necessarily pressing on us in dividing the whole country into districts have often made it impossible to continue District Auditors against whom no complaint has been made, but whose retention of office would have disturbed the general arrangements which we were called upon to make. In such cases we have reluctantly been compelled to allow the Act to take its course, and the services of persons so situated, as well as of the Auditors for single Unions, have terminated, or will necessarily terminate, as fresh districts are declared. With regard to the Auditors for single Unions, we have in some instances, in which the Board of Guardians have expressed confidence in them, felt especial regret at our inability to continue them. Upon the whole, however, the sacrifice of individual interest in each case is so trifling as to make the operation of the Act in respect of the Auditors for single Unions of less importance, inasmuch as their salary is always inconsiderable, and their duties as Auditor have occupied but a small portion of their time.

Number of Districts declared.—49. Since the passing of the Act we have declared twenty-four districts for the purpose of audit: of these, sixteen are districts in which we have thought it right to continue the services of an Auditor already acting for more than one Union, and the remainder are districts in which an Auditor either has been or will be elected by the Chairmen and Vice chairmen of the several Boards of Guardians. With regard to these latter districts, we insert in the Appendix a copy of the order directing the mode of election; which we have endeavoured to frame so as to give the least possible trouble to the electors, and to leave in the hands of our Assistant Commissioner, acting as returning officer, as little discretion as is compatible with the proper conduct of the election.

Order relating to Election of Guardians.—50. Some important amendments of the law in matters relating to the election of Guardians (particularly in the scale of voting for owners and rate-payers) were made by the Act of last session; and we accordingly, in January last, issued a general order, regulating the manner of conducting the elections of Guardians, in which all the provisions are adapted to the altered state of the law.

Modification of Kensington Union.—51. By the 66th section of the Act we were empowered to separate parishes from, or annex them to, existing Unions, without the consent of the Board of Guardians, required by the Poor Law Amendment Act. In pursuance of this provision, we have detached the parishes of Kensington and Paddington from the former Kensington Union, and have placed them under separate Boards of Guardians; the other two parishes of the Union, Fulham and Hammersmith, remain together, as the Fulham Union. Our attention has likewise been directed to other Unions in different parts of the country, which appeared to be inconveniently large, or otherwise to require modification, with a view to the exercise of the power just adverted to. We have reason to believe that some of the Unions in Lincolnshire, in particular, contain too large an area, and that the local circumstances will in several cases admit of their reduction. The recent continued increase of pauperism in that county has, as it appears to us, been partly caused by the difficulty of inspection, which arises from the extent of the district placed under the superintendence of a single Board of Guardians.

Alteration in number of Guardians for certain Parishes.—52. We have likewise exercised in many cases the power conferred upon us by the same Act (sec. 18), of altering the number of Guardians elected by a parish. In general this alteration has been effected by authorising the election of an additional Guardian or Guardians, the object being to remove slight inequalities in the representation, which had either existed from the formation of the Union, or had been produced by the disproportionate increase of population in different parishes.

Discharge of outstanding balances.—53. The 34th section of the Act gave the Commissioners the power of consenting to the discharge by the Auditor of any outstanding balance struck against an officer before the passing of the Act, provided no proceedings had been taken for its recovery. We have been applied to for our consent to the discharge of such balances in many cases, and in the majority of them this consent has been given. In some we have felt a difficulty in interpreting the words which occur in the middle of the clause, and have hesitated to assume a power respecting which some doubt may exist. In one or two cases only we have reluctantly refused on different grounds; that is to say, because it appeared that the balance due arose from illegal payments knowingly persevered in after notice of their illegality. We have thought that it was the intention of the Legislature to relieve from embarrassment those officers only who had been exposed to loss through inadvertence or ignorance of the law, not such as had intentionally violated its provisions.

Appointment of Collectors and Assistant Overseers.—54. The powers in the Act (sections 61 and 62) for the appointment of collectors and assistant overseers, and the provisions with respect to their duties and the security to be given by them, have been found very useful. Applications are constantly made to us from Boards of Guardians and from parishes to be allowed to avail themselves of the power of appointment in section 62. Although this portion of the administration of the Poor Laws is still encumbered with some difficulties, we entertain a confident hope that there will gradually be established a degree of regularity and of responsibility on the part of those officers such as has not hitherto existed.

55. We have only, in conclusion, to state that, with the exception of the points expressly mentioned above, the statute of the 7th and 8th Vic., c. 101, is now in operation, without having deranged, in any important respect, the previous administration of the Poor Laws, and without any prospect, so far as we can see, of its provisions acting otherwise than beneficially, both as regards the poor and the rate-payers.

General Medical Order.—56. In our last Annual Report we stated that the difficulties which we had experienced in enforcing the provisions of our general medical order, of March, 1842, had principally arisen in connexion with one of the three following subjects, viz.—1. The qualifications of the medical officers. 2. The maximum amount of the area and population of medical districts. 3. The rates of payments for medical officers in certain surgical and midwifery cases.

57. During the last year, the size of the medical districts has not undergone much modification; a few districts, in which the previous arrangements were susceptible of improvement, have been divided, or otherwise altered. The rates of the surgical and midwifery fees have continued in several unions to create objection; but these payments are now generally acquiesced in, since the Boards of Guardians have learnt by experience that the increase of expenditure, and the various evils, which they anticipated from the introduction of the fees in question, have not, in fact, been produced. The following is the amount of the expenditure for medical relief in each year since 1838;—

Years ending Lady-day.	Amount of Medical Relief.	Years ending Lady-day.	Amount of Medical Relief.
1838	£136,775	1842	£152,006
1839	148,652	1843	160,726
1840	151,781	1844	166,257
1841	154,054		

Medical Salaries.—58. In regulating the remuneration for medical relief, our object has been to secure to the medical officer such a payment as would enable him to discharge his duty to his pauper patients, and to furnish them with proper medicines. In fixing this amount, however, it is necessary that we should keep in view the value at which the services of a medical man are attainable for this purpose, under the existing circumstances of the profession. If the Commissioners were to attempt, by their regulations, to fix the salaries of medical officers at a rate higher than that which competent medical men are willing to accept the office and perform its duties, the result would be that the medical offices of unions would become the subjects of sale, more or less concealed, and the pauper patients would derive no benefit from the excessive payment. A case, which affords an illustration of this principle, has recently occurred in the South Dublin Union. It appears that upon the resignation of one of the medical officers for the workhouse, an arrangement was made by the retiring officer with another medical gentleman that the latter, if elected his successor, would pay him a sum of 300*l.*; the annual salary of the office being 100*l.* We insert in the Appendix the correspondence relating to the case. We think that the transaction to which we now refer affords a sufficient proof that the mere act of fixing a higher salary by the Commissioners or the Guardians cannot, as a matter of course, bring about the result that the increase of salary to a medical officer will secure more attention to the duties of the office which he holds. The increase, instead of acting as a constant stimulus to the exertions of the medical man from day to day, with reference to the persons to be placed under his care, may have passed out of his pocket by anticipation, and have gone simply to enrich his predecessor; nay, he may by this very payment be left encumbered with debts and difficulties which would rather impede than facilitate the discharge of his duties, especially if he had to provide medicines at his own cost.

59. The subject of medical relief is surrounded with great practical difficulties, and it has accordingly occupied a large share of our attention. We do not, however, anticipate at present any serious obstacle to the administration of this branch of relief under the provisions of our general medical order. The questions which at present create the chief embarrassment in connexion with medical relief, and which admit of the least satisfactory solution, are those which arise from the inconvenient, intricate, and obscure state of the law respecting medical qualifications.

Vaccination.—60. In our last Annual Report (par. 40) we noticed the increase which had then taken place in the mortality from small-pox. It was with regret that we perceived from the Registrar-General's Quarterly Tables of Mortality that the deaths from this cause continued on the increase, nothwithstanding the extent to which vaccination was carried on throughout England and Wales.

61. Towards the end of the year we caused a form of return to be prepared and transmitted to the clerks of the several Unions and parishes, calling for a statement of the numbers vaccinated in each during the year ending 29th September, 1844. We have since received returns from 542 Unions and parishes, an abstract from which will be found in the Appendix to this Report. The returns distinguish the number of children which have been successfully vaccinated; they also distinguish the places where the parties were vaccinated. In order that we might the more readily judge whether vaccination had kept pace in each Union with the increase and probable wants of the population in that respect, we required the clerks to state the number of births in their respective Unions during the year. We also invited the remarks of the Guardians and public vaccinators on the working of the Vaccination Extension Act.

Number of Children vaccinated.—62. The births in the 542 Unions from which returns were received (after estimating the births for those Unions the returns for which were imperfect), amounted to 452,235. Of the children born in the year 1842, 8 and seven-tenths per cent. died under the age of three months. Assuming therefore that the ratio of deaths of children under that age in the 542 Unions during the year ended 29th September, 1844, was the same, 39,344 children died in that year before attaining the age at which vaccination is most usually performed. This leaves 412,891 children requiring to be vaccinated in the course of the year. By the abstract of the returns referred to, it appears that there were 290,453 persons vaccinated by the public vaccinators, leaving only 122,438 children to be vaccinated by private medical practitioners and at public institutions. We are aware that the children vaccinated were not all born within the year ended 29th September, 1844, indeed that many adults are included in the number, and also that there may have been a considerable number of cases of re-vaccination; but we think we may assume that the relation which the number of births bears to the number vaccinated is a tolerably correct measure of the efficiency of the arrangements for promoting the object of the Act.

63. Whenever we found that the births in any Union greatly exceeded the numbers vaccinated, we requested the Guardians to call the attention of the vaccinators to the subject, with a view to the further extension of vaccination in their respective districts; and where we found that few or none had been vaccinated at the appointed stations, we suggested that the vaccinators should be directed, as opportunities offered, to visit the houses of the poorer classes for the purpose of vaccinating any unvaccinated children. We have also, where it was stated that great prejudice prevailed against vaccination, recommended the

Guardians to address circular letters to the clergymen within the Union, requesting them to co-operate with the public vaccinators in the extension of vaccination: and we believe that the clergy have in many instances rendered important service in removing the objections of their poorer parishioners. We have also the satisfaction of knowing, from the information supplied to us by the vaccinators, that although many of the more ignorant are still averse to their children being vaccinated, from the erroneous apprehension that other eruptive and cutaneous diseases may thereby be communicated to them, the prejudice does not now prevail to so great an extent as it did in previous years.

64. The public vaccinators return 3954 cases of small-pox attended by them during the year, out of which they state that 1283 were previously vaccinated. The information which the returns supply, in respect to the deaths from small-pox, on comparison with the mortality as published by the Registrar-General, proved to be so inaccurate that we have altogether omitted it from the abstract.

65. In the 542 Unions referred to there are 2614 public vaccinators, and the number of stations appointed is 7075, which number includes the vaccinators' residences; but, in many instances, the out-stations have been given up in consequence of the neglect of the people to take their children to them. In such cases the vaccinators perform the operation either at their own residences, or visit the parties' houses for that purpose. Of the 290,453 persons vaccinated, the vaccinators returned 278,192 as successful; so that, of the total number vaccinated, only 12,261, or 4 per cent., on inspection, proved unsuccessful.

Mortality from Small-pox.—66. The following table is a continuation of the one contained in our last Annual Report of the Mortality from Small-pox in the Metropolis, since 1840:—

Years.	March.	June.	September.	December.	Total.
1840	104	170	253	708	1,235
1841	605	252	128	68	1,053
1842	71	59	126	104	360
1843	144	105	75	114	438
1844	252	425	556	571	1,804
1845	481	...	...	...	...

It is satisfactory to observe a decrease in the mortality of the March quarter of 1845, as compared with the two preceding quarters; and we trust that the steps which we have taken, with the view of increasing the diligence of the public vaccinators, and calling public attention to the subject of vaccination, will have the effect of lessening the mortality from this disease.

The mortality from small-pox in England and Wales, during the years 1840, 1841, and 1842, was as follows:—

1840 10,434; 1841 6,368; 1842 2,715

67. The fees paid to the public vaccinators in England and Wales, during the year ended 25th March, 1844, amounted to 16,694*l.*, being an increase of 675*l.* upon the amount paid in the previous year.

Omission in some Unions to provide for Vaccination.—68. We regret to be compelled to state that, in some few Unions in Wales, and in the Todmorden and Hayfield Unions, the Guardians have omitted to make provision for the gratuitous vaccination of the residents generally. We believe, however, that in these Unions the medical officers vaccinate all poor persons who apply to them, without charge; and are required, in terms of their appointment, to vaccinate the children of all the paupers. In very few of the parishes which are not in union, or governed under the provisions of local Acts, have the parish officers contracted expressly for vaccination.

Issue of Orders to Local Act Parishes.—69. Since the date of our last Annual Report, we have issued our Workhouse Regulations to Chester, Southampton, Chichester, Exeter, and St. Mary's Newington, all which places are governed by Boards of Guardians appointed under the provisions of local Acts. We have likewise issued a general order to several of the metropolitan parishes, requiring the clerks to make a weekly return of the number of paupers relieved, and certain other particulars, to the Assistant Commissioner of the district. We subjoin a copy of this order in the Appendix. Our general order on pauper apprenticeship (see above, par. 32) was likewise issued to the Unions and parishes under local Acts; and we have included several places similarly situated, in districts for the audit of accounts.

70. In all the above orders which we have issued to Unions and parishes under local Acts, we have, acting upon the spirit of the decision of the Court of Queen's Bench in the case of the parish of St. Pancras, carefully abstained from interfering with the constitution of the Board of Guardians, and the mode of its appointment. Our regulations have been confined to a control of the powers exercised by the local Board. We have found that the strict observance of this distinction, coupled with the explanations which we have given in our recent Annual Reports, has removed much of the misunderstanding which previously existed in many of the local Act Boards, with respect to the extent of the powers of the Commissioners. The decision of the Court of Queen's Bench, in the case of the Queen *v.* the Guardians of the Poor of the city of Oxford, in Easter Term, 1844, has likewise placed out of all doubt the power of the Commissioners to regulate the proceedings of Boards of Guardians appointed under a local Act. In this case (of which the material facts are stated in our last Annual Report, par. 50), the Court of Queen's Bench decided, upon argument, that an order issued by the Poor Law Commissioners to the Oxford Guardians (who are elected under a local Act), directing them to appoint a master of the workhouse, was valid and must be

obeyed.* We have likewise the satisfaction of stating that the difficulties to which we adverted in our last Annual Report, as having arisen in the parish of Birmingham, with respect to the regulations which we had issued to the Guardians, have since that time been removed.

Appointment of Chairman and Vice-chairman of Local Boards.—71. The 64th section of the 7 and 8 Vic. c. 101, provides that whenever, under any local Act, there is no person particularly designated or authorised to act as chairman or vice-chairman, the Guardians shall appoint annually a chairman or vice-chairman. In consequence of this provision, we issued a circular to the Boards of Guardians under local Acts, inquiring whether a chairman and vice-chairman had been appointed accordingly, and we believe that this direction of the statute has generally been complied with.

Formation of Ashbourne Union.—72. A considerable number of parishes in Derbyshire and Staffordshire had been left under the provisions of the 43 Eliz., in consequence of their vicinity to the Alstonefield Union, formed under Gilbert's Act. Having ascertained that many of the parishes which assumed to belong to this Union had not been included in it according to the forms prescribed by the statute, we submitted a case to the Solicitor-General and Mr. Tomlinson; and, upon the authority of their opinion, we issued an order, dated the 4th of January last, by which we formed the Ashbourne Union out of the two classes of parishes just described. We have likewise annexed to the Uttoxeter and Bakewell Unions some other of the parishes which claimed to be a part of the Alstonefield Union. Since the date of our order, two elections of Guardians for the Ashbourne Union have taken place; and the Board have appointed their officers and divided the Union into districts for general and medical relief. We have, however, received notice on behalf of some of the parishes which consider themselves members of the Alstonefield Union, that it is their intention to apply for a writ of *certiorari* to bring up our order before the Court of Queen's Bench.

Order for Election of Board of Guardians for Leeds.—73. In the township of Leeds, containing a population of 88,741 persons, the relief of the poor had been administered by a body of overseers, appointed under a provision in a local Act for lighting and cleansing the town. By an Order, dated the 21st of November, 1844, we placed the administration of relief in that township under a Board of Guardians; and by the same Order we divided the township into wards for the election of Guardians, in pursuance of the powers contained in s. 19 of the 7 and 8 Vic., c. 101. Some questions have arisen in consequence of the transfer of power from the overseers to the Board of Guardians; but we have the satisfaction of stating that the operations of the newly appointed Board of Guardians have been conducted in such a manner as to lead us to anticipate much benefit to this important town from the change.

Proceedings respecting Rochdale Union.—74. We have stated in former Reports that there are in Lancashire three Unions (viz., the Rochdale, Ashton, and Oldham Unions,) which were formed in the year 1837, for the purposes of the Act for registering births, deaths, and marriages, but which had never been put in operation for the administration of relief to the poor. Having come to the conclusion that it was desirable to put an end to the anomalous state in which these Unions remained, we issued, in October last, an Order to the Rochdale Guardians, directing them to take upon themselves the administration of relief to the poor. As this Order was not complied with, we caused an application to be made to the Court of Queen's Bench for a writ of mandamus to compel the Guardians to obey its directions. The mandamus was granted by the Court, and a return to it was made by the Guardians; which return was traversed on the part of the Crown, and the issues thus framed were tried at the last assizes at Liverpool. A verdict was, under the direction of the judge, given for the Crown upon all the issues, with a power to the defendants to move to set it aside. This motion has since been made in Easter Term, and a rule *nisi* has been obtained. As soon as the judgment of the Court upon the points reserved (which relate to merely formal questions) shall have been given, we shall be able to take such further steps as may be requisite for bringing the general law into operation in this Union.

Orders respecting Religious Worship in Royston Workhouse.—75. The Guardians of the Royston Union have never appointed a chaplain for their workhouse; and complaints having been made to us with respect to the attendance of Protestant dissenting ministers upon members of the Established Church, being inmates of the workhouse (which complaints were afterwards investigated,) we issued in February, and afterwards in April, 1842, an Order directing that "no child under the age of 16 years, being a pauper and an inmate of the workhouse of the Royston Union, who shall be a member of the Established Church, should be compelled, required, or permitted to attend the religious service or instruction of any minister dissenting from the principles of such Established Church, either in or out of such workhouse."

76. In the letter which accompanied our General Workhouse Order (dated February, 1842,) we made the following remarks in reference to the restrictions which we thought it advisable to place upon the presence of members of the Established Church at the religious services of dissenting ministers in the workhouse:—

* A full report of the case is given in "The Justice of the Peace," for October 26, 1844.

"It appears to the Commissioners that the section of the Poor Law Amendment Act just quoted (s. 19) does not contemplate the attendance of members of the Established Church at the Divine service performed by a dissenting minister in a workhouse. If any adult members of the Established Church should desire to attend the service of a dissenting minister, the Commissioners would not interfere to prevent their attendance, provided that no improper influence was used to induce them to attend, although they consider it objectionable: but the Commissioners think that children, being members of the Established Church, should never be permitted to attend on such occasions, and they would, in case of necessity, prohibit any such practice by an Order."

We still think that a considerable difference exists between the cases of children and adults; and we are reluctant, without strong reasons, to interfere for the purpose of controlling the religious discretion of adults in a workhouse. But the peculiar circumstances of the Royston workhouse, and the complaints which we continued to receive after the issue of the Order to which we have above referred, induced us to issue a further Order to this Union in January last, extending the provisions of the former Order to *all* pauper inmates of the workhouse, without reference to their age.

77. We have subsequently received a memorial from the Board of Guardians, containing a strong remonstrance against the last-mentioned Order. The chief ground upon which the Guardians rely in this memorial, is that the prohibition of adult inmates of a workhouse, belonging to the Established Church, from attendance upon the religious service of a dissenting minister, is an infraction of their religious liberty. It appears to us, however, that no serious invasion of the religious liberty of the adult inmates of workhouses can be said to have taken place, so long as every such inmate can change his religious profession whenever he thinks fit, and can cause the register of his religious creed to be altered upon a simple notice to the Guardians. It is, moreover, necessary that, in framing regulations on this subject, we should look to the state of things in the Irish as well as the English workhouses; and we fear that serious inconveniences might arise in Ireland, if the adult inmates of a workhouse were to be permitted, without restriction, sometimes to attend the religious services of the Protestant and sometimes of the Roman Catholic chaplain.

Employment of Inmates of Workhouses in Needlework.—78. Representations were some time ago made to us that the quantity of needlework executed in the metropolitan workhouses by the pauper inmates was sufficient to affect the market price of the article, and to lower the wages of the women who were employed by the trade. We accordingly instructed our Assistant-Commissioner, Mr. Hall, to make inquiry into the subject; and we insert in the Appendix his Report, containing the results of his investigation. It appears from his Report that the value of the needlework performed in the metropolitan workhouses is not sufficient to affect the general market price, inasmuch as the total average value of such work done in the 28 metropolitan workhouses under our regulations does not amount to 14*l.* per week. For further details we refer to Mr. Hall's Report, which we insert in the Appendix.

State of Cottages of Paupers in Honiton Union.—79. We likewise insert in the Appendix a communication which we received from the Guardians of the Honiton Union, in Devonshire, containing a report, prepared by several of the Guardians, of the state of the cottages inhabited by paupers in a portion of their Union. Much advantage would, we think, be produced by a similar inspection of this class of cottages in other Unions.

Emigration.—80. With reference to the subject of the emigration of paupers during the past year, we have to state that the number of emigrants to Canada who went out under our regulations exceeded that of the previous year.

81. Mr. Buchanan, in his Report on emigration for the year 1843, set forth 659 emigrants as having been sent out under the superintendence of the Poor Law Commissioners; while in a list appended to his Report for the last year, a copy of which has been forwarded to us by the Colonial Land and Emigration Commissioners, 813 persons are stated to have been sent out under our orders. We do not readily trace 50 of these, according to the names of the ships which are given by Mr. Buchanan; but we have occasionally some difficulty in doing so where the contracts for the passage are not entered into with the merchants usually engaged in the carriage of emigrants to the colonies.

82. In the course of last autumn one vessel was sent out to Australia, under the directions of the Colonial Land and Emigration Commissioners, as a bounty ship, and it contained many pauper emigrants, who were assisted by their parishes under our authority. Another vessel is about to sail this spring, and several pauper emigrants will proceed in it.

83. We have no knowledge of any intention on the part of the Colonial Land and Emigration Commissioners to recommend the resumption of the bounty emigration to the Australian colonies; we observe, however, that though in their Fifth General Report, which has been lately presented to Parliament, they state, in reference to New South Wales, that there was still much demand for shepherds and agricultural labourers, the following passage occurs:—"At Port Philip the prospect for *single men* is described as good, although the immigration of married people with young children was considered very unadvisable." As for the most part pauper emigrants consist of families, it is of much importance that this recommendation should be attended to by persons who may be disposed to forward the emigration of persons of that class.

84. There is one subject connected with the emigration of paupers to which we referred in our Eighth

Annual Report, p. 37 (8vo. edition,) and which we consider it highly desirable to notice again. We there described a practice of men quitting England and procuring a passage to the United States, leaving their families to be forwarded to that country by the parish officers or private individuals; and we stated that we objected to sanction the emigration to the United States, and added our strong opinion of the great inexpediency of rendering the assistance to the families of persons so circumstanced, which it is the object of the parties to obtain by the desertion of their families.

Emigration.—85. The remarks there made have been frequently supposed to refer simply to the emigration of parties to the United States, and we have been often requested to sanction the emigration of the wives and children of men who have deserted them and have emigrated to Canada. It has appeared to us, however, that the strongest objections exist to defraying from the funds of the parish the charges of emigration for families left destitute in this country by the husband or father. If anything were wanting to show the importance of adhering to a general rule with regard to such cases, we would refer to the following passage in the extract from the Annual Report of the Chief Agent for Emigration in Canada, dated Quebec, 20th December, 1844, which is printed in the Appendix to the Report of the Colonial Land and Emigration Commissioners above referred to, No. 8, p. 36:—

"There is another class of our emigration in almost every instance requiring assistance from this department on arrival. I find, on referring to the books of the office at this place, that 173 widows, accompanied by 488 children and grandchildren, came out this season to join their sons or daughters; *and* 245 *women having* 713 *children, came out to join their husbands*, all of whom received more or less assistance from their relatives here to enable them to reach this port."

This extract gives information only as to those who have been sent for by their husbands and fathers and we are left in ignorance as to the numbers who have been totally deserted, or who, in the expectation of being summoned to the colony, are left either in charge upon the parochial funds or their poor relations.

86. In the allowances which we have sanctioned from the parish funds for the emigration of paupers, we have deemed it advisable to make an addition, to enable the Guardians to provide an outfit of bedding and utensils for the voyage. It was generally found that the emigrants arrived at the vessel unprovided with these requisites; and as the shipper's contract did not stipulate for the providing of them, they were to be purchased on the spot. This purchase not being according to the terms of our order, often led to many irregularities. We might have required the shipper's contract to include these articles; but as it appeared that the emigrants might frequently have what was wanted, it was considered inexpedient to make a provision which would operate universally, though not always required.

87. We deem it right to advert to the provision in the statute of the last Session of Parliament, contained in sec. 29, which enables the Guardians of the parish or Union to apply the money raised for the purpose of defraying the expenses of emigration in such parish, or in any parish in the Union. We have been informed that some misapprehension has arisen upon the effect of this clause, and that some Boards of Guardians have entertained an idea that they could apply any money for emigration purposes when it seemed fit to them to do so. It is however, we believe, quite clear that they have no power to act in this matter, except to carry into effect the resolution of the rate-payers and owners of property who agree to the expenditure.

[*The portion of the Report which relates to "Proceedings in Ireland," is omitted.*]

We have the honour to be, &c. &c.

(Signed) George Nicholls.
George Cornewall Lewis.
(L. S.) Edmund Walker Head.

Printed by Order of the Poor Law Commissioners, by Blackburn and Pardon, 6, Hatton Garden, and Published by Charles Knight and Co., 22, Ludgate Street, Publishers to the Poor Law Commissioners.

AN

OFFICIAL CIRCULAR

OF PUBLIC DOCUMENTS AND INFORMATION:

DIRECTED BY THE POOR LAW COMMISSIONERS TO BE PRINTED, CHIEFLY FOR THE USE OF THE MEMBERS AND PERMANENT OFFICERS OF BOARDS OF GUARDIANS, UNDER THE POOR LAW AMENDMENT ACT.

No. 48. CIRCULAR ISSUED JUNE 1ST, 1845.

THE Poor Law Commissioners directed that the following documents be printed and circulated for the information of Guardians and Officers of the several Unions, viz.

(Signed) By Order of the Board,
EDWIN CHADWICK, *Secretary.*

I.—BASTARDY.

1. RELIEF OF A BASTARD CHILD BY OVERSEERS.

March 15th, 1845.

Overseers of Fareham, Fareham Union—Requested the Commissioners' advice in a case where they, the overseers, had been summoned to appear before justices to answer the complaint of E. M. for refusing her relief, on account of a bastard child, aged eleven years and ten months. The putative father, on whom an order was made in June, 1833, had recently ceased to contribute towards the maintenance of the child.

Ans.—The Commissioners direct your attention to the 54th section of the Poor Law Amendment Act, which restricts the powers of overseers, as to granting relief, to cases of sudden and urgent necessity; and which also restricts the powers of justices, as to ordering relief, to certain cases of refusal or neglect on the part of overseers to give relief, and to cases of sudden and dangerous illness. It does not appear from your letter, that the case of the bastard child referred to was one of sudden and urgent necessity, or of sudden and dangerous illness. If the case was not of either the one or the other character, and the child nevertheless was in need of relief, the application for such relief should have been made to the board of guardians, or the relieving officer. And if the child still needs relief, that would now be the proper course to pursue. The Commissioners have further to point out, that the order of affiliation made in 1833, on the reputed father of the illegitimate child, does not impose any liability on the overseers to give relief to the mother of the child. Such order is only for the indemnity of the parish, and its protection in case relief should be given to the child.

2. RELIEF TO MOTHER OF BASTARD.

Clerk of Honiton Union—The board of guardians ordered relief (two shillings in money, and four pounds of bread per week,) to the mother of an illegitimate child, lately confined, during her illness; and declared that the same should be by way of loan. Subsequent to this, the justices made an order on the father for payment of a sum of money weekly to the mother, to commence from the birth of the child; whereupon the mother repaid to the relieving officer the money advanced to her by way of loan. Inquired, whether this, on the part of the relieving officer, is a receiving of money "in respect of a bastard child under an order of petty sessions," which is declared by the 7th sec. of the 7 and 8 Vic. cap. 101, to be illegal.

Ans.—The granting of relief to the mother of a bastard child on loan, and the repayment of that relief by the mother, out of money received by her from the putative father, under an order of justices, does not seem to the Commissioners to be prohibited by the 7th sec. of the 7 and 8 Vic. c. 101. That sec. forbids "any officer of any parish or union to receive any money in respect of any bastard child under an order of petty session as aforesaid." In the case above described it would not be the officers of the parish or union, but the mother herself, who would receive the money under the orders.

3. DITTO.

March 15th, 1845.

Clerk of Evesham Union—A single woman and her two illegitimate children are inmates of the union workhouse: with the youngest child she receives, under an order in bastardy made in 1844, the sum of one shilling and three-pence weekly. Inquired whether the guardians can demand this sum from the woman towards the maintenance of herself and children while in the workhouse.

Ans.—The guardians have no claim upon the woman for the money received under the bastardy order mentioned in your letter, though she and her children are relieved in the workhouse. The fact of the mother being in receipt of this money, however, constitutes in her a partial ability to maintain herself and her family. It may, therefore, be proper for the guardians to consider how far the mother can be regarded a destitute person so as to justify the continuance of relief, especially if the circumstances be such as to show that she could increase that ability by her personal exertions or labour.

4. DITTO.

Clerk of Newport (Salop) Union—Inquired, in reference to the clauses relating to bastardy in the Act of 7 and 8 Vic. c. 101,—1. Whether the guardians were empowered to grant relief out of the workhouse to a pregnant woman, unable to work and in a state of destitution. 2. In case the woman is confined in the workhouse, whether the guardians could afterwards recover from the putative father the fee paid to the midwife. 3. Where the medical officer is ordered to attend a woman in her confinement of an illegitimate child out of the workhouse, how are the guardians to obtain repayment of the fee paid to him?

Ans.—1st. If a woman pregnant with a bastard child apply to the guardians, in a destitute condition, for relief, it will be their duty, in giving such relief, to conform to the provisions of the General Prohibitory Order. Where the applicant is able-bodied, the relief can lawfully be given only in the workhouse, pursuant to Article 1 of that order. If, however, the case should fall within any of the exceptions to Article 1, the guardians can in their discretion give out-relief. The Commissioners would observe, they do not think that the mere fact of pregnancy brings the case within the 2nd exception to that article. 2nd and 3rd. If the woman be confined in the workhouse, or if the necessary relief in such case be given out of the workhouse, the guardians have no claim on the putative father for the fee paid to the midwife or for the cost of the relief, medical or otherwise, given in the case. But should the guardians (as it is competent to them to do) grant the relief as a loan to the mother, there would be nothing to prevent their enforcing the liability of such mother to repay the loan, in the event of the justices including in any order they may make, under the 3rd sec. of 7 and 8 Vic. c. 101, the fee to the midwife. The Commissioners would add, that, it would be proper for the guardians to continue the relief, so long as the inability of the mother to provide for herself and child existed, without reference to the probability or otherwise of an order being ultimately made upon the putative father.

II.—CHARGEABILITY.

March 17th, 1845.

Clerk of Hereford Union—A. H., who had resided for many years in a cottage in the parish of Lugwardine, in this union, was lately, with her child, turned out of her dwelling, her tenancy having expired: whereupon she and her child went into the parish of Fownhope, about four miles distant, to seek relief, under the impression that Fownhope was her parish, she having been removed there about ten years since by one of the city parishes, and she there found the relieving officer who was going his rounds, who does not however reside in that parish, but in the parish of Withington, about three miles from Lugwardine. The relieving officer gave her an order for the workhouse, and she was admitted as chargeable to Fownhope, the place where she saw the relieving officer, and received the order. The guardian of Fownhope contended that the relieving officer had no right to charge the pauper to Fownhope, inasmuch as, having for years resided in Lugwardine, she went to Fownhope to see him; and the board of guardians have transferred the charge to Lugwardine. The guardian of Lugwardine however urges that, inasmuch as the pauper had given up her residence in Lugwardine, and had not received any relief from that parish, and having been removed some years since to Fownhope, and gone into that parish to apply for relief, she was properly entered by the relieving officer as chargeable to that parish. Inquired—1st. To which of the two parishes should the relieving officer have made the pauper chargeable. 2nd. Whether the board had any power to transfer the charge from Fownhope to Lugwardine.

Ans.—The guardians are certainly not concluded on a question of chargeability by an error of their relieving officer. If the relieving officer have charged the relief in any case to the wrong parish, the Commissioners see no reason to suppose that the guardians cannot rectify the mistake in charging the relief for that quarter to the second parish. With respect to the present case, the Commissioners desire to point out that, if the parish officers of Fownhope acknowledge A. H. to be settled in that parish, the guardians may, if they think fit, charge her relief to that parish, in consideration of such settlement. It is stated that she was removed thither about ten years ago, (as the Commissioners presume, under an order of justices;) if this be so, and if she has acquired no settlement since that time, there would seem to be no ground for avoiding that acknowledgment. If, however, the question of her chargeability is to be determined irrespectively of her settlement, the Commissioners would feel some difficulty in expressing an opinion thereon, without further information as to her reasons for going to Fownhope, when turned out of her cottage in Lugwardine. The Commissioners would be glad to know whether she went to Fownhope with the expectation and for the purpose of seeing the relieving officer; or whether she went thither from any other consideration, and met with the relieving officer by chance when there. Although the relieving officer lives at Withington, she might have known he would be at Fownhope on that occasion, and have gone thither accordingly.

April 17th, 1845.

The Clerk of same Union—A. H. went into the parish of Fownhope for the purpose of obtaining relief, and not for any other consideration.

Ans.—The general rule for determining the chargeability of paupers is this:—a pauper is chargeable to that parish, in which, being destitute, he applies for and obtains relief. But where a pauper, destitute in one parish of a union, is obliged, by the nature of the union arrangements, to go into another parish of the union (for example, where the relieving officer lives, or where the workhouse stands,) in order to make his application for relief, the Commissioners think that such application must be regarded as being constructively made, not in the parish where it actually takes place, but in the parish in which the pauper was destitute, and in which he would have applied for relief, but for the union arrangements. It appears to the Commissioners, that this is required by the 26 sec. of the Poor Law Amendment Act, which renders every parish in a union chargeable with the relief of "its own poor," that is, as the Commissioners conceive, the poor with which it would have been chargeable irrespectively of the union. If, therefore, A. H. being destitute in Lugwardine, was obliged, by the arrangement for relief in Hereford Union, to go into Fownhope parish in order to make her application for relief, she would, in the Commissioners' opinion, be chargeable to Lugwardine. But the Commissioners do not gather from your letters on the subject, whether this was really the case, or not. In your letter of the 1st ult., you state that A. H. went into Fownhope to seek relief, "under the impression that Fownhope was her proper parish, having been removed there about ten years since by one of the city parishes. She there found the relieving officer, who was going his rounds," &c. In the same letter you mention, that the guardian of Fownhope objected to her being charged to that parish, "inasmuch as, having been for years residing in Lugwardine, she only went to Fownhope, to see the relieving officer;" and in your letter of the 26th ult. you say, "that A. H. went into the parish of Fownhope for the purpose of obtaining relief, and not for any other consideration." The question appears to the Commissioners to be, not whether A. H. went to Fownhope for the purpose of obtaining relief, but, whether she went there, in consequence of the union arrangements, in order to make her application for relief. If she went there merely on account of her "impression that Fownhope was her proper parish," she did not go there in consequence of the union arrangements; and the Commissioners consider that she would be chargeable to Fownhope accordingly. Under a similar impression she might have gone into a parish in another union, or into a parish not included in any union. But if she went there solely with a view to meet the relieving officer, and make that application to him there which she would have made to him at Lugwardine, had he been in the latter parish, then the Commissioners think that her application was constructively made at Lugwardine, and that her relief would be chargeable to that parish on the principle above laid down.

2. CHARGEABILITY OF BASTARD CHILD.

March 7th, 1845.

Clerk of Wincanton Union—In February, 1843, W. H. and Elizabeth his wife, and R. M. a bastard child of the wife, born two months before the passing of the Poor Law Amendment Act, were admitted into the union workhouse as paupers belonging to the parish of Bruton. But, upon inquiry, it was ascertained that R. M. was born in the parish of St. Giles in the Fields, Middlesex. The parties left the workhouse and went to reside in the parish of Balcary, in the Langport Union, and whilst there, W.H. deserted his wife and the child, who did not, however, apply for relief in that parish, but came to Wincanton, in which parish the union workhouse is situated, to apply to the relieving officer for Bruton, who also resides in Wincanton, for relief. The officer ascertained from the woman that she and her child slept in the parish of Blackford within the Wincanton Union the night before she applied to him for relief on her road from Balcary to make her application, but it does not appear that she applied to any one for assistance from the parish of Blackford. The relieving officer for Bruton and Wincanton gave her an order for the workhouse for herself and the child, but did not in the order name the parish from which they were to be received. Inquired to what parish the relief of the mother and child ought to be charged, it being the opinion of some that the child should be charged to the mother's parish of Bruton, others, that it should be charged to Blackford, the mother and child having slept in that parish the night before applying for relief.

Ans.—The Commissioners see no ground whatever for charging the relief of R. M. to the parish of Bruton. He is not settled in that parish, nor was he destitute in that parish, at the time of his applying for relief. The fact of his mother's being settled in Bruton is immaterial, with reference to the question of his chargeability. Then, as between the parishes of Blackford and Wincanton, the Commissioners are disposed to think that he is properly chargeable to Wincanton. The mere circumstance of his having slept in Blackford the night before he applied for relief, would not, of itself, be sufficient ground for charging that parish. The Commissioners certainly consider that, when a person is destitute in one parish, and is obliged by the union arrangements to go into another parish, in order to apply for relief, he must be regarded as having constructively made the application in the parish in which his destitution occasioned his seeking the relief. But it appears, in the present case, that Robert Mules went to Wincanton, not because the relieving officer for Blackford lived there, but because he was travelling with his mother, who had her own reasons for going thither. Under these circumstances, the Commissioners incline to the opinion that Wincanton was the parish in which, being destitute, he applied for and obtained relief, and to which, therefore, such relief should be charged.

---

3. PROOF OF CHARGEABILITY.

April 29th, 1845.

Clerk of Bourn Union—Inquired whether it is necessary, and, if so, whether it is the duty of the workhouse master or relieving officer (as the case may be) to attend before justices for the purpose of identifying the parties described in certificates of chargeability, and of proving that they are actually chargeable at the time of their examination. If the relieving officer is bound to attend, he is obviously not only taken from the duties for which he was appointed, but he also incurs expenses which it is considered the parties who require his attendance ought to repay.

Ans.—It is undoubtedly necessary that the justices should be satisfied that the parties brought before them for the purpose of removal are the same as those described in the certificate of the guardians as being chargeable to the parish. The master of the workhouse, in the case of in-door paupers, and the relieving officer, in the case of persons relieved out of the workhouse, seem to be the proper persons to prove the identity in the respective cases. The Commissioners consider, however, they are fairly entitled to be reimbursed by the parish obtaining the order, any actual expenses they may be put to in such attendance before the justices. Where the certificate, made in conformity with the statute, is produced before the justices, the Commissioners consider no further evidence of actual chargeability at the time of examination is necessary to give the justices jurisdiction in the case. The 69th section of 7 and 8 Vic. c. 101, expressly declares "that, for the purpose of making any order of removal or other order, no further or other evidence of chargeability than such certificate shall be required, provided that every such order bear date within twenty-one days next after the day of the date of such certificate." This undoubtedly is equivalent to a declaration that a chargeability, declared to have existed before the certificate, is sufficiently alleged for the purposes of every order of removal made within twenty-one days after the certificate.

III.—CONSTABLES' CHARGES.

Jan. 28th, 1845.

Auditor of —— Union—A farm servant summoned his master for the non-payment of his wages. On hearing of the summons the master paid the wages, and the justices ordered the overseers of the township of —— to pay to the constable of the township certain fees "under the statutes 5 and 6 Vic. c. 109." The fees are for the service of the summons; mileage; attendance before the justice; and for the order of the justices. Inquired whether these fees are properly payable out of the poor-rates.

Ans.—The Commissioners presume that the proceedings were taken by the servant in this case, under the 1 sec. of the 20 Geo. 2, c. 19. It appears to the Commissioners that the provisions of that sec. are of a remedial, not of a penal, character: and the Commissioners are disposed to consider that the fees payable to constables out of the poor-rates under the 5 and 6 Vic. c. 109, s. 17, are only payable in regard to criminal matters, and not in cases of civil remedies. The Commissioners are therefore inclined to the opinion that the order of justices referred to in your letter is not a valid one.

---

2. EXPENSES INCURRED BY CONSTABLES IN APPREHENDING VAGRANTS.

Overseer of Thirfield, Royston Union—Inquired, whether the overseers are bound to pay costs incurred by rural police constables without the sanction or knowledge of the overseers.

Ans.—In the case of Reg. *v.* The Churchwardens and Overseers of Chelmsford, 3 Gale and Dav. 357, it was decided, that a constable appointed under 2 and 3 Vic. c. 93, (an Act for the appointment of County and District Constables) is entitled to be reimbursed by each parish in his division, for fees paid by him to a justice's clerk in respect of proceeding against vagrants apprehended in such parish. It does not appear from that case that the vagrants were apprehended at the instance or by the direction of the overseers, but the court, nevertheless, held that the county or district constable was entitled to be repaid from the poor-rates, the expenses incurred in this respect, when he has presented his account pursuant to the 18th Geo. 3, c. 19, sec. 4. That statute requires that constables, &c. shall, every three months, deliver to the overseers, &c. of the parish, on account of the money expended or received by them, on account of the parish. In case such account is approved of by the majority of the inhabitants, the overseers are to pay it out of the poor-rates; if it is not approved of, the constables may take it before a justice, who is to settle what shall paid, and by the 5th section the overseers may appeal from his decision to the quarter sessions.

IV.—COUNTY RATE.

May 9th, 1845.

Clerk of the Manchynlleth Union—The treasurers of the counties of Merioneth and Cardigan, within which the union is situate, have consented to allow the county rate to be paid, in the case of Merioneth, to the Dolgelly branch of the National and Provincial Bank; and in the case of Cardigan to the Aberystwith branch of the same bank. As the Manchynlleth branch of this bank, through which the guardians pay the rate, charge a small commission, inquired in what way the commission should be charged to the several parishes, and whether it could be apportioned in the same way as the establishment expenses.

Ans.—It is the business of the guardians to cause the money for the county rates to be paid to the county treasurer at the expense of the several parishes on whose behalf the rate is to be paid. The payment of the commission to the bank, is a fair and economical arrangement for the purpose. That commission ought to be divided amongst the parishes, not in proportion to the averages or establishment expenses, but in proportion to the sums respectively paid to the county treasurer on behalf of the parishes.

2. DITTO.

January 1st, 1845.

Clerk of Atcham Union—Inquired, in reference to the Act 7 and 8 Vic. c. 33, relating to the collection of county rates,—1st. Whether the orders of the guardians on the overseers for the payment of the sums required by the precept of the justices must specify the subject for which the demand is made, viz., "county rate," &c.; or, will it be sufficient to make such orders in the usual form of contribution order prescribed by the Commissioners? 2. Whether such orders must be confined to the amou ts specified in the precept, to be paid by each parish; or, will it be sufficient to include such amounts with "the sums ordered for relief and general purposes of the union?" 3. Whether, in the event of the overseers of any parish neglecting to pay the amount ordered by the guardians, within the time specified in the order, it will be their duty to proceed against such overseers for the neglect in the same manner as they would for neglect to pay an ordinary contribution; or, will the guardians return the parish in arrear to the county treasurer, and leave the justices to make the order on the overseers with the ten per cent. addition thereto, without any further notice of the matter by the guardians? 4. Whether the moneys received and paid by the treasurer for county rates, &c., are to be entered as a part of the ordinary cash accounts of the union, and be debited and credited to the respective parishes in common with the other items of receipt and expenditure; or, are they to form a separate and distinct account? 5. Whether these items are to be accounted for by the overseers in their quarterly statement, as cash paid to the treasurer of the union; or, as at present, under the head of county rate, &c.; and in the quarterly abstract are they to be entered as at present in form B 12, or to be transferred to a new column to be inserted in form B 11?

Ans.—The words of the 1st sec. of 7 and 8 Vic. c. 33, "and such guardians shall raise the moneys required by such precepts to be paid in like manner, as the money required by such guardians for the relief of the poor," appear to the Commissioners to contemplate the making of a distinct order upon the overseers, for raising the amount required. The Commissioners, however, are not prepared to say, that the moneys might not be lawfully raised by including the amount required for this purpose in the general contribution order. The Commissioners think the former of these courses the most desirable to be followed, and, where it is adopted, it will be necessary that the order should show on the face of it for what purpose the demand is made. The Commissioners are disposed to think that the remedy given by the 2 and 3 Vic. c. 84, would be available for the recovery of the moneys required of overseers under the recent Act. The former statute, sec. 1, provides for the recovery of any contribution by overseers of moneys required by the boards of guardians for the performance of the duties (*i.e.*, duties of the guardians) which may be in arrear. The moneys which the guardians call for under the 7 and 8 Vic. c. 33, are unquestionably moneys required by the guardians for the performance of their duty, viz., that of satisfying the precept issued to them by the justices. It is further to be observed that, by the very terms of the 1st sec., the money which the guardians are directed to raise, is to be "paid *in like manner* as money required by the guardians for the relief of the poor." Still, the Commissioners do not advise hat, where the overseers neglect to make the payments for county rate, pursuant to the orders made upon them, the guardians should take any further steps in the matter, but rather leave it to the justices to pursue the particular course provided by the statute, (see section 2.) It appears to the Commissioners, that the treasurer need not keep a separate account of the moneys paid for county rate. The debits and credits for these sums will appear in his general account, and they should also be recorded in the account of the particular parish in the ledger. The payments made by the overseers, in obedience to the precepts of the guardians, should be entered in the quarterly statements under the head "county rate;" they should likewise be entered in form B 12, as they have been hitherto entered. The payments made by the guardians on account of county rate, should be entered in a separate column to be added to form B 11.

---

3. RECEIPTS FROM THE COUNTY TREASURER FOR THE COUNTY RATE.

Clerk of Wincanton Union—Inquired, 1st, whether it is the duty of the clerk of the guardians, on paying money to the county treasurer, under the 7and 8 Vic. c. 33, on behalf of several parishes in the union, to obtain a receipt for the amount paid in respect of each parish separately; or, will one receipt for the whole amount paid be sufficient. 2nd. Whether the receipts given by the county treasurer must be on proper stamps; and, in case of the payment to him of a sum of £5, the auditor would be justified in allowing the payment without the production of a stamped receipt.

Ans.—1st. The Commissioners consider that the county treasurer will doubtless be justified in giving one receipt for the sum actually paid to him by the guardians, and they will be able to apply the payment to the sum specified in the precept according as they pay the whole amount specified therein, or the sum chargeable to some one or more of the parishes name therein. 2nd. The language of the statute requires the county treasurer to give a receipt for the sum received by him. This receipt, therefore, he must provide, and as there is no exemption from the payment of stamps in reference to this matter, and as it would be unlawful in the county treasurer to sign an unstamped receipt where a stamp is required, the Commissioners presume that the difficulty suggested by the clerk will not arise. But though a receipt is the most convenient evidence of the making of a payment, (and it is therefore desirable that it should be obtained in all cases,) the Commissioners are nevertheless of opinion, that if evidence of the payment other than the written receipt were produced to the auditor, he would not be justified in disallowing the payment, although an unstamped receipt were produced. There might not perhaps in some case be evidence of the payment between the party paying the money and the guardians, if a stamped receipt were not produceable.

V.—ELECTION OF GUARDIANS.

CONSTRUCTION OF 15 SEC. OF 7 AND 8 VIC. c. 101.

January 2, 1845.

J. P., Toxteth Park, West Derby Union—1. Stated, that section 15 of the Act 7 and 8 Vic. c. 101, seemed to require that the statement to be given by owners of property to overseers, in order to entitle such owners to vote under the provisions of the Poor Law Amendment Act, should contain a description of the nature of the interest or estate the owner may have in such property. It had been suggested that under these words will be required a statement, whether the property is mortgaged or not. If each owner be required to state this fact, very few of the owners of property in Toxteth Park would claim to vote, where at least five-sixths of the property there is mortgaged. Inquired whether it will be necessary for the owners of property, in cases where the property is mortgaged, to state that fact in the claim to vote. 2. Observed also, that the recent Act provides that "no appointment of proxy shall remain in force for a longer period than two years from the making thereof;" inquired whether it will be necessary for an owner who appointed a proxy to give to the overseers the statement above referred to *every year*. 3. Inquired also, whether there must be new forms of "owners' claim to vote," "appointment of proxy," and the "proxy's statement;" or whether the forms that have been employed for several years back will be sufficient.

Ans.—The 15th section of the Act above referred to does not require that any owner should in his statement describe any charge that may have been made upon his interest or estate. He is merely required to describe the nature of the interest, or of the estate, by virtue of which he claims to be owner, &c. 1. An owner is not called on to describe any tenants but those who pay him a rent-service, *i. e.*, a rent for the right of occupation; nor is he called upon to describe any out-goings, but such rent-service; and, therefore, he is neither called on to describe any tenant by mortgage, nor any interest which he may pay to a mortgagee. Moreover, mortgagees are not recognised as owners, except when they are in possession; (4 and 5 Wm. 4, c. 76, s. 109;) and there is therefore no possible conflict of claim between the mortgagor in possession and his mortgagee; and consequently no such advantage derivable from this statement as is contemplated in so much of the provisions of the 7 and 8 Vic. c. 108, s. 15, as requires the description of the particulars of the rights of persons who are declared "owners" (by 4 and 5 Wm. 4, c. 76, s. 109) in respect of the proportion of rack-rent they may be entitled to receive and retain. Mortgagees not in possession are therefore out of the purview of the Act, and their interest is foreign to the objects of the whole of the provisions; and when a mortgagor has conveyed by way of mortgage all his estate or interest, it would appear to be quite consistent with the purview of the Act that he should still describe his estate or interest according to its nature, as it is in equity and irrespective of the mortgage—adopting in this, the view taken by courts of common law, as by Lord Mansfield, chief justice, who says, (in the King *v.* St. Michael's, 2 Doug. 632,) "If the estate on which a person resides is substantially his property, that is sufficient, whatever forms of conveyance there may be; and therefore a mortgagor in possession gains a settlement because the mortgagee, notwithstanding the form, has but a chattel, and the mortgage is only a security. It is an affront to common sense to say the mortgagor is not the real owner." (See further the King *v.* Edington, 1 East, 293.) When the mortgage is of a term of years, less than the estate of the mortgagor, as this grant involves no receipt of rent-service, there is still less occasion than might, in a strict and technical view, have appeared necessary in the case just referred to, for adverting to the mortgage. 2. The owner is not obliged to make his statement of ownership again, while a former statement continues correctly to represent his relation to the property. He is, therefore, not obliged to renew his statement when he makes a new appointment of proxy. 3. The form heretofore in use for "owners' statements," will not apply to the present requirements of the law. The "appointment of proxy," and the "proxy's statement" require no alteration.

VI.—JUSTICES.—THEIR POWER.

Feb. 15th, 1845.

Clerk of New Romney Union—It is presumed that there is not any legal objection to two justices, rated in the parish of A, allowing a poor-rate for that parish; but can they, with reference to the case of The Queen *v.* the Justices of Hertfordshire, and other decisions, on the complaint of the collector of the rates against an occupier in the *same* parish for not-payment of his rate, lawfully issue a summons, hear and adjudicate on the case, and, if necessary, grant a warrant of distress for recovery of the rate?

Ans.—The competency of the justices to act in the enforcement of the rate under the circumstances suggested is perfectly clear with reference to the 16 Geo. 2, c. 18. But for that express provision, empowering justices to act in certain cases relating to parishes to the rates or taxes of which they are rated, the case of Reg. *v.* the Justices of Hertfordshire to which you advert, would certainly suggest a doubt as to their competency.

VII.—MEDICAL RELIEF.

May 23rd, 1845.

Clerk of Newton Abbot—Inquired whether an able-bodied person in the receipt of full agricultural wages, say from nine shillings to twelve shillings per week, having a wife, or any one or more of his children ill, is entitled to medical relief, when other relief is not applied for. 2. Whether such able-bodied person, who is a member of a sick club, and entitled to receive ten shillings a-week as bed pay, (having a wife and three, four, five, or six children, principally dependent on him,) is, when ill, entitled to "Medical Relief," although he does not apply for other relief.

Ans.—As every case must depend upon the circumstances peculiar to it, it is not possible for the Commissioners to lay down any general rule which shall be applicable to all cases. The Commissioners, can only point out that if a person is able to provide himself and his family with food, lodging, and clothing, while they are in health, but is unable, in case of sickness, to provide medical

Bench Formulist Specimen Page of Information to ground Summary Conviction.

(i.) VENUE. See above, p. 5. *County of*

The information must be laid as in the county where the matter constituting the charge in truth happened. Whether or not justices may receive informations out of their counties, they certainly have no power further to entertain a charge thereout.

(ii.) COMPLAINANT'S DESIGNATION. See above, p. 19. *The complaint and information of A. C.* [name], *of* [abode and addition]

In general any one may inform. But where the penalty, or part of it, is given to the informer, a material witness should not inform; for an informer interested in the penalty is not a competent witness at hearing, unless by the recent Act;—above, pp 43, 44, and below, "Evidence." As to the case of the penalty or damages being given to the party aggrieved, see Variation, below, p. 166.

Oath.—See the Jurat. below. *who on his oath saith,*

(iii.) DEFENDANT'S DESIGNATION. See above, p. 19. *that N. O.* [name] *of* [abode and addition]

(iv.) ARTICLES OF CHARGE.

Time.—There is no general Act of limitation, except Stat. 31 Eliz. c. 5, s. 5, as to informations, &c. in cases where the Crown has the whole or part of the penalty. As to limitation, interval, and hour, see above, p. 85, and *R.* v. *Tolly*, 3 East, 467. In computing a period of time, it is the safer rule to consider that the day of committing the offence is included.—*Lester* v. *Garland*, 15 Ves. 248. If the period be of "months," lunar months are understood. The Court takes judicial notice of the calendar.—*R.* v. *Brown*, 1 Mo. and M. 163. As to whether the repeated commission of the act prohibited on the same day constitutes several offences, or only one offence, see *Crepps* v. *Durden*, Cowp. 640; *Brooks* v. *Milliken*, 3 T. R. 509.

on the day of in the year one thousand eight hundred and [or *within next before the day of exhibiting this information, namely, on, &c.*] [or, *between the day of and the day of*],

Place.—As to cases where the parish must be named, see above, pp. 34, 36. The offence must be alleged to have happened within the county, or other limit of the magistrate's jurisdiction.—*R.* v. *Johnson*, 1 Stra. 261. Or if it happened out of the local limits of jurisdiction, facts must be alleged to shew that the case comes within their authority.—*Kite* and *Lane's* case, 1 B. and C. 101; *Talbot* v. *Hubble*, 2 Stra. 1154; and see above, pp. 11, 34, 85. *Margin*,—see above, p. 8.

at in the county named in the margin

Character of Defendant.—See above, p. 19. Where the matter is an offence, as being done or committed by a person in a certain condition of life, office, class, or situation, it must appear that the defendant filled the character; *e.g.* that of "British subject," in certain smuggling offences.—*Ex parte* Hawkins, 2 B. and C. 31. And where there is a further qualification, it must be stated from the statute, as "hawker going from town to town," for hawker alone would be insufficient.—*R.* v. *Little*, 1 Bur. 613. And where there is a distinction between classes, &c., the defendant must be described in terms of the distinction, "as a person other than a servant, &c., under the degree of a gentleman," and not as of a particular trade, &c., according to the Swearing Act, 6 and 7 Wm. III. c. 11; *R.* v. *Sparling*, 1 Stra. 497; as an unqualified person, in a charge under 5 Ann, c. 14, s. 4, for keeping a dog to kill and destroy game.—*Reason* v. *Lisle*, Com. 576. The above form of description refers to the time of the deed. See above, p. 19, and *R.* v. *Somerton*, 7 B. and C. 463.

he then and there being, &c.

aid, he is entitled to receive medical relief, at the charge of the poor-rates. Although he does not apply for any other sort of relief, he has not the less a claim to that kind of relief which he actually stands in need of. Whether he has or has not the means of procuring for himself medical aid, is a question which it is entirely within the province of the guardians to decide; and one which will depend upon the varying circumstances of each particular case.

VIII.—MEDICAL OFFICER.—REFUSAL OF PAUPER TO SUBMIT TO AN OPERATION.

Feb. 8th, 1845.

Clerk of Solihull Union—Stated that a pauper inmate of the union workhouse, who is a person of weak mind, is under the care of the medical officer with a diseased leg; the medical officer represented to the guardians that the leg would probably get well, if the pauper would allow it to be opened, which he absolutely refused to do, and that it was in danger of causing his death if this was not done. Inquired whether the medical officer would be justified in using force in order to accomplish the operation.

Ans.—The question appears to the Commissioners to turn upon the point, whether the pauper is competent to exercise a discretion of his own. If any medical practitioner (not the medical officer of the workhouse) can certify that the pauper is not of sound mind, the Commissioners think that the guardians would be justified in authorising those means to be used which they are informed can alone save his life: on the other hand, if the patient is of sound mind, he must be allowed to judge for himself in the matter in question.

IX.—OFFICERS' SALARIES—GENERAL ORDER.

To the Guardians of the Poor of the several Unions and Incorporations named in the Schedule hereunto annexed;—

To the Churchwardens and Overseers of the Poor of the several Parishes and Places comprised within the said Unions and Incorporations respectively;—

To the Clerk or Clerks to the Justices of the Petty Sessions held for the Division or Divisions in which the said Unions and Incorporations are situate;—

To the Treasurers of the said Unions and Incorporations respectively;—

And to all others whom it may concern.

Whereas the Poor Law Commissioners, by various Orders under their Hands and Seal, respectively issued to the Unions and Incorporations named in the Schedule hereunto annexed, the dates whereof are set forth in the said Schedule, having provided for the audit of the accounts of such Unions and Incorporations, and the several parishes therein, quarterly, as in such Orders is fully set forth, did Order and direct, that each paid Officer of the Union or Incorporation, or any of the parishes comprised therein, who was bound to account under any of such Orders, should be entitled to receive his salary quarterly, as soon after the termination of the quarter as his accounts for such quarter should have been duly audited and allowed by the Auditor; and that the fact of such audit and allowance should be duly recorded in the minute book, and be a warrant for the payment of the salary of such Officer.

And whereas, by certain other Orders, bearing date respectively the Tenth, Eleventh, and Twenty-first days of January, the Eighth, Twelfth, Nineteenth, and Twenty-fifth days of February, the Seventh, Tenth, Eleventh, and Twentieth days of March, and the Second, Twelfth, and Seventeenth days of April, One thousand eight hundred and forty-five, the Poor Law Commissioners have made certain Provisions, under the authority of the statute passed in the eighth year of the reign of Her present Majesty Queen Victoria, intituled "*An Act for the further Amendment of the Laws relating to the Poor in England*," whereby the said Unions and Incorporations, named in the said Schedule, have been combined into Districts for the audit of accounts, and the Poor Law Commissioners have thereby directed that the Auditor to be appointed to each of such Districts shall, twice in every year, that is to say, as soon as may be after the Twenty-fifth day of March, and the Twenty-ninth day of September, examine, audit, and allow or disallow, the accounts of the several Unions and Incorporations so thereby combined, and of the several Parishes comprised therein, according to the laws in force for the time being for the Administration of the Relief of the Poor; and it is expedient to alter the above-recited provision for the payment of the salaries of the paid Officers of the said Unions and Incorporations and of the Parishes comprised therein.

Now, therefore, We, the Poor Law Commissioners, do hereby alter so much of the said several Orders herein first recited as provides for the payment of the salaries of the Officers as aforesaid.

And We do Order, that the Guardians of the Poor of the said several Unions and Incorporations may, if they think fit, pay to each Officer, other than the Auditor, entitled to receive payment of any salary from them, whether by way of annual stipend, poundage, or other emolument, on account of such salary, the amount which shall be due at the expiration of the quarters ending at Midsummer and Christmas in every year, provided the accounts of such Officer shall have been presented by him to such Guardians, duly made up and balanced, at a meeting of the Guardians, and such Officer shall receive the balance of his salary due at Lady Day and Michaelmas Day, so soon as his accounts have been audited and allowed by the Auditor, after those days respectively, but not before.

SCHEDULE to which the above Order refers.

Names of the Unions and Incorporations.	Dates of the Orders firstly above referred to.
Aberaeron	11 August 1837
Albans, Saint	13 August 1836
Ampthill	17 August 1836
Ashby-de-la-Zouch	23 July 1836
Atherstone	11 August 1836
Axminster	8 August 1836
Aylsham	11 August 1836
Bakewell	17 October 1838
Barnet	13 August 1836
Barnstaple	13 August 1836
Barrow-upon-Soar	9 February 1838
Basford	5 August 1836
Bedford	19 August 1836
Belper	9 May 1837
Berkhampstead	13 August 1836
Bideford	12 August 1836
Biggleswade	19 August 1836
Billesdon	11 August 1836
Bingham	6 August 1836
Bishop's Stortford	20 August 1836
Blaby	31 August 1836
Blofield	29 August 1836
Blything	19 August 1836
Bosmere and Claydon	22 August 1836
Boston	12 October 1836
Bourn	11 August 1836
Brecknock	4 November 1836
Bridgend and Cowbridge	31 December 1836
Bromley	10 August 1836
Builth	4 May 1837
Buntingford	18 August 1836
Burton-upon-Trent	28 April 1837
Caistor	20 December 1836
Cambridge	19 August 1836
Cardiff	2 August 1836
Cardigan	11 August 1837
Carmarthen	2 August 1836
Caxton and Arrington	18 August 1836
Cheadle	25 May 1837
Chesterfield	7 December 1837
Chesterton	8 August 1836
Cosford	18 August 1836
Crediton	11 August 1836
Croydon	3 August 1836
Depwade	8 August 1836
Derby	13 April 1837
Docking	17 August 1836
Downham	2 September 1836
Dulverton	3 August 1836
East Retford	25 July 1836
Ely	6 August 1836
Erpingham	9 August 1836
Faith's, Saint	13 August 1836
Hundreds of East and West Flegg	30 January 1838
Hundred of Forehoe	31 January 1838
Freebridge Lynn	11 August 1836
Gainsborough	24 January 1837
Glanford Brigg	19 January 1837
Grantham	12 August 1836
Greenwich	7 March 1837
Guiltcross	31 August 1836
Hartismere	16 August 1836
Hatfield	13 August 1836
Haverfordwest	17 May 1837
Hay	28 October 1836
Hemel Hempstead	13 August 1836
Henstead	10 August 1836
Hertford	18 August 1836
Hinckley	11 August 1836
Hitchin	19 August 1836
Holbeach	9 August 1836
Honiton	8 August 1836
Horncastle	17 January 1837
Hoxne	18 August 1836
Huntingdon	1 September 1836
Ipswich	16 August 1836
Ives, Saint	12 August 1836
Kingsbridge	1 August 1836
King's Lynn	22 August 1836
Lampeter	16 August 1837
Leek	13 February 1838
Leicester	1 August 1836
Leighton Buzzard	18 August 1836
Lewisham	3 April 1837

Names of the Unions and Incoporations.	Dates of the Orders firstly above referred to.
Lichfield	18 March 1837
Lincoln	22 December 1836
Linton	18 August 1836
Llandilo Fawr	4 March 1837
Llandovery	3 April 1837
Llanelly	7 November 1836
Loddon and Clavering	1 September 1836
London, City of	16 September 1837
London, East	16 January 1838
London, West	17 January 1838
Loughborough	9 February 1838
Louth	5 May 1837
Luton	15 August 1836
Lutterworth	31 August 1836
Mansfield	23 July 1836
Market Bosworth	16 August 1836
Market Harborough	13 August 1836
Melton Mowbray	12 August 1836
Merthyr Tydvil	28 February 1837
Mildenhall	12 August 1836
Mitford and Launditch	4 August 1836
Hundreds of Mutford and Lothingland	3 January 1838
Narberth	2 August 1837
Neath	2 September 1836
Neot's, Saint	30 August 1836
Newark	12 August 1836
Newcastle in Emlyn	22 December 1837
Newcastle-under-Lyme	12 June 1838
Newmarket	6 August 1836
Newport Pagnell	30 August 1836
Newton Abbot	1 August 1836
North Witchford	5 August 1836
Nottingham	25 July 1836
Oakham	5 August 1836
Okehampton	9 August 1836
Pembroke	4 May 1837
Penkridge	20 October 1836
Peterborough	13 August 1836
Plomesgate	30 August 1836
Radford	27 July 1836
Risbridge	31 August 1836
Royston	15 August 1836
Hundred of Samford	1 February 1838
Shardlow	5 April 1837
Sleaford	13 October 1836
South Molton	13 August 1836
Southwell	5 August 1836
Spalding	10 August 1836
Spilsby	8 May 1837
Stafford	29 October 1836
Stamford	12 August 1836

Names of the Unions and Incorporations.	Dates of the Orders firstly above referred to.
Stone	20 February 1838
Stow	31 August 1836
Stratton	14 February 1837
Sudbury	30 August 1836
Swaffham	22 August 1836
Swansea	20 December 1836
Tamworth	12 August 1836
Thetford	9 August 1836
Thingoe	31 August 1836
Thomas, Saint	8 August 1836
Tiverton	12 August 1836
Torrington	12 August 1836
Totnes	1 August 1836
Tregaron	20 December 1837
Hundreds of Tunstead and Happing	11 January 1838
Uppingham	6 August 1836
Uttoxeter	25 May 1837
Walsingham	9 August 1836
Wangford	15 August 1836
Ware	20 August 1836
Watford	13 August 1836
Wayland	27 August 1836
Welwyn	13 August 1836
Wisbeach	6 August 1836
Woburn	16 August 1836
Wolstanton and Burslem	12 June 1838
Woodbridge	29 August 1836
Worksop	25 July 1836

Given under our Hands and Seal of Office, this Twenty-fourth day of May, in the year One thousand eight hundred and forty-five.

(Signed) GEO. NICHOLLS.
L. S. G. C. LEWIS.
EDMUND W. HEAD.

X.—PENSION — WHETHER ASSIGNABLE TO MEET PAYMENTS UNDER AN ORDER IN BASTARDY.

January 4th, 1845.

——— *Esq., Droitwich Union*—Inquired whether, in the case of a person who is entitled to a pension from Chelsea Hospital, part of such pension can be assigned to make the payments under an order made upon him by the justices to contribute towards the support of an illegitimate child.

Ans.—The Commissioners conclude that the order was made since the passing of 7 and 8 Vic. c. 101, (9th Aug. 1844,) and consequently under the authority of that Act. Upon referring to the 2 and 3 Vic. c. 51, you will perceive that the object of the assignment of the pension is to reimburse the parish the cost of the relief given to the pensioner, his wife, or his family; and it therefore only enables the guardians to retain so much of the pension as may be necessary to cover the charge. It would not be competent to them to retain the costs which they might incur in enforcing payment of an order in bastardy, even assuming that they had any duty or concern in respect to such enforcement, as that would obviously not be the cost of relief to the pensioner, or to or on account of his wife or his family. But it is to be borne in mind that the remedy given to the mother of an illegitimate child, by the 7 and 8 Vic. c. 101, is entirely personal, and the order being made for her benefit and not for the indemnity of the parish, neither the guardians nor overseers are the parties to look to the enforcement of the order.

XI.—PENSIONERS.

May 30th, 1845.

Clerk of Seven Oaks Union—Inquired whether parties who are in receipt of pensions from the army, sufficient for their maintenance, are liable to be proceeded against under the Vagrant Act, if they become chargeable, in consequence of an improper expenditure of their incomes. The justices entertain a doubt upon the point.

Ans.—The provisions for recovering the cost of relief from pensioners, in no way interfere with their liability to the provisions of the Vagrant Act. What the justices had in view was, probably, a case where the pension had actually been assigned for the relief of the family. In such a case, the man would not have neglected to maintain his family, but would have supplied a lawful means to their support, and consequently would not be liable to be punished as a vagrant. But where the guardians have not required or taken an assignment of the pension, and it is shown that the pensioner has neglected to maintain his family, and they thereby become chargeable, there appears to be no doubt of the pensioner's liability to be punished under the Vagrant Act.

XII.—POOR-RATES.—COST OF RECOVERING POOR-RATES.

April 16th, 1845.

Clerk of Hendon Union—The justices have refused to award to the overseers of the several parishes in the union costs incurred by them in the recovery of the poor-rates, it being the opinion of the justices that neither the Act of 43 Elizabeth, c. 2 nor any other Act authorised them to do so. The 1st section of the 18th Geo. 3, c. 19, does not, the justices conceive, apply to the case of a public officer, because he is not the party injured. Requested the Commissioners' advice.

Ans.—The Commissioners quite concur in the views of the justices, that there is no power given by the 43 Eliz. c. 2, to award to the overseers the costs of the summons and proceedings before justices in the recovery of the poor-rate. But the Commissioners apprehend that, since the decision in Skingley *v.* Surridge, 3 Meeson and Welsby, 503, no reasonable doubt can be entertained that the 18th Geo. 3, c. 19, sec. 1, applies to the case, and that an information before justices of the non-payment of the poor-rate is a "complaint out of sessions" within the meaning of sec. 1 of that statute, and that the overseer is a person "injured" by reason of the non-payment of the rate. In Skingley *v.* Surridge, one of the objections to the distress for poor-rate was, that it was illegal, because 11*s.* 6*d.*, the costs of the summons and hearing before two justices who granted the warrant, were included; and that the claim for these costs was not warranted by law. The Commissioners understand the decision of the court to have been that, though not recoverable under the statute of Elizabeth, the sum was nevertheless due, under 18 Geo. 3, c. 19, and that a distress for that amount would have been good, if there had been an award of costs in the form given by that statute. The Commissioners think it probable that the intention of the justices may not have been called to the decision referred to. If not, it is undoubtedly desirable that this should be done.

XIII.—RATING.

1. RENT-CHARGE.

April 5th, 1845.

Churchwarden of —— Union—Inquired how the tithe rent-charge should be rated to the relief of the poor, and whether, in case the value of the rent-charge be in any year reduced by a variation in the average price of corn below the amount at which the rent-charge was commuted, the overseers, in rating the rent-charge for that year, should take such reduction into consideration.

Ans.—It would be the duty of the overseers to rate the owner of the rent-charge on the value of such rent-charge for the current year. The value of the rent-charge will vary every year according to the average price of corn, that average being ascertained and declared in the manner provided by the 6 and 7 Will. 4, c. 71, sec. 56.

When the average price of corn so declared in any year is shown to be less than the average declared in the preceding year, the value of the rent-charge to the tithe-owner for the ensuing year will be proportionably diminished, and in estimating the value of the rent-charge, for the purposes of the poor-rate, it will, of course, be necessary to have regard to this alteration in the value of the rent-charge, and to give the tithe owner the benefit of it.

2. DITTO.

April 10th, 1845.

The Rev. —— —Inquired whether his presentation fees can legally be deducted from the rent-charge before assessing it to the poor-rate.

Ans.—The ecclesiastical dues which may be allowed for in assessing the rate in respect to tithes, are those several or periodical dues which reduce the annual value of the benefice. The Commissioners do not understand that the fees payable in connexion with the admission to a benefice can be deducted in any year subsequent to the year of the clerk's admission, and they entertain a doubt whether they are in any case a subject of deduction.

3. DITTO.

March 28th, 1845.

Mr. ——, Inquired whether the annual instalments and the interest thereon payable in respect of a sum of money borrowed by the rector of ——, under the Tithe Commutation Act, to defray the commutation expenses, form a proper deduction to be made on assessing the rent-charge to the relief of the poor.

Ans.—The Commissioners consider that the repayment in question is clearly not a tenant's tax, within the meaning of the 1st section of the Parochial Assessments Act, nor can it be considered as an expense incurred in keeping up the value of the rent-charge so as to bring the case within the last clause of that section—" other expenses," &c. The Commissioners are of opinion, therefore, that no such deduction could be lawfully made from the gross value of the rent-charge in ascertaining the rateable value.

4. DEER PARK.

Feb. 13th, 1845.

Mr.———, *Andover Union*—Inquired whether a deer park is rateable to the poor-rate as pasture land; and if not, on what principle it should be rated.

Ans.—The deer park is liable to be assessed like all other rateable properties, at its estimated annual value to let as a deer park, according to the 1st sec. of the Parochial Assessments Act. If the property in question be a deer park and nothing more, the Commissioners do not see on what ground it can be rated in any other character. If, however, any part of it be used for the purposes of general pasture, it would, of course, be proper to take that circumstance into account, in forming an estimate of its annual value.

XIV.—RELIEF.

1. TO AN ABLE-BODIED MAN.—POWER TO TAKE POSSESSION OF HIS GOODS IN THE CUSTODY OF HIS WIFE.

Feb. 12th, 1845.

Clerk of Dorking Union— A. B., an able-bodied man, whose wife refuses to allow him to go into his own house, where his goods are, or to render him any assistance, being out of work and in a state of destitution, has applied for admission into the workhouse, or for out-door relief. Requested the Commissioners' opinion as to the course which the guardians ought to adopt in reference to the application; and whether they would be justified in taking the man's goods in the possession of the wife.

Ans.—The Commissioners are willing to this case being excepted from the provisions of the Prohibitory Order, and to relief being afforded to the man by admitting him into the workhouse without his wife, if the guardians think the course desirable. With regard to the goods which are alleged to belong to him, but to be in the possession of his wife, the Commissioners are of opinion that any person might, under the authority of the husband, take them. They would not, however, advise that the guardians should make themselves his agents for this purpose. But the relief may be afforded to him by loan, in order that it may afterwards be repaid from the property which he possesses.

2. RELIEF TO A YEARLY HIRED SERVANT IN SICKNESS.

March 4th, 1845.

Clerk of Bodmin Union—J. B., a yearly hired servant residing under his master's roof, being sick, the master had applied to the guardians for medical relief, and payment of the amount alleged to be due for the servant's maintenance during his sickness, and the charges of the nurse for attending on him. Inquired whether the guardians would be justified in acceding to the application, or, whether the master was bound to provide for his servant in sickness.

Ans.—In the case of a yearly hired servant, if he fall sick during that period, the master is not entitled to put the servant away, or abate his wages. (Dalt. c. 58, p. 141 ; R. *v.* Subbrooke, 1 Smith's Rep. 59.) But though he cannot refuse to support his servant under such circumstances, the master is not bound to provide his servant with medical attendance or with medicines ; (see Sellon *v.* Norman, 4 C. and P. 80. Newby *v.* Wiltshire, 2 Esp. 739, and other cases.) There may be cases in which the earnings of a yearly hired servant are so small, as to be obviously insufficient to enable him to procure medical attendance at his own cost. The Commissioners, therefore, are not prepared to say that, in every case of this kind which can be conceived, relief at the cost of the poor-rates would be improperly afforded. But, as a general rule, the Commissioners do not think that persons in the situation and circumstances described, can be considered as proper objects for relief, and such as ought to receive medical aid at the charge of the poor-rates. If, however, the guardians should consider that the circumstances were such as to warrant them in providing medical aid to J. B., they are clearly not liable in law to the demand made upon them by the master for the cost of his maintenance and the nurse's charges.

---

3. REFUSAL OF MOTHER, WHOSE CHILDREN ARE IN THE WORKHOUSE, TO GO IN HERSELF, OR TO TAKE HER CHILDREN OUT.

May 23rd, 1845.

Clerk of Highworth and Swindon Union—M. H. having become the mother of an illegitimate child during her widowhood, the board of guardians discontinued the out-door relief which she had previously been receiving on account of her three legitimate children, and offered the workhouse to her and her family. The three legitimate children have since been received into the workhouse ; but the mother has refused to go in, or to maintain her children, alleging that she was not able to do so. Requested the Commissioners' instructions as to how to deal with the case.

Ans.—It is undoubtedly competent to the guardians, if they think that M.H. is in a situation to maintain her legitimate children, to discharge them from the workhouse. But the children should not be allowed to suffer from destitution, so far as the guardians may have the means of preventing it ; and the above course could not, therefore, be advised, unless there is a reasonable prospect of the mother's being able to support them. If the workhouse be offered to the mother, and she refuse to avail herself of it, allowing her children to be maintained therein, it would be for the justices to consider whether the offer to maintain the widow in the workhouse, in return for work there provided for her, and her refusal to accept such work on those terms, would be a wilful refusal or neglect of a person wholly or in part able to maintain herself and family by work, or other means; by which refusal or neglect, her family, whom she is bound to maintain, are allowed to be chargeable. The Commissioners are advised that this would be an offence within the meaning of the 3rd section of the Vagrant Act.

XV.—RELIEVING OFFICERS' DUTIES.

January 10th, 1845.

Clerk of ——— *Union*—Inquired whether he was empowered to require the attendance of the relieving officers, with their books, on the business of the union, at any reasonable time in the intervals between the sittings of the board of guardians, provided it be not at hours when the relieving officers must, of necessity, be engaged in attending their several stations, or visiting paupers.

Ans.—The latter part of the Article 20, No. 11, of the General Order of the Commissioners on "Duties of Officers" makes it the duty of the relieving officer to balance his account weekly, "and to present the same to the clerk for his inspection and authentication before every ordinary meeting of the board of guardians." The Commissioners do not think that this Article gives the clerk a discretionary power as to what particular time the relieving officer shall produce such books and accounts. The Commissioners also refer you to Article 20, No. 15, of the same order, which makes it the duty of the relieving officer "to observe and execute all lawful orders and directions of the guardians applicable to his office." If, therefore, the guardians order the relieving officer to attend upon the clerk for the purpose above mentioned, at any particular time between their ordinary sittings, it is his duty to do so ; but care must be taken not to interfere with the more important duties of the relieving officer's district.

XVI.—SETTLEMENT.

1. BY ESTATE.

March 15th, 1845.

Clerk of Weobley Union—E. S., an aged woman, residing in the parish of Eardisland, in the Weobley Union, but whose husband has been for many years an inmate of the union workhouse at the charge of the parish of Dilwyn, also in the Weobley Union, has applied to the guardians for relief. E. S.'s husband had been living separate from her for several years before his admission into the workhouse. Although the husband has been for several years maintained at the charge of Dilwyn, and his settlement has been acknowledged to be in that parish, it is now alleged that he has acquired a settlement by estate in Eardisland; the tenement in which the wife resides having been left to her by her deceased father's will. This, however, occurred subsequent to the separation of the parties, and the husband has never resided in the tenement. Inquired to which of the two parishes named the relief to be given to the wife should be charged.

Ans.—You state that E. S.'s husband is acknowledged to belong to Dilwyn parish, unless it is considered that he has gained a settlement by estate in Eardisland, under the circumstances which you describe. If, from your statement that the husband "has never resided in such tenement with his wife since it came into her possession for life," the Commissioners are to understand that he has not resided in the parish in which the estate is situated, it is clear that he has not gained any settlement in that parish in respect of such estate; (Berkhampstead *v.* Saint Mary, Northchurch, 2 Bott. 33.) If so, it appears that he belongs to the parish of Dilwyn; and as his wife cannot acquire any settlement independently of him, she must belong to that parish also; (see the case above cited.) The parish officers of Dilwyn cannot consent to acknowledge the husband, and refuse to accept the wife; and therefore, so long as the husband's settlement is admitted to be in Dilwyn, the Commissioners think that the guardians may, if they think fit, charge the wife's relief to that parish. As, however, the wife is living in Eardisland, that parish it primarily liable for her support: and the Commissioners would not advise the guardians to charge her relief to Dilwyn, if the overseers, notwithstanding their previous admission of the husband's settlement, should now adduce good grounds for believing that his present settlement is in Eardisland. If he really has resided forty days in Eardisland, since his wife became possessed of the estate in question, he has doubtless gained a settlement there.

2. DITTO.

Assistant Overseer of Bishop Auckland—R. formerly possessed a cottage in the town of Bishop Auckland, in which he resided for some years, and thereby gained a settlement in the township: he disposed of the cottage upwards of twenty years ago, but he has continued to live in the township up to the present time; he has a son, who was born in the cottage above-mentioned, and who is now married, and become chargeable to another township in the Auckland Union. Not having gained any settlement in his own right, the son claims one in Bishop Auckland, as derived from his father under the circumstances above stated. Inquired, whether the father, by the sale of his property, lost the settlement acquired by it, and then fell back on his previous settlement. If the father still retains his settlement in Bishop Auckland, inquired whether the son's settlement is also in that township.

Ans.—Assuming the elder R. to have gained a settlement by estate in Bishop Auckland, the mere circumstance of his disposing of the property would not of itself deprive him of such settlement; and if he has not acquired any other settlement since, nor ceased to inhabit within ten miles, (See Poor Law Amendment Act, sec. 68,) he still continues to retain his settlement in Bishop Auckland. And as he seems to have gained this settlement before his son's emancipation, such son derived it from him; and, not having acquired any other, still retains it. It has been decided by the courts (R. *v.* Hendon, 2 Gale and Dav. 394,) that the 68th section of the Poor Law Amendment Act does not extend to derivate settlements; and consequently, the younger R., even if he has ceased to inhabit within the ten miles, would not thereby lose the settlement derived from his father in Bishop Auckland.

XVII.—TAXATION OF LAW BILLS.

May 26th, 1845.

THE following reply was given by the Commissioners to questions submitted to them on this subject:—

The taxation by the clerk of the peace of any

attorney's bill, exonerates the auditor from the responsibility of deciding on the reasonableness of the charges in such bill, but it is not, in the opinion of the Commissioners, conclusive as between the attorney and his clients, and does not interfere with the right of a party to have a bill taxed by the usual taxing officer, and in the usual manner: when the more conclusive course is resorted to by the parties, of a taxation by the master of the Crown Office, or other officer authorised by the 6 and 7 Vic. c. 73, the Commissioners think that the auditor, although not obliged to do so, would exercise a sound discretion in being guided by this taxation, rather than by that of the clerk of the peace.

XVIII.—TREASURER.—CANNOT ACT AS AN EX-OFFICIO GUARDIAN OF THE UNION OF WHICH HE IS TREASURER.

——— *Union*—Inquired whether the treasurer of the ——— Union, who has recently been made a justice of the peace, could act as an ex-officio guardian of the union while he continues to hold the office of treasurer.

Ans.—The Commissioners think that the treasurer of a union is a paid officer engaged in the administration of the laws for the relief of the poor, within the meaning of the 14th section of the 5 and 6 Vic. c. 57; and consequently that any person holding that office is thereby rendered incapable of serving as a guardian. The Commissioners further consider that the words used in that section, "serving as a guardian," standing as they do without limitation, would include an *ex-officio* as well as an elected guardian, and that a person holding the office of treasurer in a union is therefore, so long as he retains that office, incapable of acting as an *ex-officio* guardian.

XIX. — WORKHOUSES. — WHETHER THE WIFE CAN BE DETAINED IN THE WORKHOUSE WHILST THE HUSBAND IS AN INMATE THEREIN.

May 12th, 1845.

Clerk of Alton Union—A. B., and C. his wife, are both inmates of Alton Union Workhouse. The husband, who is seventy-four years of age, is bedridden from paralysis; but the wife, who is sixty-two years of age, is in good health, and she has latterly been called to attend upon her afflicted husband. A few days since she applied for permission to quit the house, leaving her husband behind her. Her conduct appearing so unreasonable and unnatural, her application was refused, but she persisted in her desire to leave. The guardians requested to be informed whether they were empowered to enforce the attendance of the wife on the husband, under the circumstances.

Ans.—The Commissioners are not aware that the guardians have any power to restrain the wife from leaving the workhouse. The refusal of the wife to remain in the workhouse with her husband and her family is not an offence for which she would be punishable under the Vagrant Act, inasmuch as the legal obligation to maintain the family attaches to the husband, and relief to or on account of the family is relief to him, (sec. 56 P. L. A. Act.) In the case of A. B. it does not appear that he has any children dependent upon him for support, but this makes no difference as regards the power of the guardians to restrain the wife. The Commissioners are of opinion that a woman may be restrained by the control of her husband from leaving the workhouse, and, if he declines to use his marital control, it is in the power of the guardians to dismiss the husband. But whether it is expedient or judicious to pursue such a course, must depend on the peculiar circumstance which each individual case presents. One consideration is particularly important in dealing with any case of this description—this is, whether the husband is in a condition practically to exercise his control over his wife. Where he is not, it would be very unadvisable, in the opinion of the Commissioners, to make it a condition of the relief of the husband or of his children (if he have any) that he should exercise an authority over his wife which practically he cannot exercise.

LONDON:
Printed by Order of the Poor Law Commissioners, by BLACKBURN and PARDON, 6, Hatton Garden, and Published by CHARLES KNIGHT and Co., 22, Ludgate Street, Publishers to the Poor Law Commissioners.

AN

OFFICIAL CIRCULAR

OF PUBLIC DOCUMENTS AND INFORMATION:

DIRECTED BY THE POOR LAW COMMISSIONERS TO BE PRINTED, CHIEFLY FOR THE USE OF THE MEMBERS AND PERMANENT OFFICERS OF BOARDS OF GUARDIANS, UNDER THE POOR LAW AMENDMENT ACT.

No. 49. CIRCULAR ISSUED JULY 1st, 1845.

The Poor Law Commissioners directed that the following documents be printed and circulated for the information of Guardians and Officers of the several Unions, viz.

(Signed) By Order of the Board,
Edwin Chadwick, *Secretary.*

I.—ACCOUNTS.—AUDIT OF.

March 15th, 1845.

Auditor of —— District.—Referred to the case of Reg. *v.* St. Andrew's Holborn, and inquired—1st, how far it is the duty of the auditor to call upon the overseers to account for rates made for the separate purpose of county rates, borough rates, lunatic asylum rates, and lighting and watching rates, in cases where separate rates for the relief of the poor are separately made and duly accounted for. 2nd. Whether the amount of maintenance of paupers under orders of removal, during the twenty-one days of the pendency of the notice previous to removal, when paid by overseers, should form an item in the overseers' accounts, or should be repaid to the overseers by the relieving officer, and form an item in the relieving officer's weekly relief list. 3rd. Instances have occurred in which small quantities of lime and other articles have been supplied for the use of the Union by persons who are guardians; in one instance at a sale, by the guardians, by public auction, of hogs kept at the workhouse, a hog has been bought by a guardian. He presumed that the several parties were liable to penalties under the 55 Geo. 3, c. 90, if prosecuted, but inquired what will be his duty in regard to accounts for such articles of sale when they are presented to him as auditor. 4th. In some parishes the proprietor of tithes is rated for his commuted tithes, which he is entitled to receive half yearly; by arrangement he receives his tithes yearly, and, in consideration thereof, he is not called upon to pay his several poor rates until the end of the year; by this means occupiers of houses, &c. not liable to the payment of tithes, are called upon to pay an undue proportion of poor rates during the intermediate part of the year. In case the justices allow new rates to be made whilst such arrears of the assessment on the tithes are unpaid, inquired what will be his duty and power in regard to such arrears at each quarter. 5th. The order of the Commissioners directs the medical officer to keep an annual index; inquired whether the medical officers are bound to keep such index posted up and produced to the auditor at each quarterly audit, or only at the end of the year. 6. Inquired further whether, as a general rule, boards of guardians are authorised to make any new erections, to any and what extent, without the order of the Commissioners.

Ans.—It appears to the Commissioners that the decision in Reg. *v.* St. Andrew, Holborn, establishes no more than that overseers (or other officers) are bound to account to the auditor, under the 46th and 47th sec. of the Poor Law Amendment Act, for all money raised by them as *poor-rate*. It does not determine that, where separate rates are levied for objects which are in some places provided for out of the money raised as poor-rate, the officers are bound to account to the auditor for such separate rates. And the Commissioners are disposed to think that there is nothing either in the Poor Law Amendment Act, or in the 7th and 8th Vic. c. 101, which requires such an account to be rendered to the auditor. 2. With regard to the "mode of charging out-relief paid under orders of removal," the Commissioners do not clearly perceive whether your question refers to relief given before removal, or to the repayment of such relief after the removal of the pauper. If the latter, the Commissioners think that, although the 84th sec. of the Poor Law Amendment Act is not distinct upon this point, yet, as all the other duties in connexion with removals still devolve upon the overseers, it is most proper for the overseers to make the repayment of relief required by that section; and, of course, if such repayment be made by them, it must be charged in their accounts. At the same time, the Commissioners see no objection (if the overseers and the guardians prefer such an arrangement) to the repayment being made by the relieving officer (either in person or through the overseers), and charged by him in his accounts accordingly. 3. Without a full statement of each case it is difficult for the Commissioners to say whether any of the guardians to whom you allude as having supplied goods to the union, have rendered themselves liable to penalties. Certainly, the Commissioners think that the enactments on this subject do not prevent a guardian *buying* a hog sold by the board of guardians, by public auction; which is clearly a very different case from that of a guardian *selling* any article to the Union. The Commissioners do not think that *coffins* are within the terms of the 6th sec. of the 55th Geo. 3, c. 137; which speaks of "goods, materials, or provisions, for the use of any workhouse, or otherwise for the support and maintenance of the poor," although they might, perhaps, be held to come within the scope of the 77th sec. of the Poor Law Amendment Act, which relates to "goods, materials, or provisions, ordered to be given in parochial relief." With regard to the lime, the straw, and the bricks you advert to, the Commissioners are not prepared, without further information, to express any definite opinion; but they direct your attention to the several decisions of the courts on the construction of the 55th Geo. 3, c. 137, sec. 6, especially the cases of Proctor *v.* Mainwaring (8 B. and A. 145) and Henderson *v.* Sherborne (2 Mees. and W. 236.) The Commissioners will add, however, that they consider it to be your duty as auditor to disallow any payments really made in contravention of the enactments in question. 4. The Commissioners do not consider that the overseers are justified in purposely allowing any rates duly assessed and actually recoverable, to continue in arrear, but, on the other hand, the Commissioners do not see in what way the auditor could interfere in such a case as that which you describe as occurring in certain parishes with regard to the collection of the poor-rates on the tithes. 5. The Commissioners desire to observe that the medical officer is not required to make up the annual index (Form C) to his weekly register (Form B) until the year's end. Indeed, it would be impossible to arrange the names in strict alphabetical order, if the index were prepared from time to time during the year. 6. The guardians should obtain the Commissioners' sanction to all additions or alterations in the workhouse; but there are cases where the work and the cost are comparatively trifling, in which the Commissioners do not feel it incumbent upon them to issue a formal order as an authority for the expense.

II.—BASTARDY.

TRANSMISSION OF DUPLICATES OF ORDERS IN, TO CLERKS TO GUARDIANS.

Clerk of —— *Union*—Wrote to the clerk to the justices at ————, calling his attention to that part of the 5th section of the 7 and 8 Vic. c. 101, which directs the clerks to justices to send a duplicate of any order made on the putative father of a bastard child, or appointment of any person to have the custody of such child, to the clerk to the guardians of the Union or parish in which the mother of such bastard child resided at the time of making such order or appointment, and requesting him to forward duplicates of such orders as had been made in conformity with the provisions of the Act. The clerk to the justices replied that the section above referred to was applicable only to cases of death, unsoundness of mind, or criminal punishment of the mother or persons appointed to have the care of illegitimate children, and that as no cases of that kind had occurred, no duplicates had been sent: but that the guardians might have duplicates of such orders as had been made on payment of his charge. The guardians are of opinion that the section in question refers not only to those cases mentioned by the clerk to the justices, but to "any order made on the putative father of a bastard child;" and as regards the payment of the charge of the justices' clerk, for the duplicates of orders, the guardians think no claim can be made upon them; but that such charge would be properly included in the costs on the putative father under the following words of the 3rd section of the Act, viz., "in such costs as may have been incurred in the obtaining of such order." The guardians requested the Commissioners' opinion on the subject.

Ans.—The Commissioners do not concur in the interpretation put by the clerk to the justices at ————, on the 5th section of the 7 and 8 Vic. c. 101. In regard to the point in question, the terms in the section are, "the clerk to the justices making *any* order on the putative father of a bastard child * * * * as herein-before provided, shall, as soon as may be, send by post, or otherwise, a duplicate of *such* order," &c. The Commissioners understand this provision to require that the clerk to the justices shall furnish duplicates of *all* such orders, without exception; and the Commissioners see nothing in any other part of the statute, or in the nature of the subject matter, to limit that requirement in any way. With regard to the payment of fees to the justices' clerk for such duplicates, the Commissioners desire to point out that there is no provision for such payment in the 7 and 8 Vic. c. 101. The duty is imposed absolutely on the clerk of the justices for public purposes; and he appears to have no specific claim for remuneration for this service. This, however, will probably be borne in mind by justices in settling the table of fees which he may take in the course of the previous proceedings. At all events, the duty is so easy, that the payments which he may claim at present for the performance of his duties must be very closely adjusted to his services, if they do not compensate him also for this additional labour.

2. RELIEF TO BASTARDS.

Clerk of Bath Union—Inquired, whether the guardians are justified in refusing relief, either in or out of the workhouse, to a bastard child, who has been affiliated under the provisions of 7 and 8 Vic. c. 101; and if the mother (being destitute) and child are admitted into the workhouse to whom the weekly allowance ordered by the justices is to be paid; or whether the putative father becomes exonerated from such payment.

Ans.—Where in any case the mother of an illegitimate child may apply for relief for her child, and an order on the reputed father may have been made, under the statute 7 and 8 Vic. c. 101, it would be proper for the guardians, in considering whether the woman is or is not destitute so as to require relief, to take into consideration the existence of such order on the reputed father for the indemnity of the mother. There may be cases in which it would not be advisable that relief should be refused to the mother merely from the circumstance that the father makes the weekly payments required by the order. Each case must, therefore, the Commissioners consider, be dealt with by reference to its peculiar circumstances, and especially as to the means or opportunities afforded to the mother of maintaining her child independently of the aid derived under the order. Generally, the existence of an order under the statute, and the payment of money under it by the putative father, are to be regarded as evidence of ability upon the part of the mother to maintain the child. Where the mother is relieved in the workhouse with her child (which will be the proper course if the mother be an able-bodied person, and relief be necessary in the case) the moneys payable under the order will still be due to the mother, and should be paid to her. The 5th sec. of the 7 and 8 Vic. c. 101, enumerates the cases or circumstances in which the custody of the child can be transferred to persons other than the mother, and the payments made to such persons. But chargeability is not one of those cases. The chargeability of the child does not exonerate the reputed father from liability under the order.

III.—BURIAL OF PAUPERS.—WORKHOUSE CHAPLAIN NOT ENTITLED TO A FEE.

April 12th, 1845.

Clerk of ——— *Union*—T. S. residing at S. in this union, became chargeable to that parish in consequence of his wife's sickness. The wife subsequently died and was buried in that parish; and a bill for burial fees, including the fee of the minister, who is the chaplain of the union workhouse, was presented to the board of guardians for payment. The board declined to order the payment of the minister's fee, conceiving that the 31st section of the Act 7 and 8 Vic. 101, rendered the payment illegal. Inquired, whether the guardians decided correctly in the case, and also whether, in the event of the burial of a pauper in the parish of S. by any other than the minister of the parish, the minister's fee can be legally paid by this board.

Ans.—In the case of T. S., as stated in your letter, the Commissioners consider that the chaplain was prevented, by the 31st sec. of the 7 and 8, c. 101, from taking any burial fee. The terms of the sec. are, "It shall not be lawful for any officer connected with the relief of the poor, to receive any money for the burial of the body of any poor person which may be within the parish, &c., in which the death may have occurred." The Commissioners are advised, that a chaplain to a union workhouse is an officer connected with the relief of the poor, within the meaning of this provision. It appears that the wife of T. S. died in S. and was buried there; so that the case was in fact that of the burial of the body of a poor person within the parish in which the death occurred. In reply to your inquiry whether, in the event of any other minister officiating in such cases, the usual fee could lawfully be paid, the Commissioners desire to observe that they think the fee might be paid, under such circumstances, to the officiating minister, but, that it would not be lawful for the chaplain to receive it, directly or indirectly.

The Commissioners, in another case similar to the above, have replied as follows—It appears impossible to maintain that the chaplain is not "an officer connected with the relief of the poor;" and consequently within the prohibition contained in the proviso to the 31st section of the Poor Law Amendment Act. But the proviso has reference to the general enactment which precedes it, relating to the payment of fees for burial by the guardians or overseers. The prohibition contained in the proviso, therefore, only prohibits the receipt of the fee in the cases where it is to be paid by the guardians or overseers, and does not affect the case where paupers are buried otherwise than by the direction and at the expense of the guardians or overseers.

IV.—CHARGEABILITY—CERTIFICATE OF.

July 4th, 1845.

Clerk of Great Boughton Union—Inquired whether in a certificate of chargeability made under the 69th sec. of the 7th and 8th Vic. 101, the first day on which the pauper became chargeable, or the day on which the certificate was signed, should be stated as the date of his chargeability.

Ans.—The Commissioners do not think it necessary that, where such a certificate is given, the pauper should be actually chargeable when the order of removal is made. Such certificate, according to the form in Schedule C. to the Act, certifies that on a certain day the pauper became chargeable; and this is all that it does certify. Consequently, there is nothing in the certificate to show that the pauper is chargeable, even at the date of the certificate.

V.—CONTRIBUTION ORDERS.

April 18th, 1845.

Clerk of Shipston-on-Stour Union—Orders were made on the overseers of the several parishes in the Union, for the usual quarterly contributions on the 1st March, and served a few days afterwards. The payments were to be made on the 29th March. The sums were intended to be applied, partly to meet the expenses of the then current quarter, and partly to meet the expenses of the quarter ending June. Some of the parish officers having refused to obey these orders, inquired, whether the parish officers upon whom the orders were served can legally resist the payment upon the ground that the money was not required to be wholly expended during their year of office.

Ans.—If the orders of contribution in the present instance were in conformity with the form prescribed by the orders of the Commissioners, the Commissioners do not see how the objection adverted to in your letter could be raised, as the orders, on the face of them, not purporting to be made for any particular period, there would be nothing to show that the money called for was not wanted to meet the present wants of the guardians. But assuming that the objection as to the prospective nature of the orders could be properly raised before the justices by the overseers, the Commissioners do not consider it valid. The guardians are made responsible for the relief of the poor, and this duty cannot be effectually discharged by them unless they are provided with the funds by anticipation: of the sums necessary for this purpose the guardians and not the overseers are the judges. The overseers on their part are responsible for providing and supplying to the guardians the moneys necessary for the relief of the poor and the other purposes of the Union, (see 7 and 8 Vic. c. 101, sec. 61,) and this obligation is not discharged until they have satisfied the prospective orders of the guardians. Accordingly the law has furnished the overseers with the requisite powers of making poor rates to meet future charges. If the guardians were (as appears to be supposed) restrained from requiring overseers to pay a greater sum by way of contribution than was actually necessary for the relief of the poor, during the period of office of such overseers, the result would be that there would be an interval during which the guardians would be without funds, and during which the poor would consequently go unrelieved; for, on this supposition, the funds of the guardians would be exhausted on the overseers quitting office, and no further supplies could be obtained until the guardians could make an order on the succeeding overseers, and until a reasonable time had elapsed to allow of their raising the funds necessary to comply with such orders. The Commissioners would add, however, that if (as they suppose) the overseers upon whom the orders of contribution were made are no longer in office, it would seem that they cannot now be proceeded against under the 2 and 3 Vic. c. 84, sec. 1. But the difficulty of so proceeding is quite independent of the objection raised in the present case, and is occasioned by the terms of the statute, which appear to the Commissioners to confine the remedy to persons who are overseers or acting as such at the time the proceedings are taken for the recovery.

VI.—COUNTY RATE.

1. ACCOUNTS.

June 21st, 1845.

Clerk of Preston Union—Inquired in what way the payments to be made under the Act 7 and 8 Vic. c. 33, to the county, are to be debited to the townships, so as to appear in the Union quarterly abstracts, in place of the parochial abstracts as heretofore.

Ans.—As regards the overseers of the several parishes, they should continue, as heretofore, to enter in their receipt and payment books, the payments made by them for county rates; the only change effected by the law as respects such payments by the overseers, consists in the fact that they are now made to the board of guardians instead of the high constable. These payments should also appear in their appropriate column, in the parochial quarterly abstracts, B. 12, as before. As regards the Union accounts, it will be necessary to open, in the Union ledger, a separate account with the county treasurer; and the payments made to him by the board of guardians, on account of the several parishes, should be entered in the Union quarterly abstract, B. 11, for which purpose a new column must be added.

2. COUNTY TREASURER REQUIRED TO GIVE STAMPED RECEIPTS.

June 3rd, 1845.

Clerk of Windsor Union—Inquired whether the board of guardians will be justified in paying any county-rate without a receipt from the county treasurer for the same on a stamp.

Ans.—By the 7th and 8th Vic. c. 33, sec. 1, the treasurer of the county is required to give a receipt for any sum of moneys received by him from any person on behalf of the guardians in payment of county rate. Such receipt being a memorandum or note given to a person upon the payment of money by which a debt or demand is acknowledged to be discharged or satisfied, appears to be subject to stamp duty under 55th Geo. 3, c. 184, in all cases where the demand is of the amount of £5. The Commissioners do not perceive that payments in respect of county rate are included in the list of exemptions from the duties on receipts. The Commissioners, therefore, consider the guardians should require to be furnished with receipts on stamps for the payments they may make under 7 and 8 Vic. c. 33.

VII.—GAS RATES.

ON WORKHOUSE.

Clerk of —— *Union*—The parishioners of —— in which the workhouse is situate, have adopted the provisions of the 3 and 4 Will. 4, c. 90, for a part of the parish (under the 73rd section,) for the purpose of lighting the town of —— with gas, that town being in the above parish. A district has accordingly been formed which includes the Union workhouse and premises. Inquired whether the guardians are liable to pay the sum of £1. 9*s*. 2*d*., now claimed from them as a gas-rate, at 2*d*. in the pound on the rateable value of the Union house and premises.

Ans.—It appears to the Commissioners, that the 33rd sec. of 3 and 4 Will. 4, c. 90, contemplates that the same description of property which is subject to the poor-rate should contribute to the rate which the overseers of the parish by which the Act may be adopted, are empowered to levy for the purposes of the Act. The section provides that "the sum shall be assessed upon the full and fair annual value, to which lands, houses, buildings, and other property within the said parish shall be rated or shall be rateable, according to the last valuation made and acted upon for the rate for the relief of the poor within the said parish." These terms clearly include the Union workhouse. It makes no difference, the Commissioners apprehend, as regards the question of liability, that the Act may in the present case have been adopted for a part of the parish only. The overseers have still power to levy the rate within such part, (see sec. 73.)

VIII.—GUARDIANS.

1. RIGHT OF INDIVIDUAL GUARDIAN TO TAKE COPIES OF OFFICIAL DOCUMENTS.

Clerk of —— *Union*—Inquired whether individual guardians have a right, during the sitting of the board, to take copies of, or extracts from, any letters, minutes, or other documents belonging to the board.

Ans.—The books, in which are recorded the proceedings of the guardians, communications made to the guardians by the Commissioners and others, and copies of the answers of the guardians to these communications, are the property of the guardians as a board:—no individual guardian possesses, by virtue of his office, any right to take copies or make extracts from those documents; but the guardians can expressly authorise any member of the board to make a copy of, or extract from, any document in their custody. The Commissioners believe, however, that the common practice is to allow such copies, or extracts, to be taken by a guardian, without express authority, nor are they aware of any inconveniences having arisen from the existence of this practice.

2. MINUTES OF THE PROCEEDINGS OF GUARDIANS.

Clerk of ——— *Union*—Inquired whether it is the duty of the clerk of the guardians to record on the minutes, a motion which is made and seconded at a meeting of the board, but which the chairman refuses to put to the vote.

Ans.—By the Commissioners' general order of the 21st April, 1842, (Art. 17, No. 1,) the clerk to the guardians is required to keep "a true record of the proceedings of the board." The Commissioners are disposed to consider that a motion not put to the board (though made and seconded) cannot be properly regarded as "a proceeding of the board," and that consequently the clerk is not bound by the Commissioners' regulations to enter such a motion on the minutes. At the same time, it appears to the Commissioners to be competent to the guardians in any such case to determine and direct that the motion so made and seconded, but not put, shall be entered on the minutes; and the Commissioners think that it would be the duty of the clerk to obey such direction, if given by the board.

3. QUALIFICATION OF EX-OFFICIO GUARDIAN.

J. H. —— *Union*—Inquired whether he is qualified to act as an *ex-officio* guardian of the —— Union, under the 24th section of the 7 and 8 Vic. c. 101, being a justice of the peace acting for the liberty and soke of P——, in the county of N——, (in which liberty the —— Union is situate), but residing at A——, in the county of H——, a parish within the —— Union.

Ans.—The latter part of section 24 of the 7 and 8 Vic. c. 101, provides that "every justice of the peace residing in any parish within such a Union, and acting for any *county*, *riding*, or *division*, in which any part of such Union is situated, shall be *ex-officio* a guardian of such Union." It appears that J. H. resides at A——, in the county of H. a parish within the —— Union, and therefore complies with the first of the two conditions imposed by this provision. But J. H. states—"I am a justice of the peace acting for the liberty and soke of P——, in the county of N——." The Commissioners are not precisely aware of the exact nature of the arrangements for the administration of justice in P——, but they presume that J. H.'s commission as a justice of the peace does not enable him to act in that character for the county of N—— generally, but is, in fact, confined to the limits of the soke or liberty of P——. As that liberty does not appear to be a county of itself, the only question seems to be, whether it is a "division" of a county, within the meaning of the above-cited section. The signification of the word "division," in its application to territ... districts, is not very certain or defini... regard to the decision i... Stevens," (4 T... mi... ...e; but having ... Evans, *qui tam*, against ... Term. Rep., 224 and 459,) the Com... ...ssioners are disposed to consider that the soke or liberty of P—— would probably not be held to be ... the meaning of the section in question. The decision in Evans *v.* Stevens turned upon the construction of this word, as used in the phrase "county, riding, or division," in 22 Geo. 3, c. 41. Lord Kenyon observed, (4 T. R. 227,) "The word *division* in this Act stands with county and riding, and therefore must mean something analogous to them; and the word *division* applies to the county of Lincoln, in the same manner that *riding* does to the county of York." And again, (4 T. R. 462,) "There are legal divisions which satisfy and directly apply to each of these words; *county* applies to every county in the kingdom, except two; *riding* to Yorkshire, and *division* to Lincolnshire, where there are three divisions, and three separate commissions of the peace, three quarter sessions, and three distinct rates."

IX.—JUSTICES.

1. SERVICE OF SUMMONS ON, TO ATTEND SPECIAL SESSIONS.

Clerk of —— *Union*—The overseers of some of the parishes in the —— Union being in arrear with their contributions, the necessary steps have been taken, under the 2 and 3 Vic. c. 84, s. 1, to compel payment of such arrears; and the clerk to the magistrates has summoned the magistrates to attend a special sessions, by *personal* service of such summons on each magistrate within the division, thereby causing a very considerable delay, as well as great expense for messengers and horse-hire. Inquired whether it is necessary that each magistrate should be summoned by personal service of the summons.

Ans.—There is no doubt that, to constitute a legal special sessions, reasonable notice must be given to all the magistrates of the division, the notice specifying the particular purpose for which the special sessions is convened, Rex *v.* Justices of Worcestershire, 2 B. and Ald. 228. As to the manner of giving the notice, it seems to be laid down by the authorities that the notice must be personally served on the justices by the high constable or his agent, (see Dickenson's Qu... Sessions by Talfourd; and Rex *v.* Ju... Suffolk, 6 B. and C. 110.)

...rter ...stices of

2. JURISDICTI... ...N OF JUSTICES.

Feb. 15*th*, 1845.

Clerk of Corwen Union—Inquired whether the justices acting in and for the county of Merioneth, can proceed against overseers of parishes situated in the portion of the Corwen Union, which lies in the county of Denbigh, for neglecting to pay money to the treasurer, pursuant to orders of contributions issued to them by the guardians. The guardians meet, and the treasurer resides, in the part of the union situated in Merionethshire.

Ans.—Assuming the proceeding to be taken under 2 and 3 Vic. c. 84, there appears to be no question that, upon the terms of that statute, the justices who act for the district, or jurisdiction in which the parish in arrear is situate, would be alone competent to entertain it. Again, if it be sought to inflict a penalty upon the overseers for the neglect under the 95th or 98th sections of the Poor Law Amendment Act, the Commissioners still think that the proceeding should be taken before the justices of Denbighshire, in which county the defaulting parishes are situate. For, as the offence of the overseers consists, not in the commission of any specific act, but in the omission to perform a duty, the Commissioners consider that it can only be regarded as taking place where the overseers themselves, who omit the duty, happen to be; and not in some other place in which they ought to have performed the duty, but whither they neglect to go: (see the King *v.* Hazell, 13 East, 139.) The question is, however, one for the justices to decide, as affecting their own jurisdiction.

3. POWERS OF JUSTICES.

Auditor of —— *Union*—At the petty sessions of ———— five fishermen were fined £25, on an information of the conservators of the ———— fisheries, for using illegal nets, under 1 Geo. 1, c. 18, which directs that one moiety of the fine shall go to the informers, the other moiety to the poor. The overseer of ———, who received one moiety of the above fine, (minus the expenses,) has not debited himself with the amount in his accounts; but states that he has received the magistrates' directions to distribute the amount in bread to the ... of the parish, and that he has already done ... extent of more than one-half of the sum ... quired whether the magistrates have poor ... ring the distribution of money so so to the ... r's discretion. received. In... observe that the 1 the power of orde... moiety of the received at the overse... the

Ans.—The Commission... one ... Geo. 1, st. 2, s. 18, directs ... penalty in such cases as those de...scribed ... auditor's letter, to be given "*to the poor of the parish*" where the offence was committed. The Act, however, does not specify what particular class of persons are to be considered "the poor of the parish," nor by whom, nor in what way, the money is to be distributed among them. With regard to charitable gifts, it has been expressly held that, where such gifts are left for the relief of the poor of a parish, they ought to be applied exclusively to *the poor not receiving parochial relief*, (Attorney Gen. *v.* Wilkinson, 1 Beaven, 370; 1 Lumley's Cases, 73.) But the Commissioners are disposed to consider that this principle would not be held to apply to the interpretation of the phrase "the poor of the parish," as used not only in the statute above-mentioned, but in several other statutes containing similar provisions. The Commissioners conceive that in these cases it was the intention of the legislature that the penalty should be appropriated in aid of the poor-rates. The Commissioners believe that the word "poor" is usually employed in the statutes as having reference to persons receiving or requiring parochial relief.

X.—MEDICAL ORDER.

1. CONSTRUCTION OF PROVISO IN ARTICLE 10.

Clerk of the ——*Union*—A woman having applied for an order for medical relief, the medical officer was directed to attend her, which he accordingly did, and after some time amputated her thigh, from which she has now recovered, and the medical officer claims the fee of £5, as fixed by the General Medical Order. Although the woman was fit to be removed prior to the operation, (as far as the guardians have been able to learn,) the medical officer never suggested to his patient that she should be sent to the general infirmary; but the woman states, that, had such a proposal been made to her, she should have refused to go. The concluding proviso in Article 10 of the Medical Order requires, "that *before* performing" any of the operations before recited, such medical officer shall "obtain, at his own cost, the advice of some member of the Royal College of Surgeons of London, or some fellow or licentiate of the Royal College of Physicians of London, and shall produce to the board of guardians a certificate from such member of the Royal College of Surgeons, or such fellow or licentiate, stating that in his opinion it was right and proper that such amputation or operation should be then performed." Inquired whether such *certificate* ought to be obtained previous to the operation ...ing performed; or whether, if the required ... took place prior to the operation, a ...ct. although obtained some ... sufficient to enable ... consultation ... certificate to that e... months afterwards, would be ... the payment to be legally ...

Ans.—The Commissioners do not consider that the proviso in Article 10 of the General Medical Order, which requires that the medical officer shall produce to the board of guardians a certificate, to the effect that it was right and proper that amputation or operation should be performed, is a condition *precedent* to the performance of the operation.

2. MIDWIFERY CASE.

July 14th, 1845.

Clerk of Bromsgrove Union—Inquired whether in case of attendance on the confinement of a woman whose name is on the permanent pauper list (and who is in possession of a ticket for the supply of medical relief,) the medical officer who attends her is entitled to be paid the midwifery fee allowed by Article 12 of the General Medical Order of the Commissioners, although he may not have received any special order for his attendance.

Ans.—Seeing that Article 18 declares that the medical officer shall, on the exhibition to him of the ticket, and on application made on behalf of the party to whom such ticket was given, be held responsible for affording such advice, attendance, and medicines, as he may be bound to supply, in the same manner as if he had received in each case a special order from the board of guardians, or from any officer, to afford such advice, &c., it appears to the Commissioners that the medical officer so attending, would, if the case be one of childbirth, be entitled to be paid the usual midwifery fee. It must be understood that this answer only applies to the case of a person who is named on the list required to be made out by Article 16 of the order, and who shall be in possession of the ticket required to be given by Article 17, and shall have caused such ticket to be exhibited to the medical officer as provided by Article 18. The Commissioners desire at the same time to point out that the order provides that the medical officer shall be paid the usual midwifery fee, for attendance in childbirth in the case of any woman actually receiving relief (or whom the guardians may decide to have been in a destitute condition) under circumstances of difficulty or danger, without any order.

3. EXTRA FEES UNDER ARTICLE 10.

E. M. ——*Union*—Inquired whether a medical officer is entitled to the fee allowed by the General Medical Order for fracture of the arm, in cases of the fracture of the clavicle and of the acromion scapulæ.

Ans.—The surgical cases mentioned in E. M.'s letter do not come within the terms of the General Medical Order, art. 10, and the medical officer is not entitled to a special fee under that order for the treatment of them.

4. DITTO.

J. J., Medical Officer of —— *Union*—Inquired whether he can charge a fee, under the Medical Order, for his attendance in a case of compound fracture of the metacarpal bones of the hand.

Ans.—The case does not come within the provisions of article 10 of the General Medical Order, and a medical officer is not entitled to an extra fee for his attendance in such a case.

5. DITTO.

Clerk of Union—One of the medical officers has charged two fees in a case of fracture, where, after the fracture had been reduced, and the splints removed, a second fracture of the same limb occurred, through the patient getting out of bed. Inquired whether the two fees should be allowed.

Ans.—The Commissioners think that this can only be considered as one case, under the General Medical Order, and consequently as entitling the medical officer to only one fee for his attendance on the pauper.

6. DITTO.

Clerk of —— *Union*—A pauper named W. A. having sustained a compound fracture of the thigh, was attended by one of the medical officers, who has been paid the fee of £5 allowed by the General Medical Order for attendance in such cases. About two weeks ago, the man, while on his way home from a walk, fell again, and broke his thigh in the same place in which the former fracture occurred. The medical officer now makes a claim for a fee of £3 for a simple fracture of the thigh, which the guardians do not think he is entitled to, as he had not ceased to attend the pauper on account of the first accident at the time the second occurred. Inquired whether the medical officer is entitled to the second fee of £3.

Ans.—The Commissioners are of opinion that the case of W. A. was not complete at the time when the second fracture occurred; and as the second fracture took place in the same place as the first fracture, and as the medical officer was still in attendance on the patient, the Commissioners think that there is no sufficient ground for his claiming a second fee, in addition to the original fee of £5 which was paid him by the guardians.

7. DITTO.

Clerk of —— *Union*—Inquired whether a medical officer is entitled to two fees, of £3 each, for his attendance upon a pauper, in a case of lateral dislocation of the knee joint, and an oblique simple fracture of the tibia and fibula, both injuries being in the same leg.

Ans.—The Commissioners are of opinion that the medical officer is entitled to be paid two fees for his attendance in the case of the pauper alluded to.

8. DITTO.

Clerk of —— *Union*—Two of the medical officers of the —— Union have claimed fees of £1 and £3 respectively, under the General Medical Order; the former for a case of dislocation of the patella, the latter for one of dislocation of the hip-joint. Inquired whether they are entitled to the fees which they respectively claim for the cases above referred to.

Ans.—1. The Commissioners consider a dislocation of the thigh-bone, at the hip-joint, to be a dislocation of the thigh, and that the medical officer is in such a case entitled to a fee of £3 under the General Medical Order.—2. A dislocation of the patella is not within the cases for which fees are prescribed by the order; but the Commissioners are willing to sanction the allowance of some extra remuneration to the medical officer, if the guardians should wish to make him such an allowance.

XI.—OFFICERS.

LIABILITY OF COLLECTOR.

Auditor of —— *Union*—An assistant-overseer of the parish of —— took a £5 note, in payment of poor-rate of a bank which stopped payment in a week after, and while the note was still in his possession. Inquired whether the assistant-overseer is personally liable for the loss, or whether it should be charged to the parish on account of which the money was collected.

Ans.—The Commissioners cannot state any invariable rule to be observed in cases where officers have taken bad money, or notes of banks which have subsequently stopped payment. In some cases the Commissioners think the loss will fall on the officer, in others upon the public; and in determining which of those consequences is applicable to any case, the auditor will find occasion for great vigilance and judgment. The Commissioners will proceed to state their general views upon the subject, but must leave the application of them to the auditor's decision. As a general rule, the officer is to be held responsible for taking good and lawful money in discharge of the claims of the parish. If he takes base coin, it is through a defect of vigilance. If he takes or keeps in his possession private notes, it is at his own option; he is under no obligation or legal necessity to do so. To regard him as exonerated generally from private loss, if he takes base money or private notes of insolvent banks, in payment of the demands of the parish, would, when he acts *bonâ fide*, encourage a most dangerous habit of negligence, and would in other cases enable an unscrupulous officer to cast on the parish losses incurred in his private business. In one parish, where it was the custom to allow regularly a certain sum for bad money taken, the parish officers were known to give to their friends good money for base coin. It will, before any relaxation is allowed of the general responsibility of an officer, therefore, be necessary that the auditor should be thoroughly satisfied that the base coin, or unpaid notes, came into the officer's hands in the *bonâ fide* exercise of his office. But though an officer is generally responsible for taking good money in liquidation of public demands, the Commissioners do not think that his responsibility extends beyond the duty of exercising such a caution as a prudent man would exercise in his own business. The caution of an ordinary person in his own concerns does not satisfy the exigences of a special trust in the case of common bailments or deposits of property, powers of collection and receipt, and the like; and certainly nothing less than such caution as a prudent person would use in his own concerns can exonerate an officer when any injury is incurred by his defaults. But the Commissioners think, that where an officer is shown to have acted *bonâ fide*, and to have neglected no precaution adopted by prudent persons in the protection of their personal interests, he may generally be considered to have done all that his office requires of him, and to be discharged from liability to personal loss or penalty, if injury is suffered, which such caution and good faith would not have prevented. The Commissioners would observe, with reference to the taking of country bankers' notes, that a question will arise between the collector and the payer of the rates; because if the collector has not been guilty of laches, or negligence in presenting the note for payment, he is entitled to recover the amount of the note from the party paying it. Hence, the collector would have no loss to charge to the parish, and as he will only discharge the payer by negligence, it will seem that such negligence must necessarily render him responsible to the parish.

---

2. Powers of Collector.

Clerk of —— Union—Requested the Commissioners' opinion as to whether the power of a paid collector of poor-rates appointed under the 62nd section of the 7th and 8th Vict. c. 101, extended beyond the collection of the rates, and more particularly to the summoning of defaulters in the payment of the rates.

Ans.—The Commissioners apprehend that the collectors appointed under the above section would be empowered to take proceedings against defaulters to the extent of laying the necessary information as to non-payment before the justices: the warrant of distress, however, should be directed to the churchwardens and overseers and the constable. But the Commissioners are not aware that the collector would have any other powers, except such, indeed, as are necessarily incident to the office, viz., the power to make a valid demand of the rate, and the power to give a valid discharge for the payment of the same.

---

3. Medical Officer, also Coroner.

May 20th, 1845.

The Commissioners having been informed that Mr. ——, medical officer of a district in the —— Union was also coroner of a division of the county of ——, informed him that they were in the habit of considering the two offices of coroner and medical officer as incompatible; and that they did not think it desirable that he should continue to hold both.

---

4. Appointment of Overseers.

Clerk of —— Union—A difficulty has arisen in obtaining the contribution of the township of —— to the expenses of the Union for the present quarter, under the following circumstances. The overseers acting for the township last year, returned two gentlemen to the magistrates to be appointed as overseers for the present year in the usual form, and they were accordingly appointed. In the return, they are described as C. S. S., and J. T., householders, but in fact neither of them are householders or residents in the township; Mr. S. being a clergyman of the established church, and vicar of the parish of W. (of which the township forms a part), and Mr. T. agent to the owner of the great tithes of the parish of W., but not even rated to the relief of the poor in the township. These gentlemen will not act, indeed Mr. T. resides a great distance from the township. The words "being substantial householders of the township of" have been erased from the appointment, and, it is believed, since it was signed by the magistrates. A question arises, therefore, what course should be adopted; the case of Rex *v.* Great Marlow, 2 East, 244, decided that the magistrates having made an appointment, were *functus officii,* and could not therefore make another. In that case, however, the appointment was good in the first instance, but one of the parties subsequently obtained an appointment, which exempted him from serving the office of overseer. Requested the Commissioners' opinion, whether the magistrates may, in this case, treat the appointment of Messrs. S. and T. as void, and appoint fresh overseers, on a representation of the facts being made to them by the board of guardians; and, if not, whether the board of guardians should tae anand w at steps in the matter.

Ans.—If the persons named in the warrant are not householders in the township of —— there is no doubt that the justices had no authority to appoint them overseers of the township. (Rex *v.* Morris, 4 T. R. 550.) You state that one of the persons so named is a clergyman of the established church; if so, this of itself would apparently be a ground of exemption. (Anon Gibs Codex, 215, 6 Mod. 140, 1 Bott. 12.) The appointment would appear to be void on the former ground, and, as the Commissioners apprehend, could not be enforced. The fact of their not being householders would be a defence to any proceeding (an indictment for instance) for not taking upon themselves the office. If the persons were householders in the township, and the objection were that they were not "substantial householders," this would be a point for the sessions to determine on appeal. The Commissioners see nothing to prevent the justices now proceeding to make an appointment, which can be done, though the period limited by the statute has expired. (Rex *v.* Sparrow, 2 Sess. Ca. 140, 2 Str. 1123, 1.) The case of Rex *v.* Great Marlow, 2 East 243, is not opposed to this course. There a good appointment of overseers had been made for the parish of Marlow; and the court held, that other magistrates had no jurisdiction to make another appointment. That obstacle does not exist in the present case, as it must be taken that no appointment of overseers has yet been made.

5. POWERS OF OVERSEERS.

July 29th, 1845.

Guardian of ——— *Union*—Inquired whether the auditor was empowered to allow any charge for law expenses incurred in any legal proceedings, either relative to appeals in settlement cases, or otherwise, without such proceedings having received not only the sanction of a vestry, but that of the board of guardians also.

Ans.—Notwithstanding the general powers as to the administration of relief conferred upon the guardians of unions by the Poor Law Amendment Act, there are certain powers and duties relating to the execution of the Poor Laws, which still belong to the overseers of the several parishes, independently of the guardians. Such, for example, are the assessment of the poor-rates, and the removal of paupers to the parishes of their settlement. In incurring any legal expenses in matters of this kind, the overseers are under no obligation to consult the guardians, and the guardians have no power to control the overseers.

6. OVERSEERS, WHETHER ACCOUNTABLE FOR THE WHOLE AMOUNT OF THE RATES ALLOWED BY JUSTICES.

Auditor of——*Union*—Inquired whether he is, as auditor, bound to insist on the overseers charging themselves with the whole amount of each poor-rate allowed by the justices, or only with so much thereof as they may have actually collected.

Ans.—Where the overseers of any given year do not collect the whole of the rates allowed during such year, the arrears remaining due on such rates may, and should, be collected by the succeeding overseers. (See 17 Geo. 2, c. 38, s. 11.) It appears to the Commissioners, therefore, that the overseers for the year in which such arrears originate are not responsible to their successors for such arrears as for a money balance; in other words, they are not bound to pay over to their successors, in cash, the amount of such arrears, which it is open to their successors to gather in from the parties assessed. This being, as the Commissioners conceive, the state of the law with regard to the liabilities of the overseers in this matter, the precise mode of entering the facts in any particular case in the overseers' accounts is a point of practice which the Commissioners leave to the auditor's discretion. If the overseers enter in their "receipt and payment book" only so much on the one side as they actually receive, and on the other side as they actually disburse, the balance will, of course, exhibit the exact sum of money actually due from them to their successors; and if the "rate book" is at the same time treated as a separate account, the difference between the "total amount to be collected" and the aggregate of the two columns, "amount actually collected," and "amount not recoverable, or legally excused," will of course be the sum of the arrears to be collected by such successors. If, on the other hand, the whole amount of the rate is entered to the debit of the overseers in their "receipt and payment book," credit must likewise be given them in that book for the "amount not recoverable, or legally excused;" and the balance appearing on the face of the account should of course be subdivided, according to the proportions of money and arrears of which it may really consist. The Commissioners, however, think it right to add, that they quite concur in the auditor's remark, that the poor-rates ought to be collected, if possible, by the overseers for the year in which the rates are made.

XII.—PAUPER.

PROPERTY OF DECEASED PAUPER.

March 7th, 1845.

Clerk of —— *Union*—A pauper who died lately had been in receipt of regular relief for upwards of seven years, amounting to about £40. On his death it was found that he had secreted a sum of £44. 3*s.* 2½*d.* He owed £8. 10*s.* for rent, and his funeral and other expenses amounted to about £5. Inquired whether the parish officers, after paying the funeral expences and arrears of rent, may retain the balance of the £44. 3*s.* 2½*d.* towards the repayment of the relief given to the deceased.

Ans.—If the relief afforded to J. W., was given to him expressly by way of loan, the guardians of —— Union may repay themselves out of his effects, the relief so given; but if the relief was not granted upon loan, the Commissioners do not see that the guardians have any legal claim to such repayment, except so far as regards the funeral expenses, which the guardians may, like any other person, repay themselves out of the effects of the deceased, although such expenses were not advanced as a loan.

XIII.—POOR ALLOTMENTS.

RECOVERY OF RENTS.

Clerk to the Magistrates of ——.—Under the provisions of the Act of 1 and 2 Will. 4, c. 42, s. 2, certain waste and common lands in the parish of A——, containing about twenty acres, were, in the year 1832, inclosed by the churchwardens and overseers of that parish, with the consent of the lord of the manor, and the major part in value of the persons having right of common thereupon, signified by writing under their hands and seals, in accordance with the provisions of the above section. The churchwardens and overseers have for several years past, let portions of the inclosed lands, in quantities varying from thirty to fifty rods, to the poor and industrious inhabitants of the parish, at fair and moderate rents, viz., at the rate of about 32*s*. per acre, the land being of good quality. Arrears of rent being now due from some of the tenants, the churchwardens and overseers have demanded payment, which has been refused, and application to the justices to enforce payment has become necessary. Inquired whether the churchwardens and overseers alone can make application to the justices, under the 11th section of the 2nd Will. 4, c. 42, for the recovery of the arrears of rent, the lands having been inclosed and let prior to the passing of the 5 and 6 Will. 4, c. 69, or whether the powers and provisions of the 2 Will. 4, c. 42, (so far as the same extend to the recovery of the said rents or otherwise,) are by virtue of the 4th sec. of 5 and 6 Will. 4, c. 69, subjected to the rules, orders, and regulations of the Poor Law Commissioners, and can only be exercised by the board of guardians of the Union in which the said parish of A—— is comprised, and not by the churchwardens and overseers of that parish. And if the latter, what steps should be taken for the recovery of the arrears of rent in question.

Ans.—The Commissioners feel some difficulty in determining the exact effect of the 5 and 6 Will. 4, c. 69, sec. 6, upon the statutes 59 Geo. 3, c. 12, and 1 and 2 Will. 4, c. 42, and c. 59, and the 2 and 3 Will. 4, c. 42. But they think that the former statute only gives to the guardians the power of making the same inclosures, or obtaining the same allotments, as the parish officers could previously have done, and consequently that the guardians have nothing to do with allotments which have been taken and let by the parish officers, and the vestry, previous to the passing of the 5 and 6 Will. 4, c. 69. It appears that in the present case, the lands were taken under the 1 and 2 Will. 4, c. 42, and consequently they are brought under the operation of the 2 and 3 Will. 4, c. 42, by sec. 9. According to this latter Act, the rent of the land, when received, is to be applied in the purchase of fuel to be distributed among the poor parishioners. And if this be the correct construction of the Act, the rent of the land in question is not to be brought into the general accounts of the parish, nor mixed up with the general poor-rate. However this may be, the Commissioners see no reason to doubt the power of the churchwardens and overseers to recover the arrears of rent by the summary process referred to.

XIV.—POOR RATES.

1. RECOVERY OF WHEN QUASHED.

Clerk of —— *Union*—The churchwardens and overseers of the parish of ——, made a rate for the relief of the poor in August last, which was duly signed, allowed, and published. The vicar of the parish, at the last quarter sessions for the county, appealed against the assessment on his tithe, and succeeded in quashing the rate. Subsequently, the overseers summoned a defaulter in payment of the same rate, before a bench of magistrates, who, upon hearing evidence that the rate was quashed, refused to enforce the amount claimed against this person. Inquired, 1st, Whether the justices were right in refusing to enforce payment of the rate in question. 2dly, In what manner the parish officers are to obtain funds for the purposes of the parish, during the period occupied in making a new valuation. 3dly, Whether the parish officers can make another rate, and enforce the same, on the valuation upon which the quashed rate was founded.

Ans.—The 1st section of the 41 Geo. 3, c. 23, expressly provides, that the court of quarter sessions, if they deem it necessary, may quash a poor-rate which has been appealed against, "but nevertheless, all and every sum, &c., by such rate or assessment charged on any person or persons, shall and may be levied and recovered by such ways and means, &c., as if no appeal had been made against such rate." It further provides, that the sums so recovered shall be treated as payments on account of the next effective rate or rates. The 3rd section, however, empowers the court of quarter sessions, where a rate is quashed, "to order any sum, &c., by such rate or assessment charged on any person, &c. not to be paid;" in which case, no proceedings shall be commenced or continued for the recovery thereof. Unless such an order has been made by the court of quarter sessions, the Commissioners do not see why the justices should have refused to enforce payment of the poor-rate referred to in your letter, as having been quashed upon appeal. With regard to any future rates, the Commissioners desire to point out that it is the duty of the overseers to provide the necessary funds for the relief of the poor, and for this purpose to make the requisite rates to the best of their ability; which rates, if appealed against, may nevertheless be levied in accordance with the statute above alluded to, 41 Geo. 3, c. 23.

2. COST OF MAKING COPIES OF ENTRIES OF BAPTISMS, &C. NOT PAYABLE OUT OF THE POOR RATES.

April 2nd, 1845.

Auditor of ——— *Union*—Inquired whether he will be justified in allowing, in the accounts of the parish officers of ———, a payment of six guineas made to the rector for furnishing manuscripts of the baptisms and burials for three years to the bishop's registry.

Ans.—The 52nd Geo. 3, c. 146, sec. 6, requires that, at the expiration of two months after every year, copies of all the entries of baptisms, marriages, and burials, in the year preceding, are to be made by the officiating minister, or church or chapel-warden's clerk, or other person under his direction, on parchment, to be provided by the parishes; and when so made and properly verified and attested, to be transmitted by the church or chapel-wardens to the registrars of the diocese. The Commissioners presume that the charge of six guineas in the present case was for making copies of the church registers pursuant to the statute cited. The statute, it will be seen, throws the charge of providing the parchments on which the copies are to be made on the parish concerned. But it does not go on to specify "any fund" from which the payment is to be made. The question, therefore, arises whether the poor-rate can be lawfully resorted to for the purpose, and the Commissioners are of opinion that it cannot, and for these reasons. The object is one wholly unconnected with the relief of the poor or the administration of the Poor Laws. The persons charged with the duty of making the copies are ecclesiastical officers. It is true that churchwardens (who are mentioned in the 6th sec.) are, by virtue of their office, overseers of the poor; but it is clear, both from the nature of the duty itself, as well as from the terms of the statute, that it is in their character of ecclesiastical officers that the duty is cast upon the churchwardens. It is possible therefore that they might be justified in making the payment out of any church-rate raised in the parish. On this, however, the Commissioners are not called upon to give an opinion, and they can only say they consider the poor-rate is not liable.

XV.—RATING.

July, 1845.

———Inquired—1. Whether machinery, such as is usual in paper mills, roperies, and manufactories (other than the moving power) is rateable. 2. Whether the justices in petty sessions have power to amend a rate, by increasing or decreasing the rates of parties who have had no notice on an appeal for inequality by other parties, or whether the rate must be entirely quashed. 3. Whether the overseers are bound to assess all the small tenements in the parish, although occupied by poor persons, and if they are omitted in the rate whether that circumstance will be a good ground of appeal to the quarter sessions, it being presumed that, by the proviso to the 6th sec. of the Parochial Assessment Act, the petty sessions could not be appealed to on such an objection.

Ans.—1. It is clear, from all the decisions which have been given by the courts on the subject, that, where machinery is fixed to real property and occupied with it, such property is rateable to the poor-rate at its increased value, arising from the combination of such machinery with it. Those decisions do not distinctly point out the limits of this principle in its practical application; but the Commissioners believe it to be the general practice, to include in the assessment only so much of the machinery as constitutes the "moving power." 2. The question, whether the justices in special session, under the 6th sec. of the Parochial Assessments Act, have power to amend a poor-rate as to parties other than the appellant, where no notice has been given to such other parties, is a question of considerable difficulty, and one on which the Commissioners are not prepared to express any positive opinion. The 6th sec. itself empowers the justices to hear and determine *all* objections to the rate, "on the ground of inequality, unfairness, or incorrectness, in the valuation of *any* hereditaments included therein," provided only that notice be previously given by the appellant "to the collector, overseers, or other persons by whom such rate was made." So far, therefore, as the 6th sec. is concerned, notice to parties assessed does not appear to be required; but as the 7th sec. gives the justices in special session all the power of *amending* a rate, which any court of quarter sessions has upon appeals, it may be contended that such powers of amendment can only be exercised in the one case under the same conditions as in the other, and that, consequently, the justices in special session cannot amend the rate as to parties other than the appellant, unless notice has been given to such other parties, according to the provisions of the 41 Geo. 3, c. 23, sec. 6. 3. The overseers are bound to include in every poor-rate all the properties in the parish which are legally liable to be assessed; and the omission of any such properties from the rate, would certainly be a good ground of appeal against it, to the quarter session, though not to the justices in special session under the Parochial Assessments Act. With regard to the rating of small tenements, however, the Commissioners direct your attention to the 59 Geo. 3, c. 12, sec. 19.

XVI.—REGISTRATION.

May 5th, 1845.

Clerk of the Westbury-upon-Severn Union.—In June, 1838, the registrar-general by his order directed that a certain part of the Forest of Dean should be, for the purposes of registration, part of the Newnham registrar's district in the Westbury-upon-Severn Union. In 1842, the Forest of Dean was, by an Act 5 and 6 Vict. c. 48, parochialised and divided into two townships, namely, East Dean and West Dean; the former township was added to the Westbury-upon-Severn Union, and the latter to the Monmouth Union. The Newnham registrar's district includes some parts both of East Dean and of West Dean, and the expenses attendant upon the registration in the district, cannot therefore be levied upon such district, but they have been defrayed out of the general funds of the Westbury-upon-Severn Union, and consequently, the proportion which East Dean pays towards its own registration expenses is very small. Suggested that the registrar-general should revise the order of June, 1838, and direct that for the future the township of East Dean shall form a district of itself, and, like a parish, pay the total expenses of its own registration; and also that West Dean should be formed into a district of itself in a similar manner.

Ans.—The general intention of the Registration Act is clearly this, that each parish shall bear its own burden in respect of registration; and this is so consonant with legal principles, that any construction which would defeat this end, would not, except where it was absolutely inevitable, be admitted. The inconvenience and inequality involved in the subsisting arrangement respecting the township of East Dean as described in your communication, appear therefore to afford a reason for supposing that it could not be the intention of the Act of Parliament to sanction it, where the more equitable and convenient arrangement under the general provisions of the Registration Acts, applicable to parochial divisions, was capable of being applied. It is clear that the power under the Act 1 Vict. c. 22, s. 9, can only be used originally in places not included in districts under boards of guardians; and the purview of the provision appears merely to be, to make arrangements applicable to places not under boards of guardians, and to have no object applicable to a place under a board of guardians. It seems therefore to the Commissioners that when East Dean became a township and was included in a Union, it acquired all the rights and obligations of a township in a Union, and that the provision specifically applicable to it as a non parochial place out of the control of a board of guardians, ceased to have effect, and that the provisions applicable to it as a township in a Union became *ipso facto* in force then. Consequently, that the registrar-general's order of June, 1838, ceased then to be in operation there. This being so, the revocation of that order is not necessary. Adverting to the suggestion respecting West Dean, the Commissioners wish to add that the cases of East and West Dean appear to be identical in principle, and therefore the above remarks would seem to apply equally to both cases.

XVII.—SETTLEMENT.

BY HIRING AND SERVICE.

Feb. 8th, 1845.

The Rev. ——. —The widow of a man who belonged to a distant parish came to the parish of —— about thirty years ago, where she continued for many years in the service of a farmer as his housekeeper, and received as wages four guineas per annum. She now applies for relief. Inquired therefore whether she gained a settlement in that parish by hiring and service; or, whether she is settled in her late husband's parish.

Ans.—The mere circumstance of the woman referred to being a widow, would not prevent her from acquiring a settlement by hiring and service. The words of the statute 3 Will. and Mary, c. 11, s. 7, are, "If any unmarried person, not having a child or children," &c. These words would certainly apply to a widow; and in the case of R. *v.* Hensingham, (Cald. 206) a widow was held to be within the statute. The Commissioners presume from your statement that a contract of hiring took place, and that there was a year's service under it prior to the 14th August, 1834, (see Poor Law Amendment Act, se. 64, 65.)

XVIII.—VACCINATION.

March 7th, 1845.

Clerk of —— *Union*—Inquired whether the guardians would be justified in withholding relief from all paupers having children who have not been vaccinated, as a means of compelling them to have their children vaccinated.

Ans.—The guardians would not be justified in withholding relief from paupers on this ground, inasmuch as to constitute a valid claim for relief and an obligation on the authorities to grant all necessary relief, it is only required that the party applying be destitute and resident within the Union, or casually destitute therein. The Commissioners think that as so few persons have been vaccinated in the Union during the past year, as compared with the number of births, it would be advisable for the guardians to direct the vaccinators, as opportunities may offer to them, to visit the houses of the humbler classes, where they know there are unvaccinated children, and endeavour to obtain the consent of the parents of such children to their being vaccinated.

XIX.—VAGRANT ACT.

Refusal of Man to maintain his Family.

Clerk of —— *Union*—In November, J. O. was convicted as an idle and disorderly person, under the Vagrant Act, for refusing to maintain his wife and family, then and now in the workhouse; the conviction, however, being quashed on appeal. The wife and family were admitted into the workhouse in consequence of J. O. having been committed to prison on a charge of stealing corn from his master, of which charge he was subsequently acquitted. During this time his master, who was also his landlord, distrained upon his goods for rent. J. O. is in work at twelve shillings per week, and has a house, but it is believed little or no furniture. He refuses either to take his family out of the workhouse, or to provide for them in any way. Inquired whether the guardians should at once discharge the wife and children from the workhouse; or whether they should direct the overseer of the parish to which the paupers are chargeable to take them from the workhouse, and convey them in a cart to J. O.'s residence; or whether they should proceed against J. O. for refusing to maintain his family.

Ans.—Assuming the circumstances of the case to remain unaltered, it appears to the Comissioners that the guardians would be justified in discharging J.O.'s wife and family from the workhouse, as it appears that J. O. is in receipt of sufficient wages to enable him to maintain them, and is also provided with a habitation. If this course is taken, it would be advisable that the family should be conveyed (if the distance requires it) and delivered to J. O. If he still refuse, or neglect, to discharge his legal obligation with respect to his family, and in consequence of such refusal it should be necessary to re-admit the family, the case should then be dealt with under the Vagrant Act, sec. 3. It would perhaps be sufficient to sustain a conviction, under that Act, if the guardians caused a notice to be given to J. O. that his wife and family were chargeable, and required him to contribute to their support, and he should then make a default in doing so, and should also neglect or refuse to remove his family from the workhouse. But the former course will avoid any question which might possibly be raised under the 3rd section, as to whether the chargeability arose from the refusal to maintain.

XX. WORKHOUSE CHAPEL, Licensing.

Jan. 16th, 1845.

Clerk of the Isle of Thanet Union—Inquired whether it was customary for chapels belonging to Union workhouses to be licensed by the diocesan.

Ans.—It is not usual for workhouse chapels to be licensed by the diocesan; and if no other persons than the paupers and inmates of the workhouse be admitted, the Commissioners apprehend that it is not necessary that a workhouse chapel should be registered and certified according to the provisions of the 52 Geo. 3, c. 155, s. 2.

LONDON:
Printed by order of the Poor Law Commissioners, by Blackburn and Pardon, 6, Hatton Garden, and Published by Charles Knight and Co., 22, Ludgate Street, Publishers to the Poor Law Commissioners.

AN

OFFICIAL CIRCULAR

OF PUBLIC DOCUMENTS AND INFORMATION:

DIRECTED BY THE POOR LAW COMMISSIONERS TO BE PRINTED CHIEFLY FOR THE USE OF THE MEMBERS AND PERMANENT OFFICERS OF BOARDS OF GUARDIANS, UNDER THE POOR LAW AMENDMENT ACT.

No. 50. CIRCULAR ISSUED AUGUST 1ST, 1845.

THE Poor Law Commissioners directed that the following documents be printed and circulated for the information of Guardians and Officers of the several Unions, viz.

(Signed) By Order of the Board,
EDWIN CHADWICK, *Secretary*.

I.—BASTARDY—ORDERS IN.

March 27th, 1845.

Clerk of ——— *Union*—Inquired whether the guardians will be justified in paying the clerk to the justices of the sessions the sum of 2*s*. 6*d*. for each duplicate order in bastardy delivered to the board in pursuance of the

7th and 8th Vic. c. 101, sec. 5; and if they are bound to make the payment, to what fund the same is to be charged.

Ans.—The statute adverted to simply imposes upon the clerk to the justices the duty of sending the duplicate order to the guardians, but makes no provision for remunerating him for the service. It is not information furnished to the guardians on their request, or in reference to any application in which they are parties concerned. The Commissioners apprehend, therefore, that the justices' clerk has no claim in law upon the guardians for the fee in question.

II.—BURIAL—OF PAUPERS.

Clerks of Wareham and Purbeck Union—Inquired to which parish the funeral expenses of a pauper should be charged, in a case where such pauper has been residing and has also died in one parish, but has been relieved at the cost of another parish, within the same Union. And whether the board of guardians have the power, under sections 31 and 56 of the 7 and 8 Vic. c. 101, of charging the funeral expenses of a pauper who has died in the workhouse, either to the parish in which such workhouse is situate, or to the parish to which he was chargeable.

Ans.—The alternative words in the 31st section of 7 and 8 Vic. c. 101,—"charge the expense thereof (*i. e.*, of burial) to any parish under their control to which such person may have been chargeable, or in which he may have died, or otherwise in which such body may be,"—do not, in the opinion of the Commissioners, give the guardians the discretion of charging the expenses to whichever of the three parishes they may think fit. These words are to be taken *reddendo singula singulis*, and as applicable singly to each of the several cases which are distinguished. The Commissioners, therefore, conclude that when a person has been chargeable to a parish, the cost of his interment should be charged to that parish, in two cases—1st, whenever the person may have died within the Union; 2nd, whenever his body may, after his decease, be brought within the Union. Where the deceased person was *not chargeable* in his lifetime, the cost of the burial should be charged to the parish within the Union in which he may have died, if such parish be known. But if such parish be not known, and the body may nevertheless be found within the Union, or where, though it may be known that the death did not occur within the Union, the body may, nevertheless, be brought within it, (as sometimes occurs in the cases of persons found drowned or accidentally killed,) the body should be buried at the charge of the parish where such body may be; that being *ex necessitate* the only parish having any concern in the burial. The Commissioners would add, that though the guardians are clearly authorised, by section 31, in the case of a person dying in the Union workhouse but chargeable to a different parish, to direct (in the absence of any wish expressed by the deceased person in his lifetime or by his relations) that the body shall be buried, either in the parish in which the death actually occurred, or in the parish of the chargeability, (in which, by operation of section 56, it may be considered as having constructively occurred,) the guardians have not, in the opinion of the Commissioners, the power in such case to charge the former parish with the cost of the burial.

III.—COUNTY-RATE.

ASSESSED UPON TOWNSHIPS SEPARATED FROM ONE, AND ADDED TO ANOTHER, COUNTY.

Clerk of Bromsgrove Union—At the general quarter sessions of the peace, held for the county of Salop, on the 14th of October, 1844, a county-rate of three-farthings in the pound was made upon all parishes and places within the county, comprising the townships of Hunnington and Rowsley, within this Union. These townships, which at that time were detached parts of the county of Salop, though locally situate within the county of Worcester, were, on the 21st of October, declared to form part of the latter county, under the 7 and 8 Vic. c. 61. The warrants or precepts to collect this rate were not issued until the 12th of November. The precept to the guardians of this Union, requiring them to pay the amount assessed upon the two townships above named, to the treasurer of the county of Salop, before the 30th of December following, was not received by the clerk to the guardians until the 16th of November. Inquired whether the guardians can, under the circumstances, legally pay the amount thus demanded of them.

Ans.—The question raised in your letter is not clear of legal difficulty, although the course for the guardians to adopt is plain. The Commissioners, however, will state their views of the whole of the difficulty, in order that the guardians may communicate to the officers of the townships of Hunnington and Rowsley suggestions of the course which those officers should pursue. When the rate was made in quarter sessions, on the 14th October, the townships of Hunnington and Rowsley being within the county of Salop and the jurisdiction of the justices of the county for the purpose of making county-rates, it appears that there was at least an inchoate, if not a perfect, right in the county to enforce the rate in those townships. The obligation, however, on those townships to pay was not complete while the precepts remained unissued. Consequently, their obligation to pay was not completed while they remained within the jurisdiction of the justices of Salop. Under these circumstances, the power of the justices of Salop to enforce payment by their warrant, appears to have ceased when the townships were included in the county of Worcester. This remedy failing, it is questionable whether the Court of Queen's Bench would issue a mandamus to the township officers to pay; inasmuch as the right of the county of Salop, even if sustainable in strict law, could not be enforced without a hardship on those townships; for it is to be presumed that the county of Salop had already in hand funds sufficient for the purposes of the county up to the time when, by the justices' precept, payment was required, viz., till the 30th of December. If this be so, the townships of Hunnington and Rowsley would have already paid, by anticipation, to the county of Salop their fair shares of contribution for several months subsequent to their severance from that county. As the enforcement of the strict right of the county would not, under these circumstances, be equitable, it may be anticipated that the Court of Queen's Bench would not issue its writ of mandamus for that purpose. It therefore appears to the Commissioners, that the guardians should use their legal option, so as to leave to the townships the opportunity to raise the question, if the justices of Salop should think it right to urge their claim. The guardians can do this by refusing to pay the sums assessed by those justices on the townships of Hunnington and Rowsley. The justices can then claim, if they think proper, those sums of the officers of those townships; and the whole question may thus be raised for the decision of the proper tribunal.

IV.—DESERTERS OF FAMILIES.

1. CONSTRUCTION OF SEC. 59 OF 7 AND 8 VIC. c. 101.

June 30th, 1845.

Clerk of Oakham Union—The overseers of B— having been directed by the guardians, in the month of March last, to take the necessary proceedings to apprehend a pauper belonging to that parish, for neglecting to maintain his wife and family and leaving them chargeable to their parish, a reward of £1 was offered for his apprehension, which was effected. This sum, and £2. 6*s*. the constable's expenses attendant upon the apprehension and committal of the pauper, were allowed by the parishioners in assembled vestry, and charged in the overseers' accounts; but the auditor has disallowed the payments on the ground that, under the 59th section of 7 and 8 Vic. cap. 101, they could only be made by the guardians out of the funds in their hands, *and that they should be charged to the establishment*. The guardians think the auditor is right as to the payment being made by them, but they consider that the section adverted to renders it necessary to have the Commissioners' approval, as to whether the expenses shall be charged to the common funds of the Union, or to the parish concerned. Requested the Commissioners' opinion upon the matter, for the guidance of the guardians in this and similar cases.

Ans.—The Commissioners concur in the view expressed by the auditor, that the expenses of prosecuting persons charged with offences under the Vagrant Act, when the proceedings are instituted under the direction of the guardians, should be paid by the guardians, and charged by them in the mode which the 59th section of 7 and 8 Vic. c. 101, contemplates. Where a constable is employed in any case of this kind to apprehend an offender, the Commissioners do not mean to say that, in default of payment by the guardians of his (the constable's) costs, he might not include them in his accounts against the parish for which he acts, pursuant to 18th Geo. 3, c. 19, s. 4, (see Reg. *v.* Churchwardens of Chelmsford, 3 Gale and Dav. 357.) The Commissioners would add, that the guardians are correct in their impression that the 59th section renders it necessary that the Commissioners should first approve of the mode of charging the expenses incurred in any particular case, to render the charge by the guardians a valid one. With respect to the principle which should regulate the charging of the expenses of prosecuting persons who neglect to maintain their families, and suffer them to become chargeable, (whether to the common fund, or to any particular parish,) the Commissioners desire to observe, that the proceeding in this case is partly of a penal, and partly of a remedial nature; for, in the conviction and punishment of the offender, one of the objects (if not the chief) sought to be effected, is the discharge or performance for the future, of the person's legal obligations towards his family, and as a consequence, the relief of the parish from the charge of maintaining the family. This ground will, therefore, generally justify the charging the costs to the parish immediately interested in the conviction of the offender. But there may, nevertheless, in some cases, exist strong reasons for making the costs of the apprehension and conviction an establishment, or common, charge; and it will be seen, that such a mode of charging the costs is contemplated by the 59th section.

---

2. LIABILITY OF WIFE OF MARINE TO BE PROSECUTED FOR DESERTING HER FAMILY.

Clerk of Honiton Union— Inquired whether the guardians can take proceeding against S. P. the wife of a marine, for having deserted her children, who are now chargeable to the parish. The husband, when last heard of, was either on board ship off Ireland or in that country.

Ans.—It does not appear from your letter to be distinctly known where the husband of S. P. is *at the present time;* and unless it can be shown that he is "beyond the seas," the case does not seem to be one to which the 25th section of the 7 and 8 Vic. c. 101 would apply. If, however, he is *now* in Ireland, or on board ship off its coasts, the Commissioners believe that, according to the legal meaning of the phrase, he is "beyond the seas," and that his wife is liable accordingly under the above-mentioned section.

V.—GUARDIANS.

EX-OFFICIO — POWER OF TO HEAR APPLICATIONS FROM PARISHES IN THEIR OWN UNION.

Clerk of Romney Marsh Union—Inquired—1st, whether justices of the peace for the town of Lydd, who are also guardians of the Romney Marsh Union, can hear an application for, and make an order of affiliation on the putative father of the bastard child of a woman residing in the parish of Lydd. 2nd. Whether a justice of the peace for the town of Lydd, who is a paid officer of the Romney Marsh Union, can join in hearing a like application, and make a like order. 3rd. Whether two justices of the peace for the town of Lydd, being rated inhabitants of the parish of Lydd, can, within the liberty of such town, take the examination of a person chargeable to that parish, as to his settlement, and make a valid order of removal.

Ans. — In reply to your first inquiry, the Commissioners desire to point out that the obtaining of orders in bastardy, under the 7 and 8 Vic. c. 101, is not a matter in which the guardians of Romney Marsh Union are interested as such guardians; the remedy against the putative father, provided by that statute, being a personal remedy, in favour of the mother—not of the parish or union. The Commissioners, therefore, do not see that an ex-officio guardian of the union would have, in that character, any such interest in the matter, as would prevent his acting as a justice of the peace, in making an order on a putative father under the above-named statute. In reply to your second inquiry, the Commissioners would state that they do not perceive anything in the 7th section of the 7 and 8 Vic. c. 101, to prevent a paid officer of Romney Marsh Union from acting as a justice of the peace, in making orders in bastardy, under the provisions of that statute, in cases occurring in that union. You will observe that the prohibitions in that section apply only to the receiving of money under the order, the conducting of applications for making or enforcing the order, and the interfering to cause the application, or to procure evidence in support of it. The prohibitions do not extend to receiving the application, or hearing evidence, or making the order. And the Commissioners do not see that a paid officer of a union has any such interest, as such officer, in the obtaining of the order, as would prevent his acting as a justice of the peace in making it. With reference to your third question, the Commissioners direct your attention to the 16 Geo. 2, c. 18, which enables any justice of the peace to act in matters connected with the relief, maintenance, and settlement of the poor, &c., notwithstanding he may be a rate-payer in the parish concerned in such acts.

VI.—JUSTICES.

POWER OF JUSTICES OF COUNTY OF A TOWN TO HOLD SPECIAL SESSIONS.

Feb. 15th, 1845.

Clerk to the Justices of ——,—The town of A. is a county of itself, independently of the county of B., in which it is locally situated. It has its court of assize and court of quarter sessions, (in which magistrates preside under Her Majesty's Commission,) and its own lord lieutenant and custos rotulorum. In fact, it has all the privileges of a county at large. The magistrates hold petty sessions for the whole of the county of the town, but they hold no divisional petty sessions. They have hitherto held special petty sessions, under the 6 and 7 Will. 4, c. 96, s. 6, to hear and determine appeals against poor-rates; but looking at pages 84, 86, and 288, of the Commissioners' Report on Local Taxation, doubts have arisen, as to the power of the magistrates of the county of the town of A. to hold such special sessions. Inquired whether the view taken by the Commissioners in the above-mentioned report, has been strengthened by any decision of the courts of common law; and whether the Commissioners now see any reason to adopt a different view to that expressed in that report, so far as such view would affect the county of the town of A.

Ans.—The Commissioners were, in the first instance, inclined to the opinion that, wherever petty sessions were, in fact, held, the place for which they were so held was, whether it was the whole district of the jurisdiction of the justices, or a part of such district, a petty sessions division within the meaning of the Parochial Assessments Act. But it was, without any decision being had, or any case being laid, so far as the Commissioners know, before counsel, understood to be the opinion of the profession, and generally the opinion of the magistrates concerned in the question, that the Act only applied where there was a territorial division for the purpose of holding petty and special sessions. This opinion was so far admitted by the mover of the Parochial Assessments Act, and by the House of Commons, that Mr. Poulett Scrope obtained permission to bring in a bill to extend the provisions of the Act to places not divided, and he brought in his bill accordingly, which however was never passed. There can be no doubt that the short and literal construction of the Act accords with the conclusion stated in the Report on Local Taxation, and the Commissioners still remain of the opinion there stated, on the same grounds; but without any decided conviction that that opinion is correct.

VII.—MEDICAL ORDER.

1. DEFINITION OF TERM "COMPOUND FRACTURE."

Clerk of Bridgewater Union—A medical officer having been directed to attend an infirm pauper, aged seventy nine, who had met with an accident, found, upon examination, that she had broken both bones of the leg about the centre, that the large one had torn and penetrated the surrounding flesh, and that both bones were freely communicating with the external air. He succeeded in setting the fracture, but great constitutional irritation soon came on, increased by her infirm and weak condition, and, in spite of every attention, she died at the end of ten days. Inquired whether the case was one of "compound fracture," as the woman had a sore on her leg previous to the accident, through which the bone protruded, and not through the *skin.*

Ans.—The Commissioners having communicated with an eminent surgeon on the subject received from him the following opinion:—"A fracture is called 'compound' when the end or ends of the bone or bones have penetrated the soft parts, so as to come in contact with the external air, which alters the whole of the processes set up by nature for the cure of a simple fracture; giving rise, at the same time, to such degree of constitutional irritation as usually leads to the death of old people. The case is rather worse, than better, if the sufferer should have no skin, inasmuch as a tear in the skin can sometimes be induced to unite, although rarely, and the case be thus reduced to that of a simple fracture, which I do not apprehend would be the case if muscular and tendinous parts were torn and exposed by the bone without such usual covering."

The Commissioners therefore think that the case referred to must be considered as one of "compound fracture."

2. DITTO—FEES UNDER ARTICLE 10.

Clerk of Williton Union—One of the medical officers has sent in a claim of £2 to the guardians, under Article 10, No. 7, of the General Medical Order, in the following form; namely, "Reduction and cure of a fracture of the arm in the case of W. V., £1; reducing a dislocation of the radius, a bone of the arm, and case of severe injury of the elbow joint, for the same man, £1." The guardians are doubtful whether it was the intention of the medical order to allow more than £1 for one and the same accident, although there may be a dislocation of a joint and fracture of a bone of the same arm, arising from such accident. The medical officer contends that, as there is a *fracture* of one bone of the arm, and a dislocation at the elbow joint of the other bone, the cases are distinct, and that he is entitled to the fee of £1 for each case. Requested the Commissioners' opinion on the subject.

Ans.—The Commissioners are of opinion that the fracture and the dislocation, in the case described, are two distinct injuries; for each of which the medical officer is entitled to be paid the fees prescribed by Article 10 of the General Medical Order; namely, £1 in each case. The case is different from a fracture of the same bone in two places.

VIII.—OVERSEER.

SUPPLYING HORSES FOR PAUPER FUNERALS.

May 2nd, 1845.

Mr. —— stated that he had, for several years past, been engaged to supply the board of guardians of the —— Union with horses to convey the deceased paupers to their several parishes for burial; and inquired, (as he is now appointed an overseer of the poor,) whether he can continue to do so, without subjecting himself to penalties.

Ans.—The Commissioners are disposed to consider that such an agreement as you describe, would not be a supply of "goods, materials, or provisions, for the use of any workhouse, or otherwise for the support and maintenance of the poor;" nor a supply of "goods, materials, or provisions, ordered to be given in parochial relief, or for, or in respect of the money ordered to be given in parochial relief;" and that, consequently, your continuing to supply the horses in the cases you refer to, would not subject you to penalties, either under the 55 Geo. 3, cap. 137, sec. 6, or under the Poor Law Amendment Act, sec. 77, notwithstanding your appointment as overseer. The Commissioners, however, consider it doubtful, whether your continuing to do so would not expose you to the penalty mentioned in the proviso to the 31st section of the 7 and 8 Vic. c. 101. That proviso is as follows:—"Provided always, that it shall not be lawful for any officer connected with the relief of the poor to receive any money for the burial of the body of any poor person which may be within the parish, &c., in which the death may have occurred, or to act as undertaker for personal gain or reward in the burial of any such body, or to receive any money from any dissecting school, &c., to whom any such body may be delivered, *or to derive any personal emolument whatever for, or in respect of, the burial or disposal of any such body.*" The Commissioners apprehend that receiving payment for conveying the body to the burial place, is deriving emolument in respect of the burial.

IX.—PAUPERS.

EMPLOYMENT OF WHILE UNDER ORDERS OF REMOVAL.

Clerk of Reading Union—Inquired whether the guardians have power to direct the pauper inmates of the workhouse, who are under orders of removal to their places of settlement, to be set to work.

Ans.—The Commissioners are of opinion, that as long as persons are maintained in the workhouse, they are subject to the rules and discipline of the establishment, and are bound to perform any work or labour required of them suitable to their strength and capacity. This obligation on the part of paupers, to conform, and the power of the guardians to require them to work, appear to the Commissioners to be in no way affected by the consideration that such paupers are under orders of removal, and that the cost of their maintenance in the house may be ultimately repaid by the parishes of the settlement. If the parish primarily charged with the relief of the pauper were credited with the profit derived from the labour of such pauper, (assuming that a profit were made,) instead of the common fund, this might possibly be considered as giving the parish of the settlement a claim to have the cost of relief and maintenance diminished to the extent of the profit realised. But this (assuming the claim to be well founded) would be a question entirely between the removing parish and the parish of the settlement, and could not in any way affect the power of the guardians to set such persons to work in common with the other inmates of the establishment.

X.—POOR-RATES.

1. CHARGES UPON.

Auditor of Pershore Union—Four men committed a breach of the peace in parish C., and were apprehended and conveyed before the justices in petty sessions, by a police constable. The justices directed the police constable, who was appointed under the 2 and 3 Vic. c. 88, to prosecute the offenders; and they were severally convicted of drunkenness, and committed to the county gaol, in default of finding sureties to keep the peace. The justices intend to make an order upon the overseers of parish C., under the 18th Geo. 3, c. 19, s. 4, for the payment of the expenses incurred by the police constable in the prosecution. Inquired whether such expenses should be allowed in the accounts of the overseers of parish C.

Ans.—The Commissioners observe that, in the case of Reg. *v.* Chelmsford, part of the expenses in question consisted of fees paid to the justices' clerk in respect of drunkards, (12 L. J. R., n. s., M. C. 139.) But as Lord Denman, in delivering judgment, did not advert to these, but confined his remarks exclusively to the charges for vagrants, the Commissioners presume that the point raised in your letter cannot be regarded as directly decided by that case, though it may be affected by it indirectly. The Commissioners are disposed to think that the costs of prosecuting vagrants, and those of prosecuting drunkards, stand upon a similar footing. By the 6th section of the Vagrant Act, the constable, or other peace officer of the place, is bound to take into custody offenders against that Act; and by the 7th section of the 4th Jac. 1, c. 5, the constables, &c. are required to present the offences contrary to that statute. In Reg. *v.* Chelmsford, the circumstance of the constable's being bound to apprehend the vagrants, and being consequently unable to avoid the attendant expenses, seems to have formed a prominent part of Lord Denman's argument. The like obligation, and the like consequence, occur with regard to drunkards. By a similar analogy, the expenses in question, in the present case, though incurred by a county or district constable appointed under the 2nd and 3rd Vic. c. 93, and 3rd and 4th Vic. c. 88, would appear to be payable by the parish and not by the division. The Commissioners observe that the expenses specified in your letter are not restricted to justices' clerks' fees. They incline to think, however, that the decision in Reg. *v.* Chelmsford, supposing it to justify inferentially the payment of any such costs at all, would authorise the payment of all such costs in the matter as the constable unavoidably incurs. How far the payments to the witnesses are, under the circumstances of the particular case, expenses of this kind, the Commissioners express no opinion. But they apprehend that the item described "Paid to the Police 8*s*.," is not the reimbursement of an expense, but the payment of a remuneration to the constable. If so, it would not come within the scope of the 18th Geo. 3, c. 19, s. 4.

2. ENFORCEMENT OF POOR-RATE AGAINST OUT-GOING TENANTS.

Auditor of —— *District*—Inquired what course he should pursue in regard to the collection of poor-rates from persons who have been assessed thereto, but who leave their houses a few days after the rate has been allowed; an opinion prevailing amongst collectors of poor-rates that it would be unreasonable to require payment from persons who leave their occupations within a day or two after the making of the rate.

Ans.—The general law for the division of the rate between out-going and in-coming tenants is contained in the 17th Geo. 2, c. 38, s. 12. That law only provides in terms for the case where a tenant succeeds the out-going tenant. On a strict construction the case is not provided for where no tenant succeeds during the currency of the rate in force when the out-going tenant leaves; and it might, therefore, be held that, in such a case, the previous law, that an occupier was liable prospectively for the whole rate,—remains in force. Still it is not probable that the courts would give so strict a construction to the statute, but would uphold the extension of its principle to all cases where an occupier leaves during the currency of a rate. This construction would make it the duty of the overseers to obtain, in all cases, a part of the rate, proportionate to the term during which the occupier was in occupation. When, however, the proportionate part would be so small as not to justify a resort to the justices, in case of dispute, it would appear to be a fair case for the auditor's consideration, whether the abandonment of the rate, with a view to avoid greater expense in making application to the justices, and enforcing payment, be, or be not, under the circumstances of such case, a reasonable course.

3. PUBLICATION OF POOR-RATE.

Clerk of Cardigan Union—Inquired whether the suspension of the rate-book itself on the church-door, during the hours of Divine service, on the first Sunday after the allowance of the rate by the justices, is a sufficient publication thereof.

Ans.—As regards the publication of the poor-rate, the Commissioners direct your attention to the 1 Vic. c. 45. The Commissioners think that the mere suspension of the rate-book itself on the door of the church would not be a sufficient compliance with that statute.

4. Recovery of Poor Rate.

Assistant Overseer of Hitchin, Hitchin Union—Inquired whether he is bound, as assistant overseer, to execute personally distress warrants which he may obtain against rate-payers for non-payment of their poor-rates; or whether he can employ, at his own cost, a bailiff, to distrain upon the goods of such defaulters; as the cottagers lock their doors to prevent the execution of such warrants by him.

Ans.—The 4th section of the 43rd Eliz. c. 2, provides as follows:—"That it shall be lawful, as well for the present as subsequent churchwardens and overseers, or any of them, by warrant from two justices of peace as is aforesaid, to levy . . . the said sums of money, and all arrearages, of every one that shall refuse to contribute according as they shall be assessed, by distress and sale of the offender's goods, . . . rendering to the parties the overplus; and in defect of such distress, it shall be lawful for any such two justices of the peace to commit him or them to the common jail of the county, there to remain without bail or mainprize, until payment of the said sum," &c. Under this provision, therefore, the distress is to be made, under the warrant of the justices, by the churchwardens and overseers. Whether you have the same powers and duties in this particular matter as overseers, depends upon the terms of your appointment as assistant overseer. The Commissioners are not aware of anything to prevent overseers from employing a bailiff to distrain on their behalf, whose costs would be recoverable, according to the provisions of the statutes 57 Geo. 3, c. 93, and 7 and 8 Geo. 4, c. 17; and it appears to be the common practice for overseers to employ persons duly licensed to act as brokers, for the purpose of making such distresses. You will perceive that the statute provides for commitment to "prison in defect of such distress." The Commissioners believe that where access to the premises cannot be obtained, there is such a defect of the distress as would come within the meaning of the statute. In a case of non-payment of rent, it was held by Lord Tenterden that the words "no sufficient distress" must mean "no sufficient distress which can be got at. In this case," (his Lordship observed,) "the doors are locked up, so that the landlord cannot get at the premises to distrain; there is, consequently, no sufficient distress, for there is no available distress." (Doe *v.* Dyson, Mood and Malk. 77.) The Commissioners also direct your attention to the provisions of the 17 Geo. 2, c. 38, 33 Geo. 3, c. 55, and 54 Geo. 3, c. 170, relative to distraints for poor-rates beyond the limits of the particular parish concerned.

XI.—RATING.

1. Houses in certain cases.

Overseer of Newton Abbott Union—Inquired, first, whether a house unoccupied, but having furniture, is assessable to the poor-rate; secondly, whether a house occupied by a servant to take care of it, but having no furniture in it except the servant's, is assessable to the poor-rate; and thirdly, whether a house occupied by a gentleman only during the winter, he residing in another house during the summer, is assessable to the poor-rate, both houses continuing furnished during the proprietor's absence.

Ans.—Where a house is occupied merely for its preservation, or for the purpose of answering inquiries, in the intervals of letting, by persons lodging there solely for that purpose, the Commissioners are of opinion that there is no such beneficial occupation of the property as would render it rateable. But where a house is left by the proprietor, or tenant, in the intervals of his own residence therein, the house remaining furnished, and in the care of servants, the Commissioners think that the proprietor or tenant still continues, during such intervals, to be the beneficial occupier, and is rateable accordingly.

2. Rating Alms-Houses.

Overseer of Ringwood—Six alms-houses, to which are attached an acre and forty perches of land, have recently been erected in the parish of Ringwood; and are occupied by twelve inmates, who are allowed 2*s.* a-week each. Inquired whether these alms-houses are rateable to the relief of the poor.

Ans.—Having regard to the decisions in R. *v.* Green, 9 B. and C. 203, and R. *v.* Munday, 1 East 584, it seems most probable that, notwithstanding the charitable nature of the institution, the inmates of the alms-houses to which you allude would be held rateable to the roor-rate, as beneficial occupiers of the property.

3. Rating Salt and Sulphur Springs, &c.

Overseer of Rhosferrig, Builth Union—Inquired—whether salt and sulphur springs are rateable to the poor-rate; and also whether "fishing in different rivers, and shooting over different farms, all of which produce rent for a few months in the year, during the time when each is in season, being occupied by young single men having neither house nor harbour in the parish, but living in lodgings out of it"—are rateable to the poor-rate.

Ans.—Where the value of any land is increased by sulphur, salt, or other springs, the land is rateable according to such increased value, (See R. *v.* New River Company, 1 M. and S. 503; R. *v.* Miller, 3 Cowp. 619.) With regard to the "fishing in different rivers, and shooting over different farms, all of which produce rent for a few months in the year, during the time each is in its season, ... and are occupied by young single men having neither house nor harbour in the parish," the Commissioners conceive that, where any land may let at an increased rent by reason of a right of fishing, or killing game, the occupier of such land would be rateable for the value at which the land with these advantages would let. If he grant the mere privilege of fishing or shooting to some other person for a consideration, the Commissioners consider that he would still be rateable on the above principle, and that such other person would in no case be liable to assessment, simply on account of the right of fishing or license to shoot.

XII.—REGISTRATION FEES.

ON BIRTHS AND DEATHS IN WORKHOUSES.

Clerk of Clifton Union — By the 7 and 8 Vic. cap. 101, sec. 56, it is enacted that "all fees for registering births and deaths in any such workhouse or building, shall be charged, by the guardians, to the parish or union to which the person dying, or the mother of the child respectively, is chargeable." The workhouse for the able-bodied paupers in this union is situate in the parish of St. Philip and Jacob, and the registrar, in making out his bill of fees for paupers dying in that workhouse, charges all parties dying therein to the parish of St. Philip, and refuses to make any memorandum, at the time of registering the death, of the parish to which such person was chargeable, so that, in making out his account, he may state to what parish each fee is to be charged. Inquired what course should be pursued under the above circumstances.

Ans.—It appears to the Commissioners that, as section 56 of the 7 and 8 Vic. c. 101, directs the guardians to charge the fees above referred to to the parish to which the person dying, or the mother of the child, is chargeable, it is necessary for the guardians to ascertain, first, what cases have actually been registered from the workhouse; and, secondly, to what parishes the parties were chargeable, in such cases respectively. It seems to the Commissioners that the requisite information on both these points may be obtained by the guardians, from the registers of births and deaths required to be kept by the master of the workhouse. (Order of Accounts, Sched. C, Forms No. 16 and No. 17.) As to the first point, it would, no doubt, be convenient for the guardians to receive from the registrar (in addition to, and as a check upon, the workhouse master's statement) a specification of the particular cases actually registered from the workhouse. But looking to the terms of the 29th sec. of the Registration Act, relating to the registrar's quarterly account, the Commissioners think that the registrar is not bound to give this detailed information, and that it rests with him to do so or not, as he may think fit. As to the second point, some doubt may perhaps arise from the heading of one of the columns in the workhouse master's register of births, and also in his register of deaths. The heading here referred to is in these terms: "To what parish *belonging*;" which should be read as meaning, "To what parish *chargeable*." The Commissioners think that the statements made in these columns, of the parishes of the chargeability, in the cases of births and deaths occurring in the workhouse, should be examined and verified by the clerk to the guardians, before the guardians proceed to distribute the charge of the registration fees among such parishes. The Commissioners certainly consider that it does not, in any way, belong to the registrar to specify the parishes of the chargeability; and indeed, that, if he voluntarily does so, it would not be proper to rely upon his statement, as it is obvious that he has no direct means of ascertaining the facts. To the foregoing general remarks, however, the Commissioners think that one exception must be made. The 29th sec. of the Registration Act provides for two classes of payments to the registrar; viz., half-a-crown for each of the first twenty entries in the year, and a shilling for each of the remaining entries. In distributing the charge of the registration fees on cases arising in the workhouse, among the parishes indicated by the 56 sec. of the 7 and 8 Vic. cap. 101, it is clearly indispensable that the guardians should know whether such cases form part of the first twenty entries or not; in other words, whether the fees to be charged upon the above-mentioned parishes are half-crown or shilling fees. The guardians cannot well ascertain this point from any one but the registrar himself; and the Commissioners accordingly consider that the registrar should specify in his account the particular cases registered from the workhouse (if there be any such) which form part of the first twenty entries. The trouble involved in this necessary statement must be so slight, that the Commissioners do not suppose that any registrar will refuse to perform the duty; but if any difficulty should occur in the Union on the subject, the Commissioners would be prepared to take the matter into their further consideration.

XIII.—REGISTRATION.

RECOVERY OF EXPENSES OF FROM PARISHES UNDER GILBERT'S ACT.

Clerk of Hinckley Union—The parishes of —— and ———, which are under Gilbert's Act, have, since the year 1837, been united to the several parishes in the ——— Union, for registration purposes; but the guardians have been unable to recover any portion of the fees paid to the district registrar from the former parish since the above year, and from the latter during the last four years. Inquired by what means the guardians can recover the money so advanced on behalf of these parishes.

Ans.—Under the 29th section of the 6th and 7th Wm. 4, c. 86, the registrar is to be paid by "the guardians or overseers of the parish, township, or place, in or for which he shall be registrar." The general tenor of the statute shows that the guardians here mentioned are guardians appointed under the Poor Law Amendment Act. As the parishes of ——— and ——— are managed under the provisions of Gilbert's Act, and not of the Poor Law Amendment Act; and as the guardians of ——— Union, therefore, whatever may be the arrangement of the registration districts, are not, in fact, guardians of the above-mentioned parishes, it appears to the Commissioners that the registrar "in or for" those parishes is to be paid (according to the 29th section of the Registration Act) not by the guardians of ——— Union, but by the overseers of such parishes respectively; but having regard to the terms of the 7th section of the 22nd Geo. 3, c. 83, which seem completely to place the guardians appointed thereunder in the room of the overseers, except as to making and collecting rates, the Commissioners presume that the payment might properly be made, not by the overseers of the said parishes, but by the guardians appointed for such parishes under the provisions of Gilbert's Act. The Commissioners would add that, whichever of these may be the proper parties to satisfy the claim of the district registrar, the Commissioners apprehend that, in the event of a refusal to pay, the claim can only be enforced by mandamus.

XIV.—RELATIONS.

LIABILITY OF APPRENTICE TO SUPPORT HIS WIFE AND CHILD.

Clerk of Sheffield Union—E. H., aged twenty-two, has applied to the guardians, for relief for herself and infant child, on the ground that she cannot procure a maintenance from her husband, who is a minor, is apprenticed to a mechanic in Sheffield, and is in the receipt of no wages. Inquired what course the guardians should pursue under these circumstances.

Ans.—The husband is liable to all the same consequences of the relief to his wife and child, as if he were not an apprentice; and therefore, if he have the means of supporting them, and neglect to do so, he is liable to be punished under the Vagrant Act. Whether he have any such means, is a matter of fact which in this case appears doubtful; and if he have none, his remaining under his articles of apprenticeship, though it should involve his absence from his family, and his not providing for them by his labour, would constitute a wilful neglect or desertion of his family.

XV.—RELIEF.

TO A PERSON POSSESSED OF A COW AND HEIFER.

Clerk of Llandilo Union—Application having been made to the guardians for an increase of the out-relief granted to E. S., aged eighty-two, it was discovered during the discussion that she was in possession of a cow and a heifer. Inquired whether the guardians will be justified in continuing the allowance of out-relief to the pauper while she is possessed of the above property.

Ans.—The Commissioners are of opinion that, as a general principle, persons possessed of property cannot be considered as proper objects for relief, not being in that destitute condition which constitutes the title to relief; cases may, however, occur in which persons may have an interest in property, and yet, being incapable of labour, may be without the means necessary for their support. In such cases it is for the board of guardians to exercise their discretion as to giving relief. The question is, whether the property possessed by a person in such a case is available for the supply of the wants which such person applies to the guardians to relieve; and of this the guardians must judge according to the circumstances of the case. They, however, cannot compel the pauper to sell the cow and heifer, although they might refuse to afford relief. But, in a case where the person is notoriously without the means of maintaining himself or herself, and is unwilling to dispose of the property, the Commissioners think that the guardians might incur a serious responsibility by refusing relief, supposing the necessities of such person to be urgent, until the property were disposed of.

XVI.—RELIGIOUS INSTRUCTION.

Clerk of Isle of Thanet Union—Inquired whose duty it is to prepare the pauper children in the Union workhouse, and to give them certificates to present to the bishop, for the purpose of confirmation.

Ans.—The Commissioners consider the religious instruction of those children in the workhouse who are members of the Established Church, to be under the direction of the chaplain, (see Workhouse Order, Art. 76, No. 2.) It is competent to the schoolmaster, or schoolmistress, to assist in the religious instruction of these children, under the guidance and control of the chaplain; for example, to teach them the Church Catechism, or to explain the verbal meaning of passages in the Bible, (see Workhouse Order, Articles 22 and 77, No. 1.) With regard to certificates for confirmation, the Commissioners think that these ought to be given by the chaplain, as being best acquainted with the religious proficiency of the children. The Commissioners, however, do not doubt that the incumbent of the parish in which the workhouse is situate might properly give these certificates if he thought fit to do so. The decision, however, as to what certificate would be deemed sufficient must necessarily rest with the bishop.

XVII.—REMOVAL—CHARGEABILITY.

1. OF FAMILY OF IMPRISONED VAGRANT.

June 9th, 1845.

Clerk of Wimborne and Cranborne Union—On the 12th March last, S. W. C. was committed to the house of correction at Dorchester, for deserting his wife and family, leaving them chargeable to the parish of Wimborne Minster. On the 16th May, orders were obtained for the removal of the wife and two children, of the ages of ten and eight years, to the parish of Melcombe Regis, and on the same day the execution of the orders was suspended on account of the dangerous illness of the wife. The orders were served on the 23rd May; on the 25th May the wife died. The overseers of Melcombe Regis refused to receive the children until after the expiration of the twenty-one days from the service of the order. As the term of S. W. C.'s imprisonment will expire on the 11th of June, and the children cannot be legally removed before the 13th of June, it is possible that he may return to Wimborne Minster, and take the children under his care without their being further chargeable. Inquired, 1st, whether, in the event of his doing so, the overseers of Wimborne Minster would be justified in removing the children to Melcombe Regis against the consent of the father. 2nd. Whether relief given to the children during the father's imprisonment is a sufficient chargeability of the father to justify the magistrates in compelling him to be examined for the purpose of removing him to his settlement, without a fresh chargeability arising after the expiration of his imprisonment; and would the circumstance of the children ceasing to reside in the removing parish affect this question. 3rd. Whether it would be sufficient to treat the vagrancy as the actual chargeability under 5 Geo. 4, c. 83, s. 20, and whether in that case, a certificate of the conviction must be obtained from the clerk of the peace. It is presumed that, to render him liable to be removed on this ground, he must return to and reside in the parish. 4th. Whether after issuing a summons to the father to attend at a petty sessions to be examined as to his settlement, and he disobeys it, two magistrates would be justified in granting a warrant to bring him to petty sessions for that purpose, and in case of his refusing to be examined, to commit him; (R. *v.* Jackson and another, 1 J. R. 653.)

Ans.—1. Assuming that the order of justices for the removal of S. W. C.'s wife and children was in the first instance a valid order, (and the Commissioners see nothing in your statement of the case to show that it was not,) the Commissioners consider that it would still continue to be a valid and effective order, notwithstanding the return of S. W. C. himself to the parish of Wimborne Minster, and that consequently it might be duly executed by the overseers of that parish, notwithstanding any objection which might be made by S. W. C. to its execution. The Commissioners are not aware of any ground for supposing that such return or objection on the part of the father would affect the validity of the justices' order, or necessarily render it inoperative. At the same time, the Commissioners apprehend that the overseers of Wimborne Minster would not be bound to receive the children if in their discretion they should think fit to abandon the order; see Reg. *v.* St. Pancras, (12 L. J. R. n. s. M. C. 42,) in which Lord Denman observed, "An order of removal is merely a warrant to enable the officers to remove the paupers, but they are not obliged to carry it into effect." 2. The Commissioners do not think that S. W. C. could be removed to Melcombe Regis, in respect of the chargeability of his children to Wimborne Minster, during his imprisonment at Dorchester. It is true that, under the 56th sec. of the Poor Law Amendment Act, the relief given to the children would render him constructively chargeable to Wimborne Minster: but the 1st sec. of the 35 Geo. 3, c. 101, requires that a pauper, in order to be removable, shall be chargeable to the parish in which he shall be then inhabiting; and certainly S. W. C. while in prison at Dorchester, was not inhabiting in Wimborne Minster. If, however, the children should continue to be chargeable to the last-named parish, after S. W. C.'s return there, the case would obviously be different. 3. The Commissioners think that S. W. C.'s case comes within the 20th sec. of the Vagrant Act, but they feel some difficulty in construing that section, with regard to the parish of the pauper's residence. The terms of the section are—"Every person, &c. shall be deemed to be actually chargeable to the parish, &c. in which such person shall reside." It does not clearly appear to what time such residence is to have relation; but the Commissioners consider that the statute must be understood to mean the parish in which the party is resident at some time subsequent to the conviction. Whether this applies simply to the parish where the vagrant concludes his term of imprisonment, or generally to any parish in which he may subsequently reside, is by no means free from doubt: a certified copy of the conviction obtained from the clerk of the peace, under 5 Geo. 4, c. 83, sec. 17, will be sufficient evidence of the conviction. 4 and 5. With respect to your last inquiries, the Commissioners direct your attention to the cases of Ware *v.* Stanstead (2 Bott. 816,) and R. *v.* Wykes, (2 Bott. 819,) in addition to that of R. *v.* Jackson, to which you allude. In Ware *v.* Stanstead, it was said by Gould, J.—"The statute directs, and the practice is, to make complaint to one justice, and then he grants his warrant to bring the poor man before two justices, and then those two justices are to examine and remove."

2. Removal of a Pauper without an Order.

Clerk of Merthyr Tydvil Union—Some time ago, M. H. an aged woman was brought by her granddaughter from the parish of A. in the —Union, where her husband then lived and still lives, to the parish of B. in this Union. It appears that, after residing some time with her granddaughter, in the parish of B. she was sent to the house of her son-in-law, in the same parish, who, being unable to support her, applied to the relieving officer of the district in which the parish of B. is situated for relief, which was granted, and M. H. has continued chargeable to the parish of B. ever since. The guardians are aware of the liability of M. H.'s husband under the 56th section of the Poor Law Amendment Act, and they believe he is open to proceedings under the Vagrant Act; but as he is very aged, and very likely to be either a pauper on the parish of A. or a pensioner on a benefit club, they are not disposed to take proceedings against him. Inquired whether there would be any objection to the guardians providing means for conveying M. H. to the residence of her husband, in the parish of A.; as, if all the formalities required by law for her removal are to be adopted, difficulties present themselves to the guardians which appear insurmountable.

Ans.—If A. is the parish of M. H.'s husband's (and consequently of her own) settlement, the Commissioners see nothing in your statement of the case to prevent her removal, under an order of justices, from B. to A. If there is some difficulty as to the woman's settlement, it is possible she might be removed to her husband by an order of justices made under the general power described in 2 Nolan's P. L. 245. The Commissioners, however, can hardly advise that recourse should be had to a power which is scarcely ever exercised, and is very imperfectly defined.

3. Removal of the Wife without the Husband.

Clerk of Wem Union—On the 28th of March, 1843, an order was made by the magistrates for the borough of ——— for the removal of W. G. and his wife from the parish of M. to the parish of W., which order was on the same day suspended, on account of the illness of the pauper's wife. On the 11th of March, 1845, the suspension was taken off, and £26. 10*s*. 2½*d*. ordered to be paid by the parish of W. for the expenses under the suspension. On the 9th of May, 1845, (nearly two months after the suspension was taken off,) the pauper's wife was removed to W. by, or by the direction of, M. parish, without her husband, it being then stated by the officer who brought her, that the husband could not be found; and she has ever since continued in the ——— Union workhouse. The wife's mother came over to the workhouse to see her daughter, and states that when the relieving officer of M. was about removing her daughter to W., and indeed several times before that period, she apprised him, and also the other relieving officer, that her husband was residing at Y., eighteen miles from M., he having left her about twelve months back, and that the officer *said that when they removed the wife, W. parish would see after the husband.* Inquired whether the removal of the wife without the husband was legal; and if not, whether the £26. 10*s*. 2½*d*. is recoverable by M. parish from W. parish.

Ans.—The Commissioners are of opinion that the order of removal referred to might, under the circumstances stated in your letter, be lawfully executed as regards the wife alone; and that the overseers of W. would have rendered themselves liable to a penalty, under the 3rd W. and M. c. 11, sec. 10, had they refused to receive her. The Commissioners, therefore, consider that the overseers of W. cannot lawfully refuse to obey the order of justices, as to the payment of the costs incurred by the suspension of the order of removal, solely on the ground that the wife was removed without the husband, both being included in the order of removal.

---

4. RECOVERY OF EXPENSES UNDER SUSPENDED ORDER OF REMOVAL.

Clerk of Hartley Wintney Union—About seven years ago a suspended order of removal was served by the parish officers of Chester upon the parish officers of Heckfield, for the removal of a pauper named E. H. No removal under this order has taken place, but once a year the parish officers of Chester have been in the habit of sending a letter to the overseers of Heckfield, containing an account of the money expended in the relief of E. H., and stating that she was still too ill to be removed. The total amount is now very considerable. No order, or allowance of magistrates, for these sums has been furnished. The parish officers of Heckfield do not dispute the settlement of the pauper, but they do not like the accumulation of debt, and have therefore applied to the guardians for advice, and the guardians are desirous of having the Commissioners' opinion of the case.

Ans.—The 2nd section of the 35 Geo. 3, c. 101, does not enable the justices to order repayment of the charges incurred by the suspension of an order of removal, in any other event than the removal or the death of the paupers. (Rex. *v*. Clagford, 4 B. & A. 235.) As E. H. has not yet been removed, and is still living, the justices have at present no power to order the overseers of Heckfield to repay the charges hitherto incurred on her account by the parish officers of Chester. The Commissioners, however, are not aware of anything to prevent the overseers of Heckfield from making such repayment, or from continuing to repay, from time to time, the expenses which may arise hereafter, if the overseers think fit to do so. The points for consideration are these:—On the one hand, the parish officers of Chester, so long as the pauper is living and unremoved, cannot enforce the repayment, and the overseers of Heckfield are under no legal obligation to make it; on the other hand, the debt is accumulating against the parish of Heckfield, and in the event of the removal or death of the pauper, may some day fall with undue weight upon the rate-payers of the particular year in which such event occurs. With these remarks the Commissioners leave it for the guardians of Hartley Wintney Union and the overseers of Heckfield to decide upon the course which ought to be pursued, bearing in mind, however, that immediate payment will deprive the parish of the advantage of the proof on oath, and the opportunity to appeal, as to the amount of the charges, which are provided by the statute for the protection of the parish liable to repay.

---

5. VALIDITY OF ORDER OF REMOVAL.

Clerk of Northallerton Union—G. F., a pauper belonging to B., in the ——— Union, but residing at C. with his four children, having been committed to gaol for deserting his family, an order was taken out for the removal of himself and his family to B., but was *suspended* on the ground, as therein stated, that "G. F. is unable to travel by reason of his *confinement in the House of Correction at W.*" After G. F. was released out of prison, the suspension was taken off, and an order made directing the overseers of B. to pay the overseers of C. £3. 12*s.* 6*d.* "*for charges necessarily incurred by the township of C., by the suspension of the said order of removal.*" On the 23rd day from the date of the order of removal, the paupers were removed to N., and left there with the relieving officer, who gave an order for their admission into the workhouse. The four children were in the workhouse at C. at the time the order of removal was made, and remained there until removed with their father. No demand has yet been made upon the overseers of B. to pay the £3. 12*s.* 6*d.*; but the guardians being of opinion that the order of removal could not be legally suspended on the ground stated therein, and, consequently, that payment of the £3. 12*s.* 6*d.* ought not to be submitted to, (although it may be enforced by distress if not paid within three days after demand thereof, or notice of appeal given within the same time, under the 35 Geo. 3, c. 101, s. 2,) requested the Commissioners' opinion, whether the order for suspension, and the subsequent order, for payment of the charges alleged to have been incurred thereby, are legal.

Ans.—The terms of the 2nd section of the 35 Geo. 3, c. 101, obviously do not authorise the suspension of an order of removal, on the ground of the pauper being in prison at the time. The object of that section is distinctly defined by the terms of the preamble, "And whereas poor persons are often removed or passed to the place of their settlement, *during the time of their sickness, to the great danger of their lives. For remedy thereof,* be it further enacted," &c. And the substantive enactment is limited, in like manner, to cases in which "it shall appear to the justices that such poor person *is unable to travel, by reason of sickness or other infirmity,* or that it would be *dangerous* for him or her so to do." The Commissioners think, therefore, that under the circumstances described by the clerk in the case of G. F., the suspension of the order of removal and the subsequent order for costs were simply nullities, being made by the justices without any authority whatever; and that, consequently, the overseers of B. should pay no regard to them. If the overseers of C. endeavour to enforce the order of costs by distress, they will do so at their own peril. It would clearly not be proper for the overseers of B. to appeal against an order which is wholly null and void; but it does not appear that the order of removal itself was in any way invalid; and as the suspension was simply a nullity, such order will stand on the same footing as other common orders of removal. The 79th section of the Poor Law Amendment Act provides that no pauper shall be removed under an order until twenty-one days after a notice in writing of his chargeability, accompanied by a copy of the order for his removal, and a copy of the examination on which such order was made, shall have been sent to the overseers of the parish of his alleged settlement. You state that the order in the present case was made on the 24th of July last; but you do not mention when the notice of chargeability, &c. was sent to the overseers of B. The order, it appears, was executed on the 16th of August, twenty-three days after its date. The Commissioners think that, under the 84th section of the same Act, the costs of maintenance during the twenty-one days from the sending of the notice of chargeability, &c., may be recovered from the parish of B.

6. WHEN ORDER OF REMOVAL SHOULD BE SUSPENDED.

Clerk of Tunstead and Happing Incorporation—The parish authorities of Great Yarmouth having obtained an order, on the 2nd Dec., 1843, for the removal of a pauper to the parish of Witton, in the Tunstead and Happing Incorporation, gave notice of their intention to remove such pauper after the expiration of twenty-one days, but on the same day that the order was obtained it was suspended, and the pauper was not removed until the 11th Jan. 1844; when a charge of £4. 9*s.* 6*d.* was made for his maintenance, and for the expenses incurred in the suspension of the order. The guardians have no objection to make to the charge for the maintenance of the pauper; but they think that the order ought not to have been suspended until the twenty-one days had expired. Requested the Commissioners' advice as to whether the parish of Great Yarmouth can enforce payment of the above sum of £4. 9*s.* 6*d.*

Ans.—The suspending of the order before the expiration of the twenty-one days, or receipt of an admission of settlement, is entirely unnecessary; inasmuch as the officers are already prohibited from executing the order, and there is no reason apparent that the execution will be injurious to the paupers at the end of twenty-one days. As far, therefore, as the expense of such suspension at the time of obtaining the order is concerned, the Commissioners think that it could be successfully resisted. It is more doubtful whether the suspension is altogether void; and the Commissioners would not (except with a view to try the question, where any parties were desirous of doing so) advise that expenses incurred in maintaining a pauper after the time of execution (*i. e.* twenty-one days) under colour of such suspension, should be resisted. In the present case the part of the £4. 9*s.* 6*d.* expended during the twenty-one days would be payable under the order, independently of the suspension; and this part, whatever it may be, should in any case be tendered.

XVIII.—SETTLEMENT.

June 30th, 1845.

————, *Dover Union*—R. R., residing in the parish of St. Mary, Dover, during the years 1831, 1832, 1833, 1834, 1835, was acknowledged to belong to, and to have received relief from, the parish of Hurstmonceux now in the Hailsham Union, during two of those years, viz., 1832, 1833: he occupied a house, at a rent of £8. 15*s.*, and land, at a rent of £1. 7*s.*; together, £10. 2*s.*; both situate in the parish of St. Mary, Dover. R. R. is now become chargeable to that parish, and the parish of Hurstmonceux declines to acknowledge him. St. Mary, Dover, has therefore sought to have the pauper's examination taken, but the justices refuse to examine him, because they have no doubt that he has gained a settlement in St. Mary's, by hiring, notwithstanding that he received relief, subsequently to such hiring, from the parish of Hurstmonceux. Inquired, to which of the parishes the pauper belongs; and also, whether the magistrates were justified in refusing to take his examination.

Ans.—With regard to the first question asked by you, viz., "To which parish the pauper belongs," the Commissioners do not feel that the statement of facts contained in your letter is sufficiently complete to enable them to answer the inquiry. It may be remarked, however, that the tenement in respect of which a settlement may be acquired need not be one entire tenement; a house and land, hired of the same or different landlords, may be made contributory to a settlement. The tenement in the present case, appears to have been rented (*i. e.* the land and the house taken together) for the sum of £10 a-year, and if the other conditions were complied with by the pauper, that is, if the tenement was actually occupied by the person hiring it, if £10 of the year's rent was paid by the person hiring it, and if the party resided forty days in the parish of St. Mary, Dover, during the year's occupation, then a settlement was undoubtedly acquired in that parish. Then, presuming the acquisition of a settlement by the pauper in 1832 and 1833, in St. Mary, Dover, the fact of the pauper having subsequently received relief from Hurstmonceux will not defeat or supersede the settlement gained in St. Mary, Dover. The fact of a parish giving relief to a pauper residing out of it, only shows the opinion of the parish giving the relief that the pauper is settled in such parish. But this, at the utmost, is only *primâ facie* evidence of a settlement in such parish, and does not conclude it: it is open to the overseers to show that the relief was given under a misapprehension (see Reg. *v.* Bedingham, 8 Jurist 378, also Burn's Justice by Chitty, 1845, vol. iv. p. 1132.) With respect to the second question, "Are the magistrates justified in refusing to take the pauper's examination?" the Commissioners would refer you to the case of Reg. *v.* Rogers, 12 Law Journal Reports, new series (magistrates' cases) p. 50. The Commissioners collect from that decision, that justices are not justified in refusing to take the examination of a pauper as to his settlement, if applied to do so; and that the court of Queen's Bench would issue a mandamus in any case where the justices might perversely refuse to take the examination, though the court (as the case shows) will not compel justices, when they have taken the examination, to make the order of removal.

2. SETTLEMENT—MARRIAGE AT GRETNA GREEN.

Rev. ——, *Bolton Union*—H. S., a pauper belonging to the parish of Caton, and M. B., a pauper belonging to the township of Bolton, were married while "on tramp" at Gretna Green, on the 19th of March last, "after the manner," as the printed certificate states, "of the Church of England, and agreeably to the laws of Scotland." M. B. had, previous to this marriage, three unaffiliated illegitimate children, maintained at the cost of Bolton. Inquired—1st. Will the woman gain a settlement in H. S.'s parish by the marriage? 2nd. Will the burden of maintaining the children fall upon the township of Caton, or upon the parish of Bolton, H. S. being unable to maintain them?

Ans.—The Commissioners apprehend, that if H. S. and M. B. were really married (as the certificate states) at Gretna Green, "agreeably to the laws of Scotland," their marriage would be held by the English courts to be valid, (see Rogers's Eccles. Law tit. Marriage.) The Commissioners think that the woman would consequently acquire her husband's parochial settlement in England, according to the usual rule. With regard to the woman's bastard children, it is not stated whether they were born before or after the passing of the Poor Law Amendment Act. If born subsequently to the passing of that Act, the 71st section would confer upon them the settlement acquired by their mother through her marriage, (Reg. *v.* St. Mary, Newington; 2 Gale and Dav. 686.) The Commissioners presume that the children were born in England.

XIX.—VAGRANT ACT.

CONSTRUCTION OF SECTION 4.

Clerk of Eton Union—Inquired whether able-bodied women, deserted by their husbands, are punishable, under the Vagrant Act, for discharging themselves from the workhouse and leaving their children chargeable to the parish.

Ans.—The Commissioners understand the effect of the 25th sec. of the Act 7 and 8 Vic. c. 101, in enabling (in the cases to which that section applies) the relief to be given, "to the wife in the same manner, and subject to the same conditions as if she were a widow," to subject her to the provisions of the Vagrant Act (sec. 4,) if she run away and leave her children chargeable to the parish. But the mere desertion of the husband (where he is not beyond the seas) would not bring the case within the 25th section.

XX.—VAGRANTS.—PUNISHMENT OF.

Clerk of Wolverhampton Union—Some weeks since the guardians made an order that every able-bodied vagrant casually relieved with lodging for the night and a breakfast in the morning, should break a certain quantity of stones in return for such relief. On a recent occasion, three vagrants so relieved refused to perform the required task of work. As the guardians' order has not been reported for the Commissioners' sanction, a question arises, as to whether vagrants refusing to obey it can be punished by the magistrates, under 5 and 6 Vic. c. 57, s. 5, which authorises the guardians to make such an order "subject always to the powers of the Poor Law Commissioners." If not, can they be punished under any other enactment? And can they be dealt with by the workhouse master in the same manner as refractory paupers who are not casual poor?

Ans.—The power of the guardians to prescribe a task of work does not require the express sanction of the Commissioners; but if the Commissioners judge it proper, they can, in any case, regulate the exercise of the power of the guardians. If the Commissioners do not regulate such power, the disobedience of the guardians' prescription is a complete offence under the 5th sec. of the Act referred to, and the punishment of course legal. But the provision in the 5th sec. is a cumulative provision, which adds to the previous powers of the guardians and liabilities of paupers relieved. Before that provision, a pauper relieved in any workhouse was liable, whether settled or not settled, resident or vagrant, ordinary or casual, to be imprisoned for twenty-one days, with hard labour, for refusing to do any work suited to his age, strength, and capacity, 55 Geo. 3, c. 137, s. 3. This provision is in full force, as is also the provision of the Vagrant Act, 5 Geo. 4, c. 83, s. 3, under which it has been the general practice to commit persons who refused to earn their maintenance, wholly or partly, according to their ability, by doing such work as the guardians or parish officers set to them. In ordinary cases where the pauper receives relief of any kind, and does not require to quit the workhouse, or to go away before his task is done, the above provisions, particularly that in 55 Geo. 3, c. 137, are sufficient for the purpose of punishing all paupers refusing to work. The purpose of the recent enactment was to give the guardians a power to prescribe a task of work absolutely so, that the pauper could not lawfully require to leave the workhouse before it is completed, the period of detention not exceeding four hours after breakfast on the day succeeding that of his admission. This enactment therefore, though applicable to the cases where paupers are maintained in a workhouse, is more particularly applicable to the cases of vagrants and other paupers who would otherwise be at liberty to leave the house before there was time to complete the task. There seems to be no other difference between the vagrant and the resident and settled poor to be observed in the cases described, except that it will be more economical to cause the vagrants who offend to be proceeded against before justices, inasmuch as the power to restrain or punish that class by the discipline of the workhouse would very rarely be found sufficient.

LONDON:
Printed by order of the Poor Law Commissioners, by BLACKBURN and PARDON, 6, Hatton Garden, and Published by CHARLES KNIGHT and Co., 22, Ludgate Street, Publishers to the Poor Law Commissioners.

AN

OFFICIAL CIRCULAR

OF PUBLIC DOCUMENTS AND INFORMATION:

DIRECTED BY THE POOR LAW COMMISSIONERS TO BE PRINTED, CHIEFLY FOR THE USE OF THE MEMBERS AND PERMANENT OFFICERS OF BOARDS OF GUARDIANS, UNDER THE POOR LAW AMENDMENT ACT.

No. 51. CIRCULAR ISSUED SEPTEMBER 1, 1845.

Poor Law Commission Office,
Somerset House, Sept. 1st, 1845.

THE Poor Law Commissioners directed that the following documents be printed and circulated for the information of Guardians and Officers of the several Unions, viz.

(Signed) By Order of the Board,
EDWIN CHADWICK, *Secretary.*

I.—APPRENTICING POOR CHILDREN.

1. CIRCULAR ON THE MODIFICATION OF THE GENERAL ORDER.

Poor Law Commission Office,
Somerset House, May 5th, 1845.

SIR,—The Poor Law Commissioners have had under consideration certain Objections made to the Order relating to the Apprenticeship of Poor Children, recently issued by them, and they propose, in consequence of the representations made to them, to modify the Provisions contained in Articles 2 and 18 of that Order.

The Commissioners intend to make the alterations in question before the end of the month of June, and they will be ready, before that time, to consider any observations which the Board of Guardians may be desirous of offering upon these, or any other Articles in the Order.

The Regulations which it is proposed to modify are the following:—

Article 2.—"No premium other than clothing for the apprentice shall be given upon the binding of any person above the age of *fourteen,* unless such person be maimed, deformed, or suffering from some personal bodily infirmity, so that the nature of the work or trade which such person is fit to perform or exercise is restricted."

Proposed Alteration—For "fourteen," insert "sixteen."

Article 18.—No. 8.—" Where the apprentice continues bound after the age of *seventeen* years, the master shall pay to such apprentice, for and in respect of every week that he duly and properly serves the said master, as a remuneration, a sum to be inserted in the indenture, or to be agreed upon by the guardians and the said master when that time arrives, or, if they cannot agree, to be settled by some person to be then chosen by the said master and such guardians, and until such sum be agreed upon or settled, not less than one-*fourth* of the amount then commonly paid as wages to journeymen in the said trade, business, or employment."

Proposed Alteration—" Provided that the board of guardians, or parties binding, may dispense with any such stipulation if they see fit."

Article 18.—No. 10.—"The master shall not cause the said apprentice to work or live more than *ten miles* from the place or places mentioned in the indenture, according to Article 16, without the leave of the guardians so binding him, to be given under their common seal."

Proposed Alteration—" Provided that the licence of the board of guardians, or party binding, if once given, shall, if they think fit, authorise the master at any time afterwards during the apprenticeship, to change the place of the apprentice's abode or service."

Signed by Order of the Board,
EDWIN CHADWICK, *Secretary*.

To the Clerk to the Board of Guardians.

---

2. GENERAL ORDER ISSUED TO UNIONS, AND PARISHES UNDER BOARDS OF GUARDIANS, AMENDING AN ORDER DATED 31ST DEC. 1844.

To the Guardians of the Poor of the several Unions and of the several Parishes under a Board of Guardians, named in the Schedules hereunto annexed, and the Officers of such Unions and Parishes ;—

To the Churchwardens and Overseers of the several Parishes and Places comprised within the said Unions, and of the several other Parishes named in the said Schedule ;—

To the Clerk or Clerks to the Justices of the Petty Sessions held for the Division or Divisions in which the Parishes and Places comprised within the said Unions, and the said other Parishes named in the said Schedule, are situate ;—

And to all others whom it may concern.

Whereas the Poor Law Commissioners, in pursuance of the powers vested in them by an Act passed in the fifth year of the reign of His late Majesty King William the Fourth, intituled "*An Act for the Amendment and better Administration of the Laws relating to the Poor in England and Wales*," and an Act passed in the eighth year of the reign of Her present Majesty Queen Victoria, intituled "*An Act for the further Amendment of the Laws relating to the Poor in England*," by an Order under their Hands and Seal, bearing date the Thirty-first day of December last, and addressed to the Guardians of the Poor of the several Unions named in the Schedule A, hereunto annexed, and of the Parishes named in the Schedule B, hereunto annexed, did make certain Rules and Regulations in regard to the apprenticing of Poor Children, and it is expedient that certain alterations should be made therein.

Now, therefore, We, the Poor Law Commissioners, acting under the authority of the Statutes aforesaid, do hereby alter the said Order, in the manner hereinafter mentioned, and do Order,—

First, That it shall be lawful for the Guardians of the Poor of the said Unions and Parishes respectively to give a premium, other than clothing, upon the binding as an apprentice of any person not above the age of sixteen years ;

Secondly, That the Guardians who shall bind any poor person apprentice may dispense with the condition by the said Order required to be inserted in the indenture of apprenticeship, providing for the payment of the remuneration to the apprentice after the age of seventeen years ;

Thirdly, That to the condition, by the said Order required to be inserted in the said indenture, providing that the master shall not cause the said apprentice to work or live more than ten miles from the place or places mentioned in the indenture, according to Article 16 of the said recited Order, without the leave of the Guardians so binding him, to be given under their common seal, shall be annexed the proviso following; that is to say,

Provided, That such Guardians may in such licence so to be given under their Common Seal, by express words to that effect, if they think fit, authorise the master, at any time during the residue of the term of the apprenticeship, to change the place of the abode or service of the apprentice, without any further application to them or their successors.

And We do hereby Order, that all the terms contained in this Order shall be construed in the same manner as the same terms are required to be construed in the Order above cited.

[*Schedules A and B annexed to this Order consist of the names of the Unions and Parishes that are set forth in No.* 43, *of the Official Circular, pages* 15,16.]

Given under our Hands and Seal of Office, this Fifteenth day of August, in the year One thousand eight hundred and forty-five.

(Signed) GEO. NICHOLLS.
L. S. EDMUND W. HEAD.

3. GENERAL ORDER ISSUED to UNIONS AND PARISHES GOVERNED UNDER LOCAL ACTS, AMENDING AN ORDER DATED 29TH JANUARY, 1845.

To the Guardians of the Poor of the several Unions and of the several Parishes under a Board of Guardians named in the Schedules A. and B. hereunto annexed, and the Officers of such Unions and Parishes;—

To the Churchwardens and Overseers of the several Parishes and Places comprised within the said Unions, and of the several other Parishes named in the said Schedule;—

To the Clerk or Clerks to the Justices of the Petty Sessions held for the Division or Divisions in which the Parishes and Places comprised within the said Unions, and the said other Parishes named in the said Schedule B., are situate;—

And to all others whom it may concern.

Whereas the Poor Law Commissioners, in pursuance of the powers vested in them by an Act passed in the fifth year of the reign of His late Majesty King William the Fourth, intituled "*An Act for the Amendment and better Administration of the Laws relating to the Poor in England and Wales,*" and an Act passed in the eighth year of the reign of Her present Majesty Queen Victoria, intituled "*An Act for the further Amendment of the Laws relating to the Poor in England,*" by an Order under their Hands and Seal, bearing date the Twenty-ninth day of January last, and addressed to the Guardians of the Poor of the several Unions named in the Schedule A. hereunto annexed, and of the Parishes named in the Schedule B. hereunto annexed, did make certain Rules and Regulations in regard to the apprenticing of Poor Children, and it is expedient that certain alterations should be made therein.

Now, therefore, We, the Poor Law Commissioners, acting under the Authority of the Statutes aforesaid, do hereby alter the said Order, in the manner hereinafter mentioned, and do Order,—

First, That it shall be lawful for the Guardians of the Poor of the said Unions and Parishes respectively to give a premium, other than clothing, upon the binding as an apprentice of any person not above the age of sixteen years;

Secondly, That the Guardians who shall bind any poor person apprentice, may dispense with the condition by the said Order required to be inserted in the indenture of apprenticeship, providing for the payment of the remuneration to the apprentice after the age of seventeen years;

Thirdly, That to the condition, by the said Order required to be inserted in the said indenture, providing that the master shall not cause the said apprentice to work or live more than ten miles from the place or places mentioned in the indenture, according to Article 16 of the said recited Order, without the leave of the Guardians so binding him, or their successors, shall be annexed the proviso following; that is to say,

Provided, That such Guardians may in such licence so to be given, by express words to that effect, if they think fit, authorise the master at any time during the residue of the term of the apprenticeship, to change the place of the abode or service of the apprentice, without any further application to them or their successors.

And We do hereby Order, that all the terms contained in this Order shall be construed in the same manner as the same terms are required to be construed in the Order above cited.

And, in pursuance of the provisions contained in the said first-recited Act, We do Direct, that whenever any Justice or Justices shall, under any authority of law, assent or consent, order or allow, of the binding of any poor child as apprentice, and the provisions herein contained shall be adopted on such binding, such Justice or Justices shall certify at the foot of the indenture and the counterpart thereof, in the form and manner following; that is to say,

"I, *or* We, *(as the case may be,)* Justice *or* Justices of the Peace of and in the County *(or other jurisdiction as the case may be,)* of , who have assented to, ordered, *or* allowed the above binding, do hereby certify, that we have examined and ascertained that the Rules, Orders, and Regulations of the Poor Law Commissioners, for the binding of poor children apprentices, and applicable to the above-named Parish, *(or other place, as the case may be,)* contained in their General Orders bearing date respectively the Twenty-ninth day of January, and the Twenty-second day of August, One thousand eight hundred and forty-five, have been complied with.

"Signed this day of

Signature."

[*Schedules A. and B. annexed to this Order consist of the names of the Unions and Parishes which are set forth in No.* 43 *of the Official Circular, pages* 15, 16.]

Given under our Hands and Seal of Office, this Twenty-second day of August, in the year One thousand eight hundred and forty-five.

(Signed) GEO. NICHOLLS.
L. S. G. C. LEWIS.
EDMUND W. HEAD.

---

4. GENERAL ORDER ISSUED TO PARISHES NOT IN UNIONS AND NOT GOVERNED BY BOARDS OF GUARDIANS, AMENDING AN ORDER DATED 29TH JANUARY, 1845.

To the Churchwardens and Overseers of the several Parishes and Places named in the Schedule hereunto annexed;—

To the Clerk or Clerks to the Justices of the Petty Sessions held for the Division or Divisions in which the Parishes and Places named in the said Schedule are situate;—

And to all others whom it may concern.

Whereas the Poor Law Commissioners, in pursuance of the powers vested in them by an Act passed in the fifth year of the reign of His late Majesty King William the Fourth, intituled "*An Act for the Amendment and better Administration of the Laws relating to the Poor in England and Wales,*" and an Act passed in the eighth year of the reign of Her present Majesty Queen Victoria, intituled "*An Act for the further Amendment of the Laws relating to the Poor in England,*" by an Order under their Hands and Seal, bearing date the Twenty-ninth day of January last, and addressed to the Churchwardens and Overseers of the Poor of the several Parishes and Places named in the Schedule hereunto annexed, did make certain Rules and Regulations in regard to the apprenticing of Poor Children, and it is expedient that certain alterations should be made therein.

Now, therefore, We, the Poor Law Commissioners, acting under the Authority of the Statutes aforesaid, do hereby alter the said Order, in the manner hereinafter mentioned, and do Order,—

First, That it shall be lawful for the Overseers of the Poor of the said Parishes and Places respectively to give a premium, other than clothing, upon the binding as an apprentice of any person not above the age of sixteen years;

Secondly, That the Overseers who shall bind any poor person apprentice, may dispense with the condition, by the said Order required to be inserted in the indenture of apprenticeship, providing for the payment of the remuneration to the apprentice after the age of seventeen years;

Thirdly, That to the condition, by the said Order required to be inserted in the said indenture, providing that the master shall not cause the said apprentice to work or live more than ten miles from the place or places mentioned in the indenture, according to Article 16 of the said recited Order, without the leave of the Overseers so binding him or their successors, shall be annexed the proviso following; that is to say,

Provided, That such Overseers may in such licence so to be given, by express words to that effect, if they think fit, authorise the master, at any time during the residue of the term of the apprenticeship, to change the place of the abode or service of the apprentice, without any further application to them or their successors.

And We do hereby Order, that all the terms contained in this Order shall be construed in the same manner as the same terms are required to be construed in the Order above cited.

And in pursuance of the provisions contained in the said first-recited Act, We do Direct, that whenever any Justice or Justices shall, under any authority of law, assent or consent, order or allow, of the binding of any poor child as apprentice, and the provisions herein contained shall be adopted on such binding, such Justice or Justices shall certify at the foot of the indenture and the counterpart thereof, in the form and manner following; that is to say,

"I, or We, *(as the case may be)* Justice or Justices of the Peace of and in the County *(or other jurisdiction, as the case may be,)* of , who have assented to, ordered, or allowed the above binding, do hereby certify, that we have examined and ascertained that the Rules, Orders, and Regulations of the Poor Law Commissioners, for the binding of poor children apprentices, and applicable to the above named Parish, *(or other place, as the case may be,)* contained in their General Orders bearing date respectively the Twenty-ninth day of January, and the Twenty-second day of August, One thousand eight hundred and forty-five, have been complied with.

"Signed this day of

Signature."

[*The Schedule annexed to this Order consists of the names of the Parishes and Places set forth in No.* 43 *of the Official Circular, pages* 15, 16.]

Given under our Hands and Seal of Office, this Twenty-second day of August, in the year One thousand eight hundred and forty-five.

(Signed) GEO. NICHOLLS.
L. S. G. C. LEWIS.
EDMUND W. HEAD.

5. CIRCULAR ACCOMPANYING THE ABOVE ORDERS

Poor Law Commission Office,
Somerset House, 30th August, 1845.

Amended Apprenticing Order.

SIR,—I am directed by the Poor Law Commissioners to inform you, that, in conformity with their Circular Letter of the 5th May last, respecting certain objections which had been made to the Order relating to the Apprenticeship of Poor Children, recently issued by the Commissioners, they have modified such Order in the manner proposed in that Circular, and herewith I am to transmit to you Two Sealed Copies of the amended Order which the Commissioners have thus issued relating to the several Places contained in the Schedule annexed to the Order.

As the Order appears to come within the definition of a General Rule given by the Poor Law Amendment Act, it will not operate until the expiration of forty days from the period of the same having been transmitted to One of Her Majesty's Principal Secretaries of State, as required by the Sixteenth Section of that Act.

I am further directed to state, that a Copy of the Order was forwarded by the Commissioners to the Right Honourable Sir James Graham, Bart., Her Majesty's Principal Secretary of State for the Home Department, on the Twenty-third day of August instant, and it will consequently come into operation on the Third day of October next.

I am, &c.,
W. G. LUMLEY,
Assistant Secretary.

To the Clerk to the Guardians.

II.—AUDIT DISTRICTS.

FORM OF THE ORDERS FOR CREATING AUDIT DISTRICTS AND PRESCRIBING THE MODE OF ELECTING AUDITORS.

} Audit District.

To the Guardians of the poor of the ——— unions.

To the churchwardens and overseers of the poor of the several parishes and places comprised in the said unions;—

To the treasurers of the said unions respectively;—

To the clerk or clerks to the justices of the petty sessions held for the division or divisions in which the said unions are situate;—

And to all others whom it may concern.

I.—*Creation of District.*

Article 1.—We, the Poor Law Commissioners, acting under the authority of an Act passed in the fifth year of the reign of His late Majesty King William the Fourth, intituled "An Act for the Amendment and better Administration of the Laws relating to the Poor in England and Wales," and of an Act passed in the eighth year of the reign of Her present Majesty Queen Victoria, intituled "An Act for the further Amendment of the Laws relating to the Poor in England," do hereby combine the following unions, viz. —— Unions, into a district for the audit of accounts, to be termed "The Berkshire and Hampshire Audit District," and do order and direct, that one person shall be appointed as the auditor of the said district.

II.—*Mode of Election.*

Article 2.—And we do hereby prescribe the time and manner in which such auditor shall be elected, as follows; that is to say,

On some day or days *between the* ——— *and days of* ——— *next,* and on some day *within thirty days* after the happening of any vacancy in the said office, an Assistant Poor Law Commissioner, to be determined by the Poor Law Commissioners, shall cause an advertisement to be inserted in one of the newspapers published in the cities of London or Westminster, and in two or more newspapers published within the counties in which the said unions or some of them are situated, giving notice of the vacancy, and inviting persons desirous to become candidates for the office of auditor to send to him, at some place to be therein specified, their names in full, their profession or occupation, their age and residence, within a time *not exceeding fourteen days* from the first insertion of such notice in such newspapers as aforesaid.

Article 3.—On the expiration of the said term of fourteen days, the Assistant Poor Law Commissioner shall cause a list to be made of such persons as may have duly offered themselves as candidates, and may have forwarded the information herein-before required; and such Assistant Poor Law Commissioner shall send copies of such list, with the other particulars herein-before required, to each of the several chairmen and vice-chairmen of the boards of guardians of the before-mentioned unions respectively, and to such other persons as may be qualified to vote at the election of the auditor for the district, and shall request each elector to return to him, in some writing signed by such elector, on or before a day to be specified by such Assistant Poor Law Commissioner, being *not less than seven days, nor more than fourteen days*, after the date of such list, the name of the candidate in such list for whom such elector votes.

Article 4.—On the day next after the day specified by such Assistant Poor Law Commissioner for the return of such names, the said Assistant Poor Law Commissioner shall examine the returns then received by him, and shall cast up the numbers, and shall enter on the said list so made out by him as aforesaid, against the name of each candidate, the names of the several electors who shall have voted for such candidate.

Article 5.—If any candidate shall have obtained the majority of the votes of the said electors, the Assistant Poor Law Commissioner shall certify in writing at the foot of such list, that such candidate hath been duly elected the auditor for such district.

Article 6.—If no candidate have received the votes of the majority of the electors, the Assistant Poor Law Commissioner shall again send the names of the two candidates who have received the greatest number of votes to each of the several electors, with a request that each elector will return, in some writing signed by him, the name of one of such two persons to the said Assistant Poor Law Commissioner, on or before a day to be specified, being *not less than seven days, nor more than fourteen days*, after the date of such request.

Article 7.—On the day next after the day specified for the second return, the Assistant Poor Law Commissioner shall examine the returns then received by him, and shall proceed, as on the former occasion, to cast up the number of the votes, and to enter the names of the persons voting, and to certify in writing that the candidate who then has the greater number of votes is elected the auditor of the district.

Article 8.—If on the return to the copies of the list first sent out by the said Assistant Poor Law Commissioner it be found that no candidate has a majority of the votes of the electors, and that the votes are equal in favour of the three candidates, who have received the largest number of votes, or in favour of any two of such three candidates, he shall forward on the second occasion the names of all such three candidates, and shall proceed as if the names of the candidates so sent were sent for the first time, except that, in the event of there being an equality of votes on the second voting, the election shall be deemed to have failed, and proceedings shall take place as on a new vacancy.

Article 9.—If only one candidate shall offer himself to the Assistant Poor Law Commissioner, the name and address of such person shall be sent by such Assistant Poor Law Commissioner to all the persons qualified to vote as aforesaid, and such Assistant Poor Law Commissioner shall request such persons to inform him in writing, on or before a day to be specified, being *not less than seven days, nor more than fourteen days* from the date of such request, whether such persons assent or object to such candidate being elected as an auditor, and if the greater number of the electors then entitled to vote shall signify their assent to the election of such person, but not otherwise, the said Assistant Poor Law Commissioner shall declare the candidate to be duly elected.

Article 10.—The Assistant Poor Law Commissioner shall cause copies of the lists showing the names of the voters who shall have voted for each candidate, or, in case of no contest, of the electors who shall have expressed their assent to the election of the person nominated, with the name of the person elected as auditor duly certified at the foot thereof, to be printed forthwith, and shall transmit to the guardians of the several unions respectively printed copies thereof, and shall communicate to the person so elected auditor the fact of his having been so elected, and shall advertise the result of the election in some one or more newspaper or newspapers published in the district.

III.—*Continuance in Office.*

Article 11.—And we do determine that the officer so appointed shall continue in office until he shall die or resign, or be removed therefrom by the Poor Law Commissioners. And in case of such death, resignation, or removal, another auditor shall be appointed in manner aforesaid.

IV.—*Duties of the Auditor.*

Article 12.—The auditor shall, twice in every year, that is to say, as soon as may be after the twenty-fifth day of March, and the twenty-ninth day of September, examine, audit, and allow or disallow, the accounts of the several unions herein-before combined, and of the several parishes comprised in the said unions, according to the laws in force for the time being for the administration of the relief to the poor.

V.—*Remuneration of Auditor.*

Article 13.—And we do regulate the amount of the salary payable to such officer, and the time and mode of payment thereof, and the proportions in which such respective unions shall contribute to such payment, as follows:—

We order, that the said auditor shall be paid for the performance of his duties an annual salary, commencing on the day when the Assistant Poor Law Commissioner shall certify his election as aforesaid, after the rate of three hundred and forty-one pounds per annum, such sum to be paid by two proportionate payments, one thereof to be made on the first day of January and the other to be made on the first day of July in each year, in respect of each union for which the last audit shall have been completed by him, or so soon after the aforesaid days as such audit shall have been completed.

Provided nevertheless, that if it shall happen that the person for the time being filling the said office of district auditor shall cease to be such auditor, after having completed the audit of some one or more of the above-mentioned unions, but before he shall have completed the audit of the whole of them, the guardians of every union whose accounts shall have been completely audited shall pay their share of the salary so payable to the said auditor, in the manner aforesaid.

Article 14.—And we do hereby order, that the said several unions shall contribute to the said sum of three hundred and forty-one pounds in the manner following; that is to say,

	£
The —— union shall contribute the sum of -	
The —— union shall contribute the sum of -	
The —— union shall contribute the sum of -	

VI.—*Explanation of Terms.*

Article 15.—Whenever the majority of electors is spoken of in this order, it is to be taken to mean the majority of those electors whose assents to, or dissents from, a candidate on any list sent out as aforesaid are received in due form, and within the proper time.

Article 16.—Whenever any notice or list or other document is required to be sent, it shall be sufficient if the same be sent by the post, and the date of the delivery of the same to the Post-office shall be taken to be the date of sending the same.

Article 17.—If, by any accident, error, or other cause, a majority of the whole number of votes to be given has not been received on the day appointed for the receipt thereof, the election shall be deemed to have failed.

Article 18.—The word *Parishes* in this order shall be taken to include all places maintaining their own poor, whether parochial or extra-parochial.

Given under our Hands and Seal of Office, this day of in the year one thousand eight hundred and forty-five.

(Signed) GEO. NICHOLLS.
L. S. G. C. LEWIS.

III.—AUDITOR.

TERMINATION OF THE POWERS OF A UNION AUDITOR, AND THE COMMENCEMENT OF THOSE OF A DISTRICT AUDITOR.

The Poor Law Commissioners have addressed the following circular letter to the Clerks of the Guardians of those Unions formed into Audit Districts:—

Poor Law Commission Office,
Somerset House, 1845.

SIR,

THE Poor Law Commissioners having observed that considerable doubt occasionally prevails, as to the precise time when the powers of an Union Auditor cease, and those of a District Auditor begin, after the issue of an Order either for the election of a District Auditor, or for the continuance of such an officer, under the provisions of the Act 7 and 8 Vict. c. 101, the Commissioners desire to state, for your information and guidance, that they consider that in a district for which an Auditor is to be elected under the 32nd section of the Act referred to, the powers of the Union Auditor will continue up to the day on which the District Auditor shall be appointed; that is to say, the day on which it is declared that an auditor for that district has been duly elected, in pursuance of the Order of the Commissioners.

The powers of the District Auditor will commence from the day on which he is declared to be elected.

The declaration that an auditor has been elected for a district will be made by the Assistant Commissioner conducting the election; and will be publicly notified by means of advertisements inserted in one or more of the local or other newspapers published or circulated in the district.

When the Commissioners issue an Order under the 37th section of the 7th and 8th Vict. c. 101, "continuing" an Auditor of more than one Union in his office, and thereby making him a "District Auditor," within the meaning of that Act—the powers of the Union Auditor will continue until that Order takes effect, and then cease.

On the Order taking effect, the powers of the District Auditor will arise.

As such an Order must necessarily be directed to, and affect more than one Union at the time of issuing the same, it will be a "General Rule" within the terms of the 109th section of the 4th and 5th Wm. IV. c. 76, and therefore it will not take effect until the expiration of forty days after the same shall have been sent by the Commissioners to one of Her Majesty's Principal Secretaries of State.

With regard to the Salaries of the Auditors, the Commissioners wish to remark that the Salary of the Union Auditor will be due, and ought to be paid to him up to the day on which he ceases to hold the Office, on being superseded by the District Auditor.

The District Auditor's Salary will accrue from that day.

I am, Sir, &c.

EDWIN CHADWICK, *Secretary*.

To the Clerk to the Board of Guardians.

IV.—BASTARDY.

COST OF SUMMONING THE PUTATIVE FATHER.

28th July, 1845.

Assistant Overseer of Hedon, Sculcoates Union—Inquired whether the overseers were bound to pay the cost of serving a summons, under the Act of 7th and 8th Vic. c. 101, on the putative father of a bastard child, the justices having made an order on the overseers calling on them to pay such costs.

Ans.—The Commissioners are of opinion that the justices have no power to order the overseers of a parish to pay the constable for serving a summons on the putative father of a bastard child, under the 7th and 8th Vic. c. 101. It appears to the Commissioners that the remedy given to the mother of a bastard child by that statute, is entirely of a private and personal nature; and that when she obtains a summons upon the putative father to appear before the justices, it rests with her to procure it to be served, as she may think fit. If she employs the constable to serve it, she must so employ him as her private agent; and she may be reimbursed the expense thereby incurred, under the order for costs, which the justices are empowered to make on the putative father, under the third section of the Act. But as the summons does not relate to any question of parochial concern, or any matter affecting the preservation of the peace, and the service of it is not a duty which the justices can require the constable to perform, the Commissioners think that the case does not come within the seventeenth section of the 5th and 6th Vic. c. 109, (the Parish Constables Act,) and that consequently no fee or allowance in relation to it can legally be charged upon the poor-rates of the parish. The Commissioners accordingly consider that the Order in question is of no effect.

V.—CHARGEABILITY—REMOVAL.

June 6th, 1845.

The Rev. Mr. ———. The sole occupier and the holder of all the parochial offices of the adjoining parish of A, took a house at a rent of ten pounds a-year in the parish of B, for a sickly pauper belonging to the parish of A, with the acknowledged object of his gaining a settlement in that parish. Immediately on the pauper completing his twelve months' occupancy, he was dismissed from his employment in the parish of A, and told to look to the parish of B for work and relief. He then applied to the overseers of that parish, who gave him temporary assistance; and shortly after, he and his family were admitted into the union workhouse, where they remained two days. On the clerk of the guardians being applied to for a certificate of chargeability, with a view to the removal of the pauper, he refused to give it, on the ground that it could be of no avail as the pauper had ceased to be chargeable, he having left the workhouse a quarter of an hour before. The certificate was, however, obtained subsequently; but the justices taking the same view of the matter as the clerk, declined to take the examination of the pauper. Inquired, whether this view of the matter is a correct one; and also whether an action will not lie against Mr. ——— for a fraudulent attempt to settle the pauper on the parish of B.

Ans.—As regards the certificate of chargeability which has been already obtained in the case referred to by you, it would, in the opinion of the Commissioners, be sufficient for the purposes of the order of removal, provided that such order were made within the period of twenty-one days from the date of the certificate. Where a certificate in the form of the statute 7 and 8 Vic. c. 101, is produced to the justices, and the period of twenty-one days from the date of such certificate has not elapsed, the Commissioners do not understand that it is necessary, with a view to making the order of removal, that other evidence should be given of the pauper's being *then* actually chargeable. In order to avoid the necessity of the more distinct allegations of chargeability and relief before required, the 69th section of the act above cited, provides that, "for the purpose of making any order of removal or other order, no further or other evidence of chargeability than such certificate shall be required, provided that every such order bear date within twenty-one days next after the day of the date of such certificate." This is evidently equivalent to a declaration that a chargeability declared to have existed before the certificate, is sufficiently alleged for the purposes of every order of removal made within twenty-one days *after* the certificate. With respect to the circumstances detailed in the first part of your letter, and the conduct attributed to Mr. ———, I am to observe that the Commissioners do not perceive that such conduct, assuming it could be clearly established, affords any ground of action against him. In Rex *v.* Edwards, 8 Mod. 321, 1 Bott. 374, it appears to have been laid down by the court that a conspiracy by parish officers to procure a settlement for a pauper in order to bring a charge upon another parish, is an indictable offence. The circumstances of the present case, as detailed in your letter, do not, however, appear to be such as would support an indictment for conspiracy. You observe that Mr. ——— is the sole occupier in A, and holds all the parish offices in that parish. It does not appear, therefore, to be likely that he combined or conspired with any other person to effect the purpose of charging the parish of B, unless, indeed, the pauper be shown to be a party to the conspiracy. Enough is not stated to enable the Commissioners to form a judgment on this part of the question. It is, however, very questionable whether a settlement was obtained under the circumstances in the parish of B. The Commissioners conclude, from your statement, that Mr. ——— filled the office of overseer in A at the period when the hiring took place at B: and it is stated, he took the house for the pauper. If this were so—if there were not an actual hiring of the house by the pauper—no settlement was acquired by the mere occupation of the tenement. To gain a settlement under the united operation of 6th Geo. 4, and 1st Wm. 4, c. 18, the tenement must be actually occupied for a year by the person hiring it. Further, it is stated by you, that "the pauper admits having received the money to make the quarterly payments, from Mr. ———." Now, the statutes referred to, not only require that the renting should be bonâ fide, but that the payment of the rent should also be bonâ fide. If the payments made to the pauper in this case were fraudulent, *i. e.* not with a view to his relief, but to get rid of the pauper—to enable him to pay his rent for the tenement in B, and so to acquire a settlement in that parish—then it is clear, according to the decisions of Rex *v.* The inhabitants of Tillingham, 1 B. and Ad. 180, and Rex *v.* St. Sepulchre, Cambridge, 1 B. and Ad. 924, that no settlement was acquired.

VI.—JUSTICES.—THEIR JURISDICTION.—RECOVERY OF CONTRIBUTIONS.

5th August, 1845.

Clerk of North Aylesford Union.—The parochial affairs of Strood, one of the parishes in the North Aylesford Union, are managed by a body of trustees under a Local Act, who may sue and be sued in the name of their clerk, and the order of the guardians for contributions from the parish to the union are therefore addressed not to the overseers but to the trustees and their clerk, and are served on that officer. Owing to the non-payment of the contributions of the parish, proceedings were taken under 2 and 3 Vic. c. 84, to enforce payment; and on the hearing of the complaint, the clerk to the trustees objected to the authority of the justices of Rochester to act in the case, on the ground that the parish of Strood was not wholly within their jurisdiction, while he admitted that the greater portion of the parish was so. The justices, however, overruled the objection, and made their order for payment of the amount,—the greater part of which has since been paid. As it is possible that it may be necessary to take proceedings to enforce payment of future orders, requested the Commissioners' opinion as to whether the justices for the city and borough of Rochester, or the justices for the county of Kent at large, have jurisdiction in the matter. The parish is divided into three parts; Strood intra, Strood media, and Strood extra. Strood intra, being that part of the parish which was anciently within the limits and jurisdiction of the city of Rochester; Strood media, that part which, by the Parliamentary Boundary Act, is placed within the boundary of the city and borough of Rochester; and Strood extra, that part which remains without the boundary and jurisdiction of Rochester. The poor-rates for the parish are made by the trustees, and, as directed by the Local Act, allowed by the justices for Rochester as to that part which is within their jurisdiction, and by the justices for the county, for that part which is without such jurisdiction. The parish church and nearly the whole population are within the boundary of the city and borough, as is also the union workhouse; and the clerk to the trustees also resides within the borough.

Ans.—Having regard to the nature of the question raised in your letter, and to the provisions of the Municipal Corporations Act, (5 and 6 Wm. 4, c. 76,) the Commissioners presume that the justices for the county of Kent have no jurisdiction within the city of Rochester. Under the 1st sec. of the 2 and 3 Vic. c. 84, the proceedings for the recovery of contributions from any parish, are to be taken before "two justices acting within the *district* wherein such parish shall be situate." The precise meaning of the word "district," as used in this section, appears to the Commissioners to be open to considerable doubt; whenever consulted on this point, they have stated it as their opinion, that it would be the safest course to construe the word as referring to the particular petty sessional division, which comprises the parish in arrear. From any point of view, they see great difficulty in giving such an interpretation to the word, as would bring the case of Strood parish within the provisions of the statute. If the word is taken as referring to a petty sessional division, then it would seem that the parish of Strood is not wholly within any one such *division*. if, as referring to the limits of the jurisdiction of the justices, it would likewise seem that the entire parish is not within any one such *jurisdiction*, and if the *entire* parish is not within any one such division, (or jurisdiction,) the Commissioners apprehend that it cannot be considered as situated within the district (whether the jurisdiction or division,) so as to come within the terms—"the district *wherein such parish* shall be situate." The Commissioners are disposed to think that the situation of only a part of the parish within the district would not be sufficient to give the justices of such a district authority to act in the case. If the word "district" were here used synonymously with "union," the justices for the city of Rochester might act in the case, inasmuch as they are justices acting within the union wherein the parish of Strood is situate. But the Commissioners do not think that such an interpretation can be supported; for (among other reasons) it would obviously exclude from the statute the cases of single parishes under separate boards of guardians, cases which are expressly mentioned in the previous portion of the clause as coming within its provisions. On the whole, therefore, the Commissioners are unable to say, either that the justices of Kent, or that the justices of Rochester, can deal with this matter. The Commissioners see nothing in the local Acts that affects the construction of the 2 and 3 Vic. c. 84. Under these circumstances, the Commissioners can only advise that if the trustees of Strood should in future refuse or neglect to pay the contributions required of them by the guardians of North Aylesford Union, the guardians should proceed against the trustees penally, either under the 95th sec. of the Poor Law Amendment Act, for a disobedience of the order of the guardians, or under the 98th sec. of that act, for a disobedience of the orders of the Commissioners. Having regard to the doubts which some persons entertain, as to the construction of the 95th sec., the Commissioners in such cases usually recommend that resort should be had to the provisions of the 98th.

VII.—MEDICAL OFFICERS.—CIRCULAR.

Poor Law Commission Office, Somerset House, 21st July, 1845.

SIR,—The Poor Law Commissioners have learnt that the Registrar General has addressed a circular letter, dated the 10th July instant, to "Physicians, Surgeons, and Apothecaries, legally qualified, practising medicine in England," with the view of obtaining an accurate and uniform return of the causes of death; and the Commissioners, being desirous that all the medical officers appointed under the Poor Law Amendment Act should render their best assistance in securing so important an object, have directed me to request that you will be good enough, in the case of the death of every pauper attended by you, to comply with the wishes of the Registrar General in this matter, by making the return of the cause of such death in the form referred to in the above-mentioned circular,—which form will be supplied to you by the Registrar of the district where you reside.

I am, Sir, your most obedient servant,

EDWIN CHADWICK, *Secretary*.

To the Medical Officer

VIII.—MERCHANT SERVICE.

ACT OF 8 AND 9 VICT. c. 116.—CIRCULAR.

Poor Law Commission Office, Somerset House, Aug. 20th, 1845.

SIR,—I am directed by the Poor Law Commissioners to state, that they have ascertained that various persons have lately made applications to boards of guardians to procure lads for the merchant service, upon various terms and stipulations, not being themselves either masters of vessels or ship-owners.

The Commissioners have reason to believe that very serious evils have resulted from this species of brokerage, and that many of the persons engaged in the procuring of hands for that service have adopted a course of proceeding highly demoralising and injurious to the health and condition of the persons for whom they have undertaken to procure situations.

The attention of the legislature has been drawn to the subject; and during the last session of parliament an Act was passed, entitled, *An Act for the Protection of Seamen entering on board Merchant Ships*, (8 and 9 Vic. c. 116.)

It will be seen that it is thereby provided that persons may, after the first of September next, be licensed by the Board of Trade to provide seamen for merchant ships: and that after the first of November next, no person, not being so licensed, or the owner, master, person in charge of a ship, or ship's husband, shall provide any seamen for a merchant ship.

Should, therefore, any application be made to the guardians for lads to be placed on board merchant ships, it will be necessary for them to ascertain that the applicants are legally authorised to make such application.

The guardians will observe, that by section 8 of the Act, if any person receive from any person other than the owner, master, or ship's husband, any remuneration, either directly or indirectly, for the providing of any seaman, he will forfeit the sum of £5.

If the guardians consider it expedient to bind any children to the sea service, they must not lose sight of the provisions contained in the 7 and 8 Vic. c. 112, for the binding of poor children as apprentices to that service, and must abide strictly by the regulations therein prescribed, which statute, it may be observed, expressly enables the guardians to provide for the cost of the outfit of the lads, while it does not appear that the same could be supplied by the guardians under other circumstances.

I am, &c.,

W. G. LUMLEY, *Assistant Secretary*.

To the Clerk to the Guardians.

IX.—RATING COAL MINES.

13th Jan., 1845.

J. C., Darlington Union—Submitted for the Commissioners' opinion, the following case:

A. B. is the lessee of certain coal mines in the county of Durham. The lessor is C. D., who in the year 1830 advertised the coal-beds or seams of coal to be let for the best annual rent that could be obtained. A. B. became lessee, and entered into the usual covenants; the rents to be paid were £500 certain rent, whether any coals were wrought and vended or not, and a further rent of 25*s*. for every fifty tons of coals which should be wrought and vended over and above twenty thousand tons, which at 25*s*. per fifty tons was the equivalent for the £500 certain rent. A. B. expended £40,000 in clearing the mine of water, and in bringing the mine into a working condition—laying railways and making the needful erections. The lease was for a term of twenty-five years. Owing to sundry hinderances and disappointments, the mine was not brought into regular work till the year 1835: there then remained twenty years of the lease unexpired. Owing to various difficulties, the mine was worked without profit till the year 1840. There then remained sixteen years of the lease: and a profitable occupation may be said to have then commenced. Under the operation of the Income Tax, the profits of the mine in the years 1842, 1843, were assessed at £5500, which was thus made up:—Rent paid by lessees to lessor, £1500; profits on working and vending coals £4000=£5500. The mine was regularly rated by the parochial authorities in the township wherein it was mainly situated, to poor's rate, county rate, church rate, &c., at the sum of £1000 per annum. In 1844, the magistrates for the county, desirous of regulating the county rate, and being of opinion that the mining property was not fairly rated, entered upon an inquiry, in order to ascertain that fact; and having possessed themselves of the assessments made under the Property and Income Tax, resolved to enforce a rating equal in amount to those returns, less an abatement of 25 per cent. for what they term, tenant's risk and contingencies. The assessment upon A. B.'s colliery was directed to be made at £4125. Thus: lessor's rent, about which there can be no dispute, £1500, less 25 per cent., £375=£1125. Profit (not as profits, but as showing, it is said, the annual value of the mine to the present occupant at the present moment,) £4000, less 25 per cent. £1000=£3000; making together £4125. The whole of the mine not being in one township, about £1250 was paid as rent in respect of the part in one township; and £250 in respect of the part in another township. It will be seen that £1250 bore the same relation to the former assessment of £1000, as that now proposed by the magistrates; but the question of assessment upon profits, (not as profits, but as increased value ascertained as above,) remained untouched. The parochial officers, however, consider that no alteration has taken place in the value of mineral property, and have resolved that the colliery had been fairly let; that the sum paid to the lessor was the full and fair annual value of the colliery to let; that the profits were no more now than ought to be received for the capital expended and sunk, and for meeting all the serious risks of mining. A capital of £40,000 was expended, the interest on which is £2,000 per annum; for 10 years the mine was wholly unprofitable, and the loss augmented. When the lease expires, there will remain about £10,000 in value of removable stock; £30,000 will have been redeemed by annual profits or will have been entirely lost; £2000 per annum will be required to redeem the money expended on the mine, which will leave the lessees for the interest of capital, all his time, labour, skill, and risks, over and above the ordinary risk of commercial adventure, just 5 per cent. on his capital; without this investment, no rent whatever could be obtained. The magistrates require, that all collieries whose rents and profits have been ascertained, shall be rated at the gross amount of such rents and profits, subject to a deduction of 25 per cent. thereon for tenant's right, risk, and contingencies; parties claiming further deductions to be heard by themselves and witnesses before a barrister.—Inquired, 1st, What is the principle of rating now recognised as just and legal in such a case? 2nd, Should the magistrates under the powers conferred upon them, by employing valuers other than the parochial officers, amend the rate, and augment the levy, what redress have the lessees? 3rd, If proprietors of collieries are rateable to the extent contended for by the magistrates, are not farmers, market-gardeners, and others in like manner rateable for profits, or rather should not their rents be increased, in case they are found to have made profits beyond the actual rent?

Ans.—It is the imposition of the county rate which is directly in question in this case. But inasmuch as that rate appears to be raised by the overseers (and not by the constable, as would be more regular in the county of Durham) and is presumably paid out of the poor rates, it does not appear to be foreign to the Commissioners' duties to state their opinion in reply to the questions addressed to them. There can be no ground for imposing a county rate on a parish or township in respect of any property which is not liable to be rated to the poor's rate. The county rate is only to be levied in such places upon "the messuages, lands, tenements, and hereditaments rateable to the relief of the poor," 55 Geo. III. c. 51, s. 1. These terms might be held to have excluded profits of trade or business, while such profits were liable to the poor's rate, but certainly could not be used to support the imposition of the county rate on such profits, while, as is the case at present, they are exempt from poor's rate. There is, therefore, no authority to include in the county rate, in any parish or township, the value of any profits, other than the net rent of messuages, lands, tenements, and hereditaments. But as the Income Tax includes the whole of the net profits of a business, it includes profits not subject to taxation by the county rate or poor's rate, while, at the same time, the assessment does not distinguish profits of business from what may be the profits derived from a beneficial interest in a rateable tenement. It follows, that the assessment of a tenant to the Income Tax, cannot be properly adopted as the ground of his assessment to the poor or county rate. At the same time it appears to the Commissioners, by the statement in this case, that the lessees are liable to be rated on a larger sum than the rent they pay. The actual rent is no criterion of rateable value. The rateable value consists of the rent at which the tenement, in its existing state, might be reasonably expected to let for, allowance being made for payment by the tenant of taxes, repairs, &c., 6 and 7 Will. IV. c. 96, s. 1. It is quite immaterial by whom or by what expenditure a rateable tenement has been brought to its present value. The expenditure may have been profitable or not, it may have been made by the lessees, or the lessor; but all this is immaterial. The sole question for the valuer is, what is the rent for which it would let in its existing state to an occupier who should have the benefit of all its existing advantages. He can make no deduction for the interest of capital expended in bringing the tenement to its present value, and he can allow nothing as a sinking fund to replace the value to an occupier at the end of his term. He could, therefore, not take into consideration the amount spent in the present case, in bringing the mine into working condition, laying rails, or making erections. The rent which he is to estimate, is one which allows for future risks of the failure of productiveness or ruin of the tenement, for the real value is estimated on the principle of assuring the rent which remains, after payment of all expenses of repairs and insurance, and otherwise necessary to maintain the tenement in a state to command the supposed rent, 6 and 7 Will. IV. c. 96, s. 1. The elements are not shown which would enable the Commissioners to state what, in their opinion, is the present rateable value of the mine; but it will be easy for those who know the facts of the case to make application of the principles discussed above. 2. The lessees have no direct redress against an improper valuation to the county rate by the justices, whether that valuation be made at petty sessions under the 55 Geo. III. c. 51, sect. 1, or be adopted in quarter sessions as the ground of the county rate. The assessment to the county rate is a subject of appeal; but this is made on the whole parish or township, and the appeal against the county rate is given to the overseer, or the other rating officer, on behalf of the whole parish or township, 12 Geo. II. c. 29, s. 12: 55 Geo. III. c. 51, s. 14. The lessee's remedy is against the poor's rate, if his property is overvalued to that rate. But if he is fairly valued in the poor's rate itself, he does not appear to have any appeal against it, on the ground that the overseers have been over-assessed, and have paid too much to the county rate. 3. As above stated, proprietors of collieries are only rateable for the net value of their tenements, as they exist at the time of the rate, and not for profits of their business, independent of the existing letting value of the tenement. The same rule applies to gardeners and others. If they, as occupiers, improve the value of the tenement, they are rateable in respect of the improved letting value; but not in respect of the profits made from their exertions, skill, floating capital employed in wages, and other casual expenses, or any other way.

X.—RATING TITHES.

Mr. ———, *Wycombe Union*— Stated that the tithe commutation rent charge in the parish of A— having been duly settled and apportioned, the overseers were about to rate the tithe owners. There is a rent charge in lieu of vicarial tithes; also one in lieu of impropriate tithes, payable to an individual in respect of (say) 100 acres of land. The impropriate tithes of the remainder of the land in the parish are merged. Section 1 of the 6 and 7 Wm. 4, c. 96, enacts that no rate shall be of any force "which shall not be made upon an estimate of the net annual value of the hereditaments rated thereunto; that is to say, of the rent at which the same might reasonably be expected to let from year to year, free of all usual tenants' rates and taxes, and tithe commutation rent charge, if any, and deducting," &c. By the Commissioners' minute of the 29th November, 1841, it seems they consider that the "tithe commutation rent charge" should not form one of the deductions from the gross estimated rental in the same manner as the usual tenants' rates and taxes. The words, "tithe commutation rent charge, if any," in the act appear to have no meaning unless they bear the same construction as the words "usual tenants' rates and taxes," as to the deduction. It may be said that the words "usual tenants, &c." apply as well to "tithe commutation rent charge, if any," as to the words "rates and taxes;" but presuming that *all* tithes are alike chargeable upon the *land*, the true meaning of the clause seems to be that *all* tithe commutation rent charge whatever, is to be deducted from the gross estimated rental of land, as well as the usual tenants' rates and taxes; and that the words, "if any" have reference to houses, &c., which pay no tithe rent charge, and cannot claim a deduction in respect thereof. In point of *principle*, it matters not whether the tithe rent charge be considered as an impost upon the landlord or the tenant; for whatever is raised *from* the *land*, whether in the shape of rates or of tithes, they all equally affect the landlords' interest; and consequently *all* should form items of deduction with reference to the poor rate assessment; thus placing the proprietor of land upon the same footing as the tithe owner in regard to outgoings. Requested the Commissioners' opinion.

Ans.—The Commissioners agree that all tithe commutation rent charge is to be deducted from the gross value of the property to be rated. But they cannot understand that it is to be deducted from the gross value of property, except that upon which a rent charge is actually imposed. The Commissioners understand the hypothetical language of the 6 and 7 Wm. 4, c. 96, s. 1, as meaning this—that rent charge, if there be any charged on a given property, is to be deducted; if there be none fixed on the given property, it is not to be deducted. The purpose of this is apparently twofold:—1. To rate each property only on the annual net value of it to its possessor: for which purpose rent charge, which is no property of his, must be omitted:—2. To avoid rating double—which would be affected, the tithe owner being rateable independently, if the value of the rent charge was also rated in the value of the properties out of which it issues. Where a property is not burdened with the charge, as when the tithes are merged, then the owner of the property is rateable for its value without deduction. He in this case bears as much additional rate as if he were the owner of the rent charge, which appears just as regards him. The parish, and the other ratepayers, lose nothing, and gain nothing by this arrangement: the entire taxation remaining the same, notwithstanding the merging of the tithe and the consequent merging of the rate on the tithe in the land, and the rate in the land.

XI.—RELIEF.

1. CONSTRUCTION OF ARTICLE 1, EXCEPTION 2, OF PROHIBITORY ORDER.

———, adverting to Art. 1 of the Prohibitory Order, Except. 2, and the Art. 3, Except. 2, inquired whether the Commissioners are of opinion that the exceptions in question only permit out-relief, or non-resident relief, to the amount reasonably required to cover the particular case of sickness, &c., under consideration. For instance, a man, having a wife and five children to maintain, is out of work at the time of his wife's confinement, or of a child's illness; are the guardians justified in allowing out-relief for the man and the whole family because of the wife's or the child's sickness without reporting the case under Article 4, of the above order?

Ans.—The Commissioners in reply desire to point out that Article 1, of the above-named order, contains a positive provision to the effect that all able-bodied paupers and their families, shall be relieved wholly in the workhouse, "save and except in the following cases," *i. e.*, the cases enumerated in the several exceptions thereafter specified. The Commissioners understand this expression, 'save and except, &c.' as simply taking the cases adverted to, out of the operation of the positive provision of the Article; and consequently leaving such cases to be dealt with by the guardians, in the same manner in which the guardians might have dealt with them, if the order had not been issued. The 2nd exception is in these terms, "where such person shall require relief on account of any sickness, &c., affecting such person, or any of his or her family." It appears to the Commissioners to follow, from the view above explained, that where an able-bodied pauper requires relief, on account of any such sickness as is here described, his case is taken out of the operation of Art. 1 entirely, and not merely to the extent to which he may need relief, on account of such sickness alone. The provision in Art. 1 is unlimited. "Every able-bodied person, &c. shall be relieved wholly in the workhouse, &c., together with *such of the family* of every such able-bodied person *as may be resident with him, &c.*" If a case comes at all within this provision, it must be so entirely. If an able-bodied man requires relief at the same time on two grounds—sickness in his family, and want of employment for himself; it cannot, consistently, be said that the guardians are bound to deal with his case, under Art. 1—*i. e.*, to take him and the *whole of his family* into the workhouse; and that they are also at liberty to treat it as coming within Except. 2, as far as the sickness is concerned,—*i. e.*, to relieve the *sick part of his family* out of the workhouse. The Commissioners need scarcely add that they consider these remarks applicable, *mutatis mutandis*, to Except. 2 to Art. 3 as regards non-resident relief.

---

2. DEFICIENCY OF FUNDS TO SUPPLY RELIEF. —DUTY OF GUARDIANS.

Clerk of Louth Union—Inquired, 1st, whether the guardians would be justified in withholding relief from paupers, where the overseers of the parishes to which they are chargeable have neglected to supply funds to the guardians for their maintenance. 2. Whether the guardians are the proper parties to proceed against the overseers so offending, under the 63rd section of the 7 and 8 Vic. c. 101; or whether they can be proceeded against under the provisions of the Poor Law Amendment Act, if the guardians prefer that course.

Ans.—1. With regard to your first question, the Commissioners desire to observe that it is obviously fair and proper that the guardians should obtain beforehand money from each parish in proportion, as nearly as possible, to the anticipated wants of each, and that they should never allow any parish to be in arrear, and its obligations provided for at the expense of other parishes. Nevertheless, though this is the only fair and proper course for the guardians to pursue, it can scarcely be said that they are bound to abstain so rigidly from applying temporarily the funds in their hands originally derived from one parish to the purposes of another, as to be under the necessity of refusing or withholding relief, in urgent cases, solely on that ground. It may be remarked, that if relief be granted under such circumstances, the charge will of course be thrown, at the end of the quarter, upon the parish liable in respect of it, and the next order for contribution from that parish should be made accordingly. But although the guardians may be justified, by circumstances, in thus applying moneys of one parish to the concerns of another, they are under no absolute obligation to do so. Each parish is, by the 26th section of the Poor Law Amendment Act, made separately chargeable with and liable to defray the expense of its own poor. 2. With reference to your second question, the Commissioners in the first place desire to point out that the 63rd section of the 7 and 8 Vic. c. 101, does not apply to cases of mere neglect on the part of the overseers to supply funds for the maintenance of the poor, but only to cases in which, in consequence of such neglect, "any relief directed by the board of guardians to be given to any poor person is delayed or withheld during a period of seven days." In cases to which the provision does apply, the section does not confine the institution of proceedings against the overseers to any particular parties; and the Commissioners think that it is open to the guardians (as well as other persons) to take such proceedings, and to charge the costs upon the poor-rates, under the 59th section of the same statute. 3. In reply to your third inquiry, the Commissioners desire to state that the 63rd section of the 7 and 8 Vic. c. 101, does not in any way interfere with the liabilities of the overseers, under the Poor Law Amendment Act, for disobeying the orders of the guardians.

XII.—RETURNS RELATING TO THE ADMINISTRATION OF THE POOR LAW MADE TO PARLIAMENT DURING THE SESSION OF 1845.

Agricultural Statistics.—Copy of Correspondence between the Board of Trade and other Public Departments, relative to Agricultural Statistics. (265.) Moved for by Mr. Hutt. Presented 30th April.

Medical Officers.—A Return containing the description of the Diplomas, Licences, or other Letters Testimonial, that are admitted and sanctioned by the Poor Law Commissioners as legal qualifications which entitle Medical Practitioners to be appointed Medical Officers of Poor Law Unions in England and Wales. (53.) Moved for by Mr. Wakley. Presented 20th February.

Medical Poor Relief.—Report from the Select Committee of the House of Commons on Medical Poor Relief Committee, 1844, appointed to investigate the allegations of the petitions of D. Philipps and J. Parrott, Esq. (619.) Presented 5th August, and Index to the said Report.

Newington Workhouse.—Chaplain.—A Copy of all Correspondence between the Rector of Newington, (Surrey,) the Churchwardens, Overseers, or Guardians of the Poor, and the Poor Law Commissioners, relating to the appointment of a Chaplain to the Workhouse, between the 1st day of January, 1844, and the present time.

(613.) Moved for by Mr. Hawes. Presented 4th August.

Pauper Lunatics.—A Return of the number of Pauper Lunatics and Idiots chargeable to each of the Unions in England and Wales, and also to those places under Local Acts, in the month of August, 1844, (in pursuance of the Acts 5 and 6 Vic. c. 57, and 7 and 8 Vic. c. 101,) distinguishing those maintained in County Lunatic Asylums, in Licensed Houses, and elsewhere; with the average weekly cost per head of maintenance and clothing: together with the population of each Union in 1841, and the estimated number of Lunatics and Idiots for other places not under the Poor Law Amendment Act. (333.) Moved for by Lord Ashley. Presented 28th May.

Poor Law Commissioners.—Eleventh Annual Report of the Commissioners, together with Appendices. Presented (H. of C.) by command.

— Copies of several General Rules issued by the Poor Law Commissioners to Unions and Parishes in England and Wales since the last Session of Parliament. (8.) Presented 11th February.

— A Return of the number of days each Poor Law Commissioner has sat in discharge of his official duty at the office appointed for such official sittings, or at any other place for the same purpose; and a similar Return of the number of days each Assistant Poor Law Commissioner has been engaged in the discharge of his official duty: the place and periods at which those have been performed respectively, whether at the office of the Central Board of Commissioners, or in visits and inspections, or other matters of official duty, at the different Unions or Union Workhouses throughout England and Wales; the number of days employed therein; and the amount of expense incurred by each Assistant Poor Law Commissioner in travelling or in other incidental expenses relating thereto. (179.) Moved for by Colonel Sibthorp. Presented 1st April.

Poor's Rate and County Rate.—Return showing the total amount of Money levied for Poor Rate and County Rate in England and Wales, and the amount expended thereout for the relief and maintenance of the Poor for the years ended Lady-day, 1813 to 1844, both inclusive. (30.) Moved for by Sir James Graham. Presented 13th February.

Removal.—Return from the Clerks of the Peace of all Appeals to the Quarter Sessions against Orders of Removal, in the years 1841, 1842, and 1843, distinguishing how many have been quashed on the merits or on points of form. (13.) Moved for by Mr. Tatton Egerton. Presented 7th February.

Removal of Paupers.—A Return of the sums paid by Counties, Cities, Boroughs, Towns Corporate, Divisions, or Liberties, for the removal of Poor Persons born in Scotland and Ireland, and chargeable to Parishes in England, under the provisions of the Act 3 and 4 Wm. IV., c. 40, for three years ending the 31st day of December, 1844, distinguishing the amount paid in each year. (363.) Moved for by Mr. Alderman Copeland. Presented 10th June.

Rochdale Union.—Copy of a Memorial from the Board of Guardians of the Union of Rochdale, addressed to the Secretary of State for the Home Department, against the Introduction of the New Poor Laws into that District; and of the Answer to said Memorial:—and also Copy of a similar Memorial from the Ratepayers of Rochdale (with a Note of the number of Signatures attached to it;) and Copy of the Answer to that Memorial. (122.) Moved for by Mr. Sharman Crawford. Presented 13th March.

Workhouses.—A Return of all Union Workhouses under the Poor Law Amendment Act, in which the Pauper Inmates thereof are, or have been, since the formation of such Unions, employed in grinding or crushing Bones by means of Mills, Machinery, or otherwise, together with the Date of such Erection of Mills or other machinery; and the names of the Chairman and Vice-Chairman of the Board of Guardians of every such Union at the period; also the cost of the said Bones, including all expenses of carriage and other incidental expenses, and the amount which the same have produced in their manufactured state, and whether the same have been sold by tender or at a fixed price, or otherwise. (41.) Moved for by Captain Pechell. Presented 18th February.

LONDON:

Printed by Order of the Poor Law Commissioners, by BLACKBURN and PARDON, 6, Hatton Garden, and Published by CHARLES KNIGHT and Co., 22, Ludgate Street, Publishers to the Poor Law Commissioners.

AN

OFFICIAL CIRCULAR

OF PUBLIC DOCUMENTS AND INFORMATION:

DIRECTED BY THE POOR LAW COMMISSIONERS TO BE PRINTED, CHIEFLY FOR THE USE OF THE MEMBERS AND PERMANENT OFFICERS OF BOARDS OF GUARDIANS, UNDER THE POOR LAW AMENDMENT ACT.

No. 52. CIRCULAR ISSUED OCTOBER 1ST, 1845.

Poor Law Commission Office,
Somerset House, Oct. 1st, 1845.

THE Poor Law Commissioners directed that the following documents be printed and circulated for the information of Guardians and Officers of the several Unions, viz.

(Signed) By Order of the Board,
EDWIN CHADWICK, *Secretary.*

I.—ASYLUM DISTRICTS.

BY the Act 7 and 8 Vic. c. 101, s. 41, the Poor Law Commissioners are empowered, "as, and when they may see fit, by order under their hands and seal, to declare so many parishes or unions, or parishes and unions, any part of which may be within the district of the Metropolitan Police, or the City of London, or within the limits respectively of the city, towns, or boroughs" of Liverpool, Manchester, Bristol, Leeds, and Birmingham, "to be combined into districts for the purpose of providing and managing asylums for the temporary relief and setting to work therein of destitute houseless poor, who are not charged with any offence, and who may apply for relief, or become chargeable to the poor's-rate within such parish or union."

Sect. 42 of the Act provides that a Board shall be constituted for every district so to be formed, and directs the Commissioners to fix the qualification of the members of such board.

Sect. 43 empowers the Commissioners to regulate the proceedings of the district boards, and to direct and regulate the appointment, duties, remuneration, and removal of paid officers to be appointed by any such board.

The Commissioners under these powers have combined the unions and parishes hereafter named into districts, denominated *the Central Metropolitan Asylum District; the North-Eastern Metropolitan Asylum District; the South-Western Metropolitan Asylum District; the Western Metropolitan Asylum District; the South-Eastern Metropolitan Asylum District; and the North-Western Metropolitan Asylum District.*

And the Commissioners have also prescribed regulations for their management.

1. GENERAL ORDER CREATING THE CENTRAL METROPOLITAN ASYLUM DISTRICT, UNDER THE ACT 7 AND 8 VIC. C. 101.

To the Guardians of the Poor of the Holborn, Strand, City of London, East London, and West London Unions;—

To the Churchwardens and Overseers of the Poor of the several Parishes and Places comprised in the said Unions;—

To the Guardians and Governors of the Poor of the Parish of Saint James Clerkenwell, in the County of Middlesex;—

To the Directors of the Poor of the Parishes of Saint Giles in the Fields and Saint George Bloomsbury, in the said County of Middlesex;—

To the Guardians of the Poor of the Parish of Saint Luke, in the said County of Middlesex;—

To the Trustees of the Parish of Saint Mary, Islington, in the said County of Middlesex;—

To the Directors of the Poor of the Parish of Saint Pancras, in the said County of Middlesex;—

To the Churchwardens and Overseers of the Poor of the said several Parishes respectively;—

To the Clerk or Clerks to the Justice or Justices of the Petty Sessions held for the Division or Divisions in which the said Unions and Parishes respectively are situate;—

And to all others whom it may concern.

We, the Poor Law Commissioners, under the authority of an Act passed in the fifth year of the reign of His late Majesty King William the Fourth, intituled, "*An Act for the Amendment and better Administration of the Laws relating to the Poor in England and Wales,*" and of an Act passed in the eighth year of the reign of Her present Majesty, intituled, "*An Act for the further Amendment of the Laws relating to the Poor in England,*" do hereby declare as follows:

Article I.—That the following unions, that is to say, the Holborn and Strand Unions, being respectively situated within the district of the Metropolitan Police, the City of London, the East London, and the West London Unions, being respectively situated within the City of London, and the several parishes of Saint Giles in the Fields and Saint George Bloomsbury, Saint James Clerkenwell, Saint Luke Middlesex, Saint Mary Islington, and Saint Pancras, in the County of Middlesex, which said several parishes are respectively situated within the said district of the Metropolitan Police, shall be combined into a district, to be termed "*The Central Metropolitan Asylum District,*" for the purpose of providing and managing one or more asylum or asylums for the temporary relief and setting to work therein of destitute houseless poor persons, who are not charged with any offence, and who may apply for relief, or become chargeable to the poor's-rate, within any of the unions or parishes above mentioned.

Article II.—That a Board of Management shall be constituted for the said district, which shall consist of the ex-officio members entitled to act according to the provisions of the last-recited Act, and of seventeen members to be elected as hereinafter prescribed; so that

For the Holborn Union shall be elected One Guardian.

For the Strand Union shall be elected One Guardian.

For the City of London Union shall be elected Two Guardians.

For the East London Union shall be elected One Guardian.

For the West London Union shall be elected One Guardian.

For the Parish of Saint James Clerkenwell shall be elected Two Guardians.

For the Parishes of Saint Giles in the Fields and Saint George Bloomsbury shall be elected Two Guardians.

For the Parish of Saint Mary Islington shall be elected Two Guardians.

For the Parish of Saint Luke Middlesex shall be elected Two Guardians.

For the Parish of Saint Pancras shall be elected Three Guardians.*

Article III.—That the qualification for each person to be elected as a member of the said district, shall consist in the being rated within the said district upon a net annual value of not less than thirty pounds.

Article IV.—That the manner of the election of each member shall be as follows; the Guardians of the several Unions and Parishes in the said district, shall, at their first ordinary meeting after the fifth day of September next, elect some duly qualified person or persons, as the case may be, according to the number prescribed above, to be the member or members of the said Board, on behalf of the respective union or parish, the candidate or candidates being respectively nominated

* By an order, dated 27th Sept. 1845, this Parish is directed to elect *four* Guardians.

and seconded by Guardians at such meeting, and elected by a majority of the Guardians present thereat, who shall vote by a show of hands, to be counted by the presiding Chairman of such meeting.

Article V.—That the first-elected members of the Board of Management shall continue to serve as such, from the day of the election as aforesaid, until the twenty-fifth day of March, One thousand eight hundred and forty-seven.

Article VI.—That each Board of Guardians of the said Unions and Parishes shall, on one of the last two ordinary meetings before the twenty-fifth day of March, in the year One thousand eight hundred and forty-seven, and in every subsequent year, proceed, in the manner herein-before prescribed, to elect the member or members, as the case may be, for their union or parish, to serve for the year next ensuing such twenty-fifth day of March.

Given under our hands and seal of office, this twenty-sixth day of July, in the year One thousand eight hundred and forty-five.

(Signed) G. NICHOLLS.
G. C. LEWIS.

---

2. GENERAL ORDER PRESCRIBING REGULATIONS FOR THE CENTRAL METROPOLITAN DISTRICT ASYLUM.

To the Board of Management of the Central Metropolitan District Asylum:—

To the Churchwardens and Overseers of the Poor of the several Parishes respectively comprised in the said District:

To the Clerk or Clerks to the Justice or Justices of the Petty Sessions held for the Division or Divisions in which the said District and Parishes respectively are situate:—

And to all others whom it may concern.

Whereas, by an order bearing date the Twenty-sixth day of July instant, the Poor Law Commissioners did order and declare, that the following unions, that is to say, the Holborn and Strand Unions, being situated within the district of the Metropolitan Police,—the City of London, the East London, and the West London Unions, being situated within the City of London,—and the several parishes of Saint Giles in the Fields and Saint George Bloomsbury, Saint James Clerkenwell, Saint Luke Middlesex, Saint Mary Islington, and Saint Pancras, in the County of Middlesex, which said several parishes are situated within the said district of the Metropolitan Police, should be combined into a district, to be termed *"The Central Metropolitan Asylum District,"* for the purpose of providing and managing one or more asylum or asylums for the temporary relief and setting to work therein of destitute houseless poor persons, who are not charged with any offence, and who may apply for relief or become chargeable to the poor's-rates within any of the unions or parishes above mentioned.

And the said Commissioners did thereby order and declare, that a Board of Management should be constituted for the said district, which should consist of the ex-officio members entitled to act according to the provisions of the last-recited Act, and of certain members to be elected as therein prescribed.

And whereas it is expedient that the rules and regulations hereinafter set forth should be observed by the Board of Management of the said district; and also that proper officers should be appointed to carry into effect the orders and directions of the said board, and to assist in the administration of the relief of the poor in the said district.

Now, therefore, We, the Poor Law Commissioners, in pursuance of the authorities vested in us by an Act of Parliament passed in the fifth year of the reign of His late Majesty King William the Fourth, intituled *"An Act for the Amendment and better Administration of the Laws relating to the Poor in England and Wales,"* and by another Act passed in the eighth year of the reign of Her present Majesty Queen Victoria, intituled *"An Act for the further Amendment of the Laws relating to the Poor in England,"* do hereby order and direct as follows; that is to say:—

Meetings of the Board of Management.

Article 1.—The first meeting of the said Board of Management shall be held at the *Board Room of the City of London Union, situated at No.* 35, *Cannon Street, London, on Wednesday the Twenty-fourth day of September next,* and shall commence at eleven o'clock in the forenoon, or as soon after such day or hour as may be.

Article 2.—No manager shall act in virtue of his office, except as a member, and at a meeting of the Board of Management.

Article 3.—The board shall meet *once at the least in every month* for the execution of their duties, and shall at their first meeting so to be held as aforesaid, determine upon some fixed day of the week, and upon some fixed hour, for holding such monthly meetings; and it shall be competent to the said managers, when they think fit, to change the time or place for the holding of such meetings, and notice shall forthwith be given to the Poor Law Commissioners of every such change.

Article 4.—The managers shall, at their first meeting to be held as aforesaid, and at the first meeting after every annual election of managers, elect out of the whole number of managers a chairman and a vice-chairman, who shall continue respectively to act as such until the next annual election of managers shall take place, if they so long continue respectively to be managers.

Article 5.—If a chairman or a vice-chairman cease to be a manager, or refuse or become incapable to act as chairman or vice-chairman, before the expiration of the term of office, the managers shall, at one of the two meetings within two months next after the occurrence of the vacancy, refusal, or incapacity, elect some other manager to be chairman or vice-chairman, as the case may be.

Article 6.—No act of any meeting of the district board shall be valid unless three managers be present, and concur therein.

Article 7.—If three managers be not present at any meeting, an entry of that fact shall be made in the minute book, by the clerk to the district board, and the time for holding such meeting shall be deemed to have expired as soon as the said entry shall have been made; but one hour at least shall be allowed to elapse from the time fixed for the commencement of the meeting, before such entry shall be made.

Article 8.—If three, or four, or more managers be present at any ordinary meeting, such three, or the majority of such four or more managers may adjourn the same to the day of the next ordinary meeting, or to some other day previous to the next ordinary meeting.

Article 9.—An extraordinary meeting of the board may be summoned to be held at any time, upon the requisition of any two managers, addressed to the clerk to the managers. Every such requisition shall be made in writing, according to the Form A, hereunto annexed, and no business, other than the business specified in the said requisition, shall be transacted at such extraordinary meeting.

Article 10.—Notice of every change in the time or place of holding any meeting, and notice of the adjournment of any meeting, and notice of every extraordinary meeting, shall be given in writing to the Poor Law Commissioners, and to every manager. Every such notice to a manager shall be respectively according to the Forms B, C, and D, hereunto annexed, and shall be given or sent by the clerk to every manager, or left at his place of abode, two days, if practicable, before the day appointed for the meeting to which it relates.

Article 11.—If any case of emergency arise, requiring that a meeting of the managers should immediately take place, they, or any three of them, shall meet at the ordinary place of meeting, and take such case into consideration, and may make an order or orders thereon.

Proceedings of the Board.

Article 12.—At every meeting the chairman, or, in his absence, a vice-chairman shall preside; and if at the commencement of any meeting the chairman and vice-chairman, or vice-chairmen, be absent, the managers present shall elect one of themselves to preside at such meeting as chairman thereof, until the chairman, or a vice-chairman, may take the chair.

Article 13.—All questions at any meeting consisting of more than three managers shall be determined by a majority of the votes of the managers present thereat.

Article 14.—At every ordinary meeting of the managers the minutes of the last ordinary meeting, and of any other meeting of the board or of any committee which may have been held since such ordinary meeting, shall be read to the board, and signed by the chairman presiding at the meeting at which such minutes are read; and an entry of the same having been so read shall be made in the minutes of the day when read. All reports of the state of the asylum or asylums shall be read, and the board shall proceed to give the necessary directions respecting the same. They shall examine all books and accounts relative to the relief of the paupers of the district in the asylum, and give all needful directions concerning the management and discipline of the asylum or asylums. They shall make the necessary orders on the proper authorities of the several unions and parishes comprised in the said district, for providing such sums as may be lawfully required by the board on account of the district; and they shall transact any such business applicable to their duties as may not fall within any of the above classes.

Article 15.—The managers may at any time appoint from themselves one or more committee or committees, consisting of not less than three nor more than five persons, which committee or committees shall have such powers and authorities as the said managers shall delegate to them.

Contracts.

Article 16.—All contracts to be entered into on behalf of the district relating to the management and relief of the poor, or for any other purpose connected therewith, shall be made and entered into by the board of management.

Article 17.—The managers shall require tenders to be made in some sealed paper for the supply of all matters the consumption of which may be estimated, one month with another, to exceed ten pounds per month, and of all matters the cost of which may be reasonably estimated to exceed fifty pounds in a single sum, to be paid for by the managers, and shall purchase the same upon contracts to be entered into after the receipt of such tenders.

Article 18.—Any work or repairs to be executed for the said district in any asylum belonging to the said district, or on the premises connected with the asylum, or any fittings to be put up therein, which shall respectively be reasonably estimated to exceed the cost of fifty pounds in one sum, shall be contracted for by the managers on sealed tenders, in the manner prescribed in articles 17 and 19.

Article 19.—Notice of the nature and conditions of the contract to be entered into, of the last day on which tenders will be received, and the day on which the tenders will be opened, shall be given in some newspaper circulating in the district, not less than ten days previous to the last day on which such tenders shall be received, and no tender shall be opened by the clerk, or any manager, or other person, prior to the day specified in such notice, or otherwise than at a meeting of the said managers.

Article 20.—When any tender shall be accepted, the party making the tender shall, in pursuance of these regulations, enter into a contract, in writing, with the board of management, containing the terms, conditions, and stipulations mutually agreed upon, and whenever the board shall deem it advisable, the party contracting shall in like manner find one or more surety or sureties, who shall enter into a bond, in such penalty as the board shall think fit, conditioned for the due performance of the contract, or shall otherwise secure the same.

Article 21.—Provided always, that if, from the peculiar nature of any furniture, goods, materials, or fittings to be supplied, or of any work or repairs to be executed, it shall appear to the managers desirable that a specific person or persons be employed to supply or execute the same, without requiring sealed tenders as herein-before directed, it shall be lawful for the board of management, with the consent of the Poor Law Commissioners first had and obtained, to enter into a contract with such person or persons as may be deemed best qualified to supply or execute the same, and to require such sureties and securities as are specified in article 20.

Orders for Contributions and Payments.

Article 22.—The board of management shall from time to time make orders on the proper authorities of the several unions and parishes in the said district, for the payment to the board of such sums as may be required by the board for the contributions of each union or parish to the common fund of the board.

Article 23.—Every such order shall be given according to the form E, hereunto annexed, and shall be signed by the presiding chairman of the meeting, and two other managers present thereat, and shall be countersigned by the clerk to the board.

Article 24.—The board shall pay every sum greater than three pounds by an order which shall be drawn upon the treasurer of the district, and shall be signed by the acting chairman and two other of such managers at a meeting, and shall be countersigned by the clerk or the person for the time being acting as the clerk to the managers.

Security of Officers.

Article 25.—The board shall require every officer to supply forthwith a fresh surety, in place of any surety who may die, or become bankrupt, or insolvent, or be released from his obligation.

Article 26.—The board shall, once in every year, that is to say, at the audit next after the twenty-fifth day of March, cause every person having the custody of bonds given by any officer of the district to produce such bonds to the Auditor (when any such shall be) for his inspection, and the fact of such inspection, and any defects apparent in the said bonds, shall be reported by such auditor to the said board.

And with reference to the several officers of the said board, we, the Poor Law Commissioners do hereby order as follows, that is to say :—

Article 27.—The board shall, within *forty days from their first meeting,* appoint a fit and proper person to be the clerk to the said board, and on the happening of any vacancy hereafter, shall in like manner appoint another person to fill the said office.

Article 28.—And we do further order and direct, that the said board shall, within the like period of *forty days from their first meeting*, and from time to time whenever the said office shall be vacant, appoint a fit person to be the treasurer of the said district.

Article 29.—The said officers shall respectively perform such duties as may be required of them by the rules and regulations of the Poor Law Commissioners, in force at the time, together with all such other duties, conformable with the nature of their respective offices, as the said board of management may lawfully require them to perform.

Mode of Appointment.

Article 30.—Every officer to be appointed under this order shall be appointed by a majority of the managers present at any meeting of the board, and every such appointment shall, as soon as the same shall have been made, be reported to the Poor Law Commissioners by the clerk.

Article 31.—No appointment to the office of clerk or treasurer, other than the first, shall be made under this order, unless notice that such appointment will be made shall have been given at one of the two ordinary meetings of the board next preceding the meeting at which the appointment shall be made, or unless an advertisement, giving notice of such appointment, shall have appeared in some public paper, by the direction of the managers, at least seven days before the day on which such appointment shall be made.

Salaries of the Officers.

Article 32.—The Board of Management shall pay to the officers appointed to any office or employment under this order, such salaries or remuneration as the Poor Law Commissioners may from time to time direct or approve.

Article 33.—The salary of every officer appointed under this order, shall be payable up to the day on which he ceases to hold such office, and no longer.

Security.

Article 34.—Every person appointed to the office of clerk or treasurer, shall respectively give a bond in such penal sum as the board shall think fit, with two sufficient sureties, conditioned for the due and faithful performance of the duties of the office; and every such officer shall give immediate notice to the Board of Management of the death, insolvency, or bankruptcy of either of such sureties, and shall, when required by the managers, supply a fresh surety in the place of any such surety who may die, or become bankrupt or insolvent.

Continuance in Office, and Suspension of Officers—Supply of Vacancies..

Article 35.—Every officer appointed under this order, shall continue to hold the same until he shall die, or resign, or be removed by the Poor Law Commissioners.

Article 36.—If any officer appointed under this order, be at any time prevented by sickness or accident, or other sufficient reason, from the performance of his duties, the managers may appoint a fit person to act as his temporary substitute, and may pay him a reasonable compensation for his services; and every such appointment shall be reported to the Poor Law Commissioners as soon as the same shall have been made.

Article 37.—The Vice-Chairman, or some manager to be appointed by the Board of Management, may perform any of the duties assigned to the clerk until any vacancy in the office shall have been filled, or until a substitute be appointed in the case of the sickness, accident, or absence of the clerk.

Article 38.—When any officer appointed under this order shall die, or resign, the board shall, as soon as conveniently may be after such death or resignation, give notice thereof to the Poor Law Commissioners, and shall proceed to make a new appointment in the manner prescribed by the above regulations.

Duties of the Officers.

Article 39.—And we do hereby define and specify the duties of the several officers appointed under this order, and direct the execution thereof to be as follows :—

Duties of the Clerk to the Board.

Article 40.—The duties of the Clerk to the Board shall be :—

No. 1.—To attend all meetings of the board, and to keep punctually minutes of the proceedings at every meeting, to enter the said minutes in a book, and to submit the same so entered in the said book to the presiding chairman at the succeeding meeting, to be authenticated by the signature of such chairman, as a true record of the proceedings of the board.

No. 2.—To keep all accounts, books of accounts, minutes, books, and other documents, as required of him by the regulations of the Poor Law Commissioners, or relating to the business of the board, and from time to time to produce all such books, other documents, and vouchers for the same, together with the bonds of any officers, which may be in his custody, to the auditor of the said district, at such place and time, and in such manner, as may be required by the regulations of the said Commissioners in force at the time.

No. 3.—To peruse and conduct the correspondence of the board according to their directions, and to preserve the same, and all letters, books, papers, and documents belonging to the board, or entrusted to him by the said board, and to make all necessary copies thereof.

No. 4.—To receive all requisitions of managers for extraordinary meetings, and to summon such meetings accordingly, and to make, sign, and send all notices required to be given to the managers, by any order of the Poor Law Commissioners.

No. 5.—To countersign all orders legally made by the said board, for the payment of money, and all orders legally drawn by the board upon the treasurer of the said district.

No. 6.—To communicate to the several officers and persons engaged under the said board in the administration of relief within the district, all orders and directions of the Poor Law Commissioners, or of the said board, and, so far as may be, to give the instructions requisite for the prompt and correct execution of all such orders and directions, and to examine and report on any neglect or failure therein which may come to his knowledge.

No. 7.—To conduct all applications necessary to be made by or on behalf of the said board, to any magistrate, justice, or justices, at their special, petty, or general sessions, and, if he be an attorney or solicitor, to perform and execute all legal business connected with the board, or in which the board shall be engaged, except actions at law or suits in equity, without charge for any thing beyond disbursements.

No. 8.—To prepare a weekly statement in the form F, hereunto annexed, and punctually to transmit the same to the Assistant Poor Law Commissioner having the superintendence of the District.

No. 9.—To prepare and transmit all answers or returns as to any question or matter connected with or relating to the administration of the laws for the relief of the poor in the district, or to any other business of the district, which the Poor Law Commissioners, or any Assistant Commissioner, may lawfully require from the said board, or from himself.

No. 10.—To observe and execute all lawful orders and directions of the board applicable to his office.

Duties of the Treasurer.

Article 41.—The duties of the treasurer shall be :—

No. 1.—To receive all monies tendered to be paid on account of the said board, and to place the same to their credit.

No. 2.—To pay out of any monies for the time being in his hands belonging to the said board all orders for money which shall be drawn upon him, on behalf of such board, and shall be signed by the chairman and two other of the managers, and shall be countersigned by the clerk, or the person for the time being acting as the clerk, as and when the same shall be presented at the house or usual place of business of the treasurer.

No. 3.—To keep an account, under the proper dates, of all monies received and paid by him as such treasurer, and to render an account thereof to the said board, when received by them, or by any regulation of the Poor Law Commissioners, to do so.

No. 4.—Whenever there shall not be funds belonging to the board in his hands as treasurer of the district, to report in writing the fact of such deficiency to the Poor Law Commissioners, and to the clerk to the said board.

No. 5.—To submit the above-mentioned account to the auditor at the periods of audit, duly notified in pursuance of the regulations of the Poor Law Commissioners in force at the time.

FORMS REFERRED TO IN THE ABOVE ORDER.

FORM A.

To the Clerk to the Board of Management of the Central Metropolitan District Asylum.

Requisition for an Extraordinary Meeting of the Board.

We, the undersigned, being two of the Managers of

the Central Metropolitan District Asylum, do hereby require an Extraordinary Meeting of the Board of the said Asylum to be summoned, to be holden at on the day of 18 , at o'clock in the forenoon, to take into consideration [set out the motion.]

} Managers.

FORM B.

Notice of Change of Time, or Place of Meeting.

To A. B. ( ) Manager of the Central Metropolitan District Asylum.

Sir,—You are hereby informed, that the next Ordinary Meeting of the Board of Management of the Central Metropolitan District Asylum will take place at on the day of 18 , at o'clock in the forenoon, for the transaction of business; and that meetings of the said Board will henceforth be held at the same place, on in every [as the case may be,] at the same hour of in the noon.

(Signed)
Clerk to the said Board.

FORM C.

Notice of an Adjourned Meeting of the Board.

To A. B. ( ) Manager of the Central Metropolitan District Asylum.

Sir,—This is to give you notice, that an Adjourned Meeting of the Board of Management of the Central Metropolitan District Asylum will be held at on the day of 18 , to take into consideration [set out the motion,] which meeting you are hereby requested to attend.

(Signed)
Clerk to the said Board.

FORM D.

Notice of an Extraordinary Meeting of the Board.

To A. B. ( ) Manager of the Central Metropolitan District Asylum.

Sir,—I am directed by C. D. and E. F., two of the Managers of the Central Metropolitan District Asylum, to summon an Extraordinary Meeting of the Board of the said Asylum, at on the day of 18 , at o'clock in the noon, to take into consideration [set out the motion,] which meeting you are hereby requested to attend.

(Signed)
Clerk to the said Board.

FORM E.

To the Guardians of the Poor of the Union, in the Central Metropolitan Asylum District.

To A. B. and C. D., Churchwardens and Overseers (or) of the Parish of in the Central Metropolitan Asylum District.

You are hereby ordered and directed to pay to F. G. of on behalf of the Board of Management of the Central Metropolitan District Asylum, on the day of at the sum of Pounds Shillings and Pence, as the Contribution of the said Union or Parish to the common fund of the Board of Management, and such other expenses as are chargeable by the said Board on the said Union or Parish, and to take the Receipt of the said F. G. for the said Sum of £ *s.* *d.*

Given under our Hands, at a Meeting of the Board of Management of the Central Metropolitan District Asylum, held on the day of 18 .

(Counter-signature of the Clerk to the said Board.)

(Signed) X. Y. Presiding Chairman.
W. X. } Managers.
U. V. }

[See FORM F, at page 153.]

Given under our hands and seal of office, this Twenty-ninth day of July, in the year One thousand eight hundred and forty-five.

L. S. (Signed) { GEO. NICHOLLS.
G. C. LEWIS.

3. THE NORTH-EASTERN METROPOLITAN ASYLUM DISTRICT, formed under an order dated 31st July, 1845, consists of the Hackney Union, the Poplar Union, the Stepney Union, the West Ham Union, the Whitechapel Union, the parish of St. George in the East, the parish of St. Leonard, Shoreditch, and the parish of St. Matthew, Bethnal Green. The parish of St. Leonard, Shoreditch, is entitled to elect two members of the Board of Management, and each of the other unions and parishes, one member.

The qualification of a member consists in being rated within the district upon a net annual value of not less than £30.

The order prescribing Regulations for the Board of Management, dated 15th August, 1845, is similar, in all respects, to the one issued to the "Central Metropolitan Asylum District," and set forth above, as are those also issued to the other districts.

4. THE SOUTH-WESTERN METROPOLITAN ASYLUM DISTRICT, formed under an order, dated 30th July, 1845, consists of the St. Saviour's Union, Wandsworth and Clapham Union, (each of which unions is entitled to elect Two Guardians,) the parish of St. Mary, Lambeth, the parish of St.

CENTRAL METROPOLITAN ASYLUM DISTRICT.

RETURN of DESTITUTE PERSONS relieved during the Week ended Saturday the day of 184

FORM F.

ASYLUM situated at †	*SUNDAY					MONDAY					TUESDAY					WEDNESD.					THURSDAY					FRIDAY					SATURDAY				
	In the Asylum	Admitted	Discharged	Dead	Remaining in the Asylum	In the Asylum	Admitted	Discharged	Dead	Remaining in the Asylum	In the Asylum	Admitted	Discharged	Dead	Remaining in the Asylum	In the Asylum	Admitted	Discharged	Dead	Remaining in the Asylum	In the Asylum	Admitted	Discharged	Dead	Remaining in the Asylum	In the Asylum	Admitted	Discharged	Dead	Remaining in the Asylum	In the Asylum	Admitted	Discharged	Dead	Remaining in the Asylum
MEN...... Able-bodied																																			
Temporarily disabled																																			
Old and infirm																																			
YOUTHS.. From Seven to Fifteen Years																																			
BOYS..... From Two to Seven Years																																			
WOMEN.. Able-bodied																																			
Temporarily disabled																																			
Old and infirm																																			
GIRLS.... From Seven to Fifteen Years																																			
From Two to Seven Years																																			
INFANTS.. Under Two Years																																			
Born																																			
TOTAL																																			
Detained under Punishment																																			
Awaiting decision of Board or Committee																																			
Sick																																			
Others																																			
TOTAL																																			

In the event of more room being required for the answer to either of these questions, insert the observation on the next page, and refer thereto.

1.—Is there any Remark in the Visiting Committee's Book concerning any defect in the discipline or internal economy of the Asylum? If so, furnish a copy of the remark - -

2.—Did the Number of Paupers in the Asylum at any one time exceed that fixed or sanctioned by the Poor Law Commissioners? If so, state on what night, and to what extent the number was exceeded - - - - - -

(Signed) Clerk to the Board of Management of the Central Metropolitan Asylum District.

To

Assistant Poor Law Commissioner. Sent this day of 184 .

* It is to be understood, in respect of this Form, that the day begins at Twelve o'clock at noon, and lasts for twenty-four hours, and that Sunday ends at noon on Monday.
† A separate Return is required to be made for each Asylum in the District.

Mary, Newington, each of which parishes is entitled to elect Three Guardians.

The qualification consists in being rated within the district upon a net annual value of not less than £25.

The order prescribing Regulations for the Board of Management is dated 30 Aug. 1845.

---

5. THE WESTERN METROPOLITAN ASYLUM DISTRICT, formed under an order dated 31 July, 1845, consists of the Brentford Union, which is to elect Four Guardians; the Fulham Union, which is to elect Three Guardians; and the Richmond Union, which is to elect Two Guardians.

The qualification to be the same as in the last-mentioned district.

The order prescribing Regulations for the Board of Management is dated 26 Aug. 1845.

---

6. THE SOUTH-EASTERN METROPOLITAN ASYLUM DISTRICT, formed under an order dated 30th July, 1845, consists of the Greenwich Union, the Lewisham Union, the St. Olave's Union, the parish of St. Giles, Camberwell, the parish of St. Mary Magdalen, Bermondsey, and the parish of St. Mary, Rotherhithe. The Greenwich Union is entitled to elect Two Guardians, and each of the other unions and parishes One.

The qualification, £30.

The order prescribing Regulations for the Board of Management is dated 26 Aug. 1845.

---

7. THE NORTH-WESTERN METROPOLITAN ASYLUM DISTRICT, formed under an order dated 31 July, 1845, consists of the parish of St. George, Hanover-square, which is to elect Two Guardians; the parish of St. James, Westminster, which is to elect Two Guardians; the parish of St. Mary Abbott's, Kensington, which is to elect One Guardian; the parish of St. Luke, Chelsea, which is to elect Two Guardians; the parishes of St. Margaret, and St. John the Evangelist, Westminster, which are to elect Two Guardians; the parish of St. Mary-le-Bone, which is to elect Three Guardians; and the parish of Paddington, which is to elect One Guardian.

The qualification, £30.

The order prescribing Regulations for the Board of Management is dated 12 Aug. 1845.

The chairman of every Board of Guardians constituted under the Poor Law Amendment Act shall, if he consents thereto, be ex-officio a member of the District Board of Management.

II.—LUNATIC PAUPERS.—REMOVAL OF SCOTCH AND IRISH PAUPERS.

1. CIRCULAR LETTER DIRECTING ATTENTION TO THE ACTS 8 AND 9 VIC. C. 100, 117, AND 126.

Poor Law Commission Office,
Somerset House, Sept. 5, 1845.

SIR,—I am directed by the Poor Law Commissioners to call the attention of the Guardians to two measures relating to the Administration of the Relief to the Poor, which have been passed by the Legislature in the last Session of Parliament.

They relate to Pauper Lunatics, and the removal of Poor Persons born in Scotland, Ireland, and the Islands of Man, Scilly, Jersey, and Guernsey. The Statutes 8 and 9 Vict. c. 100, and c. 126, apply to the former subject, and the 8 and 9 Vict. c. 117 to the latter.

PAUPER LUNATICS.

The statute 8 and 9 Vict. c. 100 relates to Houses Licensed for the Reception of Lunatics of all classes, and to Public Hospitals in which Lunatics are received. The 8 and 9 Vict. c. 126 relates to the providing of additional Asylums for Lunatics in Counties and Boroughs. Various provisions are contained in these Statutes to which it is particularly necessary that the attention of the Guardians and their Officers should be directed.

1. *As to Licensed Houses.*

The statute 8 and 9 Vict. c. 100 establishes a Permanent Commission in Lunacy, and not only confers upon the Commissioners the Power of granting Licenses to Houses for the Reception of Lunatics within a limited distance of the Metropolis, but also imposes upon them the duty of visiting, and to a certain extent controlling, all such Houses in England and Wales.

Hospitals in which Lunatics are received are also required to be Registered, and Visited by such Commissioners. § 43.

In all Counties and Boroughs of England, not comprised within the limit above referred to, the Justices at the Quarter Sessions are empowered to License such Houses, and at the Michaelmas Sessions are directed to appoint Visitors of the Houses Licensed in their respective Counties and Boroughs, which Visitors are to visit all Licensed Houses within their jurisdiction four times at least in every year, and to examine the state and condition of the Houses and the Inmates.

Power is given to the Commissioners and the

Visitors to determine and regulate the *Dietary* of the *Pauper Lunatics* in these Houses and in Registered Hospitals, and where the regulations of the Visitors and Commissioners differ, those prescribed by the latter shall prevail; it is, however, provided, that such Regulations shall not take effect so as to affect any Contract existing on the 1st of June last for the maintenance of Pauper Lunatics, before the 1st of June next, or the expiration of the Contract, whichever shall first happen. § 82.

Two or more of the Commissioners, one at least being a Physician or Surgeon, and one a Barrister, shall and may once or oftener in each year, on such day or days, and such hours in the day, and for such length of time as they shall think fit, *visit every Parish or Union Workhouse* in which there are, or are alleged to be, any Lunatics, and shall inquire whether the provisions of the Law as to Lunatics have been carried out as to the arrangement, visitation, and management of such Workhouse, and as to the dietary, accommodation, and treatment of the Lunatics in such Workhouse, and shall report in writing thereon to the Poor Law Commissioners. § 111.

Any one of the Commissioners may at any time give an Order in writing, under his hand, for the *admission*, to any Patient confined in any house or place authorised to be visited by the Commissioners, of any relation or friend of such Patient (or of any Medical or other person whom any relation or friend of such Patient shall desire to be admitted to him,) and such order of admission may be either for a single admission, or for an admission for any limited number of times, or for admission generally at all reasonable times; and a penalty of a sum not exceeding £20 is imposed upon any person refusing or preventing the admission of such person. § 85.

It will not be necessary to bring under the particular notice of the Guardians any of the provisions contained in the statute for the regulation of such Licensed Houses, or the various duties which are imposed upon the Proprietors; but it is important that their attention should be directed to the subject of the *admission* and *discharge* of Pauper Lunatics into and from Licensed Houses and Hospitals.

First, in regard to the *admission* of Pauper Lunatics. §§ 48, 49.

It is enacted, that no Pauper shall be *received* into or *detained* in any Licensed House or Hospital without an *Order* and *Statement* according to the Form, and stating the particulars required in the schedule to the Act, under the hands of one Justice or an Officiating Clergyman, *with* the Relieving Officer or one of the Overseers of the Union or Parish from which such Pauper shall be sent (which said Justice or which said Clergyman and Relieving Officer or Overseer, as the case may be, shall have personally examined such Pauper previously to signing such Order,) nor without a Medical Certificate according to a form set forth in the schedule, and dated not more than seven days previously to the reception of such Pauper into such House or Hospital. The Certificate is to be signed by a Physician, Surgeon, or Apothecary (not being the Medical Officer of the Parish or Union) on the day he shall examine such Pauper. § 48.

The receipt of any Pauper without such Order and Medical Certificate is made a misdemeanor. *Ib.*

No Physician, Surgeon, or Apothecary who, or whose Father, Brother, Son, or Partner, is wholly or partly the Proprietor of or a regular professional Attendant in a Licensed House or an Hospital shall sign any Certificate for the reception of a Patient into such House or Hospital, and no Physician, Surgeon, or Apothecary, who, or whose Father, Brother, Son, or Partner, shall have signed any *Order* for the reception, shall sign any *Certificate* for the same Patient. § 49.

Secondly, in regard to the *Discharge* of the Pauper. §§ 74, 75.

The Guardians of any Parish or Union may, by a Minute of their Board, direct that any Pauper Patient belonging to such Parish or Union and detained in any Licensed House or any Hospital, shall be *discharged* or *removed* therefrom, and may direct the mode of such discharge or removal; and if a Copy of such Minute be produced to the Proprietor or Superintendent of such Licensed House or Hospital, he shall forthwith discharge or remove such Patient accordingly, or cause or suffer him to be discharged or removed. § 74.

But no such Patient shall be so discharged or removed from any Licensed House or Hospital, if the Physician, Surgeon, or Apothecary who keeps the same, or shall be the regular Medical Attendant thereof thereat, certify that such Patient is *dangerous and unfit to be at large*, unless the Commissioners or Visitors shall consent, in writing, thereto. § 75.

Powers are given, under certain restrictions, to the Commissioners and Visitors to discharge individual Patients, whether Paupers or not; but it is required that they shall make two visits before they do so, and they are to give seven days' notice prior to the second visit, a copy whereof is to be sent, in the case of a Pauper to the Guardians of the Parish or Union. §§ 76, 80.

It seems therefore, that the Guardians would have an opportunity of expressing to the Commissioners or Visitors any objection which they may entertain to the discharge of any such particular Pauper.

It may be well here to observe, that the 8 and 9 Vict. c. 126, s. 54, enables any two Visiting Justices of any Asylum, by an Order in writing under their hands and seals, to direct any Overseer or Relieving or other Officer of any Parish or Union, contributing to any Asylum, to remove any Pauper Lunatic chargeable to such Parish or Union, now or at any time hereafter in any Registered Hospital or Licensed House, to an Asylum, and such Lunatic shall be removed at the expense of such Parish or Union accordingly, and the Overseer or Relieving Officer who, for fourteen days, shall neglect or refuse to remove any Lunatic accordingly, will be liable to a penalty of not more than £20, nor less than £2.

2. AS TO LUNATIC ASYLUMS FOR COUNTIES AND BOROUGHS.

The 8 and 9 Vict. c. 126, proceeds in the first place to make provisions for enforcing the erection and establishment of Pauper Lunatic Asylums in Counties and Boroughs, and for the appointment of Committees of Visitors to superintend, regulate, and visit these Asylums.

A series of regulations is then enacted to secure the removal of Pauper Lunatics to Asylums.

By section 47, a return is required to be made by the Clerks of the Board of Guardians of all Pauper Lunatics, chargeable to the Parish or Union, on the *1st of January* in each year, to be laid before the Visitors of the Asylum, and copies to be transmitted to the Clerk of the Peace, the Commissioners in Lunacy, and the Poor Law Commissioners, the return required to be made by the 5 & 6 Vict. c. 57, § 6, on the 15th of August being henceforth dispensed with.

Admission of Pauper Lunatics.

Section 48 requires every Medical Officer of the Parish or Union, who has knowledge that any person chargeable to any Parish in the Union is deemed to be Lunatic, to give notice thereof within three days to the Overseers, if the Parish be not in Union, and to the Relieving Officer if it be in Union.

The Overseer or Relieving Officer, who shall have like knowledge, whether by such notice or otherwise, must, within three days, give notice thereof to some Justices of the County or Borough within which such Parish is situate. *Ib.*

Thereupon such Justice, by order under his hand and seal, shall require the Overseer or Relieving Officer to bring such Lunatic before him or some other Justice of the County or Borough within three days. *Ib.*

The Justice is to examine the Lunatic when brought before him, and to call to his assistance a Physician, Surgeon, or Apothecary, *not being the Medical Officer of such Union or Parish;* and if such Physician sign a Certificate as to the insanity of the Pauper, the Justice shall direct such person to be received into the Asylum of the County or Borough in which the Parish shall be situate, or if there be no such Asylum, or if it be full, then into some Licensed House or Registered Hospital. *Ib.*

Such Overseer or Relieving Officer shall immediately convey such Lunatic, or cause such Lunatic to be conveyed, to the Asylum, House, or Hospital. *Ib.*

If the Pauper, on account of his health or other cause, cannot be brought before the Justice, he may be examined at his own abode, or elsewhere, by a Justice or an Officiating Clergyman of the Parish, with the Overseer or Relieving Officer, who, in like manner, shall call a Medical man to their assistance, and if he certifies as to the insanity, such Justice or Officiating Clergyman, with the Overseer or Relieving Officer may direct the Pauper to be sent to such Asylum, House, or Hospital, as above. *Ib.*

In this case there is no such restriction, as in the former, upon the Medical Officer of the Parish or Union certifying as to the state of sanity. *Ib.*

If the Medical man certify that the Pauper is not in a fit state to be removed, the removal shall be suspended until a Certificate be obtained that he can be removed with safety. *Ib.*

Section 49 provides for two classes of Lunanatics — one *Wandering Lunatics,* and the other of *Lunatics not chargeable to any Parish, but under the care of relatives, or other persons who neglect or cruelly treat them, so that they are not properly taken care of.*

Any Overseer or Relieving Officer who has knowledge that any person *wandering* within his District, Parish, or Union, is deemed to be Lunatic, is required to apprehend such person and take him before a Justice, who is to call in the assistance of the Medical Practitioner, and take the same steps as in the former section, and, *if he think fit*, shall issue an Order for the removal of such Wandering Lunatic to an Asylum, Licensed House, or Registered Hospital. § 49.

If any Overseer or Relieving Officer has notice of any Lunatic not chargeable, who is neglected or cruelly treated as above stated, he shall, within three days, give notice to a Justice, who upon receipt of such notice in writing, and a statement on oath, may require the Overseer or Relieving Officer to bring such person before him and some other Justice, within three days. Such two Justices are in like manner to call in the assistance of a Medical Practitioner, and take such steps as above stated; and upon proof of neglect or cruel treatment, may, *if they think fit*, direct the Lunatic to be removed to the Asylum, Licensed House, or Hospital aforesaid. *Ib.*

The Overseer or Relieving Officer, in either case must convey the Lunatic, or cause such Lunatic to be conveyed, according to the Order. *Ib.*

There is no restriction upon the Medical Officer of the Parish or Union in these cases. *Ib.*

If the Lunatic in these cases cannot be brought before the Justice or Justices, the Lunatic may be examined by him or them at his own abode with the same assistance, and if satisfied that the party is a Lunatic, and if not chargeable, has been neglected or cruelly treated, the Justice or Justices shall make an Order as above stated. *Ib.*

In reference to these last-mentioned Lunatics, the Justice or Justices, or a Visiting Justice of the Asylum, are required to make an Order upon the Treasurer of the Guardians of the Union, or upon the Overseer of the Poor of the Parish from which the Lunatic is taken, for the payment of the charges of the Examination, Removal, Lodging, Maintenance, Clothing, Medicine, and care of such Lunatic, and in case it shall afterwards appear that the Lunatic is chargeable to any other Parish, then upon the Treasurer of the Guardians of the Union in which such other Parish is situate, or upon the Overseers of such other Parish. *Ib.*

Provision is made, as in the last section, for suspending the removal in case the Lunatic shall not be capable of being removed. *Ib.*

Another provision is introduced to enable the property of the Lunatic, if he have any, to be made applicable to the charge of his maintenance, similar to that which is contained in the previous statutes of the 9 Geo. IV. c. 40, and the 7 and 8 Vict. c. 101, § 27. *Ib.*

The power of any relation or friend to retain or take charge of the Lunatic, upon giving proper assurance for good treatment, is preserved. *Ib.*

Penalties are imposed upon any Medical Officer omitting for three days, after obtaining knowledge of a chargeable Lunatic, to give the notice above required; and upon the Overseer or Relieving Officer omitting for three days to give the notices in respect of chargeable Lunatics, and other Lunatics not chargeable but neglected or ill-treated, or to apprehend wandering Lunatics, as above described. § 50.

The reception of a Pauper Lunatic, or any such Lunatic as already referred to, into any Asylum, Registered Hospital, or Licensed House, without an Order of a Justice or of an Officiating Clergyman with one of the Overseers or the Relieving Officer, and a Medical Certificate, is prohibited.

Beside the above order for the payment of the costs and charges, expenses and cost of maintenance, the statute contains some other provisions upon the same subject in regard to other Pauper Lunatics.

It is provided in the first place that the Pauper Lunatic shall be deemed to belong to the Parish from which he shall have been sent until it shall be adjudged that he is settled in some other Parish, or that it cannot be ascertained in what Parish he is settled. § 57.

Two Justices are empowered at any time to adjudicate as to the settlement of any Pauper sent to a Lunatic Asylum, Hospital, or House. § 58.

If the pauper be not settled in the Parish from which he has been sent, and it cannot be ascertained in which Parish he is settled, the Relieving Officer of the Union, or the Overseers, shall give notice to the Clerk of the Peace to appear before two Justices, who are empowered to adjudge the Pauper to be chargeable to the County. § 59.

The Guardians, their Clerk or Relieving Officer, or the Overseers, and every person duly authorised by them, are to have access to the Lunatic for the purpose of examining him with reference to the question of his settlement in the presence of the medical attendant. § 60.

The Justice or Justices by whom the Lunatic has been sent to the Asylum, Hospital, or House, or any two of the Visitors of the Asylum, may make an order upon the Treasurer of the Guardians, *or other Officer*, of the Union or Parish, or the Overseers of the Parish from which such Lunatic shall have been sent, for payment to the Treasurer, Officer, or Proprietor of the Asylum, Hospital, or House, of the reasonable charges of the lodging, maintenance, medicine, clothing, and care of such Lunatic, in such Asylum, Hospital, or House, and such Treasurer or Overseer shall pay out of the moneys coming to his hands from time to time to the said Treasurer, Officer, or Proprietor, the charges aforesaid. § 61.

If the Lunatic be adjudged to belong to some other Parish than that from which he shall have been sent, two Justices may make an Order upon such other Parish or Union to repay the moneys already paid within twelve months, by the first Union or Parish, and for the payment of future charges to the Treasurer, Officer, or Proprietor of the Asylum, Hospital, or House. Against this order there may be an appeal, as in cases of removal. § 62.

If it be ascertained or adjudged that the Lunatic is chargeable to a County, then an Order is to be made upon the Treasurer of a County, to pay the moneys incurred by any Union or Parish already paid, within the same time, to the said Union or Parish, and for the payment of future charges to the Treasurer, Officer, or Proprietor of the Asylum, Hospital, or House. § 63.

If after a Lunatic has been adjudged to be chargeable to a County, it shall be adjudged that he is settled in any Parish, a similar order may be made by two Justices for the reimbursement of the County, upon the Treasurer of the Guardians, or the Overseer, who shall, out of any moneys which come to his hands by virtue of his office, pay the moneys ordered to be paid by him. § 64.

If any Treasurer of a Board of Guardians, or Relieving Officer, or Overseer, upon any order for the payment of money under the provisions of the Act, shall have been made, shall for twenty days after notice thereof refuse or neglect to pay the sum ordered to be paid, the same with costs shall be recovered by a warrant of distress under the hands of two Justices, or by an action at law against such Treasurer, Overseer, or Relieving Officer. § 68.

Such are the provisions in respect of the payment for the maintenance of Pauper Lunatics in confinement.

It is to be noticed, that power is given to any Medical Practitioner appointed by the Guardians of any Union or Parish, and also to the Guardians or any appointed members of the Guardians or Parish, and also to the Overseers of any Parish, between the hours of eight in the morning and six at night, to visit and examine any Pauper Lunatic belonging to such Union or Parish, confined in any Asylum, Hospital, or House, unless the Medical Officer of the Asylum is of opinion that such visit and examination will be injurious to such Lunatic. § 79.

Removal and Discharge.

Any three Members of the Committee of Visitors of any Asylum may, by writing, order the removal or discharge of any person confined in any Asylum, whether recovered or not; and may permit any person convalescent to be absent wholly or partly from the Asylum upon trial; and to allow him to the extent of his cost in the Asylum, and may discharge therefrom any person whose recovery is certified by the Medical Officer thereof. And every person who shall have been sent to a Lunatic Asylum as a Pauper Lunatic shall be safely kept therein until such order for his removal, trial, or discharge, shall have been given. § 71.

On the regular discharge or removal of any Pauper from any Asylum the necessary expenses attending his discharge or removal shall be borne by the Union or Parish to which such Pauper shall then be deemed to belong, or if chargeable to the County, by such County, and the amount of the expenses, when allowed by the Justices of the County, shall be paid by the Guardians of the Union or Parish, or the Treasurer of the County. § 72.

Although the statute appears to require the removal of every Pauper Lunatic into some Asylum, yet from various causes, but principally from the present want of accommodation, many Lunatics must remain for some time at large, or not under confinement in any Asylum, Licensed House, or Hospital.

These Lunatics are not to be allowed to remain unnoticed or unattended to.

Accordingly, it is required that every Pauper Lunatic chargeable to any Parish, who shall not be in an Asylum, Hospital, or Licensed House, shall be *visited* once in every three months by the Medical Officer of the Union or Parish to which such Lunatic shall belong. § 55.

And a list of all such Lunatics shall be sent once in every three months by such Medical

Officer to the Clerk of the Peace, and to the Visitors of the Asylum for the County, and to the Commissioners of Lunacy, according to a Form in the Schedule to the Act. *Ib.*

In that list the Medical Officer shall state whether any such Lunatic is or is not fit to be at large, and is properly taken care of. *Ib.*

It is then provided, that after an Asylum shall be established for any County or Borough under the provisions of this Act, no Pauper who shall have *lately* become Lunatic (whether such Pauper shall or shall not have been previously confined in an Asylum) shall be received, lodged, or detained in any house or place other than a County or Borough Lunatic Asylum, Hospital, or Licensed House, for a longer period than shall be requisite for obtaining an order for the removal of such Lunatic to such Asylum. *Ib.*

And the statute proceeds to enact, that if any Medical Officer shall return any *such* Pauper in any such list *as fit to be at large*, or shall knowingly sign any such list untruly setting forth any of the particulars required by this Act, he shall forfeit a sum not less than *ten*, and not exceeding *fifty* pounds. *Ib.*

The object of this last provision is to secure as early attention as possible to cases of *recent* insanity, which are the most likely to be curable.

In all future arrangements to be made with Medical Officers, these new duties must be borne in mind.

3. REMOVAL OF SCOTCH AND IRISH PAUPERS.

The 8 and 9 Vict. c. 117, provides for the removal of poor persons born in Scotland or Ireland, the Isle of Man, or the Channel Islands, who, not being settled in England, become chargeable to Parishes in England.

All previous statutes upon the subject are repealed, and permanent provisions are made for the future.

If any such person become chargeable to any parish in England, by reason of relief given to himself or herself, or to his wife, or to any legitimate or bastard child, such person, his wife, and any child so chargeable, shall be liable to be removed to Scotland, Ireland, the Isle of Man, Scilly, Jersey, or Guernsey. § 2.

And if the guardians of such parish, or of any union in which the same may be comprised, or where there are no such guardians, if the overseers of such parish complain thereof to any one justice, such justice may summon the person to come before any two justices at any time or place, and any two justices may hear the complaint, and issue a warrant to remove such person forthwith, at the expense of such union or parish. *Ib.*

Persons executing such warrants of removal, are to have the authority of constables for the purposes of the Act, in all Counties and Places through which they may pass. § 3.

Section 4, requires the Justices of the Peace to make new regulations for the removal of such poor persons, which are to be approved of by one of the Secretaries of State, and when they have been so approved, they are to be observed by all Justices, Guardians, Overseers, Constables, and other persons, in the removal of such poor persons; but until such regulations have been made and approved of, the regulations heretofore made shall continue in force.

Section 5, provides for the cost of removals which may be incurred by some few Parishes of population under 30,000, which are not in any Union.

To these Parishes the cost of the Removal will be repaid by the County or Borough in which they are situated, but all Unions will have to defray the cost of removals of such poor persons which are effected at the instance of the Guardians as a common charge. All parishes not in any Union the population whereof exceeds 30,000, will bear the cost without any power of recovering the same from the County or Borough.

Section 6, provides that, if Boards of Guardians, of any Union in Ireland, and the Heritors and Kirk Session or Borough Magistrates in Scotland, forward a statement of their case and give security to the Commissioners for payment of costs, the Poor Law Commissioners may appeal against the warrant of removal to the Quarter Sessions, giving notice to the Guardians or Overseers on whose application the warrant was obtained.

The Quarter Session shall then hear and determine the appeal, and if the warrant be reversed such Guardians or Overseers shall pay the costs, and the expenses incurred by or on account of the Board of Guardians, or Kirk Session, or Borough Magistrates, in conveying the poor person, removed under the same, back. *Ib.*

The amount may be recovered, after a refusal or neglect to pay within seven days, as Penalties and Forfeitures. *Ib.*

Power is given to the Guardians or Overseers

to abandon the warrant of removal, but they shall thereupon pay the expenses incurred by reason of such warrant. *Ib.*

The Statute supplies Forms which may be adopted.

I am, your obedient Servant,
W. G. LUMLEY, *Assistant Secretary.*

To the Clerk of the Guardians.

---

2. LUNATIC PAUPERS—CIRCULAR.

Poor Law Commission Office, Somerset House, August 14th, 1845.

SIR,—I am directed by the Poor Law Commissioners to inform you that by the 8 and 9 Vict. c. 126, sec. 47, it is enacted that so much of the Statute of the 5 and 6 Vict. c. 57, as required the clerks to boards of guardians to make out the return of pauper lunatics on the 15th day of August, is repealed.

It will be seen, however, that a return to the same effect as was required by that statute, must be made by the clerks to boards of guardians on the first of January in every year, or as soon after as may be, and copies thereof must be sent on or before the first of February ensuing, to the Commissioners in Lunacy, and to the Poor Law Commissioners.

I am, &c.,
W. G. LUMLEY, *Assistant Secretary.*

To the Clerk to the Guardians.

---

3. LUNATIC PAUPERS—CIRCULAR.

Poor Law Commission Office, Somerset House, August 25th, 1845.

SIR,—I am directed by the Poor Law Commissioners to call your attention, as a medical officer of the Union, to the provision in the recent Statute relating to pauper lunatics, 8 and 9 Vict. c. 126, sec. 55; which is as follows:—

"Be it Enacted, that every Pauper Lunatic, chargeable to any Parish, who shall not be in an Asylum, or a Registered Hospital, or a house duly licensed for the reception of Pauper Lunatics, shall be *visited* once in every *Three months* by the *Medical Officer* of the Parish or Union to which such Lunatic shall belong; and a *List* of all such Lunatics shall be sent once in every Three Months by such Medical Officer *to the Clerk of the Peace* of the County or Borough to which such Lunatic shall belong, or in which he shall be resident, to be by him laid before the Justices acting for such County at their next General or Quarter Sessions, or before the Justices of such Borough, *and* to the Visitors of the Asylum for the County in which such Parish or Union shall be situate, *and* to the Commissioners in Lunacy, according to the Form in Schedule (F), to this Act annexed:

"And the said List shall state whether any such Lunatic is or is not, in the opinion of such Medical Officer, fit to be at large, and is properly taken care of:

"And such List of such Lunatics shall be prepared and signed by the Medical Officer required to make the same.

"Provided, nevertheless, That after an Asylum shall be established for any County or Borough under the Provisions of this Act, no Pauper, who shall have *lately become lunatic* (whether such Pauper shall or shall not have been previously confined in an Asylum,) shall be received, lodged, or detained in any House or Place, other than a County or Borough Lunatic Asylum, or a Public Hospital, or a House duly licensed for the Reception of Pauper Lunatics, for a longer period than shall be requisite for obtaining an Order for the Removal of such Lunatic to such Asylum:

"And if any Medical Officer shall return any *such Pauper* in any such List as fit to be at large, or shall knowingly sign any such List, *untruly* setting forth any of the Particulars required by this Act, he shall, for every such Offence, forfeit any sum not less than *Ten*, and not exceeding *Fifty* Pounds."

I am, &c.,
W. G. LUMLEY, *Assistant Secretary.*

To the Medical Officer.

LONDON:
Printed by Order of the Poor Law Commissioners, by BLACKBURN and PARDON, 6, Hatton Garden, and Published by CHARLES KNIGHT and Co., 22, Ludgate Street, Publishers to the Poor Law Commissioners.

AN

OFFICIAL CIRCULAR

OF PUBLIC DOCUMENTS AND INFORMATION:

DIRECTED BY THE POOR LAW COMMISSIONERS TO BE PRINTED, CHIEFLY FOR THE USE OF THE MEMBERS AND PERMANENT OFFICERS OF BOARDS OF GUARDIANS, UNDER THE POOR LAW AMENDMENT ACT.

No. 53. CIRCULAR ISSUED NOVEMBER 10, 1845.

Poor Law Commission Office,
Somerset House, Nov. 10, 1845.

THE Poor Law Commissioners directed that the following documents and Minutes of Correspondence, be printed and circulated for the information of Guardians and Officers of the several Unions, viz.

(Signed) By Order of the Board,
EDWIN CHADWICK, *Secretary.*

I. POTATOE CROPS IN AMERICA—

AFFECTED BY DISEASE.

IN one of the "Executive Documents," (Document No. 177,) issued by the American Congress in 1844, is found a report on the State of the Potatoe Crops, in the United States, in the preceding year. By this report, it appears that the potatoes, in several of the states, were affected by a disease similar to that which has attacked this important vegetable in this country.

"In Otsego and Schoharie counties," the report states, "the potatoes are said to have been subject to a dry-rot, attacking some in the hill and some in the heap, and fatal to the whole, wherever it made its appearance, causing them to rot and to emit a very offensive stench. Those who undertook to feed them out after the rot commenced, found the injury to the cattle greater than the loss of the vegetables. Although the crop was originally good as usual, there will be a great scarcity of the article. In the eastern section of the state they were, also, much lighter than usual, and somewhat diseased, and rotted after being secured, owing to the unfavourable weather for gathering the crop. The estimate of the deficiency, in some counties, is even as high as fifty per cent., while in others it is about twelve to fifteen per cent. They have black spots, and rot in the hill and on the way to market.

"One who is esteemed high authority on this subject, speaking of the crop, says, that 'through nearly the entire extent of the state, (and it is said, also, in portions of Connecticut, New Jersey, and Pennsylvania,) it is rendered almost valueless by a disease new to farmers here, which, in most cases, attacked the potatoes before they were dug. Many crops were worthless when dug from the ground; and almost all crops began to decay immediately after drying, and rapidly decayed till they were an extremely offensive putrid mass. The diseased potatoes are said to be poisonous, and to have caused the death of hogs fed upon them. In this section of the state, the disease is not as universal as it is represented to be in other places. I have heard of no injurious effects from feeding them; my hogs have eaten them freely, uncooked, down to the present time, (December, 1843,) without injury.' Another person, also, who enjoyed great advantages for ascertaining the condition of the crops, remarks, that 'potatoes suffered greatly from the dry weather of June and

July, and the early crop was a very light one, though good in quality. The latter ones seem to have been injured by the long-protracted rains of August and through the fall, and did not sufficiently ripen, but proved green and watery; and hence, in my opinion, the fatal disease among them. The early snows prevented their being properly gathered in the northern and western parts of the state, and there has been a great loss in consequence.' The potatoe crop of New Jersey, likewise, as has been mentioned, suffered from the same cause; they were 'of a very inferior quality,' the deficiency is estimated to 'have been twenty per cent.' By some it is thought that the crop is even 'one-third less than an average one.'

"Pennsylvania in 1842, stood next to New York, in the quantity of potatoes raised; and the crop there was a good one; but the past year there has been a very great falling-off, and the crop is at least thirty per cent. less than that of 1842. The particular accounts correspond well to the general estimate. In no case have we heard of an increased crop, but the language, as applied to different sections, is—'nearly fifty per cent. less, owing to a rot which seized them before the time for taking them out of the ground;' 'fifty per cent. less, owing to a rot produced by a long drought, followed by heavy rains;' 'seventy-five per cent. less; they rotted in the ground when ripe, from a week's excessive heat, day and night, while the ground was constantly wet, from which fermentation ensued, except only in dry soils;' 'an averege crop, but a total loss, owing to rot, supposed to be caused by the excessive amount of rain and the extreme hot weather in August; the potatoes rotted in the ground to a great extent, the residue rotted after being gathered.' Another says, 'forty per cent. less, and the quality very inferior—spoiling.' Another, 'thirty-three per cent. less, occasioned by dry weather.' Another still: 'twenty-five per cent. less,' and assigns a similar cause for the deficiency. The disease mentioned above, seems also to have equally injured the crop in Delaware, as according to the information obtained, although there might be in some sections, perhaps, 'a fair average,' and even 'a large one,' yet, when they came to be gathered, they were not more than 'one-half or three-quarters of a crop,' as they 'rotted in the ground,' and so offensive, after being gathered, that it became necessary to remove them from the cellars. * * * *

"It is said that, in the vicinity of Philadelphia, 'where farmers have planted from one or two to ten or fifteen acres, they have lost them almost bodily,' and, in some instances, '1500 or 1200 bushels have decayed after they were dug.' In an agricultural journal of high standing, it is affirmed that the potatoes which are brought from the eastward are occasionally so heated in the vessel, as to become unfit for planting.' As an instance of this, 'some very fine mercer potatoes were obtained on board a vessel from Maine. They were planted, but about one-fourth of them only ever vegetated. Johnston, in his lectures on agricultural chemistry, remarks, in reference to this subject: 'The seeds of all cultivated plants are known at times to fail, and the necessity of an occasional change of seed is recognised in almost every district.' He mentions, that in the Lowlands of Scotland, 'potatoes brought from the Highlands are generally preferred for seed;' and that 'on the banks of the Tyne, Scottish potatoes bring a higher price for seed than those of native growth.' He adds, that 'this superior quality is supposed by some to arise from the less perfect ripening of the upland potatoes;' and alludes, in conformity with this view, to the extensive failures which have taken place during the summer of 1843, and which 'have been ascribed to the unusual degree of ripeness attained by the potatoes during the warm dry autumn of the past year.' 'This,' he says, 'may in part, be a true explanation of the fact, if, as is said, the ripest potatoes always contain the largest proportion of starch; since some very interesting observations of Mr. Shrrat, of Paisley, would seem to indicate that *'whatever increases the per centage of starch, increases also the risk of failure in potatoes that are to be used for seed.'*

"Mr. Shrrat gives it as his conclusion, that 'if farmers were careful in raising their own seed-potatoes from land that has lain long in a state of rest, or, where that cannot be had, by bringing new soil to the surface by trenching as much as is necessary,—or by the use of the sub-soil plough, failures of the potatoe crop, from the seed not being good, would become much less frequent.' Professor Johnston, however, doubts 'whether the relative proportions of starch are to be considered as the cause of the relative values of different samples of seed potatoes.' He speaks of the value of saline matter, and says that it is 'beautifully illustrated by the observations of Mr. Fleming, that potatoes dressed with sulphate and nitrate of soda in 1841, and used for seed in 1842, presented a remarkable contrast to the same variety of potatoe planted alongside of them, but which had not been so dressed in the previous season. These last came away weak, and of a yellowish colour, and, under the same treatment in every respect, did not produce so good a crop by fifteen colls (three tons and three-quarters) an acre.'

"The disease with which, as has been mentioned above, the potatoe crop has been attacked has excited more than usual attention. The cause is generally attributed to the peculiarity of the weather. In one agricultural paper, we find the disease ascribed to a 'premature ripening,' which caused the first set of tubers to sprout for the second crop. In another, it is mentioned thus: 'The cause of the disease, or sudden decay, has not as yet been satisfactorily accounted for. It has generally been attributed to their not ripening perfectly, and having been harvested prematurely. Our opinion, however, is, that it was caused by the superabundant moisture of the soil, in which they were allowed to remain too long. In support of this view, we would observe that, in one of our fields, which is low and of a retentive soil, we were compelled to leave a part of it ten or twelve days after the first part were harvested, before we could finish; and many of those last dug were affected, and soon rotted after exposure to the air. The tops of our potatoes, in one field, which were planted early, withered and dried long before we supposed the roots had ripened. They were dug early, and immediately stored in the cellar, with very little exposure to the sun; and no trace of disease, as yet, (December,) has been discovered; while others, in the same neighbourhood, under the same circumstances, but left until a later period before they were dug, have nearly all been destroyed. It does not appear to be confined to any variety; but the pink-eyes and the mercers have suffered most. In some cases, where the diseased potatoes have been fed to hogs and cattle, death ensued.'

"In another agricultural paper, we find the opinion expressed that the potatoe crop is almost a total failure; and the doubt is stated, if, in the general average of the entire country, the crop will turn out from one-fourth to one-fifth the usual product of former years. The editor says, 'we have heard of several, which, on being dug, did not yield one-fifth the quantity which the ground appropriated to their growth should have produced.' He further remarks, 'of the cause there is no diversity of opinion. All refer the decay of the roots to the frequent heavy rains; and we apprehend that of the propriety of this reference, there can be no doubt as, from the superabundant supply of water thus afforded to the vines, the tubers were prematurely forced in ripeness; and the same cause, existing under a greatly reduced temperature of the earth, proceeding from its supersaturated condition, and the atmospheric heat arising from the obscuration of the sun, on reaching the point of ripeness, instead of commencing a *second growth*, (as would have been the case, had there been sufficient sunshine and heat to bring out germination,) the tubers commenced the process of decomposition weeks before the regular time of harvesting them; and, in many instances, were found to be so many masses of rottenness when they were attempted to be dug, throwing out such an intolerable stench, that, in several cases, we have heard, the hands had to desist from digging them. Had these potatoes been dug just at the point of time at which they were ripe, there can be no question that they could have been saved from rotting.' The remedy suggested is later planting than usual; for the late-planted potatoes are said to have fared much better than the early planted. Another writer says, 'It is a fact not generally known, that the cause of the failure of the potatoe crop last summer was not caused by an excess of rainy weather, so much as the manner of ploughing the ground to receive slips. Farmers who ploughed their fields deep, and those particularly who used the subsoil plough, had a full average crop, and were more than compensated by thus deepening and pulverising the substratum; on the contrary, when the reverse was the case, two-thirds of the potatoes were found to be rotten, which was caused by water having no vent settling around them. The subsoil plough obviates this difficulty, and also, in event of a drought, allows the moisture to ascend, by which the plants are nourished, and an abundant crop realised.' An eminent agriculturalist also gives it as his opinion that the disease 'is a fungus belonging to the vegetable growth, as rust and smut in wheat and corn, and mould and mildew.' He recommends that 'all diseased potatoes be carefully taken out, and thrown away; and that, finally, pulverised *lime*, either slaked or unslaked, be sprinkled among the healthy potatoes, just enough to whiten their surfaces lightly.' No experiments to this effect, of course, have yet been tried.

"Another, also of high authority on agricultural subjects, writes: 'Potatoes on old ploughed highlands and alluvial grounds are liable to rust:

in 1843 rust was more common and prevalent than usual. High pasture lands, without manure, yield the best potatoes; these do not fail to work well. Potatoes struck with rust before they are ripe, are invariably watery and unpalatable. This was the case with four-fifths of the potatoes at the lower end of the state. On high grounds, broken from the sod, the potatoes are always good. I this year raised 1000 bushels nearly on five acres of alluvial sward land, where they were not injured by rust, and produced 200 bushels to the acre. These were planted in the sward, on a direct line, between every third furrow. The manure was all spread upon the sward, which was cut and turned over to the depth of from eight to ten inches; the manure was all out of sight. The roots of the potatoes derived all their necessary aid from the manure, the whole strength of which, for future crops, was retained in the ground. The potatoe vines continued green until fully ripe. Will some curious observer describe the disease of rust, and prescribe the best remedy? Four acres of the above were stirred with the subsoil plough, eight inches below the turning over of the surface plough, making sixteen inches in depth.'

"A gentleman, to whom we are indebted for much valuable information, mentions that he heard, two or three years ago, from one of the foreign ministers in this country, that a similar disease had attacked the potatoes in his country, but, as yet, we have been unable to find any notice of the same in any European publication. We find the following description of the appearance and progress of the disease in an agricultural journal: 'The pink-eyes are almost universally affected. The disease first manifests itself by a black spot on the surface of the potatoe, which rapidly spreads, till the whole root becomes soft and worthless. Many farmers have lost their entire crops; the disease, in many cases, destroying the roots while in the ground; and in others, the potatoes, after having been carefully stowed away in the cellar, apparently free from disease, and sound, in a few weeks were thrown away, utterly lost.'

"Again, another person says: 'The potatoes, when dug, appeared to look as fine as usual; but when put in heaps in the field, and covered as usual, they become a rotten mass. In a dry cellar they hold their usual appearance tolerably well, except somewhat darkened, and a little shrivelled; but on breaking them open, it was found that their surface, about a quarter of an inch in thickness, was of a dark brown, and some of them entirely through were of the same colour.' On feeding his hogs with them, he soon found that 'they began to cough, pant, and appear as if worried in a hot day; in about a week after they were taken, they refused to eat; and finally, after a few days, died—no doubt from their having been fed on these diseased potatoes.'

"Another gentleman, in writing on the same subject, says: 'This disease has spread through the whole of this crop with an amazing rapidity, from one potatoe to another, until the whole are more or less affected. I have frequently seen a small, dark, mortified kind of a spot, the size of a finger-nail, on the potatoe, whence issued bubbles of matter; soon the potatoe would be entirely soft, filled with yellowish matter, slimy, and somewhat resembling the rot of an egg. The touch of other potatoes would spread the disease through the whole of them.'

"Frozen potatoes are usually supposed to be unfit for use; but if they have not been permitted to thaw, and if they are at once, while frozen, thrown into a kettle of boiling water, the frost being in them, they are said to be equally as palatable and nutritious as those which have not been frozen.

"The following table, showing the analysis of different sorts of potatoes, is quoted from Accum (a bushel of potatoes weighs about sixty-four pounds.)

SORT.	Fibrine.	Starch.	Vegetable Albumen.	Gum.	Acids & Salts.	Water.	By whom Analysed.
Red Potatoes ..	7·0	15·0	1·4	4·1	5·1	75·0	Einhoff
Red Potatoes germinated	6·8	15·2	1·3	3·7		73·0	Ditto
Potatoe Sprouts	2·8	0·4	0·4	3·3		93·0	Ditto
Kidney Potatoes	8·8	9·1	0·8			81·3	Ditto
Large red Potatoes	6·0	12·9	0·7			78·0	Ditto
Sweet Potatoes..	8·2	15·1	0·8			74·3	Ditto
Potatoe of Peru	5·2	15·0	1·9	1·9		76·0	Lamped
Potatoe of England	6·8	12·9	1·1	1·7		77·5	Ditto
Onion Potatoe..	8.4	18·7	0·9	1·7		70·3	Ditto
Voigtland......	7·1	15·4	1·2	2·0		74·3	Ditto
Cultivated in the environs of Paris	6·79	13·3	0·92	3·3	1·4	73·12	Henry

"It is well known that there is a difference in the parts of the potatoe, as used for seed. An experiment on this point, is mentioned in some of the agricultural journals, in which the seed potatoes were cut in four equal parts, and the butt end, seed end, and two centre pieces, were separately planted. The result was, from the butt end were raised forty pounds, from the seed end sixty-two pounds, and from the centre pieces together one hundred and sixty pounds—showing the superiority of the centre pieces by fifty-eight pounds in the quantity planted; probably owing to the greater nutriment afforded. Whole potatoes are better than the eyes only for seed.

"The following experiment for raising potatoes in the winter, without great care or cost, in the open air, is mentioned in the Berlin Polytechnic Archives as having been tried with success at Frankfort-on-the-Maine.

"On the 26th of July, and 1st of August of the former year, two fields were planted with potatoes from three-fourths to one foot deep, and one and a half to two feet from each other; which, after they were hoed and hilled, blossomed in the end of October. When the cold weather began, the stalk was cut off half a foot above the earth, and then it was placed in one place, with leaves and manure, and covered in another with some straw; and, lastly, some earth was thrown over it. In both places the potatoes were gathered on the 10th of March; they had a perfectly fine appearance, and were of good taste."

---

2. POTATOE CROP IN ENGLAND.—EXTRACTION OF FARINA FROM DISEASED POTATOES.—DIRECTIONS ISSUED BY THE HADLEIGH FARMERS' CLUB.*

Oct. 10, 1845.

1. Thoroughly wash the potatoes. It is unnecessary to peel them, unless a very superior article is required.

2. Rasp them to a fine pulp with a common bread grater; such as may be procured for 5½*d.*, or may be made by punching a piece of tin with a nail. The more finely the pulp has been rasped, the more flour will be obtained.

3. Place some of the pulp (say about a quarter of a pailful at a time) into a pail. Fill the pail with water and stir up the whole well, in order to work the flour out of the pulp. The water will soon become thick from the quantity of flour it will hold in suspension.

4. Pour the contents of the pail (before it has had time to settle) upon a horse-hair or other sieve placed over a large rub. The water will readily pass through the sieve with most of the flour in suspension, whilst the pulp remains behind, and may be emptied from the sieve into another pail, to undergo a second or a third washing, after all the pulp has been similarly treated. This plan is better than putting the pulp first on the sieve and then pouring water upon it. As some small portion of the pulp often finds its way through the sieve, it may be removed at once by allowing the water to fall upon a loose coarse cloth stretched over the tub; but in this case the water must be continually stirred whilst it is filtering through the cloth, otherwise the flour is apt to clot and fill up the passages.

5. The flour will rapidly subside in the tub, and in less than ten minutes there will be a compact layer formed at the bottom. But as the finest particles remain suspended in the water much longer than the rest during this first part of the process, it is advisable to let the whole stand for three or four hours, when the water may be poured off.

6. The flour thus procured should be washed at least once or twice more, by filling the tub with fresh water, stirring it up well, and then allowing it to settle again, which it will now do very rapidly; and as soon as the water above is clear, it may be poured off.

7. The flour, on being removed from the tub, may be spread out in thin layers to dry, upon cloths, which may be changed and dried before the fire once or twice a-day. But the flour itself must not be exposed to any great heat, and even the temperature of boiling water will change it, whilst it is wet, into a mass of dough. As the process of drying is tedious, and this method of spreading out the flour troublesome, it will generally be advisable to adopt a method which has been found to be perfectly efficacious, and which gives very little trouble or inconvenience. The flour may be collected from the tub into bags of linen or calico, and these hung up in a warm or airy situation. The water then drains from the flour, which gradually dries without injury. The bags may be taken down in two or three days, and pressed and shaken, in order to break the lumps into which the flour may have collected, and then hung up again. Temporary bags may readily be made out of table-cloths, sheets, or pillow-cases.

8. When the flour is thoroughly dry, it may

---

* See, however, the report of the 29th Oct., at page 169.

be kept in a dry place for any number of years fit for use, in bags, jars, or casks.

Upon the whole, it will be found that this method is more to be recommended than the plan of not passing the water through a sieve; but where no great nicety is required, or no sieve at hand, the pulp may be thrown into a large tub filled with water, and the whole stirred up and allowed to settle. In two or three minutes most of the pulp will have fallen to the bottom, whilst the heavier flour—from its being composed of so much finer particles—is still held in suspension in the water. By degrees, however, the flour, owing to its greater specific gravity, finds its way past the pulp, and at length settles below it. The water and pulp may then be poured off together, and the flour will be found in a compact mass at the bottom of the tub. These effects are readily to be seen, and may be better appreciated by a little experiment in which glass tumblers may be substituted for pail and tub. If the potatoe flour be mixed with wheat flour in any proportion, it will make wholesome bread: but as it is not so well calculated for making bread as for some other purposes, it is advisable not to add more than from a sixth to a third of the flour of the potatoes in this mixture. It serves better for puddings, &c. Its best use as food, is under the forms to which arrow-root may be applied; and it is well understood that a very high per centage of what is sold in the shops under the name of arrow-root, is nothing more than this very flour of potatoes. It is also passed off in London under about a dozen different names, as an important and nutritious article of diet.

To prepare a cup as arrow-root, take about a tablespoonful of the flour, add a little cold water to it, and stir it up to the consistency of cream. Now pour on it water absolutely boiling, (for if cooler it will not answer,) and keep stirring it till the cup is nearly full, when it will suddenly pass to a transparent paste-like jelly. This jelly is nearly tasteless, but may be rendered very palatable in several ways. By adding salt and a very little piece of butter, it proves to be a grateful dish to the poor. With sugar and nutmeg, it is extremely pleasant to most palates, and more especially so if a little white wine is added to it. Some children of the labourers prefer it with salt and butter to having it prepared with sugar and nutmeg; also with sugar and milk it seems to be highly approved by them. A good basonful of this jelly may be prepared *in less than ten minutes from a single raw potatoe.* It takes not two minutes to wash and grate it; not a minute to stir the pulp in water and pass it over the sieve. If the strained water be then left to stand for six or seven minutes in a bason and then poured out again, a firm layer of the flour will already have settled at the bottom, and if this be stirred up whilst boiling water is poured upon it, the bason is presently filled with a mass of most excellent jelly. It would be better to re-wash the flour and allow it to settle again, as it has not been thoroughly cleaned of the crude juice of the potatoe, which might sometimes impart a flavour to the jelly; but if the experiment be tried in the way suggested, it proves very attractive and inviting to further inquiry, with persons who might not otherwise feel disposed to attend to the process.

Among several facts which have been named in favour of the process recommended for extracting and saving the wholesome flour contained in bad potatoes, the following may be selected.

Mr. J. Rand, the vice-president of the club, has employed women to grate about thirty sacks of bad potatoes, (grown on his own farm,) at a cost of two shillings the sack. He has ascertained that from one sack he obtained seventeen pounds of flour.

Mr. A. Smith, clerk of Layham, has extracted thirty pounds of flour from about five bushels of bad potatoes, part of the produce of his allotment, and has refused sixpence the pound, which was offered him for his sample.

Mr. W. Baker, carpenter at Hitcham, has long been in the habit of procuring arrow-root from the shops at one shilling and four-pence per pound for an invalid wife, who uses a good deal of it; but he now finds that he can prepare for himself, from his bad potatoes, an article equal to what he has been accustomed to buy.

At the Cosford Union House, about forty sacks of potatoes, grown on the premises, proved too bad for use; these are undergoing the process, and a large quantity of the flour has already been procured from them.

Since a bushel of sound potatoes, in the early part of the season, may be made to produce from eleven to twelve pounds of this flour of a most superior quality, quite equal to what is sold very frequently as arrow-root, &c., from one shilling and sixpence to two shillings and sixpence the pound; and since the prime cost of a bushel of potatoes may be estimated, in most seasons (to the growers themselves) at sixpence to a shilling, it should seem, that whilst the potatoe flour may command a marketable value which would remunerate the labour bestowed in its manufacture, it may often be prepared by the growers themselves, for home use, at a prime cost of a halfpenny or penny per pound.

---

3. POTATOE CROP IN IRELAND.—CONVERTING POTATOES INTO FARINA.—LETTER TO THE POOR LAW COMMISSIONERS.

Waterford Poor Law Board Room,
Oct. 17, 1845.

GENTLEMEN,—I returned here last night, after having travelled through a part of the counties of Tipperary and Limerick; where, from personal observation as well as information, I have ascertained that the apprehensions relating to the prevailing disease in the potatoe are of a very serious character; and it appears to me, that if immediate steps be not taken to avert the consequences of a general decay of the potatoe, it would necessarily follow that serious distress and poverty would be the result. I, from past experience, dread the effects of the disease in the pit, more than, as at present, in the ground. For some years past, I have turned my attention to the very important consideration of securing a portion of our potatoe crop, so as to be available for consumption for any number of years, in the shape of farina, and erected machinery at a neighbouring mill for the purpose, where I was very successful in producing flour or potatoe farina of excellent quality. However, such were the mistaken ideas of some, and the prejudices of others, that I failed in my endeavours to persuade every farmer or cottier to take some ten, twenty, or thirty barrels of their potatoes to be converted into farina. The case is now altered. The time has arrived to awaken *all* to its importance; and with this view, a special meeting of our board will meet on Monday next, to take this matter into its consideration. I therefore most respectfully submit, that it would be advisable that all boards throughout the land, should do the same. It may be useful to be generally known, the mode of converting the potatoe into farina. It is very simple. For example: Take thirty barrels of potatoes; let them be thoroughly washed; they then fall into a hopper, (similar to that used for grinding apples for cider,) the pulp is received into a wire turning cylinder of about ten feet long, sixteen inches diameter, over the length of which, is a tin pipe perforated with holes, through which flows a constant supply of pure water. By this process, the farina is extracted from the pulp, and passes with the water through a pipe that leads to the vats in another apartment, while the pulp passes to the waste-room. The farina becomes deposited at the bottom of each vat or tub, from which the clear water is drawn off by plug-holes. The farina is then taken by clean spades from the bottom, in the heavy mass, and immediately placed in boxes or (for better dispatch) placed on sheets of calico spread on a kiln to dry. When dry, it is taken to the loft and spread open to the air. It becomes beautifully white and fit for packing in sacks, and will keep for years. Thirty barrels will make one ton of farina; but they must be sound to do so. For consumption, one-third part of oatmeal or wheaten flour should be added, when it will make excellent and substantial *griddle-cake* bread. I have ventured to offer the foregoing observations, believing they may be of some use; and I would strongly recommend generally, as I intend to do, at our next meeting, that all persons of influence throughout the country should, without loss of time, secure the small mills of the country, with the view of carrying out this object at the least possible expense to the poor.

I have, &c.,

SIMON NEWPORT, Poor Law Guardian.

To the Poor Law Commissioners, Dublin.

REPORTS OF THE COMMISSIONERS APPOINTED BY HER MAJESTY'S GOVERNMENT TO EXAMINE INTO THE STATE OF THE POTATOE CROP IN IRELAND.

Board Room, Royal Dublin Society,
24th October, 1845.

MY LORD,

We, the undersigned Commissioners appointed by Her Majesty's Government to report to your Excellency on the state of disease in the potatoe crop, and on the means of its prevention, have the honour to inform your Excellency that we are pursuing our inquiries with unremitting attention.

We are fully sensible of the important and difficult nature of the inquiry, and therefore are unwilling to offer, at the present moment, any final recommendations, as we are still receiving evidence, and awaiting the results of various experiments now in progress. But at the same time, we ought to state to your Excellency, that we have reason to hope that the progress of the disease may be retarded by the application of simple means, which we trust may appear worthy of adoption, until we are enabled to offer further recommendations.

In the present communication, we avoid entering into any account of the origin or nature of the disease; but we would particularly direct attention to the ascertained facts, that moisture hastens its progress, and that it is capable of being communicated to healthy potatoes when they are in contact with such as are already tainted. A knowledge of these facts, determined as they have been by experiment, and agreeing with the scientific information obtained as to the causes and nature of the disease, lead us to propose the adoption of the following plan for diminishing the evils arising from the destructive malady :—

In the event of a continuance of dry weather, and in soils tolerably dry, we recommend that the potatoes should be allowed, for the present, to remain in the land ; but if wet weather intervene, or if the soil be naturally wet, we consider that they should be removed from the ground without delay.

When the potatoes are dug out of the ground, we are decidedly of opinion that they should not be pitted in the usual way, as the circumstances under which potatoes are placed in ordinary pits, are precisely those which tend to hasten their decay.

We recommend that potatoes when dug should be spread over the field, and not collected into heaps, and if the weather continue dry and free from frost, that they should be allowed to lie upon the field for a period of time not exceeding three days.

The potatoes, after being thus dried and improved in their power of resisting disease by the means proposed, should then be sorted by carefully separating those which show any tendency to decay. Those potatoes which appear to be sound, should then be placed about two inches apart in a layer, and over each layer of potatoes should be placed a layer of turf ashes, or dry turf-mould, or dry sand, or burned clay, to the depth of a few inches. Thus will be formed a bed of potatoes, each potatoe being completely separated from the other by a dry absorptive material; upon this bed, another layer of potatoes should be spread in like manner, and be also covered with the dry materials employed ; as many as four layers may thus be placed one above the other, and when the heap is completed, it should be covered with dry clay, straw, heath, or any other material adapted to protect it from rain.

In the event of the weather becoming wet, these recommendations are not applicable. In that case, we would advise the potatoes to be packed in small heaps, with either straw or heath interposed, and well covered; in such a situation they should become as well dried as seems practicable under the circumstances. When out-buildings exist, it would be advisable that this mode of temporary packing should be carried on in those places. If there be no out-houses, the heaps may be left in the open field. We, however, particularly recommend that potatoes should not be removed into inhabited rooms.

With regard to the treatment of potatoes already attacked with the disease, we have to state that in this early stage of our investigation, we do not feel justified in proposing to your Excellency any mode of positive treatment,—this subject we reserve for a future report; but we may remark that exposure to light and dryness, in all cases retards the progress of alterations, such as the disease in question, and we therefore suggest that all such potatoes should, as far as possible, be so treated.

We do not mean to represent that these recommendations, if carried into effect, will prevent the occurrence of disease in potatoes; but we feel assured that the decay will extend less extensively under these circumstances, than if the potatoes when taken from the ground, be at once pitted in the usual manner. Neither do we offer these suggestions to your Excellency as a final means of securing the crop, but merely as a method of retarding the progress of an enemy whose history and habits are as yet but imperfectly known, whilst we endeavour to ascertain the means of more completely counteracting its injurious effects, if any such can be discovered.

All which we submit to your Excellency's consideration, and remain,

Your Excellency's obedient and faithful servants,

Robert Kane,
John Lindley,
Lyon Playfair.

To His Excellency Baron Heytesbury,
Lord Lieutenant of Ireland,
&c. &c. &c.

Board Room, Royal Dublin Society,

29th October, 1845.

MY LORD—Having submitted to your Excellency, in a former report, some preliminary instructions intended to prevent improper treatment of the potatoe crop still remaining unaffected, we now have the honour to lay before your Excellency our views regarding some processes of treatment for the potatoe, which appear to us to be of practical value and importance.

We are deeply sensible of the incompleteness of form which this mode of presenting our results to your Excellency, necessarily assumes; but the exigencies of the case are such, that we consider it our highest duty to bring at once under the notice of Her Majesty's Government such principles or modes of practice as, upon due consideration, we feel ourselves authorised to recommend.

We have been engaged in the investigation of various plans for preserving diseased potatoes, as proposed by other persons, or suggested by ourselves, and we have been collecting precise information as to the experience of others in their endeavours to arrest the progress of the disease. From all the results that we have obtained, we feel justified in submitting to your Excellency the following observations:—

Plans of treatment have been proposed by persons possessing more or less of chemical knowledge, in which, by some, acids are to be employed; in others, alkaline liquors; and in a third class, gases such as chlorine. These processes we dismiss from further consideration, as, even did they, in the laboratory, answer the intended purpose, they are totally inapplicable to the circumstances of the produce of an entire country, and to a population such as that for whose welfare your Excellency is so deeply anxious. Other methods, apparently more practical, consist in the treatment of the potatoes with chloride of lime (bleaching powder) and salt, either separate or in mixture. The result of our own experiments, and the evidence we have received concerning trials made by persons in whom we have full confidence, authorise us at once to recommend the rejection of those materials. We have found the decomposition of the potatoe to be decidedly accelerated by their application. With respect to lime, the results of our own experiments are not yet decisive; nor is the experience of others as yet satisfactory. We therefore reserve this point for further consideration.

Whilst the disease is not yet very far advanced in the potatoe, it is certain, that after being boiled or steamed, it may be employed as food for immediate use, both for man and other animals, without prejudice to health.

When the disease is more advanced, so as to have invaded a large part of the potatoe, and when the tubers have acquired a disagreeable smell, their influence on the system is more questionable. We have put in operation a series of experiments, in order to determine this point, and will, in due time, report the result to your Excellency. As, however, the potatoe, when once affected, quickly runs into total decomposition if left to itself, it is evident that its consumption merely for the purpose of food cannot be sufficiently rapid; and it therefore becomes necessary to consider to what other uses it may be applied.

The extraction of starch from potatoes, and its use as food, having strongly attracted public attention, and conflicting, and, in many cases, inaccurate opinions having been entertained on this subject, we consider it of paramount importance at once to direct your Excellency's attention to the actual state of knowledge regarding this material. It is recognised that the potatoe, in relation either to its weight or bulk, is one of the most inferior articles of food. In its ordinary state of sound constitution, every hundred pounds by weight of potatoes contain, on an average, seventy-four pounds of water; of skin and fibrous matter, eight pounds; and of starch, sixteen pounds; whilst of gluten, the most nutritious of vegetable matters, and which predominates in corn, there is not more than two pounds in the above quantity. It is quite certain that starch, or materials corresponding to it, exist to a certain amount in every variety of useful food; but it is equally certain that in food starch is not the material which serves for the support of the animal frame; and an animal fed merely on starch dies of starvation nearly, if not quite, as soon, as if totally deprived of food. Hence, starch extracted from the potatoe cannot be viewed as a substitute for the potatoe itself; and we consider it of great importance that whilst the attention of the people is directed to the real value of starch and the uses to which it may be advantageously applied, they should not be allowed to rest their hopes of nourishment during the succeeding season upon any store of it alone.

With this preliminary caution, we have to state to your Excellency that probably the best use to which diseased potatoes may be applied, is the extraction of starch. In a commercial point of view, the starch represents a considerable proportion of the value of the potatoe, although it is not present in as large a quantity in the unsound tubers, as in those which are free from disease. The extraction is simple, and consists in processes which we need not here describe, as they are given in the current publications of the day, and indeed are already practised in most parts of the country.

Your Excellency is aware that we are directing our attention to the manner in which starch can be advantageously employed. It can be worked off, and with utility, as food, when mixed with proportions of oatmeal, bean-meal, or peas-meal; and such intermixture forms an excellent and economical article of food. It is also to be remarked, that the pulp remaining after the extraction of the starch from the diseased potatoes, contains a considerable quantity of nutritive material; and as the decomposing substance is, to a very great extent, washed out during the preparation, the pulp may, when dried, be applied with confidence to the nourishment of animals. Further, if the dried starch, extracted from the potatoe, be mixed up with the dry residual pulp, a material will be produced really representing the potatoe, equivalent to it as food, and, if kept dry, capable of being preserved for a considerable length of time: it, of course, must be prepared for use by cooking or baking in the ordinary way.

The manufacture of the pulp and starch, on an extensive scale, in accordance with these suggestions, we venture to consider worthy of your Excellency's attention. It is an operation not suited to the circumstances of isolated cotters, and just now might not be a proper object for mere commercial speculation. But arrangements might possibly be made for carrying out this recommendation, through the agency of the poor law unions, and other government establishments, in which mechanical power and intelligent superintendence could be speedily and economically applied. We feel, however, that even these facilities for the conversion of the tubers may not be sufficient to keep pace with the progressive injury which, it is to be feared, the potatoe crop is sustaining. We, therefore, recommend a mode by which we believe the process of decomposition may be retarded. In our preliminary report, we mentioned to your Excellency the important influence exercised upon the disease by moisture and dryness. Our subsequent investigations have confirmed this opinion, and we believe where means exist for a more complete drying of the tubers, such a method will prove the most efficacious plan for preserving the potatoe from further decay. This more perfect drying cannot, however, be effected in this climate by mere exposure to air,—it requires artificial heat, applied in some form of kiln; and without entering into mechanical details, we may name some simple contrivances which seem well adapted to the purpose.

The corn kilns extensively distributed through the country may at once be applied to the drying of the potatoes, which will, however, demand a temperature, rendered gradually higher than that required for corn. But as in many cases those kilns are at present fully occupied, we would represent that every lime kiln may be adapted to the purpose, without interfering with its ordinary operations, by erecting over it, at a suitable height above its mouth, a frame-work of hurdles, upon which the potatoes may be spread in a thin layer, fresh potatoes being added as the others become dry and are removed. In localities where the previous means do not exist, or may not be on a sufficiently extensive scale, potatoes might be spread on a frame-work of hurdles, supported on a few props of stone, two or three feet high: one or more turf fires burning slowly under the hurdles, would effect the same object. There need be no fear of the potatoes becoming slightly browned, as they are not injured thereby for future use; and the turf smoke would act favourably on the potatoes rather than otherwise.

In all these modes of drying, the potatoe should be cut into two, or if very large, into three pieces, so as to allow the water to escape.

Potatoes dried in any of the modes above described are certainly capable of being preserved when kept in a dry place, and stored, with the precautions described in our first report, until suitable opportunities arise for using them directly as food, or for converting them into starch or meal, according to the degree in which they were affected by the disease.

It is gratifying to us to find that our own opinion as to the advantages of thoroughly drying the potatoe in the manner we have recommended, and by processes such as those above described, are confirmed by the experience of highly intelligent persons, who have simultaneously directed their attention to the subject.

We shall not hesitate to bring under the notice

of your Excellency, our further conclusions, and,
We have the honour to be,
Your Excellency's obedient and faithful servants,
ROBERT KANE,
JOHN LINDLEY,
LYON PLAYFAIR.
To His Excellency Baron Heytesbury,
Lord Lieutenant of Ireland, &c.

Board Room, Royal Dublin Society,
3rd November, 1845.

MY LORD—We have had the honour to lay before your Excellency, reports on the diseases in the potatoe crop, which have been distributed extensively throughout the country. Representations, however, have been made to us, that the recommendations being in the form of reports, are not likely to be of that use which the more simple form of instructions might enable them to be. We have, therefore, thought it advisable to prepare the accompanying directions, in the hope that the methods recommended may be easily understood and promptly carried into execution.

We shall immediately lay before your Excellency our views upon the course which should be pursued with regard to seed for a future year.

We have the honour to be,
Your faithful and obedient servants,
ROBERT KANE,
JOHN LINDLEY,
LYON PLAYFAIR.
To His Excellency Baron Heytesbury,
Lord Lieutenant of Ireland, &c.

TO THE FARMERS AND TO THE PEASANTRY OF IRELAND.

The dreadful disease that has attacked your potatoes is one, the effects of which you can only stop by strict attention to the advice of those interested in your welfare. Many plans have been proposed, and, after examining them all, we recommend the following as the best.

All competent persons are of opinion, that the first things to bear in mind are the following directions:—

1. Dig your potatoes in dry weather, if you can, and if you cannot, get them dry somehow as fast as you can.
2. Keep them DRY and cool.
3. Keep the bad potatoes separate from the good.
4. Do not pit your potatoes as you have been accustomed to do in former years.
5. Recollect that if they get damp, nothing can make them keep; and do not consider them dry unless the mould which sticks to them is like dust.
6. Do not take them into your houses unless you want them for immediate use.

Digging and Drying.

As you dig the potatoes, leave them in the sun all day; and, if you can, throw them upon straw, turning them over two or three times. At night you may gather them together and cover them with straw, so as to keep off frost. Next day take off the straw, spread them out, and give them the sun again. Do this for three days running, if the weather permit. If you put straw enough upon them at night they will not suffer.

If the weather be unfavourable, and you have a dry loft, or out-house large enough to hold them, you may spread them thinly on the floor, allowing a free circulation of air so as to dry them there.

They MUST be got DRY.

Sorting the Potatoes.

As soon as they are dry, you must sort them. Pick them one by one, and put in one heap the very bad ones, in another, those which are not so bad, and in a third, those that are sound. Treat the bad potatoes as shall afterwards be directed, and store the sound ones according to the directions given in the next paragraph. You will know the very bad potatoes by their unpleasant smell, and the second set by their skin looking brown, or dull, and not bright, as it generally does; a very little practice will teach you how to distinguish them easily from each other.

Storing.

When the potatoes are quite dry, and well sorted, proceed to store them thus:—Mark out on the ground a space six feet wide, and as long as you please. Dig a shallow trench two feet wide all round, and throw the mould upon the space; then level it, and cover it with a floor of turf-sods, set on their edges. On this sift or spread, very thinly, the dry mixtures, or any of the dry materials described below, and which you may call the *packing stuff*. Also, get some dry slacked lime, and dust all the potatoes with it as well as you can. Then put one row of turf-sods, laid flat, on the top of the floor, all round the sides, so as to form a broad edge, and within this, spread the dry potatoes, mixed well with the packing stuff, so as not to touch one another. When you have covered the floor in this manner, up to the top of the sods, lay another row of sods all round the first, so that half of each sod may rest on the bed of potatoes, and the other half on the first layer of sods; this will make another edge one sod deep, which must be filled up with dry potatoes and dry packing stuff, as before. Then lay another edge of sods in the same way, fill it again, and so go on till the heap is made. When the building of this pit is finished, it may be covered with sods at the top, and will be ready for thatching. If rightly made, it will look like the roof of a cottage cut into steps, as shown in this sketch,

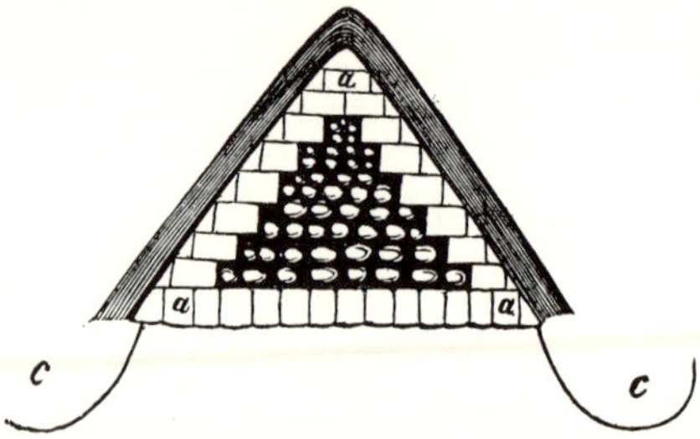

in which *a a* are sods, and *c c* the ditch all round the heap; potatoes and packing stuff, are the white and black space in the middle.

If you do not understand this, ask your landlord or your clergyman to explain its meaning, and we are sure that they will give you every assistance; also recollect that the recommendation applies only to sound potatoes, after being well dried.

You will lose nothing by applying these materials in storing, for the turf can be burnt as you use up the potatoes; and the mixture of lime with dry sand, dry clay or ashes, which you are afterwards directed to employ, will form a good manure after having saved the potatoes. The only difference is, that you must get what you want now instead of waiting till another time.

After you have completed the heap, thatch it so as to throw off the waters into the ditch, and keep out the frost.

In districts where there may not be spare turf sufficient to form the pits in the above way, make them as follows:—Mark out the spot, and make the trench as before. Lay on the ground a floor of stones, about as large as apples, and over them as much heath, brushwood, or twigs, as will just cover the stones. On this floor form the heaps of potatoes, and packing stuff, just as described, for the turf-pit. Cover the sides of the potatoes with more of the packing stuff, and thatch in the usual way.

We must again impress upon you that to pit potatoes in your usual way is certain destruction to them.

Packing Stuff.

This, which is of the greatest consequence, may be prepared in either of the following ways,—some of you may prefer the one, some the other:—

First way.—Mix a barrel of freshly burned unslacked lime, with two barrels of sand or earth, as dry as you can possibly get it. The lumps of lime should be broken into pieces as large as marbles, and the mixture should be left twenty-four hours; at the end of that time, turn the heap well over, mixing together the lime and sand (or other dry materials) till no lumps of lime can be found.

Second way.—Mix well equal quantities of earth and broken turf, or dry sawdust, put a few sods of lighted turf on the ground, place the mixture on them by degrees till a large heap is made, in a few hours the fire will have spread through the heap, which is then to be covered with earth so as to put out the fire. In fact, this is to be managed just as if you were burning land. This burned mixture forms a very good kind of packing stuff, perhaps as good as the mixture of lime with dry materials.

What to do with bad Potatoes.

When potatoes are only slightly diseased, that is, when the disease shows itself only under the skin in small dark spots, or at most, spreading into the substance of the potatoe for about a quarter of an inch deep, with a yellow or light brown, or blackish colour, and without any smell, they may be eaten by the family without danger. They should be peeled and the diseased parts pared off before they are boiled; the parts cut off should be kept for making starch. Potatoes thus treated are wholesome and palatable, but should be used for food as quickly as possible, as it is not quite certain that they will keep long, with the greatest care.

It is a pity to destroy potatoes for starch if they will otherwise keep. Cut out the diseased parts, if it can easily be done, and dust over the cut parts with lime and the potatoe also. Get them dry as soon as you possibly can, and if you have outhouses or sheds, you should keep the potatoes in them also, using the packing materials. In such cases you should allow the air to circulate freely in the sheds, and should frequently examine your potatoes, which should not be laid in layers above two or three feet in height. If you turn them frequently during the first two or three weeks and keep them VERY DRY, in this way they will probably keep. Although sheds or outhouses are to be preferred, if you have them not, and cannot construct them out of cheap materials, you should store the diseased potatoes by themselves just as we have recommended you to store the sound ones.

If, with all your care, the diseased potatoes still get worse, dry them thoroughly in kilns, or on hurdles placed over lime kilns, or on screens or hurdles placed over low turf fires, after having cut the potatoes into two or three slices. It is only very bad potatoes that you should break up into starch.

How to save the value of very bad Potatoes.

Although nobody knows how to make bad potatoes into good ones, or to prevent many of them from becoming worse, yet it is possible to extract from bad potatoes, or from bad parts of them, a great deal which is good. For this purpose proceed as follows:—Provide yourselves with the following things, a rasp or grater, which may be made of a sheet of tin or even of sheet iron bent round, and punched full of holes, with a nail—a common coarse linen cloth, or hair sieve, hand sieve, or common cloth strainer—and a pail, or tub or two to hold water.

To make the bad potatoes useful, wash them clean, and then rasp them into one of the tubs of water; the finer they are rasped the more food will you procure from them. Having rasped a good many, take the cloth and place it on another tub, then put the pulp on the cloth, and pour water on it, allowing the water to run through. You have now two things to attend to—the pulp and the starch.

First,—Attend to the pulp, squeeze out as much water as you can from what remains on the cloth. You should wash it, however, till no smell remains. After you have squeezed it pretty dry, complete the drying on a griddle, over a slack fire, and when it is dry put it aside for use.

Next look to the milky water; it will then become clear, and the milkiness, which is starch, will have settled to the bottom. Pour off the water gently till the starch is tolerably well drained; then add more water, stir the whole well up, and let it settle again. As soon as it is again clear, pour off the water, and when you have got rid of as much as you can, put the wet lumps of starch on a shelf or other place to dry. In a few days it will be fit to pack up.

Good wholesome bread may be made by mixing the starch with the dried pulp, peasmeal, beanmeal, oatmeal, or flour. You must bear in mind, that starch is not food by itself.

There will be, of course, a good deal of trouble in doing all that we have recommended, and perhaps you will not succeed very well at first; but we are confident that all true Irishmen will exert themselves, and never let it be said, that in Ireland the inhabitants wanted courage to meet difficulties against which other nations are successfully struggling.

ROBERT KANE,
JOHN LINDLEY,
LYON PLAYFAIR.

II. LUNATIC PAUPERS.

1. CONSTRUCTION OF 8 & 9 VIC. C. 100 AND C. 126.

6th October, 1845.

Clerk of Strand Union—Stated, that by the 8 and 9 Vict. cap. 100, s. 48, and by another Act of the same Session, cap. 126, it is provided that no pauper shall be received into any house or hospital for lunatics without a certificate signed by a physician, surgeon, or apothecary, not being the medical officer of the Union. But in the latter statute exception is made in cases of lunatics found wandering, or neglected, or cruelly treated by their relatives or friends. No provision, however, appears to be made under either of the statutes in question for the payment of any medical man (not being a Union officer) who may furnish such certificate, or render the service required by the Acts. The magistrates have, of course, no funds at their disposal out of which they can pay any remuneration for such assistance. The guardians would be willing, under the Commissioners' sanction, to pay such remuneration out of the poor-rates; but a difficulty would in that case arise as to the nomination of a gentleman to furnish such certificate, as, if he were to be employed by the guardians, such employment emanating from them might constitute him a medical officer, and thereby disqualify him for the discharge of the particular duty. In the event, however, of these difficulties being removed, the rate of payment per case will have to be decided on; and it seems desirable that the maximum amount to be given in such cases should be fixed by the Commissioners.

Ans.—Although no express provision is made in the Act 8 and 9 Vic. c. 126, for the payment of a fee to the medical man called in by the justice to his assistance, under the 48th section, yet it appears to the Commissioners that such medical man is entitled to demand a reasonable remuneration for his services. The Act requires the justice to call in a medical man to his assistance, but it does not require the medical man to render such assistance gratuitously. A difficulty may sometimes arise in settling the amount of the fee. In the absence of any positive enactment on the subject, the Commissioners think that this point must be arranged in each case between the justice and the medical man. With regard to the parties by whom the fee is to be paid, the Commissioners are disposed to consider that it must be paid by the officers acting on behalf of the parish to which the pauper lunatic, in the particular case, is chargeable; that is to say, in respect of any parish in the Strand Union, by the guardians of that union. The Commissioners rest this opinion on the grounds that the expenses of the examination of a pauper lunatic, and of his removal to an asylum, &c. are, as they conceive, chargeable on the parish from which he is receiving relief at the time; and that the fee to the medical man is one of those expenses. The Commissioners direct your attention to the 57th section of the statute, which provides that when any pauper lunatic shall be confined under the provisions of the Act he shall continue chargeable to the parish from which he was sent, until such parish shall, in due course of law, have established that such lunatic is settled in some other parish, or that it cannot be ascertained in what parish such lunatic is settled. In the latter case the lunatic will become chargeable to the county, according to section 59. If he is settled elsewhere, the parish of his settlement may be required to repay to the parish from which he was sent to the asylum, "all expenses incurred by or on behalf of such parish, in or about the examination of such lunatic, and his conveyance to the asylum," (sect. 62). If he becomes chargeable to the county, the repayment of these expenses may be obtained from the county treasurer, (sect. 63,) and if his settlement is afterwards discovered, the county treasurer may procure the reimbursement of the charge by the parish in which he is settled, (sect. 64.) Although the statute does not expressly authorise the parish from which the lunatic is sent to the asylum to defray the cost of his examination and removal, the power to do so seems to follow from the duty of taking those proceedings; and at all events the provisions above cited, with regard to the repayment of the expenses, clearly imply that the parish from which the pauper is sent, is to be called upon in the first instance to provide for the change. On the whole, therefore, the Commissioners think that in the cases in question occurring, under the 8th and 9th Vic. c. 126, the medical man is entitled to a fee of reasonable amount, and that such fee must be paid by the parish to which the lunatic is chargeable when taken before the justice, as one of the expenses of his examination. With regard to the 48th section of the 8th and 9th Vic. c. 100, the Commissioners are disposed to consider that it does not raise or affect any question as to the payment of the medical men to whose certificate it refers; inasmuch as it appears to the Commissioners to be merely of a prohibitory or conditional character, and not to authorise of itself the origination of any proceedings. The Commissioners apprehend that all cases of pauper lunatics are to be dealt with under the 48th section of the 8th and 9th Vic. c. 126: although the Commissioners confess that they feel great difficulty in construing the 51st sect. of that statute in connexion with the 48th sect. of the 8th and 9th Vict. c. 100.

---

2. DITTO.

6th October, 1845.

Medical Officer of Northallerton Union—Inquired whether it was his duty, under the Act 8 and 9 Vict. c. 126, sect. 55, to visit all the lunatics which actually belong, and are chargeable to the several parishes in his district as medical officer; that is, those who are not in any registered or licensed hospital; and also, whether he was entitled to any fee for such examination, or travelling expenses in attending to make the same, as he will in some instances have to go out of his district.

Ans.—The terms of the section are, "That *every* pauper lunatic, *chargeable to any parish,* who shall not be in an asylum, &c., shall be visited once in every three months by *the medical officer of the parish or union to which such lunatic shall belong.*" The Commissioners think it clear that this provision casts upon you, as medical officer, the duty of visiting *every* pauper lunatic who "belongs" to any parish within your district. It is provided by the Interpretation clause (sect. 84) that the word "lunatic" shall mean every insane person, and every person being an idiot or lunatic, or of unsound mind. The question then arises, what meaning is to be attached to the word "belong," as used in the sentence above cited. The Commissioners have had occasion to communicate on this subject with the Commissioners in Lunacy, who state their views in the following terms: "The Commissioners in Lunacy apprehend that the word 'belong' will be satisfied by holding, for the purpose of that the medical officer of the union within which the pauper resides, and through the relieving officer of which, as the Commissioners assume, the weekly payments are made, is the proper medical officer to visit the pauper." As the duties imposed by the 55th sect. are cast upon you as medical officer by the statute, which makes no provision for any special payment on that account, the Commissioners think that you are not entitled to any separate fee for the performance of this particular service; but as this additional labour was not contemplated when your appointment took place, it may be a matter for consideration by the guardians, whether they will deem it right to recommend any increase in your remuneration.

---

3. DITTO.

Oct. 10*th*, 1845.

Clerk of Thetford Union—Stated, that a pauper residing in the workhouse and unable to be examined out of it, is about to be removed to a Lunatic Asylum under the 48th section of the 8 and 9 Vict. 126. The justice will make the order under the proviso, in which no restriction is made as to the surgeon being a medical officer of the union; but by the 48th section of the 8 and 9 Vict. c. 100, no pauper can be received into a "Licensed House or Hospital" without a certificate from a surgeon, not being the medical officer of the union. The interpretation clause of the 8 & 9 Vict. c. 126, declares that "Asylum" shall mean any house, &c. Inquired whether it was necessary to obtain the certificate of a surgeon not being a medical officer of the union.

Ans.—If in the case to which you refer, it is intended to send the pauper to the *County Asylum,* it appears to the Commissioners that the medical certificate required under the proviso to section 48 of 8 and 9 Vict. c. 126, may be signed by a medical officer of the union. In that proviso, there is no restriction excluding the medical officer from certifying; nor is there any such restriction in section 51 of the same statute; and the restriction in section 48 of the 8 and 9 Vic. c. 100, has reference, not to *County Asylums* but to *Registered Hospitals* and *Licensed Houses* exclusively. If, however, there is no county asylum, and the pauper is to be sent to a licensed house or registered hospital, the case would apparently be different, and the Commissioners apprehend that it would be necessary to obtain a certificate from a medical man not a medical officer of the union, in accordance with the provisions of the 48th section of the 8 and 9 Vict. c. 100.

---

4. DITTO.

Oct. 17*th*, 1845.

Medical Officer of St. Neots Union—Inquired in reference to the Act of 8 and 9 Vic. c. 126,—1. Of whom he is to learn the names and residences of the pauper lunatics residing in his district. 2. What is the proper time for making the returns required in section 55 of the Act? 3. Whether the term, "fit to be at large," can be properly applied to any other than harmless idiots? 4. In the case of a pauper becoming insane within the union workhouse, is it sufficient notice, under section 48, to make an entry of insanity in the Form C, or to give notice to the master of the workhouse? 5. Whether he is under section 48, as medical officer of the workhouse, or of a district of the union, prohibited from signing a certificate of the insanity of any pauper, residing either in his own, or in any other district, of the union? 6. Whether, under section 49, he is, although a medical officer, at liberty, if required by a magistrate, to certify the insanity of a wandering lunatic?

Ans.—1. The relieving officer, or the guardians, or the overseers will doubtless give you the information as to the pauper lunatics who are residing in your district. 2. No time is specified in the Act for making the return; it must be made within every three months; and, consequently, it would seem most convenient that the return should be made at the end of each three months. 3. The Commissioners are not prepared to give any general instruction as to the meaning of the words "fit to be at large," as it is incumbent upon the medical officer to make a specific report upon each particular case. But they observe, that the Legislature appears to have contemplated that other than *harmless idiots* may be fit to be at large, as the term actually used is *lunatics*, which includes, according to the interpretation clause, *insane persons, and persons of unsound mind,* as well as *idiots*. 4. In regard to the lunatic pauper in the workhouse, it appears that so far as the medical officer is concerned, he must give notice, in writing, under section 48, to the relieving officer of the union, in which the parish to which the pauper is chargeable, is comprised; and this relieving officer must take the requisite proceedings under the statute. It is manifest, therefore, that no entry in the Form C, nor any notice to the master, will be a compliance with this provision. 5. The Commissioners consider that you cannot certify as to the insanity of any lunatic paupers, who are taken before the justices, whether they belong to your own district, or any other district in the union, such paupers not being wandering lunatics. 6. It does not appear that there is any restriction upon your certifying as to the insanity of any wandering lunatic brought before the justices, under the 49th section.

5. DITTO.

8th Sept. 1845.

Medical Officer of Kingsbridge Union—Stated, that the recent statute relating to pauper lunatics appears to be at variance with the Commissioners' Circular, dated August 25, 1845. From the Act, he understands that he is, as medical officer, to report to the relieving officer all persons who are either lunatic, idiotic, or imbecile, whether they be dangerous or not, in order that they may be within three days brought before a magistrate, and be examined by another medical man, not connected with the union, as to their state of mind; thus imposing on him the most disagreeable part of the duty, without providing any emolument.

Ans.—The Commissioners, in their letter of the 25th August last, have only sought to put you in possession of one of the clauses of the Act which particularly imposes certain duties upon you. They are aware that there is another clause which requires you to perform another duty, apparently somewhat inconsistent with the one brought under your notice. On a careful consideration of the clauses, it does not appear that they are so inconsistent as to neutralise each other. It is required that the medical officer shall give notice to the overseer of every lunatic person, of whose lunacy he shall have knowledge, so that steps may be taken to procure his removal to an asylum. If the lunatic be so removed, no necessity will exist for the medical officer's visiting; but if, notwithstanding he has given such notice, the lunatic from any cause be not removed, it will be his duty to visit such lunatic, in the manner prescribed in the statute. The Commissioners being aware that there are many pauper lunatics not in any asylum, or licensed house, have deemed it advisable to point out to the medical officers of unions the new duties applicable to them in reference to such lunatics. Upon the provision in the statute, which prohibits the medical officer of the union from giving the requisite certificate of the insanity of the pauper, the Commissioners have only to observe that the Legislature has deemed it right to make this exclusion, and so far as the prohibition extends in the Act, it must be submitted to.

LONDON:
Printed by Order of the Poor Law Commissioners, by BLACKBURN and PARDON, 6, Hatton Garden, and Published by CHARLES KNIGHT and Co., 22, Ludgate Street, Publishers to the Poor Law Commissioners.

AN

OFFICIAL CIRCULAR

OF PUBLIC DOCUMENTS AND INFORMATION:

DIRECTED BY THE POOR LAW COMMISSIONERS TO BE PRINTED, CHIEFLY FOR THE USE OF THE MEMBERS AND PERMANENT OFFICERS OF BOARDS OF GUARDIANS, UNDER THE POOR LAW AMENDMENT ACT.

No. 54. CIRCULAR ISSUED DECEMBER 1ST, 1845.

THE Poor Law Commissioners directed that the following documents be printed and circulated for the information of Guardians and Officers of the several Unions, viz.

(Signed) By Order of the Board,
EDWIN CHADWICK, *Secretary*.

I.—POTATOE CROP.

1. REPORTS OF THE COMMISSIONERS APPOINTED BY HER MAJESTY'S GOVERNMENT TO EXAMINE INTO THE STATE OF THE POTATOE CROP IN IRELAND.

Board Room, Royal Dublin Society,
7th November, 1845.

MY LORD,—Having laid before Your Excellency our views as to the best means of storing the potatoe, and converting to useful purposes such as are too much diseased to offer a probability of being preserved, we now have the honour to bring under your consideration the question of seed for a future year. If, in our former Reports, we have found it difficult to determine what course, under the peculiar circumstances of Ireland, it might be most advisable to pursue, we are still more embarrassed, on the present occasion, in consequence of the conflicting testimony that has been presented to us, and the absence of all decisive evidence as to the cause of the potatoe disease. The want of experience, derived from previous visitations of the same nature, also renders it impossible to affirm in what manner the potatoe may be affected in the course of the next few months.

We have, however, endeavoured to ascertain all that is positively known upon these subjects, by the examination of a great variety of published documents, both foreign and domestic; by personal observation, and by inquiries addressed to persons of practical experience or scientific reputation.

It is a very general opinion, and one entertained by men whose extensive knowledge entitles it to respect, that parasitical fungi, similar in their nature to those which produce mildew and dry-rot, are the real cause of the malady. It is stated that one of these plants belonging to the genus "Botrytis," and similar to that which some years since produced great mischief among the silk-worms of France and Italy, has attacked the potatoe crop. It is described as entering the potatoe plant by the breathing pores of its leaves, and then passing down through the interior of the stem into the tubers, in which its mycelium or spawn fixes itself, traversing the cellular mass, separating the cells themselves, causing alterations in their chemical condition, and thus producing decay. In other cases where the spawn is not apparently distinguishable in diseased portions of potatoes, even by the most practised observers, it is suggested that the juices of the plant may be vitiated by the parasite which destroyed the leaves, and that particles of it, too obscure to be distinguished by the eye, may be circulating with the juices and producing disease by irritation. The presence of the parasite is not to be detected by the naked eye, unless it makes its appearance on the outside of the potatoe in the form of mouldy tufts; but its spawn may be detected in the diseased portions by the microscope, whether any external indications of its presence can be perceived or not; hence it is inferred that it is produced exclusively from within. It is, however, within our knowledge, that when apparently sound potatoes are pitted in places where the mouldiness of a diseased potatoe is able to appear, that mouldiness rapidly establishes itself on the sound potatoes at every point where their surface has been wounded or bruised; and that under such circumstances, the disease is immediately extended through the entire mass.

That the spawn or fungi is present in large quantity in diseased potatoes is undoubted: the evidence of the best microscopical observers would be with us conclusive on that point, even if we had not verified the fact by personal examination. We also regard it as well ascertained, that these parasites spread rapidly in warm and damp situations, producing infinite mischief under such circumstances, and that their advance is only to be successfully resisted by dryness. But it does not appear to us, that their being the original cause of the disease has been well established; if it were so, it is difficult to conceive why fields of potatoes placed very near each other should be differently affected, or why certain varieties of this plant should be much less injured than others—the Irish apple potatoe for instance, which appears to have suffered more extensively than any other. We are also unable to reconcile with the theory of the potatoe disease being caused by parasitical fungi, the remarkable fact that in its present form it is certainly of modern origin. That it may have always existed is possible, though of this we have no proof; but at least there can be no doubt that it has only manifested itself to any considerable degree within the last few years. We cannot suppose the botrytis, which observers find to be a kind of fungus that attacks the potatoe, to be a recent creation. We must assume it to have been co-existent with the potatoe itself; and therefore we must conclude that some recent causes have come into operation favourable to its increase to the present alarming degree.

Without pretending to decide what that cause really was, we may state that it seems to be connected with the cold, cloudy, ungenial weather, which has characterised the present year over the north of Europe; conditions highly unsuited to the constitution of a plant, which like the potatoe, is a native of a warm, dry, sunny country, and insufficient for the ripening of the tubers. Without adverting to solitary cases, which require to be examined with more care than we have the means of giving to them, we may state, that amidst the mass of conflicting evidence which we have obtained, the following facts appear to be established:—

First. That potatoes planted early in the season, are more healthy than those planted later.

Second. That the crop has suffered less in dry, elevated, sandy districts, when the influence of the season was mitigated by slowness of growth, or compensated for by the natural warmth of the soil.

Third. That the late varieties of potatoes are more diseased than early ones.

Fourth. That the present disease seems to be confined to the northern parts of Europe and North America, and to be unknown in the countries to the southward.

If we are right in the conclusion at which we have thus arrived, there will not be cause for serious alarm as to the crop of another year, unless an equally unfavourable season should be experienced, or the supply of healthy seed should be insufficient, or that the parasite should be found to have so entirely taken possession of this year's plants, as to overcome the natural power of living bodies to repel the attacks of such enemies to healthy vegetation.

To Providence we must turn in the hope, that a second season like this may not be visited upon us. Should the Almighty in his infinite mercy avert such a misfortune, we entertain confident hopes, that the two other sources of danger may be guarded against by human foresight and diligence.

In providing seed for a future year, we may look with confidence to such potatoes of home growth as shall have resisted all tendency to decay during the winter, and we trust, that a considerable quantity of them will be found remaining where the precautions for storing which we have recommended shall have been observed. We do not anticipate any danger in the use of them, if they are planted early, especially if, before being planted, they are exposed to light till they become green. Another source of supply may doubtless be found in the southern parts of Europe, where we have reason to believe that disease has not shown itself; and we would strongly advise the public to lose no time in securing what may be procurable from that quarter.

It is stated by M. Séringe, secretary to the commission appointed in the department of the Rhone, in a report just published by him on the potatoe disease, that it is unknown at Genoa, and in the warmer countries. Our own advices describe the crops about Marseilles as being perfectly healthy, and therefore we may conclude, that mercantile enterprise will make up by importations, a large part of the deficiency to be apprehended.

It has also been ascertained by actual experiments that potatoes, although diseased, will grow and produce apparently healthy plants. The Reverend Mr. Berkely, a gentleman eminent above all other naturalists of the United Kingdom, in his knowledge of the habits of fungi, and whom we have consulted on this occasion, states, that although there would certainly be some risk of raising a diseased progeny from a diseased stock, yet the growth of fungi so evidently depends on atmospheric conditions, that it does not follow that because germs are present they should be developed.

We cannot, however, recommend the use of diseased tubers for seed, except by way of experiment, or in cases of absolute necessity, and it will always be prudent to dust them with powdered lime before they are used. It would indeed be proper to do so even when sets, however sound in appearance, are employed; for this process will destroy the minute seeds of parasitical fungi, which may be sticking to the sets, and assist in repelling those which are lying in the ground; of course those potatoes being selected which, on careful inspection, show no sign of disease, and hence afford the fairest prospect of a sound and healthy growth.

Where home-grown sets are to be employed for another crop, we would suggest with very great confidence, the adoption of the system of autumn planting, a method of cultivation which has been proved advantageous in regard to the crop, which is attended with no unusual expense, and which seems particularly adapted to the circumstances of the present case. It has been shown by Mr. Grey of Dilson, that in Northumberland, his potatoe crop has been considerably increased in quantity by this practice, and that he has no disease in it this year. In 1844, his autumn-planted crop produced a hundred and eleven loads, when the same quantity of spring-planted land yielded but eighty loads under the same circumstances. And in the present season, this gentleman states, that his autumn-planted is one-third better than his spring-planted crop. There can, therefore, be no doubt that autumn planting may be safely practised. On this occasion, it has these peculiar advantages, that it offers an additional chance of security against renewed attacks from parasitical fungi. On this point, the evidence of Mr. Brokeley is positive. "Autumn planting," he states, "seems to me to offer the best chance of obtaining healthy sets. What are now planted will produce their tubers before the atmospheric conditions requisite for the growth of the parasite in the leaves can be realised, and without such growth, the particles, if present, will be too few to cause much evil. I think, under existing circumstances, the Commissioners cannot do a greater service than by encouraging and enforcing as much as possible, autumn planting." Concurring, as we entirely do, in this recommendation, we trust that the planters of potatoes who have it in their power to adopt it will do so at once.

All that we conceive it necessary to state with reference to this practice, is, that it should be performed at any time before the end of January; that the sets should be thoroughly dried by exposure to light and air; that they should also be well dusted with lime; and that they should be planted in drills six inches deep, with farmyard manure below the sets. We also recommend that where the potatoes are not large, they should be planted whole, and even large potatoes should be cut into not more than two pieces.

We have ascertained that autumn planting has already been practised throughout Fingal, for the early supply of the Dublin market, and that, although the practice has been nearly discontinued, that has not happened for any reason that affects the present question. Neither do we learn that the early period at which the leaves appear above the ground in spring, is attended with any greater risk than what attends precarious crops like the potatoe in any season. The effect to be anticipated from autumn planting consists not merely in a probable increase of quantity in next year's supply, but in the saving of potatoes which may perish before spring, if the slow growth which goes on during winter is arrested, and in the early ripening of next year's crop, in the event of a second unfavourable season supervening. We may add, that experience has shown the small refuse potatoes of the year to be suited to autumn planting, if sound, and prepared in the manner we have recommended.

It has been supposed by many persons that the potatoe has arrived at a state of general debility, and that the crop will continue liable to disease like the present, until new varieties shall have been raised from seed. We do not find any satisfactory evidence to support this opinion. It is doubtless true that great constitutional differences exist among the varieties of the potatoe, and that some are much more delicate than others ; but we do not find that the oldest varieties are the most tender, or the newest the most hardy. On the contrary, it is within our own knowledge, that, in the present season, very healthy varieties, recently raised, have suffered much more than kinds that have been long in cultivation.

While, however, we withhold our assent to the proposition, that newly-raised varieties of the potatoe are exempt in any peculiar degree from the attacks of disease, we fully admit the fact that some varieties are much more subject to it than others, and we therefore recommend the cultivation of the tender kinds to be discontinued, and that those alone be used for future cropping which the experience of the present year shows to be best suited to unfavourable seasons; and on this point we may further remark, that concurrent testimony points out the Irish "Cup" variety as that which has suffered least from the attacks of the disease.

We are also of opinion that it will be imprudent to plant potatoes for the next crop, in land which has been just cleared of them. The latter is in all probability filled with the seeds of fungi, countless myriads of which must have been scattered over the tainted field ; and, although they probably have been borne by the winds to every portion of the country, yet it may be conceived that the soil will be more impregnated where diseased potatoes have just been growing, than in fields in which decaying matter was not actually present.

Under these circumstances, we are decidedly of opinion, that, prior to putting any kind of crop, for the coming year, into land that has been this season under potatoes, it will be prudent, if not absolutely necessary, that the ground should be turned up and exposed to the action of the atmosphere with care, and that it should be thoroughly manured with lime. We have already recommended that the potatoes, whether whole or cuttings, used for seed, should be dusted over with lime, previous to planting ; and we further urge, that, in the case of corn or seed crops of every kind, the seeds should be steeped in lime-water, or in the solution of blue stone and salt, well known to farmers. Evidence has already been laid before us of injurious effects, where precautions such as we have described have been neglected.

We forbear from adverting to the possibility of replenishing the diminished supply of potatoes by sowing the seeds formed by the flower. This is an operation which can only be carried on successfully in a garden—is unsuited to the means of the small cultivator—cannot in any way affect the question of immediate supply—and may be safely left to the intelligence of the gardeners scattered through the country.

Hitherto we have laid before your Excellency, for the purposes of publication, several reports, in a merely popular form, suited to the present emergency. We are confident that the recommendations contained in them, if carried into effect, will tend to mitigate the evils arising from the attacks of the disease in the potatoe crop. We now propose to proceed forthwith to apply ourselves to the investigation of the important scientific questions involved in the subject; and to report, in due time, the results of our inquiries, in order that from past experience we may derive knowledge for future guidance. These investigations will occupy us for a considerable time; and while we do not contemplate the necessity of publishing further popular directions, we shall hold ourselves in readiness to give our immediate attention to any question which your Excellency may submit for our consideration, or to report from time to time for your Excellency's private information. We have the honour to be,

Your faithful and obedient servants,

ROBERT KANE.
JOHN LINDLEY.
LYON PAYFAIR.

To His Excellency Baron Heytesbury,
Lord Lieutenant of Ireland, &c.

Board Room, Royal Dublin Society,
12th November, 1845.

My Lord,—Having been requested to submit to Your Excellency a detailed description of the methods which we propose should be employed, under the authority of the Government, for utilising the diseased potatoes, and rendering available to the people all that may remain of the substance fit for food, we have to report as follows :—

We have mentioned to Your Excellency in a previous report, that our early chemical investigations led us to the recognition of two important facts—1stly, That by the action of water, the diseased parts of the potatoes were capable of being wholly removed; and, 2ndly, The pulpy material which remains is rich in the most valuable elements of food. Upon these principles are founded the processes by which we propose to render the bad potatoes useful for wholesome food. The simplicity of their practical working has been approved of by the judgment of persons of practical experience, from whose co-operation we have derived very considerable advantage.

The potatoes which we suppose to be employed in the following processes, are such as, being in great part or deeply infected with the disease, present an appearance too repulsive to allow of their being used directly for human food, and do not admit of the diseased parts being peeled off previous to cooking, without the sacrifice of a large portion of their substance. In such condition, we propose that the potatoes should be first washed from adherent dirt; this is very easily effected, when the quantity operated on is not very large, by the means everywhere adopted, in the farm-house or cottage. But when, as in Government Establishments, Poor Law Unions, or other places, it might be desirable to carry on the operations on a greater scale, it would be proper to wash the potatoes, by placing them in a cylindrical vessel formed of wooden bars, and working partially immersed in a vessel of water. This mode, which is adopted in all well-conducted factories for such purposes, will clean a large quantity of potatoes in a very short time.

The cleaned potatoes are next to be grated down by some one or other of the machines adapted for that operation. We have had occasion to direct the attention of Government to certain forms of these machines, which we consider best suited to the object, among those exhibited to the Royal Agricultural Improvement Society, and the Royal Dublin Society. The size and structure of the machine, of course, will differ, according as it is destined for cottage or for farm use, or for employment in extensive opreations; but in every case the machine derives great simplification from the fact, that the processes we recommend do not involve the separating of starch, but only the breaking down the structure of the potatoe; hence the pulp need not be so fine as if starch were to be extracted, and consequently the graters may be stronger and rougher; hence also the complex and expensive arrangement of sieves and cloths, for separating starch, are altogether dispensed with; the machine being reduced to the mere condition of a hopper, to hold the potatoes upon the grater, the grater itself, and a barrel, into which the broken down substance may be delivered.

When the potatoe has thus been obtained in the form of a pulpy mass, it is to be washed with water; the diseased portions of tissue, and all the peculiar substances produced by the disease, are in great part dissolved by the water, and render it thick and slimy, and dark reddish brown coloured; this is to be again poured off, and more water poured on, agitated moderately, and when the pulpy mass has subsided, this second liquid is to be poured off also. In general the second washing will fully cleanse out the diseased portion, but if necessary a third water may be used; in this way all that part of the potatoe that might prove injurious, may be washed out, and the residue that settles at the bottom of the vessel is to be used as food, in the way described below.

It is to be remarked that by much or continued washing, the starch, which it is our object to leave in the pulp, and which, in fact, must remain in the pulp to produce the article of food that we purpose to employ, may be washed out, and such washing out is the process by which potatoe starch is commonly prepared; it is, therefore, indispensable that the washing should be so managed as to suffice to remove the light and partly soluble diseased matter, but not enough to take out any quantity of the denser and insoluble starch. This is in practice perfectly easy; once performing the operation will fully show the point at which the washing, when properly conducted, should be arrested.

When the pulpy substance of the potatoe has settled down at the bottom of the vessel, it will form a mass, which, on examination, will be found usually not to be quite the same all through. If the washing the dirt from the potatoes had not been thoroughly well done, there may be found at the bottom of the mass some grit, sand, or clay, which can then be perfectly removed; at the top of the mass there will be found a quantity of starch which has been loosened from the broken down tissue of the potatoe; any grit, or clay, having been removed, the wet pulp, with its adhering starch, is to be put into a vessel where it may be mixed with a quantity of oatmeal, in such proportions, that the pulpy mass, when dried, should be two parts to one of oatmeal: this will be obtained by taking three parts of the moist pulp; the dry oatmeal and the wet pulp mixed well into a doughy mass, is to be then flattened into a cake and heated upon a plate or floor, so that they shall be at once dried and baked thoroughly.

The drying and baking process can be carried on in the cottage or farm-house, with complete success and facility. In large establishments, the plan which we propose to be applied, consists in the formation of a plate iron floor, heated by one or two fires, the flues from which, should circulate under the plates and bring every part to the proper temperature; on this floor the cakes, which should not exceed three-eighths of an inch in thickness, when dry, should be spread, and the drying and baking will proceed with ease and rapidity.

There will be then obtained from the diseased potatoes an article of food, which, from a number of trials, and from its constitution, we do consider may be relied upon as wholesome, nutritive, and capable of being preserved for any length of time. This nutritious matter is well adapted for food, and may be preserved without being mixed with oatmeal; it forms a matter which when dried and ground is very similar in appearance and taste to oatmeal, although not so rich in nutritious matter as the latter. In this ground form it may be kept like ordinary meal, and be converted into bread, soup, or stirabout, in the cottages of the poor.

Your Excellency will remark that even when the bread is at once made, the process consists of five operations, all of the simplest kind, and but one of these requiring the aid of fire:—

1st—Washing the potatoes.
2nd—Grating them down to pulp.
3rd—Washing the pulpy mass.
4th—Stirring in the oatmeal.
5th—Baking the cakes.

The only machinery necessary in the cottage or farm-house is a grater, a tub or bucket, and a griddle. In the large manufacturing establishments or Poor Law Unions, of course a more mechanical arrangement is desirable; but even then the process is one of extreme simplicity. The instruments are:—

1st—A hollow revolving cylinder to wash the potatoes.
2nd—A grating machine for reducing them to pulp.
3rd—Barrels or vats for washing the pulp.
4th—A floor for mixing pulp and oatmeal.
5th—A heated floor or oven for baking the cakes.

As it will, for many reasons, be desirable frequently to manufacture the potatoe meal, which we have described, without mixing it with oatmeal or baking it, the above processes will, in such cases, be reduced and simplified.

We have attached to this report a brief statement, in the form of directions, for the use of cottiers or farmers, of how the process is to be carried on, on a small scale. Such is the plan that we have the honour to propose for the utilisation of diseased potatoes, and which we submit for Your Excellency's judgment. We believe it to be the cheapest, simplest, and most certain process by which that vegetable may be rescued from the destruction which now, in great part, threatens it, and its valuable nutritious material placed in a form where it may be preserved by the people for food, without being liable to loss or deterioration.

Several processes for converting diseased potatoes into food have been placed under our notice, either by the parties themselves proposing them, or by Her Majesty's Government, to whom they had been transmitted. We have carefully examined their respective merits, and we do not consider any of them to possess the necessary qualities for adapting them to the actual circumstances of this country. Of these plans, there are, however, two, which, as they approach somewhat to the character of the material we propose to be employed, we feel that we should expressly give our reasons for not recommending them to Your Excellency.

The first of these plans consists in boiling the potatoes, after cutting out the diseased portions, and afterwards drying the boiled mass by the application of heat, and preserving the dried mass in air-tight canisters or barrels.

The second plan consists in steaming the potatoes after they are peeled, with or without the diseased parts being cut out, and ramming down the potatoes thus softened into air-tight barrels, and closing them with air-tight lids.

Both these plans may be made to succeed, and the materials produced by their operation form an agreeable and useful food. But, at the same time, Your Excellency is aware that the advantages of such processes must depend upon their simplicity, and their adaptation to the circumstances of this country. The first of these plans differs from the second, in requiring twice the expenditure of fuel required either in the second plan, or that which we have proposed to Your Excellency. And it also differs from both, by the waste caused in cutting out the diseased parts, which, if they are at all to be economised, must be exposed to the tedious and expensive processes of making starch, with the loss of the nutritious pulp still undestroyed. In the process of steaming potatoes, it is proposed to preserve the diseased parts, which is objectionable, not only from the appearance given to the prepared part, but also from other reasons to which we have, on former occasions, directed Your Excellency's attention.

Both the plans under consideration involve a feature which we consider quite sufficient to prevent their general adoption, namely, the necessity for large and costly air-tight vessels to preserve the potatoes mashed in the manner proposed. Unless the products are preserved in tight vessels, well secured from air and moisture, they cannot be preserved in the manner indicated. The immense expense which would necessarily be incurred in applying such methods to the produce of an entire country is sufficient, in our opinion, to prevent their general adoption.

The plan which we have recommended to Your Excellency, unites the advantages of the previous plans, and at the same time introduces simplicity into the processes, with a less expenditure of labour and fuel, with a machinery certainly equally cheap, and with facilities of application much more universal. In offering a plan for converting all the nutriment existing in the diseased potatoe, into the form of a nutritious meal, as capable of preservation as ordinary oatmeal or flour, Your Excellency will perceive that it is highly important that the potato, however preserved, should be capable of being converted into hot soups or stirabout, so as to compensate for the loss of hot diet to which the peasant was accustomed in the potatoe. We have had practical experience, that the potatoe meal, such as we have suggested, made into soup, with any such vegetables as can be procured, forms a palatable accompaniment to the potatoe bread, at an expense not exceeding one penny for five pints, and therefore within the means of the poorest peasant.

We would further lay before Your Excellency, that the plan as proposed by us, is equally applicable to the cottier as it is to the large establishments, for which it is mainly intended. When applied to the home of the cotter, we would suggest the circulation of the following simple directions which accompany this Report.

We have the honour to be,

Your Excellency's obedient and faithful servants,

ROBERT KANE,
LYON PLAYFAIR.

To His Excellency Baron Heytesbury,
Lord Lieutenant of Ireland, &c. &c. &c.

TO THE FARMERS AND PEASANTRY OF IRELAND.

Directions for making Wholesome Food from Diseased Potatoes.

1st.—The potatoes should be well washed with water, so as to cleanse them from all dirt.

2nd.—Grate down the potatoes by means of a grater, which may be made of a piece of sheet-iron, or tin punched up into holes and fastened on a board; or a better machine may be had for four or five shillings, consisting of a cylinder of punched sheet-iron turned by the hand, with a hopper to hold the potatoes. This grater should dip nearly half into a bucket or tub of water, into which the pulp will fall according as it is produced.

3rd.—When the pulp has settled completely down, pour off the dirty reddish water, and put more fresh water on. Stir up all well together, and then let the pulp settle down again, and pour off the liquor. If necessary, this is to be done again, if the liquor comes away reddish or brownish; but two washings will usually be enough to leave the pulp clean and free from the diseased parts, which all go off with the water.

4th.—Recollect that the starch is not to be washed out of the pulp, but only the reddish diseased stuff. The starch must be let to settle down along with the pulp, for they are both required in the food.

5th.—The wet pulp is then to be taken out of the tub and is to be freed as well as you can from water, by draining and pressing it. To every three stone weight of this wet pulp is to be mixed one stone of oatmeal, and as much salt as you may think well. The mass is then to be rolled out into a thin cake, and this is to be baked on a griddle until it is quite dry and slightly browned on the outside.

6th.—These cakes will keep for a very long time without souring or spoiling, if moderate care be taken to keep them dry. A good way is to put them on a string and hang them up to the ceiling near the fire.

7th.—If you do not like to make all the potatoes into this sort of bread, dry the pulp on the griddle without the oatmeal, and do not let it brown. You will then get the pure potatoe meal, which will keep if you do not let damp get at it. This meal will serve very well for making broth and soup, and for mixing with oatmeal to make bread.

In this way almost every diseased potatoe can be made into wholesome food.

2. Circular which accompanied the Official Circular, No. 53.

Poor Law Commission Office,
Somerset House, 10th November, 1845.

Sir,—The enclosed number of the Official Circular of the Poor Law Commissioners contains some papers relating to the disease now prevailing among the potatoes in the United Kingdom. The first document is extracted from a report made in the year 1843, by the Commissioner of Patents in the United States, and is chiefly important as showing the wide range of the disease, and its existence in America before the present year.

The other papers relate principally to the mode in which diseased potatoes may be made in some degree available for human food. The Poor Law Commissioners particularly request attention to the reports of the Commission appointed by Her Majesty's Government in Ireland to investigate the subject.

It appears to the Poor Law Commissioners, that no objection exists to the inmates of a workhouse being employed on the premises, in performing such processes as are necessary for extracting the farina or starch from diseased potatoes. The guardians would be as much justified in purchasing every utensil necessary for setting them to work in this manner, as they would be in purchasing tools or other instruments for employing them in any other kind of labour.

The Commissioners make this suggestion, not with the intention that farina so procured should be manufactured for the use of the workhouse, or consumed therein, but that an opportunity should be given to such poor persons in the neighbourhood, as may be desirous of availing themselves of it, of bringing diseased potatoes to be scraped or bruised, and washed, as recommended in the enclosed papers. The actual produce of such potatoes should be given back to the parties without any diminution, and the Commissioners do not think it necessary that any charge should be made for the labour performed. The guardians should employ no persons except paupers in performing the work.

The Commissioners trust that this subject will be brought under the consideration of the board of guardians at an early meeting, and that no time will be lost in taking such steps as the condition of the crop in the union and other circumstances may make desirable.

Signed by order of the Board,
Edwin Chadwick, *Secretary.*

To the Clerk to the Board of Guardians.

3. Circular—Modification of Dietaries where Potatoes are prescribed.

Poor Law Commission Office,
Somerset House, 10th November, 1845.

Sir,—I am directed by the Poor Law Commissioners to state, that in consequence of the failure of the potatoe crop, the guardians may find it impracticable or inexpedient to supply the inmates of the workhouse of your union with the article of potatoes as prescribed by the dietary. The Commissioners will, therefore, be prepared to entertain any proposition for such modification of the dietary, as will enable the guardians to substitute any other article instead of potatoes.

I am to request that the subject may be immediately brought under the consideration of the board of guardians.

I am, Sir, your most obedient servant,
Edwin Chadwick, *Secretary.*

To the Clerk of the Board of Guardians.

II.—AUDIT DISTRICTS.

The Bedfordshire and Hertfordshire Audit District, formed under an order dated 8th February, 1845.

Auditor, *Daniel Goodson Adey, Esq.*, St. Albans, continued in office under an order dated 7th February, 1845.

Unions comprised in the District,—St. Albans, Ampthill, Barnet, Bedford, Berkhampstead, Biggleswade, Bishop's Stortford, Buntingford, Hatfield, Hemel Hempstead, Hertford, Hitchin, Leighton Buzzard, Luton, Newport Pagnell, Ware, Watford, Welwyn, and Woburn.

THE BERKSHIRE AND HAMPSHIRE AUDIT DISTRICT, formed under an order dated 15th July, 1845.

AUDITOR, *George Barnes, Esq.*, *Newbury*, elected under the above order.

UNIONS comprised in the District,—Abingdon, Alton, Basingstoke, Bradfield, Cookham, Easthampstead, Eton, Hartley Wintney, Henley, Kingsclere, Newbury, Reading, Wallingford, Whitchurch, and Wokingham.

THE BUCKINGHAMSHIRE AND NORTHAMPTONSHIRE AUDIT DISTRICT, formed under an order dated 1st May, 1845.

AUDITOR, *Alfred Hayward, Esq.*, Brackley, elected under the above order.

UNIONS, &c. comprised in the District Incorporation,—Amersham, Aylesbury, Bicester, Brackley, Brixworth, Buckingham, Daventry, Hardingstone, Headington, Kettering, Northampton, Oundle, Potterspury, Thame, Thrapston, Towcester, Wellingborough, Winslow, and Wycombe Unions, and Oxford Incorporation.

THE CAMBRIDGESHIRE AND HUNTINGDONSHIRE AUDIT DISTRICT, formed under an order dated 17th April, 1845.

AUDITOR, *Charles Brent Wale, Esq.*, Barrister-at-Law, Little Shelford, Cambridgeshire, elected under the above order.

UNIONS comprised in the District,—Cambridge, Caxton and Arrington, Chesterton, Ely, Huntingdon, St. Ives, Linton, St. Neots, Newmarket, North Witchford, Risbridge, Royston, and Whittlesea.

THE CHESHIRE AND DENBIGHSHIRE AUDIT DISTRICT, formed under an order dated 10th July, 1845.

AUDITOR, *Thomas Kyffin Roberts, Esq.*, St. Asaph, elected under the above order.

UNIONS, &c., comprised in the District,—St. Asaph, Great Boughton, Holywell, Nantwich, Northwich, Runcorn, Ruthin, Wirrall, and Wrexham Unions, and Chester Incorporation.

THE CORNWALL AND DEVONSHIRE AUDIT DISTRICT, formed under an order dated 23rd July, 1845.

AUDITOR, *William Hughes, Esq.*, 2, Alfred-place, Plymouth, elected under the above order.

UNIONS, &c., comprised in the District,—St. Austell, Bodmin, Camelford, St. Columb Major, Falmouth, St. Germans, Helston, Launceston, Liskeard, Penzance, Plympton St. Mary, Redruth, Tavistock, and Truro Unions, East Stonehouse, and Stoke Damerell Parishes, and Plymouth Incorporation.

THE EAST CUMBERLAND AND WESTMORELAND AUDIT DISTRICT, formed under an order dated 17th June, 1845.

AUDITOR, *John Bell, Esq.*, Appleby, Westmoreland, continued in office under an order dated 16th June, 1845.

UNIONS, &c., comprised in the District,— —Brampton, Carlisle, East Ward, Longtown, Penrith, Sedbergh, and West Ward Unions, and Alston with Garrigill Parish.

THE WEST CUMBERLAND AUDIT DISTRICT, formed under an order dated 24th June, 1845.

AUDITOR, *Robert Francis Yarker, Esq.*, Ulverstone, continued in office under an order dated 23rd June, 1845.

UNIONS comprised in the District,—Bootle, Cockermouth, Kendal, Ulverstone, Whitehaven, and Wigton.

THE CENTRAL DEVONSHIRE AUDIT DISTRICT, formed under an order dated 2nd April, 1845.

AUDITOR, *John Tyrrell, Esq.*, Exeter, continued in office under an order dated 1st April, 1845.

UNIONS comprised in the District,—Crediton, Okehampton, and Saint Thomas Unions, and Exeter Incorporation.

THE NORTH DEVONSHIRE AUDIT DISTRICT, formed under an order dated 12th April, 1845.

AUDITOR, *Charles Wm. Johnson*, Esq., Torrington, continued in office under an order dated 11th April, 1845.

UNIONS comprised in the District,—Barnstaple, Bideford, Dulverton, Holsworthy, South Molton, Stratton, Tiverton, and Torrington.

THE SOUTH-EAST DEVONSHIRE AUDIT DISTRICT, formed under an order dated 20th March, 1845.

AUDITOR, *Robert Tucker, Esq.*, Ashburton, continued in office under an order dated 19th March, 1845.

UNIONS comprised in the District,—Axminster, Honiton, Kingsbridge, Newton Abbott, and Totnes.

THE DURHAM AUDIT DISTRICT, formed under an order dated 1st July, 1845.

AUDITOR, *Thomas Christopher Maynard, Esq.*, Solicitor, Durham, continued in office under an order dated 30th June, 1845.

UNIONS comprised in the District,—Chester le Street, Durham, Easington, Gateshead, Houghton le Spring, Lanchester, South Shields, Sunderland. and Weardale.

THE DURHAM AND YORKSHIRE AUDIT DISTRICT, formed under an order dated 3rd July, 1845.

AUDITOR, *James Hunton, Esq.*, Richmond, Yorkshire, continued in office under an order dated 2nd July, 1845.

UNIONS in the District,—Auckland, Darlington, Leyburn, Reeth, Richmond (York,) Sedgefield, and Teesdale.

THE ESSEX AUDIT DISTRICT, formed under an order dated 13th June, 1845.

AUDITOR, *Edward Wilson Banks, Esq.*, Witham, elected under the above order.

UNIONS comprised in the District,—Billericay, Braintree, Chelmsford, Colchester, Dunmow, Epping, Halsted, Lexden and Winstree, Maldon, Ongar, Orsett, Rochford, Romford, Saffron Walden, Tendring, West Ham, and Witham.

THE GLOUCESTERSHIRE AND MONMOUTHSHIRE AUDIT DISTRICT, formed under an order dated 28th May, 1845.

AUDITOR, *Edward Murrell, Esq.*, Pershore, elected under the above order.

UNIONS comprised in the District,—Abergavenny, Cheltenham, Chepstow, Crickhowel, Gloucester, Ledbury, Martley, Monmouth, Newent, Newport (Monmouth,) Pontypool, Ross, Tewkesbury, Upton on Severn, Westbury on Severn, and Winchcombe.

THE HAMPSHIRE AND SUSSEX AUDIT DISTRICT, formed under an order dated 30th June, 1845.

AUDITOR, *Thomas Hoskins, Esq.*, 3, High-st., Gosport, elected under the above order.

UNIONS, &c., comprised in the District,—Catherington, Droxford, Fareham, Guildford, Hambledon, Havant, Petersfield, Petworth, and Portsea Island Unions, and Chichester and Isle of Wight Incorporations.

THE HAMPSHIRE AND WILTSHIRE AUDIT DISTRICT, formed under an order dated 30th June, 1845.

AUDITOR, *William James Paterson, Esq*, 87, Guildford-street, Russell-square, elected under the above order.

UNIONS, &c., comprised in the District,—Alderbury, Alresford, Amesbury, Andover, Christchurch, Fordingbridge, Hursley, Lymington, New Forest, Poole, Ringwood, Romsey, South Stoneham, Stockbridge, Wareham and Purbeck, Wilton, Wimborne and Cranborne, and New Winchester Unions, Southampton Incorporation, and United Parishes of New Sarum.

THE HEREFORDSHIRE AUDIT DISTRICT, formed under an order dated 15th May, 1845.

AUDITOR, *Jonathan Green, Esq.*, Kington, elected under the above order.

UNIONS comprised in the District,—Bromyard, Dore, Hereford, Kington, Leominster, Presteign, Tenbury, and Weobley.

Addition made to District by an order dated 15th September, 1845, of the Knighton Union.

THE EAST KENT AUDIT DISTRICT, formed under an order dated 31st October, 1844.

AUDITOR, *Richard Bathurst, Esq.*, Faversham, continued in office under an order dated 30th October, 1844.

UNIONS, &c., comprised in the District,—East Ashford, West Ashford, Blean, Bridge, Dover, Eastry, Elham, Faversham, Milton, Sheppey, Isle of Thanet Unions, and Canterbury Incorporation.

THE WEST KENT AUDIT DISTRICT, formed under an order dated 13th November, 1844.

AUDITOR, *Thomas Patten, Esq.*, Rochester, continued in office under an order dated 12th November, 1844.

UNIONS comprised in the District,—North Aylesford, Dartford, Gravesend and Milton, Hollingbourn, Hoo, Maidstone, Malling, Medway, Sevenoaks, and Tonbridge.

THE WEST AND NORTH LANCASHIRE AUDIT DISTRICT, formed under an order dated 12th August, 1845.

AUDITOR, *William Rees, Esq.*, Standishgate, Wigan, elected under the above order.

UNIONS, &c., comprised in the District,—Blackburn, Chorley, Clitheroe, Fylde, Garstang, Lancaster, Ormskirk, Prescot, Preston, Warrington, West Derby, and Wigan Unions, and Liverpool Parish.

THE SOUTH LANCASHIRE AND CHESHIRE AUDIT DISTRICT, formed under an order dated 22nd July, 1845.

AUDITOR, *Charles Mott, Esq.*, Ashton, Warrington, elected under the above order.

UNIONS comprised in the District—Altrincham, Bolton, Bury, Chapel en le Frith, Chorlton, Congleton, Glossop, Haslingden, Hayfield, Leigh, Macclesfield, Manchester, Salford, and Stockport.

THE LEICESTERSHIRE AND NOTTINGHAMSHIRE AUDIT DISTRICT, formed under an order dated 21st January, 1845.

AUDITOR, *William Power, Esq.*, Freazley, Polesworth, near Fazeley, Staffordshire, elected under the above order.

UNIONS comprised in the District,—Ashby de

la Zouch, Atherstone, Barrow-upon-Soar, Basford, Billesdon, Bingham, Blaby, Hinckley, Leicester, Loughborough, Lutterworth, Mansfield, Market Bosworth, Market Harborough, Melton Mowbray, Nottingham, Radford, Southwell, and Tamworth.

THE LINCOLNSHIRE AND RUTLANDSHIRE AUDIT DISTRICT, formed under an order dated 10th January, 1845.

AUDITOR, *Sturton Johnson, Esq.*, Barrister at Law, 1, Mitre-court Buildings, Temple, and 29, Gordon-street, Gordon-square, elected under the above order.

UNIONS comprised in the District,—Boston, Bourn, Caistor, East Retford, Gainsborough, Glanford Brigg, Grantham, Holbeach, Horncastle, Lincoln, Louth, Newark, Oakham, Peterborough, Sleaford, Spalding, Spilsby, Stamford, Uppingham, and Worksop.

THE LONDON AUDIT DISTRICT, formed under an order dated 10th March, 1845.

AUDITOR, *Joseph Gibbs, Esq.*, Barrister-at-Law, 5, Hare-court, Temple, elected under the above order.

UNIONS comprised in the District,—City of London, East London, and West London.

THE NORTH-EAST METROPOLITAN AUDIT DISTRICT, formed under an order dated 17th December, 1844.

AUDITOR, *Blomfield Burnell, Esq.*, 58, Fenchurch-street, continued in office under an order dated 16th December, 1844.

UNIONS, &c., comprised in the District,—Edmonton, Hackney, Poplar, Stepney, and Whitechapel Unions, St. Matthew Bethnal Green, St. George in the East, St. Leonard's Shoreditch, and St. Luke Middlesex Parishes.

Addition made by order dated 31 Oct. 1845,—Epsom Union.

THE SOUTH-EAST METROPOLITAN AUDIT DISTRICT, formed under an order dated 11th Jan. 1845.

AUDITOR, *William Fossett, Esq.*, Charlotte-row, Walworth, continued in office under an order dated 10th January, 1845.

UNIONS, &c., comprised in the District,—Bromley, Croydon, Greenwich, and Lewisham Unions, and St. Giles' Camberwell Parish.

THE SOUTH-WEST METROPOLITAN AUDIT DISTRICT, formed under an order dated 4th Jan. 1845.

AUDITOR, *John Clarke Meymott, Esq.*, 86, Blackfriars-road, continued in office under an order dated 3rd January, 1845.

UNIONS, &c., comprised in the District,—St. Olave's, St. Saviour's, and Wandsworth and Clapham Unions, Bermondsey, Lambeth, Newington, Rotherhithe, and St. George the Martyr Southwark Parishes.

Addition made by order dated 31st October, 1845, of the following Unions,—Chertsey and Kingston.

THE NORTH-WEST METROPOLITAN AUDIT DISTRICT, formed under an order dated 4th June, 1845.

AUDITOR, *James Hales Mitchener, Esq.*, Staines, continued in office under an order dated 3rd June, 1845.

UNIONS, &c., comprised in the District,—Brentford, Fulham, Hendon, Holborn, Richmond (Surrey,) Staines, Strand, Uxbridge, and Windsor Unions, Clerkenwell, Chelsea, Islington, Kensington, St. Martin in the Fields, Paddington, and St. Margaret and St. John the Evangelist Westminster Parishes.

THE EAST NORFOLK AUDIT DISTRICT, formed under an order dated 11th March, 1845.

AUDITOR, *Robert Rising, Esq.*, Horsey, Norfolk, continued in office under an order dated 10th March, 1845.

UNIONS, &c., comprised in the District,—Blofield and Erpingham Unions, East and West Flegg, Mutford and Lothingland, and Tunstead and Happing Incorporated Hundreds, and Great Yarmouth Parish.

THE WEST NORFOLK AUDIT DISTRICT, formed under an order dated 11th March, 1845.

AUDITOR, *Wales Christopher Hotson, Esq.*, Barrister-at-Law, Long Stratton, Norfolk, continued in office under an order dated 10th March, 1845.

UNIONS, &c., comprised in the District,—Aylsham, Blything, Depwade, Docking, Downham, St. Faiths, Freebridge Lynn, Guiltcross, Henstead, Kings Lynn, Loddon and Clavering, Mitford and Launditch, Swaffham, Thetford, Walsingham, Wayland, Wangford, and Wisbeach Unions, Forehoe Hundred, and Norwich Incorporation.

THE NORTHUMBERLAND AUDIT DISTRICT, formed under an order dated 6th June, 1845.

AUDITOR, *Robert Usher, Esq.*, 5, Low Swinburne-place, Newcastle-upon-Tyne, elected under the above order.

UNIONS comprised in the District,—Alnwick,

Belford, Bellingham, Berwick-upon-Tweed, Castle Ward, Glendale, Haltwhistle, Hexham, Morpeth, Newcastle-upon-Tyne, Rothbury, and Tynemouth.

THE OXFORDSHIRE AND WARWICKSHIRE AUDIT DISTRICT, formed under an order dated 24th April, 1845.

AUDITOR, *James Hunt, Esq.*, Oxford, elected under the above order.

UNIONS comprised in the District,—Alcester, Banbury, Chipping Norton, Coventry, Droitwich, Evesham, Foleshill, Northleach, Pershore, Rugby, Shipston-on-Stour, Solihull, Southam, Stow-on-the-Wold, Stratford-on-Avon, Warwick, Witney, Woodstock, and Worcester.

THE WEST SOMERSETSHIRE AUDIT DISTRICT, formed under an order dated 29th July, 1845.

AUDITOR, *John Payne, Esq.*, Solicitor, Milverton, Somerset, continued in office under an order dated 28th July, 1845.

UNIONS comprised in the District—Beaminster, Blandford, Bridgwater, Bridport, Cerne, Chard, Dorchester, Langport, Shaftesbury, Sherborne, Sturminster, Taunton, Wellington (Somerset,) Weymouth, Williton, and Yeovil.

THE SHROPSHIRE AND MONTGOMERYSHIRE AUDIT DISTRICT, formed under an order dated 15th July, 1845.

AUDITOR, *Robert Fisher, jun., Esq.*, Newport, Salop, elected under the above order.

UNIONS, &c., comprised in the District,—Atcham, Bridgnorth, Church Stretton, Clun, Ellesmere, Llanfyllin, Ludlow, Madeley, Newport (Salop,) Newtown and Llanidloes, Wellington (Salop,) Wem, and Whitchurch (Salop,) Unions, and Montgomery and Pool, Oswestry, and Shrewsbury Incorporations.

THE SOMERSETSHIRE AND WILTSHIRE AUDIT DISTRICT, formed under an order dated 19th July, 1845.

AUDITOR, *Alfred Whitaker, Esq.*, Solicitor, Frome, elected under the above order.

UNIONS, &c., comprised in the District,—Axbridge, Bath, Bedminster, Bradford (Wilts,) Calne, Chippenham, Clifton, Clutton, Frome, Keynsham, Melksham, Mere, Shepton Mallett, Tisbury, Warminster, Wells, Westbury and Whorwelsdown, and Wincanton Unions, and Bristol City.

THE STAFFORDSHIRE AND DERBYSHIRE AUDIT DISTRICT, formed under an order dated 7th March, 1845.

AUDITOR, *Richard Stone, Esq.*, 11, St. Mary's Gate, Derby, elected under the above order.

UNIONS, &c., comprised in the District,—Ashbourne, Bakewell, Belper, Burton-upon-Trent, Cheadle, Chesterfield, Derby, Leek, Lichfield, Newcastle-under-Lyme, Penkridge, Shardlow, Stafford, Stone, Uttoxeter, and Wolstanton and Burslem Unions, and Stoke-upon-Trent Parish.

THE STAFFORDSHIRE AND WORCESTERSHIRE AUDIT DISTRICT, formed under an order dated 9th May, 1845.

AUDITOR, *Thomas Stonor Simkiss, Esq.*, Wolverhampton, continued in office under an order dated 8th May, 1845.

UNIONS, &c., comprised in the District,—Aston, Bromsgrove, Cleobury Mortimer, Drayton, Dudley, Kidderminster, King's Norton, Meriden, Nuneaton, Seisdon, Shiffnal, Stourbridge, Walsall, West Bromwich, and Wolverhampton Unions, and Birmingham Parish.

THE NORTH WEST SUFFOLK AUDIT DISTRICT, formed under an order dated 25th February, 1845.

AUDITOR, *Edgar Rout Buchanan, Esq.*, Stowmarket, continued in office by the above order.

UNIONS comprised in the District and Burgh,—Mildenhall, Sudbury, and Thingoe Unions, and Burgh of Bury St. Edmunds.

THE EAST SUFFOLK AUDIT DISTRICT, formed under an order dated 12th February, 1845.

AUDITOR, *Francis William Ellis, Esq.*, Southwold, Suffolk, continued in office under an order dated 11th February, 1845.

UNIONS, &c., comprised in the District,—Hartismere, Hoxne, Ipswich, Plomesgate, and Woodbridge Unions, and Samford Hundred.

THE WEST SUFFOLK AUDIT DISTRICT, formed under an order dated 19th February, 1845.

AUDITOR, *Charles Gross, jun., Esq.*, Ipswich, continued in office under the above order.

UNIONS comprised in the District,—Bosmere and Claydon, Cosford, and Stow.

THE WEST SUSSEX AUDIT DISTRICT, formed under an order dated 27th September, 1845.

AUDITOR, *William Mason, Esq.*, Chichester, continued in office under the above order.

UNIONS comprised in the District,—Midhurst, Steyning, Thakeham, Westbourne, and Westhampnett.

THE SUSSEX AND KENT AUDIT DISTRICT, formed under an order dated 14th August, 1845.

AUDITOR, *Nathaniel Polhill Kell, Esq.*, Solicitor, Battle, continued in office under an order dated 13th August, 1845.

UNIONS comprised in the District,—Battle, Cranbrook, Eastbourne, Hailsham, Hastings, Romney Marsh, Rye, Tenterden, and Ticehurst.

THE EAST SURREY AND SUSSEX AUDIT DISTRICT, formed under an order dated 18th July, 1845.

AUDITOR, *George Turner, Esq.*, Fletching, Uckfield, elected under the above order.

UNIONS, &c., comprised in the District,—Chailey, Cuckfield, Dorking, East Grinstead, Godstone, Horsham, Lewes, Newhaven, Reigate, Uckfield, and West Firle Unions, and Brighthelmston Parish.

THE WILTSHIRE AND GLOUCESTERSHIRE AUDIT DISTRICT, formed under an order dated 19th July, 1845.

AUDITOR, *George Symons White, Esq.*, Fairford, Gloucestershire, elected under the above order.

UNIONS comprised in the District,—Chipping Sodbury, Cirencester, Cricklade and Wootton Bassett, Devizes, Dursley, Farringdon, Highworth and Swindon, Hungerford, Malmesbury, Marlborough, Pewsey, Stroud, Tetbury, Thornbury, Wantage, and Wheatenhurst.

THE NORTH-EAST YORKSHIRE AUDIT DISTRICT, formed under an order dated 6th June, 1845.

AUDITOR, *Robert Corney Weatherill, Esq.*, Lazenby, Guisborough, elected under the above order.

UNIONS comprised in the District,—Bedale, Bridlington, Driffield, Easingwold, Guisborough, Helmsley Blackmoor, Malton, Pocklington, Northallerton, Pickering, Scarborough, Stockton, Stokesley, Thirsk, Whitby, York.

THE SOUTH YORKSHIRE AUDIT DISTRICT, formed under an order dated 27th August, 1845.

AUDITOR, *John Brewin, Esq.*, Cote Field, Wortley, Sheffield, elected under the above order.

UNIONS, &c., comprised in the District,—Beverley, Doncaster, Ecclesall Bierlow, Goole, Howden, Patrington, Rotherham, Sculcoates, Selby, Sheffield, Skirlaugh, Thorne, and Wortley Unions, and Town of Kingston-upon-Hull.

THE WEST YORKSHIRE AUDIT DISTRICT, formed under an order dated 21st August, 1845.

AUDITOR, *John Manwaring, Esq.*, Pateley Bridge, elected under the above order.

UNIONS, &c., comprised in the District,—Bradford (Yorks.) Burnley, Dewsbury, Halifax, Huddersfield, Keighley, Pateley Bridge, Settle, Skipton, Todmorden, and Wakefield Unions, and Leeds Township.

THE NORTH WALES AUDIT DISTRICT, formed under an order dated 10th July, 1845.

AUDITOR, *William Prichard Lloyd, Esq.*, Llwydiarth, Anglesey, elected under the above order.

UNIONS comprised in the District,—Aberystwith, Anglesey, Bala, Bangor and Beaumaris, Carnarvon, Conway, Corwen, Dolgelly, Festiniog, Llanrwst, Machynlleth, Pwllheli, and Rhayader.

THE SOUTH WALES AUDIT DISTRICT, formed under an order dated 20th March, 1845.

AUDITOR, *Thomas Bowen, Esq.*, Carmarthen, continued in office under an order dated 19th March, 1845.

UNIONS comprised in the District,—Aberaeron, Brecknock, Bridgend and Cowbridge, Builth, Cardiff, Cardigan, Carmarthen, Haverfordwest, Hay, Lampeter, Llandilo Fawr, Llandovery, Llanelly, Merthyr Tidvil, Narberth, Neath, Newcastle in Emlyn, Pembroke, Swansea, and Tregaron.

III.—DISORDERLY HOUSES—PROSECUTION UNDER 25 GEO. 2, c. 36.

4*th Nov.* 1845.

Vestry Clerk of St. George the Martyr.—For several years past the parish officers have been appealed to respecting certain disorderly houses complained against as great nuisances to the neighbourhood; but they have, from the difficulties connected with indictments in such cases, and the expenses of such prosecutions, declined to interfere: recently, however, two rated inhabitants gave notice to the beadle, as parish constable, that they intended to prosecute certain parties under the 5th sect. of the 25 Geo. 2, cap. 36. The recognisances required were entered into by these inhabitants, and an indictment was preferred against two persons for keeping a bawdy-house, to which they pleaded guilty at the last Surrey session; but having abated the nuisance, they were permitted by the court to enter into their own recognisances to appear for judgment when called upon. At the time the notice was given to the constable, a notice was also served upon the vestry clerk, and he attended before the justices, stating that the parish officers themselves declined to prosecute, but that they would not oppose any attempt to abate the nuisance. Two bills of costs are now claimed, amounting to £32 10*s.* 10*d.*, and the parties undertake to forego the two ten pounds penalties, provided these bills are immediately settled. Inquired whether the notice served upon the vestry clerk was a sufficient notice to the overseers, and such as is required under the 7th section of the 58th George 3, cap. 70; taking into account his appointment as assistant overseer, under 59th George 3, cap. 12, and also that the parish officers had before refused to interfere.

Ans.—The 7th sec. of the 58 George 3, cap. 70, requires "that a copy of the notice which shall be given to the constable, shall also be served on, or left at the places of abode of the overseers of the poor of such parish or place, or one of them," &c: you state that in the present case the notice was served upon yourself, and that you are an assistant overseer of the parish appointed under the 59th Geo. 3, c. 12. sec. 7. The question is, therefore, whether such service of the notice upon yourself is a service of the notice upon "one of the overseers," within the meaning of the statute. If your appointment as assistant overseer is unrestricted, and empowers you to execute all the duties of the office of overseer, the Commissioners are disposed to consider that the notice would be held to be sufficiently served; but, as the Commissioners are not aware of the precise terms of your appointment, they are not prepared to express a positive opinion on the point. The Commissioners would observe that they collect from your statement that the two inhabitants who entered into the recognisances before the justices, were the parties who prosecuted the present case. You state that "two rated inhabitants gave notice to the beadle as parish constable, that they intended to prosecute certain parties under the 5th sec. of 25 Geo. 2, c. 36," and further, that "the parties (apparently meaning the inhabitants previously mentioned) are willing to forego the two rewards of £10 each, provided the costs of the prosecution are paid. The Commissioners think it necessary to call your attention to the case of Clarke *v.* Rice, reported in 1 Bar. and Ald. 694, which you will perceive related to a similar claim made by certain inhabitants of the parish of St. George the Martyr, Southwark. This case decided in effect that the inhabitants are not the proper parties to carry on the prosecution under the statute, but the parish constable, and that, except where the prosecution has been conducted by that officer, no claim can be made on the overseers either for the reward of £10, or the expenses of the prosecution. Assuming, however, that the Commissioners are incorrect in this impression, and that the prosecution in the present case was in *fact* conducted by the parish constable, then, as far as this objection is concerned, there is no obstacle to the payment of the expenses incurred by him, or of the £10 to the inhabitants. What may be the effect of the parties not having been called up for judgment, the Commissioners are not prepared to say. It may be, that until this is done, there is no obligation on the overseers to pay the rewards or other expences: see the case of Burgess *v.* Boetefleur and Brown, 22 Law Journal Repts. M. C. 122. The Commissioners, in making these observations, desire to be understood as not wishing to throw any difficulties in the way of the settlement of the costs, presuming that there is a legal foundation for them as against the parish. It is right, however, that the overseers, before they make any payment, should be fully satisfied of their authority to do so.

IV.—LUNATIC PAUPERS.—CONSTRUCTION OF 8 AND 9 VIC. c. 101, s. 27.

20th Oct. 1845.

Clerk of Nantwich Union—Stated that E. B., an idiot, chargeable to the parish of Minshull Vernon, has been for several years past an inmate of the Nantwich Union Workhouse: that there is in the Northwich Savings-bank a sum of £17, belonging to, and standing in the name of the idiot, which was left to her by a relative; and the overseers being advised that under the 7th and 8th Vict. c. 101, sect. 27, they were entitled to receive the money to defray the cost of her maintenance in the workhouse, obtained the order of two justices, directing the trustees of the savings-bank to pay to the overseers the above amount. A doubt is entertained as to the power of the trustees to comply with the order. Requested, therefore, the opinion of the Commissioners on the point.

Ans.—It will be quite lawful for the trustees of the savings-bank to pay over to the guardians of the Nantwich Union, or to the overseers of Minshull Vernon, the money in their hands belonging to E. B., to defray the cost of her maintenance by the parish; and it is clear that if they do so, the receipt of the clerk or the overseers, as the case may be, will be a good discharge to such trustees: (see sec. 27, 7 and 8 Vic. cap. 101.) But the Commissioners do not perceive that the trustees could be compelled to pay over the money. The case does not, as the Commissioners are advised, fall within the former part of the section cited, which gives power to justices, under certain circumstances, to direct the overseers to seize the property of a lunatic, or idiot, who is chargeable.

The Commissioners apprehend that the money there spoken of, which the overseers may seize with the authority of the justices, must be in the actual possession or power of the lunatic, or idiot; as distinguished from money which may be in the possession or custody of other persons, and held in trust for the lunatic or idiot. Otherwise the power expressly given to trustees to pay in the cases last mentioned, would have been superfluous, if the justices had power to direct the payment or seizure; for the order of the justices would in itself have been a sufficient indemnity or discharge to the trustees.

V.—MEDICAL OFFICER. —CONVEYANCE OF MEDICINES TO SICK PAUPERS.

10 *Oct.* 1845.

Clerk of Darlington Union—Inquired whether the medical officers are required, under the General Medical Order, to forward to the residences of the paupers under their care, the medicines prescribed for them. If not, inquired how are paupers to procure such medicine who are unable to go themselves, and have no friends to go for them.

Ans.—The General Medical Order issued by the Commissioners does not contain any regulation on the subject referred to; and the Commissioners are of opinion that the medical officers are not bound, under the provisions of that order, to forward to the residences of the sick paupers under their care; the medicines prescribed for them by such medical officers. If the paupers are able to go themselves for the medicines, or can send for them by any member of their family, or other available means, they may be reasonably expected to do so; the Commissioners also believe that in general the medical officers co-operate in forwarding the medicine to the paupers, in so far as the means of sending medicines in their general practice may be available for the like purpose as regards their pauper patients, without incurring additional expense. But if the paupers themselves are unable to go, or send for the medicine, and if the medical officer cannot forward them without employing a special messenger for the purpose, it then becomes the duty of the relieving officer, under the direction of the board of guardians, to provide for the due conveyance of the medicine to the paupers; as in no case must the latter be left without the medicine prescribed for them by the medical officer. The subject is one of detail, depending on local and temporary circumstances, which ought in general to be regulated according to the discretion of the board of guardians, when any difficulty arises.

VI.—POOR LAW UNIONS' GAZETTE.

THE Poor Law Commissioners have received resolutions from several Unions, expressive of the opinion of the Boards of Guardians of the utility of this publication, which is issued weekly by Mr. Mallett, at No. 59, Wardour Street, London, for advertising, gratuitously, persons who abscond, leaving their families chargeable to parishes.

The Commissioners understand that 112 deserters, who had left 470 persons chargeable to parishes within the 215 Unions subscribing for the publication, were discovered by its means, during the last twelve months.

In a communication which the Commissioners addressed to Mr. Mallett on the 17th Sept. 1843, they have stated that they "consider the publication of the *Poor Law Unions' Gazette* useful and desirable, as tending to facilitate the apprehension of persons who have deserted their families, and left them chargeable to the poor-rates; and, looking to the object of the publication, they are of opinion that any Board of Guardians would be justified in purchasing the same, and charging the expense to the common fund of the union."

VII.—WORKHOUSES.

1. GENERAL ORDER PROHIBITING THE EMPLOYMENT OF PAUPERS IN WORKHOUSES IN POUNDING BONES.

To the Guardians of the Poor of the several Unions and of the several Parishes under a Board of Guardians named in the Schedules hereunto annexed, and the several Officers of such Unions and Parishes:—

To the Churchwardens and Overseers of the Poor of the several Parishes and Places comprised within the said Unions, and of the several other Parishes named in the said Schedules:—

To the Clerk or Clerks to the Justices of the Petty Sessions held for the Division or Divisions in which the Parishes and Places comprised within the said Unions, and the said other Parishes named in the said Schedules, are situate:—

And to all others whom it may concern.

Whereas it is expedient to regulate the mode in which the poor who are relieved in the workhouses of unions or parishes are set to work.

Now, therefore, We, the Poor Law Commissioners, in pursuance of the authorities vested in Us by an Act passed in the fifth year of the reign of His late Majesty King William the Fourth, intituled "*An Act for the Amendment and better Administration of the Laws relating to the Poor in England and Wales*," do hereby Order, Direct, and Declare, with respect to each and every of the Unions named in the Schedule A, hereunto annexed, and of the Parishes named in the Schedule B, hereunto annexed, That from and after the *First of January next*, no pauper, who shall be in any Workhouse under the management and control of any Board of Guardians shall be employed or set to work by the said Guardians, or any of their Officers or Servants, in pounding, grinding, or otherwise breaking bones, or in preparing bone dust.

And we do further Order, that—

The word "*Union*" in this Order shall be taken to include not only an Union of parishes formed under the provisions of the herein-before recited Act, but also an Union of Parishes incorporated or united for the relief or maintenance of the poor under any Local Act of Parliament.

The word "*Guardians*" in this Order shall be taken to include not only Guardians appointed or entitled to act under the provisions of the said herein-before recited Act, but also any Governors, Deputy Governors, Assistants, Directors, Managers, Acting Guardians, Trustees of the Poor, or Select Vestrymen, entitled to act in the ordering of relief to the Poor from the poor rate under any Local Act of Parliament, and the Churchwardens and Overseers of the poor of the several Parishes in the city of Salisbury.

The word "*Parish*" in this Order shall be taken to include any place maintaining its own Poor, whether parochial or extra-parochial.

[*Schedules A and B contain the names of all the Unions and Parishes under Boards of Guardians in England and Wales.*]

Given under our Hands and Seal of Office, this eighth day of November, in the year One thousand eight hundred and forty-five.

(Signed) G. C. LEWIS.
L. S. EDMUND W. HEAD.

---

2. CIRCULAR ACCOMPANYING THE ABOVE ORDER.

Poor Law Commission Office,
Somerset House, November 8th, 1845.

SIR,—The Poor Law Commissioners have, for some time, had under their consideration the expediency of issuing a General Rule, prohibiting the employment of paupers in workhouses, in grinding, pounding, or breaking bones.

The Commissioners are aware that there is considerable difficulty in finding work for the able-bodied inmates of a workhouse, which shall not interfere with the market for independent labour, and which shall not, at the same time, involve some loss to the rate-payers. They have been moreover unwilling, in any case where the exercise of their authority is not absolutely necessary, to restrict the discretion as to the sorts of labour which the guardians, as the immediate managers of the workhouse, may reasonably be supposed to possess.

The Commissioners believe, that in the majority of unions where this kind of labour has been employed, no serious inconvenience has resulted from its use, owing to the care with which it has been superintended by the guardians. Moreover, in the cases in which its introduction, even for vagrants and trampers, has been brought before the Commissioners, they have constantly required a certificate from the medical officer, that no injury to the health of the inmates of the workhouse was to be apprehended from its adoption.

Notwithstanding these considerations, the Commissioners, looking to the serious objections to which this mode of employment is liable, have, after mature deliberation, decided on issuing a General Rule, prohibiting bone-crushing in all workhouses, a copy of which is herewith transmitted to you. The Order, for this purpose, will come into operation on the first day of January next.

The Commissioners will only add, that they will be ready to afford any assistance or advice to the guardians in meeting the difficulties which may result from the discontinuance of bone-crushing in those workhouses where it has hitherto been carried on.

I am, Sir, your most obedient servant,
EDWIN CHADWICK, *Secretary.*

LONDON:
Printed by Order of the Poor Law Commissioners, by BLACKBURN and PARDON, 6, Hatton Garden, and Published by CHARLES KNIGHT and Co., 22, Ludgate Street, Publishers to the Poor Law Commissioners.

VOLUME VI
[1846]

AN

OFFICIAL CIRCULAR

OF PUBLIC DOCUMENTS AND INFORMATION:

DIRECTED BY THE POOR LAW COMMISSIONERS TO BE PRINTED, CHIEFLY FOR THE USE OF THE MEMBERS AND PERMANENT OFFICERS OF BOARDS OF GUARDIANS, UNDER THE POOR LAW AMENDMENT ACT.

No. 55. CIRCULAR ISSUED JANUARY 1st, 1846.

THE Poor Law Commissioners directed that the following documents be printed and circulated for the information of Guardians and Officers of the several Unions, viz.

(Signed) By Order of the Board,
EDWIN CHADWICK, *Secretary.*

I.—APPRENTICESHIP—OF POOR CHILDREN TO THE SEA SERVICE.

Oct. 6th, 1845.

Clerk of St. Alban's Union—Requested the advice of the Commissioners as to the best course of proceeding to get boys out as apprentices to the merchant service.

Ans.—It appears to the Commissioners that the guardians might advertise in the public papers if they have any lads fit for the service; and they might also communicate with the secretary of the Admiralty on the subject. It may be useful to direct the attention of the guardians to the Act which was passed last session, (8 and 9 Vic. c. 116,) "for the protection of seamen entering on board merchant ships." That act authorised the Committee of Council for trade and foreign plantations, from and after the 1st of September, 1845, to license agents for providing merchant ships with seamen. If the guardians have any lads ready to be apprenticed, they might inform such agents accordingly.

II.—BURIAL OF PAUPERS.

September 15th, 1845.

Clerk of Bridgwater Union—The board of guardians of the Bridgwater Union have been applied to by the board of guardians of the Williton Union, to give them an undertaking to repay the funeral expenses of all paupers belonging to parishes in the Bridgwater Union, who may happen to die in the Williton Union, whilst in the receipt of non-resident relief. Inquired, whether such an arrangement would be legal.

Ans.—The Commissioners are of opinion, that the funeral expenses of paupers belonging to the Bridgwater Union, who die out of it, cannot legally be repaid out of the poor-rates of that union. The power of guardians to bury the bodies of poor persons at the charge of the rates is given by sec. 31 of the 7 and 8 Vic. c. 101. The words of that section are, "to bury the body of any poor person which may be *within* their parish or union respectively, and charge the expense thereof to any parish under their control," &c. If, therefore, the guardians of the Bridgwater Union were to give the undertaking sought by the guardians of the Williton Union, they would be clearly taking upon themselves an obligation which attaches to the guardians of the Williton Union, and this, without any authority to charge the expense upon any parish in the Bridgwater Union; for the power to charge only exists where there is a prior obligation or duty to bury.

2. BURIAL OF PAUPERS.

Dec. 24*th*, 1845.

Clerk of ——— *Union*—The friends of a deceased pauper, who, up to her death, resided and was settled in the parish of B., applied to the relieving officer for a coffin for her, and he gave a note addressed to the Union contractors for a coffin accordingly, and also a note addressed to the parish clerk for the burial fees; which, as usual in such cases, was intended to comprehend the vicar's and the sexton's fees. The relieving officer, at the next meeting of the board of guardians, reported these orders, and the amount was allowed on the supposition that the burial had taken place in the church-yard of the parish, instead of in an unconsecrated burial-ground in the parish, as it afterwards appeared to have been the case. The relieving officer's note was handed over by the friends of the deceased to the sexton of the unconsecrated burial-ground, and on its production to the relieving officer he paid the fees to such sexton. Inquired whether these fees could, under the circumstances, be legally charged to the poor-rates.

Ans.—Under the 31st sect. of the 7th and 8th Vict. c. 101, the guardians may bury the body of any poor person, &c., and charge the expense *thereof* to *any* parish, &c., that is to say, they may charge the expense of the burial in cases in which they bury the body. The same section also enacts that, in all cases of burial, *under the direction* of the guardians, they shall pay the lawful fees. Consequently, their authority to charge the expense, and their obligation to pay the fees, depend upon the question, whether the body is buried by them or under their direction. In the particular case referred to in your letter, the Commissioners do not think that the body can be considered to have been buried by the guardians, or under their direction. According to your statement, all that the relieving officer did was to give to the applicants a note on the contractor for the coffin, and a note on the parish clerk for the fees. He gave no directions as to the place or mode of burial, and did not provide for the funeral in any way, beyond furnishing the coffin and undertaking to pay the fees. The Commissioners, therefore, think it cannot be said, either that he buried the body, or that the burial took place under his direction; and they accordingly consider that the terms of the 31st sect. do not authorise the payment of the fees or of any other expense connected with the burial in this case out of the poor-rates. The question then arises, whether any expense incurred in this matter can be regarded and charged as relief given to the friends of the deceased, who applied to the relieving officer for assistance. The Commissioners are not sufficiently acquainted with the circumstances of the case to be able to express any decisive opinion on this point. They think it right, however, to direct your attention to the decision in Reg. *v.* Steward, 12 Ad. and Ell. 773, which may, perhaps, bear upon the question.

3. BURIAL OF PAUPERS.

Dec. 1*st*, 1845.

Clerk of ——— *Union*—One of the relieving officers of the Union having been applied to by a widow in receipt of out-door relief for assistance towards the burial of her child in a cemetery belonging to dissenters, refused to comply with the application, conceiving that he was not justified in giving assistance for the burial of paupers in any other place than the church-yard of the parish. Requested the Commissioners' opinion on the case.

Ans.—The 31st sec. of the 7th and 8th Vic. c. 101, certainly leaves it discretionary with the guardians whether they will or will not, in any case bury the body of a deceased person at the expense of the poor-rates. The terms of the section are, that "it shall be lawful" for the guardians to do so, not that it shall be compulsory. At the same time the Commissioners apprehend there could be no doubt that it is the duty of the guardians to exercise this power, whenever a proper occasion arises: what is a proper occasion for its exercise, must, of course, be judged of according to the circumstances of each individual case. The Commissioners, however, will state generally, that in their opinion the guardians, in determining whether the burial of any person shall take place at the expense of the poor-rates, ought to be guided by a consideration of the *necessity* which may exist for their assistance in the case, and that where such necessity really exists, they ought not to withhold such assistance, solely on account of the religious persuasion to which the deceased may have belonged. With regard to the place of burial, the 31st sect. enacts that, except where the guardians direct the body of a pauper to be buried in the parish to which he was chargeable, "every dead body which the guardians, or any of their officers duly authorised shall direct to be buried at the expense of the poor-rates, shall (*unless the deceased person, or the husband or wife or next of kin of such deceased person, have otherwise desired*) be buried in the church-yard or other consecrated burial ground in or belonging to the parish, &c., in which the death may have occurred." The exception in italics appears to the Commissioners to have been intended to secure, on the part of the guardians, a due consideration of the wishes of the persons interested, and not to aid the guardians in establishing any undue distinctions between persons of different religious persuasions of the poor, which are entitled to respect. The Commissioners therefore consider that the relieving officer, in the case stated in your letter, acted very improperly in refusing to give the widow any assistance towards the burial of her child, except upon condition that the child should be buried in a place to which she conscientiously objected.

III.—CHARGEABILITY.

1. Certificates of.

Sept. 18*th*, 1845.

Clerk of Machynlleth Union—The parish of Machynlleth is divided into three places, each of which maintains its own poor, viz., the township of Is-y-garreg, the township of Uwch-y-garreg, and the town and liberties of Machynlleth. Inquired whether in filling up the form of certificate of chargeability (Schedule C, 7 and 8 Vic. c. 101) for any of these places it is necessary to strike out the word parish and substitute "township" or "town and liberties" as the case may be.

Ans.—The word "parish," as used in the form of the certificate in Schedule C, includes, according to the definition of the term in the Poor Law Amendment Act (sec. 109) any place maintaining its own poor. There would, consequently, be no incorrectness in retaining this word in the certificate, even with reference to a township, or other district, if it maintained its own poor separately. On the other hand the Commissioners consider that the substitution of "township," &c. for "parish," would not invalidate the certificate, and that it might be done accordingly without impropriety, if deemed desirable. The 69th sec. only requires the certificate to be "in the form *or to the effect* contained in the schedule." The substitution of "township," &c. for "parish" does not appear to the Commissioners to be necessary, except where some doubt or ambiguity might arise from the use of the latter term. Thus in your case, where the whole parish and part of the parish have the same name of the "town and liberties of Machynlleth," were it described as "the parish of Machynlleth," it would be uncertain what district was meant; and, therefore, it would be proper to alter the prescribed form of the certificate by inserting in place of the word "parish," a precisely accurate and unambiguous description of the district referred to.

2. Ditto.

Sept. 19*th*, 1845.

Clerk of Basford Union—It is the practice of the justices of Derbyshire and Nottinghamshire to require the attendance of the relieving officers upon questions of settlement, to prove the amount of relief administered by them to paupers about to be removed, as also to produce the certificate of chargeability provided by the 69 section of the 7 and 8 Vict. c. 101. Inquired, whether the attendance of the relieving officer in such cases is necessary; or, whether the certificate in question alone is not sufficient under the above section.

Ans.—The course taken by the magistrates is that which was requisite in all cases before the 5 and 6 Vict. c. 57, s. 17, and the 7 and 8 Vict. c. 101, s. 69, and is still requisite where certificates of chargeability under those statutes are not produced. Before these statutes, and now without such certificates, the chargeability of a pauper for the purpose of removal was and is a conclusion to be established by evidence of certain facts, viz. the relief of the pauper in a certain manner. See the Queen *v.* the Inhabitants of High Bickington, L. J. v. 22, p. 3, p. 74. But the object of the statutes referred to, and as the Commissioners conceive the undoubted effect of them, is, where a certificate of chargeability is produced, to dispense with all detailed and specific evidence of the facts on which the conclusion of chargeability must otherwise be grounded; accordingly the Commissioners entertain no doubt, that where such certificate is produced, there is no legal necessity for the attendance of the relieving officer to prove the amount of relief administered. Where the relieving officer does so attend and proves the relief, then the certificate is unnecessary; for the certificate is not an additional proof required, but was only provided in substitution for the proof which was previously required.

IV.—CONTRIBUTION.—CHURCHWARDEN'S LIABILITY.

Sept. 18*th*, 1845.

Churchwarden of —— Inquired whether he, as churchwarden, was liable for the neglect of the overseers in not paying the contribution ordered by the board of guardians of the —— Union.

Ans.—By the 43 Eliz. c. 2, the churchwardens of every parish are expressly constituted overseers of the poor; and as such they are liable to the same obligations, and subject to the same responsibilities as other overseers. Generally speaking, therefore, you, as churchwarden, are equally responsible with your fellow-officers for the payment of the contributions required from your parish by the guardians of ——— Union; but what may be the extent of your liability in the present instance, the Commissioners, not being informed of all the circumstances, are of course unable to say.

V.—JERSEY.—APPREHENSION OF A PERSON IN.

Sept. 8*th*, 1845.

Clerk of Cerne Union—C. W. having gone to reside in Jersey, leaving his wife and four children chargeable to the parish of Cerne Abbas, inquired what steps will be necessary to give effect to a justices' warrant under the Vagrant Act, with a view to his apprehension at that place.

Ans.—The Islands of Jersey and Guernsey are only affected by English acts of parliament when specially named. The vagrancy laws do not, therefore, extend to those islands. For the same reason, the provisions of the several statutes for backing, in Ireland and Scotland, warrants issued by justices in England do not apply to them. There appears, therefore, to be no available remedy against C. W. described as having left his family chargeable to Cerne Abbas, while he continues to reside in Jersey.

VI.—LUNATIC PAUPERS.

Oct. 6*th*, 1845.

Clerk of Lymington Union—1. Inquired, whether a medical officer of one district in a Union is prohibited by the 48th sect. of the 8th and 9th Vic. c. 126, from certifying as to pauper lunatics residing in other districts in the Union. All the medical practitioners at Lymington are medical officers of the Union, with the exception of one, and he is an elected guardian of the Union. Inquired whether, in the event of the medical officer's not being allowed to give the required certificate, such medical practitioner, who is a guardian, would be allowed to do so. 2. A labouring man, whose wife is a lunatic, refuses to allow her to be brought before a justice for examination, and has stated his determination to resist any attempt to remove her to an asylum. Inquired whether the relieving officer, having the summons of the justice to bring the lunatic before him, can compel her attendance against the expressed determination of the husband that she shall not be examined or removed to an asylum.

Ans.—1. In the Commissioners' opinion, the 48th sec. prohibits every medical officer of every district in the Lymington Union from giving the certificate required, by the section, with reference to any lunatic pauper of any parish in that union. The terms of the section are, "such physician, surgeon, or apothecary, not being *the medical officer of such Union or parish.*" The Commissioners understand these terms to refer to the medical officer of the Union, where the parish to which the lunatic is chargeable is within a Union, and to the medical officer of the parish, where the parish is not within a Union. This distinction between parishes in union and parishes not in union, appears to the Commissioners to be the one kept up throughout the whole section. "The medical officer of *every parish and union* who, &c., that any person chargeable *to such parish* or to any parish *within such Union*, &c., to the overseer of the poor of the parish, *if the parish be not within a Union*, and to the relieving officer of *the Union, if the parish be within a Union*, &c." And the

Commissioners see no reason to doubt that the medical officer of a district within a Union is a medical officer of such Union, within the meaning of the section. The Commissioners do not think that he can be regarded as a medical officer of the parish, in the sense in which the section employs those terms. There is a parallel expression in the same section, viz., "the relieving officer of the Union, if the parish be within a Union;" which, certainly, as it seems to the Commissioners, cannot be construed as limited to those relieving officers who respectively act for entire Unions. The Commissioners, therefore, consider that in the case of a pauper lunatic chargeable to any parish within a Union, no medical officer appointed by the guardians of such Union can give the certificate mentioned in the section with reference to such pauper. The Commissioners, however, are not aware that the mere circumstance of a medical man being also an elected guardian of the Union would operate in law to prevent his giving the certificate referred to. 2. With regard to the case you allude to, in which the husband refuses to allow his lunatic wife to be brought before the justice for examination, the section provides as follows:—"And thereupon the said justice shall, by an order under his hand and seal, require the overseer or relieving officer of the parish or union to bring such person before him, or some other justice of the said county or borough, at such time and place (within three days from the time of such notice being given to such justice) as shall be appointed by the said order." If in the case in question the justice has made an order to this effect, it is clear that the husband, in opposing such order, would be resisting the law; and the Commissioners apprehend that the relieving officer would be justified in taking such measures as might be necessary to enforce obedience. At the same time the Commissioners direct your attention to the proviso, which relates to cases where the lunatic cannot, "on account of his health or other cause, be safely taken before any justice."

2. LUNATIC PAUPERS.

Nov. 27th, 1845.

Clerk of Devizes Union—A pauper who has been some time in the Union workhouse and considered a harmless idiot, refuses to speak or to take any nourishment. The board of guardians think it necessary to call in the aid of a medical man to see the pauper, with a view, if possible, to the application of a suitable remedy to his case. Inquired whether the board would be justified in giving remuneration to the medical man called in, and whether the amount should be charged to the common fund of the Union, or to the parish to which the pauper belongs.

Ans.—If the circumstances of the case are such as to render it necessary that medical advice should be obtained, in addition to that of the medical officer of the workhouse, the Commissioners think that the guardians would be justified in calling in the aid of another medical man, and paying him a proper remuneration at the expence of the particular parish to which the pauper is chargeable. As such additional assistance would be relief to the individual pauper, and the medical man called in for the occasion would not be an officer of the Union, the Commissioners see no ground for charging his remuneration on the common fund.

3. LUNATIC PAUPERS.

Dec. 12th, 1845.

Clerk of the —— Union—Several pauper lunatics belonging to this Union having to be removed from the county asylum, the clergyman of —— (in the absence of a justice) attended, and, in conjunction with a relieving officer and a surgeon, examined the paupers, and made the necessary orders for their removal. The clergyman demanded a fee of £1. 1*s*. for his attendance. Inquired whether he is entitled to such fee.

Ans.—The Commissioners are of opinion that the clergyman is no more entitled to any fee for these orders than the justice would have been if he had made them.

4. LUNATIC PAUPERS.

Sept. 26th, 1845.

Overseer of Rotherhithe Parish—The parish of Rotherhithe being under a Board of Guardians, and not within a Union, inquired whether it is the duty of the overseers, or of the relieving officer, to act in carrying out the 48th section of 8 and 9 Vic. c. 126.

Ans.—Looking to the phraseology of the section in question, the Commissioners are of opinion that, in the case of the parish of Rotherhithe, the statute requires the overseers of the parish, and not the relieving officer, to take the proceedings to which the section has reference. You will observe, in the first place, that the section requires the medical officer to give the notice "to the overseers of the poor of the parish, if the parish *be not within a union,* and to the relieving officer of the union, if the parish *be within a union.*" It then goes on to direct that "every such overseer and relieving officer, who shall have knowledge, &c. that any person chargeable *to the parish of such overseer,* or to any parish within *the union of such relieving officer, &c.*" The only distinction here made is obviously that between parishes which are included within unions, and parishes which are not so included; and the same distinction, and that alone, is kept up throughout the whole section. For instance, provision is subsequently made for an examination of the pauper "by an officiating clergyman of the parish in which he shall be resident, together with an *overseer of such parish, or the relieving officer of the union* to which the same shall belong." It appears to the Commissioners, therefore, that where a parish is *not* within a union, even although it may be under a board of guardians, the overseers, according to the terms of the statute, are the parties whose duty it is to take the proceedings pointed out in the section. The Commissioners, of course, express no opinion as to the reasons which may have induced the Legislature to make this difference between unions and parishes under boards of guardians; they confine themselves to a statement of what appears to them to be the clear and obvious import of the language employed.

5. LUNATIC PAUPERS.

Dec. 29th, 1845.

Mr. —— Inquired—1st, whether the appointment of medical officer to superintend lunatic asylums is vested in the board of guardians, it appearing to him to be the effect of the 8 and 9 Vict. cap. 126. s. 69; 2ndly, whether it is incumbent on them to make such appointment forthwith, or at any other time suiting their wants or convenience; 3rdly, whether he can (as a duly qualified surgeon) holding office as a guardian of the Union, be eligible for the appointment.

Ans.—The 69 sec. of the 8 and 9 Vict. c. 126, does not empower the guardians of a Union to appoint (as you seem to suppose) a "medical officer to superintend lunatic asylums," it merely enables them to appoint a physician, surgeon, or apothecary, "to visit and examine any or every pauper lunatic belonging to such Union, confined in any asylum, registered hospital, or licensed house." It appears to the Commissioners that the guardians of the —— Union are not bound to make any such appointment forthwith, but that they may wait until occasion arises. With regard to your legal competency to receive the appointment, being yourself a guardian of the Union, the Commissioners direct your attention to the 14 sec. of the 5 and 6 Vict. c. 57, which provides that "no person receiving any fixed salary or emolument from the poor-rates in any parish or Union, shall be capable of serving as a guardian in such parish or Union." If a person were appointed generally to visit and examine the lunatics of a parish or Union at a fixed salary, he would come within this provision. If the appointment were only for the occasion, the Commissioners do not think that it would be incompatible with the office of guardian.

6. LUNATIC PAUPERS.

Dec. 4th, 1845.

Clerk of Newcastle-upon-Tyne Union—Requested the Commissioners' opinion and advice on the following case:—

On the 8th of September, 1845, two justices of the borough and town and county of Newcastle-upon-Tyne, made an order for sending to a licensed house for the reception of lunatics, situate within the borough and town and county, one J. R., an Irish woman, and she was accordingly sent thither, at the charge of the parish of All Saints, in the Newcastle-upon-Tyne Union, as being chargeable to that parish, no adjudication as to her settlement, nor order of maintenance having been at that time made. On the 10th of October following, the overseers of All Saints, having given to the clerk of the peace due notice as required by 8 and 9 Vic. c. 126, s. 59, made an application to two justices of the borough and town and county for an order under sec. 63, upon the treasurer of the borough, for the maintenance of the lunatic in the asylum, on the ground of her not having gained a settlement in England. The clerk of the peace appeared by his deputy, and the correctness of the notice, and that the lunatic had no settlement in England, were admitted; but the justices, alleging that inasmuch as no borough-rate was assessed or levied within the borough, they could not legally make an order of maintenance upon the treasurer, and refused to do so, until they had further legal advice on the case. Prior to the passing of the Municipal Reform Act, that portion of the present extended borough of Newcastle-upon-Tyne, comprised within the ancient corporate limits, and then designated "the town and county of the town of Newcastle-upon-Tyne," formed a distinct county of itself, similar to Hull, and many other large towns; the mayor, recorder, and aldermen were justices of the peace, had a court of quarter sessions, appointed a county treasurer, and levied a county rate, which was applied to all the purposes to which a county rate was by law applicable. Since the passing of the Municipal Act, the justices of the borough and town and county have been appointed by the crown; they hold a court of quarter sessions, of which the recorder is the sole judge. It is true that no borough rate has, since the latter period, been assessed or levied, the funds of the corporation, together with fines imposed under their bye-laws having been found sufficient for, and have been applied to the maintenance of the gaol and house of correction, the payment of the expenses of prosecutions, and all other purposes to which by law a county rate is applicable. On reference to the interpretation clause of the before-mentioned Act, it will be found thus:—"*County*" shall mean every county, riding, and division of a county, *county of a city, county of a town*, &c. "*Borough rate*," shall mean a borough fund or rate, and any funds assessed upon or raised in, or *belonging to any borough*, and applicable to the purposes to which borough rates are applicable. "*County rate*" shall mean a county rate, and any funds assessed upon, or raised in, *or belonging to*, any county in the nature of county rate, and applicable to the purposes to which county rates are applicable. Taking these three clauses together, the overseers submitted to the justices that the borough fund, although not raised by assessment, yet as *belonging to* the borough, was applicable to the maintenance of the lunatic, and that they therefore ought to make the order applied for. On the part of the clerk of the peace it was contended, that the justices could not, consistently with the following portion of the interpretation clause, make an order upon the treasurer of the borough, as he had not the custody of any money raised by a borough rate,—"*Treasurer of the borough*" shall mean every officer who has the custody of any moneys raised by a borough rate.

Ans.—The Commissioners understand that, on the 8th of September, 1845, J. R. was sent by an order of two justices of the borough of Newcastle-upon-Tyne, from the parish of All Saints, which is within that borough, and to which she was then chargeable, to a licensed house for lunatics, situated within the borough. This, it would seem, the justices referred to were quite competent to do, as the 48th section of the 8 and 9 Vic. c. 126, gives authority to act in such cases, to any "justice of the county or borough" within which the parish whence the lunatic is sent may be situate. The questions then arise, Who is liable for the costs of the pauper's maintenance in such licensed house? And how is that liability to be enforced? It is stated that J. R. is an Irish-woman, and has gained no settlement in England. If showing that the lunatic has no settlement at all, is to be regarded as tantamount to establishing "that it cannot be ascertained in what parish such lunatic is settled," the Commissioners are disposed to think that the case comes within the scope of the 59th section. That section, it is true, refers to *counties* only, and *not to boroughs;* but as Newcastle-upon-Tyne, under the combined operation of the 5 and 6 Will. 4, c. 76, and 2 and 3 Will. 4, c. 64, is not only a "borough," but also a "county of a town," and as the word "county," in the 8 and 9 Vic. c. 126, (see sec. 84,) includes a "county" of a town, it appears to the Commissioners that Newcastle-upon-Tyne is subject to the provisions of sec. 59, as a "county," though it would not have been so merely as a "borough." Under these circumstances the Commissioners think, that the justices of the county of the town of Newcastle-upon-Tyne are bound to adjudge J. R. to be chargeable to that county. The 63rd section applies to cases in which, after a lunatic has been sent to a licensed house, "it shall be ascertained or adjudged in due course of law, that such lunatic is chargeable to a county." It is, therefore, applicable to the case of J. R., and its provisions, so far as they bear upon that case, are as follows:—"It shall be lawful for any two justices of the county in which such licensed house is situate, to make an order or orders upon the *treasurer of such county* so chargeable as aforesaid, for payment to the treasurer of the guardians of any Union, of all expenses incurred by such Union in or about the examination of such lunatic, and his conveyance to the licensed house; and of all moneys paid by the treasurer of the guardians of such Union to the proprietor of the licensed house, for the lodging, &c. of such lunatic, and incurred within twelve calendar months previous to the date of such order, and also for payment to the proprietor of the licensed house, of the reasonable charges of the future lodging, &c. of such lunatic; and *every such treasurer of a county*, on whom any such order shall be made, shall, *out of any moneys which may come into his hands by virtue of his office,* immediately pay to the treasurer of the guardians of such Union the amount of the expenses and moneys by such order directed to be paid to him, and from time to time pay to the said proprietor of the licensed house the future charges aforesaid." It is stated that the licensed house to which J. R. was sent, is situated within the county of the town of Newcastle-upon-Tyne; consequently, the justices of that county may make the order in the case as is referred to in the provision recited above. That order must be made "upon the treasurer of such county." Some doubt appears to be raised, in the present case, as to whether there is any such officer, within the meaning of the statute, in Newcastle-upon-Tyne; and reference is made in support of such doubt, to the interpretation clause, sec. 84. In that clause it is enacted, that the words "treasurer of the county" shall mean every officer who has the custody of any county rate; and that the words "county rate," shall mean a county rate, and any funds assessed upon, or raised in, or belonging to, any county, in the nature of county rates, and applicable to the purposes to which county rates are applicable. The Commissioners understand that there is an officer who acts as the treasurer of the county of the town of Newcastle-upon-Tyne, and who, when any rates in the nature of county rates are raised in that county, has the custody thereof. In order to render such an officer a "treasurer of the county," within the meaning of the Act, it does not appear to the Commissioners to be necessary that the proceeds of a county rate should be in his hands at any particular moment; it seems to them to be sufficient, if such a rate is capable of being made within the county, and if such rate, when made, would be confided to the custody of the officer in question. The Commissioners accordingly consider that the justices of Newcastle-upon-Tyne are authorised, and therefore bound to make such an order as the case requires, upon the treasurer of that county, and that such treasurer will be bound to make the payments "out of any moneys which may come into his hands by virtue of his office."

7. LUNATIC PAUPERS.

Oct. 24th, 1845.

Overseers of Mile End New Town Hamlet, Whitechapel Union—B. S., a lunatic, with his children, became some time since chargeable to the hamlet of Mile End New Town. He is wholly maintained in a lunatic asylum at the expense of the hamlet, and his children receive weekly relief. It has been ascertained that he is possessed of about £900 stock in the Bank of England, on which there are several years' dividends due, and that he is also entitled to a freehold house in which his mother resides, who takes care of his children who reside with her, in consequence of which they receive less relief than if they were at the expense of a lodging. The cost of the maintenance of the lunatic and the relief to his children would wholly exhaust the dividends to arise from the Bank stock, and the rent of the house if let to a tenant. Inquired whether the justices could make an order on the governor and company of the Bank of England under the authority of the Act 7 and 8 Vict. cap. 101, sec. 27, to pay over the dividends due and to become due on the stock, and to empower the overseers to let the house. The words of the section seem to refer to the case of an insane person, &c., having an estate *more* than sufficient to maintain his family, &c.

Ans.—It is certainly very desirable that this property should be made available for B. S.'s maintenance; but the question is how that can be done. As regards the stock, and the dividends due thereon, it must be observed, that the first part of the 7 and 8 Vict. c. 101, sec. 27 cannot apply to them, inasmuch as such stock and dividends are not money, nor goods and chattels capable of being seised. The latter part of that section would, however, *empower* the governor and company of the Bank of England to pay the dividends to the overseers of the poor of the hamlet, or to the guardians of the Whitechapel Union, in discharge of the cost of the maintenance of the lunatic. Such a proceeding would, however, be quite voluntary on the part of the governor and company, and no order could be issued to compel them to adopt it. In regard to the house, the Commissioners observe, that it does not appear that *any rent* is received in respect of it with which the justices can deal under the section above referred to, while it certainly is not shown that the case is one to which the clause is applicable in regard to the sufficiency of the estate for the maintenance of the family.

8. LUNATIC PAUPERS.

Oct. 7th, 1845.

Clerk of Totnes Union—The board of guardians are in doubt whether the 48th sec. of the 8 and 9

Vic. c. 126, taken in conjunction with the interpretation of the word "lunatic" in sec. 84 of that act, renders it imperative that every pauper of unsound mind, however harmless and however unnecessary it might be to confine him, should be at once sent to the county asylum. While the provisions of the act seem to contemplate the removal of every pauper of unsound mind, some of the forms in the schedule to the act refer to lunatics maintained in places other than asylums. Requested the Commissioners' opinion for the guidance of the board of guardians.

Ans.—The Commissioners in Lunacy [with whom the Poor Law Commissioners have communicated upon the subject] concur with the guardians of the Totnes Union, in thinking that the requisitions of the statute will be satisfied if such lunatics, idiots, and persons of unsound mind, only, as their medical officer may deem "proper to be confined," (agreeably to the express terms of the order and certificate set forth in Schedule E. No. 1,) shall be sent to an asylum.

---

9. Lunatic Paupers.

Dec. 5th, 1845.

Clerk of Honiton Union—Several pauper lunatics have been lately taken before the justices of the Woodbury Division, in which a part of this Union lies. The clerk to the justices has made in each case a charge of 10*s.*, and on being applied to by the board of guardians for the particulars of the charge, he disputed the right of the board to question it, and declined to furnish any particulars. Inquired whether the board are bound to pay this charge without such particulars.

Ans.—The Commissioners think that the guardians and their officers, having no authority to expend the moneys committed to their charge, except for definite and legal purposes, are bound to ascertain that any payments they may be called upon to make, are lawful before they make them, and that they ought therefore to refuse compliance with any such demand as that which you refer to, if the nature and the grounds of it be not specified.

Dec. 23rd, 1845.

Clerk of the same Union—Transmitted the following account furnished to the guardians by the clerk to the justices,—"Order for bringing up lunatic: examination before the magistrate: certificate of medical man: filling up particulars as required for the signature of the relieving officer: and order for admission. In each case, 10*s.*"—(there being three cases) £1. 10*s.* Inquired whether the guardians were bound to pay this charge without a more specific account.

Ans.—The legality of the demand made by the justices' clerk for the fees alluded to, depends entirely upon the question, whether such fees are authorised by the table of fees established for the district under the 26 Geo. 2, c. 14. The only mode of ascertaining this, would be by a detailed comparison of the specific charges made by Mr. C., with the items included in such table. The Commissioners observe that in each of the cases comprised in Mr. C.'s account, there are five distinct documents charged for, and only one sum (10*s.*) charged. This sum may be either the amount of a single fee allowed by the table for the whole of these documents collectively, or the total amount of separate fees allowed by the table for the several documents respectively.

---

10. Lunatic Paupers.

Dec. 18th, 1845.

Clerk of Chepstow Union—Inquired, if the Commissioners would issue some general instructions on the new duties which are imposed on the relieving officers of unions, by the 48th section of the 8 and 9 Vic. c. 126, in regard to lunatic paupers; and observed that the Act does not distinguish the relieving officer of one district from that of another.

Ans.—The enactment referred to, is express in its terms as to the duties of the relieving officer; and no power of making regulations for carrying it into effect, is given to the Poor Law Commissioners. They will, however, be ready to give their opinion on any particular case in which difficulty may occur in this respect. With regard to your remark, that the Act does not distinguish the relieving officers of the several districts in a union, that remark is correct; but the abovementioned duties would naturally seem to belong to each relieving officer in respect of the chargeable lunatics residing in his district, and probably this will be generally understood; although it must still be borne in mind that, by the terms of the Act, the duty is imposed generally on all the relieving officers in the union.

---

11. Lunatic Paupers.

January, 1846.

Medical Officer of ——— *Union*—Inquired—1st, whether it is necessary to make a quarterly return of the names of those lunatics who are not dangerous, but who have been placed in the workhouse because they had no friends or relations either capable or willing to take charge of them. 2nd. Whether in a case where the son is a medical officer of the Union, and in partnership with his father, who holds no union appointment, the father would be competent to give certificates affecting lunatics residing in or belonging to the Union.

Ans.—The quarterly lists of lunatics to be made by medical officers of Unions for their respective districts, under the 55th section of the 8th and 9th Vic. c. 126, are to include "every pauper lunatic chargeable to any parish, who shall not be in an asylum, or a registered hospital, or a house duly licensed for the reception of pauper lunatics." Consequently the list must comprise all pauper lunatics in union workhouses. The Commissioners think that the restriction placed by the 8th and 9th Vic. c. 126, and also by the 8th and 9th Vic. c. 100, sec. 48, upon medical officers of unions in regard to certificates as to pauper lunatics, does not extend to any other person even where such person may be in partnership with any such officer.

12. LUNATIC PAUPERS.

Dec. 24th, 1845.

Clerk of Bedminster Union — Inquired whether in the case of an in-door pauper alleged to be lunatic, the medical officer should give the notice to the master of the workhouse or to a relieving officer; and whether it is the duty of a relieving officer to take any steps on the receipt by him of notice from the medical officer that a pauper in the workhouse is lunatic. Inquired also whether the board of guardians are now authorised to send pauper lunatics to an asylum without an application to justices.

Ans.—The 48th sec. of the 8th and 9th Vic. c. 126, draws no distinction between lunatic paupers receiving out-door, and those receiving in-door relief; and consequently both classes must be dealt with under that section in the same manner. The Commissioners are of opinion that the guardians have no authority to send a pauper lunatic to an asylum otherwise than under the provisions of the Act.

13. LUNATIC PAUPERS—CONSTRUCTION OF 8 AND 9 VIC. C. 100, SEC. 126.

Dec. 23rd, 1845.

Clerk of Conway Union—A lunatic (or an idiot), in destitute circumstances, was found wandering in the parish of Eglwysrhos in the Conway Union, but it has not been possible to ascertain his name or where he comes from, as he cannot give any account of himself, or, in fact, give a coherent answer to any question put to him. There is no county asylum for the county in which the parish of Eglwysrhos is situate, and there will be a difficulty in obtaining an order from a justice for admission into Haydock Lodge, or any other licensed house, in consequence of the inability to make the statement, and give the particulars required in Schedule E, annexed to the 8 and 9 Vic. c. 126. And it is apprehended that if an order were made for a person "name unknown," and omitting the other particulars required, he would not be received into any licensed house, as the 8 and 9 Vic. c. 100, s. 48, provides that no pauper shall be received without an order and statement to that effect, according to the form in Schedule D. Requested the Commissioners' advice as to the proper course to be adopted under the circumstances. Inquired also whether it will be necessary that a medical man, not being the medical officer of the Union, should sign the requisite certificate, as there is no medical man besides the medical officer residing within the Union.

Ans.—The above questions were submitted by the Poor Law Commissioners to the Commissioners in Lunacy, who gave the following answer thereto :—" The provision of the Act will be satisfied if the statement appended to the order of admission be filled up, so far as the particulars required to be inserted are known, or can, without difficulty or delay, be ascertained. It very frequently happens, especially in the case of paupers, that the statement is of necessity imperfectly filled up. The lunatic referred to may be properly described as of 'name unknown.' With reference to the question of medical certificates, the 48th section of the Act is imperative. The certificate cannot legally be signed by medical officers of the union from which the pauper is sent. A certificate must be obtained from some medical man not connected with that union.

VII.—PERAMBULATION OF PARISHES—7 AND 8 VIC. C. 101, SEC. 60.

Nov. 27th, 1845.

Mr. E. Murrell, District Auditor—The overseers of the parish of ——— have entered in their accounts the following charges incurred in the perambulation of the parish :—" Four constables, £2; S. and J. N., axe carriers, £1. 6s.; banner, £2. 12s., band, £7; wands, 8s. 6d.; beer, constables, 5s.; man swimming through lake, 12s.; cups, 18s. 6d.; horses, 18s.; Preston, 10s.; Vines, £1; refreshments, £45. 17s.; Mathews, 15s.; Gregory, £1. 2s.; boys, 3s.; Mr. P. £4. 4s.; Garn, 10s.; ringers, £1. 1s.; man and paint, and constable, 16s.; Mr. P. 2s. 6d.; waiters, £1;—together, £73. 0s. 6d." As this amount appears to be unreasonable, and several of the charges unnecessarily incurred, requested the opinion of the Commissioners, as to how far he would be justified, under section 60 of the Act 7 and 8 Vic. c. 101, in allowing the above charges in the overseers' account.

Ans.—The expenses which may be allowed for this object in the overseers' accounts, under the authority of the statute referred to (sect. 60) are "all expenses properly incurred by the same officers (*i. e.* officers of the parish) on the perambulation of the parish, and in setting up and keeping in proper repair the boundary stones of the parish (provided that such perambulations do not arise more than once in three years)." By the words "properly incurred on the perambulation," are meant, as the Commissioners conceive, such expenses as are fairly incident to the ascertaining the boundaries of the parish by the officers, and are in their nature necessary and unavoidable. Thus any reasonable payment to any person whose evidence or services on such an inquiry might be actually necessary, would, the Commissioners consider, be properly incurred. So also the cost of necessary refreshments to the persons employed by the officers, and provided during the progress of the perambulation, would probably be held to be allowable under the section. The Commissioners apprehend that by far the larger portion of the charges incurred in the present instance are not such as the statute authorises. It is not apparent to the Commissioners that the use of banners, the attendance of a band of music, or the employment of ringers, are legal or reasonable requisites on the occasion of a perambulation. The Commissioners are led to suppose, from the large amount of the item in the bill for refreshments, that the practice which formerly prevailed in some parishes of providing an expensive entertainment to the officers and others, has been followed on the present occasion. If so, they conceive that such an expenditure is quite unauthorised, that it is not, in the words of the statute, "properly incurred." There are other items in the bill which, in the absence of explanation, seem open to objection. Such are the payments made to sundry persons, without a statement of the particular service rendered by them. The Commissioners would observe, generally, that where the expense incurred is in its nature a proper one, the reasonableness of the amount must be judged of and determined by yourself, having regard to the circumstances of each case, as the law does not invest the Commissioners with any power to control your decision, except where the lawfulness of the grounds of such decision are impugned, and the case is brought before the Commissioners by appeal, under 36th sect. of 7 and 8 Vic. c. 101.

VIII.—RELATIONS.

1. ORDER FOR MAINTENANCE.

May 19*th*, 1845.

Clerk of Milton Union—C. M. and his wife have become chargeable to a parish in this union. C. M. has a family both by a former and his present wife, three of whom, one by his first, and two by his present wife, are contributing, under orders of justices, towards the support of their father and mother. C. M.'s wife has also a son, W. D. by a former husband, who is in possession of considerable freehold property, and at the time of making the orders alluded to, he also appeared before the justices, and voluntarily offered to contribute one shilling per week towards his mother's maintenance, which the justices acquiesced in, having some doubt whether they could legally make an order on him to support his mother, in consequence of her being a married woman. W. D. has paid the shilling a-week for a short time, but he now refuses to do so, alleging inability. The board of guardians, however, do not consider this a valid excuse, and are desirous of obtaining an order of justices to compel the payment. Inquired whether under the circumstances stated, such an order would legally be made.

Ans.—The Commissioners are not aware of any ground for supposing that the mere circumstance of Mrs. M. being a married woman would release her son from his liability to contribute to the extent of his means towards her support, under the 43 Eliz. c. 2, s. 7.

August 13*th*, 1845.

Clerk of same Union.—The justices, requiring the production of authorities in support of the liability of W. D. to contribute towards the maintenance of his mother, requested the Commissioners to refer the guardians to such authorities. The justices contend that, in consequence of Mrs. M. being a married woman, W. D. cannot contribute towards her exclusive support, and that she could not if required give a legal discharge for such contribution. If the Commissioners should still be of opinion that W. D. is liable to support his mother, inquired whether the order should be in favour of the guardians, or the churchwardens and overseers. Inquired also whether, in cases where the guardians intend to apply for orders of maintenance, it is the safest way in all cases to receive the parties requiring relief into the workhouse previous to taking any steps to obtain an order.

Ans.—The Commissioners are not aware of any case in which this point has been decided by the courts; after consideration of the subject, however, the Commissioners retain the opinion which they expressed in their letter of 19th May last. With regard to the arguments which appear to have weighed with the justices that Mrs. M. cannot give a legal discharge for a contribution under the order, the Commissioners would observe that they do not see what discharge (assuming the order were made) she would be required to give. The order could not be made at all, unless Mrs. M. be actually chargeable to the parish, then the order would be in favour of the churchwardens and overseers of the parish, (Rex *v.* Tripping, 1 Bott, 430, Reg. *v.* Toke, 8 A and E, 227,) and therefore the person to give the discharge for the payments under the order would be the churchwardens and overseers. The order would, the Commissioners apprehend, confer no right on Mrs. M., it would simply be an indemnification of the parish against the charge. The Commissioners conceive that the order could not be legally made in favour of the guardians of the union. The chargeability (the foundation of the order) should be a lawful chargeability, and to effect this, the relief given in the case should be lawful relief. The relief, to be lawful, must be in conformity with the orders of the Commissioners in force in the union; relief in the workhouse would, under any circumstances, be lawful relief, though relief out of the workhouse would be equally so in those cases which constitute the exceptions to Art. 1 of the Prohibitory Order.

IX.—RELIEF.

1. To Railway Labourers.

Sept. 27*th*, 1845.

——— In consequence of the railway running through the parish of Ringwood, a number of excavators are already employed, and many more will be required in constructing the line for some considerable period. Inquired—1st, what steps should be taken in case such men or their families become destitute and require relief in the Union, through accident, sickness, or other cause. 2nd. Whether the relief that may be given should be charged to the parish of Ringwood alone, (that parish being the only one that will ultimately derive an advantage from rating the railway,) or generally against all the parishes in the Union. 3rd. Whether if any accident should happen in an adjoining extra-parochial place, the master will be bound to receive the person disabled into the workhouse on an application being made for that purpose.

Ans.—The parish in which a man or his family are destitute, is liable for their relief so long as they remain destitute within that parish, or until they are legally removed therefrom. But if the accident happen in an extra-parochial place, there is clearly no fund there on which the relief of the man can be charged. In such a case the parish into which the man was first brought in a destitute condition would be liable while he remained there, the same as if the accident happened in the parish. There is no general fund on which the relief of this class of paupers can be charged, and the probable future assessment of the railway, in the parish of Ringwood, furnishes no ground whatever for charging the relief to that parish, if the accident happen in another.

---

2. Recovery of Relief by way of Loan.

August 14*th*, 1845.

Clerk of Witham Union—Inquired whether the board of guardians had the power to compel the overseers or an assistant overseer to take proceedings for the recovery of relief granted by way of loan.

Ans.—The 59th sec. Poor Law Amendment Act, enables the justices to proceed in the recovery of loans "upon the application of the overseers or guardians of the parish or union providing the relief." The terms would apparently render it competent either to the guardians of the union, or to the overseers of the particular parish charged with the relief given to the pauper, to make the necessary application for the recovery. At all events, the guardians are empowered to do so, and an application by any officer whom they may duly authorise for the purpose (see 7 and 8 Vic. c. 101, sections 68 and 69,) would be a good application. But the Commissioners do not perceive that the law has invested the guardians with any powers of compelling the overseers to act in the recovery; and if the guardians have no authority in this respect over the overseers, neither would they have over an assistant overseer appointed under the 59 Geo. 3, c. 12.

3. NON-RESIDENT RELIEF ORDER.

Nov. 28th, 1845.

Clerk of —— Union—Urging the Commissioners to make their general orders relating to non-settled and non-resident relief obligatory on all Unions, with a view to securing greater accuracy in the accounts and better supervision of the poor.

Ans.—The Commissioners cannot compel one board of guardians to become the agent or to employ the agency of another board of guardians, in administering non-resident relief to any pauper. The order of the Commissioners only declares that if a board of guardians of a Union undertakes to administer relief to a non-settled poor person resident therein, on behalf of another board of guardians, or authorises relief by any other board of guardians on their behalf, to a non-resident pauper, certain regulations which are laid down in that order shall be observed. The order, however, does not prevent the guardians from transmitting relief to a poor person who is non-resident, in cases where the same may be lawfully given through any private channel, or any means other than the officers of another Union.

4. RELIEF TO A PAUPER WHOSE WIFE IS POSSESSED OF PROPERTY.

Sept. 6th, 1845.

Clerk of the Dolgelly Union — A pauper named T. J. S., and his children, have become chargeable to the parish of Llanegryn in this union, and are likely to remain so: the pauper's wife is in the actual receipt of an income from lands and houses of about £80 a year clear, settled upon her (as is believed) beyond the control of her husband. The pauper and his wife have been separated about two years, and she refuses to contribute anything towards the support of her children; but she offers to take and maintain three of the children, which offer is refused on the part of the husband, because she is an habitual drunkard; and she recently so abused her eldest child that she was bound over to keep the peace. Inquired—1. Whether under the circumstances the board of guardians are empowered to proceed against the pauper's wife, under the Vagrant Act, or any other act, in order to compel her to contribute towards the support of her children. 2. Whether the board can legally compel the pauper to deliver up any of his children to his wife, or to any other person, there being no workhouse in the union in which they can be placed.

Ans.—1. The Commissioners consider that T. J. S.'s wife cannot be proceeded against under the Vagrant Act, or any other statute, for the omission or neglect to maintain her children. Such neglect on her part is not legally an offence, inasmuch as, her husband being alive, the legal obligation to maintain attaches to him. The case would, of course, be different as regards the question of liability, if the circumstances were such as to bring it within the 25th sec. of 7 and 8 Vic. c. 101. 2. The board of guardians have clearly no power of compelling T. J. S. to deliver up his children to his wife, or to any other person for the purpose of maintenance. The father of a child is entitled to the custody of it, though this right to the possession is subject to the control of the Court of Chancery; but the reported cases show that that court will not interfere where there is nothing to prove that the custody of the father is improper.

5. GENERAL ORDER RESPECTING NON-RESIDENT RELIEF.

August 14th, 1845.

Relieving Officer of Preston Union—Inquired whether, under the General Order relating to non-resident relief, the repayment of the relief advanced by other unions to the non-resident poor of this union, should be included in his account for the quarter in which the relief is given, or in the following quarter, when the repayment of such relief is actually made by him.

Ans.—Where the relief to a non-resident pauper is paid through the relieving officer of the board of guardians allowing such relief, the pauper's name will appear in the relief list kept by such relieving officer, as a matter of course; and such relief will be charged by the relieving officer to the parish to which the pauper may belong, in the same way as relief to a resident settled pauper would be. But where such relief is paid by cheque, or by other means, as prescribed by the Commissioners' order relating to non-resident relief, it is clear that the relieving officer of the union to which the paupers relieved may belong, has nothing whatever to do with the matter; and after the proper authority on the minutes the relief will be a credit to the treasurer, and a debit to the parish against which it is charged. In fact, you will only have to enter in your books the cases of those paupers belonging to other unions, but residing in your district, whose relief goes through your hands: this will not be the case with those belonging to your district, but residing in other unions, who are relieved in accordance with the terms of the order by the relieving officers of other unions, and whose relief is repaid through the treasurers of the respective unions. The relief granted to non-resident and non-settled paupers should be charged in the account of the quarter during which the payments for such relief is actually made. The true dates of the payments should always appear.

X.—REMOVAL.

1. RESOLUTIONS PASSED AT A MEETING OF THE BOARD OF GUARDIANS OF THE STRAND UNION, HELD ON 9TH DECEMBER, 1845.

"That heavy and oppressive expenses have been heretofore incurred by unions and parishes in the metropolis in respect of appeals against removals, founded on technical objections, and not on substantial merits—that this board, with a view to avoid such unnecessary outlay, and to the establishment of that friendly and rational intercourse between unions and parishes, by which their mutual interests may be secured, have resolved, that in future no appeal shall be commenced or opposition determined on, until the facts and circumstances of such appeal shall have been submitted to, and fully considered by this board, by whom it is further resolved that every equitable means shall be adopted to avoid litigation and the inevitable expenses consequent thereon.

"That this board, in the spirit of the foregoing resolution, desires it may be communicated to the unions and parishes in and near the metropolis, that in future every case in which the settlement may clearly appear to be in any parish in this union, this board will accept such case without imposing upon the parish to which the same is chargeable, the trouble and expense of removing the parties according to the formalities of law; and this board earnestly invites other unions and parishes to pursue the same amicable and beneficial course, whereby heavy burdens on the rates may be avoided, and a friendly feeling between unions and parishes cultivated and maintained."

2. REMOVAL.—JURISDICTION OF JUSTICES.
August 5th, 1845.

Clerk of Atcham Union—The Atcham Union, comprising forty-three parishes and townships, separately maintaining their own poor, is situated in the counties of Salop and Montgomery. Two of those townships only, viz., Bauseley and Criggion, are in the latter county: and the workhouse of the union is situate in the former. A pauper in the workhouse, chargeable to Bauseley, but having a legal settlement in a parish not within the union, is now ill; and it is doubtful whether he can, at present, be removed therefrom with safety. The petty sessions for the division of Montgomery, in which Bauseley is situate, is held at a greater distance from the workhouse than the place of the pauper's settlement. Inquired—1. Whether two justices for the division of the county of *Salop*, in which the workhouse is situate, can make an order for the removal of the pauper to the place of his settlement, and suspend the execution thereof, if found necessary. 2. Whether two justices for the county of *Montgomery* can make an order for such removal at the said workhouse. 3. Whether in case the pauper is unable to attend the petty sessions to be examined, can such examination be taken at the workhouse by a justice for the county Salop, and reported to the justices in petty sessions for Montgomery; and if so, whether the report must be made in person, or by writing.

Ans.—1. The justices of Salop, in which county the workhouse of the Atcham Union is situate, would have no power to make an order for the removal of the pauper to the place of his settlement, inasmuch as the township to which the pauper is chargeable, and which can alone make the necessary complaint, is not within the jurisdiction of the justices of Salop. 2. The Commissioners apprehend that the justices for the county of Montgomery are competent to make the order: to give them jurisdiction, it is necessary that the pauper should be inhabiting in, and chargeable to some parish or township in the county of Montgomery. It is stated that the relief given to the pauper is charged to Bauseley, which is in the county of Montgomery. Then, though the workhouse in which the pauper is at present maintained is actually situate in the county of Salop, still by virtue of sec. 56 of

7 and 8 Vic. c. 101, the pauper is constructively inhabiting in Bauseley. That section enacts that for "the purposes of relief, settlement, and removal of poor persons, &c., the workhouse of any union, &c., shall be considered as situated in the parish to which each poor person respectively to be relieved, removed, &c., is or has been chargeable." This constructive residence is, therefore, rendered sufficient to give the justices jurisdiction in making the order of removal. 3. Presuming the pauper to be unable from sickness to attend before the justices of Montgomery for this purpose, the Commissioners are not aware that the justices of Salop are empowered to take the examination, and report to the justices of the former jurisdiction. The provision contained in the 49 Geo. 3, c. 124, s. 4, only enables a magistrate of the district where an infirm or sick pauper may be, to take the examination of such pauper and report the same to two magistrates acting for the same district. It does not extend to enable justices acting for another jurisdiction to act upon such report. The Commissioners are not, however, prepared to say that the power might not be usefully extended to meet such a case as you have brought under their notice.

XI.—SMALL POX.—AS TO THE PROPRIETY OF SENDING A PERSON LABOURING UNDER SMALL POX INTO A WORKHOUSE.

Sept. 27th, 1845.

Clerk of —— Union—The child of a male vagrant who had been lodging for several nights at a vagrant house in the borough of L. was found to be labouring under small-pox of a malignant kind. This becoming known caused alarm, and both the parent and child were turned out, or threatened to be turned out of doors by the keeper of the house. The overseers, on finding the vagrant and his child in a sad state of destitution, and about to be, or, as has been reported, actually turned into the street, at once caused both father and child to be conveyed to the union workhouse. The master on their admission placed them in a ward within the walls of the workhouse, but somewhat detached from the main building. Notwithstanding this caution, several cases of small-pox occurred in the workhouse in consequence of the introduction of the child in question, and in two instances it proved fatal. The guardians generally are of opinion that the child ought not to have been sent into the workhouse. At the same time they are not aware of any statute or of any order of the Commissioners prohibiting the admission of paupers labouring under contagious diseases into the workhouse. Inquired whether the overseers of L. were justified in conveying the child under the circumstances to the workhouse, and if not, what course they should have taken in reference to the case.

Ans.—The Commissioners cannot but lament the introduction of this case of small-pox into the workhouse of a union, especially as the most serious consequences appear to have resulted from it. But they do not see that the overseers of L. necessarily adopted an improper course in sending the paupers to the workhouse in the circumstances in which they were placed. The case being one of sudden and urgent necessity, the overseers were bound to relieve the paupers, who manifestly could not be left in a state of destitution where they were: the workhouse being the lodging which the law most especially puts at the disposal of the overseers, it appears to the Commissioners that the overseers acted rightly in sending the paupers there, if, as would seem likely, it was very difficult if not quite impracticable, to obtain lodging for them elsewhere. The man and his child could not be left to die in the street, merely because the child was suffering from small-pox. If the overseers had altogether neglected the case they would have acted both inhumanly and illegally, and would have incurred very serious responsibility by so gross a dereliction of their duty; and the Commissioners, as at present informed, do not see what other course the overseers could adopt in dealing with the case than the one which they actually pursued. If there was any small-pox hospital to which the child might have been sent, that would certainly have been preferable, but the Commissioners presume that there was no such institution within reach. The occurrence of this case shews two things. 1st. The extreme importance of promoting vaccination by all means in the power of the guardians. 2ndly. That it is of the utmost consequence that provision should be made at the workhouse by separate infectious wards for the reception of cases of this description without endangering the health of all in the house.

XII.—VAGRANTS.

1. REFUSING TO LEAVE THE WORKHOUSE.

September 8th, 1845.

Clerk of Tonbridge Union—Stated that tramps

and Irish vagrants, usually relieved in the workhouse, are in the constant practice of refusing to leave the house when required to do so, and requested the Commissioners' directions as to how the guardians should act in regard to such cases.

Ans.—To meet cases of this class of paupers, the guardians should be enabled to rely on their arrangements for setting voluntary paupers to work, as a protection against the burden of maintaining them permanently. But when the guardians are satisfied that a claim to relief is wholly unfounded, and that the applicant has the means of self-support, it is open to them to refuse relief, or the continuance of relief, and to remove the applicant from the workhouse, for which purpose, if resistance is offered, they will be justified in the use of the necessary force. Probably, however, it will rarely be the case that vagrants and tramps have the present means of supporting themselves; and when they have not, it will be necessary to set them to labour. The Commissioners cannot, in general, recommend that recourse be had to ejecting the person from the house. If a definite offer of work be made at wages sufficient to maintain a pauper, and that is refused, such a person is of course punishable as a vagrant.

---

2. SETTING VAGRANTS TO WORK IN WORKHOUSE.

Clerk of the Bicester Union—1. The 5th and 6th Vic. c. 57, sec. 5, enacts that "it shall be lawful for the guardians, &c., to prescribe a task of work to be done by any person relieved in any workhouse, in return for the food and lodging afforded to such person." Inquired whether in case of any wayfaring paupers accepting "*lodging*" but refusing "*food,*" they can be legally required to perform a reasonable task of work. 2. The some section provides that "it shall not be lawful to detain any person against his will, for the performance of such work for any time exceeding four hours from the hour of breakfast in the morning succeeding the admission of such person into the workhouse; and if any such person refuse or neglect to perform such task of work, &c., he shall be deemed an *idle and disorderly person.*" Inquired whether any such wayfaring pauper can be legally set to work at any other time than the four hours after breakfast in the morning succeeding his admission into the workhouse.

Ans.—1. The phrase, "in return for the food and lodging afforded to such person," appears to the Commissioners to be a general expression of the ground on which the guardians are empowered to prescribe the taskwork for the inmates of the workhouse, and not a specific enumeration of the conditions on which alone such work can be required to be performed in each individual case. The Commissioners conceive, therefore, that *any person relieved in the workhouse,* refusing to perform the task of work duly required of him under the provisions of the sec. in question, would be punishable for such refusal under the Vagrant Act. 2. There is nothing in the sec. as it seems to the Commissioners, which would prevent any pauper relieved in the workhouse from being *set to work,* under the guardians' regulations, at night or in the morning before breakfast; although he could not be *detained in the workhouse,* for the performance of such work, for more than four hours after the breakfast hour.

XIII.—WORKHOUSE—REFUSAL OF A WIFE TO QUIT.

Oct. 16th, 1845.

Assistant Overseer, Bishop Auckland — A woman, with her two children, having been deserted by her husband, became chargeable to the parish of Bishop Auckland, and has been, for some time, an inmate of the union workhouse. The husband has now returned, and offers to take his wife and children out of the workhouse and to provide for them. The wife, however, obstinately refuses to leave the workhouse. Inquired by what means the woman could be compelled to do so.

Ans.—Unless there is an apparent danger that the wife and children to whom you refer will suffer immediately from destitution or violence, nothing will justify the union or parish officers in giving harbour to them, when the husband and father requires that they should be given up to him. If the man is able to support his wife and children, and is willing to receive them, they should be delivered into his hands. He may be required to come to the workhouse to receive them, and the officer, under the direction of the guardians, may then compel them to quit the workhouse. This course should be pursued, even if the man is likely to require relief; and the application for such relief should then be received as coming from the man himself. If, however, the woman alleges that she entertains the fear of personal violence from her husband, she should be taken before justices to see whether the husband should not be bound over to keep the peace.

LONDON:
Printed by Order of the Poor Law Commissioners, by BLACKBURN and PARDON, 6, Hatton Garden, and Published by CHARLES KNIGHT and Co., 22, Ludgate Street, Publishers to the Poor Law Commissioners.

AN

OFFICIAL CIRCULAR

OF PUBLIC DOCUMENTS AND INFORMATION:

DIRECTED BY THE POOR LAW COMMISSIONERS TO BE PRINTED, CHIEFLY FOR THE USE OF THE MEMBERS AND PERMANENT OFFICERS OF BOARDS OF GUARDIANS, UNDER THE POOR LAW AMENDMENT ACT.

No. 56. CIRCULAR ISSUED FEBRUARY 2, 1846.

The Poor Law Commissioners directed that the following documents be printed and circulated for the information of Guardians and Officers of the several Unions, viz.: Page

(Signed) By Order of the Board,
EDWIN CHADWICK, *Secretary*.

I.—ACCOUNTS.

PAYMENTS BY WAY OF DEPOSITS TO HOSPITALS.

Dec. 18th, 1845.

District Auditors—The Commissioners observing that in the accounts of a union there was comprised under the head,—"money expended for all other purposes," an item charged as "caution money to ——— Hospital," inquired of the clerk to the guardians the meaning of the item. The clerk replied that such sum was a deposit for paupers admitted into the hospital, to indemnify the institution in case of death or other contingency happening to the paupers sent there, and that in general the principal part of the deposits is returned on the discharge of the patients therefrom.

The Commissioners having reason to believe that such payments are made to a large extent through the whole of the county of ———, by parishes, as well as by boards of guardians, addressed a circular to the district auditors calling their attention to the subject, and stating, that, considered as a subscription to an hospital, the payment in question may be legal, if made by the board of guardians, but it is clearly illegal if made by the overseers of parishes in unions.

II.—CONTRACT.

FOR SUPPLY OF GOODS TO WORKHOUSE—LIMITATION OF.

October 4th, 1845.

Clerk of West Ashford Union—A contractor for supplying flour to the paupers having agreed with the guardians "*from the 25th day of March last, to the 25th day of September instant,*" contends that his contract ceases on the evening of the 24th September, but the guardians conceive that he is bound to supply them up to the evening of the 25th. Inquired Commissioners' opinion thereon.

Ans.—Unless there is some evidence to show that the intention of the parties was different, it would appear that both the 25th of March, and the 25th of September, are by the words of the contract excluded. "From the 25th day" excludes the 25th day; Clayton's case, 5 Rep. 1. For the same reason ,though there is no express authority for the conclusion, "to the 25th day" would exclude that day; "from," and "to," evidently denoting only the intervals lying between objects named as terms, and having no operation in common or legal language, of including these objects.

III.—COUNTY AND POLICE RATES.

WHETHER RECEIPTS FOR ARE EXEMPT FROM STAMP DUTY.

6th January, 1846.

Clerk of Cleobury Mortimer Union—Inquired whether the receipt of the county treasurer for the amounts of police and county rates paid to him should be given on a stamp; and referred the Commissioners to the latter part of the first section of the 7 & 8 Vic. c. 33, and to the General Stamp Act.

Ans.—The Commissioners are disposed to think that the particular exemption to the duties charged in the schedule 55 Geo. 3, c. 184, referred to by county treasurer, applies to such a case as the present, *i. e.*, that a check drawn on the union treasurer and transmitted to the county treasurer is a security for money within the terms of the exemption, and that a letter acknowledging the safe arrival of such check satisfies the provision in the 7th and 8th Vict. c. 33, which requires the county treasurer to give a receipt for monies tendered by or on behalf of the guardians in respect of county rate.

IV.—DIETARY.

ALLOWANCE OF PORTER TO SICK, INFIRM, AND LABOURING IN-DOOR PAUPERS.

January 9, 1846.

Clerk of Poplar Union—The medical officer recommended that an allowance of porter be made to others than sick paupers in the workhouse, their names being stated in a book kept for that purpose. Many of such other persons are nurses, others employed as carpenters, laundresses, bed-room cleaners, &c., and the rest infirm persons, requiring it on account of their health. The allowance to nurses and work-people to be given to them only when acting in their several capacities, and discontinued when others are employed in their stead. The allowance is thus a daily one, varying according to circumstances.

Ans.—The Commissioners are of opinion that the case does not come within the proviso to the 17th art. of the workhouse rules. If the medical officer thinks that on account of the infirm health of any individual pauper, without reference to his wish, an allowance of porter is necessary for him, there should be a recommendation of the medical officer for the allowance of it in the case of such individual. With regard to paupers employed as nurses, carpenters, laundresses, or in other household work, there is a special provision in the Workhouse Rules, Art. 21, as the guardians are aware, which authorises the allowance to them of extra food, but it is expressly directed, that they shall not be allowed fermented or spirituous liquors. But if any person so employed is so far infirm, or in such a state of health, that the work in which he is employed, when considered with his infirmity or state of health, appears to the medical officer to render an allowance of fermented liquors necessary, then the medical officer can, without doubt, recommend such an allowance for that person. Such an allowance would be bona fide made on the ground of the person's health, although when he was not so employed it might be unnecessary. But it is evident that every order of the medical officer made on these principles, must be an order affecting the individual, and not an order applicable to a class of persons employed in a particular kind of work.

V. LUNATICS.

WHETHER MEDICAL OFFICER'S PARTNER CAN GIVE CERTIFICATE.

31st Jan. 1846.

Mr. R. Smith, Medical Officer, Chertsey Union—Inquired whether his partner, who is not a medical officer of the Chertsey union, can give a certificate, under section 48 of the 8 and 9 Vic.

c. 126, relative to the state of mind of a lunatic, to enable a justice to make an order for such lunatic's admission into an asylum.

Ans.—Although a medical officer is prohibited by the provisions of section 48 of the 8 and 9 Vic. c. 126, from signing the certificate required before an order is made by a justice for the admission of a lunatic pauper into a lunatic asylum, the Commissioners are of opinion that this prohibition does not extend to the partner of a medical officer; and that such partner is, therefore, not legally disqualified to give a certificate in the case adverted to.

VI.—MEDICAL ORDER.

FEES UNDER ART. 10.—FRACTURE OF THE THUMB.

January 7th, 1846.

Medical Officer of —— *Union*—Inquired whether he is entitled to an extra fee for reducing a compound fracture and dislocation of the thumb, which he attended under an order from the relieving officer. The man did not live in his district, but having met with the accident near his house, had applied to him. The injury, though to a small joint, was a dangerous one, since lock-jaw often succeeds lacerated wounds of the thumb; and the joint being torn open and the bones protruding, it was important to reduce the parts without delay.

Ans.—As a fracture of the thumb cannot be considered a fracture of the arm, you are not legally entitled to payment of an extra fee for your treatment of the case. If, however, in any special case not coming within Art. 10 of the General Medical Order, the guardians should be of opinion that the medical officer is fairly entitled to some extra remuneration, the Commissioners would consider any proposition which the guardians might make to them with that view.

VII.—OVERSEERS.

1. PROCEEDINGS AGAINST ASSISTANT OVERSEERS FOR EMBEZZLEMENT.

January 7th, 1846.

Clerk of Caxton and Arrington Union—E. N., an assistant overseer, who was appointed by the parishioners in vestry, and his appointment approved by the justices, has absconded with £80 of the parish money. Inquired, 1. Whether the parish officers can offer a reward for his apprehension; 2. Whether they can indict him for embezzlement, it being considered useless to proceed against him for penalties as he has no property to distrain upon, and gave no security upon entering on his office; and, 3. Whether the overseers are personally responsible for the loss which the parishioners have incurred by his misconduct.

Ans.—The Commissioners are disposed to consider that the guardians might, if the circumstances render it expedient, offer a reward for the capture of E. N., and pay it out of the funds in their hands, under the 59th section of the 7 and 8 Vic. c. 101, as part of the reasonable costs of apprehending a person charged with embezzling, &c., property applicable to the relief of the poor. If apprehended, he may be proceeded against under the 97th sect. of the 4 and 5 Wm. 4, c. 76. It is, however, a question for the consideration of the legal advisers of the guardians whether he can be indicted for the felonious embezzlement under the 7 and 8 Geo. 4, c. 29. It has not yet been expressly decided that an assistant overseer is a clerk or servant of the overseers. He is not appointed by them, but by the justices on the nomination of the vestry: but it does not appear to be an objection that a person is appointed by other persons than those he serves. (R. *v.* Jenson Moo. C. C. R., 434: Callahan's case, 8 C. and P. 154.) He is, in some respects, an officer acting under a statutory authority: but so was the collector in Callahan's case, where this objection was held to be of no force. Any loss that may be sustained through E. N.'s default will fall upon the parish generally, who omitted to protect themselves by requiring security, and not upon the overseers personally, unless the latter are culpably implicated.

2. ELIGIBILITY OF FEMALES TO SERVE THE OFFICE OF OVERSEER.

January 15th, 1846.

Overseer of Kingswear, Totnes Union—Inquired whether females being rate-payers of the parish, in which the number of males suitable for the office is very limited, can be compelled to serve the office of overseer, or to procure substitutes.

Ans.—It has been decided that there is

nothing in the nature of the office of overseer which renders a female incompetent to it, if she be a substantial householder in the parish (Rex *v.* Stubbs, 2 Term Rep. 395). It seems, however, manifestly undesirable that a woman should be appointed to that office, where there are persons of the opposite sex in the parish, legally competent to fill the office.

VIII.—PAUPERS.

RIGHT TO PROPERTY OF DECEASED PAUPERS.

Aug. 4th, 1845.

Vice-Chairman of ——— *Union*— Inquired, whether the father of a woman, who had been recently buried at the expense of the parish to which she had been chargeable, is entitled to her clothes.

Ans.—Unless relief was given to the young woman you allude to expressly as a loan, the guardians cannot retain the property she has left in their possession, for the purpose of repaying themselves such relief. They may, however, retain so much thereof as may be necessary to provide for the charges of her funeral. What should be done with any residue that might remain after defraying those charges, would depend upon the circumstances of the case: the father would not necessarily be entitled to receive it; at the same time the Commissioners see nothing in your letter to show that it would be improper for the guardians to give it to him.

IX.—POOR'S RATE.

1.—EXCUSED RATES AFTERWARDS COLLECTED AND MISAPPLIED BY COLLECTOR.

January 31st, 1846.

————Certain persons are legally excused from the payment of a poor's-rate; the rate is balanced and closed, the sums so excused being carried to account. The collector, who is appointed by the board of guardians, afterwards demands and obtains payment of the rate from the persons excused, and applies the money so obtained to his own use. Inquired, 1. Whether the overseers or the guardians would be justified in prosecuting the collector, on behalf of the poor persons whom he has defrauded, and paying the expences out of the poor's-rate. 2. Whether the monies so obtained should be regarded as belonging to the parish or union, notwithstanding the excusal, so that proceedings may be taken against the collector under the 97th sec. of the Poor Law Amendment Act, on the ground of misapplication.

Ans.—The Commissioners consider it useless to advert to the remedy by action, which would undoubtedly be open to the poor people referred to. The proper course appears to the Commissioners to be to indict the offender for extortion. As the offence is committed *colore officii,* and is an abuse of his office, (which is in the administration of the Poor Laws,) it would be one for which the guardians might provide the expences out of the funds in their hands. The definition of extortion is perfectly apt, and the cases are of very wide application. (See Hawk. P. c. c. 68; Co. Lit. 368; 10 Rep. 102; 1 Sid. 307; Lord Raym. 159; 4 Mood. 101, and many others.)

IX. (a)—POOR RATES—MEDICAL RELIEF—LOCAL TAXATION.

1. THE AMOUNT of Money levied for POOR RATES, in *England* and *Wales,* (exclusive of the Counties of *Kent, Middlesex,* and *Surrey,*) during each of the Years ended Lady-day 1826 and 1841; distinguishing the Amount levied on Landed Property, Dwelling-houses, and all other Property.

Years ended Lady-day.	On Landed Property.	Proportion per cent. to Total.	Dwelling-houses.	Proportion per Cent. to Total.	All other Property.	Proportion per Cent. to Total.	Total Amount of Money Levied.
	£.		£.		£.		£.
1826	4,404,529	77	1,057,215	18	278, 692	5	5,740,436
1841	3,113,180	60	1,451,316	28	589, 856	12	5,154,352
AGGREGATE TOTALS of Kent, Middlesex, and Surrey, not included in the above Totals:							
1826	390,953	32	757,013	62	77,754	6	1,225,720
1841	203,413	17	923,905	77	70,158	6	1,197,476

2. THE AMOUNT of Money Expended for MEDICAL RELIEF in Unions and single Parishes, under the Regulations of the Poor Law Commissioners; together with the Total Cost of RELIEF to the Poor during the Years ended Lady-day 1843, 1844, & 1845.

NAMES of COUNTIES.	Number of Unions in each County in 1845.	YEARS ENDED LADY-DAY: 1843. Amount expended for Medical Relief.	1843. Total Cost of Relief to the Poor, including Medical Relief.	1844. Amount expended for Medical Relief.	1844. Total Cost of Relief to the Poor, including Medical Relief.	1845. Amount expended for Medical Relief.	1845. Total Cost of Relief to the Poor, including Medical Relief.
ENGLAND:		£.	£.	£.	£.	£.	£.
Bedford	6	1,862	43,265	1,709	40,736	1,719	42,934
Berks	12	[illegible]	77,357	3,719	74,224	3,492	78,179
Buckingham	7	2,574	77,627	2,742	[illegible]	[illegible]	79,983
Cambridge	9	2,441	71,900	2,747	70,319	2,959	74,537
Chester	9	2,652	87,130	2,299	78,338	2,676	73,948
Cornwall	13	2,259	80,333	2,356	74,962	2,416	77,945
Cumberland	9	976	37,560	1,071	35,513	1,133	36,921
Derby	8	1,172	56,973	1,315	52,259	1,326	51,281
Devon	17	5,219	170,140	5,469	156,438	5,879	159,936
Dorset	12	3,006	83,657	3,232	79,051	3,328	82,721
Durham	14	1,529	79,143	1,848	80,564	1,460	72,210
Essex	17	8,022	164,865	7,892	159,817	7,695	168,251
Gloucester	16	3,716	117,675	3,817	112,490	3,889	118,145
Hereford	8	2,011	43,868	2,019	42,755	2,242	45,198
Hertford	13	3,331	63,673	3,623	60,505	3,878	63,338
Huntingdon	3	1,091	25,816	1,118	24,135	1,155	1,016
Kent	27	6,889	195,787	7,591	189,073	7,427	190,746
Lancaster	26	7,743	354,595	6,519	323,369	7,339	289,555
Leicester	11	2,395	83,839	2,605	77,537	2,502	76,308
Lincoln	14	3,373	110,708	3,952	112,930	4,089	115,375
Middlesex	19	6,960	306,037	7,682	284,026	8,287	291,669
Monmouth	5	1,043	28,432	1,091	28,062	1,259	27,479
Norfolk	21	6,159	165,903	5,520	164,416	5,606	174,430
Northampton	12	3,077	90,724	3,061	88,081	2,846	91,006
Northumberland	12	1,390	69,829	1,501	71,383	1,694	76,377
Nottingham	9	2,131	32,717	2,638	69,404	2,424	60,655
Oxford	8	2,761	73,043	2,891	71,772	2,401	76,454
Rutland	2	300	7,495	317	7,741	338	7,834
Salop	13	2,408	52,653	2,493	56,740	2,720	54,594
Somerset	17	6,028	166,351	6,512	158,783	6,427	164,732
Southampton	23	6,065	129,049	5,322	124,274	5,597	114,492
Stafford	16	3,087	118,382	3,646	112,274	3,565	108,756
Suffolk	17	5,453	139,919	5,132	135,820	5,573	145,809
Surrey	18	5,776	188,725	6,274	178,298	6,765	179,538
Sussex	20	4,889	120,472	5,268	111,393	5,570	114,995
Warwick	11	2,114	66,420	2,332	62,297	2,331	67,947
Westmorland	3	514	19,309	589	18,702	643	18,176
Wilts	17	4,510	137,847	4,713	131,316	4,825	134,545
Worcester	13	3,190	68,424	3,504	66,522	3,311	69,867
York, East Riding	9	1,443	57,050	1,541	56,784	1,606	57,810
,, North Riding	14	1,529	58,646	1,703	57,759	1,639	58,590
,, West Riding	19	3,679	226,761	3,949	208,727	*4,408	*202,027
TOTAL of England	549	140,293	4,350,099	145,322	4,185,319	149,371	4,196,309
WALES:							
Anglesey	1	267	17,781	261	17,452	285	18,778
Brecon	4	565	18,279	646	18,974	717	19,636
Cardigan	5	397	18,084	407	17,099	404	17,520
Carmarthen	5	820	33,547	830	31,446	1,067	31,789
Carnarvon	4	703	22,717	676	22,897	781	23,754
Denbigh	3	603	30,625	632	29,754	600	30,947
Flint	2	467	19,600	486	19,550	542	19,821
Glamorgan	5	913	42,115	749	41,726	1,015	43,807
Merioneth	4	474	14,865	473	14,850	491	15,035
Montgomery	3	810	24,286	751	23,116	1,141	22,262
Pembroke	3	713	23,732	752	22,638	753	23,847
Radnor	3	238	10,626	244	10,187	242	10,770
TOTAL of Wales	42	6,970	276,257	6,907	269,678	8,038	277,966
TOTAL of England & Wales	591	147,263	4,626,356	152,229	4,455,017	157,409	4,474,275

* In this year the township of Leeds was included with the Unions, but not included in the former years. The amount of Medical Relief in 1845 being 558*l*., and the Relief to the Poor, 20,799*l*.

3. THE POPULATION, the Amount Levied for POOR RATES, &c., and the Ratio which the Amount Levied for Poor Rates, &c. bore to the Population, during each of the Years ended Lady-day 1813, 1824, 1834, and 1844.

COUNTIES.	Population, 1811.	Total Money Levied for Poor Rate, County Rate, &c., Year ended Lady-day 1813.	Rate per Head on the Population.	Population, 1821.	Total Money Levied for Poor Rate, County Rate, &c., Year ended Lady-day 1824.	Rate per Head on the Population.	Population, 1831.	Total Money Levied for Poor Rate, County Rate, &c., Year ended Lady-day 1834.	Rate per Head on the Population.	Population, 1841.	Total Money Levied for Poor Rate, County Rate, &c., Year ended Lady-day 1844.	Rate per Head on the Population.
ENGLAND.		£.	s. d.		£.	s. d.		£.	s. d.		£.	s. d.
Bedford	70,213	80,788	23 —	83,716	74,787	17 10	95,483	92,046	19 3	107,936	53,907	10 —
Berks	118,277	188,418	31 10	131,977	109,137	16 6	145,389	127,229	17 6	161,147	98,331	12 2
Buckingham	117,650	162,376	27 7	134,068	124,065	18 6	146,529	153,040	20 11	155,983	94,260	12 1
Cambridge	101,109	106,661	21 1	121,909	99,776	16 4	143,955	120,763	16 9	164,459	93,877	11 5
Chester	227,031	159,510	14 1	270,098	116,488	8 8	334,391	138,229	8 3	395,660	113,880	5 9
Cornwall	216,667	133,889	12 4	257,447	111,087	8 8	300,938	118,322	7 10	341,279	95,710	5 7
Cumberland	133,744	67,390	10 1	156,124	54,200	6 11	169,681	57,920	6 11	178,038	44,926	5 1
Derby	185,487	126,892	13 8	213,333	91,570	8 7	237,170	107,837	9 1	272,217	83,229	6 1
Devon	383,308	305,188	15 11	439,040	232,935	10 7	494,478	250,270	10 1	533,460	218,532	8 2
Dorset	124,693	130,046	20 0	144,499	92,598	12 10	159,252	102,616	12 11	175,043	94,011	10 9
Durham	177,625	104,475	11 9	207,673	93,533	9 —	253,910	107,648	8 6	324,284	111,026	6 10
Essex	252,473	367,237	29 1	289,424	286,868	19 10	317 507	291,010	18 4	344,979	212,776	12 4
Gloucester	285,514	212,954	14 11	335,843	167,485	10 —	387,019	205,025	10 7	431,383	194,249	9 —
Hereford	94,073	103,567	22 —	103,243	62,496	12 1	111,211	67,267	12 1	113,878	55,442	9 9
Hertford	111,654	113,622	20 4	129,714	95,488	14 9	143,341	108,190	15 1	157,207	86,281	11 —
Huntingdon	42,208	48,534	23 —	48,771	43,825	18 —	53,192	45,500	17 1	58,549	36,076	12 4
Kent	373,095	402,229	21 7	426,016	377,699	17 9	479,155	418,786	17 6	548,337	258,166	9 5
Lancaster	828,309	460,420	11 1	1,052,859	327,724	6 2	1,336,854	428,770	6 5	1,667,054	530,490	6 4
Leicester	150,419	154,410	20 6	174.571	103,368	11 10	197,003	133,812	13 7	215.867	103,718	9 7
Lincoln	237,891	227,681	19 2	283,058	206,411	14 7	317,465	228,238	14 5	362,602	151,999	8 5
Middlesex	953,276	627,853	13 2	1,144,531	572,955	10 —	1,358,330	939,890	13 10	1,576.636	758,160	9 7
Monmouth	62,127	37,939	12 4	71,833	28,243	7 10	98,130	37,707	7 8	134,855	44,598	6 8
Norfolk	291,999	361,633	24 9	344.368	305,254	17 9	390,054	355,685	18 3	412,664	228,377	11 1
Northampton	141,353	173,317	24 6	162,483	141,327	17 5	179,336	166,713	18 7	199,228	113,725	11 5
Northumberland	172,161	99,519	11 7	198,965	80,495	8 1	222,912	95,665	8 7	250,278	84,402	6 9
Nottingham	162,900	127,562	15 8	186,873	82,542	8 10	225,327	101,236	9 —	249,910	87,770	7 —
Oxford	119,191	170,614	28 8	136,971	122,579	17 10	152,156	150,335	19 9	161,643	91,065	11 3
Rutland	16,380	18,241	22 3	18,487	12,196	13 2	19,385	13,394	13 10	21,302	9,763	9 2
Salop	194,298	137,895	14 2	206,153	88,869	8 7	222,938	105,863	9 6	239,048	95,684	8 —
Somerset	303,180	245,969	16 3	355,314	171,447	9 8	404,200	221,841	11 —	435,982	203,622	9 4
Southampton	245,080	260,335	21 3	283,298	210,463	14 10	314,280	243,526	15 6	355,004	179,195	10 1
Stafford	295,153	169,810	11 6	341,040	139,523	8 2	410,512	171,330	8 4	510,504	172,965	6 9
Suffolk	234,211	279,925	23 11	270,542	279,808	20 8	296,317	290,131	19 7	315,073	173,829	11 —
Surrey	323,851	280,327	17 4	398,658	263,481	13 3	486,334	357,299	14 8	582,678	299,718	10 3
Sussex	190,083	350,610	36 11	233,019	266,748	22 11	272,340	299,621	22 —	299,753	174,984	11 8
Warwick	228,735	220,575	19 3	274,392	142,744	10 5	336,610	185,715	11 —	401,715	170,412	8 6
Westmorland	45,922	28,946	12 7	51,359	26,080	10 2	55,041	29,291	10 8	5[illegible],454	21,538	7 8
Wilts	193,828	272,493	28 1	222,157	174,114	15 8	240,156	210,769	17 7	258,733	167,249	12 11
Worcester	160,546	124,956	15 7	184,424	83,352	9 —	211,365	107,506	10 2	233,336	101,311	8 8
York, East Riding	167,353	130,363	15 7	190,449	107,613	11 4	204,253	124,112	12 2	233,257	94,861	8 2
,, North Riding	152,445	113,834	14 11	183,381	87,757	9 7	190,756	103,707	10 10	204,122	74,640	7 4
,, West Riding	653,315	463,566	14 2	799,357	289,595	7 3	976,350	359,329	7 4	1,154,101	405,382	7 —
Total of England	9,538,827	8,342,569	17 6	11,261,437	6,548,725	11 8	13,091,005	7,973,183	12 2	14,995,138	6,479,136	8 8
WALES.												
Anglesey	37,045	12,523	6 9	45,063	15,379	14 7	48,325	20,332	8 5	50,891	21,476	8 5
Brecon	37,735	20,182	10 8	43,613	19,902	18 6	47,763	23,721	9 11	55,603	24,887	8 11
Cardigan	50,260	18,154	7 3	57,784	17,234	12 4	64,780	22,686	7 —	68,766	21,947	6 5
Carmarthen	77,217	34,195	8 10	90,239	32,234	14 10	100,740	43,994	8 9	106,326	43.230	8 2
Carnarvon	49,336	16,308	6 7	57,958	18,437	12 11	66,448	25,555	7 8	81,093	29,812	7 4
Denbigh	64,240	40,000	12 5	76,511	36,062	19 7	83,629	41,532	9 11	88,866	41,827	9 5
Flint	46,518	26,578	11 5	53,784	20,909	17 2	60,012	26,964	9 —	66,919	26,123	7 10
Glamorgan	85,067	43,258	10 2	101,737	38,968	16 2	126,612	51,958	8 2	171,188	60,057	7 —
Merioneth	30,924	14,536	9 5	34,382	14,895	18 4	35,315	18,040	10 3	39,332	17,284	8 9
Montgomery	51,931	36,443	14 —	59,899	32,471	23 —	66,482	42,606	12 10	69,219	39,756	11 6
Pembroke	60,615	26,784	8 10	74,009	24,453	14 2	81,425	31,281	7 8	88,044	28,636	6 6
Radnor	20,900	15,311	14 8	22,459	13,961	24 9	24,651	16,227	13 2	25,356	13,034	10 3
Total of Wales	611,788	304 272	9 11	717,438	284,905	16 8	806,182	364,896	9 1	911,603	368,069	8 1
Totals of England and Wales	10,150,615	8,646,841	17 —	11,978,875	6,833,630	11 5	13,897,187	8,338,079	12 0	15,906,741	6,847,205	8 6

4.—AMOUNT of MONEY levied for POOR RATES in *England* and *Wales*, for each of the Years ended Lady-day, 1826, 1833, and 1841, distinguishing the Amount levied on Landed Property, Dwelling-houses, and "all other kinds of Property."

AMOUNT OF MONEY LEVIED BY ASSESSMENT.

Years ended Lady-day.	On Landed Property.	Proportion per Cent.	Dwelling-houses	Proportion per cent.	All other Property.	Proportion per Cent.	TOTAL Amount levied.
	£.		£.		£.		£.
* 1826	4,795,482	69	1,814,228	26	356,447	5	6,966,157
† 1833	5,434,890	63	2,635,258	31	536,353	6	8,606,501
‡ 1841	3,316,593	52	2,375,221	37	660,014	11	6,351,828
Average	4,515,655	62	2,273,902	31	517,605	7	7,308,162

* From Parliamentary Paper, No. 120, Session 1827.
† From Parliamentary Paper, No. 335, Session 1834.
‡ Ascertained from Return of Real Property, Parliamentary Paper, No. 235, Session 1842.

5.—ANNUAL VALUE of REAL PROPERTY Assessed to the Poor Rate in *England* and *Wales*, in the Year ended Lady-day 1841, distinguishing Landed Property, Dwelling-houses, and all other kinds of Property.

Landed Property.	Proportion per cent.	Dwelling-houses.	Proportion per cent.	All other Property.	Proportion per cent.	TOTAL Annual Value.
£.		£.		£.		
*32,655,137	52	23,386,401	37	6,498,492	11	62,540,030

* From Return of Real Property, Parliamentary Paper, No. 235, Session 1842.

6.—A STATEMENT of the TOTAL AMOUNT of LOCAL TAXATION in *Great Britain* and *Ireland*, so far as it can be ascertained from Documents in the Office of the Poor Law Commissioners,—the latest available information being taken in each case.

ENGLAND AND WALES.

	£	£
RATES:—		
Poor Rate, year ending 25th March, 1844:		
Expenditure for the Poor	4,976,093	
Expenditure for miscellaneous purposes	567,567	
	5,543,660	
Paid for County, Police, and Borough Rate	1,356,457	
		6,900,117
Workhouse Building Rate; Survey and Valuation Rate	not levied separately, their purposes being provided for out of the Poor Rate	
Gaol Fees Rate		unknown.
Constables' Rate		unknown.
Highway Rates, 1839		1,169,891
Lighting and Watching Rate		unknown.
Militia Rate	not levied now, the Militia being disembodied	
Church Rates	year ending Easter 1839	506,812

			£	£
	Brought forward . . .		8,576,820	
Sewers Rates .	estimated for the Metropolis, at per annum . . .		75,000	
Drainage and Inclosure Rates			unknown.	
* County and Police Rates:		£		
Year ending Michaelmas 1844		963,223	*See* above, Poor Rate.	
Borough Rates, . .	year ending 31st August 1843 .	246,743	*See* above, Poor Rates.	
Shire Hall Rate County Lunatic Asylum Rate County Burial Rate	probably not levied separately; but their purposes provided for out of the County Rates.			
Hundred Rate . .	only levied when occasion arises, to compensate for damage done in riots.			
				8,651,820
TOLLS, DUES and FEES:				
† Borough Tolls and Dues .	year ending 31st August 1843 . .		172,911	
City of London, 1841 .	. . . .		188,521	
‡ Turnpike Tolls . . .	year ending 31st December 1843 . .		1,348,084	
§ Light Dues . . .	year 1843		243,023	
‖ Port Dues . . .	annual income of all the ports in England .		525,000	
Fees in administration of Justice	to Justices' clerks, annual average 1830 to 1834		57,668	
	to other officers		unknown.	
				2,535,207
				£11,187,027

* The amount of the County and County Police Rates are taken from a Return to the House of Commons in 1845; Parliamentary Paper, 331. The amount of the Borough Rates (which seem to include all the rates raised in Boroughs), is taken from an Abstract printed by the House of Commons in 1844; Parliamentary Paper, 593. It is impossible to reconcile these amounts with the Poor Rate Returns; from which it appears, that in the year ending 25th March 1844, the sum of £1,356,457 was paid out of the Poor Rate towards the several County and Borough Rates. Yet these Rates are not derived entirely from the Poor Rate.

† From Abstract printed by House of Commons in 1844; Parliamentary Paper, 593.

‡ From Abstract printed by House of Commons in 1845; Parliamentary Paper, 648.

§ From Report of Select Committee on Lighthouses; House of Commons, 1845; Parliamentary Paper, 607, page 22.

‖ From First Report of Tidal Harbours Commissioners, 1845; Appendix, page 195. The amount is an approximate one.

SCOTLAND.

		£	£
RATES:			
* Poor Rate, 1841 . .	Legal Assessment	129,335	
	Voluntary Assessment	23,564	
	Kirk Collections	37,466	
	Other Receipts . . .	28,116	
			218,481
Statute Labour Rate			unknown.
Church and Manse Rate			unknown.
School Rate			unknown.
Lighting and Watching Rates			unknown.
Militia Rate			unknown.
Bridge-money Rate			unknown.
Prisons Rate:			
The Assessments on the several counties, for building Prisons under the General Board of Directors, in the year 1842, is stated by them (Fourth Rep. App. No. 15) to have been			47,290

			£	£
		Brought forward	265,771	
It is stated, in the Tenth Annual Report of the Inspector of Prisons for Scotland, that the cost of the Prisons in Scotland in the year 1843-44 (exclusive of that of building new Prisons), after deducting the money received for prisoners' work, was somewhat more than			36,000	
Rogue-money Rate			unknown.	
Rural Police Rate			unknown.	
Burgh Cess	1829		8,777	
Borough Police Rate			unknown.	
				310,548
DUES:				
† Light Dues	1843		44,117	
‡ Port Dues	Annual Income of all the Ports in Scotland		176,000	
				220,117
				£530,665

IRELAND.

		£	£
RATES:			
§ Poor Rate	collected in the year ended 29th September 1844	256,658	
‖ County Cess	average annual amount ordered to be levied in the three years, 1841, 1842, and 1843	1,158,198	
			1,414,856
DUES:			
† Light Dues	1843	53,335	
Port Dues	Annual Income of all the Ports in Ireland	93,000	
			146,335
			£1,561,191

TOTAL.

		£	£
ENGLAND and WALES	Rates	8,651,820	
	Dues	2,535,207	
			11,187,027
SCOTLAND	Rates	310,548	
	Dues	220,117	
			530,665
IRELAND	Rates	1,414,856	
	Dues	146,335	
			1,561,191
			£13,278,883

* From Returns printed by the House of Commons in 1843; Parliamentary Paper, 361, pages 10 and 35.

† From Report of Select Committee on Lighthouses, House of Commons, 1845; Parl. Paper, 607, page 22.

‡ From First Report of Tidal Harbour Commissioners, 1845, Appendix page 195. The amounts are approximate ones.

§ From Eleventh Annual Report of the Poor Law Commissioners.

‖ From Report of Commissioners of Inquiry as to Occupation of Land in Ireland, 1845, Appendix No. 8, pages 54, 55.

X.—RATING.

GAS WORKS.

January 30th, 1846.

J. S.—Inquired whether the assessment of gas works should be on the buildings, gasometers, &c., or upon the amount of profit the company divide after all the expenses are paid.

Ans.—Assuming the company to be rateable for these works, (with reference to which point the Commissioners direct your attention to the decision in R. *v.* the Commissioners for lighting Beverley, 6 Adol. and Ellis, 645,) the Commissioners desire to point out, that the rate must be laid upon the annual value of the land occupied by the company, as improved by the erection of their works, the laying down of the pipes, and so forth, according to the provisions of the 1st sec. of the Parochial Assessments Act, 6 and 7 Wm. 4., c. 96. This rateable annual value will be the sum which the land in question, as so improved, would probably let for, to a tenant taking it for the same purposes to which it is now applied; subject, of course, to the deductions specified in the enactment just mentioned. You would doubtless derive much information on the subject, by referring to the decisions of the courts in the following cases:—R. *v.* Birmingham Gaslight Company, 1 Barn. and Cres., 506. R. *v.* Brighton Gas and Coke Company, 5 Barn. and Cres., 466. R. *v.* Birmingham and Staffordshire Gas Company, 6 Adol. and Ellis, 634. R. *v.* Cambridge Gas Company, 8 Adol. and Ellis, 73.

XI. — REGISTRATION. — CHARGES FOR COUNTY REGISTRATION—CIRCULAR.

Poor Law Commission Office,
Somerset House,
October 29th, 1845.

SIR,—I am directed by the Poor Law Commissioners to state that it has been represented to them that in many places there is an unnecessary and wasteful expenditure of money from the poor-rates for the county registration.

The Commissioners are, therefore, desirous of drawing your attention to the subject, with the view to your making due inquiry as to the propriety of any charges under this head, which may be contained in the accounts submitted to you for audit, before the same are allowed by you. The Commissioners desire to point out that the proper voucher should in all cases be produced for the charges in question. They refer you to the Act of 6 and 7 Vic. c. 18, section 57, which authorises an account of all expenses incurred by the overseers of every parish or township in carrying into effect the provisions of the Act, to be laid before the Revising Barrister, and provides that the Revising Barrister shall sign and give to the said overseers a certificate of the sum which he shall allow to be due to them in respect of the said expenses; and that it shall be lawful for the said overseers to receive the sum so due to them, out of the first moneys thereafter to be collected for the relief of the poor in the same parish or township. If, therefore, the overseers produce to you the certificate of the Revising Barrister, it will be a sufficient voucher for the sum allowed therein.

I am, Sir,
Your most obedient servant,
E. CHADWICK, *Secretary.*

To
Auditor of the District.

XII.—RELIEF—MEDICAL.

IN CASE OF ACCIDENT WHICH PARISH LIABLE.

December 2nd, 1845.

Clerk of Liskeard Union—J. T., a labourer, was lodging in the town of Callington, and was employed in the parish of South-hill, in this union, and occasionally in the parish of Stokeclimsland, in the Launceston Union, going daily to his work from his lodging in Callington. Whilst at work in the parish of Stokeclimsland, he fractured his leg, and was conveyed to his lodgings in Callington, as the most convenient place to which he could be taken. His settlement is in South-hill, which has been acknowledged by his receiving relief from that parish before and after the accident. The fracture was reduced whilst he was in Callington, from which place a medical man could most conveniently be sent to him, had he been sent to any house in Stokeclimsland, where the accident happened. All the expenses, except reducing the fractured leg, has been defrayed by South-hill. Inquired the Commissioners' opinion as to which parish the surgeon's fee is to be charged.

Ans.—The Commissioners are of opinion that the guardians will be justified in charging the surgeon's fee for reducing the fracture to Callington. Though the accident happened in Stokeclimsland, in the Launceston Union, yet it seems the pauper was removed without fraud on the part of the officers of that parish to his own residence in Callington, as being the most convenient place to which he could be taken; and it further appears, that the medical attendance was given and the fracture reduced at the pauper's lodgings at Callington. Under these circumstances, the Commissioners think, on the authority of Lamb *v.* Bunce, 4 M. and S. 275, that Callington became liable to the medical relief afforded to the pauper. In that case, it was held by Lord Ellenborough, that there is no ground for saying that there is an exclusive liability attaching to the parish in which the accident happens, to give the relief, but that the law raises an obligation against the parish where the pauper lies *sick*, as casual poor, to look to the supply of his necessities. But although under the authority of this decision, the guardians would be clearly warranted in charging the medical fee to Callington, yet the Commissioners think it would likewise be competent to adopt the alternative course of holding the parish of the pauper's settlement (South-hill) liable for all the relief given in consequence of the accident. Where a pauper is clearly settled in one parish within the union, but resident in some other parish of such union, the guardians are empowered to give relief to the pauper while so resident at the charge of the first parish. It is stated that all expenses except reducing the fractured leg, had been defrayed by South-hill. It seems to the Commissioners, that the reasons which would warrant the charging any relief whatever given since the accident to South-hill, would apply with equal force to the charging of the medical expenses.

2. DITTO.

January 21*st*, 1846.

Clerk of Ticehurst Union—M. H. fractured her arm in the parish of T. in this union, where she temporarily resided as a hop-picker. On the day of the accident, the relieving officer of the district comprising the parish of T., was administering relief in the neighbouring parish of B., to which parish the woman went and obtained an order for the medical officer of B. parish to attend her. The pauper remained some time in the latter parish under the care of the medical officer, then returned to the parish of T., and from thence to her usual place of abode in the west of Sussex. There is a medical officer for the parish of T. as well as for the parish of B. Inquired which of the two parishes is liable for payment of the medical officer's fee.

Ans.—The general rule which determines the chargeability of a pauper, is, that he is chargeable to the parish in which, being destitute, he applies for and obtains relief. To this general rule, however, an apparent exception occurs in the case of persons who, being destitute in one parish, are compelled by the union arrangements to go into another parish for the purpose of making the application for relief, as where the relieving officer's residence, or the place where he attends weekly to relieve the district, the guardians' place of meeting, or the union workhouse is situate in such other parish. In these cases the relief is chargeable not to the parish in which the application is actually made, but to the parish in which the necessity for relief arose, and in which it must be deemed to have been constructively made. In the present case it appears that the pauper was destitute, and required medical aid, in the parish of T., where she met with the accident, but that she went into the parish of B., merely because the relieving officer was there administering relief. If this be so, the case falls within the exception above stated, *i.e.*, that the application for relief, though in fact made in B., is to be regarded as constructively made in T., where the necessity for relief arose, and that the latter parish is consequently liable for the relief, medical or otherwise, given to the pauper.

XIII.—REMOVAL.

1. CHARGES UNDER SUSPENDED ORDER.

August 13*th*, 1845.

Clerk of Tunstead and Happing Incorporated Hundreds—Inquired whether a parish, to which a pauper has been removed under an order of justices, is bound to pay the gross amount of the charges incurred in consequence of the suspension of such order, without being furnished with the several particulars of the expenditure.

Ans.—The charges claimed in this instance are, it would seem, those ordered by the justices to be paid, in pursuance of the power conferred on them in this respect, by the 35th Geo. 3, c. 101. The Commissioners are not aware that the parish ordered to pay the amount, can insist upon being furnished with particulars. The justices, who order the payment, are to satisfy themselves that the costs claimed have actually been incurred by the removing parish, in consequence of the suspension, but their order (except where the sum claimed exceeds £20) appears to be conclusive upon the parish to which the removal is made. The Commissioners, however, consider it is but reasonable that the particulars of the gross amount claimed under suspended orders of removal should be furnished; and, as regards the present case, the Commissioners cannot suppose that the authorities of the parish can have any objection to furnish the details. The Commissioners would, therefore, recommend that they should be applied to on the subject.

---

2. EXECUTION OF ORDER, PENDING A CASE GRANTED FOR THE COURT OF QUEEN'S BENCH.

August 29th, 1845.

Clerk of Whittlesey Union—In the month of April, 1845, an order of justices was obtained by the parish officers of Whittlesey, for the removal of a man and his family from that parish to the parish of Farcet, in the Peterborough Union, and was afterwards suspended on account of the man's illness. Notice of appeal, and the grounds thereof, having been duly served by the parish officer of Farcet, within twenty-one days from the date of the notice of chargeability, as required by statute, the case came on for hearing on the 2nd of July, at the quarter sessions held for the Isle of Ely, when the court confirmed the order, but granted the appellants a case for the Court of Queen's Bench, principally upon the objection that the parishes of Whittlesey were not united for the purposes of settlement. The solicitor for the parish of Farcet informed the assistant overseer of Whittlesey, that he should recommend his clients to receive the paupers, and pay the costs ordered by the court, as the man and one child were dead and the widow was not likely to be very troublesome. The parish officers of Whittlesey waited one week, and not hearing from the officers of Farcet, obtained the justices' order for costs, and for the removal of the suspension; and the wife and children were accordingly removed and delivered at the house of an overseer, (who was ill in bed,) together with a copy of the order, the original being shown to the overseer's wife. A day or two afterwards, the overseer alluded to sent for the pauper, (who had remained in the village with a relative,) and delivered to her the copy of the order for her removal, and told her to return to Whittlesey, and remain there until the case was decided. The pauper returned to Whittlesey, and has again applied to the board of guardians for relief; but being a strong young woman and in full employ, with only two children aged six and three years, relief has been refused her. If hereafter relief actually becomes necessary, the guardians will have no alternative but to grant it. Inquired—1stly, whether the parish officers of Whittlesey acted wrong in removing the family to Farcet, before they were officially informed whether the parish officers of Farcet declined removing the case into the court of Queen's Bench. 2ndly, Whether the parish officers of Farcet acted legally in giving the copy of the removal order to the pauper, and directing her to return to Whittlesey, before the case was finally decided. 3dly, In what manner the guardians should act if the pauper again applies for relief. 4thly, Whether the parish officers of Whittlesey could recover the amount of relief granted to the pauper pending the decision of the Court of Queen's Bench, if that decision should be in favour of Whittlesey.

Ans.—The 79th sec. 4 and 5 Will. 4, c. 76, provides "that if notice of appeal against such order of removal shall be received by the overseers or guardians of the parish from which such poor person is directed in such order to be removed, within the said period of twenty-one days, it shall not be lawful to remove such poor person, until after the time for prosecuting such appeal shall have expired, or in case such appeal shall be duly prosecuted, until after the *final determination of such appeal.*" The Commissioners are not aware of any decision of the courts on the meaning of the latter words, but the Commissioners apprehend they must mean the determination of the appeal by the highest tribunal to which the matter can be carried, inasmuch as that alone can be final. If, therefore, in the present case, the sessions confirmed the order granting a case for the superior court, the result of which may be the quashing or reversing the order of sessions, the decision of the sessions cannot, in the language of the statute, be said to be "the final determination of the appeal." It appears, therefore, to the Commissioners, in answer to your specific inquiries—1st. That the parish officers of Whittlesey acted erroneously in removing the pauper to Farcet before they were officially informed, whether the officers of the latter declined removing the case into the court of Queen's Bench. The time allowed for issuing out the *certiorari* is six months. 2dly. The Commissioners cannot undertake to say that the officers of Farcet acted illegally under the circumstances, in sending the copy order of the justices back, and directing the pauper to return to Whittlesey. 3dly. If the pauper again applies for relief to the guardians of the Whittlesey Union, the Commissioners would recommend the guardians to give needful relief, if the pauper is considered to be destitute. 4thly. The Commissioners consider the parish of Whittlesey will be entitled, under the 84th sec. of the Poor Law Amendment Act, to recover back from Farcet the costs of relieving the pauper pending the decision of the Court of Queen's Bench, assuming such decision to be in favour of the former parish.

XIV.—SETTLEMENT.

1. BY RENTING A POST-MILL.

Aug. 4th, 1845.

Clerk of Hinckley Union—A. B. occupied a post-mill, which was removeable without being taken to pieces, together with a dwelling-house, in the parish of Barwell, at a rent of upwards of £30 a-year; but the dwelling-house itself was worth only £5 a-year. Inquired whether A. B. gained a settlement by such occupation.

Ans.—If the post mill occupied in Barwell parish by G. was not affixed to the land, or to something connected with the land, it was a mere chattel, and not a parcel of a tenement the occupation of which conferred a settlement, (see Rex *v.* Londonthorpe, 6 T. R. 377, Rex *v.* Ottley, B. and Ad. 161.) On the contrary, if the post mill were affixed to the freehold, or to something annexed to the soil, as to a foundation of brick, it was undoubtedly a tenement in law, and the occupation of the mill in connection with the dwelling-house, (if rented and occupied for the required period,) according to Rex *v.* Ottley, conferred a settlement. Assuming that the post-mill rented in Barwell was not a tenement, the occupation of the dwelling-house alone being but of the value of £5 was insufficient.

---

2. BY RENTING A TENEMENT.

Sept., 1845.

Mr. B. J., ——— *Union*—At Michaelmas 1810, T. J. took a house and land in the parish of Llandyssal, in the county of Cardigan, at a rent of £8. 8*s.* per annum, (but considered to be worth more,) and a private bridge, called Pontlwny (which crossed the river Tivy, the boundary between the parishes of Llandyssal and Llanllwny) at a rent of £4 a-year, receiving a penny from each person that passed over the bridge. T. J. rented the house and bridge for eleven or twelve years, when the bridge was thrown open to the public, but he continued in the occupation of the house at the same rent, until Michaelmas, 1833, having paid rates and taxes for the house during the whole of the time. He then rented a house, a mill, and some land in the parish of Llanllwny, at a rent of £19 per annum, and continued in the occupation of the same for seven years, but during that period he was not assessed to the poor-rate, inasmuch as the mill and land formed part of the farm of Gelli, the occupier of which underlet the mill, &c. to T. J. and paid the poor-rates for the same, along with those for the farm. Requested the Commissioners' opinion as to the settlement of T. J.

Ans.—Before the passing of the 59th Geo. 3, c. 12, (July 1819,) the settlement depended, not upon the rent, but upon the value of the tenement. If, therefore, the yearly value of the tenement, the house and land rented by the pauper in Llandyssal, was £10, he gained a settlement in that parish, by the occupation and residence, though the rent was only £8. 8*s*. But, however this might have been, it seems that the pauper, in addition to the tenement in Llandyssal, rented, under the same landlord, a private bridge, for £4 yearly, that this bridge was over the river Tivy, and that the middle of the river formed the boundary between the parishes of Llandyssal and Llanllwny, and that the bridge formed the communication between the two places. There is no doubt that the tolls of a bridge are in law a tenement, and when rented by a valid title, under a proper demise, it was held in several cases, that this kind of tenement, prior to the 59th Geo. 3, c. 12, conferred a settlement. But, in the present case, the tenement by itself was not of a sufficient yearly value to confer a settlement. But distinct tenements under different landlords, and lying in different parishes, if together of the yearly value of £10, have been held to gain a settlement. In the present instance, assuming that the pauper rented the tolls of the bridge by a valid title, this, taken together with the house and land rented in Llandyssal, was, as it appears to the Commissioners, a sufficient tenement within the meaning of the statute, and that the pauper accordingly gained a settlement in Llandyssal, where it seems he resided. You state that the pauper continued to occupy the house and land in Llandyssal until Michaelmas, 1833, when he commenced renting a house, mill, and land, in Llanllwny, but that he was not assessed to the poor-rate in respect to the house, mill, and land. If such were the case, it would appear to the Commissioners that the pauper gained no settlement in Llanllwny, by renting a tenement. The 4 and 5 Will. 4, c. 76, s. 66, provides " that, from and after the passing of this Act, no settlement shall be acquired or completed by occupying a tenement, unless the person occupying the same shall have been assessed to the poor-rate, and shall have paid the same, in respect of such tenement for one year." This Act passed on the 14th August, 1834; at that time the pauper had not occupied the tenement for twelve months, and had not, therefore, acquired a settlement. The section, it will be seen, prevents any settlement, not then acquired, from being completed, unless the conditions as to rating and paying rates for the required period have been complied with.

XV.—STAMPED RECEIPTS.

WHETHER REQUIRED TO BE GIVEN FOR PAYMENTS MADE BY GUARDIANS.

December 10*th*, 1845.

Clerk of Northallerton Union—It being doubted whether stamped receipts were requisite for payments made by the guardians to tradesmen, for goods purchased for the use of the union, or for the salaries of officers,—requested the Commissioners' opinion on the point; and referred to the case of the guardians of the Banbury union *v.* Robinson—1 Dav. and Mer. p. 92.

Ans.—It appears to the Commissioners that stamped receipts are requisite in the cases mentioned in your letter, assuming that the sums paid amount in each case, to £5, and that the guardians should require such receipts from the officers, and other parties to whom monies are paid. To establish an exemption from stamp-duty, the case must be brought within the 86th sec. of 4th and 5th Wm. 4, c. 76, that is, the instrument must be shown to be an instrument made in pursuance of that Act. The Commissioners do not at present see how the receipt or discharge, given by a tradesman for money paid him by the guardians, for goods furnished in the one case, or by an officer for salary received in the other, can be said to be an instrument made in pursuance of that Act. The Commissioners have referred to the case of the guardians of the Banbury union *v.* Robinson, 1 Dav. and Mer. p. 92, but they see nothing in the opinions expressed by the court in that case as to the meaning of the word "instrument," to lead them to think that such meaning would be extended to such a case as the present.

XVI.—VACCINATION.

INOCULATION FOR SMALL POX.—COSTS OF DETECTING OFFENDERS.

November 11*th*, 1845.

Clerk of Watford Union—There is a very strong impression that several children in the union have been inoculated, and that the disease has been communicated to others by exposing the healthy to those who had the disease. Inquired whether the guardians would be justified in offering a reward to informants, who would assist in prosecuting to conviction, parties who have offended, or who may offend, against the statute.

Ans.—The Commissioners collect from your inquiry that the guardians wish to be informed more particularly as to their power to pay, out of the funds in their control, any sum which they might see fit to offer for the object stated. The Act 4th and 5th Vic., cap. 32, from which the guardians derive their power to pay any expenses connected with vaccination out of the poor-rates, provides, " that it shall be, and be deemed to have been lawful for the guardians of any parish or union in England and Ireland, &c. by whom the contracts for vaccination may respectively be, or have been made under the provisions of the said Act, to defray the expenses incident to the execution of the said Act, out of any rates or monies which may come, or may have come, into their hands respectively for the relief of the poor." If the words " expenses incident to the execution of the Act," are to be understood as referring solely to such things as the guardians are required to do or perform in execution of the 3rd and 4th Vic., cap. 29, then it would seem clear that the cost of proceeding against persons under the 8th section of that act could not be paid out of the poor-rates, as it is not made any part of the duty of guardians, as such, to enforce the statute against offenders. But if the words cited have a more extended meaning, and are to be construed as including the costs incurred in effecting any of the objects or purposes of the statute, the case would apparently be different as regards the power to defray the expenses last referred to, as one of the objects of the statute is the punishment of persons who attempt to produce by inoculation the disease of small pox. The Commissioners are themselves disposed to think that the latter construction might be supported by the courts, though they admit the case is by no means free from doubt. But assuming the clause to have the effect of enabling the guardians to defray the expenses of proceeding against any persons summarily before the justices, under the 8th section, the Commissioners are of opinion that the power would not be held to extend to the payment of sums offered as an inducement to persons to give information as to offenders against the statute.

XVII.—VAGRANTS.

POWER OF GUARDIANS TO PROCEED AGAINST DESERTERS OF FAMILIES, WITHOUT THE INTERVENTION OF PARISH OFFICERS.

November 22nd, 1845.

Clerk of Mitford and Launditch Union—Inquired whether the guardians could by their relieving officers, or otherwise, and without the assistance of parish officers, take proceedings under the Vagrant Act, (5 Geo. 4, c. 83,) for the punishment of parties deserting their families, and leaving them chargeable to the parish.

Ans.—In the opinion of the Commissioners, the guardians are clearly authorised to take steps through their officers for the apprehension and punishment (under 5th Geo. 4, cap. 83,) of persons who are guilty of the offence of deserting their families, and suffering them to become chargeable. See the 59th sec. of 7th and 8th Vic. cap. 101. But even before the passing of that Act, the overseers had no special duty or exclusive province in regard to taking such proceedings; the prosecution being a criminal matter, it was apparently open to any one acquainted with the facts, and in a situation to prove the chargeability, to institute the proceedings. The practical difficulty in the way of such proceedings being taken by the overseers, was that the law did not enable *them* to defray the costs out of the poor-rate, and that difficulty yet remains in regard to the overseers, for the statute last referred to merely enables the *guardians* to pay the costs out of the funds in their hands.

XVIII.—VALUATION.

EXPENSES OF OCCASIONAL SURVEYS, ETC. FOR RATING.

January 13th, 1846.

Clerk of Tamworth Union—A new house was built in a parish of the Union, and the overseers, to avoid unnecessary expense, rated it to the best of their ability. The owner being dissatisfied with the valuation, appealed to the justices, who recommended that a surveyor should be employed. The overseers accordingly employed the surveyor who had formerly valued the whole parish, and his charge was two guineas. The overseers paid the charge, but the auditor has disallowed it in their accounts. Inquired how surveyors, who are employed by order or recommendation of the justices, to value new property in parishes, are to be paid.

Ans.—The Commissioners are not aware of any legal mode by which the overseers can procure the aid of a surveyor, for occasional surveys and valuations of property, prior to its assessment to the poor's rate. If the rate once made be appealed against, the overseers may employ a surveyor, to give evidence of the value, and thereby obtain an estimate by which they may learn the value of the particular property, and alter or abide by the rate accordingly. The justices have no power to order the overseers to have any property surveyed and valued for the purposes of poor rate assessment. It is incumbent upon the justices to act upon the evidence produced before them.

XIX.—VESTRY MEETINGS.

1. POWER IN REGARD TO MAKING RATES, ETC.

January 16, 1846.

Mr. ——, *Newmarket Union*—Notice was given of a parish vestry to be held "for the purpose of granting the churchwardens and overseers a rate for the relief of the poor, and for other purposes." Inquired, 1, whether any alteration in the assessment of any rate-payer, proposed and carried at such vestry meeting, would be legal. 2. Whether any other business than that of granting a rate could be legally transacted thereat.

Ans.—The vestry of a parish has no authority to determine the amount at which any person shall be assessed in the poor's rate for such parish. It rests with the overseers of the poor, on their own responsibility, to assess every rate-payer at such amount as they think right, having due regard to the requirements of the law. The commissioners do not mean to say that the overseers may not derive very material aid from the vestry in forming their own opinions on the points alluded to; but they are bound to state that the vestry has no legal power to control the overseers in the matter. With regard to your question whether any other business besides that of granting a poor's rate can lawfully be transacted at a vestry meeting convened in the manner described, the Commissioners desire to observe that it would not come within their province to express any opinion thereon, unless the "other business" you advert to, be connected with the administration of the poor laws.

---

2. PUBLICATION OF NOTICES.

Clerk to Guardians of —— Union—It is proposed by the guardians to recommend the inhabitants in vestry, to appoint the collector of poor-rates for this parish, to act as assistant overseer, but it is expected that obstacles will be thrown in the way of the appointment. Inquired whether notices for calling the vestry should be published on the doors of the dissenting chapels, as well as of those of the established church, as stated in a late number of The Justice of the Peace.

Ans.—Having regard to what the Commissioners believe to be the ordinary legal meaning of the word "chapel," and to what appears to be the general tenor of the statute, 1 Vic. cap. 45, the Commissioners are disposed to consider that the chapels referred to in that statute are chapels belonging to the established church, and not places of worship used by dissenting congregations. The Commissioners do not concur in the view taken by the "Justice of the Peace," (in the article to which you refer,) as to the effect of the decision in Reg. *v.* Whipp, (4 Ad. and Ell. n. s. 141, 3 Gal. and Dav. 372.) It is true that the existence of dissenting chapels in the parish, is mentioned as one of the facts in that case, but there is nothing in the judgment, as reported, to show that this circumstance had any effect upon the decision of the court, which might, for aught that appears, have proceeded upon the ground that the rate was not published in all the "churches and chapels" belonging to the established church. At the same time, if any question on the point is likely to be raised in any instance, the Commissioners see nothing to prevent the publication at the dissenting chapels, so as to guard against any subsequent dispute.

Printed by Order of the Poor Law Commissioners, by BLACKBURN AND PARDON, 6, Hatton Garden, and Published by CHARLES KNIGHT and Co., 22, Ludgate Street, Publishers to the Poor Law Commissioners.

AN

OFFICIAL CIRCULAR

OF PUBLIC DOCUMENTS AND INFORMATION:

DIRECTED BY THE POOR LAW COMMISSIONERS TO BE PRINTED, CHIEFLY FOR THE USE OF THE MEMBERS AND PERMANENT OFFICERS OF BOARDS OF GUARDIANS, UNDER THE POOR LAW AMENDMENT ACT.

No. 57. CIRCULAR ISSUED MARCH 2ND, 1846.

THE Poor Law Commissioners directed that the following documents be printed and circulated for the information of Guardians and Officers of the several Unions, viz.

(Signed) By order of the Board,

EDWIN CHADWICK, *Secretary*.

I.—ACCOUNTS.

1. SEPARATE ACCOUNT OF IN-MAINTENANCE OF SICK, &c.

Oct. 18*th*, 1845.

Clerk of the Hay Union.—The guardians are desirous of classifying and charging the cost of in-maintenance in the following manner—1st class, Actual cost of in-maintenance of the sick, aged, and infirm; 2nd class, Actual cost of those on the ordinary dietary. The alteration appears the more necessary because it has been the practice to crowd the house with the aged, infirm, and sick, the cost of whose maintenance ranges considerably higher than that of the other classes of inmates, and consequently raising the average. The average cost per head per week for all classes, including extras, being about 2*s.*, whilst the average cost under the ordinary dietary would be about 1*s.* 6*d.* The object of the guardians is not to diminish the extras or comfort allowed to the aged, but to avoid the increase in the cost of maintenance of the younger classes which the present system of averaging effects.

Ans.—One principle laid down in the order of accounts is, that the cost of maintenance charged should be regulated in each case by the actual number of days during which each parish has had paupers in the workhouse; but it does not follow necessarily that the cost of each such pauper should be the same. If the guardians, therefore, think that they can satisfactorily separate the extras from the ordinary expenses of maintenance, so as to correctly distinguish the actual cost of maintaining each of the classes of paupers, the Commissioners would offer no objection to that course.

2. APPLICATION OF BALANCE RECOVERED FROM PAST OVERSEER.

November 8*th*, 1846.

District Auditor — (*Ashbourne Union*) — Inquired, whether the amount of balance certified by him to be due from the late overseers of one of the parishes in the union, and which had been paid over by them to the union treasurer, could be appropriated by the present overseers towards the payment of the next call made upon them by the board of guardians.

Ans.—The 23nd sec. of the 7th and 8th Vic., cap. 101, after directing that the money certified by the auditor to be due from any person shall be paid to the treasurer of the union, if there be one, proceeds to enact that "in case of a union, such money shall be applied by the guardians to the use of all or any of the parishes included in such union, according as all or any of such parishes may be interested in the sum so paid." Consequently, the sum paid over by the late overseers of ———— to the treasurer of the Ashbourne Union, now lies at the disposal of the guardians of the union, and not of the present overseers of the parish. It must be applied by the guardians to the use of such parish, and may insofar diminish the amount of contribution which it may be requisite for the guardians to demand of the present overseers; but it cannot be applied by those overseers, to the payment of any sum demanded of them by the guardians.

3. AUDIT.—DUTY OF OVERSEERS TO ATTEND AUDIT AT THE PLACE APPOINTED.

February 21*st*, 1846.

Clerk of the Alton Union—Some overseers thought that the legislature intended by sec. 33 of 7 and 8 Vic. c. 101, to relieve them from attending any audit not held within their respective parishes, and to prevent their coming from a distance. Inquired the Commissioners' opinion whether, under that clause, the overseers are compelled to attend any audit out of their parishes.

Ans.—The auditor is not required by the statute, 7 and 8 Vic. c. 101, to attend in every parish in his district to audit the overseers' accounts; but it is the duty of the overseers to attend at the place appointed by the auditor for the purpose.

4. COST OF CLOTHING, HOW TO BE CHARGED.

February 27*th*, 1846.

Clerk of the Falmouth Union.—The guardians purchased a quantity of cloth at a cost of £69, and placed it in stock with a view to its being expended as occasion required. Several of the guardians consider that some parishes would be prejudiced by the cost of the cloth being charged under the head of clothing, and that it should be borne by the establishment. The object of making the purchase was to provide an uniform dress for the pauper inmates. Requested the Commissioners' opinion.

Ans.—The amount paid for the cloth in question should be debited to the clothing account in the ledger, but it would obviously not be equitable to charge the whole of this amount against the parishes happening to have paupers in the workhouse during the quarter in which the expenditure was incurred. The most simple mode of distributing the cost of clothing amongst the several parishes in a union, and that which is most commonly adopted, is to charge against the parishes whose paupers have been in the workhouse during the quarter, the cost of all *new clothing given out of store* during that quarter.

II.—APPRENTICESHIP.

JUSTICES' CERTIFICATE OF SATISFACTION ON THE INDENTURE.

October 23*rd*, 1845.

Clerk of the Whitechapel Union.—Inquired whether it was necessary in case of apprenticeship under the Commissioners' general order of the 31st December, 1844, that the justices should certify at the foot of the indenture, that the Commissioners' regulations had been complied with, and whether the indenture would be valid without such certificate.

Ans. The Commissioners consider it is not necessary that the justices should so certify. The 31st sec. of the Poor Law Amendment Act provides, that the justices are to certify in such form and manner as the Commissioners, by any orders, or regulations issued by them, may have directed. Though the Commissioners have, by the order referred to in your letter, regulated the mode of apprenticing poor children by the guardians, in the Whitechapel Union, they have not thought it necessary to prescribe any form in which the justices are to certify that the regulations have been complied with by the guardians. The absence of the certificate will not, therefore, in the opinion of the Commissioners, invalidate the contract, or indenture of apprenticeship. The Commissioners would add, for the information of the guardians, that since the allowance or assent of justices to the indenture of apprenticeship, is expressly dispensed with by the 12th sec. of 7th and 8th Vic., cap. 101, it seems to the Commissioners, that there are no longer any justices who can certify under the 61st section of 4th and 5th Wm. 4, cap. 76. The justices who are to certify under that section as to the observance of the Commissioners' regulations, are (it will be seen) the same justices who assent to the binding and allow the indentures; but in the case of bindings by the guardians, there are no justices who can so assent and allow, and it follows, therefore, there are none who can certify.

III.—AUDITORS.

1. DUTY OF—IN EXAMINING RATE-BOOKS.

October 20*th*, 1845.

A Guardian of the Clifton Union—Inquired whether the auditor is to call for the rate-books of the respective parishes to inspect them and see that the amount of the rate is accounted for by the collector, and if necessary to make a thorough examination of the rate.

Ans.—The Commissioners consider the auditor will not properly discharge his duty under the order of accounts unless he examine the rate-books in such a manner as will show whether the rate is duly accounted for. It will thus be necessary that he should see that the entries are duly made in the appropriate column, and that the columns are correctly cast up. By this means the rate will be balanced, *i. e.*, it will be made to appear on the face of the rate, what portion of the rate as originally made and allowed, has been obtained, and what portion still remains to be accounted for. Upon this subject, the Commissioners would direct your attention to an opinion expressed by them in answer to a somewhat similar inquiry, and which will be found at page 35 of the *Official Circular*, No. 23.

2. REPAYMENT OF POSTAGE PAID BY AUDITORS ON ACCOUNT OF PARISHES.

December 24*th*, 1845.

Auditor of the ——— *District*—Inquired Commissioners' opinion with respect to the repayment to the auditor of expenses incurred by him for postage, on account of the several parishes comprised in the unions in his district.

Ans.—As you are not bound to pay the postage of the notices sent by you, to the parish officers, of the day of audit, the Commissioners think the charge is not one which you are liable to bear. But as the charge will be double, if the letters are not prepaid, the Commissioners think it better that you should, in the first instance, pay the postage, and that the amount should be refunded to you, and debited to each parish, either by the clerk in the union accounts, or by the overseers.

IV.—BASTARDY.

ORDERS CANNOT BE ENFORCED THROUGH THE INABILITY OF MOTHERS OF BASTARDS TO PAY JUSTICES' CLERK'S FEES.

February 24*th*, 1846.

Clerk of Hayfield Union—Two young women, each having a bastard child, have entered the workhouse, not being able to maintain themselves and children. Orders have been made upon the putative fathers, who are well able to pay the amount ordered, but the women cannot pay the fees charged by the clerk to justices for making out the orders and summonses, and therefore the orders will not be given up to the women, and they cannot, in consequence, take proceedings against the putative fathers. He was not aware of any way in which he could use the duplicates of the orders, which he held under sec. 5, of 7 and 8 Vic. c. 101. Inquired what course he should pursue in relieving the parishes from the burden of maintaining in the workhouse the women and their children.

Ans.—The Commissioners do not see that the guardians can lawfully interfere to assist the mothers in procuring the orders. To advance the means to pay the demand of the clerk to justices would probably not be an offence under the 7th sec. of 7 and 8 Vic. c. 101, seeing that the orders have been made; but the advance of such moneys from the poor's-rate would clearly be an illegal application of that fund. Neither do the Commissioners see that the duplicates of the orders which the guardians hold, under sec. 5 of the Act cited, would be available for the purpose of securing the payment of the sums mentioned in the orders, seeing that the putative fathers have not been served with the orders made on them by the justices. Upon the whole, the Commissioners see no remedy unless the mothers are able, themselves, to provide the means for paying the demand of the clerk to the justices. The necessity for payment of fees to justices' clerks, is incident to every species of complaint thus pursued. The proceeding is, at any rate, the simplest and cheapest known to the law of this country.

V.—CONTRACTORS.

Remedy against contractor supplying bread of an inferior quality.

December 6th, 1845.

Clerk of the Honiton Union—Inquired as to the best mode of proceeding, in cases where the bread delivered by the contractors appeared, at first to be good, but after a space of twenty-four hours, proved to be of inferior quality, it being almost impossible to return the bread, as some of it had been consumed, and nearly all distributed to the various paupers.

Ans. The better course would appear to be that the guardians should ascertain the quality of the bread, and get good evidence on the subject, and being satisfied that it is not of the quality contracted for, should employ some other person to supply the bread, according to the provisions of the contract, at the cost (if the price exceed that contracted for with the original contractor,) of such contractor, and in case he fails to pay this difference, to sue him and his sureties on the contract.

VI.—CONTRIBUTION.

Re-payment of loan to parish officers for the purpose of meeting call for contribution.

October 7th, 1845.

Late Auditor of ——— *Union*—Pending a dispute as to making a rate for the use of the poor, in consequence of the recent new valuation of ——— parish not being satisfactory, the parish officers applied to the magistrates as to providing funds for the parish, and especially to pay £150 to the treasurer of the union, in pursuance of the contribution warrant of the guardians, until a rate was made and allowed by justices. The magistrates advised the parish officers to borrow £200 until a rate was made. The loan was procured, and the parish officers gave their note of hand for the amount. As it is now proposed to repay the amount of the loan out of the poor's-rate, inquired whether, as auditor, he would be warranted in allowing the same in the accounts.

Ans.—Payments to the guardians, by the overseers, in pursuance of the orders of the former, are made in anticipation of expenditure by the guardians. A payment at the end of a year in compliance with a demand of the guardians during that year, and for their purposes during the following year, is not like a payment made for the purposes of the expiring year, and does not appear to the Commissioners to come within the principle of Tawney's case, 2 Salk. 531, 2 Ld. Raymond, 1009, which decided in effect, that the rates of one year could not be applied to the payment of debts incurred in a preceding year. The real question which arises in the present case, is, whether the contribution required by the guardians of the ——— Union of the overseers of ———, (to meet which the sum of £200 was borrowed of the bankers,) was for the purposes of the past or the present year. If for the latter, there would be no legal difficulty in discharging the debt incurred by the overseers out of the rates of the present year. In like manner, if part of the contribution only were required for the purposes of the present year, the power to discharge the debt would apply to such part. On the other hand, if the contribution were required for the purposes of the year ended 25th March last, of course the principle of

Tawney's case would apply, and there would, as the Commissioners consider, be a legal obstacle to the charging any portion of the sum borrowed upon the present rate-payers, seeing that the overseers of the last year failed to turn over a balance sufficient to meet the debt. The Commissioners perceive that the order of the guardians was made on the 21st of February last, and was not operative on the overseers until the 19th of March. The probability, therefore, is, that it was required for the most part to meet the demands of the ensuing year.

VII.—CONTRIBUTION ORDERS.

1. FORM OF MAKING—LIABILITY OF CHURCHWARDENS TO OBEY.

Oct. 13th, 1845.

Clerk of the Wellington (Salop) Union—Inquired—1. Whether the names of the overseers need be specified in the contribution order, and whether the churchwardens are to be included in and served with the order? 2. Whether, in case it is necessary to enforce the order, the churchwardens, as well as the overseers, should be summoned? 3. Whether succeeding overseers or churchwardens are liable to orders made during the term of office of their predecessors? 4. Whether the proof of service upon each overseer, &c., of the order, is necessary on the hearing of summons before justices, especially where any payment has been made to the treasurer on account of such order.

Ans.—1. The names of the overseers as well as the churchwardens should be specified in the order of contribution, and a copy of such order should be served on each of such officers. 2. In any proceedings taken to enforce the order, the churchwardens as well as the overseers should be summoned. 3. The Commissioners are of opinion that succeeding overseers are not liable in respect of orders of contribution made upon their predecessors; and such orders cannot be enforced against such succeeding overseers. 4. The Commissioners are advised that it is proper that all the churchwardens and overseers should be personally served, though, possibly, in a case where the order had been in part satisfied and payments in respect of it made to the treasurer of the union, the proof of service as regards the overseers making the payments, would be unnecessary.

---

2. POWER OF JUSTICES, WHERE OVERSEERS DISOBEY.

February 14th, 1846.

Clerk of the Walsingham Union.—The guardians have great difficulty in obtaining the contributions from one of the parishes in the union, and on a recent occasion, proceedings were taken against them before justices. The justices would have issued a distress warrant against the goods of the parish officers, but the latter produced the receipt of the treasurer, by which it appeared that they had paid him the contribution, the day previous to the hearing of the complaint. The justices, thereupon, adjudged that the overseers should pay a fine of £5, under the provisions of 4 and 5 Wm. 4, cap. 76, sec. 95, but it was objected, that as no separate complaint had been made in writing against the overseers, at the instance of the board of guardians, they could not enforce payment of the fine, and further, that the parish officers had not wilfully disobeyed the legal and reasonable orders of such justices *and* guardians. That to give the justices jurisdiction, there must be a separate complaint in writing exhibited, and proof on the hearing, that the parish officers had not obeyed the legal and reasonable orders of the justices and guardians, and, therefore, that although the parish officers had been summoned for non-payment of the contribution, the justices had no power to enforce the penalty, as *no order* had been made *by them*, by reason of the parish officers having paid the treasurer the contribution, the day before the hearing, which was several weeks after it should have been paid, and several days after the service of the summonses. Requested the Commissioners' advice as to the best mode of dealing with the parish officers, who were likely to treat future orders in the same manner.

Ans. The Commissioners collect that the proceeding taken against the overseers, was under the 2nd and 3rd Vic., c. 84, for the recovery of money in arrear. If so, the Commissioners conceive the objection taken at the hearing of the case, namely, that the justices could not without a separate complaint, or information, proceed to convict the overseers of an offence under the 95th sec. of the Poor Law Amendment Act, is a valid objection. Of course the justices in a proceeding under the former of these statutes, are prevented from issuing their warrant against the goods of the overseers, where, on the hearing of the complaint, evidence is given of the previous payment to the treasurer of the union, of the money called for by the guardians. But though no warrant can issue under such circumstances, as the overseers have been guilty of the offence of disobedience to the orders of the guardians, proceedings under the 95th sec. could still be taken, but as before stated, there must be a distinct complaint, and a summons must issue to the overseers to answer such complaint. The Commissioners entirely dissent from the view that, to support a conviction under that section, evidence must be given that the overseers have disobeyed the order of the justices and guardians, meaning by that, the joint order of such justices and guardians. The Commissioners were advised by the late Attorney General (Sir J. Campbell,) and are themselves of opinion, that the words, "orders of such justices and guardians," in the 95th sec., are to be taken distributively, *reddendo singula singulis*—as referring to the orders which the justices and guardians respectively, but not conjointly, are enabled to make. This, indeed, is the only reasonable interpretation; any other construction would render the provision inoperative, there being no case in which, as far as the Commissioners are aware, the justices and guardians are empowered or required to concur in making an order on the overseers.

VIII.—GUARDIANS.

1. POWER OF COMMITTEE OF GUARDIANS TO EXAMINE BOOKS OF THE UNION.

February 11*th*, 1846.

A Guardian of the Wellington (*Salop*) *Union*—Inquired, whether the finance and visiting committee of the guardians have a right to call for the minute book and ledger, to enable them to compare tradesmen's bills and vouchers,—in effect, to audit the accounts, including the balance sheet, previous to the payment of the officers' salaries.

Ans.—The committee of the guardians have not the power to call for and examine the books described, unless the board of guardians expressly authorise such committee so to do. The guardians cannot, however, confer any authority to audit the accounts in the sense of finally allowing or disallowing items.

2. PROCEEDINGS OF.—ENTRY OF GUARDIANS' PROTESTS ON THE MINUTES.

February 26, 1846.

A Guardian of the ——— *Union*—Inquired whether the dissent of individual guardians in disputed points can be claimed to be entered on the minutes of the proceedings of the board.

Ans.—The minutes of the guardians being a record of the proceedings of the board, and as the protest of individual guardians do not form a part of such proceedings, the Commissioners think that the guardians protesting cannot require their protest to be entered on the minutes.

IX.—JUSTICES.

JURISDICTION OVER PARISH SITUATED IN TWO COUNTIES.

October 24*th*, 1845.

Clerk of the Wimborne and Cranborne Union—Part of the parish of Hampreston, in this union, is situate in the county of Southampton, and the remainder, in the county of Dorset. The parish church is in Dorset, and the magistrates of that county have always appointed the overseers, who act for the whole parish, and assess all the property in one poor-rate. In the Poor Law Commissioners' orders, the parish has been treated as if wholly in Dorset. The parish contributes to the county rates of both counties. A question has arisen, whether the magistrates of Dorset have jurisdiction to make an order for the removal of a pauper living in that part of the parish, which is in Hants, or to take proceedings for the recovery of rates assessed on property in that part. He is aware of the provision in section 9 of the 43rd Elizabeth, cap. 2, but cannot find any decision since R. *v.* Merryman, in Hilary Term, 1770. Requested to have Commissioners' opinion for the guidance of the parish officers who are desirous of proceeding to recover some arrears of poor-rates.

Ans.—The Commissioners think it clear that the justices of Dorset are not empowered to take proceedings for the recovery of poor-rates in that portion of the parish of Hampreston which is in Hants. In cases where a parish extends into more counties than one, sec. 9 of 43rd Elizabeth, c. 2, only enables justices to intermeddle in so much of the parish as may be within their respective jurisdictions. To this extent each set of justices may grant warrants of distress for non-payment of poor-rates. As regards, therefore, persons who are rated, and who reside in that part which is in Dorset, application should be made to the justices of Dorset, and the like application should be made to the justices of Hants, in respect to the persons in Hants. With respect to the making of orders of removal, the Commissioners would observe that they have not been able to find the case of R. *v.* Merryman, cited in your letter, nor indeed anything in point. The case is obviously not met by the provisions in the 43rd Elizabeth, above referred to, as the power to remove poor persons to their settlement was not given until 13th and 14th Charles 2nd. The Commissioners, however, do not at present see anything to prevent the justices of Dorset making an order of removal in respect of a pauper chargeable to Hampreston, but residing in that part of the parish which is in Dorset. If this be so, a like power could be exercised by the justices of Hants, in respect of persons residing in Hants. As the overseers act for the whole of the parish, there can be no doubt of their power to make the necessary complaint of chargeability, in whichever portion of the parish the pauper to be removed may reside. The Commissioners would observe, further, that the order of removal should, in their opinion, be made to conform to the facts of the case, *i.e.*, it should be stated that the pauper resides in that portion of the parish which is in the county for which the removing justices act.

November 15*th*, 1845.

Same writer—Inquired further, whether, as the poor-rate for Hampreston parish is allowed by magistrates of Dorset only, the justices of Hants could enforce it as regarded property in that county, or should the rate be allowed by justices of both counties? Also, if able-bodied paupers residing in that part of Hampreston which is in Hants, became chargeable to that parish, and were admitted into the union workhouse at Wimborne, Dorset, could the magistrates of Dorset remove them to their place of settlement?

Ans.—1. The Commissioners are disposed to think that the rate for Hampreston parish should have the consent or allowance of the justices of both counties, *i.e.*, of Hants and Dorset, and that a rate could not be enforced by the justices of the former county, as regards the property in that county, where it had been allowed by the justices of Dorset only. 2. The workhouse for the purpose of removal is deemed to be situated in the parish to which the poor person to be removed is or has been chargeable (sec. 56, 7th and 8th Victoria, c. 101.) A person in the workhouse, may, therefore, be removed in the same manner, as if he were actually in the parish which is charged with his relief. It is not indeed clear that the ordinary place of residence of the pauper is material in this case. Still it would be better, for the avoidance of all dispute, to obtain the warrant of removal from justices acting for the county in which the ordinary residence of the pauper is situate.

X.—LAW BILLS.

INCURRED IN FORMER YEARS, HOW TO BE DISCHARGED.—CLAIM OF JUSTICES' CLERKS TO PROFESSIONAL FEES FROM PARISHES.

September 13*th*, 1845.

Clerk of *Union*—Law bills extending over a period of nearly six years, (commencing in 1839,) have been delivered by Mr. ——— to the overseers of a parish in the union. The charges in the bills are all for attendance and advice upon questions of settlement, which have been given (with very few exceptions) at the place where Mr. ——— has been at the same time acting as clerk to the magistrates. The overseers, when they have been referred to Mr. ———, by the magistrates, were not aware that they were consulting him as an attorney, but in his official capacity as magistrates' clerk. As similar bills have been delivered to every parish in the union which has had any business to transact with Mr. ———, inquired how far the parish is liable for the payment of such bills, under the circumstances above described.

Ans.—As the bills were not incurred during the period of office of the present overseers, they are under no legal obligation to satisfy the demand of Mr. ———. Assuming the claim to be a lawful and proper one in other respects, the present overseers of ——— would be justified in discharging (though they could not be compelled) so much of the claim as was incurred during the period of office of their immediate predecessors, if the latter left a balance in money, or arrears of rates, sufficient to meet this, and all other liabilities incurred by them, but not satisfied when they left office. But with regard to such of the bills as were incurred before the period last mentioned, it seems to the Commissioners, that the present overseers have no authority to discharge such bills out of the current rates. The rule of law, established in Tawney's case, and recognised in numerous recent decisions, shows that the present rate-payers cannot be called upon to pay the debts incurred at former periods. The charges contained in the bills appear to be of two kinds, first, the amount of fees claimed in the several cases as clerk to the justices. Second, charges for advising the parish officers professionally, in the same cases. Upon the first of these points, there is no doubt that Mr. ——— was entitled to be paid by the overseers such fees as the table of fees sanctioned, but the Commissioners do not understand that any objection is raised to the bills in this regard. On the second point, as to the claims for professional advice, the Commissioners think that Mr. ———'s title is not so clear. Generally it may be observed, when overseers come to a justices' clerk, they may fairly presume that he is able to form a good notion of what evidence will support the justices' order. When the clerk is a professional man, there can be no good reason to presume that in taking his advice, the overseers separate his character of clerk, from that of a professional man, and seek to avail themselves of his judgment in the latter capacity. If in any of the cases to which the bills relate, the overseers sought the advice of the clerk before the time of meeting, and at another place than where acting as clerk to the justices, there would be reason to consider them as consulting him professionally.

XI.—LUNATICS.

REMUNERATION TO CLERK TO GUARDIANS FOR PREPARING ANNUAL LUNATIC RETURN.

February 16th, 1846.

Clerk of the ——— Union—Inquired whether he was intitled to make a charge for filling up the necessary forms of returns of lunatics.

Ans.—In the opinion of the Commissioners, the clerk of a union cannot make any charge for this additional duty which the legislature has thought fit to cast upon him.

XII.—MEDICAL RELIEF.

PAYMENT OF MIDWIFERY FEE, WHERE ORDER GIVEN BY OVERSEERS. — MEDICAL TICKETS, HOW FAR AVAILABLE.

October 11th, 1845.

Clerk of the Scarborough Union—A medical officer of the union has been refused payment by the board of guardians of the midwifery fee, for attendance on the wife of an able-bodied labouring man, under the written order of an overseer. The board considered that the overseer ought not to have given the order, as the husband was in such employment, as, with ordinary frugality, would have enabled him to pay for medical attendance. Inquired. 1st. Whether the guardians are bound to pay all the orders given by the overseers for medical attendance in labour cases. 2nd. Whether, when the husband has a medical ticket for himself, or any of his family, the medical officer is required to attend the wife during labour, and entitled to his fee for so doing.

Ans.—1st. Where the overseer is legally qualified to make the order, that is, in cases of sudden and urgent necessity, the guardians are bound to pay the fee, under Article 12 of the General Medical Order. But if the guardians think the overseer was not legally authorised to give such order, they may decline to pay the fee, and the overseer will then make the payment himself, and include the same in his accounts, subject to the allowance or disallowance of the item, by the auditor. 2nd. The medical tickets provided for by Articles 17 and 18 of the General Medical Order, are intended to be given only to aged and infirm persons, or persons permanently sick, or disabled. The Commissioners are of opinion that, for attendance on the wife of any pauper in childbirth, a separate order should be given to the medical officer. At the same time, if the wife's name is inserted in the medical ticket, and the medical officer has attended her in childbirth without any further order, the Commissioners think that looking to the terms of Article 18, which provides that the medical officer, on the exhibition to him of the ticket, and an application made on behalf of the party to whom the ticket was given, shall be held responsible for affording advice, attendance and medicines "in the same manner as if he had received in each case a special order," the medical officer would be entitled to the payment of a fee for his attendance.

XIII.—OVERSEERS.

1. SUPPLY OF GOODS TO WORKHOUSE BY.

October 27th, 1845.

Clerk of Whittlesey Union—The guardians being about to contract for stoves and other fixtures required for the union workhouse, and the only ironmonger in the town of any note being the overseer for the current year,—inquired whether the board of guardians would be considered *criminis particeps* if such party were contracted with.

Ans.—I am to call your attention to the exception contained in section 6 of 55th Geo. 3rd, cap. 137, as to the case where there is no person (other than an overseer) to be found within a convenient distance from the workhouse, competent and willing to supply goods required for the use of the workhouse, in which case justices are authorised by certificate to permit an overseer to contract for the supply of the goods. The Commissioners cannot undertake to say whether the circumstances of the present case are such as to bring it within that exception—this is a point to be determined by the justices. The Commissioners would observe, however, that if the justices do not think fit to give the overseer the express benefit of the exception in the statute, there can be no doubt that he would be subjecting himself to the penalties provided by the former part of the section referred to, if he were concerned in the supply of the goods required; and the guardians would be participating in an unlawful act in entering into a contract with such overseer for the supply.

---

2. WHERE PARISH DIVIDED BETWEEN TWO OVERSEERS FOR COLLECTION OF THE RATES,—REMEDY AGAINST ONE OVERSEER OMITTING TO ACCOUNT FOR RATES COLLECTED.

January 12th, 1846.

A Guardian of the ——— Union—The non-payment by the overseers of the parish of ——— of the money ordered by the board of guardians, has caused great trouble to the guardians. The parish being divided into two parts for the convenience of collecting, one of the overseers, who has always readily paid the full amount of the rates of his division (being the west side) of the parish, frequently has had to advance money of his own, to make up the deficiency of the other overseer, who collects the east side of the parish, and who holds a balance of about fifty pounds. It is believed that the board of guardians could not proceed against the defaulting overseer without involving the other, and the late auditor was not able to render the assistance required. Inquired what proceedings can be taken to compel the defaulting overseer to account for the balance due from him to the overseer who is in advance; and also if any means can be used to deter the defaulting overseer from collecting the rate for the ensuing quarter of the year, so that the other overseer may collect the whole, and thereby be enabled to pay the treasurer of the union, according to the order of the board of guardians.

Ans.—The overseer of the east side of the parish in question cannot be prevented from collecting the rates, if he thinks fit to do so: indeed, it is clearly his duty, under the circumstances stated in your letter, to collect the rates with all possible speed. At the same time, the officer who collects for the other division of the parish, (the west side,) is entitled to collect in the east side, and on refusal to pay by any rate-payer, he is empowered to take proceedings to compel payment, there being nothing in the existing arrangement as to the division of the parish for collection, which, in any way, deprives the overseers of their authority over every part of the parish. If in any proceedings that the guardians may think fit to take against the overseer who is in default, they should wish to protect the other overseer of the parish, "who is in advance," it would be easy to do so. If on a summons for default to the order of the board of guardians, it was shown by him, and admitted by them, that he had done his share of the duty of collecting the rate, and that the default arose entirely from the neglect of the other overseer, the distress might be levied solely on the other overseer.

XIV.—PAUPERS.

1. CHARGED WITH FELONY—DETENTION OF, IN WORKHOUSE.

October 10th, 1845.

Clerk of the West London Union.—Three of the male inmates of the workhouse have been given into the custody of the police, charged with an act of felony, committed in the workhouse. The magistrate, before whom they were taken, adjourned the hearing to a future day, and directed that in the mean time the persons charged should be taken back to the workhouse, and there confined in the black-hole, or refractory ward. This was accordingly done. The master of the workhouse, however, feeling some doubt, whether such a proceeding on the magistrate's part was sanctioned by law, and whether he was legally justified in obeying such a direction, applied to the clerk for advice upon the subject. Inquired the Commissioners' opinion, whether the proceeding referred to was legal, or whether the remand ought not to have been made, as is ordinarily the case, to a prison within the jurisdiction of the magistrate.

Ans. After the expiration of the twenty-four hours, during which a pauper inmate of a workhouse may be confined, for an offence, or misbehaviour, under the 54th Geo. 3, cap. 170, s. 7, it is not lawful to detain such pauper longer in the workhouse against his will. The Commissioners think that in such a case as the one you refer to, the remand of the paupers would not constitute an authority to the master of the workhouse to detain them—although it would do so to a peace officer, or a jailor.

2. DESERTION FROM WORKHOUSE WITH UNION CLOTHING.

October 14*th*, 1845.

Clerk of the South Stoneham Union—Inquired whether a pauper inmate who absconded from the workhouse with the union clothing, which he was then wearing, and returned, after three months' absence, bringing back a part only of the clothing, alleging that the remainder was worn out, was punishable, and by what proceeding.

Ans.—The Commissioners think the case falls directly within the 2nd section of 55th Geo. 3, cap. 137, that is to say, that there was both such a desertion from the workhouse, and such a carrying away of the union property, as that provision contemplates. The Commissioners do not think it is necessary to show that there was such a conversion of the property upon the part of the pauper to his own purposes, as would be necessary to establish a case of felony against him.

3. OVERSEERS PROVIDING PAUPERS WITH COTTAGES IN OTHER UNIONS — POOR'S-RATES THEREON.

February 24*th*, 1846.

Clerk of the Carnarvon Union—Inquired, what remedy the guardians have against overseers of parishes in other unions taking houses for their paupers in this union, and not providing them with the means of paying their poor's-rates.

Ans.—The Commissioners do not see that the law affords any remedy which the guardians themselves can resort to in such cases. The overseers of parishes in other unions would certainly be acting unlawfully in furnishing paupers residing in the Carnarvon Union with the means of paying their poor's-rates.

XV.—POOR'S RATE.

ABANDONMENT OF RATE ON ACCOUNT OF NEW VALUATION OF PARISH BEING MADE.

January 20*th*, 1846.

Overseers of St. Giles, Durham Union.—A rate of 6*d*. in the pound was made, and signed by the justices in October last, but a valuation of the parish being in progress at the time, the overseers, to avoid dissatisfaction on the part of the ratepayers, omitted to collect that rate. The new valuation was completed in November, and a rate of 1*s*. in the pound was made upon it in December. Part of the last-named rate was collected, but some of the ratepayers objected to pay it, offering to pay the former rate of 6*d*. in the pound. Requested the Commissioners' advice as to the course the overseers should pursue.

Ans.—The Court of Queen's Bench has expressly decided that a poor rate, when duly made, allowed, and published, cannot be abandoned by the overseers. (R. *v*. The Justices of Cambridge, 2 A. and E. 370.) If, therefore, the October rate referred to in your letter was duly made, allowed, and published, it is your duty to collect it, and you will be accordingly responsible for the neglect of that duty. If it was not duly made, allowed, and published, of course the case would be different.

XVI.—PROPERTY AND INCOME TAX.

ASSESSMENT OF WORKHOUSE THERETO—WORKHOUSE OFFICERS' SALARIES.

November 10*th*, 1845.

Clerk of the Cambridge Union—Referred to the Commissioners' Circular of the 24th June, 1843, relating to the assessment of workhouses, under the Property and Income Tax Act, wherein it was stated, that " if the total income of the officers occupying apartments in such workhouse is under £150 (including the value of such occupation) the assessment may be altogether discharged."—(Vide *Official Circular*, No. 26, p. 111.) The workhouse of the Cambridge Union has been assessed at the sum of £400, against which the board of guardians intend to appeal, and requested the Commissioners' opinion whether the aggregate amount of the salaries of all the officers of the workhouse may be considered as making such assessment, or whether it is necessary that the salary of one of the officers should amount to that sum to render the workhouse liable to be assessed.

Ans.—The Commissioners are of opinion that by the above words, quoted from their circular, must be understood the aggregate amount of the income of all the officers of the workhouse, and not the amount of the income of any single officer. They also presume, that income must be held to mean the salary of the officers, including the annual value of the apartments occupied by them in the workhouse. The Commissioners desire to add that the matter appears to them to be one for communication with the Commissioners of Stamps and Taxes, at Somerset House, rather than for appeal under the statute.

XVII.—RATING.

1. TITHE OF HOPS.

September 22*nd*, 1846.

Mr. ————, *East Retford Union*—Inquired

whether, in making a valuation for a parish, he should assess the vicar for parochial rates, upon the sum received by him as extraordinary rent-charge upon hops, over and above the sum received by the tithe owners as for arable land.

Ans.—The Commissioners are not aware of any reason for supposing that the vicar is not liable to be rated for his tithe of hops, and the Commissioners do not see that the distinction between the ordinary and extraordinary charge required by the Act 6 and 7 Wm. 4. c. 71, s. 42, to be made in the commutation of such tithe, in any way affects that liability. The 69th sec. of that Act expressly provides, that every rent-charge payable instead of tithes shall be subject to all parochial, county, and other rates, in like manner as the tithes commuted for such rent-charge have previously been subject.

2. EASTER OFFERINGS, WHERE COMMUTED.

Jan. 22nd, 1846.

Vicar of ———.—It is stated to be the intention of the overseers of ———, to assess him to the poor's-rates for the rent-charge, in lieu of Easter offerings, which were commuted; but as he had never paid rates for such offerings before commutation, nor been considered liable to do so by the parish authorities, he considers he is exempted by the 69th section of the Commutation Act, (6 and 7 Wm. 4, c. 71.) Requested the Commissioners' opinion thereon.

Ans.—Whether oblations are rateable under the law as it stood, before the passing of the Act referred to, (6 and 7 Wm. 4, c. 71,) as constituting a part of "the ability of the parson, or vicar," is a point perhaps not quite free from doubt. It is necessary to bear in mind that parsons and vicars under the statute of Elizabeth, are not rateable in respect of tithe as tithe, but are rateable generally, in respect of their ability, and tithe, as usually constituting the chief source of their ability, is also, by consequence, usually the chief subject of consideration, in rating the clergy. Accordingly before the Tithe Commutation Act was passed, a rent charge in lieu of tithes was rateable. Some authorities also exist for rating the clergy for oblations and offerings, which are said to be liable to the rate (see 1 Nol. 145.) In the case of Rex *v.* Carlyon, 3 Term Rep. 385, it was distinctly said by Lord Kenyon, "oblations and other offerings which constitute the rectorial or vicarial dues are rateable." Assuming that Easter offerings were so rateable, and the Commissioners are disposed (on the authority of the case last referred to) to think they were, they see nothing in the 69th section of the Act cited by you, which operates as an exemption from such liability. That section renders "every rent charge payable instead of tithes, subject to all parliamentary, parochial, and county and other rates, charges, and assessments, in like manner as the tithes commuted for such rent charge have heretofore been subject." It, therefore, confines the liability to the rate, in virtue of that provision, to rent charge payable in lieu of *tithes,*—the case of rent charge payable in lieu of oblations, offerings, or other customary payments is not provided for. The provision, therefore, appears to the Commissioners, to leave the liability of a rector or vicar to be rated in respect of oblations, or offerings, as it stood before the commutation was effected.

XVIII.—REGISTER BOOKS.

COST OF PROVIDING, WHERE CHURCH-RATE REFUSED—POOR'S-RATE NOT LIABLE.

February 23rd, 1846.

Rev. ——— —In the township of which he is incumbent, they had been unable for several years to obtain a church-rate, and, therefore, he had provided the baptismal and burial register books at his own expense, but he could not any longer provide them. There is no other place for interment within the township, and a burial register-book is urgently wanted. Inquired whether the select vestry (under Sturges Bourne's Act,) of the township is empowered to provide register books out of monies coming into their hands, and can they, upon refusal, be compelled to do so. The registrar-general states that "the Act of 6 and 7 Wm. 4, c. 86, s. 1, has repealed so much only of the Act of 52 Geo. 3, c. 146, as relates to the registration of marriages — the second section of that act, therefore, is still in full force, so far as it relates to the registration of baptisms and burials."

Ans. For the purposes of an ecclesiastical register for baptism, (not births) and deaths, the law on the subject, as regulated by 52 Geo. 3, c. 116, has not been altered by the late Act of 6 and 7 Wm. 4, c. 86. The former of these Acts (sec. 2) provides, that books, *i.e.*, registers, in conformity with the forms in the schedules to the Acts, are to be furnished by the church or chapel-wardens, at the expense of the parish or chapelry, whenever required by the rector, vicar, curate or officiating minister. The statute, it will be seen, while it throws the charge of providing the books for the register on the parishes concerned, does not go on to specify *any fund* from which the payment is to be made. The question arises, therefore, whether the poor's-rate can be lawfully resorted to for the purpose, and the Commissioners are of opinion that it cannot, and for these reasons:—The object is one wholly unconnected with the relief of the poor, or the administration of the Poor Laws. The persons charged with the duty of providing the books, are ecclesiastical officers. It is true that churchwardens, who are mentioned, are by virtue of their office, overseers of the poor, but it is clear both from the nature of the duty itself, as well as from the terms of the statute, that it is in their character as ecclesiastical officers, that the duty is cast upon the churchwardens. It is possible, therefore, that they might be justified in making the payment out of any church-rate raised in the parish; on this, however, the Commissioners are not called upon to give an opinion. The Commissioners apprehend, that a select vestry appointed under Sturges Bourne's Act, 59 Geo. 3, c. 12, are clearly not bound to provide the register books you speak of, neither are the monies at their control, as a select vestry, available for the purpose. The only fund over which they have a control, is the poor's-rate, and that fund is not, for the reasons already assigned, in the opinion of the Commissioners, liable.

XIX.—REGISTRATION.

DIVISION OF EXPENSE OF ENTRIES IN CERTIFIED COPIES OF MARRIAGES PERFORMED IN PARISH CHURCH, OF PERSONS LIVING IN DIFFERENT TOWNSHIPS.

December 24th, 1845.

Clerk of the —— Union—The parish church of R., is situate in the township of C. At this church, parties have been married who were resident in the different townships in the union, and some of them even out of the union. As persons from townships not in the union, could be married at this church;—inquired whether, in the accounts, he could divide the sum paid to the clergyman for entries in the certified copies of marriages, amongst the several townships in the union, according to the averages, or, as the marriages had all taken place in the township of C., the whole sum should go to the debit of that township; if so, it would be felt as an injustice to the township.

Ans. The 1st Vic., c. 22, provides that "the said superintendent registrar shall pay, or cause to be paid to the said rector, vicar, or curate, the sum of 6d. for every entry contained in such certified copy, which sum shall be reimbursed to the said superintendent registrar, by the guardians or overseers of the union, parish, or place for which he shall be appointed superintendent registrar, as aforesaid, in like manner as by the said act (6 and 7 Wm. 4, c. 86,) is provided for the payment of the registrar, on production of his accounts to the superintendent registrar." This enactment, however, omits to provide for the apportionment of the fees so paid among the places comprised in a union. In ordinary cases there is no difficulty in apportioning the fees amongst the parishes or townships in a union, in respect of which the charges are respectively incurred. In the present case, which is quite anomalous, the apportionment amongst the several townships, cannot be calculated by reference to any principle applicable in ordinary cases. The Commissioners recommend, therefore, that the guardians should pay the money as a common charge, and not attempt an apportionment, which it would be impossible to support.

XX.—RELATIONS.

1. LIABILITY OF GRANDCHILDREN TO SUPPORT GRANDFATHER.

February 17th, 1846.

A. R.—He is seventy-nine years of age, and in destitute circumstances, but having a grandson, who is able to contribute to his maintenance, inquired, whether the grandson was compellable, by law, to make such contribution.

Ans. It is doubtful whether a grandchild is liable, in law, to support the grandfather. The terms of the 7th sec. of the 43rd Eliz., c. 2, impose the obligation upon "children" merely, and it remains to be decided, whether the word "children," as employed in that sec., is to be taken to include "grandchildren." It is true that in Waltham v. Sparks, 1 Bott. 439,—Holt, C. J. said, that the word "children" in this statute, included grandchildren, but there has never been any express decision on the point. The Commissioners desire to add, that if you are destitute, the officers acting on behalf of the parish in which you are residing, will be bound to relieve you, if you apply to them.

2. MAINTENANCE OF STEPMOTHER.

February 23rd, 1846.

Clerk of the Easingwold Union—Stated, that out-relief of 5*s*. per week is granted by one of the townships in the union to a pauper and his wife on account of the age and sickness of the man. Application has been made to the pauper's son for repayment of the relief, but although of sufficient ability, he refused to pay more than 3*s*. per week, being the relief, as he asserts, actually paid to his father, the other 2*s*. being relief given to the wife, who is only step-mother to the son. Inquired whether the son had good grounds for refusing to repay the whole relief, the township contending that the relief of 5*s*. was given to the husband entirely, and proceedings before justices were about to be taken.

Ans.—The 7th sec. of the 43 Eliz. c. 2, is held by the courts to apply exclusively to natural relations. It has been decided, for example, that a man is not liable under that sec. to support his mother-in-law, (R. *v*. Munday, 1 Strange, 190,) and the Commissioners apprehend that, on the same principle, he is under no obligation to maintain his step-mother. But of the amount to be paid for the support of the father, the justices are to decide.

3. PROCEEDINGS TO ENFORCE MAINTENANCE BY.

Feb. 28th, 1846.

Clerk of the Alderbury Union.—A poor person became chargeable to the union, who has relatives capable of supporting him, but refuse to do so. Inquired, 1. whether the board of guardians should relieve the pauper and apply for an order of maintenance against the relatives; 2, whether the maintenance ordered to be paid by the relatives should be received by the overseers or by the relieving officer; and 3, whether the board, taking into consideration the sum to be contributed by the relatives, should regulate the amount of relief to be given to the pauper, and leave him to get the deficiency from the relatives.

Ans.—In cases such as you have described, it seems to the Commissioners, that the guardians should give needful relief to the poor person; for, until chargeable to the parish, no order on the relatives under the 43rd Eliz. c. 2, and 59th Geo. 3, c. 12, can be made. The order should be in favour of the churchwardens and overseers of the parish which is charged with the relief, (Reg. *v*. Toke, 8 Adol. and Ellis, 227). It seems to the Commissioners that the person ordered to be maintained, cannot obtain, under the order, from the relatives who are to maintain, the weekly payments directed by the order. The order being in favour of the overseers, or rather of the parish, the overseers can alone enforce the order, after the parish has in fact been charged. Where in a case in which an order has been made, the relatives made liable by such order are willing to make an allowance to the poor relation equal to that named in the order, without the intervention of the parish authorities, all the guardians will have to consider will be—whether the allowance is sufficient for the support of the poor person, and, if not, to supply the deficiency. But where such an arrangement between the parties to maintain and to be maintained respectively cannot be made, but the enforcement of the order becomes necessary, then it will be for the guardians to fix the amount of the relief with reference to the actual necessities of the poor person, without taking into consideration the liabilities of the relatives as regards the parish. This liability, as already explained, will be subsequently enforced by the overseers.

XXI.—RELIEF.

1. OF NON-SETTLED IRISHMAN, CHANGING PLACE OF RESIDENCE.

September 8th, 1845.

Clerk of the Richmond (York) Union—T. C., an Irishman, not having any settlement in England, became chargeable to the parish of Richmond, on account of sickness, and has received relief for nearly three years; a few months ago he left Richmond and went to reside in the township of Hepswell, in the same union, his relief being charged to the parish of Richmond, during part of his residence in Hepswell. The guardians of Richmond now object to the relief being charged to their parish, and Hepswell also object to its being charged to that township. Inquired to which parish or township during the pauper's residence in Hepswell should his relief be charged, both places appearing unwilling to remove him to his own country.

Ans.—As the pauper had no legal settlement in the Richmond union, the only ground which could justify the charging of the relief given to him, to the parish of Richmond in the first instance, was the fact of the pauper having become destitute in Richmond during his residence there, and requiring relief. But this liability on the part of Richmond to afford the relief could not continue longer than the pauper's continuance in the parish. When the pauper went to reside in Hepswell, and in like manner required relief while there on the ground of destitution, the same reasons which warranted the charging of the relief to Richmond, would warrant the charging of the relief given subsequent to the removal, to Hepswell. It appears to the Commissioners to be immaterial whether on the pauper's leaving Richmond there was an actual interruption to the receipt of relief, or not. If, indeed, there were at this time a cessation of the relief, and a new application were made in Hepswell, the case would be stronger against the latter township, but otherwise the Commissioners think the guardians cannot legally continue to charge Richmond with the relief given while the pauper is in Hepswell; at all events, not without the concurrence of the overseers of Richmond.

2. OF FEMALE PAUPER COMMITTED TO PRISON AND HAVING A CHILD BORN THEREIN.

January 28th, 1846.

Clerk of the Warminster Union—The governor of the county gaol had, by direction of the magistrates at quarter sessions, applied to the master of the workhouse for baby-linen for a child of which E. P. had been delivered, while a prisoner for the offence of deserting her children, by leaving them in the workhouse. Her term of imprisonment has now expired, and she will be well enough in a day or two to be removed to the workhouse. Inquired the Commissioners' opinion on the case.

Ans.—While the child continues in the county gaol with its mother, it cannot be said to be destitute in the sense of the Poor Laws; and, consequently, the guardians are under no legal obligation to afford relief to the child, or to furnish the clothing or linen which is stated to be required by the mother in her present circumstances. The fact that the mother was committed for the offence of deserting her children and leaving them chargeable to the parish, *i.e.*, for an offence against the Vagrant Laws, is, in the view of the Commissioners, an entirely unimportant circumstance, so far, at least, as it may be supposed to cast a liability on the parish to comply with the present demand, which would not otherwise have existed. That the mother during her term of imprisonment is to be maintained at the charge of the county is sufficiently clear from the 10th section of the 4 Geo. 4, c. 64. And as the child, by reason of its tender years, cannot be separated from the mother, an obligation to provide for its actual wants seems necessarily to rest on the authorities of the gaol. But, however this may be, it appears to the Commissioners that persons while resident in a gaol are in a situation which does not give the guardians any direction or control over them, or the administration of relief to them, or any duties or responsibilities connected with such relief. The Commissioners would add, that if, upon the discharge of the mother, she should become destitute in the parish in which the gaol is situate, or in any other parish of the Warminster Union, it would of course be the duty of the guardians, or their officers, to afford such relief to her or to her child as may be required by the circumstances of her situation.

3. OF SEAMAN IN THE FOREIGN SERVICE, WHO HAD MET WITH AN ACCIDENT.

February 9th, 1846.

Captain Hamilton, R.N., Admiralty—Transmitted copies of correspondence, relative to the case of a seaman, in a Dutch East Indiaman, which had been driven into an English port, through stress of weather—the seaman having met with a severe accident, by a fall from the fore-yard, it became necessary, in order to save the man's life, that he should be admitted into a hospital, or infirmary, on shore. Inquired whether, if the accident had happened to an English subject, he would have been admitted to the infirmary of a union workhouse, and, also, whether a foreigner would be admissible.

Ans. As far as the right to relief is concerned, a foreigner is in the same condition as an Englishman. If a foreigner is landed in this country and becomes destitute, he is entitled to relief at the charge of the parish in which he is destitute. In such a case as that described, he would be attended by the parish, or union medical officer, and if that were judged by the guardians the most convenient and safe course, he would be received into the workhouse provided for the parish, or union. Until, however, he is landed and within the boundaries of an English parish, and in a condition, therefore, to make the necessary application for relief, no legal obligation, on the part of the parish, or of the authorities, arises, to afford such relief. A foreigner having no settlement in England, is incapable of removal, as in the case of an Englishman having no known settlement. The parish in which, therefore, he first became destitute, on his landing, would be bound to continue the relief, medical or otherwise, so long as the destitution might continue.

XXII.—REMOVAL.

1. OF MOTHER WITH CHILD BORN AFTER ORDER MADE BUT NOT EXECUTED.

May 8th, 1845.

Clerk of the Buntingford Union—An order was made for the removal of a pauper with his wife and four children, but on the day the removal was to take place, the woman was delivered of a child. Inquired whether under such order if suspended, the removal can take place, or the child being an increase in the number of the family specified in the order, it would be necessary to commence proceedings *de novo*.

Ans.—It does not appear to the Commissioners necessary that in the case to which your letter refers, a fresh order of removal should be obtained. The existing order can be suspended, if the mother is unable to travel, and, upon the removal of the suspension, can be executed as to the persons mentioned in it. The child which has been born since the order was obtained cannot be separated from the mother. If the mother is removed, the child must accompany her as a matter of course, though not mentioned in the order.

2. OF SCOTCH AND IRISH PAUPERS UNDER 8 AND 9 VIC., C. 117.

November 20th, 1845.

Clerk of the Rochdale Union—Inquired by whom and in what way the expences of removals of Scotch, or Irish, &c. paupers, under the Act of last session (including the expences of the magistrate's summons and order) should be paid and charged?

Ans.—The second section of the Act of 8 and 9 Vic., cap. 117, appears to the Commissioners to require that the expense should be borne by the union, in the case of a pauper chargeable to a parish within the union, and by the parish, in the case of a pauper chargeable to a parish not in a union. The section enacts that a pauper shall be removed "at the expense of such union, or parish," and the Commissioners think that these words are not to be read as merely alternate expressions, but that they are to be referred to their antecedents, according to the rule "reddendo singula singulis," so that the union shall be charged where there is a union, and the parish where there is no union.

XXIII.—SETTLEMENT.

1. OF WIFE AND CHILDREN OF IRISHMAN.—ORDER FOR THE REMOVAL OF A WOMAN BEFORE MARRIAGE LOST,—PROOF NECESSARY.

October 11th, 1845.

Overseers of Llanbeblig, Carnarvon Union—Four children, who had been deserted by their parents, had been relieved by the parish for about two years. D. W., the father, is an Irishman, and his wife, A. W., is a Welshwoman, and they had been in the receipt of relief for several years from the parish of Llangeinwen, in this union, being the wife's maiden settlement, in right of her father. About thirty years ago, A. W., when single, was removed by order of justices, as part of her father's family, from Llanbeblig to Llangeinwen, against which order there was no appeal. The order cannot now be found, but proof can be given that it was in existence, and that relief had been granted under it by the former parish officers of Llangeinwen, such relief being continued to D. W. and his wife and children up to the end of 1843, when the parish officers of Llangeinwen discontinued it. Neither D. W., nor his wife, ever held a house, lodging, or room, in the parish of Llanbeblig, but resided there a very few days, in passing from one place to another. Inquired whether the children could be removed to the mother's maiden settlement.

Ans.—If, as is probable, the father, being an Irishman, has no settlement in England, then the children can be removed to the settlement which their mother had prior to her marriage. This is stated by you, to be Llangeinwen. You state, also, that about thirty years since, A. W., while single, was removed by an order of justices from Llanbeblig to Llangeinwen, as a part of her father's family, against which there was no appeal. The order, therefore, is not only conclusive of the settlement adjudicated by it (*i.e.*, as the Commissioners collect from your statement, the settlement of A. W.,) but also, of her children, who derive a settlement from her. (Rex *v.* Catterall, 6 M. and S. 83.) Of course, if the order be in existence, it should be produced before the justices who may now be applied to to remove the parties, together with proof that the order was put in execution; but if the order be really lost, and proof of due search and of the loss be given, other evidence is admissible to prove the making of the order by the justices, and its due execution by the officers of the parish in whose favour it was made. It will likewise be necessary that the examination should set out, either that the order of removal was produced before the removing justices, or that evidence was given to show that it was lost, or could not be obtained. The Commissioners would add, that relief given by the overseers of one parish to paupers resident in another parish, is evidence of a settlement in the relieving parish, and where (as in the present instance) relief has been so given for a number of years, cogent evidence. It is not, however, conclusive, and it is open to Llangeinwen, the parish which gave the relief to A. W. and her family, while residing elsewhere, to show, if they can, that it was given under a mistake.

2. BY ESTATE. NECESSITY OF RESIDENCE IN THE PARISH IN WHICH THE ESTATE IS SITUATE.

January 24th, 1846.

Rev. O. J. Humphreys, Corwen Union—A pauper named J. P., chargeable to the parish of Llansantfraid Glyn Ceiriog, in this union, came into possession, on the death of his father, of a small freehold farm in the parish of Llangadwaladr. The farm, being mortgaged, was sold by the said J. P. He never resided at the farm after it came into his possession, and consequently did not pay rates or taxes. He had since become chargeable to the first-named parish, in which he resided. J. P. did not reside in the parish in which the estate was situate, while his interest in the estate continued, but he always resided within two miles of the estate, except on one occasion, that he was imprisoned in Ruthin Gaol, which was above ten miles from the estate. Inquired whether the pauper had acquired a settlement in the parish in which the estate was situate.

Ans.—No settlement has acquired by the mere possession of the property, it being necessary to the acquisition of a settlement by estate that the owner should reside for forty days in the parish in which the estate lies, whilst his interest in the estate continues, (R. *v.* Sowton, Burr, S.C. 125, 2 Bott. 675, R. *v.* St. Nyott's, Burr, S. C. 132.) But had the case been otherwise, had there been such a residence in the parish of Llangadwaladr, as, coupled with the possession of the property, was sufficient to have conferred a settlement by estate, it would appear that the pauper lost it when he was committed to Ruthin Gaol, by which circumstance (though the act of the law,) he ceased to reside within ten miles of the parish in which the estate was situate. (Reg. *v.* Whissendine, 1 G. and D. 560.)

3. BY ESTATE. ON MARRIAGE, PASSES TO THE HUSBAND.

February 16th, 1846.

Clerk of Chipping Sodbury Union—J. W. built a house on the waste, in the parish of A., about twenty years ago. The lord of the manor afterwards took possession, but granted a lease for lives at a nominal rent. J. W. died, leaving the property to his son, W. W., who also died, leaving his wife with three children, in possession of the property. W. W., the son's widow, afterwards married a man named P., belonging to the parish of B., who resided with the woman in the house. He was in gaol for theft, leaving his wife and children chargeable to the parish in which the property was situate. Inquired whether the man's settlement was transferred to the woman, or the woman's transferred to the man.

Ans.—As the estate referred to was merely a leasehold, in both J. and W. W's. case, and the rental was under £10 a year, neither of these acquired any settlement in respect of it, (6 Geo. 4, c. 57.) For the same reasons, neither W. W.'s widow, nor his children, gained any settlement by the possession of this property. But on the widow's marriage with P., her share of the estate passed to her husband by operation of law, and if he resided within the parish for forty days, he acquired a settlement in respect of such estate accordingly, (R. *v.* North Cerney, 3 B. and Ad. 463.) If he has continued to reside since his marriage, within ten miles of the parish, he still retains that settlement, but otherwise he has lost it (4 and 5 Wm. 4, c. 76, s. 68.) The wife follows her husband's settlement, and therefore, on P.'s acquiring the settlement by estate, such settlement was communicated to his wife, although the estate itself was not such as to confer a settlement upon her before the marriage (see R. *v.* North Cerney, already cited.)

LONDON:
Printed by order of the Poor Law Commissioners, by BLACKBURN and PARDON, 6, Hatton Garden, and Published by CHARLES KNIGHT and Co., 22, Ludgate Street, Publishers to the Poor Law Commissioners.

AN

OFFICIAL CIRCULAR

OF PUBLIC DOCUMENTS AND INFORMATION:

DIRECTED BY THE POOR LAW COMMISSIONERS TO BE PRINTED, CHIEFLY FOR THE USE OF THE MEMBERS AND PERMANENT OFFICERS OF BOARDS OF GUARDIANS, UNDER THE POOR LAW AMENDMENT ACT.

No. 58.] CIRCULAR ISSUED APRIL 1, 1846.

Poor Law Commission Office, Somerset House, April 1, 1846.

THE Poor Law Commissioners directed that the following documents be printed and circulated for the information of Guardians and Officers of the several Unions, viz.

(Signed) By order of the Board,
EDWIN CHADWICK, *Secretary*.

I.—ACCOUNTS.

1. CONSTABLES' EXPENSES—LAW BILLS.

March 17th, 1846.

Clerk of the ——— Union—The magistrates, under the recent statute, require the constables to bring before them bills for all business done by such constables within their parishes. The magistrates, when they approve of any such bills, sign them, and make an order upon the parish officers, to pay them; but the auditor refuses to allow any charges that may not be for parish business. The guardians are of opinion that the auditor has not taken a correct view of the statute. In parish appeals, also, the auditor refuses to pass any solicitor's bill, that has not been taxed by the clerk of the peace. The board of guardians are of opinion that it is optional for the parish or the solicitor to have the bill taxed by the clerk of the peace, and that when it is not taxed it is the duty of the auditor himself to strike out anything that may be objectionable, and to allow the remainder; but this he refuses to do, and the parish officers, having paid the bills, are without any remedy.

Ans.—In reference to the question of constables' expenses, the Commissioners direct attention to Number 30 of the *Official Circular*, p. 164, which contains the opinion of the late Sir Wm. Follett and Mr. Tomlinson, upon a case submitted to them by the Commissioners respecting the construction of the Parish Constables' Act, 5th & 6th Vict. c. 109, sec. 17, as to what fees could be properly paid to parish constables out of the poor-rates under that section. It will be seen that the purport of such opinion is, that the fees or allowances to constables out of the poor-rates under that Act, are not limited to those cases in which the constable's services have been required in a matter of parochial concern. The Commissioners, when applied to on this subject, have always suggested that the view expressed in that opinion should be acquiesced in by overseers, auditors, and others. Upon the second point adverted to, the Commissioners do not see that the auditor can insist on the taxation of an attorney's bill, which has not been taxed, when the account containing the payment comes before him. It is bills which are due to any solicitor or attorney in respect of business performed on behalf of any parish or union which are to be taxed by the clerk of the peace on application, (see sec. 39, 7 & 8 Vict. c. 101.) But when any such account has been paid by an overseer, without taxation, (and it must have been paid before the charge can appear in the accounts,) then it is no longer a bill "due to any solicitor or attorney." Where a bill is not taxed previously to its discharge by the overseers or guardians, the auditor will very properly exercise his judgment with respect to the bill, and judge for himself of the reasonableness and legality of the charges; and his decision (as the 39th section of 7 & 8 Vict. c. 101, shows,) is final in such case. In such case, any deduction made from the bill by the auditor will be the loss of the officer who has paid the account, and, for his own protection, therefore, he should previously insist upon the taxation of the bill by the competent authority.

---

2. EXAMINATION OF ACCOUNTS BY GUARDIANS.
February 3rd, 1846.

Clerk of Carnarvon Union—Inquired, what is the duty of the guardians in reference to the examination of the union accounts; and to what extent, as to time, their attention should be directed to them.

Ans.—The Commissioners presume, that this inquiry has reference to the regulation in Article 14 of their General Order on the Proceedings of Boards of Guardians, which directs (*inter alia*) that the guardians "shall examine all books and accounts relative to the relief of the paupers of the union." The books and accounts more especially referred to by that Regulation, are those mentioned in the following Articles of the General Order on the Duties of Officers, namely: Article 19, No. 3, which directs the treasurer to render an account of all monies received and paid by him, as such treasurer, when required of the guardians to do so. This must, in fact, be done at every meeting, as entries of all money transactions should appear on the minutes. Article 19, No. 3, which directs medical officers to make a weekly return to the board of guardians, in Form B, annexed to the General Order. Article 20, No. 11, which requires the relieving officer to keep a separate, full, and true account of all monies received and disbursed by him, for, or on account of, the relief of the poor of each parish in the district for which he acts; to balance such account weekly, and submit the same to the guardians at every ordinary meeting of the board for their approval. Article 74, No. 17, of the General Workhouse Rules, which requires the master of the workhouse to submit all books of accounts which he is required to keep, to the board of guardians at their meetings. With respect to the extent, as to time, to which the guardians should devote their attention to this part of their duties, the Commissioners cannot lay down any definite rule; it is a matter on which the guardians must act on their own judgment and discretion, according to circumstances. The Commissioners would merely remark, that it is (as the guardians are, doubtless, aware) a point of great importance, with a view to the interests of both the ratepayers and the paupers, and to ensure a correct discharge of their duties by the respective officers, that the books and accounts of the latter should be regularly and carefully examined and checked by the guardians, at short intervals. They are on the spot, and are cognizant of all the details which enable them at the moment to clear up any doubtful point, and correct any inaccuracy. When the clerk inspects the books of the officers, as required by Article 20, No. 11, of the Order on the Duties of Officers, and Section II. No. 12, of the General Order of Accounts, he should point out any errors or false entries which he may discover, to the board of guardians at their next meeting.

II.—APPRENTICESHIP—Power of guardians to apprentice orphan who is not a pauper.

March 22nd, 1845.

Clerk of Preston Union—Inquired whether the guardians have power to apprentice an orphan boy who is not chargeable to any parish in the union.

Ans.—The 43rd Eliz. does not require the child to be chargeable before he is apprenticed, the overseers being empowered to put out as apprentices the children of such parents as they believe to be unable to maintain them. If previous chargeability may be dispensed with in the case of a child whose parents are living, there seems to be no reason why it must be insisted on in the case of an orphan.

III.—CLERK—Whether bound to attend to give evidence in settlement cases.

Jan. 19th, 1846.

Clerk of Marlborough Union—Inquired whether he is bound by any regulation of the Commissioners to attend in order to give evidence, at a distance of between thirty and forty miles, on the examination of a pauper as to his settlement, to prove the fact of relief having been administered to some ancestor of such pauper; and whether he must furnish any books, papers, or accounts, that may be asked for in relation to this case.

Ans.—The Commissioners have issued no order which requires the clerk of the board of guardians to attend as a witness, on any inquiry as to the settlement of a pauper. He is under the same obligation to obey the subpœna in this case as in any other, but no more. It seems clear, from the decision of the court of Queen's Bench, in the Queen *v.* Greenway, and the Queen *v.* Carey, 14 L. J. R. n. s., M. C., 490, that if you are served with a subpœna, *duces tecum*, you must take all such books, documents, and papers as are in your possession.

IV.—CONTRIBUTION—Levy of, upon overseers' goods.

February 27th, 1846.

Clerk of Newport (Monmouth) Union—Inquired whether the landlord of an overseer on whose goods a distress has been levied for the recovery of contributions due to the Union, can distrain on the same goods for rent, and thereby supersede the proceedings of the guardians.

Ans.—The Commissioners think that a distress issued against the overseers under the 2 and 3 Vic. c. 84, for non-payment of a contribution order, is a taking of goods by execution within the statute 8 Anne, c. 14, s. 1, and that such distress is so far controlled by that provision as to give the landlord, if he have a claim for rent, the prior right to have such claim satisfied if it do not exceed one year's rent. The proper course, as will be seen by the provision contained in the statute of Anne, is for the person executing the distress before he removes the goods from the premises to pay the amount of the claim. If, however, one overseer has not sufficient assets, the other overseer or overseers can still be proceeded against for the amount in arrear.

V.—CORONER—Claim of, to fees out of the poor-rates.

Jan. 9th, 1847.

Mr. ———, *District Auditor*—Inquired whether coroners can claim to be paid fees out of the poor-rates for inquests in which verdicts of felo-de-se or manslaughter have been returned; a coroner in his district having claimed such fees under the authority of the 3rd of Hen. 7, c. 1, and the 12th of Geo. 2, c. 29.

Ans.—The statute which ought to have been cited as providing for the payment of the fee to the coroner in such cases, is the 25 Geo. 2, cap. 29, sec. 3, which continues the statute 3 Hen. 7, cap. 1. The latter statute provides that the coroner's fee of thirteen shillings and fourpence shall be paid out of the goods and chattels of the slayer, or, out of the amerciament upon the township; which amerciament is imposed when the slayer escapes. The act 1 Vict. cap. 68, provides further for the expenses of the coroner's inquest to be paid out of the county rate. But none of the statutes impose any charge upon the poor-rates in respect of such expenses.

VI.—ELECTION OF GUARDIANS.

1.—DEFINITION OF ART. 29 OF THE GENERAL ELECTION ORDER OF JANUARY 27TH, 1845—CIRCULAR.

Poor Law Commission Office,
Somerset House,
March 9th, 1846.

SIR,—I am directed by the Poor Law Commissioners to call your attention to Art. 29 in their General Election Order, which provides that whenever the day appointed therein for the performance of any act shall be a Sunday, such act shall be performed on the day following.

The Commissioners are informed that some misunderstanding prevails as to the extent of this provision, and desire me to point out to you that it is only the act which is to be done on the day which happens to be Sunday in any particular year which is postponed. All the other proceedings must take place on the days specified in the order.

Thus in the present year, as the 15th of March will fall on a Sunday, the notice of the election, if not published before the 16th, may be published on that day, and, as the 5th of April will fall on a Sunday, the voting papers must be delivered on the 6th and collected on the 7th.

I am, Sir, your obedient servant,
W. G. LUMLEY,
Assistant Secretary.

The Clerk to the Guardians.

2. NOMINATION PAPERS.

March 28th, 1846.

Clerk of Cheltenham Union—Has received two nominations of guardians from a parish in the union entitled to elect *two* guardians. One nomination paper contained the names of *two* persons and the other the names of *three* persons. Inquired whether the nomination containing the names of three persons should be treated as a nullity?

Ans.—The Commissioners think that a nomination paper containing the names of a greater number of candidates than there are guardians to be elected for the parish, is void for uncertainty, and should, therefore, be rejected by you.

3. OWNERS' CLAIMS.

February 27th, 1846.

Clerk of Northampton Union—Inquired whether it is necessary that owners registered last year claiming to vote at the election of guardians, should claim and be registered again previous to voting at any subsequent election; the qualification remaining the same. The Commissioners had expressed an opinion, (*Official Circular*, No. 26, p. 102,) that owners need not send in a fresh claim, but that opinion having been given before the passing of the 7 and 8 Vic. c. 101, the inquiry is made with reference to the 15th sec. of that act.

Ans.—The Commissioners do not think it necessary under sec. 15 of 7 and 8 Vic. c. 101, that persons duly registered last year as owners, claiming to vote at the election of guardians, should claim and be registered again to entitle them to vote at the election in the present or any subsequent year, the qualification of such persons to vote as owners remaining the same.

4. QUALIFICATION OF GUARDIAN WHOSE NAME IS OMITTED IN RATE-BOOK.

March 24th, 1846.

A ratepayer, Sheppey Union— Mr. B—., a guardian of the union, was, from some unknown cause, omitted from the poor-rate in the last quarter. In the last rate, however, the overseers rated him again to the same property. Inquired whether Mr. B. is disqualified from sitting as guardian for the parish for the ensuing year, through the omission in the former rate.

Ans.—If Mr. B. is actually rated to the poor-rate in some parish in the union, when the election of guardians for the ensuing year takes place, he will be eligible to be elected a guardian, presuming, of course, that he is rated in respect of hereditaments of the annual value or rental required as a qualification for a guardian of the Sheppey Union. The fact of his name having been omitted from a poor-rate during the last quarter, will not at all affect his eligibility to be elected a guardian, if he is rated as above stated, at the time when the election takes place.

5. TIME FOR DECLARING NEWLY-ELECTED GUARDIANS.

March 21st, 1846.

Clerk of Reading Union—Inquired when, in the

event of there being no contest for any of the parishes in the union, will be the latest period after the 26th March, that he must declare the newly-nominated board of guardians for the ensuing year. A meeting of the board is to be held on the 2nd April for the purpose of examining the bills for the quarter ended 31st March, and for the election of a registrar for one of the districts of the union; and the inquiry is more particularly made with a view to ascertain in whom, under the circumstances, the election of a registrar is vested—in the present board of guardians, or the guardians which may be elected for the ensuing year.

Ans.—If there is no contest in any of the parishes of the Reading Union, *i.e.*, if no more persons are put in nomination than there are persons to be elected for the parishes, of course the persons nominated (if otherwise qualified) will be the elected guardians for the ensuing year. Their election is complete under the order on the 26th March, the last day on which nominations can be received. The necessary notification to the guardians elected should, therefore, be made as soon after the 26th instant, as it can be done. Upon the supposition that there is no contest, the newly-elected guardians will be entitled to sit at the meeting of the board on the 2nd April. If, however, there is a contested election in any of the parishes, the declaration of the election generally should be delayed until such contested elections are brought to a close.

VII.—GUARDIAN.

1. HIGH CONSTABLE ELIGIBLE FOR THE OFFICE.

March 21st, 1846.

Mr. ———,—Inquired whether a person serving the office of high constable, and receiving his whole salary from the county rates, is eligible to be a guardian within the union he is resident in.

Ans.—There is nothing in the circumstance of a person serving the office of high constable, and receiving a salary from the source stated in your letter, which renders him legally ineligible for the office of guardian.

2. LIABILITY OF GUARDIAN, SUPPLYING GOODS TO RELIEVING OFFICER FOR THE USE OF THE POOR, TO A PENALTY.

Jan. 30th, 1846.

Chairman of Worcester Union—It frequently occurs that relieving officers are obliged to purchase a little tea and sugar, or a small quantity of meat, for the families of paupers in cases of urgent want. Inquired whether a guardian of the union would render himself liable to the penalty imposed by the 77th section of the Poor Law Amendment Act, if he supplied such articles to the relieving officer, for the purpose above adverted to.

Ans.—The terms of section 77 of the Act 4 & 5 Wm. 4, c. 76, clearly extend to, and include, a guardian of the poor. Whether, however, the fact of a guardian supplying the relieving officer with goods or provisions, under such circumstances as are described in your letter, would be an offence against the provision, is a point not free from doubt. If the relieving officer, in any case, gave a written or printed order on the guardian, to supply the pauper with provisions on the account, or credit, of such relieving officer, such a case would be directly within the provision cited, and the guardian would be liable to the penalty. But where, as in the case put, no such order is given, but the relieving officer himself purchases the provisions, with the intention of applying them in the relief of some destitute person, and the provisions are so given, or applied, it is certainly by no means clear that the guardian, by supplying the goods, would be offending against the statute; unless the circumstances should show that, at the time of the purchase, the guardian had a knowledge that the articles purchased were to be given in relief. It is certainly difficult to suppose a case in which a guardian would not know something as to the intended application of the provisions purchased under such circumstances by a relieving officer, if, indeed, such a knowledge on his part is not, by reason of the office he fills, in all cases to be presumed. Seeing, therefore, the doubt which exists, the Commissioners could not advise that articles required in cases of sudden and urgent necessity, should be purchased by the relieving officer of a person who fills the office of guardian or overseer of the poor.

3. POWER OF GUARDIANS TO REQUIRE PRODUCTION OF MINUTES OF VESTRY—PAYMENT OF REMUNERATION TO GUARDIAN FOR SERVING OFFICE.

September 19th, 1845.

Cardigan Union—The Commissioners having received a protest against Mr. ——— acting as guardian for the parish of A., on the ground that he received £20 per annum for executing the officer of guardian, overseer, and surveyor of highways, caused a letter to be written to the guardians, requesting information on the subject. The guardians replied that they were unable to give the information asked for, in consequence of the Vestry Minute Book of the parish of A. being in the custody of the person against whom the protest had been made as overseer of that parish, and of his refusal to produce it to the guardians.

Ans.—(*To the Clerk*)—The guardians certainly have no means of compelling the production of the Vestry Minutes, which are officially in the possession of an overseer, and are, moreover, documents with which the functions of the guardians may be in no wise concerned. It is not alleged that Mr. —— is an assistant overseer. If he be not an assistant overseer, he does not appear to be disqualified from being guardian, on account of anything apparent in the protest of Mr. ——. For Mr. —— cannot be lawfully a paid overseer; nor can he be lawfully paid as a guardian, and any money he may affect to take from the poor's rate as remuneration for the execution of either of those offices or of surveyor of highways is recoverable from him, and is in no sense a payment of salary or emolument to him, and cannot, therefore, disqualify him under the 5 & 6 Vict. c. 57, s. 14.

VIII.—LUNATIC—RECEPTION OF WANDERING LUNATIC INTO WORKHOUSE.

March 10*th*, 1846.

———,—Two police constables found a person *wandering about* the town of C., in a "high state of insanity," whom they conveyed to the workhouse, two miles off, and the master, under the apprehension that they would leave him "raving" at the gates, was induced to take him in. Inquired whether the master acted rightly, as it is conceived that he was under no obligation to relieve the police from the custody of a madman.

Ans.—The master of the workhouse can, upon his own authority, admit a pauper who may be brought there in a destitute state, *i. e.*, if the case be that of a sudden and urgent necessity; and, therefore, when the occasion arises, it is his duty so to admit. In the present case the Commissioners are not prepared to say that the master did wrong in admitting the man brought to the workhouse in the mode described, though "he was in a high state of insanity." Speaking generally, the workhouse is not a fit place for the reception of dangerous lunatics, but under some circumstances, it may be the only available course, there may be no other place to which the lunatic can with safety be taken. Whether the police ought not to have taken the man elsewhere, is not a question for the Commissioners. Of course the master in any such case would do right in giving notice at once to the relieving officer, who, under section 48 of 8th and 9th Vic., c. 126, should bring the case before the justice, to be dealt with under that provision.

IX. — MEDICAL OFFICER OF WORKHOUSE—WHETHER ENTITLED TO FEES FOR POST MORTEM EXAMINATIONS, BY ORDER OF CORONER.

March 18*th*, 1846.

Medical Officer of —— *Union Workhouse*—Inquired, Whether in his capacity of medical officer to the union workhouse, it is part of his duty, by order of the coroner, to make *post mortem* examinations of bodies, and give evidence at inquests, without being paid the fees allowed by law to medical men in general for such services. A young woman was brought into the workhouse labouring under symptoms of poisoning by arsenic, the drug having been secretly taken several hours before her admission, and from the effects of which she died. He was ordered by the coroner to inspect the body, and give evidence at the inquest, both of which orders he obeyed. The coroner informed him that no remuneration was allowed by law to medical officers of union workhouses, for performing autopsies, and attending at inquests; that they came under the same denomination as surgeons of gaols, lunatic asylums, hospitals, &c.

Ans.—The Commissioners are not aware that the medical officer of the workhouse, when required by the coroner to make a *post mortem* examination of the body of a person dying in the union workhouse, is by law restrained from demanding or receiving the fees which, by 6 & 7 Wm. 4, c. 89, are directed to be paid by the coroner to medical practitioners ordered to make such examinations. The Commissioners think it probable that the coroner may have grounded his refusal to order payment of the usual fees in the case referred to, upon the following provision in the statute cited, sect. 5: "And be it enacted, that when any inquest shall be holden on the body of any person who has died in any public hospital or infirmary, or any building or place belonging thereunto, or used for the reception of the patients thereof, or who has died in any county or other lunatic asylum, or in any public infirmary, or other public medical institution, whether the same be supported by endowments, or by voluntary subscriptions, then, and in such case, nothing herein contained shall be construed to entitle the medical officer whose duty it may have been to attend the deceased person as a medical officer of such institution as aforesaid to the fees or remuneration herein provided." If this be so, the Commissioners can only say, that they do not concur in the construction which would extend the provision to the medical officer of a union workhouse. A union workhouse does not appear to be a public hospital or infirmary, within the meaning of the statute. It appears probable, that, in considering whether a public institution comes within the description of the statute, the general character and object of such institution should be looked at, and not the use which is incidentally made of it. By the word "infirmary," is meant a place established for, and applied to, the reception and medical treatment of persons infirm through sickness, and to such persons only. A workhouse, on the other hand, is intended for the reception and employment of destitute persons. It is true, that persons who are sick as well as destitute are admitted, but it is because they are destitute, and not because they are sick.

X.—MEDICAL ORDER—MODE OF CHARGING FEES PAYABLE UNDER.

March 2nd, 1846.

Clerk of Devizes Union — Requested to be informed of the grounds on which the Commissioners think that the fees, payable under Articles 10, 12, and 13, of the General Medical Order, should be charged to the respective parishes to which the paupers belong, instead of to the establishment.

Ans.—The provisions which must govern the Commissioners and guardians in this matter are, first, the declaration in section 26 of the Poor Law Amendment Act, that each parish in a union shall be separately chargeable with the expense of its own poor; and, secondly, the definition in section 28, of the purposes for which charges may be made on the common fund, the material parts of which are the terms, "for the payment, or allowance of the officers of the union, and for any other expense to be incurred for the common use or benefit, or on the common account of the parishes." As to the first provision, there seems to be no doubt that the fee of the medical officer, for a service to any pauper, is an expense of one of the poor of the parish to which such pauper is chargeable; and is, therefore, under the 26th section, (unless the 28th section alters the effect) to be charged to the particular parish, and as regards the 28th section, all the purposes enumerated, are purposes in which the share of the expense of each parish cannot be, at the time of payment, defined or ascertained. They are all strictly *common purposes*, the respective shares in which are (without the adoption of an arbitrary rule,) indefinite. The words "payment or allowance of the officers of the union," are used in the singular, and imply one payment or allowance for the whole service,—not distant payments for each particular service; and the context, which relates only to aggregate payments for common purposes, strengthens this implication. For these reasons, the Commissioners think that the 28th section does not affect the requirements of the 26th in this respect, and that, in accordance with the latter section, the fees referred in your letter should be charged to the respective parishes, and not to the establishment or common fund.

XI.—OVERSEERS—LIABILITY OF, FOR THE DEFAULT OF ASSISTANT OVERSEER IN PAYMENT OF CONTRIBUTIONS, ETC.

March 23rd, 1846.

Clerk of Bury (Lancaster) Union—In the year 1841 the ratepayers of a township in the union appointed W. W., a small farmer, as assistant overseer, at a salary of £8 a year, and the duty of collecting the rate, and paying the various calls, and other parochial business, have devolved wholly upon him, with scarcely any superintendence. No bond was required on his appointment to the office. Some time ago application was made to the overseers for payment of the calls due to the board of guardians, and upon the assistant overseer informing the other overseers that part of the money had been paid, and that the remainder would be attended to, no further notice was taken of the subject until a warrant of distress was issued against the overseers' goods. On the overseers getting possession of the books, they found that the sum of £200 was unaccounted for by the assistant overseer, besides smaller sums, which he had received and not debited himself with. The overseers also found that, on the 26th January last, their assistant obtained from one of the principal ratepayers the sum of £17, under the pretence that a new rate had been made on the

23rd of that month. Inquired, 1st. As a warrant of distress had been issued against the overseers, for the non-payment of their calls, whether the guardians have the power under that warrant to sell the assistant overseer's effects. 2. Whether the overseers could and ought to proceed against the assistant overseer for embezzling the money of the township. 3. Whether money obtained under pretence of a new rate, when there really was no such rate, was a fraud upon the township, or should the loss fall upon the party making the payment.

Ans.—Whether the effects of the assistant overseer are liable, in common with those of the overseers, to be distrained under the warrant, for non-payment of the contribution, depends upon circumstances which are not stated in your communication. An assistant overseer has only such duties and powers as are expressed in the warrant for his appointment. It does not follow necessarily that it is a part of the duty of the assistant overseer to pay the calls made by the guardians, so as in case of non-payment to render his goods liable to be distrained under a proceeding taken under 2 & 3 Vict. c. 84. Before the Commissioners could answer the inquiry put, it would be necessary to know the precise terms of W. W.'s appointment as assistant overseer. Whether the contribution order was addressed to him by name, as well as to the overseers, and whether in the proceedings taken for the recovery of the amount, he was summoned, and if so, whether he is included in the warrant. 2. The Commissioners are not able to say whether a charge of embezzlement could be established against W. W. If the offence do not amount to embezzlement, it would certainly seem that there has been a misapplication of the moneys of the township, within the meaning of the 97th sec. of the Poor Law Amendment Act, and the Commissioners think that if the overseers are prepared with evidence to prove the alleged misapplication by W. W., they should lose no time in proceeding to obtain a conviction under that section. It will be seen, that a person convicted under that section, is liable to pay for the offence, a sum not exceeding £20, and also treble the amount or value of the money, goods, or chattels, purloined, embezzled, wasted, or misapplied. 3. It appears to the Commissioners, that the money obtained from a ratepayer, under the pretence of a new rate, when in fact there was no such rate, was not a fraud upon the township, but upon the party who paid the money, who has his remedy (either criminal or civil) against W. W.

XII.—PARISH COTTAGES—HOW TO OBTAIN POSSESSION OF.

Jan. 7th, 1846.

Mr. ———.—The overseers have for some years hired certain cottages joining each other, but without internal communication, which appear to have been used for some of the purposes of a workhouse. In one of these cottages, consisting of but one room, and a sort of cellar at the back, the overseers have allowed a man of the name of F., aged from 50 to 55, and his daughter, who is blind and slightly paralytic, aged 29, to live rent free, for the last four years. The overseers have done this to afford relief to F. and his daughter, but they have given them no other assistance. The little furniture in the cottage belongs to the inmates. The occupation of the cottage by the paupers can, it is apprehended, be put an end to at any moment, inasmuch as they have none of the rights of tenants, their occupation being merely parochial relief, liable to be terminated at the discretion of the authority giving it. The guardians took upon themselves the administration of relief in the union, on the 25th December last, up to which day it had remained with the overseers of the several parishes and townships. F.'s case will come before the board at its first meeting, the 8th instant, in order that the guardians may, as far as they have authority, remove him from the cottage. No question will arise as to the relative legal rights of the overseers and the guardians in the cottages over the occupiers, but all that the board will have to do will be to refuse to continue to the paupers the kind of relief they have been receiving, viz. residing in the cottage in question, and to substitute for it some other description of assistance.

Ans.—It appears that these persons occupy the cottage free of rent, and consequently, to that extent, receive relief from the township. The guardians may forthwith give directions that relief shall not be given to these persons in the shape of allowing them to occupy the house rent-free, and therefore the overseers would be bound to require the parties to pay rent for the house, and, if such rent be refused, then summary proceedings may be taken under the 59 Geo. 3, c. 12, for the recovery of the possession of the cottage. That statute requires a month's notice to be given, and a demand of possession to be made before these proceedings can be taken. If the overseers decline to take these steps, the auditor will probably feel himself bound to charge them with the amount of the rent which ought to be received for the property.

XIII.—PAUPERS.

1. EMPLOYMENT OF, IN OAKUM-PICKING.

February 14th, 1846.

Clerk of Romsey Union—The guardians being desirous of introducing the picking of oakum as employment for the in-door paupers, requested the Commissioners' sanction thereto, and to be furnished with any information the Commissioners were able to give on that kind of employment.

Ans.—The Commissioners see no objection to the employment of the inmates of the workhouse in picking oakum as the guardians propose. The Commissioners have had occasion to make inquiry as to the terms upon which junk for picking is purchased, and the amount obtained for the oakum, and they learn that when the junk is sent by the dealers to be picked, they pay the guardians from £3. 10*s*. to £4. 10*s*. per ton for picking it. When the junk is bought by the guardians, the price usually obtained for the oakum is about that amount, plus the cost price of the junk. The Commissioners believe that an able-bodied man, if accustomed to the work, may pick four pounds per diem, and women from two to three pounds per diem.

2. REFUSAL TO LEAVE THE WORKHOUSE AND ACCEPT WORK, FOR WANT OF A RESIDENCE IN THE PARISH.

March 17th, 1846.

Overseers of ———.—W. H., an able-bodied man, at present (with his wife and four children under sixteen years of age) an inmate of the union workhouse, has been offered work for himself, at which other men are earning from 9*s*. to 10*s*. per week, and also for his wife (an able-bodied woman) at which she might earn from 4*s*. to 5*s*. per week. The children are of an age that they do not require the constant care of their mother. W. H. refuses to leave the workhouse, and alleges that he cannot get a residence in his own parish, which is believed to be correct, but there are many houses unoccupied in a town which is only two miles from the spot where he has been offered employment. Inquired as to the best means of compelling the pauper to support himself and family.

Ans.—The law has undoubtedly invested the guardians with full power to withhold relief from the man, if they are satisfied he is not destitute, and has the means to maintain himself, and those dependent upon him, or uses an "ordinary and daily trade of life to get his living by," (see 43rd Eliz. cap. 2, sec. 1.) It must however be added, that the inability to obtain a dwelling is one species of destitution, and may entitle the person so circumstanced to relief. It does not appear to the Commissioners to be material that such dwelling should be in the same parish as that in which work is offered, if it be within a reasonable distance of the employment. The Commissioners are of opinion, therefore, that in point of law, if a pauper be offered work, suitable to his strength and capacity, at wages sufficient to afford the means of providing for the support and *lodging* of himself and family, and refuses to accept such offer, he would be liable to be dealt with under the 3rd section of the Vagrant Act. The guardians are clearly under no obligation, and, in fact, have no power, to provide a habitation for the pauper under such circumstances. If the pauper alleges his inability to procure maintenance and lodging for his family at the wages offered to him, the case will remain for the decision of the justices on the facts before them, if proceedings be taken against the pauper, under the Vagrant Act. The Commissioners think it more advisable, in general, to adopt proceedings under the Vagrant Act, after making the man a definite offer of work at specific wages, than discharging him and his family from the workhouse.

XIV.—POOR-RATE.

1. WHETHER GUARDIANS CAN PAY POOR-RATES FOR PERMANENT PAUPERS.

March 6th, 1847.

Clerk of Chertsey Union—When a rate is made in a parish in the union, the relieving officer, at the request of the overseers, makes out a list of the permanent paupers belonging to that parish, with the amount of rate due from each pauper. This list is submitted to the guardians, and if approved of, the rates are paid to the overseers by the relieving officer, and charged against the respective parties in the out-relief list. Requested the Commissioners' opinion on the legality of this proceeding.

Ans.—The Commissioners are of opinion that the practice described in your letter is not authorised by law. The guardians are not empowered to advance, from the funds at their disposal, to any rate-payer (though such rate-payer may be in the permanent receipt of relief from the parish) the means of paying the sums assessed on him as poor-rate. It certainly may be that persons who are recognised as permanent paupers are not in a condition to pay rates; but of their inability to do this, the law has constituted the justices, in conjunction with the parochial authorities, the judges; and to the former belongs the exclusive power of ordering a discharge from the payment.

---

2. Delay in making poor-rate, and borrowing money to meet calls.

March 26th, 1846.

Overseer of Titchmarsh, Thrapstone Union—In consequence of the difficulty in assessing a railway passing through the parish, and not previously assessed to the poor's-rate, it was determined to postpone making a rate; and in order to meet the calls for contribution to the relief of the poor, and for county and police expenses, the vestry agreed to obtain a loan for the purpose. Requested the Commissioners' sanction, which he had been informed by the auditor was necessary before such loan could be legally obtained.

Ans.—If the law does not authorise an overseer to borrow money and to charge the poor-rates with interest, the Commissioners could not by any assent or sanction of theirs render the proceeding lawful. The Commissioners think the auditor's view that as an overseer is not authorised in his official character to borrow money at interest, he is not intitled to enter the transaction in his account, is legally correct. Such a transaction is altogether of a private nature, and it is not one of the matters or things of which the overseer is to give an account to the parish. Of course any payments for parochial objects which an overseer may make out of any monies which he may obtain on loan, he is entitled to enter in his accounts, and if at the end of his year of office, it should appear from the account that he has advanced money to the parish, the succeeding overseers may collect the arrears of rates turned over by such overseer, and out of such arrears reimburse him the sums which he has laid out.

---

3. Dividing parishes for the purposes of rating.

June 16th, 1845.

Mr. W. Snell, Callington—There being a great distinction in the amount of the poor-rate levied in the parish of Callington as between the town and agricultural parts of the parish, inquired, 1. Whether the Commissioners are empowered to divide parishes for the purposes of rating. 2. What proportion of the rate should be borne by the house property and the farms.

Ans.—The law has not invested the Commissioners with any power to divide parishes for the purposes of rating. Such an object (assuming it to be desirable in any case) could only be now effected by a special enactment for the purpose. It seems to the Commissioners that the law, as it at present exists, is calculated to secure equality of assessment, even in parishes in the situation of Callington. All property is by law rateable on the same principle, viz., at what it may be worth to let from year to year for the particular purpose or use to which it is adapted (see the 1st s. of 6 & 7 Wm. 4, c. 96.) If this principle be equally applied both to houses and farms, neither description of property will contribute in a greater proportion than the other to the burdens of the parish. If, however, practically one description of property is rated at its net annual value as defined by the statute cited, while another is assessed only on a portion of that value, no doubt an injustice is thereby effected. But for this the law provides a remedy, as it enables the justices to correct the inequality on appeal against the rate.

---

4. Publication of poor-rate on church doors, etc.

March 18th, 1846.

H. Shaw, Esq. J. P.—Wigan Union—In the township of Ashton there are two churches of the establishment, St. Thomas and Holy Trinity Church, with several chapels belonging to different denominations. Notice of a poor's rate, signed by himself and another county magistrate, was placed upon a board, and exhibited from some time before the commencement, until the conclusion of the morning service on the following Sunday, on the outer door of St. Thomas' Church only. At the conclusion of the service the notice was removed, on the ground, that having been exhibited for one hour, it was a sufficient publication. Inquired what is the duty of overseers with reference to the directions of the Act 1 Vic. c. 45, s. 2, and whether, under the circumstances stated, the justices could sign warrants of distress for non-payment of the rate so published.

Ans.—Having regard to the ordinary legal meaning of the word "chapel," and to what appears to be the general tenor of the 1 Vic. c. 45, the Commissioners consider that the chapels referred to in that statute are chapels belonging to the Established Church, and that consequently it is not necessary, in order to give due publication to a poor rate, that notice of it should be affixed on places of worship used by dissenting congregations. At the same time the Commissioners think it clear that the notice must be "affixed on or near to the doors of *all* the churches and chapels" of the Established Church, within the parish or place. In the case referred to, there are two churches in the township, St. Thomas and Holy Trinity, and the notice was posted on St. Thomas's only. The Commissioners think that this was not a sufficient publication of the rate within the meaning of the 17 Geo. 2, c. 3, s. 1, and 1 Vic. c. 45, s. 2, and that therefore the rate in question cannot legally be enforced by warrants of distress. (See Reg. *v.* Whipp, 4 Ad. & Ell. n. s. 141.) The notice of a poor's rate, when duly affixed on or near to the doors of all the churches and chapels in the parish, ought not to be removed, but should be allowed by the officers to remain there until at least the oceasion for the notice has passed away. The statute, 1 Vic. c. 45, expressly directs that the notice shall be so "affixed;" but it is silent as to its removal. It may be inferred that the notice was intended to remain so long as the occasion for it continued.

XV.—PROPERTY AND INCOME TAX.

COST OF MAINTENANCE OF WORKHOUSE OFFICERS TO BE ASSESSED.

March 22nd, 1846.

Clerk of Stone Union—Inquired, with reference to the Commissioners' Circular on the assessment of workhouses to the Income Tax, (*Official Circular*, No. 25, page 111,) whether by the words "total income of the officers occupying apartments," the cost of maintenance should be added and considered with the salary as the total income in question.

Ans.—In estimating the income of workhouse officers, for the purposes of the Income Tax, the Commissioners understand that the cost of maintenance of the officers should be added to and considered, with the salary, as the total income of the officers, derived from the union.

XVI.—RATING.

1. RAILWAY AND APPURTENANCES.

March 6th, 1846.

Mr. ——— —A railway runs through the parish of L., which is divided into two hamlets, each hamlet separately maintaining its own poor. Two miles of the railway passes through the middle division, or hamlet, for which the company is rated, but on that line of two miles a weighing machine belonging to the railway is set up, which is not rated to the poor's-rate. The length of railway in this division of the parish is rated at £100 per mile, but the receipts of the whole line, which is eighteen miles in length, is about £7000, or £388 per mile per annum. The weighing machine, however, constitutes a source of profit, the small tolls at which, from casual traffic, amount to about £10 per month. It is composed of a platform placed on the railway, and in a house adjacent is placed a yard, or balance, which determines the weight. Every waggon going over the railway in the neighbourhood of the machine is weighed there, and a certain sum per mile is charged. Inquired, 1, whether the machine is liable to be rated separately from the two miles of railway on which it is set up, or can the assessment be made upon "railway and weighing machine," in the same way as "land and buildings" ordinarily are, and an additional amount charged upon the extent of railway in consequence of having such machine set up thereon. 2. Whether all the miles in the length of railway can be rated alike.

Ans.—The Commissioners do not think that the weighing machine described should be separately assessed to the poor's-rate. It does not appear to them to be a distinct subject of occupation by the company, but to be a part of one entire property occupied by the company for the purposes of the railway,—analogous to the case to which you compare it, of buildings appurtenant to a farm. With reference to the question, whether in assessing the railway "all miles in its length can be rated alike," the Commissioners desire to direct your attention to the following remark made by Lord Denman, in the case of the Queen *v.* the Directors of the London and South Western Railway Company, (1 Adol. and Ell. n. s. 558,) "Another question was raised, as to the mode of measuring the rate, namely, whether it was to be measured according to the proportion which the mileage of the railway in the parish bears to the whole length of the way, assuming the profits to arise equally through the whole, or according to the actual earnings in the parish. It was conceded ultimately that the *latter* was the proper mode."

2. RENT-CHARGE—DEDUCTIONS FOR CURATES' STIPENDS.

April, 1846.

Rev. ———, *Cardiff Union*—As vicar of the parish of ———, he is entitled to the rent-charge in lieu of vicarial tithes for the parishes of ——— and ———, but there is an annual stipend payable thereout, by endowment, to the respective perpetual curates of those parishes. Inquired whether he is intitled to deduct from the assessment on his rent charge in those parishes respectively the amount of stipend payable out of the rent charge to the curate of each such parish.

Ans.—The case is essentially the same, though it differs in the manner in which the stipend is charged, as the ordinary one, of the payment by the incumbent of a curate's stipend. The incumbent is, in consideration of the living, bound to provide for the service of the church and cure of souls, and is not intitled to any deduction of rate on account of such service. Where the incumbent does not in his own person perform the duties of incumbency, but receives the profits of the benefice, he is rateable for the full amount of the net value of the living, without deduction for any charges incurred in procuring the performance of those duties.

XVII.—RELATIONS—LIABILITY OF STEP-SON FOR THE SUPPORT OF HIS FATHER AND STEP-MOTHER.

February 23rd, 1846.

Mr. ——— *Uckfield Union*—Stated that the justices have made an order upon him for the support of his father and step-mother, the former of whom he is willing to maintain, but not the latter. Inquired whether the justices can make a distress upon his goods for the amount which they have ordered him to pay.

Ans.—As the facts are stated by you, the Commissioners are not prepared to say that the justices, in making the order upon you, of which you complain, have exceeded the powers conferred upon them by the 43 Eliz. c. 2, and the 59th Geo. 3, c. 12. Disobedience to an order of justices so made subjects the person disobeying to a penalty of 20*s*. a month, and such penalty can be recovered by distress and sale of the goods of such person. The disobedience is also punishable as a misdemeanour at common law, *i.e.*, by indictment.

XVIII.—RELIEF—OF ABLE-BODIED—DISCRETION OF RELIEVING OFFICERS, ETC., TO GIVE ORDERS FOR THE WORKHOUSE.

March 11th, 1846.

Clerk of the Southwell Union—Inquired whether relieving officers or overseers can refuse orders to the workhouse to able-bodied men, when destitute, particularly to those who appear at the time to be under the influence of liquor, or those who have had them previously within a short time, and returned upon their round of vagrancy.

Ans.—It is competent to the overseers to give orders of admission to the workhouse under circumstances of "sudden and urgent necessity." The relieving officers in the intervals between the meetings of the board are empowered to provide medical or surgical relief in cases of sickness or accident requiring such relief, and in every case of sudden and urgent necessity, to afford requisite relief to the destitute person, either by giving such person an order of admission to the workhouse, and conveying him there, or by affording relief out of the workhouse. These are the rules which are to guide the officers, and they must apply them according to the circumstances of each case, on their own judgment and responsibility. Admission to the workhouse should not be refused because the applicant is an able-bodied man, or has recently been an inmate, or that he is under the influence of liquor. The question is that of destitution, and this the officers must decide for themselves. If any person seeking relief is in a state of intoxication, he can be given into the custody of the police and taken before the magistrates, and this would be the proper course.

XIX.—REMOVAL.

1. COST OF MAINTENANCE—PENDING APPEAL AGAINST ORDERS OF.

March 5th, 1846.

Parish Officers of Towcester, Towcester Union—About three years ago a family was removed under orders of removal to Towcester, from the parish of S., also in the same union. An appeal was made against the orders, at the ensuing quarter sessions, when the court confirmed them, subject to the opinion of the Court of Queen's Bench upon a reserved point. The Court of Queen's Bench afterwards reversed the decision of the quarter sessions, and quashed the orders. The paupers, thereupon, became again chargeable to the parish of S., from whence they were removed. Applications have been made to the last-named parish for repayment of the cost of maintenance by the parish of Towcester, pending the trials, amounting to £76. 12*s.* 3½*d.*, but the parish of S. refuses the payment. Inquired whether the parish of S. is liable to repay the cost of maintenance.

Ans.—Sec. 84 of the 4 and 5 Wm. 4, c. 76, provides "that the parish to which any poor person whose settlement shall be in question at the time of granting relief, shall be admitted, or finally adjudged to belong, shall be chargeable with, and liable to pay the cost and expense of the relief and maintenance of such poor person, and such cost and expense may be recovered against such parish in the same manner as any penalties or forfeitures are by this Act recoverable." If, therefore, in the present case, the pauper has been adjudged to belong to S. the remedy against that parish for the costs of maintenance of the paupers pending the determination of the appeal, appears to be that pointed out in the 84th sec. of the Poor Law Amendment Act. Sec. 99 and 101 point out the mode of recovering penalties: any two justices having jurisdiction may be applied to for the purpose.

---

2. EXPENSES UNDER ORDER OF REMOVAL.

March 28th, 1846.

Clerk of Martley Union — Inquired, 1, whether the amount expended under suspended orders of removal, and allowed by justices, is to be paid by the relieving officer of the Union, or by the overseers of the parish to which the pauper is to be removed. 2. Whether under orders of removal not suspended, the amount expended for the twenty-one days from the serving of the order to the removal of the pauper, is to be paid by the relieving officer, or by the overseers. 3. Whether in cases of suspended orders of removal, the charges for taking the examination of the pauper, orders of removal, service of the order, &c. can be charged by the removing parish as part of the expenses incurred by reason of the suspension of the order of removal.

Ans.—1. The amount expended under suspended orders of removal, and allowed by the justices, is to be paid by the overseers of the parish to which the pauper is directed to be removed. By 35 Geo. 3, c. 101, the goods of the overseers are liable to be distrained in case the amount is not paid within three days after demand. 2. In cases of orders of removal not suspended, the amount expended in the maintenance of the pauper during the period of notice (twenty-one days,) is, as in the former case, to be paid by the overseers of the parish to which the order is directed. 3. In cases of suspended orders of removal, only such charges can be recovered by the removing parish, as can be said to be incurred by reason or in consequence of the suspension. The charge for taking the examination of the pauper, and the order of removal itself, cannot be said to be a consequence of the suspension, and cannot therefore be recovered. The cost of effecting personal service of the order when suspended, appears to the Commissioners to be one of the consequences of the suspension, inasmuch as in an ordinary case, transmission by the post would be sufficient, (see sec. 79 of the Poor Law Amendment Act.) Such an expense can therefore be included in the costs ordered to be paid under 35 Geo. 3, c. 101.

XX.—SETTLEMENT.

1. REMOVAL OF CHILD OF MARRIED WOMAN BY A FORMER HUSBAND.

February 23rd, 1845.

Clerk of Stokesley Union — A pauper belonging to Bishop Auckland, but residing at Hutton Rudly, about five years ago married a woman, having a legitimate daughter, eleven years old, and settled in Faceley. The husband being unable to maintain the child, inquired 1. Whether the child can be removed to Faceley according to the decision in R. *v.* Inhabitants of Wendron, 7 Ad. and Ell. 819. 2. Can the child be separated from the mother; or, 3. Can the child be removed with the mother and her husband to Bishop Auckland?

Ans.—The child by the former husband can now be removed to Faceley, assuming that the mother was settled in that parish prior to her marriage with her present husband. The case of R. *v.* Walthamstow 6 A. and E. 301, shows that the children by the first marriage do not gain a new settlement by their mother's second marriage, and that they cannot be removed by order of justices with their mother and her husband to the place of such husband's settlement. In the present case the child is above the age of nurture, and the Commissioners are not aware of any legal hindrance (however objectionable this course may be on other grounds) to the child being removed to its place of settlement, which, as already observed, is unchanged by the marriage. The Commissioners understand this to be the effect of the case referred to, but see the more recent decision of Reg. *v.* Inhabitants of Leeds, Queen's Bench Rep. Vol. 5, part 4, p. 916, in which an order removing a married woman with her four children to the place of her maiden settlement, was confirmed as to the two children above the age of nurture, but quashed as to the wife and children under that age, there appearing to be no sufficient consent on the part of the wife to be removed without her husband.

---

2. REMOVAL OF A BASTARD CHILD WHOSE MOTHER AFTERWARDS MARRIED.

February 18*th*, 1846.

Clerks of Wareham and Purbeck Union—J. H., who was settled in the parish of Corfe Castle subsequently to the passing of the Poor Law Amendment Act, (4 and 5 Wm. IV. c. 76,) married S. S., who was settled in the parish of Steeple, she having at the time a bastard child born since the passing of the above act. The mother is since dead, and J. H. threatens to cease maintaining the child. Inquired, 1st. whether the child belongs to Corfe Castle or Steeple, and until what period. 2nd. With reference to Sec. 71 of the Poor Law Amendment Act, whether an illegitimate child retains its mother's last settlement, (after 16,) acquired by marriage, until it gains a settlement in its own right, or reverts back to its former settlement, supposing it to have had one?

Ans.—The child appears to belong to the parish of Corfe Castle. It was expressly decided, in Reg. *v.* St. Mary, Newington, (2 Gal. and Dav. 686,) that the settlement which the mother of a bastard child may acquire by marriage, presents no exception to the rule laid down in the 71st sec. of the 4 and 5 Wm. 4. c. 76.—that bastard children born after the passing of that Act, shall have and follow their mother's settlement. With reference to your last enquiry, the Commissioners incline to the opinion that the child in question will, on attaining the age of sixteen, retain the last settlement derived from its mother, unless it previously acquire a settlement in its own right. The Commissioners are disposed to consider that the word "have," in the 71st sec. must be construed to mean "take," and that the subsequent limitation ("until," &c.,) has reference to the word "follow," and will not deprive the bastard at sixteen, of a settlement then actually acquired from its mother. The Commissioners admit, however, that the point is not free from doubt.

---

3. REMOVAL OF WIFE OF TRANSPORTED FELON, AND OF HER CHILDREN BY RE-MARRIAGE.

February 18*th*, 1846.

Clerk of New Forest Union—J. D., who was settled in the parish of M. in this union, was transported for felony in 1827, leaving his wife M. D. and four children in England. In 1833 M. D. intermarried with A. B., by whom she had nine children. The youngest and two eldest of these children were born in the parish of M., and the others in the parish of E., also in this union, the two eldest being born previous to her marriage with A. B. The woman and her children are now residing in and chargeable to the parish of M., between which parish and E. (where A. B. is settled,) there is a dispute as to which is liable for the relief of the woman and her children, M. contending that the paupers take a settlement by the marriage with A. B., whilst the parish of E. disputes the validity of the second marriage, and consequently the legitimacy of the children, who are, therefore, settled in M.,—the woman by her marriage with J. D., and the children by their illegitimacy, the two eldest being born in M. prior to the passing of the Poor Law Amendment Act, and the others who were born subsequently, following the settlement of the mother. M. D. was twice removed, whilst pregnant with her two eldest children, from E. to M., and the orders of removal were not appealed against. J. D. was living at the time of his wife's second marriage, as proved by letters received from him, and by a certificate of his being alive in the year 1844, obtained from the Home Office. Inquired the Commissioners' opinion as to the place of settlement of the woman and her children.

Ans.—The children born to M. D. by A. B., being, according to the statement, illegitimate, (the marriage contracted in 1833 being invalid, as M. D.'s husband was then alive) such of the children as were born before the 14th of

August, 1834, are settled in the parish in which they were respectively born, (Whitechapel *v.* Stepney, 2 Bott. 1, Rex *v.* Spitalfields, Lord Raym. 567, Rex *v.* St. Nicholas, Leicester, 2 B. and C., 889,) but such as have been born since that date, and have not by any act of their own acquired a settlement, are settled in the parish in which their mother is now settled, (see 71 sec. of 4 and 5 Wm. 4, c. 76.) M. D. acquired no settlement by the supposed marriage with A. B., (Rex *v.* Lubbenham, 4 T. R. 251,) and unless, therefore, she has herself done some act to acquire a settlement since the date of her removal by order of justices to M., that parish would appear to be the place of her present settlement,—such order (not having been appealed against) being conclusive. If this be so, the illegitimate children born since the 14th August, 1834, are also settled in the parish of M. It is stated that the two eldest children were born before that date, and in the parish of M.—if so, that is their present place of settlement. If letters were received from J. D. subsequently to his wife's marriage with A. B., the case cited (R. *v.* Harborne, 2 A. and E. 540,) would certainly seem to show that such letters must be received as evidence of the existence of the first husband, and therefore establishing the invalidity of the second marriage.

XXI.—VAGRANCY—NEGLECT TO MAINTAIN FAMILY—PROOF OF CHARGEABILITY.

February 10th, 1846.

A Guardian of ———— *Union*—R. T. an able-bodied labourer in good employ, being a widower, with a family grown up, refuses to provide for a daughter, who is ill and destitute, and proceedings are about being taken before magistrates to compel him to support her. The writer applied to the clerk to the guardians for a certificate of her chargeability, who said that such certificate would not be available except in a case of disputed settlement, and that the relieving officer who pays the relief to the daughter must attend. This appeared hard, as the relieving officer lives eight miles from the place where the magistrates meet, and, of course, he would make a considerable charge if he attended. Inquired, whether any remedy can be provided.

Ans.—If it is intended to proceed against R. T. under 5 Geo. 4, c. 83, for the neglect to maintain his family, the Commissioners concur in the view, that the certificate of chargeability which the guardians can make under s. 69 of 7 & 8 Vict. c. 101, would not be sufficient to enable the justices to convict, in the absence of other evidence of the fact of chargeability. In such a case the justices are not empowered to make an order on the person neglecting to maintain, but only to convict him for the offence where the neglect or refusal is proved. The 69th section only provides, "that for the purpose of making any order of removal, or other order, no further or other evidence of chargeability than such certificate shall be required." If, however, the proceeding proposed to be taken against R. T. is for an order of maintenance under 43 Eliz. c. 2, s. 7, then it appears to the Commissioners that the certificate of the guardians as to the chargeability of the party to be maintained (if made in due form) would be available, for the words of the section cited, "or other order," clearly apply to such a case.

XXII.—VAGRANTS.

1. PAYMENT OF INSPECTOR OF VAGRANTS' LODGING HOUSES.

January 27th, 1846.

Assistant Overseer of St. Chad's, Shrewsbury—Inquired whether the salary of a person appointed to visit the small lodging houses for vagrants in that town, could be allowed in the overseers' accounts.

Ans.—If authority could be given to a constable to inspect lodging houses, an arrangement could be made for paying him a salary. But at present the law confers no such authority of visitation, and there is, therefore, no means of attaining the end proposed by you.

---

2. PERSON DESERTING FAMILY, DISCHARGED BY JUSTICES, ON GIVING SECURITY FOR REPAYMENT OF RELIEF.

February 23rd, 1846.

Clerk of Sheffield Union—H. B. was committed to prison for neglecting to maintain his family, and on his liberation, went to Ireland, assumed another name, and lived in adultery, his family being left chargeable in Sheffield. Steps were taken for his apprehension, when he was brought back in custody, and taken before justices, who ultimately agreed to discharge the man on payment by him of the expense of apprehending and conveying him back to England, and on giving a note of hand jointly with two sureties for the payment, by weekly instalments, to the relieving officer of the union of the amount of relief given to his family, when deserted by him. Inquired as to the legality of the order to discharge a prisoner under the circumstances stated, and in case of the non-payment of the instalments secured by the note, whether the guardians could take legal proceedings for the recovery of the amount.

Ans.—In proceedings taken under the Vagrant Act, the law certainly vests a discretion in the justices whether they will convict or not. It is not for the Commissioners (who have not the evidence before them,) to say whether the justices have, or have not, exercised their discretion wisely. Apparently the justices were not satisfied in the present case, that the evidence adduced at the hearing, warranted a conviction. It seems, however, that they discharged H. B., on payment of the expenses of his apprehension, and giving a security for £10. 13*s*., relief given to his wife and children during his absence. Whether it was competent to the justices to impose a condition of this kind, may, perhaps, admit of doubt; but, however this may be, the arrangement made was much more advantageous to the union or parish, than if there had been a conviction. As regards the note which was given, supposing it to be duly stamped, the Commis ioners see no reason to doubt that the relieving officer (the obligation being to him) is entitled to sue on the note for the instalments due. If the obligation had been to the guardians, they would have been entitled to recover. The guardians may, however, require the relieving officer to sue on the note at their cost, or to allow his name to be used, he being indemnified from costs.

XXIII.—VESTRY MEETINGS—QUALIFICATION OF VOTERS—PROXY.

March 25th, 1846.

Mr. ———, *Cardigan Union*—Inquired, 1. Whether the vote of a blind man is legal at a vestry, and, if not, whether he can legally vote by proxy. 2. Whether a female ratepayer has a vote at vestry meetings, and, if she has, whether she can legally appoint a proxy to vote for her.

Ans.—1. The fact of a ratepayer being blind does not legally disqualify him to vote at a vestry

meeting. 2. A female ratepayer is legally entitled to vote at a vestry meeting, equally with male ratepayers. Ratepayers generally are not authorised to vote by proxy in a parish vestry; but where corporations or companies are charged to the rate for the relief of the poor in any parish, they may authorise their clerk, secretary, or agent to be present at any vestry of the parish, and vote on behalf of the corporation or company as the case may be.

XXIV.—WORKHOUSE—EXAMINATION OF VISITORS TO—PROHIBITION OF ARTICLES BEING CARRIED INTO.

February 3rd, 1846.

J. S. an inmate of the ——— *Union Workhouse.* The inmates are prohibited from receiving trifling articles of food, &c., from their friends, and the practice of searching by the porter prevents the friends of the inmates visiting them. Requested the Commissioners to relax the workhouse rules in this respect. Complained also of the practice of searching and of taking away from the inmates such articles on their return to the workhouse after leave of absence, &c.

Ans.—The Commissioners have prohibited articles of food being admitted into the workhouse on the occasion of visits to paupers, because the guardians are empowered and bound to provide everything necessary for the inmates, according to their age and state of health, and to vary that provision from time to time when circumstances may require it. There is no authority given by the workhouse rules for searching persons who present themselves as visitors to inmates. But the porter is authorised to search any pauper whom he may suspect to have possession of any spirits or prohibited articles, and to require all other persons to satisfy him that they have none. This authority is requisite to ensure the observance of the prohibitory rule. The Commissioners are not prepared to vary the regulations in either respect.

Printed by Order of the Poor Law Commissioners, by BLACKBURN AND PARDON, 6, Hatton Garden, and Published by CHARLES KNIGHT and Co., 22, Ludgate Street, Publishers to the Poor Law Commissioners.

AN

OFFICIAL CIRCULAR

OF PUBLIC DOCUMENTS AND INFORMATION:

DIRECTED BY THE POOR LAW COMMISSIONERS TO BE PRINTED, CHIEFLY FOR THE USE OF THE MEMBERS AND PERMANENT OFFICERS OF BOARDS OF GUARDIANS, UNDER THE POOR LAW AMENDMENT ACT.

No. 59. CIRCULAR ISSUED MAY 1, 1846.

Poor Law Commission Office,
Somerset House,
May 1, 1846.

THE Poor Law Commissioners have directed that their Twelfth Annual Report be printed and circulated for the information of Guardians and Officers of the several Unions.

By Order of the Board,
EDWIN CHADWICK, *Secretary.*

TO THE RIGHT HON. SIR JAMES GRAHAM, BART. Her Majesty's Principal Secretary of State for the Home Department.

Poor Law Commission Office, Somerset House, May 1, 1846.

SIR,

Amount of Poor-rate levied and expended in the year ended at Lady-day, 1845.—1. In our last Annual Report we submitted to you an account of the moneys received as poor-rate, and expended for the relief of the poor, and the other purposes to which that fund is applicable, in England and Wales, for the parochial year ending at Lady-day, 1844. We will commence this Report by laying before you a similar account for the parochial year ending at Lady-day, 1845.

An Account of the Receipt and Expenditure of the Poor's Rate for the year ended Lady-day, 1845.

Receipt.	£.
Amount of money levied by assessment	6,791,006
Received from other sources in aid of poor rate	218,505
Total receipt	£7,009,511
Expenditure.	
For relief to the poor	5,039,703
Law charges, parochial and Union	95,397
Expenses before magistrates, and constables' expenses (parochial and Union)	57,988
Payments under the Parochial Assessments Act (for surveys, valuations, &c.) and loans repaid under the same	22,877
Expenses under the Vaccination Act	25,905
Expenses under the Act for Registering Births, Deaths, and Marriages	57,388
Payments for county and borough rate, and for county and local police forces	1,279,962
Costs of voters, burgesses, and jury lists	20,153
Expenses of parish property	14,752
Money expended for all other purposes	243,277
Total expenditure	6,857,402

2. The results exhibited in this statement do not differ materially from the corresponding amounts for the preceding year. In the total amount of moneys received as poor's rate, there has been a diminution of 57,286*l.*; in the total expenditure from the poor's rate, there has been a diminution of 42,715*l.*; in the expenditure for the relief of the poor, there has been an increase of 63,610*l.*

Years ending Lady-day.	Total Amount received as Poor's Rate.
1844	£7,066,797
1845	7,000,511
Diminution	57,286

Years ending Lady-day.	Total Amount expended from the Poor's Rate.
1844	£6,900,117
1845	6,857,402
Diminution	42,715

Years ending Lady-day.	Total Expenditure for the Relief of the Poor.
1844	£4,976,093
1845	5,039,703
Increase	63,610

3. Considering the uncertain and fluctuating nature of the expenditure for the relief of the poor, as well as of most of the other expenses charged upon the poor's rate, these variations are so slight that the receipt and the expenditure may be considered as having been stationary during the two parochial years ending at Lady-day, 1844 and 1845. The expenditure for the relief of the poor in the parochial year 1845, was less than that in the parochial year 1843, but greater than that in each of the years from 1836 to 1842 inclusive. We annex to this Report (page 80) a table, containing a complete statement of the receipt and expenditure of the poor's rate since 1834, from which these and other comparisons can be obtained. As compared with the cost of the relief of the poor in 1834, the parochial year immediately preceding the passing of the Poor Law Amendment Act, the amount for 1844 stands thus:—

Years ending Lady-day.	Total Expenditure for the Relief of the Poor.
1834	£6,317,255
1845	5,039,703
Diminution	1,277,552

If to this amount we add the saving under the heads of law charges and the miscellaneous expenditure for "other purposes," which (as we explained in our last Annual Report, par. 17) has resulted from the Poor Law Amendment Act, the total reduction of expenditure in 1845, as compared with 1834, due to the reform of the law, may be taken at nearly two millions sterling, without making any allowance for the increase of population.

4. But although the expenditure for relief of the poor in the parochial year 1845 scarcely differed (as we have already stated) from that in the preceding year, yet the expenditure in particular counties was not stationary. In some parts of the kingdom the expense of the relief of the poor increased, in others it diminished in 1845 as compared with 1844. The following table will exhibit some of these differences.

Total Amount expended for Relief to the Poor.

	Years ended Lady-day.		Decrease per cent. in 1845 compared with 1844.	Increase per cent. in 1845 compared with 1844.
	1844.	1845.		
	£	£.		
Nottingham	74,291	65,540	12	...
York, West Riding	208,805	186,321	11	...
Lancaster	231,648	211,694	9	...
Chester	80,413	76,124	5	...
Durham	79,863	75,824	5	...
Stafford	103,105	98,266	5	...
Huntingdon	22,991	25,658	...	12
Warwick	59,840	64,992	...	9
Anglesey	13,289	14,253	...	7
Cambridge	75,349	80,665	...	7
Brecon	20,221	21,354	...	6
Suffolk	136,658	144,964	...	6
Oxford	72,735	77,395	...	6
Norfolk	160,586	169,769	...	6

It will be perceived, upon an inspection of this table, that the diminution has chiefly occurred in the manufacturing, and the increase in the agricultural, districts. Thus, whilst in the West Riding of York, an important seat of manufacture, there was a decrease of 11 per cent., in the East Riding, which is purely agricultural, there was an increase of one per cent. This difference was mainly owing to the fact stated in our last Annual Report (par. 23), that whereas the demand for labour in the manufacturing districts was extensive and constant during the parochial year 1845, an interruption in the employment of the agricultural labourers was caused by the drought in the summer of 1844, and the length and severity of the cold during the winter of 1844-5.

5. The following table exhibits the principal heads of the poor relief expenditure in the parochial year 1845, for that part of the country in which there are boards of guardians appointed under the Poor Law Amendment Act. From the rest of the country (including parishes under Local Acts, Gilbert Unions, and ununited parishes under the Act of Eliz., whose expenditure for the relief of the poor amounted in that year to 622,730*l.*), we do not receive returns which can be reduced to this form.

Expenditure of 585 Unions and Parishes under Boards of Guardians.

Years ended Lady-day.	In-Maintenance.	Out-Relief.	Establishment Charges and Salaries.	Workhouse Loan Repaid.	Other Charges connected with Relief to the Poor.	Total Expenditure for Relief, &c. to the Poor.	Rate per Head of Total on Population.
	£.	£.	£.	£.	£.	£.	*s. d.*
1844	705,253	2,726,451	748,985	183,898	5,584	4,370,171	6 5½
1845	714,523	2,767,903	750,372	177,603	6,572	4,416,973	6 6¾
Increas	9,270	41,452	1,387	...	988	46,802	0 1¼
Decrease	...	...	...	6,295	...	...	...

Number of persons relieved.—6. As the expenditure for the relief of the poor in the two last years remained nearly stationary, so the number of persons relieved underwent little variation.

Comparative Statement of the Number of In-door and Out-door Paupers relieved in England and Wales, during each of the Quarters ended Lady-day 1844 and 1845.

Quarters ended Lady-Day.	Number of Paupers Relieved.			Rate per Cent. of Total Number of Paupers on Population in 1841.
	In-door.	Out-door.	Total.	
1844	230,818	1,246,743	1,477,561	9·3
1845	215,325	1,255,645	1,470,970	9·2
Decrease	15,493	...	6,591	0·1
Increase	...	8,902	...	...

Population in 1841 ... ... 15,906,741.

NOTE.—An Estimate is made of the number of Paupers relieved in places not in Union, and included in the above Totals.

7. The following table exhibits the number of persons returned to the Commissioners as relieved, both in and out of the workhouse, in the several Lady-day quarters, since the year 1840.

Summary of Returns, showing the Number of Paupers relieved in England and Wales, during the Quarters ended at Lady-Day, 1840, 1841, 1842, 1843, 1844, and 1845, with the proportion per Cent. which the Number of In-door and Out-door Paupers relieved bear to the Total Number.

Quarters ended Lady-Day.	Number of Paupers Relieved.				
	In-door.	Proportion per Cent. to Total.	Out-door.	Proportion per Cent. to Total.	Total In-door and Out-door.
1840	169,232	14	1,030,297	86	1,199,529
1841	192,106	15	1,106,942	85	1,299,048
1842	222,642	16	1,204,545	84	1,427,187
1843	238,560	15	1,300,930	85	1,539,490
1844	230,818	16	1,246,743	84	1,477,561
1845	215,325	15	1,255,645	85	1,470,970

NOTE.—An Estimate is made for those places not under the provisions of the Poor Law Amendment Act.

8. With regard, however, to the statements of the total number of persons who have been relieved in a quarter, which are transmitted to us by the clerks to the guardians, it is to be observed that their *absolute* accuracy cannot be safely relied on, owing to the difficulty of preventing the same person, if he becomes chargeable on several occasions, or in different Unions, from being counted more than once. Their *relative* accuracy, for the purpose of comparing one period with another, may, as the enumeration is made on uniform principles, be assumed without danger of serious error.

9. In the number of able-bodied paupers relieved in the workhouse during the parochial year 1845, there was (as appears from the subjoined table) a diminution of 10 per cent., as compared with the previous year. In the number of able-bodied paupers who received out-door relief on account of temporary sickness or accident, there was an increase of more than 5 per cent.; but in the number of the same class who received out-door relief, on account of all other causes, including vagrants, there was a decrease of nearly 6 per cent. In the total number of able-bodied persons relieved in the parochial year 1845, there was a diminution of 2 7-10ths per cent.

Comparative Statement of the Number of Able-bodied Paupers relieved in England and Wales, during each of the Quarters ended Lady-Day, 1844 and 1845.

Quarters ended Lady-Day.	In-door.			Out-door.			
	On Account of temporary Sickness or Accident.	All other causes including Vagrants.	Total In-door.	On Account of temporary Sickness or Accident.	All other causes including Vagrants.	Total Out-door.	Total, In-door and Out-door.
1844	11,458	86,327	97,785	158,280	175,419	333,699	431,484
1845	11,406	76,199	87,605	167,234	165,044	332,278	419,883
Increase per cent.	...	...	...	5 · 7	...	...	...
Decrease per cent.	0 · 5	11 · 7	10 · 4	...	5 · 9	0 · 4	2 · 7

NOTE.—An Estimate is made for places not in Union under the Poor Law Amendment Act. The above results are obtained from the Union Quarterly Abstracts.

Employment and wages of working classes.—10. We have not yet received complete returns of the receipt and expenditure of the poor rate for the year ending at Lady-day 1846; but we can state generally that, throughout England and Wales, the working classes have, during this period, been steadily employed at wages rather above than below the average rates, as well in the agricultural as the manufacturing parts of the country. The demand for hands in the manufacturing districts has been constant, and the employment of the agricultural labourers was much facilitated by the unusual mildness of the winter. During last winter, scarcely any workhouse in a rural Union was so full as to necessitate the allowance of out-door relief to the able-bodied.

Failure of potato crop.—11. The partial failure of the potato crop for 1845, through a species of vegetable epidemic disease, (the effects of which began to manifest themselves in the autumn,) induced us to issue, in the month of November last, two circular letters to the Boards of Guardians, suggesting certain precautionary measures in relation to this subject. In one of these we indicated the extraction of farina from diseased potatoes as a mode of employment in workhouses; in the other we pointed out the expediency of substituting in the workhouse dietaries some article for potatoes. This substitution has been made in certain cases; but the failure of the potato, to the extent to which it has proceeded, has not, in England, produced any important influence on the food of the people. From a few Unions in Devonshire and Somersetshire we have received applications to permit the out-door relief of the able-bodied on account of the failure of the potatoes. We insert in the Appendix a report from our Assistant Commissioner, Mr. Tufnell, relative to the effects of the potato disease in that part of the country.

Order prohibiting bone-crushing in workhouses.—12. In the course of last year, we considered it necessary to issue a general order prohibiting the crushing of bones as a kind of labour to be performed in workhouses. This order will be found in the Appendix to our Report, and we think it our duty to state fully the circumstances under which it was issued.

13. The position of the Commissioners is such that, on the one hand, they often necessarily incur the reproach of interfering too much with the discretion of the local authorities, whilst, on the other, they are held responsible for practices which do not originate with themselves: practices which they would not themselves have introduced, but which are, nevertheless, consistent with the law, and have been deliberately adopted by Boards of Guardians in the exercise of the powers vested in them. The Commissioners do not consider it is their duty to interpose, by regulation or remonstrance, in every instance in which a Board of Guardians may sanction an act or practice of which the Commissioners may not approve, provided that such act or practice be not contrary to the regu

lations of the Commissioners, or otherwise illegal. Experience may, however, show, in particular cases, the necessity of interfering with the discretion thus left to the Boards of Guardians when a manifest tendency to abuse it is visible, and when obloquy and discredit may be thrown on the general administration of the law, for the sake of local or temporary convenience.

14. With respect to the kind of work to be performed in workhouses the Commissioners had interfered but little. The 21st Article of their Workhouse Regulations provides that—

"The paupers of the several classes shall be kept employed according to their capacity and ability, and no pauper shall receive any compensation for his labour."

It appeared to us that local knowledge and experience were peculiarly requisite for determining what species of labour could be best resorted to for the employment of the able-bodied inmates in each particular workhouse. We have always discouraged the Guardians from selecting their mode of labour with a view to pecuniary profit; but we have, for the most part, left the regulation of the details to each Board of Guardians. The members of that Board necessarily know the habits of the labourers who are likely to form the mass of able-bodied inmates in the house. They are conversant with the means of employment which the materials of the neighbourhood can furnish. In some parts of the country, for instance, stone-breaking is inapplicable, because the roads are mended with gravel; in others, the vicinity of a sea-port will make the picking of oakum a kind of work readily accessible. Persons on the spot, too, can alone know how far a particular sort of labour may interfere injuriously with the independent workman. It appears never to have been the intention of the Poor Law Amendment Act that the control of the Commissioners should entirely supersede the judgment of the authorities on the spot, without some just and manifest reason of a general character, and which, from its general character, may possibly not be apparent to a large number of single Boards acting each in its own particular neighbourhood.

Discretion left to Boards of Guardians as to the mode of employment in workhouses.—15. Upon the grounds which we have just stated, we had, by our regulations, left a discretion to the Guardians, with respect to the mode of employment in workhouses. Many of the Boards, especially in the west of England, in the exercise of that discretion, adopted the breaking and pounding of bones, by hand or by machinery, as work which was advantageous in itself, and interfered little with the labour market out of the workhouse. This mode of employment had been in many places strongly recommended, and in some few instances it had been brought under the direct notice of the Commissioners. On the other hand, objections were raised to its adoption in a particular form, which induced the Commissioners, on the 10th of November, 1842, to write a letter of caution to a considerable number of Unions, requesting them to consult with their medical officers as "to the nature of the bones usually obtained, the instrument employed, and the place where the work was carried on."

Resolutions as to task of work under 5 & 6 Vict., c. 5.—16. After the passing of the 5 and 6 Vict., c. 57, empowering Boards of Guardians to detain casual poor or trampers for a short time, to perform a task of work, and to fix such task of work by a resolution sanctioned by the Poor Law Commissioners, the case was somewhat different, so far at least, as regarded the application of labour of this description to that particular class for the period of four hours.

When resolutions, imposing a task of bone crushing, were forwarded to us for our approval, in pursuance of the statute, we requested that the medical officer might be called on to state in each case whether he objected to the adoption of this species of employment as likely to be injurious to the persons employed on it, or to affect the healthiness of the inmates generally. We withheld our sanction to the resolutions until we were satisfied that no objection was raised by the medical officer. Our correspondence on this subject with the Board of Guardians of the Andover Union is annexed as an example in the Appendix to this Report.

In a letter to the Guardians of the Plympton St. Mary Union, dated 29th August, 1844, we expressed ourselves as follows:—

"The Commissioners desire to state that they see no objection to the erection of a shed and room at the Union workhouse, for the employment of the able-bodied. The Commissioners, however, much doubt whether bone crushing is the best form of affording such employment, and they object to its adoption altogether, without the opinion of the medical officer of the workhouse having been obtained, that no prejudicial consequences of any kind are to be apprehended from the effluvia of the bones."

In the Torrington Union the Guardians proposed to us oakum picking and bone crushing as a mode of employing the paupers in the workhouse. We admitted the first, and objected to the second, until we received a special report from our Assistant Commissioner, on the subject of the arrangement.

17. Thus it will be seen that whilst we avoided as far as possible any undue interference with the discretion of the several Boards of Guardians with reference to the labour resorted to in the workhouses, we did not for the most part assent to the adoption of bone crushing without such conditions and such precautions as we thought sufficient to guard against abuse.

18. We were aware that many persons entertained strong objections to this kind of work. Nevertheless, we did not feel justified in interposing by any general regulation to put an end to the particular mode of

employment in these workhouses, until the occurrence of certain painful circumstances connected with it in the Andover Union, added to the objections already expressed, showed that a great and paramount expediency required us to overrule the discretion hitherto exercised in this matter by the several Boards of Guardians. We, therefore, issued the order referred to above; from which, however, one of the Commissioners dissented, and recorded his dissent upon the minutes, according to the provision of the Poor Law Amendment Act.

The remonstrances which we subsequently received from many Boards of Guardians, by whom the practice had been sanctioned, evince the reluctance with which it was abandoned, and the conviction which was entertained in many places that this kind of labour was unobjectionable in itself. In some instances, where there was machinery which would have suddenly stood idle, and where there was a stock of bones in hand, or where some very special circumstances existed, on the application of the Guardians, we suspended the operation of our general order until the 1st of April. That day having now passed, it has become illegal to employ paupers in workhouses in the breaking or pounding of bones. We trust that no serious difficulty will be experienced by those Boards where bone crushing was hitherto employed, in providing work which shall be free from the real objections applicable to that now abandoned; and we will direct our own attention, and that of our Assistant Commissioners, to the consideration of the various expedients which may be resorted to with advantage for this purpose.

Cases of infanticide.—19. Our attention has been recently called to two cases of infanticide committed by mothers of illegitimate children, who had left the workhouse without a sufficient provision of clothing for their infants. We will proceed to state the facts of these cases, as ascertained by us upon inquiry.

Case of Harriet Bowkett.—20. The first case was that of Harriet Bowkett, which occurred in the Ledbury Union. The following explanation was furnished to us by the clerk to the Ledbury Guardians, in a letter dated the 30th of January last:—

"Harriet Bowkett is a single woman, about 23 years of age; she was admitted into the Ledbury Union Workhouse with her bastard child, about six weeks old, on the 2nd of May, 1843, and was discharged on the 15th day of July, 1843. She was again admitted into the Ledbury Union Workhouse in a state of pregnancy, on the 22nd day of August, 1845, (she having left her child with her mother), she was delivered of her second child, in the workhouse, on the 12th of November, 1845. About a fortnight after her confinement, she gave notice to leave the house in consequence of the nurse having reproved her for neglecting and ill-treating her infant, but the matron would not allow her to leave the house, at the same time informing her that she was not in a fit state to quit her room.

"On the 29th day of November, about nine o'clock in the morning, she again gave notice to quit the house. At about 11 o'clock the medical officer visited the house, when the matron asked him if Harriet Bowkett was well enough to leave the house; he said she was, if she wished it. The matron and the nurse then reminded the woman of her not having any clothing for her child, and begged her to remain in the house until Tuesday, the 2nd of December, when the master would bring her case before the Board. She replied, that she had plenty of clothes at her mother's, and would go. She then converted her own cotton night-gown, flannel petticoat, and night-cap into clothing for her infant, in which she dressed it, and then wrapped her shawl round the child; she then dressed herself in the remainder of her own clothes, which consisted of a cotton chemise, stays, a cotton petticoat with a body to it, a gown, stockings, shoes, and bonnet, all in good condition. She quitted the workhouse about one o'clock (the day being very mild for the time of year.) After leaving the workhouse, the matron followed her to the outer garden gate of the workhouse, and again entreated her to return to the house, and remain until Tuesday, and offered to send some one to her mother. She replied 'that she was going to a glover in the town to get two dozen of gloves to take home with her to make: that she could get 6*s*. per week.'

"The woman's mother is a widow, keeping a turnpike-gate in the parish of Mathon, about six miles from the Ledbury Union Workhouse, where the woman's other child was: also clothing for the infant. On her way home, about a mile and a half from her mother's abode, she stripped the child, and left it naked under a hedge; then went to her mother, who asked her where the child was, she replied, 'It was where she wished it to be—it was dead.'

"I also beg to state, that the said Harriet Bowkett, during the whole of the time she was in the Ledbury Union Workhouse, never made any application to the Board of Guardians (who meet every Tuesday), nor to any one of their officers, for relief of any kind out of the house. Had she applied to the Board of Guardians, and made it known to them that she had no clothing for her child, nor the money to procure it, an order would have been given to the master of the workhouse to furnish her with what was requisite.

"The Board of Guardians were wholly ignorant of the case until they met on the following Tuesday, the 2nd of December; the woman was then committed to prison."

Case of Elizabeth Butcher.—21. The second case was that of Elizabeth Butcher, in the Cricklade and Wootton Bassett Union. With reference to this case, we insert a statement of the facts, as ascertained upon personal inquiry by our Assistant Commissioner, Mr.

Grenville Pigott (from a Report dated the 31st January last).

"As regards the individual case of Elizabeth Butcher, she gave notice of her intention to quit the house at eight o'clock, A. M. on the 9th of January, and did quit it at eleven o'clock, A. M. The Board of Guardians, although sitting, were not informed of the fact, because she had made no application of any kind to be laid before them, and because her departure from the house was of her own free will, and could not be prevented by them. The matron and Jane Cook advised Elizabeth Butcher to stay, but she refused to do so, and said that she wanted to go to her aunt for her own clothes, and that she had baby linen. Jane Cook advised her to send to her aunt for clothes for the baby before she took it away, but she refused to do so. Her residence was at Tokenham, six miles from the workhouse. The matron and Jane Cook were both of opinion that the child, as it was wrapped up, might have been safely taken that distance on that day, which was mild. The master and matron both bear a high character for humanity, and Elizabeth Butcher made no complaint of her treatment whilst in the house.

"On the other hand, it is to be feared that the clothing was not sufficient for herself and her child; and although she made no application to the Guardians, who she knew were sitting, for additional clothing, it is admitted by the master that it was generally understood amongst the female paupers that any such application would have been refused."

Supply of clothing to paupers leaving the workhouse.—22. The supply of clothing to paupers leaving the workhouse is a subject which has frequently been under the consideration of the Commissioners. The following remarks in relation to it, occur in a minute of the Commissioners, dated the 29th of October, 1839, inserted in their sixth Annual Report (App. A., No. 3):—

"With respect to allowances of clothing to paupers in the workhouse, it is desirable that persons residing a short time in the workhouse should not on leaving it be furnished, except under very particular circumstances, with a fresh suit of clothes. * * * * * Persons permanently domiciled in the workhouse, and especially children who have remained in it from an early age, must on quitting it be furnished with a decent outfit of clothing. Young persons who have been brought up in the workhouse, and who leave it for service or apprenticeship, ought, in the opinion of the Commissioners, to be furnished with an outfit of clothing as is usually possessed by young persons not being paupers in a similar condition."

Supply of clothing for infants born in the workhouse.—We are not aware that the practice of the Guardians with respect to the supply of clothing to infants born in the workhouse, and leaving it with their mothers, was ever brought specifically under our attention until the occurrence of the two cases above-mentioned. The supply of clothing to an infant leaving the workhouse with its parents if legitimate, and with its mother if illegitimate, is relief to the parent, and will, in general, come under the regulations with respect to relief of the able-bodied. If the parents of any infant child in the workhouse are, when about to leave the workhouse, desirous of obtaining an allowance of clothing for the child, they can apply to the Board of Guardians, who, if they think fit, can make the allowance as for a case of emergency. The Guardians can, moreover, empower the relieving officers, or the master of the workhouse, to allow clothing, in cases of urgency, to persons suddenly leaving the workhouse in the interval between the sittings of the Board. And it appears to us that the master and matron ought not to suffer any infant to leave the workhouse, under such circumstances, without sufficient covering to protect it against the consequences of exposure to the air.

Number and salaries of Union officers.—23. One of the principal functions imposed upon the Commisioners by the Poor Law Amendment Act consists in authorising the appointment, defining the duties, and regulating the salaries of the paid officers of unions and parishes. A large part of the business of the Commissioners likewise consists in the superintendence of the body of paid officers, and in the decision of the various questions, to which new appointments, proposed increases or diminutions of salary, charges of misconduct, &c., give rise. The following statement shows the total number of each class of paid officers in the unions and parishes under the regulations of the Commissioners, with the total amount of their salaries:—

Return showing the Number of Officers of each Class, employed in 591 Unions of England and Wales, with the amount to them in fixed Salaries for the Year 1844-5.

Description of Officers.	No.	Salaries.
		£
Clerks	590	59,431
Chaplains	415	19,140
Medical officers	2,680	124,532
Relieving officers	1,257	103,881
Masters and matrons	1,238	44,369
Schoolmasters	284	7,423
Schoolmistresses	423	7,009
Porters	347	6,340
Nurses	171	2,161
Taskmasters	20	936
Collectors or assistant-overseers	499	23,026
Treasurers	52	973
Other officers	264	7,747
Total	8,240	406,968
District auditors	50	12,933
Total inclusive of auditors	8,290	419,901

NOTE.—Officers that are not paid by *fixed* salaries are excluded; also assistant-overseers and collectors not appointed under the Board's orders.

*** The salary of the district auditors includes remuneration for some Parishes not in Union.

Proceedings under 7 *and* 8 *Vict. c.* 101.—24. In our last Annual Report, we gave a detailed account of our proceedings, under the authority of the Act of 7 and 8 Vic. c. 101. We now continue that account with respect to those proceedings which were not completed at the date of that Report.

Division of Metropolis into districts for relief of casual poor.—25. We stated in our last Annual Report, par. 44, that we had then framed a scheme for the division of the metropolis into districts for the relief of casual poor, in pursuance of the provisions in the Act of 7 and 8 Vic. c. 101. This scheme was in substance founded upon the recommendations of our Assistant Commissioner, Mr. Hall, whom we had instructed to investigate the subject, and whose Reports, containing the result of his inquiries, we insert in the Appendix. In the months of July and August last, we issued a series of orders, dividing the metropolis and its vicinity into six districts, named respectively as follows, viz.:—The Central, the North-Eastern, the South-Western, the Western, the South-Eastern, the North-Western, and Metropolitan Asylum Districts. We likewise, at the same time, fixed the number of members which each union and parish, included in a district, was to return to the District Board of Management, and we defined the manner in which the election was to be conducted. We issued also other orders regulating the mode of proceedings to be pursued by the Board of Management, and authorising the appointment of certain paid officers, with specified powers and duties. The following table contains a statement of the most important particulars relative to each of the above-named six districts:—

SOUTH-EASTERN METROPOLITAN ASYLUM DISTRICT.

Name of Union or Parish.	Population.	Valuation of Property.	Number of Managers. Elected.	Ex-officio.
		£		
Greenwich	80,811	178,787	2	1
Lewisham	23,013	107,382	1	1
St. Mary, Rotherhithe	13,916	49,806	1	1
St. Mary Magdalen, Bermondsey	34,947	88,492	1	1
St. Olave, Southwark	18,427	84,076	1	1
St. Giles, Camberwell	39,867	153,278	1	1
			7	6
Totals	210,981	661,821	13	

SOUTH-WESTERN METROPOLITAN ASYLUM DISTRICT.

Name of Union or Parish.	Population.	Valuation of Property.	Number of Managers. Elected.	Ex-officio.
		£		
St. Saviour	32,980	84,372	2	1
St. George-the-Martyr	46,622	119,963	2	1
St. Mary, Newington	54,606	161,802	3	0
St. Mary, Lambeth	115,883	449,142	3	1
Wandsworth and Clapham	39,853	204,357	2	1
			12	4
Totals	289,944	1,019,636	16	

NORTH-EASTERN METROPOLITAN ASYLUM DISTRICT.

Name of Union or Parish.	Population.	Valuation of Property.	Number of Managers. Elected.	Ex-officio.
		£		
Hackney	42,274	160,981	1	1
Poplar	31,091	160,657	1	1
Stepney	90,657	212,603	1	1
West Ham	26,919	88,950	1	1
Whitechapel	71,758	197,524	1	1
St. George-in-the-East	41,351	141,301	1	1
St. Matthew, Bethnal Grn.	74,087	95,549	1	1
St. Leonard, Shoreditch	83,432	169,133	2	0
			9	7
Totals	461,569	1,226,698	16	

CENTRAL METROPOLITAN ASYLUM DISTRICT.

Name of Union or Parish.	Population.	Valuation of Property.	Number of Managers. Elected.	Ex-officio.
		£		
Holborn	43,700	182,860	1	1
Strand	43,894	211,521	1	1
City of London	55,967	613,883	2	1
East London	39,655	140,139	1	1
West London	33,629	108,089	1	1
St. James, Clerkenwell	56,756	176,338	2	0
St. Giles, and St. George, Bloomsbury	54,292	236,970	2	0
St. Mary, Islington	55,690	212,283	2	0
St. Luke, Middlesex	49,829	131,676	2	0
St. Pancras	128,479	582,000	4	0
			18	5
Totals	561,891	2,595,759	23	

WESTERN METROPOLITAN ASYLUM DISTRICT.

Name of Union or Parish.	Population.	Valuation of Property.	Number of Managers. Elected.	Ex-officio.
		£		
Fulham	22,772	82,308	3	1
Brentford	37,054	130,204	4	1
Richmond	13,558	61,221	2	1
			9	3
Totals	73,384	273,733	12	

NORTH-WESTERN METROPOLITAN ASYLUM DISTRICT.

Name of Union or Parish.	Population.	Valuation of Property.	Number of Managers. Elected.	Ex-officio.
		£		
St. George, Hanover-squ.	66,453	604,176	2	0
St. James, Westminster	37,398	240,648	2	0
St. Mary Abbots, Kensington	26,830	148,368	1	1
St. Luke, Chelsea	40,177	123,200	2	1
St. Margaret, and St. John the Evangelist, Westm.	56,481	168,440	2	0
St. Martin-in-the-Fields	25,195	239,996	1	1
St. Marylebone	138,164	816,480	3	0
Paddington	25,173	209,076	1	1
			14	4
Totals	415,871	2,550,384	18	

Appointment of Boards of Management, and refusal of three parishes to elect Managers.—26. At the proper times appointed by the orders in question, elections of members for the several Boards of Management took place, and a Board was constituted in each district. The local Boards of three parishes, (viz., Marylebone and St. Luke, Chelsea, in the north-western district, and St. Giles, Camberwell, in the south-eastern district,) refused, however, to proceed to an election. With these exceptions, every Union and parish comprised in the orders has returned members to its district Board. All the Boards of Management have held meetings, and three of them have taken the first steps in execution of the powers conferred upon them.

Appointment of Select Committee of the House of Commons on the Asylum Districts.—27. We have already stated that the Directors and Guardians of the parish of Marylebone, a parish important from its population and wealth, declined to return members to the district Board. In September and January last, deputations from this parish communicated to the Commissioners their wish that it should be exempted from the plan, and continue to maintain its casual poor separately as heretofore. The Commissioners stated to these deputations, their opinion that there were no grounds for excepting Marylebone, which did not apply to all large parishes under local Acts, and that the plan ought to be founded on a division of the entire metropolis. They, therefore, declined to modify their order in the manner indicated by these deputations. In the early part of this Session of Parliament, a Select Committee of the House of Commons was appointed to inquire into the manner in which the Poor Law Commissioners have carried into effect the provisions of the 7th and 8th Vic., relating to district asylums; and since the appointment of this Select Committee, the Commissioners have abstained from taking any active steps for carrying these provisions into effect; inasmuch as they thought it desirable to wait until it appears whether any alteration of the existing law relative to the relief of the wandering and houseless poor is likely to result from the inquiries and recommendations of the Committee.

Course pursued by the Commissioners respecting relief of casual poor in the Metropolis since the establishment of the Commission.—28. Having described the nature of the plan which we have formed for the division of the Metropolis into asylum districts under the 7th and 8th Vic. c. 101, we will take this opportunity of shortly stating the course which the Commissioners have pursued with respect to the relief of the houseless poor in the metropolitan Unions and parishes, since the first establishment of the Poor Law Commission.

Relief of casual Poor in the Metropolis.—29. In August, 1837, the Commissioners of Metropolitan Police addressed a letter to the Poor Law Commissioners, enclosing returns of persons found by the police in a state of destitution, and stating that difficulties still occurred with respect to obtaining immediate relief from the parochial authorities, in cases of urgency. The Police Commissioners desired to receive from the Poor Law Commissioners such suggestions as would enable the police to act more effectually in cases of destitute persons, of whom they were obliged to take cognizance. The Poor Law Commissioners, in answer to this communication, addressed a letter to the Police Commissioners, (dated 6th September, 1837,) in which they explained the state of the law on the subject, showing that destitute persons, though not settled in a parish, were nevertheless entitled to relief from it; and that relief ought, therefore, to precede inquiry into settlement. In the same letter, they indicated the duties of the local Poor Law Officers, with respect to the relief of the casual poor; they likewise suggested that professional beggars should be dealt with under the Vagrant Act.

The following are extracts from this letter:—

"If any person state that he has no food, and that he is destitute, or otherwise express or signify that he is in danger of perishing unless relief be given to him, then any officer charged with the relief is bound, unless he have presented to him some facts or reasonable evidence to rebut such statement, to give relief to such destitute person in the mode prescribed by the law."

* * * *

"On the occurrence of any case of destitution, or of sudden and pressing emergency, the better course will be to apply to the nearest paid officer of the Union, the Relieving Officer, or the Master of the Workhouse, who best know the most efficient remedies applicable for the relief of such cases, and who have the best means of applying them. The Commissioners will feel it their duty to make those officers responsible in their situations for any serious neglect—for the bad consequences of any omission to give prompt and adequate relief in any case of real destitution and emergency. For relief to be effectual, it must be given at the time when the emergency shall occur to the destitute person. The question as to any existing means of repayment, or as to the place to which the destitute person may be chargeable, it will be the duty of the officer to reserve for investigation after the pressing want shall have been relieved."

* * * *

"All persons who are not casually destitute, but who beg as a profession, the Poor Law Commissioners submit should be dealt with under the Vagrant Act, and be apprehended by the police, and taken before the magistrate for his award of punishment. In those cases which the Union or Parish officers find to be cases of imposture, or where, after the destitution shall have been relieved, it is ascertained to have been brought about by misconduct or by any act of vagrancy, then it will be the duty of those officers to give the offenders into the custody of the police, that they may be taken before the magistrate.

That which the Commissioners are most anxious to have made known is, that the relief of actual destitution, in cases of emergency, should always precede the investigation of any question as to its cause, or as to the liability of any other parties than the parish to contribute to it."

The preceding correspondence was published in the Fourth Annual Report of the Poor Law Commissioners, Appendix A. No. 2.

The Poor Law Commissioners, by a circular letter, dated the 12th of December, 1838, and sent to the Boards of Guardians in the metropolis, called attention to this correspondence, as printed in their Fourth Annual Report, and pressed upon the attention of the Guardians the views expressed in their letter to the Commissioners of Police. They further recommended the relief of the casually destitute in workhouses, where they could be employed in suitable labour, (Fifth Annual Report, App. A., No. 10.) By a similar circular letter to the Metropolitan Boards of Guardians, dated the 7th of December, 1839, they renewed the expression of their opinion as to the obligation of the parish to give immediate relief to casually destitute persons, and they enforced their remarks by the following declaration:—

"The Commissioners request the Board of Guardians to warn their officers that no consideration of past services will be deemed by the Commissioners a sufficient reason for their hesitating to remove any officer, who, after this period, shall have neglected his primary duty in relieving any case of urgent casual destitution brought under his notice, by affording such relief within the workhouse in all cases in which there is ability to labour, or in which relief within the workhouse is desirable, such as cases of houseless destitution and casualty, or by affording such relief as may be appropriate in other cases, in articles of absolute necessity." (Sixth Annual Report, App. A., No. 6.)

In their Eighth Annual Report, presented in May, 1842, the Commissioners stated fully the law with respect to the relief of wayfaring and casual poor, and explained the nature of the difficulties which had arisen on this subject in the metropolis and other large towns. They there expressed an opinion that the object to be aimed at was to secure immediate relief to this class of poor without reference to the place of their settlement, and at the same time to avoid, as far as possible, affording encouragement to habitual vagrancy, (par. 67—73.)

In their Tenth Annual Report, presented in May, 1844, the Commissioners further considered the subject in reference to London, and stated an opinion favourable to the establishment of separate asylums for the vagrant poor, at the cost of the poor rates, in the metropolis, (par. 13—29.) In the same year the Act of 7 and 8 Vict. was passed, containing the provisions relative to district asylums, upon which our orders have been founded.

30. In adopting the course just described, with respect to the relief of casual poor in the metropolis, both before and after the passing of the Act of 7 and 8 Vic., the Commissioners have been guided by the following considerations.

31 The laws relating to the relief of the poor confer a right to relief irrespective of settlement. All destitute persons have a right to be relieved at the cost of the parish in which they are. This right, in the first instance, is absolute; but if a person so relieved has a settlement in another parish, the officers of the parish to which he has become chargeable can, if they think fit, remove him to the place of his settlement.* According, therefore, to the established law, a wandering poor person who applies for relief in a parish, metropolitan or rural, although he has not acquired any settlement in it, must, if he be destitute, there receive parochial relief.

32. It is doubtless desirable, as far as possible, to avoid all encouragement of habitual mendicancy and vagrancy, by affording undue facilities for obtaining relief to persons leading a life of this sort, which is always accompanied with laziness and vice, and almost always with crime. But a wandering mendicant, if he becomes destitute and applies for relief, has as good a legal right to it as any other poor person in a similar condition. If a wanderer of this sort died of starvation or exposure to the cold, in consequence of the refusal of relief, the local Poor Law officers would be held responsible for the result. Nor does a repetition of applications for relief constitute any offence against the law, or render the person liable to the penalties of the Vagrant Act. The 5th Geo. 4, c. 83, contains only three enactments applicable to habitual beggars. In sec. 3, it declares, that "every person wandering about, and placing himself or herself in any public place, street, highway, court, or passage, to beg or gather alms, or causing, or procuring, or encouraging any child or children so to do, shall be deemed an idle and disorderly person within the true intent and meaning of this Act." In sec. 4, it declares, that "every person wandering abroad, and lodging in any barn or outhouse, or in any deserted or unoccupied building, or in the open air, or under a tent, or in any cart or waggon, not having any visible means of subsistence, and not giving a good account of himself or herself;" and that "every person wandering abroad and endeavouring, by the exposure of wounds or deformities, to obtain or gather alms, shall be deemed a rogue and vagabond within the true intent and meaning of this Act." Unless a wandering beggar, applying for relief at a workhouse, has committed some act falling within one of the above descriptions, and can be proved by legal evidence, to the satisfaction of a justice, to have committed it, he cannot be transferred to the police and proceeded against under the Vagrant Act, but must be relieved like any other destitute person.

It appears, therefore, that the obligation imposed by the existing law to relieve wanderers and houseless strangers applying for relief on account of destitution, in a parish in which they have not a settlement, is unquestionable. This obligation extends

* See Minute on Relief of persons not resident within their Union, 7th Ann. Rep., App. A., No. 2.

equally over all parts of the country, and is binding upon rural not less than metropolitan parishes. Before the interference of the Poor Law Commissioners in the years 1837, 1838, and 1839, (as already stated,) it was a general practice in the metropolitan parishes to refuse relief to wanderers, on the ground that they had no settlement in the parish. This practice has, to a considerable extent, been changed in consequence of the measures taken by the Commissioners; and less distinction has been made between settled and other poor with respect to relief. But the measures taken by the Commissioners altered not the *law*, but the *practice* which had been established in the London parishes; on the contrary, their interference was, as they stated in their letters, founded on a desire to bring the practice into accordance with the law.

33. The distribution of workhouses at short distances over the entire country, and the regular enforcement of the right of strangers and wayfarers to relief, may, in some cases, unduly encourage wandering habits among the poor, notwithstanding the provision of the 5th and 6th Vic. c. 57, which authorises the detention of this class of paupers in a workhouse for four hours in the morning, in order that they may be set to work. Nevertheless, this disadvantage, as far as it exists, appears to be a necessary incident to the existing law, which (rightly, as it seems to us) extends the benefit of relief to *all* destitute persons, without reference to their settlement or place of residence.

34. In the majority of the country workhouses the number of applications from vagrants is not in general so great as to cause material inconvenience, provided there be proper wards for their reception, and adequate means of setting them to work. If the burthen of this class of poor, which is now in general concentrated upon the parish in which the workhouse is situate, were distributed over the entire union, we believe that the practical grievance arising from this branch of relief in rural unions would not be great. As respects the metropolis, the inconveniences and injustice produced by the present mode of relief will, as it appears to us, be materially alleviated by the adoption of separate establishments for the reception of the houseless poor, according to the plan which we have above described. This plan proceeds upon the assumption that the right to relief possessed by this class of poor will remain on its present footing. It involves no new principle of relief; it merely makes a different distribution of the existing workhouse arrangements and the costs of the maintenance. Instead of there being a ward for vagrants in each metropolitan workhouse, there will be a separate building devoted exclusively to the reception of this class of poor, and common to a district of unions and parishes. In this building (which will be a cheap workhouse for a limited purpose,) the houseless and wandering poor will be alone admitted, and will be relieved and set to work according to prescribed regulations. Moreover, the total expenses of their relief will be divided among the several parishes and unions comprised in each asylum district, according to their respective valuations. In this manner the costs of the casual poor, which are now capriciously and unjustly accumulated upon certain parishes and unions, will be distributed equally over the entire metropolis.

35. With respect to proposals for strengthening the penal provisions against vagrants, and for rendering it more difficult for wanderers and habitual mendicants to obtain relief, it is to be observed that legal enactments on this subject would be inoperative, unless they were in accordance with public opinion; and, even under the present law, there is, on the part of magistrates, much reluctance to convict for begging, as well as great difficulty on the part of the police in obtaining the requisite evidence. Moreover, it should be borne in mind that the current of modern legislation has run in the direction of affording additional facilities for the free circulation of labour; and it is generally admitted to be an object of public policy that the law of settlement should not oppose any unnecessary obstacles to an unemployed labourer who is *bonâ fide* in search of work. If any change of the law, in the manner indicated, is to be made, it appears to us that the best course would be to enlarge the power of detention in the workhouse, conferred by the 5th and 6th Vic. c. 57, in cases where a casual pauper had applied for relief more than once in the union within a certain number of days.

Appointment of District Auditors, and arrangement of Audit Districts.—36. In our last Annual Report (par. 45—49) we referred to the provisions made by the statute 7 and 8 Vic. c. 101, for the appointment of district auditors, and we described the steps which we had then taken for giving effect to those provisions.

Since our last Report, the audit arrangements have been completed throughout the country, although some few additions will probably be made to the existing districts.

The general results of this arrangement are as follow:—

Total number of Orders issued relating to District Auditors.	Number of such Orders for continuance of existing Auditors, and altering their Districts.	Number of such Orders for the Election of new Auditors.	Average number of Unions to each Auditor.	Average Salary of each Auditor.
				£. s. d.
72	44	28	12·38	259 10 4¾

In 1842, before the appointment of district auditors under the recent statute, the number of auditors in England and Wales was 454, and the average amount of salary for each Union was 22*l.* Under the existing arrangement, the difficulty of obtaining efficient officers for the discharge of their most important duty, is diminished and the average salary for each Union is reduced, being 21*l.* At the same time the aggregate sum paid for the audit has slightly increased; the number of places, the accounts of which are subjected to audit, being larger. In 1842, the number of Unions subject to audit was 585, and the aggregate payment was 12,816*l.*; at present the number of Unions is 619, and the amount paid is 12,976*l.* being an increase of 169*l.* The average size of the districts would have been larger, but for our unwillingness to disturb so large a number of auditors already acting for more than one Union. We had to take our choice between two evils, that of unnecessarily removing persons fit for their duty, or that of exercising the powers conferred by the Act of Parliament, in such a manner, as in many cases to deprive the Chairman and Vice-Chairman of Boards of Guardians of their vote at the first appointment of a district auditor. Their right, however, remains unimpaired, as to all future elections, and we could not have effected the object which the law appeared to contemplate, without this temporary inconvenience. That object, we assume to have been the formation of proper districts of sufficient size so as to secure the due and satisfactory audit of the accounts at as early a period as possible. Whenever we deemed it compatible with other arrangements to do so, we have continued existing auditors with a smaller district, rather than infringe upon the rights, even for one election, of the Chairman and Vice-Chairman of the several Boards. In other instances, however, it was not deemed by us expedient to do so, and we regret to find that some dissatisfaction has existed in consequence.

Efficiency of District Auditors.—37. Our experience of the efficiency of the district auditors is highly in favour of the alteration effected by the statute. Many illegal practices have been checked; irregularities in the accounts of officers are more strictly investigated; greater punctuality in sending in the accounts of solicitors and others, so that the charge may fall on the rate-payers of the year in which it is incurred, is gradually being enforced, and finally a system of checking the expenditure of parish officers and Boards of Guardians, on more uniform principles, will without doubt, gradually establish itself.

Legal proceedings as to appointment of District Auditors in Eton and Winslow Unions.—38. One or two legal points connected with the appointment of district auditors and the provisions of the recent statute have come before the superior courts. The auditor of the Eton Union was also the auditor of the Amersham Union, and having audited the accounts of the parish of Burnham in the former Union, had been required to set forth his reasons for allowing certain items, but had declined to do so. A *certiorari* having been moved for in the Court of Queen's Bench to bring up this allowance, he objected that he had not been continued by the Poor Law Commissioners as an auditor under the statute; and, therefore, that the provisions therein contained relative to the *certiorari* did not apply to him. The Court of Queen's Bench, however, made the rule absolute for a *certiorari*, intimating a strong opinion that he could not make such an objection. We are informed that the then auditor has since made a return to the writ, and raised this objection in his formal return.

39. The decision was supposed by some persons to imply that all persons who were auditors for more than one Union, and had not been expressly removed by the Commissioners immediately after the statute was passed, became, by implication of the Act, district auditors, and that it was not competent for the Commissioners subsequently to cause the Unions under the control of such an auditor to be included in a district newly formed. The Winslow Union, acting on this opinion, refused to submit their accounts to the district auditor appointed in pursuance of our order. We felt it our duty to apply to the Court of Queen's Bench for a rule to compel them to conform in this matter with what we conceived to be the requisitions of the rule absolute, without thinking it necessary to hear our counsel in support of the statute. The Court, after hearing counsel in answer to the application, made the rule. We are bound, however, to say, that we believe the Board of Guardians to have acted in this matter in perfect good faith, and to have resisted the right of the district auditor because they believed the law to be on their side.

40. We believe that this institution of district auditors has established a class of officers whose services may readily be made available for the superintendence and control of other local expenditure—officers for the most part conversant with accounts and with the consideration of legal questions, and who will, from day to day, gain by the experience which necessarily attends the constant discharge of their duties.

Discharge of outstanding Balances, under 7 and 8 Vic. c. 101.—41. Section 34 of the Statute 7 and 8 Vic. c. 101, conferred on the Commissioners the power, in certain cases, of consenting to the discharge of outstanding balances which had been struck against officers, provided they had not been paid over, or proceedings taken to recover them before the passing of the Act. This provision was of a remedial character, and was calculated to set right certain irregularities apparent on the face of some accounts, as well as to relieve from the hardship of re-payment officers who might, unknowingly, have offended against the law. The power of relief was, however, restricted by certain conditions necessary to prevent the re-opening of transactions already closed, and which must *primâ facie* be taken to have been lawful, or its interference with proceedings already before the proper tribunal, and, therefore, to be determined in due course of law. These conditions, imposed by the statute, have prevented our exercising this power of relief, in certain cases, which no doubt have appeared to the parties themselves to be cases of hardship. We could not enter into the consideration of their merits or demerits, since they did not come within the letter of the statute: one such instance there has been in the large and populous parish of Lambeth, in which we had, as we are advised, no discretion conferred on us by the Act. With regard to cases coming within the provisions of the Act, the course which we have hitherto pursued has been to consent to the discharge of such balances as had arisen from ignorance of the state of the law on the part of the overseers, and in reference to which the officers had acted in good faith at the time of incurring the expense. We have declined, in a few instances, to consent to the discharge, where there had been deliberate and wilful perseverance in illegal payments.

Audit of Accounts changed from quarterly to half-yearly.—42. We have, under the powers conferred upon us by Section 38 of the 7th and 8th Vict. c. 101, by orders issued during the last year, directed the auditors to audit the accounts of the unions and parishes in their respective districts twice in every year. This change in the period of audit, from quarterly to half-yearly, has rendered some modification in several of the books of account and forms prescribed by the Commissioners in 1836, necessary. The experience of ten years in the working of the accounts then prescribed, has also suggested many improvements in the arrangement of the books and forms, whereby a more satisfactory check on the parties accounting may be attained, without increasing the labour of keeping the accounts. We have, therefore, availed ourselves of the occasion which the change in the period of audit has presented, for taking the whole of the present order under our consideration, with a view to revising all the books and forms, and introducing such provisions as may appear best adapted for securing proper accounting. We purpose issuing the revised order with as little delay as may be compatible with that mature consideration which the importance of its provisions demands.

Election of Guardians.—43. Although the questions which have annually been submitted to us in relation to the election of guardians have been very numerous, we have not found it necessary to exercise the power vested in us by the 8th section of the Act of 5th and 6th Vict., c. 57, for determining such questions by orders under seal, in more than three cases. One of these cases occurred in the Cambridge Union, another in the Kensington Union, and the third in the West Bromwich Union.

Modification of Apprenticeship Order.—44. In our last Annual Report (par. 34), we adverted to objections which had been made to certain provisions of the General Order issued by us on the 31st of December, 1844,* for regulating the Apprenticing of Pauper Children. In consequence of such objections, we addressed a circular to the boards of guardians, intimating that we proposed to make some modifications in that order, and should be ready to receive any observations which they might wish to offer thereon. Having duly considered the numerous communications made to us upon the subject by boards of guardians, we issued an order on the 15th of August, 1845, modifying the first-mentioned Order, by enabling boards of guardians to give premiums, other than clothing, in certain cases, and to dispense with the condition requiring the payment of a remuneration to an apprentice after the age of 17 years, and also to authorise the master to change the place of abode or service of the apprentice.

Remodelling of the Wycombe Union.—45. We stated in our last Annual Report, par. 51, our belief that some unions in different parts of the country might be advantageously reduced in size, by means of the powers contained in the 7th and 8th Vict., c. 101, and we particularly indicated the Lincolnshire Unions, as likely to derive benefit from such a modification. During the last year, we have remodelled the Wycombe Union, and we have directed the attention of our assistant-Commissioner, Mr. Weale, to the large size of some of the Lincolnshire Unions; but we find so much local opposition to any change in the existing boundaries of Unions, that we have only exercised this power in a few cases.

Formation of Farnham Union.—46. By an order, dated the 27th February last, we formed the parish of Farnham, which had previously been administered under Gilbert's Act, together with the parishes of Aldershott, Dockenfield, Frensham, and Frimley, into a Union, named the Farnham Union, and we have subsequently added to the Union the Ville of Waverley. We insert in the Appendix the statistical particulars relating to it. A Board of Guardians for the Union has been elected, and we have every reason to anticipate a favourable result from their administration of the law.

Medical Relief.—47. Upon the subject of Medical Relief, we have nothing material to state in addition to the explanations in our Annual Reports since 1842. The expenditure under this head has increased in the parochial year 1845, as appears from the following Table:—

Years ending Lady-day.	Amount of Medical Relief. £.
1838	136,775
1839	148,652
1840	151,781
1841	154,054
1842	152,006
1843	160,726
1844	166,257
1845	174,330

Vaccination.—48. From the steps which we took, as detailed in our last Report, we anticipated that the Vaccination Returns for the year ended 29th September, 1845, would show a large increase in the number of persons vaccinated by the public vaccinators of the several Unions; and it will be seen by the summary of these returns, contained in the

* Appendix A., No. 2, of the Eleventh Annual Report.

Appendix to this Report, that the progress of vaccination during that year has been highly satisfactory, there having been 362,087 persons vaccinated, and the operation having proved successful in 347,765 cases, the successful cases being equal to 96 per cent. on the number vaccinated.

49. The following table shows the number vaccinated, and the births in the unions from which returns have been received for the years ended respectively 29th September, 1844 and 1845:—

Years.	No. of Unions and Parishes.	No. of Persons Vaccinated.	No. of Persons successfully Vaccinated.	No. of Registered Births.	Ratio of Persons Vaccinated to the No. of Births.	Ratio of Persons successfully Vaccinated to the No. of Births.
1844	542	290,453	278,192	452,235	100 in 156	100 in 163
1845	580	362,087	347,765	486,632	100 in 134	100 in 140

50. In order to ascertain whether the number of children vaccinated under one year of age approximated to the number of births, we framed the form of return so as to show the number vaccinated under and above that age; and we find that the numbers were as follows:—

——	Under one Year.	Above one Year.	Total.*
Vaccinated	154,031	204,242	362,087
Successfully vaccinated	147,958	196,216	347,765

The number vaccinated under one year of age is 43 per cent. upon the total number vaccinated, and 32 per cent. upon the number of births.

In every union in which we found that the number vaccinated under one year of age did not nearly approximate to the number of births, or in which a falling off had taken place in the number vaccinated, as compared with the previous year, we requested the guardians of the union to call the attention of the vaccinators to the subject, and to urge upon them the importance of extending the practice of vaccination in their districts. Though the number of children vaccinated under one year of age is only 32 per cent. upon the number of births, we still think that the relation which the births bear to the number vaccinated is a tolerably correct measure of the efficiency of the arrangements for promoting the object of the Vaccination Extension Act, as from the communication which we have received from boards of guardians and vaccinators, we learn that vaccination is very frequently deferred till the child attains its second or third year.

51. During the past year small pox has not prevailed to such an extent as it did in the year 1844, the deaths in the metropolis in 1845 being only 909, whilst in 1844 they were 1804.

* These totals do not correspond, in consequence of the ages of the persons vaccinated not being distinguished in some of the returns.

The Registrars of the 115 districts, comprised in the Quarterly Tables of Mortality published by the Registrar-General, are required when the deaths are above the average, to state whether any epidemic disease has been prevailing in the districts, or if there be any other known circumstance which will account for the increase. We are thus enabled to ascertain in what localities small pox has recently been prevalent, and we then place ourselves in communication with the boards of guardians of the unions in which the deaths occurred, and request that the public vaccinators may be instructed to use every means in their power to extend the practice of vaccination in their respective districts, and that the attention of the residents of the union may be especially directed to the arrangements which have been made for vaccination. At the same time we feel bound to state, that the boards of guardians and vaccinators generally appear to be fully sensible of the importance of giving full effect to the provisions of the Vaccination Extension Act, and manifest great zeal in the extension of the practice of vaccination. The amount paid in fees to the vaccinators during the year ended 25th March, 1845, was £25,905, being an increase of £9025, or of 35 per cent. upon the amount paid in the previous year.

Legal Proceedings connected with formation of the Ashbourne Union.—52. In our last report we stated that we had received notice on behalf of some of the parishes which considered themselves members of the Alstonefield Union, of their intention to apply for a writ of *certiorari* to bring up our order, forming the Ashbourne Union, before the Court of Queen's Bench. That notice was abandoned, and another notice having been afterwards served, was acted upon, and a rule *nisi* for the writ was obtained in Trinity Term last. In the same term cause was shown by our counsel, and the rule was discharged with costs, the Court being satisfied that the several parishes which claimed to belong to the Alstonefield Union had never been legally added to it. By this decision the validity of the order forming the Ashbourne Union was established, and all the parishes comprised in it have been brought under the operation of the general law.

Proceedings for bringing the Rochdale Union into operation.—53. We also stated in our last Report the circumstances connected with the legal proceedings which took place in respect of the order which we issued to the Rochdale Union in October, 1844, and that a rule *nisi* had been obtained for setting aside the verdict, which we had obtained at the assizes on the trial of the traverse of the *mandamus*. We considered that the decision of the question, which was one purely of form, could not be obtained according to the ordinary course of the proceedings in that court until after a long interval. In the mean time the administration of the law for the relief of the poor in the union was in a state of great embarrassment, in regard to the legality of any proceedings which could take place in the matter. As there had been no election of guardians at the time for the last annual election, there was no board of guardians to which we could issue a fresh order. The case, therefore, was one to which the provision in the 38th section of the Poor Law Amendment Act, which requires the *ex-officio* guardians to act, applied. We accordingly called upon them to do so, and at the same time issued an order, requiring the several townships in the union to proceed to an extraordinary election of guardians. The justices proceeded to act in conformity with the law, and took upon themselves the administration of the law for the relief of the poor, until guardians having been elected in some of the townships, a portion of those guardians proceeded to carry out the provisions of the law, and during the last winter and up to the present time have acted in the complete discharge of their duties. The object of the *mandamus* having been thus obtained, we considered that no benefit would have resulted from our continuing the litigation in which it was involved, and consequently the proceedings were stayed at Christmas last by the ordinary course of a *stet processus*.

Ashton-under-Line Union brought into operation.—54. In furtherance of our intention to bring the Ashton-under-Line and Oldham Unions into operation for the administration of the law, we issued an order to the former union, dated the 30th of September last, directing an election of guardians to take place, and another on the 14th of December, directing the guardians forthwith to assume the administration of the relief of the poor. Both orders were readily obeyed, and that union is now in full operation.

Proceedings in Oldham Union.—55. In the Oldham Union, which was also originally formed in 1837, inasmuch as no board of guardians ever met for the discharge of their duties, there was no clerk who could conduct the election; consequently a question arose as to the best mode of procuring such election in this union; and we considered it advisable to direct the several parish officers to meet, and elect a person to act as a relieving officer, to conduct the election of guardians for the several townships of which the union is composed. This order was issued on the 15th day of November last, and directed the overseers to make the appointment on the 2nd day of December last. Some of the overseers attended at the appointed place of meeting; but as the greater part of them abstained from so doing, no election was made. We applied in last term to the Court of Queen's Bench for a writ of *mandamus* to the several overseers in this union to meet and elect a returning officer, and obtained a rule *nisi*, which has been made absolute this Easter term. An affidavit had been made in answer by the parties who represented the township of Oldham, in which they questioned our power to direct the appointment of the returning officer, but no cause was shown against the rule, as it was proposed by the defendants to argue the question, whatever it may be, on the return to the writ, which we shall forthwith cause to be prepared and served.

Act of 8 *and* 9 *Vict.* c. 10.—56. As it was found that considerable difficulty existed in framing proceedings under the new provisions relating to Bastardy in the 7 and 8 Vict. c. 101, so as to be free from technical objections, the Legislature passed, in the commencement of the session of 1845, a short Act (8 and 9 Vict. c. 10) upon the subject, which supplied a complete series of forms to be used in such proceedings, and also removed some few doubts which had arisen in the construction of the former statute.

Acts of 8 *and* 9 *Vict.*, *c.* 100 *and* 126 *(Lunacy Acts), and Acts of* 8 *and* 9 *Vict. c.* 117 (*Act for removal of Scotch and Irish paupers.*)—57. But there were three Acts of the last session to which, as they affected the relief of paupers, we deemed it necessary to give particular attention. We allude to the Acts for the Licensing of Houses for the reception of Lunatics, and for enforcing the establishment of Lunatic Asylums, and the Act for the removal of Scotch and Irish Paupers. Those Acts determined the course of proceedings which had previously prevailed in regard to the relief and removal of the classes of paupers to which they applied, and introduced many new regulations. We thought it expedient to prepare and circulate a letter to all boards of guardians, containing an exposition of such of the regulations and provisions of those statutes as appeared to us to require the attention of the guardians and their officers, in reference to the performance of their several duties in the administration of the relief to the poor. We also directed the attention of the medical officers to the duty imposed upon them, in regard to visiting and reporting upon lunatic paupers, by a separate communication.

Act of 8 *and* 9 *Vict.*, *c.* 116.—58. The Act of the last session, for the protection of Seamen entering on board Merchant Ships, (8 and 9 Vict. c. 116,) containing provisions prohibiting the engagement of seamen by other than licensed persons, appeared to affect the unions and parishes in certain districts, from which lads are frequently sought for engagement into that service. We therefore deemed it expedient to transmit a copy of this statute, with a brief reference to its provisions, to the different boards of guardians.

Act of 9 *and* 10 *Vict.*, *c.* 10.—59. We may mention likewise, that a Statute of the present Session of Parliament (9 and 10 Vict., c. 10) having altered the mode which had been established for the repayment of Greenwich and Chelsea Pensioners, who by themselves or by their families receive parochial relief, we have taken means to communicate to the different boards of guardians the new provision, which will, we believe, remove much of the mischief that has resulted from the mode of dealing with the pensions of these persons.

Sales of Parish Property.—60. Before we conclude the account of our proceedings in England, we think it right to advert to the subject of parish property. Although the sales of this property have been much diminished for some time past, they have by no means ceased. We regret to find that, in many places there is a determined resolution on the part of the parishioners to retain their old workhouses, as receptacles into which they allow paupers receiving out-door relief to be crowded, instead of such paupers being relieved by the guardians to the extent, or in the manner requisite to secure them adequate and proper lodging. Too many families are thus congregated in places which cannot be regulated or kept in proper order and repair, where no control exists, and where many evils affecting both the health and the morals of the inmates are engendered or aggravated. We constantly remonstrate with boards of guardians and parish officers upon this state of things, but have had little success in carrying into effect the only sound remedy. The appearance of a saving to the parish by allowing a pauper to reside in such dilapidated buildings rather than supply the means of providing proper lodging, or causing them to be received into the workhouse, proves to be an unsurmountable barrier to the course which is obviously desirable—namely, the disposal of such property to persons competent and willing to attend to and improve it.

61. It is sometimes urged that the property is a profitable investment for the parish, as it may be let out to labourers at rents to be paid over in aid of the poor rates. But it is only under very peculiar circumstances that this can be the result. The parish overseers are seldom strict or accurate receivers, and the labourer who occupies the cottages is so little above the class of paupers, that the exaction of the payment of the rent would too often bring him into that condition. The rent is therefore excused, and the tenant loses that habit of punctual payment which is so important to be preserved by him. In an application which we lately received from a parish in a northern union for the sale of some cottages, occur the following expressions:

"The cottages act as a bounty upon pauperism; the occupiers are in a worse condition than the generality of labourers in the village; they are more insubordinate. As soon as a vacancy occurs, or is in prospect, the overseers are subject to great annoyance by numbers of applications, chiefly persons with large families, who threaten that unless a house is provided for them, they will throw themselves and families upon the poor rate, *a great and increasing evil.*"

We believe this to be a correct representation. We have, in many instances, stated to the district auditors, that it is their duty to enforce from the overseers an account of the rents of such property, as we consider that the law does not empower them to dispense with the payment of those rents.

Emigration.—62. The emigration of poor persons during the last year has not been so extensive as in former periods, in consequence of the greater demand for labour in this country. The number who have emigrated will appear in the table in the Appendix applicable to this subject. One of the shipowners usually engaged in emigration made Southampton the port of embarcation for all the emigrants who were carried by him, instead of the port of London, which has been customarily the port of embarcation for emigrants from the south-eastern counties. Some advantages undoubtedly resulted from this course, but we are not prepared to express any opinion in favour of its universal adoption.

63. The Colonial Land and Emigration Commissioners were enabled, by means of arrangements with the Colonial Governments of New South Wales and the Cape of Good Hope, to resume gratuitous emigration to Australia, and to provide the same to a limited extent to the Cape, and some of the persons who emigrated under the authority of our orders, availed themselves of the opportunity thus afforded to them of proceeding to those colonies. We have not been accustomed to favour or forward emigration to the Cape, as we were not assured that this colony required additional labourers, and consequently felt a difficulty in satisfying ourselves of the proper reception of emigrants of the class referred to. At the same time, the cost of the passage was generally so great as to prevent parishes from assenting to the outlay. But when the Commissioners above referred to were enabled to propose and carry out this emigration, though to a small extent, we readily approved of the various applications made to us to sanction the trifling expenditure from the parochial funds, which was sometimes required to enable the parties to accept the offers of the Commissioners. As there appeared to be no doubt of the emigrants being instantly engaged on their arrival at the Cape, we withdrew our requisite of the landing money in this instance, as we had previously done in regard to Australia. We have reason to believe that the emigrants, on arrival at the Cape, obtained immediate employment.

Proposed Fund for Superannuated Officers.—64. In our 10th Annual Report, we expressed our opinion in favour of the establishment, under the sanction of the Legislature, of a fund for superannuated workhouse masters, to be created by receiving a proportionate part of the salaries of these officers, who would have a contingent claim upon it. Since that period a more comprehensive arrangement of the same kind has been in the contemplation of parish and union officers in England. Our Assistant-Commissioner, Mr. Hall, has been consulted on the subject; and it appears from papers communicated to him, that more than 1030 paid officers have signified their assent to the formation of a superannuation fund on the principle of deduction from their salaries; and that 22 boards of guardians have passed resolutions in favour of such an arrangement. We also perceive from the printed votes of both Houses of Parliament, that several petitions have been presented, praying the Legislature to facilitate the establishment of such a fund. We observe that in the Act to amend the Laws for the provision and regulation of Lunatic Asylums in Counties and Boroughs, (8 and 9 Vict. c. 126,) it is provided in the 43rd section, that such superannuation annuities, payable out of the county rates, may be granted by the justices to any officers of such lunatic asylums, on their becoming incapacitated from confirmed sickness, age, or infirmity, as they (the justices) may in their discretion think proportionate to their merits and time of services, not, however, exceeding in amount two-thirds of the salaries payable to them at the time of their retirements. We refer to this provision as evidencing the disposition of Parliament in favour of the genera principle of granting superannuation allowances tc incapacitated officers on their retirement from situations, being similar to those of officers concerned in the administration of the relief of the poor. The particular manner which we are prepared to approve would, in its principles and details, resemble rather the system of the Police Act than that of the Lunacy Act; and we advert to the subject on this occasion, in order to express our readiness to assist in the preparation of any such measure, believing that it would be for the advantage of the paid officers and the rate-payers, as well as that of the recipients of relief.

We have the honour to be,

Sir,

Your very faithful and obedient Servants,

(Signed) GEORGE NICHOLLS,
GEORGE CORNEWALL LEWIS,
EDMUND W. HEAD,
E. T. B. TWISLETON.

[*The portion of the Report which relates to "Proceedings in Ireland," is omitted.*]

AMOUNT of MONEY Levied, and Received from other Sources in aid of POOR'S RATE, and expended for the RELIEF ar MAINTENANCE of the POOR, and for other Purposes, in England and Wales, during the Years ended 25th March, 1834 to 184 with the Average Price of Wheat per Quarter in each Year.

Years ended at Lady-day.	Receipt.			Expenditure.												
	Amount of Money levied by Assessment.	Received from all other Sources in aid of Poor's Rate.	Total Amount of Money received as Poor's Rate.	Amount of Money expended in Relief, &c. of the Poor.*	Amount of Money expended in Law Charges (Parochial and Union.)	Amount of Fees paid to the Vaccinators under the Vaccination Extension Act.	Payments on account of the Registration Act; viz. Fees to Clergymen and Registrars, Outlay for Register Offices, Books and Forms.	Payments under the Parochial Assessments' Act, (for Surveys, Valuation, &c.,) and Loans repaid under the same.	Enumeration & other Payments made under the Act for taking an Account of the Census of 1841.	Payments for or towards the County or Borough Rate.	Payments for or towards the County & Local Police Forces (if any), and if not paid out of the County or Borough Rate.	Money expended for all other purposes.	Total Parochial Rates expended.	Medical Relief.	Average Price of Wheat per
	£.	£.	£.	£.	£.	£.	£.	£.	£.	£.	£.	£.	£.	£.	s.
1834†	8,338,079	... ...	... ...	6,317,255	258,604	...	...	... ...	...	691,518	.. ...	1,021,941	8,289,348	...	5
1835	7,373,807	... ...	... ...	5,526,418	220,527	...	... ...	... ...	...	705,711	... ...	935,362	7,370,018	...	4
1836	6,354,538	... ...	... ...	4,717,630	172,432	...	... ...	... ...	...	699,845	... ...	823,213	6,413,120	...	3
1837	5,294,566	... ...	... ...	4,044,741	126,951	...	... ...	... ...	...	604,203	... ...	637,043	5,412,938	...	5.
1838	5,186,389	... ...	... ...	4,123,604	93,982	...	35,662	25,680	...	681,842	... ...	507,929	5,468,699	136,775	5.
1839	5,613,939	273,139	5,887,078	4,406,907	63,412	...	52.306	56,846	...	741,407	... ...	493,703	5,814,581	148,652	6
1840	6,014,605	227,966	6,242,571	4,576,965	67,020	...	51,228	49,963	...	855,552	... ...	466,698	6,067,426	151,781	6.
1841	6,351,828	226,984	6,578,812	4,760,929	69,942	11,661	53,728	43,157	...	1,026,035	... ...	527,717	6,493,172	154,054	6.
1842	6,552,890	201,514	6,754,404	4,911,498	68,051	33,744	52,379	40,178	57,111	1.003,651	227 067	318,092	6,711,771	153,481	6
1843	7,085,595	219,006	7,304,601	5,208,027	84,730	16,425	53,896	30,420	...	1,051,878	243,738	346,007	7,035,121	160,726	5
1844	6,847,205	219,592	7,066.797	4,976,093	105,304	16,980	56,094	30,083	...	1,111,236	245,221	359,106	6,900,117	166.257	5
1845	6,791,006	218,505	7,009,511	5,039,703	95,397	25,905	57,388	22,877	...	1,046,412	233,550	336,170	6,857,402	174,330	4

* Including in-door and out-door relief and establishment charges; and since the passing of the Poor Law Amendment Act, in addition thereto, bui and emigration loans repaid, furnishing of Union Workhouses, &c.

† The last parochial year previous to the passing of the Poor Law Amendment Act.

NOTE.—The above results are obtained from the Annual Poor Rate Return received from the Clerks of Unions and Overseers of the Poor.

Printed by Order of the Poor Law Commissioners, by BLACKBURN AND PARDON, 6, Hatton Garden, and Published by CHARLES KNIGHT and Co., 22, Ludgate Street, Publishers to the Poor Law Commissioners.

AN

OFFICIAL CIRCULAR

OF PUBLIC DOCUMENTS AND INFORMATION:

DIRECTED BY THE POOR LAW COMMISSIONERS TO BE PRINTED, CHIEFLY FOR THE USE OF THE MEMBERS AND PERMANENT OFFICERS OF BOARDS OF GUARDIANS UNDER THE POOR LAW AMENDMENT ACT.

No. 60.] CIRCULAR ISSUED JULY 1, 1846.

Poor Law Commission Office, Somerset House, July 1st, 1846.

THE Poor Law Commissioners directed that the following documents be printed and circulated for the information of Guardians and Officers of the several Unions, viz.

Page

(Signed) By order of the Board,
EDWIN CHADWICK, *Secretary.*

I.—AUDITOR—WHETHER PRINTING AND POSTAGE EXPENSES OF, SHOULD BE PAID BY THE UNIONS.

April 21st, 1846.

Clerk of ——— *Union*—Inquired whether the guardians are bound to pay a proportionate share of the printing and postage expenses of the district auditor, who has sent in a small account of that kind for the past year, which the guardians do not object to pay, provided the Commissioners think it should be paid by the union.

Ans.—The Commissioners consider that the district auditor should pay the expenses of any printing which may be incurred by him, as also of stationery; but he need not pay postage, and it is better therefore that the guardians should pay it, to prevent double postage.

II.—BASTARDY—LIABILITY OF PARISH FOR EXPENCES OF APPREHENDING PUTATIVE FATHERS.

April 28th, 1846.

Mr. ——, *Glanford Brigg Union*—A girl, living in the parish of H., but not belonging to it, having affiliated her bastard child to a man residing in a distant parish, and he having absconded, the justices issued a warrant for his apprehension, and placed it in the hands of a constable, who apprehended the man and lodged him in gaol. The constable has now brought a bill, of upwards of £3, with a justices' order for payment, against the overseers of the parish of H. Inquired whether they are bound to pay the bill.

Ans.—The Commissioners consider the question as subject to doubt, but, on the whole, they incline to think that the payment for executing the warrant of the magistrates in the case to which you advert may be charged to the poor-rate.

III.—BURIAL.

1. FEES ON BURIAL OF ROMAN CATHOLIC PAUPERS.

June 6th, 1846.

The Roman Catholic Pastor of ———, —Inquired, whether the Poor Law Act allows him to have the Catholic paupers buried in his own churchyard, adjoining the Roman Catholic chapel, at the parish expense; and whether he can demand the usual fee paid to the Protestant clergyman on the burial of paupers.

Ans.—Under the 31st section of the 7 and 8 Vic. c. 101, Roman Catholic paupers may undoubtedly be buried at the parish expense. That section empowers the guardians to bury the body of any poor person at the charge of the poor-rate; and it draws no distinction whatever, in this respect, between paupers of different religious persuasions. With regard to the *place* of burial, the same section enacts that if the guardians do not direct the body to be buried in the parish to which the deceased was chargeable, the body shall (unless the deceased, or the husband, or wife, or next of kin, desire otherwise,) "be buried in the churchyard, or other consecrated burial ground, in or belonging to the parish, &c., in which the death may have occurred." In the section adverted to, there is a clause specially providing for the payment of burial fees, on the interment of paupers. That clause, however, only authorises the payment of such fees to the persons who, by the custom of the place, or by Act of Parliament, may be entitled to receive them. The Commissioners are advised that these terms appear to point exclusively to the incumbent of the living, or other person standing in his place, or in an analogous position in relation to the Established Church; and that a custom certainly cannot, and probably no local act does, recognise any person as entitled to burial fees, but a minister of the Established Church. The Commissioners, however, think it right to add that, although a Roman Catholic priest or dissenting minister has no such claim to burial fees under this particular clause of the section, as a clergyman of the Established Church derives from it, yet it appears to them that, where the body of a pauper is buried, under the directions of the guardians, in the burial ground of a Roman Catholic or dissenting chapel, the sums claimed by the priest or minister, or the proprietor of the ground, as the condition of the interment, may be considered as forming part of the necessary expenses of the funeral, (inasmuch as the guardians have no power to insist that the body shall be buried there,) and may accordingly be paid by the guardians under that clause of the 31st section, which authorises them to charge on the poor-rate the expenses of the burial of paupers.

---

2. THE PARISH OF BURIAL.

June 25th, 1846.

Clerk of Bodmin Union—Inquired whether the Commissioners concur in the view of the law, relating to the burial of paupers, stated to have been recently expressed by the Archdeacon of ——, namely, that clergymen are required to authorise the burial of paupers who may die in union workhouses, in the respective parishes of such paupers, and not, as heretofore, in the parishes in which they happen to die.

Ans.—The Commissioners do not quite understand what is meant by the words "required to authorise." It will probably be sufficient if they state their own view of the operation of the Act apparently alluded to. The recent provision of 7 and 8 Vic. c. 101, sec. 31, undoubtedly authorises that the bodies of paupers who die in one parish of a union, but are chargeable to some other parish, in the same union, should be buried in the latter, where the guardians may so direct. The Commissioners conceive it is a matter wholly in the discretion of the guardians, and dependent upon the direction they may give respecting the interment. The 31st section provides, that "unless the guardians, in compliance with the desire expressed by such person in his lifetime, or by any of his relations, or for any other cause, direct the body of such poor person to be buried in the churchyard, or burial ground, of the parish to which such person has been chargeable, (which they are hereby authorised to do,) every dead body which the guardians, or any of their officers duly authorised, shall direct to be buried at the expense of the poor-rates, shall (unless, &c.) be buried in the churchyard, or other consecrated burial ground, in, or belonging to, the parish, division of parish, chapelry, or place, in which the death may have occurred." The ordinary rule laid down is clearly, that a body is to be buried in the churchyard of the parish where the death occurred; the burial in the parish of the chargeability, is made the exceptional case, *i.e.*, where the guardians, for any of the specific reasons assigned in the section, or other sufficient cause, may see fit to direct, or authorise that course. The Commissioners apprehend that the clergyman of the parish in which the death actually occurs, whether it occur in or out of the workhouse, cannot legally refuse to bury the body. His obligation so to inter is, the Commissioners consider, sufficiently apparent both from the terms of the canon, (68,) and the requirements of the 31st section, already referred to.

IV.—CLERK TO GUARDIANS.

1. DUTY OF, TO MAKE CALCULATION REQUIRED BY GUARDIANS OF COST PER HEAD OF PAUPERS.

May 9th, 1846.

Clerk of —— *Union* — Inquired whether it forms part of his duty to make the calculation required in the following order of the guardians, namely, "The clerk is requested to furnish to the board of guardians, at their next meeting, a return of the cost per head, for the year ending the 25th of March, 1846, on the population of each separate parish, for the maintenance of the poor."

Ans.—It appears to the Commissioners that the order referred to is a lawful order of the guardians, applicable to the clerk's office; and one which you are, therefore, bound to obey under Article 17, No. 11, of the General Order of the Commissioners on the Duties of Officers.

2. DUTIES OF CLERKS, AS TO EXAMINING TRADESMEN'S BILLS.

April 21st, 1846.

Clerk of —— *Union*—Some of the guardians contend that it forms a part of his (the clerk's) duty to examine the tradesmen's bills in order to test the propriety of the charges made therein, (as, for instance, the prices charged for stationery, &c., not supplied by contract,) which would require a knowledge of the prices proper to be charged by various tradesmen, with the nature of whose business he has not the slightest acquaintance. It is also asserted that he is bound personally to examine the accounts with the vouchers; that it is not sufficient for him to produce such accounts and vouchers previously checked by his clerk, whom he considers fully competent to perform that duty, and who keeps the union books under his superintendence. Inquired what is the precise extent of the duties of the clerk in relation to the matters above adverted to.

Ans.—The only order in force in the —— Union which bears upon the point is the General Order respecting the Duties of Officers, Art. 17. In this, there is nothing imposing upon the clerk the duty of examing invoices of goods supplied to the union, (not upon contract,) to ascertain whether the charges are correct. That duty rather lies upon the guardians themselves. As to discharging the duty of examining the accounts with the vouchers, personally, the Commissioners consider that it is not required so long as the clerk is personally responsible for the examination being correct, which is the case in the present instance. Adverting, however, to No. 11 of Art. 17 of the order above referred to, the Commissioners are not prepared to say that, if the guardians should direct the clerk to discharge the duties personally, such duties would not be "applicable to his office," except so far as regards a technical knowledge of the prices of the goods.

3. RIGHT OF CLERK TO A FEE FOR CERTIFICATES OF CHARGEABILITY.

April 17th, 1846.

Clerk of Dorchester Union—He has of late been required by several parishes to grant certificates for the purpose of proving the chargeability of paupers previous to their removal; and, as such certificates are given to save the expense of witnesses at the examination, as well as at the hearing of an appeal; he requested the Commissioners' opinion as to his right to demand a fee for such certificates.

Ans.—If the certificates to which you refer are those authorised by the 5 & 6 Vict. c. 57, they are to be issued by the board of guardians, and you only countersign them as the officer of the guardians; consequently, your filling up the certificate, and transmitting it to the parties applying are part of your official duties, for which no extra fee is payable.

V.—CLERKS TO JUSTICES— PAYMENT OF FEES TO.

May 23rd, 1846.

Mr. ——, District Auditor—The clerk to the justices has been in the habit, in addition to his duties as such clerk, of going journeys to make inquiries respecting the settlement of paupers, and also of transacting other business usually done by attorneys and assistant overseers. Inquired whether any charge for payment to him as justices' clerk, beyond what the table of fees allowed by the judges sanctions, should be allowed in the overseers' accounts.

Ans.—You would certainly not be justified in allowing in the overseers' accounts any payment made to a clerk of the justices, for services rendered by him as such clerk beyond what may be authorised by the established table of fees. If the same individual affords to the overseers any advice or assistance as an attorney, his payment by them, and the allowance of such payment in their accounts, will, of course, depend upon the same considerations that would govern the compensation of any other attorney in the like case. Whether his services in any instance have been rendered to the overseers in his character of clerk to the justices, or in that of attorney, is a question that must be decided according to the particular circumstances. The Commissioners desire to add that, if he is paid for doing any duty as an assistant overseer, the legality of the payment will, in the first place, depend upon the question, whether he is duly appointed to that office.

VI.—CLOTHING —ALLOWANCE OF TO BASTARD CHILDREN BORN IN THE WORKHOUSE, ON QUITTING SAME.

May 25th, 1846.

Clerk of Bideford Union—Inquired, whether the guardians can legally refuse to permit able-bodied women, who have been delivered of bastard children in the workhouse, on quitting, to take with them the clothing with which such children have been supplied therein.

Ans.—As the guardians cannot separate the child from its mother, if the latter gives notice to leave the workhouse, and has no clothes for her child, (the child having been born in the workhouse,) the case appears to the Commissioners to be one of such urgency as would bring it within the 1st Exception to Article 1 of the Out-Relief Prohibitory Order. The Commissioners assume that the mother is able-bodied and in health. If, however, in any case, the circumstances should not be such as would render it one of sudden and urgent necessity, the guardians might give the relief under Article 6 of the Order, and report the same to the Commissioners within fifteen days. The relief, if approved by the Commissioners, would then be lawful. With reference to the inquiry of the guardians, whether they can legally refuse the allowance of such relief, I am to state that if the mother has no other means of providing clothing for her child, the allowance of at least some covering for the child appears to be necessary. But the guardians are the judges of the necessity in this as in all other cases of relief. The Commissioners refer the guardians to the observations on the subject contained in their last Annual Report, par. 22. See Official Circular, No. 59.

VII.—COLLECTOR—APPOINTMENT OF AS OVERSEER.

June 18th, 1846.

Clerk of Chorlton Union—T. R., collector of poor-rates for the township of Chorlton-upon-Medlock, has been appointed overseer for that township, but he has not resigned his former office. How far are the two offices compatible?

Ans.—The offices of collector of poor-rates and overseer of the poor of the same parish are incompatible; or, in other words, cannot legally be held by the same person at the same time. An overseer of the poor is bound by law to discharge the duties of his office without remuneration, and one of those duties is certainly the collection of the poor-rates. If, therefore, he were to be paid as collector for the discharge of a duty which he is bound as overseer to perform gratuitously, it is obvious that such an arrangement would be a mere evasion of the law. Moreover, by the 61st section of 7 & 8 Vict. c. 101, every such collector is bound to obey the directions of the majority of the overseers; and, if he were at the same time one of the overseers, he would of course stand in the anomalous position of being subordinate to himself. On the whole, therefore, the Commissioners consider that the two offices cannot be held together; and that as his appointment to the office of overseer has been made and acted upon by him, such appointment to it must be considered as vacating that of collector. Under these circumstances, it appears to the Commissioners that T. R. has ceased to be a collector of poor-rates for the parish of Chorlton-upon-Med lock, and cannot be re-appointed to that office so long as he continues overseer of that parish.

VIII.—CONSTABLE.

REFUSAL OF OVERSEER TO PAY BILL OF CONSTABLE FOR REMOVING VAGRANTS.

May 2nd, 1846.

Clerks to Justices, Maidstone—A complaint has been made to the justices of the East Aylesford Bench, by W. M., a constable appointed for the parish of B., under the Parish Constables Act, (5 and 6 Vic. c. 109,) that the overseers of that parish refuse to pay him his bill, amounting to £1. 18*s*. 4*d*., for moving vagrants out of the parish. The bill has been presented to the inhabitants in vestry, in pursuance of the 18th Geo. 3, c. 19, s. 4, and allowed by them, but the overseer has refused to pay it, on the ground that the auditor had, on a previous occasion, refused to pass a similar account, unless it was allowed by the justices. The justices to whom the complaint was preferred in this instance, finding that the inhabitants had allowed the bill, considered that they had, in consequence thereof, no jurisdiction in regard to the question; their interference only arising in case the inhabitants had disallowed it; but, thinking the case one of hardship, they wish the Commissioners' attention to be directed to it.

Ans.—The Commissioners think it probably admits of question whether a constable appointed under 5 & 6 Vic. c. 109, for whose remuneration special provision is made, (sec: 17,) is entitled to claim, under 18th Geo. 3, c. 19, sec. 4, to be reimbursed any sums which he may expend on account of the parish or township. The view which the Commissioners are disposed to take is that, so far at least as the fees or allowances contemplated by sec. 17, of 5 & 6 Vic. c. 109, are within the 18th Geo. 3, c. 19, sec. 4, the latter statute may be considered as virtually repealed, but that where the table of fees and allowances settled under the 5 & 6 Vic. c. 109, makes no provision for the case, and a constable appointed under the latter Act is put to charge in doing the business of the parish or township, his right to reimbursement under 18th Geo. 3, c. 19, s. 4, is preserved. With respect to the particular case to which your letter immediately relates, in which the constable of B. has made a claim under the last-mentioned Act on the overseers, it appears to the Commissioners that the vestry cannot, by their acquiescence in, or approval of the account of the constable, make it a lawful charge on the poor-rates, if the sums entered in the account be not in their nature such as the 18th Geo. 3, c. 19, warrants. The Commissioners conceive, however, that where the account containing items in their nature lawful has been allowed by the vestry, the statute makes it incumbent on the overseers to discharge the bill. In the account of the constable of B. an item or charge of 1*s*. 3*d*. "for moving vagrants on the hill" frequently occurs. The Commissioners do not at present see that this is warranted by 18th Geo. 3, c. 19, s. 4. It is unquestionably the duty of the constable to relieve the parish from the burden of vagrants, but this duty does not consist in moving them on, or sending them into the next parish, but in apprehending them and taking them before a magistrate. A claim upon the parish for any expenses which the constable might actually be put to in performing this duty would be a legal demand, under 18 Geo. 3, c. 19, sec. 4, (see Reg. *v.* Churchwardens of Chelmsford, 3 Gal. & Dav. 357,) *i.e.*, assuming no provision is otherwise made for the case by the table of fees and allowances settled under the Parish Constables Act. Moreover, the charge of 1*s*. 3*d*. does not appear to be an expense which the constable incurs, but a recompense for the service: on this ground also the item is not warranted by 18th Geo. 3, c. 19, s. 4, which, as the Commissioners are advised, contemplates only the reimbursements of the constable the sums which he actually disburses on account of the parish or township. The Commissioners would further observe, that (assuming the propriety of the items) they do not see that the justices have jurisdiction in the case to order payment of the account. It is only where the bill or account is not approved by the inhabitants in the vestry that the justices (on the application of the constable) are to determine what is to be paid to him. The case does not appear to the Commissioners to be one in which they can give directions as to the payment of the constable. The payment depends entirely upon the legal considerations applicable to the case, and not upon any approval or sanction of the Commissioners.

IX.—DESERTION—THE HUSBAND LIVING IN ADULTERY AND THE WIFE LEAVING HIS HOME IN CONSEQUENCE.

May 28th, 1846.

Chairman of Bridgnorth Union—Requested the Commissioners' advice with reference to the case of a man against whom the guardians are about to take proceedings for deserting his wife, who has left his house and become an inmate of the workhouse in consequence of her husband having brought home a woman with whom he is now living in a state of adultery.

Ans.—The Commissioners think that the husband, under the circumstances described in your letter, is liable to be proceeded against for the refusal or neglect to maintain his wife, by which refusal or neglect it appears she is now chargeable to the parish. The Commissioners collect from your statement that there is no imputation on the wife, but that she has been compelled to leave her husband's roof for a reasonable cause, *i.e.*, his conduct, or rather mode of living, has rendered his home unfit for a modest woman to reside in it. It was held in Aldis *v.* Chapman, 1 Selwyn N. P. 281, (and to the same effect are the subsequent cases: see Houliston *v.* Smith, 3 Bing. 127; 10 Moore 482; 2 C. and P. 22,) that where a husband, by bringing another woman under his roof, renders his house unfit for the residence of his wife, and she, thereupon, removes and lives apart from him, he is bound to provide her with necessaries during the separation. Such treatment on the part of the husband is equivalent to turning his wife out of the house, (per Lord Kenyon in the case of Hodges *v.* Hodges, 1 Esp. N. P. C. 441.) The question, however, is, whether the husband, under such circumstances, is criminally answerable under 5th Geo. 4, cap. 83, sec. 3; in other words, whether his civil obligation and his criminal liability stand on the same footing. The Commissioners consider that they do, and that the ground in both cases is "the legal obligation to maintain." The case of Rex *v.* Flinton, 1 B. and Adol. 227, appears to establish thus much. The husband there was held not to have committed an offence under sec. 3 of 5th Geo. 4, cap. 83, because the obligation to maintain his wife was not made out, she having left him without sufficient cause, and having committed adultery. Had the case been otherwise, *i.e.*, had the husband been civilly liable for his wife's contracts, it would seem that the conviction would have been upheld. Justice Littledale observes: "I do not see the distinction attempted between the parish and an individual supplying necessaries. If the husband is not obliged to answer for his wife's contracts, or to receive her into his house, it cannot be said that he is legally bound to maintain her." The inference from this is, that if the husband had been liable for his wife's contracts, and bound to receive her, he would have been equally bound to have maintained her, within the meaning of 3 Geo. 4, cap. 83. The Commissioners entertain some doubt whether the husband could be proceeded against under sec. 4 of 5th Geo. 4, cap. 83, for the offence of desertion. It, probably, could not be made out that he had run away, and left his wife. The terms of the 3rd section are different, and apply simply to a neglect to maintain.

X.—ELECTION OF GUARDIANS.

1. DUTY OF CLERK WHERE HE BELIEVES A NOMINATION PAPER TO BE A FORGERY.

April 2nd, 1846.

Clerk of —— Union—Inquired what course he should pursue in the case of a nomination for the office of guardian, in which he has some doubts whether the signature to the nomination paper is that of the person purporting to have signed it; whether he can call upon the person whose signature it purports to be, to speak to the fact, or allow an objection to be taken on the point at any stage of the election.

Ans.—The Commissioners think that if you are satisfied that the signature attached to a nomination paper is a forgery, it will be your duty to treat such nomination as invalid. The Commissioners consider, however, that the proper time for taking the objection is before the day arrives for issuing the voting papers. With regard to the evidence of the supposed forgery, the Commissioners can only say that you must satisfy yourself upon the point by the best testimony you can obtain.

2. QUALIFICATION TO VOTE OF PERSONS ON THE RATE-BOOK, BUT WHOSE RATES ARE PAID BY THEIR LANDLORDS—NON-RESIDENT VOTER.

April 1*st*, 1846.

Clerk of Lutterworth Union—Requested the Commissioners' opinion on the following points, with reference to the election of guardians; namely,—1st, Whether occupiers of cottages, whose names appear in the rate-book, the rates, however, being paid by the landlord, are entitled to vote. 2ndly, Whether the incumbent of the parish, who is non-resident, can authorise his agent (who pays the rates for him) to receive his voting paper, and fill it up and sign it; or, if not, can the agent send the paper to the incumbent to fill up, and, on its return, deliver it to the person appointed to receive the voting papers, and thus secure the incumbent's vote.

Ans.—1st. The 46th section of the Poor Law Amendment Act requires, as the condition of voting as rate-payer, that the person should have been rated for a given period (a year), and should have paid the rates for such period. The payment here required is undoubtedly either a direct payment by the party himself, or by some one who can be considered as his agent for the purpose. The circumstances of the case, as stated by you, are very similar to those in Reg. *v.* Inhabitants of South Kilvington, in which it was held, that a payment of the rate by the landlord was not a payment by the tenant within the meaning of the 3rd and 4th William and Mary, c. 11, s. 6. The Commissioners cannot, however, undertake to advise as to the sufficiency of the payment in the present case, as a payment by the occupiers, or parties assessed, unless informed more particularly of the facts of the case, and the precise nature of the arrangement which may have been entered into between such occupiers and the landlords. 2nd. A voter who can write cannot authorise an agent to sign the voting paper for him. A voter who does not reside in the Union may name a place of address in the parish at which the voting paper may be delivered. The paper, when delivered at such address, might be transmitted to the voter for signature, and returned by the latter in sufficient time to allow of the paper being given to the person authorised to call at the place of address for the same. If a non-resident voter does not name a place of address, he may himself apply to the clerk for a voting paper in the manner provided by Article 19 of the Order of Election.

3. VOTING: CHANGE OF RESIDENCE FROM ONE WARD TO ANOTHER.

March 30*th*, 1846.

Clerk of Leeds Township—It frequently happens that rate-payers remove out of one ward to another between the periods at which a poor-rate may have been made and the time at which an election of guardians may occur. By the Commissioners' Election Order for Leeds, which divides the township into wards for the election of guardians, it is directed under 7 & 8 Vic. c. 101, that such ward shall, for the purposes of the election of guardians, be considered as a separate parish, so that, for the purposes of such election, a person who has removed his residence into another ward since the half-yearly, November, poor-rate for 1844 was laid, will not now have been rated in such other ward for the twelve months required by law. The election order requires the voting paper to be delivered at the residence in the ward of the voter, which cannot be done if a person who is qualified to vote for the north ward only, removes his residence before the day of election into the west ward, or any other ward of the township, in which he has not previously been rated. Inquired whether a person thus circumstanced would be entitled to vote in the ward into which he may have removed, or from which he may have removed: whether a person who may have so removed is bound to give the notice prescribed by sec. 21 of 7 & 8 Vic. c. 101, in order to preserve his right to vote in the ward from which he has removed: whether also he would be bound to give the like notice before he could vote in the ward into which he has removed, in the event of the right of voting enuring to him notwithstanding such removal. Further, whether a rate-payer is entitled to nominate in a ward in which he is not entitled to vote.

Ans.—Looking to the language of the 7 & 8 Vic. c. 101, sec. 21, it appears that no person can vote in any other ward than that in which he resides, unless, being entitled to vote in respect of property in such other ward, he have given the notice required to enable him to exercise the right in such other ward. It also appears that the qualification in any ward must be in respect of property in that ward. Consequently, it seems to the Commissioners, that a party who has not been rated in respect of property in the ward in which he resides at the time of the election, cannot vote as rate-payer in that ward. If a party, being qualified in respect of property in any ward, removes into another ward before the time of election, he may, in some cases, continue to be qualified in the former ward, as he may be still on the rate in respect of the property for which he had been rated; and in this case, if he give the notice prescribed by the 21st sec., he would be entitled to vote in the ward where he was so qualified. But if he were off the rate, in respect of that property at the time of the election, then he would not be entitled to vote in that ward although he give the notice. It appears, therefore, that no person can vote out of the ward in which he resides, except he give the notice referred to, and that no such notice will be available except where the party continues to be qualified in respect of property in the ward to which the notice applies up to the time of the election. Where there is not a right to vote there is not a right to nominate. Consequently, where the vote would be disallowed the nomination by the same person is invalid.

XI.—GUARDIANS.

1. APPOINTMENT OF CHAIRMAN AND VICE-CHAIRMAN.

April 14th, 1846.

Clerk of Lincoln Union—Inquired whether the guardians were authorised in making the appointment of a chairman and vice-chairman of the board for the ensuing year at their last meeting, a contest for the election of a guardian in one of the parishes in the union being then pending.

Ans.—The Commissioners direct your attention to their General Order of the 20th of April, 1842, which provides that "the guardians shall *at the first meeting after every annual election of guardians*, elect out of the whole number of guardians a chairman and a vice-chairman." It appears to the Commissioners that, under the circumstances mentioned in your letter, the annual election of guardians for the Lincoln Union for the present year was not complete on the first of April; and that, consequently, the meeting held by the guardians on that day was not the first meeting after such election, within the meaning of the order. The Commissioners, therefore, consider that the appointments referred to are altogether null and void.

2. WHETHER A GUARDIAN, WHO IS AN ATTORNEY, CAN CONDUCT PAROCHIAL BUSINESS.

May 19th, 1846.

Messrs. ———, *Solicitors*—Inquired, whether their firm, one of its members being a guardian of the ——— Union, can legally conduct professional business for the overseers of a parish in the union.

Ans.—The Commissioners are not aware of any legal objection to a guardian of a union being retained as the attorney for one of the parishes in that union, in conducting appeals, or other similar matters, which relate solely to the affairs of the parish.

XII.—JUSTICES—THEIR POWER TO ACT IN CASES IN WHICH THE UNIONS, OF WHICH THEY ARE EX-OFFICIO GUARDIANS, ARE INTERESTED.

May 23rd, 1846.

Clerk of Bakewell Union—Can justices acting as ex-officio guardians in this union, and as justices in the Bakewell division of the union, legally commit, under the Vagrant Act, a man resident within the union who has deserted his family.

Ans.—The 15th sec. of the 5 & 6 Vic. c. 57, removes any doubts as to the competency of justices to act as such, at petty, special, or quarter sessions, in matters in which the guardians of the union are complainants or are otherwise interested or concerned, merely on the ground that they are ex-officio members of the board of guardians so complaining, interested or concerned in such matter, and have acted as ex-officio members of such board. In the case put in your letter, (namely, in a proceeding under the Vagrant Act for desertion of family,) the Commissioners do not see any reason to doubt the power of the justices, being ex-officio members of the board of guardians of the Bakewell Union, to entertain and adjudicate in the matter.

XIII.—INQUEST—EXPENSES OF WITNESSES AT.

February 28th, 1846.

Clerk of Mitford and Launditch Union—A pauper belonging to the parish of Great Dunham, in this union, was found drowned in a pond under suspicious circumstances. A very minute investigation was made both by the coroner and the magistrates, which required the attendance of several witnesses for some days. As there is no public fund from which the expenses incurred in the investigation can be paid, requested the Commissioners' sanction to their being paid out of the poor-rates of the parish.

Ans.—The Commissioners do not see that the poor-rates could be lawfully applied to the payment of the expenses attending the inquiry by the coroner and magistrates in the case described by you, or that the sanction of the Commissioners, if given, would give validity to such a payment. The circumstance of the person whose death was inquired into being a pauper did not alter the character of the inquiry, which was apparently instituted for the simple purpose of furthering the ends of justice, and such as would, therefore, have taken place had not the deceased been chargeable to the parish in his lifetime. However proper and necessary such an inquiry may have been, the Commissioners are not aware of any authority which would justify the proposed payment out of the poor-rates.

XIV.—LUNATIC PAUPER.

1. DUTY OF MEDICAL OFFICER WITH REGARD TO.

June 10th, 1846.

Medical Officer, Linton Union—Inquired whether he is bound, under the 8 and 9 Vic. c. 126, to visit and report to the clerk of the peace, upon the case of a pauper lunatic, whom he is not attending.

Ans.—The 55th section of the 8 and 9 Vic. c. 126, requires every pauper lunatic, chargeable to any parish, not in an asylum, hospital, or licensed house, to be visited and reported on by the medical officer of the parish, or union, to which such pauper belongs. If, therefore, the pauper lunatic in question be chargeable to one of the parishes comprised in your district, it is your duty to visit and report such lunatic, without any order from the relieving officer, or the board of guardians.

2. SERVICE OF ORDERS OF MAINTENANCE OF LUNATICS, UNDER SEC. 62, OF 8 & 9 VIC. C. 126.

April 27th, 1846.

Clerk of Erpingham Union—Inquired whether the orders made under the 62nd section of the 8 & 9 Vic. c. 126, for repayment of the costs of the maintenance of pauper lunatics, should be served by the post, or personally, upon the boards of guardians and overseers to whom they are directed.

Ans.—The Commissioners find no provision in the statute referred to for the service of orders or other documents, though there is such a provision in the Act 8 & 9 Vic. c. 100. The Commissioners believe, therefore, that the service of such an order by the post will not suffice, and that personal service is, in strictness, necessary. Section 68 contemplates that the officer shall have *due notice* of the order before he can be made responsible for any neglect in obeying it. It may be sufficient in the first instance to send by post a copy of the order, and if the union or parish upon which it is made will not recognise or obey it, a copy of the original order must be served personally on the party to whom it is addressed.

XV.—MEDICAL RELIEF.

1. ORDERED BY OVERSEER, WITHOUT REPORTING IT TO RELIEVING OFFICER.

February 6th, 1846.

Clerk of ——— *Union*—The guardians' attention has been called to three cases entered in the book of the medical officer of the workhouse, in which the overseer of ——— had given orders for medical relief, without reporting the same to the relieving officer. Requested the Commissioners' opinion on the matter, with a view to protect the medical officer from being called upon to attend to cases in which the overseers are not, in the opinion of the guardians, empowered to order medical relief; and to be informed whether the overseer alluded to has not rendered himself liable to the penalty imposed by the 98th section of the 4 & 5 Wm. 4, c. 76, for improperly ordering the relief in question.

Ans.—If any proceedings are taken against the overseer in question in reference to this matter, the Commissioners think it should be for not reporting the cases in which he had given orders for medical relief to the relieving officer, or to the board of guardians under Article 1 of the General Order of the Commissioners on the Duties of Overseers, dated 22nd April, 1842. The omission of that article from the printed copy of the overseer's instructions given to him by the magistrates on his appointment to the office is immaterial as affecting his liability to report under the Commissioners' General Order above mentioned. With regard to the hardship on the medical officer in being called upon to attend upon such cases, the Commissioners think, that if the overseer has given orders which he was not empowered to give, the medical officer might, no doubt, recover the cost of his attendance, &c., from the overseer.

2. WHETHER BOUND TO ATTEND, ON THE ORDER OF AN ASSISTANT OVERSEER, PERSONS WHO ARE NOT DESTITUTE.

May 8th, 1846.

Clerk of ——— Union—One of the medical officers of the union has informed the guardians that he had received an order (which he attended to) from an assistant overseer in his district, to visit the sick wife of an able-bodied man, who rents a house of £10 a year, and who keeps two cows, and is in constant work at wages of 10*d*. per day. Inquired whether the medical officer is bound to attend to cases similar to the one alluded to if directed to do so by persons duly authorised.

Ans.—It is the duty of the medical officer to attend cases such as that alluded to by you if so directed by the board of guardians, or by the overseers, or relieving officers. The board of guardians are, however, the judges of the destitution of the person, and if satisfied that he is not in a condition to need medical relief at the expense of the ratepayers, the guardians may, and ought, to direct the medical officer not to attend the person on their account.

XVI.—OVERSEERS.

1. HIRING OF ROOM BY OVERSEERS FOR TRANSACTION OF PARISH BUSINESS.

February 20th, 1846.

Overseers of Edgbaston, King's Norton Union—Requested the Commissioners' sanction to the payment of a sum of £20 per annum, for the rent of a room in which to transact the general business of the parish.

Ans.—Seeing that the statutes relating to the inspection of Poor Rates, the Parochial Accounts, &c., apparently contemplate other places besides the vestry or the overseers' house, in which such inspection may be made, (see 17 Geo. 2, c. 38, s. 13; 7 & 8 Vict. c. 101, s. 33,) the Commissioners are disposed to think it may be lawful under certain circumstances, to provide, at the expense of the poor-rates, a place or room suitable for the purpose, and which would likewise be available for the transaction of other business incident to the office of overseer. It will, of course, always be a question in each case whether there is an actual necessity for providing such a place; and, if so, whether the expense proposed to be incurred for the object be reasonable; though these are points upon which it will be necessary for the auditor to decide.

2. DUTY OF OVERSEERS UNDER LIGHTING AND WATCHING ACT.

May 16th, 1846.

Overseers of Penrith—Are the overseers of the poor bound to collect the lighting and watching rate when ordered to do so by the inspectors appointed under the 3 & 4 Wm. 4, c. 90, (the Lighting and Watching Act.) The overseers think, that as the Poor Law Amendment Act was passed subsequently to the above-mentioned Act, their duties were changed by being placed under the authority of the Poor Law Commissioners, who have from time to time issued rules for their guidance, and it did not appear that they had to collect any other rates than those required for the relief of the poor. Inquired the Commissioners' opinion as to the overseers' duty under the Act.

Ans.—The duties of overseers in regard to the collection of lighting and watching rates under the 3 & 4 Wm. 4, c. 90, are not in any way altered by the Poor Law Amendment Act, 4 & 5 Wm. 4, c. 76. The overseers are still bound to comply with the orders of the inspectors, issued under the 32nd section of the Lighting and Watching Act; and are still subject to be proceeded against in case of default, as described in the 38th section.

3. WHETHER DUTY OF ASSISTANT-OVERSEER TO COLLECT LIGHTING-RATE.

May 19th, 1845.

Assistant Overseer, Penzance Union—Inquired whether it is part of his duty to collect the lighting-rate for the town and parish for which he acts as assistant-overseer, his appointment having been made by the guardians, and his bond specifying the usual duties, with the following addition; namely, "to perform all such of the other duties of overseers of such of the said parishes for which they shall be respectively appointed assistant-overseers as relate to the administration of the laws for the relief of the poor."

Ans.—The former part of the additional clause referred to by you is very general in its terms, and would, but for the words in the concluding part, certainly impose upon the assistant-overseer the obligation of performing any duty which, by law, is cast upon an overseer of the poor. Those words, however, clearly contain a limitation, and define the duties as those "which relate to the administration of the laws for the relief of the poor." The Commissioners cannot say that the collection of the lighting-rate, though a duty expressly cast upon the overseers by the 3 & 4 of Wm. 4, c. 90, "relates to the administration of the laws for the relief of the poor." The lighting rate is a distinct rate from the poor-rate, and cannot, unlike some other rates, (the county-rate, for instance,) be collected as a part of the poor-rate. Moreover, a distinct and separate account is required to be kept and yielded of the moneys raised under it. The Commissioners, therefore, think that, under the terms of your appointment, it is no part of your duty to collect the lighting-rate.

---

4. WHETHER A BLIND MAN CAN BE APPOINTED TO THE OFFICES OF CHURCHWARDEN OR OVERSEER.

April 9th, 1846.

Mr. ———, *Cardigan Union* — Inquired, whether a blind man can be appointed to serve the office either of churchwarden or overseer of a parish.

Ans.—The appointment of fit persons for the discharge of the office of overseer, is a discretionary power, vested in the justices, who are to select such householders as they may think most proper, having respect to the circumstances of the place and the condition of the individual. The law requires that they should be substantial householders. A blind person does not certainly seem a very fit one for the office, even though he should be a substantial householder; for, there are many duties imposed upon an overseer of the poor, which a person who is blind could scarcely perform. The Commissioners will not say that such an appointment would be void, but the choice, they think, would be improper, if there were other substantial persons in the parish capable of serving the office; and, possibly, the quarter sessions, on appeal, would quash such an appointment. As regards churchwardens, they are chosen usually, one by the parishioners, and one by the clergyman. As regards the persons to be selected, the same objections that would apply to the appointment of a blind person to the office of overseer would equally apply to that of churchwarden. If, however, an unfit person be chosen by the parishioners, there appears to be no remedy.

---

5. DUTY OF OVERSEERS OF PLACES WHERE THERE ARE NO POOR TO SUBMIT ACCOUNTS TO AUDITOR.

May 25th, 1846.

Mr. ——, *District Auditor*—Several townships and extra-parochial places separately liable to maintain their own poor, avoid contributing to the general fund of the union by inserting the words, "no poor" in the columns of the declared averages. They respectively return a guardian whose qualification must of necessity be, an assessment for the relief of the poor, but the replies of the overseers are, "no poor, no account," and consequently refuse to render any account. The county rate is paid by them on the order of the guardians to the union treasurers, some part of which is supposed to be for the relief of poor prisoners. Inquired whether the overseers should be required to submit their accounts for audit.

Ans.—You should summon the overseers of every parish or other place within your district, to attend you at the audit. If any of such overseers, when so in attendance, decline to produce to you any accounts, on the ground that they have none to render, the question will arise, how far that is a valid excuse under the circumstances of the particular case. If it should appear, on due inquiry, that they have no accounts to render, because, in point of fact, nothing has occurred in respect of which they would be liable to account, then, of course, there would be an end of the matter. But, if their excuse be not a true one, it will be your duty to make such inquiry into the circumstances, as may enable you to deal effectually with the case. Upon so general a statement as that contained in your letter, the Commissioners find it difficult to express any precise opinion. They will observe, however, that the mere circumstance of there being "no poor" in any parish, in any half year, would not necessarily exonerate the overseers of that parish from the obligation to submit their accounts to you for such half year.

---

6. APPOINTMENT OF OVERSEERS.

April 13, 1846.

Mr. —— inquired whether the list of persons nominated for overseers made by the vestry, or that made by the outgoing overseers, should be submitted to the justices.

Ans.—By the statute of the 43rd Eliz. c. 2, s. 1, the power of appointing overseers is vested in the justices alone. It is not competent, either to the outgoing overseers or to the vestry, to make any selection which shall be binding on the justices; though there is nothing to prevent their making suggestions to the justices on the subject.

7. EXPENSES OF OVERSEERS BEFORE REVISING BARRISTER.

April 17*th*, 1846.

Clerk of Kendal Union—At the last court held by the barrister appointed to revise the Lists of Parliamentary Voters, application was made by the overseers of the different townships for the usual certificate of expenses, which the revising barrister declined to give, on the ground that the auditor would allow such expenses without a certificate; but the auditor refuses to do so, and the revising barrister now states that he has no authority to sign certificates after the last day of October. Requested that the Commissioners will, if they have the power, direct the auditor to allow the charges made by the overseers on the usual scale.

Ans.—The Commissioners think that the auditor was right in law in requiring the production of the certificate of the revising barrister, as the condition of the allowance by him of any expences incurred by the overseers in carrying into effect the statute 6 & 7 Vict. c. 18. The Commissioners apprehend that the poor-rates cannot be lawfully charged for the purpose, except where the sum has been certified by the revising barrister in the manner provided by section 57 of that statute. Whether it is open to the revising barrister in this case, now to certify upon an investigation of the several claims, the Commissioners will offer no opinion; but if it is not, the refusal of the barrister to certify in accordance with the express direction of the statute when applied to by the overseers, has certainly inflicted a great hardship upon them. The Commissioners have, as they believe, no discretion in the matter, and their sanction would not render the payment lawful if otherwise unlawful.

XVII.—POOR-RATES.

1. PROCEEDINGS TO ENFORCE PAYMENT OF.

April 19*th*, 1845.

The Rev. —— *J. P.*—The overseers of —— having summoned several small holders for the nonpayment of poor-rates, inquired whether, in the event of the magistrates authorising the overseers to pay the costs of the proceedings, the same could be allowed in their accounts; and, if not, whether a distress will be legal if made for the precise amount of rate and a given sum for the costs up to the time of distraining, and also for those afterwards incurred for the holding and selling.

Ans.—The Commissioners entertain no doubt that the costs incurred previously to the issuing of the warrant of distress for nonpayment of poor-rates, may, in all cases where the rates sought to be recovered are legally due, be paid by the overseers, and by them charged in their accounts. But no order of justices appears necessary to enable the overseers to do this. It must be considered as established by several decisions, that the expenses incidental to the discharge of an official duty (where the public officer has exercised reasonable skill and prudence in its discharge) are such as he is entitled to be reimbursed out of the funds which he administers. This applies with full force to such a case as the present, it being the unquestioned duty of the overseers to take proceedings for the enforcement of a valid poor-rate. It is to be observed with regard to the costs incurred previously to the distress, that they are incurred at the instance of the overseers and on their application; the claim of the justices' clerk would, therefore, in the first instance be against the overseers. But the Commissioners understand the recent case of Skingley *v.* Surridge, 11 Meeson & Welsby, 503, to decide that the justices, in circumstances such as those stated in your letter, are empowered to award costs to the overseers under the 18 Geo. 3, c. 19, s. 4, as a party injured. The justices have, therefore, the means, where they may think the circumstances call for it, to relieve the parish, in fact, from the payment of the costs by ordering the party complained against (the person in arrear) to pay as costs, an amount to the overseers equivalent to that which the latter have incurred in the recovery of the rate. The Commissioners further understand the effect of the above decision to be, that the costs so awarded ought not to be included in the warrant for the recovery of the rate itself. It was there observed by Mr. Baron Parke, "it was urged that this sum [11*s*. 6*d*. admitted in the preceding part of the judgment to have been due under 18 Geo. 3, c. 19] could not be recovered by distress under the statute of Elizabeth, nor could it; nor could the distress for it be justified under the general form given by that statute, which is equally true." The Commissioners apprehend that where there is an intention to award costs, the statute, 18 Geo. 3, c. 19, s. 4, must be pursued, and there must be a distinct award of costs (see the form) and a distinct warrant for their recovery. With respect to your question, therefore, "Can a distress be considered legal when made for the precise amount of rate, and a given sum for the costs up to the time of distraining, and also for those costs afterwards incurred for the holding and selling?" the Commissioners apprehend the correct answer is, that, as regards the former costs, the distress (if levied by warrant) would not be lawful, but, as regards the latter, it would; although the former would be recoverable by a separate process as already pointed out.

---

2. APPLICATION OF POOR-RATE TO THE PURCHASE OF SEED POTATOES FOR THE POOR.

May 23rd, 1846.

Clerk of Carmarthen Union—Stated that the board of guardians purposed taking into consideration the propriety of purchasing a quantity of potatoes to be distributed for seed among the poorer classes in the union, and requested Commissioners' directions thereon.

Ans.—However desirable it may be to supply the poor with seed potatoes, the Commissioners think that, in the present state of the law, the poor-rates cannot legally be applied to such a purpose; the rates being only applicable, except where otherwise expressly provided by statute, to the relief of actual destitution.

---

3. PUBLICATION OF POOR-RATE ON DOOR OF CHAPEL OF EASE.

May 4th, 1846.

Overseers of ———, —The overseers having made a rate for the relief of the poor, after allowance duly published it upon the door of the parish church, being the only place where a rate has been published from time immemorial in the parish, an objection was raised in consequence of the rate not having been published on the door of a chapel of ease in the parish; which is distant about two miles from the parish church, and in which service has been performed for several years; although it has never been usual to affix any notice on the door. Inquired whether the rate is, in consequence of the above circumstance, invalid.

Ans.—The 2nd section of the 1st Vict. c. 45, expressly requires the notice of a poor-rate to be affixed on or near to the doors of all the churches and chapels within the parish or place. The Commissioners are disposed to consider that the word "chapels," as here employed, does not apply to places of worship used by dissenting congregations; but they certainly think it includes chapels of ease belonging to the Established Church. As the notice of the poor-rate to which you refer was not affixed at the chapel of ease in the parish of ———, on the Sunday after its allowance, the Commissioners are of opinion that it was not sufficiently published, and, consequently, cannot be collected or enforced, (see 17 Geo. 2, c. 3, s. 1.)

---

4. RECOVERY OF POOR-RATE FROM BANKRUPT.

May 13th, 1846.

Clerk of Uppingham Union—A. B. was gazetted as a bankrupt, in the month of November last, but continues to occupy his farm as usual. The overseers of the poor laid a rate to meet the necessary expenses of the parish, in January last, which was allowed by the justices, on the 31st of that month, and duly published; in which rate, A. B. is assessed for the farm he occupies. The rate was demanded of him, when he refused payment. The overseers then summoned him before the justices, to show cause why he should not pay the rate, but the bench dismissed the complaint. The official assignee has been applied to, but he states he has no money in hand. There is stock on the farm, which A. B. deals with, apparently as his own.—Inquired what course should be adopted for the recovery of the rate due on the farm occupied by A. B.

Ans.—It is, of course, a question of fact, whether or not the bankrupt, who, it appears, resides in the farm, and carries on the farming operations as usual, is, or is not, the beneficial occupier. If the assignees were the occupiers of the farm when the January rate was made, (the farming operations being merely carried on by A. B. on their account,) the assignees, and not A. B., should have been rated, and not having been so rated, the rate cannot now be recovered It may be, however, that A. B. is the actual occupier; if so, and if since the fiat was issued, he has become possessed of any goods or effects, it appears to the Commissioners, that such goods and effects could be lawfully distrained upon for the January rate, in case of its non-payment.

XVIII.—RELIEF.

1. POWER OF GUARDIANS TO PAY THE COST OF MAINTAINING A PAUPER IN A PENITENTIARY.

April 5th, 1846.

Clerk of — Union—E. H. aged eighteen years, a pauper, chargeable to —— parish, in the —— union, has made an application to the guardians to be sent to a penitentiary, or refuge for the destitute, such as that in the Hackney-road, or the Philanthropic Asylum. For the pauper's maintenance at either of those places the guardians would have to pay 7*s.* a week.—Inquired whether the guardians have power to comply with the application, by making an advance by way of loan or otherwise.

Ans.—However desirable it may be, under the circumstances of E. H.'s case, that she should be placed in some asylum, or institution of the nature of those mentioned, the Commissioners are of opinion that the guardians cannot lawfully expend the poor-rates for such a purpose.

2. RELIEF TO THE WIFE AND FAMILY OF A MAN WHO HAS ENTERED THE ARMY.

February 23rd, 1846.

Clerk of Kingston Union—An application has been made to the guardians, by the wife of a man who has enlisted in the army, for relief, on the ground that she and her family are destitute. The guardians have communicated with the War Office, for the purpose of ascertaining whether any part of the man's pay can be set apart for the maintenance of his family; and they wish to have the Commissioners' advice as to the course they should pursue with the woman and her family.

Ans.—Unless the authorities of the War Office can interfere under the circumstances to protect the parish, by requiring a part of the husband's pay to be applied to the maintenance of his family, the Commissioners are not aware that there is any available remedy. The Commissioners have reason to believe that it is not the practice of the War Office so to interfere. The Commissioners are advised that the husband is protected by the provisions of the Mutiny Act from being proceeded against for the offence of deserting his family and suffering them to become chargeable. If the wife have not the means of supporting herself and family, the guardians will do right in giving needful relief. The absence of the husband will not prevent the removal of the wife and family to their place of settlement if not settled within the union, if that step be advisable under the circumstances.

3. RECOVERY OF RELIEF GRANTED TO NON-RESIDENT PAUPERS RELIEVED BY THEIR PARISHES.

May 5th, 1846.

Clerk of Wincanton Union—In a recent account delivered by the guardians of the Shepton Mallet Union, for relief advanced by them to paupers residing in their union, but belonging to parishes in the Wincanton Union, there is a charge for a fee of £1. 10*s.* for medical attendance on a pauper (J. F.) belonging to the latter union. Inquired whether such fees should not be paid by the union or parish in which the paupers are resident.

Ans.—The Commissioners do not understand you so much to raise the question as to the actual liability of the guardians of the Wincanton Union to repay the medical relief under the circumstances of the particular case of J. F., as to inquire generally whether medical relief stands on the same footing as other relief with respect to its repayment and recovery in the cases of non-resident paupers. Where the actual cost of medical relief given in a specific case can be ascertained, the union in which the pauper is settled may undertake to repay it if they think proper, as they may any other non-resident relief which is lawful; but there is no obligation on such union to do so. On the contrary, the obligation to afford medical relief rests, in the first instance, on the union where the pauper resides, and, in most cases, the cost, forming part of the gross salary of the medical officer, cannot be separately stated. Probably in J. F.'s case the liability to repay the cost of medical relief will turn on the question whether the union of her settlement undertook to repay it.

4. RELIEF TO AN ENGLISH PAUPER RESIDENT IN SCOTLAND.

May 29th, 1846.

Clerk of Dartford Union—The guardians for the parish of Bexley, in the Dartford Union, have received a communication from the inspector of the poor for the parish of Cargill, in Scotland, stating that a person named J. D. has become chargeable to that parish. As the pauper belongs to Bexley, and the practicability of giving relief at Cargill is excluded by the Commissioners' Order relating to Non-resident Relief, the guardians wish to know if any mode is open to them to grant relief to the pauper, at Cargill, on account of the parish of Bexley.

Ans.—The Non-resident Relief Order of the Commissioners does not bear upon the case at all. If J. D. is within the exceptions to Article 3 of the Out-relief Order, it is competent to the guardians to give him relief while resident in Scotland. The Commissioners, however, believe that it has never been the practice for English parishes to give relief to persons resident out of England; and no such system of relief appears to have been contemplated by the statutes.

---

5. RELIEF BY PURCHASE OF A PAUPER'S GOODS SEIZED FOR RENT.

May 23rd, 1846.

Clerk of ——— *Union*—The guardians feel some difficulty as to the proper course for them to pursue in the cases of paupers, relieved under the Out-door Labour Test Order, whose goods have been distrained for rent, as the workhouses of the union are full, and the order alluded to prohibits the guardians from paying paupers' rents. The guardians perceive no other alternative than purchasing goods for such paupers as have had their goods seized for rent; but they wish to have the Commissioners' advice as to how far they would be justified in buying the goods of the paupers at the sale.

Ans.—The Out-door Labour Test Order of the Commissioners prohibits the payment of rent, as such, to able-bodied paupers, a practice which often leads to abuse by causing money to be paid from the poor-rates, not as relief to the pauper to provide for his present wants, but as a mode of discharging arrears due to the landlord. But though rent cannot be paid as such, the guardians are, without doubt, bound to make such allowance to a pauper destitute of lodging, as will enable him to procure lodging during such time as the allowance is intended to cover. The Commissioners do not, however, think that the guardians can legally buy in at a sale the goods of persons distrained upon for rent professedly as a means of relieving those persons. If, in consequence of any such distress and sale of the goods, any person become so destitute as to require relief, the relieving officer may be directed to supply any bedding or similar articles which may be found necessary. This should be done out of the stores of the union, and, in many instances, such supply may be made by way of loan.

XIX.—RELIEVING OFFICERS — NOT INCLUDED IN THE WORDS "OTHER OFFICERS" IN 7 AND 8 VICT. c. 101, s. 33.

May 18th, 1846.

Clerk of Merthyr Tydvil Union—Inquired whether the term "other officers," as used in section 33 of the 7 & 8 Vict. c. 101, extends to relieving officers.

Ans.—The Commissioners are of opinion that the term "other officers," as used in the 7 & 8 Vict. c. 101, s. 33, means the parochial officers, and does not extend to the relieving officers.

XX.—REMOVAL—OF SCOTCH AND IRISH POOR.

October 30th, 1845.

Clerk of Newcastle-upon-Tyne Union—1. Inquired whether the expense of removing a poor person, under sections 2 and 3 of the 8 and 9 Vic. c. 117, is to be paid by the parish to which such person is chargeable, or out of the common fund of the union; and by whom the expense of an appeal, under section 6 of the above Act, is to be borne. 2. Whether justices have the power to commit to prison, or otherwise punish, paupers who refuse to be sworn when brought before them for the purpose of being removed to Ireland, &c.

Ans.—1. The Commissioners are disposed to consider that the terms of the 2nd section of the 8 and 9 Vic. c. 117, require the expense of removing a pauper under that section to be borne by *the union*, in the case of a pauper chargeable to a parish within a union, and by the *parish*, in the case of a pauper chargeable to a parish not in a union. The section directs that the pauper shall be removed "at the expense of *such union or parish*;" and the Commissioners think that these words are not to be read as merely alternative expressions, but that they are to be referred to their antecedents according to the rule, "*reddendo singula singulis*," so that the union shall be charged, where there is a union, and the parish, where there is no union. The expenses of an appeal, under the 6th section of the Act are, when the warrant of removal is reversed, to be paid *by the guardians or overseers* on whose application such warrant was obtained. In the case of a pauper removed from a parish within a union, the Commissioners apprehend that, as the expenses of his removal will (upon the foregoing opinion) be chargeable to the union, so also will the expenses of the appeal, when required to be paid by the guardians. 2. The Commissioners direct your attention to the case of R. *v.* Jackson (1 Term Rep. 653), which seems to show that justices, where hey have power to examine, have also the power to commit the party for refusing to be examined.

XXI.—SETTLEMENT.

April 7th, 1846.

Clerk of Calne Union—L. C., a girl aged ten years, has become chargeable to the united parishes of the city of Coventry. She is the illegitimate daughter of H. C., who has been dead about three months, and whose maiden settlement was at Yatesbury, in this union. Subsequent to the birth of the child, H. C. married a man named W., belonging to Leek, who maintained the child up to the mother's death. He has now ceased to do so. The girl is living with her grandmother at Coventry, who is not able to support her. Inquired whether W.'s liability to maintain the child ceased at the death of her mother, and occasioned the child's original settlement at Yatesbury to revive; or, whether the child will take the settlement of W.

Ans.—The Commissioners think that the husband's liability to maintain the child ceased on the death of the mother. The statute which imposes the liability on the husband (4 & 5 Wm. 4, c. 76, s. 57,) defines also the extent or duration of such liability to be, "until such child shall attain the age of sixteen years, or until the death of the mother of such child." The latter of these contingencies has, in the present instance, arisen. As regards the settlement of the child, the Commissioners apprehend, on the authority of Reg. *v.* St. Mary, Newington, 2 Gale & Dav. 686, that it is now settled in the parish in which the husband is settled. That case decided in effect, that the case where the mother acquires a settlement by marriage is no exception to the rule prescribed by section 71 of 4 & 5 Wm. 4, c. 76, viz., "that an illegitimate child born since the passing of that Act shall have and follow the settlement of the mother until such child shall attain the age of sixteen, or shall acquire a settlement in its own right." It is clear from this provision that the illegitimate child, in the case stated, does not now revert to the settlement which the mother had before the marriage with W.

XXII.—STAMPED RECEIPTS.

1. DUTY OF CHIEF CONSTABLE TO GIVE STAMPED RECEIPTS FOR COUNTY RATE.

June 16th. 1846.

Mr. ———, *District Auditor*—Stated that some of the chief constables in his district refuse to give receipts on a stamp for county rate, where the sum paid exceeds £5 in amount; and that at the last audit, he directed several of the overseers to tender the stamp for signature, and demand repayment of the cost of it. This was

Ans.—There appears to the Commissioners to be no possible question as to the obligation of the high constable to give a receipt. His receipt is expressly declared to be a discharge of the overseers, &c., (see 12 Geo. 2, cap. 29, sec. 2,) and the overseers are entitled, on tender of a paper duly stamped, to have the receipt or acquittance required, and to be repaid the price of the stamp duty. The high constable refusing to give such receipt, and to repay the stamp duty, is liable to a penalty of £10 under the Act 43rd Geo. 3, c. 126, s. 5.

2. WHETHER WORKHOUSE MASTER SHOULD REQUIRE STAMPED RECEIPTS FROM GUARDIANS FOR MONEY RECEIVED FOR THEM.

May 14th, 1846.

Master of the Workhouse, South Stoneham Union—Inquired, whether he is authorised to require a stamped receipt from the guardians for moneys which he may receive for them from various sources, and which are afterwards credited to the establishment account.

Ans.—The Commissioners think that these sums referred to by the master, should be paid to the treasurer of the union, in which case, the money being paid, not in satisfaction of a demand of the treasurer, but as a sum to be accounted for by him, an acknowledgment of it to that effect is exempt from stamp duty. The same would be the effect if paid to any other officer or person accountable to the guardians. But in all such cases the acknowledgment should be of the receipt of the money "to be accounted for," (see Tomkins *v.* Ashley, 6 B. & C. 542.) In case the sums are paid to the guardians directly, and not to some person accountable to them, there is more difficulty. The money received by the master of the workhouse, is the money or property of the guardians, the property being in them, though the possession is in the master. The transfer from one servant to another of the same owner, or from a servant to his employer, the owner, is not, before some default of the servant, the "payment" or "settlement," "balance," "discharge," or "satisfaction" on a "debt" or "demand." Before any default by the servant, which default has turned that possession which he had for his master into a debt, or demand, it would appear, that the delivery of the money from the servant to the master, is not a case in which a stamped receipt can be required.

LONDON:
Printed by order of the Poor Law Commissioners, by BLACKBURN and PARDON, 6, Hatton Garden, and Published by CHARLES KNIGHT and Co., 22, Ludgate Street, Publishers to the Poor Law Commissioners.

AN

OFFICIAL CIRCULAR

OF PUBLIC DOCUMENTS AND INFORMATION:

DIRECTED BY THE POOR LAW COMMISSIONERS TO BE PRINTED, CHIEFLY FOR THE USE OF THE MEMBERS AND PERMANENT OFFICERS OF BOARDS OF GUARDIANS, UNDER THE POOR LAW AMENDMENT ACT.

No. 61.] CIRCULAR ISSUED SEPTEMBER 1ST, 1846.

Poor Law Commission Office, Somerset House, September 1, 1846.

THE Poor Law Commissioners have directed that the following information be printed and circulated for the information of Guardians and Officers of the several Unions.

By Order of the Board,

EDWIN CHADWICK, *Secretary.*

I.—ACCOUNTS—WHETHER AUDITORS SHOULD DISALLOW ITEMS FOR GOODS SUPPLIED TO A UNION BY A GUARDIAN.

July 8th, 1846.

Mr. ———, —In the accounts of the ——— Union, for the half-year ended the 25th of March last, the following sums have been paid to one of the guardians; namely, £48. 8*s.* 6*d.* for printing, £1. 15*s.* for coffins, and £31. 6*s.* for a wall and gates at the union workhouse. These items were objected to as being illegal. The auditor, although he admitted the impropriety of a guardian supplying goods, &c., to the union for his own profit, did not believe that such a proceeding was illegal, and refused to disallow the items in the accounts. Inquired whether the objection to these items is valid.

Ans.—The Commissioners have had occasion to consult counsel on a similar case, and were advised by him that, although a guardian might have rendered himself liable to a penalty for supplying goods for his own profit, the auditor had no authority to disallow the payments made to him by the guardians for goods which they had actually received, on the ground of the illegality of the supply. The auditor, therefore, appears, in the present case, to have taken the proper course in allowing the items.

II.—BAPTISMS—REGISTRATION OF, IN THE CASES OF CHILDREN BORN IN THE WORKHOUSE.

July 7th, 1846.

Chaplain of Horncastle Union — Inquired whether it is necessary to insert the baptisms which take place in the union workhouse in the Horncastle parish register-book of baptisms, as well as in the register-book provided for that purpose at the workhouse.

Ans.—Article 74, No. 15, of the Commissioners' general workhouse rules, applies to the registration of births of children born in the workhouse. The Commissioners do not contemplate baptisms in the workhouse, except in cases of emergency, where the child might be baptized in a private house. It appears to the Commissioners that the minister of the parish should deal with the baptisms of children in the workhouse exactly as he does with those of other children in the parish. The register of births does not dispense with the register of baptisms.

III.—BASTARDY.

1. ORDER OF MAINTENANCE UNDER 7 & 8 VICT. c. 101.

August 16th, 1846.

Clerk of Lancaster Union—A question has arisen as to whether the justices in a case where the mother of a bastard child has been confined in a workhouse, and has been attended by the workhouse medical officer, are empowered to comprehend in their order on the putative father, made under the 3rd section of the Act, 7 & 8 Vict. c. 101, the weekly payments from the date of the child's birth, and include also in the order the medical officer's fee for attending the confinement. It has been suggested that the relief granted to the mother might be granted by way of loan, to be recovered under the Poor Law Amendment Act, or that she might repay the same voluntarily. Requested the Commissioners' opinion on the point.

Ans.—The Commissioners are of opinion that the justices are empowered, on application made to them, under the 3rd section of the 7 & 8 Vict. c. 101, to make an order on the putative father to pay a weekly sum, to be calculated from the birth of the child, although the woman should be attended in her confinement at the charge of the union or parish. If the woman receive the money ordered to be paid by the justices, she is under no obligation to pay the amount over to the guardians or overseers. There is certainly nothing to prevent her doing so voluntarily, but whether the guardians can recover the amount from her under the power contained in the 4 & 5 Wm. 4, c. 76, sec. 58, in return for relief supplied to her, depends upon whether the Commissioners had authorised relief to be given to such woman in the particular union by way of loan, which does not appear in the case. The Commissioners cannot give any opinion as to the propriety of the justices making the order on the putative father. The above observations only apply to the expenses of the midwife. The Commissioners refer the guardians to the 7th sec. of the 7 & 8 Vict. c. 101, which renders it unlawful for any officer of a parish or union to receive any money in respect of a bastard child under an order of petty session.

---

2. ENFORCEMENT OF ORDER OF MAINTENANCE IN BASTARDY, THE MOTHER BEING DEAD.

July 16th, 1846.

Clerk of Tetbury Union — Some months since an order of filiation and maintenance was made upon R. P., then a resident in Tetbury, whereby he was ordered to pay to E. P., the mother of a bastard child, the weekly sum of 1*s.* 6*d.* R. P. paid such weekly sum up to the time of the death of E. P.; but he has made no payment since that time, and the child has become chargeable to the parish of S——, in the Tetbury Union. That parish officers wish to enforce the order of maintenance against R. P., pursuant to sec. 7 of the 7 & 8 Vict. c. 101, but they are unable to procure a suitable person to take charge of the child for the weekly sum directed to be paid by the order. The justices' clerk is of opinion, that a person must be appointed to take charge of the child before proceedings can be taken against the putative father, and that the person so appointed, and not the guardians, should make the application for the enforcement of the order. Requested the Commissioners' opinion as to the recovery of the arrears due from R. P., and the enforcement of the order.

Ans.—It appears to the Commissioners, that unless a person be appointed by the justices to have the custody of the child, pursuant to sec. 5 of the 7 & 8 Vict. c. 101, the power given to the guardians by sec. 7 to make application to the justices for the enforcement of the order does not come into operation, inasmuch as it is provided that the payments made in pursuance of such application are to be made to the person appointed by the justices. In the absence of such appointment there is no person authorised to receive the money, and no payments can therefore be due under the order. No appointment can be made but with the consent of the person selected; accordingly, if from the smallness of the weekly sum to be contributed by the reputed father under the order, or for any other cause, no person can be induced to undertake the custody of the child, the result will be, that the child must, from the necessity of the case, continue chargeable to the parish. Certainly, it would not be competent to the guardians to make from the poor-rates any addition to the weekly sum paid by the reputed father; their doing so would, in fact, prevent the enforcement of the order against the reputed father (sec. 7.) Assuming, however, that the difficulty as to the appointment of a guardian for the child can be got over, the point whether during the interval between the decease of the mother and the appointment of the person to the custody, anything can be recovered from the reputed father under the order certainly arises. It appears, that in the case put in your letter, the putative father has not in fact during such period continued to make the weekly payments for the child's support, though the order was duly performed up to the time of the decease of the mother. The Commissioners are disposed to consider that no arrears are legally due from the reputed father. The order in this case was, it would seem, made since the passing of the 8 & 9 Vict. c. 10, (8th May, 1845:) such order, therefore, it is to be presumed, is in the form given by the schedule to that Act (No. 8), and in conformity with the 7 & 8 Vict. c. 101, sec. 3; if so, the order only required a weekly sum to be paid to the mother so long as she should live, or to the person who might be appointed to have the custody of the child. Now it is clear that the obligation imposed by the order towards the mother terminates with her life; and, until a person be appointed by the justices to have the custody of the child, nothing can be due to such person. In short, it appears to the Commissioners, that in the interval occurring between the decease of the mother and the appointment of the guardian, or person to have the custody of the child, there is no one to whom the weekly payments are due, or can be made; and, consequently, there are no arrears. It is true, that the guardians, by the 7th sec. (*i.e.*, where the child becomes chargeable) "may make such application for the enforcement of the order as might have been made by the mother of such bastard child if alive." Possibly, therefore, if at the time of the mother's decease, any payments were in arrear, the guardians might recover the amount; inasmuch as the mother, if alive, might have made an application for the recovery. But the guardians can have no claim in a case where it has been shown that by the terms of the order imposing the obligation on the putative father, nothing is due to the mother, or any other person. The Commissioners have only to add, that it appears to them that where an appointment is made in pursuance of sec. 5, that the person appointed must (*i.e.*, if the child be not chargeable) make application for the recovery of the payments, and that such person is alone entitled to apply. If, however, the child be chargeable, such person has no longer power to apply for the enforcement, but the guardians can alone do so under sec. 7, although some practical difficulty appears to arise in carrying this provision into effect.

IV.—BURIAL.

1. IN ROMAN CATHOLIC BURIAL GROUND.

July 21st, 1846.

The Roman Catholic Pastor of ——— —Inquired, whether the guardians are bound to bury a Roman Catholic pauper in a burial ground of that persuasion, if there should be one in the parish, and he has made a request that he might be buried there.

Ans.—It is necessary to premise that unless a pauper dies in any workhouse in the occupation or use of the guardians, the guardians are under no legal obligation to inter the body, (Reg. *v.* Steward, 12 A. and E. 773.) The 31st sec. of 7 and 8 Vic. c. 101, gives, indeed, an unrestricted *power* to the guardians to bury the body "of any poor person which may be within their parish or union." But though the guardians may, (*i. e.*, it is lawful for them to do this,) they are not (except in the particular case adverted to) compelled to do so. The Commissioners must, therefore, understand your inquiry, whether the guardians can be compelled to bury a Catholic in his own churchyard, to apply to a case in which, for the reasons assigned in Reg. *v.* Steward, a duty is cast upon the guardians to bury the body of the deceased person. You will observe, upon reference to the 31st section, that where the guardians adopt the alternative course of burying the body in the parish to which the deceased was chargeable, the interment must, by the provision, take place in the churchyard, or burial ground, of the parish. If, therefore, there be any burial-ground of the parish, the provision certainly allows of the guardians burying the body therein; but it does not justify the burial in any burial-ground situate in the parish of the chargeability, (as distinguished from that in which the body is at the time, or in which the death occurred,) which does not belong to such parish. If, however, the guardians do not adopt the alternative of burying the body in the parish to which the deceased was chargeable, then the section provides that "every dead body which the guardians, or any of their officers duly authorised, shall direct to be buried at the expense of the poor-rates, shall (unless the deceased person, or the husband, or wife, or next of kin, of such deceased person have otherwise desired,) be buried in the churchyard, or other consecrated burial-ground, in or belonging to the parish, division of parish, chapelry, or place in which the death may have occurred." The Commissioners understand the effect of the provision to be, that, assuming that the guardians would, where such a desire has been so expressed, be restrained from interring the body in the churchyard, or consecrated burial-ground, in or belonging to the parish referred to, *i. e.*, the parish of the death, (a proposition which may not be admitted to be clearly established,) it is apparently still a matter in the discretion of the guardians, as to where else the body shall be buried, that is, they are not compelled to inter in any particular burial-ground in the parish which the deceased or his relatives may have selected. The Commissioners, however, have no hesitation in stating their opinion, that the guardians would act most advisedly in causing the interment to take place in that burial-ground in the parish which shall be conformable with the feelings of the relatives of the deceased, according as they or such deceased person shall have expressed their wishes, unless indeed in any case it can be shown that such interment would be improper, on grounds wholly irrespective of the particular religious belief or persuasion of the deceased or his relatives.

---

2. EXPENSES OF BURIAL OF NON-SETTLED POOR, HOW TO BE CHARGED.

July 18th, 1846.

Clerk of Kingsclere Union—A man residing in parish A. obtained relief from the guardians for the purpose of burying one of his children who had died in that parish. The man was not settled in A., and was not actually chargeable to any parish at the time of his child's death; but during the preceding six months, and whilst residing in A., he was several times relieved by the guardians, at the cost of parish B. The man afterwards died in the former parish, not being at the time in the receipt of relief from any parish. Inquired to which parish, in each case, the burial expenses should be charged.

Ans.—The 31st section of the 7 & 8 Vic. c. 101, enables the guardians to bury the body of any person "which may be within their parish or union respectively, and to charge the expense thereof to any parish under their control to which such person may have been chargeable, or in which he may have died, or otherwise in which such body may be." By the words "may have been chargeable," and by the words "has been chargeable," subsequently used in the same section, the Commissioners think is meant "was chargeable at the time of the poor person's decease." This appears to the Commissioners the only reasonable construction; for if a chargeability occurring some time antecedent to the period of the death of the person would suffice at all, as the foundation for charging the costs of burial to the parish, there is, apparently, no limit to the period. If the guardians could go back a month, then they might go back a year, or any number of years. This could not have been intended, and the Commissioners therefore consider, that the clause does not authorise the guardians to charge a parish with the costs of the burial merely because the pauper, at some time prior to his decease, had been chargeable to such parish, though not so chargeable at the time of his decease. In the cases put, therefore, the Commissioners think that the guardians have no alternative but to charge the cost to the parish in which the death actually took place.

---

3. EXPENSES OF BURIAL OF PAUPERS DYING IN THE WORKHOUSE, HOW TO BE CHARGED.

November 27th, 1845.

Clerk of Lymington Union—Inquired whether the cost of the coffin and the burial fees for a pauper dying in the union workhouse should be debited to the establishment account, or be paid by the relieving officer, and debited by him, in the out-relief list, to the parish to which the pauper was chargeable in his lifetime.

Ans.—If the cost of the coffin and burial fees is paid by the relieving officer, it should go into the relief list, and be charged as relief to the head of the family, if the deceased was a child or wife dependent on such head. If a single person, the name of the deceased must be entered as a pauper. If the pauper resided in the union, the relief should be charged to the parish to which he was chargeable, but in no case should it be charged to the establishment account.

V. — CHARGEABILITY — OF RELIEF TO CASUAL PAUPER.

April 15th, 1846.

Clerk of Truro Union—E. T., a widow, with two children, came from the parish of Camborne, in the Redruth Union, on Tuesday, the 6th of January last, and applied at the house of the relieving officer of the Truro Union, which is situate in the parish of Saint Clement, for relief. The relieving officer offered her an order for the workhouse for the night, telling her, at the same time, that he could give her no other relief, but would bring her case before the guardians on the following day. The woman declined to enter the workhouse, and slept at a house in the parish of Kenwyn ; which is also in the Truro Union. On the following day she appeared before the board of guardians, in the parish of Saint Mary, when she received an order for the workhouse, where she went and still remains. Assuming the widow to be a casual pauper, inquired to which of the above parishes her relief should be charged ; and, whether all casual paupers who apply at the house of the relieving officer, in the parish of St. Clement, for relief, should be charged to that parish.

Ans.—There appears from the statement to be no ground for supposing that the pauper is settled in any parish in the Truro Union. The question of chargeability must be determined, therefore, by considerations wholly irrespective of settlement. The Commissioners conceive, that what occurred on Tuesday, 6th January last, *i.e.*, the application then made by the pauper to the relieving officer in the St. Clement parish, the offer of the workhouse and the refusal of that offer, must be put out of the question in determining the chargeability ; and for this reason : As the pauper did not, in fact, accept the relief, it must be considered that she was not in such a condition, at that time at least, as to require it; indeed, what subsequently took place shows that she had another resource. It seems that she then went to a friend's house at Kenwyn, and slept there on Tuesday night, and on the following day appeared at the meeting of the board in the parish of St. Mary, Truro. It appears to the Commissioners that the liability for the relief given on this second application rests upon one or other of these parishes ; and the question is, which parish, under the circumstances, is liable—Kenwyn, where the pauper slept the night preceding the application, or St. Mary, in which the application was actually made and the relief granted. The general rule undoubtedly is, that a pauper is chargeable to that parish in which, being destitute, he applies for, and obtains relief. But the exception to this rule is, where a pauper being destitute in one parish in a union, is compelled by the nature of the union arrangements to go into another parish for the purpose of making the application for the requisite relief, as where the union workhouse, or the relieving officer's residence, is in a different parish. In this case the application, though made in the latter parish, must be regarded as constructively made in the former. If (as seems probable) the pauper were destitute and required relief in Kenwyn, on the morning on which she went to St. Mary to attend the meeting of the board, Kenwyn would, in the opinion of the Commissioners, be liable ; though the application was actually made in St. Mary. The Commissioners would observe that the mere fact of sleeping in a parish, the night previous to the application, is not in itself a sufficient ground for charging that parish with the relief. It is the fact of the pauper being destitute in any given parish, not that of his having slept there, which creates the liability to afford relief. It will no doubt sometimes occur, that the pauper is destitute in the parish in which he last slept ; and where that is so, as already stated, the fact of the application for the necessary relief being made in another parish, under the circumstances above referred to, will not (in a union) release the parish in which the sleeping took place, from the obligation of giving relief.

VI.—CLERK TO GUARDIANS—REMUNERATION OF, FOR DUTIES CONNECTED WITH NEW VALUATION OF A PARISH.

July 31st, 1846.

Clerk of Ringwood Union—Stated that he has been called upon to advise the overseers of Ringwood, and to attend their meetings, and also to attend special and adjourned meetings of the board of guardians, on the subject of a new valuation of that parish; and that the correspondence, contracts, and other business consequent upon the carrying into effect the resolution of the guardians for a new valuation, will, for a time, add to his duties. Inquired whether he can claim some remuneration for these additional duties.

Ans.—The Commissioners think that you have a right to make a charge against the individuals who have engaged you to advise them as to the legal proceedings necessary for providing a new valuation of the rateable property in the parish of Ringwood; but whether your charges in this respect can be paid by those individuals out of the poor-rates, is a matter for the consideration and the decision of the auditor. So far, however, as you have assisted the board of guardians in the matter, the Commissioners think no extra charge can be made; and that such assistance must be taken to be compensated by your salary as clerk.

VII.—CONSTABLES—POWER OF JUSTICES TO ORDER PAYMENT OF FEES TO.

June 27th, 1846.

Mr. ———, *District Auditor*—Some justices in his district contend that they are empowered to direct fees to be paid out of the poor-rates to constables under the Constabulary Act, 5 & 6 Vic. c. 109, for all duties for the discharge of which such constables may fail to obtain payment from any other source; that they alone are the judges in such cases as to what should be paid; and that the district auditor is bound to allow whatever they may order, even when, as they do in some cases, they make orders on the parish officers for payment of gross sums, without any explanation of the business done. Inquired whether such orders of justices for the payment of gross sums are legal orders; and, if not, what course he should adopt in such cases in future; and whether he or the justices are to decide on the legality of the fees claimed by constables.

Ans.—The Commissioners think that the order of the justices in petty sessions is not conclusive upon the auditor, *i.e.*, does not restrain him from entering upon the inquiry, whether the sums directed by the order to be paid to the constable by the overseer, are in accordance with the prescribed Table of Fees and Allowances, and the provisions of 5 & 6 Vic. c. 109. The 17th section of that Act, it will be seen, does not give an unlimited power to the justices to order payment to the constable out of the poor-rates. The power given by the section is, in its exercise, subject to the restrictions, first, that the payment must be in respect of some duty required of the constable; next, that the duty should be one, for the performance of which some fee or allowance shall have been previously settled by the quarter sessions, for which the payment is not by law charged upon the county rates. If, therefore, the justice should include in an order of this kind any payment to the constable not relating to a duty performed by him; or, if in respect of such a duty, if the payment is not in accordance with the prescribed table, they would clearly exceed their jurisdiction, and the order (as the Commissioners are advised) cannot be binding upon the overseers. Where, however, a fee or allowance included in any order of justices, purporting to have been made under the statute, agrees with the table settled by the justices at quarter sessions, and confirmed by the Secretary of State, the Commissioners are of opinion that the auditor cannot properly disallow any such fee or allowance, even though he may doubt whether the case for which the table makes provision be one contemplated by the 17th sec. Generally, therefore, all that it will be needful for the auditor to do when any payment to parish constables is included in the accounts of the overseers, will be to refer to the established table of fees and allowances, to see whether it provides for the cases in which fees or allowances have been ordered by the justices in petty sessions; and, if so, whether the amount accords with the table: where it does so accord, the auditor's duty will be clear, *i. e.* to allow the payment; where it does not, to reject it, or rather so much of it as is not borne out by the table. There will no doubt be cases in which a sum is ordered to be paid to the constable for the performance of some duty or service, which duty is not specifically mentioned in the table, and no fee or allowance fixed in reference to it, but the amount is claimed under some general words in the table, as "for any other occasional duty performed by order, or with the sanction of the justices." In such a case as this, the auditor's course will be attended with some difficulty, as he may, perhaps, entertain a doubt whether it was, in strictness, a part of the duty of the constable to render the service to which the payment relates. Unless, however, the case is most manifestly one not contemplated by the statute, the Commissioners think the safer course for the auditor to pursue will be to acquiesce in the decision of the justices; as it cannot be doubted that it is properly within the jurisdiction of the justices to inquire and determine whether a duty has been performed by the constable in any case for which he is entitled to payment from the poor rates; though their finding or conclusion, on this point, may possibly be erroneous. With reference to the other questions suggested by your letter, the Commissioners are of opinion that the justices cannot properly make an order under the 17th sec., for the payment of an aggregate amount of fees and allowances without any specification of the separate particulars, and that the auditor would be justified in disallowing a payment made by the overseers under such an order. The statute, indeed, appears to contemplate a separate order for each fee; but if several fees are included in one order, for the sake of convenience, they might certainly be distinctly particularised. So also, there ought to be a separate order in respect of each separate constable. With respect to the kind of fees and allowances which may be paid to parish constables out of the poor rate, under the 5 & 6 Vic. c. 109, s. 17, the Commissioners direct your attention to an opinion on that subject, given by the late Sir William Follett and Mr. Tomlinson, and contained in the accompanying copy of the Official Circular, No. 30. They also inclose a copy of their Official Circular, No. 51, which contains a communication respecting the payment of the expenses of serving the summonses on the putative father in cases of bastardy. (See page 136.)

VIII.—ELECTION OF GUARDIANS—

DELIVERY OF VOTING PAPERS.

March 18th, 1846.

Clerk of Leeds Township—The General Election Order, dated the 16th January, 1845, Article 18, requires the voting papers to be delivered "at the address in each parish of the voter;" but the article bearing the same number in the Election Order of the 22nd February, 1845, addressed to the township of Leeds, requires the voting papers to be left "at the residence in the ward of the voter." In the Official Circular, vol. 4, p. 54, it seems that the Commissioners hold that it is sufficient, if the place of business of a person nominated as guardian is inserted in the column headed "residence of the person nominated." Inquired whether he would be warranted in delivering a voting-paper at the place of business of a rate-payer, in any ward for which an election might be going on, if such rate-payer do not reside thereat.

Ans.—There is some distinction between the 4 & 5 Wm. 4, c. 76, s. 40, and the 7 & 8 Vic. c. 101, s. 21. The former speaks of the *address* of parties claiming to vote; the latter requires the voter to vote in the ward in which he *resides*. The language therefore of the two Orders of the Commissioners relating to the election of guardians differs, and the Commissioners are not prepared to admit that the *place of business* will satisfy their direction for the delivery of the voting paper at the *residence*, if in fact the party does not reside at his place of business. In the late case of Q. *v.* Deighton, 5 Ad. & El. Rep. n. s. 896, the Court of Queen's Bench held that the statement of the place of business of a party nominated as an alderman of a borough, did not satisfy the statute which required his place of abode to be set out.

IX.—GUARDIAN.

1. WITHDRAWAL OF REFUSAL TO SERVE AS GUARDIANS.

April 1st, 1846.

Clerk of Wortley Union—Mr. J., one of the guardians for the parish of E. for the past year, having been nominated for the same office for the present year, sent a letter, (not being aware at the time that he had been nominated,) stating that it was his intention to decline standing again should he be put in nomination; but, being subsequently induced to alter his intention, he wrote another letter, consenting to stand for the office. Inquired whether, under the above circumstances, the first letter is such a refusal to serve the office of guardian as cannot be recalled or withdrawn by the person nominated.

Ans.—In the opinion of the Commissioners Mr. J.'s letter, containing his provisional refusal to act, was a refusal within the meaning of the 9th section of the 5 & 6 Vic. c. 57; and, consequently, cannot be withdrawn. That section speaks of the refusal of "any person put in nomination for the office of guardian;" and it appears, from your statement, that at the time when Mr. J. wrote the letter in question, he was, in fact, a person put in nomination, although he was not aware of it. The Commissioners therefore think, so far as regards Mr. J., the election ought not to be further proceeded with.

2. QUALIFICATION FOR THE OFFICE OF GUARDIAN.

April 2nd, 1846.

Clerk of Llanelly Union—H. W. has been nominated for the office of guardian for one of the parishes of the union. The annual value of the property for which he is rated is £15; but his wife, who lives apart from him, is assessed to the poor-rate, in her own name, for the house in which she resides, and the annual value of the two houses would give him a qualification. Inquired whether H. W. has a sufficient qualification for the office of guardian under the circumstances above stated.

Ans.—The point appears to the Commissioners to admit of considerable doubt; but they are, on the whole, disposed to consider that, as H. W. is not, in point of fact, assessed to the poor-rate in respect of the house occupied by his wife, the value of that house cannot be included in the calculation of his qualification. If you consider that H. W. is not duly qualified, you should pursue the course pointed out in the 12th Article of the Election Order.

X.—LUNATIC PAUPERS—DUTY OF MEDICAL OFFICER AS TO VISITING AND MAKING RETURNS OF.

June 22nd, 1846.

Mr. ——, *Bury Union*—Inquired, with reference to the recent statutes relating to pauper lunatics,—1st, Whether idiots are to be included in the quarterly returns of the medical officers of Unions. 2ndly, Whether such medical officers are bound to visit, once a quarter, the pauper lunatics belonging to parishes in their respective districts, but resident out of the Union.

Ans.—The Commissioners have had occasion to communicate with the Commissioners in Lunacy on the second point raised in your letter, and the Commissioners in Lunacy seem to be of opinion that the requisitions of the statute will be satisfied if non-resident paupers, receiving relief through the agency of the officers of the Union in which they live, are visited by the medical officer of such Union: consequently, you will not be required to go out of your district to visit non-resident pauper lunatics in such cases. The Poor Law Commissioners apprehend, with reference to your first question, that, according to the meaning given to the word "lunatic," by the interpretation clause, 8 & 9 Vic. c. 126, s. 84, it is the duty of the medical officer to visit, under section 55, every pauper who may come within the description in that section, and who is either an "insane person," or an "idiot," or a "lunatic," or a person of "unsound mind."

XI.—MEDICAL RELIEF.

TO ABLE-BODIED MEN'S WIVES IN CONFINEMENT.

Dec. 21st, 1844.

Clerk of Ringwood Union—The guardians experience great difficulty in deciding upon the applications of able-bodied men for medical relief during their wives' confinement. The guardians are aware that the decision in each case ought, and in fact must, depend upon the particular circumstances of such case, and it is their practice to refuse the relief applied for where the husbands are in regular employment, and have less than four children; but, at the same time, they think that some general rule should be adopted for the guidance of the relieving officers when applied to for medical relief in such cases. Requested the Commissioners' opinion upon the subject.

Ans.—The Commissioners are of opinion that it is impossible to regulate this matter by general rule. The discretion as to whether or not an order shall be given, as the guardians very truly state, must be exercised in the individual cases by the guardians themselves and their relieving officers. It is conceivable that the urgency of a case may outweigh all considerations of how many children the man has, and what he ought to have saved out of his earnings for this purpose. The difficulty of such cases is a difficulty inherent in all detailed administration of a poor law, whatever may be the system pursued, or the constitution of the authorities to whom the discretion to give the order is entrusted.

March 28th, 1846.

Clerk of Ringwood Union—I. Application has been made to the guardians for an order on the medical officer to attend the wife of an able-bodied bricklayer, who generally earns 18*s.* per week, but is now out of work, and has a wife and four children dependent upon him for support. 2. A single woman, aged 19, has applied for an order for the medical officer to attend her, and has been offered admission into the workhouse, where she will receive medical attendance, but she refuses to accept the offer made to her. Requested some explicit instructions for the guidance of the guardians in the first case; and, as regards the second, to be informed whether the guardians would be justified in refusing the order for the medical officer to attend at the applicant's lodgings, she being in a condition to go, or be removed, to the workhouse.

Ans.—With respect to the first case, the Commissioners refer the guardians to the above letter of Dec. 21st, 1844. The Commissioners are unable to add anything to the opinion (which they still hold,) expressed in that letter, except to remark that in any such case in which there may be a doubt as to the destitution of the applicant, the Commissioners think that the guardians might direct that the medical relief be given by way of loan; in which case, it is necessary that the relief be declared to be a loan, at the time it is given, and that the pauper be at the same time so informed. With respect to the second case above-mentioned, (in which the inability of the applicant to procure the necessary medical attendance for herself appears to be admitted,) the Commissioners are of opinion that an offer of an order of admission into the workhouse, where the pauper would receive the attendance of the medical officer in her confinement, is a sufficient offer of relief, so long as the pauper is in a fit state to go, or be removed, to the workhouse. If, however, in such a case, the pauper persist in refusing to avail herself of the offer of admission to the workhouse, and an order for the attendance of the medical officer on the pauper at her lodgings be withheld, the guardians should direct the relieving officer carefully to watch the case; as, if the application for medical relief be renewed, or the guardians or relieving officer are otherwise aware of the destitution of the applicant, at a later period, when she might be in an unfit state to be removed to the workhouse, it would then become the duty of the relieving officer to give an order for the attendance of the medical officer at the pauper's lodgings, and this notwithstanding her previous refusal of an order of admission to the workhouse. The Commissioners desire to add that the guardians will observe that the second exception to art. 1 of the general prohibitory order leaves it to the discretion of the guardians to grant relief out of the workhouse, where a person shall require relief on account of any sickness, &c., affecting such person or any of his family.

XII.—MIDWIVES—EMPLOYMENT OF TO ATTEND PAUPERS.

May 8th, 1846.

Clerk of Isle of Wight Incorporation—Inquired if the guardians are acting illegally in giving out relief to paupers for the payment of midwives; and in paying fees to their medical officers to instruct such midwives in their duties, so as to enable them to attend the wives of paupers during their confinement.

Ans.—The Commissioners are of opinion that there is nothing in the provisions of the general law, or of the local act, relating to the administration of relief to the poor within the Isle of Wight, which makes it imperative on the guardians to employ their medical officers in cases of women in labour, or which prevents the guardians from employing midwives to attend in such cases. The Commissioners, moreover, see no objection to the employment of midwives in cases of ordinary labours, provided that the persons employed in that capacity be competent to discharge properly the duty which they undertake. To ensure this, as far as practicable, they should be selected with care; and the guardians would do well to ascertain from the medical officers of the respective districts, whether they are aware of any objection to the particular persons proposed to be employed. The guardians should impress upon the midwives who may be employed by them that the medical officer is to be called in in all cases of emergency. With respect to the guardians paying fees to their surgeons for instructing and qualifying midwives to attend the wives of paupers, the Commissioners are not aware of any provision of the law which will authorise them in saying that such fees can be legally paid out of the poor-rates.

XIII.—OVERSEERS.

1. EXCESSIVE RATE MADE BY OVERSEER, REMEDY OF RATE-PAYERS.

June 16, 1846.

Clerk of ——— *Union*—The guardians of

the parish of ——— have complained to the board of guardians that the overseers of that parish have made a rate which will leave in their hands a balance of £50, after paying all demands upon the parish for the present quarter. He has advised the board of guardians that they have nothing to do with the matter, and that the only remedy for the rate-payers is by appeal to the justices. Requested the Commissioners' opinion on the subject.

Ans.—The matter is not one within the control of the board of guardians. The law requires the overseers to raise by rate sufficient funds for the relief of the poor, but they are not, therefore, justified in making an excessive rate. The rule is thus stated by Lord Kenyon in the case of Durant *v.* Boys, 6 Term. Rep. 580. "A rate may be made prospectively, not indeed ***wantonly***, but such as is adapted for the probable exigencies of the parish." The Commissioners apprehend that the remedy for an excessive rate is by appeal against it. But the overseers are also punishable by indictment for any abuse of their office: for instance, if the overseer do not provide for the poor he is indictable, (Tawney's case Viner's ab. title Poor, p. 415,) and it would seem equally an offence to tax the ratepayers improperly and without a sufficient reason for so doing. It must, of course, be shown, in a case of this kind, that the overseer acted wilfully: an error in judgment, or mere inadvertence, would not expose him to an indictment.

---

2. ERECTION OF PARISH STOCKS.

Aug. 25th, 1846.

Mr. ———, *Pontypool Union*—Inquired whether the overseers of ——— can provide new stocks for that parish, in the place of the old stocks which have been removed for the purpose of erecting buildings on the ground on which they stood.

Ans.—It is not the duty of the overseers of the poor to provide and maintain the stocks, as they are not liable for payments chargeable at common law on parishes. The liability for the provision and maintenance of the stocks appears to the Commissioners to be a matter of some obscurity; but probably it may be considered as an obligation resting on the constable. If he incur any expense in discharging this obligation, he may introduce that expense into his accounts, and submit it to the vestry in accordance with the provisions of the 18 Geo. 3, c. 19, sec. 4; and if passed by them, it will be payable by the overseers, but not otherwise.

XIV.—PARISH—PERAMBULATION OF BOUNDARY OF.

August 1st, 1846.

Mr. ———, *Ringwood Union*—Inquired whose duty it is to perambulate the boundary of a parish; how often it should be done; and from what fund the expenses are to be paid.

Ans.—The Commissioners are not aware of any provision of law which requires any particular parish officer to perambulate the parish at any time—still less at any particular time. But the 7 & 8 Vict. c. 101, s. 60, provides that "all expenses properly incurred by the same officers (*i.e.* the parish officers) on the perambulation of the parish, and in setting up and keeping in proper repair the boundary stones of the parish, provided that such perambulations do not arise more than once in every three years," shall be paid and allowed to the parish officers out of the poor-rates of the parish.

XV.—PAUPERS.

1. CUTTING THE HAIR OF, ON ADMISSION INTO THE WORKHOUSE.

July 9th, 1846.

Master of Workhouse, Aylesbury Union—Inquired, whether the Commissioners have issued any order with respect to the cutting of the hair of paupers (adults and children) who come into the workhouse with their heads in a dirty state, and infested with vermin; and requested the Commissioners' advice and instructions for his guidance.

Ans.—The master of a workhouse is not justified in law in forcibly cutting the hair of any adult pauper against his or her expressed wish. It was held in the case of Ford against Skinner, (4 Carr and Payne's Reports, p. 239,) that an overseer could not justify the cutting of a pauper's hair in the workhouse by force. On the ground of this decision the Commissioners, some years back, directed proceedings to be taken against the master of the Croydon Union workhouse for having used undue violence in cutting a pauper's hair immediately before he left the workhouse. On the other hand, the Regulations of the Commissioners prescribe that a pauper should be *thoroughly cleansed* on admission into the workhouse; and, if a pauper refuse to submit to anything *absolutely necessary* to cleanse his person, he is guilty of a breach of the rules; and would be punishable as disorderly, he being thereby guilty of misbehaviour within the meaning of the Act of 55 Geo. 3, c. 137. Cutting the hair is not, however, the only mode of cleansing the head, nor is it (except in very rare cases) absolutely essential to that operation. With regard to children, the Commissioners think that the guardians may cause their hair to be cut whenever it may be necessary or proper.

2. CLAIM TO PROPERTY OF DECEASED PAUPERS.

March 5th, 1846.

Mr. —— *St. Leonard's, Hythe*—A widow, named R., having died in 1832, and apparently without any kin, the overseers of St. Leonard's Hythe buried her and took possession of her effects, which they sold, and, having paid the expenses of her funeral out of the proceeds, there remained a balance of £5. 2*s*. 1½*d*. This balance was placed to the general account of the parish, in order that it might be paid to any lawful claimant who should subsequently come forward to demand it. The widow's son, who was absent from England at the time of her death, has now made application to be paid the amount of the balance, and the Commissioners' advice is requested upon the subject.

Ans.—The Commissioners collect from your statement that the overseers of 1832 brought the money which is now claimed by the son of the widow R., into the general account of the parish, pursuant to the resolution of the vestry; that is, they used it for the purposes of that year. Now the parish had no claim whatever to this balance, and the overseers of the period, therefore, certainly acted without legal authority in so applying the money. It seems to the Commissioners that the present overseers have no concern with the claim now made; neither can the present rate-payers (who had no benefit from the application of the money) be called upon to pay the amount claimed in this case.

3. PUNISHMENT OF PAUPERS.

Dec. 15*th*, 1845.

Clerk of Rochford Union—1. A female pauper, who has an illegitimate child, having been guilty of great indecency in the workhouse, was put on an allowance of bread and water for twenty-four hours by the master, and desired to pick a small quanty of oakum. When the time of punishment expired, the pauper refused to do the work assigned to her, and she was in consequence taken before a justice of the peace as a refractory pauper and committed to the house of correction for seven days. She was sent to prison in the union clothes; and the master having learned that she committed the offence for the purpose of being sent to gaol, in order that when the term of her imprisonment expired, she might quit the place and leave her child in the workhouse, applied for instructions to the guardians, who directed him to attend at the gaol at the expiration of the pauper's imprisonment for the purpose of receiving her from the gaoler and restoring her to her duties in the workhouse. Requested the Commissioners' opinion as to the legality of the course pursued by the master in compliance with the guardians' directions. 2. The justices for the petty sessional division in which the Rochford Union is situate, object to hear any complaint against a pauper brought from the workhouse unless such complaint be made in writing, by the master or matron, and a summons served upon the pauper in the usual manner. Inquired whether a summons is necessary in such cases.

Ans. — 1. The Commissioners think that neither the guardians nor the master of the workhouse, acting under their directions, had any authority to hold the pauper in custody, and to require her return to the workhouse upon her discharge from gaol at the expiration of the term for which she was imprisoned. It is entirely in the discretion of the pauper, in such case, whether she will return or not. It is altogether a different question, whether if, after her discharge she allowed her child (for whose support she was legally liable) to continue chargeable in the workhouse, she having the ability in whole or in part to maintain such child, she could be punished under 5th Geo. 4, c. 83, for the neglect to maintain it. The Commissioners think she could be so punished. 2. If the pauper is guilty of the refusal to work, or any other of the offences to which section 5 of 5th and 6th Vic. c. 57 applies, then it is not necessary, either that there should be a written complaint, or that a summons should precede the hearing of the case. Any person offending under the section cited, is to be deemed to be an idle and disorderly person within the meaning of the Act 5th Geo. 4, c. 83—An Act for the punishment of idle and disorderly persons, and rogues and vagabonds, *i.e.*, that the offender is punishable in the same manner as offenders under 5th Geo. 4, c. 83, are punishable. Now as regards such persons, the 6th section of that Act provides "that it shall be lawful for any person whatsoever to apprehend any person who shall be found offending against this Act, and forthwith to take and convey him or her before some justice of the peace, to be dealt with in such a manner as hereinbefore directed." The master might, therefore, as the Commissioners consider, take any inmate persisting in his refusal to perform his appointed task of work, at once before the justices, without the intervention of a summons or a warrant. The case may be, and the Commissioners are inclined to think is, different where it is sought to punish a pauper for misbehaviour in the workhouse under the 55th Geo. 3, c. 137, sec. 5. There is no power given by that Act to the master to apprehend the pauper, and he cannot, therefore, compel his attendance before the justices until furnished with a summons or warrant. But the Commissioners are not satisfied that in such a case the complaint upon which the summons or warrant might be founded need be in writing.

XVI.—POOR-RATES.

1. AUDITOR'S DUTY WITH REGARD TO.

June 13th, 1846.

Mr. —— *District Auditor*—Inquired what is his duty with respect to passing poor-rates which have not been signed by the churchwardens or overseers, or allowed by the justices; and to the correction of errors contained in such rates.

Ans.—Where a rate or assessment has not been allowed by justices, and is not capable, therefore, of being enforced, all that will be necessary on your part as auditor will be to debit the overseers in their accounts with the sums which they collect on such rate or assessment, the overseer being accountable for all moneys professedly raised as poor-rate, and applicable to the relief of the poor. You cannot, however, hold the overseer responsible for what they do not collect under such an informal rate, as not being binding upon the persons included in it, there is no power of recovery. Where a rate is duly signed by the overseers, allowed by the justices, and published, though defective in some particulars, you have no power, as the Commissioners consider, to correct errors in the amounts entered in the column "Rate at —— in the £ —," or where there may be an omission to insert in that column the amount assessed on any property, to supply such omission. If, however, the totals of that or any other column be incorrectly cast up or calculated, you can, and, indeed, should, correct the error, as such a correction is obviously not an alteration of the rate, *i.e.*, of the sum or proportion assessed on any occupier.

2. WHETHER THE COST OF ERECTING A "DEAD-HOUSE" MAY BE CHARGED ON POOR-RATES.

May 6th, 1846.

Mr. ————.—The rector of W. has given notice of his intention to prevent dead bodies, cast ashore in that parish, being removed to a place called the "bone-house," situate in the churchyard, and has called upon the churchwardens and overseers to erect a suitable place for the reception of such bodies. Inquired whether the expenses of erecting such a building can be paid out of the poor-rates.

Ans.—The Commissioners are not aware of any authority under which the overseers of W. could lawfully apply the poor-rates of the parish to the erection of such a building as you advert to, however desirable it may be that such a building should be available for the use of the parish.

XVII.—RATING.

1. TITHE RENT-CHARGE—DEDUCTIONS FOR PAYMENTS TO PERPETUAL CURATES.

July 10th, 1846.

Clerk of Wells Union—Inquired whether, in assessing the tithe rent-charge of a parish to the poor-rate, deductions should be made therefrom on account of payments which the vicar is bound to make to the perpetual curates of three chapels of ease in the parish.

Ans.—The Commissioners think these payments do not form part of the deductions which can be lawfully made or allowed for in such case. These payments are nothing more, apparently, than a division of the net value of the tithe or rent-charge, between the tithe-owner, (the vicar) and other persons to whom he thinks proper, or may have been, in some peculiar manner, liable to pay them. The cases establish the principle that the overseers, in assessing the poor-rate upon any property, are to look to those who immediately receive the whole profit or value, without reference to the subsequent distribution of that profit, or value, amongst different persons. In the case of Rex *v.* Woking, 4 Adol. and Ellis 40,) it was held that, in estimating the profits of a canal for the purposes of the poor-rate, the compensation made to certain persons out of the profits derived by the company were not deductable before the rate was assessed, as such compensations were "in the nature of a rent charge." The principle of that decision seems applicable to the present case, and the Commissioners desire to refer you to it accordingly, and to the judgment of Lord Denman.

2. RATING TOLL HOUSES.

August 26th, 1846.

Mr. ——— *District Auditor* — Toll-bar keepers, who are generally paid a small sum for their services, (often not more than five shillings per week,) live in the toll-houses rent-free, and are permitted to carry on any trade, avocation, or employment, for their own profit, provided it does not take them away from their attendance on the gate. Inquired whether this employment carried on by the toll-bar keepers for their own profit, creates a beneficial occupancy distinct from the exemption given in the 4 Geo. 4, c. 95, s. 31; and whether it renders these houses liable to be rated, if not to their full value, at least to a reduced amount, according to circumstances; and further, whether the exemption in the above-cited Act extends to any garden or land attached to such toll-houses.

Ans.—Your inquiries seem to relate generally to toll-houses of every description on turnpike roads; but the 4 Geo. 4, c. 95, s. 31, to which you allude, has reference exclusively to "any house or building erected or used by the trustees of any turnpike-road for the residence or accommodation of persons appointed for weighing any waggons or other carriages." Under this enactment, the Commissioners are disposed to think that the houses and buildings thus described, are exempted absolutely from the rate; and that, while they are used for the residence or accommodation of the persons appointed for weighing waggons, the fact of their being also applied to some other use would not render them rateable. But the Commissioners think it possible to construe the 51st section of the 3 Geo. 4, c. 126, somewhat differently. That enactment provides, that no toll-house erected, or to be erected, for the purpose of collecting the tolls on any turnpike-road, shall be assessed. So far, therefore, as such toll-houses are erected for the sole purpose of collecting the tolls, they are exempt; but it seems to the Commissioners that, if such houses afford any accommodation beyond what is fairly required for the collection, the occupiers might be rateable for such excess of accommodation, on the principle of the decision in R. *v.* Terrott, (1 Bott. 213; 3 East. 506.) The Commissioners are of opinion that neither the 3 Geo. 4, c. 126, sec. 51, nor the 4 Geo. 4, c. 95, s. 31, has the effect of releasing any garden or other land (not used for the purpose of weighing, or the collection of tolls) attached to the toll-houses, from the rate.

XVIII.—RELIEF.

1. POWER OF RELIEVING OFFICER AND OF GUARDIANS IN THE CHARGING OF.

August 11th, 1846.

Clerk of Colchester Union—If a pauper, residing in parish A., applies to the relieving officer for relief, stating that he belongs to B., can that officer debit the latter parish with the relief given in the case? Can the guardians transfer the cost of the relief of a pauper from parish A. to parish B., with the consent of the officers of the latter parish, who, at the time they give such consent, believe the pauper to belong to their parish?

Ans.—The relieving officer has no authority finally to determine the relative liabilities of parishes in a union in respect of relief given to paupers who become destitute in such union. Where persons are relieved by the relieving officer in the intervals of the weekly meetings of the board of guardians, it is the duty of the relieving officer, when he reports to the guardians the fact of the relief, and seeks their confirmation of his act, also to take their instructions as to the charging of the relief; the relieving officer may indeed make a provisional entry of the relief as against some parish, but it must await the confirmation of the guardians, whose province it is to determine the parish liable for the relief—having regard to the facts and the law of the case. The law does not, however, invest the guardians with any power to determine or adjudicate questions of settlement; and if in any case, therefore, it be proposed to charge the relief of a pauper to a parish on the ground of a presumed settlement in such parish, an admission of the settlement in such parish, and the concurrence of such overseers in the proposed charge must be first obtained.

2. POWER OF JUSTICE TO ORDER RELIEF TO SICK PERSONS.

July 30th, 1846.

Clerk of St. Thomas Union.—A. H., a person in service at Littleham, having become ill, obtained an order upon the Devon and Exeter Hospital for medical assistance, and has been made an out-patient of that hospital, and directed to reside in Exeter, in order that she may have the benefit of frequent attendance on the medical officers. She requires relief, but as it is asserted that she neither belongs to Littleham nor to

Exeter, the former place objects to relieve her, and the latter, if she becomes chargeable, will take steps to remove her to the place in which she is legally settled. A justices' order, made under the Exeter local Act, has been served upon the overseers of Littleham, directing them to pay her 3*s*. 6*d*. a week, which order the overseers refuse to obey, on the ground that she is not settled in that parish. Inquired what steps the guardians should take in this and similar cases.

Ans.—The Commissioners are not prepared to say how far the overseers are justified in resisting the order made on them by the justice in the case of A. H., merely on the ground that they dispute the fact adjudged in the order, that A. H. is legally settled in the parish of Littleham. But the Commissioners are disposed to consider, that the order is not binding upon the overseers upon another ground, and which probably may not have occurred to the justice who made the order. The 54th sec. 4 & 5 Wm. 4, c. 76, it will be seen, gives to the guardians, where they exist, the exclusive ordering, giving, and directing of all relief to the poor of any parish for which such guardians act, (except in the particular instances defined by the section, in which overseers and justices may do so,) and concludes with this proviso, "but it shall not be lawful for any justice, or justices, to order relief to any person or persons from the poor-rates of any such parish, except as hereinbefore provided." Now the cases so provided for are—1. Where the overseer, in a case of sudden and urgent necessity, may have neglected to give relief, then the justice, by writing under his hand and seal, may order the overseer to give such temporary relief, in articles of absolute necessity, as the case may require, but not in money. 2. A justice may give an order for medical relief (only) to any parishioner, as well as out-parishioner, where any case of sudden and dangerous illness may require it. It appears to the Commissioners that in the case of a union, or a parish, otherwise under the control of guardians, the 54th section operates as a repeal of the particular provision in the Exeter local Act, 25 Geo. 3, c. 21, sec. 10 & 11, (under which latter statute the order in the present instance purports to have been made,) and that, as regards any poor person settled in such union or parish, a justice is not now empowered by the local Act, last mentioned, to order out-relief *in money*. There is a manifest repugnancy in the two provisions. The power given to the justice by the local Act, 25 Geo. 3, c. 21, secs. 10 & 11, to order an out-patient of the Devon and Exeter Hospital to be relieved, in such manner as the exigency of his or her case may require, by the overseers of the parish of the settlement, (though such out-patient be residing out of such parish,) is clearly at variance with the latter provision, giving to or vesting in the guardians of such parish, or of the union in which such parish is comprised, the exclusive ordering of relief, and expressly limiting the power of the justices in this respect to certain specified cases, of which the ordering of relief in money to a non-resident pauper is not one. The two powers cannot, as it appears to the Commissioners, subsist together, and they think that the negative or restraining words in the proviso of the 54th sec., already cited, do, in effect, repeal the provision in the local Act. The Commissioners do not see, as the facts are stated in your letter, that the guardians of the St Thomas Union are called upon to interfere in the case. The order of the justice, supposing it to be legal, is binding upon the parties to whom it is addressed, (*i.e.*, the overseers of Littleham,) and not on the guardians. But if the order cannot be sustained, the guardians, certainly, cannot of their own authority give relief to A. H. while she continues to reside out of the union at the charge of Littleham, as the alleged settlement of the pauper in that parish, is a fact not admitted by the overseers of Littleham.

---

3. Relief advanced by guardians of one union to paupers belonging to another.

April 2nd, 1846.

Clerk of Boston Union—The guardians of the Boston Union are frequently requested by the guardians of other unions to advance relief to paupers who are about to remove into that union. Inquired whether the Boston guardians can legally advance the relief required; and whether they can recover the amounts so advanced if the auditor should refuse to allow the same in the accounts.

Ans.—So far as the Commissioners are concerned, they are never desirous of raising the point of the legality of an allowance to non-resident poor in the case of the union where it is paid, but in that in which the allowance is ordered. It is for the board of guardians, ordering the allowance, to satisfy the board consenting to act as agents in the matter as to the legality of the relief to be paid. If this is not done, the Boston board of guardians may properly refuse to act as the agents of the board allowing the relief, if they think right to do so. Whether in the case of an illegal allowance the board of guardians acting as agents could recover the money, depends upon the nature of the guarantee under which they act.

XIX.—REMOVALS.

1. MODE OF CHARGING EXPENSES OF REMOVING IRISH POOR.

May 23rd, 1846.

Clerk of West London Union—Inquired whether the expenses incurred in the removal of poor persons to Ireland, under the 8th and 9th Vic. c. 117, should be charged, under the 2nd section of that Act, to the establishment account, or to the account of the particular parish to which such poor person may have been chargeable.

Ans.—The Commissioners are disposed to consider that the terms of the 2nd section of the 8th and 9th Vic. c. 117, require the expense of removing a pauper under that section, to be borne by the union in the case of a pauper chargeable to a parish within a union; and by the parish in the case of a pauper chargeable to a parish not in union. The section directs that the pauper shall be removed "at the expense of such union or parish;" and the Commissioners think that these words are not to be read as merely alternative expressions, but that they are to be referred to their antecedents according to the rule "reddendo singula singulis," so that the union (*i.e.* the common fund) shall be charged where there is a union, and the parish where there is no union.

2. REMOVAL OF DESERTED WIFE AND CHILDREN TO SCOTLAND.

August 21st, 1846.

Clerk of Louth Union—Inquired whether a woman, whose husband has deserted her, can be removed, with her children, to the place of her birth in Scotland, under the provisions of the 8th and 9th Vic. c. 117; both husband and wife being natives of Scotland, and not having gained a settlement in England.

Ans.—The Commissioners think the question, which depends upon the proper construction of the Act referred to, is by no means free from doubt. The language of the statute does not clearly warrant the removal of the children of a man, except in the case where the man is also removed; and as the removal is an act depriving a party of liberty to a certain extent, the courts would not give any extension to the language of the statute. The Commissioners can only state, therefore, that the justices must satisfy themselves of their authority in the matter, which, to say the least, is open to question.

XX.—SETTLEMENT—BY ESTATE.

July 24th, 1846.

Clerk of Festiniog Union—A. D., whose maiden settlement was in the parish of Beddgelert, resided for several years prior to, and down to the time of her first marriage, with her mother (a widow), at a cottage, in the parish. The cottage was rented in the mother's name, though A. D. paid half the rent, owned most of the furniture, and considered that she had an equal interest in the cottage with her mother. About sixteen years ago A. D. married W. R., who thereupon came to reside with his wife and mother-in-law in the above-mentioned cottage, where he continued to live up to the time of his death (three years subsequently), and paid one moiety of the rent. Three years after W. R.'s death A. D. married J. D., who then came to reside in the cottage with his wife and mother-in-law, the latter dying twelve months afterwards. J. D. paid half the rent of the cottage up to his mother-in-law's death, and some arrears of rent due from her at her death. After this he rented the cottage on his own account, and continued therein for the following twelve months, when he removed to the village of Penmorfa. He stayed there two years, when he removed to Nantmor, in the parish of Beddgelert, where he remained for a year, and then deserted his wife, and went to North America. A. D. continued in the cottage at Nantmor for twelve months after her husband had left her, and received relief during half that time from the parish of Beddgelert. She afterwards went into service in the parish of Llanfrothen, where she continued for two years, and left in May, 1845. She was also in service for several months last year in the parish of Ynyscynhaiarn; from thence she went to Liverpool to see her son-in-law, and after remaining there a fortnight, visited her aunt at Pynllan, in the parish of Dolbenmaen, with whom she continued two or three weeks, and then removed to Llanfrothen, where she stopped a week. She afterwards went to Beddgelert for one night, and then returned to Dolbenmaen, where she resided for a week, but left, in consequence of the guardian of that parish objecting to her longer residence there, and went direct to the workhouse, which is in the parish of Llanfihangel-y-traethau. She obtained an order for admission into the workhouse, but returned to Dolbenmaen, and on the guardian of that parish again objecting to her residence there she entered the workhouse, where she now is. A. D.'s second husband, so long as he continued with her, resided within ten miles of the parish of Beddgelert, and she has also resided within that distance, except during her journey to Liverpool. Inquired to what parish the cost of the relief of A. D. should be charged.

Ans.—If, as the Commissioners suppose, A.D. was sole next of kin, and was in possession of the cottage in Beddgelert when her mother died, it would seem, according to the decisions, that on such death taking place—though letters of administration were not taken out by A. D., she had such an estate in the property as is recognised by the law as one which would have conferred a settlement. This estate being an interest in a term of years vested in her husband by operation of law, and therefore it seems that he gained a settlement by forty days' residence upon it. But J. D. certainly lost the settlement so acquired when he ceased to inhabit within ten miles of the parish; and the question arises, did A. D. lose her settlement also? The Commissioners are disposed to think that she did; not, however, by the operation of the 68th section, but of the general law. In Reg. *v.* Wendon, 2 Gale & Dav. 394, the 65th section was held only to extend to a settlement gained by the party's own possession of the property in the parish, and not to a derivative settlement. Now the settlement which A. D. had in Beddgelert was derived from her husband. The mere fact of her ceasing to inhabit within ten miles of Beddgelert did not in itself, according to the decision referred to, affect or destroy her settlement. But the rule of law established by a series of decisions (and to which the Commissioners are aware of no exception) is, that where a man has a known settlement, that is, the settlement of his wife, a wife cannot gain a settlement separate and distinct from her husband during the coverture. J. D. having lost his settlement in Beddgelert by non-residence, is referred by the 68th section to the settlement which he acquired by his inhabitancy in Beddgelert. The case, as regards him, is as though he never gained a settlement in that parish. The same, in the opinion of the Commissioners, holds as to the wife, who cannot retain what her husband has lost, otherwise she would have a settlement distinct from her husband; a position for which the Commissioners know of no authority, and which is at variance with the tenor of the decisions and opposed to the policy of the law. The Commissioners, on the whole, think that A. D., if chargeable to any parish in the Festiniog Union, is removable to the parish to which the husband, if chargeable, could be removed, and to that parish only. With respect to the parish liable for the relief of A. D. by her admission into the workhouse, the Commissioners are disposed to consider that, as the facts are stated, Dolbenmaen is liable. The pauper, it seems, was residing there, and apparently was destitute in that parish, inasmuch as it seems she went direct from that parish to the union workhouse, situate in Llanfihangel. Her only object in going to Llanfihangel was to obtain the relief which she stood in need of while in Dolbenmaen, in which latter parish the application would, no doubt, have been made, if the union arrangements had allowed of it; *i. e.* if the workhouse had been situate, or the relieving officers of the district had resided therein. If, however, on further inquiry, the facts should show that the pauper was not destitute in Dolbenmaen, but was destitute for the first time when she came to Llanfihangel, the latter parish would be liable as the parish in which both the destitution occurred and the application for relief was actually made.

XXI.—VACCINATION—CHARGING COST OF TO PARISHES TO WHICH PAUPERS BELONG.

July 6th, 1846.

Clerk of Hungerford Union—Requested to be referred to an authority (if any such exists,) for charging the cost of vaccinating the pauper inmates of the workhouse to the several parishes of the union, to which such paupers respectively belong.

Ans.—Although perhaps the vaccination of a pauper in the workhouse might possibly have been considered as relief to such pauper, and if so, the cost would, according to the 56th section of the Act 7 & 8 Vic. c. 101, be chargeable to the parish to which the pauper relieved is chargeable, yet the Act 4 and 5 Vic. c. 32, sec. 2, expressly declares that it shall not be deemed to be parochial relief. The Commissioners therefore see no ground for charging the cost in question "to the parishes to which the inmates vaccinated are chargeable."

LONDON:
Printed by order of the Poor Law Commissioners, by BLACKBURN and PARDON, 6, Hatton Garden, and Published by CHARLES KNIGHT and Co., 22, Ludgate Street, Publishers to the Poor Law Commissioners.

SUPPLEMENT.

RETURNS RELATING TO THE ADMINISTRATION OF THE POOR LAW, MADE TO PARLIAMENT DURING THE SESSION OF 1846.

Andover Union.—Report of the Select Committee appointed to inquire into the administration of the Poor Laws in the Andover Union, and into the management of the union workhouse, and into the conduct of the Poor Law Commissioners, and their late Assistant Commissioner, Mr. Parker, with reference to the two investigations held at Andover, and into all the circumstances under which the Poor Law Commissioners called upon Mr. Parker to resign his Assistant Commissionership; and who were instructed to inquire into all the circumstances under which Mr. Day was called upon to resign his office of Assistant Poor Law Commissioner; and who were empowered to report the minutes of evidence taken before them, together with their observations and opinions thereupon, to the House. (H. of C. 663.) Ordered to be printed 20th Aug. 1846.

Andover Union.—A copy of the depositions taken before Mr. Pigott, the Assistant Poor Law Commissioner, at the late investigation into the conduct of Mr. M'Dougall, jun., the schoolmaster of the Andover Union. (708.) Moved for by Mr. Etwall. Presented 28th Aug. 1846.

Atcham Union — Compulsory resignation of Relieving Officer.—Copies of all correspondence of the Poor Law Commissioners relative to the compulsory resignation of Mr. Forester Cross, formerly a relieving officer of the Atcham Union. (429.) Moved for by Mr. Christie. Presented 19th June, 1846.

Barrow-upon-Soar Union—Treatment of Aged Paupers in Workhouse.—Copies of the depositions taken by Mr. Weale, Assistant Poor Law Commissioner, in an inquiry into the treatment of aged paupers in the Barrow Workhouse, and of Mr. Weale's Report, and of Correspondence of the Poor Law Commissioners on the subject. (430.) Moved for by Mr. Christie. Presented 19th June, 1846.

Bone-Pounding in Workhouses.—Copy of any letter and general rule issued by the Poor Law Commissioners relative to the employment of paupers in pounding, grinding, or otherwise breaking bones, or in preparing bone-dust, with copies of any answers from the several boards of guardians remonstrating against such general rules. (75.) Moved for by Captain Pechell. Presented 20th February, 1846.

Bone-Pounding in Workhouses.—Copy of the minute recording the dissent of one of the Poor Law Commissioners to the issue of the order of the 8th day of Nov. 1845, prohibiting the employment of paupers in workhouses in pounding bones.

Copy of a Report of the secretary of the Poor Law Commissioners on bone-crushing. (432.) Moved for by Captain Pechell. Presented 16th June, 1846.

Bromley Union—Dietary Table.—A copy of the diet table now in use in the Bromley Union Workhouse, stating the quantity of meat in the meat pudding allowed once a week to the able-bodied labourer:—Also a copy of any correspondence between the guardians and Commissioners on the subject of increasing the diet. (554.) Moved for by Mr. Wakley. Presented 30th July, 1846.

Cerne Union—Dismissal of Workhouse Master.—Copies of the minutes of the board of guardians of the Cerne Union, in the county of Dorset; and all correspondence of the Poor Law Commissioners relative to the dismissal of the late master of the union workhouse at Cerne. (549.) Moved for by Mr. Sheridan. Presented 30th July, 1846.

Clothes for Infants on leaving Workhouse—Cricklade and Wootton Bassett Union.—Copy of letter written by the Poor Law Commissioners to the guardians of the Cricklade and Wootton Bassett Union, on the subject of allowing clothes for infants born in the workhouse, on their leaving, if otherwise unprovided. (234.) Moved for by Mr. Christie. Presented 23rd April, 1846.

Clothes for Infants on leaving Workhouse.—Copies of all correspondence of the Poor Law Commissioners with the guardians of the Ledbury Union, or with the Rev. Edward Higgins, an ex-officio guardian of the union, relative to a resolution of the board for giving a discretionary power to the master or matron of the workhouse of supplying clothes for new-born infants, otherwise unprovided with clothes, on their being taken out of the workhouse; and of any other correspondence relative to the case of Harriett Boukett, whose infant was stripped of its clothing on being taken out of the workhouse.

Copies of all correspondence with the guardians of the Cricklade and Wootton Bassett Union, or with the Assistant Commissioner of the district, relative to a similar case in that union.

Copies of any circular letter to boards of guardians on the subject of providing clothes for infants born in workhouses, on their being taken out, and of all communications received from boards of guardians on the subject of such letter.

Return of all applications addressed to the Poor Law Commissioners on the subject of providing clothes for infants born in workhouses, on their being taken out, and of all answers given since the passing of the Poor Law Amendment Act. (481.) Moved for by Mr. Christie. Presented 16th June, 1846.

District Asylums.—Report of select committee appointed to inquire into the manner in which the Poor Law Commissioners have exercised the power for the establishment of district asylums for the houseless poor in the metropolis, confided to them by the Statute 7 & 8 Vic. c. 101; and also to inquire into the effects of any asylums, supported by voluntary subscriptions, which may have been framed for the same purpose; and who were empowered to report the minutes of evidence taken before them. (388.) Ordered to be printed 12th June, 1846.

Farnham Parish.—Copies of any instructions issued by the Poor Law Commissioners for the purpose of uniting the parish of Farnham in Surrey, now under Gilbert's Act, with certain other parishes under the Poor Law Act.

Of any memorial to the Poor Law Commissioners from the rate-payers of the parish of Farnham, remonstrating against such union, or any interference whatever. (93.) Moved for by Capt. Pechell. Presented 26th February, 1846.

Guardian—Liability of to Penalties as Contractor for the Poor.—A copy "of correspondence of the Poor Law Commissioners with the clerk of the Chesterfield Union on the liability of a guardian to penalties under the Act 55 Geo. 3, cap. 137, as a contractor for the poor."

A copy "of correspondence of the Poor Law Commissioners in March, 1844, on the liability of a guardian to like penalties if concerned in the maintenance of pauper lunatics chargeable to his union." (454.) Moved for by Mr. Christie. Presented 26th June, 1846.

Keighley Workhouse, State of.—Copy of letter from the Poor Law Commissioners to Alfred Austin, Esq., Assistant Poor Law Commissioner.

Report from Alfred Austin, Esq. to the Poor Law Commissioners. (H. of C. 413.) Presented by command. Ordered to be printed 19th June, 1846.

Local Taxation.—Return relative to local taxation, viz.: poor rates, county rates, highways and church rates, being No. 562 of 1839. (17.) Moved for by Mr. Wodehouse. Ordered to be reprinted 3rd February, 1846.

Lunatic Paupers — Haydock Lodge Lunatic Asylum.—A return of the number of patients for which Haydock Lodge Asylum is licensed.

The number of patients confined in Haydock Lodge on the 1st day of January, 1846, distinguishing the pauper patients from private, and the places from which the pauper patients were received.

Also, the greatest number of patients admitted at one time into Haydock Lodge since 1844.

Number of deaths, with the dates of each, since the 1st day of January, 1845, distinguishing private from pauper, and the length of time each patient had been previously in the asylum.

The number of resident medical attendants in the asylum at Haydock.

The number of keepers and nurses for pauper patients on the 1st day of January, 1845 and 1846 respectively.

Number of Welsh pauper patients.

If any medical attendants or keepers and nurses understand and speak Welsh, and how many, male or female, were in the asylum on the 1st day of January, 1845 and 1846.

If the pauper patients were in the habit of working on any farm, and to whom such farm belonged. (567.) Moved for by Mr. W. O. Stanley. Presented 24th June, 1846.

Copy of correspondence relative to the treatment

of lunatics in an asylum at Haydock Lodge, in the county of Lancaster.

Copy of further report of the Commissioners relative to the treatment of lunatics at Haydock Lodge. (H. of C. 567.) Presented by command 24th June, 1846.

Lunatics—Paupers.—A return of the pauper lunatics and idiots chargeable to each of the unions in England and Wales, and also to parishes not under the Poor Law Amendment Act, on the 1st day of January, 1846, (in pursuance of the Act 8 & 9 Vic. cap. 126) distinguishing those maintained in county lunatic asylums, in licensed houses, and elsewhere: with the average cost per head of maintenance and clothing; together with the population of each union in 1841. (551.) Moved for by Mr. Estcourt. Presented 28th July, 1846.

Macclesfield and Bolton Unions.—A copy of reports received by the Poor Law Commissioners in 1841, on the state of the Macclesfield and Bolton Unions. (661.) Moved for by Mr. Christie. Presented 14th August, 1846. [See also, Return, (293) presented to the House of Lords 20th August, 1846.]

Marlborough House, Peckham, Lunatic Asylum.—Extracts from correspondence between the Poor Law Commissioners and the guardians of the City of London Union, relative to Marlborough House, Peckham.

Copy of report on the state of Marlborough House, Peckham. (H. of C. 534.) Presented by command 29th July, 1846.

Medical Relief — Winkfield Parish, Easthampstead Union.—Copies of all correspondence between the rate-payers of the parish of Winkfield, in the county of Berks, and the Poor Law Commissioners, as to the inefficiency of medical relief and the inadequacy of their representation at the board of guardians of the Easthampstead Union.

Also, copy of a memorial from the said parish, addressed to Sir James Graham, on the 2nd day of January, 1842. (600.) Moved for by Capt. Pechell. Presented 29th July, 1846.

Pauperism—Able-bodied Paupers.—Return of the number of able-bodied paupers receiving relief in the Poor Law unions of England and Wales in each of the weeks in January, 1845, and January, 1846, distinguishing those receiving in-door and out-door relief. (279.) Moved for by Mr. Manners Sutton. Presented 5th May, 1846.

Poor Law, Abuses of, in the Norfolk and Suffolk Unions.—Copy of a report presented by Sir John Walsham, Assistant Poor Law Commissioner, to the Poor Law Commissioners, on certain alleged abuses in the administration of the Poor Law in Norfolk and Suffolk, and of any correspondence between the Poor Law Commissioners and the Home Office, on the subject of the report. (409.) Moved for by Mr. Christie. Presented 16th June, 1846.

Poor Law Commissioners.—Return, showing whether the Poor Law Commissioners have made annually a return of the proceedings of their Board, according to the provisions of the act 4 & 5 Wm. 4, cap. 76, clause 4, to the Secretary of State; if so, whether that Annual Report has been made according to the strict letter of the act; if not, in what years no returns have been made, and in what matter such reports shall have been deficient. (390.) Moved for by Mr. Miles. Presented 10th June, 1846.

Poor Law Commissioners.—A statement of the nature of the official record, from which a return of attendances of the Poor Law Commissioners of 1843 and 1844, presented to this House on the 31st March, 1845, was prepared as stated in the Return in the following words: "The days included in the number stated in this Return, are limited to those of which there exists an official record." (498.) Moved for by Mr. Christie. Presented 16th June, 1846.

Poor Law Commission.—A Return of the name and date of Appointment of each Assistant Poor Law Commissioner acting in England and Wales in the years 1840, 1841, 1842, 1843, 1844, 1845, and 1846; and of the amount of public money paid to each of them in each of those years; distinguishing salary and other allowances; also, a distinctive return of the date of any resignation of, or removal from, such appointment.

Statement of any service not connected with the administration of the Poor Law in England and Wales, in which any such Assistant Commissioner may have been employed during each of those years.

Similar returns and statements as to the secretaries and assistant secretaries to the Poor Law Commissioners.

Return of the name and of the date and duration of appointment of each Assistant Commissioner appointed by the Poor Law Commissioners, for the purpose of conducting any special inquiry; together with a statement of the nature of such inquiry. (572.) Moved for by Mr. Arkwright. Presented 3rd August, 1846.

Poor Rates and Local Taxation.—1. An account of the amount of money levied for poor rates in England and Wales for each of the years ended Lady Day, 1826, 1833, and 1841, respectively, distinguishing the amount levied on landed property in dwelling-houses, and all other kinds of property.

2. An account of the annual value of real property assessed to the poor-rate in England and Wales, in the year ended Lady Day, 1841, distinguishing landed property, dwelling-houses, and all other kinds of property.

3. Return of the total amount of local taxation in Great Britain and Ireland, as far as can be ascertained from official documents. (14.) Moved for by Sir James Graham. Presented 2nd February, 1846. (H. of L. 15.) Presented 9th February, 1846.

Poor Rates—Medical Relief.—Return, showing the population, the amount of money levied for poor rates, and the ratio which the amount levied for poor rates bore to the population in each of the counties of England and Wales during each of the years ended Lady Day, 1813, 1824, 1834, and 1844; also a return of the amount levied for poor-rates in England and Wales, (exclusive of the counties of Kent, Middlesex, and Surrey,) for each of the years ended Lady Day, 1826 and 1841; distinguishing the amount levied on landed property, dwelling-houses, and all other kinds of property, with the proportion per cent. which the amount levied on each description of property bears to the total amount levied.

Account of the expenses of medical relief in each union and parish of England and Wales, under the regulations of the Poor Law Commissioners for the years ending Lady Day, 1843, 1844, and 1845; together with the total cost of relief to the poor in each union. (64.) Moved for by Mr. Wodehouse. Presented 13th February, 1846.

Provisions.—Contract prices of bread and flour and meat, with the average prices for each year, for the unions, for the relief of the poor in England and Wales, from the year 1835 to the end of 1845. (H. of L. 167.) Presented 4th June, 1846.

Relief.—Return of any examination of special reports relating to the relief in Macclesfield, Leek, Stockport, Chorlton, Bolton, and Manchester, received by the Poor Law Commissioners between April and June, 1841. (H. of L. 293.) Presented 20th August, 1846. [See also Return (661.) Presented to the House of Commons 14th August, 1846.]

Relief to the Non-settled Poor.—Returns of the several unions and parishes included in an order of the Poor Law Commissioners, dated the 21st day of December, 1844 (relative to the poor persons who reside in such unions or parishes, but are not settled therein (distinguishing such of the same unions and parishes as have agreed, from such of them as have refused, to administer relief, through their officers, to any non-settled poor, on behalf of the unions or parishes to which they belong:)—Of the number of poor persons belonging to such of the said unions and parishes, respectively, as have refused so to administer such relief, who, at any time between the date of the said Order and the 25th day of March following, were receiving non-resident relief from the union or parish to which they belonged; and showing also how many of such last-mentioned persons continued to receive relief from the unions or parishes to which they belonged at any time between the said 25th day of March, and the 24th day of June following; and whether as resident or non-resident poor; and showing as to such of them as were resident, whether out-door or in-door relief was given; and stating as to such of them as were so relieved being non-resident, by what species of agency such relief was administered. (197.) Moved for by Mr. Ludlow Bruges. Presented 3rd April, 1846.

Removal.—Return specifying the number of families and persons removed by any local order, or other authority, to their place of settlement, from each manufacturing town in Yorkshire, Lancashire, and Cheshire, during the years 1841, 1842, and 1843; the date of such removal, the name of the parish to which removed, and the occupation or trade, and length of residence in the town from which such families and persons were so removed. (209.) Moved for by Mr. Thos. Duncombe. Presented 6th April, 1846. Further return in the above matter. (209—II.) Presented 15th May, 1846.

Sudbury Union, Division of.—Copy of a letter addressed by the Poor Law Commissioners to the clerk of the Sudbury Union, in April, 1843, on a resolution of the board of guardians to divide the board for the examination of paupers. (416.) Moved for by Mr. Christie. Presented 18th June, 1846.

Ware Union—Compulsory resignation of Clerk—Copies of all letters to and from the Poor Law Commissioners and their Assistant Commissioner, Mr. Hall, relative to the compulsory resignation of Mr. Palmer, late clerk and superintendent registrar of the Ware Union. (428.) Moved for by Mr. Christie. Presented 19th June, 1846.

Ware Union—Compulsory Resignation of Clerk—Supplementary Return.—Copies of all letters to and from the Poor Law Commissioners and their Assistant Commissioner, Mr. Hall, relative to the compulsory resignation of Mr. Palmer, late clerk and superintendent registrar of the Ware Union. Omitted by mistake in former return, 428. (524.) Moved for by Mr. Christie. Presented 24th July, 1846.

Workhouses, Money borrowed for building and altering—Settlement, Law Expenses in respect of.—Statement of the sums borrowed for the purposes of an Act intituled "An Act for the Amendment and better Administration of the Laws relating to the Poor in England and Wales," by each of the unions comprised in the Account of the Population of Unions, ordered to be printed on the 22nd May, 1837.

Also, Statement of the sums expended in the years 1836, 1837, and 1838 respectively, on account of legal proceedings relative to the settlement of poor persons by each of the said unions.

And also, statement of the average annual expenditure on account of such proceedings in the parishes comprised in the said unions for the three years previous to the formation thereof. (H. of L. 272.) Ordered to be printed 10th August, 1846.

Vagrants.—Return of the vagrants, or wandering poor, received into the union workhouses, irrespective of the metropolitan districts, for the last five years, 1841, 1842, 1843, 1844, and 1845, distinguishing the number of males and females, and specifying where any records have been kept, the numbers of males between the ages of eighteen and forty. (391.) Moved for by Mr. Evelyn Denison. Ordered to be printed 15th June, 1846.

Vagrants, Relief to in the Metropolis.—Return of the number of casual poor relieved with lodging, food, clothing, and other necessaries, in the unions and parishes comprised in the asylum district, formed by the Poor Law Commissioners in the years 1842, 1843, 1844, and 1845, with the cost of such relief in each year. Moved for by Mr. Pattison. (174.) Presented 30th March, 1846.

Supplemental return, comprising returns from certain metropolitan parishes not included in the above return. (174—II.) Presented 7th April, 1846.

London: Printed by Order of the Poor Law Commissioners, by S. Blackburn, 90½ Holborn Hill, and Published by CHARLES KNIGHT, 90, Fleet Street.